ABC Thumb Index

With the help of the ABC Thumb Index at the edge of this page you can quickly find the letter you are looking for in the English-German or German-English section of this Dictionary.

You place your thumb on the letter you want at the edge of this page, then flip through the Dictionary till you come to the appropriate pages in the English-German or German-English section.

Left-handed people should use the ABC Thumb Index at the end of the book.

A
B
C
D
E
F
G
H
I
J
K
L
M
N
O
P
Q
R
S
T
U
V
W
Z

LANGENSCHEIDT'S POCKET GERMAN DICTIONARY

GERMAN-ENGLISH
ENGLISH-GERMAN

Edited by
THE LANGENSCHEIDT
EDITORIAL STAFF

LANGENSCHEIDT

NEW YORK · BERLIN · MUNICH · VIENNA · ZURICH

© *1970, 1987 Langenscheidt KG, Berlin and Munich*

Printed in Germany

Preface

For over 130 years Langenscheidt's bilingual dictionaries have been essential tools for the student of languages. For several decades Langenscheidt's German-English dictionaries have been used not only for academic work, but in all walks of life.

However, languages are in a constant process of change. To keep you abreast of these changes, Langenscheidt has compiled this new Dictionary. Many words which have entered the German and English languages in the last few years have been included in the vocabulary.

The Dictionary has been considerably <u>enlarged</u>, not only to accommodate the new words, but also to make space for a number of <u>user-friendly innovations.</u> The demands for more detailed notes for the user have now been met. The somewhat abstract short notes have been replaced by a more detailed and graphic explanation of the peculiarities of the Dictionary.

The Dictionary also provides clear answers to questions of declension and conjugation in more than 15,000 German noun and verb entries.

The phonetic transcription of the German and English headwords follows the principles laid down by the International Phonetic Association (IPA).

In addition to the vocabulary, this Dictionary contains <u>special quick-reference sections</u> of proper names, abbreviations, weights and measures, and an <u>alphabetical list of German and English irregular verbs.</u>

Designed for the widest possible variety of uses, this Dictionary, with its <u>more than 48,000 entries and phrases,</u> will be of great value to students, teachers and tourists, and will find a place in home and office libraries alike.

Contents

How do you use the Dictionary?

Don't be afraid of words you don't know!

This Dictionary does all that it can to make it as easy as possible for you to look up and become familiar with a word.

How and where do you find a word?

Strict alphabetical order has been maintained throughout the Dictionary. The principle parts (infinitive, preterite, and past participle) of the irregular German and English verbs as well as the irregular plural forms of English nouns have also been given in their proper alphabetical order, e.g.:

> **gebissen** *p.p. of beißen*
> **bitten** *p.p. von bite*
> **men** *pl. von man*

In the German-English section we have treated the umlauts *ä ö ü* as *a o u*, rather than as *ae oe ue*.

When trying to locate a particular German or English word, you can use the boldface **catchwords** at the top corner of each page as a guide. These catchwords show you (on the left-hand side) the *first* boldface word on the left-hand page and (on the right-hand side) the *last* boldface word on the right-hand page, e.g. **Konflikt – köstlich** on page 188 and 189.

How do you spell the word?

As in a monolingual dictionary you can check the spelling of any word in this Dictionary. In the German-English section the American spelling has been given in the following ways:

> *theat|re, Am. -er, defen|ce, Am. -se*
> *council(l)or, hono(u)r*
> *plough, Am. plow*

and in the English-German section as follows:

> *centre, Am. -ter – theatre, Am. -ter*
> *dialogue, Am. -log – programme, Am. -gram*
> *colo(u)r – hono(u)r – travel(l)er*

In a very few cases a letter in round brackets indicates that a particular word can be spelled in two different ways: *judg(e)ment = judgment* or *judgement*.

In the English-German section the dots within a head-word indicate syllabification breaks.

What do the various typefaces mean?

All German and English headwords are printed **in bold face**, as are the Arabic numerals used to distinguish the various parts of speech and grammatical forms of a word:

> **klopfen 1.** *v/i. heart, pulse*: beat; ... **2.** *v/t.* knock, drive (*nail, etc.*)
>
> **feed** ... **1.** Futter *n*; ... **2.** (*fed*) *v/t.* füttern; **~·back** ...

Italics are used a) for grammatical and subject label abbreviations: *adj., adv., v/i., v/t., econ., pol., zo.,* etc.; b) to indicate the gender of a German word: *m, f, n*; c) for any details added to give more precise information about a word or a particular meaning of a word, e.g.:

> **mild** ... *weather, punishment, etc.*: mild
>
> **schälen** ... pare, peel (*fruit, potatoes, etc.*)
>
> **file**[1] ... *Computer*: Datei *f*
>
> **page** ... Seite *f* (*e-s Buches, e-r Zeitung etc.*)

Lightface type is used for all idiomatic phrases:

> **gut** ... *ganz* ~ not bad
>
> **Lage** ... *in der* ~ *sein zu inf.* be able to *inf.*
>
> **depend** ... *it* ~*s* F es kommt (ganz) darauf an
>
> **line** ... *hold the* ~ *teleph.* am Apparat bleiben

All translations are printed in normal type.

How do you pronounce the word?

The phonetic transcription of a word indicates how you should pronounce it. So that *everyone* could know precisely which signs represent which sounds, an international phonetic alphabet was established. As the signs used by the International Phonetic Association are considered standard, we now talk of the **IPA phonetic alphabet**.

The phonetic symbols in square brackets – [ ] – are used in the Dictionary to describe how you should pronounce the German or English headword, e.g.:

> **fest** [fɛst] – **Hilfe** ['hilfə]
>
> **coat** [kəʊt] – **message** ['mesɪdʒ]

Guide to Pronunciation
for the German-English Section

The length of vowels is indicated by [:] following the vowel symbol, the stress by ['] preceding the stressed syllable. The glottal stop [ʔ] is the forced stop between one word or syllable and a following one beginning with a vowel, as in *unentbehr-lich* [un'ɛnt'beːrliç]. No transcription of compounds is given if the parts appear as separate headwords.

A. Vowels

[a] as in French *carte*: *Mann* [man].

[ɑ:] as in *father*: *Wagen* ['vɑːgən].

[e] as in *bed*: *Edikt* [e'dikt].

[e:] resembles the sound in *day*: *Weg* [veːk].

[ə] unstressed e as in *ago*: *Bitte* ['bitə].

[ɛ] as in *fair*: *männlich* ['mɛnliç], *Geld* [gɛlt].

[ɛ:] same sound but long: *zählen* ['tsɛːlən].

[i] as in *it*: *Wind* [vint].

[i:] as in *meet*: *hier* [hiːr].

[ɔ] as in *long*: *Ort* [ɔrt].

[ɔ:] same sound but long as in *draw*: *Komfort* [kɔm'fɔːr].

[o] as in *molest*: *Moral* [mo'rɑːl].

[o:] resembles the English sound in *go* [gəʊ] but without the [ʊ]: *Boot* [boːt].

[ø:] as in French *feu*. The sound may be acquired by saying [e] through closely rounded lips: *schön* [ʃøːn].

[ø] same sound but short: *Ökono-mie* [økono'miː].

[œ] as in French *neuf*. The sound resembles the English vowel in *her*. Lips, however, must be well rounded as for [ɒ]: *öffnen* ['œfnən].

[u] as in *book*: *Mutter* ['mutər].

[u:] as in *boot*: *Uhr* [uːr].

[y] almost like the French u as in *sur*. It may be acquired by saying [ɪ] through fairly closely rounded lips: *Glück* [glyk].

[y:] same sound but long: *führen* ['fyːrən].

B. Diphthongs

[aɪ] as in *like*: *Mai* [maɪ].

[aʊ] as in *mouse*: *Maus* [maʊs].

[ɔy] as in *boy*: *Beute* ['bɔytə], *Läufer* ['lɔyfər].

C. Consonants

[b] as in *better*: *besser* ['bɛsər].

[d] as in *dance*: *du* [duː].

[f] as in *find*: *finden* ['findən], *Vater* ['fɑːtər], *Philosoph* [filo'zoːf].

[g] as in *gold*: *Gold* [gɔlt], *Geld* [gɛlt].

[ʒ] as in *measure*: *Genie* [ʒe'niː], *Journalist* [ʒurna'list].

[h] as in *house* but not aspirated: *Haus* [haʊs].

[ç] an approximation to this sound may be acquired by assuming the mouth-configuration for [ɪ] and emitting a strong current of breath: *Licht* [liçt], *Mönch* [mœnç], *lustig* ['lustiç].

[x] as in Scottish *loch*. Whereas [ç] is pronounced at the front of the mouth, [x] is pronounced in the throat: *Loch* [lɔx].

[j] as in *year*: *ja* [jɑː].

[k] as in *kick*: *keck* [kɛk], *Tag* [tɑːk], *Chronist* [kro'nist], *Café* [ka'feː].

[l] as in *lump*. Pronounced like English initial "clear l": *lassen* ['lasən].

[m] as in *mouse*: *Maus* [maʊs].

[n] as in *not*: *nein* [naɪn].

[ŋ] as in *sing*, *drink*: *singen* ['ziŋən], *trinken* ['triŋkən].

[p] as in *pass*: *Paß* [pas], *Trieb* [triːp], *obgleich* [ɔp'glaɪç].

[r]	as in *rot*. There are two pronunciations: the frontal or lingual r and the uvular r (the latter unknown in England): *rot* [ro:t].	[ʃ]	as in *ship*: *Schiff* [ʃif], *Charme* [ʃarm], *Spiel* [ʃpi:l], *Stein* [ʃtam].
[s]	as in *miss*. Unvoiced when final, doubled, or next a voiceless consonant: *Glas* [gla:s], *Masse* ['masə], *Mast* [mast], *naß* [nas].	[t]	as in *tea*: *Tee* [te:], *Thron* [tro:n], *Stadt* [ʃtat], *Bad* [ba:t], *Findling* ['fintliŋ], *Wind* [vint].
		[v]	as in *vast*: *Vase* ['va:zə], *Winter* ['vintər].
[z]	as in *zero*. S voiced when initial in a word or syllable: *Sohn* [zo:n], *Rose* ['ro:zə].	[ã, ɛ̃, õ]	are nasalized vowels. Examples: *Ensemble* [ã'sã:bəl], *Terrain* [tɛ'rɛ̃:], *Bonbon* [bõ'bõ:].

List of Suffixes

The German suffixes are not transcribed unless they are parts of headwords.

-bar	[-ba:r]	-ist	[-ist]
-chen	[-çən]	-keit	[-kait]
-d	[-t]	-lich	[-liç]
-de	[-də]	-ling	[-liŋ]
-ei	[-ai]	-losigkeit	[-lo:ziçkait]
-en	[-ən]	-nis	[-nis]
-end	[-ənt]	-sal	[-za:l]
-er	[-ər]	-sam	[-za:m]
-haft	[-haft]	-schaft	[-ʃaft]
-heit	[-hait]	-sieren	[-zi:rən]
-ie	[-i:]	-ste	[-stə]
-ieren	[-i:rən]	-tät	[-tɛ:t]
-ig	[-iç]	-tum	[-tu:m]
-ik	[-ik]	-ung	[-uŋ]
-in	[-in]	-ungs-	[-uŋs-]
-isch	[-iʃ]		

Guide to the Phonetic Transcriptions in the English-German Section

A. Vowels and Diphthongs

[i:]	see	[si:]		[ə]	consist	[kən'sist]
[ɪ]	it	[ɪt]		[ɜ:]	bird	[bɜ:d]
[e]	get	[get]		[eɪ]	day	[deɪ]
[æ]	cat	[kæt]		[əʊ]	go	[gəʊ]
[ɑ:]	father	['fɑ:ðə]		[aɪ]	fly	[flaɪ]
[ɒ]	not	[nɒt]		[aʊ]	how	[haʊ]
[ɔ:]	saw	[sɔ:]		[ɔɪ]	boy	[bɔɪ]
[ʊ]	put	[pʊt]		[ɪə]	sheer	[ʃɪə]
[u:]	too	[tu:]		[ʊə]	tour	[tʊə]
[ʌ]	up	[ʌp]		[eə]	vary	['veərɪ]

The length of a vowel is indicated by the symbol [:], e.g. *ask* [ɑ:sk], *astir* [ə'stɜ:].

The following French nasal sounds are used occasionally: [ã] as in French *blanc,* [ɔ̃] as in French *bonbon* and [ɛ̃] as in French *vin.*

B. Consonants

[r]	bright	[braɪt]		[z]	zone	[zəʊn]
[ŋ]	ring	[rɪŋ]		[ʃ]	ship	[ʃɪp]
[ŋk]	ink	[ɪŋk]		[ʒ]	measure	[ˈmeʒə]
[j]	yes	[jes]		[tʃ]	chicken	[ˈtʃɪkɪn]
[f]	fat	[fæt]		[dʒ]	judge	[dʒʌdʒ]
[v]	very	[ˈverɪ]		[θ]	thin	[θɪn]
[w]	well	[wel]		[ð]	then	[ðen]
[s]	soul	[səʊl]				

To save space in the individual entries, we shall limit ourselves to a short note here on the ending -ed* and the plural -s** of the English headwords. These endings will then appear in the vocabulary without phonetics, unless they are exceptions to the rules.

* [-d] after vowels and voiced consonants; [-t] after unvoiced consonants; [-ɪd] after final d and t.

** [-z] after vowels and voiced consonants; [-s] after unvoiced consonants.

Stress

In the German and English headwords the sign ' (the stress accent) preceding a syllable indicates that this syllable is stressed.

> **durchschlagen** [ˈdurçʃlɑːgən] – **durchschlagen** [durçˈʃlɑːgən]
>
> **'nachsehen** – **ˌ∼senden**
>
> **record** [rɪˈkɔːd] – **record** [ˈrekɔːd]
>
> **gamekeeper** [ˈgeɪmkiːpə]

If in an English entry the headword is followed by a word which has the same stress, no stress accent is given for the second word – it is always stressed in exactly the same way as the word preceding it, e.g.:

> **helper** [ˈhelpə] – **helpful** [∼fl = ˈhelpfl]

What do the abbreviations and symbols tell you?

Wherever possible, we have used pictorial symbols and/or abbreviations to indicate the subject area from which a headword and/or some of its meanings are taken. A pictorial symbol or an abbreviation placed immediately after a headword applies to all translations given in the entry. Any symbol or abbreviation preceding an individual translation refers to this translation only. If the abbreviation is followed by a colon, it applies to all the following translations. Thus in the German-English section an F placed before the German or English part of an example sentence indicates that only that part of the sentence is used familiarly. On the other hand, an F: placed before the German part indicates that the example and translation belong to the same linguistic usage level.

Labels denoting figurative usage have been placed between the example phrases or sentences and their translations. This is also sometimes the case with other labels.

F	*familiar*, umgangssprachlich.	🚂	*railway*, *railroad*, Eisenbahn.
V	*vulgar*, vulgär.	✈	*aviation*, Flugwesen.
†	*archaic*, veraltet.	✉	*postal affairs*, Postwesen.
⌀	*rare, little used*, selten.	♪	*musical term*, Musik.
⚏	*scientific term*, wissenschaftlich.	🏛	*architecture*, Architektur.
♀	*botany*, Botanik, Pflanzenkunde.	⚡	*electrical engineering*, Elektrotechnik.
⊕	*engineering*, Technik; *handicraft*, Handwerk.		
		⚖	*legal term*, Rechtswissenschaft.
⚒	*mining*, Bergbau.	♟	*mathematics*, Mathematik.
⚔	*military term*, militärisch.	✔	*farming*, Landwirtschaft.
⚓	*nautical term*, Schiffahrt.	⚗	*chemistry*, Chemie.
✝	*commercial term*, Handelswesen.	✚	*medicine*, Medizin.

In addition, the English-German section contains the sign ⚠, which is intended as a warning against typical mistakes:

actual ... ⚠ *nicht aktuell*

A further symbol is the box: □. When placed after an English adjective, this box means that the corresponding adverb is formed regularly by adding -*ly* to the adjective or by transforming -*le* to -*ly* or -*y* to -*ily*, e.g.:

beautiful □ = *beautifully*
acceptable □ = *acceptably*
happy □ = *happily*

Adverbs can also be formed by adding -*ally* to the adjective form. Such cases have been treated as follows:

authentic ... (~*ally*) = *authentically*

What does the **tilde (~)** mean?

One symbol which you will meet constantly in the entries is a sign indicating repetition, the tilde (~ ⚲, ~ ⚲). The boldface tilde (~) replaces either the whole headword or the part of the headword preceding the vertical bar (|). The lightface tilde (~) represents the entry immediately preceding it, which itself might have been formed with the help of a boldface tilde:

Ski ... **~fahrer** (= *Skifahrer*), **~läufer** (= *Skiläufer*)
ab|blasen ... **~bringen:** *j-n* ~ (= *abbringen*) *von* ...
foot ... **~ball** (= *football*)
happi|ly ... **~ness** (= *happiness*)

When the initial letter of an entry changes in a run-on entry from small to capital or vice versa, the simple tilde (~) is replaced by the following symbol ♀:

dick ... **♀kopf** (= *Dickkopf*)
Geschicht|e ... **♀lich** (= *geschichtlich*)
representative ... *House of* ♀s
(= *House of Representatives*)

The same procedure has been used in the phonetics. The simple tilde is used for the whole word or for the part of the word which is repeated unchanged. Only the syllables or letters which change are added:

bewegen¹ [bə'veːɡən] – **bewegen²** [~]
Beweis [bə'vaɪs] ... **♀en** [~zən]
chap¹ [tʃæp] – **chap²** [~] – **chap³** [~]
per|suade [pə'sweɪd] ... **~suasion** [~ʒn]
destruc|tion [dɪ'strʌkʃn] ... **~tive** [~tɪv]

In addition to the symbols, you will find the following **abbreviations** for grammatical terms and special subject areas:

a.	*also*, auch.	*b.s.*	*bad sense*, in schlechtem Sinne.
abbr.	*abbreviation*, Abkürzung.		
acc.	*accusative (case)*, Akkusativ.	*bsd.*	*especially*, besonders.
adj.	*adjective*, Adjektiv.		
adv.	*adverb*, Adverb.	*cj.*	*conjunction*, Konjunktion.
allg.	*commonly*, allgemein.	*co.*	*comic(al)*, scherzhaft.
Am.	*American English*, amerikanisches Englisch.	*coll.*	*collectively*, als Sammelwort.
		comp.	*comparative*, Komparativ.
anat.	*anatomy*, Anatomie.	*contp.*	*contemptuously*, verächtlich.
appr.	*approximately*, etwa.		
arch.	*architecture*, Architektur.	*dat.*	*dative (case)*, Dativ.
art.	*article*, Artikel.	*dem.*	*demonstrative*, hinweisend.
ast.	*astronomy*, Astronomie.		
attr.	*attributively*, attributiv.	*ea.*	*one another, each other*, einander.
biol.	*biology*, Biologie.	*eccl.*	*ecclesiastical*, kirchlich.
Brit.	*British*, britisch.	*econ.*	*economics*, Wirtschaft.
Brt.	*British English*, britisches Englisch.	*e-e, e-e, e-e a(n)*, eine.	
		e.g.	*for example*, zum Beispiel.

12

e-m, *e-m, e-m to a(n)*, einem.		n	*neuter*, sächlich.
e-n, *e-n, e-n a(n)*, einen.		nom.	*nominative (case)*, Nominativ.
engS.	*in narrower sense*, in engerem Sinne.	npr.	*proper name*, Eigenname.
e-r, *e-r, e-r of a(n)*, *to a(n)*, einer.		od.	*or*, oder.
e-s, *e-s, e-s of a(n)*, eines.		opt.	*optics*, Optik.
esp.	*especially*, besonders.	orn.	*ornithology*, Ornithologie.
et., *et., et. something*, etwas.		o.s.	*oneself*, sich.
etc., *etc. and so on*, und so weiter.			
		P.	*person*, Person.
f	*feminine*, weiblich.	p.	*person*, Person.
fig.	*figuratively*, bildlich.	paint.	*painting*, Malerei.
frz.	*French*, französisch.	parl.	*parliamentary term*, parlamentarischer Ausdruck.
gen.	*genitive (case)*, Genitiv.	pass.	*passive voice*, Passiv.
geogr.	*geography*, Geographie.	pers.	*personal*, persönlich.
geol.	*geology*, Geologie.	pharm.	*pharmacy*, Pharmazie.
geom.	*geometry*, Geometrie.	phls.	*philosophy*, Philosophie.
ger.	*gerund*, Gerundium.	phot.	*photography*, Photographie.
Ggs.	*antonym*, Gegensatz.	phys.	*physics*, Physik.
gr.	*grammar*, Grammatik.	physiol.	*physiology*, Physiologie.
		pl.	*plural*, Plural.
h	*have*, haben.	poet.	*poetry*, Dichtung.
hist.	*history*, Geschichte.	pol.	*politics*, Politik.
hunt.	*hunting*, Jagdwesen.	poss.	*possessive*, besitzanzeigend.
		p.p.	*past participle*, Partizip Perfekt.
ichth.	*ichthyology*, Ichthyologie.	p.pr.	*present participle*, Partizip Präsens.
impers.	*impersonal*, unpersönlich.		
indef.	*indefinite*, unbestimmt.	pred.	*predicative*, prädikativ.
inf.	*infinitive (mood)*, Infinitiv.	pres.	*present*, Präsens.
int.	*interjection*, Interjektion.	pret.	*preterit(e)*, Präteritum.
interr.	*interrogative*, fragend.	print.	*printing*, Buchdruck.
iro.	*ironically*, ironisch.	pron.	*pronoun*, Pronomen.
irr.	*irregular*, unregelmäßig.	prov.	*provincialism*, Provinzialismus.
j., *j., j. someone*, jemand.		prp.	*preposition*, Präposition.
j-m, *j-m, j-m to s.o.*, jemandem.		psych.	*psychology*, Psychologie.
j-n, *j-n, j-n someone*, jemanden.			
j-s, *j-s, j-s someone's*, jemandes.		refl.	*reflexive*, reflexiv.
		rel.	*relative*, Relativ...
konkr.	*concretely*, konkret.	rhet.	*rhetoric*, Rhetorik.
ling.	*linguistics*, Sprachwissenschaft.	S., S.	*thing*, Sache.
lit.	*literary*, nur in der Schriftsprache vorkommend.	s.	*see, refer to*, siehe.
		schott.	*Scottish*, schottisch.
		s-e, *s-e, s-e his, one's*, seine.
m	*masculine*, männlich.	sep.	*separable*, abtrennbar.
m-e, *m-e, m-e my*, meine.		sg.	*singular*, Singular.
m-r	*of my, to my*, meiner.	sl.	*slang*, Slang.
metall.	*metallurgy*, Metallurgie.	s-m, *s-m, s-m to his, to one's*, seinem.
meteor.	*meteorology*, Meteorologie.	s-n, *s-n, s-n his, one's*, seinen.
min.	*mineralogy*, Mineralogie.	s.o., *s.o., s.o. someone*, jemand(en).
mot.	*motoring*, Kraftfahrwesen.	s-r, *s-r, s-r of his, of one's, to his, to one's*, seiner.
mount.	*mountaineering*, Bergsteigen.		
mst	*mostly, usually*, meistens.	s-s, *s-s, s-s of his, of one's*, seines.
myth.	*mythology*, Mythologie.	s.th., *s.th., s.th. something*, etwas.

subj.	*subjunctive* (*mood*), Konjunktiv.	*vet.*	*veterinary medicine*, Tiermedizin.
sup.	*superlative*, Superlativ.	*vgl.*	*compare*, vergleiche.
surv.	*surveying*, Landvermessung.	*v/i.*	*intransitive verb*, intransitives Verb.
tel.	*telegraphy*, Telegraphie.		
teleph.	*telephony*, Fernsprechwesen.	*v/refl.*	*reflexive verb*, reflexives Verb.
thea.	*theatre*, Theater.	*v/t.*	*transitive verb*, transitives Verb.
TM	*trademark*, Warenzeichen.		
TV	*television*, Fernsehen.	*weitS.*	*in a wider sense*, in weiterem Sinne.
typ.	*typography*, Typographie.		
u., u.	*and*, und.	*z.B.*	*for example*, zum Beispiel.
univ.	*university*, Hochschulwesen, Studentensprache.	*zo.*	*zoology*, Zoologie.
		zs., zs.,	*zs. together*, zusammen.
v/aux.	*auxiliary verb*, Hilfsverb.	*Zssg(n)*	*compound word(s)*, Zusammensetzung(en).
vb.	*verb*, Verb.		

A few words on the translations

You will no doubt have already noticed that it is very rare for there to be only one translation after any headword. In most cases the headword has several translations which are related in meaning and are separated from one another by a comma. However, the headword itself can also have several very different meanings, depending on the context in which it is used.

When a word has several meanings, a semicolon is used to separate them from one another. But the various meanings of a word are often so far apart from one another that it is not enough simply to separate them by a semicolon. In such cases we use several different methods to separate the translations:

a) the headword is repeated and given a superior number:

leben[1] ... live   **chap**[1] ... Riß *m*
Leben[2] *n* ... life   **chap**[2] ... Kerl *m*
Tor[1] *n* ... gate   **chap**[3] ... Kinnbacke *f*
Tor[2] *m* ... fool

b) When a headword can be several different parts of speech (a noun, verb, adjective, etc.) the various translations are distinguished by boldface Arabic numerals:

böse ... **1.** bad (*adjective*)
          2. ♀ *n* evil (*noun*)
work ... **1.** Arbeit *f* (*noun*)
          2. *v/i.* arbeiten (*verb*)
green ... **1.** grün (*adjective*)
          2. Grün *n* (*noun*)

In the German-English section boldface Arabic numerals are also used to distinguish transitive, intransitive and reflexive verbs (if this affects their translation) and to indicate the different meanings of nouns which can occur in more than one gender:

> **bohren** ... **1.** *v/t.* bore
> **2.** *v/i.* drill
> **Bund** ... **1.** *m* ...; **2.** *n* ...

Boldface Arabic numerals are also used to show that where there is a change of meaning a noun or verb may be differently inflected or conjugated:

> **Bau** ... *m* **1.** (-[e]s/*no pl.*) ...; **2.** (-[e]s/-ten) ...; **3.** (-[e]s/-e) ...
> **schwimmen** *v/i.* (*irr.*, *ge-*) **1.** (*sein*) ...; **2.** (*h*) ...

If grammatical indications come before the subdivision they refer to all translations following:

> **Alte** (-*n*/-*n*) **1.** *m* ...; **2.** *f* ...
> **humpeln** ... *v/i.* (*ge-*) **1.** (*sein*) ...; **2.** (*h*) ...

As you know, British and American English sometimes use different terms to denote the same thing. The American *sidewalk* and the British *pavement* are both "Bürgersteig" in German, whereas only in American English does *fall* have the meaning "Herbst". In this Dictionary words which are chiefly used in British English are marked *Brt.* and those which are more typically American *Am.*

Grammar in the Dictionary, too?

It is often possible for you to arrive at the correct grammatical use of a word from the "additional information" which belongs to it. If, for instance, a headword (a verb, adjective or noun) is governed by certain prepositions, these are given together with the English or German translations and placed next to the appropriate translation. If the German or English preposition is the same for all or several translations, it is given only once before or after the first translation and then also applies to the translations which follow it.

The following methods are used to relate the prepositions to their appropriate headwords:

> **abrücken** ... **1.** *v/t.* move away (*von* from) ...
> **befestigen** ... *v/t.* fasten (*an dat.* to), fix (to), attach (to) ...

dissent ... anderer Meinung sein (*from* als) ...
dissimilar ... (*to*) unähnlich (*dat.*); verschieden (von) ...

With German prepositions which can take the dative or the accusative, the case is given in brackets:

enter ... (ein)treten in (*acc.*) ...

Notes on special grammatical conventions used in the German-English section:

a) **nouns**

The inflectional forms (*genitive singular | nominative plural*) follow immediately after the indication of gender. No forms are given for compounds if the parts appear as separate headwords.

The horizontal stroke replaces the part of the word which remains unchanged in the inflexion:

Affe *m* (-*n*/-*n*) – **Affäre** *f* (-/-*n*)

The sign ⸚ indicates that an umlaut appears in the inflected form in question:

Blatt *n* (-[*e*]*s*/⸚*er*).

b) **verbs** (see also the list of irregular German verbs on page 744)

Verbs have been treated in the following ways:

1. bändigen *v/t.* (*ge-, h*)

The past participle of this verb is formed by means of the prefix *ge-* and the auxiliary verb *haben*: *er hat gebändigt*.

2. abfassen *v/t.* (*sep., -ge-, h*)

In conjugation the prefix *ab* must be separated from the primary verb *fassen*: *er faßt ab*; *er hat abgefaßt*.

3. verderben *v/i.* (*irr., no -ge-, sein*)

irr. following the verb refers the reader to the list of irregular German verbs in the appendix (page 744) for the principal parts of this particular verb: *es verdarb*; *es ist verdorben*.

4. abfallen *v/i.* (*irr. fallen, sep., -ge-, sein*)

A reference such as *irr. fallen* indicates that the compound verb *abfallen* is conjugated in exactly the same way as the primary verb *fallen* as given in the list of irregular verbs: *er fiel ab; er ist abgefallen*.

5. sieden *v/t. and v/i.* ([*irr.,*] ge-, h)

The square brackets indicate that *sieden* can be treated as a regular or irregular verb: *er siedete or er sott; er hat gesiedet or er hat gesotten*.

In the English-German section of the Dictionary, round brackets can be found in some entries after the square brackets for the phonetics. These round brackets indicate that the headword has a grammatical peculiarity in one of the following points:

a) **irregular plural**

    child ... (*pl. children*) – **to·ma·to** ... (*pl. -toes*)

    a·nal·y·sis ... (*pl. -ses* [-si:z])

b) **irregular verbs** (see also the list of irregular English verbs on page 746)

    go ... (*went, gone*) – **shut** ... (*shut*)

    learn ... (*learned or learnt*)

    out·grow ... (*-grew, -grown*)

c) **doubling of the final consonant**

    hit ... (*-tt-*) – **trav·el** ... (*esp. Brt. -ll-, Am. a. -l-*)

c and b)

shut ... (*-tt-; shut*) – **out·bid** ... (*-dd-; -bid*)

d) **final –c becomes –ck–**

    frol·ic ... (*-ck-*) = *frolicking*

e) **comparative and superlative forms**

    good ... (*better, best*)

    an·gry ... (*-ier, -iest*) – **sore** ... (*~r, ~st*)

You will have seen from these notes that this Dictionary offers more than simply word-for-word equivalents as are to be found in the vocabulary sections of textbooks.

PART I

GERMAN-ENGLISH
DICTIONARY

A

Aal *ichth.* [ɑːl] *m* (-[e]s/-e) eel; '**⁀-glatt** *adj.* (as) slippery as an eel.

Aas [ɑːs] *n* **1.** (-es/⁀-e) carrion, carcass; **2.** *fig.* (-es/Äser) beast; '**⁀-geier** *orn. m* vulture.

ab [ap] **1.** *prp.* (*dat.*): ~ *Brüssel* from Brussels onwards; ~ *Fabrik, Lager etc.* ✝ ex works, warehouse, *etc.*; **2.** *prp.* (*dat.*, ✝ *F acc.*): ~ *erstem or ersten März* from March 1st, on and after March 1st; **3.** ✝ *prp.* (*gen.*) less; ~ *Unkosten* less charges; **4.** *adv. time:* *von jetzt* ~ from now on, in future; ~ *und zu* from time to time, now and then; *von da* ~ from that time forward; *space:* *thea.* exit, *pl.* exeunt; *von da* ~ from there (on).

abänder|n ['ap⁀-] *v/t.* (*sep.*, -ge-, *h*) alter, modify; *parl.* amend; '**⁀ung** *f* alteration, modification; *parl.* amendment (*to bill, etc.*); '**⁀ungsantrag** *parl. m* amendment.

abarbeiten ['ap⁀-] *v/t.* (*sep.*, -ge-, *h*) work off (*debt*); *sich* ~ drudge, toil.

Abart ['ap⁀-] *f* variety.

'**Abbau** *m* **1.** (-[e]s/*no pl.*) pulling down, demolition (*of structure*); dismantling (*of machine, etc.*); dismissal, discharge (*of personnel*); reduction (*of staff, prices, etc.*); cut (*of prices, etc.*); **2.** ⚒ (-[e]s/-e) working, exploitation; '**⁀en** *v/t.* (*sep.*, -ge-, *h*) pull or take down, demolish (*structure*); dismantle (*machine, etc.*); dismiss, discharge (*personnel*); reduce (*staff, prices, etc.*); cut (*prices, etc.*); ⚒ work, exploit.

'**ab|beißen** *v/t.* (*irr.* beißen, *sep.*, -ge-, *h*) bite off; '**⁀bekommen** *v/t.* (*irr.* kommen, *sep.*, *no* -ge-, *h*) get off; *s-n Teil or et.* ~ get one's share; *et.* ~ be hurt, get hurt.

abberuf|en *v/t.* (*irr.* rufen, *sep.*, *no* -ge-, *h*) recall; '**⁀ung** *f* recall.

'**ab|bestellen** *v/t.* (*sep.*, *no* -ge-, *h*) countermand, cancel one's order for (*goods, etc.*); cancel one's subscription to, discontinue (*news-*

paper, *etc.*); '**⁀biegen** *v/i.* (*irr.* biegen, *sep.*, -ge-, *sein*) *p.* turn off; *road:* turn off, bend; *nach rechts* (*links*) ~ turn right (left); *von e-r Straße* ~ turn off a road.

'**Abbild** *n* likeness; image; '**⁀en** ['⁀dən] *v/t.* (*sep.*, -ge-, *h*) figure, represent; *sie ist auf der ersten Seite abgebildet* her picture is on the front page; '**⁀ung** ['⁀duŋ] *f* picture, illustration.

'**abbinden** *v/t.* (*irr.* binden, *sep.*, -ge-, *h*) untie, unbind, remove; 🩹 ligate, tie up.

'**Abbitte** *f* apology; ~ *leisten or tun* make one's apology (*bei j-m wegen et.* to s.o. for s.th.); '**⁀n** *v/t.* (*irr.* bitten, *sep.*, -ge-, *h*): *j-m et.* ~ apologize to s.o. for s.th.

'**ab|blasen** *v/t.* (*irr.* blasen, *sep.*, -ge-, *h*) blow off (*dust, etc.*); call off (*strike, etc.*), cancel; ⚔ break off (*attack*); '**⁀blättern** *v/i.* (*sep.*, -ge-, *sein*) paint, *etc.*: scale, peel (off); *skin:* desquamate; 🌿 shed the leaves; '**⁀blenden** (*sep.*, -ge-, *h*) **1.** *v/t.* screen (*light*); *mot.* dim, dip (*headlights*); **2.** *v/i. mot.* dim or dip the headlights; *phot.* stop down; '**⁀blitzen** *F v/i.* (*sep.*, -ge-, *sein*) meet with a rebuff; ~ *lassen* snub; '**⁀brausen** (*sep.*, -ge-) **1.** *v/refl.* (*h*) have a shower(-bath), douche; **2.** *F v/i.* (*sein*) rush off; '**⁀brechen** (*irr.* brechen, *sep.*, -ge-) **1.** *v/t.* (*h*) break off (*a. fig.*); pull down, demolish (*building, etc.*); strike (*tent*); *fig.* stop; *das Lager* ~ break up camp, strike tents; **2.** *v/i.* (*sein*) break off; **3.** *fig. v/i.* (*h*) stop; '**⁀bremsen** *v/t. and v/i.* (*sep.*, -ge-, *h*) slow down; brake; '**⁀brennen** (*irr.* brennen, *sep.*, -ge-) **1.** *v/t.* (*h*) burn down (*building, etc.*); let *or* set off (*firework*); **2.** *v/i.* (*sein*) burn away *or* down; *s. abgebrannt*; '**⁀bringen** *v/t.* (*irr.* bringen, *sep.*, -ge-, *h*) get off; *j-n* ~ *von* argue s.o. out of; dissuade s.o. from; '**⁀bröckeln** *v/i.* (*sep.*, -ge-, *sein*) crumble (*a.* ✝).

'Abbruch *m* pulling down, demolition (*of building, etc.*); rupture (*of relations*); breaking off (*of negotiations, etc.*); *fig.* damage, injury; j-m ~ tun damage s.o.

'**ab|brühen** *v/t.* (*sep.*, -ge-, h) scald; *s.* abgebrüht; '**~bürsten** *v/t.* (*sep.*, -ge-, h) brush off (*dirt, etc.*); brush (*coat, etc.*); '**~büßen** *v/t.* (*sep.*, -ge-, h) expiate, atone for (*sin, etc.*); serve (*sentence*). [bet.]

Abc [a:be:'tse:] *n* (-/-) ABC, alphabet.

'**abdank|en** *v/i.* (*sep.*, -ge-, h) resign; *ruler:* abdicate; '**2ung** *f* (-/-en) resignation; abdication.

'**ab|decken** *v/t.* (*sep.*, -ge-, h) uncover; untile (*roof*); unroof (*building*); clear (*table*); cover; '**~dichten** *v/t.* (*sep.*, -ge-, h) make tight; seal up (*window, etc.*); ⊕ pack (*gland, etc.*); '**~dienen** *v/t.* (*sep.*, -ge-, h): s-e Zeit ~ ✗ serve one's time; '**~drängen** *v/t.* (*sep.*, -ge-, h) push aside; '**~drehen** (*sep.*, -ge-, h) **1.** *v/t.* twist off (*wire*); turn off (*water, gas, etc.*); ✗ switch off (*light*); **2.** ⚓, ✗ *v/i.* change one's course; '**~drosseln** *mot. v/t.* (*sep.*, -ge-, h) throttle.

'**Abdruck** *m* (-[e]s/⁻e) impression, print, mark; cast; '**2en** *v/t.* (*sep.*, -ge-, h) print; publish (*article*).

'**abdrücken** (*sep.*, -ge-, h) **1.** *v/t.* fire (*gun, etc.*); F hug *or* squeeze affectionately; *sich* ~ leave an impression *or* a mark; **2.** *v/i.* pull the trigger.

Abend ['a:bənt] *m* (-s/-e) evening; am ~ in the evening, at night; heute abend tonight; morgen (gestern) abend tomorrow (last) night; *s.* essen; '**~anzug** *m* evening dress; '**~blatt** *n* evening paper; '**~brot** *n* supper, dinner; '**~dämmerung** *f* (evening) twilight, dusk; '**~essen** *n* s. Abendbrot; '**~gesellschaft** *f* evening party; '**~kasse** *thea. f* box-office; '**~kleid** *n* evening dress *or* gown; '**~land** *n* (-[e]s/*no pl.*) the Occident; **2ländisch** *adj.* ['~lɛndiʃ] western, occidental; '**~mahl** *eccl. n* (-[e]s/-e) the (Holy) Communion, the Lord's Supper; '**~rot** *n* evening *or* sunset glow.

abends *adv.* ['a:bənts] in the evening.

'**Abend|schule** *f* evening school, night-school; '**~sonne** *f* setting

sun; '**~toilette** *f* evening dress; '**~wind** *m* evening breeze; '**~zeitung** *f* evening paper.

Abenteu|er ['a:bəntɔyər] *n* (-s/-) adventure; '**2erlich** *adj.* adventurous; *fig.*: strange; wild, fantastic; '**~rer** ['~ɔyrər] *m* (-s/-) adventurer.

aber ['a:bər] **1.** *adv.* again; Tausende und ~ Tausende thousands upon thousands; **2.** *cj.* but; *oder* ~ otherwise, (or) else; **3.** *int.:* ~! now then!; ~, ~! come, come!; ~ nein! no!, on the contrary!; **4.** ♀ *n* (-s/-) but.

'**Aber|glaube** *m* superstition; **2gläubisch** *adj.* ['~ɡlɔybiʃ] superstitious.

aberkenn|en ['ap²-] *v/t.* (*irr.* kennen, *sep.*, *no* -ge-, h): j-m et. ~ deprive s.o. of s.th. (*a.* ⚖); dispossess s.o. of s.th.; '**2ung** *f* (-/-en) deprivation (*a.* ⚖); dispossession.

aber|malig *adj.* ['a:bərma:liç] repeated; '**~mals** *adv.* ['~s] again, once more.

'**ab|ernten** ['ap²-] *v/t.* (*sep.*, -ge-, h) reap, harvest; '**~essen** ['ap²-] (*irr.* essen, *sep.*, -ge-, h) **1.** *v/t.* clear (*plate*); **2.** *v/i.* finish eating; '**~fahren** (*irr.* fahren, *sep.*, -ge-) **1.** *v/i.* (sein) leave (nach for), depart (for), start (for); set out *or* off (for); **2.** *v/t.* (h) carry *or* cart away (*load*).

'**Abfahrt** *f* departure (nach for), start (for); setting out *or* off (for); *skiing:* downhill run; '**~sbahnsteig** *m* departure platform; '**~slauf** *m* *skiing:* downhill race; '**~ssignal** *n* starting-signal; '**~szeit** *f* time of departure; ⚓ *a.* time of sailing.

'**Abfall** *m* defection (von from), falling away (from); *esp. pol.* secession (from); *eccl.* apostasy (from); *often* Abfälle *pl.* waste, refuse, rubbish, *Am. a.* garbage; ⊕ clippings *pl.*, shavings *pl.*; *at butcher's:* offal; '**~eimer** *m* dust-bin, *Am.* ash can; '**2en** *v/i.* (*irr.* fallen, *sep.*, -ge-, sein) leaves, *etc.*: fall (off); ground, *etc.*: slope (down); *fig.* fall away (von from); *esp. pol.* secede (from); *eccl.* apostatize (from); ~ gegen come off badly by comparison with, be inferior to; '**~erzeugnis** *n* waste product; by-product.

'**abfällig** *adj.* judgement, *etc.*: adverse, unfavo(u)rable; *remark:* disparaging, depreciatory.

'Abfallprodukt n by-product; waste product.

'ab|fangen v/t. (irr. fangen, sep., -ge-, h) catch; snatch (ball, etc.); intercept (letter, etc.); △, ✗ prop; ✗ check (attack); ✗ flatten out; mot., ✗ right; **'∼färben** v/i. (sep., -ge-, h): der Pullover färbt ab the colo(u)r of the pull-over runs (auf acc. on); ∼ auf (acc.) influence, affect.

'abfass|en v/t. (sep., -ge-, h) compose, write, pen; catch (thief, etc.); **'2ung** f composition; wording.

'ab|faulen v/i. (sep., -ge-, sein) rot off; **'∼fegen** v/t. (sep., -ge-, h) sweep off; **'∼feilen** v/t. (sep., -ge-, h) file off.

abfertig|en ['apfɛrtigən] v/t. (sep., -ge-, h) dispatch (a. 🚂); customs: clear; serve, attend to (customer); j-n kurz ∼ snub s.o.; **'2ung** f (-/-en) dispatch; customs: clearance; schroffe ∼ snub.

'abfeuern v/t. (sep., -ge-, h) fire (off), discharge.

'abfind|en v/t. (irr. finden, sep., -ge-, h) satisfy, pay off (creditor); compensate; sich mit et. ∼ resign o.s. to s.th.; put up with s.th.; **'2ung** f (-/-en) settlement; satisfaction; compensation; **'2ung(ssumme)** f indemnity; compensation.

'ab|flachen v/t. and v/refl. (sep., -ge-, h) flatten; **'∼flauen** v/i. (sep., -ge-, sein) wind, etc.: abate; interest, etc.: flag; ✝ business: slacken; **'∼fliegen** v/i. (irr. fliegen, sep., -ge-, sein) leave by plane; ✗ take off, start; **'∼fließen** v/i. (irr. fließen, sep., -ge-, sein) drain or flow off or away.   [parture.]

'Abflug ✗ m take-off, start, de-[parture.]

'Abfluß m flowing or draining off or away; discharge (a. ✗); drain (a. fig.); sink; outlet (of lake, etc.).

'abfordern v/t. (sep., -ge-, h): j-m et. ∼ demand s.th. of or from s.o.

Abfuhr ['apfu:r] f (-/-en) removal; fig. rebuff.

'abführ|en (sep., -ge-, h) **1.** v/t. lead off or away; march (prisoner) off; pay over (money) (an acc. to); **2.** ✗ v/i. purge (the bowels), loosen the bowels; **'∼end** ✗ adj. purgative, aperient, laxative; **'2mittel** ✗ n purgative, aperient, laxative.

'abfüllen v/t. (sep., -ge-, h) decant;

in Flaschen ∼ bottle; Bier in Fässer ∼ rack casks with beer.

'Abgabe f sports: pass; casting (of one's vote); sale (of shares, etc.); mst ∼n pl. taxes pl.; rates pl., Am. local taxes pl.; duties pl.; **'2frei** adj. tax-free; duty-free; **'2npflichtig** adj. taxable; dutiable; liable to tax or duty.

'Abgang m departure; start; thea. exit (a. fig.); retirement (from a job); loss, wastage; deficiency (in weight, etc.); ✗ discharge; ✗ miscarriage; nach ∼ von der Schule after leaving school.

'abgängig adj. missing.

'Abgangszeugnis n (school-)leaving certificate, Am. a. diploma.

'Abgas n waste gas; esp. mot. exhaust gas.   [toil-worn, worn-out.]

abgearbeitet adj. ['apgə'arbaitət]]

'abgeben v/t. (irr. geben, sep., -ge-, h) leave (bei, an dat. at); hand in (paper, etc.); deposit, leave (luggage); cast (one's vote); sports: pass (ball, etc.); sell, dispose of (goods); give off (heat, etc.); e-e Erklärung ∼ make a statement; s-e Meinung ∼ express one's opinion (über acc. on); j-m et. ∼ von et. give s.o. some of s.th.; e-n guten Gelehrten ∼ make a good scholar; sich ∼ mit occupy o.s. with s.th.; sie gibt sich gern mit Kindern ab she loves to be among children.

'abge|brannt adj. burnt down; F fig. hard up, sl. broke; **∼brüht** fig. adj. ['∼bry:t] hardened, callous; **'∼droschen** adj. trite, hackneyed; **∼feimt** adj. ['∼faimt] cunning, crafty; **'∼griffen** adj. worn; book: well-thumbed; **∼härtet** adj. ['∼hertet] hardened (gegen to), inured (to); **∼härmt** adj. ['∼hermt] care-worn.

'abgehen (irr. gehen, sep., -ge-) **1.** v/i. (sein) go off or away; leave, start, depart; letter, etc.: be dispatched; post: go; thea. make one's exit; side-road: branch off; goods: sell; button, etc.: come off; stain, etc.: come out; ✗ be discharged; (von e-m Amt) ∼ give up a post; retire; von der Schule ∼ leave school; ∼ von digress from (main subject); deviate from (rule); alter, change (one's opinion); relinquish (plan, etc.); diese Eigenschaft geht ihm ab he lacks this quality; gut ∼ end well, pass off well; *hiervon geht or gehen ... ab* ✝ less, minus; **2.** *v/t.* (*h*) measure by steps; patrol.

abge|hetzt *adj.* ['apgəhetst] harassed; exhausted; run down; breathless; **~kartet** F *adj.* ['~kartət]: ~e *Sache* prearranged affair, put-up job; '**~legen** *adj.* remote, distant; secluded; out-of-the-way; **~macht** ['~maxt]: ~*l* it's a bargain *or* deal!; **~magert** *adj.* ['~ma:gərt] emaciated; **~neigt** *adj.* ['~naıkt] disinclined (*dat.* for *s.th.*; *zu tun to do*), averse (*to*; *from* doing), unwilling (*zu tun to do*); **~nutzt** *adj.* ['~nutst] worn-out.

Abgeordnete ['apgəʔordnətə] *m, f* (*-n/-n*) deputy, delegate; *in Germany*: member of the Bundestag *or* Landtag; *Brt.* Member of Parliament, *Am.* Representative.

'**abgerissen** *fig. adj.* ragged; shabby; *style, speech*: abrupt, broken.

'**Abgesandte** *m, f* (*-n/-n*) envoy; emissary; ambassador.

'**abgeschieden** *fig. adj.* isolated; secluded, retired; '**2heit** *f* (*-/-en*) seclusion; retirement.

'**abgeschlossen** *adj. flat*: self-contained; *training, etc.*: complete.

abgeschmackt *adj.* ['apgəʃmakt] tasteless; tactless; '**2heit** *f* (*-/-en*) tastelessness; tactlessness.

'**abgesehen** *adj.*: ~ *von* apart from, *Am. a.* aside from.

abge|spannt *fig. adj.* ['apgəʃpant] exhausted, tired, run down; '**~standen** *adj.* stale, flat; '**~storben** *adj.* numb; dead; **~stumpft** *adj.* ['~ʃtumpft] blunt(ed); *fig.* indifferent (*gegen* to); '**~tragen** *adj.* worn-out; threadbare, shabby.

'**abgewöhnen** *v/t.* (*sep.*, *-ge-*, *h*): *j-m et.* ~ break *or* cure s.o. of s.th.; *sich das Rauchen* ~ give up smoking.

abgezehrt *adj.* ['apgətse:rt] emaciated, wasted.

'**abgießen** *v/t.* (*irr. gießen*, *sep.*, *-ge-*, *h*) pour off; 🜍 decant; ⊕ cast.

'**Abglanz** *m* reflection (*a. fig.*).

'**abgleiten** *v/i.* (*irr. gleiten*, *sep.*, *-ge-*, *sein*) slip off; slide off; glide

Abgott *m* idol. [off.\]

abgöttisch *adv.* ['apgœtiʃ]: *j-n* ~ *lieben* idolize *or* worship s.o.; dote (up)on s.o.

'**ab|grasen** *v/t.* (*sep.*, *-ge-*, *h*) graze; *fig.* scour; '**~grenzen** *v/t.* (*sep.*,

-ge-, *h*) mark off, delimit; demarcate (*a. fig.*); *fig.* define.

'**Abgrund** *m* abyss; precipice; chasm, gulf; *am Rande des* ~*s* on the brink of disaster.

'**Abguß** *m* cast.

'**ab|hacken** *v/t.* (*sep.*, *-ge-*, *h*) chop *or* cut off; '**~haken** *fig. v/t.* (*sep.*, *-ge-*, *h*) tick *or* check off; '**~halten** *v/t.* (*irr. halten*, *sep.*, *-ge-*, *h*) hold (*meeting, examination, etc.*); keep out (*rain*); *j-n von der Arbeit* ~ keep s.o. from his work; *j-n davon* ~ *et. zu tun* keep *or* restrain s.o. from doing s.th.; *et. von j-m* ~ keep s.th. away from s.o.; '**~handeln** *v/t.* (*sep.*, *-ge-*, *h*) discuss; treat; *j-m et.* ~ bargain s.th. out of s.o.

abhanden *adv.* [ap'handən]: ~ *kommen* get lost.

'**Abhandlung** *f* treatise (*über acc.* [up]on), dissertation ([up]on, concerning); essay. [clivity.\]

'**Abhang** *m* slope, incline; de-\

'**abhängen 1.** *v/t.* (*sep.*, *-ge-*, *h*) take down (*picture, etc.*); 🚋 uncouple; **2.** *v/i.* (*irr. hängen*, *sep.*, *-ge-*, *h*): ~ *von* depend (up)on.

abhängig *adj.* ['aphεnıç]: ~ *von* dependent (up)on; '**2keit** *f* (*-/no pl.*) dependence (*von* [up]on).

ab|härmen ['aphεrmən] *v/refl.* (*sep.*, *-ge-*, *h*) pine away (*über acc.* at); '**~härten** *v/t.* (*sep.*, *-ge-*, *h*) harden (*gegen* to), inure (*to*); ~ harden o.s. (*gegen* to), inure o.s. (*to*); '**~hauen** (*irr. hauen*, *sep.*, *-ge-*) **1.** *v/t.* (*h*) cut *or* chop off; **2.** F *v/i.* (*sein*) be off; *hau ab! sl.* beat it!, scram!; '**~häuten** *v/t.* (*sep.*, *-ge-*, *h*) skin, flay; '**~heben** (*irr. heben*, *sep.*, *-ge-*, *h*) **1.** *v/t.* lift *or* take off; *teleph.* lift (*receiver*); (with)draw (*money*); *sich* ~ *von* stand out against; *fig. a.* contrast with; **2.** *v/i.* cut (the cards); *teleph.* lift the receiver; '**~heilen** *v/i.* (*sep.*, *-ge-*, *sein*) heal (up); '**~helfen** *v/i.* (*irr. helfen*, *sep.*, *-ge-*, *h*): *e-m Übel* ~ cure *or* redress an evil; *dem ist nicht abzuhelfen* there is nothing to be done about it; '**~hetzen** *v/refl.* (*sep.*, *-ge-*, *h*) tire o.s. out; rush, hurry.

'**Abhilfe** *f* remedy, redress, relief; ~ *schaffen* take remedial measures.

'**abhobeln** *v/t.* (*sep.*, *-ge-*, *h*) plane (away, down).

abhold *adj.* [ˈaphɔlt] averse (*dat.* to *s.th.*); ill-disposed (towards *s.o.*).

'**ab|holen** *v/t.* (*sep.*, -ge-, h) fetch; call for, come for; *j-n von der Bahn* ~ go to meet s.o. at the station; '~**holzen** *v/t.* (*sep.*, -ge-, h) fell, cut down (*trees*); deforest; '~**horchen** *⚕ v/t.* (*sep.*, -ge-, h) auscultate, sound; '~**hören** *v/t.* (*sep.*, -ge-, h) listen in to, intercept (*telephone conversation*); *e-n Schüler* ~ hear a pupil's lesson.

Abitur [abiˈtuːr] *n* (-s/⚕-e) school-leaving examination (*qualifying for university entrance*).

'**ab|jagen** *v/t.* (*sep.*, -ge-, h): *j-m et.* ~ recover s.th. from s.o.; '~**kanzeln** F *v/t.* (*sep.*, -ge-, h) reprimand, F tell s.o. off; '~**kaufen** *v/t.* (*sep.*, -ge-, h): *j-m et.* ~ buy *or* purchase s.th. from s.o.

Abkehr *fig.* [ˈapkeːr] *f* (-/*no pl.*) estrangement (*von* from); withdrawal (from); '**2en** *v/t.* (*sep.*, -ge-, h) sweep off; *sich* ~ *von* turn away from; *fig.*: take no further interest in; become estranged from; withdraw from.

'**ab|klingen** *v/i.* (*irr.* klingen, *sep.*, -ge-, sein) fade away; *pain, etc.*: die down; *pain, illness*: ease off; '~**klopfen** *v/t.* (*sep.*, -ge-, h) **1.** *v/t.* knock (*dust, etc.*) off; dust (*coat, etc.*); *⚕* sound, percuss; **2.** *v/t.* *conductor*: stop the orchestra; '~**knicken** *v/t.* (*sep.*, -ge-, h) snap *or* break off; bend off; '~**knöpfen** *v/t.* (*sep.*, -ge-, h) unbutton; F *j-m Geld* ~ get money out of s.o.; '~**kochen** *v/t.* (*sep.*, -ge-, h) **1.** boil; scald (*milk*); **2.** *v/i.* cook in the open air (*a.* ⚒); '~**kommandieren** ⚔ *v/t.* (*sep.*, *no* -ge-, h) detach, detail; second (*officer*).

Abkomme [ˈapkɔmə] *m* (-n/-n) descendant.

'**abkommen 1.** *v/i.* (*irr.* kommen, *sep.*, -ge-, sein) come away, get away *or* off; *von e-r Ansicht* ~ change one's opinion; *von e-m Thema* ~ digress from a topic; *vom Wege* ~ lose one's way; **2.** **2** *n* (-s/-) agreement.

abkömm|lich *adj.* [ˈapkœmliç] dispensable; available; *er ist nicht* ~ he cannot be spared; **2ling** [ˈ~liŋ] *m* (-s/-e) descendant.

'**ab|koppeln** *v/t.* (*sep.*, -ge-, h) un-couple; '~**kratzen** (*sep.*, -ge-) **1.** *v/t.* (h) scrape off; **2.** *sl. v/i.* (sein) kick the bucket; '~**kühlen** *v/t.* (*sep.*, -ge-, h) cool; refrigerate; *sich* ~ cool down (*a. fig.*).

Abkunft [ˈapkunft] *f* (-/⚕-e) descent; origin, extraction; birth.

'**abkürz|en** *v/t.* (*sep.*, -ge-, h) shorten, abbreviate (*word, story, etc.*); *den Weg* ~ take a short cut; '**2ung** *f* (-/-en) abridgement; abbreviation; short cut.

'**abladen** *v/t.* (*irr.* laden, *sep.*, -ge-, h) unload; dump (*rubbish, etc.*).

'**Ablage** *f* place of deposit; filing tray; files *pl.*; cloak-room.

'**ab|lagern** (*sep.*, -ge-) **1.** *v/t.* (h) season (*wood, wine*); age (*wine*); *sich* ~ settle; be deposited; **2.** *v/i.* (sein) *wood, wine*: season; *wine*: age; '~**lassen** (*irr.* lassen, *sep.*, -ge-, h) **1.** *v/t.* let (*liquid*) run off; let off (*steam*); drain (*pond, etc.*); **2.** *v/i.* leave off (*von et.* [*doing*] s.th.).

'**Ablauf** *m* running off; outlet, drain; *sports*: start; *fig.* expiration, end; *nach* ~ *von* at the end of; '**2en** (*irr.* laufen, *sep.*, -ge-) **1.** *v/i.* (sein) run off; drain off; *period of time*: expire; † *bill of exchange*: fall due; *clock, etc.*: run down; *thread, film*: unwind; *spool*: run out; *gut* ~ end well; **2.** *v/t.* (h) wear out (*shoes*); scour (*region, etc.*); *sich die Beine* ~ run one's legs off; *s.* Rang.

'**Ableben** *n* (-s/ *no pl.*) death, decease (⚖, ⚖); ⚖ demise.

'**ab|lecken** *v/t.* (*sep.*, -ge-, h) lick (off); '~**legen** (*sep.*, -ge-, h) **1.** *v/t.* take off (*garments*); leave off (*garments*); give up, break o.s. of (*habit*); file (*documents, letters, etc.*); make (*confession, vow*); take (*oath, examination*); *Zeugnis* ~ bear witness (*für* to; *von* of); *s.* Rechenschaft; **2.** *v/i.* take off one's (hat and) coat.

'**Ableger** ⚘ *m* (-s/-) layer, shoot.

'**ablehn|en** (*sep.*, -ge-, h) **1.** *v/t.* decline, refuse; reject (*doctrine, candidate, etc.*); turn down (*proposal, etc.*); **2.** *v/i.* decline; *dankend* ~ decline with thanks; '~**end** *adj.* negative; '**2ung** *f* (-/-en) refusal; rejection.

'**ableit|en** *v/t.* (*sep.*, -ge-, h) divert (*river, etc.*); drain off *or* away (*water, etc.*); *gr.*, ⚗, *fig.* derive (*aus*, von from); *fig.* infer (from); **'₂ung** *f* diversion; drainage; *gr.,* Ⓐ derivation (*a. fig.*).

'ab|lenken *v/t.* (*sep.,* -ge-, h) turn aside; divert (*suspicion, a.*) (von from); *phys., etc.:* deflect (*rays, etc.*); *j-n von der Arbeit* ~ distract s.o. from his work; **'∼lesen** *v/t.* (*irr. lesen, sep.,* -ge-, h) read (*speech, etc.*); read (off) (*values from instruments*); **'∼leugnen** *v/t.* (*sep.,* -ge-, h) deny, disavow, disown.

'abliefer|n *v/t.* (*sep.,* -ge-, h) deliver; hand over; surrender; **'₂ung** *f* delivery.

'ablöschen *v/t.* (*sep.,* -ge-, h) blot (up) (*ink*); Ⓔ temper (*steel*).

'ablös|en *v/t.* (*sep.,* -ge-, h) detach; take off; ⚔, *etc.:* relieve; supersede (*predecessor in office*); discharge (*debt*); redeem (*obligation*); *sich* ~ come off; *fig.* alternate, take turns; **'₂ung** *f* detachment; ⚔, *etc.:* relief; *fig.* supersession; discharge; redemption.

'abmach|en *v/t.* (*sep.,* -ge-, h) remove, detach; *fig.* settle, arrange (*business, etc.*); agree (up)on (*price, etc.*); **'₂ung** *f* (-/-en) arrangement, settlement; agreement.

'abmager|n *v/i.* (*sep.,* -ge-, sein) lose flesh; grow lean *or* thin; **'₂ung** *f* (-/-en) emaciation.

'ab|mähen *v/t.* (*sep.,* -ge-, h) mow (off); **'∼malen** *v/t.* (*sep.,* -ge-, h) copy.

'Abmarsch *m* start; ⚔ marching off; **'₂ieren** *v/i.* (*sep., no* -ge-, sein) start; ⚔ march off.

'abmeld|en *v/t.* (*sep.,* -ge-, h): *j-n von der Schule* ~ give notice of the withdrawal of a pupil (from school); *sich polizeilich* ~ give notice to the police of one's departure (from town, *etc.*); **'₂ung** *f* notice of withdrawal; notice of departure.

'abmess|en *v/t.* (*irr. messen, sep.,* -ge-, h) measure; **'₂ung** *f* (-/-en) measurement.

'ab|montieren *v/t.* (*sep., no* -ge-, h) disassemble; dismantle, strip (*machinery*); remove (*tyre, etc.*); **'∼mühen** *v/refl.* (*sep.,* -ge-, h) drudge, toil; **'∼nagen** *v/t.* (*sep.,* -ge-, h) gnaw off; pick (*bone*).

Abnahme ['apnɑːmə] *f* (-/∼-n) taking off; removal; ⚕ amputation; † taking delivery; † purchase; †

sale; Ⓔ acceptance (*of machine, etc.*); administering (*of oath*); decrease, diminution; loss (*of weight*).

'abnehm|en (*irr. nehmen, sep.,* -ge-, h) **1.** *v/t.* take off; remove; *teleph.* lift (*receiver*); ⚕ amputate; gather (*fruit*); Ⓔ accept (*machine, etc.*); *j-m et.* ~ take s.th. from s.o.; † *a.* buy *or* purchase s.th. from s.o.; *j-m zuviel* ~ overcharge s.o.; **2.** *v/i.* decrease, diminish; decline; lose weight; *moon:* wane; *storm:* abate; *days:* grow shorter; **'₂er** † *m* (-s/-) buyer; customer; consumer.

'Abneigung *f* aversion (*gegen* to); disinclination (to); dislike (to, of, for); antipathy (against, to).

abnorm *adj.* [ap'nɔrm] abnormal; anomalous; exceptional; **₂i'tät** *f* (-/-en) abnormality; anomaly.

'abnötigen *v/t.* (*sep.,* -ge-, h): *j-m et.* ~ extort s.th. from s.o.

'ab|nutzen *v/t. and v/refl.* (*sep.,* -ge-, h), **'∼nützen** *v/t. and v/refl.* (*sep.,* -ge-, h) wear out; **'₂nutzung** *f,* **'₂nützung** *f* (-/-en) wear (and tear).

Abonn|ement [abɔn(ə)'mãː] *n* (-s/ -s) subscription (*auf acc.* to); **∼ent** [∼'nɛnt] *m* (-en/-en) subscriber; **₂ieren** [∼'niːrən] *v/t.* (*no* -ge-, h) subscribe to (*newspaper*); **₂iert** *adj.* [∼'niːrt]: ~ *sein auf* (*acc.*) take in (*newspaper, etc.*).

abordn|en ['ap⁹-] *v/t.* (*sep.,* -ge-, h) depute, delegate, *Am. a.* deputize; **'₂ung** *f* delegation, deputation.

Abort [a'bɔrt] *m* (-[e]s/-e) lavatory, toilet.

'ab|passen *v/t.* (*sep.,* -ge-, h) fit, adjust; watch for, wait for (*s.o., opportunity*); waylay *s.o.*; **'∼pflük-ken** *v/t.* (*sep.,* -ge-, h) pick, pluck (off), gather; **'∼plagen** *v/refl.* (*sep.,* -ge-, h) toil; **'∼platzen** *v/i.* (*sep.,* -ge-, sein) burst off; fly off; **'∼pral-len** *v/i.* (*sep.,* -ge-, sein) rebound, bounce (off); ricochet; **'∼putzen** *v/t.* (*sep.,* -ge-, h) clean (off, up); wipe off; polish; **'∼raten** *v/i.* (*irr. raten, sep.,* -ge-, h): *j-m* ~ *von* dissuade s.o. from, advise s.o. against; **'∼räumen** *v/t.* (*sep.,* -ge-, h) clear (away); **'∼reagieren** *v/t.* (*sep., no* -ge-, h) work off (*one's anger, etc.*); *sich* ~ F *a.* let off steam.

'abrechn|en (*sep.,* -ge-, h) **1.** *v/t.* deduct; settle (*account*); **2.** *v/i.:* mit *j-m* ~ settle with s.o.; *fig.* settle (accounts) with s.o., F get even with s.o.; '2**ung** f settlement (of accounts); deduction, discount.

'**Abrede** f: in ~ stellen deny or question s.th.

'**abreib**|**en** v/t. (irr. reiben, sep., -ge-, h) rub off; rub down (body); polish; '2**ung** f rub-down; F fig. beating.

'**Abreise** f departure (nach for); '2**n** v/i. (sep., -ge-, sein) depart (nach for), leave (for), start (for), set out (for).

'**abreiß**|**en** (irr. reißen, sep., -ge-) **1.** v/t. (h) tear or pull off; pull down (building); s. abgerissen; **2.** v/i. (sein) break off; button, etc.: come off; '2**kalender** m tear-off calendar.

'**ab**|**richten** v/t. (sep., -ge-, h) train (animal), break (horse) (in); '~**riegeln** v/t. (sep., -ge-, h) bolt, bar (door); block (road).

'**Abriß** m draft; summary, abstract; (brief) outlines pl.; brief survey.

'**ab**|**rollen** (sep., -ge-) v/t. (h) and v/i. (sein) unroll; uncoil; unwind, unreel; roll off; '~**rücken** (sep., -ge-) **1.** v/t. (h) move off or away (von from), remove; **2.** ✕ v/i. (sein) march off, withdraw.

'**Abruf** m call; recall; auf ~ ✝ on call; '2**en** v/t. (irr. rufen, sep., -ge-, h) call off (a. ✝), call away; recall; 📞 call out.

'**ab**|**runden** v/t. (sep., -ge-, h) round (off); '~**rupfen** v/t. (sep., -ge-, h) pluck off.

abrupt adj. [ap'rupt] abrupt.

'**abrüst**|**en** ✕ v/i. (sep., -ge-, h) disarm; '2**ung** ✕ f disarmament.

'**abrutschen** v/i. (sep., -ge-, sein) slip off, glide down; 🎿 skid.

'**Absage** f cancellation; refusal; '2**n** (sep., -ge-, h) **1.** v/t. cancel, call off; refuse; recall (invitation); **2.** v/i. guest: decline; j-m ~ cancel one's appointment with s.o.

'**absägen** v/t. (sep., -ge-, h) saw off; F fig. sack s.o.

'**Absatz** m stop, pause; typ. paragraph; ✝ sale; heel (of shoe); landing (of stairs); '2**fähig** ✝ adj. saleable, marketable; '~**markt** ✝ m market, outlet; '~**möglichkeit** ✝ f opening, outlet.

'**abschaben** v/t. (sep., -ge-, h) scrape off.

'**abschaff**|**en** v/t. (sep., -ge-, h)

abolish; abrogate (law); dismiss (servants); '2**ung** f (-/-en) abolition; abrogation; dismissal.

'**ab**|**schälen** v/t. (sep., -ge-, h) peel (off), pare; bark (tree); '~**schalten** v/t. (sep., -ge-, h) switch off, turn off or out; ⚡ disconnect.

'**abschätz**|**en** v/t. (sep., -ge-, h) estimate; value; assess; '2**ung** f valuation; estimate; assessment.

'**Abschaum** m (-[e]s/no pl.) scum; fig. a. dregs pl.

'**Abscheu** m (-[e]s/no pl.) horror (vor dat. of), abhorrence (of); loathing (of); disgust (for).

'**abscheuern** v/t. (sep., -ge-, h) scour (off); wear out; chafe, abrade.

abscheulich adj. [ap'ʃɔʏlɪç] abominable, detestable, horrid; 2**keit** f (-/-en) detestableness; atrocity.

'**ab**|**schicken** v/t. (sep., -ge-, h) send off, dispatch; ✉ post, esp. Am. mail; '~**schieben** v/t. (irr. schieben, sep., -ge-, h) push or shove off.

Abschied ['apʃiːt] m (-[e]s/✕-e) departure; parting, leave-taking, farewell; dismissal, ✕ discharge; ~ nehmen take leave (von of), bid farewell (to); j-m den ~ geben dismiss s.o.; ✕ discharge s.o.; s-n ~ nehmen resign, retire; '~**feier** f farewell party; '~**sgesuch** n resignation.

'**ab**|**schießen** v/t. (irr. schießen, sep., -ge-, h) shoot off; shoot, discharge, fire (off) (fire-arm); launch (rocket); kill, shoot; (shoot or bring) down (aircraft); s. Vogel; '~**schinden** v/refl. (irr. schinden, sep., -ge-, h) toil and moil, slave, drudge; '~**schirmen** v/t. (sep., -ge-, h) shield (gegen from); screen (from), screen off (from); '~**schlachten** v/t. (sep., -ge-, h) slaughter, butcher.

'**Abschlag** ✝ m reduction (in price); auf ~ on account; 2**en** ['~ɡən] v/t. (irr. schlagen, sep., -ge-, h) knock off, beat off, strike off; cut off (head); refuse (request); repel (attack).

abschlägig adj. ['apʃlɛːgɪç] negative; ~e Antwort refusal, denial.

'**Abschlagszahlung** f payment on account; instal(l)ment.

'**abschleifen** v/t. (irr. schleifen, sep., -ge-, h) grind off; fig. refine, polish.

'**Abschlepp**|**dienst** mot. m towing service, Am. a. wrecking service;

'**Зen** v/t. (sep., -ge-, h) drag off; *mot.* tow off.

'**abschließen** (irr. schließen, sep., -ge-, h) **1.** v/t. lock (up); ⊕ seal (up); conclude (letter, etc.); settle (account); balance (the books); effect (insurance); contract (loan); fig. seclude, isolate; e-n Handel ~ strike a bargain; sich ~ seclude o.s.; **2.** v/i. conclude; '**_d 1.** adj. concluding; final; **2.** adv. in conclusion.

'**Abschluß** m settlement; conclusion; ⊕ seal; '**_prüfung** f final examination, finals pl., Am. a. graduation; '**_zeugnis** n leaving certificate; diploma.

'**ab|schmeicheln** v/t. (sep., -ge-, h): j-m et. ~ coax s.th. out of s.o.; '**_schmelzen** (irr. schmelzen, sep., -ge-) v/t. (h) and v/i. (sein) melt (off); ⊕ fuse; '**_schmieren** ⊕ v/t. (sep., -ge-, h) lubricate, grease; '**_schnallen** v/t. (sep., -ge-, h) unbuckle; take off (ski, etc.); '**_schneiden** (irr. schneiden, sep., -ge-, h) **1.** v/t. cut (off); slice off; den Weg ~ take a short cut; j-m das Wort ~ cut s.o. short; **2.** v/i.: gut ~ come out or off well.

'**Abschnitt** m ⚔ segment; † coupon; typ. section, paragraph; counterfoil, Am. a. stub (of cheque, etc.); stage (of journey); phase (of development); period (of time).

'**ab|schöpfen** v/t. (sep., -ge-, h) skim (off); '**_schrauben** v/t. (sep., -ge-, h) unscrew, screw off.

'**abschrecken** v/t. (sep., -ge-, h) deter (von from); scare away; '**_d** adj. deterrent; repulsive, forbidding.

'**abschreib|en** (irr. schreiben, sep., -ge-, h) **1.** v/t. copy; write off (debt, etc.); plagiarize; in school: crib; **2.** v/i. send a refusal; '**Зer** m copyist; plagiarist; '**Зung** † f (-/-en) depreciation.

'**abschreiten** v/t. (irr. schreiten, sep., -ge-, h) pace (off); e-e Ehrenwache ~ inspect a guard of hono(u)r.

'**Abschrift** f copy, duplicate.

'**abschürf|en** v/t. (sep., -ge-, h) graze, abrade (skin); '**Зung** f (-/-en) abrasion.

'**Abschuß** m discharge (of fire-arm); launching (of rocket); hunt. shooting; shooting down, downing (of aircraft); '**_rampe** f launching platform.

'**abschüssig** adj. ['apʃysiç] sloping; steep.

'**ab|schütteln** v/t. (sep., -ge-, h) shake off (a. fig.); fig. get rid of; '**_schwächen** v/t. (sep., -ge-, h) weaken, lessen, diminish; '**_schweifen** v/i. (sep., -ge-, sein) deviate; fig. digress; '**_schwenken** v/i. (sep., -ge-, sein) swerve; ✕ wheel; '**_schwören** v/i. (irr. schwören, sep., -ge-, h) abjure; forswear; '**_segeln** v/i. (sep., -ge-, sein) set sail, sail away.

'**abseh|bar** adj. ['apze:baːr]: in ~er Zeit in the not-too-distant future; '**_en** (irr. sehen, sep., -ge-, h) **1.** v/t. (fore)see; j-m et. ~ learn s.th. by observing s.o.; es abgesehen haben auf (acc.) have an eye on, be aiming at; **2.** v/i.: ~ von refrain from; disregard.

'**abseits** ['apzaɪts] **1.** adv. aside, apart; football, etc.: off side; **2.** prp. (gen.) aside from; off (the road).

'**absend|en** v/t. ([irr. senden,] sep., -ge-, h) send off, dispatch; ✉ post, esp. Am. mail; '**Зer** ✉ m sender.

'**absengen** v/t. (sep., -ge-, h) singe off.

'**Absenker** ♀ m (-s/-) layer, shoot.

'**absetz|en** (sep., -ge-, h) **1.** v/t. set or put down, deposit; deduct (sum); take off (hat); remove, dismiss (official); depose, dethrone (king); drop, put down (passenger); † sell (goods); typ. set up (in type); thea.: ein Stück ~ take off a play; **2.** v/i. break off, stop, pause; '**Зung** f (-/-en) deposition; removal, dismissal.

'**Absicht** f (-/-en) intention, purpose, design; '**Зlich 1.** adj. intentional; **2.** adv. on purpose.

'**absitzen** (irr. sitzen, sep., -ge-) **1.** v/i. (sein) rider: dismount; **2.** v/t. (h) serve (sentence), F do (time).

absolut adj. [apzo'luːt] absolute.

absolvieren [apzɔl'viːrən] v/t. (no -ge-, h) absolve; complete (studies); get through, graduate from (school).

'**absonder|n** v/t. (sep., -ge-, h) separate; ✎ secrete; sich ~ withdraw; '**Зung** f (-/-en) separation; ✎ secretion.

ab|sorbieren [apzɔr'biːrən] v/t. (no -ge-, h) absorb; '**_speisen** fig. v/t. (sep., -ge-, h) put s.o. off.

abspenstig adj. ['apʃpɛnstiç]: ~

machen entice away (*von* from).

'absperr|en *v/t.* (*sep.*, -*ge*-, *h*) lock; shut off; bar (*way*); block (*road*); turn off (*gas, etc.*); **'~hahn** *m* stop-cock.

'ab|spielen *v/t.* (*sep.*, -*ge*-, *h*) play (*record, etc.*); play back (*tape record-ing*); *sich* ~ happen, take place; **'~sprechen** *v/t.* (*irr. sprechen, sep.*, -*ge*-, *h*) deny; arrange, agree; **'~springen** *v/i.* (*irr. springen, sep.*, -*ge*-, *sein*) jump down *or* off; ⚓ jump, bale out, (*Am. only*) bail out; rebound.   [off.\

'Absprung *m* jump; *sports*: take-/

'abspülen *v/t.* (*sep.*, -*ge*-, *h*) wash up; rinse.

'abstamm|en *v/i.* (*sep.*, -*ge*-, *sein*) be descended; *gr.* be derived (*both*: *von* from); **'2ung** *f* (-/-en) descent; *gr.* derivation.

'Abstand *m* distance; interval; ~ compensation, indemnification; ~ *nehmen von* desist from.

ab|statten ['apʃtatən] *v/t.* (*sep.*, -*ge*-, *h*) *e-n Besuch* ~ pay a visit; *Dank* ~ return *or* render thanks; **'~stauben** *v/t.* (*sep.*, -*ge*-, *h*) dust.

'abstech|en (*irr. stechen, sep.*, -*ge*-, *h*) **1.** *v/t.* cut (*sods*); stick (*pig, sheep, etc.*); stab (*animal*); **2.** *v/i.* contrast (*von* with); **'2er** *m* (-*s*/-) excursion, trip; detour.

'ab|stecken *v/t.* (*sep.*, -*ge*-, *h*) unpin, undo; fit, pin (*dress*); *surv.* mark out; **'~stehen** *v/i.* (*irr. stehen, sep.*, -*ge*-, *h*) stand off; stick out, pro-trude; *s. abgestanden;* **'~steigen** *v/i.* (*irr. steigen, sep.*, -*ge*-, *sein*) descend; alight (*von* from) (*car-riage*); get off, dismount (from) (*horse*); put up (*in dat.* at) (*hotel*); **'~stellen** *v/t.* (*sep.*, -*ge*-, *h*) put down; stop, turn off (*gas, etc.*); park (*car*); *fig.* put an end to *s.th.*; **'~stempeln** *v/t.* (*sep.*, -*ge*-, *h*) stamp; **'~sterben** *v/i.* (*irr. sterben, sep.*, -*ge*-, *sein*) die off; *limb*: mor-tify.

Abstieg ['apʃtiːk] *m* (-[e]s/-e) de-scent; *fig.* decline.

abstimm|en (*sep.*, -*ge*-, *h*) **1.** *v/i.* vote; **2.** *v/t.* tune in (*radio*); *fig.*: harmonize; time; ♪ balance (*books*); **'2ung** *f* voting; vote; tuning.

Abstinenzler [apsti'nɛntslər] *m* (-*s*/-) teetotal(l)er.

'abstoppen (*sep.*, -*ge*-, *h*) **1.** *v/t.*

stop; slow down; *sports*: clock, time; **2.** *v/i.* stop.

'abstoßen *v/t.* (*irr. stoßen, sep.*, -*ge*-, *h*) knock off; push off; clear off (*goods*); *fig.* repel; *sich die Hör-ner* ~ sow one's wild oats; **'~d** *fig. adj.* repulsive.

abstrakt *adj.* [ap'strakt] abstract.

'ab|streichen *v/t.* (*irr. streichen, sep.*, -*ge*-, *h*) take *or* wipe off; **'~streifen** *v/t.* (*sep.*, -*ge*-, *h*) strip off; take *or* pull off (*glove, etc.*); slip off (*dress*); wipe (*shoes*); **'~strei-ten** *v/t.* (*irr. streiten, sep.*, -*ge*-, *h*) contest, dispute; deny.

'Abstrich *m* deduction, cut; ⚕ swab.

'ab|stufen *v/t.* (*sep.*, -*ge*-, *h*) gradu-ate; gradate; **'~stumpfen** (*sep.*, -*ge*-) **1.** *v/t.* (*h*) blunt; *fig.* dull (*mind*); **2.** *fig. v/i.* (*sein*) become dull.

'Absturz *m* fall; ⚓ crash.

'ab|stürzen *v/i.* (*sep.*, -*ge*-, *sein*) fall down; ⚓ crash; **'~suchen** *v/t.* (*sep.*, -*ge*-, *h*) search (*nach* for); scour *or* comb (*area*) (for).

absurd *adj.* [ap'zurt] absurd, pre-posterous.

Abszeß ⚕ [aps'tsɛs] *m* (*Abszesses/ Abszesse*) abscess.

Abt [apt] *m* (-[e]s/-e) abbot.

'abtakeln ⚓ *v/t.* (*sep.*, -*ge*-, *h*) unrig, dismantle, strip.

Abtei [ap'taɪ] *f* (-/-en) abbey.

Ab|'teil 🚇 *n* compartment; **2teilen** *v/t.* (*sep.*, -*ge*-, *h*) divide; △ par-tition off; **'~teilung** *f* division; **~'teilung** *f* department; ward (*of hospital*); compartment; ✕ detach-ment; **~'teilungsleiter** *m* head of a department.

'abtelegraphieren *v/i.* (*sep., no -ge-*, *h*) cancel a visit, *etc.* by telegram.

Äbtissin [ɛp'tɪsɪn] *f* (-/-nen) abbess.

'ab|töten *v/t.* (*sep.*, -*ge*-, *h*) destroy, kill (*bacteria, etc.*); **'~tragen** *v/t.* (*irr. tragen, sep.*, -*ge*-, *h*) carry off; pull down (*building*); wear out (*garment*); pay (*debt*).

abträglich *adj.* ['aptrɛːklɪç] injuri-ous, detrimental.

'abtreib|en (*irr. treiben, sep.*, -*ge*-) **1.** *v/t.* (*h*) drive away *or* off; *ein Kind* ~ procure abortion; **2.** ⚓, ✕ *v/i.* (*sein*) drift off; **'2ung** *f* (-/-en) abortion.

'abtrennen *v/t.* (*sep.*, -*ge*-, *h*) de-tach; separate; sever (*limbs, etc.*); take (*trimmings*) off (*dress*).

'abtret|en (irr. treten, sep., -ge-) 1. v/t. (h) wear down (heels); wear out (steps, etc.); fig. cede, transfer; 2. v/i. (sein) retire, withdraw; resign; thea. make one's exit; 'Qer m (-s/-) doormat; 'Qung f (-/-en) cession, transfer.

'ab|trocknen (sep., -ge-) 1. v/t. (h) dry (up); wipe (dry); sich ~ dry oneself, rub oneself down; 2. v/i. (sein) dry up, become dry; '~tropfen v/i. (sep., -ge-, sein) liquid: drip; dishes, vegetables: drain.

abtrünnig adj. ['aptrʏnɪç] unfaithful, disloyal; eccl. apostate; 2e ['~gə] m (-n/-n) deserter; eccl. apostate.

'ab|tun v/t. (irr. tun, sep., -ge-, h) take off; settle (matter); fig.: dispose of; dismiss; '~urteilen ['apʔ-] v/t. (sep., -ge-, h) pass sentence on s.o.; '~wägen v/t. ([irr. wägen,] sep., -ge-, h) weigh (out); fig. consider carefully; '~wälzen v/t. (sep., -ge-, h) roll away; fig. shift; '~wandeln v/t. (sep., -ge-, h) vary, modify; '~wandern v/i. (sep., -ge-, sein) wander away; migrate (von from).

'Abwandlung f modification, variation.

'abwarten (sep., -ge-, h) 1. v/t. wait for, await; s-e Zeit ~ bide one's time; 2. v/i. wait.

abwärts adv. ['apvɛrts] down, downward(s).

'abwaschen v/t. (irr. waschen, sep., -ge-, h) wash (off, away); bathe; sponge off; wash up (dishes, etc.).

'abwechseln (sep., -ge-, h) 1. v/t. vary; alternate; 2. v/i. vary; alternate; mit j-m ~ take turns; '~d adj. alternate.

'Abwechs(e)lung f (-/-en) change; alternation; variation; diversion; zur ~ for a change.

'Abweg m: auf ~e geraten go astray; 2ig adj. ['~gɪç] erroneous, wrong.

'Abwehr f defen|ce, Am. -se; warding off (of thrust, etc.); '~dienst ✗ m counter-espionage service; '2en v/t. (sep., -ge-, h) ward off; avert; repulse, repel, ward off (attack, enemy).

'abweich|en v/i. (irr. weichen, sep., -ge-, sein) deviate (von from), swerve (from); differ (from); compass-needle: deviate; '2ung f (-/-en) deviation; difference; deflexion, (Am. only) deflection.

'abweiden v/t. (sep., -ge-, h) graze.

'abweis|en v/t. (irr. weisen, sep., -ge-, h) refuse, reject; repel (a. ✗); rebuff; '~end adj. unfriendly, cool; '2ung f refusal, rejection; repulse (a. ✗); rebuff.

'ab|wenden v/t. ([irr. wenden,] sep., -ge-, h) turn away; avert (disaster, etc.); parry (thrust); sich ~ turn away (von from); '~werfen v/t. (irr. werfen, sep., -ge-, h) throw off; ✗ drop (bombs); shed, cast (skin, etc.); shed (leaves); yield (profit).

'abwert|en v/t. (sep., -ge-, h) devaluate; '2ung f devaluation.

abwesen|d adj. ['apvezənt] absent; '2heit f (-/✗ -en) absence.

'ab|wickeln v/t. (sep., -ge-, h) unwind, unreel, wind off; transact (business); '~wiegen v/t. (irr. wiegen, sep., -ge-, h) weigh (out) (goods); '~wischen v/t. (sep., -ge-, h) wipe (off); '~würgen v/t. (sep., -ge-, h) strangle, throttle, choke; mot. stall; '~zahlen v/t. (sep., -ge-, h) pay off; pay by instal(l)ments; '~zählen v/t. (sep., -ge-, h) count (out, over).

'Abzahlung f instal(l)ment, payment on account; '~sgeschäft n hire-purchase.

'abzapfen v/t. (sep., -ge-, h) tap, draw off.

'Abzehrung f (-/-en) wasting away, emaciation; ✗ consumption.

'Abzeichen n badge; ✗ marking.

'ab|zeichnen v/t. (sep., -ge-, h) copy, draw; mark off; initial; tick off; sich ~ gegen stand out against; '~ziehen (irr. ziehen, sep., -ge-) 1. v/t. (h) take off, remove; ⅄ subtract; strip (bed); bottle (wine); phot. print (film); typ. pull (proof); take out (key); das Fell ~ skin (animal); 2. v/i. (sein) go away; ✗ march off; smoke: escape; thunderstorm, clouds: move on.

'Abzug m departure; ✗ withdrawal, retreat; ⊕ drain; outlet; deduction (of sum); phot. print; typ. proof (-sheet).

abzüglich prp. (gen.) ['aptsy:klɪç] less, minus, deducting.

'Abzugsrohr n waste-pipe.

'abzweig|en ['aptsvaɪgən] (sep., -ge-) 1. v/t. (h) branch; divert (money); sich ~ branch off; 2. v/i. (sein) branch off; '2ung f (-/-en) branch; road-junction.

ach *int.* [ax] oh!, ah!, alas!; ~ *so!* oh, I see!

Achse ['aksə] *f* (-/-n) axis; ⊕: axle; shaft; axle(-tree) (*of carriage*); *auf der ~* on the move.

Achsel ['aksəl] *f* (-/-n) shoulder; *die ~n zucken* shrug one's shoulders; '~höhle *f* armpit.

acht¹ [axt] **1.** *adj.* eight; *in ~ Tagen* today week, this day week; *vor ~ Tagen* a week ago; **2.** ♀ *f* (-/-en) (figure) eight.

Acht² [~] *f* (-/*no pl.*) ban, outlawry; attention; *außer acht lassen* disregard; *sich in acht nehmen* be careful; be on one's guard (*vor j-m or et.* against s.o. *or* s.th.); look out (*for* s.o. *or* s.th.).

'**achtbar** *adj.* respectable.

'**achte** *adj.* eighth; ♀l ['~əl] *n* (-s/-) eighth (part).

'**achten** (*ge-, h*) **1.** *v/t.* respect, esteem; regard; **2.** *v/i.: ~ auf* (*acc.*) pay attention to; *achte auf meine Worte* mark *or* mind my words; *darauf ~, daß* see to it that, take care that.

ächten ['ɛçtən] *v/t.* (*ge-, h*) outlaw, proscribe; ban.

'**Achter** *m* (-s/-) *rowing:* eight.

achtfach *adj.* ['axtfax] eightfold.

'**achtgeben** *v/i.* (*irr. geben, sep., -ge-, h*) be careful; pay attention (*auf acc.* to); take care (of); *gib acht!* look *or* watch out!, be careful!

'**achtlos** *adj.* inattentive, careless, heedless.

Acht'stundentag *m* eight-hour day.

'**Achtung** *f* (-/*no pl.*) attention; respect, esteem, regard; ~*!* look out!, ✕ attention!; ~ *Stufe!* mind the step!; ♀svoll *adj.* respectful.

'**achtzehn** *adj.* eighteen; ~te *adj.* ['~tə] eighteenth.

achtzig *adj.* ['axtsiç] eighty; '~ste *adj.* eightieth.

ächzen ['ɛçtsən] *v/i.* (*ge-, h*) groan, moan.

Acker ['akər] *m* (-s/ᵘ) field; '~bau *m* agriculture; farming; ♀bau-treibend *adj.* agricultural, farming; '~geräte *n/pl.* farm implements *pl.*; '~land *n* arable land; ♀n *v/t. and v/i.* (*ge-, h*) plough, till, *Am.* plow.

addi|eren [a'di:rən] *v/t.* (*no -ge-, h*) add (up); ♀tion [adi'tsjo:n] *f* (-/-en) addition; adding up.

Adel ['a:dəl] *m* (-s/*no pl.*) nobility, aristocracy; '♀ig *adj.* noble; '♀n *v/t.* (*ge-, h*) ennoble (*a. fig.*); *Brt.* knight, raise to the peerage; '~s-stand *m* nobility; aristocracy; *Brt.* peerage.

Ader ['a:dər] *f* (-/-n) ✗, *wood, etc.:* vein; *anat.:* vein; artery; *zur ~ lassen* bleed.

adieu *int.* [a'djø:] good-bye, farewell, adieu, F cheerio.

Adjektiv *gr.* ['atjɛkti:f] *n* (-s/-e) adjective.

Adler *orn.* ['a:dlər] *m* (-s/-) eagle; '~nase *f* aquiline nose.

adlig *adj.* ['a:dliç] noble; ♀e ['~gə] *m* (-n/-n) nobleman, peer.

Admiral ⚓ [atmi'ra:l] *m* (-s/-e, ⁼e) admiral.

adopt|ieren [adɔp'ti:rən] *v/t.* (*no -ge-, h*) adopt; ♀ivkind [~'ti:f-] *n* adopted child.

Adressat [adrɛ'sa:t] *m* (-en/-en) addressee; consignee (*of goods*).

Adreßbuch [a'drɛs-] *n* directory.

Adress|e [a'drɛsə] *f* (-/-n) address; direction; *per ~* care of (*abbr.* c/o); ♀ieren [~'si:rən] *v/t.* (*no -ge-, h*) address, direct; ✝ consign; *falsch ~* misdirect.

adrett *adj.* [a'drɛt] smart, neat.

Adverb *gr.* [at'vɛrp] *n* (-s/-ien) adverb.

Affäre [a'fɛ:rə] *f* (-/-n) (love) affair; matter, business, incident. [key.\

Affe *zo.* ['afə] *m* (-n/-n) ape; mon-\

Affekt [a'fɛkt] *m* (-[e]s/-e) emotion; passion; ♀iert *adj.* [~'ti:rt] affected.

'**affig** F *adj.* foppish; affected; silly.

Afrikan|er [afri'ka:nər] *m* (-s/-) African; ♀isch *adj.* African.

After *anat.* ['aftər] *m* (-s/-) anus.

Agent [a'gɛnt] *m* (-en/-en) agent; broker; *pol.* (secret) agent; ~ur [~'tu:r] *f* (-/-en) agency.

aggressiv *adj.* [agrɛ'si:f] aggressive.

Agio ✝ ['a:ʒio] *n* (-s/*no pl.*) agio, premium.

Agitator [agi'ta:tɔr] *m* (-s/-en) agitator. [brooch.\

Agraffe [a'grafə] *f* (-/-n) clasp;\

agrarisch *adj.* [a'gra:riʃ] agrarian.

Ägypt|er [ɛ:'gyptər] *m* (-s/-) Egyptian; ♀isch *adj.* Egyptian.

ah *int.* [a:] ah!

aha *int.* [a'ha] aha!, I see!

Ahle ['a:lə] *f* (-/-n) awl, pricker; punch.

Ahn [ɑːn] *m* (-[e]s, -en/-en) ancestor; ~en *pl. a.* forefathers *pl.*

ähneln ['ɛːnəln] *v/i.* (ge-, h) be like, resemble.

ahnen ['ɑːnən] *v/t.* (ge-, h) have a presentiment of *or* that; suspect; divine.

ähnlich *adj.* ['ɛːnliç] like, resembling; similar (*dat.* to); *iro.*: *das sieht ihm* ~ that's just like him; **'2keit** *f* (-/-en) likeness, resemblance; similarity.

Ahnung ['ɑːnuŋ] *f* (-/-en) presentiment; foreboding; notion, idea; **'2slos** *adj.* unsuspecting; **'2svoll** *adj.* full of misgivings.

Ahorn ♀ ['ɑːhɔrn] *m* (-s/-e) maple (-tree).

Ähre ♀ ['ɛːrə] *f* (-/-n) ear, head; spike; ~n *lesen* glean.

Akademi|e [akadə'miː] *f* (-/-n) academy, society; ~ker [~'deːmikər] *m* (-s/-) university man, *esp. Am.* university graduate; **2sch** *adj.* [~'deːmiʃ] academic.

Akazie [a'kɑːtsjə] *f* (-/-n) acacia.

akklimatisieren [aklimati'ziːrən] *v/t. and v/refl.* (no -ge-, h) acclimatize, *Am.* acclimate.

Akkord [a'kɔrt] *m* (-[e]s/-e) ♪ chord; ✝: contract; agreement; composition; *im* ~ ✝ by the piece *or* job; ~arbeit *f* piece-work; ~arbeiter *m* piece-worker; ~lohn *m* piecewages *pl.*

akkredit|ieren [akredi'tiːrən] *v/t.* (no -ge-, h) accredit (*bei* to); **2iv** [~'tiːf] *n* (-s/-e) credentials *pl.*; ✝ letter of credit.

Akku F ⊕ ['aku] *m* (-s/-s), ~mulator [~mu'lɑːtɔr] *m* (-s/-en) accumulator, (storage-)battery.

Akkusativ *gr.* ['akuzatiːf] *m* (-s/-e) accusative (case). [acrobat.]

Akrobat [akro'bɑːt] *m* (-en/-en)

Akt [akt] *m* (-[e]s/-e) act(ion), deed; *thea.* act; *paint.* nude.

Akte ['aktə] *f* (-/-n) document, deed; file; ~n *pl.* records *pl.*, papers *pl.*; deeds *pl.*, documents *pl.*; files *pl.*; *zu den* ~n to be filed; *zu den* ~n *legen* file; '~ndeckel *m* folder; '~nmappe *f*, '~ntasche *f* portfolio; briefcase; '~nzeichen *n* reference *or* file number.

Aktie ✝ ['aktsjə] *f* (-/-n) share, *Am.* stock; ~n *besitzen* hold shares, *Am.* hold stock; '~nbesitz *m* share-

holdings *pl.*, *Am.* stockholdings *pl.*; '~ngesellschaft *f* *appr.* joint-stock company, *Am.* (stock) corporation; '~nkapital *n* share-capital, *Am.* capital stock.

Aktion [ak'tsjoːn] *f* (-/-en) action; activity; *pol., etc.*: campaign, drive; ⚔ operation; ~är [~'nɛːr] *m* (-s/-e) shareholder, *Am.* stockholder.

aktiv *adj.* [ak'tiːf] active.

Aktiv|a ✝ [ak'tiːva] *n/pl.* assets *pl.*; ~posten [~'tiːf-] *m* asset (*a. fig.*).

aktuell *adj.* [aktu'ɛl] current, present-day, up-to-date, topical.

Akust|ik [a'kustik] *f* (-/*no pl.*) acoustics *sg., pl.*; **2isch** *adj.* acoustic.

akut *adj.* [a'kuːt] acute.

Akzent [ak'tsɛnt] *m* (-[e]s/-e) accent; stress; **2uieren** [~u'iːrən] *v/t.* (no -ge-, h) accent(uate); stress.

Akzept ✝ [ak'tsɛpt] *n* (-[e]s/-e) acceptance; ~ant ✝ [~'tant] *m* (-en/-en) acceptor; **2ieren** [~'tiːrən] *v/t.* (no -ge-, h) accept.

Alarm [a'larm] *m* (-[e]s/-e) alarm; ~ *blasen or schlagen* ⚔ sound *or* give the alarm; ~bereitschaft *f*: *in* ~ *sein* stand by; **2ieren** [~'miːrən] *v/t.* (no -ge-, h) alarm.

Alaun 🜛 [a'laun] *m* (-[e]s/-e) alum.

albern *adj.* ['albərn] silly, foolish.

Album ['album] *n* (-s/*Alben*) album.

Alge ♀ ['algə] *f* (-/-n) alga, seaweed.

Algebra 🝡 ['algebra] *f* (-/*no pl.*) algebra.

Alibi 🝮 ['ɑːlibi] *n* (-s/-s) alibi.

Alimente 🝮 [ali'mɛntə] *pl.* alimony.

Alkohol ['alkohɔl] *m* (-s/-e) alcohol; **'2frei** *adj.* non-alcoholic, *esp. Am.* soft; ~es *Restaurant* temperance restaurant; ~iker [~'hoːlikər] *m* (-s/-) alcoholic; **2isch** *adj.* [~'hoːliʃ] alcoholic; '~schmuggler *m* liquor-smuggler, *Am.* bootlegger; '~verbot *n* prohibition; '~vergiftung *f* alcoholic poisoning.

all¹ [al] **1.** *pron.* all; ~e everybody; ~es *in* ~em on the whole; *vor* ~em first of all; **2.** *adj.* all; every, each; any; ~e *beide* both of them; *auf* ~e *Fälle* in any case, at all events; ~e *Tage* every day; ~e *zwei Minuten* every two minutes.

All² [~] *n* (-s/*no pl.*) the universe.

'alle F *adj.* all gone; ~ *werden* come to an end; *supplies, etc.*: run out.

Allee [a'leː] *f* (-/-n) avenue; (tree-lined) walk.

allein [a'laın] **1.** *adj.* alone; single; unassisted; **2.** *adv.* alone; only; **3.** *cj.* yet, only, but, however; 2**berechtigung** *f* exclusive right; 2**besitz** *m* exclusive possession; 2**herrscher** *m* absolute monarch, autocrat; dictator; **~ig** *adj.* only, exclusive, sole; 2**sein** *n* loneliness, solitariness, solitude; **~stehend** *adj.* p.: alone in the world; single; *building, etc.*: isolated, detached; 2**verkauf** *m* exclusive sale; monopoly; 2**vertreter** *m* sole representative *or* agent; 2**vertrieb** *m* sole distributors *pl.*

allemal *adv.* ['alə'mɑ:l] always; *ein für ~* once (and) for all.

'allen'falls *adv.* if need be; possibly, perhaps; at best.

allenthalben † *adv.* ['alənt'halbən] everywhere.

'aller'best 1. best ... of all, very best; **~dings** *adv.* ['~'dıŋs] indeed; to be sure; **~!** certainly!, *Am.* F sure!; **~'erst 1.** *adj.* first ... of all, very first; foremost; **2.** *adv.*: *zu ~* first of all.

Allergie ✹ [aler'gi:] *f* (-/-n) allergy.

'aller'hand *adj.* of all kinds *or* sorts; F *das ist ja ~!* F I say!; *sl.* that's the limit!; **'2'heiligen** *n* (-/*no pl.*) All Saints' Day; **~lei** *adj.* ['~'laı] of all kinds *or* sorts; '2'**lei** *n* (-s/-s) medley; **~'letzt 1.** *adj.* last of all, very last; latest (*news, fashion, etc.*); **2.** *adv.*: *zu ~* last of all; **'~'liebst 1.** *adj.* dearest of all; (most) lovely; **2.** *adv.*: *am ~en* best of all; **'~'meist 1.** *adj.* most; **2.** *adv.*: *am ~en* mostly, chiefly; **'~'nächst** *adj.* very next; **'~'neu(e)st** *adj.* the very latest; **'2'seelen** *n* (-/*no pl.*) All Souls' Day; **'~'seits** *adv.* on all sides; universally; **'~'wenigst** *adv.*: *am ~en* least of all.

'alle'samt *adv.* one and all, all together; **'~'zeit** *adv.* always, at all times, for ever.

'all'gegenwärtig *adj.* omnipresent, ubiquitous; **'~ge'mein 1.** *adj.* general; common; universal; **2.** *adv.*: *im ~en* in general, generally; **'2ge-meinheit** *f* (-/*no pl.*) generality; universality; general public; 2'**heilmittel** *n* panacea, cure-all (*both a. fig.*).

Allianz [ali'ants] *f* (-/-en) alliance.

alli'ier|en *v/refl.* (*no* -ge-, *h*) ally

o.s. (*mit* to, with); 2**te** *m* (-n/-n) ally.

'all|'jährlich 1. *adj.* annual; **2.** *adv.* annually, every year; '2**macht** *f* (-/*no pl.*) omnipotence; **~'mächtig** *adj.* omnipotent, almighty; **~mählich** [~'mɛ:lıç] **1.** *adj.* gradual; **2.** *adv.* gradually, by degrees.

Allopathie ✦ [alopa'ti:] allopathy.

all|'seitig *adj.* universal; all-round; '2**strom** ⚡ *m* (-[e]s/*no pl.*) alternating current/direct current (*abbr.* A.C./D.C.); '2**tag** *m* workday; week-day; *fig.* everyday life, daily routine; **~'täglich** *adj.* daily; *fig.* common, trivial; '2**tags-leben** *n* (-s/*no pl.*) everyday life; **~'wissend** *adj.* omniscient; '2'**wissenheit** *f* (-/*no pl.*) omniscience; **~'wöchentlich** *adj.* weekly; **~zu** *adv.* (much) too; **'~zu'viel** *adv.* too much. [alp.]

Alm [alm] *f* (-/-en) Alpine pasture.

Almosen ['almo:zən] *n* (-s/-) alms; ~ *pl.* alms *pl.*, charity.

Alp|druck ['alp-] *m* (-[e]s/⸚e), **'~drücken** *n* (-s/*no pl.*) nightmare.

Alpen ['alpən] *pl.* Alps *pl.*

Alphabet [alfa'be:t] *n* (-[e]s/-e) alphabet; **2isch** *adj.* alphabetic(al).

'Alptraum *m* nightmare.

als [als] *cj.* than; as, like; (in one's capacity) as; but, except; *temporal*: after, when; as; ~ *ob* as if, as though; *so viel ~* as much as; *er ist zu dumm, ~ daß er es verstehen könnte* he is too stupid to understand it; **~'bald** *adv.* immediately; **~'dann** *adv.* then.

also ['alzo:] **1.** *adv.* thus, so; **2.** *cj.* therefore, so, consequently; *na ~!* there you are!

alt¹ *adj.* [alt] old; aged; ancient; antique; stale; second-hand.

Alt² ♪ [~] *m* (-s/-e) alto, contralto.

Altar [al'ta:r] *m* (-[e]s/⸚e) altar.

Alteisen ['alt²-] *n* scrap-iron.

'Alte (-n/-n) **1.** *m* old man; F: *der ~* the governor; *hist.*: *die ~n pl.* the ancients *pl.*; **2.** *f* old woman.

'Alter *n* (-s/-) age; old age; seniority; *er ist in meinem ~* is my age; *von mittlerem ~* middle-aged.

älter *adj.* ['ɛltər] older; senior; *der ~e Bruder* the elder brother.

altern ['altərn] *v/i.* (ge-, *h*, *sein*) grow old, age.

Alternative [alterna'ti:və] f (-/-n) alternative; *keine ~ haben* have no choice.

'**Alters|grenze** f age-limit; retirement age; '**~heim** n old people's home; '**~rente** f old-age pension; '2**schwach** adj. decrepit; senile; '**~schwäche** f decrepitude; '**~versorgung** f old-age pension.

Altertum ['altərtu:m] n **1.** (-/no pl.) antiquity; **2.** (-s/-er) mst Altertümer pl. antiquities pl.

altertümlich adj. ['altərty:mliç] ancient, antique, archaic.

'**Altertums|forscher** m arch(a)eologist; '**~kunde** f arch(a)eology.

ältest adj. ['eltəst] oldest; eldest (*sister, etc.*); earliest (*recollections*); '2**e** m (-n/-n) elder; senior; *mein ~r* my eldest (son).

Altistin ♪ [al'tistin] f (-/-nen) alto-singer, contralto-singer.

'**altklug** adj. precocious, forward.

ältlich adj. ['eltliç] elderly, oldish.

'**Alt|material** n junk, scrap; salvage; '**~meister** m doyen, dean, F Grand Old Man (*a. sports*); *sports*: ex-champion; '2**modisch** adj. old-fashioned; '**~papier** n waste paper; '**~philologe** m classical philologist *or* scholar; '**~stadt** f old town *or* city; '**~warenhändler** m second-hand dealer; '**~weibersommer** m Indian summer; gossamer.

Aluminium 🜊 [alu'mi:njum] n (-s/no pl.) aluminium, *Am.* aluminum.

am prp. [am] = *an dem.*

Amateur [ama'tø:r] m (-s/-e) amateur. [*bosse*) anvil.]

Amboß ['ambɔs] m (Ambosses/Am-)

ambulan|t ♮ adj. [ambu'lant]: ~ *Behandelter* out-patient; 2**z** [~ts] f (-/-en) ambulance.

Ameise zo. ['a:maizə] f (-/-n) ant; '**~nhaufen** m ant-hill.

Amerikan|er [ameri'ka:nər] m (-s/-), **~erin** f (-/-nen) American; 2**isch** adj. American.

Amme ['amə] f (-/-n) (wet-)nurse.

Amnestie [amnɛs'ti:] f (-/-n) amnesty, general pardon.

Amor ['a:mɔr] m (-s/no pl.) Cupid.

Amortis|ation [amɔrtiza'tsjo:n] f (-/-en) amortization, redemption; 2**ieren** [~'zi:rən] v/t. (no -ge-, h) amortize, redeem; pay off.

Ampel ['ampəl] f (-/-n) hanging lamp; traffic light.

Amphibie zo. [am'fi:bjə] f (-/-n) amphibian.

Ampulle [am'pulə] f (-/-n) ampoule.

Amput|ation ♮ [amputa'tsjo:n] f (-/-en) amputation; 2**ieren** ♮ [~'ti:rən] v/t. (no -ge-, h) amputate; **~ierte** m (-n/-n) amputee. [bird.]

Amsel orn. ['amzəl] f (-/-n) black-)

Amt [amt] n (-[e]s/-er) office; post; charge; office, board; official duty, function; (telephone) exchange; 2**ieren** [~'ti:rən] v/i. (no -ge-, h) hold office; officiate; '2**lich** adj. official; '**~mann** m district administrator; *hist.* bailiff.

'**Amts|arzt** m medical officer of health; '**~befugnis** f competence, authority; '**~bereich** m jurisdiction; '**~bezirk** m jurisdiction; '**~blatt** n gazette; '**~eid** m oath of office; '**~einführung** f inauguration; '2**führung** f administration; '**~geheimnis** n official secret; '**~gericht** n appr. district court; '**~geschäfte** n/pl. official duties pl.; '**~gewalt** f (official) authority; '**~handlung** f official act; '**~niederlegung** f(-/-en) resignation; '**~richter** m appr. district court judge; '**~siegel** n official seal; '**~vorsteher** m head official.

Amulett [amu'lɛt] n (-[e]s/-e) amulet, charm.

amüs|ant adj. [amy'zant] amusing, entertaining; **~ieren** [~'zi:rən] v/t. (no -ge-, h) amuse, entertain; *sich ~* amuse *or* enjoy o.s., have a good time.

an [an] **1.** prp. (dat.) at; on, upon; in; against; to; by, near, close to; ~ *der Themse* on the Thames; ~ *der Wand* on *or* against the wall; *es ist* ~ *dir zu inf.* it is up to you to inf.; *am Leben* alive; *am 1. März* on March 1st; *am Morgen* in the morning; **2.** prp. (acc.) to; on; on to; at; against; about; *bis* ~ as far as, up to; **3.** adv. on; *von heute* ~ from this day forth, from today; *von nun or jetzt* ~ from now on.

analog adj. [ana'lo:k] analogous (dat. or zu to, with).

Analphabet [an(?)alfa'be:t] m (-en/-en) illiterate (person).

Analys|e [ana'ly:zə] f (-/-n) analysis; 2**ieren** [~'zi:rən] v/t. (no -ge-, h) analy|se, *Am.* -ze.

Anämie 🐟 [anɛˈmiː] f (-/-) an(a)e-
mia.

Ananas [ˈananas] f (-/-, -se) pine-
apple.

Anarchie [anarˈçiː] f (-/-n) anarchy.

Anatom|ie [anatoˈmiː] f (-/no pl.)
anatomy; **ℒisch** adj. [~ˈtoːmiʃ]
anatomical.

'anbahnen v/t. (sep., -ge-, h) pave
the way for, initiate; open up; **sich
~** be opening up.

'Anbau m 1. ✔ (-[e]s/no pl.) cultivation; 2. △ (-[e]s/-ten) outbuilding,
annex, extension, addition; **ℒen**
v/t. (sep., -ge-, h) ✔ cultivate, grow;
△ add (an acc. to); **'~fläche** ✔ f
arable land.

'anbehalten v/t. (irr. halten, sep., no
-ge-, h) keep (garment, etc.) on.

an'bei ✝ adv. enclosed.

'an|beißen (irr. beißen, sep., -ge-, h)
1. v/t. bite into; 2. v/i. fish: bite;
'~bellen v/t. (sep., -ge-, h) bark at;
~beraumen [ˈ~bərauˌmən] v/t.
(sep., no -ge-, h) appoint, fix; **'~be-
ten** v/t. (sep., -ge-, h) adore, worship.

'Anbetracht m: in ~ considering, in
consideration of.

'anbetteln v/t. (sep., -ge-, h) beg
from, solicit alms of.

'Anbetung f (-/⅍-en) worship,
adoration; **ℒswürdig** adj. adorable.

'an|bieten v/t. (irr. bieten, sep.,
-ge-, h) offer; **'~binden** v/t. (irr.
binden, sep., -ge-, h) bind, tie (up);
~ an (dat., acc.) tie to; s. angebunden; **'~blasen** v/t. (irr. blasen, sep.,
-ge-, h) blow at or (up)on.

'Anblick m look; view; sight, aspect; **ℒen** v/t. (sep., -ge-, h) look
at; glance at; view; eye.

'an|blinzeln v/t. (sep., -ge-, h) wink
at; **'~brechen** (irr. brechen, sep.,
-ge-) 1. v/t. (h) break into (provisions, etc.); open (bottle, etc.); 2. v/i.
(sein) begin; day: break, dawn;
'~brennen (irr. brennen, sep., -ge-)
1. v/t. (h) set on fire; light (cigar,
etc.); 2. v/i. (sein) catch fire; burn;
'~bringen v/t. (irr. bringen, sep.,
-ge-, h) bring; fix (an dat. to), attach (to); place; ✝ dispose of
(goods); lodge (complaint); s. ange-
bracht.

'Anbruch m (-[e]s/no pl.) beginning; break (of day).

'anbrüllen v/t. (sep., -ge-, h) roar at.

Andacht ['andaxt] f (-/-en) devo-
tion(s pl.); prayers pl.

andächtig adj. ['andɛçtiç] devout.

'andauern v/i. (sep., -ge-, h) last,
continue, go on.

'Andenken n (-s/-) memory, remembrance; keepsake, souvenir;
zum ~ an (acc.) in memory of.

ander adj. ['andər] other; different; next; opposite; am ~en Tag
(on) the next day; e-n Tag um den
~en every other day; ein ~er Freund
another friend; nichts ~es nothing
else.

andererseits adv. ['andərər'zaits]
on the other hand.

ändern ['endərn] v/t. (ge-, h) alter;
change; ich kann es nicht ~ I can't
help it; sich ~ alter; change.

'andern'falls adv. otherwise, else.

anders adv. ['andərs] otherwise;
differently (als from); else; j. ~
somebody else; ich kann nicht ~,
ich muß weinen I cannot help crying; ~ werden change.

'ander'seits adv. s. andererseits.

'anders'wo adv. elsewhere.

anderthalb adj. ['andərt'halp] one
and a half.   [tion.]

'Änderung f (-/-en) change, altera-

ander|wärts adv. ['andər'verts]
elsewhere; **'~weitig** 1. adj. other;
2. adv. otherwise.

'andeut|en v/t. (sep., -ge-, h) indi-
cate; hint; intimate; imply; suggest; **ℒung** f intimation; hint;
suggestion.

'Andrang m rush; 🐟 congestion.

andre adj. ['andrə] s. andere.

'andrehen v/t. (sep., -ge-, h) turn
on (gas, etc.); ⚡ switch on (light).

'androh|en v/t. (sep., -ge-, h): j-m
et. ~ threaten s.o. with s.th.; **ℒung**
f threat.

aneignen ['anʔ-] v/refl. (sep., -ge-,
h) appropriate; acquire; adopt;
seize; usurp.

aneinander adv. [anʔai'nandər] together; **~geraten** v/i. (irr. raten,
sep., no -ge-, sein) clash (mit with).

anekeln ['anʔ-] v/t. (sep., -ge-, h)
disgust, sicken.

Anerbieten ['anʔ-] n (-s/-) offer.

anerkannt adj. ['anʔ-] acknowledged, recognized.

anerkenn|en ['anʔ-] v/t. (irr. ken-
nen, sep., no -ge-, h) acknowledge
(als as), recognize; appreciate; own

(*child*); hono(u)r (*bill*); '**Qung** f (-/-en) acknowledgement; recognition; appreciation.

'**anfahr|en** (*irr. fahren, sep., -ge-*) **1.** v/i. (sein) start; ✗ descend; *angefahren kommen* drive up; **2.** v/t. (h) run into; carry, convey; *j-n ~* let fly at s.o.; '**Qt** f approach; drive.

'**Anfall** ✗ m fit, attack; '**Qen** (*irr. fallen, sep., -ge-*) **1.** v/t. (h) attack; assail; **2.** v/i. (sein) accumulate; *money*: accrue.

anfällig adj. ['anfeliç] susceptible (*für* to); prone to (*diseases, etc.*).

'**Anfang** m beginning, start, commencement; ~ *Mai* at the beginning of May, early in May; '**Qen** v/t. *and* v/i. (*irr. fangen, sep., -ge-, h*) begin, start, commence.

Anfäng|er ['anfeŋər] m (-s/-) beginner; '**Qlich 1.** adj. initial; **2.** adv. in the beginning.

anfangs adv. ['anfaŋs] in the beginning; '**Qbuchstabe** m initial (letter); *großer ~* capital letter; '**Qgründe** ['~gryndə] m/pl. elements pl.

'**anfassen** (*sep., -ge-, h*) **1.** v/t. seize; touch; handle; **2.** v/i. lend a hand.

anfecht|bar adj. ['anfeçtbaːr] contestable; '**~en** v/t. (*irr. fechten, sep., -ge-, h*) contest, dispute; ⚖ avoid (*contract*); '**Qung** f (-/-en) contestation; ⚖ avoidance; *fig.* temptation.

an|fertigen ['anfertiɡən] v/t. (*sep., -ge-, h*) make, manufacture; '**~feuchten** v/t. (*sep., -ge-, h*) moisten, wet, damp; '**~feuern** v/t. (*sep., -ge-, h*) fire, heat; *sports:* cheer; *fig.* encourage; '**~flehen** v/t. (*sep., -ge-, h*) implore; '**~fliegen** ✗ v/t. (*irr. fliegen, sep., -ge-, h*) approach, head for (*airport, etc.*); '**Qflug** ✗ m approach (flight); *fig.* touch, tinge.

'**anforder|n** v/t. (*sep., -ge-, h*) demand; request; claim; '**Qung** f demand; request; claim.

'**Anfrage** f inquiry; '**Qn** v/i. (*sep., -ge-, h*) ask (*bei* j-m) inquire (*bei* j-m *nach et.* of s.o. about s.th.).

an|freunden ['anfrɔyndən] v/refl. (*sep., -ge-, h*): *sich ~ mit* make friends with; '**~frieren** v/i. (*irr. frieren, sep., -ge-, sein*) freeze on (*an dat. or acc.* to); '**~fügen** v/t. (*sep., -ge-, h*) join, attach (*an acc.* to); '**~fühlen** v/t. (*sep., -ge-, h*) feel, touch; *sich ~ feel*.

Anfuhr ['anfuːr] f (-/-en) conveyance, carriage.

'**anführ|en** v/t. (*sep., -ge-, h*) lead; allege; ✗ command; quote, cite (*authority, passage, etc.*); dupe, fool, trick; '**Qer** m (ring)leader; '**Qungszeichen** n/pl. quotation marks pl., inverted commas pl.

'**Angabe** f declaration; statement; instruction; F *fig.* bragging, showing off.

'**angeb|en** (*irr. geben, sep., -ge-, h*) **1.** v/t. declare; state; specify; allege; give (*name, reason*); ✝ quote (*prices*); denounce, inform against; **2.** v/i. *cards:* deal first; F *fig.* brag, show off, *Am.* blow; '**Qer** m (-s/-) informer; F braggart, *Am.* blowhard; '**~lich** adj. ['~pliç] supposed; pretended, alleged.

'**angeboren** adj. innate, inborn; ✗ congenital.

'**Angebot** n offer (*a.* ✝); *at auction sale:* bid; ✝ supply.

'**ange|bracht** adj. appropriate, suitable; well-timed; '**~bunden** adj.: *kurz ~ sein* be short (*gegen* with).

'**angehen** (*irr. gehen, sep., -ge-, h*) **1.** v/i. (sein) begin; *meat, etc.:* go bad, go off; *es geht an* it will do; **2.** v/t. (h): *j-n ~* concern s.o.; *das geht dich nichts an* that is no business of yours.

'**angehör|en** v/i. (*sep., no -ge-, h*) belong to; '**Qige** ['~iɡə] m, f (-n/-n): *seine ~n* pl. his relations pl.; *die nächsten ~n* pl. the next of kin.

Angeklagte ⚖ ['angəklaːktə] m, f (-n/-n) *the* accused; prisoner (at the bar); defendant.

Angel ['aŋəl] f (-/-n) hinge; fishing-tackle, fishing-rod.

'**angelegen** adj.: *sich et. ~ sein lassen* make s.th. one's business; '**Qheit** f business, concern, affair, matter.

'**Angel|gerät** n fishing-tackle; '**Qn** (*ge-, h*) **1.** v/i. fish (*nach* for), angle (for) (*both a. fig.*); ~ *in* fish (*river, etc.*); **2.** v/t. fish (*trout*); '**~punkt** *fig.* m pivot.

'**Angel|sachse** m Anglo-Saxon; '**Q-sächsisch** adj. Anglo-Saxon.

'**Angelschnur** f fishing-line.

'**ange|messen** adj. suitable, appropriate; reasonable; adequate; '**~nehm** adj. pleasant, agreeable, pleasing; *sehr ~!* glad *or* pleased to meet you; **∼regt** adj. [ˈ∼reːkt] stimulated; discussion: animated, lively; **∼sehen** adj. respected, esteemed.

ˈAngesicht n (-[e]s/-er, -e) face, countenance; von ∼ zu ∼ face to face; **ˈ∼s** prp. (gen.) in view of.

angestammt adj. [ˈangəʃtamt] hereditary, innate.

Angestellte [ˈangəʃtɛltə] m, f (-n/-n) employee; die ∼n pl. the staff.

ˈange|trunken adj. tipsy; **∼wandt** adj. [ˈ∼vant] applied; **∼wiesen** adj.: ∼ sein auf (acc.) be dependent or thrown (up)on.

angewöhnen v/t. (sep., -ge-, h): j-m et. ∼ accustom s.o. to s.th.; sich et. ∼ get into the habit of s.th.; take to (smoking).

ˈAngewohnheit f custom, habit.

Angina ✚ [aŋˈgiːna] f (-/Anginen) angina; tonsillitis.

ˈangleichen v/t. (irr. gleichen, sep., -ge-, h) assimilate (an acc. to, with), adjust (to); sich ∼ an (acc.) assimilate to or with, adjust or adapt o.s. to.

Angler [ˈaŋlər] m (-s/-) angler.

ˈangliedern v/t. (sep., -ge-, h) join; annex; affiliate.

Anglist [aŋˈglist] m (-en/-en) professor or student of English, Angli(ci)st.

ˈangreif|en v/t. (irr. greifen, sep., -ge-, h) touch; draw upon (capital, provisions); attack; affect (health, material); ✚ corrode; exhaust; **ˈ∼er** m (-s/-) aggressor, assailant.

ˈangrenzend adj. adjacent; adjoining.

ˈAngriff m attack, assault; in ∼ nehmen set about; **ˈ∼skrieg** m offensive war; **ˈ∼slustig** adj. aggressive.

Angst [aŋst] f (-/⁎e) fear; anxiety; anguish; ich habe ∼ I am afraid (vor dat. of); **ˈ∼hase** m coward.

ängstigen [ˈɛŋstigən] v/t. (ge-, h) frighten, alarm; sich ∼ be afraid (vor dat. of); be alarmed (um about).

ängstlich adj. [ˈɛŋstliç] uneasy, nervous; anxious; afraid; scrupulous; timid; **ˈ∼keit** f (-/no pl.) anxiety; scrupulousness; timidity.

ˈan|haben v/t. (irr. haben, sep., -ge-, h) have (garment) on; das kann mir nichts ∼ that can't do me any harm; **ˈ∼haften** v/i. (sep., -ge-, h) stick, adhere (dat. to); **ˈ∼haken** v/t. (sep., -ge-, h) hook on; tick (off), Am. check (off) (name, item).

ˈanhalten (irr. halten, sep., -ge-, h) **1.** v/t. stop; j-n ∼ zu et. keep s.o. to s.th.; den Atem ∼ hold one's breath; **2.** v/i. continue, last; stop; um ein Mädchen ∼ propose to a girl; **ˈ∼d** adj. continuous; persevering.

ˈAnhaltspunkt m clue.

Anhang m appendix, supplement (to book, etc.); followers pl., adherents pl.

ˈanhäng|en (sep., -ge-, h) **1.** v/t. hang on; affix, attach, join; add; couple (on) (coach, vehicle); **2.** v/i. (irr. hängen) adhere to; **ˈ∼er** m (-s/-) adherent, follower; pendant (of necklace, etc.); label, tag; trailer (behind car, etc.).

anhänglich adj. [ˈanhɛŋliç] devoted, attached; **ˈ∼keit** f (-/no pl.) devotion, attachment.

Anhängsel [ˈanhɛŋzəl] n (-s/-) appendage.

ˈanhauchen v/t. (sep., -ge-, h) breathe on; blow (fingers).

ˈanhäuf|en v/t. and v/refl. (sep., -ge-, h) pile up, accumulate; **ˈ∼ung** f accumulation.

ˈan|heben v/t. (irr. heben, sep., -ge-, h) lift, raise; **ˈ∼heften** v/t. (sep., -ge-, h) fasten (an acc.); stitch (to).

anˈheim|fallen v/i. (irr. fallen, sep., -ge-, sein): j-m ∼ fall to s.o.; **∼stellen** v/t. (sep., -ge-, h): j-m et. ∼ leave s.th. to s.o.

ˈAnhieb m: auf ∼ at the first go.

ˈAnhöhe f rise, elevation, hill.

ˈanhören v/t. (sep., -ge-, h) listen to; sich ∼ sound.

Anilin ✚ [aniˈliːn] n (-s/no pl.) anilin(e).

ˈankämpfen v/i. (sep., -ge-, h): ∼ gegen struggle against.

ˈAnkauf m purchase.

Anker ⚓ [ˈaŋkər] m (-s/-) anchor; vor ∼ gehen cast anchor; **ˈ∼kette** ⚓ f cable; **ˈ∼n** ⚓ v/t. and v/i. (ge-, h) anchor; **ˈ∼uhr** f lever watch.

ˈanketten v/t. (sep., -ge-, h) chain (an dat. or acc. to).

ˈAnklage f accusation, charge; ⚖ a. indictment; **ˈ∼n** v/t. (sep., -ge-, h) accuse (gen. or wegen of), charge (with); ⚖ a. indict (for).

ˈAnkläger m accuser; öffentlicher ∼ ⚖ public prosecutor, Am. district attorney.

ˈanklammern v/t. (sep., -ge-, h)

clip *s.th.* on; *sich* ~ cling (*an dat. or acc.* to).

'**Anklang** *m*: ~ *an* (*acc.*) suggestion of; ~ *finden* meet with approval.

'**an**|**kleben** *v/t.* (*sep.*, -ge-, *h*) stick on (*an dat. or acc.* to); glue on (to); paste on (to); gum on (to); '~**klei-den** *v/t.* (*sep.*, -ge-, *h*) dress; *sich* ~ dress (o.s.); '~**klopfen** *v/i.* (*sep.*, -ge-, *h*) knock (*an acc.* at); '~**knipsen** *⚡ v/t.* (*sep.*, -ge-, *h*) turn *or* switch on; '~**knüpfen** (*sep.*, -ge-, *h*) **1.** *v/t.* tie (*an dat. or acc.* to); *fig.* begin; *Verbindungen* ~ form connexions *or* (*Am. only*) connections; **2.** *v/i.* refer (*an acc.* to); '~**kommen** *v/i.* (*irr. kommen, sep.*, -ge-, *sein*) arrive; ~ *auf* (*acc.*) depend (up)on; *es darauf* ~ *lassen* run the risk, risk it; *darauf kommt es an* that is the point; *es kommt nicht darauf an* it does not matter.

Ankömmling ['ankœmliŋ] *m* (-s/-e) new-comer, new arrival.

'**ankündig**|**en** *v/t.* (*sep.*, -ge-, *h*) announce; advertise; '2**ung** *f* announcement; advertisement.

Ankunft ['ankunft] *f* (-/*no pl.*) arrival.

'**an**|**kurbeln** *v/t.* (*sep.*, -ge-, *h*) mot. crank up; *die Wirtschaft* ~ F boost the economy; '~**lächeln** *v/t.* (*sep.*, -ge-, *h*), '~**lachen** *v/t.* (*sep.*, -ge-, *h*) smile at.

'**Anlage** *f* construction; installation; ⊕ plant; grounds *pl.*, park; plan, arrangement, layout; enclosure (*to letter*); ✝ investment; talent; predisposition, tendency; *öffentliche* ~*n pl.* public gardens *pl.*; '~**kapital** ✝ *n* invested capital.

'**anlangen** (*sep.*, -ge-) **1.** *v/i.* (*sein*) arrive at; **2.** *v/t.* (*h*) F touch; concern; *was mich anlangt* as far as I am concerned, (speaking) for myself.

Anlaß ['anlas] *m* (*Anlasses/Anlässe*) occasion; *ohne allen* ~ without any reason.

'**anlass**|**en** *v/t.* (*irr. lassen, sep.*, -ge-, *h*) F leave *or* keep (*garment, etc.*) on; leave (*light, etc.*) on; ⊕ start, set going; *sich gut* ~ promise well; '2**er** *mot. m* (-s/-) starter.

anläßlich *prp.* (*gen.*) ['anlɛsliç] on the occasion of.

'**Anlauf** *m* start, run; '2**en** (*irr. laufen, sep.*, -ge-) **1.** *v/i.* (*sein*) run up;

start; tarnish, (grow) dim; ~ *gegen* run against; **2.** ⚓ *v/t.* (*h*) call *or* touch at (*port*).

'**an**|**legen** (*sep.*, -ge-) **1.** *v/t.* put (*an acc.* to, against); lay out (*garden*); invest (*money*); level (*gun*); put on (*garment*); found (*town*); ⚚ apply (*dressing*); lay in (*provisions*); *Feuer* ~ *an* (*acc.*) set fire to; **2.** *v/i.* ⚓: land; moor; ~ *auf* (*acc.*) aim at; '~**lehnen** *v/t.* (*sep.*, -ge-, *h*) lean (*an acc.* against); leave *or* set (*door*) ajar; *sich* ~ *an* (*acc.*) lean against *or* on.

Anleihe ['anlaɪə] *f* (-/-n) loan.

'**anleit**|**en** *v/t.* (*sep.*, -ge-, *h*) guide (*zu* to); instruct (*in dat.* in); '2**ung** *f* guidance, instruction; guide.

'**Anliegen** *n* (-s/-) desire, request.

'**an**|**locken** *v/t.* (*sep.*, -ge-, *h*) allure, entice; decoy; '~**machen** *v/t.* (*sep.*, -ge-, *h*) fasten (*an acc.* to), fix (to); make, light (*fire*); ⚡ switch on (*light*); dress (*salad*); '~**malen** *v/t.* (*sep.*, -ge-, *h*) paint.

'**Anmarsch** *m* approach.

anmaß|**en** ['anmaːsən] *v/refl.* (*sep.*, -ge-, *h*) arrogate *s.th.* to o.s.; assume (*right*); presume; '~**end** *adj.* arrogant; '2**ung** *f* (-/-en) arrogance, presumption.

'**anmeld**|**en** *v/t.* (*sep.*, -ge-, *h*) announce, notify; *sich* ~ *bei* make an appointment with; '2**ung** *f* announcement, notification.

'**anmerk**|**en** *v/t.* (*sep.*, -ge-, *h*) mark; note down; *j-m et.* ~ observe *or* perceive *s.th.* in s.o.; '2**ung** *f* (-/-en) remark; note; annotation; comment.

'**anmessen** *v/t.* (*irr. messen, sep.*, -ge-, *h*): *j-m e-n Anzug* ~ measure s.o. for a suit; *s. angemessen*.

'**Anmut** *f* (-/*no pl.*) grace, charm, loveliness; '2**ig** *adj.* charming, graceful, lovely.

'**an**|**nageln** *v/t.* (*sep.*, -ge-, *h*) nail on (*an acc.* to); '~**nähen** *v/t.* (*sep.*, -ge-, *h*) sew on (*an acc.* to).

annäher|**nd** *adj.* ['annɛːərnt] approximate; '2**ung** *f* (-/-en) approach.

Annahme ['annaːmə] *f* (-/-n) acceptance; receiving-office; *fig.* assumption, supposition.

'**annehm**|**bar** *adj.* acceptable; *price*: reasonable; '~**en** (*irr. nehmen, sep.*, -ge-, *h*) **1.** *v/t.* accept, take; *fig.*:

suppose, take it, *Am.* guess; assume; contract (*habit*); adopt (*child*); *parl.* pass (*bill*); *sich* ~ (*gen.*) ~ attend to *s.th.*; befriend *s.o.*; **2.** *v/i.* accept; **'2lichkeit** *f* (*-/-en*) amenity, agreeableness.

Annexion [anɛkˈsjoːn] *f* (*-/-en*) annexation.

Annonce [aˈnõːsə] *f* (*-/-n*) advertisement.   [mous.]

anonym *adj.* [anoˈnyːm] anony-]

anordn|en [ˈanʔ-] *v/t.* (*sep.,* -ge-, *h*) order; arrange; direct; **'2ung** *f* arrangement; direction; order.

'anpacken *v/t.* (*sep.,* -ge-, *h*) seize, grasp; *fig.* tackle.

'anpass|en *v/t.* (*sep.,* -ge-, *h*) fit, adapt, suit; adjust; try or fit (*garment*) on; *sich* ~ adapt o.s. (*dat.* to); **'2ung** *f* (*-/-en*) adaptation; **'~ungsfähig** *adj.* adaptable.

'anpflanz|en *v/t.* (*sep.,* -ge-, *h*) cultivate, plant; **'2ung** *f* cultivation; plantation.

Anprall [ˈanpral] *m* (*-[e]s/*~*-e*) impact; **'2en** *v/i.* (*sep.,* -ge-, *sein*) strike (*an acc.* against).

'anpreisen *v/t.* (*irr.* preisen, *sep.,* -ge-, *h*) commend, praise; boost, push.

'Anprobe *f* try-on, fitting.

'an|probieren *v/t.* (*sep.,* no -ge-, *h*) try *or* fit on; **'~raten** *v/t.* (*irr.* raten, *sep.,* -ge-, *h*) advise; **'~rechnen** *v/t.* (*sep.,* -ge-, *h*) charge; *hoch* ~ value highly.

'Anrecht *n* right, title, claim (*auf acc.* to).

'Anrede *f* address; **'2n** *v/t.* (*sep.,* -ge-, *h*) address, speak to.

'anreg|en *v/t.* (*sep.,* -ge-, *h*) stimulate; suggest; **'~end** *adj.* stimulative, stimulating; suggestive; **'2ung** *f* stimulation; suggestion.

'Anreiz *m* incentive; **'2en** *v/t.* (*sep.,* -ge-, *h*) stimulate; incite.

'an|rennen *v/i.* (*irr.* rennen, *sep.,* -ge-, *sein*): ~ *gegen* run against; *angerannt kommen* come running; **'~richten** *v/t.* (*sep.,* -ge-, *h*) prepare, dress (*food, salad*); cause, do (*damage*).

anrüchig *adj.* [ˈanryçiç] disreputable.

'anrücken *v/i.* (*sep.,* -ge-, *sein*) approach.

'Anruf *m* call (*a. teleph.*); **'2en** *v/t.* (*irr.* rufen, *sep.,* -ge-, *h*) call (*zum*

Zeugen to witness); *teleph.* ring up, F phone, *Am.* call up; hail (*ship*); invoke (*God, etc.*); appeal to (*s.o.'s help*).

'anrühren *v/t.* (*sep.,* -ge-, *h*) touch; mix.

'Ansage *f* announcement; **'2n** *v/t.* (*sep.,* -ge-, *h*) announce; **'~r** *m* (*-s/-*) announcer; compère, *Am.* master of ceremonies.

'ansammeln *v/t.* (*sep.,* -ge-, *h*) collect, gather; accumulate, amass; *sich* ~ collect, gather; accumulate.

ansässig *adj.* [ˈanzɛsiç] resident.

'Ansatz *m* start.

'an|schaffen *v/t.* (*sep.,* -ge-, *h*) procure, provide; purchase; *sich et.* ~ provide *or* supply o.s. with s.th.; **'~schalten** ⚡ *v/t.* (*sep.,* -ge-, *h*) connect; switch on (*light*).

'anschau|en *v/t.* (*sep.,* -ge-, *h*) look at, view; **'~lich** *adj.* clear, vivid; graphic.

'Anschauung *f* (*-/-en*) view; perception; conception; intuition; contemplation; **'~smaterial** *n* illustrative material; **'~sunterricht** [ˈanʃauuŋsʔ-] *m* visual instruction, object-lessons *pl.*; **'~svermögen** *n* intuitive faculty.

'Anschein *m* (*-[e]s/no pl.*) appearance; **'2end** *adj.* apparent, seeming.

'an|schicken *v/refl.* (*sep.,* -ge-, *h*): *sich* ~, *et. zu tun* get ready for s.th.; prepare for s.th.; set about doing s.th.; **'~schirren** [ˈ~ʃirən] *v/t.* (*sep.,* -ge-, *h*) harness.

'Anschlag ⚙ *m* stop, catch; ♩ touch; notice; placard, poster, bill; estimate; calculation; plot; *e-n* ~ *auf j-n verüben* make an attempt on s.o.'s life; **'~brett** [ˈ~k-] *n* notice-board, *Am.* bulletin board; **2en** [ˈ~gən] (*irr.* schlagen, *sep.,* -ge-, *h*) **1.** *v/t.* strike (*an dat. or acc.* against), knock (against); post up (*bill*); ♩ touch; level (*gun*); estimate, rate; **2.** *v/i.* strike (*an acc.* against), knock (against); *dog:* bark; ♩ take (effect); *food:* agree (*bei* with); **'~säule** [ˈ~k-] *f* advertising pillar; **'~zettel** [ˈ~k-] *m* placard, poster, bill.

'anschließen *v/t.* (*irr.* schließen, *sep.,* -ge-, *h*) fix with a lock; join, attach, annex; ⊕, ⚡ connect; *sich j-m* ~ join s.o.; *sich e-r Meinung* ~ follow an opinion; **'~d** *adj.* adjacent (*an acc.* to); subsequent (to).

'Anschluß m joining; 🚂, ⚡, teleph., gas, etc.: connexion, (Am. only) connection; ~ haben an (acc.) 🚂, boat: connect with; 🚂 run in connexion with; ~ finden make friends (an acc. with), F pal up (with); teleph.: ~ bekommen get through; **'~dose** ⚡ f (wall) socket; **'~zug** 🚂 m connecting train, connexion.

'an|schmiegen v/refl. (sep., -ge-, h): sich ~ an (acc.) nestle to; **'~schmie-ren** v/t. (sep., -ge-, h) (be)smear, grease; F fig. cheat; **'~schnallen** v/t. (sep., -ge-, h) buckle on; bitte ~! 🚗 fasten seat-belts, please!; **'~schnauzen** F v/t. (sep., -ge-, h) snap at, blow s.o. up, Am. a. bawl s.o. out; **'~schneiden** v/t. (irr. schneiden, sep., -ge-, h) cut; broach (subject).

'Anschnitt m first cut or slice.

'an|schrauben v/t. (sep., -ge-, h) screw on (an dat. or acc. to); **'~schreiben** v/t. (irr. schreiben, sep., -ge-, h) write down; sports, games: score; et. ~ lassen have s.th. charged to one's account; buy s.th. on credit; **'~schreien** v/t. (irr. schreien, sep., -ge-, h) shout at.

'Anschrift f address.

an|schuldigen ['anʃuldigən] v/t. (sep., -ge-, h) accuse, incriminate; **'~schwärzen** v/t. (sep., -ge-, h) blacken; fig. a. defame.

'anschwell|en (irr. schwellen, sep., -ge-) 1. v/i. (sein) swell; increase, rise; 2. v/t. (h) swell; **'2ung** f swelling.

anschwemm|en ['anʃvɛmən] v/t. (sep., -ge-, h) wash ashore; geol. deposit (alluvium); **'2ung** f (-/-en) wash; geol. alluvial deposits pl., alluvium.

'ansehen 1. v/t. (irr. sehen, sep., -ge-, h) (take a) look at; view; regard, consider (als as); et. mit ~ witness s.th.; ~ für take for; man sieht ihm sein Alter nicht an he does not look his age; **2.** 2 n (-s/no pl.) authority, prestige; respect; F appearance, aspect.

ansehnlich adj. ['anzeːnliç] considerable; good-looking.

'an|seilen mount. v/t. and v/refl. (sep., -ge-, h) rope; **'~sengen** v/t. (sep., -ge-, h) singe; **'~setzen** (sep., -ge-, h) **1.** v/t. put (an acc. to); add (to); fix, appoint (date); rate; fix,

quote (prices); charge; put forth (leaves, etc.); put on (flesh); put (food) on (to boil); Rost ~ rust; **2.** v/i. try; start; get ready.

'Ansicht f (-/-en) sight, view; fig. view, opinion; meiner ~ nach in my opinion; zur ~ ✝ on approval; **'~s-(post)karte** f picture postcard; **'~ssache** f matter of opinion.

ansied|eln v/t. and v/refl. (sep., -ge-, h) settle; **'2ler** m settler; **'2-lung** f settlement.

'Ansinnen n (-s/-) request, demand.

'anspann|en v/t. (sep., -ge-, h) stretch; put or harness (horses, etc.) to the carriage, etc.; fig. strain, exert; **'2ung** fig. f strain, exertion.

anspeien v/t. (irr. speien, sep., -ge-, h) spit (up)on or at.

'anspiel|en v/i. (sep., -ge-, h) cards: lead; sports: lead off; football: kick off; ~ auf (acc.) allude to, hint at; **'2ung** f (-/-en) allusion, hint.

'anspitzen v/t. (sep., -ge-, h) point, sharpen.

'Ansporn m (-[e]s/⚡ -e) spur; **'2en** v/t. (sep., -ge-, h) spur s.o. on.

'Ansprache f address, speech; e-e ~ halten deliver an address.

'ansprechen v/t. (irr. sprechen, sep., -ge-, h) speak to, address; appeal to; **'~d** adj. appealing.

'an|springen (irr. springen, sep., -ge-) **1.** v/i. engine: start; **2.** v/t. (h) jump (up)on, leap at; **'~spritzen** v/t. (sep., -ge-, h) splash (j-n mit et. s.th. on s.o.); (be-) sprinkle.

'Anspruch m claim (a. ⚖) (auf acc. to), pretension (to); ⚖ title (to); ~ haben auf (acc.) be entitled to; in ~ nehmen claim s.th.; Zeit in ~ nehmen take up time; **'2slos** adj. unpretentious; unassuming; **'2svoll** adj. pretentious.

'an|spülen v/t. (sep., -ge-, h) s. an-schwemmen; **'~stacheln** v/t. (sep., -ge-, h) goad (on).

Anstalt ['anʃtalt] f (-/-en) establishment, institution; ~en treffen zu make arrangements for.

'Anstand m **1.** (-[e]s/⚡e) hunt. stand; objection; **2.** (-[e]s/⚡⚡e) good manners pl.; decency, propriety.

anständig adj. ['anʃtɛndiç] decent; respectable; price: fair, handsome; **'2keit** f (-/⚡-en) decency.

'Anstands|gefühl n sense of propri-

ety; tact; **'ₒlos** adv. unhesitatingly.
'anstarren v/t. (sep., -ge-, h) stare or gaze at.
anstatt prp. (gen.) and cj. [an'ʃtat] instead of.
'anstaunen v/t. (sep., -ge-, h) gaze at s.o. or s.th. in wonder.
'ansteck|en v/t. (sep., -ge-, h) pin on; put on (ring); 💉 infect; set on fire; kindle (fire); light (candle, etc.); **'₋end** adj. infectious; contagious; fig. a. catching; **'ₒung** 💉 f (-/-en) infection; contagion.
'an|stehen v/i. (irr. stehen, sep., -ge-, h) queue up (nach for), Am. stand in line (for); **'₋steigen** v/i. (irr. steigen, sep., -ge-, sein) ground: rise, ascend; fig. increase.
'anstell|en v/t. (sep., -ge-, h) engage, employ, hire; make (experiments); draw (comparison); turn on (light, etc.); manage; sich ₋ queue up (nach for), Am. line up (for); sich dumm ₋ set about s.th. stupidly; **'₋ig** adj. handy, skil(l)ful; **'ₒung** f place, position, job; employment.
Anstieg [an'ti:k] m (-[e]s/-e) ascent.
'anstift|en v/t. (sep., -ge-, h) instigate; **'ₒer** m instigator; **'ₒung** f instigation.
'anstimmen v/t. (sep., -ge-, h) strike up (tune).
'Anstoß m football: kick-off; fig. impulse; offen|ce, Am. -se; ₋ erregen give offence (bei to); ₋ nehmen an (dat.) take offence at; ₋ geben zu et. start s.th., initiate s.th.; **'ₒen** (irr. stoßen, sep., -ge-) 1. v/t. (h) push, knock (acc. or an against); nudge; 2. v/i. (sein) knock (an acc. against); border (on, upon; adjoin; 3. v/i. (h): mit der Zunge ₋ lisp; auf j-s Gesundheit ₋ drink (to) s.o.'s health; **'ₒend** adj. adjoining.
anstößig adj. ['anʃtøːsiç] shocking.
'an|strahlen v/t. (sep., -ge-, h) illuminate; floodlight (building, etc.); fig. beam at s.o.; **'₋streben** v/t. (sep., -ge-, h) aim at, aspire to, strive for.
'anstreich|en v/t. (irr. streichen, sep., -ge-, h) paint; whitewash; mark; underline (mistake); **'ₒer** m (-s/-) house-painter; decorator.
anstrengen ['anʃtrɛŋən] v/t. (sep., -ge-, h) exert (eyes); fatigue; Prozeß ₋ bring an action (gegen j-n

against s.o.); sich ₋ exert o.s.; **'₋end** adj. strenuous; trying (für to); **'ₒung** f (-/-en) exertion, strain, effort.
'Anstrich m paint, colo(u)r; coat (-ing); fig.: tinge; air.
'Ansturm m assault; onset; ₋ auf (acc.) rush for; ⚓ run on (bank).
'anstürmen v/i. (sep., -ge-, sein) storm, rush.
'Anteil m share, portion; ₋ nehmen an (dat.) take an interest in; sympathize with; **'₋nahme** ['₋naː-mə] f (-/no pl.) sympathy; interest; **'₋schein** ✝ m share-certificate.
Antenne [an'tɛnə] f (-/-n) aerial.
Antialkoholiker [anti'alko'hoːlikər, '₋'] m (-s/-) teetotaller.
antik adj. [an'tiːk] antique.
Antilope zo. [anti'loːpə] f (-/-n) antelope.
Antipathie [antipa'tiː] f (-/-n) antipathy.
antippen F v/t. (sep., -ge-, h) tap.
Antiquar [anti'kvaːr] m (-s/-e) second-hand bookseller; **₋iat** [₋ar-'jaːt] n (-[e]s/-e) second-hand bookshop; **ₒisch** adj. and adv. [₋'kvaːriʃ] second-hand.
Antiquitäten [antikvi'tɛːtən] f/pl. antiques pl.
'Anti-Rakete f anti-ballistic missile.
antiseptisch 💉 adj. [anti'zɛptiʃ] antiseptic.
Antlitz ['antlits] n (-es/₍ -e) face, countenance.
Antrag ['antraːk] m (-[e]s/⸚e) offer, proposal; application; request; parl. motion; ₋ stellen auf (acc.) make an application for; parl. put a motion for; **'₋steller** m (-s/-) applicant; parl. mover; ⚖ petitioner.
'an|treffen v/t. (irr. treffen, sep., -ge-, h) meet with. find; **'₋treiben** (irr. treiben, sep., -ge-) 1. v/i. (sein) drift ashore; 2. v/t. (h) drive (on); fig. impel; **'₋treten** (irr. treten, sep., -ge-) 1. v/t. (h) enter upon (office); take up (position); set out on (journey); enter upon. take possession of (inheritance); 2. v/i. (sein) take one's place; ⚔ fall in.
'Antrieb m motive, impulse; ⊕ drive, propulsion.
'Antritt m (-[e]s/₍ -e) entrance (into office); taking up (of position); setting out (on journey); entering into possession (of inheritance).

'antun v/t. (irr. tun, sep., -ge-, h): j-m et. ~ do s.th. to s.o.; sich et. ~ lay hands on o.s.

'Antwort f (-/-en) answer, reply (auf acc. to); '2en (ge-, h) 1. v/i. answer (j-m s.o.), reply (j-m to s.o.; both: auf acc. to); 2. v/t. answer (auf acc. to), reply (to); '~schein m (international) reply coupon.

an|vertrauen v/t. (sep., no -ge-, h): j-m et. ~ (en)trust s.o. with s th., entrust s.th. to s.o.; confide s.th. to s.o.; '2wachsen v/i. (irr. wachsen, sep., -ge-, sein) take root; fig. increase; ~ an (acc.) grow on o.s.

Anwalt ['anvalt] m (-[e]s/=e) lawyer; solicitor, Am. attorney; counsel; barrister, Am. counsel(l)or; fig. advocate.

Anwandlung f fit; impulse.

Anwärter m candidate, aspirant; expectant.

Anwartschaft ['anvartʃaft] f (-/-en) expectancy; candidacy; prospect (auf acc. of).

'anweis|en v/t. (irr. weisen, sep., -ge-, h) assign; instruct; direct; s. angewiesen; '2ung f assignment; instruction; direction; ✝: cheque, Am. check; draft; s. Postanweisung.

'anwend|en v/t. ([irr. wenden,] sep., -ge-, h) employ, use; apply (auf acc. to); s. angewandt; '2ung f application.

'anwerben v/t. (irr. werben, sep., -ge-, h) ✕ enlist, enrol(l); engage.

Anwesen n estate; property.

'anwesen|d adj. present; '2heit f (-/no pl.) presence.

'Anzahl f (-/no pl.) number; quantity.

'anzahl|en v/t. (sep., -ge-, h) pay on account; pay a deposit; '2ung f (first) instal(l)ment; deposit.

'anzapfen v/t. (sep., -ge-, h) tap.

'Anzeichen n symptom; sign.

Anzeige ['antsaɪɡə] f (-/-n) notice, announcement; ✝ advice; advertisement; ⚖ information; '2n v/t. (sep., -ge-, h) announce, notify; ✝ advise; advertise; indicate; ⊕ instrument: indicate, show; thermometer: read (degrees); j-n ~ denounce s.o., inform against s.o.

'anziehen (irr. ziehen, sep., -ge-, h) 1. v/t. draw, pull; draw (rein); tighten (screw); put on (garment);

dress; fig. attract; 2. v/i. draw; prices: rise; '~d adj. attractive, interesting.

'Anziehung f attraction; '~skraft f attractive power; attraction.

'Anzug m 1. (-[e]s/=e) dress; suit; 2. (-[e]s/no pl.): im ~ sein storm: be gathering; danger: be impending.

anzüglich adj. ['antsy:klɪç] personal; '2keit f (-/-en) personality.

'anzünden v/t. (sep., -ge-, h) light, kindle; strike (match); set (building) on fire.

apathisch adj. [a'pɑ:tiʃ] apathetic.

Apfel ['apfəl] m (-s/=) apple; '~mus n apple-sauce; ~sine [~'zi:nə] f (-/-n) orange; '~wein m cider.

Apostel [a'pɔstəl] m (-s/-) apostle.

Apostroph [apɔ'stro:f] m (-s/-e) apostrophe.

Apotheke [apo'te:kə] f (-/-n) chemist's shop, pharmacy, Am. drugstore; ~r m (-s/-) chemist, Am. druggist, pharmacist.

Apparat [apa'rɑ:t] m (-[e]s/-e) apparatus; device; teleph.: am ~! speaking!; teleph.: am ~ bleiben hold the line.

Appell [a'pɛl] m (-s/-e) ✕: roll-call; inspection; parade; fig. appeal (an acc. to); 2ieren [~'li:rən] v/i. (no -ge-, h) appeal (an acc. to).

Appetit [ape'ti:t] m (-[e]s/-e) appetite; 2lich adj. appetizing, savo(u)ry, dainty.

Applaus [a'plaʊs] m (-es/✎ -e) applause.

Aprikose [apri'ko:zə] f (-/-n) apricot.

April [a'pril] m (-[s]/-e) April.

Aquarell [akva'rɛl] n (-s/-e) water-colo(u)r (painting), aquarelle.

Aquarium [a'kvɑ:rium] n (-s/ Aquarien) aquarium

Äquator [ɛ'kvɑ:tɔr] m (-s/✎ -e) equator.

Ära ['ɛ:ra] f (-/✎ Ären) era.

Arab|er ['arabər] m (-s/-) Arab; 2isch adj. [a'rɑ:biʃ] Arabian, Arab(ic).

Arbeit ['arbaɪt] f (-/-en) work; labo(u)r, toil; employment; job; task; paper; workmanship; bei der ~ at work; sich an die ~ machen, an die ~ gehen set to work; (keine) ~ haben be in (out of) work; die ~ niederlegen stop work, down tools;

'²en (ge-, h) **1.** v/i. work; labo(u)r, toil; **2.** v/t. work; make.

'**Arbeiter** m (-s/-) worker; workman, labo(u)rer, hand; '**~in** f (-/-nen) female worker; working woman, workwoman; '**~klasse** f working class(es pl.); '**~partei** f Labo(u)r Party; '**~schaft** f (-/-en), '**~stand** m working class(es pl.), labo(u)r.

'**Arbeit|geber** m (-s/-), '**~geberin** f (-/-nen) employer; '**~nehmer** m (-s/-), '**~nehmerin** f (-/-nen) employee.

'**arbeitsam** adj. industrious.

'**Arbeits|amt** n labo(u)r exchange; '**~anzug** m overall; '**~beschaffung** f (-/-en) provision of work; '**~bescheinigung** f certificate of employment; '**~einkommen** n earned income; '²fähig adj. able to work; '**~gericht** n labo(u)r or industrial court; '**~kleidung** f working clothes pl.; '**~kraft** f working power; worker, hand; Arbeitskräfte pl. a. labo(u)r; '**~leistung** f efficiency; power (of engine); output (of factory); '**~lohn** m wages pl., pay; '²los adj. out of work, unemployed; '**~lose** m (-n/-n): die ~n pl. the unemployed pl.; '**~losenunterstützung** f unemployment benefit; ~ beziehen F be on the dole; '**~losigkeit** f (-/no pl.) unemployment; '**~markt** m labo(u)r market; '**~minister** m Minister of Labour, Am. Secretary of Labor; '**~nachweis(stelle** f) m employment registry office, Am. labor registry office; '**~niederlegung** f (-/-en) strike, Am. F a. walkout; '**~pause** f break, intermission; '**~platz** m place of work; job; '**~raum** m workroom; '²scheu adj. work-shy; '**~scheu** f aversion to work; '**~schutzgesetz** n protective labo(u)r law; '**~tag** m working day, workday; '²unfähig adj. incapable of working; disabled; '**~weise** f practice, method of working; '**~willige** m (-n/-n) non-striker; '**~zeit** f working time; working hours pl.; '**~zeug** n tools pl.; '**~zimmer** n workroom; study.

Archäo|loge [arçɛo'lo:gə] m (-n/-n) arch(a)eologist; '**~logie** [~o'gi:] f (-/no pl.) arch(a)eology.

Arche ['arçə] f (-/-n) ark.

Architekt [arçi'tɛkt] m (-en/-en) architect; **~ur** [~'tu:r] f (-/-en) architecture.

Archiv [ar'çi:f] n (-s/-e) archives pl.; record office.

Areal [are'a:l] n (-s/-e) area.

Arena [a're:na] f (-/Arenen) arena; bullring; (circus-)ring.

arg adj. [ark] bad; wicked; gross.

Ärger ['ɛrgər] m (-s/no pl.) vexation, annoyance; anger; '²lich adj. vexed, F mad, angry (auf, über acc. at s.th., with s.o.); annoying, vexatious; '²n v/t. (ge-, h) annoy, vex, irritate, fret; bother; sich ~ feel angry or vexed (über acc. at, about s.th.; with s.o.); '**~nis** n (-ses/-se) scandal, offen|ce, Am. -se.

Arg|list f (-/no pl.) cunning, craft (-iness); '²**listig** adj. crafty, cunning; '²**los** adj. guileless; artless, unsuspecting; **~wohn** ['~vo:n] m (-[e]s/no pl.) suspicion; ²**wöhnen** ['~vø:nən] v/t. (ge-, h) suspect; ²**wöhnisch** adj. suspicious.

Arie ♪ ['a:rjə] f (-/-n) aria.

Aristokrat [aristo'kra:t] m (-en/-en), **~in** f (-/-nen) aristocrat; **~ie** [~kra'ti:] f (-/-n) aristocracy.

Arkade [ar'ka:də] f (-/-n) arcade.

arm[1] adj. [arm] poor.

Arm[2] [~] m (-[e]s/-e) arm; branch (of river, etc.); F: j-n auf den ~ nehmen pull s.o.'s leg.

Armaturenbrett [arma'tu:rənbrɛt] n instrument board, dash-board.

Arm|band n bracelet; **~banduhr** ['armbant?~] f wrist watch; **~bruch** m fracture of the arm.

Armee [ar'me:] f (-/-n) army.

Ärmel ['ɛrməl] m (-s/-) sleeve; '**~kanal** m the (English) Channel.

Armen|haus n alms-house, Brt. a. workhouse; '**~pflege** f poor relief; '**~pfleger** m guardian of the poor; welfare officer; '**~unterstützung** f poor relief.

ärmlich adj. ['ɛrmliç] s. armselig.

'**armselig** adj. poor; wretched; miserable; shabby; paltry.

Armut ['armu:t] f (-/no pl.) poverty.

Aroma [a'ro:ma] n (-s/Aromen, Aromata, -s) aroma, flavo(u)r; fragrance.

Arrest [a'rɛst] m (-es/-e) arrest; confinement; seizure (of goods); detention (of pupil, etc.); ~ bekommen be kept in.

Art [ɑːrt] f (-/-en) kind, sort; ♀, zo. species; manner, way; nature; manners pl.; breed, race (of animals); auf die(se) ~ in this way; 'Qen v/i. (ge-, sein): ~ nach take after. [artery.]

Arterie anat. [ar'te:rjə] f (-/-n)]

artig adj. ['a:rtiç] good, well-behaved; civil, polite; 'Qkeit f (-/-en) good behavio(u)r; politeness; civility, a. civilities pl.

Artikel [ar'ti:kəl] m (-s/-) article; commodity.

Artillerie [artilə'ri:] f (-/-n) artillery.

Artist [ar'tist] m (-en/-en), ~in f (-/-nen) circus performer.

Arznei [arts'naɪ] f (-/-en) medicine, F physic; ~kunde f (-/no pl.) pharmaceutics; ~mittel n medicine, drug.

Arzt [a:rtst] m (-es/ⁿe) doctor, medical man; physician.

Ärztin ['ɛ:rtstin] f (-/-nen) woman or lady doctor.

ärztlich adj. ['ɛ:rtstliç] medical.

As [as] n (-ses/-se) ace.

Asche ['aʃə] f (-/-n) ash(es pl.); '~bahn f sports: cinder-track, mot. dirt-track; '~becher m ash-tray; '~nbrödel [-nbrøːdəl] n, '~nputtel ['nputəl] n 1. (-s/no pl.) Cinderella; 2. (-s/-) drudge.

Ascher'mittwoch m Ash Wednesday.

'**asch'grau** adj. ash-grey, ashy, Am. ash-gray.

äsen hunt. ['ɛ:zən] v/i. (ge-, h) graze, browse.

Asiat [az'jɑːt] m (-en/-en), ~in f (-/-nen) Asiatic, Asian; Qisch adj. Asiatic, Asian.

Asket [as'keːt] m (-en/-en) ascetic.

Asphalt [as'falt] m (-[e]s/-e) asphalt; Qieren [ti:rən] v/t. (no -ge-, h) asphalt.

aß [a:s] pret. of essen.

Assistent [asis'tent] m (-en/-en), ~in f (-/-nen) assistant.

Ast [ast] m (-es/ⁿe) branch, bough; knot (in timber); '~loch n knot-hole.

Astro|naut [astro'naut] m (-en/-en) astronaut; ~nom [no:m] m (-en/-en) astronomer.

Asyl [a'zyːl] n (-s/-e) asylum; fig. sanctuary.

Atelier [atə'lje:] n (-s/-s) studio.

Atem ['a:təm] m (-s/no pl.) breath;

außer ~ out of breath; 'Qlos adj. breathless; '~not ♂ f difficulty in breathing; '~pause f breathing-space; '~zug m breath, respiration.

Äther ['ɛ:tər] m 1. (-s/no pl.) the ether; 2. ♎ (-s/-) ether; Qisch adj. [ɛ'te:riʃ] ethereal, etheric.

Athlet [at'le:t] m (-en/-en), ~in f (-/-nen) athlete; ~ik f (-/no pl.) athletics mst sg.; Qisch adj. athletic.

atlantisch adj. [at'lantiʃ] Atlantic.

Atlas ['atlas] m 1. geogr. (-/no pl.) Atlas; 2. (-, -ses/-se, Atlanten) maps: atlas; 3. (-, -ses/-se) textiles: satin.

atmen ['a:tmən] v/i. and v/t. (ge-, h) breathe.

Atmosphär|e [atmo'sfɛ:rə] f (-/-n) atmosphere; Qisch adj. atmospheric.

'**Atmung** f (-/-en) breathing, respiration.

Atom [a'to:m] n (-s/-e) atom; Qar adj. [ato'mɑ:r] atomic; ~bombe f atomic bomb, atom-bomb, A-bomb; ~energie f atomic or nuclear energy; ~forschung f atomic or nuclear research; ~kern m atomic nucleus; ~kraftwerk n nuclear power station; ~meiler m atomic pile, nuclear reactor; ~physiker m atomic physicist; ~reaktor m nuclear reactor, atomic pile; ~versuch m atomic test; ~waffe f atomic or nuclear weapon; ~wissenschaftler m atomic scientist; ~zeitalter n atomic age.

Attent|at [atɛn'tɑːt] n (-[e]s/-e) (attempted) assassination; fig. outrage; ~äter [ɛ:tər] m (-s/-) assailant, assassin.

Attest [a'test] n (-es/-e) certificate; Qieren [ti:rən] v/t. (no -ge-, h) attest, certify.

Attraktion [atrak'tsjo:n] f (-/-en) attraction.

Attrappe [a'trapə] f (-/-n) dummy.

Attribut [atri'bu:t] n (-[e]s/-e) attribute; gr. attributive.

ätz|en ['etsən] v/t. (ge-, h) corrode; ♂ cauterize; etch (metal plate); '~end adj. corrosive, caustic (a. fig.); 'Qung f (-/-en) corrosion, cauterization; etching.

au int. [au] oh!; ouch!

auch cj. [aux] also, too, likewise; even; ~ nicht neither, nor; wo ~ (immer) wher(eso)ever; ist es ~ wahr? is it really true?

Audienz [audiˈɛnts] f (-/-en) audience, hearing.

auf [auf] **1.** prp. (dat.) (up)on; in; at; of; by; ~ dem Tisch (up)on the table; ~ dem Markt in the market; ~ der Universität at the university; ~ e-m Ball at a ball; **2.** prp. (acc.) on; in; at; to; towards (a. ~ ... zu); up; ~ deutsch in German; ~ e-e Entfernung von at a range of; ~ die Post etc. gehen go to the post-office, etc.; ~ ein Pfund gehen 20 Schilling 20 shillings go to a pound; es geht ~ neun it is getting on to nine; ~ ... hin on the strength of; **3.** adv. up(wards); ~ und ab gehen walk up and down or to and fro; **4.** cj.: ~ daß (in order) that; ~ daß nicht that not, lest; **5.** int.: ~! up!

auf|arbeiten [ˈauf⁹-] v/t. (sep., -ge-, h) work off (arrears of work); furbish up; F do up (garments); **~atmen** fig. [ˈauf⁹-] v/i. (sep., -ge-, h) breathe again.

'Aufbau m (-[e]s/no pl.) building up; construction (of play, etc.); F esp. Am. setup (of organization); mot. body of car, etc.; **'2en** v/t. (sep., -ge-, h) erect, build up; construct.

'auf|bauschen v/t. (sep., -ge-, h) puff out; fig. exaggerate; **'~beißen** v/t. (irr. beißen, sep., -ge-, h) crack; **'~bekommen** v/t. (irr. kommen, sep., -ge-, h) get open (door); be given (a task); **'~bessern** v/t. (sep., -ge-, h) raise (salary); **'~bewahren** v/t. (sep., no -ge-, h) keep; preserve; **'~bieten** v/t. (irr. bieten, sep., -ge-, h) summon; exert; ✗ raise; **'~binden** v/t. (irr. binden, sep., -ge-, h) untie; **'~bleiben** v/i. (irr. bleiben, sep., -ge-, sein) sit up (door, etc.: remain open; **'~blenden** (sep., -ge-, h) **1.** mot. v/i. turn up the headlights; **2.** v/t. fade in (scene); **'~blicken** v/i. (sep., -ge-, h) look up; raise one's eyes; **'~blitzen** v/i. (sep., -ge-, h, sein) flash (up); **'~blühen** v/i. (sep., -ge-, sein) bloom; flourish.

'aufbrausen fig. v/i. (sep., -ge-, sein) fly into a passion; **'~d** adj. hot-tempered.

'auf|brechen (irr. brechen, sep., -ge-) **1.** v/t. (h) break open; force open; **2.** v/i. (sein) burst open; set

out (nach for); **'~bringen** v/t. (irr. bringen, sep., -ge-, h) raise (money, troops); capture (ship); rouse or irritate s.o.

'Aufbruch m departure, start.

'auf|bügeln v/t. (sep., -ge-, h) iron; **'~bürden** v/t. (sep., -ge-, h): j-m et. ~ impose s.th. on s.o.; **'~decken** v/t. (sep., -ge-, h) uncover; spread (cloth), fig. disclose; **'~drängen** v/t. (sep., -ge-, h) force, obtrude (j-m [up]on s.o.); **'~drehen** v/t. (sep., -ge-, h) turn on (gas, etc.).

'aufdringlich adj. obtrusive.

'Aufdruck m (-[e]s/-e) imprint; surcharge.

'aufdrücken v/t. (sep., -ge-, h) impress.

aufeinander adv. [aufʔaiˈnandər] one after or upon another; **2folge** f succession; **'~folgend** adj. successive.

Aufenthalt [ˈaufɛnthalt] m (-[e]s/-e) stay; residence; delay; 🚂 stop; **'~genehmigung** f residence permit.

auferlegen [ˈaufʔɛrleˈgən] v/t. (sep., no -ge-, h) impose (j-m on s.o.).

auferstehen [ˈaufʔɛrʃteˈən] v/i. (irr. stehen, sep., no -ge-, sein) rise (from the dead); **2ung** f (-/-en) resurrection.

auf|essen [ˈaufʔ-] v/t. (irr. essen, sep., -ge-, h) eat up; **'~fahren** v/i. (irr. fahren, sep., -ge-, sein) ascend; start up; fig. fly out; ⚓ run aground; mot. drive or run (auf acc. against, into).

'Auffahrt f ascent; driving up; approach; drive, Am. driveway; **'~srampe** f ramp.

'auf|fallen v/i. (irr. fallen, sep., -ge-, sein) be conspicuous; j-m ~ strike s.o.; **'~fallend** adj., **'~fällig** adj. striking; conspicuous; flashy.

'auffangen v/t. (irr. fangen, sep., -ge-, h) catch (up); parry (thrust).

'auffass|en v/t. (sep., -ge-, h) conceive; comprehend; interpret; **'2ung** f conception; interpretation; grasp.

'auffinden v/t. (irr. finden, sep., -ge-, h) find, trace, discover, locate.

'aufforder|n v/t. (sep., -ge-, h) ask, invite; call (up)on; esp. ✗ summon; **'2ung** f invitation; esp. ⚖ summons.

'auffrischen (sep., -ge-) **1.** v/t. (h) freshen up, touch up; brush up (*knowledge*); revive; **2.** *v/i.* (*sein*) *wind*: freshen.

'auffÜhr|en *v/t.* (*sep.*, -ge-, *h*) *thea.* represent, perform, act; enumerate; enter (*in list*); *einzeln* ~ specify, *Am.* itemize; *sich* ~ behave; **'2ung** *f thea.* performance; enumeration; entry; specification; conduct.

'Aufgabe *f* task; problem; *school*: homework; posting, *Am.* mailing (*of letter*); booking (*of luggage*), *Am.* checking (*of baggage*); resignation (*from office*); abandonment; giving up (*business*); *es sich zur* ~ *machen* make it one's business.

'Aufgang *m* ascent; *ast.* rising; staircase.

'aufgeben (*irr. geben, sep.*, -ge-, *h*) **1.** *v/t.* give up, abandon; resign from (*office*); insert (*advertisement*); post, *Am.* mail (*letter*); book (*luggage*), *Am.* check (*baggage*); hand in, send (*telegram*); ✝ place (*order*); set, *Am.* assign (*homework*); set (*riddle*); **2.** *v/i.* give up *or* in.

'Aufgebot *n* public notice; ✗ levy; *fig.* array; banns *pl.* (*of marriage*).

'aufgehen *v/i.* (*irr. gehen, sep.*, -ge-, *sein*) open; ⚕ leave no remainder; *sewing*: come apart; *paste, star, curtain*: rise; *seed*: come up; ~ *in* (*dat.*) be merged in; *fig.* be devoted to (*work*); *in Flammen* ~ go up in flames.

aufgeklärt *adj.* ['aufgəkle:rt] enlightened; **'2heit** *f* (-/*no pl.*) enlightenment.

'Aufgeld ✝ *n* agio, premium.

aufge|legt *adj.* ['aufgəle:kt] disposed (*zu* for); in the mood (*zu inf.* for *ger.*, *zu inf.*); *gut* (*schlecht*) ~ in a good (bad) humo(u)r; **'~schlossen** *fig. adj.* open-minded; **~weckt** *fig. adj.* ['~vekt] bright.

'auf|gießen *v/t.* (*irr. gießen, sep.*, -ge-, *h*) pour (on); make (*tea*); **'~greifen** *v/t.* (*irr. greifen, sep.*, -ge-, *h*) snatch up, *fig.* take up; seize.

'Aufguß *m* infusion.

'auf|haben (*irr. haben, sep.*, -ge-, *h*) **1.** *v/t.* have on (*hat*); have open (*door*); have to do (*task*); **2.** F *v/i.*: *das Geschäft hat auf* the shop is open; **'~haken** *v/t.* (*sep.*, -ge-, *h*) unhook; **'~halten** *v/t.* (*irr. halten, sep.*, -ge-, *h*) keep open; stop, detain, delay; hold up (*traffic*); *sich* ~ stay;

sich ~ *bei* dwell on; *sich* ~ *mit* spend one's time on; **'~hängen** *v/t.* (*irr. hängen, sep.*, -ge-, *h*) hang (up); ⊕ suspend.

'aufheb|en *v/t.* (*irr. heben, sep.*, -ge-, *h*) lift (up), raise; pick up; raise (*siege*); keep, preserve; cancel, annul, abolish; break off (*engagement*); break up (*meeting*); *sich* ~ neutralize; *die Tafel* ~ rise from the table; *gut aufgehoben sein* be well looked after; *viel Aufhebens machen* make a fuss (*von* about); **'2ung** *f* (-/-*en*) raising; abolition; annulment; breaking up.

'auf|heitern *v/t.* (*sep.*, -ge-, *h*) cheer up; *sich* ~ *weather*: clear up; *face*: brighten; **'~hellen** *v/t. and v/refl.* (*sep.*, -ge-, *h*) brighten.

'aufhetz|en *v/t.* (*sep.*, -ge-, *h*) incite, instigate *s.o.*; **'2ung** *f* (-/-*en*) instigation, incitement.

'auf|holen *v/t.* (*sep.*, -ge-, *h*) **1.** *v/t.* make up (for); ⚓ haul up; **2.** *v/i.* gain (*gegen* on); pull up (to); **'~hören** *v/i.* (*sep.*, -ge-, *h*) cease, stop; *Am.* quit (*all: zu tun* doing); F: *da hört* (*sich*) *doch alles auf!* that's the limit!, *Am.* that beats everything!; **'~kaufen** *v/t.* (*sep.*, -ge-, *h*) buy up.

'aufklär|en *v/t.* (*sep.*, -ge-, *h*) clear up; enlighten (*über acc.* on); ✗ reconnoit|re, *Am.* -er; *sich* ~ clear up; **'2ung** *f* enlightenment; ✗ reconnaissance.

'auf|kleben *v/t.* (*sep.*, -ge-, *h*) paste on, stick on, affix on; **'~klinken** *v/t.* (*sep.*, -ge-, *h*) unlatch; **'~knöpfen** *v/t.* (*sep.*, -ge-, *h*) unbutton.

'aufkommen **1.** *v/i.* (*irr. kommen, sep.*, -ge-, *sein*) rise; recover (*from illness*); come up; come into fashion or use; *thought*: arise; ~ *für et.* answer for s.th.; ~ *gegen* prevail against *s.o.*; **2.** ♀ *n* (-*s*/*no pl.*) rise; recovery.

auf|krempeln ['aufkrempəln] *v/t.* (*sep.*, -ge-, *h*) turn up, roll up; tuck up; **'~lachen** *v/i.* (*sep.*, -ge-, *h*) burst out laughing; **'~laden** *v/t.* (*irr. laden, sep.*, -ge-, *h*) load; ⚡ charge.

'Auflage *f* edition (*of book*); circulation (*of newspaper*); ⊕ support.

'auf|lassen *v/t.* (*irr. lassen, sep.*, -ge-, *h*) F leave open (*door, etc.*); F keep on (*hat*); ⚓ cede; '**~lauern** *v/i.* (*sep.*, -ge-, h): j-m ~ lie in wait for s.o.

'**Auflauf** *m* concourse; riot; *dish*: soufflé; '**2en** *v/i.* (*irr. laufen, sep.*, -ge-, sein) interest: accrue; ⚓ run aground.

'**auflegen** (*sep.*, -ge-, h) **1.** *v/t.* put on, lay on; apply (*auf acc.* to); print, publish (*book*) *teleph.* hang up; **2.** *teleph.* ring off.

'**auflehn|en** *v/t.* (*sep.*, -ge-, h) lean (on); *sich* ~ lean (on); *fig.* rebel, revolt (*gegen* against); '**2ung** *f* (-/-en) rebellion.

'**auf|lesen** *v/t.* (*irr. lesen, sep.*, -ge-, h) gather, pick up; '**~leuchten** *v/i.* (*sep.*, -ge-, h) flash (up); '**~liegen** *v/i.* (*irr. liegen, sep.*, -ge-, h) lie (*auf dat.* on).

'**auflös|bar** *adj.* (dis)soluble; '**~en** *v/t.* (*sep.*, -ge-, h) undo (*knot*); break up (*meeting*); dissolve (*salt*, *etc.*; *marriage, business, Parliament, etc.*); solve (⚗, *riddle*); disintegrate; *fig.* aufgelöst upset; '**2ung** *f* (dis-)solution; disintegration.

'**aufmach|en** *v/t.* (*sep.*, -ge-, h) open; undo (*dress, parcel*); put up (*umbrella*); make up, get up; *sich* ~ wind: rise; set out (*nach acc.* for); make for; *die Tür* ~ answer the door; '**2ung** *f* (-/-en) make-up, get-up.

'**aufmarschieren** *v/i.* (*sep.*, no -ge-, sein) form into line; ~ *lassen* ⚔ deploy.

'**aufmerksam** *adj.* attentive (*gegen* to); j-n ~ *machen auf* (*acc.*) call s.o.'s attention to; '**2keit** *f* (-/-en) attention; token.

'**aufmuntern** *v/t.* (*sep.*, -ge-, h) rouse; encourage; cheer up.

Aufnahme ['aufnaːmə] *f* (-/-n) taking up (*of work*); reception; admission; *phot.*: taking; photograph, shot; shooting (*of a film*); '**2fähig** *adj.* capable of absorbing; *mind*: receptive (*für* of); '**~gebühr** *f* admission fee; '**~gerät** *n phot.* camera; recorder; '**~prüfung** *f* entrance examination.

'**aufnehmen** *v/t.* (*irr. nehmen, sep.*, -ge-, h) take up; pick up; take in; take down (*dictation, etc.*); take s.th. in (*mentally*); receive (*guests*); admit; raise, borrow (*money*); draw up, record; shoot (*film*); *phot.* take

(*picture*); gut (übel) ~ take well (ill); es ~ mit be a match for.

aufopfer|n ['auf?-] *v/t.* (*sep.*, -ge-, h) sacrifice; '**2ung** *f* sacrifice.

'**auf|passen** *v/i.* (*sep.*, -ge-, h) attend (*auf acc.* to); watch; *at school*: be attentive; look out; ~ *auf* (*acc.*) take care of; '**~platzen** *v/i.* (*sep.*, -ge-, sein) burst (open); '**~polieren** *v/t.* (*sep.*, no -ge-, h) polish up; '**~prallen** *v/i.* (*sep.*, -ge-, sein): auf den Boden ~ strike the ground; '**~pumpen** *v/t.* (*sep.*, -ge-, h) blow up (*tyre*, *etc.*); '**~raffen** *v/t.* (*sep.*, -ge-, h) snatch up; *sich* ~ rouse o.s. (*zu for*); muster up one's energy; '**~räumen** (*sep.*, -ge-, h) **1.** *v/t.* put in order; tidy (up), clear away; *Am.* straighten up; clear away; **2.** *v/i.* tidy up; ~ *mit* do away with.

'**aufrecht** *adj. and adv.* upright (*a. fig.*), erect; '**~erhalten** *v/t.* (*irr. halten, sep.*, no -ge-, h) maintain, uphold; '**2erhaltung** *f* (-/no pl.) maintenance.

'**aufreg|en** *v/t.* (*sep.*, -ge-, h) stir up, excite; *sich* ~ get excited *or* upset (über acc. about); aufgeregt excited; upset; '**2ung** *f* excitement, agitation.

'**auf|reiben** *v/t.* (*irr. reiben, sep.*, -ge-, h) chafe (*skin, etc.*); *fig.*: destroy; exhaust, wear s.o. out; '**~reißen** (*irr. reißen, sep.*, -ge-, h) **1.** *v/t.* (h) rip *or* tear up *or* open; fling open (*door*); open (*eyes*) wide; **2.** *v/i.* (sein) split open, burst.

'**aufreiz|en** *v/t.* (*sep.*, -ge-, h) inc.te, stir up; '**~end** *adj.* provocative; '**2ung** *f* instigation.

'**aufrichten** *v/t.* (*sep.*, -ge-, h; set up, erect; *sich* ~ stand up; straighten; sit up (*in bed*).

'**aufrichtig** *adj.* sincere, candid; '**2keit** *f* sincerity, cando(u)r.

'**aufriegeln** *v/t.* (*sep.*, -ge-, h) un-)

'**Aufriß** △ *m* elevation.   [bolt.)

'**aufrollen** *v/t. and v/refl.* (*sep.*, -ge-, h) roll up; unroll.

'**Aufruf** *m* call, summons; '**2en** *v/t.* (*irr. rufen, sep.*, -ge-, h) call up; call on s.o.

Aufruhr ['aufruːr] *m* (-[e]s/-e) uproar, tumult; riot, rebellion.

'**aufrühr|en** *v/t.* (*sep.*, -ge-, h) stir up; revive; *fig.* rake up; '**2er** *m* (-s/-) rebel; '**~erisch** *adj.* rebellious.

'**Aufrüstung** ⚔ f (rc)armament.

'**auf|rütteln** v/t. (sep., -ge-, h) shake up; rouse; '**~sagen** v/t. (sep., -ge-, h) say, repeat; recite.

aufsässig adj. ['aufzɛsiç] rebellious.

'**Aufsatz** m essay; composition; ⊕ top.

'**auf|saugen** v/t. (sep., -ge-, h) suck up; 🔬 absorb; '**~scheuchen** v/t. (sep., -ge-, h) scare (away); disturb; rouse; '**~scheuern** v/t. (sep., -ge-, h) scour; 🎯 chafe; '**~schichten** v/t. (sep., -ge-, h) pile up; '**~schieben** v/t. (irr. schieben, sep., -ge-, h) slide open; fig.: put off; defer, postpone; adjourn.

'**Aufschlag** m striking; impact; additional or extra charge; facing (on coat), lapel (of coat); cuff (on sleeve); turn-up (on trousers); tennis: service; '2en ['~gən] (irr. schlagen, sep., -ge-) . v/t. (h) open; turn up (sleeve, etc.); take up (abode); pitch (tent); raise (prices); cut (one's knee) open; 2. v/i. (sein) strike, hit; 🔺 rise, go up (in price); tennis: serve.

'**auf|schließen** v/t. (irr. schließen, sep., -ge-, h) unlock, open; '**~schlitzen** v/t. (sep., -ge-, h) slit or rip open.

'**Aufschluß** fig. m information.

'**auf|schnallen** v/t. (sep., -ge-, h) unbuckle; '**~schnappen** (sep., -ge-) 1. v/t. (h) snatch; fig. pick up; 2. v/i. (sein) snap open; '**~schneiden** (irr. schneiden, sep., -ge-) 1. v/t. cut open; cut up (meat); 2. fig. v/i. brag, boast.

'**Aufschnitt** m (slices pl. of) cold meat, Am. cold cuts pl.

'**auf|schnüren** v/t. (sep., -ge-, h) untie; unlace; '**~schrauben** v/t. (sep., -ge-, h) screw (auf acc. on); unscrew; '**~schrecken** (sep., -ge-) 1. v/t. (h) startle; 2. v/i. (irr. schrecken, sein) start (up).

'**Aufschrei** m shriek, scream; fig. outcry.

'**auf|schreiben** v/t. (irr. schreiben, sep., -ge-, h) write down; '**~schreien** v/i. (irr. schreien, sep., -ge-, h) cry out, scream.

'**Aufschrift** f inscription; address, direction (on letter); label.

'**Aufschub** m deferment; delay; adjournment; respite.

'**auf|schürfen** v/t. (sep., -ge-, h)

graze (skin); '**~schwingen** v/refl. (irr. schwingen, sep., -ge-, h) soar, rise; sich zu et. ~ bring o.s. to do s.th.

'**Aufschwung** m fig. rise, Am. upswing; 🔺 boom.

'**auf|sehen 1.** v/i. (irr. sehen, sep., -ge-, h) look up; 2. 2 n (-s/no pl.) sensation; ~ erregen cause a sensation; '**~erregend** adj. sensational.

'**Aufseher** m overseer; inspector.

'**aufsetzen** (sep., -ge-, h) 1. v/t. set up; put on (hat, countenance); draw up (document); sich ~ sit up; 2. 🔺 v/i. touch down.

'**Aufsicht** f (-/-en) inspection, supervision; store: shopwalker, Am. floorwalker; '**~sbehörde** f board of control; '**~srat** m board of directors.

'**auf|sitzen** v/i. (irr. sitzen, sep., -ge-, h) rider: mount; '**~spannen** v/t. (sep., -ge-, h) stretch; put up (umbrella); spread (sails); '**~sparen** v/t. (sep., -ge-, h) save; fig. reserve; '**~speichern** v/t. (sep., -ge-, h) store up; '**~sperren** v/t. (sep., -ge-, h) open wide; '**~spielen** (sep., -ge-, h) 1. v/t. and v/i. strike up; 2. v/refl. show off; sich ~ als set up for; '**~spießen** v/t. (sep., -ge-, h) pierce; with horns: gore; run through, spear; '**~springen** v/i. (irr. springen, sep., -ge-, sein) jump up; door: fly open; crack; skin: chap; '**~spüren** v/t. (sep., -ge-, h) hunt up; track down; '**~stacheln** fig. v/t. (sep., -ge-, h) goad; incite, instigate; '**~stampfen** v/i. (sep., -ge-, h) stamp (one's foot).

'**Aufstand** m insurrection; rebellion; uprising, revolt.

aufständisch adj. ['aufʃtɛndiʃ] rebellious; '2e m (-n/-n) insurgent, rebel.

'**auf|stapeln** v/t. (sep., -ge-, h) pile up; 🔺 store (up); '**~stechen** v/t. (irr. stechen, sep., -ge-, h) puncture; prick open; 🎯 lance; '**~stecken** v/t. (sep., -ge-, h) pin up; put up (hair); '**~stehen** v/i. (irr. stehen, sep., -ge-) 1. (sein) stand up; rise, get up; revolt; 2. F (h) stand open; '**~steigen** v/i. (irr. steigen, sep., -ge-, sein) rise, ascend; 🪁 take off; rider: mount.

'**aufstellen** v/t. (sep., -ge-, h) set up, put up; ⚔ draw up; post (sentries); make (assertion); set (example); erect (column); set (trap);

nominate (*candidate*); draw up
(*bill*); lay down (*rule*); make out
(*list*); set up, establish (*record*);
'**2ung** *f* putting up; drawing up;
erection; nomination; ✝ statement;
list.

Aufstieg ['auf∫ti:k] *m* (-[e]s/-e)
ascent, *Am. a.* ascension; *fig.* rise.
'**auf|stöbern** *fig. v/t.* (*sep.*, -ge-, *h*)
hunt up; '**~stoßen** (*irr. stoßen, sep.*,
-ge-) **1.** *v/t.* (*h*) push open; ~ auf
(*acc.*) knock against; **2.** *v/i.* (*h, sein*)
of *food:* rise, repeat; belch; '**~strei-
chen** *v/t.* (*irr. streichen, sep.*, -ge-,
h) spread (*butter*).

'**Aufstrich** *m* spread (*for bread*).
'**auf|stützen** *v/t.* (*sep.*, -ge-, *h*) prop
up, support *s.th.*; *sich* ~ *auf* (*acc.*)
lean on; '**~suchen** *v/t.* (*sep.*, -ge-, *h*)
visit (*places*); go to see *s.o.*, look
s.o. up.

'**Auftakt** *m* ♩ upbeat; *fig.* prelude,
preliminaries *pl.*
'**auf|tauchen** *v/i.* (*sep.*, -ge-, *sein*)
emerge, appear, turn up; '**~tauen**
(*sep.*, -ge-) **1.** *v/t.* (*h*) thaw; **2.** *v/i.*
(*sein*) thaw (*a. fig.*); '**~teilen** *v/t.*
(*sep.*, -ge-, *h*) divide (up), share.

Auftrag ['auftra:k] *m* (-[e]s/-̈e)
commission; instruction; mission;
⚖ mandate; ✝ order; **2en** ['~ɡən]
v/t. (*irr. tragen, sep.*, -ge-, *h*) serve
(up) (*meal*); lay on (*paint*); wear
out (*dress*); *j-m et.* ~ charge *s.o.*
with *s.th.*; **~geber** ['~k-] *m* (-s/-)
employer; customer; principal; **~s-
erteilung** ['~ks᾿ɛrtaɪluŋ] *f* (-/-e)
placing of an order.

'**auf|treffen** *v/i.* (*irr. treffen, sep.*,
-ge-, *sein*) strike, hit; '**~treiben** *v/t.*
(*irr. treiben, sep.*, -ge-, *h*) hunt up;
raise (*money*); '**~trennen** *v/t.* (*sep.*,
-ge-, *h*) rip; unstitch (*seam*).

'**auftreten 1.** *v/i.* (*irr. treten, sep.*,
-ge-, *sein*) tread; *thea., witness, etc.:*
appear (*als* as); behave, act; *difficulties:* arise; **2.** **2** *n* (-s/*no pl.*) appearance; occurrence (*of events*);
behavio(u)r.
'**Auftrieb** *m phys. and fig.* buoyancy; 🜨 lift; *fig.* impetus.
'**Auftritt** *m thea.* scene (*a. fig.*);
appearance (*of actor*).
'**auf|trumpfen** *fig. v/i.* (*sep.*, -ge-, *h*)
put one's foot down; '**~tun** *v/t./v.*(*irr.
tun, sep.*, -ge-, *h*) open; *sich* ~ open;
chasm: yawn; *society:* form; '**~tür-
men** *v/t.* (*sep.*, -ge-, *h*) pile *or* heap

up; *sich* ~ tower up; pile up; *difficulties:* accumulate; '**~wachen** *v/i.*
(*sep.*, -ge-, *sein*) awake, wake up;
'**~wachsen** *v/i.* (*irr. wachsen, sep.*,
-ge-, *sein*) grow up.

'**Aufwallung** *f* ebullition, surge.
Aufwand ['aufvant] *m* (-[e]s/*no pl.*)
expense, expenditure (*an dat.* of);
pomp; splendid *or* great display (*of
words, etc.*).
'**aufwärmen** *v/t.* (*sep.*, -ge-, *h*)
warm up.
'**Aufwarte|frau** *f* charwoman, *Am.
a.* cleaning woman; '**2n** *v/i.* (*sep.*,
-ge-, *h*) wait (up)on *s.o.*, attend on
s.o.; wait (at table).
aufwärts *adv.* ['aufvɛrts] upward(s).
'**Aufwartung** *f* attendance; visit;
j-m s-e ~ *machen* pay one's respects
to *s.o.*, call on *s.o.*
'**aufwasch|en** *v/t.* (*irr. waschen,
sep.*, -ge-, *h*) wash up; '**2wasser** *n*
dish-water.
'**auf|wecken** *v/t.* (*sep.*, -ge-, *h*)
awake(n), wake (up); '**~weichen**
(*sep.*, -ge-) **1.** *v/t.* (*h*) soften; soak;
2. *v/i.* (*sein*) soften, become soft;
'**~weisen** *v/t.* (*irr. weisen, sep.*,
-ge-, *h*) show, exhibit; produce;
'**~wenden** *v/t.* ([*irr. wenden*], *sep.*,
-ge-, *h*) spend; *Mühe* ~ take pains;
'**~werfen** *v/t.* (*irr. werfen, sep.*,
-ge-, *h*) raise (*a. question*).
'**aufwert|en** *v/t.* (*sep.*, -ge-, *h*) re-
valorize; revalue; '**2ung** *f* revalor-
ization; revaluation.
'**aufwickeln** *v/t. and v/refl.* (*sep.*,
-ge-, *h*) wind up, roll up.
aufwiegel|n ['aufvi:ɡəln] *v/t.* (*sep.*,
-ge-, *h*) stir up, incite, instigate;
'**2ung** *f* (-/-en) instigation.
'**aufwiegen** *fig. v/t.* (*irr. wiegen,
sep.*, -ge-, *h*) make up for.
Aufwiegler ['aufvi:ɡlər] *m* (-s/-)
agitator; instigator.
'**aufwirbeln** (*sep.*, -ge-) **1.** *v/t.* (*h*)
whirl up; raise (*dust*); *fig. viel Staub*
~ create a sensation; **2.** *v/i.* (*sein*)
whirl up.
'**aufwisch|en** *v/t.* (*sep.*, -ge-, *h*)
wipe up; '**2lappen** *m* floor-cloth.
'**aufwühlen** *v/t.* (*sep.*, -ge-, *h*) turn
up; *fig.* stir.
'**aufzähl|en** *v/t.* (*sep.*, -ge-, *h*) count
up; *fig.* enumerate, *Am. a.* call off;
specify, *Am.* itemize; '**2ung** *f*
(-/-en) enumeration; specification.
'**auf|zäumen** *v/t.* (*sep.*, -ge-, *h*)

bridle; '**~zehren** v/t. (sep., -ge-, h) consume.

'**aufzeichn|en** v/t. (sep., -ge-, h) draw; note down; record; '2**ung** f note; record.

'**auf|zeigen** v/t. (sep., -ge-, h) show; demonstrate; point out (mistakes, etc.); disclose; '**~ziehen** (irr. ziehen, sep., -ge-) **1.** v/t. (h) draw or pull up; (pull) open; hoist (flag); bring up (child); mount (picture); wind (up) (clock, etc.); j-n ~ tease s.o., pull s.o.'s leg; Saiten auf e-e Violine ~ string a violin; **2.** v/i. (sein) ✕ draw up; storm: approach.

'**Aufzucht** f rearing, breeding.

'**Aufzug** m ⊕ hoist; lift, Am. elevator; thea. act; attire; show.

'**aufzwingen** v/t. (irr. zwingen, sep., -ge-, h): j-m et. ~ force s.th.upon

Augapfel ['auk?-] m eyeball. [s.o.]

Auge ['augə] n (-s/-n) eye; sight; ♀ bud; in meinen ~n in my view; im ~ behalten keep an eye on; keep in mind; aus den ~n verlieren lose sight of; ein ~ zudrücken turn a blind eye (bei to); ins ~ fallen strike the eye; große ~n machen open one's eyes wide; unter vier ~n face to face, privately; kein ~ zutun not to get a wink of sleep.

'**Augen|arzt** m oculist, eye-doctor; '**~blick** m moment, instant; '2**blicklich 1.** adj. instantaneous; momentary; present; **2.** adv. instant(aneous)ly; at present; '**~braue** f eyebrow; '**~entzündung** ♀ f inflammation of the eye; '**~heilkunde** f ophthalmology; '**~klinik** f ophthalmic hospital; '**~leiden** ♀ n eye-complaint; '**~licht** n eyesight; '**~lid** n eyelid; '**~maß** n: ein gutes ~ a sure eye; nach dem ~ by eye; **~merk** ['~mɛrk] n (-[e]s/no pl.): sein ~ richten auf (acc.) turn one's attention to; have s.th. in view; '**~schein** m appearance; in ~ nehmen examine, view, inspect; '2**scheinlich** adj. evident; '**~wasser** n eyewash, eye-lotion; '**~wimper** f eyelash; '**~zeuge** m eyewitness.

August [au'gust] m (-[e]s, - /-e) August.

Auktion [auk'tsjoːn] f (-/-en) auction; **~ator** [~o'naːtɔr] m (-s/-en) auctioneer.

Aula ['aula] f (-/Aulen, -s) (assembly) hall, Am. auditorium.

aus [aus] **1.** prp. (dat.) out of; from; of; by; for; in; ~ Achtung out of respect; ~ London kommen come from London; ~ diesem Grunde for this reason; ~ Ihrem Brief ersehe ich I see from your letter; **2.** adv. out; over; die Schule ist ~ school is over; F: von mir ~ for all I care; auf et. ~ sein be keen on s.th.; es ist ~ mit ihm it is all over with him; das Spiel ist ~! the game is up!; er weiß weder ein noch ~ he is at his wit's end; on instruments, etc.: an — ~ on — off.

ausarbeit|en ['aus?-] v/t. (sep., -ge-, h) work out; elaborate; '2**ung** f (-/-en) working-out; elaboration; composition.

aus|arten ['aus?-] v/i. (sep., -ge-, sein) degenerate; get out of hand; **~atmen** ['aus?-] (sep., -ge-, h) **1.** v/i. breathe out; **2.** v/t. breathe out; exhale (vapour, etc.); '**~baggern** v/t. (sep., -ge-, h) dredge (river, etc.); excavate (ground).

'**Ausbau** m (-[e]s/-ten) extension; completion; development; '2**en** v/t. (sep., -ge-, h) develop; extend; finish, complete; ⊕ dismantle (engine). [sep., no -ge-, h) stipulate.]

'**ausbedingen** v/t. (irr. bedingen,

'**ausbesser|n** v/t. (sep., -ge-, h) mend, repair, Am. F a. fix; '2**ung** f repair, mending.

'**Ausbeut|e** f (-/%-n) gain, profit; yield; ✕ output; '2**en** v/t. (sep., -ge-, h) exploit; sweat (workers); '**~ung** f (-/-en) exploitation.

'**ausbild|en** v/t. (sep., -ge-, h) form, develop; train; instruct; educate; ✕ drill; '2**ung** f development; training; instruction; education; ✕ drill.

'**ausbitten** v/t. (irr. bitten, sep., -ge-, h): sich et. ~ request s.th.; insist on s.th.

'**ausbleiben 1.** v/i. (irr. bleiben, sep., -ge-, sein) stay away, fail to appear; **2.** ~ n (-s/no pl.) non-arrival, non-appearance; absence.

'**Ausblick** m outlook (auf acc. over, on), view (of), prospect (of); fig. outlook (on).

'**aus|bohren** v/t. (sep., -ge-, h) bore, drill; '**~brechen** (irr. brechen, sep., -ge-) **1.** v/t. (h) break out; vomit; **2.** v/i. (sein) break out; fig. burst out (laughing, etc.).

'**ausbreit|en** v/t. (sep., -ge-, h) spread (out); stretch (out) (arms, wings); display; sich ~ spread; '**2ung** f (-/~-en) spreading.

'**ausbrennen** (irr. brennen, sep., -ge-) 1. v/t. (h) burn out; ♯ cauterize; 2. v/i. (sein) burn out.

'**Ausbruch** m outbreak; eruption (of volcano); escape (from prison); outburst (of emotion).

'**aus|brüten** v/t. (sep., -ge-, h) hatch (a. fig.); '**~bürgern** v/t. (sep., -ge-, h) denationalize, expatriate.

'**Ausdauer** f perseverance; '**2nd** adj. persevering; ♀ perennial.

'**ausdehn|en** v/t. and v/refl. (sep., -ge-, h) extend (auf acc. to); expand; stretch; '**2ung** f expansion; extension; extent.

'**aus|denken** v/t. (irr. denken, sep., -ge-, h) think s.th. out, Am. a. think s.th. up, contrive, devise, invent; imagine; '**~dörren** v/t. (sep., -ge-, h) dry up; parch; '**~drehen** v/t. (sep., -ge-, h) turn off (radio, gas); ♭ turn out, switch off (light).

'**Ausdruck** m 1. (-[e]s/no pl.) expression; 2. (-[e]s/~e) expression; term.

'**ausdrück|en** v/t. (sep., -ge-, h) press, squeeze (out); stub out (cigarette); fig. express; '**~lich** adj. express, explicit.

'**ausdrucks|los** adj. inexpressive, expressionless; blank; '**~voll** adj. expressive; '**2weise** f mode of expression; style.

'**Ausdünstung** f (-/-en) exhalation; perspiration; odo(u)r, smell.

auseinander adv. [aus?ar'nandər] asunder, apart; separate(d); **~bringen** v/t. (irr. bringen, sep., -ge-, h) separate, sever; **~gehen** v/i. (irr. gehen, sep., -ge-, sein) meeting, crowd: break up; opinions: differ; friends: part; crowd: disperse; roads: diverge; **~nehmen** v/t. (irr. nehmen, sep., -ge-, h) take apart or to pieces; ⊕ disassemble, dismantle; **~setzen** v/t. (sep., -ge-, h) explain; sich mit j-m ~ ✝ compound with s.o.; argue with s.o.; have it out with s.o.; sich mit e-m Problem ~ get down to a problem; come to grips with a problem; **2setzung** f (-/-en) explanation; discussion; settlement (with creditors, etc.); kriegerische ~ armed conflict.

auserlesen adj. ['aus?-] exquisite, choice; select(ed).

auserwählen ['aus?-] v/t. (sep., no -ge-, h) select, choose.

'**ausfahr|en** (irr. fahren, sep., -ge-) 1. v/i. (sein) drive out, go for a drive; ⊕ leave (port); 2. v/t. (h) take (baby) out (in pram); take s.o. for a drive; rut (road); ✈ lower (undercarriage); '**2t** f drive; excursion; way out, exit (of garage, etc.); gateway; departure.

'**Ausfall** m falling out; ✝: loss; deficit; **2en** v/i. (irr. fallen, sep., -ge-, sein) fall out; not to take place; turn out, prove; ~ lassen drop; cancel; die Schule fällt aus there is no school; '**2end** adj. offensive, insulting.

'**aus|fasern** v/i. (sep., -ge-, sein) ravel out, fray; '**~fegen** v/t. (sep., -ge- h) sweep (out).

ausfertig|en ['ausfertigən] v/t. (sep., -ge-, h) draw up (document); make out (bill, etc.); issue (passport); '**2ung** f (-/-en) drawing up; issue; draft; copy; in doppelter ~ in duplicate. [chen find out; discover.

ausfindig adj. ['ausfindiç]: ~ ma-∫

'**Ausflucht** f (-/~-e) excuse, evasion, shift, subterfuge.

'**Ausflug** m trip, excursion, outing.

Ausflügler ['ausfly:klər] m (-s/-) excursionist, tripper, tourist.

'**Ausfluß** m flowing out; discharge (a. ♯); outlet, outfall.

'**aus|fragen** v/t. (sep., -ge-, h) interrogate, Am. a. quiz; sound; '**~fransen** v/i. (sep., -ge-, sein) fray.

Ausfuhr ✝ f (-/-en) export(ation); '**~artikel** ✝ m export (article).

'**ausführ|bar** adj. practicable; ✝ exportable; '**~en** v/t. (sep., -ge-, h) execute, carry out, perform, Am. a. fill; ✝ export; explain; j-n ~ take s.o. out.

'**Ausfuhr|genehmigung** f export permit; '**~handel** m export trade.

'**ausführlich** 1. adj. detailed; comprehensive; circumstantial; 2. adv. in detail, at (some) length; **2keit** f (-/no pl.) minuteness of detail; particularity; comprehensiveness; copiousness.

'**Ausführung** f execution, performance; workmanship; type, make;

explanation; '**~sbestimmungen** † f/pl. export regulations pl.

'**Ausfuhr|verbot** n embargo on exports; '**~waren** f/pl. exports pl.; '**~zoll** m export duty.

'**ausfüllen** v/t. (sep., -ge-, h) fill out or up; fill in, complete (form); Am. fill out (blank).

'**Ausgabe** f distribution; edition (of book); expense, expenditure; issue (of shares, etc.); issuing office.

'**Ausgang** m going out; exit; way out; outlet; end; result; '**~skapital** † n original capital; '**~spunkt** m starting-point; '**~sstellung** f starting-position.

'**ausgeben** v/t. (irr. geben, sep., -ge-, h) give out; spend (money); issue (shares, etc.); sich ~ für pass o.s. off for, pretend to be.

ausge|beult adj. ['ausgəbɔylt] baggy; **~bombt** adj. ['~bɔmpt] bombed out; **~dehnt** adj. ['~de:nt] expansive, vast, extensive; **~dient** adj. ['~di:nt] worn out; superannuated; retired, pensioned off; **~er** Soldat ex-serviceman, veteran; '**~fallen** fig. adj. odd, queer, unusual.

'**Aushang** m notice, placard, poster.

'**aushänge|n 1.** v/t. (sep., -ge-, h) hang or put out; unhinge (door); **2.** v/i. (irr. hängen, sep., -ge-, h) have been hung or put out; '**2-schild** n signboard.

aus|harren ['ausharən] v/i. (sep., -ge-, h) persevere; hold out; '**~hauchen** v/t. (sep., -ge-, h) breathe out, exhale; '**~heben** v/t. (irr. heben, sep., -ge-, h) dig (trench); unhinge (door); recruit, levy (soldiers); excavate (earth); rob (nest); clean out, raid (nest of criminals); '**~helfen** v/i. (irr. helfen, sep., -ge-, h) help out.

'**Aushilf|e** f (temporary) help or assistance; sie hat e-e ~ she has s.o. to help out; '**2sweise** adv. as a makeshift; temporarily.

'**aushöhl|en** v/t. (sep., -ge-, h) hollow out; '**2ung** f hollow.

'**aus|holen** (sep., -ge-, h) **1.** v/i. raise one's hand (as if to strike); weit ~ go far back (in narrating s.th.); **2.** v/t. sound, pump s.o.; '**~horchen** v/t. (sep., -ge-, h) sound, pump s.o.; '**~hungern** v/t. (sep., -ge-, h) starve (out); '**~husten** v/t. (sep., -ge-, h) cough up; '**~kennen** v/refl. (irr. kennen, sep., -ge-, h) know one's way (about place); be well versed, be at home (in subject); er kennt sich aus he knows what's what; '**~kleiden** v/t. (sep., -ge-, h) undress; ⊕ line, coat; sich ~ undress; '**~klopfen** v/t. (sep., -ge-, h)

compromise; compensation; † settlement; sports: equalization (of score); tennis: deuce (score of 40 all); '**2en** v/t. (irr. gleichen, sep., -ge-, h) equalize; compensate (loss); † balance.

'**aus|gleiten** v/i. (irr. gleiten, sep., -ge-, h) slip, slide; '**~graben** v/t. (irr. graben, sep., -ge-, h) dig out or up (a. fig.); excavate; exhume (body).

Ausguck ⚓ ['ausguk] m (-[e]s/-e) look-out.

'**Ausguß** m sink; '**~eimer** m slop-pail.

'**aus|haken** v/t. (sep., -ge-, h) unhook; '**~halten** (irr. halten, sep., -ge-, h) **1.** v/t. endure, bear, stand; ♪ sustain (note); **2.** v/i. hold out; last; '**~händigen** ['~hɛndigən] v/t. (sep., -ge-, h) deliver up, hand over, surrender.

'**ausge|lassen** fig. adj. frolicsome, boisterous; '**~nommen** prp. **1.** (acc.) except (for); **2.** (nom.): Anwesende ~ present company excepted; **~prägt** adj. ['~prɛːkt] marked, pronounced; '**~rechnet** fig. adv. ['~rɛçnət] just; ~ er least of all people; ~ heute today of all days; '**~schlossen** fig. adj. impossible.

'**ausgestalten** v/t. (sep., no -ge-, h) arrange (celebration); et. zu et. ~ develop or turn s.th. into s.th.

ausge|sucht fig. adj. ['ausgəzuːxt] exquisite, choice; '**~wachsen** adj. full-grown; **~zeichnet** fig. adj. ['~tsaiçnət] excellent.

'**ausgiebig** adj. ['ausgiːbiç] abundant, plentiful; meal: substantial.

'**ausgießen** v/t. (irr. gießen, sep., -ge-, h) pour out.

Ausgleich ['ausglaiç] m (-[e]s/-e)

beat (out); dust (*garment*); knock out (*pipe*); ~klügeln ['~kly:gəln] v/t. (*sep.*, -ge-, *h*) work s.th. out; contrive; puzzle s.th. out.

'**auskommen 1.** v/i. (*irr.* kommen, *sep.*, -ge-, *sein*) get out; escape; ~ mit manage with s.th.; get on with s.o.; ~ ohne do without; mit dem Geld ~ make both ends meet; **2.** ♀ n (-s/no pl.) competence, competency.

'**auskundschaften** v/t. (*sep.*, -ge-, *h*) explore; ✕ reconnoit|re, *Am.* -er, scout.

Auskunft ['auskunft] f (-/=e) information; inquiry office, inquiries pl., *Am.* information desk; ~**sstelle** f inquiry office, inquiries pl., *Am.* information bureau.

'**aus|lachen** v/t. (*sep.*, -ge-, *h*) laugh at, deride; '~**laden** v/t. (*irr.* laden, *sep.*, -ge-, *h*) unload; discharge (*cargo from ship*); cancel s.o.'s invitation, put off (*guest*).

'**Auslage** f display, show (*of goods*); in der ~ in the (shop) window; ~n pl. expenses pl.

'**Ausland** n (-[e]s/no pl.): das ~ foreign countries pl.; ins ~, im ~ abroad.

Ausländ|er ['auslɛndər] m (-s/-), ~**erin** f (-/-nen) foreigner; alien; '♀**isch** adj. foreign; ♀, zo. exotic. '**Auslandskorrespondent** m foreign correspondent.

'**auslass|en** v/t. (*irr.* lassen, *sep.*, -ge-, *h*) let out (*water*); melt (down) (*butter*); render down (*fat*); let out (*garment*); let down (*hem*); leave out, omit (*word*); cut s.th. out; miss or cut out (*meal*); miss (*dance*); s-n Zorn an j-m ~ vent one's anger on s.o.; sich ~ über (*acc.*) say s.th. about; express one's opinion about; '♀**ung** f (-/-en) omission; remark, utterance; '♀**ungszeichen** gr. n apostrophe.

'**aus|laufen** v/i. (*irr.* laufen, *sep.*, -ge-, *sein*) run or leak out (aus et. of s.th.); leak; end (*in s.th.*); *machine*: run down; ♣ (set) sail; '~**leeren** v/t. (*sep.*, -ge-, *h*) empty; ✗ evacuate (*bowels*).

'**ausleg|en** v/t. (*sep.*, -ge-, *h*) lay out; display (*goods*); explain, interpret; advance (*money*); '♀**ung** f (-/-en) explanation, interpretation.

'**aus|leihen** v/t. (*irr.* leihen, *sep.*, -ge-, *h*) lend (out), esp. *Am.* loan;

'~**lernen** v/i. (*sep.*, -ge-, *h*) finish one's apprenticeship; man lernt nie aus we live and learn.

'**Auslese** f choice, selection; *fig.* pick; '♀**n** v/t. (*irr.* lesen, *sep.*, -ge-, *h*) pick out, select; finish reading (*book*).

'**ausliefer|n** v/t. (*sep.*, -ge-, *h*) hand or turn over, deliver (up); extradite (*criminal*); ausgeliefert sein (*dat.*) be at the mercy of; '♀**ung** f delivery; extradition.

'**aus|liegen** v/i. (*irr.* liegen, *sep.*, -ge-, *h*) be displayed, be on show; '~**löschen** v/t. (*sep.*, -ge-, *h*) put out, switch off (*light*); extinguish (*fire*) (*a. fig.*); efface (*word*); wipe out, erase; '~**losen** v/t. (*sep.*, -ge-, *h*) draw lots for.

'**auslös|en** v/t. (*sep.*, -ge-, *h*) ⊕ release; redeem, ransom (*prisoner*); redeem (*from pawn*); *fig.* cause, start; arouse (*applause*); '♀**er** m (-s/-) ⊕ release, esp. *phot.* trigger.

'**aus|lüften** v/t. (*sep.*, -ge-, *h*) air, ventilate; '~**machen** v/t. (*sep.*, -ge-, *h*) make out, sight, spot; *sum:* amount to; constitute, make up; put out (*fire*); ⚡ turn out, switch off (*light*); agree on, arrange; settle; es macht nichts aus it does not matter; würde es Ihnen et. ~, wenn ...? would you mind (*ger.*) ...?; '~**malen** v/t. (*sep.*, -ge-, *h*) paint; sich et. ~ picture s.th. to o.s., imagine s.th.

'**Ausmaß** n dimension(s pl.), measurement(s pl.); *fig.* extent.

'**aus|mergeln** ['ausmergəln] v/t. (*sep.*, -ge-, *h*) emaciate; exhaust; ~**merzen** ['~mertsən] v/t. (*sep.*, -ge-, *h*) eliminate; eradicate; ~**messen** v/t. (*irr.* messen, *sep.*, -ge-, *h*) measure.

Ausnahm|e ['ausna:mə] f (-/-n) exception; ♀**sweise** adv. by way of exception; exceptionally.

'**ausnehmen** v/t. (*irr.* nehmen, *sep.*, -ge-, *h*) take out; draw (*fowl*); F fleece s.o.; *fig.* except, exempt; '~**d 1.** adj. exceptional; **2.** adv. exceedingly.

'**aus|nutzen** v/t. (*sep.*, -ge-, *h*) utilize; take advantage of; esp. ♋, ✕ exploit; ~**packen** (*sep.*, -ge-, *h*) **1.** v/t. unpack; **2.** F *fig.* v/i. speak one's mind; ~**pfeifen** thea. v/t. (*irr.* pfeifen, *sep.*, -ge-, *h*) hiss; ~**plaudern** v/t. (*sep.*, -ge-, *h*) blab *or* let out; '**~polstern** *v/t.* (*sep.*, -ge-, *h*) stuff, pad; wad; '**~probieren** *v/t.* (*sep.*, *no* -ge-, *h*) try, test.

Auspuff *mot.* ['aʊspʊf] *m* (-[e]s/-e) exhaust; '**~gas** *mot. n* exhaust gas; '**~rohr** *mot. n* exhaust-pipe; '**~topf** *mot. m* silencer, *Am.* muffler.

'**aus|putzen** *v/t.* (*sep.*, -ge-, *h*) clean; '**~quartieren** *v/t.* (*sep.*, *no* -ge-, *h*) dislodge; ⚔ billet out; '**~radieren** *v/t.* (*sep.*, *no* -ge-, *h*) erase; '**~rangieren** *v/t.* (*sep.*, *no* -ge-, *h*) discard; '**~rauben** *v/t.* (*sep.*, -ge-, *h*) rob; ransack; '**~räumen** *v/t.* (*sep.*, -ge-, *h*) empty, clear (out); remove (*furniture*); '**~rechnen** *v/t.* (*sep.*, -ge-, *h*) calculate, compute; reckon (out), *Am.* figure out *or* up (*all a. fig.*).

'**Ausrede** *f* excuse, evasion, subterfuge; '**2n** (*sep.*, -ge-, *h*) **1.** *v/i.* finish speaking; ~ *lassen* hear *s.o.* out; **2.** *v/t.*: *j-m et.* ~ dissuade s.o. from s.th.

'**ausreichen** *v/i.* (*sep.*, -ge-, *h*) suffice; '**~d** *adj.* sufficient.

'**Ausreise** *f* departure; ⚓ voyage out.

'**ausreiß|en** (*irr. reißen*, *sep.*, -ge-) **1.** *v/t.* (*h*) pull *or* tear out; **2.** *v/i.* (*sein*) run away; '**2er** *m* runaway.

aus|renken ['aʊsrɛŋkən] *v/t.* (*sep.*, -ge-, *h*) dislocate; '**~richten** *v/t.* (*sep.*, -ge-, *h*) straighten; ⚔ dress; adjust; deliver (*message*); do, effect; accomplish; obtain; arrange (*feast*); *richte ihr e-n Gruß von mir aus!* remember me to her!; **~rotten** ['~rɔtən] *v/t.* (*sep.*, -ge-, *h*) root out; *fig.* extirpate, exterminate.

'**Ausruf** *m* cry; exclamation; '**2en** (*irr. rufen*, *sep.*, -ge-,*h*) **1.** *v/i.* cry out, exclaim; **2.** *v/t.* proclaim; '**~ezeichen** *n* exclamation mark, *Am. a.* exclamation point; '**~ung** *f* (-/-en) proclamation; '**~ungszeichen** *n s. Ausrufezeichen.*

'**ausruhen** *v/i.*, *v/t. and v/refl.* (*sep.*, -ge-, *h*) rest.

'**ausrüst|en** *v/t.* (*sep.*, -ge-, *h*) fit out; equip; '**2ung** *f* outfit, equipment, fittings *pl.*

'**aussäen** *v/t.* (*sep.*, -ge-, *h*) sow; *fig.* disseminate.

'**Aussage** *f* statement; declaration; ⚖ evidence; *gr.* predicate; '**2n** (*sep.*, -ge-, *h*) **1.** *v/t.* state, declare; ⚖ depose; **2.** ⚖ *v/i.* give evidence.

'**Aussatz** ⚕ *m* (-es/*no pl.*) leprosy.

'**aus|saugen** *v/t.* (*sep.*, -ge-, *h*) suck (out); *fig.* exhaust (*land*); '**~schalten** *v/t.* (*sep.*, -ge-, *h*) eliminate; ⚡ cut out, switch off, turn off *or* out (*light*).

Ausschank ['aʊsʃaŋk] *m* (-[e]s/⸗e) retail (*of alcoholic drinks*); public house, F pub.

'**Ausschau** *f* (-/*no pl.*): ~ *halten nach* be on the look-out for, watch for.

'**ausscheid|en** (*irr. scheiden*, *sep.*, -ge-) **1.** *v/t.* (*h*) separate; ⚗, ⚗, *physiol.* eliminate; ⚕ secrete; **2.** *v/i.* (*sein*) retire; withdraw; *sports*: drop out; '**2ung** *f* separation; elimination (*a. sports*); ⚕ secretion.

'**aus|schiffen** *v/t. and v/refl.* (*sep.*, -ge-, *h*) disembark; '**~schimpfen** *v/t.* (*sep.*, -ge-, *h*) scold, tell *s.o.* off, berate; **~schirren** ['~ʃirən] *v/t.* (*sep.*, -ge-, *h*) unharness; '**~schlachten** *v/t.* (*sep.*, -ge-, *h*) cut up; cannibalize (*car*, *etc.*); *fig.* exploit, make the most of; '**~schlafen** (*irr. schlafen*, *sep.*, -ge-, *h*) **1.** *v/i.* sleep one's fill; **2.** *v/t.* sleep off (*effects of drink*, *etc.*).

'**Ausschlag** *m* ⚕ eruption, rash; deflexion (*of pointer*); *den* ~ *geben* settle it; **2en** ['~gən] (*irr. schlagen*, *sep.*, -ge-) **1.** *v/t.* (*h*) knock *or* beat out; line; refuse, decline; **2.** *v/i.* (*h*) *horse*: kick; *pointer*: deflect; **3.** *v/i.* (*h*, *sein*) bud; **2gebend** *adj.* ['~k-] decisive.

'**ausschließ|en** *v/t.* (*irr. schließen*, *sep.*, -ge-, *h*) shut *or* lock out; *fig.*: exclude; expel; *sports*: disqualify; '**~lich** *adj.* exclusive.

'**Ausschluß** *m* exclusion; expulsion; *sports*: disqualification.

'**ausschmücken** *v/t.* (*sep.*, -ge-, *h*) adorn, decorate; *fig.* embellish.

'**Ausschnitt** *m* cut; décolleté, (low) neck (*of dress*); cutting, *Am.* clipping (*from newspaper*); *fig.* part, section.

'**ausschreib|en** *v/t.* (*irr. schreiben*, *sep.*, -ge-, *h*) write out; copy; write out (*word*) in full; make out (*invoice*); announce; advertise; '**2ung** *f* (-/-en) announcement; advertisement.

'**ausschreit|en** (*irr. schreiten*, *sep.*, -ge-) **1.** *v/i.* (*sein*) step out, take long strides; **2.** *v/t.* (*h*) pace (*room*), measure by steps; '**2ung** *f* (-/-en) excess; ~*en pl.* riots *pl.*

'**Ausschuß** *m* refuse, waste, rubbish; committee, board.

'**aus|schütteln** *v/t.* (*sep.*, -ge-, *h*) shake out; '**~schütten** *v/t.* (*sep.*, -ge-, *h*) pour out; spill; ✝ distribute (*dividend*); j-m sein Herz ~ pour out one's heart to s.o.; '**~schwärmen** *v/i.* (*sep.*, -ge-, *sein*) swarm out; ~ (*lassen*) ✕ extend, deploy.

'**ausschweif|end** *adj.* dissolute; '**2ung** *f* (-/-en) debauchery, excess.

'**ausschwitzen** *v/t.* (*sep.*, -ge-, *h*) exude.

'**aussehen** **1.** *v/i.* (*irr. sehen, sep.*, -ge-, *h*) look; wie sieht er aus? what does he look like?; es sieht nach Regen aus it looks like rain; **2.** 2 *n* (-s/ *no pl.*) look(s *pl.*), appearance.

außen *adv.* ['ausən] (on the) outside; von ~ her from (the) outside; nach ~ (hin) outward(s); '**2aufnahme** *f* film: outdoor shot; '**2bordmotor** *m* outboard motor.

'**aussenden** *v/t.* (*irr. senden,*] *sep.*, -ge-, *h*) send out.

'**Außen|hafen** *m* outport; '**~handel** *m* foreign trade; '**~minister** *m* foreign minister; Foreign Secretary, *Am.* Secretary of State; '**~ministerium** *n* foreign ministry; Foreign Office, *Am.* State Department; '**~politik** *f* foreign policy; '**2politisch** *adj.* of *or* referring to foreign affairs; '**~seite** *f* outside, surface; '**~seiter** *m* (-s/-) outsider; '**~stände** ✝ ['~ʃtɛndə] *pl.* outstanding debts *pl.*, *Am.* accounts *pl.* receivable; '**~welt** *f* outer *or* outside world.

außer ['ausər] **1.** *prp.* (*dat.*) out of; beside(s), *Am.* aside from; except; ~ sich sein be beside o.s. (vor Freude with joy); **2.** *cj.*: ~ daß except that; ~ wenn unless; '**~dem** *cj.* besides, moreover.

äußere ['ɔysərə] **1.** *adj.* exterior, outer, external, outward; **2.** 2 *n* (Äußer[e]n/*no pl.*) exterior, outside, outward appearance.

'**außer|gewöhnlich** *adj.* extraordinary; exceptional; '**~halb** **1.** *prp.* (*gen.*) outside, out of; beyond; **2.** *adv.* on the outside.

äußerlich *adj.* ['ɔysərliç] external, outward; '**2keit** *f* (-/-en) superficiality; formality.

äußern ['ɔysərn] *v/t.* (ge-, *h*) utter, express; advance; sich ~ matter:

manifest itself; *p.* express o.s.

'**außer'ordentlich** *adj.* extraordinary.

äußerst ['ɔysərst] **1.** *adj.* outermost; *fig.* utmost, extreme; **2.** *adv.* extremely, highly.

außerstande *adj.* [ausər'ʃtandə] unable, not in a position.

'**Äußerung** *f* (-/-en) utterance, remark.

'**aussetz|en** (*sep.*, -ge-, *h*) **1.** *v/t.* set *or* put out; lower (*boat*); promise (*reward*); settle (*pension*); bequeath; expose (*child*); expose (*dat.* to); et. ~ an (*dat.*) find fault with; **2.** *v/i.* intermit; fail; *activity:* stop; suspend; *mot.* misfire; '**2ung** *f* (-/-en) exposure (of child, to weather, etc.) (a. 🏛).

'**Aussicht** *f* (-/-en) view (auf *acc.* of); *fig.* prospect (of), chance (of); in ~ haben have in prospect; '**2slos** *adj.* hopeless, desperate; '**2sreich** *adj.* promising, full of promise.

'**aussöhn|en** ['ausøːnən] *v/t.* (*sep.*, -ge-, *h*) reconcile *s.o.* (mit to *s.th.*, with *s.o.*); sich ~ reconcile o.s. (to *s.th.*, with *s.o.*); '**2ung** *f* (-/-en) reconciliation.

'**aussondern** *v/t.* (*sep.*, -ge-, *h*) single out; separate.

'**aus|spannen** (*sep.*, -ge-, *h*) **1.** *v/t.* stretch, extend; 𝕱 *fig.* steal (*s.o.'s girl friend*); unharness (*draught animal*); **2.** *fig. v/i.* (take a) rest, relax; '**~speien** *v/t.* and *v/i.* (*irr. speien, sep.*, -ge-, *h*) spit out.

'**aussperr|en** *v/t.* (*sep.*, -ge-, *h*) shut out; lock out (*workmen*); '**2ung** *f* (-/-en) lock-out.

'**aus|spielen** (*sep.*, -ge-, *h*) **1.** *v/t.* play (*card*); **2.** *v/i.* at cards: lead; er hat ausgespielt he is done for; '**~spionieren** *v/t.* (*sep., no* -ge-, *h*) spy out.   [cent; discussion.|

'**Aussprache** *f* pronunciation, ac-]

'**aussprechen** (*irr. sprechen, sep.*, -ge-, *h*) **1.** *v/t.* pronounce, express; sich ~ für (gegen) declare o.s. for (against); **2.** *v/i.* finish speaking.

'**Ausspruch** *m* utterance; saying; remark.

'**aus|spucken** *v/i.* and *v/t.* (*sep.*, -ge-, *h*) spit out; '**~spülen** *v/t.* (*sep.*, -ge-, *h*) rinse.

'**Ausstand** *m* strike, *Am.* F a. walkout; in den ~ treten go on strike, *Am.* F a. walk out.

ausstatt|en ['aʊsʃtatən] v/t. (sep., -ge-, h) fit out, equip; furnish; supply (mit with); give a dowry to (daughter); get up (book); **'2ung** f (-/-en) outfit, equipment; furniture; supply; dowry; get-up (of book).

'aus|stechen v/t. (irr. stechen, sep., -ge-, h) cut out (a. fig.); put out (eye); **'~stehen** (irr. stehen, sep., -ge-, h) **1.** v/i. payments: be outstanding; **2.** v/t. endure, bear; **'~steigen** v/i. (irr. steigen, sep., -ge-, sein) get out or off, alight.

'ausstell|en v/t. (sep., -ge-, h) exhibit; make out (invoice); issue (document); draw (bill); **'2er** m (-s/-) exhibitor; drawer; **'2ung** f exhibition, show; **'2ungsraum** m show-room.

'aussterben v/i. (irr. sterben, sep., -ge-, sein) die out; become extinct.

'Aussteuer f trousseau, dowry.

'ausstopfen v/t. (sep., -ge-, h) stuff, wad, pad.

'ausstoß|en v/t. (irr. stoßen, sep., -ge-, h) thrust out, eject; expel; utter (cry); heave (sigh); ✕ cashier; **'2ung** f (-/-en) expulsion.

'aus|strahlen v/t. and v/i. (sep., -ge-, h) radiate; **'~strecken** v/t. (sep., -ge-, h) stretch (out) **'~streichen** v/t. (irr. streichen, sep., -ge-, h) strike out; smooth (down); **'~streuen** v/t. (sep., -ge-, h) scatter; spread (rumours); **'~strömen** (sep., -ge-) **1.** v/i. (sein) stream out; gas, light: emanate; gas, steam: escape; **2.** v/t. (h) pour (out); **'~suchen** v/t. (sep., -ge-, h) choose, select.

'Austausch m exchange; **'2bar** adj. exchangeable; **'2en** v/t. (sep., -ge-, h) exchange.

'austeil|en v/t. (sep., -ge-, h) distribute; deal out (blows); **'2ung** f distribution.

Auster zo. ['aʊstər] f (-/-n) oyster.

'austragen v/t. (irr. tragen, sep., -ge-, h) deliver (letters, etc.); hold (contest).

Austral|ier [aʊ'straːliər] m (-s/-) Australian; **2isch** adj. Australian.

'austreib|en v/t. (irr. treiben, sep., -ge-, h) drive out; expel; **'2ung** f (-/-en) expulsion.

'aus|treten (irr. treten, sep., -ge-) **1.** v/t. (h) tread or stamp out; wear out (shoes); wear down (steps);

2. v/i. (sein) emerge, come out; river: overflow its banks; retire (aus from); F ease o.s.; **~ aus** leave (society, etc.); **'~trinken** (irr. trinken, sep., -ge-, h) **1.** v/t. drink up; empty, drain; **2.** v/i. finish drinking; **'2tritt** m leaving; retirement; **'~trocknen** (sep., -ge-) **1.** v/t. (h) dry up; drain (land); parch (throat, earth); **2.** v/i. (sein) dry up.

'ausüb|en v/t. (sep., -ge-, h) exercise; practi|se, Am. -ce (profession); exert (influence); **'2ung** f practice; exercise.

'Ausverkauf ✝ m selling off or out (of stock); sale; **'2t** ✝, thea. adj. sold out; theatre notice: 'full house'.

'Auswahl f choice; selection; ✝ assortment. [choose, select.]

'auswählen v/t. (sep., -ge-, h)]

'Auswander|er m emigrant; **'2n** v/i. (sep., -ge-, sein) emigrate; **'~ung** f emigration.

auswärt|ig adj. ['aʊsvɛrtiç] out-of-town; non-resident; foreign; das Auswärtige Amt s. Außenministerium; **~s** adv. ['~s] outward(s); out of doors; out of town; abroad; **~ essen** dine out.

'auswechseln v/t. (sep., -ge-, h) exchange; change; replace; **2 n** (-s/no pl.) exchange; replacement.

'Ausweg m way out (a. fig.); outlet; fig. expedient.

'ausweichen v/i. (irr. weichen, sep., -ge-, sein) make way (for); fig. evade, avoid; **'~d** adj. evasive.

Ausweis ['aʊsvaɪs] m (-es/-e) (bank) return; identity card, Am. identification (card); **2en** ['~zən] v/t. (irr. weisen, sep., -ge-, h) turn out, expel; evict; deport; show, prove; sich **~** prove one's identity; **'~papiere** n/pl. identity papers pl.; **'~ung** ['~zuŋ] f expulsion; **'~ungsbefehl** m expulsion order.

'ausweiten v/t. and v/refl. (sep., -ge-, h) widen, stretch, expand.

'auswendig 1. adj. outward, outside; **2.** adv. outwardly, outside; fig. by heart.

'aus|werfen v/t. (irr. werfen, sep., -ge-, h) throw out, cast; eject; ✄ expectorate; allow (sum of money); **'~werten** v/t. (sep., -ge-, h) evaluate; analyze, interpret; utilize, exploit; **'~wickeln** v/t. (sep., -ge-, h) unwrap; **'~wiegen** v/t. (irr. wiegen, *sep.*, -ge-, *h*) weigh out; '**~wirken** *v/refl.* (*sep.*, -ge-, *h*) take effect, operate; *sich ~ auf* (*acc.*) affect; '**Ꞇwirkung** *f* effect; '**~wischen** *v/t.* (*sep.*, -ge-, *h*) wipe out, efface; '**~wringen** *v/t.* (*irr.* wringen, *sep.*, -ge-, *h*) wring out.

'**Auswuchs** *m* excrescence, outgrowth (*a. fig.*), protuberance.

'**Auswurf** *m* ⚕ expectoration; *fig.* refuse, dregs *pl.*

'**aus|zahlen** *v/t.* (*sep.*, -ge-, *h*) pay out; pay *s.o.* off; '**~zählen** *v/t.* (*sep.*, -ge-, *h*) count out.

'**Auszahlung** *f* payment.

'**Auszehrung** *f* (-/-en) consumption.

'**auszeichn|en** *v/t.* (*sep.*, -ge-, *h*) mark (out); *fig.* distinguish (*sich o.s.*); '**Ꞇung** *f* marking; distinction; hono(u)r; decoration.

'**auszieh|en** (*irr.* ziehen, *sep.*, -ge-) **1.** *v/t.* (*h*) draw out, extract; take off (*garment*); *sich ~* undress; **2.** *v/i.* (*sein*) set out; move (out), remove, move house; '**Ꞇplatte** *f* leaf (*of table*).

'**Auszug** *m* departure; ✕ marching out; removal; extract, excerpt (*from book*); summary; ✝ statement (of account). [tic, genuine.\

authentisch *adj.* [au'tɛntiʃ] authen-\

Auto ['auto] *n* (-s/-s) (motor-)car, *Am. a.* automobile; *~ fahren* drive, motor; '**~bahn** *f* motorway, auto-bahn; '**~biographie** *f* autobiography; '**~bus** ['-bus] *m* (-ses/-se) (motor-)bus; (motor) coach; '**~bus-**

haltestelle *f* bus stop; **~didakt** [-di'dakt] *m* (-en/-en) autodidact, self-taught person; '**~droschke** *f* taxi(-cab), *Am.* cab; '**~fahrer** *m* motorist; **~'gramm** *n* autograph; **~'grammjäger** *m* autograph hunter; '**~händler** *m* car dealer; '**~kino** *n* drive-in cinema; **~krat** [-'kra:t] *m* (-en/-en) autocrat; **~kratie** [-a-'ti:] *f* (-/-en) autocracy; **~mat** [-'ma:t] *m* (-en/-en) automaton; slot-machine, vending machine; **~'matenrestaurant** *n* self-service restaurant, *Am.* automat; **~mation** ⊕ [-ma'tsjo:n] *f* (-/*no pl.*) automation; **Ꞇ'matisch** *adj.* automatic; **~'mechaniker** *m* car mechanic; **~mobil** [-mo'bi:l] *n* (-s/-e) *s.* Auto; **Ꞇnom** *adj.* [-'no:m] autonomous; **~nomie** [-o'mi:] *f* (-/-en) autonomy.

Autor ['autor] *m* (-s/-en) author.

'**Autoreparaturwerkstatt** *f* car repair shop, garage. [thor(ess).\

Autorin [au'to:rin] *f* (-/-nen) au-\

autori|sieren [autori'zi:rən] *v/t.* (*no* -ge-, *h*) authorize; **~tär** *adj.* [-'tɛ:r] authoritarian; **Ꞇ'tät** *f* (-/-en) authority.

'**Auto|straße** *f* motor-road; '**~vermietung** *f* (-/-en) car hire service.

avisieren ✝ [avi'zi:rən] *v/t.* (*no* -ge-, *h*) advise.

Axt [akst] *f* (-/⸚e) ax(e).

Azetylen 🜊 [atsety'le:n] *n* (-s/*no pl.*) acetylene. [Ꞇn *adj.* azure.\

Azur [a'tsu:r] *m* (-s/*no pl.*) azure;\

B

Bach [bax] *m* (-[e]s/⸚e) brook, *Am. a.* run.   [port.\

Backbord ⚓ ['bak-] *n* (-[e]s/-e)\

Backe ['bakə] *f* (-/-n) cheek.

backen ['bakən] (*irr.*, ge-, *h*) **1.** *v/t.* bake; fry; dry (*fruit*); **2.** *v/i.* bake; fry.

'**Backen|bart** *m* (side-)whiskers *pl.*, *Am. a.* sideburns *pl.*; '**~zahn** *m* molar (tooth), grinder.

Bäcker ['bɛkər] *m* (-s/-) baker; **~ei** [-'rai] *f* (-/-en) baker's (shop), bakery.

'**Backfisch** *m* fried fish; *fig.* girl in her teens, teenager, *Am. a.* bobby soxer; '**~obst** *n* dried fruit; '**~ofen**

m oven; '**~pflaume** *f* prune; '**~pulver** *n* baking-powder; '**~stein** *m* brick; '**~ware** *f* baker's ware.

Bad [ba:t] *n* (-[e]s/⸚er) bath; *in river, etc.*: *a.* bathe; *s.* Badeort; *ein ~ nehmen* take *or* have a bath.

Bade|anstalt ['ba:də-] *f* (public swimming) baths *pl.*; '**~anzug** *m* bathing-costume, bathing-suit; '**~hose** *f* bathing-drawers *pl.*, (bathing) trunks *pl.*; '**~kappe** *f* bathing-cap; '**~kur** *f* spa treatment; '**~mantel** *m* bathing-gown, *Am.* bathrobe; '**~meister** *m* bath attendant; swimming-instructor; '**Ꞇn** (ge-, *h*) **1.** *v/t.* bath (*baby, etc.*); bathe (*eyes, etc.*);

2. v/i. bath, tub; have or take a bath; in river, etc.: bathe; ~ gehen go swimming; '~ofen m geyser, boiler, Am. a. water heater; '~ort m watering-place; spa; seaside resort; '~salz n bath-salt; '~strand m bathing-beach; '~tuch n bath-towel; '~wanne f bath-tub; '~zimmer n bathroom.

Bagatell|e [baga'tɛlə] f (-/-n) trifle, trifling matter, bagatelle; 2i'sieren v/t. (no -ge-, h) minimize (the importance of), Am. a. play down.

Bagger ['bagər] m (-s/-) excavator; dredge(r); '2n v/i. and v/t. (ge-, h) excavate; dredge.

Bahn [baːn] f (-/-en) course; path; 🚂 railway, Am. railroad; mot. lane; trajectory (of bullet, etc.); ast. orbit; sports: track, course, lane; skating: rink; bowling: alley; '2brechend adj. pioneer(ing), epoch-making; art: avant-gardist; '~damm m railway embankment, Am. railroad embankment; '2en v/t. (ge-, h) clear, open (up) (way); den Weg ~ prepare or pave the way (dat. for); sich e-n Weg ~ force or work or elbow one's way; '~hof m (railway-)station, Am. (railroad-)station; '~linie f railway-line, Am. railroad line; '~steig m platform; '~steigkarte f platform ticket; '~übergang m level crossing, Am. grade crossing.

Bahre ['baːrə] f (-/-n) stretcher, litter; bier.

Bai [baɪ] f (-/-en) bay; creek.

Baisse [ˈbɛːs(ə)] f (-/-n) depression (on the market); fall (in prices); auf ~ spekulieren ✝ bear, speculate for a fall, Am. sell short; '~spekulant m bear.

Bajonett ✗ [bajoˈnɛt] n (-[e]s/-e) bayonet; das ~ aufpflanzen fix the bayonet.

Bake ['baːkə] f (-/-n) ⚓ beacon; 🚂 warning-sign.

Bakterie [bakˈteːrjə] f (-/-n) bacterium, microbe, germ.

bald adv. [balt] soon; shortly; before long; ~ almost, nearly; early; so ~ als möglich as soon as possible; ~ hier, ~ dort now here, now there; '~ig adj. ['~dɪç] speedy; ~e Antwort ✝ early reply. [valerian.]

Baldrian ['baldriaːn] m (-s/-e)

Balg [balk] **1.** m (-[e]s/¨e) skin; body (of doll); bellows pl.; **2.** F m, n (-[e]s/¨er) brat, urchin; 2en ['balgən] v/refl. (ge-, h) scuffle (um for), wrestle (for).

Balken ['balkən] m (-s/-) beam; rafter.

Balkon [balˈkõː; ~ˈkoːn] m (-s/-s; -s/-e) balcony; thea. dress circle, Am. balcony; ~tür f French window.

Ball [bal] m (-[e]s/¨e) ball; geogr., ast. a. globe; ball, dance; auf dem ~ at the ball. [lad.]

Ballade [baˈlaːdə] f (-/-n) bal-

Ballast ['balast] m (-es/~-e) ballast; fig. burden, impediment; dead weight.

'ballen¹ v/t. (ge-, h) (form into a) ball; clench (fist); sich ~ (form into a) ball; cluster.

'Ballen² m (-s/-) bale; anat. ball; ~ Papier ten reams pl.

Ballett [baˈlɛt] n (-[e]s/-e) ballet; ~änzer [baˈlɛtɛntsər] m (-s/-) ballet-dancer.

ball|förmig adj. ['balfœrmiç] ball-shaped, globular; '2kleid n ball-dress.

Ballon [baˈlõː; ~ˈoːn] m (-s/-s; -s/-e) balloon.

'Ball|saal m ball-room; '~spiel n ball-game, game of ball.

Balsam ['balzaːm] m (-s/-e) balsam, balm (a. fig.); 2ieren [~aˈmiːrən] v/t. (no -ge-, h) embalm.

Balz [balts] f (-/-en) mating season; display (by cock-bird).

Bambus ['bambus] m (-ses/-se) bamboo; '~rohr n bamboo, cane.

banal adj. [baˈnaːl] commonplace, banal, trite; trivial; 2ität [~aliˈtɛːt] f (-/-en) banality; commonplace; triviality.

Banane [baˈnaːnə] f (-/-n) banana; ~nstecker ⚡ m banana plug.

Band [bant] **1.** m (-[e]s/¨e) volume; **2.** n (-[e]s/¨er) band; ribbon; tape; anat. ligament; **3.** fig. n (-[e]s/-e) bond, tie; **4.** 2 pret. of binden.

Bandage [banˈdaːʒə] f (-/-n) bandage; 2ieren [~aˈʒiːrən] v/t. (no -ge-, h) (apply a) bandage.

Bande ['bandə] f (-/-n) billiards: cushion; fig. gang, band.

bändigen ['bɛndigən] v/t. (ge-, h) tame; break in (horse); subdue (a. fig.); fig. restrain, master.

Bandit [ban'diːt] m (-en/-en) bandit.

'Band|maß n tape measure; **'~säge** f band-saw; **'~scheibe** anat. f intervertebral disc; **'~wurm** zo. m tapeworm.

bang adj. [baŋ], **~e** adj. ['~ə] anxious (um about), uneasy (about), concerned (for); mir ist ~ I am afraid (vor dat. of); j-m bange machen frighten or scare s.o.; **~e** v/i. (ge-, h) be anxious or worried (um about).

Bank [baŋk] f **1.** (-/ᵂe) bench; school: desk; F durch die ~ without exception, all through); auf die lange ~ schieben put off, postpone; shelve; **2.** ✝ (-/-en) bank; Geld auf der ~ money in the bank; **'~anweisung** f cheque, Am. check; **'~ausweis** m bank return or statement; **'~beamte** m bank clerk or official; **'~einlage** f deposit.

Bankett [baŋ'kɛt] n (-[e]s/-e) banquet.

'Bank|geheimnis n banker's duty of secrecy; **'~geschäft** ✝ n bank (-ing) transaction, banking operation; **'~haus** n bank(ing-house).

Bankier [baŋk'jeː] m (-s/-s) banker.

'Bank|konto n bank(ing) account; **'~note** f (bank) note, Am. (bank) bill.

bankrott [baŋ'krɔt] **1.** adj. bankrupt; **2.** ♀ m (-[e]s/-e) bankruptcy, insolvency, failure; ~ machen fail, go or become bankrupt.

'Bankwesen n banking.

Bann [ban] m (-[e]s/-e) ban; fig. spell; eccl. excommunication; **'~en** v/t. (ge-, h) banish (a. fig.); exorcize (devil); avert (danger); eccl. excommunicate; spellbind.

Banner ['banər] n (-s/-) banner (a. fig.); standard; **'~träger** m standard-bearer.

'Bann|fluch m anathema; **'~meile** f precincts pl.; ⚖ area around government buildings within which processions and meetings are prohibited.

bar¹ [baːr] **1.** adj.: e-r Sache ~ destitute or devoid of s.th.; ~es Geld ready money, cash; ~er Unsinn sheer nonsense; **2.** adv.: ~ bezahlen pay in cash, pay money down.

Bar² [.] f (-/-s) bar; night-club.

Bär [bɛːr] m (-en/-en) bear; j-m e-n ~en aufbinden hoax s.o.

Baracke [ba'rakə] f (-/-n) barrack; **~nlager** n hutment.

Barbar [bar'baːr] m (-en/-en) barbarian; **~ei** [~a'raɪ] f (-/-en) barbarism; barbarity; **²isch** [~'baːrɪʃ] adj. barbarian; barbarous; art, taste: barbaric.

'Bar|bestand m cash in hand; **'~betrag** m amount in cash.

'Bärenzwinger m bear-pit.

barfuß adj. and adv. ['baːr-], **~füßig** adj. and adv. ['~fyːsɪç] barefoot.

barg [bark] pret. of bergen.

'Bar|geld n cash, ready money; **'²geldlos** adj. cashless; **'~er Zahlungsverkehr** cashless money transfers pl.; **²häuptig** adj. and adv. ['~hɔyptɪç] bare-headed, uncovered.

Bariton ♪ ['baːritɔn] m (-s/-e) baritone. [launch.]

Barkasse ⚓ [bar'kasə] f (-/-n)

barmherzig adj. [barm'hɛrtsɪç] merciful, charitable; der ~e Samariter the good Samaritan; ²e Schwester Sister of Mercy or Charity; **²keit** f (-/-en) mercy, charity.

Barometer [baro'-] n barometer.

Baron [ba'roːn] m (-s/-e) baron; **~in** f (-/-nen) baroness.

Barre ['barə] f (-/-n) bar.

Barren ['barən] m (-s/-) metall. bar, ingot, bullion; gymnastics: parallel bars pl.

Barriere [bar'jɛːrə] f (-/-n) barrier.

Barrikade [bari'kaːdə] f (-/-n) barricade; **~n errichten** raise barricades.

barsch adj. [barʃ] rude, gruff, rough.

'Bar|schaft f (-/-en) ready money, cash; **'~scheck** ✝ m open cheque, Am. open check.

barst [barst] pret. of bersten.

Bart [baːrt] m (-[e]s/ᵂe) beard; bit (of key); sich e-n ~ wachsen lassen grow a beard.

bärtig adj. ['bɛːrtɪç] bearded.

'bartlos adj. beardless.

'Barzahlung f cash payment; nur gegen ~ ✝ terms strictly cash.

Basis ['baːzɪs] f (-/Basen) base; fig. basis.

Baß ♪ [bas] m (Basses/Bässe) bass; **'~geige** f bass-viol.

Bassist [ba'sɪst] m (-en/-en) bass (singer).

Bast [bast] m (-es/-e) bast; velvet (on antlers).

Bastard ['bastart] m (-[e]s/-e) bas-

B

tard; half-breed; *zo.*, ⚭ hybrid.
bast|eln ['bastəln] (ge-, h) **1.** *v/t.*
build, F rig up; **2.** *v/i.* build; **Ṣler**
m (-s/-) amateur craftsman, do-it-
yourself man.

bat [baːt] *pret. of* **bitten.**

Bataillon [batal'joːn] *n* (-s/-e)
battalion.

Batist [ba'tist] *m* (-[e]s/-e) cambric.

Batterie ⨯, ⚡ [batə'riː] *f* (-/-n)
battery.

Bau [bau] *m* **1.** (-[e]s/*no pl.*) building, construction; build, frame;
2. (-[e]s/-ten) building, edifice;
3. (-[e]s/-e) burrow, den (*a. fig.*),
earth.

'Bau|arbeiter *m* workman in the
building trade; **'∼art** *f* architecture,
style; method of construction;
mot. type, model.

Bauch [baux] *m* (-[e]s/=e) *anat.*
abdomen, belly; paunch; *ship:*
bottom; **'Ṣig** *adj.* big-bellied, bulgy;
'∼landung *f* belly landing; **'∼red-
ner** *m* ventriloquist; **'∼schmerzen**
m/pl., **'∼weh** *n* (-s/*no pl.*) belly-ache,
stomach-ache.

bauen ['bauən] (ge-, h) **1.** *v/t.* build,
construct; erect, raise; build, make
(*nest*); make (*violin, etc.*); **2.** *v/i.*
build; ∼ auf (*acc.*) trust (in); rely
or count or depend on.

Bauer ['bauər] **1.** *m* (-n, -s/-n)
farmer; peasant, countryman; *chess:*
pawn; **2.** *n*, *m* (-s/-) (bird-)cage.

Bäuerin ['bɔʏərɪn] *f* (-/-nen) farmer's wife; peasant woman.

Bauerlaubnis ['bau'ʔ-] *f* building
permit.

bäuerlich *adj.* ['bɔʏərlɪç] rural,
rustic.

Bauern|fänger *contp.* ['bauərn-
fɛŋər] *m* (-s/-) trickster, confidence
man; **'∼haus** *n* farm-house; **'∼hof**
m farm.

'bau|fällig *adj.* out of repair,
dilapidated; **'Ṣgerüst** *n* scaffold
(-ing); **'Ṣhandwerker** *m* craftsman
in the building trade; **'Ṣherr** *m*
owner; **'Ṣholz** *n* timber, *Am.* lumber; **'Ṣjahr** *n* year of construction;
∼ *1969* 1969 model or make; **'Ṣka-
sten** *m* box of bricks; **'Ṣkunst** *f*
architecture.

'baulich *adj.* architectural; struc-
tural; *in gutem ∼en Zustand* in good
repair.

Baum [baum] *m* (-[e]s/=e) tree.

'Baumeister *m* architect.

baumeln ['bauməln] *v/i.* (ge-, h)
dangle, swing; *mit den Beinen* ∼
dangle or swing one's legs.

'Baum|schere *f* (*eine a pair of*)
pruning-shears *pl.*; **'∼schule** *f*
nursery (*of young trees*); **'∼stamm**
m trunk; **'∼wolle** *f* cotton; **'Ṣwol-
len** *adj.* (made of) cotton.

'Bau|plan *m* architect's or building
plan; **'∼platz** *m* building plot or site,
Am. location; **'∼polizei** *f* Board of
Surveyors.

Bausch [bauʃ] *m* (-es/-e, =e) pad;
bolster; wad; *in* ∼ *und Bogen* alto-
gether, wholesale, in the lump;
'Ṣen *v/t.* (ge-, h) swell; *sich* ∼ bulge,
swell out, billow (out).

'Bau|stein *m* brick, building stone;
building block; *fig.* element; **'∼-
stelle** *f* building site; **'∼stil** *m* (architectural) style; **'∼stoff** *m* building material; **'∼unternehmer** *m*
building contractor; **'∼zaun** *m*
hoarding.

Bay|er ['baiər] *m* (-n/-n) Bavarian;
'Ṣ(e)risch *adj.* Bavarian.

Bazill|enträger ⚕ [ba'tsilən-] *m*
(germ-)carrier; **∼us** [∼us] *m* (-/Ba-
zillen) bacillus, germ.

beabsichtigen [bə'apzɪçtɪɡən] *v/t.*
(*no* -ge-, h) intend, mean, propose
(*zu tun* to do, doing).

be'acht|en *v/t.* (*no* -ge-, h) pay at-
tention to; notice; observe; **∼ens-
wert** *adj.* noteworthy, remarkable;
∼lich *adj.* remarkable; considerable; **Ṣung** *f* attention; consideration; notice; observance.

Beamte [bə'amtə] *m* (-n/-n) official,
officer, *Am. a.* officeholder; functionary; Civil Servant. [quieting.\
be'ängstigend *adj.* alarming, dis-\]
beanspruch|en [bə'anʃpruxən] *v/t.*
(*no* -ge-, h) claim, demand; require
(*efforts, time, space, etc.*); ⊕ stress;
Ṣung *f* (-/-en) claim; demand (*gen.*
on); ⊕ stress, strain.

beanstand|en [bə'anʃtandən] *v/t.*
(*no* -ge-, h) object to; **Ṣung** *f* (-/-en)
objection (*gen.* to).

beantragen [bə'antraːɡən] *v/t.* (*no*
-ge-, h) apply for; ⚖, *parl.* move,
make a motion; propose.

be'antwort|en *v/t.* (*no* -ge-, h) an-
swer (*a. fig.*), reply to); **Ṣung** *f*
(-/-en) answer, reply; *in* ∼ (*gen.*) in
answer or reply to.

be'arbeit|en v/t. (no -ge-, h) work; ✎ till; dress (leather); hew (stone); process; 🜍 treat; ⚖ be in charge of (case); edit, revise (book); adapt (nach from); esp. ♪ arrange; j-n ~ work on s.o.; batter s.o.; ℒung f (-/-en) working; revision (of book); thea. adaptation; esp. ♪ arrangement; processing; 🜍 treatment.

be'argwöhnen v/t. (no -ge-, h) suspect, be suspicious of.

beaufsichtig|en [bə'aufziçtigən] v/t. (no -ge-, h) inspect, superintend, supervise, control; look after (child); ℒung f (-/-en) inspection, supervision, control.

be'auftrag|en v/t. (no -ge-, h) commission (zu inf. to inf.), charge (mit with); ℒte [⸗ktə] m (-n/-n) commissioner; representative; deputy; proxy.

be'bauen v/t. (no -ge-, h) ⚒ build on; ✎ cultivate.

beben ['be:bən] v/i. (ge-, h) shake (vor dat. with), tremble (with); shiver (with); earth: quake.

Becher ['beçər] m (-s/-) cup (a. fig.).

Becken ['bekən] n (-s/-) basin, Am. a. bowl; ♪ cymbal(s pl.); anat. pelvis.

bedacht adj. [bə'daxt]: ~ sein auf (acc.) look after, be concerned about, be careful or mindful of; darauf ~ sein zu inf. be anxious to inf.

bedächtig adj. [bə'deçtiç] deliberate.

bedang [bə'daŋ] pret. of bedingen.

be'danken v/refl. (no -ge-, h): sich bei j-m für et. ~ thank s.o. for s.th.

Bedarf [bə'darf] m (-[e]s/no pl.) need (an dat. of), want (of); ✝ demand (for); ~sartikel [bə'darfs²-] m/pl. necessaries pl., requisites pl.

bedauerlich adj. [bə'dauərliç] regrettable, deplorable.

be'dauern 1. v/t. (no -ge-, h) feel or be sorry for s.o.; pity s.o.; regret, deplore s.th.; 2. ℒ n (-s/no pl.) regret; pity; ~swert adj. pitiable, deplorable.

be'deck|en v/t. (no -ge-, h) cover; ✕ escort; ♨ convoy; ~t adj. sky: overcast; ℒung f cover(ing); ✕ escort; ♨ convoy.

be'denken 1. v/t. (irr. denken, no -ge-, h) consider; think s.th. over;

j-n in s-m Testament ~ remember s.o. in one's will; 2. ℒ n (-s/-) consideration; objection; hesitation; scruple; ~los adj. unscrupulous.

be'denklich adj. doubtful; character: a. dubious; situation, etc.: dangerous, critical; delicate; risky.

Be'denkzeit f time for reflection; ich gebe dir e-e Stunde ~ I give you one hour to think it over.

be'deut|en v/t. (no -ge-, h) mean, signify; stand for; ~end adj. important, prominent; sum, etc. considerable; ~sam adj. significant.

Be'deutung f meaning, significance; importance; ℒslos adj. insignificant; meaningless; ℒsvoll adj. significant; ~swandel ling. m semantic change.

be'dien|en (no -ge-, h) 1. v/t. serve; wait on; ⊕ operate, work (machine); ✕ serve (gun); answer (telephone); sich ~ at table: help o.s.; 2. v/i. serve; wait (at table); cards: follow suit; ℒung f (-/-en) service, esp. ✝ attendance; in restaurant, etc.: service; waiter, waitress; shop assistant(s pl.).

beding|en [bə'diŋən] v/t. ([irr.,] no -ge-, h) condition; stipulate; require; cause; imply; ~t adj. conditional (durch on); restricted; ~ sein durch be conditioned by; ℒung f (-/-en) condition; stipulation; ~en pl. ✝ terms pl.; ~ungslos adj. unconditional.

be'dräng|en v/t. (no -ge-, h) press hard, beset; ℒnis f (-/-se) distress.

be'droh|en v/t. (no -ge-, h) threaten; menace; ~lich adj. threatening; ℒung f threat, menace (gen. to).

be'drück|en v/t. (no -ge-, h) oppress; depress; deject; ℒung f (-/-en) oppression; depression; dejection.

bedungen [bə'duŋən] p.p. of bedingen.

be'dürf|en v/i. (irr. dürfen, no -ge-, h): e-r Sache ~ need or want or require s.th.; ℒnis n (-ses/-se) need, want, requirement; sein ~ verrichten relieve o.s. or nature; ℒnisanstalt [bə'dyrfnis²-] f public convenience, Am. comfort station; ~tig adj. needy, poor, indigent.

be'ehren v/t. (no -ge-, h) hono(u)r, favo(u)r; ich beehre mich zu inf. I have the hono(u)r to inf.

beeilen

be'eilen v/refl. (no -ge-, h) hasten, hurry, make haste, *Am.* F a. hustle.

beeindrucken [bə'aɪndrukən] v/t. (no -ge-, h) impress, make an impression on.

beeinfluss|en [bə'aɪnflusən] v/t. (no -ge-, h) influence; affect; *parl.* lobby; **2ung** f (-/-en) influence; *parl.* lobbying.

beeinträchtig|en [bə'aɪntrɛçtɪgən] v/t. (no -ge-, h) impair, injure, affect (adversely); **2ung** f (-/-en) impairment (gen. of); injury (to).

be'end|en v/t. (no -ge-, h), **~igen** [~ɪgən] v/t. (no -ge-, h) (bring to an) end, finish, terminate; **2igung** [~ɪguŋ] f (-/-en) ending, termination.

beengt adj. [bə'ɛŋkt] *space*: narrow, confined, cramped; sich ~ fühlen feel cramped (for room) or feel oppressed or uneasy.

be'erben v/t. (no -ge-, h): j-n ~ be s.o.'s heir.

beerdig|en [bə'eːrdɪgən] v/t. (no -ge-, h) bury; **2ung** f (-/-en) burial, funeral.

Beere ['beːrə] f (-/-n) berry.

Beet ✗ [beːt] n (-[e]s/-e) bed.

befähig|en [bə'fɛːɪgən] v/t. (no -ge-, h) enable (zu inf. to inf.); qualify (für, zu for); **~t** adj. [~çt] (cap)able; **2ung** f (-/-en) qualification; capacity.

befahl [bə'faːl] pret. of befehlen.

befahr|bar adj. [bə'faːrbaːr] passable, practicable, trafficable; ⚓ navigable; **~en** v/t. (irr. fahren, no -ge-, h) drive or travel on; ⚓ navigate (river).

be'fallen v/t. (irr. fallen, no -ge-, h) attack; befall; *disease:* a. strike; *fear:* seize.

be'fangen adj. embarrassed; self-conscious; prejudiced (a. ⚖); ⚖ bias(s)ed; **2heit** f (-/-en) embarrassment; self-consciousness; ⚖ bias, prejudice.

be'fassen v/refl. (no -ge-, h): sich ~ mit occupy o.s. with; engage in; attend to; deal with.

Befehl [bə'feːl] m (-[e]s/-e) command (über acc. of); order; **2en** (irr., no -ge-, h) **1.** v/t. command; order; **2.** v/i. command; **2igen** ✗ [~ɪgən] v/t. (no -ge-, h) command.

Be'fehlshaber m (-s/-) commander(-in-chief); **2isch** adj. imperious.

be'festig|en v/t. (no -ge-, h) fasten (an dat. to), fix (to), attach (to); ✗ fortify; *fig.* strengthen; **2ung** f (-/-en) fixing, fastening; ✗ fortification; *fig.* strengthening.

be'feuchten v/t. (no -ge-, h) moisten, damp; wet.

be'finden **1.** v/refl. (irr. finden, no -ge-, h) be; **2.** **2** n (-s/no pl.) (state of) health.

be'flaggen v/t. (no -ge-, h) flag.

be'flecken v/t. (no -ge-, h) spot, stain (a. fig.); fig. sully.

beflissen adj. [bə'flɪsən] studious; **2heit** f (-/no pl.) studiousness, assiduity.

befohlen [bə'foːlən] p.p. of befehlen.

be'folg|en v/t. (no -ge-, h) follow, take (advice); obey (rule); adhere to (principle); **2ung** f (-/✗-en) observance (of); adherence (to).

be'förder|n v/t. (no -ge-, h) convey, carry; haul (goods), transport; forward; ⚓ ship (a. ⚓); promote (to be) (a. ✗); **2ung** f conveyance, transport(ation), forwarding; promotion; **2ungsmittel** n (means of) transport, *Am.* (means of) transportation.

be'fragen v/t. (no -ge-, h) question, interview; interrogate.

be'frei|en v/t. (no -ge-, h) (set) free (von from); liberate (nation, mind, etc.) (from); rescue (captive) (from); exempt s.o. (from); deliver s.o. (aus, von from); **2er** m liberator; **2ung** f (-/-en) liberation, deliverance; exemption.

Befremden [bə'frɛmdən] n (-s/ no pl.) surprise.

befreund|en [bə'frɔyndən] v/refl. (no -ge-, h): sich mit j-m ~ make friends with s.o.; sich mit et. ~ get used to s.th., reconcile o.s. to s.th.; **~et** adj. friendly; on friendly terms; ~ sein be friends.

befriedig|en [bə'friːdɪgən] v/t. (no -ge-, h) satisfy; appease (hunger); meet (expectations, demand); pay off (creditor); **~end** adj. satisfactory; **2ung** f (-/-en) satisfaction.

be'fristen v/t. (no -ge-, h) set a time-limit.

be'frucht|en v/t. (no -ge-, h) fertilize; fructify; fecundate; impregnate; **2ung** f (-/-en) fertilization; fructification; fecundation; impregnation.

Befug|nis [bə'fu:knis] f (-/-se) authority, warrant; *esp.* ⚖ competence; **2t** adj. authorized; competent.

be'fühlen v/t. (no -ge-, h) feel; touch, handle, finger.

Be'fund m (-[e]s/-e) result; finding(s pl.); ⚕ diagnosis.

be'fürcht|en v/t. (no -ge-, h) fear, apprehend; suspect; **2ung** f (-/-en) fear, apprehension, suspicion.

befürworten [bə'fy:rvɔrtən] v/t. (no -ge-, h) plead for, advocate.

begab|t adj. [bə'ga:pt] gifted, talented; **2ung** [.bʊŋ] f (-/-en) gift, talent(s pl.).

begann [bə'gan] pret. of *beginnen*.

be'geben v/t. (irr. geben, no -ge-, h) ✝ negotiate (*bill of exchange*); sich ~ happen; sich ~ nach go to, make for; sich in Gefahr ~ expose o.s. to danger.

begegn|en [bə'ge:gnən] v/i. (no -ge-, sein) meet s.o. or s.th., meet with; *incident*: happen to; anticipate, prevent; **2ung** f (-/-en) meeting.

be'gehen v/t. (irr. gehen, no -ge-, h) walk (on); inspect; celebrate (*birthday, etc.*); commit (*crime*); make (*mistake*); ein Unrecht ~ do wrong.

begehr|en [bə'ge:rən] v/t. (no -ge-, h) demand, require; desire, crave (for); long for; **.lich** adj. desirous, covetous.

begeister|n [bə'gaɪstərn] v/t. (no -ge-, h) inspire, fill with enthusiasm; sich ~ für feel enthusiastic about; **2ung** f (-/no pl.) enthusiasm, inspiration.

Be'gier f, **.de** [.də] f (-/-n) desire (*nach* for), appetite (for); concupiscence; **2ig** adj. eager (*nach* for, auf acc. for; zu inf. to inf.), desirous (*nach* of; zu inf. to inf.), anxious (zu inf. to inf.).

be'gießen v/t. (irr. gießen, no -ge-, h) water; baste (*roasting meat*); F wet (*bargain*).

Beginn [bə'gin] m (-[e]s/no pl.) beginning, start, commencement; origin; **2en** v/t. and v/i. (irr. no -ge-, h) begin, start, commence.

beglaubig|en [bə'glaubiɡən] v/t. (no -ge-, h) attest, certify; legalize, authenticate; **2ung** f (-/-en) attestation, certification; legalization; **2ungsschreiben** n credentials pl.

be'gleichen ✝ v/t. (irr. gleichen, no -ge-, h) pay, settle (*bill, debt*).

be'gleit|en v/t. (no -ge-, h) accompany (a. ♪ auf dat. on), escort; attend (a. fig.); see (s.o. home, etc.); **2er** m (-s/-) companion, attendant, escort; ♪ accompanist; **2erscheinung** f attendant symptom; **2-schreiben** n covering letter; **2ung** f (-/-en) company; attendants pl., retinue (of sovereign, etc.); esp. ✕ escort; ⚓, ✕ convoy; ♪ accompaniment.

be'glückwünschen v/t. (no -ge-, h) congratulate (zu on).

begnadig|en [bə'gna:diɡən] v/t. (no -ge-, h) pardon; pol. amnesty; **2ung** f (-/-en) pardon; pol. amnesty.

begnügen [bə'gny:ɡən] v/refl. (no -ge-, h): sich ~ mit content o.s. with, be satisfied with.

begonnen [bə'gɔnən] p.p. of *beginnen*.

be'graben v/t. (irr. graben, no -ge-, h) bury (a. fig.); inter.

Begräbnis [bə'grɛ:pnis] n (-ses/-se) burial; funeral, obsequies pl.

begradigen [bə'gra:diɡən] v/t. (no -ge-, h) straighten (*road, frontier, etc.*).

be'greif|en v/t. (irr. greifen, no -ge-, h) comprehend, understand; **.lich** adj. comprehensible.

be'grenz|en v/t. (no -ge-, h) bound, border; fig. limit; **2theit** f (-/-en) limitation (of knowledge); narrowness (of mind); **2ung** f (-/-en) boundary; bound, limit; limitation.

Be'griff m idea, notion, conception; comprehension; im ~ sein zu inf. be about or going to inf.

be'gründ|en v/t. (no -ge-, h) establish, found; give reasons for, substantiate (*claim, charge*); **2ung** f establishment, foundation; fig. substantiation (of claim or charge); reason.

be'grüß|en v/t. (no -ge-, h) greet, welcome; salute; **2ung** f (-/-en) greeting, welcome; salutation.

begünstig|en [bə'gynstiɡən] v/t. (no -ge-, h) favo(u)r; encourage; patronize; **2ung** f (-/-en) f favo(u)r; encouragement; patronage.

begutachten [bə'gu:t⁹-] v/t. (no -ge-, h) give an opinion on; examine; ~ lassen obtain expert opinion on, submit s.th. to an expert.

B

begütert adj. [bə'gy:tərt] wealthy, well-to-do.

be'haart adj. hairy.

behäbig adj. [bə'hɛ:biç] phlegmatic, comfort-loving; *figure:* portly.

be'haftet adj. afflicted (*with disease, etc.*).

behag|en [bə'ha:gən] **1.** v/i. (no -ge-, h) please or suit s.o.; **2.** ♀ n (-s/no pl.) comfort, ease; **~lich** adj. [~k-] comfortable; cosy, snug.

be'halten v/t. (irr. halten, no -ge-, h) retain; keep (für sich to o.s.); remember.

Behälter [bə'hɛltər] m (-s/-) container, receptacle; box; *for liquid:* reservoir; *for oil, etc.:* tank.

be'hand|eln v/t. (no -ge-, h) treat; deal with (a. subject); ⊕ process; ⚕ treat; dress (wound); **♀lung** f treatment; handling; ⊕ processing.

be'hängen v/t. (no -ge-, h) hang, drape (mit with); sich ~ mit cover or load o.s. with (jewellery).

beharr|en [bə'harən] v/i. (no -ge-, h) persist (auf dat. in); **~lich** adj. persistent; **♀lichkeit** f (-/no pl.) persistence.

be'hauen v/t. (no -ge-, h) hew; trim (wood).

behaupt|en [bə'hauptən] v/t. (no -ge-, h) assert; maintain; **♀ung** f (-/-en) assertion; statement.

Behausung [bə'hauzuŋ] f (-/-en) habitation; lodging.

Be'helf m (-[e]s/-e) expedient, (make)shift; s. *Notbehelf;* **♀en** v/refl. (irr. helfen, no -ge-, h): sich ~ mit make shift with; sich ~ ohne do without; **~sheim** n temporary home.

behend adj. [bə'hent], **~e** adj. [~də] nimble, agile; smart; **♀igkeit** [~d-] f (-/no pl.) nimbleness, agility; smartness. [lodge, shelter.]

be'herbergen v/t. (no -ge-, h)

be'herrsch|en v/t. (no -ge-, h) rule (over), govern; command (situation, etc.); have command of (language); sich ~ control o.s.; **♀er** m ruler (gen. over, of); **♀ung** f (-/-en) command, control.

beherzigen [bə'hɛrtsigən] v/t. (no -ge-, h) take to heart, (bear in) mind.

be'hexen v/t. (no -ge-, h) bewitch.

be'hilflich adj.: j-m ~ sein help s.o. (bei in).

be'hindern v/t. (no -ge-, h) hinder, hamper, impede; handicap; obstruct (a. traffic, etc.).

Behörde [bə'hø:rdə] f (-/-n) authority, mst authorities pl.; board; council.

be'hüten v/t. (no -ge-, h) guard, preserve (vor dat. from).

behutsam adj. [bə'hu:tza:m] cautious, careful; **♀keit** f (-/no pl.) caution.

bei prp. (dat.) [bai] address: ~ Schmidt care of (abbr. c/o) Schmidt; ~m Buchhändler at the bookseller's; ~ uns with us; ~ der Hand nehmen take by the hand; ich habe kein Geld ~ mir I have no money about or on me; ~ der Kirche near the church; ~ guter Gesundheit in good health; wie es ~ Schiller heißt as Schiller says; die Schlacht ~ Waterloo the Battle of Waterloo; ~ e-m Glase Wein over a glass of wine; ~ alledem for all that; Stunden nehmen ~ take lessons from or with; ~ günstigem Wetter weather permitting.

'beibehalten v/t. (irr. halten, sep., no -ge-, h) keep up, retain.

'Beiblatt n supplement (zu to).

'beibringen v/t. (irr. bringen, sep., -ge-, h) bring forward; produce (witness, etc.) to s.o.; teach s.o. s.th.; j-m et. ~ impart (news, etc.) to s.o.; teach s.o. s.th.; inflict (defeat, wound, etc.) on s.o.

Beichte ['baiçtə] f (-/-n) confession; **'♀n** v/t. and v/i. (ge-, h) confess.

beide adj. ['baidə] both; nur wir ~ just the two of us; in ~n Fällen in either case.

beider|lei adj. ['baidərlai] of both kinds; ~ Geschlechts of either sex; **'~seitig** 1. adj. on both sides; mutual; 2. adv. mutually; **'~seits** 1. prp. on both sides (gen. of); 2. adv. mutually.

'Beifahrer m (-s/-) (front-seat) passenger; assistant driver; motor racing: co-driver.

'Beifall m (-[e]s/no pl.) approbation; applause; cheers pl.

'beifällig adj. approving; favo(u)rable.

'Beifallsruf m acclaim; ~e pl. cheers pl.

'beifügen v/t. (sep., -ge-, h) add; enclose.

'Beigeschmack m (-[e]s/no pl.)

slight flavo(u)r; smack (of) (*a. fig.*).

'**Beihilfe** *f* aid; allowance; *for study:* grant; *for project:* subsidy; ♈ aiding and abetting; *j-m* ~ **leisten** ♈ aid and abet s.o.

'**beikommen** *v/i.* (*irr.* kommen, *sep.*, *-ge-*, *sein*) get at.

Beil [baɪl] *n* (-[e]s/-e) hatchet; chopper; cleaver; ax(e).

'**Beilage** *f* supplement (*to newspaper*); F trimmings *pl.* (*of meal*); vegetables *pl.*

beiläufig *adj.* ['baɪlɔyfiç] casual; incidental.

'**beileg**|**en** *v/t.* (*sep.*, *-ge-*, *h*) add (*dat.* to); enclose; settle (*dispute*); **Չung** *f* (-/-en) settlement.

Beileid ['baɪlaɪt] *n* condolence; *j-m* sein ~ **bezeigen** condole with s.o. (zu on, upon).

'**beiliegen** *v/i.* (*irr.* liegen, *sep.*, *-ge-*, *h*) be enclosed (*dat.* with).

'**beimessen** *v/t.* (*irr.* messen, *sep.*, *-ge-*, *h*) attribute (*dat.* to), ascribe (to); attach (*importance*) (to).

'**beimisch**|**en** *v/t.* (*sep.*, *-ge-*, *h*): e-r *Sache et.* ~ mix s.th. with s.th.; **Չung** *f* admixture.

Bein [baɪn] *n* (-[e]s/-e) leg; bone.

'**beinah**(**e**) *adv.* almost, nearly.

'**Beiname** *m* appellation; nickname.

'**Beinbruch** *m* fracture of the leg.

beiordnen ['baɪ⁹-] *v/t.* (*sep.*, *-ge-*, *h*) adjoin; co-ordinate (*a. gr.*).

'**beipflichten** *v/i.* (*sep.*, *-ge-*, *h*) agree with *s.o.*; assent to *s.th.*

'**Beirat** *m* (-[e]s/⸚e) adviser, counsel(l)or; advisory board.

be'irren *v/t.* (*no* -ge-, *h*) confuse.

beisammen *adv.* [baɪ'zamən] together.

'**Beisein** *n* presence; *im* ~ (*gen.*) *or* *von* **in the presence of** *s.o.*, in *s.o.*'s presence.

bei'seite *adv.* aside, apart; *Spaß* ~! joking apart!

'**beisetz**|**en** *v/t.* (*sep.*, *-ge-*, *h*) bury, inter; **Չung** *f* (-/-en) burial, funeral.

'**Beisitzer** ♈ *m* (-s/-) assessor; associate judge; member (*of committee*).

'**Beispiel** *n* example, instance; *zum* ~ for example *or* instance; '**Չhaft** *adj.* exemplary; '**Չlos** *adj.* unprecedented, unparalleled; unheard of.

beißen ['baɪsən] (*irr.*, *ge-*, *h*) **1.** *v/t.* bite; *fleas, etc.:* bite, sting; **2.** *v/i.* bite (*auf acc.* on; *in acc.* into);

fleas, etc.: bite, sting; *smoke:* bite, burn (*in dat.* in); *pepper, etc.:* bite, burn (*auf dat.* on); '~**d** *adj.* biting, pungent (*both a. fig.*); *pepper, etc.:* hot.

'**Beistand** *m* assistance.

'**beistehen** *v/i.* (*irr.* stehen, *sep.*, *-ge-*, *h*): *j-m* ~ stand by *or* assist *or* help s.o.

'**beisteuern** *v/t.* and *v/i.* (*sep.*, *-ge-*, *h*) contribute (zu to).

Beitrag ['baɪtrɑːk] *m* (-[e]s/⸚e) contribution; share; subscription, *Am.* dues *pl.*; article (*in newspaper, etc.*).

'**bei**|**treten** *v/i.* (*irr.* treten, *sep.*, *-ge-*, *sein*) join (*political party, etc.*); '**Չtritt** *m* joining.

'**Beiwagen** *m* side-car (*of motorcycle*); trailer (*of tram*).

'**Beiwerk** *n* accessories *pl.*

'**beiwohnen** *v/i.* (*sep.*, *-ge-*, *h*) assist *or* be present at, attend.

bei'zeiten *adv.* early; in good time.

beizen ['baɪtsən] *v/t.* (*ge-*, *h*) corrode; *metall.* pickle; bate (*hides*); stain (*wood*); ⚕ cauterize; *hunt.* hawk.

bejahen [bə'jɑːən] *v/t.* (*no* -ge-, *h*) answer in the affirmative, affirm; '~**d** *adj.* affirmative.

be'jahrt *adj.* aged.

Bejahung *f* (-/-en) affirmation, affirmative answer; *fig.* acceptance.

be'jammern *s.* beklagen.

be'kämpfen *v/t.* (*no* -ge-, *h*) fight (against); combat; *fig.* oppose.

bekannt *adj.* [bə'kant] known (*dat.* to); *j-n mit j-m* ~ **machen** introduce s.o. to s.o.; **Չe** *m, f* (-n/-n) acquaintance, *mst* friend; '~**lich** *adv.* as you know; ~**machen** *v/t.* (*sep.*, *-ge-*, *h*) make known; **Չmachung** *f* (-/-en) publication; public notice; **Չschaft** *f* (-/-en) acquaintance.

be'kehr|**en** *v/t.* (*no* -ge-, *h*) convert; **Չte** *m, f* (-n/-n) convert; **Չung** *f* (-/-en) conversion (zu to).

be'kenn|**en** *v/t.* (*irr.* kennen, *no* -ge-, *h*) admit; confess; *sich schuldig* ~ ♈ plead guilty; *sich* ~ *zu* declare o.s. for; profess *s.th.*; **Չtnis** *n* (-ses/ -se) confession; creed.

be'klagen *v/t.* (*no* -ge-, *h*) lament, deplore; *sich* ~ complain (*über acc.* of, about); ~**swert** *adj.* deplorable, pitiable.

Beklagte [bə'klɑːktə] *m, f* (-n/-n) *civil case:* defendant, *the* accused.

B

be'klatschen v/t. (no -ge-, h) applaud, clap.

be'kleben v/t. (no -ge-, h) glue or stick s.th. on s.th.; mit Etiketten ~ label s.th.; mit Papier ~ paste s.th. up with paper; e-e Mauer mit Plakaten ~ paste (up) posters on a wall.

be'kleckern F [bə'klɛkərn] v/t. (no -ge-, h) stain (garment); sich ~ soil one's clothes. [daub; blot.]

be'klecksen v/t. (no -ge-, h) stain,]

be'kleid|en v/t. (no -ge-, h) clothe, dress; hold, fill (office, etc.); ~ mit invest with; ℒung f clothing, clothes pl.

be'klemm|en v/t. (no -ge-, h) oppress; ℒung f (-/-en) oppression; anguish, anxiety.

be'kommen (irr. kommen, no -ge-) 1. v/t. (h) get, receive; obtain; get, catch (illness); have (baby); catch (train, etc.); Zähne ~ teethe, cut one's teeth; 2. v/i. (sein): j-m (gut) ~ agree with s.o.; j-m nicht or schlecht ~ disagree with s.o.

bekömmlich adj. [bə'kœmlɪç] wholesome (dat. to).

beköstig|en [bə'kœstɪgən] v/t. (no -ge-, h) board, feed; ℒung f (-/‑en) board(ing).

be'kräftig|en v/t. (no -ge-, h) confirm; ℒung f (-/-en) confirmation.

be'kränzen v/t. (no -ge-, h) wreathe; festoon. [criticize.]

be'kritteln v/t. (no -ge-, h) carp at,]

be'kümmern v/t. (no -ge-, h) afflict, grieve; trouble; s. kümmern.

be'laden v/t. (irr. laden, no -ge-, h) load; fig. burden.

Belag [bə'la:k] m (-[e]s/⸚e) covering; ⊕ coat(ing); surface (of road); foil (of mirror); 🦷 fur (on tongue); (slices of) ham, etc. (on bread); filling (of roll).

Belager|er [bə'la:gərər] m (-s/-) besieger; ℒn v/t. (no -ge-, h) besiege, beleaguer; ℒung f siege.

Belang [bə'laŋ] m (-[e]s/-e) importance; ~e pl. interests pl.; ℒen v/t. (no -ge-, h) concern; 🏛 sue; ℒlos adj. unimportant; ~losigkeit f (-/-en) insignificance.

be'lasten v/t. (no -ge-, h) load; fig. burden; 🏛 incriminate; mortgage (estate, etc.); j-s Konto (mit e-r Summe) ~ † charge or debit s.o.'s account (with a sum).

belästig|en [bə'lɛstɪgən] v/t. (no -ge-, h) molest; trouble, bother; ℒung f molestation; trouble.

Be'lastung f (-/-en) load (a. 𝆕, ⊕); fig. burden; † debit; encumbrance; 🏛 incrimination; erbliche ~ hereditary taint; ~szeuge 🏛 m witness for the prosecution.

be'laufen v/refl. (irr. laufen, no -ge-, h): sich ~ auf (acc.) amount to.

be'lauschen v/t. (no -ge-, h) overhear, eavesdrop on s.o.

be'leb|en fig. v/t. (no -ge-, h) enliven, animate; stimulate; ~t adj. street: busy, crowded; stock exchange: brisk; conversation: lively, animated.

Beleg [bə'le:k] m (-[e]s/-e) proof; 🏛 (supporting) evidence; document; voucher; ℒen [~gən] v/t. (no -ge-, h) cover; reserve (seat, etc.); prove, verify; univ. enrol(l) or register for, Am. a. sign up for (course of lectures, term); ein Brötchen mit et. ~ put s.th. on a roll, fill a roll with s.th.; ~schaft f (-/-en) personnel, staff; labo(u)r force; ~stelle f reference; ℒt adj. engaged, occupied; hotel, etc.: full; voice: thick, husky; tongue: coated, furred; ~es Brot (open) sandwich.

be'lehr|en v/t. (no -ge-, h) instruct, inform; sich ~ lassen take advice; ~end adj. instructive; ℒung f (-/-en) instruction; information; advice.

beleibt adj. [bə'laɪpt] corpulent, stout, bulky, portly.

beleidig|en [bə'laɪdɪgən] v/t. (no -ge-, h) offend (s.o.; ear, eye, etc.); insult; ~end adj. offensive; insulting; ℒung f (-/-en) offen|ce, Am. -se; insult.

be'lesen adj. well-read.

be'leucht|en v/t. (no -ge-, h) light (up), illuminate (a. fig.); fig. shed or throw light on; ℒung f (-/-en) light(ing); illumination; ℒungskörper m lighting appliance.

be'licht|en phot. v/t. (no -ge-, h) expose; ℒung phot. f exposure.

Be'lieb|en n (-s/no pl.) will, choice; nach ~ at will; es steht in Ihrem ~ I leave it to you; ℒig 1. adj. any; jeder ~e anyone; 2. adv. at pleasure; ~ viele as many as you like; ℒt adj. [~pt] popular (bei with); ~theit f (-/no pl.) popularity.

be'liefer|n v/t. (no -ge-, h) supply,

bereden

bellen ['bɛlən] v/i. (ge-, h) bark.

belobigen [bə'lo:bigən] v/t. (no -ge-, h) commend, praise.

be'lohn|en v/t. (no -ge-, h) reward; recompense; 2ung f (-/-en) reward; recompense. [j-n ~ lie to s.o.]

be'lügen v/t. (irr. lügen, no -ge-, h):)

belustig|en [bə'lustigən] v/t. (no -ge-, h) amuse, entertain; sich ~ amuse o.s.; 2ung f (-/-en) amusement, entertainment.

bemächtigen [bə'mɛçtigən] v/refl. (no -ge-, h): sich e-r Sache ~ take hold of s.th., seize s.th.; sich e-r Person ~ lay hands on s.o., seize s.o.

be'malen v/t. (no -ge-, h) cover with paint; paint; daub.

bemängeln [bə'mɛŋəln] v/t. (no -ge-, h) find fault with, cavil at.

be'mannen v/t. (no -ge-, h) man.

be'merk|bar adj. perceptible; ~en v/t. (no -ge-, h) notice, perceive; remark, mention; ~enswert adj. remarkable (wegen for); 2ung f (-/-en) remark.

bemitleiden [bə'mitlaɪdən] v/t. (no -ge-, h) pity, commiserate (with); ~swert adj. pitiable.

be'müh|en v/t. (no -ge-, h) trouble (j-n in or wegen et. s.o. about s.th.); sich ~ trouble o.s.; endeavo(u)r; sich um e-e Stelle ~ apply for a position; 2ung f (-/-en) trouble; endeavo(u)r, effort.

be'nachbart adj. neighbo(u)ring; adjoining, adjacent (to).

benachrichtig|en [bə'na:xriçtigən] v/t. (no -ge-, h) inform, notify; ✝ advise; 2ung f (-/-en) information, notification; ✝ advice.

benachteilig|en [bə'na:xtaɪligən] v/t. (no -ge-, h) place s.o. at a disadvantage, discriminate against s.o.; handicap; sich benachteiligt fühlen feel handicapped or at a disadvantage; 2ung f (-/-en) disadvantage; discrimination; handicap.

be'nehmen 1. v/refl. (irr. nehmen, no -ge-, h) behave (o.s.); **2.** 2 n (-s/no pl.) behavio(u)r, conduct.

be'neiden v/t. (no -ge-, h) envy (j-n um et. s.o. s.th.); ~swert adj. enviable.

be'nennen v/t. (irr. nennen, no -ge-, h) name. [rascal; urchin.)

Bengel ['bɛŋəl] m (-s/-) (little))

benommen adj. [bə'nɔmən] bemused, dazed, stunned; ~ sein be in a daze. [require, want.)

be'nötigen v/t. (no -ge-, h) need,)

be'nutz|en v/t. (no -ge-, h) use (a. patent, etc.); make use of; avail o.s. of (opportunity); take (tram, etc.); 2ung f use.

Benzin [bɛn'tsi:n] n (-s/-e) 🜛 benzine; mot. petrol, F juice, Am. gasoline, F gas; ~**motor** m petrol engine, Am. gasoline engine; s. Tank.

beobacht|en [bə'o:baxtən] v/t. (no -ge-, h) observe; watch; police: shadow; 2er m (-s/-) observer; 2ung f (-/-en) observation.

beordern [bə'ɔrdərn] v/t. (no -ge-, h) order, command.

be'packen v/t. (no -ge-, h) load (mit with). [(mit with).)

be'pflanzen v/t. (no -ge-, h) plant)

bequem adj. [bə'kve:m] convenient; comfortable; p.: easy-going; lazy; ~en v/refl. (no -ge-, h): sich ~ zu condescend to; consent to; 2lichkeit f (-/-en) convenience; comfort, ease; indolence.

be'rat|en (irr. raten, no -ge-, h) **1.** v/t. advise s.o.; consider, debate, discuss s.th.; sich ~ confer (mit j-m with s.o.; über et. on or about s.th.); **2.** v/i. confer; über et. ~ consider, debate, discuss s.th., confer on or about s.th.; 2er m (-s/-) adviser, counsel(l)or; consultant; ~schlagen (no -ge-, h) **1.** v/i. s. beraten 2; **2.** v/refl. confer (mit j-m with s.o.; über et. on or about s.th.); 2ung f (-/-en) advice; debate; consultation; conference; 2ungsstelle f advisory bureau.

be'raub|en v/t. (no -ge-, h) rob, deprive (gen. of); 2ung f (-/-en) robbery, deprivation.

be'rauschen v/t. (no -ge-, h) intoxicate (a. fig.).

be'rechn|en v/t. (no -ge-, h) calculate; ✝ charge (zu at); ~end adj. calculating, selfish; 2ung f calculation.

berechtig|en [bə'rɛçtigən] v/t. (no -ge-, h) j-n ~ zu entitle s.o. to; authorize s.o. to; ~t adj. [~çt] entitled (zu to); qualified (to); claim: legitimate; 2ung f (-/-en) title (zu to); authorization.

be'red|en v/t. (no -ge-, h) talk s.th.

B

over; persuade *s.o.*; gossip about *s.o.*; ₂**samkeit** [˶tzaːmkaɪt] *f* (-/*no pl.*) eloquence; ˷**t** *adj.* [˶t] eloquent (*a. fig.*).

Be'reich *m, n* (-[e]s/-e) area; reach; *fig.* scope, sphere; *science, etc.*: field, province; ₂**ern** *v/t.* (*no -ge-, h*) enrich; *sich* ˷ enrich o.s.; ˷**erung** *f* (-/-en) enrichment.

be'reif|en *v/t.* (*no -ge-, h*) hoop (*barrel*); tyre, (*Am. only*) tire (*wheel*); ₂**ung** *f* (-/-en) (set of) tyres *pl.*, (*Am. only*) (set of) tires *pl.*

be'reisen *v/t.* (*no -ge-, h*) tour (in), travel (over); *commercial traveller*: cover (*district*).

bereit *adj.* [bə'raɪt] ready, prepared; ˷**en** *v/t.* (*no -ge-, h*) prepare; give (*joy, trouble, etc.*); ˷**s** *adv.* already; ₂**schaft** *f* (-/-en) readiness; *police*: squad; ˷**stellen** *v/t.* (*sep., -ge-, h*) place *s.th.* ready; provide; ₂**ung** *f* (-/-en) preparation; ˷**willig** *adj.* ready, willing; ₂**willigkeit** *f* (-/*no pl.*) readiness, willingness.

be'reuen *v/t.* (*no -ge-, h*) repent (of); regret, rue.

Berg [bɛrk] *m* (-[e]s/-e) mountain; hill; ˷**e** *pl. von F* heaps *pl.* of, piles *pl.* of; *über den* ˷ *sein* be out of the wood, *Am.* be out of the woods; *über alle* ˷**e** off and away; *die Haare standen ihm zu* ˷**e** his hair stood on end; ₂**'ab** *adv.* downhill (*a. fig.*); ₂**'an** *adv. s.* bergauf; ˷**'arbeiter** *m* miner; ₂**'auf** *adv.* uphill (*a. fig.*); ˷**bahn** 🚋 *f* mountain railway; ˷**bau** *m* (-[e]s/*pl.*) mining.

bergen ['bɛrgən] *v/t.* (*irr., ge-, h*) save; rescue *s.o.*; ⚓ salvage, salve. [hilly.]

bergig *adj.* ['bɛrgɪç] mountainous,]

'Berg|kette *f* mountain chain or range; ˷**mann** ⚒ *m* (-[e]s/*Bergleute*) miner; ˷**predigt** *f* (-/*no pl.*) *the* Sermon on the Mount; ˷**recht** *n* mining laws *pl.*; ˷**rennen** *mot. n* mountain race; ˷**rücken** *m* ridge; ˷**rutsch** *m* landslide, landslip; ˷**spitze** *f* mountain peak; ˷**steiger** *m* (-s/-) mountaineer; ˷**sturz** *m s.* Bergrutsch.

'Bergung *f* (-/-en) ⚓ salvage; rescue; ˷**sarbeiten** ['bɛrguŋsˀ-] *f/pl.* salvage operations *pl.*; rescue work.

'Bergwerk *n* mine; ˷**saktien** ['bɛrk- verksˀ-] *f/pl.* mining shares *pl.*

Bericht [bə'rɪçt] *m* (-[e]s/-e) report

(*über acc.* on); account (of); ₂**en** (*no -ge-, h*) **1.** *v/t.* report; *j-m et.* ˷ inform s.o. of s.th.; tell s.o. about s.th.; **2.** *v/i.* report (*über acc.* on); *journalist: a.* cover (*über acc.* s.th.); ˷**erstatter** *m* (-s/-) reporter; correspondent; ˷**erstattung** *f* reporting; report(s *pl.*).

berichtig|en [bə'rɪçtɪgən] *v/t.* (*no -ge-, h*) correct (*s.o.*; *error, mistake, etc.*); put right (*mistake*); emend (*corrupt text*); ✝ settle (*claim, debt, etc.*); ₂**ung** *f* (-/-en) correction; emendation; settlement.

be'riechen *v/t.* (*irr.* riechen, *no -ge-, h*) smell or sniff at.

Berliner [bɛr'liːnər] **1.** *m* (-s/-) Berliner; **2.** *adj.* (of) Berlin.

Bernstein ['bɛrnʃtaɪn] *m* amber; *schwarzer* ˷ jet.

bersten ['bɛrstən] *v/i.* (*irr., ge-, sein*) burst (*fig. vor dat.* with).

berüchtigt *adj.* [bə'rʏçtɪçt] notorious (*wegen* for), ill-famed.

berücksichtig|en [bə'rʏkzɪçtɪgən] *v/t.* (*no -ge-, h*) take *s.th.* into consideration, pay regard to *s.th.*; consider *s.o.*; ₂**ung** *f* (-/-en) consideration; regard.

Beruf [bə'ruːf] *m* (-[e]s/-e) calling; profession; vocation; trade; occupation; ₂**en 1.** *v/t.* (*irr.* rufen, *no -ge-, h*): *j-n zu e-m Amt* ˷ appoint s.o. to an office; *sich auf j-n* ˷ refer to s.o.; **2.** *adj.* competent; qualified; ₂**lich** *adj.* professional; vocational.

Be'rufs|ausbildung *f* vocational or professional training; ˷**beratung** *f* vocational guidance; ˷**kleidung** *f* work clothes *pl.*; ˷**krankheit** *f* occupational disease; ˷**schule** *f* vocational school; ˷**spieler** *m* sports: professional (player); ₂**tätig** *adj.* working; ˷**tätige** [˷gə] *pl.* working people *pl.*

Be'rufung *f* (-/-en) appointment (*zu* to); 🏛 appeal (*bei dat.* to); reference (*auf acc.* to); ˷**sgericht** *n* court of appeal.

be'ruhen *v/i.* (*no -ge-, h*): ˷ *auf* (*dat.*) rest or be based on; *et. auf sich* ˷ *lassen* let a matter rest.

beruhig|en [bə'ruːɪgən] *v/t.* (*no -ge-, h*) quiet, calm; soothe; *sich* ˷ calm down; ₂**ung** *f* (-/-en) calming (down); soothing; comfort; ₂**ungs- mittel** 💊 *n* sedative.

berühmt adj. [bə'ry:mt] famous (wegen for); celebrated; **2heit** f (-/-en) fame, renown; famous or celebrated person, celebrity; person of note.

be'rühr|en v/t. (no -ge-, h) touch (a. fig.); touch (up)on (subject); **2ung** f (-/-en) contact; touch; in ~ kommen mit come into contact with.

be'sag|en v/t. (no -ge-, h) say; mean, signify; **~t** adj. [~kt] (afore-)said; above(-mentioned).

besänftigen [bə'zɛnftigən] v/t. (no -ge-, h) appease, calm, soothe.

Be'satz m (-es/^ue) trimming; braid.

Be'satzung f ⚔ occupation troops pl.; ⚔ garrison; ⚓, ✈ crew; ~s-**macht** f ⚔ occupying power.

be'schädig|en v/t. (no -ge-, h) damage, injure; **2ung** f damage, injury (gen. to).

be'schaffen 1. v/t. (no -ge-, h) procure; provide; raise (money); **2.** adj.: gut (schlecht) ~ sein be in good (bad) condition or state; **2heit** f(-/-en)state,condition;properties pl.

beschäftig|en [bə'ʃɛftigən] v/t. (no -ge-, h) employ, occupy; keep busy; sich ~ occupy or busy o.s.; **2ung** f (-/-en) employment; occupation.

be'schäm|en v/t. (no -ge-, h) (put to) shame, make s.o. feel ashamed; **~end** adj. shameful; humiliating; **~t** adj. ashamed (über acc. of); **2ung** f (-/-en) shame; humiliation.

beschatten [bə'ʃatən] v/t. (no -ge-, h) shade; fig. shadow s.o., Am. sl. tail s.o.

be'schau|en v/t. (no -ge-, h) look at, view; examine, inspect (goods, etc.); **~lich** adj. contemplative, meditative.

Bescheid [bə'ʃaɪt] m (-[e]s/-e) answer; ⚖ decision; information (über acc. on, about); ~ geben let s.o. know; ~ bekommen be informed or notified; ~ hinterlassen leave word (bei with, at); ~ wissen be informed, know, F be in the know.

bescheiden adj. [bə'ʃaɪdən] modest, unassuming; **2heit** f (-/no pl.) modesty.

bescheinig|en [bə'ʃaɪnigən] v/i. (no -ge-, h) certify, attest; den Empfang ~ acknowledge receipt; es wird hiermit bescheinigt, daß this is to certify that; **2ung** f (-/-en) certification, attestation; certificate; receipt; acknowledgement.

be'schenken v/t. (no -ge-, h): j-n ~ make s.o. a present; j-n mit et. ~ present s.o. with s.th.; j-n reichlich ~ shower s.o. with gifts.

be'scher|en v/t. (no -ge-, h): j-n ~ give s.o. presents (esp. for Christmas); **2ung** f (-/-en) presentation of gifts; F fig. mess.

be'schieß|en v/t. (irr. schießen, no -ge-, h) fire or shoot at or on; bombard (a. phys.), shell; **2ung** f (-/-en) bombardment.

be'schimpf|en v/t. (no -ge-, h) abuse, insult; call s.o. names; **2ung** f (-/-en) abuse; insult, affront.

be'schirmen v/t. (no -ge-, h) shelter, shield, guard, protect (vor dat. from); defend (against).

be'schlafen v/t. (irr. schlafen, no -ge-, h): et. ~ sleep on a matter, take counsel of one's pillow.

Be'schlag m ⊕ metal fitting (s pl.); furnishing (s pl.) (of door, etc.); shoe (of wheel, etc.); (horse)shoe; ⚖ seizure, confiscation; in ~ nehmen, mit ~ belegen seize; ⚖ seize, attach (real estate, salary, etc.); confiscate (goods, etc.); monopolize s.o.'s attention.

be'schlagen 1. v/t. (irr. schlagen, no -ge-, h) cover (mit with); ⊕ fit, mount; shoe (horse); hobnail (shoe); **2.** v/i. (irr. schlagen, no -ge-, h) window, wall, etc.: steam up; mirror, etc.: cloud or film over; **3.** adj. windows, etc.: steamed-up; fig. well versed (auf, in dat. in).

Beschlagnahme [bə'ʃla:kna:mə] f (-/-n) seizure; confiscation (of contraband goods, etc.); ⚖ sequestration, distraint (of property); ⚔ requisition (of houses etc.); embargo, detention (of ship); **2n** v/t. (no -ge-, h) seize; attach (real estate); confiscate; ⚖ sequestrate, distrain upon (property); ⚔ requisition; ⚓ embargo.

beschleunig|en [bə'ʃlɔʏnigən] v/t. (no -ge-, h) mot. accelerate; hasten, speed up; s-e Schritte ~ quicken one's steps; **2ung** f (-/-en) acceleration.

be'schließen v/t. (irr. schließen, no -ge-, h) end, close, wind up; resolve, decide.

Be'schluß m decision, resolution, Am. a. resolve; ⚖ decree; **2fähig** adj.: ~ sein form or have a quorum;

B

~**fassung** f (passing of a) resolution.

be'**schmieren** v/t. (no -ge-, h) (be)smear (with grease, etc.).

be'**schmutzen** v/t. (no -ge-, h) soil (a. fig.), dirty; bespatter.

be'**schneiden** v/t. (irr. schneiden, no -ge-, h) clip, cut; lop (tree); trim, clip (hair, hedge, etc.); dress (vinestock, etc.); fig. cut down, curtail, F slash.

beschönig|en [bə'ʃøːnigən] v/t. (no -ge-, h) gloss over, palliate; 2**ung** f (-/-en) gloss, palliation.

beschränk|en [bə'frɛŋkən] v/t. (no -ge-, h) confine, limit, restrict, Am. a. curb; sich ~ auf (acc.) confine o.s. to; ~**t** fig. adj. of limited intelligence; 2**ung** f (-/-en) limitation, restriction.

be'**schreib|en** v/t. (irr. schreiben, no -ge-, h) write on (piece of paper, etc.), cover with writing; describe, give a description of; 2**ung** f (-/-en) description; account.

be'**schrift|en** v/t. (no -ge-, h) inscribe; letter; 2**ung** f (-/-en) inscription; lettering.

beschuldig|en [bə'ʃuldigən] v/t. (no -ge-, h) accuse (gen. of [doing] s.th.), esp. ⚖ charge (with); 2**te** [~ktə] m, f (-n/-n) the accused; 2**ung** f (-/-en) accusation, charge.

Be'**schuß** m (Beschusses/no pl.) bombardment.

be'**schütz|en** v/t. (no -ge-, h) protect, shelter, guard (vor dat. from); 2**er** m (-s/-) protector; 2**ung** f (-/-en) protection.

be'**schwatzen** v/t. (no -ge-, h) talk s.o. into (doing) s.th., coax s.o. into (doing s.th.).

Beschwerde [bə'ʃveːrdə] f (-/-n) trouble; ⚕ complaint; complaint (über acc. about); ⚖ objection (gegen to); ~**buch** n complaints book.

beschwer|en [bə'ʃveːrən] v/t. (no -ge-, h) burden (a. fig.); weight (loose sheets, etc.); lie heavy on (stomach); weigh on (mind, etc.); sich ~ complain (über acc. about, of; bei to); ~**lich** adj. troublesome.

beschwichtigen [bə'ʃviçtigən] v/t. (no -ge-, h) appease, calm (down), soothe.

be'**schwindeln** v/t. (no -ge-, h) tell

a fib or lie; cheat, F diddle (um out of).

be'**schwipst** F adj. tipsy.

be'**schwör|en** v/t. (irr. schwören, no -ge-, h) take an oath on s.th.; implore or entreat s.o.; conjure (up), invoke (spirit); 2**ung** f (-/-en) conjuration.

be'**seelen** v/t. (no -ge-, h) animate, inspire.

be'**sehen** v/t. (irr. sehen, no -ge-, h) look at; inspect; sich et. ~ look at s.th.; inspect s.th.

beseitig|en [bə'zaitigən] v/t. (no -ge-, h) remove, do away with; 2**ung** f (-/-en) removal.

Besen ['beːzən] m (-s/-) broom; ~**stiel** m broomstick.

be'**sessen** adj. [bə'zɛsən] obsessed, possessed (von by, with); wie ~ like mad; 2**e** m, f (-n/-n) demoniac.

be'**setz|en** v/t. (no -ge-, h) occupy (seat, table, etc.); fill (post, etc.); man (orchestra); thea. cast (play); ✗ occupy; trim (dress, etc.); set (crown with jewels, etc.); ~**t** adj. engaged, occupied; seat: taken; F bus, etc.: full up; hotel: full; teleph. engaged, Am. busy; 2**ung** f (-/-en) thea. cast; ✗ occupation.

besichtig|en [bə'ziçtigən] v/t. (no -ge-, h) view, look over; inspect (a. ✗); visit; 2**ung** f (-/-en) sightseeing; visit (gen. to); inspection (a. ✗).

be'**sied|eln** v/t. (no -ge-, h) colonize, settle; populate; 2**lung** f (-/-en) colonization, settlement.

be'**siegeln** v/t. (no -ge-, h) seal (a. fig.).

be'**siegen** v/t. (no -ge-, h) conquer; defeat, beat (a. sports).

be'**sinn|en** v/refl. (irr. sinnen, no -ge-, h) reflect, consider; sich ~ auf (acc.) remember, think of; ~**lich** adj. reflective, contemplative.

Be'**sinnung** f (-/no pl.) reflection; consideration; consciousness; (wieder) zur ~ kommen recover consciousness; fig. come to one's senses; 2**slos** adj. unconscious.

Be'**sitz** m possession; in ~ nehmen, ~ ergreifen von take possession of; 2**anzeigend** gr. adj. possessive; 2**en** v/t. (irr. sitzen, no -ge-, h) possess; ~**er** m (-s/-) possessor, owner, proprietor; den ~ wechseln change hands; ~**ergreifung** f taking possession (*von* of), occupation; ~**tum** n (-s/-¨er), ~**ung** f (-/-en) possession; property; estate.

be'**sohlen** v/t. (no -ge-, h) sole.

besold|en [bə'zɔldən] v/t. (no -ge-, h) pay a salary to (*civil servant, etc.*); pay (*soldier*); 2**ung** f (-/-en) pay; salary.

besonder adj. [bə'zɔndər] particular, special; peculiar; separate; 2**heit** f (-/-en) particularity; peculiarity; ~**s** adv. especially, particularly; chiefly, mainly; separately.

besonnen adj. [bə'zɔnən] sensible, considerate, level-headed; prudent; discreet; 2**heit** f (-/no pl.) considerateness; prudence; discretion; presence of mind.

be'sorg|en v/t. (no -ge-, h) get (j-m et. s.o. s.th.), procure (s.th. for s.o.); do, manage; 2**nis** [~knis] f (-/-se) apprehension, fear, anxiety, concern (*über* acc. about; at); ~**niserregend** adj. alarming; ~**t** adj. [~kt] uneasy (*um* about); worried (about), concerned (about); anxious (*um* for, about); 2**ung** f (-/-en) procurement; management; errand; ~**en machen** go shopping.

be'sprech|en v/t. (irr. sprechen, no -ge-, h) discuss, talk *s.th.* over; arrange; review (*book, etc.*); sich ~ **mit** confer with (*über* acc. about); 2**ung** f (-/-en) discussion; review; conference.

be'spritzen v/t. (no -ge-, h) splash, (be)spatter.

besser ['besər] 1. adj. better; superior; 2. adv. better; ~**n** v/t. (ge-) (h) (make) better, improve; reform; sich ~ get or become better, improve, change for the better; mend one's ways; 2**ung** f (-/-en) improvement; change for the better; reform (*of character*); ✞ improvement, recovery; gute ~! I wish you a speedy recovery!

best [best] 1. adj. best; der erste ~**e** (just) anybody; ~**en Dank** thank you very much; sich von s-r ~**en Seite zeigen** be on one's best behavio(u)r; 2. adv. best; am ~**en** best; aufs ~**e**, ~**ens** in the best way possible; zum ~**en geben** recite (*poem*), tell (*story*), oblige with (*song*); j-n zum ~**en haben** or **halten** make fun of s.o., F pull s.o.'s leg; ich danke ~**ens!** thank you very much!

Be'**stand** m (continued) existence; continuance; stock; ✞ stock-in-trade; ✞ cash in hand; ~ haben be lasting, last.

be'**ständig** adj. constant, steady; lasting; continual; *weather*: settled; 2**keit** f (-/-en) constancy, steadiness; continuance.

Bestand|saufnahme ✞ [bə-'ʃtants?-] f stock-taking, Am. inventory; ~**teil** m component, constituent; element, ingredient; part.

be'**stärken** v/t. (no -ge-, h) confirm, strengthen, encourage (*in* dat. in).

bestätig|en [bə'ʃteːtigən] v/t. confirm (a. ⚖ verdict, ✞ order); attest; verify (*statement, etc.*); ratify (*law, treaty*); ✞ acknowledge (*receipt*); 2**ung** f (-/-en) confirmation; attestation; verification; ratification; acknowledgement.

bestatt|en [bə'ʃtatən] v/t. (no -ge-, h) bury, inter; 2**ung** f (-/-en) burial, interment; funeral; 2**ungsinstitut** [bə'ʃtatuŋs?-] n undertakers pl.

'Beste 1. n (-n/no pl.) the best (thing); zu deinem ~**n** in your interest; zum ~**n der Armen** for the benefit of the poor; das ~ **daraus machen** make the best of it; 2. m, f (-n/-n): er ist der ~ **in s-r Klasse** he is the best in his class.

Besteck [bə'ʃtɛk] n (-[e]s/-e) 𝄂 (case or set of) surgical instruments pl.; (single set of) knife, fork and spoon; (complete set of) cutlery, Am. a. flatware.

be'**stehen** 1. v/t. (irr. stehen, no -ge-, h) come off victorious in (*combat, etc.*); have (*adventure*); stand, undergo (well) (*test, trial*); pass (*test, examination*); 2. v/i. (irr. stehen, no -ge-, h) be, exist; continue, last; ~ **auf** (dat.) insist (up)on; ~ **aus** consist of; 3. 2 n (-s/no pl.) existence; continuance; passing.

be'**stehlen** v/t. (irr. stehlen, no -ge-, h) steal from, rob.

be'**steig|en** v/t. (irr. steigen, no -ge-, h) climb (up) (*mountain, tree, etc.*); mount (*horse, bicycle, etc.*); ascend (*throne*); get into or on, board (*bus, train, plane*); 2**ung** f ascent; accession (*to* throne).

be'**stell|en** v/t. (no -ge-, h) order; ✞ a. place an order for; subscribe to (*newspaper, etc.*); book, reserve (*room, seat, etc.*); make an appoint-

B

ment with *s.o.*; send for (*taxi, etc.*); cultivate, till (*soil, etc.*); give (*message, greetings*); *j-n zu sich* ~ send for s.o.; 2**ung** *f* order; subscription (to); booking, *esp. Am.* reservation; ✓ cultivation; message.

'**besten'falls** *adv.* at (the) best.

be'steuer|n *v/t.* (*no* -ge-, *h*) tax; 2**ung** *f* taxation.

besti|alisch *adj.* [bɛst'jɑːlɪʃ] bestial; brutal; inhuman; *weather, etc.*: F beastly; 2**e** ['~jə] *f* (-/-n) beast; *fig.* brute, beast, inhuman person.

be'stimmen (*no* -ge-, *h*) **1.** *v/t.* determine, decide; fix (*date, place, price, etc.*); appoint (*date, time, place, etc.*); prescribe; define (*species, word, etc.*); *j-n für or zu et.* ~ designate *or* intend s.o. for s.th.; **2.** *v/i.*: ~ *über* (*acc.*) dispose of.

be'stimmt 1. *adj. voice, manner, etc.*: decided, determined, firm; *time, etc.*: appointed, fixed; *point, number, etc.*: certain; *answer, etc.*: positive; *tone, answer, intention, idea*: definite (*a. gr.*); ~ *nach* ⚓, ✈ bound for; **2.** *adv.* certainly, surely; 2**heit** *f* (-/-en) determination, firmness; certainty.

Be'stimmung *f* determination; destination (*of s.o. for the church, etc.*); designation, appointment (*of s.o. as successor, etc.*); definition; ⚖ provision (*in document*); (*amtliche*) ~**en** *pl.* (official) regulations *pl.*; ~**sort** [bə'ʃtimuŋsˀ-] *m* destination.

be'straf|en *v/t.* (*no* -ge-, *h*) punish (*wegen, für* for; *mit* with); 2**ung** *f* (-/-en) punishment.

be'strahl|en *v/t.* (*no* -ge-, *h*) irradiate (*a.* ⚕); 2**ung** *f* irradiation; ⚕ ray treatment, radiotherapy.

Be'streb|en *n* (-s/*no pl.*), ~**ung** *f* (-/-en) effort, endeavo(u)r.

be'streichen *v/t.* (*irr. streichen, no* -ge-, *h*) coat, cover; spread; *mit Butter* ~ butter.

be'streiten *v/t.* (*irr. streiten, no* -ge-, *h*) contest, dispute, challenge (*point, right, etc.*); deny (*facts, guilt, etc.*); defray (*expenses, etc.*); fill (*programme*).

be'streuen *v/t.* (*no* -ge-, *h*) strew, sprinkle (*mit* with); *mit Mehl* ~ flour; *mit Zucker* ~ sugar.

be'stürmen *v/t.* (*no* -ge-, *h*) storm, assail (*a. fig.*); pester, plague (*s.o. with questions, etc.*).

be'stürz|t *adj.* dismayed, struck with consternation (*über acc.* at); 2**ung** *f* (-/-en) consternation, dismay.

Besuch [bə'zuːx] *m* (-[e]s/-e) visit (*gen., bei, in dat.* to); call (*bei* on; *in dat.* at); attendance (*gen.* at) (*lecture, church, etc.*); visitor(s *pl.*), company; 2**en** *v/t.* (*no* -ge-, *h*) visit; call on, go to see; attend (*school, etc.*); frequent; ~**er** *m* visitor, caller; ~**szeit** *f* visiting hours *pl.*

be'tasten *v/t.* (*no* -ge-, *h*) touch, feel, finger; ⚕ palpate.

betätigen [bə'tɛːtigən] *v/t.* (*no* -ge-, *h*) ⊕ operate (*machine, etc.*); put on, apply (*brake*); *sich* ~ *als* act *or* work as; *sich politisch* ~ dabble in politics.

betäub|en [bə'tɔʏbən] *v/t.* (*no* -ge-, *h*) stun (*a. fig.*), daze (*by blow, noise, etc.*); deafen (*by noise, etc.*); *slaughtering*: stun (*animal*); ⚕ an(a)esthetize; 2**ung** *f* (-/-en) ⚕ an(a)esthetization; ⚕ an(a)esthesia; *fig.* stupefaction; 2**ungsmittel** ⚕ *n* narcotic, an(a)esthetic.

beteilig|en [bə'taɪligən] *v/t.* (*no* -ge-, *h*): *j-n* ~ give s.o. a share (*an dat.* in); *sich* ~ take part (*an dat., bei* in), participate (*a.* ⚖) (in); 2**te** [~çtə] *m, f* (-n/-n) person *or* party concerned; 2**ung** *f* (-/-en) participation (*a.* ⚖, ✝), partnership; share, interest (*a.* ✝).

beten ['beːtən] *v/i.* (ge-, *h*) pray (*um* for), say one's prayers; *at table*: say grace.

be'teuer|n *v/t.* (*no* -ge-, *h*) protest (*one's innocence*); swear (to *s.th.*; that); 2**ung** *f* protestation; solemn declaration.

be'titeln *v/t.* (*no* -ge-, *h*) entitle (*book, etc.*); style (*s.o. 'baron', etc.*).

Beton ⊕ [be'tõː; be'toːn] *m* (-s/-s; -s/-e) concrete.

be'tonen *v/t.* (*no* -ge-, *h*) stress; *fig. a.* emphasize.

betonieren [beto'niːrən] *v/t.* (*no* -ge-, *h*) concrete.

Be'tonung *f* (-/-en) stress; emphasis.

betör|en [bə'tøːrən] *v/t.* (*no* -ge-, *h*) dazzle; infatuate, bewitch; 2**ung** *f* (-/-en) infatuation.

Betracht [bə'traxt] *m* (-[e]s/*no pl.*): *in* ~ *ziehen* take into consideration; (*nicht*) *in* ~ *kommen* (not to) come into question; 2**en** *v/t.* (*no* -ge-, *h*) view; contemplate; *fig. a.* consider.

beträchtlich *adj.* [bə'trɛçtliç] considerable.

Be'trachtung *f* (-/-en) view; contemplation; consideration.

Betrag [bə'tra:k] *m* (-[e]s/⁼e) amount, sum; **2en** [‿gən] **1.** *v/t.* (*irr. tragen, no -ge-, h*) amount to; **2.** *v/refl.* (*irr. tragen, no -ge-, h*) behave (o.s.); **3.** **2** *n* (-s/*no pl.*) behavio(u)r, conduct.

be'trauen *v/t.* (*no -ge-, h*): j-n mit et. ‿ entrust or charge s.o. with s.th.

be'trauern *v/t.* (*no -ge-, h*) mourn (for, over).

Betreff [bə'trɛf] *m* (-[e]s/-e) *at head of letter:* reference; **2en** *v/t.* (*irr. treffen, no -ge-, h*) befall; refer to; concern; *was ... betrifft* as for, as to; **2end** *adj.* concerning; *das ‿e Geschäft* the business referred to or in question; **2s** *prp.* (*gen.*) concerning; as to.

be'treiben 1. *v/t.* (*irr. treiben, no -ge-, h*) carry on (*business, etc.*); pursue (*one's studies*); operate (*railway line, etc.*); **2.** **2** *n* (-s/*no pl.*): *auf ‿ von* at or by *s.o.'s* instigation.

be'treten 1. *v/t.* (*irr. treten, no -ge-, h*) step on; enter (*room, etc.*); **2.** *adj.* embarrassed, abashed.

betreu|en [bə'trɔyən] *v/t.* (*no -ge-, h*) look after; attend to; care for; **2ung** *f* (-/*no pl.*) care (*gen.* of, for).

Betrieb [bə'tri:p] *m* (-[e]s/-e) working, running, *esp. Am.* operation; business, firm, enterprise; plant, works *sg.*; workshop, *Am. a.* shop; *fig.* bustle; *in ‿* working; **2sam** *adj.* active; industrious.

Be'triebs|anleitung *f* operating instructions *pl.*; **‿ausflug** *m* firm's outing; **‿ferien** *pl.* (firm's, works) holiday; **‿führer** *m s.* Betriebsleiter; **‿kapital** *n* working capital; **‿kosten** *pl.* working expenses *pl.*, *Am.* operating costs *pl.* **‿leiter** *m* (works) manager, superintendent; **‿leitung** *f* management; **‿material** *n* working materials *pl.*; 🚄 rolling stock; **‿rat** *m* works council; **2sicher** *adj.* safe to operate; foolproof; **‿störung** *f* breakdown; **‿unfall** *m* industrial accident, accident while at work.

be'trinken *v/refl.* (*irr. trinken, no -ge-, h*) get drunk.

betroffen *adj.* [bə'trɔfən] afflicted (*von* by), stricken (with); *fig.* disconcerted.

be'trüben *v/t.* (*no -ge-, h*) grieve, afflict.

Be'trug *m* cheat(ing); fraud (*a.* 🏛); [deceit.\]

be'trüg|en *v/t.* (*irr. trügen, no -ge-, h*) deceive; cheat (*a. at games*); defraud; F skin; **2er** *m* (-s/-) cheat, deceiver, impostor, confidence man, swindler, trickster; **‿erisch** *adj.* deceitful, fraudulent.

be'trunken *adj.* drunken; *pred.* drunk; **2e** *m* (-n/-n) drunk(en man).

Bett [bet] *n* (-[e]s/-en) bed; **‿bezug** *m* plumeau case; **'‿decke** *f* blanket; bedspread, coverlet.

Bettel|brief ['betəl-] *m* begging letter; **‿ei** [‿'laɪ] *f* (-/-en) begging, mendicancy; **'2n** *v/i.* (*ge-, h*) beg (*um* for); ‿ *gehen* go begging; **'‿stab** *m*: *an den ‿ bringen* reduce to beggary.

'Bett|gestell *n* bedstead; **2lägerig** *adj.* ['‿lɛːgəriç] bedridden, confined to bed, *Am. a.* bedfast; **'‿laken** *n* sheet.

Bettler ['betlər] *m* (-s/-) beggar, *Am. sl.* panhandler.

'Bett|überzug *m* plumeau case; **‿uch** ['bettuːx] *n* sheet; **'‿vorleger** *m* bedside rug; **'‿wäsche** *f* bedlinen; **'‿zeug** *n* bedding.

be'tupfen *v/t.* (*no -ge-, h*) dab.

beug|en ['bɔygən] *v/t.* (*ge-, h*) bend, bow; *fig.* humble, break (pride); *gr.* inflect (*word*), decline (*noun, adjective*); *sich ‿* bend (*vor dat.* to), bow (to); **2ung** *f* (-/-en) bending; *gr.* inflection, declension.

Beule ['bɔylə] *f* (-/-n) bump, swelling; boil; *on metal, etc.:* dent.

beunruhig|en [bə'ʊnruːɪgən] *v/t.* (*no -ge-, h*) disturb, trouble, disquiet, alarm; *sich ‿ über* (*acc.*) be uneasy about, worry about; **2ung** *f* (-/*no pl.*) disturbance; alarm; uneasiness.

beurkund|en [bə'uːrkʊndən] *v/t.* (*no -ge-, h*) attest, certify, authenticate; **2ung** *f* (-/-en) attestation, authentication.

beurlaub|en [bə'uːrlaʊbən] *v/t.* (*no -ge-, h*) give or grant *s.o.* leave (of absence); give *s.o.* time off; suspend (*civil servant, etc.*); **2ung** *f* (-/-en) leave (of absence); suspension.

B

beurteil|en [bə'urtaɪlən] *v/t.* (*no -ge-, h*) judge (*nach* by); **2ung** *f* (*/-en*) judg(e)ment.

Beute ['bɔytə] *f* (*-/no pl.*) booty, spoil(s *pl.*); loot; prey; *hunt.* bag; *fig.* prey, victim (*gen.* to).

Beutel ['bɔytəl] *m* (*-s/-*) bag; purse; pouch.

'Beutezug *m* plundering expedition.

bevölker|n [bə'fœlkərn] *v/t.* (*no -ge-, h*) people, populate; **2ung** *f* (*/-en*) population.

bevollmächtig|en [bə'fɔlmɛçtɪɡən] *v/t.* (*no -ge-, h*) authorize, empower; **2te** [-çtə] *m,f* (*-n/-n*) authorized person *or* agent, deputy; *pol.* plenipotentiary; **2ung** *f* (*/-en*) authorization.

be'vor *cj.* before.

bevormund|en fig. [bə'fo:rmundən] *v/t.* (*no -ge-, h*) patronize, keep in tutelage; **2ung** fig. *f* (*/-en*) patronizing, tutelage.

be'vorstehen *v/i.* (*irr.* stehen, *sep.*, *-ge-, h*) be approaching, be near; *crisis, etc.*: be imminent; *j-m* ~ be in store for s.o., await s.o.; **~d** *adj.* approaching; imminent.

bevorzug|en [bə'fo:rtsu:ɡən] *v/t.* (*no -ge-, h*) prefer; favo(u)r; **2t** privilege; **2ung** *f* (*/-en*) preference.

be'wach|en *v/t.* (*no -ge-, h*) guard, watch; **2ung** *f* (*/-en*) guard; escort.

bewaffn|en [bə'vafnən] *v/t.* (*no -ge-, h*) arm; **2ung** *f* (*/-en*) armament; arms *pl.*

be'wahren *v/t.* (*no -ge-, h*) keep, preserve (*mst fig.*: *secret, silence, etc.*).

be'währen *v/refl.* (*no -ge-, h*) stand the test, prove a success; *sich* ~ *als* prove o.s. (as) (*a good teacher, etc.*); *sich* ~ *in* prove o.s. efficient in (*one's profession, etc.*); *sich nicht* ~ prove a failure.

be'wahrheiten *v/refl.* (*no -ge-, h*) prove (to be) true; *prophecy, etc.*: come true.

be'währt *adj.* *friend, etc.*: tried; *solicitor, etc.*: experienced; *friendship, etc.*: long-standing; *remedy, etc.*: proved, proven.

Be'währung *f* 🏛️ probation; *in Zeiten der* ~ in times of trial; *s. bewähren*; **~sfrist** 🏛️ *f* probation.

bewaldet *adj.* [bə'valdət] wooded, woody, *Am. a.* timbered.

bewältigen [bə'vɛltɪɡən] *v/t.* (*no*

-ge-, h) overcome (*obstacle*); master (*difficulty*); accomplish (*task*).

be'wandert *adj.* (well) versed (*in dat.* in), proficient (in); *in e-m Fach gut* ~ *sein* have a thorough knowledge of a subject.

be'wässer|n *v/t.* (*no -ge-, h*) water (*garden, lawn, etc.*); irrigate (*land, etc.*); **2ung** *f* (*/-en*) watering; irrigation.

bewegen¹ [bə've:ɡən] *v/t.* (*irr.*, *no -ge-, h*): *j-n* ~ *zu* induce *or* get s.o. to.

beweg|en² [~] *v/t. and v/refl.* (*no -ge-, h*) move, stir; **2grund** [~k-] *m* motive (*gen.*, *für* for); **~lich** *adj.* [~k-] movable; *p., mind, etc.*: agile, versatile; active; **2lichkeit** [~k-] *f* (*-/no pl.*) mobility; agility, versatility; **~t** *adj.* [~kt] *sea*: rough, heavy; *fig.* moved, touched; *voice*: choked, trembling; *life*: eventful; *times, etc.*: stirring, stormy; **2ung** *f* (*/-en*) movement; motion (*a. phys.*); *fig.* emotion; *in* ~ *setzen* set going *or* in motion; **~ungslos** *adj.* motionless, immobile.

be'weinen *v/t.* (*no -ge-, h*) weep *or* cry over; lament (for, over).

Beweis [bə'vaɪs] *m* (*-es/-e*) proof (*für* of); evidence (*esp.* 🏛️); **2en** [~zən] *v/t.* (*irr.* weisen, *no -ge-, h*) prove; show (*interest, etc.*); **~führung** *f* argumentation; **~grund** *m* argument; **~material** *n* evidence; **~stück** *n* (piece of) evidence; 🏛️ exhibit. [leave it at that.]

be'wenden *vb.*: *es dabei* ~ *lassen⌋*

be'werb|en *v/refl.* (*irr.* werben, *no -ge-, h*): *sich* ~ *um* apply for, *Am.* run for; stand for; compete for (*prize*); court (*woman*); **2er** *m* (*-s/-*) applicant (*um* for); candidate; competitor; suitor; **2ung** *f* application; candidature; competition; courtship; **2ungsschreiben** *n* (letter of) application.

bewerkstelligen [bə'vɛrkʃtɛlɪɡən] *v/t.* (*no -ge-, h*) manage, effect, bring about.

be'wert|en *v/t.* (*no -ge-, h*) value (*auf acc.* at; *nach* by); **2ung** *f* valuation.

bewillig|en [bə'vilɪɡən] *v/t.* (*no -ge-, h*) grant, allow; **2ung** *f* (*/-en*) grant, allowance.

be'wirken *v/t.* (*no -ge-, h*) cause; bring about, effect.

be'wirt|en v/t. (no -ge-, h) entertain; **~schaften** v/t. (no -ge-, h) farm (land); ✓ cultivate (field); manage (farm, etc.); ration (food, etc.); control (foreign exchange, etc.); 2ung f (-/-en) entertainment; hospitality.

bewog [bə'vo:k] pret. of bewegen¹.
~en [bə'vo:gən] p.p. of bewegen¹.

be'wohn|en v/t. (no -ge-, h) inhabit, live in; occupy; 2er m (-s/-) inhabitant; occupant.

bewölk|en [bə'vœlkən] v/refl. (no -ge-, h) sky: cloud up or over; brow: cloud over, darken; **~t** adj. sky: clouded, cloudy, overcast; brow: clouded, darkened; 2ung f (-/no pl.) clouds pl.

be'wunder|n v/t. (no -ge-, h) admire (wegen for); **~nswert** adj. admirable; 2ung f (-/-en) admiration.

bewußt adj. [bə'vust] deliberate, intentional; sich e-r Sache ~ sein be conscious or aware of s.th.; die ~e Sache the matter in question; **~los** adj. unconscious; 2sein n (-s/no pl.) consciousness.

be'zahl|en (no -ge-, h) 1. v/t. pay; pay for (s.th. purchased); pay off, settle (debt); 2. v/i. pay (für for); 2ung f payment; settlement.

be'zähmen v/t. (no -ge-, h) tame (animal); restrain (one's anger, etc.); sich ~ control or restrain o.s.

be'zauber|n v/t. (no -ge-, h) bewitch, enchant (a. fig.); fig. charm, fascinate; 2ung f (-/-en) enchantment; spell; fascination.

be'zeichn|en v/t. (no -ge-, h) mark; describe (als as), call; **~end** adj. characteristic, typical (für of); 2ung f indication (of direction, etc.); mark, sign, symbol; name, designation, denomination.

be'zeugen v/t. (no -ge-, h) ⚖ testify to, bear witness to (both a. fig.); attest.

be'zieh|en v/t. (irr. ziehen, no -ge-, h) cover (upholstered furniture, etc.); put cover on (cushion, etc.); move into (flat, etc.); enter (university); draw (salary, pension, etc.); get, be supplied with (goods); take in (newspaper, etc.); sich ~ sky: cloud over; sich ~ auf (acc.) refer to; 2er m (-s/-) subscriber (gen. to).

Be'ziehung f relation (zu et. to s.th.; zu j-m with s.o.); connexion, (Am. only) connection (zu with); in die-

ser ~ in this respect; 2sweise adv. respectively; or rather.

Bezirk [bə'tsirk] m (-[e]s/-e) district, Am. a. precinct; s. Wahlbezirk.

Bezogene † [bə'tso:gənə] m (-n/-n) drawee.

Bezug [bə'tsu:k] m cover(ing), case; purchase (of goods); subscription (to newspaper); in ~ auf (acc.) = nehmen auf (acc.) refer to, make reference to.

bezüglich [bə'tsy:kliç] 1. adj. relative, relating (both: auf acc. to); 2. prp. (gen.) regarding, concerning.

Be'zugsbedingungen † f/pl. terms pl. of delivery.

be'zwecken v/t. (no -ge-, h) aim at; ~ mit intend by.

be'zweifeln v/t. (no -ge-, h) doubt, question.

be'zwing|en v/t. (irr. zwingen, no -ge-, h) conquer (fortress, mountain, etc.); overcome, master (feeling, difficulty, etc.); sich ~ keep o.s. under control, restrain o.s.; 2ung f (-/-en) conquest; mastering.

Bibel ['bi:bəl] f (-/-n) Bible.
Biber zo. ['bi:bər] m (-s/-) beaver.
Bibliothek [biblio'te:k] f (-/-en) library; **~ar** [~e'ka:r] m (-s/-e) librarian.

biblisch adj. ['bi:bliʃ] biblical, scriptural; **~e** Geschichte Scripture.

bieder adj. ['bi:dər] honest, upright, worthy (a. iro.); simple-minded; '2-keit f (-/no pl.) honesty, uprightness; simple-mindedness.

bieg|en ['bi:gən] (irr., ge-) 1. v/t. (h) bend; 2. v/refl. (h) bend; sich vor Lachen ~ double up with laughter; 3. v/i. (sein): um e-e Ecke ~ turn (round) a corner; **~sam** adj. ['bi:kza:m] wire, etc.: flexible; body: lithe, supple; pliant (a. fig.); '2samkeit f (-/no pl.) flexibility; suppleness; pliability; '2ung f (-/-en) bend, wind (of road, river); curve (of road, arch).

Biene zo. ['bi:nə] f (-/-n) bee; **~n-königin** f queen bee; **~nkorb** m (bee)hive; **~nschwarm** m swarm of bees; **~nstock** m (bee)hive; **~n-zucht** f bee-keeping; **~nzüchter** m bee-keeper.

Bier [bi:r] n (-[e]s/-e) beer; helles ~ pale beer, ale; dunkles ~ dark beer;

stout, porter; '~**brauer** m brewer; '~**brauerei** f brewery; '~**garten** m beer-garden; '~**krug** m beer-mug, Am. stein.

Biest [bi:st] n (-es/-er) beast, brute.

bieten ['bi:tən] (irr., ge-, h) **1.** v/t. offer; ✝ at auction sale: bid; sich ~ opportunity, etc.: offer itself, arise, occur; **2.** ✝ v/i. at auction sale: bid.

Bigamie [biga'mi:] f (-/-n) bigamy.

Bilanz [bi'lants] f (-/-en) balance; balance-sheet, Am. a. statement; fig. result, outcome; die ~ ziehen strike a balance; fig. take stock (of one's life, etc.).

Bild [bilt] n (-[e]s/-er) picture; image; illustration; portrait; fig. idea, notion; '~**bericht** m press: picture story.

bilden ['bildən] v/t. (ge-, h) form; shape; fig.: educate, train (s.o., mind, etc.); develop (mind, etc.); form, constitute (obstacle, etc.); sich ~ form; fig. educate o.s., improve one's mind; sich e-e Meinung ~ form an opinion.

Bilder|buch ['bildər-] n picture-book; '~**galerie** f picture-gallery; '~**rätsel** n rebus.

'**Bild|fläche** f: F auf der ~ erscheinen appear on the scene; F von der ~ verschwinden disappear (from the scene); '~**funk** m radio picture transmission; television; '~**hauer** m (-s/-) sculptor; ~**hauerei** [~'raɪ] f (-/-en) sculpture; '2**lich** adj. pictorial; word, etc.: figurative; '~**nis** n (-ses/-se) portrait; '~**röhre** f picture or television tube; '~**säule** f statue; '~**schirm** m (television) screen; '2**schön** adj. most beautiful; '~**seite** f face, head (of coin); '~**streifen** m picture or film strip; '~**telegraphie** f (-/no pl.) phototelegraphy.

'**Bildung** f (-/-en) forming, formation (both a. gr.: of plural, etc.); constitution (of committee, etc.); education; culture; (good) breeding. [sg.; billiard-table.)

Billard ['biljart] n (-s/-e) billiards)

billig adj. ['biliç] just, equitable; fair; price: reasonable, moderate; goods: cheap, inexpensive; recht und ~ right and proper; '~**en** [~gən] v/t. (ge-, h) approve of, Am. a. approbate; '2**keit** f (-/no pl.) justness,

equity; fairness; reasonableness, moderateness; 2**ung** ['~gun] f (-/~-en) approval, sanction.

Binde ['bində] f (-/-n) band; tie; ✚ bandage; (arm-)sling; s. Damenbinde; '~**gewebe** anat. n connective tissue; '~**glied** n connecting link; '~**haut** anat. f conjunctiva; '~**hautentzündung** ✚ f conjunctivitis; '2**n** (irr., ge-, h) **1.** v/t. bind, tie (an acc. to); bind (book, etc.); make (broom, wreath, etc.); knot (tie); sich ~ bind or commit or engage o.s.; **2.** v/i. bind; unite; ⊕ cement, etc.: set, harden; '~**strich** m hyphen; '~**wort** gr. n (-[e]s/-er) conjunction.

Bindfaden ['bint-] m string; packthread.

'**Bindung** f (-/-en) binding (a. of ski); ♪ slur, tie, ligature; fig. commitment (a. pol.); engagement; ~en pl. bonds pl., ties pl.

binnen prp. (dat., a. gen.) ['binən] within; ~ kurzem before long.

'**Binnen|gewässer** n inland water; '~**hafen** m close port; '~**handel** m domestic or home trade, Am. domestic commerce; '~**land** n inland, interior; '~**verkehr** m inland traffic or transport.

Binse ♀ ['binzə] f (-/-n) rush; F: in die ~n gehen go to pot; '~**nwahrheit** f, '~**nweisheit** f truism.

Biochemie [bioçe'mi:] f (-/no pl.) biochemistry.

Biograph|ie [biogra'fi:] f (-/-n) biography; 2**isch** adj. [~'grɑ:fiʃ] biographic(al).

Biolog|ie [biolo'gi:] f (-/no pl.) biology; 2**isch** adj. [~'lo:giʃ] biological.

Birke ♀ ['birkə] f (-/-n) birch(-tree).

Birne ['birnə] f (-/-n) ♀ pear; ∮ (electric) bulb; fig. sl. nob, Am. bean.

bis [bis] **1.** prp. (acc.) space: to, as far as; time: till, until, by; zwei ~ drei two or three, two to three; ~ auf weiteres until further orders, for the meantime; ~ vier zählen count up to four; alle ~ auf drei all but or except three; **2.** cj. till, until.

Bisamratte zo. ['bi:zam-] f muskrat.

Bischof ['biʃɔf] m (-s/-e) bishop.

bischöflich adj. ['biʃøfliç] episcopal.

bisher *adv.* [bis'he:r] hitherto, up to now, so far; **~ig** *adj.* until now; hitherto existing; former.

Biß [bis] **1.** *m* (*Bisses/Bisse*) bite; **2.** ♀ *pret. of* beißen.

bißchen ['bisçən] **1.** *adj.*: ein ~ a little, a (little) bit of; **2.** *adv.*: ein ~ a little (bit).

Bissen ['bisən] *m* (-s/-) mouthful; morsel; bite.

'bissig *adj.* biting (*a. fig.*); *remark*: cutting; *Achtung*, ~*er Hund!* beware of the dog!

Bistum ['bistu:m] *n* (-s/~er) bishopric, diocese.

bisweilen *adv.* [bis'vaɪlən] sometimes, at times, now and then.

Bitte ['bitə] *f* (-/-n) request (*um* for); entreaty; *auf j-s ~* (*hin*) at s.o.'s request.

'bitten (*irr.*, ge-, h) **1.** *v/t.*: j-n um et. ~ ask *or* beg s.o. for s.th.; j-n um Entschuldigung ~ beg s.o.'s pardon; *dürfte ich Sie um Feuer ~*? may I trouble you for a light?; *bitte* please; (*wie*) *bitte?* (I beg your) pardon?; *bitte!* offering *s.th.*: (please,) help yourself, (please,) do take some *or* one; *danke (schön) — bitte (sehr)!* thank you — not at all, you're welcome, don't mention it, F that's all right; **2.** *v/i.*: um et. ~ ask *or* beg for s.th.

bitter *adj.* ['bitər] bitter (*a. fig.*); *frost*: sharp; **2keit** *f* (-/-en) bitterness; *fig. a.* acrimony; **'~lich** *adv.* bitterly.

'Bitt|gang *eccl. m* procession; **'~schrift** *f* petition; **'~steller** *m* (-s/-) petitioner.

bläh|en ['blɛ:ən] (ge-, h) **1.** *v/t.* inflate, distend, swell out; belly (out), swell out (*sails*); *sich ~ sails*: belly (out), swell out; *skirt*: balloon out; **2.** ⚕ *v/i.* cause flatulence; **'~end** *adj.* flatulent; **'2ung** *f* (-/-en) flatulence; F wind.

Blam|age [bla'ma:ʒə] *f* (-/-n) disgrace, shame; **2ieren** [~'mi:rən] *v/t.* (*no* -ge-, *h*) make a fool of *s.o.*, disgrace; *sich ~* make a fool of o.s.

blank *adj.* [blaŋk] shining, shiny, bright; polished; F *fig.* broke.

blanko ✝ ['blaŋko] **1.** *adj. form*, *etc.*: blank, not filled in; in blank; **2.** *adv.*: ~ *verkaufen stock exchange*: sell short; **2scheck** *m* blank cheque, *Am.* blank check; **'2unterschrift** *f*

blank signature; **'2vollmacht** *f* full power of attorney, carte blanche.

Bläschen ⚕ ['blɛ:sçən] *n* (-s/-) vesicle, small blister.

Blase ['bla:zə] *f* (-/-n) bubble; blister (*a.* ⚕); *anat.* bladder; bleb (*in glass*); ⊕ flaw; **'~balg** *m* (*ein a pair of*) bellows *pl.*; **'2n** (*irr.*, ge-, *h*) **1.** *v/t.* blow; blow, sound; play (*wind-instrument*); **2.** *v/i.* blow.

Blas|instrument ♩ ['bla:s-] *n* wind-instrument; **'~kapelle** *f* brass band.

blaß *adj.* [blas] pale (*vor dat.* with); ~ *werden* turn pale; *keine blasse Ahnung* not the faintest idea.

Blässe ['blɛsə] *f* (-/*no pl.*) paleness.

Blatt [blat] *n* (-[e]s/~er) leaf (*of book*, ⚘); petal (*of flower*); leaf, sheet (*of paper*); ♩ sheet; blade (*of oar, saw, airscrew, etc.*); hand (*of metal*); *cards*: hand; (*news*)paper.

Blattern 𝒔 ['blatərn] *pl.* smallpox.

blättern ['blɛtərn] *v/i.* (ge-, *h*): in e-m Buch ~ leaf through a book, thumb a book.

'Blatternarb|e *f* pock-mark; **'2ig** *adj.* pock-marked.

'Blätterteig *m* puff paste.

'Blatt|gold *n* gold-leaf, gold-foil; **'~laus** *zo.* *f* plant-louse; **'~pflanze** *f* foliage plant.

blau [blau] **1.** *adj.* blue; F *fig.* drunk, tight, boozy; ~*er Fleck* bruise; ~*es Auge* black eye; *mit e-m ~en Auge davonkommen* get off cheaply; **2.** ♀ *n* (-s/*no pl.*) blue (colo[u]r); *Fahrt ins ~* mystery tour. [blue.\]

bläuen ['blɔyən] *v/t.* (ge-, *h*) (dye)\

'blau|grau *adj.* bluish grey; **'2jacke** ⚓ *f* bluejacket, sailor.

'bläulich *adj.* bluish.

'Blausäure 🜍 *f* (-/*no pl.*) hydrocyanic *or* prussic acid.

Blech [blɛç] *n* (-[e]s/-e) sheet metal; metal sheet, plate; F *fig.* balderdash, rubbish, *Am. sl. a.* baloney; **'~büchse** *f* tin, *Am.* can; **'2ern** *adj.* (of) tin; *sound*: brassy; *sound, voice*: tinny; **'~musik** *f* brass-band music; **'~waren** *f/pl.* tinware.

Blei [blaɪ] *n* (-[e]s/-e) **1.** *n* lead; **2.** F *n, m* (lead) pencil.

bleiben ['blaɪbən] *v/i.* (*irr.*, ge-, *sein*) remain, stay; be left; *ruhig ~* keep calm; ~ *bei* keep to *s.th.*, stick to *s.th.*; *bitte bleiben Sie am Apparat teleph.* hold the line, please; **'~d**

adj. lasting, permanent; '~**lassen** *v/t.* (*irr.* lassen, *sep.*, *no* -ge-, *h*) leave *s.th.* alone; *laß das bleiben!* don't do it!; leave it alone!; stop that (*noise*, *etc.*)!

bleich *adj.* [blaɪç] pale (*vor dat.* with); '~**en** (ge-) **1.** *v/t.* (*h*) make pale; bleach; blanch; **2.** *v/i.* (*irr.*, *sein*) bleach; lose colo(u)r, fade; '~**süchtig** ✍ *adj.* chlorotic, greensick.

'**bleiern** *adj.* (of) lead, leaden (*a. fig.*).

'**Blei**|**rohr** *n* lead pipe; '~**soldat** *m* tin soldier; '~**stift** *m* (lead) pencil; '~**stifthülse** *f* pencil cap; '~**stift- spitzer** *m* (-s/-) pencil-sharpener; '~**vergiftung** ✍ *f* lead-poisoning.

Blend|**e** ['blɛndə] *f* (-/-n) *phot.* diaphragm, stop; △ blind *or* sham window; '2**en** (ge-) **1.** *v/t.* blind; dazzle (*both a. fig.*); **2.** *v/i. light:* dazzle the eyes; ~**laterne** ['blɛnt-] *f* dark lantern.

blich [blɪç] *pret. of* bleichen 2.

Blick [blɪk] *m* (-[e]s/-e) glance, look; view (*auf acc.* of); *auf den ersten* ~ at first sight; *ein böser* ~ an evil *or* angry look; '2**en** *v/i.* (ge-) (*h*) look, glance (*auf acc., nach* at); '~**fang** *m* eye-catcher.

blieb [bliːp] *pret. of* bleiben.

blies [bliːs] *pret. of* blasen.

blind *adj.* [blɪnt] blind (*a. fig.:* gegen, für to; *vor dat.* with); *metal:* dull, tarnished; *window:* opaque (*with age, dirt*); *mirror:* clouded, dull; *cartridge:* blank; ~er *Alarm* false alarm; ~er *Passagier* stowaway; *auf e-m Auge* ~ blind in one eye.

'**Blinddarm** *anat. m* blind gut; appendix; '~**entzündung** ✍ *f* appendicitis.

Blinde ['blɪndə] (-n/-n) **1.** *m* blind man; **2.** *f* blind woman; ~**nanstalt** ['blɪndən⁹-] *f* institute for the blind; '~**nheim** *n* home for the blind; '~**nhund** *m* guide dog, *Am. a.* seeing-eye dog; '~**nschrift** *f* braille.

'**blind**|**fliegen** ✈ (*irr.* fliegen, *sep.*, -ge-) *v/t.* (*h*) *and v/i.* (*sein*) fly blind *or* on instruments; '2**flug** ✈ *m* blind flying *or* flight; '2**gänger** *m* ✖ blind shell, dud; *F fig.* washout; '2**heit** *f* (-/*no pl.*) blindness; ~**lings** *adv.* ['~lɪŋs] blindly; at random; '2**schleiche** *zo. f* (-/-/-) slow-worm,

blind-worm; '~**schreiben** *v/t. and v/i.* (*irr.* schreiben, *sep.*, -ge-, *h*) touch-type.

blink|**en** ['blɪŋkən] *v/i.* (ge-, *h*) star, light: twinkle; *metal, leather, glass, etc.:* shine; signal (with lamps), flash; '2**er** *mot. m* (-s/-) flashing indicator; '2**feuer** *n* flashing light.

blinzeln ['blɪntsəln] *v/i.* (ge-, *h*) blink (*at light, etc.*); wink.

Blitz [blɪts] *m* (-es/-e) lightning; '~**ableiter** *m* (-s/-) lightning-conductor; '2**en** *v/i.* (ge-, *h*) flash; es *blitzt* it is lightening; '~**gespräch** *teleph. n* special priority call; '~**licht** *phot. n* flash-light; '2**schnell** *adv.* with lightning speed; '~**strahl** *m* flash of lightning.

Block [blɔk] *m* **1.** (-[e]s/⁼e) block; slab (*of cooking chocolate*); block, log (*of wood*); ingot (*of metal*); *parl., pol.,* ✝ bloc; **2.** (-[e]s/⁼e, -s) block (*of houses*); pad, block (*of paper*); ~**ade** ✖ ⚓ [~'kaːdə] *f* (-/-n) blockade; ~**adebrecher** *m* (-s/-) blockade-runner; ~**haus** *n* log cabin; 2**ieren** [~'kiːrən] (*no* -ge-, *h*) **1.** *v/t.* block (up); lock (*wheel*); **2.** *v/i.* brakes, *etc.*: jam.

blöd *adj.* [bløːt], ~**e** *adj.* ['~də] imbecile; stupid, dull; silly; '2**heit** *f* (-/-en) imbecility; stupidity, dullness; silliness; '2**sinn** *m* imbecility; rubbish, nonsense; '~**sinnig** *adj.* imbecile; idiotic, stupid, foolish.

blöken ['bløːkən] *v/i.* (ge-, *h*) *sheep, calf:* bleat.

blond *adj.* [blɔnt] blond, fair (-haired).

bloß [bloːs] **1.** *adj.* bare, naked; mere; ~**e** *Worte* mere words; *mit dem* ~**en** *Auge wahrnehmbar* visible to the naked eye; **2.** *adv.* only, merely, simply, just.

Blöße ['bløːsə] *f* (-/-n) bareness, nakedness; *fig.* weak point *or* spot; *sich e-e* ~ *geben* give o.s. away; lay o.s. open to attack; *keine* ~ *bieten* be invulnerable.

'**bloß**|**legen** *v/t.* (*sep.*, -ge-, *h*) lay bare, expose; '~**stellen** *v/t.* (*sep.*, -ge-, *h*) expose, compromise, unmask; *sich* ~ compromise o.s.

blühen ['blyːən] *v/i.* (ge-, *h*) blossom, flower, bloom; *fig.* flourish, thrive, prosper; ✝ boom.

Blume ['bluːmə] *f* (-/-n) flower; *wine:* bouquet; *beer:* froth.

'Blumen|beet n flower-bed; **'~blatt** n petal; **'~händler** m florist; **'~strauß** m bouquet or bunch of flowers; **'~topf** m flowerpot; **'~zucht** f floriculture.

Bluse ['blu:zə] f (-/-n) blouse.

Blut [blu:t] n (-[e]s/no pl.) blood; **~ vergießen** shed blood; **böses ~ machen** breed bad blood; **'~andrang** ⚕ m congestion; **'arm** adj. bloodless; **** an(a)emic; **'~armut** ⚕ f an(a)emia; **'~bad** n carnage, massacre; **'~bank** f blood bank; **'~blase** f blood blister; **'~druck** m blood pressure; **dürstig** adj. ['~dyrstɪç] bloodthirsty.

Blüte ['bly:tə] f (-/-n) blossom, bloom, flower; esp. fig. flower; prime, heyday (of life).

Blutegel ['blu:tʔe:gəl] m (-s/-) leech.

'bluten v/i. (ge-, h) bleed (aus from); aus der Nase ~ bleed at the nose.

Bluterguß ⚕ ['blu:tʔ-] m effusion of blood.

'Blütezeit f flowering period or time; fig. a. prime, heyday.

'Blut|gefäß anat. n blood-vessel; **~gerinnsel** ['~gərinzəl] n (-s/-) clot of blood; **'~gruppe** f blood group; **'~hund** zo. m bloodhound; **'blutig** adj. bloody, blood-stained; es ist mein ~er Ernst I am dead serious; ~er Anfänger mere beginner, F greenhorn.

Blut|körperchen ['blu:tkœrpərçən] n (-s/-) blood corpuscle; **'~kreislauf** m (blood) circulation; **'~lache** f pool of blood; **leer** adj., **los** adj. bloodless; **'~probe** f blood test; **'~rache** f blood feud or revenge or vengeance, vendetta; **'rot** adj. blood-red; crimson; **rünstig** adj. ['~rynstɪç] bloodthirsty; bloody; **'~schande** f incest; **'~spender** m blood-donor; **stillend** adj. blood-sta(u)nching; **'~sturz** ⚕ m h(a)emorrhage; **sverwandt** adj. related by blood (mit to); **'~sverwandtschaft** f blood-relationship, consanguinity; **'~übertragung** f blood-transfusion; **'~ung** f (-/-en) bleeding, h(a)emorrhage; **unterlaufen** adj.: blood-shot; **'~vergießen** n bloodshed; **'~vergiftung** f blood-poisoning.

Bö [bø] f (-/-en) gust, squall.

Bock [bɔk] m (-[e]s/e) deer, hare, rabbit: buck; he-goat, F billy-goat; sheep: ram; gymnastics: buck; e-n ~ schießen commit a blunder, sl. commit a bloomer; den ~ zum Gärtner machen set the fox to keep the geese; **en** v/i. (ge-, h) horse: buck; child: sulk; p. be obstinate or refractory; mot. move jerkily, Am. F a. buck; **ig** adj. stubborn, obstinate, pigheaded; **'~sprung** m leap-frog; gymnastics: vault over the buck; Bocksprünge machen caper, cut capers.

Boden ['bo:dən] m (-s/) ground; ⚚ soil; bottom; floor; loft; **'~kammer** f garret, attic; **los** adj. bottomless; fig. enormous; unheard-of; **'~personal** ✈ n ground personnel or staff, Am. ground crew; **'~reform** f land reform; **'~satz** m grounds pl., sediment; **~schätze** ['~ʃɛtsə] m/pl. mineral resources pl.; **ständig** adj. native, indigenous.

bog [bo:k] pret. of biegen.

Bogen ['bo:gən] m (-s/-,) bow, bend, curve; ⚚ arc; △ arch; skiing: turn; skating: curve; sheet (of paper); **förmig** adj. arched; **'~gang** △ m arcade; **'~lampe** ⚡ f arc-lamp; **'~schütze** m archer, bowman.

Bohle ['bo:lə] f (-/-n) thick plank, board.

Bohne ['bo:nə] f (-/-n) bean; grüne ~n pl. French beans pl., Am. string beans pl.; weiße ~n pl. haricot beans pl.; F blaue ~n pl. bullets pl.; **~nstange** f beanpole (a. F fig.).

bohnern ['bo:nərn] v/t. (ge-, h) polish (floor, etc.), (bees)wax (floor).

bohr|en ['bo:rən] (ge-, h) **1.** v/t. bore, drill (hole); sink, bore (well, shaft); bore, cut, drive (tunnel, etc.); **2.** v/i. drill (a. dentistry); bore; **'er** ⊕ m (-s/-) borer, drill.

'böig adj. squally, gusty; ✈ bumpy.

Boje ['bo:jə] f (-/-n) buoy.

Bollwerk ✕ ['bɔlvɛrk] n bastion, bulwark (a. fig.).

Bolzen ⊕ ['bɔltsən] m (-s/-) bolt.

Bombard|ement [bɔmbardə'mã:] n (-s/-s) bombardment; bombing; shelling; **ieren** [~'di:rən] v/t. (no -ge-, h) bomb; shell; bombard (a. fig.).

Bombe ['bɔmbə] f (-/-n) bomb; fig. bomb-shell; **nsicher** adj. bomb-

B

proof; F *fig.* dead sure; '**~nschaden** *m* bomb damage; '**~r** ✕⚔ *m* (-s/-) bomber.

Bon † [bõ:] *m* (-s/-s) coupon; vouch-

Bonbon [bõ'bõ:] *m, n* (-s/-s) sweet (-meat), bon-bon, F goody, *Am.* candy. [*Am. a.* big shot.\

Bonze F ['bɔntsə] *m* (-n/-n) bigwig,\

Boot [bo:t] *n* (-[e]s/-e) boat; '**~shaus** *n* boat-house; '**~smann** *m* (-[e]s/ *Bootsleute*) boatswain.

Bord [bɔrt] (-[e]s/-e) **1.** *n* shelf; **2.** ⚓, ⚔ *m:* an ~ on board, aboard (*ship, aircraft, etc.*); über ~ overboard; von ~ gehen go ashore; '**~funker** ⚓, ⚔ *m* wireless *or* radio operator; '**~stein** *m* kerb, *Am.* curb.

borgen ['bɔrgən] *v/t.* (ge-, h) borrow (*von, bei* from, of); lend, *Am. a.* loan (≈-m *et.* s.th. to s.o.).

Borke ['bɔrkə] *f* (-/-n) bark (*of tree*).

borniert *adj.* [bɔr'ni:rt] narrowminded, of restricted intelligence.

Borsalbe ['bo:r-] *f* boracic ointment.

Börse ['bœrzə] *f* (-/-n) purse; †‡ stock exchange; stock-market; money-market; '**~nbericht** *m* market report; '**~nfähig** *adj.* stock: negotiable on the stock exchange; '**~nkurs** *m* quotation; '**~nmakler** *m* stock-broker; '**~nnotierung** *f* (official, stock exchange) quotation; '**~npapiere** *n/pl.* listed securities *pl.*; '**~nspekulant** *m* stockjobber; '**~nzeitung** *f* financial newspaper.

Borst|e ['bɔrstə] *f* (-/-n) bristle (*of hog or brush, etc.*); '**2ig** *adj.* bristly.

Borte ['bɔrtə] *f* (-/-n) border (*of carpet, etc.*); braid, lace.

'**bösartig** *adj.* malicious, vicious; ✗ malignant; '**2keit** *f* (-/-en) viciousness; ✗ malignity.

Böschung ['bœʃuŋ] *f* (-/-en) slope; embankment (*of railway*); bank (*of river*).

böse ['bø:zə] **1.** *adj.* bad, evil, wicked; malevolent, spiteful; angry (über *acc.* at, about; *auf* j-n with s.o.); er meint es nicht ~ he means no harm; **2.** ≈ *n* (-n/*no pl.*) evil; 2wicht ['~viçt] *m* (-[e]s/-er, -e) villain, rascal.

bos|haft *adj.* ['bo:shaft] wicked; spiteful; malicious; '**2heit** *f* (-/-en) wickedness; malice; spite.

'**böswillig** *adj.* malevolent; ~e Ab-

sicht ‡‡ malice prepense; ~es Verlassen ‡‡ wilful desertion; '**2keit** *f* (-/-en) malevolence.

bot [bo:t] *pret. of bieten.*

Botan|ik [bo'ta:nik] *f* (-/*no pl.*) botany; '**~iker** *m* (-s/-) botanist; **2isch** *adj.* botanical.

Bote ['bo:tə] *m* (-n/-n) messenger; '**~ngang** *m.* errand; *Botengänge machen* run errands.

Botschaft *f* (-/-en) message; *pol.* embassy; '**~er** *m* (-s/-) ambassador; *in British Commonwealth countries:* High Commissioner.

Bottich ['bɔtiç] *m* (-[e]s/-e) tub; wash-tub; *brewing:* tun. vat.

Bouillon [bu'ljõ:] *f* (-/-s) beef tea.

Bowle ['bo:lə] *f* (-/-n) *vessel:* bowl; *cold drink consisting of fruit, hock and champagne or soda-water: appr.* punch.

box|en ['bɔksən] **1.** *v/i.* (ge-, h) box; **2.** *v/t.* (ge-, h) punch *s.o.*; **3.** 2 *n* (-s/*no pl.*) boxing; pugilism; '**2er** *m* (-s/-) boxer; pugilist; '**2handschuh** *m* boxing-glove; '**2kampf** *m* boxing-match, bout, fight; '**2sport** *m* boxing.

Boykott [bɔy'kɔt] *m* (-[e]s/-e) boycott; **2ieren** [~'ti:rən] *v/t.* (*no* -ge-, h) boycott.

brach [bra:x] **1.** *pret. of brechen;* **2.** ✓ *adv.* fallow; uncultivated (*both a. fig.*).

brachte ['braxtə] *pret. of bringen.*

Branche † ['brã:ʃə] *f* (-/-n) line (*of business*), trade; branch.

Brand [brant] *m* (-[e]s/⸚e) burning; fire, blaze; ✗ gangrene; ⚚, ✓ blight, smut, mildew; '**~blase** *f* blister; '**~bombe** *f* incendiary bomb; **2en** ['~dən] *v/i.* (ge-, h) surge (*a. fig.*), break (*an acc.*, gegen against); '**~fleck** *m* burn; **2ig** *adj.* ['~diç] ⚚, ✓ blighted, smutted; ✗ gangrenous; '**~mal** *n* brand; *fig.* stigma, blemish; '**2marken** *v/t.* (ge-, h) brand (*animal*); *fig.* brand *or* stigmatize *s.o.*; '**~mauer** *f* fire (-proof) wall; '**~schaden** *m* damage caused by *or* loss suffered by fire; '**2schatzen** *v/t.* (ge-, h) lay (*town*) under contribution; sack, pillage; '**~stätte** *f,* '**~stelle** *f* scene of fire; '**~stifter** *m* incendiary, *Am.* F *a.* firebug; '**~stiftung** *f* arson; **~ung** ['~duŋ] *f* (-/-en) surf, surge, breakers *pl.*; '**~wache** *f* fire-watch;

'~wunde f burn; scald; **'~zeichen** n brand.

brannte ['brantə] pret. of brennen.

Branntwein ['brantvaɪn] m brandy, spirits pl.; whisk(e)y; gin; **'~brennerei** f distillery.

braten ['braːtən] 1. v/t. (irr., ge-, h) in oven: roast; grill; in frying-pan: fry; bake (apple); am Spieß ~ roast on a spit, barbecue; 2. v/i. (irr., ge-, h) roast; grill; fry; in der Sonne ~ p. roast or grill in the sun; 3. ♀ m (-s/-) roast (meat); joint; **'♀fett** n dripping; **'♀soße** f gravy.

'Brat|fisch m fried fish; **'~hering** m grilled herring; **'~huhn** n roast chicken; **'~kartoffeln** pl. fried potatoes pl.; **'~ofen** m (kitchen) oven; **'~pfanne** f frying-pan, Am. a. skillet; **'~röhre** f s. Bratofen.

Brauch [braux] m (-[e]s/¤e) custom, usage; use, habit; practice; **'♀bar** adj. p., thing: useful; p. capable, able; thing: serviceable; **'♀en** (h) 1. v/t. (ge-) need, want; require; take (time); use; 2. v/aux. (no -ge-): du brauchst es nur zu sagen you only have to say so; er hätte nicht zu kommen ~ he need not have come; **'~tum** n (-[e]s/¤er) custom; tradition; folklore.

Braue ['brauə] f (-/-n) eyebrow.

brau|en ['brauən] v/t. (ge-, h) brew; **'♀er** m (-s/-) brewer; **♀erei** [~'raɪ] f (-/-en) brewery; **'♀haus** n brewery.

braun adj. [braun] brown; horse: bay; ~ werden get a tan (on one's skin).

Bräune ['brɔynə] f (-/no pl.) brown colo(u)r; (sun) tan; **'♀n** (ge-, h) 1. v/t. make or dye brown; sun: tan; 2. v/i. tan.

'Braunkohle f brown coal, lignite.

'bräunlich adj. brownish.

Brause ['brauzə] f (-/-n) rose, sprinkling-nozzle (of watering can); s. Brausebad; s. Brauselimonade; **'~bad** n shower(-bath); **'~limonade** f fizzy lemonade; **'♀n** v/i. (ge-, h) wind, water, etc.: roar; rush; have a shower(-bath); **'~pulver** n effervescent powder.

Braut [braut] f (-/¤e) fiancée; on wedding-day: bride; **'~führer** m best man.

Bräutigam ['brɔytigam] m (-s/-e) fiancé; on wedding-day: bridegroom, Am. a. groom.

'Braut|jungfer f bridesmaid; **'~kleid** n wedding-dress; **'~kranz** m bridal wreath; **'~leute** pl., **'~paar** n engaged couple; on wedding-day: bride and bridegroom; **'~schleier** m bridal veil.

brav adj. [braːf] honest, upright; good, well-behaved; brave.

bravo int. ['braːvo] bravo!, well done!

Bravour [bra'vuːr] f (-/no pl.) bravery, courage; brilliance.

Brecheisen ['brɛçʔ-] n crowbar; (burglar's) jemmy, Am. a. jimmy.

'brechen (irr., ge-) 1. v/t. (h) break; pluck (flower); refract (ray, etc.); fold (sheet of paper); quarry (stone); vomit; die Ehe ~ commit adultery; sich ~ break (one's arm, etc.); opt. be refracted; 2. v/i. (h) break; vomit; mit j-m ~ break with s.o.; 3. v/i. (sein) break, get broken; bones: break, fracture.

'Brech|mittel 𝄐 n emetic; F fig. sickener; **'~reiz** m nausea; **'~stange** f crowbar, Am. a. pry; **'~ung** opt. f (-/-en) refraction.

Brei [braɪ] m (-[e]s/-e) paste; pulp; mash; pap (for babies); made of oatmeal: porridge; (rice, etc.) pudding; **'♀ig** adj. pasty; pulpy; pappy.

breit adj. [braɪt] broad, wide; zehn Meter ~ ten metres wide; ~e Schichten der Bevölkerung large sections of or the bulk of the population; **'~beinig 1.** adj. with legs wide apart; 2. adv.: ~ gehen straddle.

Breite ['braɪtə] f (-/-n) breadth, width; ast., geogr. latitude; **'♀n** v/t. (ge-, h) spread; **'~ngrad** m degree of latitude; **'~nkreis** m parallel (of latitude).

'breit|machen v/refl. (sep., -ge-, h) spread o.s.; take up room; **'~schlagen** v/t. (irr. schlagen, sep., -ge-, h): F j-n ~ persuade s.o.; F j-n zu et. ~ talk s.o. into (doing) s.th.; **'♀seite** ♣ f broadside.

Bremse ['brɛmzə] f (-/-n) zo. gadfly; horse-fly; ⊕ brake; **'♀n** (ge-, h) v/i. brake, put on the brakes; slow down; 2. v/t. brake, put on the brakes; slow down; fig. curb.

'Brems|klotz m brake-block; 𝌏 wheel chock; **'~pedal** n brake pedal; **'~vorrichtung** f brake-mechanism; **'~weg** m braking distance.

brennbar

brenn|bar adj. ['brɛnbɑːr] combustible, burnable; **≈dauer** f burning time; **≈en** (irr., ge-, h) **1.** v/t. burn; distil(l) (brandy); roast (coffee); bake (brick, etc.); **2.** v/i. burn; be ablaze, be on fire; wound, eye: smart, burn; nettle: sting; vor Ungeduld ≈ burn with impatience; F darauf ≈ zu inf. be burning to inf.; es brennt! fire!

'Brenn|er m (-s/-) p. distiller; fixture: burner; **≈essel** ['brɛnnɛsəl] f stinging nettle; **≈glas** n burning glass; **≈holz** n firewood; **≈material** n fuel; **≈öl** n lamp-oil; fuel-oil; **≈punkt** m focus, focal point; in den ≈ rücken bring into focus (a. fig.); im ≈ des Interesses stehen be the focus of interest; **≈schere** f curling-tongs pl.; **≈spiritus** m methylated spirit; **≈stoff** m combustible; mot. fuel.

brenzlig ['brɛntslıç] **1.** adj. burnt; matter: dangerous; situation: precarious; ≈er Geruch burnt smell, smell of burning; **2.** adv.: es riecht ≈ it smells of burning.

Bresche ['brɛʃə] f (-/-n) breach (a. fig.), gap; in die ≈ springen help s.o. out of a dilemma.

Brett [brɛt] n (-[e]s/-er) board; plank; shelf; spring-board; **≈spiel** n game played on a board.

Brezel ['breːtsəl] f (-/-n) pretzel.

Brief [briːf] m (-[e]s/-e) letter; **≈aufschrift** f address (on a letter); **≈beschwerer** m (-s/-) paperweight; **≈bogen** m sheet of notepaper; **≈geheimnis** n secrecy of correspondence; **≈karte** f correspondence card (with envelope); **≈kasten** m letter-box; pillar-box; Am. mailbox; **≈lich** adj. and adv. by letter, in writing; **≈marke** f (postage) stamp; **≈markensammlung** f stamp-collection; **≈öffner** m letter-opener; **≈ordner** m letter-file; **≈papier** n notepaper; **≈porto** n postage; **≈post** f mail, post; **≈tasche** f wallet, Am. a. billfold; **≈taube** f carrier pigeon, homing pigeon, homer; **≈träger** m postman, Am. mailman; **≈umschlag** m envelope; **≈waage** f letter-balance; **≈wechsel** m correspondence; **≈zensur** f postal censorship.

brief [briːt] pret. of braten.

Brikett [bri'kɛt] n (-[e]s/-s) briquet (-te).

Brillant [bril'jant] **1.** m (-en/-en) brilliant, cut diamond; **2.** ♀ adj. brilliant; **≈ring** m diamond ring.

Brille ['brılə] f (-/-n) (eine a pair of) glasses pl. or spectacles pl.; goggles pl.; lavatory seat; **≈nfutteral** n spectacle-case; **≈nträger** m person who wears glasses.

bringen ['brıŋən] v/t. (irr., ge-, h) bring; take; see (s.o. home, etc.); put (in order); make (sacrifice); yield (interest); an den Mann ≈ dispose of, get rid of; j-n dazu ≈, et. zu tun make or get s.o. to do s.th.; et. mit sich ≈ involve s.th.; j-n um et. ≈ deprive s.o. of s.th.; j-n zum Lachen ≈ make s.o. laugh.

Brise ['briːzə] f (-/-n) breeze.

Brit|e ['briːtə] m (-n/-n) Briton, Am. a. Britisher; die ≈n pl. the British pl.; **≈isch** adj. British.

bröckeln ['brœkəln] v/i. (ge-, h) crumble; become brittle.

Brocken ['brɔkən] **1.** m (-s/-) piece; lump (of earth or stone, etc.); morsel (of food); F ein harter ≈ a hard nut; **2.** ♀ v/t. (ge-, h): Brot in die Suppe ≈ break bread into soup.

brodeln ['broːdəln] v/i. (ge-, h) bubble, simmer.

Brombeer|e ['brɔm-] f blackberry; **≈strauch** m blackberry bush.

Bronch|ialkatarrh ♀ [brɔnçi'ɑːl-katar] m bronchial catarrh; **≈ien** anat. f/pl. bronchi(a) pl.; **≈itis** ♀ [≈'çiːtıs] f (-/Bronchitiden) bronchitis.

Bronze ['brõːsə] f (-/-n) bronze; **≈medaille** f bronze medal.

Brosche ['brɔʃə] f (-/-n) brooch.

broschier|en [brɔ'ʃiːrən] v/t. (no -ge-, h) sew, stitch (book); **≈t** adj. book: paper-backed, paper-bound; fabric: figured.

Broschüre [brɔ'ʃyːrə] f (-/-n) booklet; brochure; pamphlet.

Brot [broːt] n (-[e]s/-e) bread; loaf; sein ≈ verdienen earn one's living; **≈aufstrich** m spread.

Brötchen ['brøːtçən] n (-s/-) roll.

'Brot|korb m: j-m den ≈ höher hängen put s.o. on short allowance; **≈los** fig. adj. unemployed; unprofitable; **≈rinde** f crust; **≈schneidemaschine** f bread-cutter; **≈schnitte** f slice of bread;

'**studium** n utilitarian study; '**teig** m bread dough.

Bruch [brux] (-[e]s/-̈e) break(ing); breach; ⚙ fracture (of bones); ⚕ hernia; crack; fold (in paper); crease (in cloth); split (in silk); A̋ fraction; breach (of promise); violation (of oath, etc.); violation, infringement (of law, etc.); '**band** ⚙ n truss.

brüchig adj. ['bryçiç] fragile; brittle; voice: cracked.

'**Bruch|landung** ✈ f crash-landing; '**rechnung** f fractional arithmetic, F fractions pl.; '**strich** Ą m fraction bar; '**stück** n fragment (a. fig.); '**teil** m fraction; im ~ e-r Sekunde in a split second; '**zahl** f fraction(al) number.

Brücke f ['brykə] (-/-n) bridge; carpet: rug; sports: bridge; e-e ~ schlagen über (acc.) build or throw a bridge across, bridge (river); '**nkopf** ✕ m bridge-head; '**npfeiler** m pier (of bridge).

Bruder ['bru:dər] m (-s/-̈) brother; eccl. (lay) brother, friar; '**krieg** m fratricidal or civil war; '**kuß** m fraternal kiss.

brüderlich ['bry:dərliç] **1.** adj. brotherly, fraternal; **2.** adv.: ~ teilen share and share alike; '**2keit** f (-/no pl.) brotherliness, fraternity.

Brühe ['bry:ə] f (-/-n) broth; stock; beef tea; F dirty water; drink: F dishwater; '**2heiß** adj. scalding hot; '**würfel** m beef cube.

brüllen ['brylən] v/i. (ge-, h) roar; bellow; cattle: low; bull: bellow; vor Lachen ~ roar with laughter; '**des Gelächter** roar of laughter.

brumm|en ['brumən] v/i. (ge-, h) p. speak in a deep voice, mumble; growl (a. fig.); insect: buzz; engine: buzz, boom; fig. grumble, Am. F grouch; mir brummt der Schädel my head is buzzing; '**2bär** fig. m grumbler, growler, Am. F grouch; '**2er** m (-s/-) bluebottle; dung-beetle; '**ig** adj. grumbling, Am. F grouchy. [brunette.\]

brünett adj. ['bry'nɛt] woman: \

Brunft hunt. [brunft] f (-/-̈e) rut; '**zeit** f rutting season.

Brunnen ['brunən] m (-s/-) well; spring; fountain (a. fig.); e-n ~ graben sink a well; '**wasser** n pump-water, well-water.

'**Brunst** [brunst] f (-/-̈e) zo. rut (of male animal), heat (of female animal); lust, sexual desire.

brünstig adj. ['brynstiç] zo. rutting, in heat; lustful.

Brust [brust] f (-/-̈e) chest, anat. thorax; breast; (woman's) breast(s pl.), bosom; aus voller ~ at the top of one's voice, lustily; '**bild** n half-length portrait.

'**Brust|fell** anat. n pleura; '**fellentzündung** ⚕ f pleurisy; '**kasten** m, '**korb** m chest, anat. thorax; '**schwimmen** n (-s/no pl.) breast-stroke.

Brüstung ['brystuŋ] f (-/-en) balustrade, parapet.

'**Brustwarze** anat. f nipple.

Brut [bru:t] f (-/-en) brooding, sitting; brood; hatch; fry, spawn (of fish); fig. F brood, (bad) lot.

brutal adj. [bru'tɑ:l] brutal; 2ität [...ali'tɛ:t] f (-/-en) brutality.

Brutapparat zo. ['bru:t?-] m incubator.

brüten ['bry:tən] v/i. (ge-, h) brood, sit (on egg); incubate; ~ über (dat.) brood over s.th.

'**Brutkasten** ⚕ m incubator.

brutto ✝ adv. ['bruto] gross; '**2gewicht** n gross weight; '**2registertonne** ✝ f gross register ton; '**2verdienst** m gross earnings pl.

Bube ['bu:bə] m (-n/-n) boy, lad; knave, rogue; cards: knave, jack; '**nstreich** m, '**nstück** n boyish prank; knavish trick.

Buch [bu:x] n (-[e]s/-̈er) book; volume; '**binder** m (book-)binder; '**drucker** m printer; '**druckerei** [..'rai] f printing; printing-office, Am. print shop.

Buche ♀ ['bu:xə] f (-/-n) beech.

buchen ['bu:xən] v/t. (ge-, h) book, reserve (passage, flight, etc.); book-keeping: book (item, sum), enter (transaction) in the books; et. als Erfolg ~ count s.th. as a success.

Bücher|abschluß ✝ ['by:çər-] m closing of or balancing of books; '**brett** n bookshelf; '**ei** [..'rai] f (-/-en) library; '**freund** m book-lover, bibliophil(e); '**revisor** ✝ m (-s/-en) auditor; accountant; '**schrank** m bookcase; '**wurm** m bookworm.

B

'Buch|fink *orn. m* chaffinch; '~halter *m* (-s/-) book-keeper; '~haltung *f* book-keeping; '~handel *m* book-trade; '~händler *m* bookseller; '~handlung *f* bookshop, *Am.* bookstore.

Büchse ['byksə] *f* (-/-n) box, case; tin, *Am.* can; rifle; '~nfleisch *n* tinned meat, *Am.* canned meat; '~nöffner [byksən⁹-] *m* tin-opener, *Am.* can opener.

Buchstab|e ['bu:xʃta:bə] *m* (-n/-n) letter, character; *typ.* type; Qieren [~a'bi:rən] *v/t.* (*no* -ge-, *h*) spell.

buchstäblich ['bu:xʃtɛ:pliç] 1. *adj.* literal; 2. *adv.* literally; word for word.

Bucht [buxt] *f* (-/-en) bay; bight; creek, inlet.

'Buchung *f* (-/-en) booking, reservation; *book-keeping*: entry.

Buckel ['bukəl] 1. *m* (-s/-) hump, hunch; humpback, hunchback; boss, stud, knob; 2. *f* (-/-n) boss, stud, knob.

'buckelig *adj. s.* bucklig.

bücken ['bykən] *v/refl.* (ge-, *h*) bend (down), stoop.

bucklig *adj.* ['bukliç] humpbacked, hunchbacked.

Bückling ['byklin] *m* (-s/-e) bloater, red herring; *fig.* bow.

Bude ['bu:də] *f* (-/-en) stall, booth; hut, cabin, *Am.* shack; F: place; den; (student's, *etc.*) digs *pl.*

Budget [by'dʒe:] *n* (-s/-s) budget.

Büfett [by'fe:; by'fɛt] *n* (-[e]s/-s, -[e]s/-e) sideboard, buffet; buffet, bar, *Am. a.* counter; *kaltes ~* buffet supper or lunch.

Büffel ['byfəl] *m* (-s/-) *zo.* buffalo; F *fig.* lout, blockhead.

Bug [bu:k] *m* (-[e]s/-e) ⏚ bow; ✂ nose; fold; (sharp) crease.

Bügel ['by:gəl] *m* (-s/-) bow (*of spectacles, etc.*); handle (*of handbag, etc.*); coat-hanger; stirrup; '~brett *n* ironing-board; '~eisen *n* (flat-)iron; '~falte *f* crease; Qn *v/t.* (ge-, *h*) iron (*shirt, etc.*), press (*suit, skirt, etc.*).

Bühne ['by:nə] *f* (-/-n) platform (*a.* ⊕); scaffold; *thea.* stage; *fig.*: *die ~* the stage; *die politische ~* the political scene; '~nanweisungen ['by:-nən-] *f/pl.* stage directions *pl.*; '~nbild *n* scene(ry); décor; stage design; '~ndichter *m* playwright,

dramatist; '~nlaufbahn *f* stage career; '~nstück *n* stage play.

buk [bu:k] *pret. of* backen.

Bull|auge ⏚ ['bul-] *n* porthole, bull's eye; '~dogge *zo. f* bulldog.

Bulle ['bulə] 1. *zo. m* (-n/-n) bull; 2. *eccl. f* (-/-n) bull.

Bummel F ['buməl] *m* (-s/-) stroll; spree, pub-crawl, *sl.* binge; '~ei [~'lai] *f* (-/-en) dawdling; negligence; '2n *v/i.* (ge-) 1. (*sein*) stroll, saunter; pub-crawl; 2. (*h*) dawdle (*on way, at work*), waste time; '~streik *m* go-slow (strike), *Am.* slowdown; '~zug *m* slow train, *Am.* way train.

Bummler ['bumlər] *m* (-s/-) saunterer, stroller; loafer, *Am.* F *a.* bum; dawdler.

Bund [bunt] 1. *m* (-[e]s/⁰e) *pol.* union, federation, confederacy; (waist-, neck-, wrist)band; 2. *n* (-[e]s/-e) bundle (*of faggots*); bundle, truss (*of hay or straw*); bunch (*of radishes, etc.*).

Bündel ['byndəl] *n* (-s/-) bundle, bunch; '2n *v/t.* (ge-, *h*) make into a bundle, bundle up.

Bundes|bahn ['bundəs-] *f* Federal Railway(s *pl.*); '~bank *f* Federal Bank; '~genosse *m* ally; '~gerichtshof *m* Federal Supreme Court; '~kanzler *m* Federal Chancellor; '~ministerium *n* Federal Ministry; '~post *f* Federal Postal Administration; '~präsident *m* President of the Federal Republic; '~rat *m* Bundesrat, Upper House of German Parliament; '~republik *f* Federal Republic; '~staat *m* federal state; confederation; '~tag *m* Bundestag, Lower House of German Parliament.

bündig *adj.* ['byndiç] *style, speech*: concise, to the point, terse.

Bündnis ['byntnis] *n* (-ses/-se) alliance; agreement.

Bunker ['buŋkər] *m* (-s/-) ⚒, coal, fuel, *etc.*: bunker; bin; air-raid shelter; ✂ bunker, pill-box; ⏚ (submarine) pen.

bunt *adj.* [bunt] (multi-)colo(u)red, colo(u)rful; motley; *bird, flower, etc.*: variegated; bright, gay; *fig.* mixed, motley; full of variety; '2druck *m* colo(u)r-print(ing); '2stift *m* colo(u)r pencil, crayon.

Bürde ['byrdə] f (-/-n) burden (a. fig.: für j-n to s.o.), load.

Burg [burk] f (-/-en) castle; fortress; citadel (a. fig.).

Bürge ['byrgə] m (-n/-n) guarantor, security, surety, bailsman; sponsor; **'2n** v/i. (ge-, h): für j-n ~ stand guarantee or surety or security for s.o., Am. a. bond s.o.; stand bail for s.o.; vouch or answer for s.o.; sponsor s.o.; für et. ~ stand security for s.th., guarantee s.th.; vouch or answer for s.th.

Bürger ['byrgər] m (-s/-) citizen; townsman; **'_krieg** m civil war.

'bürgerlich adj. civic, civil; ~e Küche plain cooking; Verlust der ~en Ehrenrechte loss of civil rights; Bürgerliches Gesetzbuch German Civil Code; **'2e** m (-n/-n) commoner.

'Bürger|meister m mayor; in Germany: a. burgomaster; in Scotland: provost; **'_recht** n civic rights pl.; citizenship; **'_schaft** f (-/-en) citizens pl.; **'_steig** m pavement, Am. sidewalk; **'_wehr** f militia.

Bürgschaft ['byrkʃaft] f (-/-en) security; bail; guarantee.

Büro [by'ro:] n (-s/-s) office; **'_angestellte** m, f (-n/-n) clerk; **'_arbeit** f office-work; **'_klammer** f paper-clip; **'_krat** [ʊo'kra:t] m (-en/-en) bureaucrat; **'_kratie** [ʊo-kra'ti:] f (-/-n) bureaucracy; red tape; **'_kratisch** adj. [ʊo'kra:tiʃ] bureaucratic; **'_stunden** f/pl. office hours pl.; **'_vorsteher** m head or senior clerk.

Bursch [burʃ] m (-en/-en), **'_e** ['_ə] m (-n/-n) boy, lad, youth; F chap, Am. a. guy; ein übler ~ a bad lot, F a bad egg.

burschikos adj. [burʃi'ko:s] free and easy; esp. girl: boyish, unaffected, hearty.

Bürste ['byrstə] f (-/-n) brush; **'2n** v/t. (ge-, h) brush.   [shrub.]

Busch [buʃ] m (-es/⸚e) bush,

Büschel ['byʃəl] n (-s/-) bunch; tuft, handful (of hair); wisp (of straw or hair).

'Busch|holz n brushwood, underwood; **'2ig** adj. hair, eyebrows, etc.: bushy, shaggy; covered with bushes or scrub, bushy; **'_messer** n bushknife; machete; **'_neger** m maroon; **'_werk** n bushes pl., shrubbery, Am. a. thicket.

Busen ['bu:zən] m (-s/-) bosom, breast (esp. of woman); fig. bosom, heart; geog. bay, gulf; **'_freund** m bosom friend.

Bussard orn. ['busart] m (-[e]s/-e) buzzard.

Buße ['bu:sə] f (-/-n) atonement (for sins), penance; repentance; satisfaction; fine; ~ tun do penance.

büßen ['by:sən] (ge-, h) **1.** v/t. expiate, atone for (sin, crime); er mußte es mit s-m Leben ~ he paid for it with his life; das sollst du mir ~! you'll pay for that!; **2.** v/i. atone, pay (für for).

'Büßer m (-s/-) penitent.

'buß|fertig adj. penitent, repentant, contrite; **'2fertigkeit** f (-/no pl.) repentance, contrition; **'2tag** m day of repentance; Buß- und Bettag day of prayer and repentance.

Büste ['bystə] f (-/-n) bust; **'_n-halter** m (-s/-) brassière, F bra.

Büttenpapier ['bytən-] n handmade paper.

Butter ['butər] f (-/no pl.) butter; **'_blume** ♀ f buttercup; **'_brot** n (slice or piece of) bread and butter; F: für ein ~ for a song; **'_brotpapier** n greaseproof paper; **'_dose** f butter-dish; **'_faß** n butter-churn; **'_milch** f buttermilk; **'2n** v/i. (ge-, h) churn.

C

Café [ka'fe:] n (-s/-s) café, coffeehouse.

Cape [ke:p] n (-s/-s) cape.

Cell|ist ♪ [tʃe'list] m (-en/-en) violoncellist, (')cellist; **'_o** ♪ ['_o] n (-s/-s, Celli) violoncello, (')cello.

Celsius ['tsɛlzius]: 5 Grad ~ (abbr. 5° C) five degrees centigrade.

Chaiselongue [ʃɛz(ə)'lõ:] f (-/-n, -s) chaise longue, lounge, couch.

Champagner [ʃam'panjər] m (-s/-) champagne.

Champignon

Champignon ♀ ['ʃampinjõ] m (-s/-s) champignon, (common) mushroom.

Chance ['ʃãːs(ə)] f (-/-n) chance; *keine ~ haben* not to stand a chance; *sich eine ~ entgehen lassen* miss a chance *or* an opportunity; *die ~n sind gleich* the chances *or* odds are even.

Chaos ['kaːɔs] n (-/no pl.) chaos.

Charakter [ka'raktər] m (-s/-e) character; nature; **~bild** n character (sketch); **~darsteller** thea. m character actor; **~fehler** m fault in s.o.'s character; **2fest** adj. of firm *or* strong character; **2i'sieren** v/t. (no -ge-, h) characterize, describe (*als acc.* as); **~i'sierung** f (-/-en) characterization; **~istik** [~'ristik] f (-/-en) characterization; **2istisch** adj. [~'ristiʃ] characteristic *or* typical (*für* of); **2lich** adj. of *or* concerning (the) character; **2los** adj. characterless, without (strength of) character, spineless; **~rolle** thea. f character role; **~zug** m characteristic, feature, trait.

charm|ant adj. [ʃar'mant] charming, winning; **2e** [ʃarm] m (-s/no pl.) charm, grace.

Chassis [ʃa'siː] n (-/-) mot., radio: frame, chassis.

Chauffeur [ʃɔ'føːr] m (-s/-e) chauffeur, driver.

Chaussee [ʃo'seː] f (-/-n) highway, (high) road.

Chauvinismus [ʃovi'nismus] m (-/no pl.) jingoism; chauvinism.

Chef [ʃɛf] m (-s/-s) head, chief; ✝ principal, F boss; senior partner.

Chem|ie [çe'miː] f (-/no pl.) chemistry; **~iefaser** f chemical fib|re, Am. -er; **~ikalien** [~i'kaːljən] f/pl. chemicals pl.; **~iker** ['çeːmikər] m (-s/-) (analytical) chemist; **2isch** adj. ['çeːmiʃ] chemical.

Chiffr|e ['ʃifər] f (-/-n) number; cipher; *in advertisement:* box number; **2ieren** [ʃi'friːrən] v/t. (no -ge-, h) cipher, code (*message, etc.*); write in code *or* cipher.

Chines|e [çi'neːzə] m (-n/-n) Chinese, *contp.* Chinaman; **2isch** adj. Chinese.

Chinin ♁ [çi'niːn] n (-s/no pl.) quinine.

Chirurg [çi'rurk] m (-en/-en) surgeon; **~ie** [~'giː] f (-/-n) surgery; **2isch** adj. [~giʃ] surgical.

Chlor ♁ [kloːr] n (-s/no pl.) chlo-

rine; **2en** v/t. (ge-, h) chlorinate (*water*); **~kalk** ♁ m chloride of lime.

Chloroform ♁ [kloro'fɔrm] n (-/no pl.) chloroform; **2ieren** ♁ [~'miːrən] v/t. (no -ge-, h) chloroform.

Cholera ♁ ['koːləra] f (-/no pl.) cholera.

cholerisch adj. [ko'leːriʃ] choleric, irascible.

Chor [koːr] m **1.** △ a. n (-[e]s/-e, ⁓e) chancel, choir; (organ-)loft; **2.** (-[e]s/⁓e) *in drama:* chorus; *singers:* choir, chorus; *piece of music:* chorus; **~al** [ko'raːl] m (-s/⁓e) choral(e); hymn; **~gesang** m choral singing, chorus; **~sänger** m member of a choir; chorister.

Christ [krist] m (-en/-en) Christian; **~baum** m Christmas-tree; **~enheit** f (-/no pl.): *die ~* Christendom; **~entum** n (-s/no pl.) Christianity; **~kind** n (-[e]s/no pl.) Christ-child, Infant Jesus; **2lich** adj. Christian.

Chrom ♁ [kroːm] n (-s/no pl.) metal: chromium; *pigment:* chrome.

chromatisch ♪, opt. adj. [kro'maː-tiʃ] chromatic.

Chronik ['kroːnik] f (-/-en) chronicle.

chronisch adj. ['kroːniʃ] disease: chronic (a. fig.).

Chronist [kro'nist] m (-en/-en) chronicler.

chronologisch adj. [krono'loːgiʃ] chronological.

circa adv. ['tsirka] about, approximately.

Clique ['klikə] f (-/-n) clique, set, group, coterie; **~nwirtschaft** f (-/no pl.) cliquism.

Conférencier [kõferã'sjeː] m (-s/-s) compère, Am. master of ceremonies.

Couch [kautʃ] f (-/-es) couch.

Coupé [ku'peː] n (-s/-s) mot. coupé; ♠ ⊞ compartment.

Couplet [ku'pleː] n (-s/-s) comic *or* music-hall song.

Coupon [ku'põː] m (-s/-s) coupon; dividend-warrant; counterfoil.

Courtage ✝ [kur'taːʒə] f (-/-n) brokerage.

Cousin [ku'zɛ̃] m (-s/-s), **~e** [~'ziːnə] f (-/-n) cousin.

Creme [kreːm, krɛːm] f (-/-s) cream (a. fig.: only sg.).

Cut [kœt, kat] m (-s/-s), **~away** ['kœtəveˑ, 'katəveˑ] m (-s/-s) cutaway (coat), morning coat.

D

da [da:] **1.** *adv. space:* there; ~ *wo* where; *hier und* ~ here and there; ~ *bin ich* here I am; ~ *haben wir's!* there we are!; *von* ~ *an* from there; *time:* ~ *erst* only then, not till then; *von* ~ *an* from that time (on), since then; *hier und* ~ now and then *or* again; **2.** *cj. time:* as, when, while; *nun,* ~ *du es einmal gesagt hast* now (that) you have mentioned it; *causal:* as, since, because; ~ *ich krank war, konnte ich nicht kommen* as *or* since I was ill I couldn't come.

dabei *adv.* [da'baɪ, *when emphatic:* 'da:baɪ] near (at hand), by; about, going (*zu inf.* to *inf.*), on the point (of *ger.*); besides; nevertheless, yet, for all that; *was ist schon* ~? what does it matter?; *lassen wir es* ~ let's leave it at that; ~ *bleiben* stick to one's point, persist in it.

da'bei|bleiben *v/i.* (*irr. bleiben, sep., -ge-, sein*) stay with it *or* them; **~sein** *v/i.* (*irr. sein, sep., -ge-, sein*) be present *or* there; **~stehen** *v/i.* (*irr. stehen, sep., -ge-, h*) stand by *or* near.

'dableiben *v/i.* (*irr. bleiben, sep., -ge-, sein*) stay, remain.

da capo *adv.* [da'ka:po] *at opera, etc.*: encore.

Dach [dax] *n* (-[e]s/⁻er) roof; *fig.* shelter; **'~antenne** *f* aerial; **'~decker** *m* (-s/-) roofer; tiler; slater; **'~fenster** *n* skylight; dormer window; **'~garten** *m* roofgarden; **'~gesellschaft** *f* holding company; **'~kammer** *f* attic, garret; **'~pappe** *f* roofing felt; **'~rinne** *f* gutter, eaves *pl.*

dachte ['daxtə] *pret. of* denken.

Dachs *zo.* [daks] *m* (-es/-e) badger; **'~bau** *m* (-[e]s/-e) badger's earth.

'Dach|sparren *m* rafter; **'~stube** *f* attic, garret; **'~stuhl** *m* roof framework; **'~ziegel** *m* (roofing) tile.

dadurch [da'dʊrç, *when emphatic:* 'da:dʊrç] **1.** *adv.* for this reason, in this manner *or* way; by it *or* that; **2.** *cj.:* ~, *daß* owing to (the fact that), because; by *ger.*

dafür *adv.* [da'fy:r, *when emphatic:* 'da:fy:r] for it *or* that; instead (of it); in return (for it), in exchange; ~ *sein* to be in favo(u)r of it; ~ *sein zu*

inf. be for *ger.*, be in favo(u)r of *ger.*; *er kann nichts* ~ it is not his fault; ~ *sorgen, daß* see to it that.

Da'fürhalten *n* (-s/*no pl.*): *nach meinem* ~ in my opinion.

dagegen [da'ge:gən, *when emphatic:* 'da:ge:gən] **1.** *adv.* against it *or* that; in comparison with it, compared to it; ~ *sein* be against it, be opposed to it; *ich habe nichts* ~ I have no objection (to it); **2.** *cj.* on the other hand, however.

daheim *adv.* [da'haɪm] at home.

daher [da'he:r, *when emphatic:* 'da:he:r] **1.** *adv.* from there; *prefixed to verbs of motion:* along; *fig.* from this, hence; ~ *kam es, daß* thus it happened that; **2.** *cj.* therefore; that is (the reason) why.

dahin *adv.* [da'hɪn, *when emphatic:* 'da:hɪn] there, to that place; gone, past; *prefixed to verbs of motion:* along; *j-n* ~ *bringen, daß* induce s.o. to *inf.*; *m-e Meinung geht* ~, *daß* my opinion is that.

da'hingestellt *adj.:* ~ *sein lassen* (,ob) leave it undecided (whether).

dahinter *adv.* [da'hɪntər, *when emphatic:* 'da:hɪntər] behind it *or* that, at the back of it; *es steckt nichts* ~ there is nothing in it.

da'hinterkommen *v/i.* (*irr. kommen, sep., -ge-, sein*) find out about it.

damal|ig *adj.* ['da:ma:lɪç] then, of that time; *der* ~e *Besitzer* the then owner; **'~s** *adv.* then, at that time.

Damast [da'mast] *m* (-es/-e) damask.

Dame ['da:mə] *f* (-/-n) lady; *dancing, etc.:* partner; *cards, chess:* queen; *s.* Damespiel; **'~brett** *n* draught-board, *Am.* checkerboard.

'Damen|binde *f* (woman's) sanitary towel, *Am.* sanitary napkin; **'~doppel** *n* tennis: women's doubles *pl.*; **'~einzel** *n* tennis: women's singles *pl.*; **'²haft** *adj.* ladylike; **'~konfektion** *f* ladies' ready-made clothes *pl.*; **'~mannschaft** *f* sports: women's team; **'~schneider** *m* ladies' tailor, dressmaker.

'Damespiel *n* (game of) draughts *pl.*, *Am.* (game of) checkers *pl.*

damit **1.** *adv.* [da'mɪt, *when emphatic:* 'da:mɪt] with it *or* that, therewith, herewith; by it or that; *was will er ~ sagen?* what does he mean by it?; *wie steht es ~?* how about it?; *~ einverstanden sein* agree to it; **2.** *cj.* (in order) that, in order to *inf.*; *so (that)*; *~ nicht lest,* (so as) to avoid that; for fear that (*all with subjunctive*). [asinine.)

dämlich F *adj.* ['dɛ:mliç] silly,)

Damm [dam] *m* (-[e]s/ᵤe) dam; dike, dyke; 🚢 embankment; embankment, *Am.* levee (*of river*); roadway; *fig.* barrier; **'~bruch** *m* bursting of a dam or dike.

dämmer|ig *adj.* ['dɛmərɪç] dusky; **'2licht** *n* twilight; **'~n** *v/i.* (ge-, h) dawn (*a. fig.*: F *j-m* on s.o.); grow dark or dusky; **'2ung** *f* (-/-en) twilight, dusk; *in the morning:* dawn.

Dämon ['dɛ:mɔn] *m* (-s/-en) demon; **2isch** *adj.* [dɛ'mo:niʃ] demoniac(al).

Dampf [dampf] *m* (-[e]s/ᵤe) steam; vapo(u)r; **'~bad** *n* vapo(u)r-bath; **'~boot** *n* steamboat; **'2en** *v/i.* (ge-, h) steam.

dämpfen ['dɛmpfən] *v/t.* (ge-, h) deaden (*pain, noise, force of blow*); muffle (*bell, drum, oar*); damp (*sound, oscillation, fig. enthusiasm*); ♪ mute (*stringed instrument*); soften (*colour, light*); attenuate (*wave*); steam (*cloth, food*); stew (*meat, fruit*); *fig.* suppress, curb (*emotion*).

'Dampfer *m* (-s/-) steamer, steamship.

'Dämpfer *m* (-s/-) damper (*a.* ♪ *of piano*); ♪ mute (*for violin, etc.*).

'Dampf|heizung *f* steam-heating; **'~kessel** *m* (steam-)boiler; **'~maschine** *f* steam-engine; **'~schiff** *n* steamer, steamship; **'~walze** *f* steam-roller.

danach *adv.* [da'nɑ:x, *when emphatic:* 'dɑ:nɑ:x] after it or that; afterwards; subsequently; accordingly; *ich fragte ihn ~* I asked him about it; *iro. er sieht ganz ~ aus* he looks very much like it.

Däne ['dɛ:nə] *m* (-n/-n) Dane.

daneben *adv.* [da'ne:bən, *when emphatic:* 'dɑ:ne:bən] next to it or that; beside it or that; besides, moreover; beside the mark.

da'nebengehen F *v/i.* (*irr.* gehen, sep., -ge-, sein) *bullet, etc.:* miss the target or mark; *remark, etc.:* miss one's effect, F misfire.

daniederliegen [da'ni:dər-] *v/i.* (*irr.* liegen, sep., -ge-, h) be laid up (*an dat.* with); *trade:* be depressed.

dänisch *adj.* ['dɛ:niʃ] Danish.

Dank [daŋk] **1.** *m* (-[e]s/*no pl.*) thanks *pl.*, gratitude; reward; *j-m ~ sagen* thank s.o.; *Gott sei ~!* thank God!; **2.** ♀ *prp.* (*dat.*) owing or thanks to; **'2bar** *adj.* thankful, grateful (*j-m* to s.o.; *für* for); profitable (*j-m* to s.o.); **'2barkeit** *f* (-/*no pl.*) gratitude; **'2en** *v/i.* (ge-, h) thank (*j-m für et.* s.o. for s.th.); *danke (schön)!* thank you (very much)!; *danke* thank you; *nein, danke* no, thank you; *nichts zu ~* don't mention it; **'2enswert** *adj. thing:* one can be grateful for; *efforts, etc.:* kind; *task, etc.:* rewarding, worth-while; **'~gebet** *n* thanksgiving (*prayer*); **'~schreiben** *n* letter of thanks.

dann *adv.* [dan] then; *~ und wann* (every) now and then.

daran *adv.* [da'ran, *when emphatic:* 'dɑ:ran] at (or by, in, on, to) it or that; *sich ~ festhalten* hold on tight to it; *~ festhalten* stick to it; *nahe ~ sein zu inf.* be on the point or verge of *ger.*

da'rangehen *v/i.* (*irr.* gehen, sep., -ge-, sein) set to work; set about *ger.*

darauf *adv.* [da'rauf, *when emphatic:* 'dɑ:rauf] *space:* on (top of) it or that; *time:* thereupon, after it or that; *am Tage ~* the day after, the next or following day; *zwei Jahre ~* two years later; *~ kommt es an* that's what matters; **~hin** *adv.* [darauf'hin, *when emphatic:* 'dɑ:-rauf'hin] thereupon.

daraus *adv.* [da'raus, *when emphatic:* 'dɑ:raus] out of it or that; from it or that; *~ folgt* hence it follows; *was ist ~ geworden?* what has become of it?; *ich mache mir nichts ~* I don't care or mind (about it).

darben ['darbən] *v/i.* (ge-, h) suffer want; starve.

darbiet|en ['dɑ:r-] *v/t.* (*irr.* bieten, sep., -ge-, h) offer, present; perform; **'2ung** *f* (-/-en) *thea., etc.:* performance.

'darbringen *v/t.* (*irr.* bringen, sep., -ge-, h) offer; make (*sacrifice*).

darein *adv.* [da'rain, *when em-*

phatic: ['dɑːraɪn] into it *or* that, therein.

da'rein|finden *v/refl.* (*irr.* finden, *sep.*, -ge-, h) put up with it; **~mischen** *v/refl.* (*sep.*, -ge-, h) interfere (with it); **~reden** *v/i.* (*sep.*, -ge-, h) interrupt; *fig.* interfere.

darin *adv.* [da'rɪn, *when emphatic:* 'dɑːrɪn] in it *or* that; therein; es war nichts ~ there was nothing in it *or* them.

darleg|en ['dɑːr-] *v/t.* (*sep.*, -ge-, h) lay open, expose, disclose; show; explain; demonstrate; point out; '**2ung** *f* (-/-en) exposition; explanation; statement.

Darlehen ['dɑːrleːən] *n* (-s/-) loan.

Darm [darm] *m* (-[e]s/ʋe) gut, *anat.* intestine; (sausage-)skin; Därme *pl.* intestines *pl.*, bowels *pl.*

'**darstell|en** *v/t.* (*sep.*, -ge-, h) represent; show, depict; delineate; describe; *actor:* interpret (*character*, *part*), represent (*character*); *graphic arts:* graph, plot (*curve*, *etc.*); '**2er** *thea. m* (-s/-) interpreter (*of a part*); actor; '**2ung** *f* representation; *thea.* performance.

'**dartun** *v/t.* (*irr.* tun, *sep.*, -ge-, h) prove; demonstrate; set forth.

darüber *adv.* [da'ryːbər, *when emphatic:* 'dɑːryːbər] over it *or* that; across it; in the meantime; ~ werden Jahre vergehen it will take years; wir sind ~ hinweg we got over it; ein Buch ~ schreiben write a book about it.

darum [da'rʊm, *when emphatic:* 'dɑːrʊm] **1.** *adv.* around it *or* that; er kümmert sich nicht ~ he does not care; es handelt sich ~ zu inf. the point is to *inf.*; **2.** *cj.* therefore, for that reason; ~ ist er nicht gekommen that's (the reason) why he hasn't come.

darunter *adv.* [da'rʊntər, *when emphatic:* 'dɑːrʊntər] under it *or* that; beneath it; among them; less; zwei Jahre und ~ two years and under; was verstehst du ~? what do you understand by it?

das [das] *s.* der.

dasein ['dɑː-] **1.** *v/i.* (*irr.* sein, *sep.*, -ge-, sein) be there *or* present; exist; **2.** **2** *n* (-s/no *pl.*) existence; life; being.

daß *cj.* [das] that; ~ nicht less; es sei denn, ~ unless; ohne ~ with-

out *ger.*; nicht ~ ich wüßte not that I know of.

'**dastehen** *v/i.* (*irr.* stehen, *sep.*, -ge-, h) stand (there).

Daten ['dɑːtən] *pl.* data *pl.* (*a.* ⊕), facts *pl.*; particulars *pl.*; '**~verarbeitung** *f* (-/-en) data processing.

datieren [da'tiːrən] *v/t. and v/i.* (*no* -ge-, h) date.   [(case).]

Dativ *gr.* ['dɑːtiːf] *m* (-s/-e) dative|

Dattel ['datəl] *f* (-/-n) date.

Datum ['dɑːtum] *n* (-s/Daten) date.

Dauer ['dauər] *f* (-/no *pl.*) length, duration; continuance; auf die ~ in the long run; für die ~ von for a period *or* term of; von ~ sein last well; '**2haft** *adj.* peace, *etc.*: lasting; *material, etc.*: durable; *colour*, *dye*: fast; '**~karte** *f* season ticket, *Am.* commutation ticket; '**~lauf** *m* jog-trot; endurance-run; '**2n** *v/i.* (ge-, h) continue, last; take (*time*); '**~welle** *f* permanent wave, F perm.

Daumen ['daumən] *m* (-s/-) thumb; j-m den ~ halten keep one's fingers crossed (for s.o.); '**~abdruck** *m* (-[e]s/ʋe) thumb-print.

Daune ['daunə] *f* (-/-n): ~(n *pl.*) down; '**~ndecke** *f* eiderdown (quilt).

davon *adv.* [da'fɔn, *when emphatic:* 'dɑːfɔn] of it *or* that; thereof; from it *or* that; off, away; was habe ich ~? what do I get from it?; das kommt ~! it serves you right!

da'von|kommen *v/i.* (*irr.* kommen, *sep.*, -ge-, sein) escape, get off; **~laufen** *v/i.* (*irr.* laufen, *sep.*, -ge-, sein) run away.

davor *adv.* [da'foːr, *when emphatic:* 'dɑːfoːr] *space:* before it *or* that, in front of it *or* that; er fürchtet sich ~ he is afraid of it.

dazu *adv.* [da'tsuː, *when emphatic:* 'dɑːtsuː] to it *or* that; for it *or* that; for that purpose; in addition to that; noch ~ at that; ~ gehört Zeit it requires time.

da'zu|gehörig *adj.* belonging to it; **~kommen** *v/i.* (*irr.* kommen, *sep.*, -ge-, sein) appear (on the scene); find time.

dazwischen *adv.* [da'tsvɪʃən] between (them), in between; **~kommen** *v/i.* (*irr.* kommen, *sep.*, -ge-, sein) *thing:* intervene, happen.

Debatt|e [de'batə] *f* (-/-n) debate; **2ieren** [~'tiːrən] (*no* -ge-, h) **1.** *v/t.*

discuss; debate; **2.** *v/i.* debate (*über acc.* on).

Debüt [de'by:] *n* (-s/-s) first appearance, début.

dechiffrieren [deʃi'fri:rən] *v/t.* (*no* -ge-, *h*) decipher, decode.

Deck ⚓ [dek] *n* (-[e]s/-s, ⚓ -e) deck; '**adresse** *f* cover (address); '**bett** *n* feather bed.

Decke ['dekə] *f* (-/-n) cover(ing); blanket; (travel[l]ing) rug; ceiling; '**l** *m* (-s/-) lid, cover (*of box or pot, etc.*); lid (*of piano*); (book-)cover; '**n** (ge-, *h*) **1.** *v/t.* cover; *den Tisch* ~ lay the table; **2.** *v/i. paint:* cover.

'**Deck**|**mantel** *m* cloak, mask, disguise; '**name** *m* assumed name, pseudonym; '**ung** *f* (-/-en) cover; security.

defekt [de'fekt] **1.** *adj.* defective, faulty; **2.** ♀ *m* (-[e]s/-e) defect, fault.

defin|**ieren** [defi'ni:rən] *v/t.* (*no* -ge-, *h*) define; **ℒition** [ʌi'tsjo:n] *f* (-/-en) definition; **ʌitiv** *adj.* [ʌi'ti:f] definite; definitive.

Defizit ♀ ['de:fitsit] *n* (-s/-e) deficit, deficiency.

Degen ['de:gən] *m* (-s/-) sword; *fencing:* épée.

degradieren [degra'di:rən] *v/t.* (*no* -ge-, *h*) degrade, *Am. a.* demote.

dehn|**bar** *adj.* [de:nba:r] extensible; elastic; *metal:* ductile; *notion, etc.:* vague; '**en** *v/t.* (ge-, *h*) extend; stretch; '**ℒung** *f* (-/-en) extension; stretch(ing).

Deich [daiç] *m* (-[e]s/-e) dike, dyke.

Deichsel ['daiksəl] *f* (-/-n) pole, shaft.

dein *poss. pron.* [dain] your; *der (die, das)* ~e yours; *ich bin* ~ I am yours; *die Deinen pl.* your family; '**erseits** *adv.* ['ʌər'zaits] for *or* on your part; '**es**'**gleichen** *pron.* your like, your (own) kind, F the like(s) of you.

Dekan *eccl. and univ.* [de'ka:n] *m* (-s/-e) dean.

Deklam|**ation** [deklama'tsjo:n] *f* (-/-en) declamation; reciting; **ℒieren** [ʌ'mi:rən] *v/t. and v/i.* (*no* -ge-, *h*) recite; declaim.

Deklin|**ation** *gr.* [deklina'tsjo:n] *f* (-/-en) declension; **ℒieren** *gr.* [ʌ-'ni:rən] *v/t.* (*no* -ge-, *h*) decline.

Dekor|**ateur** [dekora'tø:r] *m* (-s/-e) decorator; window-dresser; *thea.*

scene-painter; **ʌation** [ʌ'tsjo:n] *f* (-/-en) decoration; (window-)dressing; *thea.* scenery; **ℒieren** [ʌ'ri:rən] *v/t.* (*no* -ge-, *h*) decorate; dress (*window*).

Dekret [de'kre:t] *n* (-[e]s/-e) decree.

delikat [deli'ka:t] delicate (*a. fig.*); delicious; *fig.* ticklish; **ℒesse** [ʌ'tesə] *f* (-/-n) delicacy; dainty.

Delphin *zo.* [del'fi:n] *m* (-s/-e) dolphin.

Dement|**i** [de'menti] *n* (-s/-s) (formal) denial; **ℒieren** [ʌ'ti:rən] *v/t.* (*no* -ge-, *h*) deny, give a (formal) denial of.

'**dem**|**entsprechend** *adv.*, '**gemäß** *adv.* correspondingly, accordingly; '**nach** *adv.* therefore, hence; accordingly; '**nächst** *adv.* soon, shortly, before long.

demobili'sier|**en** (*no* -ge-, *h*) **1.** *v/t.* demobilize; disarm; **2.** *v/i.* disarm; **ℒung** *f* (-/-en) demobilization.

Demokrat [demo'kra:t] *m* (-en/-en) democrat; **ℒie** [ʌa'ti:] *f* (-/-n) democracy; **ℒisch** *adj.* [ʌ'kra:tiʃ] democratic.

demolieren [demo'li:rən] *v/t.* (*no* -ge-, *h*) demolish.

Demonstr|**ation** [demonstra'tsjo:n] *f* (-/-en) demonstration; **ℒieren** [ʌ'stri:rən] *v/t. and v/i.* (*no* -ge-, *h*) demonstrate.

Demont|**age** [demon'ta:ʒə] *f* (-/-n) disassembly; dismantling; **ℒieren** [ʌ'ti:rən] *v/t.* (*no* -ge-, *h*) disassemble; dismantle.

Demut ['de:mu:t] *f* (-/*no pl.*) humility, humbleness.

demütig *adj.* ['de:my:tiç] humble; **en** ['ʌgən] *v/t.* (ge-, *h*) humble, humiliate.

denk|**bar** ['deŋkba:r] **1.** *adj.* conceivable, thinkable, imaginable; **2.** *adv.:* ~ *einfach* most simple; '**en** (*irr.,* ge-, *h*) **1.** *v/i.* think; ~ *an* (*acc.*) think of; remember; ~ *über* (*acc.*) think about; *j-m zu* ~ *geben* set s.o. thinking; **2.** *v/t.* think; *sich et.* ~ imagine *or* fancy s.th.; *das habe ich mir gedacht* I thought as much; '**ℒmal** *n* monument; memorial; '**ℒschrift** *f* memorandum; memoir; '**ℒstein** *m* memorial stone; '**würdig** *adj.* memorable; '**ℒzettel** *fig. m* lesson.

denn [den] **1.** *cj.* for; *mehr* ~ *je* more than ever; **2.** *adv.* then; *es sei* ~,

daß unless, except; *wieso* ~? how so.
dennoch *cj.* ['dɛnnɔx] yet, still, nevertheless; though.
Denunz|iant [denun'tsjant] *m* (-en/-en) informer; ~iation [~'tsjo:n] *f* (-/-en) denunciation; 2ieren [~'tsi:rən] *v/t.* (*no* -ge-, *h*) inform against, denounce.
Depesche [de'pɛʃə] *f* (-/-n) dispatch; telegram, *Am. ✝* wire; wireless.
deponieren [depo'ni:rən] *v/t.* (*no* -ge-, *h*) deposit.
Deposi|ten ✝ [depo'zi:tən] *pl.* deposits *pl.*; ~bank *f* deposit bank.
der [de:r], **die** [di:], **das** [das] **1.** *art.* the; **2.** *dem. pron.* that; this; he, she, it; **die** *pl.* these, those, they, them; **die** *pl.* these, those, they, them; **3.** *rel. pron.* who, which, that.
'der'artig *adj.* such, of such a kind, of this *or* that kind.
derb *adj.* [dɛrp] *cloth*: coarse, rough; *shoes, etc.*: stout, strong; *ore, etc.*: massive; *p.*: sturdy; rough; *food*: coarse; *p., manners*: rough, coarse; *way of speaking*: blunt, unrefined; *joke*: crude; *humour*: broad.
der'gleichen *adj.* such, of that kind; *used as a noun*: the like, such a thing; *und* ~ and the like; *nichts* ~ nothing of the kind.
der- ['de:rjenigə], **'die-**, **'dasjenige** *dem. pron.* he *who*, she *who*, that *which*; **diejenigen** *pl.* those *who*, those *which*.
der- [de:r'zɛlbə], **die-**, **das'selbe** *dem. pron.* the same; he, she, it.
Desert|eur [dezɛr'tø:r] *m* (-s/-e) deserter; 2ieren [~'ti:rən] *v/i.* (*no* -ge-, *sein*) desert.
desgleichen [dɛs'glaɪçən] **1.** *dem. pron.* such a thing; **2.** *cj.* likewise.
deshalb ['dɛshalp] **1.** *cj.* for this *or* that reason; therefore; **2.** *adv.*: *ich tat es nur* ~, *weil* I did it only because. [(*no* -ge-, *h*) disinfect.]
desinfizieren [dɛs'ʔinfi'tsi:rən] *v/t.*]
Despot [dɛs'po:t] *m* (-en/-en) despot; 2isch *adj.* despotic.
destillieren [dɛsti'li:rən] *v/t.* (*no* -ge-, *h*) distil.
desto *adv.* ['dɛsto] (all, so much) the; ~ *besser* all the better; ~ *erstaunter* (all) the more astonished.
deswegen *cj. and adv.* ['dɛs've:gən] *s. deshalb*.
Detail [de'taɪ] *n* (-s/-s) detail.
Detektiv [detɛk'ti:f] *m* (-s/-e) detective.

deuten ['dɔʏtən] (ge-, *h*) **1.** *v/t.* interpret; read (*stars, dream, etc.*); **2.** *v/i.*: ~ *auf* (*acc.*) point at.
'deutlich *adj.* clear, distinct, plain.
deutsch *adj.* [dɔʏtʃ] German; 2e *m, f* (-n/-n) German.
'Deutung *f* (-/-en) interpretation, explanation.
Devise [de'vi:zə] *f* (-/-n) motto; ~n *pl. ✝* foreign exchange *or* currency.
Dezember [de'tsɛmbər] *m* (-[s]/-) December.
dezent *adj.* [de'tsɛnt] *attire, etc.*: decent, modest; *literature, etc.*: decent; *behaviour*: decent, proper; *music, colour*: soft, restrained; *lighting, etc.*: subdued.
Dezernat [detsɛr'nɑ:t] *n* (-[e]s/-e) (administrative) department.
dezimal *adj.* [detsi'mɑ:l] decimal; 2bruch *m* decimal fraction; 2stelle *f* decimal place.
dezi'mieren *v/t.* (*no* -ge-, *h*) decimate; *fig. a.* reduce (drastically).
Diadem [dia'de:m] *n* (-s/-e) diadem.
Diagnose [dia'gno:zə] *f* (-/-n) diagnosis.
diagonal *adj.* [diago'nɑ:l] diagonal; 2e *f* (-/-n) diagonal.
Dialekt [dia'lɛkt] *m* (-[e]s/-e) dialect; 2isch *adj.* dialectical.
Dialog [dia'lo:k] *m* (-[e]s/-e) dialogue, *Am. a.* dialog.
Diamant [dia'mant] *m* (-en/-en) diamond.
Diät [di'ɛ:t] *f* (-/*no pl.*) diet; *diät leben* live on a diet.
dich *pers. pron.* [diç] you; ~ (*selbst*) yourself.
dicht [diçt] **1.** *adj.* *fog, rain, etc.*: dense; *fog, forest, hair*: thick; *eyebrows*: bushy, thick; *crowd*: thick, dense; *shoe, etc.*: (water)tight; **2.** *adv.*: ~ *an* (*dat.*) *or bei* close to.
'dichten[1] *v/t.* (ge-, *h*) make tight.
'dicht|en[2] (ge-, *h*) **1.** *v/t.* compose, write; **2.** *v/i.* compose *or* write poetry; 2er *m* (-s/-) poet; author; ~erisch *adj.* poetic(al); 2kunst *f* poetry.
'Dichtung[1] ⊕ *f* (-/-en) seal(ing).
'Dichtung[2] *f* (-/-en) poetry; fiction; poem, poetic work.
dick *adj.* [dik] *wall, material, etc.*: thick; *book*: thick, bulky; *p.* fat, stout; 2e *f* (-/-en) thickness; bulkiness; *p.* fatness, stoutness; '~fellig *adj. p.* thick-skinned; '~flüssig *adj.*

thick; viscid, viscous, syrupy; ²**icht** ['ɪçt] n (-[e]s/-e) thicket; '²**kopf** m stubborn person, F pig-headed person; **~leibig** adj. ['~laɪbɪç] corpulent; fig. bulky.

die [diː] s. der.

Dieb [diːp] m (-[e]s/-e) thief, Am. F a. crook; **~erei** [diːbə'raɪ] f (-/-en) thieving, thievery.

Diebes|bande ['diːbəs-] f band of thieves; '**~gut** n stolen goods pl.

dieb|isch adj. ['diːbɪʃ] thievish; fig. malicious; ²**stahl** ['diːp-] m (-[e]s/ ⁼e) theft, ⁿⁿ mst larceny.

Diele ['diːlə] f (-/-n) board, plank; hall, Am. a. hallway.

dienen ['diːnən] v/i. (ge-, h) serve (j-m s.o.; als as; zu for; dazu, zu inf. to inf.); womit kann ich ~? what can I do for you?

'**Diener** m (-s/-) (man-, domestic) servant; fig. bow (vor dat. to); '**~in** f (-/-nen) (woman-)servant; maid; '**~schaft** f (-/-en) servants pl.

'**dienlich** adj. useful, convenient; expedient; suitable.

Dienst [diːnst] m (-es/-e) service; duty; employment; ~ haben be on duty; im (außer) ~ on (off) duty.

Dienstag ['diːnstaːk] m (-[e]s/-e) Tuesday.

'**Dienst|alter** n seniority, length of service; '²**bar** adj. subject (j-m to s.o.); '**~bote** m domestic (servant), Am. help; '²**eifrig** adj. (over-)eager (in one's duty); '²**frei** adj. off duty; ~er Tag day off; '**~herr** m master; employer; '**~leistung** f service; '²**lich** adj. official; '**~mädchen** n maid, Am. help; '**~mann** m (street-)porter; '**~stunden** f/pl. office hours pl.; '²**tauglich** adj. fit for service or duty; '²**tuend** adj. ['~tuːənt] on duty; '²**untauglich** adj. unfit for service or duty; '**~weg** m official channels pl.; '**~wohnung** f official residence.

dies [diːs], **~er** ['diːzər], **~e** ['diːzə], **~es** ['diːzəs] adj. and dem. pron. this; diese pl. these; dieser Tage one of these days; used as a noun: this one; he, she, it; diese pl. they.

Dieselmotor ['diːzəl-] m Diesel engine.

dies|jährig adj. ['diːsjɛːrɪç] this year, this year's; '**~mal** adv. this time; for (this) once; **~seits** ['~zaɪts]

1. adv. on this side; 2. prp. (gen.) on this side of.

Dietrich ['diːtrɪç] m (-s/-e) skeleton key; picklock.

Differenz [dɪfə'rɛnts] f (-/-en) difference; disagreement.

Diktat [dɪk'taːt] n (-[e]s/-e) dictation; nach ~ at or from dictation; **~or** [~ɔr] m (-s/-en) dictator; ²**orisch** adj. [~a'toːrɪʃ] dictatorial; **~ur** [~a'tuːr] f (-/-en) dictatorship.

dik'tieren v/t. and v/i. (no -ge-, h) dictate.

Dilettant [dile'tant] m (-en/-en) dilettante, dabbler; amateur.

Ding [dɪŋ] n (-[e]s/-e) thing; guter ~e in good spirits; vor allen ~en first of all, above all.

Diphtherie ⅋ [dɪfte'riː] f (-/-n) diphtheria.

Diplom [di'ploːm] n (-[e]s/-e) diploma, certificate.

Diplomat [diplo'maːt] m (-en/-en) diplomat; diplomatist; **~ie** [~a'tiː] f (-/no pl.) diplomacy; ²**isch** adj. [~'maːtɪʃ] diplomatic (a. fig.).

dir pers. pron. [diːr] (to) you.

direkt [di'rɛkt] 1. adj. direct; ~er Wagen ⚙ through carriage, Am. through car; 2. adv. direct(ly); ²**ion** [~'tsjoːn] f (-/-en) direction; management; board of directors; ²**or** [di'rɛktɔr] m (-s/-en) director; manager; headmaster, Am. principal; ²**orin** [~'toːrɪn] f (-/-nen) headmistress, Am. principal; ²**rice** [~'triːs(ə)] f (-/-n) directress; manageress.

Dirig|ent ♪ [diri'gɛnt] m (-en/-en) conductor; ²**ieren** ♪ [~'giːrən] v/t. and v/i. (no -ge-, h) conduct.

Dirne ['dɪrnə] f (-/-n) prostitute.

Disharmon|ie ♪ [dɪsharmo'niː] f (-/-n) disharmony, dissonance (both a. fig.); ²**isch** adj. [~'moːnɪʃ] discordant, dissonant.

Diskont ✝ [dɪs'kɔnt] m (-s/-e) discount; ²**ieren** [~'tiːrən] v/t. (no -ge-, h) discount.

diskret adj. [dɪs'kreːt] discreet; ²**ion** [~e'tsjoːn] f (-/no pl.) discretion.

Disku|ssion [dɪsku'sjoːn] f (-/-en) discussion, debate; ²'**tieren** (no -ge-, h) 1. v/t. discuss, debate; 2. v/i.: ~ über (acc.) have a discussion about, debate (up)on.

dispo|nieren [dɪspo'niːrən] v/i. (no

-ge-, h) make arrangements; plan ahead; dispose (über acc. of); **2si-tion** [ˌziˈtsjoːn] f (-/-en) disposition; arrangement; disposal.

Distanz [diˈstants] f (-/-en) distance (a. fig.); **2ieren** [ˌtsiːrən] v/refl. (no -ge-, h): sich ~ von dis(as)sociate o.s. from.

Distel ⚘ [ˈdistəl] f (-/-n) thistle.

Distrikt [diˈstrikt] m (-[e]s/-e) district; region; area.

Disziplin [distsiˈpliːn] f (-/-en) discipline.

Divid|ende ✝ [diviˈdɛndə] f (-/-n) dividend; **2ieren** [ˌdiːrən] v/t. (no -ge-, h) divide (durch by).

Diwan [ˈdiːvaːn] m (-s/-e) divan.

doch [dɔx] **1.** cj. but, though; however, yet; **2.** adv. in answer to negative question: yes; bist du noch nicht fertig? — ~! aren't you ready yet? — yes, I am; also ~! I knew it!, I was right after all!; komm ~ herein! do come in!; nicht ~! don't!

Docht [dɔxt] m (-[e]s/-e) wick.

Dock ⚓ [dɔk] n (-[e]s/-s) dock.

Dogge zo. [ˈdɔgə] f (-/-n) Great Dane.

Dohle orn. [ˈdoːlə] f (-/-n) (jack)daw.

Doktor [ˈdɔktɔr] m (-s/-en) doctor.

Dokument [dokuˈmɛnt] n (-[e]s/-e) document; ⚖ instrument; **~arfilm** [ˌtaːr-] m documentary (film).

Dolch [dɔlç] m (-[e]s/-e) dagger; poniard; **~stoß** m dagger-thrust.

Dollar [ˈdɔlar] m (-s/-s) dollar.

dolmetsch|en [ˈdɔlmɛtʃən] v/i. and v/t. (ge-, h) interpret; **2er** m (-s/-) interpreter.

Dom [doːm] m (-[e]s/-e) cathedral.

Domäne [doˈmɛːnə] f (-/-n) domain (a. fig.); province.

Domino [ˈdɔːmino] (-s/-s) **1.** m domino; **2.** n (game of) dominoes pl.

Donner [ˈdɔnər] m (-s/-) thunder; **2n** v/i. (ge-, h) thunder (a. fig.); **~schlag** m thunderclap (a. fig.); **~stag** m Thursday; **~wetter** n thunderstorm; F fig. telling off; F: ~! my word!, by Jove!; F zum ~! F confound it!, sl. damn it!

Doppel [ˈdɔpəl] n (-s/-) duplicate; tennis, etc.: double, Am. doubles pl.; **~bett** n double bed; **~decker** m (-s/-) ⚒ biplane; double-decker (bus); **~ehe** f bigamy; **~gänger** [ˈˌgɛŋər] m (-s/-) double; **~punkt**

m colon; **~sinn** m double meaning, ambiguity; **2sinnig** adj. ambiguous, equivocal; **~stecker** ⚡ m two-way adapter; **2t 1.** adj. double; **2.** adv. doubly; twice; **~zentner** m quintal; **2züngig** adj. [ˈˌtsyŋiç] two-faced.

Dorf [dɔrf] n (-[e]s/ⁿer) village; **~be-wohner** m villager.

Dorn [dɔrn] m **1.** (-[e]s/-en) thorn (a. fig.), prickle, spine; j-m ein ~ im Auge sein be a thorn in s.o.'s flesh or side; **2.** (-[e]s/-e) tongue (of buckle); spike (of running-shoe, etc.); ⊕ punch; **2ig** adj. thorny (a. fig.).

dörr|en [ˈdœrən] v/t. (ge-, h) dry; **2fleisch** n dried meat; **2gemüse** n dried vegetables pl.; **2obst** n dried fruit.

Dorsch ichth. [dɔrʃ] m (-es/-e) cod(fish).

dort adv. [dɔrt] there; over there; **~her** adv. from there; **~hin** adv. there, to that place; **~ig** adj. there, in or of that place.

Dose [ˈdoːzə] f (-/-n) box; tin, Am. can; **~nöffner** [ˈdoːznˀ-] m (-s/-) tin-opener, Am. can opener.

Dosis [ˈdoːzis] f (-/Dosen) dose (a. fig.).

dotieren [doˈtiːrən] v/t. (no -ge-, h) endow.

Dotter [ˈdɔtər] m, n (-s/-) yolk.

Dozent [doˈtsɛnt] m (-en/-en) (university) lecturer, Am. assistant professor.

Drache [ˈdraxə] m (-n/-n) dragon; **~n** m (-s/-) kite; fig. termagant, shrew, battle-axe.

Dragoner [draˈgoːnər] m (-s/-) ✗ dragoon (a. fig.).

Draht [draːt] m (-[e]s/ⁿe) wire; **2en** v/t. (ge-, h) telegraph, wire; **~ge-flecht** n (-[e]s/-e) wire netting; **~hindernis** ✗ n wire entanglement; **2ig** adj. p. wiry; **2los** adj. wireless; **~seilbahn** f funicular (railway); **~stift** m wire tack; **~zieher** F fig. m (-s/-) wire-puller.

drall adj. [dral] girl, legs, etc.: plump; woman: buxom.

Drama [ˈdraːma] n (-s/Dramen) drama; **~tiker** [draˈmaːtikər] m (-s/-) dramatist; **2tisch** adj. [draˈmaːtiʃ] dramatic.

dran F adv. [dran] s. daran; er ist gut (übel) ~ he's well (badly) off; ich bin ~ it's my turn.

Drang [draŋ] **1.** *m* (-[e]s/‿e) pressure, rush; *fig.* urge; **2.** ⚲ *pret. of dringen.*

drängen ['drɛŋən] (ge-, h) **1.** *v/t.* press (*a. fig.*), push; *fig.* urge; *creditor:* dun; *sich* ~ crowd, throng; **2.** *v/i.* press, be pressing *or* urgent.

drangsalieren [draŋza'li:rən] *v/t.* (*no* -ge-, h) harass, vex, plague.

drastisch *adj.* ['drastiʃ] drastic.

drauf F *adv.* [drauf] *s.* darauf; ~ *und dran sein zu inf.* be on the point of *ger.*; **⚲gänger** ['‿gɛŋər] *m* (-s/-) dare-devil, *Am. sl. a.* go-getter.

draus F *adv.* [draus] *s.* daraus.

draußen *adv.* ['drausən] outside; out of doors; abroad; out at sea.

drechseln ['drɛksəln] *v/t.* (ge-, h) turn (*wood, etc.*); **‿ler** ['‿slər] *m* (-s/-) turner.

Dreck F [drɛk] *m* (-[e]s/*no pl.*) dirt; mud; filth (*a. fig.*); *fig.* trash; F ~ *am Stecken haben* not to have a clean slate; F *das geht dich einen* ~ *an* that's none of your business; **⚲ig** *adj.* dirty; filthy.

Dreh|bank ['dre:-] *f* (-/‿e) (turning-) lathe; **'⚲bar** *adj.* revolving, rotating; **'‿bleistift** *m* propelling pencil; **'‿buch** *n* scenario; script; **'‿bühne** *thea. f* revolving stage; **'⚲en** *v/t.* (ge-, h) turn; shoot (*film*); roll (*cigarette*); *es dreht sich darum zu inf.* it is a matter of *ger.*; *sich* ~ turn; **'‿kreuz** *n* turnstile; **'‿orgel** *f* barrel-organ; **'‿punkt** *m* ⊕ centre of rotation, *Am.* center of rotation, pivot (*a. fig.*); **'‿strom** ⚡ *m* three-phase current; **'‿stuhl** *m* swivel-chair; **'‿tür** *f* revolving door; **'‿ung** *f* (-/-en) turn; rotation.

drei *adj.* [drai] three; **'‿beinig** *adj.* three-legged; **'⚲eck** *n* triangle; **'‿eckig** *adj.* triangular; **‿erlei** ['‿ər'lai] *adj.* of three kinds *or* sorts; **'‿fach** *adj.* ['‿fax] threefold, treble, triple; **'‿farbig** *adj.* three-colo(u)r(ed); **'⚲fuß** *m* tripod; **'‿jährig** *adj.* ['‿jɛːriç] three-year-old; triennial; **'‿mal** *adv.* three times; **'‿malig** *adj.* done *or* repeated three times; three; **⚲'meilenzone** ⚓, ⚖ *f* three-mile limit; **'⚲rad** *n* tricycle; **'‿seitig** *adj.* three-sided; trilateral; **'‿silbig** *adj.* trisyllabic.

dreißig *adj.* ['draisiç] thirty; **'‿ste** *adj.* thirtieth.

dreist *adj.* [draist] bold, audacious;

cheeky, saucy; **'⚲igkeit** *f* (-/-en) boldness, audacity; cheek, sauciness.

'drei|stimmig ♩ *adj.* for *or* in three voices; **‿tägig** *adj.* ['‿tɛːgiç] three-day; **'‿teilig** *adj.* in three parts, tripartite; **'‿zehn(te)** *adj.* thirteen(th).

dreschen ['drɛʃən] *v/t. and v/i.* (*irr.*, ge-, h) thresh; thrash; **'⚲flegel** *m* flail; **'⚲maschine** *f* threshing-machine.

dressieren [drɛ'si:rən] *v/t.* (*no* -ge-, h) train; break in (*horse*).

drillen ⚔, ✎ ['drilən] *v/t.* (ge-, h) drill.

Drillinge ['driliŋə] *m/pl.* triplets *pl.*

drin F *adv.* [drin] *s.* darin.

dringen ['driŋən] *v/i.* (*irr.*, ge-) **1.** (sein): ~ *durch* force one's way through *s.th.*, penetrate *or* pierce *s.th.*; ~ *aus* break forth from *s.th.*; *noise:* come from; ~ *in* (*acc.*) penetrate into; *in j-n* ~ urge *or* press s.o.; *an die Öffentlichkeit* ~ get abroad; **2.** (h): ~ *auf* (*acc.*) insist on, press for; **'‿d** *adj.* urgent, pressing; *suspicion:* strong.

'dringlich *adj.* urgent, pressing; **⚲keit** *f* (-/*no pl.*) urgency.

drinnen *adv.* ['drinən] inside; indoors.

dritt|e *adj.* ['dritə] third; **'⚲el** *n* (-s/-) third; **'‿ens** *adv.* thirdly; **'‿letzt** *adj.* last but two.

Drog|e ['dro:gə] *f* (-/-n) drug; **‿erie** [drogə'ri:] *f* (-/-n) chemist's (shop), *Am.* drugstore; **‿ist** [dro-'gist] *m* (-en/-en) (retail pharmaceutical) chemist.

drohen ['dro:ən] *v/i.* (ge-, h) threaten, menace.

Drohne ['dro:nə] *f* (-/-n) *zo.* drone (*a. fig.*).

dröhnen ['drø:nən] *v/i.* (ge-, h) *voice, etc.:* resound; *cannon, drum, etc.:* roar; *voice, cannon:* boom.

Drohung ['dro:uŋ] *f* (-/-en) threat, menace.

drollig *adj.* ['drɔliç] amusing, quaint, comical.

Dromedar *zo.* ['dromə'da:r] *n* (-s/-e) dromedary.

drosch [drɔʃ] *pret. of* dreschen.

Droschke ['drɔʃkə] *f* (-/-n) taxi (-cab), *Am. a.* cab; hack; **'‿nkutscher** *m* cabman, driver, *Am. a.* hackman.

Drossel *orn.* ['drɔsəl] *f* (-/-n) thrush; '≈**n** ⊕ *v/t.* (ge-, *h*) throttle.

drüben *adv.* ['dry:bən] over there, yonder.

drüber F *adv.* ['dry:bər] *s.* darüber.

Druck [druk] *m* **1.** (-[e]s/≈e) pressure; squeeze (*of hand, etc.*); **2.** *typ.* (-[e]s/-e) print(ing); '~**bogen** *m* printed sheet; '~**buchstabe** *m* block letter.

drucken ['drukən] *v/t.* (ge-, *h*) print; ~ *lassen* have *s.th.* printed, publish.

drücken ['drykən] (ge-, *h*) **1.** *v/t.* press; squeeze (*hand, etc.*); force down (*prices, wages, etc.*); lower (*record*); press, push (*button, etc.*); F *sich* ~ *vor* (*dat.*) *or von* shirk (*work, etc.*); **2.** *v/i.* shoe: pinch.

'**Drucker** *m* (-s/-) printer.

'**Drücker** *m* (-s/-) door-handle; trigger.

Drucker|ei [drukə'raɪ] *f* (-/-en) printing office, *Am.* printery, print shop; '~**schwärze** *f* printer's *or* printing-ink.

'**Druck|fehler** *m* misprint; '~**fehlerverzeichnis** *n* errata *pl.*; '≈**fertig** *adj.* ready for press; '~**kammer** *f* pressurized cabin; '~**knopf** *m* patent fastener, snap-fastener; ∮ push-button; '~**luft** *f* compressed air; '~**pumpe** *f* pressure pump; '~**sache(n** *pl.*) ⅋ *f* printed matter, *Am. a.* second-class *or* third-class matter; '~**schrift** *f* block letters; publication; '~**taste** *f* press key.

drum F *adv.*, *cj.* [drum] *s.* darum.

drunter F *adv.* ['druntər] *s.* darunter.

Drüse *anat.* ['dry:zə] *f* (-/-n) gland.

du *pers. pron.* [du:] you.

Dublette [du'blɛtə] *f* (-/-n) duplicate.

ducken ['dukən] *v/refl.* (ge-, *h*) duck, crouch; *fig.* cringe (*vor dat.* to, before).

Dudelsack ∮ ['du:dəl-] *m* bagpipes *pl.*

Duell [du'ɛl] *n* (-s/-e) duel; ≈**ieren** [due'li:rən] *v/refl.* (*no* -ge-, *h*) (fight a) duel (*mit* with).

Duett ∮ [du'ɛt] *n* (-[e]s/-e) duet.

Duft [duft] *m* (-[e]s/≈e) scent, fragrance, perfume; '≈**en** *v/i.* (ge-, *h*) smell, have a scent, be fragrant; '≈**end** *adj.* fragrant; '≈**ig** *adj.* dainty, fragrant.

duld|en ['duldən] (ge-, *h*) **1.** *v/t.*

bear, stand, endure, suffer (*pain, grief, etc.*); tolerate, put up with; **2.** *v/i.* suffer; '~**sam** *adj.* ['⌣t-] tolerant; '≈**samkeit** *f* (-/*no pl.*) tolerance; ≈**ung** ['⌣duŋ] *f* (-/⅋-en) toleration; sufferance.

dumm *adj.* [dum] stupid, dull, *Am.* F dumb; '≈**heit** *f* (-/-en) stupidity, dullness; stupid *or* foolish action; '≈**kopf** *m* fool, blockhead, *Am. sl. a.* dumbbell.

dumpf *adj.* [dumpf] smell, air, etc.: musty, fusty; *atmosphere:* stuffy, heavy; *sound, sensation, etc.:* dull; '~**ig** *adj.* cellar, etc.: damp, musty.

Düne ['dy:nə] *f* (-/-n) dune, sandhill.   [manure.\

Dung [duŋ] *m* (-[e]s/*no pl.*) \

dünge|n ['dyŋən] *v/t.* (ge-, *h*) dung, manure; fertilize; '≈**r** *m* (-s/-) *s.* Dung; fertilizer.

dunkel ['duŋkəl] **1.** *adj.* dark; dim; *fig.* obscure; *idea, etc.:* faint, vague; **2.** ≈ *n* (-s/*no pl.*) *s.* Dunkelheit.

Dünkel ['dyŋkəl] *m* (-s/*no pl.*) conceit, arrogance; ≈**haft** *adj.* conceited, arrogant.

'**Dunkel|heit** *f* (-/*no pl.*) darkness (*a. fig.*); *fig.* obscurity; '~**kammer** *phot.* f dark-room; '≈**n** *v/i.* (ge-, *h*) grow dark, darken.

dünn *adj.* [dyn] paper, *material, voice, etc.:* thin; *hair, population, etc.:* thin, sparse; *liquid:* thin, watery; *air:* rare(fied).

Dunst [dunst] *m* (-es/≈e) vapo(u)r; haze, mist; fume.

dünsten ['dynstən] (ge-, *h*) **1.** *v/t.* steam (*fish, etc.*); stew (*fruit, etc.*); **2.** *v/i.* steam.

'**dunstig** *adj.* vaporous; hazy.

Duplikat [dupli'ka:t] *n* (-[e]s/-e) duplicate.

Dur ∮ [du:r] *n* (-/-) major.

durch [durç] **1.** *prp.* (*acc.*) through; **2.** *adv.:* *die ganze Nacht* ~ all night long; ~ *und* ~ through and through; thoroughly.

durcharbeiten ['durç⸗-] (*sep.*, -ge-, *h*) **1.** *v/t.* study thoroughly; *sich* ~ *durch* work through (*book, etc.*); **2.** *v/i.* work without a break.

durch'aus *adv.* through and through; thoroughly; by all means; absolutely, quite; ~ *nicht* not at all, by no means.

'**durch|biegen** *v/t.* (*irr.* biegen, *sep.*,

-ge-, h) bend; deflect (*beam*, *etc*.); *sich ~ beam*, *etc*.: deflect, sag; '**_blättern** v/t. (*sep.*, -ge-, h) glance or skim through (*book*, *etc*.), *Am.* thumb through, skim; '**Qblick** m: ~ *auf* (*acc*.) view through to, vista over, view of; '**_blicken** v/i. (*sep.*, -ge-, h) look through; ~ *lassen*, daß give to understand that.

durch|'bluten v/t. (*no* -ge-, h) supply with blood; **_'bohren** v/t. (*no* -ge-, h) pierce; perforate; *mit Blicken ~* look daggers at *s.o.*

'**durch|braten** v/t. (*irr.* braten, *sep.*, -ge-, h) roast thoroughly; **_'brechen** (*irr.* brechen) **1.** ['_brɛçən] v/i. (*sep.*, -ge-, sein) break through or apart; **2.** ['_] v/t. (*sep.*, -ge-, h) break apart or in two; **3.** [_'brɛçən] v/t. (*no* -ge-, h) break through, breach; run (*blockade*); crash (*sound barrier*); '**_brennen** v/i. (*irr.* brennen, *sep.*, -ge-, sein) **∮** *fuse*: blow; F *fig.* run away; *woman*: elope; '**_bringen** v/t. (*irr.* bringen, *sep.*, -ge-, h) bring or get through; dissipate, squander (*money*); '**Qbruch** m ✕ breakthrough; rupture; breach; *fig.* ultimate success.

durch|'denken v/t. (*irr.* denken, *no* -ge-, h) think *s.th.* over thoroughly; '**durch|drängen** v/refl. (*sep.*, -ge-, h) force or push one's way through; **_dringen** (*irr.* dringen) **1.** ['_drɪŋən] v/i. (*sep.*, -ge-, sein) penetrate (through); win acceptance (*mit* for) (*proposal*); **2.** [_'drɪŋən] v/t. (*no* -ge-, h) penetrate, pierce; *water*, *smell*, *etc*.: permeate.

durcheinander [durç⁹aɪ'nandər] **1.** *adv.* in confusion or disorder; pell-mell; **2.** ⚲ n (-s/-) muddle, mess, confusion; **_bringen** v/t. (*irr.* bringen, *sep.*, -ge-, h) confuse *s.o.*; mix (*things*) up; **_werfen** v/t. (*irr.* werfen, *sep.*, -ge-, h) throw into disorder; *fig.* mix up.

durchfahr|en (*irr.* fahren) **1.** ['_fa:rən] v/i. (*sep.*, -ge-, sein) go or pass or drive through; **2.** [_'fa:rən] v/t. (*no* -ge-, h) go or pass or travel or drive through; traverse (*tract of country*, *etc*.); '**Qt** f passage (through); gate(way); **_verboten!** no thoroughfare!

'**Durchfall** m ✱ diarrh(o)ea; F *fig.* failure, *Am. a.* flunk; **Qen** (*irr.* fallen) **1.** ['_falən] v/i. (*sep.*, -ge-, sein)

fall through; fail, F get ploughed (*in examination*); *thea.* be a failure, *sl.* be a flop; ~ *lassen* reject, F plough; **2.** [_'falən] v/t. (*no* -ge-, h) fall or drop through (*space*).

'**durch|fechten** v/t. (*irr.* fechten, *sep.*, -ge-, h) fight or see *s.th.* through; '**_finden** v/refl. (*irr.* finden, *sep.*, -ge-, h) find one's way (through).

durch|'flechten v/t. (*irr.* flechten, *no* -ge-, h) interweave, intertwine; **_'forschen** v/t. (*no* -ge-, h) search through, investigate; explore (*region*, *etc*.).

'**Durchfuhr** ✝ f (-/-en) transit.

durchführ|bar adj. ['durçfy:rba:r] practicable, feasible, workable; **_en** v/t. (*sep.*, -ge-, h) lead or take through or across; *fig.* carry out or through; realize; '**Qungsbestimmung** f (implementing) regulation.

'**Durchgang** m passage; ✝ transit; *sports*: run; '**_sverkehr** m through traffic; ✝ transit traffic; '**_szoll** m transit duty.

'**durchgebraten** adj. well done.

'**durchgehen** (*irr.* gehen, *sep.*, -ge-) **1.** v/i. (sein) go or walk through; *bill*: pass, be carried; run away or off; abscond; *woman*: elope; *horse*: bolt; **2.** v/t. (sein) go through (*street*, *etc*.); **3.** v/t. (h, sein) go or look or read through (*work*, *book*, *etc*.); '**_d 1.** adj. continuous; **_er** Zug through train; **2.** adv. generally; throughout.

durch'geistigt adj. spiritual.

'**durch|greifen** v/i. (*irr.* greifen, *sep.*, -ge-, h) put one's hand through; *fig.* take drastic measures or steps; '**_greifend** adj. drastic, radical, sweeping; '**_halten** (*irr.* halten, *sep.*, -ge-, h) **1.** v/t. keep up (*pace*, *etc*.); **2.** v/i. hold out; '**_hauen** v/t. (*irr.* hauen, *sep.*, -ge-, h) cut or chop through; *fig.* give *s.o.* a good hiding; '**_helfen** v/i. (*irr.* helfen, *sep.*, -ge-, h) help through (*a. fig.*); '**_kämpfen** v/t. (*sep.*, -ge-, h) fight out; *sich ~* fight one's way through; '**_kneten** v/t. (*sep.*, -ge-, h) knead or work thoroughly; '**_kommen** v/i. (*irr.* kommen, *sep.*, -ge-, sein) come or get or pass through; *sick person*: pull through; *in examination*: pass.

durch'kreuzen v/t. (*no* -ge-, h) cross, foil, thwart (*plan*, *etc*.).

Durch|laß ['durçlas] *m* (*Durch-lasses/Durchlässe*) passage; **'₂las-sen** *v/t.* (*irr. lassen, sep., -ge-, h*) let pass, allow to pass, let through; *Wasser* ~ leak; **'₂lässig** *adj.* pervious (to), permeable (to); leaky.

durchlaufen (*irr. laufen*) **1.** ['ˌlau-fən] *v/i.* (*sep., -ge-, sein*) run *or* pass through; **2.** ['ˌ] *v/t.* (*sep., -ge-, h*) wear out (*shoes, etc.*); **3.** [ˌ'laufən] *v/t.* (*no -ge-, h*) pass through (*stages, departments, etc.*); *sports:* cover (*distance*). [live through.)

durch'leben *v/t.* (*no -ge-, h*) go *or*)

'durchlesen *v/t.* (*irr. lesen, sep., -ge-, h*) read through.

durchleuchten (*h*) **1.** ['ˌlɔyçtən] *v/i.* (*sep., -ge-*) shine through; **2.** [ˌ'lɔyçtən] *v/t.* (*no -ge-*) ✧ X-ray; *fig.* investigate.

durchlöchern [durç'lœçərn] *v/t.* (*no -ge-, h*) perforate, make holes into *s.th.*

'durchmachen *v/t.* (*sep., -ge-, h*) go through (*difficult times, etc.*); undergo (*suffering*). [through.)

'Durchmarsch *m* march(ing))

'Durchmesser *m* (*-s/-*) diameter.

durch'nässen *v/t.* (*no -ge-, h*) wet through, soak, drench.

'durchnehmen *v/t.* (*irr. nehmen, sep., -ge-, h*) go through *or* over (*subject*) through; **~pausen** *v/t.* (*sep., -ge-, h*) trace, calk (*design, etc.*).

durchqueren [durç'kve:rən] *v/t.* (*no -ge-, h*) cross, traverse.

'durch|rechnen *v/t.* (*sep., -ge-, h*) (re)calculate, check; **'₂reise** *f* journey *or* way through; **~reisen 1.** ['ˌ-raizən] *v/i.* (*sep., -ge-, sein*) travel *or* pass through; **2.** [ˌ'raizən] *v/t.* (*no -ge-, h*) travel over *or* through *or* across; **'₂reisende** *m, f* (*-n/-n*) person travel(l)ing through, *Am. a.* transient; 🚞 through passenger; **'~reißen** (*irr. reißen, sep., -ge-*) **1.** *v/i.* (*sein*) tear, break; **2.** *v/t.* (*h*) tear asunder, tear in two; **~schauen** (*h*) **1.** ['ˌʃauən] *v/i. and v/t.* (*sep., -ge-*) look through; **2.** *fig.* [ˌ'ʃauən] *v/t.* (*no -ge-*) see through.

'durchscheinen *v/i.* (*irr. scheinen, sep., -ge-, h*) shine through; **'~d** *adj.* translucent; transparent.

'durchscheuern *v/t.* (*sep., -ge-, h*) rub through; **~schießen** (*irr. schie-ßen*) **1.** [ˌ'ʃi:sən] *v/i.* (*sep., -ge-, h*) shoot through; **2.** ['ˌ] *v/i.* (*sep.,*

-ge-, sein) *water:* shoot *or* race through; **3.** [ˌ'ʃi:sən] *v/t.* (*no -ge-, h*) shoot *s.th.* through; *typ.:* space out (*lines*); interleave (*book*).

'Durchschlag *m* colander, strainer; carbon copy; **₂en** (*irr. schlagen*) **1.** ['ˌʃla:gən] *v/t.* (*sep., -ge-, h*) break *or* pass through; strain (*peas, etc.*); *sich* ~ get along, make one's way; **2.** ['ˌ] *v/i.* (*sep., -ge-, h*) *typ.* come through; take *or* have effect; **3.** [ˌ'ʃla:gən] *v/t.* (*no -ge-, h*) pierce; *bullet:* penetrate; **'₂end** *adj.* effective, telling; **~papier** ['ˌk-] *n* copying paper.

durchschneiden *v/t.* (*irr. schneiden, h*) **1.** ['ˌʃnaidən] (*sep., -ge-*) cut through; **2.** [ˌ'ʃnaidən] (*no -ge-*) cut through, cut in two.

'Durchschnitt *m* cutting through; ⊕ section, profile; ⋀ intersection; *fig.* average; *im* ~ on an average; **'₂lich 1.** *adj.* average; normal; **2.** *adv.* on an average; normally; **'~swert** *m* average value.

'durch|sehen (*irr. sehen, sep., -ge-, h*) **1.** *v/i.* see *or* look through; **2.** *v/t.* see *or* look through *s.th.*; look *s.th.* over, go over *s.th.*; **'~seihen** *v/t.* (*sep., -ge-, h*) filter, strain; **~setzen** *v/t.* (*h*) **1.** ['ˌzetsən] (*sep., -ge-*) put (*plan, etc.*) through; force through; *seinen Kopf* ~ have one's way; *sich* ~ *opinion, etc.*: gain acceptance. **2.** [ˌ'zetsən] (*no -ge-*) intersperse.

'Durchsicht *f* looking through *or* over; examination; correction; *typ.* reading; **'₂ig** *adj. glass, water, etc.*: transparent; *fig.* clear, lucid; **'~ig-keit** *f* (*-/no pl.*) transparency; *fig.* clarity, lucidity.

'durch|sickern *v/i.* (*sep., -ge-, sein*) seep *or* ooze through; *news, etc.*: leak out; **~sieben** *v/t.* (*h*) **1.** ['ˌzi:-bən] (*sep., -ge-*) sieve, sift; bolt (*flour*); **2.** [ˌ'zi:bən] (*no -ge-*) riddle (*with bullets*); **'~sprechen** *v/t.* (*irr. sprechen, sep., -ge-, h*) discuss, talk over; **~stechen** *v/t.* (*irr. stechen, h*) **1.** ['ˌʃteçən] (*sep., -ge-*) stick (*needle, etc.*) through *s.th.*; stick through *s.th.*; **2.** [ˌ'ʃteçən] (*no -ge-*) pierce; cut through (*dike, etc.*); **'~stecken** *v/t.* (*sep., -ge-, h*) pass *or* stick through.

'Durchstich *m* cut(ting).

durch'stöbern *v/t.* (*no -ge-, h*) ransack (*room, pockets, etc.*); rummage through (*drawers, papers,* etc.).

'durchstreichen v/t. (*irr. streichen, sep., -ge-, h*) strike *or* cross out, cancel.

durch'streifen v/t. (*no -ge-, h*) roam *or* wander through *or* over *or* across.

durch'such|en v/t. (*no -ge-, h*) search (*a.* 🏛️); **2ung** f (*-/-en*) search.

durchtrieben adj. [durç'tri:bən] cunning, artful; **2heit** f (*-/no pl.*) cunning, artfulness.

durch'wachen v/t. (*no -ge-, h*) pass (*the night*) waking.

durch'wachsen adj. bacon: streaky.

durchwandern 1. ['ˌvandərn] v/i. (*sep., -ge-, sein*) walk *or* pass through; **2.** [ˌ'vandərn] v/t. (*no -ge-, h*) walk *or* pass through (*place, area,* etc.).

durch'weben v/t. (*no -ge-, h*) interweave; *fig. a.* intersperse.

durchweg adv. ['durçvɛk] throughout, without exception.

durch'weichen 1. ['ˌvaiçən] v/i. (*sep., -ge-, sein*) soak; **2.** [ˌ'vaiçən] v/t. (*no -ge-, h*) soak, drench; **'ˌwinden** v/refl. (*irr. winden, sep., -ge-, h*) worm *or* thread one's way through; **ˌwühlen** (*h*) **1.** fig. ['ˌvy:lən] v/refl. (*sep., -ge-*) work one's way through; **2.** [ˌ'vy:lən] v/t. (*no -ge-*) rummage; **'ˌzählen** v/t. (*sep., -ge-, h*) count; **'ˌziehen** (*irr. ziehen*) **1.** ['ˌtsi:ən] v/i. (*sep., -ge-, sein*) pass *or* go *or* come *or* march through; **2.** ['ˌ] v/t. (*sep., -ge-, h*) pull (*thread,* etc.) through; **3.** [ˌ'tsi:ən] v/t. (*no -ge-, h*) go *or* travel through; *scent,* etc.: fill, pervade (*room,* etc.).

durch'zucken v/t. (*no -ge-, h*) flash through.

'Durchzug m passage through; draught, *Am.* draft.

'durchzwängen v/refl. (*sep., -ge-, h*) squeeze o.s. through.

dürfen ['dyrfən] (*irr., h*) **1.** v/i. (*ge-*): ich darf (nicht) I am (not) allowed to; **2.** v/aux. (*no -ge-*): ich darf inf. I am permitted *or* allowed to inf.; I may inf.; du darfst nicht inf. you must not inf.; iro.: wenn ich bitten darf if you please.

durfte ['durftə] pret. of dürfen.

dürftig adj. ['dyrftiç] poor; scanty.

dürr adj. [dyr] wood, leaves, etc.: dry; land: barren, arid; p. gaunt, lean, skinny; **'2e** f (*-/-n*) dryness; barrenness; leanness.

Durst [durst] m (*-es/no pl.*) thirst (nach for); ~ haben be thirsty.

dürsten ['dyrstən] v/i. (*ge-, h*): ~ nach thirst for.

'durstig adj. thirsty (nach for).

Dusche ['duʃə] f (*-/-n*) shower (-bath); **'2n** v/refl. and v/i. (*ge-, h*) have a shower(-bath).

Düse ['dy:zə] f (*-/-n*) ⊕ nozzle; ✈ jet; **ˌnantrieb** ['ˌn⁹-] m jet propulsion; mit ~ jet-propelled; **'ˌnflugzeug** n (*jet-propelled*) aircraft, F jet; **'ˌnjäger** ✈ m jet fighter.

düster adj. ['dy:stər] dark, gloomy (both a. fig.); light: dim; fig.: sad; depressing; **'2heit** f (*-/no pl.*), **'2keit** f (*-/no pl.*) gloom(iness).

Dutzend ['dutsənt] n (*-s/-e*) dozen; ein ~ Eier a dozen eggs; ~e von Leuten dozens of people; **'2weise** adv. by the dozen, in dozens.

Dynam|ik [dy'na:mik] f (*-/no pl.*) dynamics; **2isch** adj. dynamic(al).

Dynamit [dyna'mi:t] n (*-s/no pl.*) dynamite.

Dynamo [dy'ha:mo] m (*-s/-s*), **~maschine** f dynamo, generator.

D-Zug ['de:tsu:k] m express train.

E

Ebbe ['ɛbə] f (*-/-n*) ebb(-tide); low tide; **'2n** v/i. (*ge-, sein*) ebb.

eben ['e:bən] **1.** adj. even, plain, level, flat; 🔬 plane; zu ~er Erde on the ground floor, *Am.* on the first floor; **2.** adv. exactly; just; ~

erst just now; **'2bild** n image, likeness; **ˌbürtig** adj. ['ˌbyrtiç] of equal birth; j-m ~ sein be a match for s.o., be s.o.'s equal; **'ˌda** adv., **'ˌdaˈselbst** adv. at the very (same) place, just there; quoting books:

ibidem (*abbr.* ib., ibid.); '**~der**, '**~die**, '**~das** *dem. pron.* = '**~der'selbe**, '**~die'selbe**, '**~das'selbe** *dem. pron.* the very (same); '**~des'wegen** *adv.* for that very reason.

Ebene ['e:bənə] *f* (-/-n) plain; ⅄ plane; *fig.* level.

'**eben|erdig** *adj. and adv.* at street level; on the ground floor, *Am.* on the first floor; '**~falls** *adv.* likewise; '**2holz** *n* ebony; '**~maß** *n* symmetry; harmony; regularity (*of features*); '**~mäßig** *adj.* symmetrical; harmonious; regular; '**~so** *adv.* just so; just as ...; likewise; '**~sosehr** *adv.*, '**~soviel** *adv.* just as much; '**~sowenig** *adv.* just as little *or* few (*pl.*), no more.

Eber *zo.* ['e:bər] *m* (-s/-) boar; '**~esche** ⚘ *f* mountain-ash.

ebnen ['e:bnən] *v/t.* (ge-, h) level; *fig.* smooth.

Echo ['ɛço] *n* (-s/-s) echo.

echt *adj.* [ɛçt] genuine; true; pure; real; *colour:* fast; *document:* authentic; '**2heit** *f* (-/*no pl.*) genuineness; purity; reality; fastness; authenticity.

Eck [ɛk] *n* (-[e]s/-e) *s.* Ecke; '**~ball** *m* sports: corner-kick; '**~e** *f* (-/-n) corner; edge; *fig.* angular; *fig.* awkward; '**~platz** *m* corner-seat; '**~stein** *m* corner-stone; '**~zahn** *m* canine tooth.

edel *adj.* ['e:dəl] noble; *min.* precious; *organs of the body:* vital; '**~denkend** *adj.* noble-minded; '**2mann** *m* nobleman; '**2mut** *m* generosity; '**~mütig** *adj.* ['~my:tiç] noble-minded, generous; '**2stein** *m* precious stone; gem.

Edikt [e'dikt] *n* (-[e]s/-e) edict.

Efeu ⚘ ['e:fɔy] *m* (-s/*no pl.*) ivy.

Effekt [ɛ'fɛkt] *m* (-[e]s/-e) effect; '**~en** *pl.* effects *pl.*; ✝: securities *pl.*; stocks *pl.*; '**~hascherei** [~haʃə'raɪ] *f* (-/-en) claptrap; '**2iv** *adj.* [~'ti:v] effective; '**2uieren** [~u'i:rən] *v/t.* (*no* -ge-, h) effect; execute, *Am. a.* fill; '**2voll** *adj.* effective, striking.

egal *adj.* [e'ga:l] equal; F all the same.

Egge ['ɛgə] *f* (-/-n) harrow; '**2n** *v/t.* (ge-, h) harrow.

Egois|mus [ego'ismus] *m* (-/*Egois-* men) ego(t)ism; **~t** *m* (-en/-en) ego(t)ist; **2tisch** *adj.* selfish, ego(t)istic(al).

ehe[1] *cj.* ['e:ə] before.

Ehe[2](**~**) *f*(-/-*n*) marriage; matrimony; '**~anbahnung** *f* (-/-en) matrimonial agency; '**~brecher** *m* (-s/-) adulterer; '**~brecherin** *f* (-/-nen) adulteress; '**2brecherisch** *adj.* adulterous; '**~bruch** *m* adultery; '**~frau** *f* wife; '**~gatte** *m*, '**~gattin** *f* spouse; '**~leute** *pl.* married people *pl.*; '**2lich** *adj.* conjugal; *child:* legitimate; '**~losigkeit** *f* (-/*no pl.*) celibacy; single life.

ehemal|ig *adj.* ['e:əma:lıç] former, ex-...; old; '**~s** *adv.* formerly.

'**Ehe|mann** *m* husband; '**~paar** *n* married couple.

'**eher** *adv.* sooner; rather; more likely; je ~, desto besser the sooner the better.

'**Ehering** *m* wedding ring.

ehern *adj.* ['e:ərn] brazen, of brass.

'**Ehe|scheidung** *f* divorce; '**~schlie-ßung** *f* (-/-en) (contraction of) marriage; '**~stand** *m* (-[e]s/*no pl.*) married state, matrimony; '**~stifter** *m*, '**~stifterin** *f* (-/-nen) matchmaker; '**~vermittlung** *f s.* Eheanbahnung; '**~versprechen** *n* promise of marriage; '**~vertrag** *m* marriage contract.

Ehrabschneider ['e:rʔapʃnaɪdər] *m* (-s/-) slanderer.

'**ehrbar** *adj.* hono(u)rable, respectable; modest; '**2keit** *f* (-/*no pl.*) respectability; modesty.

Ehre ['e:rə] *f* (-/-n) hono(u)r; zu **~**n (*gen.*) in hono(u)r of; '**2n** *v/t.* (ge-, h) hono(u)r; esteem.

'**ehren|amtlich** *adj.* honorary; '**2-bürger** *m* honorary citizen; '**2dok-tor** *m* honorary doctor; '**2erklä-rung** *f* (full) apology; '**2gast** *m* guest of hono(u)r; '**2gericht** *n* court of hono(u)r; '**~haft** *adj.* hono(u)rable; '**2kodex** *m* code of hono(u)r; '**2legion** *f* Legion of Hono(u)r; '**2mann** *m* (-/*no pl.*) Legion of Hono(u)r; '**2mann** *m* man of hono(u)r; '**2mitglied** *n* honorary member; '**2platz** *m* place of hono(u)r; '**2recht** *n:* bürgerliche **~**e *pl.* civil rights *pl.*; '**2rettung** *f* rehabilitation; '**~rührig** *adj.* defamatory; '**2sache** *f* affair of hono(u)r; point of hono(u)r; '**~voll** *adj.* hono(u)rable; '**~wert** *adj.* hono(u)rable;

'Ꞇwort n (-[e]s/-e) word of hono(u)r.

ehr|erbietig adj. ['e:r⁹ɛrbi:tɪç] respectful; **'Ꞇerbietung** f (-/-en) reverence; **'Ꞇfurcht** f (-/~-en) respect; awe; **'~furchtgebietend** adj. awe-inspiring, awesome; **~fürchtig** adj. ['~fʏrçtɪç] respectful; **'Ꞇgefühl** n (-[e]s/no pl.) sense of hono(u)r; **'Ꞇgeiz** m ambition; **'~geizig** adj. ambitious.

'ehrlich adj. honest; commerce, game: fair; opinion: candid; ~ während am längsten honesty is the best policy; **'Ꞇkeit** f (-/no pl.) honesty; fairness.

'ehrlos adj. dishono(u)rable, infamous; **'Ꞇigkeit** f (-/-en) dishonesty, infamy.

'ehr|sam adj. s. ehrbar; **'Ꞇung** f (-/-en) hono(u)r (conferred on s.o.); **'~vergessen** adj. dishono(u)rable, infamous; **'Ꞇverlust** ⚖ m (-es/no pl.) loss of civil rights; **'~würdig** adj. venerable, reverend.

ei¹ int. [aɪ] ah!, indeed!

Ei² [~] n (-[e]s/-er) egg; physiol. ovum.

Eibe ♀ ['aɪbə] f (-/-n) yew(-tree).

Eiche ♀ ['aɪçə] f (-/-n) oak(-tree); **'~l** ['~l] f (-/-n) ♀ acorn; cards: club; **'~lhäher** orn. ['~hɛ:ər] m (-s/-) jay.

eichen¹ ['aɪçən] v/t. (ge-, h) ga(u)ge.

eichen² adj. [~] oaken, of oak.

Eich|hörnchen zo. ['aɪçhœrnçən] n (-s/-) squirrel; **'~maß** n standard.

Eid [aɪt] m (-es/-e) oath; **'Ꞇbrüchig** adj.: ~ werden break one's oath.

Eidechse zo. ['aɪdɛksə] f (-/-n) lizard.

eidesstattlich ⚖ adj. ['aɪdəs-] in lieu of (an) oath; ~e Erklärung statutory declaration.

'eidlich 1. adj. sworn; **2.** adv. on oath.

'Eidotter m, n yolk.

'Eier|kuchen m omelet(te), pancake; **'~schale** f egg-shell; **'~stock** anat. m ovary; **'~uhr** f egg-timer.

Eifer ['aɪfər] m (-s/no pl.) zeal; eagerness; ardo(u)r; **'~er** m (-s/-) zealot; **'~sucht** f (-/no pl.) jealousy; **'Ꞇsüchtig** adj. jealous (auf acc. of).

eifrig adj. ['aɪfrɪç] zealous, eager; ardent.

eigen adj. ['aɪgən] own; particular; strange, odd; in compounds: ...-owned; peculiar (dat. to); **'Ꞇart** f peculiarity; **'~artig** adj. peculiar;

singular; **'Ꞇbrötler** ['~brø:tlər] m (-s/-) odd or eccentric person, crank; **'Ꞇgewicht** n dead weight; **'~händig** adj. and adv. ['~hɛndɪç] with one's own hands; **'Ꞇheim** n house of one's own; homestead; **'Ꞇheit** f (-/-en) peculiarity; oddity; of language: idiom; **'Ꞇliebe** f self-love; **'Ꞇlob** n self-praise; **'~mächtig** adj. arbitrary; **'Ꞇname** m proper name; **~nützig** adj. ['~nʏtsɪç] self-interested, selfish; **'~s** adv. expressly, specially; on purpose.

'Eigenschaft f (-/-en) quality (of s.o.); property (of s.th.); in s-r ~ als in his capacity as; **'~swort** gr. n (-[e]s/~er) adjective.

'Eigensinn m (-[e]s/no pl.) obstinacy; **'Ꞇig** adj. wil(l)ful, obstinate.

'eigentlich 1. adj. proper; actual; true, real; **2.** adv. properly (speaking).

'Eigentum n (-s/~er) property.

Eigentüm|er ['aɪgəntʏ:mər] m (-s/-) owner, proprietor; **'Ꞇlich** adj. peculiar; odd; **'~lichkeit** f (-/-en) peculiarity.

'Eigentums|recht n ownership; copyright; **'~wohnung** f freehold flat. [individual.]

'eigenwillig adj. self-willed; fig. in-

eign|en ['aɪgnən] v/refl. (ge-, h): sich ~ für be suited for; **'Ꞇung** f (-/-en) aptitude, suitability.

'Eil|bote ⚑ m express messenger; durch ~n by special delivery; **'~brief** ⚑ m express letter, Am. special delivery letter.

Eile ['aɪlə] f (-/no pl.) haste, speed; hurry; **'Ꞇn** v/i. (ge-, sein) hasten, make haste; hurry; letter, affair: be urgent; **'Ꞇnds** adv. ['~ts] quickly, speedily.

'Eil|fracht f, **'~gut** n express goods pl., Am. fast freight; **'Ꞇig** adj. hasty, speedy; urgent; es ~ haben be in a hurry.

Eimer ['aɪmər] m (-s/-) bucket, pail.

ein [aɪn] **1.** adj. one; **2.** indef. art. a, an.

einander adv. [aɪ'nandər] one another; each other.

ein|arbeiten ['aɪn⁹-] v/t. (sep., -ge-, h): j-n ~ in (acc.) make s.o. acquainted with; **~armig** adj. ['aɪn⁹-] one-armed; **~äschern** ['aɪn⁹ɛʃərn] v/t. (sep., -ge-, h) burn to ashes; cremate (dead body); **'Ꞇäscherung**

f (-/-en) cremation; **~atmen** ['aɪn'-] *v/t.* (*sep.*, -ge-, *h*) breathe, inhale; **~äugig** *adj.* ['aɪn'ɔʏgɪç] one-eyed.

'**Einbahnstraße** *f* one-way street.

'**einbalsamieren** *v/t.* (*sep.*, no -ge-, *h*) embalm.

'**Einband** *m* (-[e]s/ÿe) binding; cover.

'**ein|bauen** *v/t.* (*sep.*, -ge-, *h*) build in; install (*engine, etc.*); **~behalten** *v/t.* (*irr. halten, sep.*, no -ge-, *h*) detain; **~berufen** *v/t.* (*irr. rufen, sep.*, no -ge-, *h*) convene; ✕ call up, *Am.* induct.

'**einbett|en** *v/t.* (*sep.*, -ge-, *h*) embed; '**2zimmer** *n* single(-bedded) room.

'**einbild|en** *v/refl.* (*sep.*, -ge-, *h*) fancy, imagine; '**2ung** *f* imagination, fancy; conceit.

'**einbinden** *v/t.* (*irr. binden, sep.*, -ge-, *h*) bind (*books*).

'**Einblick** *m* insight (*in acc.* into).

'**einbrechen** (*irr. brechen, sep.*, -ge-) 1. *v/t.* (*h*) break open; 2. *v/i.* (*sein*) break in; *of night, etc.*: set in; ~ *in* (*acc.*) break into (*house*).

'**Einbrecher** *m* at night: burglar; by day: housebreaker.

'**Einbruch** *m* ✕ invasion; housebreaking, burglary; *bei ~ der Nacht* at nightfall; '**~(s)diebstahl** *m* house-breaking, burglary.

'**einbürger|n** ['aɪnbʏrgərn] *v/t.* (*sep.*, -ge-, *h*) naturalize; '**2ung** *f* (-/-en) naturalization.

'**Ein|buße** *f* loss; '**2büßen** *v/t.* (*sep.*, -ge-, *h*) lose, forfeit.

'**ein|dämmen** ['aɪndɛmən] *v/t.* (*sep.*, -ge-, *h*) dam (up); embank (*river*); *fig.* check; '**~deutig** *adj.* unequivocal; clear, plain.

'**eindring|en** *v/i.* (*irr. dringen, sep.*, -ge-, *sein*) enter; penetrate; intrude; ~ *in* (*acc.*) penetrate (into); force one's way into; invade (*country*); '**~lich** *adj.* urgent; **2ling** ['~lɪŋ] *m* (-s/-e) intruder; interloper.

'**Eindruck** *m* (-[e]s/ÿe) impression.

'**ein|drücken** *v/t.* (*sep.*, -ge-, *h*) press in; crush (in) (*hat*); break (*pane*); '**~drucksvoll** *adj.* impressive; **~engen** ['aɪn'-] *v/t.* (*sep.*, -ge-, *h*) narrow; *fig.* limit.

ein|er[1] ['aɪnər], '**~e**, '**~(e)s** *indef. pron.* one.

Einer[2] [~] *m* (-s/-) ♣ unit, digit; *rowing*: single sculler, skiff.

einerlei ['aɪnər'laɪ] 1. *adj.* of the same kind; immaterial; *es ist mir ~* it is all the same to me; 2. **2** *n* (-s/no *pl.*) sameness; monotony; humdrum (*of one's existence*).

einerseits *adv.* ['aɪnər'zaɪts] on the one hand.

einfach *adj.* ['aɪnfax] simple; single; plain; *meal*: frugal; *ticket*: single, *Am.* one-way; '**2heit** *f* (-/no *pl.*) simplicity.

einfädeln ['aɪnfɛːdəln] *v/t.* (*sep.*, -ge-, *h*) thread; *fig.* start, set on foot; contrive.

'**Einfahrt** *f* entrance, entry.

'**Einfall** *m* ✕ invasion; idea, inspiration; '**2en** *v/i.* (*irr. fallen, sep.*, -ge-, *sein*) fall in; collapse; break in (*on a conversation*), interrupt, cut short; chime in; ♪ join in; invade; *j-m ~* occur to s.o.

Ein|falt ['aɪnfalt] *f* (-/no *pl.*) simplicity; silliness; **2fältig** *adj.* ['~-fɛltɪç] simple; silly; '**~faltspinsel** *m* simpleton, *Am.* F sucker.

'**ein|farbig** *adj.* one-colo(u)red, uni-colo(u)red; plain; '**~fassen** *v/t.* (*sep.*, -ge-, *h*) border; set (*precious stone*); '**2fassung** *f* border; setting; '**~fetten** *v/t.* (*sep.*, -ge-, *h*) grease; oil; '**~finden** *v/refl.* (*irr. finden, sep.*, -ge-, *h*) appear; arrive; !**~flechten** *fig. v/t.* (*irr. flechten, sep.*, -ge-, *h*) put in, insert; '**~fließen** *v/i.* (*irr. fließen, sep.*, -ge-, *sein*) flow in; ~ *in* (*acc.*) flow into; **~** *lassen* mention in passing; '**~flößen** *v/t.* (*sep.*, -ge-, *h*) infuse.

'**Einfluß** *m* influx; *fig.* influence; '**2reich** *adj.* influential.

ein|förmig *adj.* ['aɪnfœrmɪç] uniform; monotonous; **~frieden** ['~-friːdən] *v/t.* (*sep.*, -ge-, *h*) fence, enclose; '**2friedung** *f* (-/-en) enclosure; '**~frieren** (*irr. frieren, sep.*, -ge-) 1. *v/i.* (*sein*) freeze (in); 2. *v/t.* (*h*) freeze (*food*); '**~fügen** *v/t.* (*sep.*, -ge-, *h*) put in; *fig.* insert; *sich ~* fit in.

Einfuhr ✝ ['aɪnfuːr] *f* (-/-en) import(ation); '**~bestimmungen** *f/pl.* import regulations *pl.*

'**einführen** *v/t.* (*sep.*, -ge-, *h*) ✝ import; introduce (*s.o., custom*); insert; initiate; install (*s.o. in an office*).

'**Einfuhrwaren** ✝ *f/pl.* imports *pl.*

'**Eingabe** f petition; application.

'**Eingang** m entrance; entry; arrival (of goods); nach ∼ on receipt; '∼**buch** ✝ n book of entries.

'**eingeben** v/t. (irr. geben, sep., -ge-, h) give, administer (medicine) (dat. to); prompt, suggest (to).

'**einge|bildet** adj. imaginary; conceited (auf acc. of); '∼**boren** adj. native; '2**borene** m, f (-n/-n) native.

Eingebung ['aɪngeːbuŋ] f (-/-en) suggestion; inspiration.

einge|denk adj. ['aɪngədɛŋk] mindful (gen. of); '∼**fallen** adj. eyes, cheeks: sunken, hollow; emaciated; ∼**fleischt** fig. adj. ['∼gəflaɪʃt] inveterate; confirmed; ∼er Junggeselle confirmed bachelor.

'**eingehen** (irr. gehen, sep., -ge-) **1.** v/i. (sein) mail, goods: come in, arrive; ♀, animal: die; cease (to exist); material: shrink; ∼ auf (acc.) agree to; enter into; **2.** v/t. (h, sein) enter into (relationship); contract (marriage); ein Risiko ∼ run a risk, esp. Am. take a chance; e-n Vergleich ∼ come to terms; Verbindlichkeiten ∼ incur liabilities; e-e Wette ∼ make a bet; eingegangene Gelder n/pl. receipts pl.; '∼**d** adj. detailed; thorough; examination: close.

Eingemachte ['aɪngəmaxtə] n (-n/ no pl.) preserves pl.; pickles pl.

'**eingemeinden** v/t. (sep., no -ge-, h) incorporate (dat. into).

'**einge|nommen** adj. partial (für to); prejudiced (gegen against); von sich ∼ conceited; '2**sandt** ✍ n (-s/-s) letter to the editor; ∼**schnappt** F fig. adj. ['∼gəʃnapt] offended, touchy; '∼**sessen** adj. long-established; '2**ständnis** n confession, avowal; '∼**stehen** v/t. (irr. stehen, sep., no -ge-, h) confess, avow.

Eingeweide anat. ['aɪngəvaɪdə] pl. viscera pl.; intestines pl.; bowels pl.; esp. of animals: entrails pl.

'**einge|wöhnen** v/refl. (sep., no -ge-, h) accustom o.s. (in acc. to); acclimatize o.s., Am. acclimate o.s. (to); get used (to).

eingewurzelt adj. ['∼gəvurtsəlt] deep-rooted, inveterate.

'**eingießen** v/t. (irr. gießen, sep., -ge-, h) pour in or out.

eingleisig adj. ['aɪnglaɪziç] single-track.

'**ein|graben** v/t. (irr. graben, sep.,

-ge-, h) dig in; bury; engrave; sich ∼ ✕ dig o.s. in, entrench o.s.; fig. engrave itself (on one's memory); '∼**gravieren** v/t. (sep., no -ge-, h) engrave.

'**eingreifen 1.** v/i. (irr. greifen, sep., -ge-, h) intervene; ∼ in (acc.) interfere with; encroach on (s.o.'s rights); in die Debatte ∼ join in the debate; **2.** 2 n (-s/no pl.) intervention.

'**Eingriff** m fig. encroachment; ⚕ operation.

'**einhaken** v/t. (sep., -ge-, h) fasten; sich bei j-m ∼ take s.o.'s arm.

'**Einhalt** m (-[e]s/no pl.): ∼ gebieten (dat.) put a stop to; '2**en** fig. (irr. halten, sep., -ge-, h) **1.** v/t. observe, keep; **2.** v/i. stop, leave off (zu tun doing).

'**ein|hängen** ([irr. hängen,] sep., -ge-, h) **1.** v/t. hang in; hang up, replace (receiver); sich bei j-m ∼ take s.o.'s arm, link arms with s.o.; **2.** teleph. v/i. hang up; '∼**heften** v/t. (sep., -ge-, h) sew or stitch in.

'**einheimisch** adj. native (in dat. to), indigenous (to) (a. ♀); ∼ endemic; product: home-grown; '2**e** m, f (-n/-n) native; resident.

'**Einheit** f (-/-en) unity; oneness; ☿, phys., ✕ unit; '2**lich** adj. uniform; '∼**spreis** m standard price.

'**einheizen** (sep., -ge-, h) **1.** v/i. make a fire; **2.** v/t. heat (stove).

einhellig adj. ['aɪnhɛliç] unanimous.

'**einholen** (sep., -ge-, h) **1.** v/t. catch up with, overtake; make up for (lost time); make (inquiries); take (order); seek (advice); ask for (permission); buy; **2.** v/i.: ∼ gehen go shopping.

'**Einhorn** zo. n unicorn.

'**einhüllen** v/t. (sep., -ge-, h) wrap (up or in), envelop.

einig adj. ['aɪniç] united; ∼ sein agree; nicht ∼ sein differ (über acc. about); ∼**e** indef. pron. ['∼gə] several; some; ∼**en** ['∼igən] v/t. (ge-, h) unite; sich ∼ come to terms; ∼er**maßen** adv. ['∼gər'maːsən] in some measure; somewhat; ∼**es** indef. pron. ['∼gəs] some(thing); '2**keit** f (-/no pl.) unity; concord; 2**ung** ['∼g-] f (-/-en) union; agreement.

ein|impfen ['aɪn ?-] v/t. (sep., -ge-, h) ⚕ inoculate (a. fig.); '∼**jagen** v/t.

(*sep.*, -*ge*-, *h*): *j-m Furcht* ~ scare s.o.

'**einjährig** *adj.* ['aɪnjɛːrɪç] one-year-old; *esp.* ♃ annual; *animal*: yearling.

'**ein|kalkulieren** *v/t.* (*sep.*, *no* -*ge*-, *h*) take into account, allow for; '**~kassieren** *v/t.* (*sep.*, *no* -*ge*-, *h*) cash; collect.

'**Einkauf** *m* purchase; *Einkäufe machen s.* einkaufen 2; '**2en** (*sep.*, -*ge*-, *h*) **1.** *v/t.* buy, purchase; **2.** *v/i.* make purchases, go shopping.

'**Einkäufer** *m* buyer.

'**Einkaufs|netz** *n* string bag; '**~preis** ♥ *m* purchase price; '**~tasche** *f* shopping-bag.

'**ein|kehren** *v/i.* (*sep.*, -*ge*-, *sein*) put up *or* stop (*at an inn*); '**~kerben** *v/t.* (*sep.*, -*ge*-, *h*) notch; '**~kerkern** *v/t.* (*sep.*, -*ge*-, *h*) imprison; '**~klagen** *v/t.* (*sep.*, -*ge*-, *h*) sue for; '**~klammern** *v/t.* (*sep.*, -*ge*-, *h*) typ. bracket; put in brackets.

'**Einklang** *m* unison; harmony.

'**ein|kleiden** *v/t.* (*sep.*, -*ge*-, *h*) clothe; fit out; '**~klemmen** *v/t.* (*sep.*, -*ge*-, *h*) squeeze (in); jam; '**~klinken** (*sep.*, -*ge*-) **1.** *v/t.* (*h*) latch; **2.** *v/i.* (*sein*) latch; engage; '**~knicken** (*sep.*, -*ge*-) *v/t.* (*h*) *and* *v/i.* (*sein*) bend in, break; '**~kochen** (*sep.*, -*ge*-) **1.** *v/t.* (*h*) preserve; **2.** *v/i.* (*sein*) boil down *or* away.

'**Einkommen** *n* (-*s*/-) income, revenue; '**~steuer** *f* income-tax.

'**einkreisen** *v/t.* (*sep.*, -*ge*-, *h*) encircle.

Einkünfte ['aɪnkʏnftə] *pl.* income, revenue.

'**einlad|en** *v/t.* (*irr. laden*, *sep.*, -*ge*-, *h*) load (in) (*goods*); *fig.* invite; '**2ung** *f* invitation.

'**Einlage** *f* enclosure (*in letter*); ♥ investment; deposit (*of money*); *gambling*: stake; inserted piece; ♪ arch-support; temporary filling (*of tooth*); '**2rn** ♥ *v/t.* (*sep.*, -*ge*-, *h*) store (up).

'**Einlaß** ['aɪnlas] *m* (*Einlasses/Einlässe*) admission, admittance.

'**einlassen** *v/t.* (*irr. lassen*, *sep.*, -*ge*-, *h*) let in, admit; ~ *in* (*acc.*) ⊕ imbed in; *sich* ~ *in or auf* (*both acc.*) engage in, enter into.

'**ein|laufen** *v/i.* (*irr. laufen*, *sep.*, -*ge*-, *sein*) come in, arrive; *ship*: enter; *material*: shrink; '**~leben**

v/refl. (*sep.*, -*ge*-, *h*) accustom o.s. (*in acc.* to).

'**einlege|n** *v/t.* (*sep.*, -*ge*-, *h*) lay *or* put in; insert; ⊕ inlay; deposit (*money*); pickle; preserve (*fruit*); *Berufung* ~ lodge an appeal (*bei* to); *Ehre* ~ *mit* gain hono(u)r *or* credit by; '**2sohle** *f* insole, sock.

'**einleit|en** *v/t.* (*sep.*, -*ge*-, *h*) start; introduce; *fig.* **~end** *adj.* introductory; '**2ung** *f* introduction.

'**ein|lenken** *fig.* *v/i.* (*sep.*, -*ge*-, *h*) come round; '**~leuchten** *v/i.* (*sep.*, -*ge*-, *h*) be evident *or* obvious; '**~liefern** *v/t.* (*sep.*, -*ge*-, *h*) deliver (up); *in ein Krankenhaus* ~ take to a hospital, *Am.* hospitalize; '**~lösen** *v/t.* (*sep.*, -*ge*-, *h*) ransom (*prisoner*); redeem (*pledge*); ♥ hono(u)r (*bill*); cash (*cheque*); ♥ meet (*bill*); '**~machen** *v/t.* (*sep.*, -*ge*-, *h*) preserve (*fruit*); tin, *Am.* can.

'**einmal** *adv.* once; one day; *auf* ~ all at once; *es war* ~ once (upon a time) there was; *nicht* ~ not even; '**2eins** *n* (-/-) multiplication table; '**~ig** *adj.* single; unique.

'**Einmarsch** *m* marching in; entry; '**2ieren** *v/i.* (*sep.*, *no* -*ge*-, *sein*) march in, enter.

'**ein|mengen** *v/refl.* (*sep.*, -*ge*-, *h*), '**~mischen** *v/refl.* (*sep.*, -*ge*-, *h*) meddle, interfere (*in acc.* with), *esp. Am. sl.* butt in.

'**Einmündung** *f* junction (*of roads*); mouth (*of river*).

einmütig *adj.* ['aɪnmyːtɪç] unanimous; '**2keit** *f* (-/*no pl.*) unanimity.

Einnahme ['aɪnnaːmə] *f* (-/-*n*) ✕ taking, capture; *mst* ~*n* *pl.* takings *pl.*, receipts *pl.*

'**einnehmen** *v/t.* (*irr. nehmen*, *sep.*, -*ge*-, *h*) take (*meal*, *position*, ✕); ♥ take (*money*); ♥ earn, make (*money*); take up, occupy (*room*); *fig.* captivate; '**~d** *adj.* taking, engaging, captivating.

'**einnicken** *v/i.* (*sep.*, -*ge*-, *sein*) doze *or* drop off.

Einöde ['aɪnʔøː-] *f* desert, solitude.

'**ein|ordnen** ['aɪnʔ-] *v/t.* (*sep.*, -*ge*-, *h*) arrange in proper order; classify; file (*letters*, *etc.*); '**~packen** *v/t.* (*sep.*, -*ge*-, *h*) pack up; wrap up; '**~pferchen** *v/t.* (*sep.*, -*ge*-, *h*) pen in; *fig.* crowd, cram; '**~pflanzen** *v/t.* (*sep.*, -*ge*-, *h*) plant; *fig.* implant; '**~pökeln** *v/t.* (*sep.*, -*ge*-, *h*) pickle, salt; '~**prägen** v/t. (sep., -ge-, h) imprint; impress; sich ~ imprint itself; commit s.th. to one's memory; '~**quartieren** v/t. (sep., no -ge-, h) quarter, billet; '~**rahmen** v/t. (sep.,-ge-, h) frame; '~**räumen** fig. v/t. (sep.,-ge-, h) grant, concede; '~**rechnen** v/t. (sep.,-ge-, h) comprise, include; '~**reden** (sep., -ge-, h) **1.** v/t.: j-m ~ persuade or talk s.o. into (doing) s.th.; **2.** v/i.: auf j-n ~ talk insistently to s.o.; '~**reichen** v/t. (sep.,-ge-, h) hand in, send in, present; '~**reihen** v/t. (sep., -ge-, h) insert (unter acc. in); class (with); place (among); sich ~ take one's place.

einreihig adj. ['aɪnraɪç] jacket: single-breasted.

'**Einreise** f entry; '~**erlaubnis** f, '~**genehmigung** f entry permit.

'**ein|reißen** (irr. reißen, sep., -ge-) **1.** v/t. (h) tear; pull down (building); **2.** v/i. (sein) tear; abuse, etc.: spread; ~**renken** ['~rɛŋkən] v/t. (sep., -ge- h) ⚕ set; fig. set right.

'**einricht|en** v/t. (sep., -ge-, h) establish; equip; arrange; set up (shop); furnish (flat); es ~ manage; sich ~ establish o.s., settle down; economize; sich ~ auf (acc.) prepare for; '⁀**ung** f establishment; arrangement, esp. Am. setup; equipment; furniture; fittings pl. (of shop); institution.

'**ein|rollen** v/t. (sep., -ge-, h) roll up or in; sich ~ roll up; curl up; '~**rosten** v/i. (sep., -ge-, sein) rust; screw, etc.: rust in; '~**rücken** (sep., -ge-) **1.** v/i. (sein) enter, march in; ✕ join the army; **2.** v/t. (h) insert (advertisement in a paper); typ. indent (line, word, etc.); '~**rühren** v/t. (sep.,-ge-, h) stir (in).

eins adj. [aɪns] one.

einsam adj. lonely, solitary; '⁀**keit** f (-/⁀ -en) loneliness, solitude.

'**einsammeln** v/t. (sep., -ge-, h) gather; collect.

'**Einsatz** m inset; insertion (of piece of material); gambling: stake, pool; ♪ striking in, entry; employment; engagement (✕ ✕); ✕ action, operation; unter ~ s-s Lebens at the risk of one's life.

'**ein|saugen** v/t. (sep., -ge-, h) suck in; fig. imbibe; '~**schalten** v/t. (sep., -ge-, h) insert; ⚡ switch or

turn on; den ersten Gang ~ mot. go into first or bottom gear; sich ~ intervene; '~**schärfen** v/t. (sep., -ge-, h) inculcate (dat. upon); '~**schätzen** v/t. (sep., -ge-, h) assess, appraise, estimate (auf acc. at); value (a. fig.); '~**schenken** v/t. (sep., -ge-, h) pour in or out; '~**schicken** v/t. (sep., -ge-, h) send in; '~**schieben** v/t. (irr. schieben, sep.,-ge-, h) insert; '~**schiffen** v/t. and v/refl. (sep., -ge-, h) embark; '⁀**schiffung** f (-/-en) embarkation; '~**schlafen** v/i. (irr. schlafen, sep., -ge-, sein) fall asleep; ~**schläfern** ['~ʃlɛːfərn] v/t. (sep., -ge-, h) lull to sleep; ⚕ narcotize.

'**Einschlag** m striking (of lightning); impact (of missile); fig. touch; '⁀**en** (irr. schlagen, sep., -ge-, h) **1.** v/t. drive in (nail); break (in); smash (in); wrap up; take (road); tuck in (hem, etc.); enter upon (career); **2.** v/i. shake hands; lightning, missile: strike; fig. be a success; nicht ~ fail; (wie e-e Bombe) ~ cause a sensation; auf j-n ~ belabour s.o.

einschlägig adj. ['aɪnʃlɛːgɪç] relevant, pertinent.

'**Einschlagpapier** n wrapping-paper.

'**ein|schleichen** v/refl. (irr. schleichen, sep., -ge-, h) creep or sneak in; '~**schleppen** v/t. (sep., -ge-, h) ♧ tow in; import (disease); '~**schleusen** fig. v/t. (sep., -ge-, h) channel or let in; '~**schließen** v/t. (irr. schließen, sep.,-ge-, h) lock in or up; enclose; ✕ surround, encircle; fig. include; '~**schließlich** prp. (gen.) inclusive of; including, comprising; '~**schmeicheln** v/refl. (sep., -ge-, h) ingratiate o.s. (bei with); '~**schmeichelnd** adj. insinuating; '~**schmuggeln** v/t. (sep., -ge-, h) smuggle in; '~**schnappen** v/i. (sep., -ge-, sein) catch; fig. s. eingeschnappt; '~**schneidend** fig. adj. incisive, drastic.

'**Einschnitt** m cut, incision; notch.

'**ein|schnüren** v/t. (sep., -ge-, h) lace (up); ~**schränken** ['~ʃrɛŋkən] v/t. (sep., -ge-, h) restrict, confine; reduce (expenses); sich ~ economize; '⁀**schränkung** f (-/-en) restriction; reduction.

'**Einschreibe|brief** m registered letter; '⁀**n** v/t. (irr. schreiben, sep.,

-ge-, h) enter; book; enrol(l); ⚔
enlist, enrol(l); ⚓ register; ~ lassen
have registered; sich ~ enter one's
name.

'einschreiten 1. fig. v/i. (irr. schreiten, sep., -ge-, sein) step in, inter-
pose, intervene; take action (gegen
against); 2. ⚓ n (-s/no pl.) intervention.

'ein|schrumpfen v/i. (sep., -ge-,
sein) shrink; '~schüchtern v/t.
(sep., -ge-, h) intimidate; bully;
'⚓schüchterung f (-/-en) intimidation; '~schulen v/t. (sep., -ge-, h)
put to school.

'Einschuß m bullet-hole; ✝ invested
capital.

'ein|segnen v/t. (sep., -ge-, h) con-
secrate; confirm (children); '⚓seg-
nung f consecration; confirmation.

'einsehen 1. v/t. (irr. sehen, sep.,
-ge-, h) look into; fig.: see, com-
prehend; realize; 2. ⚓ n (-s/no pl.):
ein ~ haben show consideration.

'einseifen v/t. (sep., -ge-, h) soap;
lather (beard); F fig. humbug (s.o.).

'einseitig adj. ['aɪnzaɪtɪç] one-sided;
⚕, pol., ⚖ unilateral.

'einsend|en v/t. (irr. senden], sep.,
-ge-, h) send in; '⚓er m (-s/-)
sender; contributor (to a paper).

'einsetz|en (sep., -ge-, h) 1. v/t. set
or put in; stake (money); insert;
institute; instal(l), appoint (s.o.);
fig. use, employ; risk (one's life);
sich ~ für stand up for; 2. v/i. fever,
flood, weather: set in; ♪ strike in;
'⚓ung f (-/-en) insertion; appointment, installation.

'Einsicht f (-/-en) inspection; fig.
insight, understanding; judicious-
ness; '⚓ig adj. judicious; sensible.

'einsickern v/i. (sep., -ge-, sein)
soak in; infiltrate.

'Einsiedler m hermit.

'einsilbig adj. ['aɪnzɪlbɪç] monosyl-
labic; fig. taciturn; '⚓keit f (-/no
pl.) taciturnity.

'einsinken v/i. (irr. sinken, sep.,
-ge-, sein) sink (in).

Einspänn|er ['aɪnʃpɛnər] m (-s/-)
one-horse carriage; '⚓ig adj. one-
horse.

'ein|sparen v/t. (sep., -ge-, h) save,
economize; '~sperren v/t. (sep.,
-ge-, h) imprison; lock up, confine;
'~springen v/i. (irr. springen, sep.,
-ge-, sein) ⊕ catch; fig. step in,

help out; für j-n ~ substitute for
s.o.; '~spritzen v/t. (sep., -ge-, h)
inject; '⚓spritzung f (-/-en) injection.

'Einspruch m objection, protest,
veto; appeal; '~srecht n veto.

'einspurig adj. single-track.

einst adv. [aɪnst] once; one or some
day.

'Einstand m entry; tennis: deuce.

'ein|stecken v/t. (sep., -ge-, h) put
in; pocket; plug in; '~steigen v/i.
(irr. steigen, sep., -ge-, sein) get in;
~! 🚂 take your seats!, Am. all
aboard!

'einstell|en v/t. (sep., -ge-, h) put in;
⚔ enrol(l), enlist, Am. muster in;
engage, employ, Am. a. hire; give
up; stop, cease, Am. a. quit (payment, etc.); adjust (mechanism) (auf
acc. to); tune in (radio) (to); opt.,
focus (on) (a. fig.); die Arbeit ~ cease
working; strike, Am. a. walk out;
sich ~ appear; sich ~ auf (acc.) be
prepared for; adapt o.s. to; '⚓ung f
⚔ enlistment; engagement; ad-
justment; focus; (mental) attitude,
mentality.

'einstimm|en ♪ v/i. (sep., -ge-, h)
join in; '~ig adj. unanimous; '⚓ig-
keit f (-/no pl.) unanimity.

'einstöckig adj. ['aɪnʃtœkɪç] one-
storied.

'ein|streuen fig. v/t. (sep., -ge-, h)
intersperse; '~studieren v/t. (sep.,
no -ge-, h) study; thea. rehearse;
'~stürmen v/i. (sep., -ge-, sein):
auf j-n ~ rush at s.o.; '⚓sturz m
falling in, collapse; '~stürzen v/i.
(sep., -ge-, sein) fall in, collapse.

einst|weilen adv. ['aɪnst'vaɪlən] for
the present; in the meantime;
'~weilig adj. temporary.

'ein|tauschen v/t. (sep., -ge-, h)
exchange (gegen for); '~teilen v/t.
(sep., -ge-, h) divide (in acc. into);
classify; '~teilig adj. one-piece;
'⚓teilung f division; classification.

eintönig adj. ['aɪntø:nɪç] monoton-
ous; '⚓keit f (-/✎, -en) monotony.

'Eintopf(gericht n) m hot-pot;
stew.

'Eintracht f (-/no pl.) harmony,
concord.

einträchtig adj. ['aɪntrɛçtɪç] har-
monious.

'eintragen v/t. (irr. tragen, sep.,
-ge-, h) enter; register; bring in,

yield (*profit*); sich ~ in (*acc.*) sign.

einträglich *adj.* ['aɪntrɛːkliç] profitable.

'**Eintragung** *f* (-/-en) entry; registration.

'**ein|treffen** *v/i.* (*irr.* treffen, *sep.*, -ge-, *sein*) arrive; happen; come true; '~treiben *v/t.* (*irr.* treiben, *sep.*, -ge-, *h*) drive in *or* home; collect (*debts, taxes*); '~treten (*irr.* treten, *sep.*, -ge-) **1.** *v/i.* (*sein*) enter; occur, happen, take place; ~ für stand up for; ~ in (*acc.*) enter into (*rights*); enter upon (*possession*); enter (*room*); join (*the army, etc.*); **2.** *v/t.* (*h*) kick in (*door*); sich et. ~ run s.th. into one's foot.

'**Eintritt** *m* entry, entrance; admittance; beginning, setting-in (*of winter, etc.*); ~ frei! admission free!; ~ verboten! no admittance!; '~sgeld *n* entrance *or* admission fee; *sports*: gate money; '~skarte *f* admission ticket.

'**ein|trocknen** *v/i.* (*sep.*, -ge-, *sein*) dry (up); '~trüben *v/refl.* (*sep.*, -ge-, *h*) become cloudy *or* overcast; ~üben [aɪn⁹-] *v/t.* (*sep.*, -ge-, *h*) practi|se, *Am.* -ce *s.th.*; train *s.o.*

einver|leiben ['aɪnfɛrlaɪbən] *v/t.* ([*sep.*,] *no* -ge-, *h*) incorporate (*dat.* in); annex (to); F sich et. ~ eat *or* drink s.th.; '2nehmen *n* (-s/*no pl.*) agreement, understanding; in gutem ~ on friendly terms; '~standen *adj.*: ~ sein agree; '2ständnis *n* agreement.

'**Einwand** *m* (-[e]s/⸚e) objection (gegen to).

'**Einwander|er** *m* immigrant; '2n *v/i.* (*sep.*, -ge-, *sein*) immigrate; '~ung *f* immigration.

'**einwandfrei** *adj.* unobjectionable; perfect; faultless; *alibi*: sound.

einwärts *adv.* ['aɪnvɛrts] inward(s).

'**Einwegflasche** *f* one-way bottle, non-return bottle.

'**einweih|en** *v/t.* (*sep.*, -ge-, *h*) *eccl.* consecrate; inaugurate; ~ in (*acc.*) initiate *s.o.* into; '~ung *f* (-/-en) consecration; inauguration; initiation.

'**einwend|en** *v/t.* ([*irr.* wenden], *sep.*, -ge-, *h*) object; '2ung *f* objection.

'**einwerfen** (*irr.* werfen, *sep.*, -ge-, *h*) **1.** *v/t.* throw in (*a. fig.*); smash, break (*window-pane*); post, *Am.*

mail (*letter*); interject (*remark*); **2.** *v/i. football*: throw in.

'**einwickel|n** *v/t.* (*sep.*, -ge-, *h*) wrap (up), envelop; '2papier *n* wrapping-paper.

einwillig|en ['aɪnvɪligən] *v/i.* (*sep.*, -ge-, *h*) consent, agree (*in acc.* to); '2ung *f* (-/-en) consent, agreement.

'**einwirk|en** *v/i.* (*sep.*, -ge-, *h*): ~ auf (*acc.*) act (up)on; influence; effect; '2ung *f* influence; effect.

Einwohner ['aɪnvoːnər] *m* (-s/-), '~in *f* (-/-nen) inhabitant; resident.

'**Einwurf** *m* throwing in; *football*: throw-in; *fig.* objection; slit (*for letters, etc.*); slot (*for coins*).

'**Einzahl** *gr. f* (-/⸚-*no pl.*) singular (number); '2en *v/t.* (*sep.*, -ge-, *h*) pay in; '~ung *f* payment; deposit (*at bank*).

einzäunen ['aɪntsɔynən] *v/t.* (*sep.*, -ge-, *h*) fence in.

Einzel ['aɪntsəl] *n* (-s/-) *tennis*: single, *Am.* singles *pl.*; ~gänger ['~gɛŋər] *m* (-s/-) outsider; F lone wolf; '~handel † *m* retail trade; '~händler † *m* retailer, retail dealer; '~heit *f* (-/-en) detail, item; *en pl.* particulars *pl.*, details *pl.*; '2n **1.** *adj.* single; particular; individual; separate; *of shoes, etc.*: odd; *im ~en* in detail; **2.** *adv.*: ~ angeben *or* aufführen specify, *esp. Am.* itemize; '~nè *m* (-n/-n) *the* individual; '~verkauf *m* retail sale; '~wesen *n* individual.

'**einziehen** (*irr.* ziehen, *sep.*, -ge-) **1.** *v/t.* (*h*) draw in; *esp.* ⊕ retract; ✗ call up, *Am.* draft, induct; ⚖ seize, confiscate; make (*inquiries*) (*über acc.* on, about); **2.** *v/i.* (*sein*) enter; move in; *liquid*: soak in; ~ in (*acc.*) move into (*flat, etc.*).

einzig *adj.* ['aɪntsɪç] only; single; sole; unique; '~artig *adj.* unique, singular.

'**Einzug** *m* entry, entrance; moving in.

'**einzwängen** *v/t.* (*sep.*, -ge-, *h*) squeeze, jam.

Eis [aɪs] *n* (-es/*no pl.*) ice; ice-cream; '~bahn *f* skating-rink; '~bär *zo. m* polar bear; '~bein *n* pickled pork shank; '~berg *m* iceberg; '~decke *f* sheet of ice; '~diele *f* ice-cream parlo(u)r.

Eisen ['aɪzən] *n* (-s/-) iron.

'**Eisenbahn** *f* railway, *Am.* railroad;

Embryo

mit der ~ by rail, by train; '~**er** *m* (-s/-) railwayman; '~**fahrt** *f* railway journey; '~**knotenpunkt** *m* (railway) junction; '~**unglück** *n* railway accident; '~**wagen** *m* railway carriage, *Am.* railroad car; coach.

'**Eisen|blech** *n* sheet-iron; '~**erz** *n* iron-ore; '~**gießerei** *f* iron-foundry; '2**haltig** *adj.* ferruginous; '~**hütte** *f* ironworks *sg.*, *pl.*; '~**waren** *f/pl.* ironmongery, *esp. Am.* hardware; '~**warenhändler** *m* ironmonger, *esp. Am.* hardware dealer.

eisern *adj.* ['aɪzərn] iron, of iron.

'**Eis|gang** *n* breaking up of the ice; ice-drift; '2**gekühlt** *adj.* ['~gəky:lt] iced; '2**grau** *adj.* hoary; '~**hockey** *n* ice-hockey; '2**ig** *adj.* ['aɪzɪç] icy; '2'**kalt** *adj.* icy (cold); '~**kunstlauf** *m* figure-skating; '~**lauf** *m*, '~**laufen** *n* (-s/*no pl.*) skating; skate; '~**läufer** *m* skater; '~**meer** *n* polar sea; '~**schnellauf** *m* speed-skating; '~**scholle** *f* ice-floe; '~**schrank** *m* s. *Kühlschrank*; '~**vogel** *orn. m* kingfisher; '~**zapfen** *m* icicle; '~**zeit** *geol. f* ice-age.

eitel *adj.* ['aɪtəl] vain (*auf acc.* of); conceited; mere; '2**keit** *f* (-/-en) vanity.

Eiter *s* ['aɪtər] *m* (-s/*no pl.*) matter, pus; '~**beule** *s f* abscess; '2**ig** *s adj.* purulent; '2**n** *s v/i.* (ge-, h) fester, suppurate; '~**ung** *s f* (-/-en) suppuration.

eitrig *s adj.* ['aɪtrɪç] purulent.

'**Eiweiß** *n* (-es/-e) white of egg; *m* albumen; '2**haltig** *m adj.* albuminous.

'**Eizelle** *f* egg-cell, ovum.

Ekel ['e:kəl] 1. *m* (-s/*no pl.*) disgust (*vor dat.* at), loathing; aversion; *s* nausea; 2. F *n* (-s/-) nasty person; '2**erregend** *adj.* nauseating, sickening; '2**haft** *adj.*, '2**ig** *adj.* revolting; *fig.* disgusting; '2**n** *v/refl.* (ge-, h): *sich* ~ be nauseated (*vor dat.* at); *fig.* be or feel disgusted (at).

eklig *adj.* ['e:klɪç] s. *ekelhaft*.

elasti|sch *adj.* [e'lastiʃ] elastic; 2**zität** [~tsi'tɛ:t] *f* (-/*no pl.*) elasticity.

Elch *zo.* [ɛlç] *m* (-[e]s/-e) elk; moose.

Elefant *zo.* [ele'fant] *m* (-en/-en) elephant.

elegan|t *adj.* [ele'gant] elegant;

smart; 2**z** [~ts] *f* (-/*no pl.*) elegance.

elektrifizier|en [elɛktrifi'tsi:rən] *v/t.* (*no -ge-, h*) electrify; 2**ung** *f* (-/-en) electrification.

Elektri|ker [e'lɛktrikər] *m* (-s/-) electrician; 2**sch** *adj.* electric(al); 2**sieren** [~zi:rən] *v/t.* (*no -ge-, h*) electrify.

Elektrizität [elɛktritsi'tɛ:t] *f* (-/*no pl.*) electricity; ~**sgesellschaft** *f* electricity supply company; ~**s-werk** *n* (electric) power station, power-house, *Am.* power plant.

Elektrode [elɛk'tro:də] *f* (-/-n) electrode.

Elektro|gerät [e'lɛktro-] *n* electric appliance; ~**lyse** [~'ly:zə] *f* (-/-n) electrolysis.

Elektron *s* [e'lɛktrɔn] *n* (-s/-en) electron; ~**engehirn** [~'tro:nən-] *n* electronic brain; ~**ik** [~'tro:nik] *f* (-/*no pl.*) electronics *sg.*

Elektro|technik *f* electrical engineering; ~**er** *m* electrical engineer.

Element [ele'mɛnt] *n* (-[e]s/-e) element.

elementar *adj.* [elemɛn'ta:r] elementary; 2**schule** elementary *or* primary school, *Am.* grade school.

Elend ['e:lɛnt] 1. *n* (-[e]s/*no pl.*) misery; need, distress; 2. 2 *adj.* miserable, wretched; needy, distressed; '~**sviertel** *n* slums *pl.*

elf[1] [ɛlf] 1. *adj.* eleven; 2. 2 *f* (-/-en) eleven (*a. sports*).

Elf[2] [~] *m* (-en/-en), ~**e** ['ɛlfə] *f* (-/-n) elf, fairy.

'**Elfenbein** *n* (-[e]s/~-e) ivory; '2**ern** *adj.* ivory.

Elf'meter *m* *football*: penalty kick; ~**marke** *f* penalty spot.

'**elfte** *adj.* eleventh.

Elite [e'li:tə] *f* (-/-n) élite.

'**Ellbogen** *anat. m* (-s/-) elbow.

Elle ['ɛlə] *f* (-/-n) yard; *anat.* ulna.

Elster *orn.* ['ɛlstər] *f* (-/-n) magpie.

elter|lich *adj.* ['ɛltərlɪç] parental; '2**n** *pl.* parents *pl.*; '~**nlos** *adj.* parentless, orphaned; '2**nteil** *m* parent. [(-/-n) enamel.)

Email [e'ma:j] *n* (-s/-s), ~**le** [~] *f*)

Emanzipation [emantsipa'tsjo:n] *f* (-/-en) emancipation.

Embargo [ɛm'bargo] *n* (-s/-s) embargo. [bolism.)

Embolie *s* [ɛmbo'li:] *f* (-/-n) em-)

Embryo *biol.* ['ɛmbryo] *m* (-s/-s, -nen) embryo.

Emigrant [emi'grant] *m* (-en/-en) emigrant.

empfahl [ɛm'pfɑːl] *pret. of* empfehlen.

Empfang [ɛm'pfaŋ] *m* (-[e]s/ᵁe) reception (*a. radio*); receipt (*of s.th.*); *nach or bei* ~ on receipt; '**2en** *v/t.* (*irr.* fangen, *no -ge-, h*) receive; welcome; conceive (*child*).

Empfänger [ɛm'pfɛŋər] *m* (-s/-) receiver, recipient; payee (*of money*); addressee (*of letter*); † consignee (*of goods*).

em'pfänglich *adj.* susceptible (*für* to); **2keit** *f* (-/*no pl.*) susceptibility.

Em'pfangs|dame *f* receptionist; ~**gerät** *n* receiver, receiving set; ~**schein** *m* receipt; ~**zimmer** *n* reception-room.

empfehl|en [ɛm'pfeːlən] *v/t.* (*irr., no -ge-, h*) recommend; commend; ~ *Sie mich* (*dat.*) please remember me to; ~**enswert** *adj.* (re)commendable; **2ung** *f* (-/-en) recommendation; compliments *pl.*

empfinden [ɛm'pfɪndən] *v/t.* (*irr.* finden, *no -ge-, h*) feel; perceive.

empfindlich *adj.* [ɛm'pfɪntlɪç] sensitive (*a. phot.*, ⚗); (*für, gegen* to); delicate; tender; *p.*: touchy, sensitive; *cold*: severe; *pain, loss, etc.*: grievous; *pain*: acute; **2keit** *f* (-/-en) sensitivity; sensibility; touchiness; delicacy.

empfindsam *adj.* [ɛm'pfɪntzaːm] sensitive; sentimental; **2keit** *f* (-/-en) sensitiveness; sentimentality.

Empfindung [ɛm'pfɪndʊŋ] *f* (-/-en) perception; sensation; sentiment; **2slos** *adj.* insensible; *esp. fig.* unfeeling; ~**svermögen** *n* faculty of perception.

empfohlen [ɛm'pfoːlən] *p.p. of* empfehlen. [wards.\]

empor *adv.* [ɛm'poːr] up, up-\]

empören [ɛm'pøːrən] *v/t.* (*no -ge-, h*) incense; shock; *sich* ~ revolt (*a. fig.*), rebel; grow furious (*über acc.* at); empört indignant, shocked (*both: über acc.* at).

em'por|kommen *v/i.* (*irr.* kommen, *sep., -ge-, sein*) rise (in the world); **2kömmling** [~kœmlɪŋ] *m* (-s/-e) upstart; ~**ragen** *v/i.* (*sep., -ge-, h*) tower, rise; ~**steigen** *v/i.* (*irr.* steigen, *sep., -ge-, sein*) rise, ascend.

Em'pörung *f* (-/-en) rebellion, revolt; indignation.

emsig *adj.* ['ɛmzɪç] busy, industrious, diligent; '**2keit** *f* (-/*no pl.*) busyness, industry, diligence.

Ende ['ɛndə] *n* (-s/-n) end; *am* ~ at *or* in the end; after all; eventually; *zu* ~ *gehen end*; expire; run short; '**2n** *v/i.* (*ge-, h*) end; cease, finish.

end|gültig *adj.* ['ɛntɡyltɪç] final, definitive; '~**lich** *adv.* finally, at last; ~**los** *adj.* ['~loːs] endless; '**2punkt** *m* final point; '**2runde** *f* *sports*: final; '**2station** 🚇 *f* terminus, *Am.* terminal; '**2summe** *f* (sum) total.

Endung *ling.* ['ɛndʊŋ] *f* (-/-en) ending, termination.

Endzweck ['ɛnt-] *m* ultimate object.

Energie [ɛnɛr'ɡiː] *f* (-/-n) energy; **2los** *adj.* lacking in energy.

e'nergisch *adj.* vigorous; energetic.

eng *adj.* [ɛŋ] narrow; *clothes*: tight; close; intimate; *im* ~*eren Sinne* strictly speaking.

engagieren [ãɡa'ʒiːrən] *v/t.* (*no -ge-, h*) engage, *Am. a.* hire.

Enge ['ɛŋə] *f* (-/-n) narrowness; *fig.* straits *pl.*

Engel ['ɛŋəl] *m* (-s/-) angel.

'**engherzig** *adj.* ungenerous, petty.

Engländer ['ɛŋlɛndər] *m* (-s/-) Englishman; *die* ~ *pl.* the English *pl.*; '~**in** *f* (-/-nen) Englishwoman.

englisch *adj.* ['ɛŋlɪʃ] English; British.

'**Engpaß** *m* defile, narrow pass, *Am. a.* notch; *fig.* bottle-neck.

en gros † *adv.* [ɑ̃'ɡroː] wholesale.

En'groshandel † *m* wholesale trade.

'**engstirnig** *adj.* narrow-minded.

Enkel ['ɛŋkəl] *m* (-s/-) grandchild; grandson; ~**in** *f* (-/-nen) granddaughter.

enorm *adj.* [e'nɔrm] enormous; F *fig.* tremendous.

Ensemble *thea.*, ♪ [ã'sãːbəl] *n* (-s/-s) ensemble; company.

entart|en [ɛnt'aːrtən] *v/i.* (*no -ge-, sein*) degenerate; **2ung** *f* (-/-en) degeneration.

entbehr|en [ɛnt'beːrən] *v/t.* (*no -ge-, h*) lack; miss; want; do without; ~**lich** *adj.* dispensable; superfluous; **2ung** *f* (-/-en) want, privation.

ent'bind|en (*irr.* binden, *no -ge-, h*)

1. *v/t.* dispense, release (*von* from); deliver (*of a child*); **2.** *v/i.* be confined; ♀ung *f* dispensation, release; delivery; ♀ungsheim *n* maternity hospital.

ent'blöß|en *v/t.* (*no -ge-*, h) bare, strip; uncover (*head*); ~t *adj.* bare.

ent'deck|en *v/t.* (*no -ge-*, h) discover; detect; disclose; ~er *m* (*-s/-*) discoverer; ♀ung *f* discovery.

Ente ['entə] *f* (*-/-n*) *orn.* duck; *false report:* F canard, hoax.

ent'ehr|en *v/t.* (*no -ge-*, h) dishono(u)r; ♀ung *f* degradation; rape.

ent'eign|en *v/t.* (*no -ge-*, h) expropriate; dispossess; ♀ung *f* expropriation; dispossession.

ent'erben *v/t.* (*no -ge-*, h) disinherit.

entern ['entərn] *v/t.* (*ge-*, h) board, grapple (*ship*).

ent'fachen *v/t.* (*no -ge-*, h) kindle; *fig. a.* rouse (*passions*); ~'fallen *v/i.* (*irr. fallen*, *no -ge-*, sein): *j-m* ~ escape s.o.; *fig.* slip s.o.'s memory; *auf j-n* ~ fall to s.o.'s share; *s. wegfallen*; ~'falten *v/t.* (*no -ge-*, h) unfold; *fig.*: develop; display; *sich* ~ unfold; *fig.* develop (*zu* into).

ent'fern|en *v/t.* (*no -ge-*, h) remove; *sich* ~ withdraw; ~t *adj.* distant, remote (*both a. fig.*); ♀ung *f* (*-/-en*) removal; distance; range; ♀ungsmesser *phot. m* (*-s/-*) range-finder.

ent'flammen (*no -ge-*) *v/t.* (h) and *v/i.* (sein) inflame; ~'fliehen *v/i.* (*irr. fliehen*, *no -ge-*, sein) flee, escape (*aus* or *dat.* from); ~'fremden *v/t.* (*no -ge-*, h) estrange; alienate (*j-m* from s.o.).

ent'führ|en *v/t.* (*no -ge-*, h) abduct, kidnap; run away with; ♀er *m* abductor, kidnap(p)er; ♀ung *f* abduction, kidnap(p)ing.

ent'gegen **1.** *prp.* (*dat.*) in opposition to, contrary to; against; **2.** *adv.* towards; ~gehen *v/i.* (*irr. gehen*, *sep.*, -ge-, sein) go to meet; ~gesetzt *adj.* opposite; *fig.* contrary; ~halten *v/t.* (*irr. halten*, *sep.*, -ge-, h) hold out; *fig.* object; ~kommen *v/i.* (*irr. kommen*, *sep.*, -ge-, sein) come to meet; *fig.* meet s.o.('s wishes) halfway; ♀kommen *n* (*-s/no pl.*) obligingness; ~kommend *adj.* obliging; ~nehmen *v/t.* (*irr. nehmen*, *sep.*, -ge-, h) accept, receive; ~sehen *v/i.* (*dat.*) (*irr. sehen*, *sep.*, -ge-, h) await; look forward to; ~setzen *v/t.* (*sep.*, -ge-, h) oppose; ~stehen *v/i.* (*irr. stehen*, *sep.*, -ge-, h) be opposed (*dat.* to); ~strecken *v/t.* (*sep.*, -ge-, h) hold or stretch out (*dat.* to); ~treten *v/i.* (*dat.*) (*irr. treten*, *sep.*, -ge-, sein) step up to *s.o.*; oppose; face (*danger*).

entgegn|en [ent'ge:gnən] *v/i.* (*no -ge-*, h) reply; return; retort; ♀ung *f* (*-/-en*) reply; retort.

ent'gehen *v/i.* (*irr. gehen*, *no -ge-*, sein) escape.

entgeistert *adj.* [ent'gaɪstərt] aghast, thunderstruck, flabbergasted.

Entgelt [ent'gelt] *n* (*-[e]s/no pl.*) recompense; ♀en *v/t.* (*irr. gelten*, *no -ge-*, h) atone or suffer or pay for.

ent'gleis|en [ent'glaɪzən] *v/i.* (*no -ge-*, sein) run off the rails, be derailed; *fig.* (make a) slip; ♀ung *f* (*-/-en*) derailment; *fig.* slip.

ent'gleiten *v/i.* (*irr. gleiten*, *no -ge-*, sein) slip (*dat.* from).

ent'halt|en *v/t.* (*irr. halten*, *no -ge-*, h) contain, hold, include; *sich* ~ (*gen.*) abstain or refrain from; ~sam *adj.* abstinent; ♀samkeit *f* (*-/no pl.*) abstinence; ♀ung *f* abstention.   [decapitate.]

ent'haupten *v/t.* (*no -ge-*, h) behead,

ent'hüll|en *v/t.* (*no -ge-*, h) uncover; unveil; *fig.* reveal, disclose; ♀ung *f* (*-/-en*) uncovering; unveiling; *fig.* revelation, disclosure.

Enthusias|mus [entuzi'asmus] *m* (*-/no pl.*) enthusiasm; ~t *m* (*-en/-en*) enthusiast; *film*, *sports:* F fan; ♀tisch *adj.* enthusiastic.

ent'kleiden *v/t.* and *v/refl.* (*no -ge-*, h) undress.

ent'kommen **1.** *v/i.* (*irr. kommen*, *no -ge-*, sein) escape (*j-m* s.o.; *aus* from), get away or off; **2.** ♀ *n* (*-s/no pl.*) escape.

entkräft|en [ent'kreftən] *v/t.* (*no -ge-*, h) weaken, debilitate; *fig.* refute; ♀ung *f* (*-/-en*) weakening; debility; *fig.* refutation.

ent'lad|en (*irr. laden*, *no -ge-*, h) unload; *esp.* ⚡ discharge; explode; *sich* ~ *esp.* ⚡ discharge; *gun:* go off; *anger:* vent itself; ♀ung *f* unloading; *esp.* ⚡ discharge; explosion.

ent'lang **1.** *prp.* (*dat.*; *acc.*) along; **2.** *adv.* along; *er geht die Straße* ~ he goes along the street.

ent'larven *v/t.* (*no -ge-*, h) unmask; *fig. a.* expose.

ent'lass|en *v/t.* (*irr. lassen, no -ge-,* *h*) dismiss, discharge; F give *s.o.* the sack, *Am. a.* fire; ℒung *f* (*-/-en*) dismissal, discharge; ℒungsgesuch *n* resignation.

ent'lasten *v/t.* (*no -ge-, h*) unburden; ⚖ exonerate, clear (*from suspicion*).

Ent'lastung *f* (*-/-en*) relief; discharge; exoneration; ⸗sstraße *f* by-pass (road); ⸗szeuge *m* witness for the defen|ce, *Am.* -se.

ent'|laufen *v/i.* (*irr. laufen, no -ge-,* *sein*) run away (*dat.* from); ⸗ledigen [⸗'le:digən] *v/refl.* (*gen.*) (*no -ge-, h*): rid o.s. of *s.th.*, get rid of *s.th.*; acquit o.s. of (*duty*); execute (*orders*); ⸗'leeren *v/t.* (*no -ge-, h*) empty. [of-the-way.\]

ent'legen *adj.* remote, distant, out-\]

ent'|lehnen *v/t.* (*no -ge-, h*) borrow (*dat. or aus* from); ⸗'locken *v/t.* (*no -ge-, h*) draw, elicit (*dat.* from); ⸗'lohnen *v/t.* (*no -ge-, h*) pay (off); ⸗'lüften *v/t.* (*no -ge-, h*) ventilate; ⸗militarisieren [⸗militari'zi:rən] *v/t.* (*no -ge-, h*) demilitarize; ⸗mutigen [⸗'mu:tigən] *v/t.* (*no -ge-, h*) discourage; ⸗'nehmen *v/t.* (*irr. nehmen, no -ge-, h*) take (*dat.* from); ⸗ *aus* (*with*)draw from; *fig.* gather or learn from; ⸗'rätseln *v/t.* (*no -ge-, h*) unriddle; ⸗'reißen *v/t.* (*irr. reißen, no -ge-, h*) snatch away (*dat.* from); ⸗'richten *v/t.* (*no -ge-, h*) pay; ⸗'rinnen *v/i.* (*irr. rinnen, no -ge-, sein*) escape (*dat.* from); ⸗'rollen *v/t.* (*no -ge-, h*) unroll; ⸗'rücken *v/t.* (*no -ge-, h*) remove (*dat.* from), carry off or away; ⸗'rückt *adj.* entranced; lost in thought.

ent'rüst|en *v/t.* (*no -ge-, h*) fill with indignation; *sich* ⸗ become angry or indignant (*über acc. at s.th.*, with *s.o.*); ⸗et *adj.* indignant (*über acc.* at *s.th.*, with *s.o.*); ℒung *f* indignation.

ent'sag|en *v/i.* (*no -ge-, h*) renounce, resign; ℒung *f* (*-/-en*) renunciation, resignation.

ent'schädig|en *v/t.* (*no -ge-, h*) indemnify, compensate; ℒung *f* indemnification, indemnity; compensation.

ent'scheid|en (*irr. scheiden, no -ge-,* *h*) **1.** *v/t.* decide; *sich* ⸗ question, *etc.*: be decided; *p.*: decide (*für for*; *gegen*

against; *über acc.* on); come to a decision; **2.** *v/i.* decide; ⸗end *adj.* decisive; crucial; ℒung *f* decision.

entschieden *adj.* [ent'ʃi:dən] decided; determined, resolute; ℒheit *f* (*-/no pl.*) determination.

ent'schließen *v/refl.* (*irr. schließen,* *no -ge-, h*) resolve, decide, determine (*zu on s.th.*; *zu inf.* to *inf.*), make up one's mind (*zu inf.* to *inf.*).

ent'schlossen *adj.* resolute, determined; ℒheit *f* (*-/no pl.*) resoluteness.

ent'schlüpfen *v/i.* (*no -ge-, sein*) escape, slip (*dat.* from).

Ent'schluß *m* resolution, resolve, decision, determination.

entschuldig|en [ent'ʃuldigən] *v/t.* (*no -ge-, h*) excuse; *sich* ⸗ apologize (*bei* to; *für* for); *sich* ⸗ *lassen* beg to be excused; ℒung *f* (*-/-en*) excuse; apology; *ich bitte* (*Sie*) *um* ⸗ I beg your pardon.

ent'senden *v/t.* (*irr. senden, no -ge-,* *h*) send off, dispatch; delegate, depute.

ent'setz|en **1.** *v/t.* (*no -ge-, h*) dismiss (*from a position*); ✗ relieve; frighten; *sich* ⸗ be terrified or shocked (*über acc.* at); **2.** ℒ *n* (*-/no pl.*) horror, fright; ⸗lich *adj.* horrible, dreadful, terrible, shocking.

ent'sinnen *v/refl.* (*gen.*) (*irr. sinnen,* *no -ge-, h*) remember or recall *s.o.*, *s.th.*

ent'spann|en *v/t.* (*no -ge-, h*) relax; unbend; *sich* ⸗ relax; *political situation:* ease; ℒung *f* relaxation; *pol.* détente.

ent'sprech|en *v/i.* (*irr. sprechen,* *no -ge-, h*) answer (*description, etc.*); correspond to; meet (*demand*); ⸗end *adj.* corresponding; appropriate; ℒung *f* (*-/-en*) equivalent.

ent'springen *v/i.* (*irr. springen, no* *-ge-, sein*) escape (*dat.* from); *river:* rise, *Am.* head; *s.* entstehen.

ent'stammen *v/i.* (*no -ge-, sein*) be descended from; come from or of, originate from.

ent'steh|en *v/i.* (*irr. stehen, no -ge-,* *sein*) arise, originate (*both: aus* from); ℒung *f* (*-/-en*) origin.

ent'stell|en *v/t.* (*no -ge-, h*) disfigure; deface, deform; distort; ℒung *f* disfigurement; distortion, misrepresentation.

ent'täusch|en *v/t.* (*no -ge-, h*) dis-

appoint; **2ung** f disappointment.
ent'thronen v/t. (no -ge-, h) dethrone.
entvölker|n [ɛnt'fœlkərn] v/t. (no -ge-, h) depopulate; **2ung** f (-/-en) depopulation.
ent'wachsen v/i. (irr. wachsen, no -ge-, sein) outgrow.
entwaffn|en [ɛnt'vafnən] v/t. (no -ge-, h) disarm; **2ung** f (-/-en) disarmament.
ent'warnen v/i. (no -ge-, h) civil defence: sound the all-clear (signal).
ent'wässer|n v/t. (no -ge-, h) drain; **2ung** f (-/-en) drainage; **♒** dehydration.
ent'weder cj.: ~ ... oder either ... or.
ent|'weichen v/i. (irr. weichen, no -ge-, sein) escape (aus from); ~'**weihen** v/t. (no -ge-, h) desecrate, profane; ~'**wenden** v/t. (no -ge-, h) pilfer, purloin (j-m et. s.th. from s.o.); ~'**werfen** v/t. (irr. werfen, no -ge-, h) draft, draw up (document); design; sketch, trace out, outline; plan.
ent'wert|en v/t. (no -ge-, h) depreciate, devaluate; cancel (stamp); **2ung** f depreciation, devaluation; cancellation.
ent'wickeln v/t. (no -ge-, h) develop (a. phot.); evolve; sich ~ develop.
Entwicklung [ɛnt'viklʊŋ] f (-/-en) development; evolution; ~**shilfe** f development aid.
ent|'wirren v/t. (no -ge-, h) disentangle, unravel; ~'**wischen** v/i. (no -ge-, sein) slip away, escape (j-m [from] s.o.; aus from); j-m ~ give s.o. the slip; ~**wöhnen** [~'vø:nən] v/t. (no -ge-, h) wean.
Ent'wurf m sketch; design; plan; draft.
ent|'wurzeln v/t. (no -ge-, h) uproot; ~'**ziehen** v/t. (irr. ziehen, no -ge-, h) deprive (j-m et. s.o.o of s.th.); withdraw (dat. from); sich ~ avoid, elude; evade (responsibility); ~'**ziffern** v/t. (no -ge-, h) decipher, make out; tel. decode.
ent'zücken 1. v/t. (no -ge-, h) charm, delight; 2. **2** n (-s/no pl.) delight, rapture(s pl.), transport(s pl.).   [ing.\
ent'zückend adj. delightful; charm-\
Ent'zug m (-[e]s/no pl.) withdrawal; cancellation (of licence); deprivation.

entzünd|bar adj. [ɛnt'tsʏntbɑːr] (in)flammable; ~**en** v/t. (no -ge-, h) inflame (a. ♒), kindle; sich ~ catch fire; **♒** become inflamed; **2ung** f **♒** inflammation.
ent'zwei adv. asunder, in two, to pieces; ~**en** v/t. (no -ge-, h) disunite, set at variance; sich ~ quarrel, fall out (both: mit with); ~**gehen** v/i. (irr. gehen, sep., -ge-, sein) break, go to pieces; **2ung** f (-/-en) disunion.
Enzian ♀ ['ɛntsjaːn] m (-s/-e) gentian.
Enzyklopädie [ɛntsyklopɛ'diː] f (-/-n) (en)cyclop(a)edia.
Epidemie ♒ [epide'miː] f (-/-n) epidemic (disease).
Epilog [epi'loːk] m (-s/-e) epilog(ue).
episch adj. ['eːpiʃ] epic.
Episode [epi'zoːdə] f (-/-n) episode.
Epoche [e'pɔxə] f (-/-n) epoch.
Epos ['eːpɔs] n (-/Epen) epic (poem).
er pers. pron. [eːr] he.
erachten [ɛr'-] 1. v/t. (no -ge-, h) consider, think, deem; 2. **2** n (-s/no pl.) opinion; m-s ~s in my opinion.
erbarmen [ɛr'barmən] 1. v/refl. (gen.) (no -ge-, h) pity or commiserate s.o.; 2. **2** n (-s/no pl.) pity, compassion, commiseration; mercy; ~**swert** adj. pitiable.
erbärmlich adj. [ɛr'bɛrmliç] pitiful, pitiable; miserable; behaviour: mean.
erbarmungslos adj. pitiless, merciless, relentless.
er'bau|en v/t. (no -ge-, h) build (up), construct, raise; fig. edify; **2er** m (-s/-) builder; constructor; ~**lich** adj. edifying; **2ung** fig. f (-/-en) edification, Am. uplift.
Erbe ['ɛrbə] 1. m (-n/-n) heir; 2. n (-s/no pl.) inheritance, heritage.
er'beben v/i. (no -ge-, sein) tremble, shake, quake.
'erben v/t. (ge-, h) inherit.
er'beuten v/t. (no -ge-, h) capture.
er'bieten v/refl. (irr. bieten, no -ge-, h) offer, volunteer.
'Erbin f (-/-nen) heiress.
er'bitten v/t. (irr. bitten, no -ge-, h) beg or ask for, request, solicit.
er'bitter|n v/t. (no -ge-, h) embitter, exasperate; **2ung** f (-/♒ -en) bitterness, exasperation.
Erbkrankheit ♒ ['ɛrp-] f hereditary disease.

erblassen [ɛr'blasən] v/i. (no -ge-, sein) grow or turn pale, lose colo(u)r.

Erblasser [ˈɛrplasər] m (-s/-) testator; '**~in** f (-/-nen) testatrix.

er'bleichen v/i. (no -ge-, sein) s. erblassen.

erblich adj. [ˈɛrpliç] hereditary; **2keit** physiol. f (-/no pl.) heredity.

er'blicken v/t. (no -ge-, h) perceive, see; catch sight of.

erblind|en [ɛr'blindən] v/i. (no -ge-, sein) grow blind; **2ung** f (-/-en) loss of sight.

er'brechen 1. v/t. (irr. brechen, no -ge-, h) break or force open; vomit; sich ~ ✻ vomit; **2.** 2 n (-s/no pl.) vomiting.

Erbschaft [ˈɛrpʃaft] f (-/-en) inheritance, heritage.

Erbs|e ♀ [ˈɛrpsə] f (-/-n) pea; '**~nbrei** m pease-pudding, Am. pea purée; '**~nsuppe** f pea-soup.

Erb|stück [ˈɛrp-] n heirloom; '**~sünde** f original sin; '**~teil** n (portion of an) inheritance.

Erd|arbeiter [ˈeːrt-] m digger, navvy; '**~ball** m globe; '**~beben** n (-s/-) earthquake; '**~beere** ♀ f strawberry; '**~boden** m earth; ground, soil; **~e** [ˈeːrdə] f (-/✻ -n) earth; ground; soil; world; '**2en** ⚡ v/t. (ge-, h) earth, ground.

er'denklich adj. imaginable.

Erdgeschoß [ˈeːrt-] n ground-floor, Am. first floor.

er'dicht|en v/t. (no -ge-, h) invent, feign; **~et** adj. fictitious.

erdig adj. [ˈeːrdiç] earthy.

Erd|karte [ˈeːrt-] f map of the earth; '**~kreis** m earth, world; '**~kugel** f globe; '**~kunde** f geography; '**~leitung** ⚡ f earth-connexion, earth-wire, Am. ground wire; '**~nuß** f peanut; '**~öl** n mineral oil, petroleum.

er'dolchen v/t. (no -ge-, h) stab (with a dagger).

Erdreich [ˈeːrt-] n ground, earth.

er'dreisten v/refl. (no -ge-, h) dare, presume.

er'drosseln v/t. (no -ge-, h) strangle, throttle.

er'drücken v/t. (no -ge-, h) squeeze or crush to death; '**~d** fig. adj. overwhelming.

Erd|rutsch [ˈeːrt-] m landslip; landslide (a. pol.); '**~schicht** f layer of earth, stratum; '**~teil** m

part of the world; geogr. continent.

er'dulden v/t. (no -ge-, h) suffer, endure.

er'eifern v/refl. (no -ge-, h) get excited, fly into a passion.

er'eignen v/refl. (no -ge-, h) happen, come to pass, occur.

Ereignis [ɛr'aiknis] n (-ses/-se) event, occurrence; **2reich** adj. eventful.

Eremit [ere'miːt] m (-en/-en) hermit, anchorite.

ererbt adj. [ɛr'ɛrpt] inherited.

er'fahr|en 1. v/t. (irr. fahren, no -ge-, h) learn; hear; experience; **2.** adj. experienced, expert, skil(l)ful; **2ung** f (-/-en) experience; practice; skill.

er'fassen v/t. (no -ge-, h) grasp (a. fig.), seize, catch; cover; register, record.

er'find|en v/t. (irr. finden, no -ge-, h) invent; **2er** m inventor; **~erisch** adj. inventive; **2ung** f (-/-en) invention.

Erfolg [ɛr'folk] m (-[e]s/-e) success; result; **2en** [~gən] v/i. (no -ge-, sein) ensue, follow; happen; **2los** adj. [~k-] unsuccessful; vain; **2reich** adj. [~k-] successful.

er'forder|lich adj. necessary, required; **~n** v/t. (no -ge-, h) require, demand; **2nis** n (-ses/-se) requirement, demand, exigence, exigency.

er'forsch|en v/t. (no -ge-, h) inquire into, investigate; explore (country); **2er** m investigator; explorer; **2ung** f investigation; exploration.

er'freu|en v/t. (no -ge-, h) please; delight; gratify; rejoice; sich e-r Sache ~ enjoy s.th.; **~lich** adj. delightful, pleasing, pleasant, gratifying.

er'frier|en v/i. (irr. frieren, no -ge-, sein) freeze to death; **2ung** f (-/-en) frost-bite.

er'frisch|en v/t. (no -ge-, h) refresh; **2ung** f (-/-en) refreshment.

er'froren adj. limb: frost-bitten.

er'füll|en v/t. (no -ge-, h) fill; fig. fulfil(l); perform (mission); comply with (s.o.'s wishes); meet (requirements); **2ung** f fulfil(l)ment; performance; compliance; **2ungsort** ✝, ⚖ [ɛr'fylʊŋs?-] m place of performance (of contract).

ergänz|en [ɛr'gɛntsən] v/t. (no -ge-,

h) complete, complement; supplement; replenish (*stores, etc.*); **~end** *adj.* complementary, supplementary; **2ung** *f* (-/-en) completion; supplement; replenishment; *gr.* complement; **2ungsband** *m* (-[e]s/=e) supplementary volume.

er'geben 1. *v/t.* (*irr.* geben, *no* -ge-, *h*) yield, give; prove; *sich ~* surrender; *difficulties:* arise; devote o.s. to *s.th.*; *sich ~ aus* result from; *sich ~ in* (*acc.*) resign o.s. to; **2.** *adj.* devoted (*dat.* to); **~st** *adv.* respectfully; **2heit** *f* (-/no *pl.*) devotion.

Ergeb|nis [ɛr'geːpnɪs] *n* (-ses/-se) result, outcome; *sports:* score; **~ung** [~bʊŋ] *f* (-/-en) resignation; ⚔ surrender.

er'gehen *v/i.* (*irr.* gehen, *no* -ge-, *sein*) be issued; *~ lassen* issue, publish; *über sich ~ lassen* suffer, submit to; *wie ist es ihm ergangen?* how did he come off?; *sich ~ in* (*dat.*) indulge in. [rich.\

ergiebig *adj.* [ɛr'giːbɪç] productive.\

er'gießen *v/refl.* (*irr.* gießen, *no* -ge-, *h*) flow (*in acc.* into; *über acc.* over).

er'götz|en 1. *v/t.* (*no* -ge-, *h*) delight; *sich ~ an* (*dat.*) delight in; **2. 2** *n* (-s/no *pl.*) delight; **~lich** *adj.* delightful.

er'greif|en *v/t.* (*irr.* greifen, *no* -ge-, *h*) seize; grasp; take (*possession, s.o.'s part, measures, etc.*); take to (*flight*); take up (*profession, pen, arms*); *fig.* move, affect, touch; **2ung** *f* (-/⚘ -en) seizure.

Er'griffenheit *f* (-/no *pl.*) emotion.

er'gründen *v/t.* (*no* -ge-, *h*) fathom; *fig.* penetrate, get to the bottom of.

Er'guß *m* outpouring; effusion.

er'haben *adj.* elevated; *fig.* exalted, sublime; *~ sein über* (*acc.*) be above; **2heit** *f* (-/⚘ -en) elevation; *fig.* sublimity.

er'halt|en 1. *v/t.* (*irr.* halten, *no* -ge-, *h*) get; obtain; receive; preserve, keep; support, maintain; *sich ~ von* subsist on; **2.** *adj.:* *gut ~* in good repair *or* condition; **2ung** *f* preservation; maintenance. [able.\

erhältlich *adj.* [ɛr'hɛltlɪç] obtain-\

er'|härten *v/t.* (*no* -ge-, *h*) hang; **~'härten** *v/t.* (*no* -ge-, *h*) harden; *fig.* confirm; **~'haschen** *v/t.* (*no* -ge-, *h*) snatch, catch.

er'heb|en *v/t.* (*irr.* heben, *no* -ge-, *h*) lift, raise; elevate; exalt; levy, raise, collect (*taxes, etc.*); *Klage ~* bring an action; *sich ~* rise; *question, etc.:* arise; **~end** *fig. adj.* elevating; **~lich** *adj.* [~p-] considerable; **2ung** [~bʊŋ] *f* (-/-en) elevation; levy (*of taxes*); revolt; rising ground.

er'|heitern *v/t.* (*no* -ge-, *h*) cheer up, amuse; **~'hellen** *v/t.* (*no* -ge-, *h*) light up; *fig.* clear up; **~'hitzen** *v/t.* (*no* -ge-, *h*) heat; *sich ~* get *or* grow hot; **~'hoffen** *v/t.* (*no* -ge-, *h*) hope for.

er'höh|en *v/t.* (*no* -ge-, *h*) raise; increase; **2ung** *f* (-/-en) elevation; rise (*in prices, wages*); advance (*in prices*); increase.

er'hol|en *v/refl.* (*no* -ge-, *h*) recover; (take a) rest, relax; **2ung** *f* (-/-en) recovery; recreation; relaxation; **2ungsurlaub** [ɛr'hoːluŋs-] *m* holiday, *Am.* vacation; recreation leave; ⚕ convalescent leave, sick-leave. [(request.)\

er'hören *v/t.* (*no* -ge-, *h*) hear; grant\

erinner|n [ɛr'ɪnərn] *v/t.* (*no* -ge-, *h*): *j-n ~ an* (*acc.*) remind s.o. of; *sich ~* (*gen.*), *sich ~ an* (*acc.*) remember s.o. *or* s.th., recollect s.th.; **2ung** *f* (-/-en) remembrance; recollection; reminder; **~en** *pl.* reminiscences *pl.*

er'kalten *v/i.* (*no* -ge-, *sein*) cool down (*a. fig.*), get cold.

erkält|en [ɛr'kɛltən] *v/refl.* (*no* -ge-, *h*): *sich (sehr) ~* catch (a bad) cold; **2ung** *f* (-/-en) cold.

er'kennen *v/t.* (*irr.* kennen, *no* -ge-, *h*) recognize (*an dat.* by); perceive, discern; realize.

er'kenntlich *adj.* perceptible; *sich ~ zeigen* show one's appreciation; **2keit** *f* (-/-en) gratitude; appreciation.

Er'kenntnis 1. *f* perception; realization; **2.** ⚖ *n* (-ses/-se) decision, sentence, finding.

Erker ['ɛrkər] *m* (-s/-) bay; **'~fenster** *n* bay-window.

er'klär|en *v/t.* (*no* -ge-, *h*) explain; account for; declare, state; *sich ~* declare (*für* for; *gegen* against); **~lich** *adj.* explainable, explicable; **~t** *adj.* professed, declared; **2ung** *f* explanation; declaration.

er'klingen *v/i.* (*irr.* klingen, *no* -ge-, *sein*) (re)sound, ring (out).

erkoren *adj.* [ɛr'koːrən] (s)elect, chosen.

er'krank|en v/i. (no -ge-, sein) fall ill, be taken ill (an dat. of, with); become affected; ♀**ung** f (-/-en) illness, sickness, falling ill.

er|'kühnen v/refl. (no -ge-, h) venture, presume, make bold (zu inf. to inf.); **~'kunden** v/t. (no -ge-, h) explore; ✕ reconnoit|re, Am. -er.

erkundig|en [ɛr'kundigən] v/refl. (no -ge-, h) inquire (über acc. after; nach after or for s.o.; about s.th.); ♀**ung** f (-/-en) inquiry.

er|'lahmen fig. v/i. (no -ge-, sein) grow weary, tire; slacken; interest: wane, flag; **~'langen** v/t. (no -ge-, h) obtain, get.

Er|laß [ɛr'las] m (Erlasses/Erlasse) dispensation, exemption; remission (of debt, penalty, etc.); edict, decree; ♀**'lassen** v/t. (irr. lassen, no -ge-, h) remit (debt, penalty, etc.); dispense (j-m et. s.o. from s.th.); issue (decree); enact (law).

erlauben [ɛr'laubən] v/t. (no -ge-, h) allow, permit; sich et. ~ indulge in s.th.; sich ~ zu inf. ✝ beg to inf.

Erlaubnis [ɛr'laupnis] f (-/no pl.) permission; authority; **~schein** m permit.

er|'läutern v/t. (no -ge-, h) explain, illustrate; comment (up)on; ♀**ung** f explanation, illustration; comment.

Erle ♀ ['ɛrlə] f (-/-n) alder.

er|'leben v/t. (no -ge-, h) (live to) see; experience; go through; ♀**nis** [~pnis] n (-ses/-se) experience; adventure.

erledig|en [ɛr'le:digən] v/t. (no -ge-, h) dispatch; execute; settle (matter); **~t** adj. [~çt] finished, settled; fig.: played out; F done for; F: du bist für mich ~ I am through with you; ♀**ung** [~gun] f (-/-en) dispatch; settlement.

er|'leichter|n v/t. (no -ge-, h) lighten (burden); fig.: make easy, facilitate; relieve; ♀**ung** f (-/-en) ease; relief; facilitation; **~en** pl. facilities pl.

er|'leiden v/t. (irr. leiden, no -ge-, h) suffer, endure; sustain (damage, loss); **~'lernen** v/t. (no -ge-, h) learn, acquire.

er'leucht|en v/t. (no -ge-, h) illuminate; fig. enlighten; ♀**ung** f (-/-en) illumination; fig. enlightenment.

er'liegen v/i. (irr. liegen, no -ge-, sein) succumb (dat. to). [true.]

erlogen adj. [ɛr'lo:gən] false, un-

Erlös [ɛr'løːs] m (-es/-e) proceeds pl.

erlosch [ɛr'lɔʃ] pret. of erlöschen; **~en 1.** p.p. of erlöschen; **2.** adj. extinct.

er'löschen v/i. (irr., no -ge-, sein) go out; fig. become extinct; contract: expire.

er'lös|en v/t. (no -ge-, h) redeem; deliver; ♀**er** m (-s/-) redeemer, deliverer; eccl. Redeemer, Saviour; ♀**ung** f redemption; deliverance.

ermächtig|en [ɛr'mɛçtigən] v/t. (no -ge-, h) authorize; ♀**ung** f (-/-en) authorization; authority; warrant.

er'mahn|en v/t. (no -ge-, h) admonish; ♀**ung** f admonition.

er'mangel|n v/i. (no -ge-, h) be wanting (gen. in); ♀**ung** f (-/no pl.): in ~ (gen.) in default of, for want of, failing.

er'mäßig|en v/t. (no -ge-, h) abate, reduce, cut (down); ♀**ung** f (-/-en) abatement, reduction.

er'matt|en (no -ge-) **1.** v/t. (h) fatigue, tire, exhaust; **2.** v/i. (sein) tire, grow weary; fig. slacken; ♀**ung** f (-/↙ -en) fatigue, exhaustion.

er'messen 1. v/t. (irr. messen, no -ge-, h) judge; **2.** ♀ n (-s/no pl.) judg(e)ment; discretion.

er'mitt|eln v/t. (no -ge-, h) ascertain, find out; 🕸 investigate; ♀(**e)lung** [~(ə)lun] f (-/-en) ascertainment; inquiry; 🕸 investigation.

er'möglichen v/t. (no -ge-, h) render or make possible.

er'mord|en v/t. (no -ge-, h) murder; assassinate; ♀**ung** f (-/-en) murder; assassination.

er'müd|en (no -ge-) **1.** v/t. (h) tire, fatigue; **2.** v/i. (sein) tire, get tired or fatigued; ♀**ung** f (-/↙ -en) fatigue, tiredness.

er'munter|n v/t. (no -ge-, h) rouse, encourage; animate; ♀**ung** f (-/-en) encouragement, animation.

ermutig|en [ɛr'mu:tigən] v/t. (no -ge-, h) encourage; ♀**ung** f (-/-en) encouragement.

er'nähr|en v/t. (no -ge-, h) nourish, feed; support; ♀**er** m (-s/-) breadwinner, supporter; ♀**ung** f (-/↙ -en) nourishment; support; physiol. nutrition.

er'nenn|en v/t. (irr. nennen, no -ge-, h) nominate, appoint; ♀**ung** f nomination, appointment.

er'neu|ern v/t. (no -ge-, h) renew,

renovate; revive; **Ꝗerung** f renewal, renovation; revival; **~t** adv. once more.

erniedrig|en [ɛrˈniːdriɡən] v/t. (no -ge-, h) degrade; humiliate, humble; **Ꝗung** f (-/-en) degradation; humiliation.

Ernst [ɛrnst] 1. m (-es/no pl.) seriousness; earnest(ness); gravity; im ~ in earnest; 2. Ꝗ adj. = **'Ꝗhaft** adj., **'Ꝗlich** adj. serious; earnest; grave.

Ernte [ˈɛrntə] f (-/-n) harvest; crop; **~'dankfest** n harvest festival; **'Ꝗn** v/t. (ge-, h) harvest, gather (in), reap (a. fig.).

er'nüchter|n v/t. (no -ge-, h) (make) sober; fig. disillusion; **Ꝗung** f (-/-en) sobering; fig. disillusionment.

Er'ober|er m (-s/-) conqueror; **Ꝗn** v/t. (no -ge-, h) conquer; **~ung** f (-/-en) conquest.

er'öffn|en v/t. (no -ge-, h) open; inaugurate; disclose (j-m et. s.th. to s.o.); notify; **Ꝗung** f opening; inauguration; disclosure.

erörter|n [ɛrˈʔœrtərn] v/t. (no -ge-, h) discuss; **Ꝗung** f (-/-en) discussion.

Erpel orn. [ˈɛrpəl] m (-s/-) drake.

erpicht adj. [ɛrˈpɪçt]: ~ auf (acc.) bent or intent or set or keen on.

er'press|en v/t. (no -ge-, h) extort (von from); blackmail; **Ꝗer** m (-s/-), **Ꝗerin** f (-/-nen) extort(ion)er; blackmailer; **Ꝗung** f (-/-en) extortion; blackmail.

er'proben v/t. (no -ge-, h) try, test.

erquick|en [ɛrˈkvɪkən] v/t. (no -ge-, h) refresh; **Ꝗung** f (-/-en) refreshment.

er|'raten v/t. (irr. raten, no -ge-, h) guess, find out; **~'rechnen** v/t. (no -ge-, h) calculate, compute, work out.

erreg|bar adj. [ɛrˈreːkbaːr] excitable; **~en** [~ɡən] v/t. (no -ge-, h) excite; cause; **Ꝗer** [~ɡər] m (-s/-) exciter (a. ⚡); ⚕ germ, virus; **Ꝗung** [~ɡʊŋ] f excitation; excitement.

er'reich|bar adj. attainable; within reach or call; **~en** v/t. (no -ge-, h) reach; fig. achieve, attain; catch (train); come up to (certain standard).

er'rett|en v/t. (no -ge-, h) rescue; **Ꝗung** f rescue.

er'richt|en v/t. (no -ge-, h) set up, erect; establish; **Ꝗung** f erection; establishment.

er|'ringen v/t. (irr. ringen, no -ge-, h) gain, obtain; achieve (success); **~'röten** v/i. (no -ge-, sein) blush.

Errungenschaft [ɛrˈrʊŋənʃaft] f (-/-en) acquisition; achievement.

Er'satz m (-es/no pl.) replacement; substitute; compensation, amends sg., damages pl.; indemnification; s. Ersatzmann, Ersatzmittel; ~ leisten make amends; **~mann** m substitute; **~mine** f refill (for pencil); **~mittel** n substitute, surrogate; **~reifen** mot. m spare tire, (Am. only) spare tire; **~teil** ⊕ n, m spare (part).

er'schaff|en v/t. (irr. schaffen, no -ge-, h) create; **Ꝗung** f (-/no pl.) creation.

er'schallen v/i. ([irr. schallen,] no -ge-, sein) (re)sound; ring.

er'schein|en 1. v/i. (irr. scheinen, no -ge-, sein) appear; 2. Ꝗ n (-s/no pl.) appearance; **Ꝗung** f (-/-en) appearance; apparition; vision.

er|'schießen v/t. (irr. schießen, no -ge-, h) shoot (dead); **~'schlaffen** v/i. (no -ge-, sein) tire; relax; fig. languish, slacken; **~'schlagen** v/t. (irr. schlagen, no -ge-, h) kill, slay; **~'schließen** v/t. (irr. schließen, no -ge-, h) open; open up (new market); develop (district).

er'schöpf|en v/t. (no -ge-, h) exhaust; **Ꝗung** f exhaustion.

erschrak [ɛrˈʃraːk] prét. of erschrecken 2.

er'schreck|en 1. v/t. (no -ge-, h) frighten, scare; 2. v/i. (irr., no -ge-, sein) be frightened (über acc. at); **~d** adj. alarming, startling.

erschrocken [ɛrˈʃrɔkən] 1. p.p. of erschrecken 2; 2. adj. frightened, terrified.

erschütter|n [ɛrˈʃʏtərn] v/t. (no -ge-, h) shake; fig. shock, move; **Ꝗung** f (-/-en) shock; fig. emotion; ⚕ concussion; ⊕ percussion.

er'schweren v/t. (no -ge-, h) make more difficult; aggravate.

er'schwing|en v/t. (irr. schwingen, no -ge-, h) afford; **~lich** adj. within s.o.'s means; prices: reasonable.

er|'sehen v/t. (irr. sehen, no -ge-, h) see, learn, gather (all: aus from); **~'sehnen** v/t. (no -ge-, h) long for; **~'setzen** v/t. (no -ge-, h) repair; make up for, compensate (for); replace; refund.

er'sichtlich *adj.* evident, obvious.

er'sinnen *v/t.* (*irr.* sinnen, *no* -ge-, h) contrive, devise.

er'spar|en *v/t.* (*no* -ge-, h) save; *j-m et.* ~ spare s.o. s.th.; **2nis** *f* (*-/-se*) saving.

er'sprießlich *adj.* useful, beneficial.

erst [e:rst] **1.** *adj.:* der (die, das) ~e the first; **2.** *adv.* first; at first; only; not ... till *or* until.

er'starr|en *v/i.* (*no* -ge-, sein) stiffen; solidify; congeal; set; grow numb; *fig. blood:* run cold; **~t** *adj.* benumbed; **2ung** *f* (*-/-en*) numbness; solidification; congealment; setting.

erstatt|en [ɛr'ʃtatən] *v/t.* (*no* -ge-, h) restore; *s. ersetzen; Bericht* ~ (make a) report; **2ung** *f* (*-/-en*) restitution.

'Erstaufführung *f thea.* first night *or* performance, premiere; *film:* a. first run.

er'staun|en 1. *v/i.* (*no* -ge-, sein) be astonished (*über acc.* at); **2.** *v/t.* (*no* -ge-, h) astonish; **3.** **2** *n* astonishment; *in* ~ setzen astonish; **~lich** *adj.* astonishing, amazing.

er'stechen *v/t.* (*irr.* stechen, *no* -ge-, h) stab.

er'steig|en *v/t.* (*irr.* steigen, *no* -ge-, h) ascend, climb; **2ung** *f* ascent.

erstens *adv.* ['e:rstəns] first, firstly.

er'stick|en (*no* -ge-) *v/t.* (h) *and v/i.* (sein) choke, suffocate; stifle; **2ung** *f* (*-/-en*) suffocation. [rate, F A 1.]

'erstklassig *adj.* first-class, first-]

er'streben *v/t.* (*no* -ge-, h) strive after *or* for; **~swert** *adj.* desirable.

er'strecken *v/refl.* (*no* -ge-, h) extend; *sich* ~ *über* (*acc.*) cover.

er'suchen 1. *v/t.* (*no* -ge-, h) request; **2.** **2** *n* (*-s/-*) request.

er'tappen *v/t.* (*no* -ge-, h) catch, surprise; *a. frisch;* **~tönen** *v/i.* (*no* -ge-, sein) (re)sound.

Ertrag [ɛr'traːk] *m* (*-[e]s/-̈e*) produce, yield; proceeds *pl.*, returns *pl.*; **⚒** output; **2en** [~gən] *v/t.* (*irr.* tragen, *no* -ge-, h) bear, endure; suffer; stand. [able.]

erträglich *adj.* [ɛr'trɛːklɪç] toler-]

er'tränken *v/t.* (*no* -ge-, h) drown; **~trinken** *v/i.* (*irr.* trinken, *no* -ge-, sein) be drowned, drown; **~übrigen** [ɛr'yːbrɪgən] *v/t.* (*no* -ge-, h) save; spare (*time*); *sich* ~ be unnecessary; **~wachen** *v/i.* (*no* -ge-, sein) awake, wake up.

er'wachsen 1. *v/i.* (*irr.* wachsen, *no* -ge-, sein) arise (*aus* from); **2.** *adj.* grown-up, adult; **2e** *m, f* (*-n/-n*) grown-up, adult.

er'wäg|en *v/t.* (*irr.* wägen, *no* -ge-, h) consider, think s.th. over; **2ung** *f* (*-/-en*) consideration.

er'wählen *v/t.* (*no* -ge-, h) choose, elect.

er'wähn|en *v/t.* (*no* -ge-, h) mention; **2ung** *f* (*-/-en*) mention.

er'wärmen *v/t.* (*no* -ge-, h) warm, heat; *sich* ~ warm (up).

er'wart|en *v/t.* (*no* -ge-, h) await, wait for; *fig.* expect; **2ung** *f* expectation.

er'wecken *v/t.* (*no* -ge-, h) wake, rouse; *fig.* awake; cause (*fear*); arouse (*suspicion*); **~wehren** *v/refl.* (*gen.*) (*no* -ge-, h) keep *or* ward off; **~weichen** *v/t.* (*no* -ge-, h) soften; *fig.* move; **~weisen** *v/t.* (*irr.* weisen, *no* -ge-, h) prove; show (*respect*); render (*service*); do, pay (*honour*); do (*favour*).

er'weiter|n *v/t. and v/refl.* (*no* -ge-, h) expand, enlarge, extend, widen; **2ung** *f* (*-/-en*) expansion, enlargement, extension.

Erwerb [ɛr'vɛrp] *m* (*-[e]s/-e*) acquisition; living; earnings *pl.*; business; **2en** [~bən] *v/t.* (*irr.* werben, *no* -ge-, h) acquire; gain; earn.

erwerbs|los *adj.* [ɛr'vɛrpsloːs] unemployed; **~tätig** *adj.* (gainfully) employed; **~unfähig** *adj.* [ɛr-'vɛrps?-] incapable of earning one's living; **2zweig** *m* line of business.

Erwerbung [ɛr'vɛrbʊŋ] *f* acquisition.

erwider|n [ɛr'viːdərn] *v/t.* (*no* -ge-, h) return; answer, reply; retort; **2ung** *f* (*-/-en*) return; answer, reply.

er'wischen *v/t.* (*no* -ge-, h) catch, trap, get hold of.

er'wünscht *adj.* desired; desirable; welcome.

er'würgen *v/t.* (*no* -ge-, h) strangle, throttle. [brass.]

Erz **⚒** [eːrts] *n* (*-es/-e*) ore; *poet.*]

er'zähl|en *v/t.* (*no* -ge-, h) tell; relate; narrate; **2er** *m*, **2erin** *f* (*-/-nen*) narrator; writer; **2ung** *f* narration; (short) story, narrative.

'Erz|bischof *eccl. m* archbishop; **~bistum** *eccl. n* archbishopric; **~engel** *eccl. m* archangel.

er'zeug|en v/t. (no -ge-, h) beget; produce; make, manufacture; 2**er** m (-s/-) father (of child); ⚙ producer; 2**nis** n produce; production; ⊕ product; 2**ung** f production.

'**Erz|feind** m arch-enemy; '**~herzog** m archduke; '**~herzogin** f archduchess; '**~herzogtum** n archduchy.

er'ziehe|n v/t. (irr. ziehen, no -ge-, h) bring up, rear, raise; educate; 2**r** m (-s/-) educator; teacher, tutor; 2**rin** f (-/-nen) teacher; governess; **~risch** adj. educational, pedagogic (-al).

Er'ziehung f (-/~ -en) upbringing; breeding; education; **~sanstalt** [ɛr'tsi:uŋs²-] f reformatory, approved school; **~swesen** n (-s/no pl.) educational matters pl. or system.

er'ziel|en v/t. (no -ge-, h) obtain; realize (price); achieve (success); sports: score (points, goal); **~'zürnen** v/t. (no -ge-, h) make angry, irritate, enrage; **~'zwingen** v/t. (irr. zwingen, no -ge-, h) (en)force; compel; extort (von from).

es pers. pron. [ɛs] 1. pers.: it, he, she; wo ist das Buch? — ~ ist auf dem Tisch where is the book? — it is on the table; das Mädchen blieb stehen, als ~ seine Mutter sah the girl stopped when she saw her mother; 2. impers.: it; ~ gibt there is, there are; ~ ist kalt it is cold; ~ klopft there is a knock at the door.

Esche ♣ ['ɛʃə] f (-/-n) ash(-tree).

Esel zo. ['e:zəl] m (-s/-) donkey; esp. fig. ass; ~**ei** [~'laɪ] f (-/-en) stupidity, stupid thing, folly; '**~sbrücke** f at school: crib, Am. pony; '**~sohr** ['e:zəls²-] n dog's ear (of book).

Eskorte [ɛs'kɔrtə] f (-/-n) ✕ escort; ⚓ convoy.

Espe ♣ ['ɛspə] f (-/-n) asp(en).

'**eßbar** adj. eatable, edible.

Esse ['ɛsə] f (-/-n) chimney.

essen ['ɛsən] 1. v/i. (irr. essen, -ge-, h) eat; zu Mittag ~ (have) lunch; dine, have dinner; zu Abend ~ dine, have dinner; esp. late at night: sup, have supper; auswärts ~ eat or dine out; 2. v/t. (irr. essen, -ge-, h) eat; et. zu Mittag etc. ~ have s.th. for lunch, etc.; 3. 2 n (-s/-) eating; food; meal; dish; midday meal: lunch, dinner; evening meal: dinner; last meal of the day:

supper; '2**szeit** f lunch-time; dinner-time; supper-time.

Essenz [ɛ'sɛnts] f (-/-en) essence.

Essig ['ɛsiç] m (-s/-e) vinegar; '**~gurke** f pickled cucumber, gherkin.

'**Eß|löffel** m soup-spoon; '**~nische** f dining alcove, Am. dinette; '**~tisch** m dining-table; '**~waren** f/pl. eatables pl., victuals pl., food; '**~zimmer** n dining-room.

etablieren [eta'bli:rən] v/t. (no -ge-, h) establish, set up.

Etage [e'ta:ʒə] f (-/-n) floor, stor(e)y; **~nwohnung** f flat, Am. a. apartment.

Etappe [e'tapə] f (-/-n) ✕ base; fig. stage, leg.

Etat [e'ta:] m (-s/-s) budget, parl. the Estimates pl.; **~sjahr** n fiscal year. [or sg.]

Ethik ['e:tik] f (-/~ -en) ethics pl.)

Etikett [eti'kɛt] n (-[e]s/-e, -s) label, ticket; tag; gummed: Am. a. sticker; **~e** f (-/-en) etiquette; 2**ieren** [~'ti:rən] v/t. (no -ge-, h) label, ticket.

etliche indef. pron. ['ɛtliçə] some, several.

Etui [e'tvi:] n (-s/-s) case.

etwa adv. ['ɛtva] perhaps, by chance; about, Am. a. around; **~ig** adj. ['~²iç] possible, eventual.

etwas ['ɛtvas] 1. indef. pron. something; anything; 2. adj. some; any; 3. adv. somewhat; 4. 2 n (-/-): das gewisse ~ that certain something.

euch pers. pron. [ɔʏç] you; ~ (selbst) yourselves.

euer poss. pron. ['ɔʏər] your; der (die, das) eu(e)re yours.

Eule orn. ['ɔʏlə] f (-/-n) owl; **~n** nach Athen tragen carry coals to Newcastle.

euresgleichen pron. ['ɔʏrəs'glaɪçən] people like you, F the likes of you.

Europä|er [ɔʏro'pɛ:ər] m (-s/-) European; 2**sch** adj. European.

Euter ['ɔʏtər] n (-s/-) udder.

evakuieren [evaku'i:rən] v/t. (no -ge-, h) evacuate.

evangeli|sch adj. [evaŋ'ge:liʃ] evangelic(al); Protestant; Lutheran; 2**um** [~jum] n (-s/Evangelien) gospel.

eventuell [eventu'ɛl] 1. adj. possible; 2. adv. possibly, perhaps.

ewig adj. ['e:viç] eternal, everlasting; perpetual; auf ~ for ever;

'**2keit** f (-/-en) eternity; F: *seit e-r ~* for ages.

exakt adj. [ɛ'ksakt] exact; **2heit** f (-/-en) exactitude, exactness; accuracy.

Exam|en [ɛ'ksaːmən] n (-s/-, Examina) examination, F exam; **2inieren** [~ami'niːrən] v/t. (no -ge-, h) examine.

Exekutive [ɛksəku'tiːvə] f (-/no pl.) executive power.

Exempel [ɛ'ksɛmpəl] n (-s/-) example, instance.

Exemplar [ɛksɛm'plaːr] n (-s/-e) specimen; copy (of book).

exerzier|en ✕ [ɛksɛr'tsiːrən] v/i. and v/t. (no -ge-, h) drill; **2platz** ✕ m drill-ground, parade-ground.

Exil [ɛ'ksiːl] n (-s/-e) exile.

Existenz [ɛksis'tɛnts] f (-/-en) existence; living, livelihood; **~minimum** n subsistence minimum.

exis'tieren v/i. (no -ge-, h) exist; subsist.

exotisch adj. [ɛ'ksoːtiʃ] exotic.

exped|ieren [ɛkspe'diːrən] v/t. (no -ge-, h) dispatch; **2ition** [~i'tsjoːn] f (-/-en) dispatch, forwarding; expedition; † dispatch or forwarding office.

Experiment [ɛksperi'mɛnt] n (-[e]s/-e) experiment; **2ieren** [~'tiːrən] v/i. (no -ge-, h) experiment.

explo|dieren [ɛksplo'diːrən] v/i. (no -ge-, sein) explode, burst; **2sion** [~'zjoːn] f (-/-en) explosion; **~siv** adj. [~'ziːf] explosive.

Export [ɛks'pɔrt] m (-[e]s/-e) export(ation); **2ieren** [~'tiːrən] v/t. (no -ge-, h) export.

extra adj. ['ɛkstra] extra; special; '**2blatt** n extra edition (of newspaper), Am. extra. [tract.]

Extrakt [ɛks'trakt] m (-[e]s/-e) ex-)

Extrem [ɛks'treːm] 1. n (-s/-e) extreme; 2. **2** adj. extreme.

Exzellenz [ɛkstse'lɛnts] f (-/-en) Excellency.

exzentrisch adj. [ɛks'tsɛntriʃ] eccentric.

Exzeß [ɛks'tsɛs] m (Exzesses/Exzesse) excess.

F

Fabel ['faːbəl] f (-/-n) fable (a. fig.); plot (of story, book, etc.); '**2haft** adj. fabulous; marvellous; '**2n** v/i. (ge-, h) tell (tall) stories.

Fabrik [fa'briːk] f (-/-en) factory, works sg., pl., mill; **~ant** [~i'kant] m (-en/-en) factory-owner, mill-owner; manufacturer; **~arbeit** f factory work; s. Fabrikware; **~arbeiter** m factory worker or hand; **~at** [~i'kaːt] n (-[e]s/-e) make; product; **~ationsfehler** [~a'tsjoːns-] m flaw; **~besitzer** m factory-owner; **~marke** f trade mark; **~stadt** f factory or industrial town; **~ware** f manufactured article; **~zeichen** n s. Fabrikmarke.

Fach [fax] n (-[e]s/⸚er) section, compartment, shelf (of bookcase, cupboard, etc.); pigeon-hole (in desk); drawer; fig. subject; s. Fachgebiet; '**~arbeiter** m skilled worker; '**~arzt** m specialist (für in); '**~ausbildung** f professional training; '**~ausdruck** m technical term.

fächeln ['fɛçəln] v/t. (ge-, h) fan s.o.

Fächer ['fɛçər] m (-s/-) fan; **2förmig** adj. ['~fœrmiç] fan-shaped.

'**Fach|gebiet** n branch, field, province; '**~kenntnisse** f/pl. specialized knowledge; '**~kreis** m: in ⸚en among experts; '**2kundig** adj. competent, expert; '**~literatur** f specialized literature; '**~mann** m expert; **2männisch** adj. ['~mɛniʃ] expert; '**~schule** f technical school; '**~werk** △ n framework.

Fackel ['fakəl] f (-/-n) torch; '**2n** F v/i. (ge-, h) hesitate, F shilly-shally; '**~zug** m torchlight procession.

fad adj. [faːt], **~e** adj. ['faːdə] food: insipid, tasteless; stale; p. dull, boring.

Faden ['faːdən] m (-s/⸚) thread (a. fig.); fig.: an e-m ~ hängen hang by a thread; '**~nudeln** f/pl. vermicelli pl.; '**2scheinig** adj. ['~ʃainiç] threadbare; excuse, etc.: flimsy, thin.

fähig adj. ['fɛːiç] capable (zu inf. of ger.; gen. of); able (to inf.); '**2keit** f (-/-en) (cap)ability; talent, faculty.

F

fahl adj. [fɑːl] pale, pallid; colour: faded; complexion: leaden, livid.

fahnd|en ['faːndən] v/i. (ge-, h): nach j-m ~ search for s.o.; '2ung f (-/-en) search.

Fahne ['faːnə] f (-/-n) flag; standard; banner; ♣, ✗, fig. colo(u)rs pl.; typ. galley-proof.

'**Fahnen|eid** m oath of allegiance; '~flucht f desertion; '2flüchtig adj.: ~ werden desert (the colo[u]rs); '~stange f flagstaff, Am. a. flagpole.

'**Fahr|bahn** f, '~damm m roadway.

Fähre ['fɛːrə] f (-/-n) ferry(-boat).

fahren ['faːrən] (irr., ge-) 1. v/i. (sein) driver, vehicle, etc.: drive, go, travel; cyclist: ride, cycle; ♣ sail; mot. motor; mit der Eisenbahn ~ go by train or rail; spazieren~ go for or take a drive; mit der Hand ~ über (acc.) pass one's hand over; ~ lassen let go or slip; gut (schlecht) ~ bei do or fare well (badly) at or with; er ist gut dabei gefahren he did very well out of it; 2. v/t. (h) carry, convey; drive (car, train, etc.); ride (bicycle, etc.).

'**Fahrer** m (-s/-) driver; '~flucht f (-/no pl.) hit-and-run offence, Am. hit-and-run offense.

'**Fahr|gast** m passenger; in taxi: fare; '~geld n fare; '~gelegenheit f transport facilities pl.; '~gestell n mot. chassis; ✈ undercarriage, landing gear; '~karte f ticket; '~kartenschalter m booking-office, Am. ticket office; '2lässig adj. careless, negligent; '~lässigkeit f (-/-en) carelessness, negligence; '~lehrer mot. m driving instructor; '~plan m timetable, Am. a. schedule; '2planmäßig 1. adj. regular, Am. scheduled; 2. adv. on time, Am. a. on schedule; '~preis m fare; '~rad n bicycle, F bike; '~schein m ticket; '~schule mot. f driving school, school of motoring; '~stuhl m lift, Am. elevator; '~stuhlführer m lift-boy, lift-man, Am. elevator operator; '~stunde mot. f driving lesson.

Fahrt [faːrt] f (-/-en) ride, drive; journey; voyage, passage; trip; ~ ins Blaue mystery tour; in voller ~ (at) full speed.

Fährte ['fɛːrtə] f (-/-n) track (a. fig.); auf der falschen ~ sein be on the wrong track.

'**Fahr|vorschrift** f rule of the road; '~wasser n ♣ navigable water; fig. track; '~weg m roadway; '~zeug n vehicle; ♣ vessel.

Fakt|or ['faktɔr] m (-s/-en) factor; ~otum [~'toːtʊm] n (-s/-s, Faktoten) factotum; ~ur † [~'tuːr] f (-/-en), ~ura † [~'tuːra] f (-/Fakturen) invoice.

Fakultät univ. [fakʊl'tɛːt] f (-/-en) faculty.

Falke orn. ['falkə] m (-n/-n) hawk, falcon.

Fall [fal] m (-[e]s/⸚e) fall (of body, stronghold, city, etc.); gr., ♫, ⚖ case; gesetzt den ~ suppose; auf alle Fälle at all events; auf jeden ~ in any case, at any rate; auf keinen ~ on no account, in no case.

Falle ['falə] f (-/-n) trap (a. fig.); pitfall (a. fig.); e-e ~ stellen set a trap (j-m for s.o.).

fallen ['falən] 1. v/i. (irr., ge-, sein) fall, drop; ✗ be killed in action; shot: be heard; flood water: subside; auf j-n ~ suspicion, etc.: fall on s.o.; ~ lassen drop (plate, etc.); 2. 2 n (-s/no pl.) fall(ing).

fällen ['fɛlən] v/t. (ge-, h) fell, cut down (tree); ✗ lower (bayonet); ♫ pass (judgement), give (decision).

fallenlassen v/t. (irr. lassen, sep., no -ge-, h) drop (plan, claim, etc.).

fällig adj. ['fɛliç] due; payable; '2keit f (-/⸚-en) maturity; '2keitstermin m date of maturity.

'**Fall|obst** n windfall; '~reep ♣ ['~reːp] n (-[e]s/-e) gangway.

falls cj. [fals] if; in the event of ger.; in case.

'**Fall|schirm** m parachute; '~schirmspringer m parachutist; '~strick m snare; '~tür f trap door.

falsch [falʃ] 1. adj. false; wrong; bank-note, etc.: counterfeit; money: base; bill of exchange, etc.: forged; p. deceitful; 2. adv.: ~ gehen watch: go wrong; ~ verbunden! teleph. sorry, wrong number.

fälsch|en ['fɛlʃən] v/t. (ge-, h) falsify; forge, fake (document, etc.); counterfeit (bank-note, coin, etc.); fake (calculations, etc.); tamper with (financial account); adulterate (food, wine); '2er m (-s/-) forger, faker; adulterator.

'**Falsch|geld** n counterfeit or bad or base money; '~heit f (-/-en) falseness, falsity; duplicity, deceitfulness; '~**meldung** f false report; '~**münzer** m (-s/-) coiner; '~**münzerwerkstatt** f coiner's den; 'Q**spielen** v/i. (sep., -ge-, h) cheat (at cards); '~**spieler** m cardsharper.

'**Fälschung** f (-/-en) forgery; falsification; fake; adulteration.

Falt|boot ['falt-] n folding canoe, Am. foldboat, faltboat; ~**e** ['~ə] f (-/-n) fold; pleat (in skirt, etc.); crease (in trousers); wrinkle (on face); 'Q**en** v/t. (ge-, h) fold; clasp or join (one's hands); 'Q**ig** adj. folded; pleated; wrinkled.

Falz [falts] m (-es/-e) fold; rabbet (for woodworking, etc.); bookbinding: guard; 'Q**en** v/t. (ge-, h) fold; rabbet. [informal.]

familiär adj. [famil'jε:r] familiar.]

Familie [fa'mi:ljə] f (-/-n) family (a. zo., ♀).

Fa'milien|angelegenheit f family affair; ~**anschluß** m: ~ haben live as one of the family; ~**nachrichten** f/pl. in newspaper: birth, marriage and death announcements pl.; ~**name** m family name, surname, Am. a. last name; ~**stand** m marital status.

Fanati|ker [fa'na:tikər] m (-s/-) fanatic; Q**sch** adj. fanatic(al).

Fanatismus [fana'tismus] m (-/no pl.) fanaticism.

fand [fant] pret. of finden.

Fanfare [fan'fɑ:rə] f (-/-n) fanfare, flourish (of trumpets).

Fang [faŋ] m (-[e]s/¨e) capture, catch(ing); hunt. bag; 'Q**en** v/t. (irr. ge-, h) catch (animal, ball, thief, etc.); '~**zahn** m fang (of dog, wolf, etc.); tusk (of boar).

Farb|band ['farp-] n (typewriter) ribbon; ~**e** ['~bə] f (-/-n) colo(u)r; paint; dye; complexion; cards: suit; Q**echt** adj. ['farp⁹-] colo(u)rfast.

färben ['fɛrbən] v/t. (ge-, h) colo(u)r (glass, food, etc.); dye (material, hair, Easter eggs, etc.); tint (hair, paper, glass); stain (wood, fabrics, glass, etc.); sich ~ take on or assume a colo(u)r; sich rot ~ turn or go red.

'**farben|blind** adj. colo(u)r-blind; 'Q**druck** m (-[e]s/-e) colo(u)r print; '~**prächtig** adj. splendidly colo(u)rful.

Färber ['fɛrbər] m (-s/-) dyer.

Farb|fernsehen ['farp-] n colo(u)r television; '~**film** m colo(u)r film; Q**ig** adj. ['~biç] colo(u)red; glass: tinted, stained; fig. colo(u)rful; Q**los** adj. ['~p-] colo(u)rless; '~**photographie** f colo(u)r photography; '~**stift** m colo(u)red pencil; '~**stoff** m colo(u)ring matter; '~**ton** m tone; shade, tint.

Färbung ['fɛrbuŋ] f (-/-en) colo(u)ring (a. fig.); shade (a. fig.).

Farnkraut ♀ ['farnkraut] n fern.

Fasan orn. [fa'za:n] m (-[e]s-e[n]) pheasant. [val.]

Fasching ['faʃiŋ] m (-s/-e, -s) carni-]

Fasel|ei [fɑ:zə'lai] f (-/-en) drivelling, waffling; twaddle; 'Q**n** v/i. (ge-, h) blather; F waffle.

Faser ['fɑ:zər] f (-/-n) anat., ♀, fig. fib|re, Am. -er; cotton, wool, etc.: staple; 'Q**ig** adj. fibrous; 'Q**n** v/i. (ge-, h) wool: shed fine hairs.

Faß [fas] n (Fasses/Fässer) cask, barrel; tub; vat; '~**bier** n draught beer.

Fassade △ [fa'sɑ:də] f (-/-n) façade, front (a. fig.); ~**nkletterer** m (-s/-) cat burglar.

fassen ['fasən] (ge-, h) 1. v/t. seize, take hold of; catch, apprehend (criminal); hold; s. einfassen; fig. grasp, understand, believe; pluck up (courage); form (plan); make (decision); sich ~ compose o.s.; sich kurz ~ be brief; 2. v/i.: ~ nach reach for. [ceivable.]

'**faßlich** adj. comprehensible, con-]

'**Fassung** f (-/-en) setting (of jewels); ∮ socket; fig.: composure; draft (-ing); wording, version; die ~ verlieren lose one's self-control; aus der ~ bringen disconcert; '~**kraft** f (powers of) comprehension, mental capacity; '~**svermögen** n (holding) capacity; fig. s. Fassungskraft.

fast adv. [fast] almost, nearly; ~ nichts next to nothing; ~ nie hardly ever.

fasten ['fastən] v/i. (ge-, h) fast; abstain from food and drink; 'Q**zeit** f Lent.

'**Fast|nacht** f (-/no pl.) Shrovetide; carnival; '~**tag** m fast-day.

fatal adj. [fa'tɑ:l] situation, etc.: awkward; business, etc.: unfortunate; mistake, etc.: fatal.

fauchen ['fauxən] v/i. (ge-, h) cat, etc.: spit; F p. spit (with anger); locomotive, etc.: hiss.

faul adj. [faul] fruit, etc.: rotten, bad; fish, meat: putrid, bad; fig. lazy, indolent, idle; fishy; ～e Ausrede lame excuse; '**～en** v/i. (ge-, h) rot, go bad, putrefy.

faulenze|n ['faulentsən] v/i. (ge-, h) idle, laze, loaf; '2r m (-s/-) idler, sluggard, F lazy-bones.

'Faul|heit f (-/no pl.) idleness, laziness; '2ig adj. putrid.

Fäulnis ['fɔylnɪs] f (-/no pl.) rottenness; putrefaction; decay.

'Faul|pelz m s. Faulenzer; '**～tier** n zo. sloth (a. fig.).

Faust [faust] f (-/ˈe) fist; auf eigene ～ on one's own initiative; '**～handschuh** m mitt(en); '**～schlag** m blow with the fist, punch, Am. F a. slug.

Favorit [favoˈriːt] m (-en/-en) favo(u)rite.

Faxe ['faksə] f (-/-n): ～n machen (play the) fool; ～n schneiden pull or make faces.

Fazit ['faːtsit] n (-s/-e, -s) result, upshot; total; das ～ ziehen sum or total up.

Februar ['feːbruaːr] m (-[s]/-e) February.

fecht|en ['fɛçtən] v/i. (irr., ge-, h) fight; fenc. fence; '2er m (-s/-) fencer.

Feder ['feːdər] f (-/-n) feather; (ornamental) plume; pen; ⊕ spring; '**～bett** n feather bed; '**～busch** m tuft of feathers; plume; '**～gewicht** n boxing, etc.: featherweight; '**～halter** m (-s/-) penholder; '**～kiel** m quill; '**～kraft** f elasticity, resilience; '**～krieg** m paper war; literary controversy; '2**leicht** adj. (as) light as a feather; '**～lesen** n (-s/no pl.): nicht viel ～s machen mit make short work of; '**～messer** n penknife; '2n v/i. (ge-, h) be elastic; '2nd adj. springy, elastic; '**～strich** m stroke of the pen; '**～vieh** n poultry; '**～zeichnung** f pen-and-ink drawing.

Fee [feː] f (-/-n) fairy.

Fegefeuer ['feːgəˌfɔyər] n purgatory.

fegen ['feːgən] v/t. (ge-, h) sweep, clean.

Fehde ['feːdə] f (-/-n) feud; private war; in ～ liegen be at feud; F be at daggers drawn.

Fehl [feːl] m: ohne ～ without fault or blemish; '**～betrag** m deficit, deficiency.

fehlen ['feːlən] v/i. (ge-, h) be absent; be missing or lacking; do wrong; es fehlt ihm an (dat.) he lacks; was fehlt Ihnen? what is the matter with you?; weit gefehlt! far off the mark!

Fehler ['feːlər] m (-s/-) mistake, error, F slip; fault; ⊕ defect, flaw; '2**frei** adj., '2**los** adj. faultless, perfect; ⊕ flawless; '2**haft** adj. faulty; defective; incorrect.

'Fehl|geburt f miscarriage, abortion; '2**gehen** v/i. (irr. gehen, sep., -ge-, sein) go wrong; '**～griff** fig. m mistake, blunder; '**～schlag** fig. m failure; '2**schlagen** fig. v/i. (irr. schlagen, sep., -ge-, sein) fail, miscarry; '**～schuß** m miss; '2**treten** v/i. (irr. treten, sep., -ge-, sein) make a false step; '**～tritt** m false step; slip; fig. slip, fault; '**～urteil** tⁱⁱ n error of judg(e)ment; '**～zündung** mot. f misfire, backfire.

Feier ['faiər] f (-/-n) ceremony; celebration; festival; festivity; '**～abend** m finishing or closing time; ～ machen finish, F knock off; '2**lich** adj. promise, oath, etc.: solemn; act: ceremonial; '**～lichkeit** f (-/-en) solemnity; ceremony; '2n (ge-, h) 1. v/t. hold (celebration); celebrate, observe (feast, etc.); 2. v/i. celebrate; rest (from work), make holiday; '**～tag** m holiday; festive day.

feig adj. [faik] cowardly.

feige¹ adj. ['faigə] cowardly.

Feige² [～] f (-/-n) fig; '**～nbaum** ♀ m fig-tree; '**～nblatt** n fig-leaf.

Feig|heit ['faikhait] f (-/no pl.) cowardice, cowardliness; **～ling** ['～lɪŋ] m (-s/-e) coward.

feil adj. [fail] for sale, to be sold; fig. venal; '**～bieten** v/t. (irr. bieten, sep., -ge-, h) offer for sale.

Feile ['failə] f (-/-n) file; '2n (ge-, h) 1. v/t. file (a. fig.); fig. polish; 2. v/i.: ～ an (dat.) file (at); fig. polish (up).

feilschen ['failʃən] v/i. (ge-, h) bargain (um for), haggle (for, about), Am. a. dicker (about).

fein adj. [fain] meal, material, etc.: high-grade; wine, etc.: choice; fabric, etc.: delicate, dainty; manners: polished; p. polite; distinction: subtle.

Feind [faɪnt] m (-[e]s/-e) enemy (a. ✕); 'Qlich adj. hostile, inimical; '~schaft f (-/-en) enmity; animosity, hostility; 'Qselig adj. hostile (gegen to); '~seligkeit f (-/-en) hostility; malevolence.

'fein|fühlend adj., '~fühlig adj. sensitive; 'Qgefühl n sensitiveness; delicacy; 'Qgehalt m (monetary) standard; 'Qheit f (-/-en) fineness, delicacy, daintiness; politeness; elegance; 'Qkost f high-class groceries pl., Am. delicatessen; '~mechanik f precision mechanics; 'Qschmecker m (-s/-) gourmet, epicure; '~sinnig adj. subtle.

feist adj. [faɪst] fat, stout.

Feld [fɛlt] n (-[e]s/-er) field (a. ✕, ✕, sports); ground, soil; plain; chess: square; △, ⊕ panel, compartment; ins ~ ziehen take the field; '~arbeit f agricultural work; '~bett n camp-bed; '~blume f wild flower; '~dienst ✕ m field service; '~flasche f water-bottle; '~frucht f fruit of the field; '~geschrei n war-cry, battle-cry; '~herr m general; '~kessel m camp-kettle; '~lazarett ✕ n field-hospital; '~lerche orn. f skylark; '~marschall m Field Marshal; 'Qmarschmäßig ✕ adj. in full marching order; '~maus zo. f field-mouse; '~messer m (land) surveyor; '~post ✕ f army postal service; '~schlacht ✕ f battle; '~stecher m (-s/-) (ein a pair of) field-glasses pl.; '~stuhl m camp-stool; '~webel ['~ve:bəl] m (-s/-) sergeant; '~weg m (field) path; '~zeichen ✕ n standard; '~zug m ✕ campaign (a. fig.), (military) expedition; Am. fig. a. drive.

Felge ['fɛlgə] f (-/-n) felloe (of cart-wheel); rim (of car wheel, etc.).

Fell [fɛl] n (-[e]s/-e) skin, pelt, fur (of dead animal); coat (of cat, etc.); fleece (of sheep).

Fels [fɛls] m (-en/-en), ~en ['~zən] m (-s/-) rock; '~block ['fɛls-] m rock; boulder; 'Qig adj. ['~zɪç] rocky.

Fenchel ♀ ['fɛnçəl] m (-s/no pl.) fennel.

Fenster ['fɛnstər] n (-s/-) window; '~brett n window-sill; '~flügel m casement (of casement window); sash (of sash window); '~kreuz n cross-bar(s pl.);

'~rahmen m window-frame; '~riegel m window-fastener; '~scheibe f (window-)pane; '~sims m, n window-sill.

Ferien ['fe:rjən] pl. holiday(s pl.), esp. Am. vacation; leave, Am. a. furlough; parl. recess; ⚖ vacation, recess; '~kolonie f children's holiday camp.

Ferkel ['fɛrkəl] n (-s/-) young pig; contp. p. pig.

fern [fɛrn] **1.** adj. far (off), distant; remote; **2.** adv. far (away); von ~ from a distance.

'Fernamt teleph. n trunk exchange, Am. long-distance exchange.

'fernbleiben **1.** v/i. (irr. bleiben, sep., -ge-) stay away (dat. from); **2.** Q n (-s/no pl.) absence (from school, etc.); absenteeism (from work).

Fern|e ['fɛrnə] f (-/-n) distance; remoteness; aus der ~ from or at a distance; 'Qer **1.** adj. farther; fig.: further; future; **2.** adv. further (-more), in addition, also; ~ liefen ... also ran ...; '~flug ✈ m long-distance flight; 'Qgelenkt adj. ['~gəlɛŋkt] missile: guided; aircraft, etc.: remote-control(l)ed; '~gespräch teleph. n trunk call, Am. long-distance call; 'Qgesteuert adj. s. ferngelenkt; '~glas n binoculars pl.; 'Qhalten v/t. and v/refl. (irr. halten, sep., -ge-, h) keep away (von from); '~heizung f district heating; '~laster F mot. m long-distance lorry, Am. long haul truck; '~lenkung f (-/-en) remote control; 'Qliegen v/i. (irr. liegen, sep., -ge-, h): es liegt mir fern zu inf. I am far from ger.; '~rohr n telescope; '~schreiber m teletypewriter, Am. teletypewriter; '~sehen **1.** n (-s/no pl.) television; **2.** Q v/i. (irr. sehen, sep., -ge-, h) watch television; '~seher m television set; p. television viewer, televiewer; '~sehsendung f television broadcast, telecast; '~sicht f visual range.

'Fernsprech|amt n telephone exchange, Am. a. central; '~anschluß m telephone connection; '~er m telephone; '~leitung f telephone line; '~zelle f telephone box.

'fern|stehen v/i. (irr. stehen, sep., -ge-, h) have no real (point of) contact with (dat. with); 'Qsteuerung f

s. Fernlenkung; '⁰unterricht *m* correspondence course *or* tuition; '⁰verkehr *m* long-distance traffic.
Ferse ['fɛrzə] *f* (-/-n) heel.
fertig *adj.* ['fɛrtiç] ready; *article, etc.*: finished; *clothing*: ready-made; mit et. ~ werden get s.th. finished; mit et. ~ sein have finished s.th.; '⁀bringen *v/t.* (*irr.* bringen, *sep.*, -ge-, *h*) bring about; manage; '⁰keit *f* (-/-en) dexterity; skill; fluency (*in the spoken language*); '⁀machen *v/t.* (*sep.*, -ge-, *h*) finish, complete; get *s.th.* ready; *fig.* finish, settle *s.o.'s* hash; sich ~ get ready; '⁰stellung *f* completion; '⁰waren *f/pl.* finished goods *pl. or* products *pl.*

fesch F *adj.* [fɛʃ] hat, dress, *etc.*: smart, stylish, chic; dashing.
Fessel ['fɛsəl] *f* (-/-n) chain, fetter, shackle; *vet.* fetlock; *fig.* bond, fetter, tie; '⁀ballon *m* captive balloon; '⁰n *v/t.* (ge-, *h*) chain, fetter, shackle; *j-n* ~ hold *or* arrest *s.o.'s* attention; fascinate *s.o.*
fest [fɛst] **1.** *adj.* firm; solid; fixed; fast; *principle*: firm, strong; *sleep*: sound; *fabric*: close; **2.** ⁰ *n* (-es/-e) festival, celebration; holiday, *eccl.* feast; '⁀binden *v/t.* (*irr.* binden, *sep.*, -ge-, *h*) fasten, tie (*an dat.* to); '⁰essen *n* banquet, feast; '⁀fahren *v/refl.* (*irr.* fahren, *sep.*, -ge-, *h*) get stuck; *fig.* reach a deadlock; '⁰halle *f* (festival) hall; '⁀halten (*irr.* halten, *sep.*, -ge-, *h*) **1.** *v/i.* hold fast *or* tight; ~ *an* (*dat.*) adhere *or* keep to; **2.** *v/t.* hold on to; hold tight; sich ~ *an* (*dat.*) hold on to; ⁀igen ['⁀igən] *v/t.* (ge-, *h*) consolidate (*one's position, etc.*); strengthen (*friendship, etc.*); stabilize (*currency*) '⁰igkeit ['⁀ç-] *f* (-/no *pl.*) firmness; solidity; '⁰land *n* mainland, continent; '⁀legen *v/t.* (*sep.*, -ge-, *h*) fix, set; sich auf et. ~ commit o.s. to s.th.; '⁀lich *adj.* meal, day, *etc.*: festive; *reception, etc.*: ceremonial; '⁰lichkeit *f* (-/-en) festivity; festive character; '⁀machen (*sep.*, -ge-, *h*) **1.** *v/t.* fix, fasten, attach (*an dat.* to); ⚓ moor; **2.** ⚓ *v/i.* moor; put ashore; '⁰mahl *n* banquet, feast; ⁰nahme ['⁀naːmə] *f* (-/-n) arrest; '⁀nehmen *v/t.* (*irr.* nehmen, *sep.*, -ge-, *h*) arrest, take into custody; '⁰rede *f* speech

of the day; '⁀setzen *v/t.* (*sep.*, -ge-, *h*) fix, set; sich ~ *dust, etc.*: become ingrained; *p.* settle (down); '⁰spiel *n* festival; '⁀stehen *v/i.* (*irr.* stehen, *sep.*, -ge-, *h*) stand firm; *fact*: be certain; '⁀stehend *adj.* fixed, stationary; *fact*: established; '⁀stellen *v/t.* (*sep.*, -ge-, *h*) establish (*fact, identity, etc.*); ascertain, find out (*fact, s.o.'s whereabouts, etc.*); state; see, perceive (*fact, etc.*); '⁰stellung *f* establishment; ascertainment; statement; '⁰tag *m* festive day; festival, holiday; *eccl.* feast; '⁰ung ⚔ *f* (-/-en) fortress; '⁰zug *m* festive procession.

fett [fɛt] **1.** *adj.* fat; fleshy; *voice*: oily; *land, etc.*: rich; **2.** ⁰ *n* (-[e]s/-e) fat; grease (*a.* ⊕); '⁰druck *typ. m* bold type; '⁀fleck *m* grease-spot; '⁀ig *adj.* hair, skin, *etc.*: greasy, oily; *fingers, etc.*: greasy; *substance*: fatty.
Fetzen ['fɛtsən] *m* (-s/-) shred; rag, *Am. a.* frazzle; scrap (*of paper*); in ~ in rags.

feucht *adj.* [fɔyçt] *climate, air, etc.*: damp, moist; *air, zone, etc.*: humid; '⁰igkeit *f* (-/no *pl.*) moisture (*of substance*); dampness (*of place, etc.*); humidity (*of atmosphere, etc.*).
Feuer ['fɔyər] *n* (-s/-) fire; light; *fig.* ardo(u)r; ~ fangen catch fire; *fig.* fall for (*girl*); '⁀alarm *m* fire alarm; '⁀beständig *adj.* fire-proof, fire-resistant; '⁀bestattung *f* cremation; '⁀eifer *m* ardo(u)r; '⁰fest *adj. s.* feuerbeständig; '⁰gefährlich *adj.* inflammable; '⁀haken *m* poker; '⁀löscher *m* (-s/-) fire extinguisher; '⁰n (ge-, *h*) **1.** ⚔ *v/i.* shoot, fire (auf *acc.* at, on); **2.** F *fig.* *v/t.* hurl; '⁀probe *fig. f* crucial test; '⁰rot *adj.* fiery (red), (as) red as fire; '⁀sbrunst *f* conflagration; '⁀schiff ⚓ *n* lightship; '⁀schutz *m* fire prevention; ⚔ covering fire; '⁀sgefahr *f* danger *or* risk of fire; '⁰speiend *adj.*: ~er Berg volcano; '⁀spritze *f* fire engine; '⁀stein *m* flint; '⁀versicherung *f* fire insurance (company); '⁀wache *f* fire station, *Am. a.* firehouse; '⁀wehr *f* fire-brigade, *Am. a.* fire department; '⁀wehrmann *m* fireman; '⁀werk *n* (display of) fireworks *pl.*; '⁀werkskörper *m* firework; '⁀~

zange f (e-e a pair of) firetongs pl.; '~zeug n lighter.

feurig adj. ['fɔyrɪç] fiery (a. fig.); fig. ardent.

Fiasko [fi'asko] n (-s/-s) (complete) failure, fiasco; sl. flop. [primer.\

Fibel ['fiːbəl] f (-/-n) spelling-book.\

Fichte ♀ ['fɪçtə] f (-/-n) spruce; '~nnadel f pine-needle.

fidel adj. [fi'deːl] cheerful, merry, jolly, Am. F a. chipper.

Fieber ['fiːbər] n (-s/-) temperature, fever; ~ haben have or run a temperature; '~anfall m attack or bout of fever; '2haft adj. feverish (a. fig.); febrile; '2krank adj. ill with fever; '~mittel n febrifuge; '2n v/i. (ge-, h) have or run a temperature; ~ nach crave or long for; '~schauer m chill, shivers pl.; '~tabelle f temperature-chart; '~thermometer n clinical thermometer.

fiel [fiːl] pret. of fallen.

Figur [fi'guːr] f (-/-en) figure; chess: chessman, piece.

figürlich adj. [fi'gyːrlɪç] meaning, etc.: figurative. [pork, etc.).\

Filet [fi'leː] n (-s/-s) fillet (of beef,\

Filiale [fil'jaːlə] f (-/-n) branch.

Filigran(arbeit f) [fili'graːn(ʔ-)] n (-s/-e) filigree.

Film [fɪlm] m (-[e]s/-e) film, thin coating (of oil, wax, etc.); film, (moving) picture, Am. a. motion picture, F movie; e-n ~ einlegen phot. load a camera; '~atelier n film studio; '~aufnahme f filming, shooting (of a film); film (of sporting event, etc.); '2en (ge-, h) 1. v/t. film, shoot (scene, etc.); 2. v/i. film, make a film; '~gesellschaft f film company, Am. motion-picture company; '~kamera f film camera, Am. motion-picture camera; '~regisseur m film director; '~reklame f screen advertising; '~schauspieler m film or screen actor, Am. F movie actor; '~spule f (film) reel; '~streifen m film strip; '~theater n cinema, Am. motion-picture or F movie theater; '~verleih m (-[e]s/-e) film distributors pl.; '~vorführer m projectionist; '~vorstellung f cinema performance, Am. F movie performance.

Filter ['fɪltər] (-s/-) 1. m (coffee-, etc.) filter; 2. ⊕ n filter; '2n v/t. (ge-, h) filter (water, air, etc.); filtrate (water, impurities, etc.); strain (liquid); '~zigarette f filter-tipped cigarette.

Filz [fɪlts] m (-es/-e) felt; fig. F skinflint; '2ig adj. felt-like; of felt; fig. F niggardly, stingy; '~laus f crab louse.

Finanz|amt [fi'nantsʔamt] n (inland) revenue office, office of the Inspector of Taxes; '~en f/pl. finances pl.; 2iell adj. [~'tsjɛl] financial; 2ieren [~'tsiːrən] v/t. (no -ge-, h) finance (scheme, etc.); sponsor (radio programme, etc.); '~lage f financial position; '~mann m financier; ~minister m minister of finance; Chancellor of the Exchequer, Am. Secretary of the Treasury; ~ministerium n ministry of finance; Exchequer, Am. Treasury Department; ~wesen n (-s/no pl.) finances pl.; financial matters pl.

Findelkind ['fɪndəl-] n foundling.

finden ['fɪndən] (irr., ge-, h) 1. v/t. find; discover, come across; think, consider; wie ~ Sie ...? how do you find ...?; sich ~ thing: be found; 2. v/i.: ~ zu find one's way to. [finder's reward.\

'**Finder** m (-s/-) finder; '~lohn m\

'**findig** adj. resourceful, ingenious.

Findling ['fɪntlɪŋ] m (-s/-e) foundling; geol. erratic block, boulder.

fing [fɪŋ] pret. of fangen.

Finger ['fɪŋər] m (-s/-) finger; sich die ~ verbrennen burn one's fingers; er rührte keinen ~ he lifted no finger; '~abdruck m fingerprint; '~fertigkeit f manual skill; '~hut m thimble; ♀ foxglove; '2n v/i. (ge-, h): ~ nach fumble for; '~spitze f finger-tip; '~spitzengefühl fig. n sure instinct; '~übung ♪ f finger exercise; '~zeig ['~tsaɪk] m (-[e]s/-e) hint, F pointer.

Fink orn. [fɪŋk] m (-en/-en) finch.

finster adj. ['fɪnstər] night, etc.: dark; shadows, wood, etc.: sombre; night, room, etc.: gloomy, murky; person, nature: sullen; thought, etc.: sinister, sombre, gloomy; '2nis f (-/no pl.) darkness, gloom.

Finte ['fɪntə] f (-/-n) feint; fig. a. ruse, trick.

Firma ✝ ['fɪrma] f (-/Firmen) firm, business, company.

firmen eccl. ['fɪrmən] v/t. (ge-, h) confirm.

'**Firmen|inhaber** m owner of a firm; '**~wert** m goodwill.

Firn [firn] m (-[e]s/-e) firn, névé.

First △ [first] m (-es/-e) ridge; '**~ziegel** m ridge tile.

Fisch [fiʃ] m (-es/-e) fish; '**~dampfer** n trawler; '**2en** v/t. and v/i. (ge-, h) fish; '**~er** m (-s/-) fisherman; '**~erboot** n fishing-boat; '**~erdorf** n fishing-village; **~erei** [~'raɪ] f (-/-en) fishery; fishing; '**~fang** m fishing; '**~geruch** m fishy smell; '**~gräte** f fish-bone; '**~grätenmuster** n herring-bone pattern; '**~händler** m fishmonger, Am. fish dealer; '**2ig** adj. fishy; '**~laich** m spawn; '**~leim** m fish-glue; '**~mehl** n fish-meal; '**~schuppe** f scale; '**~tran** m train-oil; '**~vergiftung** ♣ f fish-poisoning; '**~zucht** f pisci-culture, fish-hatching; '**~zug** m catch, haul, draught (of fish).

fiskalisch adj. [fis'kɑ:liʃ] fiscal, governmental.

Fiskus ['fiskus] m (-/⚥ -se, Fisken) Exchequer, esp. Am. Treasury; government.

Fistel ♣ ['fistəl] f (-/-n) fistual; '**~stimme** ♪ f falsetto.

Fittich ['fitiç] m (-[e]s/-e) poet. wing; j-n unter s-e ~e nehmen take s.o. under one's wing.

fix adj. [fiks] salary, price, etc.: fixed; quick, clever, smart; e-e ~e Idee an obsession; e-er Junge a smart fellow; **2ierbad** phot. [fi-'ksi:rba:t] n fixing bath; **~ieren** [fi'ksi:rən] v/t. (no -ge-, h) fix (a. phot.); fix one's eyes (up)on, stare at s.o.; '**2stern** ast. m fixed star; '**2um** n (-s/Fixa) fixed or basic salary.

flach adj. [flax] roof, etc.: flat; ground, etc.: flat, level, even; water, plate, fig.: shallow; ∆ plane.

Fläche ['flɛçə] f (-/-n) surface, ∆ a. plane; sheet (of water, snow, etc.); geom. area; tract, expanse (of land, etc.); **~ninhalt** ∆ ['flɛçənˀ-] m (surface) area; '**~nmaß** n square or surface measure.

'**Flach|land** n plain, flat country; '**~rennen** n turf: flat race.

Flachs ⚘ [flaks] m (-es/no pl.) flax.

flackern ['flakərn] v/i. (ge-, h) light, flame, etc.: flicker, wave; voice: quaver, shake.

Flagge ⚓ ['flagə] f (-/-n) flag,

colo(u)rs pl.; '**2n** v/i. (ge-, h) fly or hoist a flag; signal (with flags).

Flak ⚔ [flak] f (-/-, -s) anti-aircraft gun; anti-aircraft artillery.

Flamme ['flamə] f (-/-n) flame; blaze; '**~nmeer** n sea of flames; '**~nwerfer** ⚔ m (-s/-) flame-thrower.

Flanell [fla'nɛl] m (-s/-e) flannel; **~anzug** m flannel suit; '**~hose** f flannel trousers pl., flannels pl.

Flank|e ['flaŋkə] f (-/-n) flank (a. ∆, ⊕, ⚔, mount.); side; **2ieren** [~'ki:rən] v/t. (no -ge-, h) flank.

Flasche ['flaʃə] f (-/-n) bottle; flask.

'**Flaschen|bier** n bottled beer; '**~hals** m neck of a bottle; '**~öffner** m (-s/-) bottle-opener; '**~zug** ⊕ m block and tackle.

flatter|haft adj. ['flatərhaft] girl, etc.: fickle, flighty; mind: fickle, volatile; '**~n** v/i. (ge-) 1. (h, sein) bird, butterfly, etc.: flutter (about); bird, bat, etc.: flit (about); 2. (h) hair, flag, garment, etc.: stream, fly; mot. wheel: shimmy, wobble; car steering: judder; 3. (sein): auf den Boden ~ flutter to the ground.

flau adj. [flau] weak, feeble, faint; sentiment, reaction, etc.: lukewarm; drink: stale; colour: pale, dull; ✝ market, business, etc.: dull, slack; ~e Zeit slack period.

Flaum [flaum] m (-[e]s/no pl.) down, fluff; fuzz.

Flau|s [flaus] m (-es/-e), **~sch** [~ʃ] m (-es/-e) tuft (of wool, etc.); napped coating.

Flausen F ['flauzən] f/pl. whims pl., fancies pl., (funny) ideas pl.; F fibs pl.; j-m ~ in den Kopf setzen put funny ideas into s.o.'s head; j-m ~ vormachen tell s.o. fibs.

Flaute ['flautə] f (-/-n) ♣ dead calm; esp. ✝ dullness, slack period.

Flecht|e ['flɛçtə] f (-/-n) braid, plait (of hair); ⚘ lichen; ♣ herpes; '**2en** v/t. (irr., ge-, h) braid, plait (hair, ribbon, etc.); weave (basket, wreath, etc.); wreath (flowers); twist (rope, etc.); '**~werk** n wickerwork.

Fleck [flɛk] m (-[e]s/-e, -en) 1. mark (of dirt, grease, etc.; zo.); spot (of grease, paint, etc.); smear (of oil, blood, etc.); stain (of wine, coffee, etc.); blot (of ink); place, spot; fig. blemish, spot, stain; 2. patch (of material); bootmaking: heel-piece;

'**~en** m (-s/-) s. Fleck 1; small (market-)town, townlet; '**~enwasser** n spot or stain remover; '**~fieber** ⚕ n (epidemic) typhus; '**2ig** adj. spotted; stained.

Fledermaus zo. ['fle:dər-] f bat.

Flegel ['fle:gəl] m (-s/-) flail; fig. lout, boor; **~ei** [~'laɪ] f (-/-en) rudeness; loutishness; '**~haft** adj. rude-ill-mannered; loutish; '**~jahre** pl. awkward age.

flehen ['fle:ən] **1.** v/i. (ge-, h) entreat, implore (zu j-m s.o.; um et. s.th.); **2.** ⚕ n (-s/no pl.) supplication; imploration, entreaty.

Fleisch [flaɪʃ] n (-es/no pl.) flesh; meat; ⚕ pulp; '**~brühe** f meat-broth; beef tea; '**~er** m (-s/-) butcher; **~erei** [~'raɪ] f (-/-en) butcher's (shop), Am. butcher shop; '**~extrakt** m meat extract; '**2fressend** adj. carnivorous; '**~hackmaschine** f mincing machine, mincer, Am. meat grinder; '**2ig** adj. fleshy; ⚕ pulpy; '**~konserven** f/pl. tinned or potted meat, Am. canned meat; '**~kost** f meat (food); '**2lich** adj. desires, etc.: carnal, fleshly; '**2los** adj. meatless; '**~pastete** f meat pie, Am. a. potpie; '**~speise** f meat dish; '**~vergiftung** f meat or ptomaine poisoning; '**~ware** f meat (product); '**~wolf** m s. Fleischhackmaschine.

Fleiß [flaɪs] m (-es/no pl.) diligence, industry; '**2ig** adj. diligent, industrious, hard-working.

fletschen ['fletʃən] v/t. (ge-, h): die Zähne ~ animal: bare its teeth; p. bare one's teeth.

Flicken ['flikən] **1.** m (-s/-) patch; **2.** ⚕ v/t. (ge-, h) patch (dress, tyre, etc.); repair (shoe, roof, etc.); cobble (shoe).

'**Flick|schneider** m jobbing tailor; '**~schuster** m cobbler; '**~werk** n (-[e]s/no pl.) patchwork.

Flieder ⚕ ['fli:dər] m (-s/-) lilac.

Fliege ⚕ ['fli:gə] f (-/-n) zo. fly; bow-tie.

'**fliegen 1.** v/i. (irr., ge-, sein) fly; go by air; **2.** v/t. (irr., ge-, h) fly, pilot (aircraft, etc.); convey (goods, etc.) by air; **3.** ⚕ n (-s/no pl.) flying; ✈ a. aviation.

Fliegen|fänger ['fli:gənfɛŋər] m (-s/-) fly-paper; '**~fenster** n fly-screen; '**~gewicht** n boxing, etc.:

flyweight; '**~klappe** f fly-flap, Am. fly swatter; '**~pilz** ⚕ m fly agaric.

'**Flieger** m (-s/-) flyer; ✈ airman, aviator; pilot; F plane, bomber; cycling: sprinter; '**~abwehr** ⚕ f anti-aircraft defen|ce, Am. -se; '**~alarm** ⚕ m air-raid alarm or warning; '**~bombe** ⚕ f aircraft bomb; '**~offizier** ⚕ m air-force officer.

flieh|en ['fli:ən] (irr., ge-) **1.** v/i. (sein) flee (vor dat. from), run away; **2.** v/t. (h) flee, avoid, keep away from; '**2kraft** phys. f centrifugal force. [(floor-)tile.]

Fliese ['fli:zə] f (-/-n) (wall-)tile.

Fließ|band ['fli:s-] n (-[e]s/⁼er) conveyor-belt; assembly-line; '**2en** v/i. (irr., ge-, sein) river, traffic, etc.: flow; tap-water, etc.: run; '**2end 1.** adj. water: running; traffic: moving; speech, etc.: fluent; **2.** adv.: ~ lesen (sprechen) read (speak) fluently; '**~papier** n blotting-paper.

Flimmer ['flimər] m (-s/-) glimmer, glitter; '**2n** v/i. (ge-, h) glimmer, glitter; television, film: flicker; es flimmert mir vor den Augen everything is dancing in front of my eyes.

flink adj. [fliŋk] quick, nimble, brisk.

Flinte ['flintə] f (-/-n) shotgun; die ~ ins Korn werfen throw up the sponge.

Flirt [flœrt] m (-es/-s) flirtation; '**2en** v/i. (ge-, h) flirt (mit with).

Flitter ['flitər] m (-s/-) tinsel (a. fig.), spangle; '**~kram** m cheap finery; '**~wochen** pl. honeymoon.

flitzen F ['flitsən] v/i. (ge-, sein) whisk, scamper; dash (off, etc.).

flocht [flɔxt] pret. of flechten.

Flock|e ['flɔkə] f (-/-n) flake (of snow, soap, etc.); flock (of wool); '**2ig** adj. fluffy, flaky.

flog [flo:k] pret. of fliegen.

floh¹ [flo:] pret. of fliehen.

Floh² zo. [~] m (-[e]s/⁼e) flea.

Flor [flo:r] m (-s/-e) bloom, blossom; fig. bloom, prime; gauze; crêpe, crape.

Florett fenc. [flo'rɛt] n (-[e]s/-e) foil.

florieren [flo'ri:rən] v/i. (no -ge-, h) business, etc.: flourish, prosper, thrive.

Floskel ['flɔskəl] f (-/-n) flourish; empty phrase.

floß¹ [flɔs] pret. of fließen.

Floß² [flo:s] n (-es/⁼e) raft, float.

Flosse ['flɔsə] f (-/-n) fin; flipper (of penguin, etc.).

flöß|en ['flø:sən] v/t. (ge-, h) raft, float (timber, etc.); **'2er** m (-s/-) rafter, raftsman.

Flöte ♩ ['flø:tə] f (-/-n) flute; **'2n** (ge-, h) **1.** v/i. (play the) flute; **2.** v/t. play on the flute.

flott adj. [flɔt] ⚓ floating, afloat; pace, etc.: quick, brisk; music, etc.: gay, lively; dress, etc.: smart, stylish; car, etc.: sporty, racy; dancer, etc.: excellent.

Flotte ['flɔtə] f (-/-n) ⚓ fleet; ✗ navy; **'⁓nstützpunkt** ✗ m naval base.

Flotille ⚓ ['flø'tiljə] f (-/-n) flotilla.

Flöz geol., ⚒ [flø:ts] n (-es/-e) seam, layer, stratum.

Fluch [flu:x] m (-[e]s/-e) curse, malediction; eccl. anathema; curse, swear-word; **'2en** v/i. (ge-, h) swear, curse.

Flucht [fluxt] f (-/-en) flight (vor dat. from); escape (aus dat. from); line (of windows, etc.); suite (of rooms); flight (of stairs).

flücht|en ['flYçtən] v/i. (ge-, h) (sein and v/refl. (h) flee (nach, zu to); run away; escape; **'⁓ig** adj. fugitive (a. fig.); thought, etc.: fleeting; fame, etc.: transient; p. careless, superficial; 🜍 volatile; **2ling** ['⁓lɪŋ] m (-s/-e) fugitive; pol. refugee; **'2-lingslager** n refugee camp.

Flug [flu:k] m (-[e]s/-e) flight; im ⁓(e) rapidly; quickly; **'⁓abwehrra-kete** f anti-aircraft missile; **'⁓bahn** f trajectory (of rocket, etc.); ✈ flight path; **'⁓ball** m tennis, etc.: volley; **'⁓blatt** n handbill, leaflet, Am. a. flier; **'⁓boot** ✈ n flying-boat; **'⁓dienst** ✈ m air service.

Flügel ['fly:gəl] m (-s/-) wing (a. △, ✈, ✗); blade, vane (of propeller, etc.); s. Fensterflügel, Türflügel, Lungenflügel; sail (of windmill, etc.); ♩ grand piano; **'⁓fenster** △ n casement-window; **'2lahm** adj. broken-winged; **'⁓mann** ✗ m marker; flank man; **'⁓tür** △ f folding door.

Fluggast ['flu:k-] m (air) passenger.

flügge adj. ['flYgə] fledged; ⁓ wer-den fledge; fig. begin to stand on one's own feet.

Flug|hafen m airport; **'⁓linie** f ✈ air route; airline; **'⁓platz** m air-field, aerodrome, Am. a. airdrome;

airport; **'⁓sand** geol. m wind-blown sand; **'⁓schrift** f pamphlet; **'⁓-sicherung** f air traffic control; **'⁓sport** m sporting aviation; **'⁓-wesen** n aviation, aeronautics.

'Flugzeug n aircraft, aeroplane, F plane, Am. a. airplane; **'⁓bau** m aircraft construction; **'⁓führer** m pilot; **'⁓halle** f hangar; **'⁓rumpf** m fuselage, body; **'⁓träger** m aircraft carrier, Am. sl. flattop; **'⁓un-glück** n air crash or disaster.

Flunder ichth. ['flʊndər] f (-/-n) flounder.

Flunker|ei F [flʊŋkə'raɪ] f (-/-en) petty lying, F fib(bing); **'2n** v/i. (ge-, h) F fib, tell fibs.

fluoreszieren [fluorɛs'tsi:rən] v/i. (no -ge-, h) fluoresce.

Flur [flu:r] **1.** f (-/-en) field, meadow; poet. lea; **2.** m (-[e]s/-e) (entrance-)hall.

Fluß [flus] m (Flusses/Flüsse) river, stream; flow(ing); fig. fluency, flux; **2'abwärts** adv. downriver, downstream; **2'aufwärts** adv. up-river, upstream; **'⁓bett** n river bed.

flüssig adj. ['flYsiç] fluid, liquid; metal: molten, melted; 🜚 money, capital, etc.: available, in hand; style: fluent, flowing; **2keit** f (-/-en) fluid, liquid; fluidity, liquidity; availability; fluency.

'Fluß|lauf m course of a river; **'⁓-mündung** f mouth of a river; **'⁓-pferd** zo. n hippopotamus; **'⁓-schiffahrt** f river navigation or traffic.

flüstern ['flYstərn] v/i. and v/t. (ge-, h) whisper.

Flut [flu:t] f (-/-en) flood; high tide, (flood-)tide; fig. flood, torrent, deluge; **'2en** (ge-) **1.** v/i. (sein) water, crowd, etc.: flood, surge (über acc. over); **2.** v/t. (h) flood (dock, etc.); **'⁓welle** f tidal wave.

focht [fɔxt] pret. of fechten.

Fohlen zo. ['fo:lən] **1.** n (-s/-) foal; male: colt; female: filly; **2.** 2 v/i. (ge-, h) foal.

Folge ['fɔlgə] f (-/-n) sequence, succession (of events); instalment, part (of radio series, etc.); consequence, result; series; set, suit; future; ⁓n pl. aftermath.

'folgen v/i. (dat.) (ge-, sein) follow; succeed (j-m s.o.; auf acc. to); follow, ensue (aus from); obey (j-m

s.o.); **~dermaßen** *adv.* ['~dərmaː-
sən] as follows; '**~schwer** *adj.* of
grave consequence, grave.
'**folgerichtig** *adj.* logical; consistent.
folger|n ['fɔlgərn] *v/t.* (ge-, h) infer,
conclude, deduce (*aus* from);
'**2ung** *f* (-/-en) inference, conclusion, deduction.
'**folgewidrig** *adj.* illogical; incon-
sistent.
folglich *cj.* ['fɔlkliç] therefore, consequently.
folgsam *adj.* ['fɔlkzaːm] obedient;
'**2keit** *f* (-/no pl.) obedience.
Folie ['foːljə] *f* (-/-n) foil.
Folter ['fɔltər] *f* (-/-n) torture; *auf
die* ~ *spannen* put to the rack; *fig.*
F *a.* keep on tenterhooks; '**2n** *v/t.*
(ge-, h) torture, torment; '**~qual** *f*
torture, *fig. a.* torment.
Fonds † [fõː] *m* (-/-) fund (*a. fig.*);
funds *pl.*
Fontäne [fɔn'tɛːnə] *f* (-/-n) fountain.
foppen ['fɔpən] *v/t.* (ge-, h) tease,
F pull s.o.'s leg; hoax, fool.
forcieren [fɔr'siːrən] *v/t.* (no -ge-, h)
force (up).
'**Förder|band** *n* (-[e]s/⸚er) con-
veyor-belt; '**2lich** *adj.* conducive
(*dat.* to), promotive (of); '**~korb**
⚒ *m* cage.
fordern ['fɔrdərn] *v/t.* (ge-, h) demand; claim (*compensation, etc.*);
ask (*price, etc.*); challenge (*to duel*).
fördern ['fœrdərn] *v/t.* (ge-, h)
further, advance, promote; ⚒ haul,
raise (*coal, etc.*); *zutage* ~ reveal,
bring to light.
'**Forderung** *f* (-/-en) demand;
claim; charge; challenge.
'**Förderung** *f* (-/-en) furtherance,
advancement, promotion; ⚒ haul-
age; output.   [trout.]
Forelle *ichth.* [fo'rɛlə] *f* (-/-n))
Form [fɔrm] *f* (-/-en) form, figure,
shape; model; ⊕ mo(u)ld; *sports*:
form, condition; **2al** *adj.* [~'maːl]
formal; **~alität** [~ali'tɛːt] *f* (-/-en)
formality; **~at** [~'maːt] *n* (-[e]s/-e)
size; *von* ~ of distinction; **~el** ['~əl]
f (-/-n) formula; **2ell** *adj.* [~'mɛl]
formal; '**2en** *v/t.* (ge-, h) form (*object, character, etc.*); shape, fashion
(*wood, metal, etc.*); mo(u)ld (*clay,
character, etc.*); '**~enlehre** *gr. f* ac-
cidence; '**~fehler** *m* informality; ⚖

flaw; **2ieren** [~'miːrən] *v/t.* (no
-ge-, h) form; draw up, line up;
sich ~ line up.
förmlich *adj.* ['fœrmliç] formal;
ceremonious; '**2keit** *f* (-/-en) formality; ceremoniousness.
'**formlos** *adj.* formless, shapeless;
fig. informal.
Formular [fɔrmu'laːr] *n* (-s/-e)
form, *Am. a.* blank.
formu'lieren *v/t.* (no -ge-, h) for-
mulate (*question, etc.*); word, phrase
(*question, contract, etc.*).
forsch *adj.* [fɔrʃ] vigorous, energetic; smart, dashing.
forsch|en ['fɔrʃən] *v/i.* (ge-, h): ~
nach (*dat.*) search for or after; ~ *in*
(*dat.*) search (through); '**2er** *m*
(-s/-) researcher, research worker.
'**Forschung** *f* (-/-en) research
(work); '**~sreise** *f* (exploring) expedition; '**~sreisende** *m* explorer.
Forst [fɔrst] *m* (-es/-e[n]) forest; '**~-
aufseher** *m* (forest-)keeper, game-
keeper.   [ranger.]
Förster ['fœrstər] *m* (-s/-) forester;)
'**Forst|haus** *n* forester's house; '**~-
revier** *n* forest district; '**~wesen** *n*,
'**~wirtschaft** *f* forestry.
Fort[1] ⚔ [foːr] *n* (-s/-s) fort.
fort[2] *adv.* [fɔrt] away, gone; on;
gone, lost; *in e-m* ~ continuously;
und so ~ and so on or forth; *s. a.*
weg.
'**fort|bestehen** *v/i.* (*irr.* stehen, sep.,
no -ge-, h) continue, persist; '**~be-
wegen** *v/t.* (sep., no -ge-, h) move
(on, away); *sich* ~ move, walk; '**2-
dauer** *f* continuance; '**~dauern** *v/i.*
(sep., -ge-, h) continue, last; '**~fah-
ren** *v/i.* (*irr.* fahren, sep., -ge-) **1.**
(sein) depart, leave; drive off; **2.** (h)
continue, keep on (et. *zu tun* doing
s.th.); '**~führen** *v/t.* (sep., -ge-, h)
continue, carry on; '**2gang** *m* departure, leaving; continuance; '**~-
gehen** *v/i.* (*irr.* gehen, sep., -ge-,
sein) go (away), leave; '**~geschrit-
ten** *adj.* advanced; '**2kommen** *n*
(-s/no pl.) progress; '**~laufend** *adj.*
consecutive, continuous; '**~pflan-
zen** *v/t.* (sep., -ge-, h) propagate;
sich ~ biol. propagate, reproduce;
phys., disease, rumour: be propa-
gated; '**2pflanzung** *f* propagation;
reproduction; '**~reißen** *v/t.* (*irr.
reißen, sep., -ge-, h) avalanche, etc.:
sweep or carry away; '**~schaffen**

v/t. (*sep.*, *-ge-*, *h*) get *or* take away, remove; **'~schreiten** *v/i.* (*irr. schreiten*, *sep.*, *-ge-*, *sein*) advance, proceed, progress; **'~schreitend** *adj.* progressive; **'Qschritt** *m* progress; **'~schrittlich** *adj.* progressive; **'~setzen** *v/t.* (*sep.*, *-ge-*, *h*) continue, pursue; **'Qsetzung** *f* (*-/-en*) continuation, pursuit; **'~** folgt to be continued; **'~während 1.** *adj.* continual, continuous; perpetual; **2.** *adv.* constantly, always.

Forum ['fo:rum] *n* (*-s/Foren*, *Fora* *and* *-s*) forum.

Foto... ['fo:to-] *s.* Photo...

Foyer [foa'je:] *n* (*-s/-s*) *thea.* foyer, *Am. and parl.* lobby; *hotel:* foyer, lounge.

Fracht [fraxt] *f* (*-/-en*) goods *pl.*; 🚂 carriage, freight; ⚓, ✈ freight (*-age*), cargo; **'~brief** *m* ⚓ consignment note, *Am.*, ⚓ bill of lading; **'~dampfer** *m* cargo steamer, freighter; **'~er** *m* (*-s/-*) freighter; **'Qfrei** *adj.* carriage *or* freight paid; **'~führer** *m* carrier, *Am. a.* teamster; **'~geld** *n* carriage charges *pl.*, 🚂, ⚓, *Am.* freight; **'~gut** *n* goods *pl.*, freight; **'~stück** *n* package.

Frack [frak] *m* (*-[e]s/⁼e*, *-s*) dress coat, tail-coat, F tails; **'~anzug** *m* dress-suit.

Frag|e ['fra:gə] *f* (*-/-n*) question, *gr.*, *reth.* interrogation; problem, point; *e-e ~ stellen* ask a question; *in ~ stellen* question; **'~ebogen** *m* questionnaire; form; **'Qen** (*ge-*, *h*) **1.** *v/t.* ask; question; *es fragt sich, ob* it is doubtful whether; **2.** *v/i.* ask; **'~er** *m* (*-s/-*) questioner; **'~ewort** *gr. n* (*-[e]s/⁼er*) interrogative; **'~ezeichen** *n* question-mark, point of interrogation, *Am. mst* interrogation point; **Qlich** *adj.* ['fra:k-] doubtful, uncertain; in question; **Qlos** *adv.* ['fra:k-] undoubtedly, unquestionably. [fragment.]

Fragment [fra'ment] *n* (*-[e]s/-e*)

fragwürdig *adj.* ['fra:k-] doubtful, dubious, questionable.

Fraktion *parl.* [frak'tsjo:n] *f* (*-/-en*) (parliamentary) group.

frank|ieren [fraŋ'ki:rən] *v/t.* (*no* *-ge-*, *h*) prepay, stamp; **'~o** *adv.* ['~o] free; post(age) paid; *parcel:* carriage paid.

Franse ['franzə] *f* (*-/-n*) fringe.

Franz|ose [fran'tso:zə] *m* (*-n/-n*)

Frenchman; *die ~n* *pl.* the French *pl.*; **~ösin** [~'ø:zin] *f* (*-/-nen*) Frenchwoman; **Qösisch** *adj.* [~'ø:ziʃ] French.

fräs|en ⊕ ['frɛ:zən] *v/t.* (*ge-*, *h*) mill; **Qmaschine** ['frɛ:s-] *f* milling-machine.

Fraß [fra:s] **1.** F *m* (*-es/-e*) *sl.* grub; **2.** **Q** *pret. of* fressen.

Fratze ['fratsə] *f* (*-/-n*) grimace, F face; *~n schneiden* make grimaces.

Frau [frau] *f* (*-/-en*) woman; lady; wife; *~ X* Mrs X.

'Frauen|arzt *m* gyn(a)ecologist; **'~klinik** *f* hospital for women; **'~rechte** *n/pl.* women's rights *pl.*; **'~stimmrecht** *pol. n* women's suffrage; **'~zimmer** *mst contp. n* female, woman.

Fräulein ['frɔylain] *n* (*-s/-*, F *-s*) young lady; teacher; shop-assistant; waitress; *~ X* Miss X.

'fraulich *adj.* womanly.

frech *adj.* [frɛç] impudent, insolent, F saucy, cheeky, *Am.* F *a.* sassy, *sl.* fresh; *lie, etc.*: brazen; *thief, etc.*: bold, daring; **'Qheit** *f* (*-/-en*) impudence, insolence; F sauciness, cheek; boldness.

frei *adj.* [frai] free (*von* from, of); *position:* vacant; *field:* open; *parcel:* carriage-paid; *journalist, etc.*: free-lance; liberal; candid, frank; licentious; *~ Haus* ⚓ franco domicile; *~er Tag* day off; *im Freien* in the open air.

'Frei|bad *n* open-air bath; **~beuter** ['~bɔytər] *m* (*-s/-*) freebooter; **'Qbleibend** ✝ *adj.* price, *etc.*: subject to alteration; *offer:* conditional; **'~brief** *m* charter; *fig.* warrant; **'~denker** *m* (*-s/-*) freethinker.

Freier ['fraiər] *m* (*-s/-*) suitor.

'Frei|exemplar *n* free *or* presentation copy; **'~frau** *f* baroness; **'~gabe** *f* release; **'Qgeben** (*irr. geben*, *sep.*, *-ge-*, *h*) **1.** *v/t.* release; give (*s.o. an hour, etc.*) off; **2.** *v/i.*: *j-m ~* give s.o. time off; **'Qgebig** *adj.* generous, liberal; **'~gebigkeit** *f* (*-/-en*) generosity, liberality; **'~gepäck** *n* free luggage; **'Qhaben** *v/i.* (*irr. haben*, *sep.*, *-ge-*, *h*) have a holiday; have a day off; **'~hafen** *m* free port; **'Qhalten** *v/t.* (*irr. halten*, *sep.*, *-ge-*, *h*) keep free *or* clear; *in restaurant, etc.*: treat; **'~handel** *m* free trade.

'**Freiheit** f (-/-en) liberty; freedom; *dichterische ~* poetic licence, *Am.* poetic license.

'**Frei|herr** m baron; '**~karte** f free (*thea. a.* complimentary) ticket; '**Ωlassen** v/t. (*irr. lassen, sep., -ge-, h*) release, set free *or* at liberty; *gegen Kaution ~* ⚖ release on bail; '**~lassung** f (-/-en) release; '**~lauf** m free-wheel.

'**freilich** adv. indeed, certainly, of course; admittedly.

'**Frei|lichtbühne** f open-air stage *or* theat|re, *Am.* -er; '**Ωmachen** v/t. (*sep., -ge-, h*) ✉ prepay, stamp (*letter, etc.*); *sich ~* undress, take one's clothes off; '**~marke** f stamp; '**~maurer** m freemason; '**~maure-rei** [~'raɪ] f (-/no pl.) freemasonry; '**~mut** m frankness; '**Ωmütig** adj. ['~my:tɪç] frank; '**Ωschaffend** adj.: *~er Künstler* free-lance artist; '**~schärler** ⚔ ['~ʃɛːrlər] m (-s/-) volunteer, irregular; '**~schein** m licen|ce, *Am.* -se; '**Ωsinnig** adj. liberal; '**Ωsprechen** v/t. (*irr. spre-chen, sep., -ge-, h*) *esp. eccl.* absolve (*von* from); ⚖ acquit (*of*); release (*apprentice*) from his articles; '**~sprechung** f (-/-en) *esp. eccl.* absolution; release from articles; = '**~spruch** ⚖ m acquittal; '**~staat** *pol.* m free state; '**Ωstehen** v/i. (*irr. stehen, sep., -ge-, h*) house, *etc.*: stand empty; *es steht Ihnen frei zu inf.* you are free *or* at liberty to *inf.*; '**Ωstellen** v/t. (*sep., -ge-, h*): *j-n ~* exempt s.o. (*von* from) (*a.* ⚔); *j-m et. ~* leave s.th. open to s.o.; '**~stoß** m *football:* free kick; '**~tag** m Fri-day; '**~tod** m suicide; '**Ωtragend** △ adj. cantilever; '**~treppe** f outdoor staircase; '**Ωwillig 1.** adj. voluntary; **2.** adv. a. of one's own free will; '**~willige** ['~vɪlɪgə] m (-n/-n) volun-teer; '**~zeit** f free *or* spare *or* leisure time; **Ωzügig** adj. ['~tsy:gɪç] free to move; '**~zügigkeit** f (-/no pl.) freedom of movement.

fremd adj. [frɛmt] strange; foreign; alien; extraneous; '**~artig** adj. strange; exotic.

Fremde ['frɛmdə] **1.** f (-/no pl.) distant *or* foreign parts; *in der ~* far away from home, abroad; **2.** m, f (-n/-n) stranger; foreigner; '**~n-buch** n visitors' book; '**~nführer** m guide, cicerone; '**~nheim** n

boarding house; '**~nindustrie** ['frɛmdən?-] f tourist industry; '**~nlegion** ⚔ f Foreign Legion; '**~nverkehr** m tourism, tourist traffic; '**~nzimmer** n spare (bed-)room; *tourism:* room.

'**Fremd|herrschaft** f fofeign rule; '**~körper** ⚕ m foreign body; '**Ωländisch** adj. ['~lɛndɪʃ] foreign, exotic; '**~sprache** f foreign lan-guage; '**Ωsprachig** adj., '**Ωsprach-lich** adj. foreign-language; '**~wort** n (-[e]s/~er) foreign word.

Frequenz *phys.* [fre'kvɛnts] f (-/-en) frequency.

fressen ['frɛsən] **1.** v/t. (*irr., ge-, h*) eat; *beast of prey:* devour; F *p.* devour, gorge; **2.** v/i. (*irr., ge-, h*) eat; F *p.* gorge; **3.** ⚕ n (-s/no pl.) feed, food.

'**Freß|gier** f voracity, gluttony; '**~napf** m feeding dish.

Freude ['frɔydə] f (-/-n) joy, glad-ness; delight; pleasure; *~ haben an* (*dat.*) find *or* take pleasure in.

'**Freuden|botschaft** f glad tidings *pl.*; '**~fest** n happy occasion; '**~feuer** n bonfire; '**~geschrei** n shouts *pl.* of joy; '**~tag** m day of rejoicing, red-letter day; '**~taumel** m transports *pl.* of joy.

'**freud|estrahlend** adj. radiant with joy; '**Ωig** adj. joyful; happy; '**~es Ereignis** happy event; '**~los** adj. ['frɔytlo:s] joyless, cheerless.

freuen ['frɔyən] v/t. (*ge-, h*): *es freut mich, daß* I am glad *or* pleased (that); *sich ~ über* (*acc.*) be pleased about *or* with, be glad about; *sich ~ auf* (*acc.*) look forward to.

Freund [frɔynt] m (-es/-e) (boy-)friend; '**~in** ['~dɪn] f (-/-nen) (girl-)friend; '**Ωlich** adj. friendly, kind, nice; cheerful, bright; *climate:* mild; '**~lichkeit** f (-/-en) friend-liness, kindness; '**~schaft** f (-/-en) friendship; *~ schließen* make friends (*mit* with); '**Ωschaftlich** adj. friendly.

Frevel ['fre:fəl] m (-s/-) outrage (*an dat., gegen* on), crime (*against*); '**Ωhaft** adj. wicked, outrageous; impious; '**Ωn** v/i. (*ge-, h*) commit a crime *or* outrage (*gegen* against).

Frevler ['fre:flər] m (-s/-) evil-doer, offender; blasphemer.

Friede(n) ['fri:də(n)] m (*Friedens/Frieden*) peace; *im Frieden* in peace-

time; *laß mich in Frieden!* leave me
alone!

Friedens|bruch *m* violation of
(the) peace; '**~stifter** *m* peace-
maker; '**~störer** *m* (-s/-) disturber
of the peace; '**~verhandlungen** *f/pl.*
peace negotiations *pl.*; '**~vertrag**
m peace treaty.

'**ried|fertig** *adj.* ['fri:t-] peaceable,
peace-loving; '**2hof** *m* cemetery,
graveyard; churchyard; '**~lich** *adj.
s.* friedfertig; peaceful; '**~liebend**
adj. peace-loving.

~rieren ['fri:rən] *v/i.* (*irr.*, ge-)
1. (sein) *liquid*: freeze, become
frozen; *river, etc.*: freeze (over, up);
window-pane, etc.: freeze over;
2. (h) be *or* feel cold; *mich friert
or ich friere an den Füßen* my feet
are cold.

Fries ⚠ [fri:s] *m* (-es/-e) frieze.

frisch [friʃ] **1.** *adj. food, flowers,
etc.*: fresh; *egg*: new-laid; *linen, etc.*:
clean; *auf ~er Tat ertappen* catch
red-handed; **2.** *adv.*: *~ gestrichen!*
wet paint!, *Am.* fresh paint!; **2e**
['~ə] *f* (-/no *pl.*) freshness.

Friseu|r [fri'zø:r] *m* (-s/-e) hair-
dresser; (*men's*) barber; '**~se** [~zə] *f*
(-/-n) (woman) hairdresser.

fri'sier|en *v/t.* (*no* -ge-, h): *j-n ~*
do *or* dress s.o.'s hair; F: *einen
Wagen ~ mot.* tune up *or* soup up *or*
hot up a car; *sich ~* do one's hair;
2kommode *f* dressing-table; **2sa-
lon** *m* hairdressing saloon; **2tisch**
m s. Frisierkommode.

Frist [frist] *f* (-/-en) (fixed *or* limited)
period of time; time allowed; term;
⚖ prescribed time; ⚖, ⸸ respite,
grace; '**2en** *v/t.* (ge-, h): *sein
Dasein ~* scrape along, scrape a
living.

Frisur [fri'zu:r] *f* (-/-en) hair-style,
hair-do, coiffure.

frivol *adj.* [fri'vo:l] frivolous, flippant; **2ität** [~oli'tɛ:t] *f* (-/-en)
frivolity, flippancy.

froh [fro:] *adj.* joyful, glad; cheerful; happy; gay (*a. colour*).

fröhlich *adj.* ['frø:liç] gay, merry,
cheerful, happy, *Am.* F *a.* chipper;
'**2keit** *f* (-/~ -en) gaiety, cheerfulness; merriment.

froh'locken *v/i.* (*no* -ge-, h) shout
for joy, be jubilant; exult (*über acc.*
at, in); gloat (over); '**2sinn** *m*
-[e]s/no *pl.*) gaiety, cheerfulness.

fromm *adj.* [frɔm] *p.* pious, religious; *life, etc.*: godly; *prayer, etc.*:
devout; *horse, etc.*: docile; *~e Lüge*
white lie; *~er Wunsch* wishful
thinking, idle wish.

Frömmelei [frœmə'laɪ] *f* (-/-en)
affected piety, bigotry.

'**Frömmigkeit** *f* (-/-en) piety,
religiousness; godliness; devout-
ness.

Fron [fro:n] *f* (-/-en), '**~arbeit** *f*,
'**~dienst** *hist. m* forced *or* compulsory labo(u)r *or* service; *fig.*
drudgery.

frönen ['frø:nən] *v/i.* (*dat.*) (ge-, h)
indulge in; be a slave to.

Front [front] *f* (-/-en) ⚙ front,
façade, face; ⚔ front (line), line;
pol., ⸸, *etc.*: front.

fror [fro:r] *pret. of* frieren.

Frosch *zo.* [frɔʃ] *m* (-es/¨e) frog;
'**~perspektive** *f* worm's-eye view.

Frost [frɔst] *m* (-es/¨e) frost; chill;
'**~beule** *f* chilblain.

frösteln ['frœstəln] *v/i.* (ge-, h)
feel chilly, shiver (with cold).

'**frostig** *adj.* frosty (*a. fig.*); *fig.* cold,
frigid, icy.

'**Frost|salbe** ⚕ *f* chilblain ointment;
'**~schaden** *m* frost damage; '**~-
schutzmittel** *mot. n* anti-freezing
mixture; '**~wetter** *n* frosty weather.

frottier|en [frɔ'ti:rən] *v/t.* (*no* -ge-,
h) rub; **2(hand)tuch** *n* Turkish
towel.

Frucht [fruxt] *f* (-/¨e) ⚘ fruit (*a.
fig.*); corn; crop; *fig.* reward,
result; '**2bar** *adj.* fruitful (*esp. fig.*);
fertile (*a. biol.*); '**~barkeit** *f* (-/no
pl.) fruitfulness; fertility; '**2brin-
gend** *adj.* fruit-bearing; *fig.* fruitful; '**2en** *v/i.* (ge-, h) be of use;
'**~knoten** ⚘ *m* ovary; '**2los** *adj.*
fruitless; *fig. a.* ineffective.

früh [fry:] **1.** *adj.* early; *am ~en
Morgen* in the early morning; *~es
Aufstehen* early rising; *~e Anzeichen*
early symptoms; *~er former*; **2.** *adv.*
in the morning; *~ aufstehen* rise
early; *heute ~* this morning; *morgen
~* tomorrow morning; *~er* earlier;
formerly, in former times; *~estens*
at the earliest; '**2aufsteher** *m* (-s/-)
early riser, F early bird; '**2e** *f* (-/no
pl.): *in aller ~* very early in the
morning; '**2geburt** *f* premature
birth; premature baby *or* animal;
'**2gottesdienst** *m* early service;

'Ωjahr n, Ωling ['ːliŋ] m (-s/-e) spring; 'ːmorgens adv. early in the morning; 'ːreif fig. adj. precocious; 'Ωsport m early morning exercises; 'Ωstück n breakfast; 'ːstücken (ge-, h) **1.** v/i. (have) breakfast; **2.** v/t. have s.th. for breakfast; 'Ωzug 🚂 m early train.

Fuchs [fuks] m (-es/ːe) zo. fox (a. fig.); horse: sorrel.

Füchsin zo. ['fyksin] f (-/-nen) she-fox, vixen.

'**Fuchs|jagd** f fox-hunt(ing); 'ːpelz m fox-fur; 'Ωʹrot adj. foxy-red, sorrel; 'ːschwanz m foxtail; ⊕ pad-saw; ♀ amaranth(h); 'Ωʹteufels-**wild** F adj. mad with rage, F hopping mad.

fuchteln ['fuxtəln] v/i. (ge-, h): ː mit (dat.) wave (one's hands) about.

Fuder ['fuːdər] n (-s/-) cart-load; tun (of wine).

Fuge ['fuːgə] f (-/-n) ⊕ joint; seam; [♩ fugue.]

füg|en ['fyːgən] v/refl. (ge-, h) submit, give in, yield (dat.; in acc. to); comply (with); ːsam adj. ['fyːk-] (com)pliant; manageable.

'**fühl|bar** adj. ['fyːlbaːr] tangible, palpable; fig. sensible, noticeable; 'ːen (ge-, h) **1.** v/t. feel; be aware of; sich glücklich ː feel happy; **2.** v/i.: mit j-m ː feel for or sympathize with s.o.; 'Ωer m (-s/-) feeler (a. fig.); 'Ωung f (-/-en) touch, contact (a. ✕); ː haben be in touch (mit with); ː verlieren lose touch.

fuhr [fuːr] pret. of fahren.

Fuhre ['fuːrə] f (-/-n) cart-load.

führen ['fyːrən] (ge-, h) **1.** v/t. lead, guide (blind person, etc.); show (zu dat. to); wield (paint-brush, etc.); ✕ command (regiment, etc.); have, bear (title, etc.); carry on (conversation, etc.); conduct (campaign, etc.); ✝ run (shop, etc.); deal in (goods); lead (life); keep (diary, etc.; ⚖ try (case); wage (war) (mit, gegen against); ː durch show round; sich ː conduct, behave (o.s.); **2.** v/i. path, etc.: lead, run, go (nach, zu to); sports, etc.: (hold the) lead, be ahead; ː zu lead to, result in; 'ːd adj. leading, prominent, Am. a. banner.

'**Führer** m (-s/-) leader (a. pol., sports); guide(-book); 'ːraum ✈ m cockpit; 'ːschein mot. m driving licence, Am. driver's license; 'ːsitz

m mot. driver's seat, ✈ pilot's seat 'ːstand 🚂 m (driver's) cab.

'**Fuhr|geld** n, 'ːlohn m cartage carriage; 'ːmann m (-[e]s/ːer, Fuhr-leute) carter, carrier, wag(g)oner driver; 'ːpark m fleet (of lorries) Am. fleet (of trucks).

'**Führung** f (-/-en) leadership; conduct, management; guidance; conduct, behavio(u)r; sports, etc.: lead 'ːszeugnis n certificate of good conduct.

'**Fuhr|unternehmer** m carrier, haulage contractor, Am. a. trucker, teamster; 'ːwerk n (horse-drawn) vehicle; cart, wag(g)on.

Fülle ['fylə] f (-/no pl.) fullness (a. fig.); corpulence, plumpness, stout-ness; fig. wealth, abundance, profusion.

füllen¹ ['fylən] v/t. (ge-, h) fill (a. tooth); stuff (cushion, poultry, etc.).

Füllen² zo. [ː] n (-s/-) foal; male: colt; female: filly.

'**Füll|er** F m (-s/-), 'ːfeder(halter m) f fountain-pen; 'ːhorn n horn of plenty; 'ːung f (-/-en) filling; panel (of door, etc.).

Fund [funt] m (-[e]s/-e) finding, discovery; find.

Fundament [funda'ment] n (-[e]s/-e) ⚖ foundation; fig. basis.

'**Fund|büro** n lost-property office; 'ːgegenstand m object found; 'ːgrube fig. f rich source, mine.

fünf adj. [fynf] five; 'Ωeck n pentagon; 'ːfach adj. ['ːfax] fivefold, quintuple; 'Ωkampf m sports: pentathlon; Ωlinge ['ːliŋə] m/pl. quintuplets pl.; 'ːte adj. fifth; 'Ωtel n (-s/-) fifth (part); 'ːtens adv. fifthly, in the fifth place; 'ːzehn(te) adj. fifteen(th); 'Ωzig adj. ['ːtsiç] fifty; 'ːzigste adj. fiftieth.

fungieren [fuŋ'giːrən] v/i. (no -ge-, h): ː als officiate or act as.

Funk [fuŋk] m (-s/no pl.) radio, wireless; 'ːanlage f radio or wire-less installation or equipment; 'ːbastler m do-it-yourself radio ham; 'ːbild n photo-radiogram.

Funke ['fuŋkə] m (-ns/-n) spark; fig. a. glimmer.

'**funkeln** v/i. (ge-, h) sparkle, glitter; star: twinkle, sparkle.

'**Funken¹** esp. fig. m (-s/-) s. Funke.

'**funken²** v/t. (ge-, h) radio, wireless, broadcast.

Funk|er m (-s/-) radio or wireless operator; **˷gerät** n radio (communication) set; **˷spruch** m radio or wireless message; **˷station** f radio or wireless station; **˷stille** f radio or wireless silence; **˷streifen-wagen** m radio patrol car.

Funktion [fuŋk'tsjo:n] f (-/-en) function; **˷är** [˷tsjo'nɛ:r] m (-s/-e) functionary, official; **2ieren** [˷o-'ni:rən] v/i. (no -ge-, h) function, work.

Funk|turm m radio or wireless tower; **˷verkehr** m radio or wireless communication; **˷wagen** m radio car; **˷wesen** n (-s/no pl.) radio communication.

für prp. (acc.) [fy:r] for; in exchange or return for; in favo(u)r of; in s.o.'s place; Schritt ˷ Schritt step by step; Tag ˷ Tag day after day; ich ˷ meine Person ... as for me, I ...; das Für und Wider the pros and cons pl.

'Fürbitte f intercession.

Furche ['furçə] f (-/-n) furrow (a. in face); rut; ⊕ groove; **2n** v/t. (ge-, h) furrow (a. face); ⊕ groove.

Furcht [furçt] f (-/no pl.) fear, dread; aus ˷ vor for fear of; **2bar** adj. awful, terrible, dreadful.

fürchten ['fyrçtən] (ge-, h) **1.** v/t. fear, dread; sich ˷ vor (dat.) be afraid or scared of; **2.** v/i.: ˷ um fear for.

'fürchterlich adj. s. furchtbar.

furcht|los adj. fearless; **2losig-keit** f (-/no pl.) fearlessness; **˷sam** adj. timid, timorous; **2samkeit** f (-/no pl.) timidity.

Furie ['fu:rjə] f (-/-n) fury.

Furnier ⊕ [fur'ni:r] n (-s/-e) veneer; **2en** v/t. (no -ge-, h) veneer.

'Für|sorge f care; öffentliche ˷ public welfare work; **˷sorgeamt** n welfare department; **˷sorgeer-ziehung** f corrective training for juvenile delinquents; **˷sorger** m (-s/-) social or welfare worker; **2sorglich** adj. considerate, thoughtful, solicitous; **˷sprache** f intercession (für for, bei with); **˷sprecher** m intercessor.

Fürst [fyrst] m (-en/-en) prince; sovereign; **˷enhaus** n dynasty; **˷enstand** m prince's rank; **˷en-**

tum n (-s/˷er) principality; **2lich 1.** adj. princely (a. fig.), royal; fig. magnificent, sumptuous; **2.** adv.: ˷ leben live like a lord or king; **˷lich-keiten** f/pl. royalties pl.

Furt [furt] f (-/-en) ford.

Furunkel ⚕ [fu'ruŋkəl] m (-s/-) boil, furuncle.

'Fürwort gr. n (-[e]s/˷er) pronoun.

Fusel F ['fu:zəl] m (-s/-) low-quality spirits, F rotgut.

Fusion ✝ [fu:'zjo:n] f (-/-en) merger, amalgamation.

Fuß [fu:s] m (-es/˷e) foot; ˷ fassen find a foothold; fig. become established; auf gutem (schlechtem) ˷ stehen mit be on good (bad) terms with; zu ˷ on foot; zu ˷ gehen walk; gut zu ˷ sein be a good walker; **˷abstreifer** m (-s/-) door-scraper, door-mat; **˷angel** f mantrap; **˷ball** m (association) football, F and Am. soccer; **˷ballspieler** m football player, footballer; **˷bank** f footstool; **˷bekleidung** f foot-wear, footgear; **˷boden** m floor (-ing); **˷bodenbelag** m floor cover-ing; **˷bremse** mot. f foot-brake; **2en** v/i. (ge-, h): ˷ auf (dat.) be based or founded on; **˷gänger** ['˷gɛŋər] m (-s/-) pedestrian; **˷ge-lenk** anat. n ankle joint; **˷note** f footnote; **˷pfad** m footpath; **˷sack** m foot-muff; **˷sohle** anat. f sole of the foot; **˷soldat** ✕ m foot-soldier, infantryman; **˷spur** f foot-print; track; **˷stapfe** ['˷ʃtapfə] f (-/-n) footprint, fig. a. footstep; **˷steig** m footpath; **˷tritt** m kick; **˷wanderung** f walking tour, hike; **˷weg** m footpath.

Futter ['futər] n **1.** (-s/no pl.) food, sl. grub, Am. F a. chow; feed, fodder; **2.** (-s/-) lining; △ casing.

Futteral [futə'ra:l] n (-s/-e) case (for spectacles, etc.); cover (of um-brella); sheath (of knife).

'Futtermittel n feeding stuff.

füttern ['fytərn] v/t. (ge-, h) feed; line (dress, etc.); △ case.

'Futter|napf m feeding bowl or dish; **˷neid** fig. m (professional) jealousy; **˷stoff** m lining (material).

'Fütterung f (-/-en) feeding; lining; △ casing.   [(tense).\]

Futur gr. [fu'tu:r] n (-s/-e) future]

G

gab [ɡɑːp] *pret. of* geben.

Gabe ['ɡɑːbə] *f* (-/-n) gift, present; alms; donation; ♂ dose; talent.

Gabel ['ɡɑːbəl] *f* (-/-n) fork; '**2n** *v*/*refl.* (ge-, h) fork, bifurcate; '**~ung** *f* (-/-en) bifurcation.

gackern ['ɡakərn] *v*/*i.* (ge-, h) cackle.

gaffen ['ɡafən] *v*/*i.* (ge-, h) gape, stare.

Gage ['ɡɑːʒə] *f* (-/-n) salary, pay.

gähnen ['ɡɛːnən] **1.** *v*/*i.* (ge-, h) yawn; **2.** **2** *n* (-s/*no pl.*) yawning.

Gala ['ɡala] *f* (-/*no pl.*) gala; *in* ~ *in* full dress.

galant *adj.* [ɡa'lant] gallant; courteous; **2erie** [~ə'riː] *f* (-/-n) gallantry; courtesy.

Galeere ⚓ [ɡa'leːrə] *f* (-/-n) galley.

Galerie [ɡaləˈriː] *f* (-/-n) gallery.

Galgen ['ɡalɡən] *m* (-s/-) gallows, gibbet; '**~frist** *f* respite; '**~gesicht** *n* gallows-look, hangdog look; '**~humor** *m* grim humo(u)r; '**~strick** *m*, '**~vogel** *m* gallows-bird, hangdog.

Galle *anat.* ['ɡalə] *f* (-/-n) bile (*of person*); gall (*of animal*; *a. fig.*); '**~nblase** *anat.* *f* gall-bladder; '**~nleiden** ♂ *n* bilious complaint; '**~nstein** ♂ *m* gall-stone, bile-stone.

gallig *fig. adj.* bilious.

Galopp [ɡa'lɔp] *m* (-s/-s, -e) gallop; canter; **2ieren** [~pi'riːrən] *v*/*i.* (*no* -ge-, *sein*) gallop; canter.

galt [ɡalt] *pret. of* gelten.

galvani|sch *adj.* [ɡal'vɑːniʃ] galvanic; **~sieren** [~ani'-] *v*/*t.* (*no* -ge-, h) galvanize.

Gang¹ [ɡaŋ] *m* (-[e]s/-e) walk; *s.* Gangart; *fig.* motion; running, working (*of machine*); errand; way; course (*of events, of a meal, etc.*); passage(-way); alley; corridor, gallery; *in vehicle, between seats:* gangway, *esp. Am.* aisle; ⚓ corridor, *Am.* aisle; *fencing:* pass; *anat.* duct; *mot.* gear; *erster (zweiter, dritter, vierter)* ~ low or bottom (second, third, top) gear; *in* ~ *bringen or setzen* set going or in motion, *Am.* operate; *in* ~ *kommen* get going, get started; *im* ~ *sein* be in motion; ⊕ be working or running; *fig.* be

in progress; in vollem ~ *in full swing.*

gang² *adj.* [~]: ~ *und gäbe* customary, traditional.

'**Gang|art** *f* gait, walk (*of person*); pace (*of horse*); ♞ road: practicable, passable; *money:* current; ♣ *goods:* marketable; *s.* **gängig**.

Gängelband ['ɡɛŋəl-] *n* leading-strings *pl.*; *am* ~ *führen* keep in leading-strings, lead by the nose.

gängig *adj.* ['ɡɛŋiç] *money:* current; ♣ *goods:* marketable; **~er** *Ausdruck* current word or phrase.

Gans *orn.* [ɡans] *f* (-/-e) goose.

Gänse|blümchen ♣ ['ɡɛnzəblyːmçən] *n* (-s/-) daisy; '**~braten** *m* roast goose; '**~feder** *f* goose-quill; '**~füßchen** ['~fyːsçən] *n*/*pl.* quotation marks *pl.*, inverted commas *pl.*; '**~haut** *f* goose-skin; *fig. a.* goose-flesh, *Am. a.* goose pimples *pl.*; '**~klein** *n* (-s/*no pl.*) (goose-)giblets *pl.*; '**~marsch** *m* single or Indian file; **~rich** *orn.* ['~riç] *m* (-s/-e) gander; '**~schmalz** *n* goose-grease.

ganz [ɡants] **1.** *adj.* all; entire, whole; complete, total, full; *den* ~*en Tag* all day (long); **2.** *adv.* quite; entirely, *etc.* (*s.* 1.); very; ~ *Auge (Ohr)* all eyes (ears); ~ *und gar* wholly, totally; ~ *und gar nicht* not at all; *im* ~*en* on the whole, generally; in all; ♣ in the lump; '**2e** *n* (-n/*no pl.*) whole; totality; *aufs* ~ *gehen* go all out, *esp. Am. sl.* go the whole hog.

gänzlich *adj.* ['ɡɛntsliç] complete, total, entire.

'**Ganztagsbeschäftigung** *f* full-time job or employment.

gar [ɡɑːr] **1.** *adj. food:* done; **2.** *adv.* quite, very; even; ~ *nicht* not at all.

Garage [ɡa'rɑːʒə] *f* (-/-n) garage.

Garantie [ɡaran'tiː] *f* (-/-n) guarantee, warranty, ⚖ guaranty; **2ren** *v*/*t.* (*no* -ge-, h) guarantee, warrant.

Garbe ['ɡarbə] *f* (-/-n) sheaf.

Garde ['ɡardə] *f* (-/-n) guard.

Garderobe [ɡardə'roːbə] *f* (-/-n) wardrobe; cloakroom, *Am.* checkroom; *thea.* dressing-room; **~nfrau** *f* cloak-room attendant, *Am.* hat-check girl; **~nmarke** *f* check; **~nschrank** *m* wardrobe; **~nständer**

m coat-stand, hat-stand, hall-stand.

Garderobiere [gardəro'bjɛːrə] *f* (-/-n) *s.* **Garderobenfrau;** *thea.* wardrobe mistress.

Gardine [gar'diːnə] *f* (-/-n) curtain.

gär|en ['gɛːrən] *v/i.* (*irr.*, ge-, *h*, *sein*) ferment; **⁀mittel** *n* ferment.

Garn [garn] *n* (-[e]s/-e) yarn; thread; cotton; net; *j-m ins ⁀ gehen* fall into s.o.'s snare.

Garnele *zo.* [gar'neːlə] *f* (-/-n) shrimp.

garnieren [gar'niːrən] *v/t.* (*no* -ge-, *h*) trim; garnish (*esp. a dish*).

Garnison ⚔ [garni'zoːn] *f* (-/-en) garrison, post.

Garnitur [garni'tuːr] *f* (-/-en) trimming; ⊕ fittings *pl.*; set.

garstig *adj.* [garstiç] nasty, bad; ugly.

'Gärstoff *m* ferment.

Garten ['gartən] *m* (-s/⁀) garden; **⁀anlage** *f* gardens *pl.*, park; **⁀arbeit** *f* gardening; **⁀bau** *m* horticulture; **⁀erde** *f* (garden-)mo(u)ld; **⁀fest** *n* garden-party, *Am. a.* lawn party; **⁀geräte** *n/pl.* gardening-tools *pl.*; **⁀stadt** *f* garden city.

Gärtner ['gɛrtnər] *m* (-s/-) gardener; **⁀ei** [⁀'raɪ] *f* (-/-en) gardening, horticulture; nursery; **⁀in** *f* (-/-nen) gardener.   [tation.]

Gärung ['gɛːruŋ] *f* (-/-en) fermen-

Gas [gaːs] *n* (-es/-e) gas; *⁀ geben mot.* open the throttle, *Am.* step on the gas; **⁀anstalt** *f* gas-works, *Am. a.* gas plant; **⁀behälter** *m* gasometer, *Am.* gas tank *or* container; **⁀beleuchtung** *f* gaslight; **⁀brenner** *m* gas-burner, ⁀**förmig** *adj.* [⁀'fœrmiç] gaseous; **⁀hahn** *m* gas-tap; **⁀herd** *m* gas-stove, *Am.* gas range; **⁀leitung** *f* gas-mains *pl.*; **⁀messer** *m* (-s/-) gas-meter; **⁀ofen** *m* gas-oven; **⁀pedal** *mot. n* accelerator (pedal), *Am.* gas pedal.

Gasse ['gasə] *f* (-/-n) lane, by-street, alley(-way); **⁀nhauer** *m* (-s/-) street ballad, popular song; **⁀njunge** *m* street arab.

Gast [gast] *m* (-es/⁀e) guest; visitor; customer (*of public house, etc.*); *thea.*: guest (artist); guest star; **⁀arbeiter** *m* foreign worker; **⁀bett** *n* spare bed.

Gäste|buch ['gɛstə-] *n* visitors' book; **⁀zimmer** *n* guest-room; spare (bed)room; *s.* **Gaststube.**

'gast|freundlich *adj.* hospitable; ⁀**freundschaft** *f* hospitality; ⁀**geber** *m* (-s/-) host; ⁀**geberin** *f* (-/-nen) hostess; ⁀**haus** *n*, ⁀**hof** *m* restaurant; inn, hotel; ⁀**hörer** *univ. m* guest student, *Am. a.* auditor.

gastieren [gas'tiːrən] *v/i.* (*no* -ge-, *h*) appear as a guest.

'gast|lich *adj.* hospitable; ⁀**mahl** *n* feast, banquet; ⁀**recht** *n* right of *or* to hospitality; ⁀**rolle** *thea. f* guest part; starring part *or* role; ⁀**spiel** *thea. n* guest appearance *or* performance; starring (performance); ⁀**stätte** *f* restaurant; ⁀**stube** *f* taproom; restaurant; ⁀**wirt** *m* innkeeper, landlord; ⁀**wirtin** *f* innkeeper, landlady; ⁀**wirtschaft** *f* inn, public house, restaurant; ⁀**zimmer** *n s.* **Gästezimmer.**

'Gas|uhr *f* gas-meter; **⁀werk** *n s.* **Gasanstalt.**

Gatte ['gatə] *m* (-n/-n) husband; spouse, consort.

Gatter ['gatər] *n* (-s/-) lattice; railing, grating.

Gattin *f* (-/-nen) wife; spouse, consort.

Gattung ['gatuŋ] *f* (-/-en) kind; sort; type; species; genus.

gaukeln ['gaʊkəln] *v/i.* (ge-, *h*) juggle; *birds, etc.*: flutter.

Gaul [gaʊl] *m* (-[e]s/⁀e) (old) nag.

Gaumen *anat.* ['gaʊmən] *m* (-s/-) palate.

Gauner ['gaʊnər] *m* (-s/-) scoundrel, swindler, sharper, *sl.* crook; **⁀ei** [⁀'raɪ] *f* (-/-en) swindling, cheating, trickery.

Gaze ['gaːzə] *f* (-/-n) gauze.

Gazelle *zo.* [ga'tsɛlə] *f* (-/-n) gazelle.

Geächtete [gə'ɛçtətə] *m, f* (-n/-n) outlaw.

Gebäck [gə'bɛk] *n* (-[e]s/-e) baker's goods *pl.*; pastry; fancy cakes *pl.*

ge'backen *p.p. of* **backen.**

Gebälk [gə'bɛlk] *n* (-[e]s/*no pl.*) framework, timber-work; beams *pl.*

gebar [gə'baːr] *pret. of* **gebären.**

Gebärde [gə'bɛːrdə] *f* (-/-n) gesture; ⁀**n** *v/refl.* (*no* -ge-, *h*) conduct o.s., behave; **⁀nspiel** *n* (-[e]s/*no pl.*) gesticulation; dumb show, pantomime; **⁀nsprache** *f* language of gestures.

Gebaren [gə'baːrən] *n* (-s/*no pl.*) conduct, deportment, behavio(u)r.

G

gebären [gə'bɛːrən] v/t. (irr., no -ge-, h) bear, bring forth (a. fig.); give birth to.

Ge|bäude [gə'bɔydə] n (-s/-) building, edifice, structure; **~bell** [ˌˈbɛl] n (-[e]s/no pl.) barking.

geben ['geːbən] v/t. (irr., ge-, h) give (j-m et. s.o. s.th.); present (s.o. with s.th.); put; yield s.th.; deal (cards); pledge (one's word); von sich ~ emit; utter (words); bring up, vomit (food); et. (nichts) ~ auf (acc.) set (no) great store by; sich geschlagen ~ give in; sich zufrieden ~ content o.s. (mit with); sich zu erkennen ~ make o.s. known; es gibt there is, there are; was gibt es? what is the matter?; thea.: gegeben werden be on.

Gebet [gə'beːt] n (-[e]s/-e) prayer.

ge'beten p.p. of bitten.

Gebiet [gə'biːt] n (-[e]s/-e) territory; district; region; area; fig.: field; province; sphere.

ge'biet|en (irr. bieten, no -ge-, h) **1.** v/t. order, command; **2.** v/i. rule; **2er** m (-s/-) master, lord, governor; **2erin** f (-/-nen) mistress; **~erisch** adj. imperious; commanding.

Gebilde [gə'bildə] n (-s/-) form, shape; structure; **2t** adj. educated; cultured, cultivated.

Gebirg|e [gə'birgə] n (-s/-) mountains pl.; mountain chain or range; **2ig** adj. mountainous; **~sbewohner** m mountaineer; **~szug** m mountain range.

Ge'biß n (Gebisses/Gebisse) (set of) teeth; (set of) artificial or false teeth, denture; harness: bit.

ge|'bissen p.p. of beißen; **~'blasen** p.p. of blasen; **~'blichen** p.p. of bleichen 2; **~blieben** [ˌˈbliːbən] p.p. of bleiben; **~blümt** adj. [ˌˈblyːmt] pattern, design: flowered; material: sprigged; **~'bogen** 1. p.p. of biegen; 2. adj. bent, curved; **~boren** [ˌˈboːrən] 1. p.p. of gebären; 2. adj. born; ein ~er Deutscher German by birth; **~e** Schmidt née Smith.

ge'borgen 1. p.p. of bergen; 2. adj. safe, sheltered; **2heit** f (-/no pl.) safety, security.

geborsten [gə'bɔrstən] p.p. of bersten.

Ge'bot n (-[e]s/-e) order; command; bid(ding), offer; eccl.: die Zehn ~e

---

pl. the Ten Commandments pl.; **2en** p.p. of bieten.

ge|bracht [gə'braxt] p.p. of bringen; **~brannt** [ˌˈbrant] p.p. of brennen; **~'braten** p.p. of braten.

Ge'brauch m **1.** (-[e]s/no pl.) use; ⚕ application; **2.** (-[e]s/ᵘe) usage, practice; custom; **2en** v/t. (no -ge-, h) use, employ; **2t** adj. clothes, etc.: second-hand.

gebräuchlich adj. [gə'brɔyçliç] in use; usual, customary.

Ge'brauchs|anweisung f directions pl. or instructions pl. for use; **~artikel** m commodity, necessary, requisite; personal article; **2fertig** adj. ready for use; coffee, etc.: instant; **~muster** ✝ n sample; registered design.

Ge'braucht|wagen mot. m used car; **~waren** f/pl. second-hand articles pl.

Ge'brechen n (-s/-) defect, infirmity; affliction.

ge'brechlich adj. fragile; p.: frail, weak; infirm; **2keit** f (-/-en) fragility, infirmity. [chen.\

gebrochen [gə'brɔxən] p.p. of bre-

Ge|brüder [gə'bryːdər] pl. brothers pl.; **~brüll** [ˌˈbryl] n (-[e]s/no pl.) roaring; lowing (of cattle).

Gebühr [gə'byːr] f (-/-en) due; duty; charge; rate; fee; **~en** pl. fee(s pl.), dues pl.; **2en** v/i. (no -ge-, h) be due (dat. to); sich ~ be proper or fitting; **2end** adj. due; becoming; proper; **2enfrei** adj. free of charge; **2enpflichtig** adj. liable to charges, chargeable.

gebunden [gə'bundən] **1.** p.p. of binden; **2.** adj. bound.

Geburt [gə'buːrt] f (-/-en) birth; **~enkontrolle** f, **~enregelung** f birth-control; **~enziffer** f birth-rate.

gebürtig adj. [gə'byrtiç]: ~ aus a native of.

Ge'burts|anzeige f announcement of birth; **~fehler** m congenital defect; **~helfer** m obstetrician; **~hilfe** f obstetrics, midwifery; **~jahr** n year of birth; **~land** n native country; **~ort** m birth-place; **~schein** m birth certificate; **~tag** m birthday; **~urkunde** f birth certificate.

Gebüsch [gə'byʃ] n (-es/-e) bushes pl., undergrowth, thicket.

gedacht [gə'daxt] p.p. of denken.

Gedächtnis [gə'dɛçtnis] n (-ses/-se) memory; remembrance, recollection; im ~ behalten keep in mind; zum ~ (gen.) in memory of; **~feier** f commemoration.

Gedanke [gə'daŋkə] m (-ns/-n) thought; idea; in ~n (versunken or verloren) absorbed in thought; sich ~n machen über (acc.) worry about. **Ge'danken|gang** m train of thought; **~leser** m, **~leserin** f (-/-nen) thought-reader; **~los** adj. thoughtless; **~strich** m dash; **~voll** adj. thoughtful.

Ge|därm [gə'dɛrm] n (-[e]s/-e) mst pl. entrails pl., bowels pl., intestines pl.; **~deck** [~'dɛk] n (-[e]s/-e) cover; menu; ein ~ auflegen lay a place.

gedeihen [gə'daɪən] 1. v/i. (irr., no -ge-, sein) thrive, prosper; 2. 2 n (-s/no pl.) thriving, prosperity.

ge'denken 1. v/i. (gen.) (irr. denken, no -ge-, h) think of; remember, recollect; commemorate; mention; ~ zu inf. intend to inf.; 2. 2 n (-s/no pl.) memory, remembrance (an acc. of).

Ge'denk|feier f commemoration; **~stein** m memorial stone; **~tafel** f commemorative or memorial tablet. **Ge'dicht** n (-[e]s/-e) poem.

gediegen adj. [gə'di:gən] solid; pure; **2heit** f (-/no pl.) solidity; purity.

gedieh [gə'di:] pret. of gedeihen; **~en** p.p. of gedeihen.

Gedräng|e [gə'drɛŋə] n (-s/no pl.) crowd, throng; **2t** adj. crowded, packed, crammed; style: concise.

ge|droschen [gə'drɔʃən] p.p. of dreschen; **~'drückt** fig. adj. depressed; **~drungen** [~'druŋən] 1. p.p. of dringen; 2. adj. compact; squat, stocky, thickset.

Geduld [gə'dult] f (-/no pl.) patience; **2en** [~dən] v/refl. (no -ge-, h) have patience; **2ig** adj. [~diç] patient.

ge|dunsen adj. [gə'dunzən] bloated; **~durft** [~'durft] p.p. of dürfen 1; **~ehrt** adj. [~'e:rt] hono(u)red; correspondence: Sehr ~er Herr N.! Dear Sir, Dear Mr N.; **~eignet** adj. [~'aɪgnət] fit (für, zu, als for s.th.); suitable (to for s.th.); qualified (for). **Gefahr** [gə'fa:r] f (-/-en) danger, peril; risk; auf eigene ~ at one's

own risk; ~ laufen zu inf. run the risk of ger.

gefährden [gə'fɛːrdən] v/t. (no -ge-, h) endanger; risk.

ge'fahren p.p. of fahren.

gefährlich adj. [gə'fɛːrliç] dangerous.

ge'fahrlos adj. without risk, safe.

Gefährt|e [gə'fɛːrtə] m (-en/-en), **~in** f (-/-nen) companion, fellow.

Gefälle [gə'fɛlə] n (-s/-) fall, slope, incline, descent, gradient, esp. Am. a. grade; fall (of river, etc.).

Ge'fallen 1. m (-s/-) favo(u)r; **2.** n (-s/no pl.): ~ finden an (dat.) take (a) pleasure in, take a fancy to or for; **3.** 2 v/i. (irr. fallen, no -ge-, h) please (j-m s.o.); er gefällt mir I like him; sich et. ~ lassen put up with s.th.; **4.** 2 p.p. of fallen.

gefällig adj. [gə'fɛliç] pleasing, agreeable; p.: complaisant, obliging; kind; **2keit** f (-/~en) complaisance, kindness; favo(u)r; **~st** adv. (if you) please.

ge'fangen 1. p.p. of fangen; **2.** adj. captive, imprisoned; **2e** m (-n/-n), f (-n/-n) prisoner, captive; **2en-lager** n prison(ers') camp; **2-nahme** f (-/no pl.) capture; seizure, arrest; **2nehmen** v/t. (irr. nehmen, sep., -ge-, h) take prisoner; fig. captivate; **2schaft** f (-/no pl.) captivity; imprisonment; **2setzen** v/t. (sep., -ge-, h) put in prison.

Gefängnis [gə'fɛŋnis] n (-ses/-se) prison, jail, gaol, Am. a. penitentiary; **~direktor** m governor, warden; **~strafe** f (sentence or term of) imprisonment; **~wärter** m warder, gaoler, jailer, (prison) guard.

Gefäß [gə'fɛːs] n (-es/-e) vessel.

gefaßt adj. [gə'fast] composed; ~ auf (acc.) prepared for.

Ge|fecht [gə'fɛçt] n (-[e]s/-e) engagement, combat, fight; action; **~fieder** [~'fiːdər] n (-s/-) plumage, feathers pl.

ge|fleckt adj. spotted; **~flochten** [~'flɔxtən] p.p. of flechten; **~flogen** [~'floːgən] p.p. of fliegen; **~flohen** [~'floːən] p.p. of fliehen; **~flossen** [~'flɔsən] p.p. of fließen.

Ge'flügel n (-s/no pl.) fowl; poultry; **~flüster** [~'flystər] n (-s/no pl.) whisper(ing). [ten.)

gefochten [gə'fɔxtən] p.p. of fech-)

Ge'folg|e n (-s/no pl.) retinue, train, followers pl.; attendants pl.; **~schaft** [~kʃaft] f (-/-en) followers pl.

gefräßig adj. [gə'frɛːsiç] greedy, voracious; **2keit** f (-/no pl.) greediness, gluttony, voracity.

ge'fressen p.p. of fressen.

ge'frier|en v/i. (irr. frieren, no -ge-, sein) congeal, freeze; **2fleisch** n frozen meat; **2punkt** m freezing-point; **2schutz(mittel** n) m anti-freeze.

gefroren [gə'froːrən] p.p. of frieren. **2e** [~ə] n (-n/no pl.) ice-cream.

Gefüge [gə'fyːgə] n (-s/-) structure; texture.

ge'fügig adj. pliant; **2keit** f (-/no pl.) pliancy.

Gefühl [gə'fyːl] n (-[e]s/-e) feeling; touch; sense (für of); sensation; **~los** adj. unfeeling, insensible (gegen to); **2sbetont** adj. emotional; **2voll** adj. (full of) feeling; tender; sentimental.

ge'funden [gə'fundən] p.p. of finden; **~gangen** [~'gaŋən] p.p. of gehen.

ge'geben p.p. of geben; **~enfalls** adv. in that case; if necessary.

gegen prp. (acc.) ['geːgən] space, time: towards; against, ⚖ versus; about, Am. around; by; compared with; (in exchange) for; remedy: for; freundlich sein ~ be kind to (-wards); ~ bar for cash.

'Gegen|angriff m counter-attack; **'~antrag** m counter-motion; **'~antwort** f rejoinder; **'~befehl** m counter-order; **'~beschuldigung** f countercharge; **'~besuch** m return visit; **'~bewegung** f counter-movement; **'~beweis** m counter-evidence.

Gegend ['geːgənt] f (-/-en) region; area.

'Gegen|dienst m return service, service in return; **'~druck** m counter-pressure; fig. reaction; **2ei'nander** adv. against one another or each other; **'~erklärung** f counter-statement; **'~forderung** f counter-claim; **'~frage** f counter-question; **'~geschenk** n return present; **'~gewicht** n counterbalance, counterpoise; **'~gift** ⚗ n antidote; **'~kandidat** m rival candidate; **'~klage** f coun16charge; **'~leistung**

f return (service), equivalent; **~lichtaufnahme** phot. ['gɔːgənliçt9-] f back-lighted shot; **'~liebe** f requited love; keine ~ finden meet with no sympathy or enthusiasm; **'~maßnahme** f counter-measure; **'~mittel** n remedy (gegen for), antidote (against, for); **'~partei** f opposite party; **'~probe** f check-test; **'~satz** m contrast; opposition; im ~ zu in contrast to or with, in opposition to; **2sätzlich** adj. ['~zetsliç] contrary, opposite; **'~seite** f opposite side; **2seitig** adj. mutual, reciprocal; **'~seitigkeit** f (-/no pl.): auf ~ assurance: mutual; auf ~ beruhen be mutual; **'~spieler** m games, sports: opponent; antagonist; **'~spionage** f counter-espionage; **'~stand** m object; subject, topic; **'~strömung** f counter-current; **'~stück** n counterpart; match; **'~teil** n contrary, reverse; im ~ on the contrary; **2teilig** adj. contrary, opposite; **2'über 1.** adv. opposite; **2.** prp. (dat.) opposite (to); to (-wards); as against; face to face with; **~'über** n (-s/-) vis-à-vis; **2'überstehen** v/i. (irr. stehen, sep., -ge-, h) (dat.) be faced with; face; **~'überstellung** esp. ⚖ f confrontation; **'~vorschlag** m counter-proposal; **~wart** ['~vart] f (-/no pl.) presence; present time; gr. present tense; **2wärtig** ['~vertiç] **1.** adj. present; actual; **2.** adv. at present; **'~wehr** f defen|ce, Am. -se; resistance; **'~wert** m equivalent; **'~wind** m contrary wind, head wind; **'~wirkung** f counter-effect; reaction; **2zeichnen** v/t. (sep., -ge-, h) countersign; **'~zug** m counter-move (a. fig.); 🚃 corresponding train.

ge'gessen [gə'gɛsən] p.p. of essen; **~glichen** [~'gliçən] p.p. of gleichen; **~gliedert** adj. articulate, jointed; **~glitten** [~'glitən] p.p. of gleiten; **~glommen** [~'glɔmən] p.p. of glimmen.

Gegner ['geːgnər] m (-s/-) adversary, opponent; **~schaft** f (-/-en) opposition.

ge'golten [gə'gɔltən] p.p. of gelten; **~goren** [~'goːrən] p.p. of gären; **~gossen** [~'gɔsən] p.p. of gießen; **~'graben** p.p. of graben; **~griffen** [~'grifən] p.p. of greifen; **~habt** [~'haːpt] p.p. of haben.

Gehalt [gə'halt] **1.** m (-[e]s/-e) contents pl.; capacity; merit; **2.** n (-[e]s/-^er) salary; **2en** p.p. of halten; **2los** [.lo:s] adj. empty; **~empfänger** [gə'halts^ʔ-] m salaried employee or worker; **~serhöhung** [gə'halts^ʔ-] f rise (in salary), Am. raise; **2voll** adj. rich; substantial; wine: racy.

gehangen [gə'haŋən] p.p. of hängen 1.

gehässig adj. [gə'hesiç] malicious, spiteful; **2keit** f (-/-en) malice, spitefulness.

ge'hauen p.p. of hauen.

Ge'häuse [gə'hɔyzə] n (-s/-) case, box; cabinet; shell; core (of apple, etc.); **~hege** [.'he:gə] n (-s/-) enclosure.

geheim adj. [gə'haim] secret; **2-dienst** m secret service.

Ge'heimnis n (-ses/-se) secret; mystery; **~krämer** m mystery-monger; **2voll** adj. mysterious.

Ge'heim|polizei f secret police; **~polizist** m detective; plain-clothes man; **~schrift** f cipher; tel. code.

ge'heißen p.p. of heißen.

gehen ['ge:ən] v/i. (irr., ge-, sein) go; walk; leave; machine: go, work; clock, watch: go; merchandise: sell; wind: blow; paste: rise; wie geht es Ihnen? how are you (getting on)?; das geht nicht that won't do; in sich ~ repent; wieviel Pfennige ~ auf e-e Mark? how many pfennigs go to a mark?; das Fenster geht nach Norden the window faces or looks north; es geht nichts über (acc.) there is nothing like; wenn es nach mir ginge if I had my way.

Geheul [gə'hɔyl] n (-[e]s/no pl.) howling.

Ge'hilf|e m (-n/-n), **~in** f (-/-nen) assistant; fig. helpmate.

Ge'hirn n (-[e]s/-e) brain(s pl.); **~erschütterung** ⚕ f concussion (of the brain); **~schlag** ⚕ m cerebral apoplexy.

gehoben [gə'ho:bən] **1.** p.p. of heben; **2.** adj. speech, style: elevated; **~e Stimmung** elated mood.

Gehöft [gə'hø:ft] n (-[e]s/-e) farm (-stead).

geholfen [gə'hɔlfən] p.p. of helfen.

Gehölz [gə'hœlts] n (-es/-e) wood, coppice, copse.

Gehör [gə'hø:r] n (-[e]s/no pl.)

hearing; ear; nach dem ~ by ear; j-m ~ schenken lend an ear to s.o.; sich ~ verschaffen make o.s. heard.

ge'horchen v/i. (no -ge-, h) obey (j-m s.o.).

ge'hör|en v/i. (no -ge-, h) belong (dat. or zu to); es gehört sich it is proper or fit or right or suitable; das gehört nicht hierher that's not to the point; **~ig 1.** adj. belonging (dat. or zu to); fit, proper, right; due; F good; **2.** adv. duly; F thoroughly.

gehorsam [gə'ho:rza:m] **1.** adj. obedient; **2.** 2 m (-s/no pl.) obedience.

'Geh|steig m, **'~weg** m pavement, Am. sidewalk; **'~werk** ⊕ n clockwork, works pl.

Geier orn. ['gaiər] m (-s/-) vulture.

Geige ♪ ['gaigə] f (-/-n) violin, F fiddle; (auf der) ~ spielen play (on) the violin; **'~nbogen** ♪ m (violin-) bow; **'~nkasten** ♪ m violin-case; **'~r** ♪ m (-s/-), **'~rin** ♪ f (-/-nen) violinist.

'Geigerzähler phys. m Geiger counter.

geil adj. [gail] lascivious, wanton; luxuriant.

Geisel ['gaizəl] f (-/-n) hostage.

Geiß zo. [gais] f (-/-en) (she-, nanny-)goat; **'~blatt** ♀ n (-[e]s/no pl.) honeysuckle, woodbine; **'~bock** zo. m he-goat, billy-goat.

Geißel ['gaisəl] f (-/-n) whip, lash; fig. scourge; **'2n** v/t. (ge-, h) whip, lash; fig. castigate.

Geist [gaist] m (-es/-er) spirit; mind, intellect; wit; ghost; sprite.

'Geister|erscheinung f apparition; **'2haft** adj. ghostly.

'geistes|abwesend adj. absent-minded; **'2arbeiter** m brain-worker, white-collar worker; **'2-blitz** m brain-wave, flash of genius; **'2gabe** f talent; **'2gegenwart** f presence of mind; **'2gegenwärtig** adj. alert; quick-witted; **'~gestört** adj. mentally disturbed; **'~krank** adj. insane, mentally ill; **'2krankheit** f insanity, mental illness; **'~schwach** adj. feeble-minded, imbecile; **'~verwandt** adj. congenial; **'2wissenschaften** f/pl. the Arts pl., the Humanities pl.; **'2zustand** m state of mind.

'geistig adj. intellectual, mental;

spiritual; ~e Getränke n/pl. spirits pl.

'**geistlich** adj. spiritual; clerical; sacred; ²**e** m (-n/-n) clergyman; minister; '²**keit** f (-/no pl.) clergy.

'**geist|los** adj. spiritless; dull; stupid; '~**reich** adj., '~**voll** adj. ingenious, spirited.

Geiz [gaɪts] m (-es/no pl.) avarice; '~**hals** m miser, niggard; '²**ig** adj. avaricious, stingy, mean.

Gejammer [gə'jamər] n (-s/no pl.) lamentation(s pl.), wailing.

gekannt [gə'kant] p.p. of kennen.

Geklapper [gə'klapər] n (-s/no pl.) rattling.

Geklirr [gə'klɪr] n (-[e]s/no pl.), ~**e** [~ə] n (-s/no pl.) clashing, clanking.

ge|klungen [gə'kluŋən] p.p. of klingen; ~**kniffen** p.p. of kneifen; ~'**kommen** p.p. of kommen; ~**konnt** [~'kɔnt] p.p. of können 1, 2.

Ge|kreisch [gə'kraɪʃ] n (-es/no pl.) screaming, screams pl.; shrieking; ~**kritzel** [~'krɪtsəl] n (-s/no pl.) scrawl(ing), scribbling, scribble.

ge|krochen [gə'krɔxən] p.p. of kriechen; ~**künstelt** adj. [~'kyn-stəlt] affected.

Gelächter [gə'leçtər] n (-s/-) laughter.

ge'laden p.p. of laden.

Ge'lage n (-s/-) feast; drinking-bout.

Gelände [gə'lendə] n (-s/-) ground; terrain; country; area; ²**gängig** mot. adj. cross-country; ~**lauf** m sports: cross-country race or run.

Geländer [gə'lendər] n (-s/-) railing, balustrade; banisters pl.

ge'lang pret. of gelingen.

ge'langen v/i. (no -ge-, sein): ~ an (acc.) or in (acc.) arrive at, get or come to; ~ zu attain (to), gain.

ge'lassen 1. p.p. of lassen; 2. adj. calm, composed.

Gelatine [ʒela'ti:nə] f (-/no pl.) gelatin(e).

ge|'laufen p.p. of laufen; ~**läufig** adj. [~'lɔyfɪç] current; fluent, easy; tongue: voluble; familiar; ~**launt** adj. [~'launt] in a (good, etc.) humo(u)r or Am. mood.

Geläut [gə'lɔyt] n (-[e]s/-e), ~**e** [~ə] n (-s/-) ringing (of bells); chimes pl. (of church bells).

gelb adj. [gelp] yellow; '~**lich** adj.

yellowish; '²**sucht** ♀ f (-/no pl.) jaundice.

Geld [gelt] n (-[e]s/-er) money; im ~ schwimmen be rolling in money; zu ~ machen turn into cash; '~**an-gelegenheit** f money-matter; '~**anlage** f investment; '~**ausgabe** f expense; '~**beutel** m purse; '~**ent-wertung** f devaluation of the currency; '~**erwerb** m money-making; '~**geber** m (-s/-) financial backer, investor; '~**geschäfte** n/pl. money transactions pl.; '²**gierig** adj. greedy for money, avaricious; '~**mittel** n/pl. funds pl., resources pl.; '~**schein** m bank-note, Am. bill; '~**schrank** m strong-box, safe; '~**sendung** f remittance; '~**strafe** f fine; '~**stück** n coin; '~**tasche** f money-bag; notecase, Am. billfold; '~**überhang** m surplus money; '~**umlauf** m circulation of money; '~**umsatz** m turnover (of money); '~**verlegenheit** f pecuniary embarrassment; '~**wechsel** m exchange of money; '~**wert** m (-[e]s/no pl.) value of money, money value.

Gelee [ʒə'le:] n, m (-s/-s) jelly.

ge'legen 1. p.p. of liegen; 2. adj. situated, Am. a. located; convenient, opportune; ²**heit** f (-/-en) occasion; opportunity; chance; facility; bei ~ on occasion.

Ge'legenheits|arbeit f casual or odd job, Am. a. chore; ~**arbeiter** m casual labo(u)rer, odd-job man; ~**kauf** m bargain.

ge'legentlich 1. adj. occasional; 2. prp. (gen.) on the occasion of.

ge'lehr|ig adj. docile; ²**igkeit** f (-/no pl.) docility; ²**samkeit** f (-/no pl.) learning; ~**t** adj. [~t] learned; ²**te** [~ə] m (-n/-n) learned man, scholar.

Geleise [gə'laɪzə] n (-s/-) rut, track; ⚏ rails pl., line, esp. Am. tracks pl.

Geleit [gə'laɪt] n (-[e]s/-e) escort; attendance; j-m das ~ geben accompany s.o.; ²**en** v/t. (no -ge-, h) accompany, conduct; escort; ~**zug** ⚓ m convoy.

Gelenk anat., ⊕, ♀ [gə'leŋk] n (-[e]s/-e) joint; ²**ig** adj. pliable, supple.

ge|'lernt adj. worker: skilled; trained; ~**lesen** p.p. of lesen.

Geliebte [gə'li:ptə] (-n/-n) 1. m lover; 2. f mistress, sweetheart.

geliehen [gə'li:ən] *p.p. of leihen.*

ge'linde 1. *adj.* soft, smooth; gentle; **2.** *adv.:* gelinde gesagt to put it mildly, to say the least.

gelingen [gə'liŋən] **1.** *v/i.* (irr., no -ge-, sein) succeed; *es gelingt mir zu inf.* I succeed in *ger.;* **2.** ♀ *n* (-s/no pl.) success.

ge'litten *p.p. of leiden.*

gellen ['gɛlən] (ge-, h) **1.** *v/i.* shrill; yell; *of ears:* ring, tingle; **2.** *v/t.* shrill; yell; '~d *adj.* shrill, piercing.

ge'loben *v/t.* (no -ge-, h) vow, promise.

Gelöbnis [gə'lø:pnis] *n* (-ses/-se) promise, pledge; vow.

ge'logen *p.p. of lügen.*

gelten ['gɛltən] (*irr.,* ge-, h) **1.** *v/t.* be worth; **2.** *v/i.* be of value; be valid; ♀ count; *money:* be current; *maxim, etc.:* hold (good *or* true); *et.* ~ have credit *or* influence; *j-m* ~ concern s.o.; ~ *für or als* pass for, be reputed *or* thought *or* supposed to be; ~ *für* apply to; ~ *lassen* let pass, allow; ~d *machen* maintain, assert; *s-n Einfluß bei j-m* ~d *machen* bring one's influence to bear on s.o.; *das gilt nicht* that is not fair; that does not count; *es galt unser Leben* our life was at stake; '♀ung *f* (-/-, -en) validity; value; currency; authority (*of person*); *zur* ~ *kommen* tell; take effect; show; '♀ungsbedürfnis *n* desire to show off.   [ise; vow.\

Gelübde [gə'lypdə] *n* (-s/-) prom-\

gelungen [gə'luŋən] **1.** *p.p. of gelingen;* **2.** *adj.* successful; amusing, funny; F: *das ist ja* ~! that beats everything!

gemächlich *adj.* [gə'mɛ:çlɪç] comfortable, easy; ♀keit *f* (-/no pl.) ease, comfort.

Gemahl [gə'ma:l] *m* (-[e]s/-e) consort; husband.

ge'mahlen *p.p. of mahlen.*

Gemälde [gə'mɛ:ldə] *n* (-s/-) painting, picture; ~galerie *f* picture-gallery.

gemäß *prp.* (*dat.*) [gə'mɛ:s] according to; ~igt *adj.* moderate; temperate (*a. geogr.*).

gemein *adj.* [gə'maɪn] common; general; low, vulgar, mean, coarse; *et.* ~ *haben mit* have s.th. in common with.

Gemeinde [gə'maɪndə] *f* (-/-n)

community; parish; municipality; *eccl.* congregation; ~bezirk *m* district; municipality; ~rat *m* municipal council; ~steuer *f* rate, *Am.* local tax; ~vorstand *m* district council.

ge'mein|gefährlich *adj.* dangerous to the public; ~er Mensch public danger, *Am.* public enemy; ♀heit *f* (-/-en) vulgarity; meanness; mean trick; ~nützig *adj.* of public utility; ♀platz *m* commonplace; ~sam *adj.* common; joint; mutual; ♀schaft *f* (-/-en) community; intercourse; ~schaftlich *adj. s.* gemeinsam; ♀-schaftsarbeit [gə'maɪnʃafts9-] *f* team-work; ♀sinn *m* (-[e]s/no pl.) public spirit; ~verständlich *adj.* popular; ♀wesen *n* community; ♀wohl *n* public welfare.

Ge'menge *n* (-s/-) mixture.

ge'messen 1. *p.p. of messen;* **2.** *adj.* measured; formal; grave.

Gemetzel [gə'mɛtsəl] *n* (-s/-) slaughter, massacre.

gemieden [gə'mi:dən] *p.p. of meiden.*

Gemisch [gə'mɪʃ] *n* (-es/-e) mixture; 🜍 compound, composition.

ge|mocht [gə'mɔxt] *p.p. of mögen;* ~molken [gə'mɔlkən] *p.p. of melken.*

Gemse *zo.* ['gɛmzə] *f* (-/-n) chamois.

Gemurmel [gə'murməl] *n* (-s/no pl.) murmur(ing).

Gemüse [gə'my:zə] *n* (-s/-) vegetable(s *pl.*); greens *pl.;* ~anbau *m* vegetable gardening, *Am.* truck farming; ~garten *m* kitchen garden; ~händler *m* greengrocer.

gemußt [gə'must] *p.p. of müssen* 1.

Gemüt [gə'my:t] *n* (-[e]s/-er) mind; feeling; soul; heart; disposition; temper; ♀lich *adj.* good-natured; genial; comfortable, snug, cosy, cozy; ♀lichkeit *f* (-/no pl.) snugness, cosiness; easy-going; genial temper.

Ge'müts|art *f* disposition, nature, temper, character; ~bewegung *f* emotion; ♀krank *adj.* emotionally disturbed; melancholic; depressed; ~krankheit *f* mental disorder; melancholy; ~ruhe *f* composure; ~verfassung *f,* ~zustand *m* state of mind, humo(u)r.

ge'mütvoll *adj.* emotional; full of feeling.

G

genannt [gə'nant] *p.p. of* nennen.

genas [gə'naːs] *pret. of* genesen.

genau *adj.* [gə'nau] exact, accurate; precise; strict; es ~ nehmen (*mit*) be particular (about); ~eres full particulars *pl.*; ~igkeit *f* (-/-en) accuracy, exactness; precision; strictness.

genehm *adj.* [gə'neːm] agreeable, convenient; ~igen [~igən] *v/t.* (*no* -ge-, *h*) grant; approve (of); ~igung *f* (-/-en) grant; approval; licen|ce, *Am.* -se) permit; permission; consent.

geneigt *adj.* [gə'naikt] well disposed (*j-m* towards s.o.); inclined (zu to).

General ✕ [gene'raːl] *m* (-s/-e, -e) general; ~bevollmächtigte *m* chief representative *or* agent; ~direktor *m* general manager, managing director; ~feldmarschall ✕ *m* field-marshal; ~intendant *thea. m* (artistic) director; ~konsul *m* consul-general; ~konsulat *n* consulate-general; ~leutnant ✕ *m* lieutenant-general; ~major ✕ *m* major-general; ~probe *thea. f* dress rehearsal; ~stab ✕ *m* general staff; ~stabskarte ✕ *f* ordnance (survey) map, *Am.* strategic map; ~streik *m* general strike; ~versammlung *f* general meeting; ~vertreter *m* general agent; ~vollmacht *f* full power of attorney.

Generation [genəra'tsjoːn] *f* (-/-en) generation.

generell *adj.* [genə'rɛl] general.

genes|en [gə'neːzən] **1.** *v/i.* (*irr.*, *no* -ge-, *sein*) recover (*von* from); **2.** *p.p. of* 1; ~ende *m*, *f* (-n/-n) convalescent; ~ung *f* (-/~, -en) recovery.

genial *adj.* [gen'jaːl] highly gifted, ingenious; ~ität [~ali'tɛːt] *f* (-/*no pl.*) genius.

Genick [gə'nik] *n* (-[e]s/-e) nape (of the neck), (back of the) neck.

Genie [ʒe'niː] *n* (-s/-s) genius.

ge|nieren *v/t.* (*no* -ge-, *h*) trouble, bother; *sich* ~ feel *or* be embarrassed *or* shy; be self-conscious.

genießen [gə'niːsən] *v/t.* (*irr.*, *no* -ge-, *h*) enjoy; eat; drink; et. ~ take some food *or* refreshments; *j-s Vertrauen* ~ be in s.o.'s confidence.

Genitiv *gr.* ['geːnitiːf] *m* (-s/-e) genitive (case); possessive (case).

ge|nommen [gə'nɔmən] *p.p. of* nehmen; ~normt *adj.* standardized; ~noß [~'nɔs] *pret. of* genießen.

Genoss|e [gə'nɔsə] *m* (-n/-n) companion, mate; comrade (*a. pol.*); ~en *p.p. of* genießen; ~enschaft *f* (-/-en) company, association; co(-)operative (society); ~in *f* (-/-nen) (female) companion; comrade (*a. pol.*). [cient.]

genug *adj.* [gə'nuːk] enough, suffi-]

Genüg|e [gə'nyːgə] *f* (-/*no pl.*): zur ~ enough, sufficiently; ~en *v/i.* (*no* -ge-, *h*) be enough, suffice; *das genügt* that will do; *j-m* ~ satisfy s.o.; ~end *adj.* sufficient; ~sam *adj.* [~k-] easily satisfied; frugal; ~samkeit [~k-] *f* (-/*no pl.*) modesty; frugality.

Genugtuung [gə'nuːktuːʊŋ] *f*(-/-en) satisfaction. [gender.]

Genus *gr.* ['geːnus] *n* (-/Genera)]

Genuß [gə'nus] *m* (Genusses/Genüsse) enjoyment; pleasure; use; consumption; taking (*of food*); *fig.* treat; ~mittel *n* semi-luxury; ~sucht *f* (-/*no pl.*) thirst for pleasure; ~süchtig *adj.* pleasure-seeking.

Geo|graph [geo'graːf] *m* (-en/-en) geographer; ~graphie [~a'fiː] *f* (-/*no pl.*) geography; ~graphisch *adj.* [~'graːfiʃ] geographic(al); ~loge [~'loːgə] *m* (-n/-n) geologist; ~logie [~lo'giː] *f* (-/*no pl.*) geology; ~logisch *adj.* [~lo'giʃ] geologic(al); ~metrie [~me'triː] *f* (-/-en) geometry; ~metrisch *adj.* [~'meːtriʃ] geometric(al).

Gepäck [gə'pɛk] *n* (-[e]s/*no pl.*) luggage, ✕ *or Am.* baggage; ~annahme *f* luggage (registration) counter, *Am.* baggage (registration) counter; ~aufbewahrung *f* (-/-en) left-luggage office, *Am.* checkroom; ~ausgabe *f* luggage delivery office, *Am.* baggage room; ~netz *n* luggage-rack, *Am.* baggage rack; ~schein *m* luggage-ticket, *Am.* baggage check; ~träger *m* porter, *Am.* a. redcap; *on bicycle:* carrier; ~wagen *m* luggage van, *Am.* baggage car.

ge|pfiffen [gə'pfifən] *p.p. of* pfeifen; ~pflegt *adj.* ['pfleːkt] *appearance:* well-groomed; *hands, garden, etc.:* well cared-for; *garden, etc.:* well-kept.

Gepflogenheit [gə'pfloːgənhait] *f* (-/-en) habit; custom; usage.

Ge|plapper [gə'plapər] n (-s/no pl.) babbling, chattering; **~plauder** [~'plaudər] n (-s/no pl.) chatting, small talk; **~polter** [~'pɔltər] n (-s/no pl.) rumble; **~präge** [~'prɛː-gə] n (-s/-) impression; stamp (a. fig.).

ge|priesen [gə'priːzən] p.p. of preisen; **~quollen** [~'kvɔlən] p.p. of quellen.

gerade [gə'raːdə] **1.** adj. straight (a. fig.); number, etc.: even; direct; bearing: upright, erect; **2.** adv. just; er schrieb ~ he was (just) writing; nun ~ now more than ever; ~ an dem Tage on that very day; **3.** ♀ f (-n/-n) Å straight line; straight (of race-course); linke (rechte) ~ boxing: straight left (right); **~'aus** adv. straight on or ahead; **~'he'raus** adv. frankly; **~nwegs** adv. [~nve:ks] directly; **~stehen** v/i. (irr. stehen, sep., -ge-, h) stand erect; ~ für answer for s.th.; **~wegs** adv. [~ve:ks] straight, directly; **~'zu** adv. straight; almost; downright.

ge'rannt p.p. of rennen.

Gerassel [gə'rasəl] n (-s/no pl.) clanking; rattling.

Gerät [gə'rɛːt] n (-[e]s/-e) tool, implement, utensil; ⊕ gear; teleph., radio: set; apparatus; equipment; elektrisches ~ electric(al) appliance.

ge'raten 1. v/i. (irr. raten, no -ge-, sein) come or fall or get (an acc. by, upon; auf acc. on, upon; in acc. in, into); (gut) ~ succeed, turn out well; in Brand ~ catch fire; ins Stocken ~ come to a standstill; in Vergessenheit ~ fall or sink into oblivion; in Zorn ~ fly into a passion; **2.** p.p. of raten.

Gerate'wohl n: aufs ~ at random.

geräumig [gə'rɔymiç] spacious.

Geräusch [gə'rɔʏʃ] n (-es/-e) noise; ♀loss adj. noiseless; ♀voll adj. noisy.

gerb|en ['gɛrbən] v/t. (ge-, h) tan; **'♀er** m (-s/-) tanner; ♀**erei** [~'raɪ] f (-/-en) tannery.

ge'recht adj. just; righteous; ~ werden (dat.) do justice to; be fair to; meet; please s.o.; fulfil (requirements); ♀**igkeit** f (-/no pl.) justice; righteousness; j-m ~ widerfahren lassen do s.o. justice.   [rumo(u)r.]

Ge'rede n (-s/no pl.) talk; gossip;]

ge'reizt adj. irritable, irritated; ♀**heit** f (-/no pl.) irritation.

ge'reuen v/t. (no -ge-, h): es gereut mich I repent (of) it, I am sorry for it.

Gericht [gə'riçt] n (-[e]s/-e) dish, course; s. Gerichtshof; mst rhet. and fig. tribunal, ♀**lich** adj. judicial, legal.

Ge'richts|barkeit f (-/-en) jurisdiction; **~bezirk** m jurisdiction; **~diener** m (court) usher; **~gebäude** n court-house; **~hof** m lawcourt, court of justice; **~kosten** pl. (law-)costs pl.; **~saal** m courtroom; **~schreiber** m clerk (of the court); **~stand** m (legal) domicile; venue; **~tag** m court-day; **~verfahren** n legal proceedings pl., lawsuit; **~verhandlung** f (court) hearing; trial; **~vollzieher** m (-s/-) (court-)bailiff.

gerieben [gə'riːbən] p.p. of reiben.

gering adj. [gə'rɪŋ] little, small; trifling, slight; mean, low; poor; inferior; **~achten** v/t. (sep., -ge-, h) think little of; disregard; **~er** adj. inferior. less, minor; **~fügig** adj. insignificant, trifling; slight; **~schätzen** v/t. (sep., -ge-, h) s. geringachten; **~schätzig** adj. disdainful, contemptuous, slighting; ♀**schätzung** f (-/no pl.) disdain; disregard; **~st** adj. least; nicht im ~en not in the least.

ge'rinnen v/i. (irr. rinnen, no -ge-, sein) curdle (a. fig.); congeal; coagulate, clot.

Ge'rippe n (-s/-) skeleton (a. fig.); ⊕ framework.

ge'rissen [gə'rɪsən] **1.** p.p. of reiß\n; **2.** fig. adj. cunning, crafty, smart; **~ritten** [~'rɪtən] p.p. of reiten.

germanis|ch adj. [gɛr'maːnɪʃ] Germanic, Teutonic; ♀**t** [~a'nɪst] m (-en/-en) Germanist, German scholar; student of German.

gern(e) adv. ['gɛrn(ə)] willingly, gladly; ~ haben or mögen be fond of, like; er singt ~ he is fond of singing, he likes to sing.

ge'rochen p.p. of riechen.

Geröll [gə'rœl] n (-[e]s/-e) boulders pl.

geronnen [gə'rɔnən] p.p. of rinnen.

Gerste ♀ ['gɛrstə] f (-/-n) barley; **'~nkorn** n barleycorn; ♣ sty(e).

Gerte ['gɛrtə] f (-/-n) switch, twig.

Geruch [gə'rux] m (-[e]s/-e) smell, odo(u)r; scent; fig. reputation; ♀**los**

adj. odo(u)rless, scentless; **~ssinn** *m* (-[e]s/ *no pl.*) sense of smell.

Gerücht [gə'rγçt] *n* (-[e]s/-e) rumo(u)r.

ge'ruchtilgend *adj.*: **~es** *Mittel* deodorant.

ge'rufen *p.p. of* rufen.

ge'ruhen *v/i.* (*no* -ge-, h) deign, condescend, be pleased.

Gerümpel [gə'rγmpəl] *n* (-s/*no pl.*) lumber, junk.

Gerundium *gr.* [gə'rundjum] *n* (-s/*Gerundien*) gerund.

gerungen [gə'ruŋən] *p.p. of* ringen.

Gerüst [gə'ryst] *n* (-[e]s/-e) scaffold(ing); stage; trestle.

ge'salzen *p.p. of* salzen.

gesamt *adj.* [gə'zamt] whole, entire, total, all; **2ausgabe** *f* complete edition; **2betrag** *m* sum total; **~deu sch** *adj.* all-German.

gesand *t* [gə'zant] *p.p. of* senden; **2e** [~ə] *m* (-n/-n) envoy; **2schaft** *f* (-/-en) legation.

Ge'sang *m* (-[e]s/ᵉe) singing; song; **~buch** *eccl. n* hymn-book; **~slehrer** *m* singing-teacher; **~verein** *m* choral society, Am. glee club.

Gesäß *anat.* [gə'zɛːs] *n* (-es/-e) seat, buttocks *pl.*, posterior, F bottom, behind.

ge'schaffen *p.p. of* schaffen 1.

Geschäft [gə'ʃɛft] *n* (-[e]s/-e) business; transaction; affair; occupation; shop, Am. store; **2ig** *adj.* busy, active; **~igkeit** *f* (-/*no pl.*) activity; **2lich 1.** *adj.* business ...; commercial; **2.** *adv.* on business.

Ge'schäfts|bericht *m* business report; **~brief** *m* business letter; **~frau** *f* business woman; **~freund** *m* business friend, correspondent; **~führer** *m* manager; **~haus** *n* business firm; office building; **~inhaber** *m* owner or holder of a business; shopkeeper; **~jahr** *n* financial or business year, Am. fiscal year; **~lage** *f* business situation; **~leute** *pl.* businessmen *pl.*; **~mann** *m* businessman; **2mäßig** *adj.* business-like; **~ordnung** *f* standing orders *pl.*; rules *pl.* (of procedure); **~papiere** *n/pl.* commercial papers *pl.*; **~partner** *m* (business) partner; **~räume** *m/pl.* business premises *pl.*; **~reise** *f* business trip; **~reisende** *m* commercial travel(l)er, Am. travel(l)ing salesman; **~schluß** *m*

closing-time; *nach* ~ *a.* after business hours; **~stelle** *f* office; **~träger** *m pol.* chargé d'affaires; ✝ agent, representative; **2tüchtig** *adj.* efficient, smart; **~unternehmen** *n* business enterprise; **~verbindung** *f* business connexion *or* connection; **~viertel** *n* business cent|re, Am. -er; Am. downtown; shopping cent|re, Am. -er; **~zeit** *f* office hours *pl.*, business hours *pl.*; **~zimmer** *n* office, bureau; **~zweig** *m* branch (of business), line (of business).

geschah [gə'ʃaː] *pret. of* geschehen.

geschehen [gə'ʃeːən] **1.** *v/i.* (*irr.*, *no* -ge-, *sein*) happen, occur, take place; be done; *es geschieht ihm recht* it serves him right; **2.** *p.p. of* 1; **3.** **2** *n* (-s/-) events *pl.*, happenings *pl.*

gescheit *adj.* [gə'ʃait] clever, intelligent, bright.

Geschenk [gə'ʃɛŋk] *n* (-[e]s/-e) present, gift; **~packung** *f* gift-box.

Geschicht|e [gə'ʃiçtə] *f* **1.** (-/-n) story; tale; *fig.* affair; **2.** (-/*no pl.*) history; **2lich** *adj.* historical; **~sforscher** *m*, **~sschreiber** *m* historian.

Ge'schick *n* **1.** (-[e]s/-e) fate; destiny; **2.** (-[e]s/*no pl.*) = **~lichkeit** *f* (-/-en) skill; dexterity; aptitude; **2t** *adj.* skil(l)ful; dexterous; apt; clever.

ge'schieden [gə'ʃiːdən] *p.p. of* scheiden; **~schienen** [~'ʃiːnən] *p.p. of* scheinen.

Geschirr [gə'ʃir] *n* (-[e]s/-e) vessel; dishes *pl.*; china; earthenware, crockery; service; *horse*: harness.

ge'schlafen *p.p. of* schlafen; **~'schlagen** *p.p. of* schlagen.

Ge'schlecht *n* (-[e]s/-er) sex; kind; species; race; family; generation; *gr.* gender; **2lich** *adj.* sexual.

Ge'schlechts|krankheit ♂ *f* venereal disease; **~reife** *f* puberty; **~teile** *anat. n/pl.* genitals *pl.*; **~trieb** *m* sexual instinct *or* urge; **~verkehr** *m* (-[e]s/*no pl.*) sexual intercourse; **~wort** *gr. n* (-[e]s/ᵉer) article.

ge'schlichen [gə'ʃliçən] *p.p. of* schleichen; **~schliffen** [~'ʃlifən] **1.** *p.p. of* schleifen; **2.** *adj. jewel:* cut; *fig.* polished; **~schlossen**

[~'ʃləsən] **1.** *p.p.* of schließen; **2.** *adj. formation:* close; collective; ~**e Gesellschaft** private party; **~schlungen** [~'ʃluŋən] *p.p.* of schlingen.

Geschmack [gə'ʃmak] *m* (-[e]s/~e, *co.* ~er) taste (*a. fig.*); flavo(u)r; ~ **finden an** (*dat.*) take a fancy to; **2los** *adj.* tasteless; *pred. fig.* in bad taste; ~(**s**)**sache** *f* matter of taste; **2voll** *adj.* tasteful; *pred. fig.* in good taste.

ge|schmeidig *adj.* [gə'ʃmaidiç] supple, pliant; **~schmissen** [~'ʃmisən] *p.p.* of schmeißen; **~schmolzen** [~'ʃmɔltsən] *p.p.* of schmelzen.

Geschnatter [gə'ʃnatər] *n* (-s/*no pl.*) cackling (*of geese*); chatter(ing) (*of girls, etc.*).

ge|schnitten [gə'ʃnitən] *p.p.* of schneiden; **~schoben** [~'ʃo:bən] *p.p.* of schieben; **~scholten** [~'ʃɔltən] *p.p.* of schelten.

Geschöpf [gə'ʃœpf] *n* (-[e]s/-e) creature.

ge'schoren *p.p.* of scheren.

Geschoß [gə'ʃɔs] *n* (Geschosses/Geschosse) projectile; missile; stor(e)y, floor. [*Ben.*\

geschossen [gə'ʃɔsən] *p.p.of schie-*\

Ge'schrei *n* (-[e]s/*no pl.*) cries *pl.*; shouting; *fig.* noise, fuss.

ge|schrieben [gə'ʃri:bən] *p.p.* of schreiben; **~schrie(e)n** [~'ʃri:(ə)n] *p.p.* of schreien; **~schritten** [~'ʃritən] *p.p.* of schreiten; **~schunden** [~'ʃundən] *p.p.* of schinden.

Geschütz ⚔ [gə'ʃyts] *n* (-es/-e) gun, cannon; ordnance.

Geschwader ⚔ [gə'ʃva:dər] *n* (-s/-) ⚓ squadron; ✈ wing, *Am.* group.

Geschwätz [gə'ʃvɛts] *n* (-es/*no pl.*) idle talk; gossip; **2ig** *adj.* talkative.

geschweige *cj.* [gə'ʃvaigə]: ~ (denn) not to mention; let alone, much less.

geschwiegen [gə'ʃvi:gən] *p.p.* of schweigen.

geschwind *adj.* [gə'ʃvint] fast, quick, swift; **2igkeit** [~diçkait] *f* (-/-en) quickness; speed, pace; *phys.* velocity; rate; **mit e-r ~ von ...** at the rate of ...; **2igkeitsbegrenzung** *f* speed limit.

Geschwister [gə'ʃvistər] *n* (-s/-): ~ *pl.* brother(s *pl.*) and sister(s *pl.*).

ge|schwollen [gə'ʃvɔlən] **1.** *p.p.* of schwellen; **2.** *adj. language:* bom-

bastic, pompous; **~schwommen** [~'ʃvɔmən] *p.p.* of schwimmen.

geschworen [gə'ʃvo:rən] *p.p.* of schwören; **2e** [~ə] *m, f* (-n/-n) juror; **die ~n** *pl.* the jury; **2engericht** *n* jury.

Geschwulst ⚕ [gə'ʃvulst] *f* (-/~e) swelling; tumo(u)r.

ge|schwunden [gə'ʃvundən] *p.p.* of schwinden; **~schwungen** [~'ʃvuŋən] *p.p.* of schwingen.

Geschwür ⚕ [gə'ʃvy:r] *n* (-[e]s/-e) abscess, ulcer.

ge'sehen *p.p.* of sehen.

Gesell 🔨 [gə'zɛl] *m* (-en/-en), **~e** [~ə] *m* (-n/-n) companion, fellow; ⊕ journeyman; **2en** *v/refl.* (*no -ge-, h*) associate, come together; *sich zu j-m ~* join s.o.; **2ig** *adj.* social; sociable.

Ge'sellschaft *f* (-/-en) society; company (*a.* ✝); party; *j-m ~ leisten* keep s.o. company; **~er** *m* (-s/-) companion; ✝ partner; **~erin** *f* (-/-nen) (lady) companion; ✝ partner; **2lich** *adj.* social.

Ge'sellschafts|dame *f* (lady) companion; **~reise** *f* party tour; **~spiel** *n* party or round game; **~tanz** *m* ball-room dance.

gesessen [gə'zɛsən] *p.p.of* sitzen.

Gesetz [gə'zɛts] *n* (-es/-e) law; statute; **~buch** *n* code; statute-book; **~entwurf** *m* bill; **~eskraft** *f* legal force; **~essammlung** *f* code; **2gebend** *adj.* legislative; **~geber** *m* (-s/-) legislator; **~gebung** *f* (-/-en) legislation; **2lich 1.** *adj.* lawful, legal; **2.** *adv.*: ~ geschützt patented, registered; **2los** *adj.* lawless; **2mäßig** *adj.* legal; lawful.

ge'setzt 1. *adj.* sedate, staid; sober; mature; **2.** *cj.*: ~ den Fall, (daß) ... suppose or supposing (that) ...

ge'setzwidrig *adj.* unlawful, illegal.

Ge'sicht *n* (-[e]s/-er) face; countenance; *fig.* character; *zu ~ bekommen* catch sight of or a glimpse of; set eyes on.

Ge'sichts|ausdruck *m* (facial) expression; **~farbe** *f* complexion; **~kreis** *m* horizon; **~punkt** *m* point of view, viewpoint, aspect, *esp. Am.* angle; **~zug** *m mst* Gesichtszüge *pl.* feature(s *pl.*), lineament(s *pl.*).

Ge'sims *n* ledge.

Gesinde [gə'zində] *n* (-s/-) (domestic) servants *pl.*; **~l** [~l] *n* (-s/*no pl.*) rabble, mob.

ge'sinn|t *adj. in compounds*: ...-minded; *wohl* ~ well disposed (*j-m* towards s.o.); **²ung** *f* (-/-en) mind; conviction; sentiment(s *pl.*); opinions *pl.*

gesinnungs|los *adj.* [gə'zinuŋslo:s] unprincipled; **~treu** *adj.* loyal; **²wechsel** *m* change of opinion; *esp. pol.* volte-face.

ge|sittet *adj.* [gə'zitət] civilized; well-bred, well-mannered; **~'soffen** *p.p. of saufen*; **~sogen** [~'zo:gən] *p.p. of saugen*; **~sonnen 1.** *p.p. of sinnen*; **2.** *adj.* minded, disposed; **~sotten** [~'zɔtən] *p.p. of sieden*; **~'spalten** *p.p. of spalten*.

Ge'spann *n* (-[e]s/-e) team, *Am. a.* span; *oxen*: yoke; *fig.* pair, couple.

ge'spannt *adj.* tense (*a. fig.*); *rope*: tight, taut; *fig.* intent; *attention*: close; *relations*: strained; ~ *sein auf* (*acc.*) be anxious for; *auf* ~*em Fuß* on bad terms; **²heit** *f* (-/*no pl.*) tenseness, tension.

Gespenst [gə'ʃpɛnst] *n* (-es/-er) ghost, spect|re, *Am.* -er; **²isch** *adj.* ghostly.

Ge'spiel|e *m* (-n/-n), **~in** *f* (-/-nen) playmate.

gespien [gə'ʃpi:n] *p.p. of speien*.

Gespinst [gə'ʃpinst] *n* (-es/-e) web, tissue (*both a. fig.*); spun yarn.

gesponnen [gə'ʃpɔnən] *p.p. of spinnen*.

Gespött [gə'ʃpœt] *n* (-[e]s/*no pl.*) mockery, derision, ridicule; *zum* ~ *der Leute werden* become a laughing-stock.

Gespräch [gə'ʃprɛ:ç] *n* (-[e]s/-e) talk, conversation; *teleph.* call; dialogue; **²ig** *adj.* talkative.

ge|sprochen [gə'ʃrɔxən] *p.p. of sprechen*; **~'sprossen** *p.p. of sprießen*; **~sprungen** [~'ʃpruŋən] *p.p. of springen*.

Gestalt [gə'ʃtalt] *f* (-/-en) form, figure, shape; stature; **²en** *v/t. and v/refl.* (*no* -ge-, *h*) form, shape; **~ung** *f* (-/-en) formation; arrangement, organization.

gestanden [gə'ʃtandən] *p.p. of stehen*.

ge'ständ|ig *adj.*: ~ *sein* confess; **²nis** [~t-] *n* (-ses/-se) confession.

Ge'stank *m* (-[e]s/*no pl.*) stench.

gestatten [gə'ʃtatən] *v/t.* (*no* -ge-, *h*) allow, permit.

Geste ['gɛstə] *f* (-/-n) gesture.

ge'stehen (*irr.* stehen, *no* -ge-, *h*) **1.** *v/t.* confess, avow; **2.** *v/i.* confess.

Ge|'stein *n* (-[e]s/-e) rock, stone; **~stell** [~'ʃtɛl] *n* (-[e]s/-e) stand, rack, shelf; frame; trestle, horse.

gestern *adv.* ['gɛstərn] yesterday; ~ *abend* last night.

gestiegen [gə'ʃti:gən] *p.p. of steigen*.

Ge'stirn *n* (-[e]s/-e) star; *astr.* constellation; **²t** *adj.* starry.

ge|stoben [gə'ʃto:bən] *p.p. of stieben*; **~stochen** [~'ʃtɔxən] *p.p. of stechen*; **~stohlen** [~'ʃto:lən] *p.p. of stehlen*; **~storben** [~'ʃtɔrbən] *p.p. of sterben*; **~'stoßen** *p.p. of stoßen*; **~strichen** [~'ʃtriçən] *p.p. of streichen*.

gestrig *adj.* ['gɛstriç] of yesterday, yesterday's ...

ge'stritten *p.p. of streiten*.

Gestrüpp [gə'ʃtryp] *n* (-[e]s/-e) brushwood; undergrowth.

gestunken [gə'ʃtuŋkən] *p.p. of stinken*.

Gestüt [gə'ʃty:t] *n* (-[e]s/-e) stud farm; *horses kept for breeding, etc.*: stud.

Gesuch [gə'zu:x] *n* (-[e]s/-e) application, request; petition; **²t** *adj.* wanted; sought-after; *politeness*: studied.

gesund *adj.* [gə'zunt] sound, healthy; salubrious; wholesome (*a. fig.*); **~er** *Menschenverstand* common sense; **~en** [~dən] *v/i.* (*no* -ge-, *sein*) recover.

Ge'sundheit *f* (-/*no pl.*) health (-iness); wholesomeness (*a. fig.*); *auf j-s* ~ *trinken* drink (to) s.o.'s health; **²lich** *adj.* sanitary; ~ *geht es ihm gut* he is in good health.

Ge'sundheits|amt *n* Public Health Department; **~pflege** *f* hygiene; public health service; **²schädlich** *adj.* injurious to health, unhealthy, unwholesome; **~wesen** *n* Public Health; **~zustand** *m* state of health, physical condition.

ge|sungen [gə'zuŋən] *p.p. of singen*; **~sunken** [~'zuŋkən] *p.p. of sinken*; **~tan** [~'ta:n] *p.p. of tun*.

Getöse [gə'tø:zə] *n* (-s/*no pl.*) din, noise.

ge'tragen 1. *p.p. of tragen*; **2.** *adj.* solemn.

Getränk [gə'trɛŋk] *n* (-[e]s/-e) drink, beverage. [venture.]

ge'trauen *v/refl.* (*no* -ge-, *h*) dare,)

Getreide [gə'traɪdə] n (-s/-) corn, esp. Am. grain; cereals pl.; ~(an)bau m corn-growing, esp. Am. grain growing; ~pflanze f cereal plant; ~speicher m granary, grain silo, Am. elevator.

ge'treten p.p. of treten.

ge'treu(lich) adj. faithful, loyal, true.

Getriebe [gə'tri:bə] n (-s/-) bustle; ⊕ gear(ing); ⊕ drive.

ge|trieben [gə'tri:bən] p.p. of treiben; ~**troffen** [~'trɔfən] p.p. of treffen; ~**trogen** [~'tro:gən] p.p. of trügen.

ge'trost adv. confidently.

ge'trunken p.p. of trinken.

Ge|tue [gə'tu:ə] n (-s/no pl.) fuss; ~**tümmel** [~'tyməl] n (-s/-) turmoil; ~**viert** [~'fi:rt] n (-[e]s/-e) square.

Gewächs [gə'vɛks] n (-es/-e) growth (a. ♂️); plant; vintage; ~**haus** n greenhouse, hothouse, conservatory.

ge|'wachsen 1. p.p. of wachsen; **2.** adj.: j-m ~ sein be a match for s.o.; e-r Sache ~ sein be equal to s.th.; sich der Lage ~ zeigen rise to the occasion; ~**wagt** adj. [~'va:kt] risky; bold; ~**wählt** adj. [~'vɛ:lt] style: refined; ~'**wahr** adj.: ~ werden (acc. or gen.) perceive s.th.; become aware of s.th.; ~ werden, daß become aware that.

Gewähr [gə'vɛ:r] f (-/no pl.) guarantee, warrant, security; 2en v/t. (no -ge-, h) grant, allow; give, yield, afford; j-n ~ lassen let s.o. have his way; leave s.o. alone; 2**leisten** v/t. (no -ge-, h) guarantee.

Ge'wahrsam m (-s/-e) custody, safe keeping.

Ge'währsmann m informant, source.

Gewalt [gə'valt] f (-/-en) power; authority; control; force, violence; höhere ~ act of God; mit ~ by force; ~**herrschaft** f despotism, tyranny; 2ig adj. powerful, mighty; vehement; vast; ~**maßnahme** f violent measure; 2**sam 1.** adj. violent; **2.** adv. a. forcibly; ~ öffnen force open; open by force; ~**tat** f act of violence; 2**tätig** adj. violent.

Gewand [gə'vant] n (-[e]s/⁼er) garment; robe; esp. eccl. vestment.

ge'wandt 1. p.p. of wenden 2; **2.** adj. agile, nimble, dexterous, adroit; clever; 2**heit** f (-/no pl.) agility, nimbleness; adroitness, dexterity; cleverness.

ge'wann pret. of gewinnen.

Gewäsch F [gə'vɛʃ] n (-es/no pl.) twaddle, nonsense.

ge'waschen p.p. of waschen.

Gewässer [gə'vɛsər] n (-s/-) water(s pl.).

Gewebe [gə've:bə] n (-s/-) tissue (a. anat. and fig.); fabric, web; texture.

Ge'wehr n gun; rifle; ~**kolben** m (rifle-)butt; ~**lauf** m (rifle-, gun-)barrel.

Geweih [gə'vaɪ] n (-[e]s/-e) horns pl., head, antlers pl.

Gewerbe [gə'vɛrbə] n (-s/-) trade, business, industry; ~**freiheit** f freedom of trade; ~**schein** m trade licen|ce, Am. -se; ~**schule** f technical school; ~**steuer** f trade tax; 2**treibend** adj. carrying on a business, engaged in trade; ~**treibende** m (-n/-n) tradesman.

gewerb|lich adj. [gə'vɛrplɪç] commercial, industrial; ~**mäßig** adj. professional.

Ge'werkschaft f (-/-en) trade(s) union, Am. labor union; ~**ler** m (-s/-) trade(s)-unionist; 2**lich** adj. trade-union; ~**sbund** m Trade Union Congress, Am. Federation of Labor.

ge|wesen [gə've:zən] p.p. of sein; ~**wichen** [~'vɪçən] p.p. of weichen.

Gewicht [gə'vɪçt] n (-[e]s/-e) weight, Am. F a. heft; e-r Sache ~ beimessen attach importance to s.th.; ~ haben carry weight (bei dat. with); ~ legen auf et. lay stress on s.th.; ins ~ fallen be of great weight, count, matter; 2ig adj. weighty (a. fig.).

ge|wiesen [gə'vi:zən] p.p. of weisen; ~**willt** adj. [~'vɪlt] willing.

Ge|wimmel [gə'vɪməl] n (-s/no pl.) swarm; throng; ~**winde** ⊕ [~'vɪndə] n (-s/-) thread.

Gewinn [gə'vɪn] m (-[e]s/-e) gain; † gains pl.; profit; lottery ticket: prize; game: winnings pl.; ~**anteil** m dividend; ~**beteiligung** f profit-sharing; 2**bringend** adj. profitable; 2**en** (irr., no -ge-, h) **1.** v/t. win; gain; get; **2.** v/i. win; gain; fig. improve; 2**end** adj. manner, smile: winning, engaging; ~**er** m (-s/-) winner.

G

Ge'wirr n (-[e]s/-e) tangle, entanglement; *streets*: maze; *voices*: confusion.

gewiß [gə'vis] **1.** *adj.* certain; *ein gewisser Herr N.* a certain Mr. N., one Mr. N.; **2.** *adv.*: ∼! certainly!, to be sure!, *Am.* sure!

Ge'wissen n (-s/-) conscience; **2haft** *adj.* conscientious; **2los** *adj.* unscrupulous; **∼sbisse** m/pl. remorse, pangs pl. of conscience; **∼sfrage** f question of conscience.

gewissermaßen *adv.* [gəvisər-'ma:sən] to a certain extent.

Ge'wißheit f (-/-en) certainty; certitude.

Gewitter [gə'vitər] n (-s/-) (thunder)storm; **2n** v/i. (no -ge-, h): es gewittert there is a thunderstorm; **∼regen** m thunder-shower; **∼wolke** f thundercloud.

ge|woben [gə'vo:bən] p.p. of weben; **∼wogen 1.** p.p. of wägen and wiegen¹; **2.** adj. (dat.) well or kindly disposed towards, favo(u)rably inclined towards.

gewöhnen [gə'vø:nən] v/t. (no -ge-, h) accustom, get used (an acc. to).

Gewohnheit [gə'vo:nhait] f (-/-en) habit; custom; **2smäßig** adj. habitual.

ge'wöhnlich adj. common; ordinary; usual, customary; habitual; common, vulgar.

ge'wohnt adj. customary, habitual; (es) ∼ sein zu inf. be accustomed or used to inf.

Gewölbe [gə'vœlbə] n (-s/-) vault.

ge|wonnen [gə'vɔnən] p.p. of gewinnen; **∼worben** [∼'vɔrbən] p.p. of werben; **∼worden** [∼'vɔrdən] p.p. of werden; **∼worfen** [∼'vɔrfən] p.p. of werfen; **∼wrungen** [∼'vruŋən] p.p. of wringen.

Gewühl [gə'vy:l] n (-[e]s/no pl.) bustle; milling crowd.

gewunden [gə'wundən] **1.** p.p. of winden; **2.** adj. twisted; winding.

Gewürz [gə'vyrts] n (-es/-e) spice; condiment; **∼nelke** ⚘ f clove.

ge'wußt p.p. of wissen.

Ge|'zeit f: mst ∼en pl. tide(s pl.); **∼'zeter** n (-s/no pl.) (shrill) clamo(u)r.

ge|'ziert adj. affected; **∼zogen** [∼'tso:gən] p.p. of ziehen.

Gezwitscher [gə'tsvitʃər] n (-s/no pl.) chirping, twitter(ing).

gezwungen [gə'tsvuŋən] **1.** p.p. of zwingen; **2.** adj. forced, constrained.

Gicht ⚕ [giçt] f (-/no pl.) gout; **2isch** ✦ adj. gouty; **∼knoten** ⚕ m gouty knot.

Giebel ['gi:bəl] m (-s/-) gable(-end).

Gier [gi:r] f (-/no pl.) greed(iness) (nach for); **2ig** adj. greedy (nach for, of).

'Gießbach m torrent.

gieß|en ['gi:sən] (irr., ge-, h) **1.** v/t. pour; ⊕ cast, found; water (flowers); **2.** v/i.: es gießt it is pouring (with rain); **2er** m (-s/-) founder; **2erei** [∼'rai] f (-/-en) foundry; **'2kanne** f watering-can or -pot.

Gift [gift] n (-[e]s/-e) poison; venom (esp. of snakes) (a. fig.); malice, spite; **2ig** adj. poisonous; venomous; malicious, spiteful; **'∼schlange** f venomous or poisonous snake; **'∼zahn** m poison-fang.

Gigant [gi'gant] m (-en/-en) giant.

Gimpel orn. ['gimpəl] m (-s/-) bullfinch.

ging [giŋ] pret. of gehen.

Gipfel ['gipfəl] m (-s/-) summit, top; peak; **'∼konferenz** pol. f summit meeting or conference; **'2n** v/i. (ge-, h) culminate.

Gips [gips] m (-es/-e) min. gypsum; ⊕ plaster (of Paris); **'∼abdruck** m, **'∼abguß** m plaster cast; **'2en** v/t. (ge-, h) plaster; **'∼verband** ⚕ m plaster (of Paris) dressing.

Giraffe zo. [gi'rafə] f (-/-n) giraffe.

girieren † [ʒi'ri:rən] v/t. (no -ge-, h) endorse, indorse (bill of exchange)

Girlande [gir'landə] f (-/-n) garland.

Giro † ['ʒi:ro] n (-s/-s) endorsement, indorsement; **'∼bank** f clearing-bank; **'∼konto** n current account.

girren ['girən] v/i. (ge-, h) coo.

Gischt [giʃt] m (-es/✦ -e) and f (-/✦ -en) foam, froth; spray; spindrift.

Gitarre ♪ [gi'tarə] f (-/-n) guitar.

Gitter ['gitər] n (-s/-) grating; lattice; trellis; railing; **'∼bett** n crib; **'∼fenster** n lattice-window.

Glacéhandschuh [gla'se:-] m kid glove.

Glanz [glants] m (-es/no pl.) brightness; lust|re, Am. -er; brilliancy; splendo(u)r.

glänzen ['glɛntsən] v/i. (ge-, h) glitter, shine; '**~d** adj. bright, brilliant; fig. splendid.

'**Glanz|leistung** f brilliant achievement or performance; '**~papier** n glazed paper; '**~punkt** m highlight; '**~zeit** f golden age, heyday.

Glas [glaːs] n (-es/ɯer) glass; **~er** ['ɯzər] m (-s/-) glazier.

gläsern adj. ['glɛːzərn] of glass; fig. glassy.

'**Glas|glocke** f (glass) shade or cover; globe; bell-glass; '**~hütte** f glassworks sg., pl.

glasieren [gla'ziːrən] v/t. (no -ge-, h) glaze; ice, frost (cake).

glasig adj. ['glaːziç] glassy, vitreous.

'**Glasscheibe** f pane of glass.

Glasur [gla'zuːr] f (-/-en) glaze, glazing; enamel; icing, frosting (on cakes).

glatt [glat] **1.** adj. smooth (a. fig.); even; lie, etc.: flat, downright; road, etc.: slippery; **2.** adv. smoothly, evenly; ~ anliegen fit closely or tightly; ~ rasiert clean-shaven; et. ~ ableugnen deny s.th. flatly.

Glätte ['glɛtə] f (-/-n) smoothness; road, etc.: slipperiness.

'**Glatteis** n glazed frost, icy glaze, Am. glaze; F: j-n aufs ~ führen lead s.o. up the garden path.

'**glätten** v/t. (ge-, h) smooth.

Glatze ['glatsə] f (-/-n) bald head.

Glaube ['glaubə] m (-ns/~ɯ) faith, belief (an acc. in); '**2n** (ge-, h) **1.** v/t. believe; think, suppose, Am. a. guess; **2.** v/i. believe (j-m s.o.; an acc. in).

'**Glaubens|bekenntnis** n creed, profession or confession of faith; '**~lehre** f, '**~satz** m dogma, doctrine.

glaubhaft adj. ['glaup-] credible, plausible; authentic.

gläubig adj. ['glɔybiç] believing, faithful; **2e** ['ɯgə] m, f (-n/-n) believer; **2er** † ['ɯgər] m (-s/-) creditor.

glaubwürdig adj. ['glaup-] credible.

gleich [glaiç] **1.** adj. equal (an dat. in); the same; like; even, level; in ~er Weise likewise; zur ~en Zeit at the same time; es ist mir ~ it's all the same to me; das ~e the same; as much; er ist nicht (mehr) der ~e

he is not the same man; **2.** adv. alike, equally; immediately; presently, directly, at once; just; es ist ~ acht (Uhr) it is close on or nearly eight (o'clock); **~altrig** adj. ['ɯaltriç] (of) the same age; '**~artig** adj. homogeneous; similar; uniform; '**~bedeutend** adj. synonymous; equivalent (to); tantamount (mit to); '**~berechtigt** adj. having equal rights; '**~bleibend** adj. constant, steady; '**~en** v/i. (irr., ge-, h) equal; resemble.

'**gleich|falls** adv. also, likewise; '**~förmig** adj. ['ɯfœrmiç] uniform; '**~gesinnt** adj. like-minded; '**2gewicht** n balance (a. fig.); equilibrium, equipoise; pol.: ~ der Kräfte balance of power; '**~gültig** adj. indifferent (gegen to); es ist mir ~ I don't care; ~, was du tust no matter what you do; '**2gültigkeit** f indifference; '**2heit** f (-/-en) equality; likeness; '**2klang** m unison; consonance, harmony; '**~kommen** v/i. (irr. kommen, sep., -ge-, sein): e-r Sache ~ amount to s.th.; j-m ~ equal s.o.; '**~laufend** adj. parallel; '**~lautend** adj. consonant; identical; '**~machen** v/t. (sep., -ge-, h) make equal (dat. to), equalize (to or with); '**2maß** n regularity; evenness; fig. equilibrium; '**~mäßig** adj. equal; regular; constant; even; '**2mut** m equanimity; '**~mütig** adj. even-tempered; calm; **~namig** adj. ['ɯnaːmiç] of the same name; '**2nis** n (-ses/-se) parable; rhet. simile; '**~sam** adv. as it were, so to speak; '**~schalten** v/t. (sep., -ge-, h) ⊕ synchronize; pol. co-ordinate, unify; '**~seitig** adj. equilateral; '**~setzen** v/t. (sep., -ge-, h) equate (dat. or mit with); '**~stehen** v/i. (irr. stehen, sep., -ge-, h) be equal; '**~stellen** v/t. (sep., -ge-, h) equalize, equate (dat. with); put s.o. on an equal footing (with); '**2stellung** f equalization, equation; '**2strom** m ≠ direct current; '**2ung** ♉ f (-/-en) equation; '**~wertig** adj. equivalent, of the same value, of equal value; '**~zeitig** adj. simultaneous; synchronous; contemporary.

Gleis [glais] n (-es/-e) s. Geleise.

gleiten ['glaitən] v/i. (irr., ge-, sein) glide, slide.

'**Gleit|flug** m gliding flight, glide,

volplane; **'~schutzreifen** *m* non-skid tyre, (*Am. only*) non-skid tire; **'~schutz(vorrichtung** *f*) *m* anti-skid device.

Gletscher ['glɛtʃər] *m* (-s/-) glacier; **~spalte** *f* crevasse.

glich [gliç] *pret. of* gleichen.

Glied [gli:t] *n* (-[e]s/-er) *anat.* limb; member (*a. anat.*); link; ✕ rank, file; **2ern** ['~dərn] *v/t.* (ge-, h) joint, articulate; arrange; divide (*in acc.* into); **'~erung** *f* (-/-en) articulation; arrangement; division; formation; **~maßen** ['~tmɑːsən] *pl.* limbs *pl.*, extremities *pl.*

glimmen ['glimən] *v/i.* ([*irr.*,] ge-, h) *fire*: smo(u)lder (*a. fig.*); glimmer, glow.

glimpflich ['glimpfliç] **1.** *adj.* lenient, mild; **2.** *adv.*: ~ *davonkommen* get off lightly.

glitschig *adj.* ['glitʃiç] slippery.

glitt [glit] *pret. of* gleiten.

glitzern ['glitsərn] *v/i.* (ge-, h) glitter, glisten.

Globus ['gloːbus] *m* (-, -ses/Globen, Globusse) globe.

Glocke ['glɔkə] *f* (-/-n) bell; shade; (glass) cover.

'Glocken|schlag *m* stroke of the clock; **'~spiel** *n* chime(s *pl.*); **'~stuhl** *m* bell-cage; **'~turm** *m* bell tower, belfry.

Glöckner ['glœknər] *m* (-s/-) bell-ringer.

glomm [glɔm] *pret. of* glimmen.

Glorie ['gloːrjə] *f* (-/-n) glory; **'~n-schein** *fig. m* halo, aureola.

glorreich *adj.* ['gloːr-] glorious.

glotzen F ['glɔtsən] *v/i.* (ge-, h) stare.

Glück [glyk] *n* (-[e]s/*no pl.*) fortune; good luck; happiness, bliss, felicity; prosperity; *auf gut* ~ on the off chance; ~ *haben* be lucky, succeed; *das* ~ *haben zu inf.* have the good fortune to *inf.*; *j-m* ~ *wünschen* congratulate s.o. (*zu* on); *viel* ~! good luck!; *zum* ~ fortunately; **2bringend** *adj.* lucky.

Glucke *orn.* ['glukə] *f* (-/-n) sitting hen. [gen.]

'glücken *v/i.* (ge-, sein) *s.* gelin-]

gluckern ['glukərn] *v/i.* (ge-, h) *water, etc.*: gurgle.

'glücklich *adj.* fortunate; happy; lucky; **'~er'weise** *adv.* fortunately.

'Glücksbringer *m* (-s/-) mascot.

glück'selig *adj.* blissful, blessed, happy. [gurgle.]

glucksen ['gluksən] *v/i.* (ge-, h)]

'Glücks|fall *m* lucky chance, stroke of (good) luck; **~göttin** *f* Fortune; **~kind** *n* lucky person; **~pfennig** *m* lucky penny; **~pilz** *m* lucky person; **~spiel** *n* game of chance; *fig.* gamble; **~stern** *m* lucky star; **~tag** *m* happy *or* lucky day, red-letter day.

'glück|strahlend *adj.* radiant(ly happy); **2wunsch** *m* congratulation, good wishes *pl.*; compliments *pl.*; ~ *zum Geburtstag* many happy returns (of the day).

Glüh|birne ⚡ ['gly:-] *f* (electric-light) bulb; **2en** *v/i.* (ge-, h) glow; **2end** *adj.* glowing; *iron*: red-hot; *coal*: live; *fig.* ardent, fervid; **2(end)'heiß** *adj.* burning hot; **~lampe** *f* incandescent lamp; **~wein** *m* mulled wine; **~würm-chen** *zo.* ['~vyrmçən] *n* (-s/-) glow-worm.

Glut [glu:t] *f* (-/-en) heat, glow (*a. fig.*); glowing fire, embers *pl.*; *fig.* ardo(u)r.

Gnade ['gnɑːdə] *f* (-/-n) grace; favo(u)r; mercy; clemency; pardon; ✕ quarter.

'Gnaden|akt *m* act of grace; **~brot** *n* (-[e]s/*no pl.*) bread of charity; **~frist** *f* reprieve; **~gesuch** *n* petition for mercy.

gnädig *adj.* ['gnɛːdiç] gracious; merciful; *address*: 2e *Frau* Madam.

Gnom [gnoːm] *m* (-en/-en) gnome, goblin.

Gobelin [gobə'lɛ̃ː] *m* (-s/-s) Gobelin tapestry.

Gold [gɔlt] *n* (-[e]s/*no pl.*) gold; **~barren** *m* gold bar, gold ingot, bullion; **~borte** *f* gold lace; **2en** *adj.* ['~dən] gold; *fig.* golden; **~feder** *f* gold nib; **~fisch** *m* goldfish; **2gelb** *adj.* golden(-yellow); **~gräber** ['~grɛːbər] *m* (-s/-) gold-digger; **~grube** *f* gold-mine; **2haltig** *adj.* gold-bearing, containing gold; **2ig** *fig. adj.* ['~diç] sweet, lovely, *Am.* F *a.* cute; **~mine** *f* gold-mine; **~münze** *f* gold coin; **~schmied** *m* goldsmith; **~schnitt** *m* gilt edge; *mit* ~ gilt-edged; **~stück** *n* gold coin; **~waage** *f* gold-balance; **~wäh-rung** *f* gold standard.

149   **Graupe**

Golf¹ *geogr.* [gɔlf] *m* (-[e]s/-e) gulf.
Golf² [~] *n* (-s/*no pl.*) golf; '**~platz**
m golf-course, (golf-)links *pl.*;
'**~schläger** *m* golf-club; '**~spiel** *n*
golf; '**~spieler** *m* golfer.
Gondel ['gɔndəl] *f* (-/-n) gondola;
✈ *mst* car.
gönnen ['gœnən] *v/t.* (ge-, h): j-m
et. ~ allow *or* grant *or* not to grudge
s.o. s.th.
'**Gönner** *m* (-s/-) patron; *Am. a.*
sponsor; '**2haft** *adj.* patronizing.
gor [goːr] *pret. of* gären.
Gorilla *zo.* [go'rila] *m* (-s/-s) gorilla.
goß [gɔs] *pret. of* gießen.
Gosse ['gɔsə] *f* (-/-n) gutter (*a. fig.*).
Gott [gɔt] *m* (-es, ✝ -s/⸚er) God;
god, deity; '**2ergeben** *adj.* resigned
(to the will of God).
'**Gottes|dienst** *eccl. m* (divine)
service; '**2fürchtig** *adj.* godfearing;
'**~haus** *n* church, chapel; '**~läste-
rer** *m* (-s/-) blasphemer; '**~läste-
rung** *f* blasphemy.
'**Gottheit** *f* (-/-en) deity, divinity.
Göttin ['gœtin] *f* (-/-nen) goddess.
göttlich *adj.* ['gœtliç] divine.
gott|'lob *int.* thank God *or* good-
ness!; '**~los** *adj.* godless; impious;
F *fig. deed*: unholy, wicked; '**2ver-
trauen** *n* trust in God.
Götze ['gœtsə] *m* (-n/-n) idol;
'**~bild** *n* idol; '**~ndienst** *m* idolatry.
Gouvern|ante [guvɛr'nantə] *f* (-/-n)
governess; **~eur** [~'nøːr] *m* (-s/-e)
governor.
Grab [graːp] *n* (-[e]s/⸚er) grave,
tomb, sepulchre, *Am. -er.*
Graben ['graːbən] **1.** *m* (-s/⸚) ditch;
✗ trench; **2.** 2 *v/t.* (*irr.*, ge-, h)
dig; *animal*: burrow.
'**Grab|gewölbe** ['graːp-] *n* vault,
tomb; '**~mal** *n* monument; tomb,
sepulchre, *Am. -er*; '**~rede** *f* funeral
sermon; funeral oration *or* address;
'**~schrift** *f* epitaph; '**~stätte** *f*
burial-place; grave, tomb; '**~stein**
m tombstone; gravestone.
Grad [graːt] *m* (-[e]s/-e) degree;
grade, rank; *15* ~ *Kälte* 15 degrees
below zero; '**~einteilung** *f* graduation; '**~messer** *m* (-s/-) graduated
scale, graduator; *fig.* criterion;
'**~netz** *n* map: grid.
Graf [graːf] *m* (-en/-en) *in Britain:*
earl; count.
Gräfin ['grɛːfin] *f* (-/-nen) countess.
'**Grafschaft** *f* (-/-en) county.

Gram [graːm] **1.** *m* (-[e]s/*no pl.*)
grief, sorrow; **2.** 2 *adj.*: j-m ~
sein bear s.o. ill will *or* a grudge.
grämen ['grɛːmən] *v/t.* (ge-, h)
grieve; *sich* ~ grieve (*über acc.* at,
for, over).
Gramm [gram] *n* (-s/-e) gramme,
Am. gram.
Grammati|k [gra'matik] *f* (-/-en)
grammar; **2sch** *adj.* grammatical.
Granat *min.* [gra'naːt] *m* (-[e]s/-e)
garnet; **~e** ✗ *f* (-/-n) shell; grenade;
~splitter ✗ *m* shell-splinter;
~trichter ✗ *m* shell-crater; **~wer-
fer** ✗ *m* (-s/-) mortar.
Granit *min.* [gra'niːt] *m* (-s/-e)
granite.
Granne ♀ ['granə] *f* (-/-n) awn,
beard.
Graphi|k ['graːfik] *f* (-/-en) graphic
arts *pl.*; **2sch** *adj.* graphic(al).
Graphit *min.* [gra'fiːt] *m* (-s/-e)
graphite.
Gras ♀ [graːs] *n* (-es/⸚er) grass;
2bewachsen *adj.* ['~bəvaksən]
grass-grown, grassy; **2en** ['~zən]
v/i. (ge-, h) graze; '**~halm** *m* blade
of grass; '**~narbe** *f* turf, sod;
'**~platz** *m* grass-plot, green.
grassieren [gra'siːrən] *v/i.* (*no* ge-,
h) rage, prevail.
gräßlich *adj.* ['grɛsliç] horrible;
hideous, atrocious.
Grassteppe ['graːs-] *f* prairie,
savanna(h).
Grat [graːt] *m* (-[e]s/-e) edge, ridge.
Gräte ['grɛːtə] *f* (-/-n) (fish-)bone.
Gratifikation [gratifika'tsjoːn] *f*
(-/-en) gratuity, bonus.
gratis *adv.* ['graːtis] gratis, free of
charge.
Gratul|ant [gratu'lant] *m* (-en/-en)
congratulator; **~ation** [~'tsjoːn] *f*
(-/-en) congratulation; **~ieren** [~-
'liːrən] *v/i.* (*no* ge-, h) congratulate (*j-m zu* et. s.o. on s.th.); *j-m zum
Geburtstag* ~ wish s.o. many happy
returns (of the day).
grau *adj.* [grau] grey, *esp. Am.* gray.
'**grauen**¹ *v/i.* (ge-, h) *day*: dawn.
'**grauen**² **1.** *v/i.* (ge-, h): *mir graut
vor* (*dat.*) I shudder at, I dread;
2. 2 *n* (-s/*no pl.*) horror (*vor dat.* of);
'**~erregend** *adj.*, '**~haft** *adj.*, '**~voll**
adj. horrible, dreadful.
gräulich *adj.* ['grɔyliç] greyish, *esp.
Am.* grayish.
Graupe ['graupə] *f* (-/-n) (peeled)

barley, pot-barley; '**∼ln 1.** f/pl. sleet; **2.** e-e v/i. (ge-, h) sleet.

'**grausam** adj. cruel; **2keit** f (-/-en) cruelty.

'**grausen** ['grauzən] **1.** v/i. (ge-, h) s. **grauen²** 1; **2.** 2 n (-s/no pl.) horror (vor dat. of).

'**grausig** adj. horrible. [graver.]

Graveur [gra'vø:r] m (-s/-e) en-]

gravieren [gra'vi:rən] v/t. (no -ge-, h) engrave; **∼d** fig. adj. aggravating.

gravitätisch adj. [gravi'tɛ:tiʃ] grave; dignified; solemn; stately.

Grazie ['grɑːtsjə] f (-/-n) grace(fulness).

graziös adj. [gra'tsjø:s] graceful.

greifen ['graifən] (irr., ge-, h) **1.** v/t. seize, grasp, catch hold of; ♪ touch (string); **2.** v/i.: an den Hut ∼ touch one's hat; ∼ nach grasp or snatch at; um sich ∼ spread; j-m unter die Arme ∼ give s.o. a helping hand; zu strengen Mitteln ∼ resort to severe measures; zu den Waffen ∼ take up arms.

Greis [grais] m (-es/-e) old man; **2enhaft** adj. ['∼zən-] senile (a. ♣); **∼in** f ['∼zin] f (-/-nen) old woman.

grell adj. [grɛl] light: glaring; colour: loud; sound: shrill.

Grenze ['grɛntsə] f (-/-n) limit; territory: boundary; state: frontier, borders pl.; e-e ∼ ziehen draw the line; **2n** v/i. (ge-, h): ∼ an (acc.) border on (a. fig.); fig. verge on; **2nlos** adj. boundless.

'**Grenz|fall** m border-line case; '**∼land** n borderland; '**∼linie** f boundary or border line; '**∼schutz** m frontier or border protection; frontier or border guard; '**∼stein** m boundary stone; '**∼übergang** m frontier or border crossing(-point).

Greuel ['grɔyəl] m (-s/-) horror; abomination; atrocity; '**∼tat** f atrocity.

Griech|e ['gri:çə] m (-n/-n) Greek; **2isch** adj. Greek; ♣, features: Grecian.

griesgrämig adj. ['gri:sgrɛ:miç] morose, sullen.

Grieß [gri:s] m (-es/-e) gravel (a. ♣), grit; semolina; '**∼brei** m semolina pudding.

Griff [grif] **1.** m (-[e]s/-e) grip, grasp, hold; ♪ touch; handle (of knife, etc.); hilt (of sword); **2.** 2 pret. of greifen.

Grille ['grilə] f (-/-n) zo. cricket; fig. whim, fancy; **2nhaft** adj. whimsical.

Grimasse [gri'masə] f (-/-n) grimace; ∼n schneiden pull faces.

Grimm [grim] m (-[e]s/no pl.) fury, rage; **2ig** adj. furious, fierce, grim.

Grind [grint] m (-[e]s/-e) scab, scurf.

grinsen ['grinzən] **1.** v/i. (ge-, h) grin (über acc. at); sneer (at); **2.** 2 n (-s/no pl.) grin; sneer.

Grippe ♣ ['gripə] f (-/-n) influenza, F flu(e), grippe.

grob adj. [grɔp] coarse; gross; rude; work, skin: rough; **2heit** f (-/-en) coarseness; grossness; rudeness; ∼en pl. rude things pl.

grölen F ['grø:lən] v/t. and v/i. (ge-, h) bawl.

Groll [grɔl] m (-[e]s/no pl.) grudge, ill will; **2en** v/i. (ge-, h) thunder rumble; j-m ∼ bear s.o. ill will or a grudge.

Gros¹ † [grɔs] n (-ses/-se) gross.

Gros² [gro:] n (-/-) main body.

Groschen ['grɔʃən] m (-s/-) penny.

groß adj. [gro:s] great; large; big; figure: tall; huge; fig. great, grand; heat: intense; cold: severe; loss: heavy; die 2en pl. the grown-ups pl.; im ∼en wholesale, on a large scale; im ∼en (und) ganzen on the whole; ∼er Buchstabe capital (letter); das ∼e Los the first prize; ich bin kein ∼er Tänzer I am not much of a dancer; '**∼artig** adj. great, grand, sublime; first-rate; '**2aufnahme** f film: close-up.

Größe ['grø:sə] f (-/-n) size; largeness; height, tallness; quantity (esp. ♣); importance: greatness; p. celebrity; thea. star.

'**Großeltern** pl. grandparents pl.

'**großenteils** adv. to a large or great extent, largely.

'**Größenwahn** m megalomania.

'**Groß|grundbesitz** m large landed property; '**∼handel** † m wholesale trade; '**∼handelspreis** m wholesale price; '**∼händler** † m wholesale dealer, wholesaler; '**∼handlung** † f wholesale business; '**∼herzog** m grand duke; '**∼industrielle** m big industrialist.

Grossist [grɔ'sist] m (-en/-en) s. Großhändler.

groß|jährig adj. ['gro:sjɛ:riç] of age;

~ werden come of age; '2jährigkeit f (-/no pl.) majority, full (legal) age; '2kaufmann m wholesale merchant; '2kraftwerk ⚡ n superpower station; '2macht f great power; '2maul n braggart; '2mut f (-/no pl.) generosity; ~mütig adj. ['~my·tiç] magnanimous, generous; '2mutter f grandmother; '2neffe m great-nephew, grandnephew; '2nichte f great-niece, grand-niece; '2onkel m great-uncle, grand-uncle; '2schreibung f (-/-en) use of capital letters; capitalization; '~sprecherisch adj. boastful; '~spurig adj. arrogant; '2stadt f large town or city; '~städtisch adj. of or in a large town or city; '2tante f great-aunt, grandaunt.

größtenteils adv. ['grø:stəntaɪls] mostly, chiefly, mainly.

'groß|tun v/i. (irr. tun, sep., -ge-, h) swagger, boast; sich mit et. ~ boast or brag of or about s.th.; '2vater m grandfather; '2verdiener m (-s/-) big earner; '2wild n big game; '~ziehen v/t. (irr. ziehen, sep., -ge-, h) bring up (child); rear, raise (child, animal); ~zügig adj. ['~tsy·giç] liberal; generous; broad-minded; planning: a. on a large scale.

grotesk adj. [gro'tɛsk] grotesque.

Grotte ['grɔtə] f (-/-n) grotto.

grub [gru:p] pret. of graben.

Grübchen ['gry:pçən] n (-s/-) dimple.

Grube ['gru:bə] f (-/-n) pit; ⚒ mine, pit.

Grübel|ei [gry:bə'laɪ] f (-/-en) brooding, musing, meditation; '2n ['~ln] v/i. (ge-, h) muse, meditate, ponder (all: über acc. on, over), Am. F a. mull (over).

'Gruben|arbeiter ⚒ m miner; '~gas ⚒ n fire-damp; '~lampe ⚒ f miner's lamp.

Gruft [gruft] f (-/⁔e) tomb, vault.

grün [gry:n] 1. adj. green; ~er Hering fresh herring; ~er Junge greenhorn; ~ und blau schlagen beat s.o. black and blue; vom ~en Tisch aus armchair (strategy, etc.); 2. 2 n (-s/no pl.) green; verdure.

Grund [grunt] m (-[e]s/⁔e) ground; soil; bottom (a. fig.); land, estate; foundation; fig.: motive; reason; argument; von ~ auf thoroughly, fundamentally; '~ausbildung f basic instruction; ✗ basic (military) training; '~bedeutung f basic or original meaning; '~bedingung f basic or fundamental condition; '~begriff m fundamental or basic idea; ~e pl. principles pl.; rudiments pl.; '~besitz m land(ed property); '~besitzer m landowner; '~buch n land register.

gründ|en ['gryndən] v/t. (ge-, h) establish; ✝ promote; sich ~ auf (acc.) be based or founded on; '2er m (-s/-) founder; ✝ promoter.

'grund|falsch adj. fundamentally wrong; '~farbe f ground-colo(u)r; opt. primary colo(u)r; '2fläche f base; area (of room, etc.); '2gebühr f basic rate or fee; flat rate; '2gedanke m basic or fundamental idea; '2gesetz n fundamental law; ⚖ appr. constitution; '2kapital ✝ n capital (fund); '2lage f foundation, basis; '~legend adj. fundamental, basic.

gründlich adj. ['gryntliç] thorough; knowledge: profound.

'Grund|linie f base-line; '2los adj. bottomless; fig.: groundless; unfounded; '~mauer f foundationwall. [Thursday.]

Grün'donnerstag eccl. m Maundy

'Grund|regel f fundamental rule; '~riß m △ ground-plan; outline; compendium; '~satz m principle; 2sätzlich ['~zetsliç] 1. adj. fundamental; 2. adv. in principle; on principle; '~schule f elementary or primary school; '~stein m △ foundation-stone; fig. corner-stone; '~steuer f land-tax; '~stock m basis, foundation; '~stoff m element; '~strich m down-stroke; '~stück n plot (of land); ⚖ (real) estate; premises pl.; '~stücksmakler m real estate agent, Am. realtor; '~ton m ♪ keynote; ground shade.

'Gründung f (-/-en) foundation, establishment.

'grund|ver'schieden adj. entirely different; '2wasser geol. n (under-)ground water; '2zahl gr. f cardinal number; '2zug m main feature, characteristic.

'grünlich adj. greenish.

'Grün|schnabel fig. m greenhorn; whipper-snapper; '~span m (-[e]s/no pl.) verdigris.

grunzen ['gruntsən] v/i. and v/t. (ge-, h) grunt.

Grupp|e ['grupə] f (-/-n) group; ✗ section, Am. squad; 2**ieren** [~'piːrən] v/t. (no -ge-, h) group, arrange in groups; sich ~ form groups.

Gruselgeschichte ['gruːzəl-] f tale of horror, spine-chilling story or tale, F creepy story or tale.

Gruß [gruːs] m (-es/⁎e) salutation; greeting; esp. ✗, ⚓ salute; mst **Grüße** pl. regards pl.; respects pl., compliments pl.

grüßen ['gryːsən] v/t. (ge-, h) greet, esp. ✗ salute; hail; ~ **Sie ihn von mir** remember me to him; **j-n ~ lassen** send one's compliments or regards to s.o.

Grütze ['grytsə] f (-/-n) grits pl., groats pl.

guck|en ['gukən] v/i. (ge-, h) look; peep, peer; 2**loch** n peep- or spy-hole.

Guerilla [ge'ril(j)a] f (-/-s) guer(r)illa war.

gültig adj. ['gyltiç] valid; effective, in force; legal; coin: current; ticket: available; 2**keit** f (-/no pl.) validity; currency (of money); availability (of ticket).

Gummi ['gumi] n, m (-s/-s) gum; (india-)rubber; '~**ball** m rubber ball; '~**band** n elastic (band); rubber band; '~**baum** ♀ m gum-tree; (india-)rubber tree.

gum'mieren v/t. (no -ge-, h) gum. '**Gummi|handschuh** m rubber glove; '~**knüppel** m truncheon, Am. club; '~**schuhe** m/pl. rubber shoes pl., Am. rubbers pl.; '~**sohle** f rubber sole; '~**stiefel** m wellington (boot), Am. rubber boot; '~**zug** m elastic; elastic webbing.

Gunst [gunst] f (-/no pl.) favo(u)r, goodwill; **zu ~en** (gen.) in favo(u)r of.

günst|ig adj. ['gynstiç] favo(u)rable; omen: propitious; im ⁎**sten Fall** at best; **zu ~en Bedingungen** ✝ on easy terms; 2**ling** ['~liŋ] m (-s/-e) favo(u)rite.

Gurgel ['gurgəl] f (-/-n): **j-m an die ~ springen** leap or fly at s.o.'s throat; 2**n** v/i. (ge-, h) ♪ gargle; gurgle.

Gurke ['gurkə] f (-/-n) cucumber; pickled: gherkin.

gurren ['gurən] v/i. (ge-, h) coo.

Gurt [gurt] m (-[e]s/-e) girdle; harness: girth; strap; belt.

Gürtel ['gyrtəl] m (-s/-) belt; girdle; geogr. zone.

Guß [gus] m (Gusses/Güsse) ⊕ founding, casting; typ. fount, Am. font; rain: downpour, shower; '~**eisen** n cast iron; 2**eisern** adj. cast-iron; '~**stahl** m cast steel.

gut[1] [guːt] **1.** adj. good; ⁎**e Worte** fair words; ⁎**es Wetter** fine weather; ⁎**er Dinge** or ⁎**en Mutes sein** be of good cheer; ⁎**e Miene zum bösen Spiel machen** grin and bear it; ~ **so!** good!, well done!; ⁎ **werden** get well, heal; fig. turn out well; **ganz ~ not bad; schon ~!** never mind!, all right!; **sei so ~ und ...** (will you) be so kind as to inf.; **auf ~ deutsch** in plain German; **j-m ~ sein** love or like s.o.; **2.** adv. well; **ein ~ gehendes Geschäft** a flourishing business; **du hast ~ lachen** it's easy or very well for you to laugh; **es ~ haben** be lucky; be well off.

Gut[2] [~] n (-[e]s/⁎er) possession, property; (landed) estate; ✝ goods pl.

'**Gut|achten** n (-s/-) (expert) opinion; '~**achter** m (-s/-) expert; consultant; 2**artig** adj. good-natured; ✿ benign; '~**dünken** ['~dynkən] n (-s/no pl.): **nach ~** at discretion or pleasure.

'**Gute 1.** n (-n/no pl.) the good; ~**s tun** do good; **2.** m, f (-n/-n): **die ~n** pl. the good pl.

Güte ['gyːtə] f (-/no pl.) goodness, kindness; ✝ class, quality; **in ~** amicably; F: **meine ~!** good gracious!; **haben Sie die ~ zu** inf. be so kind as to inf.

'**Güter|abfertigung** f dispatch of goods; = '~**annahme** f goods office, Am. freight office; '~**bahnhof** m goods station, Am. freight depot or yard; '~**gemeinschaft** 🜨 f community of property; '~**trennung** 🜨 f separation of property; '~**verkehr** m goods traffic, Am. freight traffic; '~**wagen** m (goods) wag(g)on, Am. freight car; **offener ~** (goods) truck; **geschlossener ~** (goods) van, Am. boxcar; '~**zug** m goods train, Am. freight train.

'**gut|gelaunt** adj. good-humo(u)red;

'**~gläubig** adj. acting or done in good faith; s. leichtgläubig; '**~haben** v/t. (irr. haben, sep., -ge-, h) have credit for (sum of money); '♀haben ✝ n credit (balance); '**~heißen** v/t. (irr. heißen, sep., -ge-, h) approve (of); '**~herzig** adj. good-natured, kind-hearted.

'**gütig** adj. good, kind(ly).

'**gütlich** adv.: sich ~ einigen settle s.th. amicably; sich ~ tun an (dat.) regale o.s. on.

'**gut|machen** v/t. (sep., -ge-, h) make up for, compensate, repair; **~mütig** adj. ['~my:tiç] good-natured; '♀mütigkeit f (/♀ -en) good nature.   [of an estate.]

'**Gutsbesitzer** m landowner; owner]

'**Gut|schein** m credit note, coupon;

voucher; '♀**schreiben** v/t. (irr. schreiben, sep., -ge-, h): j-m e-n Betrag ~ put a sum to s.o.'s credit; '**~schrift** ✝ f credit(ing).

'**Guts|haus** n farm-house; manor house; '**~herr** m lord of the manor; landowner; '**~hof** m farmyard; estate, farm; '**~verwalter** m (landlord's) manager or steward.

'**gutwillig** adj. willing; obliging.

Gymnasi|albildung [gymna'zja:l-] f classical education; **~ast** [~ast] m (-en/-en) appr. grammar-school boy; **~um** [~'na:zjum] n (-s/Gymnasien) appr. grammar-school.

Gymnasti|k [gym'nastik] f (-/no pl.) gymnastics pl.; ♀**sch** adj. gymnastic.   [(-n/-n) gyn(a)ecologist.]

Gynäkologe ✹ [gyne:ko'lo:gə] m]

H

Haar [ha:r] n (-[e]s/-e) hair; sich die ~e kämmen comb one's hair; sich die ~e schneiden lassen have one's hair cut; aufs ~ to a hair; um ein ~ by a hair's breadth; '**~ausfall** m loss of hair; '**~bürste** f hairbrush; '♀**en** v/i. and v/refl. (ge-, h) lose or shed one's hairs; '**~esbreite** f: um ~ by a hair's breadth; '♀**fein** adj. (as) fine as a hair; fig. subtle; '**~gefäß** anat. n capillary (vessel); '♀**ge'nau** adj. exact to a hair; '♀**ig** adj. hairy; in compounds: ...-haired; '♀**klein** adv. to the last detail; '**~klemme** f hair grip, Am. bobby pin; '**~nadel** f hairpin; '**~nadelkurve** f hairpin bend; '**~netz** n hair-net; '**~öl** n hair-oil; '♀**scharf** 1. adj. very sharp; fig. very precise; 2. adv. by a hair's breadth; '**~schneidemaschine** f (e-e a pair of) (hair) clippers pl.; '**~schneider** m barber, (men's) hairdresser; '**~schnitt** m haircut; '**~schwund** m loss of hair; '**~spalte'rei** f (-/-en) hair-splitting; '♀**sträubend** adj. hair-raising, horrifying; '**~tracht** f hair-style, coiffure; '**~wäsche** f hair-wash, shampoo; '**~wasser** n hair-lotion; '**~wuchs** m growth of the hair; '**~wuchsmittel** n hair-restorer.

Habe ['ha:bə] f (-/no pl.) property; belongings pl.

haben ['ha:bən] 1. v/t. (irr., ge-, h) have; F fig.: sich ~ (make a) fuss; etwas (nichts) auf sich ~ be of (no) consequence; unter sich ~ be in control of, command; zu ~ ✝ goods: obtainable, to be had; da ~ wir's! there we are!; 2. ♀ ✝ n (-s/-) credit (side).

Habgier ['ha:p-] f avarice, covetousness; '♀**ig** adj. avaricious, covetous.

habhaft adj. ['ha:phaft]: ~ werden (gen.) get hold of; catch, apprehend.

Habicht orn. ['ha:biçt] m (-[e]s/-e) (gos)hawk.

Hab|seligkeiten ['ha:p-] f/pl. property, belongings pl.; '**~sucht** f s. Habgier; ♀**süchtig** adj. s. habgierig.

Hacke ['hakə] f (-/-n) ♪ hoe, mattock; (pick)axe; heel.

Hacken ['hakən] 1. m (-s/-) heel; die ~ zusammenschlagen ✕ click one's heels; 2. ♀ v/t. (ge-, h) ♪ hack (soil); mince (meat); chop (wood).

'**Hackfleisch** n minced meat, Am. ground meat.

Häcksel ['hɛksəl] n, m (-s/no pl.) chaff, chopped straw.

Hader ['ha:dər] m (-s/no pl.) dispute, quarrel; discord; '♀**n** v/i. (ge-, h) quarrel (mit with).

Hafen ['ha:fən] m (-s/⁀) harbo(u)r;

port; `~anlagen` f/pl. docks pl.; `~arbeiter` m docker, Am. a. longshoreman; `~damm` m jetty; pier; `~stadt` f seaport.

Hafer ['haːfər] m (-s/-) oats pl.; `~brei` m (oatmeal) porridge; `~flocken` f/pl. porridge oats pl.; `~grütze` f groats pl., grits pl.; `~schleim` m gruel.

Haft [haft] f (-/no pl.) custody; detention, confinement; `2bar` adj. responsible, ɪ̃ʈ liable (für for); `~befehl` m warrant of arrest; `~en` v/i. (ge-, h) stick, adhere (an dat. to); ~ für ɪ̃ʈ answer for, be liable for.

Häftling ['heftliŋ] m (-s/-e) prisoner.

Haftpflicht ɪ̃ʈ f liability; `2ig` adj. liable (für for); `~versicherung` f third-party insurance.

Haftung f (-/-en) responsibility, ɪ̃ʈ liability; mit beschränkter ~ limited.

Hagel ['haːgəl] m (-s/-) hail; fig. a. shower, volley; `~korn` n hailstone; `2n` v/i. (ge-, h) hail (a. fig.); `~schauer` m shower of hail, (brief) hailstorm.

hager adj. ['haːgər] lean, gaunt; scraggy, lank.

Hahn [haːn] m 1. orn. (-[e]s/⁼e) cock; rooster; 2. ⊕ (-[e]s/-e, -en) (stop)cock, tap, Am. a. faucet; `~enkampf` m cock-fight; `~enschrei` m cock-crow.

Hai ichth. [haɪ] m (-[e]s/-e), `~fisch` m shark.

Hain poet. [haɪn] m (-[e]s/-e) grove; wood.

häkel|n ['heːkəln] v/t. and v/i. (ge-, h) crochet; `2nadel` f crochet needle or hook.

Haken ['haːkən] 1. m (-s/⁼) hook (a. boxing); peg; fig. snag, catch; 2. ℒ v/i. (ge-, h) get stuck, jam.

hakig adj. hooked.

halb [halp] 1. adj. half; eine ~e Stunde half an hour, a half-hour; eine ~e Flasche Wein a half-bottle of wine; ein ~es Jahr half a year; ~e Note ♪ minim, Am. a. half note; ~er Ton ♪ semitone, Am. a. half tone; 2. adv. half; ~ voll half full; ~ soviel half as much; es schlug ~ it struck the half-hour.

'halb|amtlich adj. semi-official; `2bruder` m half-brother; `2dunkel` n semi-darkness; dusk, twilight; `~er` prp. (gen.) ['halbər] on

account of; for the sake of; `2fabrikat` ⊕ n semi-finished product; `~gar` adj. underdone, Am. a. rare; `2gott` m demigod; `2heit` f (-/-en) half-measure.

halbieren [hal'biːrən] v/t. (no -ge-, h) halve, divide in half; ↓ bisect.

'Halb|insel f peninsula; `~jahr` n half-year, six months pl.; `2jährig` adj. [ˈ~jeːrɪç] half-year, six months; of six months; `2jährlich` 1. adj. half-yearly; 2. adv. a. twice a year; `~kreis` m semicircle; `~kugel` f hemisphere; `2laut` 1. adj. low, subdued; 2. adv. in an undertone; `~mast` adv. (at) half-mast, Am. a. (at) half-staff; `~messer` ↓ m (-s/-) radius; `~mond` m half-moon, crescent; `2part` adv.: ~ machen go halves, F go fifty-fifty; `~schuh` m (low) shoe; `~schwester` f half-sister; `~tagsbeschäftigung` f part-time job or employment; `2tot` adj. half-dead; `2wegs` adv. ['~'veːks] half-way; fig. to some extent, tolerably; `~welt` f demi-monde; `2wüchsig` adj. ['~vyːksɪç] adolescent, Am. a. teen-age; `~zeit` f sports: half(-time). [dump.]

Halde ['haldə] f (-/-n) slope; ℅ |

half [half] pret. of helfen.

Hälfte ['helftə] f (-/-en) half, ɪ̃ʈ moiety; die ~ von half of.

Halfter ['halftər] m, n (-s/-) halter.

Halle ['halə] f (-/-n) hall; hotel: lounge; tennis: covered court; ✈ hangar.

hallen ['halən] v/i. (ge-, h) (re)sound, ring, (re-)echo.

'Hallen|bad n indoor swimming-bath, Am. a. natatorium; `~sport` m indoor sports pl.

hallo [ha'loː] 1. int. hallo!, hello!, hullo!; 2. 2 fig. n (-s/-s) hullabaloo.

Halm ♀ [halm] m (-[e]s/-e) blade; stem, stalk; straw.

Hals [hals] m (-es/⁼e) neck; throat; ~ über Kopf head over heels; auf dem ~e haben have on one's back, be saddled with; sich den ~ verrenken crane one's neck; `~abschneider` fig. m extortioner, F shark; `~band` n necklace; collar (for dog, etc.); `~entzündung` ✗ f sore throat; `~kette` f necklace; string; chain; `~kragen` m collar; `~schmerzen` m/pl.: ~ haben have a sore throat; `2starrig` adj. stubborn, obstinate; '**~tuch** n neckerchief; scarf; '**~weite** f neck size.

¦alt [halt] m (-[e]s/-e) hold; foothold, handhold; support (a. fig.); fig.: stability; security, mainstay.

¦alt 1. int. stop!; ✕ halt!; **2.** F adv. just; das ist ~ so that's the way it is.

haltbar adj. material, etc.: durable, lasting; colour: fast; fig. theory, etc.: tenable.

halten (irr., ge-, h) **1.** v/t. hold (fort, position, water, etc.); maintain (position, level, etc.); keep (promise, order, animal, etc.); make, deliver (speech); give, deliver (lecture); take in (newspaper); ~ für regard as, take to be; take for; es ~ mit side with; be fond of; kurz ~ keep s.o. short; viel (wenig) ~ von think highly (little) of; sich ~ hold out; last; food: keep; sich gerade ~ hold o.s. straight; sich gut ~ in examination, etc.: do well; p. be well preserved; sich ~ an (acc.) adhere or keep to; **2.** v/i. stop, halt; ice: bear; rope, etc.: stand the strain; ~ zu stick to or by; ~ auf (acc.) set store by, value; auf sich ~ pay attention to one's appearance; have self-respect.

Halte|punkt m 🚋, etc.: wayside stop, halt; shooting: point of aim; phys. critical point; '**~r** m (-s/-) keeper; a. owner; devices: ... holder; '**~stelle** f 🚋 station, stop; '**~signal** 🚋 n stop signal.

¦alt|los adj. ['haltlo:s] p. unsteady, unstable; theory, etc.: baseless, without foundation; '**~machen** v/i. (sep., -ge-, h) stop, halt; vor nichts ~ stick or stop; at nothing; '**Qung** f (-/-en) deportment, carriage; pose; fig. attitude (gegenüber towards); self-control; stock exchange: tone.

¦ämisch adj. ['he:miʃ] spiteful, malicious.

Hammel ['haməl] m (-s/-, =) wether; '**~fleisch** n mutton; '**~keule** f leg of mutton; '**~rippchen** n (-s/-) mutton chop.

Hammer ['hamər] m (-s/=) hammer; (auctioneer's) gavel; unter den ~ kommen come under the hammer.

¦ämmern ['hemərn] (ge-, h) **1.** v/t. hammer; **2.** v/i. hammer (a. an dat. at door, etc.); hammer away (auf dat. at piano); heart, etc.: throb (violently), pound.

Hämorrhoiden 🚋 [hɛ:mɔroˈiːdən]

f/pl. h(a)emorrhoids pl., piles pl.

Hampelmann ['hampəlman] m jumping-jack; fig. (mere) puppet.

Hamster zo. ['hamstər] m (-s/-) hamster; '**Qn** v/t. and v/i. (ge-, h) hoard.

Hand [hant] f (-/-e) hand; j-m die ~ geben shake hands with s.o.; an ~ (gen.) or von with the help or aid of; aus erster ~ first-hand, at first hand; bei der ~, zur ~ at hand; ~ und Fuß haben be sound, hold water; seine ~ im Spiele haben have a finger in the pie; '**~arbeit** f manual labo(u)r or work; (handi)craft; needlework; '**~arbeiter** m manual labo(u)rer; '**~bibliothek** f reference library; '**~breit** f (-/-) hand's breadth; **2.** ♀ adj. a hand's breadth across; '**~bremse** mot. f hand-brake; '**~buch** n manual, handbook.

Hände|druck ['hɛndə-] m (-[e]s/=e) handshake; '**~klatschen** (-s/no pl.) (hand-)clapping; applause.

Handel ['handəl] m **1.** (-s/no pl.) commerce; trade; business; market; traffic; transaction, deal, bargain; **2.** (-s/=): Händel pl. quarrels pl., contention; '**Qn** v/i. (ge-, h) act, take action; ✝ trade (mit with s.o., in goods), deal (in goods); bargain (um for), haggle (over); ~ von treat of, deal with; es handelt sich um it concerns, it is a matter of.

'**Handels|abkommen** n trade agreement; '**~bank** f commercial bank; '**Qeinig** adj.: ~ werden come to terms; '**~genossenschaft** f traders' co-operative association; '**~gericht** n commercial court; '**~gesellschaft** f (trading) company; '**~haus** n business house, firm; '**~kammer** f Chamber of Commerce; '**~marine** f mercantile marine; '**~minister** m minister of commerce; President of the Board of Trade, Am. Secretary of Commerce; '**~ministerium** n ministry of commerce; Board of Trade, Am. Department of Commerce; '**~reisende** m commercial traveller, Am. traveling salesman, F drummer; '**~schiff** n merchantman; '**~schiffahrt** f merchant shipping; '**~schule** f commercial school; '**~stadt** f commercial town; '**Qüblich** adj. customary in trade; '**~vertrag** m commercial treaty, trade agreement.

'**handeltreibend** adj. trading.
'**Hand|feger** m (-s/-) hand-brush; '**~fertigkeit** f manual skill; '**℔fest** adj. sturdy, strong; fig. well-founded, sound; '**~feuerwaffen** f/pl. small arms pl.; '**~fläche** f flat of the hand, palm; '**℔gearbeitet** adj. hand-made; '**~geld** n earnest money; ✕ bounty; '**~gelenk** anat. n wrist; '**~gemenge** n scuffle, mêlée; '**~gepäck** n hand luggage, Am. hand baggage; '**~granate** ✕ f hand-grenade; '**℔greiflich** adj. violent; fig. tangible, palpable; **~ werden** turn violent, Am. a. get tough; '**~griff** m grasp; handle, grip; fig. manipulation; '**~habe** fig. f handle; '**℔haben** v/t. (no -ge-) handle, manage; operate (machine, etc.); administer (law); '**~karren** m hand-cart; '**~koffer** m suitcase, Am. a. valise; '**~kuß** m kiss on the hand; '**~langer** m (-s/-) hodman, handy man; fig. dog's-body, henchman. [trader.]

Händler ['hɛndlər] m (-s/-) dealer,!
'**handlich** adj. handy; manageable.
Handlung ['handluŋ] f (-/-en) act, action; deed; thea. action, plot; ✝ shop, Am. store.

'**Handlungs|bevollmächtigte** m proxy; '**~gehilfe** m clerk; shop-assistant, Am. salesclerk; '**~reisende** m s. Handelsreisende; '**~weise** f conduct; way of acting.

'**Hand|rücken** m back of the hand; '**~schelle** f handcuff, manacle; '**~schlag** m handshake; '**~schreiben** n autograph letter; '**~schrift** f handwriting; manuscript; '**℔-schriftlich** 1. adj. hand-written; 2. adv. in one's own handwriting; '**~schuh** m glove; '**~streich** ✕ m surprise attack, coup de main; im ~ nehmen take by surprise; '**~tasche** f handbag, Am. a. purse; '**~tuch** n towel; '**~voll** f (-/-) handful; '**~wagen** m hand-cart; '**~werk** n (handi)craft, trade; '**~werker** m (-s/-) (handi)craftsman, artisan; workman; '**~werkzeug** n (kit of) tools pl.; '**~wurzel** anat. f wrist; '**~zeichnung** f drawing.

Hanf ⚘ [hanf] m (-[e]s/no pl.) hemp.
Hang [haŋ] m (-[e]s/ⸯe) slope, incline, declivity; hillside; fig. inclination, propensity (zu for; zu inf. to inf.); tendency (to).

Hänge|boden ['hɛŋə-] m hanging-loft; **~brücke** △ f suspension bridge; '**~lampe** f hanging lamp; '**~matte** f hammock.

hängen ['hɛŋən] 1. v/i. (irr., ge-, h) hang, be suspended; adhere, stick, cling (an dat. to); ~ an (dat.) be attached or devoted to; 2. v/t. (ge-, h) hang, suspend; '**~bleiben** v/i. (irr. bleiben, sep., -ge-, sein) get caught (up) (an dat. on, in); fig. stick (in the memory).

hänseln ['hɛnzəln] v/t. (ge-, h) tease (wegen about), F rag.
Hansestadt ['hanzə-] f Hanseatic town.
Hanswurst [hans'-] m (-es/-e, F ⸯe) merry andrew; Punch; fig. contp. clown, buffoon.
Hantel ['hantəl] f (-/-n) dumb-bell.
hantieren [han'ti:rən] v/i. (no -ge-, h) be busy (mit with); work (an dat. on).
Happen ['hapən] m (-s/-) morsel, mouthful, bite; snack.
Harfe ♪ ['harfə] f (-/-n) harp.
Harke ✍ ['harkə] f (-/-n) rake; '**℔n** v/t. and v/i. (ge-, h) rake.
harmlos adj. ['harmlo:s] harmless, innocuous; inoffensive.
Harmon|ie [harmo'ni:] f (-/-n) harmony (a. ♪); **℔ieren** v/i. (no -ge-, h) harmonize (mit with); fig. a. be in tune (with); **~ika** ♪ [~'mo:-nika] f (-/-s, Harmoniken) accordion; mouth-organ; **℔isch** adj. [~'mo:niʃ] harmonious.
Harn [harn] m (-[e]s/-e) urine; '**~blase** anat. f (urinary) bladder; '**℔en** v/i. (ge-, h) pass water, urinate.
Harnisch ['harniʃ] m (-es/-e) armo(u)r; in ~ geraten be up in arms (über acc. about).
'**Harnröhre** anat. f urethra.
Harpun|e [har'pu:nə] f (-/-n) harpoon; **℔ieren** [~u'ni:rən] v/t. (no -ge-, h) harpoon.
hart [hart] 1. adj. hard; fig. a. harsh; heavy, severe; 2. adv. hard; ~ arbeiten work hard.
Härte ['hɛrtə] f (-/-n) hardness; fig. a. hardship; severity; '**℔n** (ge-, h) 1. v/t. harden (metal); temper (steel); case-harden (iron, steel); 2. v/i. and v/refl. harden, become or grow hard; steel: temper.
'**Hart|geld** n coin(s pl.), specie; '**~gummi** m hard rubber; ✝ ebon-

ite, vulcanite; **'⊘herzig** *adj.* hard-hearted; **'⊘köpfig** *adj.* ['.kœpfiç] stubborn, headstrong; **⊘näckig** *adj.* ['.nɛkiç] *p.* obstinate, obdurate; *effort:* dogged, tenacious; *✗ ailment:* refractory.

Harz [haːrts] *n* (-es/-e) resin; *♪ rosin*; *mot.* gum; **'⊘ig** *adj.* resinous.

Hasardspiel [ha'zart-] *n* game of chance; *fig.* gamble.

haschen ['haʃən] (ge-, h) **1.** *v/t.* catch (hold of), snatch; *sich ~ children:* play tag; **2.** *v/i.: ~ nach* snatch at; *fig.* strain after (*effect*), fish for (*compliments*).

Hase ['haːzə] *m* (-n/-n) *zo.* hare; *ein alter ~* an old hand, an old-timer.

Haselnuß ⚘ ['haːzəlnus] *f* hazelnut.

'Hasen|braten *m* roast hare; **'.fuß** F *fig. m* coward, F funk; **'.panier** F *n: das ~ ergreifen* take to one's heels; **'.scharte** ⚘ *f* hare-lip.

Haß [has] *m* (Hasses/*no pl.*) hatred.

'hassen *v/t.* (ge-, h) hate.

häßlich *adj.* ['hɛsliç] ugly; *fig. a.* nasty, unpleasant.

Hast [hast] *f* (-/*no pl.*) hurry, haste; rush; *in wilder ~* in frantic haste, rush; **'⊘en** *v/i.* (ge-, sein) hurry, hasten; rush; **'⊘ig** *adj.* hasty, hurried.

hätscheln ['hɛːtʃəln] *v/t.* (ge-, h) caress, fondle, pet; pamper, coddle.

hatte ['hatə] *pret.* of *haben.*

Haube ['haubə] *f* (-/-n) bonnet (a. ⊕, *mot.*); cap; *orn.* crest, tuft; *mot. Am. a.* hood.   [howitzer.⟩

Haubitze ✗ [hau'bitsə] *f* (-/-n)⟩

Hauch [haux] *m* (-[e]s/✗ -e) breath; *fig.:* waft, whiff (*of perfume, etc.*); touch, tinge (*of irony, etc.*); **'⊘en** (ge-, h) **1.** *v/i.* breathe; **2.** *v/t.* breathe, whisper; *gr.* aspirate.

Haue ['hauə] *f* (-/-n) *⚒* hoe, mattock; pick; F hiding, spanking; **'⊘n** (*[irr.,]* ge-, h) **1.** *v/t.* hew (*coal, stone*); cut up (*meat*); chop (*wood*); cut (*hole, steps, etc.*); beat (*child*); *sich ~* (have a) fight; **2.** *v/i.: ~ nach* cut at, strike out at.

Haufen ['haufən] *m* (-s/-) heap, pile (*both* F *a. fig.*); *fig.* crowd.

häufen ['hɔyfən] *v/t.* (ge-, h) heap (up), pile (up); accumulate; *sich ~* pile up, accumulate; *fig.* become more frequent, increase.

'häufig *adj.* frequent; **'⊘keit** *f* (-/*no pl.*) frequency.

'Häufung *fig. f* (-/-en) increase, *fig.* accumulation.

Haupt [haupt] *n* (-[e]s/⁼er) head; *fig.* chief, head, leader; **'.altar** *m* high altar; **'.anschluß** *teleph. m* subscriber's main station; **'.bahnhof** 🚂 *m* main *or* central station; **'.beruf** *m* full-time occupation; **'.buch** ✝ *n* ledger; **'.darsteller** *thea. m* leading actor; **'.fach** *univ. n* main *or* principal subject, *Am. a.* major; **'.film** *m* feature (film); **'.geschäft** *n* main transaction; main shop; **'.geschäftsstelle** *f* head *or* central office; **'.gewinn** *m* first prize; **'.grund** *m* main reason; **'.handelsartikel** ✝ ['haupthandəls?-] *m* staple.   [chief(tain).⟩

Häuptling ['hɔyptlɪŋ] *m* (-s/-e)⟩

'Haupt|linie 🚂 *f* main *or* trunk line; **'.mann** ✗ *m* (-[e]s/*Hauptleute*) captain; **'.merkmal** *n* characteristic feature; **'.postamt** *n* general post office, *Am.* main post office; **'.punkt** *m* main *or* cardinal point; **'.quartier** *n* headquarters *sg. or pl.*; **'.rolle** *thea. f* lead(ing part); **'.sache** *f* main thing *or* point; **'⊘sächlich** *adj.* main, chief, principal; **'.satz** *gr. m* main clause; **'.stadt** *f* capital; **'⊘städtisch** *adj.* metropolitan; **'.straße** *f* main street; major road; **'.treffer** *m* first prize, jackpot; **'.verkehrsstraße** *f* main road; arterial road; **'.verkehrsstunden** *f/pl.*, **'.verkehrszeit** *f* rush hour(s *pl.*), peak hour(s *pl.*); **'.versammlung** *f* general meeting; **'.wort** *n* (-[e]s/⁼er) substantive, noun.

Haus [haus] *n* (-es/⁼er) house; building; home; family, household; dynasty; ✝ (business) house, firm; *parl.* House; *nach ~e* home; *zu ~e* at home, F in; **'.angestellte** *f* (-n/-n) (house-)maid; **'.apotheke** *f* (household) medicine-chest; **'.arbeit** *f* housework; **'.arrest** *m* house arrest; **'.arzt** *m* family doctor; **'.aufgaben** *f/pl.* homework, F prep; **'⊘backen** *fig. adj.* homely; **'.bar** *f* cocktail cabinet; **'.bedarf** *m* household requirements *pl.*; **'.besitzer** *m* house-owner; **'.diener** *m* (man-)servant; *hotel:* porter, boots *sg.*

hausen ['hauzən] *v/i.* (ge-, h) live; play *or* work·havoc (*in a place*).

'**Haus|flur** m (entrance-)hall, esp. Am. hallway; '**.frau** f housewife; '**.halt** m household; '**2halten** v/i. (irr. halten, sep., -ge-, h) be economical (mit with), economize (on); **.hälterin** ['.hɛltərin] f (-/-nen) housekeeper; '**.halt(s)plan** parl. m budget; '**.haltung** f housekeeping; household, family; '**.haltwaren** f/pl. household articles pl.; '**.herr** m master of the family; landlord.

hausier|en [hau'zi:rən] v/i. (no -ge-, h) hawk, peddle (mit et. s.th.); ~ **gehen** be a hawker or pedlar; **2er** m (-s/-) hawker, pedlar.

'**Haus|kleid** n house dress; '**.knecht** m boots; '**.lehrer** m private tutor.

häuslich adj. ['hɔyslɪç] domestic; domesticated; **2keit** f (-/no pl.) domesticity; family life; home.

'**Haus|mädchen** n (house-)maid; '**.mannskost** f plain fare; '**.meister** m caretaker; janitor; '**.mittel** n popular medicine; '**.ordnung** f rules pl. of the house; '**.rat** m household effects pl.; '**.recht** n domestic authority; '**.sammlung** f house-to-house collection; '**.schlüssel** m latchkey; front-door key; '**.schuh** m slipper.

Hauss|e ['ho:s(ə)] f (-/-n) rise, boom; '**.ier** [hos'je:] m (-s/-s) speculator for a rise, bull.

'**Haus|stand** m household; e-n ~ **gründen** set up house; '**.suchung** z'z f house search, domiciliary visit, Am. a. house check; '**.tier** n domestic animal; '**.tür** f front door; '**.verwalter** m steward; '**.wirt** m landlord; '**.wirtin** f (-/-nen) landlady.

Haut [haut] f (-/=e) skin; hide; film; bis auf die ~ to the skin; aus der ~ **fahren** jump out of one's skin; F e-e **ehrliche** ~ an honest soul; '**.abschürfung** & f skin abrasion; '**.arzt** m dermatologist; '**.ausschlag** & m rash; '**2eng** adj. garment: skin-tight; '**.farbe** f complexion.

Hautgout [o'gu] m (-s/no pl.) high taste.

häutig adj. ['hɔytɪç] membranous; covered with skin.

'**Haut|krankheit** f skin disease; '**.pflege** f care of the skin; '**.**

schere f (e-e a pair of) cuticle scissors pl. [age.]

Havarie ⚓ [hava'ri:] f (-/-n) average.]

H-Bombe ⚔ ['ha:-] f H-bomb.

he int. [he:] hi!, hi there!, I say!

Hebamme ['he:pˀamə] f midwife.

Hebe|baum ['he:bə-] m lever (for raising heavy objects); '**.bühne** mot. f lifting ramp; '**.eisen** n crowbar; '**.kran** m lifting crane.

Hebel ⊕ ['he:bəl] m (-s/-) lever; '**.arm** m lever arm.

heben ['he:bən] v/t. (irr., ge-, h) lift (a. sports), raise (a. fig.); heave (heavy load); hoist; recover (treasure); raise (sunken ship); fig. promote, improve, increase; sich ~ rise, go up.

Hecht ichth. [hɛçt] m (-[e]s/-e) pike.

Heck [hɛk] n (-[e]s/-e, -s) ⚓ stern; mot. rear; ✈ tail.

Hecke ['hɛkə] f (-/-n) ✿ hedge; zo. brood, hatch; '**2n** v/t. and v/i. (ge-, h) breed, hatch; '**.nrose** ✿ f dog-rose. [(hallo!)]

heda int. ['he:da:] hi (there)!,]

Heer [he:r] n (-[e]s/-e) ⚔ army; fig. a. host; '**.esdienst** m military service; '**.esmacht** f military force(s pl.); '**.eszug** m military expedition; '**.führer** m general; '**.lager** n (army) camp; '**.schar** f army, host; '**.straße** f military road; highway; '**.zug** m s. Heereszug.

Hefe ['he:fə] f (-/-n) yeast; barm.

Heft [hɛft] n (-[e]s/-e) dagger, etc.: haft; knife: handle; fig. reins pl.; exercise book; periodical, etc.: issue, number.

'**heft|en** v/t. (ge-, h) fasten, fix (an acc. on to); affix, attach (to); pin on (to); baste (seam, etc.); stitch, sew (book); '**2faden** m basting thread.

'**heftig** adj. storm, anger, quarrel, etc.: violent, fierce; rain, etc.: heavy; pain, etc.: severe; speech, desire, etc.: vehement, passionate; p. irascible; '**2keit** f (-/⚓ -en) violence, fierceness; severity; vehemence; irascibility.

'**Heft|klammer** f paper-clip; '**.pflaster** n sticking plaster.

hegen ['he:gən] v/t. (ge-, h) preserve (game); nurse, tend (plants); have, entertain (feelings); harbo(u)r (fears, suspicions, etc.).

Hehler ɹ̣̃ʒ ['heːlər] *m* (-s/-) receiver (of stolen goods); **~ei** [.'raɪ] *f* (-/-en) receiving (of stolen goods).

Heide ['haɪdə] 1. *m* (-n/-n) heathen; 2. *f* (-/-n) heath(-land); = '**~kraut** ⚘ *n* heather; '**~land** *n* heath(-land).

'**Heiden|geld** F *n* pots *pl.* of money; '**~lärm** F *m* hullabaloo; '**~spaß** F *m* capital fun; '**~tum** *n* (-s/*no pl.*) heathenism.   [(-ish).]

heidnisch *adj.* ['haɪdnɪʃ] heathen)

heikel *adj.* ['haɪkəl] *p.* fastidious, particular; *problem*, *etc.*: delicate, awkward.

heil [haɪl] 1. *adj. p.* safe, unhurt; whole, sound; 2. ⚚ *n* (-[e]s/*no pl.*) welfare, benefit; *eccl.* salvation; 3. *int.* hail!

Heiland *eccl.* ['haɪlant] *m* (-[e]s/-e) Saviour, Redeemer.

'**Heil|anstalt** *f* sanatorium, *Am. a.* sanitarium; '**~bad** *n* medicinal bath; spa; '⚚**bar** *adj.* curable; '⚚**en** (ge-) 1. *v/t.* (h) cure, heal; ~ *von* s.o. of; 2. *v/i.* (sein) heal (up); '**~gehilfe** *m* male nurse.

heilig *adj.* ['haɪlɪç] holy; sacred; solemn; ⚚*er Abend* Christmas Eve; ⚚**e** ['~gə] *m*, *f* (-n/-n) saint; **~en** ['~gən] *v/t.* (ge-, h) sanctify (*a. fig.*), hallow; '⚚**keit** *f* (-/*no pl.*) holiness; sacredness, sanctity; '**~sprechen** *v/t.* (*irr.* sprechen, sep., -ge-, h) canonize; '⚚**sprechung** *f* (-/-en) canonization; '⚚**tum** *n* (-[e]s/ᵘer) sanctuary; sacred relic; ⚚**ung** ['~gʊŋ] *f* (-/-en) sanctification (*a. fig.*), hallowing.

'**Heil|kraft** *f* healing *or* curative power; '⚚**kräftig** *adj.* healing, curative; '**~kunde** *f* medical science; '⚚**los** *fig. adj.* confusion: utter, great; '**~mittel** *n* remedy, medicament; '**~praktiker** *m* non-medical practitioner; '**~quelle** *f* medicinal spring; '⚚**sam** *adj.* curative; *fig.* salutary.   [Army.]

Heilsarmee ['haɪls-] *f* Salvation)

'**Heil|ung** *f* (-/-en) cure, healing, successful treatment; '**~verfahren** *n* therapy.

heim [haɪm] 1. *adv.* home; 2. ⚚ *n* (-[e]s/-e) home; hostel; '⚚**arbeit** *f* homework, outwork.

Heimat ['haɪmaːt] *f* (-/⚘ -en) home; own country; native land; '**~land** *n* own country, native land; '**~lich** *adj.* native; '⚚**los** *adj.* homeless;

'**~ort** *m* home town *or* village; '**~vertriebene** *m* expellee.

Heimchen *zo.* ['haɪmçən] *n* (-s/-) cricket.

'**heimisch** *adj.* trade, industry, etc.: home, local, domestic; ⚘, *zo.*, etc.: native, indigenous; ~ *werden* settle down; become established; *sich* ~ *fühlen* feel at home.

Heim|kehr ['haɪmkeːr] *f* (-/*no pl.*) return (home), homecoming; '⚚**kehren** *v/i.* (sep., -ge-, sein), '⚚**kommen** *v/i.* (*irr.* kommen, sep., -ge-, sein) return home.

'**heimlich** *adj.* plan, feeling, etc.: secret; *meeting, organization, etc.*: clandestine; *glance, movement, etc.*: stealthy, furtive.

'**Heim|reise** *f* homeward journey; '⚚**suchen** *v/t.* (sep., -ge-, h) *disaster, etc.*: afflict, strike; *ghost*: haunt; *God*: visit, punish; '**~tücke** *f* underhand malice, treachery; '⚚**tückisch** *adj.* malicious, treacherous, insidious; ⚚**wärts** *adv.* ['~vɛrts] homeward(s); '**~weg** *m* way home; '**~weh** *n* homesickness, nostalgia; ~ *haben* be homesick.

Heirat ['haɪraːt] *f* (-/-en) marriage; '⚚**en** (ge-, h) 1. *v/t.* marry; 2. *v/i.* marry, get married.

'**Heirats|antrag** *m* offer *or* proposal of marriage; '⚚**fähig** *adj.* marriageable; '**~kandidat** *m* possible marriage partner; '**~schwindler** *m* marriage impostor; '**~vermittler** *m* matrimonial agent.

heiser *adj.* ['haɪzər] hoarse; husky; '⚚**keit** *f* (-/*no pl.*) hoarseness; huskiness.

heiß *adj.* [haɪs] hot; *fig. a.* passionate, ardent; *mir ist* ~ I am *or* feel hot.

heißen ['haɪsən] (*irr.*, ge-, h) 1. *v/t.*: *e-n Lügner* ~ call s.o. a liar; *willkommen* ~ welcome; 2. *v/i.* be called; mean; *wie* ~ *Sie?* what is your name?; *was heißt das auf englisch?* what's that in English?

heiter *adj.* ['haɪtər] *day, weather*: bright; *sky*: bright, clear; *p.*, etc.: cheerful, gay; serene; '⚚**keit** *f* (-/*no pl.*) brightness; cheerfulness, gaiety; serenity.

heiz|en ['haɪtsən] (ge-, h) 1. *v/t.* heat (*room, etc.*); light (*stove*); fire (*boiler*); 2. *v/i.* stove, etc.: give out heat; turn on the heating; *mit*

Kohlen ～ burn coal; '♀er *m* (-s/-) stoker, fireman; '♀kissen *n* electric heating pad; '♀körper *m* central *heating*: radiator; ⚡ heating element; '♀material *n* fuel; '♀ung *f* (-/-en) heating.

Held [hɛlt] *m* (-en/-en) hero. **'Helden|gedicht** *n* epic (poem); '♀haft *adj.* heroic, valiant; '～mut *m* heroism, valo(u)r; ♀mütig *adj.* ['～my:tiç] heroic; '～tat *f* heroic or valiant deed; '～tod *m* hero's death; '～tum *n* (-[e]s/*no pl.*) heroism.

helfen ['hɛlfən] *v/i.* (*dat.*) (irr., ge-, h) help, assist, aid; ～ gegen be good for; *sich nicht zu* ～ *wissen* be helpless.

'Helfer *m* (-s/-) helper, assistant; '～shelfer *m* accomplice.

hell *adj.* [hɛl] *sound, voice, light, etc.*: clear; *light, flame, etc.*: bright; *hair*: fair; *colour*: light; *ale*: pale; '～blau *adj.* light-blue; '～blond *adj.* very fair; '～hörig *adj. p.* quick of hearing; *fig.* perceptive; ⚠ poorly sound-proofed; '♀seher *m* clairvoyant.

Helm [hɛlm] *m* (-[e]s/-e) ✕ helmet; ⚠ dome, cupola; ♂ helm; '～busch *m* plume.

Hemd [hɛmt] *n* (-[e]s/-en) shirt; vest; '～bluse *f* shirt-blouse, *Am.* shirtwaist.

Hemisphäre [he:mi'sfɛːrə] *f* (-/-n) hemisphere.

hemm|en ['hɛmən] *v/t.* (ge-, h) check, stop (*movement, etc.*); stem (*stream, flow of liquid*); hamper (*free movement, activity*); be a hindrance to; *psych.*: *gehemmt sein* be inhibited; '♀nis *n* (-ses/-se) hindrance, impediment; '♀schuh *m* slipper; *fig.* hindrance, F drag (*für acc.* on); '♀ung *f* (-/-en) stoppage, check; *psych.*: inhibition.

Hengst *zo.* [hɛŋst] *m* (-es/-e) stallion.

Henkel ['hɛŋkəl] *m* (-s/-) handle, ear.

Henker ['hɛŋkər] *m* (-s/-) hangman, executioner; F: *zum* ～! hang it (all)!

Henne *zo.* ['hɛnə] *f* (-/-n) hen.

her *adv.* [heːr] here; hither; *es ist schon ein Jahr* ～, *daß* ... *or seit* ... it is a year since ...; *wie lange ist es* ～, *seit* ... how long is it since ...; *hinter* (*dat.*) ～ *sein* be after; ～ *damit!* out with it!

herab *adv.* [hɛ'rap] down, downward; ～lassen *v/t.* (irr. lassen, sep., -ge-, h) let down, lower; *fig. sich* ～ condescend; ～lassend *adj.* condescending; ～setzen *v/t.* (sep., -ge-, h) take down; *fig.* belittle, disparage *s.o.*; ♱ reduce, lower, cut (*price, etc.*); ♀setzung *fig. f* (-/-en) reduction; disparagement; ～steigen *v/i.* (irr. steigen, sep., -ge-, sein) climb down, descend; ～würdigen *v/t.* (sep., -ge-, h) degrade, belittle, abase.

heran *adv.* [hɛ'ran] close, near; up; *nur* ～! come on!; ～bilden *v/t.* (sep., -ge-, h) train, educate (zu as *s.th.*, to be *s.th.*); ～kommen *v/i.* (irr. kommen, sep., -ge-, sein) come or draw near; approach; ～ an (acc.) come up to *s.o.*; measure up to; ～wachsen *v/i.* (irr. wachsen, sep., -ge-, sein) grow (up) (zu into).

herauf *adv.* [hɛ'rauf] up(wards), up here; upstairs; ～beschwören *v/t.* (irr. schwören, sep., no -ge-, h) evoke, call up, conjure up (*spirit, etc.*); *fig. a.* bring about, provoke, give rise to (*war, etc.*); ～steigen *v/i.* (irr. steigen, sep., -ge-, sein) climb up (here), ascend; ～ziehen (irr. ziehen, sep., -ge-) **1.** *v/t.* (h) pull or hitch up (*trousers, etc.*); **2.** *v/i.* (sein) cloud, *etc.*: come up.

heraus *adv.* [hɛ'raus] out, out here; *zum Fenster* ～ out of the window; ～ *mit der Sprache!* speak out!; ～bekommen *v/t.* (irr. kommen, sep., no -ge-, h) get out; get (*money*) back; *fig.* find out; ～bringen *v/t.* (irr. bringen, sep., -ge-, h) bring or get out; *thea.* stage; ～finden *v/t.* (irr. finden, sep., -ge-, h) find out; *fig. a.* discover; ♀forderer *m* (-s/-) challenger; ～fordern *v/t.* (sep., -ge-, h) challenge (*to a fight*); provoke; ♀forderung *f* (-/-en) challenge; provocation; ～geben (irr. geben, sep., -ge-, h) **1.** *v/t.* surrender; hand over; restore; edit (*periodical, etc.*); publish (*book, etc.*); issue (*regulations, etc.*); **2.** *v/i.* give change (*auf acc.* for); ♀geber *m* (-s/-) editor; publisher; ～kommen *v/i.* (irr. kommen, sep., -ge-, sein) come out; *fig. a.* appear, be published; ～nehmen *v/t.* (irr. nehmen, sep., -ge-, h) take out; *sich viel* ～ take liberties; ～putzen *v/t.* (sep.,

-ge-, h) dress up; sich ~ dress (o.s.) up; ~reden v/refl. (sep., -ge-, h) talk one's way out; ~stellen v/t. (sep., -ge-, h) put out; fig. emphasize, set forth; sich ~ emerge, turn out; ~strecken v/t. (sep., -ge-, h) stretch out; put out; ~streichen v/t. (irr. streichen, sep., -ge-, h) cross out, delete (word, etc.); fig. extol, praise; ~winden fig. v/refl. (irr. winden, sep., -ge-, h) extricate o.s. (aus from).

herb adj. [herp] fruit, flavour, etc.: tart; wine, etc.: dry; features, etc.: austere; criticism, etc.: harsh; disappointment, etc.: bitter.

herbei adv. [her'bai] here; ~! come here!; ~eilen [her'bai⁹-] v/i. (sep., -ge-, sein) come hurrying; ~führen fig. v/t. (sep., -ge-, h) cause, bring about, give rise to; ~schaffen v/t. (sep., -ge-, h) bring along; procure.

Herberge ['herbergə] f (-/-n) shelter, lodging; inn.

'**Herbheit** f (-/no pl.) tartness; dryness; fig.: austerity; harshness; bitterness.

Herbst [herpst] m (-[e]s/-e) autumn, Am. a. fall.

Herd [he:rt] m (-[e]s/-e) hearth, fireplace; stove; fig. seat, focus.

Herde ['he:rdə] f (-/-n) herd (of cattle, pigs, etc.) (contp. a. fig.); flock (of sheep, geese, etc.).

herein adv. [he'rain] in (here); ~! come in!; ~brechen fig. v/i. (irr. brechen, sep., -ge-, sein) night: fall; ~ über (acc.) misfortune, etc.: befall; ~fallen v/i. (irr. fallen, sep., -ge-, sein) be taken in.

'**her|fallen** v/i. (irr. fallen, sep., -ge-, sein): ~ über (acc.) attack (a. fig.), fall upon; F fig. pull to pieces; '2~gang m course of events, details pl.; ~geben v/t. (irr. geben, sep., -ge-, h) give up, part with, return; yield; sich ~ zu lend o.s. to; '~gebracht fig. adj. traditional; customary; '~halten v/t. (irr. halten, sep., -ge-, h) 1. v/t. hold out; 2. v/i.: ~ müssen be the one to pay or suffer (für for).

Hering ichth. ['he:riŋ] m (-s/-e) herring.

'**her|kommen** v/i. (irr. kommen, sep., -ge-, sein) come or get here; come or draw near; ~ von come from; fig. a. be due to, be caused by; ~kömmlich adj. ['~kœmliç]

traditional; customary; 2kunft ['~kunft] f (-/no pl.) origin; birth, descent; '~leiten v/t. (sep., -ge-, h) lead here; fig. derive (von from); '2leitung fig. f derivation.

Herold ['he:rolt] m (-[e]s/-e) herald.

Herr [her] m (-n, ⚔ -en/-en) lord, master; eccl. the Lord; gentleman; ~ Maier Mr Maier; mein ~ Sir; m-e ~en gentlemen; ~ der Situation master of the situation.

'**Herren|bekleidung** f men's clothing; '~einzel n tennis: men's singles pl.; '~haus n manor-house; 2~los adj. ['~lo:s] ownerless; '~reiter m sports: gentleman-jockey; '~schneider m men's tailor; '~zimmer m study; smoking-room.

herrichten ['he:r-] v/t. (sep., -ge-, h) arrange, prepare.

'**herrisch** adj. imperious, overbearing; voice, etc.: commanding, peremptory.

'**herrlich** adj. excellent, glorious, magnificent, splendid; '2keit f (-/-en) glory, splendo(u)r.

'**Herrschaft** f (-/-en) rule, dominion (über acc. of); fig. mastery; master and mistress; m-e ~en! ladies and gentlemen!; '2lich adj. belonging to a master or landlord; fig. high-class, elegant.

herrsch|en ['herʃən] v/i. (ge-, h) rule (über acc. over); monarch: reign (over); govern; fig. prevail, be; '2er m (-s/-) ruler; sovereign, monarch; '2sucht f thirst for power; '~süchtig adj. thirsting for power; imperious.

'**her|rühren** v/i. (sep., -ge-, h): ~ von come from, originate with; '~sagen v/t. (sep., -ge-, h) recite; say (prayer); '~stammen v/i. (sep., -ge-, h): ~ von or aus be descended from; come from; be derived from; '~stellen v/t. (sep., -ge-, h) place here; ✝ make, manufacture, produce; '2stellung f (-/-en) manufacture, production.

herüber adv. [he'ry:bər] over (here), across.

herum adv. [he'rum] (a)round; about; ~führen v/t. (sep., -ge-, h) show (a)round; ~ in (dat.) show over; ~lungern v/i. (sep., -ge-, h) loaf or loiter or hang about; ~reichen v/t. (sep., -ge-, h) pass or hand round; ~sprechen v/refl. (irr.

sprechen, *sep.*, *-ge-*, *h* get about, spread; **~treiben** *v/refl.* (*irr. treiben*, *sep.*, *-ge-*, *h*) F gad *or* knock about.

herunter *adv.* [hɛ'rʊntər] down (here); downstairs; *von oben* ~ down from above; **~bringen** *v/t.* (*irr. bringen*, *sep.*, *-ge-*, *h*) bring down; *fig. a.* lower, reduce; **~kommen** *v/i.* (*irr. kommen*, *sep.*, *-ge-*, *sein*) come down(stairs); *fig.*: come down in the world; deteriorate; **~machen** *v/t.* (*sep.*, *-ge-*, *h*) take down; turn (*collar*, *etc.*) down; *fig.* give *s.o.* a dressing-down; *fig.* pull to pieces; **~reißen** *v/t.* (*irr. reißen*, *sep.*, *-ge-*, *h*) pull *or* tear down; *fig.* pull to pieces; **~sein** F *fig. v/i.* (*irr. sein*, *sep.*, *-ge-*, *sein*) be low in health; **~wirtschaften** *v/t.* (*sep.*, *-ge-*, *h*) run down.

hervor *adv.* [hɛr'foːr] forth, out; **~bringen** *v/t.* (*irr. bringen*, *sep.*, *-ge-*, *h*) bring out, produce (*a. fig.*); yield (*fruit*); *fig.* utter (*word*); **~gehen** *v/i.* (*irr. gehen*, *sep.*, *-ge-*, *sein*) *p.* come (*aus* from); come off (*victorious*) (from); *fact*, *etc.*: emerge (from); be clear *or* apparent (from); **~heben** *fig. v/t.* (*irr. heben*, *sep.*, *-ge-*, *h*) stress, emphasize; give prominence to; **~holen** *v/t.* (*sep.*, *-ge-*, *h*) produce; **~ragen** *v/i.* (*sep.*, *-ge-*, *h*) project (*über acc.* over); *fig.* tower (above); **~ragend** *adj.* projecting, prominent; *fig.* outstanding, excellent; **~rufen** *v/t.* (*irr. rufen*, *sep.*, *-ge-*, *h*) *thea.* call for; *fig.* arouse, evoke; **~stechend** *fig. adj.* outstanding; striking; conspicuous.

Herz [hɛrts] *n* (*-ens/-en*) *anat.* heart (*a. fig.*); *cards*: hearts *pl.*; *fig.* courage, spirit; *sich ein ~ fassen* take heart; *mit ganzem ~en* whole-heartedly; *sich et. zu ~en nehmen* take s.th. to heart; *es nicht übers ~ bringen zu inf.* not to have the heart to *inf.*; '**~anfall** *m* heart attack.

'**Herzens|brecher** *m* (*-s/-*) ladykiller; '**~lust** *f*: *nach* ~ to one's heart's content; '**~wunsch** *m* heart's desire.

'**herz|ergreifend** *fig. adj.* heartmoving; '**fehler** 🖤 *m* cardiac defect; '**gegend** *anat. f* cardiac region; '**~haft** *adj.* hearty, good; '**~ig** *adj.* lovely, *Am. a.* cute; **infarkt** 🖤 ['~ʔɪnfarkt] *m* (*-[e]s/-e*) cardiac

infarction; '**klopfen** 🖤 *n* (*-s/no pl.*) palpitation; '**~krank** *adj.* having heart trouble; '**~lich 1.** *adj.* heartfelt; cordial, hearty; **~es Beileid** sincere sympathy; **2.** *adv.*: ~ *gern* with pleasure; '**~los** *adj.* heartless; unfeeling.

Herzog ['hɛrtsoːk] *m* (*-[e]s/ᵘe*, *-e*) duke; '**~in** *f* (*-/-nen*) duchess; '**~tum** *n* (*-[e]s/ᵘer*) dukedom; duchy.

'**Herz|schlag** *m* heartbeat; 🖤 heart failure; '**~schwäche** 🖤 *f* cardiac insufficiency; '**~verpflanzung** 🖤 *f* heart transplant; **~zerreißend** *adj.* heart-rending.

Hetz|e ['hɛtsə] *f* (*-/-n*) hurry, rush; instigation (*gegen acc.* against); baiting (of); '**en** (*ge-*) **1.** *v/t.* (*h*) course (*hare*); bait (*bear*, *etc.*); *hound*: hunt, chase (*animal*); *fig.* hurry, rush; *sich* ~ hurry, rush; *e-n Hund auf j-n* ~ set a dog at *s.o.*; **2.** *v/i.* (*h*) *fig.*: cause discord; agitate (*gegen* against); **3.** *fig. v/i.* (*sein*) hurry, rush; '**~er** *fig. m* (*-s/-*) instigator; agitator; '**erisch** *adj.* virulent, inflammatory; '**~jagd** *f* hunt(ing); *fig.*: virulent campaign; rush, hurry; '**~presse** *f* yellow press.

Heu [hɔʏ] *n* (*-[e]s/no pl.*) hay; '**~boden** *m* hayloft.

Heuchel|ei [hɔʏçə'laɪ] *f* (*-/-en*) hypocrisy; '**2n** (*ge-*) **1.** *v/t.* simulate, feign, affect; **2.** *v/i.* feign, dissemble; play the hypocrite.

'**Heuchler** *m* (*-s/-*) hypocrite; '**2isch** *adj.* hypocritical.

heuer ['hɔʏər] **1.** *adv.* this year; **2.** ♀ ⚓ *f* (*-/-n*) pay, wages *pl.*; '**~n** *v/t.* (*ge-*, *h*) hire; ⚓ engage, sign on (*crew*), charter (*ship*).

heulen ['hɔʏlən] *v/i.* (*ge-*, *h*) *wind*, *etc.*: howl; *storm*, *wind*, *etc.*: roar; *siren*: wail; F *p.* howl, cry.

'**Heu|schnupfen** 🖤 *m* hay-fever; **~schrecke** *zo.* ['~ʃrɛkə] *f* (*-/-n*) grasshopper, locust.

heut|e *adv.* ['hɔʏtə] today; ~ *abend* this evening, tonight; ~ *früh*, ~ *morgen* this morning; ~ *in acht Tagen* today *or* this day week; ~ *vor acht Tagen* a week ago today; '**~ig** *adj.* this day's, today's; present; **~zutage** *adv.* ['hɔʏttsutaːgə] nowadays, these days.

Hexe ['hɛksə] *f* (*-/-n*) witch, sorceress; *fig.*: hell-cat; hag; '**2n** *v/i.* (*ge-*,

h) practice witchcraft; F *fig.* work miracles; '⊾**nkessel** *fig. m* inferno; '⊾**nmeister** *m* wizard, sorcerer; '⊾**nschuß** *⚡ m* lumbago; ⊾**rei** [⊾-'raɪ] *f* (-/-en) witchcraft, sorcery, magic.

Hieb [hi:p] **1.** *m* (-[e]s/-e) blow, stroke; lash, cut (*of whip, etc.*); a. punch (*with fist*); *fenc.* cut; ⊾e *pl.* hiding, thrashing; **2.** ♀ *pret. of* hauen.

hielt [hi:lt] *pret. of* halten.

hier *adv.* [hi:r] here; in this place; ⊾! present!; ⊾ *entlang!* this way!

hier|an *adj.* ['hi:'ran, *when emphatic* 'hi:ran] at *or* by *or* in *or* on *or* to it *or* this; ⊾**auf** *adv.* ['hi:'rauf, *when emphatic* 'hi:rauf] on it *or* this; after this *or* that, then; ⊾**aus** *adv.* ['hi:'raus, *when emphatic* 'hi:raus] from *or* out of it *or* this; ⊾**bei** *adv.* ['hi:r'baɪ, *when emphatic* 'hi:rbaɪ] here; in this case, in connection with this; ⊾**durch** *adv.* ['hi:r'durç, *when emphatic* 'hi:rdurç] through here; by this, hereby; ⊾**für** *adv.* ['hi:r'fy:r, *when emphatic* 'hi:rfy:r] for it *or* this; ⊾**her** *adv.* ['hi:r'he:r, *when emphatic* 'hi:rhe:r] here, hither; *bis* ⊾ as far as here; ⊾**in** *adv.* ['hi:'rin, *when emphatic* 'hi:rin] in it *or* this; in here; ⊾**mit** *adv.* ['hi:r-'mit, *when emphatic* 'hi:rmit] with it *or* this, herewith; ⊾**nach** *adv.* ['hi:r'na:x, *when emphatic* 'hi:rna:x] after it *or* this; according to this; ⊾**über** *adv.* ['hi:'ry:bər, *when emphatic* 'hi:ry:bər] over it *or* this; over here; on this (subject); ⊾**unter** *adv.* ['hi:'runtər, *when emphatic* 'hi:runtər] under it *or* this; among these; by this *or* that; ⊾**von** *adv.* ['hi:r'fɔn, *when emphatic* 'hi:rfɔn] of *or* from it *or* this; ⊾**zu** *adv.* ['hi:r'tsu:, *when emphatic* 'hi:rtsu:] with it *or* this; (in addition) to this.

hiesig *adj.* ['hi:ziç] of *or* in this place *or* town, local.

hieß [hi:s] *pret. of* heißen.

Hilfe ['hilfə] *f* (-/-n) help; aid, assistance; succour; relief (*für* to); ⊾! help!; *mit* ⊾ *von* with the help *or* aid of; '⊾**ruf** *m* shout *or* cry for help.

'**hilf|los** *adj.* helpless; '⊾**reich** *adj.* helpful.

'**Hilfs|aktion** *f* relief measures *pl.*;

'⊾**arbeiter** *m* unskilled worker *or* labo(u)rer; '⚙**bedürftig** *adj.* needy, indigent; '⊾**lehrer** *m* assistant teacher; '⊾**mittel** *n* aid; device; remedy; expedient; '⊾**motor** *m*: *Fahrrad mit* ⊾ motor-assisted bicycle; '⊾**quelle** *f* resource; '⊾**schule** *f* elementary school for backward children; '⊾**werk** *n* relief organization.   [berry.]

Himbeere ♀ ['himbe:rə] *f* rasp-]

Himmel ['himəl] *m* (-s/-) sky, heavens *pl.*; *eccl., fig.* heaven; '⊾**bett** *n* tester-bed; '⚙**blau** *adj.* sky-blue; '⊾**fahrt** *eccl. f* ascension (of Christ); Ascension-day; '⚙**schreiend** *adj.* crying.

'**Himmels|gegend** *f* region of the sky; cardinal point; '⊾**körper** *m* celestial body; '⊾**richtung** *f* point of the compass, cardinal point; direction; '⊾**strich** *m* region, climate zone.

'**himmlisch** *adj.* celestial, heavenly.

hin *adv.* [hin] there; gone, lost; ⊾ *und her* to and fro, *Am.* back and forth; ⊾ *und wieder* now and again *or* then; ⊾ *und zurück* there and back.

hinab *adv.* [hi'nap] down; ⊾**steigen** *v/i.* (*irr.* steigen, *sep.*, -ge-, sein) climb down, descend.

hinarbeiten ['hin⁹-] *v/i.* (*sep.*, -ge-, h): ⊾ *auf* (acc.) work for *or* towards.

hinauf *adv.* [hi'nauf] up (there); upstairs; ⊾**gehen** *v/i.* (*irr.* gehen, *sep.*, -ge-, sein) go up(stairs); *prices, wages, etc.*: go up, rise; ⊾**steigen** *v/i.* (*irr.* steigen, *sep.*, -ge-, sein) climb up, ascend.

hinaus *adv.* [hi'naus] out; ⊾ *mit euch!* out with you!; *auf* (viele) *Jahre* ⊾ for (many) years (to come); ⊾**gehen** *v/i.* (*irr.* gehen, *sep.*, -ge-, sein) go *or* walk out; ⊾ *über* (acc.) go beyond, exceed; ⊾ *auf* (acc.) *window, etc.*: look out on, overlook; *intention, etc.*: drive *or* aim at; ⊾**laufen** *v/i.* (*irr.* laufen, *sep.*, -ge-, sein) run *or* rush out; ⊾ *auf* (acc.) come *or* amount to; ⊾**schieben** *fig. v/t.* (*irr.* schieben, *sep.*, -ge-, h) put off, postpone, defer; ⊾**werfen** *v/t.* (*irr.* werfen, *sep.*, -ge-, h) throw out (aus of); turn *or* throw *or* F chuck *s.o.* out.

'**Hin|blick** *m*: *im* ⊾ *auf* (acc.) in view of, with regard to; '⚙**bringen** *v/t.*

(*irr. bringen*, *sep.*, -ge-, *h*) take there; while away, pass (*time*).

hinder|lich *adj.* ['hindərliç] hindering, impeding; *j-m* ~ *sein* be in s.o.'s way; '~**n** *v/t.* (ge-, *h*) hinder, hamper (*bei, in dat. in*); ~ *an* (*dat.*) prevent from; '2**nis** *n* (-ses/-se) hindrance; *sports*: obstacle; *turf*, *etc.*: fence; '2**nisrennen** *n* obstacle-race.

hin'durch *adv.* through; all through, throughout; across.

hinein *adv.* [hi'nam] in; ~ *mit dir!* in you go!; ~**gehen** *v/i.* (*irr. gehen*, *sep.*, -ge-, *sein*) go in; ~ *in* (*acc.*) go into; *in den Topf gehen* ... *hinein* the pot holds *or* takes ...

'**Hin|fahrt** *f* journey *or* way there; '2**fallen** *v/i.* (*irr. fallen*, *sep.*, -ge-, *sein*) fall (down); '2**fällig** *adj. p.* frail; *regulation*, *etc.*: invalid; ~ *machen* invalidate; render invalid.

hing [hɪŋ] *pret.* of **hängen** 1.

'**Hin|gabe** *f* devotion (*an acc.* to); '2**geben** *v/t.* (*irr. geben*, *sep.*, -ge-, *h*) give up *or* away; *sich* ~ (*dat.*) give o.s. to; devote o.s. to; '~**gebung** *f* (-/-en) devotion; '2**gehen** *v/i.* (*irr. gehen*, *sep.*, -ge-, *sein*) go *or* walk there; go (*zu* to); *path*, *etc.*: lead there; lead (*zu to a place*); '2**halten** *v/t.* (*irr. halten*, *sep.*, -ge-, *h*) hold out (*object*, *etc.*); put s.o. off.

hinken ['hɪŋkən] *v/i.* (ge-) **1.** (*h*) limp (*auf dem rechten Fuß* with one's right leg), have a limp; **2.** (*sein*) limp (along).

'**hin|länglich** *adj.* sufficient, adequate; '~**legen** *v/t.* (*sep.*, -ge-, *h*) lay *or* put down; *sich* ~ lie down; '~**nehmen** *v/t.* (*irr. nehmen*, *sep.*, -ge-, *h*) accept, take; put up with; '~**raffen** *v/t.* (*sep.*, -ge-, *h*) death, *etc.*: snatch *s.o.* away, carry *s.o.* off; '~**reichen** (*sep.*, -ge-, *h*) **1.** *v/t.* reach *or* stretch *or* hold out (*dat.* to); **2.** *v/i.* suffice; '~**reißen** *fig. v/t.* (*irr. reißen*, *sep.*, -ge-, *h*) carry away; enrapture, ravish; '~**reißend** *adj.* ravishing, captivating; '~**richten** *v/t.* (*sep.*, -ge-, *h*) execute, put to death; '2**richtung** *f* execution; '~**setzen** *v/t.* (*sep.*, -ge-, *h*) set *or* put down; *sich* ~ sit down; '2**sicht** *f* regard, respect; *in* ~ *auf* (*acc.*) = '~**sichtlich** *prp.* (*gen.*) with regard to, as to, concerning; '~**stellen** *v/t.*

(*sep.*, -ge-, *h*) place; put; put down; *et.* ~ *als* represent s.th. as; make s.th. appear (as).

hintan|setzen [hɪnt'an-] *v/t.* (*sep.*, -ge-, *h*) set aside; 2**setzung** *f* (-/-en) setting aside; ~**stellen** *v/t.* (*sep.*, -ge-, *h*) set aside; 2**stellung** *f* (-/-en) setting aside.

hinten *adv.* ['hɪntən] behind, at the back; in the background; in the rear.

hinter *prp.* ['hɪntər] **1.** (*dat.*) behind, *Am. a.* back of; ~ *sich lassen* outdistance; **2.** (*acc.*) behind; 2**bein** *n* hind leg; 2**bliebenen** *pl.* [~'bli:bə-nən] *the* bereaved *pl.*; surviving dependants *pl.*; ~'**bringen** *v/t.* (*irr. bringen*, *no* -ge-, *h*): *j-m et.* ~ inform s.o. of s.th. (secretly); ~ei'**nander** *adv.* one after the other; in succession; '2**gedanke** *m* ulterior motive; ~'**gehen** *v/t.* (*irr. gehen*, *no* -ge-, *h*) deceive, F doublecross; 2'**gehung** *f* (-/-en) deception; '2**grund** *m* background (*a. fig.*); 2**halt** *m* ambush; ~**hältig** *adj.* ['~hɛltiç] insidious; underhand; 2**haus** *n* back *or* rear building; ~'**her** *adv.* behind; afterwards; '2**hof** *m* backyard; '2**kopf** *m* back of the head; ~'**lassen** *v/t.* (*irr. lassen*, *no* -ge-, *h*) leave (behind); 2'**lassenschaft** *f* (-/-en) property (left), estate; ~'**legen** *v/t.* (*no* -ge-, *h*) deposit, lodge (*bei* with); 2'**legung** *f* (-/-en) deposit(ion); 2**list** *f* deceit; craftiness; insidiousness; ~**listig** *adj.* deceitful; crafty; insidious; '2**mann** *m* ⚔ rear-rank man; *fig.*: † subsequent endorser; *pol.*: backer; wire-puller; instigator; '2**n** F *m* (-s/-) backside, behind, bottom; '2**rad** *n* rear wheel; ~**rücks** *adv.* ['~ryks] from behind; *fig.* behind his, *etc.* back; '2**seite** *f* back; '2**teil** *n* back (part); rear (part); F *s.* *Hintern*; ~'**treiben** *v/t.* (*irr. treiben*, *no* -ge-, *h*) thwart, frustrate; '2**treppe** *f* backstairs *pl.*; '2**tür** *f* back door; ~'**ziehen** ⚖ *v/t.* (*irr. ziehen*, *no* -ge-, *h*) evade (*tax, duty*, *etc.*); 2'**ziehung** *f* evasion.

hinüber *adv.* [hi'ny:bər] over (there); across.

Hin- und 'Rückfahrt *f* journey there and back, *Am.* round trip.

hinunter *adv.* [hi'nʊntər] down (there); downstairs; ~**schlucken**

v/t. (*sep.*, -ge-, *h*) swallow (down); *fig.* swallow.

'Hinweg¹ *m* way there *or* out.

hinweg² *adv.* [hin'vɛk] away, off; **~gehen** *v/i.* (*irr. gehen, sep.*, -ge- *sein*): ~ über (*acc.*) go *or* walk over *or* across; *fig.* pass over, ignore; **~kommen** *v/i.* (*irr. kommen, sep.*, -ge-, *sein*): ~ über (*acc.*) get over (*a. fig.*); **~sehen** *v/i.* (*irr. sehen, sep.*, -ge-, *h*): ~ über (*acc.*) see *or* look over; *fig.* overlook, shut one's eyes to; **~setzen** *v/refl.* (*sep.*, -ge-, *h*): sich ~ über (*acc.*) ignore, disregard, make light of.

'Hin|weis ['hinvais] *m* (-es/-e) reference (*auf acc.*): hint (at); indication (of); **'2weisen** (*irr. weisen, sep.*, -ge-, *h*) 1. *v/t.*: j-n ~ *auf* (*acc.*) draw *or* call s.o.'s attention to; 2. *v/i.*: ~ *auf* (*acc.*) point at *or* to, indicate (*a. fig.*); *fig.*: point out; hint at; **'2werfen** *v/t.* (*irr. werfen, sep.*, -ge-, *h*) throw down; *fig.*: dash off (*sketch, etc.*); say *s.th.* casually; **'2wirken** *v/i.* (*sep.*, -ge-, *h*): ~ *auf* (*acc.*) work towards; use one's influence to; **'2ziehen** (*irr. ziehen, sep.*, -ge-) 1. *fig. v/t.* (*h*) attract *or* draw there; sich ~ *space*: extend (*bis zu* to), stretch (to); *time*: drag on; 2. *v/i.* (*sein*) go *or* move there; **'2zielen** *fig. v/i.* (*sep.*, -ge-, *h*): ~ *auf* (*acc.*) aim *or* drive at.

hin'zu *adv.* there; near; in addition; **~fügen** *v/t.* (*sep.*, -ge-, *h*) add (zu to) (*a. fig.*); **2fügung** *f* (-/-en) addition; **~kommen** *v/i.* (*irr. kommen, sep.*, -ge-, *sein*) come up (zu to); supervene; be added; *es kommt* (*noch*) *hinzu, daß* add to this that, (and) moreover; **~rechnen** *v/t.* (*sep.*, -ge-, *h*) add (zu to), include (in, among); **~setzen** *v/t.* (*sep.*, -ge-, *h*) s. *hinzufügen*; **~treten** *v/i.* (*irr. treten, sep.*, -ge-, *sein*) s. *hinzukommen*; join; **~ziehen** *v/t.* (*irr. ziehen, sep.*, -ge-, *h*) call in (*doctor, etc.*).

Hirn [hirn] *n* (-[e]s/-e) *anat.* brain; *fig.* brains *pl.*; mind; **'~gespinst** *n* figment of the mind, chimera; **'2los** *fig. adj.* brainless, senseless; **'~schale** *anat. f* brain-pan, cranium; **'~schlag** *s* *m* apoplexy; **'2verbrannt** *adj.* crazy, F crack-brained, cracky.

Hirsch *zo.* [hirʃ] *m* (-es/-e) species:

deer; stag, hart; **'~geweih** *n* (stag's) antlers *pl.*; **'~kuh** *f* hind; **'~leder** *n* buckskin, deerskin.

Hirse ⚘ ['hirzə] *f* (-/-n) millet.

Hirt [hirt] *m* (-en/-en), **~e** ['~ə] *m* (-n/-n) herdsman; shepherd.

hissen ['hisən] *v/t.* (ge-, *h*) hoist, raise (*flag*); ⚓ *a.* trice up (*sail*).

Histori|ker [hi'stoːrikər] *m* (-s/-) historian; **2sch** *adj.* historic(al).

Hitz|e ['hitsə] *f* (-/no *pl.*) heat; **'2ebeständig** *adj.* heat-resistant, heat-proof; **'~ewelle** *f* heat-wave, hot spell; **'2ig** *adj. p.* hot-tempered, hot-headed; *discussion*: heated; **'~kopf** *m* hothead; **'~schlag** *s* *m* heat-stroke.

hob [hoːp] *pret. of* heben.

Hobel ⊕ ['hoːbəl] *m* (-s/-) plane; **'~bank** *f* carpenter's bench; **'2n** *v/t.* (ge-, *h*) plane.

hoch [hoːx] 1. *adj.* high; *church spire, tree, etc.*: tall; *position, etc.*: high, important; *guest, etc.*: distinguished; *punishment, etc.*: heavy, severe; *age*: great, old; hohe See open sea, high seas *pl.*; 2. *adv.*: ~ lebe ...! long live ...! 3. 2 *n* (-s/-s) cheer; toast; *meteorology*: high (-pressure area).

'hoch|achten *v/t.* (*sep.*, -ge-, *h*) esteem highly; **'2achtung** *f* high esteem *or* respect; **'~achtungsvoll** 1. *adj.* (most) respectful; 2. *adv.* *correspondence*: yours faithfully *or* sincerely, *esp. Am.* yours truly; **'2adel** *m* greater *or* higher nobility; **'2amt** *eccl. n* high mass; **'2antenne** *f* overhead aerial; **'2bahn** *f* elevated *or* overhead railway, *Am.* elevated railroad; **'2betrieb** *m* intense activity, rush; **'2burg** *fig. f* stronghold; **'~deutsch** *adj.* High *or* standard German; **'2druck** *m* high pressure (*a. fig.*); *mit* ~ *arbeiten* work at high pressure; **'2ebene** *f* plateau, tableland; **'~fahrend** *adj.* high-handed, arrogant; **'~fein** *adj.* superfine; **'2form** *f*: *in* ~ *in* top form; **'2frequenz** ⚡ *f* high frequency; **'2gebirge** *n* high mountains *pl.*; **'2genuß** *m* great enjoyment; **'2glanz** *m* high polish; **'2haus** *n* multi-stor(e)y building, skyscraper; **'~herzig** *adj.* noble-minded; generous; **'2herzigkeit** *f* (-/-en) noble-mindedness; generosity; **'2konjunktur** ⚡ *f* boom, business prosperity; '**Ωland** n upland(s pl.), highlands pl.; '**Ωmut** m arrogance, haughtiness; **~mütig** adj. ['~my:tiç] arrogant, haughty; **~näsig** F adj. ['~nɛ:ziç] stuck-up; '**Ωofen** ⊕ m blast-furnace; '**~rot** adj. bright red; '**Ωsaison** f peak season, height of the season; '**~schätzen** v/t. (sep., -ge-, h) esteem highly; '**Ωschule** f university; academy; '**Ωseefischerei** f deep-sea fishing; '**Ωsommer** m midsummer; '**Ωspannung** ⚡ f high tension or voltage; '**Ωsprung** m sports: high jump.

höchst [hø:çst] **1.** adj. highest; fig. a.: supreme; extreme; **2.** adv. highly, most, extremely.

Hochstap|elei [ho:xʃtaːpəˈlaɪ] f (-/-en) swindling; '**~ler** m (-s/-) confidence man, swindler.

höchstens adv. ['hø:çstəns] at (the) most, at best.

'**Höchst|form** f sports: top form; '**~geschwindigkeit** f maximum speed; speed limit; '**~leistung** f sports: record (performance); ⊕ maximum output (of machine, etc.); '**~lohn** m maximum wages pl.; '**~maß** n maximum; '**~preis** m maximum price.

'**hoch|trabend** fig. adj. high-flown; pompous; '**Ωverrat** m high treason; '**Ωwald** m high forest; '**Ωwasser** n high tide or water; flood; '**~wertig** adj. high-grade, high-class; '**Ωwild** n big game; '**Ωwohlgeboren** m (-s/-) Right Hono(u)rable.

Hochzeit ['hɔxtsaɪt] f (-/-en) wedding; marriage; '**Ωlich** adj. bridal, nuptial; '**~sgeschenk** n wedding present; '**~sreise** f honeymoon (trip).

Hocke ['hɔkə] f (-/-n) gymnastics: squat-vault; skiing: crouch; '**Ωn** v/i. (ge-, h) squat, crouch; '**~r** m (-s/-) stool.

Höcker ['hœkər] m (-s/-) surface, etc.: bump; camel, etc.: hump; p. hump, hunch; '**Ωig** adj. animal: humped; p. humpbacked, hunchbacked; surface, etc.: bumpy, rough, uneven.

Hode anat. ['ho:də] m (-n/-n), f (-/-n), '**~n** anat. m (-s/-) testicle.

Hof [ho:f] m (-[e]s/ᵁe) court(yard); farm; king, etc.: court; ast. halo; j-m den ~ machen court s.o.; '**~da-**

~me f lady-in-waiting; '**Ωfähig** adj. presentable at court.

Hoffart ['hɔfart] f (-/no pl.) arrogance, haughtiness; pride.

hoffen ['hɔfən] (ge-, h) **1.** v/i. hope (auf acc. for); trust (in); **2.** v/t.: das Beste ~ hope for the best; '**~t-lich** adv. it is to be hoped that, I hope, let's hope.

Hoffnung ['hɔfnuŋ] f (-/-en) hope (auf acc. for, of); in der ~ zu inf. in the hope of ger., hoping to inf.; s-e ~ setzen auf (acc.) pin one's hopes on; '**Ωslos** adj. hopeless; '**Ωsvoll** adj. hopeful; promising.

'**Hofhund** m watch-dog.

höfisch adj. ['hø:fiʃ] courtly.

höflich adj. ['hø:fliç] polite, civil, courteous (gegen to); '**Ωkeit** f (-/-en) politeness, civility, courtesy.

'**Hofstaat** m royal or princely household; suite, retinue.

Höhe ['hø:ə] f (-/-n) height; ⚓, ✈, ast., geogr. altitude; hill; peak, amount (of bill, etc.); size (of sum, fine, etc.); level (of price, etc.); severity (of punishment, etc.); ♪ pitch; in gleicher ~ mit on a level with; auf der ~ sein be up to the mark; in die ~ up(wards).

Hoheit ['ho:haɪt] f (-/-en) pol. sovereignty; title: Highness; '**~s-gebiet** n (sovereign) territory; '**~s-gewässer** n/pl. territorial waters pl.; '**~szeichen** n national emblem.

'**Höhen|kurort** m high-altitude health resort; '**~luft** f mountain air; '**~sonne** f mountain sun; ⚡ ultra-violet lamp; '**~steuer** ✈ n elevator; '**~zug** m mountain range.

'**Höhepunkt** m highest point; ast., fig. culmination, zenith; fig. a.: climax; summit, peak.

hohl adj. [ho:l] hollow (a. fig.); cheeks, etc.: sunken; hand: cupped; sound: hollow, dull.

Höhle ['hø:lə] f (-/-n) cave, cavern; den, lair (of bear, lion, etc.) (both a. fig.); hole, burrow (of fox, rabbit, etc.); hollow; cavity.

'**Hohl|maß** n dry measure; '**~raum** m hollow, cavity; '**~spiegel** m concave mirror.

Höhlung ['hø:luŋ] f (-/-en) excavation; hollow, cavity.

'**Hohlweg** m defile.

Hohn [ho:n] m (-[e]s/no pl.) scorn, disdain; derision.

höhnen ['hø:nən] *v/i.* (ge-, h) sneer, jeer, mock, scoff (*über acc.* at).

'**Hohngelächter** *n* scornful *or* derisive laughter.

'**höhnisch** *adj.* scornful; sneering, derisive.

Höker ['hø:kər] *m* (-s/-) hawker, huckster; '**2n** *v/i.* (ge-, h) huckster, hawk about.

holen ['ho:lən] *v/t.* (ge-, h) fetch; go for; *a. ~ lassen* send for; draw (*breath*); *sich e-e Krankheit ~* catch a disease; *sich bei j-m Rat ~* seek s.o.'s advice.

Holländer ['hɔlɛndər] *m* (-s/-) Dutchman.

Hölle ['hœlə] *f* (-/✎-n) hell.

'**Höllen|angst** *fig. f:* *e-e ~ haben* be in a mortal fright *or* F blue funk; '**~lärm** F *fig.* m infernal noise; '**~maschine** *f* infernal machine, time bomb; '**~pein** *fig. f* torment of hell. [*a. fig.*).\

'**höllisch** *adj.* hellish, infernal (*both*

holper|ig *adj.* ['hɔlpəriç] *surface, road, etc.:* bumpy, rough, uneven; *vehicle, etc.:* jolty, jerky; *verse, style, etc.:* rough, jerky; '**~n** (ge-) **1.** *~* (sein) *vehicle:* jolt, bump; **2.** *v/i.* (h) *vehicle:* jolt, bump, be jolty *or* bumpy.

Holunder ✎ [hɔ'lundər] *m* (-s/-) elder.

Holz [hɔlts] *n* (-es/⁀er) wood; timber, *Am.* lumber; '**~bau** ⚹ *m* wooden structure; '**~bildhauer** *m* wood-carver; '**~blasinstrument** ♪ *n* woodwind instrument; '**~boden** *m* wood(en) floor; wood-loft.

hölzern *adj.* ['hœltsərn] wooden; *fig. a.* clumsy, awkward.

'**Holz|fäller** *m* (-s/-) woodcutter, woodman, *Am.* a. lumberjack, logger; '**~hacker** *m* (-s/-) wood-chopper, woodcutter, *Am.* lumberjack; '**~händler** *m* wood *or* timber merchant, *Am.* lumberman; '**~haus** *n* wooden house, *Am.* frame house; '**2ig** *adj.* woody; '**~kohle** *f* charcoal; '**~platz** *m* wood *or* timber yard, *Am.* lumberyard; '**~schnitt** *m* woodcut, wood-engraving; '**~schnitzer** *m* wood-carver; '**~schuh** *m* wooden shoe, clog; '**~stoß** *m* pile *or* stack of wood; stake; '**~weg** *fig. m: auf dem ~ sein* be on the wrong track; '**~wolle** *f* wood-wool; fine wood shavings *pl., Am.* a. excelsior.

Homöopath ✎ [homøo'pa:t] *m* (-en/ -en) hom(o)eopath(ist); '**~ie** [~a'ti:] *f* (-/*no pl.*) hom(o)eopathy; **2isch** *adj.* [~'pa:tiʃ] hom(o)eopathic.

Honig ['ho:niç] *m* (-s/-e) honey; '**~kuchen** *m* honey-cake; ginger-bread; '**2süß** *adj.* honey-sweet, honeyed (*a. fig.*); '**~wabe** *f* honey-comb.

Honor|ar [hono'ra:r] *n* (-s/-e) fee; royalties *pl.*; salary; **~atioren** [~tsjo:rən] *pl.* notabilities *pl.*; **2ieren** [~'ri:rən] *v/t.* (*no* -ge-, h) fee, pay a fee to; ✝ hono(u)r, meet (*bill of exchange*).

Hopfen ['hɔpfən] *m* (-s/-) ✿ hop; *brewing:* hops *pl.*

hops|a *int.* ['hɔpsa] (wh)oops!; up-sa-daisy!; '**~en** F *v/i.* (ge-, sein) hop, jump.

hörbar *adj.* ['hø:rba:r] audible.

horch|en ['hɔrçən] *v/i.* (ge-, h) listen (*auf acc.* to); eavesdrop; '**2er** *m* (-s/-) eavesdropper.

Horde ['hɔrdə] *f* (-/-n) horde, gang.

hör|en ['hø:rən] (ge-, h) **1.** *v/t.* hear; listen (in to (*radio*)); attend (*lecture, etc.*); hear, learn; **2.** *v/i.* hear (*von dat.* from); listen; *~ auf (acc.)* listen to; *schwer ~* be hard of hearing; *~ Sie mal!* look here!; I say!; '**2er** *m* (-s/-) hearer; *radio:* listener(-in); *univ.* student; *teleph.* receiver; '**2erschaft** *f* (-/-en) audience; '**2ge-rät** *n* hearing aid; '**2ig** *adj.: j-m ~ sein* be enslaved to s.o.; '**2igkeit** *f* (-/*no pl.*) enslavement.

Horizont [hori'tsɔnt] *m* (-[e]s/-e) horizon; skyline; *s-n ~ erweitern* broaden one's mind; *das geht über meinen ~* that's beyond me; **2al** *adj.* [~'ta:l] horizontal.

Hormon [hɔr'mo:n] *n* (-s/-e) hormone.

Horn [hɔrn] *n* **1.** (-[e]s/⁀er) horn (*of bull*); ♪, *mot., etc.:* horn; ✗ bugle; peak; **2.** (-[e]s/-e) horn, horny matter; '**~haut** *f* horny skin; *anat.* cornea (*on eye*).

Hornisse *zo.* [hɔr'nisə] *f* (-/-n) hornet.

Hornist [hɔr'nist] *m* (-en/-en) horn-player; ✗ bugler.

Horoskop [horo'sko:p] *n* (-s/-e) horoscope; *j-m das ~ stellen* cast s.o.'s horoscope.

'**Hör|rohr** *n* ear-trumpet; ♬ steth-oscope; '**~saal** *m* lecture-hall;

'**~spiel** n radio play; '**~weite** f: in ~ within earshot.

Hose ['ho:zə] f (-/-n) (e-e a pair of) trousers pl. or Am. pants pl.; slacks pl.

'**Hosen|klappe** f flap; **~latz** ['~lats] m (-es/⸚e) flap; fly; '**~tasche** f trouser-pocket; '**~träger** m: (ein Paar) ~ pl. (a pair of) braces pl. or Am. suspenders pl.

Hospital [hɔspi'ta:l] n (-s/-e, ⸚er) hospital.

Hostie eccl. ['hɔstjə] f (-/-n) host, consecrated or holy wafer.

Hotel [ho'tɛl] n (-s/-s) hotel; **~be-sitzer** m hotel owner or proprietor; **~gewerbe** n hotel industry; **~ier** [~'je:] m (-s/-s) hotel-keeper.

Hub ⊕ [hu:p] m (-[e]s/⸚e) mot. stroke (of piston); lift (of valve, etc.); '**~raum** mot. m capacity.

hübsch adj. [hypʃ] pretty, nice; good-looking, handsome; attractive.

'**Hubschrauber** ✈ m (-s/-) helicopter.

Huf [hu:f] m (-[e]s/-e) hoof; '**~eisen** n horseshoe; '**~schlag** m hoof-beat; (horse's) kick; '**~schmied** m farrier.

Hüft|e anat. ['hyftə] f (-/-n) hip; esp. zo. haunch; '**~gelenk** n hip-joint; '**~gürtel** m girdle; suspender belt, Am. garter belt.

Hügel ['hy:gəl] m (-s/-) hill(ock); '**2ig** adj. hilly.

Huhn orn. [hu:n] n (-[e]s/⸚er) fowl, chicken; hen; junges ~ chicken.

Hühnchen ['hy:nçən] n (-s/-) chicken; ein ~ zu rupfen haben have a bone to pick (mit with).

'**Hühner|auge** ✲ ['hy:nər-] n corn; '**~ei** n hen's egg; '**~hof** m poultry-yard, Am. chicken yard; '**~hund** zo. m pointer, setter; '**~leiter** f chicken-ladder.

Huld [hult] f (-/no pl.) grace, favo(u)r; '**2igen** ['~digən] v/i. (dat.) (ge-, h) pay homage to (sovereign, lady, etc.); indulge in (vice, etc.); '**~igung** f (-/-en) homage; '**2reich** adj., '**2voll** adj. gracious.

Hülle ['hylə] f (-/-n) cover(ing), wrapper; letter, balloon, etc.: envelope; book, etc.: jacket; umbrella, etc.: sheath; '**2n** v/t. (ge-, h) wrap, cover, envelope (a. fig.); sich in Schweigen ~ wrap o.s. in silence.

Hülse ['hylzə] f (-/-n) legume, pod (of leguminous plant); husk, hull (of rice, etc.); skin (of pea, etc.); ✗ case; '**~nfrucht** f legume(n); leguminous plant; '**~nfrüchte** f/pl. pulse.

human adj. [hu'ma:n] humane; **2i-tät** [~ani'tɛ:t] f (-/no pl.) humanity.

Hummel zo. ['huməl] f (-/-n) bumble-bee.

Hummer zo. ['humər] m (-s/-) lobster.

Humor [hu'mo:r] m (-s/✲-e) humo(u)r; **~ist** [~o'rist] m (-en/-en) humorist; **2istisch** adj. [~o'ristiʃ] humorous.

humpeln ['humpəln] v/i. (ge-) **1.** (sein) hobble (along), limp (along); **2.** (h) (have a) limp, walk with a limp.

Hund [hunt] m (-[e]s/-e) zo. dog; ✗ tub; ast. dog, canis; auf den ~ kommen go to the dogs.

'**Hunde|hütte** f dog-kennel, Am. a. doghouse; '**~kuchen** m dog-biscuit; '**~leine** f (dog-)lead or leash; '**~peitsche** f dog-whip.

hundert ['hundərt] **1.** adj. a or one hundred; **2.** 2 n (-s/-e) hundred; fünf vom ~ five per cent; zu ~en by hundreds; '**~fach** adj., '**~fältig** adj. hundredfold; **2'jahrfeier** f centenary, Am. a. centennial; '**~jährig** adj. ['.~jɛ:riç] centenary, a hundred years old; '**~st** adj. hundredth.

'**Hunde|sperre** f muzzling-order; '**~steuer** f dog tax.

Hündin zo. ['hyndin] f (-/-nen) bitch, she-dog; '**2sch** adj. doggish; fig. servile, cringing.

'**hunds|ge'mein** F adj. dirty, mean, scurvy; '**~mise'rabel** F adj. rotten, wretched, lousy; '**2tage** m/pl. dog-days pl.

Hüne ['hy:nə] m (-n/-n) giant.

Hunger ['huŋər] m (-s/no pl.) hunger (fig. nach for); ~ bekommen get hungry; ~ haben be or feel hungry; '**~kur** f starvation cure; '**~leider** m (-s/-) starveling, poor devil; '**~lohn** m starvation wages pl.; '**2n** v/i. (ge-, h) hunger (fig. nach after, for); go without food; ~ lassen starve ✲.o.; '**~snot** f famine; '**~streik** m hunger-strike; '**~tod** m death from starvation; '**~tuch** fig. n: am ~ nagen have nothing to bite.

'**hungrig** adj. hungry (fig. nach for).

Hupe mot. ['hu:pə] f (-/-n) horn,

hooter; klaxon; '**Ợn** v/i. (ge-, h) sound one's horn, hoot.

hüpfen ['hypfən] v/i. (ge-, sein) hip, skip; gambol, frisk (about).

Hürde ['hyrdə] f (-/-n) hurdle; fold, pen; '**ℒnrennen** n hurdle-race.

Hure ['hu:rə] f (-/-n) whore, prostitute.   [agile, nimble.)

hurtig adj. ['hurtiç] quick, swift;)

Husar ✕ [hu'za:r] m (-en/-en) hussar.

husch int. [huʃ] in or like a flash; shoo!; '**ℒen** v/i. (ge-, sein) slip, dart; small animal: scurry, scamper; bat, etc.: flit.

hüsteln ['hy:stəln] 1. v/i. (ge-, h) cough slightly; 2. ℒ n (-s/no pl.) slight cough.

husten ['hu:stən] 1. v/i. (ge-, h) cough; 2. ℒ m (-s/ﬁ·) cough.

Hut [hu:t] 1. m (-[e]s/ﬁe) hat; den ~ abnehmen take off one's hat; ~ ab vor (dat.)! hats off to …!; 2. f (-/no pl.) care, charge; guard; auf der ~ sein be on one's guard (vor dat. against).

hüte|n ['hy:tən] v/t. (ge-, h) guard, protect, keep watch over; keep (secret); tend (sheep, etc.); das Bett ~ be confined to (one's) bed; sich ~ vor (dat.) beware of; '**Ợr** m (-s/-) keeper, guardian; herdsman.

'**Hut|futter** n hat-lining; '**ℒkrempe**

f hat-brim; '**ℒmacher** m (-s/-) hatter; '**ℒnadel** f hat-pin.

Hütte ['hytə] f (-/-n) hut; cottage, cabin; ⊕ metallurgical plant; mount. refuge; '**ℒnwesen** ⊕ n metallurgy, metallurgical engineering.

Hyäne zo. [hy'ɛ:nə] f (-/-n) hy(a)ena.

Hyazinthe ♀ [hya'tsintə] f (-/-n) hyacinth.   [hydrant.)

Hydrant [hy'drant] m (-en/-en))

Hydrauli|k phys. [hy'draulik] f (-/no pl.) hydraulics pl.; ℒ**sch** adj. hydraulic.

Hygien|e [hy'gje:nə] f (-/no pl.) hygiene; ℒ**isch** adj. hygienic(al).

Hymne ['hymnə] f (-/-n) hymn.

Hypno|se [hyp'no:zə] f (-/-n) hypnosis; ℒ**tisieren** [ˌoti'zi:rən] v/t. and v/i. (no -ge-, h) hypnotize.

Hypochond|er [hypo'xɔndər] m (-s/-) hypochondriac; ℒ**risch** adj. hypochondriac.

Hypotenuse ⅍ [hypote'nu:zə] f (-/-n) hypotenuse.

Hypothek [hypo'te:k] f (-/-en) mortgage; e-e ~ aufnehmen raise a mortgage; ℒ**arisch** adj. [ˌeˈka:riʃ]: ~e Belastung mortgage.

Hypothe|se [hypo'te:zə] f (-/-n) hypothesis; ℒ**tisch** adj. hypothetical.

Hyster|ie psych. [hyste'ri:] f (-/-n) hysteria; ℒ**isch** psych. adj. [ˌʏ'te:riʃ] hysterical.

I

ich [iç] 1. pers. pron. I; 2. ℒ n (-[s]/ -[s]) self; psych. the ego.

Ideal [ide'a:l] 1. n (-s/-e) ideal; 2. ℒ adj. ideal; ℒ**isieren** [ˌali'zi:rən] v/t. (no -ge-, h) idealize; '**ℒismus** [ˌa'lismus] m (-/Idealismen) idealism; ~**ist** [ˌa'list] m (-en/-en) idealist.

Idee [i'de:] f (-/-n) idea, notion.

identi|fizieren [identifi'tsi:rən] v/t. (no -ge-, h) identify; sich ~ identify o.s.; ~**sch** adj. [i'dentiʃ] identical; ℒ**tät** [ˌ'tɛ:t] f (-/no pl.) identity.

Ideolog|ie [ideolo'gi:] f (-/-n) ideology; ℒ**isch** adj. [ˌ'lo:giʃ] ideological.

Idiot [idi'o:t] m (-en/-en) idiot; ~**ie** [ˌo'ti:] f (-/-n) idiocy; ℒ**isch** adj. [ˌ'o:tiʃ] idiotic.

Idol [i'do:l] n (-s/-e) idol.

Igel zo. ['i:gəl] m (-s/-) hedgehog.

Ignor|ant [igno'rant] m (-en/-en) ignorant person, ignoramus; ~**anz** [ˌ'ts] f (-/no pl.) ignorance; ℒ**ieren** v/t. (no -ge-, h) ignore, take no notice of.

ihm pers. pron. [i:m] p. (to) him; thing: (to) it.

ihn pers. pron. [i:n] p. him; thing: it.

'**ihnen** pers. pron. (to) them; Ihnen sg. and pl. (to) you.

ihr [i:r] 1. pers. pron.: (2nd pl. nom.) you; (3rd sg. dat.) (to) her; 2. poss. pron.: her; their; Ihr sg. and pl. your; der (die, das) ~e hers; theirs; der (die, das) Ihre sg. and pl. yours; ~**erseits** [ˌ'ər'zaits] adv. on her part; on their part; Ihrerseits sg. and pl. on your part; '**ℒes'gleichen** pron. (of) her or their kind, her or their equal; *Ihresgleichen* sg. (of) your kind, your equal; pl. (of) your kind, your equals; '**~et'wegen** adv. for her or their sake, on her or their account; *Ihretwegen* sg. or pl. for your sake, on your account; '**~et'willen** adv.: um ~ s. ihretwegen; **~ige** poss. pron. ['~igə]: der (die, das) ~ hers; theirs; der (die, das) Ihrige yours.

illegitim adj. [ilegi'ti:m] illegitimate.

illusorisch adj. [ilu'zo:riʃ] illusory, deceptive.

illustrieren [ilu'stri:rən] v/t. (no -ge-, h) illustrate.

Iltis zo. ['iltis] m (-ses/-se) fitchew, polecat.

im prp. [im] = in dem. [inary.⟩

imaginär adj. [imagi'nɛ:r] imag-⟨

'**Imbiß** m light meal, snack; '**~stube** f snack bar.

Imker ['imkər] m (-s/-) bee-master, bee-keeper.

immatrikulieren [imatriku'li:rən] v/t. (no -ge-, h) matriculate, enrol(l); sich ~ lassen matriculate, enrol(l).

immer adv. ['imər] always; ~ mehr more and more; ~ wieder again or time and again; für ~ for ever, for good; '**2grün** ♀ n (-s/-e) evergreen; '**~hin** adv. still, yet; '**~zu** adv. always, continually.

Immobilien [imo'bi:ljən] pl. immovables pl., real estate; **~händler** m s. Grundstücksmakler.

immun adj. [i'mu:n] immune (gegen against, from); **2ität** [~uni'tɛ:t] f (-/no pl.) immunity.

Imperativ gr. ['imperati:f] m (-s/-e) imperative (mood).

Imperfekt gr. ['imperfɛkt] n (-s/-e) imperfect (tense), past tense.

Imperialis|mus [imperia'lismus] m (-/no pl.) imperialism; **~t** m (-en/-en) imperialist; **2tisch** adj. imperialistic.

impertinent adj. [imperti'nɛnt] impertinent, insolent.

impf|en ✻ ['impfən] v/t. (ge-, h) vaccinate; inoculate; '**2schein** m certificate of vaccination or inoculation; '**2stoff** ✻ m vaccine; serum; '**2ung** f (-/-en) vaccination; inoculation.

imponieren [impo'ni:rən] v/i. (no -ge-, h): j-m ~ impress s.o.

Import ✝ [im'port] m (-[e]s/-e) import(ation); **~eur** ✝ [~'tø:r] m (-s/-e) importer; **2ieren** [~'ti:rən] v/t. (no -ge-, h) import.

imposant adj. [impo'zant] imposing, impressive.

imprägnieren [imprɛ'gni:rən] v/t. (no -ge-, h) impregnate; (water-) proof (raincoat, etc.).

improvisieren [improvi'zi:rən] v/t. and v/i. (no -ge-, h) improvise.

Im'puls m (-es/-e) impuls; **2iv** adj. [~'zi:f] impulsive. [be able.⟩

imstande adj. [im'ʃtandə]: ~ sein⟨

in prp. (dat.; acc.) [in] **1.** place: in, at; within; into, in; with names of important towns: in, 🏛 at, of; with names of villages and less important towns: at; im Hause in the house, indoors, in; im ersten Stock on the first floor; ~ der Schule (im Theater) at school (the thea|tre, Am. -er); ~ die Schule (~s Theater) to school (the thea|tre, Am. -er); ~ England in England; waren Sie schon einmal in England? have you ever been to England?; **2.** time: in, at, during; within; ~ drei Tagen (with)in three days; heute ~ vierzehn Tagen today fortnight; im Jahre 1960 in 1960; im Februar in February; im Frühling in (the) spring; ~ der Nacht at night; ~ letzter Zeit lately, of late, recently; **3.** mode: ~ großer Eile in great haste; ~ Frieden leben live at peace; ~ Reichweite within reach; **4.** condition, state: im Alter von fünfzehn Jahren at (the age of) fifteen; ~ Behandlung under treatment.

'**Inbegriff** m (quint)essence; embodiment, incarnation; paragon; '**2en** adj. included, inclusive (of).

'**Inbrunst** f (-/no pl.) ardo(u)r, fervo(u)r.

'**inbrünstig** adj. ardent, fervent.

in'dem cj. whilst, while; by (ger.); ~ er mich ansah, sagte er looking at me he said.

Inder ['indər] m (-s/-) Indian.

in'des(sen) 1. adv. meanwhile; **2.** cj. while; however.

Indianer [in'dja:nər] m (-s/-) (American or Red) Indian.

Indikativ gr. ['indikati:f] m (-s/-e) indicative (mood).

'**indirekt** adj. indirect.

'**indisch** adj. ['indiʃ] Indian.

'**indiskret** adj. indiscreet; 2**ion** [‿e'tsjo:n] f (-/-en) indiscretion.

indiskutabel adj. ['indiskuta:bəl] out of the question.

individu|ell adj. [individu'ɛl] individual; 2**um** [‿'vi:duum] n (-s/ Individuen) individual.

Indizienbeweis ⚖ [in'di:tsjən-] m circumstantial evidence.

Indoss|ament † [indɔsa'ment] n (-s/-e) endorsement, indorsement; 2**ieren** † [‿'si:rən] v/t. (no -ge-, h) indorse, endorse.

Industrialisierung [industriali'zi:-ruŋ] f (-/-en) industrialization.

Industrie [indus'tri:] f (-/-n) industry; **anlage** f industrial plant; **arbeiter** m industrial worker; **ausstellung** f industrial exhibition; **erzeugnis** n industrial product; **gebiet** n industrial district or area; 2**ll** adj. [‿i'ɛl] industrial; **lle** [‿i'ɛlə] m (-n/-n) industrialist; **staat** m industrial country.

ineinander adv. [in⁹ai'nandər] into one another; **greifen** ⊕ v/i. (irr. greifen, sep., -ge-, h) gear into one another, interlock.

infam adj. [in'fɑ:m] infamous.

Infanter|ie ✕ [infantə'ri:] f (-/-n) infantry; **ist** ✕ m (-en/-en) infantryman.

Infektion ✄ [infɛk'tsjo:n] f (-/-en) infection; **skrankheit** ✄ f infectious disease.

Infinitiv gr. ['infiniti:f] m (-s/-e) infinitive (mood).

infizieren [infi'tsi:rən] v/t. (no -ge-, h) infect.   [flation.\]

Inflation [infla'tsjo:n] f (-/-en) in-\

in'folge prp. (gen.) in consequence of, owing or due to; **dessen** adv. consequently.

Inform|ation [informa'tsjo:n] f (-/-en) information; 2**ieren** [‿'mi:-rən] v/t. (no -ge-, h) inform; falsch ~ misinform.

Ingenieur [inʒe'njø:r] m (-s/-e) engineer.

Ingwer ['iŋvər] m (-s/no pl.) ginger.

Inhaber ['inha:bər] m (-s/-) owner, proprietor (of business or shop); occupant (of flat); keeper (of shop); holder (of office, share, etc.); bearer (of cheque, etc.).

'**Inhalt** m (-[e]s/-e) contents pl. (of bottle, book, etc.); tenor (of speech); geom. volume; capacity (of vessel).

'**Inhalts|angabe** f summary; 2**los** adj. empty, devoid of substance; 2**reich** adj. full of meaning; life: rich, full; **verzeichnis** n on parcel: list of contents; in book: table of contents.

Initiative [initsja'ti:və] f (-/no pl.) initiative; die ~ ergreifen take the initiative.

Inkasso † [in'kaso] n (-s/-s, Inkassi) collection.

'**inkonsequen|t** adj. inconsistent; 2**z** ['‿ts] f (-/-en) inconsistency.

In'krafttreten n (-s/no pl.) coming into force, taking effect (of new law, etc.).

'**Inland** n (-[e]s/no pl.) home (country); inland.

inländisch adj. ['inlɛndiʃ] native; inland; home; domestic; product: home-made.

Inlett ['inlɛt] n (-[e]s/-e) bedtick.

in'mitten prp. (gen.) in the midst of, amid(st).

'**inne|haben** v/t. (irr. haben, sep., -ge-, h) possess, hold (office, record, etc.); occupy (flat); **halten** v/i. (irr. halten, sep., -ge-, h) stop, pause.

innen adv. ['inən] inside, within; indoors; nach ~ inwards.

'**Innen|architekt** m interior decorator; **ausstattung** f interior decoration, fittings pl., furnishing; **minister** m minister of the interior; Home Secretary, Am. Secretary of the Interior; **ministerium** n ministry of the interior; Home Office, Am. Department of the Interior; **politik** f domestic policy; **seite** f inner side, inside; **stadt** f city, Am. downtown.

inner adj. ['inər] interior; inner; ⚗, pol. internal; 2**e** n (-n/no pl.) interior; Minister(ium) des Innern s. Innenminister(ium); 2**eien** [‿'raiən] f/pl. offal(s pl.); '**halb** 1. prp. (gen.) within; 2. adv. within, inside; '**lich** adv. inwardly; esp. ⚗ internally.

innig adj. ['iniç] intimate, close; affectionate.

Innung ['inuŋ] f (-/-en) guild, corporation.

inoffiziell adj. ['in⁹-] unofficial.

ins prp. [ins] = in das.

Insasse ['inzasə] m (-n/-n) inmate; occupant, passenger (of car).

'Inschrift f inscription; legend (on coin, etc.).

Insekt zo. [in'zɛkt] n (-[e]s/-en) insect.

Insel ['inzəl] f (-/-n) island; **'~bewohner** m islander.

Inser|at [inzə'ra:t] n (-[e]s/-e) advertisement, F ad; **2ieren** [~'ri:rən] v/t. and v/i. (no -ge-, h) advertise.

insge|'heim adv. secretly; **~'samt** adv. altogether.

in'sofern cj. so far; **~** als in so far as.

insolvent ✝ adj. ['inzɔlvɛnt] insolvent.

Inspekt|ion [inspɛk'tsjo:n] f (-/-en) inspection; **~or** [in'spɛktɔr] m (-s/-en) inspector; surveyor; overseer.

inspirieren [inspi'ri:rən] v/t. (no -ge-, h) inspire.

inspizieren [inspi'tsi:rən] v/t. (no -ge-, h) inspect (troops, etc.); examine (goods); survey (buildings).

Install|ateur [instala'tø:r] m (-s/-e) plumber; (gas- or electrical) fitter; **2ieren** [~'li:rən] v/t. (no -ge-, h) install.

instand adv. [in'ʃtant]: **~** halten keep in good order; keep up; ⊕ maintain; **~** setzen repair; **2haltung** f maintenance; upkeep.

'inständig adv.: j-n **~** bitten implore or beseech s.o.

Instanz [in'stants] f (-/-en) authority; ⟶ instance; **~enweg** ⟶ m stages of appeal; auf dem **~** through the prescribed channels.

Instinkt [in'stiŋkt] m (-[e]s/-e) instinct; **2iv** adv. [~'ti:f] instinctively.

Institut [insti'tu:t] n (-[e]s/-e) institute.

Instrument [instru'mɛnt] n (-[e]s/-e) instrument.

inszenier|en esp. thea. [instse'ni:rən] v/t. (no -ge-, h) (put on the) stage; **2ung** thea. f (-/-en) staging, production.

Integr|ation [integra'tsjo:n] f (-/-en) integration; **2ieren** [~'gri:rən] v/t. (no -ge-, h) integrate.

intellektuell adj. [intelɛktu'ɛl] intellectual, highbrow; **2e** m (-n/-n) intellectual, highbrow.

intelligen|t adj. [inteli'gɛnt] intelligent; **2z** [~ts] f (-/-en) intelligence.

Intendant thea. [inten'dant] m (-en/-en) director.

intensiv adj. [intɛn'zi:f] intensive;

interess|ant adj. [interɛ'sant] interesting; **2e** [~'rɛsə] n (-s/-n) interest (an dat., für in); **2engebiet** [~'rɛsən-] n field of interest; **2engemeinschaft** [~'rɛsən-] f community of interests; combine, pool, trust; **2ent** [~'sɛnt] m (-en/-en) interested person or party; ✝ prospective buyer, Am. prospect; **~ieren** [~'si:rən] v/t. (no -ge-, h) interest (für in); sich **~** für take an interest in.

intern adj. [in'tɛrn] internal; **2at** [~'na:t] n (-[e]s/-e) boarding-school.

international adj. [internatsjo'na:l] international.

inter|'nieren v/t. (no -ge-, h) intern; **2'nierung** f (-/-en) internment; **2'nist** ✝ m (-en/-en) internal specialist, Am. internist.

inter|pretieren [interpre'ti:rən] v/t. (no -ge-, h) interpret; **2punktion** [~puŋk'tsjo:n] f (-/-en) punctuation; **2vall** [~'val] n (-s/-e) interval; **~venieren** [~ve'ni:rən] v/i. (no -ge-, h) intervene; **2'zonenhandel** m interzonal trade; **2'zonenverkehr** m interzonal traffic.

intim adj. [in'ti:m] intimate (mit with); **2ität** [~imi'tɛ:t] f (-/-en) intimacy.

'intoleran|t adj. intolerant; **2z** ['~ts] f (-/-en) intolerance.

intransitiv gr. adj. ['intranziti:f] intransitive.

Intrig|e [in'tri:gə] f (-/-n) intrigue, scheme, plot; **2ieren** [~i'gi:rən] v/i. (no -ge-, h) intrigue, scheme, plot.

Invalid|e [inva'li:də] m (-n/-n) invalid; disabled person; **~enrente** f disability pension; **~ität** [~idi'tɛ:t] f (-/no pl.) disablement, disability.

Inventar [inven'ta:r] n (-s/-e) inventory, stock.

Inventur ✝ [inven'tu:r] f (-/-en) stock-taking; **~** machen take stock.

invest|ieren ✝ [invɛs'ti:rən] v/t. (no -ge-, h) invest; **2ition** [~i'tsjo:n] f (-/-en) investment.

inwie|'fern cj. to what extent; in what way or respect; **~'weit** cj. how far, to what extent.

in'zwischen adv. in the meantime, meanwhile.

Ion phys. [i'o:n] n (-s/-en) ion.

ird|en adj. ['irdən] earthen; **'~isch** adj. earthly; worldly; mortal.

Ire ['iːrə] *m* (-n/-n) Irishman; *die* ~*n pl.* the Irish *pl.*

irgend *adv.* ['irgənt] *in compounds*: some; any (*a.* negative and in questions); *wenn ich* ~ *kann* if I possibly can; '~**ein(e)** *indef. pron. and adj.* some(one); any(one); '~**einer** *indef. pron. s. irgend jemand*; '~**'ein(e)s** *indef. pron.* some; any; '~**etwas** *indef. pron.* something; anything; ~ **jemand** *indef. pron.* someone; anybody; '~**wann** *adv.* some time (or other); '~**wie** *adv.* somehow; anyhow; '~**wo** *adv.* somewhere; anywhere; '~**wo'her** *adv.* from somewhere; from anywhere; '~**wo'hin** *adv.* somewhere; anywhere.

'**irisch** *adj.* Irish.

Iron|ie [iro'niː] *f* (-/-n) irony; **2isch** *adj.* [i'roːniʃ] ironic(al).

irre ['irə] **1.** *adj.* confused; *ℱ* insane; mad; **2.** ⚲ *f* (-/no pl.): *in die* ~ *gehen* go astray; **3.** ⚲ *m, f* (-n/-n) lunatic; mental patient; *wie ein* ~*r* like a madman; '~**führen** *v/t.* (*sep.*, -ge-, *h*) lead astray; *fig.* mislead; '~**gehen** *v/i.* (*irr. gehen, sep.*, -ge-, *sein*) go astray, stray; lose one's way; '~**machen** *v/t.* (*sep.*, -ge-, *h*) puzzle, bewilder; perplex; confuse; '~**n 1.** *v/i.* (ge-, *h*) err; wander; **2.** *v/refl.* (ge-, *h*) be mistaken (*in dat.* in *s.o.*, about *s.th.*); be wrong.

'**Irren|anstalt** *ℱ f* lunatic asylum, mental home *or* hospital; '~**arzt** *m* alienist, mental specialist; '~**haus** *ℱ n s. Irrenanstalt.*

'**irrereden** *v/i.* (*sep.*, -ge-, *h*) rave.

'**Irr|fahrt** *f* wandering; Odyssey; '~**garten** *m* labyrinth, maze; '~**glaube** *m* erroneous belief; false doctrine, heterodoxy; heresy; '2**gläubig** *adj.* heterodox; heretical; '2**ig** *adj.* erroneous, mistaken, false, wrong.

irritieren [iri'tiːrən] *v/t.* (*no* -ge-, *h*) irritate, annoy; confuse.

'**Irr|lehre** *f* false doctrine, heterodoxy; heresy; '~**licht** *n* will-o'-the-wisp, jack-o'-lantern; '~**sinn** *m* insanity; madness; '2**sinnig** *adj.* insane; mad; *fig.*: fantastic; terrible; '~**sinnige** *m, f* (-n/-n) *s. irre 3*; '~**tum** *m* (-s/⸚er) error, mistake; *im* ~ *sein* be mistaken; 2**tümlich** ['~tyːmlɪç] **1.** *adj.* erroneous; **2.** *adv.* = '2**tümlicherweise** *adv.* by mistake; mistakenly, erroneously; '~**wisch** *m s. Irrlicht; p.* flibbertigibbet.

Ischias *ℱ* ['iʃias] *f,* F *a.: n, m* (-/no pl.) sciatica.

Islam ['islam, is'laːm] *m* (-s/no pl.) Islam.

Isländ|er ['iːslɛndər] *m* (-s/-) Icelander; '2**isch** *adj.* Icelandic.

Isolator *ℱ* [izo'laːtɔr] *m* (-s/-en) insulator.

Isolier|band *ℱ* [izo'liːr-] *n* insulating tape; 2**en** *v/t.* (*no* -ge-, *h*) isolate; ~**masse** *ℱ f* insulating compound; ~**schicht** *ℱ f* insulating layer; ~**ung** *f* (-/-en) isolation (*a. ℱ*); *ℱ* quarantine; *ℱ* insulation.

Isotop ⚛, *phys.* [izo'toːp] *n* (-s/-e) isotope.

Israeli [isra'eːli] *m* (-s/-s) Israeli.

Italien|er [ital'jeːnər] *m* (-s/-) Italian; 2**isch** *adj.* Italian.

I-Tüpfelchen *fig.* ['iːtypfəlˌçən] *n* (-s/-): *bis aufs* ~ to a T.

J

ja [jaː] **1.** *adv.* yes; ⚓, *parl.* aye, *Am. parl. a.* yea; ~ *doch,* ~ *freilich* yes, indeed; to be sure; *da ist er* ~*!* well, there he is!; *ich sagte es Ihnen* ~ I told you so; *tut es* ~ *nicht!* don't you dare do it!; *vergessen Sie es* ~ *nicht!* be sure not to forget it!; **2.** *cj.*: ~ *sogar,* ~ *selbst* nay (even); *wenn* ~, if so; *er ist* ~ *mein Freund* why, he is my friend; **3.** *int.*: ~, *weißt du*

denn nicht, daß why, don't you know that.

Jacht ⚓ [jaxt] *f* (-/-en) yacht; '~**klub** *m* yacht-club.

Jacke ['jakə] *f* (-/-n) jacket.

Jackett [ʒa'kɛt] *n* (-s/-e, -s) jacket.

Jagd [jaːkt] *f* (-/-en) hunt(ing); *with a gun*: shoot(ing); chase; *s. Jagdrevier; auf* (*die*) ~ *gehen* go hunting *or* shooting, *Am. a.* be gunning; ~ *machen auf* (*acc.*) hunt after *or* for;

'~aufseher *m* gamekeeper, *Am.* game warden; '~bomber ✕ *m* (-s/-) fighter-bomber; '~büchse *f* sporting rifle; '~flinte *f* sporting gun; fowling-piece; '~flugzeug ✕ *n* fighter (aircraft); '~geschwader ✕ *n* fighter wing, *Am.* fighter group; '~gesellschaft *f* hunting *or* shooting party; '~haus *n* shooting-box *or* -lodge; '~hund *m* hound; '~hütte *f* shooting-box, hunting-box; ~pächter *m* game-tenant; '~rennen *n* steeplechase; '~revier *n* hunting-ground, shoot; '~schein *m* shooting licen|ce, *Am.* -se; '~schloß *n* hunting seat; '~tasche *f* game-bag.

jagen ['ja:gən] (ge-, h) **1.** *v/i.* go hunting *or* shooting, hunt; shoot; rush dash; **2.** *v/t.* hunt; chase; *aus dem ~ause ~* turn *s.o.* out (of doors).

Jäger ['jɛ:gər] *m* (-s/-) hunter, huntsman, sportsman; ✕ rifleman; '~latein F *fig. n* huntsmen's yarn, tall stories *pl.*

Jaguar *zo.* ['ja:gua:r] *m* (-s/-e) jaguar.

jäh *adj.* [jɛ:] sudden, abrupt; precipitous, steep.

Jahr [ja:r] *n* (-[e]s/-e) year; *ein halbes ~* half a year, six months *pl.*; *einmal im ~* once a year; *im ~e* 1900 in 1900; *mit 18 ~en, im Alter von 18 ~en* at (the age of) eighteen; *letztes ~* last year; *das ganze ~ hindurch or über* all the year round; ♀'aus *adv.*: ~, *jahrein* year in, year out; year after year; '~buch *n* year-book, annual; ~'ein *adv. s.* jahraus.

'jahrelang **1.** *adv.* for years; **2.** *adj.*: ~e Erfahrung (many) years of experience.

jähren ['jɛ:rən] *v/refl.* (ge-, h): es jährt sich heute, daß ... it is a year ago today that ..., it is a year today since ...

'Jahres|abonnement *n* annual subscription (*to magazine, etc.*); *thea.* yearly season ticket; '~abschluß *m* annual statement of accounts; '~anfang *m* beginning of the year; *zum ~ die besten Wünsche!* best wishes for the New Year; '~bericht *m* annual report; '~einkommen *n* annual *or* yearly income; '~ende *n* end of the year; '~gehalt *n* annual salary; '~tag *m* anniversary; '~wechsel *m* turn of the year; '~zahl

f date, year; '~zeit *f* season, time of the year.

'Jahrgang *m* volume, year (*of periodical, etc.*); *p.* age-group; *univ. school*: year, class; *wine*: vintage.

Jahr'hundert *n* (-s/-e) century; ~feier *f* centenary, *Am.* centennial; ~wende *f* turn of the century.

jährig *adj.* ['jɛ:riç] one-year-old.

jährlich ['jɛ:rliç] **1.** *adj.* annual, yearly; **2.** *adv.* every year; yearly, once a year.

'Jahr|markt *m* fair; ~'tausend *n* (-s/-e) millennium; ~'tausendfeier *f* millenary; ~'zehnt *n* (-[e]s/-e) decade.

Jähzorn *m* violent (fit of) temper; irascibility; '♀ig *adj.* hot-tempered; irascible.

Jalousie [ʒalu'zi:] *f* (-/-n) (Venetian) blind, *Am. a.* window shade.

Jammer ['jamər] *m* (-s/*no pl.*) lamentation; misery; *es ist ein ~* it is a pity.

jämmerlich *adj.* ['jɛmərliç] miserable, wretched; piteous; pitiable (*esp. contp.*).

jammer|n ['jamərn] *v/i.* (ge-, h) lament (*nach, um* for; *über acc.* over); moan; wail, whine; '~schade *adj.*: *es ist ~* it is a thousand pities, it is a great shame.

Januar ['janua:r] *m* (-[s]/-e) January.

Japan|er [ja'pa:nər] *m* (-s/-) Japanese; *die ~ pl.* the Japanese *pl.*; '♀isch *adj.* Japanese.

Jargon [ʒar'gõ] *m* (-s/-s) jargon, cant, slang.

Jasmin ♀ [jas'mi:n] *m* (-s/-e) jasmin(e), jessamin(e).

'Jastimme *parl. f* aye, *Am. a.* yea.

jäten ['jɛ:tən] *v/t.* (ge-, h) weed.

Jauche ['jauxə] *f* (-/-n) ↗ liquid manure; sewage.

jauchzen ['jauxtsən] *v/i.* (ge-, h) exult, rejoice, cheer; *vor Freude ~* shout for joy.

jawohl *adv.* [ja'vo:l] yes; yes, indeed; yes, certainly; that's right; ✕, *etc.*: yes, Sir!

'Jawort *n* consent; *j-m das ~ geben* accept *s.o.*'s proposal (of marriage).

je [je:] **1.** *adv.* ever, at any time; always; *ohne ihn ~ gesehen zu haben* without ever having seen him; *seit eh und ~* since time immemorial, always; *distributive with numerals:*

~ *zwei* two at a time, two each, two by two, by *or* in twos; *sie bekamen* ~ *zwei Äpfel* they received two apples each; *für* ~ *zehn Wörter* for every ten words; *in Schachteln mit or zu* ~ *zehn Stück verpackt* packed in boxes of ten; **2.** *cj.:* ~ *nach Größe* according to *or* depending on size; ~ *nachdem* it depends; ~ *nachdem, was er für richtig hält* according as he thinks fit; ~ *nachdem, wie er sich fühlt* depending on how he feels; ~ *mehr, desto besser* the more the better; ~ *länger,* ~ *lieber* the longer the better; **3.** *prp.: die Birnen kosten e-e Mark* ~ *Pfund* the pears cost one mark a pound; *s. pro.*

jede|(r, -s) *indef. pron.* ['je:də(r, -s)] every; any; *of a group:* each; *of two persons:* either; *jeder, der who-ever*; *jeden zweiten Tag* every other day; **'~n'falls** *adv.* at all events, in any case; **'~rmann** *indef. pron.* everyone, everybody; **'~r'zeit** *adv.* always, at any time; **'~s'mal** *adv.* each *or* every time; ~ *wenn* when-ever.

jedoch *cj.* [je'dɔx] however, yet, nevertheless.

'jeher *adv.: von or seit* ~ at all times, always, from time immemorial.

jemals *adv.* ['je:ma:ls] ever, at any time.

jemand *indef. pron.* ['je:mant] someone, somebody; *with questions and negations:* anyone, anybody.

jene|(r, -s) *dem. pron.* ['je:nə(r, -s)] that (one); *jene pl.* those *pl.*

jenseitig *adj.* ['jenzaitiç] opposite.

'jenseits 1. *prp.* (*gen.*) on the other side of, beyond, across; **2.** *adv.* on the other side, beyond; **3.** ♀ *n* (-/*no pl.*) *the* other *or* next world, *the* world to come, *the* beyond.

jetzig *adj.* ['jetsiç] present, existing; *prices, etc.:* current.

jetzt *adv.* [jetst] now, at present; *bis* ~ until now; so far; *eben* ~ just now; *erst* ~ only now; *für* ~ for the present; *gleich* ~ at once, right away; *noch* ~ even now; *von* ~ *an* from now on.

jeweil|ig *adj.* ['je:vaɪliç] respective; **'~s** *adv.* ['~s] respectively, at a time; from time to time (*esp.* ⚖).

Joch [jɔx] *n* (-[e]s/-e) yoke; *in mountains:* col, pass, saddle; ♙

bay; **'~bein** *anat. n* cheek-bone.

Jockei ['dʒɔki] *m* (-s/-s) jockey.

Jod ♐ [jo:t] *n* (-[e]s/*no pl.*) iodine.

jodeln ['jo:dəln] *v/i.* (ge-, h) yodel.

Johanni [jo'hani] *n* (-/*no pl.*), **~s** [~s] *n* (-/*no pl.*) Midsummer day; **~s-beere** *f* currant; *rote* ~ red currant; **~stag** *m eccl.* St John's day; Mid-summer day.

johlen ['jo:lən] *v/i.* (ge-, h) bawl, yell, howl.

Jolle ⚓ ['jɔlə] *f* (-/-n) jolly-boat, yawl, dinghy.

Jongl|eur [ʒõ'glø:r] *m* (-s/-e) juggler; **♀ieren** *v/t. and v/i.* (no -ge-, h) juggle.

Journal [ʒur'na:l] *n* (-s/-e) journal; newspaper; magazine; diary; ⚓ log-book; **~ist** [~a'list] *m* (-en/-en) journalist, *Am. a.* newspaperman.

Jubel ['ju:bəl] *m* (-s/*no pl.*) jubila-tion, exultation, rejoicing; cheer-ing; **♀n** *v/i.* (ge-, h) jubilate; exult, rejoice (*über acc.* at).

Jubil|ar [jubi'la:r] *m* (-s/-e) person celebrating his jubilee, *etc.*; **~äum** [~ɛ:um] *n* (-s/*Jubiläen*) jubilee.

Juchten ['juxtən] *m, n* (-s/*no pl.*), **'~leder** *n* Russia (leather).

jucken ['jukən] (ge-, h) **1.** *v/i.* itch; **2.** *v/t.* irritate, (make) itch; F *sich* ~ scratch (o.s.).

Jude ['ju:də] *m* (-n/-n) Jew; **'♀-feindlich** *adj.* anti-Semitic; **'~n-tum** *n* (-s/*no pl.*) Judaism; **'~nver-folgung** *f* persecution of Jews, Jew-baiting; pogrom.

Jüd|in ['jy:din] *f* (-/-nen) Jewess; **'♀isch** *adj.* Jewish.

Jugend ['ju:gənt] *f* (-/*no pl.*) youth; **'~amt** *n* youth welfare department; **'~buch** *n* book for the young; **'~-freund** *m* friend of one's youth; school-friend; **'~fürsorge** *f* youth welfare; **'~gericht** *n* juvenile court; **'~herberge** *f* youth hostel; **'~jahre** *n/pl.* early years, youth; **'~krimi-nalität** *f* juvenile delinquency; **'♀-lich** *adj.* youthful, juvenile, young; **'~liche** *m, f* (-n/-n) young person; juvenile; young man, youth; young girl; teen-ager; **'~liebe** *f* early *or* first love, calf-love, *Am. a.* puppy love; old sweetheart *or* flame; **'~-schriften** *f/pl.* books for the young; **'~schutz** *m* protection of children and young people; **'~streich** *m* youthful prank; **'~werk** *n* early work (of *author*); ∼e *pl.* a. juvenilia *pl.*; '∼zeit *f* (time *or* days of) youth.

Jugoslav|e [ju:go'sla:və] *m* (-en/-en) Jugoslav, Yugoslav; 2isch *adj.* Jugoslav, Yugoslav.

Juli ['ju:li] *m* (-[s]/-s) July.

jung *adj.* [juŋ] young; youthful; *peas:* green; *beer, wine:* new; ∼es Gemüse young *or* early vegetables *pl.*; F *fig.* young people, small fry.

'**Junge 1.** *m* (-n/-n) boy, youngster; lad; fellow, chap, *Am.* guy; *cards:* knave, jack; **2.** *n* (-n/-n) young; puppy (*of dog*); kitten (*of cat*); calf (*of cow, elephant, etc.*); cub (*of beast of prey*); ∼ werfen bring forth young; *ein* ∼s a young one; '2**nhaft** *adj.* boyish; '∼**nstreich** *m* boyish prank *or* trick.

jünger ['jyŋər] **1.** *adj.* younger, junior; *er ist drei Jahre* ∼ *als ich* he is my junior by three years, he is three years younger than I; **2.** 2*m* (-s/-) disciple.

Jungfer ['juŋfər] *f* (-/-n): *alte* ∼ old maid *or* spinster.

'**Jungfern|fahrt** ⊕ *f* maiden voyage *or* trip; '∼**flug** ✈ *m* maiden flight; '∼**rede** *f* maiden speech.

'**Jung|frau** *f* maid(en), virgin; 2-**fräulich** *adj.* ['∼frɔʏliç] virginal; *fig.* virgin; '∼**fräulichkeit** *f* (-/no *pl.*) virginity, maidenhood; '∼**ge-selle** *m* bachelor; '∼**gesellenstand** *m* bachelorhood; '∼**gesellin** *f* (-/-nen) bachelor girl.

Jüngling ['jyŋliŋ] *m* (-s/-e) youth, young man.

jüngst [jyŋst] **1.** *adj.* youngest; *time:* (most) recent, latest; *das* 2e Ge-richt, *der* 2e Tag Last Judg(e)ment, Day of Judg(e)ment; **2.** *adv.* re-cently, lately.

'**jungverheiratet** *adj.* newly mar-ried; '2**en** *pl. the* newlyweds *pl.*

Juni ['ju:ni] *m* (-[s]/-s) June; '∼**kä-fer** *zo. m* cockchafer, June-bug.

junior ['ju:njɔr] **1.** *adj.* junior; **2.** 2*m* (-s/-en) junior (a. *sports*).

Jura ['ju:ra] *n/pl.*: ∼ studieren read *or* study law.

Jurist [ju'rist] *m* (-en/-en) lawyer; law-student; 2isch *adj.* legal.

Jury [ʒy'ri:] *f* (-/-s) jury.

justier|en [jus'ti:rən] *v/t.* (no -ge-, h) adjust; 2**ung** ⊕ *f* (-/-en) adjustment.

Justiz [ju'sti:ts] *f* (-/no *pl.*) (admin-istration of) justice; ∼**beamte** *m* judicial officer; ∼**gebäude** *n* court-house; ∼**inspektor** *m* judicial offi-cer; ∼**irrtum** *m* judicial error; ∼**minister** *m* minister of justice; Lord Chancellor, *Am.* Attorney General; ∼**ministerium** *n* minis-try of justice; *Am.* Department of Justice; ∼**mord** *m* judicial murder.

Juwel [ju've:l] *m*, *n* (-s/-en) jewel, gem; ∼**en** *pl.* jewel(le)ry; ∼**ier** [∼e-'li:r] *m* (-s/-e) jewel(l)er.

Jux F [juks] *m* (-es/-e) (practical) joke, fun, spree, lark; prank.

K

(Compare also C and Z)

Kabel ['ka:bəl] *n* (-s/-) cable.

Kabeljau *ichth.* ['ka:bəljau] *m* (-s/-e, -s) cod(fish).

'**kabeln** *v/t. and v/i.* (ge-, h) cable.

Kabine [ka'bi:nə] *f* (-/-n) cabin; *at hairdresser's, etc.:* cubicle; cage (*of lift*).

Kabinett *pol.* [kabi'nɛt] *n* (-s/-e) cabinet, government.

Kabriolett [kabrio'lɛt] *n* (-s/-e) cabriolet, convertible.

Kachel ['kaxəl] *f* (-/-n) (Dutch *or* glazed) tile; '∼**ofen** *m* tiled stove.

Kadaver [ka'da:vər] *m* (-s/-) car-cass.

Kadett [ka'dɛt] *m* (-en/-en) cadet.

Käfer *zo.* ['kɛ:fər] *m* (-s/-) beetle, chafer.

Kaffee ['kafe, ka'fe:] *m* (-s/-s) cof-fee; (')∼**bohne** ♀ *f* coffee-bean; (')∼**kanne** *f* coffee-pot; (')∼**mühle** *f* coffee-mill *or* -grinder; (')∼**satz** *m* coffee-grounds *pl.*; (')∼**tasse** *f* coffee-cup.

Käfig ['kɛ:fiç] *m* (-s/-e) cage (a. *fig.*).

kahl *adj.* [ka:l] *p.* bald; *tree, etc.:* bare; *landscape, etc.:* barren, bleak; *rock, etc.:* naked; 2**kopf** *m* bald-head, baldpate; ∼**köpfig** *adj.* ['∼-kœpfiç] bald(-headed).

Kahn [kɑ:n] *m* (-[e]s/ᵘe) boat; river-barge; ~ *fahren* go boating; '~**fahren** *n* (-s/*no pl.*) boating.

Kai [kaɪ] *m* (-s/-e, -s) quay, wharf.

Kaiser ['kaɪzər] *m* (-s/-) emperor; '~**krone** *f* imperial crown; '2**lich** *adj.* imperial; '~**reich** *n*, '~**tum** *n* (-[e]s/ᵘer) empire; '~**würde** *f* imperial status.

Kajüte ⚓ [ka'jy:tə] *f* (-/-n) cabin.

Kakao [ka'ka:o] *m* (-s/-s) cocoa; ♀ *a.* cacao.

Kakt|ee ♀ [kak'te:(ə)] *f* (-/-n), **~us** ♀ ['~us] *m* (-/Kakteen, F *Kaktusse*) cactus.

Kalauer ['kɑ:lauər] *m* (-s/-) stale joke; pun.

Kalb *zo.* [kalp] *n* (-[e]s/ᵘer) calf; 2**en** ['~bən] *v/i.* (ge-, h) calve; '~**fell** *n* calfskin; '~**fleisch** *n* veal; '~**leder** *n* calf(-leather).

'Kalbs|braten *m* roast veal; '~**keule** *f* leg of veal; '~**leder** *n* s. Kalbleder; '~**nierenbraten** *m* loin of veal.

Kalender [ka'lɛndər] *m* (-s/-) calendar; almanac; ~**block** *m* date-block; ~**jahr** *n* calendar year; ~**uhr** *f* calendar watch *or* clock.

Kali ⚗ ['kɑ:li] *n* (-s/-s) potash.

Kaliber [ka'li:bər] *n* (-s/-) calib|re, Am. -er (*a. fig.*), bore (*of firearm*).

Kalk [kalk] *m* (-[e]s/-e) lime; *geol.* limestone; '~**brenner** *m* lime-burner; '2**en** *v/t.* (ge-, h) whitewash (*wall, etc.*); ✗ lime (*field*); '2**ig** *adj.* limy; '~**ofen** *m* limekiln; '~**stein** *m* limestone; '~**steinbruch** *m* lime-stone quarry.

Kalorie [kalo'ri:] *f* (-/-n) calorie.

kalt *adj.* [kalt] *climate, meal, sweat, etc.*: cold; *p., manner, etc.*: cold, chilly, frigid; *mir ist* ~ I am cold; ~**e** *Küche* cold dishes *pl.* or meat, *etc.*; *j-m die* ~ *Schulter zeigen* give s.o. the cold shoulder; '~**blütig** *adj.* ['~bly:tiç] cold-blooded (*a. fig.*).

Kälte ['kɛltə] *f* (-/*no pl.*) cold; chill; coldness, chilliness (*both a. fig.*); *vor* ~ *zittern* shiver with cold; *fünf Grad* ~ five degrees below zero; '~**grad** *m* degree below zero; '~**welle** *f* cold spell.

'kalt|stellen *fig. v/t.* (*sep.*, -ge-, h) shelve, reduce to impotence; '2**welle** *f* cold wave.

kam [kɑ:m] *pret.* of kommen.

Kamel *zo.* [ka'me:l] *n* (-[e]s/-e) camel; ~**haar** *n* textiles: camel hair.

Kamera *phot.* ['kaməra] *f* (-/-s) camera.

Kamerad [kamə'rɑ:t] *m* (-en/-en) comrade; companion; mate, F pal, chum; ~**schaft** *f* (-/-en) comradeship, companionship; 2**schaftlich** *adj.* comradely, companionable.

Kamille ♀ [ka'milə] *f* (-/-n) camomile; ~**ntee** *m* camomile tea.

Kamin [ka'mi:n] *m* (-s/-e) chimney (*a. mount.*); fireplace, fireside; ~**sims** *m, n* mantelpiece; ~**vorleger** *m* hearth-rug; ~**vorsetzer** *m* (-s/-) fender.

Kamm [kam] *m* (-[e]s/ᵘe) comb; crest (*of bird or wave*); crest, ridge (*of mountain*).

kämmen ['kɛmən] *v/t.* (ge-, h) comb; *sich* (*die Haare*) ~ comb one's hair.

Kammer ['kamər] *f* (-/-n) (small) room; closet; *pol.* chamber; board; ⚖ division (*of court*); '~**diener** *m* valet; '~**frau** *f* lady's maid; '~**gericht** ⚖ *n* supreme court; '~**herr** *m* chamberlain; '~**jäger** *m* vermin exterminator; '~**musik** *f* chamber music; '~**zofe** *f* chambermaid.

'Kamm|garn *n* worsted (yarn); '~**rad** ⊕ *n* cogwheel.

Kampagne [kam'panjə] *f* (-/-n) campaign.

Kampf [kampf] *m* (-[e]s/ᵘe) combat, fight (*a. fig.*); struggle (*a. fig.*); battle (*a. fig.*); *fig.* conflict; *sports*: contest, match; *boxing*: fight, bout; '~**bahn** *f* *sports*: stadium, arena; '2**bereit** *adj.* ready for battle.

kämpfen ['kɛmpfən] *v/i.* (ge-, h) fight (*gegen* against; *mit* with; *um* for) (*a. fig.*); struggle (*a. fig.*); *fig.* contend, wrestle (*mit* with).

Kampfer ['kampfər] *m* (-s/*no pl.*) camphor.

Kämpfer ['kɛmpfər] *m* (-s/-) fighter (*a. fig.*); ✗ combatant, warrior.

'Kampf|flugzeug *n* tactical aircraft; '~**geist** *m* fighting spirit; '~**platz** *m* battlefield; *fig., sports*: arena; '~**preis** *m* *sports*: prize; ✝ cut-throat price; '~**richter** *m* referee, judge, umpire; '2**unfähig** *adj.* disabled.

kampieren [kam'pi:rən] *v/i.* (no -ge-, h) camp.

Kanal [ka'nɑ:l] *m* (-s/ᵘe) canal; channel (*a.* ⊕, *fig.*); *geogr. the* Channel; sewer, drain; ~**isation**

K

[ˌali‿za'tsjoːn] f (-/-en) river: canalization; town, etc.: sewerage; drainage; 2**isieren** [ˌali'ziːrən] v/t. (no -ge-, h) canalize; sewer.

Kanarienvogel orn. [ka'naːrjən-] m canary (-bird).

Kandare [kan'daːrə] f (-/-n) curb (-bit).

Kandid|at [kandi'daːt] m (-en/-en) candidate; applicant; ~**atur** [ˌa'tuːr] f (-/-en) candidature, candidacy; 2**ieren** [ˌ'diːrən] v/i. (no -ge-, h) be a candidate (für for); ~ für apply for, stand for, Am. run for (office, etc.).

Känguruh zo. ['kɛŋguru:] n (-s/-s) kangaroo.

Kaninchen zo. [ka'niːnçən] n (-s/-) rabbit; ~**bau** m rabbit-burrow.

Kanister [ka'nistər] m (-s/-) can.

Kanne ['kanə] f (-/-n) milk, etc.: jug; coffee, tea: pot; oil, milk: can; ~**gießer** F fig. m political wiseacre.

Kannibal|e [kani'baːlə] m (-n/-n) cannibal; 2**isch** adj. cannibal.

kannte ['kantə] pret. of kennen.

Kanon ♪ ['kaːnɔn] m (-s/-s) canon.

Kanon|ade ✕ [kano'naːdə] f (-/-n) cannonade; ~**e** [ˌ'noːnə] f (-/-n) ✕ cannon, gun; F fig.: big shot; esp. sports: ace, crack.

Ka'nonen|boot ✕ n gunboat; ~**donner** m boom of cannon; ~**futter** fig. n cannon-fodder; ~**kugel** f cannon-ball; ~**rohr** n gun barrel.

Kanonier ✕ [kano'niːr] m (-s/-e) gunner.

Kant|e ['kantə] f (-/-n) edge; brim; ~**en** m (-s/-) end of loaf; 2**en** v/t. (ge-, h) square (stone, etc.); set on edge; tilt; edge (skis); 2**ig** adj. angular, edged; square(d).

Kantine [kan'tiːnə] f (-/-n) canteen.

Kanu ['kaːnu] n (-s/-s) canoe.

Kanüle ✍ [ka'nyːlə] f (-/-n) tubule, cannula.

Kanzel ['kantsəl] f (-/-n) eccl. pulpit; ✈ cockpit; ✕ (gun-)turret.; '~**redner** m preacher.

Kanzlei [kants'laɪ] f (-/-en) office. '**Kanzler** m (-s/-) chancellor.

Kap geogr. [kap] n (-s/-s) headland.

Kapazität [kapatsi'tɛːt] f (-/-en) capacity; fig. authority.

Kapelle [ka'pɛlə] f (-/-n) eccl. chapel; ♪ band; ~**meister** m bandleader, conductor.

kaper|n ⚓ ['kaːpərn] v/t. (ge-, h)

capture, seize; 2**schiff** n privateer.

kapieren F [ka'piːrən] v/t. (no -ge-, h) grasp, get.

Kapital [kapi'taːl] 1. n (-s/-e, -ien) capital, stock, funds pl.; ~ und Zinsen principal and interest; 2. 2 adj. capital; ~**anlage** f investment; ~**flucht** f flight of capital; ~**gesellschaft** f joint-stock company; 2**isieren** [ˌali'ziːrən] v/t. (no -ge-, h) capitalize; ~**ismus** [ˌa'lismus] m (-/no pl.) capitalism; ~**ist** [ˌa'list] m (-en/-en) capitalist; ~**markt** [ˌ'tː-l-] m capital market; ~**verbrechen** n capital crime.

Kapitän [kapi'tɛːn] m (-s/-e) captain; ~ zur See naval captain; ~**leutnant** m (senior) lieutenant.

Kapitel [ka'piːtəl] n (-s/-) chapter (a. fig.).

Kapitul|ation ✕ [kapitula'tsjoːn] f (-/-en) capitulation, surrender; 2**ieren** [ˌ'liːrən] v/i. (no -ge-, h) capitulate, surrender.

Kaplan eccl. [ka'plaːn] m (-s/-ᵉe) chaplain.

Kappe ['kapə] f (-/-n) cap; hood (a. ⊕); bonnet; '2**n** v/t. (ge-, h) cut (cable); lop, top (tree).

Kapriole [kapri'oːlə] f (-/-n) equitation: capriole; fig.: caper; prank.

Kapsel ['kapsəl] f (-/-n) case, box; ✎, ✿, anat., etc.: capsule.

kaputt adj. [ka'put] broken; elevator, etc.: out of order; fruit, etc.: spoilt; p.: ruined; tired out, F fagged out; ~**gehen** v/i. (irr. gehen, sep., -ge-, sein) break, go to pieces; spoil.

Kapuze [ka'puːtsə] f (-/-n) hood; eccl. cowl.

Karabiner [kara'biːnər] m (-s/-) carbine.

Karaffe [ka'rafə] f (-/-n) carafe (for wine or water); decanter (for liqueur, etc.).

Karambol|age [karambo'laːʒə] f (-/-en) collision, crash; billiards: cannon, Am. a. carom; 2**ieren** v/i. (no -ge-, sein) cannon, Am. a. carom; F fig. collide.

Karat [ka'raːt] n (-[e]s/-e) carat.

Karawane [kara'vaːnə] f (-/-n) caravan.

Karbid [kar'biːt] n (-[e]s/-e) carbide.

Kardinal eccl. [kardi'naːl] m (-s/-ᵘe) cardinal.
                                     [Friday.]

Karfreitag eccl. [kaːr'-] m Good

karg adj. [kark] soil: meagre; vegetation: scant, sparse; meal: meagre, frugal; **∼en** ['∼gən] v/i. (ge-, h): ∼ mit be sparing of.

kärglich adj. ['kɛrkliç] scanty, meagre; poor.

kariert adj. [ka'ri:rt] check(ed), chequered, Am. checkered.

Karik|atur [karika'tu:r] f (-/-en) caricature, cartoon; **∼ieren** [∼'ki:-rən] v/t. (no -ge-, h) caricature, cartoon.

karmesin adj. [karme'zi:n] crimson.

Karneval ['karnəval] m (-s/-e, -s) Shrovetide, carnival.

Karo ['ka:ro] n (-s/-s) square, check; cards: diamonds pl.

Karosserie mot. [karɔsə'ri:] f (-/-n) body.

Karotte ♀ [ka'rɔtə] f (-/-n) carrot.

Karpfen ichth. ['karpfən] m (-s/-) carp.

Karre ['karə] f (-/-n) cart; wheelbarrow.

Karriere [kar'jɛ:rə] f (-/-n) (successful) career.

Karte ['kartə] f (-/-n) card; postcard; map; chart; ticket; menu, bill of fare; list.

Kartei [kar'taɪ] f (-/-en) card-index; **∼karte** f index-card, filing-card; **∼schrank** m filing cabinet.

Kartell ✝ [kar'tɛl] n (-s/-e) cartel.

'Karten|brief m letter-card; **'∼haus** n ♣ chart-house; fig. house of cards; **'∼legerin** f (-/-nen) fortune-teller from the cards; **'∼spiel** n card-playing; card-game.

Kartoffel [kar'tɔfəl] f (-/-n) potato, F spud; **∼brei** m mashed potatoes pl.; **∼käfer** m Colorado or potato beetle, Am. a. potato bug; **∼schalen** f/pl. potato peelings pl.

Karton [kar'tõ:, kar'to:n] m (-s/-s, -e) cardboard, pasteboard; cardboard box, carton.   [Kartei.\

Kartothek [karto'te:k] f (-/-en) s.\

Karussell [karu'sɛl] n (-s/-e, -s) roundabout, merry-go-round, Am. a. car(r)ousel.

Karwoche eccl. ['ka:r-] f Holy or Passion Week.

Käse ['kɛ:zə] m (-s/-) cheese.

Kasern|e ✕ [ka'zɛrnə] f (-/-n) barracks pl.; **∼enhof** m barrack-yard or -square; **∼ieren** [∼'ni:rən] v/t. (no -ge-, h) quarter in barracks, barrack.

'käsig adj. cheesy; complexion: pale, pasty.

Kasino [ka'zi:no] n (-s/-s) casino, club(-house); (officers') mess.

Kasperle ['kasperlə] n, m (-s/-) Punch; **'∼theater** n Punch and Judy show.

Kasse ['kasə] f (-/-n) cash-box; till (in shop, etc.); cash-desk, pay-desk (in bank, etc.); pay-office (in firm); thea., etc.: box-office, booking-office; cash; bei ∼ in cash.

'Kassen|abschluß ✝ m balancing of the cash (accounts); **'∼anweisung** f disbursement voucher; **'∼bestand** m cash in hand; **'∼bote** m bank messenger; **'∼buch** n cash book; **'∼erfolg** m thea., etc.: box-office success; **'∼patient** ✗ m panel patient; **'∼schalter** m bank, etc.: teller's counter.

Kasserolle [kasə'rɔlə] f (-/-n) stew-pan, casserole.

Kassette [ka'sɛtə] f (-/-n) box (for money, etc.); casket (for jewels, etc.); slip-case (for books); phot. plate-holder.

kassiere|n [ka'si:rən] (no -ge-, h) 1. v/i. waiter, etc.: take the money (für for); 2. v/t. take (sum of money); collect (contributions, etc.); annul; ⚖ quash (verdict); **♀r** m (-s/-) cashier; bank: a. teller; collector.

Kastanie ♀ [ka'sta:njə] f (-/-n) chestnut.

Kasten ['kastən] m (-s/ᵘ, ✎ -) box; chest (for tools, etc.); case (for violin, etc.); bin (for bread, etc.).

Kasus gr. ['ka:sus] m (-/-) case.

Katalog [kata'lo:k] m (-[e]s/-e) catalogue, Am. a. catalog; **♀isieren** [∼ogi'zi:rən] v/t. (no -ge-, h) catalogue, Am. a. catalog.

Katarrh ✗ [ka'tar] m (-s/-e) (common) cold, catarrh.

katastroph|al adj. [katastro'fa:l] catastrophic, disastrous; **♀e** [∼'stro:-fə] f (-/-n) catastrophe, disaster.

Katechismus eccl. [kate'çismus] m (-/Katechismen) catechism.

Katego|rie [katego'ri:] f (-/-n) category; **♀risch** adj. [∼'go:riʃ] categorical.

Kater ['ka:tər] m (-s/-) zo. male cat, tom-cat; fig. s. Katzenjammer.

Katheder [ka'te:dər] n, m (-s/-) lecturing-desk.   [cathedral.\

Kathedrale [kate'dra:lə] f (-/-n)\

Katholi|k [kato'li:k] *m* (-en/-en)
(Roman) Catholic; **2sch** *adj.*
[~'to:liʃ] (Roman) Catholic.

Kattun [ka'tu:n] *m* (-s/-e) calico;
cotton cloth *or* fabric; chintz.

Katze *zo.* ['katsə] *f* (-/-n) cat; '**~n-
jammer** F *fig. m* hangover, morn-
ing-after feeling.

Kauderwelsch ['kaudərvelʃ] *n* (-[s]/
no pl.) gibberish, F double Dutch;
'**2en** *v/i.* (ge-, h) gibber, F talk
double Dutch.   [chew.\

kauen ['kauən] *v/t. and v/i.* (ge-, h)\

kauern ['kauərn] (ge-, h) **1.** *v/i.*
crouch; squat; **2.** *v/refl.* crouch
(down); squat (down); duck (down).

Kauf [kauf] *m* (-[e]s/~e) purchase;
bargain, F good buy; acquisition;
purchasing, buying; '**~brief** *m* deed
of purchase; '**2en** *v/t.* (ge-, h) buy,
purchase; acquire (by purchase);
sich et. ~ buy o.s. s.th., buy s.th. for
o.s.   [purchaser; customer.\

Käufer ['kɔyfər] *m* (-s/-) buyer,\

'**Kauf|haus** *n* department store;
'**~laden** *m* shop, *Am. a.* store.

käuflich ['kɔyflɪç] **1.** *adj.* for sale;
purchasable; *fig.* open to bribery,
bribable; venal; **2.** *adv.*: ~ *erwerben*
(acquire by) purchase; ~ *überlassen*
transfer by way of sale.

'**Kauf|mann** *m* (-[e]s/*Kaufleute*)
businessman; merchant; trader, dealer, shopkeeper; *Am. a.* storekeeper;
2männisch *adj.* ['~menɪʃ] commercial, mercantile; '**~vertrag** *m*
contract of sale.

'**Kaugummi** *m* chewing-gum.

kaum *adv.* [kaum] hardly, scarcely,
barely; ~ *glaublich* hard to believe.

'**Kautabak** *m* chewing-tobacco.

Kaution [kau'tsjo:n] *f* (-/-en)
security, surety; ‡‡ *mst* bail.

Kautschuk ['kautʃuk] *m* (-s/-e)
caoutchouc, pure rubber.

Kavalier [kava'li:r] *m* (-s/-e) gentleman; beau, admirer.

Kavallerie ✗ [kavalə'ri:] *f* (-/-n)
cavalry, horse.

Kaviar ['ka:viar] *m* (-s/-e) caviar(e).

keck *adj.* [kek] bold; impudent,
saucy, cheeky; '**2heit** *f* (-/-en) boldness; impudence, sauciness, cheek-
iness.

Kegel ['ke:gəl] *m* (-s/-) *games:*
skittle, pin; *esp.* Å, ⊕ cone; ~
schieben s. **kegeln;** '**~bahn** *f* skittle,
alley, *Am.* bowling alley; **2förmig**

adj. ['~fœrmiç] conic(al), coniform;
tapering; '**2n** *v/i.* (ge-, h) play (at)
skittles *or* ninepins, *Am.* bowl.

Kegler ['ke:glər] *m* (-s/-) skittle-
player, *Am.* bowler.

Kehl|e ['ke:lə] *f* (-/-n) throat;
'**~kopf** *anat. m* larynx.

Kehre ['ke:rə] *f* (-/-n) (sharp) bend,
turn; '**2n** *v/t.* (ge-, h) sweep,
brush; turn (*nach oben* upwards);
j-m den Rücken ~ turn one's back
on s.o.

Kehricht ['ke:rɪçt] *m, n* (-[e]s/*no pl.*)
sweepings *pl.*, rubbish.

'**Kehrseite** *f* wrong side, reverse;
esp. fig. seamy side.

'**kehrtmachen** *v/i.* (sep., -ge-, h)
turn on one's heel; ✗ turn *or* face
about.   [chide.\

keifen ['kaifən] *v/i.* (ge-, h) scold,\

Keil [kail] *m* (-[e]s/-e) wedge, gore,
gusset; '**~e** F *f* (-/*no pl.*) thrashing,
hiding; '**~er** *zo. m* (-s/-) wild-boar;
'**~erei** F *f* (-/-en) row, scrap;
2förmig *adj.* ['~fœrmiç] wedge-
shaped, cuneiform; '**~kissen** *n*
wedge-shaped bolster; '**~schrift** *f*
cuneiform characters *pl.*

Keim [kaim] *m* (-[e]s/-e) ⚕, *biol.*
germ; ♀: seed-plant; shoot; sprout;
fig. seeds *pl.*, germ, bud; '**2en** *v/i.*
(ge-, h) seeds, *etc.*: germinate; *seeds,
plants, potatoes, etc.*: sprout; *fig.*
b(o)urgeon; '**2frei** *adj.* sterilized,
sterile; '**~träger** ⚕ *m* (germ-)car-
rier; '**~zelle** *f* germ-cell.

kein *indef. pron.* [kain] *as adj.*: ~(e)
no, not any; ~ *anderer als* none
other but; *as noun:* ~er, ~e, ~(e)s
none, no one, nobody; ~er *von
beiden* neither (of the two); ~er *von
uns* none of us; '**~es'falls** *adv.*, '**~es-
wegs** *adv.* ['~'ve:ks] by no means,
not at all; '**~mal** *adv.* not once, not
a single time.

Keks [ke:ks] *m, n* (-, -es/-, -e) biscuit, *Am.* cookie; cracker.

Kelch [kelç] *m* (-[e]s/-e) cup, goblet;
eccl. chalice, communion-cup; ♀
calyx.

Kelle ['kelə] *f* (-/-n) scoop; ladle;
tool: trowel.

Keller ['kelər] *m* (-s/-) cellar; basement; **~ei** [~'rai] *f* (-/-en) wine-vault;
'**~geschoß** *n* basement; '**~meister**
m cellarman.

Kellner ['kelnər] *m* (-s/-) waiter;
'**~in** *f* (-/-nen) waitress.

.elter ['kɛltər] f (-/-n) winepress; **2n** v/t. (ge-, h) press.

.enn|en ['kɛnən] v/t. (irr., ge-, h) know, be acquainted with; have knowledge of s.th.; **'.enlernen** v/t. (sep., -ge-, h) get or come to know; make s.o.'s acquaintance, meet s.o.; **2er** m (-s/-) expert; connoisseur; **'.tlich** adj. recognizable (an dat. by); **~ machen** mark; label; **2tnis** f (-/-se) knowledge; **~ nehmen von** take not(ic)e of; **'2zeichen** n mark, sign; mot. registration (number), Am. license number; fig. hallmark, criterion; **'.zeichnen** v/t. (ge-, h) mark, characterize.

.entern ⚓ ['kɛntərn] v/i. (ge-, sein) capsize, keel over, turn turtle.

.erbe ['kɛrbə] f (-/-n) notch, nick; slot; **'2n** v/t. (ge-, h) notch, nick, indent.

.erker ['kɛrkər] m (-s/-) gaol, jail, prison; **'.meister** m gaoler, jailer.

.erl F [kɛrl] m (-s, ⚓ -es/-e, F -s) man; fellow, F chap, bloke, esp. Am. guy.

.ern [kɛrn] m (-[e]s/-e) kernel (of nut, etc.); stone, Am. pit (of cherry, etc.); pip (of orange, apple, etc.); core (of the earth); phys. nucleus; fig. core, heart, crux; **Kern... s. a. Atom...;** **'.energie** f nuclear energy; **'.forschung** f nuclear research; **'.gehäuse** n core; **2ge'sund** adj. thoroughly healthy, F as sound as a bell; **2ig** adj. full of pips; fig.: pithy; solid; **'.punkt** m central or crucial point; **'.spaltung** f nuclear fission.

Kerze ['kɛrtsə] f (-/-n) candle; **'.nlicht** n candle-light; **'.nstärke** f candle-power.

.eß F adj. [kɛs] pert, jaunty; smart.

Kessel ['kɛsəl] m (-s/-) kettle; cauldron; boiler; hollow.

Kette ['kɛtə] f (-/-n) chain; range (of mountains, etc.); necklace; **'2n** v/t. (ge-, h) chain (an acc. to).

'Ketten|hund m watch-dog; **'.raucher** m chain-smoker; **'.reaktion** f chain reaction.

Ketzer ['kɛtsər] m (-s/-) heretic; **~ei** [~'raɪ] f (-/-en) heresy; **2isch** adj. heretical.

.euch|en ['kɔʏçən] v/i. (ge-, h) pant, gasp; **'2husten** ⚕ m (w)hooping cough.   [(of mutton, pork, etc.).\

Keule ['kɔʏlə] f (-/-n) club; leg\

keusch adj. [kɔʏʃ] chaste, pure; **'2heit** f (-/no pl.), chastity, purity.

kichern ['kɪçərn] v/i. (ge-, h) giggle, titter.

Kiebitz ['ki:bɪts] m (-es/-e) orn. pe(e)wit; F fig. kibitzer; **2en** F fig. v/i. (ge-, h) kibitz.

Kiefer ['ki:fər] **1.** anat. m (-s/-) jaw(-bone); **2.** ⚘ f (-/-n) pine.

Kiel [ki:l] m (-[e]s/-e) ⚓ keel; quill; **'.raum** m bilge, hold; **'.wasser** n wake (a. fig.).

Kieme zo. ['ki:mə] f (-/-n) gill.

Kies [ki:s] m (-es/-e) gravel; sl. fig. dough; **~el** ['.zəl] m (-s/-) pebble, flint; **'.weg** m gravel-walk.

Kilo ['ki:lo] n (-s/-[s]), **~gramm** [kilo'gram] n kilogram(me); **~hertz** [~'hɛrts] n kilocycle per second; **~'meter** n kilomet|re, Am. -er; **~'watt** n kilowatt.

Kimme ['kɪmə] f (-/-n) notch.

Kind [kɪnt] n (-[e]s/-er) child; baby. **'Kinder|arzt** m p(a)ediatrician; **~ei** ['raɪ] f (-/-en) childishness; childish trick; trifle; **'.frau** f nurse; **'.fräulein** n governess; **'.funk** m children's program(me); **'.garten** m kindergarten, nursery school; **'.lähmung** ⚕ f infantile paralysis, polio(myelitis); **2leicht** adj. very easy or simple, F as easy as winking or as ABC; **'.lied** n children's song; **2los** adj. childless; **'.mädchen** n nurse(maid); **'.spiel** n children's game; **ein ~ s. kinderleicht;** **'.stube** f nursery; fig. manners pl., upbringing; **'.wagen** m perambulator, F pram, Am. baby carriage; **'.zeit** f childhood; **'.zimmer** n children's room.

'Kindes|alter n childhood, infancy; **'.beine** n/pl.: **von ~n an** from childhood, from a very early age; **'.kind** n grandchild.

'Kind|heit f (-/no pl.) childhood; **2isch** adj. ['dɪʃ] childish; **2lich** adj. childlike.

Kinn anat. [kɪn] n (-[e]s/-e) chin; **'.backe** f, **'.backen** m (-s/-) jaw (-bone); **'.haken** m boxing: hook to the chin; uppercut; **'.lade** f jaw(-bone).

Kino ['ki:no] n (-s/-s) cinema, F the pictures pl., Am. motion-picture theater, F the movies pl.; **ins ~ gehen** go to the cinema or F pictures, Am. F go to the movies; **'.besu-**

Kinovorstellung

cher *m* cinema-goer, *Am.* F moviegoer; **'~vorstellung** *f* cinema-show, *Am.* motion-picture show.

Kippe F ['kipə] *f* (-/-n) stub, fag-end, *Am. a.* butt; *auf der ~ stehen or sein* hang in the balance; **'2n** (ge-) **1.** *v/i.* (*sein*) tip (over), topple (over), tilt (over); **2.** *v/t.* (*h*) tilt, tip over *or* up.

Kirche ['kirçə] *f* (-/-n) church.

'Kirchen|älteste *m* (-n/-n) churchwarden, elder; **'~buch** *n* parochial register; **'~diener** *m* sacristan, sexton; **'~gemeinde** *f* parish; **'~jahr** *n* ecclesiastical year; **'~lied** *n* hymn; **'~musik** *f* sacred music; **'~schiff** △ *n* nave; **'~steuer** *f* church-rate; **'~stuhl** *m* pew; **'~vorsteher** *m* churchwarden.

'Kirch|gang *m* church-going; **~gänger** ['~gɛŋər] *m* (-s/-) church-goer; **'~hof** *m* churchyard; **'2lich** *adj.* ecclesiastical; **'~spiel** *n* parish; **'~turm** *m* steeple; **~weih** ['~vaɪ] *f* (-/-en) parish fair.

Kirsche ['kirʃə] *f* (-/-n) cherry.

Kissen ['kisən] *n* (-s/-) cushion; pillow; bolster, pad.

Kiste ['kistə] *f* (-/-n) box, chest; crate.

Kitsch [kitʃ] *m* (-es/*no pl.*) trash, rubbish; **'2ig** *adj.* shoddy, trashy.

Kitt [kit] *m* (-[e]s/-e) cement; putty.

Kittel ['kitəl] *m* (-s/-) overall; smock, frock.

'kitten *v/t.* (ge-, h) cement; putt.

kitz|eln ['kitsəln] (ge-, h) **1.** *v/t.* tickle; **2.** *v/i.*: *meine Nase kitzelt* my nose is tickling; **'~lig** *adj.* ticklish (*a. fig.*).

Kladde ['kladə] *f* (-/-n) rough note-book, waste-book.

klaffen ['klafən] *v/i.* (ge-, h) gape, yawn.

kläffen ['klɛfən] *v/i.* (ge-, h) yap, yelp.

klagbar ⚖ *adj.* ['klɑːkbɑːr] *matter, etc.*: actionable; *debt, etc.*: suable.

Klage ['klɑːgə] *f* (-/-n) complaint; lament; ⚖ action, suit; **'2n** (ge-, h) **1.** complain (*über acc.* of, about; *bei* to); lament; ⚖ take legal action (*gegen* against); **2.** *v/t.*: *j-m et. ~* complain to s.o. of *or* about s.th.

Kläger ⚖ ['klɛːgər] *m* (-s/-) plaintiff; complainant.

kläglich *adj.* ['klɛːkliç] pitiful, piteous, pitiable; *cries, etc.*: plaintive *condition*: wretched, lamentable *performance, result, etc.*: miserable poor; *failure, etc.*: lamentable miserable.

klamm [klam] **1.** *adj.* hands, etc. numb *or* stiff with cold, clammy **2.** ♀ *f* (-/-en) ravine, gorge, canyon

Klammer ['klamər] *f* (-/-n) ⊕ clamp, cramp; (paper-)clip; *gr. typ.*, Å bracket, parenthesis; **'2r** (ge-, h) **1.** *v/t.* clip together; s close (*wound*) with clips; *sich ~ ar* (*acc.*) cling to (*a. fig.*); **2.** *v/i.* boxing clinch.

Klang [klaŋ] **1.** *m* (-[e]s/-e) sound tone (*of voice, instrument, etc.*); tone (*of radio, etc.*); clink (*of glasses etc.*); ringing (*of bells, etc.*); timbre **2.** ♀ *pret. of klingen*; **'~fülle** *f* sonority; **'2los** *adj.* toneless; **'2voll** *adj.* sonorous.

Klappe ['klapə] *f* (-/-n) flap; flap drop leaf (*of table, etc.*); shoulder strap (*of uniform, etc.*); tailboard (*of lorry, etc.*); ⊕, ♀, *anat.* valve; ♪ key; F *fig.*: bed; trap; **'2n** (ge- h) **1.** *v/t.*: *nach oben ~* tip up; *nach unten ~* lower, put down; **2.** *v/i.* clap, flap; *fig.* come off well, work out fine, *Am. sl. a.* click.

Klapper ['klapər] *f* (-/-n) rattle; **'2ig** *adj. vehicle, etc.*: rattly, ramshackle; *furniture, etc.*: rickety; *person, horse, etc.*: decrepit; rattletrap; **'~kasten** F *m* wretched piano; rattletrap; **'2n** (ge-, h) clatter, rattle (*mit et.* s.th.); *er klapperte vor Kälte mit den Zähnen* his teeth were chattering with cold; **'~schlange** *zo.* f rattlesnake, *Am. a.* rattler.

'Klapp|kamera *phot.* f folding camera; **'~messer** *n* clasp-knife, jack-knife, *Am.* switchblade; **'~sitz** *m* tip-up *or* flap seat; **'~stuhl** *m* folding chair; **'~tisch** *m* folding table, *Am. a.* gate-leg(ged) table; **~ult** ['klappult] *n* folding desk.

Klaps [klaps] *m* (-es/-e) smack, slap; **'2en** *v/t.* (ge-, h) smack, slap.

klar *adj.* [klɑːr] clear; bright; transparent, limpid; pure; *fig.*: clear, distinct, plain; evident, obvious; *sich ~ sein über* (*acc.*) be clear about; *~en Kopf bewahren* keep a clear head.

klären ['klɛːrən] *v/t.* (ge-, h) clarify; *fig.* clarify, clear up, elucidate.

klar|legen v/t. (sep., -ge-, h); '**~stellen** v/t. (sep., -ge-, h) clear up.
Klärung f (-/-en) clarification; fig. a. elucidation.
Klasse ['klasə] f (-/-n) class, category; school: class, form, Am. a. grade; (social) class.
Klassen|arbeit f (test) paper; '2**bewußt** adj. class-conscious; '~**bewußtsein** n class-consciousness; '~**buch** n class-book; '~**haß** m class-hatred; '~**kamerad** m classmate; '~**kampf** m class-war(fare); '~**zimmer** n classroom, schoolroom.
klassifizier|en [klasifi'tsi:rən] v/t. (no -ge-, h) classify; 2**ung** f (-/-en) classification.
Klass|iker ['klasikər] m (-s/-) classic; '2**isch** adj. classic(al).
Klatsch [klatʃ] 1. int. smack!, slap!; 2. 2 m (-es/-e) smack, slap; F fig.: gossip; scandal; 2**base** ['~ba:zə] f (-/-n) gossip; '2**e** f (-/-n) fly-flap; '~**en** (ge-, h) 1. v/t. fling, hurl; Beifall ~ clap, applaud (j-m s.o.) 2. v/i. splash; applaud, clap; F fig. gossip; '~**haft** adj. gossiping, gossipy; '2**maul** F n s. Klatschbase; '~**naß** F adj. soaking wet.
Klaue ['klauə] f (-/-n) claw; paw; fig. clutch. [cell.)
Klause ['klauzə] f (-/-n) hermitage;)
Klausel ₰₰ ['klauzəl] f (-/-n) clause; proviso; stipulation.
Klaviatur ♪ [klavja'tu:r] f (-/-en) keyboard, keys pl.
Klavier ♪ [kla'vi:r] n (-s/-e) piano (-forte); ~**konzert** n piano concert or recital; ~**lehrer** m piano teacher; ~**sessel** m music-stool; ~**stimmer** m (-s/-) piano-tuner; ~**stunde** f piano-lesson.
kleb|en ['kle:bən] (ge-, h) 1. v/t. glue, paste, stick; 2. v/i. stick, adhere (an dat. to); '~**end** adj. adhesive; '2**epflaster** n adhesive or sticking plaster; '~**rig** adj. adhesive, sticky; '2**stoff** m adhesive, glue.
Klecks [kleks] m (-es/-e) blot (of ink); mark (of dirt, grease, paint, etc.); spot (of grease, paint, etc.); stain (of wine, coffee, etc.); '2**en** (ge-) 1. v/i. (h) make a mark or spot or stain; 2. v/i. (sein) ink, etc.: drip (down); 3. v/t. et. auf et. ~ splash or spill s.th. on s.th.
Klee ♣ [kle:] m (-s/no pl.) clover, trefoil.

Kleid [klait] n (-[e]s/-er) garment; dress, frock; gown; ~**er** pl. clothes pl., 2**en** ['~dən] v/t. (ge-, h) dress, clothe; attire ~ (o.s.); j-n gut ~ suit or become s.o.
Kleider|ablage ['klaidər-] f cloakroom, Am. a. checkroom; '~**bügel** m coat-hanger; '~**bürste** f clothes-brush; '~**haken** m clothes-peg; '~**schrank** m wardrobe; '~**ständer** m hat and coat stand; '~**stoff** m dress material.
'**kleidsam** adj. becoming.
Kleidung ['klaidun] f (-/-en) clothes pl., clothing; dress; '~**sstück** n piece or article of clothing; garment.
Kleie ['klaiə] f (-/-n) bran.
klein [klain] 1. adj. little (only attr.), small; fig. a. trifling, petty; 2. adv.: ~ schreiben write with a small (initial) letter; ~ anfangen start in a small or modest way; 3. adv.: von ~ auf from an early age; '2**auto** n baby or small car; '2**bahn** f narrow-ga(u)ge railway; '2**bildkamera** f miniature camera; '2**geld** n (small) change; of little faith; '2**gläubig** adj. of little faith; '2**handel** ✝ m retail trade; '2**händler** m retailer; '2**heit** f (-/no pl.) smallness, small size; '2**holz** n firewood, matchwood, kindling.
'**Kleinigkeit** f (-/-en) trifle, triviality; '~**skrämer** m pettifogger.
'**Klein|kind** n infant; '2**laut** adj. subdued; '2**lich** adj. paltry; pedantic, fussy; '~**mut** m pusillanimity, despondency; 2**mütig** adj. ['~my:-tiç] pusillanimous; despondent; '2**schneiden** v/t. (irr. schneiden, sep., -ge-, h) cut into small pieces; '~**staat** m small or minor state; '~**stadt** f small town; '~**städter** m small-town dweller, Am. a. small-towner; '2**städtisch** adj. small-town, provincial; '~**vieh** n small livestock.
Kleister ['klaistər] m (-s/-) paste; '2**n** v/t. (ge-, h) paste.
Klemm|e ['klemə] f (-/-n) ⊕ clamp; ⚡ terminal; F in der ~ sitzen be in a cleft stick, F be in a jam; '2**en** v/t. (ge-, h) jam, squeeze, pinch; '~**er** m (-s/-) pince-nez; '~**schraube** ⊕ f set screw.
Klempner ['klempnər] m (-s/-) tin-man, tin-smith, Am. a. tinner; plumber.

Klerus [ˈkleːrus] *m* (-/*no pl.*) clergy.

Klette [ˈklɛtə] *f* (-/-n) ⚬ bur(r); *fig. a.* leech.

Kletter|er [ˈklɛtərər] *m* (-s/-) climber; '**2n** *v/i.* (ge-, sein) climb, clamber (*auf e-n Baum* [up] a tree); '**⁓pflanze** *f* climber, creeper.

Klient [kliˈɛnt] *m* (-en/-en) client.

Klima [ˈkliːma] *n* (-s/-s, -te) climate; *fig. a.* atmosphere; '**⁓anlage** *f* air-conditioning plant; **2tisch** *adj.* [⁓ˈmaːtiʃ] climatic.

klimpern [ˈklimpərn] *v/i.* (ge-, h) jingle, chink (*mit et. s.th.*); F strum *or* tinkle away (*auf acc.* on, at *piano*, *guitar*).

Klinge [ˈkliŋə] *f* (-/-n) blade.

Klingel [ˈkliŋəl] *f* (-/-n) bell, hand-bell; '**⁓knopf** *m* bell-push; '**2n** *v/i.* (ge-, h) ring (the bell); *doorbell, etc.*: ring; *es klingelt* the doorbell is ringing; '**⁓zug** *m* bell-pull.

klingen [ˈkliŋən] *v/i.* (*irr.*, ge-, h) sound; *bell, metal, etc.*: ring; *glasses, etc.*: clink; *musical instrument*: speak.

Klini|k [ˈkliːnik] *f* (-/-en) nursing home; private hospital; clinic(al hospital); '**2sch** *adj.* clinical.

Klinke [ˈkliŋkə] *f* (-/-n) latch; (door-)handle.

Klippe [ˈklipə] *f* (-/-n) cliff; reef; crag; rock; *fig.* rock, hurdle.

klirren [ˈkliːrən] *v/i.* (ge-, h) *window-pane, chain, etc.*: rattle; *chain, swords, etc.*: clank, jangle; *keys, spurs, etc.*: jingle; *glasses, etc.*: clink, chink; *pots, etc.*: clatter; **⁓** *mit* rattle; jingle.

Klistier [kliˈstiːr] *n* (-s/-e) enema.

Kloake [kloˈaːkə] *f* (-/-n) sewer, cesspool (*a. fig.*).

Klob|en [ˈkloːbən] *m* (-s/-) ⊕ pulley, block; log; '**2ig** *adj.* clumsy (*a. fig.*).

klopfen [ˈklɔpfən] (ge-, h) **1.** *v/i.* *heart, pulse*: beat, throb; knock (*at door, etc.*); tap (*on shoulder*); pat (*on cheek*); *es klopft* there's a knock at the door; **2.** *v/t.* knock, drive (*nail, etc.*).

Klöppel [ˈklœpəl] *m* (-s/-) clapper (*of bell*); *lacemaking*: bobbin; beetle; '**⁓spitze** *f* pillow-lace, bone-lace.

Klops [klɔps] *m* (·es/-e) meat ball.

Klosett [kloˈzɛt] *n* (-s/-e, -s) lavatory, (water-)closet, W.C., toilet; **⁓papier** *n* toilet-paper.

Kloß [kloːs] *m* (-es/⁺e) earth, clay, *etc.*: clod, lump; *cookery*: dumpling.

Kloster [ˈkloːstər] *n* (-s/⁺) cloister; monastery; convent, nunnery; '**⁓bruder** *m* friar; '**⁓frau** *f* nun; '**⁓gelübde** *n* monastic vow.

Klotz [klɔts] *m* (-es/⁺e) block, log (*a. fig.*).

Klub [klup] *m* (-s/-s) club; '**⁓kamerad** *m* clubmate; '**⁓sessel** *m* lounge-chair.

Kluft [kluft] *f* **1.** (-/⁺e) gap (*a. fig.*), crack, cleft; gulf, chasm (*both a. fig.*); **2.** F (-/-en) outfit, F togs *pl.*; uniform.

klug *adj.* [kluːk] clever; wise, intelligent, sensible; prudent; shrewd; cunning; '**2heit** *f* (-/*no pl.*) cleverness; intelligence; prudence; shrewdness; good sense.

Klump|en [ˈklumpən] *m* (-s/-) lump (*of earth, dough, etc.*); clod (*of earth, etc.*); nugget (*of gold, etc.*); heap; '**⁓fuß** *m* club-foot; '**2ig** *adj.* lumpy; cloddish.

knabbern [ˈknabərn] (ge-, h) **1.** *v/t.* nibble, gnaw; **2.** *v/i.* nibble, gnaw (*an dat.* at).

Knabe [ˈknaːbə] *m* (-n/-n) boy; lad; F *alter* ⁓ F old chap.

'**Knaben|alter** *n* boyhood; '**⁓chor** *m* boys' choir; '**2haft** *adj.* boyish.

Knack [knak] *m* (-[e]s/-e) crack, snap, click; '**2en** (ge-, h) **1.** *v/i.* *wood*: crack; *fire*: crackle; click; **2.** *v/t.* crack (*nut, etc.*); F crack open (*safe*); *e-e harte Nuß zu* ⁓ *haben* have a hard nut to crack; **⁓s** [⁓s] *m* (-es/-e) *s.* Knack; F *fig.* defect; '**2sen** *v/i.* (ge-, h) *s.* knacken 1.

Knall [knal] *m* (-[e]s/-e) crack, bang (*of shot*); bang (*of explosion*); crack (*of rifle or whip*); report (*of gun*); detonation, explosion, report; '**⁓bonbon** *m, n* cracker; '**⁓effekt** *fig. m* sensation; '**2en** *v/i.* (ge-, h) *rifle, whip*: crack; *fireworks, door, etc.*: bang; *gun*: fire; *cork, etc.*: pop; *explosive, etc.*: detonate.

knapp *adj.* [knap] *clothes*: tight, close-fitting; *rations, etc.*: scanty, scarce; *style, etc.*: concise; *lead, victory, etc.*: narrow; *majority, etc.*: bare; *mit* ⁓*er Not entrinnen* have a narrow escape; ⁓ *werden* run short; '**2e** ⚒ *m* (-n/-n) miner; '**⁓halten** *v/t.* (*irr.* halten, *sep.*; -ge-, h) keep *s.o.* short; '**2heit** *f* (-/*no pl.*) scarcity, shortage; conciseness; '**~schaft** ⚒ f (-/-en) miners' society.

Knarre ['knarə] f (-/-n) rattle; F rifle, gun; '**2n** v/i. (ge-, h) creak; *voice:* grate.

knattern ['knatərn] v/i. (ge-, h) crackle; *machine-gun, etc.:* rattle; *mot.* roar.

Knäuel ['knɔʏəl] m, n (-s/-) clew, ball; *fig.* bunch, cluster.

Knauf [knauf] m (-[e]s/ue) knob, pommel (*of sword*).

Knauser ['knauzər] m (-s/-) niggard, miser, skinflint; **~ei** [~'raɪ] f (-/-en) niggardliness, miserliness; '**2ig** adj. niggardly, stingy; '**2n** v/i. (ge-, h) be stingy.

Knebel ['kne:bəl] m (-s/-) gag; '**2n** v/t. (ge-, h) gag; *fig.* muzzle (*press*).

Knecht [knɛçt] m (-[e]s/-e) servant; farm-labo(u)rer, farm-hand; slave; '**2en** v/t. (ge-, h) enslave; tyrannize; subjugate; '**~schaft** f (-/no pl.) servitude, slavery.

kneif|en ['knaɪfən] (irr., ge-, h) **1.** v/t. pinch, nip; **2.** v/i. pinch; F *fig.* back out, Am. F a. crawfish; '**2er** m (-s/-) pince-nez; '**2zange** f (e-e a pair of) pincers pl. or nippers pl.

Kneipe ['knaɪpə] f (-/-n) public house, tavern, F pub, Am. a. saloon; '**2n** v/i. (ge-, h) carouse, tipple, F booze; **~rei** f (-/-en) drinking-bout, carousal.

kneten ['kne:tən] v/t. (ge-, h) knead (*dough, etc.*); 𝔰 a. massage (*limb, etc.*).

Knick [knik] m (-[e]s/-e) *wall, etc.:* crack; *paper, etc.:* fold, crease; *path, etc.:* bend; '**2en** v/t. (ge-, h) fold, crease; bend; break. [*Knauser.*]

Knicker f ['knikər] m (-s/-) s.}

Knicks [kniks] m (-es/-e) curts(e)y; e-n ~ machen = '**2en** v/i. (ge-, h) (drop a) curts(e)y (*vor dat.* to).

Knie [kni:] n (-s/-) knee; '**2fällig** adv. on one's knees; '**2kehle** anat. f hollow of the knee; '**2n** v/i. (ge-, h) kneel, be on one's knees; '**~scheibe** anat. f knee-cap, knee-pan; '**~strumpf** m knee-length sock.

Kniff [knif] m (-[e]s/-e) crease, fold; *fig.* trick, knack; **2.** *pp. of* kneifen; **2(e)lig** adj. ['~(ə)liç] tricky; intricate.

knipsen ['knipsən] (ge-, h) **1.** v/t.

clip, punch (*ticket, etc.*); F *phot.* take a snapshot of, snap; **2.** F *phot.* v/i. take snapshots.

Knirps [knirps] m (-es/-e) little man; little chap, F nipper; '**2ig** adj. very small.

knirschen ['knirʃən] v/i. (ge-, h) gravel, snow, etc.: crunch, grind; *teeth, etc.:* grate; *mit den Zähnen* ~ grind or gnash one's teeth.

knistern ['knistərn] v/i. (ge-, h) woodfire, etc.: crackle; *dry leaves, silk, etc.:* rustle.

Knoblauch ♣ ['kno:plaʊx] m (-[e]s/no pl.) garlic.

Knöchel anat. ['knœçəl] m (-s/-) knuckle; ankle.

Knoch|en anat. ['knɔxən] m (-s/-) bone; '**~enbruch** m fracture (of a bone); '**2ig** adj. bony.

Knödel ['knø:dəl] m (-s/-) dumpling.

Knolle ♣ ['knɔlə] f (-/-n) tuber; bulb.

Knopf [knɔpf] m (-[e]s/ue) button.

knöpfen ['knœpfən] v/t. (ge-, h) button.

'**Knopfloch** n buttonhole.

Knorpel ['knɔrpəl] m (-s/-) cartilage, gristle.

Knorr|en ['knɔrən] m (-s/-) knot, knag, gnarl; '**2ig** adj. gnarled, knotty.

Knospe ♣ ['knɔspə] f (-/-n) bud; '**2n** v/i. (ge-, h) (be in) bud.

Knot|en ['kno:tən] **1.** m (-s/-) knot (a. *fig.*, ♪); **2.** v/t. (ge-, h) knot; '**~enpunkt** m 🚉 junction; intersection; '**2ig** adj. knotty.

Knuff F [knuf] m (-[e]s/ue) poke, cuff, nudge; '**2en** F v/t. (ge-, h) poke, cuff, nudge.

knülle|n ['knylən] v/t. and v/i. (ge-, h) crease, crumple; '**2r** F m (-s/-) hit.

knüpfen ['knypfən] v/t. (ge-, h) make, tie (*knot, etc.*); make (*net*); knot (*carpet, etc.*); tie (*shoe-lace, etc.*); strike up (*friendship, etc.*); attach (*condition, etc.*) (an acc. to).

Knüppel ['knypəl] m (-s/-) cudgel.

knurren ['knurən] v/i. (ge-, h) growl, snarl; *fig.* grumble (*über acc.* at, over, about); *stomach:* rumble.

knusp(e)rig adj. ['knusp(ə)riç] crisp, crunchy.

K

Knute ['knuːtə] f (-/-n) knout.

Knüttel ['knʏtəl] m (-s/-) cudgel.

Kobold ['koːbɔlt] m (-[e]s/-e) (hob-) goblin, imp.

Koch [kɔx] m (-[e]s/-e) cook; '**buch** n cookery-book, Am. cookbook; '2**en** (ge-, h) **1.** v/t. boil (water, egg, fish, etc.); cook (meat, vegetables, etc.) (by boiling); make (coffee, tea, etc.); **2.** v/i. water, etc.: boil (a. fig.); do the cooking; be a (good, etc.) cook; '**er** m (-s/-) cooker.

Köcher ['kœçər] m (-s/-) quiver.

'**Koch|kiste** f haybox; '**löffel** m wooden spoon; '**nische** f kitchenette; '**salz** n common salt; '**topf** m pot, saucepan.

Köder ['køːdər] m (-s/-) bait (a. fig.); lure (a. fig.); '2n v/t. (ge-, h) bait; lure; fig. a. decoy.

Kodex ['koːdɛks] m (-es, -/-e, Kodizes) code.

Koffer ['kɔfər] m (-s/-) (suit)case; trunk; '**radio** n portable radio (set).

Kognak ['kɔnjak] m (-s/-s, ✕ -e) French brandy, cognac.

Kohl ♀ [koːl] m (-[e]s/-e) cabbage.

Kohle ['koːlə] f (-/-n) coal; charcoal; ⚡ carbon; wie auf (glühenden) ∼n sitzen be on tenterhooks.

'**Kohlen|bergwerk** n coal-mine, coal-pit, colliery; '**eimer** m coalscuttle; '**händler** m coalmerchant; '**kasten** m coal-box; '**revier** ✕ n coal-district; '**säure** ♠ f carbonic acid; '**stoff** ♠ m carbon.

'**Kohle|papier** n carbon paper; '**zeichnung** f charcoal-drawing.

'**Kohl|kopf** ♀ m (head of) cabbage; '**rübe** ♀ f Swedish turnip.

Koje ♣ ['koːjə] f (-/-n) berth, bunk.

Kokain [koka'iːn] n (-s/no pl.) cocaine, sl. coke, snow.

kokett adj. [ko'kɛt] coquettish; 2**erie** [∼ə'riː] f (-/-n) coquetry, coquettishness; **ieren** [∼'tiːrən] v/i. (no -ge-, h) coquet, flirt (mit with; a. fig.).

Kokosnuß ♀ ['koːkɔs-] f coconut.

Koks [koːks] m (-es/-e) coke.

Kolben ['kɔlbən] m (-s/-) butt (of rifle); ⊕ piston; '**stange** f piston-rod.

Kolchose [kɔl'çoːzə] f (-/-n) collective farm, kolkhoz.

Kolleg univ. [kɔ'leːk] n (-s/-s, -ien course of lectures; **e** [∼gə] n (-n/-n) colleague; **ium** [∼gjum] (-s/Kollegien) council, board; teaching staff.

Kollekt|e eccl. [kɔ'lɛktə] f (-/-n) collection; **ion** ✝ [∼'tsjoːn] f (-/-en collection, range.

Koller ['kɔlər] m (-s/-) vet. staggers pl.; F fig. rage, tantrum; '2n v/i **1.** (h) turkey-cock: gobble; pigeon coo; bowels: rumble; vet. have the staggers; **2.** (sein) ball, tears, etc.: roll.

kolli|dieren [kɔli'diːrən] v/i. (no -ge-, sein) collide; fig. clash; 2**sion** [∼'zjoːn] f (-/-en) collision; fig. clash, conflict.

Kölnischwasser ['kœlniʃ-] n eau-de-Cologne.

Kolonialwaren [kolo'njaː-] f/pl. groceries pl.; **händler** m grocer; **handlung** f grocer's (shop), Am. grocery.

Kolon|ie [kolo'niː] f (-/-n) colony; 2**isieren** [∼i'ziːrən] v/t. (no -ge-, h) colonize.

Kolonne [ko'lɔnə] f (-/-n) column; convoy; gang (of workers, etc.).

kolorieren [kolo'riːrən] v/t. (no -ge-, h) colo(u)r.

Koloß [ko'lɔs] m (Kolosses/Kolosse) colossus; 2**ssal** adj. [∼'saːl] colossal, huge (both a. fig.).

Kombin|ation [kɔmbina'tsjoːn] f (-/-en) combination; overall; ✕ flying-suit; football, etc.: combined attack; 2**ieren** [∼'niːrən] (no -ge-, h) **1.** v/t. combine; **2.** v/i. reason, deduce; football, etc.: combine, move.

Kombüse ♣ [kɔm'byːzə] f (-/-n) galley, caboose.   [comet.]

Komet ast. [ko'meːt] m (-en/-en)

Komfort [kɔm'foːr] m (-s/no pl.) comfort; 2**abel** adj. [∼ər'taːbəl] comfortable.

Komik ['koːmik] f (-/no pl.) humo(u)r, fun(niness); '**er** m (-s/-) comic actor, comedian.

komisch adj. ['koːmiʃ] comic(al), funny; fig. funny, odd, queer.

Komitee [komi'teː] n (-s/-s) committee.

Kommand|ant ✕ [kɔman'dant] m (-en/-en), **eur** ✕ [∼'døːr] m (-s/-e) commander, commanding officer; 2**ieren** [∼'diːrən] (no -ge-, h) **1.** v/i.

order, command, be in command; **2.** v/t. ✕ command, be in command of; order; **~itgesellschaft** ✝ [~'di:t-] f limited partnership; **~o** [~'mando] n (-s/-s) ✕ command, order; order(s pl.), directive(s pl.); ✕ detachment; **~obrücke** ⚓ f navigating bridge.

kommen ['kɔmən] v/i. (irr., ge-, sein) come; arrive; ~ lassen send for s.o.; order s.th.; et. ~ sehen foresee; an die Reihe ~ it is one's turn; ~ auf (acc.) think of, hit upon; remember; zu dem Schluß ~, daß decide that; hinter et. ~ find s.th. out; um et. ~ lose s.th.; zu et. ~ come by s.th.; wieder zu sich ~ come round or to; wie ~ Sie dazu! how dare you!

Komment|ar [kɔmɛn'tɑːr] m (-s/-e) commentary, comment; **~ator** [~tɔr] m (-s/-en) commentator; **~ieren** [~'tiːrən] v/t. (no -ge-, h) comment on.

Kommissar [kɔmɪ'saːr] m (-s/-e) commissioner; superintendent; pol. commissar.

Kommißbrot F [kɔ'mɪs-] n army or ration bread, Am. a. G.I. bread.

Kommission [kɔmɪ'sjoːn] f (-/-en) commission (a. ✝); committee; **~är** ✝ [~o'nɛːr] m (-s/-e) commission agent.

Kommode [kɔ'moːdə] f (-/-n) chest of drawers, Am. bureau.

Kommunis|mus pol. [kɔmu'nɪsmus] m (-/no pl.) communism; **~t** m (-en/-en) communist; **2tisch** adj. communist(ic).

Komöd|iant [kɔmø'djant] m (-en/-en) comedian; fig. play-actor; **~ie** [~'møːdjə] f (-/-n) comedy; ~ spielen play-act.

Kompagnon ✝ [kɔmpan'jɔː] m (-s/-s) (business-)partner, associate.

Kompanie ✕ [kɔmpa'niː] f (-/-n) company.

Kompaß ['kɔmpas] m (Kompasses/ Kompasse) compass.   [petent.)

kompetent adj. [kɔmpe'tɛnt] com-]

komplett adj. [kɔm'plɛt] complete.

Komplex [kɔm'plɛks] m (-es/-e) complex (a. psych.); block (of houses).

Kompliment [kɔmpli'mɛnt] n (-[e]s/-e) compliment.

Komplize [kɔm'pliːtsə] m (-n/-n) accomplice.

komplizier|en [kɔmpli'tsiːrən] v/t.

(no -ge-, h) complicate; **~t** adj. machine, etc.: complicated; argument, situation, etc.: complex; **~er Bruch** ✚ compound fracture.

Komplott [kɔm'plɔt] n (-[e]s/-e) plot, conspiracy.

kompo|nieren ♪ [kɔmpo'niːrən] v/t. and v/i. (no -ge-, h) compose; **2nist** m (-en/-en) composer; **2sition** [~zi'tsjoːn] f (-/-en) composition.

Kompott [kɔm'pɔt] n (-[e]s/-e) compote, stewed fruit, Am. a. sauce.

komprimieren [kɔmpri'miːrən] v/t. (no -ge-, h) compress.

Kompromi|ß [kɔmpro'mɪs] m (Kompromisses/Kompromisse) compromise; **2los** adj. uncompromising; **2ttieren** [~'tiːrən] v/t. (no -ge-, h) compromise.

Kondens|ator [kɔndɛn'zaːtɔr] m (-s/-en) ⚡ capacitor, condenser (a. ⚛); **2ieren** [~'ziːrən] v/t. (no -ge-, h) condense.

Kondens|milch [kɔn'dɛns-] f evaporated milk; **~streifen** ✈ m condensation or vapo(u)r trail; **~wasser** n water of condensation.

Konditor [kɔn'diːtɔr] m (-s/-en) confectioner, pastry-cook; **~ei** [~ito'raɪ] f (-/-en) confectionery, confectioner's (shop); **~eiwaren** f/pl. confectionery.

Konfekt [kɔn'fɛkt] n (-[e]s/-e) sweets pl., sweetmeat, Am. a. soft candy; chocolates pl.

Konfektion [kɔnfɛk'tsjoːn] f (-/-en) (manufacture of) ready-made clothing; **~sanzug** [kɔnfɛk'tsjoːns?-] m ready-made suit; **~sgeschäft** n ready-made clothes shop.

Konfer|enz [kɔnfe'rɛnts] f (-/-en) conference; **2ieren** [~'riːrən] v/i. (no -ge-, h) confer (über acc. on).

Konfession [kɔnfe'sjoːn] f (-/-en) confession, creed; denomination; **2ell** adj. [~o'nɛl] confessional, denominational; **~sschule** [~'sjoːns-] f denominational school.

Konfirm|and eccl. [kɔnfɪr'mant] m (-en/-en) candidate for confirmation, confirmee; **~ation** [~'tsjoːn] f (-/-en) confirmation; **2ieren** [~'miːrən] v/t. (no -ge-, h) confirm.

konfiszieren ⚖ [kɔnfɪs'tsiːrən] v/t. (no -ge-, h) confiscate, seize.

Konfitüre [kɔnfi'tyːrə] f (-/-n) preserve(s pl.), (whole-fruit) jam.

Konflikt [kɔn'flikt] *m* (-[e]s/-e) conflict. [*mit* agree *or* concur with.]

konform *adv.* [kɔn'fɔrm]: ~ *gehen*|

konfrontieren [kɔnfrɔn'tiːrən] *v/t.* (*no* -ge-, *h*) confront (*mit* with).

konfus *adj.* [kɔn'fuːs] *p., a. ideas:* muddled; *p.* muddle-headed.

Kongreß [kɔn'grɛs] *m* (Kongresses/ Kongresse) congress; *Am. parl.* Congress; **~halle** *f* congress hall.

König ['køːniç] *m* (-s/-e) king; **2lich** *adj.* ['~k-] royal; regal; **~reich** ['~k-] *n* kingdom; **~swürde** ['~ks-] *f* royal dignity, kingship; **'~tum** *n* (-s/⁻er) monarchy; kingship.

Konjug|ation [kɔnjuga'tsjoːn] *f* (-/-en); **2ieren** [~'giːrən] *v/t.* (*no* -ge-, *h*) conjugate.

Konjunkt|iv *gr.* ['kɔnjuŋktiːf] *m* (-s/-e) subjunctive (mood); **~ur** ✝ [~'tuːr] *f* (-/-en) trade *or* business cycle; economic *or* business situation.

konkret *adj.* [kɔn'kreːt] concrete.

Konkurrent [kɔnku'rɛnt] *m* (-en/ -en) competitor, rival.

Konkurrenz [kɔnku'rɛnts] *f* (-/-en) competition; competitors *pl.*, rivals *pl.*; *sports:* event; **2fähig** *adj.* able to compete; competitive; **~geschäft** *n* rival business *or* firm; **~kampf** *m* competition.

konkur'rieren *v/i.* (*no* -ge-, *h*) compete (*mit* with; *um* for).

Konkurs ✝, ⚖ [kɔn'kurs] *m* (-es/-e) bankruptcy, insolvency; failure; ~ *anmelden* file a petition in bankruptcy; *in* ~ *gehen or geraten* become insolvent, go bankrupt; **~erklärung** ⚖ *f* declaration of insolvency; **~masse** ⚖ *f* bankrupt's estate; **~verfahren** ⚖ *n* bankruptcy proceedings *pl.*; **~verwalter** ⚖ *m* trustee in bankruptcy; liquidator.

können ['kœnən] **1.** *v/i.* (*irr.*, ge-, *h*): *ich kann nicht* I can't, I am not able to; **2.** *v/t.* (*irr.*, ge-, *h*) know, understand; *e-e Sprache ~* know a language; have command of a language; **3.** *v/aux.* (*irr.*, *no* -ge-, *h*) be able to *inf.*, be capable of *ger.*; be allowed *or* permitted to *inf.*; *es kann sein* it may be; *du kannst hingehen* you may go there; *er kann schwimmen* he can swim, he knows how to swim; **4.** **2** *n* (-s/*no pl.*) ability; skill; proficiency.

Konnossement ✝ [kɔnɔsə'mɛnt] (-[e]s/-e) bill of lading.

konnte ['kɔntə] *pret. of* können.

konsequen|t *adj.* [kɔnze'kvɛnt] consistent; **2z** [~ts] *f* (-/-en) consistency; consequence; *die ~en ziehen d|* the only thing one can.

konservativ *adj.* [kɔnzerva'tiːf] conservative.

Konserven [kɔn'zervən] *f/pl.* tinned *or Am.* canned foods *pl.*; **~büchse** *f*, **~dose** *f* tin, *Am.* can; **~fabrik** *f* tinning factory, *esp. Am.* cannery; **2ieren** [kɔnzer'viːrən] *v/t.* (*no* -ge-, *h*) preserve.

Konsonant *gr.* [kɔnzo'nant] *m* (-en|| ~ consonant.

Konsortium ✝ [kɔn'zɔrtsjum] *n* (-s/Konsortien) syndicate.

konstruieren [kɔnstru'iːrən] *v/t* (*no* -ge-, *h*) *gr.* construe; ⊕: construct; design.

Konstruk|teur ⊕ [kɔnstruk'tøːr] *m* (-s/-e) designer; **~tion** ⊕ [~'tsjoːn] *f* (-/-en) construction; **~'tionsfehler** ⊕ *m* constructional defect.

Konsul *pol.* ['kɔnzul] *m* (-s/-n) consul; **~at** *pol.* [~'laːt] *n* (-[e]s/-e) consulate; **2'tieren** *v/t.* (*no* -ge-, *h*) consult, seek *s.o.*'s advice.

Konsum [kɔn'zuːm] *m* **1.** (-s/*no pl.*) consumption; **2.** (-s/-s) co-operative shop, *Am.* co-operative store, F co-op; **3.** (-s/*no pl.*) consumers' co-operative society, F co-op; **~ent** [~u'mɛnt] *m* (-en/-en) consumer; **2ieren** [~u'miːrən] *v/t.* (*no* -ge-, *h*) consume; **~verein** *m s.* Konsum 3.

Kontakt [kɔn'takt] *m* (-[e]s/-e) contact (*a.* ⚡); *in* ~ *stehen mit* be in contact *or* touch with.

Kontinent ['kɔntinɛnt] *m* (-[e]s/-e) continent.

Kontingent [kɔntiŋ'gɛnt] *n* (-[e]s/ -e) ✕ contingent, quota (*a.* ✝).

Konto ✝ ['kɔnto] *n* (-s/Konten, Kontos, Konti) account; **~auszug** ✝ *m* statement of account; **~korrentkonto** ✝ [~kɔ'rɛnt-] *n* current account.

Kontor [kɔn'toːr] *n* (-s/-e) office; **~ist** [~o'rist] *m* (-en/-en) clerk.

Kontrast [kɔn'trast] *m* (-es/-e) contrast.

Kontroll|e [kɔn'trɔlə] *f* (-/-n) control; supervision; check; **2ieren** [~'liːrən] *v/t.* (*no* -ge-, *h*) control; supervise; check.

Kontroverse [kɔntro'vɛrzə] f (-/-n) controversy.

konventionell adj. [kɔnvɛntsjo'nɛl] conventional.

Konversation [kɔnvɛrza'tsjoːn] f (-/-en) conversation; **~slexikon** n encyclop(a)edia.

Konzentr|ation [kɔntsɛntra'tsjoːn] f (-/-en) concentration; **2ieren** [~'triːrən] v/t. (no -ge-, h) concentrate, focus (attention, etc.) (auf acc. on); sich ~ concentrate (auf acc. on).

Konzern ✝ [kɔn'tsɛrn] m (-s/-e) combine, group.

Konzert ♪ [kɔn'tsɛrt] n (-[e]s/-e) concert; recital; concerto; **~saal** ♪ m concert-hall.

Konzession [kɔntsɛ'sjoːn] f (-/-en) concession; licen|ce, Am. -se; **2ie-ren** [~o'niːrən] v/t. (no -ge-, h) license.

Kopf [kɔpf] m (-[e]s/⸚e) head; top; brains pl.; pipe: bowl; ein fähiger ~ a clever fellow; ~ hoch! chin up!; j-m über den ~ wachsen outgrow s.o.; fig. get beyond s.o.; **~arbeit** f brain-work; **~bahnhof** 🚂 m terminus, Am. terminal; **~bedeckung** f headgear, headwear.

köpfen ['kœpfən] v/t. (ge-, h) behead, decapitate; football: head (ball).

Kopf|ende n head; **~hörer** m headphone, headset; **~kissen** n pillow; **2los** adj. headless; fig. confused; **~nicken** n (-s/no pl.) nod; **~rechnen** n (-s/no pl.) mental arithmetic; **~salat** m cabbage-lettuce; **~schmerzen** m/pl. headache; **~sprung** m header; **~tuch** n scarf; **2über** adv. head first, headlong; **~weh** n (-[e]s/-e) s. Kopfschmerzen; **~zerbrechen** n (-s/no pl.): j-m ~ machen puzzle s.o.

Kopie [ko'piː] f(-/-n) copy; duplicate; phot., film: print; **~rstift** m indelible pencil.

Koppel ['kɔpəl] 1. f (-/-n) hounds: couple; horses: string; paddock; 2. ⚔ n (-s/-) belt; **2n** v/t. (ge-, h) couple (a. ⊕, ♪).

Koralle [ko'ralə] f (-/-n) coral; **~n-fischer** m coral-fisher.

Korb [kɔrp] m (-[e]s/⸚e) basket; fig. refusal; Hahn im ~ cock of the walk; **~möbel** n/pl. wicker furniture.

Kordel ['kɔrdəl] f (-/-n) string,

Korinthe [ko'rintə] f (-/-n) currant.

Kork [kɔrk] m (-[e]s/-e), **~en** m (-s/-) cork; **~(en)zieher** m (-s/-) corkscrew.

Korn [kɔrn] 1. n (-[e]s/⸚er) seed; grain; 2. n (-[e]s/-e) corn, cereals pl.; 3. n (-[e]s/⚔ -e) front sight; 4. F m (-[e]s/-) (German) corn whisky.

körnig adj. ['kœrniç] granular; in compounds: ...-grained.

Körper ['kœrpər] m (-s/-) body (a. phys., 🔷 m); 2 solid; **~bau** m build, physique; **2behindert** adj. ['~bə-hindərt] (physically) disabled, handicapped; **~beschaffenheit** f constitution, physique; **~fülle** f corpulence; **~geruch** m body-odo(u)r; **~größe** f stature; **~kraft** f physical strength; **2lich** adj. physical; corporal; bodily; **~pflege** f care of the body, hygiene; **~schaft** f (-/-en) body; ☆ body (corporate), corporation; **~verletzung** ☆ f bodily harm, physical injury.

korrekt adj. [ko'rɛkt] correct; **2or** [~ɔr] m (-s/-en) (proof-)reader; **2ur** [~'tuːr] f (-/-en) correction; **2ur-bogen** m proof-sheet.

Korrespond|ent [kɔrɛspɔn'dɛnt] m (-en/-en) correspondent; **~enz** [~ts] f (-/-en) correspondence; **2ieren** [~'diːrən] v/i. (no -ge-, h) correspond (mit with).

korrigieren [kɔri'giːrən] v/t. (no -ge-, h) correct.

Korsett [kɔr'zɛt] n (-[e]s/-e, -s) corset, stays pl.

Kosename ['koːzə-] m pet name.

Kosmetik [kɔs'meːtik] f (-/no pl.) beauty culture; **~erin** f (-/-nen) beautician, cosmetician.

Kost [kɔst] f (-/no pl.) food, fare; board; diet; **2bar** adj. present, etc.: costly, expensive; health, time, etc.: valuable; mineral, etc.: precious.

kosten¹ v/t. (ge-, h) taste, try, sample.

Kosten² 1. pl. cost(s pl.); expense(s pl.), charges pl.; auf ~ (gen.) at the expense of s.o.; 2. 2 v/t. (ge-, h) cost; take, require (time, etc.); **~an-schlag** m estimate, tender; **2frei** 1. adj. free; 2. adv. free of charge; **2los** s. kostenfrei.

Kost|gänger ['kɔstgɛŋər] m (-s/-) boarder; **~geld** n board-wages pl.

köstlich adj. ['kœstliç] delicious.

¹Kost|probe *f* taste, sample (*a. fig.*); **²spielig** *adj.* [ˈ~ʃpiːliç] expensive, costly.

Kostüm [kɔsˈtyːm] *n* (-s/-e) costume, dress; suit; **~fest** *n* fancy-dress ball.

Kot [koːt] *m* (-[e]s/*no pl.*) mud, mire; excrement.

Kotelett [kot(ə)ˈlet] *n* (-[e]s/-s, **~** -e) pork, veal, lamb: cutlet; pork, veal, mutton: chop; **~en** *pl.* sidewhiskers *pl.*, *Am. a.* sideburns *pl.*

¹Kot|flügel *mot.* *m* mudguard, *Am. a.* fender; **²ig** *adj.* muddy, miry.

Krabbe *zo.* [ˈkrabə] *f* (-/-n) shrimp; crab.

krabbeln [ˈkrabəln] *v/i.* (ge-, sein) crawl.

Krach [krax] *m* (-[e]s/-e, -s) crack, crash (*a.* ✝); quarrel, *sl.* bust-up; F row; **~** *machen* kick up a row; **²en** *v/i.* (ge-) **1.** (*h*) thunder: crash; cannon: roar, thunder; **2.** (sein) crash (*a.* ✝), smash.

krächzen [ˈkrɛçtsən] *v/t. and v/i.* (ge-, *h*) croak.

Kraft [kraft] **1.** *f* (-/⁓e) strength; force (*a.* ✕); power (*a.* ✞, ⊕); energy; vigo(u)r; efficacy; in **~** sein (setzen, treten) be in (put into, come into) operation *or* force; außer **~** setzen repeal, abolish (*law*). **2.** **⁓** *prp.* (*gen.*) by virtue of; **~anlage** *f* power plant; **~brühe** *f* beef tea; **~fahrer** *m* driver, motorist; **~fahrzeug** *n* motor vehicle.

kräftig *adj.* [ˈkreftiç] strong (*a. fig.*), powerful; *fig.* nutritious, rich; **~en** [ˈ~gən] (ge-, *h*) **1.** *v/t.* strengthen; **2.** *v/i.* give strength.

¹kraft|los *adj.* powerless, feeble; weak; **²probe** *f* trial of strength; **²rad** *n* motor cycle; **²stoff** *mot.* *m* fuel; **~voll** *adj.* powerful (*a. fig.*); **²wagen** *m* motor vehicle; **²werk** ✞ *n* power station.

Kragen [ˈkraːgən] *m* (-s/-) collar; **~knopf** *m* collar-stud, *Am.* collar button.

Krähe *orn.* [ˈkreːə] *f* (-/-n) crow; **²n** *v/i.* (ge-, *h*) crow.

Kralle [ˈkralə] *f* (-/-n) claw (*a. fig.*); talon, clutch.

Kram [kraːm] *m* (-[e]s/*no pl.*) stuff, odds and ends *pl.*; *fig.* affairs *pl.*, business.

Krämer [ˈkreːmər] *m* (-s/-) shop-keeper.

Krampf ✐ [krampf] *m* (-[e]s/⁓e) cramp; spasm, convulsion; **~ader** ✐ *f* varicose vein; **²haft** *adj.* spasmodic, convulsive; *laugh*: forced.

Kran ⊕ [kraːn] *m* (-[e]s/⁓e, -e) crane.

krank *adj.* [kraŋk] sick; *organ, etc.*: diseased; **~** sein *p.* be ill, *esp. Am.* be sick; *animal*: be sick *or* ill; **~** werden *p.* fall ill *or esp. Am.* sick; *animal*: fall sick; **²e** *m, f* (-n/-n) sick person, patient, invalid.

kränkeln [ˈkreŋkəln] *v/i.* (ge-, *h*) sickly, be in poor health.

kranken *fig.* *v/i.* (ge-, *h*) suffer (*an dat.* from).

kränken [ˈkreŋkən] *v/t.* (ge-, *h*) offend, injure; wound *or* hurt *s.o.'s* feelings; sich **~** feel hurt (*über acc.* at, about).

¹Kranken|bett *n* sick-bed; **~geld** *n* sick-benefit; **~haus** *n* hospital; **~kasse** *f* health insurance (fund); **~kost** *f* invalid diet; **~lager** *n* s. Krankenbett; **~pflege** *f* nursing; **~pfleger** *m* male nurse; **~schein** *m* medical certificate; **~schwester** *f* (sick-)nurse; **~versicherung** *f* health *or* sickness insurance; **~wagen** *m* ambulance; **~zimmer** *n* sick-room.

¹krank|haft *adj.* morbid, pathological; **²heit** *f* (-/-en) illness, sickness; disease.

Krankheits|erreger ✐ *m* pathogenic agent; **~erscheinung** *f* symptom (*a. fig.*).

kränklich *adj.* sickly, ailing.

Kränkung *f* (-/-en) insult, offen|ce, *Am.* -se.

Kranz [krants] *m* (-es/⁓e) wreath; garland.

Kränzchen *fig.* [ˈkrentsçən] *n* (-s/-) tea-party, F hen-party.

kraß *adj.* [kras] crass, gross.

kratzen [ˈkratsən] (ge-, *h*) **1.** *v/i.* scratch; **2.** *v/t.* scratch; sich **~** scratch (o.s.).

kraulen [ˈkraulən] (ge-) **1.** *v/t.* (*h*) scratch gently; **2.** *v/i.* (sein) *sports*: crawl.

kraus *adj.* [kraus] curly, curled; crisp; frizzy; *die Stirn* **~** *ziehen* knit one's brow; **²e** *f* (-/-en) ruff(le), frill.

kräuseln [ˈkrɔyzəln] *v/t.* (ge-, *h*) curl, crimp (*hair, etc.*); pucker *(lips)*; *sich ~ hair:* curl; *waves, etc.:* ruffle; *smoke:* curl *or* wreath up.

Kraut ♀ [kraut] *n* **1.** (-[e]s/⁻er) plant; herb; **2.** (-[e]s/*no pl.*) tops *pl.*; cabbage; weed.

Krawall [kra'val] *m* -[e]s/-e) riot; shindy, F row, *sl.* rumpus.

Krawatte [kra'vatə] *f* (-/-n) (neck-)tie.

Kreatur [krea'tu:r] *f* (-/-en) creature.

Krebs [kre:ps] *m* (-es/-e) *zo.* cray-fish, *Am. a.* crawfish; *ast.* Cancer, Crab; ♀⁸ cancer; *~e pl.* ♀ returns *pl.*

Kredit ♀ [kre'di:t] *m* (-[e]s/-e) cred-it; *auf ~* on credit; **Qfähig** ♀ *adj.* credit-worthy.

Kreide ['kraɪdə] *f* (-/-n) chalk; *paint.* crayon.

Kreis [kraɪs] *m* (-es/-e) circle *(a. fig.)*; *ast.* orbit; ⚡ circuit; district, *Am.* county; *fig.:* sphere, field; range.

kreischen ['kraɪʃən] (ge-, h) **1.** *v/i.* screech, scream; squeal, shriek; *circular saw, etc.:* grate (on the ear); **2.** *v/t.* shriek, screech *(insult, etc.).*

Kreisel ['kraɪzəl] *m* (-s/-) (whip-ping-)top; **~kompaß** *m* gyro-com-pass.

kreisen ['kraɪzən] *v/i.* (ge-, h) (move in a) circle; revolve, rotate; ⚡, *bird:* circle; *bird:* wheel; *blood, money:* circulate.

kreis|förmig *adj.* ['kraɪsfœrmiç] circular; **Qlauf** *m physiol., money, etc.:* circulation; *business, trade:* cycle; **Qlaufstörungen** ♀ *f/pl.* circulatory trouble; **~rund** *adj.* circular; **Qsäge** ⊕ *f* circular saw, *Am. a.* buzz saw; **Qverkehr** *m* roundabout (traffic).

Krempe ['krempə] *f* (-/-n) brim *(of hat).*

Krempel F ['krempəl] *m* (-s/*no pl.*) rubbish, stuff, lumber.

krepieren [kre'pi:rən] *v/i.* (*no ge-,* sein) *shell:* burst, explode; *sl.* kick the bucket, peg *or* snuff out; *ani-mal:* die, perish.

Krepp [krep] *m* (-s/-s, -e) crêpe; crape; **~apier** ['krep|api:r] *n* crêpe paper; **'~sohle** *f* crêpe(-rubber) sole.

Kreuz [krɔʏts] **1.** *n* (-es/-e) cross *(a. fig.)*; crucifix; *anat.* small of the back; ♟⁸ sacral region; *cards:* club(s *pl.*); ♪ sharp; *zu ~(e) kriechen* eat

humble pie; **2.** ♀ *adv.:* *~ und quer* in all directions; criss-cross.

'kreuzen (ge-, h) **1.** *v/t.* cross, fold *(arms, etc.)*; ♀, *zo.* cross(-breed), hybridize; *sich ~ roads:* cross, in-tersect; *plans, etc.:* clash; **2.** ⚓ *v/i.* cruise.

'Kreuzer ⚓ *m* (-s/-) cruiser.

'Kreuz|fahrer *hist. m* crusader; **'~fahrt** *f hist.* crusade; ⚓ cruise; **'~feuer** *n* ✕ cross-fire *(a. fig.).* **Qigen** ['~gən] *v/t.* (ge-, h) crucify; **~igung** ['~iguŋ] *f* (-/-en) cruci-fixion; **'~otter** *zo. f* common viper; **'~ritter** *hist. m* knight of the Cross; **'~schmerzen** *m/pl.* back ache; **'~spinne** *zo. f* garden- *or* cross-spi-der; **'~ung** *f* (-/-en) ♀⁸, roads, *etc.:* crossing, intersection; *roads:* cross-roads; ♀, *zo.* cross-breeding, hy-bridization; **'~verhör** ♈⁸ *n* cross-examination; *ins ~ nehmen* cross-examine; **'Qweise** *adv.* crosswise, crossways; **'~worträtsel** *n* cross-word (puzzle); **'~zug** *hist. m* crusade.

kriech|en ['kri:çən] *v/i.* (*irr.,* ge-, sein) creep, crawl; *fig.* cringe (*vor dat.* to, before); **Qer** *contp. m* (-s/-) toady; **Qerei** *contp.* [~'raɪ] *f* (-/-en) toadyism.

Krieg [kri:k] *m* (-[e]s/-e) war; *im ~* at war; *s. führen.*

kriegen F ['kri:gən] *v/t.* (ge-, h) catch, seize; get.

Krieg|er ['kri:gər] *m* (-s/-) warrior; **'~erdenkmal** *n* war memorial; **'Qerisch** *adj.* warlike; militant; **'Qführend** *adj.* belligerent; **'~füh-rung** *f* warfare.

'Kriegs|beil *fig. n: das ~ begraben* bury the hatchet; **Qbeschädigt** *adj.* ['~bəʃə:diçt] war-disabled; **'~be-schädigte** *m* (-n/-n) disabled ex-serviceman; **'~dienst** ✕ *m* war service; **'~dienstverweigerer** ✕ *m* (-s/-) conscientious objector; **'~er-klärung** *f* declaration of war; **'~-flotte** *f* naval force; **'~gefangene** *m* prisoner of war; **'~gefangen-schaft** ✕ *f* captivity; **'~gericht** ♈⁸ *n* court martial; **'~gewinnler** ['~gəvinlər] *m* (-s/-) war profiteer; **'~hafen** *m* naval port; **'~kamerad** *m* wartime comrade; **'~list** *f* strat-agem; **'~macht** *f* military forces *pl.*; **'~minister** *hist. m* minister of war; Secretary of State for War,

Am. Secretary of War; '**~ministe-rium** *hist. n* ministry of war; War Office, *Am.* War Department; '**~rat** *m* council of war; '**~schauplatz** ✕ *m* theat|re *or Am.* -er of war; '**~schiff** *n* warship; '**~schule** *f* military academy; '**~teilnehmer** *m* combatant; ex-serviceman, *Am.* veteran; '**~treiber** *m* (-s/-) war-monger; '**~verbrecher** *m* war crim-inal; '**~zug** *m* (military) expedition, campaign.

Kriminal|beamte [krimiˈnɑːl-] *m* criminal investigator, *Am.* plain-clothes man; **~film** *m* crime film; thriller; **~polizei** *f* criminal inves-tigation department, **~roman** *m* detective *or* crime novel, thriller, *sl.* whodun(n)it.

kriminell *adj.* [krimiˈnɛl] criminal; Qe *m* (-n/-n) criminal.

Krippe [ˈkrɪpə] *f* (-/-n) crib, man-ger; crèche.

Krise [ˈkriːzə] *f* (-/-n) crisis.

Kristall [krɪsˈtal] **1.** *m* (-s/-e) crystal; **2.** *n* (-s/*no pl.*) crystal(-glass); Qisie-ren [~ˈiːzirən] *v/i.* and *v/refl.* (no -ge-, *h*) crystallize.

Kriti|k [kriˈtiːk] *f* (-/-en) criticism; ♪, *thea.*, etc.: review, criticism; F *unter aller ~* beneath contempt; *~ üben an* (*dat.*) *s.* kritisieren; **~ker** [ˈkriːtikər] *m* (-s/-) critic; books: re-viewer; Qsch *adj.* [ˈkriːtiʃ] critical (*gegenüber of*); Qsieren [kritiˈziː-rən] *v/t.* (no -ge-, *h*) criticize; re-view (*book*).

kritt|eln [ˈkritəln] *v/t.* (ge-, *h*) find fault (*an dat.* with), cavil (at); Qler [ˈ~lər] *m* (-s/-) fault-finder, caviller.

Kritzel|ei [krɪtsəˈlaɪ] *f* (-/-en) scrawl(ing), scribble, scribbling; Qn *v/t.* and *v/i.* (ge-, *h*) scrawl, scribble.

kroch [krɔx] *pret. of* kriechen.

Krokodil *zo.* [krokoˈdiːl] *n* (-s/-e) crocodile.

Krone [ˈkroːnə] *f* (-/-n) crown; coronet (*of duke, earl, etc.*).

krönen [ˈkrøːnən] *v/t.* (ge-, *h*) crown (*zum König* king) (*a. fig.*).

'**Kron|leuchter** *m* chandelier; lust|re, *Am.* -er; electrolier; '**~prinz** *m* crown prince; '**~prinzes-sin** *f* crown princess.

'**Krönung** *f* (-/-en) coronation, crowning; *fig.* climax, culmination.

'**Kronzeuge** ⚖ *m* chief witness;

King's evidence, *Am.* State's evi-dence.

Kropf 𝄢 [krɔpf] goit|re, *Am.* -er.

Kröte *zo.* [ˈkrøːtə] *f* (-/-n) toad.

Krücke [ˈkrykə] *f* (-/-n) crutch.

Krug [kruːk] *m* (-[e]s/⁼e) jug, pitch-er; jar; mug; tankard.

Krume [ˈkruːmə] *f* (-/-n) crumb; 🖉 topsoil.

Krümel [ˈkryːməl] *m* (-s/-) small crumb; Qn *v/t.* and *v/i.* (ge-, *h*) crumble.

krumm *adj.* [krum] *p.* bent, stoop-ing; *limb, nose, etc.*: crooked; *spine*: curved; *deal, business, etc.*: crooked; '**~beinig** *adj.* bandy- or bow-legged.

krümmen [ˈkrymən] *v/t.* (ge-, *h*) bend (*arm, back, etc.*); crook (*finger, etc.*); curve (*metal sheet, etc.*); *sich ~ person, snake, etc.*: writhe; *worm, etc.*: wriggle; *sich vor Schmerzen ~* writhe with pain; *sich vor Lachen ~* be convulsed with laughter.

'**Krümmung** *f* (-/-en) road, etc.: bend; arch, road, etc.: curve; *river, path, etc.*: turn, wind, meander; *earth's surface, spine, etc.*: curva-ture.

Krüppel [ˈkrypəl] *m* (-s/-) cripple.

Kruste [ˈkrustə] *f* (-/-n) crust.

Kübel [ˈkyːbəl] *m* (-s/-) tub; pail, bucket.

Kubik|meter [kuˈbiːk-] *n, m* cubic met|re, *Am.* -er; **~wurzel** ⅍ *f* cube root.

Küche [ˈkyçə] *f* (-/-n) kitchen; cuisine, cookery; *s. kalt.*

Kuchen [ˈkuːxən] *m* (-s/-) cake, flan; pastry.

'**Küchen|gerät** *n*, '**~geschirr** *n* kitchen utensils *pl.*; '**~herd** *m* (kitchen-)range; cooker, stove; '**~schrank** *m* kitchen cupboard *or* cabinet; '**~zettel** *m* bill of·fare, menu.

Kuckuck *orn.* [ˈkukuk] *m* (-s/-e) cuckoo.

Kufe [ˈkuːfə] *f* (-/-n) ⚡ skid; *sleigh, etc.*: runner.

Küfer [ˈkyːfər] *m* (-s/-) cooper; cellarman.

Kugel [ˈkuːgəl] *f* (-/-n) ball; ✕ bullet; ⅍, *geogr.* sphere; *sports*: shot, weight; Qförmig *adj.* [ˈ~fœr-miç] spherical, ball-shaped, globu-lar; '**~gelenk** ⊕, *anat. n* ball-and-socket joint; '**~lager** ⊕ *n* ball-bearing; '**₂n** (ge-) **1.** v/i. (sein) ball, etc.: roll; **2.** v/t. (h) roll (ball, etc.); sich ~ children, etc.: roll about; F double up (vor with laughter); '**~schreiber** m ball-(point)-pen; '**~stoßen** n (-s/no pl.) sports: putting the shot or weight.

Kuh zo. [ku:] f (-/ëe) cow.

kühl adj. [ky:l] cool (a. fig.); '**₂anlage** f cold-storage plant; '**₂e** f (-/no pl.) cool(ness); '**~en** v/t. (ge-, h) cool (wine, wound, etc.); chill (wine, etc.): fair, easy; '**₂er** mot. m (-s/-) radiator; '**₂raum** m cold-storage chamber; '**₂schrank** m refrigerator, F fridge.

kühn adj. [ky:n] bold (a. fig.), daring; audacious. [a. cow barn.]

'Kuhstall m cow-house, byre, Am.

Küken orn. ['ky:kən] n (-s/-) chick.

kulant ✝ adj. [ku'lant] firm, etc.: accommodating, obliging; price, terms, etc.: fair, easy.

Kulisse [ku'lisə] f (-/-n) thea. wing, side-scene; fig. front; ~n pl. a. scenery; hinter den ~n behind the scenes.

Kult [kult] m (-[e]s/-e) cult, worship.

kultivieren [kulti'vi:rən] v/t. (no -ge-, h) cultivate (a. fig.).

Kultur [kul'tu:r] f (-/-en) ✍ cultivation; fig.: culture; civilization; '₂ell adj. [~u'rel] cultural; '**~film** [~'tu:r-] m educational film; '**~geschichte** f history of civilization; '**~volk** n civilized people.

Kultus ['kultus] m (-/Kulte) s. Kult; '**~minister** m minister of education and cultural affairs; '**~ministerium** n ministry of education and cultural affairs.

Kummer ['kumər] m (-s/no pl.) grief, sorrow; trouble, worry.

kümmer|lich adj. ['kymərliç] life, etc.: miserable, wretched; conditions, etc.: pitiful, pitiable; result, etc.: poor; resources: scanty; '**~n** v/t. (ge-, h): es kümmert mich I bother, I worry; sich ~ um look after, take care of; see to; meddle with.

'kummervoll adj. sorrowful.

Kump|an F [kum'pa:n] m (-s/-e) companion; F mate, chum, Am. ✝ a. buddy; **~el** ['~pəl] m (-s/-, F -s) ⚒ pitman, collier; F work-mate; F 's. Kumpan.

Kunde ['kundə] **1.** m (-n/-n) cus-

tomer, client; **2.** f (-/-n) knowledge.

Kundgebung ['kunt-] f (-/-en) manifestation; pol. rally.

kündig|en ['kyndigən] (ge-, h) **1.** v/i.: j-m ~ give s.o. notice; **2.** v/t. ✝ call in (capital); ⚖ cancel (contract); pol. denounce (treaty); '**₂ung** f (-/-en) notice; ✝ calling in; ⚖ cancellation; pol. denunciation.

'Kundschaft f (-/-en) customers pl., clients pl.; custom, clientele; '**~er** ⚔ m (-s/-) scout; spy.

künftig ['kynftiç] **1.** adj. event, years, etc.: future; event, programme, etc.: coming; life, world, etc.: next; **2.** adv. in future, from now on.

Kunst [kunst] f (-/ëe) art; skill; '**~akademie** f academy of arts; '**~ausstellung** f art exhibition; '**~druck** m art print(ing); '**~dünger** m artificial manure, fertilizer; '**~fertig** adj. skilful, skilled; '**~fertigkeit** f artistic skill; '**~gegenstand** m objet d'art; '₂gerecht adj. skilful; professional, expert; '**~geschichte** f history of art; '**~gewerbe** n arts and crafts pl.; applied arts pl.; '**~glied** n artificial limb; '**~griff** m trick, dodge; artifice, knack; '**~händler** m art-dealer; '**~kenner** m connoisseur of or in art; '**~leder** n imitation or artificial leather.

Künstler ['kynstlər] m (-s/-) artist; ♪, thea. performer; '₂isch adj. artistic.

künstlich adj. ['kynstliç] eye, flower, light, etc.: artificial; teeth, hair, etc.: false; fibres, dyes, etc.: synthetic.

'Kunst|liebhaber m art-lover; '**~maler** m artist, painter; '**~reiter** m equestrian; circus-rider; '**~schätze** ['~ʃɛtsə] m/pl. art treasures pl.; '**~seide** f artificial silk, rayon; '**~stück** n feat, trick, F stunt; '**~tischler** m cabinet-maker; '**~verlag** m art publishers pl.; '₂voll adj. artistic, elaborate; '**~werk** n work of art.

kunterbunt F fig. adj. ['kuntər-] higgledy-piggledy.

Kupfer ['kupfər] n (-s/no pl.) copper; '**~geld** n copper coins pl., F coppers pl.; '₂n adj. (of) copper; '₂rot adj. copper-colo(u)red; '**~stich** m copper-plate engraving.

Kupon [ku'põ:] m (-s/-s) s. Coupon.

Kuppe ['kupə] f (-/-n) rounded hilltop; nail: head.

Kuppel △ ['kupəl] f (-/-n) dome, cupola; **~ei** ⚖ [~'laɪ] f (-/-en) procuring; **'2n** (ge-, h) **1.** v/t. s. koppeln; **2.** mot. v/i. declutch.

Kuppl|er ['kuplər] m (-s/-) pimp, procurer; **'~ung** f (-/-en) ⊕ coupling (a. ⚙); mot. clutch.

Kur [ku:r] f (-/-en) course of treatment, cure.

Kür [ky:r] f (-/-en) sports: s. Kürlauf; voluntary exercise.

Kuratorium [kura'to:rium] n (-s/ Kuratorien) board of trustees.

Kurbel ⊕ ['kurbəl] f (-/-n) crank, winch, handle; **'2n** (ge-, h) **1.** v/t. shoot (film); in die Höhe ~ winch up (load, etc.); wind up (car window, etc.); **2.** v/i. crank. [pumpkin.\

Kürbis ⚘ ['kyrbis] m (-ses/-se)\

'Kur|gast m visitor to or patient at a health resort or spa; **'~haus** n spa hotel.

Kurier [ku'ri:r] m (-s/-e) courier, express (messenger).

kurieren ⚕ [ku'ri:rən] v/t. (no -ge-, h) cure.

kurios adj. [kur'jo:s] curious, odd, strange, queer. [skating.\

'Kürlauf m sports: free (roller)\

'Kur|ort m health resort; spa; **'~pfuscher** m quack (doctor); **~pfusche'rei** f (-/-en) quackery.

Kurs [kurs] m (-es/-e) ✝ currency; ✝ rate, price; ⚓ and fig. course; course, class; **'~bericht** ✝ m market-report; **'~buch** 🚂 n railway guide, Am. railroad guide.

Kürschner ['kyrʃnər] m (-s/-) furrier.

kursieren [kur'zi:rən] v/i. (no -ge-, h) money, etc.: circulate, be in circulation; rumour, etc.: circulate, be afloat, go about.

Kursivschrift typ. [kur'zi:f-] f italics pl. [class.\

Kursus ['kurzus] m (-/Kurse) course,\

'Kurs|verlust m loss on the stock exchange; **'~wert** ✝ m market value; **'~zettel** ✝ m stock exchange list.

Kurve ['kurvə] f (-/-n) curve; road, etc.: a. bend, turn.

kurz [kurts] **1.** adj. space: short; time, etc.: short, brief; ~ und bündig brief, concise; ~e Hose shorts pl.; mit ~en Worten with a few words; den kürzeren ziehen get the worst of it; **2.** adv. in short; ~ angebunden

sein be curt or sharp; ~ und gut in short, in a word; ~ vor London short of London; sich ~ fassen be brief or concise; in ~em before long shortly; vor ~em a short time ago; zu ~ kommen come off badly, get a raw deal; um es ~ zu sagen to cut a long story short; **'2arbeit** f short-time work; **'2arbeiter** ✝ m short-time worker; **~atmig** adj. ['~ʔa:tmiç] short-winded.

Kürze ['kyrtsə] f (-/no pl.) shortness; brevity; in ~ shortly, before long; **'2n** v/t. (ge-, h) shorten (dress, etc.) (um by); abridge, condense (book, etc.); cut, reduce (expenses, etc.).

'kurz|er|hand adv. without hesitation; on the spot; **2film** m short (film); **'2form** f shortened form; **'~fristig** adj. short-term; ✝ bill, etc.: short-dated; **2geschichte** f (short) short story; **~lebig** adj. ['~le:biç] short-lived; **2nachrichten** f/pl. news summary.

kürzlich adv. ['kyrtsliç] lately, recently, not long ago.

'Kurz|schluß ⚡ m short circuit, F short; **'~schrift** f shorthand, stenography; **2sichtig** adj. short-sighted, near-sighted; **2um** adv. in short, in a word.

'Kürzung f (-/-en) shortening (of dress, etc.); abridg(e)ment, condensation (of book, etc.); cut, reduction (of expenses, etc.).

'Kurz|waren f/pl. haberdashery, Am. dry goods pl., notions pl.; **'~weil** f (-/no pl.) amusement, entertainment; **2weilig** adj. amusing, entertaining; **'~welle** ⚡ f short wave; radio: short-wave band.

Kusine [ku'zi:nə] f (-/-n) s. Cousine.

Kuß [kus] m (Kusses/Küsse) kiss; **2echt** adj. kiss-proof. [kiss.\

küssen ['kysən] v/t. and v/i. (ge-, h)\

'kußfest adj. s. kußecht.

Küste ['kystə] f (-/-n) coast; shore.

'Küsten|bewohner m inhabitant of a coastal region; **'~fischerei** f inshore fishery or fishing; **'~gebiet** n coastal area or region; **'~schiffahrt** f coastal shipping.

Küster eccl. ['kystər] m (-s/-) verger, sexton, sacristan.

Kutsch|bock ['kutʃ-] m coach-box; **'~e** f (-/-n) carriage, coach; **'~enschlag** m carriage-door, coachdoor; **'~er** m (-s/-) coachman; **2ie-**

ren [ˌ~'tʃiːrən] (*no* -ge-) **1.** *v/t.* (h) drive *s.o.* in a coach; **2.** *v/i.* (h) (drive a) coach; **3.** *v/i.* (sein) (drive *or* ride in a) coach.

Kutte ['kutə] *f* (-/-n) cowl.

Kutter ⚓ ['kutər] *m* (-s/-) cutter.
Kuvert [ku'vɛrt; ku'vɛːr] *n* (-[e]s/-e; -s/-s) envelope; *at table:* cover.
Kux ⚒ [kuks] *m* (-es/-e) mining share.

L

Lab *zo.* [laːp] *n* (-[e]s/-e) rennet.
labil *adj.* [la'biːl] unstable (*a.* ⊕, ⚓); *phys.*, ⚑ labile.
Labor [la'boːr] *n* (-s/-s, -e) *s. Laboratorium;* **~ant** [labo'rant] *m* (-en/-en) laboratory assistant; **~atorium** [labora'toːrjum] *n* (-s/ Laboratorien) laboratory; ℒ**ieren** [~o'riːrən] *v/i.* (*no* -ge-, h): ~ an (*dat.*) labo(u)r under, suffer from.
Labyrinth [laby'rint] *n* (-[e]s/-e) labyrinth, maze.
Lache ['laxə] *f* (-/-n) pool, puddle.
lächeln ['lɛçəln] **1.** *v/i.* (ge-, h) smile (*über acc.* at); *höhnisch* ~ sneer (*über acc.* at); **2.** ℒ *n* (-s/*no pl.*) smile; *höhnisches* ~ sneer.
lachen ['laxən] **1.** *v/i.* (ge-, h) laugh (*über acc.* at); **2.** ℒ *n* (-s/*no pl.*) laugh(ter).
lächerlich *adj.* ['lɛçərliç] ridiculous, laughable, ludicrous; absurd; derisory, scoffing; ~ *machen* ridicule; *sich* ~ *machen* make a fool of o.s.
Lachs *ichth.* [laks] *m* (-es/-e) salmon.
Lack [lak] *m* (-[e]s/-e) (gum-)lac; varnish; lacquer, enamel; ℒ**ieren** [la'kiːrən] *v/t.* (*no* -ge-, h) lacquer, varnish, enamel; **~leder** *n* patent leather; **~schuhe** *m/pl.* patent leather shoes *pl.*, F patents *pl.*
Lade|fähigkeit ['laːdə-] *f* loading capacity; **~fläche** *f* loading area; **~hemmung** ⚔ *f* jam, stoppage; **~linie** ⚓ *f* load-line.
laden[1] ['laːdən] *v/t.* (*irr.*, ge-, h) load; load (*gun*), charge (*a.* ⚡); freight, ship; 🏛 cite, summon; invite, ask (*guest*).
Laden[2] [~] *m* (-s/⁔) shop, *Am.* store, shutter; **~besitzer** *m s. Ladeninhaber;* **~dieb** *m* shop-lifter; **~diebstahl** *m* shop-lifting; **~hüter** *m* drug on the market; **~inhaber** *m* shopkeeper; *Am.* store-

keeper; **~kasse** *f* till; **~preis** *m* selling-price, retail price; **~schild** *n* shopsign; **~schluß** *m* closing time; *nach* ~ after hours; **~tisch** *m* counter.
'Lade|platz *m* loading-place; **'~rampe** *f* loading platform *or* ramp; **'~raum** *m* loading space; ⚓ hold; **'~schein** ⚓ *m* bill of lading.
'Ladung *f* (-/-en) loading; load, freight; ⚓ cargo; ⚡ charge (*a. of gun*); 🏛 summons.
lag [laːk] *pret. of liegen.*
Lage ['laːgə] *f* (-/-n) situation, position; site, location (*of building*); state, condition; attitude; *geol.* layer, stratum; round (*of beer, etc.*); *in der* ~ *sein zu inf.* be able to *inf.*, be in a position to *inf.*; *versetzen Sie sich in meine* ~ put yourself in my place.
Lager ['laːgər] *n* (-s/-) couch, bed; den, lair (*of wild animals*); *geol.* deposit; ⊕ bearing; warehouse, storehouse, depot; store, stock (⚑ *pl. a. Läger*); ⚔, *etc.:* camp, encampment; *auf* ~ ⚑ on hand, in stock; **~buch** *n* stock-book; **~feuer** *n* camp-fire; **~geld** *n* storage; **~haus** *n* warehouse; ℒ**n** (ge-, h) **1.** *v/i.* lie down, rest; ⚔ (en)camp; ⚑ be stored; **2.** *v/t.* lay down; ⚔ (en)camp; ⚑ store, warehouse; *sich* ~ lie down, rest; **~platz** *m* ⚑ depot; resting-place; ⚔, *etc.:* camp-site; **~raum** *m* store-room; **~ung** *f* (-/-en) storage (*of goods*).
Lagune [la'guːnə] *f* (-/-n) lagoon.
lahm *adj.* [laːm] lame; **~en** *v/i.* (ge-, h) be lame.
lähmen ['lɛːmən] *v/t.* (ge-, h) (make) lame; paraly|se, *Am.* -ze (*a. fig.*).
'lahmlegen *v/t.* (*sep.*, -ge-, h) paraly|se, *Am.* -ze; obstruct.
'Lähmung ⚕ *f* (-/-en) paralysis.
Laib [laip] *m* (-[e]s/-e) loaf.

Laich [laiç] m (-[e]s/-e) spawn; **2en** v/i. (ge-, h) spawn.

Laie ['laiə] m (-n/-n) layman; amateur; **'~nbühne** f amateur theat|re, Am. -er.

Lakai [la'kai] m (-en/-en) lackey (a. fig.), footman.

Lake ['la:kə] f (-/-n) brine, pickle.

Laken ['la:kən] n (-s/-) sheet.

lallen ['lalən] v/i. and v/t. (ge-, h) stammer; babble.

Lamelle [la'mɛlə] f (-/-n) lamella, lamina; **♀** gill (of mushrooms).

lamentieren [lamɛn'ti:rən] v/i. (no -ge-, h) lament (um for; über acc. over).

Lamm zo. [lam] n (-[e]s/⁼er) lamb; **'~fell** n lambskin; **'2fromm** adj. (as) gentle or (as) meek as a lamb.

Lampe ['lampə] f (-/-n) lamp.

'Lampen|fieber n stage fright; **'~licht** n lamplight; **'~schirm** m lamp-shade.

Lampion [lã'pjõ:] m, n (-s/-s) Chinese lantern.

Land [lant] n (-[e]s/⁼er, poet. -e) land; country; territory; ground, soil; an ~ gehen go ashore; auf dem ~e in the country; aufs ~ gehen go into the country; außer ~es gehen go abroad; zu ~e by land; **'~arbeiter** m farm-hand; **'~besitz** m landed property; **♑** real estate; **'~besitzer** m landowner, landed proprietor; **'~bevölkerung** f rural population.

Lande|bahn ✈ ['landə-] f runway; **'~deck** ⚓ n flight-deck. [land.\
land'einwärts adv. upcountry, in-\
landen ['landən] (ge-) 1. v/i. (sein) land; 2. v/t. (h) **♣** disembark (troups); **✈** land, set down (troups).

'Landenge f neck of land, isthmus.

Landeplatz ✈ ['landə-] m landing-field.

Ländereien [lɛndə'raiən] pl. landed property, lands pl., estates pl.

Länderspiel ['lɛndər-] n sports: international match.

Landes|grenze ['landəs-] f frontier, boundary; **'~innere** n interior, inland, upcountry; **'~kirche** f national church; Brt. Established Church; **'~regierung** f government; in Germany: Land government; **'~sprache** f native language, vernacular; **'2üblich** adj. customary; **'~verrat** m treason; **'~verräter** m

traitor to his country; **'~verteidigung** f national defen|ce, Am. -se.

'Land|flucht f rural exodus; **'~friedensbruch ♑** m breach of the public peace; **'~gericht** n appr. district court; **'~gewinnung** f (-/-en) reclamation of land; **'~gut** n country-seat, estate; **'~haus** n country-house, cottage; **'~karte** f map; **'~kreis** m rural district; **'2läufig** adj. ['~lɔyfiç] customary, current, common.

ländlich adj. ['lɛntliç] rural, rustic.

'Land|maschinen f/pl. agricultural or farm equipment; **'~partie** f picnic, outing, excursion into the country; **'~plage** iro. f nuisance; **'~rat** m (-[e]s/⁼e) appr. district president; **'~ratte ♣** f landlubber; **'~recht** n common law; **'~regen** m persistent rain.

'Landschaft f (-/-en) province, district, region; countryside, scenery; esp. paint. landscape; **'2lich** adj. provincial; scenic (beauty, etc.).

'Landsmann m (-[e]s/Landsleute) (fellow-)countryman, compatriot; was sind Sie für ein ~? what's your native country?

'Land|straße f highway, high road; **'~streicher** m (-s/-) vagabond, tramp, Am. sl. hobo; **'~streitkräfte** f/pl. land forces pl., the Army; ground forces pl.; **'~strich** m tract of land, region; **'~tag** m Landtag, Land parliament.

Landung ['landuŋ] f (-/-en) **♣**, **✈** landing; disembarkation; arrival; **'~sbrücke ♣** f floating: landing-stage; pier; **'~ssteg ♣** m gangway, gang-plank.

'Land|vermesser m (-s/-) surveyor; **'~vermessung** f land-surveying; **'2wärts** adv. ['~vɛrts] landward(s); **'~weg** m: auf dem ~e by land; **'~wirt** m farmer, agriculturist; **'~wirtschaft** f agriculture, farming; **'2wirtschaftlich** adj. agricultural; ~e Maschinen f/pl. s. Landmaschinen; **'~zunge** f spit.

lang [laŋ] **1.** adj. long; ℗ tall; er machte ein ~es Gesicht his face fell; **2.** adv. long; e-e Woche ~ for a week; über kurz oder ~ sooner or later; ~(e) anhaltend continuous; ~(e) entbehrt long-missed; ~(e) ersehnt long-wished-for; das ist schon ~(e) her that was a long time ago; ~ *und breit* at (full *or* great) length; *noch* ~(*e*) *nicht* not for a long time yet; *far from ger.*; *wie* ~*e lernen Sie schon Englisch?* how long have you been learning English?; '~**atmig** *adj.* ['~a:tmiç] long-winded; '~**e** *adv. s.* **lang** 2.

Länge ['lɛŋə] *f* (-/-n) length; tallness; *geogr., ast.* longitude; *der* ~ *nach* (at) full length, lengthwise.

langen ['laŋən] *v/i.* (ge-, h) suffice, be enough; ~ *nach* reach for.

'**Längen|grad** *m* degree of longitude; '~**maß** *n* linear measure.

'**länger** **1.** *adj.* longer; '~*e Zeit* (for) some time; *je* ~, *je lieber* the longer the better; **2.** *adv.* longer; *ich kann es nicht* ~ *ertragen* I cannot bear it any longer; *je* ~, *je lieber* the longer the better.

'**Langeweile** *f* (-, *Langenweile/no pl.*) boredom, tediousness, ennui.

'**lang|fristig** *adj.* long-term; '~**jährig** *adj.* of long standing; ~*e Erfahrung* (many) years of experience; '**2lauf** *m* skiing: cross-country run *or* race.

'**länglich** *adj.* longish, oblong.

'**Langmut** *f* (-/*no pl.*) patience, forbearance.

längs [lɛŋs] **1.** *prp.* (*gen., dat.*) along(side of); ~ *der Küste fahren* ⚓ (sail along the) coast; **2.** *adv.* lengthwise; '**2achse** *f* longitudinal axis.

'**lang|sam** *adj.* slow; '**2schläfer** ['~ʃlɛːfər] *m* (-s/-) late riser, lie-abed; '**2spielplatte** *f* long-playing record.

längst *adv.* [lɛŋst] long ago *or* since; *ich weiß es* ~ I have known it for a long time; '~**ens** *adv.* at the longest; at the latest; at the most.

'**lang|stielig** *adj.* long-handled; ♀ long-stemmed, long-stalked; '**2-streckenlauf** *m* long-distance run *or* race; '**2weile** *f* (-, *Langenweile/no pl.*) *s.* **Langeweile**; '~**weilen** *v/t.* (ge-, h) bore; *sich* ~ be bored; '~**weilig** *adj.* tedious, boring, dull; ~*e Person* bore; '**2welle** *f* ⚡ long wave; *radio*: long wave band; ~**wierig** *adj.* ['~viːriç] protracted, lengthy; ⚕ lingering.

Lanze ['lantsə] *f* (-/-n) spear, lance.

Lappalie [la'paːljə] *f* (-/-n) trifle.

Lapp|en ['lapən] *m* (-s/-) patch; rag; duster; (dish- *or* floor-)cloth; *anat.*, ♀ lobe; '**2ig** *adj.* flabby.

läppisch *adj.* ['lɛpiʃ] foolish, silly.

Lärche ♀ ['lɛrçə] *f* (-/-n) larch.

Lärm [lɛrm] *m* (-[e]s/*no pl.*) noise; din; ~ *schlagen* give the alarm; '**2en** *v/i.* (ge-, h) make a noise; '**2end** *adj.* noisy.

Larve ['larfə] *f* (-/-n) mask; face (*often iro.*); *zo.* larva, grub.

las [laːs] *pret. of* **lesen**.

lasch F *adj.* [laʃ] limp, lax.

Lasche ['laʃə] *f* (-/-n) strap; tongue (*of shoe*).

lassen ['lasən] (*irr.*, h) **1.** *v/t.* (ge-) let; leave; *laß das!* don't!; *laß das Weinen!* stop crying!; *ich kann es nicht* ~ I cannot help (doing) it; *sein Leben* ~ *für* sacrifice one's life for; **2.** *v/i.* (ge-): *von et.* ~ desist from s.th., renounce s.th.; do without s.th.; **3.** *v/aux.* (*no -ge-*) allow, permit, let; make, cause; *drucken* ~ have s. *th.* printed; *gehen* ~ let s.o. go; *ich habe ihn dieses Buch lesen* ~ I have made him read this book; *von sich hören* ~ send word; *er läßt sich nichts sagen* he won't take advice; *es läßt sich nicht leugnen* there is no denying (the fact).

lässig *adj.* ['lɛsiç] indolent, idle; sluggish; careless.

Last [last] *f* (-/-en) load; burden; weight; cargo, freight; *fig.* weight, charge, trouble; *zu* ~*en von* ✝ to the debit of; *j-m zur* ~ *fallen* be a burden to s.o.; *j-m et. zur* ~ *legen* lay s.th. at s.o.'s door *or* to s.o.'s charge; '~**auto** *n s.* **Lastkraftwagen**.

'**lasten** *v/i.* (ge-, h): ~ *auf* (*dat.*) weigh *or* press (up)on; '**2aufzug** *m* goods lift, *Am.* freight elevator.

Laster ['lastər] *n* (-s/-) vice.

Lästerer ['lɛstərər] *m* (-s/-) slanderer, backbiter.

'**lasterhaft** *adj.* vicious; corrupt.

'**Läster|maul** *n s.* **Lästerer**; '**2n** *v/i.* (ge-, h) slander, calumniate, defame; abuse; '~**ung** *f* (-/-en) slander, calumny.

lästig *adj.* ['lɛstiç] troublesome; annoying; uncomfortable, inconvenient.

'**Last|kahn** *m* barge, lighter; '~**kraftwagen** *m* lorry, *Am.* truck; '~**schrift** ✝ *f* debit; '~**tier** *n* pack animal; '~**wagen** *m s.* **Lastkraftwagen**.

Latein [la'taɪn] *n* (-s/*no pl.*) Latin; '**2isch** *adj.* Latin.

Laterne [la'tɛrnə] f (-/-n) lantern; street-lamp; **.npfahl** m lamp-post.

latschen F ['la:tʃən] v/i. (ge-, sein) shuffle (along).

Latte [ˈlatə] f (-/-n) pale; lath; sports: bar; **'.nkiste** f crate; **'.n-verschlag** m latticed partition; **'.nzaun** m paling, Am. picket fence.

Lätzchen ['lɛtsçən] n (-s/-) bib, feeder.

lau adj. [lau] tepid, lukewarm (a. fig.).

Laub [laup] n (-[e]s/no pl.) foliage, leaves pl.; **'.baum** m deciduous tree.

Laube ['laubə] f (-/-n) arbo(u)r, bower; **.ngang** m arcade.

'Laub|frosch zo. m tree-frog; **'.säge** f fret-saw.

Lauch ꝗ [laux] m (-[e]s/-e) leek.

Lauer ['lauər] f (-/no pl.): auf der ~ liegen or sein lie in wait or ambush, be on the look-out; **'2n** v/i. (ge-, h) lurk (auf acc. for); ~ auf (acc.) watch for; **'2nd** adj. louring, lowering.

Lauf [lauf] m (-[e]s/⁼e) run(ning); sports: a. run, heat; race; current (of water); course; barrel (of gun); ♪ run; im ~e der Zeit in (the) course of time; **'.bahn** f career; **'.bursche** m errand-boy, office-boy; **'.diszi-plin** f sports: running event.

'laufen (irr.) v/i. **1.** v/i. (sein) run; walk; flow; time: pass, go by, elapse; say: die Dinge ~ lassen let things slide; j-n ~ lassen let s.o. go; **2.** v/t. (sein, h) run; walk; **'.d** adj. running; current; regular; **.en Monats** ꝗ instant; auf dem **.en sein** be up to date, be fully informed.

Läufer ['lɔyfər] m (-s/-) runner (a. carpet); chess: bishop; football: half-back.

'Lauf|masche f ladder, Am. a. run; **'.paß** F m sack, sl. walking papers pl.; **'.planke** ꝗ f gang-board, gang-plank; **'.schritt** m: im ~ running; **'.steg** m footbridge; ꝗ gang-way.

Lauge ['laugə] f (-/-n) lye.

Laun|e ['launə] f (-/-n) humo(u)r; mood; temper; caprice, fancy, whim; guter ~ in (high) spirits; **'2enhaft** adj. capricious; **'2isch** adj. moody; wayward.

Laus zo. f [laus] f (-/⁼e) louse; **.bub**

['.bu:p] m (-en/-en) young scamp, F young devil, rascal.

lausch|en ['lauʃən] v/i. (ge-, h) listen; eavesdrop; **'.ig** adj. snug, cosy; peaceful.

laut [laut] **1.** adj. loud (a. fig.); noisy; **2.** adv. aloud, loud(ly); (sprechen Sie) ~er! speak up!, Am. louder!; **3.** prp. (gen., dat.) according to; ꝗ as per; **4.** **2** m (-[e]s/-e) sound; **'2e** ♪ f (-/-n) lute; **'.en** v/i. (ge-, h) sound; words, etc.: run; read; ~ auf (acc.) passport, etc.: be issued to.

läuten ['lɔytən] (ge-, h) **1.** v/i. ring; toll; es läutet the bell is ringing; **2.** v/t. ring; toll.

'lauter adj. pure; clear; genuine; sincere; mere, nothing but, only.

läuter|n ['lɔytərn] v/t. (ge-, h) purify; ⊕ cleanse; refine; **'2ung** f (-/-en) purification; refining.

'laut|los adj. noiseless; mute; silent; silence: hushed; **'2schrift** f phonetic transcription; **'2sprecher** m loud-speaker; **'2stärke** f sound intensity; radio: (sound-)volume; **2-stärkeregler** ['.re:glər] m (-s/-) volume control.

'lauwarm adj. tepid, lukewarm.

Lava geol. ['la:va] f (-/Laven) lava.

Lavendel [la'vɛndəl] m (-s/-) lavender.

lavieren [la'vi:rən] v/i. (no -ge-, h, sein) ꝗ tack (a. fig.).

Lawine [la'vi:nə] f (-/-n) avalanche.

lax adj. [laks] lax, loose; morals: a. easy.

Lazarett [latsa'rɛt] n (-[e]s/-e) (military) hospital.

leben[1] ['le:bən] (ge-, h) **1.** v/i. live; be alive; ~ Sie wohl! good-bye!, farewell!; j-n hochleben lassen cheer s.o.; at table: drink s.o.'s health; von et. ~ live on s.th.; hier lebt es sich gut it is pleasant living here; **2.** v/t. live (one's life).

Leben[2] [.] n (-s/-) life; stir, animation, bustle; am ~ bleiben remain alive, survive; am ~ erhalten keep alive; ein neues ~ beginnen turn over a new leaf; ins ~ rufen call into being; sein ~ aufs Spiel setzen risk one's life; sein ~ lang all one's life; ums ~ kommen lose one's life; perish.

lebendig adj. [le'bɛndiç] living; pred.: alive; quick; lively.

'Lebens|alter n age; **'.anschau-**

ung f outlook on life; '**~art** f manners pl., behavio(u)r; '**~auffassung** f philosophy of life; '**~bedingungen** f/pl. living conditions pl.; '**~beschreibung** f life, biography; '**~dauer** f span of life; ⊕ durability; '**2echt** adj. true to life; '**~erfahrung** f experience of life; '**2-fähig** adj. ⚓ and fig. viable; '**~gefahr** f danger of life; **~!** danger (of death)!; unter **~** at the risk of one's life; '**~gefährlich** adj. dangerous (to life), perilous; '**~gefährte** m life's companion; '**~größe** f life-size; in **~** at full length; '**~kraft** f vital power, vigo(u)r, vitality; '**2länglich** adj. for life, lifelong; '**~lauf** m course of life; personal record, curriculum vitae; '**2lustig** adj. gay, merry; '**~mittel** pl. food (-stuffs pl.), provisions pl., groceries pl.; '**2müde** adj. weary or tired of life; '**2notwendig** adj. vital, essential; '**~retter** m life-saver, rescuer; '**~standard** m standard of living; '**~unterhalt** m livelihood; s-n **~** verdienen earn one's living; '**~versicherung** f life-insurance; '**~wandel** m life, (moral) conduct; '**~weise** f mode of living, habits pl.; gesunde **~** regimen; '**~weisheit** f worldly wisdom; '**2wichtig** adj. vital, essential; **~e** Organe pl. vitals pl.; '**~zeichen** n sign of life; '**~zeit** f lifetime; auf **~** for life.

Leber anat. ['le:bər] f (-/-) liver; '**~fleck** m mole; '**2krank** adj., '**2-leidend** adj. suffering from a liver-complaint; '**~tran** m cod-liver oil; '**~wurst** f liver-sausage, Am. liver-wurst.

'**Lebewesen** n living being, creature.
Lebe'wohl n (-[e]s/-e, -s) farewell.
leb|haft adj. ['le:phaft] lively; vivid; spirited; interest: keen; traffic: busy; '**2kuchen** m gingerbread; '**~los** adj. lifeless; '**2zeiten** pl.: zu s-n **~** in his lifetime.

lechzen ['lɛçtsən] v/i. (ge-, h): **~** nach languish or yearn or pant for.
Leck [lɛk] **1.** n (-[e]s/-s) leak; **2.** 2 adj. leaky; **~** werden ⚓ spring a leak.

lecken ['lɛkən] (ge-, h) **1.** v/t. lick; **2.** v/i. lick, leak.
lecker adj. ['lɛkər] dainty; delicious; '**2bissen** m dainty, delicacy.
Leder ['le:dər] n (-s/-) leather; in

~ gebunden leather-bound; '**2n** adj. leathern, of leather.

ledig adj. ['le:diç] single, unmarried; child: illegitimate; **~lich** adv. ['**~**k-] solely, merely.
Lee ⚓ [le:] f (-/no pl.) lee (side).
leer [le:r] **1.** adj. empty; vacant; void; vain; blank; **2.** adv.: **~** laufen ⊕ idle; '**2e** f (-/no pl.) emptiness, void (a. fig.); phys. vacuum; '**~en** v/t. (ge-, h) empty; clear (out); pour out; '**2gut** ⚓ n empties pl.; '**2lauf** m ⊕ idling; mot. neutral gear; fig. waste of energy; '**~stehend** adj. flat: empty, unoccupied, vacant.

legal adj. [le'ga:l] legal, lawful.
Legat [le'ga:t] **1.** m (-en/-en) legate; **2.** ⚖ n (-[e]s/-e) legacy.
legen ['le:gən] (ge-, h) **1.** v/t. lay; place, put; sich **~** wind, etc.: calm down, abate; cease; Wert **~** auf (acc.) attach importance to; **2.** v/i. hen: lay.

Legende [le'gɛndə] f (-/-n) legend.
legieren [le'gi:rən] v/t. (no -ge-, h) ⊕ alloy; cookery: thicken (mit with).
Legislative [le:gisla'ti:və] f (-/-n) legislative body or power.
legitim adj. [legi'ti:m] legitimate; **~ieren** [**~**i'mi:rən] v/t. (no -ge-, h) legitimate; authorize; sich **~** prove one's identity.

Lehm [le:m] m (-[e]s/-e) loam; mud; '**2ig** adj. loamy.
Lehn|e ['le:nə] f (-/-n) support; arm, back (of chair); '**2en** (ge-, h) **1.** v/i. lean (an dat. against); **2.** v/t. lean, rest (an acc., gegen against); sich **~** an (acc.) lean against; sich **~** auf (acc.) rest or support o.s. (up-on); sich aus dem Fenster **~** lean out of the window; '**~sessel** m, '**~stuhl** m armchair, easy chair.
Lehrbuch ['le:r-] n textbook.
Lehre ['le:rə] f (-/-n) rule, precept; doctrine; system; science; theory; lesson, warning; moral (of fable); instruction, tuition; ⊕ ga(u)ge; ⊕ pattern; in der **~** sein be apprenticed (bei to); in die **~** geben apprentice, article (both: bei, zu to); '**2n** v/t. (ge-, h) teach, instruct; show.
'**Lehrer** m (-s/-) teacher; master, instructor; '**~in** f (-/-nen) (lady) teacher; (school)mistress; '**~kollegium** n staff (of teachers).
'**Lehr|fach** n subject; '**~film** m in-

structional film; '**~gang** *m* course (of instruction); '**~geld** *n* premium; '**~herr** *m* master, *sl.* boss; '**~jahre** *n/pl.* (years *pl.* of) apprenticeship; '**~junge** *m s.* Lehrling; '**~körper** *m* teaching staff; *univ.* professorate, faculty; '**~kraft** *f* teacher; professor; '**~ling** *m* (-*s*/-*e*) apprentice; '**~mädchen** *n* girl apprentice; '**~meister** *m* master; '**~methode** *f* method of teaching; '**~plan** *m* curriculum, syllabus; '**2reich** *adj.* instructive; '**~satz** *m* ❧ theorem; doctrine; *eccl.* dogma; '**~stoff** *m* subject-matter, subject(s *pl.*); '**~stuhl** *m* professorship; '**~vertrag** *m* articles *pl.* of apprenticeship, indenture(s *pl.*); '**~zeit** *f* apprenticeship.

Leib [laɪp] *m* (-[e]*s*/-*er*) body; belly, *anat.* abdomen; womb; *bei lebendigem ~e* alive; *mit ~ und Seele* body and soul; *sich j-n vom ~e halten* keep s.o. at arm's length; '**~arzt** *m* physician in ordinary, personal physician; '**~chen** *n* (-*s*/-) bodice.

Leibeigen|e ['laɪp'ʔaɪgənə] *m* (-*n*/-*n*) bond(s)man, serf; '**~schaft** *f* (-*/no pl.*) bondage, serfdom.

Leibes|erziehung ['laɪbəs-] *f* physical training; '**~frucht** *f* f(o)etus; '**~kraft** *f*: *aus Leibeskräften pl.* with all one's might; '**~übung** *f* bodily *or* physical exercise.

Leib|garde *f* body-guard; '**~gericht** *n* favo(u)rite dish; '**2haftig** *adj.* ['~haftiç]: *der ~e Teufel* the devil incarnate; '**2lich** *adj.* bodily, corpor(e)al; '**~rente** *f* life-annuity; '**~schmerzen** *m/pl.* stomach-ache, belly-ache, *f* colic; '**~wache** *f* body-guard; '**~wäsche** *f* underwear.

Leiche ['laɪçə] *f* (-/-*n*) (dead) body, corpse.

Leichen|beschauer ⚕ ['laɪçənbəʃauər] *m* (-*s*/-) *appr.* coroner; '**~bestatter** *m* (-*s*/-) undertaker, *Am. a.* mortician; '**~bittermiene** F *f* woebegone look *or* countenance; '**2blaß** *adj.* deadly pale; '**~halle** *f* mortuary; '**~schau** ⚕ *f appr.* (coroner's) inquest; '**~schauhaus** *n* morgue; '**~tuch** *n* (-[e]*s*/*er*) shroud; '**~verbrennung** *f* cremation; '**~wagen** *m* hearse. [*Leiche.*]

Leichnam ['laɪçnaːm] *m* (-[e]*s*/-*e*).s)

leicht [laɪçt] **1.** *adj.* light; easy; slight; *tobacco:* mild; **2.** *adv.*: es ~ *nehmen* take it easy; '**2athlet** *m* athlete; '**2athletik** *f* athletics *pl.*, *Am.* track and field events *pl.*; '**~fertig** *adj.* light(-minded); careless; frivolous, flippant; '**2fertigkeit** *f* levity; carelessness; frivolity, flippancy; '**2gewicht** *n* boxing: lightweight; '**~gläubig** *adj.* credulous; '**~hin** *adv.* lightly, casually; **2igkeit** ['~iç-] *f* (-/-*en*) lightness; ease, facility; '**~lebig** *adj.* easy-going; '**2metall** *n* light metal; '**2sinn** *m* (-[e]*s*/*no pl.*) frivolity, levity; carelessness; '**~sinnig** *adj.* light-minded, frivolous; careless; '**~verdaulich** *adj.* easy to digest; '**~verständlich** *adj.* easy to understand.

leid [laɪt]° **1.** *adv.*: *es tut mir ~* I am sorry (*um* for), I regret; **2.** **2** *n* (-[e]*s*/*no pl.*) injury, harm; wrong; grief, sorrow; **2en** ['~dən] (*irr.*, *ge-*, *h*) **1.** *v/i.* suffer (*an dat.* from); **2.** *v/t.*: (*nicht*) ~ *können* (dis)like; **2en** ['~dən] *n* (-*s*/-) suffering; complaint; '**~end** ♣ *adj.* ['~dənt] ailing.

'**Leidenschaft** *f* (-/-*en*) passion; '**2lich** *adj.* passionate; ardent; vehement; '**2slos** *adj.* dispassionate.

'**Leidens|gefährte** *m*, '**~gefährtin** *f* fellow-sufferer.

leid|er *adv.* ['laɪdər] unfortunately; *int.* alas!; ~ *muß ich inf.* I'm (so) sorry to *inf.*; *ich muß ~ gehen* I am afraid I have to go; '**~ig** *adj.* disagreeable; '**~lich** *adj.* ['laɪt-] tolerable; fairly well; **2tragende** ['laɪt-] *m, f* (-*n*/-*n*) mourner; *er ist der ~ dabei* he is the one who suffers for it; **2wesen** ['laɪt-] *n* (-*s/no pl.*): *zu meinem ~* to my regret.

Leier ♪ ['laɪər] *f* (-/-*n*) lyre; '**~kasten** *m* barrel-organ; '**~kastenmann** *m* organ-grinder.

Leih|bibliothek ['laɪ-] *f*, '**~bücherei** *f* lending *or* circulating library, *Am. a.* rental library; **2en** *v/t.* (*irr.*, *ge-*, *h*) lend; borrow (*von* from); '**~gebühr** *f* lending fee(s *pl.*); '**~haus** *n* pawnshop, *Am. a.* loan office; **2weise** *adv.* as a loan.

Leim [laɪm] *m* (-[e]*s*/-*e*) glue; F *aus dem ~ gehen* get out of joint; F: *auf den ~ gehen* fall for it, fall into the trap; **2en** *v/t.* (*ge-*, *h*) glue; size.

Lein ♥ [laɪn] *m* (-[e]*s*/-*e*) flax.

Leine ['laɪnə] *f* (-/-*n*) line, cord; (dog-)lead, leash.

leinen ['laɪnən] **1.** adj. (of) linen; **2.** ⚥ n (-s/-) linen; in ~ gebunden cloth-bound; '⚥**schuh** m canvas shoe.

'**Lein|öl** n linseed-oil; '~**samen** m linseed; '~**wand** f (/no pl.) linen (cloth); paint. canvas; film: screen.

leise adj. ['laɪzə] low, soft; gentle; slight, faint; ~r stellen turn down (radio).

Leiste ['laɪstə] f (-/-n) border, ledge; △ fillet; anat. groin.

leisten ['laɪstən] **1.** v/t. (ge-, h) do; perform; fulfil(l); take (oath); render (service); ich kann mir das ~ I can afford it; **2.** ⚥ ⚲ m (-s/-) last; boot-tree. Am. a. shoetree; '⚥**bruch** ⚕ m inguinal hernia.

'**Leistung** f (-/-en) performance; achievement; work(manship); result(s pl.); ⊕ capacity; output (of factory); benefit (of insurance company); '⚥**fähig** adj. productive, efficient, ⊕ a. powerful; '~**fähigkeit** f efficiency; ⊕ productivity; ⊕ capacity, producing-power.

Leit|artikel ['laɪt-] m leading article, leader, editorial; '~**bild** n image; example.

leiten ['laɪtən] v/t. (ge-, h) lead, guide; conduct (a. phys., ♪); fig. direct, run, manage, operate; preside over (meeting); '~**d** adj. leading; phys. conductive; ~e Stellung key position.

'**Leiter 1.** m (-s/-) leader; conductor (a. phys., ♪); guide; manager; **2.** f (-/-n) ladder; '~**in** f (-/-nen) leader; conductress, guide; manageress; '~**wagen** m rack-wag(g)on.

'**Leit|faden** m manual, textbook, guide; '~**motiv** ♪ n leit-motiv; '~**spruch** m motto; '~**tier** n leader; '~**ung** f (-/-en) lead(ing), conducting; guidance; management, direction, administration, Am. a. operation; phys. conduction; ⚡ lead; circuit; tel. line; mains pl. (for gas, water, etc.); pipeline; die ~ ist besetzt teleph. the line is engaged or Am. busy.

'**Leitungs|draht** m conducting wire, conductor; '~**rohr** n conduit(-pipe); main (for gas, water, etc.); '~**wasser** n (-s/⚥) tap water.

'**Leitwerk** ✈ n tail unit or group, empennage.

Lekt|ion [lɛk'tsjoːn] f (-/-en) lesson;

~**or** ['lɛktɔr] m (-s/-en) lecturer; reader; ~**üre** [√'tyːrə] f **1.** (/no pl.) reading; **2.** (-/-n) books pl.

Lende anat. ['lɛndə] f (-/-n) loin(s pl.).

lenk|bar adj. ['lɛŋkaːr] guidable, manageable, tractable; docile; ⊕ steerable, dirigible; '~**en** v/t. (ge-, h) direct, guide; turn; rule; govern; drive (car); ⚓ steer; Aufmerksamkeit ~ auf (acc.) draw attention to; '⚥**rad** mot. n steering wheel; '⚥**säule** mot. f steering column; '⚥**stange** f handle-bar (of bicycle); '⚥**ung** mot. f (-/-en) steering-gear.

Lenz [lɛnts] m (-es/-e) spring.

Leopard zo. [leo'part] m (-en/-en) leopard.

Lepra ⚕ ['leːpra] f (/no pl.) leprosy.

Lerche orn. ['lɛrçə] f (-/-n) lark.

lern|begierig adj. ['lɛrn-] eager to learn, studious; '~**en** v/t. and v/i. (ge-, h) learn; study.

Lese ['leːzə] f (-/-n) gathering; s. Weinlese; '~**buch** n reader; '~**lampe** f reading-lamp.

lesen ['leːzən] (irr., ge-, h) **1.** v/t. read; ⚲ gather; Messe ~ eccl. say mass; **2.** v/i. read; univ. (give a) lecture (über acc. on); '~**swert** adj. worth reading.

'**Leser** m (-s/-), '~**in** f (-/-nen) reader; ⚲ gatherer; vintager; '⚥**lich** adj. legible; '~**zuschrift** f letter to the editor.

'**Lesezeichen** n book-mark.

'**Lesung** parl. f (-/-en) reading.

letzt adj. [lɛtst] last; final; ultimate; ~e Nachrichten pl. latest news pl.; ~e Hand anlegen put the finishing touches (an acc. to); das ~e the last thing; der ~ere the latter; der (die, das) Letzte the last (one); zu guter Letzt last but not least; finally; '~**ens** adv., '~**hin** adv. lately, of late; '~**lich** adv. s. letztens; finally; ultimately.

Leucht|e ['lɔʏçtə] f (-/-n) (fig. shining) light, lamp (a. fig.), luminary (a. fig., esp. p.); '⚥**en** v/i. (ge-, h) (give) light, shine (forth); beam, gleam; '~**en** n (-s/no pl.) shining, light, luminosity; '⚥**end** adj. shining, bright; luminous; brilliant (a. fig.); '~**er** m (-s/-) candlestick; s. Kronleuchter; '~**feuer** n ⚓, ✈, etc.: beacon(-light), flare (light); '~**käfer** zo. m glow-worm; '~**kugel** ✕ f

Very light; flare; '**~turm** *m* lighthouse; '**~ziffer** *f* luminous figure.

leugnen ['lɔ͜ygnən] *v/t.* (ge-, h) deny; disavow; contest.

Leukämie *✦* [lɔ͜ykɛ'mi:] *f* (-/-n) leuk(a)emia.

Leumund ['lɔ͜ymunt] *m* (-[e]s/*no pl.*) reputation, repute; character; '**~szeugnis** *✝✝ n* character reference.

Leute ['lɔ͜ytə] *pl.* people *pl.*; persons *pl.*; ✗, *pol.* men *pl.*; *workers*: hands *pl.*; F folks *pl.*; domestics *pl.*, servants *pl.*

Leutnant ✗ ['lɔ͜ytnant] *m* (-s/-s, ✎ -e) second lieutenant.

leutselig *adj.* ['lɔ͜ytzε:lɪç] affable.

Lexikon ['lεksikɔn] *n* (-s/*Lexika, Lexiken*) dictionary; encyclop(a)edia.

Libelle *zo.* [li'bεlə] *f* (-/-n) dragonfly.

liberal *adj.* [libe'ra:l] liberal.

Licht [lɪçt] **1.** *n* (-[e]s/-er) light; brightness; lamp; candle; *hunt.* eye; '**~ machen** *✦* switch or turn on the light(s *pl.*); *das ~ der Welt erblicken* see the light, be born; **2.** ♀ *adj.* light, bright; clear; *~er Augenblick ✦* lucid interval; '**~anlage** *f* lighting plant; '**~bild** *n* photo (-graph); '**~bildervortrag** *m* slide lecture; '**~blick** *fig. m* bright spot; '**~bogen** *✦ m* arc; '♀**durchlässig** *adj.* translucent; '♀**echt** *adj.* fast (to light), unfading; '♀**empfindlich** *adj.* sensitive to light, *phot.* sensitive; *~ machen* sensitize.

'**lichten** *v/t.* (ge-, h) clear (*forest*); *den Anker ~ ♆* weigh anchor; *sich ~ hair, crowd:* thin.

lichterloh *adv.* ['lɪçtər'lo:] blazing, in full blaze.

'**Licht|geschwindigkeit** *f* speed of light; '**~hof** *m* glass-roofed court; patio; halo (*a. phot.*); '**~leitung** *f* lighting mains *pl.*; '**~maschine** *mot. f* dynamo, generator; '**~pause** *f* blueprint; '**~quelle** *f* light source, source of light; '**~reklame** *f* neon sign; '**~schacht** *m* well; '**~schalter** *m* (light) switch; '**~schein** *m* gleam of light; '♀**scheu** *adj.* shunning the light; '**~signal** *n* light or luminous signal; '**~spieltheater** *n s.* Filmtheater, Kino; '**~strahl** *m* ray or beam of light (*a. fig.*); '♀**undurchlässig** *adj.* opaque. [ing, glade.]

'**Lichtung** *f* (-/-en) clearing, open-

'**Lichtzelle** *f s.* Photozelle.

Lid [li:t] *n* (-[e]s/-er) eyelid.

lieb *adj.* [li:p] dear; nice, kind; *child:* good; *in letters:* ~*er Herr N.* dear Mr N.; ~*er Himmel!* good Heavens!, dear me!; *es ist mir ~, daß* I am glad that; '♀**chen** *n* (-s/-) sweetheart.

Liebe ['li:bə] *f* (-/*no pl.*) love (zu of, for); *aus ~* for love; *aus ~ zu* for the love of; '♀**n** (ge-, h) **1.** *v/t.* love; be in love with; be fond of, like; **2.** *v/i.* (be in) love; '**~nde** *m, f* (-n/-n): *die ~n pl.* the lovers *pl.*

'**liebens|wert** *adj.* lovable; charming; '**~würdig** *adj.* lovable, amiable; *das ist sehr ~ von Ihnen* that is very kind of you; '♀**würdigkeit** *f* (-/-en) amiability, kindness.

'**lieber 1.** *adj.* dearer; **2.** *adv.* rather, sooner; *~ haben* prefer, like better.

'**Liebes|brief** *m* love-letter; '**~dienst** *m* favo(u)r, kindness; good turn; '**~erklärung** *f*: *e-e ~ machen* declare one's love; '**~heirat** *f* love-match; '**~kummer** *m* lover's grief; '**~paar** *n* (courting) couple, lovers *pl.*; '**~verhältnis** *n* love-affair.

'**liebevoll** *adj.* loving, affectionate.

lieb|gewinnen ['li:p-] *v/t.* (*irr. gewinnen, sep., no* -ge-, h) get or grow fond of; '**~haben** *v/t.* (*irr. haben, sep.,* -ge-, h) love, be fond of; '♀**haber** *m* (-s/-) lover; beau; *fig.* amateur; '♀**haberei** *fig.* ['~'raɪ] *f* (-/-en) hobby; '♀**haberpreis** *m* fancy price; '♀**haberwert** *m* sentimental value; '**~kosen** *v/t.* (*no* -ge-, h) caress, fondle; '♀**kosung** *f* (-/-en) caress; '**~lich** *adj.* lovely, charming, delightful.

Liebling ['li:plɪŋ] *m* (-s/-e) darling; favo(u)rite; *esp. animals:* pet; *esp. form of address:* darling, *esp. Am.* honey; '**~sbeschäftigung** *f* favo(u)rite occupation, hobby.

lieb|los *adj.* ['li:p-] unkind; careless; '♀**schaft** *f* (-/-en) (love-)affair; '♀**ste** *m, f* (-n/-n) sweetheart; darling.

Lied [li:t] *n* (-[e]s/-er) song; tune.

liederlich *adj.* ['li:dərlɪç] slovenly, disorderly; careless; loose, dissolute.

lief [li:f] *pret. of* laufen.

Lieferant [li:fə'rant] *m* (-en/-en) supplier, purveyor; caterer.

Liefer|auto ['li:fər-] *n s.* Lieferwagen; '2**bar** adj. to be delivered; available; '**~bedingungen** f/pl. terms pl. of delivery; '**~frist** f term of delivery; '2**n** v/t. (ge-, h) deliver; j-m et. ~ furnish or supply s.o. with s.th.; '**~schein** m delivery note; '**~ung** f (-/-en) delivery; supply; consignment; instal(l)ment (of book); '**~ungsbedingungen** f/pl. s. Lieferbedingungen; '**~wagen** m deliveryvan, Am. delivery wagon.

Liege ['li:gə] f (-/-n) couch; bedchair.

liegen ['li:gən] v/i. (irr., ge-, h) lie; house, etc.: be (situated); room: face; an wem liegt es? whose fault is it? es liegt an or bei ihm zu inf. it is for him to inf.; es liegt daran, daß the reason for it is that; es liegt mir daran zu inf. I am anxious to inf.; es liegt mir nichts daran it does not matter or it is of no consequence to me; '**~bleiben** v/i. (irr. bleiben, sep., -ge-, sein) stay in bed; break down (on the road, a. mot., etc.); goods: remain on hand; '**~lassen** v/t. (irr. lassen, sep., [-ge-,] h) leave; leave behind; leave alone; leave off (work); j-n links ~ ignore s.o., give s.o. the cold shoulder; '2**schaften** f/pl. real estate.

'**Liege|stuhl** m deck-chair; '**~wagen** m couchette coach.

lieh [li:] pret. of leihen.

ließ [li:s] pret. of lassen.

Lift [lift] m (-[e]s/-e, -s) lift, Am. elevator.

Liga ['li:ga] f (-/Ligen) league.

Likör [li'kø:r] m (-s/-e) liqueur, cordial.

lila adj. ['li:la] lilac.

Lilie ['li:ljə] f (-/-n) lily.

Limonade [limo'na:də] f (-/-n) soft drink, fruit-juice; lemonade.

Limousine [limu'zi:nə] f (-/-n) mot. limousine, saloon car, Am. sedan.

lind adj. [lint] soft, gentle; mild.

Linde ['lində] f (-/-n) lime(-tree), linden(-tree).

linder|n ['lindərn] v/t. (ge-, h) soften; mitigate; alleviate; soothe; allay; ease (pain); '2**ung** f (-/~-en) softening; mitigation; alleviation; easing.

Lineal [line'a:l] n (-s/-e) ruler.

Linie ['li:njə] f (-/-n) line; '**~npapier** n ruled paper; '**~nrichter** m

sports: linesman; '2**ntreu** pol. adj.: ~ sein follow the party line.

lin(i)ieren [li'ni:rən; lini'i:rən] v/t. (no -ge-, h) rule, line.

link adj. [link] left; **~e** Seite left (-hand) side, left; of cloth: wrong side; '2**e** f (-n/-n) the left (hand); pol. the Left (Wing); boxing: the left; '**~isch** adj. awkward, clumsy.

links adv. on or to the left; 2**händer** ['~hɛndər] m (-s/-) left-hander, Am. a. southpaw.

Linse ['linzə] f (-/-n) ♀ lentil; opt. lens.

Lippe ['lipə] f (-/-n) lip; '**~nstift** m lipstick.

liquidieren [likvi'di:rən] v/t. (no -ge-, h) liquidate (a. pol.); wind up (business company); charge (fee).

lispeln ['lispəln] v/i. and v/t. (ge-, h) lisp; whisper.

List [list] f (-/-en) cunning, craft; artifice, ruse, trick; stratagem.

Liste ['listə] f (-/-n) list, roll.

'**listig** adj. cunning, crafty, sly.

Liter ['li:tər] n, m (-s/-) lit|re, Am. -er.

literarisch adj. [lite'ra:riʃ] literary.

Literatur [litera'tu:r] f (-/-en) literature; **~beilage** f literary supplement (in newspaper); **~geschichte** f history of literature; **~verzeichnis** n bibliography.

litt [lit] pret. of leiden.

Litze ['litsə] f (-/-n) lace, cord, braid; ⚡ strand(ed wire).

Livree [li'vre:] f (-/-n) livery.

Lizenz [li'tsɛnts] f (-/-en) licen|ce, Am. -se; **~inhaber** m licensee.

Lob [lo:p] n (-[e]s/no pl.) praise; commendation; 2**en** ['lo:bən] v/t. (ge-, h) praise; 2**enswert** adj. ['lo:bəns-] praise-worthy, laudable; **~gesang** ['lo:p-] m hymn, song of praise; **~hudelei** [lo:phu:də'laı] f (-/-en) adulation, base flattery.

löblich adj. ['lø:pliç] s. lobenswert.

Lobrede ['lo:p-] f eulogy, panegyric.

Loch [lɔx] n (-[e]s/̈er) hole; 2**en** v/t. (ge-, h) perforate, pierce; punch (ticket, etc.); **~er** m (-s/-) punch, perforator; '**~karte** f punch(ed) card.

Locke ['lɔkə] f (-/-n) curl, ringlet.

'**locken**[1] v/t. and v/refl. (ge-, h) curl.

'**locken**[2] v/t. (ge-, h) hunt.: bait; decoy (a. fig.); fig. allure, entice.

'**Locken|kopf** *m* curly head; **~wickler** [´~viklər] *m* (-s/-) curler, roller.

locker *adj.* [´lɔkər] loose; slack; **~n** *v/t.* (ge-, h) loosen; slacken; relax (*grip*); break up (*soil*); *sich ~* loosen, (be)come loose; give way; *fig.* relax.

'**lockig** *adj.* curly.

'**Lock|mittel** *n* s. Köder; '**~vogel** *m* decoy (a. *fig.*); *Am. a.* stool pigeon (a. *fig.*).

lodern [´lo:dərn] *v/i.* (ge-, h) flare, blaze.

Löffel [´lœfəl] *m* (-s/-) spoon; ladle; '**2n** *v/t.* (ge-, h) spoon up; ladle out; '**~voll** *m* (-/-) spoonful.

log [lo:k] *pret. of* lügen.

Loge [´lo:ʒə] *f* (-/-n) *thea.* box; *free-masonry*: lodge; '**~nschließer** *thea.* *m* (-s/-) box-keeper.

logieren [lo´ʒi:rən] *v/i.* (no -ge-, h) lodge, stay, *Am. a.* room (*all: bei* with; *in dat.* at).

logisch *adj.* [´lo:giʃ] logical; '**~erweise** *adv.* logically.

Lohn [lo:n] *m* (-[e]s/~e) wages *pl.*, pay(ment); hire; *fig.* reward; '**~büro** *n* pay-office; '**~empfänger** *m* wage-earner; '**2en** *v/t.* (ge-, h) compensate, reward; *sich ~* pay; *es lohnt sich zu inf.* it is worth while *ger.*, it pays to *inf.*; '**2end** *adj.* paying; advantageous; *fig.* rewarding; '**~erhöhung** *f* increase in wages, rise, *Am.* raise; '**~forderung** *f* demand for higher wages; '**~steuer** *f* tax on wages *or* salary; '**~stopp** *m* (-s/*no pl.*) wage freeze; '**~tarif** *m* wage rate; '**~tüte** *f* pay envelope.

lokal [lo´ka:l] **1.** *adj.* local; **2.** 2 *n* (-[e]s/-e) locality, place; restaurant; public house, F pub, F local, *Am.* saloon.

Lokomotiv|e [lokomo´ti:və] *f* (-/-n) (railway) engine, locomotive; '**~führer** [´~ti:f-] *m* engine-driver, *Am.* engineer.

Lorbeer [´lɔrbe:r] *m* (-s/-en) laurel, bay.

Lore [´lo:rə] *f* (-/-n) lorry, truck.

Los[1] [lo:s] *n* (-es/-e) lot; lottery ticket; *fig.* fate, destiny, lot; *das Große ~ ziehen* win the first prize, *Am. sl.* hit the jackpot; *durchs ~ entscheiden* decide by lot.

los[2] [~] **1.** *pred. adj.* loose; free; *was ist ~?* what is the matter?, F what's up?, *Am.* F what's cooking?; *~ sein*

be rid of; **2.** *int.*: *~!* go (on *or* ahead)!

losarbeiten [´lo:s?-] *v/i.* (sep., -ge-, h) start work(ing).

lösbar *adj.* [´lø:sba:r] soluble, A *a.* solvable.

'**los|binden** *v/t.* (irr. binden, sep., -ge-, h) untie, loosen; '**~brechen** (irr. brechen, sep., -ge-) **1.** *v/t.* (h) break off; **2.** *v/i.* (sein) break *or* burst out.

Lösch|blatt [´lœʃ-] *n* blotting-paper; '**2en** *v/t.* (ge-, h) extinguish, put out (*fire, light*); blot out (*writing*); erase (*tape recording*); cancel (*debt*); quench (*thirst*); slake (*lime*); ⚓ unload; '**~er** *m* (-s/-) blotter; '**~papier** *n* blotting-paper.

lose *adj.* [´lo:zə] loose.

'**Lösegeld** *n* ransom.

losen [´lo:zən] *v/i.* (ge-, h) cast *or* draw lots (*um* for).

lösen [´lø:zən] *v/t.* (ge-, h) loosen, untie; buy, book (*ticket*); solve (*task, doubt, etc.*); break off (*engagement*); annul (*agreement, etc.*), ⚓ dissolve; *ein Schuß löste sich* the gun went off.

'**los|fahren** *v/i.* (irr. fahren, sep., -ge-, h) depart, drive off; '**~gehen** *v/i.* (irr. gehen, sep., -ge-, h) go *or* be off; come off; get loose; *gun:* go off; begin, start; F *auf j-n ~* fly at s.o.; '**~haken** *v/t.* (sep., -ge-, h) unhook; '**~kaufen** *v/t.* (sep., -ge-, h) ransom, redeem; '**~ketten** *v/t.* (sep., -ge-, h) unchain; '**~kommen** *v/i.* (irr. kommen, sep., -ge-, sein) get loose *or* free; '**~lachen** *v/i.* (sep., -ge-, h) laugh out; '**~lassen** *v/t.* (irr. lassen, sep., -ge-, h) let go; release.

löslich ⚓ *adj.* [´lø:sliç] soluble.

'**los|lösen** *v/t.* (sep., -ge-, h) loosen, detach; sever; '**~machen** *v/t.* (sep., -ge-, h) unfasten, loosen; *sich ~* disengage (o.s.) (*von* from); '**~reißen** *v/t.* (irr. reißen, sep., -ge-, h) tear off; *sich ~* break away, *esp. fig.* tear o.s. away (*both: von* from); '**~sagen** *v/refl.* (sep., -ge-, h): *sich ~ von* renounce; '**~schlagen** (irr. schlagen, sep., -ge-, h) **1.** *v/t.* knock off; **2.** *v/i.* open the attack; *auf j-n ~* attack s.o.; '**~schnallen** *v/t.* (sep., -ge-, h) unbuckle; '**~schrauben** *v/t.* (sep., -ge-, h) unscrew, screw off; '**~sprechen** *v/t.* (irr. sprechen, *sep.*, -ge-, *h*) absolve (*von* of, from); acquit (of); free (from, of); '**stürzen** *v/i.* (*sep.*, -ge-, *sein*) $\sim$ *auf* (*acc.*) rush at.

Losung ['lo:zuŋ] *f* **1.** (-/-en) ⚔ password, watchword; *fig.* slogan; **2.** *hunt.* (-/*no pl.*) droppings *pl.*, dung.

Lösung ['lø:zuŋ] *f* (-/-en) solution; '**smittel** *n* solvent.

'**los|werden** *v/t.* (*irr.* werden, *sep.*, -ge-, *sein*) get rid of, dispose of; '**ziehen** *v/i.* (*irr.* ziehen, *sep.*, -ge-, *sein*) set out, take off, march away.

Lot [lo:t] *n* (-[e]s/-e) plumb(-line), plummet.

löten ['lø:tən] *v/t.* (ge-, *h*) solder.

Lotse ⚓ ['lo:tsə] *m* (-n/-n) pilot; '**2n** *v/t.* (ge-, *h*) ⚓ pilot (*a. fig.*).

Lotterie [lɔtə'ri:] *f* (-/-n) lottery; '**gewinn** *m* prize; '**los** *n* lottery ticket.

Lotto ['lɔto] *n* (-s/-s) numbers pool, lotto.

Löwe *zo.* ['lø:və] *m* (-n/-n) lion.

'**Löwen|anteil** F *m* lion's share; '**maul** ⚘ *n* (-[e]s/*no pl.*) snapdragon; '**zahn** ⚘ *m* (-[e]s/*no pl.*) dandelion. '**Löwin** *zo. f* (-/-nen) lioness.

loyal *adj.* [loa'ja:l] loyal.

Luchs *zo.* [luks] *m* (-es/-e) lynx.

Lücke ['lykə] *f* (-/-n) gap; blank, void (*a. fig.*); '**nbüßer** *m* stopgap; '**2nhaft** *adj.* full of gaps; *fig.* defective, incomplete; '**2nlos** *adj.* without a gap; *fig.*: unbroken, complete; $\sim$er Beweis close argument.

lud [lu:t] *pret. of* laden.

Luft [luft] *f* (-/$\sim$e) air; breeze; breath; *frische* $\sim$ *schöpfen* take the air; *an die* $\sim$ *gehen* go for an airing; *aus der* $\sim$ *gegriffen* (totally) unfounded, fantastic; *es liegt et. in der* $\sim$ there is s.th. in the wind; *in die* $\sim$ *fliegen* be blown up, explode; *in die* $\sim$ *gehen* explode, *sl.* blow one's top; *in die* $\sim$ *sprengen* blow up; F *j-n an die* $\sim$ *setzen* turn s.o. out, *Am. sl.* give s.o. the air; *sich or s-n Gefühlen* $\sim$ *machen* give vent to one's feelings.

'**Luft|alarm** *m* air-raid alarm; '**angriff** *m* air raid; '**aufnahme** *f* aerial photograph; '**ballon** *m* (air-)balloon; '**bild** *n* aerial photograph, airview; '**blase** *f* airbubble; '**brücke** *f* air-bridge; *for supplies, etc.*: air-lift.

Lüftchen ['lyftçən] *n* (-s/-) gentle breeze.

'**luft|dicht** *adj.* air-tight; '**2druck** *phys. m* (-[e]s/*no pl.*) atmospheric or air pressure; '**2druckbremse** ⊕ *f* air-brake; '**durchlässig** *adj.* permeable to air.

lüften ['lyftən] (ge-, *h*) **1.** *v/i.* air; **2.** *v/t.* air; raise (*hat*); lift (*veil*); disclose (*secret*).

'**Luft|fahrt** *f* aviation, aeronautics; '**feuchtigkeit** *f* atmospheric humidity; '**2gekühlt** ⊕ *adj.* air-cooled; '**hoheit** *f* air sovereignty; '**2ig** *adj.* airy; breezy; flimsy; '**kissen** *n* air-cushion; '**klappe** *f* air-valve; '**korridor** *m* air corridor; '**krankheit** *f* airsickness; '**krieg** *m* aerial warfare; '**kurort** *m* climatic health resort; '**landetruppen** *f/pl.* airborne troops *pl.*; '**2leer** *adj.* void of air, evacuated; $\sim$er Raum vacuum; '**linie** *f* air line, bee-line; '**loch** *n* ✈ airpocket; vent(-hole); '**post** *f* air mail; '**pumpe** *f* air-pump; '**raum** *m* airspace; '**röhre** *anat. f* windpipe, trachea; '**schacht** *m* air-shaft; '**schaukel** *f* swing-boat; '**schiff** *n* airship; '**schloß** *n* castle in the air *or* in Spain; '**schutz** *m* air-raid protection; '**schutzkeller** *m* air-raid shelter; '**sprünge** ['ʃpryŋə] *m/pl.*: $\sim$ *machen* cut capers *pl.*; gambol; '**stützpunkt** ✕ *m* air base. [ten.] '**Lüftung** *f* (-/-en) airing; ventila-[

'**Luft|veränderung** *f* change of air; '**verkehr** *m* air-traffic; '**verkehrsgesellschaft** *f* air transport company, airway, *Am.* airline; '**verteidigung** ✕ *f* air defence, *Am.* -se; '**waffe** ✕ *f* air force; '**weg** *m* airway; *auf dem* $\sim$ by air; '**zug** *m* draught, *Am.* draft.

Lüge ['ly:gə] *f* (-/-n) lie, falsehood; *j-n* $\sim$*n strafen* give the lie to s.o.

'**lügen** *v/i.* (*irr.*, ge-, *h*) (tell a) lie; '**haft** *adj.* lying, mendacious; untrue, false.

Lügner ['ly:gnər] *m* (-s/-), '**in** *f* (-/-nen) liar; '**2isch** *adj. s.* lügenhaft.

Luke ['lu:kə] *f* (-/-n) dormer- *or* garret-window; hatch.

Lümmel ['lyməl] *m* (-s/-) lout, boor; saucy fellow; '**2n** *v/refl.* (ge-, *h*) loll, lounge, sprawl.

Lump [lump] *m* (-en/-en) ragamuffin, beggar; cad, *Am. sl.* rat, heel; scoundrel.

'**Lumpen 1.** *m* (-s/-) rag; **2.** ♀ *vb.*: *sich nicht ~ lassen* come down handsomely; '**~pack** *n* rabble, riffraff; '**~sammler** *m* rag-picker.

'**lumpig** *adj.* ragged; *fig.*: shabby, paltry; mean.

Lunge ['luŋə] *f* (-/-n) *anat.* lungs *pl.*; *of animals:* a. lights *pl.*

'**Lungen|entzündung** ♀ *f* pneumonia; '**~flügel** *anat. m* lung; '**♀krank** ♀ *adj.* suffering from consumption, consumptive; '**~kranke** ♀ *m, f* consumptive (patient); '**~krankheit** ♀ *f* lung-disease; '**~schwindsucht** ♀ *f* (pulmonary) consumption.

lunge·n ['luŋən] *v/i.* (ge-, h) *s. herum·lungern.*

Lupe [lu:pə] *f* (-/-n) magnifying-glass; *unter die ~ nehmen* scrutinize, take a good look at.

Lust [lust] *f* (-/⸚e) pleasure, delight; desire; lust; ~ *haben zu inf.* have a mind to *inf.*, feel like *ger.*; *haben Sie ~ auszugehen?* would you like to go out?

lüstern *adj.* ['lystərn] desirous (*nach*

of), greedy (*of, for*); lewd, lascivious, lecherous.

'**lustig** *adj.* merry, gay; jolly, cheerful; amusing, funny; *sich ~ machen über* (*acc.*) make fun of; '**♀keit** *f* (-/*no pl.*) gaiety, mirth; jollity, cheerfulness; fun.

Lüstling ['lystliŋ] *m* (-s/-e) voluptuary, libertine.

'**lust|los** *adj.* dull, spiritless; † flat; '**♀mord** *m* rape and murder; '**♀spiel** *n* comedy.

lutschen ['lutʃən] *v/i. and v/t.* (ge-, h) suck.   [ward.]

Luv ⚓ [lu:f] *f* (-/*no pl.*) luff, wind-)

luxuriös *adj.* [luksu'rjø:s] luxurious.

Luxus ['luksus] *m* (-/*no pl.*) luxury (*a. fig.*); '**~artikel** *m* luxury; '**~ausgabe** *f* de luxe edition (*of books*); '**~ware** *f* luxury (article); fancy goods *pl.*

Lymph|drüse *anat.* ['lymf-] *f* lymphatic gland; '**~e** *f* (-/-n) lymph; ♀ vaccine; '**~gefäß** *anat. n* lymphatic vessel.

lynchen ['lynçən] *v/t.* (ge-, h) lynch.

Lyrik ['ly:rik] *f* (-/*no pl.*) lyric verses *pl.*, lyrics *pl.*; '**~er** *m* (-s/-) lyric poet.

'**lyrisch** *adj.* lyric; lyrical (*a. fig.*).

M

Maat ⚓ [ma:t] *m* (-[e]s/-e[n]) (ship's) mate.

Mache F ['maxə] *f* (-/*no pl.*) make-believe, window-dressing, *sl.* eyewash; *et. in der ~ haben* have s.th. in hand.

machen ['maxən] (ge-, h) **1.** *v/t.* make; do; produce, manufacture; give (*appetite, etc.*); sit for, undergo (*examination*); come *or* amount to; make (*happy, etc.*); *was macht das (aus)?* what does that matter?; *das macht nichts!* never mind!, that's (quite) all right!; *da(gegen) kann man nichts ~* that cannot be helped; *ich mache mir nichts daraus* I don't care about it; *mach, daß du fortkommst!* off with you!; *j-n ~ lassen, was er will* let s.o. do as he pleases; *sich ~ an* (*acc.*) go *or* set about; *sich et. ~ lassen* have s.th. made; **2.** F *v/i.*: *na, mach schon!*

hurry up!; '**♀schaften** *f/pl.* machinations *pl.*

Macht [maxt] *f* (-/⸚e) power; might; authority; control (*über acc.* of); *an der ~ pol.* in power; '**~befugnis** *f* authority, power; '**~haber** *pol. m* (-s/-) ruler.

mächtig *adj.* ['meçtiç] powerful (*a. fig.*); mighty, immense, huge; *~ sein* (*gen.*) be master of *s.th.*; have command of (*language*).

'**Macht|kampf** *m* struggle for power; '**♀los** *adj.* powerless; '**~politik** *f* power politics *sg., pl.*; policy of the strong hand; '**~spruch** *m* authoritative decision; '**♀voll** *adj.* powerful (*a. fig.*); '**~vollkommenheit** *f* authority; '**~wort** *n* (-[e]s/⸚e) word of command; *ein ~ sprechen* put one's foot down.

'**Machwerk** *n* concoction, F put-up job; *elendes ~* bungling work.

Mädchen ['mɛːtçən] n (-s/-) girl; maid(-servant); ~ für alles maid of all work; fig. a. jack of all trades; '2haft adj. girlish; '~name m girl's name; maiden name; '~schule f girls' school.

Made zo. ['maːdə] f (-/-n) maggot, mite; fruit: worm.

Mädel ['mɛːdəl] n (-s/-, F -s) girl, lass(ie).

madig adj. ['maːdiç] maggoty, full of mites; fruit: wormeaten.

Magazin [maga'tsiːn] n (-s/-e) store, warehouse; ✕, in rifle, periodical: magazine.

Magd [maːkt] f (-/⸚e) maid(-servant).

Magen ['maːgən] m (-s/⸚, a. -) stomach, F tummy; animals: maw; '~beschwerden f/pl. stomach or gastric trouble, indigestion; '~bitter m (-s/-) bitters pl.; '~geschwür ⚕ n gastric ulcer; '~krampf ⚕ m stomach cramp; '~krebs ⚕ m stomach cancer; '~leiden n gastric complaint; '~säure f gastric acid.

mager adj. ['maːgər] meag|re, Am. -er (a. fig.); p., animal, meat: lean, Am. a. scrawny; '2milch f skim milk.

Magie [ma'giː] f (-/no pl.) magic; ~r ['maːgjər] m (-s/-) magician.

magisch adj. ['maːgiʃ] magic(al).

Magistrat [magis'traːt] m (-[e]s/-e) municipal or town council.

Magnet [ma'gneːt] m (-[e]s, -en/-e[n]) magnet (a. fig.); lodestone; 2isch adj. magnetic; 2isieren [~eti'ziːrən] v/t. (no -ge-, h) magnetize; ~nadel [~'gneːt-] f magnetic needle.

Mahagoni [maha'goːni] n (-s/no pl.) mahogany (wood).

mähen ['mɛːən] v/t. (ge-, h) cut, mow, reap.

Mahl [maːl] n (-[e]s/⸚er, -e) meal, repast.

'**mahlen** (irr., ge-, h) 1. v/t. grind, mill; 2. v/i. tyres: spin.

'**Mahlzeit** f s. Mahl; F feed.

Mähne ['mɛːnə] f (-/-n) mane.

mahn|en ['maːnən] v/t. (ge-, h) remind, admonish (both: an acc. of); j-n wegen e-r Schuld ~ press s.o. for payment, dun s.o.; '2mal n(-[e]s/-e) memorial; '2ung f (-/-en) admonition; ✝ reminder, dunning; '2zettel m reminder.

Mai [maɪ] m (-[e]s, -/-e) May; '~baum m maypole; ~glöckchen ⚘ ['~glœkçən] n (-s/-) lily of the valley; '~käfer zo. m cockchafer, may-beetle, may-bug.

Mais ⚘ [maɪs] m (-es/-e) maize, Indian corn, Am. corn.

Majestät [maje'stɛːt] f (-/-en) majesty; 2isch adj. majestic; ~sbeleidigung f lese-majesty.

Major ✕ [ma'joːr] m (-s/-e) major.

Makel ['maːkəl] m (-s/-) stain, spot; fig. a. blemish, fault; '2los adj. stainless, spotless; fig. a. unblemished, faultless, immaculate.

mäkeln F ['mɛːkəln] v/i. (ge-, h) find fault (an dat. with), carp (at), F pick (at).

Makler ✝ ['maːklər] m (-s/-) broker; '~gebühr ✝ f brokerage.

Makulatur ⊕ [makula'tuːr] f (-/-en) waste paper.

Mal[1] [maːl] n (-[e]s/-e, ⸚er) mark, sign; sports: start(ing-point), goal; spot, stain, mole.

Mal[2] [~] **1.** n (-[e]s/-e) time; für dieses ~ this time; zum ersten ~e for the first time; mit e-m ~e all at once, all of a sudden; **2.** 2 adv. times, multiplied by; drei ~ fünf ist fünfzehn three times five is or are fifteen; F s. einmal.

'**malen** v/t. (ge-, h) paint; portray.

'**Maler** m (-s/-) painter; artist; ~ei [~'raɪ] f (-/-en) painting; '2isch adj. pictorial, painting; fig. picturesque.

'**Malkasten** m paint-box.

'**malnehmen** ✕ v/t. (irr. nehmen, sep., -ge-, h) multiply (mit by).

Malz [malts] n (-es/no pl.) malt; '~bier n malt beer.

Mama [ma'maː, F 'mama] f (-/-s) mamma, mammy, F ma, Am. F a. mummy, mom.

man indef. pron. [man] one, you, we; they, people; ~ sagte mir I was told.   [manager.]

Manager ['menidʒər] m (-s/-)∫

manch [manç], '~er, '~e, '~es adj. and indef. pron. many a; ~e pl. some, several; ~erlei adj. ['~ər'laɪ] diverse, different; all sorts of, ... of several sorts; auf ~ Art in various ways; used as a noun: many or various things; '~mal adv. sometimes, at times.

Mandant ⚖ [man'dant] m (-en/-en) client.

M

Mandarine

Mandarine ♀ [manda'ri:nə] f (-/-n) tangerine.

Mandat [man'dɑ:t] n (-[e]s/-e) authorization; ⚖ brief; *pol.* mandate; *parl.* seat.

Mandel ['mandəl] f (-/-n) ♀ almond; *anat.* tonsil; **'~baum** ♀ m almond-tree; **'~entzündung** ⚕ f tonsillitis. [ring, manège.)

Manege [ma'nε:ʒə] f (-/-n) (circus-)

Mangel[1] ['maŋəl] m **1.** (-s/no pl.) want, lack, deficiency; shortage; penury; *aus* ~ *an* (dat.) for want of; ~ *leiden an* (dat.) be in want of; **2.** (-s/⁓) defect, shortcoming.

Mangel[2] [⁓] f (-/-n) mangle; calender.

'mangelhaft adj. defective; deficient; unsatisfactory; **'2igkeit** f (-/no pl.) defectiveness; deficiency.

'mangeln[1] v/i. (ge-, h): *es mangelt an Brot* there is a lack or shortage of bread, bread is lacking or wanting; *es mangelt ihm an* (dat.) he is in need of or short of or wanting in, he wants or lacks.

'mangeln[2] v/t. (ge-, h) mangle (clothes, etc.); ⊕ calender (cloth, paper).

'mangels prp. (gen.) for lack or want of; *esp.* ⚖ in default of.

'Mangelware ♀ f scarce commodity; goods pl. in short supply.

Manie [ma'ni:] f (-/-n) mania.

Manier [ma'ni:r] f (-/-en) manner; **2lich** adj. well-behaved; polite, mannerly. [manifesto.)

Manifest [mani'fεst] n (-es/-e)

Mann [man] m (-[e]s/⁓er) man; husband.

'mannbar adj. marriageable; **'2-keit** f (-/no pl.) puberty, manhood.

Männchen ['mεnçən] n (-s/-) little man; *zo.* male; *birds*: cock.

'Mannes|alter n virile age, manhood; **'~kraft** f virility.

mannig|fach adj. ['maniç-], **'~fal-tig** adj. manifold, various, diverse; **'2faltigkeit** f (-/no pl.) manifoldness, variety, diversity.

männlich adj. ['mεnliç] male; *gr.* masculine; *fig.* manly; **'2keit** f (-/no pl.) manhood, virility.

'Mannschaft f (-/-en) (body of) men; ⚓ crew; *sports*: team; side; **'~sführer** m *sports*: captain; **'~s-geist** m (-es/no pl.) *sports*: team spirit.

Manöv|er [ma'nø:vər] n (-s/-) ma-nœuvre, *Am.* maneuver; **2rieren** [⁓'vri:rən] v/i. (no -ge-, h) manœu-vre, *Am.* maneuver.

Mansarde [man'zardə] f (-/-n) attic, garret; **~nfenster** n dormer-window.

mansche|n F ['manʃən] (ge-, h) **1.** v/t. mix, work; **2.** v/i. dabble (in dat. in); **2'rei** F f (-/-en) mixing, F mess; dabbling.

Manschette [man'ʃεtə] f (-/-n) cuff; **~nknopf** m cuff-link.

Mantel ['mantəl] m (-s/⁓) coat; overcoat, greatcoat; cloak, mantle (*both a. fig.*); ⊕ case, jacket; (outer) cover (*of tyre*).

Manuskript [manu'skript] n (-[e]s -e) manuscript; *typ.* copy.

Mappe ['mapə] f (-/-n) portfolio, brief-case; folder; *s. a. Schreib-mappe, Schulmappe.*

Märchen ['mε:rçən] n (-s/-) fairy-tale; *fig.* (cock-and-bull) story, fib; **'~buch** n book of fairy-tales; **'2haft** adj. fabulous (*a. fig.*). [ten.)

Marder *zo.* ['mardər] m (-s/-) mar-)

Marine [ma'ri:nə] f (-/-n) marine; ⚔ navy, naval forces pl.; **~minister** m minister of naval affairs; First Lord of the Admiralty, *Am.* Secretary of the Navy; **~ministerium** n ministry of naval affairs; *the* Admiralty, *Am.* Department of the Navy.

marinieren [mari'ni:rən] v/t. (no -ge-, h) pickle, marinade.

Marionette [mario'nεtə] f (-/-n) puppet, marionette; **~ntheater** n puppet-show.

Mark [mark] **1.** f (-/-) *coin*: mark; **2.** n (-[e]s/no pl.) *anat.* marrow; ♀ pith; *fig.* core.

markant adj. [mar'kant] characteristic; striking; (well-)marked.

Marke ['markə] f (-/-n) mark, sign, token; ⚓, *etc.*: stamp; ✝ brand, trade-mark; coupon; **'~nartikel** ✝ m branded or proprietary article.

mar'kier|en (no -ge-, h) **1.** v/t. mark (*a. sports*); brand (cattle, goods, *etc.*); **2.** F *fig.* v/i. put it on; **2ung** f (-/-en) mark(ing).

'markig adj. marrowy; *fig.* pithy.

Markise [mar'ki:zə] f (-/-n) blind, (window-)awning.

'Markstein m boundary-stone, land-mark (*a. fig.*).

maßvoll

Markt [markt] *m* (-[e]s/⁺e) ⚓ market; *s.* Marktplatz; fair; *auf den ~ bringen* ⚓ put on the market; '**~flecken** *m* small market-town; '**~platz** *m* market-place; '**~schreier** *m* (-s/-) quack; puffer.

Marmelade [marmə'laːdə] *f* (-/-n) jam; marmalade (*made of oranges*).

Marmor ['marmɔr] *m* (-s/-e) marble; **2ieren** [~o'riːrən] *v/t.* (*no* -ge-, *h*) marble, vein, grain; **2n** *adj.* ['~ɔrn] (of) marble. [whim, caprice.)

Marotte [ma'rɔtə] *f* (-/-n) fancy,)

Marsch [marʃ] **1.** *m* (-es/⁺e) march (*a.* ♪); **2.** *f* (-/-en) marsh, fen.

Marschall ['marʃal] *m* (-s/⁺e) marshal.

'**Marsch|befehl** ✗ *m* marching orders *pl.*; **2ieren** [~'ʃiːrən] *v/i.* (*no* -ge-, *sein*) march; '**~land** *n* marshy land.

Marter ['martər] *f* (-/-n) torment, torture; '**2n** *v/t.* (ge-, *h*) torment, torture; '**~pfahl** *m* stake.

Märtyrer ['mertyrər] *m* (-s/-) martyr; '**~tod** *m* martyr's death; '**~tum** *n* (-s/*no pl.*) martyrdom.

Marxis|mus *pol.* [mar'ksismus] *m* (-/*no pl.*) Marxism; **~t** *pol. m* (-en/-en) Marxian, Marxist; **2tisch** *pol. adj.* Marxian, Marxist.

März [merts] *m* (-[e]s/-e) March.

Marzipan [martsi'paːn] *n*, ✗ *m* (-s/-e) marzipan, marchpane.

Masche ['maʃə] *f* (-/-n) mesh; *knitting*: stitch; F *fig.* trick, line; '**2n-fest** *adj.* ladder-proof, *Am.* runproof.

Maschine [ma'ʃiːnə] *f* (-/-n) machine; engine.

maschinell *adj.* [maʃi'nɛl] mechanical; **~e** *Bearbeitung* machining.

Ma'schinen|bau ⊕ *m* (-[e]s/*no pl.*) mechanical engineering; **~gewehr** ✗ *n* machine-gun; **2mäßig** *adj.* mechanical; automatic; **~pistole** ✗ *f* sub-machine-gun; **~schaden** *m* engine trouble; **~schlosser** *m* (engine) fitter; **~schreiberin** *f* (-/-nen) typist; **~schrift** *f* typescript.

Maschin|erie [maʃinə'riː] *f* (-/-n) machinery; **~ist** [~'nist] *m* (-en/-en) machinist.

Masern 🔬 ['maːzərn] *pl.* measles *pl.*

Mask|e ['maskə] *f* (-/-n) mask (*a. fig.*); '**~enball** *m* fancy-dress *or* masked ball; **~erade** [~'raːdə] *f* (-/-n) masquerade; **2ieren** [~'kiː-

rən] *v/t.* (*no* -ge-, *h*) mask; *sich ~* put on a mask; dress o.s. up (*als* as).

Maß [maːs] **1.** *n* (-es/-e) measure; proportion; *fig.* moderation; **~e** *pl. und Gewichte pl.* weights and measures *pl.*; **~e** *pl.* room, *etc.*: measurements *pl.*; **2.** *f* (-/-[e]) *appr.* quart (*of beer*); **3.** **⚲** *pret. of* messen.

Massage [ma'saːʒə] *f* (-/-n) massage.

'**Maßanzug** *m* tailor-made *or* bespoke suit, *Am. a.* custom(-made) suit.

Masse ['masə] *f* (-/-n) mass; bulk; substance; multitude; crowd; ⚖ assets *pl.*, estate; *die breite ~* the rank and file; F e-e ~ a lot of, F lots *pl. or* heaps *pl.* of.

'**Maßeinheit** *f* measuring unit.

'**Massen|flucht** *f* stampede; '**~grab** *n* common grave; **~güter** ⚓ ['~gyː-tər] *n/pl.* bulk goods *pl.*; '**2haft** *adj.* abundant; '**~produktion** ⊕ *f* mass production; '**~versammlung** *f* mass meeting, *Am. a.* rally; '**2-weise** *adv.* in masses, in large numbers.

Masseu|r [ma'søːr] *m* (-s/-e) masseur; **~se** [~zə] *f* (-/-n) masseuse.

'**maß|gebend** *adj.* standard; authoritative, decisive; *board:* competent; *circles:* influential, leading; '**~hal-ten** *v/i.* (*irr. halten, sep.,* -ge-, *h*) keep within limits, be moderate.

mas'sieren *v/t.* (*no* -ge-, *h*) massage, knead.

'**massig** *adj.* massy, bulky; solid.

mäßig *adj.* ['meːsiç] moderate; *food, etc.*: frugal; ⚓ *price:* moderate, reasonable; *result, etc.*: poor; **~en** ['~gən] *v/t.* (*no* -ge-, *h*) moderate; *sich ~* moderate *or* restrain o.s.; '**2ung** *f* (-/-en) moderation; restraint.

massiv [ma'siːf] **1.** *adj.* massive, solid; **2.** **⚲** *geol. n* (-s/-e) massif.

'**Maß|krug** *m* beer-mug, *Am. a.* stein; '**2los** *adj.* immoderate; boundless; exorbitant, excessive; extravagant; '**~nahme** ['~naːmə] *f* (-/-n) measure, step, action; '**2re-geln** *v/t.* (ge-, *h*) reprimand; inflict disciplinary punishment on; '**~schneider** *m* bespoke *or Am.* custom tailor; '**~stab** *m* measure, rule(r); *maps, etc.*: scale; *fig.* yardstick, standard; '**2voll** *adj.* moderate.

M

Mast¹ ⚓ [mast] *m* (-es/-e[n]) mast.

Mast² 🗡 [~] *f* (-/-en) fattening; mast, food; '**~darm** *anat. m* rectum.

mästen ['mɛstən] *v/t.* (ge-, h) fatten, feed; stuff (*geese, etc.*).

'**Mastkorb** ⚓ *m* mast-head, crows-nest.

Material [mater'ja:l] *n* (-s/-ien) material; substance; stock, stores *pl.*; *fig.*: material, information; evidence; **~ismus** *phls.* [~a'lismus] *m* (-/*no pl.*) materialism; **~ist** [~a'list] *m* (-en/-en) materialist; **2istisch** *adj.* [~a'listiʃ] materialistic.

Materie [ma'te:rjə] *f* (-/-n) matter (*a. fig.*), stuff; *fig.* subject; **2ll** *adj.* [~er'jɛl] material.

Mathemati|k [matema'ti:k] *f* (-/*no pl.*) mathematics *sg.*; **~ker** [~'ma:tikər] *m* (-s/-) mathematician; **2sch** *adj.* [~'ma:tiʃ] mathematical.

Matinee *thea.* [mati'ne:] *f* (-/-n) morning performance.

Matratze [ma'tratsə] *f* (-/-n) mattress.

Matrone [ma'tro:nə] *f* (-/-n) matron; **2nhaft** *adj.* matronly.

Matrose ⚓ [ma'tro:zə] *m* (-n/-n) sailor, seaman.

Matsch [matʃ] *m* (-es/*no pl.*), **~e** *f* ['~ə] *f* (-/*no pl.*) pulp, squash; mud, slush; '**2ig** *adj.* pulpy, squashy; muddy, slushy.

matt *adj.* [mat] faint, feeble; *voice, etc.*: faint; *eye, colour, etc.*: dim; *colour, light,* ✝ *stock exchange, style, etc.*: dull; *metal*: tarnished; *gold, etc.*: dead, dull; *chess*: mated; 🗲 *bulb*: non-glare; ~ *geschliffen glass*: ground, frosted, matted; ~ *setzen at chess*: (check)mate *s.o.*

Matte ['matə] *f* (-/-n) mat.

'**Mattigkeit** *f* (-/*no pl.*) exhaustion, feebleness; faintness.

'**Mattscheibe** *f* *phot.* focus(s)ing screen; *television*: screen.

Mauer ['mauər] *f* (-/-n) wall; ~blümchen *fig.* ['~bly:mçən] *n* (-s/-) wall-flower; '**2n** (ge-, h) **1.** *v/i.* make a wall, lay bricks; **2.** *v/t.* build (in stone or brick); '**~stein** *m* brick; '**~werk** *n* masonry, brickwork.

Maul [maul] *n* (-[e]s/ⁿer) mouth; *sl.*: halt's ~! shut up!; '**2en** F *v/i.* (ge-, h) sulk, pout; '**~esel** *zo. m* mule, hinny; '**~held** F *m* braggart;

'**~korb** *m* muzzle; '**~schelle** F *f* box on the ear; '**~tier** *zo. n* mule; '**~wurf** *zo. m* mole; '**~wurfshügel** *m* molehill.

Maurer ['maurər] *m* (-s/-) brick-layer, mason; '**~meister** *m* master mason; '**~polier** *m* bricklayers' foreman.

Maus *zo.* [maus] *f* (-/ⁿe) mouse; **~efalle** ['~zə-] *f* mousetrap; **2en** ['~zən] (ge-, h) **1.** *v/i.* catch mice; **2.** F *v/t.* pinch, pilfer, F swipe.

Mauser ['mauzər] *f* (-/*no pl.*) mo(u)lt(ing); *in der* ~ *sein* be mo(u)lting; '**2n** *v/refl.* (ge-, h) mo(u)lt.

Maximum ['maksimum] *n* (-s/*Maxima*) maximum.

Mayonnaise [majo'nɛ:zə] *f* (-/-n) mayonnaise.

Mechani|k [me'ça:nik] *f* **1.** (-/*no pl.*) mechanics *mst sg.*; **2.** ⊕ (-/-en) mechanism; '**~ker** *m* (-s/-) mechanic; **2sch** *adj.* mechanical; **2sieren** [~ani'zi:rən] *v/t.* (*no ge-*, h) mechanize; **~smus** ⊕ [~a'nismus] *m* (-/*Mechanismen*) mechanism; *clock, watch, etc.*: works *pl.*

meckern ['mɛkərn] *v/i.* (ge-, h) bleat; *fig.* grumble (*über acc.* over, at, about), carp (at); nag (at); *sl.* grouse, *Am. sl.* gripe.

Medaill|e [me'daljə] *f* (-/-n) medal; **~on** [~'jõ:] *n* (-s/-s) medallion; locket.

Medikament [medika'ment] *n* (-[e]s/-e) medicament, medicine.

Medizin [medi'tsi:n] *f* **1.** (-/*no pl.*) (science of) medicine; **2.** (-/-en) medicine, F physic; **~er** *m* (-s/-) medical man; medical student; **2isch** *adj.* medical; medicinal.

Meer [me:r] *n* (-[e]s/-e) sea (*a. fig.*), ocean; '**~busen** *m* gulf, bay; '**~enge** *f* strait(s *pl.*); '**~esspiegel** *m* sea level; '**~rettich** 🍃 *m* horse-radish; '**~schweinchen** *zo. n* guinea-pig.

Mehl [me:l] *n* (-[e]s/-e) flour; meal; '**~brei** *m* pap; '**2ig** *adj.* floury, mealy; farinaceous; '**~speise** *f* sweet dish, pudding; '**~suppe** *f* gruel.

mehr [me:r] **1.** *adj.* more; *er hat* ~ *Geld als ich* he has (got) more money than I; **2.** *adv.* more; *nicht* ~ no more, no longer; *nicht* ~ *lange* no longer; *ich habe nichts* ~ I have nothing left; '**2arbeit** *f* additional work; overtime; '²ausgaben *f/pl.* additional expenditure; '²betrag *m* surplus; '~deutig *adj.* ambiguous; '²einnahme(n *pl.*) *f* additional receipts *pl.*; '~en *v/t.* (ge-, h) augment, increase; *sich* ~ multiply, grow; '~ere *adj. and indef. pron.* several, some; '~fach **1.** *adj.* manifold, repeated; **2.** *adv.* repeatedly, several times; '~gebot *n* higher bid; '²heit *f* (-/-en) majority, plurality; '²kosten *pl.* additional expense; '~malig *adj.* repeated, reiterated; '~mals *adv.* ['~mɑːls] several times, repeatedly; '~sprachig *adj.* polyglot; '~stimmig ♩ *adj.*: ~er *Gesang* part-song; '²verbrauch *m* excess consumption; '²wertsteuer ✝ *f* (-/no *pl.*) value-added tax; '²zahl *f* majority; *gr.* plural (form); *die* ~ (*gen.*) most of.

meiden ['maɪdən] *v/t.* (irr., ge-, h) avoid, shun, keep away from.

Meile ['maɪlə] *f* (-/-n) mile; '~nstein *m* milestone.

mein *poss. pron.* [maɪn] my; *der (die, das)* ~*e* my; *die* ²*en pl.* my family, F my people *or* folks *pl.*; *ich habe das* ~*e getan* I have done all I can; ~*e Damen und Herren!* Ladies and Gentlemen!

Meineid ⚖ ['maɪn-] *m* perjury; '²ig *adj.* perjured.

meinen ['maɪnən] *v/t.* (ge-, h) think, believe, be of (the) opinion, *Am. a.* reckon, guess; say; mean; *wie* ~ *Sie das?* what do you mean by that?; ~ *Sie das ernst?* do you (really) mean it?; *es gut* ~ mean well.

meinetwegen *adv.* ['maɪnət-] for my sake; on my behalf; because of me, on my account; for all I care; I don't mind *or* care.

'**Meinung** *f* (-/-en) opinion (*über acc.,* von about, of); *die öffentliche* ~ (the) public opinion; *meiner* ~ *nach* in my opinion, to my mind; *j-m (gehörig) die* ~ *sagen* give s.o. a piece of one's mind; '~saustausch ['maɪnuŋs-] *m* exchange of views (*über acc.* on); '~sverschiedenheit *f* difference of opinion (*über acc.* on); disagreement.

Meise *orn.* ['maɪzə] *f* (-/-n) titmouse.

Meißel ['maɪsəl] *m* (-s/-) chisel; '²n *v/t. and v/i.* (ge-, h) chisel; carve.

meist [maɪst] **1.** *adj.* most; *die* ~*en*

Leute most people; *die* ~*e Zeit* most of one's time; **2.** *adv.*: *s. meistens;* *am* ~*en* most (of all); '²bietende ['~biːtəndə] *m* (-n/-n) highest bidder; ~*ens adv.* ['~əns], '~enteils *adv.* mostly, in most cases; usually.

Meister ['maɪstər] *m* (-s/-) master, *sl.* boss; *sports:* champion; '²haft **1.** *adj.* masterly; **2.** *adv.* in a masterly manner *or* way; '²n *v/t.* (ge-, h) master; '~schaft *f* **1.** (-/no *pl.*) mastery; **2.** (-/-en) *sports:* championship, title; '~stück *n*, '~werk *n* masterpiece.

'**Meistgebot** *n* highest bid, best offer.

Melancholie [melaŋko'liː] *f* (-/-n) melancholy; '²isch *adj.* [~'koːliʃ] melancholy; ~ *sein* F have the blues.

Melde|amt *n* registration office; '~liste *f sports:* list of entries; '²n *v/t.* (ge-, h) announce; *j-m et.* ~ inform s.o. of s.th.; *officially:* notify s.th. to s.o.; *j-n* ~ enter s.o.'s name (*für, zu* for); *sich* ~ report o.s. (*bei* to); *school, etc.:* put up one's hand; answer the telephone; enter (one's name) (*für, zu* for *examination, etc.*); *sich* ~ *zu* apply for; *sich auf ein Inserat* ~ answer an advertisement.

'**Meldung** *f* (-/-en) information, advice; announcement; report; registration; application; *sports:* entry.

melke|n ['mɛlkən] *v/t.* (irr., ge-, h) milk; '²r *m* (-s/-) milker.

Melod|ie ♩ [melo'diː] *f* (-/-n) melody; tune, air; '²isch *adj.* [~'loːdiʃ] melodious, tuneful.

Melone [me'loːnə] *f* (-/-n) ♠ melon, F bowler(-hat), *Am.* derby.

Membran [mɛm'braːn] *f* (-/-en), ~*e f* (-/-n) membrane; *teleph. a.* diaphragm.

Memme F ['mɛmə] *f* (-/-n) coward; poltroon.

Memoiren [memo'ɑːrən] *pl.* memoirs *pl.*

Menagerie [menaʒə'riː] *f* (-/-n) menagerie.

Menge ['mɛŋə] *f* (-/-n) quantity; amount; multitude; crowd; *in großer* ~ in abundance; *persons, animals:* in crowds; *e-e* ~ *Geld* plenty of money, F lots *pl.* of money; *e-e* ~ *Bücher* a great many books; '²n *v/t.* (ge-, h) mix, blend; *sich* ~ mix (*unter acc.* with), mingle

M

(with); *sich* ~ *in* (acc.) meddle *or* interfere with.

Mensch [mɛnʃ] *m* (-en/-en) human being; man; person, individual; *die* ~*en pl.* people *pl.*, the world, mankind; *kein* ~ nobody.

'**Menschen|affe** *zo. m* anthropoid ape; '~**alter** *n* generation, age; '~**feind** *m* misanthropist; '2**feindlich** *adj.* misanthropic; '~**fresser** *m* (-s/-) cannibal, man-eater; '~**freund** *m* philanthropist; '2~**freundlich** *adj.* philanthropic; '~**gedenken** *n* (-s/*no pl.*): *seit* ~ from time immemorial, within the memory of man; '~**geschlecht** *n* human race, mankind; '~**haß** *m* misanthropy; '~**kenner** *m* judge of men *or* human nature; '~**kenntnis** *f* knowledge of human nature; '~**leben** *n* human life; '2**leer** *adj.* deserted; '~**liebe** *f* philanthropy; '~**menge** *f* crowd (of people), throng; '2**möglich** *adj.* humanly possible; '~**raub** *m* kidnap(p)ing; '~**rechte** *n*/*pl.* human rights *pl.*; '2**scheu** *adj.* unsocial, shy; '~**seele** *f*: *keine* ~ not a living soul; '~**verstand** *m* human understanding; *gesunder* ~ common sense, F horse sense; '~**würde** *f* dignity of man.

Menschheit *f* (-/*no pl.*) human race, mankind.

'**menschlich** *adj.* human; *fig.* humane; '2**keit** *f* (-/*no pl.*) human nature; humanity, humaneness.

Mentalität [mɛntali'tɛːt] *f* (-/-en) mentality.

merk|bar *adj.* ['mɛrkbɑːr] *s.* merklich; '2**blatt** *n* leaflet, instructional pamphlet; '2**buch** *n* notebook; '~**en** (ge-, h) **1.** *v*/*i.*: ~ *auf* (acc.) pay attention to, listen to; **2.** *v*/*t.* notice, perceive; find out, discover; *sich et.* ~ remember s.th.; bear s.th. in mind; '~**lich** *adj.* noticeable, perceptible; '2**mal** *n* (-[e]s/-e) mark, sign; characteristic, feature.

'**merkwürdig** *adj.* noteworthy, remarkable; strange, odd, curious; ~**erweise** *adv.* ['~gər'-] strange to say, strangely enough; '2**keit** *f* (-/-en) remarkableness; curiosity, peculiarity.

meßbar *adj.* ['mɛsbaːr] measurable.

Messe ['mɛsə] *f* (-/-n) ✝ fair; *eccl.* mass; ✕, ♣ mess.

messen ['mɛsən] *v*/*t.* (irr., ge-, h)

measure; ♣ sound; *sich mit j-m* ~ compete with s.o.; *sich nicht mit j-m* ~ *können* be no match for s.o.; *gemessen an* (dat.) measured against, compared with.

Messer ['mɛsər] *n* (-s/-) knife; ✗ scalpel; *bis aufs* ~ to the knife; *auf des* ~*s Schneide* on a razor-edge *or* razor's edge; '~**griff** *m* knife-handle; '~**held** *m* stabber; '~**klinge** *f* knife-blade; '~**schmied** *m* cutler; '~**schneide** *f* knife-edge; '~**stecher** *m* (-s/-) stabber; '~**stecherei** [~ʃtɛçə'raɪ] *f* (-/-en) knifing, knife-battle; '~**stich** *m* stab with a knife.

Messing ['mɛsiŋ] *n* (-s/*no pl.*) brass; '~**blech** *n* sheet-brass.

'**Meß|instrument** *n* measuring instrument; '~**latte** *f* surveyor's rod; '~**tisch** *m* surveyor's *or* plane table.

Metall [me'tal] *n* (-s/-e) metal; ~**arbeiter** *m* metal worker; 2**en** *adj.* (of) metal, metallic; ~**geld** *n* coin(s *pl.*), specie; ~**glanz** *m* metallic lust|re, *Am.* -er; 2**haltig** *adj.* metalliferous; ~**industrie** *f* metallurgical industry; ~**waren** *f*/*pl.* hardware.

Meteor *ast.* [mete'oːr] *m* (-s/-e) meteor; ~**ologe** [~oro'loːgə] *m* (-n/-n) meteorologist; ~**ologie** [~orolo'giː] *f* (-/*no pl.*) meteorology.

Meter ['meːtər] *n*, *m* (-s/-) met|re, *Am.* -er; '~**maß** *n* tape-measure.

Method|e [me'toːdə] *f* (-/-n) method; ⊕ *a.* technique; 2**isch** *adj.* methodical.

Metropole [metro'poːlə] *f* (-/-n) metropolis.

Metzel|ei [mɛtsə'laɪ] *f* (-/-en) slaughter, massacre; '2**n** *v*/*t.* (ge-, h) butcher, slaughter, massacre.

Metzger ['mɛtsgər] *m* (-s/-) butcher; ~**ei** [~'raɪ] *f* (-/-en) butcher's (shop).

Meuchel|mord ['mɔʏçəl-] *m* assassination; '~**mörder** *m* assassin.

Meute ['mɔʏtə] *f* (-/-n) pack of hounds; *fig.* gang; ~**rei** [~'raɪ] *f* (-/-en) mutiny; ~**rer** *m* (-s/-) mutineer; '2**risch** *adj.* mutinous; '2**rn** *v*/*i.* (ge-, h) mutiny (*gegen* against).

mich *pers. pron.* [miç] me; ~ (*selbst*) myself.

mied [miːt] *pret. of* meiden.

Mieder ['miːdər] *n* (-s/-) bodice; corset; '~**waren** *f*/*pl.* corsetry.

Miene ['miːnə] *f* (-/-n) countenance, air; feature; *gute* ~ *zum bösen Spiel machen* grin and bear it; ~ **machen zu** inf. offer or threaten to inf.

mies F adj. [miːs] miserable, poor; out of sorts, seedy.

Miet|e ['miːtə] f (-/-n) rent; hire; **zur ~ wohnen** live in lodgings, be a tenant; **²en** v/t. (ge-, h) rent (land, building, etc.); hire (horse, etc.); (take on) lease (land, etc.); ♙, ⚓ charter; **'~er** m (-s/-) tenant; lodger, Am. a. roomer; ⚖ lessee; **'²frei** adj. rent-free; **'~shaus** n block of flats, Am. apartment house; **'~vertrag** m tenancy agreement; lease; **'~wohnung** f lodgings pl., flat, Am. apartment.

Migräne ✶ [mi'grɛːnə] f (-/-n) migraine, megrim; sick headache.

Mikrophon [mikro'foːn] n (-s/-e) microphone, F mike.

Mikroskop [mikro'skoːp] n (-s/-e) microscope; **²isch** adj. microscopic(al).

Milbe zo. ['milbə] f (-/-n) mite.

Milch [milç] f (-/no pl.) milk; milt, soft roe (of fish); **'~bar** f milk-bar; **'~bart** fig. m stripling; **'~brötchen** n (French) roll; **'~gesicht** n baby face; **'~glas** n frosted glass; **'²ig** adj. milky; **'~kanne** f milk-can; **'~kuh** f milk cow (a. fig.); **'~mädchen** F n milkmaid, dairymaid; **'~mann** F m milkman, dairyman; **'~pulver** n milk-powder; **'~reis** m rice-milk; **'~straße** ast. f Milky Way, Galaxy; **'~wirtschaft** f dairy-farm(ing); **'~zahn** m milk-tooth.

mild [milt] **1.** adj. weather, punishment, etc.: mild; air, weather, light, etc.: soft; wine, etc.: mellow, smooth; reprimand, etc.: gentle; **2.** adv.: et. ~ **beurteilen** take a lenient view of s. th.

milde ['mildə] **1.** adj. s. mild 1; **2.** adv.: ~ **gesagt** to put it mildly; **3.** ⚥ f (-/no pl.) mildness; softness; smoothness; gentleness.

milder|n ['mildərn] v/t. (ge-, h) soften, mitigate; soothe, alleviate (pain, etc.); **~de Umstände** ⚖ extenuating circumstances; **'²ung** f (-/-en) softening, mitigation; alleviation.

'mild|herzig adj. charitable; **'²herzigkeit** f (-/no pl.) charitableness; **'~tätig** adj. charitable; **'²tätigkeit** f charity.

Milieu [mil'jøː] n (-s/-s) surroundings pl., environment; class, circles pl.; local colo(u)r.

Militär [mili'tɛːr] **1.** n (-s/no pl.) military, armed forces pl.; army; **2.** m (-s/-s) military man, soldier; **~attaché** [~ataʃeː] m (-s/-s) military attaché; **~dienst** m military service; **²isch** adj. military; **~musik** f military music; **~regierung** f military government; **~zeit** f (-/no pl.) term of military service.

Miliz ✕ [mi'liːts] f (-/-en) militia; **~soldat** ✕ m militiaman.

Milliarde [mil'jardə] f (-/-n) thousand millions, milliard, Am. billion.

Millimeter [mili'-] n, m millimet|re, Am. -er.

Million [mil'joːn] f (-/-en) million; **~är** [~o'nɛːr] m (-s/-e) millionaire.

Milz anat. [milts] f (-/-en) spleen, milt.

minder ['mindər] **1.** adv. less; **nicht** ~ no less, likewise; **2.** adj. less(er); smaller; minor; inferior; **~begabt** adj. less gifted; **~bemittelt** adj. ['~bəmitəlt] of moderate means; **'²betrag** m deficit, shortage; **'²einnahme** f shortfall in receipts; **'²gewicht** n short weight; **'²heit** f (-/-en) minority; **~jährig** adj. ['~jɛːriç] under age, minor; **'²jährigkeit** f (-/no pl.) minority; **'~n** v/t. and v/refl. (ge-, h) diminish, lessen, decrease; **'²ung** f (-/-en) decrease, diminution; **~wertig** adj. inferior, of inferior quality; **'²wertigkeit** f (-/no pl.) inferiority; ✝ inferior quality; **'²wertigkeitskomplex** m inferiority complex.

mindest adj. ['mindəst] least; slightest; minimum; **nicht die ~e Aussicht** not the slightest chance; **nicht im ~en** not in the least, by no means; **zum ~en** at least; **'²alter** n minimum age; **'²anforderungen** f/pl. minumum requirements pl.; **'²betrag** m lowest amount; **'²einkommen** n minimum income; **'~ens** adv. at least; **'²gebot** n lowest bid; **'²lohn** m minimum wage; **'²maß** n minimum; **auf ein ~ herabsetzen** minimize; **'²preis** m minimum price.

Mine ['miːnə] f (-/-n) ✕, ✕, ⚓ mine; pencil: lead; ball-point-pen: refill.

M

Mineral [minə'rɑ:l] *n* (-s/-e, -ien) mineral; ℒisch *adj.* mineral; ogie [alo'gi:] *f* (-/*no pl.*) mineralogy; wasser *n* (-s/=) mineral water.

Miniatur [minia'tu:r] *f* (-/-en) miniature; gemälde *n* miniature.

Minirock ['mini-] *m* miniskirt.

Minister [mi'nistər] *m* (-s/-) minister; Secretary (of State), *Am.* Secretary; ium ['te:rjum] *n* (-s/-Ministerien) ministry; Office, *Am.* Department; präsident *m* prime minister, premier; *in Germany, etc.*: minister president; rat *m* (-[e]s/=e) cabinet council.

minus *adv.* ['mi:nus] minus, less, deducting.

Minute [mi'nu:tə] *f* (-/-n) minute; nzeiger *m* minute-hand.

mir *pers. pron.* [mi:r] (to) me.

Misch|ehe ['miʃ⁹-] *f* mixed marriage; intermarriage; 'en *v/t.* (ge-, h) mix, mingle; blend (*coffee, tobacco, etc.*); alloy (*metal*); shuffle (*cards*); *sich in* (*acc.*) interfere in; join in (*conversation*); *sich unter* (*acc.*) mix *or* mingle with (*the crowd*); ling ['liŋ] *m* (-s/-e) half-breed, half-caste; ♀, *zo.* hybrid; masch F ['maʃ] *m* (-es/-e) hotchpotch, jumble; 'ung *f* (-/-en) mixture; blend; alloy.

miß|achten [mis'-] *v/t.* (*no* -ge-, h) disregard, ignore, neglect; slight, despise; 'ℒachtung *f* disregard, neglect; 'behagen 1. *v/i.* (*no* -ge-, h) displease; 2. ℒ *n* discomfort, uneasiness; 'ℒbildung *f* malformation, deformity; 'billigen *v/t.* (*no* -ge-, h) disapprove (of); 'billigung *f* disapproval; 'ℒbrauch *m* abuse; misuse; 'brauchen *v/t.* (*no* -ge-, h) abuse; misuse; bräuchlich *adj.* ['brɔʏçliç] abusive; improper; 'deuten *v/t.* (*no* -ge-, h) misinterpret; 'ℒdeutung *f* misinterpretation.

missen ['misən] *v/t.* (ge-, h) miss; do without, dispense with.

Miß|erfolg *m* failure; fiasco; 'ernte *f* bad harvest, crop failure.

Misse|tat ['misə-] *f* misdeed; crime; 'täter *m* evil-doer, offender; criminal.

miß|'fallen *v/i.* (*irr.* fallen, *no* -ge-, h): *j-m * displease s.o.; 'ℒfallen *n* (-s/*no pl.*) displeasure, dislike; 'fällig 1. *adj.* displeasing; shock-

ing; disparaging; 2. *adv.*: *sich äußern über* (*acc.*) speak ill of; 'ℒgeburt *f* monster, freak (of nature), deformity; *gestimmt* *fig. adj.* ['gəʃtimt] *s.* mißmutig; 'glücken *v/i.* (*no* -ge-, sein) fail; 'gönnen *v/t.* (*no* -ge-, h): *j-m et. * envy *or* grudge s.o. s.th.; 'ℒgriff *m* mistake, blunder; 'ℒgunst *f* envy, jealousy; 'günstig *adj.* envious, jealous; 'handeln *v/t.* (*no* -ge-, h) ill-treat; maul, *sl.* manhandle; ℒ'handlung *f* ill-treatment; mauling, *sl.* manhandling; ℒⁱⁱ assault and battery; 'ℒheirat *f* misalliance; 'hellig *adj.* dissonant, dissentient; 'ℒhelligkeit *f* (-/-en) dissonance, dissension, discord.

Mission [mis'jo:n] *f* (-/-en) mission (*a. pol. and fig.*); ar [o'nɑ:r] *m* (-s/-e) missionary.

'Miß|klang *m* dissonance, discord (*both a. fig.*); 'kredit *fig. m* (-[e]s/*no pl.*) discredit; *in bringen* bring discredit upon *s.o.*

miß|'lang *pret.* of mißlingen; 'lich *adj.* awkward; unpleasant; liebig *adj.* ['li:biç] unpopular; lingen ['liŋən] *v/i.* (*irr.*, *no* -ge-, sein) fail; ℒ'lingen *n* (-s/*no pl.*) failure; 'ℒmut *m* ill humo(u)r; 'mutig *adj.* ill-humo(u)red; discontented; 'raten 1. *v/i.* (*irr.* raten, *no* -ge-, sein) fail; turn out badly; 2. *adj.* wayward; ill-bred; 'ℒstand *m* nuisance; grievance; 'ℒstimmung *f* ill humo(u)r; 'ℒton *m* (-[e]s/=e) dissonance, discord (*both a. fig.*); 'trauen *v/i.* (*no* -ge-, h): *j-m * distrust *or* mistrust s.o.; 'ℒtrauen *n* (-s/*no pl.*) distrust, mistrust; 'trauisch *adj.* distrustful; suspicious; 'ℒvergnügen *n* (-s/*no pl.*) displeasure; 'vergnügt *adj.* displeased; discontented; 'ℒverhältnis *n* disproportion; incongruity; 'ℒverständnis *n* misunderstanding; dissension; 'verstehen *v/t.* (*irr.* stehen, *no* -ge-, h) misunderstand, mistake (*intention, etc.*); 'ℒwirtschaft *f* maladministration, mismanagement.

Mist [mist] *m* (-es/-e) dung, manure; dirt; F *fig.* trash, rubbish; 'beet *n* hotbed.

Mistel ♀ ['mistəl] *f* (-/-n) mistletoe.

Mist|gabel f dung-fork; '**_haufen** m dung-hill.

mit [mit] **1.** prp. (dat.) with; ~ 20 Jahren at (the age of) twenty; ~ e-m Schlage at a blow; ~ Gewalt by force; ~ der Bahn by train; **2.** adv. also, too; ~ dabeisein be there too, be (one) of the party.

Mit|arbeiter m co-worker; writing, art, etc.: collaborator; colleague; newspaper, etc.: contributor (an dat. to); '**Ωbenutzen** v/t. (sep., no -ge-, h) use jointly or in common; '**_besitzer** m joint owner; '**_bestimmungsrecht** n right of co-determination; '**_bewerber** m competitor; '**_bewohner** m co-inhabitant, fellow-lodger; '**_bringen** v/t. (irr. bringen, sep., -ge-, h) bring along (with one); **_bringsel** ['_brinzəl] n (-s/-) little present; '**_bürger** m fellow-citizen; **Ωein-ander** adv. [mit⁹ai'nandər] together, jointly; with each other, with one another; **_empfinden** ['mit⁹-] n (-s/no pl.) sympathy; '**_erbe** ['mit⁹-] m co-heir; '**_esser** ['mit⁹-] m (-s/-) blackhead; '**Ωfahren** v/i. (irr. fahren, sep., -ge-, sein): mit j-m ~ drive or go with s.o.; j-n ~ lassen give s.o. a lift; '**Ωfühlen** v/i. (sep., -ge-, h) sympathize (mit with); '**Ωgeben** v/t. (irr. geben, sep., -ge-, h) give along (dat. with); **_gefühl** n sympathy; '**Ωgehen** v/i. (irr. gehen, sep., -ge-, sein): mit j-m ~ go with s.o.; '**_gift** f (-/-en) dowry, marriage portion.

Mitglied n member; '**_erver-sammlung** f general meeting; '**_erzahl** f membership; '**_sbeitrag** m subscription; '**_schaft** f (-/no pl.) membership.

mit|'hin adv. consequently, therefore; **Ωinhaber** ['mit⁹-] m co-partner; '**Ωkämpfer** m fellow-combatant; '**_kommen** v/i. (irr. kommen, sep., -ge-, sein) come along (mit with); fig. be able to follow; '**Ωläufer** pol. m nominal member; contp. trimmer.

Mitleid n (-[e]s/no pl.) compassion, pity; sympathy; aus ~ out of pity; ~ haben mit have or take pity on; '**_enschaft** f (-/no pl.): in ~ ziehen affect; implicate, involve; damage; '**Ωig** adj. compassionate, pitiful; **Ω(s)los** adj. ['_t-] pitiless, merciless;

Ω(s)voll adj. ['_t-] pitiful, compassionate.

'**mit|machen** (sep., -ge-, h) **1.** v/i. make one of the party; **2.** v/t. take part in, participate in; follow, go with (fashion); go through (hardships); '**_mensch** m fellow creature; '**_nehmen** v/t. (irr. nehmen, sep., -ge-, h) take along (with one); fig. exhaust, wear out; j-n (im Auto) ~ give s.o. a lift; **_nichten** adv. ['_niçtən] by no means, not at all; '**_rechnen** v/t. (sep., -ge-, h) include (in the account); nicht ~ leave out of account; nicht mitge-rechnet not counting; '**_reden** (sep., -ge-, h) **1.** v/i. join in the conversation; **2.** v/t.: ein Wort or Wörtchen mitzureden haben have a say (bei in); '**_reißen** v/t. (irr. reißen, sep., -ge-, h) tear or drag along; fig. sweep along.

'**Mitschuld** f complicity (an dat. in); '**Ωig** adj. accessary (an dat. to crime); '**_ige** m accessary, accomplice.

'**Mitschüler** m schoolfellow.

'**mitspiel|en** (sep., -ge-, h) **1.** v/i. play (bei with); sports: be on the team; thea. appear, star (in a play); join in a game; matter: be involved; j-m arg or übel ~ play s.o. a nasty trick; **2.** fig. v/t. join in (game); '**Ωer** m partner.

'**Mittag** m midday, noon; heute Ω at noon today; zu ~ essen lunch, dine; '**_essen** n lunch(eon), dinner; '**Ωs** adv. at noon.

'**Mittags|pause** f lunch hour; '**_ruhe** f midday rest; '**_schlaf** m, '**_schläfchen** n after-dinner nap, siesta; '**_stunde** f noon; '**_tisch** fig. m lunch, dinner; '**_zeit** f noon-tide; lunch-time, dinner-time.

Mitte ['mitə] f (-/-n) middle; cent|re, Am. -er; die goldene ~ the golden or happy mean; aus unserer ~ from among us; ~ Juli in the middle of July; ~ Dreißig in the middle of one's thirties.

'**mitteil|en** v/t. (sep., -ge-, h): j-m et. ~ communicate s.th. to s.o.; impart s.th. to s.o.; inform s.o. of s.th.; make s.th. known to s.o.; '**_sam** adj. communicative; '**Ωung** f (-/-en) communication; information; communiqué.

Mittel ['mitəl] n (-s/-) means sg.,

M

way; remedy (*gegen* for); average; ⒜ mean; *phys.* medium; ~ *pl. a.* means *pl.*, funds *pl.*, money; ~ *pl. und Wege* ways and means *pl.*; **'~alter** *n* Middle Ages *pl.*; **'⒉alter-lich** *adj.* medi(a)eval; **'⒉bar** *adj.* mediate, indirect; **'~ding** *n*: *ein ~ zwischen ... und ...* something between ... and ...; **'~finger** *m* middle finger; **'~gebirge** *n* highlands *pl.*; **'⒉groß** *adj.* of medium height; medium-sized; **'~läufer** *m sports*: centre half back, *Am.* center half back; **'⒉los** *adj.* without means, destitute; **'⒉mäßig** *adj.* middling; mediocre; **'~mäßigkeit** *f* (-/*no pl.*) mediocrity; **'~punkt** *m* cent(re, *Am.* -er; *fig. a.* focus; **'⒉s** *prp.* (*gen.*) by (means of), through; **'~schule** *f* intermediate school, *Am.* high school; **'~smann** *m* (-[e]s/⁼er, *Mittelsleute*) mediator, go-between; **'~stand** *m* middle classes *pl.*; **'~stürmer** *m sports*: centre forward, *Am.* center forward; **'~weg** *fig. m* middle course; **'~wort** *gr.* *n* (-[e]s/⁼er) participle.

mitten *adv.* ['mitən]: ~ *in or an or auf or unter* (*acc.*/*dat.*) in the midst or middle of; ~ *entzwei* right in two; ~ *im Winter* in the depth of winter; ~ *in der Nacht* in the middle or dead of night; ~ *ins Herz* right into the heart; **'~'drin** F *adv.* right in the middle; **'~'durch** F *adv.* right through or across.

Mitter|nacht ['mitər-] *f* midnight; *um ~* at midnight; **⒉nächtig** *adj.* ['~nɛçtiç], **⒉nächtlich** *adj.* midnight.

Mittler ['mitlər] **1.** *m* (-s/-) mediator, intercessor; **2.** ⒉ *adj.* middle, central; average, medium; **'⒉weile** *adv.* meanwhile, (in the) meantime.

Mittwoch ['mitvɔx] *m* (-[e]s/-e) Wednesday; **'⒉s** *adv.* on Wednesday(s), every Wednesday.

mit|'unter *adv.* now and then, sometimes; **'⒉verantwortlich** *adj.* jointly responsible; **'⒉welt** *f* (-/*no pl.*): *die ~* our, *etc.* contemporaries *pl.*

'mitwirk|en *v/i.* (*sep.*, -ge-, h) co-operate (*bei* in), contribute (to), take part (in); **'⒉ende** *m* (-n/-n) *thea.* performer, actor, player (a. ♩); *die ~n pl.* the cast; **'⒉ung** *f* (-/*no pl.*) co(-)operation, contribution.

'Mitwisser *m* (-s/-) confidant, 🔰 accessary. [*rechnen.*]
'mitzählen *v/t.* (*sep.*, -ge-, h) *s.* mit-]
Mix|becher ['miks-] *m* (cocktail-) shaker; **⒉en** *v/t.* (ge-, h) mix; **~tur** [~'tu:r] *f* (-/-en) mixture.

Möbel ['mø:bəl] *n* (-s/-) piece of furniture; ~ *pl.* furniture; **'~händler** *m* furniture-dealer; **'~spediteur** *m* furniture-remover; **'~stück** *n* piece of furniture; **'~tischler** *m* cabinet-maker; **'~wagen** *m* pantechnicon, *Am.* furniture truck.

mobil *adj.* [mo'bi:l] ⚔ mobile; F active, nimble; ~ *machen* ⚔ mobilize; **⒉iar** [~il'ja:r] *n* (-s/-e) furniture; movables *pl.*; **~isieren** [~ili-'zi:rən] *v/t.* (*no* -ge-, h) ⚔ mobilize; ✝ realize (*property*, *etc.*); **⒉machung** ⚔ [mo'bi:lmaxuŋ] *f* (-/-en) mobilization.

möblieren [mø'bli:rən] *v/t.* (*no* -ge-, h) furnish; *möbliertes Zimmer* furnished room, F bed-sitter.

mochte ['mɔxtə] *pret.* of *mögen*.

Mode ['mo:də] *f* (-/-n) fashion, vogue; use, custom; *die neueste ~* the latest fashion; *in ~* in fashion or vogue; *aus der ~ kommen* grow or go out of fashion; *die ~ bestimmen* set the fashion; **'~artikel** *m/pl.* fancy goods *pl.*, novelties *pl.*; **'~farbe** *f* fashionable colo(u)r.

Modell [mo'dɛl] *n* (-s/-e) ⊕, *fashion*, *paint.*: model; pattern, design; ⊕ mo(u)ld; *j-m ~ stehen paint.* pose for s.o.; **~eisenbahn** *f* model railway; **⒉ieren** [~'li:rən] *v/t.* (*no* -ge-, h) model, mo(u)ld, fashion.

'Moden|schau *f* dress parade, fashion-show; **'~zeitung** *f* fashion magazine.

Moder ['mo:dər] *m* (-s/*no pl.*) must, putrefaction; **'~geruch** *m* musty smell; **'⒉ig** *adj.* musty, putrid.

modern[1] ['mo:dərn] *v/i.* (ge-, h) putrefy, rot, decay.

modern[2] *adj.* [mo'dɛrn] modern; progressive; up-to-date; fashionable; **~isieren** [~i'zi:rən] *v/t.* (*no* -ge-, h) modernize, bring up to date.

'Mode|salon *m* fashion house; **'~schmuck** *m* costume jewel(le)ry; **'~waren** *f/pl.* fancy goods *pl.*; **'~zeichner** *m* fashion-designer.

modifizieren [modifi'tsi:rən] *v/t.* (*no* -ge-, h) modify.

modisch adj. ['moːdiʃ] fashionable, stylish. [liner.]

Modistin [mo'distin] f (-/-nen) mil-}

Mogel|ei F [moːgə'laɪ] f (-/-en) cheat; '2n F v/i. (ge-, h) cheat.

mögen ['møːgən] (irr., h) 1. v/i. (ge-) be willing; ich mag nicht I don't like to; 2. v/t. (ge-) want, wish; like, be fond of; nicht ~ dislike; not to be keen on (food, etc.); lieber ~ like better, prefer; 3. v/aux. (no -ge-) may, might; ich möchte wissen I should like to know; ich möchte lieber gehen I would rather go; das mag (wohl) sein that's (well) possible; wo er auch sein mag wherever he may be; mag er sagen, was er will let him say what he likes.

möglich ['møːkliç] 1. adj. possible; practicable, feasible; market, criminal, etc.: potential; alle ~en all sorts of things; alles ~e all sorts of things; sein ~stes tun do one's utmost or level best; nicht ~! you don't say (so)!; so bald etc. wie ~ = 2. adv.:~st bald etc. as soon, etc., as possible; '~er`weise adv. possibly, if possible; perhaps; '2keit f (-/-en) possibility; chance; nach ~ if possible.

Mohammedan|er [mohame'daː-nər] m (-s/-) Muslim, Moslem, Mohammedan; 2isch adj. Muslim, Moslem, Mohammedan.

Mohn ♀ [moːn] m (-[e]s/-e) poppy.

Möhre ♀ ['møːrə] f (-/-n) carrot.

Mohrrübe ♀ ['moːr-] f carrot.

Molch zo. [mɔlç] m (-[e]s/-e) salamander; newt.

Mole ⚓ ['moːlə] f (-/-n) mole, jetty.

molk [mɔlk] pret. of melken.

Molkerei [mɔlkə'raɪ] f (-/-en) dairy; ~produkte n/pl. dairy products pl.

Moll ♪ [mɔl] n (-/-) minor (key).

mollig F adj. ['mɔliç] snug, cosy; plump, rounded.

Moment [mo'mɛnt] (-[e]s/-e) 1. m moment, instant; im ~ at the moment; 2. n motive; fact(or); ⊕ momentum; ⊕ impulse (a. fig.); 2an [~'taːn] 1. adj. momentary; 2. adv. at the moment, for the time being;~aufnahme phot. f snapshot, instantaneous photograph.

Monarch [mo'narç] m (-en/-en) monarch; ~ie [~'çiː] f (-/-n) monarchy.

Monat [moːnat] m (-[e]s/-e) month; '2elang 1. adj. lasting for months;

2. adv. for months; '2lich 1. adj. monthly; 2. adv. monthly, a month.

Mönch [mœnç] m (-[e]s/-e) monk, friar.

'**Mönchs|kloster** n monastery; '~kutte f (monk's) frock; '~leben n monastic life; '~orden m monastic order; '~zelle f monk's cell.

Mond [moːnt] m (-[e]s/-e) moon; hinter dem ~ leben be behind the times; '~fähre f lunar module; '~finsternis f lunar eclipse; '2hell adj. moonlit; '~schein m (-[e]s/no pl.) moonlight; '~sichel f crescent; '2süchtig adj. moonstruck.

Mono|log [mono'loːk] m (-s/-e) monologue, Am. a. monolog; soliloquy; '~pol ♦ n (-s/-e) monopoly; 2polisieren [~oli'ziːrən] v/t. (no -ge-, h) monopolize; 2ton adj. monotonous; ~tonie [~to'niː] f (-/-n) monotony.

Monstrum ['mɔnstrum] n (-s/Monstren, Monstra) monster.

Montag ['moːn-] m Monday; '2s adv. on Monday(s), every Monday.

Montage ⊕ [mɔn'taːʒə] f (-/-n) mounting, fitting; setting up; assemblage, assembly.

Montan|industrie [mɔn'taːn-] f coal and steel industries pl.; ~union f European Coal and Steel Community.

Mont|eur [mɔn'tøːr] m (-s/-e) ⊕ fitter, assembler; esp. mot., ⚡ mechanic; ~euranzug m overall; 2ieren [~'tiːrən] v/t. (no -ge-, h) mount, fit; set up; assemble; ~ur ⚔ [~'tuːr] f (-/-en) regimentals pl.

Moor [moːr] n (-[e]s/-e) bog; swamp; '~bad n mud-bath; '2ig adj. boggy, marshy.

Moos ♀ [moːs] n (-es/-e) moss; '2ig adj. mossy.

Moped mot. ['moːpɛt] n (-s/-s) moped.

Mops zo. [mɔps] m (-es/⸚e) pug; '2en v/t. (ge-, h) F pilfer, pinch; sl.: sich ~ be bored stiff.

Moral [mo'raːl] f (-/⸚-en) morality; morals pl.; moral; ⚔, etc.: morale; 2isch adj. moral; 2isieren [~ali'ziːrən] v/i. (no -ge-, h) moralize.

Morast [mo'rast] m (-es/-e, ⸚e) slough, morass; s. Moor; mire, mud; 2ig adj. marshy; muddy, miry.

Mord [mɔrt] m (-[e]s/-e) murder

(an dat. of); e-n ~ begehen commit murder; '**~anschlag** m murderous assault; **~en** ['~dən] v/i. (ge-, h) commit murder(s).

Mörder ['mœrdər] m (-s/-) murderer; '**~isch** adj. murderous; climate, etc.: deadly; ✝ competition: cut-throat.

'**Mord|gier** f lust of murder, bloodthirstiness; **~gierig** adj. bloodthirsty; '**~kommission** f homicide squad; '**~prozeß** ⚖ m murder trial.

'**Mords|angst** F f blue funk, sl. mortal fear; '**~glück** F n stupendous luck; '**~kerl** F m devil of a fellow; '**~spektakel** F m hullabaloo.

Morgen ['mɔrgən] **1.** m (-s/-) morning; measure: acre; am ~ s. morgens; **2.** ♀ adv. tomorrow; ~ früh (abend) tomorrow morning (evening or night); ~ in acht Tagen tomorrow week; '**~ausgabe** f morning edition; '**~blatt** n morning paper; '**~dämmerung** f dawn, daybreak; '**~gebet** n morning prayer; '**~gymnastik** f morning exercises pl.; '**~land** n (-[e]s/no pl.) Orient, East; '**~rock** m peignoir, dressing-gown, wrapper (for woman); '**~röte** f dawn; '**~s** adv. in the morning; '**~zeitung** f morning paper.

'**morgig** adj. of tomorrow.

Morphium pharm. ['mɔrfium] n (-s/no pl.) morphia, morphine.

morsch adj. [mɔrʃ] rotten, decayed; brittle.

Mörser ['mœrzər] m (-s/-) mortar (a. ✕).

Mörtel ['mœrtəl] m (-s/-) mortar.

Mosaik [moza'iːk] n (-s/-en) mosaic; **~fußboden** m mosaic or tessellated pavement.

Moschee [mɔ'ʃeː] f (-/-n) mosque.

Moschus ['mɔʃus] m (-/no pl.) musk.

Moskito zo. [mɔs'kiːto] m (-s/-s) mosquito; **~netz** n mosquito-net.

Moslem ['mɔslem] m (-s/-s) Muslim, Moslem.

Most [mɔst] m (-es/-e) must, grape-juice; of apples: cider; of pears: perry. [mustard.]

Mostrich ['mɔstriç] m (-[e]s/no pl.)

Motiv [mo'tiːf] n (-s/-e) motive, reason; paint., ♪ motif; **~ieren** [~i'viːrən] v/t. (no -ge-, h) motivate.

Motor ⚡ ['moːtɔr] m (-s/-en) engine, esp. ⚡ motor; '**~boot** n motor boat; '**~defekt** m engine or ⚡ motor

trouble; '**~haube** f bonnet, Am. hood; **~isieren** [motori'ziːrən] v/t. (no -ge-, h) motorize; **~isierung** [motori'ziːruŋ] f (-/no pl.) motorization; '**~rad** n motor (bi)cycle; '**~radfahrer** m motor cyclist; '**~roller** m (motor) scooter; '**~sport** m motoring.

Motte zo. ['mɔtə] f (-/-n) moth.

'**Motten|kugel** f moth-ball; '**~sicher** adj. mothproof; '**~zerfressen** adj. moth-eaten.

Motto ['mɔto] n (-s/-s) motto.

Möwe orn. ['møːvə] f (-/-n) sea-gull, (sea-)mew.

Mücke zo. ['mykə] f (-/-n) midge, gnat, mosquito; aus e-r ~ e-n Elefanten machen make a mountain out of a molehill; '**~nstich** m gnat-bite. [hypocrite.]

Mucker ['mukər] m (-s/-) bigot,]

müd|e adj. ['myːdə] tired, weary; e-r Sache ~ sein be weary or tired of s.th.; '**~igkeit** f (-/no pl.) tiredness, weariness.

Muff [muf] m **1.** (-[e]s/-e) muff; **2.** (-[e]s/no pl.) mo(u)ldy or musty smell; '**~e** ⊕ f (-/-n) sleeve, socket; '**~eln** F v/i. (ge-, h) munch; mumble; '**~ig** adj. smell, etc.: musty, fusty; air: close; fig. sulky, sullen.

Mühe ['myːə] f (-/-n) trouble, pains pl.; (nicht) der ~ wert (not) worth while; j-m ~ machen give s.o. trouble; sich ~ geben take pains (mit over, with s.th.); '**~los** adj. effortless, easy; '**~n** v/refl. (ge-, h) take pains, work hard; '**~voll** adj. troublesome, hard; laborious.

Mühle ['myːlə] f (-/-n) mill.

'**Müh|sal** f (-/-e) toil, trouble; hardship; '**~sam, ~selig 1.** adj. toilsome, troublesome; difficult; **2.** adv. laboriously; with difficulty.

Mulatte [mu'latə] m (-n/-n) mulatto.

Mulde ['muldə] f (-/-n) trough; depression, hollow.

Mull [mul] m (-[e]s/-e) mull.

Müll [myl] m (-[e]s/no pl.) dust, rubbish, refuse, Am. a. garbage; '**~abfuhr** f removal of refuse; '**~eimer** m dust-bin, Am. garbage can.

Müller ['mylər] m (-s/-) miller.

'**Müll|fahrer** m dust-man, Am. garbage collector; '**~haufen** m dustheap; '**~kasten** m s. Mülleimer; '**~kutscher** m s. Müllfahrer; '**~wa-**

gen m dust-cart, Am. garbage cart.
Multipli|kation ♣ [multiplika-
'tsjo:n] f (-/-en) multiplication;
Ⴒzieren ♣ [-'tsi:rən] v/t. (no -ge-,
h) multiply (mit by).
Mumie ['mu:mjə] f (-/-n) mummy.
Mumps ⚕ [mumps] m, F f (-/no pl.)
mumps.
Mund [munt] m (-[e]s/⸚er) mouth;
den ~ halten hold one's tongue;
den ~ voll nehmen talk big; sich den ~
verbrennen put one's foot in it;
nicht auf den ~ gefallen sein have a
ready or glib tongue; j-m über den ~
fahren cut s.o. short; '~art f
dialect; '2artlich adj. dialectal.
Mündel ['myndəl] m, n (-s/-), girl:
a. f (-/-n) ward, pupil; 2sicher
adj.: ~e Papiere n/pl. † gilt-edged
securities pl.
münden ['myndən] v/i. (ge-, h): ~ in
(acc.) river, etc.: fall or flow into;
street, etc.: run into.
'mund|faul adj. too lazy to speak;
'~gerecht adj. palatable (a. fig.);
'2harmonika ♪ f mouth-organ;
'2höhle anat. f oral cavity.
mündig ⚖ adj. ['myndiç] of age;
~ werden come of age; '2keit f
(-/no pl.) majority.
mündlich ['myntliç] 1. adj. oral,
verbal; 2. adv. a. by word of mouth.
'Mund|pflege f oral hygiene; '~-
raub ⚖ m theft of comestibles;
'~stück n mouthpiece (of musical
instrument, etc.); tip (of cigarette);
'2tot adj.: ~ machen silence or gag
s.o.
'Mündung f (-/-en) mouth; a. estu-
ary (of river); muzzle (of fire-arms).
'Mund|vorrat m provisions pl.,
victuals pl.; '~wasser n (-s/⸚) mouth-
wash, gargle; '~werk F fig. n: ein
gutes ~ haben have the gift of the
gab.
Munition [muni'tsjo:n] f (-/-en)
ammunition.
munkeln F ['muŋkəln] (ge-, h)
1. v/i. whisper; 2. v/t. whisper,
rumo(u)r; man munkelt there is a
rumo(u)r afloat.
munter adj. ['muntər] awake; fig.:
Münz|e ['myntsə] f (-/-n) coin,
(small) change; medal; mint; für
bare ~ nehmen take at face value;
j-m et. mit gleicher ~ heimzahlen
pay s.o. back in his own coin; '~ein-
heit f (monetary) unit, standard of

currency; '2en v/t. (ge-, h) coin,
mint; gemünzt sein auf (acc.) be
meant for, be aimed at; '~fern-
sprecher teleph. m coin-box telephone; '~fuß m standard (of coin-
age); '~wesen n monetary system.
mürbe adj. ['myrbə] tender; pastry,
etc.: crisp, short; meat: well-
cooked; material: brittle; F fig.
worn-out, demoralized; F j-n ~
machen break s.o.'s resistance; F ~
werden give in.
Murmel ['murməl] f (-/-n) marble;
'2n v/t. and v/i. (ge-, h) mumble,
murmur; '~tier zo. n marmot.
murren ['murən] v/i. (ge-, h)
grumble, F grouch (both: über acc.
at, over, about).
mürrisch adj. ['myriʃ] surly, sullen.
Mus [mu:s] n (-es/-e) pap; stewed
fruit.
Muschel ['muʃəl] f (-/-n) zo.: mus-
sel; shell, conch; teleph. ear-piece.
Museum [mu'ze:um] n (-s/Museen)
museum.
Musik [mu'zi:k] f (-/no pl.) music;
~alienhandlung [Ⴒi'ka:ljən-] f
music-shop; 2alisch adj. [Ⴒi'ka:-
liʃ] musical; ~ant [Ⴒi'kant] m (-en/
-en) musician; **~automat** m juke-
box; **~er** ['mu:zikər] m (-s/-)
musician; bandsman; **~instru-
ment** n musical instrument; **~leh-
rer** m music-master; **~stunde** f
music-lesson; **~truhe** f radio-
gram(ophone), Am. radio-phono-
graph.
musizieren [muzi'tsi:rən] v/i. (no
-ge-, h) make or have music.
Muskat ♀ [mus'ka:t] m (-[e]s/-e)
nutmeg; **~nuß** ♀ f nutmeg.
Muskel ['muskəl] m (-s/-n) muscle;
'~kater F m stiffness and soreness,
Am. a. charley horse; '~kraft f
muscular strength; '~zerrung ⚕ f
pulled muscle.
Muskul|atur [muskula'tu:r] f (-/-en)
muscular system, muscles pl.; 2ös
adj. [-'lø:s] muscular, brawny.
Muß [mus] n (-/no pl.) necessity;
es ist ein ~ it is a must.
Muße ['mu:sə] f (-/no pl.) leisure;
spare time; mit ~ at one's leisure.
Musselin [musə'li:n] m (-s/-e)
muslin.
müssen ['mysən] (irr., h) 1. v/i.
(ge-): ich muß I must; 2. v/aux.
(no -ge-): ich muß I must, I have to;

I am obliged *or* compelled *or* forced to; I am bound to; *ich habe gehen ~* I had to go; *ich müßte (eigentlich) wissen* I ought to know.

müßig *adj.* ['myːsiç] idle; superfluous; useless; ⒉**gang** *m* idleness, laziness; ⒉**gänger** ['ɡɛŋər] *m* (-s/-) idler, loafer; lazy-bones.

mußte ['mustə] *pret. of* müssen.

Muster ['mustər] *n* (-s/-) model; example, paragon; design, pattern; specimen; sample; '**betrieb** *m* model factory *or* farm; '**gatte** *m* model husband; ⒉**gültig**, ⒉**haft** 1. *adj.* model, exemplary, perfect; 2. *adv.: sich ~ benehmen* be on one's best behavio(u)r; '**kollektion** ✝ *f* range of samples; ⒉**n** *v/t.* (ge-, h) examine; eye; ⚔ inspect, review; figure, pattern (*fabric, etc.*); '**schutz** *m* protection of patterns and designs; **ung** *f* (-/-en) examination; ⚔ review; pattern (*of fabric, etc.*); '**werk** *n* standard work.

Mut [muːt] *m* (-[e]s/*no pl.*) courage; spirit; pluck; *~ fassen* pluck up courage, summon one's courage; *den ~ sinken lassen* lose courage *or* heart; *guten ~(e)s sein* be of good cheer; '⒉**ig** *adj.* courageous, plucky; '⒉**los** *adj.* discouraged; despondent; '**losigkeit** *f* (-/*no pl.*) discouragement; despondency; ⒉**maßen** ['muːmɑːsən] *v/t.* (ge-, h) suppose, guess, surmise; ⒉**maßlich** *adj.* presumable; supposed; *adv.* presumptive; '**maßung** *f* (-/-en) supposition, surmise; *bloße ~en pl.* guesswork.

Mutter ['mutər] *f* 1. (-/⸚) mother; 2. ⊕ (-/-n) nut; '**brust** *f* mother's breast; '**leib** *m* womb.

mütterlich *adj.* ['mytərliç] motherly; maternal; **erseits** *adv.* ['**ər-zaits] on *or* from one's mother's side; *uncle, etc.:* maternal.

'**Mutter|liebe** *f* motherly love; ⒉**los** *adj.* motherless; '**mal** *n* birth-mark; mole; '**milch** *f* mother's milk; '**schaft** *f* (-/*no pl.*) maternity, motherhood; '⒉**seelenal'lein** *adj.* all *or* utterly alone; **söhnchen** ['**zøːnçən] *n* (-s/-) milksop, *sl.* sissy; '**sprache** *f* mother tongue; '**witz** *m* (-es/*no pl.*) mother wit.

'**Mutwill|e** *m* wantonness; mischievousness; '⒉**ig** *adj.* wanton; mischievous; wilful.

Mütze ['mytsə] *f* (-/-n) cap.

Myrrhe ['myrə] *f* (-/-n) myrrh.

Myrte ⚘ ['myrtə] *f* (-/-n) myrtle.

mysteri|ös *adj.* [myster'jøːs] mysterious; ⒉**um** [‿'teːrjum] *n* (-s/ Mysterien) mystery.

Mystifi|kation [mystifika'tsjoːn] *f* (-/-en) mystification; ⒉**zieren** [‿'tsiːrən] *v/t.* (*no* -ge-, h) mystify.

Mysti|k ['mystik] *f* (-/*no pl.*) mysticism; ⒉**sch** *adj.* mystic(al).

Myth|e ['myːtə] *f* (-/-n) myth; '⒉**isch** *adj.* mythic; *esp. fig.* mythical; **ologie** [mytolo'giː] *f* (-/-n) mythology; ⒉**ologisch** *adj.* [myto-'loːgiʃ] mythological; **os** ['‿ɔs] *m* (-/Mythen), **us** ['‿us] *m* (-/Mythen) myth.

N

na *int.* [na] now!, then!, well!, *Am. a.* hey!

Nabe ['naːbə] *f* (-/-n) hub.

Nabel *anat.* ['naːbəl] *m* (-s/-) navel.

nach [naːx] 1. *prp.* (*dat.*) direction, striving: after; to(wards), for (*a. ~ ... hin or zu*); *succession*: after; *time*: after, past; *manner, measure, example*: according to; *~ Gewicht* by weight; *~ deutschem Geld* in German money; *e-r ~ dem andern* one by one; *fünf Minuten ~ eins* five minutes past one; 2. *adv.* after;

~ und ~ little by little, gradually; *~ wie vor* now as before, still.

nachahm|en ['naːxʔaːmən] *v/t.* (*sep.*, -ge-, h) imitate, copy; counterfeit; '**ens'wert** *adj.* worthy of imitation, exemplary; '⒉**er** *m* (-s/-) imitator; '⒉**ung** *f* (-/-en) imitation; copy; counterfeit, fake.

Nachbar ['naxbaːr] *m* (-n, -s/-n), '**in** *f* (-/-nen) neighbo(u)r; '**schaft** *f* (-/-en) neighbo(u)rhood, vicinity. [ment.|

'**Nachbehandlung** ✄ *f* after-treat-|

'nachbestell|en v/t. (sep., no -ge-, h) repeat one's order for s.th.; **'2ung** f repeat (order).

'nachbeten v/t. (sep., -ge-, h) echo.

'Nachbildung f copy, imitation; replica; dummy.

'nachblicken v/i. (sep., -ge-, h) look after.

nachdem cj. [na:x'de:m] after, when; je ~ according as.

'nachdenk|en v/i. (irr. denken, sep., -ge-, h) think (über acc. over, about); reflect, meditate (über acc. on); **'2en** n (-s/no pl.) reflection, meditation; musing; **'.lich** adj. meditative, reflecting; pensive.

'Nachdichtung f free version.

'Nachdruck m 1. (-[e]s/no pl.) stress, emphasis; 2. typ. (-[e]s/-e) reprint; unlawfully: piracy, pirated edition; **'2en** v/t. (sep., -ge-, h) reprint; unlawfully: pirate.

nachdrücklich ['na:xdryklıç] 1. adj. emphatic, energetic; forcible; positive; 2. adv.: ~ betonen emphasize.

nacheifern ['na:x'9-] v/i. (sep., -ge-, h) emulate s.o.

nacheinander adv. [na:x'9aı'nandər] one another, successively; by or in turns.

nachempfinden ['na:x'9-] v/t. (irr. empfinden, sep., no -ge-, h) s. nachfühlen.

nacherzähl|en ['na:x'9-] v/t. (sep., no -ge-, h) repeat; retell; dem Englischen nacherzählt adapted from the English; **'2ung** ['na:x'9-] f repetition; story retold, reproduction.

'Nachfolge f succession; **'2n** v/i. (sep., -ge-, sein) follow s.o.; j-m im Amt ~ succeed s.o. in his office; **'.r** m (-s/-) follower; successor.

'nachforsch|en v/i. (sep., -ge-, h) investigate; search for; **'2ung** f investigation, inquiry, search.

'Nachfrage f inquiry; † demand; **'2n** v/i. (sep., -ge-, h) inquire (nach after).

'nach|fühlen v/t. (sep., -ge-, h): es j-m ~ feel or sympathize with s.o.; **'.füllen** v/t. (sep., -ge-, h) fill up, refill; **'.geben** v/i. (irr. geben, sep., -ge-, h) give way (dat. to); fig. give in, yield (to); † surcharge; **'.gehen** v/i. (irr. gehen, sep., -ge-, sein) follow (s.o., business, trade, etc.); pursue (pleasure); attend to (business); investigate

s.th.; watch: be slow; **'2geschmack** m (-[e]s/no pl.) after-taste.

nachgiebig adj. ['na:xgi:bıç] elastic, flexible; fig. a. yielding, compliant; **'2keit** f (-/-en) flexibility; compliance.

'nachgrübeln v/i. (sep., -ge-, h) ponder, brood (both: über acc. over), muse (on).

nachhaltig adj. ['na:xhaltıç] lasting, enduring.

nach'her adv. afterwards; then; bis ~! see you later!, so long!

'Nachhilfe f help, assistance; **'.lehrer** m coach, private tutor; **'.unterricht** m private lesson(s pl.), coaching.

'nach|holen v/t. (sep., -ge-, h) make up for, make good; **'2hut** ⚔ f (-/-en) rear(-guard); die ~ bilden bring up the rear (a. fig.); **'.jagen** v/i. (sep., -ge-, sein) chase or pursue s.o.; **'.klingen** v/i. (irr. klingen, sep., -ge-, h) resound, echo.

'Nachkomme m (-n/-n) descendant; ~n pl. esp. ⚖ issue; **'2n** v/i. (irr. kommen, sep., -ge-, sein) follow; come later; obey (order); meet (liabilities); **'.nschaft** f (-/-en) descendants pl., esp. ⚖ issue.

'Nachkriegs... post-war.

Nachlaß ['na:xlas] m (Nachlasses/ Nachlasse, Nachlässe) † reduction, discount; assets pl., estate, inheritance (of deceased).

'nachlassen (irr. lassen, sep., -ge-, h) 1. v/t. reduce (price); 2. v/i. deteriorate, slacken, relax; diminish; pain, rain, etc.: abate; storm: calm down; strength: wane; interest: flag.

'nachlässig adj. careless, negligent.

'nach|laufen v/i. (irr. laufen, sep., -ge-, sein) run (dat. after); **'.lesen** v/t. (irr. lesen, sep., -ge-, h) in book: look up; ✔ glean; **'.liefern** † v/t. (sep., -ge-, h) deliver subsequently; repeat delivery of; **'.lösen** v/t. (sep., -ge-, h): e-e Fahrkarte ~ take a supplementary ticket; buy a ticket en route; **'.machen** v/t. (sep., -ge-, h) imitate (j-m et. s.o. in s.th.); copy; counterfeit, forge; **'.messen** v/t. (irr. messen, sep., -ge-, h) measure again.

'Nachmittag m afternoon; **'2s** adv. in the afternoon; **'.svorstellung** thea. f matinée.

Nach|nahme ['na:xna:mə] f (-/-n)

cash on delivery, *Am.* collect on delivery; *per ~ schicken* send C.O.D.; **'~name** *m* surname, last name; **'~porto** 🕮 *n* surcharge.

'nach|prüfen *v/t.* (*sep.*, *-ge-*, *h*) verify; check; **'~rechnen** *v/t.* (*sep.*, *-ge-*, *h*) reckon over again; check (*bill*).

'Nachrede *f: üble ~* 🕮 defamation (of character); *oral:* slander, *written:* libel; **'2n** *v/t.* (*sep.*, *-ge-*, *h*): *j-m Übles ~* slander s.o.

Nachricht ['naːxrɪçt] *f* (-/-en) news; message; report; information, notice; *~ geben s. benachrichtigen*; **'~enagentur** *f* news agency; **'~endienst** *m* news service; ✗ intelligence service; **'~ensprecher** *m* newscaster; **'~enwesen** *n* (-s/*no pl.*) communications *pl.*

'nachrücken *v/i.* (*sep.*, *-ge-*, *sein*) move along.

'Nach|ruf *m* obituary (notice); **'~ruhm** *m* posthumous fame.

'nachsagen *v/t.* (*sep.*, *-ge-*, *h*) repeat; *man sagt ihm nach, daß* he is said to *inf.*

'Nachsaison *f* dead or off season.

'nachschicken *v/t.* (*sep.*, *-ge-*, *h*) *s. nachsenden.*

'nachschlage|n *v/t.* (*irr. schlagen*, *sep.*, *-ge-*, *h*) consult (*book*); look up (*word*); **'2werk** *n* reference-book.

'Nach|schlüssel *m* skeleton key; **'~schrift** *f in letter:* postscript; **'~schub** *esp.* ✗ *m* supplies *pl.*; **'~schubweg** ✗ *m* supply line.

'nach|sehen (*irr. sehen*, *sep.*, *-ge-*, *h*) **1.** *v/i.* look after; *~*, *ob* (go and) see whether; **2.** *v/t.* look after; examine, inspect; check; overhaul (*machine*); *s. nachschlagen*; *j-m et. ~* indulge s.o. in s.th.; **'~senden** *v/t.* ([*irr. senden*,] *sep.*, *-ge-*, *h*) send after; send on, forward (*letter*) (*j-m* to s.o.).

'Nachsicht *f* indulgence; **'2ig** *adj.*, **'2svoll** *adj.* indulgent, forbearing.

'Nachsilbe *gr.* *f* suffix.

'nach|sinnen *v/i.* (*irr. sinnen*, *sep.*, *-ge-*, *h*) muse, meditate (*über acc.* [*up*]*on*); **'~sitzen** *v/i.* (*irr. sitzen*, *sep.*, *-ge-*, *h*) *pupil:* be kept in.

'Nach|sommer *m* St. Martin's summer, *esp. Am.* Indian summer; **'~speise** *f* dessert; **'~spiel** *fig. n* sequel.

'nach|spionieren *v/i.* (*sep.*, *no -ge-*, *h*) spy (*dat.* on); **'~sprechen** *v/i. and v/t.* (*irr. sprechen*, *sep.*, *-ge-*, *h*) repeat; **'~spülen** *v/t.* (*sep.*, *-ge-*, *h*) rinse; **'~spüren** *v/i.* (*sep.*, *-ge-*, *h*) (*dat.*) track, trace.

nächst [nɛːçst] **1.** *adj. succession, time:* next; *distance, relation:* nearest; **2.** *prp.* (*dat.*) next to, next after; **'2!beste** *m*, *f*, *n* (-/-*n*): *der* (*die*) *~* anyone; *das ~* anything; *er fragte den ~n* he asked the next person he met.

'nachstehen *v/i.* (*irr. stehen*, *sep.*, *-ge-*, *h*): *j-m in nichts ~* be in no way inferior to s.o.

'nachstell|en (*sep.*, *-ge-*, *h*) **1.** *v/t.* place behind; put back (*watch*); ⊕ adjust (*screw*, *etc.*); **2.** *v/i.*: *j-m ~* be after s.o.; **'2ung** *fig. f* persecution.

'Nächstenliebe *f* charity.

'nächstens *adv.* shortly, (very) soon, before long.

'nach|streben *v/i.* (*sep.*, *-ge-*, *h*) *s. nacheifern*; **'~suchen** *v/i.* (*sep.*, *-ge-*, *h*): *~ um* apply for, seek.

Nacht [naxt] *f* (-/*⸚e*) night; *bei ~*, *des ~s s. nachts*; **'~arbeit** *f* night-work; **'~asyl** *n* night-shelter; **'~ausgabe** *f* night edition (*of newspaper*); **'~dienst** *m* night-duty.

'Nachteil *m* disadvantage, drawback; *im ~ sein* be at a disadvantage; **'2ig** *adj.* disadvantageous.

'Nacht|essen *n* supper; **'~falter** *zo. m* (-*s*/-) moth; **'~gebet** *n* evening prayer; **'~geschirr** *n* chamberpot; **'~hemd** *n* night-gown, *Am. a.* night robe; *for men:* nightshirt.

Nachtigall *orn.* ['naxtigal] *f* (-/-en) nightingale.

'Nachtisch *m* (-es/*no pl.*) sweet, dessert.

'Nachtlager *n* (a) lodging for the night; bed.

nächtlich *adj.* ['nɛçtlɪç] nightly, nocturnal.

'Nacht|lokal *n* night-club; **'~mahl** *n* supper; **'~portier** *m* night-porter; **'~quartier** *n* night-quarters *pl.*

Nachtrag ['naːxtraːk] *m* (-[e]s/*⸚e*) supplement; **'2en** *v/t.* (*irr. tragen*, *sep.*, *-ge-*, *h*) carry (*j-m et. s.th.* after s.o.); add; 🕮 post up (*ledger*); *j-m et. ~* bear s.o. a grudge; **'2end** *adj.* unforgiving, resentful.

nachträglich adj. ['nɑːxtrɛːklɪç] additional; subsequent.

nachts adv. [naxts] at or by night. '**Nacht|schicht** f night-shift; '**℈schlafend** adj.: zu ~er Zeit in the middle of the night; '**~schwärmer** fig. m night-reveller; '**~tisch** m bedside table; '**~topf** m chamberpot; '**~vorstellung** thea. f night performance; '**~wache** f nightwatch; '**~wächter** m (night-) watchman; **~wandler** ['~vandlər] m (-s/-) sleep-walker; '**~zeug** n night-things pl.

'**nachwachsen** v/i. (irr. wachsen, sep., -ge-, sein) grow again.

'**Nachwahl** parl. f by-election.

'**Nachweis** ['nɑːxvaɪs] m (-es/-e) proof, evidence; '**℈bar** adj. demonstrable; traceable; **℈en** ['~ən] v/t. (irr. weisen, sep., -ge-, h) point out, show; trace; prove; '**℈lich** adj. s. nachweisbar.

'**Nach|welt** f posterity; '**~wirkung** f after-effect; consequences pl.; aftermath; '**~wort** n (-[e]s/-e) epilog(ue); '**~wuchs** m (-[e]s/no pl.) rising generation.

'**nach|zahlen** v/t. (sep., -ge-, h) pay in addition; '**~zählen** v/t. (sep., -ge-, h) count over (again), check; '**℈zahlung** f additional payment.

Nachzügler ['nɑːxtsyːklər] m (-s/-) straggler, late-comer.

Nacken ['nakən] m (-s/-) nape (of the neck), neck.

nackt adj. [nakt] naked, nude; bare (a. fig.); young birds: unfledged; truth: plain.

Nadel ['nɑːdəl] f (-/-n) needle; pin; brooch; '**~arbeit** f needlework; '**~baum** ♀ m conifer(ous tree); '**~stich** m prick; stitch; fig. pinprick.

Nagel ['nɑːgəl] m (-s/⸚) anat., ⊕ nail; of wood: peg; spike; stud; die Arbeit brennt mir auf den Nägeln it's a rush job; '**~haut** f cuticle; '**~lack** m nail varnish; '**℈n** v/t. (ge-, h) nail (an or auf acc. to); **~necessaire** [~nesesɛːr] n (-s/-s) manicure-case; '**℈neu** F adj. bran(d)-new; '**~pflege** f manicure.

nage|n ['nɑːgən] (ge-, h) **1.** v/i. gnaw; ~ an (dat.) gnaw at; pick (bone). **2.** v/t. gnaw; '**℈tier** zo. n rodent, gnawer.

nah adj. [nɑː] near, close (bei to); nearby; danger: imminent.

Näharbeit ['nɛː-ʔ-] f needlework, sewing.

'**Nahaufnahme** f film: close-up.

nahe adj. ['nɑːə] s. nah.

Nähe ['nɛːə] f (-/no pl.) nearness, proximity; vicinity; in der ~ close by.

'**nahe|gehen** v/i. (irr. gehen, sep., -ge-, sein) (dat.) affect, grieve; '**~kommen** v/i. (irr. kommen, sep., -ge-, sein) (dat.) approach; get at (truth); '**~legen** v/t. (sep., -ge-, h) suggest; '**~liegen** v/i. (irr. liegen, sep., -ge-, h) suggest itself, be obvious.

nahen ['nɑːən] **1.** v/i. (ge-, sein) approach; **2.** v/refl. (ge-, h) approach (j-m s.o.).

nähen ['nɛːən] v/t. and v/i. (ge-, h) sew, stitch.

näher adj. ['nɛːər] nearer, closer; road: shorter; das Nähere (further) particulars pl. or details pl.

'**Näherin** f (-/-nen) seamstress.

'**nähern** v/t. (ge-, h) approach (dat. to); sich ~ approach (j-m s.o.).

'**nahe'zu** adv. nearly, almost.

'**Nähgarn** n (sewing-)cotton.

'**Nahkampf** ⚔ m close combat.

nahm [nɑːm] pret. of nehmen.

'**Näh|maschine** f sewing-machine; '**~nadel** f (sewing-)needle.

nähren ['nɛːrən] v/t. (ge-, h) nourish (a. fig.), feed; nurse (child); sich ~ von live or feed on.

nahrhaft adj. ['nɑːrhaft] nutritious, nourishing.

'**Nahrung** f (-/no pl.) food, nourishment, nutriment.

'**Nahrungs|aufnahme** f intake of food; '**~mittel** n/pl. food(-stuff), victuals pl.

'**Nährwert** m nutritive value.

Naht [nɑːt] f (-/⸚e) seam; ⚕ suture.

'**Nahverkehr** m local traffic.

'**Nähzeug** n sewing-kit.

naiv adj. [naˈiːf] naïve, naive, simple; **℈ität** [naiviˈtɛːt] f (-/no pl.) naïveté, naivety, simplicity.

Name ['nɑːmə] m (-ns/-n) name; im ~n (gen.) on behalf of; dem ~n nach nominal(ly), in name only; dem ~n nach kennen know by name; die Dinge beim rechten ~n nennen call a spade a spade; darf ich um Ihren ~n bitten? may I ask your name?

'**namen|los** adj. nameless, anony-

mous; *fig.* unutterable; '**~s 1.** *adv.*
named, by the name of, called;
2. *prp.* (*gen.*) in the name of.

'**Namens|tag** *m* name-day; '**~vetter**
m namesake; '**~zug** *m* signature.

namentlich ['nɑːməntlɪç] **1.** *adj.*
nominal; **2.** *adv.* by name; especially, in particular.

'**namhaft** *adj.* notable; considerable; ~ *machen* name.

nämlich ['nɛːmlɪç] **1.** *adj.* the same;
2. *adv.* namely, that is (to say).

nannte ['nantə] *pret.* of *nennen*.

Napf [napf] *m* (-[e]s/ˑe) bowl,
basin.

Narb|e ['narbə] *f* (-/-n) scar; '**~ig**
adj. scarred; *leather*: grained.

Narko|se [naɾˈkoːzə] *f* (-/-n) narcosis; **2tisieren** [ˌotiˈziːɾən] *v/t.*
(*no* -ge-, *h*) narcotize.

Narr [nar] *m* (-en/-en) fool; jester;
zum ~*en halten* = '**2en** *v/t.* (ge-, *h*)
make a fool of, fool.

'**Narren|haus** F *n* madhouse; '**~-
kappe** *f* fool's-cap; '**2sicher** *adj.*
foolproof.

'**Narrheit** *f* (-/-en) folly.

Närrin ['nɛrɪn] *f* (-/-nen) fool,
foolish woman.

'**närrisch** *adj.* foolish, silly; odd.

Narzisse [narˈtsɪsə] *f* (-/-n) narcissus; *gelbe* ~ daffodil.

nasal *adj.* [naˈzaːl] nasal; ~*e Sprech-
weise* twang.

nasch|en ['naʃən] (ge-, *h*) **1.** *v/i.*
nibble (*an dat.* at); *gern* ~ have a
sweet tooth; **2.** *v/t.* nibble; eat *s.th.*
on the sly; **2ereien** [ˌˑraɪən] *f/pl.*
dainties pl., sweets pl.; '**~haft** *adj.*
fond of dainties *or* sweets.

Nase ['naːzə] *f* (-/-n) nose; *die* ~
rümpfen turn up one's nose (*über*
acc. at).

näseln ['nɛːzəln] *v/i.* (ge-, *h*) speak
through the nose, nasalize; snuffle.

'**Nasen|bluten** *n* (-s/*no pl.*) nose-
bleeding; '**~loch** *n* nostril; '**~spitze**
f tip of the nose.

naseweis *adj.* ['naːzəvaɪs] pert,
saucy.

nasführen ['nɑːs-] *v/t.* (ge-, *h*) fool,
dupe.

Nashorn *zo.* ['nɑːs-] *n* rhinoceros.

naß *adj.* [nas] wet; damp, moist.

Nässe ['nɛsə] *f* (-/*no pl.*) wet(ness);
moisture; 🝆 humidity; '**2n** (ge-, *h*)
1. *v/t.* wet; moisten; **2.** ☞ *v/i.* discharge.

'**naßkalt** *adj.* damp and cold, raw.

Nation [naˈtsjoːn] *f* (-/-en) nation.

national *adj.* [natsjoˈnaːl] national;
2hymne *f* national anthem; **2is-
mus** [ˌaˈlɪsmʊs] *m* (-/*Nationalis-
men*) nationalism; **2ität** [ˌaliˈtɛːt] *f*
(-/-en) nationality; **2mannschaft** *f*
national team.

Natter ['natər] *f* (-/-n) *zo.* adder,
viper; *fig.* serpent.

Natur [naˈtuːr] *f* **1.** (-/*no pl.*) nature;
2. (-/-en) constitution; temper(a-
ment), disposition, nature; *von* ~ by
nature.

Naturalien [natuˈrɑːljən] *pl.* natural produce *sg.*; *in* ~ in kind.

naturalisieren [naturaliˈziːrən] *v/t.*
(*no* -ge-, *h*) naturalize.

Naturalismus [naturaˈlɪsmʊs] *m*
(-/*no pl.*) naturalism.

Naturanlage [naˈtuːr-] *f* (natural)
disposition.

Naturell [natuˈrɛl] *n* (-s/-e) natural
disposition, nature, temper.

Na'tur|ereignis *n*, **~erscheinung** *f*
phenomenon; **~forscher** *m* natu-
ralist, scientist; **2gemäß** *adj.* natural; **~geschichte** *f* natural history;
~gesetz *n* law of nature, natural
law; **2getreu** *adj.* true to nature;
life-like; **~kunde** *f* (natural)
science.

natürlich [naˈtyːrlɪç] **1.** *adj.* natural; genuine, innate; unaffected;
2. *adv.* naturally, of course.

Na'tur|produkte *n/pl.* natural prod-
ucts *pl.* or produce *sg.*; **~schutz** *m*
wild-life conservation; **~schutzge-
biet** *n*, **~schutzpark** *m* national
park, wild-life (p)reserve; **~trieb** *m*
instinct; **~wissenschaft** *f* (natural)
science; **~wissenschaftler** *m* (natural) scientist.

Nebel ['neːbəl] *m* (-s/-) fog; mist;
haze; smoke; **2haft** *fig. adj.* nebu-
lous, hazy, dim; '**~horn** *n* fog-horn.

neben *prp.* (*dat.*; *acc.*) ['neːbən] beside, by (the side of); near to;
against, compared with; apart *or*
Am. a. aside from, besides.

neben|an *adv.* next door; close by;
2anschluß *teleph.* ['neːbən?-] *m*
extension (line); **2arbeit** ['neːbən?-]
f extra work; **2ausgaben** ['neː-
bən?-] *f/pl.* incidental expenses *pl.*,
extras *pl.*; **2ausgang** ['neːbən?-] *m*
side-exit, side-door; '**2bedeutung**
f secondary meaning, connotation;

~'bei *adv.* by the way; besides; **'2beruf** *m* side-line; **'~beruflich** *adv.* as a side-line; in one's spare time; **'2beschäftigung** *f s.* Nebenberuf; **2buhler** ['~buːlər] *m* (-s/-) rival; **~ei'nander** *adv.* side by side; **~ bestehen** co-exist; **2eingang** ['neːbənɐ-] *m* side-entrance; **2einkünfte** ['neːbənɐ-] *pl.*, **2einnahmen** ['neːbənɐ-] *f/pl.* casual emoluments *pl.*, extra income; **2erscheinung** ['neːbənɐ-] *f* accompaniment; **2fach** *n* subsidiary subject, *Am.* minor (subject); **'2fluß** *m* tributary (river); **'2gebäude** *n* annex(e); outhouse; **'2geräusch** *n* *radio:* atmospherics *pl.*, interference, jamming; **'2gleis 🚂** *n* siding, side-track; **'2handlung** *thea. f* underplot; **'2haus** *n* adjoining house; **'~her** *adv.*, **'~hin** *adv.* by his *or* her side; *s.* nebenbei; **'2kläger** 🏛 *m* co-plaintiff; **'2kosten** *pl.* extras *pl.*; **'2mann** *m* person next to one; **'2produkt** *n* by-product; **'2rolle** *f* minor part (*a. thea.*); **'2sache** *f* minor matter, side issue; **'~sächlich** *adj.* subordinate, incidental, unimportant; **'2satz** *gr. m* subordinate clause; **'~stehend** *adj.* in the margin; **'2stelle** *f* branch; agency; *teleph.* extension; **'2straße** *f* by-street, by-road; **'2strecke** 🚂 *f* branch line; **'2tisch** *m* next table; **'2tür** *f* side-door; **'2verdienst** *m* incidental *or* extra earnings *pl.*; **'2zimmer** *n* adjoining room.

'neblig *adj.* foggy, misty, hazy.

nebst *prp.* (*dat.*) [neːpst] together with, besides; including.

neck|en ['nɛkən] *v/t.* (ge-, h) tease, banter, *sl.* kid; **'2erei** [~'raɪ] *f* (-/-en) teasing, banter; **'~isch** *adj.* playful; droll, funny.

Neffe ['nɛfə] *m* (-n/-n) nephew.

negativ [nega'tiːf] **1.** *adj.* negative; **'te:t]** *f* (-/no *pl.*) nervousness.

2. **2** *n* (-s/-e) negative.

Neger ['neːgər] *m* (-s/-) negro; **'~in** *f* (-/-nen) negress.

nehmen ['neːmən] *v/t.* (irr., ge-, h) take; receive; charge (*money*); *zu sich* ~ take, have (*meal*); *j-m et.* ~ take s.th. from s.o.; *ein Ende* ~ come to an end; *es sich nicht* ~ *lassen zu inf.* insist upon *ger.*; *streng genommen* strictly speaking.

Neid [naɪt] *m* (-[e]s/no *pl.*) envy; **2en** ['naɪdən] *v/t.* (ge-, h): *j-m et.*

~ envy s.o. s.th.; **~er** ['~dər] *m* (-s/-) envious person; **~hammel** F ['naɪt-] *m* dog in the manger; **2isch** *adj.* ['~dɪʃ] envious (*auf acc.* of); **2los** *adj.* ['naɪt-] ungrudging.

Neige ['naɪgə] *f* (-/-n) decline; *barrel:* dregs *pl.*; *glass:* heeltap; *zur* ~ *gehen* (be on the) decline; *esp.* ✝ run short; **'2n** (ge-, h) **1.** *v/t. and v/refl.* bend, incline; **2.** *v/i.:* *er neigt zu Übertreibungen* he is given to exaggeration.

Neigung *f* (-/-en) inclination (*a. fig.*); slope, incline.

nein *adv.* [naɪn] no.   [tar.}

Nektar ['nɛktaːr] *m* (-s/no *pl.*) nec-}

Nelke 🌷 ['nɛlkə] *f* (-/-n) carnation, pink; *spice:* clove.

nennen ['nɛnən] *v/t.* (irr., ge-, h) name; call; term; mention; nominate (*candidate*); *sports:* enter (für for); *sich ...* ~ be called ...; **'~swert** *adj.* worth mentioning.

'Nenn|er 👶 *m* (-s/-) denominator; **'~ung** *f* (-/-en) naming; mentioning; nomination (*of candidates*); *sports:* entry; **'~wert** *m* nominal *or* face value; *zum* ~ ✝ at par.

Neon 🧪 ['neːɔn] *n* (-s/no *pl.*) neon; **'~röhre** *f* neon tube.

Nerv [nɛrf] *m* (-s/-en) nerve; *j-m auf die ~en fallen or gehen* get on s.o.'s nerves.

'Nerven|arzt *m* neurologist; **'2aufreibend** *adj.* trying; **'~heilanstalt** *f* mental hospital; **'~kitzel** *m* (-s/no *pl.*) thrill, sensation; **'2krank** *adj.* neurotic; **'2leidend** *adj.* neuropathic, neurotic; **'~schwäche** *f* nervous debility; **'2stärkend** *adj.* tonic; **'~system** *n* nervous system; **'~zusammenbruch** *m* nervous breakdown.

nerv|ig *adj.* ['nɛrvɪç] sinewy; **~ös** *adj.* [~'vøːs] nervous; **2osität** [~ozi-**'te:t]** *f* (-/no *pl.*) nervousness.

Nerz *zo.* [nɛrts] *m* (-es/-e) mink.

Nessel 🌿 ['nɛsəl] *f* (-/-n) nettle. F

Nest [nɛst] *n* (-es/-er) nest; F *fig.* bed; F *fig.* hick *or* one-horse town.

nett *adj.* F [nɛt] nice; neat, pretty, *Am. a.* cute; pleasant; kind.

netto ✝ *adv.* ['nɛto] net, clear.

Netz [nɛts] *n* (-es/-e) net; *fig.* network; **'~anschluß** ⚡ *m* mains connection, power supply; **'~haut** *anat. f* retina; **'~spannung** ⚡ *f* mains voltage.

neu adj. [nɔʏ] new; fresh; recent; modern; **~ere** Sprachen modern languages; **~este** Nachrichten latest news; von **~em** anew, afresh; ein **~es** Leben beginnen turn over a new leaf; was gibt es Neues? what is the news?, Am. what is new?

'**Neu|anschaffung** f (-/-en) recent acquisition; '**2artig** adj. novel; '**~auflage** typ. f, '**~ausgabe** typ. f new edition; reprint; '**~bau** m (-[e]s/-ten) new building; '**2bearbeitet** adj. revised; '**~e** m (-n/-n) new man; new-comer; novice; '**2entdeckt** adj. recently discovered.

neuer|dings adv. ['nɔʏər'diŋs] of late, recently; '**2er** m (-s/-) innovator.

Neuerscheinung ['nɔʏ'-] f new book or publication.

'**Neuerung** f (-/-en) innovation.

'**neu|geboren** adj. new-born; '**~gestalten** v/t. (sep., -ge-, h) reorganize; '**2gestaltung** f reorganization; '**2gier** f, **2gierde** ['~də] f (-/no pl.) curiosity, inquisitiveness; '**~gierig** adj. curious (auf acc. about, of), inquisitive, sl. nos(e)y; ich bin **~**, ob I wonder whether or if; '**2heit** f (-/-en) newness, freshness; novelty.

'**Neuigkeit** f (-/-en) (e-e a piece of) news.

'**Neu|jahr** n New Year('s Day); '**~land** n (-[e]s/no pl.): **~** erschließen break fresh ground (a. fig.); '**2lich** adv. the other day, recently; '**2ling** m (-s/-e) novice; contp. greenhorn; '**2modisch** adj. fashionable; '**~mond** m (-[e]s/no pl.) new moon.

neun adj. [nɔʏn] nine; '**~te** adj. ninth; '**2tel** n (-s/-) ninth part; '**~tens** adv. ninthly; '**~zehn** adj. nineteen; '**~zehnte** adj. nineteenth; **~zig** adj. ['~tsiç] ninety; '**~zigste** adj. ninetieth.

'**Neu|philologe** m student or teacher of modern languages; '**~regelung** f reorganization, rearrangement.

neutr|al adj. [nɔʏ'traːl] neutral; **2alität** [~ali'tɛːt] f (-/no pl.) neutrality; **2um** gr. ['nɔʏtrʊm] n (-s/Neutra, Neutren) neuter.

'**neu|vermählt** adj. newly married; die **2en** pl. the newly-weds pl.; '**2wahl** parl. f new election; '**~wertig** adj. as good as new; '**2zeit** f (-/no pl.) modern times pl.

nicht adv. [niçt] not; auch **~** nor; **~** anziehend unattractive; **~** besser no better; **~** bevollmächtigt non-commissioned; **~** einlösbar † inconvertible; **~** erscheinen fail to attend.

'**Nicht|achtung** f disregard; '**2amtlich** adj. unofficial; '**~angriffspakt** pol. m non-aggression pact; '**~annahme** f non-acceptance; '**~befolgung** f non-observance.

Nichte ['niçtə] f (-/-n) niece.

'**nichtig** adj. null, void; invalid; vain, futile; für **~** erklären declare null and void, annul; '**2keit** f (-/-en) ṭṭ nullity; vanity, futility.

'**Nichtraucher** m non-smoker.

nichts [niçts] 1. indef. pron. nothing, naught, not anything; 2. **2** n (-/no pl.) nothing(ness); fig.: nonentity void; '**~ahnend** adj. unsuspecting **~desto'weniger** adv. nevertheless **~nutzig** adj. ['~nutsiç] good-for-nothing, worthless; '**~sagend** adj insignificant; **2tuer** ['~tuːər] m (-s/-) idler; '**~würdig** adj. vile base, infamous.

'**Nicht|vorhandensein** n absence lack; '**~wissen** n ignorance.

nick|en ['nikən] v/i. (ge-, h) nod; bow; '**2erchen** F n (-s/-): ein **~** machen take a nap, have one's forty winks.

nie adv. [niː] never, at no time.

nieder ['niːdər] 1. adj. low; base mean, vulgar; value, rank: inferior 2. adv. down.

'**Nieder|gang** m decline; '**2gedrückt** adj. dejected, downcast '**2gehen** v/i. (irr. gehen, sep., -ge-, sein) go down; ✈ descend; storm: break; '**2geschlagen** adj. dejected, downcast; '**2hauen** v/t. (irr. hauen, sep., -ge-, h) cut down; '**2kommen** v/i. (irr. kommen, sep., -ge-, sein) be confined; be delivered (mit of); '**~kunft** ['~kunft] f (-/ːe) confinement, delivery; '**~lage** f defeat; † warehouse; branch; '**2lassen** v/t. (irr. lassen, sep., -ge-, h) let down; sich **~** settle (down); bird: alight; sit down; establish o.s.; settle (in dat. at); '**~lassung** f (-/-en) establishment; settlement; branch, agency; '**2legen** v/t. (sep., -ge-, h) lay or put down; resign (position); retire from (business); abdicate; die Arbeit **~** (go on) strike, down tools,

Am. F *a.* walk out; *sich* ~ lie down, go to bed; '**2machen** *v/t.* (*sep.,* -*ge*-, *h*) cut down; massacre; '~**schlag** *m* ⚡ precipitate; sediment; precipitation (*of rain, etc.*); *radioactive*: fall-out; *boxing*: knockdown, knock-out; '**2schlagen** *v/t.* (*irr.* schlagen, *sep.,* -*ge*-, *h*) knock down; *boxing*: *a.* floor; cast down (*eyes*); suppress; put down, crush (*rebellion*); ⚌ quash; *sich* ~ ⚡ precipitate; '**2schmettern** *fig. v/t.* (*sep.,* -*ge*-, *h*) crush; '**2setzen** *v/t.* (*sep.,* -*ge*-, *h*) set *or* put down; *sich* ~ sit down; *birds*: perch, alight; '**2strecken** *v/t.* (*sep.,* -*ge*-, *h*) lay low, strike to the ground, floor; '**2trächtig** *adj.* base, mean; F beastly; '~**ung** *f* (-/-*en*) lowlands *pl.*

niedlich *adj.* ['ni:tliç] neat, nice, pretty, *Am. a.* cute.   [nail.|
Niednagel ['ni:t-] *m* agnail, hang-|
niedrig *adj.* ['ni:driç] low (*a. fig.*); moderate; *fig.* mean, base.
niemals *adv.* ['ni:ma:ls] never, at no time.
niemand *indef. pron.* ['ni:mant] nobody, no one; 'one; '**2sland** *n* (-[*e*]*s*/*no pl.*) no man's land.
Niere ['ni:rə] *f* (-/-*n*) kidney; '~**nbraten** *m* loin of veal.
niesel|n F ['ni:zəln] *v/i.* (*ge*-, *h*) drizzle; '**2regen** F *m* drizzle.
niesen ['ni:zən] *v/i.* (*ge*-, *h*) sneeze.
Niet ⊕ ['ni:t] *m* (-[*e*]*s*/-*e*) rivet; '~*e f* (-/-*n*) *lottery*: blank; F *fig.* washout; '**2en** ⊕ *v/t.* (*ge*-, *h*) rivet.
Nilpferd *zo.* ['ni:l-] *n* hippopotamus.
Nimbus ['nimbus] *m* (-/-*se*) halo (*a. fig.*), nimbus.
nimmer *adv.* ['nimər] never; '~**mehr** *adv.* nevermore; '**2satt** *m* (-, -[*e*]*s*/-*e*) glutton; '**2wiedersehen** F *n*: *auf* ~ never to meet again; *er verschwand auf* ~ he left for good.   [*dat.* at).|
nippen ['nipən] *v/i.* (*ge*-, *h*) sip (*an|*
Nipp|es ['nipəs] *pl.*, '~**sachen** *pl.* (k)nick-(k)nacks *pl.*
nirgend|s *adv.* ['nirgənts], '~(*s*)**wo** *adv.* nowhere.
Nische ['ni:ʃə] *f* (-/-*n*) niche, recess.
nisten ['nistən] *v/i.* (*ge*-, *h*) nest.
Niveau [ni'vo:] *n* (-*s*/-*s*) level; *fig. a.* standard.
nivellieren [nive'li:rən] *v/t.* (*no* -*ge*-, *h*) level, grade.

Nixe ['niksə] *f* (-/-*n*) water-nymph, mermaid.
noch [nɔx] **1.** *adv.* still; yet; ~ *ein* another, one more; ~ *einmal* once more *or* again; ~ *etwas* something more; ~ *etwas?* anything else?; ~ *heute* this very day; ~ *immer* still; ~ *nicht* not yet; ~ *nie* never before; ~ *so ever so*; ~ *im 19. Jahrhundert* as late as the 19th century; *es wird* ~ *2 Jahre dauern* it will take two more *or* another two years; **2.** *cj.*: *s. weder*; ~**malig** ['~ma:liç] repeated; ~**mals** *adv.* ['~ma:ls] once more *or* again.
Nomad|e [no'ma:də] *m* (-*n*/-*n*) nomad; **2isch** *adj.* nomadic.
Nominativ *gr.* ['no:minati:f] *m* (-*s*/-*e*) nominative (case).
nominieren [nomi'ni:rən] *v/t.* (*no* -*ge*-, *h*) nominate.
Nonne ['nɔnə] *f* (-/-*n*) nun; '~**nkloster** *n* nunnery, convent.
Nord *geogr.* [nɔrt], ~**en** ['~dən] *m* (-*s*/*no pl.*) north; **2isch** *adj.* ['~diʃ] northern.
nördlich *adj.* ['nœrtliç] northern, north.
'**Nord|licht** *n* northern lights *pl.*; ~'**ost(en** *m*) north-east; '~**pol** *m* North Pole; **2wärts** *adv.* ['~vɛrts] northward(s), north; ~'**west(en** *m*) north-west.
nörg|eln ['nœrgəln] *v/i.* (*ge*-, *h*) nag, carp (*an dat.* at); grumble; **2ler** ['~lər] *m* (-*s*/-) faultfinder, grumbler.
Norm [nɔrm] *f* (-/-*en*) standard; rule; norm.
normal *adj.* [nɔr'ma:l] normal; regular; *measure, weight, time*: standard; ~**isieren** [~ali'zi:rən] *v/refl.* (*no* -*ge*-, *h*) return to normal.
'**norm|en** *v/t.* (*ge*-, *h*), ~**ieren** [~'mi:rən] *v/t.* (*no* -*ge*-, *h*) standardize.
Not [no:t] *f* (-/-*e*) need, want; necessity; difficulty, trouble; misery; danger, emergency; distress (*a.* ⊕); ~ *leiden* suffer privations; *in* ~ *geraten* become destitute, get into trouble; *in* ~ *sein* be in trouble; *zur* ~ at a pinch; *es tut not, daß* it is necessary that.   [notary.|
Notar [no'ta:r] *m* (-*s*/-*e*) (public)|
'**Not|ausgang** *m* emergency exit; '~**behelf** *m* makeshift, expedient, stopgap; '~**bremse** *f* emergency

brake; '~brücke f temporary bridge; ~durft ['~durft] f (-/no pl.): s-e ~ verrichten relieve o.s.; '2dürftig adj. scanty, poor; temporary.

Note ['no:tə] f (-/-n) note (a. ♪); pol. note, memorandum; school: mark.

'Noten|bank ✝ f bank of issue; '~schlüssel ♪ m clef; '~system ♪ n staff.

'Not|fall m case of need, emergency; '2falls adv. if necessary; '2gedrungen adv. of necessity, needs.

notier|en [no'ti:rən] v/t. (no -ge-, h) make a note of, note (down); ✝ quote; 2ung ✝ f (-/-en) quotation.

nötig adj. ['nø:tiç] necessary; ~ haben need; ~en ['~gən] v/t. (ge-, h) force, oblige, compel; press, urge (guest); '~enfalls adv. if necessary; '2ung f (-/-en) compulsion; pressing; ⚖ intimidation.

Notiz [no'ti:ts] f (-/-en) notice; note, memorandum; ~ nehmen von take notice of; pay attention to; keine ~ nehmen von ignore; sich ~en machen take notes; ~block m pad, Am. a. scratch pad; ~buch n notebook.

'Not|lage f distress; emergency; '2landen ✈ v/i. (-ge-, sein) make a forced or emergency landing; '~landung ✈ f forced or emergency landing; '2leidend adj. needy, destitute; distressed; '~lösung f expedient; '~lüge f white lie.

notorisch adj. [no'to:riʃ] notorious.

'Not|ruf teleph. m emergency call; '~signal n emergency or distress signal; '~sitz mot. m dick(e)y(-seat), Am. a. rumble seat; '~stand m emergency; '~standsarbeiten f/pl. relief works pl.; '~standsgebiet n distressed area; '~standsgesetze n/pl. emergency laws pl.; '~verband m first-aid dressing; '~verordnung f emergency decree; '~wehr f self-defen|ce, Am. -se; '2wendig adj. necessary; '~wendigkeit f (-/-en) necessity; '2zucht f (-/no pl.) rape.

Novelle [no'vɛlə] f (-/-n) short story, novella; parl. amendment.

November [no'vɛmbər] m (-[s]/-) November.

Nu [nu:] m (-/no pl.): im ~ in no

Nuance [ny'ã:sə] f (-/-n) shade.

nüchtern adj. ['nyçtərn] empty, fasting; sober (a. fig.); matter-of-fact; writings: jejune; prosaic; cool; plain; '2heit f (-/no pl.) sobriety, fig. soberness.

Nudel ['nu:dəl] f (-/-n) noodle.

null [nul] 1. adj. null; nil; tennis: love; ~ und nichtig null and void; 2. 2 f (-/-en) nought, cipher (a. fig.); zero; '2punkt m zero.

numerieren [numə'ri:rən] v/t. (no -ge-, h) number; numerierter Platz reserved seat.

Nummer ['numər] f (-/-n) number (a. newspaper, thea.); size (of shoes, etc.); thea. turn; sports: event; '~nschild mot. n number-plate.

nun [nu:n] 1. adv. now, at present; then; ~? well?; ~ also well then; 2. int. now then!; '~mehr adv. now.

nur adv. [nu:r] only; (nothing) but; merely; ~ noch only.

Nuß [nus] f (-/Nüsse) nut; '~kern m kernel; '~knacker m (-s/-) nutcracker; '~schale f nutshell.

Nüstern ['ny:stərn] f/pl. nostrils pl.

nutz [nuts] s. nütze; '2anwendung f practical application; '~bar adj. useful; '~bringend adj. profitable.

nütze adj. ['nytsə] useful; zu nichts ~ sein be of no use, be good for nothing.

Nutzen ['nutsən] 1. m (-s/-) use; profit, gain; advantage; utility; 2. 2 v/i. and v/t. (ge-, h) s. nützen.

nützen ['nytsən] (ge-, h) 1. v/i.: zu et. ~ be of use or useful for s.th.; j-m ~ serve s.o.; es nützt nichts zu inf. it is no use ger.; 2. v/t. use, make use of; put to account; avail o.s. of, seize (opportunity).

'Nutz|holz n timber; '~leistung f capacity.

nützlich adj. ['nytsliç] useful, of use; advantageous.

'nutz|los adj. useless; 2nießer ['~ni:sər] m (-s/-) usufructuary; '~nießung f (-/-en) usufruct.

'Nutzung f (-/-en) using; utilization.

Nylon ['naɪlɔn] n (-s/no pl.) nylon; ~strümpfe ['~ʃtrympfə] m/pl. nylons pl., nylon stockings pl.

Nymphe ['nymfə] f (-/-n) nymph.

O

o *int.* [o:] oh!, ah!; ~ *weh!* alas!, oh dear (me)!

Oase [o'a:zə] *f* (-/-n) oasis.

ob *cj.* [ɔp] whether, if; *als* ~ as if, as though.

Obacht ['o:baxt] *f* (-/*no pl.*): ~ *geben auf* (*acc.*) pay attention to, take care of, heed.

Obdach ['ɔpdax] *n* (-[e]s/*no pl.*) shelter, lodging; **'2los** *adj.* unsheltered, homeless; **'2lose** *m, f* (-n/-n) homeless person; **'_losenasyl** *n* casual ward.

Obduktion ⚕ [ɔpduk'tsjo:n] *f* (-/-en) post-mortem (examination), autopsy; **2zieren** ⚕ [_'tsi:rən] *v/t.* (*no -ge-, h*) perform an autopsy on.

oben *adv.* ['o:bən] above; *mountain*: at the top; *house*: upstairs; on the surface; *von* ~ from above; *von* ~ *bis unten* from top to bottom; *von* ~ *herab behandeln* treat haughtily; **'_an** *adv.* at the top; **'_auf** *adv.* on the top; on the surface; **_drein** *adv.* [_'draɪn] into the bargain, at that; **_erwähnt** *adj.* ['o:bən'ɛrvɛ:nt], **'_genannt** *adj.* above-mentioned, aforesaid; **'_hin** *adv.* superficially, perfunctorily.

ober ['o:bər] **1.** *adj.* upper, higher; *fig. a.* superior; **2.** 2 *m* (-s/-) (head) waiter; *German cards*: queen.

Ober|arm ['o:bər'-] *m* upper arm; **_arzt** ['o:bər'-] *m* head physician; **_aufseher** ['o:bər'-] *m* superintendent; **_aufsicht** ['o:bər'-] *f* superintendence; **'_befehl** ⚔ *m* supreme command; **'_befehlshaber** ⚔ *m* commander-in-chief; **'_bekleidung** *f* outer garments *pl.*, outer wear; **'_bürgermeister** *m* chief burgomaster; Lord Mayor; **'_deck** ⚓ *n* upper deck; **'_fläche** *f* surface; **2flächlich** *adj.* ['_flɛçlɪç] superficial; *fig. a.* shallow; **'2halb** *prp.* (*gen.*) above; **'_hand** *fig. f*: *die* ~ *gewinnen über* (*acc.*) get the upper hand of; **'_haupt** *n* head, chief; **'_haus** *Brt. parl. n* House of Lords; **'_hemd** *n* shirt; **'_herrschaft** *f* supremacy.

Oberin *f* (-/-nen) *eccl.* Mother Superior; *at hospital*: matron.

ober|irdisch *adj.* ['o:bər'-] over-ground, above ground; ⚡ overhead; **'2kellner** *m* head waiter; **'2kiefer** *anat. m* upper jaw; **'2körper** *m* upper part of the body; **2land** *n* upland; **2lauf** *m* upper course (*of river*); **2leder** *n* upper; **'2leitung** *f* chief management; ⚡ overhead wires *pl.*; **2leutnant** ⚔ *m* (*Am.* first) lieutenant; **'2licht** *n* skylight; **'2lippe** *f* upper lip; **2schenkel** *m* thigh; **'2schule** *f* secondary school, *Am. a.* high school.

'oberst 1. *adj.* uppermost, topmost, top; highest (*a. fig.*); *fig.* chief, principal; *rank, etc.*: supreme; **2.** 2 ⚔ *m* (-en, -en, -e) colonel.

'Ober|'staatsanwalt 🏛 *m* chief public prosecutor; **'_stimme** ♪ *f* treble, soprano.

'Oberst'leutnant ⚔ *m* lieutenant-colonel.

'Ober|tasse *f* cup; **'_wasser** *fig. n*: ~ *bekommen* get the upper hand.

obgleich *cj.* [ɔp'glaɪç] (al)though.

'Obhut *f* (-/*no pl.*) care, guard; protection; custody; *in (seine)* ~ *nehmen* take care or charge of.

obig *adj.* ['o:bɪç] above(-mentioned), aforesaid.

Objekt [ɔp'jɛkt] *n* (-[e]s/-e) object (*a. gr.*); project; ✝ *a.* transaction.

objektiv [ɔpjɛk'ti:f] **1.** *adj.* objective; impartial, detached; actual, practical; **2.** 2 *n* (-s/-e) object-glass, objective; *phot.* lens; **2ität** [_ivi'tɛ:t] *f* (-/*no pl.*) objectivity; impartiality.

obligat *adj.* [obli'ga:t] obligatory; indispensable; inevitable; **2ion** ✝ [_a'tsjo:n] *f* (-/-en) obligation; debenture; **_orisch** *adj.* [_a'to:rɪʃ] obligatory (*für on*), compulsory, mandatory.

'Obmann *m* chairman; 🏛 foreman (*of jury*); umpire; ✝ shop-steward, spokesman.

Oboe ♪ [o'bo:ə] *f* (-/-n) oboe, hautboy.

Obrigkeit ['o:brɪçkaɪt] *f* (-/-en) *the* authorities *pl.*; government; **2lich** *adj.* magisterial, official; **'_sstaat** *m* authoritarian state.

ob'schon *cj.* (al)though.

Observatorium *ast.* [ɔpzɛrva'to:rjum] *n* (-s/*Observatorien*) observatory.

Obst [o:pst] *n* (-es/*no pl.*) fruit; '**~bau** *m* fruit-culture, fruit-growing; '**~baum** *m* fruit-tree; '**~ernte** *f* fruit-gathering; fruit-crop; '**~garten** *m* orchard; '**~händler** *m* fruiterer, *Am.* fruitseller; '**~züchter** *m* fruiter, fruit-grower.

obszön *adj.* [ɔps'tsøːn] obscene, filthy.

ob'wohl *cj.* (al)though.

Ochse *zo.* ['ɔksə] *m* (-n/-n) ox; bullock; '**~nfleisch** *n* beef.

öde ['øːdə] **1.** *adj.* deserted, desolate; waste; *fig.* dull, tedious; **2.** ♀ *f* (-/-n) desert, solitude; *fig.* dullness, tedium.

oder *cj.* ['oːdər] or.

Ofen ['oːfən] *m* (-s/￼) stove; oven; kiln; furnace; '**~heizung** *f* heating by stove; '**~rohr** *n* stove-pipe.

offen *adj.* ['ɔfən] open (*a. fig.*); *position:* vacant; *hostility:* overt; *fig.* frank, outspoken.

offen'bar 1. *adj.* obvious, evident; apparent; **2.** *adv. a.* it seems that; **~en** [ɔfən'-] *v/t.* (*no* -ge-, *h*) reveal, disclose; manifest; *sich j-m* ~ open one's heart to s.o.; ♀**ung** [ɔfən'-] *f* (-/-en) manifestation; revelation; ♀**ungseid** ♈ [ɔfən'baːruŋs?-] *m* oath of manifestation.

'**Offenheit** *fig. f* (-/*no pl.*) openness, frankness.

'**offen|herzig** *adj.* open-hearted, sincere; frank; '**~kundig** *adj.* public; notorious; '**~sichtlich** *adj.* manifest, evident, obvious.

offensiv *adj.* [ɔfɛn'ziːf] offensive; ♀**e** [~və] *f* (-/-n) offensive.

'**offenstehen** *v/i.* (*irr.* stehen, sep., -ge-, *h*) stand open; ✝ *bill:* be outstanding; *fig.* be open (*j-m* to s.o.); *es steht ihm offen zu inf.* he is free or at liberty to *inf.*

öffentlich ['œfəntliç] **1.** *adj.* public; **~es Ärgernis** public nuisance; **~er Dienst** Civil Service; **2.** *adv.* publicly, in public; ~ *auftreten* make a public appearance; ♀**keit** *f* (-/*no pl.*) publicity; *the* public; *in aller* ~ in public.

offerieren [ɔfə'riːrən] *v/t.* (*no* -ge-, *h*) offer. [tender.]

Offerte [ɔ'fɛrtə] *f* (-/-n) offer;]

offiziell *adj.* [ɔfi'tsjɛl] official.

Offizier ✗ [ɔfi'tsiːr] *m* (-s/-e) (commissioned) officer; **~skorps** ✗ [~skoːr] *n* (-/-) body of officers, *the* officers *pl.*; **~smesse** *f* ✗ officers' mess; ♣ *a.* wardroom.

offiziös *adj.* [ɔfi'tsjøːs] officious, semi-official.

öffn|en ['œfnən] *v/t.* (ge-, *h*) open; *a.* uncork (*bottle*); ✿ dissect (*body*); *sich* ~ open; ♀**er** *m* (-s/-) opener; ♀**ung** *f* (-/-en) opening, aperture; ♀**ungszeiten** *f/pl.* hours *pl.* of opening, business hours *pl.*

oft *adv.* [ɔft] often, frequently.

öfters *adv.* ['œftərs] *s.* oft.

'**oftmal|ig** *adj.* frequent, repeated; '**~s** *adv. s.* oft.

oh *int.* [oː] o(h)!

ohne ['oːnə] **1.** *prp.* (*acc.*) without; **2.** *cj.:* ~ *daß*, ~ *zu inf.* without *ger.*; **~dies** *adv.* anyhow, anyway; **~glei-chen** *adv.* unequal(l)ed, matchless; **~hin** *adv. s.* ohnedies.

'**Ohn|macht** *f* (-/-en) powerlessness; impotence; ✿ faint, unconsciousness; *in* ~ *fallen* faint, swoon; **~machtsanfall** ✿ ['oːnmaxts?-] *m* fainting fit, swoon; ♀**mächtig** *adj.* powerless; impotent; ✿ unconscious; ~ *werden* faint, swoon.

Ohr [oːr] *n* (-[e]s/-en) ear; *fig. a.* hearing; *s-n* ~ *haben für* have an ear for; *ganz* ~ *sein* be all ears; F *j-n übers* ~ *hauen* cheat s.o., *sl.* do s.o. (in the eye); *bis über die* ~*en* up to the ears *or* eyes.

Öhr [øːr] *n* (-[e]s/-e) eye (*of needle*).

'**Ohren|arzt** *m* aurist, ear specialist; ♀**betäubend** *adj.* deafening; '**~leiden** *n* ear-complaint; '**~schmalz** *n* ear-wax; '**~schmaus** *m* treat for the ears; '**~schmerzen** *m/pl.* ear-ache; '**~zeuge** *m* ear-witness.

Ohr|feige *f* box on the ear(s), slap in the face (*a. fig.*); ♀**feigen** *v/t.* (ge-, *h*): *j-n* ~ box s.o.'s ear(s), slap s.o.'s face; **~läppchen** ['~lɛpçən] *n* (-s/-) lobe of ear; '**~ring** *m* earring.

Ökonom|ie [økono'miː] *f* (-/-n) economy; ♀**isch** *adj.* [~'noːmiʃ] economical.

Oktav [ɔk'taːf] *n* (-s/-e) octavo; **~e** ♪ [~və] *f* (-/-n) octave.

Oktober [ɔk'toːbər] *m* (-[s]/-) October.

Okul|ar *opt.* [oku'laːr] *n* (-s/-e) eyepiece, ocular; ♀**ieren** ✗ *v/t.* (*no* -ge-, *h*) inoculate, graft.

Öl [øːl] n (-[e]s/-e) oil; ~ ins Feuer gießen add fuel to the flames; ~ auf die Wogen gießen pour on oil on the (troubled) waters; '**~baum** ♀ m olive-tree; '**~berg** eccl. m (-[e]s/no pl.) Mount of Olives; **2en** v/t. (ge-, h) oil; ⊕ a. lubricate; '**~farbe** f oil-colo(u)r, oil-paint; '**~gemälde** n oil-painting; '**~heizung** f oil heating; '**2ig** adj. oily (a. fig.).

Oliv|e ♀ [oˈliːvə] f (-/-n) olive; **~enbaum** ♀ m olive-tree; **2grün** adj. olive(-green).

Öl|malerei f oil-painting; '**~quelle** f oil-spring, gusher; oil-well; '**~ung** f (-/-en) oiling; ⊕ a. lubrication; Letzte ~ eccl. extreme unction.

Olympi|ade [olymˈpjaːdə] f (-/-n) Olympiad; a. Olympic Games pl.; **2sch** adj. [oˈlympiʃ] Olympic; Olympische Spiele pl. Olympic Games pl.

'**Ölzweig** m olive-branch.

Omelett [ɔmˈ(ə)'lɛt] n (-[e]s/-e, -s), **~e** [ˌʔlɛt] f (-/-n) omelet(te).

Om|en [ˈoːmən] n (-s/-, Omina) omen, augury; **2inös** adj. [omiˈnøːs] ominous.

Omnibus [ˈɔmnibus] m (-ses/-se) (omni)bus; (motor-)coach; '**~haltestelle** f bus-stop.

Onkel [ˈɔŋkəl] m (-s/-, F -s) uncle.

Oper [ˈoːpər] f (-/-n) ♪ opera; opera-house.

Operat|eur [opəraˈtøːr] m (-s/-e) operator; ✠ surgeon; ✖, ✕ [ˌʔtsjoːn] f (-/-en) operation; '**~ionssaal** m ✠ operating room, Am. surgery; **2iv** adj. [ˌʔtiːf] operative.

Operette ♪ [opəˈrɛtə] f (-/-n) operetta.

operieren [opəˈriːrən] (no -ge-, h) **1.** v/t.: j-n ~ ✠ operate (up)on s.o. (wegen for); **2.** ✠, ✕ v/i. operate; sich ~ lassen ✠ undergo an operation.

'**Opern|glas** n, **~gucker** F [ˈgukər] m (-s/-) opera-glass(es pl.); '**~haus** n opera-house; '**~sänger** m opera-singer, operatic singer; '**~text** m libretto, book (of an opera).

Opfer [ˈɔpfər] n (-s/-) sacrifice; offering; victim (a. fig.); ein ~ bringen make a sacrifice; j-m zum ~ fallen be victimized by s.o.; '**~gabe** f offering; '**2n** (ge-, h) **1.** v/t. sacrifice; immolate; sich für et. ~ sacrifice o.s. for s.th.; **2.** v/i. (make a)

sacrifice (dat. to); '**~stätte** f place of sacrifice; '**~tod** m sacrifice of one's life; '**~ung** f (-/-en) sacrificing, sacrifice; immolation.

Opium [ˈoːpjum] n (-s/no pl.) opium.

opponieren [ɔpoˈniːrən] v/i. (no -ge-, h) be opposed (gegen to), resist.

Opposition [ɔpoziˈtsjoːn] f (-/-en) opposition (a. parl.); **~sführer** parl. m opposition leader; **~spartei** parl. f opposition party.

Optik [ˈɔptik] f (-/♀-en) optics; phot. lens system; fig. aspect; '**~er** m (-s/-) optician.

Optim|ismus [ɔptiˈmismus] m (-/no pl.) optimism; **~ist** m (-en/-en) optimist; **2istisch** adj. optimistic.

'**optisch** adj. optic(al); ~e Täuschung optical illusion.

Orakel [oˈraːkəl] n (-s/-) oracle; **2haft** adj. oracular; **2n** v/i. (no -ge-, h) speak oracularly; **~spruch** m oracle.

Orange [oˈrãːʒə] f (-/-n) orange; **2farben** adj. orange-colo(u)red; **~nbaum** ♀ m orange-tree.

Oratorium ♪ [oraˈtoːrjum] n (-s/ Oratorien) oratorio.

Orchester ♪ [ɔrˈkɛstər] n (-s/-) orchestra.   [orchid.\

Orchidee ♀ [ɔrçiˈdeːə] f (-/-n)\

Orden [ˈɔrdən] m (-s/-) order (a. eccl.); order, medal, decoration.

'**Ordens|band** n ribbon (of an order); '**~bruder** eccl. m brother, friar; '**~gelübde** eccl. n monastic vow; '**~schwester** eccl. f sister, nun; '**~verleihung** f conferring (of) an order.

ordentlich adj. [ˈɔrdəntliç] tidy; orderly; proper; regular; respectable; good, sound; ~er Professor univ. professor in ordinary.

ordinär adj. [ɔrdiˈnɛːr] common, vulgar, low.

ordn|en [ˈɔrdnən] v/t. (ge-, h) put in order; arrange, fix (up); settle (a. ♦ liabilities); '**2er** m (-s/-) at festival, etc.: steward; for papers, etc.: file.

'**Ordnung** f (-/-en) order; arrangement; system; rules pl., regulations pl.; class; in ~ bringen put in order.

'**ordnungs|gemäß**, '**~mäßig 1.** *adj.* orderly, regular; **2.** *adv.* duly; '**2ruf** *parl. m* call to order; '**2strafe** *f* disciplinary penalty; fine; '**~widrig** *adj.* contrary to order, irregular; '**2zahl** *f* ordinal number.

Ordonnanz ✕ [ɔrdɔ'nants] *f* (-/-en) orderly.

Organ [ɔr'ɡaːn] *n* (-s/-e) organ.

Organisat|ion [ɔrɡaniza'tsjoːn] *f* (-/-en) organization; **~ionstalent** *n* organizing ability; **~or** [~'zaːtɔr] *m* (-s/-en) organizer; **2orisch** *adj.* [~a'toːriʃ] organizational, organizing.

or'ganisch *adj.* organic.

organi'sieren *v/t.* (no -ge-, *h*) organize; *sl.* scrounge; (*nicht*) *organisiert(er Arbeiter)* (non-)unionist.

Organismus [ɔrɡa'nismus] *m* (-/Organismen) organism; ✻ *a.* system.

Organist ♪ [ɔrɡa'nist] *m* (-en/-en) organist.

Orgel ♪ ['ɔrɡəl] *f* (-/-n) organ, *Am. a.* pipe organ; '**~bauer** *m* organbuilder; '**~pfeife** *f* organ-pipe; '**~spieler** *m* ♪ organist.

Orgie ['ɔrɡjə] *f* (-/-n) orgy.

Oriental|e [orien'taːlə] *m* (-n/-n) oriental; **2isch** *adj.* oriental.

orientier|en [orien'tiːrən] *v/t.* (no -ge-, *h*) inform, instruct; *sich* ~ orient(ate) o.s. (*a. fig.*); inform o.s. (*über acc.* of); *gut orientiert sein über* (*acc.*) be well informed about, be familiar with; **2ung** *f* (-/-en) orientation; *fig. a.* information; *die* ~ *verlieren* lose one's bearings.

Origin|al [origi'naːl] **1.** *n* (-s/-e) original; **2.** **2** *adj.* original; **~alität** [~ali'tɛːt] *f* (-/-en) originality; **2ell** *adj.* [~'nel] original; *design, etc.*: ingenious.

Orkan [ɔr'kaːn] *m* (-[e]s/-e) hurricane; typhoon; **2artig** *adj. storm:* violent; *applause:* thunderous, frenzied.

Ornat [ɔr'naːt] *m* (-[e]s/-e) robe(s *pl.*), vestment.

Ort [ɔrt] *m* (-[e]s/-e) place; site; spot, point; locality; place, village, town; ~ *der Handlung thea.* scene (of action); *an* ~ *und Stelle* on the spot; *höher(e)n* ~(*e*)s at higher quarters; '**2en** *v/t.* (ge-, *h*) locate.

ortho|dox *adj.* [ɔrto'dɔks] orthodox; **2graphie** [~ɡra'fiː] *f* (-/-n) orthography; **~graphisch** *adj.* [~'ɡraːfiʃ] orthographic(al); **2päde** ✻ [~'pɛːdə] *m* (-n/-n) orthop(a)edist; **2pädie** ✻ [~pɛ'diː] *f* (-/no *pl.*) orthop(a)edics, orthop(a)edy; **~pädisch** *adj.* [~'pɛːdiʃ] orthop(a)edic.

örtlich *adj.* ['œrtliç] local; ✻ *a.* topical; '**2keit** *f* (-/-en) locality.

'**Orts|angabe** *f* statement of place; '**2ansässig** *adj.* resident, local; '**~ansässige** *m* (-n/-n) resident; '**~beschreibung** *f* topography; '**~besichtigung** *f* local inspection.

'**Ortschaft** *f* (-/-en) place, village.

'**Orts|gespräch** *teleph. n* local call; '**~kenntnis** *f* knowledge of a place; '**2kundig** *adj.* familiar with the locality; '**~name** *m* place-name; '**~verkehr** *m* local traffic; '**~zeit** *f* local time.

Öse ['øːzə] *f* (-/-n) eye, loop; eyelet (*of shoe*).

Ost *geogr.* [ɔst] east; '**~en** *m* (-s/no *pl.*) east; *the* East; *der Ferne (Nahe)* ~ *the* Far (Near) East.

ostentativ *adj.* [ɔstenta'tiːf] ostentatious.

Oster|ei ['oːstər⁹-] *n* Easter egg; '**~fest** *n* Easter; '**~hase** *m* Easter bunny *or* rabbit; '**~lamm** *n* paschal lamb; '**~n** *n* (-/-) Easter.

Österreich|er ['øːstəraiçər] *m* (-s/-) Austrian; **2isch** *adj.* Austrian.

östlich ['œstliç] **1.** *adj.* eastern; *wind, etc.:* easterly; **2.** *adv.:* ~ *von* east of.

ost|wärts *adv.* ['ɔstverts] eastward(s); '**2wind** *m* east(erly) wind.

Otter *zo.* ['ɔtər] **1.** *m* (-s/-) otter; **2.** *f* (-/-n) adder, viper.

Ouvertüre ♪ [uver'tyːrə] *f* (-/-n) overture.

oval [o'vaːl] **1.** *adj.* oval; **2.** **2** *n* (-s/-e) oval.

Ovation [ova'tsjoːn] *f* (-/-en) ovation; *j-m* ~*en bereiten* give s.o. ovations.

Oxyd 🜍 [ɔ'ksyːt] *n* (-[e]s/-e) oxide; **2ieren** [~'y'diːrən] (no -ge-) **1.** *v/t.* (*h*) oxidize; **2.** *v/i.* (sein) oxidize.

Ozean ['oːtseaːn] *m* (-s/-e) ocean.

P

Paar [pɑ:r] **1.** *n* (-[e]s/-e) pair; couple; **2.** ℒ *adj.*: ein ~ a few, some; *j-m* ein ~ *Zeilen schreiben* drop s.o. a few lines; '**℀en** *v/t.* (ge-, h) pair, couple; mate (*animals*); *sich* ~ (form a) pair; *animals*: mate; *fig.* join, unite; '**℀lauf** *m sports*: pair-skating; '**℀läufer** *m sports*: pair-skater; '℀**mal** *adv.*: ein ~ *several or a few times*; '**℀ung** *f* (-/-en) coupling; mating, copulation; *fig.* union; '℀**weise** *adv.* in pairs or couples, by twos.

Pacht [paxt] *f* (-/-en) lease, tenure, tenancy; *money payment*: rent; '℀**en** *v/t.* (ge-, h) (take on) lease; rent.

Pächter ['pɛçtər] *m* (-s/-), '**℀in** *f* (-/-nen) lessee, lease-holder; tenant.

'**Pacht|ertrag** *m* rental; '**℀geld** *n* rent; '**℀gut** *n* farm; '**℀vertrag** *m* lease; '℀**weise** *adv.* on lease.

Pack [pak] **1.** *m* (-[e]s/-e, ⁼e) *s.* *Packen²*; **2.** *n* (-[e]s/*no pl.*) rabble.

Päckchen ['pɛkçən] *n* (-s/-) small parcel, *Am. a.* package; *ein* ~ *Zigaretten* a pack(et) of cigarettes.

packen¹ ['pakən] (ge-, h) **1.** *v/t.* pack (up); seize, grip, grasp, clutch; collar; *fig.* grip, thrill; F *pack dich!* F clear out!, *sl.* beat it!; **2.** *v/i.* pack (up); **3.** ℒ *n* (-s/*no pl.*) packing.

Packen² [~] *m* (-s/-) pack(et), parcel; bale.

'**Packer** *m* (-s/-) packer; **℀ei** [~'raɪ] *f* **1.** (-/-en) packing-room; **2.** (-/*no pl.*) packing.

'**Pack|esel** *fig. m* drudge; '**℀material** *n* packing materials *pl.*; '**℀papier** *n* packing-paper, brown paper; '**℀pferd** *n* pack-horse; '**℀ung** *f* (-/-en) pack(age); packet; ⚕ pack; *e-e* ~ *Zigaretten* a pack(et) of cigarettes; '**℀wagen** *m s. Gepäckwagen.*

Pädagog|e [pɛda'go:gə] *m* (-n/-n) pedagog(ue), education(al)ist; '**℀ik** *f* (-/*no pl.*) pedagogics, pedagogy; ℒ**isch** *adj.* pedagogic(al).

Paddel ['padəl] *n* (-s/-) paddle; '**℀boot** *n* canoe; '℀**n** *v/i.* (ge-, h, sein) paddle, canoe.

Page ['pɑ:ʒə] *m* (-n/-n) page.

pah *int.* [pɑ:] pah!, pooh!, pshaw!

Paket [pa'ke:t] *n* (-[e]s/-e) parcel, packet, package; **℀annahme** ℒ *f* parcel counter; **℀karte** ℒ *f* dispatch-note; **℀post** *f* parcel post; **℀zustellung** ℒ *f* parcel delivery.

Pakt [pakt] *m* (-[e]s/-e) pact, agreement; treaty.

Palast [pa'last] *m* (-es/⁼e) palace.

Palm|e ♀ ['palmə] *f* (-/-n) palm (-tree); '**℀öl** *n* palm-oil; '**℀sonntag** *eccl. m* Palm Sunday.

panieren [pa'ni:rən] *v/t.* (*no* -ge-, h) crumb.

Pani|k ['pɑ:nik] *f* (-/-en) panic, stampede; ℒ**sch** *adj.* panic; *von* ~*em Schrecken erfaßt* panic-stricken.

Panne ['panə] *f* (-/-n) breakdown, *mot. a.* engine trouble; *tyres*: puncture; *fig.* blunder.

panschen ['panʃən] (ge-, h) **1.** *v/i.* splash (about); **2.** *v/t.* adulterate (*wine, etc.*).

Panther *zo.* ['pantər] *m* (-s/-) panther.

Pantine [pan'ti:nə] *f* (-/-n) clog.

Pantoffel [pan'tɔfəl] *m* (-s/-n, F -) slipper; *unter dem* ~ *stehen* be henpecked; **℀held** F *m* henpecked husband.

pantschen ['pantʃən] *v/i. and v/t.* (ge-, h) *s.* panschen.

Panzer ['pantsər] *m* (-s/-) armo(u)r; ⚔ tank; *zo.* shell; '**℀abwehr** ⚔ *f* anti-tank defen[c]e, *Am.* -se; '**℀glas** *n* bullet-proof glass; '**℀hemd** *n* coat of mail; '**℀kreuzer** ⚔ *m* armo(u)red cruiser; '℀**n** *v/t.* (ge-, h) armo(u)r; '**℀platte** *f* armo(u)r-plate; '**℀schiff** ⚔ *n* ironclad; '**℀schrank** *m* safe; '**℀ung** *f* (-/-en) armo(u)r-plating; '**℀wagen** *m* armo(u)red car; ⚔ tank.

Papa [pa'pɑ:, F 'papa] *m* (-s/-s) papa, F pa, dad(dy), *Am. a.* pop.

Papagei *orn.* [papa'gaɪ] *m* (-[e]s, -en/-e[n]) parrot.

Papier [pa'pi:r] *n* (-s/-e) paper; ~*e* *pl.* papers *pl.*, documents *pl.*; papers *pl.*, identity card; *ein Bogen* ~ a sheet of paper; ℒ**en** *adj.* (of) paper; *fig.* dull; **℀fabrik** *f* paper-mill; **℀geld** *n* (-[e]s/*no pl.*) paper-money; bank-notes *pl.*, *Am.* bills *pl.*; **℀korb** *m* waste-paper-basket; **℀schnitzel** F *n* or *m/pl.* scraps *pl.* of paper; ~**tüte** *f* paper-bag; ~**waren** *f/pl.* stationery.

'**Papp|band** *m* (-[e]s/=e) paperback; '~**deckel** *m* pasteboard, cardboard.

Pappe ['papə] *f* (-/-n) pasteboard, cardboard.

Pappel ♀ ['papəl] *f* (-/-n) poplar.

päppeln F ['pɛpəln] *v/t.* (ge-, h) feed (with pap).

papp|en F ['papən] (ge-, h) **1.** *v/t.* paste; **2.** *v/i.* stick; '~**ig** *adj.* sticky; '**2karton** *m*, '**2schachtel** *f* cardboard box, carton.

Papst [pɑːpst] *m* (-es/=e) pope.

päpstlich *adj.* ['pɛːpstliç] papal.

'**Papsttum** *n* (-s/*no pl.*) papacy.

Parade [pa'rɑːdə] *f* (-/-n) parade; ✕ review; *fencing:* parry.

Paradies [para'diːs] *n* (-es/-e) paradise; **2isch** *fig.* [~'diːzif] heavenly, delightful. [ical.]

paradox [para'dɔks] paradox-)

Paragraph [para'grɑːf] *m* (-en, -s/-en) article, section; paragraph; section-mark.

parallel *adj.* [para'leːl] parallel; **2e** *f* (-/-n) parallel.

Paralyse ♀ [para'lyːzə] *f* (-/-n) paralysis; **2ieren** ♀ [~y'ziːrən] *v/t.* (*no -ge-,* h) paralyse.

Parasit [para'ziːt] *m* (-en/-en) parasite.

Parenthese [paren'teːzə] *f* (-/-n) parenthesis.

Parforcejagd [par'fɔrs-] *f* hunt (-ing) on horseback (with hounds), *after hares:* coursing.

Parfüm [par'fyːm] *n* (-s/-e, -s) perfume, scent; ~**erie** [~ymə'riː] *f* (-/-n) perfumery; **2ieren** [~y'miːrən] *v/t.* (*no -ge-,* h) perfume, scent.

pari ✝ *adv.* ['pɑːri] par; *al* ~ at par.

parieren [pa'riːrən] (*no -ge-,* h) **1.** *v/t. fencing:* parry (*a. fig.*); pull up (*horse*); **2.** *v/i.* obey (*j-m s.o.*).

Park [park] *m* (-s/-s, -e) park; '~**anlage** *f* park; '~**aufseher** *m* park-keeper; '~**en** (ge-, h) **1.** *v/i.* park; ~ *verboten!* no parking!; **2.** *v/t.* park.

Parkett [par'ket] *n* (-[e]s/-e) parquet; *thea.* (orchestra) stalls *pl.*, *esp. Am.* orchestra or parquet.

'**Park|gebühr** *f* parking-fee; '~**licht** *n* parking light; '~**platz** *m* (car-)park, parking lot; '~**uhr** *mot. f* parking meter.

Parlament [parla'ment] *n* (-[e]s/-e) parliament; **2arisch** *adj.* [~'tɑːriʃ] parliamentary.

Parodie [paro'diː] *f* (-/-n) parody; **2ren** *v/t.* (*no -ge-,* h) parody.

Parole [pa'roːlə] *f* (-/-n) ✕ password, watchword; *fig.* slogan.

Partei [par'taɪ] *f* (-/-en) party (*a. pol.*); *j-s* ~ *ergreifen* take s.o.'s part, side with s.o.; ~**apparat** *pol. m* party machinery; ~**gänger** [~gɛŋər] *m* (-s/-) partisan; **2isch** *adj.*, **2lich** *adj.* partial (*für* to); prejudiced (*gegen* against); **2los** *adj.* independent; ~**mitglied** *pol. n* party member; ~**programm** *pol. n* platform; ~**tag** *pol. m* convention; ~**zugehörigkeit** *pol. f* party membership.

Parterre [par'ter] *n* (-s/-s) ground floor, *Am.* first floor; *thea.:* pit, *Am.* parterre, *Am.* parquet circle.

Partie [par'tiː] *f* (-/-n) ✝ parcel, lot; outing, excursion; *cards, etc.:* game; ♪ part; *marriage:* match.

Partitur ♪ [parti'tuːr] *f* (-/-en) score.

Partizip *gr.* [parti'tsiːp] *n* (-s/-ien) participle.

Partner ['partnər] *m* (-s/-), '~**in** *f* (-/-nen) partner; *film:* a. co-star; '~**schaft** *f* (-/-en) partnership.

Parzelle [par'tselə] *f* (-/-n) plot, lot, allotment.

Paß [pas] *m* (*Passes/Pässe*) pass; passage; *football, etc.:* pass; passport.

Passage [pa'sɑːʒə] *f* (-/-n) passage; arcade.

Passagier [pasa'ʒiːr] *m* (-s/-e) passenger, *in taxis:* a. fare; ~**flugzeug** *n* air liner.

Passah ['pasa] *n* (-s/*no pl.*), '~**fest** *n* Passover.

Passant [pa'sant] *m* (-en/-en), ~**in** *f* (-/-nen) passer-by.

'**Paßbild** *n* passport photo(graph).

passen ['pasən] (ge-, h) **1.** *v/i.* fit (*j-m s.o.;* *auf acc. or für or zu et.* s.th.); suit (*j-m s.o.*), be convenient; *cards, football:* pass; ~ *zu* go with, match (*with*); **2.** *v/refl.* be fit or proper; '~**d** *adj.* fit, suitable; convenient (*für* for).

passier|bar *adj.* [pa'siːrbaːr] passable, practicable; ~**en** (*no -ge-*) **1.** *v/i.* (sein) happen; **2.** *v/t.* (h) pass (over *or* through); **2schein** *m* pass, permit.

Passion [pa'sjo:n] *f* (-/-en) passion; hobby; *eccl.* Passion.

passiv ['pasi:f] **1.** *adj.* passive; **2.** ♀ *gr. n* (-s/⚹ -e) passive (voice); **♀a †** [pa'si:va] *pl.* liabilities *pl.*

Paste ['pastə] *f* (-/-n) paste.

Pastell [pa'stɛl] *n* (-[e]s/-e) pastel.

Pastete [pa'ste:tə] *f* (-/-n) pie; **~nbäcker** *m* pastry-cook.

Pate ['pa:tə] **1.** *m* (-n/-n) godfather; godchild; **2.** *f* (-/-n) godmother; **~nkind** *n* godchild; **~nschaft** *f* (-/-en) sponsorship.

Patent [pa'tɛnt] *n* (-[e]s/-e) patent; ⚒ commission; *ein ~ anmelden* apply for a patent; **~amt** *n* Patent Office; **~anwalt** *m* patent agent; **♀ieren** [~'ti:rən] *v/t.* (*no -ge-, h*) patent; *et. ~ lassen* take out a patent for s.th.; **~inhaber** *m* patentee; **~urkunde** *f* letters patent.

Patient [pa'tsjɛnt] *m* (-en/-en), **~in** *f* (-/-en) patient.

Patin ['pa:tin] *f* (-/-nen) godmother.

Patriot [patri'o:t] *m* (-en/-en), **~in** *f* (-/-nen) patriot.

Patron [pa'tro:n] *m* (-s/-e) patron, protector; *contp.* fellow, bloke, customer; **~at** [~o'na:t] *n* (-[e]s/-e) patronage; **~e** [pa'tro:nə] *f* (-/-n) cartridge, *Am. a.* shell.

Patrouill|e ⚒ [pa'truljə] *f* (-/-n) patrol; **♀ieren** ⚒ [~'ji:rən] *v/i.* (*no -ge-, h*) patrol.

Patsch|e F *fig.* ['patʃə] *f* (-/*no pl.*): *in der ~ sitzen* be in a fix or scrape; **♀en** F (*ge-*) **1.** *v/i.* (*h, sein*) splash; **2.** *v/t.* (*h*) slap; **♀'naß** *adj.* dripping wet, drenched.

patzig F *adj.* ['patsiç] snappish.

Pauke ♪ ['paukə] *f* (-/-n) kettledrum; **♀n** F *v/i. and v/t.* (*ge-, h*) *school:* cram.

Pauschal|e [pau'ʃa:lə] *f* (-/-n), **~summe** *f* lump sum.

Pause ['pauzə] *f* (-/-n) pause, stop, interval; *school:* break, *Am.* recess; *thea.* interval, *Am.* intermission; ♪ rest; *drawing:* tracing; **♀n** *v/t.* (*ge-, h*) trace; **♀nlos** *adj.* uninterrupted, incessant; **~nzeichen** *n wireless:* interval signal.

pau'sieren *v/i.* (*no -ge-, h*) pause.

Pavian *zo.* ['pa:via:n] *m* (-s/-e) baboon.

Pavillon ['pavíljõ] *m* (-s/-s) pavilion.

Pazifist [patsi'fist] *m* (-en/-en) pacif(ic)ist.

Pech [pɛç] *n* **1.** (-[e]s /-e) pitch; **2.** F *fig.* (-[e]s/*no pl.*) bad luck; **~strähne** F *f* run of bad luck; **~vogel** F *m* unlucky fellow.

pedantisch *adj.* [pe'dantiʃ] pedantic; punctilious, meticulous.

Pegel ['pe:gəl] *m* (-s/-) waterga(u)ge.

peilen ['paɪlən] *v/t.* (*ge-, h*) sound (*depth*); take the bearings of (*coast*).

Pein [paɪn] *f* (-/*no pl.*) torment, torture, anguish; **♀igen** ['~igən] *v/t.* (*ge-, h*) torment; **~iger** ['~igər] *m* (-s/-) tormentor.

'peinlich *adj.* painful, embarrassing; particular, scrupulous, meticulous.

Peitsche ['paɪtʃə] *f* (-/-n) whip; **♀n** *v/t.* (*ge-, h*) whip; **~nhieb** *m* lash.

Pelikan *orn.* ['pe:lika:n] *m* (-s/-e) pelican.

Pell|e ['pɛlə] *f* (-/-n) skin, peel; **♀en** *v/t.* (*ge-, h*) skin, peel; **~kartoffeln** *f/pl.* potatoes *pl.* (boiled) in their jackets *or* skins.

Pelz [pɛlts] *m* (-es/-e) fur; *garment:* mst furs *pl.*; **♀gefüttert** *adj.* fur-lined; **'~händler** *m* furrier; **'~handschuh** *m* furred glove; **'♀ig** *adj.* furry; ⚘ *tongue:* furred; **~mantel** *m* fur coat; **'~stiefel** *m* fur-lined boot; **'~tiere** *n/pl.* fur-covered animals *pl.*

Pendel ['pɛndəl] *n* (-s/-) pendulum; **♀n** *v/i.* (*ge-, h*) oscillate, swing; 🚋 shuttle, *Am.* commute; **~tür** *f* swing-door; **'~verkehr** 🚋 *m* shuttle service.

Pension [pã'sjõ:, pɛn'zjo:n] *f* (-/-en) (old-age) pension, retired pay; board; boarding-house; **~är** [~o-'nɛ:r] *m* (-s/-e) (old-age) pensioner; boarder; **~at** [~o'na:t] *n* (-[e]s/-e) boarding-school; **♀ieren** [~o'ni:rən] *v/t.* (*no -ge-, h*) pension (off); *sich ~ lassen* retire; **~sgast** *m* boarder.

Pensum ['pɛnzum] *n* (-s/Pensen, Pensa) task, lesson.

perfekt 1. *adj.* [pɛr'fɛkt] perfect; *agreement:* settled; **2.** ♀ *gr.* ['~] *n* (-[e]s/-e) perfect (tense).

Pergament [pɛrga'mɛnt] *n* (-[e]s/-e) parchment.

Period|e [pe'rjo:də] *f* (-/-n) period; ⚘ periods *pl.*; **♀isch** *adj.* periodic (-al).

Peripherie [perife'ri:] *f* (-/-n) circumference; outskirts *pl.* (*of town*).

P

Perle ['pɛrlə] f (-/-n) pearl; *of glass*: bead; **'2n** v/i. (ge-, h) sparkle; **'~nkette** f pearl necklace; **'~nschnur** f string of pearls *or* beads.

'Perl|muschel zo. f pearl-oyster; **~mutt** ['~mut] n (-s/*no pl.*), **~'mutter** f (-/*no pl.*) mother-of-pearl.

Person [pɛr'zo:n] f (-/-en) person; *thea.* character.

Personal [pɛrzo'nɑːl] n (-s/*no pl.*) staff, personnel; **~abteilung** f personnel office; **~angaben** f/pl. personal data pl.; **~ausweis** m identity card; **~chef** m personnel officer *or* manager *or* director; **~ien** [~jən] pl. particulars pl., personal data pl.; **~pronomen** gr. n personal pronoun.

Per'sonen|verzeichnis n list of persons; *thea.* dramatis personae pl.; **~wagen** m 🚂 (passenger-)carriage *or* Am. car, coach; *mot.* (motor-)car; **~zug** 🚂 m passenger train.

personifizieren [pɛrzonifi'tsiːrən] v/t. (*no* -ge-, h) personify.

persönlich adj. [pɛr'zøːnlıç] personal; *opinion, letter*: a. private; **2keit** f (-/-en) personality; personage.

Perücke [pe'rykə] f (-/-n) wig.

Pest 🐀 [pɛst] f (-/*no pl.*) plague.

Petersilie 🌿 [petɛr'ziːljə] f (-/-n) parsley.

Petroleum [pe'troːleum] n (-s/*no pl.*) petroleum; *for lighting, etc.*: paraffin, *esp. Am.* kerosene.

Pfad [pfɑːt] m (-[e]s/-e) path, track; **'~finder** m boy scout; **'~finderin** f (-/-nen) girl guide, *Am.* girl scout.

Pfahl [pfɑːl] m (-[e]s/⸗e) stake, pale, pile.

Pfand [pfant] n (-[e]s/⸗er) pledge; † deposit, security; *real estate*: mortgage; *game*: forfeit; **~brief** † m debenture (bond).

pfänden ['pfɛndən] v/t. (ge-, h) seize *s.th.*; distrain upon *s.o. or s.th.*

'Pfand|haus n s. Leihhaus; **'~leiher** m (-s/-) pawnbroker; **'~schein** m pawn-ticket. (distraint.)

'Pfändung 🔨 f (-/-en) seizure.

Pfann|e ['pfanə] f (-/-n) pan; **~kuchen** m pancake.

Pfarr|bezirk ['pfar-] m parish; **'~er** m (-s/-) parson; *Church of England*: rector, vicar; *dissenters*: minister; **'~gemeinde** f parish; **'~haus** n

parsonage; *Church of England*: rectory, vicarage; **'~kirche** f parish church; **'~stelle** f (church) living.

Pfau orn. [pfau] m (-[e]s/-en) peacock.

Pfeffer ['pfɛfər] m (-s/-) pepper; **'~gurke** f gherkin; **'2ig** adj. peppery; **'~kuchen** m gingerbread; **'~minze** 🌿 ['~mıntsə] f (-/*no pl.*) peppermint; **'~minzplätzchen** n peppermint; **'2n** v/t. (ge-, h) pepper; **'~streuer** m (-s/-) pepperbox, pepper-caster, pepper-caster.

Pfeife ['pfaıfə] f (-/-n) whistle; ✗ fife; pipe (*of organ, etc.*); (tobacco-) pipe; **'2n** (irr., ge-, h) **1.** v/i. whistle (*dat.* to, for); *radio*: howl; pipe; **2.** v/t. whistle; pipe; **'~nkopf** m pipe-bowl.

Pfeil [pfaıl] m (-[e]s/-e) arrow.

Pfeiler ['pfaılər] m (-s/-) pillar (a. fig.); pier (*of bridge, etc.*).

'pfeil|'schnell adj. (as) swift as an arrow; **'2spitze** f arrow-head.

Pfennig ['pfɛnıç] m (-[e]s/-e) *coin*: pfennig; *fig.* penny, farthing.

Pferch [pfɛrç] m (-[e]s/-e) fold, pen; **'2en** v/t. (ge-, h) fold, pen; *fig.* cram.

Pferd zo. [pfeːrt] n (-[e]s/-e) horse; *zu* ~e on horseback.

Pferde|geschirr ['pfeːrdə-] n harness; **'~koppel** f (-/-n) paddock, *Am.* a. corral; **'~rennen** n horse-race; **'~schwanz** m horse's tail; *hair-style*: pony-tail; **'~stall** m stable; **'~stärke** ⊕ f horsepower.

pfiff¹ [pfıf] *pret. of* pfeifen.

Pfiff² m (-[e]s/-e) whistle; *fig.* trick; **'2ig** adj. cunning, artful.

Pfingst|en eccl. ['pfıŋstən] n (-/-), **'~fest** eccl. n Whitsun(tide); **'~montag** eccl. m Whit Monday; **'~rose** 🌿 f peony; **'~sonntag** eccl. m Whit Sunday.

Pfirsich ['pfırzıç] m (-[e]s/-e) peach.

Pflanz|e ['pflantsə] f (-/-n) plant; **'2en** v/t. (ge-, h) plant, set; pot; **'~enfaser** f vegetable fib|re, *Am.* -er; **'~enfett** n vegetable fat; **'2enfressend** adj. herbivorous; **'~er** m (-s/-) planter; **'~ung** f (-/-en) plantation.

Pflaster ['pflastər] n (-s/-) 🩹 plaster; *road*: pavement; **'~er** m (-s/-) paver, pavio(u)r; **'2n** v/t. (ge-, h) 🩹 plaster; pave (*road*); **'~stein** m paving-stone; cobble.

Pflaume ['pflaumə] f (-/-n) plum; dried: prune.

Pflege ['pfle:gə] f (-/-n) care; nursing; cultivation (of art, garden, etc.); ⊕ maintenance; in ~ geben put out (child) to nurse; in ~ nehmen take charge of; '**2bedürftig** adj. needing care; **~befohlene** ['~bəfo:lənə] m, f (-n/-n) charge; '**~eltern** pl. foster-parents pl.; '**~heim** ⊕ n nursing home; '**~kind** n foster-child; '**2n** (ge-, h) **1.** v/t. take care of; attend (to); foster (child); ⊕ nurse; maintain; cultivate (art, garden); **2.** v/i.: ~ zu inf. be accustomed or used to inf.; ~ zu inf., be in the habit of ger.; sie pflegte zu sagen she used to say; '**~r** m (-s/-) fosterer; ⊕ male nurse; trustee; ⨯ guardian, curator; '**~rin** f (-/-nen) nurse.

Pflicht [pfliçt] f (-/-en) duty (gegen to); obligation; '**2bewußt** adj. conscious of one's duty; '**2eifrig** adj.zealous; '**~erfüllung** f performance of one's duty; '**~fach** n school, univ.: compulsory subject; '**~gefühl** n sense of duty; '**2gemäß** adj. dutiful; '**2getreu** adj. dutiful, loyal; '**2schuldig** adj. in duty bound; '**2vergessen** adj. undutiful, disloyal; '**~verteidiger** ⨯ m assigned counsel.

Pflock [pflɔk] m (-[e]s/⁼e) plug, peg.

pflücken ['pflykən] v/t. (ge-, h) pick, gather, pluck. [Am. plow.]

Pflug [pflu:k] m (-[e]s/⁼e) plough,)

pflügen ['pfly:gən] v/t. and v/i. (ge-, h) plough, Am. plow.

Pforte ['pfɔrtə] f (-/-n) gate, door.

Pförtner ['pfœrtnər] m (-s/-) gate-keeper, door-keeper, porter, janitor.

Pfosten ['pfɔstən] m (-s/-) post.

Pfote ['pfo:tə] f (-/-n) paw.

Pfropf [pfrɔpf] m (-[e]s/-e) s. Pfropfen.

'**Pfropfen 1.** m (-s/-) stopper; cork; plug; ⬥ clot (of blood); **2.** ⬥ v/t. (ge-, h) stopper; cork; fig. cram; ✗ graft.

Pfründe eccl. ['pfryndə] f (-/-n) prebend; benefice, (church) living.

Pfuhl [pfu:l] m (-[e]s/-e) pool, puddle; fig. sink, slough.

pfui int. [pfui] fie!, for shame!

Pfund [pfunt] n (-[e]s/-e) pound; **2ig** F adj. ['~diç] great, Am. swell; '**2weise** adv. by the pound.

pfusch|en F ['pfuʃən] (ge-, h) **1.** v/i. bungle; **2.** v/t. bungle, botch; **2erei** F [~'rai] f (-/-en) bungle, botch.

Pfütze ['pfytsə] f (-/-n) puddle, pool.

Phänomen [fɛno'me:n] n (-s/-e) phenomenon; **2al** adj. [~e'na:l] phenomenal.

Phantasie [fanta'zi:] f (-/-n) imagination, fancy; vision; ♪ fantasia; **2ren** (no -ge-, h) **1.** v/i. dream; ramble; ⬥ be delirious or raving; ♪ improvise; **2.** v/t. dream; ♪ improvise.

Phantast [fan'tast] m (-en/-en) visionary, dreamer; **2isch** adj. fantastic; F great, terrific.

Phase ['fa:zə] f (-/-n) phase (a. ⚡), stage.

Philanthrop [filan'tro:p] m (-en/-en) philanthropist.

Philolog|e [filo'lo:gə] m (-n/-n), '**~in** f (-/-nen) philologist; '**~ie** [~o'gi:] f (-/-n) philology.

Philosoph [filo'zo:f] m (-en/-en) philosopher; '**~ie** [~o'fi:] f (-/-n) philosophy; **2ieren** [~o'fi:rən] v/i. (no -ge-, h) philosophize (über acc. on); **2isch** adj. [~'zo:fiʃ] philosophical.

Phlegma ['flɛgma] n (-s/no pl.) phlegm; **2tisch** adj. [~'ma:tiʃ] phlegmatic.

phonetisch adj. [fo'ne:tiʃ] phonetic.

Phosphor ⌢ ['fɔsfɔr] m (-s/no pl.) phosphorus.

Photo F ['fo:to] **1.** n (-s/-s) photo; **2.** m (-s/-s) = '**~apparat** m camera.

Photograph [foto'gra:f] m (-en/-en) photographer; '**~ie** [~a'fi:] f **1.** (-/-n) photograph, F: photo, picture; **2.** (-/no pl.) as an art: photography; **2ieren** [~a'fi:rən] (no -ge-, h) **1.** v/t. photograph; take a picture of; sich ~ lassen have one's photo(graph) taken; **2.** v/i. photograph; **2isch** adj. [~'gra:fiʃ] photographic.

Photo|kopie f photostat; '**~ko'pier-gerät** n photostat; '**~zelle** f photo-electric cell.

Phrase ['fra:zə] f (-/-n) phrase.

Physik [fy'zi:k] f (-/no pl.) physics sg.; **2alisch** adj. [~i'ka:liʃ] physical; '**~er** ['fy:zikər] m (-s/-) physicist.

physisch adj. ['fy:ziʃ] physical.

Pian|ist [pia'nist] m (-en/-en) pianist; '**~o** [pi'a:no] n (-s/-s) piano.

Picke ⊕ ['pikə] f (-/-n) pick(axe).

Pickel ['pikəl] m (-s/-) ✗ pimple; ⊕

pick(axe); ice-pick; **'⚲ig** adj. pimpled; pimply.

picken ['pikən] v/i. and v/t. (ge-, h) pick, peck.

picklig adj. ['piklçç] s. pickelig.

Picknick ['piknik] n (-s/-e, -s) picnic.

piekfein F adj. ['pi:k'-] smart, tiptop, slap-up.

piep(s)en ['pi:p(s)ən] v/i. (ge-, h) cheep, chirp, peep; squeak.

Pietät ['pi:'tɛ:t] f (-/no pl.) reverence; piety; **⚲los** adj. irreverent; **⚲voll** adj. reverent.

Pik [pi:k] **1.** m (-s/-e, -s) peak; **2.** F m (-s/-e): e-n ~ auf j-n haben bear s.o. a grudge; **3.** n (-s/-s) cards: spade(s pl.).

pikant adj. [pi'kant] piquant, spicy (both a. fig.); das Pikante the piquancy.

Pike ['pi:kə] f (-/-n) pike; von der ~ auf dienen rise from the ranks.

Pilger ['pilgər] m (-s/-) pilgrim; **'~fahrt** f pilgrimage; **'⚲n** v/i. (ge-, sein) go on or make a pilgrimage; wander.

Pille ['pilə] f (-/-n) pill.

Pilot [pi'lo:t] m (-en/-en) pilot.

Pilz ⚲ [pilts] m (-es/-e) fungus, edible: mushroom, inedible: toadstool.

pimp(e)lig F adj. ['pimp(ə)liç] sickly; effeminate.

Pinguin orn. ['piŋgui:n] m (-s/-e) penguin.

Pinsel ['pinzəl] m (-s/-) brush; F fig. simpleton; **'⚲n** v/t. and v/i. (ge-, h) paint; daub; **'~strich** m stroke of the brush.

Pinzette [pin'tsetə] f (-/-n) (e-e a. pair of) tweezers pl.

Pionier [pio'ni:r] m (-s/-e) pioneer; Am. a. trail blazer; ⚔ engineer.

Pirat [pi'ra:t] m (-en/-en) pirate.

Pirsch hunt. [pirʃ] f (-/no pl.) deerstalking, Am. a. still hunt.

Piste ['pistə] f (-/-n) skiing, etc.: course; ⚓ runway.

Pistole [pis'to:lə] f (-/-n) pistol, Am. F a. gun, rod; **~ntasche** f holster.

placieren [pla'si:rən] v/t. (no -ge-, h) place; sich ~ sports: be placed (second, etc.).

Plackerei F [plakə'raɪ] f (-/-en) drudgery.

plädieren [plɛ'di:rən] v/i. (no -ge-, h) plead (für for).

Plädoyer ⚖ [plɛdoa'je:] n (-s/-s) pleading.

Plage ['pla:gə] f (-/-n) trouble, nuisance, F plague; torment; **'⚲n** v/t. (ge-, h) torment; trouble, bother; F plague; sich ~ toil, drudge.

Plagiat [plag'ja:t] n (-[e]s/-e) plagiarism; ein ~ begehen plagiarize.

Plakat [pla'ka:t] n (-[e]s/-e) poster, placard, bill; **~säule** f advertisement pillar.

Plakette [pla'ketə] f (-/-n) plaque.

Plan [pla:n] m (-[e]s/⸚e) plan; design, intention; scheme.

Plane ['pla:nə] f (-/-n) awning, tilt.

'plan|en v/t. (ge-, h) plan; scheme.

Planet [pla'ne:t] m (-en/-en) planet.

planieren ⊕ [pla'ni:rən] v/t. (no -ge-, h) level.

Planke ['plaŋkə] f (-/-n) plank, board.

plänkeln ['plɛŋkəln] v/i. (ge-, h) skirmish (a. fig.).

'plan|los 1. adj. planless, aimless, desultory; **2.** adv. at random; **'~mäßig 1.** adj. systematic, planned; **2.** adv. as planned.

planschen ['planʃən] v/i. (ge-, h) splash, paddle.

Plantage [plan'ta:ʒə] f (-/-n) plantation.

Plapper|maul F ['plapər-] n chatterbox; **'⚲n** F v/i. (ge-, h) chatter, prattle, babble.

plärren F ['plɛrən] v/i. and v/t. (ge-, h) blubber; bawl.

Plasti|k [plastik] **1.** f (-/no pl.) plastic art; **2.** f (-/-en) sculpture; ⚕ plastic; **3.** ⊕ n (-s/-s) plastic; **'⚲sch** adj. plastic; three-dimensional.

Platin [pla'ti:n] n (-s/no pl.) platinum.

plätschern ['plɛtʃərn] v/i. (ge-, h) dabble, splash; water: ripple, murmur.

platt adj. [plat] flat, level, even; fig. trivial, commonplace, trite; F fig. flabbergasted.

Plättbrett ['plɛt-] n ironing-board.

Platte ['platə] f (-/-n) plate; dish; sheet (of metal, etc.); flag, slab (of stone); mountain: ledge; top (of table); tray, salver; disc, record; F fig. bald pate; kalte ~ cold meat.

plätten ['plɛtən] v/t. (ge-, h) iron.

'Platten|spieler m record-player; **'⌐teller** m turn-table.

'Platt|form f platform; **'⌐fuß** m 🦶 flat-foot; F mot. flat; **'⌐heit** fig. f (-/-en) triviality; commonplace, platitude; Am. sl. a. bromide.

Platz [plats] m (-es/⸚e) place; spot, Am. a. point; room, space; site; seat; square; round: circus; sports: ground; tennis: court; ~ behalten remain seated; ~ machen make way or room (dat. for); ~ nehmen take a seat, sit down, Am. a. have a seat; ist hier noch ~? is this seat taken or engaged or occupied?; den dritten ~ belegen sports: be placed third, come in third; **'⌐anweiserin** f (-/-nen) usherette.

Plätzchen ['pletsçən] n (-s/-) snug place; spot; biscuit, Am. cookie.

'platzen v/i. (ge-, sein) burst; explode; crack, split.

'Platz|patrone f blank cartridge; **'⌐regen** m downpour.

Plauder|ei [plaudə'raɪ] f (-/-en) chat; talk; small talk; **'2n** v/i. (ge-, h) (have a) chat (mit with), talk (to); chatter.

plauz int. [plauts] bang!

Pleite F ['plaɪtə] **1.** f (-/-en) smash; fig. failure; **2.** 2 F adj. (dead) broke, Am. sl. bust.

Plissee [pli'se:] n (-s/-s) pleating; **⌐rock** m pleated skirt.

Plomb|e ['plɔmbə] f (-/-en) (lead) seal; stopping, filling (of tooth); **2ieren** [⸚'bi:rən] v/t. (no -ge-, h) seal; stop, fill (tooth).

plötzlich adj. ['plœtsliç] sudden.

plump adj. [plump] clumsy; **⌐s** int. plump, plop; **'⌐sen** v/i. (ge-, sein) plump, plop, flop.

Plunder F ['plundər] m (-s/no pl.) lumber, rubbish, junk.

plündern ['plyndərn] (ge-, h) **1.** v/t. plunder, pillage, loot, sack; **2.** v/i. plunder, loot. [(number).]

Plural gr. ['plu:ra:l] m (-s/-e) plural⌐

plus adv. [plus] plus.

Plusquamperfekt gr. ['pluskvamperfekt] n (-s/-e) pluperfect (tense), past perfect.

Pöbel ['pø:bəl] m (-s/no pl.) mob, rabble; **'2haft** adj. low, vulgar.

pochen ['pɔxən] v/i. (ge-, h) knock, rap, tap; heart: beat, throb, thump; auf sein Recht ~ stand on one's rights.

Pocke 🦠 ['pɔkə] f (-/-n) pock; **'⌐n** 🦠 pl. smallpox; **'2nnarbig** adj. pock-marked.

Podest [po'dest] n, m (-es/-e) pedestal (a. fig.).

Podium ['po:dium] n (-s/Podien) podium, platform, stage.

Poesie [poe'zi:] f (-/-n) poetry.

Poet [po'e:t] m (-en/-en) poet; **2isch** adj. poetic(al).

Pointe [po'ɛ̃:tə] f (-/-n) point.

Pokal [po'ka:l] m (-s/-e) goblet; sports: cup; **⌐endspiel** n sports: cup final; **⌐spiel** n football: cup-tie.

Pökel|fleisch ['pø:kəl-] n salted meat; **'2n** v/t. (ge-, h) pickle, salt.

Pol [po:l] m (-s/-e) pole; ⚡ a. terminal; **2ar** adj. [po'la:r] polar (a. 🌍).

Pole ['po:lə] m (-n/-n) Pole.

Polemi|k [po'le:mik] f (-/-en) polemic(s pl.); **2sch** adj. polemic (-al); **2sieren** [⸚emi'zi:rən] v/i. (no -ge-, h) polemize.

Police [po'li:s(ə)] f (-/-n) policy.

Polier ⊕ [po'li:r] m (-s/-e) foreman; **2en** v/t. (no -ge-, h) polish, burnish; furbish.

Politi|k [poli'ti:k] f (-/⸚ -en) policy; politics sg., pl.; **⌐ker** [po'li:tikər] m (-s/-) politician; statesman; **2sch** adj. [po'li:tiʃ] political; **2sieren** [⸚iti'zi:rən] v/i. (no -ge-, h) talk politics.

Politur [poli'tu:r] f (-/-en) polish; lust|re, Am. -er, finish.

Polizei [poli'tsaɪ] f (-/⸚ -en) police; **⌐beamte** m police officer; **⌐knüppel** m truncheon, Am. club; **⌐kommissar** m inspector; **2lich** adj. (of or by the) police; **⌐präsident** m president of police; Brt. Chief Constable, Am. Chief of Police; **⌐präsidium** n police headquarters pl.; **⌐revier** n police-station; police precinct; **⌐schutz** m: unter ~ under police guard; **⌐streife** f police patrol; police squad; **⌐stunde** f (-/no pl.) closing-time; **⌐verordnung** f police regulation(s pl.); **⌐wache** f police-station.

Polizist [poli'tsist] m (-en/-en) policeman, constable, sl. bobby, cop; **⌐in** f (-/-nen) policewoman.

polnisch adj. ['pɔlniʃ] Polish.

Polster ['pɔlstər] n (-s/-) pad; cushion; bolster; s. Polsterung; **'⌐möbel** n/pl. upholstered furniture; upholstery; **'2n** v/t. (ge-, h)

P

upholster, stuff; pad, wad; '~**sessel** m, '~**stuhl** m upholstered chair; '~**ung** f (-/-en) padding, stuffing; upholstery.

poltern ['pɔltərn] v/i. (ge-, h) make a row; rumble; p. bluster.

Polytechnikum [poly'tɛçnikum] n (-s/Polytechnika, Polytechniken) polytechnic (school).

Pommes frites [pɔm'frit] pl. chips pl., Am. French fried potatoes pl.

Pomp [pɔmp] m (-[e]s/no pl.) pomp, splendo(u)r; '2**haft** adj., 2**ös** adj. [~'pø:s] pompous, splendid.

Pony ['pɔni] **1.** zo. n (-s/-s) pony; **2.** m (-s/-s) hairstyle: bang, fringe.

popul|är adj. [popu'lɛ:r] popular; 2**arität** [~ari'tɛ:t] f (-/no pl.) popularity.

Por|e ['po:rə] f (-/-n) pore; 2**ös** adj. [po'rø:s] porous; permeable.

Portemonnaie [pɔrtmɔ'nɛ:] n (-s/-s) purse.

Portier [pɔr'tje:] m (-s/-s) s. Pförtner.

Portion [pɔr'tsjo:n] f (-/-en) portion, share; ✗ ration; helping, serving; zwei ~en Kaffee coffee for two.

Porto ['pɔrto] n (-s/-s, Porti) postage; 2**frei** adj. post-free; prepaid, esp. Am. postpaid; 2**pflichtig** adj. subject to postage.

Porträt [pɔr'trɛ:] ~t] n (-s/-s, -[e]s/-e) portrait, likeness; 2**ieren** [~ɛ'ti:rən] v/t. (no -ge-, h) portray.

Portugies|e [pɔrtu'gi:zə] m (-n/-n) Portuguese; die ~n pl. the Portuguese pl.; 2**isch** adj. Portuguese.

Porzellan [pɔrtsɛ'la:n] n (-s/-e) porcelain, china.

Posaune [po'zaunə] f (-/-n) ♩ trombone; fig. trumpet.

Pose [po'zə] f (-/-n) pose, attitude; fig. a. air.

Position [pozi'tsjo:n] f (-/-en) position; social standing; ⚓ station.

positiv adj. ['po:ziti:f] positive.

Positur [pozi'tu:r] f (-/-en) posture; sich in ~ setzen strike an attitude.

Posse thea. ['pɔsə] f (-/-n) farce.

'**Possen** m (-s/-) trick, prank; 2**haft** adj. farcical, comical; '~**reißer** m (-s/-) buffoon, clown.

possessiv gr. adj. ['pɔsɛsi:f] possessive.

pos'sierlich adj. droll, funny.

Post [pɔst] f (-/-en) post, Am. mail; mail, letters pl.; post office; mit

der ersten ~ by the first delivery; '~**amt** n post office; '~**anschrift** f mailing address; '~**anweisung** f postal order; '~**beamte** m post-office clerk; '~**bote** m postman, Am. mailman; '~**dampfer** m packet-boat.

Posten ['pɔstən] m (-s/-) post, place, station; job; ✗ sentry, sentinel; item; entry; goods: lot, parcel.

'**Postfach** n post-office box.

pos'tieren v/t. (no -ge-, h) post, station, place; sich ~ station o.s.

'**Post|karte** f postcard, with printed postage stamp: Am. a. postal card; '~**kutsche** f stage-coach; '2**lagernd** adj. to be (kept until) called for, poste restante, Am. (in care of) general delivery; '~**leitzahl** f postcode; '~**minister** m minister of post; Brt. and Am. Postmaster General; '~**paket** n postal parcel; '~**schalter** m (post-office) window; '~**scheck** m postal cheque, Am. postal check; '~**schließfach** n post-office box; '~**sparbuch** n post-office savings-book; '~**stempel** m postmark; 2**wendend** adv. by return of post; '~**wertzeichen** n (postage) stamp; '~**zug** 🚂 m mail-train.

Pracht [praxt] f (-/✗ -en, ⁼e) splendo(u)r, magnificence; luxury.

prächtig adj. ['prɛçtiç] splendid, magnificent; gorgeous; grand.

'**prachtvoll** adj. s. prächtig.

Prädikat [prɛdi'ka:t] n (-[e]s/-e) gr. predicate; school, etc.: mark.

prägen ['prɛ:gən] v/t. (ge-, h) stamp; coin (word, coin).

prahlen [po'za:lən] v/i. (ge-, h) brag, boast (mit of); ~ mit show off s.th.

'**Prahler** m (-s/-) boaster, braggart; ~**ei** [~'rai] ~i f (-/-en) boasting, bragging; 2**isch** adj. boastful; ostentatious.

Prakti|kant [prakti'kant] m (-en/-en) probationer; '~**ker** m (-s/-) practical man; expert; ~**kum** [~'kum] n (-s/Praktika, Praktiken) practical course; '2**sch** adj. practical; useful, handy; ~**er Arzt** general practitioner; 2**zieren** 🩺, 🎓 [~'tsi:rən] v/i. (no -ge-, h) practi|se, Am. -ce medicine or the law.   [prelate.]

Prälat eccl. [prɛ'la:t] m (-en/-en)]

Praline [pra'li:nə] f (-/-n) ~n pl. chocolates pl.

prall *adj.* [pral] tight; plump; *sun:* blazing; '~**en** *v/i.* (ge-, sein) bounce *or* bound (*auf acc., gegen* against).

Prämi|e ['prɛ:mjə] *f* (-/-n) ✝ premium; prize; bonus; ⚲**(i)eren** [prɛ'mi:rən, premi'i:rən] *v/t.* (*no* -ge-, h) award a prize to.

prang|en ['praŋən] *v/i.* (ge-, h) shine, make a show; '~**er** *m* (-s/-) pillory.

Pranke ['praŋkə] *f* (-/-n) paw.

pränumerando [prɛ:numə'rando] *adv.* beforehand, in advance.

Präpa|rat [prɛpa'ra:t] *n* (-[e]s/-e) preparation; *microscopy:* slide; ⚲**rieren** *v/t.* (*no* -ge-, h) prepare.

Präposition *gr.* [prɛpozi'tsjo:n] *f* (-/-en) preposition.

Prärie [prɛ'ri:] *f* (-/-n) prairie.

Präsens *gr.* ['prɛ:zɛns] *n* (-/Präsentia, Präsenzien) present (tense).

Präsi|dent [prɛzi'dɛnt] *m* (-en/-en) president; chairman; ⚲**dieren** *v/i.* (*no* -ge-, h) preside (*über acc.* over); be in the chair; ~**dium** [~'zi:djum] *n* (-s/Präsidien) presidency, chair.

prasseln ['prasəln] *v/i.* (ge-, h) *fire:* crackle; *rain:* patter.

prassen ['prasən] *v/i.* (ge-, h) feast, carouse.

Präteritum *gr.* [prɛ'te:ritum] *n* (-s/Präterita) preterite (tense); past tense.

Praxis ['praksis] *f* **1.** (-/*no pl.*) practice; **2.** (-/Praxen) practice (*of doctor or lawyer*).

Präzedenzfall [prɛtse'dɛnts-] *m* precedent; ⚖️ *a.* case-law.

präzis *adj.* [prɛ'tsi:s], ~**e** *adj.* [~zə] precise.

predig|en ['pre:digən] *v/i. and v/t.* (ge-, h) preach; '~**er** *m* (-s/-) preacher; clergyman; ⚲**t** [~'diçt] *f* (-/-en) sermon (*a. fig.*); *fig.* lecture.

Preis [prais] *m* (-es/-e) price; cost; *competition:* prize; award; reward; praise; *um jeden* ~ at any price *or* cost; '~**ausschreiben** *n* competition. [praise.

preisen ['praizən] *v/t.* (*irr.*, ge-, h)

Preis|erhöhung *f* rise *or* increase in price(s); '~**gabe** *f* abandonment; revelation (*of secret*); ⚲**geben** *v/t.* (*irr. geben, sep.,* -ge-, h) abandon; reveal, give away (*secret*); disclose, expose; ⚲**gekrönt** *adj.* prize-winning, prize (*novel, etc.*); '~**gericht** *n* jury; '~**lage** *f* range of

prices; '~**liste** *f* price-list; '~**nachlaß** *m* price cut; discount; '~**richter** *m* judge, umpire; '~**schießen** *n* (-s/-) shooting competition; '~**stopp** *m* (-s/*no pl.*) price freeze; '~**träger** *m* prize-winner; ⚲**wert** *adj.*: ~ *sein* be a bargain.

prell|en ['prɛlən] *v/t.* (ge-, h) *fig.* cheat, defraud (*um* of); *sich et.* ~ ⚕️ contuse *or* bruise s.th.; '⚲**ung** ⚕️ *f* (-/-en) contusion.

Premier|e *thea.* [prəm'jɛ:rə] *f* (-/-n) première, first night; ~**minister** [~'je:-] *m* prime minister.

Presse ['prɛsə] *f* **1.** (-/-n) ⊕, *typ.* press; squeezer; **2.** (-/*no pl.*) *newspapers generally:* the press; '~**amt** *n* public relations office; '~**freiheit** *f* freedom of the press; '~**meldung** *f* news item; '⚲**n** *v/t.* (ge-, h) press; squeeze; '~**photograph** *m* press-photographer; '~**vertreter** *m* reporter; public relations officer.

Preßluft ['prɛs-] *f* (-/*no pl.*) compressed air.

Prestige [prɛs'ti:ʒə] *n* (-s/*no pl.*) prestige; ~ *verlieren a.* lose face.

Preuß|e ['prɔysə] *m* (-n/-n) Prussian; '⚲**isch** *adj.* Prussian.

prickeln ['prikəln] *v/i.* (ge-, h) prick(le), tickle; itch; *fingers:* tingle.

Priem [pri:m] *m* (-[e]s/-e) quid.

pries [pri:s] *pret. of* preisen.

Priester ['pri:stər] *m* (-s/-) priest; '~**in** *f* (-/-nen) priestess; ⚲**lich** *adj.* priestly; sacerdotal; '~**rock** *m* cassock.

prim|a F *adj.* ['pri:ma] first-rate, F A 1; ✝ *a.* prime; F swell; ⚲**är** *adj.* [pri'mɛ:r] primary.

Primel ♀ ['pri:məl] *f* (-/-n) primrose.

Prinz [prints] *m* (-en/-en) prince; ~**essin** [~'tsɛsin] *f* (-/-nen) princess; '~**gemahl** *m* prince consort.

Prinzip [prin'tsi:p] *n* (-s/-ien) principle; *aus* ~ on principle; *im* ~ in principle, basically.

Priorität [priori'tɛ:t] *f* **1.** (-/-en) priority; **2.** (-/*no pl.*) *time:* priority.

Prise ['pri:zə] *f* (-/-n) ⚓ prize; *e-e* ~ a pinch of (*salt, snuff*).

Prisma ['prisma] *n* (-s/Prismen) prism. [bed.]

Pritsche ['pritʃə] *f* (-/-n) bat; plank-]

privat *adj.* [pri'va:t] private; ⚲**adresse** *f* home address; ⚲**mann** *m* (-[e]s/Privatmänner, Privatleute) private person *or* gentleman; ♀**patient** ♂ *m* paying patient; ♀**person** *f* private person; ♀**schule** *f* private school.

Privileg [privi'le:k] *n* (-[e]s/-ien, -e) privilege.

pro *prp.* [pro:] per; ~ *Jahr* per annum; ~ *Kopf* per head; ~ *Stück* a piece.

Probe ['pro:bə] *f* (-/-n) experiment; trial, test; *metall.* assay; sample; specimen; proof; probation; check; *thea.* rehearsal; audition; *auf* ~ on probation, on trial; *auf die* ~ *stellen* (put to the) test; '~**abzug** *typ.*, *phot.* m proof; '~**exemplar** *n* specimen copy; '~**fahrt** *f* ⚓ trial trip; *mot.* trial run; '~**flug** *m* test *or* trial flight; '♀**n** *v/t.* (ge-, *h*) exercise; *thea.* rehearse; '~**nummer** *f* specimen copy *or* number; '~**seite** *typ. f* specimen page; '~**sendung** *f* goods on approval; '♀**weise** *adv.* on trial; *p. a.* on probation; '~**zeit** *f* time of probation.

probieren [pro'bi:rən] *v/t.* (no -ge-, *h*) try, test; taste (*food.*)

Problem [pro'ble:m] *n* (-s/-e) problem; ♀**atisch** *adj.* [~e'ma:tiʃ] problematic(al).

Produkt [pro'dukt] *n* (-[e]s/-e) product (*a.* 🅰); 🖊 produce; result; ~**ion** [~'tsjo:n] *f* (-/-en) production; output; ♀**iv** *adj.* [~'ti:f] productive.

Produz|ent [produ'tsɛnt] *m* (-en/-en) producer; ♀**ieren** [~'tsi:rən] *v/t.* (no -ge-, *h*) produce; *sich* ~ perform; *contp.* show off.

professionell *adj.* [profesio'nɛl] professional, by trade.

Profess|or [pro'fɛsɔr] *m* (-s/-en) professor; ~**ur** [~'su:r] *f* (-/-en) professorship, chair.

Profi ['pro:fi] *m* (-s/-s) *sports:* professional, F pro. [*on tyre:* tread.)

Profil [pro'fi:l] *n* (-s/-e) profile;)

Profit [pro'fi:t] *m* (-[e]s/-e) profit; ♀**ieren** [~i'ti:rən] *v/i.* (no -ge-, *h*) profit (*von* by).

Prognose [pro'gno:zə] *f* (+/-n) 🖋 prognosis; *meteor.* forecast.

Programm [pro'gram] *n* (-s/-e) program(me); *politisches* ~ political program(me), *Am.* platform.

Projektion [projɛk'tsjo:n] *f* (-/-en) projection; ~**sapparat** [projɛk-'tsjo:ns⁹-] *m* projector.

proklamieren [prokla'mi:rən] *v/t.* (no -ge-, *h*) proclaim.

Prokur|a ✝ [pro'ku:ra] *f* (-/Prokuren) procuration; ~**ist** [~ku'rist] *m* (-en/-en) confidential clerk.

Proletari|er [prole'ta:rjər] *m* (-s/-) proletarian; ♀**sch** *adj.* proletarian.

Prolog [pro'lo:k] *m* (-[e]s/-e) prolog(ue).

prominen|t *adj.* [promi'nɛnt] prominent; ♀**z** [~ts] *f* (-/no pl.) notables *pl.*, celebrities *pl.*; high society.

Promo|tion *univ.* [promo'tsjo:n] *f* (-/-en) graduation; ♀**vieren** [~'vi:rən] *v/i.* (no -ge-, *h*) graduate (*an dat.* from), take one's degree.

Pronomen *gr.* [pro'no:mɛn] *n* (-s/-, *Pronomina*) pronoun.

Propeller [pro'pɛlər] *m* (-s/-) ⚓, 🛪 (screw-)propeller, screw; 🛪 air-screw.

Prophe|t [pro'fe:t] *m* (-en/-en) prophet; ♀**tisch** *adj.* prophetic; ♀**zeien** [~e'tsaiən] *v/t.* (no -ge-, *h*) prophesy; predict, foretell; ~**zeiung** *f* (-/-en) prophecy; prediction.

Proportion [propɔr'tsjo:n] *f* (-/-en) proportion.

Prosa ['pro:za] *f* (-/no pl.) prose.

prosit *int.* ['pro:zit] your health!, here's to you!, cheers!

Prospekt [pro'spɛkt] *m* (-[e]s/-e) prospectus; brochure, leaflet, folder.

prost *int.* [pro:st] *s.* prosit.

Prostituierte [prostitu'i:rtə] *f* (-n/-n) prostitute.

Protest [pro'tɛst] *m* (-es/-e) protest; ~ *einlegen* or *erheben gegen* (enter a) protest against.

Protestant *eccl.* [protɛs'tant] *m* (-en/-en) Protestant; ♀**isch** *adj.* Protestant.

protes'tieren *v/i.* (no -ge-, *h*): *gegen et.* ~ protest against s.th., object to s.th.

Prothese 🖋 [pro'te:zə] *f* (-/-n) pro(s)thesis; *dentistry:* a. denture; artificial limb.

Protokoll [proto'kɔl] *n* (-s/-e) record, minutes *pl.* (*of meeting*); *diplomacy:* protocol; *das* ~ *aufnehmen* take down the minutes; *das* ~ *führen* keep the minutes; *zu* ~ *geben* ⚖️ depose, state in evidence; *zu* ~ *nehmen* take down, record; ♀**ieren** [~'li:rən] (no -ge-, *h*) **1.** *v/t.* record, take down (on record); **2.** *v/i.* keep the minutes.

Protz *contp.* [prɔts] *m* (-en, -es/)

-e[n]) braggart, F show-off; '♀en v/i. (ge-, h) show off (mit dat. with); '♀ig adj. ostentatious, showy.

Proviant [pro'vjant] m (-s/♀-e) provisions pl., victuals pl.

Provinz [pro'vints] f (-/-en) province; fig. the provinces pl.; ♀ial adj. [∼'tsjaːl], ♀iell adj. [∼'tsjɛl] provincial.

Provis|ion ✝ [provi'zjoːn] f (-/-en) commission; ♀orisch adj. [∼'zoːriʃ] provisional, temporary.

provozieren [provo'tsiːrən] v/t. (no -ge-, h) provoke.

Prozent [pro'tsɛnt] n (-[e]s/-e) per cent; ∼satz m percentage; proportion; ♀ual adj. [∼u'aːl] percental; ∼er Anteil percentage.

Prozeß [pro'tsɛs] m (Prozesses/Prozesse) process; ⚖: action, lawsuit; trial; (legal) proceedings pl.; e-n ∼ gewinnen win one's case; e-n ∼ gegen j-n anstrengen bring an action against s.o., sue s.o.; j-m den ∼ machen try s.o., put s.o. on trial; kurzen ∼ machen mit make short work of.

prozessieren [protse'siːrən] v/i. (no -ge-, h): mit j-m ∼ go to law against s.o., have the law of s.o.

Prozession [protse'sjoːn] f (-/-en) procession.

prüde adj. ['pryːdə] prudish.

prüf|en ['pryːfən] v/t. (ge-, h) examine; try, test; quiz; check, verify; '∼end adj. look: searching, scrutinizing; '♀er m (-s/-) examiner; '♀ling m (-s/-e) examinee; '♀stein fig. m touchstone; '♀ung f (-/-en) examination; school, etc.: a. F exam; test; quiz; verification, checking, check-up; e-e ∼ machen go in for or sit for or take an examination.

'**Prüfungs|arbeit** f, '∼aufgabe f examination-paper; '∼ausschuß m, '∼kommission f board of examiners.

Prügel ['pryːgəl] 1. m (-s/-) cudgel, club, stick; 2. ∼ fig. pl. beating, thrashing; ∼ei F [∼'laɪ] f (-/-en) fight, row; '∼knabe m scapegoat; '♀n F v/t. (ge-, h) cudgel, flog; beat (up), thrash; sich ∼ (have a) fight.

Prunk [pruŋk] m (-[e]s/no pl.) splendo(u)r; pomp, show; '♀en v/i. (ge-, h) make a show (mit of), show off (mit et. s.th.); '♀voll adj. splendid, gorgeous.

Psalm eccl. [psalm] m (-s/-en) psalm.

Pseudonym [psɔʏdo'nyːm] n (-s/-e) pseudonym.

pst int. [pst] hush!

Psychi|ater [psyçi'aːtər] m (-s/-) psychiatrist, alienist; ♀sch adj. ['psyːçiʃ] psychic(al).

Psycho|analyse [psyço⁹ana'lyːzə] f (-/no pl.) psychoanalysis; ∼analytiker [∼tikər] m (-s/-) psychoanalist; ♀loge [∼'loːgə] m (-n/-n) psychologist; ∼se [∼'çoːzə] f (-/-n) psychosis; panic.

Pubertät [puber'tɛːt] f (-/no pl.) puberty.

Publikum ['puːblikum] n (-s/no pl.) the public; audience; spectators pl., crowd; readers pl.

publiz|ieren [publi'tsiːrən] v/t. (no -ge-, h) publish; ♀ist m (-en/-en) publicist; journalist.

Pudding ['pudiŋ] m (-s/-e, -s) cream.

Pudel zo. ['puːdəl] m (-s/-) poodle; '♀naß F adj. dripping wet, drenched.

Puder ['puːdər] m (-s/-) powder; '∼dose f powder-box; compact; '♀n v/t. (ge-, h) powder; sich ∼ powder o.s. or one's face; '∼quaste f powder-puff; '∼zucker m powdered sugar.

Puff F [puf] m (-[e]s/✻e, -e) poke, nudge; '♀en (ge-, h) 1. F v/t. nudge; 2. v/i. pop; '∼er 🚃 m (-s/-) buffer.

Pullover [pu'loːvər] m (-s/-) pullover, sweater.

Puls 🩺 [puls] m (-es/-e) pulse; '∼ader anat. f artery; ♀ieren [∼'ziːrən] v/i. (no -ge-, h) pulsate, throb; '∼schlag 🩺 m pulsation.

Pult [pult] n (-[e]s/-e) desk.

Pulv|er ['pulfər] n (-s/-) powder; gunpowder; F fig. cash, sl. brass, dough; ♀erig adj. powdery; ♀erisieren [∼vəri'ziːrən] v/t. (no -ge-, h) pulverize; ♀rig adj. ['∼friç] powdery.

Pump F [pump] m (-[e]s/-e): auf ∼ on tick; '∼e f (-/-n) pump; '♀en (ge-, h) 1. v/i. pump; 2. v/t. pump; F fig.: give s.th. on tick; borrow (et. von j-m s.th. from s.o.).

Punkt [puŋkt] m (-[e]s/-e) point (a. fig.); dot; typ., gr. full stop, period; spot, place; fig. item; article, clause (of agreement); der springende ∼ the

P

point; **toter** ~ deadlock, dead end; **wunder** ~ tender subject, sore point; ~ **zehn Uhr** on the stroke of ten, at 10 (o'clock) sharp; *in vielen* ~**en** on many points, in many respects; *nach* ~*en siegen sports:* win on points; **2ieren** [~'ti:rən] *v/t. (no -ge-, h)* dot, point; *ℰ* puncture, tap; *drawing, painting:* stipple.

pünktlich *adj.* ['pyŋktliç] punctual; ~ *sein* be on time; **2keit** *f* (~/*no pl.*) punctuality.

Punsch [punʃ] *m* (-es/-e) punch.

Pupille *anat.* [pu'pilə] *f* (-/-n) pupil.

Puppe ['pupə] *f* (-/-n) doll *(a. fig.);* puppet *(a. fig.); tailoring:* dummy; *zo.* chrysalis, pupa; '~**nspiel** *n* puppet-show; '~**nstube** *f* doll's room; '~**nwagen** *m* doll's pram, *Am.* doll carriage or buggy.

pur *adj.* [pu:r] pure, sheer.

Püree [py're:] *n* (-s/-s) purée, mash.

Purpur ['purpur] *m* (-s/*no pl.*) purple; '**2farben** *adj.*, '**2n** *adj.*, '**2rot** *adj.* purple.

Purzel|baum ['purtsəl-] *m* somersault; *e-n* ~ *schlagen* turn a somersault; '**2n** *v/i. (ge-, sein)* tumble.

Puste F ['pu:stə] *f* (-/*no pl.*) breath; *ihm ging die* ~ *aus* he got out of breath.

Pustel *ℰ* ['pustəl] *f* (-/-n) pustule, pimple.

pusten ['pu:stən] *v/i.* (ge-, h) puff, pant; blow.

Pute *orn.* ['pu:tə] *f* (-/-n) turkey (-hen); '~**r** *orn. m* (-s/-) turkey (-cock); '**2r'rot** *adj.* (as) red as a turkey-cock.

Putsch [putʃ] *m* (-es/-e) putsch, insurrection; riot; **2en** *v/i. (ge-, h)* revolt, riot.

Putz [puts] *m* (-es/-e) *on garments:* finery; ornaments *pl.;* trimming; **⚒** roughcast, plaster; '**2en** *v/t.* (ge-, h) clean, cleanse; polish, wipe; adorn; snuff *(candle);* polish, *Am.* shine *(shoes); sich* ~ smarten or dress o.s. up; *sich die Nase* ~ blow or wipe one's nose; *sich die Zähne* ~ brush one's teeth; '~**frau** *f* charwoman, *Am. a.* scrubwoman; '**2ig** *adj.* droll, funny; '~**lappen** *m* cleaning rag; '~**zeug** *n* cleaning utensils *pl.*

Pyjama [pi'dʒa:ma] *m* (-s/-s) *(ein* a suit of) pyjamas *pl.* or *Am. a.* pajamas *pl.*

Pyramide [pyra'mi:də] *f* (-/-n) pyramid *(a. Å); ⚔* stack *(of rifles);* **2nförmig** *adj.* [~nfœrmiç] pyramidal.

Q

Quacksalber ['kvakzalbər] *m* (-s/-) quack (doctor); '~**ei** F [~'rai] *f* (-/-en) quackery; '**2n** *v/i.* (ge-, h) (play the) quack.

Quadrat [kva'dra:t] *n* (-[e]s/-e) square; *2 Fuß im* ~ *2* feet square; *ins* ~ *erheben* square; **2isch** *adj.* square; *Å equation:* quadratic; ~**meile** *f* square mile; ~**meter** *n, m* square met|re, *Am. -er;* ~**wurzel** *Å f* square root; ~**zahl** *Å f* square number.

quaken ['kva:kən] *v/i.* (ge-, h) duck: quack; *frog:* croak.   [squeak.\

quäken ['kvɛ:kən] *v/i.* (ge-, h)\

Quäker ['kvɛ:kər] *m* (-s/-) Quaker, member of the Society of Friends.

Qual [kva:l] *f* (-/-en) pain; torment; agony.

quälen ['kvɛ:lən] *v/t.* (ge-, h) torment *(a. fig.);* torture; ago-

nize; *fig.* bother, pester; *sich* ~ toil, drudge.

Qualifikation [kvalifika'tsjo:n] *f* (-/-en) qualification.

qualifizieren [kvalifi'tsi:rən] *v/t. and v/refl. (no -ge-, h)* qualify *(zu* for).

Qualit|ät [kvali'tɛ:t] *f* (-/-en) quality; **2ativ** [~a'ti:f] **1.** *adj.* qualitative; **2.** *adv.* as to quality.

Quali'täts|arbeit *f* work of high quality; ~**stahl** *m* high-grade steel; ~**ware** *f* high-grade or quality goods *pl.*

Qualm [kvalm] *m* (-[e]s/*no pl.*) dense smoke; fumes *pl.;* vapo(u)r, steam; '**2en** *v/i.* (ge-, h) **1.** *v/i.* smoke, give out vapo(u)r or fumes; F *p.* smoke heavily; **2.** F *v/t.* puff (away) at *(cigar, pipe, etc.);* '**2ig** *adj.* smoky.

qualvoll adj. very painful; pain: excruciating; fig. agonizing, harrowing.

Quantit|ät [kvanti'tɛ:t] f (-/-en) quantity; **ℒativ** [∼a'ti:f] **1.** adj. quantitative; **2.** adv. as to quantity.

Quantum ['kvantum] n (-s/Quanten) quantity, amount; quantum (a. phys.).

Quarantäne [karan'tɛ:nə] f (-/-n) quarantine; in ∼ legen (put in) quarantine.   [curd(s pl.).\

Quark [kvark] m (-[e]s/no pl.)]

Quartal [kvar'ta:l] n (-s/-e) quarter (of a year); univ. term.

Quartett [kvar'tɛt] n (-[e]s/-e) ♪ quartet(te); cards: four.

Quartier [kvar'ti:r] n (-s/-e) accommodation; ✕ quarters pl., billet.   [(powder-)puff.\

Quaste ['kvastə] f (-/-n) tassel;]

Quatsch F [kvatʃ] m (-es/no pl.) nonsense, fudge, sl. bosh, rot, Am. sl. a. baloney; **ℒen** F v/i. (ge-, h) twaddle, blether, sl. talk rot; (have a) chat; '∼kopf F m twaddler.

Quecksilber ['kvɛk-] n mercury, quicksilver.

Quelle ['kvɛlə] f (-/-n) spring, source (a. fig.); oil: well; fig. fountain, origin; '**ℒn** v/i. (irr., ge-, sein) gush, well; **∼nangabe** ['kvɛlən⁹-] f mention of sources used; '**∼nforschung** f original research.

Quengel|ei F [kvɛŋə'laɪ] f (-/-en) grumbling, whining; nagging; '**ℒn** F v/i. (ge-, h) grumble, whine; nag.

quer adv. [kve:r] crossways, crosswise; F fig. wrong; F ∼ gehen go wrong; ∼ über (acc.) across.

'**Quer|e** f (-/no pl.): der ∼ nach crossways, crosswise; F j-m in die ∼

kommen cross s.o.'s path; fig. thwart s.o.'s plans; '**∼frage** f crossquestion; '**∼kopf** fig. m wrongheaded fellow; '**ℒschießen** F v/i. (irr. schießen, sep., -ge-, h) try to foil s.o.'s plans; '**∼schiff** △ n transept; '**∼schläger** ✕ m ricochet; '**∼schnitt** m cross-section (a. fig.); '**∼straße** f cross-road; zweite ∼ rechts second turning to the right; '**∼treiber** m (-s/-) schemer; **∼treibe'rei** f (-/-en) intriguing, machination.

Querulant [kveru'lant] m (-en/-en) querulous person, grumbler, Am. sl. a. griper.

quetsch|en ['kvɛtʃən] v/t. (ge-, h) squeeze; ✄ bruise, contuse; sich den Finger ∼ jam one's finger; '**ℒung** ✄ f (-/-en), '**ℒwunde** ✄ f bruise, contusion.

quick adj. [kvik] lively, brisk.

quieken ['kvi:kən] v/i. (ge-, h) squeak, squeal.

quietsch|en ['kvi:tʃən] v/i. (ge-, h) squeak, squeal; door-hinge, etc.: creak, squeak; brakes, etc.: screech; '**∼ver'gnügt** F adj. (as) jolly as a sandboy.

Quirl [kvirl] m (-[e]s/-e) twirlingstick; '**ℒen** v/t. (ge-, h) twirl.

quitt adj. [kvit]: ∼ sein mit j-m be quits or even with s.o.; jetzt sind wir ∼ that leaves us even; **∼ieren** [∼'ti:rən] v/t. (no -ge-, h) receipt (bill, etc.); quit, abandon (post, etc.); '**ℒung** f (-/-en) receipt; fig. answer; gegen ∼ against receipt.

quoll [kvɔl] pret. of quellen.

Quot|e ['kvo:tə] f (-/-n) quota, share, portion; **∼ient** ⅍ [kvo'tsjɛnt] m (-en/-en) quotient.

R

Rabatt ✝ [ra'bat] m (-[e]s/-e) discount, rebate.

Rabe orn. ['ra:bə] m (-n/-n) raven; '**ℒn'schwarz** F adj. raven, jet-black.

rabiat adj. [ra'bja:t] rabid, violent.

Rache ['raxə] f (-/no pl.) revenge, vengeance; retaliation.

Rachen anat. ['raxən] m (-s/-) throat, pharynx; jaws pl.

rächen ['rɛçən] v/t. (ge-, h) avenge,

revenge; sich ∼ an (dat.) revenge o.s. or be revenged on.

'**Rachen|höhle** anat. f pharynx; '**∼katarrh** ✄ m cold in the throat.

'**rach|gierig** adj., '**∼süchtig** adj. revengeful, vindictive.

Rad [ra:t] n (-[e]s/ᵘer) wheel; (bi)cycle, F bike; (ein) ∼ schlagen peacock: spread its tail; sports: turn cart-wheels; unter die Räder

kommen go to the dogs; **'~achse** f axle(-tree).

Radar ['ra:da:r, ra'da:r] m, n (-s/-s) radar.

Radau F [ra'dau] m (-s/no pl.) row, racket, hubbub.

radebrechen ['ra:də-] v/t. (ge-, h) speak (language) badly, murder (language).

radeln ['ra:dəln] v/i. (ge-, sein) cycle, pedal, F bike.

Rädelsführer ['rɛ:dəls-] m ringleader.

Räderwerk ⊕ ['rɛ:dər-] n gearing.

'rad|fahren v/i. (irr. fahren, sep-, -ge-, sein) cycle, (ride a) bicycle, pedal, F bike; **'2fahrer** m cyclist, Am. a. cycler or wheelman.

radier|en [ra'di:rən] v/t. (no -ge-, h) rub out, erase; art: etch; **2gummi** m (india-)rubber, esp. Am. eraser; **2messer** n eraser; **2ung** f (-/-en) etching.

Radieschen ♀ [ra'di:sçən] n (-s/-) (red) radish.

radikal adj. [radi'ka:l] radical.

Radio ['ra:djo] n (-s/-s) radio, wireless; im ~ on the radio, on the air; **2aktiv** phys. adj. [radjoak'ti:f] radio(-)active; **~er Niederschlag** fall-out; **'~apparat** m radio or wireless (set).

Radium ⚗ ['ra:djum] n (-s/no pl.) radium.

Radius ⊹ ['ra:djus] m (-/Radien) radius.

'Rad|kappe f hub cap; **'~kranz** m rim; **'~rennbahn** f cycling track; **'~rennen** n cycle race; **'~sport** m cycling; **'~spur** f rut, track.

raffen ['rafən] v/t. (ge-, h) snatch up; gather (dress).

raffiniert adj. [rafi'ni:rt] refined; fig. clever, cunning.

ragen ['ra:gən] v/i. (ge-, h) tower, loom.

Ragout [ra'gu:] n (-s/-s) ragout, stew, hash.

Rahe ⚓ ['ra:ə] f (-/-n) yard.

Rahm [ra:m] m (-[e]s/no pl.) cream.

Rahmen ['ra:mən] 1. m (-s/-) frame; fig.: frame, background, setting; scope; aus dem ~ fallen be out of place; 2. ♀ v/t. (ge-, h) frame.

Rakete [ra'ke:tə] f (-/-n) rocket; e-e ~ abfeuern or starten launch a rocket; dreistufige ~ three-stage rocket; **~nantrieb** [ra'ke:tən⁹-] m

rocket propulsion; mit ~ rocket-propelled; **~nflugzeug** n rocket (-propelled) plane; **~ntriebwerk** n propulsion unit.

Ramm|bär ⊕ ['ram-] m, **'~bock** m, **'~e** f (-/-n) ram(mer); **'2en** v/t. (ge-, h) ram.

Rampe ['rampə] f (-/-n) ramp, ascent; **'~nlicht** n footlights pl.; fig. limelight.

Ramsch [ramʃ] m (-es/⚹ -e) junk, trash; im ~ kaufen buy in the lump; **'~verkauf** m jumble-sale; **'~ware** f job lot.

Rand [rant] m (-[e]s/⁼er) edge, brink (a. fig.); fig. verge; border; brim (of hat, cup, etc.); rim (of plate, etc.); margin (of book, etc.); lip (of wound); Ränder pl. under the eyes: rings pl., circles pl.; vor Freude außer ~ und Band geraten be beside o.s. with joy; er kommt damit nicht zu ~e he can't manage it; **'~bemerkung** f marginal note; fig. comment.

rang¹ [raŋ] pret. of ringen.

Rang² [⚹] m (-[e]s/⁼e) rank, order; ⚔ rank; position; thea. tier; erster ~ thea. dress-circle, Am. first balcony; zweiter ~ thea. upper circle, Am. second balcony; ersten ~es first-class, first-rate; j-m den ~ ablaufen get the start or better of s.o.

Range ['raŋə] m (-n/-n), f (-/-n) rascal; romp.

rangieren [rã'ʒi:rən] (no -ge-, h) 1. 🚂 v/t. shunt, Am. a. switch; 2. fig. v/i. rank.

'Rang|liste f sports, etc.: ranking list; ⚔ army-list, navy or air-force list; **'~ordnung** f order of precedence.

Ranke ♀ ['raŋkə] f (-/-n) tendril; runner.

Ränke ['rɛŋkə] m/pl. intrigues pl.

'ranken v/refl. (ge-, h) creep, climb.

rann [ran] pret. of rinnen.

rannte ['rantə] pret. of rennen.

Ranzen ['rantsən] m (-s/-) knapsack; satchel.

ranzig adj. ['rantsiç] rancid, rank.

Rappe zo. ['rapə] m (-n/-n) black horse.

rar adj. [ra:r] rare, scarce.

Rarität [rari'tɛ:t] f (-/-en) rarity, curiosity, curio.

rasch adj. [raʃ] quick, swift, brisk; hasty; prompt.

rascheln ['raʃəln] v/i. (ge-, h) rustle.

rasen[1] ['raːzən] v/i. (ge-) **1.** (h) rage, storm; rave; **2.** (sein) race, speed; **~d** adj. raving, frenzied; speed: tearing; pains: agonizing; headache: splitting; j-n ~ machen drive s.o. mad.

Rasen[2] [~] m (-s/-) grass; lawn; turf; '**~platz** m lawn, grass-plot.

Raserei F [raːzə'raɪ] f (-/-en) rage, fury; frenzy; madness; F mot. scorching; j-n zur ~ bringen drive s.o. mad.

Rasier|apparat [ra'ziːr-] m (safety) razor; **2en** v/t. (no -ge-, h) shave; sich ~ (lassen) get a shave; **~klinge** f razor-blade; **~messer** n razor; **~pinsel** m shaving-brush; **~seife** f shaving-soap; **~wasser** n aftershave lotion; **~zeug** n shaving kit.

Rasse ['rasə] f (-/-n) race; zo. breed.

rasseln ['rasəln] v/i. (ge-, h) rattle.

Rassen|frage f (-/no pl.) racial issue; '**~kampf** m race conflict; '**~problem** n racial issue; '**~schranke** f colo(u)r bar; '**~trennung** f (-/no pl.) racial segregation; '**~unruhen** f/pl. race riots pl.

'rasserein adj. thoroughbred, purebred.

'rassig adj. thoroughbred; fig. racy.

Rast [rast] f (-/-en) rest, repose; break, pause; **2en** v/i. (ge-, h) rest, repose; '**2los** adj. restless; '**~platz** m resting-place; mot. picnic area.

Rat [raːt] m **1.** (-[e]s/~e) advice, counsel; suggestion; fig. way out; zu ~e ziehen consult; j-n um ~ fragen ask s.o.'s advice; **2.** (-[e]s/~e) council, board; council(l)or, alderman.

Rate ['raːtə] f (-/-n) instal(l)ment (a. ✝); auf ~n ✝ on hire-purchase.

'raten (irr., ge-, h) **1.** v/i. advise, counsel (j-m zu inf. s.o. to inf.); **2.** v/t. guess, divine.

'raten|weise adv. by instal(l)ments; '**2zahlung** ✝ f payment by instal(l)ments.

Rat|geber m (-s/-) adviser, counsel(l)or; '**~haus** n town hall, Am. a. city hall.

ratifizieren [ratifi'tsiːrən] v/t. (no -ge-, h) ratify.

Ration [ra'tsjoːn] f (-/-en) ration, allowance; **2ell** adj. [~o'nel] rational; efficient; economical; **2ieren** [~o'niːrən] v/t. (no -ge-, h) ration.

'rat|los adj. puzzled, perplexed, at a loss; '**~sam** adj. advisable; expedient; '**2schlag** m (piece of) advice, counsel.

Rätsel ['rɛːtsəl] n (-s/-) riddle, puzzle; enigma, mystery; '**2haft** adj. puzzling; enigmatic(al), mysterious.

Ratte zo. ['ratə] f (-/-n) rat.

rattern ['ratərn] v/i. (ge-, h, sein) rattle, clatter.

Raub [raup] m (-[e]s/no pl.) robbery; kidnap(p)ing; piracy (of intellectual property); booty, spoils pl.; '**~bau** m (-[e]s/no pl.): ~ treiben ✔ exhaust the land; ⚒ rob a mine; ~ treiben mit undermine (one's health); **2en** ['~bən] v/t. (ge-, h) rob, take by force, steal; kidnap; j-m et. ~ rob or deprive s.o. of s.th.

Räuber ['rɔybər] m (-s/-) robber; '**~bande** f gang of robbers; '**2isch** adj. rapacious, predatory.

'Raub|fisch ichth. m fish of prey; '**~gier** f rapacity; '**2gierig** adj. rapacious; '**~mord** m murder with robbery; '**~mörder** m murderer and robber; '**~tier** zo. n beast of prey; '**~überfall** m hold-up, armed robbery; '**~vogel** orn. m bird of prey; '**~zug** m raid.

Rauch [raux] m (-[e]s/no pl.) smoke; fume; '**2en** (ge-, h) **1.** v/i. smoke; fume; p. (have a) smoke; **2.** v/t. smoke (cigarette); '**~er** m (-s/-) smoker; s. Raucherabteil. [eel.]

Räucheraal 🐟 ['rɔyçər?-] m smoked]

Raucherabteil 🚬 ['rauxər?-] n smoking-car(riage), smoking-compartment, smoker.

'Räucher|hering m red or smoked herring, kipper; '**2n** (ge-, h) **1.** v/t. smoke, cure (meat, fish); **2.** v/i. burn incense.

'Rauch|fahne f trail of smoke; '**~fang** m chimney, flue; '**~fleisch** n smoked meat; '**2ig** adj. smoky; '**~tabak** m tobacco; '**~waren** f/pl. tobacco products pl.; furs pl.; '**~zimmer** n smoking-room.

Räud|e ['rɔydə] f (-/-n) mange, scab; '**2ig** adj. mangy, scabby.

Rauf|bold contp. ['raufbɔlt] m (-[e]s/-e) brawler, rowdy, Am. sl. tough; '**2en** (ge-, h) **1.** v/t. pluck, pull; sich die Haare ~ tear one's hair; **2.** v/i. fight, scuffle; **~erei** [~ə'raɪ] f (-/-en) fight, scuffle.

Q
R

rauh *adj.* [rau] rough; rugged; *weather*: inclement, raw; *voice*: hoarse; *fig.*: harsh; coarse, rude; F: in ~en Mengen galore; **'2reif** *m* (-[e]s/*no pl.*) hoar-frost, *poet.* rime.

Raum [raum] *m* (-[e]s/~e) room, space; expanse; area; room; premises *pl.*; **'~anzug** *m* space suit.

räumen ['rɔymən] *v/t.* (ge-, *h*) remove, clear (away); leave, give up, *esp.* ⨯ evacuate; vacate (*flat*).

'Raum|fahrt *f* astronautics; **'~flug** *m* space flight; **'~inhalt** *m* volume, capacity; **'~kapsel** *f* capsule.

räumlich *adj.* ['rɔymliç] relating to space, of space, spatial.

'Raum|meter *n, m* cubic met|re, *Am.* -er; **'~schiff** *n* space craft *or* ship; **'~sonde** *f* space probe; **'~station** *f* space station.

'Räumung *f* (-/-en) clearing, removal; *esp.* ✝ clearance; vacating (*of flat*), *by force*: eviction; ⨯ evacuation (*of town*); **'~sverkauf** ✝ *m* clearance sale.

raunen ['raunən] (ge-, *h*) **1.** *v/i.* whisper, murmur; **2.** *v/t.* whisper, murmur; *man raunt* rumo(u)r has it.

Raupe *zo.* ['raupə] *f* (-/-n) caterpillar; **'~nschlepper** ⊕ *m* caterpillar tractor.

raus *int.* [raus] get out!, *sl.*beat it!, [scram!]

Rausch [rauʃ] *m* (-es/~e) intoxication, drunkenness; *fig.* frenzy, transport(s *pl.*); e-n ~ haben be drunk; **'2en** *v/i.* (ge-) **1.** (*h*) leaves, rain, silk: rustle; water, wind: rush; surf: roar; applause: thunder; **2.** (sein) movement: sweep; **'~gift** *n* narcotic (drug), F dope.

räuspern ['rɔyspərn] *v/refl.* (ge-, *h*) clear one's throat.

Razzia ['ratsja] *f* (-/Razzien) raid, round-up.

reagieren [rea'giːrən] *v/i.* (*no* -ge-, *h*) react (*auf acc.* [up]on; to); *fig.* and ⊕ *a.* respond (to).

Reaktion [reak'tsjoːn] *f* (-/-en) reaction (*a. pol.*); *fig. a.* response (*auf acc.* to); **~är** [~o'nɛːr] **1.** *m* (-s/-e) reactionary; **2.** ♀ *adj.* reactionary.

Reaktor *phys.* [re'aktɔr] *m* (-s/-en) (nuclear) reactor, atomic pile.

real *adj.* [re'aːl] real; concrete; **~isieren** [reali'ziːrən] *v/t.* (*no* -ge-,

h) realize; **2ismus** [rea'lismus] *m* (-/*no pl.*) realism; **~istisch** *adj.* [rea'listiʃ] realistic; **2ität** [reali'tɛːt] *f* (-/-en) reality; **2schule** *f* nonclassical secondary school.

Rebe ⚘ ['reːbə] *f* (-/-n) vine.

Rebell [re'bɛl] *m* (-en/-en) rebel; **2ieren** [~'liːrən] *v/i.* (*no* -ge-, *h*) rebel, revolt, rise; **2isch** *adj.* rebellious.

Reb|huhn *orn.* ['rɛp-] *n* partridge; **~laus** *zo.* ['reːp-] *f* vine-fretter, phylloxera; **~stock** ⚘ ['reːp-] *m* vine.

Rechen ['reçən] *m* (-s/-) rake; grid.

Rechen|aufgabe ['reçən-] *f* sum, (arithmetical) problem; **'~fehler** *m* arithmetical error, miscalculation; **'~maschine** *f* calculating-machine; **'~schaft** *f* (-/*no pl.*): ~ ablegen give *or* render an account (*über acc.* of), account *or* answer (for); *zur* ~ *ziehen* call to account (*wegen* for); **'~schieber** A *m* slide-rule.

rechne|n ['reçnən] (ge-, *h*) **1.** *v/t.* reckon, calculate; estimate, value; charge; ~ *zu* rank with *or* among(st); **2.** *v/i.* count; ~ *auf* (*acc.*) *or* mit count *or* reckon (up)on rely (up)on; **'~risch** *adj.* arithmetical.

'Rechnung *f* (-/-en) calculation, sum, reckoning; account; bill; invoice (*of goods*); *in restaurant*: bill, *Am.* check; score; *auf* ~ on account; ~ *legen* render an account (*über acc.* of); e-r *Sache* ~ *tragen* make allowance for s.th.; *es geht auf meine* ~ *in restaurants*: it is my treat, *Am.* F this is on me; **'~sprüfer** *m* auditor.

recht¹ [reçt] **1.** *adj.* right; real; legitimate; right, correct; *zur* ~*en Zeit* in due time, at the right moment; *ein* ~*er Narr* a regular fool; *mir ist es* ~ I don't mind; ~ *haben* be right; *j-m* ~ *geben* agree with s.o.; **2.** *adv.* right(ly); well; very; rather; really; correctly; *ganz* ~! quite (so)!; *es geschieht ihm* ~ it serves him right; ~ *gern* gladly, with pleasure; ~ *gut* quite good *or* well; *ich weiß nicht* ~ I wonder.

Recht² [~] *n* (-[e]s/-e) right (*auf acc.* to), title (to), claim (on), interest (in); privilege; power, authority; ⚖ law; justice; ~ *sprechen* administer justice; *mit* ~ justly.

'**Rechte** f (-n/-n) right hand; *boxing*: right; *pol. the* Right.

Rechteck ['rɛçtʔ-] n (-[e]s/-e) rectangle; '**ǁig** adj. rectangular.

recht|fertigen ['rɛçtfɛrtɪgən] v/t. (ge-, h) justify; defend, vindicate; '**ǁfertigung** f (-/-en) justification; vindication, defen|ce, Am. -se; '**ǁgläubig** adj. orthodox; '**ǁhaberisch** adj. ['-haːbərɪʃ] dogmatic; '**ǁlich** adj. legal, lawful, legitimate; honest, righteous; '**ǁlos** adj. without rights; outlawed; '**ǁlosigkeit** f (-/no pl.) outlawry; '**ǁmäßig** adj. legal, lawful, legitimate; '**ǁmäßigkeit** f (-/no pl.) legality, legitimacy.

rechts adv. [rɛçts] on or to the right (hand).

Rechts|anspruch m legal right or claim (auf acc. on, to), title (to); '**ǁanwalt** m lawyer, solicitor; barrister, Am. attorney (at law); '**ǁaußen** m (-/-) football: outside right; '**ǁbeistand** m legal adviser, counsel.

'**recht|schaffen 1.** adj. honest, righteous; **2.** adv. thoroughly, downright, F awfully; '**ǁschreibung** f (-/-en) orthography, spelling.

'**Rechts|fall** m case, cause; '**ǁfrage** f question of law; issue of law; '**ǁgelehrte** m jurist, lawyer; '**ǁgültig** adj. s. rechtskräftig; '**ǁkraft** f (-/no pl.) legal force or validity; '**ǁkräftig** adj. valid, legal; judgement: final; '**ǁkurve** f right-hand bend; '**ǁlage** f legal position or status; '**ǁmittel** n legal remedy; '**ǁnachfolger** m assign, assignee; '**ǁperson** f legal personality; '**ǁpflege** f administration of justice, judicature.

'**Rechtsprechung** f (-/-en) jurisdiction.

'**Rechts|schutz** m legal protection; '**ǁspruch** m legal decision; judg(e)ment; sentence; verdict (of jury); '**ǁsteuerung** mot. f (-/-en) right-hand drive; '**ǁstreit** m action, lawsuit; '**ǁverfahren** n (legal) proceedings pl.; '**ǁverkehr** mot. m right-hand traffic; '**ǁverletzung** f infringement; '**ǁvertreter** m s. Rechtsbeistand; '**ǁweg** m: den **ǁ** beschreiten take legal action, go to law; unter Ausschluß des **ǁes** eliminating legal proceedings; '**ǁwidrig**

adj. illegal, unlawful; '**ǁwissenschaft** f jurisprudence.

'**recht|wink(e)lig** adj. right-angled; '**ǁzeitig 1.** adj. punctual; opportune; **2.** adv. in (due) time, punctually, Am. on time.

Reck [rɛk] n (-[e]s/-e) sports: horizontal bar.

recken ['rɛkən] v/t. (ge-, h) stretch; sich **ǁ** stretch o.s.

Redakt|eur [redak'tøːr] m (-s/-e) editor; **ǁion** [-'tsjoːn] f (-/-en) editorship; editing, wording; editorial staff, editors pl.; editor's or editorial office; **ǁionell** adj. [-tsjo'nɛl] editorial.

Rede ['reːdə] f (-/-n) speech; oration; language; talk, conversation; discourse; direkte **ǁ** gr. direct speech; indirekte **ǁ** gr. reported or indirect speech; e-e **ǁ** halten make or deliver a speech; zur **ǁ** stellen call to account (wegen for); davon ist nicht die **ǁ** that is not the point; davon kann keine **ǁ** sein that's out of the question; es ist nicht der **ǁ** wert it is not worth speaking of; '**ǁgewandt** adj. eloquent; '**ǁkunst** f rhetoric; '**ǁn** (ge-, h) **1.** v/t. speak; talk; **2.** v/i. speak (mit to); talk (to), chat (with); discuss (über et. s.th.); sie läßt nicht mit sich **ǁ** she won't listen to reason.

Redensart ['reːdəns ʔ-] f phrase, expression; idiom; proverb, saying.

redigieren [redi'giːrən] v/t. (no -ge-, h) edit; revise.

redlich ['reːtlɪç] **1.** adj. honest, upright; sincere; **2.** adv.: sich **ǁ** bemühen take great pains.

Redner ['reːdnər] m (-s/-) speaker; orator; '**ǁbühne** f platform; '**ǁisch** adj. oratorical, rhetorical; '**ǁpult** n speaker's desk.

redselig adj. ['reːtzeːlɪç] talkative.

reduzieren [redu'tsiːrən] v/t. (no -ge-, h) reduce (auf acc. to).

Reede ⚓ ['reːdə] f (-/-n) roads pl., roadstead; '**ǁr** m (-s/-) shipowner; '**ǁrei** f (-/-en) shipping company or firm.

reell [re'ɛl] **1.** adj. respectable, honest; business firm: solid; goods: good; offer: real; **2.** adv.: **ǁ** bedient werden get good value for one's money.

Refer|at [refe'raːt] n (-[e]s/-e) report; lecture; paper; ein **ǁ** halten *esp. univ.* read a paper; **~endar** [~ɛn'daːr] *m* (-s/-e) ⚖ junior lawyer; *at school*: junior teacher; **~ent** [~'rɛnt] *m* (-en/-en) reporter, speaker; **~enz** [~'rɛnts] *f* (-/-en) reference; **2ieren** [~'riːrən] *v/i.* (*no* -ge-, h) report (*über acc.* [up]on); (give a) lecture (on); *esp. univ.* read a paper (on).

reflektieren [reflɛk'tiːrən] (*no* -ge-, h) **1.** *phys. v/t.* reflect; **2.** *v/i.* reflect (*über acc.* [up]on); **~ auf** (*acc.*) ✝ think of buying; be interested in.

Reflex [re'flɛks] *m* (-es/-e) *phys.* reflection *or* reflexion; ⚡ reflex (action); **2iv** *gr. adj.* [~'ksiːf] reflexive.

Reform [re'fɔrm] *f* (-/-en) reform; **~er** *m* (-s/-) reformer; **2ieren** [~'miːrən] *v/t.* (*no* -ge-, h) reform.

Refrain [rə'frɛː] *m* (-s/-s) refrain, chorus, burden.

Regal [re'gaːl] *n* (-s/-e) shelf.

rege *adj.* ['reːgə] active, brisk, lively, busy.

Regel ['reːgəl] *f* (-/-n) rule; regulation; standard; *physiol.* menstruation, menses *pl.*; **in der ~** as a rule; **2los** *adj.* irregular; disorderly; **2mäßig** *adj.* regular; **2n** *v/t.* (ge-, h) regulate, control; arrange, settle; put in order; **2recht** *adj.* regular; **~ung** *f* (-/-en) regulation, control; arrangement, settlement; **2widrig** *adj.* contrary to the rules, irregular; abnormal; *sports*: foul.

regen[1] ['reːgən] *v/t. and v/refl.* (ge-, h) move, stir.

Regen[2] [~] *m* (-s/-) rain; **vom ~ in die Traufe kommen** jump out of the frying-pan into the fire, get from bad to worse; **2arm** *adj.* dry; **~bogen** *m* rainbow; **~bogenhaut** *anat. f* iris; **2dicht** *adj.* rain-proof; **~guß** *m* downpour; **~mantel** *m* waterproof, raincoat, mac(k)intosh, F mac; **2reich** *adj.* rainy; **~schauer** *m* shower (of rain); **~schirm** *m* umbrella; **~tag** *m* rainy day; **~tropfen** *m* raindrop; **~wasser** *n* rain-water; **~wetter** *n* rainy weather; **~wolke** *f* rain-cloud; **~wurm** *zo. m* earthworm, *Am. a.* angleworm; **~zeit** *f* rainy season.

Regie [re'ʒiː] *f* (-/-n) management; *thea., film*: direction; **unter der ~ von** directed by.

regier|**en** [re'giːrən] (*no* -ge-, h) **1.** *v/i.* reign; **2.** *v/t.* govern (*a. gr.*); rule; **2ung** *f* (-/-en) government; *Am.* administration; reign.

Re'gierungs|**antritt** *m* accession (to the throne); **~beamte** *m* government official; *Brt.* Civil Servant; **~bezirk** *m* administrative district; **~gebäude** *n* government offices *pl.*

Regiment [regi'mɛnt] *n* **1.** (-[e]s/-e) government, rule; **2.** ⚔ (-[e]s/-er) regiment.

Regisseur [reʒi'søːr] *m* (-s/-e) *thea.* stage manager, director; *film*: director.

Regist|**er** [re'gistər] *n* (-s/-) register (*a. ♪*), record; index; **~ratur** [~ra'tuːr] *f* (-/-en) registry; registration.

registrier|**en** [regis'triːrən] *v/t.* (*no* -ge-, h) register, record; **2kasse** *f* cash register.

reglos *adj.* ['reːkloːs] motionless.

regne|**n** ['reːgnən] *v/i.* (ge-, h) rain; **es regnet in Strömen** it is pouring with rain; **~risch** *adj.* rainy.

Regreß ⚖, ✝ [re'grɛs] *m* (Regresses/Regresse) recourse; **2pflichtig** ⚖, ✝ *adj.* liable to recourse.

regulär *adj.* [regu'lɛːr] regular.

regulier|**bar** *adj.* [regu'liːrbaːr] adjustable, controllable; **~en** *v/t.* (*no* -ge-, h) regulate, adjust; control.

Regung ['reːguŋ] *f* (-/-en) movement, motion; emotion; impulse; **2slos** *adj.* motionless.

Reh *zo.* [reː] *n* (-[e]s/-e) deer, roe; *female*: doe.

rehabilitieren [rehabili'tiːrən] *v/t.* (*no* -ge-, h) rehabilitate.

'Reh|**bock** *zo. m* roebuck; **2braun** *adj.*, **2farben** *adj.* fawn-colo(u)red; **~geiß** *zo. f* doe; **~kalb** *zo. n*, **~kitz** *zo.* ['~kits] *n* (-es/-e) fawn.

Reib|**e** ['raibə] *f* (-/-n), **~eisen** ['raip-] *n* grater.

reib|**en** ['raibən] (*irr.*, ge-, h) **1.** *v/i.* rub (*an dat.* [up]on); **2.** *v/t.* rub, grate; pulverize; *wund ~* chafe, gall; **2erei** F *fig.* [~'rai] *f* (-/-en) (constant) friction; **2ung** *f* (-/-en) friction; **~ungslos** *adj.* frictionless; *fig.* smooth.

reich[1] *adj.* [raiç] rich (*an dat.* in); wealthy; ample, abundant, copious.

Reich[2] [~] *n* (-es/-e) empire; kingdom (*of animals, vegetables, minerals*); *poet., rhet., fig.* realm.

reichen ['raiçən] (ge-, h) **1.** *v/t.* offer; serve (*food*); *j-m et.* **~ hand**

or pass s.th. to s.o.; *sich die Hände*
~ join hands; **2.** *v/i.* reach; extend;
suffice; *das reicht!* that will do!
reich|haltig *adj.* ['raɪçhaltɪç] rich;
abundant, copious; '**~lich 1.** *adj.*
ample, abundant, copious, plenti-
ful; ~ *Zeit* plenty of time; **2.** F *adv.*
rather, fairly, F pretty, plenty;
'**2tum** *m* (-s/ˈ̈er) riches *pl.*; wealth
(*an dat.* of).
'Reichweite *f* reach; ⚔ range; *in* ~
within reach, near at hand.
reif[1] *adj.* [raɪf] ripe, mature.
Reif[2] [~] *m* (-[e]s/*no pl.*) white *or*
hoar-frost, *poet.* rime.
Reife *f* (-/*no pl.*) ripeness, maturity.
'reifen[1] *v/i.* (ge-) **1.** (sein) ripen,
mature; **2.** (h): *es hat gereift* there
is a white *or* hoar-frost.
'Reifen[2] *m* (-s/-) hoop; ring; tyre,
(*Am. only*) tire; *as ornament*:
circlet; ~ *wechseln mot.* change
tyres; '**~panne** *mot.* f puncture,
Am. a. blowout.
'Reife|prüfung f s. *Abitur*; '**~zeug-
nis** *n s. Abschlußzeugnis.*
'reiflich *adj.* mature, careful.
Reihe ['raɪə] *f* (-/-n) row; line; rank;
series; number; *thea.* row, tier; *der*
~ *nach* by turns; *ich bin an der* ~ it
is my turn.
'Reihen|folge *f* succession, se-
quence; *alphabetische* ~ alphabetical
order; '**~haus** *n* terrace-house, *Am.*
row house; '**2weise** *adv.* in rows.
Reiher *orn.* ['raɪɐ] *m* (-s/-) heron.
Reim [raɪm] *m* (-[e]s/-e) rhyme;
'**2en** (ge-, h) **1.** *v/i.* rhyme; **2.** *v/t.*
and v/refl. rhyme (*auf acc.* with).
rein *adj.* [raɪn] pure; clean; clear;
~*e Wahrheit* plain truth; '**2ertrag** *m*
net proceeds *pl.*; '**2fall** F *m* letdown;
'**2gewicht** *n* net weight; '**2gewinn**
m net profit; '**2heit** *f* (-/*no pl.*)
purity; cleanness.
'reinig|en *v/t.* (ge-, h) clean(se);
fig. purify; '**2ung** *f* (-/-en) clean(s)-
ing; *fig.* purification; *cleaners pl.*;
chemische ~ dry cleaning; '**2ungs-
mittel** *n* detergent, cleanser.
'rein|lich *adj.* clean; cleanly; neat,
tidy; '**2machefrau** *f* charwoman;
'**~rassig** *adj.* pedigree, thoroughbred, *esp. Am.* purebred; '**2schrift**
f fair copy.
Reis[1] ♀ [raɪs] *m* (-es/-e) rice.
Reis[2] ♀ [~] *n* (-es/-er) twig, sprig.
Reise ['raɪzə] *f* (-/-n) journey, ⚓,

🐝 voyage; travel; tour; trip; passage; '**~büro** *n* travel agency *or*
bureau; '**~decke** f travel(l)ing-rug;
'**2fertig** *adj.* ready to start; '**~füh-
rer** *m* guide(-book); '**~gepäck** *n*
luggage, *Am.* baggage; '**~gesell-
schaft** f tourist party; '**~kosten** *pl.*
travel(l)ing-expenses *pl.*; '**~leiter**
m courier; '**2n** *v/i.* (ge-, sein) travel,
journey; ~ *nach* go to; *ins Ausland* ~
go abroad; '**~nde** *m, f* (-n/-n) (✚
commercial) travel(l)er; *in trains*:
passenger; *for pleasure*: tourist;
'**~necessaire** ['~nesesɛːr] *n* (-s/-s)
dressing-case; '**~paß** *m* passport;
'**~scheck** *m* traveller's cheque, *Am.*
traveler's check; '**~schreibma-
schine** f portable typewriter;
'**~tasche** f travel(l)ing-bag, *Am.*
grip(sack).
Reisig ['raɪzɪç] *n* (-s/*no pl.*) brushwood.
Reißbrett ['raɪs-] *n* drawing-board.
reißen ['raɪsən] **1.** *v/t.* (*irr.*, ge-, h)
tear; pull; *an sich* ~ seize; *sich* ~
scratch o.s. (*an dat.* with); *sich* ~
um scramble for; **2.** *v/i.* (*irr.*, ge-,
sein) break; burst; split; tear; *mir*
riß die Geduld I lost (all) patience;
3. ♀ F 🐝 *n* (-s/*no pl.*) rheumatism;
'**~d** *adj.* rapid; *animal*: rapacious;
pain: acute; *~en Absatz finden* sell
like hot cakes.
'Reiß|er F *m* (-s/-) draw, box-office
success; thriller; '**~feder** f draw-
ing-pen; '**~leine** ✈ f rip-cord;
'**~nagel** *m s. Reißzwecke*; '**~schiene**
f (T-)square; '**~verschluß** *m* zip-
fastener, zipper, *Am. a.* slide
fastener; '**~zeug** *n* drawing instruments *pl.*; '**~zwecke** f drawing-pin,
Am. thumbtack.
Reit|anzug ['raɪt-] *m* riding-dress;
'**~bahn** f riding-school, manège;
riding-track; '**2en** (*irr.*, ge-) **1.** *v/i.*
(sein) ride, go on horseback; **2.** *v/t.*
(h) ride; '**~er** *m* (-s/-) rider, horse-
man; ⚔, *police*: trooper; *filing*:
tab; '**~e'rei** f (-/-en) cavalry; '**~erin**
f (-/-nen) horsewoman; '**~gerte** f
riding-whip; '**~hose** f (riding-)
breeches *pl.*; '**~knecht** *m* groom;
'**~kunst** f horsemanship; '**~lehrer**
m riding master; '**~peitsche** f riding-whip; '**~pferd** *zo.* *n* riding-
horse, saddle-horse; '**~schule** f riding-school; '**~stiefel** *m/pl.* riding-
boots *pl.*; '**~weg** *m* bridle-path.

Reiz [raɪts] *m* (-es/-e) irritation; charm, attraction; allurement; **'2̱-bar** *adj.* sensitive; irritable, excitable, *Am.* sore; **'2̱en** (ge-, h) **1.** *v/t.* irritate (*a.* 𝔰ˢ); excite; provoke; nettle; stimulate, rouse; entice, (al)lure, tempt, charm, attract; **2.** *v/i. cards:* bid; **'2̱end** *adj.* charming, attractive; *Am.* cute; lovely; **'2̱los** *adj.* unattractive; **'̱mittel** *n* stimulus; 𝔰ˢ stimulant; **'̱ung** *f* (-/-en) irritation; provocation; **'2̱-voll** *adj.* charming, attractive.

rekeln F ['reːkəln] *v/refl.* (ge-, h) loll, lounge, sprawl.

Reklamation [reklamaˈtsjoːn] *f* (-/-en) claim; complaint, protest.

Reklame [reˈklaːmə] *f* (-/-n) advertising; advertisement, F ad; publicity; **~ machen** advertise; **~ machen für et.** advertise s.th.

rekla'mieren (*no* -ge-, h) **1.** *v/t.* (re)claim; **2.** *v/i.* complain (*wegen* about).

Rekonvaleszen|t [rekɔnvalɛsˈtsɛnt] *m* (-en/-en), **~tin** *f* (-/-nen) convalescent; **~z** [~ts] *f* (-/*no pl.*) convalescence.

Rekord [reˈkɔrt] *m* (-[e]s/-e) *sports, etc.:* record.

Rekrut ⚔ [reˈkruːt] *m* (-en/-en) recruit; **2̱ieren** ⚔ [~uˈtiːrən] *v/t.* (*no* -ge-, h) recruit.

Rektor ['rɛktɔr] *m* (-s/-en) headmaster, rector, *Am.* principal; *univ.* chancellor, rector, *Am.* president.

relativ *adj.* [relaˈtiːf] relative.

Relief [relˈjɛf] *n* (-s/-s, -e) relief.

Religi|on [reliˈgjoːn] *f* (-/-en) religion; **2̱ös** *adj.* [~ˈøːs] religious; pious, devout; **~osität** [~ozitɛːt] *f* (-/*no pl.*) religiousness; piety.

Reling ⚓ ['reːlɪŋ] *f* (-/-s, -e) rail.

Reliquie [reˈliːkviə] *f* (-/-n) relic.

Ren *zo.* [rɛn; reːn] *n* (-s/-s; -s/-e) reindeer.

Renn|bahn ['rɛn-] *f* racecourse, *Am.* race track, *horse-racing: a.* the turf; *mot.* speedway; **'̱boot** *n* racing boat, racer.

rennen ['rɛnən] **1.** *v/i.* (*irr.*, ge-, sein) run; race; **2.** *v/t.* (*irr.*, ge-, sein) run; **j-n zu Boden ~** run s.o. down; **3.** 2 *n* (-s/-) run(ning); race; heat.

'Renn|fahrer *m mot.* racing driver, racer; racing cyclist; **'̱läufer** *m* ski racer; **'̱mannschaft** *f* race-crew; **'̱pferd** *zo. n* racehorse, racer;

'̱rad *n* racing bicycle, racer; **'̱sport** *m* racing; *horse-racing: a.* the turf; **'̱stall** *m* racing stable; **'̱strecke** *f* racecourse, *Am.* race track; *mot.* speedway; distance (to be run); **'̱wagen** *m* racing car, racer.

renommiert *adj.* [renɔˈmiːrt] famous, noted (*wegen* for).

renovieren [renoˈviːrən] *v/t.* (*no* -ge-, h) renovate, repair; redecorate (*interior of house*).

rent|abel [rɛnˈtaːbəl] *adj.* profitable, paying; **2̱e** *f* (-/-n) income, revenue, annuity; (old-age) pension; rent; **2̱enempfänger** ['rɛntən?-] *m s.* Rentner; rentier.

Rentier *zo.* ['rɛn-] *n s.* Ren.

rentieren [rɛnˈtiːrən] *v/refl.* (*no* -ge-, h) pay.

Rentner ['rɛntnər] *m* (-s/-) (old-age) pensioner.

Reparatur [reparaˈtuːr] *f* (-/-en) repair; **~werkstatt** *f* repair-shop; *mot. a.* garage, service station.

repa'rieren *v/t.* (*no* -ge-, h) repair, *Am.* F fix.

Report|age [repɔrˈtaːʒə] *f* (-/-n) reporting, commentary, coverage; **~er** [reˈpɔrtər] *m* (-s/-) reporter.

Repräsent|ant [reprɛzɛnˈtant] *m* (-en/-en) representative; **~antenhaus** *Am. parl. n* House of Representatives; **2̱ieren** (*no* -ge-, h) **1.** *v/t.* represent; **2.** *v/i.* cut a fine figure.

Repressalie [reprɛˈsaːljə] *f* (-/-n) reprisal.

reproduzieren [reproduˈtsiːrən] *v/t.* (*no* -ge-, h) reproduce.

Reptil *zo.* [rɛpˈtiːl] *n* (-s/-ien, ⚔ -e) reptile.

Republik [repuˈbliːk] *f* (-/-en) republic; **~aner** *pol.* [~iˈkaːnər] *m* (-s/-) republican; **2̱anisch** *adj.* [~iˈkaːnɪʃ] republican.

Reserve [reˈzɛrvə] *f* (-/-n) reserve; **~rad** *mot. n* spare wheel.

reser'vier|en *v/t.* (*no* -ge-, h) reserve; **~ lassen** book (*seat, etc.*); **~t** *adj.* reserved (*a. fig.*).

Resid|enz [reziˈdɛnts] *f* (-/-en) residence; **2̱ieren** *v/i.* (*no* -ge-, h) reside.

resignieren [reziˈgniːrən] *v/i.* (*no* -ge-, h) resign.

Respekt [reˈspɛkt] *m* (-[e]s/*no pl.*) respect; **2̱ieren** [~ˈtiːrən] *v/t.* (*no*

-ge-, *h*) respect; **2los** *adj.* irreverent, disrespectful; **2voll** *adj.* respectful.

Ressort [rɛ'soːr] *n* (-s/-s) department; province.

Rest [rɛst] *m* (-es/-e, ✝ -er) rest, remainder; residue (*a.* 🜲); *esp.* ✝ remnant (*of cloth*); leftover (*of food*); *das gab ihm den* ~ that finished him (off).

Restaurant [rɛstoˈrãː] *n* (-s/-s) restaurant.

'Rest|bestand *m* remnant; **'.betrag** *m* remainder, balance; **2lich** *adj.* remaining; **2los** *adv.* completely; entirely; **'.zahlung** *f* payment of balance; final payment.

Resultat [rezulˈtaːt] *n* (-[e]s/-e) result, outcome; *sports:* score.

retten ['rɛtən] *v/t.* (ge-, *h*) save; deliver, rescue.

Rettich 🜲 ['rɛtiç] *m* (-s/-e) radish.

'Rettung *f* (-/-en) rescue; deliverance; escape.

'Rettungs|boot *n* lifeboat; **'.gürtel** *m* lifebelt; **2los** *adj.* irretrievable, past help or hope, beyond recovery; **'.mannschaft** *f* rescue party; **'.ring** *m* life-buoy.

Reu|e ['rɔʏə] *f* (-/no *pl.*) repentance (*über acc.* of), remorse (at); **'2en** *v/t.* (ge-, *h*): *et. reut mich* I repent (of) s.th.; **2evoll** *adj.* repentant; **2(müt)ig** *adj.* ['.(myːt)iç] repentant.

Revanche [reˈvãːʃ(ə)] *f* (-/-n) revenge; **.spiel** *n* return match.

revanˈchieren *v/refl.* (no -ge-, *h*) take *or* have one's revenge (*an dat.* on); return (*für et.* s.th.).

Revers 1. [reˈvɛːr] *n, m* (-/-) lapel (*of coat*); 2. [reˈvɛrs] *m* (-es/-e) declaration; 🜲 bond.

revidieren [reviˈdiːrən] *v/t.* (no -ge-, *h*) revise; check; ✝ audit.

Revier [reˈviːr] *n* (-s/-e) district, quarter; *s. Jagdrevier.*

Revision [reviˈzjoːn] *f* (-/-en) revision (*a. typ.*); ✝ audit; 🜲 appeal; ~ *einlegen* 🜲 lodge an appeal.

Revolt|e [reˈvɔltə] *f* (-/-en) revolt, uprising; **2ieren** [.ˈtiːrən] *v/i.* (no -ge-, *h*) revolt, rise (in revolt).

Revolution [revoluˈtsjoːn] *f* (-/-en) revolution; **.är** [.oˈnɛːr] 1. *m* (-s/-e) revolutionary. 2. 🜲 *adj.* revolutionary.

Revolver [reˈvɔlvər] *m* (-s/-) revolver, *Am.* F *a.* gun.

Revue [rəˈvyː] *f* (-/-n) review; *thea.* revue, (musical) show; ~ *passieren lassen* pass in review.

Rezens|ent [retsɛnˈzɛnt] *m* (-en/-en) critic, reviewer; **2ieren** *v/t.* (no -ge-, *h*) review, criticize; **.ion** [.ˈzjoːn] *f* (-/-en) review, critique.

Rezept [reˈtsɛpt] *n* (-[e]s/-e) ✝ prescription; *cooking:* recipe (*a. fig.*).

Rhabarber 🜲 [raˈbarbər] *m* (-s/no *pl.*) rhubarb.

rhetorisch *adj.* [reˈtoːriʃ] rhetorical.

rheumati|sch *adj.* [rɔʏˈmaːtiʃ] rheumatic; **2smus** 🜲 [.aˈtismus] *m* (-/Rheumatismen) rheumatism.

rhythm|isch *adj.* ['rʏtmiʃ] rhythmic(al); **2us** ['.us] *m* (-/Rhythmen) rhythm.

richten ['rɪçtən] *v/t.* (ge-, *h*) set right, arrange, adjust; level, point (*gun*) (*auf acc.* at); direct (*gegen* at); 🜲 judge; execute; *zugrunde* ~ ruin, destroy; *in die Höhe* ~ raise, lift up; *sich* ~ *nach* conform to, act according to; take one's bearings from; *gr.* agree with; depend on; *price:* be determined by; *ich richte mich nach Ihnen* I leave it to you.

'Richter *m* (-s/-) judge; **2lich** *adj.* judicial; **'.spruch** *m* judg(e)ment, sentence.

'richtig 1. *adj.* right, correct, accurate; proper; true; just; *ein* ~*er Londoner* a regular cockney; 2. *adv.*: ~ *gehen clock:* go right; **2keit** *f* (-/no *pl.*) correctness; accuracy; justness; **'.stellen** *v/t.* (*sep.*, -ge-, *h*) put *or* set right, rectify.

'Richt|linien *f/pl.* (general) directions *pl.*, rules *pl.*; **'.preis** ✝ *m* standard price; **'.schnur** *f* ⊕ plumb-line; *fig.* rule of conduct; guiding principle.

'Richtung *f* (-/-en) direction; course, way; *fig.* line; **.anzeiger** *mot.* ['rɪçtuŋs⁹-] *m* (-s/-) flashing indicator, trafficator; **2weisend** *adj.* directive, leading, guiding.

'Richtwaage ⊕ *f* level.

rieb [riːp] *pret.* of *reiben.*

riechen ['riːçən] (*irr.*, ge-, *h*) 1. *v/i.* smell (*nach* of; *an dat.* at); sniff (*an dat.* at); 2. *v/t.* smell; sniff.

rief [riːf] *pret.* of *rufen.* [groove.\]

riefeln ⊕ ['riːfəln] *v/t.* (ge-, *h*) flute,\]

Riegel ['riːgəl] *m* (-s/-) bar, bolt; bar, cake (*of soap*); bar (*of chocolate*).

Riemen ['riːmən] *m* (-s/-) strap, thong; belt; ⚓ oar.

Ries [riːs] *n* (-es/-e) ream.

Riese ['riːzə] *m* (-n/-n) giant.

rieseln ['riːzəln] *v/i.* (ge-) **1.** (*sein*) *small stream:* purl, ripple; trickle; **2.** (*h*): es rieselt it drizzles.

ries|engroß *adj.* ['riːzən'-], '**~enhaft** *adj.*, '**~ig** *adj.* gigantic, huge; '**²in** *f* (-/-nen) giantess.

riet [riːt] *pret. of* raten.

Riff [rif] *n* (-[e]s/-e) reef.

Rille ['rilə] *f* (-/-n) groove; ⊕ *a.* flute. [tance.\

Rimesse † [ri'mɛsə] *f* (-/-n) remit-\

Rind *zo.* [rint] *n* (-[e]s/-er) ox; cow; neat; **~er** *pl.* (horned) cattle *pl.*; zwanzig **~er** twenty head of cattle.

Rinde ['rində] *f* (-/-n) 🌿 bark; rind (*of fruit, bacon, cheese*); crust (*of bread*).

'**Rinder|braten** *m* roast beef; '**~herde** *f* herd of cattle; '**~hirt** *m* cowherd, *Am.* cowboy.

'**Rind|fleisch** *n* beef; '**~(s)leder** *n* neat's-leather, cow-hide; '**~vieh** *n* (horned) cattle *pl.*, neat *pl.*

Ring [riŋ] *m* (-[e]s/-e) ring; circle; link (*of chain*); † ring, pool, trust, *Am.* F combine; '**~bahn** *f* circular railway.

ringel|n ['riŋəln] *v/refl.* (ge-, h) curl, coil; '**²natter** *zo.* *f* ring-snake.

ring|en ['riŋən] (*irr.*, ge-, h) **1.** *v/i.* wrestle; struggle (um for); nach Atem **~** gasp (for breath); **2.** *v/t.* wring (*hands, washing*); '**²er** *m* (-s/-) wrestler.

ring|förmig *adj.* ['riŋfœrmiç] annular, ring-like; '**²kampf** *m sports:* wrestling(-match); '**²richter** *m boxing:* referee.

rings *adv.* [riŋs] around; '**~he'rum** *adv.*, '**~'um** *adv.*, '**~um'her** *adv.* round about, all (a)round.

Rinn|e ['rinə] *f* (-/-n) groove, channel; gutter (*of roof or street*); gully; '**²en** *v/i.* (*irr.*, ge-, *sein*) run, flow; drip; leak; '**~sal** ['-zaːl] *n* (-[e]s/-e) watercourse, streamlet; '**~stein** *m* gutter; sink (*of kitchen unit*).

Rippe ['ripə] *f* (-/-n) rib; 🔺 groin; bar (*of chocolate*); '**²n** *v/t.* (ge-, h) rib; '**~nfell** *anat.* *n* pleura; '**~nfellentzündung** ⚕ *f* pleurisy; '**~nstoß** *m* dig in the ribs; nudge.

Risiko ['riːziko] *n* (-s/-s, Risiken)

risk; ein **~** eingehen take a risk.

risk|ant *adj.* [ris'kant] risky; **~ieren** *v/t.* (no -ge-, h) risk.

Riß [ris] **1.** *m* (Risses/Risse) rent, tear; split (*a. fig.*); crack; *in skin:* chap; scratch; ⊕ draft, plan; *fig.* rupture; **2.** ♀ *pret. of* reißen.

rissig *adj.* ['risiç] full of rents; *skin, etc.:* chappy; **~** werden crack.

Rist [rist] *m* (-es/-e) instep; back of the hand; wrist.

Ritt [rit] **1.** *m* (-[e]s/-e) ride; **2.** ♀ *pret. of* reiten.

'**Ritter** *m* (-s/-) knight; zum **~** schlagen knight; '**~gut** *n* manor; '**²lich** *adj.* knightly, chivalrous; '**~lichkeit** *f* (-/-en) gallantry, chivalry.

rittlings *adv.* ['ritliŋs] astride (auf e-m Pferd a horse).

Ritz [rits] *m* (-es/-e) crack, chink; scratch; '**~e** *f* (-/-n) crack, chink; fissure; '**²en** *v/t.* (ge-, h) scratch; cut.

Rival|e [ri'vaːlə] *m* (-n/-n), **~in** *f* (-/-nen) rival; **²isieren** [~ali'ziːrən] *v/i.* (no -ge-, h) rival (mit j-m s.o.); **~ität** [~ali'tɛːt] *f* (-/-en) rivalry.

Rizinusöl ['riːtsinusʔ-] *n* (-[e]s/no *pl.*) castor oil.

Robbe *zo.* ['rɔbə] *f* (-/-n) seal.

Robe ['roːbə] *f* (-/-n) gown; robe.

Roboter ['rɔbɔtər] *m* (-s/-) robot.

robust *adj.* [ro'bust] robust, sturdy, vigorous.

roch [rɔx] *pret. of* riechen.

röcheln ['rœçəln] (ge-, h) **1.** *v/i.* rattle; **2.** *v/t.* gasp out (*words*).

Rock [rɔk] *m* (-[e]s/ʷe) skirt; coat, jacket; '**~schoß** *m* coat-tail.

Rodel|bahn ['roːdəl-] *f* toboggan-run; '**²n** *v/i.* (ge-, h, *sein*) toboggan, *Am.* *a.* coast; '**~schlitten** *m* sled(ge), toboggan.

roden ['roːdən] *v/t.* (ge-, h) clear (*land*); root up, stub (*roots*).

Rogen *ichth.* ['roːgən] *m* (-s/-) roe, spawn.

Roggen 🌿 ['rɔgən] *m* (-s/-) rye.

roh *adj.* [roː] raw; *fig.:* rough, rude; cruel, brutal; *oil, metal:* crude; '**²bau** *m* (-[e]s/-ten) rough brick-work; '**²eisen** *n* pig-iron.

Roheit ['roːhart] *f* (-/-en) rawness; roughness (*a. fig.*); *fig.:* rudeness; brutality.

'**Roh|ling** *m* (-s/-e) brute, ruffian; '**~material** *n* raw material; '**~produkt** *n* raw product.

Rohr [ro:r] *n* (-[e]s/-e) tube, pipe; duct; ♀: reed; cane.

Röhre ['rø:rə] *f* (-/-n) tube, pipe; duct; *radio*: valve, *Am.* (electron) tube.

'**Rohr|leger** *m* (-s/-) pipe fitter, plumber; '~**leitung** *f* plumbing; pipeline; '~**post** *f* pneumatic dispatch *or* tube; '~**stock** *m* cane; '~**zucker** *m* cane-sugar.

'**Rohstoff** *m* raw material.

Rolladen ['rɔlla:dən] *m* (-s/⁼, -) rolling shutter.

'**Rollbahn** ✈ *f* taxiway, taxi-strip.

Rolle ['rɔlə] *f* (-/-n) roll; roller; coil (*of rope, etc.*); pulley; *beneath furniture*: cast|or, -er; mangle; *thea.* part, role; *fig.* figure; ~ *Garn* reel of cotton, *Am.* spool of thread; *das spielt keine* ~ that doesn't matter, it makes no difference; *Geld spielt keine* ~ money (is) no object; *aus der* ~ *fallen* forget o.s.

'**rollen** (ge-) **1.** *v/i.* (sein) roll; ✈ taxi; **2.** *v/t.* (h) roll; wheel; mangle (*laundry*).

'**Rollenbesetzung** *thea. f* cast.

'**Roller** *m* (-s/-) *children's toy:* scooter; *mot.* (motor) scooter.

'**Roll|feld** ✈ *n* manœuvring area, *Am.* maneuvering area; '~**film** *phot. m* roll film; '~**kragen** *m* turtle neck; '~**schrank** *m* roll-fronted cabinet; '~**schuh** *m* roller-skate; '~**schuhbahn** *f* roller-skating rink; '~**stuhl** *m* wheel chair; '~**treppe** *f* escalator; '~**wagen** *m* lorry, truck.

Roman [ro'ma:n] *m* (-s/-e) novel, (work) of fiction; *novel of adventure and fig.*: romance; ~**ist** [~a'nist] *m* (-en/-en) Romance scholar *or* student; ~**schriftsteller** *m* novelist.

Romanti|k [ro'mantik] *f* (-/no *pl.*) romanticism; ⚗**sch** *adj.* romantic.

Röm|er ['rø:mər] *m* (-s/-) Roman; ⚗**isch** *adj.* Roman.

röntgen ['rœntgən] *v/t.* (ge-, h) X-ray; ⚗**aufnahme** *f*, ⚗**bild** *n* X-ray; ⚗**strahlen** *m/pl.* X-rays *pl.*

rosa *adj.* ['ro:za] pink.

Rose ['ro:zə] *f* (-/-n) ♀ rose; ✸ erysipelas.

'**Rosen|kohl** ♀ *m* Brussels sprouts *pl.*; '~**kranz** *eccl. m* rosary; ⚗**rot** *adj.* rose-colo(u)red, rosy; '~**stock** ♀ *m* (-[e]s/⁼e) rose-bush.

'**rosig** *adj.* rosy (*a. fig.*), rose-colo(u)red, roseate.

Rosine [ro'zi:nə] *f* (-/-n) raisin.

Roß *zo.* [rɔs] *n* (Rosses/Rosse, F Rösser) horse, *poet.* steed; '~**haar** *n* horsehair.

Rost [rɔst] *m* **1.** (-es/no *pl.*) rust; **2.** (-es/-e) grate; gridiron; grill; '~**braten** *m* roast joint.

'**rosten** *v/i.* (ge-, h, sein) rust.

rösten ['rø:stən] *v/t.* (ge-, h) roast, grill; toast (*bread*); fry (*potatoes*).

'**Rost|fleck** *m* rust-stain; *in cloth:* iron-mo(u)ld; ⚗**frei** *adj.* rustless, rustproof; *esp. steel:* stainless; ⚗**ig** *adj.* rusty, corroded.

rot [ro:t] **1.** *adj.* red; **2.** ⚗ *n* (-s/-, F -s) red.

Rotationsmaschine *typ.* [rota-'tsjo:ns-] *f* rotary printing machine.

'**rot|backig** *adj.* ruddy; '~**blond** *adj.* sandy.

Röte ['rø:tə] *f* (-/no *pl.*) redness, red (colo[u]r); blush; ⚗**n** *v/t.* (ge-, h) redden; paint *or* dye red; *sich* ~ redden; flush, blush.

'**rot|gelb** *adj.* reddish yellow; '~**glühend** *adj.* red-hot; ⚗**haut** *f* redskin.

rotieren [ro'ti:rən] *v/i.* (no -ge-, h) rotate, revolve.

Rot|käppchen ['ro:tkɛpçən] *n* (-s/-) Little Red Riding Hood; '~**kehlchen** *orn. n* (-s/-) robin (redbreast).

rötlich *adj.* ['rø:tliç] reddish.

'**Rot|stift** *m* red crayon *or* pencil; '~**tanne** ♀ *f* spruce (fir).

Rotte ['rɔtə] *f* (-/-n) band, gang.

'**Rot|wein** *m* red wine; claret; '~**wild** *zo. n* red deer.

Rouleau [ru'lo:] *n* (-s/-s) *s.* Rolladen; blind, *Am.* (window) shade.

Route ['ru:tə] *f* (-/-n) route.

Routine [ru'ti:nə] *f* (-/no *pl.*) routine, practice.

Rübe ['ry:bə] *f* (-/-n) beet; *weiße* ~ (Swedish) turnip, *Am. a.* rutabaga; *rote* ~ red beet, beet(root); *gelbe* ~ carrot.

Rubin [ru'bi:n] *m* (-s/-e) ruby.

ruch|bar *adj.* ['ru:xba:r]: ~ *werden* become known, get about *or* abroad; '~**los** *adj.* wicked, profligate.

Ruck [ruk] *m* (-[e]s/-e) jerk, *Am.* F yank; jolt (*of vehicle*).

'**Rück|antwort** ['ryk⁹-] *f* reply; *Postkarte mit* ~ reply postcard; *mit bezahlter* ~ *telegram:* reply paid;

Q
R

'**⃝bezüglich** *gr. adj.* reflexive; '**⃝blick** *m* retrospect(ive view) (*auf acc.* at); reminiscences *pl.*

rücken¹ ['rykən] (ge-) **1.** *v/t.* (h) move, shift; **2.** *v/i.* (sein) move; *näher* ⁓ near, approach.

Rücken² [⁓] *m* (-s/-) back; ridge (*of mountain*); '**⃝deckung** *fig. f* backing, support; '**⃝lehne** *f* back (*of chair, etc.*); '**⃝mark** *anat. n* spinal cord; '**⃝schmerzen** *m/pl.* pain in the back, back ache; '**⃝schwimmen** *n* (-s/*no pl.*) backstroke swimming; '**⃝wind** *m* following *or* tail wind; '**⃝wirbel** *anat. m* dorsal vertebra.

Rück|erstattung ['ryk⁹-] *f* restitution; refund (*of money*), reimbursement (*of expenses*); '**⃝fahrkarte** *f* return (ticket), *Am.* a. round-trip ticket; '**⃝fahrt** *f* return journey *or* voyage; *auf der* ⁓ on the way back; '**⃝fall** *m* relapse; '**⃝fällig** *adj.*: ⁓ *werden* relapse; '**⃝flug** *m* return flight; '**⃝frage** *f* further inquiry; '**⃝gabe** *f* return, restitution; '**⃝gang** *fig. m* retrogression; † recession, decline; '**⃝gängig** *adj.* retrograde; ⁓ *machen* cancel; '**⃝grat** *anat. n* (-[e]s/-e) spine, backbone (*both a. fig.*); '**⃝halt** *m* support; '**⃝haltlos** *adj.* unreserved, frank; '**⃝hand** *f* (-/*no pl.*) *tennis*: backhand (stroke); '**⃝kauf** *m* repurchase; '**⃝kehr** ['⁓ke:r] *f* (-/*no pl.*) return; '**⃝kopp(e)lung** *⌁ f* (-/-en) feedback; '**⃝lage** *f* reserve(s *pl.*), savings *pl.*; '**⃝läufig** *fig. adj.* ['⁓ɔyfiç] retrograde; '**⃝licht** *mot. n* tail-light, tail-lamp, rear-light; '**⃝lings** *adv.* backwards; from behind; '**⃝marsch** *m* march back *or* home; retreat; '**⃝porto** ⓣ *n* return postage; '**⃝reise** *f* return journey, journey back *or* home.

'**Rucksack** *m* knapsack, rucksack.

'**Rück|schlag** *m* backstroke; *fig.* setback; '**⃝schluß** *m* conclusion, inference; '**⃝schritt** *fig. m* retrogression, set-back; *pol.* reaction; '**⃝seite** *f* back, reverse; *a.* tail (*of coin*); '**⃝sendung** *f* return; '**⃝sicht** *f* respect, regard, consideration (*auf j-n* for s.o.); '**⃝sichtslos** *adj.* inconsiderate (*gegen* of), regardless (of); ruthless, reckless; ⁓*es Fahren mot.* reckless driving; '**⃝sichtsvoll**

adj. regardful (*gegen* of); considerate, thoughtful; '**⃝sitz** *mot. m* back-seat; '**⃝spiegel** *mot. m* rearview mirror; '**⃝spiel** *n sports*: return match; '**⃝sprache** *f* consultation; ⁓ *nehmen mit* consult (*lawyer*), consult with (*fellow workers*); *nach* ⁓ *mit* on consultation with; '**⃝stand** *m* arrears *pl.*; backlog; ⓣ residue; *im* ⁓ *sein mit* be in arrears *or* behind with; '**⃝ständig** *fig. adj.* old-fashioned, backward; ⁓*e Miete* arrears of rent; '**⃝stoß** *m* recoil; kick (*of gun*); '**⃝strahler** *m* (-s/-) rear reflector, cat's eye; '**⃝tritt** *m* withdrawal, retreat; resignation; '**⃝trittbremse** *f* back-pedal brake, *Am.* coaster brake; '**⃝versicherung** *f* reinsurance; '**⃝wärts** *adv.* ['⁓verts] back, backward(s); '**⃝wärtsgang** *mot. m* reverse (gear); '**⃝weg** *m* way back, return.

'**ruckweise** *adv.* by jerks.

'**rück|wirkend** *adj.* reacting; ⓣⓣⁿ *etc.*: retroactive, retrospective; '**⃝wirkung** *f* reaction; '**⃝zahlung** *f* repayment; '**⃝zug** *m* retreat.

Rüde ['ry:də] **1.** *zo. m* (-n/-n) male dog *or* fox *or* wolf; large hound; **2.** ⓠ *adj.* rude, coarse, brutal.

Rudel ['ru:dəl] *n* (-s/-) troop; pack (*of wolves*); herd (*of deer*).

Ruder ['ru:dər] *n* (-s/-) oar; rudder (*a.* ⓢ); helm; '**⃝boot** *n* row(ing)-boat; '**⃝er** *m* (-s/-) rower, oarsman; '**⃝fahrt** *f* row; '**⃝n** (ge-) **1.** *v/i.* (h, sein) row; **2.** *v/t.* (h) row; '**⃝regatta** ['⁓regata] *f* (-/*Ruderregatten*) boat race, regatta; '**⃝sport** *m* rowing.

Ruf [ru:f] *m* (-[e]s/-e) call; cry, shout; summons; *univ.* call; reputation, repute; fame; standing, credit; '**⃝en** (*irr.*, ge-, h) **1.** *v/i.* call; cry, shout; **2.** *v/t.* call; ⁓ *lassen* send for.

'**Ruf|name** *m* Christian *or* first name; '**⃝nummer** *f* telephone number; '**⃝weite** *f* (-/*no pl.*): *in* ⁓ within call *or* earshot.

Rüge ['ry:gə] *f* (-/-n) rebuke, censure, reprimand; '**⃝n** *v/t.* (ge-, h) rebuke, censure, blame.

Ruhe ['ru:ə] *f* (-/*no pl.*) rest, repose; sleep; quiet, calm; tranquillity; silence; peace; composure; *sich zur* ⁓ *setzen* retire; ⁓*!* quiet!, silence!; *immer mit der* ⁓*!* take it easy!; *lassen Sie mich in* ⁓*!* let me alone!; '**⃝bedürftig** *adj.*: ⁓ *sein* want *or* need rest; '~gehalt *n* pension; '2los *adj.* restless; '2n *v/i.* (ge-, h) rest, repose; sleep; laß die Vergangenheit ~! let bygones be bygones!; '~pause *f* pause; lull; '~platz *m* resting-place; '~stand *m* (-[e]s/no *pl.*) retirement; *im* ~ retired; *in den* ~ *treten* retire; *in den* ~ *versetzen* superannuate, pension off, retire; '~stätte *f: letzte* ~ last resting-place; '~störer *m* (-s/-) disturber of the peace, peacebreaker; '~störung *f* disturbance (of the peace), disorderly behavio(u)r, riot.

ruhig *adj.* quiet; *mind, water:* tranquil, calm; silent; ⊕ smooth.

Ruhm [ru:m] *m* (-[e]s/no *pl.*) glory, fame, renown.

rühm|en ['ry:mən] *v/t.* (ge-, h) praise, glorify; *sich e-r Sache* ~ boast of s.th.; '~lich *adj.* glorious, laudable.

'**ruhm|los** *adj.* inglorious; '~reich *adj.* glorious.

Ruhr ♂ ['ru:r] *f* (-/no *pl.*) dysentery.

Rühr|ei ['ry:rʔ-] *n* scrambled egg; '2en (ge-, h) **1.** *v/t.* stir, move; *fig.* touch, move, affect; *sich* ~ stir, move, bustle; **2.** *v/i.:* an et. ~ touch s.th.; *wir wollen nicht daran* ~ let sleeping dogs lie; '2end *adj.* touching, moving; '2ig *adj.* active, busy; enterprising; nimble; '2selig *adj.* sentimental; '~ung *f* (-/no *pl.*) emotion, feeling.

Ruin [ru'i:n] *m* (-s/no *pl.*) ruin; decay; ~e *f* (-/-n) ruin(s *pl.*); *fig.* ruin, wreck; 2ieren [rui'ni:rən] *v/t.* (no -ge-, h) ruin; destroy, wreck; spoil; *sich* ~ ruin o.s.

rülpsen ['rylpsən] *v/i.* (ge-, h) belch.

Rumän|e [ru'mɛ:nə] *m* (-n/-n) Ro(u)manian; 2isch *adj.* Ro(u)manian.

Rummel F ['ruməl] *m* (-s/no *pl.*) hurly-burly, row; bustle; revel; *in publicity:* F ballyhoo; '~platz *m* fun fair, amusement park.

rumoren [ru'mo:rən] *v/i.* (no -ge-, h) make a noise *or* row; *bowels:* rumble.

Rumpel|kammer F ['rumpəl-] *f* lumber-room; '2n F *v/i.* (ge-, h, *sein*) rumble.

Rumpf [rumpf] *m* (-[e]s/⸚e) *anat.* trunk, body; torso (*of statue*); ⛵ hull, frame, body; ✈ fuselage, body.

rümpfen ['rympfən] *v/t.* (ge-, h): *die Nase* ~ turn up one's nose, sniff (*über acc.* at).

rund [runt] **1.** *adj.* round (*a. fig.*); circular; **2.** *adv.* about; '2blick *m* panorama, view all (a)round; 2e ['rundə] *f* (-/-n) *sports:* lap; *boxing:* round; round, patrol; beat (*of policeman*); *in der or die* ~ (a)round; ~en ['~dən] *v/refl.* (ge-, h) (grow) round; '2fahrt *f* drive round (*town, etc.*); *s. Rundreise;* '2flug *m* circuit (*über of*); '2frage *f* inquiry, poll.

'**Rundfunk** *m* broadcast(ing); broadcasting service; broadcasting company; radio, wireless; *im* ~ over the wireless, on the radio *or* air; '~anstalt *f* broadcasting company; '~ansager *m* (radio) announcer; '~gerät *n* radio *or* wireless set; '~gesellschaft *f* broadcasting company; '~hörer *m* listener(-in); ~ *pl. a.* (radio) audience; '~programm *n* broadcast *or* radio program(me); '~sender *m* broadcast transmitter; broadcasting *or* radio station; '~sendung *f* broadcast; '~sprecher *m* broadcaster, broadcast speaker, (radio) announcer; '~station *f* broadcasting *or* radio station; '~übertragung *f* radio transmission, broadcast(ing); broadcast (*of programme*).

'**Rund|gang** *m* tour, round, circuit; '~gesang *m* glee, catch; '2he'raus *adv.* in plain words, frankly, plainly; '2he'rum *adv.* round about, all (a)round; '2lich *adj.* round(ish); rotund, plump; '~reise *f* circular tour *or* trip, sight-seeing trip, *Am. a.* round trip; '~schau *f* panorama; *newspaper:* review; '~schreiben *n* circular (letter); '2'weg *adv.* flatly, plainly.

Runz|el ['runtsəl] *f* (-/-n) wrinkle; '2elig *adj.* wrinkled; '2eln *v/t.* (ge-, h) wrinkle; *die Stirn* ~ knit one's brows, frown; '2lig *adj.* wrinkled.

Rüpel ['ry:pəl] *m* (-s/-) boor, lout; '2haft *adj.* coarse, boorish, rude.

rupfen ['rupfən] *v/t.* (ge-, h) pull up *or* out, pluck; pluck (*fowl*) (*a. fig.*). [*fig.* rude.]

ruppig *adj.* ['rupiç] ragged, shabby;⟩

Rüsche ['ry:ʃə] *f* (-/-n) ruffle, frill.

Ruß [ru:s] *m* (-es/no *pl.*) soot.

Q
R

Russe ['rusə] *m* (-n/-n) Russian.
Rüssel ['rysəl] *m* (-s/-) trunk (*of elefant*); snout (*of pig*). [*adj.* sooty.]
ruß|en *v/i.* (ge-, h) smoke; **~ig)**
'**russisch** *adj.* Russian.
rüsten ['rystən] (ge-, h) **1.** *v/t. and v/refl.* prepare, get ready (**zu** for); **2.** *esp.* ✗ *v/i.* arm.
rüstig *adj.* ['rystiç] vigorous, strong; '**2keit** *f* (-/*no pl.*) vigo(u)r.
'**Rüstung** *f* (-/-en) preparations *pl.*; ✗ arming, armament; armo(u)r; **~sindustrie** ['rystuŋs⁹-] *f* armament industry.

'**Rüstzeug** *n* (set of) tools *pl.*, implements *pl.*; *fig.* equipment.
Rute ['ru:tə] *f* (-/-n) rod; switch; *fox's tail:* brush.
Rutsch [rutʃ] *m* (-es/-e) (land)slide; F short trip; '**~bahn** *f*, **~e** *f* (-/-n) slide, chute; '**2en** *v/i.* (ge-, sein) glide, slide; slip; *vehicle:* skid; '**2ig** *adj.* slippery.
rütteln ['rytəln] (ge-, h) **1.** *v/t.* shake, jog; jolt; **2.** *v/i.* shake, jog; *car:* jolt; **an der Tür ~** rattle at the door; **daran ist nicht zu ~** that's a fact.

S

Saal [za:l] *m* (-[e]s/Säle) hall.
Saat 🌱 [za:t] *f* (-/-en) sowing; standing *or* growing crops *pl.*; seed (*a. fig.*); '**~feld** 🌱 *n* cornfield; '**~gut** 🌱 *n* (-[e]s/*no pl.*) seeds *pl.*; '**~kartoffel** 🌱 *f* seed-potato.
Sabbat ['zabat] *m* (-s/-e) Sabbath.
sabbern F ['zabərn] *v/i.* (ge-, h) slaver, slobber, *Am. a.* drool; twaddle, *Am. sl. a.* drool.
Säbel ['zɛːbəl] *m* (-s/-) sab|re, *Am.* -er; **mit dem ~ rasseln** *pol.* rattle the sabre; '**~beine** *n/pl.* bandy legs *pl.*; '**2beinig** *adj.* bandy-legged; '**~hieb** *m* sabre-cut; '**2n** F *fig.* *v/t.* (ge-, h) hack.
Sabot|age [zabo'ta:ʒə] *f* (-/-n) sabotage; **~eur** [~ø:r] *m* (-s/-e) saboteur; **2ieren** *v/t.* (*no* -ge-, h) sabotage.
Sach|bearbeiter ['zax-] *m* (-s/-) official in charge; *social work:* case worker; '**~beschädigung** *f* damage to property; '**2dienlich** *adj.* relevant, pertinent; useful, helpful.
'**Sache** *f* (-/-n) thing; affair, matter, concern; 🏛 case; point; issue; **~n** *pl.* things *pl.*; **beschlossene ~** foregone conclusion; **e-e ~ für sich** a matter apart; **(nicht) zur ~ gehörig** (ir)relevant, *pred. a.* to (off) the point; **bei der ~ bleiben** stick to the point; **gemeinsame ~ machen mit** make common cause with.
'**sach|gemäß** *adj.* appropriate, proper; '**2kenntnis** *f* expert knowledge; '**~kundig** *adj. s.* sachverständig; '**2lage** *f* state of affairs,

situation; '**~lich 1.** *adj.* relevant, pertinent, *pred. a.* to the point; matter-of-fact, business-like; unbias(s)ed; objective; **2.** *adv.:* **~ einwandfrei** *od.* **richtig** factually correct.
sächlich *adj.* ['zɛçliç] neuter.
'**Sachlichkeit** *f* (-/*no pl.*) objectivity; impartiality; matter-of-factness.
'**Sach|register** *n* (subject) index; '**~schaden** *m* damage to property.
Sachse ['zaksə] *m* (-n/-n) Saxon.
sächsisch *adj.* ['zɛksiʃ] Saxon.
sacht *adj.* [zaxt] soft, gentle; slow.
Sach|verhalt ['zaxfɛrhalt] *m* (-[e]s/ -e) facts *pl.* (of the case); '**2verständig** *adj.* expert; '**~verständige** *m* (-n/-n) expert, authority; 🏛 expert witness; '**~wert** *m* real value.
Sack [zak] *m* (-[e]s/⁺e) sack; bag; **mit ~ und Pack** with bag and baggage; '**~gasse** *f* blind alley, cul-de-sac, impasse (*a. fig.*), *Am. a.* dead end (*a. fig.*); *fig.* deadlock; '**~leinwand** *f* sackcloth.
Sadis|mus [za'dismus] *m* (-/*no pl.*) sadism; **~t** *m* (-en/-en) sadist; **2tisch** *adj.* sadistic.
säen ['zɛːən] *v/t. and v/i.* (ge-, h) sow (*a. fig.*).
Saffian ['zafja:n] *m* (-s/*no pl.*) morocco.
Saft [zaft] *m* (-[e]s/⁺e) juice (*of vegetables or fruits*); sap (*of plants*) (*a. fig.*); '**2ig** *adj.* *fruits, etc.:* juicy; *meadow, etc.:* lush; *plants:* sappy (*a. fig.*); *joke, etc.:* spicy, coarse; '**2los** *adj.* juiceless; sapless (*a. fig.*).

Sage ['zɑːgə] *f* (-/-n) legend, myth; *die* ~ *geht the story goes.*

Säge ['zɛːgə] *f* (-/-n) saw; '~**blatt** *n* saw-blade; '~**bock** *m* saw-horse, *Am. a.* sawbuck; '~**fisch** *ichth. m* sawfish; '~**mehl** *n* sawdust.

sagen ['zɑːgən] (ge-, *h*) **1.** *v/t.* say; *j-m et.* ~ tell s.o. s.th., say s.th. to s.o.; *j-m* ~ *lassen, daß* send s.o. word that; *er läßt sich nichts* ~ he will not listen to reason; *das hat nichts zu* ~ that doesn't matter; *j-m gute Nacht* ~ bid s.o. good night; **2.** *v/i.* say; *es ist nicht zu* ~ it is incredible or fantastic; *wenn ich so* ~ *darf* if I may express myself in these terms; *sage und schreibe* believe it or not; no less than, as much as.

'**sägen** *v/t. and v/i.* (ge-, *h*) saw.

'**sagenhaft** *adj.* legendary, mythical; F *fig.* fabulous, incredible.

Säge|**späne** ['zɛːgəʃpɛːnə] *m/pl.* sawdust; '~**werk** *n* sawmill.

sah [zɑː] *pret. of sehen.*

Sahne ['zɑːnə] *f* (-/no *pl.*) cream.

Saison [zɛ'zõː] *f* (-/-s) season; **℃bedingt** *adj.* seasonal.

Saite ['zaɪtə] *f* (-/-n) string, chord (*a. fig.*); ~**ninstrument** ['zaɪtən'-] *n* stringed instrument.

Sakko ['zako] *m, n* (-s/-s) lounge coat; '~**anzug** *m* lounge suit.

Sakristei [zakrɪs'taɪ] *f* (-/-en) sacristy, vestry.

Salat [za'lɑːt] *m* (-[e]s/-e) salad; ♉ lettuce.

Salb|**e** ['zalbə] *f* (-/-n) ointment; '**℃en** *v/t.* (ge-, *h*) rub with ointment; anoint; '~**ung** *f* (-/-en) anointing, unction (*a. fig.*); **℃ungsvoll** *fig. adj.* unctuous.

saldieren † [zal'diːrən] *v/t.* (no -ge-, *h*) balance, settle.

Saldo † ['zaldo] *m* (-s/Salden, Saldos, Saldi) balance; *den* ~ *ziehen* strike the balance; '~**vortrag** † *m* balance carried down.

Saline [za'liːnə] *f* (-/-n) salt-pit, salt-works.

Salmiak ♑ [zal'mjak] *m, n* (-s/no *pl.*) sal-ammoniac, ammonium chloride; ~**geist** *m* (-es/no *pl.*) liquid ammonia.

Salon [za'lõː] *m* (-s/-s) drawing-room, *Am. a.* parlor; ♉ saloon; **℃fähig** *adj.* presentable; '~**löwe** *fig. m* lady's man, carpet-knight;

~**wagen** 🚂 *m* salooncar, saloon carriage, *Am.* parlor car.

Salpeter ♑ [zal'peːtər] *m* (-s/no *pl.*) saltpet|re *Am.* -er; nit|re, *Am.* -er.

Salto ['zalto] *m* (-s/-s, Salti) somersault; ~ *mortale* break-neck leap; *e-n* ~ *schlagen* turn a somersault.

Salut [za'luːt] *m* (-[e]s/-e) salute; ~ *schießen* fire a salute; **℃ieren** [~u'tiːrən] *v/i.* (no -ge-, *h*) (stand at the) salute.

Salve ['zalvə] *f* (-/-n) volley; ♒ broadside; salute.

Salz [zalts] *n* (-es/-e) salt; '~**bergwerk** *n* salt-mine; '**℃en** *v/t.* ([irr.,] ge-, *h*) salt; '~**faß** *n*, **~fäßchen** ['~fɛsçən] *n* (-s/-) salt-cellar; '~**gurke** *f* pickled cucumber; '**℃haltig** *adj.* saline, saliferous; '~**hering** *m* pickled herring; '**℃ig** *adj.* salt(y); *s. salzhaltig;* '~**säure** ♑ *f* hydrochloric *or* muriatic acid; '~**wasser** *n* (-s/∺) salt water, brine; '~**werk** *n* salt-works, saltern.

Same ['zɑːmə] *m* (-ns/-n), **~n** *m* (-s/-) ♇ seed (*a. fig.*); *biol.* sperm, semen; '~**nkorn** ♇ *n* grain of seed.

Sammel|**büchse** ['zaml-] *f* collecting-box; '~**lager** *n* collecting point; *refugees, etc.:* assembly camp; '**℃n** (ge-, *h*) **1.** *v/t.* gather; collect (*stamps, etc.*); *sich* ~ gather; *fig.:* concentrate; compose o.s.; **2.** *v/i.* collect money (*für* for) '~**platz** *m* meeting-place, place of appointment ✕, ♒ rendezvous.

Samm!|**er** ['zamlər] *m* (-s/-) collector; lung *f* **1.** (-/-en) collection; **2.** *fig.* (-/no *pl.*) composure; concentration.

Samstag ['zams-] *m* Saturday.

samt[1] [zamt] **1.** *adv.*: ~ *und sonders* one and all; **2.** *prp.* (*dat.*) together *or* along with.

Samt[2] [~] *m* (-[e]s/-e) velvet.

sämtlich ['zɛmtlɪç] **1.** *adj.* all (together); complete; **2.** *adv.* all (together *or* of th[e]m).

Sanatorium [zana'toːrjum] *n* (-s/Sanatorien) sanatorium, *Am. a.* sanitarium.

Sand [zant] *m* (-[e]s/-e) sand; *j-m* ~ *in die Augen streuen* throw dust into s.o.'s eyes; *im* ~*e verlaufen* end in smoke, come to nothing.

Sandale [zan'dɑːlə] *f* (-/-n) sandal.

Sand|**bahn** *f sports:* dirt-track; '~**bank** *f* sandbank; '~**boden** *m*

S

sandy soil; '~grube f sand-pit; ~ig adj. ['~dɪç] sandy; '~korn n grain of sand; '~mann fig. m (-[e]s/no pl.) sandman, dustman; '~papier n sandpaper; '~sack m sand-bag; '~stein m sandstone.

sandte ['zantə] pret. of senden.

'Sand|torte f Madeira cake; '~uhr f sand-glass; '~wüste f sandy desert.

sanft adj. [zanft] soft; gentle, mild; smooth; slope, death, etc.: easy; ~er Zwang non-violent coercion; mit ~er Stimme softly, gently; '~mütig adj. ['~myːtɪç] gentle, mild; meek.

sang [zaŋ] pret. of singen.

Sänger ['zɛŋər] m (-s/-) singer.

Sanguini|ker [zaŋguˈiːnikər] m (-s/-) sanguine person; 2sch adj. sanguine.

sanier|en [zaˈniːrən] v/t. (no -ge-, h) improve the sanitary conditions of; esp. ✝: reorganize; readjust; 2ung f (-/-en) sanitation; esp. ✝: reorganization; readjustment.

sanitär adj. [zaniˈtɛːr] sanitary.

Sanität|er [zaniˈtɛːtər] m (-s/-) ambulance man; ⚔ medical orderly.

sank [zaŋk] pret. of sinken.

Sankt [zaŋkt] Saint, St.

sann [zan] pret. of sinnen.

Sard|elle [zarˈdɛlə] f (-/-n) anchovy; ~ine ichth. [~iːnə] f (-/-n) sardine.

Sarg [zark] m (-[e]s/ᵁe) coffin, Am. a. casket; '~deckel m coffin-lid.

Sarkas|mus [zarˈkasmus] m (-/ᵁ Sarkasmen) sarcasm; 2tisch adj. [~tɪʃ] sarcastic.

saß [zaːs] pret. of sitzen.

Satan ['zaːtan] m (-s/-e) Satan; fig. devil; 2isch fig. adj. [zaˈtaːnɪʃ] satanic.

Satellit ast., pol. [zatɛˈliːt] m (-en/-en) satellite; ~enstaat pol. m satellite state.

Satin [saˈtɛ̃ː] m (-s/-s) satin; sateen.

Satir|e [zaˈtiːrə] f (-/-n) satire; ~iker [~ikər] m (-s/-) satirist; 2isch adj. satiric(al).

satt adj. [zat] satisfied, satiated, full; colour: deep, rich; sich ~ essen eat one's fill; ich bin ~ I have had enough; F et. ~ haben be tired or sick of s.th., sl. be fed up with s.th.

Sattel ['zatəl] m (-s/ᵁ) saddle; '~gurt m girth; '2n v/t. (ge-, h) saddle.

'Sattheit f (-/no pl.) satiety, fullness; richness, intensity (of colours).

sättig|en ['zɛtigən] (ge-, h) 1. v/t. satisfy, satiate; ◠, phys. saturate; 2. v/i. food: be substantial; 2ung f (-/-en) satiation; ◠, fig. saturation.

Sattler ['zatlər] m (-s/-) saddler; ~ei [~ˈraɪ] f (-/-en) saddlery.

'sattsam adv. sufficiently.

Satz [zats] m (-es/ᵁe) gr. sentence, clause; phls. maxim; ♫ proposition, theorem; ♪ movement; tennis, etc.: set; typ. setting, composition; sediment, dregs pl., grounds pl.; rate (of prices, etc.); set (of stamps, tools, etc.); leap, bound.

'Satzung f (-/-en) statute, by-law; 2sgemäß adj. statutory.

'Satzzeichen gr. n punctuation-mark.

Sau [zau] f 1. (-/ᵁe) zo. sow; fig. contp. filthy swine; 2. hunt. (-/-en) wild sow.

sauber adj. ['zaubər] clean; neat (a. fig.), tidy; attitude: decent; iro. fine, nice; 2keit f (-/no pl.) clean(li)ness; tidiness, neatness; decency (of attitude).

säuber|n ['zɔybərn] v/t. (ge-, h) clean(se); tidy, clean up (room, etc.); clear (von of); purge (of, from) (a. fig., pol.); 2ungsaktion pol. f purge.

sauer ['zauər] 1. adj. sour (a. fig.), acid (a. ◠); cucumber: pickled; task, etc.: hard, painful; fig. morose, surly; 2. adv.: ~ reagieren auf et. take s.th. in bad part.

säuer|lich ['zɔyərlɪç] sourish, acidulous; '~n v/t. (ge-, h) (make) sour, acidify (a. ◠); leaven (dough).

'Sauer|stoff ◠ m (-[e]s/no pl.) oxygen; '~teig m leaven.

saufen ['zaufən] v/t. and v/i. (irr., ge-, h) animals: drink; F p. sl. soak, lush.

Säufer F ['zɔyfər] m (-s/-) sot, sl. soak.

saugen ['zaugən] ([irr.,] ge-, h) 1. v/i. suck (an et. s.th.); 2. v/t. suck.

säuge|n ['zɔygən] v/t. (ge-, h) suckle, nurse; 2tier n mammal.

Säugling ['zɔyklɪŋ] m (-s/-e) baby, suckling; '~sheim n baby-farm, baby-nursery.

'Saug|papier n absorbent paper; '~pumpe f suction-pump; '~wirkung f suction-effect.

Säule ['zɔylə] *f* (-/-n) △, *anat.* column (*a. ☷ of smoke, mercury, etc.*); pillar, support (*both a. fig.*); '**~ngang** *m* colonnade; '**~nhalle** *f* pillared hall; portico.

Saum [zaum] *m* (-[e]s/⸗e) seam, hem; border, edge.

säum|en ['zɔymən] *v/t.* (ge-, h) hem; border, edge; *die Straßen* ~ line the streets; '**~ig** *adj. payer:* dilatory.

'**Saum|pfad** *m* mule-track; '**~tier** *n* sumpter-mule.

Säure ['zɔyrə] *f* (-/-n) sourness; acidity (*a. ☷ of stomach*); 🜊 acid.

Saure'gurkenzeit *f* silly or slack season.

säuseln ['zɔyzəln] (ge-, h) 1. *v/i. leaves, wind:* rustle, whisper; 2. *v/t. p.* say airily, purr.

sausen ['zauzən] *v/i.* (ge-, h) 1. (sein) F rush, dash; *bullet, etc.:* whiz(z), whistle; 2. (h) *wind:* whistle, sough.

'**Saustall** *m* pigsty; F *fig. a.* horrid mess.

Saxophon ♪ [zakso'fo:n] *n* (-s/-e) saxophone.

Schab|e ['ʃa:bə] *f* (-/-n) *zo.* cockroach; ⊕ *s.* Schabeisen; '**~efleisch** *n* scraped meat; '**~eisen** ⊕ *n* scraper, shaving-tool; '**~emesser** ⊕ *n* scraping-knife; '**2en** *v/t.* (ge-, h) scrape (⊕); grate, rasp; scratch; '**~er** ⊕ *m* (-s/-) scraper.

Schabernack ['ʃa:bərnak] *m* (-[e]s/-e) practical joke, hoax, prank.

schäbig *adj.* ['ʃɛ:biç] shabby (*a. fig.*), F seedy, *Am.* F *a.* dowdy, tacky; *fig.* mean.

Schablone [ʃa'blo:nə] *f* (-/-n) model, pattern; stencil; *fig.:* routine; cliché; **2nhaft** *adj.*, **2nmäßig** *adj.* according to pattern; *fig.:* mechanical; *attr. a.* routine.

Schach [ʃax] *n* (-s/-s) chess; ~! check!; *und matt!* checkmate!; *in* or *im* ~ *halten* keep *s.o.* in check; '**~brett** *n* chessboard.

schachern ['ʃaxərn] *v/i.* (ge-, h) haggle (*um* about, over), chaffer (about, over), *Am. a.* dicker; ~ *mit* barter (away).

'**Schach|feld** *n* square; '**~figur** *f* chess-man, piece; *fig.* pawn; '**2-matt** *adj.* (check)mated; *fig.* tired out, worn out; '**~spiel** *n* game of chess.

Schacht [ʃaxt] *m* (-[e]s/⸗e) shaft; ⚒)

Schachtel ['ʃaxtəl] *f* (-/-n) box; F *alte* ~ old frump.

'**Schachzug** *m* move (at chess); *ge-schickter* ~ clever move (*a. fig.*).

schade *pred. adj.* ['ʃa:də]: *es ist* ~ it is a pity; *wie* ~! what a pity!; *zu* ~ *für* too good for.

Schädel ['ʃɛ:dəl] *m* (-s/-) skull; cranium; '**~bruch** ♂ *m* fracture of the skull.

schaden ['ʃa:dən] 1. *v/i.* (ge-, h) damage, injure, harm, hurt (*j-m* s.o.); be detrimental (to s.o.); *das schadet nichts* it does not matter, never mind; 2. ♀ *m* (-s/⸗) damage (*an dat.* to); injury, harm, infirmity; hurt; loss; '**2ersatz** *m* indemnification, compensation; damages *pl.*; ~ *verlangen* claim damages; ~ *leisten* pay damages; *auf* ~ *(ver)klagen* ⚖ sue for damages; '**2freude** *f* malicious enjoyment of others' misfortunes, schadenfreude; '**~froh** *adj.* rejoicing over others' misfortunes.

schadhaft *adj.* ['ʃa:thaft] damaged; defective, faulty; *building, etc.:* dilapidated; *pipe, etc.:* leaking; *tooth, etc.:* decayed.

schädig|en ['ʃɛ:digən] *v/t.* (ge-, h) damage, impair; wrong, harm, '**2ung** *f* (-/-en) damage (*gen.* to), impairment (of); prejudice (to).

schädli|ch *adj.* ['ʃɛ:tliç] harmful, injurious; ,noxious; detrimental, prejudicial; '**2ng** ['~ŋ] *m* (-s/-e) zo. pest; ♀ destructive weed; noxious person; ~*e pl.* ✗ *a.* vermin.

schadlos *adj.* ['ʃa:tlo:s]: *sich* ~ *halten* recoup *or* idemnify o.s. (*für* for).

Schaf [ʃa:f] *n* (-[e]s/-e) *zo.* sheep; *fig.* simpleton; '**~bock** *zo. m* ram.

Schäfer ['ʃɛ:fər] *m* (-s/-) shepherd; '**~hund** *m* sheep-dog; Alsatian (wolf-hound).

Schaffell ['ʃa:f~] *n* sheepskin.

schaffen ['ʃafən] 1. *v/t.* (irr., ge-, h) create, produce; 2. *v/t.* (ge-, h) convey, carry, move; take, bring; cope with, manage; 3. *v/i.* (ge-, h) be busy, work.

Schaffner ['ʃafnər] *m* (-s/-) 🚃 guard, *Am.* conductor; *tram, bus:* conductor.

'**Schafhirt** *m* shepherd.   [fold.]

Schafott [ʃa'fɔt] *n* (-[e]s/-e) scaf- [fold.]

'**Schaf|pelz** *m* sheepskin coat; '**~stall** *m* fold.

Schaft [ʃaft] *m* (-[e]s/ː̈e) shaft (*of lance, column, etc.*); stick (*of flag*); stock (*of rifle*); shank (*of tool, key, etc.*); leg (*of boot*); '**~stiefel** *m* high boot; ~ *pl. a.* Wellingtons *pl.*

'**Schaf|wolle** *f* sheep's wool; '**~zucht** *f* sheep-breeding, sheep-farming.

schäkern ['ʃɛːkərn] *v/i.* (ge-, h) jest, joke; flirt.

schal[1] *adj.* [ʃaːl] insipid; stale; *fig. a.* flat.

Schal[2] [~] *m* (-s/-e, -s) scarf, muffler; comforter.

Schale ['ʃaːlə] *f* (-/-n) bowl; ⊕ scale (*of scales*); shell (*of eggs, nuts, etc.*); peel, skin (*of fruit*); shell, crust (*of tortoise*); paring, peeling; F: *sich in ~ werfen* doll o.s. up.

schälen ['ʃɛːlən] *v/t.* (ge-, h) remove the peel *or* skin from; pare, peel (*fruit, potatoes, etc.*); *sich ~ skin*: peel *or* come off.

Schalk [ʃalk] *m* (-[e]s/-e, ːe) rogue, wag; '**2haft** *adj.* roguish, waggish.

Schall [ʃal] *m* (-[e]s/ː̈e, ːe) sound; '**~dämpfer** *m* sound absorber; *mot.* silencer, *Am.* muffler; silencer (*on fire-arms*); '**2en** *v/i.* ([irr.,] ge-, h) sound; ring, peal; '**2end** *adj.:* ~es Gelächter roars *pl. or* a peal of laughter; '**~mauer** *f* sound barrier; '**~platte** *f* record, disc, disk; '**~welle** *f* sound-wave.

schalt [ʃalt] *pret. of* schelten.

'**Schaltbrett** ⚡ *n* switchboard.

schalten ['ʃaltən] (ge-, h) **1.** *v/i.* ⚡ switch; *mot.* change *or* shift gears; direct, rule; **2.** *v/t.* ⊕ actuate; operate, control.

'**Schalter** *m* (-s/-) 🚉, *theatre, etc.:* booking-office; 📮, *bank, etc.:* counter; ⚡ switch; ⊕, *mot.* controller.

'**Schalt|hebel** *m mot.* gear lever; ⊕, ⚙ control lever; ⚡ switch lever; '**~jahr** *n* leap-year; '**~tafel** ⚡ *f* switchboard, control panel; '**~tag** *m* intercalary day.

Scham [ʃaːm] *f* (-/*no pl.*) shame; bashfulness, modesty; *anat.* privy parts *pl.*, genitals *pl.*

schämen ['ʃɛːmən] *v/refl.* (ge-, h) be *or* feel ashamed (*gen. or wegen* of).

'**Scham|gefühl** *n* sense of shame; '**2haft** *adj.* bashful, modest; '**~haftigkeit** *f* (-/*no pl.*) bashfulness,

modesty; '**2los** *adj.* shameless; impudent; '**~losigkeit** *f* (-/-en) shamelessness; impudence; '**2rot** *adj.* blushing; ~ *werden* blush; '**~röte** *f* blush; '**~teile** *anat. m/pl.* privy parts *pl.*, genitals *pl.*

Schande ['ʃandə] *f* (-/⚓-n) shame, disgrace.

schänden ['ʃɛndən] *v/t.* (ge-, h) dishono(u)r, disgrace; desecrate, profane; rape, violate; disfigure.

Schandfleck *fig.* ['ʃant-] *m* blot, stain; eyesore.

schändlich *adj.* ['ʃɛntliç] shameful, disgraceful, infamous; '**2keit** *f* (-/-en) infamy.

'**Schandtat** *f* infamous act(ion).

'**Schändung** *f* (-/-en) dishono(u)ring; profanation, desecration; rape, violation; disfigurement.

Schanze ['ʃantsə] *f* (-/-n) ✕ entrenchment; ⚓ quarter-deck; *sports:* ski-jump; '**2n** *v/i.* (ge-, h) throw up entrenchments, entrench.

Schar [ʃaːr] *f* (-/-en) troop, band; *geese, etc.:* flock; ⚒ ploughshare, *Am.* plowshare; '**2en** *v/t.* (ge-, h) assemble, collect; *sich ~ a.* flock (*um* round).

scharf [ʃarf] **1.** *adj.* sharp; *edge:* keen; *voice, sound:* piercing, shrill; *smell, taste:* pungent; *pepper, etc.:* hot; *sight, hearing, intelligence, etc.:* keen; *answer, etc.:* cutting; ✕ ammunition: live; ~ *sein auf* (*acc.*) be very keen on; **2.** *adv.:* ~ ansehen look sharply at; ~ *reiten* ride hard; '**2blick** *fig. m* (-[e]s/*no pl.*) clear-sightedness.

Schärfe ['ʃɛrfə] *f* (-/-n) sharpness; keenness; pungency; '**2n** *v/t.* (ge-, h) put an edge on, sharpen; strengthen (*memory*); sharpen (*sight, hearing, etc.*).

'**Scharf|macher** *fig. m* (-s/-) firebrand, agitator; '**~richter** *m* executioner; '**~schütze** ✕ *m* sharpshooter, sniper; '**2sichtig** *adj.* sharp-sighted; *fig.* clear-sighted; '**~sinn** *m* (-[e]s/*no pl.*) sagacity; acumen; '**2sinnig** *adj.* sharp-witted, shrewd; sagacious.

Scharlach ['ʃarlax] *m* **1.** (-s/-e) scarlet; **2.** 🩺 (-s/*no pl.*) scarlet fever; '**2rot** *adj.* scarlet.

Scharlatan ['ʃarlatan] *m* (-s/-e) charlatan, quack (*doctor*); mountebank.

Scharmützel [ʃar'mYtsəl] *n* (-s/-) skirmish.

Scharnier ⊕ [ʃar'niːr] *n* (-s/-e) hinge, joint.

Schärpe ['ʃɛrpə] *f* (-/-n) sash.

scharren ['ʃarən] (ge-, h) **1.** *v/i.* scrape (*mit den Füßen* one's feet); *hen*, etc.: scratch; *horse*: paw; **2.** *v/t. horse*: paw (*ground*).

Schart|e ['ʃartə] *f* (-/-n) notch, nick; *mountains*: gap, Am. notch; e-e ~ *auswetzen* repair a fault; wipe out a disgrace; '2ig *adj.* jagged, notchy.

Schatten ['ʃatən] *m* (-s/-) shadow (*a. fig.*); shade (*a. paint.*); '~bild *n* silhouette; '2haft *adj.* shadowy; '~kabinett *pol. n* shadow cabinet; '~riß *m* silhouette; '~seite *f* shady side; *fig.* seamy side.

schattier|en [ʃa'tiːrən] *v/t.* (*no* -ge-, h) shade, tint; 2ung *f* (-/-en) shading; shade (*a. fig.*), tint.

schattig *adj.* shady.

Schatz [ʃats] *m* (-es/⁺e) treasure; *fig.* sweetheart, darling; '~amt ✝ *n* Exchequer, Am. Treasury (Department); '~anweisung ✝ *f* Treasury Bond, Am. a. Treasury Note.

schätzen ['ʃɛtsən] *v/t.* (ge-, h) estimate; value (*auf acc.* at); price (at); rate; appreciate; esteem; *sich glücklich ~ zu inf.* be delighted to *inf.*; '~swert *adj.* estimable.

Schatz|kammer *f* treasury; '~meister *m* treasurer.

Schätzung *f* **1.** (-/-en) estimate, valuation; rating; **2.** (-/no pl.) appreciation, estimation; esteem.

Schatzwechsel ✝ *m* Treasury Bill.

Schau [ʃau] *f* (-/-en) inspection, show, exhibition; *zur* ~ *stellen* exhibit, display.

Schauder ['ʃaudər] *m* (-s/-) shudder(ing), shiver, tremor; *fig.* horror, terror; '2haft *adj.* horrible, dreadful; F *fig. a.* awful; '2n *v/i.* (ge-, h) shudder, shiver (*both: vor dat.* at).

schauen ['ʃauən] *v/i.* (ge-, h) look (*auf acc.* at).

Schauer ['ʃauər] *m* (-s/-) rain, etc.: shower (*a. fig.*); shudder(ing); shiver; attack, fit; thrill; '2lich *adj.* dreadful, horrible; '2n *v/i.* (ge-, h) *s. schaudern*; '~roman *m* penny dreadful, thriller.

Schaufel ['ʃaufəl] *f* (-/-n) shovel;

dust-pan; '2n *v/t. and v/i.* (ge-, h) shovel.

Schaufenster *n* shop window, Am. a. show-window; '~bummel *m*: e-n ~ *machen* go window-shopping; '~dekoration *f* window-dressing; '~einbruch *m* smash-and-grab raid.

Schaukel ['ʃaukəl] *f* (-/-n) swing; '2n (ge-, h) **1.** *v/i.* swing; *ship, etc.*: rock; **2.** *v/t.* rock (*baby, etc.*); '~pferd *n* rocking-horse; '~stuhl *m* rocking-chair, Am. a. rocker.

Schaum [ʃaum] *m* (-[e]s/⁺e) foam; *beer*, etc.: froth, head; *soap*: lather; '~bad *n* bubble bath.

schäumen ['ʃɔYmən] *v/i.* (ge-, h) foam, froth; lather; *wine*, etc.: sparkle.

Schaum|gummi *n, m* foam rubber; '2ig *adj.* foamy, frothy; '~wein *m* sparkling wine.

Schau|platz *m* scene (of action), theat|re, Am. -er; '~prozeß ✝✝ *m* show trial.

schaurig *adj.* ['ʃauriç] horrible, horrid.

Schau|spiel *n* spectacle; *thea.* play; '~spieler *m* actor, player; '~spielhaus *n* playhouse, theat|re, Am. -er; '~spielkunst *f* (-/no pl.) dramatic art, *the* drama; '~steller *m* (-s/-) showman.

Scheck ✝ [ʃɛk] *m* (-s/-s) cheque, Am. check; '~buch *n*, '~heft *n* cheque-book, Am. checkbook.

scheckig *adj.* spotted; *horse*: piebald.

scheel [ʃeːl] **1.** *adj.* squint-eyed, cross-eyed; *fig.* jealous, envious; **2.** *adv.*: *j-n* ~ *ansehen* look askance at s.o.

Scheffel ['ʃɛfəl] *m* (-s/-) bushel; '2n *v/t.* (ge-, h) amass (*money, etc.*).

Scheibe ['ʃaibə] *f* (-/-n) disk, disc (*a. of sun, moon*); *esp. ast.* orb; slice (*of bread, etc.*); pane (*of window*); *shooting*: target; '~nhonig *m* honey in combs; '~nwischer *mot. m* (-s/-) wind-screen wiper, Am. windshield wiper.

Scheide ['ʃaidə] *f* (-/-n) *sword, etc.*: sheath, scabbard; border, boundary; '~münze *f* small coin; '2n (*irr.*, ge-) **1.** *v/t.* (h) separate; ⚗ analyse; *łłł* divorce; *sich ~ lassen von łłł* divorce (*one's husband or wife*); **2.** *v/i.* (sein) depart; part (*von*

S

with); *aus dem Dienst* ~ retire from service; *aus dem Leben* ~ depart from this life; '**~wand** f partition; '**~weg** fig. m cross-roads sg.

'**Scheidung** f (-/-en) separation; ⚖ divorce; '**~sgrund** ⚖ m ground for divorce; '**~sklage** ⚖ f divorce-suit; *die* ~ *einreichen* file a petition for divorce.

Schein [ʃaɪn] m **1.** (-[e]s/no pl.) shine; sun, lamp, etc.: light; fire: blaze; fig. appearance; **2.** (-[e]s/-e) certificate; receipt; bill; (bank-)note; '**2bar** adj. seeming, apparent; '**2en** v/i. (irr., ge-, h) shine; fig. seem, appear, look; '**~grund** m pretext, preten|ce, Am. -se; '**2heilig** adj. sanctimonious, hypocritical; '**~tod** 𝄐 m suspended animation; '**2tot** adj. in a state of suspended animation; '**~werfer** m (-s/-) reflector, projector; ✕, ⚓, ✈ searchlight; mot. headlight; thea. spotlight.

Scheit [ʃaɪt] n (-[e]s/-e) log, billet.
Scheitel ['ʃaɪtəl] m (-s/-) crown or top of the head; hair: parting; summit, peak; esp. ᴀ vertex; '**2n** v/t. (ge-, h) part (hair).

Scheiterhaufen ['ʃaɪtər-] m (funeral) pile; stake.
'**scheitern** v/i. (ge-, sein) ⚓ run aground, be wrecked; fig. fail, miscarry.　　　　[box on the ear.]
Schelle ['ʃɛlə] f (-/-n) (little) bell;)
'**Schellfisch** ichth. m haddock.
Schelm [ʃɛlm] m (-[e]s/-e) rogue; '**~enstreich** m roguish trick; '**2isch** adj. roguish, arch.
Schelte ['ʃɛltə] f (-/-n) scolding; '**2n** (irr., ge-, h) **1.** v/t. scold, rebuke; **2.** v/i. scold.
Schema ['ʃeːma] n (-s/-s, -ta, Schemen) scheme; model, pattern; arrangement; **2tisch** adj. [ʃeˈmaːtiʃ] schematic.
Schemel ['ʃeːməl] m (-s/-) stool.
Schemen ['ʃeːmən] m (-s/-) phantom, shadow; '**2haft** adj. shadowy.
Schenke ['ʃɛŋkə] f (-/-n) public house, F pub; tavern, inn.
Schenkel ['ʃɛŋkəl] m (-s/-) anat. thigh; anat. shank; triangle, etc.: leg; ᴀ angle: side.
schenken ['ʃɛŋkən] v/t. (ge-, h) give; remit (penalty, etc.); j-m et. ~ give s.o. s.th., present s.o. with s.th., make s.o. a present of s.th.

'**Schenkung** ⚖ f (-/-en) donation; **~surkunde** ⚖ ['ʃɛŋkuŋs-] f deed of gift.
Scherbe ['ʃɛrbə] f (-/-n), '**~n** m (-s/-) (broken) piece, fragment.
Schere ['ʃeːrə] f (-/-n) (e-e pair of) scissors pl.; zo. crab, etc.: claw; '**2n** v/t. **1.** (irr., ge-, h) shear (a. sheep), clip; shave (beard); cut (hair); clip, prune (hedge); **2.** (ge-h): sich um et. ~ trouble about s.th.; '**~nschleifer** m (-s/-) knife-grinder; **~rei** [~'raɪ] f (-/-en) trouble, bother.
Scherz [ʃɛrts] m (-es/-e) jest, joke; ~ beiseite joking apart; im ~, zum ~ in jest or joke; ~ treiben mit make fun of; '**2en** v/i. (ge-, h) jest, joke; '**2haft** adj. joking, sportive.
scheu [ʃɔʏ] **1.** adj. shy, bashful, timid; horse: skittish; ~ machen frighten; **2.** 𝄐 f (-/no pl.) shyness; timidity; aversion (vor dat. to).
scheuchen ['ʃɔʏçən] v/t. (ge-, h) scare, frighten (away).
'**scheuen** (ge-, h) **1.** v/i. shy (vor dat. at), take fright (at); **2.** v/t. shun, avoid; fear; sich ~ vor (dat.) shy at, be afraid of.
Scheuer|lappen ['ʃɔʏər-] m scouring-cloth, floor-cloth; '**~leiste** f skirting-board; '**2n** (ge-, h) **1.** v/t. scour, scrub; chafe; **2.** v/i. chafe.
'**Scheuklappe** f blinker, Am. a. blinder.
Scheune ['ʃɔʏnə] f (-/-n) barn.
Scheusal ['ʃɔʏzaːl] n (-[e]s/-e) monster.
scheußlich ['ʃɔʏsliç] hideous, atrocious (F a. fig.), abominable (F a. fig.); '**2keit** f **1.** (-/no pl.) hideousness; **2.** (-/-en) abomination; atrocity.
Schi [ʃiː] m (-s/-er) etc. s. Ski, etc.
Schicht [ʃiçt] f (-/-en) layer; geol. stratum (a. fig.); at work: shift; (social) class, rank, walk of life; '**2en** v/t. (ge-, h) arrange or put in layers, pile up; classify; '**2weise** adv. in layers; work: in shifts.
Schick [ʃik] **1.** m (-[e]s/no pl.) chic, elegance, style; **2.** 𝄐 adj. chic, stylish, fashionable.
schicken ['ʃikən] v/t. (ge-, h) send (nach, zu to); remit (money); nach j-m ~ send for s.o.; sich ~ für become, suit, befit s.o.; sich ~ in put up with, resign o.s. to s.th.
'**schicklich** adj. becoming, proper,

seemly; '2**keit** f (-/no pl.) propriety, seemliness.

Schicksal n (-[e]s/-e) fate, destiny.

Schiebe|dach mot. ['ʃiːbə-] n sliding roof; '.**fenster** n sash-window; '2n (irr., ge-, h) 1. v/t. push, shove; shift (blame) (auf acc. on to); F fig. sell on the black market; 2. F fig. v/i. profiteer; '.**r** m (-s/-) bolt (of door); ⊕ slide; fig. profiteer, black marketeer, sl. spiv; '.**tür** f sliding door.

Schiebung fig. f (-/-en) black marketeering, profiteering; put-up job.

schied [ʃiːt] pret. of scheiden.

Schieds|gericht ['ʃiːts-] n court of arbitration, arbitration committee; '.**richter** m arbitrator; tennis, etc.: umpire; football, etc.: referee; '2**richterlich** adj. arbitral; '.**spruch** m award, arbitration.

schief [ʃiːf] 1. adj. sloping, slanting, oblique; face, mouth: wry; fig. false, wrong; ~e Ebene ⚛ inclined plane; 2. adv.: j-n ~ ansehen look askance at s.o.

Schiefer ['ʃiːfər] m (-s/-) slate; splinter; '.**stift** m slate-pencil; '.**tafel** f slate.

'**schiefgehen** v/i. (irr. gehen, sep., -ge-, sein) go wrong or awry.

schielen ['ʃiːlən] v/i. (ge-, h) squint, be cross-eyed; ~ auf (acc.) squint at; leer at.

schien [ʃiːn] pret. of scheinen.

Schienbein ['ʃiːn-] n shin(-bone), tibia.

Schiene ['ʃiːnə] f (-/-n) 🚃, etc.: rail; ⚕ splint; '2n ⚕ v/t. (ge-, h) splint.

schießen ['ʃiːsən] (irr. schießen, h) shoot; tot ~ shoot dead; ein Tor ~ score (a goal); Salut ~ fire a salute; 2. v/i. (h): auf j-n ~ shoot or fire at; gut ~ be a good shot; 3. v/i. (sein) shoot, dart, rush.

'**Schieß|pulver** n gunpowder; '.**scharte** ✕ f loop-hole, embrasure; '.**scheibe** f target; '.**stand** m shooting-gallery or -range.

Schiff [ʃif] n (-[e]s/-e) ⚓ ship, vessel; ⛪ church: nave.

Schiffahrt ['ʃiffaːrt] f (-/-en) navigation.

'**schiff|bar** adj. navigable; '2**bau** m shipbuilding; '2**bauer** m (-s/-) ship-

builder; '2**bruch** m shipwreck (a. fig.); ~ erleiden be shipwrecked; fig. make or suffer shipwreck; '.**brüchig** adj. shipwrecked; '2**brücke** f pontoon-bridge; '.**en** v/i. (ge-, sein) navigate, sail; '2**er** m (-s/-) sailor; boatman; navigator; skipper.

'**Schiffs|junge** m cabin-boy; '.**kapitän** m (sea-)captain; '.**ladung** f shipload; cargo; '.**makler** m shipbroker; '.**mannschaft** f crew; '.**raum** m hold; tonnage; '.**werft** f shipyard, esp. ✕ dockyard, Am. a. navy yard.

Schikan|e [ʃiˈkaːnə] f (-/-n) vexation, nasty trick; 2**ieren** [~kaˈniːrən] v/t. (no -ge-, h) vex, ride.

Schild [ʃilt] 1. ✕ m (-[e]s/-e) shield, buckler; 2. n (-[e]s/-er) shop, etc.: sign(board), facia; name-plate; traffic: signpost; label; cap: peak; '.**drüse** anat. f thyroid gland.

'**Schilder|haus** ✕ n sentry-box; '.**maler** m sign-painter; '2n v/t. (ge-, h) describe, delineate; '.**ung** f (-/-en) description, delineation.

'**Schild|kröte** zo. f tortoise; turtle; '.**wache** ✕ f sentinel, sentry.

Schilf 🌿 [ʃilf] n (-[e]s/-e) reed; '2**ig** adj. reedy; '.**rohr** n reed.

schillern ['ʃilərn] v/i. (ge-, h) show changing colo(u)rs; be iridescent.

Schimmel ['ʃiml] m 1. zo. (-s/-) white horse; 2. ♀ (-s/no pl.) mo(u)ld, mildew; '2**ig** adj. mo(u)ldy, musty; '2n v/i. (ge-, h) become mo(u)ldy, Am. a. mo(u)ld.

Schimmer ['ʃimər] m (-s/no pl.) glimmer, gleam (a. fig.); '2n v/i. (ge-, h) glimmer, gleam.

Schimpanse zo. [ʃimˈpanzə] m (-n/-n) chimpanzee.

Schimpf [ʃimpf] m (-[e]s/-e) insult, disgrace; mit ~ und Schande ignominiously; '2**en** (ge-, h) 1. v/i. rail (über acc., auf acc. at, against); 2. v/t. scold; j-n e-n Lügner ~ call s.o. a liar; 2**lich** adj. disgraceful (für to), ignominious (to); '.**name** m abusive name; '.**wort** n term of abuse; ~e pl. a. invectives pl.

Schindel ['ʃindəl] f (-/-n) shingle.

schinden ['ʃindən] v/t. (irr. ge-, h) flay, skin (rabbit, etc.); sweat (worker); sich ~ drudge, slave, sweat.

'**Schinder** m (-s/-) knacker; fig. sweater, slave-driver; '.**ei** fig. [~'raɪ]

S

f (-/-en) sweating; drudgery, grind.

Schinken ['ʃɪŋkən] *m* (-s/-) ham.

Schippe ['ʃɪpə] *f* (-/-n) shovel; '**2n** *v/t.* (ge-, h) shovel.

Schirm [ʃɪrm] *m* (-[e]s/-e) umbrella; parasol, sunshade; *wind, television, etc.*: screen; *lamp*: shade; *cap*: peak, visor; '**~futteral** *n* umbrella-case; '**~herr** *m* protector; patron; '**~herrschaft** *f* protectorate; patronage; *unter der ~ von event*: under the auspices of; '**~mütze** *f* peaked cap; '**~ständer** *m* umbrella-stand.

Schlacht ⚔ [ʃlaxt] *f* (-/-en) battle (*bei* of); '**~bank** *f* shambles; '**2en** *v/t.* (ge-, h) slaughter, butcher.

Schlächter ['ʃlɛçtər] *m* (-s/-) butcher.

'**Schlacht|feld** ⚔ *n* battle-field; '**~haus** *n*, '**~hof** *m* slaughter-house, abattoir; '**~kreuzer** ⚓ *m* battle-cruiser; '**~plan** *m* ⚔ plan of action (*a. fig.*); '**~schiff** ⚓ *n* battleship; '**~vieh** *n* slaughter cattle.

Schlack|e ['ʃlakə] *f* (-/-n) wood, coal: cinder; *metall.* dross (*a. fig.*); slag; *geol.* scoria; '**2ig** *adj.* drossy, slaggy; F *weather*: slushy.

Schlaf [ʃla:f] *m* (-[e]s/*no pl.*) sleep; *im ~e* in one's sleep; *e-n leichten (festen) ~ haben* be a light (sound) sleeper; *in tiefem ~e liegen* be fast asleep; '**~abteil** ⚓ *n* sleeping-compartment; '**~anzug** *m* (*ein a pair of*) pyjamas *pl. or Am.* pajamas *pl.*

Schläfchen ['ʃlɛːfçən] *n* (-s/-) doze, nap, F forty winks *pl.*; *ein ~ machen* take a nap, F have one's forty winks.

'**Schlafdecke** *f* blanket.

Schläfe ['ʃlɛːfə] *f* (-/-n) temple.

'**schlafen** *v/i.* (*irr.*, ge-, h) sleep; *~ gehen, sich ~ legen* go to bed.

schlaff *adj.* [ʃlaf] slack, loose; *muscles, etc.*: flabby, flaccid; *plant, etc.*: limp; *discipline, morals, etc.*: lax; '**2heit** *f* (-/*no pl.*) slackness; flabbiness; limpness; *fig.* laxity.

'**Schlaf|gelegenheit** *f* sleeping accommodation; '**~kammer** *f* bedroom; '**~krankheit** ⚕ *f* sleeping-sickness; '**~lied** *n* lullaby; '**2los** *adj.* sleepless; '**~losigkeit** *f* (-/*no pl.*) sleeplessness, ⚕ insomnia; '**~mittel** ⚕ *n* soporific; '**~mütze** *f* nightcap; *fig.* sleepyhead.

schläfrig *adj.* ['ʃlɛːfrɪç] sleepy, drowsy; '**2keit** *f* (-/*no pl.*) sleepiness, drowsiness.

'**Schlaf|rock** *m* dressing-gown, *Am. a.* robe; '**~saal** *m* dormitory; '**~sack** *m* sleeping-bag; '**~stelle** *f* sleeping-place; night's lodging; '**~tablette** ⚕ *f* sleeping-tablet; '**2trunken** *adj.* very drowsy; '**~wagen** ⚓ *m* sleeping-car(riage), *Am. a.* sleeper; '**~wandler** ['~vandlər] *m* (-s/-) sleep-walker, somnambulist; '**~zimmer** *n* bedroom.

Schlag [ʃlaːk] *m* (-[e]s/=e) blow (*a. fig.*); stroke (*of clock, piston*) (*a. tennis, etc.*); slap (*with palm of hand*); punch (*with fist*); kick (*of horse's hoof*); ⚡ shock; beat (*of heart or pulse*); clap (*of thunder*); warbling (*of bird*); door (*of carriage*); ⚕ apoplexy; *fig.* race, kind, sort; breed (*esp. of animals*); *Schläge bekommen get* a beating; *~ sechs Uhr* on the stroke of six; '**~ader** *anat. f* artery; '**~anfall** ⚕ *m* (stroke of) apoplexy, stroke; '**2artig 1.** *adj.* sudden, abrupt; **2.** *adv.* all of a sudden; '**~baum** *m* turnpike.

schlagen ['ʃlaːgən] (*irr.*, ge-, h) **1.** *v/t.* strike, beat, hit; punch; slap; beat, defeat; fell (*trees*); fight (*battle*); *Alarm ~* sound the alarm; *zu Boden ~* knock down; *in den Wind ~* cast *or* fling to the winds; *sich ~* (have a) fight; *sich et. aus dem Kopf or Sinn ~* put s.th. out of one's mind, dismiss s.th. from one's mind; **2.** *v/i.* strike, beat; *heart, pulse*: beat, throb; *clock*: strike; *bird*: warble; *das schlägt nicht in mein Fach* that is not in my line; *um sich ~* lay about one; '**~d** *fig. adj.* striking.

Schlager ['ʃlaːgər] *m* (-s/-) ♪ song hit; *thea.* hit, draw, box-office success; *book*: best seller.

Schläger ['ʃlɛːgər] *m* (-s/-) rowdy, hooligan; *cricket, etc.*: batsman; *horse*: kicker; *cricket, etc.*: bat; *golf*: club; *tennis, etc.*: racket; *hockey, etc.*: stick; '**~ei** [~'raɪ] *f* (-/-en) tussle, fight.

'**schlag|fertig** *fig. adj.* quick at repartee; '**~e Antwort** repartee; '**2fertigkeit** *fig. f* (-/*no pl.*) quickness at repartee; '**2instrument** ♪ *n* percussion instrument; '**2kraft** *f* (-/*no pl.*) striking power (*a.* ⚔); '**2loch** *n* pot-hole; '**2mann** *m* rowing: stroke; '**2ring** *m* knuckle-duster, *Am. a.* brass knuckles *pl.*;

'**2sahne** f whipped cream; '**2-schatten** m cast shadow; '**2seite** ⚓ f list; ~ haben ⚓ list; F fig. be half-seas-over; '**2uhr** f striking clock; '**2werk** n clock: striking mechanism; '**2wort** n catchword, slogan; '**2zeile** f headline; banner headline, Am. banner; '**2zeug** ♪ n in orchestra: percussion instruments pl.; in band: drums pl., percussion; '**2zeuger** ♪ m (-s/-) in orchestra: percussionist; in band: drummer.

schlaksig adj. ['ʃlaːksiç] gawky.

Schlamm [ʃlam] m (-[e]s/⸚-e, ⸚e) mud, mire; '**~bad** n mud-bath; '**2ig** adj. muddy, miry.

Schlämmkreide ['ʃlɛm-] f (-/no pl.) whit(en)ing.

Schlampe ['ʃlampə] f (-/-n) slut, slattern; '**2ig** adj. slovenly, slip-shod.

schlang [ʃlaŋ] pret. of schlingen.

Schlange ['ʃlaŋə] f (-/-n) zo. snake, rhet. serpent (a. fig.); fig.: snake in the grass; queue, Am. a. line; ~ stehen queue up (um for), Am. line up (for).

schlängeln ['ʃlɛŋəln] v/refl. (ge-, h): sich ~ durch person: worm one's way or o.s. through; path, river, etc.: wind (one's way) through, meander through.

'**Schlangenlinie** f serpentine line.

schlank adj. [ʃlaŋk] slender, slim; '**2heit** f (-/no pl.) slenderness, slimness; '**2heitskur** f: e-e ~ machen slim.

schlapp F adj. [ʃlap] tired, exhausted, worn out; '**2e** F f (-/-n) reverse, set-back; defeat; '**~machen** F v/i. (sep., -ge-, h) break down, faint.

schlau adj. [ʃlau] sly, cunning, crafty, clever, F cute.

Schlauch [ʃlaux] m (-[e]s/⸚e) tube; hose; car, etc.: inner tube; '**~boot** n rubber boat, pneumatic boat.

Schlaufe ['ʃlaufə] f (-/-n) loop.

schlecht [ʃlɛçt] 1. adj. bad; wicked; poor; temper: ill; quality: inferior; ~e Laune haben be in a bad temper; ~e Aussichten poor prospects; ~e Zeiten hard times; mir ist ~ I feel sick; 2. adv. badly, ill; ~erdings adv. ['~ʔərˈdiŋs] absolutely, down-right, utterly; ~**gelaunt** adj. ['~gəˈlaunt] ill-humo(u)red, in a bad temper; '**~hin** adv. plainly, simply; '**2igkeit** f (-/-en) badness; wicked-

ness; ~en pl. base acts pl., mean tricks pl.; '**~machen** v/t. (sep., -ge-, h) run down, backbite; ~**weg** adv. ['~vɛk] plainly, simply.

schleich|en ['ʃlaiçən] v/i. (irr., ge-, sein) creep (a. fig.); sneak, steal; '**2er** m (-s/-) creeper; fig. sneak; '**2handel** m illicit trade; smuggling, contraband; '**2händler** m smuggler, contrabandist; black marketeer; '**2weg** m secret path.

Schleier ['ʃlaiər] m (-s/-) veil (a. fig.); mist: a. haze; den ~ nehmen take the veil; '**2haft** fig. adj. mysterious, inexplicable.

Schleife ['ʃlaifə] f (-/-n) loop (a. ⚡); slip-knot; bow; wreath: streamer; loop, horse-shoe bend.

'**schleif|en 1.** v/t. (irr., ge-, h) whet (knife, etc.); cut (glass, precious stones); polish (a. fig.); **2.** v/t. (ge-, h) ♪ slur; drag, trail; ✗ raze (fortress, etc.); **3.** v/i. (ge-, h) drag, trail; '**2stein** m grindstone, whetstone.

Schleim [ʃlaim] m (-[e]s/-e) slime; ⚕ mucus, phlegm; '**~haut** anat. f mucous membrane; '**2ig** adj. slimy (a. fig.); mucous.

schlemm|en ['ʃlɛmən] v/i. (ge-, h) feast, gormandize; '**2er** m (-s/-) glutton, gormandizer; **2erei** [~ˈrai] f (-/-en) feasting; gluttony.

schlen|dern ['ʃlɛndərn] v/i. (ge-, sein) stroll, saunter; **2drian** ['~driaːn] m (-[e]s/no pl.) jogtrot; beaten track.

schlenkern ['ʃlɛnkərn] (ge-, h) **1.** v/t. dangle, swing; **2.** v/i.: mit den Armen ~ swing one's arms.

Schlepp|dampfer ['ʃlɛp-] m steam tug, tug(boat); '**~e** f (-/-n) train (of woman's dress); '**2en** (ge-, h) **1.** v/t. carry with difficulty, haul, Am. F a. tote; ⚓, ⚡, mot. tow, haul; ⚓ tug; ✝ tout (customers); sich ~ drag o.s.; **2.** v/i. dress: drag, trail; '**2end** adj. speech: drawling; gait: shuffling; style: heavy; conversation, etc.: tedious; '**~er** ⚓ m (-s/-) steam tug, tug(boat); '**~tau** n tow(ing)-rope; ins ~ nehmen take in or on tow (a. fig.).

Schleuder ['ʃlɔydər] f (-/-n) sling, catapult (a. ⚡), Am. a. slingshot; spin drier; '**2n** (ge-, h) **1.** v/t. fling, hurl (a. fig.); sling, catapult (a. ⚡); spin-dry (washing); **2.** mot. v/i.

S

skid; '**~preis** ✝ *m* ruinous *or* give-away price; *zu* ~*en* dirt-cheap.

schleunig *adj.* ['ʃlɔyniç] prompt, speedy, quick.

Schleuse ['ʃlɔyzə] *f* (-/-n) lock, sluice; '**~n** *v/t.* (ge-, h) lock (*boat*) (up *or* down); *fig.* manœuvre, *Am.* maneuver.

schlich [ʃliç] *pret. of* schleichen.

schlicht *adj.* [ʃliçt] plain, simple; modest, unpretentious; *hair:* smooth, sleek; '**~en** *fig. v/t.* (ge-, h) settle, adjust; settle by arbitration; '**~er** *fig. m* (-s/-) mediator; arbitrator.

schlief [ʃli:f] *pret. of* schlafen.

schließ|en ['ʃli:sən] (*irr.*, ge-, h) **1.** *v/t.* shut, close; shut down (*factory, etc.*); shut up (*shop*); contract (*marriage*); conclude (*treaty, speech, etc.*); *parl.* close (*debate*); *in die Arme* ~ clasp in one's arms; *in sich* ~ comprise, include; *Freundschaft* ~ make friends (*mit* with); **2.** *v/i.* shut, close; *school:* break up; *aus et.* ~ *auf* (*acc.*) infer *or* conclude *s.th.* from s.th.; '**2fach** & *n* postoffice box; '**~lich** *adv.* finally, eventually; at last; after all.

Schliff [ʃlif] **1.** *m* (-[e]s/-e) polish (*a. fig.*); precious stones, glass: cut; **2.** ♀ *pret. of* schleifen 1.

schlimm [ʃlim] *adj.* bad; evil, wicked, nasty; serious; F ♣ bad, sore; ~*er* worse; *am* ~*sten*, *das* ♀*ste* the worst; *es wird immer* ~*er* things are going from bad to worse; **2.** *adv.:* ~ *daran sein* be badly off; '**~sten'falls** *adv.* at (the) worst.

Schling|e ['ʃliŋə] *f* (-/-n) loop, sling (*a.* ♣); noose; coil (*of wire or rope*); *hunt.* snare (*a. fig.*); *den Kopf in die* ~ *stecken* put one's head in the noose; '**~el** *m* (-s/-) rascal, naughty boy; '**2en** *v/t.* (*irr.*, ge-, h) wind, twist; plait; *die Arme* ~ *um* (*acc.*) fling one's arms round; *sich um et.* ~ wind round; '**~pflanze** ⚘ *f* creeper, climber.

Schlips [ʃlips] *m* (-es/-e) (neck)tie.

Schlitten ['ʃlitən] *m* (-s/-) sled(ge); sleigh; *sports:* toboggan.

'**Schlittschuh** *m* skate; ~ *laufen* skate; '**~läufer** *m* skater.

Schlitz [ʃlits] *m* (-es/-e) slit, slash; slot; '**2en** *v/t.* (ge-, h) slit, slash.

Schloß [ʃlɔs] **1.** *n* (*Schlosses/Schlös-*

ser) lock (*of door, gun, etc.*); castle, palace; *ins* ~ *fallen door:* snap to; *hinter* ~ *und Riegel* behind prison bars; **2.** ♀ *pret. of* schließen.

Schlosser ['ʃlɔsər] *m* (-s/-) locksmith; mechanic, fitter.

Schlot [ʃlo:t] *m* (-[e]s/-e, ⁼e) chimney; flue; ♣, ♒ funnel; '**~feger** *m* (-s/-) chimney-sweep(er).

schlotter|ig ['ʃlɔtəriç] *adj.* shaky, tottery; loose; *garment:* hang loosely; *p.* shake, tremble (*both: vor dat.* with).

Schlucht [ʃluxt] *f* (-/-en) gorge, mountain cleft; ravine, *Am. a.* gulch.

schluchzen ['ʃluxtsən] *v/i.* (ge-, h) sob.

Schluck [ʃluk] *m* (-[e]s/-e, ⁼e) draught, swallow; mouthful, sip; '**~auf** *m* (-s/*no pl.*) hiccup(s *pl.*).

'**schlucken 1.** *v/t. and v/i.* (ge-, h) swallow (*a. fig.*); **2.** ♀ *m* (-s/*no pl.*) hiccup(s *pl.*).

schlug [ʃlu:k] *pret. of* schlagen.

Schlummer ['ʃlumər] *m* (-s/*no pl.*) slumber; '**2n** *v/i.* (ge-, h) slumber.

Schlund [ʃlunt] *m* (-[e]s/⁼e) *anat.* pharynx; *fig.* abyss, chasm, gulf.

schlüpf|en ['ʃlypfən] *v/i.* (ge-, sein) slip, slide; *in die Kleider* ~ slip on one's clothes; *aus den Kleidern* ~ slip out of *or* slip off one's clothes; '**2er** *m* (-s/-) (*ein a pair of*) knickers *pl. or* drawers *pl. or* F panties *pl.*; briefs *pl.*

Schlupfloch ['ʃlupf-] *n* loop-hole.

'**schlüpfrig** *adj.* slippery; *fig.* lascivious.

'**Schlupfwinkel** *m* hiding-place.

schlurfen ['ʃlurfən] *v/i.* (ge-, sein) shuffle, drag one's feet.

schlürfen ['ʃlyrfən] *v/t. and v/i.* (ge-, h) drink *or* eat noisily; sip.

Schluß [ʃlus] *m* (*Schlusses/Schlüsse*) close, end; conclusion; *parl.* closing (*of debate*).

Schlüssel ['ʃlysəl] *m* (-s/-) key (*zu* of; *fig.* to); ♪ clef; *fig.:* code; quota; '**~bart** *m* key-bit; '**~bein** *anat. n* collar-bone, clavicle; '**~bund** *m, n* (-[e]s/-e) bunch of keys; '**~industrie** *fig. f* key industry; '**~loch** *n* keyhole; '**~ring** *m* key-ring.

'**Schluß|folgerung** *f* conclusion, inference; '**~formel** *f in letter:* complimentary close.

schlüssig *adj.* ['ʃlysiç] *evidence:*

conclusive; sich ~ werden make up one's mind (über acc. about).

'Schluß|licht n 🚗, mot., etc.: taillight; sports: last runner; bottom club; '~runde f sports: final; '~schein † m contract-note.

Schmach [ʃmaːx] f (-/no pl.) disgrace; insult; humiliation.

schmachten ['ʃmaxtən] v/i. (ge-, h) languish (nach for), pine (for).

schmächtig adj. ['ʃmɛçtiç] slender, slim; ein ~er Junge a (mere) slip of a boy.   [miliating.]

'schmachvoll adj. disgraceful; hu-|

schmackhaft adj. ['ʃmakhaft] palatable, savo(u)ry.

schmäh|en ['ʃmɛːən] v/t. (ge-, h) abuse, revile; decry, disparage; slander, defame; '~lich adj. ignominious, disgraceful; '2schrift f libel, lampoon; '2ung f (-/-en) abuse; slander, defamation.

schmal adj. [ʃmaːl] narrow; figure: slender, slim; face: thin; fig. poor, scanty.

schmäler|n ['ʃmɛːlərn] v/t. (ge-, h) curtail; impair; belittle; '2ung f (-/-en) curtailment; impairment; detraction.

'Schmal|film phot. m substandard film; '~spur 🚗 f narrow-ga(u)ge; '~spurbahn 🚗 f narrow-ga(u)ge railway; '2spurig 🚗 adj. narrow-ga(u)ge.

Schmalz [ʃmalts] n (-es/-e) grease; lard; '2ig adj. greasy; lardy; F fig. soppy, sentimental.

schmarotz|en [ʃmaˈrɔtsən] v/i. (no -ge-, h) sponge (bei on); '2er m (-s/-) 🐛, zo. parasite; fig. a. sponge.

Schmarre F ['ʃmarə] f (-/-n) slash, cut; scar.

Schmatz [ʃmats] m (-es/-e) smack, loud kiss; '2en v/i. (ge-, h) smack (mit den Lippen one's lips'); eat noisily.

Schmaus [ʃmaʊs] m (-es/-e feast, banquet; fig. treat; 2en ['~zən] v/i. (ge-, h) feast, banquet.

schmecken ['ʃmɛkən] (ge-, h) 1. v/t. taste, sample; 2. v/i.: ~ nach taste or smack of (both a. fig.); dieser Wein schmeckt mir I like or enjoy this wine.

Schmeichel|ei [ʃmaɪçəˈlaɪ] f (-/-en) flattery; cajolery; '2haft adj. flattering; '2n v/i. (ge-, h): j-m ~ flatter s.o.; cajole s.o.

Schmeichler ['ʃmaɪçlər] m (-s/-) flatterer; '2isch adj. flattering; cajoling.

schmeiß|en F ['ʃmaɪsən] (irr., ge-, h) 1. v/t. throw, fling, hurl; slam, bang (door); 2. v/i.: mit Geld um sich ~ squander one's money; '2fliege zo. f blowfly, bluebottle.

Schmelz [ʃmɛlts] m 1. (-es/-e) enamel; 2. fig. (-es/no pl.) bloom; ♪ sweetness, mellowness; '2en (irr., ge-) 1. v/i. (sein) melt (a. fig.); liquefy; fig. melt away, dwindle; 2. v/t. (h) melt; smelt, fuse (ore, etc.); liquefy; '~erei [~ˈraɪ] f (-/-en), '~hütte f foundry; '~ofen m smelting furnace; '~tiegel m melting-pot, crucible.

Schmerbauch ['ʃmeːr-] m paunch, pot-belly, F corporation, Am. sl. a. bay window.

Schmerz [ʃmerts] m (-es/-en) pain (a. fig.); ache; fig. grief, sorrow; '2en (ge-, h) 1. v/i. pain (a. fig.), hurt; ache; 2. v/t. pain (a. fig.); hurt; fig. grieve, afflict; '2haft adj. painful; '2lich adj. painful, grievous; '2lindernd adj. soothing; '2los adj. painless.

Schmetter|ling zo. ['ʃmetərlɪŋ] m (-s/-e) butterfly; '2n (ge-, h) 1. v/t. dash (zu Boden to the ground; in Stücke to pieces); 2. v/i. crash; trumpet, etc.: bray, blare; bird: warble.

Schmied [ʃmiːt] m (-[e]s/-e) (black-)smith; ~e ['~də] f (-/-n) forge, smithy; '~eeisen ['~ʔaɪzən] n wrought iron; '~ehammer m sledge(-hammer); 2en ['~dən] v/t. (ge-, h) forge; make, devise, hatch (plans).

schmiegen ['ʃmiːgən] v/refl. (ge-, h) nestle (an to; an acc. to).

schmiegsam adj. ['ʃmiːkzaːm] pliant, flexible; supple (a. fig.); '2keit f (-/no pl.) pliancy, flexibility; suppleness (a. fig.).

Schmier|e ['ʃmiːrə] f (-/-n) grease; thea. contp. troop of strolling players, sl. penny gaff; '2en v/t. (ge-, h) smear; ⊕ grease, oil, lubricate; butter (bread); spread (butter, etc.); scrawl, scribble; painter: daub; ~enkomödiant ['~kɔmədjant] m (-en/-en) strolling actor, barnstormer, sl. ham (actor); ~erei [~ˈraɪ] f (-/-en) scrawl; paint. daub; '2ig adj. greasy; dirty; fig.: filthy;

F smarmy; '~**mittel** ⊕ *n* lubricant.

Schminke ['ʃmɪŋkə] *f* (-/-n) make-up (*a. thea.*), paint; rouge; *thea.* grease-paint; '**2en** *v/t. and v/refl.* (ge-, h) paint, make up; rouge (o.s.); put on lipstick.

Schmirgel ['ʃmɪrgəl] *m* (-s/*no pl.*) emery; '**2n** *v/t.* (ge-, h) (rub with) emery; '~**papier** *n* emery-paper.

Schmiß [ʃmɪs] **1.** *m* (*Schmisses/ Schmisse*) gash, cut; (duelling-) scar; **2.** F *m* (*Schmisses/no pl.*) verve, go, *Am. sl. a.* pep; **3.** 2 *pret. of* schmeißen.

schmollen ['ʃmɔlən] *v/i.* (ge-, h) sulk, pout; '**2winkel** *m* sulking-corner.

schmolz [ʃmɔlts] *pret. of* schmelzen.

Schmor|braten ['ʃmoːr-] *m* stewed meat; '**2en** *v/t. and v/i.* (ge-, h) stew (*a. fig.*).

Schmu·k [ʃmuk] **1.** *m* (-[e]s/*~-e*) ornament; decoration; jewel(le)ry, jewels *pl.*; **2.** 2 *adj.* neat, smart, spruce, trim.

schmücken ['ʃmykən] *v/t.* (ge-, h) adorn, trim; decorate.

'**schmuck|los** *adj.* unadorned; plain; '**2sachen** *f/pl.* jewel(le)ry, jewels *pl.*

Schmuggel ['ʃmugəl] *m* (-s/*no pl.*), **~ei** [~'laɪ] *f* (-/-en) smuggling; '**2n** *v/t. and v/i.* (ge-, h) smuggle; '**~ware** *f* contraband, smuggled goods *pl.* [smuggler.]

Schmuggler ['ʃmuglər] *m* (-s/-))

schmunzeln ['ʃmuntsəln] *v/i.* (ge-, h) smile amusedly.

Schmutz [ʃmuts] *m* (-es/*no pl.*) dirt; filth; *fig. a.* smut; '**2en** *v/i.* (ge-, h) soil, get dirty; '~**fink** *fig. m* mud-lark; '~**fleck** *m* smudge, stain; *fig.* blemish; '**2ig** *adj.* dirty; filthy; *fig. a.* mean, shabby.

Schnabel ['ʃnɑːbəl] *m* (-s/*~*) bill, *esp. bird of prey*: beak.

Schnalle ['ʃnalə] *f* (-/-n) buckle; '**2n** *v/t.* (ge-, h) buckle; strap.

schnalzen ['ʃnaltsən] *v/i.* (ge-, h): mit den Fingern *~* snap one's fingers; mit der Zunge *~* click one's tongue.

schnappen ['ʃnapən] (ge-, h) **1.** *v/i. lid, spring, etc.*: snap; *lock*: catch; nach et. *~* snap *or* snatch at; nach Luft *~* gasp for breath; **2.** F *v/t.* catch, *sl.* nab (*criminal*).

'**Schnapp|messer** *n* flick-knife; '~**schloß** *n* spring-lock; '~**schuß** *phot. m* snapshot.

Schnaps [ʃnaps] *m* (-es/*~e*) strong liquor, *Am.* hard liquor; brandy; ein (*Glas*) *~* a dram.

schnarch|en ['ʃnarçən] *v/i.* (ge-, h) snore; '**2er** *m* (-s/-) snorer.

schnarren ['ʃnarən] *v/i.* (ge-, h) rattle; jar.

schnattern ['ʃnatərn] *v/i.* (ge-, h) cackle; *fig. a.* chatter, gabble.

schnauben ['ʃnaubən] (ge-, h) **1.** *v/i.* snort; vor Wut *~* foam with rage; **2.** *v/t.*: sich die Nase *~* blow one's nose. [pant, puff, blow; wheeze.]

schnaufen ['ʃnaufən] *v/i.* (ge-, h))

Schnauz|bart ['ʃnauts-] *m* mo(u)s-tache; '~**e** *f* (-/-n) snout, muzzle; ⊕ nozzle; *teapot, etc.*: spout; *sl. fig.* potato-trap; '**2en** F *v/i.* (ge-, h) jaw.

Schnecke *zo.* ['ʃnɛkə] *f* (-/-n) snail; slug; '~**nhaus** *n* snail's shell; '~**ntempo** *n*: im *~* at a snail's pace.

Schnee [ʃneː] *m* (-s/*no pl.*) snow; '~**ball** *m* snowball; '~**ballschlacht** *f* pelting-match with snowballs; '**2bedeckt** *adj.* ['~bədɛkt] snow-covered, *mountain-top*: snow-capped; '**2blind** *adj.* snow-blind; '~**blindheit** *f* snow-blindness; '~**brille** *f* (e-e *a* pair of) snow-goggles *pl.*; '~**fall** *m* snow-fall; '~**flocke** *f* snow-flake; '~**gestöber** *n* (-s/-) snow-storm; '~**glöckchen** ♀ ['~glœkçən] *n* (-s/-) snowdrop; '~**grenze** *f* snow-line; '~**mann** *m* snow man; '~**pflug** *m* snow-plough, *Am.* snowplow; '~**schuh** *m* snow-shoe; '~**sturm** *m* snow-storm, blizzard; '~**wehe** *f* (-/-n) snow-drift; '**2weiß** *adj.* snow-white.

Schneid F [ʃnaɪt] *m* (-[e]s/*no pl.*) pluck, dash, *sl.* guts *pl.*

Schneide ['ʃnaɪdə] *f* (-/-n) edge; '~**mühle** *f* sawmill; '**2n** (*irr.*, ge-, h) **1.** *v/t.* cut; carve (*meat*); pare, clip (*finger-nails, etc.*); **2.** *v/i.* cut.

'**Schneider** *m* (-s/-) tailor; '~**ei** [~'raɪ] *f* **1.** (-/*no pl.*) tailoring; dress-making; **2.** (-/-en) tailor's shop; dressmaker's shop; '~**in** *f* (-/-nen) dressmaker; '~**meister** *m* master tailor; '**2n** (ge-, h) **1.** *v/i.* tailor; do tailoring; do dressmaking; **2.** *v/t.* make, tailor.

'**Schneidezahn** *m* incisor.

'**schneidig** *fig. adj.* plucky; dashing, keen; smart, *Am. sl. a.* nifty.

schneien ['ʃnaɪən] *v/i.* (ge-, h) snow.

S

schnell [ʃnɛl] 1. *adj.* quick, fast; rapid; swift, speedy; *reply, etc.*: prompt; sudden; 2. *adv.*: ~ **fahren** drive fast; ~ **handeln** act promptly *or* without delay; (*mach*) ~! be quick!, hurry up!

Schnelläufer ['ʃnɛlbʏfər] *m* sprinter; speed skater.

'**schnell|en** (ge-) *v/t.* (h) *and v/i.* (sein) jerk; '**2feuer** ⚔ *n* rapid fire; '**2hefter** *m* (-s/-) folder.

'**Schnelligkeit** *f* (-/*no pl.*) quickness, fastness; rapidity; swiftness; promptness; speed, velocity.

'**Schnell|imbiß** *m* snack (bar); '**~imbißstube** *f* snack bar; '**~kraft** *f* (-/*no pl.*) elasticity; '**~verfahren** *n* 🕱 summary proceeding; '**~**-high-speed process; '**~zug** 🚂 *m* fast train, express (train).

schneuzen ['ʃnɔʏtsən] *v/refl.* (ge-, h) blow one's nose.

schniegeln ['ʃniːɡəln] *v/refl.* (ge-, h) dress *or* smarten *or* spruce (o.s.) up.

Schnipp|chen ['ʃnɪpçən] *n*: F *j-m* **ein ~ schlagen** outwit *or* overreach s.o.; '**2isch** *adj.* pert, snappish, *Am.* F *a.* snippy.

Schnitt [ʃnɪt] 1. *m* (-[e]s/-e) cut; *dress, etc.*: cut, make, style; pattern; *book*: edge; 🖊 (inter)section; *fig.*: average; F profit; 2. ♀ *pret.* of **schneiden**; '**~blumen** *f/pl.* cut flowers *pl.*; '**~e** *f* (-/-en) slice; '**~er** *m* (-s/-) reaper, mower; '**~fläche** 🖊 *f* section(al plane); '**2ig** *adj.* streamline(d); '**~muster** *n* pattern; '**~punkt** *m* (point of) intersection; '**~wunde** *f* cut, gash.

Schnitzel ['ʃnɪtsəl] 1. *n* (-s/-) schnitzel; 2. F *n, m* (-s/-) chip; *paper*: scrap; ~ *pl.* ⊕ parings *pl.*, shavings *pl.*; *paper*: a. clippings *pl.*; '**2n** *v/t.* (ge-, h) chip, shred, whittle.

schnitzen ['ʃnɪtsən] *v/t.* (ge-, h) carve, cut (in wood).

'**Schnitzer** *m* (-s/-) carver; F *fig.* blunder, *Am. sl. a.* boner; '**~ei** [~'raɪ] *f* 1. (-/-en) carving, carved work; 2. (-/*no pl.*) carving.

schnöde *adj.* ['ʃnøːdə] contemptuous; disgraceful; base, vile; '**~r Mammon** filthy lucre.

Schnörkel ['ʃnœrkəl] *m* (-s/-) flourish (*a. fig.*), scroll (*a.* 🔺).

schnorr|en F ['ʃnɔrən] *v/t. and v/i.* (ge-, h) cadge; '**2er** *m* (-s/-) cadger.

schnüff|eln ['ʃnʏfəln] *v/i.* (ge-, h) sniff, nose (*both: an dat.* at); *fig.* nose about, *Am.* F *a.* snoop around; '**2ler** *fig. m* (-s/-) spy, *Am.* F *a.* snoop; F sleuth(-hound).

Schnuller ['ʃnʊlər] *m* (-s/-) dummy, comforter.

Schnulze F ['ʃnʊltsə] *f* (-/-n) sentimental song *or* film *or* play, F tear-jerker.

Schnupf|en ['ʃnʊpfən] 1. *m* (-s/-) cold, catarrh; 2. ♀ *v/i.* (ge-, h) take snuff; '**~er** *m* (-s/-) snuff-taker; '**~tabak** *m* snuff.

schnuppe F *adj.* ['ʃnʊpə]: *das ist mir* ~ I don't care (F a damn); '**2rn** *v/i.* (ge-, h) sniff, nose (*both: an dat.* at).

Schnur [ʃnuːr] *f* (-/-e, ⚡ -en) cord; string, twine; line; ⚡ flex.

Schnür|band ['ʃnyːr-] *n* lace; '**2chen** ['~çən] *n* (-s/-): *wie am* ~ like clockwork; '**2en** *v/t.* (ge-, h) lace (up); (bind with) cord, tie up.

'**schnurgerade** *adj.* dead straight.

Schnurr|bart ['ʃnʊr-] *m* m(o)ustache; '**2en** (ge-, h) 1. *v/i.* wheel, *etc.*: whir(r); *cat*: purr (*a. fig.*); F *fig.* cadge; 2. F *fig. v/t.* cadge.

Schnür|senkel ['ʃnyːrzɛŋkəl] *m* (-s/-) shoe-lace, shoe-string; '**~stiefel** *m* lace-boot.

schnurstracks *adv.* ['ʃnuːr'ʃtraks] direct, straight; on the spot, at once, *sl.* straight away.

schob [ʃoːp] *pret.* of **schieben**.

Schober ['ʃoːbər] *m* (-s/-) rick, stack.

Schock [ʃɔk] 1. *n* (-[e]s/-e) three-score; 2. ⚔ *m* (-[e]s/-s, ⚡ -e) shock; **2ieren** [~'kiːrən] *v/t.* (no -ge-, h) shock, scandalize.

Schokolade [ʃoko'laːdə] *f* (-/-n) chocolate.

scholl [ʃɔl] *pret.* of **schallen**.

Scholle ['ʃɔlə] *f* (-/-n) clod (*of earth*), *poet.* glebe; floe (*of ice*); *ichth.* plaice.

schon *adv.* [ʃoːn] already; ~ *lange* for a long time; ~ *gut!* all right!; ~ *der Gedanke* the very idea; ~ *der Name* the bare name; *hast du* ~ *einmal ...?* have you ever ...?; *mußt du* ~ *gehen?* need you go yet?; ~ *um 8 Uhr* as early as 8 o'clock.

schön [ʃøːn] 1. *adj.* beautiful; *man*: handsome (*a. fig.*); *weather*: fair, fine (*a. iro.*); *das* ~**e Geschlecht** the

fair sex; die ~en Künste the fine
arts; ~e Literatur belles-lettres *pl.*;
2. *adv.*: ~ warm nice and warm;
du hast mich ~ erschreckt you gave
me quite a start.

schonen ['ʃoːnən] *v/t.* (ge-, h) spare
(j-n *s.o.*; j-s Leben *s.o.'s* life); take
care of; husband (*strength, etc.*);
sich ~ take care of o.s., look after
o.s.

'**Schönheit** *f* 1. (-/*no pl.*) beauty;
of woman: a. pulchritude; 2. (-/-en)
beauty; beautiful woman, belle;
'**~spflege** *f* beauty treatment.

'**schöntun** *v/i.* (*irr.* tun, *sep.*, -ge-, h)
flatter (j-m *s.o.*); flirt (*dat.* with).

'**Schonung** *f* 1. (-/*no pl.*) mercy;
sparing, forbearance; careful treatment; 2. (-/-en) tree-nursery;
'**2slos** *adj.* unsparing, merciless,
relentless. [*a.* crest.]

Schopf [ʃɔpf] *m* (-[e]s/ᵘe) tuft; *orn.*]

schöpfen ['ʃœpfən] *v/t.* (ge-, h)
scoop, ladle; draw (*water at well*);
draw, take (*breath*); take (*courage*);
neue Hoffnung ~ gather fresh hope;
Verdacht ~ become suspicious.

'**Schöpf|er** *m* (-s/-) creator; '**2e-
risch** *adj.* creative; '**~ung** *f* (-/-en)
creation.

schor [ʃoːr] *pret. of* scheren.

Schorf 🗲 [ʃɔrf] *m* (-[e]s/-e) scurf;
scab, crust; '**2ig** *adj.* scurfy; scabby.

Schornstein ['ʃɔrn-] *m* chimney;
⚓, 🚂 funnel; '**~feger** *m* (-s/-)
chimney-sweep(er).

Schoß 1. [ʃoːs] *m* (-es/ᵘe) lap; womb;
coat: tail; 2. 2 [ʃɔs] *pret. of* schießen.

Schote ♀ ['ʃoːtə] *f* (-/-n) pod, husk.

Schott|e ['ʃɔtə] *m* (-n/-n) Scot,
Scotchman, Scotsman; die ~n *pl.*
the Scotch *pl.*; '**~er** *m* (-s/-) gravel;
(road-)metal; '**2isch** *adj.* Scotch,
Scottish.

schräg [ʃrɛːk] 1. *adj.* oblique, slanting; sloping; 2. *adv.*: ~ gegenüber
diagonally across (von from).

schrak [ʃraːk] *pret. of* schrecken 2.

Schramme ['ʃramə] *f* (-/-n) scratch;
skin: a. abrasion; '**2n** *v/t.* (ge-, h)
scratch; graze, abrade (*skin*).

Schrank [ʃraŋk] *m* (-[e]s/ᵘe) cupboard, *esp. Am.* closet; wardrobe.

'**Schranke** *f* (-/-n) barrier (*a. fig.*);
🚂 *a.* (railway-)gate; ⚖ bar; ~n *pl.*
fig. bounds *pl.*, limits *pl.*; '**2nlos**
fig. adj. boundless; unbridled; '**~n-
wärter** 🚂 *m* gate-keeper.

'**Schrankkoffer** *m* wardrobe trunk.

Schraube ['ʃraubə] *f* (-/-n) ⊕ screw;
⚓ screw(-propeller); '**2n** *v/t.* (ge-,
h) screw.

'**Schrauben|dampfer** ⚓ *m* screw
(steamer); '**~mutter** ⊕ *f* nut;
'**~schlüssel** ⊕ *m* spanner, wrench;
'**~zieher** ⊕ *m* screwdriver.

Schraubstock ⊕ ['ʃraup-] *m* vice,
Am. vise.

Schrebergarten ['ʃreːbər-] *m* allotment garden.

Schreck [ʃrɛk] *m* (-[e]s/-e) fright,
terror; consternation; '**~bild** *n*
bugbear; '**~en** *m* (-s/-) fright, terror;
consternation; '**2en** (ge-) 1. *v/t.* (h)
frighten, scare; 2. *v/i.* (*irr.*, sein):
only in compounds: '**~ensbotschaft**
f alarming *or* terrible news; '**~ens-
herrschaft** *f* reign of terror; '**2haft**
adj. fearful, timid; '**2lich** *adj.* terrible, dreadful (*both a.* F *fig.*);
'**~schuß** *m* scare shot; *fig.* warning
shot.

Schrei [ʃraɪ] *m* (-[e]s/-e) cry; shout;
scream.

schreiben ['ʃraɪbən] 1. *v/t. and v/i.*
(*irr.*, ge-, h) write (j-m to s.o.; über
acc. on); mit der Maschine ~
type(write); 2. *v/t.* (*irr.*, ge-, h)
spell; 3. 2 *n* (-s/-) letter.

'**Schreiber** *m* (-s/-) writer; secretary, clerk.

schreib|faul *adj.* ['ʃraɪp-] lazy in
writing; '**2feder** *f* pen; '**2fehler** *m*
mistake in writing *or* spelling; slip
of the pen; '**2heft** *n* exercise-book;
'**2mappe** *f* writing-case; '**2ma-
schine** *f* typewriter; (mit der) ~
schreiben type(write); '**2material**
n writing-materials *pl.*, stationery;
'**2papier** *n* writing-paper; '**2-
schrift** *typ. f* script; '**2tisch** *m*
(writing-)desk; **2ung** ['ʃbuŋ] *f*
(-/-en) spelling; '**2unterlage** *f*
desk pad; '**2waren** *f/pl.* writing-
materials *pl.*, stationery; '**2waren-
händler** *m* stationer; '**2zeug** *n*
writing-materials *pl.*

'**schreien** (*irr.*, ge-, h) 1. *v/t.* shout;
scream; 2. *v/i.* cry (out) (vor *dat.*
with *pain, etc.*; nach for *bread,
etc.*); shout (vor with); scream
(with); '**~d** *adj. colour:* loud; *injustice:* flagrant.

schreiten ['ʃraɪtən] *v/i.* (*irr.*, ge-,
sein) step, stride (über *acc.* across);
fig. proceed (zu to).

schrie [ʃriː] *pret. of* schreien.

schrieb [ʃriːp] *pret. of* schreiben.

Schrift [ʃrift] *f* (-/-en) (hand-)writing, hand; *typ.* type; character, letter; writing; publication; *die Heilige* ~ the (Holy) Scriptures *pl.*; **~art** *f* type; **2deutsch** *adj.* literary German; **~führer** *m* secretary; **~leiter** *m* editor; **2lich 1.** *adj.* written, in writing; **2.** *adv.* in writing; **~satz** *m* ᵗᵗ pleadings *pl.*; *typ.* composition, type-setting; **~setzer** *m* compositor, type-setter; **~sprache** *f* literary language; **~steller** *m* (-s/-) author, writer; **~stück** *n* piece of writing, paper, document; **~tum** *n* (-s/*no pl.*) literature; **~wechsel** *m* exchange of letters, correspondence; **~zeichen** *n* character, letter.

schrill *adj.* [ʃril] shrill, piercing.

Schritt [ʃrit] **1.** *m* (-[e]s/-e) step (*a. fig.*); pace (*a. fig.*); ~e *unternehmen* take steps; **2.** 2 *pret. of* schreiten; **~macher** *m* (-s/-) *sports:* pace-maker; **2weise 1.** *adj.* gradual; **2.** *adv. a.* step by step.

schroff *adj.* [ʃrɔf] rugged, jagged; steep, precipitous; *fig.* harsh, gruff; **~er** *Widerspruch* glaring contradiction.

schröpfen ['ʃrœpfən] *v/t.* (ge-, h) cup; *fig.* milk, fleece.

Schrot [ʃroːt] *m, n* (-[e]s/-e) crushed grain; small shot; **~brot** *n* wholemeal bread; **~flinte** *f* shotgun.

Schrott [ʃrɔt] *m* (-[e]s/-e) scrap (-iron *or* -metal).

schrubben ['ʃrubən] *v/t.* (ge-, h) scrub.

Schrulle ['ʃrulə] *f* (-/-n) whim, fad.

schrumpf|en ['ʃrumpfən] *v/i.* (ge-, sein) shrink (*a.* ⊕, ⚕, *fig.*); **2ung** *f* (-/-en) shrinking; shrinkage.

Schub [ʃuːp] *m* (-[e]s/⁼e) push, shove; *phys.*, ⊕ thrust; *bread, people, etc.:* batch; **~fach** *n* drawer; **~karren** *m* wheelbarrow; **~kasten** *m* drawer; **~kraft** *phys.*, ⊕ *f* thrust; **~lade** *f* (-/-n) drawer.

Schubs F [ʃups] *m* (-es/-e) push; **2en** F *v/t.* (ge-, h) push.

schüchtern *adj.* ['ʃүçtərn] shy, bashful, timid; *girl:* coy; **2heit** *f* (-/*no pl.*) shyness, bashfulness, timidity; coyness (*of girl*).

schuf [ʃuːf] *pret. of* schaffen 1.

Schuft [ʃuft] *m* (-[e]s/-e) scoundrel,

rascal; cad; **2en** F *v/i.* (ge-, h) drudge, slave, plod; **2ig** *adj.* scoundrelly, rascally; caddish.

Schuh [ʃuː] *m* (-[e]s/-e) shoe; *j-m et. in die* ~e *schieben* put the blame for s.th. on s.o.; *wissen, wo der* ~ *drückt* know where the shoe pinches ~; **~anzieher** *m* (-s/-) shoehorn; **~band** *n* shoe-lace *or* -string; **~creme** *f* shoe-cream, shoe-polish; **~geschäft** *n* shoe-shop; **~löffel** *m* shoehorn; **~macher** *m* (-s/-) shoemaker; **~putzer** *m* (-s/-) shoeblack, *Am.* ~ shoeshine; **~sohle** *f* sole; **~spanner** *m* (-s/-) shoetree; **~werk** *n*, **~zeug** F *n* foot-wear, boots and shoes *pl.*

Schul|amt *n* school-board; **~arbeit** *f* homework; **~bank** *f* (school-)desk; **~beispiel** *n* test-case, typical example; **~besuch** *m* (-[e]s/*no pl.*) attendance at school; **~bildung** *f* education; *höhere* ~ secondary education; **~buch** *n* school-book.

Schuld [ʃult] *f* **1.** (-/*no pl.*) guilt; fault, blame; *es ist s-e* ~ *it is his fault, he is to blame for it;* **2.** (-/-en) debt; ~en *machen* contract *or* incur debts; **2bewußt** *adj.* conscious of one's guilt; **2en** ['ʃuldən] *v/t.* (ge-, h): *j-m et.* ~ owe s.o. s.th.; *j-m Dank* ~ be indebted to s.o. (*für* for); **2haft** *adj.* ['~thaft] culpable.

'**Schuldiener** *m* school attendant *or* porter.

schuldig *adj.* ['ʃuldiç] guilty (*e-r Sache of* s.th.); *respect, etc.:* due; *j-m et.* ~ *sein* owe s.o. s.th.; *Dank* ~ *sein* be indebted to s.o. (*für* for); *für* ~ *befinden* ᵗᵗ find guilty; **2e** ['~gə] *m, f* (-n/-n) guilty person; culprit; **2keit** *f* (-/*no pl.*) duty, obligation.

'**Schuldirektor** *m* headmaster, *Am. a.* principal.

'**schuld|los** *adj.* guiltless, innocent; **2losigkeit** *f* (-/*no pl.*) guiltlessness, innocence; **2ner** ['~dnər] *m* (-s/-) debtor; **2schein** *m* evidence of debt, certificate of indebtedness, IOU (= I owe you); **2verschreibung** *f* bond, debt certificate.

Schule ['ʃuːlə] *f* (-/-n) school; *höhere* ~ secondary school, *Am. a.* high school; *auf or in der* ~ at school; *in die* ~ *gehen* go to school; **2n** *v/t.* (ge-, h) train, school; *pol.* indoctrinate.

Schüler ['ʃyːlər] *m* (-s/-) schoolboy; pupil; *phls., etc.*: disciple; '**~austausch** *m* exchange of pupils; '**~in** *f* (-/-nen) schoolgirl.

'**Schul|ferien** *pl.* holidays *pl.*, vacation; '**~fernsehen** *n* educational TV; '**~funk** *m* educational broadcast; '**~gebäude** *n* school(house); '**~geld** *n* school fee(s *pl.*), tuition; '**~hof** *m* playground, *Am. a.* schoolyard; '**~kamerad** *m* schoolfellow; '**~lehrer** *m* schoolmaster, teacher; '**~mappe** *f* satchel; **Ꝩmeistern** *v/t.* (ge-, h) censure pedantically; '**~ordnung** *f* school regulations *pl.*; **Ꝩpflichtig** *adj.* schoolable; '**~rat** *m* supervisor of schools, school inspector; '**~schiff** *n* training-ship; '**~schluß** *m* end of school; end of term; '**~schwänzer** *m* (-s/-) truant; '**~stunde** *f* lesson.

Schulter ['ʃultər] *f* (-/-n) shoulder; '**~blatt** *anat. n* shoulder-blade; **Ꝩn** *v/t.* (ge-, h) shoulder.

'**Schul|unterricht** *m* school, lessons *pl.*; school instruction; '**~versäumnis** *f* (-/no *pl.*) absence from school; '**~wesen** *n* educational system; '**~zeugnis** *n* report.

schummeln F ['ʃuməln] *v/i.* (ge-, h) cheat, *Am.* F *a.* chisel.

Schund [ʃunt] **1.** *m* (-[e]s/no *pl.*) trash, rubbish (*both a. fig.*); **2.** Ꝩ *pret. of* schinden; '**~literatur** *f* trashy literature; '**~roman** *m* trashy novel, *Am. a.* dime novel.

Schupp|e ['ʃupə] *f* (-/-n) scale; *~n pl.* on head: dandruff; '**~en 1.** *m* (-s/-) shed; *mot.* garage; **Ꝩ** hangar; **2.** Ꝩ *v/t.* (ge-, h) scale (*fish*); *sich ~ skin:* scale off; **Ꝩig** *adj.* scaly.

Schür|eisen ['ʃyːr²-] *n* poker; **Ꝩen** *v/t.* (ge-, h) poke; stoke; *fig.* fan, foment.

schürfen ['ʃyrfən] (ge-, h) **1.** Ꝩ *v/i.* prospect (*nach* for); **2.** *v/t.* Ꝩ prospect for; *sich den Arm ~* graze one's arm.

Schurk|e ['ʃurkə] *m* (-n/-n) scoundrel, knave; **~erei** [~'raɪ] *f* (-/-en) rascality, knavish trick; **Ꝩisch** *adj.* scoundrelly, knavish.

Schürze ['ʃyrtsə] *f* (-/-n) apron; *children:* pinafore; **Ꝩn** *v/t.* (ge-, h) tuck up (*skirt*); tie (*knot*); purse (*lips*); '**~njäger** *m* skirt-chaser, *Am. sl.* wolf.

Schuß [ʃus] *m* (Schusses/Schüsse) shot (*a. sports*); *ammunition:* round; *sound:* report; charge; *wine, etc.:* dash (*a. fig.*); *in ~ sein* be in full swing, be in full working order.

Schüssel ['ʃysəl] *f* (-/-n) basin (*for water, etc.*); bowl, dish, tureen (*for soup, vegetables, etc.*).

'**Schuß|waffe** *f* fire-arm; '**~weite** *f* range; '**~wunde** *f* gunshot wound.

Schuster ['ʃuːstər] *m* (-s/-) shoemaker; **Ꝩn** *fig. v/i.* (ge-, h) *s. pfuschen.*

Schutt [ʃut] *m* (-[e]s/no *pl.*) rubbish, refuse; rubble, debris.

Schüttel|frost **Ꝩ** ['ʃytəl-] *m* shivering-fit; **Ꝩn** *v/t.* (ge-, h) shake; *den Kopf ~* shake one's head; *j-m die Hand ~* shake hands with s.o.

schütten ['ʃytən] (ge-, h) **1.** *v/t.* pour; spill (*auf acc.* on); **2.** *v/i.*: *es schüttet* it is pouring with rain.

Schutz [ʃuts] *m* (-es/no *pl.*) protection (*gegen, vor dat.* against), defen|ce, *Am.* -se (against, from); shelter (from); safeguard; cover; '**~brille** *f* (-e *e a* pair of) goggles *pl.*

Schütze ['ʃytsə] *m* (-n/-n) marksman, shot; Ꝩ rifleman; **Ꝩn** *v/t.* (ge-, h) protect (*gegen, vor dat.* against, from), defend (against, from), guard (against, from); shelter (from); safeguard (*rights, etc.*).

Schutzengel ['ʃuts²-] *m* guardian angel.

'**Schützen|graben** Ꝩ *m* trench; '**~könig** *m* champion shot.

'**Schutz|haft** *ꝩ f* protective custody; '**~heilige** *m* patron saint; '**~herr** *m* patron, protector; '**~impfung** *ꝩ f* protective inoculation; smallpox: vaccination.

Schützling ['ʃytsliŋ] *m* (-s/-e) protégé, *female:* protégée.

'**schutz|los** *adj.* unprotected; defen|celess, *Am.* -seless; '**Ꝩmann** *m* (-[e]s/=er, *Schutzleute*) policeman, (police) constable, *sl.* bobby, *sl.* cop; '**Ꝩmarke** *f* trade mark, brand; '**Ꝩmittel** *n* preservative; *ꝩ* prophylactic; '**Ꝩpatron** *m* patron saint; '**Ꝩumschlag** *m* (dust-)jacket, wrapper; '**~zoll** *m* protective duty.

Schwabe ['ʃvaːbə] *m* (-n/-n) Swabian.

schwäbisch *adj.* ['ʃvɛːbiʃ] Swabian.

schwach [ʃvax] *resistance, team, knees* (*a. fig.*), *eyes, heart, voice, character, tea, gr. verb,* ꝩ *demand,* *etc.*: weak; *person, etc.*: infirm; *person, recollection, etc.*: feeble; *sound, light, hope, idea, etc.*: faint; *consolation, attendance, etc.*: poor; *light, recollection, etc.*: dim; *resemblance*: remote; *das ~e Geschlecht* the weaker sex; *~e Seite* weak point or side.

Schwäche ['ʃvɛçə] *f* (-/-n) weakness (*a. fig.*); infirmity; *fig.* foible; *e-e ~ haben für* have a weakness for; '**2n** *v/t.* (ge-, h) weaken (*a. fig.*); impair (*health*).

'**Schwach|heit** *f* (-/-en) weakness; *fig. a.* frailty; '**~kopf** *m* simpleton, soft(y), *Am.* F *a.* sap(head); **2köpfig** *adj.* ['~kœpfiç] weak-headed, soft, *Am. sl. a.* sappy.

schwäch|lich *adj.* ['ʃvɛçlıç] weakly, feeble; delicate, frail; '**2ling** *m* (-s/-e) weakling (*a. fig.*).

'**schwach|sinnig** *adj.* weak- or feeble-minded; '**2strom** ⚡ *m* (-[e]s/*no pl.*) weak current.

Schwadron ⚔ [ʃva'droːn] *f* (-/-en) squadron; **2ieren** [~o'niːrən] *v/i.* (*no* -ge-, h) swagger, vapo(u)r.

Schwager ['ʃvaːgər] *m* (-s/⁼) brother-in-law.

Schwägerin ['ʃvɛːgərın] *f* (-/-nen) sister-in-law.　　　　[swallow.]

Schwalbe *orn.* ['ʃvalbə] *f* (-/-n)|

Schwall [ʃval] *m* (-[e]s/-e) swell, flood; *words*: torrent.

Schwamm [ʃvam] **1.** *m* (-[e]s/⁼e) sponge; ⚘ fungus; ⚘ dry-rot; **2.** ⚘ *pret. of* schwimmen; '**2ig** *adj.* spongy; *face, etc.*: bloated.

Schwan *orn.* [ʃvaːn] *m* (-[e]s/⁼e) swan.

schwand [ʃvant] *pret. of* schwinden.

schwang [ʃvaŋ] *pret. of* schwingen.

schwanger *adj.* ['ʃvaŋər] pregnant, with child, in the family way.

schwängern ['ʃvɛŋərn] *v/t.* (ge-, h) get with child, impregnate (*a. fig.*).

'**Schwangerschaft** *f* (-/-en) pregnancy.

schwanken ['ʃvaŋkən] *v/i.* (ge-) **1.** (h) *earth, etc.*: shake, rock; ⚘ *prices*: fluctuate; *branches, etc.*: sway; *fig.* waver, oscillate, vacillate; **2.** (sein) stagger, totter.

Schwanz [ʃvants] *m* (-es/⁼e) tail (*a.* ⚘, *ast.*); *fig.* train.

schwänz|eln ['ʃvɛntsəln] *v/i.* (ge-, h) wag one's tail; *fig.* fawn (*um* [up]on); '**~en** *v/t.* (ge-, h) cut (*lecture, etc.*);

die Schule ~ play truant, *Am. a.* play hooky.

Schwarm [ʃvarm] *m* (-[e]s/⁼e) bees, *etc.*: swarm; *birds*: *a.* flight, flock; *fish*: school, schoal; *birds, girls, etc.*: bevy; F *fig.* fancy, craze; *p.*: idol, hero; flame.

schwärmen ['ʃvɛrmən] *v/i.* (ge-, h) bees, *etc.*: swarm; *fig.*: revel; rave (*von* about, of), gush (over); *~ für* be wild about, adore *s.o.*

'**Schwärmer** *m* (-s/-) enthusiast; *esp. eccl.* fanatic; visionary; *fireworks*: cracker, squib; *zo.* hawkmoth; **~ei** [~'raɪ] *f* (-/-en) enthusiasm (*für* for); idolization; ecstasy; *esp. eccl.* fanaticism; '**2isch** *adj.* enthusiastic; gushing, raving; adoring; *esp. eccl.* fanatic(al).

Schwarte ['ʃvartə] *f* (-/-n) *bacon*: rind; dirty; F *fig.* old book.

schwarz *adj.* ['ʃvarts] black (*a. fig.*); dark; dirty; *~es Brett* notice-board, *Am.* bulletin board; *~es Brot* brown bread; *~er Mann* bog(e)y; *~er Markt* black market; *~ auf weiß* in black and white; *auf die ~e Liste setzen* blacklist; '**2arbeit** *f* illicit work; '**2brot** *n* brown bread; '**2e** *m, f* (-n/-n) black.

Schwärze ['ʃvɛrtsə] *f* (-/*no pl.*) blackness (*a. fig.*); darkness; '**2n** *v/t.* (ge-, h) blacken.

'**schwarz|fahren** F *v/i.* (*irr.* fahren, *sep.*, -ge-, sein) travel without a ticket; *mot.* drive without a licence; '**2fahrer** *m* fare-dodger; *mot.* person driving without a licence; '**2fahrt** *f* ride without a ticket; *mot.* drive without a licence; '**2handel** *m* illicit trade, black marketeering; '**2händler** *m* black marketeer; '**2hörer** *m* listener without a licence.

'**schwärzlich** *adj.* blackish.

'**Schwarz|markt** *m* black market; '**~seher** *m* pessimist; *TV:* viewer without a licence; '**~sender** *m* pirate broadcasting station; '**~weiß-film** *m* black-and-white film.

schwatzen ['ʃvatsən] *v/i.* (ge-, h) chat; chatter, tattle.

schwätz|en ['ʃvɛtsən] *v/i.* (ge-, h) *s.* schwatzen; '**2er** *m* (-s/-) chatterbox; tattler, prattler; gossip.

'**schwatzhaft** *adj.* talkative, garrulous.

Schwebe *fig.* ['ʃveːbə] *f* (-/*no pl.*): *in der ~ sein* be in suspense; *law,*

S

rule, etc.: be in abeyance; '**~bahn** *f* aerial railway *or* ropeway; '²**n** *v/i.* (ge-, *h*) be suspended; *bird:* hover (*a. fig.*); glide; *fig.* be pending (*a. ⚖*); *in Gefahr* ~ be in danger.

Schwed|e ['ʃveːdə] *m* (-n/-n) Swede; '²**isch** *adj.* Swedish.

Schwefel 🜍 ['ʃveːfəl] *m* (-s/*no pl.*) sulphur, *Am. a.* sulfur; '**~säure** 🜍 *f* (-/*no pl.*) sulphuric acid, *Am. a.* sulfuric acid.

Schweif [ʃvaɪf] *m* (-[e]s/-e) tail (*a. ast.*); *fig.* train; '²**en** (ge-) **1.** *v/i.* (sein) rove, ramble; **2.** ⊕ *v/t.* (*h*) curve; scallop.

schweigen ['ʃvaɪgən] **1.** *v/i.* (*irr.*, ge-, *h*) be silent; **2.** ⑨ *n* (-s/*no pl.*) silence; '²**d** *adj.* silent.

schweigsam *adj.* ['ʃvaɪkzaːm] taciturn; '²**keit** *f* (-/*no pl.*) taciturnity.

Schwein [ʃvaɪn] *n* **1.** (-[e]s/-e) *zo.* pig, hog, swine (*all a. contp. fig.*); **2.** F (-[e]s/*no pl.*): ~ *haben* be lucky.

'**Schweine|braten** *m* roast pork; '**~fleisch** *n* pork; '**~hund** F *contp. m* swine; '**~rei** [~'raɪ] *f* (-/-en) mess; dirty trick; smut(ty story); '**~stall** *m* pigsty (*a. fig.*).

'**schweinisch** *fig. adj.* swinish; smutty.

'**Schweinsleder** *n* pigskin.

Schweiß [ʃvaɪs] *m* (-es/-e) sweat, perspiration; '²**en** ⊕ *v/t.* (ge-, *h*) weld; '**~er** ⊕ *m* (-s/-) welder; '**~fuß** *m* perspiring foot; '²**ig** *adj.* sweaty, damp with sweat.

Schweizer ['ʃvaɪtsər] *m* (-s/-) Swiss; *on farm:* dairyman.

schwelen ['ʃveːlən] *v/i.* (ge-, *h*) smo(u)lder (*a. fig.*).

schwelg|en ['ʃvɛlgən] *v/i.* (ge-, *h*) lead a luxurious life; revel; *fig.* revel (*in dat.* in); '²**er** *m* (-s/-) revel(l)er; epicure; ²**erei** [~'raɪ] *f* (-/-en) revel(ry), feasting; '**~erisch** *adj.* luxurious; revel(l)ing.

Schwell|e ['ʃvɛlə] *f* (-/-n) sill, threshold (*a. fig.*); 🚉 sleeper, *Am.* tie; '²**en 1.** *v/i.* (*irr.*, ge-, sein) swell (out); **2.** *v/t.* (ge-, *h*) swell; '**~ung** *f* (-/-en) swelling.

Schwemme ['ʃvɛmə] *f* (-/-n) watering-place; horse-pond; *at tavern, etc.*: taproom; 🍎 glut (*of fruit, etc.*).

Schwengel ['ʃvɛŋəl] *m* (-s/-) clapper (*of bell*); handle (*of pump*).

schwenk|en ['ʃvɛŋkən] (ge-) **1.** *v/t.* (*h*) swing; wave (*hat, etc.*); brandish (*stick, etc.*); rinse (*washing*); **2.** *v/i.* (sein) turn, wheel; '²**ung** *f* (-/-en) turn; *fig.* change of mind.

schwer [ʃveːr] **1.** *adj.* heavy; *problem, etc.*: hard, difficult; *illness, mistake, etc.*: serious; *punishment, etc.*: severe; *fault, etc.*: grave; *wine, cigar, etc.*: strong; ~*e Zeiten* hard times; *2 Pfund* ~ *sein* weigh two pounds; **2.** *adv.*: ~ *arbeiten* work hard; ~ *hören* be hard of hearing; '²**e** *f* (-/*no pl.*) heaviness; *phys.* gravity (*a. fig.*); severity; '**~fällig** *adj.* heavy, slow; clumsy; '²**gewicht** *n sports:* heavy-weight; *fig.* main emphasis; '²**gewichtler** *m* (-s/-) *sports:* heavy-weight; '**~hörig** *adj.* hard of hearing; '²**industrie** *f* heavy industry; '²**kraft** *phys. f* (-/*no pl.*) gravity; '**~lich** *adv.* hardly, scarcely; '²**mut** *f* (-/*no pl.*) melancholy; '**~mütig** *adj.* ['~myːtɪç] melancholy; '²**punkt** *m* centre of gravity, *Am.* center of gravity; *fig.*: crucial point; emphasis.

Schwert [ʃveːrt] *n* (-[e]s/-er) sword.

'**Schwer|verbrecher** *m* felon; '²**verdaulich** *adj.* indigestible, heavy; '²**verständlich** *adj.* difficult *or* hard to understand; '²**verwundet** *adj.* seriously wounded; '²**wiegend** *fig. adj.* weighty, momentous.

Schwester ['ʃvɛstər] *f* (-/-n) sister; 🏥 nurse.

schwieg [ʃviːk] *pret. of* schweigen.

Schwieger|eltern ['ʃviːgər-] *pl.* parents-in-law *pl.*; '**~mutter** *f* mother-in-law; '**~sohn** *m* son-in-law; '**~tochter** *f* daughter-in-law; '**~vater** *m* father-in-law.

Schwiel|e ['ʃviːlə] *f* (-/-n) callosity; '²**ig** *adj.* callous.

schwierig *adj.* ['ʃviːrɪç] difficult, hard; '²**keit** *f* (-/-en) difficulty, trouble.

Schwimm|bad ['ʃvɪm-] *n* swimming-bath, *Am.* swimming pool; '²**en** *v/i.* (*irr.*, ge-, *h*) swim; *thing:* float; *ich bin über den Fluß geschwommen* I swam across the river; *in Geld* ~ be rolling in money; **2.** (*h*) swim; *ich habe lange unter Wasser geschwommen* I swam under water for a long time; '**~gür-**

tel *m* swimming-belt; lifebelt; '**~haut** *f* web; '**~lehrer** *m* swimming-instructor; '**~weste** *f* life-jacket.
Schwindel ['ʃvindəl] *m* (-s/*no pl.*) 🏵 vertigo, giddiness, dizziness; F *fig.*: swindle, humbug, *sl.* eyewash: cheat, fraud; '**~anfall** 🏵 *m* fit of dizziness; '**Ꝺerregend** *adj.* dizzy (*a. fig.*); '**~firma** ✝ *f* long firm, *Am.* wildcat firm; '**Ꝺn** *v/i.* (ge-, h) cheat, humbug, swindle.
schwinden ['ʃvindən] *v/i.* (*irr.*, ge-, sein) dwindle, grow less; *strength, colour, etc.*: fade.
Schwindl|er *m* (-s/-) swindler, cheat, humbug; liar; '**Ꝺig** 🏵 *adj.* giddy, dizzy.
Schwind|sucht 🏵 ['ʃvint-] *f* (-/*no pl.*) consumption; '**Ꝺsüchtig** 🏵 *adj.* consumptive.
Schwing|e ['ʃviŋə] *f* (-/-n) wing, *poet.* pinion; swingle; '**Ꝺen** (*irr.*, ge-, h) **1.** *v/t.* swing; brandish (*weapon*); swingle (*flax*); **2.** *v/i.* swing; ⊕ oscillate; *sound, etc.*: vibrate; '**~ung** *f* (-/-en) oscillation, vibration.
Schwips F [ʃvips] *m* (-es/-e): e-n ~ haben be tipsy, have had a drop too much.
schwirren ['ʃvirən] *v/i.* (ge-) **1.** (sein) whir(r); *arrow, etc.*: whiz(z); *insects*: buzz; *rumours, etc.*: buzz, circulate; **2.** (h): *mir schwirrt der Kopf* my head is buzzing.
Schwitz|bad *n* sweating-bath, hot-air bath, vapo(u)r bath; '**Ꝺen** (ge-, h) **1.** *v/i.* sweat, perspire; **2.** F *fig.* *v/t.*: *Blut und Wasser* ~ be in great anxiety.
schwoll [ʃvɔl] *pret.* of *schwellen*.
schwor [ʃvoːr] *pret.* of *schwören*.
schwören ['ʃvøːrən] (*irr.*, ge-, h) **1.** *v/t.* swear; e-n *Meineid* ~ commit perjury; j-m *Rache* ~ vow vengeance against s.o.; **2.** *v/i.* swear (*bei* by); ~ *auf* (*acc.*) have great belief in, F swear by.
schwül *adj.* [ʃvyːl] sultry, oppressively hot; '**Ꝺe** *f* (-/*no pl.*) sultriness.   [bast.]
Schwulst [ʃvulst] *m* (-es/-e) bom-ᗡ
schwülstig *adj.* ['ʃvylstiç] bombastic, turgid.
Schwund [ʃvunt] *m* (-[e]s/*no pl.*) dwindling; *wireless, etc.*: fading; 🏵 atrophy.
Schwung [ʃvuŋ] *m* (-[e]s/-e) swing;

fig. verve, go; flight (*of imagination*); buoyancy; '**Ꝺhaft** ✝ *adj.* flourishing, brisk; '**~rad** ⊕ *n* fly-wheel; *watch, clock*: balance-wheel; '**Ꝺvoll** *adj.* full of energy *or* verve; *attack, translation, etc.*: spirited; *style, etc.*: racy.
Schwur [ʃvuːr] *m* (-[e]s/-e) oath; '**~gericht** ⚖ *n England, Wales*: *appr.* court of assize.
sechs [zɛks] **1.** *adj.* six; **2.** 🎱 *f* (-/-en) six; '**Ꝺeck** *n* (-[e]s/-e) hexagon; '**~eckig** *adj.* hexagonal; '**~fach** *adj.* sixfold, sextuple; '**~mal** *adv.* six times; '**~monatig** *adj.* lasting *or* of six months, six-months ...; '**~monatlich 1.** *adj.* six-monthly; **2.** *adv.* every six months; **~stündig** *adj.* ['~ʃtyndiç] lasting *or* of six hours, six-hour ...; 🎱'**tagerennen** *n cycling:* six-day race; '**~tägig** *adj.* ['~tɛːgiç] lasting *or* of six days.
sechs|te *adj.* [zɛkstə] sixth; '**Ꝺtel** *n* (-s/-) sixth (part); '**~tens** *adv.* sixthly, in the sixth place.
sech|zehn(te) *adj.* ['zɛç-] sixteen(th); '**~zig** *adj.* ['~tsiç] sixty; '**~zigste** *adj.* sixtieth.
See [zeː] **1.** *m* (-s/-n) lake; **2.** *f* (-/*no pl.*) sea; *an die* ~ *gehen* go to the seaside; *in* ~ *gehen or stechen* put to sea; *auf* ~ at sea; *auf hoher* ~ on the high seas; *zur* ~ *gehen* go to sea; **3.** *f* (-/-n) sea, billow; '**~bad** *n* seaside resort; '**~fahrer** *m* sailor, navigator; '**~fahrt** *f* navigation; voyage; '**Ꝺfest** *adj.* seaworthy; ~ *sein* be a good sailor; '**~gang** *m* (motion of the) sea; '**~hafen** *m* seaport; '**~handel** ✝ *m* maritime trade; '**~herrschaft** *f* naval supremacy; '**~hund** *zo.* *m* seal; '**Ꝺkrank** *adj.* seasick; '**~krankheit** *f* (-/*no pl.*) seasickness; '**~krieg** *m* naval war(fare).
Seele ['zeːlə] *f* (-/-n) soul (*a. fig.*); *mit or von ganzer* ~ with all one's heart.
'**Seelen|größe** *f* (-/*no pl.*) greatness of soul *or* mind; '**~heil** *n* salvation, spiritual welfare; '**Ꝺlos** *adj.* soulless; '**~qual** *f* anguish of mind, (mental) agony; '**~ruhe** *f* peace of mind; coolness.
'**seelisch** *adj.* psychic(al), mental.
'**Seelsorge** *f* (-/*no pl.*) cure of souls; ministerial work; '**~r** *m* (-s/-) pastor, minister.

S

'**See|macht** f naval power; '**~mann**
m (-[e]s/Seeleute) seaman, sailor;
'**~meile** f nautical mile; '**~not** f
(-/no pl.) distress (at sea); '**~räuber**
m pirate; '**~räuberei** [~'raɪ] f (-/-en)
piracy; '**~recht** n maritime law;
'**~reise** f voyage; '**~schiff** n sea-
going ship; '**~schlacht** f naval
battle; '**~schlange** f sea serpent;
'**~sieg** m naval victory; '**~stadt** f
seaside town; '**~streitkräfte** f/pl.
naval forces pl.; '**²tüchtig** adj.
seaworthy; '**~warte** f naval observatory; '**~weg** m sea-route; auf
dem ~ by sea; '**~wesen** n (-s/no pl.)
maritime or naval affairs pl.

Segel ['ze:gəl] n (-s/-) sail; unter ~
gehen set sail; '**~boot** n sailing-boat,
Am. sailboat; sports: yacht; '**~flie-
gen** n (-s/no pl.) gliding, soaring;
'**~flug** m gliding flight, glide;
'**~flugzeug** n glider; '**²n** (ge-)
1. v/i. (h, sein) sail; sports: yacht;
2. v/t. (h) sail; '**~schiff** n sailing-
ship, sailing-vessel; '**~sport** m
yachting; '**~tuch** n (-[e]s/-e) sail-
cloth, canvas.

Segen ['ze:gən] m (-s/-) blessing (a.
fig.), esp. eccl. benediction; '**²s-
reich** adj. blessed.

Segler ['ze:glər] m (-s/-) sailing-
vessel, sailing-ship; fast, good,
etc.: sailer; yachtsman.

segn|en ['ze:gnən] v/t. (ge-, h)
bless; '**²ung** f (-/-en) s. Segen.

sehen ['ze:ən] (irr., ge-, h) 1. v/i. see;
gut ~ have good eyes; ~ auf (acc.)
look at; be particular about; ~ nach
look for; look after; 2. v/t. see;
notice; watch, observe; '**~swert**
adj. worth seeing; '**²swürdigkeit** f
(-/-en) object of interest, curiosity;
~en pl. sights pl. (of a place).

Seher ['ze:ər] m (-s/-) seer, prophet;
'**~blick** m (-[e]s/no pl.) prophetic
vision; '**~gabe** f (-/no pl.) gift of
prophecy.

'**Seh|fehler** m visual defect; '**~
kraft** f vision, eyesight.

Sehne ['ze:nə] f (-/-n) anat. sinew,
tendon; string (of bow); Å
chord.

'**sehnen** v/refl. (ge-, h) long (nach
for), yearn (for, after); sich danach
~ zu inf. be longing to inf. [nerve.]

'**Sehnerv** anat. m (visual or optic)/

sehnig adj. sinewy (a. fig.), stringy.

'**sehn|lich** adj. longing; ardent;

passionate; '**²sucht** f longing,
yearning; '**~süchtig** adj., '**~suchts-
voll** adj. longing, yearning; eyes,
etc.: a. wistful.

sehr adv. [ze:r] before adj. and adv.:
very, most; with vb.: (very) much,
greatly.

'**Seh|rohr** ⚓ n periscope; '**~weite** f
range of sight, visual range; in ~
within eyeshot or sight.

seicht adj. [zaɪçt] shallow; fig. a.
superficial.

Seide ['zaɪdə] f (-/-n) silk.

'**seiden** adj. silk, silken (a. fig.);
'**²flor** m silk gauze; '**²glanz** m
silky lust|re, Am. -er; '**²händler** m
mercer; '**²papier** n tissue(-paper);
'**²raupe** zo. f silkworm; '**²spin-
nerei** f silk-spinning mill; '**²stoff**
m silk cloth or fabric.

'**seidig** adj. silky.

Seife ['zaɪfə] f (-/-n) soap.

'**Seifen|blase** f soap-bubble; '**~ki-
stenrennen** n soap-box derby;
'**~lauge** f (soap-)suds pl.; '**~pulver**
n soap-powder; '**~schale** f soap-
dish; '**~schaum** m lather.

'**seifig** adj. soapy.

seih|en ['zaɪən] v/t. (ge-, h) strain,
filter; '**²er** m (-s/-) strainer, colander.

Seil [zaɪl] n (-[e]s/-e) rope; '**~bahn**
f funicular or cable railway; '**~er** m
(-s/-) rope-maker; '**~tänzer** m rope-
dancer.

sein¹ [zaɪn] 1. v/i. (irr., ge-, sein)
be; exist; 2. ♀ n (-s/no pl.) being;
existence.

sein² poss. pron. [~] his, her, its
(in accordance with gender of possessor); der (die, das) ~e his, hers,
its; ~ Glück machen make one's
fortune; die Seinen pl. his family or
people.

'**seiner**|'**seits** adv. for his part; '**~zeit**
adv. then, at that time; in those
days.

'**seines**|**gleichen** pron. his equal(s
pl.); j-n wie ~ behandeln treat s.o.
as one's equal; er hat nicht ~ he has
no equal; there is no one like him.

seit [zaɪt] 1. prp. (dat.): ~ 1945 since
1945; ~ drei Wochen for three
weeks; 2. cj. since; es ist ein Jahr
her, ~ ... it is a year now since ...;
'**~dem** [~'de:m] 1. adv. since or
from that time, ever since; 2. cj.
since.

Seite ['zaɪtə] f (-/-n) side (a. fig.); flank (a. ✕, △); page (of book).

'**Seiten|ansicht** f profile, side-view; '**~blick** m side-glance; '**~flügel** △ m wing; '**~hieb** fig. m innuendo, sarcastic remark; '**2s** prp. (gen.) on the part of; by; '**~schiff** △ n church: aisle; '**~sprung** fig. m extra-marital adventure; '**~straße** f bystreet; '**~stück** fig. n counterpart (zu of); '**~weg** m by-way.

seit'her adv. since (then, that time).

'**seit|lich** adj. lateral; '**~wärts** adv. ['~verts] sideways; aside.

Sekret|är [zekre'tɛ:r] m (-s/-e) secretary; bureau; **~ariat** [~ari'a:t] n (-[e]s/-e) secretary's office; secretariat(e); **~ärin** f (-/-nen) secretary.

Sekt [zɛkt] m (-[e]s/-e) champagne.

Sekt|e ['zɛktə] f (-/-n) sect; **~ierer** [~'ti:rər] m (-s/-) sectarian.

Sektor ['zɛktɔr] m (-s/-en) ⚔, ✕, pol. sector; fig. field, branch.

Sekunde [ze'kundə] f (-/-n) second; **~nbruchteil** m split second; **~nzeiger** m second-hand.

selb adj. [zɛlp] same; **~er** F pron. ['~bər] s. selbst 1.

selbst [zɛlpst] **1.** pron. self; personally; ich ~ I myself; von ~ p. of one's own accord; thing: by itself, automatically; **2.** adv. even; **3.** 2 n (-/no pl.) (one's own) self; ego.

selbständig adj. ['zɛlpʃtɛndiç] independent; sich ~ machen set up for o.s.; **2keit** f (-/no pl.) independence.

'**Selbst|anlasser** mot. m self-starter; '**~anschluß** teleph. m automatic connection; '**~bedienungsladen** m self-service shop; '**~beherrschung** f self-command, self-control; '**~bestimmung** f self-determination; '**~betrug** m self-deception; '**2bewußt** adj. self-confident, self-reliant; '**~bewußtsein** n self-confidence, self-reliance; '**~binder** m (-s/-) tie; '**~erhaltung** f self-preservation; '**~erkenntnis** f self-knowledge; '**~erniedrigung** f self-abasement; '**2gefällig** adj. (self-)complacent; '**~gefälligkeit** f (-/no pl.) (self-)complacency; '**~gefühl** n (-[e]s/no pl.) self-reliance; '**2gemacht** adj. ['~gəmaxt] home-made; '**2gerecht** adj. self-right-

eous; '**~gespräch** n soliloquy, monolog(ue); '**2herrlich 1.** adj. high-handed, autocratic(al); **2.** adv. with a high hand; '**~hilfe** f self-help; '**~kostenpreis** † m cost price; '**~laut** gr. m vowel; '**2los** adj. unselfish, disinterested; '**~mord** m suicide; '**~mörder** m suicide; '**2mörderisch** adj. suicidal; '**2sicher** adj. self-confident, self-assured; '**~sucht** f (-/no pl.) selfishness, ego(t)ism; '**2süchtig** adj. selfish, ego(t)istic(al); '**2tätig** ⊕ adj. self-acting, automatic; '**~täuschung** f self-deception; '**~überwindung** f (-/no pl.) self-conquest; '**~unterricht** m self-instruction; '**~verleugnung** f self-denial; '**~versorger** m (-s/-) self-supporter; '**2verständlich 1.** adj. self-evident, obvious; **2.** adv. of course, naturally; ~! a. by all means!; '**~verständlichkeit** f **1.** (-/-en) matter of course; **2.** (-/no pl.) matter-of-factness; '**~verteidigung** f self-defen|ce, Am. -se; '**~vertrauen** n self-confidence, self-reliance; '**~verwaltung** f self-government, autonomy; '**2zufrieden** adj. self-satisfied; '**~zufriedenheit** f self-satisfaction; '**~zweck** m (-[e]s/no pl.) end in itself.

selig adj. ['ze:liç] eccl. blessed; late, deceased; fig. blissful, overjoyed; '**2keit** fig. f (-/-en) bliss, very great joy.

Sellerie ♀ ['zɛləri:] m (-s/-[s]), f (-/-) celery.

selten ['zɛltən] **1.** adj. rare; scarce; **2.** adv. rarely, seldom; '**2heit** f (-/-en) rarity, scarcity; rarity, curio(sity); '**2heitswert** m (-[e]s/no pl.) scarcity value.

Selterswasser ['zɛltərs-] n (-s/ᵘ) seltzer (water), soda-water.

seltsam adj. ['zɛltza:m] strange, odd.

Semester univ. [ze'mɛstər] n (-s/-) term.

Semikolon gr. [zemi'ko:lɔn] n (-s/-s, Semikola) semicolon.

Seminar [zemi'na:r] n (-s/-e) univ. seminar; seminary (for priests).

Senat [ze'na:t] m (-[e]s/-e) senate; parl. Senate.

send|en ['zɛndən] v/t. **1.** ([irr.,] ge-, h) send; forward; **2.** (ge-, h) transmit; broadcast, Am. a. radio(broad-

S

cast); telecast; **'2er** *m* (-*s*/-) transmitter; broadcasting station.

'Sende|raum *m* (broadcasting) studio; **'_zeichen** *n* interval signal.

'Sendung *f* (-/-en) ✝ consignment, shipment; broadcast; telecast; *fig.* mission. [{♀}.\

Senf [zɛnf] *m* (-[e]s/-e) mustard (*a.*)

sengen ['zɛŋən] *v/t.* (ge-, h) singe, scorch; **'_d** *adj. heat*: parching.

senil *adj.* [ze'ni:l] senile; **2ität** [_ili'tɛ:t] *f* (-/*no pl.*) senility.

senior *adj.* ['ze:niɔr] senior.

Senk|blei ['zɛŋk-] *n* ♠ plumb, plummet; ♣ *a.* sounding-lead; **'2e** *geogr. f* (-/-n) depression, hollow; **'2en** *v/t.* (ge-, h) lower; sink (*a.* voice); let down; bow (*head*); cut (*prices, etc.*); *sich _ land, buildings, etc.*: sink, subside; *ceiling, etc.*: sag; **'_fuß** ♣ *m* flat-foot; **'_fußeinlage** *f* arch support; **'_grube** *f* cesspool; **'2recht** *adj.* vertical, *esp.* ♠ perpendicular; **'_ung** *f* (-/-en) *geogr.* depression, hollow; lowering, reduction (*of prices*); ♣ sedimentation.

Sensation [zɛnza'tsjo:n] *f* (-/-en) sensation; **2ell** *adj.* [_o'nɛl] sensational; **_slust** *f* (-/*no pl.*) sensationalism; **_spresse** *f* yellow press.

Sense ['zɛnzə] *f* (-/-n) scythe.

sensi|bel *adj.* [zɛn'zi:bəl] sensitive; **2bilität** [_ibili'tɛ:t] *f* (-/*no pl.*) sensitiveness.

sentimental *adj.* [zɛntimɛn'ta:l] sentimental; **2ität** [_ali'tɛ:t] *f* (-/-en) sentimentality.

September [zɛp'tɛmbər] *m* (-[s]/-) September.

Serenade ♪ [zere'na:də] *f* (-/-n) serenade.

Serie ['ze:rjə] *f* (-/-n) series; set; *billiards*: break; **'2nmäßig 1.** *adj.* standard; **2.** *adv.:* _ herstellen produce in mass; **'_nproduktion** *f* mass production.

seriös *adj.* [ze'rjø:s] serious; trustworthy, reliable.

Serum ['ze:rum] *n* (-*s*/Seren, Sera) serum.

Service¹ [zɛr'vi:s] *n* (-*s*/-) service, set.

Service² ['zø:rvis] *m*, *n* (-/-s) service.

servier|en [zɛr'vi:rən] *v/t.* (*no* -ge-, h) serve; **2wagen** *m* trolley(-table).

Serviette [zɛr'vjɛtə] *f* (-/-n) (table-)napkin.

Sessel ['zɛsəl] *m* (-*s*/-) armchair, easy chair; **'_lift** *m* chair-lift.

seßhaft *adj.* ['zɛshaft] settled, established; resident.

Setzei ['zɛts²-] *n* fried egg.

'setzen (ge-) **1.** *v/t.* (h) set, place, put; *typ.* compose; ✎ plant; erect, raise (*monument*); stake (*money*) (*auf acc.* on); *sich _* sit down, take a seat; *bird*: perch; *foundations of house, sediment, etc.*: settle; **2.** *v/i.* (h): _ *auf* (*acc.*) back (*horse, etc.*); **3.** *v/i.* (sein): _ *über* (*acc.*) leap (*wall, etc.*); clear (*hurdle, etc.*); take (*ditch, etc.*).

'Setzer *typ. m* (-*s*/-) compositor, type-setter; **_ei** *typ.* [_'raɪ] *f* (-/-en) composing-room.

Seuche ['zɔyçə] *f* (-/-n) epidemic (disease).

seufz|en ['zɔyftsən] *v/i.* (ge-, h) sigh; **'2er** *m* (-*s*/-) sigh.

sexuell *adj.* [zɛksu'ɛl] sexual.

sezieren [ze'tsi:rən] *v/t.* (*no* -ge-, h) dissect (*a. fig.*).

sich *refl. pron.* [zɪç] oneself; *sg.* himself, herself, itself; *pl.* themselves; *sg.* yourself, *pl.* yourselves; each other, one another; *sie blickte _ um* she looked about her.

Sichel ['zɪçəl] *f* (-/-n) sickle; *s. Mondsichel.*

sicher ['zɪçər] **1.** *adj.* secure (*vor dat.* from), safe (from); proof (against); *hand*: steady; certain, sure; positive; *aus _er Quelle* from a reliable source; *e-r Sache _ sein* be sure of s.th.; **2.** *adv. s. sicherlich*; *um _ zu gehen* to be on the safe side, to make sure.

'Sicherheit *f* (-/-en) security; safety; surety, certainty; positiveness; assurance (*of manner*); *in _ bringen* place in safety; **'_snadel** *f* safety-pin; **'_sschloß** *n* safety-lock.

'sicher|lich *adv.* surely, certainly; undoubtedly; *er wird _ kommen* he is sure to come; **'_n** *v/t.* (ge-, h) secure (*a.* ⚔, ⊕); guarantee (*a.* ♠); protect, safeguard; *sich et. _* secure (*prize, seat, etc.*); **'_stellen** *v/t.* (*sep.*, -ge-, h) secure; **2ung** *f* (-/-en) securing; safeguard(ing); ✝ security, guaranty; ⊕ safety device; ⚡ fuse.

Sicht [zɪçt] *f* (-/*no pl.*) visibility;

view; *in* ~ *kommen* come in(to) view or sight; *auf lange* ~ in the long run; *auf* or *bei* ~ ✝ at sight; '2**bar** *adj.* visible; '2**en** *v/t.* (ge-, h) ⚓ sight; *fig.* sift; '2**lich** *adv.* visibly; '**ver-merk** *m* visé, visa (*on passport*).

sickern ['zɪkərn] *v/i.* (ge-, sein) trickle, ooze, seep.

sie *pers. pron.* [zi:] *nom.:* *sg.* she, *pl.* they; *acc.:* *sg.* her, *pl.* them; *Sie nom. and acc.: sg. and pl.* you.

Sieb [zi:p] *n* (-[e]s/-e) sieve; riddle (*for soil, gravel, etc.*).

sieben[1] ['zi:bən] *v/t.* (ge-, h) sieve, sift; riddle.

sieben[2] [~] **1.** *adj.* seven; **2.** 2 *f* (-/-) (number) seven; *böse* ~ shrew, vixen; '**fach** *adj.* sevenfold; '**mal** *adv.* seven times; '2'**sachen** *F f/pl.* belongings *pl.*, F traps *pl.*; '**te** *adj.* seventh; '2**tel** *n* (-s/-) seventh (part); '**tens** *adv.* seventhly, in the seventh place.

sieb|**zehn(te)** *adj.* ['zi:p-] seventeen(th); ~**zig** *adj.* ['~tsɪç] seventy; '**zigste** *adj.* seventieth.

siech *adj.* [zi:ç] sickly; 2**tum** *n* (-s/*no pl.*) sickliness, lingering illness.

Siedehitze ['zi:də-] *f* boiling-heat.

siedeln ['zi:dəln] *v/i.* (ge-, h) settle; *Am. a.* homestead.

siede|**n** ['zi:dən] *v/t. and v/i.* ([irr.,] ge-, h) boil, simmer; '2**punkt** *m* boiling-point (*a. fig.*).

Siedler ['zi:dlər] *m* (-s/-) settler; *Am. a.* homesteader; '**stelle** *f* settler's holding; *Am. a.* homestead. [ing estate.]

'**Siedlung** *f* (-/-en) settlement; hous-

Sieg [zi:k] *m* (-[e]s/-e) victory (*über acc.* over); *sports: a.* win; *den* ~ *davontragen* win the day, be victorious.

Siegel ['zi:gəl] *n* (-s/-) seal (*a. fig.*); signet; '**lack** *m* sealing-wax; '2**n** *v/t.* (ge-, h) seal; '**ring** *m* signet-ring.

sieg|**en** ['zi:gən] *v/i.* (ge-, h) be victorious (*über acc.* over), conquer *s.o.*; *sports:* win; '2**er** *m* (-s/-) conqueror, *rhet.* victor; *sports:* winner.

Siegeszeichen ['zi:gəs-] *n* trophy.

'**siegreich** *adj.* victorious, triumphant.

Signal [zɪ'gna:l] *n* (-s/-e) signal; 2**isieren** [~ali'zi:rən] *v/t.* (*no* -ge-, h) signal.

Silbe ['zɪlbə] *f* (-/-n) syllable; '**n-trennung** *f* syllabi(fi)cation.

Silber ['zɪlbər] *n* (-s/*no pl.*) silver; *s. Tafelsilber*; 2**n** *adj.* (of) silver; '**zeug** F *n* silver plate, *Am. a.* silverware.

Silhouette [zɪlu'ɛtə] *f* (-/-n) silhouette; skyline.

Silvester [zɪl'vɛstər] *n* (-s/-), ~**abend** *m* new-year's eve.

simpel ['zɪmpəl] **1.** *adj.* plain, simple; stupid, silly; **2.** 2 *m* (-s/-) simpleton.

Sims [zɪms] *m, n* (-es/-e) ledge; sill (*of window*); mantelshelf (*of fireplace*); shelf; ⌂ cornice.

Simul|**ant** [zimu'lant] *m* (-en/-en) *esp.* ✕ malingerer; 2**ieren** (*no* -ge-, h) **1.** *v/t.* sham, feign, simulate (*illness, etc.*); **2.** *v/i.* sham, feign; *esp.* ✕, ⚓ malinger.

Sinfonie ♪ [zɪnfo'ni:] *f* (-/-n) symphony.

sing|**en** ['zɪŋən] *v/t. and v/i.* (irr., ge-, h) sing; *vom Blatt* ~ sing at sight; *nach Noten* ~ sing from music; '2**sang** F *m* (-[e]s/*no pl.*) singsong; '2**spiel** *n* musical comedy; '2**stimme** ♪ *f* vocal part.

Singular *gr.* ['zɪŋgula:r] *m* (-s/-e) singular (number).

'**Singvogel** *m* song-bird, songster.

sinken ['zɪŋkən] *v/i.* (irr., ge-, sein) sink; *ship: a.* founder, go down; ✝ *prices:* fall, drop, go down; *den Mut* ~ *lassen* lose courage.

Sinn [zɪn] *m* (-[e]s/-e) sense; taste (*für* for); tendency; sense, meaning; *von* ~*en sein* be out of one's senses; *im* ~ *haben* have in mind; *in gewissem* ~*e* in a sense; '**bild** *n* symbol, emblem; '2**bildlich** *adj.* symbolic(al), emblematic; '2**en** *v/i.* (irr., ge-, h): *auf Rache* ~ meditate revenge.

'**Sinnen**|**lust** *f* sensuality; '**mensch** *m* sensualist; '**rausch** *m* intoxication of the senses.

sinnentstellend *adj.* ['zɪn?-] garbling, distorting. [world.]

'**Sinnenwelt** *f* (-/*no pl.*) material

'**Sinnes**|**änderung** *f* change of mind; '**art** *f* disposition, mentality; '**organ** *n* sense-organ; '**täuschung** *f* illusion, hallucination.

'**sinn**|**lich** *adj.* sensual; material; '2**lichkeit** *f* (-/*no pl.*) sensuality; '**los** *adj.* senseless; futile, useless;

S

'2losigkeit f (-/-en) senselessness; futility, uselessness; '~reich adj. ingenious; '~verwandt adj. synonymous.

Sipp|e ['zipə] f (-/-n) tribe; (blood-)relations pl.; family; '~schaft contp. f (-/-en) relations pl.; fig. clan, clique; die ganze ~ the whole lot.

Sirene [zi're:nə] f (-/-n) siren.

Sirup ['zi:rup] m (-s/-e) syrup, Am. sirup; treacle, molasses sg.

Sitte ['zitə] f (-/-n) custom; habit; usage; ~n pl. morals pl.; manners pl.

'**Sitten|bild** n, '~gemälde n genre (-painting); fig. picture of manners and morals; '~gesetz n moral law; '~lehre f ethics pl.; 2los adj. immoral; '~losigkeit f (-/-en) immorality; ~polizei f appr. vice squad; '~prediger m moralizer; '~richter fig. m censor, moralizer; '2streng adj. puritanic(al).

'**sittlich** adj. moral; '2keit f (-/no pl.) morality; 2keitsverbrechen n sexual crime.

'**sittsam** adj. modest; '2keit f (-/no pl.) modesty.

Situation [zitua'tsjo:n] f (-/-en) situation.

Sitz [zits] m (-es/-e) seat (a. fig.); fit (of dress, etc.).

'**sitzen** v/i. (irr., ge-, h) sit, be seated; dress, etc.: fit; blow, etc.: tell; F fig. do time; ~ bleiben remain seated, keep one's seat; '~bleiben v/i. (irr. bleiben, sep., -ge-, sein) girl at dance: F be a wallflower; girl: be left on the shelf; at school: not to get one's remove; ~ auf (dat.) be left with (goods) on one's hands; '~d adj.: ~e Tätigkeit sedentary work; '~lassen v/t. (irr. lassen, sep., [no] -ge-, h) leave s.o. in the lurch, let s.o. down; girl: jilt (lover); leave (girl) high and dry; auf sich ~ pocket (insult, etc.).

'**Sitz|gelegenheit** f seating accommodation, seat(s pl.); ~ bieten für seat; '~platz m seat; '~streik m sit-down or stay-in strike.

'**Sitzung** f (-/-en) sitting (a. parl., paint.); meeting; conference; '~periode f session.

Skala ['ska:la] f (-/Skalen, Skalas) scale (a. ♪); dial (of radio set); fig. gamut; gleitende ~ sliding scale.

Skandal [skan'da:l] m (-s/-e) scandal; row, riot; 2ös adj. [~a'lø:s] scandalous.

Skelett [ske'lɛt] n (-[e]s/-e) skeleton.

Skep|sis ['skɛpsis] f (-/no pl.) scepticism, Am. a. skepticism; ~tiker [~'tikər] m (-s/-) sceptic, Am. a. skeptic; '2tisch adj. sceptical, Am. a. skeptical.

Ski [ʃi:] m (-s/-er, ⚡-) ski; ~ laufen or fahren ski; '~fahrer m, '~läufer m skier; '~lift m ski-lift; '~sport m (-[e]s/no pl.) skiing.

Skizz|e ['skitsə] f (-/-n) sketch (a. fig.); 2ieren [~'tsi:rən] v/t. (no -ge-, h) sketch, outline (both a. fig.).

Sklav|e ['skla:və] m (-n/-n) slave (a. fig.); '~enhandel m slave-trade; '~enhändler m slave-trader; ~e'rei f (-/-en) slavery; '2isch adj. slavish.

Skonto † ['skɔnto] m, n (-s/-s, ⚡ Skonti) discount.

Skrupel ['skru:pəl] m (-s/-) scruple; '2los adj. unscrupulous.

Skulptur [skulp'tu:r] f (-/-en) sculpture.

Slalom ['sla:lɔm] m (-s/-s) skiing, etc.: slalom.

Slaw|e ['sla:və] m (-n/-n) Slav; '2isch adj. Slav(onic).

Smaragd [sma'rakt] m (-[e]s/-e) emerald; 2grün adj. emerald.

Smoking ['smo:kiŋ] m (-s/-s) dinner-jacket, Am. a. tuxedo, F tux.

so [zo:] 1. adv. so, thus; like this or that; as; ~ ein such a; ~ ... as ... as; nicht ~ ... wie not so ... as; ~ oder ~ by hook or by crook; 2. cj. so, therefore, consequently; ~ daß so that; ~bald cj. [zo'-]: ~ (als) as soon as.

Socke ['zɔkə] f (-/-n) sock; '~l m (-s/-) ⚊ pedestal, socle; socket (of lamp); '~n m (-s/-) sock; '~nhalter m/pl. suspenders pl., Am. garters pl.

Sodawasser ['zo:da-] n (-s/⚊) soda(-water).

Sodbrennen ⚕ ['zo:t-] n (-s/no pl.) heartburn.

soeben adv. [zo'-] just (now).

Sofa ['zo:fa] n (-s/-s) sofa.

sofern cj. [zo'-] if, provided that; ~ nicht unless.

soff [zɔf] pret. of saufen.

sofort adv. [zo'-] at once, immediately, directly, right or straight away; ~ig adj. immediate, prompt.

Sog [zo:k] 1. m (-[e]s/-e) suction; ⚓

wake (a. fig.), undertow; **2.** ♀ pret. of saugen.

so|gar adv. [zo'-] even; **~genannt** adj. ['zo:-] so-called; **~gleich** adv. [zo'-] s. sofort.

Sohle ['zo:lə] f (-/-n) sole; bottom (of valley, etc.); ✗ floor.

Sohn [zo:n] m (-[e]s/⸚e) son.

solange cj. [zo'-]: ~ (als) so or as long as. [such.]

solch pron. [zɔlç] such; als ~e(r) as]

Sold ✗ [zɔlt] m (-[e]s/-e) pay.

Soldat [zɔl'da:t] m (-en/-en) soldier; der unbekannte ~ the Unknown Warrior or Soldier. [cenary.]

Söldner ['zœldnər] m (-s/-) mer-]

Sole ['zo:lə] f (-/-n) brine, salt water.

solid adj. [zo'li:t] solid (a. fig.); basis, etc.: sound; † firm, etc.: sound, solvent; prices: reasonable, fair; p. steady, staid, respectable.

solidarisch adj. [zoli'da:riʃ]: sich ~ erklären mit declare one's solidarity with.

solide adj. [zo'li:də] s. solid.

Solist [zo'list] m (-en/-en) soloist.

Soll † [zɔl] n (-[s]/-[s]) debit; (output) target.

sollen (h) **1.** v/i. (ge-): ich sollte (eigentlich) I ought to; **2.** v/aux. (irr., no -ge-): er soll he shall; he is to; he is said to; ich sollte I should; er sollte (eigentlich) zu Hause sein he ought to be at home; er sollte seinen Vater niemals wiedersehen he was never to see his father again.

Solo ['zo:lo] n (-s/-s, Soli) solo.

somit cj. [zo'-] thus; consequently.

Sommer ['zɔmər] m (-s/-) summer; **~frische** f (-/-n) summer-holidays pl.; summer-resort; **~lich** adj. summer-like, summer(l)y; **~sprosse** f freckle; **2sprossig** adj. freckled; **~wohnung** f summer residence, Am. cottage, summer house; **~zeit** f **1.** (-/-en) season: summertime; **2.** (-/no pl.) summer time, Am. daylight-saving time.

Sonate ♪ [zo'na:tə] f (-/-n) sonata.

Sonde ['zɔndə] f (-/-n) probe.

Sonder|angebot ['zɔndər-] n special offer; **~ausgabe** f special (edition); **2bar** adj. strange, odd; **~beilage** f inset, supplement (of newspaper); **~berichterstatter** m special correspondent; **2lich 1.** adj. special, peculiar; **2.** adv.: nicht ~

not particularly; **~ling** m (-s/-e) crank, odd person; **2n 1.** cj. but; nicht nur, ~ auch not only, but (also); **2.** v/t. (ge-, h): die Spreu vom Weizen ~ sift the chaff from the wheat; **~recht** n privilege; **~zug** 🚂 m special (train).

sondieren [zɔn'di:rən] (no -ge-, h) **1.** v/t. ⚕ probe (a. fig.); **2.** fig. v/i. make tentative inquiries.

Sonn|abend ['zɔn⁹-] m (-s/-e) Saturday; **~e** f (-/-n) sun; **2en** v/t. (ge-, h) (expose to the) sun; sich ~ sun o.s. (a. fig. in dat. in), bask in the sun.

Sonnen|aufgang m sunrise; **~bad** n sun-bath; **~brand** m sunburn; **~bräune** f sunburn, tan, Am. (sun)tan; **~brille** f (e-e a pair of) sun-glasses pl.; **~finsternis** f solar eclipse; **~fleck** m sun-spot; **2klar** fig. adj. (as) clear as daylight; **~licht** n (-[e]s/no pl.) sunlight; **~schein** m (-[e]s/no pl.) sunshine; **~schirm** m sunshade, parasol; sun's **~segel** n awning; **~seite** f sunny side (a. fig.); **~stich** ⚕ m sunstroke; **~strahl** m sunbeam; **~uhr** f sun-dial; **~untergang** m sunset, sundown; **2verbrannt** adj. sunburnt, tanned; **~wende** f solstice.

sonnig adj. sunny (a. fig.).

Sonntag m Sunday.

Sonntags|anzug m Sunday suit or best; **~fahrer** mot. contp. m Sunday driver; **~kind** n person born on a Sunday; fig. person born under a lucky star; **~rückfahrkarte** 🚂 f week-end ticket; **~ruhe** f Sunday rest; **~staat** F co. m (-[e]s/no pl.) Sunday go-to-meeting clothes pl.

sonor adj. [zo'no:r] sonorous.

sonst [zɔnst] **1.** adv. otherwise, with pron. else; usually, normally; wer ~? who else?; wie ~ as usual; ~ nichts nothing else; **2.** cj. otherwise, or else; **~ig** adj. other; **~wie** adv. in some other way; **~wo** adv. elsewhere, somewhere else.

Sopran ♪ [zo'pra:n] m (-s/-e) soprano; sopranist; **~istin** ♪ [~a'nistin] f (-/-nen) soprano, sopranist.

Sorge ['zɔrgə] f (-/-n) care; sorrow; uneasiness, anxiety; ~ tragen für take care of; sich ~n machen um be anxious or worried about; mach dir keine ~n don't worry.

S

'**sorgen** (ge-, h) **1.** v/i.: ~ *für* care for, provide for; take care of, attend to; *dafür* ~, *daß* take care that; **2.** v/refl.: *sich* ~ *um* be anxious or worried about; '~**frei** adj., '~**los** adj. carefree, free from care; '~**voll** adj. full of cares; *face*: worried, troubled.

Sorg|falt ['zɔrkfalt] f (-/no pl.) care(fulness); 2**fältig** [~'fɛltiç] adj. careful; 2**lich** adj. careful, anxious; 2**los** adj. carefree; thoughtless; negligent; careless; 2**sam** adj. careful.

Sort|e ['zɔrtə] f (-/-n) sort, kind, species, Am. a. stripe; 2**ieren** [~'ti:rən] v/t. (no -ge-, h) (as)sort; arrange; ~**iment** [~i'mɛnt] n (-[e]s/-e) assortment.

Soße ['zo:sə] f (-/-n) sauce; gravy.

sott [zɔt] pret. of sieden.

Souffl|eurkasten thea. [su'flø:r-] m prompt-box, promter's box; ~**euse** thea. [~zə] f (-/-n) prompter; 2**ieren** thea. (no -ge-, h) **1.** v/t. prompt (j-m s.o.); **2.** v/t. prompt.

Souverän [suvə'rɛ:n] **1.** m (-s/-e) sovereign; **2.** 2 adj. sovereign; fig. superior; 2**ität** [~ɛni'tɛ:t] f (-/no pl.) sovereignty.

so|viel [zo'-] **1.** cj. so or as far as; ~ *ich weiß* so far as I know; **2.** adv.: *doppelt* ~ twice as much; ~**weit 1.** cj.: ~ *es mich betrifft* in so far as it concerns me, so far as I am concerned; **2.** adv.: ~ *ganz gut* not bad (for a start); ~**wieso** adv. [zovi'zo:] in any case, anyhow, anyway.

Sowjet [zɔ'vjɛt] m (-s/-s) Soviet; 2**isch** adj. Soviet.

sowohl cj. [zo'-]: ~ ... *als* (*auch*) ... both ... and ..., ... as well as ...

sozial adj. [zo'tsja:l] social; 2**demokrat** m social democrat; ~**isieren** [~ali'zi:rən] v/t. (no -ge-, h) socialize; 2**isierung** [~ali'zi:ruŋ] f (-/-en) socialization; 2**ist** [~a'list] m (-en/-en) socialist; ~**istisch** [~a'listiʃ] adj. socialist.

Sozius ['zo:tsjus] m (-/-se) partner; mot. pillion-rider; '~**sitz** mot. m pillion.

sozusagen adv. [zotsu'za:gən] so to speak, as it were.

Spachtel ['ʃpaxtəl] m (-s/-), f (-/-n) spatula.

spähe|n ['ʃpɛ:ən] v/i. (ge-, h) look

out (*nach* for); peer; '2**r** m (-s/-) look-out; ✕ scout.

Spalier [ʃpa'li:r] n (-s/-e) trellis, espalier; fig. lane; ~ *bilden* form a lane.

Spalt [ʃpalt] m (-[e]s/-e) crack, split, rift, crevice, fissure; '~**e** f (-/-n) s. Spalt; typ. column; 2**en** v/t. ([irr.,] ge-, h) split (a. fig. hairs), cleave (block of wood, etc.); sich ~ split (up); '~**ung** f (-/-en) splitting, cleavage; fig. split; eccl. schism.

Span [ʃpa:n] m (-[e]s/ᵘe) chip, shaving, splinter.

Spange ['ʃpaŋə] f (-/-n) clasp; buckle; clip; slide (in hair); strap (of shoes); bracelet.

Span|ier ['ʃpa:njər] m (-s/-) Spaniard; 2**isch** adj. Spanish.

Spann [ʃpan] **1.** m (-[e]s/-e) instep; **2.** 2 pret. of spinnen; '~**e** f (-/-n) span; ✕, orn. spread (of wings); ✝ margin; '2**en** (ge-, h) **1.** v/t. stretch (rope, muscles, etc.); cock (rifle); bend (bow, etc.); tighten (spring, etc.); *vor den Wagen* ~ harness to the carriage; s. *gespannt*; **2.** v/i. be (too) tight; '2**end** adj. exciting, thrilling, gripping; '~**kraft** f (-/no pl.) elasticity; fig. energy; '~**ung** f (-/-en) tension (a. fig.); ⚡ voltage; ⊕ strain, stress; △ span; fig. close attention.

Spar|büchse ['ʃpa:r-] f money-box; 2**en** (ge-, h) **1.** v/t. save (money, strength, etc.); put by; **2.** v/i. save; economize, cut down expenses; ~ *mit* be chary of (praise, etc.); '~**er** m (-s/-) saver.

Spargel ⚘ ['ʃpargəl] m (-s/-) asparagus.

'**Spar|kasse** f savings-bank; '~**konto** n savings-account.

spärlich adj. ['ʃpɛ:rliç] crop, dress, etc.: scanty; population, etc.: sparse; hair: thin.

Sparren ['ʃparən] m (-s/-) rafter, spar.

'**sparsam 1.** adj. saving, economical (mit of); **2.** adv.: ~ *leben* lead a frugal life, economize; ~ *umgehen mit* use sparingly, be frugal of; 2**keit** f (-/no pl.) economy, frugality.

Spaß [ʃpa:s] m (-es/ᵘe) joke, jest; fun, lark; amusement; *aus or zum* ~ in fun; ~ *beiseite* joking apart; *er hat nur* ~ *gemacht* he was only joking; **℃en** v/i. (ge-, h) joke, jest, make fun; *damit ist nicht zu ~* that is no joking matter; **℃haft** adj., **℃ig** adj. facetious, waggish; funny; **~macher** m (-s/-), **~vogel** m wag, joker.

spät [ʃpɛːt] **1.** adj. late; advanced; *zu ~* too late; *am ~en Nachmittag* late in the afternoon; *wie ~ ist es?* what time is it?; **2.** adv. late; *er kommt 5 Minuten zu ~* he is five minutes late (*zu for*); *~ in der Nacht* late at night.

Spaten [ˈʃpaːtən] m (-s/-) spade.

spätle|r 1. adj. later; **2.** adv. later on; afterward(s); *früher oder ~* sooner or later; **~stens** adv. [ˈ~stəns] at the latest.

Spatz orn. [ʃpats] m (-en, -es/-en) sparrow.

spazieren [ʃpaˈtsiːrən] v/i. (no -ge-, sein) walk, stroll; **~fahren** (irr. fahren, sep., -ge-) **1.** v/i. (sein) go for a drive; **2.** v/t. (h) take for a drive; take (*baby*) out (in pram); **~gehen** v/i. (irr. gehen, sep., -ge-, sein) go for a walk.

Spa'zier|fahrt f drive, ride; **~gang** m walk, stroll; *e-n ~ machen* go for a walk; **~gänger** [ˈ~gɛŋər] m (-s/-) walker, stroller; **~weg** m walk.

Speck [ʃpɛk] m (-[e]s/-e) bacon.

Spedi|teur [ʃpediˈtøːr] m (-s/-e) forwarding agent; (furniture) remover; **~tion** [ˈ~tsjoːn] f (-/-en) forwarding agent *or* agency.

Speer [ʃpeːr] m (-[e]s/-e) spear; *sports:* javelin; **~werfen** n (-s/no pl.) javelin-throw(ing); **~werfer** m (-s/-) javelin-thrower.

Speiche [ˈʃpaɪçə] f (-/-n) spoke.

Speichel [ˈʃpaɪçəl] m (-s/no pl.) spit(tle), saliva; **~lecker** fig. m (-s/-) lickspittle, toady.

Speicher [ˈʃpaɪçər] m (-s/-) granary; warehouse; garret, attic.

speien [ˈʃpaɪən] (irr. ge-, h) **1.** v/t. spit out (*blood, etc.*); volcano, *etc.:* belch (*fire, etc.*). **2.** v/i. spit; vomit, be sick.

Speise [ˈʃpaɪzə] f (-/-n) food, nourishment; meal; dish; **~eis** n ice-cream; **~kammer** f larder, pantry; **~karte** f bill of fare, menu; **℃n** (ge-, h) **1.** v/i. s. *essen 1; at restaurants:* take one's meals; **2.** v/t. feed; ⊕, ⚡ a. supply (*mit with*); **~nfolge** f menu; **~röhre** anat. f

gullet, (o)esophagus; **~saal** m dining-hall; **~schrank** m (meat-) safe; **~wagen** 🚃 m dining-car, diner; **~zimmer** n dining-room.

Spektakel F [ʃpɛkˈtaːkəl] m (-s/-) noise, din.

Spekul|ant [ʃpekuˈlant] m (-en/-en) speculator; **~ation** [ˈ~aˈtsjoːn] f (-/-en) speculation; ♥ a. venture; **℃ieren** [ˈ~ˈliːrən] v/i. (no -ge-, h) speculate (*auf acc.* on).

Spelunke [ʃpeˈluŋkə] f (-/-n) den; drinking-den, Am. F a. dive.

Spende [ˈʃpɛndə] f (-/-n) gift; alms pl.; contribution; **℃n** v/t. (ge-, h) give; donate (*money to charity, blood, etc.*); *eccl.* administer (*sacraments*); bestow (*praise*) (*dat.* on); **~r** m (-s/-) giver; donor.

spen'dieren v/t. (no -ge-, h): j-m *et. ~* treat s.o. to s.th., stand s.o. s.th.

Sperling orn. [ˈʃpɛrlɪŋ] m (-s/-e) sparrow.

Sperr|e [ˈʃpɛrə] f (-/-n) barrier; 🚃 barrier, Am. gate; toll-bar; ⊕ lock(ing device), detent; barricade; ♥, ⚓ embargo; ⚔ blockade; *sports:* suspension; **℃en** (ge-, h) **1.** v/t. close; ♥, ⚓ embargo; cut off (*gas supply, electricity, etc.*); stop (*cheque, etc.*); *sports:* suspend; **2.** v/i. jam, be stuck; **~holz** n plywood; **~konto** ♥ n blocked account; **~kreis** ⚡ m wave-trap; **~sitz** thea. m stalls pl., Am. orchestra; **~ung** f (-/-en) closing; stoppage (*of cheque, etc.*); ♥, ⚓ embargo; ⚔ blockade; **~zone** f prohibited area.

Spesen [ˈʃpeːzən] pl. expenses pl., charges pl.

Spezial|ausbildung [ʃpeˈtsjaːlˀ~] f special training; **~fach** n special(i)ty; **~geschäft** ♥ n one-line shop, Am. specialty store; **℃isieren** [ˈ~ˌaliˈziːrən] v/refl. (no -ge-, h) specialize (*auf acc.* in); **~ist** [ˈ~aˈlist] m (-en/-en) specialist; **~ität** [ˈ~aliˈtɛːt] f (-/-en) special(i)ty.

speziell adj. [ʃpeˈtsjɛl] specific, special, particular.

spezifisch adj. [ʃpeˈtsiːfɪʃ]: *~es Gewicht* specific gravity.

Sphäre [ˈsfɛːrə] f (-/-n) sphere (a. fig.).

Spick|aal [ˈʃpiːk-] m smoked eel; **℃en** (ge-, h) **1.** v/t. lard; fig. (inter-)

lard (*mit* with); F: *j-n* ~ grease s.o.'s palm; **2.** F *fig. v/i.* crib.

spie [ʃpiː] *pret.* of speien.

Spiegel ['ʃpiːgəl] *m* (-s/-) mirror (*a. fig.*), looking-glass; '~**bild** *n* reflected image; '**2blank** *adj.* mirror-like; ~**ei** ['ʃpiːgəl-] *n* fried egg; '**2glatt** *adj. water*: glassy, unrippled; *road*, *etc.*: very slippery; '**2n** (ge-, h) **1.** *v/i.* shine; **2.** *v/refl.* be reflected; '~**schrift** *f* mirror-writing.

Spieg(e)lung ['ʃpiːg(ə)luŋ] *f* (-/-en) reflection, reflexion; mirage.

Spiel [ʃpiːl] *n* (-[e]s/-e) play (*a. fig.*); game (*a. fig.*); match; ♪ playing; *ein* ~ *Karten* a pack of playing-cards, Am. a deck; *auf dem* ~ *stehen* be at stake; *aufs* ~ *setzen* jeopardize, stake; '~**art** ♀, *zo.* f variety; '~**ball** *m tennis*: game ball; *billiards*: red ball; *fig.* plaything, sport; '~**bank** f (-/-en) gaming-house; '**2en** (ge-, h) **1.** *v/i.* play; gamble; ~ *mit* play with; *fig. a.* toy with; **2.** *v/t.* play (*tennis, violin, etc.*); *thea.* act, play (*part*); *mit j-m Schach* ~ play s.o. at chess; *den Höflichen* ~ do the polite; '**2end** *fig. adv.* easily; '~**er** *m* (-s/-) player; gambler; ~**e'rei** f (-/-en) pastime; child's amusement; '~**ergebnis** *n sports*: result, score; '~**feld** *n sports*: (playing-)field; pitch; '~**film** *m* feature film or picture; '~**gefährte** *m* playfellow, playmate; '~**karte** f playing-card; '~**leiter** *m thea.* stage manager; *cinematography*: director; *sports*: referee; '~**marke** f counter, *sl.* chip; '~**plan** *m thea., etc.*: program(me); repertory; '~**platz** *m* playground; '~**raum** *fig. m* play, scope; '~**regel** f rule (of the game); '~**sachen** f/pl. playthings pl., toys pl.; '~**schuld** f gambling-debt; '~**schule** f infant-school, kindergarten; '~**tisch** *m* card-table; gambling-table; '~**uhr** f musical box, Am. music box; '~**verderber** *m* (-s/-) spoil-sport, killjoy, wet blanket; '~**waren** f/pl. playthings pl., toys pl.; '~**zeit** f thea. season; *sports*: time of play; '~**zeug** *n* toy(s pl.), plaything(s pl.).

Spieß [ʃpiːs] *m* (-es/-e) spear, pike; spit; *den* ~ *umdrehen* turn the tables; '~**bürger** *m* bourgeois, Philistine, Am. a. Babbit; '**2bürgerlich** *adj.* bourgeois, Philistine;

'~**er** *m* (-s/-) s. *Spießbürger*; '~**geselle** *m* accomplice; '~**ruten** f/pl.: ~ *laufen* run the gauntlet (*a. fig.*).

spinal *adj.* [ʃpiˈnaːl]: ~*e Kinderlähmung* ⚕ infantile paralysis, poliomyelitis, F polio.

Spinat ♀ [ʃpiˈnaːt] *m* (-[e]s/-e) spinach.

Spind [ʃpint] *n, m* (-[e]s/-e) wardrobe, cupboard; ⚔, *sports, etc.*: locker.

Spindel ['ʃpindəl] f (-/-n) spindle; '**2dürr** *adj.* (as) thin as a lath.

Spinn|**e** *zo.* ['ʃpinə] f (-/-n) spider; '**2en** (*irr.*, ge-, h) **1.** *v/t.* spin (*a. fig.*); hatch (*plot, etc.*); **2.** *v/i. cat*: purr; F *fig.* be crazy, *sl.* be nuts; '~**engewebe** *n* cobweb; '~**er** *m* (-s/-) spinner; F *fig.* silly; ~**e'rei** f (-/-en) spinning; spinning-mill; '~**maschine** f spinning-machine; '~**webe** f (-/-n) cobweb.

Spion [ʃpiˈoːn] *m* (-s/-e) spy, intelligencer; *fig.* judas; ~**age** [ʃoˈnaːʒə] f (-/*no pl.*) espionage; **2ieren** [ʃoˈniːrən] *v/i.* (*no* -ge-, h) (play the) spy.

Spiral|**e** [ʃpiˈraːlə] f (-/-n) spiral (*a.* ♣), helix; **2förmig** *adj.* [~fœrmiç] spiral, helical.
[its pl.]

Spirituosen [ʃpirituˈoːzən] *pl.* spirits.

Spiritus ['ʃpiːritus] *m* (-/-se) spirit, alcohol; '~**kocher** *m* (-s/-) spirit stove.

Spital [ʃpiˈtaːl] *n* (-s/=er) hospital; alms-house; home for the aged.

spitz [ʃpits] **1.** *adj.* pointed (*a. fig.*); ⚭ *angle*: acute; *fig.* poignant; ~*e Zunge* sharp tongue; **2.** *adj.*: ~ *zulaufen* taper (off); '**2bube** *m* thief, rogue, rascal (*both a. co.*); **2büberei** [~byˈbaˈraɪ] f (-/-en) roguery, rascality (*both a. co.*); ~**bübisch** *adj.* ['~byːbiʃ] *eyes, smile, etc.*: roguish.

'**Spitz**|**e** f (-/-n) point (*of pencil, weapon, jaw, etc.*); tip (*of nose, finger, etc.*); nib (*of tool, etc.*); spire; head (*of enterprise, etc.*); lace; *an der* ~ *liegen sports*: be in the lead; *j-m die* ~ *bieten* make head against s.o.; *auf die* ~ *treiben* carry to an extreme; '~**el** *m* (-s/-) (common) informer; '**2en** *v/t.* (ge-, h) point, sharpen; *den Mund* ~ purse (up) one's lips; *die Ohren* ~ prick up one's ears (*a. fig.*).

'**Spitzen**|**leistung** f top performance; ⊕ maximum capacity; '⟨lohn *m* top wages *pl.*

spitz|findig *adj.* subtle, captious; '⟨findigkeit *f* (-/-en) subtlety, captiousness; '⟨hacke *f* pickax(e), pick; '⟨ig *adj.* pointed; *fig. a.* poignant; '⟨marke *typ. f* head(ing); '⟨name *m* nickname.

Splitter ['ʃplitər] *m* (-s/-) splinter, shiver; chip; '⟨frei *adj. glass:* shatterproof; '⟨ig *adj.* splintery; '⟨n *v/i.* (ge-, *h, sein*) splinter, shiver; '⟨nackt F *adj.* stark naked, *Am. a.* mother-naked; '⟨partei *pol. f* splinter party.

spontan *adj.* [ʃpɔn'taːn] spontaneous.

sporadisch *adj.* [ʃpo'raːdiʃ] sporadic.

Sporn [ʃpɔrn] *m* (-[e]s/Sporen) spur; *die Sporen geben* put *or* set spurs to (*horse*); *sich die Sporen verdienen* win one's spurs; '⟨en *v/t.* (ge-, *h*) spur.

Sport [ʃpɔrt] *m* (-[e]s/⚓-e) sport; *fig.* hobby; ⟨ *treiben* go in for sports; '⟨ausrüstung *f* sports equipment; '⟨geschäft *n* sporting-goods shop; '⟨kleidung *f* sport clothes *pl.*, sportswear; '⟨lehrer *m* games-master; '⟨lich *adj.* sporting, sportsmanlike; *figure:* athletic; '⟨nachrichten *f/pl.* sports news *sg.*, *pl.*; '⟨platz *m* sports field; stadium.

Spott [ʃpɔt] *m* (-[e]s/*no pl.*) mockery; derision; scorn; (*s-n*) ⟨ *treiben mit* make sport of; '⟨billig F *adj.* dirt-cheap.

Spötte|lei [ʃpœtə'laɪ] *f* (-/-en) raillery, sneer, jeer; '⟨ln *v/i.* (ge-, *h*) sneer (*über acc.* at), jeer (at).

spotten *v/i.* (ge-, *h*) mock (*über acc.* at); jeer (at); *jeder Beschreibung* ⟨ *beggar description.*

Spötter ['ʃpœtər] *m* (-s/-) mocker, scoffer; '⟨ei [⟨'raɪ] *f* (-/-en) mockery.

spöttisch *adj.* mocking; sneering; ironical.

Spott|name *m* nickname; '⟨preis *m* ridiculous price; *für e-n* ⟨ *for a mere song;* '⟨schrift *f* lampoon, satire.

sprach [ʃpraːx] *pret. of* sprechen.

Sprache *f* (-/-n) speech; language (*a. fig.*); diction; *zur* ⟨ *bringen* bring up, broach; *zur* ⟨ *kommen* come up (for discussion).

Sprach|eigentümlichkeit *f* idiom;

'⟨fehler ⚓ *m* impediment (in one's speech); '⟨führer *m* language guide; '⟨gebrauch *m* usage; '⟨gefühl *n* (-[e]s/*no pl.*) linguistic instinct; ⟨kundig *adj.* ['⟨kundiç] versed in languages; '⟨lehre *f* grammar; '⟨lehrer *m* teacher of languages; '⟨lich *adj.* linguistic; grammatical; ⟨los *adj.* speechless; '⟨rohr *n* speaking-trumpet, megaphone; *fig.:* mouthpiece; organ; '⟨schatz *m* vocabulary; '⟨störung ⚓ *f* impediment (in one's speech); '⟨wissenschaft *f* philology, science of language; linguistics *pl.*; '⟨wissenschaftler *m* philologist; linguist; ⟨wissenschaftlich *adj.* philological; linguistic.

sprang [ʃpraŋ] *pret. of* springen.

Sprech|chor ['ʃpreç-] *m* speaking chorus; ⟨en (*irr.*, ge-, *h*) **1.** *v/t.* speak (*language, truth, etc.*); pronounce (*judgement*); say (*prayer*); *j-n zu* ⟨ *wünschen* wish to see s.o.; *j-n schuldig* ⟨ pronounce s.o. guilty; F *Bände* ⟨ speak volumes (*für* for); **2.** *v/i.* speak; talk (*both: mit* to, with; *über acc.* von, of, about); *er ist nicht zu* ⟨ you cannot see him; '⟨er *m* (-s/-) speaker; *radio:* announcer; spokesman; '⟨fehler *m* slip of the tongue; '⟨stunde *f* consulting-hours *pl.*; '⟨übung *f* exercise in speaking; '⟨zimmer *n* consulting-room, surgery.

spreizen ['ʃpraɪtsən] *v/t.* (ge-, *h*) spread (out); *a.* straddle (*legs*); *sich* ⟨ pretend to be unwilling.

Spreng|bombe ✕ ['ʃpreŋ-] *f* high-explosive bomb, demolition bomb; '⟨el *eccl. m* (-s/-) diocese, see; parish; '⟨en (ge-) **1.** *v/t.* sprinkle, water (*road, lawn, etc.*); blow up, blast (*bridge, rocks, etc.*); burst open (*door, etc.*); spring (*mine, etc.*); *gambling:* break (*bank*); break up (*meeting, etc.*); **2.** *v/i.* (*sein*) gallop; '⟨stoff *m* explosive; '⟨ung *f* (-/-en) blowing-up, blasting; explosion; '⟨wagen *m* water(ing)-cart.

Sprenkel ['ʃpreŋkəl] *m* (-s/-) speckle, spot; '⟨n *v/t.* (ge-, *h*) speckle, spot.

Spreu [ʃprɔʏ] *f* (-/*no pl.*) chaff; *s. sondern 2.*

Sprich|wort ['ʃpriç-] *n* (-[e]s/⁎er) proverb, adage; ⟨wörtlich *adj.* proverbial (*a. fig.*).

S

sprießen ['ʃpriːsən] *v/i.* (*irr.*, ge-, sein) sprout; germinate.

Spring|brunnen ['ʃpriŋ-] *m* fountain; **'2en** *v/i.* (*irr.*, ge-, sein) jump, leap; *ball*, *etc.*: bounce; *swimming*: dive; burst, crack, break; *in die Augen* ~ strike the eye; ~ *über* (*acc.*) jump (over), leap, clear; **'_er** *m* (-s/-) jumper; *swimming*: diver; *chess*: knight; **'_flut** *f* spring tide.

Sprit [ʃprit] *m* (-[e]s/-e) spirit, alcohol; F *mot.* fuel, petrol, *sl.* juice, *Am.* gasoline, F gas.

Spritze ['ʃpritsə] *f* (-/-n) syringe (*a.* 💉), squirt; ⊕ fire-engine; *j-m e-e* ~ *geben* 💉 give s.o. an injection; **'2en** (ge-) **1.** *v/t.* (h) sprinkle, water (*road*, *lawn*, *etc.*); splash (*water*, *etc.*) (*über acc.* on, over); **2.** *v/i.* (h) splash; *pen*: splutter; **3.** *v/i.* (sein) F *fig.* dash, flit; ~ *aus blood*, *etc.*: spurt *or* spout from (*wound*, *etc.*); **'_er** *m* (-s/-) splash; **'_tour** *f*: *e-e* ~ *machen* go for a spin.

spröde *adj.* ['ʃprøːdə] *glass*, *etc.*: brittle; *skin*: chapped, chappy; *esp. girl*: prudish, prim, coy.

Sproß [ʃprɔs] **1.** *m* (*Sprosses/Sprosse*) 🌿 shoot, sprout, scion (*a. fig.*); *fig.* offspring; **2.** *2 pret. of* sprießen.

Sprosse ['ʃprɔsə] *f* (-/-n) rung, round, step. [*Sproß 1.; co.* son.]

Sprößling ['ʃprœslɪŋ] *m* (-s/-e) 🌿 *s.*]

Spruch [ʃprux] *m* (-[e]s/¨e) saying; dictum; ⚖ sentence; ⚖ verdict; **'_band** *n* banner; **'2reif** *adj.* ripe for decision.

Sprudel ['ʃpruːdəl] *m* (-s/-) mineral water; **'2n** *v/i.* (ge-) **1.** (h) bubble, effervesce; **2.** (sein) ~ *aus or von* gush from.

sprüh|en ['ʃpryːən] (ge-) **1.** *v/t.* (h) spray, sprinkle (*liquid*); throw off (*sparks*); *Feuer* ~ *eyes*: flash fire; **2.** *v/i.* (h): ~ *vor* sparkle with (*wit*, *etc.*); *es sprüht* it is drizzling; **3.** *v/i.* (sein) *sparks*: fly; **'2regen** *m* drizzle.

Sprung [ʃpruŋ] *m* (-[e]s/¨e) jump, leap, bound; *swimming*: dive; crack, fissure; **'_brett** *n* *sports*: springboard; *fig.* stepping-stone; **'_feder** *f* spiral spring.

Spuck|e F ['ʃpuːkə] *f* (-/no *pl.*) spit(tle); **'2en** (ge-) **1.** *v/t.* spit (out) (*blood*, *etc.*); **2.** *v/i.* spit; *engine*: splutter; **'_napf** *m* spittoon, *Am. a.* cuspidor.

Spuk [ʃpuːk] *m* (-[e]s/-e) apparition,

ghost, *co.* spook; F *fig.* noise; **'2en** *v/i.* (ge-, h): ~ *in* (*dat.*) haunt (*a place*); *hier spukt es* this place is haunted.

Spule ['ʃpuːlə] *f* (-/-n) spool, reel; bobbin; ⚡ coil; **'2n** *v/t.* (ge-, h) spool, reel.

spülen ['ʃpyːlən] (ge-, h) **1.** *v/t.* rinse (*clothes*, *mouth*, *cup*, *etc.*); wash up (*dishes*, *etc.*); *an Land* ~ wash ashore; **2.** *v/i.* flush the toilet.

Spund [ʃpunt] *m* (-[e]s/¨e) bung; plug; **'_loch** *n* bunghole.

Spur [ʃpuːr] *f* (-/-en) trace (*a. fig.*); track (*a. fig.*); print (*a. fig.*); rut (*of wheels*); *j-m auf der* ~ *sein* be on s.o.'s track.

spür|en ['ʃpyːrən] *v/t.* (ge-, h) feel; sense; perceive; *hunt.* scent; *fig. a.* flair (*für* for).

Spurweite 🚂 *f* ga(u)ge.

sputen ['ʃpuːtən] *v/refl.* (ge-, h) make haste, hurry up.

Staat [ʃtaːt] *m* **1.** F (-[e]s/no *pl.*) pomp, state; finery; ~ *machen mit* make a parade of; **2.** (-[e]s/-en) state; government; **'_enbund** *m* (-[e]s/no *pl.*) confederacy, confederation; **'2enlos** *adj.* stateless; **'2lich** *adj.* state; national; political; public.

'Staats|angehörige *m*, *f* (-n/-n) national, citizen, *esp. Brt.* subject; **'_angehörigkeit** *f* (-/no *pl.*) nationality, citizenship; **'_anwalt** *m* public prosecutor, *Am.* prosecuting attorney; **'_beamte** *m* Civil Servant, *Am. a.* public servant; **'_begräbnis** *n* state *or* national funeral; **'_besuch** *m* official *or* state visit; **'_bürger** *m* citizen; **'_bürgerkunde** *f* (-/no *pl.*) civics *sg.*; **'_bürgerschaft** *f* (-/-en) citizenship; **'_dienst** *m* Civil Service; **'2eigen** *adj.* state-owned; **'_feind** *m* public enemy; **'2feindlich** *adj.* subversive; **'_gewalt** *f* (-/no *pl.*) supreme power; **'_haushalt** *m* budget; **'_hoheit** *f* (-/no *pl.*) sovereignty; **'_kasse** *f* treasury, *Brt.* exchequer; **'_klugheit** *f* political wisdom; **'_kunst** *f* (-/no *pl.*) statesmanship; **'_mann** *m* statesman; **2männisch** *adj.* ['~mɛnɪʃ] statesmanlike; **'_oberhaupt** *n* head of (the) state; **'_papiere** *n/pl.* Government securities *pl.*; **'_rat** *m* Privy Council; **'_recht** *n* public law; **'_schatz** *m* *s.* Staatskasse

'~schulden f/pl. national debt;
'~sekretär m under-secretary of
state; **'~streich** m coup d'état;
'~trauer f national mourning;
'~vertrag m treaty; **'~wesen** n
polity; **'~wirtschaft** f public sector
of the economy; **'~wissenschaft** f
political science; **'~wohl** n public
weal.

Stab [ʃtɑːp] m (-[e]s/-̈e) staff (a. fig.);
bar (of metal, wood); crosier, staff
(of bishop); wand (of magician);
relay-race, ♪ conducting: baton;
pole-vaulting: pole.

stabil adj. [ʃtaˈbiːl] stable (a. ✝);
health: robust.

stabilisier|en [ʃtabiliˈziːrən] v/t.
(no -ge-, h) stabilize (a. ✝); **2ung** f
(-/-en) stabilization (a. ✝).

stach [ʃtɑːx] pret. of stechen.

Stachel ['ʃtaxəl] m (-s/-n) prickle
(of plant, hedgehog, etc.); sting (of
bee, etc.); tongue (of buckle); spike
(of sports shoe); fig.: sting; goad;
'~beere ⚘ f gooseberry; **'~draht** m
barbed wire; **'2ig** adj. prickly;
'stachlig adj. s. stachelig. [thorny.]

Stadi|on ['ʃtɑːdjɔn] n (-s/Stadien)
stadium; **~um** ['~um] n (-s/Stadien)
stage, phase.

Stadt [ʃtat] f (-/-̈e) town; city.

Städt|chen ['ʃtɛːtçən] n (-s/-) small
town; **'~ebau** m (-[e]s/no pl.)
town-planning; **'~er** m (-s/-) townsman; **~ pl.** townspeople pl.

'Stadt|gebiet n urban area; **'~ge-
spräch** n teleph. local call; fig. town
talk, talk of the town; **'~haus** n
town house.

städtisch adj. ['ʃtɛːtiʃ] municipal.

'Stadt|plan m city map; plan (of a
town); **'~planung** f town-planning;
'~rand m outskirts pl. (of a town);
'~rat m (-[e]s/-̈e) town council;
town council(l)or; **'~teil** m, **'~vier-
tel** m quarter.

Staffel ['ʃtafəl] f (-/-n) relay; relay-
race; **~ei** paint. ['~'laɪ] f (-/-en)
easel; **'~lauf** m relay-race; **'2n** v/t.
(ge-, h) graduate (taxes, etc.);
stagger (hours of work, etc.).

Stahl¹ [ʃtɑːl] m (-[e]s/-̈e, -e) steel.

stahl² [~] pret. of stehlen.

stählen ['ʃtɛːlən] v/t. (ge-, h) ⊕
harden (a. fig.), temper.

'Stahl|feder f steel pen; steel
spring; **'~kammer** f strong-room;
'~stich m steel engraving.

stak [ʃtɑːk] pret. of stecken 2.

Stall [ʃtal] m (-[e]s/-̈e) stable (a.
fig.); cow-house, cowshed; pigsty;
Am. a. pigpen; shed; **'~knecht** m
stableman; **'~ung** f (-/-en) stabling;
~en pl. stables pl.

Stamm [ʃtam] m (-[e]s/-̈e) ⚘ stem
(a. gr.), trunk; fig.: race; stock;
family; tribe; **'~aktie** ✝ f ordinary
share, Am. common stock; **'~baum**
m family or genealogical tree,
pedigree (a. zo.); **'~buch** n album;
book that contains the births, deaths,
and marriages in a family; zo. stud-
book; **'2eln** (-[e]s) 1. v/t. stammer
(out); 2. v/i. stammer; **'~eltern** pl.
ancestors pl.; first parents pl.; **'2en**
v/i. (ge-, sein): ~ von or aus come
from (town, etc.), Am. a. hail from;
date from (certain time); gr. be
derived from; aus gutem Haus ~ be
of good family; **'~gast** m regular
customer or guest, ✝ regular.

stämmig adj. ['ʃtɛmɪç] stocky;
thickset, squat(ty).

'Stamm|kapital ✝ n share capital,
Am. capital stock; **'~kneipe** F f
one's favo(u)rite pub, local; **'~kun-
de** m regular customer, patron;
'~tisch m table reserved for regular
guests; **~utter** ['ʃtammʊtər] f (-/-̈)
ancestress; **'~vater** m ancestor;
'2verwandt adj. cognate, kindred;
pred. of the same race.

stampfen ['ʃtampfən] (ge-) 1. v/t.
(h) mash (potatoes, etc.); aus dem
Boden ~ conjure up; 2. v/i. (h)
stamp (one's foot); horse: paw;
3. v/i. (sein): ~ durch plod through;
♣ pitch through.

Stand [ʃtant] 1. m (-[e]s/-̈e) stand
(-ing), standing or upright position;
footing, foothold; s. Standplatz;
stall; fig.: level; state; station, rank,
status; class; profession; reading
(of thermometer, etc.); ast. position;
sports: score; auf den neuesten ~
bringen bring up to date; e-n
schweren ~ haben have a hard time
(of it); 2. ♀ pret. of stehen.

Standarte [ʃtanˈdartə] f (-/-n) standard, banner.

'Standbild n statue.

Ständchen ['ʃtɛntçən] n (-s/-) serenade; j-m ein ~ bringen serenade
s.o.

Ständer ['ʃtɛndər] m (-s/-) stand;
post, pillar, standard.

S

'**Standes|amt** n registry (office), register office; '2amtlich adj.: ~e Trauung civil marriage; '~beamte m registrar; '~dünkel m pride of place; '2gemäß adj., '2mäßig adj. in accordance with one's rank; '~person f person of rank or position; '~unterschied m social difference.

'**standhaft** adj. steadfast; firm; constant; ~ bleiben stand pat; resist temptation; '2igkeit f (-/no pl.) steadfastness; firmness.

'**standhalten** v/i. (irr. halten, sep., -ge-, h) hold one's ground; j-m or e-r Sache ~ resist s.o. or s.th.

ständig adj. ['ʃtɛndiç] permanent; constant; income, etc.: fixed.

'**Stand|ort** m position (of ship, etc.); ✕ garrison, post; '~platz m stand; '~punkt fig. m point of view, standpoint, angle, Am. a. slant; '~quartier ✕ n fixed quarters pl.; '~recht ✕ n martial law; '~uhr f grandfather's clock.

Stange ['ʃtaŋə] f (-/-n) pole; rod, bar (of iron, etc.); staff (of flag); Anzug or Kleid von der ~ sl. reach-me-down, Am. F hand-me-down.

stank [ʃtaŋk] pret. of stinken.

Stänker|(**er**) contp. ['ʃtɛŋkər(ər)] m (-s/-) mischief-maker, quarrel(l)er; '2n F v/i. (ge-, h) make mischief.

Stanniol [ʃta'njo:l] n (-s/-e) tin foil.

Stanze ['ʃtantsə] f (-/-n) stanza; ⊕ punch, stamp, die; '2n ⊕ v/t. (ge-, h) punch, stamp.

Stapel ['ʃta:pəl] m (-s/-) pile, stack; ⚓ stocks pl.; vom or von ~ lassen ⚓ launch; vom or von ~ laufen ⚓ be launched; '~lauf ⚓ m launch; '2n v/t. (ge-, h) pile (up), stack; '~platz m dump; emporium.

stapfen ['ʃtapfən] v/i. (ge-, sein) plod (durch through).

Star 1. [ʃtaːr] m (-[e]s/-e) orn. starling; ✗ cataract; j-m den ~ stechen open s.o.'s eyes; 2. [staːr] m (-s/-s) thea., etc.: star.

starb [ʃtarp] pret. of sterben.

stark [ʃtark] 1. adj. strong (a. fig.); stout, corpulent; fig.: intense; large; ~e Erkältung bad cold; ~er Raucher heavy smoker; ~e Seite strong point, forte; 2. adv. very much; ~ erkältet sein have a bad cold; ~ übertrieben grossly exaggerated.

Stärke ['ʃtɛrkə] f (-/-n) strength (a.

fig.); stoutness, corpulence; fig.: intensity; largeness; strong point, forte; ♫ starch; '2n v/t. (ge-, h) strengthen (a. fig.); starch (linen, etc.); sich ~ take some refreshment(s).

'**Starkstrom** ⚡ m heavy current.

'**Stärkung** f (-/-en) strengthening; fig. a. refreshment; '~smittel n restorative; ✚ a. tonic.

starr [ʃtar] 1. adj. rigid (a. fig.), stiff; gaze: fixed; ~ vor (dat.) numb with (cold, etc.); transfixed with (horror, etc.); dumbfounded with (amazement, etc.); 2. adv.: j-n ~ ansehen stare at s.o.; '~en v/i. (ge-, h) stare (auf acc. at); vor Schmutz ~ be covered with dirt; '2heit f (-/no pl.) rigidity (a. fig.), stiffness; '2kopf m stubborn or obstinate fellow; '~köpfig adj. ['~kœpfiç] stubborn, obstinate; '2krampf ✚ m (-[e]s/no pl.) tetanus; '2sinn m (-[e]s/no pl.) stubbornness, obstinacy; '~sinnig adj. stubborn, obstinate.

Start [ʃtart] m (-[e]s/-s, ✈ -e) start (a. fig.); ✈ take-off; '~bahn ✈ f runway; '2bereit adj. ready to start; ✈ ready to take off; '2en (ge-) 1. v/i. (sein) start; ✈ take off; 2. v/t. (h) start; fig. a. launch; '~er m (-s/-) sports: starter; '~platz m starting-place.

Station [ʃta'tsjo:n] f (-/-en) station; ward (of hospital); (gegen) freie ~ board and lodging (found); ~ machen break one's journey; ~vorsteher 🚉 m station-master, Am. a. station agent.

Statist [ʃta'tist] m (-en/-en) thea. supernumerary (actor), F super; film: extra; ~ik f (-/-en) statistics pl., sg.; ~iker m (-s/-) statistician; 2isch adj. statistic(al).

Stativ [ʃta'ti:f] n (-s/-e) tripod.

Statt [ʃtat] 1. f (-/no pl.): an Eides ~ in lieu of an oath; an Kindes ~ annehmen adopt; 2. ♀ prp. (gen.) instead of; ~ zu inf. instead of ger.; ~ meiner in my place.

Stätte ['ʃtɛtə] f (-/-n) place, spot; scene (of events).

'**statt|finden** v/i. (irr. finden, sep., -ge-, h) take place, happen; '~haft adj. admissible, allowable; legal.

'**Statthalter** m (-s/-) governor.

'**stattlich** adj. stately; impressive; sum of money, etc.: considerable.

Statue ['ʃta:tuə] f (-/-n) statue.

statuieren [ʃtatu'i:rən] v/t. (no -ge-, h): ein Exempel ~ make an example (an dat. of).

Statur [ʃta'tu:r] f (-/-en) stature, size.

Statut [ʃta'tu:t] n (-[e]s/-en) statute; ~en pl. regulations pl.; ✝ articles pl. of association.

Staub [ʃtaup] m (-[e]s/⊕ -e, ⸚e) dust; powder.

Staubecken ['ʃtau-] n reservoir.

stauben ['ʃtaubən] v/i. (ge-, h) give off dust, make or raise a dust.

stäuben ['ʃtɔybən] (ge-, h) 1. v/t. dust; 2. v/i. spray.

Staub|faden ⚘ m filament; **2ig** adj. ['-biç] dusty; **~sauger** ['-p-] m (-s/-) vacuum cleaner; **~tuch** ['-p-] n (-[e]s/⸚er) duster.

stauchen ⊕ ['ʃtauxən] v/t. (ge-, h) upset, jolt.

Staudamm m dam.

Staude ⚘ ['ʃtaudə] f (-/-n) perennial (plant); head (of lettuce).

stau|en ['ʃtauən] v/t. (ge-, h) dam (up) (river, etc.); ⚓ stow; sich ~ waters, etc.: be dammed (up); vehicles: be jammed; **2er** ⚓ m (-s/-) stevedore.

staunen ['ʃtaunən] 1. v/i. (ge-, h) be astonished (über acc. at); 2. 2 n (-s/no pl.) astonishment; **~swert** adj. astonishing. [temper.]

Staupe vet. ['ʃtaupə] f (-/-n) dis-]

Stau|see m reservoir; **~ung** f (-/-en) damming (up) (of water); stoppage; 🚧 congestion (a. of traffic); jam; ⚓ stowage.

stechen ['ʃtɛçən] (irr., ge-, h) 1. v/t. prick; insect, etc.: sting; flea, mosquito, etc.: bite; card: take, trump (other card); ⊕ engrave (in or auf acc. on); cut (lawn, etc.); sich in den Finger ~ prick one's finger; 2. v/i. prick; stab (nach at); insect, etc.: sting; flea, mosquito, etc.: bite; sun: burn; j-m in die Augen ~ strike s.o.'s eye; **~d** adj. pain, look, etc.: piercing; pain: stabbing.

Steck|brief 🚓 ['ʃtɛk-] m warrant of apprehension; **2brieflich** 🚓 adv.: er wird ~ gesucht a warrant is out against him; **~dose** ⚡ f (wall) socket; **2en 1.** v/t. (ge-, h) put; esp. ⚘ insert (in acc. into); F stick; pin (an acc. to, on); 🌱 set, plant; **2.** v/i. ([irr.,] ge-, h) be; stick, be

stuck; tief in Schulden ~ be deeply in debt; **~en** m (-s/-) stick; **2en-bleiben** v/i. (irr. bleiben, sep., -ge-, sein) get stuck; speaker, etc.: break down; **~enpferd** n hobby-horse, fig. hobby; '**~er** ⚡ m (-s/-) plug; '**~kontakt** ⚡ m s. Steckdose; '**~na-del** f pin.

Steg [ʃte:k] m (-[e]s/-e) foot-bridge; ⚓ landing-stage; '**~reif** m (-[e]s/-e): aus dem ~ extempore, offhand (both a. attr.); aus dem ~ sprechen extemporize, F ad-lib.

stehen ['ʃte:ən] v/i. (irr., ge-, h) stand; be; be written; dress: suit, become (j-m s.o.); ~ vor be faced with; gut ~ mit be on good terms with; es kam ihm or ihn teuer zu ~ it cost him dearly; wie steht's mit ...? what about ...?; wie steht das Spiel? what's the score?; ~ bleiben remain standing; '**~bleiben** v/i. (irr. bleiben, sep., -ge-, sein) stand (still), stop; leave off reading, etc.; '**~lassen** v/t. (irr. lassen, sep., [no] -ge-, h) turn one's back (up)on; leave (meal) untouched; leave (behind), forget; leave alone.

'**Steher** m (-s/-) sports: stayer.

'**Steh|kragen** m stand-up collar; '**~lampe** f standard lamp; '**~leiter** f (e-e a pair of) steps pl., step-ladder.

stehlen ['ʃte:lən] (irr., ge-, h) 1. v/t. steal; j-m Geld ~ steal s.o.'s money; 2. v/i. steal.

'**Stehplatz** m standing-room; '**~in-haber** m Am. F standee; in bus, etc.: straphanger.

steif adj. [ʃtaif] stiff (a. fig.); numb (vor Kälte with cold); '**~halten** v/t. (irr. halten, sep. -ge-, h): F die Ohren ~ keep a stiff upper lip.

Steig [ʃtaik] m (-[e]s/-e) steep path; '**~bügel** m stirrup.

steigen ['ʃtaigən] 1. v/i. (irr., ge-, sein) flood, barometer, spirits, prices, etc.: rise; mists, etc.: ascend; blood, tension, etc.: mount; prices, etc.: increase; auf e-n Baum ~ climb a tree; 2. 2 n (-s/no pl.) rise; fig. a. increase.

steigern ['ʃtaigərn] v/t. (ge-, h) raise; increase; enhance; gr. compare.

'**Steigerung** f (-/-en) raising; increase; enhancement; gr. comparison; '**~sstufe** gr. f degree of comparison.

S

Steigung ['ʃtaɪɡuŋ] f (-/-en) rise, gradient, ascent, grade.

steil adj. [ʃtaɪl] steep; precipitous.

Stein [ʃtaɪn] m (-[e]s/-e) stone (a. ♥, ♫), Am. F a. rock; s. Edel♫; '♫'**alt** adj. (as) old as the hills; '♫**bruch** m quarry; '♫**druck** m 1. (-[e]s/no pl.) lithography; 2. (-[e]s/-e) lithograph; '♫**drucker** m lithographer; '♫**ern** adj. stone-..., of stone; fig. stony; '♫**gut** n (-[e]s/-e) crockery, stoneware, earthenware; '♫**ig** adj. stony; '♫**igen** v/t. (ge-, h) stone; '♫**igung** ['♫ɡuŋ] f (-/-en) stoning; '♫**kohle** f mineral coal; pit-coal; '♫**metz** ['♫mɛts] m (-en/-en) stonemason; '♫**obst** n stonefruit; '♫'**reich** F adj. immensely rich; '♫**salz** n (-es/no pl.) rock-salt; '♫**setzer** m (-s/-) pavio(u)r; '♫**wurf** m throwing of a stone; fig. stone's throw; '♫**zeit** f (-/no pl.) stone age.

Steiß [ʃtaɪs] m (-es/-e) buttocks pl., rump; '♫**bein** anat. n coccyx.

Stelldichein co. ['ʃtɛldɪçˀaɪn] n (-[s]/-[s]) meeting, appointment, rendezvous, Am. F a. date.

Stelle ['ʃtɛlə] f (-/-n) place; spot; point; employment, situation, post, place, F job; agency, authority; passage (of book, etc.); freie ~ vacancy; an deiner ~ in your place, if I were you; auf der ~ on the spot; zur ~ sein be present.

stellen v/t. (ge-, h) put, place, set, stand; regulate (watch, etc.); set (watch, trap, task, etc.); stop (thief, etc.); hunt down (criminal); furnish, supply, provide; Bedingungen ~ make conditions; e-e Falle ~ a. lay a snare; sich ~ give o.s. up to the police); stand, place o.s. (somewhere); sich krank ~ feign or pretend to be ill.

Stellenangebot n position offered, vacancy; '♫**gesuch** n application for a post; '♫**weise** adv. here and there, sporadically.

Stellung f (-/-en) position, posture; position, situation, (place of) employment; position, rank, status; arrangement (a. gr.); ✕ position; ~ nehmen give one's opinion (zu on), comment (upon); ♫**nahme** ['♫nɑː-mə] f (-/-n) attitude (zu to[wards]); opinion (on); comment (on); '♫**slos** adj. unemployed.

stellvertretend adj. vicarious,

representative; acting, deputy; ♫**er** Vorsitzender vice-chairman, deputy chairman; '♫'**er** m representative; deputy; proxy; '♫**ung** f representation; substitution; proxy.

Stelzbein contp. ['ʃtɛlts-] n wooden leg; '♫**e** f (-/-n) stilt; '♫**en** mst iro. v/i. (ge-, sein) stalk.

stemmen ['ʃtɛmən] v/t. (ge-, h) lift (weight); sich ~ press (gegen against); fig. resist or oppose s.th.

Stempel ['ʃtɛmpəl] m (-s/-) stamp; ⊕ piston; ♀ pistil; '♫**geld** F n the dole; '♫**kissen** n ink-pad; '♫**n** (ge-, h) 1. v/t. stamp; hallmark (gold, silver); 2. v/i. F: ~ gehen be on the dole.

Stengel ♀ ['ʃtɛŋəl] m (-s/-) stalk, stem.

Steno F ['ʃteno] f (-/no pl.) s. Stenographie; ♫'**gramm** n (-s/-e) stenograph; ♫'**graph** [♫'ɡrɑːf] m (-en/-en) stenographer; ♫'**graphie** [♫aˈfiː] f (-/-n) stenography, shorthand; ♫**graphieren** [♫aˈfiːrən] (no -ge-, h) 1. v/t. take down in shorthand; 2. v/i. know shorthand; ♫**graphisch** [♫ˈɡrɑːfɪʃ] 1. adj. shorthand, stenographic; 2. adv. in shorthand; ~**typistin** [♫ˈtyˈpistin] f (-/-nen) shorthand-typist.

Stepdecke ['ʃtɛp-] f quilt, Am. a. comforter; '♫**en** (ge-, h) 1. v/t. quilt; stitch; 2. v/i. tap-dance.

Sterbebett ['ʃtɛrbə-] n deathbed; '♫**fall** m (case of) death; '♫**kasse** f burial-fund.

sterben 1. v/i. (irr., ge-, sein) die (a. fig.) (an dat. of); esp. ⚕⚖ decease; 2. ♫ n (-s/no pl.): im ~ liegen be dying.

sterblich ['ʃtɛrplɪç] 1. adj. mortal; 2. adv.: ~ verliebt sein be desperately in love (in acc. with); '♫**keit** f (-/no pl.) mortality; '♫**keitsziffer** f death-rate, mortality.

stereotyp adj. [stereoˈtyːp] typ. stereotyped (a. fig.); ♫**ieren** (no -ge-, h) [♫yˈpiːrən] v/t. (no -ge-, h) stereotype.

steril adj. [ʃteˈriːl] sterile; ~**isieren** [♫iliˈziːrən] v/t. (no -ge-, h) sterilize.

Stern [ʃtɛrn] m (-[e]s/-e) star (a. fig.); '♫**bild** ast. n constellation; '♫**deuter** m (-s/-) astrologer; '♫**deutung** f astrology; '♫**enbanner** n Star-Spangled Banner, Stars and Stripes pl., Old Glory; '♫**fahrt**

mot. *f* motor rally; '~**gucker** F *m* (-s/-) star-gazer; '2**hell** *adj.* starry, starlit; '~**himmel** *m* (-s/*no pl.*) starry sky; '~**kunde** *f* (-/*no pl.*) astronomy; '~**schnuppe** *f* (-/-n) shooting star; '~**warte** *f* observatory.

stet *adj.* [ʃteːt], '~**ig** *adj.* continual, constant; steady; '2**igkeit** *f* (-/*no pl.*) constancy, continuity; steadiness; ~**s** *adv.* always; constantly.

Steuer ['ʃtɔʏər] **1.** *n* (-s/-) ⚓ helm, rudder; steering-wheel; **2.** *f* (-/-n) tax; duty; rate, local tax; '~**amt** *n s. Finanzamt*; '~**beamte** *m* revenue officer; '~**berater** *m* (-s/-) tax adviser; '~**bord** ⚓ *n* (-[e]s/-e) starboard; '~**erhebung** *f* levy of taxes; '~**erklärung** *f* tax-return; '~**ermäßigung** *f* tax allowance; '2**frei** *adj.* tax-free; *goods*: duty-free; '~**freiheit** *f* (-/*no pl.*) exemption from taxes; '~**hinterziehung** *f* tax-evasion; '~**jahr** *n* fiscal year; '~**klasse** *f* tax-bracket; '~**knüppel** ✈ *m* control lever *or* stick; '~**mann** *m* (-[e]s/⸗er, *Steuerleute*) ⚓ helmsman, steersman, *Am. a.* wheelsman; coxwain (*a. rowing*); '2**n** (ge-) **1.** *v/t.* (h) ⚓, ✈ steer, navigate, pilot; ⊕ control; *fig.* direct, control; **2.** *v/i.* (h) check *s.th.*; **3.** *v/i.* (sein): ~ *in* (*acc.*) ⚓ enter (*harbour, etc.*); ~ *nach* ⚓ be bound for; '2**pflichtig** *adj.* taxable; *goods*: dutiable; '~**rad** *n* steering-wheel; '~**ruder** ⚓ *n* helm, rudder; '~**satz** *m* rate of assessment; '~**ung** *f* (-/-en) ⚓, ✈ steering; ⊕, ⚡ control (*a. fig.*); ✈ controls *pl.*; '~**veranlagung** *f* tax assessment; '~**zahler** *m* (-s/-) taxpayer; ratepayer.

Steven ⚓ ['ʃteːvən] *m* (-s/-) stem; stern-post.

Stich [ʃtiç] *m* (-[e]s/-e) prick (*of needle, etc.*); sting (*of insect, etc.*); stab (*of knife, etc.*); *sewing*: stitch; *cards*: trick; ⊕ engraving; ⚕ stab; ~ *halten* hold water; *im* ~ *lassen* abandon, desert, forsake.

Stichel|ei *fig.* [ʃtiçə'laɪ] *f* (-/-en) gibe, jeer; '2**n** *fig. v/i.* (ge-, h) gibe (*gegen* at), jeer (at).

'**Stich|flamme** *f* flash; '2**haltig** *adj.* valid, sound; ~ *sein* hold water; '~**probe** *f* random test *or* sample, *Am. a.* spot check; '~**tag** *m* fixed day; '~**wahl** *f* second ballot; '~**wort** *n* **1.** *typ.* (-[e]s/⸗er) headword; **2.** *thea.* (-[e]s/-e) cue; '~**wunde** *f* stab.

sticken ['ʃtikən] *v/t. and v/i.* (ge-, h) embroider.

'**Stick|garn** *n* embroidery floss; '~**husten** ⚕ *m* (w)hooping cough; '2**ig** *adj.* stuffy; close; '~**stoff** ⚗ *m* (-[e]s/*no pl.*) nitrogen.

stieben ['ʃtiːbən] *v/i.* ([*irr.*,] ge-, *h, sein*) *sparks, etc.*: fly about.

Stief... ['ʃtiːf-] step...

Stiefel ['ʃtiːfəl] *m* (-s/-) boot; '~**knecht** *m* bootjack; '~**schaft** *m* leg of a boot.

'**Stief|mutter** *f* (-/⸗) stepmother; ~**mütterchen** ⚘ ['~mytərçən] *n* (-s/-) pansy; '~**vater** *m* stepfather.

stieg [ʃtiːk] *pret. of steigen.*

Stiel [ʃtiːl] *m* (-[e]s/-e) handle; helve (*of weapon, tool*); haft (*of axe*); stick (*of broom*); ⚘ stalk.

Stier [ʃtiːr] **1.** *zo. m* (-[e]s/-e) bull; **2.** 2 *adj.* staring; '2**en** *v/i.* (ge-, h) stare (*auf acc.* at); '~**kampf** *m* bull-fight.

stieß [ʃtiːs] *pret. of stoßen.*

Stift [ʃtift] **1.** *m* (-[e]s/-e) pin; peg; tack; pencil, crayon; F *fig.*: youngster; apprentice; **2.** *n* (-[e]s/-e, -er) charitable institution; '2**en** *v/t.* (ge-, h) endow, give, *Am. a.* donate; found; *fig.* cause; make (*mischief, peace*); '~**er** *m* (-s/-) donor; founder; *fig.* author; '~**ung** *f* (-/-en) (charitable) endowment, donation; foundation.

Stil [ʃtiːl] *m* (-[e]s/-e) style (*a. fig.*); '2**gerecht** *adj.* stylish; 2**isieren** [ʃtili'ziːrən] *v/t.* (*no* -ge-, *h*) stylize; 2**istisch** *adj.* [ʃti'listiʃ] stylistic.

still *adj.* [ʃtil] still, quiet; silent; ✝ dull, slack; secret; ~! silence!; *im* ~*en* secretly; ~*er Gesellschafter* ✝ sleeping *or* silent partner; *der* 2*e Ozean* the Pacific (Ocean); '2**e** *f* (-/*no pl.*) stillness, quiet(ness); silence; *in aller* ~ quietly, silently; privately; 2**eben** *paint.* ['ʃtilleːbən] *n* (-s/-) still life; ~**egen** ['ʃtilleːgən] *v/t.* (*sep.*, -ge-, *h*) shut down (*factory, etc.*); stop (*traffic*); '~**en** *v/t.* (ge-, h) soothe (*pain*); appease (*appetite*); quench (*thirst*); sta(u)nch (*blood*); nurse (*baby*); '~**halten** *v/i.* (*irr. halten, sep.*, -ge-, *h*) keep still; ~**iegen** ['ʃtilliːgən] *v/i.* (*irr. liegen, sep.*, -ge-, *h*) *factory,*

S

etc.: be shut down; *traffic*: be suspended; *machines, etc.*: be idle.
stillos *adj.* ['ſtiːlloːs] without style.
'stillschweigen 1. *v/i.* (*irr. schweigen, sep.*, -ge-, *h*) be silent; ~ zu et. ignore s.th.; **2.** ♀ *n* (-s/*no pl.*) silence; secrecy; ~ bewahren observe secrecy; et. mit ~ übergehen pass s.th. over in silence; '**~d** *adj.* silent; agreement, *etc.*: tacit.
'Still|stand *m* (-[e]s/*no pl.*) standstill; *fig.*: stagnation (*a.* ♀); deadlock; '**♀stehen** *v/i.* (*irr. stehen, sep.*, -ge-, *h*) stop; be at a standstill; *stillgestanden!* ✗ attention!
'Stil|möbel *n/pl.* period furniture; '**♀voll** *adj.* stylish.
Stimm|band *anat.* ['ſtim-] *n* (-[e]s/⸚er) vocal c(h)ord; '**♀berechtigt** *adj.* entitled to vote; '**~e** *f* (-/-n) voice (*a.* ♪, *fig.*); vote; comment; ♪ part; '**♀en** (-ge-, *h*) **1.** *v/t.* tune (*piano, etc.*); j-n fröhlich ~ put s.o. in a merry mood; **2.** *v/i.* be true or right; *sum, etc.*: be correct; ~ für vote for; '**~enmehrheit** *f* majority or plurality of votes; '**~enthaltung** *f* abstention; '**~enzählung** *f* counting of votes; '**~gabel** ♪ *f* tuning-fork; '**~recht** *n* right to vote; *pol.* franchise; '**~ung** *f* (-/-en) ♪ tune; *fig.* mood, humo(u)r; '**♀ungsvoll** *adj.* impressive; '**~zettel** *m* ballot, voting-paper.
stinken ['ſtiŋkən] *v/i.* (*irr.*, -ge-, *h*) stink (*nach* of); F *fig.* be fishy.
Stipendium *univ.* [ſti'pɛndjum] *n* (-s/*Stipendien*) scholarship; exhibition.
stipp|en ['ſtipən] *v/t.* (-ge-, *h*) dip, steep; '**♀visite** *f* F flying visit.
Stirn [ſtirn] *f* (-/-en) forehead, brow; *fig.* face, cheek; j-m die ~ bieten make head against s.o.; *s.* runzeln; '**~runzeln** *n* (-s/*no pl.*) frown(ing).
stob [ſtoːp] *pret. of* stieben.
stöbern F ['ſtøːbərn] *v/i.* (-ge-, *h*) rummage (about) (*in dat.* in).
stochern ['ſtɔxərn] *v/i.* (-ge-, *h*): ~ *in* (*dat.*) poke (*fire*); pick (*teeth*).
Stock [ſtɔk] *m* **1.** (-[e]s/⸚e) stick; cane; ♪ baton; beehive; ♀ switch; **2.** (-[e]s/-) stor(e)y, floor; *im ersten* ~ on the first floor, *Am.* on the second floor; '**♀betrunken** F *adj.* dead drunk; '**♀blind** F *adj.* stone-blind; '**♀dunkel** F *adj.* pitch-dark.

Stöckelschuh [ˈʃtœkəl-] *m* high-heeled shoe.
'stocken *v/i.* (-ge-, *h*) stop; *liquid*: stagnate (*a. fig.*); *speaker*: break down; *voice*: falter; *traffic*: be blocked; *ihm stockte das Blut* his blood curdled.
'Stock|engländer F *m* thorough or true-born Englishman; '**♀finster** F *adj.* pitch-dark; '**~fleck** *m* spot of mildew; '**♀(fleck)ig** *adj.* foxy, mildewy; '**♀nüchtern** F *adj.* (as) sober as a judge; '**~schnupfen** ♂ *m* chronic rhinitis; '**♀taub** F *adj.* stone-deaf; '**~ung** *f* (-/-en) stop (-page); stagnation (*of liquid*) (*a. fig.*); block (*of traffic*); '**~werk** *n* stor(e)y, floor.
Stoff [ſtɔf] *m* (-[e]s/-e) matter, substance; material, fabric, textile; material, stuff; *fig.*: subject(-matter); food; '**♀lich** *adj.* material.
stöhnen ['ſtøːnən] *v/i.* (-ge-, *h*) groan, moan.
Stolle ['ſtɔlə] *f* (-/-n) loaf-shaped Christmas cake; '**~n** *m* (-s/-) *s.* Stolle; ♀ tunnel, gallery (*a.* ✗).
stolpern ['ſtɔlpərn] *v/i.* (-ge-, *sein*) stumble (*über acc.* over), trip (over) (*both a. fig.*).
stolz [ſtɔlts] **1.** *adj.* proud (*auf acc.* of) (*a. fig.*); haughty; **2.** ♀ *m* (-es/*no pl.*) pride (*auf acc.* in); haughtiness; '**♀ieren** [~'tsiːrən] *v/i.* (*no* -ge-, *sein*) strut, flaunt.
stopfen ['ſtɔpfən] (-ge-, *h*) **1.** *v/t.* stuff; fill (*pipe*); cram (*poultry, etc.*); darn (*sock, etc.*); j-m den Mund ~ stop s.o.'s mouth; **2.** ♂ *v/i.* cause constipation.
'Stopf|garn *n* darning-yarn; '**~nadel** *f* darning-needle.
Stoppel ['ſtɔpəl] *f* (-/-n) stubble; '**~bart** F *m* stubbly beard; '**♀ig** *adj.* stubbly.
stopp|en ['ſtɔpən] (-ge-, *h*) **1.** *v/t.* stop; time, F clock; **2.** *v/i.* stop; '**♀licht** *mot.* *n* stop-light; '**♀uhr** *f* stop-watch.
Stöpsel ['ſtœpsəl] *m* (-s/-) stopper, cork; plug (*a. ♀*); F *fig.* whipper-snapper; '**♀n** *v/t.* (-ge-, *h*) stopper, cork; plug (up).
Storch *orn.* [ſtɔrç] *m* (-[e]s/⸚e) stork.
stören ['ſtøːrən] (-ge-, *h*) **1.** *v/t.* disturb; trouble; *radio*: jam (*reception*); *lassen Sie sich nicht* ~! don't let me disturb you!; *darf ich Sie*

kurz ~? may I trouble you for a minute?; **2.** *v/i.* be intruding; be in the way; **2fried** ['ɪfriːt] *m* (-[e]s/-e) troublemaker; intruder.

störr|ig *adj.* ['ʃtœːrɪç], '**~isch** *adj.* stubborn, obstinate; *a. horse:* restive.

'**Störung** *f* (-/-en) disturbance; trouble (*a.* ⊕); breakdown; *radio:* jamming, interference.

Stoß [ʃtoːs] *m* (-es/¨e) push, shove; thrust (*a. fencing:*) kick; butt; shock; knock, strike; blow; *swimming, billiards:* stroke; jolt (*of car, etc.*); pile, stock, heap; '**~dämpfer** *mot. m* shock-absorber; '**2en** (*irr., ge-*) **1.** *v/t.* push, shove; thrust (*weapon, etc.*); kick; butt; knock, strike; pound (*pepper, etc.*); *sich ~ an* (*dat.*) strike *or* knock against; *fig.* take offence at; **2.** *v/i.* (*h*) thrust (*nach dat.*); kick (*at*); butt (*at*); *goat, etc.:* butt; *car:* jolt; *~ an* (*acc.*) border on; **3.** *v/i.* (*sein*) F ~ *auf* (*acc.*) come across; meet with (*opposition, etc.*); ~ *gegen* or *an* (*acc.*) knock *or* strike against.

'**Stoß|seufzer** *m* ejaculation; '**~stange** *mot. f* bumper; '**2weise** *adv.* by jerks; by fits and starts; '**~zahn** *m* tusk.

stottern ['ʃtɔtərn] (*ge-, h*) **1.** *v/t.* stutter (out); stammer; **2.** *v/i.* stutter; stammer; F *mot.* conk (out).

Straf|anstalt ['ʃtraːfʔ-] *f* penal institution; prison; *Am.* penitentiary; '**~arbeit** *f* imposition, F impo(t); '**2bar** *adj.* punishable, penal; '**~e** *f* (-/-n) punishment; ‡‡, ✝, *sports, fig.* penalty; fine; *bei ~ von* on *or* under pain of; *zur ~ as* a punishment; '**2en** *v/t.* (*ge-, h*) punish.

straff *adj.* [ʃtraf] tight; *rope:* a. taut; *fig.* strict, rigid.

'**straf|fällig** *adj.* liable to prosecution; '**2gesetz** *n* penal law; '**2gesetzbuch** *n* penal code.

'**sträf|lich** *adj.* ['ʃtrɛːflɪç] culpable, reprehensible; inexcusable; **2ling** ['~lɪŋ] *m* (-s/-e) convict, *Am. sl.* a. lag.

'**straf|los** *adj.* unpunished; '**2losigkeit** *f* (-/no *pl.*) impunity; '**2porto** *n* surcharge; '**2predigt** *f* severe lecture; *j-m e-e ~ halten* lecture s.o. severely; '**2prozeß** *m* criminal action; '**2raum** *m football:* penalty

area; '**2stoß** *m football:* penalty kick; '**2verfahren** *n* criminal proceedings *pl.*

Strahl [ʃtraːl] *m* (-[e]s/-en) ray (*a. fig.*); beam; flash (*of lightning, etc.*); jet (*of water, etc.*); '**2en** *v/i.* (*ge-, h*) radiate; shine (*vor dat.* with); *fig.* beam (*vor dat.* with), shine (with); '**~ung** *f* (-/-en) radiation, rays *pl.*

Strähne ['ʃtrɛːnə] *f* (-/-n) lock, strand (*of hair*); skein, hank (*of yarn*); *fig.* stretch.

stramm *adj.* [ʃtram] tight; *rope:* a. taut; stalwart; *soldier:* smart.

strampeln ['ʃtrampəln] *v/i.* (*ge-, h*) kick.

Strand [ʃtrant] *m* (-[e]s/⅘-e, ¨e) beach; '**~anzug** *m* beach-suit; '**2en** ['~dən] *v/i.* (*ge-, sein*) ⚓ strand, run ashore; *fig.* fail, founder; '**~gut** *n* stranded goods *pl.*; *fig.* wreckage; '**~korb** *m* roofed wicker chair for use on the beach; **~promenade** ['~promənaːdə] *f* (-/-n) promenade, *Am.* boardwalk.

Strang [ʃtraŋ] *m* (-[e]s/¨e) cord (*a. anat.*); rope; halter (*for hanging s.o.*); trace (*of harness*); ⚒ track; *über die Stränge schlagen* kick over the traces.

Strapaz|e [ʃtraˈpaːtsə] *f* (-/-n) fatigue; toil; **2ieren** [~aˈtsiːrən] *v/t.* (*no -ge-, h*) fatigue, strain (*a. fig.*); wear out (*fabric, etc.*); **2ierfähig** *adj.* [~aˈtsiːr-] long-lasting; **2iös** *adj.* [~aˈtsjøːs] fatiguing.

Straße ['ʃtraːsə] *f* (-/-n) road, highway; street (*of town, etc.*); strait; *auf der ~* on the road; in the street.

'**Straßen|anzug** *m* lounge-suit, *Am.* business suit; '**~bahn** *f* tram(way), tram-line, *Am.* street railway; streetcar line; *s. Straßenbahnwagen*; '**~bahnhaltestelle** *f* tram stop, *Am.* streetcar stop; '**~bahnwagen** *m* tram(-car), *Am.* streetcar; '**~beleuchtung** *f* street lighting; '**~damm** *m* roadway; '**~händler** *m* hawker; '**~junge** *m* street arab, *Am.* street Arab; '**~kehrer** *m* (-s/-) scavenger, street orderly; '**~kreuzung** *f* crossing, cross roads; '**~reinigung** *f* street-cleaning, scavenging; '**~rennen** *n* road-race.

strategisch *adj.* [ʃtraˈteːgiʃ] strategic(al).

sträuben ['ʃtrɔybən] *v/t.* (*ge-, h*) ruffle up (*its feathers, etc.*); *sich ~*

hair: stand on end; *sich* ~ *gegen* kick against *or* at.

Strauch [ʃtraux] *m* (-[e]s/⸗er) shrub; bush.

straucheln ['ʃtrauxəln] *v/i.* (ge-, sein) stumble (*über acc.* over, at), trip (over) (*both a. fig.*).

Strauß [ʃtraus] *m* **1.** *orn.* (-es/-e) ostrich; **2.** (-es/⸗e) bunch (*of flowers*), bouquet; strife, combat.

Strebe ['ʃtreːbə] *f* (-/-n) strut, support, brace.

streben 1. *v/i.* (ge-, h): ~ *nach* strive for *or* after, aspire *to or* after; **2.** 2 *n* (-s/*no pl.*) striving (*nach* for, after), aspiration (for, after); effort, endeavo(u)r.

Streber *m* (-s/-) pusher, careerist; *at school*: *sl.* swot.

strebsam *adj.* ['ʃtreːpzaːm] assiduous; ambitious; **2keit** *f* (-/*no pl.*) assiduity; ambition.

Strecke ['ʃtrekə] *f* (-/-n) stretch; route; tract, extent; distance (*a. sports*); course; ⚓, *etc.*: section, line; *hunt.* bag; *zur* ~ *bringen hunt.* bag, hunt down (*a. fig.*); **2n** *v/t.* (ge-, h) stretch, extend; dilute (*fluid*); *sich* ~ stretch (o.s.); *die Waffen* ~ lay down one's arms; *fig. a.* give in.

Streich [ʃtraiç] *m* (-[e]s/-e) stroke; blow; *fig.* trick, prank; *j-m e-n* ~ *spielen* play a trick on s.o.; **2eln** ['⸗əln] *v/t.* (ge-, h) stroke; caress; pat; ~ **2en** (*irr.*, ge-) **1.** *v/t.* (h) rub; spread (*butter, etc.*); paint; strike out, delete, cancel (*a. fig.*); strike, lower (*flag, sail*); **2.** *v/i.* (sein) prowl (*um round*); **3.** *v/i.* (h): *mit der Hand über et.* ~ pass one's hand over s.th.; **~holz** *n* match; **~instrument** ♪ *n* stringed instrument; **~orchester** *n* string band; **~riemen** *m* strop.

Streif [ʃtraif] *m* (-[e]s/-e) *s.* *Streifen*; **~band** *n* (-[e]s/⸗er) wrapper; **~e** *f* (-/-n) patrol; patrolman; raid.

streifen (ge-) **1.** *v/t.* (h) stripe, streak, graze, touch lightly in passing, brush; touch (up)on (*subject*); **2.** *v/i.* (sein): ~ *durch* rove, wander through; **3.** *v/i.* (h): ~ *an* (*acc.*) graze, brush; *fig.* border *or* verge on; **4.** 2 *m* (-s/-) strip; stripe; streak.

'streif|ig *adj.* striped; **2licht** *n* sidelight; **2schuß** ⚔ *m* grazing shot; **2zug** ⚔ *m* ramble; ⚔ raid.

Streik [ʃtraik] *m* (-[e]s/-s) strike, *Am.* F *a.* walkout; *in den* ~ *treten* go on strike, *Am.* F *a.* walk out; **~brecher** *m* (-s/-) strike-breaker, blackleg, scab; **2en** *v/i.* (ge-, h) (be on) strike; go on strike, *Am.* F *a.* walk out; **~ende** ['⸗əndə] *m, f* (-n/-n) striker; **~posten** *m* picket.

Streit [ʃtrait] *m* (-[e]s/-e) quarrel; dispute; conflict; ⚖ litigation; **2bar** *adj.* pugnacious; **2en** *v/i. and v/refl.* (*irr.*, ge-, h) quarrel (*mit* with; *wegen* for; *über acc.* about); **~frage** *f* controversy, (point of) issue; **2ig** *adj.* debatable, controversial; *j-m et.* ~ *machen* dispute s.o.'s right to s.th.; **~igkeiten** *pl.* quarrels *pl.*; disputes *pl.*; **~kräfte** ⚔ ['⸗krɛftə] *f/pl.* (military *or* armed) forces *pl.*; **2lustig** *adj.* pugnacious, aggressive; **2süchtig** *adj.* quarrelsome; pugnacious.

streng [ʃtreŋ] **1.** *adj.* severe; stern; strict; austere; *discipline, etc.*: rigorous; *weather, climate*: inclement; *examination*: stiff; **2.** *adv.*: ~ *vertraulich* in strict confidence; **2e** *f* (-/*no pl.*) *s.* *streng 1*: severity; sternness; strictness; austerity; rigo(u)r; inclemency; stiffness; **~genommen** *adv.* strictly speaking; **~gläubig** *adj.* orthodox.

Streu [ʃtrɔy] *f* (-/-en) litter; **2en** *v/t.* (ge-, h) strew, scatter; **~zucker** *m* castor sugar.

Strich [ʃtriç] **1.** *m* (-[e]s/-e) stroke; line; dash; tract (*of land*); *j-m e-n* ~ *durch die Rechnung machen* queer s.o.'s pitch; **2.** ♀ *pret.* of *streichen*; **~regen** *m* local shower; **2weise** *adv.* here and there.

Strick [ʃtrik] *m* ⸗(-[e]s/-e) cord; rope; halter, rope (*for hanging s.o.*); F *fig.* (young) rascal; **2en** *v/t. and v/i.* (ge-, h) knit; **~garn** *n* knitting-yarn; **~jacke** *f* cardigan, jersey; **~leiter** *f* rope-ladder; **~nadel** *f* knitting-needle; **~waren** *f/pl.* knit-wear; **~zeug** *n* knitting(-things *pl.*).

Striemen ['ʃtriːmən] *m* (-s/-) weal, wale.

Strippe F ['ʃtripə] *f* (-/-n) band; string; shoe-lace; *an der* ~ *hängen* be on the phone.

stritt [ʃtrit] *pret.* of *streiten*; **~ig** *adj.* debatable, controversial; *~er Punkt* (point of) issue.

Stroh [ʃtroː] *n* (-[e]s/*no pl.*) straw;

thatch; '~**dach** n thatch(ed roof); '~**halm** m straw; nach e-m ~ greifen catch at a straw; '~**hut** m straw hat; '~**mann** m man of straw; scarecrow; fig. dummy; '~**sack** m straw mattress; '~**witwe** F f grass widow.

Strolch [ʃtrɔlç] m (-[e]s/-e) scamp, F vagabond; '**2en** v/i. (ge-, sein): ~ durch rove.

Strom [ʃtro:m] m (-[e]s/⁼e) stream (a. fig.); (large) river; ⚡ current (a. fig.); es regnet in Strömen it is pouring with rain; **2'ab(wärts)** adv. down-stream; **2'auf(wärts)** adv. up-stream.

strömen ['ʃtrø:mən] v/i. (ge-, sein) stream; flow, run; rain: pour; people: stream, pour (aus out of; in acc. into).

'**Strom|kreis** ⚡ m circuit; '~**linienform** f (-/no pl.) streamline shape; '**2linienförmig** adj. streamline(d); '~**schnelle** f (-/-n) rapid, Am. a. riffle; '~**sperre** ⚡ f stoppage of current.   [trend, tendency.]

'**Strömung** f (-/-en) current; fig. a.]

'**Stromzähler** ⚡ m electric meter.

Strophe ['ʃtro:fə] f (-/-n) stanza, verse.

strotzen ['ʃtrɔtsən] v/i. (ge-, h): ~ von abound in; teem with (blunders, etc.); burst with (health, etc.).

Strudel ['ʃtru:dəl] m (-s/-) eddy, whirlpool; fig. whirl; '**2n** v/i. (ge-, h) swirl, whirl.   [ture.]

Struktur [ʃtruk'tu:r] f (-/-en) struc-]

Strumpf [ʃtrumpf] m (-[e]s/⁼e) stocking; '~**band** n -[e]s/⁼er) garter; '~**halter** m (-s/-) suspender, Am. garter; '~**waren** f/pl. hosiery.

struppig adj. ['ʃtrupiç] hair: rough, shaggy; dog, etc.: shaggy.

Stube ['ʃtu:bə] f (-/-n) room.

'**Stuben|hocker** fig. m (-s/-) stay-at-home; '~**mädchen** n chambermaid; '**2rein** adj. house-trained.

Stück [ʃtyk] n (-[e]s/-e) piece (a. ♪); fragment; head (of cattle); lump (of sugar); thea. play; aus freien ~en of one's own accord; in ~e gehen or schlagen break to pieces; '~**arbeit** f piece-work; '**2weise** adv. piece by piece; (by) piecemeal; ✝ by the piece; '~**werk** n fig. patchwork.

Student [ʃtu'dɛnt] m (-en/-en), ~**in** f (-/-nen) student, undergraduate.

Studie ['ʃtu:djə] f (-/-n) study (über

acc., zu of, in) (a. art, literature); paint, etc.: sketch; '~**nrat** m (-[e]s/⁼e) appr. secondary-school teacher; '~**nreise** f study trip.

studier|en [ʃtu'di:rən] (no -ge-, h) **1.** v/t. study, read (law, etc.); **2.** v/i. study; be a student; **2zimmer** n study.

Studium ['ʃtu:djʊm] n (-s/Studien) study (a. fig.); studies pl.

Stufe ['ʃtu:fə] f (-/-n) step; fig.: degree; grade; stage.

'**Stufen|folge** fig. f gradation; '~**leiter** f step-ladder; fig. scale; '**2weise** **1.** adj. gradual; **2.** adv. gradually, by degrees.

Stuhl [ʃtu:l] m (-[e]s/⁼e) chair, seat; in a church: pew; weaving: loom; ⚕ s. Stuhlgang; '~**bein** n leg of a chair; '~**gang** ⚕ m (-[e]s/no pl.) stool; motion; '~**lehne** f back of a chair.

stülpen ['ʃtylpən] v/t. (ge-, h) put (über acc. over); clap (hat) (auf acc. on).

stumm adj. [ʃtum] dumb, mute; fig. a. silent; gr. silent, mute.

Stummel ['ʃtuməl] m (-s/-) stump;]

'**Stummfilm** m silent film. [stub.]

Stümper F ['ʃtympər] m (-s/-) bungler; ~**ei** f [~'raɪ] f (-/-en) bungling; bungle; '**2haft** adj. bungling; '**2n** F v/i. (ge-, h) bungle, botch.

stumpf [ʃtumpf] **1.** adj. blunt; Ⱥ angle: obtuse; senses: dull, obtuse; apathetic; **2.** ⚙ m (-[e]s/⁼e) stump, stub; mit ~ und Stiel root and branch; '**2sinn** m (-[e]s/no pl.) stupidity, dul(l)ness; '**2sinnig** adj. stupid, dull.

Stunde ['ʃtundə] f (-/-n) hour; lesson, Am. a. period; '**2n** v/t. (ge-, h) grant respite for.

'**Stunden|kilometer** m kilometre per hour; Am. kilometer per hour; '**2lang** adj.: nach ~em Warten after hours of waiting; **2.** adv. for hours (and hours); '~**lohn** m hourly wage; '~**plan** m timetable, Am. schedule; '**2weise 1.** adj.: ~ Beschäftigung part-time employment; **2.** adv. by the hour; '~**zeiger** m hour-hand.

stündlich ['ʃtyntliç] **1.** adj. hourly; **2.** adv. hourly, every hour; at any hour.

'**Stundung** f (-/-en) respite.

stur F *adj.* [ʃtu:r] *gaze*: fixed, staring; *p.* pigheaded, mulish.

Sturm [ʃturm] *m* (-[e]s/⸚e) storm (*a. fig.*); ⚓ gale.

stürm|en [ˈʃtyrmən] (ge-) **1.** *v/t.* (h) ⚔ storm (*a. fig.*); **2.** *v/i.* (h) *wind*: storm, rage; es stürmt it is stormy weather; **3.** *v/i.* (sein) rush; ˈ**2er** *m* (-s/-) *football, etc.*: forward; ˈ**~isch** *adj.* stormy; *fig.*: impetuous; tumultuous.

ˈ**Sturm|schritt** ⚔ *m* double-quick step; ˈ**~trupp** ⚔ *m* storming-party; ˈ**~wind** *m* storm-wind.

Sturz [ʃturts] *m* (-es/⸚e) fall, tumble; overthrow (*of government, etc.*); *fig.* ruin; ✝ slump; ˈ**~bach** *m* torrent.

stürzen [ˈʃtyrtsən] (ge-) **1.** *v/i.* (sein) (have a) fall, tumble; *fig.* rush, plunge (*in acc.* into); **2.** *v/t.* (h) throw; overthrow (*government, etc.*); *fig.* plunge (*in acc.* into), precipitate (into); *j-n ins Unglück* ~ ruin s.o.; *sich in Schulden* ~ plunge into debt.

ˈ**Sturz|flug** ✈ *m* (nose)dive; ˈ**~helm** *m* crash-helmet.

Stute *zo.* [ˈʃtu:tə] *f* (-/-n) mare.

Stütze [ˈʃtytsə] *f* (-/-n) support, prop, stay (*all a. fig.*).

stutzen [ˈʃtutsən] (ge-, h) **1.** *v/t.* cut (*hedge*); crop (*ears, tail, hair*); clip (*hedge, wing*); trim (*hair, beard, hedge*); dock (*tail*); lop (*tree*); **2.** *v/i.* start (*bei* at); stop dead *or* short.

ˈ**stützen** *v/t.* (ge-, h) support, prop, stay (*all a. fig.*); ~ *auf* (*acc.*) base *or* found on; *sich* ~ *auf* (*acc.*) lean on; *fig.* rely (up)on; *argument, etc.*: be based on.

ˈ**Stutz|er** *m* (-s/-) dandy, fop, *Am. a.* dude; ˈ**2ig** *adj.* suspicious; ~ *machen* make suspicious.

ˈ**Stütz|pfeiler** ⩓ *m* abutment; ˈ**~punkt** *m phys.* fulcrum; ⚔ base.

S

Subjekt [zupˈjɛkt] *n* (-[e]s/-e) *gr.* subject; *contp.* individual; **2iv** *adj.* [~ˈti:f] subjective; **~ivität** [~iviˈtɛ:t] *f* (-/*no pl.*) subjectivity.

Substantiv *gr.* [ˈzupstanti:f] *n* (-s/-e) noun, substantive; **2isch** *gr. adj.* [ˈ~viʃ] substantival.

Substanz [zupˈstants] *f* (-/-en) substance (*a. fig.*).

subtra|hieren ⩓ [zuptraˈhi:rən] *v/t.* (*no* -ge-, h) subtract; **2ktion** ⩓ [~kˈtsjo:n] *f* (-/-en) subtraction.

Such|dienst [ˈzu:x-] *m* tracing service; ˈ**~e** *f* (-/*no pl.*) search (*nach* for); *auf der* ~ *nach* in search of; ˈ**2en** (ge-, h) **1.** *v/t.* seek (*advice, etc.*); search for; look for; *Sie haben hier nichts zu* ~ you have no business to be here; **2.** *v/i.*: ~ *nach* seek for *or* after; search for; look for; ˈ**~er** *phot. m* (-s/-) view-finder.

Sucht [zuxt] *f* (-/⸚e) mania (*nach* for), rage (for), addiction (to).

süchtig *adj.* [ˈzyçtiç] having a mania (*nach* for); ~ *sein* be a drug addict; **2e** [ˈ~gə] *m, f* (-n/-n) drug addict *or* fiend.

Süd *geogr.* [zy:t], **~en** [ˈ~dən] *m* (-s/*no pl.*) south; **~früchte** [ˈzy:t-fryçtə] *f/pl.* fruits from the south; ˈ**2lich 1.** *adj.* south(ern); southerly; **2.** *adv.*: ~ *von* (to the) south of; **~ˈost** *geogr.*, **~ˈosten** *m* (-s/*no pl.*) south-east; **2ˈöstlich** *adj.* south-east(ern); ˈ**~pol** *geogr. m* (-s/*no pl.*) South Pole; **2wärts** *adv.* [ˈ~vɛrts] southward(s); **~ˈwest** *geogr.*, **~ˈwesten** *m* (-s/*no pl.*) south-west; **2ˈwestlich** *adj.* south-west(ern); ˈ**~wind** *m* south wind.

süffig F *adj.* [ˈzyfiç] palatable, tasty.

suggerieren [zugeˈri:rən] *v/t.* (*no* -ge-, h) suggest.

suggestiv *adj.* [zugɛsˈti:f] suggestive.

Sühne [ˈzy:nə] *f* (-/-n) expiation, atonement; ˈ**2n** *v/t.* (ge-, h) expiate, atone for.

Sülze [ˈzyltsə] *f* (-/-n) jellied meat.

summ|arisch *adj.* [zuˈmɑ:riʃ] summary (*a.* ⚖); ˈ**2e** *f* (-/-n) sum (*a. fig.*); (sum) total; amount.

ˈ**summen** (ge-, h) **1.** *v/i. bees, etc.*: buzz, hum; **2.** *v/t.* hum (*song, etc.*).

sumˈmieren *v/t.* (*no* -ge-, h) sum *or* add up; *sich* ~ run up.

Sumpf [zumpf] *m* (-[e]s/⸚e) swamp, bog, marsh; ˈ**2ig** *adj.* swampy, boggy, marshy.

Sünd|e [ˈzyndə] *f* (-/-n) sin (*a. fig.*); ˈ**~enbock** F *m* scapegoat; ˈ**~er** *m* (-s/-) sinner; **2haft** [ˈ~t-] **1.** *adj.* sinful; **2.** *adv.*: F ~ *teuer* awfully expensive; **2ig** [ˈ~diç] *adj.* sinful; **2igen** [ˈ~digən] *v/i.* (ge-, h) (commit a) sin.

Superlativ [ˈzu:pɛrlati:f] *m* (-s/-e) *gr.* superlative degree; *in ~en sprechen* speak in superlatives.

Suppe ['zupə] *f* (-/-n) soup; broth.
'**Suppen|löffel** *m* soup-spoon; '~schöpfer *m* soup ladle; '~schüssel *f* tureen; '~teller *m* soup-plate.

surren ['zurən] *v/i.* (ge-, h) whir(r); *insects:* buzz.

Surrogat [zuro'ga:t] *n* (-[e]s/-e) substitute.

suspendieren [zuspɛn'di:rən] *v/t.* (*no* -ge-, h) suspend.

süß *adj.* [zy:s] sweet (*a. fig.*); '**²e** *f* (-/*no pl.*) sweetness; '~**en** *v/t.* (ge-, h) sweeten; '²**igkeiten** *pl.* sweets *pl.*, sweetmeats *pl.*, *Am. a.* candy; '~**lich** *adj.* sweetish; mawkish (*a. fig.*); '²**stoff** *m* saccharin(e); '²**wasser** *n* (-s/-) fresh water.

Symbol [zym'bo:l] *n* (-s/-e) symbol; ~**ik** *f* (-/*no pl.*) symbolism; ²**isch** *adj.* symbolic(al).

Symmetr|ie [zyme'tri:] *f* (-/-n) symmetry; ²**isch** *adj.* [~'me:trɪʃ] symmetric(al).

Sympath|ie [zympa'ti:] *f* (-/-n) liking; ²**isch** *adj.* [~'pa:tɪʃ] likable; *er ist mir* ~ I like him;

~**isieren** [~i'zi:rən] *v/i.* (*no* -ge-, h) sympathize (*mit* with).

Symphonie [zymfo'ni:] *f* (-/-n) symphony; ~**orchester** *n* symphony orchestra.

Symptom [zymp'to:m] *n* (-s/-e) symptom; ²**atisch** *adj.* [~o'ma:tɪʃ] symptomatic (*für* of). [synagogue.)

Synagoge [zyna'go:gə] *f* (-/-n)

synchronisieren [zynkroni'zi:rən] *v/t.* (*no* -ge-, h) synchronize; dub.

Syndik|at [zyndi'ka:t] *n* (-[e]s/-e) syndicate; ~**us** ['zyndikus] *m* (-/-se, *Syndizi*) syndic. [syncope.)

Synkope [zyn'ko:pə] *f* (-/-n)

synonym [zyno'ny:m] **1.** *adj.* synonymous; **2.** ² *n* (-s/-e) synonym.

Syntax *gr.* ['zyntaks] *f* (-/-en) syntax.

synthetisch *adj.* [zyn'te:tɪʃ] synthetic.

System [zys'te:m] *n* (-s/-e) system; scheme; ²**atisch** *adj.* [~e'ma:tɪʃ] systematic(al), methodic(al).

Szene ['stse:nə] *f* (-/-n) scene (*a. fig.*); *in* ~ *setzen* stage; ~**rie** [stsenə'ri:] *f* (-/-n) scenery.

T

Tabak ['ta:bak, 'tabak, ta'bak] *m* (-s/-e) tobacco; (')~**händler** *m* tobacconist; (')~**sbeutel** *m* tobacco-pouch; (')~**sdose** *f* snuff-box; (')~**waren** *pl.* tobacco products *pl.*, F smokes *pl.*

tabellarisch [tabe'la:rɪʃ] **1.** *adj.* tabular; **2.** *adv.* in tabular form.

Tabelle [ta'bɛlə] *f* (-/-n) table; schedule.

Tablett [ta'blɛt] *n* (-[e]s/-e, -s) tray; *of metal:* salver; ~**e** *pharm.* *f* (-/-n) tablet; lozenge.

Tachometer [taxo'-] *n*, *m* (-s/-) ⊕ tachometer; *mot. a.* speedometer.

Tadel ['ta:dəl] *m* (-s/-) blame; censure; reprimand, rebuke, reproof; reproach; *at school:* bad mark; ²**los** *adj.* faultless, blameless; excellent, splendid; '²**n** *v/t.* (ge-, h) blame (*wegen* for); censure; reprimand, rebuke, reprove; scold; find fault with.

Tafel ['ta:fəl] *f* (-/-n) table; plate (*a. book illustration*); slab; *on houses, etc.:* tablet, plaque; slate; black-

board; signboard, notice-board, *Am.* billboard; cake, bar (*of chocolate, etc.*); dinner-table; dinner; ²**förmig** *adj.* ['~fœrmiç] tabular; '~**geschirr** *n* dinner-service, dinner-set; '~**land** *n* tableland, plateau; '²**n** *v/i.* (ge-, h) dine; feast, banquet; '~**service** *n s. Tafelgeschirr*; '~**silber** *n* silver plate, *Am.* silverware.

Täf(e)lung ['tɛ:f(ə)luŋ] *f* (-/-en) wainscot, panelling.

Taft [taft] *m* (-[e]s/-e) taffeta.

Tag [ta:k] *m* (-[e]s/-e) day; *officially:* *a.* date; *am or bei* ~**e** by day; *eines* ~**es** one day; *den ganzen* ~ all day long; ~ *für* ~ day by day; *über* ~**e** ⚒ aboveground; *unter* ~**e** ⚒ underground; *heute vor acht* ~**en** a week ago; *heute in acht* (*vierzehn*) ~**en** today or this day week (fortnight), a week (fortnight) today; *denkwürdiger or freudiger* ~ red-letter day; *freier* ~ day off; *guten* ~! how do you do?; good morning!; good afternoon!; F hallo!, hullo!, *Am.*

hello!; *am hellichten* ~e in broad daylight; *es wird ~* it dawns; *an den* ~ *bringen (kommen)* bring (come) to light; *bis auf den heutigen ~* to this day; ℒ'**aus** *adv.*: ~, *tagein* day in, day out.

Tage|blatt ['taːgə-] *n* daily (paper); '**~buch** *n* journal, diary.

tagein *adv.* [taːk'aɪn] *s.* tagaus.

tage|lang *adv.* ['taːgə-] day after day, for days together; ℒ**lohn** *m* day's *or* daily wages *pl.*; ℒ**löhner** ['~løːnər] *m* (-s/-) day-labo(u)rer; '**~n** *v/i.* (ge-, h) dawn; hold a meeting, meet, sit; ⚖ be in session; ℒ**reise** *f* day's journey.

Tages|anbruch ['taːgəsʔ-] *m* daybreak, dawn; *bei* ~ *at* daybreak *or* dawn; '**~befehl** ✗ *m* order of the day; '**~bericht** *m* daily report, bulletin; '**~einnahme** ✝ *f* receipts *pl. or* takings *pl.* of the day; '**~gespräch** *n* topic of the day; '**~kasse** *f thea.* box-office, booking-office; *s.* Tageseinnahme; '**~kurs** ✝ *m* current rate; *stock exchange:* quotation of the day; '**~licht** *n* daylight; '**~ordnung** *f* order of the day, agenda; *das ist an der ~* that is the order of the day, that is quite common; '**~presse** *f* daily press; '**~zeit** *f* time of day; daytime; *zu jeder* ~ at any hour, at any time of the day; '**~zeitung** *f* daily (paper).

tage|weise *adv.* ['taːgə-] by the day; ℒ**werk** *n* day's work; man-day.

täglich *adj.* ['tɛːklɪç] daily.

tags *adv.* [taːks]: ~ *darauf* the following day, the day after; ~ *zuvor* (on) the previous day, the day before.

'**Tagschicht** *f* day shift.

tagsüber *adv.* ['taːksʔ-] during the day, in the day-time.

Tagung ['taːgʊŋ] *f* (-/-en) meeting.

Taille ['taljə] *f* (-/-n) waist; bodice (*of dress*).

Takel ⚓ ['taːkəl] *n* (-s/-) tackle; '**~age** ⚓ [~'laːʒə] *f* (-/-n) rigging, tackle; ℒ**n** ⚓ *v/t.* (ge-, h) rig (*ship*); '**~werk** ⚓ *n s.* Takelage.

Takt [takt] *m* 1. (-[e]s/-e) ♪ time, measure, bar; *mot.* stroke; *den ~ halten* ♪ keep time; *den ~ schlagen* ♪ beat time; 2. (-[e]s/*no pl.*) tact; ℒ**fest** *adj.* steady in keeping time; *fig.* firm; '**~ik** ✗ *f* (-/-en) tactics *pl. and sg.* (*a. fig.*); '**~iker** *m* (-s/-)

tactician; 'ℒ**isch** *adj.* tactical; 'ℒ**los** *adj.* tactless; '**~stock** *m* baton; '**~strich** ♪ *m* bar; ℒ**voll** *adj.* tactful.

Tal [taːl] *n* (-[e]s/~er) valley, *poet. a.* dale; *enges* ~ glen.

Talar [ta'laːr] *m* (-s/-e) ⚖, *eccl.*, *univ.* gown; ⚖ robe.

Talent [ta'lɛnt] *n* (-[e]s/-e) talent, gift, aptitude, ability; ℒ**iert** *adj.* [~'tiːrt] talented, gifted.

'**Talfahrt** *f* downhill journey; ⚓ passage downstream.

Talg [talk] *m* (-[e]s/-e) suet; *melted:* tallow; '**~drüse** *anat. f* sebaceous gland; ℒ**ig** *adj.* ['~gɪç] suety; tallowish, tallowy; '**~licht** *n* tallow candle.

Talisman ['taːlɪsman] *m* (-s/-e) talisman, (good-luck) charm.

'**Talsperre** *f* barrage, dam.

Tampon ✂ [tãˈpõː, 'tampɔn] *m* (-s/-s) tampon, plug.

Tang ♀ [taŋ] *m* (-[e]s/-e) seaweed.

Tank [taŋk] *m* (-[e]s/-s, -e) tank; ℒ**en** *v/i.* (ge-, h) get (some) petrol, *Am.* get (some) gasoline; '**~er** ⚓ *m* (-s/-) tanker; '**~stelle** *f* petrol station, *Am.* gas *or* filling station; '**~wagen** *m mot.* tank truck, *Am. a.* gasoline truck, tank trailer; ⚙ tank-car; **~wart** ['~vart] *m* (-[e]s/-e) pump attendant.

Tanne ♀ ['tanə] *f* (-/-n) fir(-tree).

'**Tannen|baum** *m* fir-tree; '**~nadel** *f* fir-needle; '**~zapfen** *m* fir-cone.

Tante ['tantə] *f* (-/-n) aunt.

Tantieme [tãˈtjeːmə] *f* (-/-n) royalty, percentage, share in profits.

Tanz [tants] *m* (-es/~e) dance.

tänzeln ['tɛntsəln] *v/i.* (ge-, h, sein) dance, trip, frisk. [(h) dance.]

'**tanzen** (ge-) *v/i.* (h, sein) *and v/t.*

Tänzer ['tɛntsər] *m* (-s/-), '**~in** *f* (-/-nen) dancer; *thea.* ballet-dancer; partner.

'**Tanz|lehrer** *m* dancing-master; '**~musik** *f* dance-music; '**~saal** *m* dancing-room, ball-room, dance-hall; '**~schule** *f* dancing-school; '**~stunde** *f* dancing-lesson.

Tapete [ta'peːtə] *f* (-/-n) wallpaper, paper-hangings *pl.*

tapezier|en [tapeˈtsiːrən] *v/t.* (*no -ge-*, h) paper; ℒ**er** *m* (-s/-) paper-hanger; upholsterer.

tapfer *adj.* ['tapfər] brave, valiant, heroic; courageous; 'ℒ**keit** *f* (-/*no* *pl.*) bravery, valo(u)r; heroism; courage.

tappen ['tapən] *v/i.* (ge-, *sein*) grope (about), fumble. [awkward.)

täppisch *adj.* ['tepiʃ] clumsy,)

tapsen F ['tapsən] *v/i.* (ge-, *sein*) walk clumsily.

Tara † ['taːra] *f* (-/*Taren*) tare.

Tarif [ta'riːf] *m* (-s/-e) tariff, (table of) rates *pl.*, price-list; **2lich** *adv.* according to tariff; **~lohn** *m* standard wage(s *pl.*); **~vertrag** *m* collective *or* wage agreement.

tarn|en ['tarnən] *v/t.* (ge-, h) camouflage; *esp. fig.* disguise; **'2ung** *f* (-/-en) camouflage.

Tasche ['taʃə] *f* (-/-n) pocket (*of garment*); (hand)bag; pouch; *s.* Aktentasche, Schultasche.

'Taschen|buch *n* pocket-book; **'~dieb** *m* pickpocket, *Am. sl.* dip; **'~geld** *n* pocket-money; *monthly:* allowance; **'~lampe** *f* (electric) torch, *esp. Am.* flashlight; **'~messer** *n* pocket-knife; **'~spielerei** *f* juggle(ry); **'~tuch** *n* (pocket) handkerchief; **'~uhr** *f* (pocket-)watch; **'~wörterbuch** *n* pocket dictionary.

Tasse ['tasə] *f* (-/-n) cup.

Tastatur [tasta'tuːr] *f* (-/-en) keyboard, keys *pl.*

Tast|e ['tastə] *f* (-/-n) key; **'2en** (ge-, h) **1.** *v/i.* touch; grope (*nach* for, after), fumble (for); **2.** *v/t.* touch, feel; *sich ~* feel *or* grope one's way; **'~sinn** *m* (-[e]s/*no pl.*) sense of touch.

Tat [taːt] **1.** *f* (-/-en) action, act, deed; offen|ce, *Am.* -se, crime; *in der ~* indeed, in fact, as a matter of fact, really; *auf frischer ~ ertappen* catch *s.o.* red-handed; *zur ~ schreiten* proceed to action; *in die ~ umsetzen* implement, carry into effect; **2.** 2 *pret. of* tun; **'~bestand** †† *m* facts *pl.* of the case; **'2enlos** *adj.* inactive, idle.

Täter ['tɛːtər] *m* (-s/-) perpetrator; offender, culprit.

tätig *adj.* ['tɛːtiç] active; busy; *~ sein bei* work at; *be employed with;* **~en** † ['~gən] *v/t.* (ge-, h) effect, transact; conclude; **'2keit** *f* (-/-en) activity; occupation, business, job; profession.

'Tat|kraft *f* (-/*no pl.*) energy; enterprise; **'2kräftig** *adj.* energetic, active.

tätlich *adj.* ['tɛːtliç] violent; *~ werden gegen* assault; **'2keiten** *f/pl.* (acts *pl.* of) violence; †† assault (and battery).

Tatort †† ['taːt⁹-] *m* (-[e]s/-e) place *or* scene of a crime.

tätowieren [tɛto'viːrən] *v/t.* (*no -ge-, h*) tattoo.

'Tat|sache *f* (matter of) fact; **'~sachenbericht** *m* factual *or* documentary report, matter-of-fact account; **'2sächlich** *adj.* actual, real. [pat.)

tätscheln ['tɛtʃəln] *v/t.* (ge-, h) pet,)

Tatze ['tatsə] *f* (-/-n) paw, claw.

Tau¹ [tau] *n* (-[e]s/-e) rope, cable.

Tau² [~] *m* (-[e]s/*no pl.*) dew.

taub *adj.* [taup] deaf (*fig.: gegen* to); *fingers, etc.:* benumbed, numb; *nut:* deaf, empty; *rock:* dead; *~es Ei* addle egg; *auf e-m Ohr ~ sein* be deaf of *or* in one ear.

Taube *orn.* ['taubə] *f* (-/-n) pigeon; **'~nschlag** *m* pigeon-house.

'Taub|heit *f* (-/*no pl.*) deafness; numbness; **'2stumm** *adj.* deaf and dumb; **'~stumme,** *m, f* (-n/-n) deaf mute.

tauch|en ['tauxən] (ge-) **1.** *v/t.* (h) dip, plunge; **2.** *v/i.* (h, *sein*) dive, plunge; dip; *submarine:* submerge; **'2er** *m* (-s/-) diver; **'2sieder** *m* (-s/-) immersion heater.

tauen ['tauən] *v/i.* (ge-) **1.** (h, *sein*): *der Schnee or es taut* the snow *or* it is thawing; *der Schnee ist von den Dächern getaut* the snow has melted off the roofs; **2.** (h): *es aut* dew is falling.

Taufe ['taufə] *f* (-/-n) baptism, christening; **'2n** *v/t.* (ge-, h) ba)tize, christen.

Täufling ['tɔyfliŋ] *m* (-s/-e) child *or* person to be baptized.

'Tauf|name *m* Christian name, *Am. a.* given name; **'~pate 1.** *m* godfather; **2.** *f* godmother; **'~patin** *f* godmother; **'~schein** *m* certificate of baptism.

taug|en ['taugən] *v/i.* (ge-, h) be good, be fit, be of use (*all:* zu for); (*zu*) *nichts ~* be good for nothing, be no good, be of no use; **'2enichts** *m* (-, -es/-e) good-for-nothing, *Am. sl.* dead beat; **'~lich** *adj.* ['tauk-] good, fit, useful (*all:* für, zu for,. to *inf.*); able; ✕, ✇ able-bodied.

Taumel ['tauməl] *m* (-s/*no pl.*)

giddiness; rapture, ecstasy; '2ig adj. reeling; giddy; '2n v/i. (ge-, sein) reel, stagger; be giddy.

Tausch [tauʃ] m (-es/-e) exchange; barter; '2en v/t. (ge-, h) exchange; barter (gegen for).

täuschen ['tɔʏʃən] v/t. (ge-, h) deceive, delude, mislead (on purpose); cheat; sich ~ deceive o.s.; be mistaken; sich ~ lassen let o.s. be deceived; '~d adj. deceptive, delusive; resemblance: striking.

'**Tauschhandel** m barter.

'**Täuschung** f (-/-en) deception, delusion.

tausend adj. ['tauzənt] a thousand; '~fach adj. thousandfold; '2fuß zo. m, 2füß(l)er zo. ['~fy:s(l)ər] m (-s/-) millepede, milliped(e), Am. a. wirevorm; '~st adj. thousandth; '2ste. n (-s/-) thousandth (part).

'**Tau|tropfen** m dew-drop; '~wetter n thaw.

Taxameter [taksa'-] m taximeter.

Taxe ['taksə] f (-/-n) rate; fee; estimate; s. Taxi.

Taxi ['taksi] n (-[s]/-[s]) taxi(-cab), cab, Am. a. hack.

ta'xieren v/t. (no -ge-, h) rate, estimate; officially: value, appraise.

'**Taxistand** m cabstand.

Technik ['tɛçnik] f **1.** (-/no pl.) technology; engineering; **2.** (-/-en) skill, workmanship; technique, practice; ♪ execution; '~er m (-s/-) (technical) engineer; technician; '~um ['~um] n (-s/Technika, Techniken) technical school.

'**technisch** adj. technical; ~e Hochschule school of technology.

Tee [te:] m (-s/-s) tea; '~büchse f tea-caddy; '~gebäck n scones pl., biscuits pl., Am. a. cookies pl.; '~kanne f teapot; '~kessel m tea-kettle; '~löffel m tea-spoon.

Teer [te:r] m (-[e]s/-e) tar; '2en v/t. (ge-, h) tar.

'**Tee|rose** ♀ f tea-rose; '~sieb n tea-strainer; '~tasse f teacup; '~wärmer m (-s/-) tea-cosy.

Teich [taiç] m (-[e]s/-e) pool, pond.

Teig [taik] m (-[e]s/-e) dough, paste; 2ig adj. ['~giç] doughy, pasty; '~waren f/pl. farinaceous food; noodles pl.

Teil [tail] m, n (-[e]s/-e) part; portion, share; component; ⚖ party;

zum ~ partly, in part; ich für mein ~ ... for my part I ...; '2bar adj. divisible; '~chen n (-s/-) particle; '2en v/t. (ge-, h) divide; fig. share; '2haben v/i. (irr. haben, sep., -ge-, h) participate, (have a) share (both: an dat. in); '~haber ♦ m (-s/-) partner; '~nahme f (-/no pl.) participation (an dat. in); fig.: interest (in); sympathy (with); 2nahmslos adj. ['~na:mslo:s] indifferent, unconcerned; passive; apathetic; '~nahmslosigkeit f (-/no pl.) indifference; passiveness; apathy; '2nehmen v/i. (irr. nehmen, sep., -ge-, h): ~ an (dat.) take part or participate in; join in; be present at, attend at; fig. sympathize with; '~nehmer m (-s/-) participant; member; univ., etc.: student; contestant; sports: competitor; teleph. subscriber; 2s adv. ['~s] partly; '~strecke f section; stage, leg; ☷ fare stage; '~ung f (-/-en) division; '2weise adv. partly, partially, in part; '~zahlung f (payment by) instal(l)ments.

Teint [tɛ̃:] m (-s/-s) complexion.

Tele|fon [tele'fo:n] n (-s/-e) etc. s. Telephon, etc.; '~graf [~'gra:f] m (-en/-en) etc. s. Telegraph, etc.; '~gramm [~'gram] n (-s/-e) telegram, wire; overseas: cable(gram).

Telegraph [tele'gra:f] m (-en/-en) telegraph; '~enamt [~ən?-] n telegraph office; 2ieren [~a'fi:rən] v/t. and v/i. (no -ge-, h) telegraph, wire; overseas: cable; 2isch [~'gra:fiʃ] **1.** adj. telegraphic; **2.** adv. by telegram, by wire; by cable; '~ist [~a'fist] m (-en/-en), '~istin f (-/-nen) telegraph operator, telegrapher, telegraphist.

Teleobjektiv phot. ['te:le-] n telephoto lens.

Telephon [tele'fo:n] n (-s/-e) telephone, F phone; am ~ on the (tele)phone; ans ~ gehen answer the (tele)phone; ~ haben be on the (tele)phone; '~anschluß m telephone connexion or connection; '~buch n telephone directory; '~gespräch n (tele)phone call; conversation or chat over the (tele)phone; '~hörer m (telephone) receiver, handset; 2ieren [~o'ni:rən] v/i. (no -ge-, h) telephone, F phone; mit j-m ~ ring s.o. up, Am. call s.o. up; **2isch** *adv.* [~'foːniʃ] by (tele)phone, over the (tele)phone; **~ist** [~o'nist] *m* (-en/-en), **~istin** *f* (-/-nen) (telephone) operator, telephonist; **~vermittlung** *f* s. *Telephonzentrale;* **~zelle** *f* telephone kiosk *or* box, call-box, *Am.* telephone booth; **~zentrale** *f* (telephone) exchange.

Teleskop *opt.* [tele'skoːp] *n* (-s/-e) telescope.

Teller ['tɛlər] *m* (-s/-) plate.

Tempel ['tɛmpəl] *m* (-s/-) temple.

Temperament [tɛmpəra'mɛnt] *n* (-[e]s/-e) temper(ament); *fig.* spirit(s *pl.*); **2los** *adj.* spiritless; **2voll** *adj.* (high-)spirited.

Temperatur [tɛmpəra'tuːr] *f* (-/-en) temperature; *j-s* ~ *messen* take s.o.'s temperature.

Tempo ['tɛmpo] *n* (-s/-s, *Tempi*) time; pace; speed; rate.

Tendenz [tɛn'dɛnts] *f* (-/-en) tendency; trend; **2iös** *adj.* [~'tsjøːs] tendentious.

Tennis ['tɛnis] *n* (-/no *pl.*) (lawn) tennis; **~ball** *m* tennis-ball; **~platz** *m* tennis-court; **~schläger** *m* (tennis-)racket; **~spieler** *m* tennis player; **~turnier** *n* tennis tournament.

Tenor ♩ [te'noːr] *m* (-s/ᵘe) tenor.

Teppich ['tɛpiç] *m* (-s/-e) carpet; **~kehrmaschine** *f* carpet-sweeper.

Termin [tɛr'miːn] *m* (-s/-e) appointed time *or* day; ⚖, ✝ date, term; *sports:* fixture; *äußerster* ~ final date, dead(-)line; **~geschäfte** ✝ *n/pl.* futures *pl.*; **~kalender** *m* appointment book *or* pad; ⚖ causelist, *Am.* calendar; **~liste** ⚖ *f* causelist, *Am.* calendar.

Terpentin [tɛrpən'tiːn] *n* (-s/-e) turpentine.

Terrain [tɛ'rɛ̃ː] *n* (-s/-s) ground; plot; building site.

Terrasse [tɛ'rasə] *f* (-/-n) terrace; **2nförmig** *adj.* [~nfœrmiç] terraced, in terraces.

Terrine [tɛ'riːnə] *f* (-/-n) tureen.

Territorium [tɛri'toːrjum] *n* (-s/ *Territorien*) territory.

Terror ['tɛrɔr] *m* (-s/no *pl.*) terror; **2isieren** [~ori'ziːrən] *v/t.* (no -ge-, h) terrorize.

Terz ♩ [tɛrts] *f* (-/-en) third; **~ett** ♩ [~'tsɛt] *n* (-[e]s/-e) trio.

Testament [tɛsta'mɛnt] *n* (-[e]s/-e) (last) will, (*often:* last will and) testament; *eccl.* Testament; **2arisch** [~'taːriʃ] **1.** *adj.* testamentary; **2.** *adv.* by will; **~svollstrecker** *m* (-s/-) executor; *officially:* administrator.

testen ['tɛstən] *v/t.* (ge-, h) test.

teuer *adj.* ['tɔyər] dear (*a. fig.*), expensive; *wie* ~ *ist es?* how much is it?

Teufel ['tɔyfəl] *m* (-s/-) devil; *der* ~ the Devil, Satan; *zum* ~*!* F dickens!, hang it!; *wer zum* ~*?* F who the devil *or* deuce?; *der* ~ *ist los* the fat's in the fire; *scher dich zum* ~*!* F go to hell!, go to blazes!; **~ei** [~'lai] *f* (-/-en) devilment, mischief, devilry, *Am.* deviltry; **~skerl** F *m* devil of a fellow.

'teuflisch *adj.* devilish, diabolic(al).

Text [tɛkst] *m* (-es/-e) text; words *pl.* (of song); book, libretto (of opera); **~buch** *n* book; libretto.

Textil|ien [tɛks'tiːljən] *pl.*, **~waren** *pl.* textile fabrics *pl.*, textiles *pl.*

'textlich *adv.* concerning the text.

Theater [te'aːtər] *n* **1.** (-s/-) theat|re, *Am.* -er; stage; **2.** F (-s/no *pl.*) playacting; **~besucher** *m* playgoer; **~karte** *f* theatre ticket; **~kasse** *f* box-office; **~stück** *n* play; **~vorstellung** *f* theatrical performance; **~zettel** *m* playbill.

theatralisch *adj.* [tea'traːliʃ] theatrical, stagy.

Theke ['teːkə] *f* (-/-n) *at inn:* bar, *Am. a.* counter; *at shop:* counter.

Thema ['teːma] *n* (-s/*Themen, Themata*) theme, subject; topic (of *discussion*).

Theolog|e [teo'loːgə] *m* (-n/-n) theologian, divine; **~ie** [~o'giː] *f* (-/-n) theology.

Theoret|iker [teo're:tikər] *m* (-s/-) theorist; **2isch** *adj.* theoretic(al).

Theorie [teo'riː] *f* (-/-n) theory.

Therapie ⚕ [tera'piː] *f* (-/-n) therapy.   [spa.)

Thermalbad [tɛr'maː-] *n* thermal)

Thermometer [tɛrmo'-] *n* (-s/-) thermometer; **~stand** *m* (thermometer) reading.

Thermosflasche ['tɛrmɔs-] *f* vacuum bottle *or* flask, thermos (flask).

These [teːzə] *f* (-/-n) thesis.

Thrombose ⚕ [trɔm'boːzə] *f* (-/-n) thrombosis.

Thron [troːn] *m* (-[e]s/-e) throne; **~besteigung** *f* accession to the

T

throne; '**~erbe** m heir to the throne, heir apparent; '**~folge** f succession to the throne; '**~folger** m (-s/-) successor to the throne; '**~rede** parl. f Queen's or King's Speech.

Thunfisch ichth. ['tu:n-] m tunny, tuna.

Tick F [tik] m (-[e]s/-s, -e) crotchet, fancy, kink; e-n ~ haben have a bee in one's bonnet.

ticken ['tikən] v/i. (ge-, h) tick.

tief [ti:f] **1.** adj. deep (a. fig.); fig.: profound; low; im ~sten Winter in the dead or depth of winter; **2.** adv.: bis ~ in die Nacht far into the night; das läßt ~ blicken that speaks volumes; zu ~ singen sing flat; **3.** ♀ meteor. n (-[e]s/-s) depression, low(-pressure area); '**♀bau** m civil or underground engineering; '**♀-druckgebiet** meteor. n s. Tief; '**♀e** f (-/-n) depth (a. fig.); fig. profundity; '**♀ebene** f plain, lowland; '**♀enschärfe** phot. f depth of focus; '**♀flug** m low-level flight; '**♀gang** ♣ m draught, Am. draft; '**♀gebeugt** fig. adj. ['~gəbɔʏkt] deeply afflicted, bowed down; '**~gekühlt** adj. deep-frozen; '**~greifend** adj. fundamental, radical; '**♀land** n lowland(s pl.); '**~liegend** adj. eyes: sunken; fig. deep-seated; '**♀schlag** m boxing: low hit; '**~schürfend** fig. adj. profound; thorough; '**♀see** f deep sea; '**~sinnig** adj. thoughtful, pensive; F melancholy; '**♀stand** m (-[e]s/no pl.) low level.

Tiegel ['ti:gəl] m (-s/-) saucepan, stew-pan; ⊕ crucible.

Tier [ti:r] n (-[e]s/-e) animal; beast; brute; großes ~ fig. sl. bigwig, big bug, Am. big shot; '**~arzt** m veterinary (surgeon), F vet, Am. a. veterinarian; '**~garten** m zoological gardens pl., zoo; '**~heilkunde** f veterinary medicine; '**♀isch** adj. animal; fig. bestial, brutish, savage; '**~kreis** ast. m zodiac, **~quälerei** [~kve:lə'raɪ] f (-/-en) cruelty to animals; '**~reich** n (-[e]s/no pl.) animal kingdom; '**~schutzverein** m Society for the Prevention of Cruelty to Animals.

Tiger zo. ['ti:gər] m (-s/-) tiger; '**~in** zo. f (-/-nen) tigress.

tilg|en ['tilgən] v/t. (ge-, h) extinguish; efface; wipe or blot out, erase; fig. obliterate; annul, cancel;

discharge, pay (debt); redeem (mortgage, etc.); '**♀ung** f (-/-en) extinction; extermination; cancel(l)ing; discharge, payment; redemption.

Tinktur [tiŋk'tu:r] f (-/-en) tincture.

Tinte ['tintə] f (-/-n) ink; in der ~ sitzen F be in a scrape.

'**Tinten|faß** n ink-pot, desk: inkwell; '**~fisch** ichth. m cuttle-fish; '**~fleck** m, '**~klecks** m (ink-)blot; '**~stift** m indelible pencil.

Tip [tip] m (-s/-s) hint, tip; '**♀pen** (ge-, h) **1.** v/i. F type; fig. guess; j-m auf die Schulter ~ tap s.o. on his shoulder; **2.** v/t. tip; foretell, predict; F type.

Tiroler [ti'ro:lər] **1.** m (-s/-) Tyrolese; **2.** adj. Tyrolese.

Tisch [tiʃ] m (-es/-e) table; bei ~ at table; den ~ decken lay the table or cloth, set the table; reinen ~ machen make a clean sweep (damit of it); zu ~ bitten invite or ask to dinner or supper; bitte zu ~! dinner is ready!; '**~decke** f tablecloth; '**♀fertig** adj. food: ready-prepared; '**~gast** m guest; '**~gebet** n: das ~ sprechen say grace; '**~gesellschaft** f dinner-party; '**~gespräch** n table-talk; '**~lampe** f table-lamp; desk lamp.

Tischler ['tiʃlər] m (-s/-) joiner; carpenter; cabinet-maker; **~ei** [~'raɪ] f (-/-en) joinery; joiner's workshop.

'**Tisch|platte** f top (of a table); table top; leaf (of extending table); '**~rede** f toast, after-dinner speech; '**~tennis** n table tennis, ping-pong; '**~tuch** n table-cloth; '**~zeit** f dinner-time.

Titan [ti'ta:n] m (-en/-en) Titan; **♀isch** adj. titanic.

Titel ['ti:təl] m (-s/-) title; e-n ~ (inne)haben sports: hold a title; '**~bild** n frontispiece; cover picture (of magazine, etc.); '**~blatt** n title-page; cover (of magazine); '**~halter** m (-s/-) sports: title-holder; '**~kampf** m boxing: title fight; '**~rolle** thea. f title-role.

titulieren [titu'li:rən] v/t. (no -ge-, h) style, call, address as.

Toast [to:st] m (-es/-e, -s) toast (a. fig.).

tob|en ['to:bən] v/i. (ge-, h) rage, rave, storm, bluster; children: romp; **♀sucht** ♂ ['to:p-] f (-/no pl.)

raving madness, frenzy; **~süchtig** adj. ['to:p-] raving mad, frantic.

'**ochter** ['tɔxtər] f (-/-) daughter; '**~gesellschaft** † f subsidiary company.

'od [to:t] m (-[e]s/✒-e) death; ✒ decease.

'odes|angst ['to:dəs⁹-] f mortal agony; fig. mortal fear; *Todesängste ausstehen* be scared to death, be frightened out of one's wits; '**~anzeige** f obituary (notice); '**~fall** m (case of) death; *Todesfälle pl.* deaths pl., ✗ casualties pl.; '**~kampf** m death throes pl., mortal agony; '**~strafe** f capital punishment, death penalty; *bei ~ verboten* forbidden on or under pain or penalty of death; '**~ursache** f cause of death; '**~urteil** n death or capital sentence, death-warrant.

Tod|feind m deadly or mortal enemy; '**Ọ̈krank** adj. dangerously ill.

ödlich adj. ['tø:tliç] deadly; fatal; *wound:* a. mortal.

tod|'müde adj. dead tired; '**~schick** f adj. dashing, gorgeous; '**~sicher** f adj. cock-sure; '**Ọ̈sünde** f deadly or mortal sin.

Toilette [toa'lɛtə] f (-/-n) dress(ing): toilet; lavatory, gentlemen's or ladies' room, *esp. Am.* toilet.

Toi'letten|artikel m/pl. toilet articles pl., *Am.* a. toiletry; **~papier** n toilet-paper; **~tisch** m toilet (-table), dressing-table, *Am.* a. dresser.

toleran|t adj. [tole'rant] tolerant (*gegen* of); **Ọ̈z** [~ts] f 1. (-/no pl.) tolerance, toleration (*esp. eccl.*); 2. ⊕ (-/-en) allowance.

oll [tɔl] 1. *adj.* (raving) mad, frantic; mad, crazy, wild (*all a. fig.*); fantastic; *noise, etc.:* frightful, F awful; *fig.:* (just) fine; (just) great; 2. *adv.:* es ~ treiben carry on like mad; es zu ~ treiben go too far; '**~en** v/i. (ge-, h, sein) *children:* romp; '**Ọ̈haus** fig. n bedlam; '**Ọ̈heit** f (-/-en) madness; mad trick; '**~kühn** adj. foolhardy, rash; '**Ọ̈wut** *vet.* f rabies.

Tolpatsch f ['tɔlpatʃ] m (-es/-e) awkward or clumsy fellow; '**Ọ̈ig** f adj. awkward, clumsy.

Tölpel f ['tœlpəl] m (-s/-) awkward or clumsy fellow; boob(y).

Tomate ♀ [to'ma:tə] f (-/-n) tomato.

Ton¹ [to:n] m (-[e]s/-e) clay.

Ton² [~] m (-[e]s/✒e) sound; ♪ tone (a. of language); ♪ single: note; accent, stress; fig. tone; *paint.* tone, tint, shade; *guter ~* good form; *den ~ angeben* set the fashion; *zum guten ~ gehören* be the fashion; *große Töne reden or* F *spucken* F talk big, boast; '**~abnehmer** m pick-up; '**Ọ̈angebend** adj. setting the fashion, leading; '**~arm** m pick-up arm (*of record-player*); '**~art** ♪ f key; '**~band** n recording tape; '**~bandgerät** n tape recorder.

tönen ['tø:nən] (ge-, h) 1. v/i. sound, ring; 2. v/t. tint, tone, shade.

tönern adj. ['tø:nərn] (of) clay, earthen.

'Ton|fall m *in speaking:* intonation, accent; '**~film** m sound film; '**~lage** f pitch; '**~leiter** ♪ f scale, gamut; '**Ọ̈los** adj. soundless; fig. toneless; '**~meister** m sound engineer.

Tonne ['tɔnə] f (-/-n) *large:* tun; *smaller:* barrel, cask; ⚓ *measure of weight:* ton.

'Tonsilbe gr. f accented syllable.

Tonsur [tɔn'zu:r] f (-/-en) tonsure.

'Tönung *paint.* f (-/-en) tint, tinge, shade.

'Tonwaren f/pl. s. Töpferware.

Topf [tɔpf] m (-[e]s/✒e) pot.

Töpfer ['tœpfər] m (-s/-) potter; stove-fitter; **~ei** [~'raɪ] f (-/-en) pottery; '**~ware** f pottery, earthenware, crockery.

topp¹ int. [tɔp] done!, agreed!

Topp² ⚓ [~] m (-s/-e, -s) top, masthead.

Tor¹ [to:r] n (-[e]s/-e) gate; gateway (a. fig.); *football:* goal; *skiing:* gate.

Tor² [~] m (-en/-en) fool.

Torf [tɔrf] m (-[e]s/no pl.) peat.

Torheit ['to:rhaɪt] f (-/-en) folly.

'Torhüter m gate-keeper; *sports:* goalkeeper.

töricht adj. ['tø:riçt] foolish, silly.

Törin ['tø:rin] f (-/-nen) fool(ish woman).

torkeln ['tɔrkəln] v/i. (ge-, h, sein) reel, stagger, totter.

'Tor|latte f *sports:* cross-bar; '**~lauf** m *skiing:* slalom; '**~linie** f *sports:* goal-line.

Tornister [tɔr'nistər] m (-s/-) knapsack; satchel.

T

torpedieren [tɔrpeˈdiːrən] v/t. (no -ge-, h) torpedo (a. fig.).

Torpedo [tɔrˈpeːdo] m (-s/-s) torpedo; **~boot** n torpedo-boat.

Tor|pfosten m gate-post; sports: goal-post; **~schuß** m shot at the goal; **~schütze** m sports: scorer.

Torte [ˈtɔrtə] f (-/-n) fancy cake, Am. layer cake; tart, Am. pie.

Tortur [tɔrˈtuːr] f (-/-en) torture; fig. ordeal.

Tor|wart [ˈtoːrvart] m (-[e]s/-e) sports: goalkeeper; **~weg** m gateway.

tosen [ˈtoːzən] v/i. (ge-, h, sein) roar, rage; **~d** adj. applause: thunderous.

tot adj. [toːt] dead (a. fig.); deceased; **~er Punkt** ⊕ dead cent|re, Am. -er; fig.: deadlock; fatigue; **~es Rennen** sports: dead heat.

total adj. [toˈtɑːl] total, complete.

'tot|arbeiten v/refl. (sep., -ge-, h) work o.s. to death; **'2e** (-n/-n) **1.** m dead man; (dead) body, corpse; die **~n** pl. the dead pl., the deceased pl. or departed pl.; ✗ casualties pl.; **2.** f dead woman.

töten [ˈtøːtən] v/t. (ge-, h) kill; destroy; murder; deaden (nerve, etc.).

'Toten|bett n deathbed; **'2blaß** adj. deadly or deathly pale; **'~blässe** f deadly paleness or pallor; **'2bleich** adj. s. totenblaß; **'~gräber** [ˈ~ɡrɛːbər] m (-s/-) grave-digger (a. zo.); **'~hemd** n shroud; **'~kopf** m death's-head (a. zo.); emblem of death: a. skull and cross-bones; **'~liste** f death-roll (a. ✗), esp. ✗ casualty list; **'~maske** f death-mask; **'~messe** eccl. f mass for the dead, requiem; **'~schädel** m death's-head, skull; **'~schein** m death certificate; **'2still** adj. (as) still as the grave; **'~stille** f dead(ly) silence, deathly stillness.

'tot|geboren adj. still-born; **'2geburt** f still birth; **'~lachen** v/refl. (sep., -ge-, h) die of laughing.

Toto [ˈtoːto] m, F a. n (-s/-s) football pools pl.

'tot|schießen v/t. (irr. schießen, sep., -ge-, h) shoot dead, kill; **'2schlag** ⚖ m manslaughter, homicide; **'2schlagen** v/t. (irr. schlagen, sep., -ge-, h) kill (a. time), slay; **'~schweigen** v/t. (irr. schweigen, sep., -ge-, h) hush up; **'~ste-**

chen v/t. (irr. stechen, sep., -ge-, h) stab to death; **'~stellen** v/refl. (sep., -ge-, h) feign death.

'Tötung f (-/-en) killing, slaying; ⚖ homicide; fahrlässige **~** ⚖ manslaughter.

Tour [tuːr] f (-/-en) tour; excursion trip; ⊕ turn, revolution; auf **~en kommen** mot. pick up speed; **'~wagen** mot. m touring car.

Tourist [tuˈrist] m (-en/-en), **~in** (-/-nen) tourist.

Tournee [turˈneː] f (-/-s, -n) tour.

Trab [traːp] m (-[e]s/no pl.) trot.

Trabant [traˈbant] m (-en/-en) satellite.

trab|en [ˈtraːbən] v/i. (ge-, h, sein) trot; **2rennen** [ˈtraːp-] n trotting race.

Tracht [traxt] f (-/-en) dress, costume; uniform; fashion; load; e-e (gehörige) **~ Prügel** a (sound) thrashing; **'2en** v/i. (ge-, h): **~ nach** et strive for; j-m nach dem Leben **~** seek s.o.'s life.

trächtig adj. [ˈtrɛçtɪç] (big) with young, pregnant. [tradition.\

Tradition [traditˈsjoːn] f (-/-en)\

traf [traːf] pret. of treffen.

Trag|bahre [ˈtraːk-] f stretcher, litter; **'2bar** adj. portable; dress: wearable; fig.: bearable; reasonable; **~e** [ˈ~ɡə] f (-/-n) hand-barrow; s. Tragbahre.

träge adj. [ˈtrɛːɡə] lazy, indolent; phys. inert (a. fig.).

tragen [ˈtraːɡən] (irr., ge-, h) **1.** v/t. carry; bear (costs, name, responsibility, etc.); bear, endure; support; bear, yield (fruit, ♀ interest, etc.); wear (dress, etc.); bei sich **~** have about one; sich gut **~** material: wear well; zur Schau **~** show off; **2.** v/i. tree: bear, yield; gun, voice: carry; ice: bear.

Träger [ˈtrɛːɡər] m (-s/-) carrier; porter (of luggage); holder, bearer (of name, licence, etc.); wearer (of dress); (shoulder-)strap (of slip, etc.); ⊕ support; ⚠ girder.

Trag|fähigkeit [ˈtraːk-] f carrying or load capacity; ⚓ tonnage; **'~fläche** ✈ f, **'~flügel** ✈ m wing, plane.

Trägheit [ˈtrɛːkhaɪt] f (-/no pl.) laziness, indolence; phys. inertia (a. fig.).

tragisch adj. [ˈtraːɡiʃ] tragic (a. fig.); fig. tragical.

Tragödie [tra'gøːdjə] f (-/-n) tragedy.

Trag|riemen ['traːk-] m (carrying) strap; sling (of gun); **˷tier** n pack animal; **˷tüte** f carrier-bag; **˷weite** f range; fig. import(ance), consequences pl.; von großer ˷ of great moment.

Train|er ['trɛːnər] m (-s/-) trainer; coach; ℒieren [ˌ'niːrən] (no -ge-, h) **1.** v/t. train; coach; **2.** v/i. train; **˷ing** ['ˌiŋ] n (-s/-s) training; **˷ingsanzug** m sports: track suit.

traktieren [trak'tiːrən] v/t. (no -ge-, h) treat (badly).

Traktor ⊕ ['traktɔr] m (-s/-en) tractor.

trällern ['trɛlərn] v/t. and v/i. (ge-, h) troll.

trampel|n ['trampəln] v/i. (ge-, h) trample, stamp; **ℒpfad** m beaten track.

Tran [traːn] m (-[e]s/-e) train-oil, whale-oil.

Träne ['trɛːnə] f (-/-n) tear; in ˷n ausbrechen burst into tears; **ℒn** v/i. (ge-, h) water; **˷ngas** n tear-gas.

Trank [traŋk] **1.** m (-[e]s/ᵘe) drink, beverage; ♣ potion; **2.** ℒ pret. of trinken.

Tränke ['trɛŋkə] f (-/-n) watering-place; **ℒn** v/t. (ge-, h) water (animals); soak, impregnate (material).

Trans|formator ϟ [transfɔr'maːtɔr] m (-s/-en) transformer; **˷fusion** ϟ [ˌu'zjoːn] f (-/-en) transfusion.

Transistorradio [tran'zistɔr-] n transistor radio or set.

transitiv gr. adj. ['tranzitiːf] transitive.

transparent [transpa'rɛnt] **1.** adj. transparent; **2.** ℒ n (-[e]s/-e) transparency; in political processions, etc.: banner.

transpirieren [transpi'riːrən] v/i. (no -ge-, h) perspire.

Transplantation ϟ [transplanta-'tsjoːn] f transplant (operation).

Transport [trans'pɔrt] m (-[e]s/-e) transport(ation), conveyance, carriage; ℒabel adj. [ˌ'taːbəl] m (-s/-) ⌥, ✕ portable; **˷er** m (-s/-) ⌥, ✕ (troop-)transport; ✕ transport (aircraft or plane); **ℒfähig** adj. transportable, sick person: a. trans-

ferable; ℒieren [ˌ'tiːrən] v/t. (no -ge-, h) transport, convey, carry; **˷unternehmen** n carrier.

Trapez [tra'peːts] n (-es/-e) Å trapezium, Am. trapezoid; gymnastics: trapeze.

trappeln ['trapəln] v/i. (ge-, sein) horse: clatter; children, etc.: patter.

Trass|ant ✝ [tra'sant] m (-en/-en) drawer; **˷at** ✝ [ˌ'saːt] m (-en/-en) drawee; **˷e** ⊕ ⊕ f (-/-n) line; ℒieren [ˌ'siːrən] v/t. (no -ge-, h) ⊕ lay or trace out; ˷ auf (acc.) ✝ draw on.

trat [traːt] pret. of treten.

Tratte ✝ ['tratə] f (-/-n) draft.

Traube ['traubə] f (-/-n) bunch of grapes; grape; cluster; **˷nsaft** m grape-juice; **˷nzucker** m grape-sugar, glucose.

trauen ['trauən] (ge-, h) **1.** v/t. marry; sich ˷ lassen get married; **2.** v/i. trust (j-m s.o.), confide (dat. in); ich traute meinen Ohren nicht I could not believe my ears.

Trauer ['trauər] f (-/no pl.) sorrow, affliction; for dead person: mourning; **˷botschaft** f sad news; **˷fall** m death; **˷feier** f funeral ceremonies pl., obsequies pl.; **˷flor** m mourning-crape; **˷geleit** n funeral procession; **˷gottesdienst** m funeral service; **˷kleid** n mourning (-dress); **˷marsch** m funeral march; **ℒn** v/i. (ge-, h) mourn (um for); be in mourning; **˷spiel** n tragedy; **˷weide** ♀ f weeping willow; **˷zug** m funeral procession.

Traufe ['traufə] f (-/-n) eaves pl.; gutter; s. Regen².

träufeln ['trɔyfəln] v/t. (ge-, h) drop, drip, trickle. [cosy, snug.]

traulich adj. ['traulіç] intimate;}

Traum [traum] m (-[e]s/ᵘe) dream (a. fig.); reverie; das fällt mir nicht im ˷ ein! I would not dream of (doing) it!; **˷bild** n vision; **˷deuter** m (-s/-) dream-reader.

träum|en ['trɔymən] v/i. and v/t. (ge-, h) dream; **ℒer** m (-s/-) dreamer (a. fig.); **ℒerei** [ˌ'rai] f (-/-en) dreaming; fig. a. reverie (a. ♪), day-dream, musing; **˷erisch** adj. dreamy; musing.

traurig adj. ['traurіç] sad (über acc. at), Am. F blue; wretched.

'Trau|ring m wedding-ring; **˷schein** m marriage certificate or lines pl.; **˷ung** f (-/-en) marriage, wedding; '~zeuge m witness to a marriage.

Trecker ⊕ ['trɛkər] m (-s/-) tractor.

Treff [trɛf] n (-s/-s) cards: club(s pl.).

treffen¹ ['trɛfən] (irr., ge-) **1.** v/t. (h) hit (a. fig.), strike; concern, affect disadvantageously; affect; meet; nicht ~ miss; e-e Entscheidung ~ come to a decision; Maßnahmen ~ take measures or steps; Vorkehrungen ~ take precautions or measures; sich ~ happen; meet; gather, assemble; a. have an appointment (mit with), have a date (with); das trifft sich gut! that's lucky!, how fortunate!; sich getroffen fühlen feel hurt; wen trifft die Schuld? who is to blame?; das Los traf ihn the lot fell on him; du bist gut getroffen paint., phot. this is a good likeness of you; vom Blitz getroffen struck by lightning; **2.** v/i. (h) hit; **3.** v/i. (sein): ~ auf (acc.) meet with; encounter (a. ⊗).

Treffen² [~] n (-s/-) meeting; rally; gathering; ✕ encounter; '2d adj. remark: appropriate, to the point.

'Treff|er m (-s/-) hit (a. fig.); prize; '~punkt m meeting-place.

Treibeis ['traɪp-] n drift-ice.

treiben¹ ['traɪbən] (irr., ge-) **1.** v/t. (h) drive; ⊕ put in motion, propel; drift (smoke, snow); put forth (leaves); force (plants); fig. impel, urge, press (j-n zu inf. s.o. to inf.); carry on (business, trade); Musik (Sport) ~ go in for music (sports); Sprachen ~ study languages; es zu weit ~ go too far; wenn er es weiterhin so treibt if he carries or goes on like that; was treibst du da? what are you doing there?; **2.** v/i. (sein) drive; float, drift; **3.** v/i. (h) ♀ shoot; dough: ferment, work.

Treiben² [~] n (-s/no pl.) driving; doings pl., goings-on pl.; geschäftiges ~ bustle; '2d adj.: ~e Kraft driving force.

Treib|haus ['traɪp-] n hothouse; '~holz n drift-wood; '~jagd f battue; '~riemen m driving-belt; '~stoff m fuel; propell|ant, -ent (of rocket).

trenn|en ['trɛnən] v/t. (ge-, h) separate, sever; rip (seam); teleph., ∮ cut off, disconnect; isolate, segregate; sich ~ separate (von from), part (from or with s.o.; with

s.th.); '2schärfe f radio: selectivity; '2ung f (-/-en) separation; disconne|xion, -ction; segregation (of races, etc.); '2(ungs)wand f partition (wall). [(-bit).]

Trense ['trɛnzə] f (-/-) snaffle]

Treppe ['trɛpə] f (-/-n) staircase, stairway; (e-e a flight or pair of stairs pl.; zwei ~n hoch on the second floor, Am. on the third floor.

'Treppen|absatz m landing; '~geländer n banisters pl.; '~haus n staircase; '~stufe f stair, step.

Tresor [tre'zo:r] m (-s/-e) safe; bank: strong-room, vault.

treten ['tre:tən] (irr., ge-) **1.** v/i. tread, step (j-n or j-m auf die Zehen on s.o.'s toes); **2.** v/i. (sein) tread, step (j-m auf die Zehen on s.o.'s toes); walk; ins Haus ~ enter the house; j-m unter die Augen ~ appear before s.o., face s.o.; j-m zu nahe ~ offend s.o.; zu j-m ~ step or walk up to s.o.; über die Ufer ~ overflow its banks; **3.** v/t. (h) tread; kick; mit Füßen ~ trample upon.

treu adj. [trɔʏ] faithful, loyal; '2bruch m breach of faith, perfidy; '2e f (-/no pl.) fidelity, faith(fulness), loyalty; '2händer m (-s/-) trustee; '~herzig adj. guileless, ingenuous, simpleminded; '~los adj. faithless (gegen to), disloyal (to); perfidious.

Tribüne [tri'by:nə] f (-/-n) platform; sports, etc.: (grand) stand.

Tribut [tri'bu:t] m (-[e]s/-e) tribute.

Trichter ['trɪçtər] m (-s/-) funnel; made by bomb, shell, etc.: crater; horn (of wind instruments, etc.).

Trick [trik] m (-s/-e, -s) trick; '~film m animation, animated cartoon.

Trieb [tri:p] **1.** m (-[e]s/-e) ♀ sprout, (new) shoot; driving force; impulse; instinct; (sexual) urge; desire; **2.** ♀ pret. of treiben; '~feder f main-spring; fig. driving force, motive; '~kraft f motive power; fig. driving force, motive; '~wagen 🚋 m rail-car, rail-motor; '~werk ⊕ n gear (drive), (driving) mechanism, transmission; engine.

triefen ['tri:fən] v/i. ([irr.,] ge-, h) drip (von with); eye: run.

triftig adj. ['trɪftiç] valid.

rigonometrie ♫ [trigonome'tri:] f (-/no pl.) trigonometry.

rikot [tri'ko:] (-s/-s) 1. m stockinet; **2.** n tights pl.; vest; **~agen** [~o'ta:-ʒən] f/pl. hosiery.

riller ♪ ['trilər] m (-s/-) trill, shake, quaver; **2n** ♪ v/i. and v/t. (ge-, h) trill, shake, quaver; bird: a. warble.

rink|bar adj. ['trɪŋkɑːr] drinkable; **2becher** m drinking-cup; **~en** (irr., ge-, h) 1. v/t. drink; take, have (tea, etc.); 2. v/i.⚓drink; ~ auf (acc.) drink to, toast; **2er** m (-s/-) drinker; drunkard; **2gelage** n drinking-bout; **2geld** n tip, gratuity; j-m e-e Mark ~ geben tip s.o. one mark; **2glas** n drinking-glass; **2halle** f at spa: pump-room; **2kur** f: e-e ~ machen drink the waters; **2spruch** m toast; **2wasser** n (-s/no pl.) drinking-water.

rio ['tri:o] n (-s/-s) trio (a. ♪).

rippeln ['trɪpəln] v/i.(ge-,sein) trip.

Tritt [trit] m (-[e]s/-e) tread, step; footprint; noise: footfall, (foot)step; kick; ⊕ treadle; s. Trittbrett, Trittleiter; im (falschen) ~ in (out of) step; ~ halten keep step; **~brett** n step, footboard; mot. running-board; **~leiter** f stepladder; (e-e a pair or set of) steps pl.

Triumph [tri'umf] m (-[e]s/-e) triumph; **2al** adj. [~'fa:l] triumphant; **~bogen** m triumphal arch; **2ieren** [~'fi:rən] v/i. (no -ge-, h) triumph (über acc. over).

rocken adj. ['trɔkən] dry (a. fig.); soil, land: arid; **2dock** ⚓ n dry dock; **2haube** f (hood of) hairdrier; **2heit** f (-/no pl.) dryness; drought, aridity; **~legen** v/t. (sep., -ge-, h) dry up; drain (land); change the napkins of, Am. change the diapers of (baby); **2obst** n dried fruit.

trocknen ['trɔknən] (ge-) 1. v/i. (sein) dry; 2. v/t. (h) dry.

Troddel ['trɔdəl] f (-/-n) tassel.

Trödel F ['trø:dəl] m (-s/no pl.) second-hand articles pl.; lumber, Am. junk; rubbish; **2n** F fig. v/i. (ge-, h) dawdle, loiter.

Trödler ['trø:dlər] m (-s/-) second-hand dealer, Am. junk dealer, junkman; fig. dawdler, loiterer.

troff [trɔf] pret. of triefen.

Trog[1] [tro:k] m (-[e]s/⁼e) trough.

trog[2] [~] pret. of trügen.

Trommel ['trɔməl] f (-/-n) drum; ⊕ a. cylinder, barrel; **~fell** n drumskin; anat. ear-drum; **2n** v/i. and v/t. (ge-, h) drum.

Trommler ['trɔmlər] m (-s/-) drummer.

Trompete [trɔm'pe:tə] f (-/-n) trumpet; **2n** v/i. and v/t. (no -ge-, h) trumpet; **~r** m (-s/-) trumpeter.

Tropen ['tro:pən] die ~ pl. the tropics pl.

Tropf F [trɔpf] m (-[e]s/⁼e) simpleton; armer ~ poor wretch.

tröpfeln ['trœpfəln] (ge-) 1. v/i. (h) drop, drip, trickle; tap: a. leak; es tröpfelt rain: a few drops are falling; 2. v/i. (sein): ~ aus or von trickle or drip from; 3. v/t. (h) drop, drip.

tropfen[1] ['trɔpfən] (ge-) 1. v/i. (h) drop, drip, trickle; tap: a. leak; candle: gutter; 2. v/i. (sein): ~ aus or von trickle or drip from; 3. v/t. (h) drop, drip. ~

Tropfen[2] [~] m (-s/-) drop; ein ~ auf den heißen Stein a drop in the ocean or bucket; **2förmig** adj. ['~fœrmɪç] drop-shaped; **2weise** adv. drop by drop, by drops.

Trophäe [tro'fɛ:ə] f (-/-n) trophy.

tropisch adj. ['tro:pɪʃ] tropical.

Trosse ['trɔsə] f (-/-n) cable; ⚓ a. hawser.

Trost [tro:st] m (-es/no pl.) comfort, consolation; das ist ein schlechter ~ that is cold comfort; du bist wohl nicht (recht) bei ~! F you must be out of your mind!

tröst|en ['trø:stən] v/t. (ge-, h) console, comfort; sich ~ console o.s. (mit with); ~ Sie sich! be of good comfort!, cheer up!; **~lich** adj. comforting.

'trost|los adj. disconsolate, inconsolable; land, etc.: desolate; fig. wretched; **2losigkeit** f (-/no pl.) desolation; fig. wretchedness; **2preis** m consolation prize, booby prize; **~reich** adj. consolatory, comforting.

Trott [trɔt] m (-[e]s/-e) trot; F fig. jogtrot, routine; **~el** F m (-s/-) idiot, fool, ninny; **2en** v/i. (ge-, sein) trot.

trotz [trɔts] 1. prp. (gen.) in spite of, despite; ~ alledem for all that; 2. **2** m (-es/no pl.) defiance; obstinacy; **~dem** cj. ['~de:m] nevertheless; (al)though; **~en** v/i. (ge-, *h*) (*dat.*) defy, dare; brave (*danger*); be obstinate; sulk; '**~ig** *adj.* defiant; obstinate; sulky.

trüb *adj.* [try:p], **~e** *adj.* ['**~bə**] *liquid*: muddy, turbid, thick; *mind*, *thinking*: confused, muddy, turbid; *eyes*, *etc.*: dim, dull; *weather*: dull, cloudy, dreary (*all a. fig.*); *experiences*: sad.

Trubel ['tru:bəl] *m* (*-s/no pl.*) bustle.

trüben ['try:bən] *v/t.* (*ge-, h*) make thick *or* turbid *or* muddy; dim; darken; spoil (*pleasures, etc.*); blur (*view*); dull (*mind*); sich ~ *liquid*: become thick *or* turbid *or* muddy; dim, darken; *relations*: become strained.

Trüb|sal ['try:pza:l] *f* (*-/~-e*): ~ **blasen** mope, F be in the dumps, have the blues; '**2selig** *adj.* sad, gloomy, melancholy, wretched, miserable; dreary; '**~sinn** *m* (*-[e]s/ no pl.*) melancholy, sadness, gloom; '**2sinnig** *adj.* melancholy, gloomy, sad; **~ung** ['**~buŋ**] *f* (*-/-en*) *liquid*: muddiness, turbidity (*both a. fig.*); dimming, darkening.

Trüffel ♀ ['tryfəl] *f* (*-/-n*), F *m* (*-s/-*) truffle.

Trug[1] [tru:k] *m* (*-[e]s/no pl.*) deceit, fraud; delusion (*of senses*).

trug[2] [~] *pret. of* tragen.

'**Trugbild** *n* phantom; illusion.

trüg|en ['try:gən] (*irr.*, *ge-, h*) 1. *v/t.* deceive; 2. *v/i.* be deceptive; '**~e-risch** *adj.* deceptive, delusive; treacherous.

'**Trugschluß** *m* fallacy, false conclusion.

Truhe ['tru:ə] *f* (*-/-n*) chest, trunk; *radio*, *etc.*: cabinet, console.

Trümmer ['trymər] *pl.* ruins *pl.*; rubble, debris; ♣, ✈ wreckage; '**~haufen** *m* heap of ruins *or* rubble.

Trumpf [trumpf] *m* (*-[e]s/~-e*) *cards*: trump (card) (*a. fig.*); s-n ~ *ausspielen* play one's trump card.

Trunk [truŋk] *m* (*-[e]s/~-e*) drink; draught; drinking; '**2en** *adj.* drunken; *pred.* drunk (*a. fig. von, vor* with); intoxicated; '**~enbold** *contp.* ['**~bolt**] *m* (*-[e]s/-e*) drunkard, sot; '**~enheit** *f* (*-/no pl.*) drunkenness, intoxication; ~ *am Steuer* ⚖ drunken driving, drunkenness at the wheel; '**~sucht** *f* alcoholism, dipsomania; '**2süchtig** *adj.* addicted to drink, given to drinking.

Trupp [trup] *m* (*-s/-s*) troop, band, gang; ✕ detachment.

'**Truppe** *f* (*-/-n*) ✕ troop, body; ✕ unit; *thea.* company, troupe; **~n** *pl.* ✕ troops, forces *pl.*; die **~n** *p.* ✕ the (fighting) services *pl.*, the armed forces *pl.*

'**Truppen|gattung** *f* arm, branch, division; '**~schau** *f* military review; '**~transporter** ♣, ✈ *m* (troop-transport); '**~übungsplatz** *m* training area.

Truthahn *orn.* ['tru:t-] *m* turkey (-cock).

Tschech|e ['tʃɛçə] *m* (*-n/-n*), '**~in** *f* (*-/-nen*) Czech; '**2isch** *adj.* Czech.

Tube ['tu:bə] *f* (*-/-n*) tube.

tuberkul|ös ✿ *adj.* [tuberku'lø:s] tuberculous, tubercular; **2ose** ✿ [**~o:zə**] *f* (*-/-n*) tuberculosis.

Tuch [tu:x] *n* 1. (*-[e]s/-e*) cloth, fabric; 2. (*-[e]s/~er*) *head covering*: kerchief; shawl, scarf; *round neck*: neckerchief; duster; rag; '**~füh-lung** *f* (*-/no pl.*) close touch.

tüchtig ['tyçtiç] 1. *adj.* able, fit; clever; proficient; efficient; excellent; good; thorough; 2. *adv.* vigorously; thoroughly; F awfully; '**2keit** *f* (*-/no pl.*) ability, fitness; cleverness; proficiency; efficiency; excellency.

'**Tuchwaren** *f/pl.* drapery, cloths *pl.*

Tück|e ['tykə] *f* (*-/-n*) malice, spite; '**2isch** *adj.* malicious, spiteful; treacherous.

tüfteln F ['tyftəln] *v/i.* (*ge-, h*) puzzle (*an dat.* over).

Tugend ['tu:gənt] *f* (*-/-en*) virtue; **~bold** ['**~bolt**] *m* (*-[e]s/-e*) paragon of virtue; '**2haft** *adj.* virtuous.

Tüll [tyl] *m* (*-s/-e*) tulle.

Tulpe ♀ ['tulpə] *f* (*-/-n*) tulip.

tummel|n ['tuməln] *v/refl.* (*ge-, h*) *children*: romp; hurry; bestir o.s.; '**2platz** *m* playground; *fig.* arena.

Tümmler ['tymlər] *m* (*-s/-*) *orn.* tumbler; *zo.* porpoise.

Tumor ✿ ['tu:mor] *m* (*-s/-en*) tumo(u)r.

Tümpel ['tympəl] *m* (*-s/-*) pool.

Tumult [tu'mult] *m* (*-[e]s/-e*) tumult; riot, turmoil, uproar; row.

tun [tu:n] *v/t.* (*irr.*, *ge-, h*) do; make; put (*to school, into the bag, etc.*); *dazu* ~ add to it; contribute; *ich kann nichts dazu* ~ I cannot help it; *es ist mir darum zu* ~ I am anxious about (it); zu ~ haben have to do; be busy; es tut nichts it doesn't matter; 2. v/i. (irr., ge-, h) do; make; so ~ als ob make as if; pretend to inf.; das tut gut! that is a comfort!; that's good!; 3. ♀ n (-s/no pl.) doings pl.; proceedings pl.; action; ~ und Treiben ways and doings pl.

Tünche ['tʏnçə] f (-/-n) whitewash (a. fig.); '♀n v/t. (ge-, h) whitewash.

Tunichtgut ['tu:nɪçtgu:t] m (-, -[e]s/-e) ne'er-do-well, good-for-nothing.

Tunke ['tuŋkə] f (-/-n) sauce; '♀n v/t. (ge-, h) dip, steep.

tunlichst adv. ['tu:nlɪçst] if possible.

Tunnel ['tunəl] m (-s/-, -s) tunnel; subway.

Tüpfel ['tʏpfəl] m, n (-s/-) dot, spot; '♀n v/t. (ge-, h) dot, spot.

tupfen ['tupfən] 1. v/t. (ge-, h) dab, dot, spot; 2. ♀ m (-s/-) dot, spot.

Tür [ty:r] f (-/-en) door; mit der ~ ins Haus fallen blurt (things) out; j-n vor die ~ setzen turn s.o. out; vor der ~ stehen be near or close at hand; zwischen ~ und Angel in passing; '~angel f (door-)hinge.

Turbine ⊕ [tur'bi:nə] f (-/-n) turbine; ~nflugzeug n turbo-jet.

Turbo-Prop-Flugzeug ['turbo-'prɔp-] n turbo-prop.

Tür|flügel m leaf (of a door); '~füllung f (door-)panel; '~griff m door-handle.

Türk|e ['tʏrkə] m (-n/-n) Turk; '~in f (-/-nen) Turk(ish woman); '~is min. [~'ki:s] m (-es/-e) turquoise; '♀isch adj. Turkish.

Türklinke f door-handle; latch.

Turm [turm] m (-[e]s/⁻e) tower; a. steeple (of church); chess: castle, rook.

Türm|chen ['tʏrmçən] n (-s/-) tur-

ret; '♀en (ge-) 1. v/t. (h) pile up; sich ~ tower; 2. F v/i. (sein) bolt, F skedaddle, Am. sl. a. skiddoo.

'turm|hoch adv.: j-m ~ überlegen sein stand head and shoulders above s.o.; '♀spitze f spire; '♀-springen n (-s/no pl.) swimming: high diving; '♀uhr f tower-clock, church-clock.

turnen ['turnən] 1. v/i. (ge-, h) do gymnastics; 2. ♀ n (-s/no pl.) gymnastics pl.

'Turn|er m (-s/-), '~erin f (-/-nen) gymnast; '~gerät n gymnastic apparatus; '~halle f gym(nasium); '~hemd n (gym-)shirt; '~hose f shorts pl.

Turnier [tur'ni:r] n (-s/-e) tournament.

'Turn|lehrer m gym master; '~lehrerin f gym mistress; '~schuh m gym-shoe; '~stunde f gym lesson; '~unterricht m instruction in gymnastics; '~verein m gymnastic or athletic club.

'Tür|pfosten m door-post; '~rahmen m door-case, door-frame; '~schild n door-plate.

Tusche ['tuʃə] f (-/-n) India(n) or Chinese ink; '♀ln v/i. (ge-, h) whisper; '♀n v/t. (ge-, h) draw in India(n) ink.

Tüte ['ty:tə] f (-/-n) paper-bag.

tuten ['tu:tən] v/i. (ge-, h) toot(le); mot. honk, blow one's horn.

Typ [ty:p] m (-s/-en) type; ⊕ a. model; '~e f (-/-n) typ. type; F fig. (queer) character.

Typhus ⚕ ['ty:fus] m (-/no pl.) typhoid (fever).

typisch adj. typical (für of).

Tyrann [ty'ran] m (-en/-en) tyrant; ~ei [~'naɪ] f (-/no pl.) tyranny; ♀isch adj. [ty'ranɪʃ] tyrannical; ♀isieren [~i'zi:rən] v/t. (no -ge-, h) tyrannize (over) s.o., oppress, bully.

U

U-Bahn ['u:-] f s. Untergrundbahn.

übel ['y:bəl] 1. adj. evil, bad; nicht ~ not bad, pretty good; mir ist ~ I am or feel sick; 2. adv. ill; ~ gelaunt sein be in a bad mood; es gefällt mir nicht ~ I rather like it; '♀-

3. ♀ n (-s/-) evil; s. Übelstand; das kleinere ~ wählen choose the lesser evil; '~gelaunt adj. ill-humo(u)red; '♀keit f (-/-en) sickness, nausea; '~nehmen v/t. (irr. nehmen, sep., -ge-, h) take s.th. ill or amiss; '♀-

stand *m* grievance; **'2täter** *m* evil-doer, wrongdoer.

'übelwollen 1. *v/i.* (*sep.*, -ge-, *h*): j-m ~ wish s.o. ill; be ill-disposed towards s.o.; **2.** 2 *n* (-*s*/*no pl.*) ill will, malevolence; **~d** *adj.* malevolent.

üben ['y:bən] (ge-, *h*) **1.** *v/t.* exercise; practi|se, *Am. a.* -ce; Geduld ~ exercise patience; Klavier ~ practise the piano; **2.** *v/i.* exercise; practi|se, *Am. a.* -ce.

über ['y:bər] **1.** *prp.* (*dat.*; *acc.*) over, above; across (*river, etc.*); via, by way of (*Munich, etc.*); ~ Politik sprechen talk politics; nachdenken ~ (*acc.*) think about *or* of; ein Buch schreiben ~ (*acc.*) write a book on; ~ Nacht bleiben bei stay overnight at; ~ s-e Verhältnisse leben live beyond one's income; ~ kurz oder lang sooner *or* later; **2.** *adv.*: die ganze Zeit ~ all along; j-m in et. ~ sein excel s.o. in s.th.

über'all *adv.* everywhere, anywhere, *Am. a.* all over.

über|'anstrengen *v/t.* (*no* -ge-, *h*) overstrain; sich ~ overstrain o.s.; **~'arbeiten** *v/t.* (*no* -ge-, *h*) retouch (*painting, etc.*); revise (*book, etc.*); sich ~ overwork o.s.

überaus *adv.* ['y:bər?-] exceedingly, extremely.

'überbelichten *phot. v/t.* (*no* -ge-, *h*) over-expose.

über'bieten *v/t.* (*irr.* bieten, *no* -ge-, *h*) at auction: outbid; *fig.*: beat; surpass.

Überbleibsel ['y:bərblaipsəl] *n* (-*s*/-) remnant, *Am.* F *a.* holdover; ~ *pl. a.* remains *pl.*

'Überblick *fig. m* survey, general view (*both*: über *acc.* of).

über|'blicken *v/t.* (*no* -ge-, *h*) overlook; *fig.* survey, have a general view of; **~'bringen** *v/t.* (*irr.* bringen, *no* -ge-, *h*) deliver; **2'bringer** *m* (-*s*/-) bearer; **~'brücken** *v/t.* (*no* -ge-, *h*) bridge; *fig.* bridge over s.th.; **~'dachen** *v/t.* (*no* -ge-, *h*) roof over; **~'dauern** *v/t.* (*no* -ge-, *h*) outlast, outlive; **~'denken** *v/t.* (*irr.* denken, *no* -ge-, *h*) think s.th. over.

über'dies *adv.* besides, moreover.

über|'drehen *v/t.* (*no* -ge-, *h*) overwind (*watch, etc.*); strip (*screw*).

'Überdruck *m* **1.** (-[e]*s*/-e) overprint; ⊕ *a.* surcharge; **2.** ⊕ (-[e]*s*/≈e) overpressure.

Über|druß ['y:bərdrus] *m* (Überdrusses/*no pl.*) satiety; bis zum ~ to satiety; **2drüssig** *adj.* (*gen.*) ['~y-siç] disgusted with, weary *or* sick of.

Übereif|er ['y:bər?-] over-zeal; **2rig** *adj.* ['y:bər?-] over-zealous.

über'eil|en *v/t.* (*no* -ge-, *h*) precipitate, rush; sich ~ hurry too much; **~t** *adj.* precipitate, rash.

übereinander *adv.* [y:bər?ai'nandər] one upon the other; **~schlagen** *v/t.* (*irr.* schlagen, *sep.*, -ge-, *h*) cross (*one's legs*).

über'ein|kommen *v/i.* (*irr.* kommen, *sep.*, -ge-, sein) agree; **2kommen** *n* (-*s*/-) agreement; **~stimmen** *v/i.* (*sep.*, -ge-, *h*) *p.* agree (*mit* with); *thing*: correspond (with; to); **2stimmung** *f* agreement; correspondence; in ~ mit in agreement *or* accordance with.

über|'fahren **1.** ['~fa:rən] *v/i.* (*irr.* fahren, *sep.*, -ge-, sein) cross; **2.** [-'fa:rən] *v/t.* (*irr.* fahren, *no* -ge-, *h*) run over; disregard (*traffic sign, etc.*); **2fahrt** *f* passage; crossing.

'Überfall *m* ✕ surprise; ✕ invasion (*auf acc.* of); ✕ raid; hold-up; assault [up]on).

über'fallen *v/t.* (*irr.* fallen, *no* -ge-, *h*) ✕ surprise; ✕ invade; ✕ raid; hold up; assault.

'über|fällig *adj.* overdue; **2fallkommando** *n* flying squad, *Am.* riot squad.

über'fliegen *v/t.* (*irr.* fliegen, *no* -ge-, *h*) fly over *or* across; *fig.* glance over, skim (through); den Atlantik ~ fly (across) the Atlantic.

'überfließen *v/i.* (*irr.* fließen, *sep.*, -ge-, sein) overflow.

über'flügeln *v/t.* (*no* -ge-, *h*) ✕ outflank; *fig.* outstrip, surpass.

'Über|fluß *m* (Überflusses/*no pl.*) abundance (*an dat.* of); superfluity (of); ~ haben an (*dat.*) abound in; **2flüssig** *adj.* superfluous; redundant.

über'fluten *v/t.* (*no* -ge-, *h*) overflow, flood (*a. fig.*).

'Überfracht *f* excess freight.

über|'führen *v/t.* **1.** ['~fy:rən] (*sep.*, -ge-, *h*) convey (*dead body*);

2. [ˌˈfyːrən] (no -ge-, h) s. 1; ⚖︎ convict (gen. of); ⚐**führung** f (-/-en) conveyance (of dead body); bridge, Am. overpass; ⚖︎ conviction (gen. of) [dat. of.]

Überfülle f superabundance (an)

über|füllen v/t. (no -ge-, h) overfill; cram; overcrowd; sich ~ den Magen ~ glut o.s.; **~füttern** v/t. (no -ge-, h) overfeed.

Übergabe f delivery; handing over; surrender (a. ⚔︎).

Übergang m bridge; 🚂 crossing; fig. transition (a. ♩); esp. ⚖︎ devolution; **~sstadium** n transition stage.

über|geben v/t. (irr. geben, no -ge-, h) deliver up; hand over; surrender (a. ⚔︎); sich ~ vomit, be sick; **~gehen 1.** [ˈ~geːən] v/i. (irr. gehen, sep., -ge-, sein) pass over; work, duties: devolve (auf acc. [up]on); ~ in (acc.) pass into; ~ zu et. proceed to s.th.; **2.** [ˌ~ˈgeːən] v/t. (irr. gehen, no -ge-, h) pass over, ignore.

Übergewicht n (-[e]s/no pl.) overweight; fig. a. preponderance (über acc. over).

über|gießen v/t. (irr. gießen, no -ge-, h): mit Wasser ~ pour water over s.th.; mit Fett ~ baste (roasting meat).

über|greifen v/i. (irr. greifen, sep., -ge-, h): ~ auf (acc.) encroach (up-)on (s.o.'s rights); fire, epidemic, etc.: spread to; ⚐**griff** m encroachment (auf acc. [up]on), inroad (on); **~haben** F v/t. (irr. haben, sep., -ge-, h) have (coat, etc.) on; fig. have enough of, sl. be fed up with.

über'handnehmen v/i. (irr. nehmen, sep., -ge-, h) be rampant, grow or wax rife.

über'hängen 1. v/i. (irr. hängen, sep., -ge-, h) overhang; **2.** v/t. (sep., -ge-, h) put (coat, etc.) round one's shoulders; sling (rifle) over one's shoulders.

über'häufen v/t. (no -ge-, h): ~ mit swamp with (letters, work, etc.); overwhelm with (inquiries, etc.).

über'haupt adv.: wer will denn ~, daß er kommt? who wants him to come anyhow?; wenn ~ if at all; ~ nicht not at all; ~ kein no ... whatever.

überheblich adj. [yːbərˈheːplɪç] presumptuous, arrogant; ⚐**keit** f

(-/⚘-en) presumption, arrogance.

über'|hitzen v/t. (no -ge-, h) overheat (a. ✝︎); ⊕ superheat; **~holen** v/t. (no -ge-, h) overtake (a. mot.); esp. sports: outstrip (a. fig.); overhaul, esp. Am. a. service; **~holt** adj. outmoded; pred. a. out of date; **~hören** v/t. (no -ge-, h) fail to hear, miss; ignore.

'überirdisch adj. supernatural; unearthly.

'überkippen v/i. (sep., -ge-, sein) p. overbalance, lose one's balance.

über'kleben v/t. (no -ge-, h) paste over.

'Überkleidung f outer garments pl.

'überklug adj. would-be wise, sapient.

über'kochen v/i. (sep., -ge-, sein) boil over; F leicht ~ be very irritable.

über'kommen v/t. (irr. kommen, no -ge-, h): Furcht überkam ihn he was seized with fear; **~laden** v/t. (irr. laden, no -ge-, h) overload; overcharge (battery, picture, etc.).

'Überland|flug m cross-country flight; **'~zentrale** ⚡︎ f long-distance power-station.

über'|lassen v/t. (irr. lassen, no -ge-, h): j-m et. ~ let s.o. have s.th.; fig. leave s.th. to s.o.; j-n sich selbst ~ leave s.o. to himself; j-n s-m Schicksal ~ leave or abandon s.o. to his fate; **~lasten** v/t. (no -ge-, h) overload; fig. overburden.

über'|laufen 1. [ˈ~laufən] v/i. (irr. laufen, sep., -ge-, sein) run over; boil over; ⚔︎ desert (zu to); **2.** [ˌ~ˈlaufən] v/t. (irr. laufen, no -ge-, h): es überlief mich kalt a shudder passed over me; überlaufen werden von doctor, etc.: be besieged by (patients, etc.); **3.** adj. [ˌ~ˈlaufən] place, profession, etc.: overcrowded; ⚐**läufer** m ⚔︎ deserter; pol. renegade, turncoat.

'überlaut adj. too loud.

über'leben (no -ge-, h) **1.** v/t. survive, outlive (a. fig.); **2.** v/i. survive; ⚐**de** m, f (-/n-n) survivor.

'überlebensgroß adj. bigger than life-size(d).

überlebt adj. [yːbərˈleːpt] outmoded, disused, out of date.

'überlegen¹ F v/t. (sep., -ge-, h) give (child) a spanking.

über'leg|en² v/t. and v/refl. (no

-ge-, h) consider, reflect upon, think about; *ich will es mir ~* I will think it over; *es sich anders ~* change one's mind; **2.** v/i. (*no* -ge-, *h*): *er überlegt noch* he hasn't made up his mind yet; **2.** adj. superior (*dat.* to; *an dat.* in); **2enheit** f (-/*no pl.*) superiority; preponderance; **~t** adj. [~kt] deliberate; prudent; **2ung** [~gʊn] f (-/-en) consideration, reflection; *nach reiflicher ~* after mature deliberation.

über'lesen v/t. (*irr. lesen, no* -ge-, *h*) read *s.th.* through quickly, run over *s.th.*; overlook.

über'liefer|n v/t. (*no* -ge-, *h*) hand down *or* on (*dat.* to); **2ung** f tradition.

über'listen v/t. (*no* -ge-, *h*) outwit, F outsmart.

'Über|macht f (-/*no pl.*) superiority; *esp.* ✕ superior forces *pl.*; *in der ~ sein* be superior in numbers; **'2mächtig** adj. superior.

über|'malen v/t. (*no* -ge-, *h*) paint out; **~'mannen** v/t. (*no* -ge-, *h*) overpower, overcome, overwhelm (*all. a. fig.*).

'Über|maß n (-es/*no pl.*) excess (*an dat.* of); **'2mäßig 1.** adj. excessive; immoderate; **2.** adv. excessively, Am. a. overly; *~ trinken* drink to excess.

'Übermensch m superman; **2lich** adj. superhuman.

über'mitt|eln v/t. (*no* -ge-, *h*) transmit; convey; **2lung** f (-/-en) transmission; conveyance.

'übermorgen adv. the day after tomorrow.

über'müd|et adj. overtired; **2ung** f (-/~-en) overfatigue.

'Über|mut m wantonness; frolicsomeness; **2mütig** adj. ['~my:tɪç] wanton; frolicsome.

'übernächst adj. *the* next but one; *~e Woche* the week after next.

über'nacht|en v/i. (*no* -ge-, *h*) stay overnight (*bei* at *a friend's* [*house*], *with friends*); spend the night (at, with); **2ung** f (-/-en) spending the night; *~ und Frühstück* bed and breakfast.

Übernahme ['y:bərna:mə] f (-/-n) *field of application s.* übernehmen 1: taking over; undertaking; assumption; adoption.

'übernatürlich adj. supernatural.

übernehmen v/t. **1.** [~'ne:mən] (*irr. nehmen, no* -ge-, *h*) take over (*business, etc.*); undertake (*responsibility, etc.*); take (*lead, risk, etc.*); assume (*direction of business, office, etc.*); adopt (*idea, custom, etc.*); *sich ~* overreach o.s.; **2.** ✕ ['~ne:mən] (*irr. nehmen, sep.,* -ge-, *h*) slope, shoulder (*arms*).

'über|ordnen v/t. (*sep.,* -ge-, *h*): *j-n j-m ~* set s.o. over s.o.; '**~parteilich** adj. non-partisan; '**2produktion** f over-production.

über'prüf|en v/t. (*no* -ge-, *h*) reconsider; verify; check; review; screen *s.o.*; **2ung** f reconsideration; checking; review.

über|'queren v/t. (*no* -ge-, *h*) cross; **~'ragen** v/t. (*no* -ge-, *h*) tower above (*a. fig.*), overtop; *fig.* surpass.

überrasch|en [y:bər'raʃən] v/t. (*no* -ge-, *h*) surprise; catch (*bei* at, in); **2ung** f (-/-en) surprise.

über'red|en v/t. (*no* -ge-, *h*) persuade (*zu inf.* to *inf.*, into *ger.*); talk (*into ger.*); **2ung** f (-/~-en) persuasion.

über'reich|en v/t. (*no* -ge-, *h*) present; **2ung** f (-/~-en) presentation.

über|'reizen v/t. (*no* -ge-, *h*) overexcite; **~'reizt** adj. overstrung; **~'rennen** v/t. (*irr. rennen, no* -ge-, *h*) overrun.

'Überrest m remainder; **~e** *pl.* remains *pl.*; *sterbliche ~e pl.* mortal remains *pl.*

über'rump|eln v/t. (*no* -ge-, *h*) (take) by surprise; **2(e)lung** f (-/~-en) surprise.

über'rund|en v/t. (*no* -ge-, *h*) *sports:* lap; *fig.* surpass; **2ung** f (-/-en) lapping.

übersät adj. [y:bər'zɛ:t] studded, dotted.

über'sättig|en v/t. (*no* -ge-, *h*) surfeit (*a. fig.*); 🜍 supersaturate; **2ung** f (-/-en) surfeit (*a. fig.*); 🜍 supersaturation.

'Überschallgeschwindigkeit f supersonic speed.

über|'schatten v/t. (*no* -ge-, *h*) overshadow (*a. fig.*); **~'schätzen** v/t. (*no* -ge-, *h*) overrate, overestimate.

'Überschlag m *gymnastics:* somersault; ✈ loop; ⚡ flashover; *fig.*

U V

estimate, approximate calculation; **'Ren** (irr. schlagen) **1.** [',-ʃla·gən] v/t. (sep., -ge-, h) cross (one's legs); **2.** [',-ʃla·gən] v/i. (sep., -ge-, sein) voice: become high-pitched; **3.** [,-ʃla·gən] v/t. (no -ge-, h) skip (page, etc.); make a rough estimate of (cost, etc.); sich ~ fall head over heels; car, etc.: (be) turn(ed) over; ✈ loop the loop; voice: become high-pitched; sich ~ vor (dat.) outdo (one's friendliness, etc.); **4.** adj. [,-ʃla·gən] lukewarm, tepid.

über|schnappen v/i. (sep., -ge-, sein) voice: become high-pitched; F p. go mad, turn crazy.

über|'schneiden v/refl. (irr. schneiden, no -ge-, h) overlap; intersect; **,'schreiben** v/t. (irr. schreiben, no -ge-, h) superscribe, entitle; make s.th. over (dat. to); **,'schreiten** v/t. (irr. schreiten, no -ge-, h) cross; transgress (limit, bound); infringe (rule, etc.); exceed (speed limit, one's instructions, etc.); sie hat die 40 bereits überschritten she is on the wrong side of 40.

Über|schrift f heading, title; headline; **',schuh** m overshoe.

Über|schuß m surplus, excess; profit; **Rschüssig** adj. [',-ʃysiç] surplus, excess.

über|'schütten v/t. (no -ge-, h): ~ mit pour (water, etc.) on; fig.: overwhelm with (inquiries, etc.); shower (gifts, etc.) upon.

überschwemm|en [y:bər'ʃvɛmən] v/t. (no -ge-, h) inundate, flood (both a. fig.); **Rung** f (-/-en) inundation, flood(ing).

überschwenglich adj. ['y:bərʃvɛŋliç] effusive, gushy.

Übersee: nach ~ gehen go overseas; **',dampfer** ⚓ m transoceanic steamer; **',handel** m (-s/no pl.) oversea(s) trade.

über|'sehen v/t. (irr. sehen, no -ge-, h) survey; overlook (printer's error, etc.); fig. ignore, disregard.

über|send|en v/t. (irr. senden, no -ge-, h) send, transmit; consign; **Rung** f sending, transmission; ✈ consignment.

'übersetzen¹ (sep., -ge-) **1.** v/i. (sein) cross; **2.** v/t. (h) ferry.

über|'setz|en² v/t. (no -ge-, h) translate (in acc. into), render (into); ⊕ gear; **Rer** m (-s/-) translator;

Rung f (-/-en) translation (aus from; in acc. into); rendering; ⊕ gear(ing), transmission.

'Übersicht f (-/-en) survey (über acc. of); summary; **Rlich** adj. clear(ly arranged).

über|siedeln ['y:bərzi·dəln] v/i. (sep., -ge-, sein) and [,-'zi:dəln] v/i. (no -ge-, sein) remove (nach to); **Rsiedelung** [,-'zi:dəluŋ] f (-/-en), **Rsiedlung** [',-zi:dluŋ, ,-'zi:dluŋ] f (-/-en) removal (nach to).

'übersinnlich adj. transcendental; forces: psychic.

über|'spann|en v/t. (no -ge-, h) cover (mit with); den Bogen ~ go too far; **,t** adj. extravagant; p. eccentric; claims, etc.: exaggerated; **Rtheit** f (-/,-en) extravagance, eccentricity.

über'spitzt adj. oversubtle; exaggerated.

überspringen 1. [',-ʃpriŋən] v/i. (irr. springen, sep., -ge-, h) ⚡ spark: jump; in a spark, etc.: ~ von ... zu ... jump or skip from (one subject to another); **2.** [,-'ʃpriŋən] v/t. (irr. springen, no -ge-, h) jump, clear; skip (page, etc.); jump (class).

überstehen (irr. stehen) **1.** [',-ʃte:ən] v/i. (sep., -ge-, h) jut (out or forth), project; **2.** [,-'ʃte:ən] v/t. (no -ge-, h) survive (misfortune, etc.), weather (crisis); get over (illness).

über|'steigen v/t. (irr. steigen, no -ge-, h) climb over; fig. exceed; **,'stimmen** v/t. (no -ge-, h) outvote, vote down.

'überstreifen v/t. (sep., -ge-, h) slip s.th. over.

überströmen 1. [',-ʃtrø:mən] v/i. (sep., -ge-, sein) overflow (vor dat. with); **2.** [,-'ʃtrø:mən] v/t. (no -ge-, h) flood, inundate.

'Überstunden f/pl. overtime; ~ machen work overtime.

über|'stürz|en v/t. (no -ge-, h) rush, hurry (up or on); sich ~ act rashly; events: follow in rapid succession; **,t** adj. precipitate, rash; **Rung** f (-/,-en) precipitancy.

über|'teuern v/t. (no -ge-, h) overcharge; **,'tölpeln** v/t. (no -ge-, h) dupe, take in; **,'tönen** v/t. (no -ge-, h) drown.

Übertrag ✈ ['y:bərtra:k] m (-[e]s/=e) carrying forward; sum carried forward.

über'trag|bar adj. transferable; ✝ negotiable; ♣ communicable; **~en** [~gən] **1.** v/t. (irr. tragen, no -ge-, h) ✝ carry forward; make over (property) (auf acc. to); ♣ transfuse (blood); delegate (rights, etc.) (dat. to); render (book, etc.) (in acc. into); transcribe (s.th. written in shorthand); ♣, ⊕, phys., radio: transmit; radio: a. broadcast; im Fernsehen ~ televise; ihm wurde eine wichtige Mission ~ he was charged with an important mission; **2.** adj. figurative; **2ung** [~gʊŋ] f (-/-en) field of application s. übertragen 1: carrying forward; making over; transfusion; delegation; rendering, free translation; transcription; transmission; broadcast; ~ im Fernsehen telecast.

über'treffen v/t. (irr. treffen, no -ge-, h) excel s.o. (an dat. in; in dat. in, at); surpass (in), exceed (in).

über'treib|en (irr. treiben, no -ge-, h) **1.** v/t. overdo; exaggerate, overstate; **2.** v/i. exaggerate, draw the long bow; **2ung** f (-/-en) exaggeration, overstatement.

'übertreten[1] v/i. (irr. treten, sep., -ge-, sein) sports: cross the take-off line; fig. go over (zu to); zum Katholizismus ~ turn Roman Catholic.

über'tret|en[2] v/t. (irr. treten, no -ge-, h) transgress, violate, infringe (law, etc.); sich den Fuß ~ sprain one's ankle; **2ung** f (-/-en) transgression, violation, infringement.

'Übertritt m going over (zu to); eccl. conversion (to).

übervölker|n [y:bər'fœlkərn] v/t. (no -ge-, h) over-populate; **2ung** f (-/✦-en) over-population.

über'vorteilen v/t. (no -ge-, h) overreach, F do.

über'wach|en v/t. (no -ge-, h) supervise, superintend; control; police: keep under surveillance, shadow; **2ung** f (-/✦-en) supervision, superintendence; control; surveillance.

überwältigen [y:bər'vɛltigən] v/t. (no -ge-, h) overcome, overpower, overwhelm (all a. fig.); **~d** fig. adj. overwhelming.

über'weis|en v/t. (irr. weisen, no -ge-, h) remit (money) (dat. or an acc. to); (zur Entscheidung etc.) ~

refer (to); **2ung** f (-/-en) remittance; reference (an acc. to); parl. devolution.

überwerfen (irr. werfen) **1.** ['~verfən] v/t. (sep., -ge-, h) slip (coat) on; **2.** [~'verfən] v/refl. (no -ge-, h) fall out (mit with).

über'wieg|en (irr. wiegen, no -ge-, h) **1.** v/t. outweigh; **2.** v/i. preponderate; predominate; **~'wiegend** adj. preponderant; predominant; **~'winden** v/t. (irr. winden, no -ge-, h) overcome (a. fig.), subdue; sich ~ z inf. bring o.s. to inf.; **~'wintern** v/i. (no -ge-, h) (pass the) winter.

'Über|wurf m wrap; **'~zahl** (-/✦-en) numerical superiority; in der ~ superior in numbers; **2zählig** adj. ['~tse:liç] supernumerary; surplus.

über'zeug|en v/t. (no -ge-, h) convince (von of); satisfy (of); **2ung** f (-/-en) conviction.

überziehe|n v/t. (irr. ziehen) **1.** ['~tsi:ən] (sep., -ge-, h) put on; **2.** [~'tsi:ən] (no -ge-, h) cover; put clean sheets on (bed); ✝ overdraw (account); sich ~ sky: become overcast; **'2r** m (-s/-) overcoat, topcoat.

'Überzug m cover; case, tick; ⊕ coat(ing). [ary; normal.|

üblich adj. ['y:pliç] usual, custom-

U-Boot ⚓, ✕ ['u:-] n submarine, in Germany: a. U-boat.

übrig adj. ['y:briç] left, remaining; die ~e Welt the rest of the world; die ~en pl. the others pl., the rest; im ~en for the rest; by the way; ~ haben have s.th. left; keine Zeit ~ haben have no time to spare; etwas ~ haben für care for, have a soft spot for; ein ~es tun go out of one's way; **'~bleiben** v/i. (irr. bleiben, sep., -ge-, sein) be left; remain; es blieb ihm nichts anderes übrig he had no (other) alternative (als but); **~ens** adv. ['~gəns] by the way; **~lassen** ['~ç-] v/t. (irr. lassen, sep., -ge-, h) leave; viel zu wünschen ~ leave much to be desired.

'Übung f (-/-en) exercise; practice; drill; **'~shang** m skiing: nursery slope.

Ufer ['u:fər] n (-s/-) shore (of sea, lake); bank (of river, etc.).

Uhr [u:r] f (-/-en) clock; watch; um vier ~ at four o'clock; **'~armband** n (-[e]s/✦er) watch-strap; **'~feder** f watch-spring; '**~macher** m (-s/-) watch-maker; '**~werk** n clockwork; watch-work; '**~zeiger** m hand (*of clock or watch*); '**~zeigersinn** m (-[e]s/*no pl.*): im ~ clockwise; entgegen dem ~ counter-clockwise.

Uhu *orn.* ['uːhuː] m (-s/-s) eagle-owl.

Ulk [ulk] m (-[e]s/-e) fun, lark; '**2en** v/i. (ge-, h) (sky)lark, joke; '**2ig** adj. funny.

Ulme ♀ ['ulmə] f (-/-n) elm.

Ultimatum [ulti'maːtum] n (-s/*Ultimaten*, -s) ultimatum; j-m ein ~ stellen deliver an ultimatum to s.o.

Ultimo ✝ ['ultimo] m (-s/-s) last day of the month.

Ultrakurzwelle *phys.* [ultra'-] f ultra-short wave, very-high-frequency wave.

um [um] **1.** *prp.* (*acc.*): round, about; ~ vier Uhr at four o'clock; ~ sein Leben laufen run for one's life; et. ~ einen Meter verfehlen miss s.th. by a metre; et. ~ zwei Mark verkaufen sell s.th. at two marks; **2.** *prp.* (*gen.*): ~ seinetwillen for his sake; **3.** *cj.*: ~ so besser all the better, so much the better; ~ so mehr (weniger) all the more (less); ~ zu (in order) to; **4.** *adv.*: er drehte sich ~ he turned round.

um|ändern ['um⁹-] v/t. (sep., -ge-, h) change, alter; **~arbeiten** ['um⁹-] v/t. (sep., -ge-, h) make over (*coat, etc.*); revise (*book, etc.*); ~ zu make into.

um'arm|en v/t. (*no* -ge-, h) hug, embrace; sich ~ embrace; **2ung** f (-/-en) embrace, hug.

'**Umbau** m (-[e]s/-e, -ten) rebuilding; reconstruction; '**2en** v/t. (sep., -ge-, h) rebuild; reconstruct.

'**umbiegen** v/t. (*irr. biegen*, sep., -ge-, h) bend; turn up or down.

'**umbild|en** v/t. (sep., -ge-, h) remodel, reconstruct; reorganize, reform; reshuffle (*cabinet*); '**2ung** f (-/-en) remodel(l)ing, reconstruction; reorganization, *pol.* reshuffle.

'**um|binden** v/t. (*irr. binden*, sep., -ge-, h) put on (*apron, etc.*); '**~blättern** (sep., -ge-, h) **1.** v/t. turn over; **2.** v/i. turn over the page; '**~brechen** v/t. (*irr. brechen*, sep.) **1.** ✐ ['~breçən] (sep., -ge-, h) dig, break up (*ground*); **2.** *typ.* [~'breçən] (*no* -ge-, h) make up; '**~bringen** v/t. (*irr. bringen*, sep., -ge-, h) kill; sich ~ kill o.s.;

'**2bruch** m *typ.* make-up; *fig.*: upheaval; radical change; '**~buchen** v/t. (sep., -ge-, h) ✝ transfer or switch to another account; book for another date; '**~disponieren** v/i. (sep., *no* -ge-, h) change one's plans.

'**umdreh|en** v/t. (sep., -ge-, h) turn; s. Spieß; sich ~ turn round; **2ung** [um'-] f (-/-en) turn; *phys.*, ⊕ rotation, revolution.

um|fahren (*irr. fahren*) **1.** ['~faːrən] v/t. (sep., -ge-, h) run down; **2.** ['~faːrən] v/i. (sep., -ge-, sein) go a roundabout way; **3.** [~'faːrən] v/t. (*no* -ge-, h) drive round; ⚓ sail round; ⚓ double (*cape*); '**~fallen** v/i. (*irr. fallen*, sep., -ge-, sein) fall; collapse; *vet.* ~ drop dead.

'**Umfang** m (-[e]s/*no pl.*) circumference; circuit; perimeter; girth (*of body, tree, etc.*); *fig.*: extent; volume; in großem ~ on a large scale; '**2reich** adj. extensive; voluminous; spacious.

um'fass|en v/t. (*no* -ge-, h) clasp; embrace (a. *fig.*); ✗ envelop; *fig.* comprise, cover, comprehend; **~d** adj. comprehensive, extensive; sweeping, drastic.

'**umform|en** v/t. (sep., -ge-, h) remodel, recast, transform (a. ⚡); ⚡ convert; '**2er** ⚡ m (-s/-) transformer; converter.

'**Umfrage** f poll; öffentliche ~ public opinion poll.

'**Umgang** m **1.** (-[e]s/⁼e) △ gallery, ambulatory; *eccl.* procession (*round the fields, etc.*); **2.** (-[e]s/*no pl.*) intercourse (mit with); company; ~ haben mit associate with.

umgänglich adj. ['umɡɛnliç] sociable, companionable, affable.

'**Umgangs|formen** f/pl. manners pl.; '**~sprache** f colloquial usage; in der deutschen ~ in colloquial German.

um'garnen v/t. (*no* -ge-, h) ensnare.

um'geb|en 1. v/t. (*irr. geben*, *no* -ge-, h) surround; mit e-r Mauer ~ wall in; **2.** adj. surrounded (von with, by) (a. *fig.*); **2ung** f (-/-en) environs pl. (*of town, etc.*); surroundings pl., environment (*of place, person, etc.*).

umgeh|en (*irr. gehen*) **1.** ['~ɡeːən] v/i. (sep., -ge-, sein) make a detour; *rumour, etc.*: go about, be afloat;

ghost: walk; ~ *mit* use *s.th.;* deal with *s.o.;* keep company with; *ein Gespenst soll im Schlosse ~* the castle is said to be haunted; **2.** [~ɡeːən] *v/t. (no -ge-, h)* go round; ✕ flank; bypass *(town, etc.); fig.* avoid, evade; circumvent, elude *(law, etc.);* '~**end** *adj.* immediate; **Qungsstraße** [um'ɡeːuŋs-] *f* by-pass.

umgekehrt ['umɡəkeːrt] **1.** *adj.* reverse, inverse, inverted; *in ~er Reihenfolge* in reverse order; *im ~en Verhältnis zu* in inverse proportion to; **2.** *adv.* vice versa.

'**umgraben** *v/t. (irr. graben, sep., -ge-, h)* dig (up).

um|grenzen *v/t. (no -ge-, h)* encircle; enclose; *fig.* circumscribe, limit.

'**umgruppier|en** *v/t.(sep.,no-ge-,h)* regroup; '**Qung** *f (-/-en)* regrouping.

'**um|haben** F *v/t. (irr. haben, sep., -ge-, h)* have *(coat, etc.)* on; '**Qhang** *m* wrap; cape; '~**hängen** *v/t. (sep., -ge-, h)* rehang *(pictures);* sling *(rifle)* over one's shoulder; *sich den Mantel ~* put one's coat round one's shoulders; '~**hauen** *v/t. (irr. hauen, sep., -ge-, h)* fell, cut down; F: *die Nachricht hat mich umgehauen* I was bowled over by the news.

um'her|blicken *v/i. (sep., -ge-, h)* look about (one); ~**streifen** *v/i. (sep., -ge-, h)* rove.

um'hinkönnen *v/i. (irr. können, sep., -ge-, h): ich kann nicht umhin, zu sagen* I cannot help saying.

um'hüll|en *v/t. (no -ge-, h)* wrap up *(mit in),* envelop (in); **Qung** *f (-/-en)* wrapping, wrapper, envelopment.

Umkehr ['umkeːr] *f (-/no pl.)* return; '**Qen** *(sep., -ge-)* **1.** *v/i. (sein)* return, turn back; **2.** *v/t. (h)* turn out *(one's pocket, etc.);* invert *(a. ♪);* reverse *(a. ♪, ♫);* '~**ung** *f (-/-en)* reversal; inversion.

'**umkippen** *(sep., -ge-)* **1.** *v/t. (h)* upset, tilt; **2.** *v/i. (sein)* upset, tilt (over); F faint.

um'klammer|n *v/t. (no -ge-, h)* clasp; *boxing:* clinch; **Qung** *f (-/-en)* clasp; *boxing:* clinch.

'**umkleid|en** *v/refl. (sep., -ge-, h)* change (one's clothes); '**Qeraum** *m* dressing-room.

'**umkommen** *v/i. (irr. kommen, sep., -ge-, sein)* be killed *(bei in);* die (in), perish (in); *vor Langeweile ~* die of boredom.

'**Umkreis** *m (-es/no pl.)* A circumscribed circle; *im ~ von* within a radius of.

um'kreisen *v/t. (no -ge-, h)* circle round.

'**um|krempeln** *v/t. (sep., -ge-, h)* tuck up *(shirt-sleeves, etc.);* change *(plan, etc.);* (völlig) ~ turn *s.th.* inside out; '~**laden** *v/t. (irr. laden, sep., -ge-, h)* reload; ✝, ♽ tranship.

'**Umlauf** *m* circulation; *phys.,* ⊕ rotation; circular (letter); *in ~ setzen or bringen* circulate, put into circulation; *im ~ sein* circulate, be in circulation; *rumours:* be afloat; *außer ~ setzen* withdraw from circulation; '~**bahn** *f* orbit; **Qen** *(irr. laufen)* **1.** ['~laufən] *v/t. (sep., -ge-, h)* knock over; **2.** ['~laufən] *v/i. (sep., -ge-, sein)* circulate; make a detour; **3.** [~'laufən] *v/t. (no -ge-, h)* run round.

'**Umlege|kragen** *m* turn-down collar; '**Qn** *v/t. (sep., -ge-, h)* lay down; ⊕ throw *(lever);* storm, etc.: beat down *(wheat, etc.);* re-lay *(cable, etc.);* put *(coat, etc.)* round one's shoulders; apportion *(costs, etc.); fig. sl.* do *s.o.* in.

um|leit|en *v/t. (sep., -ge-, h)* divert; '**Qung** *f* diversion, detour.

'**umliegend** *adj.* surrounding; circumjacent.

um'nacht|et *adj.: geistig ~* mentally deranged; **Qung** *f (-/~-en): geistige ~* mental derangement.

'**um|packen** *v/t. (sep., -ge-, h)* repack; ~**pflanzen** *v/t.* **1.** ['~pflantsən] *(sep., -ge-, h)* transplant; **2.** [~'pflantsən] *(no -ge-, h): ~ mit* plant *s.th.* round with; ~**pflügen** *v/t. (sep., -ge-, h)* plough, *Am.* plow.

um'rahmen *v/t. (no -ge-, h)* frame; *musikalisch ~* put into a musical setting.

umrand|en [um'randən] *v/t. (no -ge-, h)* edge, border; **Qung** *f (-/-en)* edge, border.

um'ranken *v/t. (no -ge-, h)* twine (*mit* with).

'**umrechn|en** *v/t. (sep., -ge-, h)* convert *(in acc.* into); '**Qung** *f (-/no* *pl.*) conversion; **'⟨ungskurs** *m* rate of exchange.

⟨mreißen *v/t.* (*irr. reißen*) **1.** ['⟨raɪsən] (*sep.*, *-ge-*, *h*) pull down; knock *s.o.* over; **2.** [⟨'raɪsən] (*no -ge-*, *h*) outline. [round (*a. fig.*).]

m'ringen *v/t.* (*no -ge-*, *h*) sur-⟩

Um|riß *m* outline (*a. fig.*), contour; **'⟨rühren** *v/t.* (*sep.*, *-ge-*, *h*) stir; **'⟨satteln** (*sep.*, *-ge-*, *h*) **1.** *v/t.* resaddle; **2.** F *fig. v/i.* change one's studies *or* occupation; *\~von ... auf* (*acc.*) change from ... to ...; **'⟨satz** ✝ *m* turnover; sales *pl.*; return(s *pl.*); *stock exchange*: business done.

umschalt|en (*sep.*, *-ge-*, *h*) **1.** *v/t.* ⊕ change over; ⚡ commutate; ⚡ switch; **2.** ⚡, ⊕ *v/i.* switch over; **'⟨er** *m* ⊕ change-over switch; ⚡ commutator; **'⟨ung** *f* (*-/-en*) ⊕ change-over; ⚡ commutation.

'Umschau *f* (*-/no pl.*): *\~ halten nach* look out for, be on the look-out for; **'⟨en** *v/refl.* (*sep.*, *-ge-*, *h*) look round (*nach* for); look about (for) (*a. fig.*), look about one.

'umschicht|en *v/t.* (*sep.*, *-ge-*, *h*) pile afresh; *fig.* regroup (*a.* ✠); **'⟨ig** *adv.* by *or* in turns; **'⟨ung** *fig. f* (*-/-en*) regrouping; *soziale \~en pl.* social upheavals *pl.*

um'schiff|en *v/t.* (*no -ge-*, *h*) circumnavigate; double (*cape*); **⟨ung** *f* (*-/⟨-en*) circumnavigation; doubling.

'Umschlag *m* envelope, cover, wrapper; jacket; turn-up, *Am. a.* cuff (*of trousers*); 🩹 compress; 🩹 poultice; trans-shipment (*of goods*); *fig.* change, turn; **'⟨en** (*irr. schlagen*, *sep.*, *-ge-*) **1.** *v/t.* (*h*) knock *s.o.* down; cut down, fell (*tree*); turn (*leaf*); turn up (*sleeves*, *etc.*); turn down (*collar*); trans-ship (*goods*). **2.** *v/i.* (*sein*) turn over, upset; ⚓ capsize, upset; *wine*, *etc.*: turn sour; *fig.* turn (*in acc.* into); **'⟨hafen** *m* port of trans-shipment.

um|'schließen *v/t.* (*irr. schließen*, *no -ge-*, *h*) embrace, surround (*a.* ✗), enclose; ✗ invest; **\~'schlingen** *v/t.* (*irr. schlingen*, *no -ge-*, *h*) embrace.

'um|schmeißen F *v/t.* (*irr. schmei-ßen*, *sep.*, *-ge-*, *h*) *s.* umstoßen; **'\~schnallen** *v/t.* (*sep.*, *-ge-*, *h*) buckle on.

umschreib|en *v/t.* (*irr. schreiben*) **1.** ['⟨ʃraɪbən] (*sep.*, *-ge-*, *h*) re-write; transfer (*property*, *etc.*) (*auf acc.* to); **2.** [⟨'ʃraɪbən] (*no -ge-*, *h*) ⚛ circumscribe; paraphrase; **⟨ung** *f* (*-/-en*) **1.** ['⟨ʃraɪbʊŋ] rewriting; transfer (*auf acc.* to); **2.** [⟨'ʃraɪbʊŋ] ⚛ circumscription; paraphrase.

'Umschrift *f* circumscription; *phonetics*: transcription.

'umschütten *v/t.* (*sep.*, *-ge-*, *h*) pour into another vessel; spill.

'Um|schweife *pl.*: *\~ machen* beat about the bush; *ohne \~* pointblank; **'⟨schwenken** *fig. v/i.* (*sep.*, *-ge-*, *sein*) veer *or* turn round; **'\~schwung** *fig. m* revolution; revulsion (*of public feeling*, *etc.*); change (*in the weather*, *etc.*); reversal (*of opinion*, *etc.*).

um'seg|eln *v/t.* (*no -ge-*, *h*) sail round; double (*cape*); circumnavigate (*globe*, *world*); **⟨(e)lung** *f* (*-/-en*) sailing round (*world*, *etc.*); doubling; circumnavigation.

'um|sehen *v/refl.* (*irr. sehen*, *sep.*, *-ge-*, *h*) look round (*nach* for); look about (for) (*a. fig.*), look about one; **'\~sein** F *v/i.* (*irr. sein*, *sep.*, *-ge-*, *sein*) *time*: be up; *holidays*, *etc.*: be over; **'\~setzen** *v/t.* (*sep.*, *-ge-*, *h*) transpose (*a.* ♪); 🌱 transplant; ✝ turn over; spend (*money*) (*in acc.* on *books*, *etc.*); *in die Tat \~* realize, convert into fact.

'Umsicht *f* (*-/no pl.*) circumspection; **'⟨ig** *adj.* circumspect.

'umsied|eln (*sep.*, *-ge-*, *h*) **1.** *v/t.* (*h*) resettle; **2.** *v/i.* (*sein*) (re)move (*nach*, *in acc.* to); **'⟨lung** *f* (*-/\~-en*) resettlement; evacuation; removal.

um'sonst *adv.* gratis, free of charge; in vain; to no purpose; *nicht \~ not* without good reason.

umspann|en *v/t.* **1.** ['⟨ʃpanən] (*sep.*, *-ge-*, *h*) change (*horses*); ⚡ transform; **2.** [⟨'ʃpanən] (*no -ge-*, *h*) span; *fig. a.* embrace; **'⟨er** ⚡ *m* (*-s/-*) transformer.

'umspringen *v/i.* (*irr. springen*, *sep.*, *-ge-*, *sein*) shift, veer (*round*); *\~ mit* treat badly, *etc.*

'Umstand *m* circumstance; fact, detail; *unter diesen Umständen* in *or* under the circumstances; *unter keinen Umständen* in *or* under no circumstances, on no account; *unter Umständen* possibly; *ohne*

umständlich 32

Umstände without ceremony; *in anderen Umständen sein* be in the family way.

umständlich *adj.* ['ʊmʃtɛntlɪç] *story, etc.*: long-winded; *method, etc.*: roundabout; *p.* fussy; *das ist (mir) viel zu ~* that is far too much trouble (for me); **'2keit** *f* (-/‰ -en) long-windedness; fussiness.

'Umstands|kleid *n* maternity robe; **'~wort** *gr. n* (-[e]s/‰er) adverb.

'umstehend 1. *adj.: auf der ~en Seite* overleaf; **2.** *adv.* overleaf; **2en** ['~dən] *pl. the* bystanders *pl.*

'Umsteige|karte *f* transfer; **'2n** *v/i.* (*irr. steigen, sep., -ge-, sein*) change (*nach* for); **⑤** *a.* change trains (for).

Umsteigkarte ['ʊmʃtaɪk-] *f s. Umsteigekarte.*

umstell|en *v/t.* **1.** ['~ʃtɛlən] (*sep., -ge-, h*) transpose (*a. gr.*); shift (*furniture*) about *or* round; convert (*currency, production*) (*auf acc.* to); *sich ~* change one's attitude; accommodate o.s. to new conditions; adapt o.s. (*auf acc.* to); **2.** [~'ʃtɛlən] (*no -ge-, h*) surround; **2ung** [~'ʃtɛluŋ] *f* transposition; *fig.:* conversion; adaptation; change.

'um|stimmen *v/t.* (*sep., -ge-, h*) ♪ tune to another pitch; *j-n ~* change s.o.'s mind, bring s.o. round; **'~stoßen** *v/t.* (*irr. stoßen, sep., -ge-, h*) knock over; upset; *fig.* annul; ⚖ overrule, reverse; upset (*plan*).

um|'stricken *v/t. fig.* (*no -ge-, h*) ensnare; **~stritten** *adj.* [~'ʃtrɪtən] disputed, contested; controversial.

'Um|sturz *m* subversion, overturn; **'2stürzen** (*sep., -ge-*) **1.** *v/t.* upset, overturn (*a. fig.*); *fig.* subvert; **2.** *v/i.* (*sein*) upset, overturn; fall down; **2stürzlerisch** *adj.* ['~ləriʃ] subversive.

'Umtausch *m* (-es/‰ -e) exchange; ✝ conversion (*of currency, etc.*); **'2en** *v/t.* (*sep., -ge-, h*) exchange (*gegen* for); ✝ convert.

'umtun F *v/t.* (*irr. tun, sep., -ge-, h*) put (*coat, etc.*) round one's shoulders; *sich ~ nach* look about for.

'umwälz|en *v/t.* (*sep., -ge-, h*) roll round; *fig.* revolutionize; **'~end** *adj.* revolutionary; **2ung** *fig. f* (-/-en) revolution, upheaval.

'umwand|eln *v/t.* (*sep., -ge-, h*) transform (*in acc.* into); ⚡, ✝ con-

vert (into); ⚖ commute (into); **'2lung** *f* transformation; ⚡, ✝ conversion; ⚖ commutation.

'um|wechseln *v/t.* (*sep., -ge-, h*) change; **'2weg** *m* roundabout way *or* route; detour; *auf ~en* in a roundabout way; **'~wehen** *v/t.* (*sep -ge-, h*) blow down *or* over; **'2welt** *f* (-/‰ -en) environment; **'~wenden 1.** *v/t.* (*sep., -ge-, h*) turn over **2.** *v/refl.* ([*irr. wenden,*] *sep., -ge-,* look round (*nach* for).

um|'werben *v/t.* (*irr. werben, no -ge-, h*) court, woo.

'umwerfen *v/t.* (*irr. werfen, sep. -ge-, h*) upset (*a. fig.*), overturn *sich ~ einen Mantel ~* throw a coa round one's shoulders.

um|'wickeln *v/t.* (*no -ge-, h*) *mit Draht ~* wind wire round s.th. **~wölken** [~'vœlkən] *v/refl.* (*n -ge-, h*) cloud over (*a. fig.*); **~zäu nen** [~'tsɔynən] *v/t.* (*no -ge-, h* fence (in).

umziehen (*irr. ziehen*) **1.** ['~tsiːən *v/i.* (*sep., -ge-, sein*) (re)move (*nach to*); move house; **2.** [~'tsiːən *v/refl.* (*sep., -ge-, h*) change (one' clothes); **3.** [~'tsiːən] *v/refl.* (*nc -ge-, h*) cloud over.

umzingeln [ʊm'tsiŋəln] *v/t.* (*nc -ge-, h*) surround, encircle.

'Umzug *m* procession; move (*nach to*), removal (*to*); change of resi dence.

unab|änderlich *adj.* [ʊnʔap'ɛndər lɪç] unalterable; **~hängig** ['~hɛŋɪç **1.** *adj.* independent (*von of*); **2.** *adv.: ~ von* irrespective of; **'2hän gigkeit** *f* (-/*no pl.*) independ ence (*von of*); **~kömmlich** *adj.* ['~kœmlɪç]: *er ist im Moment ~* we cannot spare him at the moment, we cannot do without him at the moment; **~lässig** *adj.* incessant, unremitting; **~sehbar** *adj.* [~'zeː baːr] incalculable; *in ~er Ferne* in a distant future; **'~sichtlich** *adj.* unintentional; inadvertent; **~wend bar** *adj.* [~'vɛntbaːr] inevitable, inescapable.

unachtsam *adj.* ['ʊnʔ-] careless, heedless; **'2keit** *f* (-/‰ -en) care lessness, heedlessness.

unähnlich *adj.* ['ʊnʔ-] unlike, dis similar (*dat.* to).

unan|fechtbar *adj.* [ʊnʔan'-] un impeachable, unchallengeable, incontestable; '~gebracht adj. inappropriate; pred. a. out of place; '~gefochten 1. adj. undisputed; unchallenged; 2. adv. without any hindrance; '~gemessen adj. unsuitable; improper; inadequate; '~genehm adj. disagreeable, unpleasant; awkward; troublesome; ~'nehmbar adj. unacceptable (für to); ~'nehmlichkeit f (-/-en) unpleasantness; awkwardness; troublesomeness; ~en pl. trouble, inconvenience; '~sehnlich adj. unsightly; plain; '~ständig adj. indecent; obscene; 'Q̈ständigkeit f (-/-en) indecency; obscenity; '~tastbar adj. unimpeachable; inviolable.

nappetitlich adj. ['un⁹-] food, etc.: unappetizing; sight, etc.: distasteful, ugly.

ʃnart ['un⁹-] 1. f bad habit; 2. m (-[e]s/-e) naughty child; 'Q̈ig adj. naughty; '~igkeit f (-/-en) naughty behavio(u)r, naughtiness.

ʃnauf|dringlich adj. ['un⁹auf-] unobtrusive; unostentatious; '~fällig adj. inconspicuous; unobtrusive; ~findbar adj. [~'fintba:r] undiscoverable, untraceable; '~gefordert ['~gəfərdərt] 1. adj. unasked; 2. adv. without being asked, of one's own accord; ~'hörlich adj. incessant, continuous, uninterrupted; '~merksam adj. inattentive; 'Q̈merksamkeit f (-/-en) inattention, inattentiveness; '~richtig adj. insincere; 'Q̈richtigkeit f (-/-en) insincerity; ~schiebbar adj. [~'ʃi:pba:r] urgent; ~ sein brook no delay.

ʃnaus|bleiblich adj. [un⁹aus'blaipliç] inevitable; das war ~ that was bound to happen; ~'führbar adj. impracticable; ~geglichen adj. ['~gəgliçən] unbalanced (a. ˦); ~'löschlich adj. indelible; fig. a. inextinguishable; ~'sprechlich adj. unutterable; unspeakable; inexpressible; ~'stehlich adj. unbearable, insupportable.

unbarmherzig adj. merciless, unmerciful; 'Q̈keit f (-/no pl.) mercilessness, unmercifulness.

ʃnbe|absichtigt adj. ['unbə⁹apziçtiçt] unintentional, undesigned; '~achtet adj. unnoticed; ~anstandet adj. ['unbə⁹-] unopposed, not

objected to; '~baut adj. ✓ untilled; land: undeveloped; '~dacht adj. inconsiderate; imprudent; '~denklich 1. adj. unobjectionable; 2. adv. without hesitation; '~deutend adj. insignificant; slight; '~dingt 1. adj. unconditional; obedience, etc.: implicit; 2. adv. by all means; under any circumstances; '~fahrbar adj. impracticable, impassable; '~fangen adj. unprejudiced, unbias(s)ed; ingenuous; unembarrassed; '~friedigend adj. unsatisfactory; ~friedigt adj. ['~çt] dissatisfied; disappointed; '~fugt adj. unauthorized; incompetent; 'Q̈fugte m (-n/-n) unauthorized person; ~n ist der Zutritt verboten! no trespassing!; '~gabt adj. untalented; ~'greiflich adj. inconceivable, incomprehensible; ~'grenzt adj. unlimited; boundless; '~gründet adj. unfounded; 'Q̈hagen n uneasiness; discomfort; '~haglich adj. uneasy; uncomfortable; ~helligt adj. [~'heliçt] unmolested; ~'herrscht adj. lacking self-control; 'Q̈herrschtheit f (-/no pl.) lack of self-control; ~'hindert adj. unhindered, free; ~'holfen adj. ['~bə-hɔlfən] clumsy, awkward; 'Q̈holfenheit f (-/no pl.) clumsiness, awkwardness; ~'irrt adj. unswerving; '~kannt adj. unknown; ~e Größe A̸ unknown quantity (a. fig.); ~'kümmert adj. unconcerned (um, wegen about), careless (of, about); '~lebt adj. inanimate; street, etc.: unfrequented; ~'lehrbar adj.: ~ sein take no advice; '~liebt adj. unpopular; sich ~ machen get o.s. disliked; '~mannt adj. unmanned; '~merkt adj. unnoticed; ~'mittelt adj. impecunious; without means; ~nommen adj. [~'nɔmən]: es bleibt ihm ~ zu inf. he is at liberty to inf.; '~nutzt adj. unused; ~'quem adj. uncomfortable, inconvenient; 'Q̈quemlichkeit f lack of comfort; inconvenience; '~rechtigt adj. unauthorized; unjustified; ~schadet prp. (gen.) [~'ʃa:dət] without prejudice to; ~schädigt adj. ['~çt] uninjured, undamaged; '~scheiden adj. immodest; ~scholten adj. ['~ʃɔltən] blameless, irreproachable; ~'schränkt adj. unrestricted; absolute; ~schreiblich

U V

adj. [~ˈʃraıplıç] indescribable; **~-**
'sehen *adv.* unseen; without inspection; **'~setzt** *adj.* unoccupied;
vacant; **~siegbar** *adj.* [~ˈziːkbɑːr]
invincible; **'~sonnen** *adj.* thought-
less, imprudent; rash; **2sonnen-**
heit *f* (-/-en) thoughtlessness,
rashness; **'~ständig** *adj.* incon-
stant; unsteady; *weather:* changeable, unsettled (*a.* ✝); *p.* erratic;
2ständigkeit *f* (-/no *pl.*) incon-
stancy; changeability; **~stätigt** *adj.*
['~çt] unconfirmed; *letter, etc.:* un-
acknowledged; **~'stechlich** *adj.* in-
corruptible; unbribable; **2stech-**
lichkeit *f* (-/no *pl.*) incorruptibil-
ity; **'~stimmt** *adj.* indeterminate
(*a.* ♱); indefinite (*a.* gr.); uncertain; *feeling, etc.:* vague; **'2-**
stimmtheit *f* (-/no *pl.*) indeter-
minateness, indetermination; indef-
initeness; uncertainty; vagueness;
~'streitbar *adj.* incontestable; in-
disputable; **'~stritten** *adj.* uncon-
tested, undisputed; **'~teiligt** *adj.*
unconcerned (*an dat.* in); indifferent; **~'trächtlich** *adj.* inconsiderable, insignificant. [flexible.)
unbeugsam *adj.* [un'bɔykzaːm] in-)
'unbe|wacht *adj.* unwatched, un-
guarded (*a. fig.*); **'~waffnet** *adj.*
unarmed; *eye:* naked; **'~weglich**
adj. immovable; motionless; **'~-**
wiesen *adj.* unproven; **'~wohnt**
adj. uninhabited; unoccupied, vacant; **'~wußt** *adj.* unconscious;
~'zähmbar *adj.* indomitable.
'Un|bilden *pl.:* ~ *der Witterung*
inclemency of the weather; **'~bil-**
dung *f* lack of education.
'un|billig *adj.* unfair; **'~blutig**
1. *adj.* bloodless; **2.** *adv.* without
bloodshed.
unbotmäßig *adj.* ['unboːt-] insubordinate; **2keit** *f* (-/-en) insubor-
dination.
'un|brauchbar *adj.* useless; **'~-**
christlich *adj.* unchristian.
und *cj.* [unt] and; F: *na* ~*?* so what?
'Undank *m* ingratitude; **'2bar** *adj.*
ungrateful (*gegen* to); *task, etc.:*
thankless; **'~barkeit** *f* ingratitude,
ungratefulness; *fig.* thanklessness.
un|'denkbar *adj.* unthinkable; in-
conceivable; **~'denklich** *adj.:* seit
~*en Zeiten* from time immemorial;
'~deutlich *adj.* indistinct; *speech:*
a. inarticulate; *fig.* vague, indis-

tinct; **'~deutsch** *adj.* un-German;
'~dicht *adj.* leaky; **2ding** *n:* es
wäre ein ~, *zu behaupten, daß ... i*
would be absurd to claim that ..
'unduldsam *adj.* intolerant; **2keit**
f intolerance.
undurch|'dringlich *adj.* impene-
trable; *countenance:* impassive; **~-**
'führbar *adj.* impracticable; **~-**
'lässig *adj.* impervious, imperme-
able; **'~sichtig** *adj.* opaque; *fig*
mysterious.
uneben *adj.* ['unʔ-] *ground:* uneven
broken; *way, etc.:* bumpy; **'2heit**
1. (-/no *pl.*) unevenness; **2.** (-/-en.
bump.
un|'echt *adj.* ['unʔ-] *jewellery, etc.:*
imitation; *hair, teeth, etc.:* false
money, jewellery, etc.: counterfeit
picture, etc.: fake; ♱ *fraction:* improper; **'~ehelich** *adj.* illegitimate
Unehr|e ['unʔ-] *f* dishono(u)r; *j-m*
~ *machen* discredit s.o.; **2enhaf**
adj. dishono(u)rable; **'2lich** *adj*
dishonest; **'~lichkeit** *f* dishonesty
uneigennützig *adj.* ['unʔ-] disin-
terested, unselfish.
uneinig *adj.* ['unʔ-]: ~ *sein* be a
variance (*mit* with); disagree (*übe*
acc. on); **2keit** *f* variance, disagreement.
un|ein'nehmbar *adj.* impregnable
'~empfänglich *adj.* insusceptible
(*für* of, to).
unempfindlich *adj.* ['unʔ-] insen-
sitive (*gegen* to); **2keit** *f* insensi-
tiveness (*gegen* to).
un'endlich 1. *adj.* endless, infinite
(*both a. fig.*); **2.** *adv.* infinitely (*a*
fig.); ~ *lang* endless; ~ *viel no enc*
of (*money, etc.*); **2keit** *f* (-/no *pl.*
endlessness, infinitude, infinity (*a*
a. fig.).
unent|behrlich *adj.* [unʔent'beːrlıç
indispensable; **~'geltlich 1.** *adj*
gratuitous, gratis; **2.** *adv.* gratis
free of charge; **~'rinnbar** *adj.* in-
eluctable; **~'schieden 1.** *adj.* undecided; ~ *enden game:* end in a
draw *or* tie; **2.** ♱ *n* (-s/-) draw, tie
'~schlossen *adj.* irresolute; **'2-**
schlossenheit *f* irresoluteness, irresolution; **~'schuldbar** *adj.* [~-
'ʃultbaːr] inexcusable; **~wegt** *adv*
[~'veːkt] untiringly; continuously
'~wirrbar *adj.* inextricable.
uner|bittlich *adj.* [unʔer'bıtlıç] in-
exorable; *fact:* stubborn; **'~fahren**

adj. inexperienced; **~findlich** *adj.* [~'fintliç] incomprehensible; **~'forschlich** *adj.* inscrutable; **~'freulich** *adj.* unpleasant; **~'füllbar** *adj.* unrealizable; **'~giebig** *adj.* unproductive (*an dat.* of); **'~heblich** *adj.* irrelevant (*für* to); inconsiderable; **~hört** *adj.* **1.** ['~hø:rt] unheard; **2.** [~'hø:rt] unheard-of; outrageous; **~'kannt** *adj.* unrecognized; **~'klärlich** *adj.* inexplicable; **~läßlich** [~'lesliç] indispensable (*für* to, for); **~laubt** *adj.* ['~laupt] unauthorized; illegal, illicit; **~e** *Handlung* ✝ tort; **~ledigt** *adj.* ['~le:diçt] unsettled (*a.* ✝); **~meßlich** *adj.* [~'mesliç] immeasurable, immense; **~müdlich** *adj.* [~'my:tliç] *p.* indefatigable, untiring; *efforts, etc.*: untiring, unremitting; **'~quicklich** *adj.* unpleasant, unedifying; **~'reichbar** *adj.* inattainable; inaccessible; *pred. a.* above or beyond or out of reach; **~'reicht** *adj.* unrival(l)ed, unequal(l)ed; **~'sättlich** *adj.* [~'zetliç] insatiable, insatiate; **~'schöpflich** *adj.* inexhaustible.

unerschrocken *adj.* ['un⁹-] intrepid, fearless; **'~heit** *f* (-/*no pl.*) intrepidity, fearlessness.

uner|schütterlich *adj.* [un⁹er'ʃytərliç] unshakable; **~'schwinglich** *adj.* *price*: prohibitive; *pred. a.* above or beyond or out of reach (*für* of); **~'setzlich** *adj.* irreplaceable; *loss, etc.*: irreparable; **~'träglich** *adj.* intolerable, unbearable; **'~wartet** *adj.* unexpected; **'~wünscht** *adj.* undesirable, undesired.

'unfähig *adj.* incapable (*zu inf.* of *ger.*); unable (to *inf.*); inefficient; **'2keit** *f* incapability (*zu inf.* of *ger.*); inability (to *inf.*); inefficiency.

'Unfall *m* accident; *e-n* **~** *haben* meet with or have an accident; **'~station** *f* emergency ward; **'~versicherung** *f* accident insurance.

un'faßlich *adj.* incomprehensible, inconceivable; *das ist mir* **~** that is beyond me.

un'fehlbar **1.** *adj.* infallible (*a. eccl.*); *decision, etc.*: unimpeachable; *instinct, etc.*: unfailing; **2.** *adv.* without fail; inevitably; **2keit** *f* (-/*no pl.*) infallibility.

'un|fein *adj.* indelicate; *pred. a.* lacking in refinement; **'~fern** *prp.* (*gen.* or *von*) not far from; **'~fertig** *adj.* unfinished; *fig. a.* half-baked; **'~flätig** *adj.* ['~fle:tiç] dirty, filthy.

'unfolgsam *adj.* disobedient; **'2keit** *f* disobedience.

un|förmig *adj.* ['unfœrmiç] misshapen; shapeless; **'~frankiert** *adj.* unstamped; *& :* unstamped; **'~frei** *adj.* not free; *&* unstamped; **'~freiwillig** *adj.* involuntary; *humour:* unconscious; **'~freundlich** *adj.* unfriendly (*zu* with), unkind (to); *climate, weather:* inclement; *room, day:* cheerless; **'2friede(n)** *m* discord.

'unfruchtbar *adj.* unfruitful, sterile; **'2keit** *f* (-/*no pl.*) unfruitfulness; sterility.

Unfug ['unfu:k] *m* (-[e]s/*no pl.*) mischief.

Ungar ['uŋgar] *m* (-n/-n) Hungarian; **'2isch** *adj.* Hungarian.

'ungastlich *adj.* inhospitable.

unge|achtet *prp.* (*gen.*) ['uŋgə⁹axtət] regardless of; despite; **~ahnt** *adj.* ['uŋgə⁹-] undreamt-of, unexpected; **~bärdig** *adj.* ['~be:rdiç] unruly; **~beten** *adj.* uninvited, unasked; **~er** *Gast* intruder, *sl.* gatecrasher; **'~bildet** *adj.* uneducated; **'~bräuchlich** *adj.* unusual; **'~braucht** *adj.* unused; **'~bührlich** *adj.* improper, undue, unseemly; **'~bunden** *adj. book:* unbound; *fig.:* free; single; **'~deckt** *adj. table:* unlaid; *sports,* ✕, ✝: uncovered; *paper currency:* fiduciary.

'Ungeduld *f* impatience; **'2ig** *adj.* impatient.

'ungeeignet *adj.* unfit (*für* for *s.th.*, *zu* do *s.th.*); *p. a.* unqualified; *moment:* inopportune.

ungefähr ['uŋgəfe:r] **1.** *adj.* approximate, rough; **2.** *adv.* approximately, roughly, about, *Am.* F *a.* around; *von* **~** *by chance;* **'~det** *adj.* unendangered, safe; **'~lich** *adj.* harmless; *pred. a.* not dangerous.

'unge|fällig *adj.* disobliging; **'~halten** *adj.* displeased (*über acc.* at); **'~hemmt** **1.** *adj.* unchecked; **2.** *adv.* without restraint; **'~heuchelt** *adj.* unfeigned.

ungeheuer ['uŋgəhɔʏər] **1.** *adj.* vast, huge, enormous; **2.** **2** *n* (-s/-) monster; **~lich** *adj.* [~'hɔʏərliç] monstrous.

'**ungehobelt** adj. not planed; fig. uncouth, rough.

'**ungehörig** adj. undue, improper; '2**keit** f (-/♀-en) impropriety.

'**ungehorsam 1.** adj. disobedient; **2.** ♀ m disobedience.

'**unge|künstelt** adj. unaffected; '~**kürzt** adj. unabridged.

'**ungelegen** adj. inconvenient, inopportune; '2**heiten** f/pl. inconvenience; trouble; j-m ~ **machen** put s.o. to inconvenience.

'**unge|lehrig** adj. indocile; '~**lenk** adj. awkward, clumsy; '~**lernt** adj. unskilled; '~**mütlich** adj. uncomfortable; room: a. cheerless; p. nasty; '~**nannt** adj. unnamed; p. anonymous.

'**ungenau** adj. inaccurate, inexact; '2**igkeit** f inaccuracy, inexactness.

'**ungeniert** adj. free and easy, unceremonious; undisturbed.

unge|nießbar adj. ['ungǝni:sba:r] uneatable; undrinkable; F p. unbearable, pred. a. in a bad humo(u)r; '~**nügend** adj. insufficient; '~**pflegt** adj. unkempt; '~**rade** adj. odd; '~**raten** adj. spoilt, undutiful.

'**ungerecht** adj. unjust (gegen to); '2**igkeit** f (-/-en) injustice.

'**un|gern** adv. unwillingly, grudgingly; reluctantly; '~**geschehen** adj.: ~ **machen** undo s.th.

'**Ungeschick** n (-[e]s/no pl.), '~**lichkeit** f awkwardness, clumsiness, maladroitness; '2**t** adj. awkward, clumsy, maladroit.

'**unge|schlacht** adj. ['ungǝʃlaxt] hulking; uncouth; '~**schliffen** adj. unpolished, rough (both a. fig.); '~**schminkt** adj. not made up; fig. unvarnished.

'**ungesetzlich** adj. illegal, unlawful, illicit; '2**keit** f (-/-en) illegality, unlawfulness.

'**unge|sittet** adj. uncivilized; unmannerly; '~**stört** adj. undisturbed, uninterrupted; '~**straft 1.** adj. unpunished; **2.** adv. with impunity; ~ **davonkommen** get off or escape scot-free.

ungestüm ['ungǝʃty:m] **1.** adj. impetuous; violent; **2.** ♀ n (-[e]s/no pl.) impetuosity; violence.

'**unge|sund** adj. climate: unhealthy; appearance: a. unwholesome; food: unwholesome; '~**teilt** adj. undivided (a. fig.); ~**trübt** adj.

['~try:pt] untroubled; unmixed; ♀**tüm** ['~ty:m] n (-[e]s/-e) monster; ~**übt** adj. ['~ʹy:pt] untrained; inexperienced; '~**waschen** adj. unwashed.

'**ungewiß** adj. uncertain; j-n im ungewissen lassen keep s.o. in suspense; '2**heit** f (-/♀-en) uncertainty; suspense.

'**unge|wöhnlich** adj. unusual, uncommon; '~**wohnt** adj. unaccustomed; unusual; '~**zählt** adj. numberless, countless; 2**ziefer** ['~tsi:-fǝr] n (-s/-) vermin; '~**ziemend** adj. improper, unseemly; '~**zogen** adj. ill-bred, rude, uncivil; child: naughty; '~**zügelt** adj. unbridled.

'**ungezwungen** adj. unaffected, easy; '2**heit** f (-/♀-en) unaffectedness, ease, easiness.

'**Unglaube(n)** m unbelief, disbelief.

'**ungläubig** adj. incredulous, unbelieving (a. eccl.); infidel; '2**e** m, f unbeliever; infidel.

unglaub|lich adj. [un'glauplɪç] incredible; '~**würdig** adj. p. untrustworthy; thing: incredible; ~**e** Geschichte cock-and-bull story.

'**ungleich 1.** adj. unequal, different; uneven; unlike; **2.** adv. (by) far, much; '~**artig** adj. heterogeneous; '2**heit** f difference, inequality; unevenness; unlikeness; '~**mäßig** adj. uneven; irregular.

'**Unglück** n (-[e]s/♀-e) misfortune; bad or ill luck; accident; calamity, disaster; misery; '2**lich** adj. unfortunate, unlucky; unhappy; 2**licher'weise** adv. unfortunately, unluckily; '2**selig** adj. unfortunate; disastrous.

'**Unglücks|fall** m misadventure; accident; '~**rabe** F m unlucky fellow.

'**Un|gnade** f (-/no pl.) disgrace, disfavo(u)r; in ~ fallen bei fall into disgrace with, incur s.o.'s disfavo(u)r; '2**gnädig** adj. ungracious, unkind.

'**ungültig** adj. invalid; ticket: not available; money: not current; ♀♀ (null and void); '2**keit** f invalidity; ♀♀ a. voidness.

'**Un|gunst** f disfavo(u)r; inclemency (of weather); zu meinen ~en to my disadvantage; '2**günstig** adj. unfavo(u)rable; disadvantageous.

'**un|gut** adj.: ~es Gefühl misgiving;

nichts für ~! no offen|ce, *Am.* -se!; '**~haltbar** *adj. shot*: unstoppable; *theory, etc.*: untenable; '**~handlich** *adj.* unwieldy, bulky.

'**Unheil** *n* mischief; disaster, calamity; '**2bar** *adj.* incurable; '**2voll** *adj.* sinister, ominous.

unheimlich 1. *adj.* uncanny (*a. fig.*), weird; sinister; F *fig.* tremendous, terrific; **2.** F *fig. adv.*: ~ *viel* heaps of, an awful lot of.

'**unhöflich** *adj.* impolite, uncivil; '**2keit** *f* impoliteness, incivility.

Unhold ['unhɔlt] *m* (-[e]s/-e) fiend.

'**un|hörbar** *adj.* inaudible; '**~hygienisch** *adj.* unsanitary, insanitary.

Uni ['uni] *f* (-/-s) F varsity.

Uniform [uni'fɔrm] *f* (-/-en) uniform.

Unikum ['u:nikum] *n* (-s/*Unika*, -s) unique (thing); queer fellow.

uninteress|ant ['un⁹-] uninteresting, boring; '**~iert** *adj.* uninterested (*an dat.* in).

Universität [univɛrzi'tɛːt] *f* (-/-en) university.

Universum [uni'vɛrzʊm] *n* (-s/*no pl.*) universe.

Unke ['uŋkə] *f* (-/-n) *zo.* fire-bellied toad; F *fig.* croaker; '**2n** F *v/i.* (ge-, h) croak.

unkennt|lich *adj.* unrecognizable; '**2lichkeit** *f* (-/*no pl.*): *bis zur* ~ past all recognition; '**2nis** *f* (-/*no pl.*) ignorance.

'**unklar** *adj.* not clear; *meaning, etc.*: obscure; *answer, etc.*: vague; *im* ~*en sein* be in the dark (*über acc.* about); '**2heit** *f* want of clearness, vagueness; obscurity.

'**unklug** *adj.* imprudent, unwise.

'**Unkosten** *pl.* cost(s) *pl.*, expenses *pl.*; *sich in (große)* ~ *stürzen* go to great expense.

'**Unkraut** *n* weed.

un|kündbar *adj.* ['unkʏntbaːr] *loan, etc.*: irredeemable; *employment*: permanent; '**~kundig** *adj.* ['~kundiç] ignorant (*gen.* of); '**~längst** *adv.* lately, recently, the other day; '**~lauter** *adj. competition*: unfair; '**~leidlich** *adj.* intolerable, insufferable; '**~leserlich** *adj.* illegible; '**~leugbar** *adj.* ['~lɔykbaːr] undeniable; '**~logisch** *adj.* illogical; '**~lösbar** *adj.* unsolvable, insoluble.

'**Unlust** *f* (-/*no pl.*) reluctance (*zu*

inf. to *inf.*); '**2ig** *adj.* reluctant.

'**un|manierlich** *adj.* unmannerly; '**~männlich** *adj.* unmanly; '**~maßgeblich** *adj.* ['~gəːpliç]: *nach m-r* ~*en Meinung* in my humble opinion; '**~mäßig** *adj.* immoderate; intemperate; '**2menge** *f* enormous or vast quantity or number.

'**Unmensch** *m* monster, brute; '**2lich** *adj.* inhuman, brutal; '**~lichkeit** *f* inhumanity, brutality.

'**un|mißverständlich** *adj.* unmistakable; '**~mittelbar** *adj.* immediate, direct; '**~möbliert** *adj.* unfurnished; '**~modern** *adj.* unfashionable, outmoded.

'**unmöglich** *adj.* impossible; '**2keit** *f* impossibility.

'**Unmoral** *f* immorality; '**2isch** *adj.* immoral.

'**unmündig** *adj.* under age.

'**un|musikalisch** *adj.* unmusical; '**2mut** *m* (-[e]s/*no pl.*) displeasure (*über acc.* at, over); '**~nachahmlich** *adj.* inimitable; '**~nachgiebig** *adj.* unyielding; '**~nachsichtig** *adj.* strict, severe; inexorable; '**~nahbar** *adj.* inaccessible, unapproachable; '**~natürlich** *adj.* unnatural; affected; '**~nötig** *adj.* unnecessary, needless; '**~nütz** *adj.* useless; '**~ordentlich** *adj.* ['un⁹-] untidy; *room, etc.*: *a.* disorderly; '**2ordnung** ['un⁹-] *f* disorder, mess.

'**unpartei|isch** *adj.* impartial, unbias(s)ed; '**2ische** *m* (-n/-n) referee; umpire; '**2lichkeit** *f* impartiality.

'**un|passend** *adj.* unsuitable; improper; inappropriate; '**~passierbar** *adj.* impassable.

unpäßlich *adj.* ['unpɛsliç] indisposed, unwell; '**2keit** *f* (-/-en) indisposition.

'**un|persönlich** *adj.* impersonal (*a. gr.*); '**~politisch** *adj.* unpolitical; '**~praktisch** *adj.* unpractical, *Am. a.* impractical; '**2rat** *m* (-[e]s/*no pl.*) filth; rubbish; *~ wittern* smell a rat.

'**unrecht 1.** *adj.* wrong; *~ haben* wrong; *j-m ~ tun* wrong s.o.; **2.** **2** *n* (-[e]s/*no pl.*): *mit or zu ~* wrongly; *ihm ist ~ geschehen* he has been wronged; '**~mäßig** *adj.* unlawful; '**2mäßigkeit** *f* unlawfulness.

'**unreell** *adj.* dishonest; unfair.

'**unregelmäßig** *adj.* irregular (*a. gr.*); '**2keit** *f* (-/-en) irregularity.

U V

'unreif *adj.* unripe, immature (*both a. fig.*); **'2e** *f* unripeness, immaturity (*both a. fig.*).

'un|rein *adj.* impure (*a. eccl.*); unclean (*a. fig.*); **'~reinlich** *adj.* uncleanly; **~'rettbar** *adv.*: ~ verloren irretrievably lost; **'~richtig** *adj.* incorrect, wrong.

Unruh ['unru:] *f* (-/-en) balance (-wheel); **'~e** *f* (-/-n) restlessness, unrest (*a. pol.*); uneasiness; disquiet(ude); flurry; alarm; ~n *pl.* disturbances *pl.*, riots *pl.*; **'2ig** *adj.* restless; uneasy; *sea*: rough, choppy.

'unrühmlich *adj.* inglorious.

uns *pers. pron.* [uns] us; *dat.*: *a.* to us; ~ (selbst) ourselves, *after prp.*: us; *ein Freund von* ~ a friend of ours.

'un|sachgemäß *adj.* inexpert; **'~sachlich** *adj.* not objective; personal; **~säglich** *adj.* [~'ze:kliç] unspeakable; untold; **'~sanft** *adj.* ungentle; **'~sauber** *adj.* dirty; *fig. a.* unfair (*a. sports*); **'~schädlich** *adj.* innocuous, harmless; **'~scharf** *adj.* blurred; *pred. a.* out of focus; **~'schätzbar** *adj.* inestimable, invaluable; **'~scheinbar** *adj.* plain, *Am. a.* homely.

'unschicklich *adj.* improper, indecent; **'2keit** *f* (-/-en) impropriety, indecency.

unschlüssig *adj.* ['unʃlysiç] irresolute; **'2keit** *f* (-/*no pl.*) irresoluteness, irresolution.

'un|schmackhaft *adj.* insipid; unpalatable, unsavo(u)ry; **'~schön** *adj.* unlovely, unsightly; *fig.* unpleasant.

'Unschuld *f* (-/*no pl.*) innocence; **'2ig** *adj.* innocent (*an dat.* of).

unselbständig *adj.* dependent (on others); **'2keit** *f* (lack of in)dependence.

unser ['unzər] **1.** *poss. pron.* our; *der (die, das)* ~e ours; *die* ~en *pl.* our relations *pl.*; **2.** *pers. pron.* of us; *wir waren* ~ *drei* there were three of us.

'unsicher *adj.* unsteady; unsafe, insecure; uncertain; **'2heit** *f* unsteadiness; insecurity, unsafeness; uncertainty.

'unsichtbar *adj.* invisible.

'Unsinn *m* (-[e]s/*no pl.*) nonsense; **'2ig** *adj.* nonsensical.

'Unsitt|e *f* bad habit; abuse; **'2lich**

adj. immoral; indecent (*a.* ♣); **'~lichkeit** *f* (-/-en) immorality.

'un|solid(e) *adj. p.* easy-going; *life*: dissipated; ♣ unreliable; **'~sozial** *adj.* unsocial, antisocial; **'~sportlich** *adj.* unsportsmanlike; unfair (*gegenüber* to).

unstatthaft *adj.* inadmissible.

'unsterblich *adj.* immortal.

Un'sterblichkeit *f* immortality.

'un|stet *adj.* unsteady; *character, life*: unsettled; **2stimmigkeit** ['~ʃtimiçkaɪt] *f* (-/-en) discrepancy; dissension; **'~sträflich** *adj.* blameless; **'~streitig** *adj.* incontestable; **'~sympathisch** *adj.* disagreeable; *er ist mir* ~ I don't like him; **'~tätig** *adj.* inactive; idle.

'untauglich *adj.* unfit (*a.* ✂); unsuitable; **'2keit** *f* (-/*no pl.*) unfitness (*a.* ✂).

un'teilbar *adj.* indivisible.

unten *adv.* ['untən] below; downstairs; *von oben bis* ~ from top to bottom.

unter ['untər] **1.** *prp.* (*dat.*; *acc.*) below, under; among; ~ *anderem* among other things; ~ *zehn Mark* (for) less than ten marks; ~ *Null* below zero; ~ *aller Kritik* beneath contempt; ~ *diesem Gesichtspunkt* from this point of view; **2.** *adj.* lower; inferior; *die* ~en *Räume* the downstair(s) rooms.

Unter|abteilung ['untər?-] *f* subdivision; **~arm** ['untər?-] *m* forearm; **'~bau** *m* (-[e]s/-ten) ⌂ substructure (*a.* ⚙), foundation.

unter'bieten *v/t.* (*irr. bieten, no -ge-, h*) underbid; ♣ undercut, undersell (*competitor*); lower (*record*); **~'binden** *v/t.* (*irr. binden, no -ge-, h*) ✿ ligature; *fig.* stop; **~'bleiben** *v/i.* (*irr. bleiben, no -ge-, sein*) remain undone; not to take place.

unter'brech|en *v/t.* (*irr. brechen, no -ge-, h*) interrupt (*a.* ∉); break, *Am. a.* stop over; ∉ break (*circuit*); **2ung** *f* (-/-en) interruption; break, *Am. a.* stopover. [mit.]

unter'breiten *v/t.* (*no -ge-, h*) sub-/

'unterbring|en *v/t.* (*irr. bringen, sep., -ge-, h*) place (*a.* ♣); accommodate, lodge; **'2ung** *f* (-/-en) accommodation; ♣ placement.

unterdessen *adv.* [untər'desən] (in the) meantime, meanwhile.

unter'drück|en v/t. (no -ge-, h) oppress (subjects, etc.); repress (revolt, sneeze, etc.); suppress (rising, truth, yawn, etc.); put down (rebellion, etc.); **2ung** f (-/-en) oppression; repression; suppression; putting down.

unterernähr|t adj. ['unter⁹-] underfed, undernourished; **2ung** f (-/no pl.) underfeeding, malnutrition.

Unter'führung f subway, Am. underpass.

'**Untergang** m (-[e]s/ᴖᴗe) ast. setting; ⚓ sinking; fig. ruin.

Unter'gebene m (-n/-n) inferior, subordinate; contp. underling.

'**untergehen** v/i. (irr. gehen, sep., -ge-, sein) ast. set; ⚓ sink, founder; fig. be ruined.

untergeordnet adj. ['untərgə⁹ɔrdnət] subordinate; importance: secondary. [underweight.]

'**Untergewicht** n (-[e]s/no pl.)]

unter'graben fig. v/t. (irr. graben, no -ge-, h) undermine.

'**Untergrund** m (-[e]s/no pl.) subsoil; '**ᴗbahn** f underground (railway), in London: tube; Am. subway; '**ᴗbewegung** f underground movement.

'**unterhalb** prp. (gen.) below, underneath.

'**Unterhalt** m (-[e]s/no pl.) support, subsistence, livelihood; maintenance.

unter'halt|en v/t. (irr. halten, no -ge-, h) maintain; support; entertain, amuse; sich ~ converse (mit with; über acc. on, about), talk (with; on, about); sich gut ~ enjoy o.s.; **2ung** f maintenance, upkeep; conversation, talk; entertainment.

'**Unterhändler** m negotiator; ✗ Parlementaire.

'**Unter|haus** parl. n (-es/no pl.) House of Commons; '**ᴗhemd** n vest, undershirt; '**ᴗholz** n (-es/no pl.) underwood, brushwood; '**ᴗhose** f (e-e a pair of) drawers pl., pants pl.; '**2irdisch** adj. subterranean, underground (both a. fig.).

unter'joch|en v/t. (no -ge-, h) subjugate, subdue; **2ung** f (-/-en) subjugation.

'**Unter|kiefer** m lower jaw; '**ᴗkleid** n slip; '**ᴗkleidung** f underclothes pl., underclothing, underwear.

'**unterkommen 1.** v/i. (irr. kommen, sep., -ge-, sein) find accommodation; find employment; **2.** **2** n (-s/ᴖᴗ -) accommodation; employment, situation.

'**unter|kriegen** F v/t. (sep., -ge-, h) bring to heel; sich nicht ~ lassen not to knuckle down or under; **2kunft** ['ᴗkunft] f (-/ᴗe) accommodation, lodging; ✗ quarters pl.; '**2lage** f base; pad; fig.: voucher; ~n pl. documents pl.; data pl.

unter'lass|en v/t. (irr. lassen, no -ge-, h) omit (zu tun doing, to do); neglect (to do, doing); fail (to do); **2ung** f (-/-en) omission; neglect; failure; **2ungssünde** f sin of omission.

unter'legen¹ v/t. (sep., -ge-, h) lay or put under; give (another meaning).

unter'legen² adj. inferior (dat. to); **2e** m (-n/-n) loser; underdog; **2heit** f (-/no pl.) inferiority.

'**Unterleib** m abdomen, belly.

unter'liegen v/i. (irr. liegen, no -ge-, sein) be overcome (dat. by); be defeated (by), sports: a. lose (to); fig.: be subject to; be liable to; es unterliegt keinem Zweifel, daß ... there is no doubt that ...

'**Unter|lippe** f lower lip; '**ᴗmieter** m subtenant, lodger, Am. a. roomer.

unter'nehm|en 1. v/t. (irr. nehmen, no -ge-, h) undertake; take (steps); **2.** **2** n (-s/-) enterprise; ✝ a. business; ✗ operation.

unter'nehm|end adj. enterprising; **2er** ✝ m (-s/-) entrepreneur; contractor; employer; **2ung** f (-/-en) enterprise, undertaking; ✗ operation; **ᴗungslustig** adj. enterprising.

'**Unter|offizier** ✗ m non-commissioned officer; '**2ordnen** v/t. (sep., -ge-, h) subordinate (dat. to); sich ~ submit (to).

Unter'redung f (-/-en) conversation, conference.

Unterricht ['untərrɪçt] m (-[e]s/ᴖᴗ -e) instruction, lessons pl.

unter'richten v/t. (no -ge-, h): ~ in (dat.) instruct in, teach (English, etc.); ~ von inform s.o. of.

'**Unterrichts|ministerium** n ministry of education; '**ᴗstunde** f lesson, (teaching) period; '**ᴗwesen** n (-s/no pl.) education; teaching.

'**Unterrock** m slip.

U
V

unter'sagen v/t. (no -ge-, h) forbid (j-m et. s.o. to do s.th.).

'Untersatz m stand; saucer.

unter'schätzen v/t. (no -ge-, h) undervalue; underestimate, underrate.

unter'scheid|en v/t. and v/i. (irr. scheiden, no -ge-, h) distinguish (zwischen between; von from); sich ~ differ (von from); **2ung** f distinction.

'Unterschenkel m shank.

'unterschieb|en v/t. (irr. schieben, sep., -ge-, h) push under; fig.: attribute (dat. to); substitute (statt for); '**2ung** f substitution.

Unterschied ['untərʃiːt] m (-[e]s/-e) difference; distinction; zum ~ von in distinction from or to; '**2lich** adj. different; differential; variable, varying; **2slos** adj. indiscriminate; undiscriminating.

unter'schlag|en v/t. (irr. schlagen, no -ge-, h) embezzle; suppress (truth, etc.); **2ung** f (-/-en) embezzlement; suppression.

'Unterschlupf m (-[e]s/⁺e, -e) shelter, refuge.

unter'schreiben v/t. and v/i. (irr. schreiben, no -ge-, h) sign.

'Unterschrift f signature.

'Untersee|boot ⚓, ✕ n s. U-Boot; '~kabel n submarine cable.

unter'setzt adj. thick-set, squat.

unterst adj. ['untərst] lowest, undermost.

'Unterstand ✕ m shelter, dug-out.

unter'stehen (irr. stehen, no -ge-, h) **1.** v/i. (dat.) be subordinate to; be subject to (law, etc.); **2.** v/refl. dare; untersteh dich! don't you dare!; **~stellen** v/t. **1.** ['⁺ʃtɛlən] (sep., -ge-, h) put or place under; garage (car); sich ~ take shelter (vor dat. from); **2.** [⁺ʃtɛlən] (no -ge-, h) (pre)suppose, assume; impute (dat. to); j-m ~ ✕ put (troops, etc.) under s.o.'s command; **2'stellung** f (-/-en) assumption, supposition; imputation; **~'streichen** v/t. (irr. streichen, no -ge-, h) underline, underscore (both a. fig.).

unter'stütz|en v/t. (no -ge-, h) support; back up; **2ung** f (-/-en) support (a. ✕); assistance, aid; relief.

unter'such|en v/t. (no -ge-, h) examine (a. ✲); inquire into, investigate (a. ⚖); explore; ⚖ try;

analy|se, Am. -ze (a. 🜍); **2ung** f (-/-en) examination (a. ✲); inquiry (gen. into), investigation (a. ⚖); exploration; analysis (a. 🜍).

Unter'suchungs|gefangene m prisoner on remand; **~gefängnis** n remand prison; **~haft** ✗ detention on remand; **~richter** m investigating judge.

Untertan ['untərtaːn] m (-s, -en/-en) subject. [missive.]

untertänig adj. ['untərtɛːnɪç] sub-]

'Unter|tasse f saucer; **2tauchen** (sep., -ge-) **1.** v/i. (sein) dive, dip; duck; fig. disappear; **2.** v/t. (h) duck.

'Unterteil n, m lower part.

unter'teil|en v/t. (no -ge-, h) subdivide; **2ung** f subdivision.

'Unter|titel m subheading; subtitle; a. caption (of film); **'~ton** m undertone; **2vermieten** v/t. (no -ge-, h) sublet.

unter'wander|n pol. v/t. (no -ge-, h) infiltrate; **2ung** pol. f infiltration.

'Unterwäsche f s. Unterkleidung.

unterwegs adv. [untər'veːks] on the or one's way.

unter'weis|en v/t. (irr. weisen, no -ge-, h) instruct (in dat. in); **2ung** f instruction.

'Unterwelt f underworld (a. fig.).

unter'werf|en v/t. (irr. werfen, no -ge-, h) subdue (dat. to), subjugate (to); subject (to); submit (to); sich ~ submit (to); **2ung** f (-/-en) subjugation, subjection; submission (unter acc. to).

unterworfen adj. [untər'vɔrfən] subject (dat. to).

unterwürfig adj. [untər'vyrfɪç] submissive; subservient; **2keit** f (-/no pl.) submissiveness; subservience.

unter'zeichn|en v/t. (no -ge-, h) sign; **2er** m signer, the undersigned; subscriber (gen. to); signatory (gen. to treaty); **2erstaat** m signatory state; **2ete** m, f (-n/-n) the undersigned; **2ung** f signature, signing.

unter'ziehen v/t. (irr. ziehen, no -ge-, h) **1.** ['⁺tsiːən] (sep., -ge-, h) put on underneath; **2.** [⁺tsiːən] (no -ge-, h) subject (dat. to); sich e-r Operation ~ undergo an operation; sich e-r Prüfung ~ go in or sit for an examination; sich der Mühe ~ zu inf. take the trouble to inf.

'Untiefe f shallow, shoal.

'Untier n monster (a. fig.).

U V

un|'tilgbar *adj.* [un'tilkba:r] indelible; † *government annuities*: irredeemable; ~'tragbar *adj.* unbearable, intolerable; *costs*: prohibitive; ~'trennbar *adj.* inseparable.

'untreu *adj.* untrue (*dat.* to), disloyal (to); *husband*, *wife*: unfaithful (to); '2e *f* disloyalty; unfaithfulness, infidelity.

un|'tröstlich *adj.* inconsolable, disconsolate; ~trüglich *adj.* [~'try:kliç] infallible, unerring.

'Untugend *f* vice, bad habit.

unüber|legt *adj.* ['un'y:bər-] inconsiderate, thoughtless; '~sichtlich *adj.* badly arranged; difficult to survey; involved; *mot. corner*: blind; ~'trefflich *adj.* unsurpassable; ~windlich *adj.* [~'vintliç] invincible; *fortress*: impregnable; *obstacle, etc.*: insurmountable; *difficulties, etc.*: insuperable.

unum|gänglich *adj.* [un'um'genliç] absolutely necessary; ~schränkt *adj.* [~'frenkt] absolute; ~stößlich *adj.* [~'ʃtø:sliç] irrefutable; incontestable; irrevocable; ~wunden *adj.* [~'vundən] frank, plain.

ununterbrochen *adj.* ['un'untərbrɔxən] uninterrupted; incessant.

unver|'änderlich *adj.* unchangeable; invariable; ~'antwortlich *adj.* irresponsible; inexcusable; ~'besserlich *adj.* incorrigible; '~bindlich *adj.* not binding or obligatory; *answer, etc.*: non-committal; ~blümt *adj.* [~'bly:mt] plain, blunt; ~bürgt *adj.* [~'byrkt] unwarranted; *news*: unconfirmed; '~dächtig *adj.* unsuspected; '~daulich *adj.* indigestible (*a. fig.*); '~dient *adj.* undeserved; '~dorben *adj.* unspoiled, unspoilt; *fig.*: uncorrupted; pure, innocent; '~drossen *adj.* indefatigable, unflagging; '~dünnt *adj.* undiluted, *Am. a.* straight; ~'einbar *adj.* incompatible; '~fälscht *adj.* unadulterated; *fig.* genuine; ~fänglich *adj.* ['~fenliç] not captious; ~froren *adj.* ['~fro:rən] unabashed, impudent; '2frorenheit *f* (-/-en) impudence, F cheek; '~gänglich *adj.* imperishable; ~'geßlich *adj.* unforgettable; ~'gleichlich *adj.* incomparable; '~hältnismäßig *adj.* disproportionate; '~heiratet *adj.* un-

married, single; '~hofft *adj.* unhoped-for, unexpected; '~hohlen *adj.* unconcealed; '~käuflich *adj.* unsal(e)able; not for sale; ~'kennbar *adj.* unmistakable; ~'letzbar *adj.* invulnerable; *fig. a.* inviolable; ~meidlich *adj.* [~'maitliç] inevitable; '~mindert *adj.* undiminished; '~mittelt *adj.* abrupt.

'Unvermögen *n* (-s/*no pl.*) inability; impotence; '2d *adj.* impecunious, without means.

'unvermutet *adj.* unexpected.

'Unver|nunft *f* unreasonableness, absurdity; '2nünftig *adj.* unreasonable, absurd; '2richterdinge *adv.* without having achieved one's object.

'unverschämt *adj.* impudent, impertinent; '2heit *f* (-/-en) impudence, impertinence.

'unver|schuldet *adj.* not in debt; through no fault of mine, *etc.*; '~sehens *adv.* unawares, suddenly, all of a sudden; '~sehrt *adj.* [~'ze:rt] uninjured; '~söhnlich *adj.* implacable, irreconcilable; '~sorgt *adj.* unprovided for; '2stand *m* injudiciousness; folly, stupidity; '~ständig *adj.* injudicious; foolish; ~'ständlich *adj.* unintelligible; incomprehensible; *das ist mir ~* that is beyond me; '~sucht *adj.*: *nichts ~ lassen* leave nothing undone; '~träglich *adj.* unsociable; quarrelsome; '~wandt *adj.* steadfast; ~'wundbar *adj.* [~'vuntba:r] invulnerable; ~wüstlich *adj.* [~'vy:stliç] indestructible; *fig.* irrepressible; '~zagt *adj.* ['~tsa:kt] intrepid, undaunted; ~'zeihlich *adj.* unpardonable; ~'zinslich *adj.* bearing no interest; non-interest-bearing; ~'züglich *adj.* [~'tsy:kliç] immediate, instant.

'unvollendet *adj.* unfinished.

'unvollkommen *adj.* imperfect; '2heit *f* imperfection.

'unvollständig *adj.* incomplete; '2keit *f* (-/*no pl.*) incompleteness.

'unvorbereitet *adj.* unprepared; extempore.

'unvoreingenommen *adj.* unbias(s)ed, unprejudiced; '2heit *f* freedom from prejudice.

'unvor|hergesehen *adj.* unforeseen; ~schriftsmäßig *adj.* irregular.

U
V

unvorsichtig *adj.* incautious; imprudent; '2keit *f* incautiousness; imprudence.

unvor'stellbar *adj.* unimaginable; '~teilhaft *adj.* unprofitable; *dress, etc.*: unbecoming. [truth.]

'unwahr *adj.* untrue; '2heit *f* un-

'unwahrscheinlich *adj.* improbable, unlikely; '2keit *f* (-/-en) improbability, unlikelihood.

'un|wegsam *adj.* pathless, impassable; '~weit *prp.* (*gen. or von*) not far from; '2wesen *n* (-s/*no pl.*) nuisance; *sein ~ treiben* be up to one's tricks; '~wesentlich *adj.* unessential, immaterial (*für* to); '2wetter *n* thunderstorm; '~wichtig *adj.* unimportant, insignificant.

unwider|legbar *adj.* [unvi:dər'le:kba:r] irrefutable; ~'ruflich *adj.* irrevocable (*a.* ✝).

unwider'stehlich *adj.* irresistible; 2keit *f* (-/*no pl.*) irresistibility.

unwieder'bringlich *adj.* irretrievable.

'Unwill|e *m* (-ns/*no pl.*), '~en *m* (-s/*no pl.*) indignation (*über acc.* at), displeasure (*at*, over); '2ig *adj.* indignant (*über acc.* at), displeased (at, with); unwilling; '2kürlich *adj.* involuntary.

'unwirklich *adj.* unreal.

'unwirksam *adj.* ineffective, inefficient; *laws, rules, etc.*: inoperative; 🜍 inactive; '2keit *f* (-/*no pl.*) ineffectiveness, inefficiency; 🜍 inactivity.

unwirsch *adj.* ['unvirʃ] testy.

'unwirt|lich *adj.* inhospitable, desolate; '~schaftlich *adj.* uneconomic(al).

'unwissen|d *adj.* ignorant; '2heit *f* (-/*no pl.*) ignorance; '~tlich *adj.* unwitting, unknowing.

'unwohl *adj.* unwell, indisposed; '2sein *n* (-s/*no pl.*) indisposition.

'unwürdig *adj.* unworthy (*gen.* of).

un|zählig *adj.* [un'tsɛ:lɪç] innumerable; '2zart *adj.* indelicate.

Unze ['untsə] *f* (-/-n) ounce.

'Unzeit *f*: *zur ~* inopportunely; '2gemäß *adj.* old-fashioned; inopportune; '2ig *adj.* untimely; unseasonable; *fruit*: unripe.

unzer|brechlich *adj.* unbreakable; ~'reißbar *adj.* untearable; ~'störbar *adj.* indestructible; ~'trennlich *adj.* inseparable.

'un|ziemlich *adj.* unseemly; '2zucht *f* (-/*no pl.*) lewdness; 🝖 sexual offen|ce, *Am.* -se; '~züchtig *adj.* lewd; obscene.

'unzufrieden *adj.* discontented (*mit* with), dissatisfied (with, at); '2heit *f* discontent, dissatisfaction.

'unzugänglich *adj.* inaccessible.

'unzulänglich *adj.* ['untsulɛnlɪç] insufficient; '2keit *f* (-/-en) insufficiency; shortcoming.

'unzulässig *adj.* inadmissible; *esp.* 🝖 *influence*: undue.

'unzurechnungsfähig *adj.* irresponsible; '2keit *f* irresponsibility.

'unzu|reichend *adj.* insufficient; '~sammenhängend** *adj.* incoherent; '~träglich *adj.* unwholesome; '~treffend *adj.* incorrect; inapplicable (*auf acc.* to).

'unzuverlässig *adj.* unreliable, untrustworthy; *friend*: *a.* uncertain; '2keit *f* unreliability, untrustworthiness.

'unzweckmäßig *adj.* inexpedient; '2keit *f* inexpediency.

'un|zweideutig *adj.* unequivocal; unambiguous; '~zweifelhaft 1.** *adj.* undoubted, indubitable; **2.** *adv.* doubtless.

üppig *adj.* ['ypɪç] ♣ luxuriant, exuberant, opulent; *food*: luxurious, opulent; *figure*: voluptuous; '2keit *f* (-/♣-en) luxuriance, luxuriancy, exuberance; voluptuousness.

ur|alt *adj.* ['u:r?alt] very old; (as) old as the hills; 2aufführung ['u:r⁹-] *f* world première.

Uran [u'ra:n] *n* (-s/*no pl.*) uranium.

urbar *adj.* ['u:rba:r] arable, cultivable; *~ machen* reclaim; '2machung *f* (-/-en) reclamation.

'Ur|bevölkerung *f* aborigines *pl.*; '~bild *n* original, prototype; '2eigen *adj.* one's very own; '~enkel *m* great-grandson; '~großeltern *pl.* great-grandparents *pl.*; '~großmutter *f* great-grandmother; '~großvater *m* great-grandfather.

'Urheber *m* (-s/-) author; '~recht *n* copyright (*an dat.* in); '~schaft *f* (-/*no pl.*) authorship.

Urin [u'ri:n] *m* (-s/-e) urine; 2ieren [~i'ni:rən] *v/i.* (*no* -ge-, *h*) urinate.

'Urkund|e *f* document; deed; '~enfälschung *f* forgery of documents; 2lich *adj.* ['~tlɪç] documentary.

Urlaub ['uːrlaup] *m* (-[e]s/-e) leave (of absence) (*a.* ✗); holiday(s *pl.*), *esp. Am.* vacation; **~er** ['~bər] *m* (-s/-) holiday-maker, *esp. Am.* vacationist, vacationer.

Urne ['urnə] *f* (-/-n) urn; ballot-box.

'ur|plötzlich 1. *adj.* very sudden, abrupt; **2.** *adv.* all of a sudden; **'2sache** *f* cause; reason; *keine ~!* don't mention it, *Am. a.* you are welcome; **'~sächlich** *adj.* causal; **'2schrift** *f* original (text); **'2-sprung** *m* origin, source; **~sprünglich** *adj.* ['~ʃpryŋliç] original; **'2stoff** *m* primary matter.

Urteil ['urtaɪl] *n* (-s/-e) judg(e)-ment; ⚖️ *a.* sentence; *meinem ~ nach* in my judg(e)ment; *sich ein ~ bilden* form a judg(e)ment (*über acc.* of, on); **'2en** *v/i.* (ge-, h) judge (*über acc.* of; *nach* by, from); **'~s-kraft** *f* (-/✗ -e) discernment.

'Ur|text *m* original (text); **'~wald** *m* primeval *or* virgin forest; **2-wüchsig** *adj.* ['~vyːksiç] original; *fig.:* natural; rough; **'~zeit** *f* primitive times *pl.*   [sils *pl.*\

Utensilien [uten'ziːljən] *pl.* uten-\

Utop|ie [uto'piː] *f* (-/-n) Utopia; **2isch** *adj.* [u'toːpiʃ] Utopian, utopian.

V

Vagabund [vaga'bunt] *m* (-en/-en) vagabond, vagrant, tramp, *Am.* hobo, F bum.

Vakuum ['vaːku°um] *n* (-s/Vakua, Vakuen) vacuum.

Valuta [va'luːta] *f* (-/Valuten) value; currency.

Vanille [va'niljə] *f* (-/no *pl.*) vanilla.

variabel *adj.* [vari'aːbəl] variable.

Varia|nte [vari'antə] *f* (-/-n) variant; **~tion** [~'tsjoːn] *f* (-/-en) variation.

Varieté [varie'teː] *n* (-s/-s) **~thea-ter** *n* variety theatre, music-hall, *Am.* vaudeville theater.

variieren [vari'iːrən] *v/i.* and *v/t.* (*no -ge-*, h) vary.

Vase ['vaːzə] *f* (-/-n) vase.

Vater ['faːtər] *m* (-s/ᵘ) father; **'~-land** *n* native country *or* land, mother country; **'~landsliebe** *f* patriotism.   [paternal.\

väterlich *adj.* ['fɛːtərliç] fatherly,\

'Vater|schaft *f* (-/no *pl.*) paternity, fatherhood; **'~unser** *eccl. n* (-s/-) Lord's Prayer.

Vati ['faːti] *m* (-s/-s) dad(dy).

Veget|arier [vege'taːrjər] *m* (-s/-) vegetarian; **2arisch** *adj.* vegetarian; **~ation** [~a'tsjoːn] *f* (-/-en) vegetation; **2ieren** [~'tiːrən] *v/i.* (*no -ge-*, h) vegetate.

Veilchen 🌸 ['faɪlçən] *n* (-s/-) violet.

Vene *anat.* ['veːnə] *f* (-/-n) vein.

Ventil [vɛn'tiːl] *n* (-s/-e) valve (*a.* ♪); ♪ stop (*of organ*); *fig.* vent,

outlet; **~ation** [~ila'tsjoːn] *f* (-/-en) ventilation; **~ator** [~i'laːtər] *m* (-s/-en) ventilator, fan.

verab|folgen [fɛr'ap-] *v/t.* (*no -ge-*, h) deliver; give; ⚕️ administer (*medicine*); **~reden** *v/t.* (*no -ge-*, h) agree upon, arrange; appoint, fix (*time, place*); *sich ~* make an appointment, *Am.* F (have a) date; **2redung** *f* (-/-en) agreement; arrangement; appointment, *Am.* F date; **~reichen** *v/t.* (*no -ge-*, h) *s. verabfolgen*; **~scheuen** *v/t.* (*no -ge-*, h) abhor, detest, loathe; **~schieden** [~'ʃiːdən] *v/t.* (*no -ge-*, h) dismiss; retire (*officer*); ✗ discharge (*troops*); *parl.* pass (*bill*); *sich ~* take leave (*von* of), say good-bye (to); **2schiedung** *f* (-/-en) dismissal; discharge; passing.

ver|achten *v/t.* (*no -ge-*, h) despise; **~ächtlich** *adj.* [~'ɛçtliç] contemptuous; contemptible; **2ach-tung** *f* contempt; **~allgemeinern** [~'algə'maɪnərn] *v/t.* (*no -ge-*, h) generalize; **~altet** *adj.* antiquated, obsolete, out of date.

Veranda [ve'randa] *f* (-/Veranden) veranda(h), *Am. a.* porch.

veränder|lich *adj.* [fɛr'ɛndərliç] changeable; variable (*a.* 🅰, *gr.*); **~n** *v/t.* and *v/refl.* (*no -ge-*, h) alter, change; vary; **2ung** *f* change, alteration (*in dat.* in; *an dat.* to); variation.   [timidated, scared.\

verängstigt *adj.* [fɛr'ɛŋstiçt] in-\

ver'anlag|en v/t. (no -ge-, h) of taxation: assess; **~t** adj. [~kt] talented; **2ung** [~gʊŋ] f (-/-en) assessment; fig. talent(s pl.); *s* predisposition.

ver'anlass|en v/t. (no -ge-, h) cause, occasion; arrange; **2ung** f (-/-en) occasion, cause; auf m-e ~ at my request or suggestion.

ver'|anschaulichen v/t. (no -ge-, h) illustrate; **~'anschlagen** v/t. (no -ge-, h) rate, value, estimate (all: auf acc. at).

ver'anstalt|en v/t. (no -ge-, h) arrange, organize; give (concert, ball, etc.); **2ung** f (-/-en) arrangement; event; sports: event, meeting, Am. meet.

ver'antwort|en v/t. (no -ge-, h) take the responsibility for; account for; **~lich** adj. responsible; j-n ~ machen für hold s.o. responsible for.

Ver'antwortung f (-/-en) responsibility; die ~ tragen be responsible; zur ~ ziehen call to account; **2slos** adj. irresponsible.

ver'|arbeiten v/t. (no -ge-, h) work up; ⊕ process, manufacture (both: zu into); digest (food) (a. fig.); **~'ärgern** v/t. (no -ge-, h) vex, annoy.

ver'arm|en v/i. (no -ge-, sein) become poor; **~t** adj. impoverished.

ver'|ausgaben v/t. (no -ge-, h) spend (money); sich ~ run short of money; fig. spend o.s.; **~'äußern** v/t. (no -ge-, h) sell; alienate.

Verb gr. [vɛrp] n (-s/-en) verb.

Ver'band m (-[e]s/-̈e) *s* dressing, bandage; association, union; X formation, unit; **~(s)kasten** m first-aid box; **~(s)zeug** n dressing (material).

ver'bann|en v/t. (no -ge-, h) banish (a. fig.), exile; **2ung** f (-/-en) banishment; exile.

ver|barrikadieren [fɛrbarika'di:-rən] v/t. (no -ge-, h) barricade; block (street, etc.); **~'bergen** v/t. (irr. bergen, no -ge-, h) conceal, hide.

ver'besser|n v/t. (no -ge-, h) improve; correct; **2ung** f improvement; correction.

ver'beug|en v/refl. (no -ge-, h) bow (vor dat. to); **2ung** f bow.

ver'biegen v/t. (irr. biegen, no -ge-, h) bend, twist, distort; **~'bieten** v/t. (irr. bieten, no -ge-, h) forbid, prohibit; **~'billigen** v/t. (no -ge-, h) reduce in price, cheapen.

ver'bind|en v/t. (irr. binden, no -ge-, h) *s* dress; tie (together); bind (up); link (mit to); join, unite, combine; connect (a. teleph.); teleph. put s.o. through (mit to); j-m die Augen ~ blindfold s.o.; sich ~ join, unite, combine (a. *m*); ich bin Ihnen sehr verbunden I am greatly obliged to you; falsch verbunden! teleph. wrong number!; **~lich** adj. [~tlɪç] obligatory; obliging; **2lichkeit** f (-/-en) obligation, liability; obligingness, civility.

Ver'bindung f union; alliance; combination; association (of ideas); connexion, union; (Am. only) connection (a. teleph., *s*, *s*, ⊕); relation; communication (a. teleph.); *m* compound; geschäftliche ~ business relations pl.; teleph.: ~ bekommen (haben) get (be) through; die ~ verlieren mit lose touch with; in ~ bleiben (treten) keep (get) in touch (mit with); sich in ~ setzen mit communicate with, esp. Am. contact s.o.; **~sstraße** f communication road, feeder road; **~stür** f communication door.

ver|bissen adj. [fɛr'bisən] dogged; crabbed; **~'bitten** v/refl. (irr. bitten, no -ge-, h) das verbitte ich mir! I won't suffer or stand that!

ver'bitter|n v/t. (no -ge-, h) embitter; **2ung** f (-/-̈en) bitterness (of heart).

verblassen [fɛr'blasən] v/i. (no -ge-, sein) fade (a. fig.).

Verbleib [fɛr'blaip] m (-[e]s/no pl.) whereabouts sg., pl.; **2en** [~bən] v/i. (irr. bleiben, no -ge-, sein) be left, remain.

ver'blend|en v/t. (no -ge-, h) Δ face (wall, etc.); fig. blind, delude; **2ung** f (-/-̈-en) Δ facing; fig. blindness, delusion. [faded.]

verblichen adj. [fɛr'blıçən] colour:|

verblüff|en [fɛr'blyfən] v/t. (no -ge-, h) amaze; perplex; puzzle; dumbfound; **2ung** f (-/-̈-en) amazement, perplexity.

ver'|blühen v/i. (no -ge-, sein) fade, wither; **~'bluten** v/i. (no -ge-, sein) bleed to death.

U V

ver'borgen *adj.* hidden; secret; **2heit** *f* (-/*no pl.*) concealment; secrecy.

Verbot [fɛr'boːt] *n* (-[e]s/-e) prohibition; **2en** *adj.* forbidden, prohibited; *Rauchen* ~ no smoking.

Ver'brauch *m* (-[e]s/⁀ ≈e) consumption (*an dat.* of); **2en** *v/t.* (*no* -ge-, *h*) consume, use up; wear out; **~er** *m* (-s/-) consumer; **2t** *adj.* air: stale; *p.* worn out.

ver'brechen 1. *v/t.* (*irr.* brechen, *no* -ge-, *h*) commit; *was hat er verbrochen?* what is his offen|ce, *Am.* -se?, what has he done?; **2.** **2** *n* (-s/-) crime, offen|ce, *Am.* -se.

Ver'brecher *m* (-s/-) criminal; **2isch** *adj.* criminal; **~tum** *n* (-s/*no pl.*) criminality.

ver'breit|en *v/t.* (*no* -ge-, *h*) spread, diffuse; shed (*light, warmth, happiness*); *sich* ~ spread; *sich* ~ *über* (*acc.*) enlarge (up)on (*theme*); **~ern** *v/t. and v/refl.* (*no* -ge-, *h*) widen, broaden; **2ung** *f* (-/⁀ -en) spread (-ing), diffusion.

ver'brenn|en (*irr.* brennen, *no* -ge-) **1.** *v/i.* (sein) burn; **2.** *v/t.* (*h*) burn (up); cremate (*corpse*); **2ung** *f* (-/-en) burning, combustion; cremation (*of corpse*); *wound:* burn.

ver'bringen *v/t.* (*irr.* bringen, *no* -ge-, *h*) spend, pass.

verbrüder|n [fɛr'bryːdərn] *v/refl.* (*no* -ge-, *h*) fraternize; **2ung** *f* (-/-en) fraternization.

ver'brühen *v/t.* (*no* -ge-, *h*) scald; *sich* ~ scald o.s.; **~'buchen** *v/t.* (*no* -ge-, *h*) book.

Verbum *gr.* ['vɛrbum] *n* (-s/Verba) verb.

verbünden [fɛr'byndən] *v/refl.* (*no* -ge-, *h*) ally o.s. (*mit* to, with).

Verbundenheit [fɛr'bundənhaɪt] *f* (-/*no pl.*) bonds *pl.*, ties *pl.*; solidarity; affection.

Ver'bündete *m*, *f* (-n/-n) ally, confederate; *die* ~*n pl.* the allies *pl.*

ver'|bürgen *v/t.* (*no* -ge-, *h*) guarantee, warrant; *sich* ~ *für* answer *or* vouch for; **~'büßen** *v/t.* (*no* -ge-, *h*): *e-e Strafe* ~ serve a sentence, serve (one's) time.

Verdacht [fɛr'daxt] *m* (-[e]s/*no pl.*) suspicion; *in* ~ haben suspect.

verdächtig *adj.* [fɛr'dɛçtiç] suspected (*gen.* of); *pred.* suspect; suspicious; **~en** [~gən] *v/t.* (*no*

-ge-, *h*) suspect *s.o.* (*gen.* of); cast suspicion on; **2ung** [~guŋ] *f* (-/-en) suspicion; insinuation.

verdamm|en [fɛr'damən] *v/t.* (*no* -ge-, *h*) condemn, damn (*a. eccl.*); **2nis** *f* (-/*no pl.*) damnation; **~t 1.** *adj.* damned; F: ~*!* damn (it)!, confound it!; **~2.** F *adv.*: ~ *kalt* beastly cold; **2ung** *f* (-/⁀ -en) condemnation; damnation.

ver|'dampfen (*no* -ge-) *v/t.* (*h*) and *v/i.* (sein) evaporate; **~'danken** *v/t.* (*no* -ge-, *h*): *j-m et.* ~ owe s.th. to *s.o.*

verdarb [fɛr'darp] *pret. of* verder- [ben.]

verdau|en ['fɛr'daʊən] *v/t.* (*no* -ge-, *h*) digest; **~lich** *adj.* digestible; *leicht* ~ easy to digest, light; **2ung** *f* (-/*no pl.*) digestion; **2ungsstörung** *f* indigestion.

Ver'deck *n* (-[e]s/-e) ♃ deck; hood (*of carriage, car, etc.*); top (*of vehicle*); **2en** *v/t.* (*no* -ge-, *h*) cover, conceal, hide.

ver'denken *v/t.* (*irr.* denken, *no* -ge-, *h*): *ich kann es ihm nicht* ~, *daß* I cannot blame him for *ger.*

Verderb [fɛr'dɛrp] *m* (-[e]s/*no pl.*) ruin; **2en** [~bən] **1.** *v/i.* (*irr.*, *no* -ge-, sein) spoil (*a. fig.*); rot; *meat, etc.:* go bad; *fig.* perish; **2.** *v/t.* (*irr.*, *no* -ge-, *h*) spoil; *fig. a.:* corrupt; ruin; *er will es mit niemandem* ~ he tries to please everybody; *sich den Magen* ~ upset one's stomach; **~en** [~bən] *n* (-s/*no pl.*) ruin; **2lich** *adj.* [~pliç] pernicious; *food:* perishable; **~nis** [~pnis] *f* (-/⁀ -se) corruption; depravity; **2t** *adj.* [~pt] corrupted, depraved.

ver|'deutlichen *v/t.* (*no* -ge-, *h*) make plain *or* clear; **~'dichten** *v/t.* (*no* -ge-, *h*) condense; *sich* ~ condense; *suspicion:* grow stronger; **~'dicken** *v/t. and v/refl.* (*no* -ge-, *h*) thicken; **~'dienen** *v/t.* (*no* -ge-, *h*) merit, deserve; earn (*money*).

Ver'dienst (-es/-e) **1.** *m* gain, profit; earnings *pl.*; **2.** *n* merit; *es ist sein* ~, *daß* it is owing to him that; **2voll** *adj.* meritorious, deserving; **~spanne** ♀ *f* profit margin.

ver'dient *adj. p.* of merit; (well-) deserved; *sich* ~ *gemacht haben um* deserve well of; **~'dolmetschen** *v/t.* (*no* -ge-, *h*) interpret (*a. fig.*); **~'doppeln** *v/t. and v/refl.* (*no* -ge-, *h*) double.

verdorben [fɛrˈdɔrbən] **1.** p.p. of verderben; **2.** adj. meat: tainted; stomach: disordered, upset; fig. corrupt, depraved.

ver|dorren [fɛrˈdɔrən] v/i. (no -ge-, sein) wither (up); **~'drängen** v/t. (no -ge-, h) push away, thrust aside; fig. displace; psych. repress; **~'drehen** v/t. (no -ge-, h) distort, twist (both a. fig.); roll (eyes); fig. pervert; j-m den Kopf ~ turn s.o.'s head; **~'dreht** F fig. adj. crazy; **~'dreifachen** v/t. and v/refl. (no -ge-, h) triple.

verdrieß|en [fɛrˈdriːsən] v/t. (irr., no -ge-, h) vex, annoy; **~lich** adj. vexed, annoyed, sulky; thing: annoying.

ver|droß [fɛrˈdrɔs] pret. of verdrießen; **~drossen** [~ˈdrɔsən] **1.** p.p. of verdrießen; **2.** adj. sulky; listless.

ver'drucken typ. v/t. (no -ge-, h) misprint.

Verdruß [fɛrˈdrus] m (Verdrusses/~Verdrusse) vexation, annoyance.

ver'dummen (no -ge-) **1.** v/t. (h) make stupid; **2.** v/i. (sein) become stupid.

ver'dunk|eln v/t. (no -ge-, h) darken, obscure (both a. fig.); black out (window); sich ~ darken; **2(e)lung** f (-/~-en) darkening; obscuration; black-out; ‡‡ collusion.

ver|'dünnen v/t. (no -ge-, h) thin; dilute (liquid); **~'dunsten** v/i. (no -ge-, sein) volatilize, evaporate; **~'dursten** v/i. (no -ge-, sein) die of thirst; **~dutzt** adj. [~ˈdutst] nonplussed.

ver'ed|eln v/t. (no -ge-, h) ennoble; refine; improve; ⚘ graft; process (raw materials); **2(e)lung** f (-/~-en) refinement; improvement; processing.

ver'ehr|en v/t. (no -ge-, h) revere, venerate; worship; admire, adore; **2er** m (-s/-) worship(p)er; admirer, adorer; **2ung** f (-/~-en) reverence, veneration; worship; adoration.

vereidigen [fɛrˈaɪdɪɡən] v/t. (no -ge-, h) swear (witness); at entrance into office: swear s.o. in.

Verein [fɛrˈaɪn] m (-[e]s/-e) union; society, association; club.

ver'einbar adj. compatible (mit with), consistent (with); **~en** v/t.

(no -ge-, h) agree upon, arrange; **2ung** f (-/-en) agreement, arrangement.

ver'einen v/t. (no -ge-, h) s. vereinigen.

ver'einfach|en v/t. (no -ge-, h) simplify; **2ung** f (-/-en) simplification.

ver'einheitlichen v/t. (no -ge-, h) unify, standardize.

ver'einig|en v/t. (no -ge-, h) unite, join; associate; sich ~ unite, join; associate o.s.; **2ung** f **1.** (-/~-en) union; **2.** (-/-en) union; society, association.

ver'ein|samen v/i. (no -ge-, sein) grow lonely or solitary; **~zelt** adj. isolated; sporadic.

ver|'eiteln v/t. (no -ge-, h) frustrate; **~'ekeln** v/t. (no -ge-, h): er hat mir das Essen verekelt he spoilt my appetite; **~'enden** v/i. (no -ge-, sein) animals: die, perish; **~enge(r)n** [~ˈɛŋə(r)n] v/t. and v/refl. (no -ge-, h) narrow.

ver'erb|en v/t. (no -ge-, h) leave, bequeath; biol. transmit; sich ~ be hereditary; sich ~ auf (acc.) descend (up)on; **2ung** f (-/~-en) biol. transmission; physiol. heredity; **2ungslehre** f genetics.

verewig|en [fɛrˈeːvɪɡən] v/t. (no -ge-, h) perpetuate; **~t** adj. [~çt] deceased, late.

ver'fahren 1. v/i. (irr. fahren, no -ge-, sein) proceed; ~ mit deal with; **2.** v/t. (irr. fahren, no -ge-, h) mismanage, muddle, bungle; sich ~ miss one's way; **3.** **2** n (-s/-) procedure; proceeding(s pl. ‡‡); ⊕ process.

Ver'fall m (-[e]s/no pl.) decay, decline; dilapidation (of house, etc.); ‡‡ forfeiture; expiration; maturity (of bill of exchange); **2en 1.** v/i. (irr. fallen, no -ge-, sein) decay; house: dilapidate; document, etc.: expire; pawn: become forfeited; right: lapse; bill of exchange: fall due; sick person: waste away; ~ auf (acc.) hit upon (idea, etc.); ~ in (acc.) fall into; j-m ~ become s.o.'s slave; **2.** adj. ruinous; addicted (dat. to drugs, etc.); **~serscheinung** [fɛrˈfalsˀ-] f symptom of decline; **~tag** m day of payment.

ver|'fälschen v/t. (no -ge-, h) falsify; adulterate (wine, etc.); **~fäng-**

lich adj. [ˈfɛnlɪç] question: captious, insidious; risky; embarrassing; **~färben** v/refl. (no -ge-, h) change colo(u)r.

ver'fass|en v/t. (no -ge-, h) compose, write; **2er** m (-s/-) author.

Ver'fassung f state, condition; pol. constitution; disposition (of mind); **2smäßig** adj. constitutional; **2swidrig** adj. unconstitutional.

ver'|faulen v/i. (no -ge-, sein) rot, decay; **~fechten** v/t. (irr. fechten, no -ge-, h) defend, advocate.

ver'fehl|en v/t. (no -ge-, h) miss; **2ung** f (-/-en) offen|ce, Am. -se.

ver|feinden [fɛrˈfaɪndən] v/t. (no -ge-, h) make enemies of; sich ~ mit make an enemy of; **~feinern** [ˈfaɪnərn] v/t. and v/refl. (no -ge-, h) refine; **~fertigen** [ˈfɛrtɪɡən] v/t. (no -ge-, h) make, manufacture, compose.

ver'film|en v/t. (no -ge-, h) film, screen; **2ung** f (-/-en) film-version.

ver'|finstern v/t. (no -ge-, h) darken, obscure; sich ~ darken; **~flachen** (no -ge-) v/i. (sein and v/refl. (h) (become) shallow (a. fig.); **~flechten** v/t. (irr. flechten, no -ge-, h) interlace; fig. involve; **~fliegen** (irr. fliegen, no -ge-) 1. v/i. (sein) evaporate; time: fly; fig. vanish; 2. v/refl. (h) bird: stray; ✗ lose one's bearings, get lost; **~fließen** v/i. (irr. fließen, no -ge-, sein) colours: blend; time: elapse; **~flossen** adj. [ˈflɔsən] time: past; F in ~er Freund a late friend, an ex-friend.

ver'fluch|en v/t. (no -ge-, h) curse, Am. F cuss; **~t** adj. damned; **~l** damn (it)!, confound it!

ver|flüchtigen [fɛrˈflʏçtɪɡən] v/t. (no -ge-, h) volatilize; sich ~ evaporate (a. fig.); F fig. vanish; **~flüssigen** [ˈflʏsɪɡən] v/t. and v/refl. (no -ge-, h) liquefy.

ver'folg|en v/t. (no -ge-, h) pursue, persecute; follow (tracks); trace; thoughts, dream: haunt; gerichtlich ~ prosecute; **2er** m (-s/-) pursuer; persecutor; **2ung** f (-/-en) pursuit; persecution; pursuance; gerichtliche ~ prosecution; **2ungswahn** ✗ m persecution mania.

ver|frachten [fɛrˈfraxtən] v/t. (no -ge-, h) freight, Am. a. ship (goods);

⚓ ship; F j-n ~ in (acc.) bundle s.o. in(to) (train, etc.); **~froren** adj. chilled through; **~früht** adj. premature.

ver'füg|bar adj. [fɛrˈfyːkbaːr] available; **~en** [ˈɡən] (no -ge-, h) 1. v/t. decree, order; 2. v/i.: ~ über (acc.) have at one's disposal; dispose of; **2ung** [ˈɡuŋ] f (-/-en) decree, order; disposal; j-m zur ~ stehen (stellen) be (place) at s.o.'s disposal.

ver'führ|en v/t. (no -ge-, h) seduce; **2er** m (-s/-) seducer; **~erisch** adj. seductive; enticing, tempting; **2ung** f seduction.

vergangen adj. [fɛrˈɡaŋən] gone, past; im ~en Jahr last year; **2heit** f (-/-en) past; gr. past tense.

vergänglich adj. [fɛrˈɡɛŋlɪç] transient, transitory.

vergas|en [fɛrˈɡaːzən] v/t. (no -ge-, h) gasify; gas s.o.; **2er** mot. m (-s/-) carburet(t)or.

vergaß [fɛrˈɡaːs] pret. of vergessen.

ver'geb|en v/t. (irr. geben, no -ge-, h) give away (an j-n to s.o.); confer (on), bestow (on); place (order); forgive; sich et. ~ compromise one's dignity; **~ens** adv. [ˈs] in vain; **~lich** [ˈplɪç] 1. adj. vain; 2. adv. in vain; **2ung** [ˈbuŋ] f (-/✗-en) bestowal, conferment (both: an acc. on); forgiveness, pardon.

vergegenwärtigen [fɛrɡeːɡənˈvɛrtiɡən] v/t. (no -ge-, h) represent; sich et. ~ visualize s.th.

ver'gehen 1. v/i. (irr. gehen, no -ge-, sein) pass (away); fade (away); ~ vor (dat.) die of; 2. v/refl. (irr. gehen, no -ge-, h): sich an j-m ~ assault s.o.; violate s.o.; sich gegen das Gesetz ~ offend against or violate the law; 3. **2** n (-s/-) offen|ce, Am. -se.

ver'gelt|en v/t. (irr. gelten, no -ge-, h) repay, requite; reward; retaliate; **2ung** f (-/-en) requital; retaliation, retribution.

vergessen [fɛrˈɡɛsən] 1. v/t. (irr., no -ge-, h) forget; leave; 2. p.p. of 1; **2heit** f (-/no pl.): in ~ geraten sink or fall into oblivion.

vergeßlich adj. [fɛrˈɡɛslɪç] forgetful.

vergeud|en [fɛrˈɡɔʏdən] v/t. (no -ge-, h) dissipate, squander, waste (*time, money*); 2ung *f* (-/♀-en) waste.

vergewaltig|en [fɛrgəˈvaltigən] *v/t.* (*no -ge-, h*) violate; rape; 2ung *f* (-/-en) violation; rape.

ver|gewissern [fɛrgəˈwisərn] *v/refl.* (*no -ge-, h*) make sure (e-r *Sache* of s.th.); ~ˈgießen *v/t.* (*irr. gießen, no -ge-, h*) shed (*tears, blood*); spill (*liquid*).

ver'gift|en *v/t.* (*no -ge-, h*) poison (*a. fig.*); *sich* ~ take poison; 2ung *f* (-/-en) poisoning.

Vergißmeinnicht ♀ [fɛrˈgismaɪnniçt] *n* (-[e]s/-[e]) forget-me-not.

vergittern [fɛrˈgitərn] *v/t.* (*no -ge-, h*) grate.

Vergleich [fɛrˈglaɪç] *m* (-[e]s/-e) comparison; ⅋⅋: agreement; compromise, composition; 2bar *adj.* comparable (*mit* to); 2en *v/t.* (*irr. gleichen, no -ge-, h*) compare (*mit* with, to); *sich* ~ *mit* ⅋⅋ come to terms with; *verglichen mit* as against, compared to; 2sweise *adv.* comparatively.

vergnügen [fɛrˈgnyːgən] 1. *v/t.* (*no -ge-, h*) amuse; *sich* ~ enjoy o.s.; 2. 2 *n* (-s/-) pleasure, enjoyment; entertainment; ~ *finden an* (*dat.*) take pleasure in; *viel* ~! have a good time! [gay.╲

vergnügt *adj.* [fɛrˈgnyːkt] merry,╱

Ver'gnügung *f* (-/-en) pleasure, amusement, entertainment; ~s-reise *f* pleasure-trip; tour; 2s-süchtig *adj.* pleasure-seeking.

ver|golden [fɛrˈgɔldən] *v/t.* (*no -ge-, h*) gild; ~göttern *fig.* [~ˈgœtərn] *v/t.* (*no -ge-, h*) idolize, adore; ~ˈgraben *v/t.* (*irr. graben, no -ge-, h*) bury (*a. fig.*); *sich* ~ bury o.s.; ~ˈgreifen *v/refl.* (*irr. greifen, no -ge-, h*) sprain (*one's hand, etc.*); *sich* ~ *an* (*dat.*) lay (violent) hands on, attack, assault; embezzle (*money*); encroach upon (*s.o.'s property*); ~griffen *adj.* [~ˈgrifən] *goods:* sold out; *book:* out of print.

vergrößer|n [fɛrˈgrøːsərn] *v/t.* (*no -ge-, h*) enlarge (*a. phot.*); *opt.* magnify; *sich* ~ enlarge; 2ung *f* 1. (-/-en) *phot.* enlargement; *opt.* magnification; 2. (-/♀-en) enlargement; increase; extension; 2ungs-glas *n* magnifying glass.

Vergünstigung [fɛrˈgynstiguŋ] *f* (-/-en) privilege.

vergüt|en [fɛrˈgyːtən] *v/t.* (*no -ge-, h*) compensate (*j-m et. s.o.* for s.th.); reimburse (*money spent*); 2ung *f* (-/-en) compensation; reimbursement.

ver'haft|en *v/t.* (*no -ge-, h*) arrest; 2ung *f* (-/-en) arrest.

ver'halten 1. *v/t.* (*irr. halten, no -ge-, h*) keep back; catch *or* hold (*one's breath*); suppress, check; *sich* ~ *thing:* be; *p.* behave; *sich ruhig* ~ keep quiet; 2. 2 *n* (-s/*no pl.*) behavio(u)r, conduct.

Verhältnis [fɛrˈhɛltnis] *n* (-ses/-se) proportion, rate; relation(s *pl.*) (*zu* with); F liaison, love-affair; F mistress; ~se *pl.* conditions *pl.*, circumstances *pl.*; means *pl.*; 2mäßig *adv.* in proportion; comparatively; ~wort *gr. n* (-[e]s/⸚er) preposition.

Ver'haltungsmaßregeln *f/pl.* instructions *pl.*

ver'hand|eln (*no -ge-, h*) 1. *v/i.* negotiate, treat (*über acc., wegen* for); ⅋⅋ try (*über et.* s.th.); 2. *v/t.* discuss; 2lung *f* negotiation; discussion; ⅋⅋ trial, proceedings *pl.*

ver'häng|en *v/t.* (*no -ge-, h*) cover (over), hang; inflict (*punishment*) (*über acc.* upon); 2nis *n* (-ses/-se) fate; ~nisvoll *adj.* fatal; disastrous.

ver'härmt *adj.* [fɛrˈhɛrmt] careworn; ~harren [~ˈharən] *v/i.* (*no -ge-, h, sein*) persist (*auf dat., bei, in dat.* in), stick (to); ~ˈhärten *v/t. and v/refl.* (*no -ge-, h*) harden; ~haßt *adj.* [~ˈhast] hated; hateful, odious; ~ˈhätscheln *v/t.* (*no -ge-, h*) coddle, pamper, spoil; ~ˈhauen *v/t.* (*irr. hauen, no -ge-, h*) thrash.

verheer|en [fɛrˈheːrən] *v/t.* (*no -ge-, h*) devastate, ravage, lay waste; ~end *fig. adj.* disastrous; 2ung *f* (-/-en) devastation.

ver'hehlen [fɛrˈheːlən] *v/t.* (*no -ge-, h*) *s.* verheimlichen; ~ˈheilen *v/i.* (*no -ge-, sein*) heal (up).

ver'heimlich|en *v/t.* (*no -ge-, h*) hide, conceal; 2ung *f* (-/♀-en) concealment.

ver'heirat|en *v/t.* (*no -ge-, h*) marry (*mit* to); *sich* ~ marry; 2ung *f* (-/♀-en) marriage.

ver'heiß|en *v/t.* (*irr. heißen, no -ge-, h*) promise; 2ung *f* (-/-en) promise; ~ungsvoll *adj.* promising.

ver'helfen *v/i.* (*irr. helfen, no -ge-,*

h): j-m zu et. ~ help s.o. to s.th.
ver'herrlich|en v/t. (no -ge-, h) glorify; 2ung f (-/~-en) glorification.

ver'|hetzen v/t. (no -ge-, h) instigate; **~'hexen** v/t. (no -ge-, h) bewitch.

ver'hinder|n v/t. (no -ge-, h) prevent; 2ung f (-/~-en) prevention.

ver'höhn|en v/t. (no -ge-, h) deride, mock (at), taunt; 2ung f (-/-en) derision, mockery.

Verhör ⚖ [fɛr'høːr] n (-[e]s/-e) interrogation, questioning (of prisoners, etc.); examination; 2en v/t. (no -ge-, h) examine, hear; interrogate; sich ~ hear it wrong.

ver'|hüllen v/t. (no -ge-, h) cover, veil; **~'hungern** v/i. (no -ge-, sein) starve; **~'hüten** v/t. (no -ge-, h) prevent.

ver'irr|en v/refl. (no -ge-, h) go astray, lose one's way; **~t** adj.: ~es Schaf stray sheep; 2ung fig. f (-/-en) aberration; error.

ver'jagen v/t. (no -ge-, h) drive away.

verjähr|en ⚖ [fɛr'jɛːrən] v/i. (no -ge-, sein) become prescriptive; 2ung f (-/-en) limitation, (negative) prescription.

verjüngen [fɛr'jʏŋən] v/t. (no -ge-, h) make young again, rejuvenate; reduce (scale); sich ~ grow young again, rejuvenate; taper off.

Ver'kauf m sale; 2en v/t. (no -ge-, h) sell; zu ~ for sale; sich gut ~ sell well.

Ver'käuf|er m seller; vendor; shop-assistant, salesman, Am. a. (sales-)clerk; **~erin** f (-/-nen) seller; vendor; shop-assistant, saleswoman, shop girl, Am. a. (sales)clerk; 2lich adj. sal(e)able; for sale.

Ver'kaufs|automat m slot-machine, vending machine; **~schlager** m best seller.

Verkehr [fɛr'keːr] m (-[e]s/~-e) traffic; transport(ation), communication; correspondence; ⚓, 🚂, ✈, etc.: service; commerce, trade; intercourse (a. sexually); aus dem ~ ziehen withdraw from service; withdraw (money) from circulation; 2en (no -ge-, h) 1. v/t. convert (in acc. into), turn (into); 2. v/i. shop, bus, etc.: run, ply (zwischen dat. between); bei j-m ~ go to or visit

s.o.'s house; ~ in (dat.) frequent (public house, etc.); ~ mit associate or mix with; have (sexual) intercourse with.

Ver'kehrs|ader f arterial road; **~ampel** f traffic lights pl., traffic signal; **~büro** n tourist bureau; **~flugzeug** n air liner; **~insel** f refuge, island; **~minister** m minister of transport; **~mittel** n (means of) conveyance or transport, Am. transportation; **~polizist** m traffic policeman or constable, sl. traffic cop; 2reich adj. congested with traffic, busy; **~schild** n traffic sign; **~schutzmann** m s. Verkehrspolizist; **~stauung** f, **~stockung** f traffic block, traffic jam; **~störung** f interruption of traffic; 🚂, etc.: breakdown; **~straße** f thoroughfare; **~teilnehmer** m road user; **~unfall** m traffic accident; **~verein** m tourist agency; **~verhältnisse** pl. traffic conditions pl.; **~vorschrift** f traffic regulation; **~wesen** n (-s/no pl.) traffic; **~zeichen** n traffic sign.

ver'|kehrt adj. inverted, upside down; fig. wrong; **~'kennen** v/t. (irr. kennen, no -ge-, h) mistake; misunderstand, misjudge.

Ver'kettung f (-/-en) concatenation (a. fig.).

ver'|klagen ⚖ v/t. (no -ge-, h) sue (auf acc., wegen for); bring an action against s.o.; **~'kleben** v/t. (no -ge-, h) paste s.th. up.

ver'kleid|en v/t. (no -ge-, h) disguise; ⊕: line; face; wainscot; encase; sich ~ disguise o.s.; 2ung f (-/-en) disguise; ⊕: lining; facing; panel(l)ing, wainscot(t)ing.

verkleiner|n [fɛr'klaɪnərn] v/t. (no -ge-, h) make smaller, reduce, diminish; fig. belittle, derogate; 2ung f (-/-en) reduction, diminution; fig. derogation.

ver'klingen v/i. (irr. klingen, no -ge-, sein) die away; **~knöchern** [~'knœçərn] (no -ge-) 1. v/t. (h) ossify; 2. v/i. (sein) ossify; fig. a. fossilize; **~'knoten** v/t. (no -ge-, h) knot; **~'knüpfen** v/t. (no -ge-, h) knot or tie (together); fig. connect, combine; **~'kohlen** (no -ge-) 1. v/t. (h) carbonize; char; F: j-n ~ pull s.o.'s leg; 2. v/i. (sein) char; **~'kommen** 1. v/i. (irr. kommen, no -ge-,

U V

sein) decay; *p.*: go downhill *or* to the dogs; become demoralized; **2.** *adj.* decayed; depraved, corrupt; **~'korken** *v/t.* (no -ge-, h) cork (up).

ver'körper|n *v/t.* (no -ge-, h) personify, embody; represent; *esp.* *thea.* impersonate; **♀ung** *f* (-/-en) personification, embodiment; impersonation.

ver|'krachen F *v/i.* (no -ge-, h) fall out (*mit* with); **~'krampft** *adj.* cramped; **~'kriechen** *v/refl.* (irr. kriechen, no -ge-, h) hide; **~-'krümmt** *adj.* crooked; **~krüp-pelt** *adj.* [~'krypəlt] crippled; stunted; **~krustet** *adj.* [~'krustət] (en)crusted; caked; **~'kühlen** *v/refl.* (no -ge-, h) catch a cold.

ver'kümmer|n *v/i.* (no -ge-, sein) ♀, ♣ become stunted; ♣ atrophy; *fig.* waste away; **~t** *adj.* stunted; atrophied; rudimentary (*a.* biol.).

verkünd|en [fɛr'kyndən] *v/t.* (no -ge-, h), **~igen** *v/t.* (no -ge-, h) announce; publish, proclaim; pronounce (*judgement*); **♀igung** *f*, **♀ung** *f* (-/-en) announcement; proclamation; pronouncement.

ver|'kuppeln *v/t.* (no -ge-, h) ⊕ couple; *fig.* pander; **~'kürzen** *v/t.* (no -ge-, h) shorten; abridge; beguile (*time, etc.*); **~'lachen** *v/t.* (no -ge-, h) laugh at; **~'laden** *v/t.* (irr. laden, no -ge-, h) load, ship; ⛟ entrain (*esp.* troops).

Verlag [fɛr'la:k] *m* (-[e]s/-e) publishing house, *the* publishers *pl.*; im ~ von publishing.

ver'lagern *v/t.* (no -ge-, h) displace, shift; *sich* ~ shift.

Ver'lags|buchhändler *m* publisher; **~buchhandlung** *f* publishing house; **~recht** *n* copyright.

ver'langen **1.** *v/t.* (no -ge-, h) demand; require; desire; **2.** *v/i.* (no -ge-, h): ~ nach ask for; long for; **3.** ♀ *n* (-s/♣ -) desire; longing (*nach* for); demand, request; *auf* ~ by request, ✝ on demand; *auf* ~ *von* at the request of, at *s.o.'s* request.

verläuger|n [fɛr'lɛŋərn] *v/t.* (no -ge-, h) lengthen; prolong, extend; **♀ung** *f* (-/-en) lengthening; prolongation, extension.

ver'langsamen *v/t.* (no -ge-, h) slacken, slow down.

ver'lassen *v/t.* (irr. lassen, no -ge-, h) leave; forsake, abandon, desert;

sich ~ *auf* (*acc.*) rely on; **♀heit** *f* (-/no pl.) abandonment; loneliness.

verläßlich *adj.* [fɛr'lɛslɪç] reliable.

Ver'lauf *m* lapse, course (*of time*); progress, development (*of matter*); course (*of disease, etc.*); im ~ (*gen.*) *or* von in the course of; e-n schlimmen ~ nehmen take a bad turn; **♀en** (irr. laufen, no -ge-) **1.** *v/i.* (sein) *time*: pass, elapse; *matter*: take its course; turn out, develop; *road, etc.*: run, extend; **2.** *v/refl.* (h) lose one's way, go astray; *crowd*: disperse; *water*: subside.

ver'lauten *v/i.* (no -ge-, sein): ~ lassen give to understand, hint; *wie verlautet* as reported.

ver'leb|en *v/t.* (no -ge-, h) spend, pass; **~t** *adj.* [~pt] worn out.

ver'leg|en 1. *v/t.* (no -ge-, h) mislay; transfer, shift, remove; ⊕ lay (*cable, etc.*); bar (*road*); put off, postpone; publish (*book*); *sich* ~ *auf* (*acc.*) apply o.s. to; **2.** *adj.* embarrassed; at a loss (*um* for *answer, etc.*); **♀enheit** *f* (-/♣-en) embarrassment; difficulty; predicament; **♀er** *m* (-s/-) publisher; **♀ung** *f* (-/-en) transfer, removal; ⊕ laying; *time*: postponement.

ver'leiden *v/t.* (no -ge-, h) s. verekeln.

ver'leih|en *v/t.* (irr. leihen, no -ge-, h) lend, *Am. a.* loan; hire *or* let out; bestow (*right, etc.*) (*j-m* on s.o.); award (*price*); **♀ung** *f* (-/-en) lending, loan; bestowal.

ver|'leiten *v/t.* (no -ge-, h) mislead; induce; seduce; ♣ suborn; **~'lernen** *v/t.* (no -ge-, h) unlearn, forget; **~'lesen** *v/t.* (irr. lesen, no -ge-, h) read out; call (*names*) over; pick (*vegetables, etc.*); *sich* ~ read wrong.

verletz|en [fɛr'lɛtsən] *v/t.* (no -ge-, h) hurt, injure; *fig. a.*: offend; violate; **~end** *adj.* offensive; **♀te** [~tə] *m, f* (-n/-n) injured person; die ~n *pl.* the injured *pl.*; **♀ung** *f* (-/-en) hurt, injury, wound; *fig.* violation.

ver'leugn|en *v/t.* (no -ge-, h) deny; disown; renounce (*belief, principle, etc.*); *sich* ~ *lassen* have o.s. denied (*vor j-m* to s.o.); **♀ung** *f* (-/-en) denial; renunciation.

verleumd|en [fɛr'lɔymdən] *v/t.* (no -ge-, h) slander, defame; **~erisch** *adj.* slanderous; **♀ung** *f* (-/-en) slander, defamation, *in writing*: libel.

ver'lieb|en *v/refl.* (*no* -ge-, h): *sich ~ in* (*acc.*) fall in love with; **~t** *adj.* [~pt] in love (*in acc.* with); amorous; **2theit** *f* (-/~-en) amorousness.

verlieren [fer'li:rən] (*irr., no* -ge-, h) **1.** *v/t.* lose; shed (*leaves, etc.*); *sich ~* lose o.s.; disappear; **2.** *v/i.* lose.

ver'lob|en *v/t.* (*no* -ge-, h) engage (*mit* to); *sich ~* become engaged; **2te** [~ptə] (-*n*/-*n*) **1.** *m* fiancé; *die ~n pl.* the engaged couple *sg.*; **2.** *f* fiancée; **2ung** [~buŋ] *f* (-/-en) engagement.

ver'lock|en *v/t.* (*no* -ge-, h) allure, entice; tempt; **~end** *adj.* tempting; **2ung** *f* (-/-en) allurement, enticement.

verlogen *adj.* [fer'lo:gən] mendacious; **2heit** *f* (-/~-en) mendacity.

verlor [fer'lo:r] *pret.* of *verlieren*; **~en 1.** *p.p.* of *verlieren*; **2.** *adj.* lost; *fig.* forlorn; **~e** *Eier* poached eggs; **~engehen** *v/i.* (*irr. gehen, sep.,* -ge-, *sein*) be lost.

ver'los|en *v/t.* (*no* -ge-, h) raffle; **2ung** *f* (-/-en) lottery, raffle.

ver'löten *v/t.* (*no* -ge-, h) solder.

Verlust [fer'lust] *m* (-es/-e) loss; **~e** *pl.* ✕ casualties *pl.*

ver'mach|en *v/t.* (*no* -ge-, h) bequeath, leave *s.th.* (*dat.* to).

Vermächtnis [fer'mɛçtnis] *n* (-ses/-se) will; legacy; bequest.

vermähl|en [fer'mɛ:lən] *v/t.* (*no* -ge-, h) marry (*mit* to); *sich ~* (*mit*) marry (*s.o.*); **2ung** *f* (-/-en) wedding, marriage.

ver'mehr|en *v/t.* (*no* -ge-, h) increase (*um* by); augment; multiply; add to; *durch Zucht ~* propagate; breed; *sich ~* increase, augment; multiply (*a. biol.*); propagate (itself), *zo.* breed; **2ung** *f* (-/~-en) increase; addition (*gen.* to); propagation.

ver'meid|en *v/t.* (*irr. meiden, no* -ge-, h) avoid; **2ung** *f* (-/~-en) avoidance.

ver|meintlich *adj.* [fer'maintliç] supposed; **~'mengen** *v/t.* (*no* -ge-, h) mix, mingle, blend.

Vermerk [fer'mɛrk] *m* (-[e]s/-e) note, entry; **2en** *v/t.* (*no* -ge-, h) note down, record.

ver'mess|en 1. *v/t.* (*irr. messen, no* -ge-, h) measure; survey (*land*); **2.** *adj.* presumptuous; **2enheit** *f* (-/~-en) presumption; **2ung** *f* (-/-en) measurement; survey (*of land*).

ver'miete|n *v/t.* (*no* -ge-, h) let, *esp. Am.* rent; hire (out); ☶ lease; *zu ~ on or* for hire; *Haus zu ~* house to (be) let; **2r** *m* landlord; ☶ lessor; letter, hirer.

ver'mindern *v/t.* (*no* -ge-, h) diminish, lessen; reduce, cut.

ver'misch|en *v/t.* (*no* -ge-, h) mix, mingle, blend; **~t** *adj.* mixed; *news, etc.*: miscellaneous; **2ung** *f* (-/~-en) mixture.

ver'mi|ssen *v/t.* (*no* -ge-, h) miss; **~ßt** *adj.* [~'mist] missing; **2ßte** *m, f* (-*n*/-*n*) missing person; *die ~n pl.* the missing *pl.*

vermitt|eln [fer'mitəln] (*no* -ge-, h) **1.** *v/t.* mediate (*settlement, peace*); procure, get; give (*impression, etc.*); impart (*knowledge*) (*j-m* to *s.o.*); **2.** *v/i.* mediate (*zwischen dat.* between); intercede (*bei* with, *für* for), intervene; **2ler** *m* mediator; go-between; † agent; **2lung** *f* (-/-en) mediation; intercession, intervention; *teleph.* (telephone) exchange.

ver'modern *v/i.* (*no* -ge-, *sein*) mo(u)lder, decay, rot.

ver'mögen 1. *v/t.* (*irr. mögen, no* -ge-, h): *~ zu inf.* be able to *inf.*; *j-s* ~ *bei j-m* have influence with *s.o.*; **2.** **2** *n* (-s/-) ability, power; property; fortune; means *pl.*; ☶ assets *pl.*; **~d** *adj.* wealthy; *pred.* well off; **2sverhältnisse** *pl.* pecuniary circumstances *pl.*

vermut|en [fer'mu:tən] *v/t.* (*no* -ge-, h) suppose, presume, *Am. a.* guess; conjecture, surmise; **~lich 1.** *adj.* presumable; **2.** *adv.* presumably; I suppose; **2ung** *f* (-/-en) supposition, presumption; conjecture, surmise.

vernachlässig|en [fer'na:xlɛsigən] *v/t.* (*no* -ge-, h) neglect; **2ung** *f* (-/~-en) neglect(ing).

ver'narben *v/i.* (*no* -ge-, *sein*) cicatrize, scar over. [with.]

ver'narrt *adj.*: *~ in* (*acc.*) infatuated

ver'nehm|en *v/t.* (*irr. nehmen, no* -ge-, h) hear, learn; examine, interrogate; **~lich** *adj.* audible, distinct;

U V

2ung ⚥ f (-/-en) interrogation, questioning; examination.

ver'neig|en v/refl. (no -ge-, h) bow (vor dat. to); **2ung** f bow.

vernein|en [fer'naɪnən] (no -ge-, h) **1.** v/t. answer in the negative; deny; **2.** v/i. answer in the negative; **~end** adj. negative; **2ung** f (-/-en) negation; denial; gr. negative.

vernicht|en [fer'nɪçtən] v/t. (no -ge-, h) annihilate; destroy; dash (hopes); **~end** adj. destructive (a. fig.); look: withering; criticism: scathing; defeat, reply: crushing; **2ung** f (-/⚥ -en) annihilation; destruction.

ver'nickeln [fer'nɪkəln] v/t. (no -ge-, h) nickel(-plate); **~'nieten** v/t. (no -ge-, h) rivet.

Vernunft [fer'nʊnft] f (-/no pl.) reason; ~ annehmen listen to or hear reason; j-n zur ~ bringen bring s.o. to reason or to his senses.

vernünftig adj. [fer'nʏnftɪç] rational; reasonable; sensible.

ver'öden (no -ge-) **1.** v/t. (h) make desolate; **2.** v/i. (sein) become desolate.

ver'öffentlich|en v/t. (no -ge-, h) publish; **2ung** f (-/-en) publication.

ver'ordn|en v/t. (no -ge-, h) decree; order (a. ⚕); ⚕ prescribe (j-m to or for s.o.); **2ung** f decree, order; ⚕ prescription.

ver'pachten v/t. (no -ge-, h) rent, ⚥ lease (building, land).

Ver'pächter m landlord, ⚥ lessor.

ver'pack|en v/t. (no -ge-, h) pack (up); wrap up; **2ung** f packing (material); wrapping.

ver|'passen v/t. (no -ge-, h) miss (train, opportunity, etc.); **~'patzen** F [~'patsən] v/t. (no -ge-, h) s. verpfuschen; **~'pesten** v/t. (no -ge-, h) fumes: contaminate (the air); **~'pfänden** v/t. (no -ge-, h) pawn, pledge (a. fig.); mortgage.

ver'pflanz|en v/t. (no -ge-, h) transplant (a. ⚕); **2ung** f transplantation; ⚕ a. transplant.

ver'pfleg|en v/t. (no -ge-, h) board; supply with food, victual; **2ung** f (-/⚥ -en) board; food-supply; provisions pl.

ver'pflicht|en v/t. (no -ge-, h) oblige; engage; **2ung** f (-/-en) obligation, duty; ✝, ⚥ liability; engagement, commitment.

ver'pfusch|en F v/t. (no -ge-, h) bungle, botch; make a mess of; **~t** adj. life: ruined, wrecked.

ver|pönt adj. [fer'pøːnt] taboo; **~'prügeln** F v/t. (no -ge-, h) thrash, flog, F wallop; **~'puffen** fig. v/i. (no -ge-, sein) fizzle out.

Ver'putz △ m (-es/⚥ -e) plaster; **2en** △ v/t. (no -ge-, h) plaster.

ver'quicken [fer'kvɪkən] v/t. (no -ge-, h) mix up; **~'quollen** adj. wood: warped; face: bloated; eyes: swollen; **~rammeln** [~'raməln] v/t. (no -ge-, h) bar(ricade).

Verrat [fer'raːt] m (-[e]s/no pl.) betrayal (an dat. of); treachery (to); ⚥ treason (to); **2en** v/t. (irr. raten, no -ge-, h) betray, give s.o. away; give away (secret); sich ~ betray o.s., give o.s. away.

Verräter [fer'rɛːtər] m (-s/-) traitor (an dat. to); **2isch** adj. treacherous; fig. telltale.

ver'rechn|en v/t. (no -ge-, h) reckon up; charge; settle; set off (mit against); account for; ~ mit offset against; sich ~ miscalculate, make a mistake (a. fig.); fig. be mistaken; sich um e-e Mark ~ be one mark out; **2ung** f settlement; clearing; booking or charging (to account); **2ungsscheck** m collection-only cheque or Am. check.

ver'regnet adj. rainy, rain-spoilt.

ver'reis|en v/i. (no -ge-, sein) go on a journey; **~t** adj. out of town; (geschäftlich) ~ away (on business).

verrenk|en [fer'rɛŋkən] v/t. (no -ge-, h) ⚕: wrench; dislocate, luxate; sich et. ~ dislocate or luxate s.th.; sich den Hals ~ crane one's neck; **2ung** ⚕ f (-/-en) dislocation, luxation.

ver|'richten v/t. (no -ge-, h) do, perform; execute; sein Gebet ~ say one's prayer(s); **~'riegeln** v/t. (no -ge-, h) bolt, bar.

verringer|n [fer'rɪŋərn] v/t. (no -ge-, h) diminish, lessen; reduce, cut; sich ~ diminish, lessen; **2ung** f (-/-en) diminution; reduction, cut.

ver|'rosten v/i. (no -ge-, sein) rust; **~rotten** [~'rotən] v/i. (no -ge-, sein) rot.

ver'rück|en v/t. (no -ge-, h) displace, (re)move, shift; **~t** adj. mad, crazy (both a. fig.: nach about); wie ~ like mad; j-n ~ machen drive

U
V

s.o. mad; ²te (-n/-n) **1.** *m* lunatic, madman; **2.** *f* lunatic, madwoman; ²heit *f* (-/-en) madness; foolish action; craze.

Ver'ruf *m* (-[e]s/*no pl.*): in ~ bringen bring discredit (up)on; in ~ kommen get into discredit; ²en *adj.* ill-reputed, ill-famed.

ver'rutsch|en *v/i.* (*no* -ge-, sein) slip; ~t *adj.* not straight.

Vers [fɛrs] *m* (-es/-e) verse.

er'sagen **1.** *v/t.* (*no* -ge-, h) refuse, deny (*j-m et.* s.o. s.th.); sich et. ~ deny o.s. s.th.; **2.** *v/i.* (*no* -ge-, h) fail, break down; *gun:* misfire; **3.** ² *n* (-s/*no pl.*) failure. [ure.]

er'sager *m* (-s/-) misfire; *p.* fail-)

ver'salzen *v/t.* (*irr.* salzen,] *no* -ge-, h) oversalt; *F fig.* spoil.

ver'samm|eln *v/t.* (*no* -ge-, h) assemble; sich ~ assemble, meet; ²lung *f* assembly, meeting.

Versand [fɛr'zant] *m* (-[e]s/*no pl.*) dispatch, *Am. a.* shipment; mailing; ~ ins Ausland *a.* export(ation). ~abteilung *f* forwarding department; ~geschäft *n*, ~haus *n* mail-order business *or* firm *or* house.

ver'säum|en *v/t.* (*no* -ge-, h) neglect (*one's duty, etc.*); miss (*opportunity, etc.*); lose (*time*); ~ zu *inf.* fail *or* omit to *inf.*; ²nis *n* (-ses/-se) neglect, omission, failure.

ver'schachern F *v/t.* (*no* -ge-, h) barter (away); ~'schaffen *v/t.* (*no* -ge-, h) procure, get; sich ~ obtain, get; raise (*money*); sich Respekt ~ make o.s. respected; ~'schämt *adj.* bashful; ~'schanzen *v/refl.* (*no* -ge-, h) entrench o.s.; sich ~ hinter (*dat.*) (take) shelter behind; ~'schärfen *v/t.* (*no* -ge-, h) heighten, intensify; aggravate; sich ~ get worse; ~'scheiden *v/i.* (*irr.* scheiden, *no* -ge-, sein) pass away; ~'schenken *v/t.* (*no* -ge-, h) give s.th. away; make a present of; ~'scherzen *v/t. and v/refl.* (*no* -ge-, h) forfeit; ~'scheuchen *v/t.* (*no* -ge-, h) frighten *or* scare away; *fig.* banish; ~'schicken *v/t.* (*no* -ge-, h) send (away), dispatch, forward.

ver'schieb|en *v/t.* (*irr.* schieben, *no* -ge-, h) displace, shift, (re)move; ⚙ shunt; put off, postpone; F *fig.* ✝ sell underhand; sich ~ shift; ²ung *f* shift(ing); postponement.

ver'schieden *adj.* [fɛr'ʃiːdən] differ-

ent (*von* from); dissimilar, unlike; *aus* ~en *Gründen* for various *or* several reasons; *Verschiedenes* various things *pl.*, *esp.* ✝ sundries *pl.*; ~artig *adj.* of a different kind, various; ²heit *f* (-/-en) difference; diversity, variety; ~tlich *adv.* repeatedly; at times.

ver'schiff|en *v/t.* (*no* -ge-, h) ship; ²ung *f* (-/⚓-en) shipment.

ver'schimmel|n *v/i.* (*no* -ge-, sein) get mo(u)ldy, *Am.* mo(u)ld; ~'schlafen **1.** *v/t.* (*irr.* schlafen, *no* -ge-, h) miss by sleeping; sleep (*afternoon, etc.*) away; sleep off (*headache, etc.*); **2.** *v/i.* (*irr.* schlafen, *no* -ge-, h) oversleep (o.s.); **3.** *adj.* sleepy, drowsy.

Ver'schlag *m* shed; box; crate; ²en [~gən] **1.** *v/t.* (*irr.* schlagen, *no* -ge-, h) board up; nail up; es verschlug ihm die Sprache it dum(b)-founded him; **2.** *adj.* cunning; *eyes:* a. shifty; ~enheit *f* (-/*no pl.*) cunning.

ver'schlechter|n [fɛr'ʃlɛçtərn] *v/t.* (*no* -ge-, h) deteriorate, make worse; sich ~ deteriorate, get worse; ²ung *f* (-/⚓-en) deterioration; change for the worse.

ver'schleiern *v/t.* (*no* -ge-, h) veil (*a. fig.*).

Verschleiß [fɛr'ʃlaɪs] *m* (-es/⚓-e) wear (and tear); ²en *v/t.* ([*irr.*,] *no* -ge-, h) wear out.

ver'schlepp|en *v/t.* (*no* -ge-, h) carry off; *pol.* displace (*person*); abduct, kidnap; delay, protract; neglect (*disease*); ~'schleudern *v/t.* (*no* -ge-, h) dissipate, waste; ✝ sell at a loss, sell dirt-cheap; ~'schließen *v/t.* (*irr.* schließen, *no* -ge-, h) shut, close; lock (*door*); lock up (*house*).

verschlimmern [fɛr'ʃlɪmərn] *v/t.* (*no* -ge-, h) make worse, aggravate; sich ~ get worse.

ver'schlingen *v/t.* (*irr.* schlingen, *no* -ge-, h) devour; wolf (down) (*one's food*); intertwine, entwine, interlace; sich ~ intertwine, entwine, interlace.

verschli|ß [fɛr'ʃlɪs] *pret. of* verschleißen; ~ssen [~sən] *p.p. of* verschleißen.

verschlossen *adj.* [fɛr'ʃlɔsən] closed, shut; *fig.* reserved; ²heit *f* (-/*no pl.*) reserve.

ver'schlucken v/t. (no -ge-, h)
swallow (up); *sich* ~ swallow the
wrong way.

Ver'schluß m lock; clasp; lid; plug;
stopper (*of bottle*); seal; fastener,
fastening; *phot.* shutter; *unter* ~
under lock and key.

ver|'schmachten v/i. (no -ge-, sein)
languish, pine away; *vor Durst* ~
die *or* be dying of thirst, be parched
with thirst; **~'schmähen** v/t. (no
-ge-, h) disdain, scorn.

ver'schmelz|en (*irr.* schmelzen, no
-ge-) v/t. (h) *and* v/i. (sein) melt,
fuse (*a. fig.*); blend; *fig.*: amalgam-
ate; merge (*mit in, into*); 2ung f
(-/~-en) fusion; ✝ merger; *fig.*
amalgamation.

ver|'schmerzen v/t. (no -ge-, h)
get over (the loss of); **~'schmieren**
v/t. (no -ge-, h) smear (over); blur;
~schmitzt adj. [~'ʃmitst] cunning;
roguish; arch; **~'schmutzen** v/t. (no
-ge-) 1. v/t. (h) soil, dirty; pollute
(*water*); 2. v/i. (sein) get dirty;
~'schnaufen F v/i. *and* v/refl. (no
-ge-, h) stop for breath; **~'schneiden** v/t. (*irr.* schneiden, no -ge-, h)
cut badly; blend (*wine, etc.*); geld,
castrate; **~'schneit** adj. covered
with snow; *mountains*: a. snow-
capped; *roofs*: a. snow-covered.

Ver'schnitt m (-[e]s/no pl.) blend.

ver'schnupf|en F *fig.* v/t. (no -ge-,
h) nettle, pique; **~t** ✗ adj.: ~ *sein*
have a cold.

ver|'schnüren v/t. (no -ge-, h) tie
up, cord; **~schollen** adj. [~'ʃɔlən]
not heard of again; missing; ✗
presumed dead; **~'schonen** v/t.
(no -ge-, h) spare; *j-n mit et.* ~
spare s.o. s.th.

verschöne(r)n [fɛr'ʃøːnə(r)n] v/t.
(no -ge-, h) embellish, beautify;
2rung f (-/-en) embellishment.

ver'schossen adj. [fɛr'ʃɔsən] *colour*:
faded; F ~ *sein in* (acc.) be madly
in love with; **~schränken** [~'ʃreŋ-
kən] v/t. (no -ge-, h) cross, fold
(*one's arms*).

ver'schreib|en v/t. (*irr.* schreiben,
no -ge-, h) use up (*in writing*); ✗
prescribe (*j-m for s.o.*); ✗ assign
(*j-m to s.o.*); *sich* ~ make a slip
of the pen; *sich e-r Sache* ~ devote
o.s. to s.th.; 2ung f (-/-en) assign-
ment; prescription.

ver|schroben adj. [fɛr'ʃroːbən] ec-

centric, queer, odd; **~'schrotten**
v/t. (no -ge-, h) scrap; **~schüch-
tert** adj. [~'ʃʏçtərt] intimidated.

ver|'schulden 1. v/t. (no -ge-, h)
be guilty of; be the cause of;
2. 2 n (-s/no pl.) fault.

ver|'schuldet adj. indebted, in
debt; **~'schütten** v/t. (no -ge-, h)
spill (*liquid*); block (up) (*road*);
bury s.o. alive; **~schwägert** adj.
[~'ʃveːgərt] related by marriage;
~'schweigen v/t. (*irr.* schweigen,
no -ge-, h) conceal (*j-m et. s.th.
from s.o.*).

verschwend|en [fɛr'ʃvɛndən] v/t.
(no -ge-, h) waste, squander (*an
acc.* on); lavish (on); 2er m (-s/-)
spendthrift, prodigal; **~erisch** adj.
prodigal, lavish (*both*: *mit* of);
wasteful; 2ung f (-/~-en) waste;
extravagance.

verschwiegen adj. [fɛr'ʃviːgən]
discreet; *place*: secret, secluded;
2heit f (-/no pl.) discretion; secrecy.

ver|'schwimmen v/i. (*irr.* schwim-
men, no -ge-, sein) become indistinct or blurred; **~'schwinden**
v/i. (*irr.* schwinden, no -ge-, sein)
disappear, vanish; F *verschwinde!*
go away!, sl. beat it!; 2'schwinden n (-s/no pl.) disappearance;
~schwommen adj. [~'ʃvɔmən]
vague (*a. fig.*); blurred; *fig.* woolly.

ver'schwör|en v/refl. (*irr.* schwö-
ren, no -ge-, h) conspire; 2er m
(-s/-) conspirator; 2ung f (-/-en)
conspiracy, plot.

ver'seh|en 1. v/t. (*irr.* sehen, no -ge-,
h) fill (*an office*); look after (*house,
etc.*); *mit et.* ~ furnish or supply
with; *sich* ~ make a mistake; *ehe
man sich's versieht* all of a sudden;
2. 2 n (-s/-) oversight, mistake, slip;
aus ~ = **~tlich** adv. by mistake;
inadvertently. [disabled person.]

Versehrte [fɛr'zeːrtə] m (-n/-n)

ver'send|en v/t. ([*irr.* senden,] no
-ge-, h) send, dispatch, forward,
Am. ship; *by water*: ship; *ins Ausl-
land* ~ a. export; 2ung f (-/~-en)
dispatch, shipment, forwarding.

ver|'sengen v/t. (no -ge-, h) singe,
scorch; **~'senken** v/t. (no -ge-, h)
sink; *sich* ~ *in* (acc.) immerse o.s.
in; **~sessen** adj. [~'zɛsən]: ~ *auf*
(acc.) bent on, mad after.

ver'setz|en v/t. (no -ge-, h) displace, remove; transfer (*officer*); *at school*: remove, move up, *Am.* promote; transplant (*tree, etc.*); pawn, pledge; F *fig.* stand (*lover, etc.*) up; ~ in (*acc.*) put *or* place into (*situation, condition*); j-m e-n Schlag ~ give *or* deal s.o. a blow; *in Angst* ~ frighten *or* terrify *s.o.*; *in den Ruhestand* ~ pension *s.o.* off, retire *s.o.*; *versetzt werden* be transferred; *at school*: go up; ~ Sie sich in m-e Lage put *or* place yourself in my position; *Wein mit Wasser* ~ mix wine with water, add water to wine; *et.* ~ reply s.th.; 2ung *f* (-/-en) removal; transfer; *at school*: remove, *Am.* promotion.

ver'seuch|en *v/t.* (*no* -ge-, *h*) infect; contaminate; 2ung *f* (-/⸚ -en) infection; contamination.

ver'sicher|n *v/t.* (*no* -ge-, *h*) assure (*a. one's life*); protest, affirm; insure (*one's property or life*); sich ~ insure *or* assure o.s.; *sich* ~ (, *daß*) make sure (that); **2te** *m, f* (-n/-n) insurant, *the* insured *or* assured, policy-holder; 2ung *f* assurance; affirmation; insurance; (life-)assurance; insurance company.

Ver'sicherungs|gesellschaft *f* insurance company; **~police** *f, ~-schein** *m* policy of assurance, insurance policy.

ver'|sickern *v/i.* (*no* -ge-, *sein*) trickle away; **~'siegeln** *v/t.* (*no* -ge-, *h*) seal (up); **~'siegen** *v/i.* (*no* -ge-, *sein*) dry up, run dry; **~'silbern** *v/t.* (*no* -ge-, *h*) silver; F *fig.* realize, convert into cash; **~'sinken** *v/i.* (*irr.* sinken, *no* -ge-, *sein*) sink; *s.* versunken; **~'sinnbildlichen** *v/t.* (*no* -ge-, *h*) symbolize.

Version [ver'zjo:n] *f* (-/-en) version.

'Versmaß *n* met|re, *Am.* -er.

versöhn|en [fer'zø:nən] *v/t.* (*no* -ge-, *h*) reconcile (*mit* to, with); *sich* (*wieder*) ~ become reconciled; **~lich** *adj.* conciliatory; 2ung *f* (-/⸚ -en) reconciliation.

ver'sorg|en *v/t.* (*no* -ge-, *h*) provide (*mit* with), supply (with); take care of, look after; **~t** *adj.* [⸚kt] provided for; 2ung *f* (-/⸚gun] *f* (-/-en) providing (*mit* with), supplying (with); supply, provision.

ver'spät|en *v/refl.* (*no* -ge-, *h*) be late; **~et** *adj.* belated, late, *Am.*

tardy; 2ung *f* (-/-en) lateness, *Am.* tardiness; ~ haben be late; *mit 2 Stunden* ~ two hours behind schedule.

ver|'speisen *v/t.* (*no* -ge-, *h*) eat (up); **~'sperren** *v/t.* (*no* -ge-, *h*) lock (up); bar, block (up), obstruct (*a. view*); **~'spielen** *v/t.* (*no* -ge-, *h*) *at cards, etc.*: lose (*money*); **~'spielt** *adj.* playful; **~'spotten** *v/t.* (*no* -ge-, *h*) scoff at, mock (at), deride, ridicule; **~'sprechen** *v/t.* (*irr.* sprechen, *no* -ge-, *h*) promise; *sich* ~ make a mistake in speaking; *sich viel* ~ *von* expect much of; 2'sprechen *n* (-s/⸚ -) promise; **~'sprühen** *v/t.* (*no* -ge-, *h*) spray; **~'spüren** *v/t.* (*no* -ge-, *h*) feel; perceive, be conscious of.

ver'staatlich|en *v/t.* (*no* -ge-, *h*) nationalize; 2ung *f* (-/⸚ -en) nationalization.

Verstand [fer'ʃtant] *m* (-[e]s/*no pl.*) understanding; intelligence, intellect, brains *pl.*; mind, wits *pl.*; reason; (common) sense.

Verstandes|kraft [fer'ʃtandəs-] *f* intellectual power *or* faculty; 2-**mäßig** *adj.* rational; intellectual; **~mensch** *m* matter-of-fact person.

verständ|ig *adj.* [fer'ʃtendiç] intelligent; reasonable, sensible; judicious; **~igen** [⸚gən] *v/t.* (*no* -ge-, *h*) inform (*von* of), notify (of); *sich mit j-m* ~ make o.s. understood to s.o.; come to an understanding with s.o.; 2igung [⸚gun] *f* (-/⸚ -en) information; understanding, agreement; *teleph.* communication; **~lich** *adj.* [⸚tliç] intelligible; understandable; *j-m* et. ~ machen make s.th. clear to s.o.; *sich* ~ machen make o.s. understood.

Verständnis [fer'ʃtentnis] *n* (-ses/⸚ -se) comprehension, understanding; insight; appreciation (*für* of); ~ haben für appreciate; 2los *adj.* uncomprehending; *look, etc.*: blank; unappreciative; 2voll *adj.* understanding; appreciative; sympathetic; *look*: knowing.

ver'stärk|en *v/t.* (*no* -ge-, *h*) strengthen, reinforce (*a.* ⊕, ✕); amplify (*radio signals, etc.*); intensify; 2er *m* (-s/-) *in radio, etc.*: amplifier; 2ung *f* (-/⸚ -en) strengthening, reinforcement (*a.* ✕); amplification; intensification.

ver|'staub|en v/i. (no -ge-, sein) get dusty; ~t adj. [~pt] dusty.

ver|'stauch|en ℱ v/t. (no -ge-, h) sprain; sich den Fuß ~ sprain one's foot; 2ung ℱ f (-/-en) sprain.

ver|'stauen v/t. (no -ge-, h) stow away.

Ver'steck [fɛr'ʃtɛk] n (-[e]s/-e) hiding-place; for gangsters, etc.: Am. F a. hide-out; ~ spielen play at hide-and-seek; 2en v/t. (no -ge-, h) hide, conceal; sich ~ hide.

ver|'stehen v/t. (irr. stehen, no -ge-, h) understand, see, F get; comprehend; realize; know (language); es ~ zu inf. know how to inf.; Spaß ~ take a joke; zu ~ geben intimate; ~ Sie? do you see?; ich ~! I see!; verstanden? (do you) understand?, F (do you) get me?; falsch ~ misunderstand; ~ Sie mich recht! don't misunderstand me!; was ~ Sie unter (dat.)? what do you mean or understand by ...?; er versteht et. davon he knows a thing or two about it; sich ~ understand one another; sich ~ auf (acc.) know well, be an expert at or in; sich mit j-m gut ~ get on well with s.o.; es versteht sich von selbst it goes without saying.

ver|'steifen v/t. (no -ge-, h) ⊕ strut, brace; stiffen; sich ~ stiffen; sich ~ auf (acc.) make a point of, insist on.

ver|'steiger|n v/t. (no -ge-, h) (sell by or Am. at) auction; 2ung f (sale by or Am. at) auction, auction-sale.

ver|'steinern (no -ge-) v/t. (h) and v/i. (sein) turn into stone, petrify (both a. fig.).

ver|'stell|bar adj. adjustable; ~en v/t. (no -ge-, h) shift; adjust; disarrange; bar, block (up), obstruct; disguise (voice, etc.); sich ~ play or act a part; dissemble, feign; 2ung f (-/~-en) disguise; dissimulation.

ver|'steuern v/t. (no -ge-, h) pay duty or tax on; ~stiegen fig. adj. [~'ʃtiːɡən] eccentric.

ver|'stimm|en v/t. (no -ge-, h) put out of tune; fig. put out of humo(u)r; ~t adj. out of tune; fig. out of humo(u)r, F cross; 2ung f ill humo(u)r; disagreement; ill feeling.

ver|'stockt adj. stubborn, obdurate; 2heit f (-/no pl.) obduracy.

verstohlen adj. [fɛr'ʃtoːlən] furtive

ver|'stopf|en v/t. (no -ge-, h) stop (up); clog, block (up), obstruct; jam, block (passage, street); ℱ constipate; 2ung ℱ f (-/~-en) constipation.

verstorben adj. [fɛr'ʃtɔrbən] late deceased; 2e m, f (-n/-n) the deceased, Am. ⚖ a. decedent; die ~n pl. the deceased pl., the departed pl.

ver|'stört adj. scared; distracted bewildered; 2heit f (-/no pl.) distraction, bewilderment.

Ver'stoß m offen|ce, Am. -se; contravention (gegen of law); infringement (on trade name, etc.) blunder; 2en (irr. stoßen, no -ge-, h) 1. v/t. expel (aus from); repudiate disown (wife, child, etc.); 2. v/i. ~ gegen offend against; contravene (law); infringe (rule, etc.).

ver|'streichen (irr. streichen, no -ge-) 1. v/i. (sein) time: pass. elapse; expire; 2. v/t. (h) spread (butter, etc.); ~'streuen v/t. (no -ge-, h) scatter.

verstümmel|n [fɛr'ʃtʏməln] v/t. (no -ge-, h) mutilate; garble (text, etc.); 2ung f (-/-en) mutilation.

ver|'stummen v/i. (no -ge-, sein) grow silent or dumb.

Verstümmlung [fɛr'ʃtʏmluŋ] f (-/-en) mutilation.

Versuch [fɛr'zuːx] m (-[e]s/-e) attempt, trial; phys., etc.: experiment; e-n ~ machen mit give s.o. or s.th. a trial; try one's hand at s.th., have a go at s.th.; 2en v/t. (no -ge-, h) try, attempt; taste; j-n ~ tempt s.o.; es ~ mit give s.o. or s.th. a trial.

Ver'suchs|anstalt f research institute; ~kaninchen fig. n guinea-pig; 2weise adv. by way of trial or (an) experiment; on trial; ~zweck m: zu ~en pl. for experimental purposes pl.

Ver'suchung f (-/-en) temptation; j-n in ~ bringen tempt s.o.; in ~ sein be tempted.

ver|'sündigen v/refl. (no -ge-, h) sin (an dat. against); ~sunken fig. adj. [~'zuŋkən]: ~ in (acc.) absorbed or lost in; ~'süßen v/t. (no -ge-, h) sweeten.

ver|'tag|en v/t. (no -ge-, h) adjourn; parl. prorogue; sich ~ adjourn, Am.

a. recess; 2ung *f* adjournment; *parl.* prorogation.

er'tauschen *v/t.* (no -ge-, h) exchange (*mit* for).

erteidig|en [fer'taɪdɪgən] *v/t.* (no -ge-, h) defend; *sich ~* defend o.s.; 2er *m* (-s/-) defender; ㅎㅎ, *fig.* advocate; ㅎㅎ counsel for the defen|ce, *Am.* -se, *Am.* attorney for the defendant *or* defense; *football:* fullback; 2ung *f* (-/~-en) defen|ce, *Am.* -se.

er'teidigungs|bündnis *n* defensive alliance; ~minister *m* minister of defence; *Brt.* Minister of Defence, *Am.* Secretary of Defense; ~ministerium *n* ministry of defence; *Brt.* Ministry of Defence, *Am.* Department of Defense.

er'teil|en *v/t.* (no -ge-, h) distribute; spread (*colour, etc.*); 2er *m* (-s/-) distributor; 2ung *f* (-/~-en) distribution.

er'teuern *v/t.* (no -ge-, h) raise *or* increase the price of.

er'tief|en *v/t.* (no -ge-, h) deepen (*a. fig.*); *sich ~* deepen; *sich ~ in* (*acc.*) plunge in(to); become absorbed in; 2ung *f* (-/-en) hollow, cavity; recess.

vertikal *adj.* [verti'ka:l] vertical.

ver'tilg|en *v/t.* (no -ge-, h) exterminate; F consume, eat (up) (*food*); 2ung *f* (-/~-en) extermination.

er'tonen ♪ *v/t.* (no -ge-, h) set to music.

Vertrag [fer'tra:k] *m* (-[e]s/~e) agreement, contract; *pol.* treaty; 2en [~gən] *v/t.* (irr. tragen, no -ge-, h) endure, bear, stand; *diese Speise kann ich nicht ~* this food does not agree with me; *sich ~ things:* be compatible *or* consistent; *colours:* harmonize; *p.:* agree; get on with one another; *sich wieder ~* be reconciled, make it up; 2lich [~klɪç] 1. *adj.* contractual, stipulated; 2. *adv.* as stipulated; *~ verpflichtet sein* to be bound by contract; *sich ~ verpflichten* contract (*zu* for s.th.; *zu inf.* to inf.).

er'träglich *adj.* [fer'trɛ:klɪç] sociable.

Ver'trags|bruch *m* breach of contract; 2brüchig *adj.:* *~ werden* commit a breach of contract; ~entwurf *m* draft agreement; ~partner *m* party to a contract.

ver'trauen 1. *v/i.* (no -ge-, h) trust (*j-m* s.o.); *~ auf* (*acc.*) trust *or* confide in; 2. 2 *n* (-s/no pl.) confidence, trust; *im ~* confidentially, between you and me; ~erweckend *adj.* inspiring confidence; promising.

Ver'trauens|bruch *m* breach *or* betrayal of trust; ~frage *parl. f:* *die ~ stellen* put the question of confidence; ~mann *m* (-[e]s/eer, *Vertrauensleute*) spokesman; shopsteward; confidential agent; ~sache *f: das ist ~* that is a matter of confidence; ~stellung *f* position of trust; 2voll *adj.* trustful, trusting; ~votum *parl. n* vote of confidence; 2würdig *adj.* trustworthy, reliable.

ver'traulich *adj.* confidential, in confidence; intimate, familiar; 2-keit *f* (-/-en) confidence; intimacy, familiarity.

ver'traut *adj.* intimate, familiar; 2e (-n/-n) 1. *m* confidant, intimate friend; 2. *f* confidante, intimate friend; 2heit *f* (-/~-en) familiarity.

ver'treib|en *v/t.* (irr. treiben, no -ge-, h) drive away; expel (*aus* from); turn out; ✝ sell, distribute (*goods*); *sich die Zeit ~* pass one's time, kill time; 2ung *f* (-/~-en) expulsion.

ver'tret|en *v/t.* (irr. treten, no -ge-, h) represent (*s.o., firm, etc.*); substitute for s.o.; attend to, look after (*s.o.'s interests*); hold (*view*); *parl.* sit for (*borough*); answer for s.th.; *j-s Sache ~* plead s.o.'s case *or* cause; *sich den Fuß ~* sprain one's foot; F *sich die Beine ~* stretch one's legs; 2er *m* (-s/-) representative; ✝ *a.* agent; proxy, agent; substitute, deputy; exponent; (sales) representative; door-to-door salesman; commercial travel(l)er, *esp. Am.* travel(l)ing salesman; 2ung *f* (-/-en) representation (*a. pol.*); ✝ agency; *in office:* substitution; *in ~* by proxy; *gen.:* acting for.

Vertrieb ✝ [fer'tri:p] *m* (-[e]s/-e) sale; distribution; ~ene [~bənə] *m, f* (-n/-en) expellee.

ver'trocknen *v/i.* (no -ge-, sein) dry up; ~'trödeln F *v/t.* (no -ge-, h) dawdle away, waste (*time*); ~'trösten *v/t.* (no -ge-, h) put off; ~'tuschen F *v/t.* (no -ge-, h) hush up; ~'übeln *v/t.* (no -ge-, h) take s.th.

amiss; ~üben v/t. (no -ge-, h) commit, perpetrate.

ver'unglück|en v/i. (no -ge-, sein) meet with or have an accident; F fig. fail, go wrong; tödlich ~ be killed in an accident; 2te m, f (-n/-n) casualty.

verun|reinigen [fer'unrainigən] v/t. (no -ge-, h) soil, dirty; defile; contaminate (air); pollute (water); ~stalten [~ʃtaltən] v/t. (no -ge-, h) disfigure.

ver'untreu|en v/t. (no -ge-, h) embezzle; 2ung f (-/-en) embezzlement.

ver'ursachen v/t. (no -ge-, h) cause.

ver'urteil|en v/t. (no -ge-, h) condemn (zu to) (a. fig.), sentence (to); convict (wegen of); 2te m, f (-n/-n) convict; 2ung f (-/-en) condemnation (a. fig.), conviction.

ver'vielfältigen [fer'fi:lfeltigən] v/t. (no -ge-, h) manifold; ~vollkommnen [~'fɔlkɔmnən] v/t. (no -ge-, h) perfect; sich ~ perfect o.s.

vervollständig|en [fer'fɔlʃtendigən] v/t. (no -ge-, h) complete; 2ung f (-/~-en) completion.

ver|'wachsen 1. v/i. (irr. wachsen, no -ge-, sein): miteinander ~ grow together; 2. adj. deformed; humpbacked, hunchbacked; ~'wackeln phot. v/t. (no -ge-, h) blur.

ver'wahr|en v/t. (no -ge-, h) keep; sich ~ gegen protest against; ~lost adj. [~lo:st] child, garden, etc.: uncared-for, neglected; degenerate; 2ung f keeping; charge; custody; fig. protest; j-m et. in ~ geben give s.th. into s.o.'s charge; in ~ nehmen take charge of. [fig. deserted.]

verwaist adj. [fer'vaist] orphan(ed);}

ver'walt|en v/t. (no -ge-, h) administer, manage; 2er m (-s/-) administrator, manager; steward (of estate); 2ung f (-/-en) administration; management.

ver'wand|eln v/t. (no -ge-, h) change, turn, transform; sich ~ change (all: in acc. into); 2lung f (-/-en) change; transformation.

verwandt adj. [fer'vant] related (mit to); languages, tribes, etc.: kindred; languages, sciences: cognate (with); pred. akin (to) (a. fig.); 2e m, f (-n/-n) relative, relation; 2schaft f (-/-en) relationship; re-

lations pl.; geistige ~ congeniality

ver'warn|en v/t. (no -ge-, h) caution; 2ung f caution.

ver'wässern v/t. (no -ge-, h) water (down), dilute; fig. water down dilute.

ver'wechs|eln v/t. (no -ge-, h) mistake (mit for); confound, mix up, confuse (all: mit with); 2(e)-lung f (-/-en) mistake; confusion

verwegen adj. [fer've:gən] daring bold, audacious; 2heit f (-/~-en) boldness, audacity, daring.

ver|'wehren v/t. (no -ge-, h): j-m et. ~ (de)bar s.o. from (doing) s.th. den Zutritt ~ deny or refuse admittance (zu to); ~'weichlicht adj. effeminate, soft.

ver'weiger|n v/t. (no -ge-, h) deny refuse; disobey (order); 2ung ʃ denial, refusal.

ver'weilen v/i. (no -ge-, h) stay linger; bei et. ~ dwell (up)on s.th.

Verweis [fer'vais] m (-es/-e) reprimand; rebuke, reproof; reference (auf acc. to); 2en [~zən] v/t. (irr weisen, no -ge-, h): j-n des Landes ~ expel s.o. from Germany, etc.; j-m et. ~ reprimand s.o. for s.th.; j-n ~ auf (acc.) or an (acc.) refer s.o. to.

ver'welken v/i. (no -ge-, sein) fade, wither (up).

ver'wend|en v/t. ([irr. wenden,] no -ge-, h) employ, use; apply (für for); spend (time, etc.) (auf acc. on); sich bei j-m ~ für intercede with s.o. for; 2ung f (-/~-en) use, employment; application; keine ~ haben für have no use for.

ver'werf|en v/t. (irr. werfen, no -ge-, h) reject; ♦♦ quash (verdict); ~lich adj. abominable.

ver'werten v/t. (no -ge-, h) turn to account, utilize.

verwes|en [fer've:zən] v/i. (no -ge-, sein) rot, decay; 2ung f (-/~-en) decay.

ver'wick|eln v/t. (no -ge-, h) entangle (in acc. in); sich ~ entangle o.s. (in) (a. fig.); ~elt fig. adj. complicated; 2(e)lung f (-/-en) entanglement; fig. a. complication.

ver'wilder|n v/i. (no -ge-, sein) run wild; ~t adj. garden, etc.: uncultivated, weed-grown; fig. wild, unruly. [-ge-, h) get over s.th.

ver'winden v/t. (irr. winden, no }

ver'wirklich|en v/t. (no -ge-, h) realize; sich ~ be realized, esp. Am. materialize; come true; 2ung f (-/%-en) realization.

ver'wirr|en v/t. (no -ge-, h) entangle; j-n ~ confuse s.o.; embarrass s.o.; ~t fig. adj. confused; embarrassed; 2ung fig. f (-/-en) confusion.

ver'wischen v/t. (no -ge-, h) wipe or blot out; efface (a. fig.); blur, obscure; cover up (one's tracks).

ver'witter|n geol. v/t. (no -ge-, sein) weather; ~t adj. geol. weathered; weather-beaten (a. fig.).

ver'witwet adj. widowed.

verwöhn|en [fɛr'vø:nən] v/t. (no -ge-, h) spoil; ~t adj. fastidious, particular.

verworren adj. [fɛr'vɔrən] ideas, etc.: confused; situation, plot: intricate.

verwund|bar adj. [fɛr'vuntba:r] vulnerable (a. fig.); ~en [~dən] v/t. (no -ge-, h) wound.

ver'wunder|lich adj. astonishing; 2ung f (-/%-en) astonishment.

Ver'wund|ete ⚔ m (-n/-n) wounded (soldier), casualty; ~ung f (-/-en) wound, injury.

ver'wünsch|en v/t. (no -ge-, h) curse; 2ung f (-/-en) curse.

ver'wüst|en v/t. (no -ge-, h) lay waste, devastate, ravage (a. fig.); 2ung f (-/-en) devastation, ravage.

verzag|en [fɛr'tsa:gən] v/i. (no -ge-, h) despond (an dat. of); ~t adj. [~kt] despondent; 2theit [~kt-] f (-/no pl.) despondency, -cy.

ver'zähl|en v/refl. (no -ge-, h) miscount; ~zärteln [~'tsɛːrtəln] v/t. (no -ge-, h) coddle, pamper; ~zaubern v/t. (no -ge-, h) bewitch, enchant, charm; ~zehren v/t. (no -ge-, h) consume (a. fig.).

ver'zeichn|en v/t. (no -ge-, h) note down; record; list; fig. distort; ~ können, zu ~ haben score (success, etc.); ~et paint. adj. out of drawing; 2is n (-ses/-se) list, catalog(ue); register; inventory; index (of book); table, schedule.

verzeih|en [fɛr'tsaɪən] (irr., no -ge-, h) 1. v/i. pardon, forgive; ~ Sie! I beg your pardon!; excuse me!; sorry!; 2. v/t. pardon, forgive (j-m et. s.o. s.th.); 2ung f (-/no pl.) pardon; ~! I beg your pardon!, sorry!

ver'zerr|en v/t. (no -ge-, h) distort; sich ~ become distorted; 2ung f distortion.

ver'zetteln v/t. (no -ge-, h) enter on cards; sich ~ fritter away one's energies.

Verzicht [fɛr'tsiçt] m (-[e]s/-e) renunciation (auf acc. of); 2en v/i. (no -ge-, h) renounce (auf et. s.th.); do without (s.th.).

verzieh [fɛr'tsi:] pret. of verzeihen.

ver'ziehen¹ (irr. ziehen, no -ge-) 1. v/i. (sein) (re)move (nach to); 2. v/t. (h) spoil (child); distort; das Gesicht ~ make a wry face, screw up one's face, grimace; ohne e-e Miene zu ~ without betraying the least emotion; sich ~ wood: warp; crowd, clouds: disperse; storm, clouds: blow over; F disappear.

ver'ziehen² p.p. of verzeihen.

ver'zier|en v/t. (no -ge-, h) adorn, decorate; 2ung f (-/-en) decoration, ornament.

verzins|en [fɛr'tsinzən] v/t. (no -ge-, h) pay interest on; sich ~ yield interest; 2ung f (-/%-en) interest.

ver'zöger|n v/t. (no -ge-, h) delay, retard; sich ~ be delayed; 2ung f (-/-en) delay, retardation.

ver'zollen v/t. (no -ge-, h) pay duty on; haben Sie et. zu ~? have you anything to declare?

verzück|t adj. [fɛr'tsykt] ecstatic, enraptured; 2ung f (-/%-en) ecstasy, rapture; in ~ geraten go into ecstasies (wegen over).

Ver'zug m (-[e]s/no pl.) delay; ✝ default; in ~ geraten ✝ come in default; im ~ sein (be in) default.

ver'zweif|eln v/i. (no -ge-, h, sein) despair (an dat. of); es ist zum Verzweifeln it is enough to drive one mad; ~elt adj. hopeless; desperate; 2lung f (-/no pl.) despair; j-n zur ~ bringen drive s.o. to despair.

verzweig|en [fɛr'tsvaɪgən] v/refl. (no -ge-, h) ramify; trees: branch (out); road: branch; business firm, etc.: branch out; 2ung f (-/-en) ramification; branching.

verzwickt adj. [fɛr'tsvikt] intricate, complicated.

Veteran [vete'ra:n] m (-en/-en) ⚔ veteran (a. fig.), ex-serviceman.

Veterinär [veteri'nɛːr] m (-s/-e) veterinary (surgeon), F vet.

Veto ['ve:to] n (-s/-s) veto; ein ~

U V

einlegen gegen put a veto on, veto *s.th.*

Vetter ['fɛtər] *m* (-s/-n) cousin; '**~nwirtschaft** *f* (-/*no pl.*) nepotism.

vibrieren [vi'briːrən] *v/i.* (*no -ge-, h*) vibrate.

Vieh [fiː] *n* (-[e]s/*no pl.*) livestock; cattle; animal, brute, beast; F *fig.* brute, beast; '**~bestand** *m* livestock; '**~händler** *m* cattle-dealer; '**~hof** *m* stockyard; '**~isch** *adj.* bestial, beastly, brutal; '**~wagen** 🚃 *m* stock-car; '**~weide** *f* pasture; '**~zucht** *f* stock-farming, cattle-breeding; '**~züchter** *m* stockbreeder, stock-farmer, cattle-breeder, *Am. a.* rancher.

viel [fiːl] **1.** *adj.* much, *~e pl.* many; a lot (of), lots of; plenty of (*cake, money, room, time, etc.*); *das ~e Geld* all that money; *seine ~en Geschäfte pl.* his numerous affairs *pl.*; *sehr ~e pl.* a great many *pl.*; *ziemlich ~* a good deal of; *ziemlich ~e pl.* a good many *pl.*; *~ zuviel* far too much; *sehr ~* a great *or* good deal; **2.** *adv.* much; *~ besser* much *or* a good deal *or* a lot better; *et. ~ lieber tun* prefer to do *s.th.*

viel|beschäftigt *adj.* ['fiːlbəʃɛftiçt] very busy; '**~deutig** *adj.* ambiguous; **~erlei** *adj.* ['~ər'lai] of many kinds, many kinds of; multifarious; **~fach** ['~fax] **1.** *adj.* multiple; **2.** *adv.* in many cases, frequently; '**~fältig** *adj.* ['~fɛltiç] multiple, manifold, multifarious; '**~leicht** *adv.* perhaps, maybe; **~mals** *adv.* ['~maːls]: *ich danke Ihnen ~* many thanks, thank you very much; *sie läßt (dich) ~ grüßen* she sends you her kind regards; *ich bitte ~ um Entschuldigung* I am very sorry, I do beg your pardon; **~mehr** *cj.* rather; '**~sagend** *adj.* significant, suggestive; '**~seitig** *adj.* ['~zaitiç] many-sided, versatile; '**~versprechend** *adj.* (very) promising.

vier *adj.* [fiːr] four; *zu ~t* four of us *or* them; *auf allen ~en* on all fours; *unter ~ Augen* confidentially, privately; *um halb ~* at half past three; '**~beinig** *adj.* four-legged; '**~eck** *n* square, quadrangle; '**~eckig** *adj.* square, quadrangular; **~erlei** *adj.* ['~ər'lai] of four different kinds, four kinds of; **~fach** *adj.* ['~fax] fourfold; *~e Ausfertigung* four

copies; **2füßer** *zo.* ['~fyːsər] *m* (-s/-) quadruped; **~füßig** *adj.* ['~fyːsiç] four-footed; *zo.* quadruped; **2füßler** *zo.* ['~fyːslər] *m* (-s/-) quadruped; **~händig** ♪ *adv.* ['~hɛndiç] *~ spielen* play a duet; **~jährig** *adj.* ['~jɛːriç] four-year-old, of four **2linge** ['~liŋə] *m/pl.* quadruplets *pl.*, F quads *pl.*; '**~mal** *adv.* four times; '**~schrötig** *adj.* ['~ʃrøːtiç] square-built, thickset; **~seitig** *adj.* ['~zaitiç] four-sided; A quadrilateral; **2sitzer** *esp. mot. m* (-s/-) four-seater; **~stöckig** *adj.* ['~ʃtœkiç] four-storeyed, four-storied; **2takt-motor** *mot. m* four-stroke engine. '**~te** *adj.* fourth; '**~teilen** *v/t.* (*ge-, h*) quarter.

Viertel ['firtəl] *n* (-s/-) fourth (part); quarter; ~ *fünf, (ein) ~ nach vier* a quarter past four; *drei ~ vier* a quarter to four; '**~jahr** *n* three months *pl.*, quarter (of a year); '**2jährlich**, **2jährlich 1.** *adj.* quarterly; **2.** *adv.* every three months, quarterly; '**~note** ♪ *f* crotchet, *Am. a.* quarter note; '**~pfund** *n*, '**~pfund** *n* quarter of a pound; '**~stunde** *f* quarter of an hour, *Am.* quarter hour.

vier|tens *adv.* ['fiːrtəns] fourthly; **2vierteltakt** ♪ *m* common time. **vierzehn** *adj.* ['firtseːn] fourteen; ~ *Tage pl.* a fortnight, *Am.* two weeks *pl.*; '**~te** *adj.* fourteenth.

vierzig *adj.* ['firtsiç] forty, '**~ste** *adj.* fortieth. [vicar.]

Vikar *eccl.* [vi'kaːr] *m* (-s/-e) curate.*)*

Villa ['vila] *f* (-/*Villen*) villa.

violett *adj.* [vio'lɛt] violet.

Violine ♪ [vio'liːnə] *f* (-/-n) violin.

Viper *zo.* ['viːpər] *f* (-/-n) viper.

virtuos *adj.* [vir'tuoːs] masterly; **2e** [~zə] *m* (-n/-n), **2in** [~zin] *f* (-/-nen) virtuoso; **2ität** [~ozi'tɛːt] *f* (-/*no pl.*) virtuosity.

Virus 🔬 ['viːrus] *n, m* (-/*Viren*) virus.

Vision [vi'zjoːn] *f* (-/-en) vision.

Visitation [vizita'tsjoːn] *f* (-/-en) search; inspection.

Visite 🔬 [vi'ziːtə] *f* (-/-n) visit; **~nkarte** *f* visiting-card, *Am.* calling card.

Visum ['viːzum] *n* (-s/*Visa, Visen*) visa, visé.

Vitalität [vitali'tɛːt] *f* (-/*no pl.*) vitality. [min.]

Vitamin [vita'miːn] *n* (-s/-e) vita-*)*

Vize|kanzler ['fi:tsə-] *m* vice-chancellor; **'~könig** *m* viceroy; **'~konsul** *m* vice-consul; **'~präsident** *m* vice-president.

Vogel ['fo:gəl] *m* (-s/=) bird; F e-n ~ haben have a bee in one's bonnet, *sl.* have bats in the belfry; den ~ abschießen carry off the prize, *Am. sl.* take the cake; **'~bauer** *n, m* (-s/-) bird-cage; **'~flinte** *f* fowling-piece; **'2frei** *adj.* outlawed; **'~futter** *n* food for birds, bird-seed; **'~kunde** *f* (-/no *pl.*) ornithology; **'~liebhaber** *m* bird-fancier; **'~nest** *n* bird's nest, bird-nest; **'~perspektive** *f* (-/no *pl.*), **'~schau** *f* (-/no *pl.*) bird's-eye view; **'~scheuche** *f* (-/-n) scarecrow (*a. fig.*); **~'Strauß-Politik** *f* ostrich policy; ~ betreiben hide one's head in the sand (like an ostrich); **'~warte** *f* ornithological station; **'~zug** *m* passage *or* migration of birds.

Vokab|el [vo'ka:bəl] *f* (-/-n) word; **~ular** [~abu'la:r] *n* (-s/-e) vocabulary.

Vokal *ling.* [vo'ka:l] *m* (-s/-e) vowel.

Volk [fɔlk] *n* **1.** (-[e]s/=er) people; nation; swarm (*of bees*) covey (*of partridges*); **2.** (-[e]s/no *pl.*) populace, *the* common people; *contp. the* common *or* vulgar herd; der Mann aus dem ~e the man in the street *or Am.* on the street.

Völker|bund ['fœlkər-] *m* (-[e]s/no *pl.*) League of Nations; **'~kunde** *f* (-/no *pl.*) ethnology; **'~recht** *n* (-[e]s/no *pl.*) international law, law of nations; **'~wanderung** *f* age of national migrations.

Volks|abstimmung *pol. f* plebiscite; **'~ausgabe** *f* popular edition (*of book*); **'~bücherei** *f* free *or* public library; **'~charakter** *m* national character; **'~dichter** *m* popular *or* national poet; **'~entscheid** *pol.* ['~ɛntʃaɪt] *m* (-[e]s/-e) referendum; plebiscite; **'~fest** *n* fun fair, amusement park *or* grounds *pl.*; public merry-making; national festival; **'~gunst** *f* popularity; **'~herrschaft** *f* democracy; **'~hochschule** *f* adult education (courses *pl.*); **'~lied** *n* folk-song; **'~menge** *f* crowd (*of people*), multitude; **'~partei** *f* people's party; **'~republik** *f* people's republic; **'~schule** *f* elementary *or* primary school, *Am.*

a. grade school; **'~schullehrer** *m* elementary *or* primary teacher, *Am.* grade teacher; **'~sprache** *f* vernacular; **'~stamm** *m* tribe, race; **'~stück** *thea. n* folk-play; **'~tanz** *m* folk-dance; **'~tracht** *f* national costume; **2tümlich** *adj.* ['~ty:mlɪç] national; popular; **'~versammlung** *f* public meeting; **'~vertreter** *parl. m* deputy, representative; member of parliament; *Brt.* Member of Parliament, *Am.* Representative; **'~vertretung** *parl. f* representation of the people; parliament; **'~wirt** *m* (political) economist; **'~wirtschaft** *f* economics, political economy; **~wirtschaftler** ['~tlər] *m* (-s/-) s. Volkswirt; **'~zählung** *f* census.

voll [fɔl] **1.** *adj.* full; filled; whole, complete, entire; *figure, face:* full, round; *figure:* buxom; ~er Knospen full of buds; aus ~em Halse at the top of one's voice; aus ~em Herzen from the bottom of one's heart; in ~er Blüte in full blossom; in ~er Fahrt at full speed; mit ~en Händen lavishly, liberally; mit ~em Recht with perfect right; um das Unglück ~zumachen to make things worse; **2.** *adv.* fully, in full; ~ und ganz fully, entirely; j-n nicht für ~ ansehen *or* nehmen have a poor opinion of s.o., think little of s.o.

'voll|auf *adv.,* **~'auf** *adv.* abundantly, amply, F plenty; **'~automatisch** *adj.* fully automatic; **'2bad** *n* bath; **'2bart** *m* beard; **'2beschäftigung** *f* full employment; **'2besitz** *m* full possession; **'2blut(pferd)** *n* thoroughbred (horse); **~'bringen** *v/t.* (*irr.* bringen, *no* -ge-, h) accomplish, achieve; perform; **'2dampf** *m* full steam; F: *mit* ~ at *or* in full blast; **~'enden** *v/t.* (*no* -ge-, h) finish, complete; **~'endet** *adj.* perfect; **~ends** *adv.* ['~ɛnts] entirely, wholly, altogether; **2'endung** *f* (-/~ -en) finishing, completion; *fig.* perfection.

Völlerei [fœlə'raɪ] *f* (-/~ -en) gluttony.

voll|'führen *v/t.* (*no* -ge-, h) execute, carry out; **'~füllen** *v/t.* (*sep.,* -ge-, h) fill (up); **'2gas** *mot. n*: ~ geben give the throttle; *mit* ~ with the throttle full open; at full speed; **~gepfropft** *adj.* ['~gəpfrɔpft]

crammed, packed; **ˡ˳gießen** v/t.
(irr. gießen, sep., -ge-, h) fill (up);
ˡ˳gummi n, m solid rubber.

völlig adj. [ˈfœliç] entire, complete;
silence, calm, etc.: dead.

vollˌjährig adj. [ˈfɔljɛːriç]: ~ sein
be of age; ~ werden come of age;
ˡ˳jährigkeit f (-/no pl.) majority;
˳kommen adj. perfect; **ˡ˳kommenheit** f (-/˳-en) perfection;
ˡ˳kornbrot n whole-meal bread;
˳machen v/t. (sep., -ge-, h) fill
(up); F soil, dirty; um das Unglück
vollzumachen to make things worse;
ˡ˳macht f (-/-en) full power,
authority; ⚖ power of attorney; ~
haben be authorized; **ˡ˳matrose** ⚓
m able-bodied seaman; **ˡ˳milch** f
whole milk; **ˡ˳mond** m full moon;
ˡ˳packen v/t. (sep., -ge-, h) stuff,
cram; **ˡ˳pension** f(-/-en) full board;
˳schenken v/t. (sep., -ge-, h) fill
(up); **ˡ˳schlank** adj. stout, corpulent; **ˡ˳ständig** adj. complete;
ˡ˳stopfen v/t. (sep., -ge-, h) stuff,
cram; sich ~ stuff o.s.; sich die
Taschen ~ stuff one's pockets;
˳strecken v/t. (no -ge-, h) execute;
ˡ˳streckung f (-/-en) execution;
ˡ˳tönend adj. sonorous, rich;
ˡ˳treffer m direct hit; **ˡ˳versammlung** f plenary meeting or assembly;
General Assembly (of the United
Nations); **˳wertig** adj. equivalent,
equal in value; full; **ˡ˳zählig** adj.
complete; **˳ziehen** v/t. (irr. ziehen,
no -ge-, h) execute; consummate
(marriage); sich ~ take place;
ˡ˳ziehung f (-/˳-en), **ˡ˳zug** m
(-[e]s/no pl.) execution.

Volontär [volɔnˈtɛːr] m(-s/-e) unpaid
assistant.

Volt ⚡ [volt] n (-, -[e]s/-) volt.

Volumen [voˈluːmən] n (-s/-, Volumina) volume.

vom prp. [fɔm] = von dem

von prp. (dat.) [fɔn] space, time:
from; instead of gen.: of; passive:
by; ~ Hamburg from Hamburg;
~ nun an from now on; ~ morgen an
from tomorrow (on), beginning
tomorrow; ein Freund ~ mir a
friend of mine; die Einrichtung ~
Schulen the erection of schools; ~
dem or vom Apfel essen eat (some)
of the apple; der Herzog ~ Edinburgh the Duke of Edinburgh; ein
Gedicht ~ Schiller a poem by

Schiller; ~ selbst by itself; ~ selbst
~ sich aus by oneself; ~ drei Meter
Länge three metres long; ein Betrag
~ 300 Mark a sum of 300 marks
e-e Stadt ~ 10 000 Einwohnern ε
town of 10,000 inhabitants; reden ~
talk of or about s.th.; speak or
(scientific subject); ~ mir aus as fa.
as I am concerned; I don't mind
for all I care; das ist nett ~ ihm tha
is nice of him; ich habe ~ ihm ge
hört I have heard of him; **˳statter**
adv. [~ˈʃtatən]: gut ~ gehen go well

vor prp. (dat.; acc.) [foːr] space: in
front of, before; time: before; ~
langer Zeit a long time ago; ~ eini
gen Tagen a few days ago; (heute) ~
acht Tagen a week ago (today); an
Tage ~ (on) the day before, on the
eve of; 5 Minuten ~ 12 five minute
to twelve, Am. five minutes o
twelve; fig. at the eleventh hour
~ der Tür stehen be imminent
be close at hand; ~ e-m Hintergrun
against a background; ~ Zeugen it
the presence of witnesses; ~ alle.
Dingen above all; (dicht) ~ den
Untergang stehen be on the brin.
or verge of ruin; ~ Hunger sterber
die of hunger; ~ Kälte zitterr
tremble with cold; schützen (ver
stecken) ~ protect (hide) from o
against; ~ sich gehen take place, pas
off; ~ sich hin lächeln smile to o.s.
sich fürchten ~ be afraid of, fear

Vorˌabend [ˈfoːrˀ-] m eve; **ˡ˳ahnun**
f presentiment, foreboding.

voran adv. [foˈran] at the head (dat
of), in front (of), before; Kopf ~
head first; **˳gehen** v/i. (irr. gehen
sep., -ge-, sein) lead the way
precede; **˳kommen** v/i. (irr. kom
men, sep., -ge-, sein) make prog
ress; fig. get on (in life).

Voranˌschlag [ˈfoːrˀan-] m (rough
estimate; **ˡ˳zeige** f advance notice
film: trailer.

vorarbeiteˌn [ˈfoːrˀ-] v/t. and v/i
(sep., -ge-, h) work in advance
ˡ˳r m foreman.

voraus adv. [foˈraus] in front (dat
of), ahead (of); im ~ in advance
beforehand; **˳bestellen** v/t. (sep.
no -ge-, h) s. vorbestellen; **˳bezahlen** v/t. (sep., no -ge-, h) pay in
advance, prepay; **˳gehen** v/i. (irr
gehen, sep., -ge-, sein) go on before
s. vorangehen; **ˡ˳sage** f prediction

prophecy; forecast (*of weather*); **~sagen** v/t. (*sep.*, *-ge-*, *h*) foretell, predict; prophesy; forecast (*weather*, *etc.*); **~schicken** v/t. (*sep.*, *-ge-*, *h*) send on in advance; *fig.* mention beforehand, premise; **~sehen** v/t. (*irr.* sehen, *sep.*, *-ge-*, *h*) foresee; **~setzen** v/t. (*sep.*, *-ge-*, *h*) (pre)suppose, presume, assume; **vorausgesetzt, daß** provided that; **2setzung** f (*-/-en*) (pre)supposition, assumption; prerequisite; **2sicht** f foresight; **aller ~ nach** in all probability; **~sichtlich** adj. presumable, probable; **2zahlung** f advance payment *or* instal(l)ment.

'Vor|bedacht 1. m (*-[e]s/no pl.*): **mit ~** deliberately, on purpose; **2.** 2 adj. premeditated; **'~bedeutung** f foreboding, omen, portent; **'~bedingung** f prerequisite.

Vorbehalt ['foːrbəhalt] m (*-[e]s/-e*) reservation, reserve; **2en 1.** v/t. (*irr.* halten, *sep.*, *no -ge-*, *h*): **sich ~** reserve (*right*, *etc.*); **2.** adj.: **Änderungen ~** subject to change (without notice); **2los** adj. unreserved, unconditional.

vorbei adv. [foːrˈbaɪ] *space*: along, by, past (*all*: an dat. s.o., s.th.); *time*: over, gone; **3 Uhr ~** past three (o'clock); **~fahren** v/i. (*irr.* fahren, *sep.*, *-ge-*, *sein*) drive past; **~gehen** v/i. (*irr.* gehen, *sep.*, *-ge-*, *sein*) pass, go by; *pain*: pass (off); *storm*: blow over; **~ an** (dat.) pass; **im Vorbeigehen** in passing; **~kommen** v/i. (*irr.* kommen, *sep.*, *-ge-*, *sein*) pass by; **F drop in; F ~ an** (dat.) get past (*obstacle*, *etc.*); **~lassen** v/t. (*irr.* lassen, *sep.*, *-ge-*, *h*) let pass.

'Vorbemerkung f preliminary remark *or* note.

'vorbereit|en v/t. (*sep.*, *no -ge-*, *h*) prepare (*für*, *auf* acc. for); **'2ung** f preparation (*für*, *auf* acc. for).

'Vorbesprechung f preliminary discussion *or* talk.

'vor|bestellen v/t. (*sep.*, *no -ge-*, *h*) order in advance; book (*room*, *etc.*); **'~bestraft** adj. previously convicted.

'vorbeug|en (*sep.*, *-ge-*, *h*) **1.** v/i. prevent (*e-r Sache* s.th.); **2.** v/t. *and* v/refl. bend forward; **'~end** adj. preventive; *s* a. prophylactic; **'2ung** f prevention.

'Vorbild n model; pattern; example; prototype; **'2lich** adj. exemplary; **~ung** ['~duŋ] f preparatory training.

'vor|bringen v/t. (*irr.* bringen, *sep.*, *-ge-*, *h*) bring forward, produce; advance (*opinion*); ⅌⅛ prefer (*charge*); utter, say, state; **'2datieren** v/t. (*sep.*, *no -ge-*, *h*) post-date.

vorder adj. ['fordər] front, fore.

'Vorder|achse f front axle; **'~ansicht** f front view; **'~bein** n foreleg; **'~fuß** m forefoot; **'~grund** m foreground (*a. fig.*); **'~haus** n front building; **'~mann** m man in front (*of s.o.*); **'~rad** n front wheel; **~radantrieb** mot. ['fordərraːt?-] m front-wheel drive; **'~seite** f front (side); obverse (*of coin*); **'~sitz** m front seat; **'2st** adj. foremost; **'~teil** n, m front (part); **'~tür** f front door; **'~zahn** m front tooth; **'~zimmer** n front room.

'vordrängen v/refl. (*sep.*, *-ge-*, *h*) press *or* push forward.

'vordring|en v/i. (*irr.* dringen, *sep.*, *-ge-*, *sein*) advance; **'~lich** adj. urgent.   [*blank.*]

'Vordruck m (*-[e]s/-e*) form, *Am. a.* |

voreilig adj. ['foːr?-] hasty, rash, precipitate; **~e Schlüsse ziehen** jump to conclusions.

voreingenommen adj. ['foːr?-] prejudiced, bias(s)ed; **'2heit** f (*-/no pl.*) prejudice, bias.

vor|enthalten ['foːr?-] v/t. (*irr.* halten, *sep.*, *no -ge-*, *h*) keep back, withhold (*j-m et.* s.th. from s.o.); **2entscheidung** ['foːr?-] f preliminary decision; **~erst** adv. ['foːr?-] for the present, for the time being.

Vorfahr ['foːrfaːr] m (*-en/-en*) ancestor.

'vorfahr|en v/i. (*irr.* fahren, *sep.*, *-ge-*, *sein*) drive up; pass; **den Wagen ~ lassen** order the car; **'2t(recht** n) f right of way, priority.

'Vorfall m incident, occurrence, event; **'2en** v/i. (*irr.* fallen, *sep.*, *-ge-*, *sein*) happen, occur.

'vorfinden v/t. (*irr.* finden, *sep.*, *-ge-*, *h*) find.

'Vorfreude f anticipated joy.

'vorführ|en v/t. (*sep.*, *-ge-*, *h*) bring forward, produce; bring (*dat.* before); show, display, exhibit; demonstrate (*use of s.th.*); show, present (*film*); **2er** m projectionist (*in cinema theatre*); '**≈ung** *f* presentation, showing; ⊕ demonstration; ⚙ production (*of prisoner*); *thea.*, *film*: performance.

'**Vor|gabe** *f* sports: handicap; *athletics*: stagger; *golf*, *etc.*: odds *pl.*; '**≈gang** *m* incident, occurrence, event; facts *pl.*; file, record(s *pl.*); *biol.*, ⊕ process; '**≈gänger** ['≈gɛŋər] *m* (-s/-), '**≈gängerin** *f* (-/-nen) predecessor; '**≈garten** *m* front garden.

'**vorgeben** *v/t.* (*irr. geben*, *sep.*, -ge-, h) sports: give (*j-m s.o.*); *fig.* pretend, allege.

'**Vor|gebirge** *n* promontory, cape, headland; foot-hills *pl.*; '**≈gefühl** *n* presentiment, foreboding.

'**vorgehen 1.** *v/i.* (*irr. gehen*, *sep.*, -ge-, sein) ⚙ advance; F lead the way; go on before; *watch*, *clock*: be fast, gain (*fünf Minuten vor*) (five minutes); take precedence (*dat.* of, over), be more important (than); take action, act; proceed (*a.* ⚙; *gegen* against); go on, happen, take place; **2.** ≈ *n* (-s/*no pl.*) action, proceeding.

'**Vor|geschmack** *m* (-[e]s/*no pl.*) foretaste; '**≈gesetzte** ['≈gəzɛtstə] *m* (-n/-n) superior; *esp. Am.* F boss; '**≈gestern** *adv.* the day before yesterday; '**≈greifen** *v/i.* (*irr. greifen*, *sep.*, -ge-, h) anticipate (*j-m or e-r Sache s.o. or s.th.*).

'**vorhaben 1.** *v/t.* (*irr. haben*, *sep.*, -ge-, h) intend, mean; be going to do *s.th.*; nichts ~ be at a loose end; *haben Sie heute abend et. vor?* have you anything on tonight?; *was hat er jetzt wieder vor?* what is he up to now?; *was hast du mit ihm vor?* what are you going to do with him?; **2.** ≈ *n* (-s/-) intention, purpose, ⚙ intent; plan; project.

'**Vorhalle** *f* vestibule, (entrance-) hall; lobby; porch.

'**vorhalt|en** (*irr. halten*, *sep.*, -ge-, h) **1.** *v/t.*: j-m et. ~ hold s.th. before s.o.; *fig.* reproach s.o. with s.th.; **2.** *v/i.* last; '**≈ung** *f* remonstrance; *j-m* ~en machen remonstrate with s.o. (*wegen* on).

'**vorhanden** *adj.* [for'handən] at hand, present; available (*a.* ⚙); ~ *sein* exist, be in stock; ≈-**sein** *n* presence, existence.

'**Vor|hang** *m* curtain; '**≈hänge-schloß** *n* padlock.

'**vorher** *adv.* before, previously; in advance, beforehand.

'**vor'her|bestellen** *v/t.* (*sep.*, *no -ge-*, h) s. vorbestellen; '**≈bestimmen** *v/t.* (*sep.*, *no -ge-*, h) determine beforehand, predetermine; '**≈gehen** *v/i.* (*irr. gehen*, *sep.*, -ge-, sein) precede; '**≈ig** *adj.* preceding, previous.

'**Vorherr|schaft** *f* predominance; '**≈schen** *v/i.* (*sep.*, -ge-, h) predominate, prevail; '**≈schend** *adj.* predominant, prevailing.

'**Vor'her|sage** *f* s. Voraussage; '**≈sa-gen** *v/t.* (*sep.*, -ge-, h) s. voraussagen; '**≈sehen** *v/t.* (*irr. sehen*, *sep.*, -ge-, h) foresee; '**≈wissen** *v/t.* (*irr. wissen*, *sep.*, -ge-, h) know beforehand, foreknow.

'**vor|hin** *adv.*, ~'**hin** *adv.* a short while ago, just now.

'**Vor|hof** *m* outer court, forecourt; *anat.* auricle (*of heart*); '**≈hut** ⚙ *f* vanguard.

'**vor|ig** *adj.* last; '**≈jährig** *adj.* ['≈jɛ:rɪç] of last year, last year's.

'**Vor|kämpfer** *m* champion, pioneer; '**≈kehrung** *f* (-/-en) precaution; ~en treffen take precautions; '**≈kenntnisse** *f/pl.* preliminary or basic knowledge (*in dat.* of); *mit guten* ~*n in* (*dat.*) well grounded in.

'**vorkommen 1.** *v/i.* (*irr. kommen*, *sep.*, -ge-, sein) be found; occur, happen; *es kommt mir vor* it seems to me; **2.** ≈ *n* (-s/-) occurrence.

'**Vor|kommnis** *n* (-ses/-se) occurrence; event; '**≈kriegszeit** *f* prewar times *pl.*

'**vorlad|en** ⚙ *v/t.* (*irr. laden*, *sep.*, -ge-, h) summon; '**≈ung** ⚙ *f* summons.

'**Vorlage** *f* copy; pattern; *parl.* bill; presentation; ⊕ production (*of document*); *football*: pass.

'**vorlassen** *v/t.* (*irr. lassen*, *sep.*, -ge-, h) let *s.o.* pass, allow *s.o.* to pass; admit.

'**Vorläuf|er** *m*, '**≈erin** *f* (-/-nen) forerunner; '**≈ig 1.** *adj.* provisional, temporary; **2.** *adv.* provisionally, temporarily; for the present, for the time being.

'**vorlaut** *adj.* forward, pert.

'**Vorleben** *n* past (life), antecedents *pl.*

'**vorlege|n** *v/t.* (*sep.*, -ge-, h) put (*lock*) on; produce (*document*); submit (*plans, etc.* for discussion, etc.); propose (*plan, etc.*); present (*bill, etc.*); j-m et. ~ lay *or* place *or* put s.th. before s.o.; show s.o. s.th.; *at table*: help s.o. to s.th.; j-m e-e Frage ~ put a question to s.o.; sich ~ lean forward; '2r m (-s/-) rug.

'**vorles**|en v/t. (*irr.* lesen, *sep.*, -ge-, h) read aloud; j-m et. ~ read (out) s.th. to s.o.; '2ung f lecture (*über acc.* on; *vor dat.* to); e-e ~ halten (give a) lecture.

'**vorletzt** *adj.* last but one; ~e Nacht the night before last.

'**Vorlieb**|e f (-/*no pl.*) predilection, preference; 2nehmen [~'li:p-] v/i. (*irr.* nehmen, *sep.*, -ge-, h) be satisfied (*mit* with); ~ mit dem, was da ist *at meals*: take pot luck.

'**vorliegen** v/i. (*irr.* liegen, *sep.*, -ge-, h) lie before *s.o.*; be there, exist; da muß ein Irrtum ~ there must be a mistake; was liegt gegen ihn vor? what is the charge against him?; '~d *adj.* present, in question.

'**vor**|**lügen** v/t. (*irr.* lügen, *sep.*, -ge-, h): j-m et. ~ tell s.o. lies; '~machen v/t. (*sep.*, -ge-, h): j-m et. ~ show s.o. how to do s.th.; *fig.* impose upon s.o.; sich (*selbst*) et. ~ fool o.s.

'**Vormacht** f (-/~e), '~stellung f predominance; supremacy; hegemony.

'**Vormarsch** ✕ m advance.

'**vormerken** v/t. (*sep.*, -ge-, h) note down, make a note of; reserve; sich ~ lassen für put one's name down for.

'**Vormittag** m morning, forenoon; '2s *adv.* in the morning.

'**Vormund** m (-[e]s/-e, ⁻er) guardian; '~schaft f (-/-en) guardianship.

vorn *adv.* [fɔrn] in front; nach ~ forward; von ~ from the front; ich sah sie von ~ I saw her face; von ~ anfangen begin at the beginning; noch einmal von ~ anfangen begin anew, make a new start.

'**Vorname** m Christian name, first name, *Am. a.* given name.

vornehm ['foːrneːm] **1.** *adj.* of (superior) rank, distinguished; aristocratic; noble; fashionable; ~e Gesinnung high character; **2.** *adv.*: ~ tun give o.s. airs; '~en v/t. (*irr.* nehmen, *sep.*, -ge-, h) take *s.th.* in

hand; deal with; make (*changes, etc.*); take up (*book*) F sich j-n ~ take s.o. to task (*wegen* for, about); sich ~ resolve (up)on *s.th.*; resolve (*zu inf.* to *inf.*), make up one's mind (*to inf.*); sich vorgenommen haben a. be determined (*zu inf.* to *inf.*); '2heit f (-/*no pl.*) refinement; elegance; high-mindedness.

'**vorn**|**herein** *adv.*, ~he'rein *adv.*: von ~ from the first *or* start *or* beginning.

Vorort ['foːrʔ-] m (-[e]s/-e) suburb; '~(s)verkehr m suburban traffic; '~(s)zug m local (train).

'**Vor**|**posten** m outpost (*a.* ✕); '~rang m (-[e]s/*no pl.*) precedence (*vor dat.* of, over), priority (over); '~rat m store, stock (*an dat.* of); Vorräte *pl. a.* provisions *pl.*, supplies *pl.*; '2rätig ['~rɛːtiç] *adj.* available; ✝ *a.* on hand, in stock; '2rechnen v/t. (*sep.*, -ge-, h) reckon up (j-m to s.o.); '~recht n privilege; '~rede f preface, introduction; '~redner m previous speaker; '~richtung ⊕ f contrivance, device; 2rücken (*sep.*, -ge-) **1.** v/t. (h) move (*chair, etc.*) forward; **2.** v/i. (sein) advance; '~runde f *sports*: preliminary round; '2sagen v/i. (*sep.*, -ge-, h): j-m ~ prompt s.o.; '~saison f off *or* dead season; '~satz m intention, purpose, design; 2sätzlich *adj.* ['~zɛtsliç] intentional, deliberate; ~er Mord ✝ wil(l)ful murder; '~schein m: zum ~ bringen bring forward, produce; zum ~ kommen appear, turn up; '2schieben v/t. (*irr.* schieben, *sep.*, -ge-, h) push *s.th.* forward; slip (*bolt*); s. vorschützen; '2schießen v/t. (*irr.* schießen, *sep.*, -ge-, h) advance (*money*).

'**Vorschlag** m proposition, proposal; suggestion; offer; 2en ['~gən] v/t. (*irr.* schlagen, *sep.*, -ge-, h) propose; suggest; offer.

'**Vor**|**schlußrunde** f *sports*: semifinal; '2schnell *adj.* hasty, rash; '2schreiben v/t. (*irr.* schreiben, *sep.*, -ge-, h): j-m et. ~ write s.th. out for s.o.; *fig.* prescribe.

'**Vorschrift** f direction, instruction; prescription (*esp.* ✝); order (*a.* ✕); regulation(s *pl.*); '2smäßig *adj.* according to regulations; ~e Kleidung regulation dress; '2swidrig *adj. and adv.* contrary to regula-

'**Vor|schub** *m*: ~ leisten (*dat.*) coun-
tenance (*fraud, etc.*); further, encourage; ⚖ aid and abet; '**~schule**
f preparatory school; '**~schuß** *m*
advance; *for barrister:* retaining fee,
retainer; '**2schützen** *v/t.* (*sep.,
-ge-, h*) pretend, plead (*sickness, etc.
as excuse*); '**2schweben** *v/i.* (*sep.,
-ge-, h*): mir schwebt et. vor I have
s.th. in mind.

'**vorseh|en** *v/t.* (*irr. sehen, sep., -ge-,
h*) plan; design; ⚖ provide; sich ~
take care, be careful; sich et. ~ vor
(*dat.*) guard against; '**2ung** *f* (*-/~
-en*) providence.

'**vorsetzen** *v/t.* (*sep., -ge-, h*) put
forward; place *or* put *or* set before,
offer:

'**Vorsicht** *f* caution; care; ~! caution!, danger!; look out!, be careful!; ~, Glas! Glass, with care!;
~, Stufe! mind the step!; '**2ig** *adj.*
cautious; careful; ~! F steady!

'**vorsichts|halber** *adv.* as a pre-
caution; '**2maßnahme** *f*, '**2maß-
regel** *f*; ~, **2**precaution(ary measure);
~n treffen take precautions.

'**Vorsilbe** *gr. f* prefix.

'**vorsingen** *v/t.* (*irr. singen, sep.,
-ge-, h*): j-m et. ~ sing s.th. to s.o.

'**Vorsitz** *m* (*-es/no pl.*) chair, presi-
dency; den ~ führen *or* haben be
in the chair, preside (*bei* over; at);
den ~ übernehmen take the chair;
~ende ['~əndə] (*-n/-n*) **1.** *m* chairman, president; **2.** *f* chairwoman.

'**Vorsorg|e** *f* (*-/no pl.*) provision,
providence; precaution; ~ treffen
make provision; '**2en** *v/i.* (*sep., -ge-,
h*) provide; **2lich** ['~kliç] **1.** *adj.*
precautionary; **2.** *adv.* as a precaution.

'**Vorspeise** *f* appetizer, hors d'œuvre.

'**vorspieg|eln** *v/t.* (*sep., -ge-, h*)
pretend; j-m et. ~ delude s.o. (with
false hopes, *etc.*); '**2(e)lung** *f* pre-
ten|ce, *Am.* -se.

'**Vorspiel** *n* prelude; '**2en** *v/t.* (*sep.,
-ge-, h*): j-m et. ~ play s.th. to s.o.

'**vor|sprechen** (*irr. sprechen, sep.,
-ge-, h*) **1.** *v/t.* pronounce (*j-m et.*
s.th. to *or* for s.o.); **2.** *v/i.* call (*bei*
on *s.o.*; at *an office*); *thea.* audition; '**~springen** *v/i.* (*irr. springen,
sep., -ge-, sein*) jump forward; project; '**2sprung** *m* △ projection;

sports: lead; *fig.* start, advantage
(*vor dat.* of:) '**2stadt** *f* suburb; '**~-
städtisch** *adj.* suburban; '**2stand**
m board of directors, managing
directors *pl.*

'**vorsteh|en** *v/i.* (*irr. stehen, sep.,
-ge-, h*) project, protrude; *fig.*:
direct; manage (*both:* e-r Sache
s.th.); '**2er** *m* director, manager;
head, chief.

'**vorstell|en** *v/t.* (*sep., -ge-, h*) put
forward; put (*clock*) on; introduce
(*j-n j-m* s.o. to s.o.); mean, stand
for; represent; sich ~ bei have an
interview with; sich et. ~ imagine
or fancy s.th.; '**2ung** *f* introduction,
presentation; interview (*of applicant for post*); *thea.* performance;
fig.: remonstrance; idea, conception; imagination; '**2ungsvermö-
gen** *n* imagination.

'**Vor|stoß** ✕ *m* thrust, advance;
'**~strafe** *f* previous conviction; '**2-
strecken** *v/t.* (*sep., -ge-, h*) thrust
out, stretch forward; advance
(*money*); '**~stufe** *f* first step *or*
stage; '**2täuschen** *v/t.* (*sep., -ge-, h*)
feign, pretend.

Vorteil ['fɔrtail] *m* advantage (*a.
sports*); profit; *tennis:* (ad)vantage;
'**2haft** *adj.* advantageous (*für* to),
profitable (to).

Vortrag ['fo:rtra:k] *m* (*-[e]s/~e*)
performance; execution (*esp.* ♪);
recitation (*of poem*); ♪ recital; lecture; report; † balance carried forward; e-n ~ halten (give a) lecture
(*über acc.* on); '**2en** ['~gən] *v/t.* (*irr.
tragen, sep., -ge-, h*) † carry forward; report on; recite (*poem*);
perform, *esp.* ♪ execute; lecture on;
state, express (*opinion*); '**~ende**
['~gəndə] *m* (*-n/-n*) performer; lecturer; speaker.

vor|trefflich *adj.* [fo:r'trɛfliç] ex-
cellent; '**~treten** *v/i.* (*irr. treten,
sep., -ge-, sein*) step forward; *fig.*
project, protrude, stick out; '**2tritt**
m (*-[e]s/no pl.*) precedence.

vorüber *adv.* [fo:ry:bər] *space:* by,
past; *time:* gone by, over; '**~gehen**
v/i. (*irr. gehen, sep., -ge-, sein*) pass,
go by; '**~gehend** *adj.* passing; temporary; '**2gehende** [~də] *m* (*-n/-n*)
passer-by; '**~ziehen** *v/i.* (*irr. ziehen,
sep., -ge-, sein*) march past, pass
by; *storm:* blow over.

Vor|übung ['fo:r°-] *f* preliminary

practice; **~untersuchung** ♈ ['fo:r⁹-] f preliminary inquiry.

Vorurteil ['fo:r⁹-] n prejudice; **'2s-los** adj. unprejudiced, unbias(s)ed.

'Vor|verkauf thea. m booking in advance; im ~ bookable (bei at); **'2verlegen** v/t. (sep., no -ge-, h) advance; **'~wand** m (-[e]s/=e) pretext, preten|ce, Am. -se.

vorwärts adv. ['fo:rverts] forward, onward, on; ~! go ahead!; **'~kommen** v/i. (irr. kommen, sep., -ge-, sein) (make) progress; fig. make one's way, get on (in life).

vorweg adv. [for'vek] beforehand; **~nehmen** v/t. (irr. nehmen, sep., -ge-, h) anticipate.

'vor|weisen v/t. (irr. weisen, sep., -ge-, h) produce, show; **'~werfen** v/t. (irr. werfen, sep., -ge-, h) throw or cast before; j-m et. ~ reproach s.o. with s.th.; **'~wiegend 1.** adj. predominant, preponderant; **2.** adv. predominantly, chiefly, mainly, mostly; **'~witzig** adj. forward, pert; inquisitive.

'Vorwort n (-[e]s/-e) preface (by author); foreword.

'Vorwurf m reproach; subject (of drama, etc.); j-m e-n ~ or Vorwürfe

machen reproach s.o. (wegen with); **'2svoll** adj. reproachful.

'vor|zählen v/t. (sep., -ge-, h) enumerate, count out (both: j-m to s.o.); **'2zeichen** n omen; **'~zeichnen** v/t. (sep., -ge-, h): j-m et. ~ draw or sketch s.th. for s.o.; show s.o. how to draw s.th.; fig. mark out, destine; **'~zeigen** v/t. (sep., -ge-, h) produce, show.

'Vorzeit f antiquity; in literature often: times of old, days of yore; **'2ig** adj. premature.

'vor|ziehen v/t. (irr. ziehen, sep., -ge-, h) draw forth; draw (curtains); fig. prefer; **'2zimmer** n antechamber, anteroom; waiting-room; **'2zug** fig. m preference; advantage; merit; priority; **~züglich** adj. [~'tsy:kliç] excellent, superior, exquisite.

'Vorzugs|aktie f preference share or stock, Am. preferred stock; **'~preis** m special price; **'2weise** adv. preferably; chiefly.

Votum ['vo:tum] n (-s/Voten, Vota) vote.

vulgär adj. [vul'gɛ:r] vulgar.

Vulkan [vul'ka:n] m (-s/-e) volcano; **2isch** adj. volcanic.

W

Waag|e ['va:gə] f (-/-n) balance, (e-e a pair of) scales pl.; die ~ halten (dat.) counterbalance; **'2erecht** adj., **2recht** adj. ['va:k-] horizontal, level; **'~schale** ['va:k-] f scale.

Wabe ['va:bə] f (-/-n) honeycomb.

wach adj. [vax] awake; hell~ wide awake; ~ werden awake, wake up; **'2e** f (-/-n) watch; guard; guardhouse, guardroom; police-station; sentry, sentinel; ~ haben be on guard; ~ halten keep watch; **'~en** v/i. (ge-, h) (keep) watch (über acc. over); sit up (bei with); **'2hund** m watch-dog.

Wacholder ♃ [va'xɔldər] m (-s/-) juniper.

'wach|rufen v/t. (irr. rufen, sep., -ge-, h) rouse, evoke; **'~rütteln** v/t. (sep., -ge-, h) rouse (up); fig. rouse, shake up.

Wachs [vaks] n (-es/-e) wax.

'wachsam adj. watchful, vigilant; **'2keit** f (-/no pl.) watchfulness, vigilance.

wachsen¹ ['vaksən] v/i. (irr., ge-, sein) grow; fig. increase.

wachsen² [~] v/t. (ge-, h) wax.

wächsern adj. ['veksərn] wax; fig. waxen, waxy.

'Wachs|kerze f, **'~licht** n wax candle; **'~tuch** n waxcloth, oilcloth.

Wachstum ['vakstu:m] n (-s/no pl.) growth; fig. increase.

Wächte mount. ['veçtə] f (-/-n) cornice.

Wachtel orn. ['vaxtəl] f (-/-n) quail.

Wächter ['veçtər] m (-s/-) watcher, guard(ian); watchman.

'Wacht|meister m sergeant; **'~turm** m watch-tower.

wackel|ig adj. ['vakəliç] shaky (a. fig.), tottery; furniture, etc.: rickety;

W

tooth, etc.: loose; '♀**kontakt** ⚡ *m* loose connexion *or* (*Am. only*) connection; '**∼n** *v/i.* (ge-, h) shake; *table, etc.*: wobble; *tooth, etc.*: be loose; *tail, etc.*: wag; ∼ *mit* wag *s.th.*

wacker *adj.* ['vakər] honest, upright; brave, gallant.

wacklig *adj.* ['vakliç] *s.* wackelig.

Wade ['vaːdə] *f* (-/-n) calf; '**∼nbein** *anat. n* fibula.

Waffe ['vafə] *f* (-/-n) weapon (*a. fig.*); ∼*n pl. a.* arms *pl.*

Waffel ['vafəl] *f* (-/-n) waffle; wafer.

Waffen|fabrik *f* armaments factory, *Am. a.* armory; '**∼gattung** *f* arm; '**∼gewalt** *f* (-/*no pl.*): *mit* ∼ by force of arms; '♀**los** *adj.* weaponless, unarmed; '**∼schein** *m* firearm certificate, *Am.* gun license; '**∼stillstand** *m* armistice (*a. fig.*), truce.

Wage|hals ['vaːgəhals] *m* daredevil; '♀**halsig** *adj.* daring, foolhardy; *attr. a.* daredevil; '**∼mut** *m* daring

wagen[1] ['vaːgən] *v/t.* (ge-, h) venture; risk, dare; *sich* ∼ venture (*an acc.* [up]on).

Wagen[2] [∼] *m* (-s/-, ⁼) carriage (*a.* 🚂); *Am.* 🚂 car; 🚂 coach; wag(g)on; cart; car; lorry, truck; van.

wägen ['vɛːgən] *v/t.* (irr.,) ge-, h) weigh (*a. fig.*).

'**Wagen|heber** *m* (-s/-) (lifting) jack; '**∼park** *m* (-[e]s/*no pl.*) fleet of vehicles; '**∼schmiere** *f* grease; '**∼spur** *f* rut.

Waggon 🚂 [va'gõː] *m* (-s/-s) (railway) carriage, *Am.* (railroad) car.

wag|halsig *adj.* ['vaːkhalsiç] *s.* waghalsig; '♀**nis** *n* (-ses/-se) venture, risk.

Wahl [vaːl] *f* (-/-en) choice; alternative; selection; *pol.* election; e-e ∼ *treffen* make a choice; *s-e* ∼ *treffen* take one's choice; *ich hatte keine (andere)* ∼ I had no choice.

wählbar *adj.* ['vɛːlbaːr] eligible; '♀**keit** *f* (-/*no pl.*) eligibility.

wahl|berechtigt *adj.* ['vaːlbəreçtiçt] entitled to vote; '♀**beteiligung** *f* percentage of voting, F turn-out; '♀**bezirk** *m* constituency.

'**wählen** (ge-, h) **1.** *v/t.* choose; *pol.* elect; *teleph.* dial; **2.** *v/i.* choose, take one's choice; *teleph.* dial (the number).

'**Wahlergebnis** *n* election return.

'**Wähler** *m* (-s/-) elector, voter; '♀**isch** *adj.* particular (*in dat.* in, about, as to), nice (about), fastidious, F choosy; '**∼schaft** *f* (-/-en) constituency, electorate.

'**Wahl|fach** *n* optional subject, *Am. a.* elective; '♀**fähig** *adj.* having a vote; eligible; '**∼gang** *m* ballot; '**∼kampf** *m* election campaign; '**∼kreis** *m* constituency; '**∼lokal** *n* polling station; '♀**los** *adj.* indiscriminate; '**∼recht** *n* (-[e]s/*no pl.*) franchise; '**∼rede** *f* electoral speech.

'**Wählscheibe** *teleph. f* dial.

'**Wahl|spruch** *m* device, motto; '**∼stimme** *f* vote; '**∼urne** *f* ballotbox; '**∼versammlung** *f* electoral rally; '**∼zelle** *f* polling-booth; '**∼zettel** *m* ballot, voting-paper.

Wahn [vaːn] *m* (-[e]s/*no pl.*) delusion, illusion; mania; '**∼sinn** *m* (-[e]s/*no pl.*) insanity, madness (*both a. fig.*); '♀**sinnig** *adj.* insane, mad (vor *dat.* with) (*both a. fig.*); **∼sinnige** ['∼gə] *m* (-n/-n) madman, lunatic; '**∼vorstellung** *f* delusion, hallucination; '**∼witz** *m* (-es/*no pl.*) madness, insanity; '♀**witzig** *adj.* mad, insane.

wahr *adj.* [vaːr] true; real; genuine; '**∼en** *v/t.* (ge-, h) safeguard (*interests, etc.*); maintain (*one's opinion*); *den Schein* ∼ keep up *or* save appearances.

'**währen** ['vɛːrən] *v/i.* (ge-, h) last, continue.

'**während 1.** *prp.* (*gen.*) during; pending; **2.** *cj.* while, whilst; while, whereas.

'**wahrhaft** *adv.* really, truly, indeed; '**∼ig** [∼'haftiç] **1.** *adj.* truthful, veracious; **2.** *adv.* really, truly, indeed.

'**Wahrheit** *f* (-/-en) truth; *in* ∼ in truth; *j-m die* ∼ *sagen* give s.o. a piece of one's mind; '♀**sgetreu** *adj.* true, faithful; '**∼sliebe** *f* (-/*no pl.*) truthfulness, veracity; '♀**sliebend** *adj.* truthful, veracious.

'**wahr|lich** *adv.* truly, really; '**∼nehmbar** *adj.* perceivable, perceptible; '**∼nehmen** *v/t.* (irr. nehmen, sep., -ge-, h) perceive, notice, avail o.s. of (*opportunity*); safeguard (*interests*); '♀**nehmung** *f* (-/-en) perception, observation; '**∼sagen** *v/i.* (sep., -ge-, h) tell *or* read fortunes;

sich ~ *lassen* have one's fortune told; '≗**sagerin** *f* (-/-nen) fortune-teller; ≗**scheinlich 1.** *adj.* probable; likely; **2.** *adv.*: ich werde ~ *gehen* I am likely to go; ≗**scheinlichkeit** *f* (-/~-en) probability, likelihood; *aller* ~ *nach* in all probability *or* likelihood.

'**Wahrung** *f* (-/no pl.) maintenance; safeguarding.

Währung ['vɛ:ruŋ] *f* (-/-en) currency; standard; '**_sreform** *f* currency *or* monetary reform.

'**Wahrzeichen** *n* landmark.

Waise ['vaɪzə] *f* (-/-n) orphan; '**_n-haus** *n* orphanage.

Wal *zo.* ['va:l] *m* (-[e]s/-e) whale.

Wald [valt] *m* (-[e]s/ᵘer) wood, forest; '**_brand** *m* forest fire; ≗**ig** *adj.* ['_dɪç] wooded, woody; ≗**reich** *adj.* ['_t-] rich in forests; '**_ung** f ['_duŋ] (-/-en) forest.

Walfänger ['va:lfɛŋər] *m* (-s/-) whaler.

walken ['valkən] *v/t.* (ge-, h) full (*cloth*); mill (*cloth, leather*).

Wall [val] *m* (-[e]s/ᵘe) ✕ rampart (*a. fig.*); dam; mound.   [ing.\

Wallach ['valax] *m* (-[e]s/-e) geld-\

wallen ['valən] *v/i.* (ge-, h, sein) hair, articles of dress, etc.: flow; simmer; boil (*a. fig.*).

wall|fahren ['valfa:rən] *v/i.* (ge-, sein) (go on a) pilgrimage; ≗**fahrer** *m* pilgrim; ≗**fahrt** *f* pilgrimage; '**_fahrten** *v/i.* (ge-, sein) (go on a) pilgrimage.

'**Wallung** *f* (-/-en) ebullition; ⚕ congestion; (*Blut*) in ~ *bringen* make s.o.'s blood boil, enrage.

Walnuß ['val-] *f* walnut; '**_baum** ♀ *m* walnut(-tree).

Walroß *zo.* ['val-] *n* walrus.

walten ['valtən] *v/i.* (ge-, h): *s-s Amtes* ~ attend to one's duties; *Gnade* ~ *lassen* show mercy.

Walze ['valtsə] *f* (-/-n) roller, cylinder; ⊕ *a.* roll; ⊕, ♪ barrel; '≗**n** *v/t.* (ge-, h) roll (*a.* ⊕).

wälzen ['vɛltsən] *v/t.* (ge-, h) roll; roll (*problem*) round in one's mind; shift (*blame*) (*auf acc.* [up]on); *sich* ~ roll; wallow (*in mud, etc.*); welter (*in blood, etc.*).

Walzer ♪ ['valtsər] *m* (-s/-) waltz.

Wand [vant] **1.** *f* (-/ᵘe) wall; partition; **2.** ≗ *pret. of* winden.

Wandel ['vandəl] *m* (-s/no pl.)

change; '≗**bar** *adj.* changeable; variable; '**_gang** *m*, '**_halle** *f* lobby; '≗**n** (ge-) **1.** *v/i.* (sein) walk; **2.** *v/refl.* (h) change.

Wander|er ['vandərər] *m* (-s/-) wanderer; hiker; '**_leben** *n* (-s/no pl.) vagrant life; '≗**n** *v/i.* (ge-, sein) wander; hike; '**_niere** ⚕ *f* floating kidney; '**_prediger** *m* itinerant preacher; '**_preis** *m* challenge trophy; '**_schaft** *f* (-/no pl.) wanderings *pl.*; *auf* (*der*) ~ on the tramp; '**_ung** *f* (-/-en) walking-tour; hike.

'**Wand|gemälde** *n* mural (painting); '**_kalender** *m* wall-calendar; '**_karte** *f* wall-map.

Wandlung ['vandluŋ] *f* (-/-en) change, transformation; *eccl.* transubstantiation; ⚖ redhibition.

'**Wand|schirm** *m* folding-screen; '**_schrank** *m* wall-cupboard; '**_spiegel** *m* wall-mirror; '**_tafel** *f* blackboard; '**_teppich** *m* tapestry; '**_uhr** *f* wall-clock.

wandte ['vantə] *pret. of* wenden 2.

Wange ['vaŋə] *f* (-/-n) cheek.

Wankel|mut ['vaŋkəlmu:t] *m* fickleness, inconstancy; ≗**mütig** *adj.* ['_my:tiç] fickle, inconstant.

wanken ['vaŋkən] *v/i.* (ge-, h, sein) totter, stagger (*a. fig.*); house, etc.: rock; *fig.* waver.

wann *adv.* [van] when; *s. dann*; *seit ~?* how long?, since when?

Wanne ['vanə] *f* (-/-n) tub; bath (-tub), F tub; '**_nbad** *n* bath, F tub.

Wanze *zo.* ['vantsə] *f* (-/-n) bug, *Am. a.* bedbug.

Wappen ['vapən] *n* (-s/-) (coat of) arms *pl.*; '**_kunde** *f* (-/no pl.) heraldry; '**_schild** *m, n* escutcheon; '**_tier** *n* heraldic animal.

wappnen *fig.* ['vapnən] *v/refl.* (ge-, h): *sich* ~ *gegen* be prepared for; *sich mit Geduld* ~ have patience.

war [va:r] *pret. of* sein¹.

warb [varp] *pret. of* werben.

Ware ['va:rə] *f* (-/-n) commodity, article of trade; **_n** *pl. a.* goods *pl.*, merchandise, wares *pl.*

'**Waren|aufzug** *m* hoist; '**_bestand** *m* stock (on hand); '**_haus** *n* department store; '**_lager** *n* stock; warehouse, *Am. a.* stock room; '**_probe** *f* sample; '**_zeichen** *n* trade mark.

warf [varf] *pret. of* werfen.

warm *adj.* [varm] warm (*a. fig.*); *meal:* hot; *schön* ~ nice and warm.

Wärme ['vɛrmə] *f* (-/♀-n) warmth; *phys.* heat; '**~grad** *m* degree of heat; '**♀n** *v/t.* (ge-, h) warm; *sich die Füße* ~ warm one's feet.

'**Wärmflasche** *f* hot-water bottle.

'**warmherzig** *adj.* warm-hearted.

Warm'wasser|heizung *f* hot-water heating; **~versorgung** *f* hot-water supply.

warn|en ['varnən] *v/t.* (ge-, h) warn (*vor dat.* of, against), caution (against); '**♀signal** *n* danger-signal (*a. fig.*); '**♀streik** *m* token strike; '**♀ung** *f* (-/-en) warning, caution; **♀ungstafel** ['varnuŋs-] *f* notice-board.

Warte *fig.* ['vartə] *f* (-/-n) point of view.

warten ['vartən] *v/i.* (ge-, h) wait (*auf acc.* for); be in store (for *s.o.*); *j-n* ~ *lassen* keep s.o. waiting.

Wärter ['vɛrtər] *m* (-s/-) attendant; keeper; (male) nurse.

'**Warte|saal** *m*, '**~zimmer** *n* waiting-room.

Wartung ⊕ ['vartuŋ] *f* (-/♀-en) maintenance.

warum *adv.* [va'rum] why.

Warze ['vartsə] *f* (-/-n) wart; nipple.

was [vas] **1.** *interr. pron.* what; ~ *kostet das Buch?* how much is this book?; F ~ *rennst du denn so (schnell)?* why are you running like this?; ~ *für (ein)* ...! what a(n) ...!; ~ *für ein* ...? what ...?; **2.** *rel. pron.* what; ~ *(auch immer)*, *alles* ~ what(so)ever; ..., ~ *ihn völlig kalt ließ* ... which left him quite cold; **3.** F *indef. pron.* something; *ich will dir mal* ~ *sagen* I'll tell you what.

wasch|bar *adj.* ['vaʃbɑːr] washable; '**♀becken** *n* wash-basin, *Am.* wash-bowl.

Wäsche ['vɛʃə] *f* (-/-n) wash(ing); laundry; linen (*a. fig.*); underwear; *in der* ~ *sein* be at the wash; *sie hat heute große* ~ she has a large wash today.

waschecht *adj.* ['vaʃ⁹-] washable; *colour:* a. fast; *fig.* dyed-in-the-wool.

'**Wäsche|klammer** *f* clothes-peg, clothes-pin; '**~leine** *f* clothes-line.

waschen *v/t.* (*irr.*, ge-, h) wash;

sich ~ (have a) wash; *sich das Haar or den Kopf* ~ wash *or* shampoo one's hair *or* head; *sich gut* ~ (*lassen*) wash well.

Wäscher|ei [vɛʃə'rai] *f* (-/-en) laundry; '**~in** *f* (-/-nen) washer-woman, laundress.

'**Wäscheschrank** *m* linen closet.

'**Wasch|frau** *f* s. *Wäscherin*; '**~haus** *n* wash-house; '**~kessel** *m* copper; '**~korb** *m* clothes-basket; '**~küche** *f* wash-house; '**~lappen** *m* face-cloth, *Am.* washrag, wash-cloth; '**~maschine** *f* washing machine, washer; '**~pulver** *n* washing powder; '**~raum** *m* lavatory, *Am.* washroom; '**~schüssel** *f* wash-basin; '**~tag** *m* wash(ing)-day; '**~ung** *f* (-/-en) ♀ wash; ablution; '**~weib** *contp. n* gossip; '**~wanne** *f* wash-tub.

Wasser ['vasər] *n* (-s/-, ♀) water; ~ *lassen* make water; *zu* ~ *und zu Land(e)* by sea and land; '**~ball** *m* **1.** beach-ball; water-polo ball; **2.** (-[e]s/*no pl.*) water-polo; '**~ball-spiel** *n* **1.** (-[e]s/*no pl.*) water-polo; **2.** water-polo match; '**~behälter** *m* reservoir, water-tank; '**~blase** ♀ *f* water-blister; '**~dampf** *m* steam; **♀dicht** *adj.* waterproof; water-tight; '**~eimer** *m* water-pail, bucket; '**~fall** *m* waterfall, cascade; cataract; '**~farbe** *f* water-colo(u)r; '**~flugzeug** *n* waterplane, seaplane; '**~glas** *n* **1.** tumbler; **2.** ♀ (-es/*no pl.*) water-glass; '**~graben** *m* ditch; '**~hahn** *m* tap, *Am.* a. faucet; '**~hose** *f* waterspout.

wässerig *adj.* ['vɛsəriç] watery; washy (*a. fig.*); *j-m den Mund* ~ *machen* make s.o.'s mouth water.

'**Wasser|kanne** *f* water-jug, ewer; '**~kessel** *m* kettle; '**~klosett** *n* water-closet, W.C.; '**~kraft** *f* water-power; '**~kraftwerk** *n* hydroelectric power station *or* plant, water-power station; '**~krug** *m* water-jug, ewer; '**~kur** *f* water-cure, hydropathy; '**~lauf** *m* water-course; '**~leitung** *f* water-supply; '**~leitungsrohr** *n* water-pipe; '**~mangel** *m* shortage of water; '**~♀n** *v/i.* (ge-, h) alight on water; splash down. [(*salted herring, etc.*).]

wässern ['vɛsərn] *v/t.* (ge-, h) soak

'**Wasser|pflanze** *f* aquatic plant; '**~rinne** *f* gutter; '**~rohr** *n* water-pipe; '**~schaden** m damage caused by water; '**~scheide** f watershed, Am. a. divide; '**~schlauch** m water-hose; '**~spiegel** m water-level; '**~sport** m aquatic sports pl.; '**~spülung** f (-/-en) flushing (system); '**~stand** m water-level; '**~standsanzeiger** ['vasɐrʃtants?-] m water-gauge; '**~stiefel** m pl. waders pl.; '**~stoff** m (-[e]s/no pl.) hydrogen; '**~stoffbombe** f hydrogen bomb, H-bomb; '**~strahl** m jet of water; '**~straße** f waterway; '**~tier** n aquatic animal; '**~verdrängung** f (-/-en) displacement; '**~versorgung** f water-supply; '**~waage** f spirit-level, water-level; '**~weg** m waterway; auf dem ~e by water; '**~welle** f water-wave; '**~werk** n waterworks sg., pl.; '**~zeichen** n watermark.

wäßrig adj. ['vɛsriç] s. wässerig.

waten ['vɑːtən] v/i. (ge-, sein) wade.

watscheln ['vɑːtʃəln] v/i. (ge-, sein, h) waddle.

Watt ⚡ [vat] n (-s/-) watt.

Watt|e ['vatə] f (-/-n) cotton-wool; surgical cotton; wadding; '**~ebausch** m wad; **2ieren** [~'tiːrən] v/t. wad, pad.

weben ['veːbən] v/t. and v/i. ([irr.,] ge-, h) weave.

'**Weber** m (-s/-) weaver; **~ei** [~'raɪ] f 1. (-/no pl.) weaving; 2. (-/-en) weaving-mill.

Webstuhl ['veːpʃtuːl] m loom.

Wechsel ['vɛksəl] m (-s/-) change; allowance; ✝ bill (of exchange); hunt. runway; eigener ~ ✝ promissory note; '**~beziehung** f correlation; '**~fälle** ['~fɛlə] pl. vicissitudes pl.; '**~fieber** ⚕ n (-s/no pl.) intermittent fever; malaria; '**~frist** ✝ f usance; '**~geld** n change; '**~kurs** m rate of exchange; '**~makler** ✝ m bill-broker; '**2n** (ge-, h) 1. v/t. change; vary; exchange (words, etc.); den Besitzer ~ change hands, die Kleider ~ change (one's clothes); 2. v/i. change; vary; alternate; '**~nehmer** ✝ m (-s/-) payee; **2seitig** adj. ['~zaɪtiç] mutual, reciprocal; '**~strom** ⚡ m alternating current; '**~stube** f exchange office; '**2weise** adv. alternately, by or in turns; '**~wirkung** f interaction.

wecke|n ['vɛkən] v/t. (ge-, h) wake (up), waken; arouse (a. fig.); '**2r** m (-s/-) alarm-clock.

wedeln ['veːdəln] v/i. (ge-, h): ~ mit wag (tail).

weder cj. ['veːdər]: ~ ... noch neither ... nor.

Weg[1] [veːk] m (-[e]s/-e) way (a. fig.); road (a. fig.); path; route; walk; auf halbem ~ half-way; am ~e by the roadside; aus dem ~e gehen steer clear of; aus dem ~e räumen remove (a. fig.); in die ~e leiten set on foot, initiate.

weg[2] adv. [vɛk] away, off; gone; geh ~! be off (with you)!; ~ mit ihm! off with him!; Hände ~! hands off!; F ich muß ~ I must be off; F ganz ~ sein be quite beside o.s.; '**~bleiben** F v/i. (irr. bleiben, sep., -ge-, sein) stay away; be omitted; '**~bringen** v/t. (irr. bringen, sep., -ge-, h) take away; a. remove (things).

wegen prp. (gen.) ['veːgən] because of, on account of, owing to.

weg|fahren ['vɛk-] (irr. fahren, sep., -ge-) 1. v/t. (h) remove; cart away; 2. v/i. (sein) leave; '**~fallen** v/i. (irr. fallen, sep., -ge-, sein) be omitted; be abolished; '**2gang** m (-[e]s/no pl.) going away, departure; '**~gehen** v/i. (irr. gehen, sep., -ge-, sein) go away or off; merchandise: sell; '**~haben** F v/t. (irr. haben, sep., -ge-, h): e-n ~ be tight; have a screw loose; er hat noch nicht weg, wie man es machen muß he hasn't got the knack of it yet; '**~jagen** v/t. (sep., -ge-, h) drive away; '**~kommen** F v/i. (irr. kommen, sep., -ge-, sein) get away; be missing; gut (schlecht) ~ come off well (badly); mach, daß du wegkommst! be off (with you)!; '**~lassen** v/t. (irr. lassen, sep., -ge-, h) let s.o. go; leave out, omit; '**~laufen** v/i. (irr. laufen, sep., -ge-, sein) run away; '**~legen** v/t. (sep., -ge-, h) put away; '**~nehmen** v/t. (sep., -ge-, h) remove; a. take out (stains); '**~müssen** F v/i. (irr. müssen 1, sep., -ge-, h): ich muß weg I must be off; **2nahme** f ['~nɑːmə] f (-/-n) taking (away); '**~nehmen** v/t. (irr. nehmen, sep., -ge-, h) take up, occupy (time, space); j-m et. ~ take s.th. away from s.o.; '**~raffen** fig. v/t. (sep., -ge-, h) carry off.

Wegrand ['veːk-] *m* wayside.
weg|räumen ['vɛk-] *v/t.* (*sep.*, -ge-, h) clear away, remove; '**~schaffen** *v/t.* (*sep.*, -ge-, h) remove; '**~schikken** *v/t.* (*sep.*, -ge-, h) send away or off; '**~sehen** *v/i.* (*irr. sehen, sep.*, -ge-, h) look away; ~ **über** (*acc.*) overlook, shut one's eyes to; '**~setzen** *v/t.* (*sep.*, -ge-, h) put away; *sich* ~ **über** (*acc.*) disregard, ignore; '**~streichen** *v/t.* (*irr. streichen, sep.*, -ge-, h) strike off or out; '**~tun** *v/t.* (*irr. tun, sep.*, -ge-, h) put away or aside.
Wegweiser ['veːkvaɪzər] *m* (-s/-) signpost, finger-post; *fig.* guide.
weg|wenden ['vɛk-] *v/t.* (*irr. wenden,* sep., -ge-, h) turn away, avert (*one's eyes*); *sich* ~ turn away; '**~werfen** *v/t.* (*irr. werfen, sep.*, -ge-, h) throw away; '**~werfend** *adj.* disparaging; '**~wischen** *v/t.* (*sep.*, -ge-, h) wipe off; '**~ziehen** (*irr. ziehen, sep.*, -ge-) **1.** *v/t.* (h) pull or draw away; **2.** *v/i.* (sein) (re)move.
weh [veː] **1.** *adj.* sore; **2.** *adv.*: ~ **tun** ache, hurt; *j-m* ~ **tun** pain or hurt s.o.; *fig. a.* grieve s.o.; *sich* ~ **tun** hurt o.s.; *mir tut der Finger* ~ my finger hurts.
Wehen[1] ['veːən] *f/pl.* labo(u)r, travail.
wehen[2] [~] (*ge-*, h) **1.** *v/t.* blow; **2.** *v/i.* blow; *es weht ein starker Wind* it is blowing hard.
weh|klagen *v/i.* (*ge-*, h) lament (*um* for, over); '**~leidig** *adj.* snivel(l)ing; *voice*: plaintive; '**2mut** *f* (-/*no pl.*) wistfulness; '**~mütig** *adj.* ['~myːtɪç] wistful.
Wehr [veːr] **1.** *f* (-/-en): *sich zur* ~ *setzen* offer resistance (*gegen* to), show fight; **2.** *n* (-[e]s/-e) weir; '**~dienst** ⚔ *m* military service; '**2en** *v/refl.* (*ge-*, h) defend o.s.; offer resistance (*gegen* to); '**2fähig** ⚔ *adj.* able-bodied; '**2los** *adj.* defenceless, *Am.* defenseless; '**~pflicht** ⚔ *f* (-/*no pl.*) compulsory military service, conscription; '**2pflichtig** ⚔ *adj.* liable to military service.
Weib [vaɪp] *n* (-[e]s/-er) woman; wife; '**~chen** *zo. n* (-s/-) female.
Weiber|feind ['vaɪbər-] *m* woman-hater; '**~held** *contp. m* ladies' man; '**~volk** *F n* (-[e]s/*no pl.*) womenfolk.

weib|isch *adj.* ['vaɪbɪʃ] womanish, effeminate; '**~lich** *adj.* ['~p-] female; *gr.* feminine; womanly, feminine.
weich [vaɪç] soft (*a. fig.*); *meat,* *etc.*: tender; *egg*: soft-boiled; ~ *werden* soften; *fig.* relent.
Weiche[1] 🚆 ['vaɪçə] *f* (-/-n) switch; ~*n pl.* points *pl.*
Weiche[2] *anat.* [~] *f* (-/-n) flank, side.
weichen[1] ['vaɪçən] *v/i.* (*irr., ge-,* sein) give way, yield (*dat.* to); *nicht von der Stelle* ~ not to budge an inch; *j-m nicht von der Seite* ~ stick to s.o.
weichen[2] [~] *v/i.* (*ge-*, h, sein) soak.
'**Weichensteller** 🚆 *m* (-s/-) points-man, switch-man.
weich|herzig *adj.* soft-hearted, tender-hearted; '**~lich** *adj.* some-what soft; *fig.* effeminate; '**2ling** ['~lɪŋ] *m* (-s/-e) weakling, milksop, molly(-coddle), *sl.* sissy; '**2tier** *n* mollusc.
Weide[1] 🌿 ['vaɪdə] *f* (-/-n) willow.
Weide[2] 🌾 [~] *f* (-/-n) pasture; *auf der* ~ out at grass; '**~land** *n* pasture(-land); '**2n** (*ge-*, h) **1.** *v/t.* feed, pasture, graze; *sich* ~ *an* (*dat.*) gloat over; feast on; **2.** *v/i.* pasture, graze.
'**Weiden|korb** *m* wicker basket, osier basket; '**~rute** *f* osier switch.
weidmännisch *hunt. adj.* ['vaɪtmɛnɪʃ] sportsmanlike.
weiger|n ['vaɪgərn] *v/refl.* (*ge-*, h) refuse, decline; '**2ung** *f* (-/-en) refusal.
Weihe *eccl.* ['vaɪə] *f* (-/-n) con-secration; ordination; '**2n** *eccl. v/t.* (*ge-*, h) consecrate; *j-n zum Prie-ster* ~ ordain s.o. priest.
Weiher ['vaɪər] *m* (-s/-) pond.
'**weihevoll** *adj.* solemn.
Weihnachten ['vaɪnaxtən] *n* (-s/*no pl.*) Christmas, Xmas.
'**Weihnachts|abend** *m* Christmas eve; '**~baum** *m* Christmas-tree; '**~ferien** *pl.* Christmas holidays *pl.*; '**~fest** *n* Christmas; '**~geschenk** *n* Christmas present; '**~gratifika-tion** *f* Christmas bonus; '**~karte** *f* Christmas card; '**~lied** *n* carol, Christmas hymn; '**~mann** *m* Father Christmas, Santa Claus; '**~markt** *m* Christmas fair; '**~zeit** *f* (-/*no pl.*) Christmas(-tide) (*in Germany beginning on the first Advent Sunday*).

'**Weih|rauch** *eccl. m* incense; '**~wasser** *eccl. n* (-s/*no pl.*) holy water.

weil *cj.* [vaɪl] because, since, as.

Weil|chen ['vaɪlçən] *n* (-s/-): ein ~ a little while, a spell; '**~e** *f* (-/*no pl.*): e-e ~ a while.

Wein [vaɪn] *m* (-[e]s/-e) wine; 🍇 vine; *wilder* ~ 🍇 Virginia creeper; '**~bau** *m* (-[e]s/*no pl.*) vine-growing, viticulture; '**~beere** *f* grape; '**~berg** *m* vineyard; '**~blatt** *n* vine-leaf.

wein|en ['vaɪnən] *v/i.* (ge-, h) weep (*um, vor dat.* for), cry (*vor dat.* for joy, *etc.*, *with hunger, etc.*); '**~erlich** *adj.* tearful, lachrymose; whining.

'**Wein|ernte** *f* vintage; '**~essig** *m* vinegar; '**~faß** *n* wine-cask; '**~flasche** *f* wine-bottle; '**~geist** *m* (-[e]s/-e) spirit(*s pl.*) of wine; '**~glas** *n* wineglass; '**~handlung** *f* wine-merchant's shop; '**~karte** *f* wine-list; '**~keller** *m* wine-vault; '**~kelter** *f* winepress; '**~kenner** *m* connoisseur of *or* in wine.

'**Weinkrampf** 🩺 *m* paroxysm of weeping.

'**Wein|kühler** *m* wine-cooler; '**~lese** *f* vintage; '**~presse** *f* winepress; '**~ranke** *f* vine-tendril; '**~rebe** *f* vine; '**2rot** *adj.* claret-colo(u)red; '**~stock** *m* vine; '**~traube** *f* grape, bunch of grapes.

weise[1] ['vaɪzə] **1.** *adj.* wise; sage; **2.** *m* (-n/-n) wise man, sage.

Weise[2] [~] *f* (-/-n) ♪ melody, tune; *fig.* manner, way; *auf diese* ~ in this way.

weisen ['vaɪzən] (*irr.*, ge-, h) **1.** *v/t.*: j-m die Tür ~ show s.o. the door; *von der Schule* ~ expel from school; *von sich* ~ reject (*idea, etc.*); deny (*charge, etc.*); **2.** *v/i.*: ~ *auf* (*acc.*) point at *or* to.

Weis|heit ['vaɪshaɪt] *f* (-/🔸-en) wisdom; *am Ende s-r* ~ *sein* be at one's wit's end; '**~heitszahn** *m* wisdom-tooth; '**2machen** (*sep.*, -ge-, h): j-m et. ~ make s.o. believe s.th.

weiß *adj.* [vaɪs] white; '**2blech** *n* tin(-plate); '**2brot** *n* white bread; '**2e** *m* (-n/-n) white (man); '**~en** *v/t.* (ge-, h) whitewash; '**~glühend** *adj.* white-hot, incandescent; '**2kohl** *m* white cabbage; '**~lich** *adj.* whitish; '**2waren** *pl.* linen goods *pl.*; '**2wein** *m* white wine.

Weisung ['vaɪzʊŋ] *f* (-/-en) direction, directive.

weit [vaɪt] **1.** *adj.* distant (*von* from); *world, garment:* wide; *area, etc.:* vast; *garment:* loose; *journey, way:* long; *conscience:* elastic; **2.** *adv.:* ~ *entfernt* far away; ~ *entfernt von* a long distance from; *fig.* far from; ~ *und breit* far and wide; ~ *über sechzig* (*Jahre alt*) well over sixty; *bei* ~em (by) far; *von* ~em from a distance.

weit|ab *adv.* ['vaɪt-] far away (*von* from); '**~aus** *adv.* (by) far, much; '**2blick** *m* (-[e]s/*no pl.*) far-sightedness; '**~blickend** *adj.* far-sighted, far-seeing; '**~en** *v/t. and v/refl.* (ge-, h) widen.

'**weiter 1.** *adj. particulars, etc.:* further; *charges, etc.:* additional, extra; ~e *fünf Wochen* another five weeks; *bis auf* ~es until further notice; *ohne* ~es without any hesitation; *off-hand;* **2.** *adv.* furthermore, moreover; ~! go on!; *nichts* ~ nothing more; *und so* ~ and so on; *bis hierher und nicht* ~ so far and no farther; '**2e** *n* (-n/*no pl.*) the rest; further details *pl.*

'**weiter|befördern** *v/t.* (*sep.*, no -ge-, h) forward; '**~bestehen** *v/i.* (*irr. stehen, sep.*, no -ge-, h) continue to exist, survive; '**~bilden** *v/t.* (*sep.*, -ge-, h) give s.o. further education; *sich* ~ improve one's knowledge; continue one's education; '**~geben** *v/t.* (*irr. geben, sep.*, -ge-, h) pass (*dat., a an acc.* to); '**~gehen** *v/i.* (*irr. gehen, sep.*, -ge-, sein) pass *or* move on, walk along; *fig.* continue, go on; '**~hin** *adv.* in (the) future; furthermore; *et.* ~ *tun* continue doing *or* to do s.th.; '**~kommen** *v/i.* (*irr. kommen, sep.*, -ge-, sein) get on; '**~können** *v/i.* (*irr. können, sep.*, -ge-, h) be able to go on; '**~leben** *v/i.* (*sep.*, -ge-, h) live on, survive (*a. fig.*); '**~machen** *v/t. and v/i.* (*sep.*, -ge-, h) carry on.

'**weit|gehend** *adj. powers:* large; *support:* generous; '**~gereist** *adj.* travel(l)ed; '**~greifend** *adj.* far-reaching; '**~herzig** *adj.* broad-minded; '**~hin** *adv.* far off; '**~läufig** ['~lɔyfɪç] **1.** *adj. house, etc.:* spacious; *story, etc.:* detailed; *relative:* distant; **2.** *adv.:* ~ *erzählen* (tell in) detail; *er ist* ~ *verwandt mit mir*

W

he is a distant relative of mine; **'⁀reichend** adj. far-reaching; **'⁀schweifig** adj. diffuse, prolix; **'⁀sichtig** adj. ⚕ far-sighted; fig. a. far-seeing; **⁀sichtigkeit** f (-/⁀-en) far-sightedness; **'⁀sprung** m (-[e]s/no pl.) long jump, Am. broad jump; **'⁀tragend** adj. ✕ long-range; fig. far-reaching; **'⁀verbreitet** adj. widespread.

Weizen ♠ ['vaitsən] m (-s/-) wheat; **'⁀brot** n wheaten bread; **'⁀mehl** n wheaten flour.

welch [velç] 1. interr. pron. what; which; ⁀er? which one?; ⁀er von beiden? which of the two?; 2. rel. pron. who; that; which, that; 3. F indef. pron.: es gibt ⁀e, die sagen, daß ... there are some who say that ...; es sollen viele Ausländer hier sein, hast du schon ⁀e gesehen? many foreigners are said to be here, have you seen any yet?

welk adj. [velk] faded, withered; skin: flabby, flaccid; **'⁀en** v/i. (ge-, sein) fade, wither. [iron.]

Wellblech ['velbleç] n corrugated⟩

Welle ['velə] f (-/-n) wave (a. fig.); ⊕ shaft.

wellen v/t. and v/refl. (ge-, h) wave; **⁀bereich** ♪ m wave-range; **⁀förmig** adj. ['⁀fœrmiç] undulating, undulatory; **⁀länge** ♪ f wavelength; **⁀linie** f wavy line; **⁀reiten** n (-s/no pl.) surf-riding.

'wellig adj. wavy.

'Wellpappe f corrugated cardboard or paper.

Welt [velt] f (-/-en) world; die ganze ⁀ the whole world, all the world; auf der ⁀ in the world, auf der ganzen ⁀ all over the world; zur ⁀ bringen give birth to, bring into the world.

'Welt|all n universe, cosmos; **'⁀anschauung** f Weltanschauung; **'⁀ausstellung** f world fair; **⁀bekannt** adj. known all over the world; **⁀berühmt** adj. world-famous; **'⁀bürger** m cosmopolite; **'⁀erschütternd** adj. world-shaking; **⁀fremd** adj. wordly innocent; **'⁀friede(n)** m universal peace; **'⁀geschichte** f (-/no pl.) universal history; **⁀gewandt** adj. knowing the ways of the world; **'⁀handel** m (-s/no pl.) world trade; **'⁀karte** f map of the world; **⁀klug** adj.

wordly-wise; **'⁀krieg** m world war; der zweite ⁀ World War II; **'⁀lage** f international situation; **'⁀lauf** m course of the world; **⁀lich** 1. adj. wordly; secular, temporal; 2. adv.: ⁀ gesinnt wordly-minded; **'⁀literatur** f world literature; **'⁀macht** f world-power; **⁀männisch** adj. ['⁀meniʃ] man-of-the-world; **'⁀markt** m (-[e]s/no pl.) world market; **'⁀meer** n ocean; **'⁀meister** m world champion; **'⁀meisterschaft** f world championship; **'⁀raum** m (-[e]s/no pl.) (outer) space; **'⁀reich** n universal empire; das Britische ⁀ the British Empire; **'⁀reise** f journey round the world; **'⁀rekord** m world record; **'⁀ruf** m (-[e]s/no pl.) world-wide reputation; **'⁀schmerz** m Weltschmerz; **'⁀sprache** f world or universal language; **'⁀stadt** f metropolis; **⁀weit** adj. world-wide; **'⁀wunder** n wonder of the world.

Wende ['vendə] f (-/-n) turn (a. swimming); fig. a. turning-point; **'⁀kreis** m geogr. tropic; mot. turning-circle.

Wendeltreppe ['vendəl-] f winding staircase, (e-e a flight of) winding stairs pl., spiral staircase.

'Wende|marke f sports: turning-point; **⁀n 1.** v/t. (ge-, h) turn (coat, etc.); turn (hay) about; 2. v/refl. (irr.) ge-, h): sich ⁀ an (acc.) turn to; address o.s. to; apply to (wegen for); 3. v/i. (ge-, h) ♻, mot. turn; bitte ⁀! please turn over!; **'⁀punkt** m turning-point.

'wend|ig adj. nimble, agile (both a. fig.); mot., ♻ easily steerable; mot. flexible; **⁀ung** f (-/-en) turn (a. fig.); ✕ facing; fig.: change; expression; idiom.

wenig ['ve:niç] 1. adj. little; ⁀e pl. few pl.; ⁀er less; ⁀er pl. fewer; ein klein ⁀ Geduld a little bit of patience; das ⁀ the little; 2. adv. little; ⁀er less; ♪ a. minus; am ⁀sten least (of all); **⁀keit** f (-/-en): meine ⁀ my humble self; **⁀stens** adv. ['⁀stəns] at least.

wenn cj. [ven] when; if; ⁀ ... nicht if ... not, unless; ⁀ auch (al)though, even though; ⁀ auch noch so however; und ⁀ nun ...? what if ...?; wie wäre es, ⁀ wir jetzt heimgingen? what about going home now?

W

wer [ve:r] **1.** *interr. pron.* who; which; ~ *von euch?* which of you?; **2.** *rel. pron.* who; ~ *auch (immer)* who(so)ever; **3.** F *indef. pron.* somebody; anybody; *ist schon ~ gekommen?* has anybody come yet?

Werbe|abteilung ['vɛrbə-] *f* advertising *or* publicity department; '**~film** *m* advertising film.

'**werb|en** (*irr.*, ge-, h) **1.** *v/t.* canvass (*votes, subscribers, etc.*); ✗ recruit, enlist; **2.** *v/i.*: ~ *für* advertise, *Am. a.* advertize; make propaganda for; canvass for; '**Qung** *f* (-/-en) advertising, publicity, *Am. a.* advertizing; propaganda; canvassing; ✗ enlistment, recruiting.

Werdegang ['ve:rdə-] *m* career; ⊕ process of manufacture.

'**werden 1.** *v/i.* (*irr.*, ge-, sein) become; get; grow; turn (*pale, sour, etc.*); *was ist aus ihm geworden?* what has become of him?; *was will er (einmal) ~?* what is he going to be?; **2.** ♀ *in* ~ (ge-, h/no pl.): *noch im* ~ *sein* in embryo.

werfen ['vɛrfən] (*irr.*, ge-, h) **1.** *v/t.* throw (*nach at*); *zo.* throw (*young*); cast (*shadow, glance, etc.*); *Falten* ~ fall in folds; set badly; **2.** *v/i.* throw; *zo.* litter; ~ *mit* throw (*auf acc., nach at*). [dockyard.]

Werft ⚓ [vɛrft] *f* (-/-en) shipyard,

Werk [vɛrk] *n* (-[e]s/-e) work; act; ⊕ works *pl.*; works *sg.*, *pl.*, factory; das ~ *e-s Augenblicks* the work of a moment; *zu ~e gehen* proceed; '**~bank** *f* work-bench; '**~meister** *m* foreman; '**~statt** ['-ʃtat] *f* (-/⁺en) workshop; '**~tag** *m* workday; '**~tätig** *adj.* working; '**~zeug** *n* tool; implement; instrument.

Wermut ['ve:rmu:t] *m* (-[e]s/no pl.) ♀ wormwood; verm(o)uth.

wert [ve:rt] **1.** *adj.* worth; worthy (*gen. of*); ~ *getan zu werden* worth doing; **2.** ♀ *m* (-[e]s/-e) value (a. ♀, ♪, *phys., fig.*); worth (a. *fig.*); *Briefmarken im* ~ *von 2 Schilling* 2 shillings' worth of stamps; *großen* ~ *legen auf* (*acc.*) set a high value (up)on.

'**Wert|brief** *m* money-letter; '**Qen** *v/t.* (ge-, h) value; appraise; '**~gegenstand** *m* article of value; '**Qlos** *adj.* worthless, valueless; '**~papiere** *n/pl.* securities *pl.*; '**~sachen** *pl.* valuables *pl.*; '**~ung** *f* (-/-en)

valuation; appraisal; *sports*: score; '**Qvoll** *adj.* valuable, precious.

Wesen ['ve:zən] *n* **1.** (-s/no pl.) entity, essence; nature, character; *viel ~s machen um* make a fuss of; **2.** (-s/-) being, creature; '**Qlos** *adj.* unreal; '**Qtlich** *adj.* essential, substantial.

weshalb [vɛs'halp] **1.** *interr. pron.* why; **2.** *cj.* that's why.

Wespe *zo.* ['vɛspə] *f* (-/-n) wasp.

West *geogr.* [vɛst] west; '**~en** *m* (-s/no pl.) west; *the* West.

Weste ['vɛstə] *f* (-/-n) waistcoat, ⁺ *and Am.* vest; *e-e reine* ~ *haben* have a clean slate.

'**west|lich** *adj.* west; westerly; western; '**Qwind** *m* west(erly) wind.

Wett|bewerb ['vɛtbəvɛrp] *m* (-[e]s/-e) competition (*a.* ⁺); '**~büro** *n* betting office; '**~e** *f* (-/-n) wager, bet; *e-e eingehen* lay *or* make a bet; '**~eifer** *m* emulation, rivalry; '**Qeifern** *v/i.* (ge-, h) vie (*mit with*; *in dat.* in; *um* for); '**Qen** (ge-, h) **1.** *v/t.* wager, bet; **2.** *v/i.*: *mit j-m um et.* ~ wager *or* bet s.o. s.th.; ~ *auf* (*acc.*) wager *or* bet on, back.

Wetter[1] ['vɛtər] *n* (-s/-) weather.

Wetter[2] [~] *m* (-s/-) better.

'**Wetter|bericht** *m* weather-forecast; '**Qfest** *adj.* weather-proof; '**~karte** *f* weather-chart; '**~lage** *f* weather-conditions *pl.*; '**~leuchten** *n* (-s/no pl.) sheet-lightning; '**~vorhersage** *f* (-/-n) weather-forecast; '**~warte** *f* weather-station.

'**Wett|kampf** *m* contest, competition; '**~kämpfer** *m* contestant; '**~lauf** *m* race; '**~läufer** *m* racer, runner; '**Qmachen** *v/t.* (*sep.*, -ge-, h) make up for; '**~rennen** *n* race; '**~rüsten** *n* (-s/no pl.) armament race; '**~spiel** *n* match, game; '**~streit** *m* contest. [sharpen.]

wetzen ['vɛtsən] *v/t.* (ge-, h) whet,

wich [viç] *pret. of* weichen[1].

Wichse ['viksə] *f* **1.** (-/-n) blacking; polish; **2.** F *fig.* (-/no pl.) thrashing; '**Qn** *v/t.* (ge-, h) black; polish.

wichtig ['viçtiç] *adj.* important; *sich ~ machen* show off; '**Qkeit** *f* (-/⁺-en) importance; '**Qtuer** ['-tu:-ər] *m* (-s/-) pompous fellow; '**~tuerisch** *adj.* pompous.

Wickel ['vikəl] *m* (-s/-) roll(er); ⚕: compress; packing; '**Qn** *v/t.* (ge-, h) wind; swaddle (*baby*); wrap.

Widder 364

Widder zo. ['vɪdər] m (-s/-) ram. **wider** prp. (acc.) ['vi:dər] against, contrary to; '~borstig adj. cross-grained; ~'fahren v/i. (irr. fahren, no -ge-, sein) happen (dat. to); '2haken m barb; 2hall ['~hal] m (-[e]s/-e) echo, reverberation; fig. response; ~hallen v/i. (sep., -ge-, h) (re-)echo (von with), resound (with); ~'legen v/t. (no -ge-, h) refute, disprove; ~'lich adj. repugnant, repulsive; disgusting; ~'natürlich adj. unnatural; ~'rechtlich adj. illegal, unlawful; 2rede f contradiction; '2ruf m 🏵 revocation; retraction; ~'rufen v/t. (irr. rufen, no -ge-, h) revoke; retract (a. 🏵); ~'ruflich adj. revocable; 2sacher ['~zaxər] m (-s/-) adversary; '2schein m reflection; ~'setzen v/refl. (no -ge-, h): sich e-r Sache ~ oppose or resist s.th.; '~setzlich adj. refractory; insubordinate; '~sinnig adj. absurd; ~spenstig adj. ['~ʃpɛnstɪç] refractory; '2spenstigkeit f (-/~-en) refractoriness; '~spiegeln v/t. (sep., -ge-, h) reflect (a. fig.); sich ~ in (dat.) be reflected in; ~'sprechen v/i. (irr. sprechen, no -ge-, h): j-m ~ contradict s.o.; '2spruch m contradiction; opposition; im ~ zu in contradiction to; '~sprüchlich adj. ['~ʃpry:çlɪç] contradictory; '~spruchslos 1. adj. uncontradicted; 2. adv. without contradiction; '2stand m resistance (a. 🏵); opposition; ~ leisten offer resistance (dat. to); auf heftigen ~ stoßen meet with stiff opposition; '~standsfähig adj. resistant (a. ⊕); ~'stehen v/i. (irr. stehen, no -ge-, h): resist (e-r Sache s.th.); ~'streben v/i. (no -ge-, h): es widerstrebt mir, dies zu tun I hate doing or to do that, I am reluctant to do that; ~'strebend adv. reluctantly; '2streit m (-[e]s/-e) antagonism; fig. conflict; ~'wärtig adj. ['~vɛrtɪç] unpleasant, disagreeable; disgusting; '2wille m aversion (gegen to, for, from); dislike (to, of, for); disgust (at, for); reluctance, unwillingness; '~willig adj. reluctant, unwilling.

widm|en ['vɪtmən] v/t. (ge-, h) dedicate; '2ung f (-/-en) dedication.

widrig adj. ['vi:drɪç] adverse; ~enfalls adv. ['~ɡən'-] failing which, in default of which.

wie [vi:] 1. adv. how; ~ alt ist er? what is his age?; ~ spät ist es? what is the time?; 2. cj.: ein Mann ~ er a man such as he, a man like him; ~ er dies hörte hearing this; ich hörte, ~ er es sagte I heard him saying so.

wieder adv. ['vi:dər] again, anew; immer ~ again and again; 2'aufbau m (-[e]s/no pl.) reconstruction; rebuilding; ~'aufbauen v/t. (sep., -ge-, h) reconstruct; ~'aufleben v/i. (sep., -ge-, sein) revive; 2'aufleben n (-s/no pl.) revival; 2'aufnahme f resumption; ~'aufnehmen v/t. (irr. nehmen, sep., -ge-, h) resume; '2beginn m recommencement; re-opening; ~'bekommen v/t. (irr. kommen, sep., no -ge-, h) get back; ~'beleben v/t. (sep., no -ge-, h) resurrect; '2belebung f (-/-en) revival; fig. a. resurrection; 2'belebungsversuch m attempt at resuscitation; ~'bringen v/t. (irr. bringen, sep., -ge-, h) bring back; restore, give back; ~'einsetzen v/t. (sep., -ge-, h) restore; ~'einstellen v/t. (sep., -ge-, h) re-engage; 2'ergreifung f reseizure; ~'erkennen v/t. (irr. kennen, sep., no -ge-, h) recognize (an dat. by); ~'erstatten v/t. (sep., no -ge-, h) restore; reimburse, refund (money); '~geben v/t. (irr. geben, sep., -ge-, h) give back, return; render, reproduce; ~'gutmachen v/t. (sep., -ge-, h) make up for; 2'gutmachung f (-/-en) reparation; ~'herstellen v/t. (sep., -ge-, h) restore; ~holen (h) 1. ['~ho:lən] (no -ge-) repeat; 2. ['~ho:lən] (sep., -ge-) fetch back; 2'holung f (-/-en) repetition; 2'käuen ['~kɔʏən] (sep., -ge-, h) 1. v/i. ruminate, chew the cud; 2. F fig. v/t. repeat over and over; 2kehr ['~ke:r] f (-/no pl.) return; recurrence; '~kehren v/i. (sep., -ge-, sein) return; recur; '~kommen v/i. (irr. kommen, sep., -ge-, sein) come back, return; '~sehen v/t. and v/refl. (irr. sehen, sep., -ge-, h) see or meet again; 2sehen n (-s/no pl.) meeting again; auf ~! good-bye!; '~tun v/t. (irr. tun, sep., -ge-, h) do again; repeat;

'**∼um** *adv.* again, anew; '**∼vereinigen** *v/t.* (*sep., no* -ge-, *h*) reunite; '**²vereinigung** *f* reunion; *pol.* reunification; '**²verheiratung** *f* remarriage; '**²verkäufer** *m* reseller; retailer; '**²wahl** *f* re-election; '**∼wählen** *v/t.* (*sep.*, -ge-, *h*) reelect; '**²zulassung** *f* readmission.

Wiege ['vi:gə] *f* (-/-n) cradle.

wiegen¹ ['vi:gən] *v/t. and v/i.* (*irr.*, ge-, *h*) weigh.

wiegen² [∼] *v/t.* (ge-, *h*) rock; *in Sicherheit* ∼ rock in security, lull into (a false sense of) security.

'**Wiegenlied** *n* lullaby.

wiehern ['vi:ərn] *v/i.* (ge-, *h*) neigh.

Wiener ['vi:nər] *m* (-s/-) Viennese; '**²isch** *adj.* Viennese.

wies [vi:s] *pret. of* weisen.

Wiese ['vi:zə] *f* (-/-n) meadow.

wie'so *interr. pron.* why; why so.

wie'viel *adv.* how much; ∼ *pl.* how many *pl.*; ∼**te** *adv.* [∼tə]: den ∼ten haben wir heute? what's the date today?

wild [vilt] **1.** *adj.* wild; savage; ∼es Fleisch 🗲 proud flesh; ∼e Ehe concubinage; ∼er Streik 🏴 wildcat strike; **2.** ♀ *n* (-[e]s/*no pl.*) game.

'**Wildbach** *m* torrent; '**∼bret** ['∼bret] *n* (-s/*no pl.*) game; venison.

Wilde ['vildə] *m* (-n/-n) savage.

Wilder|er ['vildərər] *m* (-s/-) poacher; '**²n** *v/i.* (ge-, *h*) poach.

'**Wild|fleisch** *n* s. Wildbret; '**²-fremd** F *adj.* quite strange; '**∼hüter** *m* gamekeeper; '**∼leder** *n* buckskin; '**²ledern** *adj.* buckskin; doeskin; '**∼nis** *f* (-/-se) wilderness, wild (*a. fig.*); '**∼schwein** *n* wildboar.

Wille ['vilə] *m* (-ns/♀ -n) will; s-n ∼n durchsetzen have one's way; gegen s-n ∼n against one's will; j-m s-n ∼n lassen let s.o. have his (own) way; '**²nlos** *adj.* lacking will-power.

'**Willens|freiheit** *f* (-/*no pl.*) freedom of (the) will; '**∼kraft** *f* (-/*no pl.*) will-power; '**∼schwäche** *f* (-/*no pl.*) weak will; '**²stark** *adj.* strong-willed; '**∼stärke** *f* (-/*no pl.*) strong will, will-power.

'**will|ig** *adj.* willing, ready; ∼'**kommen** *adj.* welcome; ∼'**kür** ['∼ky:r] *f* (-/*no pl.*) arbitrariness; '**∼kürlich** *adj.* arbitrary.

wimmeln ['viməln] *v/i.* (ge-, *h*) swarm (*von* with), teem (with).

wimmern ['vimərn] *v/i.* (ge-, *h*) whimper, whine.

Wimpel ['vimpəl] *m* (-s/-) pennant, pennon, streamer.

Wimper ['vimpər] *f* (-/-n) eyelash.

Wind [vint] *m* (-[e]s/-e) wind; '**∼beutel** *m* cream-puff; F *fig.* windbag.

Winde ['vində] *f* (-/-n) windlass; reel.

Windel ['vindəl] *f* (-/-n) diaper, (baby's) napkin; ∼n *pl. a.* swaddlingclothes *pl.*

'**winden** *v/t.* (*irr.*, ge-, *h*) wind; twist, twirl; make, bind (*wreath*); sich ∼ vor (*dat.*) writhe with.

'**Wind|hose** *f* whirlwind, tornado; '**∼hund** *m* greyhound; '**²ig** *adj.* ['∼diç] windy; F *fig.* excuse: thin, lame; '**∼mühle** *f* windmill; '**∼pokken** *f pl.* chicken-pox; '**∼richtung** *f* direction of the wind; '**∼rose** ♟ *f* compass card; '**∼schutzscheibe** *f* wind-screen, *Am.* windshield; '**∼stärke** *f* wind velocity; '**²still** *adj.* calm; '**∼stille** *f* calm; '**∼stoß** *m* blast of wind, gust.

'**Windung** *f* (-/-en) winding, turn; bend (*of way, etc.*); coil (*of snake, etc.*).

Wink [viŋk] *m* (-[e]s/-e) sign; wave; wink; *fig.*: hint; tip.

Winkel ['viŋkəl] *m* (-s/-) ⚔ angle; corner, nook; '**²ig** *adj.* angular; *street*: crooked; '**∼zug** *m* subterfuge, trick, shift.

'**winken** *v/i.* (ge-, *h*) make a s'gn; beckon; mit dem Taschentu·h ∼ wave one's handkerchief.

winklig *adj.* ['viŋkliç] s. win'elig.

winseln ['vinzəln] *v/i.* (·e-, *h*) whimper, whine.

Winter ['vintər] *m* (-s/-) winter; im ∼ in winter; '**²lich** *adj.* wintry; '**∼schlaf** *m* hibernation; '**∼sport** *m* winter sports *pl.*

Winzer ['vintsər] *m* (-s/-) vinedresser; vine-grower; vintager.

winzig *adj.* ['vintsiç] tiny, diminutive.

Wipfel ['vipfəl] *m* (-s/-) top.

Wippe ['vipə] *f* (-/-n) seesaw; '**²n** *v/i.* (ge-, *h*) seesaw.

wir *pers. pron.* [vi:r] we; ∼ drei the three of us.

Wirbel ['virbəl] *m* (-s/-) whirl, swirl; eddy; flurry (*of blows, etc.*); *anat.* vertebra; '**²ig** *adj.* giddy,

W

vertiginous; wild; 'Ջn v/i. (ge-, h) whirl; *drums*: roll; 'säule *anat.* f spinal *or* vertebral column; 'sturm *m* cyclone, tornado, *Am. a.* twister; 'tier *n* vertebrate; 'wind *m* whirlwind (*a. fig.*).

wirk|en ['virkən] (ge-, h) **1.** v/t. knit, weave; work (*wonders*); **2.** v/i.: ~ als act *or* function as; ~ auf (*acc.*) produce an impression on; beruhigend ~ have a soothing effect; 'lich *adj.* real, actual; true, genuine; 'Ջlichkeit f (-/-en) reality; in ~ in reality; 'sam *adj.* effective, efficacious; 'Ջsamkeit f (-/⁊-en) effectiveness, efficacy; 'Ջung f (-/-en) effect.

'Wirkungs|kreis *m* sphere *or* field of activity; 'Ջlos *adj.* ineffective, ineffiacious; 'losigkeit f (-/no pl.) ineffe:tiveness, inefficacy; 'Ջvoll *adj. s.* virksam.

wirr *adj.* [vir] confused; *speech*: incoherent; *hair*: dishevel(l)ed; 'Ջen *pl.* disorders *pl.*; troubles *pl.*; Ջwarr ['var] *m* (-s/no pl.) confusion, muddle.

Wirsingkohl ['virzin-] *m* (-[e]s/no pl.) savoy.

Wirt [virt] *m* (-[e]s/-e) host; landlord; innkeeper.

'Wirtschaft f (-/-en) housekeeping; economy; trade and industry; economics *pl.*; *s.* Wirtshaus; F mess; 'Ջen v/i. (ge-, h) keep house; economize; F bustle (about); 'erin f (-/-nen) housekeeper; 'Ջlich *adj.* economic; economical.

'Wirtschafts|geld *n* housekeeping money; 'jahr *n* financial year; 'krise f economic crisis; 'politik f economic policy; 'prüfer *m* (-s/-) chartered accountant, *Am.* certified public accountant.

'Wirtshaus *n* public house, F pub.

Wisch [viʃ] *m* (-es/-e) wisp (*of straw, etc.*); *contp.* scrap of paper; 'Ջen v/t. (ge-, h) wipe.

wispern ['vispərn] v/t. and v/i. (ge-, h) whisper.

Wiß|begierde ['vis-] f (-/no pl.) thirst for knowledge; 'Ջbegierig *adj.* eager for knowledge.

wissen ['visən] **1.** v/t. (irr., ge-, h) know; *man kann nie* ~ you never know, you never can tell; **2.** Ջ *n* (-s/no pl.) knowledge; *meines* ~s to my knowledge, as far as I know.

'Wissenschaft f (-/-en) science; knowledge; 'ler *m* (-s/-) scholar; scientist; researcher; 'Ջlich *adj.* scientific.

'Wissens|drang *m* (-[e]s/no pl.) urge *or* thirst for knowledge; 'Ջwert *adj.* worth knowing.

'wissentlich *adj.* knowing, conscious.

wittern ['vitərn] v/t. (ge-, h) scent, smell; *fig. a.* suspect.

'Witterung f (-/⁊-en) weather; *hunt.* scent; 'sverhältnisse ['sferheltnisə] *pl.* meteorological conditions *pl.* [*m* (-s/-) widower.]

Witwe ['vitvə] f (-/-n) widow; 'r}

Witz [vits] *m* **1.** (-es/no pl.) wit; **2.** (-es/-e) joke; ~e reißen crack jokes; 'blatt *n* comic paper; 'Ջig *adj.* witty; funny.

wo [vo:] **1.** *adv.* where?; **2.** *cj.*: F ach ~! nonsense!

wob [vo:p] *pret. of* weben.

wo'bei *adv.* at what?; at which; in doing so.

Woche ['voxə] f (-/-n) week; *heute in e-r* ~ today week.

'Wochen|bett *n* childbed; 'blatt *n* weekly (paper); 'ende *n* weekend; 'Ջlang **1.** *adj.*: nach ~em Warten after (many) weeks of waiting; **2.** *adv.* for weeks; 'lohn *m* weekly pay *or* wages *pl.*; 'markt *m* weekly market; 'schau f news-reel; 'tag *m* week-day.

wöchentlich ['vœçəntliç] **1.** *adj.* weekly; **2.** *adv.* weekly, every week; einmal ~ once a week.

Wöchnerin ['vœçnərin] f (-/-nen) woman in childbed.

wo|'durch *adv.* by what?, how?; by which, whereby; ~'für *adv.* for what?, what ... for?; (in return) for which. [gen!.]

wog [vo:k] *pret. of* wägen *and* wie-}

Woge ['vo:gə] f (-/-n) wave (*a. fig.*), billow; *die* ~n glätten pour oil on troubled waters; 'Ջn v/i. (ge-, h) surge (*a. fig.*), billow; *wheat:* wave; heave.

wo|'her *adv.* from where?, where ... from?; ~ wissen Sie das? how do you (come to) know that?; ~'hin *adv.* where (... to)?

wohl [vo:l] **1.** *adv.* well; *sich nicht* ~ *fühlen* be unwell; ~ *oder übel* willy-nilly; *leben Sie* ~! farewell!; *er wird* ~ *reich sein* he is rich, I suppose;

2. ♀ *n* (-[e]s/*no pl.*): ~ und Wehe weal and woe; *auf Ihr* ~! your health!, here is to you!

'Wohl|befinden *n* well-being; good health; '~behagen *n* comfort, ease; '♀behalten *adv.* safe; '♀bekannt *adj.* well-known; '~ergehen *n* (-s/*no pl.*) welfare, prosperity; ♀er-zogen *adj.* ['~°ertso·gən] well-bred, well-behaved; '~fahrt *f* (-/*no pl.*) welfare; public assistance; '~ge-fallen *n* (-s/*no pl.*) pleasure; *sein* ~ *haben an* (*dat.*) take delight in; '♀gemeint *adj.* well-meant, well-intentioned; ♀gemut *adj.* ['~gə-mu:t] cheerful; '♀genährt *adj.* well-fed; '~geruch *m* scent, perfume; '♀gesinnt *adj.* well-disposed (*j-m* towards s.o.); '♀habend *adj.* well-to-do; '♀ig *adj.* comfortable, cosy, snug; '~klang *m* (-[e]s/*no pl.*) melodious sound, harmony; '♀-klingend *adj.* melodious, harmonious; '~laut *m s.* Wohlklang; '~leben *n* (-s/*no pl.*) luxury; '♀riechend *adj.* fragrant; '♀schmeckend *adj.* savo(u)ry; '~sein *n* well-being; good health; '~stand *m* (-[e]s/*no pl.*) prosperity, wealth; '~tat *f* kindness, charity; *fig.* comfort, treat; '~täter *m* benefactor; '♀tätig *adj.* charitable, beneficent; '~tä-tigkeit *f* charity; ♀tuend *adj.* ['~tu:-ənt] pleasant, comfortable; '~tun *v/i.* (*irr.* tun, *sep.*, -ge-, h) do good; '♀verdient *adj.* well-deserved; *f.* of great merit; '~wollen *n* (-s/*no pl.*) goodwill; benevolence; favo(u)r; '♀wollen *v/i.* (*sep.*, -ge-, h) be well-disposed (*j-m* towards s.o.)

wohn|en ['vo:nən] *v/i.* (ge-, h) live (*in dat.* in, at; *bei j-m* with s.o.); reside (in, at; with); '♀haus *n* dwelling-house; block of flats, *Am.* apartment house; '~haft *adj.* resident, living; '~lich *adj.* comfortable; cosy, snug; '~ort *m* dwelling-place, residence; *esp.* ⚕ domicile; '♀sitz *m* residence; *mit* ~ *in* resident in *or* at; *ohne festen* ~ without fixed abode; '♀ung *f* (-/-en) dwelling, habitation; flat, *Am.* apartment. 'Wohnungs|amt *n* housing office; '~not *f* housing shortage; '~pro-blem *n* housing problem. 'Wohn|wagen *m* caravan, trailer; '~zimmer *n* sitting-room, *esp. Am.* living room.

wölb|en ['vœlbən] *v/t.* (ge-, h) vault; arch; *sich* ~ arch; '♀ung *f* (-/-en) vault, arch; curvature.

Wolf *zo.* [vɔlf] *m* (-[e]s/-e) wolf.

Wolke ['vɔlkə] *f* (-/-n) cloud.

'Wolken|bruch *m* cloud-burst; '~kratzer *m* (-s/-) skyscraper; '♀los *adj.* cloudless.

'wolkig *adj.* cloudy, clouded.

Woll|decke ['vɔl-] *f* blanket; '~e *f* (-/-n) wool.

wollen¹ ['vɔlən] (h) **1.** *v/t.* (ge-) wish, desire; want; *lieber* ~ prefer; *nicht* ~ refuse; *er weiß, was er will* he knows his mind; **2.** *v/i.* (ge-): *ich will schon, aber* ... I want to, but ...; **3.** *v/aux.* (*no* -ge-) be willing, intend, be going to; be about to; *lieber* ~ prefer; *nicht* ~ refuse; *er hat nicht gehen* ~ he refused to go.

'woll|en² *adj.* [~] wool(l)en; '~ig *adj.* wool(l)y; '♀stoff *m* wool(l)en.

Wol|lust ['vɔlʊst] *f* (-/*e*) voluptuousness; ♀lüstig *adj.* ['~lystiç] voluptuous.

'Wollwaren *pl.* wool(l)en goods *pl.*

wo|mit *adv.* with what?, what ... with?; with which; '~möglich *adv.* perhaps, maybe.

Wonn|e ['vɔnə] *f* (-/-n) delight, bliss; '♀ig *adj.* delightful, blissful.

wo|ran *adv.* [vo·'ran]: ~ *denkst du?* what are you thinking of?; *ich weiß nicht,* ~ *ich mit ihm bin* I don't know what to make of him; ~ *liegt es, daß* ...? how is it that ...?; '~rauf *adv.* on what?, what ... on?; whereupon, after which; ~ *wartest du?* what are you waiting for?; '~raus *adv.* from what?; what ... of?; from which; '~rin *adv.* [~'rin] in what?; in which.

Wort [vɔrt] *n* **1.** (-[e]s/*e*er) word; *er kann seine Wörter noch nicht* he hasn't learnt his words yet; **2.** (-[e]s/-e) word; term, expression; *ums* ~ *bitten* ask permission to speak; *das* ~ *ergreifen* begin to speak; *parl.* rise to speak, address the House, *esp. Am.* take the floor; *das* ~ *führen* be the spokesman; ~ *halten* keep one's word; '♀brüchig *adj.*: *er ist* ~ *geworden* he has broken his word. 'Wörter|buch *n* dictionary; '~verzeichnis *n* vocabulary, list of words.

'Wort|führer *m* spokesman; '♀ge-treu *adj.* literal; '♀karg *adj.* taci-

W

turn; **∼klauberei** [∼klaubə'raɪ] *f* (-/-en) word-splitting; **'∼laut** *m* (-[e]s/*no pl.*) wording; text. [eral.\

wörtlich *adj.* ['vœrtlɪç] verbal, lit-\
'Wort|schatz *m* (-es/*no pl.*) vocabulary; **'∼schwall** *m* (-[e]s/*no pl.*) verbiage; **'∼spiel** *n* pun (*über acc.*, *mit* [up]on), play upon words; **'∼stellung** *gr. f* word order, order of words; **'∼stamm** *ling. m* stem; **'∼streit** *m*, **'∼wechsel** *m* dispute.

wo|rüber *adv.* [vo:'ry:bər] over *or* upon what?, what ... over *or* about *or* on?; over *or* upon which, about which; **∼rum** *adv.* [∼'rum] about what?, what ... about?; about *or* for which; **∼ handelt es sich?** what is it about?; **∼runter** *adv.* [∼'runtər] under *or* among what?, what ... under?; under *or* among which, among what; **∼'von** *adv.* of *or* from what?, what ... from *or* of?; about what?, what ... about?; of *or* from which; **∼'vor** *adv.* of what?, what ... of?; of which; **∼'zu** *adv.* for what?, what ... for?; for which.

Wrack [vrak] *n* (-[e]s/-e, -s) ⚓ wreck (*a. fig.*).

wrang [vraŋ] *pret. of* wringen.

wring|en ['vriŋən] *v/t.* (*irr.*, ge-, h) wring; **'∼maschine** *f* wringing-machine.

Wucher ['vu:xər] *m* (-s/*no pl.*) usury; **∼ treiben** practise usury; **'∼er** *m* (-s/-) usurer; **'∼gewinn** *m* excess profit; **'∼isch** *adj.* usurious; **'∼n** *v/i.* (ge-, h) grow exuberantly; **'∼ung** *f* (-/-en) ⚕ exuberant growth; ⚘ growth; **'∼zinsen** *m/pl.* usurious interest.

Wuchs [vu:ks] **1.** *m* (-es/*no pl.*) growth; figure, shape; stature. **2.** ♀ *pret. of* wachsen.

Wucht [vuxt] *f* (-/⚒-en) weight; force; **'⚒ig** *adj.* heavy.

Wühl|arbeit *fig.* ['vy:l-] *f* insidious agitation, subversive activity; **'⚒en** *v/i.* (ge-, h) dig; pig: root; *fig.* agitate; **∼ in** (*dat.*) rummage (about) in; **'∼er** *m* (-s/-) agitator.

Wulst [vulst] *m* (-es/⚒e), *f* (-/⚒e) pad; bulge; △ roll(-mo[u]lding); ⊕ bead; **'⚒ig** *adj. lips:* thick.

wund *adj.* [vunt] sore; **∼e Stelle** sore; **∼er Punkt** tender spot; **⚒e** ['∼də] *f* (-/-n) wound; *alte* **∼n wieder aufreißen** reopen old sores.

Wunder ['vundər] *n* (-s/-) miracle;

fig. a. wonder, marvel; **∼ wirken** pills, *etc.*: work marvels; **kein ∼,** *wenn man bedenkt* ... no wonder, considering ...; **'⚒bar** *adj.* miraculous; *fig. a.* wonderful, marvel-(l)ous; **'∼kind** *n* infant prodigy; **'⚒lich** *adj.* queer, odd; **'⚒n** *v/t.* (ge-, h) surprise, astonish; *sich* **∼** be surprised *or* astonished (*über acc.* at); **'⚒schön** *adj.* very beautiful; **'∼tat** *f* wonder, miracle; **'∼täter** *m* wonder-worker; **'⚒tätig** *adj.* wonder-working; **'⚒voll** *adj.* wonderful; **'∼werk** *n* marvel, wonder.

'Wund|fieber *n* wound-fever; **'∼starrkrampf** ⚕ *m* tetanus.

Wunsch [vunʃ] *m* (-es/⚒e) wish, desire; request; *auf* **∼** by *or* on request; *if desired; nach* **∼** as desired; *mit den besten Wünschen zum Fest* with the compliments of the season.

Wünschelrute ['vynʃəl-] *f* divining-rod, dowsing-rod; **∼ngänger** ['∼gɛŋər] *m* (-s/-) diviner, dowser.

wünschen ['vynʃən] *v/t.* (ge-, h) wish, desire; *wie Sie* **∼** as you wish; *was* **∼** *Sie?* what can I do for you?; **'∼swert** *adj.* desirable.

'wunsch|gemäß *adv.* as requested *or* desired, according to one's wishes; **'⚒zettel** *m* list of wishes.

wurde ['vurdə] *pret. of* werden.

Würde ['vyrdə] *f* (-/-n) dignity; *unter seiner* **∼** beneath one's dignity; **'⚒los** *adj.* undignified; **'∼nträger** *m* dignitary; **'⚒voll** *adj.* dignified; grave.

'würdig *adj.* worthy (*gen.* of); dignified; grave; **∼en** ['∼gən] *v/t.* (ge-, h) appreciate, value; mention hono(u)rably; laud, praise; *j-n keines Blickes* **∼** ignore s.o. completely; **⚒ung** ['∼guŋ] *f* (-/-en) appreciation, valuation.

Wurf [vurf] *m* (-[e]s/⚒e) throw, cast; *zo.* litter.

Würfel ['vyrfəl] *m* (-s/-) die; cube (*a.* Å); **'∼becher** *m* dice-box; **'⚒n** *v/i.* (ge-, h) (play) dice; **'∼spiel** *n* game of dice; **'∼zucker** *m* lump sugar. [tile.\

'Wurfgeschoß *n* missile, projec-\
würgen ['vyrgən] (ge-, h) **1.** *v/t.* choke, strangle; **2.** *v/i.* choke; retch.

Wurm *zo.* [vurm] *m* (-[e]s/⚒er) worm; **'⚒en** F *v/t.* (ge-, h) vex; rankle (*j-n* in s.o.'s mind); **'⚒stichig** *adj.* worm-eaten.

W

Wurst [vurst] *f* (-/ⁱⁱe) sausage; F *das ist mir ganz ~* I don't care a rap.

Würstchen ['vyrstçən] *n* (-s/-) sausage; *heißes ~* hot sausage, *Am.* hot dog.

Würze ['vyrtsə] *f* (-/-n) seasoning, flavo(u)r; spice, condiment; *fig.* salt.

Wurzel ['vurtsəl] *f* (-/-n) root (*a. gr.*, Å); *~ schlagen* strike or take root (*a. fig.*); '**2n** *v/i.* (ge-, h) (strike or take) root; *~ in* (*dat.*) take one's root in, be rooted in.

'würz|en *v/t.* (ge-, h) spice, season, flavo(u)r; '**~ig** *adj.* spicy, well-seasoned, aromatic.

wusch [vuʃ] *pret. of* waschen.

wußte ['vustə] *pret. of* wissen.

Wust F [vu:st] *m* (-es/no *pl.*) tangled mass; rubbish; mess.

wüst *adj.* [vy:st] desert, waste; confused; wild, dissolute; rude; '**2e** *f* (-/-n) desert, waste; **2ling** ['ˌlɪŋ] *m* (-s/-e) debauchee, libertine, rake.

Wut [vu:t] *f* (-/no *pl.*) rage, fury; *in ~* in a rage; '**~anfall** *m* fit of rage.

wüten ['vy:tən] *v/i.* (ge-, h) rage (*a. fig.*); '**~d** *adj.* furious, enraged (*über acc.* at; *auf acc.* with), *esp. Am.* F a. mad (*über acc.*, *auf acc.* at).

Wüterich ['vy:təriç] *m* (-[e]s/-e) berserker; bloodthirsty man. [rage.]

'wutschnaubend *adj.* foaming with

X, Y

X-Beine ['ɪks-] *n/pl.* knock-knees *pl.*; '**X-beinig** *adj.* knock-kneed.

x-beliebig *adj.* [ɪksbə'li:biç] any (... you please); *jede(r, -s) ~e ...* any ...

x-mal *adv.* ['ɪks-] many times, *sl.* umpteen times.

X-Strahlen ['ɪks-] *m/pl.* X-rays *pl.*

x-te *adj.* ['ɪkstə] *zum ~n Male* for the umpteenth time.

Xylophon ♪ [ksylo'fo:n] *n* (-s/-e) xylophone.

Yacht ⚓ [jaxt] *f* (-/-en) yacht.

Z

Zacke ['tsakə] *f* (-/-n) s. Zacken.

'Zacken 1. *m* (-s/-) (sharp) point; prong; tooth (*of comb, saw, rake*); jag (*of rock*); **2.** ♀ *v/t.* (ge-, h) indent, notch; jag.

'zackig *adj.* indented, notched; *rock:* jagged; pointed; ⚔ F *fig.* smart.

zaghaft *adj.* ['tsa:khaft] timid; '**2ig-keit** *f* (-/no *pl.*) timidity.

zäh *adj.* [tsɛ:] tough, tenacious (*both a. fig.*); *liquid:* viscid, viscous; *fig.* dogged; '**~flüssig** *adj.* viscid, viscous, sticky; '**2igkeit** *f* (-/no *pl.*) toughness, tenacity (*both a. fig.*); viscosity; *fig.* doggedness.

Zahl [tsa:l] *f* (-/-en) number; figure; cipher; '**2bar** *adj.* payable.

'zählbar *adj.* countable.

zahlen ['tsa:lən] (ge-, h) **1.** *v/i.* pay; *at restaurant: ~* (, *bitte*)! the bill, please!, *Am.* the check, please!; **2.** *v/t.* pay.

zählen ['tsɛ:lən] (ge-, h) **1.** *v/t.* count; number; *~ zu* count or number among; **2.** *v/i.* count; *~ auf* (*acc.*) count up)on, rely (up)on.

'Zahlen|lotto *n* s. Lotto; '**2mäßig 1.** *adj.* numerical; **2.** *adv.: j-m ~ überlegen sein* outnumber s.o.

'Zähler *m* (-s/-) counter; Å numerator; *for gas, etc.:* meter.

'Zahl|karte *f* money-order form (*for paying direct into the postal cheque account*); '**2los** *adj.* numberless, innumerable, countless; '**~meister** ⚔ *m* paymaster; '**2reich 1.** *adj.* numerous; **2.** *adv.* in great number; '**~tag** *m* pay-day; '**~ung** *f* (-/-en) payment.

'Zählung *f* (-/-en) counting.

'Zahlungs|anweisung *f* order to pay; '**~aufforderung** *f* request for payment; '**~bedingungen** *f/pl.* terms *pl.* of payment; '**~befehl** *m* order to pay; '**~einstellung** *f* suspension of payment; '**Ɂfähig** adj. solvent; '**fähigkeit** f solvency; '**frist** f term for payment; '**mittel** n currency; gesetzliches ~ legal tender; '**schwierigkeiten** f/pl.; '**termin** m date of payment; '**Ɂunfähig** adj. insolvent; '**unfähigkeit** f insolvency.

'**Zahlwort** gr. n (-[e]s/ᵘer) numeral.

zahm adj. [tsɑːm] tame (a. fig.), domestic(ated).

zähm|en ['tsɛːmən] v/t. (ge-, h) tame (a. fig.), domesticate; '**Ɂung** f (-/ᵗ-en) taming (a. fig.), domestication.

Zahn [tsɑːn] m (-[e]s/ᵘe) tooth; ⊕ tooth, cog; Zähne bekommen cut one's teeth; '**arzt** m dentist, dental surgeon; '**bürste** f toothbrush; '**creme** f tooth-paste; '**Ɂen** v/i. (ge-, h) teethe, cut one's teeth; '**ersatz** ⚕ m fáule ['ˌfɔylə] f (-/no pl.) dental caries; '**fleisch** n gums pl.; '**füllung** f filling, stopping; '**geschwür** ⚕ n gumboil; '**heilkunde** f dentistry; 'Ɂ**los** adj. toothless; '**lücke** f gap between the teeth; **pasta** ['ˌpastaɪ] f (-/Zahnpasten); '**paste** f tooth-paste; '**rad** ⊕ n cog-wheel; '**radbahn** f rack-railway; '**schmerzen** m/pl. toothache; '**stocher** m (-s/-) toothpick.

Zange ['tsaŋə] f (-/-n) (e-e a pair of) tongs pl. or pliers pl. or pincers pl.; ⚕, zo. forceps sg., pl.

Zank [tsaŋk] m (-[e]s/no pl.) quarrel, F row; '**apfel** m bone of contention; 'Ɂ**en** (ge-, h) **1.** v/i. scold (mit j-m s.o.); **2.** v/refl. quarrel, wrangle.

zänkisch adj. ['tsɛŋkɪʃ] quarrelsome.

Zäpfchen ['tsɛpfçən] n (-s/-) small peg; anat. uvula.

Zapfen ['tsapfən] **1.** m (-s/-). plug, peg, pin; bung (of barrel); pivot; ♀ cone; **2.** Ɂ v/t. (ge-, h) tap; '**streich** ✕ m tattoo, retreat, Am. a. taps pl.

'**Zapf|hahn** m tap, Am. faucet; '**säule** mot. f petrol pump.

zappel|ig adj. ['tsapəlɪç] fidgety; '**n** v/i. (ge-, h) struggle; fidget.

zart adj. [tsɑːrt] tender; soft; gentle; delicate; '**fühlend** adj. delicate; '**gefühl** n (-[e]s/no pl.) delicacy (of feeling).

zärtlich adj. ['tsɛːrtlɪç] tender; fond, loving; 'Ɂ**keit** f **1.** (-/no pl.) tenderness; fondness; **2.** (-/-en) caress.

Zauber ['tsaubər] m (-s/-) spell, charm, magic (all a. fig.); fig.: enchantment; glamo(u)r; '**ei** [~ˈraɪ] f (-/-en) magic, sorcery; witchcraft; conjuring; '**er** m (-s/-) sorcerer, magician; conjurer; '**flöte** f magic flute; '**formel** f spell; 'Ɂ**haft** adj. magic(al); fig. enchanting; '**in** f (-/-nen) sorceress, witch; fig. enchantress; '**kraft** f magic power; '**kunststück** n conjuring trick; 'Ɂ**n** (ge-, h) **1.** v/i. practise magic or witchcraft; do conjuring tricks; **2.** v/t. conjure; '**spruch** m spell; '**stab** m (magic) wand; '**wort** n (-[e]s/-e) magic word, spell.

zaudern ['tsaudərn] v/i. (ge-, h) hesitate; linger, delay.

Zaum [tsaum] m (-[e]s/ᵘe) bridle; im ~ halten keep in check.

zäumen ['tsɔymən] v/t. (ge-, h) bridle.

'**Zaumzeug** n bridle.

Zaun [tsaun] m (-[e]s/ᵘe) fence; '**gast** m deadhead; '**könig** orn. m wren; '**pfahl** m pale.

Zebra zo. ['tseːbra] n (-s/-s) zebra; '**streifen** m zebra crossing.

Zech|e ['tsɛçə] f (-/-n) score, reckoning, bill; ✕ mine; coal-pit, colliery; F die ~ bezahlen foot the bill, F stand treat; 'Ɂ**en** v/i. (ge-, h) carouse, tipple; '**gelage** n carousal, carouse; '**preller** m (-s/-) bilk(er).

Zeh [tseː] m (-[e]s/-en), '**e** f (-/-n) toe; '**enspitze** f point or tip of the toe; auf ~n on tiptoe.

zehn adj. [tseːn] ten; 'Ɂ**er** m (-s/-) ten; coin: F ten-pfennig piece; '**fach** adj. ['~fax] tenfold; '**jährig** adj. ['~jɛːrɪç] ten-year-old, of ten (years); 'Ɂ**kampf** m sports: decathlon; '**mal** adv. ten times; '**te** ['~tə] **1.** adj. tenth; **2.** ♀ † m (-n/-n) tithe; Ɂ**tel** ['~təl] n (-s/-) tenth (part); '**tens** adv. ['~təns] tenthly.

zehren ['tseːrən] v/i. (ge-, h) make thin; ~ von live on s.th.; fig. live off (the capital); ~ an prey (up)on (one's mind); undermine (one's health).

Zeichen ['tsaɪçən] n (-s/-) sign; token; mark; indication, symptom;

signal; zum ~ (gen.) in sign of, as a sign of; '~**block** m drawing-block; '~**brett** n drawing-board; '~**lehrer** m drawing-master; '~**papier** n drawing-paper; '~**setzung** gr. f (-/no pl.) punctuation; '~**sprache** f sign-language; '~**stift** m pencil, crayon; '~**trickfilm** m animation, animated cartoon; '~**unterricht** m drawing-lessons pl.

zeichn|en ['tsaɪçnən] (ge-, h) **1.** v/t. draw (plan, etc.); design (pattern); mark; sign; subscribe (sum of money) (zu to); subscribe for (shares); **2.** v/i. draw; sie zeichnet gut she draws well; '**2er** m (-s/-) draftsman, draughtsman; designer; subscriber (gen. for shares); '**2ung** f (-/-en) drawing; design; illustration; zo. marking (of skin, etc.); subscription.

Zeige|finger ['tsaɪgə-] m forefinger, index (finger); '**2n** (ge-, h) **1.** v/t. show; point out; indicate; demonstrate; sich ~ appear; **2.** v/i.: ~ auf (acc.) point at; ~ nach point to; '~**r** m (-s/-) hand (of clock, etc.); pointer (of dial, etc.); '~**stock** m pointer.

Zeile ['tsaɪlə] f (-/-n) line; row; j-m ein paar ~n schreiben drop s.o. a line or a few lines. [siskin.]

Zeisig orn. ['tsaɪzɪç] m (-[e]s/-e)]

Zeit [tsaɪt] f (-/-en) time; epoch, era, age; period, space (of time); term; freie ~ spare time; mit der ~ in the course of time; von ~ zu ~ from time to time; vor langer ~ long ago, a long time ago; zur ~ (gen.) in the time of; at (the) present; zu meiner ~ in my time; zu s-r ~ in due course (of time); das hat ~ there is plenty of time for that; es ist höchste ~ it is high time; j-m ~ lassen give s.o. time; laß dir ~! take your time!; sich die ~ vertreiben pass the time, kill time. '**Zeit|abschnitt** m epoch, period; '~**alter** n age; '~**angabe** f exact date and hour; date; '~**aufnahme** phot. f time-exposure; '~**dauer** f length of time, period (of time); '~**enfolge** gr. f sequence of tenses; '~**geist** m (-es/no pl.) spirit of the time(s), zeitgeist; '2**gemäß** adj. modern, up-to-date; '~**genosse** m contemporary; 2**genössisch** adj. ['~gənœsɪʃ] contemporary; '~**geschichte** f contemporary history;

'~**gewinn** m gain of time; '2**ig** **1.** adj. early; **2.** adv. on time; '~**karte** f season-ticket, Am. commutation ticket; '~**lang** f: e-e ~ for some time, for a while; '2**lebens** adv. for life, all one's life; '2**lich** **1.** adj. temporal; **2.** adv. as to time; ~ zusammenfallen coincide; '2**los** adj. timeless; '~**lupe** phot. f slow motion; '~**lupenaufnahme** phot.f slow-motion picture; '2**nah** adj. current, up-to-date; '~**ordnung** f chronological order; '~**punkt** m moment; time; date; '~**rafferaufnahme** phot. f time-lapse photography; '2**raubend** adj. time-consuming; pred. a. taking up much time; '~**raum** m space (of time), period; '~**rechnung** f chronology; era; '~**schrift** f journal, periodical, magazine; review; '~**tafel** f chronological table.

'**Zeitung** f (-/-en) (news)paper, journal.

'**Zeitungs|abonnement** n subscription to a paper; '~**artikel** m newspaper article; '~**ausschnitt** m (press or newspaper) cutting, (Am. only) (newspaper) clipping; ~**kiosk** ['~kiɔsk] m (-[e]s/-e) news-stand; '~**notiz** f press item; '~**papier** n newsprint; '~**verkäufer** m newsvendor; news-boy, news-man; '~**wesen** n journalism, the press.

'**Zeit|verlust** m loss of time; '~**verschwendung** f waste of time; '~**vertreib** ['~fɛrtraɪp] m (-[e]s/-e) pastime; zum ~ to pass the time; '2**weilig** adj. ['~vaɪlɪç] temporary; '2**weise** adv. for a time; at times, occasionally; '~**wort** gr. n (-[e]s/ᵉer) verb; '~**zeichen** n time-signal.

Zell|e ['tsɛlə] f (-/-n) cell; '~**stoff** m, ~**ulose** ⊕ [~u'lo:zə] f (-/-n) cellulose.

Zelt [tsɛlt] n (-[e]s/-e) tent; '2**en** v/i. (ge-, h) camp; '~**leinwand** f canvas; '~**platz** m camping-ground.

Zement [tse'mɛnt] m (-[e]s/-e) cement; 2**ieren** [~'ti:rən] v/t. (no -ge-, h) cement. [(a. fig.).]

Zenit [tse'ni:t] m (-[e]s/no pl.) zenith]

zens|ieren [tsɛn'zi:rən] v/t. (no -ge-, h) censor (book, etc.); at school: mark, Am. a. grade; '2**or** ['~ɔr] m (-s/-en) censor; 2**ur** [~'zu:r] f **1.** (-/no pl.) censorship; **2.** (-/-en) at school: mark, Am. a. grade;

Z

(school) report, *Am.* report card.

Zentimeter [tsɛnti'-] *n*, *m* centi-met|re, *Am.* -er.

Zentner ['tsɛntnər] *m* (-s/-) (*Brt. appr.*) hundredweight.

zentral *adj.* [tsɛn'trɑːl] central; Qe (-/-n) central office; *teleph.* (telephone) exchange, *Am. a.* central; Qheizung *f* central heating.

Zentrum ['tsɛntrum] *n* (-s/Zentren) cent|re, *Am.* -er. [*Am.* -er.]

Zepter ['tsɛptər] *n* (-s/-) scept|re,

zer'beißen [tsɛr'-] *v/t.* (*irr.* beißen, *no* -ge-, *h*) bite to pieces; ~'bersten *v/i.* (*irr.* bersten, *no* -ge-, *sein*) burst asunder.

zer'brech|en (*irr.* brechen, *no* -ge-) **1.** *v/t.* (*h*) break (to pieces); *sich den Kopf* ~ rack one's brains; **2.** *v/i.* (*sein*) break; ~lich *adj.* breakable, fragile.

zer'bröckeln *v/t.* (*h*) *and v/i.* (*sein*) (*no* -ge-) crumble; ~'drücken *v/t.* (*no* -ge-, *h*) crush; crease (*dress*).

Zeremon|ie [tseremo'niː, ~'moːnjə] *f* (-/-n) ceremony; Qiell *adj.* [~o'njɛl] ceremonial; ~iell [~o'njɛl] *n* (-s/-e) ceremonial.

zer'fahren *adj.* road: rutted; *p.*: flighty, giddy; scatter-brained; absent-minded.

Zer'fall *m* (-[e]s/*no pl.*) ruin, decay; disintegration; Qen *v/i.* (*irr.* fallen, *no* -ge-, *sein*) fall to pieces; decay; disintegrate; *in mehrere Teile* ~ fall into several parts.

zer'fetzen *v/t.* (*no* -ge-, *h*) tear in or to pieces; ~'fleischen *v/t.* (*no* -ge-, *h*) mangle, lacerate; ~'fließen *v/i.* (*irr.* fließen, *no* -ge-, *sein*) melt (away); ink, *etc.*: run; ~'fressen *v/t.* (*irr.* fressen, *no* -ge-, *h*) eat away; 🜍 corrode; ~'gehen *v/i.* (*irr.* gehen, *no* -ge-, *sein*) melt, dissolve; ~'gliedern *v/t.* (*no* -ge-, *h*) dismember; *anat.* dissect; *fig.* analy|se, *Am.* -ze; ~'hacken *v/t.* (*no* -ge-, *h*) cut in(to) pieces; mince; chop (up) (*wood, meat*); ~'kauen *v/t.* (*no* -ge-, *h*) chew; ~'kleinern *v/t.* (*no* -ge-, *h*) mince (*meat*); chop up (*wood*); grind.

zer'knirsch|t *adj.* contrite; Qung *f* (-/🜍 -en) contrition.

zer'knittern *v/t.* (*no* -ge-, *h*) (c)rumple, wrinkle, crease; ~'knüllen *v/t.* (*no* -ge-, *h*) crumple up (*sheet of paper*); ~'kratzen *v/t.* (*no* -ge-, *h*) scratch; ~'krümeln *v/t.* (*no* -ge-, *h*) crumble; ~'lassen *v/t.* (*irr.* lassen, *no* -ge-, *h*) melt; ~'legen *v/t.* (*no* -ge-, *h*) take apart *or* to pieces; carve (*joint*); 🜍, *gr.*, *fig.* analy|se, *Am.* -ze; ~'lumpt *adj.* ragged, tattered; ~'mahlen *v/t.* (*irr.* mahlen, *no* -ge-, *h*) grind; ~'malmen [~'malmən] *v/t.* (*no* -ge-, *h*) crush; crunch; ~'mürben *v/t.* (*no* -ge-, *h*) wear down *or* out; ~'platzen *v/i.* (*no* -ge-, *sein*) burst; explode; ~'quetschen *v/t.* (*no* -ge-, *h*) crush, squash; mash (*esp. potatoes*).

Zerrbild ['tsɛr-] *n* caricature.

zer'reiben *v/t.* (*irr.* reiben, *no* -ge-, *h*) rub to powder, grind down, pulverize; ~'reißen (*irr.* reißen, *no* -ge-) **1.** *v/t.* (*h*) tear, rip up; *in Stücke* ~ tear to pieces; **2.** *v/i.* (*sein*) tear; *rope, string:* break.

zerren ['tsɛrən] (*ge-, h*) **1.** *v/t.* tug, pull; drag; 🜎 strain; **2.** *v/i.*: ~ *an* (*dat.*) pull at.

zer'rinnen *v/i.* (*irr.* rinnen, *no* -ge-, *sein*) melt away; *fig.* vanish.

'Zerrung 🜎 *f* (-/-en) strain.

zer'rütt|en [tsɛr'rytən] *v/t.* (*no* -ge-, *h*) derange, unsettle; disorganize; ruin, shatter (*one's health or nerves*); wreck (*marriage*); ~'sägen *v/t.* (*no* -ge-, *h*) saw up; ~schellen [~'ʃɛlən] *v/i.* (*no* -ge-, *sein*) be dashed *or* smashed; ⚓ be wrecked; ✈ crash; ~'schlagen **1.** *v/t.* (*irr.* schlagen, *no* -ge-, *h*) break *or* smash (to pieces); *sich* ~ come to nothing; **2.** *adj.* battered; *fig.* knocked up; ~'schmettern *v/t.* (*no* -ge-, *h*) smash, dash, shatter; ~'schneiden *v/t.* (*irr.* schneiden, *no* -ge-, *h*) cut in two; cut up, cut to pieces.

zer'setz|en *v/t. and v/refl.* (*no* -ge-, *h*) decompose; Qung *f* (-/🜎 -en) decomposition.

zer'spalten *v/t.* ([*irr.* spalten,] *no* -ge-, *h*) cleave, split; ~'splittern (*no* -ge-) **1.** *v/t.* (*h*) split (up), splinter; fritter away (*one's energy, etc.*); **2.** *v/i.* (*sein*) split (up), splinter; ~'sprengen *v/t.* (*no* -ge-, *h*) burst (*asunder*); disperse (*crowd*); ~'springen *v/i.* (*irr.* springen, *no* -ge-, *sein*) burst; *glass:* crack; *mein Kopf zerspringt mir* I've got a splitting headache; ~'stampfen *v/t.* (*no* -ge-, *h*) crush; pound.

Z

zer'stäub|en *v/t.* (*no* -ge-, *h*) spray; **2er** *m* (-s/-) sprayer, atomizer.
zer'stör|en *v/t.* (*no* -ge-, *h*) destroy; **2er** *m* (-s/-) destroyer (*a.* ⚓); **2ung** *f* destruction.
zer'streu|en *v/t.* (*no* -ge-, *h*) disperse, scatter; dissipate (*doubt, etc.*); *fig.* divert; *sich* ~ disperse, scatter; *fig.* amuse o.s.; **~t** *fig. adj.* absent(-minded); **2theit** *f* (-/-en) absent-mindedness; **2ung** *f* **1.** (-/-en) dispersion; diversion, amusement; **2.** *phys.* (-/*no pl.*) dispersion (*of light*).
zerstückeln [tsɛr'ʃtykəln] *v/t.* (*no* -ge-, *h*) cut up, cut (in)to pieces; dismember (*body, etc.*).
zer|'teilen *v/t. and v/refl.* (*no* -ge-, *h*) divide (*in acc.* into); **~'trennen** *v/t.* (*no* -ge-, *h*) rip (up) (*dress*); **~'treten** *v/t.* (*irr. treten, no* -ge-, *h*) tread down; crush; tread *or* stamp out (*fire*); **~'trümmern** *v/t.* (*no* -ge-, *h*) smash.
Zerwürfnis [tsɛr'vyrfnis] *n* (-ses/-se) dissension, discord.
Zettel ['tsɛtəl] *m* (-s/-) slip (of paper), scrap of paper; note; ticket; label, sticker; tag; *s. Anschlagzettel*; *s. Theaterzettel*; **'~kartei** *f*, **'~kasten** *m* card index.
Zeug [tsɔʏk] *n* (-[e]s/-e) stuff (*a. fig. contp.*), material; cloth; tools *pl.*; things *pl.*
Zeuge ['tsɔʏgə] *m* (-n/-n) witness; **'2n** (ge-, *h*) **1.** *v/i.* witness; ⚖ give evidence; *für* (*gegen, von*) *et.* ~ testify for (against, of) s.th.; ~ *von* be evidence of, bespeak (*courage, etc.*); **2.** *v/t.* beget.
'Zeugen|aussage ⚖ *f* testimony, evidence; **'~bank** *f* (-/-e) witness-box, *Am.* witness stand.
Zeugin ['tsɔʏgin] *f* (-/-nen) (female) witness.
Zeugnis ['tsɔʏknis] *n* (-ses/-se) ⚖ testimony, evidence; certificate; (school) report, *Am.* report card.
Zeugung ['tsɔʏguŋ] *f* (-/-en) procreation; **'2sfähig** *adj.* capable of begetting; **'~skraft** *f* generative power; **2sunfähig** *adj.* ['tsɔʏguŋs?-] impotent.
Zick|lein *zo.* ['tsiklaɪn] *n* (-s/-) kid; **~zack** ['~tsak] *m* (-[e]s/-e) zigzag; *im* ~ *fahren etc.* zigzag.
Ziege *zo.* ['tsi:gə] *f* (-/-n) (she-)goat, nanny(-goat).
Ziegel ['tsi:gəl] *m* (-s/-) brick; tile (*of roof*); **'~dach** *n* tiled roof; **~ei** [~'laɪ] *f* (-/-en) brickworks *sg., pl.*, brickyard; **'~stein** *m* brick.
'Ziegen|bock *zo. m* he-goat; **'~fell** *n* goatskin; **'~hirt** *m* goatherd; **'~leder** *n* kid(-leather); **'~peter** ⚕ *m* (-s/-) mumps.
Ziehbrunnen ['tsi:-] *m* draw-well.
ziehen ['tsi:ən] (*irr.*, ge-) **1.** *v/t.* (*h*) pull, draw; draw (*line, weapon, lots, conclusion, etc.*); drag; ⚘ cultivate; *zo.* breed; take off (*hat*); dig (*ditch*); draw, extract (*tooth*); ⩘ extract (*root of number*); *Blasen* ~ ⚕ raise blisters; *e-n Vergleich* ~ draw *or* make a comparison; *j-n ins Vertrauen* ~ take s.o. into one's confidence; *in Erwägung* ~ take into consideration; *in die Länge* ~ draw out; *fig.* protract; *Nutzen* ~ *aus* derive profit *or* benefit from; *an sich* ~ draw to one; *Aufmerksamkeit etc. auf sich* ~ attract attention, *etc.*; *et. nach sich* ~ entail *or* involve s.th.; **2.** *v/i.* (*h*) pull (*an dat.* at); *chimney, cigar, etc.*: draw; puff (*an e-r Zigarre* at a cigar); *tea*: infuse, draw; *play*: draw (large audiences); F ✝ *goods*: draw (customers), take; *es zieht* there is a draught, *Am.* there is a draft; **3.** *v/i.* (*sein*) move, go; march; (re)move (*nach* to); *birds*: migrate; **4.** *v/refl.* (*h*) extend, stretch, run; *wood*: warp; *sich in die Länge* ~ drag on.
'Zieh|harmonika ♪ *f* accordion; **'~ung** *f* (-/-en) drawing (of lots).
Ziel [tsi:l] *n* (-[e]s/-e) aim (*a. fig.*); mark; *sports*: winning-post, goal (*a. fig.*); target; ⚔ objective; destination (*of voyage*); *fig.* end, purpose, target, object(ive); term; *sein* ~ *erreichen* gain one's end(s *pl.*); *über das* ~ *hinausschießen* overshoot the mark; *zum* ~*e führen* succeed, be successful; *sich zum* ~ *setzen zu inf.* aim at *ger.*, *Am.* aim to *inf.*; **'~band** *n sports*: tape; **'2bewußt** *adj.* purposeful; **'2en** *v/i.* (ge-, *h*) (take) aim (*auf acc.* at); **'~fernrohr** *n* telescopic sight; **'2los** *adj.* aimless, purposeless; **'~scheibe** *f* target, butt; ~ *des Spottes* butt *or* target (of derision); **'2strebig** *adj.* purposive.
ziemlich ['tsi:mliç] **1.** *adj.* fair, tolerable; considerable; **2.** *adv.*

pretty, fairly, tolerably, rather; about.

Zier [tsi:r] f (-/no pl.), **~de** ['~də] f (-/-n) ornament; fig. a. hono(u)r (für to); **'2en** v/t. (ge-, h) ornament, adorn; decorate; sich ~ be affected; esp. of woman: be prudish; refuse; **'2lich** adj. delicate; neat; graceful, elegant; **'~lichkeit** f (-/~-en) delicacy; neatness; gracefulness, elegance; **~pflanze** f ornamental plant.

Ziffer ['tsifər] f (-/-n) figure, digit; **'~blatt** n dial(-plate), face.

Zigarette [tsiga'retə] f (-/-n) cigaret(te); **~automat** [~n²-] m cigarette slot-machine; **~netui** [~n²-] n cigarette-case; **~spitze** f cigarette-holder; **~stummel** m stub, Am. a. butt.

Zigarre [tsi'garə] f (-/-n) cigar.

Zigeuner [tsi'gɔynər] m (-s/-), **~in** f (-/-nen) gipsy, gypsy.

Zimmer ['tsimər] n (-s/-) room; apartment; **'~antenne** f radio, etc.: indoor aerial, Am. a. indoor antenna; **'~einrichtung** f furniture; **'~flucht** f suite (of rooms); **'~mädchen** n chamber-maid; **'~mann** m (-[e]s/Zimmerleute) carpenter; **'2n** (ge-, h) **1.** v/t. carpenter; fig. frame; **2.** v/i. carpenter; **'~pflanze** f indoor plant; **'~vermieterin** f (-/-nen) landlady. [prudish; affected.]

zimperlich adj. ['tsimpərliç] prim;]

Zimt [tsimt] m (-[e]s/-e) cinnamon.

Zink ⚗ [tsiŋk] n (-[e]s/no pl.) zinc; **'~blech** n sheet zinc.

Zinke ['tsiŋkə] f (-/-n) prong, tooth (of comb or fork); **'~n** m (-s/-) s. Zinke.

Zinn ⚗ [tsin] n (-[e]s/no pl.) tin.

Zinne ['tsinə] f (-/-n) 🏰 pinnacle; ✕ battlement.

Zinnober [tsi'no:bər] m (-s/-) cinnabar; **2rot** adj. vermilion.

Zins [tsins] m (-es/-e) rent; tribute; mst **~en** pl. interest; **~en tragen** yield or bear interest; **2bringend** adj. bearing interest; **~eszins** ['~əs-] m compound interest; **'2frei** adj. rent-free; free of interest; **'~fuß** m, **'~satz** m rate of interest.

Zipf|el ['tsipfəl] m (-s/-) tip, point, end; corner (of handkerchief, etc.); lappet (of garment); **'2elig** adj. having points or ends; **'~elmütze** f jelly-bag cap; nightcap.

Zirkel ['tsirkəl] m (-s/-) circle (a fig.); ⚭ (ein a pair of) compasses pl. or dividers pl.

zirkulieren [tsirku'li:rən] v/i. (no -ge-, h) circulate.

Zirkus ['tsirkus] m (-/-se) circus.

zirpen ['tsirpən] v/i. (ge-, h) chirp, cheep.

zisch|eln ['tsiʃəln] v/t. and v/i. (ge-, h) whisper; **'~en** v/i. (ge-, h) hiss; whiz(z).

ziselieren [tsize'li:rən] v/t. (no -ge-, h) chase.

Zit|at [tsi'ta:t] n (-[e]s/-e) quotation; **2ieren** [~'ti:rən] v/t. (no -ge-, h) summon; quote.

Zitrone [tsi'tro:nə] f (-/-n) lemon; **~nlimonade** f lemonade; lemon squash; **~npresse** f lemon-squeezer; **~nsaft** m lemon juice.

zittern ['tsitərn] v/i. (ge-, h) tremble, shake (vor dat. with).

zivil [tsi'vi:l] **1.** adj. civil; civilian; price: reasonable; **2.** ♀ n (-s/no pl.) civilians pl.; s. Zivilkleidung; **2bevölkerung** f civilian population, civilians pl.; **2isation** [~iliza'tsjo:n] f (-/~-en) civilization; **~isieren** [~ili'zi:rən] v/t. (no -ge-, h) civilize; **2ist** [~i'list] m (-en/-en) civilian; **2kleidung** f civilian or plain clothes pl.

Zofe ['tso:fə] f (-/-n) lady's maid.

zog [tso:k] pret. of ziehen.

zögern ['tsø:gərn] **1.** v/i. (ge-, h) hesitate; linger; delay; **2.** ♀ n (-s/no pl.) hesitation; delay.

Zögling ['tsø:kliŋ] m (-s/-e) pupil.

Zoll [tsɔl] m **1.** (-[e]s/-) inch; **2.** (-[e]s/⁻e) customs pl., duty; the Customs pl.; **'~abfertigung** f customs clearance; **'~amt** n customhouse; **'~beamte** m customs officer; **'~behörde** f the Customs pl.; **'~erklärung** f customs declaration; **2frei** adj. duty-free; **'~kontrolle** f customs examination; **2pflichtig** adj. liable to duty; **'~stock** m footrule; **'~tarif** m tariff.

Zone ['tso:nə] f (-/-n) zone.

Zoo [tso:] m (-s/-s) zoo.

Zoolog|e [tsoʔo'lo:gə] m (-n/-n) zoologist; **~ie** [~o'gi:] f (-/no pl.) zoology; **2isch** adj. [~'lo:giʃ] zoological.

Zopf [tsɔpf] m (-[e]s/⁻e) plait, tress; pigtail; alter ~ antiquated ways pl. or custom.

orn [tsɔrn] *m* (-[e]s/*no pl.*) anger;
'2ig *adj.* angry (auf j-n with s.o.;
auf et. at s.th.).

ote ['tsoːtə] *f* (-/-n) filthy *or*
smutty joke, obscenity.

ottel ['tsɔtəl] *f* (-/-n) tuft (of hair);
tassel; '2(e)lig *adj.* shaggy.

u [tsu:] **1.** *prp.* (*dat.*) *direction:* to,
towards, up to; at, in; on; in addition to, along with; *purpose:* for;
~ Beginn at the beginning *or* out-
set; ~ Weihnachten at Christmas;
zum ersten Mal for the first time;
~ e-m ... Preise at a ... price; ~
meinem Erstaunen to my surprise; ~
Tausenden by thousands; ~ Wasser by water; ~ zweien by twos;
zum Beispiel for example; **2.** *adv.*
too; *direction:* towards, to; F closed,
shut; *with inf.:* to; ich habe ~
arbeiten I have to work.

zubauen *v/t.* (*sep.*, -ge-, h) build
up *or* in; block.

'Zubehör ['tsuːbəhøːr] *n, m* (-[e]s/-e)
appurtenances *pl.*, fittings *pl.*, *Am.*
F fixings *pl.*; *esp.* ⊕ accessories *pl.*

zubereit|en *v/t.* (*sep.*, *no* -ge-, h)
prepare; '2ung *f* preparation.

'zu|billigen *v/t.* (*sep.*, -ge-, h)
grant; '~binden *v/t.* (*irr.* binden,
sep., -ge-, h) tie up; '~blinzeln *v/i.*
(*sep.*, -ge-, h) wink at s.o.; '~brin-
gen *v/t.* (*irr.* bringen, *sep.*, -ge-, h)
pass, spend (*time*).

Zucht [tsuxt] *f* **1.** (-/*no pl.*) discipline; breeding, rearing; *rearing* of
bees, *etc.:* culture; ♀ cultivation;
2. (-/-en) breed, race; '~bulle *zo.*
m bull (for breeding).

zücht|en ['tsyçtən] *v/t.* (ge-, h) breed
(*animals*), grow, cultivate (*plants*);
'2er *m* (-s/-) breeder (*of animals*);
grower (*of plants*).

Zucht|haus *n* penitentiary; *punish-
ment:* penal servitude; ~häusler
['~hɔyslər] *m* (-s/-) convict; '~-
hengst *zo. m* stud-horse, stallion.

züchtig *adj.* ['tsyçtiç] chaste, modest; ~en ['~gən] *v/t.* (ge-, h) flog.

zucht|los *adj.* undisciplined; '2lo-
sigkeit *f* (-/~) want of discipline;
'2stute *zo. f* brood-mare.

zucken ['tsukən] *v/i.* (ge-, h) jerk;
move convulsively, twitch (*all:* mit
et. s.th.); *with pain:* wince;
lightning: flash.

zücken ['tsykən] *v/t.* (ge-, h) draw
(*sword*); F pull out (*purse, pencil*).

Zucker ['tsukər] *m* (-s/*no pl.*) sugar;
'~dose *f* sugar-basin, *Am.* sugar
bowl; '~erbse ♀ *f* green pea; '~guß
m icing, frosting; '~hut *m* sugar-
loaf; '2ig *adj.* sugary; '2krank *adj.*
diabetic; '2n *v/t.* (ge-, h) sugar;
'~rohr ♀ *n* sugar-cane; '~rübe ♀ *f*
sugar-beet; '2süß *adj.* (as) sweet
as sugar; '~wasser *n* sugared
water; '~zange ⊕ *f* (e-e a pair of)
sugar-tongs *pl.*

zuckrig *adj.* ['tsukriç] sugary.

'Zuckung ✗ *f* (-/-en) convulsion.

'zudecken *v/t.* (*sep.*, -ge-, h) cover
(up).

zudem *adv.* [tsu'deːm] besides,
moreover.

'zu|drehen *v/t.* (*sep.*, -ge-, h) turn
off (*tap*); j-m den Rücken ~ turn
one's back on s.o.; '~dringlich
adj. importunate, obtrusive; '~-
drücken *v/t.* (*sep.*, -ge-, h) close,
shut; '~erkennen *v/t.* (*irr.* kennen,
sep., *no* -ge-, h) award (*a.* ⚖);
adjudge (*dat.* to) (*a.* ⚖).

zuerst *adv.* [tsu'-] first (of all); at
first; er kam ~ an he was the first
to arrive.

'zufahr|en *v/i.* (*irr.* fahren, *sep.*, -ge-,
sein) drive on; ~ auf (*acc.*) drive to
(-wards); *fig.* rush at s.o.; '2t approach; drive, *Am.* driveway;
'2tsstraße *f* approach (road).

'Zufall *m* chance, accident; durch ~
by chance, by accident; '2en *v/i.*
(*irr.* fallen, *sep.*, -ge-, sein) *eyes:*
be closing (with sleep); *door:* shut
(of) itself; j-m ~ fall to s.o.('s share).

'zufällig **1.** *adj.* accidental; *attr.*
chance; casual; **2.** *adv.* accidentally,
by chance.

'zufassen *v/i.* (*sep.*, -ge-, h) seize
(hold of) s.th.; (mit) ~ lend *or* give
a hand.

'Zuflucht *f* (-/~ *⸚*e) refuge, shelter,
resort; s-e ~ nehmen zu have recourse to s.th., take refuge in s.th.

'Zufluß *m* afflux; influx (*a.* †);
affluent, tributary (*of river*); †
supply.

'zuflüstern *v/t.* (*sep.*, -ge-, h): j-m
et. ~ whisper s.th. to s.o.

zufolge *prp.* (*gen.*; *dat.*) [tsu'fɔlgə]
according to.

zufrieden *adj.* [tsu'-] content(ed),
satisfied; 2heit *f* (-/*no pl.*) content-
ment, satisfaction; '~lassen *v/t.* (*irr.*
lassen, *sep.*, -ge-, h) let s.o. alone;

Z

~stellen v/t. (sep., -ge-, h) satisfy; **2stellend** adj. satisfactory.

'zu|frieren v/i. (irr. frieren, sep., -ge-, sein) freeze up or over; **'~fügen** v/t. (sep., -ge-, h) add; do, cause; inflict (wound, etc.) (j-m [up]on s.o.); **2fuhr** ['~fu:r] f (-/-en) supply; supplies pl.; influx; **'~führen** v/t. (sep., -ge-, h) carry, lead, bring; ⊕ feed; supply (a. ⊕).

Zug [tsu:k] m (-[e]s/≈e) draw(ing), pull(ing); ⊕ traction; ⚔ expedition, campaign; procession; migration (of birds); drift (of clouds); range (of mountains); 🚂 train; feature; trait (of character); bent, tendency, trend; draught, Am. draft (of air); at chess: move; drinking: draught, Am. draft; at cigarette, etc.: puff.

'Zu|gabe f addition; extra; thea. encore; **'~gang** m entrance; access; approach; **2gänglich** adj. ['~gεŋliç] accessible (für to); **'2geben** v/t. (irr. geben, sep., -ge-, h) add; fig.: allow; confess; admit.

zugegen adj. [tsu'-] present (bei at.).

'zugehen v/i. (irr. gehen, sep., -ge-, sein) door, etc.: close, shut; p. move on, walk faster; happen; auf j-n ~ go up to s.o., move or walk towards s.o.

'Zugehörigkeit f (-/no pl.) membership (zu to) (society, etc.); belonging (to).

Zügel ['tsy:gəl] m (-s/-) rein; bridle (a. fig.); **2los** adj. unbridled; fig.: unrestrained; licentious; **2n** v/t. (ge-, h) rein (in); fig. bridle, check.

'Zuge|ständnis n concession; **'2stehen** v/t. (irr. stehen, sep., -ge-, h) concede.

'zugetan adj. attached (dat. to).

'Zugführer 🚂 m guard, Am. conductor.   [-ge-, h) add.\

'zugießen v/t. (irr. gießen, sep.,\

zug|ig adj. ['tsu:giç] draughty, Am. drafty; **2kraft** ['~k-] f ⊕ traction; fig. attraction, draw, appeal; **~kräftig** adj. ['~k-]: ~ sein be a draw.

zugleich adv. [tsu'-] at the same time; together.

'Zug|luft f (-/no pl.) draught, Am. draft; **'~maschine** f traction-engine, tractor; **'~pflaster** 💊 n blister.

'zu|greifen v/i. (irr. greifen, sep., -ge-, h) grasp or grab at s.th.; at

table: help o.s.; lend a hand **'2griff** m grip, clutch.

zugrunde adv. [tsu'grundə]: ~ gehen perish; ~ richten ruin.

'Zugtier n draught animal, Am. draft animal.

zu|gunsten prp. (gen.) [tsu'gunstən] in favo(u)r of; **~'gute** adv.: j-m et. ~ halten give s.o. credit for s.th.; ~ kommen be for the benefit (dat.).

'Zugvogel m bird of passage. [of.]

'zuhalten v/t. (irr. halten, sep., -ge-h) hold (door) to; sich die Ohren ~ stop one's ears.   [home.]

Zuhause [tsu'hauzə] n (-/no pl.)

'zu|heilen v/i. (sep., -ge-, sein) heal up, skin over; **'~hören** v/i. (sep. -ge-, h) listen (dat. to).

'Zuhörer m hearer, listener; ~ pl audience; **'~schaft** f (-/♀ -en) audience.

'zu|jubeln v/i. (sep., -ge-, h) cheer **'~kleben** v/t. (sep., -ge-, h) paste or glue up; gum (letter) down; **'~knallen** v/t. (sep., -ge-, h) bang slam (door, etc.); **'~knöpfen** v/t (sep., -ge-, h) button (up); **'~kommen** v/i. (irr. kommen, sep., -ge-sein): auf j-n ~ come up to s.o.; j-m ~ be due to s.o.; j-m et. ~ lassen let s.o. have s.th.; send s.o. s.th.; **'~korken** v/t. (sep., -ge-, h) cork (up).

Zu|kunft ['tsu:kunft] f (-/no pl.) future; gr. future (tense); **2künftig** 1. adj. future; ~er Vater father-to-be; 2. adv. in future.

'zu|lächeln v/i. (sep., -ge-, h) smile at or (up)on; **2lage** f extra pay, increase; rise, Am. raise (in salary or wages); **'~langen** v/i. (sep., -ge-, h) at table: help o.s.; **'~lassen** v/t. (irr. lassen, sep., -ge-, h) leave (door) shut; keep closed; fig.: admit s.o.; license; allow, suffer; admit of (only one interpretation, etc.); **'~lässig** adj. admissible, allowable; **2lassung** f (-/-en) admission; permission; licen[ce, Am. -se.

'zulegen v/t. (sep., -ge-, h) add; F sich et. ~ get o.s. s.th.

zuleide adv. [tsu'laidə]: j-m et. ~ tun do s.o. harm, harm or hurt s.o.

'zuleiten v/t. (sep., -ge-, h) let in (water, etc.); conduct to; pass on to s.o.

zu|letzt adv. [tsu'-] finally, at last; er kam ~ an he was the last to

Z

arrive; **⁓'liebe** adv.: j-m ⁓ for s.o.'s sake.

zum prp. [tsum] = zu dem.

zumachen v/t. (sep., -ge-, h) close, shut; button (up) (coat); fasten.

zumal cj. [tsu'-] especially, particularly.   [up.]

zumauern v/t. (sep., -ge-, h) wall.

zumut|en ['tsu:mu:tən] v/t. (sep., -ge-, h): j-m et. ⁓ expect s.th. of s.o.; sich zuviel ⁓ overtask o.s., overtax one's strength, etc.; **ℒung** f (-/-en) exacting demand, exaction; fig. impudence.

zunächst [tsu'-] **1.** prp. (dat.) next to; **2.** adv. first of all; for the present.

zu|nageln v/t. (sep., -ge-, h) nail up; **⁓nähen** v/t. (sep., -ge-, h) sew up; **ℒnahme** ['⁓nɑ:mə] f (-/-n) increase, growth; **ℒname** m surname.

zünden ['tsyndən] v/t. (ge-, h) kindle; esp. mot. ignite; fig. arouse enthusiasm.

Zünd|holz ['tsynt-] n match; '**⁓kerze** mot. f spark(ing)-plug, Am. spark plug; '**⁓schlüssel** mot. m ignition key; '**⁓schnur** f fuse; '**⁓stoff** fig. m fuel; **⁓ung** mot. ['⁓duŋ] f (-/-en) ignition.

zunehmen v/i. (irr. nehmen, sep., -ge-, h) increase (an dat. in); grow; put on weight; moon: wax; days: grow longer.

zuneig|en (sep., -ge-, h) **1.** v/i. incline to(wards); **2.** v/refl. incline to(wards); sich dem Ende ⁓ draw to a close; **ℒung** f (-/⁓ -en) affection.

Zunft [tsunft] f (-/⁓e) guild, corporation.

Zunge ['tsuŋə] f (-/-n) tongue.

züngeln ['tsyŋəln] v/i. (ge-, h) play with its tongue; flame: lick.

zungen|fertig adj. voluble; '**ℒfertigkeit** f (-/no pl.) volubility; '**ℒspitze** f tip of the tongue.

zunichte adv. [tsu'niçtə]: ⁓ machen or werden bring or come to nothing.

zunicken v/i. (sep., -ge-, h) nod to.

zunutze adv. [tsu'nutsə]: sich et. ⁓ machen turn s.th. to account, utilize s.th.; **⁓'oberst** adv. at the top, uppermost.

zupfen ['tsupfən] (ge-, h) **1.** v/t. pull, tug, twitch; **2.** v/i. pull, tug, twitch (all: an dat. at).

zur prp. [tsu:r] = zu der.

'zurechnungsfähig adj. of sound mind; ⚖ responsible; '**ℒkeit** ⚖ f (-/no pl.) responsibility.

zurecht|finden [tsu'-] v/refl. (irr. finden, sep., -ge-, h) find one's way; **⁓kommen** v/i. (irr. kommen, sep., -ge-, sein) arrive in time; ⁓ (mit) get on (well) (with); manage s.th.; **⁓legen** v/t. (sep., -ge-, h) arrange; sich e-e Sache ⁓ think s.th. out; **⁓machen** F v/t. (sep., -ge-, h) get ready, prepare, Am. F fix; adapt (für to, for purpose); sich ⁓ of woman: make (o.s.) up; **⁓weisen** v/t. (irr. weisen, sep., -ge-, h) reprimand; **ℒweisung** f reprimand.

'zu|reden v/i. (sep., -ge-, h): j-m ⁓ try to persuade s.o.; encourage s.o.; **⁓reiten** v/t. (irr. reiten, sep., -ge-, h) break in; '**⁓riegeln** v/t. (sep., -ge-, h) bolt (up).

zürnen ['tsyrnən] v/i. (ge-, h) be angry (j-m with s.o.).

zurück adv. [tsu'ryk] back; backward(s); behind; **⁓behalten** v/t. (irr. halten, sep., no -ge-, h) keep back, retain; **⁓bekommen** v/t. (irr. kommen, sep., no -ge-, h) get back; **⁓bleiben** v/i. (irr. bleiben, sep., -ge-, sein) remain or stay behind; fall behind, lag; **⁓blicken** v/i. (sep., -ge-, h) look back; **⁓bringen** v/t. (irr. bringen, sep., -ge-, h) bring back; **⁓datieren** v/t. (sep., no -ge-, h) date back, antedate; **⁓drängen** v/t. (sep., -ge-, h) push back; fig. repress; **⁓erobern** v/t. (sep., no -ge-, h) reconquer; **⁓erstatten** v/t. (sep., no -ge-, h) restore, return; refund (expenses); **⁓fahren** (irr. fahren, sep., -ge-) **1.** v/i. (sein) drive back; fig. start; **2.** v/t. (sein) drive back; **⁓fordern** v/t. (sep., -ge-, h) reclaim; **⁓führen** v/t. (sep., -ge-, h) lead back; ⁓ auf (acc.) reduce to (rule, etc.); refer to (cause, etc.); **⁓geben** v/t. (irr. geben, sep., -ge-, h) give back, return, restore; **⁓gehen** v/i. (irr. gehen, sep., -ge-, sein) go back; return; **⁓gezogen** adj. retired; **⁓greifen** fig. v/i. (irr. greifen, sep., -ge-, h): ⁓ auf (acc.) fall back (up)on; **⁓halten** (irr. halten, sep., -ge-, h) **1.** v/t. hold back; **2.** v/i.: ⁓ mit keep back; **⁓haltend** adj. reserved; **ℒhaltung** f (-/⁓ -en) reserve; **⁓kehren** v/i. (sep., -ge-, sein) return; **⁓kommen**

v/i. (*irr.* kommen, *sep.*, -ge-, *sein*) come back; return (*fig.* auf *acc.* to); **~lassen** *v/t.* (*irr.* lassen, *sep.*, *h*) leave (behind); **~legen** *v/t.* (*sep.*, -ge-, *h*) lay aside; cover (*distance*, *way*); **~nehmen** *v/t.* (*irr.* nehmen, *sep.*, -ge-, *h*) take back; withdraw, retract (*words, etc.*); **~prallen** *v/i.* (*sep.*, -ge-, *sein*) rebound; start; **~rufen** *v/t.* (*irr.* rufen, *sep.*, -ge-, *h*) call back; *sich ins Gedächtnis* ~ recall; **~schicken** *v/t.* (*sep.*, -ge-, *h*) send back; **~schlagen** (*irr.* schlagen, *sep.*, -ge-, *h*) 1. *v/t.* drive (*ball*) back; repel (*enemy*); turn down (*blanket*); 2. *v/i.* strike back; **~schrecken** *v/i.* (*sep.*, -ge-, *sein*) 1. (*irr.* schrecken) shrink back (*vor dat.* from *spectacle, etc.*); 2. shrink (*vor dat.* from *work, etc.*); **~setzen** *v/t.* (*sep.*, -ge-, *h*) put back; *fig.* slight, neglect; **~stellen** *v/t.* (*sep.*, -ge-, *h*) put back (*a. clock*); *fig.* defer, postpone; **~strahlen** *v/t.* (*sep.*, -ge-, *h*) reflect; **~streifen** *v/t.* (*sep.*, -ge-, *h*) turn *or* tuck up (*sleeve*); **~treten** *v/i.* (*irr.* treten, *sep.*, -ge-, *sein*) step *or* stand back; *fig.*: recede; resign; withdraw; **~weichen** *v/i.* (*irr.* weichen, *sep.*, -ge-, *sein*) fall back; recede (*a. fig.*); **~weisen** *v/t.* (*irr.* weisen, *sep.*, -ge-, *h*) decline, reject; repel (*attack*); **~zahlen** *v/t.* (*sep.*, -ge-, *h*) pay back (*a. fig.*); **~ziehen** (*irr.* ziehen, *sep.*, -ge-) 1. *v/t.* (*h*) draw back; *fig.* withdraw; *sich* ~ retire, withdraw; ✗ retreat; 2. *v/i.* (*sein*) move *or* march back.

'**Zuruf** *m* call; '2**en** *v/t.* (*irr.* rufen, *sep.*, -ge-, *h*) call (out), shout (*j-m et.* s.th. to s.o.).

'**Zusage** *f* promise; assent; '2**en** (*sep.*, -ge-, *h*) 1. *v/t.* promise; 2. *v/i.*: promise to come; *j-m* ~ *food, etc.*: agree with s.o.; accept s.o.'s invitation; suit s.o.

zusammen *adv.* [tsu'zamən] together; at the same time; *alles* ~ (all) in all; ~ *betragen* amount to, total (up to); 2**arbeit** *f* (-/*no pl.*) co-operation; team-work; **~arbeiten** *v/i.* (*sep.*, -ge-, *h*) work together; co-operate; **~beißen** *v/t.* (*irr.* beißen, *sep.*, -ge-, *h*): *die Zähne* ~ set one's teeth; **~brechen** *v/i.* (*irr.* brechen, *sep.*, -ge-, *sein*) break down; collapse; 2**bruch** *m* breakdown; collapse; **~drücken** *v/t.*

(*sep.*, -ge-, *h*) compress, press together; **~fahren** *fig. v/i.* (*irr.* fahren, *sep.*, -ge-, *sein*) start (*bei* at; *vor dat* with); **~fallen** *v/i.* (*irr.* fallen, *sep.*, -ge-, *sein*) fall in, collapse; coincide ~**falten** *v/t.* (*sep.*, -ge-, *h*) fold up; **~fassen** *v/t.* (*sep.*, -ge-, *h*) summarize, sum up; 2**fassung** *f* (-/-en) summary; **~fügen** *v/t.* (*sep.*, -ge-, *h*) join (together); **~halten** (*irr.* halten, *sep.*, -ge-, *h*) 1. *v/t.* hold together; 2. *v/i.* hold together; *friends:* F stick together; 2**hang** *m* coherence, coherency, connection; context; **~hängen** (*sep.*, -ge-, *h*) 1. *v/i.* (*irr.* hängen) cohere; *fig.* be connected; 2. *v/t.* hang together; **~klappen** *v/t.* (*sep.*, -ge-, *h*) fold up; close (*clasp-knife*); **~kommen** *v/i.* (*irr.* kommen, *sep.*, -ge-, *sein*) meet; 2**kunft** [~kunft] *f* (-/̈e) meeting; **~laufen** *v/i.* (*irr.* laufen, *sep.*, -ge-, *sein*) run *or* crowd together; ✗ converge; *milk:* curdle; **~legen** *v/t.* (*sep.*, -ge-, *h*) lay together; fold up (*money*) (together); **~nehmen** *fig. v/t.* (*irr.* nehmen, *sep.*, -ge-, *h*) collect (*one's wits*); *sich* ~ be on one's good behavio(u)r; pull o.s. together; **~packen** *v/t.* (*sep.*, -ge-, *h*) pack up; **~passen** *v/i.* (*sep.*, -ge-, *h*) match, harmonize; **~rechnen** *v/t.* (*sep.*, -ge-, *h*) add up; **~reißen** F *v/refl.* (*irr.* reißen, *sep.*, -ge-, *h*) pull o.s. together; **~rollen** *v/t. and v/refl.* (*sep.*, -ge-, *h*) coil (up); **~rotten** *v/refl.* (*sep.*, -ge-, *h*) band together; **~rücken** (*sep.*, -ge-) 1. *v/t.* (*h*) move together; 2. *v/i.* (*sein*) close up; **~schlagen** (*irr.* schlagen, *sep.*, -ge-) 1. *v/t.* (*h*) clap (*hands*) (together); F smash to pieces; beat *s.o.* up; 2. *v/i.* (*sein*): ~ *über* (*dat.*) close over; **~schließen** *v/refl.* (*irr.* schließen, *sep.*, -ge-, *h*) join; unite; 2**schluß** *m* union; **~schrumpfen** *v/i.* (*sep.*, -ge-, *sein*) shrivel (up), shrink; **~setzen** *v/t.* (*sep.*, -ge-, *h*) put together; compose; compound (*a.* ⌐, *word*); ⊕ assemble; *sich* ~ *aus* consist of; 2**setzung** *f* (-/-en) composition; compound; ⊕ assembly; **~stellen** *v/t.* (*sep.*, -ge-, *h*) put together; compile; combine; 2**stoß** *m* collision (*a. fig.*); ✗ encounter; *fig.* clash; **~stoßen** *v/i.* (*irr.* stoßen, *sep.*, -ge-, *sein*) collide (*a. fig.*); adjoin; *fig.* clash;

Z

~ mit knock (heads, etc.) together; ~stürzen v/i. (sep., -ge-, sein) collapse; house, etc.: fall in; ~tragen v/t. (irr. tragen, sep., -ge-, h) collect; compile (notes); ~treffen v/i. (irr. treffen, sep., -ge-, sein) meet; coincide; 2treffen n (-s/no pl.) meeting; encounter (of enemies); coincidence; ~treten v/i. (irr. treten, sep., -ge-, sein) meet; parl. a. convene; ~wirken v/i. (sep., -ge-, h) co-operate; 2wirken n (-s/no pl.) co-operation; ~zählen v/t. (sep., -ge-, h) add up, count up; ~ziehen v/t. (irr. ziehen, sep., -ge-, h) draw together; contract; concentrate (troops); sich ~ contract.

'Zusatz m addition; admixture, metall. alloy; supplement.

zusätzlich adj. ['tsu:zetslɪç] additional.

'zuschau|en v/i. (sep., -ge-, h) look on (e-r Sache at s.th.); j-m ~ watch s.o. (bei et. doing s.th.); '2er m (-s/-) spectator, looker-on, onlooker; '2erraum thea. m auditorium.

'zuschicken v/t. (sep., -ge-, h) send (dat. to); mail; consign (goods).

'Zuschlag m addition; extra charge; excess fare; ⚓ surcharge; at auction: knocking down; 2en ['~gən] (irr. schlagen, sep., -ge-) 1. v/i. (h) strike; 2. v/i. (sein) door: slam (to); 3. v/t. (h) bang, slam (door) (to); at auction: knock down (dat. to).

'zu|schließen v/t. (irr. schließen, sep., -ge-, h) lock (up); ~schnallen v/t. (sep., -ge-, h) buckle (up); '~schnappen (sep., -ge-) 1. v/i. (h) dog: snap; 2. v/i. (sein) door: snap to; ~schneiden v/t. (irr. schneiden, sep., -ge-, h) cut up; cut (suit) (to size); '2schnitt m (-[e]s/✧-e) cut; style; '~schnüren v/t. (sep., -ge-, h) lace up; cord up) '~schrauben v/t. (sep., -ge-, h) screw up or tight; '~schreiben v/t. (irr. schreiben, sep., -ge-, h): j-m et. ~ ascribe or attribute s.th. to s.o.; '2schrift f letter.

zuschulden adv. [tsu'~]: sich et. ~ kommen lassen make o.s. guilty of s.th.

'Zu|schuß m allowance; subsidy, grant (of government); '2schütten v/t. (sep., -ge-, h) fill up (ditch); F add; '2sehen v/i. (irr. sehen, sep., -ge-, h) s. zuschauen; ~, daß see (to

it) that; 2sehends adv. ['~ts] visibly; '2senden v/t. ([irr. senden,] sep., -ge-, h) s. zuschicken; '2setzen (sep., -ge-, h) 1. v/t. add; lose (money); 2. v/i. lose money; j-m ~ press s.o. hard.

'zusicher|n v/t. (sep., -ge-, h): j-m et. ~ assure s.o. of s.th.; promise s.o. s.th.; '2ung f promise, assurance.

'zu|spielen v/t. (sep., -ge-, h) sports: pass (ball) (dat. to) '~spitzen v/t. (sep., -ge-, h) point; sich ~ taper (off); fig. come to a crisis; '2spruch m (-[e]s/no pl.) encouragement; consolation; ✝ custom; '2stand m condition, state; in gutem ~ house: in good repair.

zustande adv. [tsu'ʃtandə]: ~ bringen bring about; ~ kommen come about; nicht ~ kommen not to come off.   [(-/-en) competence.)

'zuständig adj. competent; '2keit f)

zustatten adv. [tsu'ʃtatn]: j-m ~ kommen be useful to s.o.

'zustehen v/i. (irr. stehen, sep., -ge-, h) be due (dat. to).

'zustell|en v/t. (sep., -ge-, h) deliver (a. ✉); ⚖ serve (j-m on s.o.); '2ung f delivery; ⚖ service.

'zustimm|en v/i. (sep., -ge-, h) agree (dat.: to s.th.; with s.o.); consent (to s.th.); '2ung f consent.

'zustoßen fig. v/i. (irr. stoßen, sep., -ge-, sein): j-m ~ happen to s.o.

zutage adv. [tsu'ta:gə]: ~ treten come to light.

Zutaten ['tsu:ta:tən] f/pl. ingredients pl. (of food); trimmings pl. (of dress).   [fall to s.o.'s share.)

zuteil adv. [tsu'taɪl]: j-m ~ werden)

'zuteil|en v/t. (sep., -ge-, h) allot, apportion; '2ung f allotment, apportionment; ration.

'zutragen v/refl. (irr. tragen, sep., -ge-, h) happen.

'zutrauen 1. v/t. (sep., -ge-, h): j-m et. ~ credit s.o. with s.th.; sich zuviel ~ overrate o.s.; 2. 2 n (-s/no pl.) confidence (zu in).

'zutraulich adj. confiding, trustful, trusting; animal: friendly, tame.

'zutreffen v/i. (irr. treffen, sep., -ge-, h) be right, be true; ~ auf (acc.) be true of; '~d adj. right, correct; applicable.

'zutrinken v/i. (irr. trinken, sep., -ge-, h): j-m ~ drink to s.o.

Z

Zutritt

38

'Zutritt m (-[e]s/no pl.) access; admission; ~ *verboten!* no admittance! [bottom.]

zuunterst adv. [tsu'-] right at the

zuverlässig adj. ['tsu:ferlɛsiç] reliable; certain; **'2keit** f (-/no pl.) reliability; certainty.

Zuversicht ['tsu:ferziçt] f (-/no pl.) confidence; **'2lich** adj. confident.

zuviel adv. [tsu'-] too much; e-r ~ one too many.

zuvor adv. [tsu'-] before, previously; first; **~kommen** v/i. (irr. kommen, sep., -ge-, sein): j-m ~ anticipate s.o.; e-r Sache ~ anticipate or prevent s.th.; **~kommend** adj. obliging; courteous.

Zuwachs ['tsu:vaks] m (-es/no pl.) increase; **'2en** v/i. (irr. wachsen, sep., -ge-, sein) become overgrown; wound: close.

zu|wege adv. [tsu've:gə]: ~ bringen bring about; **~weilen** adv. sometimes.

'zu|weisen v/t. (irr. weisen, sep., -ge-, h) assign; **~wenden** v/t. ([irr. wenden,] sep., -ge-, h) (dat.) turn to(wards); fig.: give; bestow on; sich ~ (dat.) turn to(wards).

zuwenig adv. [tsu'-] too little.

'zuwerfen v/t. (irr. werfen, sep., -ge-, h) fill up (pit); slam (door) (to); j-m ~ throw (ball, etc.) to s.o.; cast (look) at s.o.

zuwider prp. (dat.) [tsu'-] contrary to, against; repugnant, distasteful; **~handeln** v/i. (sep., -ge-, h) (dat.) act contrary or in opposition to; esp. ṭṭ contravene; **2handlung** ṭṭ f contravention.

'zu|winken v/i. (sep., -ge-, h) (dat.) wave to; beckon to; **~zahlen** v/t. (sep., -ge-, h) pay extra; **~zählen** v/t. (sep., -ge-, h) add; **~ziehen** (irr. ziehen, sep., -ge-) **1.** v/t. (h) draw together; draw (curtains); consult (doctor, etc.); sich ~ incur (s.o.'s displeasure, etc.); ṣ̌ catch (disease); **2.** v/i. (sein) move in; **~züglich** prp. (gen.) ['~tsy:k-] plus.

Zwang [tsvaŋ] **1.** m (-[e]s/ʽ̶e) compulsion, coercion; constraint; ṭṭ duress(e); force; sich ~ antun check or restrain o.s.; **2.** 2 pret. of zwingen.

zwängen ['tsvɛŋən] v/t. (sep.-, h) press, force.

'zwanglos fig. adj. free and easy,

informal; **'2igkeit** f (-/-en) ease informality.

'Zwangs|arbeit f hard labo(u)r **~jacke** f strait waistcoat or jacket **~lage** f embarrassing situation **2läufig** fig. adj. ['~lɔyf-] necessary **~maßnahme** f coercive measure **~vollstreckung** ṭṭ f distraint execution; **'~vorstellung** ṣ̌ obsession, hallucination; **2weise** adv. by force; **~wirtschaft** (-/ʽ̶-en) controlled economy.

zwanzig adj. ['tsvantsiç] twenty **~ste** adj. ['~stə] twentieth.

zwar cj. [tsva:r] indeed, it is true und ~ and that, that is.

Zweck [tsvɛk] m (-[e]s/-e) aim, end object, purpose; design; keinen ~ haben be of no use; s-n ~ erfüllen answer its purpose; zu dem ~ (gen. for the purpose of; **'2dienlich** adj serviceable, useful, expedient.

Zwecke ['tsvɛkə] f (-/-n) tack drawing-pin, Am. thumbtack.

'zweck|los adj. aimless, purposeless useless; **~mäßig** adj. expedient suitable; **'2mäßigkeit** f (-/no pl. expediency.

zwei adj. [tsvaɪ] two; **'~beinig** adj two-legged; **'2bettzimmer** n double (bedroom); **~deutig** adj. ['~dɔy-tiç] ambiguous; suggestive; **~erlei** adj. ['~ər'laɪ] of two kinds, two kinds of; **~fach** adj. ['~fax] double, twofold.

Zweifel ['tsvaɪfəl] m (-s/-) doubt; **2haft** adj. doubtful, dubious; **2los** adj. doubtless; **'2n** v/i. (ge-, h) doubt (an e-r Sache s.th.; an j-m s.o.).

Zweig [tsvaɪk] m (-[e]s/-e) branch (a. fig.); kleiner ~ twig; **'~geschäft** n, **'~niederlassung** f, **~stelle** f branch.

zwei|jährig adj. ['tsvaɪjɛːriç] two-year-old, of two (years); **'2kampf** m duel, single combat; **'~mal** adv. twice; **'~malig** adj. (twice) repeated; **~motorig** adj. ['~moto:riç] two-or twin-engined; **'~reihig** adj. having two rows; suit: double-breasted; **'~schneidig** adj. double-or two-edged (both a. fig.); **'~seitig** adj. two-sided; contract, etc.: bilateral; fabric: reversible; **2sitzer** esp. mot. m (-s/-) two-seater; **'~sprachig** adj. bilingual; **'~stimmig** adj. for two voices; **~stöckig**

adj. ['∿ʃtœkiç] two-stor|eyed, -ied; '∿**stufig** ⊕ *adj.* two-stage; ∿**stün-dig** *adj.* ['∿ʃtyndiç] of *or* lasting two hours, two-hour.

'**weit** *adj.* [tsvaıt] second; *ein* ∿*er* another; *aus* ∿*er Hand* second-hand; *zu* ∿ *by twos; wir sind zu* ∿ there are two of us.   [engine.\

Zweitaktmotor *mot. m* two-stroke\

zweit'best *adj.* second-best.

zweiteilig *adj. garment:* two-piece.

'**weitens** *adv.* [tsvaıtəns] secondly.

zweitklassig *adj.* second-class, second-rate.

Zwerchfell *anat.* ['tsverç-] *n* dia-phragm.

Zwerg [tsverk] *m* (-[e]s/-e) dwarf; **∿enhaft** *adj.* ['∿gən-] dwarfish.

Zwetsch(g)e ['tsvetʃ(g)ə] *f* (-/-n) plum.

Zwick|el ['tsvikəl] *m* (-s/-) *sewing:* gusset; '∿**en** *v/t. and v/i.* (ge-, h) pinch, nip; '∿**er** *m* (-s/-) (*ein a pair of*) eye-glasses *pl.*, pince-nez; '∿**mühle** *fig. f* dilemma, quandary, fix.

Zwieback ['tsvi:bak] *m* (-[e]s/∿e, -e) rusk, zwieback.

Zwiebel ['tsvi:bəl] *f* (-/-n) onion; bulb (*of flowers, etc.*).

Zwie|gespräch ['tsvi:-] *n* dialog(ue); '∿**licht** *n* (-[e]s/*no pl.*) twilight; '∿**spalt** *m* (-[e]s/-e, ∿e) disunion; conflict; **⒉spältig** *adj.* ['∿ʃpeltiç] disunited; *emotions:* conflicting; '∿**tracht** *f* (-/*no pl.*) discord.

Zwilling|e ['tsviliŋə] *m/pl.* twins *pl.*); '∿**sbruder** *m* twin brother; '∿**sschwester** *f* twin sister.

Zwinge ['tsviŋə] *f* (-/-n) ferrule (*of stick, etc.*); ⊕ clamp; '⒉**n** *v/t. (irr.,* ge-, h) compel, constrain; force; '⒉**nd** *adj.* forcible; *arguments:* cogent, compelling; *imperative:* '∿**r** *m* (-s/-) outer court; kennel(s *pl.*); bear-pit.

zwinkern ['tsviŋkərn] *v/i.* (ge-, h) wink, blink.

Zwirn [tsvirn] *m* (-[e]s/-e) thread, cotton; '∿**sfaden** *m* thread.

zwischen *prp. (dat.; acc.)* ['tsviʃən] between (*two*); among (*several*); '⒉**bilanz** † *f* interim balance; '⒉**deck** ⚓ *n* steerage; ∿**durch** F *adv.* in between; for a change; '⒉**ergebnis** *n* provisional result; '⒉**fall** *m* incident; '⒉**händler** *m* middleman; '⒉**landung** ✈ *f* inter-mediate landing, stop, *Am. a.* stop-over; (*Flug*) *ohne* ∿ non-stop (flight); '⒉**pause** *f* interval, intermission; '⒉**prüfung** *f* intermediate examina-tion; '⒉**raum** *m* space, interval; '⒉**ruf** *m* (loud) interruption; '⒉**spiel** *n* interlude; '∿**staatlich** *adj.* inter-national; *Am. between States:* inter-state; '⒉**station** *f* intermediate sta-tion; '⒉**stecker** ⚡ *m* adapter; '⒉**stück** *n* intermediate piece, con-nexion, (*Am. only*) connection; '⒉**stufe** *f* intermediate stage; '⒉**wand** *f* partition (wall); '⒉**zeit** *f* interval; *in der* ∿ in the meantime.

Zwist [tsvist] *m* (-es/-e), '∿**igkeit** *f* (-/-en) discord; disunion; quarrel.

zwitschern ['tsvitʃərn] *v/i.* (ge-, h) twitter, chirp.

Zwitter ['tsvitər] *m* (-s/-) hermaph-rodite.

zwölf *adj.* [tsvœlf] twelve; *um* ∿ (*Uhr*) at twelve (o'clock); (*um*) ∿ *Uhr mittags* (at) noon; (*um*) ∿ *Uhr nachts* (at) midnight; '⒉**fingerdarm** *anat. m* duodenum; '∿**te** *adj.* ['∿tə] twelfth.

Zyankali [tsyan'ka:li] *n* (-s/*no pl.*) potassium cyanide.

Zyklus ['tsy:klus, 'tsyk-] *m* (-/Zyklen) cycle; course, set (*of lectures, etc.*).

Zylind|er [tsi'lindər, tsy'-] *m* (-s/-) Å, ⊕ cylinder; chimney (*of lamp*); top hat; ⒉**risch** *adj.* [∿driʃ] cylindrical.

Zyni|ker ['tsy:nikər] *m* (-s/-) cynic; '⒉**isch** *adj.* cynical; ∿**smus** [tsy-'nismus] *m* (-/Zynismen) cynicism.

Zypresse ♀ [tsy'presə] *f* (-/-n) cypress.

Zyste ⚕ ['tsystə] *f* (-/-n) cyst.

PART II

ENGLISH-GERMAN
DICTIONARY

A

a [ə, *betont:* eɪ], *vor Vokal:* **an** [ən, *betont:* æn] *unbestimmter Artikel:* ein(e); per, pro, je; *not a(n)* kein(e); *all of a size* alle gleich groß; *£ 10 a year* zehn Pfund im Jahr; *twice a week* zweimal die od. in der Woche.

A 1 F ['eɪ'wʌn] Ia, prima.

a·back [ə'bæk]: *taken ~ fig.* überrascht, verblüfft; bestürzt.

a·ban·don [ə'bændən] auf-, preisgeben; verlassen; überlassen; **~ed:** *be found ~* verlassen aufgefunden werden (*Fahrzeug etc.*).

a·base [ə'beɪs] erniedrigen, demütigen; **~ment** [~mənt] Erniedrigung *f*, Demütigung *f*.

a·bashed [ə'bæʃt] verlegen.

a·bate [ə'beɪt] *v/t.* verringern; *Mißstand* abstellen; *v/i.* abnehmen, nachlassen; **~ment** [~mənt] Verminderung *f*; Abschaffung *f*.

ab·at·toir ['æbətwɑː] Schlachthof *m*.

ab·bess ['æbɪs] Äbtissin *f*.

ab·bey ['æbɪ] Kloster *n*; Abtei *f*.

ab·bot ['æbət] Abt *m*.

ab·bre·vi·ate [ə'briːvɪeɪt] (ab)kürzen; **~a·tion** [əbriːvɪ'eɪʃn] Abkürzung *f*, Kurzform *f*.

ABC ['eɪbiː'siː] Abc *n*, Alphabet *n*.

ABC weap·ons *pl.* ABC-Waffen *f/pl.*

ab·di·cate ['æbdɪkeɪt] *Amt, Recht etc.* aufgeben, verzichten auf (*acc.*); ~ (*from*) *the throne* abdanken; **~ca·tion** [æbdɪ'keɪʃn] Verzicht *m*; Abdankung *f*.

ab·do·men *anat.* ['æbdəmən] Unterleib *m*; **ab·dom·i·nal** *anat.* [æb'dɒmɪnl] Unterleibs...

ab·duct ਝਝ [æb'dʌkt] *j-n* entführen.

a·bet [ə'bet] (*-tt-*): *aid and ~* ਝਝ Beihilfe leisten (*dat.*); begünstigen; **~tor** [~ə] Anstifter *m*; (Helfers)Helfer *m*.

a·bey·ance [ə'beɪəns] Unentschiedenheit *f*; *in ~* in der Schwebe.

ab·hor [əb'hɔː] (*-rr-*) verabscheuen; **~rence** [əb'hɒrəns] Abscheu *m* (*of* vor *dat.*); **~rent** [~t] zuwider (*to* *dat.*); abstoßend.

a·bide [ə'baɪd] *v/i.: ~ by the law, etc.*

sich an das Gesetz *etc.* halten; *v/t.: I can't ~ him* ich kann ihn nicht ausstehen.

a·bil·i·ty [ə'bɪlətɪ] Fähigkeit *f*.

ab·ject □ ['æbdʒekt] verächtlich, erbärmlich; *in ~ poverty* in äußerster Armut.

ab·jure [əb'dʒʊə] abschwören; entsagen (*dat.*).

a·blaze [ə'bleɪz] in Flammen; *fig.* glänzend, funkelnd (*with* vor *dat.*).

a·ble □ ['eɪbl] fähig; geschickt; *be ~ to do* imstande sein zu tun; tun können; **~bod·ied** kräftig; *~ seaman* Vollmatrose *m*.

ab·nor·mal □ [æb'nɔːml] abnorm, ungewöhnlich; anomal.

a·board [ə'bɔːd] an Bord; *all ~!* ♣ alle Mann od. Reisenden an Bord!; 🚃 alles einsteigen!; *~ a bus* in e-m Bus; *go ~ a train* in e-n Zug einsteigen.

a·bode [ə'bəʊd] *a. place of ~* Aufenthaltsort *m*, Wohnsitz *m*; *of* (od. *with*) *no fixed ~* ohne festen Wohnsitz.

a·bol·ish [ə'bɒlɪʃ] abschaffen, aufheben.

ab·o·li·tion [æbə'lɪʃn] Abschaffung *f*, Aufhebung *f*; **~ist** *hist.* [~ʃənɪst] Gegner *m* der Sklaverei.

A-bomb ['eɪbɒm] = *atom(ic) bomb.*

a·bom·i·na·ble □ [ə'bɒmɪnəbl] abscheulich, scheußlich; **~nate** [~eɪt] verabscheuen; **~na·tion** [əbɒmɪ'neɪʃn] Abscheu *m*.

ab·o·rig·i·nal [æbə'rɪdʒənl] **1.** □ eingeboren, Ur...; **2.** Ureinwohner *m*; **~ne** [~niː] Ureinwohner *m* (*bsd. Australiens*).

a·bort [ə'bɔːt] ♀ e-e Fehlgeburt herbeiführen bei od. haben; *Raumflug etc.* abbrechen; *fig.* fehlschlagen, scheitern; **a·bor·tion** ♀ [~ʃn] Fehlgeburt *f*; Schwangerschaftsunterbrechung *f*, -abbruch *m*, Abtreibung *f*; *have an ~* abtreiben (lassen); **a·bor·tive** □ *fig.* [~ɪv] mißlungen, erfolglos.

a·bound [ə'baʊnd] reichlich vorhanden sein; Überfluß haben, reich sein (*in an dat.*); voll sein (*with* von).

a·bout [ə'baʊt] **1.** *prp.* um (...herum);

bei (*dat.*); (irgendwo) herum in (*dat.*); um, gegen, etwa; im Begriff, dabei; über (*acc.*); *I had no money ~ me* ich hatte kein Geld bei mir; *what are you ~?* was macht ihr da?; **2.** *adv.* herum, umher; in der Nähe; etwa, ungefähr.

a·bove [əˈbʌv] **1.** *prp.* über, oberhalb; *fig.* über, erhaben über; *~ all* vor allem; **2.** *adv.* oben; darüber; **3.** *adj.* obig, obenerwähnt.

a·breast [əˈbrest] nebeneinander; *keep od. be ~ of fig.* Schritt halten mit.

a·bridge [əˈbrɪdʒ] (ab-, ver)kürzen; **a·bridg(e)·ment** [~mənt] (Ab-, Ver)Kürzung *f*; Kurzfassung *f*; Abriß *m*.

a·broad [əˈbrɔːd] im *od.* ins Ausland; überall(hin); *the news soon spread ~* die Nachricht verbreitete sich rasch.

a·brupt □ [əˈbrʌpt] abrupt; jäh; zusammenhanglos; schroff.

ab·scess ⚕ [ˈæbsɪs] Abszeß *m*.

ab·scond [əbˈskɒnd] sich davonmachen.

ab·sence [ˈæbsəns] Abwesenheit *f*; Mangel *m*.

ab·sent 1. □ [ˈæbsənt] abwesend; fehlend; nicht vorhanden; *be ~* fehlen (*from school* in der Schule; *from work* am Arbeitsplatz); **2.** [æbˈsent]: *~ o.s. from* fernbleiben (*dat.*) *od.* von; **~·mind·ed** □ [ˈæbsəntˈmaɪndɪd] zerstreut, geistesabwesend.

ab·so·lute □ [ˈæbsəluːt] absolut; unumschränkt; vollkommen; ♫ rein, unvermischt; unbedingt.

ab·so·lu·tion *eccl.* [æbsəˈluːʃn] Absolution *f*.

ab·solve [əbˈzɒlv] frei-, lossprechen; △ *nicht absolvieren*.

ab·sorb [əbˈsɔːb] absorbieren, auf-, einsaugen; *fig.* ganz in Anspruch nehmen; **~·ing** *fig.* [~ɪŋ] fesselnd, packend.

ab·sorp·tion [əbˈsɔːpʃn] Absorption *f*; *fig.* Vertieftsein *n*.

ab·stain [əbˈsteɪn] sich enthalten (*from gen.*).

ab·ste·mi·ous □ [æbˈstiːmɪəs] enthaltsam; mäßig.

ab·sten·tion [əbˈstenʃn] Enthaltung *f*; *pol.* Stimmenthaltung *f*.

ab·sti·nence [ˈæbstɪnəns] Abstinenz *f*, Enthaltsamkeit *f*; **~·nent** □ [~t] abstinent, enthaltsam.

ab·stract 1. □ [ˈæbstrækt] abstrakt; **2.** [~] *das* Abstrakte; Auszug *m*; **3.** [æbˈstrækt] abstrahieren; entwenden; *e-n wichtigen Punkt aus e-m Buch etc.* herausziehen; **~·ed** □ *fig.* zerstreut; **ab·strac·tion** [~kʃn] Abstraktion *f*; abstrakter Begriff.

ab·struse □ [æbˈstruːs] dunkel, schwer verständlich.

ab·surd □ [əbˈsɜːd] absurd; lächerlich.

a·bun|dance [əˈbʌndəns] Überfluß *m*; Fülle *f*; Überschwang *m*; **~·dant** □ [~t] reich(lich).

a·buse 1. [əˈbjuːs] Mißbrauch *m*; Beschimpfung *f*; **2.** [~z] mißbrauchen; beschimpfen; **a·bu·sive** □ [~sɪv] ausfallend, Schimpf...

a·but [əˈbʌt] (*-tt-*) (an)grenzen (*on* an).

a·byss [əˈbɪs] Abgrund *m* (*a. fig.*).

ac·a·dem·ic [ækəˈdemɪk] **1.** Hochschullehrer *m*; △ *nicht Akademiker*; **2.** (*~ally*) akademisch; **a·cad·e·mi·cian** [əkædəˈmɪʃn] Akademiemitglied *n*; △ *nicht Akademiker*.

a·cad·e·my [əˈkædəmɪ] Akademie *f*; *~ of music* Musikhochschule *f*.

ac·cede [ækˈsiːd]: *~ to* zustimmen (*dat.*); *Amt* antreten; *Thron* besteigen.

ac·cel·e|rate [əkˈseləreɪt] *v/t.* beschleunigen; *v/i.* schneller werden, *mot. a.* beschleunigen, Gas geben; **~·ra·tion** [əkseləˈreɪʃn] Beschleunigung *f*; **~·ra·tor** [əkˈseləreɪtə] Gaspedal *n*.

ac·cent 1. [ˈæksənt] Akzent *m* (*a. gr.*); **2.** [ækˈsent] = **ac·cen·tu·ate** [ækˈsentjʊeɪt] akzentuieren, betonen.

ac·cept [əkˈsept] annehmen; akzeptieren; hinnehmen; **ac·cep·ta·ble** □ [~əbl] annehmbar; **~·ance** [~əns] Annahme *f*; Aufnahme *f*.

ac·cess [ˈækses] Zugang *m* (*to* zu); *fig.* Zutritt *m* (*to* bei, zu); *easy of ~* zugänglich (*Person*); *~ road* Zufahrtsstraße *f*; (Autobahn)Zubringerstraße *f*.

ac·ces·sa·ry ⚖ [əkˈsesərɪ] *s.* accessory 2 ⚖.

ac·ces|si·ble □ [əkˈsesəbl] (leicht) zugänglich; **~·sion** [~ʃn] Zuwachs *m*, Zunahme *f*; Antritt *m* (*e-s Amtes*); *~ to power* Machtübernahme *f*; *~ to the throne* Thronbesteigung *f*.

ac·ces·so·ry [əkˈsesərɪ] **1.** zusätzlich; **2.** ⚖ Kompli|ze *m*, -zin *f*, Mitschuldige(r m) f; mst accessories pl. Zubehör n, Mode a. Accessoires pl.; ⊕ Zubehör(teile pl.) n.

ac·ci·dent ['æksɪdənt] Zufall m; Un(glücks)fall m; by ~ zufällig; ~**den·tal** □ [æksɪ'dentl] zufällig; versehentlich.

ac·claim [ə'kleɪm] freudig begrüßen.

ac·cla·ma·tion [æklə'meɪʃn] lauter Beifall; Lob n.

ac·cli·ma·tize [ə'klaɪmətaɪz] (sich) akklimatisieren od. eingewöhnen.

ac·com·mo·date [ə'kɒmədeɪt] (sich) anpassen (to dat. od. an acc.); unterbringen, beherbergen; Platz haben für; j-m aushelfen (with mit Geld); ~**da·tion** [əkɒmə'deɪʃn] Anpassung f; Unterbringung f, (Platz m für) Unterkunft f, Quartier n.

ac·com·pa·ni·ment ♪ [ə'kʌmpənimənt] Begleitung f; ~**ny** [ə'kʌmpəni] begleiten (a. ♪); accompanied with verbunden mit.

ac·com·plice [ə'kʌmplɪs] Komplize m, -zin f.

ac·com·plish [ə'kʌmplɪʃ] vollenden; ausführen; Zweck erreichen; ~**ed** vollendet, perfekt; ~**ment** [~mənt] Vollendung f, Ausführung f; Fähigkeit f, Talent n.

ac·cord [ə'kɔːd] 1. Übereinstimmung f; △ nicht Akkord; of one's own ~ aus eigenem Antrieb; with one ~ einstimmig; 2. v/i. übereinstimmen; v/t. gewähren; ~**ance** [~əns] Übereinstimmung f; in ~ with laut (gen.), gemäß (dat.); ~**ant** [~t] übereinstimmend; ~**ing** [~ɪŋ]: ~ to gemäß (dat.), nach; ~**ing·ly** [~ɪŋli] (dem-)entsprechend.

ac·cost [ə'kɒst] j-n bsd. auf der Straße ansprechen.

ac·count [ə'kaʊnt] 1. econ. Rechnung f, Berechnung f; econ. Konto n; Rechenschaft f; Bericht m; by all ~s nach allem, was man so hört; of no ~ ohne Bedeutung; on no ~ auf keinen Fall; on ~ of wegen; take into ~, take ~ of in Betracht od. Erwägung ziehen, berücksichtigen; turn s.th. to (good) ~ et. (gut) ausnutzen; keep ~s die Bücher führen; call to ~ zur Rechenschaft ziehen; give (an) ~ of Rechenschaft ablegen über (acc.); give an ~ of Bericht erstatten über (acc.); 2. v/i.: ~ for Rechenschaft über et. ablegen; (sich) erklären; **ac·count·a·ble** □ [~əbl] verant-

wortlich; erklärlich; **ac·count·ant** [~ənt] Buchhalter m; ~**ing** [~ɪŋ] Buchführung f.

ac·cu·mu·late [ə'kjuːmjʊleɪt] (sich) (an)häufen od. ansammeln; ~**la·tion** [əkjuːmjʊ'leɪʃn] Ansammlung f.

ac·cu·ra·cy ['ækjʊrəsi] Genauigkeit f; ~**rate** □ [~rət] genau; richtig.

ac·cu·sa·tion [ækjuː'zeɪʃn] Anklage f; An-, Beschuldigung f.

ac·cu·sa·tive gr. [ə'kjuːzətɪv] a. ~ case Akkusativ m.

ac·cuse [ə'kjuːz] anklagen; beschuldigen; the ~d der od. die Angeklagte, die Angeklagten; **ac·cus·er** [~ə] Ankläger(in); **ac·cus·ing** □ [~ɪŋ] anklagend, vorwurfsvoll.

ac·cus·tom [ə'kʌstəm] gewöhnen (to an acc.); ~**ed** gewöhnt, üblich; gewöhnt (to an acc., zu inf.).

ace [eɪs] As n (a. fig.); have an ~ up one's sleeve, Am. have an ~ in the hole fig. (noch) e-n Trumpf in der Hand haben; within an ~ um ein Haar.

ache [eɪk] 1. schmerzen, weh tun; 2. anhaltender Schmerz.

a·chieve [ə'tʃiːv] zustande bringen; Ziel erreichen; ~**ment** [~mənt] Zustandebringen n, Ausführung f; Leistung f.

ac·id ['æsɪd] 1. sauer; fig. beißend, bissig; ~ rain saurer Regen; 2. 🔬 Säure f; **a·cid·i·ty** [ə'sɪdəti] Säure f.

ac·knowl·edge [ək'nɒlɪdʒ] anerkennen; zugeben; Empfang bestätigen; ~**ment**, ~**edg(e)ment** [~mənt] Anerkennung f; (Empfangs)Bestätigung f; Eingeständnis n.

a·corn ♀ ['eɪkɔːn] Eichel f.

a·cous·tics [ə'kuːstɪks] pl. Akustik f (e-s Raumes).

ac·quaint [ə'kweɪnt] bekannt machen; ~ s.o. with s.th. j-m et. mitteilen; be ~ed with kennen; ~**ance** [~əns] Bekanntschaft f; Bekannte(r m) f.

ac·qui·esce [ækwɪ'es] (in) hinnehmen (acc.); einwilligen (in acc.).

ac·quire [ə'kwaɪə] erwerben; sich aneignen (Kenntnisse).

ac·qui·si·tion [ækwɪ'zɪʃn] Erwerb m; Erwerbung f; Errungenschaft f.

ac·quit [ə'kwɪt] (-tt-) ⚖ j-n freisprechen (of a charge von e-r Anklage); ~ o.s. of e-e Pflicht erfüllen; ~ o.s. well s-e Sache gut machen; ~**tal** ⚖ [~tl] Freispruch m.

a·cre [ˈeɪkə] Acre *m* (4047 *qm*).

ac·rid [ˈækrɪd] scharf, beißend.

a·cross [əˈkrɒs] **1.** *adv.* (quer) hin- *od.* herüber; querdurch; drüben, auf der anderen Seite; über Kreuz; **2.** *prp.* (quer) über (*acc.*); (quer) durch; auf der anderen Seite von (*od. gen.*), jenseits (*gen.*); über (*dat.*); come ~, run ~ stoßen auf (*acc.*).

act [ækt] **1.** *v/i.* handeln; sich benehmen; wirken; funktionieren; (Theater) spielen (*a. fig.*), auftreten; *v/t. thea.* spielen (*a. fig.*), Stück aufführen; ~ *out* szenisch darstellen, vorspielen; **2.** Handlung *f*, Tat *f*, Maßnahme *f*, Akt *m*; *thea.* Akt *m*; Gesetz *n*, Beschluß *m*; Urkunde *f*, Vertrag *m*; ~**ing** [ˈæktɪŋ] **1.** Handeln *n*; *thea.* Spiel(en) *n*; **2.** tätig; amtierend.

ac·tion [ˈækʃn] Handlung *f* (*a. thea.*), Tat *f*; Action *f* (*spannende Handlung*); Aktion *f*; Tätigkeit *f*, Funktion *f*; (Ein)Wirkung *f*; ⚖ Klage *f*, Prozeß *m*; ✗ Gefecht *n*, Kampfhandlung *f*; ⊕ Mechanismus *m*; *take* ~ Schritte unternehmen, handeln.

ac·tive [ˈæktɪv] aktiv; tätig, rührig, lebhaft, rege; wirksam; *econ.* lebhaft; ~ *voice* gr. Aktiv *n*, Tatform *f*; **ac·tiv·ist** [~vɪst] Aktivist(in); **ac·tiv·i·ty** [ækˈtɪvətɪ] Tätigkeit *f*; Aktivität *f*; Betriebsamkeit *f*; *bsd.* econ. Lebhaftigkeit *f*.

ac·tor [ˈæktə] Schauspieler *m*; **ac·tress** [~trɪs] Schauspielerin *f*.

ac·tu·al □ [ˈæktʃʊəl] wirklich, tatsächlich, eigentlich; △ *nicht aktuell*.

a·cute □ [əˈkjuːt] (~r, ~st) spitz; scharf(sinnig); brennend (*Frage*); 🌡 akut.

ad F [æd] = *advertisement*.

ad·a·mant □ *fig.* [ˈædəmənt] unerbittlich.

a·dapt [əˈdæpt] anpassen (to *dat. od.* an *acc.*); Text bearbeiten (*from* nach); ⊕ umstellen (to auf *acc.*); umbauen (to für); **ad·ap·ta·tion** [ædæpˈteɪʃn] Anpassung *f*; Bearbeitung *f*; **a·dapt·er**, **a·dapt·or** ⚡ [əˈdæptə] Adapter *m*.

add [æd] *v/t.* hinzufügen; ~ *up* zusammenzählen, addieren; *v/i.*: ~ *to* vermehren, beitragen zu, hinzukommen zu; ~ *up fig.* F e-n Sinn ergeben.

ad·dict [ˈædɪkt] Süchtige(r *m*) *f*; *alcohol* (*drug*) ~ Alkohol- (Drogen-*od.* Rauschgift)Süchtige(r *m*) *f*; *Fuß-*

ball- etc. Fanatiker(in), *Film-* etc. Narr *m*; ~**ed** [əˈdɪktɪd] süchtig, abhängig (to von); *be* ~ *to* alcohol (*drugs, television, etc.*) alkohol-(drogen-, fernseh- *etc.*)süchtig sein; **ad·dic·tion** [~ʃn] Sucht *f*, Zustand *a.* Süchtigkeit *f*.

ad·di·tion [əˈdɪʃn] Hinzufügen *n*; Zusatz *m*; Zuwachs *m*; Anbau *m*; ⅍ Addition *f*; *in* ~ außerdem; *in* ~ *to* außer (*dat.*); ~**al** [~l] zusätzlich.

ad·dress [əˈdres] **1.** Worte richten (to an *acc.*), *j-n* anreden od. ansprechen; **2.** Adresse *f*, Anschrift *f*; Rede *f*; Ansprache *f*; ~**ee** [ædreˈsiː] Empfänger(in).

ad·ept [ˈædept] **1.** erfahren, geschickt (*at*, *in* in *dat.*); **2.** Meister *m*, Experte *m* (*at*, *in* in *dat.*).

ad·e·qua·cy [ˈædɪkwəsɪ] Angemessenheit *f*; ~**quate** □ [~kwət] angemessen.

ad·here [ədˈhɪə] (to) kleben, haften (an *dat.*); *fig.* festhalten (an *dat.*); **ad·her·ence** [~rəns] Anhaften *n*; *fig.* Festhalten *n*; **ad·her·ent** [~rənt] Anhänger(in).

ad·he·sive [ədˈhiːsɪv] **1.** □ klebend; ~ *plaster* Heftpflaster *m*; ~ *tape* Klebestreifen *m*; *Am.* Heftpflaster *n*; **2.** Klebstoff *m*.

ad·ja·cent □ [əˈdʒeɪsnt] angrenzend, anstoßend (*to* an *acc.*); benachbart.

ad·jec·tive gr. [ˈædʒɪktɪv] Adjektiv *n*, Eigenschaftswort *n*.

ad·join [əˈdʒɔɪn] (an)grenzen an (*acc*).

ad·journ [əˈdʒɜːn] verschieben, (*v/i.* sich) vertagen; ~**ment** [~mənt] Vertagung *f*, -schiebung *f*.

ad·just [əˈdʒʌst] anpassen; in Ordnung bringen; *Streit* beilegen; *Mechanismus u. fig.* einstellen (*to* auf *acc.*); ~**ment** [~mənt] Anpassung *f*; Ordnung *f*; ⊕ Einstellung *f*; Beilegung *f*.

ad·min·is·ter [ədˈmɪnɪstə] verwalten; spenden; *Arznei* geben, verabreichen; ~ *justice* Recht sprechen; ~**tra·tion** [ədmɪnɪˈstreɪʃn] Verwaltung *f*; *pol. bsd. Am.* Regierung *f*; *bsd. Am.* Amtsperiode *f* (*e-s Präsidenten*); ~**tra·tive** □ [ədˈmɪnɪstrətɪv] Verwaltungs...; ~**tra·tor** [~reɪtə] Verwaltungsbeamte(r) *m*.

ad·mi·ra·ble □ [ˈædmərəbl] bewundernswert; großartig.

ad·mi·ral [ˈædmərəl] Admiral *m*.

ad·mi·ra·tion [ædmə'reɪʃn] Bewunderung f.

ad·mire [əd'maɪə] bewundern; verehren; **ad·mir·er** [~rə] Verehrer m.

ad·mis·si·ble □ [əd'mɪsəbl] zulässig; **~sion** [~ʃn] Zulassung f; Eintritt(sgeld n) m; Eingeständnis n; **~ free** Eintritt frei.

ad·mit [əd'mɪt] (-tt-) v/t. (her)einlassen (to, into in acc.), eintreten lassen; zulassen (to zu); zugeben; **~tance** [~əns] Einlaß m, Ein-, Zutritt m; **no ~** Zutritt verboten.

ad·mix·ture [æd'mɪkstʃə] Beimischung f, Zusatz m.

ad·mon·ish [əd'mɒnɪʃ] ermahnen; warnen (of, against vor dat.); **ad·mo·ni·tion** [ædmə'nɪʃn] Ermahnung f; Warnung f.

a·do [ə'duː] (pl. -dos) Getue n, Lärm m; without much od. more od. further ~ ohne weitere Umstände.

ad·o·les·cence [ædə'lesns] Adoleszenz f, Reifezeit f; **~cent** [~t] 1. jugendlich, heranwachsend; 2. Jugendliche(r m) f.

a·dopt [ə'dɒpt] adoptieren; sich zu eigen machen, übernehmen; **~ed child** Adoptivkind n; **a·dop·tion** [~pʃn] Adoption f; **a·dop·tive** □ [~tɪv] adoptiert; angenommen; **~ child** Adoptivkind n; **~ parents** pl. Adoptiveltern pl.

a·dor·a·ble □ [ə'dɔːrəbl] anbetungswürdig; F entzückend; **ad·o·ra·tion** [ædə'reɪʃn] Anbetung f, Verehrung f; **a·dore** [ə'dɔː] anbeten, verehren.

a·dorn [ə'dɔːn] schmücken, zieren; **~ment** [~mənt] Schmuck m.

a·droit □ [ə'drɔɪt] geschickt.

ad·ult [æd'ʌlt] 1. erwachsen; 2. Erwachsene(r m) f; **~ education** Erwachsenenbildung f.

a·dul·ter·ate [ə'dʌltəreɪt] verfälschen; **~er** [~rə] Ehebrecher m; **~ess** [~rɪs] Ehebrecherin f; **~ous** □ [~rəs] ehebrecherisch; **~y** [~rɪ] Ehebruch m.

ad·vance [əd'vɑːns] 1. v/i. vorrücken, -dringen; vorrücken (Zeit); steigen; Fortschritte machen; v/t. vorrücken; Ansicht etc. vorbringen; Geld vorauszahlen; vorschießen; (be)fördern; Preis erhöhen; beschleunigen; 2. Vorrücken n, Vorstoß m (a. fig.); Fortschritt m; Vorschuß m; Erhöhung f; in ~ im voraus; **~d** fortgeschritten; **~ for one's years** weit od.

reif für sein Alter; **~ment** [~mənt] Förderung f; Fortschritt m.

ad·van·tage [əd'vɑːntɪdʒ] Vorteil m; Überlegenheit f; Gewinn m; take ~ of ausnutzen; **~ta·geous** □ [ædvən'teɪdʒəs] vorteilhaft.

ad·ven·ture [əd'ventʃə] Abenteuer n, Wagnis n; Spekulation f; **~tur·er** [~rə] Abenteurer m; Spekulant m; **~tur·ess** [~rɪs] Abenteu(r)erin f; **~tur·ous** □ [~rəs] abenteuerlich; verwegen, kühn.

ad·verb gr. ['ædvɜːb] Adverb n, Umstandswort n.

ad·ver·sa·ry ['ædvəsərɪ] Gegner(in), Feind(in); **ad·verse** □ ['ædvɜːs] widrig; feindlich; ungünstig, nachteilig (to für); **ad·ver·si·ty** [əd'vɜːsətɪ] Unglück n.

ad·ver·tise ['ædvətaɪz] ankündigen, bekanntmachen; inserieren; Reklame machen (für); **~tise·ment** [əd'vɜːtɪsmənt] Anzeige f, Ankündigung f, Inserat n; Reklame f; **~tis·ing** ['ædvətaɪzɪŋ] 1. Reklame f, Werbung f; 2. Anzeigen..., Reklame..., Werbe...; ~ agency Anzeigenannahme f; Werbeagentur f.

ad·vice [əd'vaɪs] Rat(schlag) m; Nachricht f, Meldung f; take medical ~ e-n Arzt zu Rate ziehen; take my ~ hör auf mich.

ad·vis·a·ble □ [əd'vaɪzəbl] ratsam; **ad·vise** [əd'vaɪz] v/t. j-n beraten; j-m raten; bsd. econ. benachrichtigen; avisieren; v/i. sich beraten; **ad·vis·er**, Am. a. **ad·vi·sor** [~ə] Berater m; **ad·vi·so·ry** [~ərɪ] beratend.

ad·vo·cate 1. [ə'dvəkət] Anwalt m; Verfechter m; Befürworter m; 2. [~keɪt] verteidigen, befürworten.

aer·i·al ['eərɪəl] 1. □ luftig; Luft...; ~ view Luftaufnahme f; 2. Antenne f.

aer·o- ['eərəʊ] Aero..., Luft...

aer·o·bics [eə'rəʊbɪks] sg. Sport: Aerobic n; **~drome** bsd. Brt. ['eərədrəʊm] Flugplatz m; **~dy·nam·ic** [eərəʊdaɪ'næmɪk] (~ally) aerodynamisch; **~dy·nam·ics** sg. Aerodynamik f; **~nau·tics** [eərə'nɔːtɪks] sg. Luftfahrt f; **~plane** Brt. ['eərəplein] Flugzeug n.

aes·thet·ic [iːs'θetɪk] ästhetisch; **~s** sg. Ästhetik f.

a·far [ə'fɑː] fern, weit (weg).

af·fa·ble □ ['æfəbl] leutselig.

af·fair [ə'feə] Geschäft n, Angelegenheit f, Sache f; F Ding n,

Sache *f*; Liebesaffäre *f*, Verhältnis *n*.

af·fect [ə'fekt] (ein- *od.* sich aus-) wirken auf (*acc.*); rühren; *Gesundheit* angreifen; lieben, vorziehen; nachahmen; vortäuschen; **af·fec·ta·tion** [æfek'teɪʃn] Vorliebe *f*; Affektiertheit *f*; Verstellung *f*; ~**ed** □ gerührt; befallen (*von Krankheit*); angegriffen (*Augen etc.*); geziert, affektiert; **af·fec·tion** [ʌkʃn] Zuneigung *f*; **af·fec·tion·ate** □ [ʌʃnət] liebevoll.

af·fil·i·ate [ə'fɪlɪeɪt] *als Mitglied* aufnehmen; angliedern; ~**d company** *econ.* Tochtergesellschaft *f*.

af·fin·i·ty [ə'fɪnətɪ] (geistige) Verwandtschaft *f*; **♠** Affinität *f*; Neigung *f* (*for*, *to* zu).

af·firm [ə'fɜːm] versichern; beteuern; bestätigen; **af·fir·ma·tion** [æfə'meɪʃn] Versicherung *f*; Beteuerung *f*; Bestätigung *f*; **af·fir·ma·tive** [ə'fɜːmətɪv] **1.** □ bejahend; **2.** *answer in the* ~ bejahen.

af·fix [ə'fɪks] (*to*) anheften, -kleben (an *acc.*), befestigen (an *dat.*); bei-, hinzufügen (*dat.*).

af·flict [ə'flɪkt] betrüben, heimsuchen, plagen; **af·flic·tion** [ʌkʃn] Betrübnis *f*; Gebrechen *n*; Elend *n*, Not *f*.

af·flu·ence ['æfluəns] Überfluß *m*; Wohlstand *m*; ~**ent** [ʌt] **1.** □ reich (-lich); ~ *society* Wohlstandsgesellschaft *f*; **2.** Nebenfluß *m*.

af·ford [ə'fɔːd] sich leisten; gewähren, bieten; *I can* ~ *it* ich kann es mir leisten.

af·front [ə'frʌnt] **1.** beleidigen; **2.** Beleidigung *f*.

a·field [ə'fiːld] im Feld; (weit) weg.

a·float [ə'fləʊt] **♣** *u. fig.* flott; schwimmend; auf See; *set* ~ **♣** flottmachen; in Umlauf bringen.

a·fraid [ə'freɪd]: *be* ~ *of* sich fürchten *od.* Angst haben vor (*dat.*); *I'm* ~ *she won't come* ich fürchte, sie wird nicht kommen; *I'm* ~ *I must go now* leider muß ich jetzt gehen.

a·fresh [ə'freʃ] von neuem.

Af·ri·can ['æfrɪkən] **1.** afrikanisch; **2.** Afrikaner(in); *Am. a.* Neger(in).

af·ter ['ɑːftə] **1.** *adv.* hinterher, nachher, danach; **2.** *prp.* nach; hinter (*dat.*) (... her); ~ *all* schließlich (doch); **3.** *cj.* nachdem; **4.** *adj.* später; Nach...; ~**ef·fect** **♂** Nachwirkung *f*

(*a. fig.*); *fig.* Folge *f*; ~**glow** Abendrot *n*; ~**math** [ʌmæθ] Nachwirkungen *pl.*, Folgen *pl.*; ~**noon** [ɑːftə'nuːn] Nachmittag *m*; *this* ~ heute nachmittag; *good* ~! guten Tag!; ~**taste** ['ɑːfteteɪst] Nachgeschmack *m*; ~**thought** nachträglicher Einfall; ~**wards**, *Am. a.* ~**ward** [ʌwəd(z)] nachher, später.

a·gain [ə'gen] wieder(um); ferner; ~ *and* ~, *time and* ~ immer wieder; *as much* ~ noch einmal soviel.

a·gainst [ə'genst] gegen; *räumlich*: gegen; an, vor (*dat. od. acc.*); *fig.* im Hinblick auf (*acc.*); *as* ~ verglichen mit; *he was* ~ *it* er war dagegen.

age [eɪdʒ] **1.** (Lebens)Alter *n*; Zeit (-alter *n*) *f*; Menschenalter *n*; (*old*) ~ (hohes) Alter; (*come*) *of* ~ mündig *od.* volljährig (werden); *be over* ~ die Altersgrenze überschritten haben; *under* ~ minderjährig; unmündig; *wait for* ~*s* F e-e Ewigkeit warten; **2.** alt werden *od.* machen; ~**d** ['eɪdʒɪd] alt, betagt; [eɪdʒd]: ~ *twenty* 20 Jahre alt; ~**less** ['eɪdʒlɪs] zeitlos; ewig jung.

a·gen·cy ['eɪdʒənsɪ] Tätigkeit *f*; Vermittlung *f*; Agentur *f*, Büro *n*.

a·gen·da [ə'dʒendə] Tagesordnung *f*.

a·gent ['eɪdʒənt] Handelnde(r *m*) *f*; (Stell)Vertreter *m*; Agent *m* (*a. pol.*); Wirkstoff *m*, Mittel *n*, Agens *n*.

ag·glom·er·ate [ə'glɒməreɪt] (sich) zusammenballen; (sich) (an)häufen.

ag·gra·vate ['ægrəveɪt] erschweren, verschlimmern; F ärgern.

ag·gre·gate 1. ['ægrɪgeɪt] (sich) anhäufen; vereinigen (*to* mit); sich belaufen auf (*acc.*); **2.** [ʌgət] (an)gehäuft; gesamt; **3.** [ʌ] Anhäufung *f*; Gesamtmenge *f*, Summe *f*; Aggregat *n*.

ag·gres·sion [ə'greʃn] Angriff *m*; ~**sive** □ [ʌsɪv] aggressiv, Angriffs...; *fig.* energisch; ~**sor** [ʌsə] Angreifer *m*.

ag·grieved [ə'griːvd] verletzt, gekränkt.

a·ghast [ə'gɑːst] entgeistert, entsetzt.

ag·ile □ ['ædʒaɪl] flink, behend; **a·gil·i·ty** [ə'dʒɪlətɪ] Behendigkeit *f*.

ag·i·tate ['ædʒɪteɪt] *v/t.* hin u. her bewegen, schütteln; *fig.* aufregen; erörtern; *v/i.* agitieren; ~**ta·tion** [ædʒɪ'teɪʃn] heftige Bewegung, Erschütterung *f*; Aufregung *f*; Agitation *f*; ~**ta·tor** ['ædʒɪteɪtə] Agitator *m*, Aufwiegler *m*.

a·glow [ə'gləʊ] glühend; *be* ~ strahlen (*with* vor).

a·go [ə'gəʊ]: *a year* ~ vor e-m Jahr.

ag·o·nize ['ægənaɪz] (sich) quälen.

ag·o·ny ['ægənɪ] heftiger Schmerz, *a. seelische* Qual; Pein *f*; Agonie *f*, Todeskampf *m*.

a·grar·i·an [ə'greərɪən] Agrar...

a·gree [ə'griː] *v/i*. übereinstimmen; sich vertragen; einig werden, sich einigen (*on*, *upon* über *acc.*); übereinkommen; ~ *to* zustimmen (*dat.*), einverstanden sein mit; ~**a·ble** [ə'grɪəbl] (*to*) angenehm (für); übereinstimmend (mit); ~**ment** [ə'griːmənt] Übereinstimmung *f*; Vereinbarung *f*; Abkommen *n*; Vertrag *m*.

ag·ri·cul·tur·al [ægrɪ'kʌltʃərəl] landwirtschaftlich; ~**e** ['ægrɪkʌltʃə] Landwirtschaft *f*; ~**ist** [ægrɪ'kʌltʃərɪst] Landwirt *m*.

a·ground ⚓ [ə'graʊnd] gestrandet; *run* ~ stranden, auf Grund laufen.

a·head [ə'hed] vorwärts, voraus; vorn; *go* ~! nur zu!, mach nur!; *straight* ~ geradeaus.

aid [eɪd] **1.** helfen (*dat.*; *in* bei *et.*); fördern; **2.** Hilfe *f*, Unterstützung *f*.

ail [eɪl] *v/i* kränkeln; *v/t.* schmerzen, weh tun (*dat.*); *what* ~*s him?* was fehlt ihm?; ~**ing** ['eɪlɪŋ] leidend; ~**ment** [~mənt] Leiden *n*.

aim [eɪm] **1.** *v/i.* zielen (*at* auf *acc.*, nach); ~ *at fig.* beabsichtigen; *be* ~*ing to do s.th.* vorhaben, et. zu tun; *v/t.* ~ *at Waffe etc.* richten auf *od.* gegen (*acc.*); **2.** Ziel *n* (*a. fig.*); Absicht *f*; *take* ~ *at* zielen auf (*acc.*) *od.* nach; ~**less** □ ['eɪmlɪs] ziellos.

air¹ [eə] **1.** Luft *f*; Luftzug *m*; Miene *f*, Aussehen *n*; *by* ~ auf dem Luftwege; *in the open* ~ im Freien; *on the* ~ im Rundfunk *od.* Fernsehen; *be on the* ~ senden (*Sender*); in Betrieb sein (*Sender*); *go off the* ~ die Sendung beenden (*Person*); sein Programm beenden (*Sender*); *give o.s.* ~*s*, *put on* ~*s* vornehm tun; **2.** (aus)lüften; *fig.* an die Öffentlichkeit bringen; erörtern.

air² ♪ [~] Arie *f*, Weise *f*, Melodie *f*.

air·base ✈ ['eəbeɪs] Luftstützpunkt *m*; ~**bed** Luftmatratze *f*; ~**borne** in der Luft (*Flugzeug*); ✈ Luftlande...; ~**brake** ⊕ Druckluftbremse *f*; ~**con·di·tioned** mit Klimaanlage;

~**craft** (*pl.* -*craft*) Flugzeug *n*; ~**craft car·ri·er** Flugzeugträger *m*; ~**field** Flugplatz *m*; ~**force** ✕ Luftwaffe *f*; ~**host·ess** ✈ Stewardess *f*; ~**jack·et** Schwimmweste *f*; ~**lift** ✈ Luftbrücke *f*; ~**line** ✈ Fluggesellschaft *f*; ~**lin·er** ✈ Verkehrsflugzeug *n*; ~**mail** Luftpost *f*; *by* ~ mit Luftpost; ~**man** (*pl.* -*men*) Flieger *m* (*Luftwaffe*); ~**plane** *Am.* Flugzeug *n*; ~**pock·et** ✈ Luftloch *n*; ~**pol·lu·tion** Luftverschmutzung *f*; ~**port** Flughafen *m*; ~ **raid** Luftangriff *m*; ~**raid pre·cau·tions** *pl.* Luftschutz *m*; ~**raid shel·ter** Luftschutzraum *m*; ~**route** ✈ Flugroute *f*; ~**sick** luftkrank; ~**space** Luftraum *m*; ~**strip** (behelfsmäßige) Start- u. Landebahn; ~**ter·mi·nal** Flughafenabfertigungsgebäude *n*; ~**tight** luftdicht; ~**traf·fic** Flugverkehr *m*; ~**traf·fic con·trol** ✈ Flugsicherung *f*; ~**traf·fic con·trol·ler** ✈ Fluglotse *m*; ~**way** ✈ Fluggesellschaft *f*; ~**wor·thy** flugtüchtig.

air·y □ ['eərɪ] (-*ier*, -*iest*) luftig; *contp.* überspannt.

aisle *arch.* [aɪl] Seitenschiff *n*; Gang *m*.

a·jar [ə'dʒɑː] halb offen, angelehnt.

a·kin [ə'kɪn] verwandt (*to* mit).

a·lac·ri·ty [ə'lækrətɪ] Munterkeit *f*; Bereitwilligkeit *f*, Eifer *m*.

a·larm [ə'lɑːm] **1.** Alarm(zeichen *n*) *m*; Wecker *m*; Angst *f*; **2.** alarmieren; beunruhigen; ~**clock** Wecker *m*.

al·bum ['ælbəm] Album *n*.

al·bu·mi·nous [æl'bjuːmɪnəs] eiweißhaltig.

al·co·hol ['ælkəhɒl] Alkohol *m*; ~**ic** [ælkə'hɒlɪk] **1.** alkoholisch; **2.** Alkoholiker(in); ~**is·m** ['ælkəhɒlɪzəm] Alkoholismus *m*.

al·cove ['ælkəʊv] Nische *f*; Laube *f*.

al·der·man ['ɔːldəmən] (*pl.* -*men*) Ratsherr *m*, Stadtrat *m*.

ale [eɪl] Ale *n* (*helles, obergäriges Bier*).

a·lert [ə'lɜːt] **1.** □ wachsam; munter; **2.** Alarm(bereitschaft *f*) *m*; *on the* ~ auf der Hut; in Alarmbereitschaft; **3.** warnen (*to* vor *dat.*), alarmieren.

al·i·bi ['ælɪbaɪ] Alibi *n*; F Entschuldigung *f*, Ausrede *f*.

a·li·en ['eɪljən] **1.** fremd; ausländisch; **2.** Fremde(r *m*) *f*, Ausländer(in);

~**ate** [~eɪt] veräußern; entfremden (*from dat.*).

a·light [əˈlaɪt] **1.** in Flammen; erhellt; **2.** ab-, aussteigen; ✈ niedergehen, landen; sich niederlassen (*on, upon* auf *dat. od. acc.*).

a·lign [əˈlaɪn] (sich) ausrichten (*with* nach); ~ *o.s. with* sich anschließen an (*acc.*).

a·like [əˈlaɪk] **1.** *adj.* gleich; **2.** *adv.* gleich, ebenso.

al·i·men·ta·ry [ælɪˈmentərɪ] nahrhaft; ~ *canal* Verdauungskanal *m.*

al·i·mo·ny ⚖ [ˈælɪmənɪ] Unterhalt *m.*

a·live [əˈlaɪv] lebendig; (noch) am Leben; empfänglich (*to* für); lebhaft; belebt (*with* von).

all [ɔːl] **1.** *adj.* all; ganz; jede(r, -s) **2.** *pron.* alles; alle *pl.*; **3.** *adv.* ganz, völlig; *Wendungen:* ~ *at once* auf einmal; ~ *the better* desto besser; ~ *but* beinahe, fast; ~ *in Am.* F fertig, ganz erledigt; ~ *right* (alles) in Ordnung; *for* ~ *that* dessenungeachtet, trotzdem; *for* ~ *(that) I care* meinetwegen; *for* ~ *I know* soviel ich weiß; *at* ~ überhaupt; *not at* ~ überhaupt nicht; *the score was two* ~ das Spiel stand zwei zu zwei.

all-A·mer·i·can [ˈɔːləˈmerɪkən] rein amerikanisch; die ganzen USA vertretend.

al·lay [əˈleɪ] beruhigen; lindern.

al·le·ga·tion [ælɪˈɡeɪʃn] *unerwiesene* Behauptung.

al·lege [əˈledʒ] behaupten; ~**d** ☐ angeblich.

al·le·giance [əˈliːdʒəns] (Untertanen)Treue *f.*

al·ler|gic [əˈlɜːdʒɪk] allergisch; ~**gy** [ˈælədʒɪ] Allergie *f.*

al·le·vi·ate [əˈliːvɪeɪt] lindern, vermindern.

al·ley [ˈælɪ] (enge *od.* schmale) Gasse; Garten-, Parkweg *m*; *Bowling, Kegeln:* Bahn *f*; △ *nicht* Allee.

al·li·ance [əˈlaɪəns] Bündnis *n.*

al·lo·cate [ˈæləkeɪt] zuteilen, anweisen; ~**ca·tion** [æləˈkeɪʃn] Zuteilung *f.*

al·lot [əˈlɒt] (-tt-) zuteilen, an-, zuweisen; ~**ment** [~mənt] Zuteilung *f*; Parzelle *f.*

al·low [əˈlaʊ] erlauben, bewilligen, gewähren; zugeben; ab-, anrechnen, vergüten; ~ *for* berücksichtigen (*acc.*); ~**a·ble** ☐ [əˈlaʊəbl] erlaubt,

zulässig; ~**ance** Erlaubnis *f*; Bewilligung *f*; Taschengeld *n*, Zuschuß *m*; Vergütung *f*; fig. Nachsicht *f*; *make* ~(*s*) *for s.th.* et. in Betracht ziehen.

al·loy 1. [ˈælɔɪ] Legierung *f*; **2.** [əˈlɔɪ] legieren.

all-round [ˈɔːlraʊnd] vielseitig; ~**er** [ɔːlˈraʊndə] Alleskönner *m*; *Sport:* Allroundsportler *m*, -spieler *m.*

al·lude [əˈluːd] anspielen (*to* auf *acc.*).

al·lure [əˈljʊə] (an-, ver)locken; ~**ment** [~mənt] Verlockung *f.*

al·lu·sion [əˈluːʒn] Anspielung *f.*

al·ly 1. [əˈlaɪ] sich vereinigen, verbünden (*to, with* mit); **2.** [ˈælaɪ] Verbündete(r *m*) *f*, Bundesgenosse *m*, -in *f*; *the Allies pl.* die Alliierten *pl.*

al·ma·nac [ˈɔːlmənæk] Almanach *m.*

al·might·y [ɔːlˈmaɪtɪ] allmächtig; *the* ♀ der Allmächtige.

al·mond ♀ [ˈɑːmənd] Mandel *f.*

al·mo·ner *Brt.* [ˈɑːmənə] Sozialarbeiter(in) im Krankenhaus.

al·most [ˈɔːlməʊst] fast, beinah(e).

alms [ɑːmz] *pl.* Almosen *n.*

a·loft [əˈlɒft] (hoch) (dr)oben.

a·lone [əˈləʊn] allein; *let od. leave* ~ in Ruhe *od.* bleiben lassen; *let* ~ ... abgesehen von ...

a·long [əˈlɒŋ] **1.** *adv.* weiter, vorwärts; da; dahin; *all* ~ die ganze Zeit; ~ *with* (zusammen) mit; *come* ~ mitkommen, -gehen; *get* ~ vorwärts-, weiterkommen; auskommen, sich vertragen (*with s.o.* mit j-m); *take* ~ mitnehmen; **2.** *prp.* entlang, längs; ~**side** [~ˈsaɪd] an Seite; neben.

a·loof [əˈluːf] abseits; reserviert, zurückhaltend.

a·loud [əˈlaʊd] laut.

al·pha·bet [ˈælfəbɪt] Alphabet *n.*

al·pine [ˈælpaɪn] alpin, (Hoch)Gebirgs...

al·read·y [ɔːlˈredɪ] bereits, schon.

al·right [ɔːlˈraɪt] = *all right.*

al·so [ˈɔːlsəʊ] auch, ferner; △ *nicht* also.

al·tar [ˈɔːltə] Altar *m.*

al·ter [ˈɔːltə] (sich) (ver)ändern; ab-, umändern; ~**a·tion** [ɔːltəˈreɪʃn] Änderung *f* (*to an dat.*), Veränderung *f.*

al·ter|nate 1. [ˈɔːltɜːneɪt] abwechseln (lassen); *alternating current* ⚡ Wechselstrom *m*; **2.** ☐ [ɔːlˈtɜːnət] abwechselnd; **3.** *Am.* [~] Stellvertreter *m*; ~**na·tion** [ɔːltəˈneɪʃn] Abwechslung *f*; Wechsel *m*; ~**na·tive**

[ɔːlˈtɜːnətɪv] **1.** ☐ alternativ, wahlweise; ~ *society* alternative Gesellschaft; **2.** Alternative *f*, Wahl *f*, Möglichkeit *f*.

al·though [ɔːlˈðəʊ] obwohl, obgleich.

al·ti·tude [ˈæltɪtjuːd] Höhe *f*; *at an* ~ *of* in e-r Höhe von.

al·to·geth·er [ɔːltəˈgeðə] im ganzen, insgesamt; ganz (u. gar), völlig.

a·lu·min·i·um [æljʊˈmɪnjəm], *Am.* **a·lu·mi·num** [əˈluːmɪnəm] Aluminium *n*.

al·ways [ˈɔːlweɪz] immer, stets.

am [æm; *im Satz* əm] *1. sg. pres. von* be.

a·mal·gam·ate [əˈmælɡəmeɪt] amalgamieren; verschmelzen.

a·mass [əˈmæs] an-, aufhäufen.

am·a·teur [ˈæmətə] Amateur *m*; Dilettant(in).

a·maze [əˈmeɪz] in Erstaunen setzen, verblüffen; **~·ment** [~mənt] Staunen *n*, Verblüffung *f*; **a·maz·ing** ☐ [~ɪŋ] erstaunlich, verblüffend.

am·bas·sa·dor *pol.* [æmˈbæsədə] Botschafter *m* (*to* in e-*m Land*); Gesandte(r) *m*; **~·dress** *pol.* [~drɪs] Botschafterin *f* (*to* in e-*m Land*).

am·ber *min.* [ˈæmbə] Bernstein *m*.

am·bi·gu·i·ty [æmbɪˈɡjuːɪtɪ] Zwei-, Mehrdeutigkeit *f*; **am·big·u·ous** ☐ [æmˈbɪɡjʊəs] zwei-, vieldeutig; doppelsinnig.

am·bi·tion [æmˈbɪʃn] Ehrgeiz *m*; Streben *n*; **~·tious** ☐ [~ʃəs] ehrgeizig; begierig (*of* nach).

am·ble [ˈæmbl] **1.** Paßgang *m*; **2.** im Paßgang gehen *od.* reiten; schlendern.

am·bu·lance [ˈæmbjʊləns] ✕ Feldlazarett *n*; Krankenwagen *m*.

am·bush [ˈæmbʊʃ] **1.** Hinterhalt *m*; *be od. lie in* ~ *for s.o.* j-m auflauern; **2.** auflauern (*dat.*); überfallen.

a·me·lio·rate [əˈmiːljəreɪt] *v/t.* verbessern; *v/i.* besser werden.

a·men *int.* [ɑːˈmen] amen.

a·mend [əˈmend] verbessern, berichtigen; *Gesetz* abändern, ergänzen; **~·ment** [~mənt] Besserung *f*; Verbesserung *f*; *parl.* Abänderungs-, Ergänzungsantrag *m* (*zu e-m Gesetz*); *Am.* Zusatzartikel *m* zur Verfassung; **~s** *pl.* (Schaden)Ersatz *m*; *make* ~ Schadenersatz leisten; *make* ~ *to s.o. for s.th.* j-n für et. entschädigen.

a·men·i·ty [əˈmiːnətɪ] *oft* amenities

pl. Annehmlichkeiten *pl.*

A·mer·i·can [əˈmerɪkən] **1.** amerikanisch; ~ *plan* Vollpension *f*; **2.** Amerikaner(in); **~·ism** [~ɪzəm] Amerikanismus *m*; **~·ize** [~aɪz] (sich) amerikanisieren.

a·mi·a·ble ☐ [ˈeɪmjəbl] liebenswürdig, freundlich.

am·i·ca·ble ☐ [ˈæmɪkəbl] freundschaftlich; gütlich.

a·mid(st) [əˈmɪd(st)] inmitten (*gen.*), (mitten) in *od.* unter.

a·miss [əˈmɪs] verkehrt, falsch, übel; *take* ~ übelnehmen.

am·mo·ni·a [əˈməʊnjə] Ammoniak *n*.

am·mu·ni·tion [æmjʊˈnɪʃn] Munition *f*.

am·nes·ty [ˈæmnɪstɪ] **1.** Amnestie *f* (*Straferlaß*); **2.** begnadigen.

a·mok [əˈmɒk]: *run* ~ Amok laufen.

a·mong(st) [əˈmʌŋ(st)] (mitten) unter, zwischen.

am·o·rous ☐ [ˈæmərəs] verliebt (*of* in *acc.*).

a·mount [əˈmaʊnt] **1.** (*to*) sich belaufen (auf *acc.*); hinauslaufen (auf *acc.*); **2.** Betrag *m*, (Gesamt)Summe *f*; Menge *f*.

am·ple ☐ [ˈæmpl] (~*r*, ~*st*) weit, groß, geräumig; reich(lich), beträchtlich.

am·pli·fi·ca·tion [æmplɪfɪˈkeɪʃn] Erweiterung *f*; *rhet.* weitere Ausführung; *phys.* Verstärkung *f*; **~·fi·er** *&* [ˈæmplɪfaɪə] Verstärker *m*; **~·fy** [~faɪ] erweitern; *&* verstärken; weiter ausführen; **~·tude** [~tjuːd] Umfang *m*, Weite *f*, Fülle *f*.

am·pu·tate [ˈæmpjʊteɪt] amputieren.

a·muck [əˈmʌk] = amok.

a·muse [əˈmjuːz] (*o.s.* sich) amüsieren, unterhalten, belustigen; **~·ment** [~mənt] Unterhaltung *f*, Vergnügen *n*, Zeitvertreib *m*; **a·mus·ing** ☐ [~ɪŋ] amüsant, unterhaltend.

an [æn, ən] *unbestimmter Artikel vor vokalisch anlautenden Wörtern:* ein(e).

a·nae·mi·a *&* [əˈniːmjə] Blutarmut *f*, Anämie *f*.

an·aes·thet·ic [ænɪsˈθetɪk] **1.** (~*ally*) betäubend, Narkose...; **2.** Betäubungsmittel *n*.

a·nal *anat.* [ˈeɪnl] anal, Anal...

a·nal·o·gous ☐ [əˈnæləɡəs] analog, entsprechend; **~·gy** [~dʒɪ] Analogie *f*, Entsprechung *f*.

an·a·lyse *bsd. Brt.,* *Am.* **-lyze** ['ænəlaɪz] analysieren; zerlegen; **a·nal·y·sis** [ə'næləsɪs] (*pl.* **-ses** [-si:z]) Analyse *f.*

an·arch·y ['ænəkɪ] Anarchie *f*, Gesetzlosigkeit *f*; Chaos *n.*

a·nat·o·mize [ə'nætəmaɪz] ⚕ zergliedern; zergliedern; **~my** [⁓ɪ] Anatomie *f*; Zergliederung *f*, Analyse *f.*

an·ces·tor ['ænsestə] Vorfahr *m*, Ahn *m*; **~tral** [æn'sestrəl] angestammt; **~tress** ['ænsestrɪs] Ahne *f*; **~try** [⁓rɪ] Abstammung *f*; Ahnen *pl.*

an·chor ['æŋkə] **1.** Anker *m*; *at* ~ vor Anker; **2.** verankern; **~age** [⁓rɪdʒ] Ankerplatz *m.*

an·cho·vy *zo.* ['æntʃəvɪ] An(s)chovis *f*, Sardelle *f.*

an·cient ['eɪnʃənt] **1.** alt, antik; uralt; **2.** *the* ~s *pl. hist.* die Alten, die antiken Klassiker.

and [ænd, ənd] und.

a·ne·mi·a *Am.* = anaemia.

an·es·thet·ic *Am.* = anaesthetic.

a·new [ə'nju:] von neuem.

an·gel ['eɪndʒəl] Engel *m*; △ *nicht* Angel.

an·ger ['æŋgə] **1.** Zorn *m*, Ärger *m* (*at* über *acc.*); **2.** erzürnen, (ver)ärgern.

an·gi·na ⚕ [æn'dʒaɪnə] Angina *f*, Halsentzündung *f.*

an·gle ['æŋgl] **1.** Winkel *m*; *fig.* Standpunkt *m*; **2.** angeln (*for* nach); **~r** [⁓ə] Angler(in).

An·gli·can ['æŋglɪkən] **1.** *eccl.* anglikanisch; *Am.* britisch, englisch; **2.** *eccl.* Anglikaner(in).

An·glo-Sax·on ['æŋgləʊ'sæksən] **1.** angelsächsisch; **2.** Angelsachse *m*; *ling.* Altenglisch *n.*

an·gry □ ['æŋgrɪ] (*-ier, -iest*) zornig, verärgert, böse (*at, with* über *acc.*, *mit dat.*).

an·guish ['æŋgwɪʃ] (Seelen)Qual *f*, Schmerz *m*; **~ed** [⁓ʃt] qualvoll.

an·gu·lar □ ['æŋgjʊlə] winkelig, Winkel...; knochig.

an·i·mal ['ænɪml] **1.** Tier *n*; **2.** tierisch.

an·i·mate ['ænɪmeɪt] beleben, beseelen; aufmuntern, anregen; △ *nicht animieren*; **~ma·ted** lebendig; lebhaft, angeregt; ~ *cartoon* Zeichentrickfilm *m*; **~ma·tion** [ænɪ'meɪʃn] Leben *n*, Lebhaftigkeit *f*, Feuer *n*; Animation *f*, Herstellung *f* von (Zeichen)Trickfilmen; (Zeichen)Trickfilm *m.*

an·i·mos·i·ty [ænɪ'mɒsətɪ] Animosität *f*, Feindseligkeit *f.*

an·kle *anat.* ['æŋkl] (Fuß)Knöchel *n.*

an·nals ['ænlz] *pl.* Jahrbücher *pl.*

an·nex 1. [ə'neks] anhängen; annektieren; **2.** ['æneks] Anhang *m*; Anbau *m*; **~a·tion** [ænæk'seɪʃn] Annexion, Einverleibung *f.*

an·ni·hi·late [ə'naɪəlaɪt] vernichten.

an·ni·ver·sa·ry [ænɪ'vɜːsərɪ] Jahrestag *m*; Jahresfeier *f.*

an·no·tate ['ænəʊteɪt] mit Anmerkungen versehen; kommentieren; **~ta·tion** [ænəʊ'teɪʃn] Kommentieren *n*; Anmerkung *f.*

an·nounce [ə'naʊns] ankündigen, bekanntgeben; *Rundfunk, TV:* ansagen; durchsagen; △ *nicht annoncieren*; **~ment** [⁓mənt] Ankündigung *f*; Bekanntgabe *f*; *Rundfunk, TV:* Ansage *f*; Durchsage *f*; **an·nounc·er** [⁓ə] *Rundfunk, TV:* Ansager(in), Sprecher(in).

an·noy [ə'nɔɪ] ärgern; belästigen; **~ance** [⁓əns] Störung *f*, Belästigung *f*; Ärgernis *n*; **~ing** [⁓ɪŋ] ärgerlich; lästig.

an·nu·al ['ænjʊəl] **1.** □ jährlich, Jahres...; **2.** ♀ einjährige Pflanze; Jahrbuch *n.*

an·nu·i·ty [ə'nju:ɪtɪ] (Jahres)Rente *f.*

an·nul [ə'nʌl] (*-ll-*) für ungültig erklären, annullieren; **~ment** [⁓mənt] Annullierung *f*, Aufhebung *f.*

an·o·dyne ⚕ ['ænəʊdaɪn] **1.** schmerzstillend; **2.** schmerzstillendes Mittel.

a·noint [ə'nɔɪnt] salben.

a·nom·a·lous □ [ə'nɒmələs] anomal, abnorm, regelwidrig.

a·non·y·mous □ [ə'nɒnɪməs] anonym, ungenannt.

an·o·rak ['ænəræk] Anorak *m.*

an·oth·er [ə'nʌðə] ein anderer; ein zweiter; noch eine(r, -s).

an·swer ['ɑːnsə] **1.** *v/t. et.* beantworten; *j-m* antworten; entsprechen (*dat.*); *Zweck* erfüllen; ⊕ *dem Steuer* gehorchen; *e-r Vorladung* Folge leisten; *e-r Beschreibung* entsprechen; ~ *the bell od. door* (die Haustür) aufmachen; ~ *the telephone* ans Telefon gehen; *v/i.* antworten (*to* auf *acc.*); entsprechen (*to dat.*); ~ *back* freche Antworten geben; widersprechen; ~ *for* einstehen für; **2.** Antwort *f* (*to* auf *acc.*); **~a·ble** [⁓rəbl] verantwortlich.

ant *zo.* [ænt] Ameise *f.*

an·tag·o·nis·m [æn'tægənɪzəm] Widerstreit m; Widerstand m; Feindschaft f; **~nist** [~ɪst] Gegner(in); **~nize** [~naɪz] ankämpfen gegen; sich j-n zum Feind machen.

an·te·ced·ent [æntɪ'siːdənt] **1.** □ vorhergehend, früher (*to* als); **2.** **~s** pl. Vorgeschichte f; Vorleben n.

an·te·lope zo. ['æntɪləʊp] Antilope f.

an·ten·na¹ zo. [æn'tenə] (pl. -nae [-niː]) Fühler m.

an·ten·na² Am. [~] Antenne f.

an·te·ri·or [æn'tɪərɪə] vorhergehend, früher (*to* als); vorder.

an·te·room ['æntɪrʊm] Vorzimmer n; Wartezimmer n.

an·them ♪ ['ænθəm] Hymne f.

an·ti·... [æntɪ] Gegen..., gegen ... eingestellt od. wirkend, Anti..., anti...; **~·air·craft** ✕ Flieger-, Flugabwehr...; **~·bi·ot·ic** [~baɪ'ɒtɪk] Antibiotikum n.

an·tic·i·pate [æn'tɪsɪpeɪt] vorwegnehmen; teilnahmslos, zuvorkommen (*dat.*); voraussehen, (-)ahnen; erwarten; **an·tic·i·pa·tion** [æntɪsɪ'peɪʃn] Vorwegnahme f; Zuvorkommen n; Voraussicht f; Erwartung f; *in* ~ im voraus.

an·ti·clock·wise Brt. [æntɪ'klɒkwaɪz] entgegen dem Uhrzeigersinn.

an·tics ['æntɪks] pl. Gekasper n; Mätzchen pl.; △ *nicht* antik, Antike.

an·ti·dote ['æntɪdəʊt] Gegengift n, -mittel n; **~·freeze** Frostschutzmittel n; **~·mis·sile** ✕ [æntɪ'mɪsaɪl] Raketenabwehr...

an·tip·a·thy [æn'tɪpəθɪ] Abneigung f.

an·ti·quat·ed ['æntɪkweɪtɪd] veraltet, altmodisch.

an·tique [æn'tiːk] **1.** antik, alt; **2.** Antiquität f; △ *nicht* Antike; ~ dealer Antiquitätenhändler(in); ~ shop, *bsd.* Am. ~ store Antiquitätenladen m; **an·tiq·ui·ty** [æn'tɪkwətɪ] Altertum n, Vorzeit f.

an·ti·sep·tic [æntɪ'septɪk] **1.** antiseptisch; **2.** antiseptisches Mittel.

ant·lers ['æntləz] pl. Geweih n.

a·nus anat. ['eɪnəs] After m.

an·vil ['ænvɪl] Amboß m.

anx·i·e·ty [æŋ'zaɪətɪ] Angst f; Sorge f (*for* um); ❀ Beklemmung f.

anx·ious ['æŋkʃəs] besorgt, beunruhigt (*about* wegen); △ *nicht* ängstlich; begierig, gespannt (*for* auf *acc.*); bestrebt (*to do* zu tun).

an·y ['enɪ] **1.** adj. u. pron. (irgend-) eine(r, -s), (irgend)welche(r, -s); (irgend) etwas; jede(r, -s) (beliebige); einige pl., welche pl.; *not* ~ keiner; **2.** adv. irgend(wie), ein wenig, etwas, (noch) etwas; **~·bod·y** (irgend) jemand; jeder; **~·how** irgendwie; trotzdem, jedenfalls; wie dem auch sei; **~·one** = anybody; (irgend) etwas; alles; ~ *but* alles andere als; ~ *else?* sonst noch etwas?; *not* ~ nichts; **~·way** = anyhow; **~·where** irgendwo(hin); überall.

a·part [ə'pɑːt] einzeln, getrennt, für sich; beiseite; △ *nicht* apart; ~ *from* abgesehen von.

a·part·heid [ə'pɑːtheɪt] Apartheid f, Politik f der Rassentrennung.

a·part·ment [ə'pɑːtmənt] Zimmer n; Am. Wohnung f; **~s** pl. Brt. (möblierte) (Miet)Wohnung f; ~ *house* Am. Mietshaus n.

ap·a·thet·ic [æpə'θetɪk] (~ally) apathisch, teilnahmslos, gleichgültig; **~·thy** ['æpəθɪ] Apathie f, Teilnahmslosigkeit f, Gleichgültigkeit f.

ape [eɪp] **1.** zo. (Menschen)Affe m; **2.** nachäffen.

a·pe·ri·ent [ə'pɪərɪənt] Abführmittel n.

ap·er·ture ['æpətjʊə] Öffnung f.

a·pi·a·ry ['eɪpɪərɪ] Bienenhaus n; **~·cul·ture** [~kʌltʃə] Bienenzucht f.

a·piece [ə'piːs] für jedes od. pro Stück, je.

ap·o·log·et·ic [əpɒlə'dʒetɪk] (~ally) verteidigend; rechtfertigend; entschuldigend; **~·gize** [ə'pɒlədʒaɪz] sich entschuldigen (*for* für; *to* bei); **~·gy** [~ɪ] Entschuldigung f; Rechtfertigung f; *make* od. *offer s.o.* an ~ (*for s.th.*) sich bei j-m (für et.) entschuldigen.

ap·o·plex·y ['æpəpleksɪ] Schlag(anfall) m.

a·pos·tle [ə'pɒsl] Apostel m.

a·pos·tro·phe ling. [ə'pɒstrəfɪ] Apostroph m.

ap·pal(l) [ə'pɔːl] (-*ll*-) erschrecken, entsetzen; **~·ling** □ [~ɪŋ] erschreckend, entsetzlich.

ap·pa·ra·tus [æpə'reɪtəs] Apparat m, Vorrichtung f, Gerät n.

ap·par·el [ə'pærəl] Kleidung f.

ap·par·ent □ [ə'pærənt] sichtbar; anscheinend; offenbar.

ap·pa·ri·tion [æpə'rɪʃn] Erscheinung f, Gespenst n.

ap·peal [ə'piːl] **1.** ⚖ Berufung od.

Revision einlegen, Einspruch erheben, Beschwerde einlegen; appellieren, sich wenden (to an ~acc.); ~ to gefallen (dat.), zusagen (dat.), wirken auf (acc.); j-n dringend bitten (for um); 2. ⚖ Revision f, Berufung f; Beschwerde f; Einspruch m; Appell m (to an acc.); Aufruf m; ⚔ Appell; Wirkung f, Reiz m; Bitte f (to an acc.; for um); ~ for mercy ⚖ Gnadengesuch n; ~ing □ [~ɪŋ] flehend; ansprechend.

ap·pear [ə'pɪə] (er)scheinen; sich zeigen; öffentlich auftreten; sich ergeben od. herausstellen; ~ance [~rəns] Erscheinen n; Auftreten n; Äußere(s) n, Erscheinung f, Aussehen n; Anschein m, äußerer Schein; to all ~(s) allem Anschein nach.

ap·pease [ə'piːz] beruhigen; beschwichtigen; stillen; mildern; beilegen.

ap·pend [ə'pend] an-, hinzu-, beifügen; ~age [~ɪdʒ] Anhang m, Anhängsel n, Zubehör n.

ap·pen·di·ci·tis [əpendɪ'saɪtɪs] Blinddarmentzündung f; ~dix [ə'pendɪks] (pl. -dixes, -dices [-dɪsiːz]) Anhang m; a. vermiform ~ ⚕ Wurmfortsatz m, Blinddarm m.

ap·per·tain [æpə'teɪn] gehören (to zu).

ap·pe·tite ['æpɪtaɪt] (for) Appetit m (auf acc.); fig. Verlangen n (nach); ~tiz·er [~zə] Appetithappen m, pikante Vorspeise; ~tiz·ing □ [~ɪŋ] appetitanregend.

ap·plaud [ə'plɔːd] applaudieren, Beifall spenden; loben; **ap·plause** [~z] Applaus m, Beifall m.

ap·ple ☘ ['æpl] Apfel m; ~cart: upset s.o.'s ~ ⊦ j-s Pläne über den Haufen werfen; ~ pie (warmer) gedeckter Apfelkuchen; in ~-pie order ⊦ in schönster Ordnung; ~ sauce Apfelmus n; Am. sl. Schmus m, Quatsch m.

ap·pli·ance [ə'plaɪəns] Vorrichtung f; Gerät n; Mittel n.

ap·plic·a·ble □ ['æplɪkəbl] anwendbar (to auf acc.).

ap·pli·cant ['æplɪkənt] Antragsteller(in), Bewerber(in) (for um); ~ca·tion [æplɪ'keɪʃn] (to) Anwendung f (auf acc.); Bedeutung f (für); Gesuch n (for um); Bewerbung f (for um).

ap·ply [ə'plaɪ] v/t. (to) (auf)legen,

auftragen (auf acc.); anwenden (auf acc.); verwenden (für); ~ o.s. to sich widmen (dat.); v/i. (to) passen, zu treffen, sich anwenden lassen (auf acc.); gelten (für); sich wenden (an acc.); sich bewerben (for um), beantragen (for acc.).

ap·point [ə'pɔɪnt] bestimmen, festsetzen; verabreden; ernennen (s.o. governor j-n zum ...); berufen (to auf e-n Posten); ~ment [~mənt] Bestimmung f; Verabredung f; Termin m (geschäftlich, beim Arzt etc.); Ernennung f, Berufung f; Stelle f; ~ book Terminkalender m.

ap·por·tion [ə'pɔːʃn] ver-, zuteilen; ~ment [~mənt] Ver-, Zuteilung f.

ap·prais·al [ə'preɪzl] (Ab)Schätzung f; ~e [ə'preɪz] (ab)schätzen, taxieren

ap·pre·ci·a·ble □ [ə'priːʃəbl] nennenswert, spürbar; ~ci·ate [~ʃɪeɪt] v/t. schätzen, würdigen; dankbar sein für; v/i. im Wert steigen; ~ci·a·tion [əpriːʃɪ'eɪʃn] Schätzung f, Würdigung f; Anerkennung f; Verständnis n (of für); Einsicht f; Dankbarkeit f; econ. Wertsteigerung f.

ap·pre·hend [æprɪ'hend] ergreifen fassen; begreifen; befürchten; ~hen·sion [~ʃn] Ergreifung f, Festnahme f; Besorgnis f; ~hen·sive □ [~sɪv] ängstlich, besorgt (for um; that daß).

ap·pren·tice [ə'prentɪs] 1. Auszubildende(r m) f, Lehrling m; 2. in die Lehre geben; ~ship [~ʃɪp] Lehrzeit f, Lehre f; Ausbildung f.

ap·proach [ə'prəʊtʃ] 1. v/i. näherkommen, sich nähern; v/t. sich nähern (dat.); herangehen od. herantreten an (acc.); 2. (Heran)Nahen n; Ein-, Zu-, Auffahrt f; Annäherung f; Methode f.

ap·pro·ba·tion [æprə'beɪʃn] Billigung f, Beifall m.

ap·pro·pri·ate 1. [ə'prəʊprɪeɪt] sich aneignen; verwenden; parl. bewilligen; 2. □ [~ɪt] (for, to) angemessen (dat.), passend (für, zu).

ap·prov·al [ə'pruːvl] Billigung f; Anerkennung f, Beifall m; ~e [~v] billigen, anerkennen; ~d bewährt.

ap·prox·i·mate 1. [ə'prɒksɪmeɪt] sich nähern; 2. □ [~mət] annähernd, ungefähr.

a·pri·cot ☘ ['eɪprɪkɒt] Aprikose f.

A·pril ['eɪprɪl] April m.

a·pron ['eɪprən] Schürze f; ~string

Schürzenband *n*; *be tied to one's wife's (mother's)* ~*s fig.* unterm Pantoffel stehen (der Mutter am Schürzenzipfel hängen).

apt □ [æpt] geeignet, passend; treffend; begabt; ~ *to* geneigt zu; **ap·ti·tude** [ˈæptɪtjuːd] *(for)* Begabung *f* (für), Befähigung *f* (für), Talent *n* (zu); ~ *test* Eignungsprüfung *f*.

a·quat·ic [əˈkwætɪk] Wassertier *n*, -pflanze *f*; ~*s sg.* Wassersport *m*.

aq·ue·duct [ˈækwɪdʌkt] Aquädukt *m*.

aq·ui·line [ˈækwɪlaɪn] Adler...; gebogen; ~ *nose* Adlernase *f*.

Ar·ab [ˈærəb] Araber(in); **Ar·a·bic** [~ɪk] **1.** arabisch; **2.** *ling.* Arabisch *n*.

ar·a·ble [ˈærəbl] anbaufähig; Acker...

ar·bi|tra·ry □ [ˈɑːbɪtrərɪ] willkürlich, eigenmächtig; ~**trate** [~reɪt] entscheiden, schlichten; ~**tra·tion** [ɑːbɪˈtreɪʃn] Schlichtung *f*; ~**tra·tor** [ˈɑːbɪtreɪtə] Schiedsrichter *m*; Schlichter *m*.

ar·bo(u)r [ˈɑːbə] Laube *f*.

arc [ɑːk] (*ɟ Licht*)Bogen *m*; **ar·cade** [ɑːˈkeɪd] Arkade *f*; Bogen-, Laubengang *m*; Durchgang *m*, Passage *f*.

arch¹ [ɑːtʃ] **1.** Bogen *m*; Gewölbe *n*; *anat.* Rist *m*, Spann *m* (*Fuß*); **2.** (sich) wölben; krümmen; ~ *over* überwölben.

arch² [~] erste(r, -s), oberste(r, -s), Haupt..., Erz...

arch³ □ [~] schelmisch.

ar·cha·ic [ɑːˈkeɪɪk] (~*ally*) veraltet.

arch|an·gel [ˈɑːkeɪndʒəl] Erzengel *m*; ~**bish·op** [ˈɑːtʃbɪʃəp] Erzbischof *m*.

ar·cher [ˈɑːtʃə] Bogenschütze *m*; ~**y** [~rɪ] Bogenschießen *n*.

ar·chi|tect [ˈɑːkɪtekt] Architekt *m*; Urheber(in), Schöpfer(in); ~**tec·ture** [~ktʃə] Architektur *f*, Baukunst *f*.

ar·chives [ˈɑːkaɪvz] *pl.* Archiv *n*.

arch·way [ˈɑːtʃweɪ] (Bogen)Gang *m*.

arc·tic [ˈɑːktɪk] **1.** arktisch, nördlich, Nord...; Polar...; **2.** *Am.* wasserdichter Überschuh.

ar·dent □ [ˈɑːdənt] heiß, glühend; *fig.* leidenschaftlich, heftig; eifrig.

ar·do(u)r *fig.* [ˈɑːdə] Leidenschaft (-lichkeit) *f*, Heftigkeit *f*, Feuer *n*; Eifer *m*.

ar·du·ous □ [ˈɑːdjʊəs] mühsam; zäh.

are [ɑː, *unbetont:* ə] *pres. pl. u.* 2. *sg. von* be.

ar·e·a [ˈeərɪə] Areal *n*; (Boden)Fläche

f, Flächenraum *m*; Gegend *f*, Gebiet *n*, Zone *f*; Bereich *m*; ~ *code Am. teleph.* Vorwählnummer *f*, Vorwahl *f*.

Ar·gen·tine [ˈɑːdʒəntaɪn] **1.** argentinisch; **2.** Argentinier(in).

a·re·na [əˈriːnə] Arena *f*.

ar·gue [ˈɑːgjuː] *v/t.* (das Für u. Wider) erörtern, diskutieren; *v/i.* streiten; argumentieren, Gründe (für u. wider) anführen, Einwendungen machen.

ar·gu·ment [ˈɑːgjʊmənt] Argument *n*, Beweis(grund) *m*; Streit *m*, Wortwechsel *m*, Auseinandersetzung *f*.

ar·id □ [ˈærɪd] dürr, trocken (*a. fig.*).

a·rise [əˈraɪz] (*arose, arisen*) entstehen; auftauchen, -treten, -kommen; **a·ris·en** [əˈrɪzn] *p.p von* arise.

ar·is|toc·ra·cy [ærɪˈstɒkrəsɪ] Aristokratie *f*, Adel *m*; ~**to·crat** [ˈærɪstəkræt] Aristokrat(in); ~**to·crat·ic** (~*ally*) [ærɪstəˈkrætɪk] aristokratisch.

a·rith·me·tic [əˈrɪθmətɪk] Rechnen *n*.

ark [ɑːk] Arche *f*.

arm¹ [ɑːm] Arm *m*; Armlehne *f*; *keep s.o. at* ~*s length* sich j-n vom Leibe halten; *infant in* ~*s* Säugling *m*.

arm² [~] **1.** *mst* ~*s pl.* Waffen *pl.*; Waffengattung *f*; ~*s control* Rüstungskontrolle *f*; ~*s race* Wettrüsten *n*, Rüstungswettlauf *m*; *up in* ~*s* kampfbereit; *fig.* in Harnisch; **2.** (sich) bewaffnen; (sich) wappnen *od.* rüsten.

ar·ma·da [ɑːˈmɑːdə] Kriegsflotte *f*.

ar·ma·ment [ˈɑːməmənt] (Kriegsaus)Rüstung *f*; Aufrüstung *f*.

ar·ma·ture *ɟ* [ˈɑːmətjʊə] Anker *m*.

arm·chair [ˈɑːmˈtʃeə] Lehnstuhl *m*, Sessel *m*.

ar·mi·stice [ˈɑːmɪstɪs] Waffenstillstand *m* (*a. fig.*).

ar·mo(u)r [ˈɑːmə] **1.** ✕ Rüstung *f*, Panzer *m* (*a. fig.*, *zo.*); **2.** panzern; ~*ed car* gepanzertes Fahrzeug (*für Geldtransporte etc.*); ~**y** [~rɪ] Waffenkammer *f*; Waffenfabrik *f*.

arm·pit [ˈɑːmpɪt] Achselhöhle *f*.

ar·my [ˈɑːmɪ] Heer *n*, Armee *f*; *fig.* Menge *f*; ~ *chaplain* Militärgeistliche(r) *m*.

a·ro·ma [əˈrəʊmə] Aroma *n*, Duft *m*.

ar·o·mat·ic [ærəˈmætɪk] (~*ally*) aromatisch, würzig.

a·rose [əˈrəʊz] *pret. von* arise.

a·round [əˈraʊnd] **1.** *adv.* (rings)herum, (rund)herum, ringsumher, überall; umher, herum; in der Nähe; da; **2.** *prp.* um, um ... herum, rund um; in (*dat.*) ... herum; ungefähr, etwa.

a·rouse [əˈraʊz] (auf)wecken; *fig.* aufrütteln, erregen.

ar·range [əˈreɪndʒ] (an)ordnen; in die Wege leiten, arrangieren; vereinbaren, ausmachen; ♩ arrangieren, bearbeiten (*a. thea.*); **~·ment** [~mənt] Anordnung *f*, Zusammenstellung *f*, Verteilung *f*, Disposition *f*; Vereinbarung *f*, Absprache *f*; ♩ Arrangement *n*, Bearbeitung *f* (*a. thea.*); make ~s Vorkehrungen *od.* Vorbereitungen treffen.

ar·ray [əˈreɪ] ✗ Schlachtordnung *f*; Schar *f*, Aufgebot *n*.

ar·rear [əˈrɪə] *mst* ~s *pl.* Rückstand *m*, Rückstände *pl.*; Schulden *pl.*

ar·rest [əˈrest] **1.** ✠ Verhaftung *f*, Festnahme *f*; △ *nicht* Arrest (*Schule etc.*); **2.** ✠ verhaften, festnehmen, an-, aufhalten; *fig.* fesseln.

ar·riv·al [əˈraɪvl] Ankunft *f*; Erscheinen *n*; Ankömmling *m*; ~s *pl.* ankommende Züge *pl. od.* Schiffe *pl. od.* Flugzeuge *pl.*; **ar·rive** [~v] (an)kommen, eintreffen, erscheinen; ~ *at* die erreichen (*acc.*).

ar·ro·gance [ˈærəgəns] Arroganz *f*, Anmaßung *f*, Überheblichkeit *f*; **~·gant** □ [~t] arrogant, anmaßend, überheblich.

ar·row [ˈærəʊ] Pfeil *m*; **~·head** Pfeilspitze *f*.

ar·se·nal [ˈɑːsənl] Arsenal *n*, Zeughaus *n*.

ar·se·nic 🜭 [ˈɑːsnɪk] Arsen *n*.

ar·son 🜂 [ˈɑːsn] Brandstiftung *f*.

art [ɑːt] Kunst *f*; *fig.* List *f*; Kniff *m*; △ *nicht* Art; ~s *pl.* Geisteswissenschaften *pl.*; *Faculty of* 2s, *Am.* 2s *Department* philosophische Fakultät *f*.

ar·te·ri·al [ɑːˈtɪərɪəl] *anat.* Schlagader...; ~ *road* Hauptstraße *f*; **ar·te·ry** [ˈɑːtərɪ] *anat.* Arterie *f*, Schlag-, Pulsader *f*; *fig.* Verkehrsader *f*.

art·ful □ [ˈɑːtfl] schlau, verschmitzt.

ar·ti·cle [ˈɑːtɪkl] Artikel *m* (*a. gr.*).

ar·tic·u·late 1. [ɑːˈtɪkjʊleɪt] deutlich (aus)sprechen; zusammenfügen; **2.** □ [~lət] deutlich; 🜭 *zo.* gegliedert; **~·la·tion** [ɑːtɪkjʊˈleɪʃn] (deutliche)

Aussprache; *anat.* Gelenk(verbindung *f*) *n*.

ar·ti·fice [ˈɑːtɪfɪs] Kunstgriff *m*, List *f*; **~·fi·cial** □ [ɑːtɪˈfɪʃl] künstlich, Kunst...; ~ *person* juristische Person.

ar·til·le·ry [ɑːˈtɪlərɪ] Artillerie *f*.

ar·ti·san [ɑːtɪˈzæn] Handwerker *m*.

art·ist [ˈɑːtɪst] Künstler(in); *variety* ~ Artist(in); **ar·tis·tic** [ɑːˈtɪstɪk] (~*ally*) künstlerisch, Kunst...

art·less □ [ˈɑːtlɪs] ungekünstelt, schlicht; arglos.

as [æz, əz] **1.** *adv.* so, ebenso; wie; (*in der Eigenschaft*) als; **2.** *cj.* (gerade) wie, so wie; ebenso wie; als, während; obwohl, obgleich; da; weil; *besondere Wendungen:* ~ ... ~ (eben)so ... wie; ~ *for*, ~ *to* was ... (an)betrifft; ~ *from* von e-m *Zeitpunkt* an, ab; ~ *it were* sozusagen; ~ *Hamlet* als Hamlet.

as·cend [əˈsend] *v/i.* (auf-, empor-, hinauf)steigen; *v/t.* be-, ersteigen; *Fluß etc.* hinauffahren.

as·cen·dan·cy, as·cen·den·cy [əˈsendənsɪ] [~nsɪ] Überlegenheit *f*, Einfluß *m*; **~·sion** [~ʃn] Aufsteigen *n* (*bsd. ast.*); Aufstieg *m* (*e-s Ballons etc.*); 2 (*Day*) Himmelfahrt(stag *m*) *f*; **~·t** [~t] Aufstieg *m*; Steigung *f*.

as·cer·tain [æsəˈteɪn] ermitteln.

as·cet·ic [əˈsetɪk] (~*ally*) asketisch.

as·cribe [əˈskraɪb] zuschreiben (*to dat.*).

a·sep·tic 🜂 [æˈseptɪk] **1.** aseptisch, keimfrei; **2.** aseptisches Mittel.

ash[1] [æʃ] ♀ Esche *f*; Eschenholz *n*.

ash[2] [~] *a.* ~*es pl.* Asche *f*; *Ash Wednesday* Aschermittwoch *m*.

a·shamed [əˈʃeɪmd] beschämt; *be* ~ *of* sich schämen für (*od. gen.*).

ash can *Am.* [ˈæʃkæn] = dustbin.

ash·en [ˈæʃn] Aschen...; aschfahl.

a·shore [əˈʃɔː] am *od.* ans Ufer *od.* Land; *run* ~ stranden.

ash·tray [ˈæʃtreɪ] Asch(en)becher *m*; **~·y** [~ɪ] (-*ier*, -*iest*) = ashen.

A·sian [ˈeɪʃn, ˈeɪʒn], **A·si·at·ic** [eɪʃɪˈætɪk] **1.** asiatisch; **2.** Asiat(in).

a·side [əˈsaɪd] **1.** beiseite (*a. thea.*), seitwärts; ~ *from Am.* abgesehen von; **2.** *thea.* Aparte *n*.

ask [ɑːsk] *v/t.* fragen (*s.th.* nach et.); verlangen (*of, from s.o.* von j-m); bitten (*s.o.* [*for*] *s.th.* j. um et.; *that* darum, daß); erbitten; ~ (*s.o.*) *a question* (j-m) e-e Frage stellen;

v/i.: ~ *for* bitten um; fragen nach; *he ~ed for it od. for* trouble er wollte es ja so haben; *to be had for the ~ing* umsonst zu haben.

·skance [ə'skæns]: *look ~ at s.o.* j-n von der Seite ansehen; j-n schief *od.* mißtrauisch ansehen.

·skew [ə'skju:] schief.

·sleep [ə'sli:p] schlafend; *be (fast, sound) ~* (fest) schlafen; *fall ~* einschlafen.

s·par·a·gus ♀ [ə'spærəgəs] Spargel *m*.

s·pect ['æspekt] Lage *f*; Aspekt *m*, Seite *f*, Gesichtspunkt *m*.

s·phalt ['æsfælt] **1.** Asphalt *m*; **2.** asphaltieren.

s·pic ['æspɪk] Aspik *m*, Gelee *n*.

s·pi·rant [ə'spaɪərənt] Bewerber(in); **~·ra·tion** [æspə'reɪʃn] Ambition *f*, Bestrebung *f*.

s·pire [ə'spaɪə] streben, trachten (*to*, *after* nach).

ss *zo.* [æs] Esel *m*; △ *nicht* As.

s·sail [ə'seɪl] angreifen; *be ~ed with doubts* von Zweifeln befallen werden; **as·sai·lant** [~ənt] Angreifer(in).

s·sas·sin [ə'sæsɪn] Mörder(in) (aus politischen Gründen), Attentäter(in); **~·ate** *bsd. pol.* [~eɪt] ermorden; *be ~d* e-m Attentat *od.* Mordanschlag zum Opfer fallen; **~·a·tion** [əsæsɪ'neɪʃn] (*of*) *bsd.* politischer Mord (*an dat.*), Ermordung *f* (*gen.*), (geglücktes) Attentat (auf *acc.*).

s·sault [ə'sɔ:lt] **1.** Angriff *m*; **2.** angreifen, überfallen; ⚖ tätlich angreifen *od.* beleidigen.

s·say [ə'seɪ] **1.** (Erz-, Metall)Probe *f*; **2.** *v*/t. prüfen, untersuchen.

s·sem·blage [ə'semblɪdʒ] (An-)Sammlung *f*; ⊕ Montage *f*; **~·ble** [~bl] (sich) versammeln; ⊕ montieren; **~·bly** [~ɪ] Versammlung *f*, Gesellschaft *f*; ⊕ Montage *f*; *~ line* ⊕ Fließband *n*.

s·sent [ə'sent] **1.** Zustimmung *f*; **2.** (*to*) zustimmen (*dat.*); billigen.

s·sert [ə'sɜ:t] behaupten; geltend machen; *~ o.s.* sich behaupten *od.* durchsetzen; **as·ser·tion** [ə'sɜ:ʃn] Behauptung *f*; Erklärung *f*; Geltendmachung *f*.

s·sess [ə'ses] *Kosten etc.* festsetzen; (zur Steuer) veranlagen (*at* mit); *fig.* abschätzen, beurteilen; **~·ment** [~mənt] Festsetzung *f*, (Steuer-)

Veranlagung *f*; *fig.* Einschätzung *f*.

as·set ['æset] *econ.* Aktivposten *m*; *fig.* Plus *n*, Gewinn *m*; **~s** *pl.* Vermögen *n*; *econ.* Aktiva *pl.*; ⚖ Konkursmasse *f*.

as·sid·u·ous □ [ə'sɪdjʊəs] emsig, fleißig; aufmerksam.

as·sign [ə'saɪn] an-, zuweisen; bestimmen; zuschreiben; **as·sig·na·tion** [æsɪg'neɪʃn] (*bsd.* heimliches) Treffen (*e-s Liebespaares*); = **~·ment** [ə'saɪnmənt] An-, Zuweisung *f*; Aufgabe *f*; Auftrag *m*; ⚖ Übertragung *f*.

as·sim·i·late [ə'sɪmɪleɪt] (sich) angleichen *od.* anpassen (*to, with dat.*); **~·la·tion** [əsɪmɪ'leɪʃn] Assimilation *f*, Angleichung *f*, Anpassung *f*.

as·sist [ə'sɪst] *j-m* beistehen, helfen; unterstützen; **~·ance** [~əns] Beistand *m*, Hilfe *f*; **as·sis·tant** [~t] **1.** stellvertretend, Hilfs...; **2.** Assistent(in), Mitarbeiter(in); *shop ~ Brt.* Verkäufer(in).

as·siz·es *Brt. hist.* [ə'saɪzɪz] *pl.* Sitzung(en *pl.*) *f* des periodischen Geschworenengerichts.

as·so·ci·ate 1. [ə'səʊʃɪeɪt] vereinigen, -binden; assoziieren; *~ with* verkehren mit; **2.** [~ʃɪət] verbunden; *~ member* außerordentliches Mitglied; **3.** [~] Kollege *m*, -in *f*; Teilhaber(in); **~·a·tion** [əsəʊsɪ'eɪʃn] Vereinigung *f*, Verbindung *f*; Verein *m*; Assoziation *f*.

as·sort [ə'sɔ:t] sortieren, aussuchen, zusammenstellen; **~·ment** [~mənt] Sortieren *n*; *econ.* Sortiment *n*, Auswahl *f*.

as·sume [ə'sju:m] annehmen; vorgeben; übernehmen; **as·sump·tion** [ə'sʌmpʃn] Annahme *f*; Übernahme *f*; ♀ (*Day*) *eccl.* Mariä Himmelfahrt *f*.

as·sur·ance [ə'ʃʊərəns] Zu-, Versicherung *f*; Zuversicht *f*; Sicherheit *f*, Gewißheit *f*; Selbstsicherheit *f*; (*life*) *~ bsd. Brt.* (Lebens)Versicherung *f*; **~·e** [ə'ʃʊə] versichern; *bsd. Brt. j-s Leben* versichern; **~·ed 1.** (*adv.* **~·ed·ly** [~rɪdlɪ]) sicher; **2.** Versicherte(r *m*) *f*.

asth·ma ♂ ['æsmə] Asthma *n*.

a·stir [ə'stɜ:] auf(gestanden); auf den Beinen; voller *od.* in Aufregung.

as·ton·ish [ə'stɒnɪʃ] in Erstaunen setzen; *be ~ed* erstaunt sein (*at* über *acc.*); **~·ing** □ [~ɪŋ] erstaunlich;

~ment [~mənt] (Er)Staunen *n*, Verwunderung *f*.

as·tound [əˈstaʊnd] verblüffen.

a·stray [əˈstreɪ]: *go* ~ vom Weg abkommen; *fig.* auf Abwege geraten; irregehen; *lead* ~ *fig.* irreführen, verleiten; vom rechten Weg abbringen.

a·stride [əˈstraɪd] rittlings (*of* auf *dat.*).

as·trin·gent ♣ [əˈstrɪndʒənt] **1.** □ adstringierend; **2.** Adstringens *n*.

as·trol·o·gy [əˈstrɒlədʒɪ] Astrologie *f*.

as·tro·naut [ˈæstrənɔːt] Astronaut *m*, (Welt)Raumfahrer *m*.

as·tron·o·my [əˈstrɒnəmɪ] Astronomie *f*.

as·tute □ [əˈstjuːt] scharfsinnig; schlau; **~ness** [~nɪs] Scharfsinn *m*.

a·sun·der [əˈsʌndə] auseinander; entzwei.

a·sy·lum [əˈsaɪləm] Asyl *n*.

at [æt, *unbetont:* ət] *prp.* an; auf; aus; bei; für; in; mit; nach; über; um; von; vor; zu; ~ *school* in der Schule; ~ *the age of* im Alter von.

ate [et] *pret. von* eat 1.

a·the·is·m [ˈeɪθɪɪzəm] Atheismus *m*.

ath·lete [ˈæθliːt] (*bsd.* Leicht)Athlet *m*; **~let·ic** [æθˈletɪk] (*~ally*) athletisch; **~let·ics** *sg. od. pl.* (*bsd.* Leicht)Athletik *f*.

At·lan·tic [ətˈlæntɪk] **1.** atlantisch; **2.** *a.* ~ *Ocean* Atlantik *m*.

at·mo·sphere [ˈætməsfɪə] Atmosphäre *f* (*a. fig.*); **~spher·ic** [ætməsˈferɪk] (*~ally*) atmosphärisch.

at·om [ˈætəm] Atom *n* (*a. fig.*); ~ **bomb** Atombombe *f*.

a·tom·ic [əˈtɒmɪk] (*~ally*) atomar, Atom...; ~ **age** Atomzeitalter *n*; ~ **bomb** Atombombe *f*; ~ **en·er·gy** Atomenergie *f*; ~ **pile** Atomreaktor *m*; ~ **pow·er** Atomkraft *f*; **~pow·ered** atomgetrieben; ~ **waste** Atommüll.

at·om·ize [ˈætəmaɪz] in Atome auflösen; atomisieren; zerstäuben; **~iz·er** [~ə] Zerstäuber *m*.

a·tone [əˈtəʊn]: ~ *for et.* wiedergutmachen; **~ment** [~mənt] Buße *f*, Sühne *f*.

a·tro·cious [əˈtrəʊʃəs] scheußlich, gräßlich; grausam; **~ci·ty** [əˈtrɒsətɪ] Scheußlichkeit *f*, Gräßlichkeit *f*; Greueltat *f*, Greuel *m*.

at·tach [əˈtætʃ] *v/t.* (*to*) anheften, ankleben (an *acc.*), befestigen, anbringen (an *dat.*); *Wert, Wichtigkeit etc* beimessen (*dat.*); ~ *o.s. to* sich anschließen (*dat.*, an *acc.*); **~ed** zugetan; **~ment** [~mənt] Befestigung *f* ~ *for*, ~ *to* Bindung *f* an (*acc.*) Anhänglichkeit *f* an (*acc.*), Neigung zu.

at·tack [əˈtæk] **1.** angreifen (*a. fig.*) befallen (*Krankheit*); *Arbeit* in Angriff nehmen; **2.** Angriff *m*; ♣ Anfall *m*; Inangriffnahme *f*.

at·tain [əˈteɪn] *Ziel* erreichen, erlangen; **~ment** [~mənt] Erreichung *f* Erlangen *n*; **~s** *pl.* Kenntnisse *pl.* Fertigkeiten *pl.*

at·tempt [əˈtempt] **1.** versuchen; **2.** Versuch *m*; Attentat *n*.

at·tend [əˈtend] *v/t.* begleiten; bedienen; pflegen; ♣ behandeln; *j-n* aufwarten; beiwohnen (*dat.*), anwesend sein bei, teilnehmen an, *Schule etc.* besuchen; *e-e Vorlesung etc.* hören; *v/i.* achten, hören (*to* auf *acc.*); *to* erledigen; **~ance** [~əns] Begleitung *f*; Dienst *m*; (Auf)Wartung *f* Pflege *f*; ♣ Behandlung *f*; Anwesenheit *f* (*at* bei); Besuch *m* (*der Schule etc.*); Besucher(zahl *f*) *pl.*; **~ant** [~t] Aufseher(in); ⊕ Bedienungsmann *m*.

at·ten·tion [əˈtenʃn] Aufmerksamkeit *f* (*a. fig.*); **~tive** □ [~tɪv] aufmerksam.

at·tic [ˈætɪk] Dachboden *m*; Dachstube *f*.

at·tire [əˈtaɪə] **1.** kleiden; **2.** Kleidung *f*.

at·ti·tude [ˈætɪtjuːd] (Ein)Stellung *f*; Haltung *f*.

at·tor·ney [əˈtɜːnɪ] Bevollmächtigte(r) *m*; *Am.* Rechtsanwalt *m*; *power of* ~ Vollmacht *f*; ♀ *General Brt.* erster Kronanwalt; *Am.* Justizminister *m*.

at·tract [əˈtrækt] anziehen, *Aufmerksamkeit* erregen; *fig.* reizen; **at·trac·tion** [~kʃn] Anziehung(skraft) *f*, Reiz *m*; Attraktion *f*, *thea. etc.* Zugnummer *f*, -stück *n*; **at·trac·tive** [~tɪv] anziehend; attraktiv; reizvoll; **at·trac·tive·ness** [~nɪs] Reiz *m*.

at·trib·ute¹ [əˈtrɪbjuːt] beimessen, zuschreiben; zurückführen (*to* auf *acc.*).

at·tri·bute² [ˈætrɪbjuːt] Attribut *n* (*a. gr.*), Eigenschaft *f*, Merkmal *n*.

at·tune [əˈtjuːn]: ~ *to fig.* einstellen auf (*acc.*).

au·burn ['ɔ:bən] kastanienbraun.

auc·tion ['ɔ:kʃn] **1.** Auktion *f*; *sell by* (*Am. at*) ~ versteigern; *put up for* (*Am. at*) ~ zur Versteigerung anbieten; **2.** *mst* ~ *off* versteigern; **~·tio·neer** [~kʃə'nɪə] Auktionator *m*.

au·da·cious □ [ɔ:'deɪʃəs] kühn; dreist; **~·ci·ty** [ɔ:'dæsɪtɪ] Kühnheit *f*; Dreistigkeit *f*.

au·di·ble □ ['ɔ:dəbl] hörbar.

au·di·ence ['ɔ:djəns] Publikum *n*, Zuhörer(schaft *f*) *pl.*, Zuschauer *pl.*, Besucher *pl.*, Leser(kreis *m*) *pl.*; Audienz *f*; *give* ~ *to* Gehör schenken (*dat.*).

au·di·o·cas·sette ['ɔ:dɪəʊkæ'set] Text-, Tonkassette *f*; **~·vis·u·al** [ɔ:dɪəʊ'vɪʒʊəl]: ~ *aids pl.* audiovisuelle Unterrichtsmittel *pl.*

au·dit *econ.* ['ɔ:dɪt] **1.** Bücherrevision *f*, **2.** *Rechnungen* prüfen; **au·di·tor** [~ə] (Zu)Hörer(in); *econ.* Bücherrevisor *m*, Buchprüfer *m*; **au·di·to·ri·um** [ɔ:dɪ'tɔ:rɪəm] Zuschauerraum *m*; *Am.* Vortrags-, Konzertsaal *m*.

au·ger ['ɔ:gə] *großer* Bohrer.

aught [ɔ:t] (irgend) etwas; *for* ~ *I care* meinetwegen; *for* ~ *I know* soviel ich weiß.

aug·ment [ɔ:g'ment] vergrößern.

au·gur ['ɔ:gə]: ~ *ill* (*well*) ein schlechtes (*gutes*) Zeichen *od.* Omen sein (*for für*).

Au·gust¹ ['ɔ:gəst] August *m*.

au·gust² □ [ɔ:'gʌst] erhaben.

aunt [ɑ:nt] Tante *f*; **~·ie**, **~·y** ['ɑ:ntɪ] Tantchen *n*.

aus·pices ['ɔ:spɪsɪz] *pl.* Schirmherrschaft *f*; **~·pi·cious** □ [ɔ:'spɪʃəs] günstig.

aus·tere □ [ɒ'stɪə] streng; herb; hart; einfach; **~·ter·i·ty** [ɒ'sterɪtɪ] Strenge *f*; Härte *f*; Einfachheit *f*.

Aus·tra·li·an [ɒ'streɪljən] **1.** australisch; **2.** Australier(in).

Aus·tri·an ['ɒstrɪən] **1.** österreichisch; **2.** Österreicher(in).

au·then·tic [ɔ:'θentɪk] (~*ally*) authentisch; zuverlässig; echt.

au·thor ['ɔ:θə] Urheber(in); Autor(in), Verfasser(in); **~·i·ta·tive** □ [ɔ:'θɒrɪtətɪv] maßgebend; gebieterisch; zuverlässig; **~·i·ty** [~rətɪ] Autorität *f*; (*Amts*)Gewalt *f*; Nachdruck *m*, Gewicht *n*; Vollmacht *f*; Einfluß *m* (*over od. acc.*); Ansehen *n*; Quelle *f*; Fachmann *m*; *mst authorities pl.* Behörde *f*; **~·ize**

[ˈɔ:θəraɪz] *j-n* autorisieren, ermächtigen, bevollmächtigen, berechtigen; *et.* gutheißen; **~·ship** [~ʃɪp] Urheberschaft *f*.

au·to·graph ['ɔ:təɡrɑ:f] Autogramm *n*.

au·to·mat *TM* ['ɔ:təmæt] Automatenrestaurant *n* (*in den USA*).

au·to·mate ['ɔ:təmeɪt] automatisieren; **~·mat·ic** [ɔ:tə'mætɪk] (~*ally*) **1.** automatisch; **2.** Selbstladepistole *f*, -gewehr *n*; *mot.* Auto *n* mit Automatik; **~·ma·tion** [~'meɪʃn] Automation *f*; **~·m·a·ton** *fig.* [ɔ:'tɒmətən] (*pl.* -*ta* [-tə], -*tons*) Roboter *m*.

au·to·mo·bile *bsd. Am.* ['ɔ:təməbi:l] Auto *n*, Automobil *n*.

au·ton·o·my [ɔ:'tɒnəmɪ] Autonomie *f*.

au·tumn ['ɔ:təm] Herbst *m*; **au·tum·nal** □ [ɔ:'tʌmnəl] herbstlich, Herbst...

aux·il·i·a·ry [ɔ:g'zɪljərɪ] helfend, Hilfs...

a·vail [ə'veɪl] **1.** ~ *o.s. of sich e-r Sache* bedienen, et. nutzen; **2.** Nutzen *m*; *of od. to no* ~ nutzlos; **a·vai·la·ble** □ [~əbl] verfügbar, vorhanden; erreichbar; *econ.* lieferbar, vorrätig, erhältlich.

av·a·lanche ['ævəlɑ:nʃ] Lawine *f*.

av·a·rice ['ævərɪs] Habsucht *f*; **~·ri·cious** □ [ævə'rɪʃəs] habgierig, -süchtig.

a·venge [ə'vendʒ] rächen; **a·veng·er** [~ə] Rächer(in).

av·e·nue ['ævənju:] Allee *f*; Boulevard *m*, Prachtstraße *f*.

a·ver [ə'vɜ:] (-*rr*-) behaupten.

av·e·rage ['ævərɪdʒ] **1.** Durchschnitt *m*; ⚓ Havarie *f*; **2.** □ durchschnittlich, Durchschnitts...; **3.** durchschnittlich betragen (ausmachen, haben, leisten, erreichen *etc.*); *a.* ~ *out* den Durchschnitt ermitteln.

a·verse [ə'vɜ:s] abgeneigt (*to dat.*); **a·ver·sion** [~ʃn] Widerwille *m*, Abneigung *f*.

a·vert [ə'vɜ:t] abwenden (*a. fig.*).

a·vi·a·ry ['eɪvɪərɪ] Vogelhaus *n*, Voliere *f*.

a·vi·a·tion ✈ [eɪvɪ'eɪʃn] Luftfahrt *f*; **~·tor** ['eɪvɪeɪtə] Flieger *m*.

av·id □ ['ævɪd] gierig (*for nach*); begeistert, passioniert.

a·void [ə'vɔɪd] (ver)meiden; ausweichen; **~·ance** [~əns] Vermeidung *f*.

a·vow [ə'vaʊ] bekennen, (ein)gestehen; anerkennen; **~al** [~əl] Bekenntnis *n*, (Ein)Geständnis *n*; **~ed·ly** [~ɪdlɪ] eingestandenermaßen.

a·wait [ə'weɪt] erwarten.

a·wake [ə'weɪk] **1.** wach, munter; *be ~ to* sich e-r *Sache* (voll) bewußt sein; **2.** *a.* **a·wak·en** [~ən] (*awoke od. awaked, awaked od. awoken*) *v/t.* (auf)wecken; *~ s.o. to s.th.* j-m et. zum Bewußtsein bringen; *v/i.* auf-, erwachen; **a·wak·en·ing** [~ənɪŋ] Erwachen *n*.

a·ward [ə'wɔːd] **1.** Belohnung *f*; Preis *m*, Auszeichnung *f*; **2.** zuerkennen, *Preis etc.* verleihen.

a·ware [ə'weə]: *be ~ of s.th.* von et. wissen, sich e-r *Sache* bewußt sein; *become ~ of s.th.* et. gewahr werden *od.* merken.

a·way [ə'weɪ] (hin)weg, fort; entfernt; immer weiter, d(a)rauflos; *Sport:* auswärts; **~** (*game*) Auswärtsspiel *n*; **~** (*win*) Auswärtssieg *m*.

awe [ɔː] **1.** Ehrfurcht *f*, Scheu *f*, Furcht *f*; **2.** (Ehr)Furcht einflößen (*dat.*).

aw·ful □ [ˈɔːfl] furchtbar, schrecklich.

a·while [ə'waɪl] e-e Weile.

awk·ward □ [ˈɔːkwəd] ungeschickt, unbeholfen, linkisch; unangenehm; dumm, ungünstig (*Zeitpunkt etc.*).

awl [ɔːl] Ahle *f*, Pfriem *m*.

aw·ning [ˈɔːnɪŋ] Plane *f*; Markise *f*.

a·woke [ə'wəuk] *pret. von awake* 2; *a.* **a·wok·en** [~ən] *p.p. von awake* 2.

a·wry [ə'raɪ] schief; *fig.* verkehrt.

ax(e) [æks] Axt *f*, Beil *n*.

ax·is [ˈæksɪs] (*pl. -es* [-siːz]) Achse *f*.

ax·le ⊕ [ˈæksl] *a.* **~-tree** (Rad)Achse *f*, Welle *f*.

ay(e) [aɪ] Ja *n*; *parl.* Jastimme *f*; *the ~s have it* der Antrag ist angenommen.

az·ure [ˈæʒə] azur-, himmelblau.

B

bab·ble [ˈbæbl] **1.** stammeln; plappern, schwatzen; plätschern (*Bach*); **2.** Geplapper *n*, Geschwätz *n*.

babe [beɪb] kleines Kind, Baby *n*; *Am.* F Puppe *f* (*Mädchen*).

ba·boon *zo.* [bə'buːn] Pavian *m*.

ba·by [ˈbeɪbɪ] **1.** Säugling *m*, kleines Kind, Baby *n*; *Am.* F Puppe *f* (*Mädchen*); **2.** Baby..., Kinder...; klein; **~ car·riage** *Am.* Kinderwagen *m*; **~·hood** [~hud] frühe Kindheit, Säuglingsalter *n*; **~·mind·er** *Brt.* [~maɪndə] Tagesmutter *f*; **~·sit** (*-tt-, -sat*) babysitten; **~·sit·ter** [~ə] Babysitter(in).

bach·e·lor [ˈbætʃələ] Junggeselle *m*; *univ.* Bakkalaureus *m* (*Grad*).

back [bæk] **1.** Rücken *m*; Rückseite *f*; Rücklehne *f*; Hinterende *n*; *Fußball:* Verteidiger *m*; **2.** *adj.* Hinter..., Rück..., hintere(r, -s), rückwärtig; entlegen; rückläufig; rückständig; alt, zurückliegend (*Zeitung etc.*); **3.** *adv.* zurück; rückwärts; **4.** *v/t.* mit e-m Rücken versehen; (*a. ~ up*) unterstützen; hinten grenzen an

(*acc.*); zurückbewegen, zurückstoßen mit (*Auto*); wetten *od.* setzen auf (*acc.*); *econ.* Scheck indossieren; *v/i.* sich rückwärts bewegen, zurückgehen *od.* -treten *od.* -fahren, *mot. a.* zurückstoßen; **~ al·ley** *Am.* finstere Seitengasse; **~·bite** [ˈbækbaɪt] (*-bit, -bitten*) verleumden; **~·bone** Rückgrat *n*; **~·break·ing** [~ɪŋ] erschöpfend, mörderisch (*Arbeit*); **~·comb** *Haar* toupieren; **~·er** [~ə] Unterstützer(in); Wetter(in); **~·fire** *mot.* Früh-, Fehlzündung *f*; **~·ground** Hintergrund *m*; **~·hand** *Sport:* Rückhand *f*; **~·ing** [~ɪŋ] Unterstützung *f*; ⊕ versteifende Ausfütterung, Verstärkung *f*; ♪ Begleitung *f* (*e-s Popsängers*); **~ num·ber** alte Nummer (*e-r Zeitung*); **~ seat** Rücksitz *m*; **~·side** Gesäß *n*, Hintern *m*, Po *m*; **~ stairs** Hintertreppe *f*; **~ street** Seitenstraße *f*; **~·stroke** *Sport:* Rückenschwimmen *n*; **~ talk** *Am.* F freche Antwort(en *pl.*); **~·track** *fig.* e-n Rückzieher machen; **~·ward** [~wəd] **1.** *adj.* Rück-

(wärts)...; langsam; zurückgeblieben; rückständig; zurückhaltend; **2.** *adv.* (*a.* **~·wards** [~wədz]) rückwärts, zurück; **~·yard** *Brt.* Hinterhof *m*; *Am.* Garten *m* hinter dem Haus.

ba·con ['beɪkən] Speck *m*.

bac·te·ri·a *biol.* [bæk'tɪərɪə] *pl.* Bakterien *pl.*

bad □ [bæd] (*worse, worst*) schlecht, böse, schlimm; *go* ~ schlecht werden, verderben; *he is in a* ~ *way* es geht ihm schlecht, er ist übel dran; *he is ~ly off* es geht ihm sehr schlecht; *~ly wounded* schwerverwundet; *want ~ly* F dringend brauchen.

bade [beɪd] *pret. von* bid 1.

badge [bædʒ] Abzeichen *n*; Dienstmarke *f*.

bad·ger ['bædʒə] **1.** *zo.* Dachs *m*; **2.** plagen, *j-m* zusetzen.

bad·lands ['bædlændz] *pl.* Ödland *n*.

baf·fle ['bæfl] *j-n* verwirren; *Plan etc.* vereiteln, durchkreuzen.

bag [bæg] **1.** Beutel *m*, Sack *m*; Tüte *f*; Tasche *f*; ~ *and baggage* (mit) Sack und Pack; **2.** (*-gg-*) in e-n Beutel *etc.* tun; in e-n Beutel verpacken *od.* abfüllen; *hunt.* zur Strecke bringen; (sich) bauschen.

bag·gage *bsd. Am.* ['bægɪdʒ] (Reise)Gepäck *n*; **~·car** 🚃 Gepäckwagen *m*; **~ check** *Am.* Gepäckschein *m*; **~ room** *Am.* Gepäckaufbewahrung *f*.

bag·gy F ['bægɪ] (*-ier, -iest*) sackartig; schlaff (herunterhängend); ausgebeult (*Hose*).

bag·pipes ['bægpaɪps] *pl.* Dudelsack *m*.

bail [beɪl] **1.** Bürge *m*; Bürgschaft *f*; Kaution *f*; *admit to* ~ ⚖ gegen Kaution freilassen; *go od. stand* ~ *for s.o.* ⚖ für *j-n* Kaution stellen; **2.** ~ *out* ⚖ *j-n* gegen Kaution freibekommen; *Am.* ✈ (mit dem Fallschirm) abspringen.

bai·liff ['beɪlɪf] ⚖ *bsd.* Gerichtsvollzieher *m*; (Guts)Verwalter *m*.

bait [beɪt] **1.** Köder *m* (*a. fig.*); **2.** mit e-m Köder versehen; *fig.* ködern; *fig.* quälen, piesacken.

bake [beɪk] backen, im (Back)Ofen braten; *Ziegel* brennen; dörren; *~d beans pl.* Bohnen *pl.* in Tomatensoße; *~d potatoes pl.* ungeschälte, im Ofen gebackene Kartoffeln; Folienkartoffel *pl.*; **bak·er** ['beɪkə] Bäcker

m; **bak·er·y** [~ərɪ] Bäckerei *f*; **bak·ing-pow·der** [~ɪŋpaʊdə] Backpulver *n*.

bal·ance ['bæləns] **1.** Waage *f*; Gleichgewicht *n* (*a. fig.*); Harmonie *f*; *econ.* Bilanz *f*; *econ.* Saldo *m*, Kontostand *m*, Guthaben *n*; F Rest *m*; *a.* ~ *wheel* Unruh *f* (*der Uhr*); *keep one's* ~ das Gleichgewicht halten; *lose one's* ~ das Gleichgewicht verlieren; *fig.* die Fassung verlieren; ~ *of payments econ.* Zahlungsbilanz *f*; ~ *of power pol.* Kräftegleichgewicht *n*; ~ *of trade* (Außen)Handelsbilanz *f*; **2.** *v/t.* (ab-, er)wägen; im Gleichgewicht halten, balancieren; ausgleichen; *v/i.* balancieren, sich ausgleichen.

bal·co·ny ['bælkənɪ] Balkon *m* (*a. thea.*).

bald □ [bɔːld] kahl; *fig.* dürftig; *fig.* unverblümt; △ *nicht* bald.

bale¹ *econ.* [beɪl] Ballen *m*.

bale² *Brt.* ✈ [~]: ~ *out* (mit dem Fallschirm) abspringen.

bale·ful □ ['beɪlfl] verderblich; unheilvoll; haßerfüllt (*Blick*).

balk [bɔːk] **1.** 🌾 (Furchen)Rain *m*; Balken *m*; Hindernis *n*; **2.** *v/t.* (ver)hindern, vereiteln; *v/i.* stutzen; scheuen.

ball¹ [bɔːl] **1.** Ball *m*; Kugel *f*; *anat.* (Hand-, Fuß)Ballen *m*; Knäuel *m, n*; Kloß *m*; ~*s pl.* V Eier *pl.* (*Hoden*); *keep the* ~ *rolling* das Gespräch *od.* die Sache in Gang halten; *play* ~ F mitmachen; **2.** (sich) (zusammen-) ballen.

ball² [~] Ball *m*, Tanzveranstaltung *f*.

bal·lad ['bæləd] Ballade *f*; Lied *n*.

bal·last ['bæləst] **1.** Ballast *m*; Schotter *m*; **2.** mit Ballast beladen; beschottern.

ball-bear·ing ⊕ ['bɔːl'beərɪŋ] Kugellager *n*.

bal·let ['bæleɪ] Ballett *n*.

bal·lis·tics ✕, *phys.* [bə'lɪstɪks] *sg.* Ballistik *f*.

bal·loon [bə'luːn] **1.** Ballon *m*; **2.** im Ballon aufsteigen; sich blähen.

bal·lot ['bælət] **1.** Wahl-, Stimmzettel *m*; geheime Wahl; **2.** (geheim) abstimmen; ~ *for* losen um; **~·box** Wahlurne *f*.

ball-point (pen) ['bɔːlpɔɪnt('pen)] Kugelschreiber *m*.

ball·room ['bɔːlrʊm] Ball-, Tanzsaal *m*.

balm

balm [bɑːm] Balsam *m* (*a. fig.*).
balm·y □ ['bɑːmɪ] (*-ier, -iest*) lind,
mild (*Wetter*); *bsd. Am. sl.* bekloppt,
verrückt.
ba·lo·ney *Am. sl.* [bə'ləʊnɪ] Quatsch
m.
bal·us·trade [bælə'streɪd] Balustrade
f, Brüstung *f*, Geländer *n*.
bam·boo ♀ [bæm'buː] (*pl. -boos*)
Bambus(rohr *n*) *m*.
bam·boo·zle F [bæm'buːzl] betrügen, übers Ohr hauen.
ban [bæn] **1.** (amtliches) Verbot,
Sperre *f*; *eccl.* Bann *m*; **2.** (*-nn-*)
verbieten.
ba·nal [bə'nɑːl] banal, abgedroschen.
ba·na·na ♀ [bə'nɑːnə] Banane *f*.
band [bænd] **1.** Band *n*; Streifen *m*;
Schar *f*, Gruppe *f*; (*bsd. Räuber*)Ban-
de *f*; ♪ Kapelle *f*, (Tanz-, Unterhaltungs)Orchester *n*, (Jazz-, Rock-)
Band *f*; △ *nicht* Buch-Band, Tonband; **2.** ~ *together* sich zusammentun od. zusammenrotten.
ban·dage ['bændɪdʒ] **1.** Binde *f*; Verband *m*; **2.** bandagieren; verbinden.
ban·dit ['bændɪt] Bandit *m*.
band|-mas·ter ['bændmɑːstə] Ka-
pellmeister *m*; ~**stand** Musikpavil-
lon *m*, -podium *n*; ~**wa·gon** *m*.
Wagen *m* mit Musikkapelle; *jump
on the* ~ sich der erfolgversprechen-
den Sache anschließen.
ban·dy¹ ['bændɪ]: ~ *words* (*with s.o.*)
sich (mit j-m) streiten; ~ *about Gerüchte etc.* in Umlauf setzen *od.* wei-
tererzählen.
ban·dy² [~] (*-ier, -iest*) krumm; ~**-
legged** säbel-, O-beinig.
bane [beɪn] Ruin *m*, Fluch *m*; ~**ful** □
['beɪnfl] verderblich.
bang [bæŋ] **1.** heftiger Schlag; Knall
m; *mst* ~*s pl.* Ponyfrisur *f*; **2.** dröh-
nend (zu)schlagen.
ban·ish ['bænɪʃ] verbannen; ~**ment**
[~mənt] Verbannung *f*.
ban·is·ter ['bænɪstə] *a.* ~*s pl.* Trep-
pengeländer.
bank [bæŋk] **1.** Damm *m*; Ufer *n*;
(Fels-, Sand-, Wolken-, ⚓ Blut-
etc.)Bank *f*; *econ.* Bank(haus *n*) *f*; ~ *of
issue* Notenbank *f*; △ *nicht* Sitz-
Bank; **2.** *v/t.* eindämmen; *econ.* Geld
auf e-r Bank einzahlen; ⚓ *Blut etc.*
konservieren u. aufbewahren; *v/i.*
econ. Bankgeschäfte machen; *econ.*
ein Bankkonto haben; ~ *on* sich
verlassen auf (*acc.*); ~**bill** ['bæŋkbɪl]

Bankwechsel *m*; *Am.* = *banknote*;
~**book** Kontobuch *n*, *a.* Sparbuch
n; ~**er** [~ə] Bankier *m*; ~ **hol·i·day**
Brt. Bankfeiertag *m* (*gesetzlicher
Feiertag*); ~**ing** [~ɪŋ] Bankgeschäft
n, Bankwesen *n*; *attr.* Bank...; ~**note**
Banknote *f*, Geldschein *m*; ~ **rate**
Diskontsatz *m*.
bank·rupt ⚖ ['bæŋkrʌpt] **1.** Zah-
lungsunfähige(r *m*) *f*; **2.** bankrott,
zahlungsunfähig; *go* ~ in Konkurs
gehen, Bankrott machen; **3.** bankrott
machen; ~**cy** ⚖ [~sɪ] Bankrott *m*,
Konkurs *m*.
ban·ner ['bænə] Banner *n*; Fahne *f*.
banns [bænz] *pl.* Aufgebot *n*.
ban·quet ['bæŋkwɪt] Bankett *n*, Festessen *n*.
ban·ter ['bæntə] necken.
bap|tis·m ['bæptɪzəm] Taufe *f*; ~**-
tize** [bæp'taɪz] taufen.
bar [bɑː] **1.** Stange *f*, Stab *m*; Barren
m; Riegel *m*; Schranke *f*; Sandbank
f; (*Ordens*)Spange *f*; ♪ Takt(strich)
m; dicker Strich; ⚖ (Gerichts-)
Schranke *f*; ⚖ Anwaltschaft *f*; Bar *f*
(*im Hotel etc.*); *fig.* Hindernis *n*; **2.**
(*-rr-*) zu-, verriegeln; versperren;
einsperren; (ver)hindern; ausschließen.
barb [bɑːb] Widerhaken *m*.
bar·bar·i·an [bɑː'beərɪən] **1.** barba-
risch; **2.** Barbar(in).
bar·be·cue ['bɑːbɪkjuː] **1.** Bratrost *m*,
Grill *m*; Grillfleisch *n* (*bsd. Ochse*);
Grillparty *f*; **2.** *bsd. Ochse* auf dem
Rost braten, grillen.
barbed wire [bɑːbd 'waɪə] Stachel-
draht *m*.
bar·ber ['bɑːbə] (Herren)Friseur *m*.
bare [beə] **1.** (~*r*, ~*st*) nackt, bloß;
kahl; bar, leer; **2.** entblößen; ~**faced**
□ ['beəfeɪst] frech; ~**foot**, ~**footed**
barfuß; ~**head·ed** barhäuptig; ~**ly**
[~lɪ] kaum.
bar·gain ['bɑːgɪn] **1.** Vertrag *m*, Abmachung *f*; Geschäft *n*, Handel *m*,
Kauf *m*; vorteilhafter Kauf; *a* (*dead*)
~ spottbillig; *it's a* ~! abgemacht!;
into the ~ obendrein; **2.** (ver)han-
deln; übereinkommen; ~ **sale** Ausverkauf *m*.
barge [bɑːdʒ] **1.** Flußboot *n*, Last-
kahn *m*; Hausboot *n*; **2.** ~ *in(to)*
hereinplatzen in (*acc.*).
bark¹ [bɑːk] **1.** ♀ Borke *f*, Rinde *f*; **2.**
abrinden; *Knie* abschürfen.
bark² [~] **1.** bellen; ~ *up the wrong*

tree F auf dem Holzweg sein; an der falschen Adresse sein; **2.** Bellen *n*.

bar·ley ♀ ['bɑːlɪ] Gerste *f*; Graupe *f*.

barn [bɑːn] Scheune *f*; (Vieh)Stall *m*; **~storm** Am. pol. ['bɑːnstɔːm] herumreisen u. (Wahl)Reden halten.

ba·rom·e·ter [bə'rɒmɪtə] Barometer *n*.

bar·on ['bærən] Baron *m*; Freiherr *m*; **~ess** [~ɪs] Baronin *f*; Freifrau *f*.

bar·racks ['bærəks] *sg*. ⚔ Kaserne *f*; *contp*. Mietskaserne *f*; ⚠ *nicht* Baracke.

bar·rage ['bærɑːʒ] Staudamm *m*; ⚔ Sperrfeuer *n*; *fig*. Hagel *m*, (Wort-, Rede)Schwall *m*.

bar·rel ['bærəl] **1.** Faß *n*, Tonne *f*; (*Gewehr*)Lauf *m*; ⊕ Trommel *f*, Walze *f*; **2.** in Fässer füllen; **~or·gan** ♪ Drehorgel *f*.

bar·ren □ ['bærən] unfruchtbar; dürr, trocken; tot (*Kapital*).

bar·ri·cade [bærɪ'keɪd] **1.** Barrikade *f*; **2.** verbarrikadieren; sperren.

bar·ri·er ['bærɪə] Schranke *f* (*a. fig.*), Barriere *f*, Sperre *f*; Hindernis *n*.

bar·ris·ter *Brt*. ['bærɪstə] (plädierender) Rechtsanwalt, Barrister *m*.

bar·row ['bærəʊ] Karre *f*.

bar·ter ['bɑːtə] **1.** Tausch(handel) *m*; **2.** tauschen (*for gegen*).

base¹ □ [beɪs] (*~r, ~st*) gemein.

base² [~] **1.** Basis *f*; Grundlage *f*; Fundament *n*; Fuß *m*; ⚠ Base *f*; ⚔ Standort *m*; ⚔ Stützpunkt *m*; **2.** gründen, stützen (*on, upon* auf *acc*.).

base·ball ['beɪsbɔːl] Baseball(spiel *n*) *m*; **~board** Am. Scheuerleiste *f*; **~less** ['beɪslɪs] grundlos; **~ment** [~mənt] Fundament *n*; Kellergeschoß *n*.

base·ness ['beɪsnɪs] Gemeinheit *f*.

bash·ful □ ['bæʃfl] schüchtern.

ba·sic¹ ['beɪsɪk] **1.** grundlegend, Grund...; ⚠ basisch; **2.** ~s *pl*. Grundlagen *pl*.

BA·SIC² [~] BASIC *n* (*e-e Computersprache*)

ba·sic·al·ly ['beɪsɪkəlɪ] im Grunde.

ba·sin ['beɪsn] Becken *n*, Schale *f*, Schüssel *f*; Tal-, Wasser-, Hafenbecken *n*.

ba·sis ['beɪsɪs] (*pl. -ses* [-siːz]) Basis *f*; Grundlage *f*.

bask [bɑːsk] sich sonnen (*a. fig.*).

bas·ket ['bɑːskɪt] Korb *m*; **~ball** Basketball(spiel *n*) *m*.

bass¹ ♪ [beɪs] Baß *m*.

bass² *zo*. [bæs] (Fluß-, See)Barsch *m*.

bas·tard ['bɑːstəd] **1.** □ unehelich; unecht; Bastard...; **2.** Bastard *m*.

baste¹ [beɪst] *Braten* mit Fett begießen.

baste² [~] (an)heften.

bat¹ [bæt] *zo*. Fledermaus *f*; *as blind as a* ~ stockblind.

bat² [~] *Sport*: **1.** Schlagholz *n*, Schläger *m*; **2.** (*-tt-*) *den Ball* schlagen; *am* Schlagen *od*. dran sein.

batch [bætʃ] Schub *m* (*Brote*); Stoß *m*, Stapel *m* (*Briefe etc*.).

bate [beɪt]: *with ~d breath* mit angehaltenem Atem.

bath [bɑːθ] **1.** (*pl. baths* [~ðz]) (Wannen)Bad *n*; *have a* ~ *Brt.*, *take a* ~ *Am.* baden, ein Bad nehmen; *~s pl.* Bad *n*; Badeanstalt *f*; Badeort *m*; **2.** *Brt. v/t. Kind etc.* baden; *v/i.* baden, ein Bad nehmen.

bathe [beɪð] *v/t. Wunde etc.*, *bsd. Am. Kind etc.* baden; *v/i.* baden; schwimmen; *bsd. Am.* baden, ein Bad nehmen.

bath·ing ['beɪðɪŋ] Baden *n*; *attr.* Bade...; **~suit** Badeanzug *m*.

bath·robe ['bɑːθrəʊb] Bademantel *m*; *Am.* Morgen-, Schlafrock *m*; **~room** Badezimmer *n*; **~tow·el** Badetuch *n*; **~tub** Badewanne *f*.

bat·on ['bætən] Stab *m*; ♪ Taktstock *m*; Schlagstock *m*, Gummiknüppel *m*.

bat·tal·i·on ⚔ [bə'tæljən] Bataillon *n*.

bat·ten ['bætn] Latte *f*.

bat·ter ['bætə] **1.** *Sport*: Schläger *m*; Rührteig *m*; **2.** heftig schlagen; *Ehefrau*, *Kind etc.* mißhandeln; verbeulen; ~ *down od. in* Tür einschlagen; **~y** [~rɪ] Batterie *f*; *assault and* ~ ⚖ tätlicher Angriff; **~y-op·e·rat·ed** batteriebetrieben.

bat·tle ['bætl] **1.** Schlacht *f* (*of bei*); **2.** streiten, kämpfen; **~ax(e)** Streitaxt *f*; F alter Drachen (*bösartige Frau*); **~field**, **~ground** Schlachtfeld *n*; **~ments** [~mənts] *pl.* Zinnen *pl.*; **~plane** ⚔ Kampfflugzeug *n*; **~ship** ⚔ Schlachtschiff *n*.

baulk [bɔːk] = **balk.**

Ba·var·i·an [bə'veərɪən] **1.** bay(e)risch; **2.** Bayer(in).

bawd·y ['bɔːdɪ] (*-ier, -iest*) obszön.

bawl [bɔːl] brüllen, schreien, grölen; ~ *out Befehl* brüllen.

bay¹ [beɪ] **1.** rotbraun; **2.** Braune(r) *m* (*Pferd*).

bay² [~] Bai *f*, Bucht *f*; Erker *m*.

bay³ ♥ [~] *a.* ~ *tree* Lorbeer(baum) *m*.

bay⁴ [~] **1.** bellen, Laut geben (*Hund*); **2.** *hold a.* keep at ~ *j-n* in Schach halten; *et.* von sich fernhalten.

bay·o·net ✗ [ˈbeɪənɪt] Bajonett *n*.

bay·ou *Am.* [ˈbaɪuː] sumpfiger Fluß-arm.

bay win·dow [ˈbeɪˈwɪndəʊ] Erker-fenster *n*; *Am. sl.* Vorbau *m* (*Bauch*).

ba·za(a)r [bəˈzɑː] Basar *m*.

be [biː, bɪ] (*was od. were, been*) sein; *zur Bildung des Passivs*: werden; stattfinden; werden (*beruflich*); *he wants to* ~ ... er möchte ... werden; *how much are the shoes?* was ko-sten die Schuhe? ~ *reading* im Lesen sein, gerade lesen; *there is, there are es* gibt.

beach [biːtʃ] **1.** Strand *m*; **2.** ⚓ auf den Strand setzen *od.* ziehen; ~ **ball** Wasserball *m*; ~ **bug·gy** *mot.* Strand-buggy *m*; ~ **comb·er** *fig.* [ˈbiːtʃ-kəʊmə] Nichtstuer *m*.

bea·con [ˈbiːkən] Leuchtfeuer *n*; Funkfeuer *n*.

bead [biːd] (*Glas- etc.*)Perle *f*; Trop-fen *m*; ~**s** *pl. a.* Rosenkranz *m*; ~**y** [ˈbiːdɪ] (*-ier, -iest*) klein, rund u. glänzend (*Augen*).

beak [biːk] Schnabel *m*; ⊕ Tülle *f*.

bea·ker [ˈbiːkə] Becher *m*.

beam [biːm] **1.** Balken *m*; Waage-balken *m*; Strahl *m*; ✏ (Funk)Leit-, Richtstrahl *m*; **2.** ausstrahlen, strah-len (*a. fig. with* vor *dat.*).

bean [biːn] ♥ Bohne *f*; *Am. sl.* Birne *f* (*Kopf*); *be full of* ~**s** F voller Le-ben(skraft) stecken.

bear¹ *zo.* [beə] Bär *m*.

bear² [~] (*bore, borne od. pass. gebo-ren* [*werden*]: *born*) *v/t.* tragen; ge-bären; *ein Gefühl* hegen; ertragen; aushalten; *mst nativ*: ausstehen, leiden; ~ *down* überwinden, bewäl-tigen; ~*out* bestätigen; *v/i.* tragen; *zo.* trächtig sein; ~**a·ble** □ [ˈbeərəbl] erträglich.

beard [bɪəd] Bart *m*; ♥ Grannen *pl.*; ~**ed** [ˈbɪədɪd] bärtig.

bear·er [ˈbeərə] Träger(in); *econ.* Überbringer(in), (*Wertpapier*)Inha-ber(in).

bear·ing [ˈbeərɪŋ] (Er)Tragen *n*; Be-tragen *n*; *fig.* Beziehung *f*; Lage *f*, Richtung *f*, Orientierung *f*; *take one's* ~**s** sich orientieren; *lose one's* ~**s** die Orientierung verlieren.

beast [biːst] Vieh *n*, Tier *n*; Bestie *f*; ~**ly** [ˈbiːstlɪ] (*-ier, -iest*) scheußlich.

beat [biːt] (*beat, beaten od. beat*) *v/t.* schlagen; (ver)prügeln; besie-gen; übertreffen; ~ *it!* F hau ab!; *that* ~*s all!* das ist doch der Gipfel *od.* die Höhe!; *that* ~*s me* das ist mir zu hoch; ~ *down econ.* Preis drücken, herunterhandeln; ~ *out* Melodie etc. trommeln; *Feuer* ausschlagen; ~ *up j-n* zusammenschlagen; *v/i.* schla-gen; ~ *about the bush* wie die Katze um den heißen Brei herumschlei-chen; **2.** Schlag *m*; ♪ Takt(schlag) *m*; *Jazz:* Beat *m*; Pulsschlag *m*; Runde *f*, Revier *n* (*e-s Polizisten*); **3.** (*dead*) ~ F wie erschlagen, fix u. fertig; ~**en** [ˈbiːtn] *p.p. von beat 1*; vielbegangen (*Weg*); *off the* ~ *track* abgelegen; *fig.* ungewohnt.

beau·ti·cian [bjuːˈtɪʃn] Kosmetikerin *f*; ~**ful** □ [ˈbjuːtəfl] schön; ~**fy** [ˈtɪfaɪ] schön(er) machen.

beau·ty [ˈbjuːtɪ] Schönheit *f*; *Sleep-ing* ♀ Dornrös·chen *n*; ~ *parlo(u)r*, ~ *shop* Schönheitssalon *m*.

bea·ver [ˈbiːvə] *zo.* Biber *m*; Biber-pelz *m*.

be·came [bɪˈkeɪm] *pret. von become*.

be·cause [bɪˈkɒz] weil; ~ *of* wegen.

beck·on [ˈbekən] (zu)winken.

be·come [bɪˈkʌm] (*-came, -come*) *v/i.* werden (*of* aus); *v/t.* sich schik-ken für; *j-m* stehen, *j-n* kleiden; △ *nicht bekommen*; **be·com·ing** □ [~ɪŋ] passend; schicklich; kleidsam.

bed [bed] **1.** Bett *n*; Lager *n* (*e-s Tieres*); ♪ Beet *n*; Unterlage *f*; ~ *and breakfast* Zimmer *n* mit Frühstück; **2.** (*-dd-*): ~ *down* sein Nachtlager aufschlagen; ~**clothes** [ˈbedkləʊðz] *pl.* Bettwäsche *f*; ~**ding** [~ɪŋ] Bett-zeug *n*; Streu *f*.

bed·lam [ˈbedləm] Tollhaus *n*.

bed·rid·den [ˈbedrɪdn] bettlägerig; ~**room** Schlafzimmer *n*; ~**side**: *at the* ~ am (*a. Kranken*)Bett; ~**side lamp** Nachttischlampe *f*; ~**sit** F, ~**sit·ter** [~ə], ~**sit·ting room** [~ɪŋ] *Brt.* möbliertes Zimmer *n*; Einzimmer-ap-partement *n*; ~**spread** Tagesdecke *f*; ~**stead** Bettgestell *n*; ~**time** Schlafenszeit *f*.

bee [biː] *zo.* Biene *f*; *have a* ~ *in one's bonnet* F e-n Tick haben.

beech ♥ [biːtʃ] Buche *f*; ~**nut** Buch-ecker *f*.

beef [biːf] **1.** Rindfleisch *n*; **2.** F

meckern (*about* über *acc.*); **~ tea** Fleischbrühe *f*; **~·y** ['biːfɪ] (*-ier, -iest*) fleischig; kräftig, bullig.

bee·hive ['biːhaɪv] Bienenkorb *m*, -stock *m*; **~·keep·er** Bienenzüchter *m*, Imker *m*; **~·line** kürzester Weg; **make a ~ for** schnurstracks losgehen auf (*acc.*).

been biːn, bɪn *p.p. von* be.

beer [bɪə] Bier *n*.

beet ♀ [biːt] (Runkel)Rübe *f*, Bete *f*; *Am.* = beetroot.

bee·tle¹ *zo.* ['biːtl] Käfer *m*.

bee·tle² [~] **1.** überhängend; buschig (*Brauen*); **2.** *v/i.* überhängen.

beet·root ♀ ['biːtruːt] Rote Bete *od.* Rübe.

be·fall [bɪˈfɔːl] (*-fell, -fallen*) *v/t. j-m* zustoßen; △ *nicht befallen*; *v/i.* sich ereignen.

be·fit [bɪˈfɪt] (*-tt-*) sich schicken für.

be·fore [bɪˈfɔː] **1.** *adv. räumlich:* vorn, voran; *zeitlich:* vorher, früher, schon (früher); **2.** *cj.* bevor, ehe, bis; **3.** *prp.* vor; **~·hand** zuvor, (im) voraus.

be·friend [bɪˈfrend] sich *j-s* annehmen; △ *nicht befreunden.*

beg [beg] (*-gg-*) *v/t. et.* erbetteln; erbitten (*of* von), bitten um; *j-n* bitten; *v/i.* betteln; bitten, flehen; betteln gehen; *iro.* sich erlauben.

be·gan [bɪˈgæn] *pret. von* begin.

be·get [bɪˈget] (*-tt-; -got, -gotten*) (er)zeugen.

beg·gar ['begə] **1.** Bettler(in); F Kerl *m*; △ arm machen; *fig.* übertreffen; *it ~s all description* es spottet jeder Beschreibung.

be·gin [bɪˈgɪn] (*-nn-; began, begun*) beginnen, anfangen; **~·ner** [~ə] Anfänger(in); **~·ning** Beginn *m*, Anfang *m*.

be·gone *int.* [bɪˈgɒn] fort!

be·got [bɪˈgɒt] *pret. von* beget; **~·ten** [~tn] *p.p. von* beget.

be·grudge [bɪˈgrʌdʒ] mißgönnen.

be·guile [bɪˈgaɪl] täuschen; betrügen (*of, out of* um); sich *die Zeit* vertreiben.

be·gun [bɪˈgʌn] *p.p. von* begin.

be·half [bɪˈhɑːf]: *on* (*Am. a. in*) *~ of* im Namen von (*od. gen.*).

be·have [bɪˈheɪv] sich (gut) benehmen.

be·hav·io(u)r [bɪˈheɪvjə] Benehmen *n*, Betragen *n*, Verhalten *n*; **~·al** *psych.* [~rəl] Verhaltens...

be·head [bɪˈhed] enthaupten.

be·hind [bɪˈhaɪnd] **1.** *adv.* hinten, dahinter; zurück; **2.** *prp.* hinter; **3.** F Hinterteil *n*, Hintern *m*; **~·hand** im Rückstand.

be·hold [bɪˈhəʊld] (*-held*) **1.** erblicken, sehen; △ *nicht behalten*; **2.** *int.* siehe (da)!; **~·er** [~ə] Betrachter(in).

be·ing ['biːɪŋ] (Da)Sein *n*; Wesen *n*; *in ~* wirklich (vorhanden).

be·lat·ed [bɪˈleɪtɪd] verspätet.

belch [beltʃ] **1.** aufstoßen, rülpsen; ausspeien; **2.** Rülpser *m*.

be·lea·guer [bɪˈliːgə] belagern.

bel·fry ['belfrɪ] Glockenturm *m*, -stuhl *m*.

Bel·gian ['beldʒən] **1.** belgisch; **2.** Belgier(in).

be·lie [bɪˈlaɪ] Lügen strafen.

be·lief [bɪˈliːf] Glaube *m* (*in* an *acc.*).

be·liev·a·ble □ [bɪˈliːvəbl] glaubhaft.

be·lieve [bɪˈliːv] glauben (*in* an *acc.*); **be·liev·er** *eccl.* [~ə] Gläubige(r *m*) *f*.

be·lit·tle *fig.* [bɪˈlɪtl] herabsetzen.

bell [bel] Glocke *f*; Klingel *f*; **~·boy** *Am.* ['belbɔɪ] (Hotel)Page *m*.

belle [bel] Schöne *f*, Schönheit *f*.

bell·hop *Am.* ['belhɒp] (Hotel)Page *m*.

~·bel·lied ['belɪd] ...bäuchig.

bel·lig·er·ent [bɪˈlɪdʒərənt] **1.** kriegführend; kampflustig; aggressiv; **2.** kriegführendes Land.

bel·low ['beləʊ] **1.** brüllen; **2.** Gebrüll *n*; **~s** *pl.* Blasebalg *m*.

bel·ly ['belɪ] **1.** Bauch *m*; **2.** sich bauchen; (an)schwellen; bauschen; **~·ache** F Bauchweh *n*.

be·long [bɪˈlɒŋ] gehören; *~ to* gehören *dat. od.* zu; **~·ings** [~ɪŋz] *pl.* Habseligkeiten *pl.*

be·loved [bɪˈlʌvd] **1.** (innig) geliebt; **2.** Geliebte(r *m*) *f*.

be·low [bɪˈləʊ] **1.** *adv.* unten; **2.** *prp.* unter.

belt [belt] **1.** Gürtel *m*; ⚔ Koppel *n*; Zone *f*, Gebiet *n*; ⊕ Treibriemen *m*; **2.** *a. ~ up* den Gürtel (*gen.*) zumachen; **~·ed** ['beltɪd] mit e-m Gürtel.

be·moan [bɪˈməʊn] betrauern, beklagen.

bench [bentʃ] (Sitz)Bank *f*; Richterbank *f*; Richter *m od. pl.*; Werkbank *f*.

bend [bend] **1.** Biegung *f*, Kurve *f*; *drive s.o. round the ~* F j-n noch wahnsinnig machen; **2.** (*bent*) (sich) biegen; *Gedanken etc.* richten (*to, on* auf *acc.*); (sich) beugen; sich neigen.

B

be·neath [bɪˈniːθ] = below.

ben·e·dic·tion [benɪˈdɪkʃn] Segen m.

ben·e·fac·tor [ˈbenɪfæktə] Wohltäter m.

be·nef·i·cent □ [bɪˈnefɪsnt] wohltätig.

ben·e·fi·cial □ [benɪˈfɪʃl] wohltuend, zuträglich, nützlich.

ben·e·fit [ˈbenɪfɪt] **1.** Nutzen m, Vorteil m; Wohltätigkeitsveranstaltung f; (Sozial-, Versicherungs- etc.)Leistung f; Rente f; Unterstützung f; **2.** nützen; begünstigen; ~ by od. from Vorteil haben von od. durch, Nutzen ziehen aus.

be·nev·o|lence [bɪˈnevələns] Wohlwollen n; **~lent** □ [~t] wohlwollend; gütig, mildtätig.

be·nign □ [bɪˈnaɪn] freundlich, gütig; ⚕ gutartig.

bent [bent] **1.** pret. u. p.p. von bend 2; ~ on doing entschlossen zu tun; **2.** fig. Hang m, Neigung f; Veranlagung f.

ben·zene ⚗ [ˈbenziːn] Benzol n.

ben·zine ⚗ [ˈbenziːn] Leichtbenzin n; △ nicht Benzin.

be·queath ⚖ [bɪˈkwiːð] vermachen.

be·quest ⚖ [bɪˈkwest] Vermächtnis n.

be·reave [bɪˈriːv] (bereaved od. bereft) berauben.

be·reft [bɪˈreft] pret. u. p.p. von bereave.

be·ret [ˈbereɪ] Baskenmütze f.

ber·ry ♀ [ˈberɪ] Beere f.

berth [bɜːθ] **1.** ⚓ Liege-, Ankerplatz m; ⚓ Koje f; 🚃 (Schlafwagen)Bett n; **2.** v/t. ⚓ vor Anker legen; v/i. ⚓ anlegen.

be·seech [bɪˈsiːtʃ] (besought od. beseeched) (inständig) bitten (um); anflehen.

be·set [bɪˈset] (-tt-; beset) heimsuchen, bedrängen; ~ with difficulties mit vielen Schwierigkeiten verbunden; △ nicht besetzen.

be·side prp. [bɪˈsaɪd] neben; ~ o.s. außer sich (with vor); ~ the point, ~ the question nicht zur Sache gehörig; **~s** [~z] **1.** adv. außerdem; **2.** prp. abgesehen von, außer.

be·siege [bɪˈsiːdʒ] belagern; △ nicht besiegen.

be·smear [bɪˈsmɪə] beschmieren.

be·sought [bɪˈsɔːt] pret. u. p.p. von beseech.

be·spat·ter [bɪˈspætə] bespritzen.

best [best] **1.** adj. (sup. von good 1) beste(r, -s) höchste(r, -s), größte(r, -s), meiste; (sup. von well[2] 1) am besten; **3.** der, die, das Beste; All the ~! Alles Gute!, Viel Glück!; to the ~ of ... nach bestem ...; make the ~ of das Beste machen aus; at ~ bestenfalls; be at one's ~ in Hochod. Höchstform sein.

bes·ti·al □ [ˈbestjəl] tierisch, viehisch.

be·stow [bɪˈstəʊ] geben, schenken, verleihen (on, upon dat.).

best·sell·er [bestˈselə] Bestseller m, Verkaufsschlager m (bsd. Buch).

bet [bet] **1.** Wette f; **2.** (-tt-; bet od. betted) wetten; you ~ F und ob!

be·tray [bɪˈtreɪ] verraten (a. fig.); verleiten; **~al** [~əl] Verrat m; **~er** [~ə] Verräter(in).

bet·ter [ˈbetə] **1.** adj. (comp. von good 1) besser; he is ~ es geht ihm besser; **2.** das Bessere; ~s pl. Höherstehende pl., Vorgesetzte pl.; get the ~ of die Oberhand gewinnen über (acc.); et. überwinden; **3.** adv. (comp. von well[2] 1) besser; so much the ~ desto besser; you had ~ (Am. F you ~) go es wäre besser, wenn du gingest; **4.** v/t. verbessern; v/i. sich bessern.

be·tween [bɪˈtwiːn] **1.** adv. dazwischen; few and far ~ F (ganz) vereinzelt; **2.** prp. zwischen; unter; ~ you and me unter uns od. im Vertrauen (gesagt).

bev·el [ˈbevl] (bsd. Brt. -ll-, Am. -l-) abkanten, abschrägen.

bev·er·age [ˈbevərɪdʒ] Getränk n.

bev·y [ˈbevɪ] Schwarm m, Schar f.

be·wail [bɪˈweɪl] be-, wehklagen.

be·ware [bɪˈweə] (of) sich in acht nehmen (vor dat.), sich hüten (vor dat.); △ nicht bewahren; ~ of the dog! Warnung vor dem Hunde!

be·wil·der [bɪˈwɪldə] verwirren, irremachen; **~ment** [~mənt] Verwirrung f.

be·witch [bɪˈwɪtʃ] bezaubern, behexen.

be·yond [bɪˈjɒnd] **1.** adv. darüber hinaus; **2.** prp. jenseits; über ... (acc.) hinaus.

bi– [baɪ] zwei(fach, -mal).

bi·as [ˈbaɪəs] **1.** adj. u. adv. schief, schräg; **2.** Neigung f; Vorurteil n; **3.** (-s-, -ss-) mst ungünstig beeinflussen; **~(s)ed** bsd. ⚖ befangen.

bi·ath|lete [baɪˈæθliːt] *Sport:* Biathlet *m;* **~lon** [~ɔn] *Sport:* Biathlon *n.*

bib [bɪb] (Sabber)Lätzchen *n.*

Bi·ble [ˈbaɪbl] Bibel *f.*

bib·li·cal □ [ˈbɪblɪkl] biblisch, Bibel...

bib·li·og·ra·phy [bɪblɪˈɒɡrəfɪ] Bibliographie *f.*

bi·car·bon·ate ⚗ [baɪˈkɑːbənɪt] *a.* ~ of soda doppeltkohlensaures Natron.

bi·cen|te·na·ry [baɪsenˈtiːnərɪ] *Am.* **~ten·ni·al** [~ˈtenɪəl] Zweihundertjahrfeier *f,* zweihundertjähriges Jubiläum.

bi·ceps *anat.* [ˈbaɪseps] Bizeps *m.*

bick·er [ˈbɪkə] (sich) zanken; flackern; plätschern; prasseln.

bi·cy·cle [ˈbaɪsɪkl] **1.** Fahrrad *n;* **2.** radfahren, radeln.

bid [bɪd] (-dd-; *bid od. bade, bid od.* bidden) gebieten, befehlen; (ent)bieten; *Karten:* reizen; ~ farewell Lebewohl sagen; **2.** *econ.* Gebot *n,* Angebot *n; Karten:* Reizen *n;* **~den** [bɪd] *p.p. von* bid 1.

bide [baɪd] (bode *od.* bided, bided): ~ one's time den rechten Augenblick abwarten.

bi·en·ni·al □ [baɪˈenɪəl] zweijährlich; zweijährig (*Pflanzen*); **~ly** [~lɪ] alle zwei Jahre.

bier [bɪə] (Toten)Bahre *f;* △ *nicht* Bier.

big [bɪɡ] (-gg-) groß; erwachsen; (hoch)schwanger; F wichtig(tuerisch); ~ business Großunternehmertum *n;* ~ shot F hohes Tier (*Person*); talk ~ den Mund vollnehmen.

big·a·my [ˈbɪɡəmɪ] Bigamie *f.*

big·ot [ˈbɪɡət] selbstgerechte *od.* intolerante Person; **~ed** selbstgerecht, intolerant.

big·wig F [ˈbɪɡwɪɡ] hohes Tier (*Person*).

bike F [baɪk] (Fahr)Rad *n.*

bi·lat·er·al □ [baɪˈlætərəl] bilateral.

bile [baɪl] Galle *f* (*a. fig.*).

bi·lin·gual [baɪˈlɪŋɡwəl] zweisprachig.

bil·i·ous □ [ˈbɪljəs] gallig; *fig.* gereizt.

bill¹ [bɪl] Schnabel *m;* Spitze *f.*

bill² [~] *econ.* **1.** Rechnung *f; pol.* Gesetzentwurf *m;* ⚖ Klageschrift *f; a.* ~ of exchange *econ.* Wechsel *m;* Plakat *n; Am.* Banknote *f,* Geldschein *m;* ~ of fare Speisekarte *f;* ~ of

lading Seefrachtbrief *m,* Konnossement *n;* ~ of sale ⚖ Verkaufsurkunde *f;* **2.** (durch Anschlag) ankündigen.

bill·board *Am.* [ˈbɪlbɔːd] Reklametafel *f.*

bill·fold *Am.* [ˈbɪlfəʊld] Brieftasche *f.*

bil·li·ards [ˈbɪljədz] *sg.* Billiard(spiel) *n.*

bil·li·on [ˈbɪljən] Milliarde *f.*

bil·low [ˈbɪləʊ] Woge *f;* (*Rauch- etc.*) Schwade *f;* **~y** [~ɪ] wogend; in Schwaden ziehend; gebläht, gebauscht.

bil·ly *Am.* [ˈbɪlɪ] (Gummi)Knüppel *m;* **~goat** *zo.* Ziegenbock *m.*

bin [bɪn] (großer) Behälter.

bind [baɪnd] (bound) *v/t.* (an-, ein-, um-, auf-, fest-, ver)binden; *a.* vertraglich binden, verpflichten; *Saum* einfassen; *v/i.* binden; **~er** [ˈbaɪndə] (*bsd. Buch*)Binder(in); Einband *m,* (Akten- *etc.*)Deckel *m,* Hefter *m;* **~ing** [~ɪŋ] **1.** bindend, verbindlich; **2.** (Buch)Einband *m;* Einfassung *f,* Borte *f.*

bi·noc·u·lars [bɪˈnɒkjʊləz] *pl.* Feldstecher *m,* Fern-, Opernglas *n.*

bi·o·chem·is·try [baɪəʊˈkemɪstrɪ] Biochemie *f.*

bi·og·ra|pher [baɪˈɒɡrəfə] Biograph *m;* **~phy** [~ɪ] Biographie *f.*

bi·o·log·i·cal □ [baɪəʊˈlɒdʒɪkl] biologisch; **bi·ol·o·gy** [baɪˈɒlədʒɪ] Biologie *f.*

bi·ped *zo.* [ˈbaɪped] Zweifüßer *m.*

birch [bɜːtʃ] **1.** ♀ Birke *f;* (Birken-)Rute *f;* **2.** (mit der Rute) züchtigen.

bird [bɜːd] Vogel *m;* ~ of prey Raubvogel *m;* ~ sanctuary Vogelschutzgebiet *n;* **~'s-eye** [ˈbɜːdzaɪ]: ~ view Vogelperspektive *f.*

bi·ro *TM* [ˈbaɪrəʊ] (*pl.* -ros) Kugelschreiber *m.*

birth [bɜːθ] Geburt *f;* Ursprung *m,* Entstehung *f;* Herkunft *f;* give ~ to gebären, zur Welt bringen; **~·con·trol** Geburtenregelung *f;* **~day** [ˈbɜːθdeɪ] Geburtstag *m;* **~mark** Muttermal *n;* **~place** Geburtsort *m;* ~ rate Geburtenziffer *f.*

bis·cuit *Brt.* [ˈbɪskɪt] Keks *m, n,* Plätzchen *n;* △ *nicht* Biskuit.

bish·op [ˈbɪʃəp] Bischof *m; Schach:* Läufer *m;* **~ric** [~rɪk] Bistum *n.*

bi·son *zo.* [ˈbaɪsn] Bison *m,* Amer. Büffel; Europäischer Wisent *m.*

bit [bɪt] **1.** Bißchen *n,* Stück(chen) *n;*

B

Gebiß n (am Zaum); (Schlüssel)Bart m; Computer: Bit n; a (little) ~ ein (kleines) bißchen; **2.** pret. von bite 2.

bitch [bɪtʃ] zo. Hündin f; contp. Miststück n, -weib n.

bite [baɪt] **1.** Beißen n; Biß m; Bissen m, Happen m; ⊕ Fassen n; **2.** (bit, bitten) (an)beißen; stechen (Insekt); brennen (Pfeffer); schneiden (Kälte); beißen (Rauch); ⊕ fassen; fig. verletzen.

bit·ten [ˈbɪtn] p.p. von bite 2.

bit·ter [ˈbɪtə] **1.** □ bitter; fig. verbittert; **2.** ~s pl. Magenbitter m.

biz F[bɪz] = business.

blab F [blæb] (-bb-) (aus)schwatzen.

black [blæk] **1.** □ schwarz; dunkel; finster; ~ eye blaues Auge; have s.th. in ~ and white et. schwarz auf weiß haben od. besitzen; be ~ and blue blaue Flecken haben; beat s.o. ~ and blue j-n grün u. blau schlagen; **2.** schwärzen; wichsen; ~ out verdunkeln; **3.** Schwarz n; Schwärze f; Schwarze(r m) f, Neger(in); **~·ber·ry** ♀ [ˈblækberɪ] Brombeere f; **~·bird** zo. Amsel f; **~·board** (Schul-, Wand)Tafel f; △ nicht Schwarzes Brett; **~·en** [~ən] v/t. schwärzen; fig. anschwärzen; v/i. schwarz werden; **~·guard** [ˈblægɑːd] **1.** Lump m, Schuft m; **2.** □ gemein, schuftig; **~·head** ♂ Mitesser m; ~ ice Glatteis n; **~·ing** [~ɪŋ] schwarze Schuhwichse; **~·ish** □ [~ɪʃ] schwärzlich; **~·jack** bsd. Am. Totschläger m (Waffe); **~·leg** Brt. Streikbrecher m; **~·let·ter** print. Fraktur f; **~·mail 1.** Erpressung f; **2.** j-n erpressen; **~·mail·er** [~ə] Erpresser(in); **~ mar·ket** schwarzer Markt; **~·ness** [~nɪs] Schwärze f; **~·out** Verdunkelung f; thea., ♂, Raumfahrt: Blackout n, m; ♂ Ohnmacht f; ~ **pud·ding** Blutwurst f; ~ **sheep** fig. schwarzes Schaf; **~·smith** Grobschmied m.

blad·der anat. [ˈblædə] Blase f.

blade [bleɪd] ♀ Blatt n, Halm m; (Säge-, Schulter- etc.)Blatt n; (Propeller)Flügel m; Klinge f.

blame [bleɪm] **1.** Tadel m; Schuld f; **2.** tadeln; be to ~ for schuld sein an (dat.); △ nicht blamieren; **~·less** □ [~lɪs] untadelig.

blanch [blɑːntʃ] bleichen; erbleichen (lassen).

blanc·mange [bləˈmɒnʒ] Pudding m.

bland □ [blænd] mild, sanft.

blank [blæŋk] **1.** □ leer; unausgefüllt, unbeschrieben; econ. Blanko...; verdutzt; △ nicht blank (glänzend); ~ cartridge ✗ Platzpatrone f; ~ cheque (Am. check) econ. Blankoscheck m; **2.** Leere f; leerer Raum, Lücke f; unbeschriebenes Blatt, Formular n; Lotterie: Niete f.

blan·ket [ˈblæŋkɪt] **1.** (Woll)Decke f; wet ~ Spielverderber m; **2.** zudecken.

blare [bleə] brüllen, plärren (Radio etc.), schmettern (Trompete).

blas·pheme [blæsˈfiːm] lästern; **~·phe·my** [ˈblæsfəmɪ] Gotteslästerung f.

blast [blɑːst] **1.** Windstoß m; Ton m (e-s Blasinstruments); ⊕ Gebläse(luft f) n; Druckwelle f; ♀ Mehltau m; **2.** v/t. vernichten; sprengen; ~ off (into space) Rakete, Astronauten in den Weltraum schießen; v/i.: ~ off abheben, starten (Rakete); ~! verdammt!; **~·fur·nace** ⊕ [ˈblɑːstfɜːnɪs] Hochofen m; **~·off** Start m (Rakete).

bla·tant □ [ˈbleɪtənt] lärmend; kraß; unverhohlen.

blaze [bleɪz] **1.** Flamme n pl.) f, Feuer n; heller Schein; fig. Ausbruch m; go to ~s! zum Teufel mit dir!; **2.** brennen, flammen, lodern; leuchten; △ nicht blasen.

blaz·er [ˈbleɪzə] Blazer m.

bla·zon [ˈbleɪzn] Wappen n.

bleach [bliːtʃ] bleichen.

bleak □ [bliːk] öde, kahl; rauh; fig. trüb, freudlos, finster.

blear·y □ [ˈblɪərɪ] (-ier, -iest) trübe, verschwommen; **~·eyed** mit trüben Augen; verschlafen.

bleat [bliːt] **1.** Blöken n; **2.** blöken.

bled [bled] pret. u. p.p. von bleed.

bleed [bliːd] (bled) v/i. bluten; v/t. ♂ zur Ader lassen; fig. F schröpfen; **~·ing** [ˈbliːdɪŋ] **1.** ♂ Bluten n, Blutung f; ♂ Aderlaß m; **2.** sl. verflixt.

bleep [bliːp] **1.** Piepton m; **2.** j-n anpiepsen (über Funkrufempfänger).

blem·ish [ˈblemɪʃ] **1.** (a. Schönheits-) Fehler m; Makel m; **2.** entstellen.

blend [blend] **1.** (sich) (ver)mischen; Wein etc. verschneiden; △ nicht blenden; **2.** Mischung f; econ. Verschnitt m; **~·er** [ˈblendə] Mixer m, Mixgerät n.

bless [bles] (blessed od. blest) segnen; preisen; be ~ed with gesegnet sein mit; (God) ~ you! alles Gute!;

Gesundheit!; ～ *me!*, ～ *my heart!*, ～ *my soul!* F du meine Güte!; ～**ed** *adj.* □ ['blesɪd] glückselig, gesegnet; ～**ing** [～ɪŋ] Segen *m.*

blest [blest] *pret. u. p.p. von* bless.

blew [bluː] *pret. von* blow¹ 1.

blight [blaɪt] 1. ♣ Mehltau *m;* *fig.* Gifthauch *m;* 2. vernichten.

blind □ [blaɪnd] 1. blind (*fig.* to gegen[über]); verborgen, geheim; schwererkennbar; ～ *alley* Sackgasse *f;* ～*ly fig.* blindlings; 2. Rouleau *n,* Rollo *n;* *the* ～ *pl.* die Blinden *pl.;* 3. blenden; blind machen (*to* für, gegen); ～**ers** *Am.* ['blaɪndəz] *pl.* Scheuklappen *pl.;* ～**fold** 1. blindlings; 2. *j-m* die Augen verbinden; 3. Augenbinde *f;* ～**worm** *zo.* Blindschleiche *f.*

blink [blɪŋk] 1. Blinzeln *n;* Schimmer *m;* 2. v/i. blinzeln, zwinkern; blinken; schimmern; v/t. *fig.* ignorieren; ～**ers** ['blɪŋkəz] *pl.* Scheuklappen *pl.*

bliss [blɪs] Seligkeit *f,* Wonne *f.*

blis|ter ['blɪstə] 1. Blase *f* (*auf der Haut, im Lack*); ♣ Zugpflaster *n;* 2. Blasen hervorrufen auf (*dat.*); Blasen ziehen.

blitz [blɪts] 1. heftiger (Luft)Angriff; 2. schwer bombardieren; △ *nicht* Blitz; blitzen.

bliz|zard ['blɪzəd] Schneesturm *m.*

bloat|ed ['bləʊtɪd] (an)geschwollen, (auf)gedunsen; *fig.* aufgeblasen; ～**er** [～ə] Bückling *m.*

block [blɒk] 1. Block *m,* Klotz *m;* Baustein *m;* Verstopfung *f,* (Verkehrs)Stockung *f;* a. ～ *of flats* Brt. Wohn-, Mietshaus *n;* *Am.* (Häuser-) Block *m;* 2. formen; verhindern; *a.* ～ *up* (ab-, ver)sperren, blockieren.

block|ade [blɒ'keɪd] 1. Blockade *f;* 2. blockieren.

block|head ['blɒkhed] Dummkopf *m;* ～ **let|ters** *pl.* Blockschrift *f.*

bloke *Brt.* F ['bləʊk] Kerl *m.*

blond [blɒnd] 1. Blonde(r) *m;* 2. blond; hell (*Haut*); ～**e** [～] 1. blond; 2. Blondine *f.*

blood [blʌd] Blut *n;* *fig.* Blut *n;* Abstammung *f; attr.* Blut...; *in cold* ～ kaltblütig; ～**cur|dling** ['blʌdkɜː-dlɪŋ] grauenhaft; ～**shed** Blutvergießen *n;* ～**shot** blutunterlaufen; ～**thirst|y** □ blutdürstig; ～**ves|sel** *anat.* Blutgefäß *n;* ～**y** □ [～ɪ] (-*ier,* -*iest*) blutig; *Brt.* F verdammt, verflucht.

bloom [bluːm] 1. *poet.* Blume *f,* Blüte *f; fig.* Blüte(zeit) *f;* △ *nicht allg.* Blume; 2. blühen; *fig.* (er)strahlen.

blos|som ['blɒsəm] 1. Blüte *f;* 2. blühen.

blot [blɒt] 1. Klecks *m; fig.* Makel *m;* 2. (-*tt*-) v/t. beklecksen, beflecken; (ab)löschen; ausstreichen; v/i. klecksen.

blotch [blɒtʃ] Klecks *m;* Hautfleck *m;* ～**y** ['blɒtʃɪ] (-*ier,* -*iest*) fleckig (*Haut*).

blot|ter ['blɒtə] (Tinten)Löscher *m;* *Am.* Eintragungsbuch *n;* ～**ting-pa|per** [～ɪŋpeɪpə] Löschpapier *n.*

blouse [blaʊz] Bluse *f.*

blow¹ [bləʊ] Schlag *m,* Stoß *m.*

blow² [～] 1. (blew, blown) v/i. blasen, wehen; schnaufen; platzen (*Reifen*); ✂ durchbrennen (*Sicherung*); ～ *up* in die Luft fliegen; ～ *one's nose* sich die Nase putzen; ～ *one's top* F an die Decke gehen (*vor Wut*); ～ *out* ausblasen; ～ *up* sprengen; *Foto* vergrößern; 2. Blasen *n,* Wehen *n;* ～**dry** ['bləʊdraɪ] fönen; ～**fly** *zo.* Schmeißfliege *f;* ～**n** [bləʊn] *p.p. von* blow² 1; ～**pipe** ['bləʊpaɪp] ⊕ Lötrohr *n;* Blasrohr *n;* ～**up** Explosion *f; phot.* Vergrößerung *f.*

blud|geon ['blʌdʒən] Knüppel *m.*

blue [bluː] 1. blau; F melancholisch, traurig, schwermütig; 2. Blau *n; out of the* ～ *aus* heiterem Himmel; ～**ber|ry** ♣ ['bluːbərɪ] Blau-, Heidelbeere *f;* ～**bot|tle** *zo.* Schmeißfliege *f;* ～**col|lar work|er** (Fabrik)Arbeiter(in).

blues [bluːz] *pl. od. sing.* ♪ Blues *m;* F Melancholie *f; have the* ～ F den Moralischen haben.

bluff [blʌf] 1. □ schroff, steil; derb; 2. Steilufer *n;* Bluff *m;* 3. bluffen.

blu|ish ['bluːɪʃ] bläulich.

blun|der ['blʌndə] 1. Fehler *m,* Schnitzer *m;* 2. e-n (groben) Fehler machen; stolpern; verpfuschen; △ *nicht* plündern.

blunt [blʌnt] 1. □ stumpf (*a. fig.*); grob, rauh; 2. abstumpfen; ～**ly** ['blʌntlɪ] frei heraus.

blur [blɜː] 1. Fleck *m;* undeutlicher Eindruck, verschwommene Vorstellung; 2. (-*rr*-) v/t. beflecken; verwischen, -schmieren; *phot., TV* verwackeln, -zerren; *Sinn* trüben.

blurt [blɜːt]: ～ *out* herausplatzen mit.

blush [blʌʃ] 1. Schamröte f; Erröten n; 2. erröten, rot werden.

blus·ter [ˈblʌstə] 1. Brausen n, Toben n (a. fig.); fig. Poltern n; 2. brausen; fig. poltern, toben.

boar zo. [bɔː] Eber m; Keiler m.

board [bɔːd] 1. Brett n; (Anschlag-) Brett n; Konferenztisch m; Ausschuß m, Kommission f; Behörde f; Verpflegung f; Pappe f, Karton m; Sport: (Surf)Board n; ⚠ nicht Bücher-Bord; on ~ a train in e-m Zug; ~ of directors econ. Verwaltungsrat m; ⚲ of Trade Brt. Handelsministerium n, Am. Handelskammer f; 2. v/t. dielen, verschalen; beköstigen; an Bord gehen; ⚓ entern; einsteigen in (ein Fahr- od. Flugzeug); v/i. in Kost sein, wohnen; **~·er** [ˈbɔːdə] Kostgänger(in), Pensionsgast m; Internatsschüler(in); **~·ing-house** [~ɪŋhaʊs] Pension f, Fremdenheim n; **~·ing-school** [~ɪŋskuːl] Internat n; **~·walk** bsd. Am. Strandpromenade f.

boast [bəʊst] 1. Prahlerei f; 2. (of, about) sich rühmen (gen.), prahlen (mit); **~·ful** □ [ˈbəʊstfl] prahlerisch.

boat [bəʊt] Boot n; Schiff n; **~·ing** [ˈbəʊtɪŋ] Bootsfahrt f.

bob [bɒb] 1. Quaste f; Ruck m; Knicks m; kurzer Haarschnitt; Brt. F hist. Schilling m; 2. (-bb-) v/t. Haar kurz schneiden; **~·bed hair** Bubikopf m; v/i. springen, tanzen; knicksen.

bob·bin [ˈbɒbɪn] Spule f (a. ⚡).

bob·by Brt. F [ˈbɒbɪ] Bobby m (Polizist).

bob·sleigh [ˈbɒbsleɪ] Sport: Bob m.

bode [bəʊd] pret. von bide.

bod·ice [ˈbɒdɪs] Mieder n; Oberteil n (e-s Kleides).

bod·i·ly [ˈbɒdɪlɪ] körperlich.

bod·y [ˈbɒdɪ] Körper m, Leib m; Leiche f; Körperschaft f; Hauptteil m; mot. Karosserie f; ✗ Truppenkörper m; **~·guard** Leibwache f; **~·work** Karosserie f.

Boer [ˈbəʊə] Bure m; attr. Buren...

bog [bɒg] 1. Sumpf m, Moor n; 2. (-gg-): get **~·ged down** fig. sich festfahren.

bo·gus [ˈbəʊgəs] falsch; Schwindel...

boil¹ ⚕ [bɔɪl] Geschwür n, Furunkel m, n.

boil² [~] 1. kochen, sieden; 2. Kochen n, Sieden n; **~·er** [ˈbɔɪlə] (Dampf-) Kessel m; Boiler m; **~·er suit** Overall m; **~·ing** [~ɪŋ] kochend, siedend; **~·ing-point** Siedepunkt m (a. fig.).

bois·ter·ous □ [ˈbɔɪstərəs] ungestüm; heftig, laut; lärmend.

bold □ [bəʊld] kühn; keck, dreist, unverschämt; steil; as ~ as brass F frech wie Oskar; **~·ness** [ˈbəʊldnɪs] Kühnheit f; Keckheit f; Dreistigkeit f.

bol·ster [ˈbəʊlstə] 1. Keilkissen n; Nackenrolle f; ⚠ nicht Polster; 2. ~ up fig. (unter)stützen, j-m Mut machen.

bolt [bəʊlt] 1. Bolzen m; Riegel m; Blitz(strahl) m; plötzlicher Satz, Fluchtversuch m; 2. adv.: ~ upright kerzengerade; 3. v/t. verriegeln; F hinunterschlingen; v/i. davonlaufen, ausreißen; scheuen; durchgehen (Pferd).

bomb [bɒm] 1. Bombe f; the ~ die Atombombe; 2. bombardieren.

bom·bard [bɒmˈbaːd] bombardieren (a. fig.).

bomb|-proof [ˈbɒmpruːf] bombensicher; **~·shell** Bombe f (a. fig.).

bond [bɒnd] econ. Schuldverschreibung f, Obligation f; ⊕ Haftzeitigkeit f; **~·s** pl. Bande (der Freundschaft etc.); in ~ econ. unter Zollverschluß; **~·age** lit. [ˈbɒndɪdʒ] Hörigkeit f; Knechtschaft f.

bone [bəʊn] 1. Knochen m; Gräte f; ⚠ nicht Bein; **~·s** pl. a. Gebeine pl.; ~ of contention Zankapfel m; have a ~ to pick with s.o. mit j-m ein Hühnchen zu rupfen haben; make no **~·s** about nicht lange fackeln mit; keine Skrupel haben hinsichtlich (gen.); 2. die Knochen auslösen (aus); entgräten.

bon·fire [ˈbɒnfaɪə] Feuer n im Freien; Freudenfeuer n.

bon·net [ˈbɒnɪt] Haube f; Brt. Motorhaube f.

bon·ny bsd. schott. [ˈbɒnɪ] (-ier, -iest) hübsch; rosig (Baby); gesund.

bo·nus econ. [ˈbəʊnəs] Bonus m, Prämie f; Gratifikation f.

bon·y [ˈbəʊnɪ] (-ier, -iest) knöchern knochig.

boob sl. [buːb] Blödmann m; Brt (grober) Fehler; **~·s** pl. F Titten pl (Busen).

boo·by [ˈbuːbɪ] Trottel m.

book [bʊk] 1. Buch n; Heft n; Liste f Block m; 2. buchen; eintragen

bouquet

Fahrkarte etc. lösen; *Platz etc.* (vor-)bestellen, reservieren lassen; *Gepäck* aufgeben; ~ *in bsd. Brt.* sich (*im Hotel*) eintragen; ~ *in at* absteigen in (*dat.*); ~*ed up* ausgebucht, -verkauft, belegt (*Hotel*); ~**case** ['bʊkeɪs] Bücherschrank *m*; ~**ing** [~ɪŋ] Buchen *n*, (Vor)Bestellung *f*; ~**ing-clerk** Schalterbeamt|e(r) *m*, -in *f*; ~**ing-office** Fahrkartenausgabe *f*, -schalter *m*; *thea.* Kasse *f*; ~**keep·er** Buchhalter(in); ~**keep·ing** Buchhaltung *f*, -führung *f*; ~**let** [~lɪt] Büchlein *n*, Broschüre *f*; ~**mark(·er)** [~ə] Lesezeichen *n*; ~**sell·er** Buchhändler(in); ~**shop**, *Am.* ~**store** Buchhandlung *f*.

boom[1] [buːm] **1.** *econ.* Boom *m*, Aufschwung *m*, Hochkonjunktur *f*, Hausse *f*; **2.** in die Höhe treiben *od.* gehen.

boom[2] [~] dröhnen, donnern.

boon [buːn] Segen *m*, Wohltat *f*.

boor *fig.* [bʊə] Bauer *m*, Lümmel *m*; ~**ish** □ ['bʊərɪʃ] bäuerisch, ungehobelt.

boost [buːst] hochschieben; *Preise* in die Höhe treiben; *Wirtschaft* ankurbeln; verstärken (*a. ⚡*); *fig.* fördern, Auftrieb geben.

boot[1] [buːt]: *to* ~ obendrein.

boot[2] [~] Stiefel *m*; *Brt. mot.* Kofferraum *m*; △ *nicht* Boot; ~**ee** ['buːtiː] (*Damen*)Halbstiefel *m*.

booth [buːð] (Markt- *etc.*)Bude *f*; (Messe)Stand *m*; (Wahl-, *etc.*) Kabine *f*; (Fernsprech)Zelle *f*.

boot|**lace** ['buːtleɪs] Schnürsenkel *m*; ~**leg·ger** [~legə] Alkoholschmuggler *m*.

boot·y ['buːtɪ] Beute *f*, Raub *m*.

booze F [buːz] **1.** saufen; **2.** Alkohol *m* (*Getränk*); Sauferei *f*.

bop·per ['bɒpə] = *teeny-bopper*.

bor·der ['bɔːdə] **1.** Rand *m*, Saum *m*, Einfassung *f*; Rabatte *f*; Grenze *f*; **2.** einfassen; (um)säumen; grenzen (*on, upon an acc.*).

bore[1] [bɔː] **1.** Bohrloch *n*; Kaliber *n*; *fig.* langweiliger Mensch; langweilige Sache; *Brt.* F lästige Sache; **2.** bohren; langweilen; *j-m* lästig sein.

bore[2] [~] *pret. von* bear[2].

bor·ing □ ['bɔːrɪŋ] langweilig.

born [bɔːn] *p.p. von* bear[2] gebären.

borne [bɔːn] *p.p. von* bear[2] tragen.

bo·rough ['bʌrə] Stadtteil *m*; Stadtgemeinde *f*; Stadtbezirk *m*.

bor·row ['bɒrəʊ] (sich) *et.* borgen *od.* (aus)leihen; △ *nicht j-m et.* borgen.

bos·om ['bʊzəm] Busen *m*; *fig.* Schoß *m*.

boss F [bɒs] **1.** Boss *m*, Chef *m*; *bsd. Am. pol.* (Partei-, Gewerkschafts-) Bonze *m*; **2.** *a.* ~ *about*, ~ *around* herumkommandieren; ~**y** F ['bɒsɪ] (*-ier, -iest*) herrisch.

bo·tan·i·cal □ [bə'tænɪkl] botanisch; **bot·a·ny** ['bɒtənɪ] Botanik *f*.

botch [bɒtʃ] **1.** Pfusch(arbeit *f*) *m*; **2.** verpfuschen.

both [bəʊθ] beide(s); ~ ... *and* sowohl ... als (auch).

both·er ['bɒðə] **1.** Belästigung *f*, Störung *f*, Plage *f*, Mühe *f*; **2.** belästigen, stören, plagen; *don't* ~! bemühen Sie sich nicht!

bot·tle ['bɒtl] **1.** Flasche *f*; **2.** in Flaschen abfüllen; ~**neck** Flaschenhals *m*, Engpaß *m* (*e-r Straße*) (*a. fig.*).

bot·tom ['bɒtəm] unterster Teil, Boden *m*, Fuß *m*, Unterseite *f*; Grund *m*; F Hintern *m*, Popo *m*; *be at the* ~ *of hinter e-r Sache* stecken; *get to the* ~ *of s.th.* e-r Sache auf den Grund gehen.

bough [baʊ] Ast *m*, Zweig *m*.

bought [bɔːt] *pret. u. p.p. von* buy.

boul·der ['bəʊldə] Geröllblock *m*, Findling *m*.

bounce [baʊns] **1.** Aufprall(en *n*) *m*, Aufspringen *n* (*e-s Balles etc.*); Schwung *m* (*Lebensfreude, -kraft*); **2.** aufprallen *od.* springen (lassen) (*Ball*); F platzen (*ungedeckter Scheck*); *she* ~*d the baby on her knee* sie ließ das Kind auf den Knien reiten; **bounc·ing** ['baʊnsɪŋ] stramm (*Baby*).

bound[1] [baʊnd] **1.** *pret. u. p.p. von* bind; **2.** *adj.* verpflichtet; bestimmt, unterwegs (*for nach*).

bound[2] [~] *mst* ~*s pl.* Grenze *f*, *fig. a.* Schranke *f*.

bound[3] [~] **1.** Sprung *m*; **2.** (hoch-) springen; auf-, abprallen.

bound·a·ry ['baʊndərɪ] Grenze *f*.

bound·less □ ['baʊndlɪs] grenzenlos.

boun|te·ous □ ['baʊntɪəs], ~**ti·ful** □ [~fl] freigebig, reichlich.

boun·ty ['baʊntɪ] Mildtätigkeit *f*, Freigebigkeit *f*; Spende *f*; Prämie *f*.

bou·quet [bʊ'keɪ] Bukett *n*, Strauß *m*; Blume *f* (*des Weins*).

bout [baut] *Boxen, Ringen, Fechten:* Kampf *m*; (Verhandlungs)Runde *f*; ✗ Anfall *m*; (Trink)Gelage *n*.

bou·tique [bu:'ti:k] Boutique *f*.

bow[1] [bau] 1. Verbeugung *f*; 2. *v/i*. sich verbeugen *od.* -neigen (*to vor dat.*); *fig.* sich beugen *od.* unterwerfen (*to dat.*); *v/t*. biegen; beugen, neigen.

bow[2] ♄ [~] Bug *m*.

bow[3] [bau] 1. Bogen *m*; Schleife *f*; 2. geigen; *~-legged* O-beinig.

bow·els ['bauəlz] *pl. anat.* Eingeweide *pl.*; *das* Innere.

bowl[1] [bəul] Schale *f*, Schüssel *f*; Napf *m*; (Pfeifen)Kopf *m*; *geogr.* Becken *n*; *Am.* Stadion *n*; △ *nicht* Bowle (*Getränk*).

bowl[2] [~] 1. (*Bowling-, Kegel- etc.*) Kugel *f*; 2. *v/t*. rollen; *Bowlingkugel, Kricketball* werfen; *v/i*. bowlen, Bowling spielen; kegeln; *Kricket:* werfen; *~·ing* ['bəulɪŋ] Bowling *n*; Kegeln *n*.

box[1] [bɒks] ♀ Buchsbaum *m*; Kasten *m*, Kiste *f*; Büchse *f*, Schachtel *f*; ⊕ Gehäuse *n*; *thea.* Loge *f*; Box *f*; 2. in Kästen *etc.* tun.

box[2] [~] 1. *Sport:* boxen; *~ s.o.'s ears* j-n ohrfeigen; 2. *~ on the ear* Ohrfeige *f*; *~·er* ['bɒksə] Boxer *m*; *~·ing* [~ɪŋ] Boxen *n*, Boxsport *m*; 2·ing Day *Brt.* der zweite Weihnachtsfeiertag.

box-of·fice ['bɒksɒfɪs] Theaterkasse *f*.

boy [bɔɪ] Junge *m*, Knabe *m*, Bursche *m*; *~friend* Freund *m*; *~ scout* Pfadfinder *m*.

boy·cott ['bɔɪkɒt] boykottieren.

boy|hood ['bɔɪhʊd] Knabenalter *n*, Kindheit *f*, Jugend(zeit) *f*; *~·ish* □ ['bɔɪɪʃ] jungenhaft.

bra [brɑ:] BH *m* (*Büstenhalter*).

brace [breɪs] 1. ⊕ Strebe *f*, Stützbalken *m*; Klammer *f*; Paar *n* (*a. Wild, Geflügel*); (*a. a pair of*) *~s pl. Brt.* Hosenträger *pl.*; 2. verstreben, -steifen, stützen; spannen; *fig.* stärken.

brace·let ['breɪslət] Armband *n*.

brack·et ['brækɪt] 1. ⊕ Träger *m*, Halter *m*, Stütze *f*; (Wand)Arm (*e-r Leuchte*); Winkelstütze *f*; *arch.* Konsole *f*; *print.* (*mst eckige*) Klammer; (*bsd. Alters-, Steuer*)Klasse *f*; *lower income ~* niedrige Einkommensgruppe; 2. einklammern; *fig.* gleichstellen.

brack·ish ['brækɪʃ] brackig, salzig.

brag [bræg] 1. Prahlerei *f*; 2. (*-gg-*) prahlen (*about, of mit*).

brag·gart ['brægət] 1. Prahler *m*; 2. prahlerisch.

braid [breɪd] 1. (Haar)Flechte *f*, Zopf *m*; Borte *f*, Tresse *f*; 2. flechten; mit Borte besetzen.

brain [breɪn] *anat.* Gehirn *n*; *oft ~s pl. fig.* Gehirn *n*, Verstand *m*, Intelligenz *f*, Kopf *m*; *~s trust Brt., Am. ~ trust* ['breɪn(z)trʌst] Gehirntrust *m* (*bsd. politische od. wirtschaftliche Beratergruppe*); *~·wash* j-n e-r Gehirnwäsche unterziehen; *~·wash·ing* Gehirnwäsche *f*; *~·wave* F Geistesblitz *m*.

brake [breɪk] 1. ⊕ Bremse *f*; 2. bremsen.

bram·ble ♀ ['bræmbl] Brombeerstrauch *m*.

bran [bræn] Kleie *f*.

branch [brɑ:ntʃ] 1. Ast *m*, Zweig *m*; Fach *n*; Linie *f* (*des Stammbaumes*); Zweigstelle *f*; 2. sich verzweigen; abzweigen.

brand [brænd] 1. *econ.* (Handels-, Schutz)Marke *f*, Warenzeichen *n*; Sorte *f*, Klasse *f* (*e-r Ware*); Brandmal *n*; △ *nicht* Brand; *~ name* Markenbezeichnung *f*, -name *m*; 2. einbrennen; brandmarken.

bran·dish ['brændɪʃ] schwingen.

bran(d)-new ['bræn(d)'nju:] nagelneu.

bran·dy ['brændɪ] Kognak *m*, Weinbrand *m*.

brass [brɑ:s] Messing *n*; F Unverschämtheit *f*; *~ band* Blaskapelle *f*; *~ knuckles pl. Am.* Schlagring *m*.

bras·sière ['bræsɪə] Büstenhalter *m*.

brat *contp.* [bræt] Balg *m*, *n*, Gör *n* (*Kind*).

brave [breɪv] 1. □ (*~r, ~st*) tapfer, mutig, unerschrocken; △ *nicht* brav; 2. trotzen; mutig begegnen (*dat.*); *brav·er·y* ['breɪvərɪ] Tapferkeit *f*.

brawl [brɔ:l] 1. Krawall *m*; Rauferei *f*; 2. Krawall machen; raufen.

brawn·y ['brɔ:nɪ] (*-ier, -iest*) muskulös.

bray [breɪ] 1. Eselsschrei *m*; 2. schreien; schmettern; dröhnen.

bra·zen □ ['breɪzn] unverschämt, unverfroren, frech.

Bra·zil·ian [brə'zɪljən] 1. brasilianisch; 2. Brasilianer(in).

breach [briːtʃ] **1.** Bruch *m*; *fig.* Verletzung *f*; ✗ Bresche *f*; **2.** e-e Bresche schlagen in (*acc.*).

bread [bred] Brot *n*; *brown* ~ Schwarzbrot *n*; *know which side one's* ~ *is buttered* F s-n Vorteil (er)kennen.

breadth [bredθ] Breite *f*, Weite *f*; *fig.* Größe *f*; (*Tuch*)Bahn *f*.

break [breɪk] **1.** Bruch *m*; Lücke *f*; Pause *f* (*Brt. a. Schule*), Unterbrechung *f*; *econ.* (*Preis- etc.*)Sturz *m*; (*Tages*)Anbruch *m*; *fig.* Zäsur *f*, Einschnitt *m*; *bad* ~ F Pech *n*; *lucky* ~ F Dusel *m*, Schwein *n* (*Glück*); *without a* ~ ununterbrochen; **2.** (*broke, broken*) *v/t.* ab-, auf-, durchbrechen; *v/t.* (zer)brechen; unterbrechen; übertreten; *Tier* abrichten; *Pferd* zureiten; *Bank* sprengen; *Vorrat* anbrechen; *Nachricht* (schonend) mitteilen; ruinieren; *v/i.* brechen; eindringen *od.* -brechen in (*acc.*); (zer)brechen; aus-, los-, an-, auf-, hervorbrechen; umschlagen (*Wetter*); *mit Adverbien:* ~ *away* ab-, losbrechen; sich losmachen *od.* losreißen; ~ *down* ein-, niederreißen; *Haus* abbrechen; zusammenbrechen (*a. fig.*); versagen; ~ *in* einbrechen, -dringen; ~ *off* abbrechen; *fig. a.* Schluß machen mit; ~ *out* ausbrechen; ~ *through* durchbrechen; *fig.* den Durchbruch schaffen; ~ *up* abbrechen, beendigen, schließen; (sich) auflösen; zerbrechen, auseinandergehen (*Ehe etc.*); **~·a·ble** [ˈbreɪkəbl] zerbrechlich; **~·age** [~ɪdʒ] Bruch *m*; **~·a·way** Trennung *f*, Bruch *m*; *Brt.* Splitter...; **~·down** Zusammenbruch *m* (*a. fig.*); ⊕ Maschinenschaden *m*; *mot.* Panne *f*.

break·fast [ˈbrekfəst] **1.** Frühstück *n*; **2.** frühstücken.

break|through *fig.* [ˈbreɪkθruː] Durchbruch *m*; **~·up** Auflösung *f*; Zerfall *m*; Zerrüttung *f*; Zusammenbruch *m*.

breast [brest] Brust *f*; Busen *m*; *fig.* Herz *n*; *make a clean* ~ *of s.th.* et. offen bekennen; **~·stroke** [ˈbreststrəʊk] *Sport:* Brustschwimmen *n*.

breath [breθ] Atem(zug) *m*; Hauch *m*; *waste one's* ~ s-e Worte verschwenden.

breath·a·lyse, *Am.* **-lyze** [ˈbreθəlaɪz] *Verkehrsteilnehmer* (ins Röhrchen) blasen *od.* pusten lassen; **~·lys·er,**

Am. **-lyz·er** [~ə] Alkoholtestgerät *n*, F Röhrchen *n*.

breathe [briːð] *v/i.* atmen; leben; *v/t.* (aus-, ein)atmen; hauchen; flüstern.

breath|less ☐ [ˈbreθlɪs] atemlos; **~·tak·ing** atemberaubend.

bred [bred] *pret. u. p.p. von breed* 2.

breech·es [ˈbrɪtʃɪz] *pl.* Knie-, Reithosen *pl.*

breed [briːd] **1.** Zucht *f*, Rasse *f*; (*Menschen*)Schlag *m*; **2.** (*bred*) *v/t.* erzeugen; auf-, erziehen; züchten; *v/i.* sich fortpflanzen; **~·er** [ˈbriːdə] Züchter(in); **~·ing** [~ɪŋ] (Tier)Zucht *f*; Erziehung *f*; (gutes) Benehmen.

breeze [briːz] Brise *f*; **breez·y** [ˈbriːzɪ] (*-ier, -iest*) windig, luftig; heiter, unbeschwert.

breth·ren [ˈbreðrən] *pl.* Brüder *pl.*

brev·i·ty [ˈbrevətɪ] Kürze *f*.

brew [bruː] **1.** *v/t. u. v/i.* brauen; zubereiten; *fig.* aushecken; **2.** Gebräu *n*; **~·er** [ˈbruːə] (Bier)Brauer *m*; **~·er·y** [ˈbrʊərɪ] Brauerei *f*.

bri·ar [ˈbraɪə] = *brier*.

bribe [braɪb] **1.** Bestechung(sgeld *n*, -geschenk *n*) *f*; **2.** bestechen; **brib·er·y** [ˈbraɪbərɪ] Bestechung *f*.

brick [brɪk] **1.** Ziegel(stein) *m*; *drop a* ~ *Brt.* F ins Fettnäpfchen treten; **2.** ~ *up od. in* zumauern; **~·lay·er** [ˈbrɪkleɪə] Maurer *m*; **~·works** *sg.* Ziegelei *f*.

brid·al ☐ [ˈbraɪdl] Braut...

bride [braɪd] Braut *f*; **~·groom** [ˈbraɪdɡrʊm] Bräutigam *m*; **~·s·maid** [~zmeɪd] Brautjungfer *f*.

bridge [brɪdʒ] **1.** Brücke *f*; **2.** e-e Brücke schlagen über (*acc.*); *fig.* überbrücken.

bri·dle [ˈbraɪdl] **1.** Zaum *m*; Zügel *m*; **2.** *v/t.* (auf)zäumen; zügeln; *v/i. a.* ~ *up* den Kopf zurückwerfen; **~·path** Reitweg *m*.

brief [briːf] **1.** ☐ kurz, bündig; **2.** ⚖ schriftliche Instruktion; △ *nicht Brief;* **3.** kurz zusammenfassen; instruieren; **~·case** [ˈbriːfkeɪs] Aktenmappe *f*.

briefs [briːfs] *pl.* (*a pair of* ~ ein) Slip (*kurze Unterhose*).

bri·er ♦ [ˈbraɪə] Dorn-, Hagebuttenstrauch *m*; Wilde Rose.

bri·gade ✗ [brɪˈɡeɪd] Brigade *f*.

bright ☐ [braɪt] hell, glänzend; klar; heiter; lebhaft; gescheit; △ *nicht breit;* **~·en** [ˈbraɪtn] *v/t.* auf-, erhel-

len; polieren; aufheitern; *v/i.* sich
aufhellen; **~ness** [~nɪs] Helligkeit *f*;
Glanz *m*; Klarheit *f*; Heiterkeit *f*;
Aufgewecktheit *f*, Intelligenz *f*.

bril|liance, **~lian·cy** ['brɪljəns, ~sɪ]
Glanz *m*; durchdringender Verstand; **~liant** [~t] **1.** □ glänzend;
hervorragend, brillant; **2.** Brillant *m.*

brim [brɪm] **1.** Rand *m*; Krempe *f*; **2.**
(*-mm-*) bis zum Rande füllen *od.* voll
sein; **~ful(l)** ['brɪm'fʊl] randvoll.

brine [braɪn] Salzwasser *n*; Sole *f.*

bring [brɪŋ] (*brought*) (mit-, her-)
bringen; △ *nicht fort-, wegbringen*;
j-n veranlassen; *Klage* erheben;
Grund etc. vorbringen; **~ about** zustande bringen; bewirken; **~ back**
zurückbringen; **~ forth** hervorbringen; **~ home to** *j-n* überzeugen; **~ in**
(her)einbringen; ⚖ *Spruch* fällen; **~
off** *et.* fertigbringen, schaffen; **~ on**
verursachen; **~ out** herausbringen; **~
round** wieder zu sich bringen; *Kranken* durchbringen; **~ up** auf-, großziehen; erziehen; zur Sprache bringen; *bsd. Brt. et.* (er)brechen.

brink [brɪŋk] Rand *m* (*a. fig.*).

brisk □ [brɪsk] lebhaft, munter;
frisch; flink; belebend.

bris|tle ['brɪsl] **1.** Borste *f*; **2.** (sich)
sträuben; hochfahren, zornig werden; **~ with** *fig.* starren von; **~tly** [~lɪ]
(*-ier, -iest*) stopp(e)lig, Stoppel...

Brit·ish ['brɪtɪʃ] britisch; *the ~ pl.* die
Briten *pl.*

brit·tle ['brɪtl] zerbrechlich, spröde.

broach [brəʊtʃ] *Thema* anschneiden.

broad □ [brɔːd] breit; weit; hell
(*Tag*); deutlich (*Wink etc.*); derb
(*Witz*); allgemein; weitherzig; liberal; **~cast** ['brɔːdkɑːst] **1.** (*-cast od.
-casted*) *fig.* Nachricht verbreiten;
im Rundfunk *od.* Fernsehen bringen, ausstrahlen, übertragen; senden; im Rundfunk *od.* Fernsehen
sprechen *od.* auftreten; **2.** Rundfunk-, Fernsehsendung *f*; **~cast·er**
[~ə] Rundfunk-, Fernsehsprecher(in); **~en** [~dn] verbreitern, erweitern; **~ jump** *Am. Sport:* Weitsprung *m*; **~mind·ed** liberal.

bro·cade [brə'keɪd] Brokat *m.*

bro·chure ['brəʊʃə] Broschüre *f*,
Prospekt *m.*

brogue [brəʊg] derber Straßenschuh.

broil *bsd. Am.* [brɔɪl] = *grill* 1.

broke [brəʊk] **1.** *pret. von break* 2;

2. F pleite, abgebrannt; **bro·ken**
['brəʊkən] **1.** *p.p. von break* 2; **2.** ~
health zerrüttete Gesundheit; **~-
hearted** verzweifelt, untröstlich.

bro·ker *econ.* ['brəʊkə] Makler *m.*

bron·co *Am.* ['brɒŋkəʊ] (*pl. -cos*)
(halb)wildes Pferd.

bronze [brɒnz] **1.** Bronze *f*; **2.** bronzen, Bronze...; **3.** bronzieren.

brooch [brəʊtʃ] Brosche *f*, Spange *f.*

brood [bruːd] **1.** Brut *f*; *attr.* Brut...;
2. brüten (*a. fig.*); **~er** ['bruːdə]
Brutkasten *m.*

brook [brʊk] Bach *m.*

broom [brʊm] Besen *m*; **~stick**
['brʊmstɪk] Besenstiel *m.*

broth [brɒθ] Fleischbrühe *f.*

broth·el ['brɒθl] Bordell *n.*

broth·er ['brʌðə] Bruder *m*; ~(*s*) *and
sister(s)* Geschwister *pl.*; **~hood**
[~hʊd] Bruderschaft *f*; Brüderlichkeit *f*; **~in-law** [~rɪnlɔː] (*pl. -s-in-
law*) Schwager *m*; **~ly** [~lɪ] brüderlich.

brought [brɔːt] *pret. u. p.p. von bring.*

brow [braʊ] (Augen)Braue *f*; Stirn *f*;
Rand *m* (*e-s Steilhanges*). **~beat**
['braʊbiːt] (*-beat, -beaten*) einschüchtern; tyrannisieren.

brown [braʊn] **1.** braun; **2.** Braun *n*;
3. bräunen; braun werden.

browse [braʊz] **1.** Grasen *n*; *fig.*
Schmökern; **2.** grasen, weiden; *fig.*
schmökern.

bruise [bruːz] **1.** ⚕ Quetschung *f*,
Prellung *f*, Bluterguß *m*; **2.** (zer-)
quetschen; *j-n* grün u. blau schlagen.

brunch F [brʌntʃ] Brunch *m* (*spätes
reichliches Frühstück, das das Mittagessen ersetzt*).

brunt [brʌnt]: *bear the ~ of* die
Hauptlast von *et.* tragen.

brush [brʌʃ] **1.** Bürste *f*; Pinsel *m*;
(*Fuchs*)Rute *f*; Scharmützel *n*; Unterholz *n*; **2.** bürsten; fegen; streifen;
~ against s.o. *j-n* streifen; **~ away**, **~
off** wegbürsten, abwischen; **~ aside**,
~ away *fig. et.* abtun; **~ up** *Kenntnisse* aufpolieren, -frischen; **~up**
['brʌʃʌp]: *give one's English a ~* s-e
Englischkenntnisse aufpolieren;
~wood Gestrüpp *n*, Unterholz *n.*

brusque □ [brʊsk] brüsk, barsch.

Brus·sels sprouts ♀ ['brʌsl'spraʊts]
pl. Rosenkohl *m.*

bru·tal □ ['bruːtl] viehisch; brutal,
roh; **~i·ty** [bruː'tælətɪ] Brutalität *f*,

Roheit f; **brute** [bruːt] **1.** tierisch; unvernünftig; brutal, roh; **2.** Vieh n; F Untier n, Scheusal n.

bub·ble ['bʌbl] **1.** Blase f; fig. Schwindel m; **2.** sprudeln.

buc·ca·neer [bʌkə'nɪə] Seeräuber m.

buck [bʌk] **1.** zo. Bock m; Am. sl. Dollar m; **2.** v/i. bocken; ~ up! Kopf hoch!; v/t. ~ off Reiter (durch Bocken) abwerfen.

buck·et ['bʌkɪt] Eimer m, Kübel m.

buck·le ['bʌkl] **1.** Schnalle f, Spange f; △ nicht Buckel (=.); **2.** v/t. a. ~ up zu-, festschnallen; ~ on anschnallen; v/i. ⊕ sich (ver)biegen; ~ down to a task F sich hinter e-e Aufgabe klemmen.

buck|shot hunt. ['bʌkʃɒt] Rehposten m; **~skin** Wildleder n.

bud [bʌd] **1.** ♀ Knospe f; fig. Keim m; **2.** (-dd-) v/i. knospen, keimen; a ~ding lawyer ein angehender Jurist.

bud·dy Am. F ['bʌdɪ] Kamerad m.

budge [bʌdʒ] (sich) bewegen.

bud·ger·i·gar zo. ['bʌdʒərɪgɑː] Wellensittich m.

bud·get ['bʌdʒɪt] Vorrat m; Staatshaushalt m; Etat m, Finanzen pl.

bud·gie zo. ['bʌdʒɪ] = budgerigar.

buff¹ [bʌf] **1.** Ochsenleder n; Lederfarbe f; **2.** lederfarben.

buff² F [~] Film- etc. Fan m.

buf·fa·lo ['bʌfələʊ] (pl. -loes, -los) Büffel m.

buff·er ['bʌfə] ⊕ Puffer m; Prellbock m (a. fig.).

buf·fet¹ ['bʌfɪt] **1.** (Faust)Schlag m; **2.** schlagen; ~ about durchrütteln, -schütteln.

buf·fet² [~] Büfett n, Anrichte f.

buf·fet³ ['bʊfeɪ] Büfett n, Theke f; Tisch mit Speisen u. Getränken.

buf·foon [bə'fuːn] Possenreißer m.

bug [bʌg] **1.** zo. Wanze f; Am. zo. Insekt n; F Bazillus m; F Abhörvorrichtung f, Wanze f; Computer: Fehler m im Programm (in Soft- od. Hardware); **2.** (-gg-) F Gespräch abhören; F Wanzen anbringen in (dat.); Am. F ärgern, wütend machen.

bug·gy ['bʌgɪ] mot. Buggy m (Freizeitauto); Am. Kinderwagen m.

bu·gle ['bjuːgl] Wald-, Signalhorn n.

build [bɪld] **1.** (built) (er)bauen, errichten; △ nicht bilden; **2.** Körperbau m, Figur f; **~·er** ['bɪldə] Erbauer m, Baumeister m; Bauunternehmer

m; **~ing** [~ɪŋ] (Er)Bauen n; Bau m, Gebäude n; attr. Bau...

built [bɪlt] pret. u. p.p. von build 1.

bulb [bʌlb] ♀ Zwiebel f, Knolle f; ≴ (Glüh)Birne f.

bulge [bʌldʒ] **1.** (Aus)Bauchung f; Anschwellung f; **2.** sich (aus)bauchen; hervorquellen.

bulk [bʌlk] Umfang m; Masse f; Hauptteil m; ♣ Ladung f; in ~ econ. lose; in großer Menge; **~·y** ['bʌlkɪ] (-ier, -iest) umfangreich; unhandlich, sperrig.

bull¹ zo. [bʊl] Bulle m, Stier m.

bull² [~] päpstliche Bulle.

bull·dog zo. ['bʊldɒg] Bulldogge f.

bull|doze ['bʊldəʊz] terrorisieren; **~doz·er** ⊕ [~ə] Bulldozer m, Planierraupe f.

bul·let ['bʊlɪt] Kugel f; **~·proof** kugelsicher.

bul·le·tin ['bʊlɪtɪn] Bulletin n, Tagesbericht m; ~ board Am. Schwarzes Brett.

bul·lion ['bʊljən] Gold-, Silberbarren m; Gold-, Silberlitze f.

bul·ly ['bʊlɪ] **1.** Maulheld m; Tyrann m; **2.** einschüchtern, tyrannisieren.

bul·wark ['bʊlwək] Bollwerk n (a. fig.).

bum Am. F [bʌm] **1.** Nichtstuer m, Herumtreiber m, Gammler m; **2.** v/t. (-mm-) schnorren; ~ around herumgammeln.

bum·ble-bee zo. ['bʌmblbiː] Hummel f.

bump [bʌmp] **1.** heftiger Schlag od. Stoß; Beule f; **2.** stoßen; zusammenstoßen (mit), rammen; ~ into j-n zufällig treffen; ~ off F j-n umlegen, umbringen.

bum·per¹ ['bʌmpə] **1.** volles Glas (Wein); **2.** riesig; ~ crop Rekordernte f.

bum·per² mot. [~] Stoßstange f; ~-to-~ Stoßstange an Stoßstange.

bump·y ['bʌmpɪ] (-ier, -iest) holp(e)rig.

bun [bʌn] süßes Brötchen; (Haar-) Knoten m.

bunch [bʌntʃ] **1.** Bund n, Büschel n; Haufen m; ~ of grapes Weintraube f; **2.** a. ~ up bündeln.

bun·dle ['bʌndl] **1.** Bündel n (a. fig.), Bund n; **2.** v/t. a. ~ up bündeln.

bung [bʌŋ] Spund m.

bun·ga·low ['bʌŋgələʊ] Bungalow m.

bun·gle ['bʌŋgl] **1.** Stümperei f,

B

Pfusch(arbeit f) m; 2. (ver)pfuschen.

bun·ion ♣ ['bʌnjən] entzündeter Fußballen.

bunk [bʌŋk] Schlafkoje f.

bun·ny ['bʌni] Häschen n.

buoy ⚓ [bɔi] 1. Boje f; 2. ~ed up fig. von neuem Mut erfüllt; **~ant** □ ['bɔiənt] schwimmfähig; tragend (Wasser etc.); fig. heiter.

bur·den ['bɜːdn] 1. Last f; Bürde f; ⚓ Tragfähigkeit f; 2. belasten; **~some** [~səm] lästig, drückend.

bu·reau ['bjuərəu] (pl. -reaux, -reaus) Büro n, Geschäftszimmer n; Brt. Schreibtisch m, -pult n; Am. (bsd. Spiegel)Kommode f; **~·cra·cy** [bjuə'rɒkrəsi] Bürokratie f.

bur·glar ['bɜːɡlə] Einbrecher m; **~·glar·ize** Am. [~raiz] = burgle; **~·gla·ry** [~ri] Einbruch(sdiebstahl) m; **~·gle** [~ɡl] einbrechen (in acc.).

bur·i·al ['beriəl] Begräbnis n.

bur·ly ['bɜːli] (-ier, -iest) stämmig, kräftig.

burn [bɜːn] 1. ♣ Brandwunde f; verbrannte Stelle; 2. (burnt od. burned) (ver-, an)brennen; ~ down ab-, niederbrennen; ~ out ausbrennen; ~ up auflodern; verbrennen; verglühen (Rakete etc.); **~·ing** ['bɜːniŋ] brennend (a. fig.).

bur·nish ['bɜːniʃ] polieren.

burnt [bɜːnt] pret. u. p.p. von burn 2.

burp F [bɜːp] rülpsen, aufstoßen; ein Bäuerchen machen (lassen) (Baby).

bur·row ['bʌrəu] 1. Höhle f, Bau m; 2. (sich ein-, ver)graben.

burst [bɜːst] 1. Bersten n; Riß m; fig. Ausbruch m; 2. (burst) v/i. bersten, platzen; zerspringen; explodieren; ~ from sich losreißen von; ~ in on od. upon hereinplatzen bei j-m; ~ into tears in Tränen ausbrechen; ~ out herausplatzen; v/t. (auf)sprengen.

bur·y ['beri] be-, vergraben; beerdigen.

bus [bʌs] (pl. -es, -ses) (Omni)Bus m.

bush [buʃ] Busch m; Gebüsch n.

bush·el ['buʃl] Scheffel m (= Brt. 36,37 l, Am. 35,24 l).

bush·y ['buʃi] (-ier, -iest) buschig.

busi·ness ['biznis] Geschäft n; Beschäftigung f; Beruf m; Angelegenheit f; Aufgabe f; econ. Handel m; ~ of the day Tagesordnung f; on ~ geschäftlich; you have no ~ doing

(od. to do) that Sie haben kein Recht, das zu tun; this is none of your ~ das geht Sie nichts an; s. mind 2; **~ hours** pl. Geschäftszeit f; **~·like** geschäftsmäßig, sachlich; **~·man** (pl. -men) Geschäftsmann m; **~·trip** Geschäftsreise f; **~·wom·an** (pl. -women) Geschäftsfrau f.

bust¹ [bʌst] Büste f.

bust² Am. F [~] Pleite f.

bus·tle ['bʌsl] 1. Geschäftigkeit f; geschäftiges Treiben; 2. ~ about geschäftig hin u. her eilen.

bus·y □ ['bizi] 1. (-ier, -iest) beschäftigt; geschäftig; fleißig (at bei, an dat.); lebhaft; Am. teleph. besetzt; 2. (mst ~ o.s.) sich beschäftigen (with mit); **~·bod·y** aufdringlicher Mensch, Gschaftlhuber m.

but [bʌt, bət] 1. cj. aber, jedoch, sondern; außer, als; ohne daß; dennoch; a. ~ that daß nicht; he could not ~ laugh er mußte einfach lachen; 2. prp. außer; all ~ him alle außer ihm; the last ~ one der vorletzte; the next ~ one der übernächste; nothing ~ nichts als; ~ for wenn nicht ... gewesen wäre, ohne; 3. nach Negation: der (die od. das) nicht; there is no one ~ knows es gibt niemand, der es nicht weiß; 4. adv. nur; erst, gerade; all ~ fast, beinahe.

butch·er ['butʃə] 1. Fleischer m, Metzger m; 2. (fig. ab-, hin)schlachten; **~·y** [~ri] Schlachthaus n; fig. Gemetzel n.

but·ler ['bʌtlə] Butler m.

butt¹ [bʌt] 1. Stoß m; (dickes) Ende (e-s Baumes etc.); Stummel m, Kippe f; (Gewehr)Kolben m; Schießstand m; fig. Zielscheibe f; 2. (mit dem Kopf) stoßen; ~ in F sich einmischen (on in acc.).

butt² [~] Wein-, Bierfaß n; Regentonne f.

but·ter ['bʌtə] 1. Butter f; F Schmeichelei f; 2. mit Butter bestreichen; **~·cup** ♣ Butterblume f; **~·fly** zo. Schmetterling m; **~·y** [~ri] butter(-artig), Butter...

but·tocks ['bʌtəks] pl. Gesäß n, F od. zo. Hinterteil n.

but·ton ['bʌtn] 1. Knopf m; ♣ Knospe f; 2. mst ~ up zuknöpfen; **~·hole** Knopfloch n.

but·tress ['bʌtris] 1. Strebepfeiler m; fig. Stütze f; 2. (unter)stützen.

bux·om ['bʌksəm] drall, stramm.

buy [baɪ] **1.** F Kauf *m*; **2.** (*bought*) *v/t.* (an-, ein)kaufen (*of, from* von; *at* bei); ~ *out j-n* abfinden, auszahlen; *Firma* aufkaufen; ~ **up** aufkaufen; ~**er** [ˈbaɪə] (Ein)Käufer(in).

buzz [bʌz] **1.** Summen *n*; Surren *n*; Stimmengewirr *n*; **2.** *v/i.* summen, surren; ~ *Richtung:* durch, über; an (*dat.*) entlang *od.* vorbei; *zeitlich:* an, bei; *off!* *Brt.* F schwirr ab!, hau ab!

buz·zard *zo.* [ˈbʌzəd] Bussard *m.*

buzz·er ⚡ [ˈbʌzə] Summer *m.*

by [baɪ] **1.** *prp. räumlich:* bei; an, neben; *Richtung:* durch, über; an (*dat.*) entlang *od.* vorbei; *zeitlich:* an, bei; spätestens bis, bis zu; *Urheber, Ursache:* von, durch (*bsd. beim Passiv*); *Mittel, Werkzeug:* durch, mit; *Art u. Weise:* bei; *Schwur:* bei; *Maß:* um, bei; *Richtschnur:* gemäß, bei; ~ *the dozen* dutzendweise; ~ *o.s.* allein; ~ *land* zu Lande; ~ *rail* per

Bahn; *day* ~ *day* Tag für Tag; ~ *twos* zu zweien; **2.** *adv.* dabei; vorbei; beiseite; ~ *and* ~ bald; nach u. nach; ~ *the* ~ nebenbei bemerkt; ~ *and large* im großen u. ganzen.

by- [baɪ] Neben...; Seiten...

bye *int.* F [baɪ], *a.* **bye-bye** [ˌ~ˈbaɪ] Wiedersehen!, Tschüs!

by·e·lec·tion [ˈbaɪlekʃn] Nachwahl *f*; ~**gone** [~] **1.** vergangen; **2.** *let* ~*s be* ~*s* laß(t) das Vergangene ruhen; ~**pass 1.** Umgehungsstraße *f*; ⚡ Bypass *m*; **2.** umgehen; vermeiden; ~**path** Seitenstraße *f*; ~**prod·uct** Nebenprodukt *n*; ~**road** Seitenstraße *f*; ~**stand·er** Zuschauer(in); ~**street** Neben-, Seitenstraße *f.*

byte [baɪt] *Computer:* Byte *n.*

by·way [ˈbaɪweɪ] Seitenstraße *f*; ~**word** Sprichwort *n*; Inbegriff *m*; *be a* ~ *for* gleichbedeutend sein mit.

C

cab [kæb] Droschke *f*, Taxi *n*; Führerstand *m* (*Lokomotive*); Fahrerhaus *n* (*Lastwagen*), Führerhaus *n* (*a. Kran*).

cab·bage ♀ [ˈkæbɪdʒ] Kohl *m.*

cab·in [ˈkæbɪn] Hütte *f*; ♣ Kabine *f* (*a. Seilbahn*), Kajüte *f*; ✈ Kanzel *f*; ~**boy** ♣ junger Kabinensteward; ~ **cruis·er** ♣ Kabinenkreuzer *m.*

cab·i·net [ˈkæbɪnɪt] *pol.* Kabinett *n*; Schrank *m*, Vitrine *f*; (Radio)Gehäuse *n*; ~ *meeting* Kabinettssitzung *f*; ~**mak·er** Kunsttischler *m.*

ca·ble [ˈkeɪbl] **1.** Kabel *n*; ♣ Ankertau *n*; **2.** telegrafieren; *j-m Geld* telegrafisch anweisen; ~**car** *Seilbahn:* Kabine *f*, Wagen *m* (*Übersee*)Telegramm *n*; ~ **tel·e·vi·sion** Kabelfernsehen *n.*

cab·rank [ˈkæbræŋk], ~**stand** Taxi-, Droschkenstand *m.*

ca·ca·o ♀ [kəˈkɑːəʊ] (*pl. -os*) Kakaobaum *m*, -bohne *f.*

cack·le [ˈkækl] **1.** Gegacker *n*, Geschnatter *n*; **2.** gackern, schnattern.

cad [kæd] Schuft *m*, Schurke *m.*

ca·dav·er [kəˈdeɪvə] Leichnam *m*; ⚠ *nicht Kadaver.*

ca·dence [ˈkeɪdəns] ♪ Kadenz *f*; Tonfall *m*; Rhythmus *m.*

ca·det ✗ [kəˈdet] Kadett *m.*

caf·é, caf·e [ˈkæfeɪ] Café *n.*

caf·e·te·ri·a [kæfɪˈtɪərɪə] Selbstbedienungsrestaurant *n.*

cage [keɪdʒ] **1.** Käfig *m*; ✗ Förderkorb *m*; **2.** einsperren.

cag·ey ☐ F [ˈkeɪdʒɪ] (*-gier, -giest*) verschlossen; vorsichtig; *Am.* schlau, gerissen.

ca·jole [kəˈdʒəʊl] *j-m* schmeicheln; *j-n* beschwatzen.

cake [keɪk] **1.** Kuchen *m*, Torte *f*; Tafel *f* (*Schokolade*), Riegel *m* (*Seife*); **2.** ~*d with mud* schmutzverkrustet.

ca·lam·i·tous ☐ [kəˈlæmɪtəs] katastrophal; ~**ty** [~tɪ] großes Unglück, Katastrophe *f.*

cal·cu·late [ˈkælkjʊleɪt] *v/t.* kalkulieren; be-, aus-, errechnen; *Am.* F vermuten; *v/i.* rechnen (*on, upon* mit, auf *acc.*); ~**la·tion** [kælkjʊˈleɪʃn] Berechnung *f* (*a. fig.*), Ausrechnung *f*; *econ.* Kalkulation *f*; Überlegung *f*; ~**la·tor** [ˈkælkjʊleɪtə] Rechner *m* (*Gerät*).

C

cal·dron ['kɔːldrən] = **cauldron**.

cal·en·dar ['kælɪndə] 1. Kalender m; Liste f; 2. registrieren.

calf¹ [kaːf] (pl. calves [~vz]) Wade f.

calf² [~] (pl. calves) Kalb n; **~skin** Kalb(s)fell n.

cal·i·bre, Am. **-ber** ['kælɪbə] Kaliber n.

cal·i·co ['kælɪkəʊ] (pl. -coes, -cos) Kaliko m.

call [kɔːl] 1. Ruf m; teleph. Anruf m, Gespräch n; Ruf m, Berufung f (to in ein Amt; auf e-n Lehrstuhl); Aufruf m, Aufforderung f; Signal n; (kurzer) Besuch; Kündigung f (von Geldern); on ~ auf Abruf; make a ~ telefonieren; 2. v/t. (herbei)rufen; (ein)berufen; teleph. j-n anrufen; berufen, ernennen (to zu); nennen; Aufmerksamkeit lenken (to auf acc.); be ~ed heißen; ~ s.o. names j-n beschimpfen, beleidigen; ~ up teleph. anrufen; v/i. rufen; teleph. anrufen; e-n (kurzen) Besuch machen (on s.o., at s.o.'s [house] bei j-m); ~ at a port e-n Hafen anlaufen; ~ for rufen nach; et. anfordern; et. abholen; to be ~ed for postlagernd; ~ on s.o. j-n besuchen; ~ on, ~ upon sich an j-n wenden (for wegen), appellieren an (acc.); (to do zu tun); ~·box ['kɔːlbɒks] Am. Fernsprechzelle f; ~·er ['kɔːlə] teleph. Anrufer(in); ~·girl Callgirl n; ~·ing ['~ɪŋ] Rufen n; Berufung f; Beruf m.

cal·lous □ ['kæləs] schwielig; fig. dickfellig, herzlos.

cal·low ['kæləʊ] nackt (ungefiedert); fig. unerfahren.

calm [kaːm] 1. □ still, ruhig; 2. (Wind)Stille f, Ruhe f; 3. oft ~ down besänftigen, (sich) beruhigen.

cal·o·rie phys. ['kælərɪ] Kalorie f; ~·con·scious kalorienbewußt.

ca·lum·ni·ate [kə'lʌmnɪeɪt] verleumden; **cal·um·ny** ['kæləmnɪ] Verleumdung f.

calve [kaːv] kalben.

calves [kaːvz] pl. von calf¹,².

cam·bric ['keɪmbrɪk] Kambrik m (feines Gewebe).

came [keɪm] pret. von come.

cam·el zo., ♣ ['kæml] Kamel n.

cam·e·ra ['kæmərə] Kamera f, Fotoapparat m; in ~ 🕸 unter Ausschluß der Öffentlichkeit.

cam·o·mile ♣ ['kæməmaɪl] Kamille f.

cam·ou·flage ⊠ ['kæmʊflɑːʒ] 1. Tarnung f; 2. tarnen.

camp [kæmp] 1. Lager n; ⊠ Feldlager n; ~ bed Feldbett n; 2. lagern; ~ out zelten, campen.

cam·paign [kæm'peɪn] 1. ⊠ Feldzug m; fig. Kampagne f, Feldzug m, Aktion f; pol. Wahlkampf m; 2. ⊠ ar e-m Feldzug teilnehmen; fig. kämpfen, zu Felde ziehen; pol. sich am Wahlkampf beteiligen, Wahlkampf machen; Am. kandidieren (for für).

camp|ground ['kæmpgraʊnd], ~·site Lagerplatz m; Zelt-, Campingplatz m.

cam·pus ['kæmpəs] Campus m, Universitätsgelände n.

can¹ v/aux. [kæn, kən] (pret. could: verneint: cannot, can't) ich, du etc. kann(st) etc.; dürfen, können.

can² [~] 1. Kanne f; (Blech-, Konserven)Dose f, (-)Büchse f; 2. (-nn-) (in Büchsen) einmachen, eindosen.

Ca·na·di·an [kə'neɪdjən] 1. kanadisch; 2. Kanadier(in).

ca·nal [kə'næl] Kanal m (a. anat.).

ca·nard [kæ'nɑːd] (Zeitungs)Ente f.

ca·nar·y zo. [kə'neərɪ] Kanarienvogel m.

can·cel ['kænsl] (bsd. Brt. -ll-, Am. -l-) (durch-, aus)streichen, entwerten; rückgängig machen; absagen; be ~(l)ed ausfallen.

can·cer ['kænsə] Krebs m; ~·ous ['~rəs] krebsartig; krebsbefallen.

can·did □ ['kændɪd] aufrichtig, offen.

can·di·date ['kændɪdət] Kandidat(in) (for für), Bewerber(in) (for um).

can·died ['kændɪd] kandiert.

can·dle ['kændl] Kerze f; Licht n; burn the ~ at both ends mit s-r Gesundheit Raubbau treiben; ~·stick Kerzenleuchter m.

can·do(u)r ['kændə] Aufrichtigkeit f, Offenheit f.

can·dy ['kændɪ] 1. Kandis(zucker) m; Am. Süßigkeiten pl.; 2. v/t. kandieren.

cane [keɪn] 1. ♣ Rohr n; (Rohr)Stock m; 2. (mit dem Stock) züchtigen.

ca·nine ['keɪnaɪn] Hunde...

canned Am. [kænd] Dosen-, Büchsen...

can·ne·ry Am. ['kænərɪ] Konservenfabrik f.

can·ni·bal [ˈkænɪbl] Kannibale *m*.

can·non [ˈkænən] Kanone *f*.

can·not [ˈkænɒt] *s. can*¹.

can·ny □ [ˈkænɪ] (*-ier, -iest*) gerissen, schlau.

ca·noe [kəˈnuː] **1.** Kanu *n*, Paddelboot *n*; **2.** Kanu fahren, paddeln.

can·on [ˈkænən] Kanon *m*; Regel *f*, Richtschnur *f*; **~ize** [ˌaɪz] heiligsprechen.

can·o·py [ˈkænəpɪ] Baldachin *m*; *arch.* Vordach *n*.

cant [kænt] Fachsprache *f*; Gewäsch *n*; frömmlerisches Gerede.

can't [kɑːnt] = *cannot*.

can·tan·ker·ous □ [kænˈtæŋkərəs] zänkisch, mürrisch.

can·teen [kænˈtiːn] ✕ Feldflasche *f*; Kantine *f*; ✕ Kochgeschirr *n*; Besteck(kasten *m*) *n*.

can·ter [ˈkæntə] **1.** Kanter *m* (*kurzer, leichter Galopp*); **2.** kantern.

can·vas [ˈkænvəs] Segeltuch *n*; Zelt-, Packleinwand *f*; Segel *pl.*; *paint.* Leinwand *f*; Gemälde *n*.

can·vass [ˌ] **1.** *pol.* Wahlfeldzug *m*; *econ.* Werbefeldzug *m*; **2.** *v/t.* eingehend untersuchen *od.* erörtern *od.* prüfen; *pol.* werben um (*Stimmen*); *v/i. pol.* e-n Wahlfeldzug veranstalten.

can·yon [ˈkænjən] Cañon *m*.

cap [kæp] **1.** Kappe *f*; Mütze *f*; Haube *f*; *arch.* Aufsatz *m*; Zündkappe *f*; ✸ Pessar *n*; **2.** (*-pp-*) (mit e-r Kappe *etc.*) bedecken; *fig.* krönen; übertreffen.

ca·pa|bil·i·ty [keɪpəˈbɪlətɪ] Fähigkeit *f*; **~ble** □ [ˈkeɪpəbl] fähig (*of a.*).

ca·pa·cious □ [kəˈpeɪʃəs] geräumig.

ca·pac·i·ty [kəˈpæsətɪ] (Raum)Inhalt *m*; Fassungsvermögen *n*; Kapazität *f*; Aufnahmefähigkeit *f*; *geistige* (*od.* ✪ Leistungs)Fähigkeit *f* (*for ger. zu inf.*); *in my* ~ *as* in meiner Eigenschaft als.

cape¹ [keɪp] Kap *n*, Vorgebirge *n*.

cape² [ˌ] Cape *n*, Umhang *m*.

ca·per [ˈkeɪpə] **1.** Kapriole *f*, Luftsprung *m*; *cut* ~*s* = **2.** Freuden- *od.* Luftsprünge machen.

ca·pil·la·ry *anat.* [kəˈpɪlərɪ] Haar-, Kapillargefäß *n*.

cap·i·tal [ˈkæpɪtl] **1.** □ Kapital...; Tod(es)...; Haupt...; großartig, prima; ~ *crime* Kapitalverbrechen *n*; ~ *punishment* Todesstrafe *f*; **2.** Hauptstadt *f*; Kapital *n*; *mst* ~ *letter*

Großbuchstabe *m*; ~**is·m** [ˌɪzəm] Kapitalismus *m*; ~**ist** [ˌɪst] Kapitalist *m*; ~**ize** [ˌaɪz] kapitalisieren; groß schreiben.

ca·pit·u·late [kəˈpɪtjʊleɪt] kapitulieren (*to vor dat.*).

ca·price [kəˈpriːs] Laune *f*; **ca·pri·cious** □ [ˌɪʃəs] kapriziös, launisch.

Cap·ri·corn *ast.* [ˈkæprɪkɔːn] Steinbock *m*.

cap·size [kæpˈsaɪz] *v/i.* kentern; *v/t.* zum Kentern bringen.

cap·sule [ˈkæpsjuːl] Kapsel *f*; (Raum)Kapsel *f*.

cap·tain [ˈkæptɪn] (An)Führer *m*; Kapitän *m*; ✕ Hauptmann *m*.

cap·tion [ˈkæpʃn] Überschrift *f*, Titel *m*; Bildunterschrift *f*; *Film:* Untertitel *m*.

cap|ti·vate *fig.* [ˈkæptɪveɪt] gefangennehmen, fesseln; ~**tive** [ˈkæptɪv] **1.** gefangen; gefesselt; *hold* ~ gefangenhalten; *take* ~ gefangennehmen; **2.** Gefangene(r *m*) *f*; ~·**tiv·i·ty** [kæpˈtɪvətɪ] Gefangenschaft *f*.

cap·ture [ˈkæptʃə] **1.** Eroberung *f*; Gefangennahme *f*; **2.** fangen; erobern; erbeuten; ⚓ kapern.

car [kɑː] Auto *n*, Wagen *m*; (Eisenbahn-, Straßenbahn)Wagen *m*; Gondel *f* (*e-s Ballons etc.*); Kabine *f* (*e-s Aufzugs*); *by* ~ mit dem Auto, im Auto.

car·a·mel [ˈkærəmel] Karamel *m*; Karamelle *f*.

car·a·van [ˈkærəvæn] Karawane *f*; *Brt.* Wohnwagen *m*, -anhänger *m*; ~ *site* Campingplatz *m* für Wohnwagen.

car·a·way ♀ [ˈkærəweɪ] Kümmel *m*.

car·bine ✕ [ˈkɑːbaɪn] Karabiner *m*.

car·bo·hy·drate ♠ [ˈkɑːbəʊˈhaɪdreɪt] Kohle(n)hydrat *n*.

car·bon [ˈkɑːbən] ♠ Kohlenstoff *m*; *a.* ~ *copy* Durchschlag *m*; *a.* ~ *paper* Kohlepapier *n*.

car·bu·ret·tor, *a.* **-ret·ter** *bsd. Brt.*, *Am.* **-ret·or**, *a.* **-ret·er** ⊕ [kɑːbjʊˈretə] Vergaser *m*.

car·case, car·cass [ˈkɑːkəs] Kadaver *m*, Aas *n*; *Fleischerei:* Rumpf *m*.

card [kɑːd] Karte *f*; *have a* ~ *up one's sleeve fig.* (noch) e-n Trumpf in der Hand haben; ~**board** [ˈkɑːdbɔːd] Pappe *f*; ~ *box* Pappkarton *m*.

car·di·ac ✱ [ˈkɑːdɪæk] Herz...

car·di·gan [ˈkɑːdɪgən] Strickjacke *f*.

car·di·nal [ˈkɑːdɪnl] **1.** □ Grund...,

Haupt..., Kardinal...; scharlachrot; ~ *number* Grundzahl *f*; **2.** *eccl.* Kardinal *m*.

card-in·dex ['kɑːdɪndeks] Kartei *f*.

card-sharp·er ['kɑːdʃɑːpə] Falschspieler *m*.

care [keə] **1.** Sorge *f*; Sorgfalt *f*; Vorsicht *f*; Obhut *f*, Pflege *f*; *medical* ~ ärztliche Behandlung; ~ *of* (*abbr.* c/o) ... per Adresse, bei ...; *take* ~ *of* aufpassen auf (*acc.*); *with* ~! Vorsicht!; **2.** Lust haben (*to inf.* zu); ~ *for* sorgen für, sich kümmern um; sich etwas machen aus; *I don't* ~! F meinetwegen!; *I couldn't* ~ *less* F es ist mir völlig egal; *well* ~d-*for* gepflegt.

ca·reer [kəˈrɪə] **1.** Karriere *f*, Laufbahn *f*; **2.** Berufs...; Karriere...; **3.** rasen.

care·free ['keəfriː] sorgenfrei, sorglos.

care·ful □ ['keəfl] vorsichtig; sorgsam bedacht (*of auf acc.*); sorgfältig; *be* ~! gib acht!; ~**ness** [~nɪs] Vorsicht *f*; Sorgfalt *f*.

care·less □ ['keəlɪs] sorglos; nachlässig; unachtsam; leichtsinnig; ~**ness** [~nɪs] Sorglosigkeit *f*; Nachlässigkeit *f*; Fahrlässigkeit *f*.

ca·ress [kəˈres] **1.** Liebkosung *f*; **2.** liebkosen, streicheln.

care·tak·er ['keəteɪkə] Hausmeister *m*; (Haus- *etc.*)Verwalter *m*.

care·worn ['keəwɔːn] abgehärmt.

car·go ['kɑːgəʊ] (*pl.* -goes, *Am. a.* -gos) Ladung *f*.

car·i·ca·ture ['kærɪkətʃʊə] **1.** Karikatur *f*; **2.** karikieren; ~**tur·ist** [~rɪst] Karikaturist *m*.

car·mine ['kɑːmaɪn] Karmin(rot) *n*.

car·nal □ ['kɑːnl] fleischlich; sinnlich.

car·na·tion [kɑːˈneɪʃn] ♀ (Garten-) Nelke *f*; Blaßrot *n*.

car·ni·val ['kɑːnɪvl] Karneval *m*.

car·niv·o·rous ♀ *zo.* [kɑːˈnɪvərəs] fleischfressend.

car·ol ['kærəl] Weihnachtslied *n*.

carp *zo.* [kɑːp] Karpfen *m*.

car-park *Brt.* ['kɑːpɑːk] Parkplatz *m*; Parkhaus *n*.

car·pen·ter ['kɑːpɪntə] Zimmermann *m*; ~**try** [~rɪ] Zimmerhandwerk *n*; Zimmermannsarbeit *f*.

car·pet ['kɑːpɪt] **1.** Teppich *m*; *bring on the* ~ aufs Tapet bringen; **2.** mit e-m Teppich belegen.

car|pool ['kɑːpuːl] Fahrgemeinschaft *f*; ~**port** überdachter Abstellplatz *m* (*für Autos*).

car·riage ['kærɪdʒ] Beförderung *f*, Transport *m*; Fracht(gebühr) *f*; Kutsche *f*; *Brt.* ♒ (Personen)Wagen *m*; ⊕ Fahrgestell *n* (*a.* 🞥); (Körper-) Haltung *f*; ~**way** Fahrbahn *f*.

car·ri·er ['kærɪə] Spediteur *m*; Träger *m*; Gepäckträger *m*; ~**bag** Trag(e)tasche *f*, -tüte *f*; ~ **pi·geon** Brieftaube *f*.

car·ri·on ['kærɪən] Aas *n*; *attr.* Aas...

car·rot ♀ ['kærət] Karotte *f*, Möhre, Mohrrübe *f*.

car·ry ['kærɪ] *v/t. wohin* bringen, führen, tragen (*a. v/i.*), fahren, befördern; (*bei sich*) haben *od.* tragen; *Ansicht* durchsetzen; *Gewinn, Preis* davontragen; *Ernte, Zinsen* tragen; (weiter)führen; *Mauer* ziehen; *Antrag* durchbringen; *be carried* angenommen werden (*Antrag*); ~ *the day* den Sieg davontragen; ~ *s.th. too far* et. übertreiben, et. zu weit treiben; *get carried away* fig. die Kontrolle über sich verlieren; ~ *forward*, ~ *over econ.* übertragen; ~ *on* fortsetzen, weiterführen; *Geschäft etc.* betreiben; ~ *out*, ~ *through* durchausführen; ~**cot** *Brt.* ['kærɪkɒt] (Baby)Trag(e)tasche *f*.

cart [kɑːt] **1.** Karren *m*; Wagen *m*; *put the* ~ *before the horse* fig. das Pferd beim Schwanz aufzäumen; **2.** karren, fahren.

car·ti·lage *anat.* ['kɑːtɪlɪdʒ] Knorpel *m*.

car·ton ['kɑːtən] Karton *m*; *a* ~ *of cigarettes* e-e Stange Zigaretten.

car·toon [kɑːˈtuːn] Cartoon *m*, *n*; Karikatur *f*; Zeichentrickfilm *m*; ~**ist** [~ɪst] Karikaturist *m*.

car·tridge ['kɑːtrɪdʒ] Patrone *f*; *phot.* (Film)Patrone *f* (*e-r Kleinbildkamera*), (Film)Kassette *f* (*e-r Film- od. Kassettenkamera*); ~**pen** Patronenfüllhalter *m*.

cart-wheel ['kɑːtwiːl] Wagenrad *n*; *turn* ~*s* radschlagen.

carve [kɑːv] *Fleisch* vorschneiden, zerlegen; schnitzen; meißeln; **car·ver** ['kɑːvə] (Holz)Schnitzer *m*; Bildhauer *m*; Tranchierer *m*; Tranchiermesser *n*; **carv·ing** [~ɪŋ] Schnitzerei *f*.

car wash ['kɑːwɒʃ] Autowäsche *f*; Waschanlage *f*, -straße *f*.

cas·cade [kæˈskeɪd] Wasserfall *m*.

case¹ [keɪs] **1.** Behälter *m*; Kiste *f*, Kasten *m*; Etui *n*; Gehäuse *n*; Schachtel *f*; (*Glas*)Schrank *m*; (*Kissen*)Bezug *m*; ⊕ Verkleidung *f*; **2.** in ein Gehäuse *od.* Etui stecken; ⊕ verkleiden.

case² [~] Fall *m* (*a.* ♔); *gr.* Kasus *m*, Fall *m*; ♨ (*Krankheits*)Fall *m*, Patient(in); F komischer Kauz; Sache *f*, Angelegenheit *f*.

case·ment [ˈkeɪsmənt] Fensterflügel *m*; *a.* ~ *window* Flügelfenster *n*.

cash [kæʃ] **1.** Bargeld *n*; Barzahlung *f*; ~ *down* gegen bar; ~ *on delivery* Lieferung *f* gegen bar; (per) Nachnahme *f*; **2.** *Scheck etc.* einlösen; ~**book** [ˈkæʃbʊk] Kassenbuch *n*; ~**desk** Kasse *f* (*im Warenhaus etc.*); ~**di·spens·er** Geldautomat *m*, Bankomat *m*; ~**ier** [kæˈʃɪə] Kassierer(in); ~'s desk *od.* office Kasse *f*; ~**less** [~lɪs] bargeldlos; ~**o·mat** [kæʃəʊˈmæt] = ~ *dispenser*; ~ **re·gis·ter** Registrierkasse *f*.

cas·ing [ˈkeɪsɪŋ] (Schutz)Hülle *f*; Verschalung *f*, -kleidung *f*, Gehäuse *n*.

cask [kɑːsk] Faß *n*.

cas·ket [ˈkɑːskɪt] Kästchen *n*; *Am.* Sarg *m*.

cas·se·role [ˈkæsərəʊl] Kasserolle *f*.

cas·sette [kəˈset] (Film-, Band-*etc.*)Kassette *f*; △ *nicht Geld- etc. Kassette*; ~**deck** Kassettendeck *n*; ~**ra·di·o** Radiorecorder *m*; ~**re·cord·er** Kassettenrecorder *m*.

cas·sock *eccl.* [ˈkæsək] Soutane *f*.

cast [kɑːst] **1.** Wurf *m*; ⊕ Guß(form *f*) *m*; Abguß *m*, Abdruck *m*; Schattierung *f*, Anflug *m*; Form *f*, Art *f*; Auswerfen *n* (*der Angel etc.*); *thea.* Besetzung *f*; **2.** (*cast*) *v/t.* (ab-, aus-, hin-, um-, weg)werfen; *zo.* Haut *etc.* abwerfen; *Zähne etc.* verlieren; verwerfen; gestalten; ⊕ gießen; *a.* ~ *up* ausrechnen, zusammenzählen; *thea. Stück* besetzen; *Rollen* verteilen (*to* an *acc.*); ~ *in a lawsuit* ♔ e-n Prozeß verlieren; ~ *lots* losen (*for* um); ~ *in one's lot with s.o.* j-s Los teilen; ~ *aside Gewohnheit etc.* ablegen; *Freund etc.* fallenlassen; ~ *away* wegwerfen; *be* ~ *away* ♣ verschlagen werden; *be* ~ *down* niedergeschlagen sein; ~ *off Kleidung* ausrangieren; *Freund etc.* fallenlassen; *Stricken etc.:* Maschen abnehmen;

v/i. ⊕ sich gießen lassen; sich (ver-)werfen (*Holz*); ~ *about for*, ~ *around for* suchen (nach), *fig. a.* sich umsehen nach.

cas·ta·net [kæstəˈnet] Kastagnette *f*.

cast·a·way [ˈkɑːstəweɪ] **1.** ausgestoßen; ausrangiert, abgelegt (*Kleidung etc.*); ♣ schiffbrüchig; **2.** Ausgestoßene(r *m*) *f*; ♣ Schiffbrüchige(r *m*) *f*.

caste [kɑːst] Kaste *f* (*a. fig.*).

cast·er [ˈkɑːstə] = *castor²*.

cas·ti·gate [ˈkæstɪgeɪt] züchtigen; *fig.* geißeln.

cast i·ron [ˈkɑːstˈaɪən] Gußeisen *n*; **cast-i·ron** gußeisern.

cas·tle [ˈkɑːsl] Burg *f*, Schloß *n*; *Schach:* Turm *m*.

cas·tor¹ [ˈkɑːstə]: ~ *oil* Rizinusöl *n*.

cas·tor² [~] Laufrolle *f* (*unter Möbeln*); (Salz-, Zucker- *etc.*)Streuer *m*.

cas·trate [kæˈstreɪt] kastrieren.

cas·u·al □ [ˈkæʒjʊəl] zufällig; gelegentlich; flüchtig; lässig; ~ *wear* Freizeitkleidung *f*; ~**ty** [~ʧɪ] Unfall *m*; Verunglückte(r *m*) *f*, Opfer *n*; ✕ Verwundete(r), Gefallene(r) *m*; *casualties pl.* Opfer *pl.*, ✕ *mst* Verluste *pl.*; ~ *ward*, ~ *department* Unfallstation *f*.

cat *zo.* [kæt] Katze *f*.

cat·a·logue, *Am.* **-log** [ˈkætəlɒg] **1.** Katalog *m*; *Am. univ.* Vorlesungsverzeichnis *n*; **2.** katalogisieren.

cat·a·pult [ˈkætəpʌlt] *Brt.* Schleuder *f*; Katapult *n m*.

cat·a·ract [ˈkætərækt] Wasserfall *m*; Stromschnelle *f*; ♨ grauer Star.

ca·tarrh ♨ [kəˈtɑː] Katarrh *m*; Schnupfen *m*.

ca·tas·tro·phe [kəˈtæstrəfɪ] Katastrophe *f*.

catch [kæʧ] **1.** Fangen *n*; Fang *m*, Beute *f*; Stocken *n* (*des Atems*); Halt *m*, Griff *m*; ⊕ Haken *m*; (Tür)Klinke *f*; Verschluß *m*; *fig.* Haken *m*; **2.** (*caught*) *v/t.* (auf-, ein)fangen; packen, fassen, ergreifen; überraschen, ertappen; *Blick etc.* auffangen; *Zug etc.* (noch) kriegen; erwischen; erfassen, verstehen; einfangen (*Atmosphäre*); sich *e-e Krankheit* holen; ~ (*a*) *cold* sich erkälten; ~ *the eye* ins Auge fallen; ~ *s.o.'s eye* j-s Aufmerksamkeit auf sich lenken; ~ *s.o. up* j-n einholen; *be caught up in* verwickelt sein in (*acc.*); **3.** *v/i.* sich verfangen, hängenbleiben; fassen, greifen; ineinandergreifen (*Räder*);

klemmen; einschnappen (*Schloß etc.*); ~ *on* F einschlagen, Anklang finden; F kapieren; ~ *up with* einholen; ~**er** ['kætʃə] Fänger *m*; ~**ing** [~ɪŋ] packend; 🐾 ansteckend; ~**word** Schlagwort *n*; Stichwort *n*; ~**y** □ [~ɪ] (*-ier, -iest*) eingängig (*Melodie*).

cat·e·chis·m ['kætɪkɪzəm] Katechismus *m*.

ca·te·gor·i·cal □ [kætɪ'gɒrɪkl] kategorisch; ~**go·ry** ['kætɪgərɪ] Kategorie *f*.

ca·ter ['keɪtə]: ~ *for* Speisen u. Getränke liefern für; *fig.* sorgen für.

cat·er·pil·lar ['kætəpɪlə] *zo.* Raupe *f*; *TM* Raupenfahrzeug *n*; ~ *tractor TM* Raupenschlepper *m*.

cat·gut ['kætgʌt] Darmsaite *f*.

ca·the·dral [kə'θiːdrəl] Dom *m*, Kathedrale *f*.

Cath·o·lic ['kæθəlɪk] **1.** katholisch; **2.** Katholik(in).

cat·kin ['kætkɪn] Kätzchen *n*.

cat·tle ['kætl] Vieh *n*.

cat·ty F ['kætɪ] (*-ier, iest*) boshaft, gehässig.

caught [kɔːt] *pret. u. p.p. von* **catch** 2.

caul·dron ['kɔːldrən] großer Kessel.

cau·li·flow·er 🌱 ['kɒlɪflaʊə] Blumenkohl *m*.

caus·al □ ['kɔːzl] ursächlich.

cause [kɔːz] **1.** Ursache *f*; Grund *m*; ⚖ Klagegrund *m*; ⚖ Fall *m*, Sache *f*; Angelegenheit *f*, Sache *f*; **2.** verursachen; veranlassen; ~**less** □ ['kɔːzlɪs] grundlos.

cause·way ['kɔːzweɪ] Damm *m*.

caus·tic ['kɔːstɪk] (~*ally*) ätzend; *fig.* beißend, scharf.

cau·tion ['kɔːʃn] **1.** Vorsicht *f*; Warnung *f*; Verwarnung *f*; △ *nicht Kaution*; **2.** warnen; verwarnen; ⚖ belehren.

cau·tious □ ['kɔːʃəs] behutsam, vorsichtig; ~**ness** [~nɪs] Behutsamkeit *f*, Vorsicht *f*.

cav·al·ry *bsd. hist.* ✕ ['kævlrɪ] Kavallerie *f*.

cave [keɪv] **1.** Höhle *f*; **2.** *v/i.* ~ *in* einstürzen; klein beigeben.

cav·ern ['kævən] (große) Höhle; ~**ous** *fig.* [~əs] hohl.

cav·i·ty ['kævətɪ] Höhle *f*; Loch *n*.

caw [kɔː]: **1.** krächzen; **2.** Krächzen *n*.

cease [siːs] *v/i.* aufhören, zu Ende gehen; *v/t.* aufhören (*to do, doing* zu tun); ~**fire** ✕ ['siːsfaɪə] Feuerein-

stellung *f*; Waffenruhe *f*; ~**less** □ [~lɪs] unaufhörlich.

cede [siːd] abtreten, überlassen.

cei·ling ['siːlɪŋ] (Zimmer-)Decke *f*; *fig.* Höchstgrenze *f*; ~ *price* Höchstpreis *m*.

cel·e·brate ['selɪbreɪt] feiern; ~**brat·ed** gefeiert, berühmt (*for* für, wegen); ~**bra·tion** [selɪ'breɪʃn] Feier *f*.

ce·leb·ri·ty [sɪ'lebrətɪ] Berühmtheit *f*.

ce·ler·i·ty [sɪ'lerətɪ] Geschwindigkeit *f*.

cel·e·ry 🌱 ['selərɪ] Sellerie *m*, *f*.

ce·les·ti·al □ [sɪ'lestjəl] himmlisch.

cel·i·ba·cy ['selɪbəsɪ] Ehelosigkeit *f*.

cell [sel] Zelle *f*; ⚡ *a.* Element *n*.

cel·lar ['selər] Keller *m*.

cel·list ♪ ['tʃelɪst] Cellist(in); ~**lo** [~əʊ] (*pl. -los*) (Violon)Cello *n*.

cel·lo·phane *TM* ['seləʊfeɪn] Zellophan *n*.

cel·lu·lar ['seljʊlə] Zell(en)...

Cel·tic ['keltɪk] keltisch.

ce·ment [sɪ'ment] **1.** Zement *m*; Kitt *m*; **2.** zementieren; (ver)kitten.

cem·e·tery ['semɪtrɪ] Friedhof *m*.

cen·sor ['sensə] **1.** Zensor *m*; **2.** zensieren; ~**ship** [~ʃɪp] Zensur *f*.

cen·sure ['senʃə] **1.** Tadel *m*, Verweis *m*; △ *nicht Zensur*; **2.** tadeln.

cen·sus ['sensəs] Volkszählung *f*.

cent [sent] Hundert *n*; *Am.* Cent *m* (= $^1/_{100}$ *Dollar*); *per* ~ Prozent *n*.

cen·te·na·ry [sen'tiːnərɪ] Hundertjahrfeier *f*, hundertjähriges Jubiläum.

cen·ten·ni·al [sen'tenjəl] **1.** hundertjährig; **2.** *Am.* = *centenary*.

cen·ter *Am.* ['sentə] = *centre*.

cen·ti·grade ['sentɪgreɪd]: **10** *degrees* ~ 10 Grad Celsius; ~**me·tre**, *Am.* ~**me·ter** Zentimeter *m*, *n*; ~**pede** *zo.* [~piːd] Tausendfuß(l)er *m*.

cen·tral □ ['sentrəl] zentral; Haupt..., Zentral...; Mittel...; ~ *heating* Zentralheizung *f*; ~**ize** [~aɪz] zentralisieren.

cen·tre, *Am.* ~**ter** ['sentə] **1.** Zentrum *n*, Mittelpunkt *m*; ~ *of gravity phys.* Schwerpunkt *m*; **2.** (sich) konzentrieren; zentrieren.

cen·tu·ry ['sentʃʊrɪ] Jahrhundert *n*.

ce·ram·ics [sɪ'ræmɪks] *pl.* Keramik *f*, keramische Erzeugnisse *pl.*

ce·re·al ['sɪərɪəl] **1.** Getreide...; **2.** Getreide(pflanze *f*) *n*; Getreideflokken(gericht *n*) *pl.*, Frühstückskost *f* (*aus Getreide*).

cer·e·bral *anat.* ['serıbrəl] Gehirn...

cer·e·mo·ni·al [serı'məunjəl] **1.** □ zeremoniell; **2.** Zeremoniell *n*; **~ous** □ [~jəs] zeremoniell; förmlich; **~ny** ['serımənı] Zeremonie *f*; Feier(lichkeit) *f*; Förmlichkeit(en *pl.*) *f*.

cer·tain □ ['sɜ:tn] sicher, gewiß; zuverlässig; bestimmt; gewisse(r, -s); **~ly** [~lı] sicher, gewiß; *in Antworten*: sicherlich, bestimmt, natürlich; **~ty** [~tı] Sicherheit *f*, Bestimmtheit *f*, Gewißheit *f*.

cer·tif·i·cate 1. [sə'tıfıkıt] Zeugnis *n*; Bescheinigung *f*; **~** *of birth* Geburtsurkunde *f*; *General ♀ of Education advanced level* (*A level*) *Brit. Schule: etwa* Abitur(zeugnis) *n*; *General ♀ of Education ordinary level* (*O level*) *Schule: etwa* mittlere Reife; *medical* **~** ärztliches Attest; **2.** [~keıt] bescheinigen; **~ti·fy** ['sɜ:tıfaı] *et.* bescheinigen; beglaubigen.

cer·ti·tude ['sɜ:tıtju:d] Sicherheit *f*, Bestimmtheit *f*, Gewißheit *f*.

ces·sa·tion [se'seıʃn] Aufhören *n*.

chafe [tʃeıf] *v/t.* (auf)scheuern, wund scheuern; ärgern; *v/i.* sich aufscheuern *od.* wund scheuern; scheuern; sich ärgern.

chaff [tʃɑ:f] **1.** Spreu *f*; Häcksel *n*; F Neckerei *f*; F necken.

chaf·finch *zo.* ['tʃæfıntʃ] Buchfink *m*.

cha·grin ['ʃægrın] **1.** Ärger *m*; **2.** ärgern.

chain [tʃeın] **1.** Kette *f*; *fig.* Fessel *f*; **~ reaction** Kettenreaktion *f*; **~smoke** Kette rauchen; **~smoker** Kettenraucher *m*; **~ store** Kettenladen *m*; **2.** (an)ketten; fesseln.

chair [tʃeə] Stuhl *m*; Lehrstuhl *m*; Vorsitz *m*; *be in the* **~** den Vorsitz führen; **~ lift** ['tʃeəlıft] Sessellift *m*; **~man** (*pl. -men*) Vorsitzende(r) *m*, Präsident *m*; **~man·ship** [~ʃıp] Vorsitz *m*; **~wom·an** (*pl. -women*) Vorsitzende *f*.

chal·ice ['tʃælıs] Kelch *m*.

chalk [tʃɔ:k] **1.** Kreide *f*; **2.** mit Kreide schreiben *od.* zeichnen; **~ up** *Sieg* verbuchen.

chal·lenge ['tʃælındʒ] **1.** Herausforderung *f*; ✗ Anruf *m*; *bsd.* ✗ Ablehnung *f*; **2.** herausfordern; anrufen; ablehnen; anzweifeln.

cham·ber ['tʃeımbə] *parl.*, *zo.*, ♀, ⊕, Kammer *f*; **~s** *pl.* Geschäfts-

räume *pl.*; **~maid** Zimmermädchen *n*.

cham·ois ['ʃæmwɑ:] Gemse *f*; *a.* **~** *leather* [*mst.* 'ʃæmıleðə] Wildleder *n*.

champ F [tʃæmp] = *champion* (*Sport*).

cham·pagne [ʃæm'peın] Champagner *m*.

cham·pi·on ['tʃæmpjən] **1.** Verfechter *m*, Fürsprecher *m*; *Sport:* Sieger *m*; Meister *m*; **2.** verfechten, eintreten für, verteidigen; **3.** Meister...; **~ship** *Sport:* Meisterschaft *f*.

chance [tʃɑ:ns] **1.** Zufall *m*; Schicksal *n*; Risiko *n*; Chance *f*, (günstige) Gelegenheit; Aussicht *f* (*of auf acc.*); Möglichkeit *f*; *by* **~** zufällig; *take a* **~** es darauf ankommen lassen; *take no* **~s** nichts riskieren (wollen); **2.** zufällig; **3.** *v/i.* (unerwartet) eintreten *od.* geschehen; *I* **~***d to meet her* zufällig traf ich sie; *v/t.* riskieren.

chan·cel·lor ['tʃɑ:nsələ] Kanzler *m*.

chan·de·lier [ʃændə'lıə] Kronleuchter *m*.

change [tʃeındʒ] **1.** Veränderung *f*, Wechsel *m*; Abwechslung *f*; Wechselgeld *n*, Kleingeld *n*; *for a* **~** zur Abwechslung; **~** *for the better* (*worse*) Besserung *f* (Verschlechterung *f*); **2.** *v/t.* (ver)ändern, umändern; (aus)wechseln; (aus-, ver)tauschen (*for gegen*); *mot.* ✗ schalten; **~** *over* umschalten; umstellen; **~** *trains* umsteigen; *v/i.* sich (ver)ändern, sich umziehen; **~a·ble** □ ['tʃeındʒəbl] veränderlich; **~less** □ [~lıs] unveränderlich; **~o·ver** Umstellung *f*.

chan·nel ['tʃænl] **1.** Kanal *m*; Flußbett *n*; Rinne *f*; (*Fernseh- etc.*)Kanal *m*, (-)Programm *n*; *fig.* Kanal *m*, Weg *m*; **2.** (*bsd. Brt. -ll-; Am. -l-*) furchen; aushöhlen; *fig.* lenken.

chant [tʃɑ:nt] **1.** (Kirchen)Gesang *m*; Singsang *m*; **2.** singen; in Sprechchören rufen; Sprechchöre anstimmen.

cha·os ['keıɒs] Chaos *n*.

chap¹ [tʃæp] **1.** Riß *m*, Sprung *m*; **2.** (*-pp-*) rissig machen *od.* werden.

chap² [~] Bursche *m*, Kerl *m*, Junge *m*.

chap³ [~] Kinnbacke(n *m*) *f*; Maul *n*.

chap·el ['tʃæpl] Kapelle *f*; Gottesdienst *m*.

chap·lain ['tʃæplın] Kaplan *m*.

chap·ter ['tʃæptə] Kapitel *n*.

char [tʃɑː] (-rr-) verkohlen.

char·ac·ter [ˈkærəktə] Charakter *m*; Eigenschaft *f*; Schrift(zeichen *n*) *f*; Persönlichkeit *f*; *Roman etc.*: Figur *f*, Gestalt *f*; *thea.* Rolle *f*; *fig.* guter Ruf; Zeugnis *n*; **~·is·tic** [kærəktəˈrɪstɪk] **1.** (~ally) charakteristisch (*of* für); **2.** Kennzeichen, Merkmal *n*; **~·ize** [ˈkærəktəraɪz] charakterisieren.

char·coal [ˈtʃɑːkəʊl] Holzkohle *f*.

charge [tʃɑːdʒ] **1.** Ladung *f*; (Spreng)Ladung *f*; *bsd. fig.* Last *f*; Verantwortung *f*; Aufsicht *f*, Leitung *f*; Obhut *f*; Schützling *m*; ✗ Angriff *m*; Beschuldigung *f*, ⚖ *a.* (Punkt *m* der) Anklage *f*; Preis *m*, Kosten *pl.*; Gebühr *f*; *free of* ~ kostenlos; *be in* ~ *of* verantwortlich sein für; *have* ~ *of* in Obhut *od.* Verwahrung haben, betreuen; *take* ~ die Leitung *etc.* übernehmen, die Sache in die Hand nehmen; **2.** *v/t.* laden; beladen, belasten; beauftragen; belehren; ⚖ beschuldigen, anklagen (*with gen.*); in Rechnung stellen; berechnen; (als Preis) fordern; ✗ angreifen; *v/i.* stürmen; ~ *at s.o.* auf j-n losgehen.

char·i·ot *poet. od. hist.* [ˈtʃærɪət] Streit-, Triumphwagen *m*.

char·i·ta·ble ☐ [ˈtʃærɪtəbl] mild (-tätig), wohltätig.

char·i·ty [ˈtʃærɪtɪ] Nächstenliebe *f*; Wohltätigkeit *f*; Güte *f*; Nachsicht *f*; milde Gabe.

char·la·tan [ˈʃɑːlətən] Scharlatan *m*; Quacksalber *m*, Kurpfuscher *m*.

charm [tʃɑːm] **1.** Zauber *m*; Charme *m*, Reiz *m*; Talisman *m*, Amulett *n*; **2.** bezaubern, entzücken; **~ing** ☐ [ˈtʃɑːmɪŋ] charmant, bezaubernd.

chart [tʃɑːt] **1.** ⚓ Seekarte *f*; Tabelle *f*; ~s *pl.* Charts *pl.*, Hitliste(n *pl.*) *f*; **2.** auf e-r Karte einzeichnen.

char·ter [ˈtʃɑːtə] **1.** Urkunde *f*, Freibrief *m*; Chartern *n*; **2.** konzessionieren; ⚓, ✈ chartern, mieten; **~ flight** Charterflug *m*.

char·wom·an [ˈtʃɑːwʊmən] (*pl. -women*) Putzfrau *f*, Raumpflegerin *f*.

chase [tʃeɪs] **1.** Jagd *f*; Verfolgung *f*; gejagtes Wild; **2.** jagen, hetzen; Jagd machen auf (*acc.*); rasen, rennen.

chasm [ˈkæzəm] Kluft *f*, Abgrund *m* (*a. fig.*); Riß *m*, Spalte *f*.

chaste ☐ [tʃeɪst] rein, keusch, unschuldig; schlicht (*Stil*).

chas·tise [tʃæˈstaɪz] züchtigen.

chas·ti·ty [ˈtʃæstətɪ] Keuschheit *f*.

chat [tʃæt] **1.** Geplauder *n*, Schwätzchen *n*, Plauderei *f*; **2.** plaudern.

chat·tels [ˈtʃætlz] *pl. mst goods and* ~ bewegliches Eigentum.

chat·ter [ˈtʃætə] **1.** plappern; schnattern; klappern; **2.** Geplapper *n*; Klappern *n*; **~·box** F Plappermaul *n*; **~·er** [~ə] Schwätzer(in).

chat·ty [ˈtʃætɪ] (*-ier, -iest*) gesprächig.

chauf·feur [ˈʃəʊfə] Chauffeur *m*.

chau·vi F [ˈʃəʊvɪ] Chauvi *m*; **~·vin·ist** [~nɪst] Chauvinist *m*.

cheap ☐ [tʃiːp] billig; *fig.* schäbig, gemein; **~en** [ˈtʃiːpən] (sich) verbilligen; *fig.* herabsetzen.

cheat [tʃiːt] **1.** Betrug *m*, Schwindel *m*; Betrüger(in); **2.** betrügen.

check [tʃek] **1.** Schach(stellung *f*) *n*; Hemmnis *n*, Hindernis *n* (*on* für); Einhalt *m*; Kontrolle *f* (*on gen.*); Kontrollabschnitt *m*, -schein *m*; *Am.* Gepäckschein *m*; *Am.* = Garderobenmarke *f*; *Am. econ.* = cheque; *Am.* Rechnung *f* (*im Restaurant od. Kaufhaus*); karierter Stoff; **2.** *v/i.* an-, innehalten; *Am.* e-n Scheck ausstellen; ~ *in* sich (*in e-m Hotel*) anmelden; einstempeln; ✈ einchecken; ~ *out* (*aus e-m Hotel*) abreisen; ausstempeln; ~ *up* (*on*) F (*e-e Sache*) nachprüfen, (*e-e Sache, j-n*) überprüfen; *v/t.* hemmen, hindern, aufhalten; zurückhalten; kontrollieren, über-, nachprüfen; *Am. auf e-r Liste* abhaken; *Am. Kleider* in der Garderobe abgeben; *Am. Gepäck* aufgeben; ~ *card Am. econ.* [ˈtʃekkɑːd] Scheckkarte *f*; **~ed,** [~t] kariert; **~ers** *Am.* [~əz] *sg.* Damespiel *n*; **~·in** Anmeldung *f* (*in e-m Hotel*); Einstempeln *n*; ✈ Einchecken *n*; ~ *counter od. desk* ✈ Abfertigungsschalter *m*; **~·ing ac·count** *Am. econ.* Girokonto *n*; **~·list** Check-, Kontroll-, Vergleichsliste *f*; **~·mate 1.** (Schach)Matt *n*; **2.** (schach)matt setzen; **~·out** Abreise *f* (*aus e-m Hotel*); Ausstempeln *n*; *a.* ~ *counter* Kasse *f* (*bsd. im Supermarkt*); **~·point** Kontrollpunkt *m*; **~·room** *Am.* Garderobe *f*; Gepäckaufbewahrung *f*; **~·up** Überprüfung *f*, Kontrolle *f*; ☤ Check-up *m*, (umfangreiche) Vorsorgeuntersuchung *f*.

cheek [tʃiːk] Backe *f*, Wange *f*; F

Unverschämtheit f; **~y** □ F ['tʃi:kɪ] (-ier, -iest) frech.

cheer [tʃɪə] **1.** Stimmung f, Fröhlichkeit f; Hoch(ruf m) n, Beifall(sruf m); ~s! prost!; *three ~s!* dreimal hoch!; **2.** v/t. mit Beifall begrüßen; a. ~ *on* anspornen; a. ~ *up* aufheitern; v/i. hoch rufen, jubeln; a. ~ *up* Mut fassen; ~ *up!* Kopf hoch!; **~ful** ['tʃɪəfl] vergnügt; **~i·o** *int.* F ['tʃɪrɪ'əʊ] mach's gut!, tschüs!; **~less** [~lɪs] freudlos; **~y** □ [~rɪ] (-ier, -iest) vergnügt.

cheese [tʃiːz] Käse m.

chee·tah *zo.* ['tʃiːtə] Gepard m.

chef [ʃef] Küchenchef m; Koch m; △ *nicht Chef.*

chem·i·cal ['kemɪkl] **1.** □ chemisch; **2.** Chemikalie f.

che·mise [ʃə'miːz] (Damen)Hemd n.

chem·ist ['kemɪst] Chemiker(in); Apotheker(in); Drogist(in); *~'s shop* Apotheke f; Drogerie f; **~is·try** [~rɪ] Chemie f.

cheque *Brt. econ.* [tʃek] (*Am.* check) Scheck m; *crossed~* Verrechnungsscheck m; **~ac·count** *Brt. econ.* Girokonto n; ~ *card Brt. econ.* Scheckkarte f.

chequer *Brt.* ['tʃekə] Karomuster n.

cher·ish ['tʃerɪʃ] *Andenken an j-n etc.* hochhalten; hegen, pflegen.

cher·ry ['tʃerɪ] Kirsche f.

chess [tʃes] Schach(spiel) n; *a game of ~* e-e Partie Schach; **~board** ['tʃesbɔːd] Schachbrett n; **~man** (*pl.* -men), **~piece** Schachfigur f.

chest [tʃest] Kiste f, Kasten m, Truhe f; *anat.* Brustkasten m; *get s.th. off one's ~* F sich et. von der Seele reden; ~ *of drawers* Kommode f.

chest·nut ['tʃesnʌt] **1.** ⚜ Kastanie f; **2.** kastanienbraun.

chew [tʃuː] kauen; nachsinnen, grübeln (*on, over* über *acc.*); **~ing-gum** ['tʃuːɪŋgʌm] Kaugummi m.

chick [tʃɪk] Küken n, junger Vogel; F Biene f, Puppe f (*Mädchen*).

chick·en ['tʃɪkɪn] Huhn n; Küken n; (*Brat*)Hähnchen n, (-)Hühnchen n; **~heart·ed** furchtsam, feige; **~pox** [~pɒks] Windpocken *pl.*

chic·o·ry ⚜ ['tʃɪkərɪ] Chicorée f, m.

chief [tʃiːf] **1.** □ oberste(r, -s); Ober..., Haupt...; wichtigste(r, -s); ~ *clerk* Bürovorsteher m; **2.** Oberhaupt n, Chef m; Häuptling m; *...-in-chief* Ober...; **~ly** ['tʃiːflɪ]

hauptsächlich; **~tain** [~tən] Häuptling m.

chil·blain ['tʃɪlbleɪn] Frostbeule f.

child [tʃaɪld] (*pl. children*) Kind n; *from a ~* von Kindheit an; *with ~* schwanger; **~a·buse** ⚖ Kindesmißhandlung f; **~birth** ['tʃaɪldbɜːθ] Geburt f, Niederkunft f; **~hood** [~hʊd] Kindheit f; **~ish** □ [~ɪʃ] kindlich; kindisch; **~like** kindlich; **~mind·er** *Brt.* [~maɪndə] Tagesmutter f; **chil·dren** ['tʃɪldrən] *pl. v.* child.

chill [tʃɪl] **1.** eisig, frostig; **2.** Frost m, Kälte f; ✳ Fieberschauer m; Erkältung f; **3.** abkühlen; *j-n* frösteln lassen; *gechüllt* gekühlt; **~y** [tʃɪlɪ] (-ier, -iest) kalt, frostig.

chime [tʃaɪm] **1.** Glockenspiel n; Geläut n; *fig.* Einklang m; **2.** läuten; ~ *in* sich (ins Gespräch) einmischen.

chim·ney ['tʃɪmnɪ] Schornstein m; Rauchfang m; (Lampen)Zylinder m; **~sweep** Schornsteinfeger m.

chimp *zo.* [tʃɪmp], **chim·pan·zee** *zo.* [~ən'ziː] Schimpanse m.

chin [tʃɪn] **1.** Kinn n; (*keep your*) ~ *up!* Kopf hoch!, halt die Ohren steif!

chi·na ['tʃaɪnə] Porzellan n.

Chi·nese [tʃaɪ'niːz] **1.** chinesisch; **2.** Chinese m, -in f; *ling.* Chinesisch n; *the ~ pl.* die Chinesen *pl.*

chink [tʃɪŋk] Ritz m, Spalt m.

chip [tʃɪp] **1.** Splitter m, Span m, Schnitzel m, n; dünne Scheibe; Spielmarke f; *Computer:* Chip m; *have a ~ on one's shoulder* F sich ständig angegriffen fühlen; e-n Komplex haben (*about* wegen); ~s *pl. Brt.* Pommes frites *pl.*; *Am.* (Kartoffel)Chips *pl.*; **2.** (-pp-) v/t. schnitzeln; an-, abschlagen; v/i. abbröckeln; **~munk** *zo.* ['tʃɪpmʌŋk] nordamerikanisches gestreiftes Eichhörnchen.

chirp [tʃɜːp] **1.** zirpen, zwitschern, piepsen; **2.** Gezirp n, Zwitschern n, Piepsen n.

chis·el ['tʃɪzl] **1.** Meißel m; **2.** (*bsd. Brt. -ll-, Am. -l-*) meißeln.

chit-chat ['tʃɪttʃæt] Plauderei f.

chiv·al·rous □ ['ʃɪvlrəs] ritterlich; **~ry** [~ɪ] *hist.* Rittertum n; Ritterlichkeit f.

chive(s *pl.*) ⚜ [tʃaɪv(z)] Schnittlauch m.

chlo·ri·nate ['klɔːrɪneɪt] *Wasser etc.* chloren; **~rine** [~riːn] Chlor n; **chlor·o·form** ['klɒrəfɔːm]

1. 🔥, 🜊 Chloroform *n*; **2.** chloroformieren.

choc·o·late ['tʃɒkələt] Schokolade *f*; Praline *f*; ∼s *pl.* Pralinen *pl.*, Konfekt *n*.

choice [tʃɔɪs] **1.** Wahl *f*; Auswahl *f*; **2.** □ auserlesen, ausgesucht, vorzüglich.

choir ['kwaɪə] Chor *m*.

choke [tʃəʊk] **1.** *v/t.* (er)würgen, (*a. v/i.*) ersticken; ∼ *back Ärger etc.* unterdrücken, *Tränen* zurückhalten; ∼ *down* hinunterwürgen; *a.* ∼ *up* verstopfen; **2.** *mot.* Choke *m*, Luftklappe *f*.

choose [tʃuːz] (*chose, chosen*) (aus-)wählen, aussuchen; ∼ *to do* vorziehen zu tun.

chop [tʃɒp] **1.** Hieb *m*, Schlag *m*; Kotelett *n*; **2.** (-pp-) *v/t.* hauen, hacken, zerhacken; ∼ *down* fällen; *v/i.* hacken; ∼**per** ['tʃɒpə] Hackmesser *n*, -beil *n*; F Hubschrauber *m*; *Am. sl.* Maschinengewehr *n*; ∼**py** [∼ɪ] (*-ier, -iest*) unruhig (*See*); ∼**stick** Eßstäbchen *n*.

cho·ral □ ['kɔːrəl] Chor...; ∼**(e)** ♪ [kɒˈrɑːl] Choral *m*.

chord ♪ [kɔːd] Saite *f*; Akkord *m*.

chore *Am.* [tʃɔː] schwierige *od.* unangenehme Aufgabe; *mst* ∼s *pl.* Hausarbeit *f*.

cho·rus ['kɔːrəs] Chor *m*; Kehrreim *m*, Refrain *m*; Tanzgruppe *f* (*e-r Revue*).

chose [tʃəʊz] *pret. von* choose; **chosen** ['tʃəʊzn] *p.p. von* choose.

Christ [kraɪst] Christus *m*; △ *nicht der Christ*.

chris·ten ['krɪsn] taufen; ∼**ing** [∼ɪŋ] Taufe *f*; *attr.* Tauf...

Chris|tian ['krɪstjən] **1.** christlich; ∼ *name* Vorname *m*; **2.** Christ(in); ∼**·ti·an·i·ty** [krɪstɪˈænətɪ] Christentum *n*.

Christ·mas ['krɪsməs] Weihnachten *n u. pl.*; *at* ∼ zu Weihnachten; ∼ **Day** der erste Weihnachtsfeiertag; ∼ **Eve** Heiliger Abend.

chrome [krəʊm] Chrom *n*; **chromi·um** 🜊 ['krəʊmjəm] Chrom *n*; ∼**-plated** verchromt.

chron|ic ['krɒnɪk] (∼*ally*) chronisch (*mst* 🜊); dauernd; ∼**·i·cle** [∼l] **1.** Chronik *f*; **2.** aufzeichnen.

chron·o·log·i·cal □ [krɒnəˈlɒdʒɪkl] chronologisch; **chro·nol·o·gy** [krəˈnɒlədʒɪ] Zeitrechnung *f*; Zeitfolge *f*.

chub·by F ['tʃʌbɪ] (*-ier, -iest*) rundlich; pausbäckig.

chuck F [tʃʌk] werfen, schmeißen; ∼ *out j-n* rausschmeißen; *et.* wegschmeißen; ∼ *up Job etc.* hinschmeißen.

chuck·le ['tʃʌkl] **1.** ∼ (*to o.s.*) (stillvergnügt) in sich hineinlachen; **2.** leises Lachen.

chum F [tʃʌm] Kamerad *m*, Kumpel *m*; ∼**·my** F ['tʃʌmɪ] (*-ier, -iest*) dick befreundet.

chump [tʃʌmp] Holzklotz *m*; F Trottel *m*.

chunk [tʃʌŋk] Klotz *m*, Klumpen *m*.

church [tʃɜːtʃ] Kirche *f*; *attr.* Kirch(en)...; ∼ *service* Gottesdienst *m*; ∼**·war·den** ['tʃɜːtʃˈwɔːdn] Kirchenvorsteher *m*; ∼**·yard** Kirchhof *m*.

churl·ish □ ['tʃɜːlɪʃ] grob, flegelhaft.

churn [tʃɜːn] **1.** Butterfaß *n*; **2.** buttern; aufwühlen.

chute [ʃuːt] Stromschnelle *f*; Rutsche *f*, Rutschbahn *f*; F Fallschirm *m*.

ci·der ['saɪdə] (*Am. hard* ∼) Apfelwein *m*; (*sweet*) ∼ *Am.* Apfelmost *m*, -saft *m*.

ci·gar [sɪˈɡɑː] Zigarre *f*.

cig·a·rette, *Am. a.* **-ret** [sɪɡəˈret] Zigarette *f*.

cinch F [sɪntʃ] todsichere Sache.

cin·der ['sɪndə] Schlacke *f*; ∼s *pl.* Asche *f*; **Cin·de·rel·la** [sɪndəˈrelə] Aschenbrödel *n*, -puttel *n*; ∼**·path**, ∼**·track** *Sport*: Aschenbahn *f*.

cin·e|cam·e·ra ['sɪnɪkæmərə] (Schmal)Filmkamera *f*; ∼**·film** Schmalfilm *m*.

cin·e·ma *Brt.* ['sɪnəmə] Kino *n*; Film *m*.

cin·na·mon ['sɪnəmən] Zimt *m*.

ci·pher ['saɪfə] Ziffer *f*; Null *f* (*a. fig.*); Geheimschrift *f*, Chiffre *f*.

cir·cle ['sɜːkl] **1.** Kreis *m*; *Bekanntetc.* Kreis *m*; *fig.* Kreislauf *m*; *thea.* Rang *m*; Ring *m*; **2.** (um)kreisen.

cir|cuit ['sɜːkɪt] Kreislauf *m*; ⚡ Stromkreis *m*; Rundreise *f*; *Sport*: Zirkus *m*; *short* ∼ ⚡ Kurzschluß *m*; ∼**·cu·i·tous** □ [səˈkjuːɪtəs] weitschweifig; ∼ *route* Umweg *m*.

cir·cu·lar ['sɜːkjʊlə] **1.** □ kreisförmig; Kreis...; ∼ *letter* Rundschreiben *n*; **2.** Rundschreiben *n*, Umlauf *m*.

cir·cu·late ['sɜːkjʊleɪt] *v/i.* umlaufen, zirkulieren; *v/t.* in Umlauf setzen;

~·lat·ing [~ɪŋ]: ~ *library* Leihbücherei *f*; **~·la·tion** [sɜːkjʊ'leɪʃn] Zirkulation *f*, Kreislauf *m*; (Blut)Kreislauf *m*; *fig.* Umlauf *m*; Verbreitung *f*; Auflage(nhöhe) *f* (*e-r Zeitung, e-s Buches etc.*).

cir·cum-... ['sɜːkəm] (her)um; **~·fer·ence** [sə'kʌmfərəns] (Kreis)Umfang *m*, Peripherie *f*; **~·nav·i·gate** [sɜːkəm'nævɪgeɪt] umschiffen; **~·scribe** ['sɜːkəmskraɪb] Åv umschreiben; *fig.* begrenzen; **~·spect** □ [~spekt] um-, vorsichtig; **~·stance** [~stəns] Umstand *m*, Einzelheit *f*; **~s** *pl. a.* Verhältnisse *pl.*; *in od. under no* **~s** unter keinen Umständen, auf keinen Fall; *in od. under the* **~s** unter diesen Umständen; **~·stan·tial** □ [sɜːkəm'stænʃl] umständlich; **~** *evidence* ᵗᵗ Indizien(beweis *m*) *pl.*; **~·vent** [~'vent] überlisten; vereiteln.

cir·cus ['sɜːkəs] Zirkus *m*; (runder) Platz.

cis·tern ['sɪstən] Wasserbehälter *m*; Spülkasten *m* (*in der Toilette*).

ci·ta·tion [saɪ'teɪʃn] ᵗᵗ Vorladung *f*; Anführung *f*, Zitat *n*; **cite** [saɪt] ᵗᵗ vorladen; anführen; zitieren.

cit·i·zen ['sɪtɪzn] (Staats)Bürger(in); Städter(in); **~·ship** [~ʃɪp] Bürgerrecht *n*; Staatsbürgerschaft *f*.

cit·y ['sɪtɪ] **1.** (Groß)Stadt *f*; *the* **♎** die (Londoner) City; **2.** städtisch, Stadt...; **~** *centre Brt.* Innenstadt *f*, City *f*; **~** *council(l)or* Stadtrat(smitglied *n*) *m*; **~** *editor Am.* Lokalredakteur *m*; *Brt.* Wirtschaftsredakteur *m*; **~** *hall* Rathaus *n*; *bsd. Am.* Stadtverwaltung *f*.

civ·ic ['sɪvɪk] (staats)bürgerlich; städtisch; **~s** *sg.* Staatsbürgerkunde *f*.

civ·il ['sɪvl] staatlich, Staats...; (staats)bürgerlich, Bürger...; Zivil...; ᵗᵗ zivilrechtlich; höflich; **~** *rights pl.* (Staats)Bürgerrechte *pl.*; **~** *rights activist* Bürgerrechtler(in); **~** *rights movement* Bürgerrechtsbewegung *f*; **~** *servant* Staatsbeamte(r) *m*; **~** *service* Staatsdienst *m*, öffentlicher Dienst *m*; Beamtenschaft *f*; **~** *war* Bürgerkrieg *m*.

ci·vil·i·an [sɪ'vɪljən] Zivilist *m*; **~·ty** [~lətɪ] Höflichkeit *f*.

civ·i·li·za·tion [sɪvɪlaɪ'zeɪʃn] Zivilisation *f*, Kultur *f*; **~ze** ['sɪvɪlaɪz] zivilisieren.

clad [klæd] **1.** *pret. u. p.p. von clothe*; **2.** *adj.* gekleidet.

claim [kleɪm] **1.** Anspruch *m*; Anrecht *n* (*to auf acc.*); Forderung *f*; *Am.* Stück *n* Staatsland; *Am.* Claim *m*; **2.** beanspruchen; fordern; behaupten; **clai·mant** ['kleɪmənt] Ansprucherhebende(r *m*) *f*.

clair·voy·ant [kleə'vɔɪənt] Hellseher(in).

clam·ber ['klæmbə] klettern.

clam·my □ ['klæmɪ] (*-ier, -iest*) feuchtkalt, klamm.

clam·o(u)r ['klæmə] **1.** Geschrei *n*, Lärm *m*; **2.** schreien (*for* nach).

clamp ⊕ [klæmp] **1.** Klammer *f*; **2.** mit Klammer(n) befestigen.

clan [klæn] Clan *m*, Sippe *f* (*a. fig.*).

clan·des·tine □ [klæn'destɪn] heimlich, Geheim...

clang [klæŋ] **1.** Klang *m*, Geklirr *n*; **2.** schallen (lassen).

clank [klæŋk] **1.** Gerassel *n*, Geklirr *n*; **2.** rasseln *od.* klirren (mit).

clap [klæp] **1.** Klatschen *n*; Schlag *m*, Klaps *m*; **2.** (*-pp-*) schlagen *od.* klatschen (mit).

clar·et ['klærət] roter Bordeaux; Rotwein *m*; Weinrot *n*; *sl.* Blut *n*.

clar·i·fy ['klærɪfaɪ] *v/t.* (auf)klären, erhellen, klarstellen; *v/i.* sich (auf-)klären, klar werden.

clar·i·net ♪ [klærɪ'net] Klarinette *f*.

clar·i·ty ['klærətɪ] Klarheit *f*.

clash [klæʃ] **1.** Geklirr *n*; Zusammenstoß *m*; Widerstreit *m*, Konflikt *m*; **2.** klirren (mit); zusammenstoßen; nicht zusammenpassen *od.* harmonieren.

clasp [klɑːsp] **1.** Haken *m*, Klammer *f*; Schnalle *f*, Spange *f*; *fig.* Umklammerung *f*, Umarmung *f*; **2.** ein-, zuhaken; *fig.* umklammern, umfassen; **~·knife** ['klɑːspnaɪf] Taschenmesser *n*.

class [klɑːs] **1.** Klasse *f*; (Bevölkerungs)Schicht *f*; (Schul)Klasse *f*; (Unterrichts)Stunde *f*; Kurs *m*; *Am. univ.* Studenten *pl. e-s Jahrgangs*; **~·mate** Mitschüler(in); **~·room** Klassenzimmer *n*; **2.** (in Klassen) einteilen, einordnen.

clas|sic ['klæsɪk] **1.** Klassiker *m*; **2.** *adj.* (**~ally**) erstklassig; klassisch; **~·si·cal** □ [~kl] klassisch.

clas·si·fi·ca·tion [klæsɪfɪ'keɪʃn] Klassifizierung *f*, Einteilung *f*; **~·fy** ['klæsɪfaɪ] klassifizieren, einstufen.

clat·ter ['klætə] 1. Geklapper *n*; 2. klappern (mit).

clause [klɔːz] ⚖ Klausel *f*, Bestimmung *f*; *gr.* Satz(teil *n*) *m*.

claw [klɔː] 1. Klaue *f*, Kralle *f*, Pfote *f*; (*Krebs*)Schere *f*; 2. (zer)kratzen; umkrallen, packen.

clay [kleɪ] Ton *m*; Erde *f*.

clean [kliːn] 1. *adj.* □ rein; sauber, glatt, eben; *sl.* clean (*nicht mehr drogenabhängig*); 2. *adv.* völlig, ganz u. gar; 3. reinigen, säubern, putzen; ~ *out* reinigen; ~ *up* gründlich reinigen; aufräumen; **~·er** ['kliːnə] Reiniger *m*; Rein(e)machefrau *f*; *mst* ~**s** *pl.*, ~'s (chemische) Reinigung (*Geschäft*); **~·ing** [∪ŋ] Reinigung *f*, Putzen *n*; *do the* ~ saubermachen, putzen; *spring-cleaning* Frühjahrsputz *m*; **~·li·ness** ['klenlɪnɪs] Reinlichkeit *f*; **~·ly** 1. *adv.* ['kliːnlɪ] rein; sauber; 2. *adj.* ['klenlɪ] (*-ier, -iest*) reinlich.

cleanse [klenz] reinigen, säubern; **cleans·er** ['klenzə] Reinigungsmittel *n*.

clear [klɪə] 1. □ klar; hell; rein; frei (*of* von); ganz, voll; *econ.* rein, netto; 2. *v/t.* reinigen (*of, from* von); *Wald* lichten, roden; wegräumen (*a.* ~ *away*); *Tisch* abräumen; räumen, leeren; *Hindernis* nehmen; *econ.* verzollen; ⚖ freisprechen; ~ *out* säubern; ausräumen u. wegtun; ~ *up* aufräumen; aufklären; *v/i.* aufklaren (*Wetter*); ~ *out* F abhauen; ~ *up* aufräumen; sich aufhellen, aufklaren (*Wetter*); **~·ance** ['klɪərəns] Räumung *f*; Rodung *f*; ⊕ lichter Abstand; *econ.* Zollabfertigung *f*; Freigabe *f*; ⚓ Auslaufgenehmigung *f*; **~·ing** [∪rɪŋ] Aufklärung *f*; Lichtung *f*, Rodung *f*.

cleave [kliːv] (*cleaved od. cleft od. clove, cleaved od. cleft od. cloven*) spalten.

cleav·er ['kliːvə] Hackmesser *n*.

clef ♪ [klef] Schlüssel *m*.

cleft [kleft] 1. Spalt *m*, Spalte *f*; 2. *pret. u. p.p. von* cleave.

clem·en·cy ['klemənsɪ] Milde *f*, Gnade *f*; **~t** □ [∪t] mild.

clench [klentʃ] *Lippen etc.* (fest) zusammenpressen; *Zähne* zusammenbeißen; *Faust* ballen.

cler·gy ['klɜːdʒɪ] Geistlichkeit *f*; **~·man** (*pl.* -men) Geistliche(r) *m*.

cler·i·cal □ ['klerɪkl] geistlich; Schreib(er)...

clerk [klɑːk] Schriftführer(in), Sekretär(in); kaufmännische(r) Angestellte(r), (Büro- *etc.*) Angestellte(r *m*) *f*, (Bank-, Post)Beamt|e(r) *m*, -in *f*; *Am.* Verkäufer(in).

clev|er □ ['klevə] klug, gescheit; geschickt.

click [klɪk] 1. Klicken *n*, Knacken *n*; ⊕ Sperrhaken *m*, -klinke *f*; 2. klicken, knacken; zu-, einschnappen; *mit der Zunge* schnalzen.

cli·ent ['klaɪənt] ⚖ Klient(in), Mandant(in); Kund|e *m*, -in *f*.

cliff [klɪf] Klippe *f*, Felsen *m*.

cli·mate ['klaɪmɪt] Klima *n*.

cli·max ['klaɪmæks] 1. *rhet.* Steigerung *f*; Gipfel *m*, Höhepunkt *m*; *physiol. a.* Orgasmus *m*; 2. (sich) steigern.

climb [klaɪm] klettern; (er-, be)steigen; **~·er** ['klaɪmə] Kletterer *m*, Bergsteiger(in); *fig.* Aufsteiger *m*; ♣ Kletterpflanze *f*; **~·ing** [∪ŋ] Klettern *n*; *attr.* Kletter...

clinch [klɪntʃ] 1. ⊕ Vernietung *f*; *Boxen:* Clinch *m*; F Umarmung *f*; 2. *v/t.* vernieten; festmachen; (vollends) ⊕ entscheiden; *v/i. Boxen:* clinchen.

cling [klɪŋ] (*clung*) (*to*) festhalten (an *dat.*), sich klammern (an *acc.*); sich (an)schmiegen (an *acc.*).

clin·ic ['klɪnɪk] Klinik *f*; **~·i·cal** □ [∪l] klinisch.

clink [klɪŋk] 1. Klirren *n*, Klingen *n*; 2. klingen *od.* klirren (lassen); klimpern mit.

clip¹ [klɪp] 1. Schneiden *n*; Schur *f*; F (*Faust*)Schlag *m*; 2. (*-pp-*) (be)schneiden; ab-, ausschneiden; *Schafe etc.* scheren.

clip² [∪] 1. Klipp *m*, Klammer *f*, Spange *f*; 2. (*-pp-*) *a.* ~ *on* befestigen, anklammern.

clip|per ['klɪpə]: (*a pair of*) ~**s** *pl.* (e-e) Haarschneide-, Schermaschine *f*, (*Nagel- etc.*) Schere *f*; ⚓ Klipper *m*; ⚵ Clipper *m*; **~·pings** [∪ɪŋz] *pl.* Abfälle *pl.*, Schnitzel *pl.*; *bsd. Am.* (*Zeitungs- etc.*) Ausschnitte *pl.*

clit·o·ris *anat.* ['klɪtərɪs] Klitoris *f*.

cloak [kləʊk] 1. Mantel *m*; 2. *fig.* verhüllen; **~·room** ['kləʊkrʊm] Garderobe *f*; *Brt.* Toilette *f*.

clock [klɒk] 1. (Wand-, Stand-, Turm)Uhr *f*; 2. die Zeit (*e-s Läufers*) stoppen; ~ *in*, ~ *on* einstempeln; ~ *out*, ~ *off* ausstempeln; **~·wise**

['klɔkwaɪz] im Uhrzeigersinn;
~·work Uhrwerk *n; like ~* wie am
Schnürchen.

clod [klɔd] (Erd)Klumpen *m.*

clog [klɔg] **1.** Klotz *m;* Holzschuh *m,*
Pantine *f;* **2.** (-*gg*-) (be)hindern;
hemmen; (sich) verstopfen; klumpig
werden.

clois·ter ['klɔɪstə] Kreuzgang *m;* Kloster *n.*

close 1. *adj.* □ [kləʊs] knapp, kurz,
geschlossen, *nur pred.:* zu; verborgen; verschwiegen; knapp; nah;
eng; knapp, kurz, bündig; dicht;
genau (*Übersetzung*); schwül; geizig,
knaus(e)rig; *keep a ~ watch on*
scharf im Auge behalten (*acc.*); ~
fight Handgemenge *n; ~ season*
hunt. Schonzeit *f;* **2.** *adv.* eng, nahe,
dicht; *~ by, ~ to* ganz in der Nähe,
nahe *od.* dicht bei; **3.** [kləʊz] Schluß
m; (Ab)Schluß *m; come od. draw to*
a ~ sich dem Ende nähern; [kləʊs]
Einfriedung *f;* Hof *m;* **4.** [kləʊz] *v/t.*
(ab-, ver-, zu)schließen; *Straße*
(ab)sperren; *v/i.* (sich) schließen;
handgemein werden; *mit Adverbien:*
~ *down* schließen; stillegen; stillgelegt werden; *Rundfunk, TV:* das
Programm beenden, Sendeschluß
haben; ~ *in* bedrohlich nahekom-
men; hereinbrechen (*Nacht*); kürzer
werden (*Tage*); ~ *up* (ab-, ver-, zu-)
schließen; blockieren; aufschließen,
-rücken; **~d** geschlossen, *pred.* zu.

clos|et ['klɔzɪt] **1.** (Wand)Schrank *m;*
△ *nicht Klosett;* **2.** *be ~ed with* mit
j-m geheime Besprechungen führen.
close-up ['kləʊsʌp] *phot., Film:*
Großaufnahme *f.*

clos·ing-time ['kləʊzɪŋtaɪm] La-
den-, Geschäftsschluß *m;* Polizei-
stunde *f* (*e-s Pubs*).

clot [klɔt] **1.** Klumpen *m,* Klümp-
chen *n; Brt.* F Trottel *m;* **2.** (-*tt*-)
gerinnen; Klumpen bilden.

cloth [klɔθ] (*pl.* cloths [~θs, ~ðz])
Stoff *m,* Tuch *n;* Tischtuch *n; the ~*
der geistliche Stand; *lay the ~* den
Tisch decken; *~-bound* in Leinen
gebunden.

clothe [kləʊð] (*clothed od. clad*) (an-,
be)kleiden; einkleiden.

clothes [kləʊðz] *pl.* Kleider *pl.,* Kleidung *f;* Wäsche *f;* **~-bas·ket**
['kləʊðzbɑːskɪt] Wäschekorb *m;* **~-**
horse Wäscheständer *m;* **~-line**
Wäscheleine *f;* **~·peg** *Brt., Am.*

~·pin Wäscheklammer *f.*

cloth·ing ['kləʊðɪŋ] (Be)Kleidung *f.*

cloud [klaʊd] **1.** Wolke *f* (*a. fig.*);
Trübung *f,* Schatten *m;* **2.** (sich) be-,
umwölken (*a. fig.*); (sich) trüben;
~·burst ['klaʊdbɜːst] Wolkenbruch
m; **~·less** □ [~lɪs] wolkenlos; **~·y** □
[~ɪ] (-*ier, -iest*) wolkig, bewölkt;
Wolken...; trüb; unklar.

clout F [klaʊt] Schlag *m; bsd. Am.*
Macht *f,* Einfluß *m.*

clove¹ [kləʊv] (Gewürz)Nelke *f; ~ of*
garlic Knoblauchzehe *f.*

clove² [~] *pret. von* cleave¹; **clo·ven**
['kləʊvn] **1.** *p.p. von* cleave¹; **2.** ~
hoof zo. Huf *m* der Paarzeher.

clo·ver ⚘ ['kləʊvə] Klee *m.*

clown [klaʊn] Clown *m,* Hanswurst
m; Bauer *m,* ungehobelter Kerl;
~·ish □ ['klaʊnɪʃ] clownisch.

club [klʌb] **1.** Keule *f;* (Gummi-)
Knüppel *m;* (Golf)Schläger *m;* Klub
m; **~s** *pl.* Karten: Kreuz *n;* **2.** (-*bb*-)
v/t. einknüppeln auf (*acc.*), (nieder-)
knüppeln; *v/i.:* ~ *together* sich zusammentun; **~·foot** (*pl.* -feet)
['klʌb'fʊt] Klumpfuß *m.*

cluck [klʌk] **1.** gackern; glucken; **2.**
Gackern *n;* Glucken *n.*

clue [kluː] Anhaltspunkt *m,* Finger-
zeig *m,* Spur *f.*

clump [klʌmp] **1.** Klumpen *m,*
(*Baum- etc.*)Gruppe *f;* **2.** trampeln.

clum·sy □ ['klʌmzɪ] (-*ier, -iest*) unbeholfen, ungeschickt, plump.

clung [klʌŋ] *pret. u. p.p. von* cling.

clus·ter ['klʌstə] **1.** Traube *f;* Büschel
n; Haufen *m;* **2.** büschelartig wachsen; sich drängen.

clutch [klʌtʃ] **1.** Griff *m;* ⊕ Kupplung *f;* Klaue *f;* **2.** (er)greifen.

clut·ter ['klʌtə] **1.** Wirrwarr *m;* Unordnung *f;* **2.** *a.* ~ *up* zu voll machen
od. stellen; überladen.

coach [kəʊtʃ] **1.** Kutsche *f; Brt.* 🚌
(Personen)Wagen *m;* Omnibus, *bsd.*
Reisebus *m;* Einpauker *m; Sport:*
Trainer *m;* **2.** einpauken; *Sport:* trai-
nieren; **~·man** ['kəʊtʃmən] (*pl.*
-men) Kutscher *m.*

co·ag·u·late [kəʊˈæɡjʊleɪt] gerinnen
(lassen).

coal [kəʊl] (Stein)Kohle *f; carry ~s to*
Newcastle Eulen nach Athen tra-
gen.

co·a·lesce [kəʊəˈles] verschmelzen,
zusammenwachsen; sich vereinigen
od. verbinden.

co·a·li·tion [kəʊəˈlɪʃn] **1.** *pol.* Koalition *f;* Bündnis *n,* Zusammenschluß *m;* **2.** *pol.* Koalitions...

coal|-mine [ˈkəʊlmaɪn], **~pit** Kohlengrube *f.*

coarse □ [kɔːs] (*~r, ~st*) grob; ungeschliffen.

coast [kəʊst] **1.** Küste *f; Am.* Rodelbahn *f;* **2.** die Küste entlangfahren; im Leerlauf (*Auto*) *od.* im Freilauf (*Fahrrad*) fahren; *Am.* rodeln; **~er** [ˈkəʊstə] *Am.* Rodelschlitten; ♣ Küstenfahrer *m;* **~ guard** Küstenwache *f,* **~guard** Angehörige(r) *m* der Küstenwache; **~line** Küstenlinie *f,* **-strich** *m.*

coat [kəʊt] **1.** Jackett *n,* Jacke *f,* Rock *m;* Mantel *m;* **2.** Pelz *m,* Fell *n,* Haut *f,* Gefieder *n;* Überzug *m,* Anstrich *m,* Schicht *f;* **~ of arms** Wappen (-schild *m, n*) *n;* **2.** überziehen; beschichten; (an)streichen; **~hang·er** [ˈkəʊthæŋə] Kleiderbügel *m;* **~ing** [ˈkəʊtɪŋ] Überzug *m,* Anstrich *m,* Schicht *f;* Mantelstoff *m.*

coax [kəʊks] überreden, beschwatzen.

cob [kɒb] kleines starkes Pferd; Schwan *m;* Maiskolben *m.*

cob|bled [ˈkɒbld] **~ street** Straße *f* mit Kopfsteinpflaster; **~bler** [~ə] (Flick)Schuster *m;* Stümper *m.*

cob·web [ˈkɒbweb] Spinn(en)gewebe *n.*

co·caine [kəʊˈkeɪn] Kokain *n.*

cock [kɒk] **1.** *zo. etc.* Hahn *m;* (An-) Führer *m;* Heuhaufen *m;* **2.** *a.* **~ up** aufrichten; *Gewehrhahn* spannen.

cock·a·too *zo.* [kɒkəˈtuː] Kakadu *m.*

cock·chaf·er [ˈkɒktʃeɪfə] Maikäfer *m.*

cock-eyed F [ˈkɒkaɪd] schielend; (krumm *u.*) schief.

cock|ney [ˈkɒknɪ] *mst* 2 Cockney *m,* waschechter Londoner.

cock·pit [ˈkɒkpɪt] ✈, ♣ Cockpit *n* (*a. e-s Rennwagens*); Hahnenkampfplatz *m.*

cock|roach *zo.* [ˈkɒkrəʊtʃ] Schabe *f.*

cock|sure F [ˈkɒkˈʃʊə] absolut sicher; anmaßend; **~tail** Cocktail *m;* **~·y** F [ˈkɒkɪ] (*-ier, -iest*) großspurig, anmaßend.

co·co ♀ [ˈkəʊkəʊ] (*pl. -cos*) Kokospalme *f.*

co·coa [ˈkəʊkəʊ] Kakao *m.*

co·co·nut [ˈkəʊkənʌt] Kokosnuß *f.*

co·coon [kəˈkuːn] (*Seiden*)Kokon *m.*

cod *zo.* [kɒd] Kabeljau *m,* Dorsch *m.*

cod·dle [ˈkɒdl] verhätscheln.

code [kəʊd] **1.** Gesetzbuch *n;* Kodex *m;* (*Telegramm-*)Schlüssel *m;* Code *m,* Chiffre *f;* **2.** verschlüsseln, kodieren, chiffrieren.

cod|fish *zo.* [ˈkɒdfɪʃ] = *cod;* **~·liv·er oil** Lebertran *m.*

co·ed F [ˈkəʊˈed] Schülerin *f od.* Studentin *f* e-r gemischten Schule; **~u·ca·tion** [kəʊedjuːˈkeɪʃn] Koedukation *f,* Gemeinschaftserziehung *f.*

co·erce [kəʊˈɜːs] (er)zwingen.

co·ex·ist [ˈkəʊɪgˈzɪst] gleichzeitig *od.* nebeneinander bestehen *od.* leben. **~ence** [~əns] Koexistenz *f.*

cof·fee [ˈkɒfɪ] Kaffee *m;* **~ bean** Kaffeebohne *f;* **~pot** Kaffeekanne *f.* **~set** Kaffeeservice *n;* **~ta·ble** Couchtisch *m.*

cof·fer [ˈkɒfə] (*Geld- etc.*)Kasten *m.*

cof·fin [ˈkɒfɪn] Sarg *m.*

cog ⊕ [kɒg] (*Rad*)Zahn *m.*

co·gent □ [ˈkəʊdʒənt] zwingend.

cog·i·tate [ˈkɒdʒɪteɪt] (nach)denken.

cog·wheel ⊕ [ˈkɒgwiːl] Zahnrad *n.*

co·her|ence [kəʊˈhɪərəns] Zusammenhang *m;* **~ent** [~t] zusammenhängend.

co·he·sion [kəʊˈhiːʒn] Zusammenhalt *m;* **~sive** [~sɪv] (fest) zusammenhaltend.

coif·fure [kwɑːˈfjʊə] Frisur *f.*

coil [kɔɪl] **1.** *a.* **~ up** aufwickeln; (sich) zusammenrollen; **2.** Rolle *f;* Spirale *f;* Wicklung *f;* Spule *f;* Windung *f;* ⊕ (*Rohr*)Schlange *f.*

coin [kɔɪn] **1.** Münze *f;* **2.** prägen (*a. fig.*); münzen.

co·in|cide [kəʊɪnˈsaɪd] zusammentreffen; übereinstimmen; **~ci·dence** [kəʊˈɪnsɪdəns] Zusammentreffen *n;* Zufall *m; fig.* Übereinstimmung *f.*

coke¹ [kəʊk] Koks *m* (*a. sl. = Kokain*).

Coke² TM F [~] Coke *n,* Cola *n, f,* Coca *n, f* (*Coca-Cola*).

cold [kəʊld] **1.** □ kalt; **2.** Kälte *f,* Frost *m;* Erkältung *f;* **~blood·ed** [~ˈblʌdɪd] kaltblütig; **~heart·ed** kalt-, hartherzig; **~ness** [ˈkəʊldnɪs] Kälte *f;* **~ war** *pol.* kalter Krieg.

cole·slaw [ˈkəʊlslɔː] Krautsalat *m.*

col·ic ♣ [ˈkɒlɪk] Kolik *f.*

col·lab·o·rate [kəˈlæbəreɪt] zusammenarbeiten; **~ra·tion** [kəlæbəˈreɪʃn] Zusammenarbeit *f; in ~ with* gemeinsam mit.

col|lapse [kə'læps] **1.** zusammen-, einfallen; zusammenbrechen; **2.** Zusammenbruch m; **~lap·si·ble** [~əbl] zusammenklappbar.

col·lar ['kɒlə] **1.** Kragen m; Halsband n; Kummet n; **2.** beim Kragen packen; j-n festnehmen, F schnappen; **~bone** anat. Schlüsselbein n.

col·league ['kɒliːg] Kolleg|e m, -in f, Mitarbeiter(in).

col·lect 1. eccl. ['kɒlekt] Kollekte f; **2.** v/t. [kə'lekt] (ein)sammeln; Gedanken etc. sammeln; einkassieren; abholen; v/i. sich (ver)sammeln; **~·ed** □ fig. gefaßt; **~·lec·tion** [~kʃn] Sammlung f; econ. Eintreibung f; eccl. Kollekte f; **~·lec·tive** □ [~tɪv] gesammelt; Sammel...; ~ bargaining econ. Tarifverhandlungen pl.; **~·lec·tive·ly** [~lɪ] insgesamt; zusammen; **~·lec·tor** [~ə] Sammler(in); Steuereinnehmer m; 🚆 Fahrkartenabnehmer m; ⚡ Stromabnehmer m.

col·lege ['kɒlɪdʒ] College n (Teil e-r Universität); Hochschule f; höhere Lehranstalt.

col·lide [kə'laɪd] zusammenstoßen.

col·li·er ['kɒlɪə] Bergmann m; ⚓ Kohlenschiff n; **~·lie·ry** [~jərɪ] Kohlengrube f.

col·li·sion [kə'lɪʒn] Zusammenstoß m, -prall m, Kollision f.

col·lo·qui·al □ [kə'ləʊkwɪəl] umgangssprachlich, familiär.

col·lo·quy □ ['kɒləkwɪ] Gespräch n.

co·lon ['kəʊlən] Doppelpunkt m.

co·lo·nel ✕ ['kɜːnl] Oberst m.

co·lo·ni·al □ [kə'ləʊnjəl] Kolonial...; **~·is·m** pol. [~lɪzəm] Kolonialismus m.

col·o·nize ['kɒlənaɪz] kolonisieren, besiedeln; sich ansiedeln; **~·ny** [~nɪ] Kolonie f; Siedlung f.

co·los·sal □ [kə'lɒsl] kolossal, riesig.

col·o·u(r) ['kʌlə] **1.** Farbe f; fig. Anschein m; Vorwand m; **~s** pl. Fahne f, Flagge f; what ~ is ...? welche Farbe hat ...?; **2.** v/t. färben; an-, bemalen, anstreichen; fig. beschönigen; v/i. sich (ver)färben; erröten; **~·bar** Rassenschranke f; **~·blind** farbenblind; **~·ed** **1.** bunt; farbig; ~ man Farbige(r) m; **2.** oft contp. Farbige(r m) f; **~·fast** farbecht; ~ film phot. Farbfilm m; **~·ful** [~fl] farbenreich, -freudig; lebhaft; **~·ing** [~rɪŋ] Färbemittel n; Gesichtsfarbe f;

fig. Beschönigung f; **~·less** □ [~lɪs] farblos; ~ line Rassenschranke f; ~ set Farbfernseher m; **~ tel·e·vi·sion** Farbfernsehen n.

colt [kəʊlt] Hengstfüllen n, -fohlen n.

col·umn ['kɒləm] Säule f; print. Spalte f; ✕ Kolonne f; **~·ist** [~nɪst] Kolumnist(in).

comb [kəʊm] **1.** Kamm m; (Flachs-) Hechel f; **2.** v/t. kämmen; striegeln; Flachs hecheln.

com·bat ['kɒmbæt] **1.** Kampf m; single ~ Zweikampf m; **2.** (-tt-, Am. a. -t-) kämpfen gegen, bekämpfen; **~·ba·tant** [~ənt] Kämpfer m.

com·bi·na·tion [kɒmbɪ'neɪʃn] Verbindung f; mst ~s pl. Hemdhose f mit langem Bein; **~·bine** [kəm'baɪn] (sich) verbinden od. vereinigen.

com·bus·ti·ble [kəm'bʌstəbl] **1.** brennbar; **2.** Brennstoff m, -material n; **~·tion** [~tʃən] Verbrennung f.

come [kʌm] (came, come) kommen; to ~ künftig, kommend; ~ about passieren, geschehen; ~ across auf j-n od. et. stoßen; F kommen (Rede etc.); ~ along mitkommen; ~ apart auseinanderfallen; ~ at auf j-n od. et. losgehen; ~ back zurückkommen; ~ by et. bekommen; ~ down herunterkommen (a. fig.); einstürzen; sinken (Preis); überliefert werden; ~ down with F erkranken an (dat.); ~ for abholen kommen, kommen wegen; ~ loose sich ablösen, abgehen; ~ off ab-, losgehen, sich lösen; stattfinden; ~ on! los!, vorwärts!, komm!; ~ over vorbeikommen (Besucher); ~ round vorbeikommen (Besucher); wiederkehren; F wieder zu sich kommen; anders überlegen; ~ through durchkommen; Krankheit etc. überstehen, -leben; ~ to sich belaufen auf; wieder zu sich kommen; what's the world coming to? wohin ist die Welt geraten?; ~ to see besuchen; ~ up to entsprechen (dat.), heranreichen an (acc.); **~·back** ['kʌmbæk] Comeback n.

co·me·di·an [kə'miːdjən] Komödienschauspieler(in); Komiker(in); Lustspieldichter m.

com·e·dy ['kɒmədɪ] Komödie f, Lustspiel n.

come·ly ['kʌmlɪ] (-ier, -iest) attraktiv, gutaussehend.

com·fort ['kʌmfət] **1.** Behaglichkeit f; Trost m; Wohltat f, Erquickung f;

a. ~s *pl.* Komfort *m;* **2.** trösten; **com·for·ta·ble** □ [~əbl] komfortabel, behaglich, bequem; tröstlich; **~er** [~ə] Tröster *m;* Wollschal *m; bsd. Brt.* Schnuller *m; Am.* Steppdecke *f;* **~·less** □ [~lɪs] unbequem; trostlos; **~ sta·tion** *Am.* Bedürfnisanstalt *f.*

com·ic ['kɒmɪk] (~*ally*) komisch; Komödien..., Lustspiel...

com·i·cal □ ['kɒmɪkl] komisch, spaßig.

com·ics ['kɒmɪks] *pl.* Comics *pl.,* Comic-Hefte *pl.*

com·ing ['kʌmɪŋ] **1.** kommend; künftig; **2.** Kommen *n.*

com·ma ['kɒmə] Komma *n.*

com·mand [kə'mɑːnd] **1.** Herrschaft *f,* Beherrschung *f* (*a. fig.*); Befehl *m;* ⚔ Kommando *n; be* (*have*) *at* ~ zur Verfügung stehen (haben); **2.** befehlen; ⚔ kommandieren; verfügen über (*acc.*); beherrschen; **~er** [~ə] Kommandeur *m,* Befehlshaber *m;* ⚓ Fregattenkapitän *m;* **~·er-in-chief** ⚔ [~ərɪn'tʃiːf] (*pl. commanders-in-chief*) Oberbefehlshaber *m;* **~ing** □ [kə'mɑːndɪŋ] kommandierend, befehlshabend; gebieterisch; **~ment** [~mənt] Gebot *n;* **~ mod·ule** Raumfahrt: Kommandokapsel *f.*

com·man·do ⚔ [kə'mɑːndəʊ] (*pl. -dos, -does*) Kommando *n.*

com·mem·o·rate [kə'meməreɪt] gedenken (*gen.*), *j-s* Gedächtnis feiern; **~ra·tion** [kəmemə'reɪʃn]: *in* ~ *of* zum Gedenken *od.* Gedächtnis an (*acc.*); **~·ra·tive** □ [kə'memərətɪv] Gedenk..., Erinnerungs...

com·mence [kə'mens] anfangen, beginnen; **~ment** [~mənt] Anfang *m,* Beginn *m.*

com·mend [kə'mend] empfehlen; anvertrauen.

com|ment ['kɒment] **1.** Kommentar *m;* Erläuterung *f;* Bemerkung *f;* Stellungnahme *f; no* ~! kein Kommentar!; **2.** (*on, upon*) erläutern (*acc.*); sich (kritisch) äußern (über *acc.*); **~·men·ta·ry** ['kɒməntərɪ] Kommentar *m;* **~·men·tate** [~teɪt]: ~ *on* Rundfunk, *TV:* kommentieren (*acc.*); **~·men·ta·tor** [~ə] Kommentator *m,* Rundfunk, *TV: a.* Reporter *m.*

com·merce ['kɒmɜːs] Handel *m;* Verkehr *m.*

com·mer·cial □ [kə'mɜːʃl] **1.** kauf-

männisch, Handels..., Geschäfts... handelsüblich; ~ *travel(l)er* Handlungsreisende(r) *m;* **2.** Rundfunk *TV:* Werbespot *m,* -sendung *f;* **~·ize** [~ʃəlaɪz] kommerzialisieren, vermarkten.

com·mis·e·rate [kə'mɪzəreɪt]: ~ *with* Mitleid empfinden mit; **~·ra·tion** [kəmɪzə'reɪʃn] Mitleid *n* (*for* mit).

com·mis·sa·ry ['kɒmɪsərɪ] Kommissar *m.*

com·mis·sion [kə'mɪʃn] **1.** Auftrag *m;* Übertragung *f* (*von Macht etc.*); Begehung *f* (*e-s Verbrechens*); Provision *f;* Kommission *f;* ⚔ (Offiziers-) Patent *n;* **2.** beauftragen, bevollmächtigen; *et.* in Auftrag geben; *j-n* zum Offizier ernennen; ⚓ *Schiff in* Dienst stellen; **~er** [~ə] Bevollmächtigte(r *m*) *f;* (Regierungs)Kommissar *m.*

com·mit [kə'mɪt] (*-tt-*) anvertrauen übergeben; ⚖ *j-n* einweisen; ⚖ *j-n* übergeben; *Verbrechen* begehen; bloßstellen; ~ (*o.s.* sich) verpflichten; **~ment** [~mənt] Verpflichtung *f;* **~tal** ⚖ [~l] Einweisung *f;* **~·tee** [~l] Ausschuß *m,* Komitee *n.*

com·mod·i·ty [kə'mɒdətɪ] Ware *f* Gebrauchsartikel *m.*

com·mon ['kɒmən] **1.** □ allgemein gewöhnlich; gemein(sam), gemeinschaftlich; öffentlich; gewöhnlich minderwertig; F ordinär; ⚘ *Counci* Gemeinderat *m;* **2.** Gemeindeland *n in* ~ gemeinsam; *in* ~ *with* genau wie **~er** [~ə] Bürgerliche(r *m*) *f;* **~ law** (ungeschriebenes englisches) Gewohnheitsrecht; ⚘ **Mar·ket** *econ pol.* Gemeinsamer Markt; **~·place 1** Gemeinplatz *m;* **2.** alltäglich; abgedroschen; **~s** *pl. das* gemeine Volk *House of* ⚘ *parl.* Unterhaus *n;* **~ sense** gesunder Menschenverstand; **~·wealth** [~welθ] Gemeinwesen *n* Staat *m;* Republik *f;* the ⚘ (*o Nations*) das Commonwealth.

com·mo·tion [kə'məʊʃn] Aufruhr *m,* Erregung *f.*

com·mu·nal □ ['kɒmjʊnl] Gemeinde..., Gemeinschafts...

com·mune 1. [kə'mjuːn] sich vertraulich besprechen; **2.** ['kɒmjuːn] Kommune *f;* Gemeinde *f.*

com·mu·ni·cate [kə'mjuːnɪkeɪt] *v/t.* mitteilen; *v/i.* sich besprechen; sich in Verbindung setzen (*with s.o. mi* *j-m*); (durch e-e Tür) verbunden sein; **~·ca·tion** [kəmju:nɪˈkeɪʃn] Mitteilung f; Verständigung f; Verbindung f; ~s pl. Verbindung f, Verkehrswege pl.; ~s satellite Nachrichtensatellit m; **~·ca·tive** [kəˈmju:nɪkətɪv] mitteilsam, gesprächig.

com·mu·nion [kəˈmju:njən] Gemeinschaft f; ♀ eccl. Kommunion f, Abendmahl n.

com·mu·nis|m [ˈkɒmjʊnɪzəm] Kommunismus m; **~t** [~ɪst] **1.** Kommunist(in); **2.** kommunistisch.

com·mu·ni·ty [kəˈmju:nətɪ] Gemeinschaft f; Staat m.

com|mute [kəˈmju:t] ½½ Strafe *mildernd* umwandeln; ⬚ etc. pendeln; **~·mut·er** [~ə] Pendler(in); ~ train Pendler-, Vorort-, Nahverkehrszug m.

com·pact 1. [ˈkɒmpækt] Vertrag m; Puderdose f; Am. mot. Kompaktauto n; **2.** [kəmˈpækt] adj. dicht, fest; knapp, bündig; ~ disc Compact Disc f (Schallplatte); **3.** v/t. fest verbinden.

com·pan|ion [kəmˈpænjən] Begleiter(in); Gefährt|e m, -in f; Gesellschafter(in); Handbuch n, Leitfaden m; **~·io·na·ble** [~əbl] gesellig; **~·ion·ship** [~ʃɪp] Gesellschaft f.

com·pa·ny [ˈkʌmpənɪ] Gesellschaft f; Begleitung f; ✕ Kompanie f; econ. (Handels)Gesellschaft f; ♺ Mannschaft f; thea. Truppe f; have ~ Gäste haben; keep ~ with verkehren mit.

com|pa·ra·ble [ˈkɒmpərəbl] vergleichbar; **~·par·a·tive** [kəmˈpærətɪv] **1.** □ vergleichend; verhältnismäßig; **2.** a. ~ degree gr. Komparativ m; **~·pare** [~ˈpeə] **1.** beyond ~, without ~, past ~ unvergleichlich; **2.** v/t. vergleichen; (as) ~d with im Vergleich zu; v/i. sich vergleichen (lassen); **~·pa·ri·son** [~ˈpærɪsn] Vergleich m.

com·part·ment [kəmˈpɑ:tmənt] Abteilung f, Fach n; ♺ Abteil n.

com·pass [ˈkʌmpəs] Bereich m; ♪ Umfang m; Kompaß m; pair of ~es pl. Zirkel m.

com·pas·sion [kəmˈpæʃn] Mitleid n; **~·ate** [~ʃ(ə)nət] mitleidig.

com·pat·i·ble [kəmˈpætəbl] vereinbar; ⚕ verträglich; passend.

com·pat·ri·ot [kəmˈpætrɪət] Landsmann m, -männin f.

com·pel [kəmˈpel] (-ll-) (er)zwingen; **~·ling** □ [~ɪŋ] zwingend.

com·pen|sate [ˈkɒmpenseɪt] j-n entschädigen; et. ersetzen; ausgleichen; **~·sa·tion** [kɒmpenˈseɪʃn] Ersatz m; Ausgleich m; (Schaden)Ersatz m, Entschädigung f; Am. Bezahlung f, Gehalt n.

com|père, ~·pere Brt. [ˈkɒmpeə] **1.** Conférencier m; **2.** konferieren, ansagen.

com·pete [kəmˈpi:t] sich (mit-) bewerben (for um); konkurrieren.

com·pe|tence [ˈkɒmpɪtəns] Können n, Fähigkeit f; ½½ Zuständigkeit f; **~·tent** □ [~t] hinreichend; (leistungs)fähig, tüchtig; sachkundig.

com·pe·ti·tion [kɒmpɪˈtɪʃn] Wettbewerb m; Konkurrenz f.

com·pet·i·tive □ [kəmˈpetətɪv] konkurrierend; ~ price Mitbewerber(in); Konkurrent(in); Sport: (Wettbewerbs)Teilnehmer(in).

com·pile [kəmˈpaɪl] zusammentragen, zusammenstellen, sammeln.

com·pla|cen·cy, ~·cen·cy [kəmˈpleɪsns, ~sɪ] Selbstzufriedenheit f, -gefälligkeit f; **~·cent** □ [~nt] selbstzufrieden, -gefällig.

com·plain [kəmˈpleɪn] sich beklagen od. beschweren; klagen (of über acc.); **~t** [~t] Klage f; Beschwerde f; ⚕ a. Leiden n.

com·plai·sant □ [kəmˈpleɪzənt] gefällig, entgegenkommend.

com·ple·ment 1. [ˈkɒmplɪmənt] Ergänzung f; a. full ~ volle Anzahl; **2.** [~mənt] ergänzen; **~·men·ta·ry** [kɒmplɪˈmentərɪ] (sich gegenseitig) ergänzend.

com·plete [kəmˈpli:t] **1.** □ vollständig, ganz, vollkommen; vollzählig; **2.** vervollständigen; vervollkommnen; abschließen; **~·ple·tion** [~:ˈpli:ʃn] Vervollständigung f; Abschluß m; Erfüllung f.

com·plex [ˈkɒmpleks] **1.** □ zusammengesetzt; komplex, vielschichtig; kompliziert; **2.** Gesamtheit f; Komplex m (a. psych.); **~·ion** [kəmˈplekʃn] Aussehen n, Charakter m; Gesichtsfarbe f, Teint m; **~·i·ty** [~sətɪ] Vielschichtigkeit f.

com·pli|ance [kəmˈplaɪəns] Einwilligung f; Einverständnis n; in ~ with gemäß; **~·ant** □ [~t] willfährig, unterwürfig.

com·pli|cate [ˈkɒmplɪkeɪt] komplizieren; **~·cat·ed** kompliziert; **~·ca·tion** [kɒmplɪˈkeɪʃn] Komplikation f (a. 🐍); Kompliziertheit f.

com·plic·i·ty [kəmˈplɪsətɪ] Mitschuld f (in an dat.).

com·pli·ment 1. [ˈkɒmplɪmənt] Kompliment n; Empfehlung f; Gruß m; **2.** [~ment] v/t. (on) beglückwünschen (zu); j-m ein Kompliment machen (wegen); **~·men·ta·ry** [kɒmplɪˈmentərɪ] höflich.

com·ply [kəmˈplaɪ] sich fügen; nachkommen, entsprechen (with dat.).

com·po·nent [kəmˈpəʊnənt] Bestandteil m; ⊕, ⚡ Bauelement n.

com·pose [kəmˈpəʊz] zusammensetzen od. -stellen; ♪ komponieren; verfassen; ordnen; print. (ab)setzen; ~ o.s. sich beruhigen; **~·posed** □ ruhig, gesetzt; **~·pos·er** [~ə] Komponist(in); Verfasser(in); **~·pos·ite** [ˈkɒmpəzɪt] zusammengesetzt, gemischt; **~·po·si·tion** [kɒmpəˈzɪʃn] Zusammensetzung f; Abfassung f; Komposition f; Schriftstück n, Dichtung f; Aufsatz m; **~·po·sure** [kəmˈpəʊʒə] Fassung f, (Gemüts-) Ruhe f.

com·pound¹ [ˈkɒmpaʊnd] Lager n; Gefängnishof m; (Tier)Gehege n.

com·pound² 1. [~] zusammengesetzt; ~ interest Zinseszinsen pl.; Zusammensetzung f; Verbindung f; gr. zusammengesetztes Wort; **3.** [kəmˈpaʊnd] v/t. zusammensetzen; steigern, bsd. verschlimmern.

com·pre·hend [kɒmprɪˈhend] umfassen; begreifen, verstehen.

com·pre·hen·si·ble □ [kɒmprɪˈhensəbl] verständlich; **~·sion** [~ʃn] Begreifen n, Verständnis n; Fassungskraft f, Begriffsvermögen n, Verstand m, Einsicht f; past ~ unfaßbar, unfaßlich; **~·sive** [~sɪv] **1.** □ umfassend; **2.** a. ~ school Brt. Gesamtschule f.

com·press [kəmˈpres] zusammendrücken; **~ed air** Druckluft f; **~·pres·sion** [~ʃn] phys. Verdichtung f; ⊕ Druck m.

com·prise [kəmˈpraɪz] einschließen, umfassen, enthalten.

com·pro·mise [ˈkɒmprəmaɪz] **1.** Kompromiß m, n; **2.** v/t. (o.s. sich) bloßstellen; v/i. e-n Kompromiß schließen.

com·pul·sion [kəmˈpʌlʃn] Zwang m; **~·sive** □ [~sɪv] zwingend, Zwangs...;

psych. zwanghaft; **~·so·ry** □ [~ˈsərɪ] obligatorisch; Zwangs...; Pflicht...

com·punc·tion [kəmˈpʌŋkʃn] Gewissensbisse pl.; Reue f; Bedenken pl.

com·pute [kəmˈpjuːt] (be-, er)rechnen; schätzen.

com·put·er [kəmˈpjuːtə] Computer m, Rechner m; **~·con·trolled** computergesteuert; **~·ize** [~raɪz] mit Computern ausstatten, auf Computer umstellen; *Information* in e-m Computer speichern.

com·rade [ˈkɒmreɪd] Kamerad m; (Partei)Genosse m.

con¹ abbr. [kɒn] = contra.

con² f [~] (-nn-) reinlegen, betrügen.

con·ceal [kənˈsiːl] verbergen; verheimlichen.

con·cede [kənˈsiːd] zugestehen, einräumen; gewähren; nachgeben.

con·ceit [kənˈsiːt] Einbildung f, Dünkel m; gesuchte Metapher; **~·ed** □ eingebildet (of auf acc.).

con·cei·va·ble □ [kənˈsiːvəbl] denkbar, begreiflich; **~·ve** [kənˈsiːv] v/i. schwanger werden; v/t. Kind empfangen; sich denken; planen, ausdenken.

con·cen·trate [ˈkɒnsəntreɪt] **1.** (sich) zusammenziehen, vereinigen; (sich) konzentrieren; **2.** Konzentrat n.

con·cept [ˈkɒnsept] Begriff m; Gedanke m; △ nicht Konzept.

con·cep·tion [kənˈsepʃn] Begreifen n; Vorstellung f, Begriff m, Idee f; biol. Empfängnis f.

con·cern [kənˈsɜːn] **1.** Angelegenheit f; Interesse n; Sorge f; Beziehung f (with zu); Geschäft n, (industrielles) Unternehmen; △ nicht Konzern; **2.** betreffen, angehen, interessieren; beunruhigen; interessieren, beschäftigen; **~·ed** □ interessiert, beteiligt (in an dat.); besorgt; **~·ing** prp. [~ɪŋ] betreffend, über, wegen, hinsichtlich.

con·cert 1. [ˈkɒnsət] Konzert n; **2.** [~ˈsɜːt] Einverständnis n; **~·ed** □ [kənˈsɜːtɪd] gemeinsam; ♪ mehrstimmig.

con·ces·sion [kənˈseʃn] Zugeständnis n; Konzession f.

con·cil·i·ate [kənˈsɪlɪeɪt] aus-, versöhnen; **~·a·to·ry** [~ɪətərɪ] versöhnlich, vermittelnd.

con·cise □ [kənˈsaɪs] kurz, bündig, knapp; **~·ness** [~nɪs] Kürze f.

con·clude [kənˈkluːd] schließen, beschließen, beenden; abschließen; folgern, schließen (*from* aus); sich entscheiden; *to be* ~d Schluß folgt.

con·clu·sion [kənˈkluːʒn] Schluß *m*, Ende *n*; Abschluß *m*; Schluß *m*, (Schluß)Folgerung *f*; Beschluß *m*; *s. jump*; ~**sive** □ [~sɪv] überzeugend; endgültig.

con·coct [kənˈkɒkt] zusammenbrauen; *fig.* aushecken, sich ausdenken; ~**coc·tion** [~kʃn] Gebräu *n*; *fig.* Erfindung *f*.

con·cord [ˈkɒŋkɔːd] Eintracht *f*; Übereinstimmung *f* (*a. gr.*); ♪ Harmonie *f*.

con·course [ˈkɒŋkɔːs] Zusammen-, Auflauf *m*; Menge *f*; freier Platz.

con·crete [ˈkɒŋkriːt] 1. □ fest; konkret; Beton...; 2. Beton *m*; 3. betonieren.

con·cur [kənˈkɜː] (-*rr*-) übereinstimmen; ~**rence** [~ˈkʌrəns] Zusammentreffen *n*; Übereinstimmung *f*; △ *nicht* Konkurrenz.

con·cus·sion [kənˈkʌʃn]: ~ *of the brain* ⚕ Gehirnerschütterung *f*.

con|demn [kənˈdem] verdammen; ⚖ *u. fig.* verurteilen (*to death* zum Tode); für unbrauchbar *od.* unbewohnbar *etc.* erklären; ~**dem·na·tion** [kɒndemˈneɪʃn] ⚖ *u. fig.* Verurteilung *f*; Verdammung *f*, Mißbilligung *f*.

con|den·sa·tion [kɒndenˈseɪʃn] Verdichtung *f*; ~**dense** [kənˈdens] (sich) verdichten; ⊕ kondensieren; zusammenfassen, kürzen; ~**dens·er** ⊕ [~ə] Kondensator *m*.

con·de·scend [kɒndɪˈsend] sich herablassen, geruhen; ~**scen·sion** [~ʃn] Herablassung *f*.

con·di·ment [ˈkɒndɪmənt] Würze *f*.

con·di·tion [kənˈdɪʃn] 1. Zustand *m*; (körperlicher *od.* Gesundheits)Zustand *m*; *Sport*: Kondition *f*, Form *f*; Bedingung *f*; ~*s pl.* Verhältnisse *pl.*, Umstände *pl.*; *on* ~ *that* unter der Bedingung, daß; *out of* ~ in schlechter Verfassung, in schlechtem Zustand; 2. bedingen; in einen bestimmten Zustand bringen; ~**al** [~l] 1. □ bedingt (*on*, *upon* durch) Bedingungs...; 2. *a.* ~ *clause gr.* Bedingungs-, Konditionalsatz *m*; *a.* ~ *mood gr.* Konditional *m*.

con·dole [kənˈdəʊl] kondolieren (*with dat.*); ~**do·lence** [~əns] Beileid *n*.

con·done [kənˈdəʊn] verzeihen, vergeben.

con·du·cive [kənˈdjuːsɪv] dienlich, förderlich (*to dat.*).

con|duct 1. [ˈkɒndʌkt] Führung *f*; Verhalten *n*, Betragen *n*; 2. [kənˈdʌkt] führen; ♪ dirigieren; ~*ed tour* (*of*) Führung *f* (durch); Gesellschaftsreise (durch); ~**duc·tion** [~kʃn] Leitung *f*; ~**duc·tor** [~tə] Führer *m*; Leiter *m*; Schaffner *m*; *Am.* ☎ Zugbegleiter *m*; ♪ (Orchester)Dirigent *m*, (Chor)Leiter *m*; ⚡ Blitzableiter *m*.

cone [kəʊn] Kegel *m*; Eistüte *f*; ⚘ Zapfen *m*.

con·fec·tion [kənˈfekʃn] Konfekt *n*; △ *nicht* Konfektion; ~**er** [~nə] Konditor *m*; ~**er·y** [~ərɪ] Süßigkeiten *pl.*, Süß-, Konditoreiwaren *pl.*; Konfekt *n*; Konditorei *f*; Süßwarengeschäft *n*.

con·fed·e|ra·cy [kənˈfedərəsɪ] Bündnis *n*; *the* ⌘ *Am. hist.* die Konföderation; ~**rate 1.** [~rət] verbündet; 2. [~] Bundesgenosse *m*; 3. [~reit] (sich) verbünden; ~**ra·tion** [kənfedəˈreɪʃn] Bund *m*, Bündnis *n*; Staatenbund *m*.

con·fer [kənˈfɜː] (-*rr*-) *v/t.* übertragen, verleihen; *v/i.* sich besprechen.

con·fe·rence [ˈkɒnfərəns] Konferenz *f*.

con|fess [kənˈfes] bekennen, gestehen; beichten; ~**fes·sion** [~ʃən] Geständnis *n*; Bekenntnis *n*; Beichte *f*; ~**fes·sion·al** [~nl] Beichtstuhl *m*; ~**fes·sor** [~esə] Bekenner *m*; Beichtvater *m*.

con·fide [kənˈfaɪd] *v/t.* anvertrauen; *v/i.* ~ *in s.o.* j-m vertrauen.

con·fi·dence [ˈkɒnfɪdəns] Vertrauen *n*; Zuversicht *f*; ~ *man* (*pl. -men*) Betrüger *m*; ~ *trick* aufgelegter Schwindel.

con·fi|dent [ˈkɒnfɪdənt] zuversichtlich; ~**den·tial** □ [kɒnfɪˈdenʃl] vertraulich.

con·fid·ing □ [kənˈfaɪdɪŋ] vertrauensvoll.

con·fine [kənˈfaɪn] begrenzen; beschränken; einsperren; *be* ~*d of* entbunden werden von; *be* ~*d to bed* das Bett hüten müssen; ~**ment** [~mənt] Haft *f*; Beschränkung *f*; Entbindung *f*.

con|firm [kənˈfɜːm] (be)kräftigen; bestätigen; *eccl.* konfirmieren; *eccl.*

C

firmen; **~·fir·ma·tion** [kɒnfə-'meɪʃn] Bestätigung f; eccl. Konfirmation f; eccl. Firmung f.

con·fis|cate ['kɒnfɪskeɪt] beschlagnahmen; **~·ca·tion** [kɒnfɪ'skeɪʃn] Beschlagnahme f.

con·fla·gra·tion [kɒnflə'greɪʃn] (bsd. Groß)Brand.

con·flict 1. ['kɒnflɪkt] Konflikt m; **2.** [kən'flɪkt] in Konflikt stehen; **~·ing** [~ɪŋ] widersprüchlich.

con·form [kən'fɔ:m] (sich) anpassen (to dat., an acc.).

con·found [kən'faʊnd] j-n verwirren, -blüffen; ~ it! F verdammt!; **~·ed** □ F verdammt.

con|front [kən'frʌnt] gegenübertreten, -stehen (dat.); sich stellen (dat.); konfrontieren; **~·fron·ta·tion** [kɒnfrʌn'teɪʃn] Konfrontation f.

con|fuse [kən'fju:z] verwechseln; verwirren; **~·fused** □ verwirrt; verlegen; verworren; **~·fu·sion** [~u:ʒn] Verwirrung f; Verlegenheit f; Verwechslung f.

con|geal [kən'dʒi:l] erstarren (lassen); gerinnen (lassen).

con|gest·ed [kən'dʒestɪd] überfüllt; verstopft; **~·ges·tion** [~tʃən] Blutandrang m; a. traffic ~ Verkehrsstockung f, -stauung f.

con·glom·e·ra·tion [kənɡlɒmə'reɪʃn] Anhäufung f; Konglomerat n.

con·grat·u·late [kən'grætjuleɪt] beglückwünschen, j-m gratulieren; **~·la·tion** [kənɡrætjʊ'leɪʃn] Glückwunsch m; ~s! ich gratuliere!, herzlichen Glückwunsch!

con·gre|gate ['kɒnɡrɪɡeɪt] (sich) (ver)sammeln; **~·ga·tion** [kɒnɡrɪ-'ɡeɪʃn] Versammlung f; eccl. Gemeinde f.

con·gress ['kɒnɡres] Kongreß m; 2 Am. parl. der Kongreß; 2·**man** (pl. -men) Am. parl. Kongreßabgeordnete(r) m; 2·**wom·an** (pl. -women) Am. pl. Kongreßabgeordnete f.

con|ic bsd. ⊕ ['kɒnɪk], **~·i·cal** □ [~kl] konisch, kegelförmig.

co·ni·fer ⊕ ['kɒnɪfə] Nadelbaum m.

con·jec·ture [kən'dʒektʃə] **1.** Mutmaßung f; **2.** mutmaßen.

con·ju·gal □ ['kɒndʒʊɡl] ehelich.

con·ju|gate gr. ['kɒndʒʊɡeɪt] konjugieren, beugen; **~·ga·tion** gr. [kɒndʒʊ'ɡeɪʃn] Konjugation f, Beugung f.

con·junc·tion [kən'dʒʌŋkʃn] Verbindung f; gr. Konjunktion f.

con·junc·ti·vi·tis [kəndʒʌŋktɪ'vaɪtɪs] Bindehautentzündung f.

con|jure ['kʌndʒə] Teufel etc. beschwören; zaubern; **~·jur·er** [~rə] Zauber|er m, -in f, Zauberkünstler(in); **~·jur·ing trick** [~rɪŋ trɪk] Zauberkunststück n; **~·jur·or** [~rə] = conjurer.

con|nect [kə'nekt] verbinden; ⚡ anschließen, (zu)schalten; 🚂, 🚋 etc. Anschluß haben (with an acc.); **~·nect·ed** □ verbunden; (logisch) zusammenhängend (Rede etc.); be well ~ gute Beziehungen haben; **~·nec·tion**, Brt. a. **~·nex·ion** [~kʃn] Verbindung f; ⚡ Schaltung f; Anschluß m; Zusammenhang m; Verwandtschaft f.

con|quer ['kɒŋkə] erobern; (be)siegen; **~·or** [~rə] Eroberer m.

con·quest ['kɒŋkwest] Eroberung f (a. fig.); erobertes Gebiet; Besiegung f; Bezwingung f.

con·science ['kɒnʃəns] Gewissen n.

con·sci·en·tious □ [kɒnʃɪ'enʃəs] gewissenhaft; Gewissens...; **~ objector** Wehrdienstverweigerer m (aus Überzeugung); **~·ness** [~nɪs] Gewissenhaftigkeit f.

con·scious □ ['kɒnʃəs] bei Bewußtsein; bewußt; be ~ of sich bewußt sein (gen.); **~·ness** [~nɪs] Bewußtsein n.

con|script ⚔ **1.** [kən'skrɪpt] einziehen, -berufen; **2.** ['kɒnskrɪpt] Wehrpflichtige(r) m; **~·scrip·tion** ⚔ [kən'skrɪpʃn] Einberufung f, Einziehung f.

con·se|crate ['kɒnsɪkreɪt] weihen, einsegnen; widmen; **~·cra·tion** [kɒnsɪ'kreɪʃn] Weihe f; Einsegnung f.

con·sec·u·tive □ [kən'sekjʊtɪv] aufeinanderfolgend; fortlaufend.

con·sent [kən'sent] **1.** Zustimmung f; **2.** einwilligen, zustimmen.

con·se|quence ['kɒnsɪkwəns] Folge f, Konsequenz f; Einfluß m; Bedeutung f; **~·quent·ly** [~tlɪ] folglich, daher.

con·ser|va·tion [kɒnsə'veɪʃn] Erhaltung f; Naturschutz m; Umweltschutz m; **~·tion·ist** [~ʃnɪst] Naturschützer(in); Umweltschützer(in); **~·tive** □ [kən'sɜ:vətɪv] **1.** erhaltend; konservativ; vorsichtig; **2.** 2 pol.

Konservative(r *m*) *f*; **~·to·ry** [kɒn-ˈsɜːvətɪ] Treib-, Gewächshaus *n*; ♪
Konservatorium *n*; **con·serve** [kənˈsɜːv] erhalten.

con·sid·er [kənˈsɪdə] *v/t.* betrachten; sich überlegen, erwägen; in Betracht ziehen, berücksichtigen; meinen; *v/i.* nachdenken, überlegen; **~·er·a·ble** □ [~rəbl] ansehnlich, beträchtlich; **~·er·a·bly** [~lɪ] bedeutend, ziemlich, (sehr) viel; **~·er·ate** [~rət] rücksichtsvoll; **~·er·a·tion** [kənsɪdəˈreɪʃn] Betrachtung *f*, Erwägung *f*, Überlegung *f*; Rücksicht *f*; Gesichtspunkt *m*; *take into ~* in Erwägung *od.* in Betracht ziehen, berücksichtigen; **~·er·ing** □ [kənˈsɪdərɪŋ] **1.** *prp.* in Anbetracht (*gen.*); **2.** *adv.* F den Umständen entsprechend.

con·sign [kənˈsaɪn] übergeben; anvertrauen; *econ. Waren* zusenden; **~·ment** *econ.* [~mənt] Über-, Zusendung *f*; (Waren)Sendung *f*.

con·sist [kənˈsɪst]: *~ in* bestehen in (*dat.*); *~ of* bestehen *od.* sich zusammensetzen aus.

con·sis·tence, ~·ten·cy [kənˈsɪstəns, ~sɪ] Konsistenz *f*, Beschaffenheit *f*; Übereinstimmung *f*; Konsequenz *f*; **~·tent** □ [~ənt] übereinstimmend, vereinbar (*with* mit); konsequent; *Sport etc.*: beständig (*Leistung*).

con·so·la·tion [kɒnsəˈleɪʃn] Trost *m*; **~·sole** [kənˈsəʊl] trösten.

con·sol·i·date [kənˈsɒlɪdeɪt] festigen; *fig.* zusammenschließen, -legen.

con·so·nant [ˈkɒnsənənt] **1.** □ übereinstimmend; **2.** *gr.* Konsonant *m*, Mitlaut *m*.

con·spic·u·ous □ [kənˈspɪkjʊəs] sichtbar; auffallend; hervorragend; *make o.s. ~* sich auffällig benehmen.

con·spir·a·cy [kənˈspɪrəsɪ] Verschwörung *f*; **~·spi·ra·tor** [~tə] Verschwörer *m*; **~·spire** [~ˈspaɪə] sich verschwören.

con·sta·ble *Brt.* [ˈkʌnstəbl] Polizist *m* (auf Streife), Wachtmeister *m*; **~·stab·u·la·ry** [kənˈstæbjʊlərɪ] Polizei(truppe) *f*.

con·stan·cy [ˈkɒnstənsɪ] Standhaftigkeit *f*; Beständigkeit *f*; **~·stant** □ [~t] beständig, unveränderlich; treu.

con·ster·na·tion [kɒnstəˈneɪʃn] Bestürzung *f*.

con·sti·pat·ed ♪ [ˈkɒnstɪpeɪtɪd] ver-

stopft; **~·pa·tion** ♪ [kɒnstɪˈpeɪʃn] Verstopfung *f*.

con·sti·tu·en·cy [kənˈstɪtjʊənsɪ] Wählerschaft *f*; Wahlkreis *m*; **~·ent** [~t] **1.** e-n (Bestand)Teil bildend; *pol.* konstituierend; **2.** (wesentlicher) Bestandteil; *pol.* Wähler(in).

con·sti·tute [ˈkɒnstɪtjuːt] ein-, errichten; ernennen; bilden, ausmachen.

con·sti·tu·tion [kɒnstɪˈtjuːʃn] *pol.* Verfassung *f*, Konstitution *f*, körperliche Verfassung; Zusammensetzung *f*; **~·al** □ [~nl] **1.** □ konstitutionell; *pol.* verfassungsmäßig; **2.** (Verdauungs)Spaziergang *m*.

con·strain [kənˈstreɪn] zwingen; **~·ed** gezwungen, unnatürlich; **~·t** [~t] Zwang *m*.

con·strict [kənˈstrɪkt] zusammenziehen; **~·stric·tion** [~kʃn] Zusammenziehung *f*.

con·struct [kənˈstrʌkt] bauen, errichten, konstruieren; *fig.* bilden; **~·struc·tion** [~kʃn] Konstruktion *f*; Bau *m*; *fig.* Auslegung *f*; *~ site* Baustelle *f*; **~·struc·tive** □ [~tɪv] aufbauend, schöpferisch, konstruktiv, positiv; **~·struc·tor** [~ə] Erbauer *m*, Konstrukteur *m*.

con·strue [kənˈstruː] *gr.* konstruieren; auslegen, auffassen.

con·sul [ˈkɒnsl] Konsul *m*; **~·gen·er·al** Generalkonsul *m*; **~·su·late** [~sjʊlət] Konsulat *n* (*a. Gebäude*).

con·sult [kənˈsʌlt] *v/t.* konsultieren, um Rat fragen; in *e-m Buch* nachschlagen; *v/i.* sich beraten.

con·sul·tant [kənˈsʌltənt] (fachmännische[r]) Berater(in); *Brt.* Facharzt *m* (*an e-m Krankenhaus*); **~·ta·tion** [kɒnslˈteɪʃn] Konsultation *f*, Beratung *f*, Rücksprache *f*; *~ hour* Sprechstunde *f*; **~·ta·tive** [kənˈsʌltə-tɪv] beratend.

con·sume [kənˈsjuːm] *v/t.* essen, trinken; verbrauchen; zerstören, vernichten (*durch Feuer*); *fig.* verzehren (*durch Haß etc.*); **~·sum·er** [~ə] *econ.* Verbraucher(in).

con·sum·mate 1. □ [kənˈsʌmɪt] vollendet; **2.** [ˈkɒnsəmeɪt] vollenden.

con·sump·tion [kənˈsʌmpʃn] Verbrauch *m*; *veraltet* ♪ Schwindsucht *f*; **~·tive** □ [~tɪv] verzehrend; *veraltet* ♪ schwindsüchtig.

con·tact [ˈkɒntækt] **1.** Berührung *f*; Kontakt *m*; *make ~s* Verbindungen

anknüpfen *od.* herstellen; ~ *lenses*
pl. Haft-, Kontaktschalen *pl.*; **2.** sich
in Verbindung setzen mit, Kontakt
aufnehmen mit.

con·ta·gious □ ♂ [kən'teɪdʒəs] ansteckend (*a. fig.*).

con·tain [kən'teɪn] enthalten, (um-)
fassen; ~ *o.s.* an sich halten, sich
beherrschen; **~er** [~ə] Behälter *m*;
econ. Container *m*; **~er·ize** *econ.*
[~əraɪz] auf Containerbetrieb umstellen; in Containern transportieren.

con·tam·i·nate [kən'tæmɪneɪt] verunreinigen; infizieren, vergiften; (*a.*
radioaktiv) verseuchen; **~na·tion**
[kəntæmɪ'neɪʃn] Verunreinigung *f*;
Vergiftung *f*; (*a.* radioaktive) Ver-
seuchung.

con·tem·plate ['kɒntempleɪt] betrachten; beabsichtigen, vorhaben;
~pla·tion [kɒntem'pleɪʃn] Betrachtung *f*; Nachdenken *n*; **~pla·tive** □
['kɒntempleɪtɪv] nachdenklich;
[kən'templətɪv] beschaulich.

con·tem·po·ra·ne·ous □ [kəntem-
pə'reɪnjəs] gleichzeitig; **~ry** [kən-
'tempərərɪ] **1.** zeitgenössisch; **2.**
Zeitgenoss|e *m*, -in *f*.

con·tempt [kən'tempt] Verachtung
f; **~temp·ti·ble** □ [~əbl] verachtenswert; **~temp·tu·ous** □ [~juəs]
geringschätzig, verächtlich.

con·tend [kən'tend] *v/i.* kämpfen,
ringen (*for* um); *v/t.* behaupten; **~er**
[~ə] *bsd. Sport:* Wettkämpfer(in).

con·tent [kən'tent] **1.** zufrieden; **2.**
befriedigen; ~ *o.s.* sich begnügen; **3.**
Zufriedenheit *f*; *to one's heart's* ~
nach Herzenslust; ['kɒntent] Gehalt
m; **~s** *pl.* (*stofflicher*) Inhalt; **~ed** □
[kən'tentɪd] zufrieden.

con·ten·tion [kən'tenʃn] Streit *m*;
Argument *n*, Behauptung *f*.

con·tent·ment [kən'tentmənt] Zufriedenheit *f*.

con|test 1. ['kɒntest] Streit *m*; Wett-
kampf *m*; **2.** [kən'test] sich bewerben
um, kandidieren für; (be)streiten;
anfechten; um *et.* streiten; **~tes·**
tant [~ənt] Wettkämpfer(in), (Wettkampf)Teilnehmer(in).

con·text ['kɒntekst] Zusammenhang
m.

con·ti|nent ['kɒntɪnənt] **1.** □ enthalt-
sam, mäßig; **2.** Kontinent *m*, Erdteil
m; *the* ♀ *Brt.* das (europäische) Festland; **~nen·tal** [kɒntɪ'nentl] **1.** □

kontinental, Kontinental...; **2.** Kon-
tinentaleuropäer(in).

con·tin·gen|cy [kən'tɪndʒənsɪ] Zu-
fälligkeit *f*; Möglichkeit *f*, Eventua-
lität *f*; **~t** [~t] **1.** □: *be* ~ *on od. upon*
abhängen von; **2.** Kontingent *n*.

con·tin|u·al □ [kən'tɪnjuəl] fortwäh-
rend, unaufhörlich; **~u·a·tion** [kən-
tɪnjʊ'eɪʃn] Fortsetzung *f*; Fortdauer
f; ~ *school* Fortbildungsschule *f*; ~
training berufliche Fortbildung;
~ue [kən'tɪnjuː] *v/t.* fortsetzen,
-fahren mit; beibehalten; *to be* ~*d*
Fortsetzung folgt; *v/i.* fortdauern;
andauern, anhalten; fortfahren, weitermachen; **con·ti·nu·i·ty** [kɒntɪ-
'njuːətɪ] Kontinuität *f*; **~u·ous** □
[kən'tɪnjʊəs] ununterbrochen; ~
form gr. Verlaufsform *f*.

con|tort [kən'tɔːt] verdrehen, verzer-
ren; **~tor·tion** [~ɔːʃn] Verdrehung
f; Verzerrung *f*.

con·tour ['kɒntʊə] Umriß *m*.

con·tra ['kɒntrə] wider, gegen.

con·tra·band *econ.* ['kɒntrəbænd]
unter Ein- *od.* Ausfuhrverbot ste-
hende Ware.

con·tra·cep|tion ♂ [kɒntrə'sepʃn]
Empfängnisverhütung *f*; **~tive** ♂
[~tɪv] empfängnisverhütend(es Mittel).

con|tract 1. [kən'trækt] *v/t.* zusam-
menziehen; sich *e-e Krankheit* zuziehen; *Schulden* machen; *e-e Ehe*
etc. schließen; *v/i.* sich zusammenziehen, schrumpfen; ♊ e-n Vertrag
schließen; sich vertraglich verpflichten; **2.** ['kɒntrækt] Kontrakt *m*,
Vertrag *m*; **~trac·tion** [kən'trækʃn]
Zusammenziehung *f*; *gr.* Kurzform
f; **~trac·tor** [~ə] *a: building* ~
Bauunternehmer *m*.

con·tra|dict [kɒntrə'dɪkt] widerspre-
chen (*dat.*); **~dic·tion** [~kʃn] Widerspruch *m*; **~dic·to·ry** □ [~tərɪ]
(sich) widersprechend.

con·tra·ry ['kɒntrərɪ] **1.** □ entgegengesetzt; widrig; ~ *to* im Gegensatz
zu; ~ *to expectations* wider Erwarten; **2.** Gegenteil *n*; *on the* ~ im
Gegenteil.

con·trast 1. ['kɒntrɑːst] Gegensatz
m; Kontrast *m*; **2.** [kən'trɑːst] *v/t.*
gegenüberstellen, vergleichen; *v/i.*
sich unterscheiden, abstechen (*with*
von).

con|trib·ute [kən'trɪbjuːt] beitragen,
-steuern; spenden (*to* für); **~tri·**

bu·tion [kɔntrɪ'bjuːʃn] Beitrag *m*; Spende *f*; **~·trib·u·tor** [kən'trɪbjʊtə] Beitragende(r *m*) *f*; Mitarbeiter(in) (*an e-r Zeitung*); **~·trib·u·to·ry** [~ərɪ] beitragend.

con|trite □ ['kɔntraɪt] zerknirscht; **~·tri·tion** [kən'trɪʃn] Zerknirschung *f*.

con·trive [kən'traɪv] ersinnen, (sich) ausdenken, planen; zustande bringen; es fertigbringen (*to inf.* zu *inf.*); **~d** gekünstelt (*Freundlichkeit etc.*).

con·trol [kən'trəʊl] **1.** Kontrolle *f*, Herrschaft *f*, Macht *f*, Gewalt *f*, Beherrschung *f*; Aufsicht *f*; ⊕ Steuerung *f*; *mst* **~s** *pl.* ⊕ Steuervorrichtung *f*; △ *nicht Kontrolle* (*Überprüfung*); *lose ~* die Herrschaft *od.* Gewalt *od.* Kontrolle verlieren; **2.** (*-ll-*) beherrschen, die Kontrolle haben über (*acc.*); *e-r Sache* Herr werden, (erfolgreich) bekämpfen; kontrollieren, überwachen; *econ.* (staatlich) lenken, *Preise* binden; ⚡, ⊕ steuern, regeln, regulieren; △ *nicht kontrollieren* (*überprüfen*); **~·desk** ⚡ Schalt-, Steuerpult *n*; **~ pan·el** ⚡ Schalttafel *f*; Bedienungsfeld *n*; **~ tow·er** ✈ Kontrollturm *m*, Tower *m*.

con·tro·ver·sial □ [kɔntrə'vɜːʃl] umstritten; **~·sy** ['kɔntrəvɜːsɪ] Kontroverse *f*, Streit *m*.

con·tuse ⚕ [kən'tjuːz] quetschen.

con·va|lesce [kɔnvə'les] gesund werden, genesen; **~·les·cence** [~ns] Rekonvaleszenz *f*, Genesung *f*; **~·les·cent** [~t] **1.** □ genesend; **2.** Rekonvaleszent(in), Genesende(r *m*) *f*.

con·vene [kən'viːn] (sich) versammeln; zusammentreten (*Parlament etc.*); einberufen.

con·ve·ni|ence [kən'viːnjəns] Bequemlichkeit *f*; Angemessenheit *f*; Vorteil *m*; *Brt.* Toilette *f*; *all* (*modern*) **~s** *pl.* aller Komfort; *at your earliest ~* möglichst bald; **~·ent** □ [~t] bequem; günstig.

con·vent ['kɔnvənt] (Nonnen)Kloster *n*.

con·ven·tion [kən'venʃn] Versammlung *f*; Konvention *f*, Übereinkommen *n*, Abkommen *n*; Sitte *f*; **~·al** □ [~nl] herkömmlich, konventionell.

con·verge [kən'vɜːdʒ] konvergieren; zusammenlaufen, -strömen.

con·ver·sant [kən'vɜːsənt] vertraut.

con·ver·sa·tion [kɔnvə'seɪʃn] Gespräch *n*, Unterhaltung *f*; **~·al** □ [~nl] Unterhaltungs...; umgangssprachlich.

con·verse 1. □ ['kɔnvɜːs] umgekehrt; **2.** [kən'vɜːs] sich unterhalten.

con·ver·sion [kən'vɜːʃn] Um-, Verwandlung *f*; *econ.* ⊕ Umstellung *f*; ⊕ Umbau *m*; ⚡ Umformung *f*; *eccl.* Konversion *f*; *pol.* Übertritt *m*; *econ.* Konvertierung *f*; Umstellung *f* (*e-r Währung etc.*).

con|vert 1. ['kɔnvɜːt] Bekehrte(r *m*) *f*, *eccl. a.* Konvertit(in); **2.** [kən'vɜːt] (sich) um- *od.* verwandeln; *econ.* ⊕ umstellen (*to auf acc.*); ⊕ umbauen (*into* zu); ⚡ umformen; *eccl.* bekehren; *econ.* konvertieren, umwandeln; *Währung etc.* umstellen; **~·vert·er** ⚡ [~ə] Umformer *m*; **~·vert·i·ble 1.** □ [~əbl] um-, verwandelbar; *econ.* konvertierbar; **2.** *mot.* Kabrio(lett) *n*.

con·vey [kən'veɪ] befördern, transportieren, bringen; überbringen, -mitteln; übertragen; mitteilen; **~·ance** [~əns] Beförderung *f*, Transport *m*; Übermittlung *f*; Verkehrsmittel *n*; ⚖ Übertragung *f*; **~·er**, **~·or** ⊕ [~ɪə] = **~·er belt** Förderband *n*.

con|vict 1. ['kɔnvɪkt] Strafgefangene(r) *m*, Sträfling *m*; **2.** ⚖ [kən'vɪkt] *j-n* überführen; **~·vic·tion** [~kʃn] ⚖ Verurteilung *f*; Überzeugung *f*.

con·vince [kən'vɪns] überzeugen.

con·viv·i·al □ [kən'vɪvɪəl] gesellig.

con·voy ['kɔnvɔɪ] **1.** ⚓ Geleitzug *m*, Konvoi *m*; (Wagen)Kolonne *f*; (Geleit)Schutz *m*; **2.** Geleitschutz geben (*dat.*), eskortieren.

con·vul|sion ⚕ [kən'vʌlʃn] Zuckung *f*, Krampf *m*; **~·sive** □ [~sɪv] krampfhaft, -artig, konvulsiv.

coo [kuː] gurren.

cook [kʊk] **1.** Koch *m*; Köchin *f*; **2.** kochen; *F Bericht etc.* frisieren; **~ up** *F* sich ausdenken, erfinden; **~·book** *Am.* ['kʊkbʊk] Kochbuch *n*; **~·er** *Brt.* [~ə] Ofen *m*, Herd *m*; **~·e·ry** [~ərɪ] Kochen *n*; Kochkunst *f*; **~·book** *Brt.* Kochbuch *n*; **~·ie** *Am.* [~ɪ] (süßer) Keks, Plätzchen *n*; **~·ing** [ɪŋ] Küche *f* (*Kochweise*); **~·y** *Am.* [~ɪ] = cookie.

cool [kuːl] **1.** □ kühl; *fig.* kaltblütig, gelassen; unverfroren; *bsd. Am. F* klasse, prima, cool; **2.** Kühle *f*; *F*

(Selbst)Beherrschung f; **3.** (sich) ab- kühlen; **~ down**, **~ off** sich beruhigen.

coon zo. F [ku:n] Waschbär m.

coop [ku:p] **1.** Hühnerstall m; **2. ~ up**, **~ in** einsperren, -pferchen.

co-op F [ˈkəʊɒp] Co-op m (Genossen- schaft u. Laden).

co(-)operate [kəʊˈɒpəreɪt] mitwir- ken; zusammenarbeiten; **~ration** [kəʊɒpəˈreɪʃn] Mitwirkung f; Zu- sammenarbeit f; **~rative** [kəʊˈɒpə- rətɪv] **1.** □ zusammenarbeitend; mitarbeitend; **2.** a. **~ society** Genos- senschaft f; Co-op m, Konsum- verein m; a. **~ store** Co-op m, Kon- sumladen m; **~rator** [~reɪtə] Mit- arbeiter(in).

co(-)ordinate 1. □ [kəʊˈɔːdɪnət] koordiniert, gleichgeordnet; **2.** [~neɪt] koordinieren, aufeinander abstimmen; **~nation** [kəʊɔːdɪ- ˈneɪʃn] Koordination f; harmoni- sches Zusammenspiel.

cop F [kɒp] Bulle m (Polizist).

cope [kəʊp]: **~ with** gewachsen sein, fertig werden mit.

copier [ˈkɒpɪə] Kopiergerät n, Ko- pierer m; = copyist.

copious [ˈkəʊpjəs] reich(lich); weitschweifig.

copper¹ [ˈkɒpə] **1.** min. Kupfer n; Kupfermünze f; **2.** kupfern, Kupfer...

copper² F [~] Bulle m (Polizist).

coppice, copse [ˈkɒpɪs, kɒps] Unter- holz n, Dickicht n.

copy [ˈkɒpɪ] **1.** Kopie f; Abschrift f; Nachbildung f; Durchschlag m; Muster n; Exemplar n (e-s Buches); (Zeitungs)Nummer f; druckfertiges Manuskript; fair od. clean ~ Reinschrift f; **2.** kopieren; abschrei- ben; Computer: Daten übertragen; nachbilden; nachahmen; **~book** Schreibheft n; **~ing** [~ɪŋ] Kopier...; **~ist** [~ɪst] Abschreiber m, Kopist m; **~right** Urheberrecht n, Copyright n.

coral zo. [ˈkɒrəl] Koralle f.

cord [kɔːd] Schnur f, Strick m; anat. Band n, Schnur f, Strang m; **2.** (zu)schnüren, binden.

cordial [ˈkɔːdjəl] **1.** □ herzlich; **~** stärkend; **2.** belebendes Mittel, Stär- kungsmittel n; Fruchtsaftkonzentrat n; Likör m; **~ity** [kɔːdɪˈælətɪ] Herz- lichkeit f.

cordon [ˈkɔːdn] **1.** Kordon m, Po-

stenkette f; **2. ~ off** abriegeln, absper- ren.

corduroy [ˈkɔːdərɔɪ] Kord(samt) m; (a pair of) **~s** pl. (e-e) Kordhose.

core [kɔː] **1.** Kerngehäuse n; fig. Herz n, Mark n, Kern m; **2.** entkernen.

cork [kɔːk] **1.** Kork m; **2.** a. **~ up** zu-, verkorken; **~screw** [ˈkɔːkskruː] Korkenzieher m.

corn [kɔːn] **1.** (Samen-, Getreide-) Korn n; Getreide n; a. Indian **~** Am. Mais m; **~** Hühnerauge n; **2.** (ein-) pökeln.

corner [ˈkɔːnə] **1.** Ecke f; Winkel m; Kurve f; Fußball etc.: Eckball m, Ecke f; fig. schwierige Lage, Klem- me f, Enge f; **2.** Eck...; **~kick** Fuß- ball: Eckstoß m; **3.** in die Ecke (fig. Enge) treiben; econ. aufkaufen; **~ed** ...eckig.

cornet [ˈkɔːnɪt] ♪ Kornett n; Brt. Eistüte f.

cornflakes [ˈkɔːnfleɪks] pl. Corn- flakes pl.

cornice arch. [ˈkɔːnɪs] Gesims n, Sims m.

coronary anat. [ˈkɒrənərɪ] koro- nar; **~ artery** Koronar-, Kranzarterie f.

coronation [kɒrəˈneɪʃn] **1.** Krö- nung f.

coroner ⟨z⟩ [ˈkɒrənə] Coroner m (richterlicher Beamter zur Untersu- chung der Todesursache in Fällen ge- waltsamen od. unnatürlichen Todes); **~'s** inquest gerichtliches Verfahren zur Untersuchung der Todesursache.

coronet [ˈkɒrənɪt] Adelskrone f.

corporal [ˈkɔːpərəl] **1.** □ körper- lich; **2.** ⟨×⟩ Unteroffizier m; **~ration** [kɔːpəˈreɪʃn] Körperschaft f; Stadt- verwaltung f; Vereinigung f, Gesell- schaft f; Am. Aktiengesellschaft f.

corpse [kɔːps] Leichnam m, Leiche f.

corpulence, **~lency** [ˈkɔːpjʊləns, ~sɪ] Beleibtheit f; **~lent** [~t] beleibt.

corral Am. [kɔːˈrɑːl, Am. kəˈræl] Korral m, Hürde f, Pferch m; **2.** (-ll-) Vieh in e-n Pferch treiben.

correct [kəˈrekt] **1.** adj. □ korrekt, richtig; **2.** v/t. korrigieren; zurecht- weisen; strafen; **~rection** [~kʃn] Berichtigung f; Korrektur f; Ver- weis m; Strafe f; house of **~** (Jugend-) Strafanstalt f; (-)Gefängnis n.

corre spond [kɒrɪˈspɒnd] entspre- chen (with, to dat.); korrespondie- ren; **~spondence** [~əns] Übereinstimmung f; Korrespondenz f, Briefwechsel m; **~ course** Fernkurs m; **~·spon·dent** [~t] **1.** □ entsprechend; **2.** Briefpartner(in) Korrespondent(in); **~·spon·ding** □ [~ɪŋ] entsprechend.

or·ri·dor ['kɒrɪdɔ:] Korridor m, Gang m; **~ train** D-Zug m.

or·rob·o·rate [kə'rɒbəreɪt] bekräftigen, bestätigen.

or·rode [kə'rəʊd] zerfressen; ⊕ korrodieren; **~·ro·sion** [~ʒn] Zerfressen n; ⊕ Korrosion f; Rost m; **~·ro·sive** [~sɪv] **1.** □ zerfressend, ätzend; **2.** Korrosions-, Ätzmittel n.

or·ru·gate ['kɒrʊgeɪt] runzeln; **~d iron** Wellblech n.

or·rupt [kə'rʌpt] **1.** □ verdorben, korrupt, bestechlich, käuflich; **2.** v/t. verderben; bestechen; v/i. verderben; **~·rupt·i·ble** □ [~əbl] verderblich; korrupt, bestechlich, käuflich; **~·rup·tion** [~pʃn] Verdorbenheit, Verworfenheit f; Fäulnis f; Korruption f, Bestechlichkeit f; Verfälschung f.

or·set ['kɔ:sɪt] Korsett n.

os·met·ic [kɒz'metɪk] **1.** (**~ally**) kosmetisch, Schönheits...; **2.** kosmetisches Mittel, Schönheitsmittel n; **~·me·ti·cian** [kɒzmə'tɪʃn] Kosmetiker(in).

os·mo·naut ['kɒzmənɔ:t] Kosmonaut m, (sowjetischer) (Welt)Raumfahrer.

os·mo·pol·i·tan [kɒzmə'pɒlɪtən] **1.** kosmopolitisch; **2.** Weltbürger(in).

ost [kɒst] **1.** Preis m; Kosten pl.; Schaden m; △ nicht Kost (Essen); **~ of living** Lebenshaltungskosten pl.; **2.** (cost) kosten; **~·ly** [~lɪ] (**-ier**, **-iest**) kostspielig; teuer erkauft.

os·tume ['kɒstju:m] Kostüm n, Kleidung f, Tracht f.

o·sy ['kəʊzɪ] **1.** □ (**-ier**, **-iest**) behaglich, gemütlich; **2.** = egg-cosy, tea-cosy.

ot [kɒt] Feldbett n; Brt. Kinderbett n.

ot·tage ['kɒtɪdʒ] Cottage n, (kleines) Landhaus; Am. Ferienhaus n; **~·house** n; **~ cheese** Hüttenkäse m; **~·tag·er** [~ə] Cottagebewohner(in); Am. Urlauber(in) in e-m Ferienhaus.

ot·ton ['kɒtn] **1.** Baumwolle f; Baumwollstoff m; (Baumwoll)Garn n, (-)Zwirn m; **2.** baumwollen,

Baumwoll...; **3.** ~ **on to** et. kapieren, verstehen; **~·wood** ♦ e-e amer. Pappel; **~ wool** Brt. (Verband)Watte f.

couch [kaʊtʃ] **1.** Couch f, Sofa n; Liege f; **2.** (ab)fassen, formulieren.

cou·chette 🚃 [ku:'ʃet] Liegewagenplatz m; a. ~ **coach** Liegewagen m.

cou·gar zo. ['ku:gə] Puma m.

cough [kɒf] **1.** Husten m; **2.** husten.

could [kʊd] pret. von can[1].

coun·cil ['kaʊnsl] Rat(sversammlung f) m; ~ **house** Brt. gemeindeeigenes Wohnhaus (mit niedrigen Mieten); **~·ci(l)·lor** [~sələ] Ratsmitglied n, Stadtrat m, Stadträtin f.

coun·sel ['kaʊnsl] **1.** Beratung f; Rat(schlag) m; Brt. ⚖ (Rechts)Anwalt m; ~ **for the defence** (Am. **defense**) Verteidiger m; ~ **for the prosecution** Anklagevertreter m; **2.** (bsd. Am., Am. **-l-**) j-n beraten; j-m raten; **~·se(l)·lor** [~sələ] Berater m; a. **~-at-law** Am. ⚖ (Rechts)Anwalt m.

count[1] [kaʊnt] Graf m (nicht britisch).

count[2] [~] **1.** Rechnung f, Zählung f; ⚖ Anklagepunkt m; **2.** v/t. zählen aus-, berechnen; fig. halten für; ~ **down Geld** hinzählen; (a. v/i.) den Countdown durchführen (für e-e Rakete etc.), letzte (Start)Vorbereitungen treffen (für); v/i. zählen, rechnen; (on, upon) zählen, sich verlassen (auf acc.); gelten (for little wenig); **~·down** ['kaʊntdaʊn] Countdown m, n (beim Raketenstart etc.), letzte (Start)Vorbereitungen pl.

coun·te·nance ['kaʊntɪnəns] Gesichtsausdruck m; Fassung f.

count·er[1] ['kaʊntə] Zähler m; Zählgerät n; Brt. Spielmarke f.

coun·ter[2] [~] Ladentisch m; Theke f; (Bank-, Post)Schalter m.

coun·ter[3] [~] **1.** (ent)gegen, Gegen...; **2.** entgegentreten (dat.), entgegnen (dat.), bekämpfen; abwehren.

coun·ter·act [kaʊntə'rækt] entgegenwirken (dat.); neutralisieren; bekämpfen.

coun·ter·bal·ance 1. ['kaʊntəbæləns] Gegengewicht n; **2.** [kaʊntə'bæləns] aufwiegen, ausgleichen.

coun·ter·clock·wise [kaʊntə-'klɒkwaɪz] = anticlockwise.

coun·ter·es·pi·o·nage ['kaʊntər'espɪənɑ:ʒ] Spionageabwehr f.

coun·ter·feit ['kaʊntəfɪt] **1.** □ nach-

gemacht, falsch, unecht; **2.** Fälschung *f*; Falschgeld *n*; **3.** *Geld,
Unterschrift etc.* fälschen.

coun·ter·foil [ˈkaʊntəfɔɪl] Kontrollabschnitt *m*.

coun·ter·mand [kaʊntəˈmɑːnd]
widerrufen; *Ware* abbestellen.

coun·ter·pane [ˈkaʊntəpeɪn] = *bedspread*.

coun·ter·part [ˈkaʊntəpɑːt] Gegenstück *n*; genaue Entsprechung.

coun·ter·sign [ˈkaʊntəsaɪn] gegen-
zeichnen, mit unterschreiben.

coun·tess [ˈkaʊntɪs] Gräfin *f*.

count·less [ˈkaʊntlɪs] zahllos.

coun·try [ˈkʌntrɪ] **1.** Land *n*; Gegend
f; Heimatland *n*; **2.** Land..., ländlich; ~**man** (*pl. -men*) Landbewoh-
ner *m*; Bauer *m*; *a.* **fellow** ~ Landsmann *m*; ~ **road** Landstraße *f*;
~**side** (ländliche) Gegend; Landschaft *f*; ~**wom·an** (*pl. -women*)
Landbewohnerin *f*; Bäuerin *f*; *a.
fellow* ~ Landsmännin *f*.

coun·ty [ˈkaʊntɪ] *Brt.* Grafschaft *f*;
Am. (Land)Kreis *m* (*einzelstaatlicher
Verwaltungsbezirk*); ~ **seat** *Am.*
Kreis(haupt)stadt *f*; ~ **town** *Brt.*
Grafschaftshauptstadt *f*.

coup [kuː] Coup *m*; Putsch *m*.

cou·ple [ˈkʌpl] **1.** Paar *n*; a ~ of F ein
paar; **2.** (zusammen)koppeln; ⊕
kuppeln; *zo.* (sich) paaren.

coup·ling ⊕ [ˈkʌplɪŋ] Kupplung *f*.

cou·pon [ˈkuːpɒn] Gutschein *m*;
Kupon *m*, Bestellzettel *m*.

cour·age [ˈkʌrɪdʒ] Mut *m*; **cou·ra·
geous** □ [kəˈreɪdʒəs] mutig, beherzt.

cou·ri·er [ˈkʊrɪə] Kurier *m*, Eilbote
m; Reiseleiter *m*.

course [kɔːs] **1.** Lauf *m*, Gang *m*; Weg
m; ⚓, ⚔, *fig.* Kurs *m*; *Sport:* (Renn-)
Bahn *f*, (-)Strecke *f*, (*Golf*)Platz *m*;
Gang *m* (*Speisen*); Reihe *f*; Folge *f*;
Kurs *m*; ♂ Kur *f*; *of* ~ natürlich,
selbstverständlich; **2.** hetzen, jagen;
strömen (*Tränen etc.*).

court [kɔːt] **1.** Hof *m* (*a. e-s Fürsten*);
kleiner Platz; *Sport:* Platz *m*,
(Spiel)Feld *n*; ⚖ Gericht(shof *m*) *n*;
Gerichtssaal *m*; **2.** *j-m* den Hof machen; werben um.

cour·te·ous □ [ˈkɜːtjəs] höflich; ~**sy**
[~ɪsɪ] Höflichkeit *f*; Gefälligkeit *f*.

court-house [ˈkɔːtˈhaʊs] Gerichts-
gebäude *n*; ~**ier** [~jə] Höfling *m*; ~**ly**
[~lɪ] höfisch; höflich; ~ **mar·tial** (*pl.*

~**s martial**, ~ **martials**) Kriegsgerich
n; ~**mar·tial** [~ˈmɑːʃl] (*bsd. Brt. -ll-
Am. -l-*) vor ein Kriegsgericht stel
len; ~**room** Gerichtssaal *m*; ~**shi**
[ˈkɔːtʃɪp] Werben *n*; ~**yard** Hof *m*

cous·in [ˈkʌzn] Cousin *m*, Vetter *m*
Cousine *f*, Kusine *f*.

cove [kəʊv] kleine Bucht.

cov·er [ˈkʌvə] **1.** Decke *f*; Deckel *m*
(Buch)Deckel *m*, Einband *m*; Ein
schlag *m*; Hülle *f*; Schutzhaube *f*
-platte *f*; Abdeckhaube *f*; Briefum
schlag *m*; Deckung *f*; Schutz *m*
Dickicht *n*; Decke *f*, Mantel *m* (*Be
reifung*); *fig.* Deckmantel *m*; *take* ~ i
Deckung gehen; *under plain* ~ i
neutralem Umschlag; *under sepa
rate* ~ mit getrennter Post; **2.** (be-
zu)decken; einschlagen, -wickel
verbergen, -decken; schützen; *We*
zurücklegen; *econ.* decken; *mit e-
Schußwaffe* zielen auf (*acc.*); ⚔ *Ge*
lände bestreichen; umfassen; *fig.* er
fassen; *Presse, Rundfunk, TV:* be
richten über (*acc.*); ~ *up* ab-, zu
decken; *fig.* verbergen, -heimlichen
~ *up for s.o.* j-n decken; ~**age** [~rɪdʒ
Berichterstattung *f* (*of* über *acc.*); .

girl Covergirl *n*, Titelblattmädche
n; ~**ing** [~rɪŋ] Decke *f*; Überzug *m*
(*Fußboden*)Belag *m*; ~ **sto·ry** Titel
geschichte *f*.

cov·ert □ [ˈkʌvət] heimlich, ver
steckt.

cov·et [ˈkʌvɪt] begehren; ~**ous** □
[~əs] (be)gierig; habsüchtig.

cow[1] *zo.* [kaʊ] Kuh *f*.

cow[2] [~] einschüchtern, ducken.

cow·ard [ˈkaʊəd] **1.** □ feig(e); **2**
Feigling *m*; ~**ice** [~ɪs] Feigheit *f*; ~**ly**
[~lɪ] feig(e).

cow·boy [ˈkaʊbɔɪ] Cowboy *m*.

cow·er [ˈkaʊə] kauern; sich ducken.

cow·herd [ˈkaʊhɜːd]Kuhhirt *m*
~**hide** Rind(s)leder *n*; ~**house**
Kuhstall *m*.

cowl [kaʊl] Mönchskutte *f* (*mit Ka
puze*); Kapuze *f*; Schornsteinkappe
f.

cow|shed [ˈkaʊʃed] Kuhstall *m*
~**slip** ♀ Schlüsselblume *f*; *Am*
Sumpfdotterblume *f*.

cox [kɒks] = *coxswain*.

cox·comb [ˈkɒkskəʊm] Geck *m*.

cox·swain [ˈkɒkswein, ⚓ *mst* ˈkɒksn
Bootsführer *m*; *Rudern:* Steuermann
m.

coy □ [kɔɪ] schüchtern; spröde.

coy·ote zo. ['kɔɪəʊt] Kojote m, Prärie-wolf m.

co·zy Am. □ ['kəʊzɪ] (-ier, -iest) = cosy.

crab [kræb] Krabbe f, Taschenkrebs m; F Nörgler(in).

crack [kræk] **1.** Krach m, Knall m; Spalte f, Spalt m, Schlitz m; F derber Schlag; F Versuch m; Witz m; **2.** erstklassig; **3.** v/t. knallen mit, knacken lassen; zerbrechen; (zer-)sprengen; schlagen, hauen; (auf-)reißen; ~ a joke e-n Witz reißen; v/i. krachen, knallen, knacken; (zer-)springen, (-)platzen; überschlagen (Stimme); a. ~ up fig. zusammenbre-chen; get ~ing F loslegen; **~·er** ['krækə] Cracker m, Kräcker m (ungesüßtes, keksartiges Kleingebäck); Schwärmer m, Frosch m (Feuerwerkskörper); **~·le** [~kl] knattern, knistern, krachen.

cra·dle ['kreɪdl] **1.** Wiege f; fig. Kind-heit f; **2.** wiegen; betten.

craft[1] [krɑːft] ♣ Boot(e pl.) n, Schiff(e pl.) n; ✈ Flugzeug(e pl.) n; (Welt)Raumfahrzeug(e pl.) n.

craft[2] [~] Handwerk n, Gewerbe n; Schlauheit f, List f; △ nicht Kraft; **~s·man** ['krɑːftsmən] (pl. -men) (Kunst)Handwerker m; **~·y** □ [~ɪ] (-ier, -iest) gerissen, listig, schlau.

crag [kræg] Klippe f, Felsenspitze f.

cram [kræm] (-mm-) (voll)stopfen; nudeln, mästen; mit j-m pauken; für e-e Prüfung pauken.

cramp [kræmp] **1.** Krampf m; ⊕ Klammer f; fig. Fessel f; **2.** einen-gen, hemmen.

cran·ber·ry ♀ ['krænbərɪ] Preisel-beere f.

crane [kreɪn] **1.** zo. Kranich m; ⊕ Kran m; **2.** den Hals recken; ~ one's neck sich den Hals verrenken (for nach).

crank [kræŋk] **1.** ⊕ Kurbel f; ⊕ Schwengel m; F Spinner m, komi-scher Kauz; **2.** (an)kurbeln; **~·shaft** ⊕ ['kræŋkʃɑːft] Kurbelwelle f; **~·y** [~ɪ] (-ier, -iest) wacklig; verschro-ben; Am. schlechtgelaunt.

cran·ny ['krænɪ] Riß m, Ritze f.

crape [kreɪp] Krepp m, Flor m.

craps Am. [kræps] sg. ein Würfelspiel.

crash [kræʃ] **1.** Krach(en n) m; Unfall m, Zusammenstoß m; ✈ Absturz m; bsd. econ. Zusammenbruch m, (Börsen)Krach m; **2.** v/t. zertrüm-

mern; e-n Unfall haben mit; ✈ abstürzen mit; v/i. (krachend) zer-bersten, -brechen; krachend ein-stürzen, zusammenkrachen; bsd. econ. zusammenbrechen; krachen (against, into gegen); mot. zusam-menstoßen, verunglücken; ✈ ab-stürzen; **3.** Schnell-, Sofort...; ~ **bar·ri·er** ['kræʃbærɪə] Leitplanke f; ~ **course** Schnell-, Intensivkurs m; ~ **di·et** radikale Schlankheitskur; ~ **hel·met** Sturzhelm m; **~·land** ✈ e-e Bruchlandung machen (mit); ~ **land·ing** ✈ Bruchlandung f.

crate [kreɪt] (Latten)Kiste f.

cra·ter ['kreɪtə] Krater m; Trichter m.

crave [kreɪv] v/t. dringend bitten od. flehen um; v/i. sich sehnen (for nach); **crav·ing** ['kreɪvɪŋ] heftiges Verlangen.

craw·fish zo. ['krɔːfɪʃ] Flußkrebs m.

crawl [krɔːl] **1.** Kriechen n; **2.** krie-chen; schleichen; wimmeln; krib-beln; Schwimmen: kraulen; it makes one's flesh ~ man bekommt e-e Gänsehaut davon.

cray·fish zo. ['kreɪfɪʃ] Flußkrebs m.

cray·on ['kreɪən] Zeichenstift m, Pastellstift m.

craze [kreɪz] Verrücktheit f, Fim-mel m; be the ~ Mode sein; **cra·zy** □ ['kreɪzɪ] (-ier, -iest) verrückt (about nach).

creak [kriːk] knarren, quietschen.

cream [kriːm] **1.** Rahm m, Sahne f; Creme f; Auslese f, das Beste; **2.** a. ~ off den Rahm abschöpfen von, ab-sahnen (a. fig.); **~·e·ry** ['kriːmərɪ] Molkerei f; Milchgeschäft n; **~·y** [~ɪ] (-ier, -iest) sahnig; weich.

crease [kriːs] **1.** (Bügel)Falte f; **2.** (zer)knittern.

cre·ate [kriːˈeɪt] (er)schaffen; her-vorrufen; verursachen; kreieren; **~·a·tion** [~ˈeɪʃn] (Er)Schaffung f; Erzeugung f; Schöpfung f; **~·a·tive** □ [~ˈeɪtɪv] schöpferisch; **~·a·tor** [~ə] Schöpfer m; Er·schaffer m; **crea·ture** ['kriːtʃə] Geschöpf n; Kreatur f.

crèche [kreɪʃ] (Kinder)Krippe f.

cre·dence ['kriːdns] Glaube m; **~·den·tials** [krɪˈdenʃlz] pl. Beglaubi-gungsschreiben n; Referenzen pl.; Zeugnis pl.; (Ausweis)Papiere pl.

cred·i·ble □ ['kredəbl] glaubwürdig; glaubhaft.

cred|it [ˈkredɪt] **1.** Glaube(n) *m*; Ruf *m*, Ansehen *n*; Verdienst *n*; *econ.* Guthaben *n*; *econ.* Kredit *m*; ~ **card** *econ.* Kreditkarte *f*; *j-m* glauben; *j-m* trauen; *econ.* gutschreiben; ~ *s.o. with s.th.* j-m et. zutrauen; j-m et. zuschreiben; ~**i·ta·ble** □ ╎~əbl╎ achtbar, ehrenvoll (*to* für); ~**i·tor** [~ə] Gläubiger *m*; ~**u·lous** □ ╎~jʊləs╎ leichtgläubig.

creed [kriːd] Glaubensbekenntnis *n*.
creek [kriːk] *Brt.* kleine Bucht; *Am.* Bach *m*.
creel [kriːl] Fischkorb *m*.
creep [kriːp] (*crept*) kriechen; schleichen (*a. fig.*); ~ *in* (sich) hinein- *od.* hereinschleichen; sich einschleichen (*Fehler etc.*); *it makes my flesh* ~ ich bekomme e-e Gänsehaut davon; ~**er** ♀ [ˈkriːpə] Kriech-, Kletterpflanze *f*; ~**s** *pl.* F: *the sight gave me the* ~ bei dem Anblick bekam ich e-e Gänsehaut.
crept [krept] *pret. u. p.p. von creep.*
cres·cent [ˈkresnt] **1.** zunehmend; halbmondförmig; **2.** Halbmond *m.*
cress ♀ [kres] Kresse *f.*
crest [krest] (Hahnen-, Berg- *etc.*) Kamm *m*; Mähne *f*; Federbusch *m*; *family* ~ *Heraldik:* Familienwappen *n*; ~**fal·len** [ˈkrestfɔːlən] niedergeschlagen.
cre·vasse [krɪˈvæs] (Gletscher)Spalte *f*; *Am.* Deichbruch *m.*
crev·ice [ˈkrevɪs] Riß *m*, Spalte *f.*
crew¹ [kruː] ♣, ✈ Besatzung *f*, ♣ *a.* Mannschaft *f*; (*Arbeits*)Gruppe *f*; Belegschaft *f.*
crew² [~] *pret. von crow².*
crib [krɪb] **1.** Krippe *f*; *Am.* Kinderbett *n*; F Schule: Klatsche *f*, Spickzettel *m*; **2.** (*-bb-*) F abschreiben, spicken.
crick [krɪk] *a* ~ *in one's back* (*neck*) ein steifer Rücken (Hals).
crick·et [ˈkrɪkɪt] *zo.* Grille *f*; *Sport:* Kricket *n*; *not* ~ F nicht fair.
crime [kraɪm] ⚖ Verbrechen *n*; *coll.* Verbrechen *pl.*; ~ *novel* Kriminalroman *m.*
crim·i·nal [ˈkrɪmɪnl] **1.** □ verbrecherisch; Kriminal..., Straf...; **2.** Verbrecher(in), Kriminelle(r *m*) *f.*
crimp [krɪmp] kräuseln.
crim·son [ˈkrɪmzn] karmesinrot; puterrot.
cringe [krɪndʒ] sich ducken.
crin·kle [ˈkrɪŋkl] **1.** Falte *f*, im Ge-

sicht: Fältchen *n*; **2.** (sich) kräuseln; knittern.
crip·ple [ˈkrɪpl] **1.** Krüppel *m*; **2.** zum Krüppel machen; *fig.* lähmen.
cri·sis [ˈkraɪsɪs] (*pl. -ses* [-siːz]) Krisis *f*, Krise *f*; Wende-, Höhepunkt *m.*
crisp [krɪsp] **1.** □ kraus; knusp(e)rig, mürbe (*Gebäck*); frisch; klar; steif; **2.** (sich) kräuseln; knusp(e)rig machen *od.* werden; **3.** ~ *s pl., a. potato* ~ *s pl. Brt.* (Kartoffel)Chips *pl.*; ~**bread** [ˈkrɪspbred] Knäckebrot *n.*
criss-cross [ˈkrɪskrɒs] **1.** Netz *n* sich schneidender Linien; **2.** (durch-)kreuzen.
cri·te·ri·on [kraɪˈtɪərɪən] (*pl. -ria* [-rɪə], *-rions*) Kriterium *n.*
crit·ic [ˈkrɪtɪk] Kritiker(in); △ *nicht Kritik*; ~**i·cal** □ [~kl] kritisch; bedenklich; ~**i·cis·m** [~ɪsɪzəm] Kritik *f* (*of an dat.*); ~**i·cize** [~saɪz] kritisieren; kritisch beurteilen; tadeln.
cri·tique [krɪˈtiːk] kritischer Essay, Kritik *f.*
croak [krəʊk] krächzen; quaken.
cro·chet [ˈkrəʊʃeɪ] **1.** Häkelei *f*; Häkelarbeit *f*; **2.** häkeln.
crock·e·ry [ˈkrɒkərɪ] Geschirr *n.*
croc·o·dile *zo.* [ˈkrɒkədaɪl] Krokodil *n.*
crone F [krəʊn] altes Weib.
cro·ny F [ˈkrəʊnɪ] alter Freund.
crook [krʊk] **1.** Krümmung *f*; Haken *m*; Hirtenstab *m*; F Gauner *m*; **2.** (sich) krümmen *od.* (ver)biegen; ~**ed** [ˈkrʊkɪd] krumm; bucklig; F unehrlich; [krʊkt] Krück...
croon [kruːn] schmalzig singen; summen; ~**er** [ˈkruːnə] Schnulzensänger(in).
crop [krɒp] **1.** *zo.* Kropf *m*; Peitschenstiel *m*; Reitpeitsche *f*; (Feld-)Frucht *f*, *bsd.* Getreide *n*; Ernte *f*; kurzer Haarschnitt; **2.** (*-pp-*) abfressen, abweiden; *Haar* kurz schneiden; ~ *up* *fig.* plötzlich auftauchen.
cross [krɒs] **1.** Kreuz *n* (*a. fig. Leiden*); Kreuzung *f*; **2.** □ sich kreuzend, quer (liegend, laufend *etc.*); ärgerlich, böse; entgegengesetzt; Kreuz..., Quer...; **3.** *v/t.* kreuzen; überqueren; *fig.* durchkreuzen; *j-m* in die Quere kommen; ~ *off*, ~ *out* aus-, durchstreichen; ~ *o.s.* sich bekreuzigen; *keep one's fingers* ~*ed* den Daumen halten; *v/i.* sich kreuzen; ~**bar** [ˈkrɒsbɑː] *Fußball:* Torlatte *f*; ~**breed** (Rassen)Kreuzung

f; **~·coun·try** Querfeldein..., Gelände...; ~ *skiing* Skilanglauf *m*; ~

ex·am·i·na·tion Kreuzverhör *n*; ~
ex·am·ine ins Kreuzverhör nehmen; **~eyed** schielend; *be* ~ schielen; **~·ing** [-ɪŋ] Kreuzung *f*; Übergang *m*; ♆ Überfahrt *f*; **~road** Querstraße *f*; **~roads** *pl. od. sg.* Straßenkreuzung *f*; *fig.* Scheideweg *m*; **~sec·tion** Querschnitt *m*; **~walk** *Am.* Fußgängerüberweg *m*; **~wise** kreuzweise; **~word (puz·zle)** Kreuzworträtsel *n*.

crotch [krɒtʃ] Schritt *m* (*des Körpers, der Hose*).

crotch·et [ˈkrɒtʃɪt] Haken *m*; *bsd. Br.* ♩ Viertelnote *f*.

crouch [krautʃ] 1. sich ducken; 2. Hockstellung *f*.

crow [krəʊ] 1. *zo.* Krähe *f*; Krähen *n*; 2. (*crowed od. crew, crowed*) krähen; (*crowed*) F prahlen (*about* mit).

crow·bar [ˈkrəʊbɑː] Brecheisen *n*.

crowd [kraʊd] 1. Masse *f*, Menge *f*, Gedränge *n*; F Bande *f*; 2. sich drängen; *Straßen etc.* bevölkern, vollstopfen; **~ed** [ˈkraʊdɪd] überfüllt, voll.

crown [kraʊn] 1. Krone *f*; Kranz *m*; Gipfel *m*; Scheitel *m*; 2. krönen; *Zahn* überkronen; *to* ~ *it all* zu allem Überfluß.

cru·cial □ [ˈkruːʃl] entscheidend, kritisch.

cru·ci·fix [ˈkruːsɪfɪks] Kruzifix *n*; **~·fix·ion** [kruːsɪˈfɪkʃn] Kreuzigung *f*; **~fy** [ˈkruːsɪfaɪ] kreuzigen.

crude □ [kruːd] roh; unfertig; unreif; unfein; grob; Roh...; grell.

cru·el □ [krʊəl] (**-ll-**) grausam; roh, gefühllos; **~ty** [ˈkrʊəltɪ] Grausamkeit *f*; ~ *to animals* Tierquälerei *f*; ~ *to children* Kindesmißhandlung *f*.

cru·et [ˈkruːɪt] Essig-, Ölfläschchen *n*.

cruise ♆ [kruːz] 1. Kreuzfahrt *f*, Seereise *f*; ~ *missile* ⚔ ✕ Marschflugkörper *m*; 2. kreuzen, e-e Kreuzfahrt machen; mit Reisegeschwindigkeit fliegen *od.* fahren; **cruis·er** [ˈkruːzə] ♆ ✕ Kreuzer *m*; Jacht *f*; Kreuzfahrtschiff *n*; *Am.* (Funk-)Streifenwagen *m*.

crumb [krʌm] 1. Krume *f*; Brocken *m*; 2. panieren; zerkrümeln; **crum·ble** [ˈkrʌmbl] (zer)bröckeln; *fig.* zugrunde gehen.

crum·ple [ˈkrʌmpl] *v/t.* zerknittern;

v/i. knittern; zusammengedrückt werden.

crunch [krʌntʃ] (zer)kauen; zermalmen; knirschen.

cru·sade [kruːˈseɪd] Kreuzzug *m* (*a. fig.*); **~sad·er** *hist.* [~ə] Kreuzfahrer *m*.

crush [krʌʃ] 1. Druck *m*; Gedränge *n*; (*Frucht*)Saft *m*; F Schwärmerei *f*; *have a* ~ *on s.o.* in j-n verliebt *od.* verknallt sein; 2. *v/t.* (zer-, aus)quetschen; zermalmen; *fig.* vernichten; *v/i.* sich drängen; **~·bar·ri·er** [ˈkrʌʃbærɪə] Barriere *f*, Absperrung *f*.

crust [krʌst] 1. Kruste *f*; Rinde *f*; 2. verkrusten; verharschen.

crus·ta·cean [krʌsˈteɪʃn] Krebs-, Krusten-, Schalentier *n*.

crust·y □ [ˈkrʌstɪ] (*-ier, -iest*) krustig; *fig.* mürrisch, barsch.

crutch [krʌtʃ] Krücke *f*.

cry [kraɪ] 1. Schrei *m*; Geschrei *n*; Ruf *m*; Weinen *n*; Gebell *n*; 2. schreien; (aus)rufen; weinen; ~ *for* verlangen nach.

crypt [krɪpt] Gruft *f*; **cryp·tic** [ˈkrɪptɪk] (*~ally*) verborgen, geheim; rätselhaft.

crys·tal [ˈkrɪstl] Kristall *m*; *Am.* Uhrglas *n*; **~·line** [~təlaɪn] kristallen; **~·lize** [~aɪz] kristallisieren.

cub [kʌb] 1. Junge(s) *n*; Flegel *m*; Anfänger *m*; 2. (Junge) werfen.

cube [kjuːb] Würfel *m* (*a. ℞*); *phot.* Blitzwürfel *m*; ℞ Kubikzahl *f*; ~ *root* ℞ Kubikwurzel *f*; **cu·bic** [ˈkjuːbɪk] (*~ally*), **cu·bi·cal** □ [~kl] würfelförmig, kubisch; Kubik...

cu·bi·cle [ˈkjuːbɪkl] Kabine *f*.

cuck·oo *zo.* [ˈkʊkuː] (*pl.* **-oos**) Kuckuck *m*.

cu·cum·ber [ˈkjuːkʌmbə] Gurke *f*; *as cool as a* ~ *fig.* eiskalt, gelassen.

cud [kʌd] wiedergekäutes Futter; *chew the* ~ wiederkäuen; *fig.* überlegen.

cud·dle [ˈkʌdl] *v/t.* an sich drücken; schmusen (mit).

cud·gel [ˈkʌdʒəl] 1. Knüppel *m*; 2. (*bsd. Brt. -ll-, Am. -l-*) prügeln.

cue [kjuː] *Billard*: Queue *n*; *thea. etc.*, *a. fig.* Stichwort *n*; Wink *m*.

cuff [kʌf] 1. Manschette *f*; Handschelle *f*; (Ärmel-, *Am. a.* Hosen-)Aufschlag *m*; Schlag *m* (mit der offenen Hand); Klaps *m*; 2. (mit der flachen Hand) schlagen.

cui·sine [kwɪ'ziːn] Küche f (*Koch-kunst*).

cul·mi·nate ['kʌlmɪneɪt] gipfeln (*in* in *dat.*).

cu·lottes [kjuːˈlɒts] *pl.* (a pair of ein) Hosenrock m.

cul·pa·ble □ ['kʌlpəbl] strafbar.

cul·prit ['kʌlprɪt] Angeklagte(r m) f; Schuldige(r m) f, Täter(in).

cul·ti·vate ['kʌltɪveɪt] ✔ kultivieren, bestellen, an-, bebauen (*Freund-schaft etc.* pflegen; **~·vat·ed** ✔ bebaut; *fig.* gebildet, kultiviert; **~·va-tion** [kʌltɪ'veɪʃn] ✔ Kultivierung f, (An-, Acker)Bau m; *fig.* Pflege f.

cul·tur·al □ ['kʌltʃərəl] kulturell; Kultur...

cul·ture ['kʌltʃə] Kultur f; Zucht f; **~d** kultiviert (*a. fig.*); Zucht...

cum·ber·some ['kʌmbəsəm] lästig, hinderlich; klobig.

cu·mu·la·tive □ ['kjuːmjʊlətɪv] sich (an-, auf)häufend; anwachsend; Zusatz...

cun·ning ['kʌnɪŋ] 1. □ schlau, listig, gerissen; geschickt; *Am.* niedlich; 2. List f, Schlauheit f, Gerissenheit f; Geschicklichkeit f.

cup [kʌp] 1. Tasse f; Becher m; Schale f; Kelch m; *Sport:* Cup m, Pokal m; **~ final** Pokalendspiel n; **~ winner** Pokalsieger m; 2. (**-pp-**) *die Hand* hohl machen; *she* ~*ped her chin in her hand* sie stützte das Kinn in die Hand; **~·board** ['kʌbəd] (Geschirr-, Speise-, *Brt. a.* Wäsche-, Kleider-) Schrank m; **~ bed** Schrankbett n.

cu·pid·i·ty [kjuːˈpɪdətɪ] Habgier f.

cu·po·la ['kjuːpələ] Kuppel m.

cur [kɜː] Köter m; Schurke m.

cu·ra·ble ['kjʊərəbl] heilbar.

cu·rate ['kjʊərət] Hilfsgeistliche(r) m.

curb [kɜːb] 1. Kandare f (*a. fig.*); *bsd. Am.* = **kerb**(*stone*); 2. an die Kandare legen (*a. fig.*); *fig.* zügeln.

curd [kɜːd] 1. Quark m; 2. *mst* **cur·dle** ['kɜːdl] gerinnen (lassen); *the sight made my blood* ~ bei dem Anblick erstarrte mir das Blut in den Adern.

cure [kjʊə] 1. Kur f; Heilmittel n; Heilung f; Seelsorge f; Pfarre f; 2. heilen; pökeln; räuchern; trocknen.

cur·few ✕ ['kɜːfjuː] Ausgangsverbot n, -sperre f.

cu·ri·o ['kjʊərɪəʊ] (*pl.* -os) Rarität f; **~·os·i·ty** [kjʊərɪ'ɒsətɪ] Neugier f; Rarität f; **~·ous** □ ['kjʊərɪəs] neu-

gierig; wißbegierig; seltsam, merk-würdig.

curl [kɜːl] 1. Locke f; 2. (sich) kräuseln *od.* locken; **~·er** ['kɜːlə] Locken-wickler m; **~·y** [~ɪ] (*-ier*, *-iest*) ge-kräuselt; gelockt, lockig.

cur·rant ['kʌrənt] ♀ Johannisbeere f; Korinthe f.

cur·ren·cy ['kʌrənsɪ] Umlauf m; *econ.* Laufzeit f; *econ.* Währung f; *foreign* ~ Devisen *pl.*; **~·rent** [~t] 1. □ umlaufend; *econ.* gültig (*Geld*) allgemein (bekannt); geläufig; laufend (*Jahr etc.*); gegenwärtig, aktuell; 2. Strom m (*a.* ⚡); Strömung (*a. fig.*); (*Luft*)Zug m; **~·rent ac-count** *econ.* Girokonto n.

cur·ric·u·lum [kəˈrɪkjʊləm] (*pl.* -*la* [-lə], -*lums*) Lehr-, Stundenplan m; ~ **vi·tae** [~'vaɪtɪ:] Lebenslauf m.

cur·ry¹ ['kʌrɪ] Curry m, n.

cur·ry² [~] *Pferd* striegeln.

curse [kɜːs] 1. Fluch m; ⚠ *nicht* Kurs; 2. (ver)fluchen; strafen; **curs·ed** □ ['kɜːsɪd] verflucht.

cur·sor ['kɜːsə] ✒ Läufer m, Schieber m (*am Rechenschieber*); *Computer:* Positionsanzeiger m (*auf dem Bild-schirm*).

cur·so·ry □ ['kɜːsrɪ] flüchtig, ober-flächlich.

curt □ [kɜːt] kurz, knapp; barsch.

cur·tail [kɜː'teɪl] beschneiden; *fig.* beschränken; kürzen (*of* um).

cur·tain ['kɜːtn] 1. Vorhang m, Gar-dine f; *draw the* ~*s* den Vorhang *od.* die Vorhänge zuziehen *od.* aufzie-hen; 2. ~ *off* mit Vorhängen abteilen

curt·s(e)y ['kɜːtsɪ] 1. Knicks m; 2. knicksen (*to* vor *dat.*).

cur·va·ture ['kɜːvətʃə] Krümmung f

curve [kɜːv] 1. Kurve f; Krümmung f; 2. (sich) krümmen *od.* biegen.

cush·ion ['kʊʃn] 1. Kissen n, Polster n; *Billardtisch:* Bande f; 2. polstern

cuss F [kʌs] 1. Fluch m; 2. (ver)flu-chen.

cus·tard ['kʌstəd] Eiercreme f.

cus·to·dy ['kʌstədɪ] Haft f; Gewahr-sam m; Obhut f.

cus·tom ['kʌstəm] Gewohnheit f; Brauch m, Sitte f; *econ.* Kundschaft f; **~·a·ry** □ [~ərɪ] gewöhnlich, üb-lich; **~·built** nach Kundenangaben gefertigt; **~·er** [~ə] Kunde m, -in f; F Bursche m; **~·house** Zollamt n; **~ made** maßgefertigt, Maß...

cus·toms ['kʌstəmz] *pl.* Zoll m; ~

clear·ance Zollabfertigung f; ~ **of·fi·cer**, ~ **of·fi·cial** Zollbeamte(r) m.

cut [kʌt] **1.** Schnitt m; Hieb m; Stich m; (Schnitt)Wunde f; Einschnitt m; Graben m; Kürzung f; Ausschnitt m; Wegabkürzung f (mst short-~); (Holz)Schnitt m; (Kupfer)Stich m; Schliff m; Schnitte f, Scheibe f; Karten: Abheben n; cold ~s pl. Küche: Aufschnitt m; give s.o. the ~ direct F j-n ostentativ schneiden; **2.** (-tt-; cut) schneiden; schnitzen; gravieren; ab-, an-, auf-, aus-, be-, durch-, zer-, zuschneiden; kürzen; Edelstein etc. schleifen; Karten abheben; j-n beim Begegnen schneiden; ~ teeth zahnen; ~ short j-n unterbrechen; ~ across quer durch... gehen (um abzukürzen); ~ back Pflanze beschneiden, stutzen; kürzen; einschränken; herabsetzen; ~ down Bäume fällen; verringern, einschränken, reduzieren; ~ in F sich einschalten; ~ in on s.o. mot. j-n schneiden; ~ off abschneiden; teleph. Teilnehmer trennen; j-n enterben; ~ out ausschneiden; Am. Vieh aussondern (aus der Herde); fig. j-n ausstechen; be ~ out for das Zeug zu et. haben; ~ up zerschneiden; be ~ up F tief betrübt sein; ~**back** [ˈkʌtbæk] Kürzung f; Herabsetzung f, Verringerung f.

cute □ F [kjuːt] (~r, ~st) schlau; Am. niedlich, süß.

cu·ti·cle [ˈkjuːtɪkl] Nagelhaut f.

cut·ler·y [ˈkʌtlərɪ] (Tisch-, Eß)Besteck n.

cut·let [ˈkʌtlɪt] Schnitzel n; Hacksteak n.

cut|-price econ. [ˈkʌtpraɪs], ~**rate** ermäßigt, herabgesetzt; Billig...; ~**ter** [~ə] (Blech-, Holz)Schneider m; Schnitzer m; Zuschneider(in); (Glas- etc.)Schleifer m; Film: Cutter(in); ⊕ Schneidewerkzeug n, -maschine f; ⚓ Kutter m; Am. leichter Schlitten; ~**throat** Mörder m; Killer m; ~**ting** [~ɪŋ] **1.** □ schneidend; scharf; ⊕ Schneid..., Fräs...; **2.** Schneiden n; ⚙ etc. Einschnitt m; ⚘ Steckling m; bsd. Brt. (Zeitungs-)Ausschnitt m; ~s pl. Schnipsel pl.; ⊕ Späne pl.

cy·cle¹ [ˈsaɪkl] Zyklus m; Kreis(lauf) m; Periode f.

cy·cle² [~] **1.** Fahrrad n; **2.** radfahren; **cy·clist** [~lɪst] Radfahrer(in); Motorradfahrer(in).

cy·clone [ˈsaɪkləʊn] Wirbelsturm m.

cyl·in·der [ˈsɪlɪndə] Zylinder m, Walze f; ⊕ Trommel f.

cym·bal ♩ [ˈsɪmbl] Becken n.

cyn|ic [ˈsɪnɪk] Zyniker m; ~**i·cal** □ [~kl] zynisch.

cy·press ⚘ [ˈsaɪprɪs] Zypresse f.

cyst ⚕ [sɪst] Zyste f.

czar hist. [zɑː] = tsar.

Czech [tʃek] **1.** tschechisch; **2.** Tscheche m, -in f; ling. Tschechisch n.

Czech·o·slo·vak [ˈtʃekəʊˈsləʊvæk] **1.** Tschechoslowake m, -in f; **2.** tschechoslowakisch.

D

dab [dæb] **1.** Klaps m; Tupfen m, Klecks m; **2.** (-bb-) leicht schlagen od. klopfen; be-, abtupfen.

dab·ble [ˈdæbl] bespritzen; betupfen; plätschern; sich oberflächlich od. (contp.) in dilettantischer Weise befassen (at, in mit).

dachs·hund zo. [ˈdækshʊnd] Dackel m.

dad F [dæd], ~**dy** F [ˈdædɪ] Papa m, Vati m.

dad·dy-long·legs zo. [ˈdædɪˈlɒŋlegz] Schnake f; Am. Weberknecht m.

daf·fo·dil ⚘ [ˈdæfədɪl] gelbe Narzisse.

daft F [dɑːft] blöde, doof.

dag·ger [ˈdægə] Dolch m; be at ~s drawn fig. auf Kriegsfuß stehen.

dai·ly [ˈdeɪlɪ] **1.** täglich; **2.** Tageszeitung f; Putzfrau f.

dain·ty [ˈdeɪntɪ] **1.** □ (-ier, -iest) lecker; zart; zierlich, niedlich, reizend; wählerisch; **2.** Leckerbissen *m*.

dair·y ['deərɪ] Molkerei *f*; Milchwirtschaft *f*; Milchgeschäft *n*; ~**cat·tle** Milchvieh *n*; ~**man** (*pl. -men*) Melker *m*; Milchmann *m*.

dai·sy ♀ ['deɪzɪ] Gänseblümchen *n*.

dale *dial. od. poet.* [deɪl] Tal *n*.

dal·ly ['dælɪ] (ver)trödeln; schäkern.

dam¹ *zo.* [dæm] Mutter(tier *n*) *f*.

dam² [~] Deich *m*, (Stau)Damm *m*; **2.** (*-mm-*) *a.* ~ **up** stauen, (ab-, ein)dämmen (*a. fig.*).

dam·age ['dæmɪdʒ] **1.** Schaden *m*, (Be)Schädigung *f*; ~**s** *pl.* ⚖ Schadenersatz *m*; **2.** (be)schädigen.

dam·ask ['dæməsk] Damast *m*.

dame *Am.* F [deɪm] Weib *n*; △ *nicht Dame*.

damn [dæm] **1.** verdammen; verurteilen; ~ (*it*)! F verflucht!, verdammt! **2.** *adj. u. adv.* F = damned; **3.** *I don't care a* ~ F das ist mir völlig gleich(gültig) *od.* egal; **dam·na·tion** [dæm'neɪʃn] Verdammung *f*; Verurteilung *f*; ~**ed** F [dæmd] verdammt; ~**ing** ['dæmɪŋ] vernichtend, belastend.

damp [dæmp] **1.** □ feucht, klamm; **2.** Feuchtigkeit *f*; **3.** *a.* ~**en** ['dæmpən] an-, befeuchten; dämpfen; ~**ness** [~nɪs] Feuchtigkeit *f*.

dance [dɑːns] **1.** Tanz *m*; Tanz(veranstaltung *f*) *m*; **2.** tanzen (lassen); **dancer** ['dɑːnsə] Tänzer(in); **dancing** [~ɪŋ] Tanzen *n*; *attr.* Tanz...

dan·de·li·on ♀ ['dændɪlaɪən] Löwenzahn *m*.

dan·dle ['dændl] wiegen, schaukeln.

dan·druff ['dændrʌf] (Kopf)Schuppen *pl.*

Dane [deɪn] Dän|e *m*, -in *f*.

dan·ger ['deɪndʒə] **1.** Gefahr *f*; *be in* ~ *of doing s.th.* Gefahr laufen et. zu tun; *be out of* ~ ⚕ über den Berg sein; **2.** Gefahren...; ~ *area*, ~ *zone* Gefahrenzone *f*, -bereich *m*; ~**ous** □ [~rəs] gefährlich.

dan·gle ['dæŋgl] baumeln (lassen).

Da·nish ['deɪnɪʃ] **1.** dänisch; **2.** *ling.* Dänisch *n*.

dank [dæŋk] feucht, naß(kalt).

dap·per ['dæpə] adrett; flink.

dap·pled ['dæpld] scheckig.

dare [deə] *v/i.* es wagen; *I* ~ *say*, *I* ~*say* ich glaube wohl; allerdings; *v/t. et.* wagen; *j-n* herausfordern; trotzen (*dat.*); ~**·dev·il** ['deədevl]

Draufgänger *m*, Teufelskerl *m*; **dar·ing** □ [~rɪŋ] **1.** kühn; waghalsig; **2.** Mut *m*, Kühnheit *f*.

dark [dɑːk] **1.** □ dunkel; brünett; geheim(nisvoll); trüb(selig); **2.** Dunkel(heit *f*) *n*; before (*at, after*) ~ vor (bei, nach) Einbruch der Dunkelheit; *keep s.o. in the* ~ *about s.th.* j-n über et. im ungewissen lassen; ⚕ **Ag·es** *pl. das* frühe Mittelalter; ~**en** ['dɑːkən] (sich) verdunkeln *od.* verfinstern; ~**ness** [~nɪs] Dunkelheit *f*, Finsternis *f*.

dar·ling ['dɑːlɪŋ] **1.** Liebling *m*; **2.** Lieblings...; geliebt.

darn [dɑːn] stopfen, ausbessern.

dart [dɑːt] **1.** Wurfspieß *m*; Wurfpfeil *m*; Sprung *m*, Satz *m*; ~**s** *sg.* Darts *n* (*Wurfpfeilspiel*); ~**board** Dartsscheibe *f*; **2.** *v/t.* werfen, schleudern; *v/i.* schießen, stürzen.

dash [dæʃ] **1.** Schlag *m*; Klatschen *n*; Schwung *m*; Ansturm *m*; *fig.* Anflug *m*; Prise *f*; Schuß *m* (*Rum etc.*); (Feder)Strich *m*; Gedankenstrich *m*; *Sport:* Sprint *m*; **2.** *v/t.* schlagen, schleudern, schmettern, werfen, schleudern; *Hoffnung* zunichte machen; *v/i.* stürzen, stürmen, jagen, rasen; schlagen; ~**board** *mot.* ['dæʃbɔːd] Armaturenbrett *n*; ~**ing** □ [~ɪŋ] schneidig, forsch, flott, F fesch.

da·ta ['deɪtə] *pl., a. sg.* Daten *pl.*, Einzelheiten *pl.*, Angaben *pl.*, Unterlagen *pl.*; *Computer:* Daten *pl.*; ~ **bank** Datenbank *f*; ~ **in·put** Dateneingabe *f*; ~ **out·put** Datenausgabe *f*; ~ **pro·cess·ing** Datenverarbeitung *f*; ~ **pro·tec·tion** Datenschutz *m*; ~ **typ·ist** Datentypist(in).

date¹ ♀ [deɪt] Dattel *f*.

date² [~] Datum *n*; Zeit(punkt *m*) *f*; Termin *m*; Verabredung *f*; *Am.* F (Verabredungs)Partner(in); *out of* ~ veraltet, unmodern; *up to* ~ zeitgemäß, modern, auf dem laufenden; **2.** datieren; *Am.* F sich verabreden mit, ausgehen mit, (*regelmäßig*) gehen mit; **dat·ed** ['deɪtɪd] veraltet, überholt.

da·tive *gr.* ['deɪtɪv] *a.* ~ *case* Dativ *m*, dritter Fall.

daub [dɔːb] (be)schmieren; (be)klecksen.

daugh·ter ['dɔːtə] Tochter *f*; ~**in-law** [~rɪnlɔː] (*pl. daughters-in-law*) Schwiegertochter *f*.

daunt [dɔːnt] entmutigen; ~**less** ['dɔːntlɪs] furchtlos, unerschrocken.

daw *zo.* [dɔː] Dohle *f.*

daw·dle F ['dɔːdl] (ver)trödeln.

dawn [dɔːn] **1.** (Morgen)Dämmerung *f*, Tagesanbruch *m*; **2.** dämmern, tagen; *it ~ed on od. upon him fig.* es wurde ihm langsam klar.

day [deɪ] Tag *m; oft ~s pl.* (Lebens-)Zeit *f; ~ off* (dienst)freier Tag; *carry od.* win *the ~* den Sieg davontragen; *any~* jederzeit; *these ~s* heutzutage; *the other ~* neulich; *this ~ week* heute in e-r Woche; heute vor e-r Woche; *let's call it a ~!* machen wir Schluß für heute!, Feierabend!; **~·break** ['deɪbreɪk] Tagesanbruch *m*; **~·light** Tageslicht *n; in broad ~* am hellichten Tag; **~·time:** *in the ~* am Tag, bei Tage.

daze [deɪz] **1.** blenden; betäuben; **2.** *in a ~* benommen, betäubt.

dead [ded] **1.** tot; unempfindlich (*to* für); matt (*Farbe etc.*); blind (*Fenster etc.*); erloschen (*Feuer*); schal (*Getränk*); tief (*Schlaf*); *econ.* still, ruhig, flau; *econ.* tot (*Kapital etc.*); völlig, absolut, total; *~ bargain* Spottpreis *m; ~ letter* unzustellbarer Brief; *~ loss* Totalverlust *m; a ~ shot* ein Meisterschütze; **2.** *adv.* gänzlich, völlig, total; plötzlich, abrupt; genau, (haar)scharf; *~ tired* todmüde; *~ against* ganz u. gar gegen; **3.** *the ~* der, die, das Tote; die Toten *pl.; in the ~ of winter* im tiefsten Winter; *in the ~ of night* mitten in der Nacht; **~·cen·tre,** *Am.* **~·cen·ter** genaue Mitte; **~·en** ['dedn] abstumpfen; dämpfen; (ab)schwächen; *~ end* Sackgasse *f* (*a. fig.*); **~·heat** *Sport:* totes Rennen; **~·line** *Am.* Sperrlinie *f*, Todesstreifen *m* (*im Gefängnis*); letzter (Ablieferungs)Termin; Stichtag *m*; **~·lock** *fig.* toter Punkt; **~·locked** *fig.* festgefahren (*Verhandlungen*); **~·ly** [~lɪ] (*-ier, -iest*) tödlich.

deaf [def] **1.** □ taub; *~ and dumb* taubstumm; **2.** *the ~ pl.* die Tauben *pl.;* **~·en** ['defn] taub machen; betäuben.

deal [diːl] **1.** Teil *n*, Menge *f; Karten:* Geben *n*; F Geschäft *n;* Abmachung *f; a good ~* ziemlich viel; *a great ~* sehr viel; **2.** (*dealt*) *v/t.* (aus-, ver-, zu)teilen; *Karten* geben; *~ a blow* versetzen; *v/i.* handeln (*in* mit *e-r Ware*); *sl.* dealen (*mit Rauschgift handeln*); *Karten:* geben; *~ with* sich befassen mit, behandeln; *econ.* Han-

del treiben mit, in Geschäftsverbindung stehen mit; **~·er** ['diːlə] *econ.* Händler(in); *Karten:* Geber(in); *sl.* Dealer *m* (*Rauschgifthändler*); **~·ing** [~ɪŋ] Verhalten *n*, Handlungsweise *f; econ.* Geschäftsgebaren *n; ~s pl.* Umgang *m*, (Geschäfts)Beziehungen *pl.;* **~t** [delt] *pret. u. p.p. von* deal 2.

dean [diːn] Dekan *m.*

dear [dɪə] **1.** □ teuer; lieb; **2.** Liebste(r *m*) *f*, Schatz *m; my ~* m-e Liebe, mein Lieber; **3.** *int.* (*oh*) *~!, ~ ~!, ~ me!* F du liebe Zeit!, ach herrje!; **~·ly** ['dɪəlɪ] innig, von ganzem Herzen; teuer (*im Preis*).

death [deθ] Tod *m*; Todesfall *m;* **~·bed** ['deθbed] Sterbebett *n;* **~·less** [~lɪs] unsterblich; **~·ly** [~lɪ] (*-ier, -iest*) tödlich; **~·war·rant** ⚖ Hinrichtungsbefehl *m; fig.* Todesurteil *n.*

de·bar [dɪ'bɑː] (*-rr-*): *~ from doing s.th. j-n* hindern et. zu tun.

de·base [dɪ'beɪs] erniedrigen.

de·ba·ta·ble □ [dɪ'beɪtəbl] strittig; umstritten; **de·bate** [dɪ'beɪt] **1.** Debatte *f*; **2.** debattieren; erörtern; sich *et.* überlegen.

de·bil·i·tate [dɪ'bɪlɪteɪt] schwächen.

deb·it *econ.* ['debɪt] **1.** Debet *n*, Soll *n;* (Konto)Belastung *f; ~ and credit* Soll *n* u. Haben *n;* **2.** *j-n*, *ein Konto* belasten.

deb·ris ['debriː] Trümmer *pl.*

debt [det] Schuld *f; be in ~* verschuldet sein; *be out of ~* schuldenfrei sein; **~·or** ['detə] Schuldner(in).

de·bug ⊕ [diː'bʌg] (*-gg-*) Fehler beseitigen (*a.* Computer).

de·bunk ['diː'bʌŋk] den Nimbus nehmen (*dat.*).

dé·but, *bsd. Am.* **de·but** ['deɪbuː] Debüt *n.*

dec·ade ['dekeɪd] Jahrzehnt *n.*

dec·a·dence ['dekədəns] Dekadenz *f*, Verfall *m;* **~·dent** [~t] dekadent.

de·caf·fein·at·ed [diː'kæfɪneɪtɪd] koffeinfrei.

de·camp [dɪ'kæmp] *bsd.* ✕ das Lager abbrechen; F verschwinden.

de·cant [dɪ'kænt] abgießen; umfüllen; **~·er** [~ə] Karaffe *f.*

de·cath·lete [dɪ'kæθliːt] *Sport:* Zehnkämpfer *m;* **~·lon** [~lɒn] *Sport:* Zehnkampf *m.*

de·cay [dɪ'keɪ] **1.** Verfall *m*; Zerfall *m;* Fäule *f*; **2.** verfallen; (ver)faulen.

de·cease bsd. 🕱 [dɪˈsiːs] **1.** Tod m, Ableben n; **2.** sterben; **~d** bsd. 🕱 **1.** the ~ der od. die Verstorbene; die Verstorbenen pl.; **2.** ver-, gestorben.

de·ceit [dɪˈsiːt] Täuschung f; Betrug m; **~·ful** □ [~fl] falsch; betrügerisch.

de·ceive [dɪˈsiːv] betrügen; täuschen; **~·ceiv·er** [~ə] Betrüger(in).

De·cem·ber [dɪˈsembə] Dezember m.

de·cen|cy [ˈdiːsnsɪ] Anstand m; **~t** □ [~t] anständig; F annehmbar, (ganz) anständig; F nett; ⚠ nicht dezent.

de·cep|tion [dɪˈsepʃn] Täuschung f; **~·tive** □ [~tɪv]: be ~ täuschen, trügen (Sache).

de·cide [dɪˈsaɪd] (sich) entscheiden; bestimmen; sich entschließen; **~·cid·ed** □ entschieden; bestimmt; entschlossen.

dec·i·mal [ˈdesɪml] a. ~ fraction Dezimalbruch m; attr. Dezimal...

de·ci·pher [dɪˈsaɪfə] entziffern.

de·ci|sion [dɪˈsɪʒn] Entscheidung f; Entschluß m; Entschlossenheit f; make a ~ e-e Entscheidung treffen; reach od. come to a ~ zu e-m Entschluß kommen; **~·sive** □ [dɪˈsaɪsɪv] entscheidend; ausschlaggebend; entschieden.

deck [dek] **1.** 🛥 Deck n (a. e-s Busses); Am. Pack m Spielkarten; Laufwerk n (e-s Plattenspielers); tape ~ Tapedeck n; **2.** ~ out schmücken; **~·chair** [ˈdektʃeə] Liegestuhl m.

de·claim [dɪˈkleɪm] deklamieren, vortragen.

de·clar·a·ble [dɪˈkleərəbl] zollpflichtig.

dec·la·ra·tion [dekləˈreɪʃn] Erklärung f; Zollerklärung f.

de·clare [dɪˈkleə] (sich) erklären, bekanntgeben; behaupten; deklarieren, verzollen.

de·clen·sion gr. [dɪˈklenʃn] Deklination f.

dec·li·na·tion [deklɪˈneɪʃn] Neigung f; Abweichung f; **de·cline** [dɪˈklaɪn] **1.** Abnahme f; Niedergang m, Verfall m; **2.** v/t. neigen; (höflich) ablehnen; gr. deklinieren; v/i. sich neigen; abnehmen; verfallen.

de·cliv·i·ty [dɪˈklɪvətɪ] Abhang m.

de·clutch mot. [ˈdiːˈklʌtʃ] auskuppeln.

de·code [ˈdiːˈkəʊd] entschlüsseln.

de·com·pose [diːkəmˈpəʊz] zerlegen; (sich) zersetzen; verwesen.

dec·o·rate [ˈdekəreɪt] verzieren, schmücken; tapezieren; (an)streichen; dekorieren; **~·ra·tion** [dekəˈreɪʃn] Verzierung f, Schmuck m, Dekoration f; Orden m; **~·ra·tive** □ [ˈdekərətɪv] dekorativ; Zier...; **~·ra·tor** [~reɪtə] Dekorateur m; Maler m u. Tapezierer m.

dec·o·rous □ [ˈdekərəs] anständig; **de·co·rum** [dɪˈkɔːrəm] Anstand m.

de·coy [dɪˈkɔɪ] **1.** Lockvogel m (a. fig.); Köder m (a. fig.); **2.** [dɪˈkɔɪ] ködern; locken (into in acc.); verleiten (into zu).

de·crease 1. [ˈdiːkriːs] Abnahme f; **2.** [diːˈkriːs] (sich) vermindern.

de·cree [dɪˈkriː] **1.** Dekret n, Verordnung f, Erlaß m; 🕱 Entscheid m; **2.** 🕱 entscheiden; verordnen, verfügen.

ded·i|cate [ˈdedɪkeɪt] widmen; **~·cat·ed** engagiert; **~·ca·tion** [dedɪˈkeɪʃn] Widmung f; Hingabe f.

de·duce [dɪˈdjuːs] ableiten; folgern.

de·duct [dɪˈdʌkt] abziehen; einbehalten; **de·duc·tion** [~kʃn] Abzug m; econ. a. Rabatt m; Schlußfolgerung f, Schluß m.

deed [diːd] **1.** Tat f; Heldentat f; 🕱 (Vertrags-, bsd. Übertragungs)Urkunde f; **2.** Am. 🕱 urkundlich übertragen (to dat., auf acc.).

deem [diːm] v/t. halten für; v/i. denken, urteilen (of über acc.).

deep [diːp] **1.** □ tief; gründlich; schlau; vertieft; dunkel (a. fig.); verborgen; **2.** Tiefe f; poet. Meer n; **~·en** [ˈdiːpən] (sich) vertiefen; (sich) verstärken; **~·freeze 1.** (-froze, -frozen) tiefkühlen, einfrieren; **2.** Tiefkühl-, Gefriergerät n; **3.** Tiefkühl..., Gefrier...; ~ cabinet Tiefkühl-, Gefriertruhe f; **~·fro·zen** tiefgefroren; ~ food Tiefkühlkost f; **~·fry** fritieren; **~·ness** [~nɪs] Tiefe f.

deer zo. [dɪə] Rotwild n; Hirsch m.

de·face [dɪˈfeɪs] entstellen, unkenntlich machen; ausstreichen.

def·a·ma·tion [defəˈmeɪʃn] Verleumdung f; **de·fame** [dɪˈfeɪm] verleumden.

de·fault [dɪˈfɔːlt] **1.** Nichterscheinen n vor Gericht; Sport: Nichtantreten n; econ. Verzug m; **2.** ~ on et. Verbindlichkeiten nicht nachkommen; im Verzug sein; nicht (vor Gericht) erscheinen; Sport: nicht antreten.

de·feat [dɪˈfiːt] **1.** Niederlage f; Besiegung *f*; Vereitelung *f*; **2.** besiegen; vereiteln, zunichte machen.

de·fect [dɪ'fekt] Defekt *m*, Fehler *m*; Mangel *m*; **de·fec·tive** □ [~ɪv] mangelhaft; schadhaft, defekt.

de·fence, *Am.* **de·fense** [dɪ'fens] Verteidigung *f*; Schutz *m*; *witness for the* ~ Entlastungszeuge *m*; **~·less** [~lɪs] schutzlos, wehrlos.

de·fend [dɪ'fend] (*from, against*) verteidigen (gegen), schützen (vor *dat.*, gegen); **de·fen·dant** [~ənt] Angeklagte(r *m*) *f*; Beklagte(r *m*) *f*; **de·fend·er** [~ə] Verteidiger(in).

de·fen·sive [dɪ'fensɪv] **1.** Defensive *f*, Verteidigung *f*, Abwehr *f*; **2.** □ defensiv; Verteidigungs..., Abwehr...

de·fer [dɪ'fɜː] (*-rr-*) auf-, verschieben; *Am.* ✕ (vom Wehrdienst) zurückstellen; sich fügen, nachgeben.

def·er·ence ['defərəns] Ehrerbietung *f*; Nachgiebigkeit *f*; **~·en·tial** □ [defə'renʃl] ehrerbietig.

de·fi·ance [dɪ'faɪəns] Herausforderung *f*; Trotz *m*; **~·ant** □ [~t] herausfordernd; trotzig.

de·fi·cien·cy [dɪ'fɪʃnsɪ] Unzulänglichkeit *f*; Mangel *m*; = *deficit*; **~·t** □ [~t] mangelhaft, unzureichend.

def·i·cit *econ.* ['defɪsɪt] Fehlbetrag *m*.

de·file **1.** ['diːfaɪl] Engpaß *m*; **2.** [dɪ'faɪl] beschmutzen.

de·fine [dɪ'faɪn] definieren; erklären, genau bestimmen; **def·i·nite** □ ['defɪnɪt] bestimmt; deutlich, genau; **def·i·ni·tion** [defɪ'nɪʃn] Definition *f*, (Begriffs)Bestimmung *f*, Erklärung *f*; **de·fin·i·tive** □ [dɪ'fɪnɪtɪv] endgültig; maßgeblich.

de·flect [dɪ'flekt] ablenken; abweichen.

de·form [dɪ'fɔːm] entstellen, verunstalten; **~ed** deformiert, verunstaltet; verwachsen; **de·for·mi·ty** [~ətɪ] Entstelltheit *f*; Mißbildung *f*.

de·fraud [dɪ'frɔːd] betrügen (*of* um).

de·frost [diː'frɒst] *v/t. Windschutzscheibe* entfrosten; *Kühlschrank etc.* abtauen; *Tiefkühlkost* auftauen; *v/i.* ab-, auftauen.

deft □ [deft] gewandt, flink.

de·fy [dɪ'faɪ] herausfordern; trotzen (*dat.*).

de·gen·e·rate **1.** [dɪ'dʒenəreɪt] entarten; **2.** □ [~rət] entartet.

deg·ra·da·tion [degrə'deɪʃn] Erniedrigung *f*; **de·grade** [dɪ'greɪd] *v/t.* erniedrigen, demütigen.

de·gree [dɪ'griː] Grad *m*; Stufe *f*, Schritt *m*; Rang *m*, Stand *m*; *by* ~*s* allmählich; *take one's* ~ e-n akademischen Grad erwerben, promovieren.

de·hy·drat·ed ['diː'haɪdreɪtɪd] Trocken...

de·i·fy ['diːɪfaɪ] vergöttern; vergöttlichen.

deign [deɪn] sich herablassen.

de·i·ty ['diːɪtɪ] Gottheit *f*.

de·ject·ed □ [dɪ'dʒektɪd] niedergeschlagen, mutlos, deprimiert; **~·tion** [~kʃn] Niedergeschlagenheit *f*.

de·lay [dɪ'leɪ] **1.** Aufschub *m*; Verzögerung *f*; **2.** *v/t.* ver-, aufschieben; verzögern; aufhalten; *v/i.* ~ *in doing s.th.* es verschieben, et. zu tun.

del·e·gate **1.** ['delɪgeɪt] abordnen; übertragen; **2.** [~gət] (*Am. parl.* Kongreß)Abgeordnete(r *m*) *f*; **~·ga·tion** [delɪ'geɪʃn] Abordnung *f*; *Am. parl.* Kongreßabgeordnete *pl.*

de·lete [dɪ'liːt] tilgen, (aus)streichen, (aus)radieren.

de·lib·e·rate [dɪ'lɪbəreɪt] *v/t.* überlegen, erwägen; *v/i.* nachdenken; beraten; □ [~rət] bedachtsam; wohlüberlegt; vorsätzlich; **~·ra·tion** [dɪlɪbə'reɪʃn] Überlegung *f*; Beratung *f*; Bedächtigkeit *f*.

del·i·ca·cy ['delɪkəsɪ] Delikatesse *f*, Leckerbissen *m*; Zartheit *f*; Schwächlichkeit *f*; Feingefühl *n*; **~·cate** □ [~kət] schmackhaft, lecker; zart; fein; schwach; heikel; empfindlich; feinfühlig; wählerisch; **~·ca·tes·sen** [delɪkə'tesn] Delikatessen *pl.*, Feinkost *f*; Delikatessen-, Feinkostgeschäft *f*.

de·li·cious □ [dɪ'lɪʃəs] köstlich.

de·light [dɪ'laɪt] **1.** Lust *f*, Freude *f*, Wonne *f*; **2.** entzücken, (sich) erfreuen; ~ *in* (große) Freude haben an (*dat.*); **~·ful** □ [~fl] entzückend.

de·lin·e·ate [dɪ'lɪnɪeɪt] entwerfen; schildern.

de·lin·quen·cy [dɪ'lɪŋkwənsɪ] Kriminalität *f*; Straftat *f*; **~t** [~t] **1.** straffällig; **2.** Straffällige(r *m*) *f*; *s. juvenile 1.*

de·lir·i·ous □ [dɪ'lɪrɪəs] 🏥 phantasierend; wahnsinnig; **~·um** [~əm] Delirium *n*.

de·liv·er [dɪ'lɪvə] befreien; über-, aus-, abliefern; *bsd. econ.* liefern; *Botschaft* ausrichten; äußern; *Rede etc.* halten; *Schlag* austeilen; werfen;

⚓ entbinden; *be ∼ed of a child* entbunden werden, entbinden; **∼ance** [∼rəns] Befreiung *f*; (Meinungs)Äußerung *f*; **∼er** [∼rə] Befreier(in); Überbringer(in); **∼y** [∼rɪ] (Ab-, Aus)Lieferung *f*; **⚓** Zustellung *f*; Übergabe *f*; Halten *n* (*e-r Rede etc.*); **⚓** Entbindung *f*; **∼y van** *Brt.* Lieferwagen *m*.

dell [del] kleines Tal.

de·lude [dɪ'luːd] täuschen; verleiten.

del·uge ['deljuːdʒ] **1.** Überschwemmung *f*; **2.** überschwemmen.

de·lu·sion [dɪ'luːʒn] Täuschung *f*, Verblendung *f*, Wahn *m*; **∼sive** □ [∼sɪv] trügerisch, täuschend.

de·mand [dɪ'mɑːnd] **1.** Verlangen *n*; Forderung *f*; Anforderung (*on an acc.*); Inanspruchnahme *f* (*on gen.*); *econ.* Nachfrage *f*, Bedarf *m*; **⚖** Rechtsanspruch *m*; **2.** verlangen, fordern; erfordern; **∼ing** □ [∼ɪŋ] fordernd; anspruchsvoll; schwierig.

de·mean [dɪ'miːn]: *∼ o.s.* sich benehmen; sich erniedrigen; **de·mea·no(u)r** [∼ə] Benehmen *n*.

de·ment·ed □ [dɪ'mentɪd] wahnsinnig.

dem·i- ['demɪ] Halb...

dem·i·john ['demɪdʒɒn] große Korbflasche, Glasballon *m*.

de·mil·i·ta·rize [diː'mɪlɪtəraɪz] entmilitarisieren.

de·mo·bi·lize [diː'məʊbɪlaɪz] demobilisieren.

de·moc·ra·cy [dɪ'mɒkrəsɪ] Demokratie *f*.

dem·o·crat ['deməkræt] Demokrat(in); **∼ic** [demə'krætɪk] (*∼ally*) demokratisch.

de·mol·ish [dɪ'mɒlɪʃ] demolieren; ab-, ein-, niederreißen; zerstören; **dem·o·li·tion** [demə'lɪʃn] Demolierung *f*; Niederreißen *n*, Abbruch *m*.

de·mon ['diːmən] Dämon *m*; Teufel *m*.

dem·on·strate ['demənstreɪt] anschaulich darstellen; beweisen; demonstrieren; **∼stra·tion** [demən'streɪʃn] Demonstration *f*; Kundgebung *f*; Demonstration *f*, Vorführung *f*; anschauliche Darstellung; Beweis *m*; (Gefühls)Äußerung *f*. **de·mon·stra·tive** □ [dɪ'mɒnstrətɪv] überzeugend; demonstrativ; *be ∼* s-e Gefühle (offen) zeigen; **∼stra·tor** ['demənstreɪtə] Demonstrant(in); Vorführer(in).

de·mote [diː'məʊt] degradieren.

de·mur [dɪ'mɜː] (*-rr-*) Einwendungen machen.

de·mure □ [dɪ'mjʊə] ernst; prüde.

den [den] Höhle *f*, Bau *m*; Bude *f*; Arbeitszimmer *n*.

de·ni·al [dɪ'naɪəl] Leugnen *n*; Verneinung *f*; abschlägige Antwort.

den·ims ['denɪmz] *pl.* Overall *m* od. Jeans *pl.* aus Köper

de·nom·i·na·tion [dɪnɒmɪ'neɪʃn] *eccl.* Sekte *f*; *eccl.* Konfession *f*; *econ.* Nennwert *m* (*von Banknoten etc.*).

de·note [dɪ'nəʊt] bezeichnen; bedeuten.

de·nounce [dɪ'naʊns] anzeigen; brandmarken; *Vertrag* kündigen.

dense □ [dens] (*∼r, ∼st*) dicht, dick (*Nebel*); beschränkt; **den·si·ty** ['densətɪ] Dichte *f*.

dent [dent] **1.** Beule *f*, Delle *f*; Kerbe *f*; **2.** ver-, einbeulen.

den·tal ['dentl] Zahn...; **∼ plaque** Zahnbelag *m*; **∼ plate** Zahnprothese *f*; **∼ surgeon** Zahnarzt *m*; **∼tist** [∼ɪst] Zahnarzt *m*, -ärztin *f*; **∼tures** [∼ʃəz] *pl.* (künstliches) Gebiß.

de·nun·ci·a·tion [dɪnʌnsɪ'eɪʃn] Anzeige *f*, Denunziation *f*; **∼tor** [dɪ'nʌnsɪeɪtə] Denunziant(in).

de·ny [dɪ'naɪ] ab-, bestreiten, (ab)leugnen; verweigern, abschlagen; *j-n* abweisen.

de·part [dɪ'pɑːt] abreisen; abfahren, abfliegen; abweichen.

de·part·ment [dɪ'pɑːtmənt] Abteilung *f*; Bezirk *m*; *econ.* Branche *f*; *pol.* Ministerium *n*; **♀ of Defense** *Am.* Verteidigungsministerium *n*; **♀ of the Environment** *Brt.* Umweltschutzministerium *n*; **♀ of the Interior** *Am.* Innenministerium *n*; **♀ of State** *Am.*, **State ♀** *Am.* Außenministerium *n*; **∼ store** Warenhaus *n*.

de·par·ture [dɪ'pɑːtʃə] Abreise *f*, **⚓** etc. Abfahrt *f*, **✈** Abflug *m*; Abweichung *f*; **∼ gate ✈** Flugsteig *m*; **∼ lounge ✈** Abflughalle *f*.

de·pend [dɪ'pend]: *∼ on*, *∼ upon* abhängen von; angewiesen sein auf (*acc.*); sich verlassen auf (*acc.*); ankommen auf (*acc.*); *it ∼s* **F** es kommt (ganz) darauf an.

de·pen·da·ble [dɪ'pendəbl] zuverlässig; **∼dant** [∼ənt] Abhängige(r *m*) *f*, *bsd.* (Familien)Angehörige(r *m*) *f*; **∼dence** [∼əns] Abhängigkeit *f*; Vertrauen *n*; **∼den·cy** [∼ənsɪ] *pol.*

desire

Schutzgebiet *n*; **~dent** [~ənt] **1.** □ (*on*) abhängig (von); angewiesen (auf *acc.*); **2.** *Am.* = *dependant*.

de·pict [dɪˈpɪkt] darstellen; schildern.

de·plor|a·ble □ [dɪˈplɔːrəbl] bedauerlich, beklagenswert; **~e** [dɪˈplɔː] beklagen, bedauern.

de·pop·u·late [diːˈpɒpjʊleɪt] (sich) entvölkern.

de·port [dɪˈpɔːt] *Ausländer* abschieben; **~** *o.s.* sich *gut etc.* benehmen; **~ment** [~mənt] Benehmen *n*.

de·pose [dɪˈpəʊz] absetzen; ♌ unter Eid aussagen.

de·pos|it [dɪˈpɒzɪt] **1.** Ablagerung *f*; Lager *n*; (*Bank*)Einlage *f*; Hinterlegung *f*; Anzahlung *f*; **make a ~** e-e Anzahlung leisten; **~ account** *Brt.* Termineinlagekonto *n*; **2.** (nieder-, ab-, hin)legen; *Geld* einzahlen; *Betrag* anzahlen; hinterlegen; (sich) ablagern; **dep·o·si·tion** [depəˈzɪʃn] Absetzung *f*; (zu Protokoll gegebene) eidliche Aussage; **~i·tor** [dɪˈpɒzɪtə] Hinterleger(in); Einzahler(in); Kontoinhaber(in).

dep·ot [ˈdepəʊ] Depot *n*; Lagerhaus *n*; *Am.* [ˈdiːpəʊ] Bahnhof *m*.

de·prave [dɪˈpreɪv] moralisch verderben.

de·pre·ci·ate [dɪˈpriːʃɪeɪt] *Wert* mindern.

de·press [dɪˈpres] (nieder)drücken; *Preise etc.* senken, drücken; deprimieren, bedrücken; **~ed** deprimiert, niedergeschlagen; **de·pres·sion** [~eʃn] Vertiefung *f*, Senke *f*; Depression *f*, Niedergeschlagenheit *f*; *econ.* Depression *f*, Flaute *f*, Wirtschaftskrise *f*; ♋ Schwäche *f*.

de·prive [dɪˈpraɪv]: **~** *s.o. of s.th.* j-m et. entziehen *od.* nehmen; **~d** benachteiligt, unterprivilegiert.

depth [depθ] Tiefe *f*; *attr.* Tiefen...

dep·u·ta·tion [depjʊˈteɪʃn] Abordnung *f*; **~tize** [ˈdepjʊtaɪz]: **~** *for s.o.* j-n vertreten; **~ty** [~ɪ] *parl.* Abgeordnete(r *m*) *f*; Stellvertreter(in), Beauftragte(r *m*) *f*; Bevollmächtigte(r *m* *f*); *a.* **~ sheriff** *Am.* Hilfssheriff *m*.

de·rail 🚊 [dɪˈreɪl] *v/i.* entgleisen; *v/t.* zum Entgleisen bringen.

de·range [dɪˈreɪndʒ] in Unordnung bringen; stören; verrückt *od.* wahnsinnig machen; **~d** geistesgestört.

der·e·lict [ˈderəlɪkt] verlassen; nachlässig.

de·ride [dɪˈraɪd] verlachen, -spotten; **de·ri·sion** [dɪˈrɪʒn] Hohn *m*, Spott *m*; **de·ri·sive** □ [dɪˈraɪsɪv] spöttisch, höhnisch.

de·rive [dɪˈraɪv] herleiten; *et.* gewinnen (*from* aus); *Nutzen etc.* ziehen (*from* aus).

de·rog·a·to·ry □ [dɪˈrɒgətərɪ] abfällig, geringschätzig.

der·rick [ˈderɪk] ⊕ Derrickkran *m*; ♎ Ladebaum *m*; Bohrturm *m*.

de·scend [dɪˈsend] (her-, hin)absteigen, herunter-, hinuntersteigen, herabkommen; ✈ niedergehen; (ab)stammen; **~ on**, **~ upon** herfallen über (*acc.*); einfallen in (*acc.*); **de·scen·dant** [~ənt] Nachkomme *m*.

de·scent [dɪˈsent] Herab-, Hinuntersteigen *n*, Abstieg *m*; ✈ Niedergehen *n*; Abhang *m*, Gefälle *n*; Abstammung *f*; *fig.* Niedergang *m*, Abstieg *m*.

de·scribe [dɪˈskraɪb] beschreiben.

de·scrip|tion [dɪˈskrɪpʃn] Beschreibung *f*, Schilderung *f*; Art *f*; **~tive** □ [~tɪv] beschreibend; anschaulich.

des·e·crate [ˈdesɪkreɪt] entweihen.

des·eg·re·gate [diːˈsegrɪgeɪt] die Rassentrennung aufheben in (*dat.*).

des·ert[1] [ˈdezət] **1.** Wüste *f*; **2.** wüsten...

de·sert[2] [dɪˈzɜːt] *v/t.* verlassen; *v/i.* desertieren; **~er** ✗ [~ə] Deserteur *m*, Fahnenflüchtige(r) *m*; **de·ser·tion** [~ʃn] (♌ *a.* böswilliges) Verlassen; ✗ Fahnenflucht *f*.

de·serve [dɪˈzɜːv] verdienen; **de·serv·ed·ly** [~ɪdlɪ] mit Recht; **de·serv·ing** [~ɪŋ] würdig (*of gen.*); verdienstvoll, verdient.

de·sign [dɪˈzaɪn] **1.** Plan *m*; Entwurf *m*, Zeichnung *f*; Muster *n*; Vorhaben *n*, Absicht *f*; *have* **~s** *on od.* *against* et. (*Böses*) im Schilde führen gegen; **2.** entwerfen, ⊕ konstruieren; gestalten; planen; bestimmen.

des·ig·nate [ˈdezɪgneɪt] bezeichnen; ernennen, bestimmen; **~na·tion** [dezɪgˈneɪʃn] Bezeichnung *f*; Bestimmung *f*, Ernennung *f*.

de·sign·er [dɪˈzaɪnə] (Muster)Zeichner(in); Designer(in); ⊕ Konstrukteur *m*; (Mode)Schöpfer(in).

de·sir|a·ble □ [dɪˈzaɪərəbl] wünschenswert; angenehm; **~e** [dɪˈzaɪə]

1. Wunsch *m*, Verlangen *n*; Begierde *f*; **2.** verlangen, wünschen; begehren; **~ous** □ [~rəs] begierig.

de·sist [dɪˈzɪst] ablassen (*from* von).

desk [desk] Pult *n*; Schreibtisch *m*.

des·o·late □ [ˈdesələt] einsam; verlassen; öde.

de·spair [dɪˈspeə] **1.** Verzweiflung *f*; **2.** verzweifeln (*of* an *dat.*); **~ing** □ [~rɪŋ] verzweifelt.

de·spatch [dɪˈspætʃ] = dispatch.

des·per|ate □ [ˈdespərət] verzweifelt; hoffnungslos; F schrecklich; **~a·tion** [despəˈreɪʃn] Verzweiflung *f*.

des·pic·a·ble □ [ˈdespɪkəbl] verachtenswert, verabscheuungswürdig.

de·spise [dɪˈspaɪz] verachten.

de·spite [dɪˈspaɪt] **1.** Verachtung *f*; *in ~ of* zum Trotz, trotz; **2.** *prp. a. ~ of* trotz.

de·spon·dent □ [dɪˈspɒndənt] mutlos, verzagt.

des·pot [ˈdespɒt] Despot *m*, Tyrann *m*; **~is·m** [~pɒtɪzəm] Despotismus *m*.

des·sert [dɪˈzɜːt] Nachtisch *m*, Dessert *n*; *attr.* Dessert...

des|ti·na·tion [destɪˈneɪʃn] Bestimmung(sort *m*) *f*; **~tined** [ˈdestɪnd] bestimmt; **~ti·ny** [~ɪ] Schicksal *n*.

des·ti·tute □ [ˈdestɪtjuːt] mittellos, notleidend; *~ of* bar (*gen.*), ohne.

de·stroy [dɪˈstrɔɪ] zerstören, vernichten; töten, *Tier a.* einschläfern; **~er** [~ə] Zerstörer(in); ♣ ✕ Zerstörer *m*.

de·struc·tion [dɪˈstrʌkʃn] Zerstörung *f*, Vernichtung *f*; Tötung *f*, *e-s Tiers a.* Einschläferung *f*; **~tive** □ [~tɪv] zerstörend, vernichtend; zerstörerisch.

des·ul·to·ry □ [ˈdesəltərɪ] unstet; planlos; oberflächlich.

de·tach [dɪˈtætʃ] losmachen, (ab)lösen; absondern; ✕ abkommandieren; **~ed** einzeln (stehend); unvoreingenommen; distanziert; **~ment** [~mənt] Loslösung *f*; (Ab)Trennung *f*; ✕ (Sonder)Kommando *n*.

de·tail [ˈdiːteɪl] **1.** Detail *n*, Einzelheit *f*; eingehende Darstellung; ✕ (Sonder)Kommando *n*; *in ~* ausführlich; **2.** genau schildern; ✕ abkommandieren; **~ed** detailliert, ausführlich.

de·tain [dɪˈteɪn] aufhalten; *j-n* in (Untersuchungs)Haft (be)halten.

de·tect [dɪˈtekt] entdecken; (auf)finden; **de·tec·tion** [~kʃn] Entdeckung

f; **de·tec·tive** [~tɪv] Kriminalbeamte(r) *m*, Detektiv *m*; *~ novel*, *~ story* Kriminalroman *m*.

de·ten·tion [dɪˈtenʃn] Vorenthaltung *f*; Aufhaltung *f*; Haft *f*.

de·ter [dɪˈtɜː] (*-rr-*) abschrecken (*from* von).

de·ter·gent [dɪˈtɜːdʒənt] Reinigungsmittel *n*; Waschmittel *n*; Geschirrspülmittel *n*.

de·te·ri·o·rate [dɪˈtɪərɪəreɪt] (sich) verschlechtern; verderben; entarten.

de·ter|mi·na·tion [dɪtɜːmɪˈneɪʃn] Entschlossenheit *f*; Entscheidung *f*, Entschluß *m*; **~mine** [dɪˈtɜːmɪn] bestimmen; (sich) entscheiden; sich entschließen; **~mined** entschlossen.

de·ter|rence [dɪˈterəns] Abschreckung *f*; **~rent** [~t] **1.** abschreckend; **2.** Abschreckungsmittel *n*.

de·test [dɪˈtest] verabscheuen; **~a·ble** □ [~əbl] abscheulich.

de·throne [dɪˈθrəun] entthronen.

de·to·nate [ˈdetəneɪt] explodieren (lassen).

de·tour [ˈdiːtuə] Umweg *m*; Umleitung *f*.

de·tract [dɪˈtrækt]: *~ from s.th.* et. beeinträchtigen, et. schmälern.

de·tri·ment [ˈdetrɪmənt] Schaden *m*.

deuce [djuːs] Zwei *f* (*im Spiel*); *Tennis:* Einstand *m*; F Teufel *m*; *how the ~* wie zum Teufel.

de·val·u·a·tion [diːvæljuˈeɪʃn] Abwertung *f*; **~e** [ˈdiːˈvæljuː] abwerten.

dev·a·state [ˈdevəsteɪt] verwüsten; **~stat·ing** □ [~ɪŋ] verheerend, -nichtend; F umwerfend; **~sta·tion** [devəˈsteɪʃn] Verwüstung *f*.

de·vel·op [dɪˈveləp] (sich) entwickeln; (sich) entfalten; *Gelände* erschließen; *Altstadt etc.* sanieren; ausbauen; (sich) zeigen; **~er** [~ə] *phot.* Entwickler *m*; (Stadt)Planer *m*; **~ing** [~ɪŋ] Entwicklungs...; *~ country econ.* Entwicklungsland *n*; **~ment** [~mənt] Entwicklung *f*; Entfaltung *f*; Erschließung *f*; Ausbau *m*; *~ aid econ.* Entwicklungshilfe *f*.

de·vi|ate [ˈdiːvɪeɪt] abweichen; **~a·tion** [diːvɪˈeɪʃn] Abweichung *f*.

de·vice [dɪˈvaɪs] Vor-, Einrichtung *f*, Gerät *n*; Erfindung *f*; Plan *m*; Kunstgriff *m*, Kniff *m*; Devise *f*, Motto *n*; *leave s.o. to his own ~s* j-n sich selbst überlassen.

dev·il ['devl] Teufel m (a. fig.); **~ish** □ [~ɪʃ] teuflisch.

de·vi·ous □ ['diːvjəs] abwegig; gewunden; unaufrichtig; take a ~ route e-n Umweg machen.

de·vise □ [dɪ'vaɪz] ausdenken, ersinnen; ⚖ vermachen.

de·void [dɪ'vɔɪd]: ~ of bar (gen.), ohne.

de·vote □ [dɪ'vəʊt] widmen, et. hingeben, opfern (to dat.); △ nicht devot; **de·vot·ed** □ ergeben; eifrig, begeistert; zärtlich; **dev·o·tee** [devəʊ'tiː] begeisterter Anhänger; **de·vo·tion** [dɪ'vəʊʃn] Ergebenheit f; Hingabe f; Frömmigkeit f, Andacht f.

de·vour [dɪ'vaʊə] verschlingen.

de·vout □ [dɪ'vaʊt] andächtig; fromm; sehnlichst.

dew [djuː] Tau m; **~·y** ['djuːɪ] (-ier, -iest) (tau)feucht.

dex·ter·i·ty [dek'sterɪtɪ] Gewandtheit f; **~·ter·ous**, **~·trous** □ ['dekstrəs] gewandt.

di·ag·nose ['daɪəgnəʊz] diagnostizieren; **~·no·sis** [daɪəg'nəʊsɪs] (pl. -ses [-siːz]) Diagnose f.

di·a·gram ['daɪəgræm] graphische Darstellung, Schema n, Plan m.

di·al ['daɪəl] 1. Zifferblatt n; teleph. Wählscheibe f; ⊕ Skala f; 2. (bsd. Brt. -ll-, Am. -l-) teleph. wählen; ~ direct durchwählen (to nach); direct ~(l)ing Durchwahl f.

di·a·lect ['daɪəlekt] Dialekt m; Mundart f.

di·a·logue, Am. **-log** ['daɪəlɒg] Dialog m, Gespräch n.

di·am·e·ter [daɪ'æmɪtə] Durchmesser m; in ~ im Durchmesser.

di·a·mond ['daɪəmənd] Diamant m; Rhombus m; Baseball: Spielfeld n; Karten: Karo n.

di·a·per Am. ['daɪəpə] Windel f.

di·a·phragm ['daɪəfræm] anat. Zwerchfell n; opt. Blende f; teleph. Membran(e) f.

di·ar·rh(o)e·a ⚕ [daɪə'rɪə] Durchfall m.

di·a·ry ['daɪərɪ] Tagebuch n.

dice [daɪs] 1. pl. von die²; 2. würfeln; **~·box** ['daɪsbɒks], **~·cup** Würfelbecher m.

dick Am. sl. [dɪk] Schnüffler m (Detektiv).

dick·(e)y(-bird) ['dɪkɪ(bɜːd)] Piepvögelchen n.

dic|tate [dɪk'teɪt] diktieren; fig. vor-

schreiben; **~·ta·tion** [~ʃn] Diktat n.

dic·ta·tor [dɪk'teɪtə] Diktator m; **~·ship** [~ʃɪp] Diktatur f.

dic·tion ['dɪkʃn] Ausdruck(sweise f) m, Stil m.

dic·tion·a·ry ['dɪkʃnrɪ] Wörterbuch n.

did [dɪd] pret. von do.

die¹ [daɪ] sterben; umkommen; untergehen; absterben; ~ away sich legen (Wind); verklingen (Ton); verlöschen (Licht); ~ down nachlassen; herunterbrennen; schwächer werden; ~ off wegsterben, ~ out aussterben (a. fig.).

die² [~] (pl. dice [daɪs]) Würfel m; (pl. dies [daɪz]) Prägestock m, -stempel m.

die-hard ['daɪhɑːd] Reaktionär m.

di·et ['daɪət] 1. Diät f; Nahrung f, Kost f; be on a ~ diät leben; 2. diät leben.

dif·fer ['dɪfə] sich unterscheiden; anderer Meinung sein (with, from als); abweichen.

dif·fe·rence ['dɪfrəns] Unterschied m; Differenz f; Meinungsverschiedenheit f; **~·rent** □ [~t] verschieden; andere(r, -s); ~ (from als); **~·ren·ti·ate** [dɪfə'renʃɪeɪt] (sich) unterscheiden.

dif·fi·cult ['dɪfɪkəlt] schwierig; **~·cul·ty** [~ɪ] Schwierigkeit f.

dif·fi·dence ['dɪfɪdəns] Schüchternheit f; **~·dent** □ [~t] schüchtern.

dif|fuse fig. [dɪ'fjuːz] verbreiten; 2. □ [~s] weitverbreitet, zerstreut (bsd. Licht); weitschweifig; **~·fu·sion** [~ʒn] Verbreitung f.

dig [dɪg] 1. (-gg-; dug) graben (in dat.); oft ~ up umgraben; oft ~ up, ~ out ausgraben (a. fig.); 2. F Ausgrabung(sstätte) f; F Puff m, Stoß m; ~s pl. Brt. F Bude f, (Studenten)Zimmer n.

di·gest 1. [dɪ'dʒest] v/t. verdauen (a. fig.); ordnen; v/i. verdauen; verdaulich sein; 2. ['daɪdʒest] Abriß m; Auslese f, Auswahl f; **~·i·ble** [dɪ'dʒestəbl] verdaulich; **di·ges·tion** [~tʃən] Verdauung f; **di·ges·tive** □ [~tɪv] verdauungsfördernd.

dig·ger ['dɪgə] (bsd. Gold)Gräber m.

di·git ['dɪdʒɪt] Ziffer f; three-~ number dreistellige Zahl; **di·gi·tal** □ [~tl] digital, Digital...; ~ clock, ~ watch Digitaluhr f.

dig·ni·fied ['dɪgnɪfaɪd] würdevoll, würdig.

dig·ni·ta·ry ['dɪgnɪtərɪ] Würdenträger(in).

dig·ni·ty ['dɪgnɪtɪ] Würde f.

di·gress [daɪ'gres] abschweifen.

dike¹ [daɪk] **1.** Deich m, Damm m; Graben m; **2.** eindeichen, -dämmen.

dike² sl. [~] Lesbe f (Lesbierin).

di·lap·i·dat·ed [dɪ'læpɪdeɪtɪd] verfallen, baufällig, klapp(e)rig.

di·late [daɪ'leɪt] (sich) ausdehnen; Augen weit öffnen; **dil·a·to·ry** □ ['dɪlətərɪ] verzögernd, hinhaltend; aufschiebend; langsam.

dil·i·gence ['dɪlɪdʒəns] Fleiß m; **~gent** [~nt] fleißig, emsig.

di·lute [daɪ'ljuːt] **1.** verdünnen; verwässern; **2.** verdünnt.

dim [dɪm] **1.** □ (-mm-) trüb(e); dunkel; matt; **2.** (-mm-) (sich) verdunkeln; abblenden; (sich) trüben; matt werden.

dime Am. [daɪm] Zehncentstück n.

di·men·sion [dɪ'menʃn] Dimension f, Abmessung f; **~s** pl. a. Ausmaß n; **~al** [~ʃnl] dimensional; **three-~** dreidimensional.

di·min·ish [dɪ'mɪnɪʃ] (sich) vermindern; abnehmen.

di·min·u·tive □ [dɪ'mɪnjʊtɪv] klein, winzig.

dim·ple ['dɪmpl] Grübchen n.

din [dɪn] Getöse n, Lärm m.

dine [daɪn] essen, speisen; bewirten; **~** in od. out zu Hause od. auswärts essen; **din·er** ['daɪnə] Speisende(r m) f; Gast m (im Restaurant); bsd. Am. 🚪 Speisewagen m; Am. Speiselokal n.

din·gy □ ['dɪndʒɪ] (-ier, -iest) schmutzig.

din·ing | **car** 🚪 ['daɪnɪŋkɑː] Speisewagen m; **~ room** Eß-, Speisezimmer n.

din·ner ['dɪnə] (Mittag-, Abend)Essen n; Festessen n; **~jack·et** Smoking m; **~par·ty** Tischgesellschaft f; **~ser·vice**, **~set** Speiseservice n, Tafelgeschirr n.

dint [dɪnt] **1.** Beule f; by **~** of kraft, vermöge (gen.); **2.** ver-, einbeulen.

dip [dɪp] **1.** (-pp-) v/t. (ein)tauchen; senken; schöpfen; **~** the headlights bsd. Brt. mot. abblenden; v/i. (unter)tauchen; sinken; sich neigen, sich senken; **2.** (Ein-, Unter)Tauchen n; F kurzes Bad; Senkung f,

Neigung f, Gefälle n; Dip m (Soße).

diph·ther·i·a 🩺 [dɪf'θɪərɪə] Diphtherie f.

di·plo·ma [dɪ'pləʊmə] Diplom n.

di·plo·ma·cy [dɪ'pləʊməsɪ] Diplomatie f.

dip·lo·mat ['dɪpləmæt] Diplomat m; **~ic** [dɪplə'mætɪk] (~ally) diplomatisch.

di·plo·ma·tist fig. [dɪ'pləʊmətɪst] Diplomat(in).

dip·per ['dɪpə] Schöpfkelle f.

dire ['daɪə] (~r, ~st) gräßlich, schrecklich.

di·rect [dɪ'rekt] **1.** adj. □ direkt; gerade; unmittelbar; offen, aufrichtig; **~ current** 𝄐 Gleichstrom m; **~ train** durchgehender Zug; **2.** adv. direkt, unmittelbar; **3.** richten; lenken, steuern; leiten; anordnen; j-n anweisen; j-m den Weg zeigen; Brief adressieren; Regie führen bei.

di·rec·tion [dɪ'rekʃn] Richtung f; Leitung f, Führung f; Adresse f (e-s Briefes etc.); Film etc.: Regie f; mst **~s** pl. Anweisung f, Anleitung f; **~s for use** Gebrauchsanweisung f; △ nicht Direktion; **~find·er** [~faɪndə] (Funk)Peiler m, Peilempfänger m; **~in·di·ca·tor** mot. Fahrtrichtungsanzeiger m, Blinker m; 🚪 Kursweiser m.

di·rec·tive [dɪ'rektɪv] richtungweisend, leitend.

di·rect·ly [dɪ'rektlɪ] **1.** adv. sofort; **2.** cj. sobald, sowie.

di·rec·tor [dɪ'rektə] Direktor m; Film etc.: Regisseur m; board of **~s** Aufsichtsrat m.

di·rec·to·ry [dɪ'rektərɪ] Adreßbuch n; telephone **~** Telefonbuch n.

dirge [dɜːdʒ] Klagelied n.

dir·i·gi·ble ['dɪrɪdʒəbl] **1.** lenkbar; **2.** lenkbares Luftschiff.

dirt [dɜːt] Schmutz m; (lockere) Erde; **~cheap** F ['dɜːt'tʃiːp] spottbillig; **~y** [~ɪ] **1.** □ (-ier, -iest) schmutzig (a. fig.); **2.** beschmutzen; schmutzig werden.

dis·a·bil·i·ty [dɪsə'bɪlətɪ] Unfähigkeit f.

dis·a·ble [dɪs'eɪbl] (✕ kampf)unfähig machen; ✕ dienstuntauglich machen; **~d** **1.** arbeits-, erwerbsunfähig, invalid(e); ✕ dienstuntauglich; ✕ kriegsversehrt; körperlich od. geistig behindert; **2.** the **~** pl. die Behinderten pl.

dis·ad·van|tage [dɪsəd'vɑ:ntɪdʒ] Nachteil *m*; Schaden *m*; **~ta·geous** □ [dɪsædvɑ:n'teɪdʒəs] nachteilig, ungünstig.

dis·a·gree [dɪsə'gri:] nicht übereinstimmen; uneinig sein; nicht bekommen (*with s.o.* j-m); **~a·ble** □ [~ɪəbl] unangenehm; **~ment** [~ɪːmənt] Verschiedenheit *f*, Unstimmigkeit *f*; Meinungsverschiedenheit *f*.

dis·ap·pear [dɪsə'pɪə] verschwinden; **~ance** [~rəns] Verschwinden *n*.

dis·ap·point [dɪsə'pɔɪnt] j-n enttäuschen; *Hoffnungen etc.* zunichte machen; **~ment** [~mənt] Enttäuschung *f*.

dis·ap·prov|al [dɪsə'pru:vl] Mißbilligung *f*; **~e** ['dɪsə'pru:v] mißbilligen; dagegen sein.

dis|arm [dɪs'ɑ:m] *v/t.* entwaffnen (*a. fig.*); *v/i.* ⚔ *pol.* abrüsten; **~ar·ma·ment** [~əmənt] Entwaffnung *f*; ⚔ *pol.* Abrüstung *f*.

dis·ar·range ['dɪsə'reɪndʒ] in Unordnung bringen.

dis·ar·ray ['dɪsə'reɪ] Unordnung *f*.

dis|as·ter [dɪ'zɑːstə] Unglück(sfall *m*) *n*, Katastrophe *f*; **~trous** □ [~trəs] katastrophal, verheerend.

dis·band [dɪs'bænd] (sich) auflösen.

dis·be|lief [dɪsbɪ'liːf] Unglaube *m*; Zweifel *m* (*in* an *dat.*); **~lieve** [~.iːv] *et.* bezweifeln, nicht glauben.

disc [dɪsk] Scheibe *f* (*a. anat.*, *zo.*, ⊕); (Schall)Platte *f*; Parkscheibe *f*; △ *nicht Diskus*; *slipped ~* 🦴 Bandscheibenvorfall *m*.

dis·card [dɪ'skɑːd] *Karten, Kleid etc.* ablegen; *Freund etc.* fallenlassen.

dis·cern [dɪ'sɜːn] wahrnehmen, erkennen; **~ing** □ [~ɪŋ] kritisch, scharfsichtig; **~ment** [~mənt] Einsicht *f*; Scharfblick *m*; Wahrnehmen *n*.

dis·charge [dɪs'tʃɑːdʒ] **1.** *v/t.* ent-, ausladen; *j-n* befreien, entbinden; *j-n* entlassen; *Gewehr etc.* abfeuern; von sich geben, ausströmen, -senden; 🦴 absondern; *Pflicht etc.* erfüllen; *Zorn etc.* auslassen (*on* an *dat.*); *Schuld* bezahlen; *Wechsel* einlösen; *v/i.* sich entladen (*sich* ergießen, münden (*Fluß*)); 🦴 eitern; **2.** Entladung *f* (*e-s Schiffes etc.*); Abfeuern *n* (*e-s Gewehrs etc.*); Ausströmen *n*; 🦴 Absonderung *f*; ⚡ Ausfluß *m*; Ausstoßen *n*; ⚡ Entladung *f*; Entlassung

f; Entlastung *f*; Erfüllung *f* (*e-r Pflicht*).

di·sci·ple [dɪ'saɪpl] Schüler *m*; Jünger *m*.

dis·ci·pline ['dɪsɪplɪn] **1.** Disziplin *f*; Bestrafung *f*; **2.** disziplinieren; bestrafen; *well ~d* diszipliniert; *badly ~d* disziplinlos, undiszipliniert.

disc jock·ey ['dɪskdʒɒkɪ] Disk-, Discjockey *m*.

dis·claim [dɪs'kleɪm] ab-, bestreiten; *Verantwortung* ablehnen; 🏛 verzichten auf (*acc.*).

dis·close [dɪs'kləʊz] bekanntgeben, -machen; enthüllen, aufdecken; **~clo·sure** [~əʊʒə] Enthüllung *f*.

dis·co F ['dɪskəʊ] **1.** (*pl.* -cos) Disko *f* (*Diskothek*); **2.** Disko...; *~ sound* Diskosound *m*.

dis·col·o(u)r [dɪs'kʌlə] (sich) verfärben.

dis·com·fort [dɪs'kʌmfət] **1.** Unbehagen *n*; Beschwerden *pl.*; **2.** j-m Unbehagen verursachen.

dis·con·cert [dɪskən'sɜːt] aus der Fassung bringen.

dis·con·nect ['dɪskə'nekt] trennen (*a.* ⚡); ⚡ auskuppeln; ⚡ *Gerät* abschalten; *Gas, Strom, Telefon* abstellen; *teleph. Gespräch* unterbrechen; **~ed** □ zusammenhang(s)los.

dis·con·so·late □ [dɪs'kɒnsələt] untröstlich, tieftraurig.

dis·con·tent ['dɪskən'tent] Unzufriedenheit *f*; **~ed** □ unzufrieden.

dis·con·tin·ue ['dɪskən'tɪnjuː] aufgeben, aufhören mit; unterbrechen.

dis·cord ['dɪskɔːd], **~ance** [~dəns] Uneinigkeit *f*; ♪ Mißklang *m*; **~ant** □ [~t] nicht übereinstimmend; ♪ unharmonisch, mißtönend.

dis·co·theque ['dɪskətek] Diskothek *f*.

dis·count ['dɪskaʊnt] **1.** *econ.* Diskont *m*; Abzug *m*, Rabatt *m*; **2.** *econ.* diskontieren; abziehen, abrechnen; *Nachricht* mit Vorsicht aufnehmen.

dis·cour·age [dɪs'kʌrɪdʒ] entmutigen; abschrecken; **~ment** [~mənt] Entmutigung *f*; Hindernis *n*, Schwierigkeit *f*.

dis·course 1. ['dɪskɔːs] Rede *f*; Abhandlung *f*; Predigt *f*; **2.** [dɪ'skɔːs] e-n Vortrag halten (*on, upon* über *acc.*).

dis·cour·te|ous □ [dɪs'kɜːtjəs] unhöflich; **~sy** [~təsɪ] Unhöflichkeit *f*.

dis·cov|er [dɪ'skʌvə] entdecken; ausfindig machen; feststellen; **~e·ry** [~ərɪ] Entdeckung *f*.

dis·cred·it [dɪs'kredɪt] **1.** Zweifel *m*; Mißkredit *m*, schlechter Ruf; **2.** nicht glauben; in Mißkredit bringen.

di·screet [dɪ'skriːt] □ besonnen, vorsichtig; diskret, verschwiegen.

di·screp·an·cy [dɪ'skrepənsɪ] Widerspruch *m*, Unstimmigkeit *f*.

di·scre·tion [dɪ'skreʃn] Besonnenheit *f*, Klugheit *f*; Takt *m*; Verschwiegenheit *f*; Belieben *n*.

di·scrim·i·nate [dɪ'skrɪmɪneɪt] unterscheiden; *~ against* benachteiligen; **~·nat·ing** □ [~ɪŋ] unterscheidend; kritisch, urteilsfähig; **~·na·tion** [dɪskrɪmɪ'neɪʃn] Unterscheidung *f*; unterschiedliche (*bsd.* nachteilige) Behandlung; Urteilskraft *f*.

dis·cus [ˈdɪskəs] *Sport*: Diskus *m*; *~ throw* Diskuswerfen *n*; *~ thrower* Diskuswerfer(in).

di·scuss [dɪ'skʌs] diskutieren, erörtern, besprechen; **di·scus·sion** [~ʌʃn] Diskussion *f*, Besprechung *f*.

dis·dain [dɪs'deɪn] **1.** Verachtung *f*; **2.** geringschätzen, verachten; verschmähen.

dis·ease [dɪ'ziːz] Krankheit *f*; **~d** krank.

dis·em·bark [ˈdɪsɪm'baːk] *v/t.* ausschiffen; *v/i.* von Bord gehen.

dis·en·chant·ed [dɪsɪn'tʃaːntɪd]: *be ~ with* sich keinen Illusionen mehr hingeben über (*acc.*).

dis·en·gage [ˈdɪsɪn'ɡeɪdʒ] (sich) freimachen *od.* lösen; ⊕ loskuppeln.

dis·en·tan·gle [ˈdɪsɪn'tæŋɡl] entwirren; herauslösen (*from* aus).

dis·fa·vo(u)r [dɪs'feɪvə] Mißfallen *n*; Ungnade *f*.

dis·fig·ure [dɪs'fɪɡə] entstellen.

dis·grace [dɪs'ɡreɪs] **1.** Ungnade *f*; Schande *f*; **2.** Schande bringen über (*acc.*), *j-m* Schande bereiten; *be ~d* in Ungnade fallen; **~·ful** □ [~fl] schändlich; skandalös.

dis·guise [dɪs'ɡaɪz] **1.** verkleiden (*as* als); verstellen; verschleiern, -bergen; **2.** Verkleidung *f*; Verstellung *f*; Verschleierung *f*; *thea. u. fig.* Maske *f*; *in ~* maskiert, verkleidet; *fig.* verkappt; *in the ~ of* verkleidet als.

dis·gust [dɪs'ɡʌst] **1.** Ekel *m*, Abscheu *m*; **2.** (an)ekeln; empören, entrüsten; **~·ing** □ [~ɪŋ] ekelhaft.

dish [dɪʃ] **1.** flache Schüssel; (Ser-

vier)Platte *f*; Gericht *n*, Speise *f*; *the ~es pl.* das Geschirr; **2.** *mst ~ up* anrichten; auftischen, -tragen; *~ out* F austeilen; **~·cloth** [ˈdɪʃklɒθ] Geschirrspültuch *n*.

dis·heart·en [dɪs'haːtn] entmutigen.

di·shev·el(l)ed [dɪ'ʃevld] zerzaust.

dis·hon·est [dɪs'ɒnɪst] unehrlich, unredlich; **~·y** [~ɪ] Unredlichkeit *f*.

dis·hon·o(u)r [dɪs'ɒnə] **1.** Unehre *f*, Schande *f*; **2.** entehren; schänden; *econ. Wechsel* nicht honorieren *od.* einlösen; **~·o(u)·ra·ble** □ [~rəbl] schändlich, unehrenhaft.

dish·rag [ˈdɪʃræɡ] = dishcloth; **~·wash·er** Spüler(in); Geschirrspülmaschine *f*, -spüler *m*; **~·wa·ter** Spülwasser *n*.

dis·il·lu·sion [dɪsɪ'luːʒn] **1.** Ernüchterung *f*, Desillusion *f*; **2.** ernüchtern, desillusionieren; *be ~ed with* sich keinen Illusionen mehr hingeben über (*acc.*).

dis·in·clined [ˈdɪsɪn'klaɪnd] abgeneigt.

dis·in·fect [ˈdɪsɪn'fekt] desinfizieren; **~·fec·tant** [~ənt] Desinfektionsmittel *n*.

dis·in·her·it [dɪsɪn'herɪt] enterben.

dis·in·te·grate [dɪs'ɪntɪɡreɪt] (sich) auflösen; ver-, zerfallen.

dis·in·ter·est·ed □ [dɪs'ɪntrəstɪd] uneigennützig, selbstlos; objektiv, unvoreingenommen; △ *mst nicht* desinteressiert.

disk [dɪsk] *bsd. Am.* = *Brt.* disc; *Computer*: Diskette *f*; *~ drive* Diskettenlaufwerk *n*, F Floppy *f*.

disk·ette [ˈdɪsket, dɪ'sket] *Computer*: Diskette *f*.

dis·like [dɪs'laɪk] **1.** Abneigung *f*, Widerwille *m* (*of*, *for* gegen); *take a ~ to s.o.* gegen *j-n* e-e Abneigung fassen; **2.** nicht mögen.

dis·lo·cate [ˈdɪsləkeɪt] ✸ verrenken; verlagern.

dis·lodge [dɪs'lɒdʒ] vertreiben, verjagen; entfernen; *Stein etc.* lösen.

dis·loy·al □ [ˈdɪs'lɔɪəl] treulos.

dis·mal □ [ˈdɪzməl] trüb(e), trostlos, elend.

dis·man·tle [dɪs'mæntl] abbrechen; niederreißen; ♣ abtakeln; ⊕ abwracken; ⊕ demontieren.

dis·may [dɪs'meɪ] **1.** Schrecken *m*, Bestürzung *f*; *in ~*, *with ~* bestürzt; *to one's ~* zu s-m Entsetzen; **2.** *v/t.* erschrecken, bestürzen.

dis·miss [dɪsˈmɪs] v/t. entlassen; wegschicken; ablehnen; *Thema etc.* fallenlassen; ⚖ abweisen; **~al** [~l] Entlassung f; Aufgabe f; ⚖ Abweisung f.

dis·mount [ˈdɪsˈmaʊnt] v/t. aus dem Sattel heben; *Reiter* abwerfen; demontieren; ⊕ auseinandernehmen; v/i. absteigen, absitzen (*from* von *Fahrrad, Pferd etc.*).

dis·o·be·di·ence [dɪsəˈbiːdjəns] Ungehorsam m; **~ent** □ [~t] ungehorsam.

dis·o·bey [ˈdɪsəˈbeɪ] nicht gehorchen, ungehorsam sein (gegen).

dis·or·der [dɪsˈɔːdə] 1. Unordnung f; Aufruhr m; ⚕ Störung f; 2. in Unordnung bringen; ⚕ stören; **~ly** [~lɪ] unordentlich; ordnungswidrig; unruhig; aufrührerisch.

dis·or·gan·ize [dɪsˈɔːgənaɪz] durcheinanderbringen; desorganisieren.

dis·own [dɪsˈɔʊn] nicht anerkennen; *Kind* verstoßen; ablehnen.

di·spar·age [dɪˈspærɪdʒ] verächtlich machen; herabsetzen; geringschätzen.

di·spar·i·ty [dɪˈspærətɪ] Ungleichheit f; ~ of od. in age Altersunterschied m.

dis·pas·sion·ate □ [dɪˈspæʃnət] leidenschaftslos; objektiv.

di·spatch [dɪˈspætʃ] 1. schnelle Erledigung; (Ab)Sendung f; Abfertigung f; Eile f; (Eil)Botschaft f; Bericht m (*e-s Korrespondenten*); 2. schnell erledigen; absenden, abschicken, *Telegramm* aufgeben, abfertigen.

di·spel [dɪˈspel] (-*ll*-) *Menge etc.* zerstreuen (*a. fig.*), *Nebel* zerteilen.

di·spen·sa·ble [dɪˈspensəbl] entbehrlich; **~ry** [~rɪ] Werks-, Krankenhaus-, Schul-,⚔ Lazarettapotheke f.

dis·pen·sa·tion [dɪspenˈseɪʃn] Austeilung f; Befreiung f (*with* von); Dispens m; *göttliche* Fügung.

di·spense [dɪˈspens] austeilen; *Recht* sprechen; *Arzneien* zubereiten u. abgeben; ~ *with* auskommen ohne u. überflüssig machen; **di·spens·er** [~ə] Spender m, *für Klebestreifen a.* Abroller m, (*Briefmarken- etc.*)Automat m.

di·sperse [dɪˈspɜːs] verstreuen; (sich) zerstreuen.

di·spir·it·ed [dɪˈspɪrɪtɪd] entmutigt.

dis·place [dɪsˈpleɪs] verschieben; ablösen, entlassen; verschleppen; ersetzen; verdrängen.

di·splay [dɪˈspleɪ] 1. Entfaltung f; (Her)Zeigen n; (protzige) Zurschaustellung; Sichtanzeige f; *econ.* Display n, Auslage f; *be on* ~ ausgestellt sein; 2. entfalten; zur Schau stellen; zeigen.

dis·please [dɪsˈpliːz] j-m mißfallen; **~pleased** ungehalten; **~plea·sure** [~pleʒə] Mißfallen n.

dis·po·sa·ble [dɪˈspəʊzəbl] Einweg...; Wegwerf...; **~pos·al** [~zl] Beseitigung f (*von Müll etc.*), Entsorgung f; Verfügung(srecht n) f; *be* (*put*) *at s.o.'s* ~ j-m zur Verfügung stehen (stellen); **~pose** [~əʊz] v/t. (an)ordnen, einrichten; geneigt machen, veranlassen; v/i. ~ of verfügen über (*acc.*); erledigen; loswerden; beseitigen; **~posed** geneigt; ...gesinnt; **~po·si·tion** [dɪspəˈzɪʃn] Disposition f; Anordnung f; Neigung f; Veranlagung f, Art f.

dis·pos·sess [ˈdɪspəˈzes] enteignen, vertreiben; berauben (*of gen.*).

dis·pro·por·tion·ate □ [ˈdɪsprəˈpɔːnət] unverhältnismäßig.

dis·prove [ˈdɪsˈpruːv] widerlegen.

di·spute [dɪˈspjuːt] 1. Disput m, Kontroverse f; Streit m; Auseinandersetzung f; 2. streiten (über *acc.*); bezweifeln.

dis·qual·i·fy [dɪsˈkwɒlɪfaɪ] unfähig od. untauglich machen; für untauglich erklären; *Sport:* disqualifizieren.

dis·qui·et [dɪsˈkwaɪət] beunruhigen.

dis·re·gard [ˈdɪsrɪˈgɑːd] 1. Nichtbeachtung f; Mißachtung f; 2. nicht beachten.

dis·rep·u·ta·ble □ [dɪsˈrepjʊtəbl] übel; verrufen; **~re·pute** [ˈdɪsrɪˈpjuːt] schlechter Ruf.

dis·re·spect [ˈdɪsrɪˈspekt] Respektlosigkeit f; Unhöflichkeit f; **~ful** □ [~fl] respektlos; unhöflich.

dis·rupt [dɪsˈrʌpt] unterbrechen.

dis·sat·is·fac·tion [ˈdɪssætɪsˈfækʃn] Unzufriedenheit f; **~fy** [ˈdɪsˈsætɪsfaɪ] nicht befriedigen; j-m mißfallen.

dis·sect [dɪˈsekt] zerlegen, -gliedern.

dis·sem·ble [dɪˈsembl] v/t. verbergen; v/i. sich verstellen, heucheln.

dis·sen·sion [dɪˈsenʃn] Meinungsverschiedenheit(en *pl.*) f, Differenz(en *pl.*) f; Uneinigkeit f; **~t** [~t]

1. abweichende Meinung; **2.** anderer Meinung sein (*from* als); **~t·er** [~ə] Andersdenkende(r m) f.

dis·si·dent ['dɪsɪdənt] **1.** andersdenkend; **2.** Andersdenkende(r m) f; pol. Dissident(in), Regime-, Systemkritiker(in).

dis·sim·i·lar □ ['dɪ'sɪmɪlə] (*to*) unähnlich (*dat.*); verschieden (von).

dis·sim·u·la·tion [dɪsɪmjʊ'leɪʃn] Verstellung f.

dis·si·pate ['dɪsɪpeɪt] (sich) zerstreuen; verschwenden; **~·pat·ed** ausschweifend, zügellos.

dis·so·ci·ate [dɪ'səʊʃɪeɪt] trennen; ~ o.s. sich distanzieren, abrücken.

dis·so·lute □ ['dɪsəluːt] ausschweifend, zügellos; **~·lu·tion** [dɪsə'luːʃn] Auflösung f; Zerstörung f; ﬆ Aufhebung f, Annullierung f.

dis·solve [dɪ'zɒlv] v/t. (auf)lösen; schmelzen; v/i. sich auflösen.

dis·so·nant □ ['dɪsənənt] ♪ dissonant, mißtönend; fig. unstimmig.

dis·suade [dɪ'sweɪd] j-m abraten (*from* von).

dis|tance ['dɪstəns] **1.** Abstand m; Entfernung f, Ferne f; Strecke f; fig. Distanz f, Zurückhaltung f; *at a ~* von weitem; in einiger Entfernung; *keep s.o. at a ~* j-m gegenüber reserviert sein; *~ race* Sport: Langstreckenlauf m; *~ runner* Sport: Langstreckenläufer(in); **2.** hinter sich lassen; **~·tant** □ [~t] entfernt; fern; zurückhaltend; Fern...; *~ control* Fernsteuerung f.

dis·taste [dɪs'teɪst] Widerwille m, Abneigung f; **~·ful** □ [~fl]: *be ~ to s.o.* j-m zuwider sein.

dis·tem·per [dɪs'tempə] Krankheit f (*bsd. von Tieren*); (Hunde)Staupe f.

dis·tend [dɪs'tend] (sich) (aus)dehnen; (auf)blähen; sich weiten.

dis·til(l) [dɪs'tɪl] (*-ll-*) herabtropfen (lassen); ⚗ destillieren; **dis·til·le·ry** [~ləri] (Branntwein)Brennerei f.

dis|tinct □ [dɪs'tɪŋkt] verschieden; getrennt; deutlich, klar, bestimmt; **~·tinc·tion** [~kʃn] Unterscheidung f; Unterschied m; Auszeichnung f; Rang m; **~·tinc·tive** □ [~tɪv] unterscheidend; kennzeichnend, bezeichnend.

dis·tin·guish [dɪs'tɪŋgwɪʃ] unterscheiden; auszeichnen; *~ o.s.* sich auszeichnen; **~ed** berühmt; ausgezeichnet; vornehm.

dis·tort [dɪs'tɔːt] verdrehen; verzerren.

dis·tract [dɪs'trækt] ablenken; zerstreuen; beunruhigen; verwirren; verrückt machen; **~ed** □ beunruhigt, besorgt; (*by, with*) außer sich (vor *dat.*); wahnsinnig (vor *Schmerzen etc.*); **dis·trac·tion** [~kʃn] Ablenkung f; Zerstreutheit f; Verwirrung f; Zerstreuung f; Raserei f.

dis·traught [dɪs'trɔːt] = distracted.

dis·tress [dɪs'tres] **1.** Qual f; Kummer m, Sorge f; Elend n, Not f; **2.** in Not bringen; quälen; beunruhigen; betrüben; j-n erschöpfen; **~ed** beunruhigt, besorgt; betrübt; notleidend; *~ area* Brt. Notstandsgebiet n.

dis|trib·ute [dɪs'trɪbjuːt] ver-, aus-, zuteilen; einteilen; verbreiten; **~·tri·bu·tion** [dɪstrɪ'bjuːʃn] Ver-, Austeilung f; Verleih m (*von Filmen*); Verbreitung f; Einteilung f.

dis·trict ['dɪstrɪkt] Bezirk m; Gegend f.

dis·trust [dɪs'trʌst] **1.** Mißtrauen n; **2.** mißtrauen (*dat.*); **~·ful** □ [~fl] mißtrauisch.

dis·turb [dɪs'tɜːb] stören; beunruhigen; **~·ance** [~əns] Störung f; Unruhe f; *~ of the peace* ﬆ Störung f der öffentlichen Sicherheit u. Ordnung; *cause a ~* für Unruhe sorgen; ruhestörenden Lärm machen; **~ed** geistig gestört; verhaltensgestört.

dis·used ['dɪs'juːzd] nicht mehr benutzt (*Maschine etc.*), stillgelegt (*Bergwerk etc.*).

ditch [dɪtʃ] Graben m.

di·van [dɪ'væn, Am. 'daɪvæn] Diwan m; *~ bed* Bettcouch f.

dive [daɪv] **1.** (*dived od. Am. a. dove, dived*) (unter)tauchen; *vom Sprungbrett* springen; e-n Hecht- od. Kopfsprung machen; hechten (*for* nach); e-n Sturzflug machen; **2.** *Schwimmen:* Springen n; Kopf-, Hechtsprung m; Sturzflug m; F Spelunke f; **div·er** ['daɪvə] Taucher(in); *Sport:* Wasserspringer(in).

di·verge [daɪ'vɜːdʒ] auseinanderlaufen; abweichen; **di·ver·gence** [~əns] Abweichung f; **di·ver·gent** □ [~t] abweichend.

di·vers ['daɪvɜːz] mehrere.

di·verse □ [daɪ'vɜːs] verschieden; mannigfaltig; **di·ver·si·fy** [~sɪfaɪ] verschieden(artig) od. abwechslungsreich gestalten; **di·ver·sion**

[ʌːʃn] Ablenkung f; Zeitvertreib m; **di·ver·si·ty** [ʌːˈsətɪ] Verschiedenheit f; Mannigfaltigkeit f.

di·vert [daɪˈvɜːt] ablenken; j-n zerstreuen, unterhalten; Verkehr umleiten.

di·vide [dɪˈvaɪd] **1.** v/t. teilen; ver-, aus-, aufteilen; trennen; einteilen; A̸ dividieren (by durch); v/i. sich teilen; zerfallen; A̸ sich dividieren lassen; sich trennen od. auflösen; **2.** geogr. Wasserscheide f; **di·vid·ed** geteilt; ~ highway Am. Schnellstraße f; ~ skirt Hosenrock m.

div·i·dend econ. [ˈdɪvɪdend] Dividende f.

di·vid·ers [dɪˈvaɪdəz] pl. (a pair of ~ ein) Stechzirkel m.

di·vine [dɪˈvaɪn] **1.** □ (~r, ~st) göttlich; ~ service Gottesdienst m; **2.** Geistliche(r) m; **3.** weissagen; ahnen.

div·ing [ˈdaɪvɪŋ] Tauchen n; Sport: Wasserspringen n; attr. Tauch..., Taucher...; ~-board Sprungbrett n; ~-suit Taucheranzug m.

di·vin·i·ty [dɪˈvɪnətɪ] Gottheit f; Göttlichkeit f; Theologie f.

di·vis·i·ble □ [dɪˈvɪzəbl] teilbar; **di·vi·sion** [~ˈvɪʒn] Teilung f; Trennung f; Abteilung f; ✕, A̸ Division f.

di·vorce [dɪˈvɔːs] **1.** (Ehe)Scheidung f; get a ~ geschieden werden (from von); **2.** Ehe scheiden; sich scheiden lassen von; they have been ~d sie haben sich scheiden lassen; **di·vor·cee** [dɪvɔːˈsiː] Geschiedene(r m) f.

diz·zy □ [ˈdɪzɪ] (-ier, -iest) schwind(e)lig.

do [duː] (did, done) v/t. tun, machen; (zu)bereiten; Zimmer aufräumen; Geschirr abwaschen; Rolle spielen; Wegstrecke zurücklegen, schaffen; ~ you know him? – no, I don't kennst du ihn? – nein; what can I ~ for you? was kann ich für Sie tun?, womit kann ich (Ihnen) dienen?; ~ London F London besichtigen; have one's hair done sich die Haare machen od. frisieren lassen; have done reading fertig sein mit Lesen; v/i. tun, handeln; sich befinden; genügen; that will ~ das genügt; how ~ you ~? guten Tag! (bei der Vorstellung); ~ be quick beeile dich doch; ~ you like London? – I ~ gefällt Ihnen London? – ja; ~ well s-e Sache gut machen; gute

Geschäfte machen; mit Adverbien u. Präpositionen: ~ away with beseitigen, weg-, abschaffen; I'm done in F ich bin geschafft; ~ up Kleid etc. zumachen; Haus etc. instand setzen; Päckchen zurechtmachen; ~ o.s. up sich zurechtmachen; I'm done up F ich bin geschafft; I could ~ with ... ich könnte ... brauchen od. vertragen; ~ without auskommen od. sich behelfen ohne.

do·cile □ [ˈdəʊsaɪl] gelehrig; fügsam.

dock¹ [dɒk] stutzen, kupieren; fig. kürzen.

dock² [~] **1.** ♣ Dock n; Kai m, Pier m; ⚖ Anklagebank f; **2.** v/t. Schiff (ein)docken; Raumschiff koppeln; v/i. ♣ anlegen; andocken, ankoppeln (Raumschiff); ~·ing [ˈdɒkɪŋ] Docking n, Ankopp(e)lung f (von Raumschiffen); ~·yard ♣ (bsd. Brt. Marine)Werft f.

doc·tor [ˈdɒktə] **1.** Doktor m; Arzt m; **2.** F verarzten; F (ver)fälschen.

doc·trine [ˈdɒktrɪn] Doktrin f, Lehre f.

doc·u·ment 1. [ˈdɒkjʊmənt] Urkunde f; **2.** [~ment] (urkundlich) belegen.

doc·u·men·ta·ry [dɒkjʊˈmentrɪ] **1.** urkundlich; Film etc.: Dokumentar...; **2.** Dokumentarfilm m.

dodge [dɒdʒ] **1.** Sprung m zur Seite; Kniff m, Trick m; **2.** (rasch) zur Seite springen, ausweichen; F sich drücken (vor dat.).

doe zo. [dəʊ] Hirschkuh f; Rehgeiß f, Ricke f; Häsin f.

dog [dɒg] **1.** zo. Hund m; **2.** (-gg-) j-n beharrlich verfolgen; ~-eared [ˈdɒgɪəd] mit Eselsohren (Buch); ~-ged □ verbissen, hartnäckig.

dog·ma [ˈdɒgmə] Dogma n; Glaubenssatz m; ~·t·ic [dɒgˈmætɪk] (~ally) dogmatisch.

dog-tired F [ˈdɒgˈtaɪəd] hundemüde.

do·ings [ˈduːɪŋz] pl. Handlungen pl., Taten pl., Tätigkeit f; Begebenheiten pl.; Treiben n, Betragen n.

do-it-your·self [duːɪtjɔːˈself] **1.** Heimwerken n; **2.** Heimwerker...

dole [dəʊl] **1.** milde Gabe; Brt. F Stempelgeld n; be od. go on the ~ Brt. F stempeln gehen; **2.** ~ out sparsam ver- od. austeilen.

dole·ful □ [ˈdəʊlfl] trübselig.

doll [dɒl] Puppe f.

dol·lar ['dɒlə] Dollar *m*.

dol·phin *zo.* ['dɒlfɪn] Delphin *m*.

do·main [dəʊ'meɪn] Domäne *f*; *fig.* Gebiet *n*, Bereich *m*.

dome [dəʊm] Kuppel *f*; △ *nicht* Dom; **~d** gewölbt.

Domes·day Book ['du:mzdeɪbʊk] *Reichsgrundbuch Englands (1086)*.

do·mes·tic [də'mestɪk] 1. (~ally) häuslich; inländisch, einheimisch; zahm; ~ *animal* Haustier *n*; ~ *flight* ✈ Inlandsflug *m*; ~ *trade* Binnenhandel *m*; 2. Hausangestellte(r *m*) *f*; ~**ti·cate** [~eɪt] zähmen.

dom·i·cile ['dɒmɪsaɪl] Wohnsitz *m*.

dom·i·nant □ ['dɒmɪnənt] (vor-) herrschend; ~**nate** [~eɪt] (be)herrschen; ~**na·tion** [dɒmɪ'neɪʃn] Herrschaft *f*; ~**neer·ing** □ [~'ɪərɪŋ] herrisch, tyrannisch; überheblich.

do·min·ion [də'mɪnjən] Herrschaft *f*; (Herrschafts)Gebiet *n*; ♀ Dominion *n* (*im Brit. Commonwealth*).

don [dɒn] anziehen; *Hut* aufsetzen.

do·nate [dəʊ'neɪt] schenken, stiften; **do·na·tion** [~eɪʃn] Schenkung *f*.

done [dʌn] 1. *p.p. von* do; 2. *adj.* getan; erledigt; fertig; gar *gekocht*.

don·key ['dɒŋkɪ] *zo.* Esel *m*; *attr.* Hilfs-.

do·nor ['dəʊnə] (♺ *bsd.* Blut-, Organ)Spender(in).

doom [du:m] 1. Schicksal *n*, Verhängnis *n*; 2. verurteilen, -dammen; ~**s·day** ['du:mzdeɪ] *till* ~ F bis zum Jüngsten Tag.

door [dɔ:] Tür *f*; Tor *n*; *next* ~ nebenan; ~**han·dle** ['dɔ:hændl] Türklinke *f*; ~**keep·er** Pförtner *m*; ~**man** (*pl.* -*men*) (livrierter) Portier; ~**step** Türstufe *f*; ~**way** Türöffnung *f*, (Tür)Eingang *m*.

dope [dəʊp] 1. Schmiere *f*; *bsd.* ✈ Lack *m*; F Stoff *m*, Rauschgift *n*; F Betäubungsmittel *n*; *Sport:* Dopingmittel *n*; *Am.* F Rauschgiftsüchtige(r *m*) *f*; *sl.* Trottel *m*; *sl.* (vertrauliche) Informationen *pl.*, Geheimtip *m*; 2. ✈ lackieren; F *j-m* Stoff geben; *Sport:* dopen; ~ **ad·dict**, ~ **fiend** F Rauschgift-, Drogensüchtige(r *m*) *f*; ~ **test** Dopingkontrolle *f*.

dorm [dɔ:m] = *dormitory*.

dor·mant *mst fig.* ['dɔ:mənt] schlafend, ruhend; untätig.

dor·mer (win·dow) ['dɔ:mə('wɪndəʊ)] stehendes Dachfenster *n*.

dor·mi·to·ry ['dɔ:mɪtrɪ] Schlafsaal

m; *bsd. Am.* Studentenwohnheim *n*.

dose [dəʊs] 1. Dosis *f*; △ *nicht* Dose; 2. *j-m* e-e Medizin geben.

dot [dɒt] 1. Punkt *m*; Fleck *m*; *on the* ~ F auf die Sekunde pünktlich; 2. (-*tt*-) punktieren; tüpfeln; *fig.* sprenkeln; ~*ted line* punktierte Linie.

dote [dəʊt]: ~ *on*, ~ *upon* vernarrt sein in (*acc.*), abgöttisch lieben (*acc.*); **dot·ing** □ ['dəʊtɪŋ] vernarrt.

dou·ble □ ['dʌbl] 1. doppelt; zu zweien; gekrümmt; zweideutig; 2. Doppelte(s) *n*; Doppelgänger(in) *f*; *Film, TV:* Double *n*; *mst* ~*s sg.*, *pl.* *Tennis:* Doppel *n*; *men's* od. *women's* ~*s sg.*, *pl.* Herren- od. Damendoppel *n*; 3. (sich) verdoppeln; *Film, TV: j-n* doubeln; *a.* ~ *up* falten; *Decke* zusammenlegen; ~ *back* kehrtmachen; ~ *up* zusammenkrümmen; sich krümmen (*with* vor *dat.*); ~**breast·ed** zweireihig (*Jackett*); ~**check** genau nachprüfen; ~ **chin** Doppelkinn *n*; ~**cross** ein doppeltes od. falsches Spiel treiben mit; ~**deal·ing** 1. betrügerisch; 2. Betrug *m*; ~**deck·er** [~ə] Doppeldecker *m*; ~**edged** zweischneidig; zweideutig; ~**en·try** *econ.* doppelte Buchführung; ~ **fea·ture** *Film:* Doppelprogramm *n*; ~**head·er** *Am.* [~ə] Doppelveranstaltung *f*; ~**park** *mot.* in zweiter Reihe parken; ~**quick** F im Eiltempo, fix.

doubt [daʊt] 1. *v/i.* zweifeln; *v/t.* bezweifeln; mißtrauen (*dat.*); 2. Zweifel *m*; *be in* ~ *about* Zweifel haben an (*dat.*); *no* ~ ohne Zweifel; ~**ful** □ ['daʊtfl] zweifelhaft; ~**less** [~lɪs] ohne Zweifel.

douche [du:ʃ] 1. Spülung *f* (*a.* ♻); Spülapparat *m*; △ *nicht Dusche*; 2. spülen (*a.* ♻); △ *nicht duschen*.

dough [dəʊ] Teig *m*; ~**nut** ['dəʊnʌt] Krapfen *m*, Berliner (Pfannkuchen) *m*, Schmalzkringel *m*.

dove[1] *zo.* [dʌv] Taube *f*.

dove[2] *Am.* [dəʊv] *pret. von* dive 1.

dow·el ⊕ ['daʊəl] Dübel *m*.

down[1] [daʊn] Daunen *pl.*; Flaum *m*; Düne *f*; ~*s pl.* Hügelland *n*.

down[2] [~] 1. *adv.* nach unten, her-, hinunter, her-, hinab, abwärts; unten; 2. *prp.* her-, hinab, her-, hinunter; ~ *the river* flußabwärts; 3. *adj.* nach unten gerichtet; deprimiert; niedergeschlagen; ~ *platform* Abfahrtsbahnsteig *m* (*in London*); ~

train Zug *m* (von London fort); **4.**
v/t. niederschlagen; *Flugzeug* abschießen; F *Getränk* runterkippen; ~
tools die Arbeit niederlegen, in den
Streik treten; **~cast** ['daʊnkɑːst]
niedergeschlagen; **~fall** Platzregen
m; fig. Sturz *m*; **~heart·ed** □ niedergeschlagen; **~hill 1.** *adv.* bergab;
2. *adj.* abschüssig; *Skisport:* Ab-
fahrts...; **3.** Abhang *m; Skisport:* Abfahrt *f;* **~pay·ment** *econ.* Anzahlung
f; **~pour** Regenguß *m*, Platzregen
m; **~right 1.** *adv.* völlig, ganz u. gar,
ausgesprochen; **2.** *adj.* glatt (*Lüge*
etc.); ausgesprochen; **~stairs** die
Treppe her- *od.* hinunter; (nach)
unten; **~stream** stromabwärts; **~
to-earth** realistisch; **~town 1.**
adv. im *od.* ins Geschäftsviertel; **2.**
adj. im Geschäftsviertel (gelegen *od.*
tätig); **3.** Geschäftsviertel *n*, Innenstadt *f*, City *f*; **~ward(s)** [~wəd(z)]
abwärts, nach unten.

down·y ['daʊnɪ] (*-ier, -iest*) flaumig.

dow·ry ['daʊərɪ] Mitgift *f*.

doze [dəʊz] **1.** dösen, ein Nickerchen
machen; **2.** Nickerchen *n*.

doz·en ['dʌzn] Dutzend *n*.

drab [dræb] trist; düster; eintönig.

draft [drɑːft] **1.** Entwurf *m; econ.*
Tratte *f;* Abhebung *f* (*von Geld*); *Am.*×
(Sonder)Kommando *n; Am.*× Ein-
berufung *f; bsd. Brit.* = **draught; 2.**
entwerfen; aufsetzen; × abkommandieren; *Am.*× einziehen, -beru-
fen; **~·ee** *Am.*× [drɑːfˈtiː] Wehr-
dienstpflichtige(r) *m;* **~s·man** *bsd.*
Am. ['drɑːftsmən] (*pl. -men*) s.
draughtsman; ~·y *Am.* [~ɪ] (*-ier,
-iest*) = **draughty**.

drag [dræg] **1.** Schleppen *n*, Zerren
n; ♣ Schleppnetz *n;* Egge *f;*
Schlepp-, Zugseil *n; fig.* Hemm-
schuh *m;* F *et.* Langweiliges *f;*
2. (*-gg-*) (sich) schleppen, zerren, ziehen, schleifen; a. ~ *behind* zurückbleiben, nachhinken; ~ *on* weiter-
schleppen; *fig.* sich dahinschleppen;
fig. sich in die Länge ziehen; **~·lift**
['dræglɪft] Schlepplift *m*.

drag·on ['drægən] Drache *m;* **~·fly**
zo. Libelle *f*.

drain [dreɪn] **1.** Abfluß(kanal *m*,
-rohr *n*) *m;* Entwässerungsgraben *m;*
fig. Belastung *f;* **2.** *v/t.* abfließen
lassen; entwässern; austrinken, leeren; *fig.* aufbrauchen, -zehren; *v/i.* ~
off, ~ away abfließen, ablaufen;

~·age ['dreɪnɪdʒ] Abfließen *n*, Ablaufen *n;* Entwässerung(sanlage *f*,
-ssystem *n*) *f;* Abwasser *n;* **~·pipe**
Abflußrohr *n*.

drake *zo.* [dreɪk] Enterich *m*, Erpel
m; △ *nicht* Drache.

dram F [dræm] Schluck *m*.

dra|ma ['drɑːmə] Drama *n;* **~·mat·ic**
[drəˈmætɪk] (*~ally*) dramatisch;
~m·a·tist ['dræmətɪst] Dramatiker
m; **~m·a·tize** [~taɪz] dramatisieren.

drank [dræŋk] *pret. von* **drink 2.**

drape [dreɪp] **1.** drapieren; in Falten
legen; **2.** *mst* ~*s pl. Am.* Gardinen *pl.;*
drap·er·y ['dreɪpərɪ] Textilhandel
m; Stoffe *pl.;* Faltenwurf *m*.

dras·tic ['dræstɪk] (*~ally*) drastisch.

draught [drɑːft] (Luft)Zug *m;* Zug
m, Schluck *m;* Fischzug *m;* ♣ Tief-
gang *m;* ~*s sg. Brt.* Damespiel *n;* **~
beer** Faßbier *n;* **~·horse** [drɑːftˈhɔːs]
Zugpferd *n;* **~s·man** [~smən] (*pl.
-men*) *Brt.* Damestein *m;* ⊕ (Kon-
struktions-, Muster)Zeichner *m;* **~·y**
[~ɪ] (*-ier, -iest*) zugig.

draw [drɔː] **1.** (*drew, drawn*) ziehen;
an-, auf-, ein-, zuziehen; & *Blut*
abnehmen; *econ.* Geld abheben;
Tränen hervorlocken; *Kunden etc.*
anziehen, anlocken; *j-s Aufmerksamkeit* lenken (*to auf acc.*); *Bier* abzapfen; ausfischen; *Tier* ausnehmen,
-weiden; *Luft* schöpfen; ziehen (lassen) (*Tee*); (in Worten) schildern;
Schriftstück ab-, verfassen; *fig.* entlocken; zeichnen, malen; ziehen,
Zug haben (*Kamin*); sich zusammenziehen; sich nähern (*to dat.*);
Sport: unentschieden spielen; ~
near sich nähern; ~ *on, ~ upon* in
Anspruch nehmen; ~ *out* in die Länge ziehen; ~ *up Schriftstück* aufsetzen; halten; vorfahren; **2.** Zug *m*
(Ziehen) *n;* *Lotterie:* Ziehung *f; Sport:*
Unentschieden *n;* Attraktion *f*,
(Kassen)Schlager *m;* **~·back** ['drɔː-
bæk] Nachteil *m*, Hindernis *n;* **~·er**
['drɔːə] Zeichner *m; econ.* Aussteller
m, Trassant *m (e-s Wechsels);* [drɔː]
Schubfach *n*, -lade *f;* (*a pair of*) ~*s pl.*
(eine) Unterhose; (ein) (Damen-)
Schlüpfer *m; mst chest of* ~*s* Kommode *f*.

draw·ing ['drɔːɪŋ] Ziehen *n;*
Zeichnen *n;* Zeichnung *f;* ~ **account** *econ.* Girokonto *n;* **~·board**
Reißbrett *n;* **~·pin** *Brt.* Reißzwecke *f*, -nagel *m*, Heftzwecke

f; **~-room** = *living room*; Salon *m*.

drawl [drɔːl] **1.** gedehnt sprechen; **2.** gedehntes Sprechen.

drawn [drɔːn] **1.** *p.p. von draw 1*; **2.** *adj. Sport*: unentschieden; abgespannt.

dread [dred] **1.** (große) Angst, Furcht *f*; **2.** (sich) fürchten; **~·ful** □ ['dredfl] schrecklich, furchtbar.

dream [driːm] **1.** Traum *m*; **2.** (*dreamed od. dreamt*) träumen; **~·er** ['driːmə] Träumer(in); **~t** [dremt] *pret. u. p.p. von dream 2*; **~·y** □ ['driːmɪ] (*-ier, -iest*) träumerisch, verträumt.

drear·y □ ['drɪərɪ] (*-ier, -iest*) trübselig; trüb(e) langweilig.

dredge [dredʒ] **1.** Schleppnetz *n*; Bagger(maschine *f*) *m*; **2.** (aus)baggern.

dregs [dregz] *pl.* Bodensatz *m*; *fig.* Abschaum *m*.

drench [drentʃ] durchnässen.

dress [dres] **1.** Anzug *m*; Kleidung *f*; Kleid *n*; **2.** (sich) ankleiden *od.* anziehen; schmücken, dekorieren; zurechtmachen; *Speisen* zubereiten; *Salat* anmachen; *Abendkleidung* anziehen; ⚓ verbinden; frisieren; **~ down** *j-m* e-e Standpauke halten; **~ up** (sich) fein machen; sich kostümieren *od.* verkleiden (*bsd. Kinder*); **~ cir·cle** *thea.* ['dres'sɜːkl] erster Rang; **~ de·sign·er** Modezeichner(in); **~·er** [~ə] Anrichte *f*; Toilettentisch *m*.

dress·ing ['dresɪŋ] An-, Zurichten *n*; Ankleiden *n*; ⚓ Verband *m*; Appretur *f*; Dressing *n* (*Salatsoße*); Füllung *f*; **~-down** Standpauke *f*; **~-gown** Morgenrock *m*, -mantel *m*; *Sport*: Bademantel *m*; **~-ta·ble** Toilettentisch *m*.

dress·mak·er ['dresmeɪkə] (Damen-) Schneider(in).

drew [druː] *pret. von draw 1*.

drib·ble ['drɪbl] tröpfeln (lassen); sabbern, geifern; *Fußball*: dribbeln.

dried [draɪd] getrocknet, Dörr...

dri·er ['draɪə] = *dryer*.

drift [drɪft] **1.** (Dahin)Treiben *n*; (Schnee)Verwehung *f*; (Schnee-, Sand)Wehe *f*; *fig.* Tendenz *f*; **2.** (dahin)treiben; wehen; aufhäufen.

drill [drɪl] **1.** Drillbohrer *m*; Furche *f*; ✓ Drill-, Sämaschine *f*; ⚔ Drill *m* (*a. fig.*); ⚔ Exerzieren *n*; **2.**

bohren; ⚔, *fig.* drillen, einexerzieren.

drink [drɪŋk] **1.** Getränk *n*; **2.** (*drank, drunk*) trinken; **~ to s.o.** *j-m* zuprosten *od.* zutrinken; **~·er** ['drɪŋkə] Trinker(in).

drip [drɪp] **1.** Tröpfeln *n*; ⚓ Tropf *m*; **2.** (*-pp-*) tropfen *od.* tröpfeln (lassen); triefen; **~-dry shirt** [drɪp'draɪ 'ʃɜːt] bügelfreies Hemd; **~·ping** ['drɪpɪŋ] Bratenfett *n*.

drive [draɪv] **1.** (Spazier)Fahrt *f*; Auffahrt *f*; Fahrweg *m*; ⊕ Antrieb *m*; *mot.* (*Links- etc.*)Steuerung *f*; *psych.* Trieb *m*; *fig.* Kampagne *f*; *fig.* Schwung *m*, Elan *m*, Dynamik *f*; **2.** (*drove, driven*) *v/t.* (an-, ein)treiben; *Auto etc.* fahren, lenken, steuern; (im *Auto etc.*) fahren; ⊕ (an)treiben; zwingen; **~ off** vertreiben; *v/i.* treiben; (*Auto*) fahren; **~ off** wegfahren; *what are you driving at?* F worauf wollen Sie hinaus?

drive-in ['draɪvɪn] **1.** Auto...; **~ cinema**, *Am.* **~ motion-picture theater** Autokino *n*; **2.** Autokino *n*; Drive-in-Restaurant *n*; Autoschalter *m*, Drive-in-Schalter *m* (*e-r Bank*).

driv·el ['drɪvl] **1.** (*bsd. Brt. -ll-, Am. -l-*) faseln; **2.** Geschwätz *n*, Gefasel *n*.

driv·en ['drɪvn] *p.p. von drive 2*.

driv·er ['draɪvə] *mot.* Fahrer(in); (*Lokomotiv*)Führer *m*; **~'s li·cense** *Am.* Führerschein *m*.

driv·ing ['draɪvɪŋ] (an)treibend; ⊕ Antriebs..., Trieb..., Trieb...; *mot.* Fahr...; **~ li·cence** Führerschein *m*.

driz·zle ['drɪzl] **1.** Sprühregen *m*; **2.** sprühen, nieseln.

drone [drəʊn] **1.** *zo.* Drohne *f* (*a. fig.*); **2.** summen; dröhnen.

droop [druːp] (schlaff) herabhängen; den Kopf hängenlassen; schwinden.

drop [drɒp] **1.** Tropfen *m*; Fallen *n*, Fall *m*; *fig.* Fall *m*, Sturz *m*; Bonbon *m*, *n*; *fruit* **~s** *pl.* Drops *m*, *n od. pl.*; **2.** (*-pp-*) *v/t.* tropfen (lassen); fallen lassen; *Bemerkung, Thema etc.* fallenlassen; *Brief* einwerfen; *Fahrgast* absetzen; senken; **~ s.o. a few lines** *pl.* *j-m* ein paar Zeilen schreiben; *v/i.* tropfen; (herab-, herunter)fallen; umsinken, fallen; **~ in** (kurz) hereinschauen; **~ off** abfallen; zurückgehen, nachlassen; F einnicken;

~ **out** herausfallen; aussteigen (*of* aus); *a.* ~ **out of school** (*university*) die Schule (das Studium) abbrechen; **~out** ['drɒpaʊt] Drop-out *m*, Aussteiger *m* (*aus der Gesellschaft*); (Schul-, Studien)Abbrecher *m*.

drought [draʊt] Trockenheit *f*, Dürre *f*.

drove [drəʊv] **1.** Herde *f* (*Vieh*); Schar *f* (*Menschen*); **2.** *pret. von* drive 2.

drown [draʊn] *v/t.* ertränken; überschwemmen; *fig.* übertönen; *v/i.* ertrinken.

drowse [draʊz] dösen; ~ **off** eindösen; **drow·sy** ['draʊzɪ] (*-ier, -iest*) schläfrig; einschläfernd.

drudge [drʌdʒ] sich (ab)placken, schuften; **drudg·e·ry** ['drʌdʒərɪ] (stumpfsinnige) Plackerei *od.* Schinderei.

drug [drʌg] **1.** Arzneimittel *n*, Medikament *n*; Droge *f*; Rauschgift *n*; **be on** (**off**) ~**s** rauschgift- *od.* drogensüchtig (clean) sein; **2.** (*-gg-*) j-m Medikamente geben; j-n unter Drogen setzen; im Betäubungsmittel beimischen (*dat.*); betäuben (*a. fig.*); ~ **a·buse** Drogenmißbrauch *m*; Medikamentenmißbrauch *m*; ~ **ad·dict** Drogen-, Rauschgiftsüchtige(r *m*) *f*; **~gist** *Am.* ['drʌgɪst] Apotheker(in); Inhaber(in) e-s Drugstores; **~store** *Am.* Apotheke *f*; Drugstore *m*.

drum [drʌm] **1.** ♪ Trommel *f*; *anat.* Trommelfell *n*; ~**s** *pl.* ♪ Schlagzeug *n*; **2.** (*-mm-*) trommeln; **~mer** ♪ ['drʌmə] Trommler *m*; Schlagzeuger *m*.

drunk [drʌŋk] **1.** *p.p. von* drink 2; **2.** *adj.* betrunken; **get** ~ sich betrinken; **3.** Betrunkene(r *m*) *f*; = **~ard** ['drʌŋkəd] Trinker(in), Säufer(in); **~en** *adj.* [~ən] betrunken; ~ **driving** Trunkenheit *f* am Steuer.

dry [draɪ] **1.** □ (*-ier, -iest*) trocken, trocken, herb (*Wein*); *F* durstig; *F* trocken (*ohne Alkohol*); ~ **goods** *pl.* Textilien *pl.*; **2.** trocknen; dörren; ~ **up** austrocknen; versiegen; **~clean** ['draɪ'kliːn] chemisch reinigen; ~ **clean·er's** chemische Reinigung *f*; **~er** [~ə] *a.* drier Trockenapparat *m*, Trockner *m*.

du·al □ ['djuːəl] doppelt, Doppel...; ~ **carriageway** *Brt.* Schnellstraße *f* (*mit Mittelstreifen*).

dub [dʌb] (*-bb-*) Film synchronisieren.

du·bi·ous □ ['djuːbjəs] zweifelhaft.

duch·ess ['dʌtʃɪs] Herzogin *f*.

duck [dʌk] **1.** *zo.* Ente *f*; Ducken *n*; *F* Schatz *m* (*Anrede, oft unübersetzt*); **2.** (unter)tauchen; (sich) ducken; **~ling** *zo.* ['dʌklɪŋ] Entchen *n*.

due [djuː] **1.** zustehend; gebührend; gehörig, angemessen; fällig; *zeitlich* fällig, erwartet; *in* ~ **time** zur rechten Zeit; ~ **to** wegen (*gen.*); **be** ~ **to** j-m gebühren, zustehen; kommen von, zurückzuführen sein auf; **2.** *adv.* direkt, genau; **3.** Recht *n*, Anspruch *m*; ~**s** *pl.* Gebühr(en *pl.*) *f*; Beitrag *m*.

du·el ['djuːəl] **1.** Duell *n*; **2.** (*bsd. Brt.* -*ll-*, *Am.* -*l-*) sich duellieren.

dug [dʌg] *pret. u. p.p. von* dig 1.

duke [djuːk] Herzog *m*.

dull [dʌl] **1.** □ dumm; träge, schwerfällig; stumpf; matt (*Auge etc.*); schwach (*Gehör*); langweilig; abgestumpft, teilnahmslos; dumpf; trüb(e); *econ.* flau; **2.** stumpf machen *od.* werden; (sich) trüben; mildern, dämpfen; *Schmerz* betäuben; *fig.* abstumpfen.

du·ly *adv.* ['djuːlɪ] ordnungsgemäß; gebührend; rechtzeitig.

dumb □ [dʌm] stumm; sprachlos; *bsd. Am.* F doof, dumm, blöd; **dum(b)·found·ed** ['dʌm'faʊndɪd] verblüfft, sprachlos.

dum·my ['dʌmɪ] Attrappe *f*; Kleider-, Schaufensterpuppe *f*; Dummy *m*, Puppe *f* (*für Unfalltests*); *Brt.* Schnuller *m*; *attr.* Schein...

dump [dʌmp] **1.** *v/t.* (hin)plumpsen *od.* (hin)fallen lassen; auskippen; *Schutt etc.* abladen; *econ.* Waren zu Dumpingpreisen verkaufen; **2.** Plumps *m*; (Schutt-, Müll)Abladeplatz *m*; ✕ Depot *n*, Lager(platz *m*) *n*; **~ing** *econ.* ['dʌmpɪŋ] Dumping *n*, Ausfuhr *f* zu Schleuderpreisen.

dune [djuːn] Düne *f*.

dung [dʌŋ] **1.** Dung *m*; **2.** düngen.

dun·ga·rees [dʌŋgə'riːz] *pl.* (*a pair of* ~ e-e) Arbeitshose.

dun·geon ['dʌndʒən] (Burg)Verlies *n*.

dunk *F* [dʌŋk] (ein)tunken.

dupe [djuːp] anführen, täuschen.

du·plex ['djuːpleks] doppelt, Doppel...; ~ (*apartment*) *Am.* Maison(n)ette(wohnung) *f*; ~ (*house*) *Am.* Doppel-, Zweifamilienhaus *n*.

du·pli·cate 1. ['djuːplɪkət] doppelt; ~ **key** Zweit-, Nachschlüssel *m*; **2.** [~]

D

Duplikat *n*; Zweit-, Nachschlüssel *m*; **3.** [ˌkeɪt] doppelt ausfertigen; kopieren, vervielfältigen.

du·plic·i·ty □ [djuːˈplɪsətɪ] Doppelzüngigkeit *f*.

dur·a·ble □ [ˈdjʊərəbl] haltbar; dauerhaft; **du·ra·tion** [djʊəˈreɪʃn] Dauer *f*.

du·ress [djʊəˈres] Zwang *m*.

dur·ing *prp.* [ˈdjʊərɪŋ] während.

dusk [dʌsk] (Abend)Dämmerung *f*; **~·y** □ [ˈdʌskɪ] (*-ier, -iest*) dämmerig, düster (*a. fig.*); schwärzlich.

dust [dʌst] **1.** Staub *m*; **2.** *v/t.* abstauben; (be)streuen; *v/i.* Staub wischen, abstauben; **~·bin** *Brt.* [ˈdʌstbɪn] Abfall-, Mülleimer *m*; Abfall-, Mülltonne *f*; **~·cart** *Brt.* Müllwagen *m*; **~·er** [~ə] Staublappen *m*, -wedel *m*; *Schule*: Tafelschwamm *m*, -tuch *n*; **~·cov·er**, **~·jack·et** (*e-s Buches*) Schutzumschlag *m*; **~·man** (*pl. -men*) *Brt.* Müllmann *m*; **~·y** □ [~ɪ] (*-ier, -iest*) staubig.

Dutch [dʌtʃ] **1.** *adj.* holländisch; **2.** *adv.*: *go ~* getrennte Kasse machen; **3.** *ling.* Holländisch *n*; *the ~* die Holländer *pl.*

du·ty [ˈdjuːtɪ] Pflicht *f*; Ehrerbietung *f*; *econ.* Abgabe *f*; Zoll *m*; Dienst *m*; *be on ~* Dienst haben; *be off ~* dienstfrei haben; **~·free** zollfrei.

dwarf [dwɔːf] **1.** (*pl. dwarfs* [~fs], *dwarves* [~vz]) Zwerg(in); **2.** verkleinern, klein erscheinen lassen.

dwell [dwel] (*dwelt od. dwelled*) wohnen; verweilen (*on, upon* bei); **~·ing** [ˈdwelɪŋ] Wohnung *f*.

dwelt [dwelt] *pret. u. p.p. von* dwell.

dwin·dle [ˈdwɪndl] (dahin)schwinden, abnehmen.

dye [daɪ] **1.** Farbe *f*; *of the deepest ~ fig.* von der übelsten Sorte; **2.** färben.

dy·ing [ˈdaɪɪŋ] **1.** sterbend; Sterbe...; **2.** Sterben *n*.

dyke [daɪk] = dike[1, 2].

dy·nam·ic [daɪˈnæmɪk] dynamisch, kraftgeladen; **~s** *mst sg.* Dynamik *f*.

dy·na·mite [ˈdaɪnəmaɪt] **1.** Dynamit *n*; **2.** (mit Dynamit) sprengen.

dys·en·te·ry ✖ [ˈdɪsntrɪ] Ruhr *f*.

dys·pep·si·a ✖ [dɪsˈpepsɪə] Verdauungsstörung *f*.

E

each [iːtʃ] jede(r, -s); *~ other* einander, sich; je, pro Person, pro Stück.

ea·ger □ [ˈiːgə] begierig; eifrig; **~·ness** [ˈiːgənɪs] Begierde *f*; Eifer *m*.

ea·gle [ˈiːgl] *zo.* Adler *m*; *Am. hist.* Zehndollarstück *n*; **~·eyed** scharfsichtig.

ear [ɪə] Ähre *f*; *anat.* Ohr *n*; Öhr *n*; Henkel *m*; *keep an ~ to* the ground die Ohren offenhalten; **~·drum** *anat.* [ˈɪədrʌm] Trommelfell *n*; **~ed** mit (...) Ohren, ...ohrig.

earl [ɜːl] *englischer* Graf.

ear·lobe [ˈɪələʊb] Ohrläppchen *n*.

ear·ly [ˈɜːlɪ] früh; Früh...; Anfangs..., erste(r, -s); bald(ig); *as ~ as May* schon im Mai; *as ~ as possible* so bald wie möglich; *~ bird* Frühaufsteher(in); *~ warning system* ✖ Frühwarnsystem *n*.

ear·mark [ˈɪəmɑːk] **1.** Kennzeichen *n*; Merkmal *n*; **2.** kennzeichnen; zurücklegen (*for* für).

earn [ɜːn] verdienen; einbringen.

ear·nest [ˈɜːnɪst] **1.** □ ernst(lich, -haft); ernstgemeint; **2.** Ernst *m*; *in ~* im Ernst; ernsthaft.

earn·ings [ˈɜːnɪŋz] *pl.* Einkommen *n*.

ear|phones [ˈɪəfəʊnz] *pl.* Ohrhörer *pl.*; Kopfhörer *pl.*; **~·piece** *teleph.* Hörmuschel *f*; **~·ring** Ohrring *m*; **~·shot**: *within (out of) ~* in (außer) Hörweite.

earth [ɜːθ] **1.** Erde *f*; Land *n*; **2.** *v/t.* ⚡ erden; **~·en** [ˈɜːθn] irden; **~·en·ware** [~nweə] **1.** Töpferware *f*; Steingut *n*; **2.** irden; **~·ly** [ˈɜːθlɪ] irdisch; F denkbar; **~·quake** Erdbeben *n*; **~·worm** *zo.* Regenwurm *m*.

ease [iːz] **1.** Bequemlichkeit *f*, Behagen *n*; Ruhe *f*; Ungezwungenheit *f*;

Leichtigkeit *f; at ~* bequem, behaglich; *ill at ~* unruhig; befangen; **2.** *v/t.* erleichtern; lindern; beruhigen; bequem(er) machen; *v/i. mst ~ off, ~ up* nachlassen, sich entspannen (*Lage*); (bei der Arbeit) kürzertreten.

ea·sel ['iːzl] Staffelei *f.*

east [iːst] **1.** Ost(en *m*); *the* ♀ der Osten, die Oststaaten *pl.* (*der USA*); *pol.* der Osten; der Orient; **2.** Ost..., östlich; **3.** ostwärts, nach Osten.

Eas·ter ['iːstə] Ostern *n; attr.* Oster...

east·er·ly ['iːstəlɪ] östlich, Ost...; nach Osten; **east·ern** [~n] östlich, Ost...; **east·ward(s)** [~wəd(z)] östlich, nach Osten.

eas·y ['iːzɪ] □ (*-ier, -iest*) leicht, einfach; bequem; frei von Schmerzen; gemächlich, gemütlich; ruhig; ungezwungen; *in ~ circumstances* wohlhabend; *on ~ street Am.* in guten Verhältnissen; *go ~, take it ~* sich Zeit lassen, langsam tun; sich nicht aufregen; *take it ~!* immer mit der Ruhe!; *~ chair* Sessel *m; ~-go-ing* gelassen.

eat [iːt] **1.** (*ate, eaten*) essen; (zer-)fressen; *~ out* auswärts essen; **2.** *~s pl.* F Fressalien *pl.;* **eat·a·ble** ['iːtəbl] **1.** eß-, genießbar; **2.** *~s pl.* Eßwaren *pl.;* **~en** ['iːtn] *p.p. von* eat 1; **~er** [~ə] Esser(in).

eaves [iːvz] *pl.* Dachrinne *f*, Traufe *f; ~drop* ['iːvzdrɒp] (*-pp-*) (heimlich) lauschen *od.* horchen.

ebb [eb] **1.** Ebbe *f; fig.* Tiefstand *m; fig.* Abnahme *f;* **2.** verebben; *fig.* abnehmen, sinken; *~ tide* ['eb'taɪd] Ebbe *f.*

eb·o·ny ['ebənɪ] Ebenholz *n.*

ec·cen·tric [ɪk'sentrɪk] **1.** (*~ally*) exzentrisch; überspannt; **2.** Exzentriker *m*, Sonderling *m.*

ec·cle·si·as·tic [ɪkliːzɪ'æstɪk] (*~ally*), **~·ti·cal** □ [~kl] geistlich, kirchlich.

ech·o ['ekəʊ] **1.** (*pl. -oes*) Echo *n;* **2.** widerhallen; *fig.* echoen, nachsprechen.

e·clipse [ɪ'klɪps] **1.** *ast.* Finsternis *f;* **2.** verfinstern; *be ~d by fig.* verblassen neben (*dat.*).

e·co·cide ['iːkəsaɪd] Umweltzerstörung *f.*

e·co·log·i·cal □ [iːkə'lɒdʒɪkl] ökologisch; **~·lo·gist** [iːˈkɒlədʒɪst] Ökologe *m; ~·lo·gy* [~ɪ] Ökologie *f.*

ec·o·nom·ic [iːkə'nɒmɪk] (*~ally*) wirtschaftlich, Wirtschafts...; *~ aid*

Wirtschaftshilfe *f; ~ growth* Wirtschaftswachstum *n; ~·i·cal* □ [~kl] wirtschaftlich, sparsam; **~·ics** *sg.* Volkswirtschaft(slehre) *f.*

e·con·o·mist [ɪ'kɒnəmɪst] Volkswirt *m; ~·mize* [~aɪz] sparsam wirtschaften (mit); **~·my** [~ɪ] **1.** Wirtschaft *f;* Wirtschaftlichkeit *f*, Sparsamkeit *f;* Einsparung *f;* **2.** Spar...; *~ class* ✈ Economyklasse *f.*

e·co·sys·tem ['iːkəʊsɪstəm] Ökosystem *n.*

ec·sta·sy ['ekstəsɪ] Ekstase *f*, Verzückung *f; ~·tic* [ɪk'stætɪk] (*~ally*) verzückt.

ed·dy ['edɪ] **1.** Wirbel *m;* **2.** wirbeln.

edge [edʒ] **1.** Schneide *f;* Rand *m;* Kante *f;* Schärfe *f;* △ *nicht* (*Straßen-, Haus*)Ecke; *be on ~* nervös *od.* gereizt sein; **2.** schärfen; (um)säumen; (sich) drängen; *~·ways, ~·wise* ['edʒweɪz, ~waɪz] seitlich, von der Seite.

edg·ing ['edʒɪŋ] Einfassung *f;* Rand *m.*

edg·y ['edʒɪ] (*-ier, -iest*) scharf(kantig); F nervös; F gereizt.

ed·i·ble ['edɪbl] eßbar.

e·dict ['iːdɪkt] Edikt *n.*

ed·i·fice ['edɪfɪs] Gebäude *n.*

ed·i·fy·ing □ ['edɪfaɪŋ] erbaulich.

ed·it ['edɪt] *Text* herausgeben, redigieren; *Zeitung* als Herausgeber leiten; **e·di·tion** [ɪ'dɪʃn] (*Buch*)Ausgabe *f;* Auflage *f;* **ed·i·tor** ['edɪtə] Herausgeber(in); Redakteur(in); **ed·i·to·ri·al** [edɪ'tɔːrɪəl] **1.** Leitartikel *m;* **2.** □ Redaktions...

ed·u·cate ['edjuːkeɪt] erziehen; unterrichten; **~·cat·ed** gebildet; **~·ca·tion** [edjuː'keɪʃn] Erziehung *f;* (Aus)Bildung *f;* Bildungs-, Schulwesen *n; Ministry of* ♀ Unterrichtsministerium *n; ~·ca·tion·al* □ [~nl] erzieherisch, Erziehungs...; Bildungs...; **~·ca·tor** ['edjuːkeɪtə] Erzieher(in).

eel *zo.* [iːl] Aal *m.*

ef·fect [ɪ'fekt] **1.** Wirkung *f;* Erfolg *m*, Ergebnis *n;* Auswirkung(en *pl.*) *f;* Effekt *m*, Eindruck *m;* ⊕ Leistung *f; ~s pl. econ.* Effekten *pl.;* persönliche Habe; *be of ~* Wirkung haben; *take ~* in Kraft treten; *in ~* tatsächlich, praktisch; *to the ~ des* Inhalts; **2.** bewirken; ausführen; **ef·fec·tive** □ [~ɪv] wirksam; eindrucksvoll; tatsächlich, wirklich; ⊕ nutz-

E

bar; ~ **date** Tag m des Inkrafttretens.

ef·fem·i·nate □ [ɪˈfemɪnət] verweichlicht; weibisch.

ef·fer|vesce [efəˈves] brausen, sprudeln; ~**ves·cent** [~nt] sprudelnd, schäumend.

ef·fi·cien|cy [ɪˈfɪʃənsɪ] Leistung(sfähigkeit) f; ~ **engineer**, ~ **expert** econ. Rationalisierungsfachmann m; ~**t** □ [~t] wirksam; leistungsfähig, tüchtig.

ef·flu·ent [ˈefluənt] Abwasser n, Abwässer pl.

ef·fort [ˈefət] Anstrengung f, Bemühung f (at um); Mühe f; without~, ~**·less** □ [~lɪs] mühelos, ohne Anstrengung.

ef·fron·te·ry [ɪˈfrʌntərɪ] Frechheit f.

ef·fu·sive □ [ɪˈfjuːsɪv] überschwenglich.

egg¹ [eg]: ~ **on** anstacheln.

egg² [~] Ei n; put all one's ~s in one basket alles auf eine Karte setzen; as sure as ~s is ~s F todsicher; ~**·co·sy** [ˈegkəʊzɪ] Eierwärmer m; ~**·cup** Eierbecher m; ~**·head** F Eierkopf m (Intellektueller).

e·go·is|m [ˈegəʊɪzəm] Egoismus m, Selbstsucht f; ~**t** [~ɪst] Egoist(in), selbstsüchtiger Mensch.

eg·o·tis|m [ˈegəʊtɪzəm] Egotismus m, Selbstgefälligkeit f; ~**t** [~ɪst] Egotist(in), selbstgefälliger od. geltungsbedürftiger Mensch.

E·gyp·tian [ɪˈdʒɪpʃn] **1.** ägyptisch; **2.** Ägypter(in).

ei·der·down [ˈaɪdədaʊn] Eiderdaunen pl.; Daunendecke f.

eight [eɪt] **1.** acht; Acht f; **eigh·teen** [ˈeɪˈtiːn] **1.** achtzehn; **2.** Achtzehn f; **eigh·teenth** [~θ] achtzehnte(r, -s); ~**·fold** [ˈeɪtfəʊld] achtfach; ~**h** [eɪtθ] **1.** achte(r, -s); **2.** Achtel n; ~**h·ly** [ˈeɪtθlɪ] achtens; **eigh·ti·eth** [ˈeɪtɪɪθ] achtzigste(r, -s); **eigh·ty** [ˈeɪtɪ] **1.** achtzig; **2.** Achtzig f.

ei·ther [ˈaɪðə; Am. ˈiːðə] jede(r, -s) (von zweien); eine(r, -s) (von zweien); beides; ~ ... or entweder ... oder; not ~ auch nicht.

e·jac·u·late [ɪˈdʒækjʊleɪt] v/t. Worte etc. aus-, hervorstoßen; physiol. Samen ausstoßen; v/i. physiol. ejakulieren, e-n Samenerguß haben.

e·ject [ɪˈdʒekt] vertreiben; hinauswerfen; entlassen, -fernen (from aus e-m Amt).

eke [iːk]: ~ **out** Vorräte etc. strecken; Einkommen aufbessern; ~ **out** a living sich (mühsam) durchschlagen.

e·lab·o·rate 1. □ [ɪˈlæbərət] sorgfältig (aus)gearbeitet; kompliziert; **2.** [~reɪt] sorgfältig ausarbeiten.

e·lapse [ɪˈlæps] verfließen, -streichen.

e·las|tic [ɪˈlæstɪk] **1.** (~ally) elastisch, dehnbar; ~ **band** Brt. = **2.** Gummiring m, -band n; ~**·ti·ci·ty** [elæˈstɪsətɪ] Elastizität f.

e·lat·ed [ɪˈleɪtɪd] begeistert, stolz.

el·bow [ˈelbəʊ] **1.** Ellbogen m; Biegung f; ⊕ Knie n; at one's ~ bei der Hand; out at ~s fig. heruntergekommen; **2.** mit den Ellbogen (weg)stoßen; ~ **one's way through** sich (mit den Ellbogen) e-n Weg bahnen durch.

el·der¹ ♀ [ˈeldə] Holunder m.

el·der² [~] **1.** ältere(r, -s); **2.** der, die Ältere; (Kirchen)Älteste(r) m; ~**·ly** [~lɪ] ältlich, ältere(r, -s).

el·dest [ˈeldɪst] älteste(r, -s).

e·lect [ɪˈlekt] **1.** gewählt; **2.** (aus-, er)wählen.

e·lec|tion [ɪˈlekʃn] **1.** Wahl f; **2.** pol. Wahl...; ~**·tor** [~tə] Wähler(in); Am. pol. Wahlmann m; hist. Kurfürst m; ~**·to·ral** [~ərəl] Wahl..., Wähler...; ~ **college** Am. pol. Wahlmänner pl.; ~**·to·rate** pol. [~ərət] Wähler(schaft f) pl.

e·lec|tric [ɪˈlektrɪk] (~ally) elektrisch, Elektro...; fig. elektrisierend; ~**·tri·cal** □ [~kl] elektrisch; Elektro...; ~ **engineer** Elektroingenieur m, -techniker m; ~ **tric chair** elektrischer Stuhl; ~**·tri·cian** [ɪlekˈtrɪʃn] Elektriker m; ~**·tri·ci·ty** [~ɪsətɪ] Elektrizität f.

e·lec·tri·fy [ɪˈlektrɪfaɪ] elektrifizieren; elektrisieren (a. fig.).

e·lec·tro- [ɪˈlektrəʊ] Elektro...

e·lec·tro·cute [ɪˈlektrəkjuːt] auf dem elektrischen Stuhl hinrichten; durch elektrischen Strom töten.

e·lec·tron [ɪˈlektrɒn] Elektron n.

e·lec·tron·ic [ɪlekˈtrɒnɪk] **1.** (~ally) elektronisch, Elektronen...; ~ **data processing** elektronische Datenverarbeitung; **2.** ~s sg. Elektronik f; pl. Elektronik f (e-s Geräts).

el·e|gance [ˈelɪgəns] Eleganz f; ~**·gant** □ [~t] elegant; geschmackvoll; erstklassig.

el·e|ment [ˈelɪmənt] Element n; Urstoff *m*; (Grund)Bestandteil *m*; ~*s pl.* Anfangsgründe *pl.*, Grundlage(n *pl.*) *f*; Elemente *pl.*, Naturkräfte *pl.*; **~men·tal** □ [elɪ'mentl] elementar; wesentlich.

el·e·men·ta·ry □ [elɪ'mentərɪ] elementar; Anfangs..; ~ *school Am.* Grundschule *f*.

el·e·phant *zo.* ['elɪfənt] Elefant *m*.

el·e·vate ['elɪveɪt] erhöhen; *fig.* erheben; **~vat·ed** erhöht; *fig.* gehoben, erhaben; ~ (*railroad*) *Am.* Hochbahn *f*; **~va·tion** [elɪ'veɪʃn] Erhebung *f*; Erhöhung *f*; Höhe *f*; Erhabenheit *f*; **~va·tor** ⊕ ['elɪveɪtə] *Am.* Lift *m*, Fahrstuhl *m*, Aufzug *m*; ✈ Höhenruder *n*.

e·lev·en [ɪ'levn] **1.** elf; **2.** Elf *f*; **~th** [~θ] **1.** elfte(r, -s); **2.** Elftel *n*.

elf [elf] (*pl.* **elves**) Elf(e *f*) *m*; Kobold *m*.

e·li·cit [ɪ'lɪsɪt] *et.* entlocken (*from dat.*); ans (Tages)Licht bringen.

el·i·gi·ble □ ['elɪdʒəbl] geeignet, annehmbar, akzeptabel; berechtigt.

e·lim·i·nate [ɪ'lɪmɪneɪt] entfernen, beseitigen; ausscheiden; **~na·tion** [ɪlɪmɪ'neɪʃn] Entfernung *f*, Beseitigung *f*; Ausscheidung *f*.

é·lite [eɪ'li:t] Elite *f*; Auslese *f*.

elk *zo.* [elk] Elch *m*.

el·lipse ᴀ [ɪ'lɪps] Ellipse *f*.

elm ♀ [elm] Ulme *f*, Rüster *f*.

el·o·cu·tion [elə'kju:ʃn] Vortrag(skunst *f*,-sweise) *f* *m*; Sprechtechnik *f*.

e·lon·gate [ɪ'lɒŋgeɪt] verlängern.

e·lope [ɪ'ləʊp] (mit s-m *od.* s-r Geliebten) ausreißen *od.* durchbrennen.

e·lo·quence ['eləkwəns] Beredsamkeit *f*; **~quent** □ [~t] beredt.

else [els] sonst, weiter; anderer(r, -s); **~where** ['els'weə] anderswo(hin).

e·lu·ci·date [ɪ'lu:sɪdeɪt] erklären.

e·lude [ɪ'lu:d] geschickt entgehen, ausweichen, sich entziehen (*alle dat.*); *fig.* nicht einfallen (*dat.*).

e·lu·sive □ [ɪ'lu:sɪv] schwerfaßbar.

elves [elvz] *pl.* von **elf**.

e·ma·ci·ated [ɪ'meɪʃɪeɪtɪd] abgezehrt, ausgemergelt.

em·a·nate ['eməneɪt] ausströmen; ausgehen (*from* von); **~na·tion** [emə'neɪʃn] Ausströmen *n*; *fig.* Ausstrahlung *f*.

e·man·ci·pate [ɪ'mænsɪpeɪt] emanzipieren; befreien; **~pa·tion** [ɪmænsɪ'peɪʃn] Emanzipation *f*; Befreiung *f*.

em·balm [ɪm'bɑ:m] (ein)balsamieren.

em·bank·ment [ɪm'bæŋkmənt] Eindämmung *f*; (Erd)Damm *m*; (Bahn-, Straßen)Damm *m*; Uferstraße *f*.

em·bar·go [em'bɑ:gəʊ] (*pl.* **-goes**) Embargo *n*, (Hafen-, Handels)Sperre *f*.

em·bark [ɪm'bɑ:k] ♻, ✈ an Bord nehmen *od.* gehen, ♻ *a.* (sich) einschiffen; *Waren* verladen; ~ *on*, ~ *upon et.* anfangen *od.* beginnen.

em·bar·rass [ɪm'bærəs] in Verlegenheit bringen, verlegen machen, in e-e peinliche Lage versetzen; **~ing** □ [~ɪŋ] unangenehm, peinlich; **~ment** [~mənt] Verlegenheit *f*.

em·bas·sy ['embəsɪ] Botschaft *f*.

em·bed [ɪm'bed] (**-dd-**) (ein)betten, (ein)lagern.

em·bel·lish [ɪm'belɪʃ] verschönern; *fig.* ausschmücken, beschönigen.

em·bers ['embəz] *pl.* Glut *f*.

em·bez·zle [ɪm'bezl] unterschlagen; **~ment** [~mənt] Unterschlagung *f*.

em·bit·ter [ɪm'bɪtə] verbittern.

em·blem ['embləm] Sinnbild *n*; Wahrzeichen *n*.

em·bod·y [ɪm'bɒdɪ] verkörpern; enthalten.

em·bo·lis·m ᵍ ['embəlɪzəm] Embolie *f*.

em·brace [ɪm'breɪs] **1.** (sich) umarmen; einschließen; **2.** Umarmung *f*.

em·broi·der [ɪm'brɔɪdə] (be)sticken; *fig.* ausschmücken; **~y** [~ərɪ] Stickerei *f*; *fig.* Ausschmückung *f*.

em·broil [ɪm'brɔɪl] (in Streit) verwickeln; verwirren.

e·men·da·tion [i:mən'deɪʃn] Verbesserung *f*, Berichtigung *f*.

em·e·rald ['emərəld] **1.** Smaragd *m*; **2.** smaragdgrün.

e·merge [ɪ'mɜ:dʒ] auftauchen; hervorgehen; *fig.* sich erheben; sich zeigen.

e·mer·gen·cy [ɪ'mɜ:dʒənsɪ] Not (-lage) *f*, **-fall** *m*, **-stand** *m*; *attr.* Not...; ~ *brake* Notbremse *f*; ~ *call* Notruf *m*; ~ *exit* Notausgang *m*; ~ *landing* ✈ Notlandung *f*; ~ *number* Notruf(nummer *f*) *m*; ~ *ward* ᵍ Notaufnahme *f*; **~gent** [~t] auftauchend; *fig.* (jung u.) aufstrebend (*Nationen*).

em·i·grant ['emɪgrənt] Auswanderer *m*, *bsd. pol.* Emigrant(in); **~grate** [~reɪt] auswandern, *bsd. pol.* emigrieren; **~·gra·tion** [emɪˈɡreɪʃn] Auswanderung *f, bsd. pol.* Emigration *f.*

em·i|nence [ˈemɪnəns] (An)Höhe *f;* hohe Stellung; Ruhm *m,* Bedeutung *f;* ♀ Eminenz *f (Titel);* **~·nent** □ [~t] *fig.* ausgezeichnet, hervorragend; **~·nent·ly** [~lɪ] ganz besonders, äußerst.

e·mit [ɪˈmɪt] (-*tt-*) aussenden, -stoßen, -strahlen, -strömen; von sich geben.

e·mo·tion [ɪˈməʊʃn] (Gemüts)Bewegung *f,* Gefühl(sregung *f*) *n;* Rührung *f;* **~·al** □ [~l] emotional; gefühlsmäßig; gefühlsbetont; **~·al·ly** [~lɪ] emotional, gefühlsmäßig; *~ disturbed* seelisch gestört; *~ ill* gemütskrank; **~·less** [~lɪs] gefühllos; unbewegt.

em·pe·ror [ˈempərə] Kaiser *m.*

em·pha|sis [ˈemfəsɪs] (*pl.* -*ses* [-siːz]) Gewicht *n;* Nachdruck *m;* **~·size** [~saɪz] nachdrücklich betonen; **~·t·ic** [ɪmˈfætɪk] (~*ally*) nachdrücklich; deutlich; bestimmt.

em·pire [ˈempaɪə] (Kaiser)Reich *n;* Herrschaft *f; the British* ♀ das britische Weltreich.

em·pir·i·cal □ [emˈpɪrɪkl] erfahrungsgemäß.

em·ploy [ɪmˈplɔɪ] **1.** beschäftigen, anstellen; an-, verwenden, gebrauchen; **2.** Beschäftigung *f,* in *the ~* of angestellt bei; **~·ee** [emplɔɪˈiː] Angestellte(*r m*) *f,* Arbeitnehmer(in); **~·er** [ɪmˈplɔɪə] Arbeitgeber(in); **~·ment** [~mənt] Beschäftigung *f,* Arbeit *f; ~ agency,* (a.) Arbeits(vermittlung(sbüro *n*) *f; ~ market* Arbeits-, Stellenmarkt *m; ~ service agency Brt.* Arbeitsamt *n.*

em·pow·er [ɪmˈpaʊə] ermächtigen; befähigen.

em·press [ˈempris] Kaiserin *f.*

emp|ti·ness [ˈemptɪnɪs] Leere *f* (*a. fig.*); **~·ty** □ [ˈemptɪ] **1.** (-*ier,* -*iest*) leer (*a. fig.*); *~ of* ohne; **2.** (aus-, ent)leeren; sich leeren.

em·u·late [ˈemjʊleɪt] wetteifern mit; nacheifern (*dat.*); es gleichtun (*dat.*).

e·mul·sion [ɪˈmʌlʃn] Emulsion *f.*

en·a·ble [ɪˈneɪbl] befähigen, es j-m ermöglichen; ermächtigen.

en·act [ɪˈnækt] verfügen, -ordnen; *Gesetz* erlassen; *thea.* aufführen.

e·nam·el [ɪˈnæml] **1.** Email(le *f*) *n; anat.* (Zahn)Schmelz *m;* Glasur *f,*

Lack *m;* Nagellack *m;* **2.** (*bsd. Brt.* -*ll-, Am.* -*l-*) emaillieren; glasieren; lackieren.

en·am·o(u)red [ɪˈnæməd]: *~ of* verliebt in.

en·camp·ment *bsd.* ✕ [ɪnˈkæmpmənt] (Feld)Lager *n.*

en·cased [ɪnˈkeɪst]: *~ in* gehüllt in (*acc.*).

en·chant [ɪnˈtʃɑːnt] bezaubern; **~·ing** □ [~ɪŋ] bezaubernd; **~·ment** [~mənt] Bezauberung *f;* Zauber *m.*

en·cir·cle [ɪnˈsɜːkl] einkreisen, umzingeln; umfassen, umschlingen.

en·close [ɪnˈkləʊz] einzäunen; einschließen; beifügen; **en·clo·sure** [~əʊʒə] Einzäunung *f;* eingezäuntes Grundstück; Anlage *f* (*zu e-m Brief*).

en·com·pass [ɪnˈkʌmpəs] umgeben.

en·coun·ter [ɪnˈkaʊntə] **1.** Begegnung *f;* Gefecht *n;* **2.** begegnen (*dat.*); auf *Schwierigkeiten etc.* stoßen; mit *j-m feindlich* zusammenstoßen.

en·cour·age [ɪnˈkʌrɪdʒ] ermutigen; fördern; **~·ment** [~mənt] Ermutigung *f;* Anfeuerung *f;* Unterstützung *f.*

en·croach [ɪnˈkrəʊtʃ] (*on, upon*) eingreifen (in *j-s Recht etc.*), eindringen (in *acc.*); über Gebühr in Anspruch nehmen (*acc.*); **~·ment** [~mənt] Ein-, Übergriff *m.*

en·cum|ber [ɪnˈkʌmbə] belasten; (be)hindern; **~·brance** [~brəns] Last *f,* Belastung *f,* Hindernis *n,* Behinderung *f; without ~* ohne (Familien-)Anhang.

en·cy·clo·p(a)e·di·a [ensaɪkləˈpiːdjə] Enzyklopädie *f.*

end [end] **1.** Ende *n;* Ziel *n,* Zweck *m; no ~* of unendlich viel(e), unzählige; *in the ~* am Ende, schließlich; *on ~* aufrecht; *stand on ~* zu Berge stehen (*Haare*); *to no ~* vergebens; *go off the deep ~ fig.* in die Luft gehen; *make both ~s meet* gerade auskommen; **2.** enden; beend(ig)en.

en·dan·ger [ɪnˈdeɪndʒə] gefährden.

en·dear [ɪnˈdɪə] beliebt machen (*to s.o.* bei j-m); **~·ing** □ [~rɪŋ] gewinnend; liebenswert; **~·ment** [~mənt] Liebkosung *f; term of ~* Kosewort *n.*

en·deav·o(u)r [ɪnˈdevə] **1.** Bestreben *n,* Bemühung *f;* **2.** sich bemühen.

end|ing [ˈendɪŋ] Ende *n;* Schluß *m; gr.* Endung *f;* **~·less** □ [~lɪs] endlos, unendlich; ⊕ ohne Ende.

en·dive ❦ ['endɪv] Endivie f.

en·dorse [ɪn'dɔːs] econ. Scheck etc. indossieren; et. vermerken (on auf der Rückseite e-r Urkunde); gutheißen; **~ment** [~mənt] Aufschrift f, Vermerk m; econ. Indossament n.

en·dow [ɪn'daʊ] fig. ausstatten; ~ s.o. with s.th. j-m et. stiften; **~ment** [~mənt] Stiftung f; mst ~s pl. Begabung f, Talent n.

en·dur·ance [ɪn'djʊərəns] Ausdauer f; Ertragen n; beyond ~, past ~ unerträglich; **~e** [ɪn'djʊə] ertragen.

en·e·my ['enəmɪ] 1. Feind m; the ♀ der Teufel; 2. feindlich.

en·er|get·ic [enə'dʒetɪk] (~ally) energisch; **~gy** ['enədʒɪ] Energie f; ~ crisis Energiekrise f.

en·fold [ɪn'fəʊld] einhüllen; umfassen.

en·force [ɪn'fɔːs] (mit Nachdruck, a. gerichtlich) geltend machen; erzwingen; aufzwingen (upon dat.); durchführen; **~ment** [~mənt] Erzwingung f; Geltendmachung f; Durchführung f.

en·fran·chise [ɪn'fræntʃaɪz] j-m das Wahlrecht verleihen; j-m die Bürgerrechte verleihen.

en·gage [ɪn'geɪdʒ] v/t. anstellen; verpflichten; Künstler etc. engagieren; in Anspruch nehmen; ✕ angreifen; be ~d verlobt sein (to mit); beschäftigt sein (in mit); besetzt sein; ~ the clutch mot. e-n Gang einlegen; v/i. sich verpflichten (to do zu tun); garantieren (for für); sich beschäftigen (in mit); ✕ angreifen; ⊕ greifen (Zahnräder); **~ment** [~mənt] Verpflichtung f; Verlobung f; Verabredung f; Beschäftigung f; ✕ Gefecht n; ⊕ Ineinandergreifen f.

en·gag·ing □ [ɪn'geɪdʒɪŋ] einnehmend; gewinnend (Lächeln etc.).

en·gine ['endʒɪn] Maschine f; Motor m; 🚂 Lokomotive f; **~-driv·er** Brt. 🚂 Lokomotivführer m.

en·gi·neer [endʒɪ'nɪə] 1. Ingenieur m; Techniker m; Mechaniker m; Am. 🚂 Lokomotivführer m; ✕ Pionier m; 2. als Ingenieur tätig sein; bauen; **~ing** [~rɪŋ] 1. Maschinen- u. Gerätebau m; Ingenieurwesen n; 2. technisch; Ingenieur...

En·glish ['ɪŋglɪʃ] 1. englisch; 2. ling. Englisch n; the ~ pl. die Engländer pl.; in plain ~ fig. unverblümt; **~man** (pl. -men) Engländer m;

~wom·an (pl. -women) Engländerin f.

en·grave [ɪn'greɪv] (ein)gravieren, (-)meißeln, (-)schnitzen; fig. einprägen; **en·grav·er** [~ə] Graveur m; **en·grav·ing** [~ɪŋ] (Kupfer-, Stahl-) Stich m; Holzschnitt m.

en·grossed [ɪn'grəʊst] (in) (voll) in Anspruch genommen (von), vertieft, -sunken (in acc.).

en·gulf [ɪn'gʌlf] verschlingen (a. fig.).

en·hance [ɪn'hɑːns] erhöhen.

e·nig·ma [ɪ'nɪgmə] Rätsel n; **en·ig·mat·ic** [enɪg'mætɪk] (~ally) rätselhaft.

en·joy [ɪn'dʒɔɪ] sich erfreuen an (dat.); genießen; did you ~ it? hat es Ihnen gefallen?; ~ o.s. sich amüsieren, sich gut unterhalten; ~ yourself! viel Spaß!; I ~ my dinner es schmeckt mir; **~·a·ble** □ [~əbl] angenehm, erfreulich; **~ment** [~mənt] Genuß m, Freude f.

en·large [ɪn'lɑːdʒ] (sich) vergrößern od. erweitern, ausdehnen; phot. vergrößern, sich vergrößern lassen; verbreiten od. auslassen (on, upon über acc.); **~ment** [~mənt] Erweiterung f; Vergrößerung f (a. phot.).

en·light·en [ɪn'laɪtn] fig. erleuchten; j-n aufklären; **~ment** [~mənt] Aufklärung f.

en·list [ɪn'lɪst] v/t. ✕ anwerben; j-n gewinnen; ~ed men pl. Am. ✕ Unteroffiziere pl. und Mannschaften pl.; v/i. sich freiwillig melden.

en·liv·en [ɪn'laɪvn] beleben.

en·mi·ty ['enmɪtɪ] Feindschaft f.

en·no·ble [ɪ'nəʊbl] adeln; veredeln.

e·nor·mi·ty [ɪ'nɔːmɪtɪ] Ungeheuerlichkeit f; **~mous** □ [~əs] ungeheuer.

e·nough [ɪ'nʌf] genug.

en·quire, en·qui·ry [ɪn'kwaɪə, ~rɪ] = inquire, inquiry.

en·rage [ɪn'reɪdʒ] wütend machen; ~d wütend (at über acc.).

en·rap·ture [ɪn'ræptʃə] entzücken, hinreißen; ~d entzückt, hingerissen.

en·rich [ɪn'rɪtʃ] be-, anreichern.

en·rol(l) [ɪn'rəʊl] (-ll-) v/t. j-n in e-e Liste eintragen, univ. j-n immatrikulieren; ✕ anwerben; aufnehmen; v/i. sich einschreiben (lassen), univ. sich immatrikulieren; **~ment** [~mənt] Eintragung f, -schreibung f, univ. Immatrikulation f; bsd. ✕ Anwerbung f; Einstellung f; Aufnahme f; Schüler-, Studenten-, Teilnehmerzahl f.

en·sign ['ensaɪn] Fahne f; Flagge f; Abzeichen n; Am. ♣ ['ensn] Leutnant m zur See.

en·sue [ɪn'sjuː] (darauf, nach)folgen.

en·sure [ɪn'ʃʊə] sichern.

en·tail [ɪn'teɪl] ⚖ als Erbgut vererben; fig. mit sich bringen.

en·tan·gle [ɪn'tæŋgl] verwickeln; ~**ment** [~mənt] Verwicklung f; ✗ Drahtverhau m.

en·ter ['entə] v/t. (hinein)gehen, (-)kommen in (acc.), (ein)treten in (acc.), betreten; einsteigen od. einfahren etc. in (acc.); eindringen in (acc.); econ. eintragen, (ver)buchen; Protest erheben; Namen eintragen, -schreiben, j-n aufnehmen; Sport: melden, nennen; ~ s.o. at school j-n zur Schule anmelden; v/i. eintreten, herein-, hineinkommen, -gehen; in ein Land einweisen; Sport: sich melden (for für); ~ into fig. eingehen auf (acc.); ~ on od. upon an inheritance e-e Erbschaft antreten.

en·ter·prise ['entəpraɪz] Unternehmen n (a. econ.); econ. Unternehmertum n; Unternehmungsgeist m; ~**pris·ing** □ [~ɪŋ] unternehmungslustig; wagemutig; kühn.

en·ter·tain [entə'teɪn] unterhalten; bewirten; in Erwägung ziehen; Zweifel etc. hegen; ~**er** [~ə] Entertainer(in), Unterhaltungskünstler(in); ~**ment** [~mənt] Unterhaltung f; Entertainment n; Bewirtung f.

en·thral(l) fig. [ɪn'θrɔːl] (-ll-) fesseln, bezaubern.

en·throne [ɪn'θrəʊn] inthronisieren.

en·thu·si·asm [ɪn'θjuːzɪæzəm] Begeisterung f; ~**t** [~st] Enthusiast(in); ~**tic** [ɪnθjuːzɪ'æstɪk] (~ally) begeistert.

en·tice [ɪn'taɪs] (ver)locken; ~**ment** [~mənt] Verlockung f, Reiz m.

en·tire □ [ɪn'taɪə] ganz, vollständig; ungeteilt; ~**ly** [~lɪ] völlig; ausschließlich.

en·ti·tle □ [ɪn'taɪtl] betiteln; berechtigen (to zu).

en·ti·ty ['entɪtɪ] Wesen n; Dasein n.

en·trails ['entreɪlz] pl. Eingeweide pl.; fig. das Innere.

en·trance ['entrəns] Eintritt m; Einfahrt f; Eingang m; Einlaß m.

en·treat [ɪn'triːt] inständig bitten,

anflehen; **en·trea·ty** [~ɪ] dringende od. inständige Bitte.

en·trench ✗ [ɪn'trentʃ] verschanzen (a. fig.).

en·trust [ɪn'trʌst] anvertrauen (s.th. to s.o. j-m et.); betrauen.

en·try ['entrɪ] Einreise f; Einlaß m, Zutritt m; Eingang m; Eintritt f; Beitritt m (into zu); Eintragung f; Sport: Meldung f, Nennung f; ~ permit Einreisegenehmigung f; ~ visa Einreisevisum n; book-keeping by double (single) ~ econ. doppelte (einfache) Buchführung; no ~! Zutritt verboten!, mot. keine Einfahrt!

en·twine [ɪn'twaɪn] ineinanderschlingen.

e·nu·me·rate [ɪ'njuːməreɪt] aufzählen.

en·vel·op [ɪn'veləp] (ein)hüllen, einwickeln.

en·ve·lope ['envələʊp] Briefumschlag m.

en·vi·a·ble □ ['envɪəbl] beneidenswert; ~**ous** □ [~əs] neidisch.

en·vi·ron·ment [ɪn'vaɪərənmənt] Umgebung f, sociol. a. Milieu n; Umwelt f (a. sociol.); ~**men·tal** □ [ɪnvaɪərən'mentl] sociol. Milieu...; Umwelt...; ~ law Umweltschutzgesetz n; ~ pollution Umweltverschmutzung f; ~**men·tal·ist** [~əlɪst] Umweltschützer(in); ~**s** ['envɪrənz] pl. Umgebung f (e-r Stadt).

en·vis·age [ɪn'vɪzɪdʒ] sich et. vorstellen.

en·voy ['envɔɪ] Gesandte(r) m.

en·vy ['envɪ] 1. Neid m; 2. beneiden.

ep·ic ['epɪk] 1. episch; 2. Epos n.

ep·i·dem·ic [epɪ'demɪk] 1. (~ally) seuchenartig; ~ disease = 2. Epidemie f, Seuche f.

ep·i·der·mis [epɪ'dɜːmɪs] Oberhaut f.

ep·i·lep·sy ✿ ['epɪlepsɪ] Epilepsie f.

ep·i·logue, Am. a. **-log** ['epɪlɒg] Nachwort n.

e·pis·co·pal □ eccl. [ɪ'pɪskəpl] bischöflich.

ep·i·sode ['epɪsəʊd] Episode f.

ep·i·taph ['epɪtɑːf] Grabinschrift f; Gedenktafel f.

e·pit·o·me [ɪ'pɪtəmɪ] Verkörperung f, Inbegriff m.

e·poch ['iːpɒk] Epoche f, Zeitalter n.

eq·ua·ble □ ['ekwəbl] ausgeglichen (a. Klima).

e·qual ['iːkwəl] 1. □ gleich; gleich-

mäßig; ~ **to** fig. gewachsen (dat.); ~
opportunities pl. Chancengleichheit
f; ~ **rights** pl. for women Gleichbe-
rechtigung f der Frau; **2.** Gleiche(r
m) f; **3.** (bsd. Brt. -ll-, Am. -l-)
gleichen (dat.); **~·i·ty** [iːˈkwɒlətɪ]
Gleichheit f; **~·i·za·tion** [iːkwəlaɪ-
ˈzeɪʃn] Gleichstellung f; Ausgleich
m; **~·ize** [ˈiːkwəlaɪz] gleichmachen,
-stellen, angleichen; Sport: ausgleichen.

equ·a·nim·i·ty [iːkwəˈnɪmətɪ]
Gleichmut m.

e·qua·tion [ɪˈkweɪʒn] Ausgleich m; ♣
Gleichung f.

e·qua·tor [ɪˈkweɪtə] Äquator m.

e·qui·lib·ri·um [iːkwɪˈlɪbrɪəm] Gleichgewicht n.

e·quip [ɪˈkwɪp] (-pp-) ausrüsten;
~·ment [~mənt] Ausrüstung f; Einrichtung f.

eq·ui·ty [ˈekwətɪ] Gerechtigkeit f,
Billigkeit f.

e·quiv·a·lent [ɪˈkwɪvələnt] **1.** □
gleichwertig; gleichbedeutend (to
mit); **2.** Äquivalent n, Gegenwert m.

e·quiv·o·cal □ [ɪˈkwɪvəkl] zweideutig; zweifelhaft.

e·ra [ˈɪərə] Zeitrechnung f; Zeitalter
n.

e·rad·i·cate [ɪˈrædɪkeɪt] ausrotten.

e·rase [ɪˈreɪz] ausradieren, -strei-
chen, löschen (a. Tonband); fig. auslöschen; **e·ras·er** [~ə] Radiergummi
m.

ere [eə] **1.** cj. ehe, bevor; **2.** prp. vor
(dat.).

e·rect [ɪˈrekt] **1.** □ aufrecht; **2.** aufrichten; Denkmal etc. errichten; aufstellen; **e·rec·tion** [~kʃn] Errichtung
f; physiol. Erektion f.

er·mine zo. [ˈɜːmɪn] Hermelin n.

e·ro·sion [ɪˈrəʊʒn] Zerfressen n; geol.
Erosion f, Auswaschung f.

e·rot·ic [ɪˈrɒtɪk] (~ally) erotisch; **~·i-
cis·m** [~ɪsɪzəm] Erotik f.

err [ɜː] (sich) irren.

er·rand [ˈerənd] Botengang m, Auftrag m, Besorgung f; go on od. run an
~ e-e Besorgung machen; **~·boy**
Laufbursche m.

er·rat·ic [ɪˈrætɪk] (~ally) sprunghaft,
unstet, unberechenbar.

er·ro·ne·ous □ [ɪˈrəʊnjəs] irrig.

er·ror [ˈerə] Irrtum m, Fehler m; ~s
excepted Irrtümer vorbehalten.

e·rupt [ɪˈrʌpt] ausbrechen (Vulkan
etc.); durchbrechen (Zähne); **e·rup-**

tion [~pʃn] (Vulkan)Ausbruch m; 🌡
Ausbruch m e-s Ausschlags; 🌡 Ausschlag m.

es·ca·late [ˈeskəleɪt] eskalieren (Krieg
etc.); steigen, in die Höhe gehen
(Preise); **~·la·tion** [eskəˈleɪʃn] Eska-
lation f.

es·ca·la·tor [ˈeskəleɪtə] Rolltreppe f.

es·ca·lope [ˈeskələʊp] (bsd. Wiener)
Schnitzel n.

es·cape [ɪˈskeɪp] **1.** entgehen; entkommen, -rinnen; entweichen; j-m
entfallen; **2.** Entrinnen n; Entweichen n; Flucht f; have a narrow ~
mit knapper Not davonkommen; ~
chute 🛫 Notrutsche f.

es·cort 1. [ˈeskɔːt] 🛡 Eskorte f; Ge-
leit(schutz m) n; **2.** [ɪˈskɔːt] 🛡 eskortieren, 🛡, ⚓ Geleit(schutz) geben;
geleiten.

es·cutch·eon [ɪˈskʌtʃən] Wappenschild m, n.

es·pe·cial [ɪˈspeʃl] besondere(r, -s);
vorzüglich; **~·ly** [~lɪ] besonders.

es·pi·o·nage [espɪəˈnɑːʒ] Spionage f.

es·pla·nade [espləˈneɪd] (bsd.
Strand)Promenade f.

es·pres·so [eˈspresəʊ] (pl. -sos) Es-
presso m (Kaffee).

Es·quire [ɪˈskwaɪə] (abbr. Esq.) auf
Briefen: John Smith Esq. Herrn
John Smith.

es·say 1. [eˈseɪ] versuchen; probieren; **2.** [ˈeseɪ] Versuch m; Aufsatz m,
kurze Abhandlung, Essay m, n.

es·sence [ˈesns] Wesen n (e-r Sache)
Essenz f; Extrakt m.

es·sen·tial [ɪˈsenʃl] **1.** □ (to für) wesentlich; wichtig; **2.** mst ~s pl. das
Wesentliche; **~·ly** [~lɪ] im wesentlichen, in der Hauptsache.

es·tab·lish [ɪˈstæblɪʃ] festsetzen; errichten, gründen; einrichten; j-n
einsetzen; ~ o.s. sich niederlassen;
2ed Church Staatskirche f; **~·ment**
[~mənt] Er-, Einrichtung f; Gründung f; the 2 das Establishment, die
etablierte Macht, die herrschende
Schicht.

es·tate [ɪˈsteɪt] (großes) Grundstück,
Landsitz m, Gut n; ⚖ Besitz m,
(Erb)Masse f, Nachlaß m; housing ~
(Wohn)Siedlung f; industrial ~ In-
dustriegebiet n; real ~ Liegenschaf-
ten pl.; (Am. real) ~ **a·gent** Grund-
stücks-, Immobilienmakler m; ~ **car**
Brt. mot. Kombiwagen m.

es·teem [ɪˈstiːm] **1.** Achtung f, An-

sehen n (with bei); 2. achten, (hoch-)
schätzen; ansehen od. betrachten
als.

es·thet·ic(s) Am. [es'θetɪk(s)] =
aesthetic(s).

es·ti·ma·ble ['estɪməbl] schätzens-
wert.

es·ti|mate 1. ['estɪmeɪt] (ab-, ein-)
schätzen; veranschlagen; **2.** [∼mɪt]
Schätzung f; (Kosten)Voranschlag
m; **~·ma·tion** [estɪ'meɪʃn] Schätzung f; Meinung f; Achtung f.

es·trange ['streɪndʒ] entfremden.

es·tu·a·ry ['estjʊərɪ] den Gezeiten
ausgesetzte weite Flußmündung.

etch [etʃ] ätzen; radieren; **~·ing**
['etʃɪŋ] Radierung f; Kupferstich m.

e·ter·nal [ɪ'tɜ:nl] immerwährend,
ewig; **~·ni·ty** [∼ətɪ] Ewigkeit f.

e·ther ['i:θə] Äther m; **e·the·re·al** □
[i:'θɪərɪəl] ätherisch (a. fig.).

eth·i·cal □ ['eθɪkl] sittlich, ethisch;
~·ics [∼s] sg. Sittenlehre f, Ethik f.

Eu·ro- ['jʊərəʊ] europäisch, Euro...

Eu·ro·pe·an [jʊərə'pɪən] **1.** europäisch; **~** (Economic) Community
Europäische (Wirtschafts)Gemein-
schaft; **2.** Europäer(in).

e·vac·u·ate [ɪ'vækjʊeɪt] entleeren;
evakuieren; Haus etc. räumen.

e·vade [ɪ'veɪd] (geschickt) ausweichen (dat.); umgehen.

e·val·u·ate [ɪ'væljʊeɪt] schätzen; abschätzen, bewerten, beurteilen.

ev·a·nes·cent [i:və'nesnt] vergänglich.

e·van·gel·i·cal □ [i:væn'dʒelɪkl]
evangelisch.

e·vap·o|rate [ɪ'væpəreɪt] verdunsten,
-dampfen (lassen); **~d** milk Kon-
densmilch f; **~·ra·tion** [ɪvæpə'reɪʃn]
Verdunstung f, -dampfung f.

e·va|sion [ɪ'veɪʒn] Entkommen n;
Umgehung f, Vermeidung f; Ausflucht f; **~·sive** □ [∼sɪv] auswei-
chend; be ~ ausweichen.

eve [i:v] Vorabend m; Vortag m; on
the ~ of unmittelbar vor (dat.), am
Vorabend (gen.).

e·ven ['i:vn] **1.** adj. □ eben, gleich;
gleichmäßig; ausgeglichen; glatt;
gerade (Zahl); unparteiisch; get ~
with s.o. fig. mit j-m abrechnen; **2.**
adv. selbst, sogar, auch; not ~ nicht
einmal; ~ though ~ if wenn auch; **3.**
ebnen, glätten; ~ out sich einpen-
deln.

eve·ning ['i:vnɪŋ] Abend m; ~ class-

es pl. Abendkurs m; ~ dress Gesellschaftsanzug m; Frack m, Smoking
m; Abendkleid n.

e·ven·song ['i:vnsɒŋ] Abendgottes-
dienst m.

e·vent [ɪ'vent] Ereignis n, Vorfall m;
sportliche Veranstaltung; Sport:
Disziplin f; Sport: Wettbewerb m;
at all ~s auf alle Fälle; in the ~ of im
Falle (gen.); **~·ful** [∼fl] ereignisreich.

e·ven·tu·al □ [ɪ'ventʃʊəl] schließlich; △ nicht eventual; **~·ly** schließlich, endlich.

ev·er ['evə] je, jemals; immer; ~ so
noch so (sehr); as soon as ~ I can
sobald ich nur irgend kann; ~ after,~
since von der Zeit an, seitdem; ~ and
again dann u. wann, hin u. wieder;
for ~ für immer, auf ewig; Yours ~,...
(Briefschluß), ~·glade ~ der sump-
figes Flußgebiet; **~·green 1.** immer-
grün; unverwüstlich, bsd. immer
wieder gern gehört; ~ song Evergreen m; **2.** immergrüne Pflanze;
~·last·ing □ ewig; dauerhaft;
~·more [∼'mɔ:] immerfort.

ev·ery ['evrɪ] jede(r, -s); alle(r, -s); ~
now and then dann u. wann; ~ one of
them jeder von ihnen; ~ other day
jeden zweiten Tag, alle zwei Tage;
~·bod·y jeder(mann); **~·day** Alltags...; **~·one** jeder(mann); **~·thing**
alles; **~·where** überall; überallhin.

e·vict [ɪ'vɪkt] ɪʦ zur Räumung zwingen; j-n gewaltsam entsetzen.

ev·i·dence ['evɪdəns] **1.** Beweis(material n) m, Beweise pl.; (Zeugen-)
Aussage f; give ~ (als Zeuge) aussagen; in ~ als Beweis; deutlich sichtbar; **2.** be~, nachweisen, zeugen von;
~·dent □ [∼t] augenscheinlich,
offenbar, klar.

e·vil ['i:vl] **1.** □ (bsd. Brt. -ll-, Am. -l-)
übel, schlimm, böse; the ♀ One der
Böse (Teufel); **2.** Übel n; das Böse; **~·
mind·ed** [∼'maɪndɪd] bösartig.

e·vince [ɪ'vɪns] zeigen, bekunden.

e·voke [ɪ'vəʊk] (herauf)beschwören;
Erinnerungen wachrufen.

ev·o·lu·tion [i:və'lu:ʃn] Evolution f,
Entwicklung f.

e·volve [ɪ'vɒlv] (sich) entwickeln.

ewe zo. [ju:] Mutterschaf n.

ex [eks] prp. econ. ab Fabrik etc.;
Börse: ohne.

ex- [∼] ehemalig, früher.

ex·act [ɪg'zækt] **1.** □ genau; **2.** Zah-

lung eintreiben; *Gehorsam* fordern; **~ing** [~ɪŋ] streng, genau; **~i·tude** [~ɪtju:d] = *exactness;* **~ly** [~lɪ] exakt, genau; *als Antwort:* ganz recht, genau; **~ness** [~nɪs] Genauigkeit *f.*

ex·ag·ge·rate [ɪɡˈzædʒəreɪt] übertreiben; **~ra·tion** [ɪɡzædʒəˈreɪʃn] Übertreibung *f.*

ex·alt [ɪɡˈzɔ:lt] erhöhen, erheben; preisen; **ex·al·ta·tion** [eɡzɔ:lˈteɪʃn] Begeisterung *f.*

ex·am F [ɪɡˈzæm] Examen *n.*

ex·am·i·na·tion [ɪɡzæmɪˈneɪʃn] Examen *n,* Prüfung *f;* Untersuchung *f;* Vernehmung *f;* **~ine** [ɪɡˈzæmɪn] untersuchen; ⚖ vernehmen, -hören; *Schule etc.:* prüfen (*in in dat.;* *on* über *acc.*).

ex·am·ple [ɪɡˈzɑ:mpl] Beispiel *n,* Vorbild *n,* Muster *n; for* ~ zum Beispiel.

ex·as·pe·rate [ɪɡˈzæspəreɪt] wütend machen; **~ra·tion** □ [~ɪŋ] ärgerlich.

ex·ca·vate [ˈekskəveɪt] ausgraben, -heben, -schachten.

ex·ceed [ɪkˈsi:d] überschreiten; übertreffen; **~ing** □ [~ɪŋ] übermäßig; **~ing·ly** [~lɪ] außerordentlich, überaus.

ex·cel [ɪkˈsel] (*-ll-*) *v/t.* übertreffen; *v/i.* sich auszeichnen; **~lence** [ˈeksələns] ausgezeichnete Qualität; hervorragende Leistung; **Ex·cel·len·cy** [~ənsɪ] Exzellenz *f;* **~lent** □ [~ənt] ausgezeichnet, hervorragend.

ex·cept [ɪkˈsept] **1.** ausnehmen, -schließen; **2.** *prp.* ausgenommen, außer; **~** *for* abgesehen von; **~ing** *prp.* [~ɪŋ] ausgenommen.

ex·cep·tion [ɪkˈsepʃn] Ausnahme *f;* Einwendung *f,* Einwand *m* (*to* gegen); *by way of* ~ ausnahmsweise; *make an* ~ e-e Ausnahme machen; *take* ~ *to* Anstoß nehmen an (*dat.*); **~al** □ [~nl] außergewöhnlich; **~al·ly** [~ʃnəlɪ] un-, außergewöhnlich.

ex·cerpt [ˈeksɜ:pt] Auszug *m.*

ex·cess [ɪkˈses] Übermaß *n;* Überschuß *m;* Ausschweifung *f; attr.* Mehr...; ~ *fare* (Fahrpreis)Zuschlag *m;* ~ *baggage bsd. Am.,* ~ *luggage bsd. Brt.* ❋ Übergepäck *n;* ~ *postage* Nachgebühr *f;* **ex·ces·sive** □ [~ɪv] übermäßig, übertrieben.

ex·change [ɪksˈtʃeɪndʒ] **1.** (aus-, ein-, um)tauschen (*for* gegen); wechseln; **2.** (Aus-, Um)Tausch *m;* (*bsd.* Geld-)

Wechsel *m; a.* bill of ~ Wechsel *m;* Börse *f;* Wechselstube *f;* Fernsprechamt *n; foreign* ~(*s pl.*) Devisen *pl.; rate of* ~, ~ *rate* Wechselkurs *m;* ~ *office* Wechselstube *f;* ~ *student* Austauschstudent(in), -schüler(in).

ex·cheq·uer [ɪksˈtʃekə] Staatskasse *f;* *Chancellor of the* ♀ *Brt.* Schatzkanzler *m,* Finanzminister *m.*

ex·cise¹ [ekˈsaɪz] Verbrauchssteuer *f.*

ex·cise² 𝒮 [~] herausschneiden.

ex·ci·ta·ble [ɪkˈsaɪtəbl] reizbar, (leicht) erregbar.

ex·cite [ɪkˈsaɪt] er-, anregen; reizen; **ex·cit·ed** □ erregt, aufgeregt; **ex·cite·ment** [~mənt] Auf-, Erregung *f;* Reizung *f;* **ex·cit·ing** □ [~ɪŋ] erregend, aufregend, spannend.

ex·claim [ɪkˈskleɪm] (aus)rufen.

ex·cla·ma·tion [ekskləˈmeɪʃn] Ausruf *m,* (Auf)Schrei *m;* ~ *mark, Am. a.* ~ *point* Ausrufe-, Ausrufungszeichen *n.*

ex·clude [ɪkˈsklu:d] ausschließen.

ex·clu·sion [ɪkˈsklu:ʒn] Ausschließung *f,* Ausschluß *m;* **~sive** □ [~sɪv] ausschließlich, exklusiv; Exklusiv...; ~ *of* abgesehen von, ohne.

ex·com·mu·ni·cate [ekskəˈmju:nɪkeɪt] exkommunizieren; **~ca·tion** [ˈekskəmju:nɪˈkeɪʃn] Exkommunikation *f.*

ex·cre·ment [ˈekskrɪmənt] Kot *m.*

ex·crete [ekˈskri:t] ausscheiden.

ex·cru·ci·at·ing □ [ɪkˈskru:ʃieɪtɪŋ] entsetzlich, scheußlich.

ex·cur·sion [ɪkˈskɜ:ʃn] Ausflug *m.*

ex·cu·sa·ble □ [ɪkˈskju:zəbl] entschuldbar; **ex·cuse 1.** [ɪkˈskju:z] entschuldigen; ~ *me* entschuldige(n Sie); **2.** [~u:s] Entschuldigung *f.*

ex·e·cute [ˈeksɪkju:t] ausführen; vollziehen; ♪ vortragen; hinrichten; *Testament* vollstrecken; **ex·e·cu·tion** [eksɪˈkju:ʃn] Ausführung *f;* Vollziehung *f;* (Zwangs)Vollstreckung *f;* Hinrichtung *f;* ♪ Vortrag *m; put od. carry a plan into* ~ e-n Plan ausführen *od.* verwirklichen; **~cu·tion·er** [~ʃnə] Henker *m,* Scharfrichter *m;* **~c·u·tive** [ɪɡˈzekjutɪv] **1.** □ vollziehend, ausübend, *pol.* Exekutiv...; *econ.* leitend; ~ *board* Vorstand *m;* ~ *committee* Exekutivausschuß *m;* **2.** *pol.* Exekutive *f,* vollziehende Gewalt; *econ.* leitender Angestellter; **~c·u·tor** [~ə] Erbschaftsverwalter *m,* Testamentsvollstrecker *m.*

E

ex·em·pla·ry □ [ɪgˈzemplərɪ] vorbildlich.

ex·em·pli·fy [ɪgˈzemplɪfaɪ] veranschaulichen.

ex·empt [ɪgˈzempt] **1.** befreit, frei; **2.** ausnehmen, befreien.

ex·er·cise [ˈeksəsaɪz] **1.** Übung *f*; Ausübung *f*; *Schule:* Übung(sarbeit) *f*, Schulaufgabe *f*; ✗ Manöver *n*; (körperliche) Bewegung *f*; *do one's* ~*s* Übung *od.* Gymnastik machen; *take* ~ sich Bewegung machen; *Am.* ~*s pl.* Feierlichkeiten *pl.*; ~ *book* Schul, Schreibheft *f*; **2.** üben; ausüben; (sich) bewegen; sich Bewegung machen; ✗ exerzieren.

ex·ert [ɪgˈzɜːt] *Einfluß etc.* ausüben; ~ *o.s.* sich anstrengen *od.* bemühen; **ex·er·tion** [~ɜːʃn] Ausübung *f*; Anstrengung *f*, Strapaze *f*.

ex·hale [eksˈheɪl] ausatmen; *Gas, Geruch etc.* verströmen; *Rauch* ausstoßen.

ex·haust [ɪgˈzɔːst] **1.** erschöpfen; entleeren; auspumpen; **2.** ⊕ Abgas *n*, Auspuffgase *pl.*; Auspuff *m*; ~ *fumes pl.* Abgase *pl.*; ~ *pipe* Auspuffrohr *n*; ~**ed** erschöpft (*a. fig.*); vergriffen (*Auflage*); **ex·haus·tion** [~tʃən] Erschöpfung *f*; **ex·haus·tive** □ [~tɪv] erschöpfend.

ex·hib·it [ɪgˈzɪbɪt] **1.** ausstellen; ⚖️ vorzeigen, *Beweise* beibringen; *fig.* zeigen; **2.** Ausstellungsstück *n*; Beweisstück *n*; **ex·hi·bi·tion** [eksɪˈbɪʃn] Ausstellung *f*; Zurschaustellung *f*; *Brt.* Stipendium *n*.

ex·hil·a·rate [ɪgˈzɪləreɪt] auf-, erheitern.

ex·hort [ɪgˈzɔːt] ermahnen.

ex·ile [ˈeksaɪl] **1.** Verbannung *f*; Exil *n*; Verbannte(r *m f*); im Exil Lebende(r *m f*); **2.** in die Verbannung *od.* ins Exil schicken.

ex·ist [ɪgˈzɪst] existieren; vorhanden sein; leben; bestehen; ~**ence** [~əns] Existenz *f*; Vorhandensein *n*, Vorkommen *n*; Leben *n*, Dasein *n*; △ *nicht* *Existenz* (*Lebensunterhalt*); ~**ent** [~t] vorhanden.

ex·it [ˈeksɪt] **1.** Abgang *m*; Ausgang *m*; (Autobahn)Ausfahrt *f*; Ausreise *f*; **2.** *thea.* (geht) ab.

ex·o·dus [ˈeksədəs] Auszug *m*; Abwanderung *f*; *general* ~ allgemeiner Aufbruch.

ex·on·er·ate [ɪgˈzɒnəreɪt] entlasten, entbinden, befreien.

ex·or·bi·tant □ [ɪgˈzɔːbɪtənt] übertrieben, maßlos; unverschämt (*Preis etc.*).

ex·or·cize [ˈeksɔːsaɪz] *böse Geister* beschwören, austreiben (*from* aus); befreien (*of* von).

ex·ot·ic [ɪgˈzɒtɪk] (~*ally*) exotisch; fremdländisch; fremd(artig).

ex·pand [ɪkˈspænd] (sich) ausbreiten; (sich) ausdehnen *od.* erweitern; ~ *on* sich auslassen über (*acc.*); **ex·panse** [~ns] Ausdehnung *f*, Weite *f*; **ex·pan·sion** [~ʃn] Ausbreitung *f*; *phys.* Ausdehnung *n*; *fig.* Erweiterung *f*, Ausweitung *f*; **ex·pan·sive** □ [~sɪv] ausdehnungsfähig; ausgedehnt, weit; *fig.* mitteilsam.

ex·pat·ri·ate [eksˈpætrɪeɪt] *j-n* ausbürgern, *j-m* die Staatsangehörigkeit aberkennen.

ex·pect [ɪkˈspekt] erwarten; F annehmen; *be* ~*ing* in anderen Umständen sein; **ex·pec·tant** □ [~ənt] erwartend (*of acc.*); ~ *mother* werdende Mutter; **ex·pec·ta·tion** [ekspekˈteɪʃn] Erwartung *f*; Hoffnung *f*, Aussicht *f*.

ex·pe·di·ent [ɪkˈspiːdjənt] **1.** □ zweckmäßig; ratsam; **2.** (Hilfs-) Mittel *n*, (Not)Behelf *m*.

ex·pe·di·tion [ekspɪˈdɪʃn] Eile *f*; ✗ Feldzug *m*; (Forschungs)Reise *f*, Expedition *f*; ~**tious** □ [~ʃəs] schnell.

ex·pel [ɪkˈspel] (-*ll*-) ausstoßen; vertreiben, -jagen; hinauswerfen, ausschließen.

ex·pend [ɪkˈspend] *Geld* ausgeben; aufwenden; verbrauchen; **ex·pen·di·ture** [~dɪtʃə] Ausgabe *f*; Aufwand *m*; **ex·pense** [ɪkˈspens] Ausgabe *f*; Kosten *pl.*; ~*s pl.* Unkosten *pl.*, Spesen *pl.*, Auslagen *pl.*; *at the* ~ *of* auf Kosten (*gen.*); *at any* ~ um jeden Preis; **ex·pen·sive** □ [~sɪv] kostspielig, teuer.

ex·pe·ri·ence [ɪkˈspɪərɪəns] **1.** Erfahrung *f*; (Lebens)Praxis *f*; Erlebnis *n*; **2.** erfahren, erleben; ~**d** erfahren.

ex·per·i·ment 1. [ɪkˈsperɪmənt] Versuch *m*; **2.** [~mənt] experimentieren; ~**men·tal** □ [eksperɪˈmentl] Versuchs...

ex·pert [ˈekspɜːt] **1.** □ [*pred.* eksˈpɜːt] erfahren, geschickt; fachmännisch; **2.** Fachmann *m*; Sachverständige(r *m f*).

ex·pi·ra·tion [ekspɪˈreɪʃn] Ausat

mung f; Ablauf m, Ende n; **ex·pire** [ɪkˈspaɪə] ausatmen; sein Leben od. s-n Geist aushauchen; ablaufen, verfallen, erlöschen.

ex·plain [ɪkˈspleɪn] erklären, erläutern; *Gründe* auseinandersetzen.

ex·pla·na·tion [ekspləˈneɪʃn] Erklärung f; Erläuterung f; **ex·plan·a·to·ry** □ [ɪkˈsplænətərɪ] erklärend.

ex·pli·ca·ble □ [ˈeksplɪkəbl] erklärlich.

ex·plic·it □ [ɪkˈsplɪsɪt] deutlich.

ex·plode [ɪkˈspləʊd] explodieren (lassen); *fig.* ausbrechen (*with* in *acc.*); platzen (*with* vor); *fig.* sprunghaft ansteigen.

ex·ploit 1. [ˈeksplɔɪt] Heldentat f; 2. [ɪkˈsplɔɪt] ausbeuten; *fig.* ausnutzen; **ex·ploi·ta·tion** [eksplɔɪˈteɪʃn] Ausbeutung f, Auswertung f, Verwertung f, Abbau m; *fig.* Ausnutzung f.

ex·plo·ra·tion [ekspləˈreɪʃn] Erforschung f; **ex·plore** [ɪkˈsplɔː] erforschen; **ex·plor·er** [~rə] Forscher(in); Forschungsreisende(r m) f.

ex·plo·sion [ɪkˈspləʊʒn] Explosion f; *fig.* Ausbruch m; *fig.* sprunghafter Anstieg; **~·sive** [~əʊsɪv] 1. □ explosiv; *fig.* aufbrausend; *fig.* sprunghaft ansteigend; 2. Sprengstoff m.

ex·po·nent [ekˈspəʊnənt] Exponent m; Vertreter m.

ex·port 1. [ekˈspɔːt] exportieren, ausführen; 2. [ˈekspɔːt] Export(artikel) m, Ausfuhr(artikel m) f; **ex·por·ta·tion** [ekspɔːˈteɪʃn] Ausfuhr f.

ex·pose [ɪkˈspəʊz] aussetzen; *phot.* belichten; ausstellen; *fig.* entlarven, bloßstellen, *et.* aufdecken; **ex·po·si·tion** [ekspəˈzɪʃn] Ausstellung f.

ex·po·sure [ɪkˈspəʊʒə] Aussetzen n; Ausgesetztsein n; *fig.* Bloßstellung f; Aufdeckung f; Enthüllung f, Entlarvung f; *phot.* Belichtung f; phot. Aufnahme f; ~ *meter* Belichtungsmesser m.

ex·pound [ɪkˈspaʊnd] erklären, auslegen.

ex·press [ɪkˈspres] 1. □ ausdrücklich, deutlich; Expreß..., Eil...; ~ *compa·ny Am.* (Schnell)Transportunternehmen n; ~ *train* Schnellzug m; 2. Eilbote m; Schnellzug m; *by* ~ = 3. *adv.* durch Eilboten, als Eilgut; 4. äußern, ausdrücken; auspressen; **ex·pres·sion** [~eʃn] Ausdruck m; **ex·pres·sion·less** [~lɪs] ausdruckslos; **ex·pres·sive** □ [~sɪv]

ausdrückend (*of acc.*); ausdrucksvoll; **~·ly** [~lɪ] ausdrücklich, eigens; **~·way** *bsd. Am.* Schnellstraße f.

ex·pro·pri·ate [eksˈprəʊprɪeɪt] enteignen.

ex·pul·sion [ɪkˈspʌlʃn] Vertreibung f; Ausweisung f.

ex·pur·gate [ˈekspɜːɡeɪt] reinigen.

ex·qui·site □ [ˈekskwɪzɪt] auserlesen, vorzüglich; fein; heftig.

ex·tant [ekˈstænt] (noch) vorhanden.

ex·tend [ɪkˈstend] *v/t.* ausdehnen; ausstrecken; erweitern; verlängern; *Hilfe etc.* gewähren; ✕ ausschwärmen lassen; *v/i.* sich erstrecken.

ex·ten·sion [ɪkˈstenʃn] Ausdehnung f; Erweiterung f; Verlängerung f; Aus-, Anbau m; *teleph.* Nebenanschluß m, Apparat m; ~ *cord* ⚡ Verlängerungsschnur f; **~·sive** [~sɪv] ausgedehnt, umfassend.

ex·tent [ɪkˈstent] Ausdehnung f, Weite f, Größe f, Umfang m; Grad m; *to the* ~ *of* bis zum Betrag von; *to some od. a certain* ~ bis zu e-m gewissen Grade, einigermaßen.

ex·ten·u·ate [ekˈstenjʊeɪt] abschwächen, mildern; beschönigen; *extenuating circumstances* ✝ mildernde Umstände *pl.*

ex·te·ri·or [ekˈstɪərɪə] 1. äußerlich, äußere(r, -s), Außen...; 2. *das* Äußere; *Film*: Außenaufnahme f.

ex·ter·mi·nate [ekˈstɜːmɪneɪt] ausrotten (*a. fig.*), vernichten, *Ungeziefer, Unkraut a.* vertilgen.

ex·ter·nal □ [ekˈstɜːnl] äußere(r, -s), äußerlich, Außen...

ex·tinct [ɪkˈstɪŋkt] erloschen; ausgestorben; **ex·tinc·tion** [~kʃn] Erlöschen n; Aussterben n, Untergang m; (Aus)Löschen n; Vernichtung f, Zerstörung f.

ex·tin·guish [ɪkˈstɪŋɡwɪʃ] (aus)löschen; vernichten; **~·er** [~ə] (Feuer-)Löschgerät n.

ex·tort [ɪkˈstɔːt] erpressen (*from* von); **ex·tor·tion** [~n] Erpressung f.

ex·tra [ˈekstrə] 1. *adj.* Extra..., außer..., Außer...; Neben..., Sonder...; ~ *pay* Zulage f; ~ *time Sport*: (Spiel-)Verlängerung f; 2. *adv.* besonders; 3. *et.* Zusätzliches, Extra n; Zuschlag m; Extrablatt n; *thea., Film*: Statist(in).

ex·tract 1. [ˈekstrækt] Auszug m; 2. [ɪkˈstrækt] (heraus)ziehen; herauslocken; ab-, herleiten; **ex·trac·tion** [⁓kʃn] (Heraus)Ziehen *n*; Herkunft *f*.

ex·tra|dite ['ekstrədaɪt] ausliefern; *j-s* Auslieferung erwirken; **⁓·di·tion** [ekstrə'dɪʃn] Auslieferung *f*.

extra·or·di·na·ry □ [ɪk'strɔːdnrɪ] außerordentlich; ungewöhnlich; außerordentlich; Sonder...

ex·tra·ter·res·tri·al □ ['ekstrətɪ're-strɪəl] außerirdisch.

ex·trav·a|gence [ɪk'strævəgəns] Übertriebenheit *f*; Verschwendung *f*; Extravaganz *f*; **⁓·gant** □ [⁓t] übertrieben, überspannt; verschwenderisch; extravagant.

ex·treme [ɪk'striːm] **1.** □ äußerste(r, -s), größte(r, -s), höchste(r, -s); außergewöhnlich; **2.** *das* Äußerste; Extrem *n*; höchster Grad; **⁓·ly** [⁓lɪ] äußerst, höchst.

ex·trem|is·m *bsd. pol.* [ɪk'striːmɪzm] Extremismus *m*; **⁓·ist** [⁓ɪst] Extremist(in).

ex·trem·i·ty [ɪk'stremətɪ] *das* Äußerste; höchste Not; äußerste Maßnahme; *extremities pl.* Gliedmaßen *pl.*, Extremitäten *pl.*

ex·tri·cate ['ekstrɪkeɪt] herauswinden, -ziehen, befreien.

ex·tro·vert ['ekstrəʊvɜːt] Extrovertierte(r *m*) *f*.

ex·u·be|rance [ɪg'zjuːbərəns] Fülle *f*; Überschwang *m*; **⁓·rant** □ [⁓t] reichlich, üppig; überschwenglich; ausgelassen.

ex·ult [ɪg'zʌlt] frohlocken, jubeln.

eye [aɪ] **1.** Auge *n*; Blick *m*; Öhr *n*; Öse *f*; *see⁓ to⁓ with s.o.* mit j-m völlig übereinstimmen; *be up to the ⁓s in work* bis über die Ohren in Arbeit stecken; *with an ⁓ to s.th.* im Hinblick auf et.; **2.** ansehen; mustern; **⁓·ball** ['aɪbɔːl] Augapfel *m*; **⁓·brow** Augenbraue *f*; **⁓·catch·ing** [⁓ɪŋ] ins Auge fallend, auffallend; **⁓d** ...äugig; **⁓·glass** Augenglas *n*; *(a pair of)* **⁓es** *pl.* (e-e) Brille; **⁓·lash** Augenwimper *f*; **⁓·lid** Augenlid *n*; **⁓·lin·er** Eyeliner *m*; **⁓·o·pen·er:** *that was an ⁓ to me* das hat mir die Augen geöffnet; **⁓·shad·ow** Lidschatten *m*; **⁓·sight** Augen(licht *n*) *pl.*, Sehkraft *f*; **⁓·strain** Ermüdung *f od.* Überanstrengung *f* der Augen; **⁓·wit·ness** Augenzeug|e *m*, -in *f*.

F

fa·ble ['feɪbl] Fabel *f*; Sage *f*; Lüge *f*.

fab|ric ['fæbrɪk] Gewebe *n*, Stoff *m*; Bau *m*; Gebäude *n*; Struktur *f*; △ *nicht* Fabrik; **⁓·ri·cate** [⁓eɪt] fabrizieren (*mst fig. = erdichten, fälschen*).

fab·u·lous □ ['fæbjʊləs] sagenhaft, der Sage angehörend; sagen-, fabelhaft.

fa·çade *arch.* [fə'sɑːd] Fassade *f*.

face [feɪs] **1.** Gesicht *n*; Gesicht(sausdruck *m*) *n*, Miene *f*; (Ober)Fläche *f*; Vorderseite *f*; Zifferblatt *n*; *⁓ to ⁓ with* Auge in Auge mit; *save od. lose one's ⁓* das Gesicht wahren *od.* verlieren; *on the ⁓ of it* auf den ersten Blick; *pull a long ⁓* ein langes Gesicht machen; *have the ⁓ to do s.th.* die Stirn haben, et. zu tun; **2.** *v/t.* ansehen; gegenüberstehen (*dat.*); (hinaus)gehen auf (*acc.*); die Stirn bieten (*dat.*); einfassen; *arch.* beklei-

den; *v/i. ⁓ about* sich umdrehen; **⁓·cloth** ['feɪsklɒθ] Waschlappen *m*; **⁓·d** *in Zssgn:* mit (e-m) ... Gesicht; **⁓·flan·nel** *Brt.* = face-cloth; **⁓·lift·ing** [⁓ɪŋ] Facelifting *n*, Gesichtsstraffung *f*; *fig.* Renovierung *f*, Verschönerung *f*.

fa·ce·tious □ [fə'siːʃəs] witzig.

fa·cial ['feɪʃl] **1.** □ Gesichts...; **2.** *Kosmetik:* Gesichtsbehandlung *f*.

fa·cile ['fæsaɪl] leicht; oberflächlich; **fa·cil·i·tate** [fə'sɪlɪteɪt] erleichtern; **fa·cil·i·ty** [⁓ətɪ] Leichtigkeit *f*; Oberflächlichkeit *f*; *mst facilities pl.* Erleichterung(en *pl.*) *f*; Einrichtung(en *pl.*) *f*, Anlage(n *pl.*) *f*.

fac·ing ['feɪsɪŋ] ⊕ Verkleidung *f*; **⁓s** *pl. Schneiderei:* Besatz *m*.

fact [fækt] Tatsache *f*, Wirklichkeit *f*, Wahrheit *f*; Tat *f*; *in ⁓* in der Tat, tatsächlich.

fac·tion *bsd. pol.* ['fækʃn] Splittergruppe *f*; Zwietracht *f*.

fac·ti·tious □ [fæk'tɪʃəs] künstlich.

fac·tor ['fæktə] *fig.* Umstand *m*, Moment *n*, Faktor *m*; Agent *m*; *Schott.* Verwalter *m*.

fac·to·ry ['fæktrɪ] Fabrik *f*.

fac·ul·ty ['fækəltɪ] Fähigkeit *f*; Kraft *f*; *fig.* Gabe *f*; *univ.* Fakultät *f*.

fad [fæd] Mode(erscheinung, -torheit) *f*; (vorübergehende) Laune.

fade [feɪd] (ver)welken (lassen), verblassen; schwinden; immer schwächer werden (*Person*); △ *nicht fade*; *Film, Rundfunk, TV*: ~ *in* auf- od. eingeblendet werden; auf- od. einblenden; ~ *out* aus- od. abgeblendet werden; aus- od. abblenden.

fag¹ [fæg] F Plackerei *f*, Schinderei *f*; *Brt. Schule:* Schüler, der für e-n älteren Dienste verrichtet.

fag² *sl.* [~] *Brt.* Glimmstengel *m* (*Zigarette*); *Am.* Schwule(r) *m* (*Homosexueller*).

fail [feɪl] **1.** *v/i.* versagen; mißlingen, fehlschlagen; versiegen; nachlassen; Bankrott machen; durchfallen (*Kandidat*); *v/t.* im Stich lassen, verlassen; *j-n* in e-r Prüfung durchfallen lassen; *he ~ed to come* er kam nicht; *he cannot* ~ *to* er muß (einfach); *2. without* ~ mit Sicherheit, ganz bestimmt; **~ing** ['feɪlɪŋ] **1.** Fehler *m*, Schwäche *f*; **2.** in Ermang(e)lung (*gen.*); **~ure** [~jə] Fehlen *n*; Ausbleiben *n*; Versagen *n*; Fehlschlag *m*, Mißerfolg *m*; Verfall *m*; Versäumnis *n*; Bankrott *m*; Versager *m*.

faint [feɪnt] **1.** □ schwach, matt; **2.** ohnmächtig werden, in Ohnmacht fallen (*with* vor); **3.** Ohnmacht *f*; **~‑heart·ed** □ ['feɪnt'hɑːtɪd] verzagt.

fair¹ [feə] **1.** *adj.* □ gerecht, ehrlich, anständig, fair; ordentlich; schön (*Wetter*), günstig (*Wind*); reichlich; hell (*Haut, Haar, Teint*), blond (*Haar*); freundlich; sauber, in Reinschrift; schön, hübsch, nett; **2.** *adv.* gerecht, ehrlich, anständig, fair; in Reinschrift; direkt.

fair² [~] (Jahr)Markt *m*; Volksfest *n*; Ausstellung *f*, Messe *f*.

fair·ly ['feəlɪ] ziemlich; völlig; **~ness** [~nɪs] Schönheit *f*; Blondheit *f*; Anständigkeit *f*, *bsd. Sport:* Fairneß *f*; Ehrlichkeit *f*; Gerechtigkeit *f*.

fai·ry ['feərɪ] Fee *f*; Zauberin *f*; Elf(e

f) *m*; **~·land** Feen-, Märchenland *n*; **~·tale** Märchen *n* (*a. fig.*):

faith [feɪθ] Glaube *m*; Vertrauen *n*; Treue *f*; **~·ful** □ ['feɪθfl] treu; ehrlich; *Yours ~ly* Mit freundlichen Grüßen (*Briefschluß*); **~·less** □ [~lɪs] treulos; ungläubig.

fake [feɪk] **1.** Schwindel *m*; Fälschung *f*; Schwindler *m*; **2.** fälschen; imitieren, nachmachen; vortäuschen, simulieren; **3.** gefälscht.

fal·con *zo.* ['fɔːlkən] Falke *m*.

fall [fɔːl] **1.** Fall(en *n*) *m*; Sturz *m*; Verfall *m*; Einsturz *m*; *Am.* Herbst *m*; Sinken *n* (*der Preise etc.*); Gefälle *n*; *mst* ~*s pl.* Wasserfall *m*; △ *nicht gr.*, **~**, ***, **~** *Fall*; **2.** (*fell, fallen*) fallen, stürzen, ab-, ein-, um-, nieder-; sinken; sich legen (*Wind*); *in* ~*e-n Zustand* verfallen; ~ *ill od. sick* krank werden; ~ *in love* sich verlieben in (*acc.*); ~ *short of* den *Erwartungen etc.* nicht entsprechen; ~ *back* zurückweichen; ~ *back on fig.* zurückgreifen auf (*acc.*); ~ *for* hereinfallen auf (*j-n, et.*); F sich in *j-n* verknallen; ~ *off* zurückgehen (*Geschäfte, Zuschauerzahlen etc.*), nachlassen; ~ *on* herfallen über (*acc.*); ~ *out* sich streiten (*with* mit); ~ *through* durchfallen (*a. fig.*); ~ *to* reinhauen, tüchtig zugreifen (*beim Essen*).

fal·la·cious □ [fə'leɪʃəs] trügerisch.

fal·la·cy ['fæləsɪ] Trugschluß *m*.

fall·en ['fɔːlən] *p.p. von* **fall** 2.

fall guy *Am.* F ['fɔːlgaɪ] *der* Lackierte, *der* Dumme.

fal·li·ble □ ['fæləbl] fehlbar.

fal·ling star *ast.* ['fɔːlɪŋstɑː] Sternschnuppe *f*.

fall·out ['fɔːlaʊt] Fallout *m*, radioaktiver Niederschlag.

fal·low ['fæləʊ] *zo.* falb; ✓ brach(liegend).

false □ [fɔːls] falsch; **~·hood** ['fɔːlshʊd], **~·ness** [~nɪs] Falschheit *f*; Unwahrheit *f*.

fal·si·fi·ca·tion [fɔːlsɪfɪ'keɪʃn] (Ver-)Fälschung *f*; **~·fy** ['fɔːlsɪfaɪ] (ver)fälschen; **~·ty** [~tɪ] Falschheit *f*, Unwahrheit *f*.

fal·ter ['fɔːltə] schwanken; stocken (*Stimme*); stammeln; *fig.* zaudern.

fame [feɪm] Ruf *m*, Ruhm *m*; **~·d** berühmt (*for* wegen).

fa·mil·i·ar [fə'mɪljə] **1.** □ vertraut; gewohnt; familiär; **2.** Vertraute(r *m*) *f*; **~·i·ty** [fəmɪlɪ'ærətɪ] Vertrautheit *f;* (plumpe) Vertraulichkeit; **~ize** [fə'mɪljəraɪz] vertraut machen.

fam·i·ly ['fæmɪlɪ] **1.** Familie *f;* **2.** Familien..., Haus...; *be in the ~ way* F in anderen Umständen sein; **~ allowance** Kindergeld *n;* **~ planning** Familienplanung *f;* **~ tree** Stammbaum *m.*

fam|ine ['fæmɪn] Hungersnot *f;* Knappheit *f* (*of an dat.*); **~ished** [~ʃt] verhungert; *be ~* F am Verhungern sein. *nicht famos.*⟩

fa·mous □ ['feɪməs] berühmt; △ ⟨

fan¹ [fæn] **1.** Fächer *m;* Ventilator *m;* **~ belt** ⊕ Keilriemen *m;* **2.** (*-nn-*) (zu)fächeln; an-, *fig.* entfachen.

fan² [~] (*Sport- etc.*)Fan *m;* **~ club** Fanklub *m;* **~ mail** Verehrerpost *f.*

fa·nat|ic [fə'nætɪk] **1.** (*~ally*), *a.* **~i·cal** □ [~kl] fanatisch; **2.** Fanatiker(in).

fan·ci·er ['fænsɪə] (*Tier-, Pflanzen-*) Liebhaber(in), (-)Züchter(in).

fan·ci·ful □ ['fænsɪfl] phantastisch.

fan·cy ['fænsɪ] **1.** Phantasie *f;* Einbildung(skraft) *f;* Schrulle *f;* Vorliebe *f;* Liebhaberei *f;* **2.** Phantasie...; Mode...; *~ ball* Kostümfest *n,* Maskenball *m;* *~ dress* (Masken)Kostüm *n;* *~ goods pl.* Modeartikel *pl.,* -waren *pl.;* **3.** sich einbilden; Gefallen finden an (*dat.*); *just ~!* denken Sie nur!; **~-free** frei u. ungebunden; **~-work** feine Handarbeit, Stickerei *f.*

fang [fæŋ] Reiß-, Fangzahn *m;* Hauer *m;* Giftzahn *m.*

fan|tas·tic [fæn'tæstɪk] (*~ally*) phantastisch; **~·ta·sy** ['fæntəsɪ] Phantasie *f.*

far [fɑː] (*farther, further; farthest, furthest*) **1.** *adj.* fern, entfernt, weit; **2.** *adv.* fern; weit; (sehr) viel; *as ~ as* bis; *in so ~ as* insofern als; **~·a·way** ['fɑːrəweɪ] weit entfernt.

fare [feə] **1.** Fahrgeld *n;* Fahrgast *m;* Verpflegung *f,* Kost *f;* **2.** *gut* leben; *he ~d well* es ge(r)ging ihm gut; **~·well** [feə'wel] **1.** *int.* lebe(n Sie) wohl!; **2.** Abschied *m,* Lebewohl *n.*

far-fetched *fig.* ['fɑː'fetʃt] weithergeholt, gesucht.

farm [fɑːm] **1.** Bauernhof *m,* Gut *n,* Gehöft *n,* Farm *f;* Züchterei *f;* *chicken ~* Hühnerfarm *f;* **2.** (ver-) pachten; *Land, Hof* bewirtschaften; *Geflügel etc.* züchten; **~·er** [~ə] Bauer *m,* Landwirt *m,* Farmer *m;* (*Geflügel- etc.*)Züchter *m;* Päch-

ter *m;* **~·hand** Landarbeiter(in); **~·house** Bauernhaus *n;* **~·ing** [~ɪŋ] **1.** Acker..., landwirtschaftlich; **2.** Landwirtschaft *f;* **~·stead** Bauernhof *m,* Gehöft *n;* **~·yard** Wirtschaftshof *m* (*e-s Bauernhofs*).

far-off ['fɑːr'ɒf] entfernt, fern; **~-sight·ed** *bsd. Am.* weitsichtig; *fig.* weitblickend.

far·ther ['fɑːðə] *comp. von far;* **~·thest** ['fɑːðɪst] *sup. von far.*

fas·ci|nate ['fæsɪneɪt] faszinieren; **~·nat·ing** [~ɪŋ] faszinierend; **~·na·tion** [fæsɪ'neɪʃn] Zauber *m,* Reiz *m,* Faszination *f.*

fas·cis|m *pol.* ['fæʃɪzəm] Faschismus *m;* **~t** *pol.* [~ɪst] **1.** Faschist *m;* **2.** faschistisch.

fash·ion ['fæʃn] **1.** Mode *f;* Art *f;* feine Lebensart; Form *f;* Schnitt *m;* *in (out of) ~* (un)modern; *~ parade, ~ show* Mode(n)schau *f;* **2.** gestalten; *Kleid* machen; **~·a·ble** □ [~nəbl] modern, elegant.

fast¹ [fɑːst] **1.** Fasten *n;* **2.** fasten.

fast² [~] schnell; fest; treu; echt, beständig (*Farbe*); flott; △ *nicht fast; be ~* vorgehen (*Uhr*); **~·back** *mot.* ['fɑːstbæk] (Wagen *m* mit) Fließheck *n;* **~·breed·er, ~-breed·er re·ac·tor** *phys.* schneller Brüter.

fas·ten ['fɑːsn] *v/t.* befestigen; anheften; fest zumachen; zubinden; *Augen etc.* heften (*on, upon auf acc.*); *v/i.* schließen (*Tür*); △ *nicht fasten;* **~ on, ~ upon** sich klammern an (*acc.*); *fig.* sich stürzen auf (*acc.*); **~·er** [~ə] Verschluß *m,* Halter *m;* **~·ing** [~ɪŋ] Verschluß *m,* Halterung *f.*

fast| food Schnellgericht(e *pl.*) *n;* **~-food res·tau·rant** Schnellimbiß *m,* -gaststätte *f.*

fas·tid·i·ous □ [fə'stɪdɪəs] anspruchsvoll, heikel, wählerisch, verwöhnt.

fast lane *mot.* Überholspur *f.*

fat [fæt] **1.** □ (*-tt-*) fett; dick; fettig; **2.** Fett *n;* **3.** (*-tt-*) fett machen *od.* werden; mästen.

fa·tal □ ['feɪtl] verhängnisvoll, fatal (*to für*); Schicksals...; tödlich; **~·i·ty** [fə'tælətɪ] Verhängnis *n;* Unglücks-, Todesfall *m;* Todesopfer *n.*

fate [feɪt] Schicksal *n;* Verhängnis *n.*

fa·ther ['fɑːðə] Vater *m;* ♀ **Christmas** *bsd. Brt.* der Weihnachtsmann, der Nikolaus; **~·hood** [~hʊd] Vaterschaft *f;* **~-in-law** [~rɪnlɔː] (*pl.*

fathers-in-law) Schwiegervater *m*; **~·less** [~lɪs] vaterlos; **~·ly** [~lɪ] väterlich.

fath·om [ˈfæðəm] **1.** ♣ Faden *m* (*Tiefenmaß*); **2.** ♣ loten; *fig.* ergründen; **~·less** [~lɪs] unergründlich.

fa·tigue [fəˈtiːg] **1.** Ermüdung*f*; Strapaze*f*; **2.** ermüden.

fat|ten [ˈfætn] fett machen *od.* werden; mästen; *Boden* düngen; **~·ty** [~tɪ] (*-ier*, *-iest*) fett(ig).

fat·u·ous [ˈfætjʊəs] albern.

fau·cet *Am.* [ˈfɔːsɪt] (Wasser)Hahn *m*.

fault [fɔːlt] Fehler *m*; Defekt *m*; Schuld *f*; *find* ~ *with* et. auszusetzen haben an (*dat.*); *be at* ~ Schuld haben; **~·less** □ [~lɪs] fehlerfrei, -los; **~·y** □ [~ɪ] (*-ier*, *-iest*) fehlerhaft, ⊕ *a.* defekt.

fa·vo(u)r [ˈfeɪvə] **1.** Gunst*f*; Gefallen *m*; Begünstigung*f*; *in* ~ *of* zugunsten von *od. gen.*; *do s.o. a* ~ j-m e-n Gefallen tun; **2.** begünstigen; bevorzugen, vorziehen; wohlwollend gegenüberstehen; *Sport:* favorisieren; beehren; **fa·vo(u)·ra·ble** □ [~rəbl] günstig; **fa·vo(u)·rite** [~rɪt] **1.** Liebling *m*; *Sport:* Favorit *m*; **2.** Lieblings...

fawn[1] [fɔːn] **1.** *zo.* (Reh)Kitz *n*; Rehbraun *n*; **2.** rehbraun.

fawn[2] [~] (mit dem Schwanz) wedeln (*Hund*); *fig.* katzbuckeln (*on*, *upon* vor *dat.*).

fear [fɪə] **1.** Furcht *f* (*of* vor *dat.*); Befürchtung*f*; Angst*f*; **2.** (be)fürchten; sich fürchten vor (*dat.*); **~·ful** □ [ˈfɪəfl] furchtsam; furchtbar; **~·less** □ [~lɪs] furchtlos.

fea·si·ble □ [ˈfiːzəbl] durchführbar.

feast [fiːst] **1.** *eccl.* Fest *n*, Feiertag *m*; Festessen *n*; *fig.* Fest *n*, (Hoch)Genuß *m*; **2.** *v/t.* festlich bewirten; *v/i.* sich gütlich tun (*on an dat.*).

feat [fiːt] (Helden)Tat *f*; Kunststück *n*.

fea·ther [ˈfeðə] **1.** Feder *f*; *a.* **~s** Gefieder *n*; *birds of a* ~ Leute vom gleichen Schlag; *in high* ~ (bei) bester Laune; *in Hochform*; **2.** mit Federn schmücken; **~ bed** Matratze *f* mit Feder- *od.* Daunenfüllung; △ *nicht Federbett*; **~·bed** (*-dd-*) verwöhnen; **~·brained**, **~·head·ed** unbesonnen; albern; **~ed** be-, gefiedert; **~·weight** *Sport:* Federgewicht(ler *m*) *n*; Leichtgewicht *n* (*Person*); *fig.* unbedeutende Person;

et. Belangloses; **~·y** [~rɪ] be-, gefiedert; feder(art)ig.

fea·ture [ˈfiːtʃə] **1.** (Gesichts-, Grund-, Haupt-, Charakter)Zug *m*; (charakteristisches) Merkmal; *Rundfunk*, *TV:* Feature *n*; *a.* ~ *article*, ~ *story Zeitung:* Feature *n*; *a.* ~ *film* Haupt-, Spielfilm *m*; **~s** *pl.* Gesicht *n*; **2.** kennzeichnen; sich auszeichnen durch; groß herausbringen *od.* -stellen; *Film:* in der Hauptrolle zeigen.

Feb·ru·a·ry [ˈfebrʊərɪ] Februar *m*.

fed [fed] *pret. u. p.p. von feed 2.*

fed·e|ral □ [ˈfedərəl] Bundes...; *USA:* Zentral..., Unions..., National...; ♀ *Bureau of Investigation* (*abbr. FBI*) amer. Bundeskriminalpolizei; ~ *government* Bundesregierung*f*; **~·rate** [~eɪt] (sich) zu e-m (Staaten)Bund zusammenschließen; **~·ra·tion** [fedəˈreɪʃn] Föderation *f* (*a. econ., pol.*); (politischer) Zusammenschluß; *econ.* (Dach)Verband *m*; *pol.* Staatenbund *m*.

fee [fiː] Gebühr *f*; Honorar *n*; (Mitglieds)Beitrag *m*; Eintrittsgeld *n*.

fee·ble □ [ˈfiːbl] (*~r*, *~st*) schwach.

feed [fiːd] **1.** Futter *n*; Nahrung *f*; Fütterung *f*; ⊕ Zuführung *f*, Speisung *f*; **2.** (*fed*) *v/t.* füttern; ernähren; ⊕ (ein)speisen; weiden lassen; *be fed up with* et. *od.* j-n satt haben; *well fed* wohlgenährt; *v/i.* (fr)essen; sich ernähren; weiden; **~·back** [ˈfiːdbæk] ⚡, *Kybernetik:* Feedback *n*, Rückkoppelung *f*; *Rundfunk*, *TV:* Feedback *n* (*mögliche Einflußnahme des Publikums auf den Verlauf e-r Sendung*); Zurückleitung *f* (*von Informationen*) (*to an acc.*); **~·er** [~ə] Fütterer *m*; *Am.* Viehmäster *m*; Esser(in); **~·er road** Zubringer (-straße *f*) *m*; **~·ing-bot·tle** [~ɪŋbɒtl] (Säuglings-, Saug)Flasche *f*.

feel [fiːl] **1.** (*felt*) (sich) fühlen; befühlen; empfinden; sich anfühlen; *I* ~ *like doing* ich möchte am liebsten tun; **2.** Gefühl *n*; Empfindung*f*; **~·er** *zo.* [ˈfiːlə] Fühler *m*; **~·ing** [~ɪŋ] Gefühl *n*.

feet [fiːt] *pl. von foot 1.*

feign [feɪn] *Interesse etc.* vortäuschen; *Krankheit a.* simulieren.

feint [feɪnt] Finte *f*; ✗ Täuschungsmanöver *n*.

fell [fel] **1.** *pret. von fall 2*; **2.** niederschlagen; fällen.

fel·low ['feləʊ] **1.** Gefährt|e *m*, -in *f*, Kamerad(in); Gleiche(r, -s); Gegenstück *n*; *univ.* Fellow *m*, Mitglied *n* e-s College; Kerl *m*, Bursche *m*, Mensch *m*; *old* ~ F alter Junge; *the* ~ *of a glove* der andere Handschuh; **2.** Mit...; ~ *being* Mitmensch *m*; ~ *countryman* Landsmann *m*; ~ *travel(l)er* Mitreisende(r) *m*, Reisegefährte *m*; ~**ship** [~ʃɪp] Gemeinschaft *f*; Kameradschaft *f*.

fel·o·ny 🏛 ['felənɪ] (schweres) Verbrechen, Kapitalverbrechen *n*.

felt¹ [felt] *pret. u. p.p. von* feel 1.

felt² [~] Filz *m*; ~ *tip*, ~*tip(ped) pen* Filzschreiber *m*, -stift *m*.

fe·male ['fiːmeɪl] **1.** weiblich; **2.** Weib *n*; *zo.* Weibchen *n*.

fem·i·nine □ ['femɪnɪn] weiblich, Frauen...; weibisch; ~**ism** [~ɪzəm] Feminismus *m*; ~**nist** [~ɪst] **1.** Feminist(in); **2.** feministisch.

fen [fen] Fenn *n*, Moor *n*; Marsch *f*.

fence [fens] **1.** Zaun *m*; F Hehler *m*; **2.** *v/t.* ~ *in* ein-, umzäunen; einsperren; ~ *off* abzäunen; *v/i.* Sport: fechten; *sl.* Hehlerei treiben; **fenc·er** ['fensə] Sport: Fechter *m*; **fenc·ing** [~ɪŋ] Einfriedung *f*; Sport: Fechten *n*; *attr.* Fecht...

fend [fend]: ~ *off* abwehren; ~ *for o.s.* für sich selbst sorgen; ~**er** ['fendə] Schutzvorrichtung *f*; Schutzblech *n*; *Am. mot.* Kotflügel *m*; Kamingitter *n*, -vorsetzer *m*.

fen·nel 🌿 ['fenl] Fenchel *m*.

fer|ment 1. ['fɜːment] Ferment *n*; Gärung *f*; **2.** [fəˈment] gären (lassen); ~**men·ta·tion** [fɜːmenˈteɪʃn] Gärung *f*.

fern 🌿 [fɜːn] Farn(kraut *n*) *m*.

fe·ro·cious □ [fəˈrəʊʃəs] wild; grausam; ~**ci·ty** [fəˈrɒsɪtɪ] Wildheit *f*.

fer·ret ['ferɪt] **1.** *zo.* Frettchen *n*; *fig.* Spürhund *m*; **2.** herumstöbern; ~ *out* aufspüren, -stöbern.

fer·ry ['ferɪ] **1.** Fähre *f*; **2.** übersetzen; ~**boat** Fährboot *n*, Fähre *f*; ~**man** (*pl. -men*) Fährmann *m*.

fer|tile □ ['fɜːtaɪl] fruchtbar; reich (*of*, *in* an *dat.*); ~**til·i·ty** [fəˈtɪlətɪ] Fruchtbarkeit *f* (*a. fig.*); ~**ti·lize** ['fɜːtɪlaɪz] fruchtbar machen; befruchten; düngen; ~**ti·liz·er** [~ə] (*bsd. Kunst*)Dünger *m*, Düngemittel *n*.

fer·vent □ ['fɜːvənt] heiß; inbrünstig, glühend; leidenschaftlich.

fer·vo(u)r ['fɜːvə] Glut *f*; Inbrunst *f*.

fes·ter ['festə] eitern; verfaulen.

fes|ti·val ['festɪvl] Fest *n*; Feier *f*; Festspiele *pl.*; ~**tive** □ [~tɪv] festlich; ~**tiv·i·ty** [feˈstɪvətɪ] Festlichkeit *f*.

fes·toon [feˈstuːn] Girlande *f*.

fetch [fetʃ] holen; *Preis* erzielen; *Seufzer* ausstoßen; ~**ing** □ F ['fetʃɪŋ] reizend.

fet·id □ ['fetɪd] stinkend.

fet·ter ['fetə] **1.** Fessel *f*; **2.** fesseln.

feud [fjuːd] Fehde *f*; Lehen *n*; ~**al** □ ['fjuːdl] feudal, Lehns...; **feu·dal·is·m** [~əlɪzəm] Feudalismus *m*, Feudalsystem *n*.

fe·ver ['fiːvə] Fieber *n*; ~**ish** □ [~rɪʃ] fieb(e)rig; *fig.* fieberhaft.

few [fjuː] wenige; *a* ~ ein paar, einige; *no* ~*er than* nicht weniger als; *quite a* ~, *a good* ~ e-e ganze Menge.

fi·an·cé [fɪˈɑːnseɪ] Verlobte(r) *m*; ~**e** [~] Verlobte *f*.

fib F [fɪb] **1.** Flunkerei *f*, Schwindelei *f*; **2.** (-*bb*-) schwindeln, flunkern.

fi·bre, *Am.* **-ber** ['faɪbə] Faser *f*; Charakter *m*; **fi·brous** □ ['faɪbrəs] faserig.

fick·le ['fɪkl] wankelmütig; unbeständig; ~**ness** [~nɪs] Wankelmut *m*.

fic·tion ['fɪkʃn] Erfindung *f*; Prosaliteratur *f*, Belletristik *f*; Romane *pl.*; ~**al** □ [~l] erdichtet; Roman...

fic·ti·tious □ [fɪkˈtɪʃəs] erfunden.

fid·dle □ ['fɪdl] **1.** Fiedel *f*, Geige *f*; *play first* (*second*) ~ *bsd. fig.* die erste (zweite) Geige spielen; (*as*) *fit as a* ~ kerngesund; **2.** ♪ fiedeln; *a.* ~ *about od. around* (*with*) herumfingern (an *dat.*), spielen (mit); ~**r** [~ə] Geiger(in); ~**sticks** *int.* dummes Zeug!

fi·del·i·ty [fɪˈdelətɪ] Treue *f*; Genauigkeit *f*.

fidg·et F ['fɪdʒɪt] **1.** nervöse Unruhe *f*; **2.** nervös machen *od.* sein; ~**y** [~ɪ] zapp(e)lig, nervös.

field [fiːld] Feld *n*; (Spiel)Platz *m*; Arbeitsfeld *n*; Gebiet *n*; Bereich *m*; *hold the* ~ das Feld behaupten; ~ *e·vents pl.* Sport: Sprung- u. Wurfdisziplinen *pl.*; ~**glass·es** *pl.* (*a pair of* ~ ein) Feldstecher *m od.* Fernglas *n*; ~ *mar·shal* ✕ Feldmarschall *m*; ~ *of·fi·cer* ✕ Stabsoffizier *m*; ~ *sports pl.* Sport *m* im Freien (*bsd. Jagen, Schießen, Fischen*); ~**work** praktische (wissenschaftliche) Arbeit, *Archäologie etc.*: *a.* Arbeit *f* im Gelände; *Markt-, Meinungsforschung*: Feldarbeit *f*.

fiend [fi:nd] Satan *m*, Teufel *m*; *in Zssgn*: Süchtige(r *m*) *f*; Fanatiker(in); △ *nicht* Feind; **~ish** □ ['fi:ndɪʃ] teuflisch, boshaft.

fierce □ [fɪəs] (*~r*, *~st*) wild; scharf; heftig; **~ness** ['fɪəsnɪs] Wildheit *f*, Schärfe *f*; Heftigkeit *f*.

fi·er·y □ ['faɪərɪ] (*-ier*, *-iest*) feurig; hitzig.

fif·teen ['fɪf'ti:n] **1.** fünfzehn; **2.** Fünfzehn *f*; **~teenth** [~'ti:nθ] fünfzehnte(r, -s); **~th** [fɪfθ] **1.** fünfte(r, -s); **2.** Fünftel *n*; **~th·ly** ['fɪfθlɪ] fünftens; **~ti·eth** ['fɪftɪɪθ] fünfzigste(r, -s); **~ty** [~tɪ] **1.** fünfzig; **2.** Fünfzig *f*; **~ty-fif·ty** halbe-halbe.

fig ♀ [fɪg] Feige(nbaum *m*) *f*.

fight [faɪt] **1.** Kampf *m*; ✗ Gefecht *n*; Schlägerei *f*; *Boxen*: Kampf *m*, Fight *m*; Kampflust *f*; **2.** (*fought*) *v/t.* bekämpfen; kämpfen gegen *od.* mit, *Sport*: *a.* boxen gegen; *v/i.* kämpfen, sich schlagen; *Sport*: boxen; **~er** ['faɪtə] Kämpfer *m*; *Sport*: Boxer *m*, Fighter *m*; *a.* **~ plane** ✗ Jagdflugzeug *n*; **~ing** [~ɪŋ] Kampf *m*.

fig·u·ra·tive □ ['fɪgjʊrətɪv] bildlich.

fig·ure ['fɪgə] **1.** Figur *f*; Gestalt *f*; Zahl *f*, Ziffer *f*; Preis *m*; *be good at* ~s ein guter Rechner sein; **2.** *v/t.* abbilden, darstellen; *Am.* meinen, glauben; sich *et.* vorstellen; **~ out** rauskriegen, *Problem* lösen; verstehen; **~ up** zusammenzählen; *v/i.* erscheinen, vorkommen; **~ on** *bsd. Am.* rechnen mit; **~ skat·er** *Sport*: Eiskunstläufer(in); **~ skat·ing** *Sport*: Eiskunstlauf *m*.

fil·a·ment ['fɪləmənt] Faden *m*, Faser *f*; ♀ Staubfaden *m*; ⚡ Glüh-, Heizfaden *m*.

fil·bert ♀ ['fɪlbət] Haselnuß *f*.

filch F [fɪltʃ] klauen, stibitzen.

file[1] [faɪl] **1.** Ordner *m*, Karteikasten *m*; Akte *f*; Akten *pl.*, Ablage *f*; *Computer*: Datei *f*; Reihe *f*; ✗ Rotte *f*; *on* ~ bei den Akten; **2.** *v/t. Briefe etc.* einordnen, ablegen, zu den Akten nehmen; *Antrag* einreichen, *Berufung* einlegen; *v/i.* hintereinander marschieren.

file[2] [~] **1.** Feile *f*; **2.** feilen.

fi·li·al □ ['fɪljəl] kindlich, Kindes...

fil·ing ['faɪlɪŋ] Ablegen *n* (*von Briefen etc.*); ~ *cabinet* Aktenschrank *m*.

fill [fɪl] **1.** (sich) füllen; an-, aus-,

erfüllen; *Auftrag* ausführen; ~ *in* einsetzen; *Am. a.* ~ *out Formular* ausfüllen; ~ *up* vollfüllen; sich füllen; ~ *her up!* F volltanken, bitte!; **2.** Füllung *f*; *eat one's* ~ sich satt essen.

fil·let, *Am. a.* **fil·et** □ ['fɪlɪt] Filet *n*.

fill·ing ['fɪlɪŋ] Füllung *f*; ✞ (Zahn-) Plombe *f*; (-)Füllung *f*; ~ *station* Tankstelle *f*.

fil·ly ['fɪlɪ] Stutenfohlen *n*; *fig.* wilde Hummel (*Mädchen*).

film [fɪlm] **1.** Häutchen *n*; Membran(e) *f*; Film *m* (*a. phot. u. bsd. Brt. Kinofilm*); Trübung *f* (*des Auges*); Nebelschleier *m*; *take od. shoot a* ~ e-n Film drehen; **2.** (ver)filmen; sich verfilmen lassen.

fil·ter ['fɪltə] **1.** Filter *m*; **2.** filtern; **~tip** Filter *m*; Filterzigarette *f*; **~tipped**: ~ *cigarette* Filterzigarette *f*.

filth [fɪlθ] Schmutz *m*; **~y** □ ['fɪlθɪ] (*-ier*, *-iest*) schmutzig; *fig.* unflätig.

fin [fɪn] *zo.* Flosse *f* (*a. sl.* = Hand).

fi·nal ['faɪnl] **1.** □ letzte(r, -s); End..., Schluß...; endgültig; ~ *storage* Endlagerung *f* (*von Atommüll etc.*); **2.** *Sport*: Finale *n*, Endkampf, -lauf *m*, -runde *f*, -spiel *n*; *mst* ~s *pl.* Schlußexamen, -prüfung *f*; **~ist** [~nəlɪst] *Sport*: Finalist(in), Endkampfteilnehmer(in); **~ly** [~lɪ] endlich, schließlich; endgültig.

fi·nance [faɪ'næns] **1.** Finanzwesen *n*; ~s *pl.* Finanzen *pl.*; **2.** *v/t.* finanzieren; *v/i.* Geldgeschäfte machen; **fi·nan·cial** □ [~nʃl] finanziell; **fi·nan·cier** [~nsɪə] Finanzier *m*.

finch *zo.* [fɪntʃ] Fink *m*.

find [faɪnd] **1.** (*found*) finden; (an-) treffen; auf-, herausfinden; ⚖ *j-n für* (*nicht*) *schuldig* erklären; beschaffen; versorgen; **2.** Fund *m*, Entdeckung *f*; **~ings** ['faɪndɪŋz] *pl.* Befund *m*; ⚖ Feststellung *f*, Spruch *m*.

fine[1] □ [faɪn] **1.** *adj.* (*~r*, *~st*) schön; fein; verfeinert; rein; spitz, dünn, scharf; geziert; vornehm; *I'm* ~ mir geht es gut; **2.** *adv.* gut, bestens.

fine[2] □ [faɪn] Geldstrafe *f*, Bußgeld *n*; **2.** zu e-r Geldstrafe verurteilen.

fi·ne·ry ['faɪnərɪ] Glanz *m*; Putz *m*, Staat *m*.

fin·ger ['fɪŋgə] **1.** Finger *m*; *s. cross* 2; **2.** betasten, (herum)fingern an (*dat.*); **~nail** Fingernagel *m*; **~print** Fingerabdruck *m*; **~tip** Fingerspitze *f*.

fin·i·cky ['fɪnɪkɪ] wählerisch.

fin·ish ['fɪnɪʃ] **1.** *v/t.* beenden, vollenden; fertigstellen; abschließen; vervollkommnen; erledigen; *v/i.* enden, aufhören; ~ **with** mit j-m, et. Schluß machen; *have* ~*ed with* j-m, et. nicht mehr brauchen; **2.** Vollendung *f*, letzter Schliff; *Sport:* Endspurt *m*, Finish *n*; Ziel *n*; ~**ing line** [~ŋlaɪn] *Sport:* Ziellinie *f*.

Finn [fɪn] Finn|e *m*, -in *f*; ~**ish** ['fɪnɪʃ] **1.** finnisch; **2.** *ling.* Finnisch *n*.

fir ♀ [fɜː] *a.* ~**-tree** Tanne *f*; ~**cone** ['fɜːkəʊn] Tannenzapfen *m*.

fire ['faɪə] **1.** Feuer *n*; *be on* ~ in Flammen stehen, brennen; *catch* ~ Feuer fangen, in Brand geraten; *set on* ~, *set* ~ *to* anzünden; **2.** *v/t.* an-, entzünden; *fig.* anfeuern; abfeuern; *Ziegel etc.* brennen; F rausschmeißen (*entlassen*); heizen; *v/i.* Feuer fangen (*a. fig.*); feuern; ~**a·larm** [~rəlɑːm] Feuermelder *m*; ~**arms** *pl.* Feuer-, Schußwaffen *pl.*; ~ **bri·gade** Feuerwehr *f*; ~**bug** F Feuerteufel *m*; ~**crack·er** Frosch *m* (*Feuerwerkskörper*); ~ **de·part·ment** *Am.* Feuerwehr *f*; ~**en·gine** [~rendʒɪn] (Feuer)Spritze *f*; ~**es·cape** [~rɪskeɪp] Feuerleiter *f*, -treppe *f*; ~**ex·tin·guish·er** [~rɪkstɪŋgwɪʃə] Feuerlöscher *m*; ~**guard** Kamingitter *n*; ~**man** Feuerwehrmann *m*; Heizer *m*; ~**place** (offener) Kamin; ~**plug** Hydrant *m*; ~**proof** feuerfest; ~**rais·ing** *Brt.* [~ɪŋ] Brandstiftung *f*; ~**side** Herd *m*; Kamin *m*; ~ **sta·tion** Feuerwache *f*; ~**wood** Brennholz *n*; ~**works** *pl.* Feuerwerk *n*.

fir·ing squad ⚔ ['faɪərɪŋskwɒd] Exekutionskommando *n*.

firm¹ [fɜːm] **1.** fest; derb; standhaft; △ *nicht* firm.

firm² [~] Firma *f*, Betrieb *m*, Unternehmen *n*.

first [fɜːst] **1.** *adj.* □ erste(r, -s); beste(r, -s); **2.** *adv.* erstens; zuerst; ~ *of all* an erster Stelle; zu allererst; **3.** Erste(r, -s); *at* ~ zuerst, anfangs; *from the* ~ von Anfang an; ~ **aid** Erste Hilfe; ~**aid** ['fɜːsteɪd] Erste-Hilfe-...; ~ **kit** Verband(s)kasten *m*, -zeug *n*; ~**born** erstgeborene(r, -s), älteste(r, -s); ~ **class** 1. Klasse (*e-s Verkehrsmittels*); ~**class** erstklassig; ~**ly** [~lɪ] erstens; ~**hand** aus erster Hand; ~ **name** Vorname *m*; Beiname *m*; ~**rate** erstklassig.

firth [fɜːθ] Förde *f*, Meeresarm *m*.

fish [fɪʃ] **1.** Fisch|e *pl.*) *m*; *a queer* ~ F ein komischer Kauz; **2.** fischen, angeln; ~ *around* kramen (*for* nach); ~**bone** ['fɪʃbəʊn] Gräte *f*.

fish|er·man ['fɪʃəmən] (*pl.* -men) Fischer *m*; ~**e·ry** [~rɪ] Fischerei *f*.

fish·ing ['fɪʃɪŋ] Fischen *n*, Angeln *n*; ~**line** Angelschnur *f*; ~**rod** Angelrute *f*; ~**tack·le** Angelgerät *n*.

fish|mon·ger *bsd. Brt.* ['fɪʃmʌŋgə] Fischhändler *m*; ~**y** □ [~ɪ] (-*ier*, *-iest*) Fisch...; F verdächtig, faul.

fis|sile ⊕ ['fɪsaɪl] spaltbar; ~**sion** ['fɪʃn] Spaltung *f*; ~**sure** ['fɪʃə] Spalt *m*, Riß *m*.

fist [fɪst] Faust *f*.

fit¹ [fɪt] **1.** □ (-*tt-*) geeignet, passend; tauglich; *Sport:* fit, in (guter) Form; **2.** (-*tt-*; *fitted*, *Am. a.* fit) *v/t.* passen für *od. dat.*; anpassen, passend machen; befähigen; geeignet machen (*for*, *to* für, zu); ~ *in* j-m e-n Termin geben, j-n, et. einschieben; *a.* ~ *on* anprobieren; *a.* ~ *out* ausrüsten, -statten, einrichten, versehen (*with* mit); *a.* ~ *up* ausrüsten, -statten, einrichten; montieren; *v/i.* passen; sitzen (*Kleid*); **3.** Sitz *m* (*Kleid*).

fit² [~] Anfall *m*; 𝄞 Ausbruch *m*; Anwandlung *f*; *by* ~*s and starts* ruckweise; *give s.o. a* ~ F j-n auf die Palme bringen; j-m e-n Schock versetzen.

fit|ful □ ['fɪtfl] ruckartig; *fig.* unstet; ~**ness** [~nɪs] Tauglichkeit *f*; *bsd. Sport:* Fitneß *f*, (gute) Form; ~**ted** zugeschnitten, nach Maß (gearbeitet); Einbau...; ~ *carpet* Spannteppich *m*, Teppichboden *m*; ~ *kitchen* Einbauküche *f*; ~**ter** [~ə] Monteur *m*; Installateur *m*; ~**ting** [~ɪŋ] **1.** passend; **2.** Montage *f*; Anprobe *f*; ~*s pl.* Einrichtung *f*; Armaturen *pl.*

five [faɪv] **1.** fünf; **2.** Fünf *f*.

fix [fɪks] **1.** *v/t.* befestigen, anheften; fixieren; *Blick etc.* heften, richten (*on* auf *acc.*); fesseln; aufstellen; bestimmen, festsetzen; reparieren, instand setzen; *bsd. Am. et.* zurechtmachen, *ein Essen* zubereiten; △ *nicht* fix; ~ *up* in Ordnung bringen, regeln; j-n unterbringen; *v/i.* fest werden; ~ *on* sich entschließen für *od. zu*; **2.** F Klemme *f*, Patsche *f*; *sl.* Schuß *m* (*Heroin etc.*); ~**ed** □ fest; bestimmt; starr; ~**ing** ['fɪksɪŋ] Befestigen *n*;

Instandsetzen n; Fixieren n; Aufstellen n, Montieren n; Besatz m, Versteifung f; Am. ~s pl. Zubehör n, Ausrüstung f; ~**ture** □ [~st/ə] fest angebrachtes Zubehörteil, feste Anlage; Inventarstück n; lighting ~ Beleuchtungskörper m.

fizz [fɪz] 1. zischen, sprudeln; 2. Zischen n; F Schampus m (Sekt).

flab·ber·gast F ['flæbəgɑːst] verblüffen; be ~ed platt sein.

flab·by □ ['flæbɪ] (-ier, -iest) schlaff.

flac·cid □ ['flæksɪd] schlaff, schlapp.

flag [flæg] 1. Flagge f; Fahne f; Fliese f; ♀ Schwertlilie f; 2. (-gg-) beflaggen; durch Flaggen signalisieren; mit Fliesen belegen; ermatten; mutlos werden; ~**pole** f ['flægpəʊl] = flagstaff.

fla·grant □ ['fleɪgrənt] abscheulich; berüchtigt; offenkundig.

flag|staff ['flægstɑːf] Fahnenstange f, -mast m; ~**stone** Fliese f.

flair [fleə] Talent n; Gespür n, (feine) Nase.

flake [fleɪk] 1. Flocke f; Schicht f; 2. (sich) flocken; abblättern; **flak·y** ['fleɪkɪ] (-ier, -iest) flockig; blätt(e)rig; ~ pastry Blätterteig m.

flame [fleɪm] 1. Flamme f (a. fig.); be in ~s in Flammen stehen; 2. flammen, lodern.

flam·ma·ble Am. u. ⊕ ['flæməbl] = inflammable.

flan [flæn] Obst-, Käsekuchen m.

flank [flæŋk] 1. Flanke f; 2. flankieren.

flan·nel ['flænl] Flanell m; Waschlappen m; ~s pl. Flanellhose f.

flap [flæp] 1. (Ohr)Läppchen n; Rockschoß m; (Hut)Krempe f; Klappe f; Klaps m; (Flügel)Schlag m; 2. v/t. ~ klatschen(d schlagen); v/i. lose herabhängen; flattern.

flare [fleə] 1. flackern; sich nach außen erweitern, sich bauschen; ~ up aufflammen; fig. aufbrausen; 2. flackerndes Licht; Lichtsignal n.

flash [flæʃ] 1. Aufblitzen n, -leuchten n, Blitz m; Rundfunk etc.: Kurzmeldung f; phot. F Blitz m (Blitzlicht); bsd. Am. F Taschenlampe f; like a ~ wie der Blitz; in a ~ im Nu; ~ of lightning Blitzstrahl m; 2. (auf)blitzen; auflodern (lassen); Blick etc. werfen; blitzen; funken; telegrafieren; it ~ed on me mir kam plötzlich der Gedanke; ~**back** ['flæʃbæk]

Film, Roman: Rückblende f; ~**light** phot. Blitzlicht n; ⚓ Leuchtfeuer; bsd. Am. Taschenlampe f; ~y □ [~ɪ] (-ier, -iest) auffallend, -fällig.

flask [flɑːsk] Taschenflasche f; Thermosflasche f.

flat [flæt] 1. □ (-tt-) flach, platt; schal; econ. flau; klar; glatt; mot. platt (Reifen); ♪ erniedrigt (Note); ~ price Einheitspreis m; 2. adv. glatt; völlig; fall ~ danebengehen; sing ~ zu tief singen; 3. Fläche f, Ebene f; Flachland n; Untiefe f; (Miet)Wohnung f; ♪ B n; F Simpel m; bsd. Am. mot. Reifenpanne f, Plattfuß m; ~**foot** ['flætfʊt] (pl. -feet) Plattfuß m (Polizist); ~**foot·ed** plattfüßig; ~**i·ron** Plätteisen n; ~**ten** [~tn] (sich) ab-, verflachen.

flat·ter ['flætə] schmeicheln (dat.); △ nicht flattern; ~**er** [~rə] Schmeichler(in); ~**y** [~rɪ] Schmeichelei f.

fla·vo(u)r ['fleɪvə] 1. Geschmack m; Aroma n; Blume f (Wein); fig. Beigeschmack m; Würze f; 2. würzen; ~**ing** [~ərɪŋ] Würze f, Aroma n; ~**less** [~lɪs] geschmacklos, fad.

flaw [flɔː] 1. Sprung m, Riß m; Fehler m; ⚓ Bö f; 2. zerbrechen; beschädigen; ~**less** □ ['flɔːlɪs] fehlerlos.

flax ♀ [flæks] Flachs m, Lein m.

flea zo. [fliː] Floh m.

fleck [flek] Fleck(en) m; Tupfen m.

fled [fled] pret. u. p.p. von flee.

fledged [fledʒd] flügge; **fledg(e)·ling** ['fledʒlɪŋ] Jungvogel m; fig. Grünschnabel m.

flee [fliː] (fled) fliehen; meiden.

fleece [fliːs] 1. Vlies n; 2. scheren; **fleec·y** ['fliːsɪ] (-ier, -iest) wollig; flockig.

fleet [fliːt] 1. □ schnell; 2. ⚓ Flotte f; 2 Street das Londoner Presseviertel; die (Londoner) Presse.

flesh [fleʃ] lebendiges Fleisch; ~**y** ['fleʃɪ] (-ier, -iest) fleischig; dick.

flew [fluː] pret. von fly 2.

flex¹ bsd. anat. [fleks] biegen.

flex² bsd. Brit. ≁ [~] (Anschluß-, Verlängerungs)Kabel n, (-)Schnur f.

flex·i·ble □ ['fleksəbl] flexibel, biegsam; fig. anpassungsfähig.

flick [flɪk] schnippen; schnellen.

flick·er ['flɪkə] 1. flackern; flattern; flimmern; 2. Flackern n, Flimmern n; Flattern n; Am. Buntspecht m.

fli·er ['flaɪə] = flyer.

flight [flaɪt] Flucht f; Flug m (a. fig.);

Schwarm *m* (*Vögel etc.*; *a.* ✈, ⚔); *a.* ~ *of stairs* Treppe *f*; *put to* ~ in die Flucht schlagen; *take* (*to*) ~ die Flucht ergreifen; **~·less** *zo.* [~lɪs] flugunfähig; **~·y** □ ['flaɪtɪ] (*-ier, -iest*) launisch.

flim·sy ['flɪmzɪ] (*-ier, -iest*) dünn; zart; *fig.* fadenscheinig.

flinch [flɪntʃ] zurückweichen; zucken.

fling [flɪŋ] **1.** Wurf *m*; Schlag *m*; *have one's od. a* ~ sich austoben; **2.** (*flung*) *v/i.* eilen; ausschlagen (*Pferd*); *fig.* toben; *v/t.* werfen, schleudern; ~ *o.s.* sich stürzen; ~ *open* aufreißen.

flint [flɪnt] Feuerstein *m*.

flip [flɪp] **1.** Klaps *m*; Ruck *m*; **2.** (*-pp-*) schnippen, schnipsen.

flip·pant □ ['flɪpənt] respektlos, schnodd(e)rig.

flip·per ['flɪpə] *zo.* Flosse *f*; *Sport:* (Schwimm)Flosse *f*.

flirt [flɜːt] **1.** flirten; = *flip 2*; **2.** *be a* ~ gern flirten; **flir·ta·tion** [flɜːˈteɪʃn] Flirt *m*.

flit [flɪt] (*-tt-*) flitzen, huschen.

float [fləʊt] **1.** Schwimmer *m*; Floß *n*; Plattformwagen *m*; **2.** *v/t.* überfluten; flößen; tragen (*Wasser*); ⚓ flott machen; *fig.* in Gang bringen; *econ.* Gesellschaft gründen; *econ.* Wertpapiere *etc.* in Umlauf bringen; verbreiten; *v/i.* schwimmen, treiben; schweben; umlaufen, in Umlauf sein; **~·ing** ['fləʊtɪŋ] **1.** schwimmend, treibend, Schwimm...; umlaufend (*Geld etc.*); flexibel (*Wechselkurs*); frei konvertierbar (*Währung*); ~ *voter pol.* Wechselwähler *m*; **2.** *econ.* Floating *n*.

flock [flɒk] **1.** Herde *f* (*bsd. Schafe od. Ziegen*) (*a. fig.*); Schar *f*; △ *nicht* Flocke; **2.** sich scharen; zs.-strömen.

floe [fləʊ] (treibende) Eisscholle.

flog [flɒg] (*-gg-*) peitschen; prügeln; **~·ging** ['flɒgɪŋ] Tracht *f* Prügel.

flood [flʌd] **1.** *a.* ~*tide* Flut *f*; Überschwemmung *f*; **2.** überfluten, überschwemmen; **~·gate** ['flʌdgeɪt] Schleusentor *n*; **~·light** ⚡ Flutlicht *n*.

floor [flɔː] **1.** (Fuß)Boden *m*; Stock (-werk *n*) *m*; Tanzfläche *f*; ♪ Tenne *f*; *first* ~ *Brt.* erster Stock, *Am.* Erdgeschoß *n*; *second* ~ *Brt.* zweiter Stock, *Am.* erster Stock; ~ *leader Am. parl.* Fraktionsvorsitzende(r) *m*; ~ *show* Nachtklubvor-

stellung *f*; *take the* ~ das Wort ergreifen; **2.** dielen; zu Boden schlagen; verblüffen; **~·board** ['flɔːbɔːd] (Fußboden)Diele *f*; **~·cloth** Putzlappen *m*; **~·ing** [~rɪŋ] Dielung *f*; Fußboden *m*; ~ **lamp** Stehlampe *f*; **~·walk·er** *Am.* = shopwalker.

flop [flɒp] **1.** (*-pp-*) schlagen; flattern; (hin)plumpsen; sich fallen lassen; F durchfallen, danebengehen, ein Reinfall sein; **2.** Plumps *m*; F Flop *m*, Mißerfolg *m*, Reinfall *m*, Pleite *f*; Versager *m*.

flor·id □ ['flɒrɪd] rot, gerötet.

flor·ist ['flɒrɪst] Blumenhändler *m*.

flounce¹ [flaʊns] Volant *m*.

flounce² [~]: ~ *off* davonstürzen.

floun·der¹ ['flaʊndə] Flunder *f*.

floun·der² [~] zappeln; strampeln; *fig.* sich verhaspeln.

flour ['flaʊə] (feines) Mehl.

flour·ish ['flʌrɪʃ] **1.** Schnörkel *m*; schwungvolle Bewegung; ♪ Tusch *m*; **2.** *v/i.* blühen, gedeihen; *v/t.* schwenken.

flout [flaʊt] (ver)spotten.

flow [fləʊ] **1.** Fließen *n*, Strömen *n* (*beide a. fig.*), Rinnen *n*; Fluß *m*, Strom *m* (*beide a. fig.*); ⚓ Flut *f*; **2.** fließen, strömen, rinnen; wallen (*Haar*).

flow·er ['flaʊə] **1.** Blume *f*; Blüte *f* (*a. fig.*); Zierde *f*; **2.** blühen; **~·bed** Blumenbeet *n*; **~·pot** Blumentopf *m*; **~·y** [~rɪ] (*-ier, -iest*) Blumen...; *fig.* blumig (*Stil*).

flown [fləʊn] *p.p. von fly 2*.

fluc·tu·ate ['flʌktjʊeɪt] schwanken; **~·a·tion** [flʌktjʊˈeɪʃn] Schwankung *f*.

flu F [fluː] Grippe *f*.

flue [fluː] Rauchfang *m*, Esse *f*.

flu·en·cy *fig.* ['fluːənsɪ] Fluß *m*; **~t** □ [~t] fließend; flüssig; gewandt (*Redner*).

fluff [flʌf] **1.** Flaum *m*; Flocke *f*; *fig.* Schnitzer *m*; **2.** *Kissen* aufschütteln; *Federn* aufplustern (*Vogel*); **~·y** ['flʌfɪ] (*-ier, -iest*) flaumig; flockig.

flu·id ['fluːɪd] **1.** flüssig; **2.** Flüssigkeit *f*.

flung [flʌŋ] *pret. u. p.p. von fling 2*.

flunk *Am. fig.* F [flʌŋk] durchfallen (lassen).

flu·o·res·cent [flʊəˈresnt] fluoreszierend.

flur·ry ['flʌrɪ] Nervosität *f*; Bö *f*;

Am. a. (Regen)Schauer *m*; Schnee-gestöber *n*.

flush [flaʃ] **1.** ⊕ in gleicher Ebene; reichlich; (über)voll; **2.** Erröten *n*; Erregung *f*; Spülung *f*; (Wasser-)Spülung *f (in der Toilette)*; **3.** *v/t. a.* ~ *out* (aus)spülen; ~ *down* hinunter-spülen; ~ *the toilet* spülen; *v/i.* erröten, rot werden; spülen *(Toilette od. Toilettenbenutzer)*.

flus·ter ['flʌstə] **1.** Aufregung *f*; **2.** nervös machen, durcheinanderbringen.

flute [flu:t] **1.** ♩ Flöte *f*; Falte *f*; **2.** (auf der) Flöte spielen; riefeln; fälteln.

flut·ter ['flʌtə] **1.** Geflatter *n*; Erregung *f*; F Spekulation *f*; **2.** *v/t.* aufregen; *v/i.* flattern.

flux *fig.* [flʌks] Fluß *m*.

fly [flaɪ] **1.** *zo.* Fliege *f*; Flug *m*; Hosenschlitz *m*; Zeltklappe *f*; **2.** *(flew, flown)* fliegen (lassen); stürmen, stürzen; flattern, wehen; verfliegen *(Zeit)*; Drachen steigen lassen; ✈ überfliegen; ~ *at s.o.* auf j-n losgehen; ~ *into a passion* od. *rage* in Wut geraten; ~·**er** ['flaɪə] Flieger *m*; *Am.* Flugblatt *n*, Reklamezettel *m*; ~·**ing** [~ɪŋ] fliegend; Flug...; ~ *saucer* fliegende Untertasse; ~ *squad* Überfallkommando *n (der Polizei)*; ~·**o·ver** *Brt.* (Straßen-, Eisenbahn)Überführung *f*; ~·**weight** Boxen: Fliegengewicht(ler *m*) *n*; ~·**wheel** Schwungrad *n*.

foal *zo.* [fəʊl] Fohlen *n*.

foam [fəʊm] **1.** Schaum *m*; ~ *rubber* Schaumgummi *m*; **2.** schäumen; ~·**y** ['fəʊmɪ] *(-ier, -iest)* schaumig.

fo·cus ['fəʊkəs] **1.** *(pl. -cuses, -ci* [-saɪ]*)* (sich) (im Brennpunkt vereinigen; *opt.* einstellen *(a. fig.)*; konzentrieren.

fod·der ['fɒdə] (Trocken)Futter *n*.

foe *poet.* [fəʊ] Feind *m*, Gegner *m*.

fog [fɒg] **1.** (dichter) Nebel; *fig.* Umnebelung *f*; *phot.* Schleier *m*; **2.** *(-gg-) mst fig.* umnebeln; *phot.* verschleiern; ~·**gy** ['fɒgɪ] *(-ier, -iest)* neb(e)lig, nebelhaft.

foi·ble *fig.* ['fɔɪbl] (kleine) Schwäche.

foil¹ [fɔɪl] Folie *f*; *fig.* Hintergrund *m*.

foil² [~] vereiteln.

foil³ [~] *Fechten:* Florett *n*.

fold¹ [fəʊld] **1.** Schafhürde *f*; *fig.* Herde *f*; **2.** einpferchen.

fold² [~] **1.** Falte *f*; Falz *m*; **2.** ...fach, ...fältig; **3.** *v/t.* falten; falzen; *Arme*

kreuzen; ~ *(up)* einwickeln; *v/i.* sich falten; *Am.* F eingehen; ~·**er** ['fəʊldə] Mappe *f*, Schnellhefter *m*; Faltprospekt *m*.

fold·ing ['fəʊldɪŋ] zusammenlegbar; Klapp...; ~ *bed* Klappbett *n*; ~ *bi·cy·cle* Klapprad *n*; ~ *boat* Faltboot *n*; ~ *chair* Klappstuhl *m*; ~ *door(s pl.)* Falttür *f*.

fo·li·age ['fəʊlɪɪdʒ] Laub(werk) *n*.

folk [fəʊk] *pl.* Leute *pl.*; ~ *pl.* Leute *pl. (Angehörige)*; △ *nicht* Volk; ~·**lore** ['fəʊklɔː] Volkskunde *f*; Volkssagen *pl.*; ~·**song** Volkslied *n*; Folksong *m*.

fol·low ['fɒləʊ] folgen *(dat.)*; folgen auf *(acc.)*; be-, verfolgen; *s-m Beruf etc.* nachgehen; ~ *through* Plan etc. bis zum Ende durchführen; *e-e Sache* nachgehen; *e-e Sache* weiterverfolgen; ~·**er** [~ə] Nachfolger(in); Verfolger(in); Anhänger(in); ~·**ing** [~ɪŋ] **1.** Anhängerschaft *f*, Anhänger *pl.*; Gefolge *n*; *the* ~ das Folgende; die Folgenden *pl.*; **2.** folgende(r, -s); **3.** im Anschluß an *(acc.)*.

fol·ly ['fɒlɪ] Torheit *f*; Narrheit *f*.

fond □ [fɒnd] zärtlich; vernarrt *(of in acc.)*; *be* ~ *of* gern haben, lieben; **fon·dle** ['fɒndl] liebkosen; streicheln; (ver)hätscheln; ~·**ness** [~nɪs] Liebe *f*, Zuneigung *f*; Vorliebe *f*.

font [fɒnt] Taufstein *m*; *Am.* Quelle *f*.

food [fuːd] Speise *f*, Nahrung *f*; Essen *n*; Futter *n*; Lebensmittel *pl.*

fool [fuːl] **1.** Narr *m*, Närrin *f*, Dummkopf *m*; *make a* ~ *of s.o.* j-n zum Narren halten; *make a* ~ *of o.s.* sich lächerlich machen; **2.** *Am.* F närrisch, dumm; **3.** *v/t.* narren; betrügen *(out of um et.)*; ~ *away* vertrödeln; *v/i.* herumalbern; (herum)spielen; ~ *(a)round bsd. Am.* Zeit vertrödeln.

fool·e·ry ['fuːlərɪ] Torheit *f*; ~·**har·dy** □ [~hɑːdɪ] tollkühn; ~·**ish** □ [~ɪʃ] dumm, töricht; unklug; ~·**ish·ness** [~ɪʃnɪs] Dummheit *f*; ~·**proof** kinderleicht; todsicher.

foot [fʊt] **1.** *(pl. feet)* Fuß *m (a. Maß = 0,3048 m)*; Füßende *n*; ✕ Infanterie *f*; *on* ~ zu Fuß; im Gange, in Gang; *mst* ~ *up* addieren; ~ *it zu* Fuß gehen; ~·**ball** ['fʊtbɔːl] *Brt.* Fußball(spiel *n*) *m*; *Am.* Football (-spiel *n*) *m*; *Brt.* Fußball *m*; *Am.* Football-Ball *m*; ~·**board** Trittbrett

n; **~bridge** Fußgängerbrücke f;
~fall Tritt m, Schritt m (Geräusch);
~gear Schuhwerk n; **~hold** fester
Stand; fig. Halt m.

foot·ing ['futɪŋ] Halt m, Stand m;
Grundlage f, Basis f; Stellung f;
fester Fuß; Verhältnis n; × Zustand
m; Endsumme f; be on a friendly ~
with s.o. ein gutes Verhältnis zu j-m
haben; lose one's ~ ausgleiten.

foot|**lights** thea. ['futlaɪts] pl. Ram-
penlicht(er pl.) n; Bühne f; **~loose**
frei, unbeschwert; ~ and fancy-free
frei u. ungebunden; **~path** (Fuß-)
Pfad m; **~print** Fußabdruck m; **~s**
pl. a. Fußspur(en pl.) f; **~sore** wund
an den Füßen; **~step** Tritt m,
Schritt m; Fußstapfe f; **~wear** =
footgear.

fop [fɒp] Geck m, Fatzke m.

for [fɔː, fə] 1. prp. mst für; Zweck, Ziel,
Richtung: zu; nach; warten, hoffen
etc. auf (acc.); sich sehnen etc. nach;
Grund, Anlaß: aus, vor (dat.), wegen; Zeitdauer: ~ three days drei
Tage (lang); seit drei Tagen; Entfernung: I walked ~ a mile ich ging eine
Meile (weit); Austausch: (an)statt; in
der Eigenschaft: I ~ one ich zum
Beispiel; ~ sure sicher!, gewiß!; 2.
cj. denn.

for·age ['fɒrɪdʒ] a. ~ about (herum-)
stöbern, (-)wühlen (in in dat.; for
nach).

for·ay ['fɒreɪ] räuberischer Einfall.

for·bear[1] [fɔː'beə] (-bore, -borne)
v/t. unterlassen; v/i. sich enthalten
(from gen.); Geduld haben.

for·bear[2] ['fɔːbeə] Vorfahr m.

for·bid [fə'bɪd] (-dd-; -bade od. -bad
[-bæd], -bidden od. -bid) verbieten;
hindern; **~ding** [~] abstoßend.

force [fɔːs] 1. Stärke f, Kraft f, Gewalt
f; Nachdruck m; Zwang m; Heer n;
Streitmacht f; in ~ in großer Zahl od.
Menge; the (police) ~ die Polizei;
armed ~s pl. (Gesamt)Streitkräfte
pl.; come (put) in(to) ~ in Kraft
treten (setzen); 2. zwingen, nötigen;
erzwingen; aufzwingen; Gewalt antun (dat.); beschleunigen; aufbrechen; künstlich reif machen; ~ open
aufbrechen; **~d**: ~ landing Notlandung f; ~ march bsd. × Gewalt-
marsch m; **~ful** □ ['fɔːsfl] energisch,
kraftvoll (Person); eindrucksvoll,
überzeugend.

for·ceps ⚕ ['fɔːseps] Zange f.

for·ci·ble □ ['fɔːsəbl] gewaltsam;
Zwangs...; eindringlich; wirksam.

ford [fɔːd] 1. Furt f; 2. durchwaten.

fore [fɔː] 1. adv. vorn; 2. Vorderteil m,
n; come to the ~ sich hervortun; 3.
adj. vorder; Vorder...; **~arm** ['fɔː-
rɑːm] Unterarm m; **~bear** ['fɔːbeə]
= forbear[2]; **~bod·ing** [fɔː'bəʊdɪŋ]
(böses) Vorzeichen; Ahnung f;
~cast ['fɔːkɑːst] 1. Vorhersage f; 2.
(-cast od. -casted) vorhersagen;
voraussagen; **~fa·ther** Vorfahr m;
~fin·ger Zeigefinger m; **~foot** (pl.
-feet) zo. Vorderfuß m; **~gone**
['fɔːgɒn] von vornherein feststen-
hend; ~ conclusion ausgemachte
Sache, Selbstverständlichkeit f;
~ground ['fɔːgraʊnd] Vordergrund
m; **~hand** 1. Sport: Vorhand(stellung
m) f; 2. Sport: Vorhand...; **~head**
['fɒrɪd] Stirn f.

for·eign ['fɒrən] fremd, ausländisch,
-wärtig, Auslands..., Außen...; ~
affairs Außenpolitik f; ~ language
Fremdsprache f; ~ minister pol. Außenminister m; ≈ Office Brt. pol.
Außenministerium n; ~ policy Außenpolitik f; ≈ Secretary Brt. pol.
Außenminister m; ~ trade econ. Au-
ßenhandel m; ~ worker Gastarbeiter
m; **~er** [~ə] Ausländer(in), Frem-
de(r m) f.

fore|**knowl·edge** ['fɔː'nɒlɪdʒ] Vor-
herwissen n; **~leg** zo. ['fɔːleg] Vor-
derbein n; **~man** (pl. -men) ⚖ Obmann m; Vorarbeiter m, (Werk-)
Meister m, Polier m, ⚒ Steiger m;
~most vorderste(r, -s), erste(r, -s);
~name Vorname m; **~run·ner**
Vorläufer(in); **~see** [fɔː'siː] (-saw,
-seen) vorhersehen; **~shad·ow**
ahnen lassen, andeuten; **~sight**
['fɔːsaɪt] fig. Weitblick m, (weise)
Voraussicht.

for·est ['fɒrɪst] 1. Wald m (a. fig.),
Forst m; ~ ranger Am. Förster m; 2.
aufforsten.

fore·stall [fɔː'stɔːl] et. vereiteln; j-m
zuvorkommen.

for·est|**er** ['fɒrɪstə] Förster m; Wald-
arbeiter m; **~ry** [~rɪ] Forstwirtschaft
f; Waldgebiet n.

fore|**taste** ['fɔːteɪst] Vorgeschmack
m; **~tell** [fɔː'tel] (-told) vorhersagen;
~thought ['fɔːθɔːt] Vorsorge f, -be-
dacht m.

for·ev·er, for ev·er [fə'revə] für immer.

fore|wom·an (pl. -women) Aufseherin f; Vorarbeiterin f; **~word** Vorwort n.

for·feit ['fɔ:fɪt] **1.** Verwirkung f; Strafe f; Pfand n; **2.** verwirken; einbüßen.

forge¹ [fɔ:dʒ] mst ~ ahead sich vor(wärts)arbeiten.

forge² [~] **1.** Schmiede f; **2.** schmieden (fig. sich ausdenken); fälschen; **forg·er** ['fɔ:dʒə] Fälscher; **for·ge·ry** [~ərɪ] Fälschen n; Fälschung f.

for·get [fə'get] (-got, -gotten) vergessen; **~ful** [~fl] vergeßlich; **~-me-not** ⚘ Vergißmeinnicht n.

for·give [fə'gɪv] (-gave, -given) vergeben, -zeihen; Schuld erlassen; **~ness** [~nɪs] Verzeihung f; **for·giv·ing** □ [~ɪŋ] versöhnlich; nachsichtig.

for·go [fɔ:'gəu] (-went, -gone) verzichten auf (acc.).

fork [fɔ:k] **1.** (Eß-, Heu-, Mistetc.)Gabel f; **2.** (sich) gabeln; **~ed** gegabelt, gespalten; **~·lift** ['fɔ:klɪft], a. **~ truck** Gabelstapler m.

for·lorn [fə'lɔ:n] verloren, -lassen.

form [fɔ:m] **1.** Form f; Gestalt f; Formalität f; Formular n; (Schul-)Bank f; (Schul)Klasse f; Kondition f; geistige Verfassung; **2.** (sich) formen, (sich) bilden, gestalten; ✕ (sich) aufstellen.

form·al □ ['fɔ:ml] förmlich; formell; äußerlich; **for·mal·i·ty** [fɔ:'mælətɪ] Förmlichkeit f; Formalität f.

for·ma·tion [fɔ:'meɪʃn] Bildung f; **~·tive** ['fɔ:mətɪv] bildend; gestaltend; ~ years pl. Entwicklungsjahre pl.

for·mer ['fɔ:mə] vorig, früher; ehemalig, vergangen; erstere(r, -s); jene(r, -s); **~·ly** [~lɪ] ehemals, früher.

for·mi·da·ble □ ['fɔ:mɪdəbl] furchtbar, schrecklich; ungeheuer.

for·mu·la ['fɔ:mjulə] (pl. -las, -lae [-li:]) Formel f; Rezept n (zur Zubereitung); △ nicht Formular; **~·late** [~leɪt] formulieren.

for·sake [fə'seɪk] (-sook, -saken) aufgeben; verlassen; **~·sak·en** [~ən] p.p. von forsake; **~·sook** [fɔ:'suk] pret. von forsake; **~·swear** [fɔ:'sweə] (-swore, -sworn) abschwören, entsagen.

fort ✕ [fɔ:t] Fort n, Festung f.

forth [fɔ:θ] vor(wärts); voran; heraus, hinaus, hervor; weiter, fort; **~·com·ing** ['fɔ:θ'kʌmɪŋ] erscheinend; bereit; bevorstehend; F entgegenkommend; **~ with** [~'wɪθ] sogleich.

for·ti·eth ['fɔ:tɪɪθ] vierzigste(r, -s).

for·ti·fi·ca·tion [fɔ:rtɪfɪ'keɪʃn] Befestigung f; **~·fy** ['fɔ:tɪfaɪ] ✕ befestigen; fig. (ver)stärken; **~·tude** [~tju:d] Seelenstärke f; Tapferkeit f.

fort·night ['fɔ:tnaɪt] vierzehn Tage.

for·tress ['fɔ:trɪs] Festung f.

for·tu·i·tous □ [fɔ:'tju:ɪtəs] zufällig.

for·tu·nate ['fɔ:tʃnət] glücklich; be ~ Glück haben; **~·ly** [~lɪ] glücklicherweise.

for·tune ['fɔ:tʃn] Glück n; Schicksal n; Zufall m; Vermögen n; **~-tell·er** Wahrsager(in).

for·ty ['fɔ:tɪ] **1.** vierzig; **~-niner** Am. kalifornischer Goldsucher von 1849; ~ winks pl. F Nickerchen n; **2.** Vierzig f.

for·ward ['fɔ:wəd] **1.** adj. vorder; bereit(willig); fortschrittlich; vorwitzig, keck; **2.** adv. a. **~s** vor(wärts); **3.** Fußball: Stürmer m; **4.** befördern, (ver)senden, schicken; Brief etc. nachsenden; **~·ing a·gent** [~ɪŋeɪdʒənt] Spediteur m.

fos·ter-child ['fɒstətʃaɪld] (pl. -children) Pflegekind n; **~-par·ents** pl. Pflegeeltern pl.

fought [fɔ:t] pret. u. p.p. von fight 2.

foul [faul] **1.** □ stinkend, widerlich, schlecht, übel(riechend); schlecht, stürmisch (Wetter); widrig (Wind); Sport: regelwidrig, unfair; fig. widerlich, ekelhaft; fig. abscheulich; gemein; △ nicht faul; Sport: Foul n, Regelverstoß m; **3.** a. ~ up be-, verschmutzen, verunreinigen; Sport: foulen.

found [faund] **1.** pret. u. p.p. von find 2. **2.** (be)gründen; stiften; ⊕ gießen.

foun·da·tion [faun'deɪʃn] arch. Grundmauer f, Fundament n; fig. Gründung f, Errichtung f; (gemeinnützige) Stiftung; fig. Grund(lage f) m, Basis f.

found·er¹ ['faundə] Gründer(in), Stifter(in).

found·er² [~] ⚓ sinken; fig. scheitern.

found·ling ['faundlɪŋ] Findling m.

foun·dry ⊕ ['faundrɪ] Gießerei f.

foun·tain ['fauntɪn] Quelle f; Springbrunnen m; **~ pen** Füllfederhalter m.

F

four [fɔː] 1. vier; 2. Vier f; *Rudern:* Vierer m; *on all* ~*s* auf allen vieren; ~**square** [fɔːˈskweə] viereckig; *fig.* unerschütterlich; ~**stroke** [ˈfɔːstrəʊk] *mot.* Viertakt...; ~**teen** [ˈfɔːˈtiːn] 1. vierzehn; 2. Vierzehn f; ~**teenth** [ˌˈtiːnθ] vierzehnte(r, -s); ~**th** [fɔːθ] 1. vierte(r, -s); 2. Viertel n; ~**th·ly** [ˈfɔːθlɪ] viertens.

fowl [faʊl] Geflügel n; Huhn n; Vogel m; ~**ing piece** [ˈfaʊlɪŋpiːs] Vogelflinte f.

fox [fɒks] 1. Fuchs m; 2. betrügen; ~**glove** ♀ [ˈfɒksglʌv] Fingerhut m; ~**y** [ˌsɪ] (-ier, -iest) fuchsartig; schlau, gerissen.

frac·tion [ˈfrækʃn] Bruch(teil) m; △ *nicht parl.* Fraktion.

frac·ture [ˈfræktʃə] 1. (*bsd.* Knochen)Bruch m; 2. brechen.

fra·gile [ˈfrædʒaɪl] zerbrechlich.

frag·ment [ˈfrægmənt] Bruchstück n.

fra|grance [ˈfreɪgrəns] Wohlgeruch m, Duft m; ~**grant** □ [ˌt] wohlriechend.

frail □ [freɪl] gebr-, zerbrechlich; zart, schwach; ~**ty** [ˈfreɪltɪ] Zartheit f; Zerbrechlichkeit f; Schwäche f.

frame [freɪm] 1. Rahmen m; Gerippe n; Gerüst n; (Brillen)Gestell n; Körper m; (An)Ordnung f; *phot.* (Einzel)Bild n; ✧ Frühbeetkasten m; ~ *of mind* Gemütsverfassung f, Stimmung f; 2. bilden, formen, bauen; entwerfen; (ein)rahmen; sich entwickeln; ~**up** *bsd. Am.* F [ˈfreɪmʌp] abgekartetes Spiel; ~**work** ⊕ Gerippe n; Rahmen m; *fig.* Struktur f, System n.

fran·chise ⚖ [ˈfræntʃaɪz] Wahlrecht n; Bürgerrecht n; *bsd. Am.* Konzession f.

frank [fræŋk] 1. □ frei(mütig), offen; 2. *Brief* maschinell frankieren.

frank·fur·ter [ˈfræŋkfɜːtə] Frankfurter Würstchen n.

frank·ness [ˈfræŋknɪs] Offenheit f.

fran·tic [ˈfræntɪk] (~*ally*) wahnsinnig.

fra·ter|nal □ [frəˈtɜːnl] brüderlich; ~**ni·ty** [ˌnətɪ] Brüderlichkeit f; Bruderschaft f; *Am. univ.* Verbindung f.

fraud [frɔːd] Betrug m; F Schwindel m; ~**u·lent** □ [ˈfrɔːdjʊlənt] betrügerisch.

fray [freɪ] (sich) abnutzen; (sich) durchscheuern, (sich) ausfransen.

freak [friːk] 1. Mißbildung f, Mißge-

burt f, Monstrosität f; außergewöhnlicher Umstand; Grille f, Laune f; *mst in Zssgn:* Süchtige(r m) f; Freak m, Narr m, Fanatiker m; ~ *of nature* Laune f der Natur; *film* ~ Kinonarr m, -fan m; 2. ~ *out* sl. ausflippen.

freck·le [ˈfrekl] Sommersprosse f; ~**d** sommersprossig.

free [friː] 1. □ (~*r*, ~*st*) frei; freigebig (*of* mit); freiwillig; *he is* ~ *to inf.* es steht ihm frei, zu *inf.*; ~ *and easy* zwanglos; sorglos; *make* ~ sich Freiheiten erlauben; *set* ~ freilassen; 2. (*freed*) befreien; freilassen; *et.* freimachen; ~**dom** [ˈfriːdəm] Freiheit f; freie Benutzung; Offenheit f; Zwanglosigkeit f; (plumpe) Vertraulichkeit; ~ *of a city* (Ehren)Bürgerrecht n; ~**hold·er** Grundeigentümer m; ~**lance** frei(beruflich tätig), freischaffend; ♀**ma·son** Freimaurer m; ~**way** *Am.* Schnellstraße f; ~**wheel** ⊕ [friːˈwiːl] 1. Freilauf m; 2. im Freilauf fahren.

freeze [friːz] 1. (*froze, frozen*) v/i. (ge)frieren; erstarren; v/t. gefrieren lassen; *Fleisch etc.* einfrieren, tiefkühlen; *econ. Preise etc.* einfrieren; 2. Frost m, Kälte f; *econ. pol.* Einfrieren n; *wage* ~, ~ *on wages* Lohnstopp m; ~**dry** [friːzˈdraɪ] gefriertrocknen; **freez·er** [ˈfriːzə] *a.* deep ~ Gefriertruhe f, Tiefkühl-, Gefriergerät n; Gefrierfach n; **freez·ing** □ [ˌɪŋ] eisig; ⊕ Gefrier...; ~ *compartment* Gefrier-, Tiefkühlfach n; ~ *point* Gefrierpunkt m.

freight [freɪt] 1. Fracht(geld n) f; *attr. Am.* Güter...; 2. be-, verfrachten; ~ **car** *Am.* 🚃 [ˈfreɪtkɑː] Güterwagen m; ~**er** [ˌə] Frachter m, Frachtschiff n; Fracht-, Transportflugzeug n; ~ **train** *Am.* Güterzug m.

French [frentʃ] 1. französisch; *take* ~ *leave* heimlich weggehen; ~ *doors pl. Am.* = *French window(s pl.)*; ~ *fries pl. bsd. Am.* Pommes frites pl.; ~ *window(s pl.)* Terrassen-, Balkontür f; 2. *ling.* Französisch n; *the* ~ *die* Franzosen pl.; ~**man** [ˈfrentʃmən] (*pl. -men*) Franzose m.

fren|zied [ˈfrenzɪd] wahnsinnig; ~**zy** [ˌɪ] wilde Aufregung; Ekstase f; Raserei f.

fre·quen|cy [ˈfriːkwənsɪ] Häufigkeit f; ⚡ Frequenz f; ~**t** 1. □ [ˌt] häufig; 2. [frɪˈkwent] (oft) besuchen.

fresh □ [freʃ] frisch; neu; unerfahren; *Am.* F frech; **~en** ['freʃn] frisch machen *od.* werden; **~ up** neuer *od.* schöner machen; **~ up** sich frisch machen; **~man** (*pl. -men*) *univ.* Student *m* im ersten Jahr; **~ness** [~nɪs] Frische *f*; Neuheit *f*; Unerfahrenheit *f*; **~ water** Süßwasser *n*; **~water** Süßwasser...

fret [fret] 1. Aufregung *f*; Ärger *m*; ♪ Bund *m*, Griffleiste *f*; 2. (-tt-) zerfressen; (sich) ärgern; (sich) grämen; **~ away**, **~ out** aufreiben.

fret·ful □ ['fretfl] ärgerlich.

fret·saw ['fretsɔ:] Laubsäge *f*.

fret·work ['fretwɜ:k] (geschnitztes) Gitterwerk; Laubsägearbeit *f*.

fri·ar ['fraɪə] Mönch *m*.

fric·tion ['frɪkʃn] Reibung *f* (*a. fig.*).

Fri·day ['fraɪdɪ] Freitag *m*.

fridge F [frɪdʒ] Kühlschrank *m*.

friend [frend] Freund(in); Bekannte(r *m f*); **make ~s with** sich anfreunden mit, Freundschaft schließen mit; **~ly** ['frendlɪ] freund(schaft)-lich; **~ship** [~ʃɪp] Freundschaft *f*.

frig·ate ⚓ ['frɪgɪt] Fregatte *f*.

fright [fraɪt] Schreck(en) *m*; *fig.* Vogelscheuche *f*; **~en** ['fraɪtn] erschrecken; **be ~ed of** s.th. vor et. Angst haben; **~en·ing** □ [~ɪŋ] furchterregend; **~ful** □ [~fl] schrecklich.

fri·gid □ ['frɪdʒɪd] kalt, frostig; *psych.* frigid(e).

frill [frɪl] Krause *f*, Rüsche *f*.

fringe [frɪndʒ] 1. Franse *f*; Rand *m*; Ponyfrisur *f*; **~ benefits** *pl. econ.* Gehalts-, Lohnnebenleistungen *pl.*; **~ event** Randveranstaltung *f*; **~ group** Soziologie: Randgruppe *f*; 2. mit Fransen besetzen.

Fri·si·an ['frɪzɪən] friesisch.

frisk [frɪsk] 1. Luftsprung *m*; 2. herumtollen; F filzen; *j-n, et.* durchsuchen; **~y** □ ['frɪskɪ] (-ier, -iest) lebhaft, munter.

frit·ter ['frɪtə] 1. Pfannkuchen *m*, Krapfen *m*. 2. **~ away** vertun, -trödeln, -geuden.

fri·vol·i·ty [frɪ'vɒlətɪ] Frivolität *f*, Leichtfertigkeit *f*; **friv·o·lous** □ ['frɪvələs] frivol, leichtfertig.

friz·zle ['frɪzl] *Küche*: brutzeln.

frizz·y □ ['frɪzɪ] (-ier, -iest) gekräuselt, kraus (*Haar*).

fro [frəʊ]: **to and ~** hin und her.

frock [frɒk] Kutte *f*; (*Frauen*)Kleid *n*; Kittel *m*; Gehrock *m*.

frog *zo.* [frɒg] Frosch *m*; **~man** ['frɒgmən] (*pl. -men*) Froschmann *m*.

frol·ic ['frɒlɪk] 1. Herumtoben *n*, -tollen *n*; Ausgelassenheit *f*; Streich *m*, Jux *m*; 2. (-ck-) herumtoben, -tollen; **~some** □ [~səm] lustig, fröhlich.

from [frɒm, frəm] von; aus, von ... her; von ... (an); aus, vor, wegen; nach, gemäß; **defend ~** schützen vor (*dat.*); **~ amidst** mitten aus.

front [frʌnt] 1. Stirn *f*; Vorderseite *f*; ✕ Front *f*; Hemdbrust *f*; Strandpromenade *f*; Kühnheit *f*, Frechheit *f*; **at the ~**, **in ~** vorn; **in ~ of** räumlich vor; 2. Vorder...; **~ door** Haustür *f*; **~ entrance** Vordereingang *m*; 3. *a.* **~ on**, **~ towards** die Front haben nach; gegenüberstehen, gegenübertreten (*dat.*); **~age** ['frʌntɪdʒ] (Vorder-) Front *f* (*e-s Hauses*); **~al** □ [~tl] Stirn...; Front..., Vorder...

fron·tier ['frʌntɪə] (Landes)Grenze *f*; *Am. hist.* Grenzland *n*, Grenze *f* (*zum Wilden Westen*); *attr.* Grenz...

front page ['frʌntpeɪdʒ] *Zeitung*: Titelseite *f*; **~-wheel drive** *mot.* Vorderradantrieb *m*.

frost [frɒst] 1. Frost *m*; *a. hoar ~*, *white ~* Reif *m*; 2. (mit Zucker) bestreuen; glasieren, mattieren; **~ed glass** Milchglas *n*; **~·bite** ['frɒstbaɪt] Erfrierung *f*; **~·bit·ten** erfroren; **~y** □ [~ɪ] (-ier, -iest) eisig, frostig (*a. fig.*).

froth [frɒθ] 1. Schaum *m*; 2. schäumen; zu Schaum schlagen; **~y** □ ['frɒθɪ] (-ier, -iest) schäumend, schaumig; *fig.* seicht.

frown [fraʊn] 1. Stirnrunzeln *n*; finsterer Blick; 2. *v/i.* die Stirn runzeln; finster blicken; **~ on** *od.* **upon** s.th. et. mißbilligen.

froze [frəʊz] *pret. von* freeze 1;

fro·zen ['frəʊzn] 1. *p.p. von* freeze 1; 2. *adj.* (eis)kalt; (ein-, zu)gefroren; Gefrier...; **~ food** Tiefkühlkost *f*.

fru·gal □ ['fru:gl] einfach; sparsam.

fruit [fru:t] 1. Frucht *f*; Früchte *pl.*; Obst *n*; 2. Frucht tragen; **~·er·er** ['fru:tərə] Obsthändler *m*; **~·ful** □ [~fl] fruchtbar; **~·less** □ [~lɪs] unfruchtbar; **~y** □ [~ɪ] (-ier, -iest) frucht-, obstartig; fruchtig (*Wein*); klangvoll, sonor (*Stimme*).

frustrate 494

frus|trate [frʌ'streɪt] vereiteln; enttäuschen; frustrieren; **~tra·tion** [~eɪ∫n] Vereitelung f; Enttäuschung f; Frustration f.

fry [fraɪ] 1. Gebratene(s) n; Fischbrut f; 2. braten, backen; **~ing-pan** ['fraɪŋpæn] Bratpfanne f.

fuch·sia ♀ ['fju:∫ə] Fuchsie f.

fuck ∨ [fʌk] 1. ficken, vögeln; ~ *it!* Scheiße!; *get ~ed!* der Teufel soll dich holen!; 2. *int.* Scheiße!; **~ing** ∨ ['fʌkɪŋ] Scheiß..., verflucht, -dammt (*oft nur verstärkend*); ~ *hell!* verdammte Scheiße!

fudge [fʌdʒ] 1. F zurechtpfuschen; 2. Unsinn m; *Art* Fondant m.

fu·el [fjʊəl] 1. Brennmaterial n; Betriebs-, mot. Kraftstoff m; 2. (*bsd. Brt.* -ll-, *Am.* -l-) mot., ✈ (auf)tanken.

fu·gi·tive ['fju:dʒɪtɪv] 1. flüchtig (a. *fig.*); 2. Flüchtling m.

ful·fil, *Am. a.* -**fill** [fʊl'fɪl] (-ll-) erfüllen; vollziehen; **~ment** [~mənt] Erfüllung f.

full [fʊl] 1. □ voll; Voll...; vollständig, völlig; reichlich; ausführlich; *of ~ age* volljährig; 2. *adv.* völlig, ganz; genau; 3. *das* Ganze; Höhepunkt m; *in ~* völlig; ausführlich; *to the ~* vollständig; **~-blood·ed** ['fʊlblʌdɪd] vollblütig; kräftig; reinrassig; **~ dress** Gesellschaftsanzug m; **~-dress** formell, Gala...; **~-fledged** *Am.* = *fully-fledged*; **~-grown** ausgewachsen, **~-length** in voller Größe; bodenlang; abendfüllend (*Film etc.*); **~ moon** Vollmond m; **~ stop** *ling.* Punkt m; **~ time** *Sport:* Spielende n; **~-time** ganztägig, Ganztags...; **~ job** Ganztagsbeschäftigung f.

ful·ly ['fʊlɪ] voll, völlig, ganz; **~-fledged** flügge; *fig.* richtig; **~-grown** = *full-grown*.

fum·ble ['fʌmbl] tasten, fummeln.

fume [fju:m] 1. rauchen; aufgebracht sein; 2. **~s** pl. Dämpfe pl., Dünste pl.

fu·mi·gate ['fju:mɪgeɪt] ausräuchern, desinfizieren.

fun [fʌn] Scherz m, Spaß m; *make ~ of* sich lustig machen über (*acc.*).

func·tion ['fʌŋk∫n] 1. Funktion f; Beruf m; Tätigkeit f; Aufgabe f; Feierlichkeit f; 2. funktionieren; **~a·ry** [~ərɪ] Funktionär m.

fund [fʌnd] 1. Fonds m; **~s** pl. Staats-

papiere pl.; Geld(mittel pl.) n; a ~ *of fig.* ein Vorrat an (*dat.*); 2. *Schuld* fundieren; *Geld* anlegen; das Kapital aufbringen für.

fun·da·men·tal □ [fʌndə'mentl] 1. grundlegend; Grund...; 2. ~s pl. Grundlage f, -züge pl., -begriffe pl.

fu·ne·ral ['fju:nərəl] Beerdigung f; *attr.* Trauer..., Begräbnis...; **~re·al** □ [fju:'nɪərɪəl] traurig, düster.

fun-fair ['fʌnfeə] Rummelplatz m.

fu·nic·u·lar [fju:'nɪkjʊlə] a. ~ *railway* (Draht)Seilbahn f.

fun·nel ['fʌnl] Trichter m; Rauchfang m; ♣, ♖ Schornstein m.

fun·nies *Am.* ['fʌnɪz] pl. Comics pl.

fun·ny ['fʌnɪ] (-ier, -iest) lustig, spaßig, komisch.

fur [fɜ:] 1. Pelz m; Belag m (*auf der Zunge*); Kesselstein m; **~s** pl. Pelzwaren pl.; 2. mit Pelz besetzt *od.* füttern.

fur·bish ['fɜ:bɪ∫] putzen, polieren.

fu·ri·ous □ ['fjʊərɪəs] wütend; wild.

furl [fɜ:l] *Fahne, Segel* auf-, einrollen; *Schirm* zusammenrollen.

fur·lough ✖ ['fɜ:ləʊ] Urlaub m.

fur·nace ['fɜ:nɪs] Schmelz-, Hochofen m; (Heiz)Kessel m.

fur·nish ['fɜ:nɪ∫] versehen (*with* mit); *et.* liefern; möblieren; ausstatten.

fur·ni·ture ['fɜ:nɪt∫ə] Möbel pl., Einrichtung f; Ausstattung f; *sectional* ~ Anbaumöbel pl.

fur·ri·er ['fʌrɪə] Kürschner m.

fur·row ['fʌrəʊ] 1. Furche f; 2. furchen.

fur·ry ['fɜ:rɪ] aus Pelz, pelzartig; belegt (*Zunge*).

fur·ther ['fɜ:ðə] 1. *comp. von* far; 2. fördern; **~ance** [~rəns] Förderung f; **~more** [~'mɔ:] ferner, überdies; **~most** [~məʊst] weiteste(r, -s), entfernteste(r, -s).

fur·thest ['fɜ:ðɪst] *sup. von* far.

fur·tive □ ['fɜ:tɪv] verstohlen.

fu·ry ['fjʊərɪ] Raserei f, Wut f; Furie f.

fuse [fju:z] 1. schmelzen; ∮ durchbrennen; 2. ∮ Sicherung f; Zünder m; Zündschnur f.

fu·se·lage ✈ ['fju:zɪlɑ:ʒ] (Flugzeug-) Rumpf m.

fu·sion ['fju:ʒn] Verschmelzung f, Fusion f; *nuclear* ~ Kernfusion f.

fuss F [fʌs] 1. Lärm m; Wesen n, Getue n; 2. viel Aufhebens machen (*about* um, von); (sich) aufregen; **~y**

☐ ['fʌsɪ] (-ier, -iest) aufgeregt, hektisch; kleinlich, pedantisch; heikel, wählerisch.

fus·ty ['fʌstɪ] (-ier, -iest) muffig; fig. verstaubt.

fu·tile ☐ ['fju:taɪl] nutz-, zwecklos.

fu·ture ['fju:tʃə] 1. (zu)künftig; 2. Zukunft f; gr. Futur n, Zukunft f; in ~ in Zukunft, künftig.

fuzz[1] [fʌz] 1. feiner Flaum; Fusseln pl.; 2. fusseln, (zer)fasern.

fuzz[2] sl. [~] Bulle m (Polizist).

G

gab F [gæb] Geschwätz n; have the gift of the ~ ein gutes Mundwerk haben.

gab·ar·dine ['gæbədi:n] Gabardine m (Wollstoff).

gab·ble ['gæbl] 1. Geschnatter n, Geschwätz n; 2. schnattern, schwatzen.

gab·er·dine ['gæbədi:n] hist. Kaftan m (der Juden); = gabardine.

ga·ble arch. ['geɪbl] Giebel m.

gad F [gæd] (-dd-): ~ about, ~ around (viel) unterwegs sein (in dat.).

gad·fly zo. ['gædflaɪ] Bremse f.

gad·get ⊕['gædʒɪt] Apparat m, Gerät n, Vorrichtung f; oft contp. technische Spielerei.

gag [gæg] 1. Knebel m (a. fig.); F Gag m; 2. (-gg-) knebeln; fig. mundtot machen.

gage Am. [geɪdʒ] = gauge; △ nicht Gage.

gai·e·ty ['geɪətɪ] Fröhlichkeit f.

gai·ly ['geɪlɪ] adv. von gay 1.

gain [geɪn] 1. Gewinn m; Vorteil m; 2. gewinnen; erreichen; bekommen; zunehmen an (dat.); vorgehen (um) (Uhr); ~ in zunehmen an (dat.).

gait [geɪt] Gang(art f) m; Schritt m.

gai·ter ['geɪtə] Gamasche f.

gal F [gæl] Mädel n.

gal·ax·y ast. ['gæləksɪ] Milchstraße f, Galaxis f.

gale [geɪl] Sturm m.

gall [gɔ:l] 1. veraltet Galle f; wundgeriebene Stelle; F Frechheit f; 2. wund reiben; ärgern.

gal·lant ['gælənt] stattlich; tapfer; galant, höflich; ~·lan·try [~rɪ] Tapferkeit f; Galanterie f.

gal·le·ry ['gælərɪ] Galerie f; Empore f.

gal·ley ['gælɪ] ⚓ Galeere f; ⚓ Kom-

büse f; a. ~ proof print. Fahne(nabzug m) f.

gal·lon ['gælən] Gallone f (4,54 Liter, Am. 3,78 Liter).

gal·lop ['gæləp] 1. Galopp m; 2. galoppieren (lassen).

gal·lows ['gæləʊz] sg. Galgen m.

ga·lore [gə'lɔ:] in rauhen Mengen.

gam·ble ['gæmbl] 1. (um Geld) spielen; 2. F Glücksspiel n; ~r [~ə] Spieler(in).

gam·bol ['gæmbl] 1. Luftsprung m; 2. (bsd. Brt. -ll-, Am. -l-) (herum-)tanzen, (-)hüpfen.

game [geɪm] 1. (Karten-, Ball- etc.)Spiel n; (einzelnes) Spiel (a. fig.); hunt. Wild n; Wildbret n; ~s pl. Spiele pl.; Schule: Sport m; 2. mutig; bereit (for zu; to do zu tun); ~·keep·er ['geɪmki:pə] Wildhüter m.

gam·mon bsd. Brt. ['gæmən] schwachgepökelter od. -geräucherter Schinken.

gan·der zo. ['gændə] Gänserich m.

gang [gæŋ] 1. (Arbeiter)Trupp m; Gang f, Bande f; Clique f; Horde f; △ nicht der Gang; 2. ~ up sich zusammentun, contp. sich zusammenrotten.

gang·ster ['gæŋstə] Gangster m.

gang·way ['gæŋweɪ] (Durch)Gang m; ⚓ Fallreep n; ⚓ Laufplanke f.

gaol [dʒeɪl], ~·bird ['dʒeɪlbɜ:d], ~·er [~ə] s. jail etc.

gap [gæp] Lücke f; Kluft f; Spalte f.

gape [geɪp] gähnen; klaffen; gaffen.

gar·age ['gærɑ:ʒ] 1. Garage f; (Reparatur)Werkstatt f (u. Tankstelle f); 2. Auto in e-r Garage ab- od. unterstellen; Auto in die Garage fahren.

gar·bage bsd. Am. ['gɑ:bɪdʒ] Abfall m, Müll m; ~ can Abfall-, Mülleimer

m; Abfall-, Mülltonne *f*; ~ truck
Müllwagen *m*.

gar·den ['gɑːdn] **1.** Garten *m*; **2.** im
Garten arbeiten; Gartenbau trei-
ben; **~er** [~ə] Gärtner(in); **~ing**
[~ɪŋ] Gartenarbeit *f*.

gar·gle ['gɑːgl] **1.** gurgeln; **2.** Gurgeln *n*; Gurgelwasser *n*.

gar·ish □ ['geərɪʃ] grell, auffallend.

gar·land ['gɑːlənd] Girlande *f*.

gar·lic ♀ ['gɑːlɪk] Knoblauch *m*.

gar·ment ['gɑːmənt] Gewand *n*.

gar·nish ['gɑːnɪʃ] garnieren; zieren.

gar·ret ['gærət] Dachstube *f*.

gar·ri·son ✕ ['gærɪsn] Garnison *f*.

gar·ru·lous □ ['gærələs] schwatzhaft.

gar·ter ['gɑːtə] Strumpfband *n*; *Am.*
Socken-, Strumpfhalter *m*.

gas [gæs] **1.** Gas *n*; *Am.* F Benzin *n*; **2.**
(-ss-) *v/t.* vergasen; *v/i.* F faseln; *a.* ~
up *Am.* F *mot.* (auf)tanken; **~e·ous**
['gæsjəs] gasförmig.

gash [gæʃ] **1.** klaffende Wunde; Hieb
m; Riß *m*; **2.** tief (ein)schneiden in
(*acc.*).

gas·ket ⊕ ['gæskɪt] Dichtung *f*.

gas|light ['gæslaɪt] Gasbeleuchtung
f; **~ me·ter** Gasuhr *f*; **~·o·lene**,
~·o·line *Am.* ['gæsəliːn] Benzin *n*.

gasp [gɑːsp] **1.** Keuchen *n*, schweres
Atmen; **2.** keuchen, ~ for breath
nach Luft schnappen, nach Atem
ringen.

gas| sta·tion *Am.* ['gæssteɪʃn] Tank-
stelle *f*; **~ stove** Gasofen *m*, -herd *m*;
~·works *sg.* Gaswerk *n*.

gate [geɪt] Tor *n*; Pforte *f*; Schranke *f*,
Sperre *f*; ⚐ Flugsteig *m*; **~·crash**
['geɪtkræʃ] uneingeladen kommen
od. (hin)gehen (zu); sich ohne zu
bezahlen hinein- *od.* hereinschmug-
geln; sich ohne zu bezahlen schmuggeln in (*acc.*); **~·post** Tor-, Türpfo-
sten *m*; **~·way** Tor(weg *m*) *n*, Einfahrt *f*.

gath·er ['gæðə] **1.** *v/t.* (ein-, ver-)
sammeln; ernten; pflücken; schlie-
ßen (from aus); zusammenziehen,
kräuseln; ~ speed schneller werden;
v/i. sich (ver)sammeln; sich vergrößern; reifen (*Abszeß*); eitern (*Wun-
de*); **2.** Falte *f*; **~·ing** [~rɪŋ] Versammlung *f*; Zusammenkunft *f*.

gau·dy □ ['gɔːdɪ] (-ier, -iest) auffällig, bunt, grell (*Farbe*); protzig.

gauge [geɪdʒ] **1.** (Normal)Maß *n*; ⊕
Lehre *f*; ∰ Spurweite *f*; Meßgerät *n*;

fig. Maßstab *m*; **2.** eichen; (aus)mes-
sen; *fig.* abschätzen.

gaunt □ [gɔːnt] hager; ausgemergelt.

gaunt·let ['gɔːntlɪt] Schutzhand-
schuh *m*; *fig.* Fehdehandschuh *m*;
run the ~ Spießruten laufen.

gauze [gɔːz] Gaze *f*.

gave [geɪv] *pret. von* give.

gav·el ['gævl] Hammer *m* (*e-s Vorsit-
zenden od. Auktionators*).

gaw·ky ['gɔːkɪ] (-ier, -iest) unbeholfen, linkisch.

gay [geɪ] **1.** lustig, fröhlich; bunt,
(farben)prächtig; F schwul (*homosexuell*); **2.** F Schwule(r) *m* (*Homosexueller*).

gaze [geɪz] **1.** (starrer) Blick; △ *nicht*
Gaze; **2.** starren; ~ at starren auf
(*acc.*), anstarren.

ga·zette [gə'zet] Amtsblatt *n*.

ga·zelle *zo.* [gə'zel] Gazelle *f*.

gear [gɪə] **1** ⊕ Getriebe *n*; *mot.* Gang
m; *mst in Zssgn*: Vorrichtung *f*, Gerät
n; *in* ~ mit eingelegtem Gang; out of
~ im Leerlauf; change ~(s), *Am.*
shift ~(s) *mot.* schalten; landing ~ ✕
Fahrgestell *n*; steering ~ ⚓ Ruder-
anlage *f*; *mot.* Lenkung *f*; **2.** einschalten; ⊕ greifen; **~·lev·er** ['grəliː-
və], *Am.* **~·shift** *mot.* Schalthebel *m*.

geese [giːs] *pl. von* goose.

geld·ing *zo.* ['geldɪŋ] Wallach *m*.

gem [dʒem] Edelstein *m*; Gemme *f*;
fig. Glanzstück *n*.

gen·der ['dʒendə] *gr.* Genus *n*, Geschlecht *n*; *coll.* ⚲ Geschlecht *n*.

gen·e·ral ['dʒenərəl] **1.** □ allgemein; allgemeingültig; ungefähr;
Haupt..., General...; ♀ Certificate of
Education s. certificate 1; ~ education *od.* knowledge Allgemeinbil-
dung *f*; ~ election *Brt. pol.* allgemeine Wahlen *pl.*; ~ practitioner
praktischer Arzt; **2.** ✕ General *m*;
Feldherr *m*; *in* ~ im allgemeinen;
~·i·ty [dʒenə'rælətɪ] Allgemeinheit *f*;
die große Masse; **~·ize** [~laɪz] verall-
gemeinern; **gen·er·al·ly** [~lɪ] im allgemeinen, überhaupt; gewöhnlich.

gen·e·rate ['dʒenəreɪt] erzeugen;
~·ra·tion [dʒenə'reɪʃn] (Er)Zeu-
gung *f*; Generation *f*; Menschenalter *n*; **~·ra·tor** ['dʒenəreɪtə] Erzeuger *m*; ⊕ Generator *m*; *bsd. Am. mot.*
Lichtmaschine *f*.

gen·e·ros·i·ty [dʒenə'rɒsətɪ] Großmut *f*; Großzügigkeit *f*; **~·rous** □
['dʒenərəs] großmütig, großzügig.

ge·ni·al □ ['dʒiːnjəl] freundlich; angenehm; wohltuend; △ *nicht genial.*

gen·i·tive *gr.* ['dʒenɪtɪv] *a.* ~ *case* Genitiv *m*, zweiter Fall.

ge·ni·us ['dʒiːnjəs] Geist *m*; Genie *n.*

gent F [dʒent] Herr *m*; ~*s sg. Brt.* F Herrenklo *n.*

gen·teel □ [dʒen'tiːl] vornehm; elegant.

gen·tile ['dʒentaɪl] **1.** heidnisch, nichtjüdisch; **2.** Heid|e *m*, -in *f.*

gen·tle □ ['dʒentl] (~*r*, ~*st*) sanft; mild; zahm; leise, sacht; vornehm; ~**·man** (*pl.* -men) Herr *m*; Gentleman *m*; ~**·man·ly** [~mənlɪ] gentlemanlike, vornehm; ~**·ness** [~nɪs] Sanftheit *f*; Milde *f*, Güte *f*, Sanftmut *f.*

gen·try ['dʒentrɪ] niederer Adel; Oberschicht *f.*

gen·u·ine □ ['dʒenjʊɪn] echt; aufrichtig.

ge·og·ra·phy [dʒɪ'ɒɡrəfɪ] Geographie *f.*

ge·ol·o·gy [dʒɪ'ɒlədʒɪ] Geologie *f.*

ge·om·e·try [dʒɪ'ɒmətrɪ] Geometrie *f.*

germ *biol.*, ⚕ [dʒɜːm] Keim *m.*

Ger·man ['dʒɜːmən] **1.** deutsch; **2.** Deutsche(r *m*) *f*; *ling.* Deutsch *n.*

ger·mi·nate ['dʒɜːmɪneɪt] keimen (lassen).

ger·und *gr.* ['dʒerənd] Gerundium *n.*

ges·tic·u·late [dʒe'stɪkjʊleɪt] gestikulieren; ~**·la·tion** [dʒestɪkjʊ'leɪʃn] Gebärdenspiel *n.*

ges·ture ['dʒestʃə] Geste *f*, Gebärde *f.*

get [get] (-*tt*-; *got, got* od. *Am.* gotten) *v/t.* erhalten, bekommen, F kriegen; besorgen; holen; bringen; erwerben; verdienen; ergreifen, fassen; fangen; (veran)lassen; *mit adv. mst* bringen, machen; *have got* haben; *have got to* müssen; ~ *one's hair cut* sich die Haare schneiden lassen; ~ *by heart* auswendig lernen; *v/i.* gelangen, geraten, kommen; gehen; werden; ~ *ready* sich fertig machen; ~ *about* auf den Beinen sein; herumkommen; sich verbreiten (*Gerücht*); ~ *ahead* vorankommen; ~ *ahead of* übertreffen (*acc.*); ~ *along* vorwärtskommen; auskommen (*with* mit); ~ *at* herankommen an (*acc.*); sagen wollen; ~ *away* loskommen; entkommen; ~ *in* einsteigen (in), ~ *off*

aussteigen (aus); ~ *on* einsteigen (in); ~ *out* heraus-, hinausgehen; aussteigen (*of* aus); ~ *over s.th.* über et. hinwegkommen; ~ *to* kommen nach; ~ *together* zusammenkommen; ~ *up* aufstehen; ~**·a·way** ['getəweɪ] Flucht *f*; ~ *car* Fluchtauto *n*; ~**·up** Aufmachung *f.*

ghast·ly ['ɡɑːstlɪ] (-*ier*, -*iest*) gräßlich; schrecklich; (toten)bleich; gespenstisch.

gher·kin ['ɡɜːkɪn] Gewürzgurke *f.*

ghost [ɡəʊst] Geist *m*, Gespenst *n*; *fig.* Spur *f*; ~**·ly** ['ɡəʊstlɪ] (-*ier*, -*iest*) geisterhaft.

gi·ant ['dʒaɪənt] **1.** riesig; **2.** Riese *m.*

gib·ber ['dʒɪbə] kauderwelschen; ~**·ish** [~rɪʃ] Kauderwelsch *n.*

gib·bet ['dʒɪbɪt] Galgen *m.*

gibe [dʒaɪb] **1.** spotten (*at* über *acc.*); **2.** höhnische Bemerkung.

gib·lets ['dʒɪblɪts] *pl.* Hühner-, Gänseklein *n.*

gid|di·ness ['ɡɪdɪnɪs] 🏥 Schwindel *m*; Unbeständigkeit *f*; Leichtsinn *m*; ~**·dy** □ ['ɡɪdɪ] (-*ier*, -*iest*) schwind(e)lig; leichtfertig; unbeständig; albern.

gift [ɡɪft] Geschenk *n*; Talent *n*; △ *nicht Gift*; ~**·ed** ['ɡɪftɪd] begabt.

gi·gan·tic [dʒaɪ'ɡæntɪk] (~*ally*) gigantisch, riesenhaft, riesig, gewaltig.

gig·gle ['ɡɪɡl] **1.** kichern; **2.** Gekicher *n.*

gild [ɡɪld] (*gilded* od. *gilt*) vergolden; verschönen; ~*ed youth* Jeunesse *f* dorée.

gill [ɡɪl] *zo.* Kieme *f*; ⚘ Lamelle *f.*

gilt [ɡɪlt] **1.** *p.p. von gild*; **2.** Vergoldung *f.*

gim·mick F ['ɡɪmɪk] Trick *m.*

gin [dʒɪn] Gin *m* (*Wacholderschnaps*).

gin·ger ['dʒɪndʒə] **1.** Ingwer *m*; rötliches od. gelbliches Braun; **2.** rötlich- od. gelblichbraun; ~**·bread** Pfefferkuchen *m*; ~**·ly** [~lɪ] zimperlich; behutsam, vorsichtig.

gip·sy ['dʒɪpsɪ] Zigeuner(in).

gi·raffe *zo.* [dʒɪ'rɑːf] Giraffe *f.*

gir·der ⊕ ['ɡɜːdə] Tragbalken *m.*

gir·dle ['ɡɜːdl] Hüfthalter *m*, -gürtel *m*, Korselett *n*, Miederhose *f.*

girl [ɡɜːl] Mädchen *n*; ~**·friend** ['ɡɜːlfrend] Freundin *f*; ~ **guide** [~ɡaɪd] Pfadfinderin *f* (*in Großbritannien*); ~**·hood** [~hʊd] Mädchenzeit *f*, Mädchenjahre *pl.*, Jugend(zeit) *f*; ~**·ish** □ [~lɪʃ] mädchenhaft; Mädchen...; ~ **scout** Pfadfinderin f (*in den USA*).

gi·ro ['dʒaɪrəʊ] **1.** Postscheckdienst m (*in Großbritannien*); **2.** Postscheck...

girth [gɜːθ] (Sattel)Gurt m; (*a. Körper*)Umfang m.

gist [dʒɪst] *das* Wesentliche.

give [gɪv] (*gave*, *given*) geben; ab-, übergeben; her-, hingeben; überlassen; zum besten geben; schenken; gewähren; von sich geben; ergeben; ~ *birth to* zur Welt bringen; ~ **and** her-, weggeben, verschenken; *j-n*, *et.* verraten; ~ *back* zurückgeben; ~ *in Gesuch* einreichen, *Prüfungsarbeit* abgeben; nachgeben; aufgeben; ~ *off Geruch* verbreiten; ausstoßen, -strömen; ~ *out* aus-, verteilen; zu Ende gehen (*Kräfte*, *Vorräte*); ~ *up* (es) aufgeben; aufhören mit; *j-n* ausliefern; ~ *o.s. up* sich (freiwillig) stellen (*to the police* der Polizei); ~ **and take** ['gɪvən'teɪk] (Meinungs)Austausch m; Kompromiß m, n; **giv·en** ['gɪvn] *p.p. von give*; **2.** *be* ~ *to* verfallen sein; neigen zu; **giv·en name** *m.* Vorname m.

gla·cial □ ['gleɪsjəl] eisig, Eis...; Gletscher...; **~·ci·er** ['glæsjə] Gletscher m.

glad □ [glæd] (*-dd-*) froh, erfreut; freudig; **~·den** ['glædn] erfreuen.

glade [gleɪd] Lichtung f; *Am.* sumpfige Niederung.

glad·ly ['glædlɪ] gern(e); **~·ness** [~nɪs] Freude f.

glam·or·ous, -our·ous □ ['glæmərəs] bezaubernd; **~·o(u)r** ['glæmə] **1.** Zauber m, Glanz m, Reiz m; **2.** bezaubern.

glance [glɑːns] **1.** (schneller *od.* flüchtiger) Blick (*at* auf *acc.*); △ *nicht Glanz*; *at a* ~ mit e-m Blick; **2.** (auf)leuchten, (-)blitzen; *mst* ~ *off* abprallen; ~ *at* flüchtig ansehen; anspielen auf (*acc.*).

gland *anat.* [glænd] Drüse f.

glare [gleə] **1.** grelles Licht; wilder, starrer Blick; **2.** grell leuchten; wild blicken; (~ *at* an)starren.

glass [glɑːs] **1.** Glas n; Spiegel m; Opern-, Fernglas n; Barometer n; (*a pair of*) ~*es pl.* (e-e) Brille f; gläsern; Glas...; **3.** verglasen; ~ *case* ['glɑːskeɪs] Vitrine f; Schaukasten m; **~·ful** [~fʊl] *ein* Glas(voll); **~·house** Treibhaus m; ✕ F Bau m;

~**ware** Glas(waren *pl.*) n; ~**y** [~ɪ] (*-ier*, *-iest*) gläsern; glasig.

glaze [gleɪz] **1.** Glasur f; **2.** *v/t.* verglasen; glasieren; polieren; *v/i.* trüb(e) *od.* glasig werden (*Auge*); **gla·zi·er** ['gleɪzjə] Glaser m.

gleam [gliːm] **1.** Schimmer m, Schein m; **2.** schimmern.

glean [gliːn] *v/t.* sammeln; *v/i.* Ähren lesen.

glee [gliː] Fröhlichkeit f; ~**ful** □ ['gliːfl] ausgelassen, fröhlich.

glen [glen] Bergschlucht f.

glib □ [glɪb] (*-bb-*) gewandt; schlagfertig.

glide [glaɪd] **1.** Gleiten n; ✈ Gleitflug m; **2.** (dahin)gleiten (lassen); e-n Gleitflug machen; **glid·er** ✈ ['glaɪdə] Segelflugzeug n; Segelflieger(in); **glid·ing** ✈ [~ɪŋ] *das* Segelfliegen.

glim·mer ['glɪmə] **1.** Schimmer m; *min.* Glimmer m; **2.** schimmern.

glimpse [glɪmps] **1.** flüchtiger Blick (*at* auf *acc.*); Schimmer m; flüchtiger Eindruck; **2.** flüchtig (er)blicken.

glint [glɪnt] **1.** blitzen, glitzern; **2.** Lichtschein m.

glis·ten ['glɪsn] glitzern, glänzen.

glit·ter ['glɪtə] **1.** glitzern, funkeln, glänzen; **2.** Glitzern n, Funkeln n, Glanz m.

gloat [gləʊt]: ~ *over* sich hämisch *od.* diebisch freuen über (*acc.*); **~·ing** □ ['gləʊtɪŋ] hämisch, schadenfroh.

globe [gləʊb] (Erd)Kugel f; Globus m.

gloom [gluːm] Düsterkeit f; Dunkelheit f; gedrückte Stimmung; Schwermut f; ~**y** □ ['gluːmɪ] (*-ier*, *-iest*) dunkel; düster; schwermütig, traurig.

glo·ri·fy ['glɔːrɪfaɪ] verherrlichen; **~·ri·ous** □ [~ɪəs] herrlich; glorreich; **~·ry** [~ɪ] **1.** Ruhm m; Herrlichkeit f, Pracht f; Glorienschein m; **2.** ~ *in* sich freuen über (*acc.*).

gloss [glɒs] **1.** Glosse f, Bemerkung f; Glanz m; **2.** Glossen machen (zu); Glanz geben (*dat.*); ~ *over* beschönigen.

glos·sa·ry ['glɒsərɪ] Glossar n, Wörterverzeichnis n (*mit Erklärungen*).

gloss·y □ ['glɒsɪ] (*-ier*, *-iest*) glänzend.

glove [glʌv] Handschuh m; ~ *compartment mot.* Handschuhfach n.

glow [gləʊ] 1. Glühen n; Glut f; 2. glühen.

glow·er ['glaʊə] finster blicken.

glow-worm zo. ['gləʊwɜ:m] Glühwürmchen n.

glu·cose ['glu:kəʊs] Traubenzucker m.

glue [glu:] 1. Leim m; 2. kleben.

glum □ [glʌm] (-mm-) bedrückt, niedergeschlagen.

glut [glʌt] (-tt-) übersättigen, -schwemmen; ~ o.s. with od. on sich vollstopfen mit.

glu·ti·nous □ ['glu:tɪnəs] klebrig.

glut·ton ['glʌtn] Unersättliche(r m) f; Vielfraß m; ~ous □ [~əs] gefräßig; ~y [~ɪ] Gefräßigkeit f.

gnarled [nɑ:ld] knorrig; knotig (Hände).

gnash [næʃ] knirschen (mit).

gnat zo. [næt] (Stech)Mücke f.

gnaw [nɔ:] (zer)nagen; (zer)fressen.

gnome [nəʊm] Gnom m; Gartenzwerg m.

go [gəʊ] 1. (went, gone) gehen, fahren, fliegen; weggehen, aufbrechen, abfahren, abreisen; verkehren (Fahrzeuge); vergehen (Zeit); werden; führen (to nach); sich erstrecken, reichen (to bis zu); ausgehen, ablaufen, ausfallen; gehen, arbeiten, funktionieren; kaputtgehen; let ~ loslassen; ~ shares teilen; I must be ~ing ich muß weg od. fort; ~ to bed ins Bett gehen; ~ to school zur Schule gehen; ~ to see besuchen; ~ ahead vorangehen; vorausgehen, -fahren; ~ ahead with s.th. et. durchführen, et. machen; ~ at losgehen auf (acc.); ~ between vermitteln (zwischen); ~ by sich richten nach; ~ for holen; ~ for a walk e-n Spaziergang machen, spazierengehen; ~ in hineingehen, eintreten; ~ in for an examination e-e Prüfung machen; ~ off fortgehen, -u weitergehen, -fahren; fig. fortfahren (doing zu tun); fig. vor sich gehen, vorgehen; ~ out hinausgehen; ausgehen (with mit) (a. Licht etc.); ~ through durchgehen; durchmachen; ~ up steigen; hinaufgehen, -steigen; ~ without sich behelfen ohne, auskommen ohne; 2. F Mode f; Schwung m, Schneid m; on the ~ auf den Beinen; im Gange; it is no ~ es geht nicht; in one ~ auf Anhieb; have a ~ at es versuchen mit.

goad [gəʊd] 1. Stachelstock m; fig. Ansporn m; 2. fig. anstacheln.

go-a·head F ['gəʊəhed] zielstrebig; unternehmungslustig.

goal [gəʊl] Mal n; Ziel n; Fußball: Tor n; ~·keep·er ['gəʊlki:pə] Torwart m.

goat zo. [gəʊt] Ziege f, Geiß f.

gob·ble ['gɒbl] 1. kollern (Truthahn); schlingen; mst ~ up verschlingen; 2. Kollern n; ~·r [~ə] Truthahn m; gieriger Esser.

go-be·tween ['gəʊbɪtwi:n] Vermittler(in), Mittelsmann m.

gob·let ['gɒblɪt] Kelchglas n; Pokal m, Becher m.

gob·lin ['gɒblɪn] Kobold m.

god [gɒd] eccl. 2 Gott m; Abgott m; ~·child ['gɒdtʃaɪld] (pl. -children) Patenkind n; ~·dess ['gɒdɪs] Göttin f; ~·fa·ther Pate m (a. fig.), Taufpate m; ~·for·sak·en contp. gottverlassen; ~·head Gottheit f; ~·less [~lɪs] gottlos; ~·like göttlich; göttlich; ~·ly [~lɪ] (-ier, -iest) gottesfürchtig; fromm; ~·moth·er (Tauf)Patin f; ~·pa·rent (Tauf)Pate m, (-)Patin f; ~·send Geschenk n des Himmels.

go-get·ter F ['gəʊ'getə] Draufgänger m.

gog·gle ['gɒgl] 1. glotzen; 2. ~s pl. Schutzbrille f; ~·box Brt. F Glotze f (Fernseher).

go·ing ['gəʊɪŋ] 1. gehend; im Gange (befindlich); be ~ to inf. im Begriff sein zu inf., gleich tun wollen od. werden; 2. Gehen n; Vorwärtskommen n; Straßenzustand m; Geschwindigkeit f, Leistung f; ~s-on F [~z'ɒn] pl. Treiben n, Vorgänge pl.

gold [gəʊld] 1. Gold n; 2. golden; ~·dig·ger Am. ['gəʊlddɪgə] Goldgräber m; ~·en mst fig. [~ən] golden, goldgelb; ~·finch zo. Stieglitz m; ~·fish zo. Goldfisch m; ~·smith Goldschmied m.

golf [gɒlf] 1. Golf(spiel) n; 2. Golf spielen; ~ club ['gɒlfklʌb] Golfschläger m; Golfklub m; ~ course, ~ links pl. od. sg. Golfplatz m.

gon·do·la ['gɒndələ] Gondel f.

gone [gɒn] 1. p.p. von go 1; 2. adj. fort; F futsch; vergangen; tot; F hoffnungslos.

good [gʊd] 1. (better, best) gut; artig; gütig; gründlich; ~ at geschickt od. gut in (dat.); 2. Nutzen m, Wert m,

Vorteil *m*; *das* Gute, Wohl *n*; **~s** *pl.* *econ.* Waren *pl.*, Güter *pl.*; *that's no* ~ das nützt nichts; *for* ~ für immer; **~·by(e)** 1. [gʊd'baɪ]: *wish s.o.* ~, *say* ~ *to s.o.* j-m auf Wiedersehen sagen; 2. *int.* ['gʊd'baɪ] (auf) Wiedersehen!; ♀ **Fri·day** Karfreitag *m*; **~·hu·mo(u)red** □ gutgelaunt; gutmütig; **~·look·ing** [~ɪŋ] gutaussehend; **~·ly** ['gʊdlɪ] anmutig, hübsch; *fig.* ansehnlich; **~·na·tured** □ gutmütig; **~·ness** [~nɪs] Güte *f*; *das* Beste; *thank ~!* Gott sei Dank!; *(my) ~!*, ~ *gracious!* du meine Güte!, du lieber Himmel!; *for* ~' *sake* um Himmels willen!; ~ *knows* weiß der Himmel; **~·will** Wohlwollen *n*; *econ.* Kundschaft *f*; *econ.* Firmenwert *m*.

good·y F ['gʊdɪ] Bonbon *m*, *n*.

goose *zo.* [guːs] *(pl. geese)* Gans *f (a. fig.)*.

goose·ber·ry ♀ ['gʊzbərɪ] Stachelbeere *f*.

goose|flesh ['guːsfleʃ], **~ pim·ples** *pl.* Gänsehaut *f*.

go·pher *zo.* ['gəʊfə] Taschenratte *f*; *Am.* Ziesel *m*.

gore [gɔː] durchbohren, aufspießen (*mit den Hörnern etc.*).

gorge [gɔːdʒ] 1. Kehle *f*, Schlund *m*; enge (Fels)Schlucht *f*; 2. (ver)schlingen; (sich) vollstopfen.

gor·geous □ ['gɔːdʒəs] prächtig.

go·ril·la *zo.* [gə'rɪlə] Gorilla *m*.

gor·y □ ['gɔːrɪ] *(-ier, -iest)* blutig; *fig.* blutrünstig.

gosh *int.* F [gɒʃ]: *by* ~ Mensch!

gos·ling *zo.* ['gɒzlɪŋ] junge Gans.

go-slow *Brt. econ.* [gəʊ'sləʊ] Bummelstreik *m*.

Gos·pel *eccl.* ['gɒspəl] Evangelium *n*.

gos·sa·mer ['gɒsəmə] Altweibersommer *m*.

gos·sip ['gɒsɪp] 1. Klatsch *m*, Tratsch *m*; Klatschbase *f*; 2. klatschen, tratschen.

got [gɒt] *pret. u. p.p. von* get.

Goth·ic ['gɒθɪk] gotisch; Schauer...; ~ *novel* Schauerroman *m*.

got·ten *Am.* ['gɒtn] *p.p. von* get.

gouge [gaʊdʒ] 1. ⊕ Hohlmeißel *m*; 2. ~ *out* ausmeißeln; ~ *out s.o.'s eye* j-m ein Auge ausstechen.

gourd ♀ [gʊəd] Kürbis *m*.

gout ♂ [gaʊt] Gicht *f*.

gov·ern ['gʌvn] *v/t.* regieren, beherrschen; lenken, leiten; *v/i.* herrschen; **~·ess** [~ɪs] Erzieherin *f*; **~·ment**

[~mənt] Regierung(sform) *f*; Herrschaft *f (of über acc.*); Ministerium *n*; *attr.* Staats...; **~·men·tal** [gʌvn'mentl] Regierungs...; **gov·er·nor** ['gʌvənə] Gouverneur *m*; Direktor *m*, Präsident *m*; F Alte(r) *m (Vater, Chef)*.

gown [gaʊn] 1. (Frauen)Kleid *n*; Robe *f*, Talar *m*; 2. kleiden.

grab [græb] 1. *(-bb-)* (hastig *od.* gierig) ergreifen, packen, fassen; 2. (hastiger *od.* gieriger) Griff; ⊕ Greifer *m*.

grace [greɪs] 1. Gnade *f*; Gunst *f*; (Gnaden)Frist *f*; Grazie *f*, Anmut *f*; Anstand *m*; Zier(de) *f*; *rel.* Tischgebet *n*; *Your* ♀ Eure Hoheit *(Herzog[in])*; Eure Exzellenz *(Erzbischof)*; 2. zieren, schmücken; begünstigen, auszeichnen; **~·ful** □ ['greɪsfl] anmutig; **~·less** □ [~lɪs] ungraziös, linkisch; ungehobelt.

gra·cious □ ['greɪʃəs] gnädig.

gra·da·tion [grə'deɪʃn] Abstufung *f*.

grade [greɪd] 1. Grad *m*, Rang *m*; Stufe *f*; Qualität *f*; *bsd. Am.* = gradient; *Am. Schule:* Klasse *f*; Note *f*; *make the* ~ es schaffen, Erfolg haben; ~ *crossing bsd. Am.* schienengleicher Bahnübergang; 2. abstufen; einstufen; ⊕ planieren.

gra·di·ent 🚗 *etc.* ['greɪdjənt] Steigung *f*.

grad·u·al □ ['grædʒʊəl] stufenweise, allmählich; **~·al·ly** [~lɪ] nach u. nach; allmählich; **~·ate** 1. [~ʊeɪt] graduieren; (sich) abstufen; die Abschlußprüfung machen; promovieren; 2. [~ʊət] *univ.* Hochschulabsolvent(in), Akademiker(in); Graduierte(r *m*) *f*; *Am.* Schulabgänger(in); **~·a·tion** [grædʒʊ'eɪʃn] Gradeinteilung *f*; *univ.*, *Am. a. Schule:* (Ab-)Schlußfeier *f*; *univ.* Erteilung *f od.* Erlangung *f* e-s akademischen Grades.

graft [grɑːft] 1. ♂ Pfropfreis *n*; *Am.* Schiebung *f*; *Am.* Schmiergelder *pl.*; 2. ♂ pfropfen; ♂ verpflanzen.

grain [greɪn] (Samen)Korn *n*; Getreide *n*; Gefüge *n*; *fig.* Natur *f*; Gran *n (Gewicht)*.

gram [græm] Gramm *n*.

gram·mar ['græmə] Grammatik *f*; **~ school** *Brt. etwa* (humanistisches) Gymnasium; *Am. etwa* Grundschule *f*.

gram·mat·i·cal □ [grə'mætɪkl] grammatisch.

gramme [græm] = **gram**.

gra·na·ry ['grænərɪ] Kornspeicher *m*.

grand □ [grænd] 1. *fig.* großartig; erhaben; groß; Groß..., Haupt...; ⚸ *Old Party Am.* Republikanische Partei; 2. *(pl. grand)* F Riese *m* (*1000 Dollar od. Pfund*); **~child** ['grænt·faɪld] *(pl. -children)* Enkel(in).

gran·deur ['grændʒə] Größe *f*, Hoheit *f*; Erhabenheit *f*.

grand·fa·ther ['grændfɑ:ðə] Großvater *m*.

gran·di·ose □ ['grændɪəʊs] großartig.

grand|moth·er ['grænmʌðə] Großmutter *f*; **~·par·ents** [~peərənts] *pl.* Großeltern *pl.*; **~ pi·an·o** ♪ *(pl. -os)* (Konzert)Flügel *m*; **~·stand** *Sport:* Haupttribüne *f*.

grange [greɪndʒ] (kleiner) Gutshof.

gran·ny F ['grænɪ] Oma *f*.

grant [grɑ:nt] 1. Gewährung *f*; Unterstützung *f*; Stipendium *n*; 2. gewähren; bewilligen; verleihen; ⚖ übertragen; zugestehen; **~ed**, zugeben, aber; *take for ~ed* als selbstverständlich annehmen.

gran|u·lat·ed ['grænjʊleɪtɪd] körnig, granuliert; **~ sugar** Kristallzucker *m*; **~·ule** [~ju:l] Körnchen *n*.

grape [greɪp] Weinbeere *f*, -traube *f*; **~·fruit** ♀ ['greɪpfru:t] Grapefruit *f*, Pampelmuse *f*; **~·vine** ♀ Weinstock *m*.

graph [græf] graphische Darstellung; **~·ic** ['græfɪk] *(~ally)* graphisch; anschaulich; **~ arts** *pl.* Graphik *f*, graphische Kunst.

grap·ple ['græpl] ringen, kämpfen; **~ with s.th.** *fig.* sich mit et. herumschlagen.

grasp [grɑ:sp] 1. Griff *m*; Bereich *m*; Beherrschung *f*; Fassungskraft *f*; 2. (er)greifen, packen; begreifen.

grass [grɑ:s] Gras *n*; Rasen *m*; Weide(land *n*) *f*; *sl.* Grass *m* (*Marihuana*); **~·hop·per** *zo.* ['grɑ:shɒpə] Heuschrecke *f*; **~ wid·ow** Strohwitwe *f*; *Am.* geschiedene Frau; *Am.* (von ihrem Mann) getrennt lebende Frau; **~ wid·ow·er** Strohwitwer *m*; *Am.* geschiedener Mann; *Am.* (von s-r Frau) getrennt lebender Mann; **gras·sy** [~ɪ] *(-ier, -iest)* grasbedeckt, Gras...

grate [greɪt] 1. (Kamin)Gitter *n*; (Feuer)Rost *m*; 2. reiben, raspeln; knirschen (mit); **~ on s.o.'s nerves** an j-s Nerven zerren.

grate·ful □ ['greɪtfʊl] dankbar.

grat·er ['greɪtə] Reibe *f*.

grat·i|fi·ca·tion [grætɪfɪ'keɪʃn] Befriedigung *f*; Freude *f*; △ *nicht Gratifikation*; **~·fy** ['grætɪfaɪ] erfreuen; befriedigen.

grat·ing¹ □ ['greɪtɪŋ] kratzend, knirschend, quietschend; schrill; unangenehm.

grat·ing² [~] Gitter(werk) *n*.

grat·i·tude ['grætɪtju:d] Dankbarkeit *f*.

gra·tu·i·tous □ [grə'tju:ɪtəs] unentgeltlich; freiwillig; **~·ty** [~'tju:ətɪ] Abfindung *f*; Gratifikation *f*; Trinkgeld *n*.

grave¹ □ [greɪv] *(~r, ~st)* ernst; (ge)wichtig; gemessen.

grave² [~] Grab *n*; **~-dig·ger** ['greɪvdɪgə] Totengräber *m* (*a. zo.*).

grav·el ['grævl] 1. Kies *m*; Schotter *m*; ♣ Harngrieß *m*; 2. *(bsd. Brt. -ll-, Am. -l-)* mit Kies bestreuen.

grave·stone ['greɪvstəʊn] Grabstein *m*; **~·yard** Friedhof *m*.

grav·i·ta·tion [grævɪ'teɪʃn] *phys.* Schwerkraft *f*; *fig.* Hang *m*, Neigung *f*.

grav·i·ty ['grævətɪ] Schwere *f*, Ernst *m*; *phys.* Schwerkraft *f*.

gra·vy ['greɪvɪ] Bratensaft *m*; Bratensoße *f*.

gray *bsd. Am.* [greɪ] grau.

graze¹ [greɪz] *Vieh* weiden (lassen); (ab)weiden; (ab)grasen.

graze² [~] 1. streifen; schrammen; *Haut* (ab-, auf)schürfen, (auf-) schrammen; 2. Abschürfung *f*, Schramme *f*.

grease 1. [gri:s] Fett *n*; Schmiere *f*; 2. [gri:z] (be)schmieren.

greas·y □ ['gri:zɪ] *(-ier, -iest)* fett(ig), ölig; schmierig.

great □ [greɪt] groß, Groß...; F großartig; **~-grand·child** [greɪt'grænt·faɪld] *(pl. -children)* Urenkel(in); **~-grand·fa·ther** Urgroßvater *m*; **~-grand·moth·er** Urgroßmutter *f*; **~-grand·par·ents** *pl.* Urgroßeltern *pl.*; **~·ly** ['greɪtlɪ] sehr; **~·ness** [~nɪs] Größe *f*; Stärke *f*.

greed [gri:d] Gier *f*; **~·y** □ ['gri:dɪ] *(-ier, -iest)* gierig (*for auf acc., nach*); habgierig; gefräßig.

Greek [gri:k] 1. griechisch; 2. Griech|e *m*, -in *f*; *ling.* Griechisch *n*.

green [gri:n] 1. □ grün (*a. fig.*); frisch (*Fisch etc.*); neu; Grün...; 2. Grün *n*; Grünfläche *f*, Rasen *m*; ~s *pl.* grünes Gemüse, Blattgemüse *n*; ~**back** *Am.* F ['gri:nbæk] Dollarschein *m*; ~**belt** Grüngürtel *m* (*um e-e Stadt*); ~**gro·cer** *bsd. Brt.* Obst- u. Gemüsehändler(in); ~**gro·cer·y** *bsd. Brt.* Obst- u. Gemüsehandlung *f*; ~**horn** Greenhorn *n*, Grünschnabel *m*; ~**house** Gewächs-, Treibhaus *n*; ~**ish** [~ɪʃ] grünlich.

greet [gri:t] grüßen; ~**ing** ['gri:tɪŋ] Begrüßung *f*, Gruß *m*; ~s *pl.* Grüße *pl.*

gre·nade ✕ [grɪ'neɪd] Granate *f*.

grew [gru:] *pret. von* grow.

grey [greɪ] 1. □ grau; 2. Grau *n*; 3. grau machen *od.* werden; ~**hound** *zo.* ['greɪhaʊnd] Windhund *m*.

grid [grɪd] 1. Gitter *n*; ✟ *etc.* Versorgungsnetz *n*; 2. ✟ Gitter...; *Am.* F Football...; ~**i·ron** ['grɪdaɪən] (Brat)Rost *m*.

grief [gri:f] Gram *m*, Kummer *m*; *come to* ~ zu Schaden kommen.

griev|ance ['gri:vns] Beschwerde *f*; Mißstand *m*; ~**e** [gri:v] *v/t.* betrüben, bekümmern; *j-m* Kummer bereiten; *v/i.* bekümmert sein; ~ *for* trauern um; ~**ous** □ ['gri:vəs] kränkend, schmerzlich; schlimm.

grill [grɪl] 1. grillen; 2. Grill *m*; Bratrost *m*; Gegrillte(s) *n*; *a.* ~**room** Grillroom *m*.

grim □ [grɪm] (-*mm*-) grimmig; schrecklich; erbittert; F schlimm.

gri·mace [grɪ'meɪs] 1. Fratze *f*, Grimasse *f*; 2. Grimassen schneiden.

grime [graɪm] Schmutz *m*; Ruß *m*; **grim·y** □ ['graɪmɪ] (-*ier*, -*iest*) schmutzig; rußig.

grin [grɪn] 1. Grinsen *n*; 2. (-*nn*-) grinsen.

grind [graɪnd] 1. (*ground*) (zer)reiben; mahlen; schleifen; *Leierkasten etc.* drehen; *fig.* schinden; mit *den Zähnen* knirschen; 2. Schinderei *f*, Schufterei *f*; △ *nicht* Grind; ~**er** ['graɪndə] (*Messer- etc.*)Schleifer *m*; ⊕ Schleifmaschine *f*; ⊕ Mühle *f*; ~**stone** Schleifstein *m*.

grip [grɪp] 1. (-*pp*-) packen, fassen (*a. fig.*); 2. Griff *m* (*a. fig.*); *fig.* Gewalt *f*, Herrschaft *f*; *Am.* Reisetasche *f*.

gripes [graɪps] *pl.* Bauchschmerzen *pl.*, Kolik *f*.

grip·sack *Am.* ['grɪpsæk] Reisetasche *f*.

gris·ly ['grɪzlɪ] (-*ier*, -*iest*) gräßlich, schrecklich.

gris·tle ['grɪsl] Knorpel *m* (*im Fleisch*).

grit [grɪt] 1. Kies *m*; Sand(stein) *m*; *fig.* Mut *m*; 2. (-*tt*-): ~ *one's teeth* die Zähne zusammenbeißen.

griz·zly (bear) ['grɪzlɪ(beə)] Grizzly (-bär) *m*, Graubär *m*.

groan [grəʊn] 1. stöhnen, ächzen; 2. Stöhnen *n*, Ächzen *n*.

gro·cer ['grəʊsə] Lebensmittelhändler *m*; ~**ies** [~rɪz] *pl.* Lebensmittel *pl.*; ~**y** [~ɪ] Lebensmittelgeschäft *n*.

grog·gy F ['grɒgɪ] (-*ier*, -*iest*) schwach *od.* wackelig (auf den Beinen).

groin *anat.* [grɔɪn] Leiste(ngegend) *f*.

groom [grʊm] 1. Pferdepfleger *m*, Stallbursche *m*; = *bridegroom*; 2. pflegen; *j-n* aufbauen, lancieren.

groove [gru:v] Rinne *f*, Furche *f*; Rille *f*, Nut *f*; **groov·y** *sl.* ['gru:vɪ] (-*ier*, -*iest*) klasse, toll.

grope [grəʊp] tasten; *sl. Mädchen* befummeln.

gross [grəʊs] 1. □ dick, fett; grob, derb; *econ.* Brutto...; 2. Gros *n* (*12 Dutzend*); *in the* ~ im ganzen.

gro·tesque □ [grəʊ'tesk] grotesk.

ground[1] [graʊnd] 1. *pret. u. p.p. von* grind[1]; 2. ~ *glass* Mattglas *n*.

ground[2] [graʊnd] 1. Grund *m*, Boden *m*; Gebiet *n*; (*Spiel- etc.*)Platz *m*; (*Beweg- etc.*)Grund *m*; ✟ Erde *f*; ~s *pl.* Grundstück *n*, Park(s *pl.*) *m*, Gärten *pl.*; (*Kaffee*)Satz *m*; *on the* ~(*s*) *of* auf Grund (*gen.*); *stand od. hold od. keep one's* ~ sich behaupten; 2. niederlegen; (be)gründen; *j-m* die Anfangsgründe beibringen; ✟ erden; ~ **crew** ✈ Bodenpersonal *n*; ~ **floor** *bsd. Brt.* [graʊnd'flɔ:] Erdgeschoß *n*; ~ **forc·es** *pl.* ✕ Bodentruppen *pl.*, Landstreitkräfte *pl.*; ~**hog** *zo.* Amer. Waldmurmeltier *n*; ~**ing** [~ɪŋ] *Am.* ✟ Erdung *f*; Grundlagen *pl.*, -kenntnisse *pl.*; ~**less** □ [~lɪs] grundlos; ~**nut** *Brt.* ♥ Erdnuß *f*; ~**staff** *Brt.* ✈ Bodenpersonal *n*; ~**sta·tion** *Raumfahrt:* Bodenstation *f*; ~**work** Grundlage *f*.

group [gru:p] 1. Gruppe *f*; 2. (sich) gruppieren.

group·ie F ['gruːpɪ] Groupie n (*aufdringlicher weiblicher Fan*).

group·ing ['gruːpɪŋ] Gruppierung f.

grove [grəʊv] Wäldchen n, Gehölz n.

grov·el ['grɒvl] (*bsd. Brt. -ll-, Am. -l-*) (am Boden) kriechen.

grow [grəʊ] (*grew, grown*) v/i. wachsen; werden; ~ *into* hineinwachsen in; werden zu, sich entwickeln zu; ~ *on j-m* lieb werden od. ans Herz wachsen; ~ *out of* herauswachsen aus; entstehen aus; ~ *up* aufwachsen, heranwachsen; sich entwickeln; v/t. 🌱 anpflanzen, anbauen, züchten; **~·er** ['grəʊə] Züchter m, Erzeuger m, *in Zssgn* ...bauer m.

growl [graʊl] knurren, brummen.

grown [grəʊn] 1. p.p. von *grow*; 2. adj. erwachsen; bewachsen; **~·up** ['grəʊnʌp] 1. erwachsen; 2. Erwachsene(r m) f; **growth** [grəʊθ] Wachstum n; (An)Wachsen n; Entwicklung f; Erzeugnis n; 🌿 Gewächs n, Wucherung f.

grub [grʌb] 1. zo. Raupe f, Larve f, Made f; F Futter n (*Essen*); 2. (*-bb-*) graben; sich abmühen; **~·by** ['grʌbɪ] (*-ier, -iest*) schmutzig.

grudge [grʌdʒ] 1. Groll m; 2. mißgönnen; ungern geben od. tun *etc.*

gru·el [grʊəl] Haferschleim m.

gruff □ [grʌf] grob, schroff, barsch.

grum·ble ['grʌmbl] 1. murren; 2. Murren n; **~·r** fig. [~ə] Brummbär m.

grunt [grʌnt] 1. grunzen; brummen; stöhnen; 2. Grunzen n; Stöhnen n.

guar·an·tee [gærən'tiː] 1. Garantie f; Bürgschaft f; Sicherheit f; Zusicherung f; 2. (sich ver)bürgen für; garantieren; **~·tor** [~'tɔː] Bürge m, Bürgin f; **~·ty** [~ərəntɪ] Garantie f; Bürgschaft f; Sicherheit f.

guard [gɑːd] 1. Wacht f; ✕ Wache f; Wächter m, Wärter m; 🚂 Schaffner m; Schutz(vorrichtung f) m; 🚂 pl. Garde f; be on ~ Wache haben; be on (off) one's ~ (nicht) auf der Hut sein; 2. v/t. bewachen, (be)schützen (*from* vor *dat.*); v/i. sich hüten (*against* vor *dat.*); **~·ed** ['gɑːdɪd] vorsichtig, zurückhaltend; **~·i·an** [~jən] Hüter m, Wächter m; 🏛 Vormund m; *attr.* Schutz...; **~·i·an·ship** 🏛 [~ʃɪp] Vormundschaft f.

gue(r)·ril·la ✕ [gə'rɪlə] Guerilla m; ~ *warfare* Guerillakrieg m.

guess [ges] 1. Vermutung f; 2. vermuten; schätzen; raten; *Am.* glau-

ben, denken; **~·ing game** Ratespiel n; **~·work** ['geswɜːk] (reine) Vermutung(en pl.).

guest [gest] 1. Gast m; 2. Gast...; **~·house** ['gesthaʊs] (Hotel)Pension f, Fremdenheim n; **~·room** Gast-, Gäste-, Fremdenzimmer n.

guf·faw [gʌ'fɔː] 1. schallendes Gelächter; 2. schallend lachen.

guid·ance ['gaɪdns] Führung f; (An-) Leitung f.

guide [gaɪd] 1. (Reise-, Fremden-) Führer(in); ⊕ Führung f; a. ~*book* (Reise- *etc.*) Führer m (*Buch*); a ~ *to London* ein London-Führer; s. *girl guide*; 2. leiten; führen; lenken; **guid·ed mis·sile** ✕ Lenkflugkörper m; **guid·ed tour** Führung f; **~·line** ['gaɪdlaɪn] Richtlinie f, -schnur f (*on gen.*).

guild hist. [gɪld] Gilde f, Zunft f; **2·hall** ['gɪld'hɔːl] Rathaus n (*von London*).

guile [gaɪl] Arglist f; **~·ful** □ ['gaɪlfl] arglistig; **~·less** □ [~lɪs] arglos.

guilt [gɪlt] Schuld f; Strafbarkeit f; **~·less** □ ['gɪltlɪs] schuldlos; unkundig; **~·y** □ [~ɪ] (*-ier, -iest*) schuldig (*of gen.*).

guin·ea ['gɪnɪ] Guinee f (*21 Schilling alter Währung*); **~·pig** zo. Meerschweinchen n.

guise [gaɪz] Erscheinung f, Gestalt f; fig. Maske f.

gui·tar ♪ [gɪ'tɑː] Gitarre f.

gulch bsd. Am. [gʌlʃ] tiefe Schlucht.

gulf [gʌlf] Meerbusen m, Golf m; Abgrund m; Strudel m.

gull zo. [gʌl] Möwe f.

gul·let anat. ['gʌlɪt] Schlund m, Speiseröhre f, Gurgel f.

gulp [gʌlp] 1. (großer) Schluck m; 2. oft ~ *down* Getränk hinunterstürzen, *Speise* hinunterschlingen.

gum [gʌm] 1. Gummi m, n; Klebstoff m; ~, Am. ~*drop* Gummibonbon m, n; ~s pl. anat. Zahnfleisch n; Am. Gummischuhe pl.; 2. (*-mm-*) gummieren; kleben.

gun [gʌn] 1. Gewehr n; Flinte f; Geschütz n, Kanone f; Am. Revolver m; big ~ F fig. hohes Tier; 2. (*-nn-*): mst ~ *down* niederschießen; ~ **bat·tle** Feuergefecht n, Schießerei f; **~·boat** ['gʌnbəʊt] Kanonenboot n; **~·fight** Am. = gun battle; **~·fire** Schüsse pl.; ✕ Geschützfeuer n; **~·li·cence** Waffenschein m; **~·man**

gunner   504

(*pl. -men*) Bewaffnete(r) *m*; Revolverheld *m*; **~ner** ✕ [~ə] Kanonier *m*; **~point**: at ~ mit vorgehaltener Waffe, mit Waffengewalt; **~powder** Schießpulver *n*; **~run·ner** Waffenschmuggler *m*; **~run·ning** Waffenschmuggel *m*; **~shot** Schuß *m*; *within (out of)* ~ in (außer) Schußweite; **~smith** Büchsenmacher *m*.
gur·gle [ˈgɜːgl] 1. glucksen, gluckern, gurgeln; 2. Glucksen *n*, Gurgeln *n*.
gush [gʌʃ] 1. Schwall *m*, Strom *m* (*a. fig.*); 2. sich ergießen, schießen (*from* aus); *fig.* schwärmen.
gust [gʌst] Windstoß *m*, Bö *f*.
gut [gʌt] *anat.* Darm *m*; ♪ Darmsaite

f; **~s** *pl.* Eingeweide *pl.*; *das* Innere; *fig.* Schneid *m*, Mumm *m*.
gut·ter [ˈgʌtə] Dachrinne *f*; Gosse *f* (*a. fig.*), Rinnstein *m*.
guy F [gaɪ] Kerl *m*, Typ *m*.
guz·zle [ˈgʌzl] saufen; fressen.
gym F [dʒɪm] = *gymnasium*; *gymnastics*; **~na·si·um** [dʒɪmˈneɪzjəm] Turn-, Sporthalle *f*; △ *nicht Gymnasium*; **~nas·tics** [~ˈnæstɪks] *sg.* Turnen *n*, Gymnastik *f*.
gy·n(a)e·col·o·gist [gaɪnɪˈkɒlədʒɪst] Gynäkologe *m*, -in *f*, Frauenarzt *m*, -ärztin *f*; **~gy** [~dʒɪ] Gynäkologie *f*, Frauenheilkunde *f*.
gyp·sy *bsd. Am.* [ˈdʒɪpsɪ] = *gipsy*.
gy·rate [dʒaɪəˈreɪt] kreisen, sich (im Kreis) drehen, (herum)wirbeln.

H

hab·er·dash·er [ˈhæbədæʃə] *Brt.* Kurzwarenhändler *m*; *Am.* Herrenausstatter *m*; **~y** [~rɪ] *Brt.* Kurzwaren(geschäft *n*) *pl.*; *Am.* Herrenbekleidungsartikel *pl.*; *Am.* Herrenmodengeschäft *n*.
hab|it [ˈhæbɪt] (An)Gewohnheit *f*; *bsd.* Ordenskleidung *f*; ~ *of mind* Geistesverfassung *f*; *drink has become a* ~ *with him* er kommt vom Alkohol nicht mehr los; **~i·ta·ble** □ [~əbl] bewohnbar.
ha·bit·u·al □ [həˈbɪtjʊəl] gewohnt, gewöhnlich; Gewohnheits...
hack¹ [hæk] (zer)hacken.
hack² [~] Reitpferd *n*; Mietpferd *n*; Klepper *m*; *a.* ~ *writer* Schreiberling *m*; **~neyed** [ˈhæknɪd] abgedroschen.
had [hæd] *pret. u. p.p. von* have.
had·dock *zo.* [ˈhædək] Schellfisch *m*.
h(a)e·mor·rhage 𝒔 [ˈheməridʒ] Blutung *f*.
hag *fig.* [hæg] häßliches altes Weib, Hexe *f*.
hag·gard □ [ˈhægəd] verhärmt.
hag·gle [ˈhægl] feilschen, schachern.
hail [heɪl] 1. Hagel *m*; (Zu)Ruf *m*; 2. (nieder)hageln (lassen); rufen; (be-)grüßen; ~ *from* stammen aus; **~stone** [ˈheɪlstəʊn] Hagelkorn *n*; **~storm** Hagelschauer *m*.

hair [heə] *einzelnes* Haar; *coll.* Haar *n*, Haare *pl.*; **~breadth** [ˈheəbredθ]: *by a* ~ um Haaresbreite; **~brush** Haarbürste *f*; **~cut** Haarschnitt *m*; **~do** (*pl. -dos*) F Frisur *f*; **~dress·er** Friseur *m*, Friseuse *f*; **~dri·er**, **dry·er** [~draɪə] Trockenhaube *f*; Haartrockner *m*; *TM* Fön *m*; **~grip** *Brt.* Haarklammer *f*, -klemme *f*; **~less** [~lɪs] ohne Haare, kahl; **~pin** Haarnadel *f*; ~ *bend* Haarnadelkurve *f*; **~rais·ing** [~reɪzɪŋ] haarsträubend; **~'s breadth** = *hairbreadth*; **~slide** *Brt.* Haarspange *f*; **~split·ting** Haarspalterei *f*; **~spray** Haarspray *m, n*; **~style** Frisur *f*; **~styl·ist** Hair-Stylist *m*, Haarstilist *m*; Damenfriseur *m*; **~y** [~rɪ] (*-ier, -iest*) behaart; haarig.
hale [heɪl]: ~ *and hearty* gesund u. munter.
half [hɑːf] 1. (*pl. halves* [~vz]) Hälfte *f*; *by halves* nur halb; *go halves* halbe-halbe machen, teilen; 2. halb; ~ *an hour* e-e halbe Stunde; ~ *a pound* ein halbes Pfund; ~ *past ten* halb elf (Uhr); ~ *way up* auf halber Höhe; **~back** [ˈhɑːfbæk] *Fußball:* Läufer *m*; **~breed** [~briːd] Halbblut *n*; **~broth·er** Halbbruder *m*; **~caste** Halbblut *n*; **~heart·ed** □

hang

[ˈhɑːtɪd] lustlos, lau; **~length:** ~
portrait Brustbild *n*; **~mast:** fly at ~
auf halbmast wehen; **~pen·ny**
[ˈhepnɪ] (*pl. -pennies, -pence*) halber Penny; **~ sis·ter** Halbschwester
f; **~term** *Brt. univ.* kurze Ferien in
der Mitte e-s Trimesters; **~time**
[ˈhɑːftaɪm] *Sport:* Halbzeit *f*; **~**
way halb; auf halbem Weg, in der
Mitte; **~wit·ted** schwachsinnig.

hal·i·but *zo.* [ˈhælɪbət] Heilbutt *m*.

hall [hɔːl] Halle *f*, Saal *m*; Flur *m*,
Diele *f*; Herrenhaus *n*; *univ.* Speise-
saal *m*; **~ of residence** Studentenwohnheim *n*.

hal·lo *Brt.* [həˈləʊ] = hello.

hal·low [ˈhæləʊ] heiligen, weihen;
ℒ**e'en** [hæləʊˈiːn] Abend *m* vor Al-
lerheiligen.

hal·lu·ci·na·tion [həluːsɪˈneɪʃn] Hal-
luzination *f*.

hall·way *bsd. Am.* [ˈhɔːlweɪ] Halle *f*,
Korridor *m*.

ha·lo [ˈheɪləʊ] (*pl. -loes, -los*) *ast.*
Hof *m*; Heiligenschein *m*.

halt [hɔːlt] **1.** Halt(estelle *f*) *m*; Stillstand *m*; **2.** (an)halten.

hal·ter [ˈhɔːltə] Halfter *m*, *n*; Strick
m.

halve [hɑːv] halbieren; **~s** [hɑːvz] *pl.*
von half *1*.

ham [hæm] Schinken *m*; **~ and eggs**
Schinken mit (Spiegel)Ei.

ham·burg·er [ˈhæmbɜːgə] *Am.* Rinderhack *n*; *a.* ℒ *steak* Hamburger *m*,
Frikadelle *f* (*aus Rinderhack*).

ham·let [ˈhæmlɪt] Weiler *m*.

ham·mer [ˈhæmə] **1.** Hammer *m*; **2.**
hämmern.

ham·mock [ˈhæmək] Hängematte *f*.

ham·per¹ [ˈhæmpə] (Trag)Korb *m*
(*mit Deckel*); Geschenk-, Freßkorb
m.

ham·per² [~] (be)hindern; stören.

ham·ster *zo.* [ˈhæmstə] Hamster
m.

hand [hænd] Hand *f* (*a. fig.*);
Handschrift *f*; Handbreite *f*; (Uhr)-
Zeiger *m*; Mann *m*, Arbeiter *m*;
Karten: Blatt *n*; *at* ~ bei der Hand;
nahe bevorstehend; *at first* ~ aus
erster Hand; *a good (poor)* ~ *at*
(un)geschickt in (*dat.*); ~ *and glove*
ein Herz und eine Seele; *change* ~*s*
den Besitzer wechseln; *lend a* ~ (mit)
anfassen; *off* ~ aus dem Handgelenk
od. Stegreif; *on* ~ *econ.* vorrätig, auf

Lager; *bsd. Am.* zur Stelle, bereit; *on*
one's ~*s* auf dem Hals; *on the one* ~
einerseits; *on the other* ~ andererseits; **2.** ein-, aushändigen, (über)ge-
ben, (-)reichen; ~ *around* herumrei-
chen; ~ *down* herunterreichen; vererben; ~ *in* et. hinein-, hereinrei-
chen; *Prüfungsarbeit etc.* abgeben;
Bericht, Gesuch einreichen; ~ *on* wei-
terreichen, -geben; ~ *out* aus-, verteilen; ~ *over* übergeben; aushändigen; ~ *up* hinauf-, heraufreichen;
~bag [ˈhændbæg] Handtasche *f*;
~bill Handzettel *m*, Flugblatt *n*;
~brake ⊕ Handbremse *f*; **~cuffs**
pl. Handschellen *pl.*; **~ful** [~fʊl]
Handvoll *f*; F Plage *f*.

hand·i·cap [ˈhændɪkæp] **1.** Handikap
n; *Sport:* Vorgabe *f*; Vorgaberennen
n, -spiel *n*, -kampf *m*; *fig.* Behinderung *f*, Benachteiligung *f*, Nachteil
m; *s. mental, physical;* **2.** (-pp-)
(be)hindern, benachteiligen, belasten; *Sport:* mit Handikap belegen;
~ped 1. gehandikapt, behindert, benachteiligt; *s. mental, physical;* **2.**
the ~ *pl.* ☒ die Behinderten *pl.*

hand·ker·chief [ˈhæŋkətʃɪf] (*pl.*
-chiefs) Taschentuch *n*.

han·dle [ˈhændl] **1.** Griff *m*; Stiel *m*;
Henkel *m*; (Pumpen- etc.)Schwengel
m; *fig.* Handhabe *f*; *fly off the* ~ F
wütend werden; **2.** anfassen; handhaben; behandeln; △ *nicht han-*
deln; **~bar(s** *pl.*) Lenkstange *f*.

hand|lug·gage [ˈhændlʌgɪdʒ] Hand-
gepäck *n*; **~made** handgearbeitet;
~rail Geländer *n*; **~shake** Hände-
druck *m*; **~some** ☐ [ˈhænsəm] (~*r*,
~*st*) ansehnlich; hübsch; anständig;
~work Handarbeit *f*; **~writ·ing**
Handschrift *f*; **~writ·ten** handge-
schrieben; **~y** ☐ [~ɪ] (*-ier, -iest*)
geschickt; handlich; nützlich; *zur*
Hand; *come in* ~ sich als nützlich
erweisen; *sehr gelegen kommen.*

hang¹ [hæŋ] **1.** (*hung*) *v/t.* hängen;
auf-, einhängen; verhängen; hängenlassen; *Tapete* ankleben; *v/i.* hängen; schweben; sich neigen; ~ *about,*
~ *around* herumlungern; ~ *back* zögern; ~ *on* sich klammern (*to* an *acc.*)
(*a. fig.*); ~ *up teleph.* einhängen,
auflegen; *she hung up on me* sie
legte einfach auf; **2.** Fall *m*, Sitz *m*
(*e-s Kleides etc.*); *get the* ~ *of s.th.* et.
kapieren, den Dreh rauskriegen (bei
et.).

hang² [~] (*hanged*) (auf)hängen; ~ o.s. sich erhängen.

han·gar ['hæŋə] Hangar *m*, Flugzeughalle *f*.

hang·dog ['hæŋdɒg] Armesünder...

hang·er ['hæŋə] Kleiderbügel *m*; ~ **on** *fig*. [~ər'ɒn] (*pl. hangers-on*) Klette *f*.

hang|-glid·er ['hæŋglaɪdə] (Flug-) Drachen *m*; Drachenflieger(in); ~ **glid·ing** [~ɪŋ] Drachenfliegen *n*.

hang·ing ['hæŋɪŋ] **1.** hängend; Hänge...; **2.** (Er)Hängen *n*; ~s Tapete *f*, Wandbehang *m*, Vorhang *m*.

hang·man ['hæŋmən] (*pl. -men*) Henker *m*.

hang·nail ♣ ['hæŋneɪl] Niednagel *m*.

hang·o·ver ['hæŋəʊvə] Katzenjammer *m*, Kater *m*.

han·ker ['hæŋkə] sich sehnen (*after, for* nach).

hap·haz·ard ['hæp'hæzəd] **1.** Zufall *m*; at ~ aufs Geratewohl; **2.** □ willkürlich, plan-, wahllos.

hap·pen ['hæpən] sich ereignen, geschehen; *he* ~*ed to be at home* er war zufällig zu Hause; ~ *on, ~ upon* zufällig treffen auf (*acc.*); ~ *in Am.* F hereinschneien; ~**ing** ['hæpnɪŋ] Ereignis *n*, Vorkommnis *n*; Happening *n*.

hap·pi·ly ['hæpɪlɪ] glücklich(erweise); ~**ness** [~nɪs] Glück(seligkeit *f*) *n*.

hap·py □ ['hæpɪ] (*-ier, -iest*) glücklich; beglückt; erfreut; erfreulich; geschickt; treffend; F beschwipst; ~**go-luck·y** unbekümmert.

ha·rangue [hə'ræŋ] **1.** Strafpredigt *f*; **2.** *v/t. j-m* e-e Strafpredigt halten.

har·ass ['hærəs] belästigen, quälen.

har·bo·u·r ['hɑːbə] **1.** Hafen *m*; Zufluchtsort *m*; **2.** beherbergen; *Gedanken, Rache etc.* hegen.

hard [hɑːd] **1.** *adj.* □ hart; schwer; mühselig; streng; ausdauernd; fleißig; heftig; hart (*Droge*), *Getränk a.* stark; ~ *of hearing* schwerhörig; **2.** *adv.* stark; tüchtig; mit Mühe; *by* nahe bei; ~ *up* in Not; ~**boiled** ['hɑː'dbɔɪld] hart(gekocht); *fig.* hart, unsentimental, nüchtern; ~ **cash** Bargeld *n*; klingende Münze; ~ **core** harter Kern (*e-r Bande etc.*); ~**core** zum harten Kern gehörend; hart (*Pornographie*); ~**cov·er** *print.* **1.** gebunden; **2.** Hard cover *n*, gebundene Ausgabe; ~**en** [~n] härten; hart ma-

chen *od.* werden; (sich) abhärten; *fig.* (sich) verhärten (*to gegen*); *econ.* sich festigen (*Preise*); ~ **hat** Schutzhelm *m* (*für Bauarbeiter etc.*); ~**head·ed** nüchtern, praktisch; *bsd. Am.* starr-, dickköpfig; ~ **la·bo·u·r** ⚖ Zwangsarbeit *f*; ~ **line** *bsd. pol.* harter Kurs; ~**line** *bsd. pol.* hart, kompromißlos; ~**heart·ed** □ hart (-herzig); ~**ly** [~lɪ] kaum; streng; mit Mühe; ~**ness** [~nɪs] Härte *f*; Schwierigkeit *f*; Not *f*; ~**ship** [~ʃɪp] Bedrängnis *f*, Not *f*; Härte *f*; ~ **shoul·der** *mot.* Standspur *f*; ~**ware** Eisenwaren *pl.*; Haushaltswaren *pl.*; *Computer:* Hardware *f* (*technisch-physikalische Teile*); *Sprachlabor:* Hardware *f*, technische Ausrüstung; **har·dy** □ [~ɪ] (*-ier, -iest*) kühn; widerstandsfähig, hart; abgehärtet; winterfest (*Pflanze*).

hare *zo.* [heə] Hase *m*; ~**bell** ♣ ['heəbel] Glockenblume *f*; ~**brained** verrückt (*Person, Plan*); ~**lip** *anat.* [~'lɪp] Hasenscharte *f*.

hark [hɑːk]: ~ *back* F zurückgreifen, -kommen, *a. zeitlich:* zurückgehen (*to* auf *acc.*).

harm [hɑːm] **1.** Schaden *m*; Unrecht *n*, Böse(s) *n*; **2.** beschädigen, verletzen; schaden, Leid zufügen (*dat.*); ~**ful** □ ['hɑːmfl] schädlich; ~**less** □ [~lɪs] harmlos; unschädlich.

har·mo·ni·ous □ [hɑː'məʊnjəs] harmonisch; ~**nize** ['hɑːmənaɪz] *v/t.* in Einklang bringen; *v/i.* harmonieren; ~**ny** [~ɪ] Harmonie *f*.

har·ness ['hɑːnɪs] **1.** Harnisch *m*; (Pferde- *etc.*)Geschirr *n*; *die in* ~ *fig.* in den Sielen sterben; **2.** anschirren; *Naturkräfte etc.* nutzbar machen.

harp [hɑːp] **1.** ♪ Harfe *f*; **2.** ♪ Harfe spielen; ~ *on fig.* herumreiten auf (*dat.*).

har·poon [hɑː'puːn] **1.** Harpune *f*; **2.** harpunieren.

har·row ✒ ['hærəʊ] **1.** Egge *f*; **2.** eggen.

har·row·ing □ ['hærəʊɪŋ] quälend; qualvoll, erschütternd.

harsh □ [hɑːʃ] rauh; herb; grell; streng; schroff; barsch.

hart *zo.* [hɑːt] Hirsch *m*.

har·vest ['hɑːvɪst] **1.** Ernte(zeit) *f*; (Ernte)Ertrag *m*; **2.** ernten; einbringen; ~**er** [~ə] *bsd.* Mähdrescher *m*.

has [hæz] *3. sg. pres. von* have.

hash¹ [hæʃ] **1.** Haschee *n*; *fig.* Durcheinander *n*; **make a ~ of** verpfuschen; 2. *Fleisch* zerhacken, -kleinern.

hash² F [~] Hasch *n* (*Haschisch*).

hash·ish ['hæʃiːʃ] Haschisch *n*.

hasp [hɑːsp] Schließband *n*, (Verschluß)Spange *f*.

haste [heɪst] Eile *f*; Hast *f*; **make ~** sich beeilen; **has·ten** ['heɪsn] *j-n* antreiben; (sich be)eilen; *et.* beschleunigen; **hast·y** □ ['heɪstɪ] (*-ier*, *-iest*) (vor)eilig; hastig; hitzig, heftig.

hat [hæt] Hut *m*.

hatch¹ [hætʃ] *a.* **~ out** ausbrüten; ausschlüpfen.

hatch² [~] ⊕, ✠ Luke *f*; Durchreiche *f* (*für Speisen*); **~·back** *mot.* ['hætʃbæk] (Wagen *m* mit) Hecktür *f*.

hatch·et ['hætʃɪt] (Kriegs)Beil *n*.

hatch·way ⊕ ['hætʃweɪ] Luke *f*.

hate [heɪt] 1. Haß *m*; 2. hassen; **~·ful** □ ['heɪtfl] verhaßt; abscheulich; **ha·tred** [~rɪd] Haß *m*.

haugh·ti·ness ['hɔːtɪnɪs] Stolz *m*; Hochmut *m*; **~·ty** □ [~ɪ] stolz; hochmütig.

haul [hɔːl] 1. Ziehen *n*; (Fisch)Zug *m*; Transport(weg) *m*; 2. ziehen; schleppen; transportieren; ✗ fördern; ⊕ abdrehen.

haunch [hɔːntʃ] Hüfte *f*; *zo.* Keule *f*; *Am. a.* **~es** *pl.* Gesäß *n*; *zo.* Hinterbacken *pl.*

haunt [hɔːnt] 1. Aufenthaltsort *m*; Schlupfwinkel *m*; 2. oft besuchen; heimsuchen; verfolgen; spuken in (*dat.*); **~·ing** □ ['hɔːntɪŋ] quälend; unvergeßlich, eindringlich.

have [hæv] (*had*) *v/t.* haben; bekommen; *Mahlzeit* einnehmen; **~ to do** tun müssen; *I had my hair cut* ich ließ mir die Haare schneiden; *he will ~ it that* ... er behauptet, daß ...; *I had better go* es wäre besser, wenn ich ginge; *I had rather go* ich möchte lieber gehen; **~ about** one bei *od.* an sich haben; **~ on** anhaben; **~ it out with** sich auseinandersetzen mit; *v/aux.* haben; *bei v/i. oft* sein; **~ come** gekommen sein.

ha·ven ['heɪvn] Hafen *m* (*mst fig.*).

hav·oc ['hævək] Verwüstung *f*; **play ~ with** verwüsten, zerstören; verheerend wirken auf (*acc.*), übel mitspielen (*dat.*).

haw ⚘ [hɔː] Mehlbeere *f*.

Ha·wai·i·an [həˈwaɪən] 1. hawai-

isch; 2. Hawaiianer(in); *ling.* Hawaiisch *n*.

hawk¹ *zo.* [hɔːk] Habicht *m*, Falke *m*.

hawk² [~] hausieren (gehen) mit; auf der Straße verkaufen.

haw·thorn ⚘ ['hɔːθɔːn] Weißdorn *m*.

hay [heɪ] 1. Heu *n*; 2. Heu machen; **~·cock** ['heɪkɒk] Heuhaufen *m*; **~·fe·ver** Heuschnupfen *m*; **~·loft** Heuboden *m*; **~·rick**, **~·stack** Heumiete *f*.

haz·ard ['hæzəd] 1. Zufall *m*; Gefahr *f*, Wagnis *n*; Hasard(spiel) *n*; 2. wagen; **~·ous** □ [~əs] gewagt.

haze [heɪz] Dunst *m*, feiner Nebel.

ha·zel ['heɪzl] 1. ⚘ Haselnuß *f*, Hasel(nuß)strauch *m*; 2. (hasel)nußbraun; **~·nut** ⚘ Haselnuß *f*.

haz·y □ ['heɪzɪ] (*-ier*, *-iest*) dunstig, diesig; *fig.* unklar.

H-bomb ✗ ['eɪtʃbɒm] H-Bombe *f*, Wasserstoffbombe *f*.

he [hiː] 1. er; 2. Er *m*; *zo.* Männchen *n*; 3. *adj. in Zssgn, bsd. zo.*: männlich; ...männchen *n*; **~·goat** Ziegenbock *m*.

head [hed] 1. Kopf *m* (*a. fig.*); Haupt *n* (*a. fig.*); *nach Zahlwort* (*pl.* ~): Kopf *m*, Person *f*, Stück *n* (*Vieh etc.*); Leiter(in); Chef *m*; Kopfende *n* (*e-s Bettes etc.*); Kopfseite *f* (*e-r Münze*); Gipfel *m*; Quelle *f*; Vorderteil *n*; ⊕ Bug *m*; Hauptpunkt *m*, Abschnitt *m*; Überschrift *f*; **come to a ~** eitern (*Geschwür*); *fig.* sich zuspitzen, zur Entscheidung kommen; **get it into one's ~ that** ... es sich in den Kopf setzen, daß; **lose one's ~** den Kopf *od.* die Nerven verlieren; **~ over heels** Hals über Kopf; 2. Ober..., Haupt..., Chef..., oberste(r, -s), erste(r, -s); 3. *v/t.* (an)führen; an der Spitze von *et.* stehen; vorausgehen (*dat.*); mit *e-r* Überschrift versehen; **~ off** ablenken; *v/i.* gehen, fahren; sich bewegen (*for auf acc.* ... *zu*); lossteuern, -gehen (*for auf acc.*); ⊕ zusteuern (*for auf acc.*); entspringen (*Fluß*); **~·ache** ['hedeɪk] Kopfweh *n*; **~·band** Stirnband *n*; **~·dress** Kopfschmuck *m*; **~·gear** Kopfbedeckung *f*; Zaumzeug *n*; **~·ing** [~ɪŋ] Brief-, Titelkopf *m*, Rubrik *f*; Überschrift *f*, Titel *m*; Kopfballspiel *n*; **~·land** [~lənd] Vorgebirge *n*, Kap *n*; **~·light** *mot.* Scheinwerfer(licht *n*) *m*; **~·line** Überschrift *f*; Schlagzeile *f*; **~s** *pl. Rundfunk, TV:* das Wichtigste

in Schlagzeilen; **~·long 1.** *adj.* unge-
stüm; **2.** *adv.* kopfüber; **~·mas·ter**
Schule: Direktor *m*, Rektor *m*;
~·mis·tress *Schule:* Direktorin *f*,
Rektorin *f*; **~·on** frontal; ~ *collision*
Frontalzusammenstoß *m*; **~·phones**
pl. Kopfhörer *pl.*; **~·quar·ters** *pl.* ✗
Hauptquartier *n*; Zentrale *f*;
~·re·straint Kopfstütze *f*; **~·set** *bsd.*
Am. Kopfhörer *pl.*; **~ start** *Sport:*
Vorgabe *f*, **~·sprung** (a. *m*);
~·strong halsstarrig; **~·wa·ters** *pl.*
Quellgebiet *n*; **~·way** *fig.* Fort-
schritt(e *pl.*) *m*; *make* ~ (gut) vorankommen; **~·word** Stichwort *n* (*in*
e-m Wörterbuch); **~·y** □ [⌐ʌɪ] (*-ier*,
-iest) ungestüm; voreilig; zu Kopfe
steigend.

heal [hiːl] heilen; ~ *over*, ~ *up* (zu-)
heilen.

health [helθ] Gesundheit *f*; ~ *club*
Fitneßclub *m*; ~ *food* Reformkost *f*;
~ *food shop* (*bsd. Am. store*) Re-
formhaus *n*; ~ *insurance* Kranken-
versicherung *f*; ~ *resort* Kurort *m*; ~
service Gesundheitsdienst *m*; **~·ful**
□ [ˈhelθfl] gesund; heilsam; **~·y** □
[⌐ʌɪ] (*-ier*, *-iest*) gesund.

heap [hiːp] **1.** Haufe(n) *m*; **2.** *a.* ~ *up*
aufhäufen, *fig. a.* anhäufen.

hear [hɪə] (*heard*) hören; erfahren;
anhören, *j-m* zuhören; erhören;
Zeugen vernehmen; *Lektion* abhören; **~·d** [hɜːd] *pret. u. p.p. von hear*;
~·er [ˈhɪərə] (Zu)Hörer(in); **~·ing**
[⌐rɪŋ] Gehör *n*; ⚖ Verhandlung *f*; ⚖
Vernehmung *f*; *bsd. pol.* Hearing *n*,
Anhörung *f*; *within* (*out of*) ~ in
(außer) Hörweite; **~·say** Gerede *n*;
by ~ vom Hörensagen *n*.

hearse [hɜːs] Leichenwagen *m*.

heart [hɑːt] *anat.* Herz *n* (*a. fig.*);
Innere(s) *n*; Kern *m*; *fig.* Liebling *m*,
Schatz *m*; *by* ~ auswendig; *out of* ~
mutlos; *cross my* ~ Hand aufs Herz,
auf Ehre u. Gewissen; *lay to* ~ sich
zu Herzen nehmen; *lose* ~ den Mut
verlieren; *take* ~ sich ein Herz fassen; **~·ache** [ˈhɑːteɪk] Kummer *m*; ~
at·tack ✿ Herzanfall *m*; ~ **Herzin-**
farkt *m*; **~·beat** Herzschlag *m*; **~·**
break Leid *n*, großer Kummer; **~·**
break·ing □ [⌐ɪŋ] herzzerreißend;
~·bro·ken gebrochen, verzweifelt;
~·burn Sodbrennen *n*; **~·en** [⌐n]
ermutigen; ~ **fail·ure** ✿ Herzinsuf-
fizienz *f*; ✿ Herzversagen *n*; **~·felt**
innig, tiefempfunden.

hearth [hɑːθ] Herd *m* (*a. fig.*).
heart|less □ [ˈhɑːtlɪs] herzlos;
~·rend·ing □ [ˈhɑːtrendɪŋ] herzzerreißend; ~ **trans·plant** ✿ Herzver-
pflanzung *f*, -transplantation *f*; **~·y**
□ [⌐ʌɪ] (*-ier*, *-iest*) herzlich; aufrichtig; gesund; herzhaft.

heat [hiːt] **1.** Hitze *f*; Wärme *f*; Eifer
m; *Sport:* Vorlauf *m*; *zo.* Läufigkeit
f; **2.** heizen; (sich) erhitzen (*a. fig.*);
~·ed □ [ˈhiːtɪd] erhitzt; *fig.* erregt;
~·er ⊕ [⌐ə] Heizgerät *n*, Ofen *m*.

heath [hiːθ] Heide *f*; ♥ Heidekraut *n*.

hea·then [ˈhiːðn] **1.** Heide *m*, -in *f*; **2.**
heidnisch.

heath·er ♥ [ˈheðə] Heidekraut *n*.

heat·ing [ˈhiːtɪŋ] Heizung *f*; *attr.*
Heiz...; **~·proof**, **~·re·sis·tant**, **~·**
re·sist·ing hitzebeständig; **~·shield**
Raumfahrt: Hitzeschild *m*; **~·stroke**
✿ Hitzschlag *m*; ~ **wave** Hitzewelle
f.

heave [hiːv] **1.** Heben *n*; **2.** (*heaved*,
bsd. ♦ *hove*) *v/t.* heben; *Seufzer*
ausstoßen; *Anker* lichten; *v/i.* sich
heben u. senken, wogen.

heav·en [ˈhevn] Himmel *m*; **~·ly** [⌐lɪ]
himmlisch.

heav·i·ness [ˈhevɪnɪs] Schwere *f*,
Druck *m*; Schwerfälligkeit *f*;
Schwermut *f*.

heav·y □ [ˈhevɪ] (*-ier*, *-iest*) schwer;
schwermütig; schwerfällig; trüb;
drückend; heftig (*Regen etc.*); un-
wegsam (*Straße*); Schwer...; ~ **cur-**
rent ⚡ Starkstrom *m*; **~·du·ty** ⊕
Hochleistungs...; strapazierfähig;
~·hand·ed □ ungeschickt; **~·heart-**
ed niedergeschlagen; **~·weight** *Bo-*
xen: Schwergewicht(ler) *n*) *m*.

He·brew [ˈhiːbruː] **1.** hebräisch; **2.**
Hebräer(in), Jude *m*, Jüdin *f*; *ling.*
Hebräisch *n*.

heck·le [ˈhekl] *j-m* zusetzen; *e-n Red-*
ner durch Zwischenrufe *od.* -fragen
aus der Fassung bringen *od.* in die
Enge treiben.

hec·tic [ˈhektɪk] (*~ally*) hektisch.

hedge [hedʒ] **1.** Hecke *f*; **2.** *v/t.* mit e-r
Hecke einfassen *od.* umgeben; *v/i.*
ausweichen, sich nicht festlegen
(wollen); **~·hog** *zo.* [ˈhedʒhɒg] Igel
m; *Am.* Stachelschwein *n*; **~·row**
Hecke *f*.

heed [hiːd] **1.** Beachtung *f*, Aufmerksamkeit *f*; *take* ~ *of*, *give od.* *pay* ~ *to*
achtgeben auf (*acc.*), beachten; **2.**
beachten, achten auf (*acc.*); **~·less** □

['hi:dlɪs] unachtsam; unbekümmert (of um).

heel [hi:l] 1. Ferse f; Absatz m; Am. sl. Lump m; head over ~s Hals über Kopf; down at ~ mit schiefen Absätzen; fig. abgerissen; schlampig; 2. Absätze machen auf.

hef·ty ['heftɪ] (-ier, -iest) kräftig, stämmig; mächtig (Schlag etc.), gewaltig.

heif·er zo. ['hefə] Färse f, junge Kuh.

height [haɪt] Höhe f; Höhepunkt m; ~en ['haɪtn] erhöhen; vergrößern.

hei·nous □ ['heɪnəs] abscheulich.

heir [eə] Erbe m; ~ apparent rechtmäßiger Erbe; ~ess ['eərɪs] Erbin f; ~loom ['eəlu:m] Erbstück n.

held [held] pret. u. p.p. von hold 2.

hel·i·cop·ter ['helɪkɒptə] Hubschrauber m, Helikopter m; ~port ⚒ Hubschrauberlandeplatz m.

hell [hel] 1. Hölle f; attr. Höllen...; what the ~...? F was zum Teufel ...?; raise ~ F e-n Mordskrach schlagen?; 2. int. F verdammt!, verflucht!; ~bent ['helbent] ganz versessen (for, on auf acc.); ~ish □ [~ɪʃ] höllisch.

hel·lo int. [hə'ləʊ] hallo!

helm ⚓ [helm] Ruder n, Steuer n; △ nicht Helm.

hel·met ['helmɪt] Helm m.

helms·man ⚓ ['helmzmən] (pl. -men) Steuermann m.

help [help] 1. Hilfe f; (Hilfs)Mittel n; (Dienst)Mädchen n; 2. helfen; ~ o.s. sich bedienen, zulangen; I cannot ~ it ich kann es nicht ändern; I could not ~ laughing ich mußte einfach lachen; ~er ['helpə] Helfer(in); ~ful □ [~fl] hilfreich; nützlich; ~ing [~ɪŋ] Portion f (Essen); ~less □ [~lɪs] hilflos; ~less·ness [~nɪs] Hilflosigkeit f.

hel·ter-skel·ter ['heltə'skeltə] 1. adv. holterdiepolter, Hals über Kopf; 2. adj. hastig, überstürzt; 3. Brt. Rutschbahn f.

helve [helv] Stiel m, Griff m.

Hel·ve·tian [hel'vi:ʃjən] Helvetier(in); attr. Schweizer...

hem [hem] 1. Saum m; 2. (-mm-) säumen; ~ in einschließen.

hem·i·sphere geogr. ['hemɪsfɪə] Halbkugel f, Hemisphäre f.

hem·line ['hemlaɪn] (Kleider)Saum m.

hem·lock ⚘ ['hemlɒk] Schierling m.

hemp ⚘ [hemp] Hanf m.

hem·stitch ['hemstɪtʃ] Hohlsaum m.

hen [hen] zo. Henne f, Huhn n; Weibchen n (von Vögeln).

hence [hens] hieraus; daher; a week ~ in od. nach e-r Woche; ~forth ['hens'fɔ:θ], ~for·ward [~'fɔ:wəd] von nun an.

hen-house ['henhaʊs] Hühnerstall m; ~pecked unter dem Pantoffel (stehend).

her [hɜː, hə] sie; ihr; ihr(e); sich.

her·ald ['herəld] 1. hist. Herold m; 2. ankündigen; ~ in einführen; ~ry [~rɪ] Wappenkunde f, Heraldik f.

herb ⚘ [hɜːb] Kraut n; **her·ba·ceous** ⚘ [hɜː'beɪʃəs] krautartig; ~ border (Stauden)Rabatte f; **herb·age** ['hɜːbɪdʒ] Gras n; Weide f; **her·biv·o·rous** □ zo. [hɜː'bɪvərəs] pflanzenfressend.

herd [hɜːd] 1. Herde f (a. fig.), wildlebender Tiere a. Rudel n; 2. v/t. Vieh hüten; v/i. a. ~ together in e-r Herde leben; sich zusammendrängen; ~s·man ['hɜːdzmən] (pl. -men) Hirt m.

here [hɪə] hier; hierher; ~ you are hier, (bitte); ~'s to you! auf dein Wohl!

here·a·bout(s) ['hɪərəbaʊt(s)] hier herum, in dieser Gegend; ~af·ter [hɪər'ɑ:ftə] 1. künftig; 2. das Jenseits; ~by ['hɪə'baɪ] hierdurch.

he·red·i·ta·ry [hɪ'redɪtərɪ] erblich; Erb...; ~ty [~ɪ] Erblichkeit f; ererbte Anlagen pl., Erbmasse f.

here·in ['hɪər'ɪn] hierin; ~of [~'ɒv] hiervon.

her·e·sy ['herəsɪ] Häresie f, Ketzerei f; ~tic [~tɪk] Häretiker(in), Ketzer(in).

here·up·on ['hɪərə'pɒn] hierauf; ~with hiermit.

her·i·tage ['herɪtɪdʒ] Erbschaft f.

her·mit ['hɜːmɪt] Einsiedler m.

he·ro ['hɪərəʊ] (pl. -roes) Held m; ~ic [hɪ'rəʊɪk] (~ally) heroisch; heldenhaft; Helden...

her·o·in ['herəʊɪn] Heroin n.

her·o·ine ['herəʊɪn] Heldin f; ~is·m [~ɪzəm] Heldenmut m, -tum n.

her·on zo. ['herən] Reiher m.

her·ring zo. ['herɪŋ] Hering m.

hers [hɜːz] der, die, das ihr(ig)e; ihr.

her·self [hɜː'self] sie selbst; ihr selbst; sich; by ~ von selbst, allein, ohne Hilfe.

hes·i|tant □ ['hezɪtənt] zögernd, zaudernd, unschlüssig; **~tate** [~eɪt] zögern, zaudern, unschlüssig sein, Bedenken haben; **~ta·tion** [hezɪ-'teɪʃn] Zögern n, Zaudern n, Unschlüssigkeit f; *without ~* ohne zu zögern, bedenkenlos.

hew [hjuː] (*hewed, hewed od. hewn*) hauen, hacken; **~ down** fällen, umhauen; **~n** [hjuːn] *p.p. von hew.*

hey *int.* [heɪ] ei!, hei!; he!, heda!

hey·day ['heɪdeɪ] Höhepunkt m, Blüte f.

hi *int.* [haɪ] hallo!; he!, heda!

hi·ber·nate *zo.* ['haɪbəneɪt] Winterschlaf halten.

hic|cup, ~·cough ['hɪkʌp] 1. Schluckauf m; 2. den Schluckauf haben.

hid *pret. von hide²;* **~·den** ['hɪdn] *p.p. von hide².*

hide¹ [haɪd] Haut f, Fell n.

hide² [~] (*hid, hidden*) (sich) verbergen, -stecken; **~-and-seek** ['haɪdn-'siːk] Versteckspiel n; **~·a·way** f [~əweɪ] Versteck n; **~·bound** engstirnig.

hid·e·ous □ ['hɪdɪəs] scheußlich.

hide·out ['haɪdaʊt] Versteck n.

hid·ing¹ f ['haɪdɪŋ] Tracht f Prügel.

hid·ing² [~] Verstecken n, -bergen n, **~·place** Versteck n.

hi-fi ['haɪ'faɪ] 1. (*pl. hi-fis*) Hi-Fi n; Hi-Fi-Anlage f; 2. Hi-Fi-...

high [haɪ] 1. *adj.* □ hoch; vornehm; gut, edel (*Charakter*); stolz; hochtrabend; angegangen (*Fleisch*); extrem; stark; üppig, flott (*Leben*); F blau (*betrunken*); F high (*im Drogenrausch; in euphorischer Stimmung*); Haupt..., Hoch..., Ober...; *with a ~ hand* arrogant, anmaßend; *in ~ spirits* guter Laune; *~ society* High-Society f, gehobene Gesellschaftsschicht; ♀ *Tech* = ♀ *Technology* Hochtechnologie f; *~ time* höchste Zeit; *~ words* heftige Worte; 2. *meteor.* Hoch n; 3. *adv.* hoch; stark, heftig; **~·ball** *Am.* ['haɪbɔːl] Highball m (*Whisky-Cocktail*); **~·brow** f 1. Intellektuelle(r m f) 2. betont intellektuell; **~·class** erstklassig; **~fi·del·i·ty** High-Fidelity f; **~·fi·del·i·ty** High-Fidelity-...; **~·grade** hochwertig; **~·hand·ed** □ anmaßend; **~ jump** *Sport:* Hochsprung m; **~ jump·er** *Sport:* Hochspringer(in); **~·land** ['haɪlənd] *mst ~s pl.* Hochland n; **~·lights** *pl. fig.* Höhe-

punkte *pl.;* **~·ly** [~lɪ] hoch; sehr; *speak ~ of s.o.* j-n loben; **~·mind·ed** hochgesinnt; hoch (*Ideale*); **~·ness** [~nɪs] Höhe f; *fig.* Hoheit f; **~·pitched** schrill (*Ton*); steil (*Dach*); **~·pow·ered** ⊕ Hochleistungs..., Groß..., stark; dynamisch; **~·pres·sure** *meteor.,* ⊕ Hochdruck...; **~·rise** 1. Hoch...; Hochhaus...; 2. Hochhaus n; **~·road** Hauptstraße f; *~ school bsd. Am.* High-School f; *~ street* Hauptstraße f; **~·strung** reizbar, nervös; **~ tea** *Brt.* (*frühes*) Abendessen; **~ wa·ter** Hochwasser n; **~·way** *bsd. Am. od.* ⚖ Highway m, Haupt(verkehrs)straße f, Luftpirat m; ♀ *Code Brt.* Straßenverkehrsordnung f; **~·way·man** (*pl. -men*) Straßenräuber m.

hi·jack ['haɪdʒæk] 1. *Flugzeug* entführen; j-n, *Geldtransport etc.* überfallen; 2. (*Flugzeug*)Entführung f; Überfall m; **~·er** [~ə] (*Flugzeug*)Entführer m, Luftpirat m; Räuber m.

hike f [haɪk] 1. wandern; 2. Wanderung f; *Am.* Erhöhung f (*Preis etc.*); **hik·er** ['haɪkə] Wanderer m; **hik·ing** [~ɪŋ] Wandern n.

hi·lar·i·ous □ [hɪ'leərɪəs] ausgelassen; **~·ty** [hɪ'lærətɪ] Ausgelassenheit f.

hill [hɪl] Hügel m, Berg m; **~·bil·ly** *Am.* f ['hɪlbɪlɪ] Hinterwäldler m; *~ music* Hillbilly-Musik f; **~·ock** ['hɪlək] kleiner Hügel; **~·side** ['hɪl'saɪd] Hang m; **~·top** Gipfel m; **~·y** ['hɪlɪ] (*-ier, -iest*) hügelig.

hilt [hɪlt] Griff m (*bsd. am Degen*).

him [hɪm] ihn; ihm; sich; **~·self** [hɪm'self] sich; sich (selbst); (er, ihm, ihn) selbst; *by ~* von selbst, allein, ohne Hilfe.

hind¹ *zo.* [haɪnd] Hirschkuh f.

hind² [~] Hinter...

hind·er¹ ['haɪndə] hintere(r, -s); Hinter...

hin·der² ['hɪndə] hindern (*from an dat.*); hemmen.

hind·most ['haɪndməʊst] hinterste(r, -s), letzte(r, -s).

hin·drance ['hɪndrəns] Hindernis n.

hinge [hɪndʒ] 1. Türangel f; Scharnier n; *fig.* Angelpunkt m; 2. *~ on, ~ upon fig.* abhängen von.

hint [hɪnt] 1. Wink m; Anspielung f; *take a ~* e-n Wink verstehen; 2. andeuten; anspielen (*at auf acc.*).

hin·ter·land ['hɪntəlænd] Hinterland *n*.

hip¹ *anat*. [hɪp] Hüfte *f*.

hip² ♀ [~] Hagebutte *f*.

hip·pie, hip·py ['hɪpɪ] Hippie *m*.

hip·po *zo*. F ['hɪpəʊ] (*pl*. -pos) = **~·pot·a·mus** *zo*. [hɪpə'pɒtəməs] (*pl*. -muses, -mi [-maɪ]) Fluß-, Nilpferd *n*.

hire ['haɪə] **1.** Miete *f*; Entgelt *n*, Lohn *m*; *for* ~ zu vermieten; frei (*Taxi*); ~ *car* Leih-, Mietwagen *m*; ~ *charge* Leihgebühr *f*; ~ *purchase Brt. econ*. Kauf *m* auf Raten- *od*. Teilzahlung; **2.** mieten; *j-n* anstellen; ~ *out* vermieten.

his [hɪz] sein(e); seine(r, -s).

hiss [hɪs] **1.** zischen; zischeln; *a*. ~ *at* auszischen; **2.** Zischen *n*.

his·to·ri·an [hɪ'stɔːrɪən] Historiker *m*; **~·tor·ic** [hɪ'stɒrɪk] (~*ally*) historisch, geschichtlich; **~·tor·i·cal** □ [~kl] historisch, geschichtlich; Geschichts...; **~·to·ry** ['hɪstərɪ] Geschichte *f*; ~ *of civilization* Kulturgeschichte *f*; *contemporary* ~ Zeitgeschichte *f*.

hit [hɪt] **1.** Schlag *m*, Stoß *m*; *fig*. (Seiten)Hieb *m*; (Glücks)Treffer *m*; Hit *m* (*Buch, Schlager etc.*); **2.** (-*tt-*; *hit*) schlagen, stoßen; treffen; auf *et*. stoßen; ~ *it off with* F sich vertragen mit; ~ *on*, ~ *upon* (zufällig) stoßen auf (*acc*.), finden; **~-and-run** [hɪtənd'rʌn] **1.** *a*. ~ *accident* Unfall *m* mit Fahrerflucht; **2.** ~ *driver* unfallflüchtiger Fahrer.

hitch [hɪtʃ] **1.** Ruck *m*; ♣ Knoten *m*; Schwierigkeit *f*, Problem *n*, Haken *m*; **2.** (ruckartig) ziehen, rücken; befestigen, festmachen, -haken, anbinden, ankoppeln; **~·hike** ['hɪtʃhaɪk] per Anhalter fahren, trampen; **~·hik·er** Anhalter(in), Tramper(in).

hith·er ['hɪðə]: ~ *and thither* hierhin u. dorthin; **~·to** bisher.

hive [haɪv] Bienenstock *m*; Bienenschwarm *m*.

hoard [hɔːd] **1.** Vorrat *m*, Schatz *m*; **2.** *a*. ~ *up* horten, hamstern.

hoard·ing ['hɔːdɪŋ] Bauzaun *m*; Brt. Reklametafel *f*.

hoar·frost ['hɔː'frɒst] (Rauh)Reif *m*.

hoarse □ [hɔːs] (~*r*, ~*st*) heiser, rauh.

hoar·y ['hɔːrɪ] (-*ier*, -*iest*) (alters)grau.

hoax [həʊks] **1.** Falschmeldung *f*; (übler) Scherz; **2.** *j-n* hereinlegen.

hob·ble ['hɒbl] **1.** Hinken *n*, Humpeln *n*; **2.** *v/i*. humpeln, hinken (*a. fig*.); *v/t*. an den Füßen fesseln.

hob·by ['hɒbɪ] *fig*. Steckenpferd *n*, Hobby *n*; **~·horse** Steckenpferd *n*; Schaukelpferd *n*.

hob·gob·lin ['hɒbgɒblɪn] Kobold *m*.

ho·bo *Am*. ['həʊbəʊ] (*pl*. -boes, -bos) Wanderarbeiter *m*; Landstreicher *m*.

hock¹ [hɒk] Rheinwein *m*.

hock² *zo*. [~] Sprunggelenk *n*.

hock·ey ['hɒkɪ] *Brt*., *Am*. *field* ~ *Sport*: Hockey *n*; *Am*. Eishockey *n*.

hoe ✔ [həʊ] **1.** Hacke *f*; **2.** hacken.

hog [hɒg] (Mast)Schwein *n*; *Am*. Schwein *n*; **~·gish** □ ['hɒgɪʃ] schweinisch; gefräßig.

hoist [hɔɪst] **1.** (Lasten)Aufzug *m*, Winde *f*; **2.** hochziehen; hissen.

hold [həʊld] **1.** Halten *n*; Halt *m*; Griff *m*; Gewalt *f*, Macht *f*, Einfluß *m*; ♣ Lade-, Frachtraum *m*; *catch* (*od. get, lay, take, seize*) ~ *of* erfassen, ergreifen; sich aneignen; *keep* ~ *of* festhalten; **2.** (*held*) halten; (fest)halten; (zurück-, einbe)halten; abhalten (*from* von); an-, aufhalten; *Wahlen, Versammlung etc.* abhalten; *Sport*: *Meisterschaft etc.* austragen; beibehalten; innehaben; besitzen; *Amt* bekleiden; *Platz* einnehmen; *Rekord* halten; fassen, enthalten; behaupten, *Ansicht* vertreten; fesseln, in Spannung halten; stand-, aushalten; (sich) festhalten; sich verhalten; anhalten, andauern (*Wetter*); ~ *one's ground*, ~ *one's own* sich behaupten; ~ *the line teleph*. am Apparat bleiben; *a*. ~ *good* (weiterhin) gelten; ~ *still* stillhalten; ~ *against j-m et*. vorhalten *od*. vorwerfen; *j-m et*. übelnehmen; ~ *back* (sich) zurückhalten; *fig*. zurückhalten mit; ~ *forth* sich auslassen *od*. verbreiten (*on* über *acc*); ~ *off* (sich) fernhalten; *et*. aufschieben; ausbleiben; ~ *on* (sich) festhalten (*to* an *dat*.); aus-, durchhalten; andauern; *teleph*. am Apparat bleiben; ~ *on to et*. behalten; ~ *over* vertagen, -schieben; ~ *together* zusammenhalten; ~ *up* hochheben; hochhalten; hinstellen (*as als Beispiel etc.*); aufhalten, verzögern; *j-n, Bank etc.* überfallen; **~·all** [hɔːl] Reisetasche *f*; **~·er** [~ə] Pächter *m*; Halter *m* (*Gerät*); Inhaber(in) (*bsd. econ.*);

~ing [~ɪŋ] Halten n; Halt m; Pachtgut n; Besitz m; ~ **company** econ. Holding-, Dachgesellschaft f; ~**up** Verzögerung f, (a. Verkehrs-)Stockung f; (bewaffneter) (Raub-)Überfall m.

hole [həʊl] **1.** Loch n; Höhle f; F fig. Klemme f; pick ~s in bekritteln; **2.** aushöhlen; durchlöchern.

hol·i·day ['hɒlədɪ] Feiertag m; freier Tag; bsd. Brt. mst ~s pl. Ferien pl., Urlaub m; ~**mak·er** Urlauber(in).

holi·ness ['həʊlɪnɪs] Heiligkeit f; His ♀ Seine Heiligkeit (der Papst).

hol·ler Am. F ['hɒlə] schreien.

hol·low ['hɒləʊ] **1.** ☐ hohl; leer; falsch; **2.** Höhle f, (Aus)Höhlung f; (Land)Senke f; **3.** ~ out aushöhlen.

hol·ly ♀ ['hɒlɪ] Stechpalme f.

hol·o·caust ['hɒləkɔːst] Massenvernichtung f, sterben n, (bsd. Brand-)Katastrophe f; the ♀ hist. der Holocaust.

hol·ster ['həʊlstə] (Pistolen)Halfter m, n.

ho·ly ['həʊlɪ] (-ier, -iest) heilig; ♀ Thursday Gründonnerstag m; ~ water Weihwasser n; ♀ Week Karwoche f.

home [həʊm] **1.** Heim n; Haus n, Wohnung f; Heimat f; Sport: Heimspiel n; Heimsieg m; at ~ zu Hause; make oneself at ~ es sich bequem machen; at ~ and abroad im In- u. Ausland; **2.** adj. (ein)heimisch, inländisch; wirkungsvoll (Schlag etc.); **3.** adv. heim, nach Hause; zu Hause, daheim; ins Ziel od. ~ Schwarze; strike ~ sitzen, treffen; ~ **com·put·er** Heimcomputer m; ♀ **Coun·ties** pl. die an London angrenzenden Grafschaften; ~ **e·co·nom·ics** sg. Hauswirtschaft(slehre) f; ~**felt** ['həʊmfelt] tief empfunden; ~**less** [~lɪs] heimatlos; ~**like** anheimelnd, gemütlich; ~**ly** [~lɪ] (-ier, -iest) freundlich (with zu); vertraut; einfach; Am. unscheinbar, reizlos; ~**made** selbstgemacht, Hausmacher...; ♀ **Of·fice** Brt. pol. Innenministerium m; ♀ **Sec·re·ta·ry** Brt. pol. Innenminister m; ~**sick:** be ~ Heimweh haben; ~**sick·ness** Heimweh n; ~**stead** Gehöft n; ♀ in USA: Heimstätte f; ~ **team** Sport: Gastgeber pl.; ~**ward** [~wəd] **1.** adj. Heim..., Rück...; **2.** adv. Am. heimwärts, nach Hause; ~**wards**

[~wədz] adv. = homeward 2; ~**work** Hausaufgabe(n pl.) f, Schularbeiten pl.

hom·i·cide ⚖ ['hɒmɪsaɪd] Tötung f; Totschlag m; Mord m; Totschläger(in); Mörder(in); ~ squad Mordkommission f.

ho·mo F ['həʊməʊ] (pl. -mos) Homo m (Homosexueller).

ho·mo·ge·ne·ous ☐ [hɒmə'dʒiːnjəs] homogen, gleichartig.

ho·mo·sex·u·al [hɒmə'seksjʊəl] **1.** ☐ homosexuell; **2.** Homosexuelle(r m) f.

hone ⊕ [həʊn] feinschleifen.

hon·est ☐ ['ɒnɪst] ehrlich, rechtschaffen; aufrichtig; echt; ~**es·ty** [~ɪ] Ehrlichkeit f, Rechtschaffenheit f; Aufrichtigkeit f.

hon·ey ['hʌnɪ] Honig m; fig. Liebling m; ~**comb** [~kəʊm] (Honig)Wabe f; ~**ed** [~ɪd] honigsüß; ~**moon 1.** Flitterwochen pl.; **2.** s-e Hochzeitsreise machen.

honk mot. [hɒŋk] hupen.

hon·ky-tonk Am. sl. ['hɒŋkɪtɒŋk] Spelunke f.

hon·or·ar·y ['ɒnərərɪ] Ehren...; ehrenamtlich.

hon·o(u)r ['ɒnə] **1.** Ehre f; fig. Zierde f; ~s pl. besondere Auszeichnung(en pl.), Ehren pl.; Your ♀ Euer Ehren; **2.** (be)ehren; econ. honorieren; ~**a·ble** ☐ [~rəbl] ehrenvoll; redlich; ehrbar; ehrenwert.

hood [hʊd] Kapuze f; mot. Verdeck n; Am. (Motor)Haube f; ⊕ Kappe f.

hood·lum Am. F ['huːdləm] Rowdy m; Ganove m.

hood·wink ['hʊdwɪŋk] j-n reinlegen.

hoof [huːf] (pl. hoofs [~fs], hooves [~vz]) Huf m.

hook [hʊk] **1.** Haken m; Angelhaken m; Sichel f; by ~ or by crook so oder so; **2.** (sich) (zu-, fest)haken; angeln (a. fig.); ~**ed** krumm, Haken...; F süchtig (on nach) (a. fig.); ~ on heroin (television) heroin- (fernseh)süchtig; ~**y** F ['hʊkɪ]: play ~ Am. F (bsd. die Schule) schwänzen.

hoo·li·gan ['huːlɪgən] Rowdy m; ~**is·m** [~ɪzəm] Rowdytum n.

hoop [huːp] **1.** (Faß- etc.) Reif(en) m; ⊕ Ring m; **2.** Fässer binden.

hoot [huːt] **1.** Schrei m (der Eule); höhnischer, johlender Schrei; mot. Hupen n; **2.** v/i. heulen; johlen; mot. hupen; v/t. auspfeifen, auszischen.

Hoo·ver *TM* ['huːvə] **1.** Staubsauger *m*; **2.** *mst* ⚥ (staub)saugen, *Teppich etc. a.* absaugen.

hooves [huːvz] *pl. von hoof.*

hop[1] [hɒp] Sprung *m*; F Tanz *m*; **2.** (*-pp-*) hüpfen; springen (über *acc.*); *be ~ping mad* F e-e Stinkwut (im Bauch) haben.

hop[2] ⚥ [⁓] Hopfen *m*.

hope [həʊp] **1.** Hoffnung *f*; **2.** hoffen (*for auf acc.*); ⁓ *in* vertrauen auf (*acc.*); **~·ful** □ ['həʊpfl] hoffnungsvoll; **~·less** □ [⁓lɪs] hoffnungslos; verzweifelt.

horde [hɔːd] Horde *f*.

ho·ri·zon [həˈraɪzn] Horizont *m*.

hor·i·zon·tal □ [hɒrɪˈzɒntl] horizontal, waag(e)recht.

horn [hɔːn] Horn *n*; Schalltrichter *m*; *mot.* Hupe *f*; ⁓*s pl.* Geweih *n*; ⁓ *of plenty* Füllhorn *n*.

hor·net *zo.* ['hɔːnɪt] Hornisse *f*.

horn·y ['hɔːnɪ] (*-ier, -iest*) hornig, schwielig; V geil (*Mann*).

hor·o·scope ['hɒrəskəʊp] Horoskop *n*.

hor·ri·ble □ ['hɒrəbl] schrecklich, furchtbar, scheußlich; F gemein; **~·rid** □ ['hɒrɪd] gräßlich, abscheulich; schrecklich; **~·ri·fy** [⁓faɪ] erschrecken; entsetzen; **~·ror** [⁓ə] Entsetzen *n*, Schauder *m*; Schrecken *m*; Greuel *m*.

horse [hɔːs] *zo.* Pferd *n*; Bock *m*, Gestell *n*; *wild ~s will not drag me there* keine zehn Pferde bringen mich dort hin; **~·back** ['hɔːsbæk]: *on ~* zu Pferde, beritten; **~ chest·nut** ⚥ Roßkastanie *f*; **~·hair** Roßhaar *n*; **~·man** (*pl. -men*) (geübter) Reiter; **~·man·ship** [⁓mənʃɪp] Reitkunst *f*; **~ op·e·ra** F Western *m* (*Film*); **~·pow·er** *phys.* Pferdestärke *f*; **~·rac·ing** Pferderennen *n od. pl.*; **~·rad·ish** Meerrettich *m*; **~·shoe** Hufeisen *n*; **~·wom·an** (*pl. -women*) (geübte) Reiterin.

hor·ti·cul·ture ['hɔːtɪkʌltʃə] Gartenbau *m*.

hose[1] [həʊz] Schlauch *m*.

hose[2] [⁓] *pl.* Strümpfe *pl.*, Strumpfwaren *pl.*; △ *nicht Hose.*

ho·sier·y ['həʊʒərɪ] Strumpfwaren *pl.*

hos·pi·ta·ble □ ['hɒspɪtəbl] gastfrei.

hos·pi·tal ['hɒspɪtl] Krankenhaus *n*, Klinik *f*; ⚔ Lazarett *n*; *in (Am. in the)* ⁓ im Krankenhaus; **~·i·ty**

[hɒspɪˈtælətɪ] Gastfreundschaft *f*, Gastlichkeit *f*; **~·ize** ['hɒspɪtəlaɪz] ins Krankenhaus einliefern *od.* -weisen.

host[1] [həʊst] Gastgeber *m*; (Gast-) Wirt *m*; *Rundfunk, TV:* Talkmaster *m*; Showmaster *m*; Moderator *m*; *your ~ was ...* durch die Sendung führte Sie ...

host[2] [⁓] Menge *f*, Masse *f*.

host[3] *eccl.* [⁓] *oft* ⚥ Hostie *f*.

hos·tage ['hɒstɪdʒ] Geisel *m, f*; *take s.o. ~* j-n als Geisel nehmen.

hos·tel ['hɒstl] *bsd. Brt.* (Studenten-, Arbeiter- *etc.*) (Wohn)Heim *n*; *mst youth ~* Jugendherberge *f*.

host·ess ['həʊstɪs] Gastgeberin *f*; (Gast)Wirtin *f*; Hostess *f*; ✈ Stewardeß *f*.

hos·tile ['hɒstaɪl] feindlich (gesinnt); ⁓ *to foreigners* ausländerfeindlich; **~·til·i·ty** [hɒˈstɪlətɪ] Feindseligkeit *f* (*to gegen*).

hot [hɒt] (*-tt-*) heiß; scharf; beißend; hitzig, heftig; eifrig; warm (*Speise, Fährte*); F heiß, gestohlen; radioaktiv; **~·bed** ['hɒtbed] Mistbeet *n*; *fig.* Brutstätte *f*.

hotch·potch ['hɒtʃpɒtʃ] Mischmasch *m*; Gemüsesuppe *f*.

hot dog [hɒtˈdɒg] Hot dog *n, m.*

ho·tel [həʊˈtel] Hotel *n*.

hot·head ['hɒthed] Hitzkopf *m*; **~·house** Treibhaus *n*; **~ line** *pol.* heißer Draht; **~·pot** Eintopf *m*; **~ spot** *bsd. pol.* Unruhe-, Krisenherd *m*; **~·spur** Hitzkopf *m*; **~·wa·ter bottle** Wärmflasche *f*.

hound [haʊnd] **1.** Jagdhund *m*; *fig.* Hund *m*; **2.** jagen, hetzen.

hour ['aʊə] Stunde *f*; Zeit *f*, Uhr *f*; **~·ly** [⁓lɪ] stündlich.

house 1. [haʊs] Haus *n*; *the* ⚥ *das* Unterhaus; die Börse; **2.** [haʊz] *v/t.* unterbringen; *v/i.* hausen; **~·a·gent** ['haʊseɪdʒənt] Häusermakler *m*; **~·bound** *fig.* ans Haus gefesselt; **~·hold** Haushalt *m*; *attr.* Haushalts...; Haus...; **~·hold·er** Hausherr *m*; **~·hus·band** *bsd. Am.* Hausmann *m*; **~·keep·er** Haushälterin *f*; **~·keep·ing** Haushaltung *f*, Haushaltsführung *f*; **~·maid** Hausmädchen *n*; **~·man** (*pl. -men*) *Brt.* ⚕ Medizinalassistent *m*; △ *nicht Hausmann*; **~·warm·ing (par·ty)** [⁓wɔːmɪŋ(pɑːtɪ)] Einzugsparty *f*;

~wife ['haʊswaɪf] (*pl.* -wives) Hausfrau *f*; ['hazɪf] Nähetui *n*; **~work** Hausarbeit *f*; △ *nicht Hausaufgabe(n).*

hous·ing ['haʊzɪŋ] Unterbringung *f*; Wohnung *f*; ~ **estate** *Brt.* Wohnsiedlung *f*.

hove [haʊv] *pret. u. p.p. von* heave 2.

hov·el ['hɒvl] Schuppen *m*; Hütte *f*.

hov·er ['hɒvə] schweben; lungern; *fig.* schwanken; **~craft** (*pl.* -craft[s]) Hovercraft *n*, Luftkissenfahrzeug *n*.

how [haʊ] wie; ~ *do you do? bei der Vorstellung:* guten Tag!; ~ *about* ...? wie steht's mit ...?

how·dy *Am. int.* F ['haʊdɪ] Tag!

how·ev·er [haʊ'evə] 1. *adv.* wie auch (immer), wenn auch noch so ...; 2. *cj.* (je)doch.

howl [haʊl] 1. heulen; brüllen; 2. Heulen *n*, Geheul *n*; **~er** F ['haʊlə] grober Schnitzer.

hub [hʌb] (Rad)Nabe *f*; *fig.* Mittel-Angelpunkt *m*.

hub·bub ['hʌbʌb] Tumult *m*.

hub·by F ['hʌbɪ] (Ehe)Mann *m*.

huck·le·ber·ry ♀ ['hʌklberɪ] amerikanische Heidelbeere.

huck·ster ['hʌkstə] Hausierer(in).

hud·dle ['hʌdl] 1. *a.* ~ *together* (sich) zusammendrängen, zusammenpressen; ~ (*o.s.*) *up* sich zusammenkauern; 2. (wirrer) Haufen, Wirrwarr *m*, Durcheinander *n*.

hue[1] [hju:] Farbe *f*; (Farb)Ton *m*.

hue[2] [~]: ~ *and cry fig.* großes Geschrei.

huff [hʌf] Verärgerung *f*; Verstimmung *f*; *be in a* ~ verärgert *od.* -stimmt sein.

hug [hʌg] 1. Umarmung *f*; 2. (-gg-) an sich drücken, umarmen; *fig.* festhalten an (*dat.*); sich dicht am *Weg etc.* halten.

huge □ [hju:dʒ] ungeheuer, riesig; **~ness** ['hju:dʒnɪs] ungeheure Größe.

hulk·ing ['hʌlkɪŋ] sperrig, klotzig; ungeschlacht, unförmig.

hull [hʌl] 1. ♀ Schale *f*, Hülse *f*; ♣ Rumpf *m*; 2. enthülsen; schälen.

hul·la·ba·loo ['hʌləbə'lu:] (*pl.* -loos) Lärm *m*.

hul·lo *int.* [hə'ləʊ] hallo!

hum [hʌm] (-mm-) summen; brummen.

hu·man ['hju:mən] 1. □ menschlich, Menschen...; △ *nicht human*; **~ly**

possible menschenmöglich; ~ *being* Mensch *m*; ~ *rights pl.* Menschenrechte *pl.*; 2. Mensch *m*; **~e** □ [hju:'meɪn] human, menschenfreundlich; **~i·tar·i·an** [hju:mænɪ'teərɪən] 1. Menschenfreund *m*; 2. menschenfreundlich; **~i·ty** [hju:'mænətɪ] die Menschheit, die Menschen *pl.*; Humanität *f*, Menschlichkeit *f*; *humanities pl.* Geisteswissenschaften *pl.*; Altphilologie *f*.

hum·ble ['hʌmbl] 1. □ (~*r*, ~*st*) demütig; bescheiden; 2. erniedrigen; demütigen.

hum·ble-bee *zo.* ['hʌmblbi:] Hummel *f*.

hum·ble·ness ['hʌmblnɪs] Demut *f*.

hum·drum ['hʌmdrʌm] eintönig.

hu·mid ['hju:mɪd] feucht, naß; **~i·ty** [hju:'mɪdətɪ] Feuchtigkeit *f*.

hu·mil·i·ate [hju:'mɪlɪeɪt] erniedrigen, demütigen; **~a·tion** [hju:mɪlɪ'eɪʃn] Erniedrigung *f*, Demütigung *f*; **~ty** [hju:'mɪlətɪ] Demut *f*.

hum·ming·bird *zo.* ['hʌmɪŋbɜ:d] Kolibri *m*.

hu·mor·ous □ ['hju:mərəs] humoristisch, humorvoll; spaßig.

hu·mo(u)r ['hju:mə] 1. Laune *f*, Stimmung *f*; Humor *m*; *das* Spaßige; *out of* ~ schlecht gelaunt; 2. *j-m* s-n Willen lassen; eingehen auf (*acc.*).

hump [hʌmp] 1. Höcker *m* (*e-s Kamels*), Buckel *m*; 2. krümmen; *Brt.* F auf den Rücken nehmen, tragen; ~ *o.s. Am. sl.* sich ranhalten; **~back(ed)** ['hʌmpbæk(t)] = hunchback(ed).

hunch [hʌntʃ] 1. = hump 1; dickes Stück; Ahnung *f*, Gefühl *n*; 2. *a.* ~ *up* krümmen; **~back** ['hʌntʃbæk] Buckel *m*; Bucklige(r *m*) *f*; **~backed** buck(e)lig.

hun·dred ['hʌndrəd] 1. hundert; 2. Hundert *n* (*Einheit*); Hundert *f* (*Zahl*); **~th** [~θ] 1. hundertste(r, -s); 2. Hundertstel *n*; **~weight** *in GB:* *appr.* Zentner *m* (= 50,8 *kg*).

hung [hʌŋ] 1. *pret. u. p.p. von* hang[1]; 2. *adj.* abgehangen (*Fleisch*).

Hun·gar·i·an [hʌŋ'geərɪən] 1. ungarisch; 2. Ungar(in); *ling.* Ungarisch *n*.

hun·ger ['hʌŋə] 1. Hunger *m* (*a. fig.*: *for* nach); 2. hungern (*for, after* nach); ~ **strike** Hungerstreik *m*.

hun·gry □ ['hʌŋgrɪ] (-ier, -iest) hungrig.

hunk [hʌŋk] dickes Stück.

hunt [hʌnt] 1. Jagd f (a. fig.: for nach); Jagd(revier n) f; Jagd(gesellschaft) f; 2. jagen; Revier bejagen; hetzen; ~ out, ~ up aufspüren; ~ after, ~ for Jagd machen auf (acc.); ~er ['hʌntə] Jäger m; Jagdpferd n; ~ing [~ɪŋ] Jagen n; attr. Jagd...; ~ing-ground Jagdrevier n.

hur·dle ['hɜːdl] Sport: Hürde f (a. fig.); ~r [~ə] Sport: Hürdenläufer(in); ~race Sport: Hürdenrennen n.

hurl [hɜːl] 1. Schleudern n; 2. schleudern; Worte ausstoßen.

hur·ri·cane ['hʌrɪkən] Hurrikan m, Wirbelsturm m; Orkan m.

hur·ried □ ['hʌrɪd] eilig; übereilt.

hur·ry ['hʌrɪ] 1. (große) Eile, Hast f; be in a (no) ~ es (nicht) eilig haben; not ... in a ~ F nicht so bald, nicht so leicht; 2. v/t. (an)treiben; drängen; et. beschleunigen; eilig schicken od. bringen; v/i. eilen, hasten; ~ up sich beeilen.

hurt [hɜːt] 1. Schmerz m; Verletzung f, Wunde f; Schaden m; 2. (hurt) verletzen, -wunden (a. fig.); schmerzen, weh tun; schaden (dat.); ~ful □ ['hɜːtfl] verletzend.

hus·band ['hʌzbənd] 1. (Ehe)Mann m; 2. haushalten mit; verwalten; ~ry [~rɪ] ✔ Landwirtschaft f; fig. Haushalten n, sparsamer Umgang (of mit).

hush [hʌʃ] 1. int. still!; 2. Stille f; 3. zum Schweigen bringen; besänftigen, beruhigen; △ nicht huschen; ~ up vertuschen; ~money ['hʌʃmʌnɪ] Schweigegeld n.

husk [hʌsk] 1. ✔ Hülse f, Schote f, Schale f (a. fig.); 2. enthülsen; **hus·ky** ['hʌskɪ] 1. □ (-ier, -iest) hülsig; trocken; heiser; F stramm, stämmig; 2. F stämmiger Kerl.

hus·sy ['hʌsɪ] Fratz m, Göre f; Flittchen n.

hus·tle ['hʌsl] 1. v/t. (an)rempeln; stoßen; drängen; v/i. (sich) drängen;

hasten, hetzen; sich beeilen; 2. ~ and bustle Gedränge n; Gehetze n; Getriebe n.

hut [hʌt] Hütte f; ✕ Baracke f.

hutch [hʌtʃ] (bsd. Kaninchen)Stall m.

hy·a·cinth ♀ ['haɪəsɪnθ] Hyazinthe f.

hy·ae·na zo. [haɪˈiːnə] Hyäne f.

hy·brid biol. ['haɪbrɪd] Bastard m, Mischling m, Kreuzung f; attr. Bastard...; Zwitter...; ~ize [~aɪz] kreuzen.

hy·drant ['haɪdrənt] Hydrant m.

hy·drau·lic ['haɪdrɔːlɪk] (~ally) hydraulisch; ~s sg. Hydraulik f.

hy·dro- ['haɪdrəʊ] Wasser...; ~car·bon Kohlenwasserstoff m; ~chlor·ic ac·id [~ə'klɒrɪk'æsɪd] Salzsäure f; ~foil ♉ [~fɔɪl] Tragflächen-, Tragflügelboot n; ~gen [~ədʒən] Wasserstoff m; ~gen bomb Wasserstoffbombe f; ~plane ✈ Wasserflugzeug n; ♉ Gleitboot n.

hy·e·na zo. [haɪˈiːnə] Hyäne f.

hy·giene ['haɪdʒiːn] Hygiene f; **hy·gien·ic** [haɪˈdʒiːnɪk] (~ally) hygienisch.

hymn [hɪm] 1. Hymne f; Lobgesang m; Kirchenlied n; 2. preisen.

hy·per- ['haɪpə] Hyper..., über..., höher, größer; ~mar·ket Groß-, Verbrauchermarkt m; ~sen·si·tive [haɪpə'sensətɪv] überempfindlich (to gegen).

hy·phen ['haɪfn] Bindestrich m; ~ate [~eɪt] mit Bindestrich schreiben.

hyp·no·tize ['hɪpnətaɪz] hypnotisieren.

hy·po·chon·dri·ac ['haɪpəʊ'kɒndrɪæk] Hypochonder m.

hy·poc·ri·sy [hɪ'pɒkrəsɪ] Heuchelei f; **hyp·o·crite** ['hɪpəkrɪt] Heuchler(in); Scheinheilige(r m) f; **hyp·o·crit·i·cal** □ [hɪpə'krɪtɪkl] heuchlerisch, scheinheilig.

hy·poth·e·sis [haɪ'pɒθɪsɪs] (pl. -ses [-siːz]) Hypothese f.

hys·te·ri·a [hɪ'stɪərɪə] Hysterie f; ~ter·i·cal □ [~'sterɪkl] hysterisch; ~ter·ics [~ɪks] pl. hysterischer Anfall; go into ~ hysterisch werden; F e-n Lachkrampf bekommen.

H

I

I [aɪ] ich; *it is* ~ ich bin es.

ice [aɪs] **1.** Eis *n*; **2.** gefrieren lassen; *a.* ~ *up* vereisen; *Kuchen* mit Zuckerguß überziehen; in Eis kühlen; ~**age** ['aɪseɪdʒ] Eiszeit *f*; ~**berg** [~bɜːg] Eisberg *m* (*a. fig.*); ~**bound** eingefroren; ~**box** Eisfach *n*; *Am.* Kühlschrank *m*; ~**cream** (Speise)Eis *n*; ~**cube** Eiswürfel *m*; ~ **floe** Eisscholle *f*; ~**lolly** *Brt.* Eis *n* am Stiel; ~ **rink** (Kunst)Eisbahn *f*; ~ **show** Eisrevue *f*.

i·ci·cle ['aɪsɪkl] Eiszapfen *m*.

ic·ing ['aɪsɪŋ] Zuckerguß *m*; Vereisung *f*.

i·cy □ ['aɪsɪ] (*-ier, -iest*) eisig (*a. fig.*); vereist.

i·dea [aɪ'dɪə] Idee *f*; Begriff *m*; Vorstellung *f*; Gedanke *m*; Meinung *f*; Ahnung *f*; Plan *m*; ~**l** [~l] **1.** □ ideell; (nur) eingebildet; ideal; **2.** Ideal *n*; ~**l·is·m** [~lɪzəm] Idealismus *m*; ~**l·ize** [~laɪz] idealisieren.

i·den·ti·cal □ [aɪ'dentɪkl] identisch, gleich(bedeutend); ~**fi·ca·tion** [aɪdentɪfɪ'keɪʃn] Identifizierung *f*; Ausweis *m*; ~**fy** [aɪ'dentɪfaɪ] identifizieren; ausweisen; erkennen; ~**ty** [~tɪ] Identität *f*; Persönlichkeit *f*; Eigenart *f*; ~ *card* (Personal)Ausweis *m*, Kennkarte *f*; ~ *disk, Am.* ~ *tag* ✗ Erkennungsmarke *f*.

i·de·o·log·i·cal □ [aɪdɪə'lɒdʒɪkl] ideologisch; ~**ol·ogy** [aɪdɪ'ɒlədʒɪ] Ideologie *f*.

id·i·om ['ɪdɪəm] Idiom *n*; Redewendung *f*; ~**o·mat·ic** [ɪdɪə'mætɪk] (~*ally*) idiomatisch.

id·i·ot ['ɪdɪət] Idiot(in), Schwachsinnige(*r m*) *f*; ~**ic** [ɪdɪ'ɒtɪk] (~*ally*) blödsinnig.

i·dle ['aɪdl] **1.** □ (~*r*, ~*st*) müßig, untätig; träge, faul; *econ.* unproduktiv, tot; ungenutzt; beiläufig; ~ *hours pl.* Mußestunden *pl.*; **2.** *v/t.* *mst* ~ *away* vertrödeln; *v/i.* faulenzen; ⊕ leer laufen; ~**ness** [~nɪs] Untätigkeit *f*, Müßiggang *m*; Faulheit *f*; Muße *f*; Zwecklosigkeit *f*.

i·dol ['aɪdl] Idol *n* (*a. fig.*), Götzenbild *n*; ~**a·trous** [aɪ'dɒlətrəs] abgöttisch; ~**a·try** Götzenanbetung *f*; *fig.* abgöttische Verehrung *f*, Vergötterung *f*; ~**ize** ['aɪdəlaɪz] abgöttisch verehren, vergöttern.

i·dyl·lic [aɪ'dɪlɪk] (~*ally*) idyllisch.

if [ɪf] **1.** wenn, falls; ob; **2.** Wenn *n*.

ig·nite [ɪg'naɪt] anzünden, (sich) entzünden; *mot.* zünden; **ig·ni·tion** [ɪg'nɪʃən] An-, Entzünden *n*; *mot.* Zündung *f*.

ig·no·ble □ [ɪg'nəʊbl] gemein, unehrenhaft.

ig·no·min·i·ous □ [ɪgnə'mɪnɪəs] schändlich, schimpflich.

ig·no·rance ['ɪgnərəns] Unwissenheit *f*; **ig·no·rant** [~t] unwissend; ungebildet; F ungehobelt; **ig·nore** [ɪg'nɔː] ignorieren, nicht beachten; ✗ verwerfen.

ill [ɪl] **1.** (*worse, worst*) krank; schlimm, schlecht, übel; böse; *fall* ~, *be taken* ~ krank werden; **2.** ~*s pl.* Übel *n*, Mißstand *m*; ~**ad·vised** ['ɪləd'vaɪzd] schlecht beraten; unbesonnen, unklug; ~**bred** schlechterzogen; ungezogen; ~ **breed·ing** schlechtes Benehmen.

il·le·gal □ [ɪ'liːgl] unerlaubt, ✗ illegal, ungesetzlich; ~ *parking* Falschparken *n*.

il·le·gi·ble □ [ɪ'ledʒəbl] unleserlich.

il·le·git·i·mate □ [ɪlɪ'dʒɪtɪmət] illegitim; unrechtmäßig; unehelich.

ill-fat·ed ['ɪl'feɪtɪd] unglücklich, Unglücks...; ~**fa·vo(u)red** häßlich; ~**hu·mo(u)red** schlechtgelaunt.

il·lib·e·ral □ [ɪ'lɪbərəl] engstirnig, intolerant; knaus(e)rig.

il·li·cit □ [ɪ'lɪsɪt] unerlaubt.

il·lit·e·rate [ɪ'lɪtərət] **1.** □ unwissend, ungebildet; **2.** Analphabet(in).

ill·judged ['ɪl'dʒʌdʒd] unbesonnen, unklug; ~**man·nered** ungezogen, mit schlechten Umgangsformen; ~**na·tured** □ boshaft, bösartig.

ill·ness ['ɪlnɪs] Krankheit *f*.

il·log·i·cal □ [ɪ'lɒdʒɪkl] unlogisch.

ill-tem·pered ['ɪl'tempəd] schlechtgelaunt, übellaunig; ~**timed** ungelegen, unpassend, zur unrechten Zeit.

il·lu·mi·nate [ɪ'ljuːmɪneɪt] be-, erleuchten (*a. fig.*); *fig.* erläutern, erklären; ~**nat·ing** [~ɪŋ] Leucht...; *fig.* aufschlußreich; ~**na·tion** [ɪljuːmɪ'neɪʃn] Er-, Beleuchtung *f*; *fig.* Erläuterung *f*, Erklärung *f*; ~*s pl.* Illumination *f*, Festbeleuchtung *f*.

ill-use ['ɪl'juːz] mißhandeln.

il·lu·sion [ɪˈluːʒn] Illusion *f*, Täuschung *f*; **~sive** [~sɪv], **~so·ry** □ [~ərɪ] illusorisch, trügerisch.

il·lus|trate [ˈɪləstreɪt] illustrieren, bebildern; erläutern; **~tra·tion** [ˈɪləˈstreɪʃn] Erläuterung *f*; Illustration *f*; Bild *n*, Abbildung *f*, **~tra·tive** □ [ˈɪləstrətɪv] erläuternd.

il·lus·tri·ous □ [ɪˈlʌstrɪəs] berühmt.

ill will [ˈɪlˈwɪl] Feindschaft *f*.

im·age [ˈɪmɪdʒ] Bild *n*; Statue *f*; Götzenbild *n*; Ebenbild *n*; Image *n*; **im·ag·er·y** [~ərɪ] Bilder *pl.*; Bildersprache *f*, Metaphorik *f*.

i·mag·i·na|ble □ [ɪˈmædʒɪnəbl] denkbar; **~ry** [~ərɪ] eingebildet, imaginär; **~tion** [ɪmædʒɪˈneɪʃn] Einbildung(skraft) *f*; **~tive** □ [ɪˈmædʒɪnətɪv] ideen-, einfallsreich; **i·ma·gine** [ɪˈmædʒɪn] sich *et.* einbilden *od.* vorstellen *od.* denken.

im·bal·ance [ɪmˈbæləns] Unausgewogenheit *f*; *pol. etc.* Ungleichgewicht *n*.

im·be·cile □ [ˈɪmbɪsiːl] 1. schwachsinnig; 2. Schwachsinnige(r *m*) *f*; *contp.* Idiot *m*, Trottel *m*.

im·bibe [ɪmˈbaɪb] trinken; *fig.* sich zu eigen machen.

im·bue *fig.* [ɪmˈbjuː] durchdringen, erfüllen (*with* mit).

im·i|tate [ˈɪmɪteɪt] nachahmen, imitieren; **~ta·tion** [ɪmɪˈteɪʃn] 1. Nachahmung *f*; Imitation *f*; 2. nachgemacht, unecht, künstlich, Kunst...

im·mac·u·late □ [ɪˈmækjʊlət] unbefleckt, rein; fehlerlos.

im·ma·te·ri·al □ [ɪməˈtɪərɪəl] unkörperlich; unwesentlich (*to* für).

im·ma·ture □ [ɪməˈtjʊə] unreif.

im·mea·su·ra·ble □ [ɪˈmeʒərəbl] unermeßlich.

im·me·di·ate □ [ɪˈmiːdjət] unmittelbar; unverzüglich, sofortig; **~ly** [~lɪ] 1. *adv.* sofort; 2. *cj.* sobald; sofort, als.

im·mense □ [ɪˈmens] riesig; *fig. a.* enorm, immens; prima, großartig.

im·merse [ɪˈmɜːs] (ein-, unter)tauchen; *fig.* versenken *od.* vertiefen (*in* in *acc.*); **im·mer·sion** [~ʃn] Ein-, Untertauchen *n*; **~ heater** Tauchsieder *m*.

im·mi|grant [ˈɪmɪgrənt] Einwander|er *m*, -in *f*, Immigrant(in); **~grate** [~greɪt] *v/i.* einwandern; *v/t.* ansiedeln (*into* in *dat.*); **~gra·tion**

[ɪmɪˈgreɪʃn] Einwanderung *f*, Immigration *f*.

im·mi·nent □ [ˈɪmɪnənt] nahe bevorstehend; **~** *danger* drohende Gefahr.

im·mo·bile [ɪˈməʊbaɪl] unbeweglich.

im·mod·e·rate □ [ɪˈmɒdərət] maßlos.

im·mod·est □ [ɪˈmɒdɪst] unbescheiden; unanständig.

im·mor·al □ [ɪˈmɒrəl] unmoralisch.

im·mor·tal [ɪˈmɔːtl] 1. □ unsterblich; 2. Unsterbliche(r *m*) *f*; **~i·ty** [ɪmɔːˈtælətɪ] Unsterblichkeit *f*.

im·mo·va·ble [ɪˈmuːvəbl] 1. □ unbeweglich; unerschütterlich; unnachgiebig; 2. **~s** *pl.* Immobilien *pl.*

im·mune [ɪˈmjuːn] (*against, from, to*) immun (gegen); geschützt (gegen), frei (von); **im·mu·ni·ty** [~tɪ] Immunität *f*; Unempfindlichkeit *f*.

im·mu·ta·ble □ [ɪˈmjuːtəbl] unveränderlich.

imp [ɪmp] Teufelchen *n*; Racker *m*.

im·pact [ˈɪmpækt] (Zusammen)Stoß *m*; Anprall *m*; Einwirkung *f*.

im·pair [ɪmˈpeə] beeinträchtigen.

im·part [ɪmˈpɑːt] (*to dat.*) geben; mitteilen; vermitteln.

im·par|tial □ [ɪmˈpɑːʃl] unparteiisch; **~ti·al·i·ty** [ˈɪmpɑːʃɪˈælətɪ] Unparteilichkeit *f*, Objektivität *f*.

im·pass·a·ble □ [ɪmˈpɑːsəbl] unpassierbar.

im·passe [æmˈpɑːs] Sackgasse *f* (*a. fig.*); *fig.* toter Punkt.

im·pas·sioned [ɪmˈpæʃnd] leidenschaftlich.

im·pas·sive □ [ɪmˈpæsɪv] teilnahmslos; unbewegt (*Gesicht*).

im·pa|tience [ɪmˈpeɪʃns] Ungeduld *f*; **~tient** □ [~t] ungeduldig.

im·peach [ɪmˈpiːtʃ] anklagen (*for, of, with gen.*); anfechten, anzweifeln.

im·pec·ca·ble □ [ɪmˈpekəbl] sünd(en)los; untadelig, einwandfrei.

im·pede [ɪmˈpiːd] (be)hindern.

im·ped·i·ment [ɪmˈpedɪmənt] Hindernis *n*.

im·pel [ɪmˈpel] (*-ll-*) (an)treiben.

im·pend·ing [ɪmˈpendɪŋ] nahe bevorstehend; **~** *danger* drohende Gefahr.

im·pen·e·tra·ble □ [ɪmˈpenɪtrəbl] undurchdringlich; *fig.* unergründlich; *fig.* unzugänglich (*to dat.*).

im·per·a·tive [ɪmˈperətɪv] **1.** □ notwendig, dringend, unbedingt erforderlich; befehlend; gebieterisch; *gr.* imperativisch; **2.** Befehl *m*; *a.* ~ **mood** *gr.* Imperativ *m*, Befehlsform *f.*

im·per·cep·ti·ble □ [ɪmpəˈseptəbl] unmerklich.

im·per·fect [ɪmˈpɜːfɪkt] **1.** □ unvollkommen; unvollendet; **2.** *a.* ~ **tense** *gr.* Imperfekt *n.*

im·pe·ri·al·ism *pol.* [ɪmˈpɪərɪəlɪzəm] Imperialismus *m*; ~**t** *pol.* [~ɪst] Imperialist *m.*

im·per·il [ɪmˈperəl] (*bsd.* Brt. *-ll-*, *Am. -l-*) gefährden.

im·pe·ri·ous □ [ɪmˈpɪərɪəs] herrisch, gebieterisch; dringend.

im·per·me·a·ble □ [ɪmˈpɜːmjəbl] undurchlässig.

im·per·son·al □ [ɪmˈpɜːsnl] unpersönlich.

im·per·son·ate [ɪmˈpɜːsəneɪt] *thea. etc.* verkörpern, darstellen.

im·per·ti|nence [ɪmˈpɜːtɪnəns] Unverschämtheit *f*, Ungehörigkeit *f*, Frechheit *f*; ~**nent** □ [~t] unverschämt, ungehörig, frech.

im·per·tur·ba·ble □ [ɪmpəˈtɜːbəbl] unerschütterlich, gelassen.

im·per·vi·ous □ [ɪmˈpɜːvjəs] unzugänglich (*to* für); undurchlässig.

im·pe·tu·ous □ [ɪmˈpetjʊəs] ungestüm, heftig; impulsiv.

im·pe·tus [ˈɪmpɪtəs] Antrieb *m*, Schwung *m.*

im·pi·e·ty [ɪmˈpaɪətɪ] Gottlosigkeit *f*; Respektlosigkeit *f.*

im·pinge [ɪmˈpɪndʒ]: ~ *on*, ~ *upon* sich auswirken auf (*acc.*), beeinflussen (*acc.*).

im·pi·ous □ [ˈɪmpɪəs] gottlos; pietätlos; respektlos.

im·plac·a·ble □ [ɪmˈplækəbl] unversöhnlich, unnachgiebig.

im·plant [ɪmˈplɑːnt] *⚕* einpflanzen; *fig.* einprägen.

im·ple·ment 1. [ˈɪmplɪmənt] Werkzeug *n*; Gerät *n*; **2.** [~ment] ausführen.

im·pli|cate [ˈɪmplɪkeɪt] verwickeln; zur Folge haben; ~**ca·tion** [ɪmplɪˈkeɪʃn] Verwick(e)lung *f*; Implikation *f*, Einbeziehung *f*; Folgerung *f.*

im·pli·cit □ [ɪmˈplɪsɪt] unausgesprochen; bedingungslos, blind (*Glaube etc.*).

im·plore [ɪmˈplɔː] inständig bitten, anflehen; (er)flehen.

im·ply [ɪmˈplaɪ] implizieren, (mit) einbegreifen; bedeuten; andeuten.

im·po·lite □ [ɪmpəˈlaɪt] unhöflich.

im·pol·i·tic □ [ɪmˈpɒlɪtɪk] unklug.

im·port 1. [ˈɪmpɔːt] *econ.* Import *m*, Einfuhr *f*; *econ.* Import-, Einfuhrartikel *m*; Bedeutung *f*; Wichtigkeit *f*; ~**s** *pl. econ.* (Gesamt)Import *m*, (-)Einfuhr *f*; Importgüter *pl.*; **2.** [ɪmˈpɔːt] *econ.* importieren, einführen; bedeuten.

im·por|tance [ɪmˈpɔːtəns] Bedeutung *f*, Wichtigkeit *f*; ~**tant** □ [~t] bedeutend, wichtig; wichtigtuerisch.

im·por·ta·tion [ɪmpɔːˈteɪʃn] *s.* import 1 *econ.*

im·por|tu·nate □ [ɪmˈpɔːtjʊnət] lästig; zudringlich; ~**tune** [ɪmˈpɔːtjuːn] dringend bitten; belästigen.

im·pose [ɪmˈpəʊz] *v/t.* auferlegen, -bürden, -drängen, -zwingen (*on*, *upon dat.*); *v/i.* ~ *on*, ~ *upon* j-m imponieren, j-n beeindrucken; j-n ausnutzen; sich j-m aufdrängen; j-m zur Last fallen; **im·pos·ing** □ [~ɪŋ] imponierend, eindrucksvoll, imposant.

im·pos·si·bil·i·ty [ɪmpɒsəˈbɪlətɪ] Unmöglichkeit *f*; ~**ble** [ɪmˈpɒsəbl] unmöglich.

im·pos·tor [ɪmˈpɒstə] Betrüger *m.*

im·po|tence [ˈɪmpətəns] Unfähigkeit *f*; Hilflosigkeit *f*; Schwäche *f*; *⚕* Impotenz *f*; ~**tent** □ [~t] unfähig; hilflos; schwach; *⚕* impotent.

im·pov·er·ish [ɪmˈpɒvərɪʃ] arm machen; *Boden* auslaugen.

im·prac·ti·ca·ble □ [ɪmˈpræktɪkəbl] unbrauchbar; unpassierbar (*Straße*).

im·prac·ti·cal □ [ɪmˈpræktɪkl] unpraktisch; theoretisch; unbrauchbar.

im·preg|na·ble □ [ɪmˈpregnəbl] uneinnehmbar; ~**nate** [ˈɪmpregneɪt] *biol.* schwängern; *🜨* sättigen; ⊕ imprägnieren.

im·press [ɪmˈpres] (auf-, ein)drücken; (deutlich) klarmachen; einschärfen; j-n beeindrucken; j-n *mit et.* erfüllen; **im·pres·sion** [~ʃn] Eindruck *m*; *print.* Abdruck *m*; Abzug *m*; Auflage *f*; *be under the* ~ *that* den Eindruck haben, daß; **im·pres·sive** □ [~sɪv] eindrucksvoll.

im·print 1. [ɪmˈprɪnt] aufdrücken, -prägen; *fig.* einprägen (*on, in dat.*); **2.** [ˈɪmprɪnt] Eindruck *m*; Stempel *m* (*a. fig.*); *print.* Impressum *n*.

im·pris·on ʒ⁄ʒ [ɪmˈprɪzn] inhaftieren; **~ment** ʒ⁄ʒ [~mənt] Freiheitsstrafe *f*, Gefängnis(strafe *f*) *n*, Haft *f*.

im·prob·a·ble □ [ɪmˈprɒbəbl] unwahrscheinlich.

im·prop·er □ [ɪmˈprɒpə] ungeeignet, unpassend; unanständig, unschicklich (*Benehmen etc.*); ungenau.

im·pro·pri·e·ty [ɪmprəˈpraɪətɪ] Unschicklichkeit *f*.

im·prove [ɪmˈpruːv] *v/t.* verbessern; veredeln, -feinern; *v/i.* sich (ver)bessern; ~, *on, upon* übertreffen; **~ment** [~mənt] (Ver)Besserung *f*; Fortschritt *m* (*on, upon* gegenüber *dat.*).

im·pro·vise [ˈɪmprəvaɪz] improvisieren.

im·pru·dent □ [ɪmˈpruːdənt] unklug.

im·pu|dence [ˈɪmpjʊdəns] Unverschämtheit *f*, Frechheit *f*; **~dent** □ [~t] unverschämt, frech.

im·pulse [ˈɪmpʌls] Impuls *m*, (An-) Stoß *m*; *fig.* (An)Trieb *m*; **im·pul·sive** □ [ɪmˈpʌlsɪv] (an)treibend; *fig.* impulsiv.

im·pu·ni·ty [ɪmˈpjuːnətɪ] Straflosigkeit *f*; *with* ~ ungestraft.

im·pure □ [ɪmˈpjʊə] unrein (*a. eccl.*), schmutzig; verfälscht; *fig.* schlecht, unmoralisch.

im·pute [ɪmˈpjuːt] zuschreiben (*to dat.*); ~ *s.th.* zu j-m *od.* e-r Sache bezichtigen; j-m et. unterstellen.

in [ɪn] **1.** *prp.* in (*dat.*), innerhalb (*gen.*); an (*dat.*) (~ *the morning*, ~ *number*, ~ *itself*, *professor* ~ *the university*); auf (*dat.*) (~ *the street*, ~ *English*); auf (*acc.*) (~ *this manner*); aus (*coat* ~ *velvet*); bei (~ *Shakespeare*, ~ *crossing the road*); mit (*engaged* ~ *reading*, ~ *a word*); nach (~ *my opinion*); über (*acc.*) (*rejoice* ~ *s.th.*); unter (*dat.*) (~ *the circumstances*, ~ *the reign of, one* ~ *ten*); vor (*dat.*) (*cry out* ~ *alarm*); zu (*grouped* ~ *tens*, ~ *excuse*, ~ *honour of*); ~ *1989 1989*; *that* ... insofern als, weil; **2.** *adv.* innen, drinnen; herein; hinein; in; in Mode; *be* ~ *for et.* zu erwarten haben; *e-e Prüfung etc.* vor sich haben; *be* ~ *with* gut mit

j-m stehen; **3.** *adj.* hereinkommend; Innen...

in·a·bil·i·ty [ɪnəˈbɪlətɪ] Unfähigkeit *f*.

in·ac·ces·si·ble □ [ɪnækˈsesəbl] unzugänglich, unerreichbar (*to* für *od. dat.*).

in·ac·cu·rate □ [ɪnˈækjʊrət] ungenau; unrichtig.

in·ac|tive □ [ɪnˈæktɪv] untätig; *econ.* lustlos, flau; ⚗ unwirksam; **~tiv·i·ty** [ɪnækˈtɪvətɪ] Untätigkeit *f*; *econ.* Lustlosigkeit *f*, Flauheit *f*; ⚗ Unwirksamkeit *f*.

in·ad·e·quate □ [ɪnˈædɪkwət] unangemessen; unzulänglich, ungenügend.

in·ad·mis·si·ble □ [ɪnədˈmɪsəbl] unzulässig, unerlaubt.

in·ad·ver·tent □ [ɪnədˈvɜːtənt] unachtsam; unbeabsichtigt, versehentlich.

in·a·lie·na·ble □ [ɪnˈeɪljənəbl] unveräußerlich.

i·nane □ *fig.* [ɪˈneɪn] leer; albern.

in·an·i·mate □ [ɪnˈænɪmət] leblos; unbelebt (*Natur*); geistlos, langweilig.

in·ap·pro·pri·ate □ [ɪnəˈprəʊprɪət] unpassend, ungeeignet.

in·apt □ [ɪnˈæpt] ungeeignet, unpassend.

in·ar·tic·u·late □ [ɪnɑːˈtɪkjʊlət] unartikuliert, undeutlich (*ausgesprochen*), unverständlich; unfähig (, *deutlich*) zu sprechen.

in·as·much [ɪnəzˈmʌtʃ]: ~ *as* insofern als.

in·at·ten·tive □ [ɪnəˈtentɪv] unaufmerksam.

in·au·di·ble □ [ɪnˈɔːdəbl] unhörbar.

in·au·gu·ral [ɪˈnɔːgjʊrəl] Antrittsrede *f*; *attr.* Antritts...; **~rate** [~reɪt] (*feierlich*) einführen; einweihen; einleiten; **~ra·tion** [ɪnɔːgjʊˈreɪʃn] Amtseinführung *f*; Einweihung *f*; Beginn *m*; ♀ *Day Am.* Tag *m* der Amtseinführung des neugewählten Präsidenten der USA (*20. Januar*).

in·born [ˈɪnˈbɔːn] angeboren.

in·built [ˈɪnbɪlt] eingebaut, Einbau...

in·cal·cu·la·ble □ [ɪnˈkælkjʊləbl] unberechenbar.

in·can·des·cent □ [ɪnkænˈdesnt] (*weiß*)glühend.

in·ca·pa·ble □ [ɪnˈkeɪpəbl] unfähig, nicht imstande (*of doing* zu tun); hilflos.

J

in·ca·pa·ci|tate [ɪnkəˈpæsɪteɪt] unfähig machen; **~ty** [~sətɪ] Unfähigkeit f.

in·car·nate [ɪnˈkɑːnət] eccl. fleischgeworden; fig. verkörpert.

in·cau·tious ☐ [ɪnˈkɔːʃəs] unvorsichtig.

in·cen·di·a·ry [ɪnˈsendjərɪ] 1. Brand...; fig. aufwiegelnd, -hetzend; 2. Brandstifter m; Aufwiegler m.

in·cense[1] [ˈɪnsens] Weihrauch m.

in·cense[2] [ɪnˈsens] in Wut bringen.

in·cen·tive [ɪnˈsentɪv] Ansporn m, Antrieb m.

in·ces·sant ☐ [ɪnˈsesnt] unaufhörlich.

in·cest [ˈɪnsest] Inzest m, Blutschande f.

inch [ɪntʃ] 1. Inch m (= 2,54 cm), Zoll m (a. fig.); by ~es allmählich; every ~ durch u. durch; 2. (sich) zentimeterweise od. sehr langsam bewegen.

in·ci·dence [ˈɪnsɪdəns] Vorkommen n; **~dent** [~t] Vorfall m, Ereignis n, Vorkommnis n; **~den·tal** ☐ [ɪnsɪˈdentl] zufällig; gelegentlich; Neben...; beiläufig; **~ly** nebenbei.

in·cin·e|rate [ɪnˈsɪnəreɪt] verbrennen; **~ra·tor** [~ə] Verbrennungsofen m; Verbrennungsanlage f.

in·cise [ɪnˈsaɪz] ein-, aufschneiden; einritzen, -schnitzen; **in·ci·sion** [ɪnˈsɪʒn] (Ein)Schnitt m; **in·ci·sive** ☐ [ɪnˈsaɪsɪv] (ein)schneidend; scharf; **in·ci·sor** [~aɪzə] anat. Schneidezahn m.

in·cite [ɪnˈsaɪt] anspornen, anregen; anstiften; **~ment** [~mənt] Anregung f; Ansporn m; Anstiftung f.

in·clem·ent ☐ [ɪnˈklemənt] rauh (Klima).

in·cli·na·tion [ɪnklɪˈneɪʃn] Neigung f (a. fig.); **in·cline** [ɪnˈklaɪn] 1. v/i. sich neigen, (schräg) abfallen; ~ to fig. zu et. neigen; v/t. neigen; geneigt machen; 2. Gefälle n; (Ab)Hang m.

in·close [ɪnˈkləʊz], **in·clos·ure** [~əʊ-ʒə] s. enclose, enclosure.

in·clude [ɪnˈkluːd] einschließen; enthalten; **in·clud·ed** eingeschlossen; mit inbegriffen; tax ~ inklusive Steuer; **in·clud·ing** einschließlich; **in·clu·sion** [~ʒn] Einschluß m, Einbeziehung f; **in·clu·sive** ☐ [~sɪv] einschließlich, inklusive (of gen.); be ~ of einschließen (acc.); ~ terms pl. Pauschalpreis m.

in·co·her|ence [ɪnkəʊˈhɪərəns] Zu-

sammenhang(s)losigkeit f; **~ent** ☐ [~t] (logisch) unzusammenhängend, unklar, unverständlich.

in·come econ. [ˈɪnkʌm] Einkommen n, Einkünfte pl.; ~ tax econ. Einkommensteuer f.

in·com·ing [ˈɪnkʌmɪŋ] hereinkommend; ankommend; nachfolgend, neu; ~ orders pl. econ. Auftragseingänge pl.

in·com·mu·ni·ca·tive ☐ [ɪnkəˈmjuːnɪkətɪv] nicht mitteilsam, verschlossen.

in·com·pa·ra·ble ☐ [ɪnˈkɒmpərəbl] unvergleichlich.

in·com·pat·i·ble ☐ [ɪnkəmˈpætəbl] unvereinbar; unverträglich.

in·com·pe|tence [ɪnˈkɒmpɪtəns] Unfähigkeit f; Inkompetenz f; **~tent** ☐ [~t] unfähig; nicht fach- od. sachkundig; unzuständig, inkompetent.

in·com·plete ☐ [ɪnkəmˈpliːt] unvollständig; unvollkommen.

in·com·pre·hen·si·ble ☐ [ɪnkɒmprɪˈhensəbl] unbegreiflich, unfaßbar; **~sion** [~ʃn] Unverständnis n.

in·con·cei·va·ble ☐ [ɪnkənˈsiːvəbl] unbegreiflich, unfaßbar; undenkbar.

in·con·clu·sive ☐ [ɪnkənˈkluːsɪv] nicht überzeugend; ergebnis-, erfolglos.

in·con·gru·ous ☐ [ɪnˈkɒŋɡruəs] nicht übereinstimmend; nicht passend.

in·con·se|quent ☐ [ɪnˈkɒnsɪkwənt] inkonsequent, folgewidrig; **~quen·tial** ☐ [ɪnkɒnsɪˈkwenʃl] unbedeutend.

in·con·sid·e|ra·ble ☐ [ɪnkənˈsɪdərəbl] unbedeutend; **~er·ate** ☐ [~rət] unüberlegt; rücksichtslos.

in·con·sis|ten·cy [ɪnkənˈsɪstənsɪ] Unvereinbarkeit f; Inkonsequenz f; **~tent** ☐ [~t] unvereinbar; widersprüchlich; unbeständig; inkonsequent.

in·con·so·la·ble ☐ [ɪnkənˈsəʊləbl] untröstlich.

in·con·spic·u·ous ☐ [ɪnkənˈspɪkjʊəs] unauffällig.

in·con·stant ☐ [ɪnˈkɒnstənt] unbeständig, veränderlich.

in·con·ti·nent ☐ [ɪnˈkɒntɪnənt] zügellos; 🞲 inkontinent.

in·con·ve·ni·ence [ɪnkənˈviːnjəns] 1. Unbequemlichkeit f; Unannehmlichkeit f; 2. belästigen, stören;

~ent □ [~t] unbequem; ungelegen, lästig.

in·cor·po·rate [ɪn'kɔːpəreɪt] (sich) verbinden *od.* -vereinigen *od.* zusammenschließen; *Idee etc.* einverleiben; aufnehmen, eingliedern, inkorporieren; *econ.*, ᵗᵗᵗ als Gesellschaft eintragen (lassen); **~rat·ed** *econ.*, ᵗᵗᵗ als (*Am.* Aktien)Gesellschaft eingetragen; **~ra·tion** [ɪnkɔː-pə'reɪʃn] Vereinigung *f*, -bindung *f*, Zusammenschluß *m*; Eingliederung *f*; *econ.*, ᵗᵗᵗ Eintragung *f* als (*Am.* Aktien)Gesellschaft.

in·cor·rect □ [ɪnkə'rekt] unrichtig, falsch; inkorrekt.

in·cor·ri·gi·ble □ [ɪn'kɒrɪdʒəbl] unverbesserlich.

in·cor·rup·ti·ble □ [ɪnkə'rʌptəbl] unbestechlich; unvergänglich.

in·crease 1. [ɪn'kriːs] zunehmen, (an)wachsen, (an)steigen, (sich) vergrößern *od.* -mehren *od.* erhöhen *od.* steigern *od.* verstärken; **2.** ['ɪnkriːs] Zunahme *f*, Vergrößerung *f*; (An-)Wachsen *n*, Steigen *n*, Steigerung *f*; Zuwachs *m*; **in·creas·ing·ly** [ɪn-'kriːsɪŋlɪ] zunehmend, immer mehr; **~** *difficult* immer schwieriger.

in·cred·i·ble □ [ɪn'kredəbl] unglaublich, unglaubhaft.

in·cre·du·li·ty [ɪnkrɪ'djuːlətɪ] Ungläubigkeit *f*; **in·cred·u·lous** □ [ɪn-'kredjʊləs] ungläubig, skeptisch.

in·crim·i·nate [ɪn'krɪmɪneɪt] beschuldigen; *j-n* belasten.

in·cu·bate ['ɪnkjʊbeɪt] ausbrüten; **~·ba·tor** [~ə] Brutapparat *m*; Brutkasten *m*.

in·cum·bent □ [ɪn'kʌmbənt] obliegend; *it is ~* on *her* es ist ihre Pflicht.

in·cur [ɪn'kɜː] (-*rr*-) sich *et.* zuziehen, auf sich laden, geraten in (*acc.*); *Schulden* machen; *Verpflichtung* eingehen; *Verlust* erleiden.

in·cu·ra·ble □ [ɪn'kjʊərəbl] unheilbar.

in·cu·ri·ous □ [ɪn'kjʊərɪəs] nicht neugierig, gleichgültig, uninteressiert.

in·cur·sion [ɪn'kɜːʃn] (feindlicher) Einfall; plötzlicher Angriff; Eindringen *n*.

in·debt·ed [ɪn'detɪd] *econ.* verschuldet; *fig.* (zu Dank) verpflichtet.

in·de·cent □ [ɪn'diːsnt] unanständig, anstößig; ᵗᵗᵗ unsittlich, unzüchtig; **~** *assault* ᵗᵗᵗ Sittlichkeitsverbrechen *n*.

in·de·ci|sion [ɪndɪ'sɪʒn] Unentschlossenheit *f*; **~·sive** □ [~'saɪsɪv] unbestimmt, ungewiß; unentschlossen, unschlüssig.

in·deed [ɪn'diːd] **1.** *adv.* in der Tat, tatsächlich, wirklich; allerdings; *thank you very much ~!* vielen herzlichen Dank!; **2.** *int.* ach! wirklich!

in·de·fat·i·ga·ble □ [ɪndɪ'fætɪgəbl] unermüdlich.

in·de·fen·si·ble □ [ɪndɪ'fensəbl] unhaltbar.

in·de·fi·na·ble □ [ɪndɪ'faɪnəbl] undefinierbar, unbestimmbar.

in·def·i·nite □ [ɪn'defɪnət] unbestimmt; unbegrenzt; unklar.

in·del·i·ble □ [ɪn'delɪbl] unauslöschlich, untilgbar; *fig.* unvergeßlich; **~** *pencil* Kopier-, Tintenstift *m.*

in·del·i·cate [ɪn'delɪkət] unfein, derb; taktlos.

in·dem·ni|fy [ɪn'demnɪfaɪ] *j-n* entschädigen (*for* für); versichern; ᵗᵗᵗ *j-m* Straflosigkeit zusichern; **~·ty** [~ətɪ] Schadenersatz *m*, Entschädigung *f*, Abfindung *f*; Versicherung *f*; ᵗᵗᵗ Straflosigkeit *f*.

in·dent [ɪn'dent] einkerben, auszacken; *print.* Zeile einrücken; ᵗᵗᵗ Vertrag mit Doppel ausfertigen; **~** *on s.o. for s.th. bsd. Brt. econ.* et. bei *j-m* bestellen.

in·den·tures *econ.*, ᵗᵗᵗ [ɪn'dentʃəz] *pl.* Ausbildungs-, Lehrvertrag *m.*

in·de·pen|dence [ɪndɪ'pendəns] Unabhängigkeit *f*; Selbständigkeit *f*; Auskommen *n*; *♀ Day Am.* Unabhängigkeitstag *m* (4. *Juli*); **~·dent** □ [~t] unabhängig; selbständig.

in·de·scri·ba·ble □ [ɪndɪ'skraɪbəbl] unbeschreiblich.

in·de·struc·ti·ble □ [ɪndɪ'strʌktəbl] unzerstörbar; unverwüstlich.

in·de·ter·mi·nate □ [ɪndɪ'tɜːmɪnət] unbestimmt; unklar, vage.

in·dex ['ɪndeks] **1.** (*pl.* -*dexes*, -*dices* [-disiːz])(Inhalts-, Namens-, Sach-, Stichwort)Verzeichnis *n*, Register *n*, Index *m*; Index-, Meßziffer *f*; ⊕ Zeiger *m*; Anzeichen *n*; *cost of living* **~** Lebenshaltungskosten-Index *m*; **2.** mit e-m Inhaltsverzeichnis versehen; in ein Verzeichnis aufnehmen; **~** *card* Karteikarte *f*; **~** *fin·ger* Zeigefinger *m.*

In·di·an ['ɪndjən] **1.** indisch; indianisch, Indianer...; **2.** Inder(in); *a.* American **~**, Red **~** Indianer(in);

I J

~ corn ♀ Mais *m*; **~ file:** *in* ~ im Gänsemarsch; **~ pud·ding** Maismehlpudding *m*; **~ sum·mer** Altweiber-, Nachsommer *m*.

In·di·a rub·ber, in·di·a-rub·ber ['ɪndjə'rʌbə] Radiergummi *m*; *attr.* Gummi...

in·di·cate ['ɪndɪkeɪt] (an)zeigen; hinweisen *od.* -deuten auf (*acc.*); andeuten; *mot.* blinken; **~·ca·tion** [ɪndɪ-'keɪʃn] (An)Zeichen *n*, Hinweis *m*, Andeutung *f*; **in·dic·a·tive** [ɪn'dɪkətɪv] *a.* ~ *mood* *gr.* Indikativ *m*; **~·ca·tor** ['ɪndɪkeɪtə] (An)Zeiger *m*; *mot.* Richtungsanzeiger *m*, Blinker *m*.

in·di·ces ['ɪndɪsiːz] *pl. von* index.

in·dict [ɪn'daɪt] anklagen (*for* wegen); **~·ment** ᵗᵗ [~mənt] Anklage *f*.

in·dif·fer|ence [ɪn'dɪfrəns] Gleichgültigkeit *f*, Interesselosigkeit *f*; **~ent** □ [~t] gleichgültig (*to* gegen), interesselos (*to* gegenüber); durchschnittlich, mittelmäßig.

in·di·gent □ [ɪn'dɪdʒənt] arm.

in·di·ges|ti·ble □ [ɪndɪ'dʒestəbl] unverdaulich; **~tion** [~tʃən] Verdauungsstörung *f*, Magenverstimmung *f*.

in·dig·nant □ [ɪn'dɪgnənt] entrüstet, empört, ungehalten (*at, over, about* über *acc.*); **~·na·tion** [ɪndɪg'neɪʃn] Entrüstung *f*, Empörung *f* (*at, over, about* über *acc.*); **~·ni·ty** [ɪn'dɪgnəti] Demütigung *f*, unwürdige Behandlung.

in·di·rect □ [ɪndɪ'rekt] indirekt (*a. gr.*); *by* ~ *means* auf Umwegen.

in·dis|creet □ [ɪndɪ'skriːt] unbesonnen; taktlos; indiskret; **~cre·tion** [~reʃn] Unbesonnenheit *f*; Taktlosigkeit *f*; Indiskretion *f*.

in·dis·crim·i·nate □ [ɪndɪ'skrɪmɪnət] unterschieds-, wahllos; willkürlich.

in·dis·pen·sa·ble □ [ɪndɪ'spensəbl] unentbehrlich, unerläßlich.

in·dis|posed [ɪndɪ'spəʊzd] indisponiert; unpäßlich; abgeneigt; **~·po·si·tion** [ɪndɪspə'zɪʃn] Abneigung *f* (*to* gegen); Unpäßlichkeit *f*.

in·dis·pu·ta·ble □ [ɪndɪ'spjuːtəbl] unbestreitbar, unstreitig.

in·dis·tinct □ [ɪndɪ'stɪŋkt] undeutlich; unklar, verschwommen.

in·dis·tin·guish·a·ble □ [ɪndɪ'stɪŋgwɪʃəbl] nicht zu unterscheiden(d).

in·di·vid·u·al [ɪndɪ'vɪdjʊəl] **1.** □ persönlich; individuell; besondere(r, -s); einzeln, Einzel...; **2.** Individuum *n*, Einzelne(r *m*) *f*; **~·is·m** [~ɪzəm] Individualismus *m*; **~·ist** [~ɪst] Individualist(in); **~·i·ty** [ɪndɪvɪdjʊ'ælɪtɪ] Individualität *f*, (persönliche) Note; **~·ly** [ɪndɪ'vɪdjʊəlɪ] einzeln, jede(r, -s) für sich.

in·di·vis·i·ble □ [ɪndɪ'vɪzəbl] unteilbar.

in·do·lent □ ['ɪndələnt] träge, faul, arbeitsscheu; ᵍ schmerzlos.

in·dom·i·ta·ble □ [ɪn'dɒmɪtəbl] unbezähmbar, nicht unterzukriegen(d).

in·door ['ɪndɔː] zu *od.* im Hause (befindlich), Haus..., Zimmer..., Innen..., *Sport:* Hallen...; **~s** ['ɪn'dɔːz] zu *od.* im Hause; im *od.* ins Haus.

in·dorse [ɪn'dɔːs] = endorse *etc.*

in·duce [ɪn'djuːs] veranlassen; hervorrufen, bewirken; **~·ment** [~mənt] Anlaß *m*; Anreiz *m*, Ansporn *m*.

in·duct [ɪn'dʌkt] einführen, -setzen; **in·duc·tion** [~kʃn] Einführung *f*, Einsetzung *f* (*in Amt, Pfründe*); ᵋ Induktion *f*.

in·dulge [ɪn'dʌldʒ] nachsichtig sein gegen, gewähren lassen, *j-m* nachgeben; ~ *in s.th.* sich et. gönnen *od.* leisten; **in·dul·gence** [~əns] Nachsicht *f*, Nachgiebigkeit *f*; Schwäche *f*, Leidenschaft *f*; **in·dul·gent** □ [~nt] nachsichtig, -giebig.

in·dus·tri·al □ [ɪn'dʌstrɪəl] industriell, Industrie..., Gewerbe..., Betriebs...; ~ *area* Industriegebiet *n*; **~·ist** *econ.* [~əlɪst] Industrielle(r *m*) *f*; **~·ize** *econ.* [~əlaɪz] industrialisieren.

in·dus·tri·ous □ [ɪn'dʌstrɪəs] fleißig; △ *nicht* Industrie...

in·dus·try ['ɪndəstrɪ] *econ.* Industrie (-zweig *m*) *f*; Gewerbe(zweig *m*) *n*; Fleiß *m*.

in·ed·i·ble □ [ɪn'edɪbl] ungenießbar, nicht eßbar.

in·ef·fa·ble □ [ɪn'efəbl] unaussprechlich, unbeschreiblich.

in·ef·fec|tive □ [ɪnɪ'fektɪv], **~·tu·al** □ [~tʃʊəl] unwirksam, wirkungslos; untauglich.

in·ef·fi·cient □ [ɪnɪ'fɪʃnt] unfähig, untauglich; leistungsschwach, unproduktiv.

in·el·e·gant □ [ɪn'elɪgənt] unelegant; schwerfällig.

in·el·i·gi·ble □ [ɪn'elɪdʒəbl] nicht

wählbar; ungeeignet; nicht berechtigt; *bsd.* ⚔ untauglich.

in·ept ☐ [ɪˈnept] unpassend; ungeschickt; albern, töricht.

in·e·qual·i·ty [ɪnɪˈkwɒlətɪ] Ungleichheit *f*.

in·ert ☐ [ɪˈnɜːt] *phys.* träge (*a. fig.*); 🜍 inaktiv; **in·er·tia** [ɪˈnɜːʃjə] Trägheit *f* (*a. fig.*).

in·es·ca·pa·ble [ɪnɪˈskeɪpəbl] unvermeidlich.

in·es·sen·tial [ɪnɪˈsenʃl] unwesentlich, unwichtig (*to* für).

in·es·ti·ma·ble ☐ [ɪnˈestɪməbl] unschätzbar.

in·ev·i·ta·ble ☐ [ɪnˈevɪtəbl] unvermeidlich; zwangsläufig.

in·ex·act ☐ [ɪnɪɡˈzækt] ungenau.

in·ex·cu·sa·ble ☐ [ɪnɪkˈskjuːzəbl] unverzeihlich, unentschuldbar.

in·ex·haus·ti·ble ☐ [ɪnɪɡˈzɔːstəbl] unerschöpflich; unermüdlich.

in·ex·o·ra·ble ☐ [ɪnˈeksərəbl] unerbittlich.

in·ex·pe·di·ent ☐ [ɪnɪkˈspiːdjənt] unzweckmäßig; nicht ratsam.

in·ex·pen·sive ☐ [ɪnɪkˈspensɪv] nicht teuer, billig, preiswert.

in·ex·pe·ri·ence [ɪnɪkˈspɪərɪəns] Unerfahrenheit *f*; **~d** unerfahren.

in·ex·pert ☐ [ɪnˈekspɜːt] unerfahren; ungeschickt.

in·ex·plic·a·ble ☐ [ɪnɪkˈsplɪkəbl] unerklärlich.

in·ex·pres·si·ble ☐ [ɪnɪkˈspresəbl] unaussprechlich, unbeschreiblich; **~ve** [~sɪv] ausdruckslos.

in·ex·tri·ca·ble ☐ [ɪnˈekstrɪkəbl] unentwirrbar.

in·fal·li·ble ☐ [ɪnˈfæləbl] unfehlbar.

in·fa|mous ☐ [ˈɪnfəməs] berüchtigt; schändlich, niederträchtig; **~my** [~ɪ] Ehrlosigkeit *f*; Schande *f*; Niedertracht *f*.

in·fan|cy [ˈɪnfənsɪ] frühe Kindheit; 🏛 Minderjährigkeit *f*; *in its ~ fig.* in den Anfängen *od.* Kinderschuhen steckend; **~t** [~t] Säugling *m*; Kleinkind *n*; 🏛 Minderjährige(r *m*) *f*.

in·fan·tile [ˈɪnfəntaɪl] kindlich; Kindes..., Kinder...; infantil, kindisch.

in·fan·try ⚔ [ˈɪnfəntrɪ] Infanterie *f*.

in·fat·u·at·ed [ɪnˈfætjʊeɪtɪd] vernarrt (*with* in *acc.*).

in·fect [ɪnˈfekt] 🜍 *j-n*, *et.* infizieren, *j-n* anstecken (*a. fig.*); verseuchen, -unreinigen; **in·fec·tion** [~kʃn] 🜍 Infektion *f*, Ansteckung *f* (*a. fig.*);

in·fec·tious ☐ [~kʃəs] 🜍 infektiös, ansteckend (*a. fig.*).

in·fer [ɪnˈfɜː] (-*rr*-) folgern, schließen (*from* aus); **~ence** [ˈɪnfərəns] (Schluß)Folgerung *f*.

in·fe·ri·or [ɪnˈfɪərɪə] **1.** (*to*) untergeordnet (*dat.*), (*im Rang*) tieferstehend, niedriger, geringer (als); minderwertig; *be ~ to s.o.* j-m untergeordnet sein; *j-m* unterlegen sein; **2.** Untergebene(r *m*) *f*; **~i·ty** [ɪnfɪərɪˈɒrɪtɪ] Unterlegenheit *f*; geringerer Wert *od.* Stand, Minderwertigkeit *f*; ~ *complex psych.* Minderwertigkeitskomplex *m*.

in·fer|nal ☐ [ɪnˈfɜːnl] höllisch, Höllen...; **~no** [~əʊ] (*pl. -nos*) Inferno *n*, Hölle *f*.

in·fer·tile [ɪnˈfɜːtaɪl] unfruchtbar.

in·fest [ɪnˈfest] heimsuchen; verseuchen, befallen; *fig.* überschwemmen (*with* mit).

in·fi·del·i·ty [ɪnfɪˈdelətɪ] (*bsd.* eheliche) Untreue.

in·fil·trate [ˈɪnfɪltreɪt] *v/t.* eindringen in (*acc.*); einsickern in (*acc.*), durchdringen; *pol.* unterwandern; *pol.* einschleusen; *v/i.* eindringen (*into* in *acc.*); *pol.* unterwandern (*into* in *acc.*), sich einschleusen (*into* in *acc.*).

in·fi·nite ☐ [ˈɪnfɪnət] unendlich.

in·fin·i·tive [ɪnˈfɪnɪtɪv] *a.* ~ *mood gr.* Infinitiv *m*, Nennform *f*.

in·fin·i·ty [ɪnˈfɪnətɪ] Unendlichkeit *f*.

in·firm ☐ [ɪnˈfɜːm] schwach; gebrechlich; **in·fir·ma·ry** [~ərɪ] Krankenhaus *n*; Krankenstube *f*, -zimmer *n* (*in Internaten etc.*); **in·fir·mi·ty** [~ətɪ] Schwäche *f* (*a. fig.*); Gebrechlichkeit *f*.

in·flame [ɪnˈfleɪm] entflammen (*mst fig.*); 🜍 (sich) entzünden; erregen; erzürnen.

in·flam·ma|ble [ɪnˈflæməbl] leicht entzündlich; feuergefährlich; **~tion** 🜍 [ɪnfləˈmeɪʃn] Entzündung *f*; **~to·ry** [ɪnˈflæmətərɪ] 🜍 entzündlich; *fig.* aufrührerisch, Hetz...

in·flate [ɪnˈfleɪt] aufpumpen, -blasen, -blähen (*a. fig.*); *econ.* Preise etc. in die Höhe treiben; **in·fla·tion** [~ʃn] Aufblähung *f*; *econ.* Inflation *f*.

in·flect *gr.* [ɪnˈflekt] flektieren, beugen; **in·flec·tion** [~kʃn] = *inflexion*.

in·flex·i·ble ☐ [ɪnˈfleksəbl] unbiegsam, starr (*a. fig.*); *fig.* unbeugsam;

~·ion *bsd. Brt.* [~kʃn] *gr.* Flexion *f*, Beugung *f*; ♪ Modulation *f*.

in·flict [ɪnˈflɪkt] (*on, upon*) Leid *etc.* zufügen (*dat.*); *Wunde etc.* beibringen (*dat.*); *Schlag* versetzen (*dat.*); *Strafe* verhängen (über *acc.*); aufbürden, -drängen (*dat.*); **in·flic·tion** [~kʃn] Zufügung *f*; Verhängung *f* (*e-r Strafe*); Plage *f*.

in·flu·ence [ˈɪnflʊəns] **1.** Einfluß *m*; **2.** beeinflussen; **~·en·tial** □ [ɪnflʊˈenʃl] einflußreich.

in·flu·en·za [ɪnflʊˈenzə] Grippe *f*.

in·flux [ˈɪnflʌks] Einströmen *n*; *econ.* (*Waren*)Zufuhr *f*; *fig.* (Zu)Strom *m*.

in·form [ɪnˈfɔːm] benachrichtigen, unterrichten (*of* von), informieren (*of* über *acc.*); ~ *against od. on od. upon s.o.* j-n anzeigen; j-n denunzieren.

in·for·mal □ [ɪnˈfɔːml] formlos, zwanglos; **~·i·ty** [ɪnfɔːˈmælətɪ] Formlosigkeit *f*; Ungezwungenheit *f*.

in·for·ma·tion [ɪnfəˈmeɪʃn] Auskunft *f*; Nachricht *f*; Information *f*; ~ *storage Computer*: Datenspeicherung *f*; **~·tive** [ɪnˈfɔːmətɪv] informativ; lehrreich; mitteilsam.

in·form·er [ɪnˈfɔːmə] Denunziant(in); Spitzel *m*.

in·fre·quent □ [ɪnˈfriːkwənt] selten.

in·fringe [ɪnˈfrɪndʒ]: ~ *on*, ~ *upon Rechte, Vertrag etc.* verletzen.

in·fu·ri·ate [ɪnˈfjʊərɪeɪt] wütend machen.

in·fuse [ɪnˈfjuːz] *Tee* aufgießen; *fig.* einflößen; *fig.* erfüllen (*with* mit); **in·fu·sion** [~ʒn] Aufguß *m*, Tee *m*; Einflößen *n*; ♪ Infusion *f*.

in·ge·ni·ous □ [ɪnˈdʒiːnjəs] genial, geist-, sinnreich; erfinderisch; raffiniert; **~·nu·i·ty** [ɪnˈdʒɪˈnjuːətɪ] Genialität *f*; Einfallsreichtum *m*.

in·gen·u·ous □ [ɪnˈdʒenjʊəs] offen, aufrichtig; unbefangen; naiv.

in·got [ˈɪŋgət] (*Gold- etc.*)Barren *m*.

in·gra·ti·ate [ɪnˈgreɪʃɪeɪt]: ~ *o.s. with s.o.* sich bei j-m beliebt machen.

in·grat·i·tude [ɪnˈgrætɪtjuːd] Undankbarkeit *f*.

in·gre·di·ent [ɪnˈgriːdjənt] Bestandteil *m*; *Küche*: Zutat *f*.

in·grow·ing [ˈɪngrəʊɪŋ] nach innen wachsend; eingewachsen.

in·hab·it [ɪnˈhæbɪt] bewohnen, leben in (*dat.*); **~·it·a·ble** [~əbl] bewohn-

bar; **~·i·tant** [~ənt] Bewohner(in); Einwohner(in).

in·hale [ɪnˈheɪl] einatmen, ♪ *a.* inhalieren.

in·her·ent □ [ɪnˈhɪərənt] anhaftend; innewohnend, angeboren, eigen (*in dat.*).

in·her·it [ɪnˈherɪt] erben; **~·i·tance** [~əns] Erbe *n*, Erbschaft *f*; *biol.* Vererbung *f*.

in·hib·it [ɪnˈhɪbɪt] hemmen (*a. psych.*), hindern; **~ed** *psych.* gehemmt; **in·hi·bi·tion** *psych.* [ɪnhɪˈbɪʃn] Hemmung *f*.

in·hos·pi·ta·ble □ [ɪnˈhɒspɪtəbl] ungastlich; unwirtlich (*Gegend etc.*).

in·hu·man □ [ɪnˈhjuːmən] unmenschlich; **~e** □ [ɪnhjuːˈmeɪn] inhuman; menschenunwürdig.

in·im·i·cal □ [ɪˈnɪmɪkl] feindselig (*to* gegen); nachteilig (*to* für).

in·im·i·ta·ble □ [ɪˈnɪmɪtəbl] unnachahmlich.

i·ni·tial [ɪˈnɪʃl] **1.** □ anfänglich, Anfangs...; **2.** Initiale *f*, (großer) Anfangsbuchstabe; **~·tial·ly** [~əlɪ] am *od.* zu Anfang; **~·ti·ate 1.** [~ʃɪət] Eingeweihte(r *m*) *f*; **2.** [~ʃɪeɪt] beginnen, in die Wege leiten; einführen, einweihen; aufnehmen; **~·ti·a·tion** [ɪnɪʃɪˈeɪʃn] Einführung *f*; Aufnahme *f*; ~ *fee bsd. Am.* Aufnahmegebühr *f* (*Vereinigung*); **~·tia·tive** [ɪˈnɪʃɪətɪv] Initiative *f*; erster Schritt; Entschlußkraft *f*, Unternehmungsgeist *m*; *take the ~* die Initiative ergreifen; *on one's own ~* aus eigenem Antrieb.

in·ject ♪ [ɪnˈdʒekt] injizieren, einspritzen; **in·jec·tion** ♪ [~kʃn] Injektion *f*, Spritze *f*.

in·ju·di·cious □ [ɪndʒuːˈdɪʃəs] unklug, unüberlegt.

in·junc·tion [ɪnˈdʒʌŋkʃn] ♪♩ gerichtliche Verfügung *f*; ausdrücklicher Befehl.

in·jure [ˈɪndʒə] verletzen, -wunden; (be)schädigen; schaden (*dat.*); kränken; **in·ju·ri·ous** □ [ɪnˈdʒʊərɪəs] schädlich; beleidigend; *be ~ to* schaden (*dat.*); ~ *to health* gesundheitsschädlich; **in·ju·ry** [ˈɪndʒərɪ] ♪ Verletzung *f*; Unrecht *n*; Schaden *m*; Kränkung *f*.

in·jus·tice [ɪnˈdʒʌstɪs] Ungerechtigkeit *f*; Unrecht *n*; *do s.o. an ~* j-m unrecht tun.

ink [ɪŋk] Tinte *f*; *mst printer's ~*

Druckerschwärze f; attr. Tinten...

ink·ling ['ɪŋklɪŋ] Andeutung f; dunkle od. leise Ahnung.

ink|pad ['ɪŋkpæd] Stempelkissen n; **~·y** [~ɪ] (-ier, -iest) voll Tinte, Tinten...; tinten-, pechschwarz.

in·laid ['ɪnleɪd] eingelegt, Einlege...; **~ work** Einlegearbeit f.

in·land 1. adj. ['ɪnlənd] inländisch, einheimisch; Binnen...; **2.** [~] das Landesinnere; Binnenland n. **3.** adv. [ɪn'lænd] landeinwärts; **~ rev·e·nue** Brt. Steuereinnahmen pl.; ♀ **Rev·e·nue** Brt. Finanzamt n.

in·lay ['ɪnleɪ] Einlegearbeit f; (Zahn-) Füllung f, Plombe f.

in·let ['ɪnlet] Meeresarm m; Flußarm m; ⊕ Einlaß m.

in·mate ['ɪnmeɪt] Insass|e m, -in f; Mitbewohner(in).

in·most ['ɪnməʊst] = innermost.

inn [ɪn] Gasthaus n, Wirtshaus n.

in·nate □ ['ɪ'neɪt] angeboren.

in·ner ['ɪnə] innere(r, -s); Innen...; verborgen; **~·most** innerste(r,-s) (a. fig.).

in·nings ['ɪnɪŋz] (pl. innings) Krikket, Baseball: Spielzeit f (e-s Spielers od. e-r Mannschaft).

inn·keep·er ['ɪnki:pə] Gastwirt(in).

in·no|cence ['ɪnəsns] Unschuld f; Harmlosigkeit f; Naivität f; **~·cent** [~t] **1.** □ unschuldig; harmlos; arglos, naiv; **2.** Unschuldige(r m) f; Einfältige(r m) f.

in·noc·u·ous □ [ɪ'nɒkjʊəs] harmlos.

in·no·va·tion [ɪnəʊ'veɪʃn] Neuerung f.

in·nu·en·do [ɪnju:'endəʊ] (pl. -does, -dos) (versteckte) Andeutung.

in·nu·me·ra·ble □ [ɪ'nju:mərəbl] unzählig, zahllos.

i·noc·u|late ♣ [ɪ'nɒkjʊleɪt] (ein)impfen; **~·la·tion** ♣ [ɪnɒkjʊ'leɪʃn] Impfung f.

in·of·fen·sive □ [ɪnə'fensɪv] harmlos.

in·op·e·ra·ble □ [ɪn'ɒpərəbl] ♣ inoperabel, nicht operierbar; undurchführbar (Plan etc.).

in·op·por·tune □ [ɪn'ɒpətju:n] inopportun, unangebracht, ungelegen.

in·or·di·nate □ [ɪ'nɔ:dɪnət] unmäßig.

in-pa·tient ♣ ['ɪnpeɪʃnt] stationärer Patient, stationäre Patientin.

in·put ['ɪnpʊt] Input m: econ. (von außen bezogene) Produktionsmittel pl.; Arbeitsaufwand m; Energiezufuhr f; ⚡ Eingang m (an Geräten); Computer: (Daten- od. Programm-) Eingabe f.

in·quest ☆ ['ɪnkwest] gerichtliche Untersuchung; coroner's **~** s. coroner.

in·quire [ɪn'kwaɪə] fragen od. sich erkundigen (nach); **~ into** untersuchen; **in·quir·ing** □ [~rɪŋ] forschend; wißbegierig; **in·quir·y** [~rɪ] Erkundigung f, Nachfrage f; Untersuchung f; Ermittlung f; make inquiries Erkundigungen einziehen.

in·qui·si·tion [ɪnkwɪ'zɪʃn] ☆ Untersuchung f; Verhör n; eccl. hist. Inquisition f; **in·quis·i·tive** □ [ɪn'kwɪzətɪv] neugierig; wißbegierig.

in·road fig. ['ɪnrəʊd] (into, on) Eingriff m (in acc.); übermäßige Inanspruchnahme (gen.).

in·sane □ [ɪn'seɪn] geisteskrank, wahnsinnig.

in·san·i·ta·ry [ɪn'sænɪtərɪ] unhygienisch.

in·san·i·ty [ɪn'sænətɪ] Geisteskrankheit f, Wahnsinn m.

in·sa·tia·ble □ [ɪn'seɪʃjəbl] unersättlich.

in·scribe [ɪn'skraɪb] (ein-, auf-) schreiben, einmeißeln, -ritzen; Buch mit e-r Widmung versehen.

in·scrip·tion [ɪn'skrɪpʃn] In-, Aufschrift f; Widmung f.

in·scru·ta·ble □ [ɪn'skru:təbl] unerforschlich, unergründlich.

in·sect zo. ['ɪnsekt] Insekt n, Kerbtier n; **in·sec·ti·cide** [ɪn'sektɪsaɪd] Insektenvertilgungsmittel n, Insektizid n.

in·se·cure □ [ɪnsɪ'kjʊə] unsicher; nicht sicher od. fest.

in·sen·si|ble □ [ɪn'sensəbl] unempfindlich (to gegen); bewußtlos; unmerklich; gefühllos, gleichgültig; **~·tive** [~sətɪv] unempfindlich, gefühllos (to gegen); unempfänglich.

in·sep·a·ra·ble □ [ɪn'sepərəbl] untrennbar; unzertrennlich.

in·sert 1. [ɪn'sɜ:t] einfügen, -setzen, -führen, (hinein)stecken; Münze einwerfen; inserieren; **2.** [~] Bei-, Einlage f; **in·ser·tion** [ɪn'sɜ:ʃn] Einfügen n, -setzen n, -führen n, Hineinstecken n; Einfügung f; Einwurf m (e-r Münze); Anzeige f, Inserat n.

in·shore ['ɪn'ʃɔː] an *od.* nahe der Küste; Küsten...

in·side ['ɪn'saɪd] **1.** Innenseite *f*; *das* Innere; *turn* ~ *out* umkrempeln; auf den Kopf stellen; **2.** *adj.* innere(r, -s), Innen...; Insider...; **3.** *adv.* im Innern, (dr)innen; ~ *of a week* F innerhalb e-r Woche; in; in ... (hinein); **in·sid·er** [~ə] Eingeweihte(r *m*) *f*, Insider *m*.

in·sid·i·ous □ ['ɪn'sɪdɪəs] heimtückisch.

in·sight □ ['ɪnsaɪt] Einsicht *f*, Einblick *m*; Verständnis *n*.

in·sig·ni·a [ɪn'sɪgnɪə] *pl.* Insignien *pl.*; Abzeichen *pl.*

in·sig·nif·i·cant [ɪnsɪg'nɪfɪkənt] bedeutungslos; unbedeutend.

in·sin·cere □ [ɪnsɪn'sɪə] unaufrichtig.

in·sin·u·ate [ɪn'sɪnjʊeɪt] andeuten, anspielen auf (*acc.*); ~·**a·tion** [ɪnsɪnjʊ'eɪʃn] Anspielung *f*, Andeutung *f*.

in·sip·id □ [ɪn'sɪpɪd] geschmacklos, fad.

in·sist [ɪn'sɪst] bestehen, beharren (*on*, *upon* auf *dat.*); **in·sis·tence** [~əns] Bestehen *n*, Beharren *n*; Beharrlichkeit *f*; **in·sis·tent** □ [~t] beharrlich, hartnäckig.

in·so·lent □ ['ɪnsələnt] unverschämt.

in·sol·u·ble □ [ɪn'sɒljʊbl] unlöslich; unlösbar (*Problem etc.*).

in·sol·vent [ɪn'sɒlvənt] zahlungsunfähig, insolvent.

in·som·ni·a [ɪn'sɒmnɪə] Schlaflosigkeit *f*.

in·spect [ɪn'spekt] untersuchen, prüfen, nachsehen; besichtigen, inspizieren; **in·spec·tion** [~kʃn] Prüfung *f*, Untersuchung *f*, Kontrolle *f*; Inspektion *f*; **in·spec·tor** [~ktə] Aufsichtsbeamte(r) *m*, Inspektor *m*; (Polizei)Inspektor *m*, (-)Kommissar *m*.

in·spi·ra·tion [ɪnspə'reɪʃn] Inspiration *f*, Eingebung *f*; **in·spire** [ɪn'spaɪə] inspirieren; hervorrufen; *Hoffnung etc.* wecken; *Respekt etc.* einflößen.

in·stall [ɪn'stɔːl] ⊕ installieren, einrichten, aufstellen, einbauen, *Leitung* legen; *in ein Amt etc.* einsetzen; **in·stal·la·tion** [ɪnstə'leɪʃn] ⊕ Installation *f*, Einrichtung *f*, -bau *m*; ⊕ *fertige* Anlage; Einsetzung *f*, -führung *f* (*in ein Amt*).

in·stal·ment, *Am. a.* **-stall-** [ɪn'stɔːlmənt] *econ.* Rate *f*; (Teil)Lieferung *f* (*e-s Buches etc.*); Fortsetzung *f* (*e-s Romans etc.*); *Rundfunk, TV*: (Sende)Folge *f*.

in·stance ['ɪnstəns] Beispiel *n*; (besonderer) Fall; ⚖ Instanz *f*; *for* ~ zum Beispiel; *at s.o.'s* ~ auf j-s Veranlassung (hin).

in·stant □ ['ɪnstənt] **1.** sofortig; unmittelbar; *econ.* Fertig...; ~ *coffee* löslicher *od.* Pulverkaffee, Instantkaffee *m*; **2.** Augenblick *m*; **in·stan·ta·ne·ous** □ [ɪnstən'teɪnjəs] sofortig, augenblicklich; Moment...; ~·**ly** ['ɪnstəntlɪ] sofort, unverzüglich.

in·stead [ɪn'sted] statt dessen, dafür; ~ *of* an Stelle von, (an)statt.

in·step *anat.* ['ɪnstep] Spann *m*, Rist *m*.

in·sti·gate ['ɪnstɪgeɪt] anstiften; aufhetzen; veranlassen; ~·**ga·tor** [~ə] Anstifter(in); (Auf)Hetzer(in).

in·stil, *Am. a.* **-still** *fig.* [ɪn'stɪl] (-*ll*-) beibringen, einflößen (*into dat.*).

in·stinct ['ɪnstɪŋkt] Instinkt *m*; **in·stinc·tive** □ [ɪn'stɪŋktɪv] instinktiv.

in·sti·tute ['ɪnstɪtjuːt] **1.** Institut *n*; (*gelehrte etc.*) Gesellschaft; **2.** einrichten, gründen; einleiten; ~·**tu·tion** [ɪnstɪ'tjuːʃn] Institut *n*, Anstalt *f*; Einführung *f*; Institution *f*, Einrichtung *f*.

in·struct [ɪn'strʌkt] unterrichten; belehren; j-m anweisen; **in·struc·tion** [~kʃn] Unterricht *m*; Anweisung *f*, Instruktion *f*; *Computer*: Befehl *m*; ~*s for use* Gebrauchsanweisung *f*; *operating* ~*s* Bedienungsanleitung *f*; **in·struc·tive** □ [~ktɪv] instruktiv, lehrreich; **in·struc·tor** [~ə] Lehrer *m*; Ausbilder *m*; *Am. univ.* Dozent *m*.

in·stru·ment ['ɪnstrʊmənt] Instrument *n*; Werkzeug *n* (*a. fig.*); ~ *panel* ⊕ Armaturenbrett *n*; ~·**men·tal** □ [ɪnstrʊ'mentl] behilflich, dienlich; ♪ Instrumental...

in·sub·or·di·nate [ɪnsə'bɔːdənət] aufsässig; ~·**na·tion** ['ɪnsəbɔːdɪ'neɪʃn] Auflehnung *f*.

in·suf·fe·ra·ble □ [ɪn'sʌfərəbl] unerträglich, unausstehlich.

in·suf·fi·cient □ [ɪnsə'fɪʃnt] unzulänglich, ungenügend.

in·su·lar □ ['ɪnsjʊlə] Insel...; *fig.* engstirnig.

in·su|late ['ɪnsjʊleɪt] isolieren; **~·la·tion** [ɪnsjʊ'leɪʃn] Isolierung *f*; Isoliermaterial *n*.

in·sult 1. ['ɪnsʌlt] Beleidigung *f*; **2.** [ɪn'sʌlt] beleidigen.

in·sur|ance [ɪn'ʃʊərəns] Versicherung *f*; Versicherungssumme *f*; ~ *company* Versicherungsgesellschaft *f*; ~ *policy* Versicherungspolice *f*; **~e** [ɪn'ʃʊə] versichern (*against* gegen).

in·sur·gent [ɪn'sɜːdʒənt] **1.** aufständisch; **2.** Aufständische(r *m*) *f*.

in·sur·moun·ta·ble □ *fig.* [ɪnsə-'maʊntəbl] unüberwindlich.

in·sur·rec·tion [ɪnsə'rekʃn] Aufstand *m*.

in·tact [ɪn'tækt] unberührt; unversehrt, intakt.

in·tan·gi·ble □ [ɪn'tændʒəbl] nicht greifbar; unbestimmt.

in·te|gral □ ['ɪntɪɡrəl] ganz, vollständig; wesentlich; **~·grate** [~eɪt] *v/t.* integrieren, zu e-m Ganzen zusammenfassen; einbeziehen, -gliedern; *Am.* die Rassenschranken aufheben zwischen; *v/i.* sich integrieren; **~·grat·ed** einheitlich; ⊕ eingebaut; ohne Rassentrennung; **~·gra·tion** [ɪntɪ'ɡreɪʃn] Integration *f*.

in·teg·ri·ty [ɪn'teɡrətɪ] Integrität *f*, Rechtschaffenheit *f*; Vollständigkeit *f*.

in·tel|lect ['ɪntəlekt] Intellekt *m*, Verstand *m*; **~·lec·tual** [ɪntə'lektjʊəl] **1.** □ intellektuell, Verstandes...; geistig; **2.** Intellektuelle(r *m*) *f*.

in·tel·li·gence [ɪn'telɪdʒəns] Intelligenz *f*, Verstand *m*; Nachrichten *pl.*, Informationen *pl.*; *a.* ~ *department* Geheimdienst *m*; **~·gent** □ [~t] intelligent, klug.

in·tel·li·gi·ble □ [ɪn'telɪdʒəbl] verständlich (*to* für).

in·tem·per·ate □ [ɪn'tempərət] unmäßig, maßlos; trunksüchtig.

in·tend [ɪn'tend] beabsichtigen, vorhaben, planen; **~ed for** bestimmt für *od.* zu.

in·tense □ [ɪn'tens] intensiv; stark, heftig; angespannt; ernsthaft.

in·ten|si·fy [ɪn'tensɪfaɪ] intensivieren; (sich) verstärken; **~·si·ty** [~sətɪ] Intensität *f*; **~·sive** [~sɪv] intensiv; stark, heftig; ~ *care unit* 🏥 Intensivstation *f*.

Absicht *f*, Vorhaben *n*; *to all* ~*s and purposes* in jeder Hinsicht; **in·ten·tion** [~ʃn] Absicht *f*; ⚖ Vorsatz *m*; **in·ten·tion·al** □ [~nl] absichtlich, vorsätzlich.

in·ter [ɪn'tɜː] (-*rr*-) bestatten.

in·ter- ['ɪntə] zwischen, Zwischen...; gegenseitig, einander.

in·ter·act [ɪntər'ækt] aufeinander (ein)wirken, sich gegenseitig beeinflussen.

in·ter·cede [ɪntə'siːd] vermitteln, sich einsetzen (*with* bei; *for* für).

in·ter·cept [ɪntə'sept] abfangen; aufhalten; **~·cep·tion** [~pʃn] Abfangen *n*; Aufhalten *n*.

in·ter·ces·sion [ɪntə'seʃn] Fürbitte *f*, -sprache *f*.

in·ter·change 1. [ɪntə'tʃeɪndʒ] austauschen; **2.** ['ɪntə'tʃeɪndʒ] Austausch *m*; kreuzungsfreier Verkehrsknotenpunkt.

in·ter·course ['ɪntəkɔːs] Verkehr *m*; *a.* sexual ~ (Geschlechts)Verkehr *m*.

in·ter|dict [ɪntə'dɪkt] untersagen, verbieten (*s.th. to s.o.* j-m et.; *s.o. from doing* j-m zu tun); **2.** ['ɪntədɪkt], **~·dic·tion** [ɪntə'dɪkʃn] Verbot *n*.

in·ter·est ['ɪntrɪst] **1.** Interesse *n* (*in an dat.*, für), (An)Teilnahme *f*; Nutzen *m*; *econ.* Anteil *m*, Beteiligung *f*; *econ.* Zins(en *pl.*) *m*; Interessenten *pl.*, Interessengruppe(n *pl.*) *f*; *take an* ~ *in* sich interessieren für; **2.** interessieren (*in* für *et.*); **~·ing** □ [~ɪŋ] interessant.

in·ter·face ['ɪntəfeɪs] *Computer*: Schnittstelle *f*.

in·ter·fere [ɪntə'fɪə] sich einmischen (*with in acc.*); stören; **~·fer·ence** [~rəns] Einmischung *f*; Störung *f*.

in·te·ri·or [ɪn'tɪərɪə] **1.** □ innere(r, -s), Innen...; Binnen...; Inlands...; ~ *decorator* Innenarchitekt(in); **2.** *das* Innere; Interieur *n*; *pol.* innere Angelegenheiten *pl.*; *Department of the* ⚷ *Am.* Innenministerium *n*.

in·ter|ject [ɪntə'dʒekt] *Bemerkung* einwerfen; **~·jec·tion** [~kʃn] Einwurf *m*; Ausruf *m*; *ling.* Interjektion *f*.

in·ter·lace [ɪntə'leɪs] (sich) (ineinander) verflechten.

in·ter·lock [ɪntə'lɒk] ineinandergreifen; (miteinander) verzahnen.

in·ter·lop·er ['ɪntələʊpə] Eindringling *m*.

J

interlude

in·ter·lude ['ɪntəlu:d] Zwischenspiel n; Pause f; ~s of bright weather zeitweilig schön.

in·ter·me·di·a·ry [ɪntə'mi:djərɪ] Vermittler(in); **~ate** □ [~ət] in der Mitte liegend, Mittel..., Zwischen...; ~ range missile Mittelstreckenrakete f.

in·ter·ment [ɪn'tɜ:mənt] Beerdigung f, Bestattung f.

in·ter·mi·na·ble □ [ɪn'tɜ:mɪnəbl] endlos.

in·ter·mis·sion [ɪntə'mɪʃn] Aussetzen n, Unterbrechung f; bsd. Am. thea., Film etc.: Pause f.

in·ter·mit·tent □ [ɪntə'mɪtənt] (zeitweilig) aussetzend, periodisch (auftretend); ~ fever ♒ Wechselfieber n.

in·tern¹ [ɪn'tɜ:n] internieren.

in·tern² Am. ♒ ['ɪntɜ:n] Medizinalassistent(in).

in·ter·nal □ [ɪn'tɜ:nl] innere(r, -s); einheimisch, Inlands...; ~combustion engine Verbrennungsmotor m.

in·ter·na·tion·al [ɪntə'næʃənl] **1.** □ international; ~ law ⚖ Völkerrecht n; **2.** Sport: Internationale m, f, Nationalspieler(in); internationaler Wettkampf; Länderspiel n.

in·ter·po·late [ɪn'tɜ:pəleɪt] einfügen.

in·ter·pose [ɪntə'pəʊz] v/t. Veto einlegen; Wort einwerfen; v/i. eingreifen.

in·ter·pret [ɪn'tɜ:prɪt] auslegen, erklären, deuten, interpretieren; dolmetschen; **~pre·ta·tion** [ɪntɜ:prɪ'teɪʃn] Auslegung f, Deutung f, Interpretation f; **~pret·er** [ɪn'tɜ:prɪtə] Dolmetscher(in); Interpret(in).

in·ter·ro·gate [ɪn'terəgeɪt] (be-, aus-)fragen; verhören; **~ga·tion** [ɪnterə'geɪʃn] Befragung f; Verhör m; Frage f; note od. mark od. point of ~ ling. Fragezeichen n; **~ga·tive** □ [ɪntə'rɒgətɪv] fragend, Frage...; gr. Interrogativ..., Frage...

in·ter·rupt [ɪntə'rʌpt] unterbrechen; **~rup·tion** [~pʃn] Unterbrechung f.

in·ter·sect [ɪntə'sekt] durchschneiden; sich schneiden od. kreuzen; **~sec·tion** [~k]n] Schnittpunkt m; (Straßen- etc.) Kreuzung f.

in·ter·sperse [ɪntə'spɜ:s] einstreuen, hier u. da einfügen.

in·ter·state Am. [ɪntə'steɪt] zwischen den einzelnen Bundesstaaten.

in·ter·twine [ɪntə'twaɪn] (sich ineinander) verschlingen.

in·ter·val ['ɪntəvl] Intervall n (a. ♪) Abstand m; Pause f; at ~s of ir Abständen von.

in·ter·vene [ɪntə'vi:n] einschreiten intervenieren; dazwischenliegen (unerwartet) dazwischenkommen **~ven·tion** [~'venʃn] Eingreifen n -griff m, Intervention f.

in·ter·view ['ɪntəvju:] **1.** Presse, TV Interview n; Unterredung f; (Vorstellungs)Gespräch n; **2.** j-n interviewen, befragen; ein Vorstellungsgespräch führen mit; **~er** [~ə] Interviewer(in); Leiter(in) e-s Vorstellungsgesprächs.

in·ter·weave [ɪntə'wi:v] (-wove, -woven) (miteinander) verweben -flechten, -schlingen.

in·tes·tate ⚖ [ɪn'testeɪt]: die ~ ohne Testament sterben.

in·tes·tine anat. [ɪn'testɪn] Darm m; ~s pl. Eingeweide pl.

in·ti·ma·cy ['ɪntɪməsɪ] Intimität f (a. sexuell), Vertrautheit f; Vertraulichkeit f.

in·ti·mate¹ ['ɪntɪmət] **1.** □ intim (a sexuell), vertraut; vertraulich; **2** Vertraute(r m) f.

in·ti·mate² ['ɪntɪmeɪt] andeuten; **~ma·tion** [ɪntɪ'meɪʃn] Andeutung f.

in·tim·i·date [ɪn'tɪmɪdeɪt] einschüchtern; **~da·tion** [ɪntɪmɪ'deɪʃn Einschüchterung f.

in·to ['ɪntu, 'ɪntə] in (acc.), in (acc.) ... hinein; gegen (acc.); ⚹ in (acc.); **4** ~ 20 goes five times 4 geht fünfmal in 20.

in·tol·e·ra·ble □ [ɪn'tɒlərəbl] unerträglich.

in·tol·e·rance [ɪn'tɒlərəns] Intoleranz f, Unduldsamkeit (of gegen); **~rant** [~t] intolerant, unduldsam (of gegen).

in·to·na·tion [ɪntəʊ'neɪʃn] gr. Intonation f, Tonfall m; ♪ Intonation f.

in·tox·i·cant [ɪn'tɒksɪkənt] **1.** berauschend; **2.** bsd. berauschendes Getränk; **~cate** [~eɪt] berauschen (a. fig.), betrunken machen; **~ca·tion** [ɪntɒksɪ'keɪʃn] Rausch m (a. fig.).

in·trac·ta·ble □ [ɪn'træktəbl] unlenksam, eigensinnig; schwer zu handhaben(d).

in·tran·si·tive □ gr. [ɪn'trænsətɪv] intransitiv.

in·tra·ve·nous ♃ [ɪntrə'viːnəs] intravenös.

in·trep·id □ [ɪn'trepɪd] unerschrocken.

in·tri·cate □ ['ɪntrɪkət] verwickelt, kompliziert.

in·trigue [ɪn'triːg] **1.** Intrige *f*; Machenschaft *f*; **2.** faszinieren, interessieren; intrigieren.

in·trin·sic [ɪn'trɪnsɪk] (~*ally*) wirklich, wahr, inner(lich).

in·tro·duce [ɪntrə'djuːs] vorstellen (*to dat.*), *j-n* bekannt machen (*to* mit); einführen; einleiten; ~**duc·tion** [~'dʌkʃn] Vorstellung *f*; Einführung *f*; Einleitung *f*; *letter of* ~ Empfehlungsschreiben *n*; ~**duc·to·ry** [~tərɪ] einleitend, Einführungs..., Einleitungs...

in·tro·spec·tion [ɪntrəʊ'spekʃn] Selbstbeobachtung *f*; ~**tive** [~tɪv] selbstbeobachtend.

in·tro·vert *psych.* ['ɪntrəʊvɜːt] introvertierter Mensch; ~**ed** *psych.* introvertiert, in sich gekehrt.

in·trude [ɪn'truːd] sich eindrängen; sich ein- *od.* aufdrängen; stören; *am I intruding?* störe ich?; **in·trud·er** [~ə] Eindringling *m*; **in·tru·sion** [~ʒn] Aufdrängen *n*; Einmischung *f*; Auf-, Zudringlichkeit *f*; Störung *f*; Verletzung *f*; **in·tru·sive** [~sɪv] aufdringlich.

in·tu·i·tion [ɪntjuː'ɪʃn] Intuition *f*; Ahnung *f*; ~**tive** □ [ɪn'tjuːɪtɪv] intuitiv.

in·un·date ['ɪnʌndeɪt] überschwemmen, -fluten (*a. fig.*).

in·vade [ɪn'veɪd] eindringen in, einfallen in, ⚔ *a.* einmarschieren in (*acc.*); *fig.* überlaufen, -schwemmen; ~**r** [~ə] Eindringling *m*.

in·val·id¹ ['ɪnvəlɪd] **1.** dienstunfähig; kränklich, invalide; Kranken...; **2.** Invalide *m, f*.

in·val·id² □ [ɪn'vælɪd] (rechts)ungültig; ~**i·date** [~eɪt] *Argument* entkräften; ⚖ ungültig machen.

in·val·u·a·ble □ [ɪn'væljʊəbl] unschätzbar.

in·var·i·a·ble □ [ɪn'veərɪəbl] unveränderlich; ~**bly** [~lɪ] ausnahmslos.

in·va·sion [ɪn'veɪʒn] Invasion *f*, Einfall *m*; *fig.* Eingriff *m*, Verletzung *f*.

in·vec·tive [ɪn'vektɪv] Schmähung *f*, Beschimpfung *f*.

in·vent [ɪn'vent] erfinden; **in·ven-** **tion** [~ʃn] Erfindung(sgabe) *f*; **in·ven·tive** □ [~tɪv] erfinderisch; **in·ven·tor** [~ə] Erfinder(in); **in·ven·tory** ['ɪnvəntrɪ] Inventar *n*; Bestandsverzeichnis *n*; *Am.* Inventur *f*.

in·verse ['ɪn'vɜːs] **1.** □ umgekehrt; **2.** Umkehrung *f*, Gegenteil *n*; **in·ver·sion** [ɪn'vɜːʃn] Umkehrung *f*; *gr.* Inversion *f*.

in·vert [ɪn'vɜːt] umkehren; *gr. Satz etc.* umstellen; ~**ed commas** *pl.* Anführungszeichen *pl.*

in·ver·te·brate *zo.* [ɪn'vɜːtɪbrət] **1.** wirbellos; **2.** wirbelloses Tier.

in·vest [ɪn'vest] investieren, anlegen.

in·ves·ti·gate [ɪn'vestɪgeɪt] untersuchen; überprüfen; Untersuchungen *od.* Ermittlungen anstellen (*into* über *acc.*), nachforschen; ~**ga·tion** [ɪnvestɪ'geɪʃn] Untersuchung *f*; Ermittlung *f*, Nachforschung *f*; ~**ga·tor** [ɪn'vestɪgeɪtə] Untersuchungs-, Ermittlungsbeamte(r) *m*; *private* ~ Privatdetektiv *m*.

in·vest·ment *econ.* [ɪn'vestmənt] Investition *f*, (Kapital)Anlage *f*.

in·vet·e·rate □ [ɪn'vetərət] unverbesserlich; unversöhnlich; hartnäckig.

in·vid·i·ous □ [ɪn'vɪdɪəs] verhaßt; gehässig, boshaft, gemein; ungerecht.

in·vig·o·rate [ɪn'vɪgəreɪt] kräftigen, stärken, beleben.

in·vin·ci·ble □ [ɪn'vɪnsəbl] unbesiegbar; unüberwindlich.

in·vi·o·la·ble □ [ɪn'vaɪələbl] unverletzlich, unantastbar; ~**te** [~lət] unverletzt; unversehrt.

in·vis·i·ble □ [ɪn'vɪzəbl] unsichtbar.

in·vi·ta·tion [ɪnvɪ'teɪʃn] Einladung *f*; Aufforderung *f*; **in·vite** [ɪn'vaɪt] einladen; auffordern; *Gefahr etc.* herausfordern; ~ *s.o. in* *j-n* hereinbitten; **in·vit·ing** □ [~ɪŋ] einladend, verlockend.

in·voice *econ.* ['ɪnvɔɪs] **1.** (Waren-) Rechnung *f*; Lieferschein *m*; **2.** in Rechnung stellen, berechnen.

in·voke [ɪn'vəʊk] anrufen; zu Hilfe rufen (*acc.*); appellieren an (*acc.*); *Geist* heraufbeschwören.

in·vol·un·ta·ry □ [ɪn'vɒləntərɪ] unfreiwillig; unabsichtlich; unwillkürlich.

in·volve [ɪn'vɒlv] verwickeln, hineinziehen (*in* in *acc.*); umfassen; zur Folge haben, mit sich bringen; betreffen; **~d** kompliziert; betroffen (*Person*); **~ment** [~mənt] Verwicklung *f*; Beteiligung *f*; Engagement *n*; (Geld)Verlegenheit *f*.

in·vul·ne·ra·ble ☐ [ɪn'vʌlnərəbl] unverwundbar; *fig.* unanfechtbar.

in·ward ['ɪnwəd] **1.** *adj.* innere(r, -s), innerlich; **2.** *adv. mst* **~s** einwärts, nach innen.

i·o·dine ⚗ ['aɪədiːn] Jod *n*.

i·on *phys.* ['aɪən] Ion *n*.

IOU ['aɪəʊ'juː] (= *I owe you*) Schuldschein *m*.

I·ra·ni·an [ɪ'reɪnjən] **1.** iranisch, persisch; **2.** Iraner(in), Perser(in); *ling.* Iranisch *n*, Persisch *n*.

I·ra·qi [ɪ'rɑːkɪ] **1.** irakisch; **2.** Iraker(in); *ling.* Irakisch *n*.

i·ras·ci·ble ☐ [ɪ'ræsəbl] jähzornig.

i·rate [aɪ'reɪt] zornig, wütend.

i·ri·des·cent [ɪrɪ'desnt] schillernd.

i·ris ['aɪərɪs] *anat.* Regenbogenhaut *f*, Iris *f*; ⚘ Schwertlilie *f*, Iris *f*.

I·rish ['aɪərɪʃ] **1.** irisch; **2.** *ling.* Irisch *n*; *the* **~** *pl.* die Iren *pl.*; **~man** (*pl. -men*) Ire *m*; **~wom·an** (*pl. -women*) Irin *f*.

irk·some ['ɜːksəm] lästig, ärgerlich.

i·ron ['aɪən] **1.** Eisen *n*; *a. flat~* Bügeleisen *n*; **~s** *pl.* Hand- u. Fußschellen *pl.*; *strike while the* **~** *is hot fig.* das Eisen schmieden, solange es heiß ist; **2.** eisern (*a. fig.*), Eisen..., aus Eisen; **3.** bügeln, plätten; **~** *out fig. et.* ausbügeln, *Schwierigkeiten* beseitigen; ⚑ **Cur·tain** *pol.* Eiserner Vorhang.

i·ron·ic [aɪ'rɒnɪk] (**~ally**), **i·ron·i·cal** ☐ [~kl] ironisch, spöttisch.

i·ron·ing ['aɪənɪŋ] Bügel-, Plättwäsche *f*; **~board** Bügel-, Plättbrett *n*; **~lung** ⚕ eiserne Lunge; **~mon·ger** *Brt.* [~mʌŋgə] Eisenwarenhändler *m*; **~mon·ger·y** *Brt.* [~ərɪ] Eisenwaren *pl.*, **~works** *sg.* Eisenhütte *f*.

i·ron·y ['aɪərənɪ] Ironie *f*.

ir·ra·tion·al ☐ [ɪ'ræʃənl] irrational; unvernünftig; vernunftlos (*Tier*).

ir·rec·on·cil·a·ble ☐ [ɪ'rekənsaɪləbl] unversöhnlich; unvereinbar.

ir·re·cov·er·a·ble ☐ [ɪrɪ'kʌvərəbl] unersetzlich; unwiederbringlich.

ir·re·fu·ta·ble ☐ [ɪ'refjʊtəbl] unwiderlegbar, nicht zu widerlegen(d).

ir·reg·u·lar ☐ [ɪ'regjʊlə] unregelmäßig; uneben; ungleichmäßig; regelwidrig; ungesetzlich; ungehörig.

ir·rel·e·vant ☐ [ɪ'reləvənt] irrele-

vant, nicht zur Sache gehörig; unerheblich, belanglos (*to* für).

ir·rep·a·ra·ble ☐ [ɪ'repərəbl] irreparabel, nicht wiedergutzumachen(d).

ir·re·place·a·ble ☐ [ɪrɪ'pleɪsəbl] unersetzlich.

ir·re·pres·si·ble ☐ [ɪrɪ'presəbl] nicht zu unterdrücken(d); unerschütterlich; un(be)zähmbar.

ir·re·proa·cha·ble ☐ [ɪrɪ'prəʊtʃəbl] einwandfrei, tadellos, untadelig.

ir·re·sis·ti·ble ☐ [ɪrɪ'zɪstəbl] unwiderstehlich.

ir·res·o·lute ☐ [ɪ'rezəluːt] unentschlossen.

ir·re·spec·tive ☐ [ɪrɪ'spektɪv]: **~** *of* ungeachtet (*gen.*), ohne Rücksicht auf (*acc.*); unabhängig von.

ir·re·spon·si·ble ☐ [ɪrɪ'spɒnsəbl] unverantwortlich; verantwortungslos.

ir·re·trie·va·ble ☐ [ɪrɪ'triːvəbl] unwiederbringlich, unersetzlich; nicht wiedergutzumachen(d).

ir·rev·e·rent ☐ [ɪ'revərənt] respektlos.

ir·rev·o·ca·ble ☐ [ɪ'revəkəbl] unwiderruflich, unabänderlich, endgültig.

ir·ri·gate ['ɪrɪgeɪt] (künstlich) bewässern.

ir·ri·ta|ble ☐ ['ɪrɪtəbl] reizbar; **~nt** [~ənt] Reizmittel *n*; **~te** [~teɪt] reizen; ärgern; **~ting** ☐ [~tɪŋ] aufreizend; ärgerlich (*Sache*); **~tion** [ɪrɪ'teɪʃn] Reizung *f*; Gereiztheit *f*, Ärger *m*.

is [ɪz] *3. sg. pres. von* be.

Is·lam ['ɪzlɑːm] der Islam.

is·land ['aɪlənd] Insel *f*; *a. traffic* **~** Verkehrsinsel *f*; **~er** [~ə] Inselbewohner(in).

isle *poet.* [aɪl] Insel *f*.

is·let ['aɪlɪt] Inselchen *n*.

i·so|late ['aɪsəleɪt] absondern; isolieren; **~lat·ed** einsam, abgeschieden; einzeln; ⚠ *nicht* ⚡ *isoliert*; **~la·tion** [aɪsə'leɪʃn] Isolierung *f*; Absonderung *f*; **~ward** ⚡ Isolierstation *f*.

Is·rae·li [ɪz'reɪlɪ] **1.** israelisch; **2.** Israeli *m*, Bewohner(in) des Staates Israel.

is·sue ['ɪʃuː] **1.** Herauskommen *n*; Herausfließen *n*; Abfluß *m*; ⚕ Nachkommen(schaft *f*) *pl.*; *econ.* Ausgabe *f* (*von Banknoten etc.*); Erteilung *f* (*von Befehlen etc.*); *print.* Ausgabe *f*, Exemplar *n* (*e-s Buches*);

print. Ausgabe *f*, Nummer *f* (*e-r Zeitung*); *bsd.* ⟨⟩ Streitfrage *f*; *fig.* Ausgang, Ergebnis *n*; *at* ~ zur Debatte stehend; *point at* ~ strittiger Punkt; 2. *v/i.* herauskommen; ausfließen, -strömen; herkommen, -rühren (*from* von); *v/t. econ.*, *Material etc.* ausgeben; *Befehl* erteilen; *Buch, Zeitung* herausgeben, veröffentlichen.

isth·mus ['ɪsməs] Landenge *f*.

it [ɪt] es; er, ihn, sie; *nach prp.*: *by* ~ dadurch; *for* ~ dafür.

I·tal·i·an [ɪ'tæljən] 1. italienisch; 2. Italiener(in); *ling.* Italienisch *n*.

i·tal·ics *print.* [ɪ'tælɪks] Kursivschrift *f*.

itch [ɪtʃ] 1. 🕱 Krätze *f*; Jucken *n*; Verlangen *n*; 2. jucken; *I* ~ *all over* es

i·tem ['aɪtəm] Punkt *m*; Gegenstand *m*; Posten *m*, Artikel *m*; *a. news* ~ (Zeitungs)Notiz *f*, (kurzer) Artikel; *Rundfunk, TV:* (kurze) Meldung; ~·**ize** [~aɪz] einzeln angeben *od.* aufführen.

i·tin·e·rant □ [ɪ'tɪnərənt] reisend; umherziehend, Reise..., Wander...; ~·**ra·ry** [aɪ'tɪnərərɪ] Reiseroute *f*; Reisebeschreibung *f*.

its [ɪts] sein(e), ihr(e), dessen, deren.

it·self [ɪt'self] sich; (sich) selbst; *by* ~ (für sich) allein; von selbst; *in* ~ an sich.

i·vo·ry ['aɪvərɪ] Elfenbein *n*.

i·vy ♀ ['aɪvɪ] Efeu *m*.

J

jab [dʒæb] 1. (*-bb-*) stechen; (zu)stoßen; 2. Stich *m*, Stoß *m*; F 🕱 Spritze *f*.

jab·ber ['dʒæbə] (daher)plappern.

jack [dʒæk] 1. ⊕ Hebevorrichtung *f*; ⊕ Wagenheber *m*; ⚡ Klinke *f*; ⚡ Steckdose *f*, Buchse *f*; ⚓ Gösch *f*, kleine Bugflagge; *Kartenspiel:* Bube *m*; 2. ~ *up Auto* aufbocken.

jack·al *zo.* ['dʒækɔ:l] Schakal *m*.

jack|ass ['dʒækæs] Esel *m* (*a. fig.*); ~·**boots** ✕ Reitstiefel *pl.*; hohe Wasserstiefel *pl.*; ~·**daw** *zo.* Dohle *f*.

jack·et ['dʒækɪt] Jacke *f*, Jackett *n*; ⊕ Mantel *m*; Schutzumschlag *m* (*e-s Buches*); *Am.* (Schall)Plattenhülle *f*.

jack|-knife ['dʒæknaɪf] 1. (*pl. -knives*) Klappmesser *n*; 2. zusammenklappen, -knicken; ~ *of all trades* Alleskönner *m*, Hansdampf in allen Gassen; ~·**pot** Haupttreffer *m*, -gewinn *m*; *hit the* ~ F den Haupttreffer machen; *fig.* das große Los ziehen.

jade [dʒeɪd] Jade *m*, *f*; Jadegrün *n*.

jag [dʒæg] Zacken *m*; ~·**ged** □ ['dʒægɪd] gezackt; zackig.

jag·u·ar *zo.* ['dʒægjʊə] Jaguar *m*.

jail [dʒeɪl] 1. Gefängnis *n*; 2. einsperren; ~·**bird** F ['dʒeɪlbɜ:d] Knastbru-

der *m*; ~·**er** [~ə] Gefängnisaufseher *m*; ~·**house** *Am.* Gefängnis *n*.

jam¹ [dʒæm] Konfitüre *f*, Marmelade *f*.

jam² [~] 1. Gedränge *n*, Gewühl *n*; ⊕ Klemmen *n*, Blockierung *f*; Stauung *f*, Stockung *f*; *traffic* ~ Verkehrsstau *m*; *be in a* ~ F in der Klemme sein; 2. (*-mm-*) ⊕ (sich) (ver)klemmen, blockieren; (hinein-) zwängen, (-)stopfen; einklemmen; pressen, quetschen; ~ *the brakes on*, ~ *on the brakes* auf die Bremse steigen.

jamb [dʒæm] (Tür-, Fenster)Pfosten *m*.

jam·bo·ree [dʒæmbə'ri:] Jamboree *n*, Pfadfindertreffen *n*.

jan·gle ['dʒæŋgl] klimpern *od.* klirren (mit); bimmeln (lassen).

jan·i·tor ['dʒænɪtə] Hausmeister *m*.

jan·u·a·ry ['dʒænjʊərɪ] Januar *m*.

Jap·a·nese [dʒæpə'ni:z] 1. japanisch; 2. Japaner(in); *ling.* Japanisch *n*; *the* ~ *pl.* die Japaner *pl.*

jar¹ [dʒɑ:] 1. Krug *m*, Topf *m*; (Marmelade- *etc.*)Glas *n*.

jar² [~] 1. (*-rr-*) knarren, kreischen, quietschen; sich nicht vertragen; erschüttern (*a. fig.*); 2. Knarren *n*,

Kreischen *n*, Quietschen *n*; Erschütterung *f* (*a. fig.*); Schock *m*.

jar·gon ['dʒɑːɡən] Jargon *m*, Fachsprache *f*.

jaun·dice ✠ ['dʒɔːndɪs] Gelbsucht *f*; **∼d** ✠ gelbsüchtig; *fig.* neidisch, eifersüchtig, voreingenommen.

jaunt [dʒɔːnt] **1.** Ausflug *m*, Spritztour *f*; **2.** e-n Ausflug machen; **jaun·ty** □ ['dʒɔːntɪ] (*-ier, -iest*) munter, unbeschwert; flott.

jav·e·lin ['dʒævlɪn] *Sport:* Speer *m*; ∼ (*throw[ing]*), *throwing the* ∼ Speerwerfen *n*; ∼ *thrower* Speerwerfer(in).

jaw [dʒɔː] *anat.* Kinnbacken *m*, Kiefer *m*; ∼*s pl.* Rachen *m*; Maul *n*; Schlund *m*; ⊕ Backen *pl.*; **∼·bone** *anat.* ['dʒɔːbəʊn] Kieferknochen *m*.

jay *zo.* [dʒeɪ] Eichelhäher *m*; **∼·walk** ['dʒeɪwɔːk] unachtsam über die Straße gehen; **∼·walk·er** unachtsamer Fußgänger.

jazz ♪ [dʒæz] Jazz *m*.

jeal·ous □ ['dʒeləs] eifersüchtig (*of* auf *acc.*); neidisch; **∼·y** [∼ɪ] Eifersucht *f*; Neid *m*; ⚠ *nicht* Jalousie.

jeans [dʒiːnz] *pl.* Jeans *pl.*

jeep *TM* [dʒiːp] Jeep *m*.

jeer [dʒɪə] **1.** Spott *m*; höhnische Bemerkung; **2.** spotten (*at* über *acc.*); verspotten, -höhnen.

jel·lied ['dʒelɪd] eingedickt (*Fruchtsaft*); in Gelee.

jel·ly ['dʒelɪ] **1.** Gallert(e *f*) *n*; Gelee *n*; **2.** gelieren; ∼ **ba·by** *Brt.* Gummibärchen *n*; **∼ bean** Gummi-, Geleebonbon *m*, *n*; **∼·fish** *zo.* Qualle *f*.

jeop·ar·dize ['dʒepədaɪz] gefährden; **∼·dy** [∼ɪ] Gefahr *f*.

jerk [dʒɜːk] **1.** (plötzlicher) Ruck; Sprung *m*, Satz *m*; ✠ Zuckung *f*, Zucken *n*; **2.** (plötzlich) ziehen, zerren, reißen (an *dat.*); schleudern; schnellen; **∼·y** □ ['dʒɜːkɪ] (*-ier, -iest*) ruckartig; holprig; abgehackt (*Sprache*).

jer·sey ['dʒɜːzɪ] Pullover *m*.

jest [dʒest] **1.** Spaß *m*; **2.** scherzen; **∼·er** [∼ə] ['dʒestə] (Hof)Narr *m*.

jet [dʒet] **1.** (Wasser-, Gas- *etc.*)Strahl *m*; ⊕ Düse *f*; ∼ *engine*, ∼ *plane*; **2.** (*-tt-*) hervorschießen, (her)ausströmen; ✗ jetten; **∼ en·gine** ⊕ Düsen-, Strahltriebwerk *n*; **∼ lag** körperliche Anpassungsschwierigkeiten *pl.* durch die Zeitverschiebung bei weiten Flugreisen; **∼ plane** Düsenflug-

zeug *n*, Jet *m*; **∼-pro·pelled** ['dʒetprəpeld] mit Düsenantrieb, Düsen...; ∼ **pro·pul·sion** ⊕ Düsen-, Strahlantrieb *m*; **∼ set** Jet-set *m*; ∼ **set·ter** Angehörige(r *m*) *f* des Jet-set.

jet·ty ♦ ['dʒetɪ] Mole *f*; Pier *m*.

Jew [dʒuː] Jude *m*, Jüdin *f*; *attr.* Juden...

jew·el ['dʒuːəl] Juwel *m*, *n*, Edelstein *m*; Schmuckstück *n*; **∼·ler**, *Am.* **∼·er** [∼ə] Juwelier *m*; **∼·lery**, *Am.* **∼·ry** [∼lrɪ] Juwelen *pl.*; Schmuck *m*.

Jew·ess ['dʒuːɪs] Jüdin *f*; **∼·ish** [∼ɪʃ] jüdisch.

jib ♦ [dʒɪb] Klüver *m*.

jif·fy F ['dʒɪfɪ]: *in a* ∼ im Nu, sofort.

jig·saw ['dʒɪɡsɔː] Laubsäge *f*; = ∼ **puz·zle** Puzzle(spiel) *n*.

jilt [dʒɪlt] *Mädchen* sitzenlassen; *Liebhaber* den Laufpaß geben.

jin·gle ['dʒɪŋgl] **1.** Geklingel *n*, Klimpern *n*; Spruch *m*, Vers *m*; *advertising* ∼ Werbespruch *m*; **2.** klingeln; klimpern (mit); klinge(l)n lassen.

jit·ters F ['dʒɪtəz] *pl.*: *the* ∼ Bammel *m*, das große Zittern.

job [dʒɒb] (ein Stück) Arbeit *f*; *econ.* Akkordarbeit *f*; Beruf *m*, Beschäftigung *f*, Stellung *f*, Stelle *f*, Arbeit *f*, Job *m*; Aufgabe *f*, Sache *f*; *by the* ∼ im Akkord; *out of* ∼ arbeitslos; **∼·ber** *Brt.* ['dʒɒbə] Börsenspekulant *m*; **∼-hop·ping** *Am.* [∼hɒpɪŋ] häufiger Arbeitsplatzwechsel; **∼ hunt·er** Arbeit(s)suchende(r *m*) *f*; **∼ hunt·ing**: *be* ∼ auf Arbeitssuche sein; **∼·less** [∼lɪs] arbeitslos; ∼ **work** Akkordarbeit *f*.

jock·ey ['dʒɒkɪ] Jockei *m*.

joc·u·lar □ ['dʒɒkjʊlə] lustig; spaßig.

jog [dʒɒg] **1.** (leichter) Stoß, Schubs; *Sport:* Dauerlauf *m*; Trott *m*; **2.** (*-gg-*) *v/t.* (an)stoßen, (*fig.* auf)rütteln; *v/i. mst* ∼ *along*, ∼ *on* dahintrotten, -zuckeln; *Sport:* Dauerlauf machen, joggen; **∼·ging** ['dʒɒgɪŋ] *Sport:* Dauerlauf *m*, Jogging *n*, Joggen *n*.

join [dʒɔɪn] **1.** *v/t.* verbinden, zusammenfügen (*to* mit); vereinigen; sich anschließen (*dat. od.* an *acc.*), sich gesellen zu; eintreten in (*acc.*), beitreten; ∼ *hands* sich die Hände reichen; *fig.* sich zusammentun; *v/i.* sich verbinden *od.* vereinigen; ∼ *in* teilnehmen an (*dat.*), mitmachen bei, sich beteiligen an (*dat.*); ∼ *up* Soldat werden; **2.** Verbindungsstelle *f*, Naht *f*.

join·er ['dʒɔɪnə] Tischler *m*, Schreiner *m*; **~·y** *bsd.* Brt. [~ərɪ] Tischlerhandwerk *n*; Tischlerarbeit *f*.

joint [dʒɔɪnt] **1.** Verbindung(sstelle) *f*; Naht(stelle) *f*; *anat.*, ⊕ Gelenk *n*; ♞ Knoten *m*; *Brt.* Braten *m*; *sl.* Spelunke *f*; *sl.* Joint *m* (*Marihuanazigarette*); *out of* ~ ausgerenkt; *fig.* aus den Fugen; **2.** □ gemeinsam; Mit...; ~ *heir* Miterbe *m*; ~ *stock econ.* Aktienkapital *n*; **3.** verbinden, zusammenfügen; *Braten* zerlegen; **~ed** ['dʒɔɪntɪd] gegliedert, Glieder...; **~·stock** *econ.* Aktien...; ~ *company* Brt. Aktiengesellschaft *f*.

joke [dʒəʊk] **1.** Witz *m*; Scherz *m*, Spaß *m*; *practical* ~ Streich *m*; **2.** scherzen, Witze machen; **jok·er** ['dʒəʊkə] Spaßvogel *m*; *Kartenspiel:* Joker *m*.

jol·ly ['dʒɒlɪ] **1.** *adj.* (*-ier, -iest*) lustig, fidel, vergnügt; **2.** *adv.* Brt. F mächtig, sehr; ~ *good* prima.

jolt [dʒəʊlt] **1.** stoßen, rütteln, holpern; *fig.* aufrütteln; **2.** Ruck *m*, Stoß *m*; *fig.* Schock *m*.

jos·tle ['dʒɒsl] **1.** (an)rempeln; drängeln; **2.** Stoß *m*, Rempelei *f*; Zusammenstoß *m*.

jot [dʒɒt] **1.** *not a* ~ keine Spur, kein bißchen; **2.** (*-tt-*): ~ *down* schnell hinschreiben od. notieren.

jour·nal ['dʒɜːnl] Journal *n*; (Fach-)Zeitschrift *f*; (Tages)Zeitung *f*; Tagebuch *n*; **~·is·m** ['dʒɜːnəlɪzəm] Journalismus *m*; **~·ist** [~ɪst] Journalist(in).

jour·ney ['dʒɜːnɪ] **1.** Reise *f*; Fahrt *f*; **2.** reisen; **~·man** (*pl. -men*) Geselle *m*.

jo·vi·al □ ['dʒəʊvjəl] heiter, jovial.

joy [dʒɔɪ] Freude *f*; *for* ~ vor Freude; **~·ful** □ ['dʒɔɪfʊl] freudig; erfreut; **~·less** □ [~lɪs] freudlos, traurig; **~·stick** ✈ Steuerknüppel *m* (F *a. für Computerspiele*).

ju·bi·lant □ ['dʒuːbɪlənt] jubelnd, überglücklich.

ju·bi·lee ['dʒuːbɪliː] Jubiläum *n*.

judge [dʒʌdʒ] **1.** ⅍ Richter *m*; Schieds-, Preisrichter *m*; Kenner(in), Sachverständige(r *m*) *f*; **2.** *v/i.* urteilen; *v/t.* ⅍ *Fall* verhandeln, die Verhandlung führen über (*acc.*); ⅍ ein Urteil fällen über (*acc.*); richten; beurteilen; halten für.

judg(e)·ment ['dʒʌdʒmənt] ⅍ Urteil *n*; Urteilsvermögen *n*; Meinung *f*, Ansicht *f*, Urteil *n*; *göttliches* (*Straf-*)Gericht; *pass* ~ *on* ⅍ ein Urteil fällen über (*acc.*); 2 *Day, Day of* 2 *eccl.* Tag *m* des Jüngsten Gerichts.

ju·di·cial □ [dʒuː'dɪʃl] ⅍ gerichtlich; Gerichts...; kritisch; unparteiisch.

ju·di·cia·ry [dʒuː'dɪʃɪərɪ] Richter (-stand *m*) *pl.*

ju·di·cious □ [dʒuː'dɪʃəs] klug, weise.

jug [dʒʌg] Krug *m*, Kanne *f*.

jug·gle ['dʒʌgl] jonglieren (mit); manipulieren, *Bücher etc.* frisieren; **~r** [~ə] Jongleur *m*; Schwindler(in).

juice [dʒuːs] Saft *m*; *mot.* Sprit *m*; **juic·y** □ [dʒuːsɪ] (*-ier, -iest*) saftig; F pikant, gepfeffert.

juke·box ['dʒuːkbɒks] Musikbox *f*, Musikautomat *m*.

Ju·ly [dʒuː'laɪ] Juli *m*.

jum·ble ['dʒʌmbl] **1.** Durcheinander *n*; **2.** *a.* ~ *together*, ~ *up* durcheinanderbringen, -werfen; ~ *sale* Brt. Wohltätigkeitsbasar *m*.

jum·bo ['dʒʌmbəʊ] *a.* ~*-sized* riesig.

jump [dʒʌmp] **1.** Sprung *m*; *the* ~*s pl.* große Nervosität; *high* (*long*) ~ *Sport:* Hoch-(Weit)sprung *m*; *get the* ~ *on* F zuvorkommen; **2.** *v/i.* springen; zusammenzucken, -fahren; ~ *at the chance* mit beiden Händen zugreifen; ~ *to conclusions* übereilte Schlüsse ziehen; *v/t.* (hinweg)springen über (*acc.*); überspringen; springen lassen; ~ *the queue* Brt. sich vordrängel(n)n; ~ *the lights* bei Rot über die Kreuzung fahren, F bei Rot drüberfahren; **~·er** ['dʒʌmpə] Springer(in); Brt. Pullover *m*; Am. Trägerkleid *n*; **~·ing jack** Hampelmann *m*; **~·y** [~ɪ] (*-ier, -iest*) nervös.

junc·tion ['dʒʌŋkʃn] Verbindung *f*; (Straßen)Kreuzung *f*; ❹ Knotenpunkt *m*; **~·ture** [~ktʃə]: *at this* ~ an dieser Stelle, in diesem Augenblick.

June [dʒuːn] Juni *m*.

jun·gle ['dʒʌŋgl] Dschungel *m*.

ju·ni·or ['dʒuːnjə] **1.** jüngere(r, -s); untergeordnet; rangniedrig; *Sport:* Junioren..., Jugend...; **2.** Jüngere(r *m*) *f*; F Junior *m*; *Am. univ.* Student (-in) im vorletzten Studienjahr.

junk¹ [dʒʌŋk] Dschunke *f*.

junk² F [~] Plunder *m*, alter Kram; *sl.* Stoff *m* (*bsd.* Heroin); ~ *food* kalo-

rienreiches aber minderwertiges Nahrungsmittel; **~ie,** **~y** sl. ['dʒʌŋkɪ] Fixer(in), Junkie m; **~ yard** Schrottplatz m.

jur·is·dic·tion ['dʒʊərɪs'dɪkʃn] Gerichtsbarkeit f; Zuständigkeit(sbereich m) f.

ju·ris·pru·dence ['dʒʊərɪs'pruːdəns] Rechtswissenschaft f.

ju·ror ᚦᚦ ['dʒʊərə] Geschworene(r m) f.

ju·ry ['dʒʊərɪ] ᚦᚦ *die Geschworenen* pl.; Jury f, Preisrichter pl.; **~·man** (pl. **-men**) ᚦᚦ Geschworene(r) m; **~·wom·an** (pl. **-women**) ᚦᚦ Geschworene f.

just □ [dʒʌst] **1.** adj. gerecht; berechtigt; angemessen; **2.** adv. gerade, (so)eben; gerade, genau, eben; gerade (noch), ganz knapp; nur, bloß; F

einfach, wirklich; **~** now gerade (jetzt); (so)eben.

jus·tice ['dʒʌstɪs] Gerechtigkeit f; Rechtmäßigkeit f; Berechtigung f, Recht n; Gerichtsbarkeit f, Justiz f; ᚦᚦ Richter m; ☿ of the Peace Friedensrichter m; court of ~ Gericht(shof m) n.

jus·ti·fi·ca·tion [dʒʌstɪfɪ'keɪʃn] Rechtfertigung f; **~·fy** ['dʒʌstɪfaɪ] rechtfertigen.

just·ly ['dʒʌstlɪ] mit od. zu Recht.

jut [dʒʌt] (*-tt-*): **~** out vorspringen, hervorragen, -stehen.

ju·ve·nile ['dʒuːvənaɪl] **1.** jung, jugendlich; Jugend...; für Jugendliche; **~** court Jugendgericht n; **~** delinquency Jugendkriminalität f; **~** delinquent jugendlicher Straftäter; **2.** Jugendliche(r m) f.

K

kan·ga·roo zo. [kæŋgə'ruː] (pl. **-roos**) Känguruh n.

keel ⚓ [kiːl] **1.** Kiel m; **2.** **~** over kieloben legen; umschlagen, kentern.

keen □ [kiːn] scharf (a. fig.); schneidend (*Kälte*); heftig; stark, groß (*Appetit etc.*); **~** on F scharf od. erpicht auf (acc.); be **~** on hunting ein leidenschaftlicher Jäger sein; **~·ness** ['kiːnnɪs] Schärfe f; Heftigkeit f; Scharfsinn m.

keep [kiːp] **1.** (Lebens)Unterhalt m; for **~**s F für immer; **2.** (kept) v/t. (auf-, [bei]be-, er-, fest-, zurück-) halten; unterhalten, sorgen für; *Gesetze etc.* einhalten, befolgen; *Ware, Tagebuch* führen; *Geheimnis* für sich behalten; *Versprechen* halten, einlösen; (auf)bewahren; abhalten, hindern (from von); *Vieh* halten; *Bett* hüten; (be)schützen; **~** s.o. company j-m Gesellschaft leisten; **~** company with verkehren mit; **~** one's head die Ruhe bewahren; **~** early hours früh zu Bett gehen; **~** one's temper sich beherrschen; **~** time richtig gehen (*Uhr*); Takt, Schritt halten; **~** s.o. waiting j-n

warten lassen; **~** away fernhalten; **~** s.th. from s.o. j-m et. vorenthalten od. verschweigen od. verheimlichen; **~** in *Schüler* nachsitzen lassen; **~** on *Kleid* anbehalten, *Hut* aufbehalten; **~** up aufrechterhalten; *Mut* bewahren; instand halten; fortfahren mit, weitermachen; nicht schlafen lassen; **~** it up so weitermachen; v/i. bleiben; sich halten; fortfahren, weitermachen; **~** doing immer wieder tun; **~** going weitergehen; **~** away sich fernhalten; **~** from doing s.th. et. nicht tun; **~** off weg-, fernbleiben; **~** on fortfahren (doing zu tun); **~** on talking weiterreden; **~** to sich halten an (acc.); **~** up stehen bleiben; andauern, anhalten; **~** up with Schritt halten mit; **~** up with the Joneses nicht hinter den Nachbarn zurückstehen (wollen).

keep|er ['kiːpə] Wärter(in), Wächter(in), Aufseher(in); Verwalter(in); Inhaber(in); **~·ing** [~ɪŋ] Verwahrung f; Obhut f; be in (out of) **~** with ... (nicht) übereinstimmen mit ...; **~·sake** [~seɪk] Andenken n (*Geschenk*).

keg [keg] Fäßchen n, kleines Faß.

ken·nel ['kenl] Hundehütte *f*; ~*s pl.* Hundezwinger *m*; Hundepension *f*.

kept [kept] *pret. u. p.p. von* keep 2.

kerb [kɜ:b], **~stone** ['kɜ:bstəʊn] Bordstein *m*.

ker·chief ['kɜ:tʃɪf] (Hals-, Kopf-) Tuch *n*.

ker·nel ['kɜ:nl] Kern *m* (*a. fig.*).

ket·tle ['ketl] (Koch)Kessel *m*; **~drum** ♪ (Kessel)Pauke *f*.

key [ki:] 1. Schlüssel *m*; (*Schreibmaschinen-, Klavier- etc.*)Taste *f*; (Druck)Taste *f*; ♪ Tonart *f*; *fig.* Ton *m*; *fig.* Schlüssel *m*, Lösung *f*; *attr.* Schlüssel...; 2. anpassen (*to an acc.*); ~*ed up* nervös, aufgeregt, überdreht; **~board** ['ki:bɔ:d] Klaviatur *f*; Tastatur *f*; **~hole** Schlüsselloch *n*; **~man** (*pl. -men*) Schlüsselfigur *f*; **~mon·ey** Brt. Abstand(ssumme *f*) *m* (*für e-e Wohnung*); **~note** ♪ Grundton *m*; *fig.* Grundgedanke *m*, Tenor *m*; **~ring** Schlüsselring *m*; **~stone** *arch.* Schlußstein *m*; *fig.* Grundpfeiler *m*; **~word** Schlüssel-, Stichwort *n*.

kick [kɪk] 1. (Fuß)Tritt *m*; Stoß *m*; F Kraft *f*, Feuer *n*; F Nervenkitzel *m*; *get a ~ out of s.th.* e-n Riesenspaß an et. haben; *for ~s* (nur) zum Spaß; 2. *v/t.* (mit dem Fuß) stoßen *od.* treten; *Fußball:* schießen, treten, kicken; ~ *off* von sich schleudern; ~ *out* hinauswerfen; ~ *up* hochschleudern; ~ *up a fuss od. row* F Krach schlagen; *v/i.* (mit dem Fuß) treten *od.* stoßen; (hinten) ausschlagen; strampeln; ~ *off Fußball:* anstoßen, den Anstoß ausführen; **~er** ['kɪkə] Fußballspieler *m*; **~off** *Fußball:* Anstoß *m*.

kid [kɪd] 1. Zicklein *n*, Kitz *n*; Ziegenleder *n*; F Kind *n*; ~ *brother* F kleiner Bruder; 2. (*-dd-*) *v/t.* j-n aufziehen; ~ *s.o.* j-m et. vormachen; *v/i.* Spaß machen; *he is only ~ding* er macht ja nur Spaß; *no ~ding!* im Ernst!; ~ *glove* Glacéhandschuh *m* (*a. fig.*).

kid·nap ['kɪdnæp] (*-pp-, Am. a. -p-*) entführen, kidnappen; **~per**, *Am. a.* **~er** [~ə] Entführer(in), Kidnapper(in); **~ping**, *Am. a.* **~ing** [~ɪŋ] Entführung *f*, Kidnapping *n*.

kid·ney ['kɪdnɪ] *anat.* Niere *f* (*a. als Speise*); ~ *bean* ♣ Weiße Bohne; ~ *machine* künstliche Niere.

kill [kɪl] 1. töten (*a. fig.*); umbringen; vernichten; beseitigen; *Tiere* schlachten; *hunt.* erlegen, schießen; *be ~ed in an accident* tödlich verunglücken; ~ *time* die Zeit totschlagen; 2. ~ *Tötung *f*; *hunt.* Jagdbeute *f*; **~er** ['kɪlə] Mörder(in), F Killer *m*; **~ing** □ [~ɪŋ] mörderisch, tödlich.

kiln [kɪln] Brenn-, Darrofen *m*.

ki·lo F ['ki:ləʊ] (*pl. -los*) Kilo *n*.

kil·o·gram(me) ['kɪləɡræm] Kilogramm *n*; **~me·tre**, *Am.* **~me·ter** Kilometer *m*.

kilt [kɪlt] Kilt *m*, Schottenrock *m*.

kin [kɪn] Verwandtschaft *f*, Verwandte *pl.*

kind [kaɪnd] 1. □ gütig, freundlich, liebenswürdig, nett; 2. Art *f*, Sorte *f*; Art *f*, Gattung *f*, Geschlecht *n*; ⚠ *nicht Kind*; *pay in ~* in Naturalien zahlen; *fig.* mit gleicher Münze heimzahlen.

kin·der·gar·ten ['kɪndəɡɑ:tn] Kindergarten *m*.

kind-heart·ed ['kaɪnd'hɑ:tɪd] gütig.

kin·dle ['kɪndl] anzünden; (sich) entzünden (*a. fig.*).

kin·dling ['kɪndlɪŋ] Material *n* zum Anzünden, Anmachholz *n*.

kind·ly ['kaɪndlɪ] *adj.* (*-ier, -iest*) *u. adv.* freundlich, liebenswürdig, nett; gütig; **~ness** [~nɪs] Güte *f*; Freundlichkeit *f*, Liebenswürdigkeit *f*; Gefälligkeit *f*.

kin·dred ['kɪndrɪd] 1. verwandt; *fig.* gleichartig; ~ *spirits pl.* Gleichgesinnte *pl.*; 2. Verwandtschaft *f*.

king [kɪŋ] König *m* (*a. fig. u. Schach, Kartenspiel*); **~dom** ['kɪŋdəm] Königreich *n*; *eccl.* Reich *n* Gottes; *animal (mineral, vegetable)* ~ Tier-(Mineral-, Pflanzen)reich *n*; **~ly** ['kɪŋlɪ] (*-ier, -iest*) königlich; **~size(d)** extrem groß.

kink [kɪŋk] Schleife *f*, Knoten *m*; *fig.* Schrulle *f*, Tick *m*, Spleen *m*; **~y** ['kɪŋkɪ] (*-ier, -iest*) schrullig, spleenig.

ki·osk ['ki:ɒsk] Kiosk *m*; *Brt.* Telefonzelle *f*.

kip·per ['kɪpə] Räucherhering *m*.

kiss [kɪs] 1. Kuß *m*; 2. (sich) küssen.

kit [kɪt] Ausrüstung *f* (*a. ✗ u. Sport*); Werkzeug(e *pl.*) *n*; Werkzeugtasche *f*, -kasten *n*; Bastelsatz *m*; *s. first-aid*; **~bag** ['kɪtbæg] Seesack *m*.

kitch·en ['kɪtʃn] Küche *f*; *attr.* Küchen...; **~ette** [kɪtʃɪ'net] Kleinküche *f*, Kochnische *f*; ~ **gar·den** ['kɪtʃɪn'ɡɑ:dn] Küchen-, Gemüsegarten *m*.

K

kite [kaɪt] (Papier-, Stoff)Drachen m; zo. Milan m.

kit·ten ['kɪtn] Kätzchen n.

knack [næk] Kniff m, Trick m, Dreh m; Geschick n, Talent n.

knave [neɪv] Schurke m, Spitzbube m; Kartenspiel: Bube m, Unter m.

knead [niːd] kneten; massieren.

knee [niː] Knie n; ⊕ Kniestück n; **~·cap** anat. ['niːkæp] Kniescheibe f; **~·deep** knietief, bis an die Knie (reichend); **~·joint** anat. Kniegelenk n (a. ⊕); **~l** [niːl] (knelt, Am. a. kneeled) knien (to vor dat.); **~·length** knielang (Rock etc.).

knell [nel] Totenglocke f.

knelt [nelt] pret. u. p.p. von kneel.

knew [njuː] pret. von know.

knick·er·bock·ers ['nɪkəbɒkəz] pl. Knickerbocker pl., Kniehosen pl.; **~s** Brt. F [~z] pl. (Damen)Schlüpfer m.

knick-knack ['nɪknæk] Nippsache f.

knife [naɪf] 1. (pl. knives [~vz]) Messer n; 2. schneiden; mit e-m Messer verletzen; erstechen.

knight [naɪt] 1. Ritter m; Schach: Springer m; 2. zum Ritter schlagen; **~·hood** ['naɪthʊd] Ritterwürde f, -stand m; Ritterschaft f.

knit [nɪt] (-tt-; knit od. knitted) v/t. stricken; a. ~ together zusammenfügen, verbinden; ~ one's brows die Stirn runzeln; v/i. stricken; zusammenwachsen (Knochen); **~·ting** ['nɪtɪŋ] Stricken n; Strickzeug n; attr. Strick...; **~·wear** Strickwaren pl.

knives [naɪvz] pl. von knife 1.

knob [nɒb] Knopf m, Knauf m; Buckel m; Brocken m.

knock [nɒk] 1. Stoß m; Klopfen (a. mot.), Pochen n; there is a ~ es klopft; 2. v/i. schlagen, pochen, klopfen; stoßen (against, into gegen); ~ about, ~ around F sich herumtreiben; F herumliegen; ~ at the door an die Tür klopfen; ~ off Feierabend od. Schluß machen, aufhören; v/t. stoßen, schlagen; F schlechtmachen, verreißen; ~ about, ~ around herumstoßen, übel zurich-

ten; ~ down niederschlagen, umwerfen; um-, überfahren; Auktion: et. zuschlagen (to s.o. j-m); Preis herabsetzen; ⊕ auseinandernehmen, zerlegen; Haus abreißen; Baum fällen; be ~ed down überfahren werden; ~ off herunterstoßen; abschlagen; F aufhören mit; F hinhauen (schnell erledigen); vom Preis abziehen, nachlassen; Brt. F ausrauben; ~ out (her)ausschlagen, (her)ausklopfen; k.o. schlagen; fig. F umwerfen, schocken; be ~ed out of ausscheiden aus (e-m Wettbewerb); ~ over umwerfen, umstoßen; um-, überfahren; be ~ed over überfahren werden; ~ up hochschlagen; Brt. F rasch auf die Beine stellen, improvisieren; **~·er** ['nɒkə] Türklopfer m; **~·kneed** [~·niːd] X-beinig; **~·out** [~kaʊt] Boxen: Knockout m, K.o. m.

knoll [nəʊl] kleiner runder Hügel; △ nicht Knolle.

knot [nɒt] 1. Knoten m; Astknorren m; ♣ Knoten m, n (Menschen); Gruppe f, Knäuel m, n (Menschen); 2. (-tt-) (ver)knoten, (-)knüpfen; **~·ty** ['nɒti] (-ier, -iest) knotig; knorrig; fig. verzwickt.

know [nəʊ] (knew, known) wissen; kennen; erfahren; (wieder)erkennen, unterscheiden; (es) können od. verstehen; ~ French Französisch können; come to ~ erfahren; get to ~ kennenlernen; ~ one's business, ~ the ropes, ~ a thing or two, ~ what's what F sich auskennen, Erfahrung haben; you ~ wissen Sie; **~·how** ['nəʊhaʊ] Know-how m, praktische (Sach-, Spezial)Kenntnis(se pl.) f; **~·ing** □ [~ɪŋ] klug; schlau; verständnisvoll; wissend; **~·ing·ly** [~lɪ] wissend; absichtlich, bewußt; **~l·edge** ['nɒlɪdʒ] Kenntnis(se pl.) f; Wissen n; to my ~ meines Wissens; **~n** [nəʊn] p.p. von know; bekannt; make ~ bekanntmachen.

knuck·le ['nʌkl] 1. (Finger)Knöchel m; 2. ~ down to work sich an die Arbeit machen.

Krem·lin ['kremlɪn]: the ~ der Kreml.

L

lab F [læb] Labor n.

la·bel ['leɪbl] **1.** Etikett n, Aufkleber m, Schild(chen) n; Aufschrift f, Beschriftung f; (Schall)Plattenfirma f; **2.** (*bsd. Brt. -ll-, Am. -l-*) etikettieren, beschriften; *fig.* abstempeln als.

la·bo·ra·to·ry [lə'brətəri] Labor(atorium) n; ∼ **assistant** Laborant(in).

la·bo·ri·ous □ [lə'bɔːriəs] mühsam; schwerfällig (*Stil*).

la·bo(u)r ['leɪbə] **1.** (schwere) Arbeit; Mühe f; ஐ Wehen pl.; Arbeiter pl., Arbeitskräfte pl.; **Labour** pol. die Labour Party; *hard* ∼ ஐ Zwangsarbeit f; **2.** Arbeiter..., Arbeits...; **3.** v/i. (schwer) arbeiten; sich abmühen, sich quälen; ∼ *under* leiden unter (*dat.*), zu kämpfen haben mit; v/t. ausführlich behandeln; ∼**ed** schwerfällig (*Stil*); ∼**er** [∼rə] bsd. ungelernter Arbeiter; **Labour Ex·change** *Brt.* F od. hist. Arbeitsamt n; **La·bour Par·ty** pol. Labour Party f; **la·bor u·ni·on** Am. pol. Gewerkschaft f.

lace [leɪs] **1.** Spitze f; Borte f; Schnürsenkel m; **2.** ∼ *up* (zu-, zusammen-) schnüren; *Schuh* zubinden; ∼*d with brandy* mit e-m Schuß Weinbrand.

la·ce·rate ['læsəreɪt] zerfleischen, -schneiden, -kratzen, aufreißen; *j-s Gefühle* verletzen.

lack [læk] **1.** (*of*) Fehlen n (von), Mangel m (an *dat.*); △ *nicht Lack*; **2.** v/t. nicht haben; *he* ∼*s money* es fehlt ihm an Geld; v/i. *be* ∼*ing* fehlen; *he is* ∼*ing in courage* ihm fehlt der Mut; ∼**·lus·tre**, Am. ∼**·lus·ter** ['læklʌstə] glanzlos, matt.

la·con·ic [lə'kɒnɪk] (∼*ally*) lakonisch, wortkarg, kurz und prägnant.

lac·quer ['lækə] **1.** Lack m; Haarspray m, n; Nagellack m; **2.** lackieren.

lad [læd] Bursche m, Junge m.

lad·der ['lædə] Leiter f; *Brt.* Laufmasche f; ∼**proof** (lauf)maschenfest (*Strumpf*).

la·den ['leɪdn] (schwer) beladen.

lad·ing ['leɪdɪŋ] Ladung f, Fracht f.

la·dle ['leɪdl] **1.** (Schöpf-, Suppen-) Kelle f, Schöpflöffel m; **2.** ∼ *out Suppe* austeilen.

la·dy ['leɪdɪ] Dame f; Lady f (a.

Titel); ∼ *doctor* Ärztin f; *Ladies('),* *Am. Ladies' room* Damentoilette f; ∼**bird** zo. Marienkäfer m; ∼**like** damenhaft; ∼**ship** [∼ʃɪp]: *her od.* *your* ∼ Ihre Ladyschaft.

lag [læg] **1.** (*-gg-*) ∼ *behind* zurückbleiben; sich verzögern; **2.** Verzögerung f; Zeitabstand m, -differenz f.

la·ger ['lɑːgə] Lagerbier n; △ *nicht Lager.*

la·goon [lə'guːn] Lagune f.

laid [leɪd] pret. u. p.p. von lay³.

lain [leɪn] p.p. von lie² 2.

lair [leə] Lager n, Höhle f, Bau m (*e-s wilden Tieres*).

la·i·ty ['leɪətɪ] Laien pl.

lake [leɪk] See m.

lamb [læm] **1.** Lamm n; **2.** lammen.

lame [leɪm] **1.** □ lahm (a. *fig.* = *unbefriedigend*); **2.** lähmen.

la·ment [lə'ment] **1.** Wehklage f; Klagelied n; **2.** (be)klagen; (be)trauern; **lam·en·ta·ble** □ ['læməntəbl] beklagenswert; kläglich; **lam·en·ta·tion** [læmən'teɪʃn] Wehklage f.

lamp [læmp] Lampe f; Laterne f.

lam·poon [læm'puːn] **1.** Schmähschrift f; **2.** verspotten, -unglimpfen.

lamp·post ['læmppəʊst] Laternenpfahl m; ∼**shade** Lampenschirm m.

lance [lɑːns] Lanze f.

land [lænd] **1.** Land n; ✈ Land n, Boden m; Land-, Grundbesitz m; Land n, Staat m, Nation f; *by* ∼ auf dem Landweg; ∼*s* pl. Ländereien pl.; **2.** landen; *Fracht* löschen; F *j-n* od. *et.* erwischen, kriegen; *j-n in Schwierigkeiten etc.* bringen; ∼**agent** ['lænderdʒənt] Gutsverwalter m; ∼**ed** Land..., Grund...; ∼**hold·er** Grundbesitzer(in).

land·ing ['lændɪŋ] Landung f; Anlegen n (*Schiff*); Anlegestelle f; Treppenabsatz m; Flur m, Gang m (*am Ende e-r Treppe*); ∼**field** ✈ Landebahn f; ∼**gear** ✈ Fahrgestell n; ∼**stage** Landungsbrücke f, -steg m.

land·la·dy ['lænleɪdɪ] Vermieterin f; Wirtin f; ∼**lord** [∼lɔːd] Vermieter m; Wirt m; Hauseigentümer m; Grundbesitzer m; ∼**lub·ber** ⚓ contp. [∼dlʌbə] Landratte f; ∼**mark** Grenzstein m; Orientierungspunkt m; Wahrzeichen n; *fig.* Markstein m; ∼**own·er** Grundbesitzer(in);

~scape ['lænskeɪp] Landschaft *f* (*a. paint.*); **~slide** Erdrutsch *m* (*a. pol.*); *a ~ victory pol.* ein überwältigender Wahlsieg; **~slip** (kleiner) Erdrutsch.

lane [leɪn] Feldweg *m*; Gasse *f*, Sträßchen *n*; ✣ (Fahrt)Route *f*; ✈ Flugschneise *f*; *mot.* Fahrbahn *f*, Spur *f*; *Sport:* (einzelne) Bahn.

lan·guage ['læŋgwɪdʒ] Sprache *f*; *~ laboratory* Sprachlabor *n*.

lan·guid □ ['læŋgwɪd] matt; träg(e).

lank □ [læŋk] dünn, dürr; strähnig (*Haar*); **~y** □ ['læŋkɪ] (*-ier*, *-iest*) schlaksig.

lan·tern ['læntən] Laterne *f*.

lap¹ [læp] Schoß *m*.

lap² [~] 1. *Sport:* Runde *f*; 2. (*-pp-*) *Sport:* Gegner überrunden; *Sport:* e-e Runde zurücklegen; wickeln; einhüllen.

lap³ [~] (*-pp-*) *v/t.:* *~ up* auflecken, -schlecken; *v/i.* plätschern (*against* gegen).

la·pel [lə'pel] Revers *n*, *m*.

lapse [læps] 1. Verlauf *m* (*der Zeit*); (kleiner) Fehler *od.* Irrtum; ⚖ Verfall *m*; 2. verfallen; ⚖ verfallen, erlöschen; abfallen (*vom Glauben*).

lar·ce·ny ⚖ ['lɑːsənɪ] Diebstahl *m*.

larch ♀ [lɑːtʃ] Lärche *f*.

lard [lɑːd] 1. Schweinefett *n*, -schmalz *n*; 2. *Fleisch* spicken; **larder** ['lɑːdə] Speisekammer *f*; Speiseschrank *m*.

large □ [lɑːdʒ] (*~r*, *~st*) groß; umfassend, weitgehend, ausgedehnt; *at ~* in Freiheit, auf freiem Fuß; ganz allgemein; in der Gesamtheit; (sehr) ausführlich; **~ly** ['lɑːdʒlɪ] zum großen Teil; im wesentlichen; **~minded** tolerant; **~ness** [~nɪs] Größe *f*.

lar·i·at *bsd. Am.* ['lærɪət] Lasso *n*, *m*.

lark¹ *zo.* [lɑːk] Lerche *f*.

lark² F [~] Jux *m*, Spaß *m*.

lark·spur ♀ ['lɑːkspɜː] Rittersporn *m*.

lar·va *zo.* ['lɑːvə] (*pl. -vae* [-viː]) Larve *f*.

lar·ynx *anat.* ['lærɪŋks] Kehlkopf *m*.

las·civ·i·ous □ [lə'sɪvɪəs] lüstern.

la·ser *phys.* ['leɪzə] Laser *m*; *~ beam* Laserstrahl *m*.

lash [læʃ] 1. Peitschenschnur *f*; Peitschenhieb *m*; Wimper *f*; 2. peitschen, schlagen; (fest)binden; *~ out* (wild) um sich schlagen; *fig.* heftig angreifen.

lass, **~ie** [læs, 'læsɪ] Mädchen *n*.

las·si·tude ['læsɪtjuːd] Mattigkeit *f*.

las·so [læ'suː] (*pl. -sos*, *-soes*) Lasso *n*, *m*.

last¹ [lɑːst] 1. *adj.* letzte(r, -s); vorige(r, -s); äußerste(r, -s); neueste(r, -s); *~ but one* vorletzte(r, -s); *~ night* gestern abend; 2. *der, die, das Letzte*; ⚠ *nicht Last*; *at ~* endlich; *to the ~* bis zum Schluß; 3. *adv.* zuletzt; *~ but not least* nicht zuletzt.

last² [~] (an-, fort)dauern; (sich) halten (*Farbe etc.*); (aus)reichen.

last³ [~] (Schuhmacher)Leisten *m*.

last·ing □ ['lɑːstɪŋ] dauerhaft; beständig.

last·ly ['lɑːstlɪ] schließlich, zum Schluß.

latch [lætʃ] 1. Klinke *f*; Schnappschloß *n*; 2. ein-, zuklinken; **~key** ['lætʃkiː] Hausschlüssel *m*.

late □ [leɪt] (*~r*, *~st*) spät; jüngste(r, -s), letzte(r, -s); frühere(r, -s), ehemalig; verstorben; *be ~* zu spät kommen, sich verspäten; *at (the) ~st* spätestens; *as ~ as* noch, erst; *of ~* kürzlich; *~r on* später; **~ly** ['leɪtlɪ] kürzlich.

la·tent □ ['leɪtənt] verborgen, latent.

lat·er·al □ ['lætərəl] seitlich, Seiten...

lath [lɑːθ] Latte *f*.

lathe ⊕ [leɪð] Drehbank *f*.

la·ther ['lɑːðə] 1. (Seifen)Schaum *m*; 2. *v/t.* einseifen; *v/i.* schäumen.

Lat·in ['lætɪn] 1. *ling.* lateinisch; romanisch; südländisch; 2. *ling.* Latein *n*; Roman|e *m*, -in *f*, Südländer(in).

lat·i·tude ['lætɪtjuːd] *geogr.* Breite *f*; *fig.* Spielraum *m*.

lat·ter ['lætə] letztere(r, -s) (*von zweien*); letzte(r, -s), spätere(r, -s); **~ly** [~lɪ] in letzter Zeit.

lat·tice ['lætɪs] Gitter *n*.

lau·da·ble □ ['lɔːdəbl] lobenswert.

laugh [lɑːf] 1. Lachen *n*, Gelächter *n*; 2. lachen; *~ at j-n* auslachen; *have the last ~* (am Ende) doch noch gewinnen; **~a·ble** □ ['lɑːfəbl] lächerlich; **~ter** [~tə] Lachen *n*, Gelächter *n*.

launch [lɔːntʃ] 1. *Schiff* vom Stapel laufen lassen; *Boot* aussetzen; schleudern; *Rakete* starten, abschießen; *fig.* in Gang setzen; 2. ✣ Barkasse *f*; = **~ing** ['lɔːntʃɪŋ] ✣ Stapellauf *m*; Abschuß *m* (*e-r Rakete*); *fig.*

Start(en n) m; ~ pad Abschußrampe f; ~ site Abschußbasis f.

laun·de·rette [lɔ:ndə'ret], bsd. Am. **~·dro·mat** ['lɔ:ndrəmæt] Waschsalon m, Münzwäscherei f; **~·dry** [~rɪ] Wäscherei f; schmutzige od. gewaschene Wäsche.

laur·el ♀ ['lɒrəl] Lorbeer m (a. fig.).

lav·a·to·ry ['lævətərɪ] Toilette f, Klosett n; public ~ Bedürfnisanstalt f.

lav·en·der ♀ ['lævəndə] Lavendel m.

lav·ish ['lævɪʃ] **1.** □ freigebig, verschwenderisch; **2.** ~ s.th. on s.o. j-n mit et. überhäufen od. überschütten.

law [lɔ:] Gesetz n; Recht n; (Spiel-) Regel f; Rechtswissenschaft f, Jura pl.; F die Polizei; ~ and order Recht od. Ruhe u. Ordnung; **~·a·bid·ing** ['lɔ:əbaɪdɪŋ] gesetzestreu; **~·court** Gericht(shof m) n; **~·ful** □ [~fl] gesetzlich; rechtmäßig, legitim; rechtsgültig; **~·less** □ [~lɪs] gesetzlos; gesetzwidrig; zügellos.

lawn [lɔ:n] Rasen m.

law|suit ['lɔ:sju:t] Prozeß m; **~·yer** [~jə] (Rechts)Anwalt m, (-)Anwältin f.

lax □ [læks] locker, lax; schlaff; lasch; **~·a·tive** ♂ ['læksətɪv] **1.** abführend; **2.** Abführmittel n.

lay¹ [leɪ] pret. von lie² 2.

lay² ♀ eccl. weltlich; Laien...

lay³ [~] (laid) v/t. legen; umlegen; Plan schmieden; Tisch decken; Eier legen; beruhigen, besänftigen; auferlegen; Klage vorbringen, Anklage erheben; Wette abschließen; Summe wetten; ~ in einlagern, sich eindecken mit; ~ low niederstrecken, -werfen; ~ off econ. Arbeiter vorübergehend entlassen, Arbeit einstellen; ~ open darlegen; ~ out ausbreiten; Garten etc. anlegen; entwerfen, planen; print. Buch gestalten; ~ up Vorräte hinlegen, sammeln; be laid up das Bett hüten müssen; v/i. (Eier) legen.

lay-by Brt. mot. ['leɪbaɪ] Parkbucht f, -streifen m; Park-, Rastplatz m.

lay·er ['leɪə] Lage f, Schicht f.

lay·man ['leɪmən] (pl. -men) Laie m.

lay|-off econ. ['leɪɒf] vorübergehende Arbeitseinstellung, Feierschicht(en pl.) f; **~·out** Anlage f; Plan m; print. Layout n, Gestaltung f.

la·zy □ ['leɪzɪ] (-ier, -iest) faul; träg(e), langsam; müde od. faul machend.

lead¹ [led] ♠ Blei n; ♣ Lot n.

lead² [li:d] **1.** Führung f; Leitung f; Spitzenposition f; Beispiel n; thea. Hauptrolle f; thea. Hauptdarsteller(in); Sport u. fig. Führung f, Vorsprung m; Kartenspiel: Vorhand f; ♪ Leitung f; (Hunde)Leine f; Hinweis m, Tip m, Anhaltspunkt m; **2.** (led) v/t. führen; leiten; (an)führen; verleiten, bewegen (to zu); Karte ausspielen; ~ on F j-n anführen, auf den Arm nehmen; v/i. führen; vorangehen; Sport: in Führung liegen; ~ off führen beginnen; ~ up to führen zu, überleiten zu.

lead·en ['ledn] bleiern (a. fig.), Blei...

lead·er ['li:də] (An)Führer(in), Leiter(in); Erste(r m) f; Brt. Leitartikel m; **~·ship** [~ʃɪp] Führung f, Leitung f.

lead-free ['ledfri:] bleifrei.

lead·ing ['li:dɪŋ] leitend; führend; Haupt...

leaf [li:f] **1.** (pl. leaves [~vz]) Blatt n; (Tür- etc.)Flügel m; (Tisch)Klappe f; **2.** ~ through durchblättern; **~·let** ['li:flɪt] Prospekt m; Broschüre f, Informationsblatt n; Merkblatt n; **~·y** [~] (-ier, -iest) belaubt.

league [li:g] Liga f (a. hist. u. Sport); Bund m.

leak [li:k] **1.** Leck n, undichte Stelle (a. fig.); **2.** lecken, leck sein; tropfen; ~ out auslaufen, -strömen, entweichen; fig. durchsickern; **~·age** ['li:kɪdʒ] Lecken n, Auslaufen n, -strömen n; fig. Durchsickern n; **~·y** [~] (-ier, -iest) leck, undicht.

lean¹ [li:n] (bsd. Brt. leant od. bsd. Am. leaned) (sich) lehnen; (sich) stützen; (sich) neigen; ~ on, ~ upon sich verlassen auf (acc.).

lean² [~] **1.** mager; **2.** das Magere (von gekochtem Fleisch).

leant bsd. Brt. [lent] pret u. p.p. von lean¹.

leap [li:p] **1.** Sprung m, Satz m; **2.** (leapt od. leaped) (über)springen; ~ at fig. sich stürzen auf; **~·t** [lept] pret. u. p.p. von leap 2; ~ year ['li:pjɜ:] Schaltjahr n.

learn [lɜ:n] (learned od. learnt) lernen; erfahren, hören; **~·ed** ['lɜ:nɪd] gelehrt; **~·er** [~ə] Anfänger(in); Lernende(r m) f; ~ driver mot. Fahrschüler(in); **~·ing** [~ɪŋ] (Er)Lernen n; Gelehrsamkeit f; **~·t** [lɜ:nt] pret. u. p.p. von learn.

lease [li:s] **1.** Pacht *f*, Miete *f*; Pacht-, Mietvertrag *m*; **2.** (ver)pachten, (ver)mieten.

leash [li:ʃ] (Hunde)Leine *f*.

least [li:st] **1.** *adj.* (*sup. von little 1*) kleinste(r, -s), geringste(r, -s), wenigste(r, -s); **2.** *adv.* (*sup. von little 2*) am wenigsten; ~ of all am allerwenigsten; **3.** *das* Geringste, *das* Mindeste, *das* Wenigste; at ~ wenigstens; to say the ~ gelinde gesagt.

leath·er [ˈleðə] **1.** Leder *n*; **2.** ledern; Leder...

leave [li:v] **1.** Erlaubnis *f*; *a.* ~ of absence Urlaub *m*; Abschied *m*; take (one's) ~ sich verabschieden; **2.** (*left*) *v/t.* (hinter-, über-, übrig-, ver-, zurück)lassen; stehen-, liegenlassen; vergessen; vermachen, -erben; *v/i.* (fort-, weg)gehen, abreisen, abfahren, abfliegen.

leav·en [ˈlevn] Sauerteig *m*; Hefe *f*.

leaves [li:vz] *pl. von leaf 1*; Laub *n*.

leav·ings [ˈli:vɪŋz] *pl.* Überreste *pl.*

lech·er·ous □ [ˈletʃərəs] lüstern.

lec·ture [ˈlektʃə] **1.** *univ.* Vorlesung *f*, Vortrag *m*; Strafpredigt *f*; △ *nicht* Lektüre; **2.** *v/i. univ.* e-e Vorlesung halten; e-n Vortrag halten; *v/t.* tadeln, abkanzeln; ~**tur·er** [~rə] *univ.* Dozent(in); Redner(in).

led [led] *pret. u. p. p. von lead² 2.*

ledge [ledʒ] Leiste *f*; Sims *m, n*; Riff *n*; (Fels)Vorsprung *m*.

led·ger *econ.* [ˈledʒə] Hauptbuch *n*.

leech [li:tʃ] *zo.* Blutegel *m*; *fig.* Blutsauger *m*, Schmarotzer *m*.

leek ♀ [li:k] Lauch *m*, Porree *m*.

leer [lɪə] **1.** anzüglicher (Seiten)Blick; **2.** anzüglich *od.* lüstern blicken; schielen (*at* nach).

lee·ward ♣ [ˈli:wəd] leewärts; ~**way** ♣ Abtrift *f*; *fig.* Rückstand *m*; *fig.* Spielraum *m*.

left¹ [left] *pret. u. p.p. von leave 2.*

left² [~] **1.** *adj.* linke(r, -s); **2.** *adv.* (nach) links; **3.** Linke *f* (*a. pol.*, *Boxen*), linke Seite; on *od.* to the ~ links; ~**hand** [ˈlefthænd] linke(r, -s); ~ drive *mot.* Linkssteuerung *f*; ~**hand·ed** □ [ˈleftˈhændɪd] linkshändig; für Linkshänder.

left-lug·gage of·fice *Brt.* ☎ [ˈleft-ˈlʌgɪdʒɒfɪs] Gepäckaufbewahrung *f*; ~**o·vers** *pl.* (Speise)Reste *pl.*; ~**wing** *pol.* linke(r, -s), linksgerichtet.

leg [leg] Bein *n*; Keule *f*; (Stiefel-)Schaft *m*; ♣ Schenkel *m*; pull s.o.'s ~ j-n auf den Arm nehmen (*hänseln*); stretch one's ~s sich die Beine vertreten.

leg·a·cy [ˈlegəsɪ] Vermächtnis *n*.

le·gal □ [ˈli:gl] legal, gesetz-, rechtmäßig; gesetz-, rechtlich; juristisch, Rechts...; ~**ize** [~aɪz] legalisieren, rechtskräftig machen.

le·ga·tion [lɪˈgeɪʃn] Gesandtschaft *f*.

le·gend [ˈledʒənd] Legende *f*, Sage *f*; Bildunterschrift *f*; **le·gen·da·ry** [~ərɪ] legendär, sagenhaft.

leg·gings [ˈlegɪŋz] *pl.* Gamaschen *pl.*; Beinlinge *pl.*, -schutz *m*.

le·gi·ble □ [ˈledʒəbl] leserlich.

le·gion *fig.* [ˈli:dʒən] Legion *f*, Heer *n*.

le·gis·la·tion [ledʒɪsˈleɪʃn] Gesetzgebung *f*; ~**tive** *pol.* [ˈledʒɪslətɪv] **1.** □ gesetzgebend, legislativ; **2.** Legislative *f*, gesetzgebende Gewalt; ~**tor** [~eɪtə] Gesetzgeber *m*.

le·git·i·mate □ [lɪˈdʒɪtɪmət] legitim; gesetz-, rechtmäßig, berechtigt; ehelich.

lei·sure [ˈleʒə] Muße *f*, Freizeit *f*; at ~ frei, unbeschäftigt; ohne Hast; ~**ly** [~lɪ] gemächlich.

lem·on ♀ [ˈlemən] Zitrone *f*; ~**ade** [lemɔˈneɪd] Zitronenlimonade *f*; ~ squash Zitronenwasser *n*.

lend [lend] (*lent*) *j-m et.* (ver-, aus)leihen, borgen; △ *nicht sich et. leihen.*

length [leŋθ] Länge *f*; Strecke *f*; (Zeit)Dauer *f*; at ~ endlich, schließlich; ausführlich; go to any *od.* great *od.* considerable ~s sehr weit gehen; ~**en** [ˈleŋθən] verlängern; länger werden; ~**ways** [~weɪz], ~**wise** [~waɪz] der Länge nach; ~**y** □ [~ɪ] (-ier, -iest) sehr lang.

le·ni·ent □ [ˈli:njənt] mild(e), nachsichtig.

lens *opt.* [lenz] Linse *f*.

lent¹ [lent] *pret. u. p.p. von lend.*

Lent² [~] Fastenzeit *f*.

len·til ♀ [ˈlentɪl] Linse *f*.

leop·ard *zo.* [ˈlepəd] Leopard *m*.

le·o·tard [ˈli:əʊtɑːd] (Tänzer)Trikot *n*; Gymnastikanzug *m*.

lep·ro·sy ♣ [ˈleprəsɪ] Lepra *f*.

les·bi·an [ˈlezbɪən] **1.** lesbisch; **2.** Lesbierin *f*, F Lesbe *f*.

less [les] **1.** *adj. u. adv.* (*comp. von little 1, 2*) kleiner, geringer, weniger; **2.** *prp.* weniger, minus, abzüglich.

less·en [ˈlesn] (sich) vermindern *od.* -ringern; abnehmen; herabsetzen.

less·er ['lesə] kleiner, geringer.

les·son ['lesn] Lektion f; (Haus)Aufgabe f; (Unterrichts)Stunde f; fig. Lektion f, Lehre f; ~s pl. Unterricht m.

lest [lest] damit nicht; daß.

let [let] (let) lassen; vermieten, -pachten; ~ alone allein lassen; geschweige denn; ~ down herab-, herunterlassen; Kleider verlängern; j-n im Stich lassen; ~ go loslassen; ~ o.s. go sich gehenlassen; ~ in (her)einlassen; ~ o.s. in for s.th. sich et. aufhalsen od. einbrocken; ~ s.o. in on s.th. j-n in et. einweihen; ~ off abschießen; j-n laufenlassen; aussteigen lassen; ~ out hinauslassen; Schrei ausstoßen; ausplaudern; vermieten; ~ up aufhören.

le·thal □ ['li:θəl] tödlich; Todes...

leth·ar·gy ['leθədʒɪ] Lethargie f.

let·ter ['letə] 1. Buchstabe m; print. Type f; Brief m, Schreiben n; ~s pl. Literatur f; attr. Brief...; 2. beschriften; ~box Briefkasten m; ~card Kartenbrief m; ~ car·ri·er Am. Briefträger m; ~ed (literarisch) gebildet; ~ing [~rɪŋ] Beschriftung f.

let·tuce ♧ ['letɪs] (bsd. Kopf)Salat m.

leu·k(a)e·mia ♂ [lju:'ki:mɪə] Leukämie f.

lev·el ['levl] 1. waag(e)recht; eben; gleich; ausgeglichen; my ~ best f mein möglichstes; ~ crossing Brt. schienengleicher Bahnübergang; 2. Ebene f, ebene Fläche; (gleiche) Höhe, (Wasser- etc.)Spiegel m, (-)Stand m; Wasserwaage f; fig. Niveau n, Stand m, Stufe f; sea ~ Meeresspiegel m; on the ~ f ehrlich, aufrichtig; 3. (bsd. Brt. -ll-, Am. -l-) ebnen, planieren; niederschlagen, fällen; ~ at Waffe richten auf (acc.); Anklage erheben gegen (acc.); ~head·ed vernünftig, nüchtern.

le·ver ['li:və] Hebel m; ~age [~rɪdʒ] Hebelkraft f, -wirkung f.

lev·y ['levɪ] 1. Steuereinziehung f; Steuer f; ✗ Aushebung f; 2. Steuern einziehen, erheben; ✗ ausheben.

lewd □ [lju:d] unanständig, obszön; schmutzig.

li·a·bil·i·ty [laɪə'bɪlətɪ] ⚖ Haftung f, Haftpflicht f; liabilities pl. Verbindlichkeiten pl.; econ. Passiva pl.

li·a·ble ['laɪəbl] ⚖ haftbar, -pflichtig; be ~ for haften für; be ~ to neigen zu; anfällig sein für.

li·ar ['laɪə] Lügner(in).

lib F [lɪb] abbr. für liberation.

li·bel ⚖ ['laɪbl] 1. Verleumdung f od. Beleidigung f (durch Veröffentlichung); 2. (bsd. Brt. -ll-, Am. -l-) (schriftlich) verleumden od. beleidigen.

lib·e·ral ['lɪbərəl] 1. □ liberal (a. pol.), aufgeschlossen; großzügig; reichlich; 2. Liberale(r m) f (a. pol.); ~i·ty [lɪbə'rælɪtɪ] Großzügigkeit f; Aufgeschlossenheit f.

lib·e·rate ['lɪbəreɪt] befreien; ~ra·tion [lɪbə'reɪʃn] Befreiung f; ~ra·tor ['lɪbəreɪtə] Befreier m.

lib·er·ty ['lɪbətɪ] Freiheit f; take liberties sich Freiheiten herausnehmen; be at ~ frei sein.

li·brar·i·an [laɪ'breərɪən] Bibliothekar(in); **li·bra·ry** ['laɪbrərɪ] Bibliothek f; Bücherei f.

lice [laɪs] pl. von louse.

li·cence, Am. **-cense** ['laɪsəns] Lizenz f, Konzession f; Freiheit f; Zügellosigkeit f; license plate Am. mot. Nummernschild n; driving ~ Führerschein m.

li·cense, -cence [~] e-e Lizenz od. Konzession erteilen; (amtlich) genehmigen od. zulassen.

li·cen·tious □ [laɪ'senʃəs] ausschweifend; zügellos.

li·chen ♧, ♂ ['laɪkən] Flechte f.

lick [lɪk] 1. Lecken n; Salzlecke f; 2. v/t. (ab-, auf-, be)lecken; F verdreschen, -prügeln; F schlagen, besiegen; v/i. lecken; züngeln (Flammen).

lic·o·rice ['lɪkərɪs] = liquorice.

lid [lɪd] Deckel m; (Augen)Lid n.

lie¹ [laɪ] 1. Lüge f; give s.o. the ~ j-n Lügen strafen; 2. lügen.

lie² [~] 1. Lage f; 2. (lay, lain) liegen; ~ behind fig. dahinterstecken; ~ down sich hinlegen; let sleeping dogs ~ fig. daran rühren wir lieber nicht; ~ down F [laɪ'daʊn] Nickerchen n; ~ in ['laɪɪn]: have a ~ Brt. F sich gründlich ausschlafen.

lieu [lju:]: in ~ statt dessen; in ~ of an Stelle von (od. gen.), anstatt (gen.).

lieu·ten·ant [lef'tenənt, ⚓ le'tenənt; Am. lu:'tenənt] Leutnant m.

life [laɪf] (pl. lives [~vz]) Leben n; Menschenleben n; Lebensbeschreibung f, Biographie f; for ~ fürs (ganze) Leben; bsd. ⚖ lebenslänglich; ~ imprisonment, ~ sentence

lebenslängliche Freiheitsstrafe; ~
as·sur·ance Lebensversicherung f;
~**belt** ['laifbelt] Rettungsgürtel m;
~**boat** Rettungsboot n; ~**guard** ⚔
Leibgarde f; Bademeister m; Rettungsschwimmer m; ~ **in·sur·ance**
Lebensversicherung f; ~**jack·et**
Schwimmweste f; ~**less** □ [~lɪs]
leblos; matt, schwung-, lustlos;
~**like** lebensecht; ~**long** lebenslang; ~ **pre·serv·er** Am. [~prɪzɜ:və]
Schwimmweste f; Rettungsgürtel
m; ~**time** Lebenszeit f.

lift [lɪft] **1.** (Hoch-, Auf)Heben n;
phys., ✈ Auftrieb m; bsd. Brt. Lift
m, Aufzug m, Fahrstuhl m; give s.o.
a ~ j-n aufmuntern; j-m Auftrieb
geben; j-n (im Auto) mitnehmen; **2.**
v/t. (hoch-, auf)heben; erheben;
Verbot aufheben; Gesichtshaut straffen; F klauen, stehlen; v/i. sich heben (Nebel); ~ **off** abheben (Rakete
etc.); ~**off** ['lɪftɔf] Start m, Abheben
n (Rakete etc.).

lig·a·ture ['lɪgətʃʊə] Binde f; ✠ Verband m.

light¹ [laɪt] **1.** Licht n (a. fig.); Lampe
f; Leuchten n, Glanz m; Aspekt m,
Gesichtspunkt m; Can you give me
a ~, please? Haben Sie Feuer?; put
a ~ to anzünden; **2.** licht, hell; blond;
3. (lit od. lighted) v/t. ~ (up) be-,
erleuchten; anzünden; v/i. sich entzünden, brennen; ~ up aufleuchten.

light² adj. □ u. adv. [~] leicht (a. fig.);
make ~ of et. leichtnehmen.

light·en¹ ['laɪtn] v/t. erhellen; aufhellen; aufheitern; v/i. hell(er) werden,
sich aufhellen.

light·en² [~] leichter machen od. werden; erleichtern.

light·er ['laɪtə] Anzünder m; Feuerzeug n; ⚓ Leichter m.

light·-head·ed ['laɪt'hedɪd] benommen, benebelt; leichtfertig, töricht;
~**heart·ed** □ fröhlich, unbeschwert; ~**house** Leuchtturm m.

light·ing ['laɪtɪŋ] Beleuchtung f; Anzünden n.

light·-mind·ed ['laɪt'maɪndɪd]
leichtfertig; ~**ness** ['laɪtnɪs] Leichtheit f; Leichtigkeit f.

light·ning ['laɪtnɪŋ] Blitz m; attr.
blitzschnell; Blitz...; ~ **con·duc·tor**,
Am. ~ **rod** ⚡ Blitzableiter m.

light·weight ['laɪtweɪt] Boxen:
Leichtgewicht(ler m) n.

like [laɪk] **1.** gleich; ähnlich; (so) wie;

F als ob; ~ that so; feel ~ Lust haben
auf od. zu; what is he ~? wie ist er?;
that is just ~ him! das sieht ihm
ähnlich!; **2.** der, die, das gleiche, et.
Gleiches; his ~ seinesgleichen; the ~
dergleichen; the ~s of you Leute wie
du; my ~s and dislikes was ich mag
und was ich nicht mag; **3.** v/t. gern
haben, (gern) mögen; gern tun etc.;
how do you ~ it? wie gefällt es dir?,
wie findest du es?; I ~ that! iro. das
hab' ich gern!; I should ~ to come ich
würde gern kommen; v/i. wollen; as
you ~ wie du willst; if you ~ wenn Sie
wollen; ~**li·hood** ['laɪklɪhʊd] Wahrscheinlichkeit f; ~**ly** [~lɪ] **1.** adj.
(-ier, -iest) wahrscheinlich; geeignet; **2.** adv. wahrscheinlich; not~!
F bestimmt nicht!

lik·en ['laɪkən] vergleichen (to mit).
like·ness ['laɪknɪs] Ähnlichkeit f;
(Ab)Bild n; Gestalt f; ~**wise** [~waɪz]
gleich-, ebenfalls; auch.

lik·ing ['laɪkɪŋ] (for) Vorliebe f (für),
Gefallen n (an dat.).

li·lac ['laɪlək] **1.** lila; **2.** ⚘ Flieder m.

lil·y ⚘ ['lɪlɪ] Lilie f; ~ of the valley
Maiglöckchen n; ~**white** schneeweiß.

limb [lɪm] (Körper)Glied n; Ast m.

lim·ber ['lɪmbə]: ~ up Sport:
Lockerungsübungen machen.

lime¹ [laɪm] Kalk m; Vogelleim m; △
nicht Leim.

lime² ⚘ [~] Linde f; Limone f.

lime·light fig. ['laɪmlaɪt] Rampenlicht n.

lim·it ['lɪmɪt] **1.** fig. Grenze f; within
~s inGrenzen; off ~s Am. Zutritt
verboten (to für); that is the ~! F das
ist der Gipfel!, das ist (doch) die
Höhe!; go to the ~ bis zum Äußersten gehen; **2.** beschränken (to auf
acc.).

lim·i·ta·tion [lɪmɪ'teɪʃn] Ein-, Beschränkung f; fig. Grenze f.

lim·it·ed ['lɪmɪtɪd] beschränkt, begrenzt; ~ (liability) company Brt.
Gesellschaft f mit beschränkter Haftung; ~**less** □ [~lɪs] grenzenlos.

limp [lɪmp] **1.** hinken, humpeln; **2.**
Hinken n, Humpeln n; **3.** schlaff,
schwach, müde; weich.

lim·pid □ ['lɪmpɪd] klar, durchsichtig.

line [laɪn] **1.** Linie f; Zeile f; Vers m;
Strich m; Falte f, Runzel f, Furche f;
Reihe f; (Menschen)Schlange f;

live

(*Ahnen-* etc.)Reihe f, Linie f; (*Bahn-*, *Verkehrs-* etc.)Linie f, Strecke f; (*Eisenbahn-*, *Verkehrs-* etc.)Gesellschaft f; tel., teleph. Leitung f; Branche f, Fach n, Gebiet n; Sport: (*Ziel-* etc.)Linie f; Leine f; (*Angel*)Schnur f; Äquator m; Richtung f; econ. Posten m (*Ware*); fig. Grenze f; ~s pl. thea. Rolle f, Text m; be in ~ for gute Aussichten haben auf (acc.); be in ~ with übereinstimmen mit; draw the ~ haltmachen; e-e Grenze ziehen (at bei); hold the ~ teleph. am Apparat bleiben; stand in ~ Am. Schlange stehen; 2. lin(i)ieren; Gesicht furchen, zeichnen; Weg etc. säumen; Kleid füttern; ⊕ auskleiden; ~ up (sich) in e-r Reihe aufstellen.

lin·e·a·ments ['lɪnɪəmənts] pl. Gesichtszüge pl.

lin·e·ar ['lɪnɪə] linear, geradlinig; Längen...

lin·en ['lɪnɪn] 1. Leinen n; (*Bett-*, *Tisch-* etc.)Wäsche f; 2. leinen, Leinen...; ~·clos·et, ~·cup·board Wäscheschrank m.

lin·er ['laɪnə] Linien-, Passagierschiff n; Verkehrsflugzeug n; = eyeliner.

lin·ger ['lɪŋgə] zögern; verweilen, sich aufhalten; dahinsiechen; a. ~ on sich hinziehen.

lin·ge·rie ['lɛ̃ːnʒəriː] Damenunterwäsche f.

lin·i·ment pharm. ['lɪnɪmənt] Liniment n, Einreibemittel n.

lin·ing ['laɪnɪŋ] Futter(stoff m) n; (*Brems*)Belag m; ⊕ Aus-, Verkleidung f.

link [lɪŋk] 1. (*Ketten*)Glied n; Manschettenknopf m; fig. (*Binde*)Glied n, Verbindung f; 2. (sich) verbinden; ~ up miteinander verbinden; *Raumschiff* (an)koppeln.

links [lɪŋks] pl. Dünen pl.; a. golf ~ Golfplatz m.

link-up ['lɪŋkʌp] Zusammenschluß m, Verbindung f; Kopplung(smanöver n) f (*Raumschiff*).

lin·seed ['lɪnsiːd] ♀ Leinsamen m; ~ oil Leinöl n.

li·on zo. ['laɪən] Löwe m; ~·ess zo. [~nɪs] Löwin f.

lip [lɪp] Lippe f; (*Tassen-* etc.)Rand m; sl. Unverschämtheit f; ~·stick ['lɪpstɪk] Lippenstift m.

liq·ue·fy ['lɪkwɪfaɪ] (sich) verflüssigen.

liq·uid ['lɪkwɪd] 1. flüssig; feucht (schimmernd) (*Augen*); 2. Flüssigkeit f.

liq·ui·date ['lɪkwɪdeɪt] liquidieren (a. econ.); *Schuld(en*) tilgen.

liq·uid·ize ['lɪkwɪdaɪz] zerkleinern, pürieren (im Mixer); ~·iz·er [~ə] Mixgerät n, Mixer m.

liq·uor ['lɪkə] Brt. alkoholische Getränk; Am. Schnaps m; ⚠ nicht Likör.

liq·uo·rice ['lɪkərɪs] Lakritze f.

lisp [lɪsp] 1. Lispeln n; 2. lispeln.

list [lɪst] 1. Liste f, Verzeichnis n; 2. (in e-e Liste) eintragen; verzeichnen, auflisten.

lis·ten ['lɪsn] (to) lauschen, horchen (auf acc.); anhören (acc.), zuhören (dat.); hören (auf acc.); ~ in (im Radio) hören (to acc.); am Telefon mithören; ~·er [~ə] Zuhörer(in); (*Rundfunk*)Hörer(in).

list·less ['lɪstlɪs] teilnahms-, lustlos.

lit [lɪt] pret. u. p.p. von light[1] 3.

lit·er·al □ ['lɪtərəl] (wort)wörtlich; buchstäblich; prosaisch.

lit·er·a·ry □ ['lɪtərərɪ] literarisch, Literatur...; ~·ture [~rətʃə] Literatur f.

lithe □ [laɪð] geschmeidig, gelenkig.

lit·i·ga·tion ⚖ [lɪtɪ'geɪʃn] Prozeß m.

li·tre, Am. **-ter** ['liːtə] Liter m, n.

lit·ter ['lɪtə] 1. Sänfte f; Tragbahre f, Trage f; Streu f; zo. Wurf m; Abfall m, bsd. herumliegendes Papier; Durcheinander n, Unordnung f; 2. v/t. zo. *Junge* werfen; verstreuen; be ~ed with übersät sein mit; v/i. zo. Junge werfen; ~ bas·ket, ~ bin Abfallkorb m.

lit·tle ['lɪtl] 1. adj. (less, least) klein; gering(fügig), unbedeutend; wenig; ~ one Kleiner m, Kleine f, Kleines n (*Kind*); 2. adv. (less, least) wenig, kaum; überhaupt nicht; 3. Kleinigkeit f; a ~ ein bißchen, etwas; ~ by ~ nach und nach; not a ~ nicht wenig.

live[1] [lɪv] v/i. leben; wohnen; ~ to see erleben; ~ off von s-m Kapital etc. leben; auf j-s Kosten leben; ~ on leben von; ~ through durchmachen, -stehen; ~ up to s-m Ruf gerecht werden, s-n Grundsätzen gemäß leben; *Versprechen* halten; *Erwartungen* erfüllen; ~ with mit j-m zusammenleben; mit et. leben; v/t. Leben führen; ~ s.th. down et. durch guten Lebenswandel vergessen lassen.

live[2] [laɪv] 1. adj. lebend, lebendig;

wirklich, richtig; aktuell; glühend; scharf (*Munition*); ⚡ stromführend, geladen; *Rundfunk, TV*: direkt, Direkt..., live, Live..., Original...; **2.** *adv. Rundfunk, TV*: direkt, live, original.

live·li·hood ['laɪvlɪhʊd] (Lebens-)Unterhalt *m*; **~·li·ness** [~nɪs] Lebhaftigkeit *f*; **~·ly** [~lɪ] (*-ier, -iest*) lebhaft, lebendig; aufregend; schnell; bewegt.

liv·er *anat.* ['lɪvə] Leber *f*.

liv·e·ry ['lɪvərɪ] Livree *f*; (Amts-)Tracht *f*.

lives [laɪvz] *pl. von* life.

live·stock ['laɪvstɒk] Vieh(bestand *m*) *n*.

liv·id □ ['lɪvɪd] bläulich; F fuchsteufelswild.

liv·ing ['lɪvɪŋ] **1.** □ lebend(ig); *the ~ image of* das genaue Ebenbild *gen.*; **2.** *das* Leben; Lebensweise *f*; Lebensunterhalt *m*; *eccl.* Pfründe *f*; *the ~ pl.* die Lebenden *pl.*; *standard of ~* Lebensstandard *m*; **~ room** Wohnzimmer *n*.

liz·ard *zo.* ['lɪzəd] Eidechse *f*.

load [ləʊd] **1.** Last *f* (*a. fig.*); Ladung *f*; Belastung *f*; **2.** (auf-, be)laden; *Schußwaffe* laden; *j-n* überhäufen (*with* mit); *~ a camera* e-n Film einlegen; **~·ing** ['ləʊdɪŋ] Laden *n*; Ladung *f*, Fracht *f*; *attr.* Lade...

loaf¹ [ləʊf] (*pl.* loaves [~vz]) Laib *m* (Brot); Brot *n*.

loaf² [~] herumlungern; **~·er** ['ləʊfə] Faulenzer(in).

loam [ləʊm] Lehm *m*; **~·y** ['ləʊmɪ] (*-ier, -iest*) lehmig.

loan [ləʊn] **1.** (Ver)Leihen *n*; Anleihe *f*; Darlehen *n*; Leihgabe *f*; *on ~* leihweise; **2.** *bsd. Am.* an *j-n* ausleihen.

loath □ [ləʊθ] abgeneigt; *be ~ to do s.th.* et. ungern tun; **~e** [ləʊð] sich ekeln vor (*dat.*); verabscheuen; **~·ing** ['ləʊðɪŋ] Ekel *m*; Abscheu *m*; **~·some** □ [~ðsəm] abscheulich, ekelhaft; verhaßt.

loaves [ləʊvz] *pl. von* loaf¹.

lob·by ['lɒbɪ] **1.** Vorhalle *f*; *thea., Film*: Foyer *n*; *parl.* Wandelhalle *f*; *pol.* Lobby *f*, Interessengruppe *f*; **2.** *pol. Abgeordnete* beeinflussen.

lobe *anat.*, ♀ [ləʊb] Lappen *m*; *a. ear~* Ohrläppchen *n*.

lob·ster *zo.* ['lɒbstə] Hummer *m*.

lo·cal □ ['ləʊkl] **1.** örtlich, Orts...;

lokal, Lokal...; *~ government* Gemeindeverwaltung *f*; **2.** Einheimische(r *m*) *f*; *a. ~ train* Nahverkehrszug *m*; *the ~ Brt.* F *bsd.* die Stammkneipe; **~·i·ty** [ləʊˈkælətɪ] Örtlichkeit *f*; Lage *f*; **~·ize** ['ləʊkəlaɪz] lokalisieren.

lo·cate [ləʊˈkeɪt] *v/t.* ausfindig machen; orten; *be ~d* eingen, sich befinden; **lo·ca·tion** [~eɪʃn] Lage *f*; Standort *m*; Platz *m* (for für); *Film*: Gelände *n* für Außenaufnahmen; *on ~* auf Außenaufnahme.

loch *schott.* [lɒk] See *m*.

lock¹ [lɒk] **1.** (Tür-, Gewehr- *etc.*) Schloß *n*; Schleuse(nkammer) *f*; ⊕ Sperrvorrichtung *f*; **2.** (ab-, ver-, zu)schließen, zu-, versperren; umschließen, umfassen; sich schließen lassen; ⊕ blockieren; *~ away* wegschließen; *~ in* einschließen, -sperren; *~ out* aussperren; *~ up* abschließen; wegschließen; einsperren.

lock² [~] (Haar)Locke *f*.

lock·er ['lɒkə] Schrank *m*, Spind *m*; Schließfach *n*; *~ room* Umkleideraum *m*; **~·et** [~ɪt] Medaillon *n*; **~-out** *econ.* Aussperrung *f*; **~·smith** Schlosser *m*; **~-up** (Haft)Zelle *f*; F Gefängnis *n*.

lo·co *Am. sl.* ['ləʊkəʊ] bekloppt.

lo·co·mo·tion [ləʊkəˈməʊʃn] Fortbewegung(sfähigkeit) *f*; **~·tive** ['ləʊkəməʊtɪv] **1.** (Fort)Bewegungs...; **2.** *a. ~ engine* Lokomotive *f*.

lo·cust *zo.* ['ləʊkəst] Heuschrecke *f*.

lodge [lɒdʒ] **1.** Häuschen *n*, Jagd-, Skihütte *f etc.*; Pförtnerhaus *n*, -loge *f*; (*Freimaurer*)Loge *f*; **2.** *v/i.* (*bsd.* vorübergehend *od.* in Untermiete) wohnen; stecken(bleiben) (*Kugel etc.*), (fest)sitzen; *v/t.* aufnehmen, beherbergen, unterbringen; *Kugel* jagen (*in* in dat.); *Schlag* versetzen; *Beschwerde* einlegen; *Klage* einreichen; **lodg·er** ['lɒdʒə] Untermieter(in); **lodg·ing** [~ɪŋ] Unterkunft *f*; *~s pl. bsd.* möbliertes Zimmer.

loft [lɒft] (Dach)Boden *m*; Heuboden *m*; Empore *f*; **~·y** □ ['lɒftɪ] (*-ier, -iest*) hoch; erhaben; stolz.

log [lɒg] (Holz)Klotz *m*, (*gefällter*) Baumstamm; ♣ Log *m*; = **~·book** ['lɒgbʊk] ♣, ✈ Logbuch *n*; *mot.* Fahrtenbuch *n*; *Brt. mot.* Kraftfahrzeugbrief *m*; **~ cab·in** Blockhaus *n*, -hütte *f*; **~·ger·head** [~əhed]: *be at ~s* sich in den Haaren liegen.

lo·gic ['lɒdʒɪk] Logik f; **~al** □ [~kl] logisch.

loins [lɔɪnz] pl. anat. Lende f; Koch-kunst: Lende(nstück n) f.

loi·ter ['lɔɪtə] trödeln, schlendern, bummeln; herumlungern.

loll [lɒl] (sich) rekeln od. lümmeln; ~ out heraushängen (Zunge).

loll·i·pop ['lɒlɪpɒp] Lutscher m; Eis n am Stiel; ~ man, ~ woman Brt. Schülerlotse m; ~·ly F ['lɒlɪ] Lutscher m; ice(d) ~ Eis n am Stiel.

lone·li·ness ['ləʊnlɪnɪs] Einsamkeit f; ~·ly [~lɪ] (-ier, -iest), ~·some □ [~səm] einsam.

long¹ [lɒŋ] **1.** (-e) lange Zeit; before ~ bald; for ~ lange; take ~ lange brauchen od. dauern; **2.** adj. lang; langfristig; in the ~ run schließlich; be ~ lange brauchen; **3.** adv. lang(e); as od. so ~ as solange, vorausgesetzt, daß; ~ ago vor langer Zeit; no ~er nicht mehr, nicht länger; so ~! F bis dann!, tschüs!

long² [~] sich sehnen (for nach).

long-dis·tance ['lɒŋ'dɪstəns] Fern...; ~ Langstrecken...; ~ call teleph. Ferngespräch n; ~ runner Sport: Langstreckenläufer m.

lon·gev·i·ty [lɒn'dʒevətɪ] Langlebigkeit f.

long·hand ['lɒŋhænd] Schreibschrift f.

long·ing ['lɒŋɪŋ] **1.** □ sehnsüchtig; **2.** Sehnsucht f, Verlangen n.

lon·gi·tude geogr. ['lɒndʒɪtjuːd] Länge f.

long jump ['lɒŋdʒʌmp] Sport: Weit-sprung m; ~·shore·man [~ʃɔːmən] (pl. -men) Hafenarbeiter m; ~-sight·ed [~'saɪtɪd] weitsichtig; ~·stand·ing seit langer Zeit bestehend; alt; ~-term langfristig, auf lange Sicht; ~ wave ≵ Langwelle f; ~-wind·ed □ langatmig.

loo Brt. F [luː] Klo n.

look [lʊk] **1.** Blick m; Miene f, (Gesichts)Ausdruck m; (good) ~s pl. gutes Aussehen; have a ~ at s.th. sich et. ansehen; I don't like the ~ of it es gefällt mir nicht; **2.** sehen, blicken, schauen (at, on auf acc., nach); nachsehen; krank etc. aussehen; aufpassen, achten; nach e-r Richtung liegen, gehen (Fenster etc.); ~ here! schau mal (her); hör mal (zu)!; ~ like aussehen wie; it ~s as if es sieht (so) aus, als ob; ~ after aufpassen auf

(acc.), sich kümmern um, sorgen für; ~ ahead nach vorne sehen; fig. vorausschauen; ~ around sich umsehen; ~ at ansehen; ~ back sich umsehen; fig. zurückblicken; ~ down herab-, heruntersehen (a. fig. on s.o. auf j-n); ~ for suchen; ~ forward to sich freuen auf (acc.); ~ in F hereinschauen (on bei) (als Besucher); F TV fernsehen; ~ into untersuchen, prüfen; ~ on zusehen, -schauen (dat.); ~ on to liegen zu, (hinaus)gehen auf (acc.) (Fenster, etc.); ~ on, ~ upon betrachten, ansehen (as als); ~ out hinaus-, heraussehen; aufpassen, sich vorsehen; Ausschau halten (for nach); ~ over et. durchsehen; j-n mustern; ~ round sich umsehen; ~ through et. durchsehen; ~ up aufblicken, -sehen; et. nachschlagen; j-n aufsuchen.

look·ing-glass ['lʊkɪŋglɑːs] Spiegel m.

look-out ['lʊkaʊt] Ausguck m; Ausschau f; fig. F Aussicht(en pl.) f; that is my ~ F das ist meine Sache.

loom [luːm] **1.** Webstuhl m; **2.** a. ~ up undeutlich sichtbar werden od. auftauchen.

loop [luːp] **1.** Schlinge f, Schleife f; Schlaufe f; Öse f; ≵ Looping m, n; Computer: Programmschleife f; **2.** v/t. in Schleifen legen; schlingen; v/i. e-e Schleife machen; sich schlingen; ~·hole ['luːphəʊl] ✗ Schießscharte f; fig. Hintertürchen n; a ~ in the law e-e Gesetzeslücke.

loose [luːs] **1.** □ (~r, ~st) los(e); locker; weit; frei; ungenau; liederlich; let ~ loslassen; freilassen; **2.** be on the ~ frei herumlaufen; **loos·en** ['luːsn] lösen, (sich) lockern; ~ up Sport: Lockerungsübungen machen.

loot [luːt] **1.** plündern; **2.** Beute f.

lop [lɒp] (-pp-) Baum beschneiden, stutzen; ~ off abhauen, abhacken; ~-sid·ed □ ['lɒp'saɪdɪd] schief; einseitig.

lo·qua·cious □ [ləʊ'kweɪʃəs] redselig, geschwätzig.

lord [lɔːd] Herr m, Gebieter m; Lord m; the ⌂ der Herr (Gott); my ~ [mɪ'lɔːd] Mylord, Euer Gnaden, Euer Ehren (Anrede); ⌂ Mayor Brt. Oberbürgermeister m; the ⌂'s Prayer das Vaterunser; ⌂'s Supper das Abendmahl; ~·ly ['lɔːdlɪ]

(-ier, -iest) vornehm, edel; gebieterisch; hochmütig, arrogant; **~ship** [~∫ɪp]: *his od.* your ~ seine *od.* Euer Lordschaft.

lore [lɔ:] Kunde *f*; Überlieferungen *pl.*

lor·ry *Brt.* ['lɒrɪ] Last(kraft)wagen *m*, Lastauto *n*, Laster *m*; 🚚 Lore *f*.

lose [lu:z] (*lost*) *v/t.* verlieren; verpassen, -säumen; *et.* nicht mitbekommen; nachgehen (*Uhr*); *j-n s-e Stellung* kosten; ~ *o.s.* sich verirren; sich verlieren; *v/i.* Verluste erleiden; verlieren; nachgehen (*Uhr*); **los·er** ['lu:zə] Verlierer(in).

loss [lɒs] Verlust *m*; Schaden *m*; *at a* ~ *econ.* mit Verlust; *be at a* ~ nicht mehr weiterwissen.

lost [lɒst] **1.** *pret. u. p.p. von lose;* **2.** *adj.* verloren; verlorengegangen; verirrt; verschwunden; verloren, -geudet (*Zeit*); versäumt (*Gelegenheit*); *be* ~ *in thought* in Gedanken versunken *od.* -tieft sein; ~ *property office* Fundbüro *n*.

lot [lɒt] Los *n*; *econ.* Partie *f*, Posten (*Ware*); *bsd. Am.* Bauplatz *m*; *bsd. Am.* Parkplatz *m*; *bsd. Am.* Filmgelände *n*; F Gruppe *f*, Gesellschaft *f*; Los *n*, Schicksal *n*; △ *nicht Lot; the* ~ F alles, das Ganze; *a* ~ *of* F, ~*s of* F viel, e-e Menge; ~*s and* ~*s of* F jede Menge; *a bad* ~ F ein übler Kerl; *cast od. draw* ~*s* losen.

loth □ [ləʊθ] = *loath.*

lo·tion ['ləʊʃn] Lotion *f*.

lot·te·ry ['lɒtərɪ] Lotterie *f*.

loud □ [laʊd] laut (*a. adv.*); *fig.* schreiend, grell (*Farben etc.*); **~speak·er** [laʊd'spiːkə] Lautsprecher *m*.

lounge [laʊndʒ] **1.** faulenzen; herumlungern; schlendern; **2.** Bummel *m*; Wohnzimmer *n*; Aufenthaltsraum *m*, Lounge *f* (*e-s Hotels*); Warteraum *m*, Lounge *f* (*e-s Flughafens*); **~ suit** Straßenanzug *m*.

louse *zo.* [laʊs] (*pl. lice* [laɪs]) Laus *f*; **lou·sy** ['laʊzɪ] (-ier, -iest) verlaust; F miserabel, saumäßig.

lout [laʊt] Flegel *m*, Lümmel *m*.

lov·a·ble □ ['lʌvəbl] liebenswert; reizend.

love [lʌv] **1.** Liebe *f* (*of, for, to, towards* zu); Liebling *m*, Schatz *m*; *Brt.* m-e Liebe, mein Lieber, mein Liebes (*Anrede*); *Tennis:* null; *be in* ~ *with s.o.* in j-n verliebt sein; *fall in*

~ *with s.o.* sich in j-n verlieben; *make* ~ sich lieben, miteinander schlafen; *give my* ~ *to her* grüße sie herzlich von mir; *send one's* ~ *to j-n* grüßen lassen; ~ *from* herzliche Grüße von (*Briefschluß*); **2.** lieben; gern mögen; ~ **af·fair** Liebesaffäre *f*; **~·ly** ['lʌvlɪ] (-ier, -iest) lieblich, wunderschön, entzückend, reizend; **lov·er** [~ə] Liebhaber *m*, Geliebte(r) *m*; Geliebte *f*; Liebhaber(in), (*Tier- etc.*)Freund(in).

lov·ing □ ['lʌvɪŋ] liebevoll, liebend.

low¹ [ləʊ] **1.** *adj.* nieder, niedrig (*a. fig.*); tief; gering(schätzig); knapp (*Vorrat*); gedämpft, schwach (*Licht*); schwach, matt; niedergeschlagen; *sozial* untere(r, -s), niedrig; gewöhnlich, niedrig (*denkend od. gesinnt*); gemein; tief (*Ton*); leise (*Ton, Stimme*); **2.** *adv.* niedrig; tief (*a. fig.*); leise; **3.** *meteor.* Tief(druckgebiet) *n*; Tiefstand *m*, -punkt *m*.

low² [~] brüllen, muhen (*Rind*).

low·brow F ['ləʊbraʊ] **1.** geistig Anspruchslose(r *m*) *f*; **2.** geistig anspruchslos.

low·er ['ləʊə] **1.** niedriger, tiefer; geringer; lesser untere(r, -s), Unter...; **2.** *v/t.* herunterlassen; niedriger machen; *Augen, Stimme, Preis etc.* senken; (ab)schwächen; *Standard* herabsetzen; erniedrigen; ~ *o.s.* sich herablassen; sich demütigen; *v/i.* fallen, sinken.

low·land ['ləʊlənd] *mst* ~*s pl.* Tiefland *n*; **~·li·ness** [~lɪnɪs] Niedrigkeit *f*; Bescheidenheit *f*; **~·ly** [~lɪ] (-ier, -iest) niedrig; bescheiden; **~-necked** (tief) ausgeschnitten (*Kleid*); **~-pitched** ♪ tief; **~-pres·sure** *meteor.* Tiefdruck...; ⊕ Niederdruck...; **~-rise** *bsd. Am.* niedrig (gebaut); **~-spir·it·ed** niedergeschlagen.

loy·al □ ['lɔɪəl] loyal, treu; **~·ty** [~tɪ] Loyalität *f*, Treue *f*.

loz·enge ['lɒzɪndʒ] Raute *f*; Pastille *f*.

lu·bri·cant ['lu:brɪkənt] Schmiermittel *n*; **~·cate** [~keɪt] schmieren, ölen; **~·ca·tion** [lu:brɪ'keɪʃn] Schmieren *n*, Ölen *n*.

lu·cid □ ['lu:sɪd] klar; deutlich.

luck [lʌk] Schicksal *n*; Glück *n*; *bad* ~, *hard* ~ Unglück *n*, Pech *n*; *good* ~ Glück *n*; *good* ~! viel Glück!; *be in* (*out of*) ~ (kein) Glück haben; **~·i·ly** ['lʌkɪlɪ] glücklicherweise, zum Glück; **~·y** □ [~ɪ] (-ier, -iest) glücklich; Glücks...; *be* ~ Glück haben.

lu·cra·tive □ [ˈluːkrətɪv] einträglich, lukrativ.

lu·di·crous □ [ˈluːdɪkrəs] lächerlich.

lug [lʌg] (-*gg*-) zerren, schleppen.

lug·gage *bsd. Brt.* [ˈlʌgɪdʒ] (Reise-) Gepäck *n*; ~ **car·ri·er** Gepäckträger *m* (*am Fahrrad*); ~ **rack** Gepäcknetz *n*, -ablage *f*; ~ **van** *bsd. Brt.* Gepäckwagen *m*.

luke·warm [ˈluːkwɔːm] lau(warm); *fig.* lau, mäßig.

lull [lʌl] 1. beruhigen; sich legen *od.* beruhigen; *mst* ~ *to sleep* einlullen; 2. Pause *f*; Flaute *f* (*a. econ.*), Windstille *f*.

lul·la·by [ˈlʌləbaɪ] Wiegenlied *n*.

lum·ba·go ☞ [lʌmˈbeɪgəʊ] Hexenschuß *m*.

lum·ber [ˈlʌmbə] 1. *bsd. Am.* Bau-, Nutzholz *n*; *bsd. Brt.* Gerümpel *n*; 2. *v/t.* ~ *s.o.* **with** *s.th. Brt.* F j-m et. aufhalsen; *v/i.* rumpeln, poltern (*Wagen*); schwerfällig gehen, trampeln; ~**jack**, ~**man** (*pl. -men*) *bsd. Am.* Holzfäller *m*, -arbeiter *m*; ~ **mill** Sägewerk *n*; ~ **room** Rumpelkammer *f*; ~**yard** Holzplatz *m*, -lager *n*.

lu·mi·na·ry [ˈluːmɪnərɪ] Himmelskörper *m*; *fig.* Leuchte *f*, Koryphäe *f*; ~**nous** □ [~əs] leuchtend, Leucht...

lump [lʌmp] 1. Klumpen *m*; Beule *f*; Stück *n* (*Zucker etc.*); △ *nicht Lump*; *in the* ~ in Bausch und Bogen; ~ *sugar* Würfelzucker *m*; ~ *sum* Pauschalsumme *f*; 2. *v/t.* zusammentun, -stellen, -legen, -werfen, -fassen; *v/i.* Klumpen bilden; ~**y** □ [~ɪ] (-*ier*, -*iest*) klumpig.

lu·na·cy [ˈluːnəsɪ] Wahnsinn *m*.

lu·nar [ˈluːnə] Mond...; ~ *module* *Raumfahrt:* Mond(lande)fähre *f*.

lu·na·tic [ˈluːnətɪk] 1. irr-, wahnsinnig; 2. Irre(r *m*) *f*, Wahnsinnige(r *m*) *f*, Geisteskranke(r *m*) *f*.

lunch [lʌntʃ], *formell* **lun·cheon** [ˈlʌntʃən] 1. Lunch *m*, Mittagessen

n; 2. zu Mittag essen; ~ **hour**, ~ **time** Mittagszeit *f*, -pause *f*.

lung *anat.* [lʌŋ] Lunge(nflügel *m*) *f*; *the* ~*s pl.* die Lunge.

lunge [lʌndʒ] 1. *Fechten:* Ausfall *m*; 2. *v/i. Fechten:* e-n Ausfall machen (*at* gegen); losstürzen (*at* auf *acc.*).

lurch [lɜːtʃ] 1. taumeln, torkeln; 2. *leave in the* ~ im Stich lassen.

lure [ljʊə] 1. Köder *m*; *fig.* Lockung *f*; 2. ködern, (an)locken.

lu·rid □ [ˈljʊərɪd] grell, schreiend (*Farben etc.*); schockierend, widerlich.

lurk [lɜːk] lauern; ~ *about*, ~ *around* herumschleichen.

lus·cious □ [ˈlʌʃəs] köstlich, lecker; üppig; knackig (*Mädchen*).

lush [lʌʃ] saftig, üppig.

lust [lʌst] 1. sinnliche Begierde, Lust *f*; Gier *f*; △ *nicht Lust* (*Freude etc.*); 2. ~ *after*, ~ *for* begehren; gierig sein nach.

lus|tre, *Am.* **-ter** [ˈlʌstə] Glanz *m*, Schimmer *m*; ~**trous** □ [~trəs] glänzend, schimmernd.

lust·y □ [ˈlʌstɪ] (-*ier*, -*iest*) kräftig, stark u. gesund, vital; kraftvoll.

lute ♪ [luːt] Laute *f*.

Lu·ther·an [ˈluːθərən] lutherisch.

lux·ate ☞ [ˈlʌkseɪt] verrenken.

lux·u|ri·ant □ [lʌgˈzjʊərɪənt] üppig; ~**ri·ate** [~ɪeɪt] schwelgen (*in* in *dat.*); ~**ri·ous** □ [~ɪəs] luxuriös, üppig; Luxus...; ~**ry** [ˈlʌkʃərɪ] Luxus *m*; Komfort *m*; Luxusartikel *m*; *attr.* Luxus...

lye [laɪ] Lauge *f*.

ly·ing [ˈlaɪɪŋ] 1. *p.pr. von* lie[1] 2 u. lie[2] 2; 2. *adj.* lügnerisch, verlogen; ~**in** [~ˈɪn] Wochenbett *n*.

lymph ☞ [lɪmf] Lymphe *f*.

lynch [lɪntʃ] lynchen; ~ *law* [ˈlɪntʃlɔː] Lynchjustiz *f*.

lynx *zo.* [lɪŋks] Luchs *m*.

lyr|ic [ˈlɪrɪk] 1. lyrisch; 2. lyrisches Gedicht *n*; ~*s pl.* Lyrik *f*; (Lied)Text *m*; ~**i·cal** □ [~kl] lyrisch, gefühlvoll; schwärmerisch.

L

M

ma F [mɑ:] Mama f, Mutti f.
ma'am [mæm] Majestät (*Anrede für die Königin*); (königliche) Hoheit (*Anrede für Prinzessinnen*); F [məm] gnä' Frau (*Anrede*).
mac *Brt.* F [mæk] = mackintosh.
ma·cad·am [məˈkædəm] Schotterdecke f (*Straßenbau*).
mac·a·ro·ni [mækəˈrəʊni] Makkaroni *pl.*
mac·a·roon [mækəˈruːn] Makrone f.
mach·i·na·tion [mækɪˈneɪʃn] (tückischer) Anschlag; ∼**s** *pl.* Ränke *pl.*
ma·chine [məˈʃiːn] 1. Maschine f; Mechanismus m; 2. maschinell herstellen *od.* drucken; mit der (Näh-)Maschine nähen; ∼**made** maschinell hergestellt.
ma·chin·e·ry [məˈʃiːnərɪ] Maschinen *pl.*; Maschinerie f; ∼**ist** [∼ɪst] Maschinenbauer m; Maschinist m; Maschinennäherin f.
mack *Brt.* F [mæk] = mackintosh.
mack·e·rel zo. [ˈmækrəl] Makrele f.
mack·in·tosh *bsd. Brt.* [ˈmækɪntɒʃ] Regenmantel m.
mac·ro· [ˈmækrəʊ] Makro..., (sehr) groß.
mad □ [mæd] wahnsinnig, verrückt; toll(wütig); F wütend; *fig.* wild; *go* ∼, *Am. get* ∼ verrückt *od.* wahnsinnig werden; *drive s.o.* ∼ j-n verrückt *od.* wahnsinnig machen; *like* ∼ wie toll, wie verrückt (*arbeiten etc.*).
mad·am [ˈmædəm] gnädige Frau, gnädiges Fräulein (*Anrede*).
mad·cap [ˈmædkæp] 1. verrückt; 2. verrückter Kerl; ∼**den** [∼dn] verrückt *od.* rasend machen; ∼**den·ing** □ [∼ɪŋ] verrückt *od.* rasend machend.
made [meɪd] *pret. u. p.p. von* make 1; ∼ *of gold* aus Gold.
mad·house [ˈmædhaʊs] Irrenhaus n; ∼**ly** [∼lɪ] wie verrückt, wie besessen; F irre, wahnsinnig; ∼**man** (*pl. -men*) Wahnsinnige(r) m, Verrückte(r) m; ∼**ness** [∼nɪs] Wahnsinn m; (Toll)Wut f; ∼**wom·an** (*pl. -women*) Wahnsinnige f, Verrückte f.
mag·a·zine [mægəˈziːn] Magazin n; (Munitions)Lager n; Zeitschrift f.
mag·got zo. [ˈmægət] Made f, Larve f.
Ma·gi [ˈmeɪdʒaɪ] *pl.*: *the* (*three*) ∼ die (drei) Weisen aus dem Morgenland, die Heiligen Drei Könige.
mag·ic [ˈmædʒɪk] 1. (∼*ally*) *a.* ∼**al** □ [∼l] magisch, Zauber...; 2. Zauberei f; Zauber m; *fig.* Wunder n; **ma·gi·cian** [məˈdʒɪʃn] Zauberer m; Zauberkünstler m.
mag·is·tra·cy [ˈmædʒɪstrəsɪ] Richteramt n; *die Richter pl.*; ∼**trate** [∼eɪt] (Polizei-, Friedens)Richter m; △ *nicht Magistrat.*
mag·na·nim·i·ty [mægnəˈnɪmətɪ] Großmut m; ∼**nan·i·mous** □ [mægˈnænɪməs] großmütig, hochherzig.
mag·net [ˈmægnɪt] Magnet m; ∼**ic** [mægˈnetɪk] (∼*ally*) magnetisch, Magnet...
mag·nif·i·cence [mægˈnɪfɪsns] Pracht f, Herrlichkeit f; ∼**i·cent** □ [∼t] prächtig, herrlich.
mag·ni·fy [ˈmægnɪfaɪ] vergrößern; ∼*ing glass* Vergrößerungsglas n, Lupe f; ∼**tude** [∼tjuːd] Größe f; Wichtigkeit f.
mag·pie zo. [ˈmægpaɪ] Elster f.
ma·hog·a·ny [məˈhɒgənɪ] Mahagoni(holz) n.
maid [meɪd] *veraltet od. lit.* (junges) Mädchen n, (junge) unverheiratete Frau; (Dienst)Mädchen n, Hausangestellte f; *old* ∼ alte Jungfer; ∼ *of all work* Mädchen n für alles; ∼ *of honour* Ehren-, Hofdame f; *bsd. Am.* (erste) Brautjungfer.
maid·en [ˈmeɪdn] 1. = maid; 2. jungfräulich; unverheiratet; *fig.* Jungfern..., Erstlings...; ∼ *name* Mädchenname m (*e-r Frau*); ∼**head** *veraltet* Jungfräulichkeit f; ∼**hood** *lit.* [∼hʊd] Jungmädchenzeit f; ∼**ly** [∼lɪ] jungfräulich; mädchenhaft.
mail[1] [meɪl] (Ketten)Panzer m.
mail[2] [∼] 1. Post(dienst m) f; Post(-sendung) f; *by* ∼ mit der Post; 2. *bsd. Am.* mit der Post schicken, aufgeben; ∼**a·ble** *Am.* [ˈmeɪləbl] postversandfähig; ∼**bag** Postsack m; *Am.* Posttasche f (*e-s Briefträgers*); ∼**box** *Am.* Briefkasten m; ∼ *car·ri·er Am.*, ∼**man** (*pl. -men*) *Am.* Briefträger m, Postbote m; ∼ **or·der** Bestellung f (*von Waren*) durch die Post; ∼**or·der firm**, *bsd. Am.* ∼**or·der house** Versandgeschäft n, -haus n.

maim [meɪm] verstümmeln, zum Krüppel machen.

main [meɪn] **1.** Haupt..., größte(r, -s), wichtigste(r, -s); hauptsächlich; *by ~ force* mit äußerster Kraft; *~ road* Haupt(verkehrs)straße *f*; **2.** *mst ~s pl.* Haupt(gas-, -wasser-, -strom)leitung *f*; (Strom)Netz *n*; *in the ~* in der Hauptsache, im wesentlichen; *~·land* [∼lənd] Festland *n*; *~·ly* [∼lɪ] hauptsächlich; *~·spring* Hauptfeder *f* (*e-r Uhr*); *fig.* Triebfeder *f*; *~·stay* ⚓ Großtag *n*; *fig.* Hauptstütze *f*; ⚳ **Street** *Am.* provinziell-materialistisch; ⚳ **Street·er** *Am.* provinzieller Spießer.

main·tain [meɪnˈteɪn] (aufrecht)erhalten, beibehalten; instand halten, ⊕ *a.* warten; unterstützen; unterhalten; behaupten.

main·te·nance [ˈmeɪntənəns] Erhaltung *f*; Unterhalt *m*; Instandhaltung *f*, ⊕ *a.* Wartung *f*.

maize *bsd. Brt.* ♀ [meɪz] Mais *m*.

ma·jes·tic [məˈdʒestɪk] (*~ally*) majestätisch; *~·ty* [ˈmædʒəstɪ] Majestät *f*; Würde *f*, Hoheit *f*.

ma·jor [ˈmeɪdʒə] **1.** größere(r, -s), *fig. a.* bedeutende, wichtig; ♪♫ volljährig; *C* ~ ♪ C-Dur *n*; ~ *key* ♪ Dur(tonart *f*) *n*; *~ league Am.* Baseball: oberste Spielklasse; ~ *road* Haupt(verkehrs)straße *f*; **2.** ✕ Major *m*; ♯♯ Volljährige(r *m*) *f*; *Am. univ.* Hauptfach *n*; ♪ Dur *m*; *~·gen·er·al* ✕ Generalmajor *m*; *~·i·ty* [məˈdʒɒrətɪ] Mehrheit *f*, Mehrzahl *f*; ♯♯ Volljährigkeit *f*; ✕ Majorsrang *m*.

make [meɪk] **1.** (*made*) *v/t.* machen; anfertigen, herstellen, erzeugen; (zu)bereiten; bilden; (er)schaffen; (aus)machen; (er)geben; machen zu; ernennen zu; *j-n* lassen, veranlassen zu, bringen zu, zwingen zu; verdienen; sich erweisen als, abgeben; schätzen auf (*acc.*); ✕ *et.* erreichen, *et.* schaffen; *Fehler* machen; *Frieden etc.* schließen; *e-e Rede* halten; F *Strecke* zurücklegen; *Uhrzeit* feststellen; ~ *s.th. do*, ~ *do with s.th.* mit et. auskommen, sich mit et. behelfen; *do you ~ one of us?* machen Sie mit?; *what do you ~ of it?* was halten Sie davon?; ~ *friends with* sich anfreunden mit; ~ *good* wiedergutmachen; *Versprechen etc.* halten, erfüllen; ~ *haste* sich beeilen; ~ *way* Platz machen; vorwärtskommen;

v/i. sich anschicken (*to do* zu tun); sich begeben; führen, gehen (*Weg etc.*); *mit Adverbien u. Präpositionen:* ~ *away with* sich davonmachen mit (*Geld etc.*); beseitigen; ~ *for* zugehen auf (*acc.*); sich aufmachen nach; ~ *into* verarbeiten zu; ~ *off* sich davonmachen, sich aus dem Staub machen; ~ *out* ausfindig machen; erkennen; verstehen; entziffern; *Rechnung etc.* ausstellen; ~ *over Eigentum* übertragen; ~ *up* ergänzen, vervollständigen; zusammenstellen; bilden, ausmachen; sich *et.* ausdenken; *Streit* beilegen; (sich) zurechtmachen *od.* schminken; ~ *up one's mind* sich entschließen; *be made up of* bestehen aus, sich zusammensetzen aus; ~ *up (for)* nach-, aufholen; für et. entschädigen; **2.** Mach-, Bauart *f*; (Körper)Bau *m*; Form *f*; Fabrikat *n*, Erzeugnis *f*; *~·be·lieve* [ˈmeɪkbɪliːv] Schein *m*, Vorwand *m*, Verstellung *f*; *~·r* [∼ə] Hersteller *m*; ♀ Schöpfer *m* (*Gott*); *~·shift* **1.** Notbehelf *m*; **2.** behelfsmäßig, Behelfs...; *~·up typ.* Umbruch *m*; Aufmachung *f*; Schminke *f*, Make-up *n*.

mak·ing [ˈmeɪkɪŋ] Machen *n*; Erzeugung *f*, Herstellung *f*; *this will be the ~ of him* damit ist er ein gemachter Mann; *he has the ~s of* er hat das Zeug *od.* die Anlagen zu.

mal- [mæl] *s. bad(ly)*.

mal·ad·just·ed [mæləˈdʒʌstɪd] schlecht angepaßt *od.* angeglichen; *~·ment* [∼mənt] schlechte Anpassung.

mal·ad·min·i·stra·tion [ˈmæləd-mɪnɪsˈtreɪʃn] schlechte Verwaltung; *pol.* Mißwirtschaft *f*.

mal·a·dy [ˈmælədɪ] Krankheit *f*.

mal·con·tent [ˈmælkəntent] **1.** unzufrieden; **2.** Unzufriedene(r *m*) *f*.

male [meɪl] **1.** männlich; Männer...; **2.** Mann *m*; *zo.* Männchen *n*.

mal·e·dic·tion [mælɪˈdɪkʃn] Fluch *m*, Verwünschung *f*.

mal·e·fac·tor [ˈmælɪfæktə] Übeltäter *m*.

ma·lev·o·lence [məˈlevələns] Bosheit *f*; *~·lent* [∼t] feindselig.

mal·for·ma·tion [mælfɔːˈmeɪʃn] Mißbildung *f*.

mal·ice [ˈmælɪs] Bosheit *f*; Groll *m*.

ma·li·cious □ [məˈlɪʃəs] boshaft; böswillig; *~·ness* [∼nɪs] Bosheit *f*.

ma·lign [məˈlaɪn] **1.** □ schädlich; **2.**

M

verleumden; **ma·lig·nant** □ [mə-'lɪgnənt] bösartig (*a. 𝒮*); boshaft; **ma·lig·ni·ty** [~əti] Bösartigkeit *f* (*a. 𝒮*); Bosheit *f*.

mall *Am.* [mɔːl, mæl] Einkaufszentrum *n*.

mal·le·a·ble ['mælɪəbl] hämmerbar; *fig.* formbar, geschmeidig.

mal·let ['mælɪt] Holzhammer *m*; (Krocket-, Polo)Schläger *m*.

mal·nu·tri·tion ['mælnju:'trɪʃn] Unterernährung *f*; Fehlernährung *f*.

mal·o·dor·ous □ [mæl'əʊdərəs] übelriechend.

mal·prac·tice ⅗ ['mæl'præktɪs] 𝒮 falsche Behandlung; Amtsvergehen *n*; Untreue (*im Amt etc.*).

malt [mɔːlt] Malz *n*.

mal·treat [mæl'triːt] schlecht behandeln; mißhandeln.

ma·ma, mam·ma [mə'mɑː] Mama *f*, Mutti *f*.

mam·mal *zo.* ['mæml] Säugetier *n*.

mam·moth ['mæməθ] **1.** Mammut *n*; **2.** riesig.

mam·my F ['mæmɪ] Mami *f*; *Am. contp.* farbiges Kindermädchen *n*.

man [mæn] **1.** [*in nachgestellten Zssgn:* -mən] (*pl. men* [men; *in nachgestellten Zssgn:* -mən]) Mann *m*; Mensch(en *pl.*) *m*; Menschheit *f*; Diener *m*; Angestellte(r) *m*; Arbeiter *m*; ✗ Mann *m*, (einfacher) Soldat *m*; (Ehe)Mann *m*; F Freund *m*; F Geliebte(r) *m*; (Schach)Figur *f*; Damestein *m*; *the ~ in* (*Am. a. on*) *the street* der Mann auf der Straße, der Durchschnittsbürger; **2.** männlich; **3.** (*-nn-*) ✗, ⚓ bemannen; *~ o.s.* sich ermannen.

man·age ['mænɪdʒ] *v/t.* handhaben; verwalten; *Betrieb etc.* leiten *od.* führen; *Gut etc.* bewirtschaften; *Künstler, Sportler* managen; mit *j-m* fertig werden; *et.* fertigbringen; F *Arbeit, Essen etc.* bewältigen, schaffen; *~ to inf.* es fertigbringen, zu *inf.*; *v/i.* die Aufsicht haben, das Geschäft führen; auskommen; F es schaffen; F es einrichten, es ermöglichen; **·a·ble** □ [~əbl] handlich; lenksam; **·ment** [~mənt] Verwaltung *f*; *econ.* Management *n*, Unternehmensführung *f*; *econ.* (Geschäfts)Leitung *f*, Direktion *f*; Bewirtschaftung *f*; Geschicklichkeit *f*, (kluge) Taktik; *~ studies* Betriebswirtschaft *f*; *labo(u)r and ~* Arbeitnehmer u. Arbeitgeber.

man·ag·er ['mænɪdʒə] Verwalter *m*; *econ.* Manager *m*; *econ.* Geschäftsführer *m*, Leiter *m*, Direktor *m*; *thea.* Intendant *m*; *thea.* Regisseur *m*; Manager *m* (*e-s Schauspielers etc.*); (Guts)Verwalter *m*; *Sport:* Cheftrainer *m*; *be a good ~* gut *od.* sparsam wirtschaften können; **·ess** [mænɪdʒə'res] Verwalterin *f*; *econ.* Managerin *f*; *econ.* Geschäftsführerin *f*, Leiterin *f*, Direktorin *f*; Managerin *f* (*e-s Schauspielers etc.*).

man·a·ge·ri·al *econ.* [mænə'dʒɪərɪəl] geschäftsführend, leitend; *~ position* leitende Stellung; *~ staff* leitende Angestellte *pl.*

man·ag·ing *econ.* ['mænɪdʒɪŋ] geschäftsführend; Betriebs...

man|date ['mændeɪt] Mandat *n*; Befehl *m*; Auftrag *m*; Vollmacht *f*; **~·da·to·ry** [~ətərɪ] vorschreibend, befehlend; obligatorisch.

mane [meɪn] Mähne *f*.

ma·neu·ver [mə'nuːvə] = *manoeuvre*.

man·ful □ ['mænfl] mannhaft, beherzt.

mange *vet.* [meɪndʒ] Räude *f*.

manger ['meɪndʒə] Krippe *f*.

man·gle ['mæŋgl] **1.** (Wäsche)Mangel *f*; **2.** mangeln; übel zurichten, zerfleischen; *fig.* verstümmeln.

mang·y □ ['meɪndʒɪ] (*-ier, -iest*) *vet.* räudig; *fig.* schäbig.

man·hood ['mænhʊd] Mannesalter *n*; Männlichkeit *f*; die Männer *pl.*

ma·ni·a ['meɪnjə] Wahn(sinn) *m*; *fig.* (*for*) Sucht *f* (*nach*), Leidenschaft *f* (*für*), Manie *f* (*für*); **~·c** ['meɪnɪæk] Wahnsinnige(r *m*) *f*; *fig.* Fanatiker *m*.

man·i·cure ['mænɪkjʊə] **1.** Maniküre *f*; **2.** maniküren.

man·i·fest ['mænɪfest] **1.** □ offenbar, -kundig, deutlich (erkennbar); **2.** *v/t.* offenbaren, kundtun, deutlich zeigen; **3.** ⚓ Ladungsverzeichnis *n*; **·fes·ta·tion** [mænɪfe'steɪʃn] Offenbarung *f*; Kundgebung *f*; △ *nicht Manifest*; **·fes·to** [mænɪ'festəʊ] (*pl. -tos, -toes*) Manifest *n*; *pol.* Grundsatzerklärung *f*, Programm *n* (*e-r Partei*).

man·i·fold ['mænɪfəʊld] **1.** □ mannigfaltig; **2.** vervielfältigen.

ma·nip·u·late [mə'nɪpjʊleɪt] manipulieren; (geschickt) handhaben; **~·la·tion** [mənɪpjʊ'leɪʃn] Manipulation f; Handhabung f, Behandlung f, Verfahren n; Kniff m.

man|jack [mæn'dʒæk]: *every ~* jeder einzelne; **~kind** [mæn'kaind] die Menschheit, die Menschen *pl.*; ['mænkaind] die Männer *pl.*; **~ly** ['mænlɪ] (*-ier, -iest*) männlich; mannhaft.

man·ner ['mænə] Art f, Weise f, Art f u. Weise f; Stil (art f) m; Art f (*sich zu geben*); *~s pl.* Benehmen n, Manieren *pl.*; Sitten *pl.*; *in a ~* gewissermaßen; **~ed** …geartet; gekünstelt; **~ly** [∼lɪ] manierlich; gesittet, anständig.

ma·noeu·vre, *Am.* **ma·neu·ver** [mə'nu:və] **1.** Manöver n (*a. fig.*); **2.** manövrieren (*a. fig.*).

man-of-war *veraltet* ['mænəv'wɔ:] (*pl.* men-of-war) Kriegsschiff n.

man·or *Brt.* ['mænə] *hist.* Rittergut n; (Land)Gut n; *sl.* Polizeibezirk m; *lord of the ~* Gutsherr m; = **~house** Herrenhaus n, -sitz m.

man·pow·er ['mænpauə] menschliche Arbeitskraft; Menschenpotential n; Arbeitskräfte *pl.*

man·ser·vant ['mænsɜːvənt] (*pl.* menservants) Diener m.

man·sion ['mænʃn] (herrschaftliches) Wohnhaus.

man·slaugh·ter ['mænslɔːtə] Totschlag m, fahrlässige Tötung.

man·tel|piece ['mæntlpiːs], **~shelf** (*pl.* -shelves) Kaminsims m.

man·tle ['mæntl] **1.** ⊕ Glühstrumpf m; *fig.* Hülle f; *a ~ of snow* e-e Schneedecke; ⚠ *nicht Mantel*; **2.** (sich) überziehen; einhüllen.

man·u·al ['mænjʊəl] **1.** ☐ Hand…; mit der Hand (gemacht); **2.** Handbuch n.

man·u·fac·ture [mænjʊ'fæktʃə] **1.** Herstellung f, Fabrikation f; Fabrikat n; **2.** (an-, ver)fertigen, erzeugen, herstellen, fabrizieren; verarbeiten; **~tur·er** [∼rə] Hersteller m, Erzeuger m; Fabrikant m; **~tur·ing** [∼ŋ] Herstellungs…; Fabrik…; Gewerbe…; Industrie…

ma·nure [mə'njʊə] **1.** Dünger m, Mist m, Dung m; **2.** düngen.

man·u·script ['mænjʊskrɪpt] Manuskript n; Handschrift f.

man·y ['menɪ] **1.** (*more, most*) viel(e); *~ (a)* manche(r, -s) manch eine(r, -s); *~ times* oft; *as ~* ebensoviel(e); *be one too ~ for s.o.* j-m überlegen sein; **2.** viele; Menge f; *a*

good *~* ziemlich viel(e); *a great ~* sehr viele.

map [mæp] **1.** (Land- *etc.*)Karte f; (Stadt- *etc.*)Plan m; ⚠ *nicht Mappe*; **2.** (*-pp-*) e-e Karte machen von; auf e-r Karte eintragen; *~ out fig.* planen; einteilen.

ma·ple ⚘ ['meɪpl] Ahorn m.

mar [mɑː] (*-rr-*) schädigen; verderben.

ma·raud [mə'rɔːd] plündern.

mar·ble ['mɑːbl] **1.** Marmor m; Murmel f; **2.** marmorn.

March¹ [mɑːtʃ] März m.

march² [∼] **1.** Marsch m; *fig.* Fortgang m; *the ~ of events* der Lauf der Dinge; **2.** marschieren (lassen); *fig.* fort-, vorwärtsschreiten.

mar·chio·ness ['mɑːʃənɪs] Marquise f.

mare [meə] *zo.* Stute f; ⚠ *nicht Mähre* m. *~'s nest fig.* Schwindel m; (Zeitungs)Ente f.

mar·ga·rine [mɑːdʒə'riːn], *Brt.* F **marge** [mɑːdʒ] Margarine f.

mar·gin ['mɑːdʒɪn] Rand m (*a. fig.*); Grenze f (*a. fig.*); Spielraum m; Verdienst-, Gewinn-, Handelsspanne f; *by a narrow ~ fig.* mit knapper Not; **~al** ☐ [∼l] am Rande (befindlich); Rand…; *~ note* Randbemerkung f.

ma·ri·na [mə'riːnə] Boots-, Jachthafen m.

ma·rine [mə'riːn] Marine f; ⚠ *nicht (Kriegs)Marine*; ♫, ✕ Marineinfanterist m; *paint.* Seestück n; *attr.* See…; Meeres…; Marine…; Schiffs…; **mar·i·ner** ['mærɪnə] Seemann m.

mar·i·tal ☐ ['mærɪtl] ehelich, Ehe…; *~ status* ⚥ Familienstand m.

mar·i·time ['mærɪtaɪm] an der See liegend *od.* lebend; See…; Küsten…; Schiffahrts…

mark¹ [mɑːk] (deutsche) Mark; ⚠ *nicht das Mark.*

mark² [∼] **1.** Marke f, Markierung f, Bezeichnung f; Zeichen n (*a. fig.*); Merkmal n; (Körper)Mal n; Ziel n (*a. fig.*); (Fuß-, Brems- *etc.*)Spur f (*a. fig.*); (Fabrik-, Waren)Zeichen n, (Schutz-, Handels)Marke f; *econ.* Preisangabe f; (Schul)Note f, Zensur f, Punkt m; *Sport:* Startlinie f; *fig.* Norm f; *fig.* Bedeutung f, Rang m; *a man of ~* e-e bedeutende Persönlichkeit; *be up to the ~* gesund-

M

heitlich auf der Höhe sein; *be wide of the ~ fig.* sich gewaltig irren; den Kern der Sache nicht treffen; *hit the ~ fig.* (ins Schwarze) treffen; *miss the ~* danebenschießen; *fig.* sein Ziel verfehlen; **2.** *v/t.* (be)zeichnen; markieren; kennzeichnen; be(ob)achten, achtgeben auf (*acc.*); sich *et.* merken; Zeichen hinterlassen auf (*dat.*); *Schule:* benoten, zensieren; notieren, vermerken; *econ. Waren* auszeichnen; *econ.* den Preis festsetzen; *Sport:* s-n *Gegenspieler* decken; *~ my words* denke an m-e Worte; *to ~ the occasion* zur Feier des Tages; *~ time* auf der Stelle treten (*a. fig.*); *~ down* notieren, vermerken; *econ.* im Preis herabsetzen; *~ off* abgrenzen; *bsd. auf e-r Liste* abhaken; *~ out durch Striche etc.* markieren, bezeichnen; *~ up econ.* im Preis heraufsetzen; *v/i.* markieren; achtgeben, aufpassen; *Sport:* decken; **~ed** □ auffallend; merklich; ausgeprägt.

mar·ket ['mɑːkɪt] **1.** Markt(platz) *m*; *Am.* (Lebensmittel)Geschäft *n*, Laden *m*; *econ.* Absatz *m*; *econ.* (*for*) Nachfrage *f* (nach), Bedarf *m* (an); *in the ~* auf dem Markt; *be on the ~* (zum Verkauf) angeboten werden; *play the ~* (an der Börse) spekulieren; **2.** *v/t.* auf den Markt bringen; verkaufen; *v/i. bsd. Am.* go *~ing* einkaufen gehen; **~·a·ble** □ [~əbl] marktfähig; -gängig; **~ gar·den** *Brt.* Handelsgärtnerei *f*; **~·ing** [~ɪŋ] *econ.* Marketing *n*, Absatzpolitik *f*; Marktbesuch *m*.

marks·man ['mɑːksmən] (*pl. -men*) guter Schütze.

mar·ma·lade ['mɑːməleɪd] *bsd.* Orangenmarmelade *f*.

mar·mot *zo.* ['mɑːmət] Murmeltier *n*.

ma·roon [mə'ruːn] **1.** kastanienbraun; **2.** *auf e-r einsamen Insel* aussetzen; **3.** Leuchtrakete *f*.

mar·quee [mɑː'kiː] Festzelt *n*.

mar·quis ['mɑːkwɪs] Marquis *m*.

mar·riage ['mærɪdʒ] Heirat *f*, Hochzeit *f*; Ehe(stand *m*) *f*; *civil ~* standesamtliche Trauung; **~·ria·gea·ble** [~dʒəbl] heiratsfähig; **~ ar·ti·cles** *pl.* Ehevertrag *m*; **~ cer·tif·i·cate**, **~ lines** *pl. bsd. Brt.* F Trauschein *m*; **~ por·tion** Mitgift *f*.

mar·ried ['mærɪd] verheiratet; ehe-

lich, Ehe...; *~ couple* Ehepaar *n*; *~ life* Ehe(leben *n*) *f*.

mar·row ['mærəʊ] *anat.* (Knochen-) Mark *n*; *fig.* Kern *m*, das Wesentlichste; (*vegetable*) *~ Brt.* ✿ Kürbis *m*.

mar·ry ['mærɪ] *v/t.* (ver)heiraten; *eccl.* trauen; *get married to* sich verheiraten mit; *v/i.* (sich ver)heiraten.

marsh [mɑːʃ] Sumpf *m*; Morast *m*.

mar·shal ['mɑːʃl] **1.** ✖ Marschall *m*; *hist.* Hofmarschall *m*; Zeremonienmeister *m*; *Am.* Branddirektor *m*; *Am.* Polizeidirektor *m*; *Am.* Bezirkspolizeichef *m*; *US ~ Am.* (Bundes-) Vollzugsbeamte(r) *m*; **2.** (*bsd. Brt. -ll-, Am. -l-*) ordnen, aufstellen; führen; 🚂 (Zug) zusammenstellen.

marsh·y ['mɑːʃɪ] (*-ier, -iest*) sumpfig, morastig.

mart [mɑːt] Markt *m*; Auktionsraum *m*.

mar·ten *zo.* ['mɑːtɪn] Marder *m*.

mar·tial □ ['mɑːʃl] kriegerisch; militärisch; Kriegs...; *~ law* ✖ Kriegsrecht *m*; (*state of*) *~ law* ✖ Ausnahmezustand *m*.

mar·tyr ['mɑːtə] **1.** Märtyrer(in) (*to gen.*); **2.** (zu Tode) martern.

mar·vel ['mɑːvl] **1.** Wunder *n*, *et.* Wunderbares; **2.** (*bsd. Brt. -ll-, Am. -l-*) sich wundern; **~·(l)ous** □ ['mɑːvələs] wunderbar; erstaunlich.

mar·zi·pan [mɑːzɪ'pæn] Marzipan *n*.

mas·ca·ra [mæ'skɑːrə] Wimperntusche *f*.

mas·cot ['mæskət] Maskottchen *m*.

mas·cu·line ['mæskjʊlɪn] männlich; Männer...

mash [mæʃ] **1.** Gemisch *n*; Maische *f*; Mengfutter *n*; **2.** zerdrücken; (ein)maischen; *~ed potatoes pl.* Kartoffelbrei *m*.

mask [mɑːsk] **1.** Maske *f*; **2.** maskieren; *fig.* verbergen; tarnen; *~ed* maskiert; *~ ball* Maskenball *m*.

ma·son ['meɪsn] Steinmetz *m*; *Am.* Maurer *m*; *mst* ♀ Freimaurer *m*; **~·ry** [~rɪ] Mauerwerk *n*.

masque *thea. hist.* [mɑːsk] Maskenspiel *n*; △ *nicht* Maske.

mas·que·rade [mæskə'reɪd] **1.** Maskenball *m*; *fig.* Maske, *f*, Verkleidung *f*; **2.** *fig.* sich maskieren.

mass [mæs] **1.** *eccl. a.* ♀ Messe *f*; Masse *f*; Menge *f*; *the ~es pl.* die (breite) Masse; ~ **media** pl. Massenmedien pl.; ~ **meeting** Massenversammlung f; **2.** (sich) (an)sammeln.

mas·sa·cre ['mæsəkə] **1.** Blutbad n; **2.** niedermetzeln.

mas·sage ['mæsɑ:ʒ] **1.** Massage f; **2.** massieren.

mas·sif ['mæsi:f] (Gebirgs)Massiv n.

mas·sive ['mæsɪv] massiv; groß u. schwer; fig. gewaltig.

mast ⚓ [mɑ:st] Mast m.

mas·ter ['mɑ:stə] **1.** Meister m; Herr m (a. fig.); Gebieter m; bsd. Brt. Lehrer m; Kapitän m (e-s Handelsschiffs); (junger) Herr (Anrede); univ. Rektor m (e-s College); ♀ of Arts (abbr. MA) Magister m Artium; ~ of ceremonies bsd. Am. Conférencier m; **2.** Meister...; Haupt..., hauptsächlich; fig. führend; **3.** Herr sein od. herrschen über (acc.); Sprache etc. meistern, beherrschen; ~**builder** Baumeister m; ~**ful** □ [~fl] herrisch; meisterhaft; ~**key** Hauptschlüssel m; ~**ly** [~lɪ] meisterhaft, virtuos; ~**piece** Meisterstück n; ~**ship** [~ʃɪp] Meisterschaft f; Herrschaft f; bsd. Brt. Lehramt n; ~**y** [~rɪ] Herrschaft f; Überlegenheit f; Oberhand f; Meisterschaft f; Beherrschung f.

mas·ti·cate ['mæstɪkeɪt] (zer)kauen.

mas·tur·bate ['mæstəbeɪt] masturbieren.

mat [mæt] **1.** Matte f; Deckchen n; Unterlage f, -setzer m; **2.** (-tt-) (sich) verflechten od. -filzen; fig. bedecken; **3.** mattiert, matt.

match¹ [mætʃ] Zünd-, Streichholz n.

match² [~] **1.** der, die, das gleiche; Partie f, Wettspiel n, -kampf m; Treffen n, Match n, m; Heirat f; be a ~ for j-m gewachsen sein; find od. meet one's ~ s-n Meister finden; **2.** v/t. passend machen, anpassen; passen zu; et. Passendes finden od. geben zu; es aufnehmen mit; passend verheiraten; be well ~ed gut zusammenpassen; v/i. zusammenpassen; gloves to ~ dazu passende Handschuhe.

match·box ['mætʃbɒks] Zünd-, Streichholzschachtel f; ~ car TM Matchbox-Auto n.

match·less □ ['mætʃlɪs] unvergleichlich, einzigartig; ~**mak·er** Ehestifter(in).

mate¹ [meɪt] s. checkmate.

mate² [~] **1.** Gefährt|e m, -in f; (Arbeits)Kamerad(in); Gatt|e m, -in f; Männchen n, Weibchen n (von Tieren); Gehilf|e m, -in f; ⚓ Maat m; **2.** (sich) verheiraten; (sich) paaren.

ma·te·ri·al □ [mə'tɪərɪəl] **1.** materiell; körperlich; materialistisch; wesentlich; **2.** Material n; Stoff m; Werkstoff m; writing ~s pl. Schreibmaterial(ien pl.) n.

ma·ter|nal □ [mə'tɜ:nl] mütterlich, Mutter...; mütterlicherseits; ~**ni·ty** [~ətɪ] **1.** Mutterschaft f; **2.** Schwangerschafts..., Umstands...; ~ hospital Entbindungsklinik f; ~ ward Entbindungsstation f.

math Am. F [mæθ] Mathe f (Mathematik).

math·e|ma·ti·cian [mæθəmə'tɪʃn] Mathematiker m; ~**mat·ics** [~'mætɪks] mst sg. Mathematik f.

maths Brt. F [mæθs] Mathe f (Mathematik).

mat·i·née thea., ♪ ['mætɪneɪ] Nachmittagsvorstellung f, Frühvorstellung f; △ nicht Matinee.

ma·tric·u·late [mə'trɪkjʊleɪt] (sich) immatrikulieren (lassen).

mat·ri·mo|ni·al □ [mætrɪ'məʊnjəl] ehelich, Ehe...; ~**ny** ['mætrɪmənɪ] Ehe(stand m) f.

ma·trix ⊕ ['meɪtrɪks] (pl. -trices [-trɪsi:z], -trixes) Matrize f.

ma·tron ['meɪtrən] Matrone f; Hausmutter f; Brt. Oberschwester f.

mat·ter ['mætə] **1.** Materie f, Material n, Substanz f, Stoff m; ✱ Eiter m; Gegenstand m; Sache f; Angelegenheit f; Anlaß m, Veranlassung f (for zu); printed ~ & Drucksache f; what's the ~ (with you)? was ist los (mit Ihnen)? no ~ es hat nichts zu sagen; no ~ who gleichgültig, wer; a ~ of course ea-e Selbstverständlichkeit; for that ~, for the ~ of that was das betrifft; a ~ of fact e-e Tatsache; **2.** von Bedeutung sein; it doesn't ~ es macht nichts; ~**-of-fact** sachlich, nüchtern.

mat·tress ['mætrɪs] Matratze f.

ma·ture [mə'tjʊə] **1.** □ (~r, ~st) reif (a. fig.); econ. fällig; fig. reiflich erwogen; **2.** v/t. zur Reife bringen; v/i. reifen; econ. fällig werden; **ma·tu·ri·ty** [~rətɪ] Reife f; econ. Fälligkeit f.

maud·lin □ ['mɔ:dlɪn] rührselig.

maul [mɔ:l] übel zurichten, roh umgehen mit; fig. verreißen.

M

Maun·dy Thurs·day *eccl.* [ˈmɔːndɪ ˈθɜːzdɪ] Gründonnerstag *m*.

mauve [məʊv] **1.** Malvenfarbe *f*; **2.** hellviolett.

maw *zo.* [mɔː] (Tier)Magen *m*, *bsd.* Labmagen *m*; Rachen *m*; Kropf *m*.

mawk·ish □ [ˈmɔːkɪʃ] rührselig, sentimental.

max·i [ˈmæksɪ] **1.** Maximode *f*; Maximantel *m*, -kleid *n*, -rock *m*; **2.** Maxi...

max·i- [ˈmæksɪ] Maxi..., riesig, Riesen...

max·im [ˈmæksɪm] Grundsatz *m*.

max·i·mum [ˈmæksɪməm] **1.** (*pl. -ma* [-mə], *-mums*) Maximum *n*, Höchstmaß *n*, -stand *m*, -betrag *m*; **2.** höchste(r, -s), maximal, Höchst...

May¹ [meɪ] Mai *m*.

may² *v/aux.* [⌢] (*pret. might*) mögen, können, dürfen.

may·be [ˈmeɪbiː] vielleicht.

may·bee·tle *zo.* [ˈmeɪbiːtl], **~bug** *zo.* Maikäfer *m*.

May Day [ˈmeɪdeɪ] der 1. Mai.

mayor [meə] Bürgermeister *m*; △ *nicht Major*.

may·pole [ˈmeɪpəʊl] Maibaum *m*.

maze [meɪz] Irrgarten *m*, Labyrinth *n*; *fig.* Verwirrung *f*; *in a* ~ = **~d** [meɪzd] verwirrt.

me [miː, mɪ] mich; mir; F ich.

mead¹ [miːd] Met *m*.

mead² *poet.* [⌢] = *meadow*.

mead·ow [ˈmedəʊ] Wiese *f*.

mea·gre, *Am.* **-ger** □ [ˈmiːgə] mager (*a. fig.*), dürr; dürftig.

meal [miːl] Mahl(zeit *f*) *n*; Essen *n*; Mehl *n*.

mean¹ □ [miːn] gemein, niedrig, gering; armselig; knauserig; schäbig; *Am.* boshaft, ekelhaft.

mean² [⌢] **1.** mittel, mittlere(r, -s); Mittel..., Durchschnitts...; **2.** Mitte *f*; ~*s pl.* (Geld)Mittel *pl.*; (*a. sg.*) Mittel *n*; *by all* ~*s* auf alle Fälle, unbedingt; *by no* ~*s* keineswegs; *by* ~*s of* mittels (*gen.*).

mean³ [⌢] (*meant*) meinen; beabsichtigen; bestimmen; bedeuten; ~ *well* (*ill*) es gut (schlecht) meinen.

mean·ing [ˈmiːnɪŋ] **1.** □ bedeutsam; **2.** Sinn *m*, Bedeutung *f*; △ *nicht Meinung*; **~·ful** □ [⌢fl] bedeutungsvoll; sinnvoll; **~·less** [⌢lɪs] bedeutungslos; sinnlos.

meant [ment] *pret. u. p.p. von mean³*.

mean|time [ˈmiːntaɪm] **1.** mittlerweile, inzwischen; **2.** *in the* ~ inzwischen; **~·while** = *meantime f*.

mea·sles 𝒮 [ˈmiːzlz] *sg.* Masern *pl.*

mea·su·ra·ble □ [ˈmeʒərəbl] meßbar.

mea·sure [ˈmeʒə] **1.** Maß *n*; Maß *n*, Meßgerät *n*; ♪ Takt *m*; Maßnahme *f*; *fig.* Maßstab *m*; ~ *of capacity* Hohlmaß *n*; *beyond* ~ über alle Maßen; *in a great* ~ großenteils; *made to* ~ nach Maß gemacht; *take* ~*s* Maßnahmen treffen *od.* ergreifen; **2.** (ab-, aus-, ver)messen; *j-m* Maß nehmen; ~ *up to* den Ansprüchen (*gen.*) genügen; **~d** gemessen; wohlüberlegt; maßvoll; **~·less** □ [⌢lɪs] unermeßlich; **~·ment** [⌢mənt] Messung *f*; Maß *n*.

meat [miːt] Fleisch *n*; *fig.* Gehalt *m*; *cold* ~ kalte Platte; **~·y** [ˈmiːtɪ] (*-ier, -iest*) fleischig; *fig.* gehaltvoll.

me·chan·ic [mɪˈkænɪk] Handwerker *m*; Mechaniker *m*; **~·i·cal** □ [⌢kl] mechanisch; Maschinen...; **~·ics** *phys. mst sg.* Mechanik *f*.

mech·a·nis·m [ˈmekənɪzəm] Mechanismus *m*; **~·nize** [⌢aɪz] mechanisieren; **~d** ✕ motorisiert, Panzer...

med·al [ˈmedl] Medaille *f*; Orden *m*; **~·(l)ist** [⌢ɪst] *Sport*: Medaillengewinner(in).

med·dle [ˈmedl] sich einmischen (*with, in* in *acc.*); **~·some** [⌢səm] zu-, aufdringlich.

me·di·a [ˈmiːdjə] *pl. die* Medien *pl.* (*Zeitung, Fernsehen, Rundfunk*).

med·i·ae·val □ [medɪˈiːvl] = *medieval*.

me·di·al □ [ˈmiːdjəl] Mittel...

me·di·an [ˈmiːdjən] die Mitte bildend *od.* einnehmend, Mittel...

me·di·ate [ˈmiːdɪeɪt] vermitteln; **~·a·tion** [miːdɪˈeɪʃn] Vermittlung *f*; **~·a·tor** [ˈmiːdɪeɪtə] Vermittler *m*.

med·i·cal □ [ˈmedɪkl] medizinisch, ärztlich; ~ *certificate* ärztliches Attest; ~ *man* F Doktor *m* (*Arzt*).

med·i·cate [ˈmedɪkeɪt] medizinisch behandeln; mit Arzneistoff(en) versetzen; **~d** *bath* medizinisches Bad.

me·di·ci·nal □ [meˈdɪsɪnl] medizinisch; heilend, Heil...; *fig.* heilsam.

medi·cine [ˈmedsɪn] Medizin *f* (*Heilkunde, Arznei*).

med·i·e·val □ [medɪˈiːvl] mittelalterlich.

me·di·o·cre [miːdɪˈəʊkə] mittelmäßig, zweitklassig.

med·i|tate ['medɪteɪt] v/i. nachdenken, überlegen; meditieren; v/t. im Sinn haben, planen, erwägen; **~ta·tion** [medɪ'teɪʃn] Nachdenken n; Meditation f; **~ta·tive** □ ['medɪtətɪv] nachdenklich, meditativ.

Med·i·ter·ra·ne·an [medɪtə'reɪnjən] Mittelmeer...

me·di·um ['miːdjəm] **1.** (pl. -dia [-djə], -diums) Mitte f; Mittel n; Vermittlung f; Medium n; (Lebens-) Element n; **2.** mittlere(r, -s), Mittel..., Durchschnitts...

med·ley ['medlɪ] Gemisch n; ♪ Medley n; Potpourri n.

meek □ [miːk] sanft-, demütig, bescheiden; **~ness** ['miːknɪs] Sanft-, Demut f.

meer·schaum ['mɪəʃəm] Meerschaum(pfeife f) m.

meet [miːt] (met) v/t. treffen (auf acc.); begegnen (dat.); abholen; stoßen auf (den Gegner), e-m Wunsch, e-r Verpflichtung etc. nachkommen; j-n kennenlernen; Am. j-m vorgestellt werden; fig. j-m entgegenkommen; v/i. sich treffen; zusammenstoßen; sich versammeln; sich kennenlernen; Sport: sich begegnen; ~ with stoßen auf (acc.); erleiden; **~ing** ['miːtɪŋ] Begegnung f; (Zusammen)Treffen n; Versammlung f; Tagung f.

mel·an·chol·y ['melənkəlɪ] **1.** Melancholie f; Schwermut f; **2.** melancholisch, traurig.

me·li·o·rate ['miːljəreɪt] (sich) (ver-) bessern.

mel·low ['meləʊ] **1.** □ mürbe; reif; weich; mild; **2.** reifen (lassen); weich machen od. werden; (sich) mildern.

me·lo·di·ous □ [mɪ'ləʊdjəs] melodisch.

mel·o|dra·mat·ic [meləʊdrə'mætɪk] melodramatisch; **~dy** ['melədɪ] Melodie f; Lied n.

mel·on ♀ ['melən] Melone f.

melt [melt] (zer)schmelzen; fig. zerfließen; Gefühl erweichen.

mem·ber ['membə] (Mit)Glied n; Angehörige(r m) f; ♀ of Parliament parl. Mitglied n des Unterhauses; **~ship** [~ʃɪp] Mitgliedschaft f; Mitgliederzahl f; ~ card Mitgliedsausweis m.

mem·brane ['membreɪn] Membran(e) f, Häutchen n.

me·men·to [mɪ'mentəʊ] (pl. -toes,

-tos) Mahnzeichen n; Andenken n.

mem·o ['meməʊ] (pl. -os) = memorandum.

mem·oir ['memwɑː] Denkschrift f; **~s** pl. Memoiren pl.

mem·o·ra·ble □ ['memərəbl] denkwürdig.

mem·o·ran·dum [memə'rændəm] (pl. -da [-də], -dums) Notiz f; pol. Note f; ⚖ Schriftsatz m.

me·mo·ri·al [mɪ'mɔːrɪəl] Denkmal n (to für); Gedenkfeier f; Denkschrift f, Eingabe f; attr. Gedächtnis..., Gedenk...

mem·o·rize ['meməraɪz] auswendig lernen, memorieren.

mem·o·ry ['memərɪ] Gedächtnis n; Erinnerung f; Andenken n; Computer: Speicher m; commit to ~ auswendig lernen; in ~ of zum Andenken an (acc.).

men [men] pl. von man 1; Mannschaft f.

men·ace ['menəs] **1.** (be)drohen; **2.** (Be)Drohung f; drohende Gefahr.

mend [mend] **1.** v/t. (ver)bessern; ausbessern, flicken; besser machen; ~ one's ways sich bessern; v/i. sich bessern; **2.** ausgebesserte Stelle; on the ~ auf dem Wege der Besserung.

men·da·cious □ [men'deɪʃəs] lügnerisch, verlogen; unwahr.

men·di·cant ['mendɪkənt] **1.** bettelnd, Bettel...; **2.** Bettler(in); Bettelmönch m.

me·ni·al ['miːnjəl] **1.** □ knechtisch; niedrig; **2.** contp. Diener(in), Knecht m.

men·in·gi·tis ⚕ [menɪn'dʒaɪtɪs] Meningitis f, Hirnhautentzündung f.

men·stru·ate physiol. ['menstrʊeɪt] menstruieren, die Regel od. Periode haben.

men·tal □ ['mentl] geistig, Geistes...; bsd. Brt. F geisteskrank, -gestört; ~ arithmetic Kopfrechnen n; ~ handicap geistige Behinderung; ~ home, ~ hospital Nervenklinik f; ~ly handicapped geistig behindert; **~i·ty** [men'tælɪtɪ] Mentalität f.

men·tion ['menʃn] **1.** Erwähnung f; **2.** erwähnen; don't ~ it! bitte (sehr)!

men·u ['menjuː] Speise(n)karte f; Speisenfolge f; △ nicht Menü.

mer·can·tile ['mɜːkəntaɪl] kaufmännisch, Handels...

mer·ce·na·ry ['mɜːsɪnərɪ] **1.** feil,

M

käuflich; gedungen; gewinnsüchtig; 2. ✕ Söldner m.

mer·cer ['mɜːsə] Seiden-, Stoffhändler m.

mer·chan·dise ['mɜːtʃəndaɪz] Ware(n pl.) f.

mer·chant ['mɜːtʃənt] 1. Kaufmann m; bsd. Am. Ladenbesitzer m, Krämer m; 2. Handels..., Kaufmanns...; **~man** (pl. **-men**) Handelsschiff n.

mer·ci·ful □ ['mɜːsɪfl] barmherzig; **~less** □ [~lɪs] unbarmherzig.

mer·cu·ry ['mɜːkjʊrɪ] Quecksilber n.

mer·cy ['mɜːsɪ] Barmherzigkeit f; Gnade f; be at the ~ of s.o. j-m auf Gedeih u. Verderb ausgeliefert sein.

mere □ [mɪə] (~r, ~st) rein; bloß; **~ly** ['mɪəlɪ] bloß, nur, lediglich.

mer·e·tri·cious □ [merɪ'trɪʃəs] protzig; bombastisch (Stil).

merge [mɜːdʒ] verschmelzen (in mit); econ. fusionieren; **merg·er** ['mɜːdʒə] Verschmelzung f; econ. Fusion f.

me·rid·i·an [mə'rɪdɪən] geogr. Meridian m; fig. Gipfel m.

mer·it ['merɪt] 1. Verdienst n; Wert m; Vorzug m; ~s pl. ⚖ Hauptpunkte pl., Wesen n (e-r Sache); 2. verdienen; **~i·to·ri·ous** □ [merɪ'tɔːrɪəs] verdienstvoll.

mer·maid ['mɜːmeɪd] Nixe f.

mer·ri·ment ['merɪmənt] Lustigkeit f; Belustigung f.

mer·ry □ ['merɪ] (-ier, -iest) lustig, fröhlich; make ~ lustig sein, feiern; **~-an·drew** Hanswurst m; **~-go-round** Karussell n; **~-mak·ing** [~meɪkɪŋ] Feiern n.

mesh [meʃ] 1. Masche f; fig. oft ~es pl. Netz n; be in ⊕ (ineinander)greifen; 2. in e-m Netz fangen.

mess¹ [mes] 1. Unordnung f; Schmutz m; F Schweinerei f; F Patsche f; △ nicht eccl. Messe; make a ~ of verpfuschen; 2. v/t. in Unordnung bringen; verpfuschen v/i. ~ about, ~ around F herummurksen; sich herumtreiben.

mess² [~] Kasino n, Messe f; △ nicht eccl. Messe.

mes·sage ['mesɪdʒ] Botschaft f (to an acc.); Mitteilung f, Bescheid m.

mes·sen·ger ['mesɪndʒə] Bote m.

mess·y □ ['mesɪ] (-ier, -iest) unordentlich; unsauber, schmutzig.

met [met] pret. u. p.p. von meet.

met·al ['metl] 1. Metall n; Brt.

Schotter m; 2. (bsd. Brt. -ll-, Am. -l-) beschottern; **me·tal·lic** [mɪ'tælɪk] (~ally) metallisch, Metall...; **~lur·gy** [me'tælədʒɪ] Hüttenkunde f.

met·a·mor·phose [metə'mɔːfəʊz] verwandeln, umgestalten.

met·a·phor ['metəfə] Metapher f.

me·te·or ['miːtjə] Meteor m.

me·te·o·rol·o·gy [miːtjə'rɒlədʒɪ] Meteorologie f, Wetterkunde f.

me·ter ⊕ ['miːtə] Messer m, Meßgerät n, Zähler; △ Brt. nicht Meter.

meth·od ['meθəd] Methode f; Art u. Weise f; Verfahren n; Ordnung f; System n; **me·thod·ic** [mɪ'θɒdɪk] (~ally), **me·thod·i·cal** □ [~kl] methodisch, planmäßig; überlegt.

me·tic·u·lous □ [mɪ'tɪkjʊləs] peinlich genau, übergenau.

me·tre, Am. **-ter** ['miːtə] Meter m, n; Versmaß n.

met·ric ['metrɪk] (~ally) metrisch; Maß...; Meter...; ~ system metrisches (Maß- u. Gewichts)System.

me·trop·o·lis [mɪ'trɒpəlɪs] Metropole f, Hauptstadt f; **met·ro·pol·i·tan** [metrə'pɒlɪtən] hauptstädtisch.

met·tle ['metl] Eifer m, Mut m, Feuer n; be on one's ~ sein Bestes tun.

mews Brt. [mjuːz] sg. veraltet Stallungen pl.; daraus entstandene Garagen pl. od. Wohnungen pl.

Mex·i·can ['meksɪkən] 1. mexikanisch; 2. Mexikaner(in).

mi·aow [mɪ'aʊ] miauen.

mice [maɪs] pl. von mouse.

Mich·ael·mas ['mɪklməs] Michaelstag m, Michaeli(s) n (29. September).

mi·cro- ['maɪkrəʊ] Mikro..., (sehr) klein.

mi·cro|phone ['maɪkrəfəʊn] Mikrophon n; **~·pro·ces·sor** Mikroprozessor m; **~·scope** Mikroskop n.

mid [mɪd] mittlere(r, -s), Mitt(el)...; in ~air (mitten) in der Luft; **~·day** ['mɪddeɪ] 1. Mittag m; 2. mittägig; Mittag(s)...

mid·dle ['mɪdl] 1. Mitte f, Mitte f (des Leibes), Taille f; △ nicht Mittel; 2. mittlere(r, -s), Mittel...; **~-aged** mittleren Alters; ♀ **2·Ag·es** pl. Mittelalter n; **~-class** Mittelstands...; ~ **class(·es** pl.) Mittelstand m; **~-man** (pl. **-men**) Mittelsmann m; **~-name** zweiter Vorname m; **~-sized** mittelgroß; ~ **weight** Boxen: Mittelgewicht(ler m) n.

mid·dling ['mɪdlɪŋ] mittelmäßig, Mittel...; leidlich.

midge zo. [mɪdʒ] kleine Mücke; **midg·et** ['mɪdʒɪt] Zwerg m, Knirps m.

mid|land ['mɪdlənd] binnenländisch; **~most** mittelste(r, -s); innerste(r, -s); **~night** Mitternacht f; **~riff** anat. ['mɪdrɪf] Zwerchfell n; **~ship·man** (pl. -men) Midshipman m; Brt. unterster Marineoffiziersrang; Am. Seeoffiziersanwärter m; **~st** [mɪdst] Mitte f; in the ~ of mitten in (dat.); **~sum·mer** ast. Sommersonnenwende f; Hochsommer m; **~way** 1. adj. in der Mitte befindlich, mittlere(r, -s); 2. adv. auf halbem Wege; **~wife** (pl. -wives) Hebamme f; **~wif·e·ry** [~wɪfərɪ] Geburtshilfe f; **~win·ter** ast. Wintersonnenwende f; Mitte f des Winters; in ~ mitten im Winter.

mien lit. [miːn] Miene f.

might [maɪt] 1. Macht f, Gewalt f; Kraft f; with ~ and main mit aller Kraft od. Gewalt; 2. pret. von may²; **~y** □ ['maɪtɪ] (-ier, -iest) mächtig, gewaltig.

mi·grate [maɪ'greɪt] (aus)wandern, (fort)ziehen (a. zo.); **mi·gra·tion** [~ʃn] Wanderung f; zo. Zug...; **mi·gra·to·ry** ['maɪɡrətərɪ] wandernd; zo. Zug...

mike F [maɪk] Mikro n (Mikrophon).

mil·age ['maɪlɪdʒ] = mileage.

mild □ [maɪld] mild; sanft; gelind; leicht.

mil·dew ♣ ['mɪldjuː] Mehltau m.

mild·ness ['maɪldnɪs] Milde f.

mile [maɪl] Meile f (1,609 km).

mile·age ['maɪlɪdʒ] zurückgelegte Meilenzahl od. Fahrtstrecke, Meilenstand m; a. ~ allowance Meilen-, appr. Kilometergeld n.

mile·stone ['maɪlstəʊn] Meilenstein m (a. fig.).

mil·i·tant □ ['mɪlɪtənt] militant; streitend; streitbar, kriegerisch; **~ta·ry** [~ərɪ] 1. □ militärisch, Militär...; Heeres..., Kriegs...; ♀ Government Militärregierung f; 2. das Militär, Soldaten pl., Truppen pl.

mi·li·tia [mɪ'lɪʃə] Miliz f, Bürgerwehr f.

milk [mɪlk] 1. Milch f; it's no use crying over spilt ~ geschehen ist geschehen; 2. v/t. melken; v/i. melken; Milch geben; **~maid** ['mɪlkmeɪd] Melkerin f; Milchmädchen n;

~man (pl. -men) Milchmann m; **~ pow·der** Milchpulver n; **~ shake** Milchmixgetränk n; **~sop** Weichling m, Muttersöhnchen n; **~y** [~kɪ] (-ier, -iest) milchig; Milch...; ♀ Way ast. Milchstraße f.

mill¹ [mɪl] 1. Mühle f; Fabrik f, Spinnerei f; 2. Korn etc. mahlen; ⊕ fräsen; Münze rändeln.

mill² Am. [~] ¹/₁₀₀₀ Dollar m.

mil·le·pede zo. ['mɪlɪpiːd] Tausendfüß(l)er m.

mill·er ['mɪlə] Müller m.

mil·let ['mɪlɪt] Hirse f.

mil·li·ner ['mɪlɪnə] Hut-, Putzmacherin f, Modistin f; **~ne·ry** [~rɪ] Putz-, Modewaren(geschäft n) pl.

mil·lion ['mɪljən] Million f; **~aire** [mɪljə'neə] Millionär(in); **~th** ['mɪljənθ] 1. millionste(r, -s); 2. Millionstel n.

mil·li·pede zo. ['mɪlɪpiːd] = millepede.

mill|-pond ['mɪlpɒnd] Mühlteich m; **~stone** Mühlstein m.

milt [mɪlt] Milch f (der Fische).

mim·ic ['mɪmɪk] 1. mimisch; Schein...; 2. Imitator m; 3. (-ck-) nachahmen; nachäffen; **~ry** [~rɪ] Nachahmung f; zo. Mimikry f.

mince [mɪns] 1. v/t. zerhacken, -stückeln; he does not ~ matters er nimmt kein Blatt vor den Mund; v/i. sich zieren; 2. a. ~d meat Hackfleisch n; **~meat** ['mɪnsmiːt] e-e süße Pastetenfüllung; **~ pie** mit mincemeat gefüllte Pastete; **minc·er** [~ə] Fleischwolf m.

mind [maɪnd] 1. Sinn m, Gemüt n, Herz n; Geist m (a. phls.); Verstand m; Meinung f, Ansicht f; Absicht f; Neigung f, Lust f; Gedächtnis n; to my ~ meiner Ansicht nach; out of one's ~, not in one's right ~ von Sinnen; change one's ~ sich anders besinnen; bear od. keep s.th. in ~ (immer) an et. denken; have (half) a ~ to (beinahe) Lust haben zu; have s.th. on one's ~ et. auf dem Herzen haben; make up one's ~ sich entschließen; s. presence; 2. merken od. achten auf (acc.); sich kümmern um; etwas (einzuwenden) haben gegen; ~! gib acht!; never ~! macht nichts!; ~ the step! Achtung, Stufe!; I don't ~ (it) ich habe nichts dagegen; do you ~ if I smoke? stört es Sie, wenn ich rauche?; would you ~ taking off your hat? würden Sie bitte den Hut abnehmen?; ~ your own business! kümmern Sie sich um Ihre Angelegenheiten!; **~ful** □ ['maɪndfl] (of) eingedenk (gen.); achtsam (auf acc.); **~less** □ [~lɪs] (of) unbekümmert (um), ohne Rücksicht (auf acc.).

mine¹ [maɪn] der, die, das meinige od. meine.

mine² [~] **1.** Bergwerk n, Mine f, Zeche f, Grube f; ✕ Mine f; fig. Fundgrube f; ✕ nicht (Kugelschreiber- etc.)Mine; **2.** v/i. graben, minieren; v/t. graben in (dat.); ✕ fördern; ✕ verminen; **min·er** ['maɪnə] Bergmann m.

min·e·ral ['mɪnərəl] **1.** Mineral n; ~s pl. Brt. Mineralwasser n; **2.** mineralisch, Mineral...

min·gle ['mɪŋgl] v/t. (ver)mischen; v/i. sich mischen od. mengen (with unter).

min·i ['mɪnɪ] **1.** Minimode f; Minimantel m, -kleid n, -rock m; **2.** Mini...

min·i- ['mɪnɪ] Mini..., Klein(st)...

min·i·a·ture ['mɪnjətʃə] **1.** Miniatur(gemälde n) f; **2.** in Miniatur; Miniatur...; Klein...; ~ camera Kleinbildkamera f.

min·i·mize ['mɪnɪmaɪz] auf ein Mindestmaß herabsetzen; als geringfügig hinstellen, bagatellisieren; **~mum** [~əm] **1.** (pl. -ma [-mə], -mums) Minimum n, Mindestmaß n, -betrag m; **2.** niedrigste(r, -s), minimal, Mindest...

min·ing ['maɪnɪŋ] Bergbau m; attr. Berg(bau)..., Bergwerks...; Gruben...

min·i·on contp. ['mɪnjən] Lakai m, Kriecher m.

min·i·skirt ['mɪnɪskɜːt] Minirock m.

min·is·ter ['mɪnɪstə] **1.** Geistliche(r) m; Minister m; Gesandte(r) m; **2.** ~ to helfen (dat.), unterstützen (acc.).

min·is·try ['mɪnɪstrɪ] geistliches Amt; Ministerium n; Regierung f.

mink zo. [mɪŋk] Nerz m.

mi·nor ['maɪnə] **1.** kleinere(r, -s), geringere(r, -s); fig. a. unbedeutend, geringfügig; ♪ Moll...; minderjährig; A ~ ♪ a-Moll n; ~ key ♪ Moll(tonart f) n; ~ league Am. Baseball: untere Spielklasse; **2.** ♪ Minderjährige(r m) f; Am. univ. Nebenfach n; ♪ Moll in ♪;

~i·ty [maɪˈnɒrətɪ] Minderheit f; ♪ Minderjährigkeit f.

min·ster ['mɪnstə] Münster n.

min·strel ['mɪnstrəl] Minnesänger m; Varietékünstler, der als Neger geschminkt auftritt.

mint¹ [mɪnt] **1.** Münze f, Münzamt n; a ~ of money e-e Menge Geld; **2.** münzen, prägen.

mint² ♀ [~] Minze f.

min·u·et ♪ [mɪnjʊˈet] Menuett n.

mi·nus ['maɪnəs] **1.** prp. minus, weniger; F ohne; **2.** adj. negativ.

min·ute¹ ['mɪnɪt] Minute f; Augenblick m; in a ~ sofort; just a ~ Moment mal!; ~s pl. Protokoll n.

mi·nute² □ [maɪˈnjuːt] sehr klein, winzig; unbedeutend; sehr genau; **~ness** [~nɪs] Kleinheit f; Genauigkeit f.

mir·a·cle ['mɪrəkl] Wunder n (übernatürliches Ereignis); **mi·rac·u·lous** □ [mɪˈrækjʊləs] wunderbar.

mi·rage ['mɪrɑːʒ] Luftspiegelung f.

mire ['maɪə] **1.** Sumpf m; Schlamm m; Kot m; **2.** mit Schlamm od. Schmutz bedecken.

mir·ror ['mɪrə] **1.** Spiegel m; **2.** (wider)spiegeln (a. fig.).

mirth [mɜːθ] Fröhlichkeit f, Heiterkeit f; **~ful** □ ['mɜːθfl] fröhlich, heiter; **~less** □ [~lɪs] freudlos.

mir·y ['maɪərɪ] (-ier, -iest) sumpfig, schlammig.

mis- [mɪs] miß..., falsch, schlecht.

mis·ad·ven·ture ['mɪsədˈventʃə] n, -betrag m; **2.** niedrigste(r, -s), Mißgeschick n; Unglück(sfall m) n.

mis·an·thrope ['mɪzənθrəʊp], **~thro·pist** [mɪˈzænθrəpɪst] Menschenfeind m.

mis·ap·ply ['mɪsəˈplaɪ] falsch anwenden.

mis·ap·pre·hend ['mɪsæprɪˈhend] mißverstehen.

mis·ap·pro·pri·ate ['mɪsəˈprəʊprɪeɪt] unterschlagen, veruntreuen.

mis·be·have ['mɪsbɪˈheɪv] sich schlecht benehmen.

mis·cal·cu·late [mɪsˈkælkjʊleɪt] falsch berechnen; sich verrechnen.

mis·car·riage [mɪsˈkærɪdʒ] Mißlingen n; Verlust m, Fehlleitung f (von Briefen etc.); ♪ Fehlgeburt f; ~ of justice Fehlspruch m, -urteil n; **~ry** [~ɪ] mißlingen, scheitern; verlorengehen (Brief); ♪ e-e Fehlgeburt haben.

mis·cel·la·ne·ous □ [mɪsɪˈleɪnjəs]

misty

ge-, vermischt; verschiedenartig; **~ny** [mɪˈselənɪ] Gemisch n; Sammelband m.

mis·chief [ˈmɪstʃɪf] Schaden m; Unfug m; Mutwille m, Übermut m; **~mak·er** Unheil-, Unruhestifter(in).

mis·chie·vous □ [ˈmɪstʃɪvəs] schädlich; boshaft, mutwillig; schelmisch.

mis·con·ceive [ˈmɪskənˈsiːv] falsch auffassen, mißverstehen.

mis·con·duct 1. [mɪsˈkɒndʌkt] schlechtes Benehmen; Eheverfehlung f; schlechte Verwaltung; **2.** [ˈmɪskənˈdʌkt] schlecht verwalten; **~ o.s.** sich schlecht benehmen; e-n Fehltritt begehen.

mis·con·strue [ˈmɪskənˈstruː] falsch auslegen, mißdeuten.

mis·deed [ˈmɪsˈdiːd] Missetat f, Vergehen n; Verbrechen n.

mis·de·mea·no(u)r ɪ̯ʒ [ˈmɪsdɪˈmiːnə] Vergehen n.

mis·di·rect [ˈmɪsdɪˈrekt] fehl-, irreleiten; e-n Brief etc. falsch adressieren.

mis·do·ing [ˈmɪsduːɪŋ] mst **~s** pl. = misdeed.

mise en scène thea. [ˈmiːzɑ̃ːnˈseɪn] Inszenierung f.

mi·ser [ˈmaɪzə] Geizhals m.

mis·e·ra·ble □ [ˈmɪzərəbl] elend; unglücklich; erbärmlich.

mi·ser·ly [ˈmaɪzəlɪ] geizig, F knick(e)rig.

mis·e·ry [ˈmɪzərɪ] Elend n, Not f.

mis·fire [ˈmɪsˈfaɪə] versagen (Waffe); mot. fehlzünden, aussetzen.

mis·fit [ˈmɪsfɪt] schlechtsitzendes Kleidungsstück; Außenseiter m, Einzelgänger m.

mis·for·tune [mɪsˈfɔːtʃən] Unglück(sfall m) n; Mißgeschick n.

mis·giv·ing [ˈmɪsˈgɪvɪŋ] böse Ahnung, Befürchtung f.

mis·guide [ˈmɪsˈgaɪd] fehl-, irreleiten.

mis·hap [ˈmɪshæp] Unglück n; Unfall m; Mißgeschick n; Panne f.

mis·in·form [ˈmɪsɪnˈfɔːm] falsch unterrichten.

mis·in·ter·pret [ˈmɪsɪnˈtɜːprɪt] mißdeuten, falsch auffassen.

mis·lay [mɪsˈleɪ] (-laid) et. verlegen.

mis·lead [mɪsˈliːd] (-led) irreführen; verleiten.

mis·man·age [ˈmɪsˈmænɪdʒ] schlecht verwalten od. führen od. handhaben.

mis·place [ˈmɪsˈpleɪs] an e-e falsche Stelle legen od. setzen; et. verlegen; falsch anbringen.

mis·print 1. [ˈmɪsˈprɪnt] verdrucken; **2.** [ˈmɪsprɪnt] Druckfehler m.

mis·read [ˈmɪsˈriːd] (-read [-red]) falsch lesen od. deuten.

mis·rep·re·sent [ˈmɪsreprɪˈzent] falsch darstellen, verdrehen.

miss¹ [mɪs] (mit nachfolgendem Namen 2) Fräulein n.

miss² [~] **1.** Fehlschlag m, -schuß m, -stoß m, -wurf m; Versäumen n, Entrinnen n; **2.** v/t. (ver)missen; verfehlen, -passen, -säumen; auslassen, übergehen; übersehen; überhören; he **~ed** ... ihm entging ...; v/i. nicht treffen; mißglücken.

mis·shap·en [ˈmɪsˈʃeɪpən] mißgebildet.

mis·sile [ˈmɪsaɪl, Am. ˈmɪsəl] **1.** (Wurf)Geschoß n; ✕ Rakete f; **2.** ✕ Raketen...

miss·ing [ˈmɪsɪŋ] fehlend, weg, nicht da; ✕ vermißt; be **~** fehlen, weg sein (Sache); vermißt sein od. werden.

mis·sion [ˈmɪʃn] pol. Auftrag m; (innere) Berufung, Sendung f, Lebensziel n; pol. Gesandtschaft f; eccl., pol. Mission f; ✕ Einsatz m, (Kampf-) Auftrag m; **~a·ry** [ˈmɪʃənrɪ] **1.** Missionar m; **2.** Missions...

mis·sive [ˈmɪsɪv] Sendschreiben n.

mis·spell [ˈmɪsˈspel] (-spelt od. -spelled) falsch buchstabieren od. schreiben.

mis·spend [ˈmɪsˈspend] (-spent) falsch verwenden; vergeuden.

mist [mɪst] **1.** (feiner od. leichter) Nebel; △ nicht Mist; **2.** (um)nebeln; sich trüben; beschlagen.

mis|take [mɪsˈteɪk] **1.** (-took, -taken) sich irren; verkennen; mißverstehen; verwechseln (for mit); **2.** Mißverständnis n; Irrtum m; Versehen n; Fehler m; **~·tak·en** □ [~ən] irrig, falsch (verstanden); be **~** sich irren.

mis·ter [ˈmɪstə] (mit nachfolgendem Namen 2) Herr m (abbr. **Mr**).

mis·tle·toe ♀ [ˈmɪsltəʊ] Mistel f.

mis·tress [ˈmɪstrɪs] Herrin f; Frau f des Hauses; bsd. Brt. Lehrerin f; Geliebte f; Meisterin f.

mis·trust 1. [ˈmɪsˈtrʌst] mißtrauen (dat.); **2.** Mißtrauen n; **~·ful** □ [~fl] mißtrauisch.

mist·y □ [ˈmɪstɪ] (-ier, -iest) neb(e)lig; unklar.

M

mis·un·der·stand ['mɪsʌndə'stænd] (-*stood*) mißverstehen; *j-n* nicht verstehen; **~ing** [~ɪŋ] Mißverständnis *n*.

mis|us·age [mɪs'ju:zɪdʒ] Mißbrauch *m*; Mißhandlung *f*; **~·use** 1. ['mɪs-'ju:z] mißbrauchen, -handeln; 2. [~s] Mißbrauch *m*.

mite [maɪt] *zo.* Milbe *f*; Würmchen *n* (*Kind*); Heller *m*; *fig.* Scherflein *n*.

mit·i·gate ['mɪtɪgeɪt] mildern, lindern.

mi·tre, *Am.* **-ter** ['maɪtə] Mitra *f*, Bischofsmütze *f*.

mitt [mɪt] *Baseball:* (Fang)Handschuh *m*; *sl.* Boxhandschuh *m*; = **mitten.**

mit·ten ['mɪtn] Fausthandschuh *m*; Halbhandschuh *m* (*ohne Finger*).

mix [mɪks] (sich) (ver)mischen; mixen; verkehren (*with* mit); **~ed** gemischt; *fig.* zweifelhaft; **~ed school** *bsd. Brt.* Koedukationsschule *f*; **~ up** durcheinanderbringen; *be ~ed up with* in *e-e Sache* verwickelt sein; **~ture** ['mɪkstʃə] Mischung *f*.

moan [məʊn] 1. Stöhnen *n*; 2. stöhnen.

moat [məʊt] Burg-, Stadtgraben *m*.

mob [mɒb] 1. Mob *m*, Pöbel *m*; 2. (-*bb-*) (lärmend) bedrängen; (in e-r Rotte) herfallen über (*acc.*) *od.* angreifen.

mo·bile ['məʊbaɪl] beweglich; ✕ mobil, motorisiert; lebhaft (*Gesichtszüge*); **~ home** *bsd. Am.* Wohnwagen *m*.

mo·bil·i·za·tion ✕ [məʊbɪlaɪ'zeɪʃn] Mobilmachung *f*; **~ze** ✕ ['məʊbɪlaɪz] mobil machen.

moc·ca·sin ['mɒkəsɪn] weiches Leder; Mokassin *m* (*Schuh*).

mock [mɒk] 1. Spott *m*; 2. Schein...; falsch, nachgemacht; 3. *v/t.* verspotten; nachmachen; täuschen; spotten (*gen.*); *v/i.* spotten (*at* über *acc.*); **~·e·ry** ['mɒkərɪ] Spott *m*, Hohn *m*, Spötterei *f*; Gespött *n*; Nachäfferei *f*; **~·ing-bird** *zo.* [~ɪŋbɜːd] Spottdrossel *f*.

mode [məʊd] (Art *f* u.) Weise *f*; (Erscheinungs)Form *f*; Mode *f*, Brauch *m*; ⚠ *nicht* (*Damen-* etc.) *Mode.*

mod·el ['mɒdl] 1. Modell *n*; Muster *n*; Vorbild *n*; Mannequin *n*, (Foto-) Modell *n*; *male ~* Dressman *m*; 2. Muster...; 3. *v/t. bsd. Brt.* (-*ll-*, *Am.* -*l-*) modellieren; (ab)formen; *Klei-*

der etc. vorführen; *fig.* formen, bilden; *v/i.* (e-m *Künstler*) Modell stehen; als Mannequin *od.* (Foto)Modell arbeiten.

mod·e|rate 1. ☐ ['mɒdərət] (mittelmäßig; gemäßigt; vernünftig, angemessen; 2. [~reɪt] (sich) mäßigen; **~·ra·tion** [mɒdə'reɪʃn] Mäßigung *f*; Mäßigkeit *f*.

mod·ern ['mɒdən] modern, neu; **~·ize** [~aɪz] modernisieren.

mod|est ☐ ['mɒdɪst] bescheiden; anständig, sittsam; **~·es·ty** [~ɪ] Bescheidenheit *f*.

mod·i·fi·ca·tion [mɒdɪfɪ'keɪʃn] Abänderung *f*; Einschränkung *f*; **~·fy** ['mɒdɪfaɪ] (ab)ändern; mildern.

mods *Brt.* [mɒdz] *pl.* betont dandyhaft gekleidete Halbstarke *pl.*

mod·u·late ['mɒdjʊleɪt] modulieren.

mod·ule ['mɒdju:l] Verhältniszahl *f*; ⊕ Baueinheit *f*; ⊕ Modul *n* (*austauschbare Funktionseinheit*), ⚡ a Baustein *m*; *Raumfahrt:* (*Kommando-* etc.)Kapsel *f*.

moi·e·ty ['mɔɪətɪ] Hälfte *f*; Teil *m*.

moist [mɔɪst] feucht; **~·en** ['mɔɪsn] *v/t.* be-, anfeuchten; *v/i.* feucht werden; **mois·ture** [~stʃə] Feuchtigkeit *f*.

mo·lar ['məʊlə] Backenzahn *m*.

mo·las·ses [mə'læsɪz] *sg.* Melasse *f*; *Am.* Sirup *m*.

mole¹ *zo.* [məʊl] Maulwurf *m*.

mole² [~] Muttermal *n*.

mole³ [~] Mole *f*, Hafendamm *m*.

mol·e·cule ['mɒlɪkju:l] Molekül *n*.

mole·hill ['məʊlhɪl] Maulwurfshügel *m*; *make a mountain out of a ~* aus e-r Mücke e-n Elefanten machen.

mo·lest [məʊ'lest] belästigen.

mol·li·fy ['mɒlɪfaɪ] besänftigen, beruhigen.

mol·ly·cod·dle ['mɒlɪkɒdl] 1. Weichling *m*, Muttersöhnchen *n*; 2. verweichlichen; -zärteln.

mol·ten ['məʊltən] geschmolzen.

mom *Am.* F [mɒm] Mami *f*, Mutti *f*.

mo·ment ['məʊmənt] Moment *m*, Augenblick *m*; Bedeutung *f*; = *momentum*; **mo·men·ta·ry** ☐ [~ərɪ] momentan, augenblicklich; vorübergehend; **mo·men·tous** ☐ [~'mentəs] bedeutend, folgenschwer; ⚠ *nicht momentan*; **mo·men·tum** *phys.* [~əm] (*pl.* -*ta* [-tə], -*tums*) Moment *n*; Triebkraft *f*.

morsel

mon|arch ['mɒnək] Monarch(in); **~ar·chy** [~ɪ] Monarchie f.
mon·as·tery ['mɒnəstrɪ] (Mönchs-)Kloster n.
Mon·day ['mʌndɪ] Montag m.
mon·e·ta·ry econ. ['mʌnɪtərɪ] Währungs...; Geld...
mon·ey ['mʌnɪ] Geld n; ready ~ Bargeld n; **~box** Sparbüchse f; **~chang·er** [~tʃeɪndʒə] (Geld)Wechsler m (Person); Am. Wechselautomat m; ~ **or·der** Postanweisung f.
mon·ger ['mʌŋgə] mst in Zusammensetzungen: Händler m, Krämer m.
mon·grel ['mʌŋgrəl] Mischling m, Bastard m; attr. Bastard...
mon·i·tor ['mɒnɪtə] ⊕, TV: Monitor m; Schule: (Klassen)Ordner m.
monk [mʌŋk] Mönch m.
mon·key ['mʌŋkɪ] 1. zo. Affe m; ⊕ Rammblock m; put s.o.'s ~ up F j-n auf die Palme bringen; ~ business F fauler Zauber; 2. ~ about, ~ around F (herum)albern; ~ (about od. around) with F herummurksen an (dat.); **~wrench** ⊕ Engländer m (Schraubenschlüssel); throw a ~ into s.th. Am. et. über den Haufen werfen.
monk·ish ['mʌŋkɪʃ] mönchisch.
mon·o F ['mɒnəʊ] (pl. -os) Radio etc.: Mono n; Monogerät n; attr. Mono...
mon·o- ['mɒnəʊ] ein(fach), einzeln.
mon·o·cle ['mɒnəkl] Monokel n.
mo·nog·a·my [mɒ'nɒgəmɪ] Einehe f.
mon·o·logue, Am. a. **~log** ['mɒnəlɒg] Monolog m.
mo·nop·o·list [mə'nɒpəlɪst] Monopolist m; **~lize** [~aɪz] monopolisieren; fig. an sich reißen; **~ly** [~ɪ] Monopol n (of auf acc.).
mo·not·o·nous □ [mə'nɒtənəs] monoton, eintönig; **~ny** [~ɪ] Monotonie f.
mon·soon [mɒn'suːn] Monsun m.
mon·ster ['mɒnstə] Ungeheuer n (a. fig.); Monstrum n; attr. Riesen...
mon|stros·i·ty [mɒn'strɒsətɪ] Ungeheuer(lichkeit f) n; **~·strous** □ ['mɒnstrəs] ungeheuer(lich), gräßlich.
month [mʌnθ] Monat m; this day ~ heute in e-m Monat; **~ly** ['mʌnθlɪ] 1. monatlich; Monats...; 2. Monatsschrift f.
mon·u·ment ['mɒnjʊmənt] Denkmal n; **~al** □ [mɒnjʊ'mentl] monumental; großartig; Gedenk...

moo [muː] muhen.
mood [muːd] Stimmung f, Laune f; **~s** pl. schlechte Laune; **~y** □ ['muːdɪ] (-ier, -iest) launisch; übellaunig; niedergeschlagen.
moon [muːn] 1. Mond m; once in a blue ~ F alle Jubeljahre (einmal); 2. ~ about, ~ around F herumirren; träumen, dösen; **~light** ['muːnlaɪt] Mondlicht n, -schein m; **~lit** mondhell; **~struck** mondsüchtig; ~ **walk** Mondspaziergang m.
Moor [1] [mʊə] Maure m, Mohr m.
moor [2] [~] Moor n; Ödland n, Heideland n.
moor [3] ⚓ [~] vertäuen; **~ings** ⚓ ['mʊərɪŋz] pl. Vertäuung f; Liegeplatz m.
moose zo. [muːs] nordamerikanischer Elch.
mop [mɒp] 1. Mop m; (Haar)Wust m; 2. (-pp-) auf-, abwischen.
mope [məʊp] den Kopf hängen lassen.
mo·ped Brt. mot. ['məʊped] Moped n.
mor·al ['mɒrəl] 1. □ moralisch; Moral..., Sitten...; 2. Moral f; Lehre f; **~s** pl. Sitten pl.; **mo·rale** [mə'rɑːl] bsd. ✕ Moral f, Stimmung f, Haltung f; **mo·ral·i·ty** [mə'rælətɪ] Moralität f; Sittlichkeit f, Moral f; **mor·al·ize** ['mɒrəlaɪz] moralisieren.
mo·rass [mə'ræs] Morast m, Sumpf m.
mor·bid □ ['mɔːbɪd] krankhaft.
more [mɔː] mehr; noch (mehr); no ~ nicht mehr; no ~ than ebensowenig wie; once ~ noch einmal, wieder; (all) the ~ so (nur) um so mehr; so much the ~ as um so mehr als.
mo·rel ♟ [mɒ'rel] Morchel f.
more·o·ver [mɔː'rəʊvə] außerdem, überdies, weiter, ferner.
morgue [mɔːg] Am. Leichenschauhaus n; F (Zeitungs)Archiv n.
morn·ing ['mɔːnɪŋ] Morgen m; Vormittag m; good ~! guten Morgen!; in the ~ morgens; morgen früh; tomorrow ~ morgen früh; ~ **dress** Anzug m (für offizielle Anlässe).
mo·ron ['mɔːrɒn] Schwachsinnige(r m) f; contp. Idiot m.
mo·rose □ [mə'rəʊs] mürrisch.
mor|phi·a ['mɔːfjə], **~phine** ['mɔː-fiːn] Morphium n.
mor·sel ['mɔːsl] Bissen m; Stückchen n, das bißchen.

M

mor·tal ['mɔːrtl] **1.** □ sterblich; tödlich; Tod(es)...; **2.** Sterbliche(r *m f*); ~**i·ty** [mɔːr'tælətɪ] Sterblichkeit *f*.

mor·tar ['mɔːtə] Mörser *m*; Mörtel *m*.

mort|gage ['mɔːɡɪdʒ] **1.** Hypothek *f*; **2.** verpfänden; ~**gag·ee** [mɔːɡə'dʒiː] Hypothekengläubiger *m*; ~**gag·er** ['mɔːɡɪdʒə], ~**ga·gor** [mɔːɡə'dʒɔː] Hypothekenschuldner *m*.

mor·tice ⊕ ['mɔːtɪs] = **mortise**.

mor·ti·cian *Am.* [mɔː'tɪʃn] Leichenbestatter *m*.

mor·ti|fi·ca·tion [mɔːtɪfɪ'keɪʃn] Kränkung *f*; Ärger *m*; ~**fy** ['mɔːtɪfaɪ] kränken; ärgern.

mor·tise ⊕ ['mɔːtɪs] Zapfenloch *n*.

mor·tu·a·ry ['mɔːtjʊərɪ] Leichenhalle *f*.

mo·sa·ic [mə'zeɪɪk] Mosaik *n*.

mosque [mɒsk] Moschee *f*.

mos·qui·to *zo.* [mə'skiːtəʊ] (*pl. -toes*) Moskito *m*; Stechmücke *f*.

moss ♀ [mɒs] Moos *n*; ~**y** ♀ ['mɒsɪ] (*-ier, -iest*) moosig, bemoost.

most [məʊst] **1.** *adj.* □ meiste(r, -s); die meisten; ~ *people pl.* die meisten Leute *pl.*; **2.** *adv.* am meisten; *vor adj.:* höchst, äußerst; *zur Bildung des Superlativs:* the ~ *important point* der wichtigste Punkt; **3.** *das meiste, das Höchste; das meiste; die meisten pl.*; *at (the)* ~ höchstens; *make the* ~ *of* möglichst ausnutzen; △ *nicht Most*; ~**ly** ['məʊstlɪ] hauptsächlich, meistens.

mo·tel [məʊ'tel] Motel *n*.

moth *zo.* [mɒθ] Motte *f*; ~**eat·en** ['mɒθiːtn] mottenzerfressen.

moth·er ['mʌðə] **1.** Mutter *f*; **2.** bemuttern; ~ **coun·try** Vater-, Heimatland *n*; ~**hood** [~hʊd] Mutterschaft *f*; ~**in-law** [~rɪnlɔː] (*pl. mothers-in-law*) Schwiegermutter *f*; ~**ly** [~lɪ] mütterlich; ~**of-pearl** [~rəv'pɜːl] Perlmutter *f*, Perlmutt *n*; ~ **tongue** Muttersprache *f*.

mo·tif [məʊ'tiːf] (Leit)Motiv *n*.

mo·tion ['məʊʃn] **1.** Bewegung *f*; Gang *m* (*a.* ⊕); *parl.* Antrag *m*; ♣ Stuhlgang *m*, *oft* ~s *pl.* Stuhl *m*; **2.** *v/t. j-m* (zu)winken, *j-m* ein Zeichen geben; *v/i.* winken; ~**less** [~lɪs] bewegungslos; ~ **pic·ture** Film *m*.

mo·ti·vate ['məʊtɪveɪt] motivieren, begründen; ~**va·tion** [məʊtɪ'veɪʃn] Motivierung *f*, Begründung *f*; Motivation *f*.

mo·tive ['məʊtɪv] **1.** Motiv *n*, Beweggrund *m*; **2.** bewegend, treibend (*a. fig.*); **3.** veranlassen.

mot·ley ['mɒtlɪ] bunt, scheckig.

mo·tor ['məʊtə] **1.** Motor *m*; Kraftwagen *m*, Auto(mobil) *n*; *anat.* Muskel *m*; *fig.* treibende Kraft; **2.** motorisch; bewegend; Motor...; Kraft...; Auto...; **3.** (*in e-m Kraftfahrzeug*) fahren; ~ **bi·cy·cle** Motorrad *n*; *Am.* Moped *n*; *Am.* Mofa *n*; ~**bike** F Motorrad *n*; *Am.* Moped *n*; *Am.* Mofa *n*; ~**boat** Motorboot *n*; ~ **bus** Autobus *m*; ~**cade** [~keɪd] Autokolonne *f*; ~ **car** (Kraft)Wagen *m*, Kraftfahrzeug *n*, Auto(mobil) *n*; ~ **coach** Reisebus *m*; ~ **cy·cle** Motorrad *n*; ~**cy·clist** Motorradfahrer(in); ~**ing** [~rɪŋ] Autofahren *n*; *school of* ~ Fahrschule *f*; ~**ist** [~rɪst] Kraft-, Autofahrer(in); ~**ize** [~raɪz] motorisieren; ~ **launch** Motorbarkasse *f*; ~**way** *Brt.* Autobahn *f*.

mot·tled ['mɒtld] gefleckt.

mo(u)ld [məʊld] ✔ Gartenerde *f*; Humus(boden) *m*; Schimmel *m*, Moder *m*; ⊕ (Guß)Form *f* (*a. fig.*); *geol.* Abdruck *m*; Art *f*; **2.** formen, gießen (*on, upon* nach).

mo(u)l·der ['məʊldə] zerfallen.

mo(u)ld·ing *arch.* ['məʊldɪŋ] Fries *m*.

mo(u)ld·y ['məʊldɪ] (*-ier, -iest*) schimm(e)lig, dumpfig, mod(e)rig.

mo(u)lt [məʊlt] (sich) mausern; Haare verlieren.

mound [maʊnd] Erdhügel *m*, -wall *m*.

mount [maʊnt] **1.** Berg *m*; Reitpferd *n*; **2.** *v/i.* (auf-, hoch)steigen; aufsitzen, aufs Pferd steigen; *v/t.* be-, ersteigen; montieren; aufziehen, -kleben; *Edelstein* fassen; ~**ed** *police* berittene Polizei.

moun·tain ['maʊntɪn] **1.** Berg *m*; ~s *pl.* Gebirge *n*; **2.** Berg..., Gebirgs...; ~**eer** [maʊntɪ'nɪə] Bergbewohner(in); Bergsteiger(in); ~**eer·ing** [~rɪŋ] Bergsteigen *n*; ~**ous** ['maʊntɪnəs] bergig, gebirgig.

moun·te·bank ['maʊntɪbæŋk] Marktschreier *m*, Scharlatan *m*.

mourn [mɔːn] (be)trauern; trauern um; ~**er** ['mɔːnə] Trauernde(r *m f*); ~**ful** □ [~fl] traurig; Trauer...; ~**ing** [~ɪŋ] Trauer *f*; *attr.* Trauer...

mouse [maʊs] (*pl. mice* [maɪs]) Maus *f*.

multiplication

mous·tache [mə'stɑːʃ], *Am.* **mus-tache** ['mʌstæʃ] Schnurrbart *m.*

mouth [mauθ] (*pl.* mouths [mauðz]) Mund *m;* Maul *n;* Mündung *f;* Öffnung *f;* **∼·ful** ['mauθful] Mundvoll *m;* **∼·or·gan** Mundharmonika *f;* **∼·piece** Mundstück *n; fig.* Sprachrohr *n.*

mo·va·ble □ ['muːvəbl] beweglich.

move [muːv] **1.** *v/t.* (fort)bewegen; in Bewegung setzen; (weg)rücken; (an)treiben; *Schach:* e-n Zug machen mit; et. beantragen; j-n et.; aufregen; *fig.* bewegen, rühren, ergreifen; *down Schüler* zurückstufen; ∼ *up Schüler* versetzen; ∼ *house Brt.* umziehen; ∼ *heaven and earth* Himmel und Hölle in Bewegung setzen; *v/i.* sich (fort)bewegen; sich rühren; *Schach:* ziehen; (um)ziehen (*to* nach) (*Mieter*); ⚗ sich entleeren (*Darm*); *fig.* voran-, fortschreiten; ∼ *away* weg-, fortziehen; ∼ *for s.th.* et. beantragen; ∼ *in* einziehen; anrücken (*Polizei etc.*); vorgehen (*on* gegen *Demonstranten etc.*); ∼ *on* weitergehen; ∼ *out* ausziehen; **2.** (Fort-)Bewegung *f,* Aufbruch *m;* Umzug *m; Schach:* Zug *m; fig.* Schritt *m; on the* ∼ in Bewegung; auf den Beinen; *get a* ∼ *on!* Tempo!, mach(t) schon!, los!; *make a* ∼ aufbrechen; *fig.* handeln; **∼·a·ble** ['muːvəbl] = *movable;* **∼·ment** [∼mənt] Bewegung *f;* ♪ Bestrebung *f,* Tendenz *f,* Richtung *f;* ♪ Tempo *n;* ♪ Satz *m;* ⊕ (Geh-)Werk *n;* ⚗ Stuhl(gang) *m.*

mov·ie *bsd. Am.* F ['muːvɪ] Film *m;* ∼*s pl.* Kino *n.*

mov·ing □ ['muːvɪŋ] bewegend (*a. fig.*); sich bewegend, beweglich; ∼ *staircase* Rolltreppe *f.*

mow [məu] (∼*ed,* ∼*n od.* ∼*ed*) mähen; **∼·er** ['məuə] Mäher(in) *f;* Mähmaschine *f, bsd.* Rasenmäher *m;* **∼·ing-ma·chine** [∼ɪŋməʃiːn] Mähmaschine *f;* **∼·n** [məun] *p.p. von* mow.

much [mʌtʃ] **1.** *adj.* (*more,* most) viel; **2.** *adv.* sehr; in *Zssgn:* viel...; *vor comp.:* viel; *vor sup.:* bei weitem; fast; ∼ *as I would like* so gern ich möchte; *I thought as* ∼ das dachte ich mir; **3.** Menge *f,* große Sache, Besondere(s) *n; make* ∼ *of* viel Wesens machen von; *I am not* ∼ *of a dancer* F ich bin kein großer Tänzer.

muck [mʌk] Mist *m* (F *a. fig.*); **∼·rake** ['mʌkreɪk] **1.** Mistgabel *f;* **2.** Skanda-le aufdecken; *contp.* im Schmutz wühlen.

mu·cus ['mjuːkəs] (Nasen)Schleim *m.*

mud [mʌd] Schlamm *m;* Kot *m,* Schmutz *m* (*a. fig.*).

mud·dle ['mʌdl] **1.** *v/t.* verwirren; *a.* ∼ *up,* ∼ *together* durcheinanderbringen; F benebeln; *v/i.* pfuschen, stümpern; ∼ *through* F sich durchwursteln; **2.** Durcheinander *n;* Verwirrung *f.*

mud·dy □ ['mʌdɪ] (*-ier, -iest*) schlammig; trüb; **∼·guard** Kotflügel *m;* Schutzblech *n.*

muff [mʌf] Muff *m.*

muf·fin ['mʌfɪn] Muffin *n* (*rundes heißes Teegebäck, mst mit Butter gegessen*).

muf·fle ['mʌfl] *oft* ∼ *up* ein-, umhüllen, umwickeln; *Stimme etc.* dämpfen; **∼·r** [∼ə] (dicker) Schal; *Am.* mot. Auspufftopf *m.*

mug¹ [mʌg] Krug *m;* Becher *m.*

mug² [∼] (*-gg-*) überfallen u. ausrauben; **∼·ger** [∼ə] Straßenräuber *m;* **∼·ging** F [∼ɪŋ] Raubüberfall *m* (*auf der Straße*).

mug·gy ['mʌgɪ] schwül.

mug·wump *Am. iro.* ['mʌgwʌmp] hohes Tier (*Person*); *pol.* Unabhängige(r) *m.*

mu·lat·to [mjuː'lætəu] (*pl. -tos, Am. -toes*) Mulatt|e *m,* -in *f.*

mul·ber·ry ⚘ ['mʌlbərɪ] Maulbeerbaum *m;* Maulbeere *f.*

mule [mjuːl] *zo.* Maultier *n,* -esel *m;* störrischer Mensch; **mu·le·teer** [mjuːlɪ'tɪə] Maultiertreiber *m...*

mull¹ [mʌl] Mull *m.*

mull² [∼]: ∼ *over* überdenken.

mulled [mʌld]: ∼ *claret,* ∼ *wine* Glühwein *m.*

mul·li·gan *Am.* F ['mʌlɪgən] Eintopfgericht *n.*

mul·li·on arch. ['mʌljən] Mittelpfosten *m* (*am Fenster*).

mul·ti- ['mʌltɪ] viel..., mehr..., ...reich, Mehrfach..., Multi...

mul·ti·far·i·ous □ [mʌltɪ'feərɪəs] mannigfaltig; **∼·form** ['mʌltɪfɔːm] vielförmig, -gestaltig; **∼·lat·e·ral** [mʌltɪ'lætərəl] vielseitig; *pol.* multilateral, mehrseitig; **∼·ple** ['mʌltɪpl] **1.** vielfach; **2.** ⚗ Vielfache(s) *n;* **∼·pli·ca·tion** [mʌltɪplɪ'keɪʃn] Vervielfachung *f;* Vermehrung *f;* ⚗ Multiplikation *f;* ∼ *table* Einmaleins

M

n; ~**pli·ci·ty** [~'plɪsətɪ] Vielfalt *f*; ~**ply** ['mʌltɪplaɪ] (sich) vermehren (*a. biol.*); vervielfältigen; & multiplizieren, malnehmen (*by* mit); ~**tude** [~tju:d] Vielheit *f*; Menge *f*; ~**tu·di·nous** [mʌltɪ'tju:dɪnəs] zahlreich.

mum¹ [mʌm] 1. still; 2. pst!

mum² *Brt.* F [~] Mami *f*, Mutti *f*.

mum·ble ['mʌmbl] murmeln, nuscheln; murmeln (*mühsam essen*).

mum·mer·y *contp.* ['mʌmərɪ] Mummenschanz *m*.

mum·mi·fy ['mʌmɪfaɪ] mumifizieren.

mum·my¹ ['mʌmɪ] Mumie *f*.

mum·my² *Brt.* F [~] Mami *f*, Mutti *f*.

mumps ✛ [mʌmps] *sg.* Ziegenpeter *m*, Mumps *m*.

munch [mʌntʃ] geräuschvoll *od.* schmatzend kauen, mampfen.

mun·dane [mʌn'deɪn] weltlich.

mu·ni·ci·pal [mju:'nɪsɪpl] städtisch, Stadt..., kommunal, Gemeinde...; ~**i·ty** [mju:nɪsɪ'pælətɪ] Stadt *f* mit Selbstverwaltung; Stadtverwaltung *f*.

mu·nif·i·cence [mju:'nɪfɪsns] Freigebigkeit *f*; ~**cent** [~t] freigebig.

mu·ni·tions ✕ [mju:'nɪʃnz] *pl.* Munition *f*.

mu·ral ['mjʊərəl] 1. Wandgemälde *n*; 2. Mauer..., Wand...

mur·der ['mɜ:də] 1. Mord *m*; 2. (er)morden; *fig.* F verhunzen; ~**er** [~rə] Mörder *m*; ~**ess** [~rɪs] Mörderin *f*; ~**ous** [~rəs] mörderisch; Mord...

murk·y [~] ['mɜ:kɪ] (-*ier*, -*iest*) dunkel, finster.

murmur ['mɜ:mə] 1. Murmeln *n*; Gemurmel *n*; Murren *n*; 2. murmeln; murren.

mur·rain ['mʌrɪn] Viehseuche *f*.

mus·cle ['mʌsl] Muskel *m*; ~**cle-bound:** *be* ~ *bei Gewichthebern etc.*: e-e starke, aber erstarrte Muskulatur haben; ~**cu·lar** ['mʌskjʊlə] Muskel...; muskulös.

Muse¹ [mju:z] Muse *f*.

muse² [~] (nach)sinnen, (-)grübeln.

mu·se·um [mju:'zɪəm] Museum *n*.

mush [mʌʃ] Brei *m*, Mus *n*; *Am.* Maisbrei *m*.

mush·room ['mʌʃrʊm] 1. ♀ Pilz *m*, *bsd.* Champignon *m*; 2. rasch wachsen; ~ *up* (wie Pilze) aus dem Boden schießen.

mu·sic ['mju:zɪk] Musik *f*; Musikstück *n*; Noten *pl.*; *set to* ~ vertonen; ~**al** [~əl] 1. Musical *n*; 2. musikalisch; Musik...; wohlklingend; ~ *box bsd. Brt.* Spieldose *f*; ~ *box bsd. Am.* Spieldose *f*; ~**hall** *Brt.* Varieté (-theater) *n*; **mu·si·cian** [mju:'zɪʃn] Musiker(in); ~**stand** Notenständer *m*; ~**stool** Klavierstuhl *m*.

musk [mʌsk] Moschus *m*, Bisam *m*; ~**deer** *zo.* ['mʌsk'dɪə] Moschustier *n*.

mus·ket ✕ *hist.* ['mʌskɪt] Muskete *f*.

musk·rat ['mʌskræt] *zo.* Bisamratte *f*; Bisampelz *m*.

mus·lin ['mʌzlɪn] Musselin *m*.

mus·quash ['mʌskwɒʃ] *zo.* Bisamratte *f*; Bisampelz *m*.

muss *Am.* F [mʌs] Durcheinander *n*.

mus·sel ['mʌsl] (Mies)Muschel *f*.

must¹ [mʌst] 1. *v/aux.* ich, du *etc.* muß(t) *etc.*, darf(st) *etc.*, *pret.* mußte(st) *etc.*, durfte(st) *etc.*; *I* ~ *not* (F *mustn't*) ich darf nicht; 2. Muß *n*.

must² [~] Schimmel *m*, Moder *m*.

must³ [~] Most *m*.

mus·tache *Am.* ['mʌstæʃ] = *moustache.*

mus·ta·chi·o [məˈstɑːʃɪəʊ] (*pl.* -*os*) *mst* ~*s pl.* Schnauzbart *m*.

mus·tard ['mʌstəd] Senf *m*.

mus·ter ['mʌstə] 1. ✕ Musterung *f*; *pass* ~ *fig.* Zustimmung finden (*with* bei); △ *nicht* (*Stoff- etc.*)*Muster*; 2. ✕ mustern; *a.* ~ *up* Mut *etc.* aufbieten, zusammennehmen; △ *nicht Stoff etc. mustern.*

must·y ['mʌstɪ] (-*ier*, -*iest*) mod(e)rig, muffig.

mu·ta·ble [~] ['mju:təbl] veränderlich; *fig.* wankelmütig; ~**tion** [mju:'teɪʃn] Veränderung *f*; *biol.* Mutation *f*.

mute [mju:t] 1. [~] stumm; 2. Stumme(r *m*) *f*); Statist(in); 3. dämpfen.

mu·ti·late ['mju:tɪleɪt] verstümmeln.

mu·ti·neer [mju:tɪ'nɪə] Meuterer *m*; ~**nous** [~] ['mju:tɪnəs] meuterisch; rebellisch; ~**ny** [~] 1. Meuterei *f*; 2. meutern.

mut·ter ['mʌtə] 1. Gemurmel *n*; Murren *n*; 2. murmeln; murren.

mut·ton ['mʌtn] Hammel-, Schaffleisch *n*; *leg of* ~ Hammelkeule *f*; ~ **chop** Hammelkotelett *n*.

mu·tu·al ['mju:tʃʊəl] gegenseitig; gemeinsam.

M

nationalize

muz·zle ['mʌzl] **1.** zo. Maul n, Schnauze f; Mündung f (e-r Feuerwaffe); Maulkorb m; **2.** e-n Maulkorb anlegen (dat.); fig. den Mund stopfen (dat.).

my [maɪ] mein(e).

myrrh ♀ [mɜː] Myrrhe f.

myr·tle ♀ ['mɜːtl] Myrte f.

my·self [maɪ'self] (ich) selbst; mir; mich; by ~ allein.

mys·te·ri·ous □ [mɪ'stɪərɪəs] geheimnisvoll, mysteriös; ~**ry** ['mɪstərɪ] Mysterium n; Geheimnis n; Rätsel n.

mys·tic ['mɪstɪk] **1.** a. ~**ti·cal** □ [~kl] mystisch; geheimnisvoll; **2.** Mystiker(in); ~**ti·fy** [~faɪ] täuschen; verwirren; in Dunkel hüllen.

myth [mɪθ] Mythe f, Mythos m, Sage f.

N

nab F [næb] (-bb-) schnappen, erwischen.

na·cre ['neɪkə] Perlmutt(er f) n.

na·dir ['neɪdɪə] ast. Nadir m (Fußpunkt); fig. Tiefpunkt m.

nag [næg] **1.** F Gaul m, Klepper m; **2.** (-gg-) v/i. nörgeln; ~ at herumnörgeln an; v/t. bekritteln; △ nicht nagen.

nail [neɪl] **1.** (Finger-, Zehen)Nagel m; ⊕ Nagel m; zo. Kralle f, Klaue f; **2.** (an-, fest)nageln; Augen etc. heften (to auf acc.); ~ **e·nam·el**, ~ **pol·ish** Am. Nagellack m; ~ **scis·sors** pl. Nagelschere f; ~ **var·nish** Brt. Nagellack m.

na·ïve □ [nɑː'iːv], **na·ive** □ [neɪv] naiv; ungekünstelt.

na·ked □ ['neɪkɪd] nackt, bloß; kahl; fig. ungeschminkt; schutz-, wehrlos; ~**ness** [~nɪs] Nacktheit f, Blöße f; Kahlheit f; Schutz-, Wehrlosigkeit f; fig. Ungeschminktheit f.

name [neɪm] **1.** Name m; Ruf m; by the ~ of ... namens ...; what's your ~? wie heißen Sie?; call s.o. ~s j-n beschimpfen; **2.** (be)nennen; erwähnen; ernennen zu; ~**less** □ ['neɪmlɪs] namenlos; unbekannt; ~**ly** [~lɪ] nämlich; ~**plate** Namens-, Tür-, Firmenschild n; ~**sake** [~seɪk] Namensvetter m.

nan·ny ['nænɪ] Kindermädchen n; ~ **goat** zo. Ziege f.

nap¹ [næp] (Tuch)Noppe f.

nap² [~] **1.** Schläfchen n; have od. take a ~ = **2**; **2.** (-pp-) ein Nickerchen machen.

nape [neɪp] mst ~ of the neck Genick n, Nacken m.

nap·kin ['næpkɪn] Serviette f; Brt. Windel f; ~**py** Brt. F [~ɪ] Windel f.

nar·co·sis ♂ [nɑː'kəʊsɪs] (pl. -ses [-siːz]) Narkose f.

nar·cot·ic [nɑː'kɒtɪk] **1.** (~ally) narkotisch, betäubend, einschläfernd; Rauschgift...; ~ addiction Rauschgiftsucht f; ~ drug Rauschgift n; **2.** Betäubungsmittel n; Rauschgift n; ~s squad Rauschgiftdezernat n.

nar·rate [nə'reɪt] erzählen; ~**ra·tion** [~ʃn] Erzählung f; ~**ra·tive** ['nærətɪv] **1.** □ erzählend; **2.** Erzählung f; ~**ra·tor** [nə'reɪtə] Erzähler(in).

nar·row ['nærəʊ] **1.** eng, schmal; beschränkt; knapp (Mehrheit, Entkommen); engherzig; **2.** ~s pl. Engpaß m; Meerenge f; **3.** (sich) verengen; beschränken; einengen; Maschen abnehmen; ~**chest·ed** schmalbrüstig; ~**mind·ed** □ engherzig, -stirnig, beschränkt; ~**ness** [~nɪs] Enge f; Beschränktheit f (a. fig.); Engherzigkeit f.

na·sal □ ['neɪzl] nasal; Nasen...

nas·ty □ ['nɑːstɪ] (-ier, -iest) schmutzig; garstig; eklig, widerlich; böse; häßlich; abstoßend, unangenehm.

na·tal ['neɪtl] Geburts...

na·tion ['neɪʃn] Nation f, Volk n.

na·tion·al ['næʃənl] **1.** □ national, National..., Landes..., Volks..., Staats...; **2.** Staatsangehörige(r m) f; ~**i·ty** [næʃə'nælətɪ] Nationalität f, Staatsangehörigkeit f; ~**ize**

['næ∫nəlaɪz] naturalisieren, einbürgern; verstaatlichen.

na·tion-wide ['neɪ∫nwaɪd] die ganze Nation umfassend, landesweit.

na·tive ['neɪtɪv] **1.** □ angeboren; heimatlich, Heimat...; eingeboren; einheimisch; ~ *language* Muttersprache f; **2.** Eingeborene(r m) f; ~-**born** gebürtig.

Na·tiv·i·ty *eccl.* [nə'tɪvətɪ] Geburt f (Christi).

nat·u·ral □ ['næt∫rəl] natürlich; angeboren; ungezwungen; unehelich (*Kind*); ~ *sience* Naturwissenschaft f; ~**ist** [~ɪst] Naturwissenschaftler(in), *bsd.* Biologe m; *phls.* Naturalist(in); ~**ize** [~aɪz] einbürgern; ~**ness** [~ɪs] Natürlichkeit f.

na·ture ['neɪt∫ə] Natur f; ~ *reserve* Naturschutzgebiet n; ~ *trail* Naturlehrpfad m.

-na·tured ['neɪt∫əd] *in Zssgn:* ...artig, ...mütig.

naught [nɔːt] Null f; *set at* ~ *et.* ignorieren, in den Wind schlagen.

naugh·ty □ ['nɔːtɪ] (*-ier, -iest*) unartig, frech, ungezogen.

nau·se|a ['nɔːsjə] Übelkeit f; Ekel m; ~**ate** ['nɔːsɪeɪt] ~ *s.o.* (*bei*) j-m Übelkeit verursachen; *be* ~*d* sich ekeln; ~**at·ing** [~ɪŋ] ekelerregend; ~**ous** □ ['nɔːsjəs] ekelhaft.

nau·ti·cal ['nɔːtɪkl] nautisch, See...

na·val ⚔ ['neɪvl] See...; Marine...; ~ *base* Flottenstützpunkt m.

nave[1] *arch.* [neɪv] (Kirchen)Schiff n.

nave[2] [~] (Rad)Nabe f.

na·vel ['neɪvl] *anat.* Nabel m; *fig.* Mittelpunkt m.

nav·i|ga·ble □ ['nævɪgəbl] schiffbar; fahrbar; lenkbar; ~**gate** [~eɪt] *v/i.* fahren, segeln; steuern; *v/t.* See etc. befahren; steuern; ~**ga·tion** [nævɪ'geɪ∫n] Schiffahrt f; Navigation f; ~**ga·tor** ['nævɪgeɪtə] ⚓ Seefahrer m; ⚓ Steuermann m; ⚔ Navigator m.

na·vy ['neɪvɪ] Kriegsmarine f.

nay Nein n; *parl.* Neinstimme f; *the* ~*s have it* der Antrag ist abgelehnt.

near [nɪə] **1.** *adj. u. adv.* nahe; kurz (*Weg*); nahe (verwandt); eng (befreundet *od.* vertraut); knapp; genau, wörtlich; sparsam, geizig; ~ *at hand* dicht dabei; **2.** *prp.* nahe, in der Nähe (von), nahe an (*dat.*) *od.* bei; **3.** sich nähern (*dat.*); ~-**by** ['nɪəbaɪ] in der Nähe (gelegen); nahe; ~**ly** [~lɪ]

nahe; fast, beinahe; annähernd; genau; ~**ness** [~nɪs] Nähe f; ~-**side** *mot.* Beifahrerseite f; ~ *door* Beifahrertür f; ~-**sight·ed** kurzsichtig.

neat □ [niːt] ordentlich; sauber; gepflegt; hübsch, adrett; geschickt; rein; *bsd. Brt.* pur (*Whisky etc.*); ~**ness** ['niːtnɪs] Sauberkeit f; Gefälligkeit f; Gewandtheit f; Reinheit f.

neb·u·lous □ ['nebjʊləs] neb(e)lig.

ne·ces|sa·ry □ ['nesəsərɪ] **1.** notwendig; unvermeidlich; **2.** *mst necessaries pl.* Bedürfnisse *pl.*; ~·**si·tate** [nɪ'sesɪteɪt] *et.* erfordern, verlangen; ~**si·ty** [~ətɪ] Notwendigkeit f; Bedürfnis n; Not f.

neck [nek] **1.** (*a. Flaschen*)Hals m; Nacken m, Genick n; Ausschnitt m (*Kleid*); ~ *and* ~ Kopf an Kopf; ~ *or nothing* auf Biegen od. Brechen; **2.** F (ab)knutschen, knutschen od. schmusen (mit); △ *nicht* **necken**; ~-**band** ['nekbænd] Halsbund m; ~-**er·chief** ['nekət∫ɪf] Halstuch n; ~**ing** F [~ɪŋ] Geschmuse n, Geknutsche n; ~-**lace** [neklɪs], ~-**let** [~lɪt] Halskette f; ~-**line** (*Kleid*)Ausschnitt m; ~-**tie** *Am.* Krawatte f, Schlips m.

nec·ro·man·cy ['nekrəʊmænsɪ] Zauberei f.

née, *Am. a.* **nee** [neɪ] *vor dem Mädchennamen:* geborene.

need [niːd] **1.** Not f; Notwendigkeit f; Bedürfnis n; Mangel m, Bedarf m; *be od. stand in* ~ *of* dringend brauchen; **2.** nötig haben, brauchen, bedürfen (*gen.*); müssen, brauchen; ~·**ful** □ [~fl] nötig, notwendig.

nee·dle ['niːdl] **1.** Nadel f; Zeiger m; **2.** nähen; *fig.* F aufziehen, reizen; *fig.* anstacheln.

need·less □ ['niːdlɪs] unnötig.

nee·dle|wom·an ['niːdlwʊmən] (*pl. -women*) Näherin f; ~-**work** Handarbeit f.

need·y □ ['niːdɪ] (*-ier, -iest*) bedürftig, arm.

ne·far·i·ous □ [nɪ'feərɪəs] schändlich.

ne·gate [nɪ'geɪt] verneinen; **ne·ga·tion** [~∫n] Verneinung f; Nichts n; **neg·a·tive** ['negətɪv] **1.** □ negativ; verneinend; **2.** Verneinung f; *phot.* Negativ n; *answer in the* ~ verneinen; **3.** verneinen; ablehnen.

ne·glect [nɪ'glekt] **1.** Vernachlässigung f; Nachlässigkeit f; **2.** vernachlässigen; ~·**ful** □ [~fl] nachlässig.

neg·li·gence ['neglɪdʒəns] Nachlässigkeit f; **~gent** □ [~t] nachlässig.

neg·li·gi·ble ['neglɪdʒəbl] nebensächlich; unbedeutend.

ne·go·ti·ate [nɪ'gəʊʃɪeɪt] verhandeln (über acc.); zustande bringen; bewältigen; Wechsel begeben; **~·a·tion** [nɪgəʊʃɪ'eɪʃn] Begegnung f (e-s Wechsels etc.); Ver-, Unterhandlung f; Bewältigung f; **~a·tor** [nɪ'gəʊʃɪeɪtə] Unterhändler m.

Ne·gress ['niːgrɪs] Negerin f; **Ne·gro** [~əʊ] (pl. -groes) Neger m.

neigh [neɪ] 1. Wiehern n; 2. wiehern.

neigh·bo(u)r ['neɪbə] Nachbar(in); Nächste(r m) f; **~hood** [~hʊd] Nachbarschaft f, Umgebung f, Nähe f; **~ing** [~rɪŋ] benachbart; **~ly** [~lɪ] nachbarlich, freundlich; **~ship** [~ʃɪp] Nachbarschaft f.

nei·ther ['naɪðə, Am. 'niːðə] 1. keine(r, -s) (von beiden); 2. noch, auch nicht; **~ ... nor** ... weder ... noch ...

ne·on ⚛ ['niːən] Neon n; **~ lamp** Neonlampe f; **~ sign** Leuchtreklame f.

neph·ew ['nevju] Neffe m.

nerve [nɜːv] 1. Nerv m; Sehne f; (Blatt)Rippe f; Kraft f, Mut m; Dreistigkeit f; lose one's ~ den Mut verlieren; get on s.o.'s ~s j-m auf die Nerven gehen; you've got a ~! F Sie haben Nerven!; 2. kräftigen; ermutigen; △ nicht nerven; **~less** □ ['nɜːvlɪs] kraftlos.

ner·vous □ ['nɜːvəs] Nerven...; nervös; nervig, kräftig; **~ness** [~nɪs] Nervigkeit f; Nervosität f.

nest [nest] 1. Nest n (a. fig.); 2. nisten.

nes·tle ['nesl] (sich) (an)schmiegen od. kuscheln (to, against an acc.); a. ~ down sich behaglich niederlassen.

net¹ [net] 1. Netz n; 2. (-tt-) mit e-m Netz fangen od. umgeben.

net² [~] 1. netto; Rein...; 2. (-tt-) netto einbringen.

neth·er ['neðə] niedere(r, -s); Unter...

net·tle ['netl] 1. ♣ Nessel f; 2. ärgern.

net·work ['netwɜːk] (Straßen-, Kanal- etc.)Netz n; Rundfunk: Sendernetz n, -gruppe f.

neu·ro·sis ♣ [njʊə'rəʊsɪs] (pl. -ses [-siːz]) Neurose f.

neu·ter ['njuːtə] 1. geschlechtslos; gr. sächlich; 2. kastriertes Tier; gr. Neutrum n.

neu·tral ['njuːtrəl] 1. neutral; unparteiisch; ~ gear mot. Leerlauf(gang) m; 2. Neutrale(r m) f; Null(punkt m) f; mot. Leerlauf(stellung f) m; **~·i·ty** [njuː'trælətɪ] Neutralität f; **~ize** ['njuːtrəlaɪz] neutralisieren.

neu·tron phys. ['njuːtrɒn] Neutron n; **~ bomb** ☒ Neutronenbombe f.

nev·er ['nevə] nie(mals); gar nicht; **~more** [~'mɔː] nie wieder; **~·the·less** [nevəðə'les] nichtsdestoweniger, dennoch.

new [njuː] neu; frisch; unerfahren; **~born** ['njuːbɔːn] neugeboren; **~com·er** [~kʌmə] Neuankömmling m; Neuling m; **~ly** ['njuːlɪ] neulich; neu.

news [njuːz] mst sg. Neuigkeit(en pl.) f, Nachricht(en pl.) f; **~a·gent** ['njuːzeɪdʒənt] Zeitungshändler m; **~boy** Zeitungsjunge m, -austräger m; **~cast** Rundfunk, TV: Nachrichtensendung f; **~cast·er** Rundfunk, TV: Nachrichtensprecher(in); **~deal·er** Am. Zeitungshändler m; **~mon·ger** Klatschmaul n; **~pa·per** [~speɪpə] Zeitung f; attr. Zeitungs...; **~print** [~zprɪnt] Zeitungspapier n; **~reel** Film: Wochenschau f; **~room** Nachrichtenredaktion f; **~stand** Zeitungskiosk m.

new year ['njuː'jɜː] Neujahr n, das neue Jahr; New Year's Day Neujahrstag m; New Year's Eve Silvester m, n.

next [nekst] 1. adj. nächste(r, -s); (the) ~ day am nächsten Tag; ~ to gleich neben od. nach; fig. fast; ~ but one übernächste(r, -s); ~ door to fig. beinahe, fast; 2. adv. als nächste(r, -s), gleich darauf; das nächste Mal; 3. der, die, das Nächste; **~door** benachbart, nebenan; **~ of kin** der, die nächste Verwandte, die nächsten Angehörigen pl.

nib·ble ['nɪbl] v/t. knabbern an (dat.); v/i. ~ at nagen od. knabbern an (dat.); fig. (herum)kritteln an (dat.).

nice □ [naɪs] (~r, ~st) fein; wählerisch; (peinlich) genau; heikel; nett; sympathisch; schön; hübsch; **~ly** ['naɪslɪ] (sehr) gut; **ni·ce·ty** [~ətɪ] Feinheit f; Genauigkeit f; Spitzfindigkeit f.

niche [nɪtʃ] Nische f.

nick [nɪk] 1. Kerbe f; in the ~ of time im richtigen Augenblick; im letzten

N O

Moment; 2. (ein)kerben; *Brt. sl.* j-n schnappen.

nick·el ['nɪkl] 1. *min.* Nickel *m (Am. a.* Fünfcentstück); 2. vernickeln.

nick-nack ['nɪknæk] = *knick-knack.*

nick-name ['nɪkneɪm] 1. Spitzname *m*; 2. *j-m* den Spitznamen ... geben.

niece [niːs] Nichte *f.*

nif·ty F ['nɪftɪ] (-ier, -iest) hübsch, schick, fesch; stinkend.

nig·gard ['nɪɡəd] Geizhals *m*; **~ly** [~lɪ] geizig, knaus(e)rig; karg.

night [naɪt] Nacht *f*; Abend *m*; at ~, by ~, in the ~ nachts; **~cap** ['naɪt-kæp] Nachtmütze *f*; Schlaftrunk *m*; **~club** Nachtklub *m*, -lokal *n*; **~dress** (Damen-, Kinder)Nachthemd *n*; **~fall** Einbruch *m* der Nacht; **~gown** *bsd. Am.*, **~ie** F [~ɪ] = *nightdress*; **nigh·tin·gale** *zo.* [~ŋɡeɪl] Nachtigall *f*; **~ly** [~lɪ] nächtlich; jede Nacht *od.* jeden Abend (stattfindend); **~mare** Alptraum *m*; **~ school** Abendschule *f*; **~shirt** (Herren)Nachthemd *n*; **~y** F [~ɪ] = *nightie.*

nil [nɪl] *bsd. Sport:* Nichts *n*, Null *f.*

nim·ble □ ['nɪmbl] (~r, ~st) flink, behend(e).

nine [naɪn] 1. neun; ~ *to five* normale Dienststunden; *a* ~*-to-five job* e-e (An)Stellung mit geregelter Arbeitszeit; 2. Neun *f*; **~pin** ['naɪnpɪn] Kegel *m*; ~*s sg.* Kegeln *n*; **~teen** ['naɪn'tiːn] 1. neunzehn; 2. Neunzehn *f*; **~teenth** [~'tiːnθ] neunzehnte(r, -s); **~ti·eth** ['naɪntɪɪθ] neunzigste(r, -s); **~ty** ['naɪntɪ] 1. neunzig; 2. Neunzig *f.*

nin·ny F ['nɪnɪ] Dummkopf *m.*

ninth [naɪnθ] 1. neunte(r, -s); 2. Neuntel *n*; **~ly** ['naɪnθlɪ] neuntens.

nip [nɪp] 1. Kneifen *n*; ⊕ Knick *m*; scharfer Frost; Schlückchen *n*; 2. (-pp-) kneifen, klemmen; schneiden (*Kälte*); *sl.* flitzen; nippen (an *dat.*); ~ *in the bud* im Keim ersticken.

nip·per ['nɪpə] *zo.* (*Krebs*)Schere *f*; (*a pair of*) ~*s pl.* (Kneif)Zange.

nip·ple ['nɪpl] Brustwarze *f.*

ni·tre, *Am.* **-ter** 🜊 ['naɪtə] Salpeter *m.*

ni·tro·gen 🜊 ['naɪtrədʒən] Stickstoff *m.*

no [nəʊ] 1. *adj.* kein(e); at ~ *time* nie; *in* ~ *time* in Nu; ~ *one* keiner; 2. *adv.* nein; nicht; 3. (*pl. noes*) Nein *n.*

no·bil·i·ty [nəʊ'bɪlətɪ] Adel *m* (*a. fig.*).

no·ble ['nəʊbl] 1. □ (~*r*, ~*st*) adlig; edel; vornehm; vortrefflich; △ *nicht* nobel; 2. Adlige(r *m*) *f*; **~man** (*pl. -men*) Adlige(r) *m*; **~mind·ed** edelmütig.

no·bod·y ['nəʊbədɪ] niemand, keiner.

noc·tur·nal [nɒk'tɜːnl] Nacht...

nod [nɒd] 1. (-dd-) nicken (mit); (*im Sitzen*) schlafen; sich neigen; ~ *off* einnicken; ~*ding acquaintance* oberflächliche Bekanntschaft; 2. Nicken *n*, Wink *m.*

node [nəʊd] Knoten *m* (a. 🜨, ♈, *ast.*); 🟉 Überbein *n*, (*Gicht*)Knoten *m.*

noise [nɔɪz] 1. Lärm *m*; Geräusch *n*; Geschrei *n*; *big* ~ *contp.* großes Tier (*Person*); 2. ~ *abroad* (*about, around*) verbreiten; **~less** □ ['nɔɪzlɪs] geräuschlos.

noi·some ['nɔɪsəm] schädlich; unangenehm; widerlich (*Geruch*).

nois·y □ ['nɔɪzɪ] (-ier, -iest) geräuschvoll; laut; lärmend; grell, aufdringlich (*Farbe*).

nom·i·nal □ ['nɒmɪnl] nominell; (nur) dem Namen nach (vorhanden); namentlich; ~ *value econ.* Nennwert *m*; **~nate** [~eɪt] ernennen; nominieren, (zur Wahl) vorschlagen; **~na·tion** [nɒmɪ'neɪʃn] Ernennung *f*; Nominierung *f*, Aufstellung *f* (*e-s Kandidaten*); **~nee** [~'niː] Kandidat(in).

nom·i·na·tive *gr.* ['nɒmɪnətɪv] *a.* ~ *case* Nominativ *m*, erster Fall.

non- [nɒn] *in Zssgn:* nicht..., Nicht..., un...

no·nage ['nəʊnɪdʒ] Minderjährigkeit *f.*

non-al·co·hol·ic ['nɒnælkə'hɒlɪk] alkoholfrei.

non-a·ligned *pol.* [nɒnə'laɪnd] blockfrei.

nonce [nɒns]: *for the* ~ nur für diesen Fall.

non-com·mis·sioned ['nɒnkə-'mɪʃnd] nicht bevollmächtigt; ~ *officer* ✕ Unteroffizier *m.*

non-com·mit·tal ['nɒnkə'mɪtl] unverbindlich.

non-con·duc·tor *bsd.* ⚡ ['nɒnkən-'dʌktə] Nichtleiter *m.*

non·con·form·ist ['nɒnkən'fɔːmɪst] Nonkonformist(in); ♀ *Brt. eccl.* Dissident(in).

non-de·script ['nɒndɪskrɪpt] nichtssagend; schwer zu beschreiben(d).

none [nʌn] 1. keine(r, -s); nichts; 2. keineswegs, gar nicht; ~ *the less* nichtsdestoweniger.

non-en-ti-ty [nɒ'nentəti] Nichtsein *n*; Unding *n*, Nichts *n*, *fig.* Null *f*.

non-ex-ist-ence ['nɒnɪg'zɪstəns] Nicht(vorhanden)sein *n*; Fehlen *n*.

non-fic-tion ['nɒn'fɪkʃn] Sachbücher *pl.*

non-par-ty ['nɒn'pɑːtɪ] parteilos.

non-per-form-ance ɡⁱⁱ ['nɒnpə'fɔːməns] Nichterfüllung *f*.

non-plus ['nɒn'plʌs] 1. Verlegenheit *f*; 2. (-ss-) *j-n* (völlig) verwirren.

non-pol-lut-ing ['nɒnpə'luːtɪŋ] umweltfreundlich, ungiftig.

non-res-i-dent ['nɒn'rezɪdənt] nicht im Haus *od.* am Ort wohnend.

non|**sense** ['nɒnsəns] Unsinn *m*; ~**sen-si-cal** [nɒn'sensɪkl] unsinnig.

non-skid ['nɒn'skɪd] rutschfest.

non-smoker ['nɒn'sməʊkə] Nichtraucher(in); ⚙ Nichtraucher(abteil *n*) *m*.

non-stop ['nɒn'stɒp] Nonstop..., ohne Halt, durchgehend (*Zug*), ohne Zwischenlandung (*Flugzeug*).

non-u-ni-on ['nɒn'juːnjən] nicht (gewerkschaftlich) organisiert.

non-vi-o-lence ['nɒn'vaɪələns] (Politik *f* der) Gewaltlosigkeit *f*.

noo-dle ['nuːdl] Nudel *f*.

nook [nʊk] Ecke *f*, Winkel *m*.

noon [nuːn] Mittag *m*; *at* (*high*) ~ um 12 Uhr mittags; ~**day** ['nuːndeɪ], ~**tide**, ~**time** *Am.* = *noon*.

noose [nuːs] 1. Schlinge *f*; 2. mit der Schlinge fangen; schlingen.

nope F [nəʊp] ne(e), nein.

nor [nɔː] noch; auch nicht.

norm [nɔːm] Norm *f*, Regel *f*; Muster *n*; Maßstab *m*; **nor-mal** □ ['nɔːml] normal; **nor-mal-ize** [~ə-laɪz] normalisieren; normen.

north [nɔːθ] 1. Nord(en *m*); 2. nördlich, Nord...; ~**east** [nɔːr'iːst] 1. Nordost(en *m*); 2. *a.* ~**east-ern** [~ən] nordöstlich; **nor-ther-ly** ['nɔːðəlɪ], **nor-thern** [~ən] nördlich, Nord...; ~**ward(s)** ['nɔːθwəd(z)] *adv.* nördlich, nordwärts; ~**west** ['nɔːθ'west] 1. Nordwest(en *m*); 2. *a.* ~**west-ern** [~ən] nordwestlich.

Nor-we-gian [nɔː'wiːdʒən] 1. norwegisch; 2. Norweger(in); *ling.* Norwegisch *n*.

nose [nəʊz] 1. Nase *f*; Spitze *f*;

Schnauze *f*; 2. *v/t.* riechen; ~ *one's way* vorsichtig fahren; *v/i.* schnüffeln; ~**bleed** ['nəʊzbliːd] Nasenbluten *n*; *have a* ~ Nasenbluten haben; ~**cone** Raketenspitze *f*; ~**dive** ✈ Sturzflug *m*; ~**gay** [~geɪ] Sträußchen *n*.

nos-ey ['nəʊzɪ] = *nosy*.

nos-tal-gia [nɒ'stældʒɪə] Nostalgie *f*, Sehnsucht *f*.

nos-tril ['nɒstrəl] Nasenloch *n*, *bsd. zo.* Nüster *f*.

nos-y F ['nəʊzɪ] (-ier, -iest) neugierig.

not [nɒt] nicht; ~ *a* kein(e).

no-ta-ble ['nəʊtəbl] 1. □ bemerkenswert; 2. angesehene Person.

no-ta-ry ['nəʊtərɪ] *mst* ~ *public* Notar *m*.

no-ta-tion [nəʊ'teɪʃn] Bezeichnung *f*.

notch [nɒtʃ] 1. Kerbe *f*, Einschnitt *m*; Scharte *f*; *Am. geol.* Engpaß *m*; 2. (ein)kerben.

note [nəʊt] 1. Zeichen *n*; Notiz *f*; *print.* Anmerkung *f*; Briefchen *n*, Zettel *m*; *bsd. Brt.* Banknote *f*; (*bsd.* Schuld)Schein *m*; Diplomatie, ♪: Note *f*; △ *nicht* (*Schul*)*Note*; ♪ Ton *m* (*a. fig.*); *fig.* Ruf *m*; Beachtung *f*; *take* ~*s* sich Notizen machen; 2. bemerken; (besonders) beachten *od.* achten *auf* (*acc.*); besonders erwähnen; *a.* ~ *down* niederschreiben, notieren; ~**book** ['nəʊtbʊk] Notizbuch *n*; **not-ed** bekannt, berühmt (*for wegen*); ~**pa-per** Briefpapier *n*; ~**wor-thy** bemerkenswert.

noth-ing ['nʌθɪŋ] 1. nichts; 2. Nichts *n*; Null *f*; ~ *but* nichts als, nur; *for* ~ umsonst; *good for* ~ zu nichts zu gebrauchen; *come to* ~ zunichte werden; *to say* ~ *of* ganz zu schweigen von; *there is* ~ *like* es geht nichts über (*acc.*).

no-tice ['nəʊtɪs] 1. Nachricht *f*, Bekanntmachung *f*; Anzeige *f*, Ankündigung *f*; Kündigung *f*; Be(ob)achtung *f*; △ *nicht* Notiz; *at short* ~ kurzfristig; *give* ~ *that* bekanntgeben, daß; *give* (*a week's*) ~ (acht Tage vorher) kündigen; *take* ~ *of* Notiz nehmen von; *without* ~ fristlos; 2. bemerken; (besonders) beachten *od.* achten auf (*acc.*); △ *nicht* notieren; ~**a-ble** □ [~əbl] wahrnehmbar; bemerkenswert; ~**board** *Brt.* Schwarzes Brett.

no-ti|fi-ca-tion [nəʊtɪfɪ'keɪʃn] Anzeige f, Meldung f; Bekanntmachung f; **~·fy** ['nəʊtɪfaɪ] et. anzeigen, melden; j-n benachrichtigen.

no·tion ['nəʊʃn] Begriff m, Vorstellung f; Absicht f; **~s** pl. Am. Kurzwaren pl.

no·to·ri·ous □ [nəʊ'tɔːrɪəs] notorisch; all-, weltbekannt; berüchtigt.

not·with·stand·ing ['nɒtwɪθ-'stændɪŋ] ungeachtet, trotz (gen.).

nought [nɔːt] Null f; poet. od. veraltet Nichts n.

noun gr. [naʊn] Substantiv n, Hauptwort n.

nour·ish ['nʌrɪʃ] (er)nähren; fig. hegen; **~·ing** [~ɪŋ] nahrhaft; **~·ment** [~mənt] Ernährung f; Nahrung(smittel n) f.

nov·el ['nɒvl] 1. neu; ungewöhnlich; 2. Roman m; △ nicht Novelle; **~·ist** [~ɪst] Romanschriftsteller(in); **no·vel·la** [nəʊ'velə] (pl. -las, -le [-liː]) Novelle f; **~·ty** ['nɒvltɪ] Neuheit f.

No·vem·ber [nəʊ'vembə] November m.

nov·ice ['nɒvɪs] Neuling m, Anfänger(in) (at auf e-m Gebiet); eccl. Novize m, f.

now [naʊ] 1. nun, jetzt; eben; just ~ gerade eben; ~ and again od. then dann u. wann; 2. cj. a. ~ that nun da.

now·a·days ['naʊədeɪz] heutzutage.

no·where ['nəʊweə] nirgends.

nox·ious □ ['nɒkʃəs] schädlich.

noz·zle ['nɒzl] Düse f; Tülle f.

nu·ance [njuː'ɑːns] Nuance f, Schattierung f.

nub [nʌb] Knötchen n; kleiner Klumpen; the ~ fig. der springende Punkt (of bei e-r Sache).

nu·cle·ar ['njuːklɪə] nuklear, Nuklear..., atomar, Atom..., Kern...; **~-free** atomwaffenfrei; **~-pow·ered** atomgetrieben; **~ pow·er sta·tion** Kernkraftwerk n; **~ re·ac·tor** Kernreaktor m; **~ war·head** ✕ Atomsprengkopf m; **~ waste** Atommüll m; **~ weap·ons** pl. Kernwaffen pl.

nu·cle·us ['njuːklɪəs] (pl. -clei [-klɪaɪ]) Kern m.

nude [njuːd] 1. nackt; 2. paint. Akt m.

nudge [nʌdʒ] 1. j-n anstoßen, (an-) stupsen; 2. Stups(er) m.

nug·get ['nʌgɪt] (bsd. Gold)Klumpen m.

nui·sance ['njuːsns] Ärgernis n, Un-

fug m, Plage f; lästiger Mensch, Nervensäge f; what a ~! wie ärgerlich!; be a ~ to s.o. j-m lästig fallen; make a ~ of o.s. den Leuten auf die Nerven gehen od. fallen.

nuke Am. sl. [njuːk] Kernwaffe f.

null [nʌl] 1. nichtssagend; ~ and void null u. nichtig; 2. ⊕, ⅋ Null f; **nul·li·fy** ['nʌlɪfaɪ] zunichte machen; aufheben, ungültig machen; **nul·li·ty** [~ətɪ] Nichtigkeit f, Ungültigkeit f.

numb [nʌm] 1. starr (with vor); taub (empfindungslos); 2. starr od. taub machen; **~ed** erstarrt.

num·ber ['nʌmbə] 1. ⅋ Zahl f; (Auto-, Haus- etc.) Nummer f; (An)Zahl f; Heft n, Ausgabe f, Nummer f (e-r Zeitschrift etc.); (Autobus- etc.)Linie f; without ~ zahllos; in ~ an der Zahl; 2. zählen; numerieren; **~·less** [~lɪs] zahllos; **~·plate** bsd. Brt. mot. Nummernschild n.

nu·me·ral ['njuːmərəl] 1. Zahl(en...); 2. ⅋ Ziffer f; ling. Numerale n, Zahlwort n; **~·rous** □ [~əs] zahlreich.

nun [nʌn] Nonne f; **~·ne·ry** ['nʌnərɪ] Nonnenkloster n.

nup·tial ['nʌpʃl] 1. Hochzeits..., Ehe...; 2. **~s** pl. Hochzeit f.

nurse [nɜːs] 1. Kindermädchen n; a. dry-~ Säuglingsschwester f; a. wet-~ Amme f; (Kranken)Pflegerin f, (Kranken)Schwester f; at ~ in Pflege; put out to ~ in Pflege geben; 2. stillen, nähren; großziehen; pflegen; hätscheln; **~·ling** ['nɜːslɪŋ] Säugling m; Pflegling m; **~·maid** Kindermädchen n; **nur·se·ry** [~sərɪ] Kinderzimmer n; ✿ Baum-, Pflanzschule f; **~ rhymes** pl. Kinderlieder pl., -reime pl.; **~ school** Kindergarten m; **~ slope** Ski: Idiotenhügel m.

nurs·ing ['nɜːsɪŋ] Stillen n; (Kranken)Pflege f; **~ bot·tle** (Säuglings-, Saug)Flasche f; **~ home** Brt. Privatklinik f.

nurs·ling ['nɜːslɪŋ] = nurseling.

nur·ture ['nɜːtʃə] 1. Pflege f; Erziehung f; 2. aufzieh(en); (er)nähren.

nut [nʌt] ⅋ Nuß f; ⊕ (Schrauben-) Mutter f; sl. verrückter Kerl; be ~s sl. verrückt sein; **~·crack·er** ['nʌtkrækə] mst ~s pl. Nußknacker m; **~·meg** ⅋ ['nʌtmeg] Muskatnuß f.

nu·tri·ment ['njuːtrɪmənt] Nahrung f.

nu·tri|tion [njuːˈtrɪʃn] Ernährung *f*; Nahrung *f*; **~tious** □ [~ʃəs], **~tive** □ [ˈnjuːtrɪtɪv] nahrhaft.

nut|shell [ˈnʌtʃel] Nußschale *f*; *in a* ~ in aller Kürze; **~ty** [ˈnʌtɪ] (*-ier*,

-iest) voller Nüsse; nußartig; *sl.* verrückt.

ny·lon [ˈnaɪlɒn] Nylon *n*; ~s *pl.* Nylonstrümpfe *pl.*

nymph [nɪmf] Nymphe *f*.

O

o [əʊ] **1.** oh!; ach!; **2.** *in Telefonnummern:* Null *f*.

oaf [əʊf] Dummkopf *m*; Tölpel *m*.

oak ♀ [əʊk] Eiche *f*.

oar [ɔː] **1.** Ruder *n*; **2.** rudern; **~s·man** [ˈɔːzmən] (*pl. -men*) Ruderer *m*.

o·a·sis [əʊˈeɪsɪs] (*pl. -ses* [-siːz]) Oase *f* (*a. fig.*).

oat [əʊt] *mst* ~s *pl.* ♀ Hafer *m*; *feel one's* ~s F groß in Form sein; *Am.* sich wichtig vorkommen; *sow one's wild* ~s sich die Hörner abstoßen.

oath [əʊθ] (*pl. oaths* [əʊðz]) Eid *m*, Schwur *m*; Fluch *m*; *be on* ~ unter Eid stehen; *take* (*make, swear*) *an* ~ e-n Eid leisten, schwören.

oat·meal [ˈəʊtmiːl] Hafermehl *n*.

ob·du·rate □ [ˈɒbdjʊrət] verstockt.

o·be·di|ence [əˈbiːdjəns] Gehorsam *m*; **~ent** □ [~t] gehorsam.

o·bei·sance [əʊˈbeɪsəns] Ehrerbietung *f*; Verbeugung *f*; *do* (*make, pay*) ~ *to* s.o. j-m huldigen.

o·bese [əʊˈbiːs] fett(leibig); **o·bes·i·ty** [~ətɪ] Fettleibigkeit *f*.

o·bey [əˈbeɪ] gehorchen (*dat.*); *Befehl etc.* befolgen, Folge leisten (*dat.*).

o·bit·u·a·ry [əˈbɪtjʊərɪ] Todesanzeige *f*; Nachruf *m*; *attr.* Todes..., Toten...

ob·ject 1. [ˈɒbdʒɪkt] Gegenstand *m*; Ziel *n*, Zweck *m*, Absicht *f*; Objekt *n* (*a. gr.*); **2.** [əbˈdʒekt] *v/t.* einwenden (*to* gegen); *v/i.* et. dagegen haben (*to ger.* daß).

ob·jec|tion [əbˈdʒekʃn] Einwand *m*, -spruch *m*; **~tio·na·ble** □ [~əbl] nicht einwandfrei; unangenehm.

ob·jec·tive [əbˈdʒektɪv] **1.** □ objektiv, sachlich; **2.** Ziel *n*; *opt.* Objektiv *n*.

ob·li·ga·tion [ɒblɪˈgeɪʃn] Verpflichtung *f*; *econ.* Schuldverschreibung *f*; *be under an* ~ *to* s.o. j-m (zu Dank)

verpflichtet sein; *be under* ~ *to inf.* die Verpflichtung haben, zu *inf.*; **ob·lig·a·to·ry** □ [əˈblɪgətərɪ] verpflichtend, (rechts)verbindlich.

o·blige [əˈblaɪdʒ] (zu Dank) verpflichten; nötigen, zwingen; ~ *s.o.* j-m e-n Gefallen tun; *much* ~*d* sehr verbunden, danke bestens; **o·blig·ing** □ [~ɪŋ] verbindlich, zuvor-, entgegenkommend, gefällig.

o·blique □ [əˈbliːk] schief, schräg.

o·blit·er·ate [əˈblɪtəreɪt] auslöschen, tilgen (*a. fig.*); *Schrift* ausstreichen; *Briefmarken* entwerten.

o·bliv·i|on [əˈblɪvɪən] Vergessen(heit *f*) *n*; **~ous** □ [~əs]: *be* ~ *of* s.th. et. vergessen haben; *be* ~ *to* s.th. blind sein gegen et., et. nicht beachten.

ob·long [ˈɒblɒŋ] länglich; rechteckig.

ob·nox·ious □ [əbˈnɒkʃəs] anstößig; widerwärtig, verhaßt.

ob·scene □ [əbˈsiːn] unanständig.

ob·scure [əbˈskjʊə] **1.** □ dunkel; *fig.* dunkel, unklar; unbekannt; **2.** verdunkeln; **ob·scu·ri·ty** [~rətɪ] Dunkelheit *f* (*a. fig.*); Unbekanntheit *f*; Niedrigkeit *f* (*der Herkunft*).

ob·se·quies [ˈɒbsɪkwɪz] *pl.* Trauerfeier(lichkeiten *pl.*) *f*.

ob·se·qui·ous □ [əbˈsiːkwɪəs] unterwürfig (*to* gegen).

ob·ser·va|ble □ [əbˈzɜːvəbl] bemerkbar; bemerkenswert; **~vance** [~ns] Befolgung *f*; Brauch *m*; **~vant** □ [~t] beachtend; aufmerksam; **~va·tion** [ɒbzəˈveɪʃn] Beobachtung *f*; Bemerkung *f*; *attr.* Beobachtungs...; Aussichts...; **~va·to·ry** [əbˈzɜːvətrɪ] Observatorium *n*, Stern-, Wetterwarte *f*.

ob·serve [əbˈzɜːv] *v/t.* be(ob)achten; sehen; *Brauch etc.* (ein)halten; *Gesetz etc.* befolgen; bemerken, äußern; *v/i.* sich äußern.

ob·sess [əb'ses] heimsuchen, quälen; ~ed by od. with besessen von; **ob·ses·sion** [~eʃn] Besessenheit f; **ob·ses·sive** □ psych. [~sɪv] zwanghaft, Zwangs...

ob·so·lete ['ɒbsəliːt] veraltet.

ob·sta·cle ['ɒbstəkl] Hindernis n.

ob·sti|na·cy ['ɒbstɪnəsɪ] Hartnäckigkeit f; Eigensinn m; ~nate □ [~t] halsstarrig; eigensinnig; hartnäckig.

ob·struct [əb'strʌkt] verstopfen, -sperren; blockieren; (be)hindern; **ob·struc·tion** [~kʃn] Verstopfung f; Blockierung f; Behinderung f; Hindernis n; **ob·struc·tive** □ [~ktɪv] blockierend; hinderlich.

ob·tain [əb'teɪn] erlangen, erhalten, erreichen, bekommen; **ob·tai·na·ble** □ [~əbl] erhältlich.

ob·trude [əb'truːd] (sich) aufdrängen (on dat.); **ob·tru·sive** □ [~sɪv] aufdringlich.

ob·tuse □ [əb'tjuːs] stumpf; dumpf; begriffsstutzig.

ob·vi·ate ['ɒbvɪeɪt] beseitigen; vorbeugen (dat.).

ob·vi·ous □ ['ɒbvɪəs] offensichtlich, augenfällig, klar, einleuchtend.

oc·ca·sion [ə'keɪʒn] 1. Gelegenheit f; Anlaß m; Veranlassung f; (festliches) Ereignis; on the ~ of anläßlich (gen.); 2. veranlassen; ~al □ [~l] gelegentlich, Gelegenheits...

Oc·ci|dent ['ɒksɪdənt] Westen m; Okzident m, Abendland n; 2·**den·tal** □ [ɒksɪ'dentl] abendländisch, westlich.

oc·cu|pant ['ɒkjʊpənt] bsd. ⚖ Besitzergreifer(in); Besitzer(in); Bewohner(in); Insass|e m, -in f; ~**pa·tion** [ɒkjʊ'peɪʃn] Besitz(nahme f) m; ⚔ Besetzung f, Besatzung f, Okkupation f; Beruf m; Beschäftigung f; ~**py** ['ɒkjʊpaɪ] einnehmen; in Besitz nehmen; ⚔ besetzen; besitzen; innehaben; bewohnen; in Anspruch nehmen; beschäftigen.

oc·cur [ə'kɜː] (-rr-) vorkommen; sich ereignen; it ~red to me mir fiel ein; ~**rence** [ə'kʌrəns] Vorkommen n; Vorfall m; Ereignis n.

o·cean ['əʊʃn] Ozean m, Meer n.

o'clock [ə'klɒk] Uhr (bei Zeitangaben); (at) five ~ (um) fünf Uhr.

Oc·to·ber [ɒk'təʊbə] Oktober m.

oc·u|lar □ ['ɒkjʊlə] Augen...; ~**list** [~lɪst] Augenarzt m.

odd □ [ɒd] ungerade (Zahl); einzeln;

nach Zahlen: und einige od. etwas darüber; überzählig; gelegentlich; sonderbar, merkwürdig; ~**i·ty** ['ɒdətɪ] Seltsamkeit f; ~**s** [ɒdz] oft sg. (Gewinn)Chancen pl.; Vorteil m; Vorgabe f (im Spiel); Verschiedenheit f; Unterschied m; Uneinigkeit f; be at ~ with s.o. mit j-m im Streit sein, uneins sein mit j-m; the ~ are that es ist sehr wahrscheinlich, daß; ~ and ends Reste pl.; Krimskrams m.

ode [əʊd] Ode f (Gedicht).

o·di·ous □ ['əʊdjəs] verhaßt, ekelhaft.

o·do(u)r ['əʊdə] Geruch m; Duft m.

of prp. [ɒv, əv] von; Ort: bei (the battle ~ Quebec); um (cheat s.o. ~ s.th.); von, an (dat.) (die ~); aus (~ charity); vor (dat.) (afraid ~); auf (acc.) (proud ~); über (acc.) (ashamed ~); nach (smell ~ roses; desirous ~); von, über (acc.) (speak ~ s.th.); an (acc.) (think ~ s.th.); Herkunft: von, aus; Material: aus, von; nimble ~ foot leichtfüßig; the city ~ London die Stadt London; the works ~ Dickens Dickens' Werke; your letter ~ ... Ihr Schreiben vom ...; five minutes ~ twelve Am. fünf Minuten vor zwölf.

off [ɒf] **1.** adv. fort, weg; ab, herunter(...), los(...); entfernt; Zeit: bis hin (3 months ~); aus(-), ab(geschaltet) (Licht etc.), zu (Hahn etc.); ab(-), los(gegangen) (Knopf etc.); frei (von Arbeit); ganz, zu Ende; econ. flau; verdorben (Fleisch etc.); fig. aus, vorbei; be ~ fort od. weg sein; (weg-) gehen; ~ and on ab u. an; ab u. zu; well (badly) ~ gut (schlecht) daran; **2.** prp. fort von, weg von; von (... ab, weg, herunter); abseits von, entfernt von; frei von (Arbeit); ⚓ auf der Höhe von; be ~ duty dienstfrei haben; be ~ smoking nicht mehr rauchen; **3.** adj. (weiter) entfernt; Seiten..., Neben...; (arbeits-, dienst-) frei; econ. flau, still, tot; int. fort!, weg!, raus!

of·fal ['ɒfl] Abfall m; ~**s** pl. bsd. Brt. Fleischerei: Innereien pl.

of·fence, Am. **-fense** [ə'fens] Angriff m; Beleidigung f, Kränkung f, Ärgernis n, Anstoß m; Vergehen n, Verstoß m; ⚖ Straftat f.

of·fend [ə'fend] beleidigen, verletzen, kränken; verstoßen (against gegen); **~er** [~ə] Übel-, Missetäter(in); ⚖️ Straffällige(r m) f; **first ~** ⚖️ nicht Vorbestrafte(r m) f, Ersttäter(in).

of·fen·sive [ə'fensɪv] **1.** □ beleidigend; anstößig; ekelhaft; Offensiv...; Angriffs...; **2.** Offensive f.

of·fer ['ɒfə] **1.** Angebot n; Anerbieten n; ~ *of marriage* Heiratsantrag m; **2.** v/t. anbieten (a. econ.); Preis, Möglichkeit etc. bieten; Preis, Belohnung aussetzen; Gebet, Opfer darbringen; sich bereit erklären zu; Widerstand leisten; v/i. sich bieten; **~ing** [~rɪŋ] eccl. Opfer(n) n; Anerbieten n, Angebot n.

off·hand ['ɒf'hænd] aus dem Stegreif, auf Anhieb; Stegreif..., unvorbereitet; ungezwungen, frei.

of·fice ['ɒfɪs] Büro n; Geschäftsstelle f; Amt n; Pflicht f; Gefälligkeit f; eccl. Gottesdienst m; ♀ Ministerium n; ~ *hours pl.* Dienststunden pl., Geschäftszeit f; **of·fi·cer** [~ə] Beamte(r m), -in f; Polizist m, Polizeibeamte(r) m; ✕ Offizier m.

of·fi·cial [ə'fɪʃl] **1.** □ offiziell, amtlich; Amts...; **2.** Beamte(r) m, -in f.

of·fi·ci·ate [ə'fɪʃɪeɪt] amtieren.

of·fi·cious □ [ə'fɪʃəs] aufdringlich, übereifrig; offiziös, halbamtlich.

off·-li·cence Brt. ['ɒflaɪsns] Schankkonzession f über die Straße; **~·print** Sonderdruck m; **~·set** ausgleichen; **~·shoot** ♀ Sproß m, Ableger m; **~·side** ['ɒf'saɪd] **1.** Sport: Abseits(stellung f, -position f) n; mot. Fahrerseite f; **~ door** Fahrertür f; **2.** Sport: abseits; **~·spring** ['ɒfsprɪŋ] Nachkomme(nschaft f) m; fig. Ergebnis n.

of·ten ['ɒfn] oft(mals), häufig.

o·gle ['əʊgl]: ~ *(at)* liebäugeln mit, schöne Augen machen (dat.).

o·gre ['əʊgə] (menschenfressender) Riese.

oh [əʊ] oh!; ach!

oil [ɔɪl] **1.** Öl n; ölen; schmieren (a. fig.); **~·cloth** ['ɔɪlklɒθ] Wachstuch n; **~ rig** (Öl)Bohrinsel f; **~·skin** Ölleinwand f; **~s** pl. Ölzeug n; **~·y** □ ['ɔɪlɪ] (-ier, -iest) ölig (a. fig.); fettig; schmierig (a. fig.).

oint·ment ['ɔɪntmənt] Salbe f.

O.K., o·kay F ['əʊ'keɪ] **1.** richtig, gut, in Ordnung; **2.** int. einverstanden!; gut!, in Ordnung!; **3.** genehmigen, zustimmen (dat.).

old [əʊld] (~er, ~est, a. elder, eldest) alt; altbekannt; erfahren; ~ *age* (das) Alter; ~ *people's home* Alters-, Altenheim n; ~ *age* ['əʊld'eɪdʒ] Alters...; **~·fash·ioned** ['əʊld'fæʃnd] altmodisch; ♀ **Glo·ry** Sternenbanner n (Flagge der U.S.A.); **~·ish** ['əʊldɪʃ] ältlich.

ol·fac·to·ry anat. [ɒl'fæktərɪ] Geruchs...

ol·ive ['ɒlɪv] ♀ Olive f; Olivgrün n.

O·lym·pic Games [ə'lɪmpɪk'geɪmz] pl. Olympische Spiele pl.; Summer (Winter) ~ pl. Olympische Sommer-(Winter)spiele pl.

om·i·nous □ ['ɒmɪnəs] unheilvoll.

o·mis·sion [əʊ'mɪʃn] Unterlassung f; Auslassung f.

o·mit [ə'mɪt] (-tt-) unterlassen; auslassen.

om·nip·o·tence [ɒm'nɪpətəns] Allmacht f; **~·tent** □ [~t] allmächtig.

om·nis·ci·ent □ [ɒm'nɪsɪənt] allwissend.

on [ɒn] **1.** prp. mst auf (dat., acc.); an (dat.) (~ *the wall, ~ the Thames*); Richtung, Ziel: auf (acc.) ... (hin), an (acc.), nach (dat.) ... (hin) (march ~ London); fig. auf (acc.) ... (hin) (~ *his authority*); Zeitpunkt: an (dat.) (~ *Sunday, ~ the 1st of April*); (gleich) nach, bei (~ *his arrival*); gehörig zu, beschäftigt bei (~ *a committee*, *the "Daily Mail"*); Zustand: in (dat.), auf (dat.), zu (~ *duty, ~ fire, ~ leave*); Thema: über (acc.) (talk ~ *a subject*); nach (dat.) (~ *this model*); von (dat.) (live ~ *s.th.*); ~ *the street* Am. auf der Straße; get ~ *a train* bsd. Am. in e-n Zug einsteigen; ~ *hearing it* als ich etc. es hörte; **2.** an(geschaltet) (Licht etc.), eingeschaltet, laufend, auf (Hahn etc.); (dar)auf(legen, -schrauben etc.); Kleidung: an(haben, -ziehen) (have a coat ~); auf(behalten) (keep one's hat ~); weiter(gehen, -sprechen etc.); and so ~ und so weiter; ~ *and* ~ immer weiter; ~ *to* ... auf (hinauf od. hinaus); be ~ im Gange sein, los sein; thea. gespielt werden; laufen (Film).

once [wʌns] **1.** adv. einmal; je(mals); einst; at ~ (so)gleich; sofort; zugleich; all at ~ plötzlich; for ~ diesmal, ausnahmsweise; ~ (and) for all ein für allemal; ~ *again*, ~ *more* noch einmal; ~ *in a while* dann und wann; **2.** cj. a. ~ *that* sobald.

one [wʌn] ein(e); einzig; eine(r, -s); man; eins; ~'s sein(e) (-); eines Tages; ~ *Smith* ein gewisser Smith; ~ *another* einander; ~ *by* ~, ~ *after another*, ~ *after the other* e-r nach dem andern; *be at* ~ *with s.o.* mit j-m einig sein; *I for* ~, *I for my part*, *the little* ~s *pl.* die Kleinen *pl.*

o·ner·ous □ ['ɒnərəs] schwer(wiegend).

one|self [wʌn'self] sich (selbst); (sich) selbst; ~**-sid·ed** □ ['wʌn'saidid] einseitig; ~**-way** ['wʌnwei]: ~ *street* Einbahnstraße *f*; ~ *ticket Am.* einfache Fahrkarte; ≉ einfaches Ticket.

on·ion ♀ ['ʌnjən] Zwiebel *f*.

on·look·er ['ɒnlʊkə] Zuschauer(in).

on·ly ['ɔʊnlɪ] **1.** *adj.* einzige(r, -s); **2.** *adv.* nur, bloß; erst; ~ *yesterday* erst gestern; **3.** *cj.* ~ (*that*) nur daß.

on·rush ['ɒnrʌʃ] Ansturm *m*.

on·set ['ɒnset], **on·slaught** ['ɒnslɔːt] Angriff *m*; Anfang *m*; ≉ Ausbruch *m* (*e-r Krankheit*).

on·ward ['ɒnwəd] **1.** *adj.* fortschreitend; **2.** *a.* ~**s** *adv.* vorwärts, weiter.

ooze [uːz] **1.** Schlamm *m*; **2.** *v/i.* sickern; ~ *away* fig. schwinden; *v/t.* ausströmen, -schwitzen.

o·paque □ [əʊ'peɪk] (~*r*, ~*st*) undurchsichtig.

o·pen ['ɔʊpən] **1.** □ offen; geöffnet, auf; frei (*Feld etc.*); öffentlich; offen, unentschieden; offen, freimütig; freigebig; *fig.* zugänglich (*to dat.*), aufgeschlossen (*to* für); **2.** *in the* ~ (*air*) im Freien; *come out into the* ~ *fig.* an die Öffentlichkeit treten; **3.** *v/t.* öffnen; eröffnen (*a. fig.*); *v/i.* sich öffnen, aufgehen; *fig.* öffnen, aufmachen, anfangen; ~ *into* führen nach (*Tür etc.*); ~ *on to* hinausgehen auf (*acc.*) (*Fenster etc.*); ~ *out* sich ausbreiten; ~**-air** ['ɔʊpən'eə] im Freien (stattfindend), Freilicht..., Freiluft...; ~**-armed** ['ɔʊpən'ɑːmd] herzlich, warm; ~**-er** ['ɔʊpnə] (*Büchsen- etc.*)Öffner *m*; ~**-eyed** ['ɔʊpən'aɪd] staunend; wach; mit offenen Augen; ~**-hand·ed** ['ɔʊpən'hændɪd] freigebig, großzügig; ~**-heart·ed** ['ɔʊpənhɑːtɪd] offen(herzig), aufrichtig; ~**-ing** ['ɔʊpnɪŋ] (Er)Öffnung *f*; freie Stelle; Gelegenheit *f*; *attr.* Eröffnungs...; ~**-mind·ed** *fig.* ['ɔʊpən'maɪndɪd] aufgeschlossen.

op·e·ra ['ɒpərə] Oper *f*; ~**-glass(·es** *pl.*) Opernglas *n*.

op·e·rate ['ɒpəreɪt] *v/t.* bewirken, (mit sich) bringen; ⊕ *Maschine* bedienen, *et.* betätigen; *Unternehmen* betreiben; *v/i.* ⊕ arbeiten, funktionieren, laufen; wirksam werden *od.* sein; ✗ operieren; ♂ operieren (*on od.* upon s.o. j-n); *operating room Am.*, *operating-theatre Brt.* Operationssaal *m*; ~**-ra·tion** [ɒpə'reɪʃn] Wirkung *f* (*on* auf *acc.*); ⊕ Betrieb *m*, Tätigkeit *f*; ♂, ✗ Operation *f*; *be in* ~ in Betrieb sein; *come into* ~ ⫱ in Kraft treten; ~**-ra·tive** ['ɒpərətɪv] **1.** □ wirksam, tätig; praktisch; ♂ operativ; **2.** Arbeiter *m*; ~**-ra·tor** ['ɒpəreɪtə] ⊕ Bedienungsperson *f*; Telephonist(in).

o·pin·ion [ə'pɪnjən] Meinung *f*; Ansicht *f*; Stellungnahme *f*; Gutachten *n*; *in my* ~ meines Erachtens.

op·po·nent [ə'pəʊnənt] Gegner *m*.

op·por|tune □ ['ɒpətjuːn] passend; rechtzeitig; günstig; ~**-tu·ni·ty** [ɒpə'tjuːnɪtɪ] (günstige) Gelegenheit *f*.

op·pose [ə'pəʊz] entgegen-, gegenüberstellen; sich widersetzen, bekämpfen; **op·posed** entgegengesetzt; *be* ~ *to* gegen ... sein; **op·po·site** ['ɒpəzɪt] **1.** □ gegenüberliegend; entgegengesetzt; **2.** *prp. u. adv.* gegenüber; **3.** Gegenteil *n*, -satz *m*; **op·po·si·tion** [ɒpə'zɪʃn] das Gegenüberstehen; Widerstand *m*; Gegensatz *m*; Widerspruch *m*; Opposition *f* (*a. pol.*).

op·press [ə'pres] be-, unterdrücken; **op·pres·sion** [~ʃn] Unterdrückung *f*; Druck *m*; Bedrängnis *f*; Bedrücktheit *f*; **op·pres·sive** □ [~sɪv] (be-)drückend; hart, grausam; schwül (*Wetter*).

op·tic ['ɒptɪk] Augen..., Seh...; = **op·ti·cal** □ [~l] optisch; **op·ti·cian** [ɒp'tɪʃn] Optiker *m*.

op·ti·mism ['ɒptɪmɪzəm] Optimismus *m*.

op·tion ['ɒpʃn] Wahl(freiheit) *f*; Alternative *f*; *econ.* Vorkaufsrecht *n*, Option *f*; ~**-al** □ [~l] freigestellt, wahlfrei.

op·u·lence ['ɒpjʊləns] (großer) Reichtum *m*, Überfluß *m*.

or [ɔː] oder; ~ *else* sonst.

o·rac·u·lar □ [ɔ'rækjʊlə] orakelhaft.

o·ral □ ['ɔːrəl] mündlich; Mund...

or·ange ['ɒrɪndʒ] **1.** Orange *n* (*Farbe*); ♀ Orange *f*, Apfelsine *f*; **2.**

orange(farben); **~ade** [ˈɒrɪndʒˈeɪd] Orangenlimonade f.

o·ra·tion [ɔːˈreɪʃn] Rede f; **or·a·tor** [ˈɒrətə] Redner m; **or·a·to·ry** [~rɪ] Redekunst f, Rhetorik f; eccl. Kapelle f.

orb [ɔːb] Ball m; Himmelskörper m; poet. Augapfel m, Auge n.

or·bit [ˈɔːbɪt] **1.** Kreis-, Umlaufbahn f; get od. put into ~ in e-e Umlaufbahn eingeben od. bringen; **2.** v/t. die Erde etc. umkreisen; Satelliten etc. auf e-e Umlaufbahn bringen; v/i. die Erde etc. umkreisen, sich auf e-r Umlaufbahn bewegen.

or·chard [ˈɔːtʃəd] Obstgarten m.

or·ches·tra [ˈɔːkɪstrə] ♪ Orchester n; Am. thea. Parkett n.

or·chid ♀ [ˈɔːkɪd] Orchidee f.

or·dain [ɔːˈdeɪn] anordnen, verfügen; zum Priester weihen.

or·deal fig. [ɔːˈdiːl] schwere Prüfung; Qual f, Tortur f.

or·der [ˈɔːdə] **1.** Ordnung f, Anordnung f, Reihenfolge f; Befehl m; econ. Bestellung f, Auftrag m; econ. Zahlungsauftrag m; parl. etc. (Geschäfts)Ordnung f; Klasse f, Rang m; Orden m (a. eccl.); take (holy) ~s in den geistlichen Stand treten; in ~ to inf. um zu inf.; in ~ that damit; out of ~ nicht in Ordnung; defekt; nicht in Betrieb; make to ~ auf Bestellung anfertigen; **2.** (an-, ✠ ver)ordnen; befehlen; econ. bestellen; j-n schicken; **~·ly** [ˈɔːdəlɪ] **1.** ordentlich; fig. ruhig; **2.** ✠ (Offiziers)Bursche m; ✕ Sanitätssoldat m; Krankenpfleger m.

or·di·nal [ˈɔːdɪnl] **1.** Ordnungs...; **2.** a. ~ number ⅋ Ordnungszahl f.

or·di·nance [ˈɔːdɪnəns] Verordnung f.

or·di·nary ☐ [ˈɔːdnrɪ] üblich, gewöhnlich, normal; △ nicht ordinär.

ord·nance ✕ [ˈɔːdnəns] Artillerie f, Geschütze pl.; Feldzeugwesen n.

ore [ɔː] Erz n.

or·gan [ˈɔːgən] ♪ Orgel f; Organ n; **~-grind·er** [~ˌgraɪndə] Leierkastenmann m; **~·ic** [ɔːˈgænɪk] (~ally) organisch; **~·ism** [ˈɔːgənɪzəm] Organismus m; **~·i·za·tion** [ɔːgənaɪˈzeɪʃn] Organisation f; **~·ize** [ˈɔːgənaɪz] organisieren; **~·iz·er** [~ə] Organisator(in).

o·ri·ent [ˈɔːrɪənt] **1.** ♀ Osten m; Orient m, Morgenland n; **2.** orientieren;

~·en·tal [ɔːrɪˈentl] **1.** ☐ orientalisch, östlich; **2.** ♀ Orientale m, -in f; **~·en·tate** [ˈɔːrɪənteɪt] orientieren.

or·i·fice [ˈɒrɪfɪs] Mündung f; Öffnung f.

or·i·gin [ˈɒrɪdʒɪn] Ursprung m; Anfang m; Herkunft f.

o·rig·i·nal [əˈrɪdʒənl] **1.** ☐ ursprünglich; originell; Original...; **2.** Original n; **~·i·ty** [ərɪdʒəˈnælətɪ] Originalität f; **~·ly** [əˈrɪdʒnəlɪ] originell; ursprünglich, zuerst.

o·rig·i·nate [əˈrɪdʒɪneɪt] v/t. hervorbringen, schaffen; v/i. entstehen; **~·na·tor** [~ə] Urheber(in).

or·na|ment 1. [ˈɔːnəmənt] Verzierung f; fig. Zierde f; **2.** [~ment] verzieren, schmücken; **~·men·tal** ☐ [ɔːnəˈmentl] schmückend, Zier...

or·nate ☐ [ɔːˈneɪt] reichverziert, reichgeschmückt; überladen.

or·phan [ˈɔːfn] **1.** Waise f; **2.** a. ~ed verwaist; **~·age** [~ɪdʒ] Waisenhaus n.

or·tho·dox ☐ [ˈɔːθədɒks] orthodox; strenggläubig; üblich, anerkannt.

os·cil·late [ˈɒsɪleɪt] schwingen; fig. schwanken.

o·si·er ♀ [ˈəʊʒə] Korbweide f.

os·prey zo. [ˈɒsprɪ] Fischadler m.

os·ten·si·ble ☐ [ɒˈstensəbl] angeblich.

os·ten·ta·tion [ɒstenˈteɪʃn] Zurschaustellung f; Protzerei f; **~·tious** ☐ [~ʃəs] großtuerisch, prahlerisch.

os·tra·cize [ˈɒstrəsaɪz] verbannen; ächten.

os·trich zo. [ˈɒstrɪtʃ] Strauß m.

oth·er [ˈʌðə] andere(r, -s); the ~ day neulich; the ~ morning neulich morgens; every ~ day jeden zweiten Tag; **~·wise** [~waɪz] anders; sonst.

ot·ter [ˈɒtə] zo. Otter m; Otterfell n.

ought v/aux. [ɔːt] (verneint: ~ not, oughtn't) ich, du etc. sollte(st) etc.; you ~ to have done it Sie hätten es tun sollen.

ounce [aʊns] Unze f (= 28,35 g).

our [ˈaʊə] unser; **~s** [ˈaʊəz] der, die, das uns(e)re; unser; **~·selves** [aʊəˈselvz] uns (selbst); wir selbst.

oust [aʊst] verdrängen, -treiben, hinauswerfen; e-s Amtes entheben.

out [aʊt] **1.** aus; hinaus(gehen, -werfen etc.); heraus(kommen etc.); aus(brechen etc.); raus; draußen; nicht zu Hause; Sport: aus, draußen; aus der Mode; vorbei; erloschen; aus(gegangen); verbraucht; (bis) zu Ende;

~ *and about* (wieder) auf den Beinen; *way* ~ Ausgang *m*; ~ *of* aus (...
heraus); hinaus; außerhalb; außer
Atem etc.; (hergestellt) aus; aus
Furcht etc.; von (*in nine cases* ~ *of
ten*); *be* ~ *of s.th.* et. nicht mehr
haben; **2.** Ausweg *m*; die ~*s* pl. parl.
die Opposition; **3.** econ. übernormal,
Über... (*Größe*); **4.** int. hinaus!,
raus!

out|bal·ance ['aʊt'bæləns] überwie-
gen, -treffen; ~·bid [aʊt'bɪd] (-*dd*-
-*bid*) überbieten; ~·board ['aʊtbɔːd]
Außenbord...; ~·break ['aʊtbreɪk]
Ausbruch *m*; ~·build·ing ['aʊtbɪl-
dɪŋ] Nebengebäude *n*; ~·burst
['aʊtbɜːst] Ausbruch *m* (*a. fig.*);
~·cast ['aʊtkɑːst] **1.** ausgestoßen; **2.**
Ausgestoßene(r *m*) *f*; ~·come ['aʊt-
kʌm] Ergebnis *n*; △ *nicht das Auskommen*; ~·cry ['aʊtkraɪ] Aufschrei
m, Schrei *m* der Entrüstung;
~·dat·ed ['aʊt'deɪtɪd] überholt, veraltet; ~·dis·tance [aʊt'dɪstəns]
(weit) überholen; ~·do [aʊt'duː]
(-*did*, -*done*) übertreffen; ~·door
['aʊtdɔː] Außen..., außerhalb des
Hauses, im Freien, draußen;
~·doors [aʊt'dɔːz] draußen, im
Freien.

out·er ['aʊtə] äußere(r, -s); Außen...;
~·most [ˌməʊst] äußerste.

out|fit ['aʊtfɪt] Ausrüstung *f*, Aus-
stattung *f*; F Haufen *m*, Trupp *m*,
(Arbeits)Gruppe *f*; *Am.* ✕ Einheit *f*;
~·fit·ter *Brt.* [ˌə] Herrenausstatter
m; ~·go·ing ['aʊtgəʊɪŋ] **1.** weg-, ab-
gehend; **2.** Ausgehen *n*; ~*s* pl.
(Geld)Ausgaben *pl.*; ~·grow ['aʊt-
'grəʊ] (-*grew*, -*grown*) herauswachsen aus (*Kleidern*); größer werden
als, hinauswachsen über (*acc.*);
~·house ['aʊthaʊs] Nebengebäude
n; *Am.* Außenabort *m*.

out·ing ['aʊtɪŋ] Ausflug *m*.

out|last ['aʊt'lɑːst] überdauern, -le-
ben; ~·law ['aʊtlɔː] Geächtete(r *m*) *f*;
~·lay ['aʊtleɪ] (Geld)Auslage(n *pl.*) *f*,
Ausgabe(n *pl.*) *f*; ~·let ['aʊtlet] Aus-
laß *m*, Abfluß *m*, Austritt *m*, Abzug
m; econ. Absatzmarkt *m*; *Am.* ∮ Anschluß *m*, Steckdose *f*; *fig.* Ventil *n*;
~·line ['aʊtlaɪn] **1.** Umriß *m*; Überblick *m*; Skizze *f*; **2.** umreißen, skizzieren; ~·live ['aʊt'lɪv] überleben;
~·look ['aʊtlʊk] Ausblick *m* (*a. fig.*);
Auffassung *f*; ~·ly·ing ['aʊtlaɪɪŋ]
entlegen; ~·match ['aʊt'mætʃ] weit

übertreffen; ~·num·ber [aʊt'nʌm-
bə] an Zahl übertreffen; ~·pa·tient
['aʊtpeɪʃnt] ambulanter Patient, am-
bulante Patientin; ~·post ['aʊtpəʊst]
Vorposten *m*; ~·pour·ing ['aʊtpɔː-
rɪŋ] (*bsd.* Gefühls)Erguß *m*; ~·put
['aʊtpʊt] Output *m*; econ. u. ⊕ Ar-
beitsertrag *m*, -leistung *f*; econ. Pro-
duktion *f*, Ausstoß *m*, Ertrag *m*; ∮
Ausgangsleistung *f*; ∮ Ausgang *m*
(*an Geräten*); *Computer*: (Daten-)
Ausgabe *f*; ~·rage ['aʊtreɪdʒ] **1.** Aus-
schreitung *f*; Gewalttat *f*; **2.** gröblich
verletzen *od.* beleidigen; Gewalt antun (*dat.*); ~·ra·geous □ [aʊt'reɪ-
dʒəs] abscheulich; empörend, unerhört; ~·reach ['aʊt'riːtʃ] weiter reichen als; ~·right [*adj.* 'aʊtraɪt, *adv.*
aʊt'raɪt] gerade heraus; völlig;
direkt; ~·run [aʊt'rʌn] (-*nn*-, -*ran*,
-*run*) schneller laufen als; *fig.* übertreffen, hinausgehen über (*acc.*);
~·set ['aʊtset] Anfang *m*; Aufbruch
m; ~·shine ['aʊt'ʃaɪn] (-*shone*) über-
strahlen; *fig. a.* in den Schatten
stellen; ~·side [aʊt'saɪd] **1.** Außen-
seite *f*; *das* Äußere; *Sport*: Außen-
stürmer *m*; *at the* (*very*) ~ (aller-)
höchstens; *attr.*: ~ *left* (*right*) *Sport*:
Links-(Rechts-)Außen *m*; **2.** *adj.*
äußere(r, -s), Außen...; außerhalb,
draußen; äußerste(r, -s) (*Preis*); **3.**
adv. draußen, außerhalb; heraus,
hinaus; **4.** *prp.* außerhalb; ~·sid·er
[ˌə] Außenseiter(in), -stehende(r *m*)
f; ~·size ['aʊtsaɪz] Übergröße *f*;
~·skirts ['aʊtskɜːts] *pl.* Außenbezir-
ke *pl.*, (Stadt)Rand *m*; ~·smart
['aʊt'smɑːt] überlisten; ~·spo·ken
[aʊt'spəʊkən] offen, freimütig; △
nicht ausgesprochen; ~·spread
['aʊt'spred] ausgestreckt, -breitet;
~·stand·ing ['aʊt'stændɪŋ] hervorragend (*a. fig.*); ausstehend (*Schuld*);
ungeklärt (*Frage*); unerledigt (*Arbeit*); ~·stretched ['aʊtstretʃt] =
outspread; ~·strip ['aʊt'strɪp] (-*pp*-)
überholen (*a. fig.*).

out·ward ['aʊtwəd] **1.** äußere(r, -s);
äußerlich; nach (dr)außen gerichtet;
2. *adv. mst* ~*s* (nach) auswärts, nach
(dr)außen; ~·ly [ˌlɪ] äußerlich; an
der Oberfläche.

out|weigh ['aʊt'weɪ] schwerer sein
als; *fig.* überwiegen; ~·wit ['aʊt'wɪt]
(-*tt*-) überlisten; ~·worn ['aʊtwɔːn]
erschöpft; *fig.* abgegriffen; überholt.

o·val ['əʊvl] **1.** □ oval; **2.** Oval n.

ov·en ['ʌvn] Backofen m.

o·ver ['əʊvə] **1.** über; hinüber; darüber; herüber; drüben; über (acc.) ...darüber(...); et. über(geben etc.); über(kochen etc.); um(fallen, -werfen etc.); herum(drehen etc.); von Anfang bis Ende, durch(lesen etc.), ganz, über u. über; (gründlich) über(legen etc.); nochmals, wieder; übermäßig, über...; darüber, mehr; übrig; zu Ende, vorüber, vorbei, aus; (all) ~ again noch einmal, (ganz) von vorn; ~ against gegenüber (dat.); all ~ ganz vorbei; ~ and again immer wieder; **2.** prp. über; über (acc.)...hin(weg); ~ and above neben, zusätzlich zu.

o·ver|act [əʊvə'ækt] e-e Rolle übertreiben; **~all** ['əʊvərɔːl] **1.** Brt. (Arbeits)Kittel m; ~s pl. Arbeitsanzug m, Overall m; **2.** gesamt, Gesamt...; **~awe** ['əʊvər'ɔː] einschüchtern; **~bal·ance** [əʊvə'bæləns] **1.** Übergewicht n; **2.** das Gleichgewicht verlieren; umkippen; aus dem Gleichgewicht bringen; überwiegen (a. fig.); **~bear·ing** □ [əʊvə'beərɪŋ] anmaßend; **~board** ♣ [əʊvə'bɔːd] über Bord; **~cast** ['əʊvəkɑːst] bewölkt; **~charge** [əʊvə'tʃɑːdʒ] **1.** ⚡, ⊕ überladen; e-n Betrag zuviel verlangen (for für); **2.** Überpreis m; Aufschlag m; **~coat** ['əʊvəkəʊt] Mantel m; **~come** [əʊvə'kʌm] (-came, -come) überwinden, -wältigen; **~crowd** [əʊvə'kraʊd] überfüllen; **~do** [əʊvə'duː] (-did, -done) zu viel tun; übertreiben; zu sehr kochen od. braten; überanstrengen; **~draw** ['əʊvə'drɔː] (-drew, -drawn) econ. Konto überziehen; fig. übertreiben; **~dress** [əʊvə'dres] (sich) übertrieben anziehen; **~due** [əʊvə'djuː] (über)fällig; **~eat** [əʊvər'iːt] (-ate, -eaten): a. ~ o.s. sich überessen; **~flow 1.** ['əʊvəfləʊ] v/t. überfluten, -schwemmen; v/i. überfließen, -laufen; **2.** ['əʊvəfləʊ] Überschwemmung f; Überschuß m; ⊕ Überlauf m; **~grow** [əʊvə'grəʊ] (-grew, -grown) v/t. überwuchern; v/i. zu groß werden; **~grown** [~n] überwuchert; übergroß; **~hang 1.** [əʊvə'hæŋ] (-hung) v/t über (dat.) hängen; v/i. überhängen; **2.** ['əʊvəhæŋ] Überhang m; **~haul** [əʊvə'hɔːl] Maschine überholen; **~head 1.**

adv. [əʊvə'hed] (dr)oben; **2.** adj. ['əʊvəhed] Hoch..., Ober...; econ. allgemein (Unkosten); **3.** mst Brt. ~s pl. econ. allgemeine Unkosten pl.; **~hear** [əʊvə'hɪə] (-heard) (zufällig) belauschen, (mit an)hören; △ nicht überhören; **~joyed** [əʊvə'dʒɔɪd] überglücklich (at über acc.); **~kill** ['əʊvəkɪl] ✕ Overkill m; fig. Übermaß n, Zuviel n (of an dat.); **~lap** [əʊvə'læp] (-pp-) übergreifen auf (acc.); sich überschneiden (mit); ⊕ überlappen; **~lay** [əʊvə'leɪ] (-laid) belegen, überziehen; **~leaf** ['əʊvə'liːf] umseitig; **~load** [əʊvə'ləʊd] überladen; **~look** [əʊvə'lʊk] übersehen (a. fig.); ~ing the sea mit Blick auf das Meer; **~much** ['əʊvə'mʌtʃ] zu viel; **~night** [əʊvə'naɪt] **1.** über Nacht; stay ~ übernachten. **2.** Nacht...; Übernachtungs...; **~pass** bsd. Am. ['əʊvəpɑːs] (Straßen-, Eisenbahn)Überführung f; **~pay** [əʊvə'peɪ] (-paid) zu viel bezahlen; **~peo·pled** [əʊvə'piːpld] übervölkert; **~plus** ['əʊvəplʌs] Überschuß m (of an dat.); **~pow·er** [əʊvə'paʊə] überwältigen; **~rate** [əʊvə'reɪt] überschätzen; **~reach** [əʊvə'riːtʃ] übervorteilen; ~ o.s. sich übernehmen; **~ride** fig. [əʊvə'raɪd] (-rode, -ridden) sich hinwegsetzen über (acc.); umstoßen; **~rule** [əʊvə'ruːl] überstimmen; ⚖ Urteil aufheben; **~run** [əʊvə'rʌn] (-nn-; -ran, -run) Land überfluten; ✕ herfallen über (acc.); überwuchern; Signal überfahren; Zeit überziehen; be ~ with wimmeln von; **~sea(s)** ['əʊvə'siː(z)] **1.** überseeisch, Übersee...; **2.** in od. nach Übersee; **~see** [əʊvə'siː] (-saw, -seen) beaufsichtigen; **~seer** ['əʊvəsɪə] Aufseher m; Vorarbeiter m; **~shad·ow** ['əʊvə'ʃædəʊ] überschatten (a. fig.); fig. in den Schatten stellen; **~sight** ['əʊvəsaɪt] Versehen n; **~sleep** [əʊvə'sliːp] (-slept) verschlafen; **~state** [əʊvə'steɪt] übertreiben; **~state·ment** [~mənt] Übertreibung f; **~strain 1.** [əʊvə'streɪn] überanstrengen; ~ o.s. sich übernehmen; **2.** ['əʊvəstreɪn] Überanstrengung f.

o·vert □ ['əʊvɜːt] offen(kundig).

o·ver|take [əʊvə'teɪk] (-took, -taken) einholen; j-n überraschen; überholen; **~tax** [əʊvə'tæks] zu hoch besteuern; *fig.* überschätzen; überfordern; **~throw** ['əʊvə'θrəʊ] (*-threw*, *-thrown*) (um)stürzen (*a. fig.*); besiegen; **2.** ['əʊvəθrəʊ] (Um-)Sturz *m*; Niederlage *f*; **~time** *econ.* ['əʊvətaɪm] Überstunden *pl.*; *be on* ~, *do* ~ Überstunden machen.

o·ver·ture ['əʊvətjʊə] ♪ Ouvertüre *f*; ♪ Vorspiel *n*; *mst* ~*s pl.* Vorschlag *m*, Antrag *m*.

o·ver·turn ['əʊvə'tɜːn] (um)stürzen (*a. fig.*); **~weight** ['əʊvə'weɪt] Übergewicht *n*; **~whelm** ['əʊvə'welm] überschütten (*a. fig.*); überwältigen (*a. fig.*); **~work** ['əʊvə'wɜːk] **1.** Überarbeitung *f*; **2.** sich überarbeiten; überanstrengen; **~wrought** ['əʊvə'rɔːt] überarbeitet; überreizt.

owe [əʊ] *Geld, Dank etc.* schulden, schuldig sein; verdanken.

ow·ing ['əʊɪŋ]: *be* ~ zu zahlen sein; ~ *to* infolge (*gen.*); wegen (*gen.*); dank (*dat.*).

owl *zo.* [aʊl] Eule *f*.

own [əʊn] **1.** eigen; selbst; einzig, (innig) geliebt; **2.** *my* ~ mein Eigentum; *a house of one's* ~ ein eigenes Haus; *hold one' s* ~ standhalten; **3.** besitzen; zugeben; anerkennen; sich bekennen (*to zu*).

own·er ['əʊnə] Eigentümer(in); **~ship** ['əʊnəʃɪp] Eigentum(srecht) *n*.

ox *zo.* [ɒks] (*pl.* oxen ['ɒksn]) Ochse *m*; Rind *n*.

ox·i·da·tion 🜨 [ɒksɪ'deɪʃn] Oxydation *f*, Oxidierung *f*; **ox·ide** 🜨 ['ɒksaɪd] Oxyd *n*; **ox·i·dize** 🜨 ['ɒksɪdaɪz] oxydieren.

ox·y·gen 🜨 ['ɒksɪdʒən] Sauerstoff *m*.

oy·ster *zo.* ['ɔɪstə] Auster *f*.

o·zone 🜨 ['əʊzəʊn] Ozon *n*.

P

pace [peɪs] **1.** Schritt *m*; Gang *m*; Tempo *n*; **2.** *v/t.* abschreiten; durchschreiten; *v/i.* (einher)schreiten; ~ *up and down* auf u. ab gehen.

pa·cif·ic [pə'sɪfɪk] (~*ally*) friedlich.

pac·i·fi·ca·tion [pæsɪfɪ'keɪʃn] Beruhigung *f*, Besänftigung *f*; **~fi·er** *Am.* ['pæsɪfaɪə] Schnuller *m*; **~fy** [~aɪ] beruhigen; besänftigen.

pack [pæk] **1.** Pack(en) *m*; Ballen *m*; Bündel *n*; *Am.* Packung *f* (*Zigaretten*); Meute *f* (*Hunde*); Rudel *n* (*Wölfe*); Pack *n*, Bande *f*; 💥, *Kosmetik*: Packung *f*; *a.* ~ *of cards* Spiel *n* Karten; ~ *of films phot.* Filmpack *n*; *a.* ~ *of lies* ein Haufen Lügen; **2.** *v/t.* (voll)packen; bepacken; vollstopfen; zusammenpferchen; *econ.* eindosen; ⊕ (ab-)dichten; *Am.* ℉ *Revolver etc.* (bei sich) tragen; *oft* ~ *up* zusammen-, ver-, ein-, abpacken; *mst* ~ *off* (rasch) fortschicken, -jagen; *v/i.* sich *par etc.* verpacken *od.* konservieren lassen; *oft* ~ *up* (zusammen)packen; *send s.o.* ~*ing* j-n fortjagen; **~age** ['pækɪdʒ] Pack *m*, Ballen *m*; Paket *n*; Packung *f*; Frachtstück *n*; ~ *tour* Pauschalreise *f*; **~er** [~ə] Packer(in); *Am.* Konservenhersteller *m*; **~et** [~ɪt] Päckchen *n*; Packung *f* (*Zigaretten*); *a.* ~*boat* ⚓ Postschiff *n*; **~ing** [~ɪŋ] Packen *n*; Verpackung *f*; **~thread** Bindfaden *m*.

pact [pækt] Vertrag *m*, Pakt *m*.

pad [pæd] **1.** Polster *n*, Kissen *n*; *Sport*: Beinschutz *m*; Schreib-, Zeichenblock *m*; Abschußrampe *f* (*für Raketen*); *a.* ink-~ Stempelkissen *n*; **2.** (-*dd*-) (aus)polstern, wattieren; **~ding** ['pædɪŋ] Polsterung *f*, Wattierung *f*.

pad·dle ['pædl] **1.** Paddel *n*; ⚓ (Rad-)Schaufel *f*; **2.** paddeln; planschen; **~wheel** ⚓ Schaufelrad *n*.

pad·dock ['pædək] (Pferde)Koppel *f*; *Pferderennsport*: Sattelplatz *m*; *Motorsport*: Fahrerlager *n*.

pad·lock ['pædlɒk] Vorhängeschloß *n*.

pa·gan ['peɪgən] **1.** heidnisch; **2.** Heide|*m*, -in *f*.

page[1] [peɪdʒ] **1.** Seite *f* (*e-s Buches, e-r Zeitung etc.*); **2.** paginieren.

page[2] [~] **1.** (Hotel)Page *m*; **2.** j-n ausrufen lassen.

pag·eant ['pædʒənt] historisches Festspiel; Festzug *m*.

paid [peɪd] *pret. u. p.p. von* pay 2.

pail [peɪl] Eimer *m*.

pain [peɪn] 1. Schmerz(en *pl.*) *m*; Kummer *m*; ~s *pl.* Mühe *f*; on *od.* under ~ of death bei Todesstrafe; be in (great) ~ (große) Schmerzen haben; take ~s sich Mühe geben; 2. *j-n* schmerzen, *j-m* weh tun; ~ful □ ['peɪnfl] schmerzhaft; schmerzlich; peinlich; mühsam; ~less □ [~lɪs] schmerzlos; ~s·tak·ing □ [~zteɪkɪŋ] sorgfältig, gewissenhaft.

paint [peɪnt] 1. Farbe *f*; Schminke *f*; Anstrich *m*; 2. (an-, be)malen; (an-) streichen; (sich) schminken; ~box ['peɪntbɒks] Malkasten *m*; ~brush (Maler)Pinsel *m*; ~er [~ə] Maler(in); ~ing [~ɪŋ] Malen *n*; Malerei *f*; Gemälde *n*, Bild *n*.

pair [peə] 1. Paar *n*; a ~ of ... ein Paar ..., ein(e) ...; a ~ of scissors e-e Schere *f*; 2. *zo.* sich paaren; zusammenpassen; ~ off Paare bilden; paarweise weggehen.

pa·ja·ma(s) *Am.* [pə'dʒɑ:mə(z)] = pyjama(s).

pal [pæl] Kumpel *m*, Kamerad *m*.

pal·ace ['pælɪs] Palast *m*, Schloß *n*.

pal·a·ta·ble □ ['pælətəbl] wohlschmeckend, schmackhaft (*a. fig.*).

pal·ate ['pælɪt] *anat.* Gaumen *m*; *fig.* Geschmack *m*.

pale[1] [peɪl] Pfahl *m*; *fig.* Grenzen *pl.*

pale[2] [~] 1. □ (~r, ~st) blaß, bleich, fahl; ~ ale helles Bier; 2. blaß *od.* bleich werden; erbleichen lassen; ~ness ['peɪlnɪs] Blässe *f*.

pal·ings ['peɪlɪŋz] *pl.* Pfahlzaun *m*.

pal·i·sade [pælɪ'seɪd] Palisade *f*; ~s *pl. Am.* Steiufer *m*.

pal·let ['pælɪt] Strohsack *m*, -lager *n*.

pal·li·ate ['pælɪeɪt] *⚕* lindern; *fig.* bemänteln; ~a·tive *⚕* [~ətɪv] Linderungsmittel *n*.

pal·lid □ ['pælɪd] blaß; ~lid·ness [~nɪs], ~lor [~ə] Blässe *f*.

palm [pɑ:m] 1. Handfläche *f*; *♀* Palme *f*; 2. in der Hand verbergen; ~ s.th. off on *od.* upon s.o. *j-m* et. andrehen; ~tree *♀* ['pɑ:mtri:] Palme *f*.

pal·pa·ble □ ['pælpəbl] fühlbar; *fig.* handgreiflich, klar, eindeutig.

pal·pi·tate *⚕* ['pælpɪteɪt] klopfen (*Herz*); ~ta·tion *⚕* [pælpɪ'teɪʃn] Herzklopfen *n*.

pal·sy ['pɔːlzɪ] 1. *⚕* Lähmung *f*; *fig.* Ohnmacht *f*; 2. *fig.* lähmen.

pal·ter ['pɔːltə] sein Spiel treiben (*with s.o.* mit *j-m*).

pal·try □ ['pɔːltrɪ] (-ier, -iest) armselig; wertlos.

pam·per ['pæmpə] verzärteln.

pam·phlet ['pæmflɪt] Broschüre *f*; (kurze, kritische) Abhandlung; △ *nicht Pamphlet.*

pan [pæn] Pfanne *f*; Tiegel *m*.

pan- [~] all..., ganz..., gesamt..., pan..., Pan...

pan·a·ce·a [pænə'sɪə] Allheilmittel *n*.

pan·cake ['pænkeɪk] Pfann-, Eierkuchen *m*.

pan·da *zo.* ['pændə] Panda *m*; ~ car *Brt.* (Funk)Streifenwagen *m*; ~ cross·ing *Brt.* Fußgängerübergang *m* mit Druckampel.

pan·de·mo·ni·um *fig.* [pændɪ'məʊnjəm] Hölle(nlärm *m*) *f*.

pan·der ['pændə] 1. Vorschub leisten (*to dat.*); *veraltet* sich als Kuppler betätigen; 2. *veraltet* Kuppler *m*.

pane [peɪn] (Fenster)Scheibe *f*.

pan·e·gyr·ic [pænɪ'dʒɪrɪk] Lobrede *f*.

pan·el ['pænl] 1. *arch.* Fach *n*, (Tür-) Füllung *f*, (*Wand*)Täfelung *f*; *♫*, ⊕ Instrumentenbrett *n*, Schalttafel *f*; *⚖* Geschworenenliste *f*; *⚖* die Geschworenen *pl.*; die Diskussionsteilnehmer *pl.*; 2. (*bsd. Brt.* -ll-, *Am.* -l-) täfeln.

pang [pæŋ] plötzlicher Schmerz; *fig.* Angst *f*, Qual *f*.

pan·han·dle ['pænhændl] 1. Pfannenstiel *m*; *Am.* schmaler Fortsatz (*e-s Staatsgebiets*); 2. *Am.* F betteln.

pan·ic ['pænɪk] 1. panisch; 2. Panik *f*; 3. (*-ck-*) in Panik geraten.

pan·sy *♀* ['pænzɪ] Stiefmütterchen *n*.

pant [pænt] *nach Luft* schnappen, keuchen, schnaufen.

pan·ther *zo.* ['pænθə] Panther *m*; *Am.* Puma *m*.

pan·ties ['pæntɪz] *pl.* (Damen-) Schlüpfer *m*; Kinderhöschen *n*.

pan·ti·hose *bsd. Am.* ['pæntɪhəʊz] Strumpfhose *f*.

pan·try ['pæntrɪ] Speisekammer *f*.

pants [pænts] *pl. bsd. Am.* Hose *f*; *bsd. Brt.* Unterhose *f*; *bsd. Brt.* Schlüpfer *m*.

pap [pæp] Brei *m*; △ *nicht Papp, Pappe.*

pa·pa [pə'pɑː] Papa *m*.

pa·pal □ ['peɪpl] päpstlich.

pa·per ['peɪpə] 1. Papier n; Zeitung f; schriftliche Prüfung; Prüfungsarbeit f; Vortrag m, Aufsatz m; ~s pl. (Ausweis)Papiere pl.; 2. tapezieren; ~·back Taschenbuch n, Paperback n; ~·bag (Papier)Tüte f; ~·clip Büroklammer f; ~·hang·er Tapezierer m; ~·mill Papierfabrik f; ~·weight Briefbeschwerer m.

pap·py ['pæpɪ] (-ier, -iest) breiig.

par [paː] econ. Nennwert m, Pari n; at ~ zum Nennwert; be on a ~ with gleich od. ebenbürtig sein (dat.).

par·a·ble ['pærəbl] Gleichnis n.

par·a|chute ['pærəʃuːt] Fallschirm m; ~·chut·ist [~ɪst] Fallschirmspringer(in).

pa·rade [pə'reɪd] 1. ✕ (Truppen-)Parade f; Zurschaustellung f, Vorführung f; (Strand)Promenade f; (Um)Zug m; make a ~ of fig. zur Schau stellen; 2. ✕ antreten (lassen); ✕ vorbeimarschieren (lassen); zur Schau stellen; ~·ground ✕ Exerzier-, Paradeplatz m.

par·a·dise ['pærədaɪs] Paradies n.

par·a·gon ['pærəgɒn] Vorbild n, Muster n.

par·a·graph ['pærəgrɑːf] print. Absatz m, Abschnitt m; kurze Zeitungsnotiz; △ nicht ⚡ Paragraph.

par·al·lel ['pærəlel] 1. parallel; 2. ⚡ Parallele f (a. fig.); Gegenstück n; Vergleich m; without (a) ~ ohnegleichen; 3. (-l-, Brt. -ll-) vergleichen; entsprechen; gleichen; parallel (ver)laufen zu.

par·a·lyse, Am. **-lyze** ['pærəlaɪz] ⚕ lähmen (a. fig.); fig. lahmlegen; machen; **pa·ral·y·sis** ⚕ [pə'rælɪsɪs] (pl. -ses [-siːz]) Paralyse f, Lähmung f.

par·a·mount ['pærəmaʊnt] höher stehend (to als), übergeordnet, oberste(r, -s); höchste(r, -s); fig. größte(r, -s).

par·a·pet ['pærəpɪt] ✕ Brustwehr f; Brüstung f; Geländer n.

par·a·pher·na·li·a [pærəfə'neɪljə] pl. Ausrüstung f; Zubehör m, n.

par·a·site ['pærəsaɪt] Schmarotzer m.

par·a·sol ['pærəsɒl] Sonnenschirm m.

par·a·troop|er ✕ ['pærətruːpə] Fallschirmjäger m; ~s ✕ [~s] pl. Fallschirmtruppen pl.

par·boil ['pɑːbɔɪl] ankochen.

par·cel ['pɑːsl] 1. Paket n, Päckchen n; Bündel n; Parzelle f; 2. (bsd. Brt. -ll-, Am. -l-) ~ out aus-, aufteilen.

parch [pɑːtʃ] rösten, (aus)dörren.

parch·ment ['pɑːtʃmənt] Pergament n.

pard Am. sl. [pɑːd] Partner m.

par·don ['pɑːdn] 1. Verzeihung f; ⚡ Begnadigung f; 2. verzeihen; ⚡ begnadigen; ~? wie bitte?; ~ me! Entschuldigung!; ~·a·ble □ [~əbl] verzeihlich.

pare [peə] (be)schneiden (a. fig.); schälen.

par·ent ['peərənt] Elternteil m, Vater m, Mutter f; fig. Ursache f; ~s pl. Eltern pl.; ~·teacher meeting Schule: Elternabend m; ~·age [~ɪdʒ] Abstammung f; **pa·ren·tal** [pə'rentl] elterlich.

pa·ren·the·sis [pə'renθɪsɪs] (pl. -ses [-siːz]) Einschaltung f; print. (runde) Klammer.

par·ing ['peərɪŋ] Schälen n; (Be-)schneiden n; ~s pl. Schalen pl.; Schnipsel pl.

par·ish ['pærɪʃ] 1. Kirchspiel n, Gemeinde f; 2. Pfarr..., Kirchen...; pol. Gemeinde...; ~ council Gemeinderat m; **pa·rish·io·ner** [pə'rɪʃənə] Gemeindemitglied n.

par·i·ty ['pærɪtɪ] Gleichheit f.

park [pɑːk] 1. Park m, Anlagen pl.; Naturschutzgebiet n, Park m; Am. (Sport)Platz m; the ~ Brt. F der Fußballplatz; mst car-~ Parkplatz m; 2. mot. parken.

par·ka ['pɑːkə] Parka f, m.

park·ing mot. ['pɑːkɪŋ] Parken n; no ~ Parkverbot, Parken verboten; ~·disc Parkscheibe f; ~·fee Parkgebühr f; ~·lot Am. Parkplatz m; ~·me·ter Parkuhr f; ~·or·bit Raumfahrt: Parkbahn f; ~·tick·et Strafzettel m (wegen falschen Parkens).

par·lance ['pɑːləns] Ausdrucksweise f, Sprache f.

par·ley ['pɑːlɪ] 1. bsd. ✕ Verhandlung f; 2. bsd. ✕ verhandeln; sich besprechen.

par·lia|ment ['pɑːləmənt] Parlament n; ~·men·tar·i·an [pɑːləmen'teərɪən] Parlamentarier(in); ~·men·ta·ry □ [pɑːlə'mentərɪ] parlamentarisch; Parlaments...

par·lo(u)r ['pɑːlə] veraltet Wohnzimmer n; Empfangs-, Sprechzimmer n; beauty ~ Am. Schönheitssalon *m*; ~ **car** *Am.* 🚃 Salonwagen *m*; ~**maid** Stuben-, Hausmädchen *n*.

pa·ro·chi·al ☐ [pəˈrəʊkjəl] Pfarr..., Kirchen..., Gemeinde...; *fig.* engstirnig, beschränkt.

pa·role [pəˈrəʊl] **1.** ⚔ Parole *f*; ⚖ bedingte Haftentlassung; ⚖ Hafturlaub *m*; *he is out on* ~ ⚖ er wurde bedingt entlassen; er hat Hafturlaub; **2.** ~ *s.o.* ⚖ j-n bedingt entlassen; j-m Hafturlaub gewähren.

par·quet [ˈpɑːkeɪ] Parkett(fußboden *m*) *n*; *Am. thea.* Parkett *n*.

par·rot [ˈpærət] **1.** *zo.* Papagei *m* (*a. fig.*); **2.** nachplappern.

par·ry [ˈpærɪ] abwehren, parieren.

par·si·mo·ni·ous ☐ [pɑːsɪˈməʊnjəs] sparsam, geizig, knaus(e)rig.

pars·ley ♣ [ˈpɑːslɪ] Petersilie *f*.

par·son [ˈpɑːsn] Pfarrer *m*; ~**age** [~ɪdʒ] Pfarrei *f*, Pfarrhaus *n*.

part [pɑːt] **1.** Teil *m, n*; Anteil *m*; Seite *f*, Partei *f*; *thea., fig.* Rolle *f*; Stimme *f*; Gegend *f*; *Am.* (*Haar*)Scheitel *m*; *a man of* (*many*) ~*s* ein fähiger Mensch; *take* ~ *in s.th.* an e-r Sache teilnehmen; *take s.th. in bad* (*good*) ~ *et.* (nicht) übelnehmen; *for my* ~ ich für mein(en) Teil; *for the most* ~ meistens; *in* ~ teilweise, zum Teil; *on the* ~ *of* von seiten, seitens (*gen.*); *on my* ~ meinerseits; **2.** *adj.* Teil...; **3.** *adv.* teils; **4.** *v/t.* (ab-, ein-, zer)teilen; trennen; *Haar* scheiteln; ~ *company* mit *j-m* sich trennen (*with* von); *v/i.* sich trennen (*with* von).

par·take [pɑːˈteɪk] [-took, -taken] teilnehmen, -haben; ~ *of Mahlzeit* einnehmen.

par·tial ☐ [ˈpɑːʃl] Teil..., teilweise, partiell; parteiisch, eingenommen (*to* für); ~**i·al·i·ty** [pɑːʃɪˈælɪtɪ] Parteilichkeit *f*; Vorliebe *f* (*for* für).

par·tic·i·pant [pɑːˈtɪsɪpənt] Teilnehmer(in); ~**pate** [~eɪt] teilnehmen, sich beteiligen (*in an dat.*); ~**pa·tion** [pɑːtɪsɪˈpeɪʃn] Teilnahme *f*, Beteiligung *f*.

par·ti·ci·ple *gr.* [ˈpɑːtɪsɪpl] Partizip *n*, Mittelwort *n*.

par·ti·cle [ˈpɑːtɪkl] Teilchen *n*.

par·tic·u·lar [pəˈtɪkjʊlə] **1.** ☐ besondere(r, -s), einzeln, Sonder...; genau, eigen; wählerisch; **2.** Einzelheit *f*; ~*s pl.* nähere Umstände *pl. od.* Angaben *pl.*; Personalien *pl.*; *in* ~ insbesondere; ~**i·ty** [pətɪkjuˈlærɪtɪ] Besonderheit *f*; Ausführlichkeit *f*;

Eigenheit *f*; ~**ly** [pəˈtɪkjʊləlɪ] besonders.

part·ing [ˈpɑːtɪŋ] **1.** Trennung *f*, Abschied *m*; (*Haar*)Scheitel *m*; ~ *of the ways bsd. fig.* Scheideweg *m*; **2.** Abschieds...

par·ti·san [pɑːtɪˈzæn] Parteigänger(in); ⚔ Partisan *m*; *attr.* Partei...

par·ti·tion [pɑːˈtɪʃn] **1.** Teilung *f*; Scheidewand *f*; Verschlag *m*; Fach *n*; **2.** ~ *off* abteilen, abtrennen.

part·ly [ˈpɑːtlɪ] teilweise, zum Teil.

part·ner [ˈpɑːtnə] **1.** Partner(in); **2.** zusammenbringen; sich zusammentun mit (*j-m*); ~**ship** [~ʃɪp] Teilhaber-, Partnerschaft *f*; *econ.* Handelsgesellschaft *f*.

part-own·er [ˈpɑːtəʊnə] Miteigentümer(in).

par·tridge *zo.* [ˈpɑːtrɪdʒ] Rebhuhn *n*.

part-time [ˈpɑːtaɪm] **1.** *adj.* Teilzeit..., Halbtags...; **2.** *adv.* halbtags.

par·ty [ˈpɑːtɪ] Partei *f*; ⚔ Abteilung *f*; (Arbeits-, Reise)Gruppe *f*; (*Rettungs- etc.*)Mannschaft *f*; Party *f*, Gesellschaft *f*; Beteiligte(*r m*) *m*; *jur.* Type *f*, Individuum *n*; △ *nicht Partie*; ~ **line** *pol.* Parteilinie *f*; ~ **pol·i·tics** *sg. od. pl.* Parteipolitik *f*.

pass [pɑːs] **1.** Passier-, Erlaubnisschein *m*; △ *nicht* (*Reise*)*Pass*; ⚔ Urlaubsschein *m*; Bestehen *n* (*e-s Examens*); *Brt. univ.* einfacher Grad; kritische Lage; *Sport*: Paß *m*, (Ball)Abgabe *f*, Vorlage *f*, Zuspiel *n*; (Gebirgs)Paß *m*; Durch-, Zugang *m*; *Karten*: Passen *n*; Handbewegung *f*, (Zauber)Trick *m*; F Annäherungsversuch *m*; *free* ~ Freikarte *f*; **2.** *v/i.* (vorbei)gehen, (-)fahren, (-)kommen, (-)ziehen *etc.*; in andere Hände übergehen, übertragen werden (*to auf acc.*); *von e-m Zustand* übergehen; herumgereicht werden, von Hand zu Hand gehen; *Sport*: (den Ball) abspielen *od.* abgeben *od.* passen (*to zu*); vergehen, vorübergehen (*Zeit, Schmerz etc.*); angenommen werden, gelten; durchkommen; (die Prüfung) bestehen; *parl.* Rechtskraft erlangen; *Karten*: passen; *bsd. biblisch*: sich zutragen, passieren, geschehen (*it came to* ~ *that* es begab sich *od.* es geschah, daß); △ *nicht passen = fit*; ~ *away* sterben; ~ *by* vorüber- *od.* vorbeigehen an (*dat.*), passieren; ~ *for od. as* gelten für *od.*

als, gehalten werden für; ~ off vonstatten gehen; ~ out F ohnmächtig werden; v/t. vorbei-, vorübergehen, -fahren, -fließen, -kommen, -ziehen etc. an (dat.); et. passieren; vorbeifahren an (dat.), überholen (a. mot.); durch-, überschreiten, durchqueren, passieren; vorbeilassen; reichen, geben; streichen (mit der Hand); Sport: Ball abspielen, abgeben, passen (to zu); Examen bestehen; Prüfling bestehen od. durchkommen lassen; et. durchgehen lassen; Zeit ver-, zubringen; Geld in Umlauf bringen; Gesetz verabschieden; Vorschlag etc. durchbringen, annehmen; Urteil abgeben; Meinung äußern; Bemerkung machen; fig. (hinaus)gehen über (acc.), übersteigen; ~·a·ble □ ['pɑːsəbl] passierbar; gangbar; gültig (Geld); leidlich.

pas·sage ['pæsɪdʒ] Durchgang m; Durchfahrt f; Durchreise f; Korridor m, Gang m; Reise f, (Über)Fahrt f, Flug m; parl. Annahme f (e-s Gesetzes); ♪ Passage f; (Text)Stelle f; bird of ~ Zugvogel m.

pass·book econ. ['pɑːsbʊk] Bankbuch n; Sparbuch n.

pas·sen·ger ['pæsɪndʒə] Passagier m, Fahr-, Fluggast m, Reisende(r m) f, (Auto- etc.)Insasse m.

pass·er-by ['pɑːsə'baɪ] (pl. passers-by) Vorbei-, Vorübergehende(r m) f, Passant(in).

pas·sion ['pæʃn] Leidenschaft f; (Gefühls)Ausbruch m; Wut f, Zorn m; 2 eccl. Passion f; 2 Week eccl. Karwoche f; ~·ate □ [~ət] leidenschaftlich.

pas·sive □ ['pæsɪv] passiv (a. gr.); teilnahmslos; untätig.

pass·port ['pɑːspɔːt] (Reise)Paß m.

pass·word ['pɑːswɜːd] Kennwort n.

past [pɑːst] **1.** vergangen, pred. vorüber; gr. Vergangenheits...; frühere(r, -s); for some time ~ seit einiger Zeit; ~ tense gr. Vergangenheit f, Präteritum n; **2.** adv. vorbei; **3.** prp. Zeit: nach, über (acc.); über ... (acc.) hinaus; an ... (dat.) vorbei; half ~ two halb drei; ~ endurance unerträglich; ~ hope hoffnungslos; **4.** Vergangenheit f (a. gr.).

paste [peɪst] **1.** Teig m; Kleister m; Paste f; **2.** (be)kleben; ~·board ['peɪstbɔːd] Pappe f; attr. Papp...

pas·tel [pæ'stel] Pastell(zeichnung f) n.

pas·teur·ize ['pæstəraɪz] pasteurisieren, keimfrei machen.

pas·time ['pɑːstaɪm] Zeitvertreib m, Freizeitbeschäftigung f.

pas·tor ['pɑːstə] Pastor m, Seelsorger m; ~·al □ [~rəl] Hirten...; idyllisch; eccl. pastoral.

pas·try ['peɪstrɪ] Kuchen m, Torte f; Konditorwaren pl., Feingebäck n; ~·cook Konditor m.

pas·ture ['pɑːstʃə] **1.** Weide(land n) f; Grasfutter n; **2.** (ab)weiden.

pat [pæt] **1.** Klaps m; Portion f (Butter); **2.** (-tt-) tätscheln; klopfen; **3.** gerade recht; parat, bereit.

patch [pætʃ] **1.** Fleck m; Flicken m; Stück n Land; ✚ Pflaster n; in ~es stellenweise; **2.** flicken; ~·work ['pætʃwɜːk] Patchwork n; contp. Flickwerk n.

pate F [peɪt] bald ~ Platte f (Glatze).

pa·tent ['peɪtənt, Am. 'pætənt] **1.** offen(kundig); patentiert; Patent...; ~ agent, Am. ~ attorney Patentanwalt m; letters ~ ['pætənt] pl. Patenturkunde f; ~ leather Lackleder n; **2.** Patent n; Privileg n, Freibrief m; Patenturkunde f; **3.** patentieren (lassen); ~·ee [peɪtən'tiː] Patentinhaber(in).

pa·ter·nal □ [pə'tɜːnl] väterlich(erseits); ~·ni·ty [~ətɪ] Vaterschaft f.

path [pɑːθ] (pl. paths [pɑːðz]) Pfad m; Weg m.

pa·thet·ic [pə'θetɪk] (~ally) kläglich, bemitleidenswert, mitleiderregend; △ nicht pathetic.

pa·thos ['peɪθɒs] Mitleid n; das Mitleiderregende; △ nicht Pathos.

pa·tience ['peɪʃns] Geduld f; Ausdauer f; Brt. Patience f (Kartenspiel); **pa·tient** [~t] **1.** □ geduldig; **2.** Patient(in).

pat·i·o ['pætɪəʊ] (pl. -os) Terrasse f; Innenhof m, Patio m.

pat·ri·mo·ny ['pætrɪmənɪ] väterliches Erbteil.

pat·ri·ot ['pætrɪət] Patriot(in); ~·ic [pætrɪ'ɒtɪk] (~ally) patriotisch.

pa·trol [pə'trəʊl] **1.** ✕ Patrouille f; (Polizei)Streife f; on ~ auf Patrouille, auf Streife; **2.** (-ll-) (ab)patrouillieren, auf Streife sein (in dat.); die Runde machen (in dat.); ~ car (Funk)Streifenwagen m; ~·man [~mæn] (pl. -men) Am. Polizist m (auf Streife); *Brt.* motorisierter Pannenhelfer (*e-s Automobilclubs*).

pa·tron ['peɪtrən] Schirmherr *m*; Gönner *m*; (Stamm)Kunde *m*; Stammgast *m*; ~ **saint** *eccl.* Schutzheilige(r) *m*; △ *nicht* Patrone; **pat·ron·age** ['pætrənɪdʒ] Schirmherrschaft *f*; Gönnerschaft *f*; Kundschaft *f*; Schutz *m*; **pat·ron·ize** [~aɪz] fördern, unterstützen; (Stamm)Kunde *od.* Stammgast sein bei; gönnerhaft *od.* herablassend behandeln.

pat·ter ['pætə] plappern; prasseln (*Regen*); trappeln (*Füße*).

pat·tern ['pætən] **1.** Muster *n* (*a. fig.*); Modell *n*; **2.** (nach)bilden, formen (*after, on* nach).

paunch [pɔːntʃ] (dicker) Bauch.

pau·per ['pɔːpə] Arme(r *m*) *f*.

pause [pɔːz] **1.** Pause *f*; △ *nicht thea., Schule:* Pause; **2.** e-e Pause machen.

pave [peɪv] pflastern; ~ **the way for** *fig.* den Weg ebnen für; **~ment** ['peɪvmənt] *Brt.* Bürgersteig *m*; Pflaster *n*; *Am.* Fahrbahn *f*.

paw [pɔː] **1.** Pfote *f*, Tatze *f*; **2.** ~ betatschen; *F* derb *od.* ungeschickt anfassen; ~ (*the ground*) (mit den Hufen *etc.*) scharren.

pawn [pɔːn] **1.** *Schach:* Bauer *m*; Pfand *n*; *in od.* at ~ verpfändet; **2.** verpfänden; **~bro·ker** ['pɔːnbrəʊkə] Pfandleiher *m*; **~shop** Leihhaus *n*.

pay [peɪ] **1.** (Be)Zahlung *f*; Sold *m*; Lohn *m*; **2.** (*paid*) *v/t.* (be)zahlen; (be)lohnen; sich lohnen für; *Aufmerksamkeit* schenken; *Besuch* abstatten; *Ehre* erweisen; *Kompliment* machen; ~ **attention** *od.* **heed** to achtgeben auf (*acc.*); ~ **down**, ~ **cash** bar bezahlen; ~ **in** einzahlen; ~ **into** einzahlen auf (*ein Konto*); ~ **off** *et.* ab(be)zahlen; *j-n* bezahlen u. entlassen; *j-n* voll auszahlen; *v/i.* zahlen; sich lohnen; ~ **for** (*fig.* für) *et.* bezahlen; **~a·ble** ['peɪəbl] zahlbar, fällig; **~day** Zahltag *m*; **~ee** [peɪ'iː] Zahlungsempfänger(in); ~ **en·vel·ope** *Am.* Lohntüte *f*; **~ing** ['peɪɪŋ] lohnend; **~mas·ter** Zahlmeister *m*; **~ment** [~mənt] (Be-, Ein-, Aus-)Zahlung *f*; Lohn *m*, Sold *m*; **~ pack·et** *Brt.* Lohntüte *f*; ~ **phone** *Brt.* Münzfernsprecher *m*; **~roll** Lohnliste *f*; ~ **slip** Lohn-, Gehalts-

streifen *m*; ~ **sta·tion** *Am.*, ~ **tel·e·phone** Münzfernsprecher *m*.

pea ⚘ [piː] Erbse *f*.

peace [piːs] Frieden *m*; Ruhe *f*; *at* ~ in Frieden; **~a·ble** □ ['piːsəbl] friedliebend, friedlich; **~ful** □ [~fl] friedlich; **~mak·er** Friedensstifter(in).

peach ⚘ [piːtʃ] Pfirsich(baum) *m*.

pea·cock *zo.* ['piːkɒk] Pfau(hahn) *m*; **~hen** *zo.* Pfauhenne *f*.

peak [piːk] Spitze *f*; Gipfel *m*; Mützenschild *n*, -schirm *m*; *attr.* Spitzen..., Höchst..., Haupt...; ~ **hours** *pl.* Hauptverkehrs-, Stoßzeit *f*; **~ed** [~t] spitz.

peal [piːl] **1.** (Glocken)Läuten *n*; Glockenspiel *n*; Dröhnen *n*; ~**s of laughter** schallendes Gelächter; **2.** erschallen (lassen); dröhnen.

pea·nut ⚘ ['piːnʌt] Erdnuß *f*.

pear ⚘ [peə] Birne *f*; Birnbaum *m*.

pearl [pɜːl] **1.** Perle *f* (*a. fig.*); *attr.* Perl(en)...; **2.** tropfen, perlen; **~y** ['pɜːlɪ] (*-ier, -iest*) perlenartig, Perl(en)...

peas·ant ['peznt] **1.** Kleinbauer *m*; **2.** kleinbäuerlich, Kleinbauern...; **~ry** [~rɪ] Kleinbauernstand *m*; *die Kleinbauern pl.*

peat [piːt] Torf *m*.

peb·ble ['pebl] Kiesel(stein) *m*.

peck [pek] **1.** Viertelscheffel *m* (= *9,087 Liter*); *fig.* Menge *f*; **2.** picken, hacken (*at* nach); *Körner etc.* aufpicken.

pe·cu·li·ar □ ['pɪ'kjuːljə] eigen(tümlich); besondere(r, -s); seltsam; **~i·ty** [pɪkjuːlɪ'ærətɪ] Eigenheit *f*; Eigentümlichkeit *f*.

pe·cu·ni·a·ry [pɪ'kjuːnjərɪ] Geld...

ped·a·gog·ics [pedə'gɒdʒɪks] *mst sg.* Pädagogik *f*; **~gogue**, *Am. a.* **~gog** ['pedəgɒg] Pädagoge *m*; *F* Pedant *m*, Schulmeister *m*.

ped·al ['pedl] **1.** Pedal *n*; *attr.* Fuß...; **3.** (*bsd. Brt. -ll-, Am. -l-*) das Pedal treten; radfahren; *Rad* fahren, treten.

pe·dan·tic [pɪ'dæntɪk] (*~ally*) pedantisch.

ped·dle ['pedl] hausieren gehen (mit); ~ **drugs** mit Drogen handeln; **~r** [~lə] *Am. = pedlar*; Drogenhändler *m*.

ped·es·tal ['pedɪstl] Sockel *m* (*a. fig.*).

pe·des·tri·an [pɪ'destrɪən] **1.** zu Fuß; *fig.* prosaisch, trocken; **2.** Fußgänger(in); ~ **cross·ing** Fußgängerübergang *m*; ~ **pre·cinct** Fußgängerzone *f*.

ped·i·gree [ˈpedɪgriː] Stammbaum *m*.

ped·lar [ˈpedlə] Hausierer *m*; Drogen-, Rauschgifthändler *m*.

peek [piːk] 1. spähen, gucken, lugen; 2. flüchtiger *od.* heimlicher Blick.

peel [piːl] 1. Schale *f*, Rinde *f*, Haut *f*; 2. *v/t.* schälen; *a.* ~ **off** abschälen; *Folie etc.* abziehen; *Kleid* abstreifen; *v/i. a.* ~ **off** sich (ab)schälen, abblättern.

peep [piːp] 1. neugieriger *od.* verstohlener Blick; Piep(s)en *n*; 2. gucken, neugierig *od.* verstohlen blicken; *a.* ~ **out** hervorschauen; *fig.* sich zeigen; piep(s)en; ~**hole** [ˈpiːphəʊl] Guckloch *n*.

peer [pɪə] 1. spähen, lugen; ~ **at** (sich) genau ansehen, anstarren; 2. Gleiche(r *m*) *f*; *Brt.* Peer *m*; ~**less** [ˈpɪəlɪs] unvergleichlich.

peev·ish □ [ˈpiːvɪʃ] verdrießlich, gereizt.

peg [peg] 1. (Holz)Stift *m*, Zapfen *m*, Dübel *m*, Pflock *m*; (*Kleider*)Haken *m*; *Brt.* (*Wäsche*)Klammer *f*; (*Zelt*-) Hering *m*; ♪ Wirbel *m*; *fig.* Aufhänger *m*; *take s.o. down a* ~ (*or two*) F j-m e-n Dämpfer aufsetzen; 2. (-*gg*-) festpflocken; *mst* ~ **out** Grenze abstecken; ~ **away**, ~ **along** F dranbleiben (*at an e-r Arbeit*); ~**top** [ˈpegtɒp] Kreisel *m*.

pel·i·can *zo.* [ˈpelɪkən] Pelikan *m*.

pel·let [ˈpelɪt] Kügelchen *n*; Pille *f*; Schrotkorn *n*.

pell-mell [ˈpelˈmel] durcheinander.

pelt [pelt] 1. Fell *n*, (rohe) Haut, (Tier)Pelz *m*; 2. *v/t.* bewerfen (*with* ~ *a*. ~ **down** (nieder)prasseln (*Regen etc.*).

pel·vis *anat.* [ˈpelvɪs] (*pl.* -vises, -ves [-viːz]) Becken *n*.

pen [pen] 1. (Schreib)Feder *f*; Federhalter *m*; Füller *m*; Kugelschreiber *m*; Pferch *m*; (Schaf)Hürde *f*; 2. (-*nn*-) schreiben; ~ **in**, ~ **up** einpferchen, -sperren.

pe·nal □ [ˈpiːnl] Straf...; strafbar; ~ **code** Strafgesetzbuch *n*; ~ **servitude** Zwangsarbeit *f*; ~**ize** [~əlaɪz] bestrafen; **pen·al·ty** [ˈpenltɪ] Strafe *f*; *Sport:* a. Strafpunkt *m*; *Fußball:* Elfmeter *m*; ~ **area** *Fußball:* Strafraum *m*; ~ **goal** *Fußball:* Elfmetertor *n*; ~ **kick** *Fußball:* Frei-, Strafstoß *m*.

pen·ance [ˈpenəns] Buße *f*.

pence [pens] *pl. von* penny.

pen·cil [ˈpensl] 1. (Blei-, Zeichen-, Farb)Stift *m*; 2. (*bsd. Brt.* -*ll*-, *Am.* -*l*-) zeichnen; (mit Bleistift) aufschreiben *od.* anzeichnen *od.* anstreichen; *Augenbrauen* nachziehen; ~**sharp·en·er** Bleistiftspitzer *m*.

pen|dant, ~**dent** [ˈpendənt] (Schmuck)Anhänger *m*.

pend·ing [ˈpendɪŋ] 1. ♣ schwebend; 2. *prp.* während; bis zu.

pen·du·lum [ˈpendjʊləm] Pendel *n*.

pen·e|tra·ble □ [ˈpenɪtrəbl] durchdringbar; ~**trate** [~eɪt] durchdringen; *fig.* ergründen; eindringen (*in acc.*); vordringen (*to bis zu*); ~**trating** □ [~ɪŋ] durchdringend, scharf (*Verstand*); scharfsinnig; ~**tra·tion** [penɪˈtreɪʃn] Durch-, Eindringen *n*; Scharfsinn *m*; ~**tra·tive** □ [ˈpenɪtrətɪv] *s. penetrating*.

pen-friend [ˈpenfrend] Brieffreund (-in).

pen·guin *zo.* [ˈpeŋgwɪn] Pinguin *m*.

pen·hold·er [ˈpenhəʊldə] Federhalter *m*.

pe·nin·su·la [pəˈnɪnsjʊlə] Halbinsel *f*.

pe·nis *anat.* [ˈpiːnɪs] Penis *m*.

pen·i|tence [ˈpenɪtəns] Buße *f*, Reue *f*; ~**tent** [~t] 1. □ reuig, bußfertig; 2. Büßer(in); ~**ten·tia·ry** *Am.* [penɪˈtenʃərɪ] (Staats)Gefängnis *n*.

pen|knife [ˈpennaɪf] (*pl.* -*knives*) Taschenmesser *n*; ~**name** Schriftstellername *m*, Pseudonym *n*.

pen·nant ♣ [ˈpenənt] Wimpel *m*.

pen·ni·less □ [ˈpenɪlɪs] ohne e-n Pfennig (Geld), mittellos.

pen·ny [ˈpenɪ] (*pl.* -*nies*, *coll. pence* [pens]) *a. new* ~ *Brt.* Penny *m* (= 1 *p* = £ 0.01); *Am.* Cent(stück *n*) *m*; *fig.* Pfennig *m*; ~**weight** *englisches* Pennygewicht (= 1,5 *g*).

pen·sion [ˈpenʃn] 1. Rente *f*, Pension *f*, Ruhegeld *n*; ⚠ *nicht* Pension (*Fremdenheim*); 2. *oft* ~ **off** pensionieren; ~**er** [~ə] Pensionär(in).

pen·sive □ [ˈpensɪv] nachdenklich.

pen·tath|lete [penˈtæθliːt] *Sport:* Fünfkämpfer(in); ~**lon** [~ɒn] *Sport:* Fünfkampf *m*.

Pen·te·cost [ˈpentɪkɒst] Pfingsten *n*.

pent·house [ˈpenthaʊs] Penthouse *n*, -haus *n*, Dachterrassenwohnung *f*; Vor-, Schutzdach *n*.

pent-up [ˈpentˈʌp] an-, aufgestaut (*Ärger etc.*).

pe·nu·ri·ous □ [pɪˈnjuərɪəs] arm; geizig; **pen·u·ry** [ˈpenjʊrɪ] Armut *f*, Not *f*; Mangel *m*.

peo·ple [ˈpiːpl] **1.** Volk *n*, Nation *f*; Leute *pl.*; Angehörige *pl.*; *coll.* die Leute *pl.*; man; **2.** besiedeln, bevölkern.

pep F [pep] **1.** Elan *m*, Schwung *m*, Pep *m*; ~ **pill** Aufputschpille *f*; **2.** (-*pp*-) *mst* ~ *up* j-n *od.* et. in Schwung bringen.

pep·per [ˈpepə] **1.** Pfeffer *m*; **2.** pfeffern; ~**mint** ♀ Pfefferminze *f*; Pfefferminzbonbon *m, n*; ~**y** [~rɪ] pfefferig; *fig.* hitzig.

per [pɜː] per, durch; pro, für, je.

per·am·bu·la·tor *bsd. Brt.* [ˈpræmbjʊleɪtə] = *pram*.

per·ceive [pəˈsiːv] (be)merken, wahrnehmen, empfinden; erkennen.

per cent, *Am.* **per·cent** [pəˈsent] Prozent *n*.

per·cen·tage [pəˈsentɪdʒ] Prozentsatz *m*; Prozente *pl.*; (An)Teil *m*.

per·cep|ti·ble □ [pəˈseptəbl] wahrnehmbar, merklich; ~**tion** [~pʃn] Wahrnehmung(svermögen *n*) *f*; Erkenntnis *f*; Auffassung(sgabe) *f*.

perch [pɜːtʃ] **1.** *zo.* Barsch *m*; Rute *f* (= 5,029 *m*); (Sitz)Stange *f* (*für Vögel*); **2.** sich setzen *od.* niederlassen, sitzen (*Vögel*); *auf et.* Hohes setzen.

per·co|late [ˈpɜːkəleɪt] *Kaffee etc.* filtern, durchsickern lassen; durchsickern (*a. fig.*); gefiltert werden; ~**la·tor** [~ə] Kaffeemaschine *f*, -automat *m*.

per·cus·sion [pəˈkʌʃn] Schlag *m*, Erschütterung *f*; ✚ Abklopfen *n*; ♪ *coll.* Schlagzeug *n*; ~ *instrument* ♪ Schlaginstrument *n*.

per·e·gri·na·tion [perɪɡrɪˈneɪʃn] Wanderschaft *f*; Wanderung *f*.

pe·remp·to·ry □ [pəˈremptərɪ] bestimmt; zwingend; herrisch.

pe·ren·ni·al □ [pəˈrenjəl] immer wiederkehrend, beständig; immerwährend; ♀ perennierend.

per|fect 1. [ˈpɜːfɪkt] □ vollkommen; vollendet; virtuos; gänzlich, völlig; **2.** [~] *a.* ~ *tense* Perfekt *n*; **3.** [pəˈfekt] vervollkommnen; vollenden; ~**fec·tion** [~kʃn] Vollendung *f*; Vollkommenheit *f*; *fig.* Gipfel *m*.

per|fid·i·ous □ [pəˈfɪdɪəs] treulos (*to*

gegen), verräterisch; ~**fi·dy** [ˈpɜːfɪdɪ] Treulosigkeit *f*, Verrat *m*.

per·fo·rate [ˈpɜːfəreɪt] durchlöchern.

per·form [pəˈfɔːm] verrichten, ausführen, tun; *Pflicht etc.* erfüllen; *thea.*, ♪ aufführen, spielen, vortragen (*a. v/i.*); ~**ance** [~əns] Verrichtung *f*, Ausführung *f*; Leistung *f*; *thea.*, ♪ Aufführung *f*, Vorstellung *f*, Vortrag *m*; ~**er** [~ə] Künstler(in).

per·fume 1. [ˈpɜːfjuːm] Duft *m*, Wohlgeruch *m*; Parfüm *n*; **2.** [pəˈfjuːm] mit Duft erfüllen, parfümieren.

per·func·to·ry □ [pəˈfʌŋktərɪ] mechanisch; oberflächlich.

per·haps [pəˈhæps, præps] vielleicht.

per·il [ˈperəl] **1.** Gefahr *f*; **2.** gefährden; ~**ous** □ [~əs] gefährlich.

pe·rim·e·ter [pəˈrɪmɪtə] ♀ Umkreis *m*; Umgrenzungslinie *f*, Grenze *f*.

pe·ri·od [ˈpɪərɪəd] Periode *f*; Zeitraum *m*; *gr. bsd. Am.* Punkt *m*; *gr.* Gliedsatz *m*, Satzgefüge *n*; (Unterrichts)Stunde *f*; *physiol.* Periode *f* (*der Frau*); ~**ic** [pɪərɪˈɒdɪk] periodisch; ~**i·cal** [~ɪkl] **1.** □ periodisch; **2.** Zeitschrift *f*.

per·ish [ˈperɪʃ] umkommen, zugrunde gehen; ~**a·ble** □ [~əbl] leicht verderblich; ~**ing** [~ɪŋ] *bsd. Brt.* F sehr kalt; F verdammt, -flixt.

per|jure [ˈpɜːdʒə]: ~ *o.s.* e-n Meineid leisten; ~**ju·ry** [~rɪ] Meineid *m*; *commit* ~ e-n Meineid leisten.

perk [pɜːk]: ~ *up v/i.* sich wieder erholen, munter werden (*Person*); *v/t.* Kopf heben, *Ohren* spitzen; schmücken, verschönern; *j-n* aufmöbeln, munter machen.

perk·y □ [ˈpɜːkɪ] (-*ier*, -*iest*) munter; keck, dreist, flott.

perm F [pɜːm] **1.** Dauerwelle *f*; **2.** *j-m* e-e Dauerwelle machen.

per·ma|nence [ˈpɜːmənəns] Dauer *f*; ~**nent** □ [~t] dauernd, ständig; dauerhaft; Dauer...; ~ *wave* Dauerwelle *f*.

per·me|a·ble □ [ˈpɜːmjəbl] durchlässig; ~**ate** [~eɪt] durchdringen; dringen (*into* in *acc.*, *through* durch).

per·mis|si·ble □ [pəˈmɪsəbl] zulässig; ~**sion** [~ʃn] Erlaubnis *f*; ~**sive** □ [~sɪv] zulässig, erlaubt; tolerant; (sexuell) freizügig; ~ *society* tabufreie Gesellschaft.

P

per·mit 1. [pə'mɪt] (*-tt-*) erlauben, gestatten; **2.** ['pɜːmɪt] Erlaubnis *f*, Genehmigung *f*; Passierschein *m*.

per·ni·cious □ [pə'nɪʃəs] verderblich, schädlich; ⚕ bösartig.

per·pen·dic·u·lar □ [pɜːpən'dɪkjʊlə] senkrecht; aufrecht; steil.

per·pe·trate ['pɜːpɪtreɪt] verüben.

per·pet·u·al □ [pə'petjʊəl] fortwährend, ständig, ewig; **~ate** [~eɪt] bewahren; verewigen.

per·plex [pə'pleks] verwirren; **~i·ty** [~ətɪ] Verwirrung *f*.

per·se·cute ['pɜːsɪkjuːt] verfolgen; **~cu·tion** [pɜːsɪ'kjuːʃn] Verfolgung *f*; **~cu·tor** ['pɜːsɪkjuːtə] Verfolger (-in).

per·se·ver·ance [pɜːsɪ'vɪərəns] Beharrlichkeit *f*, Ausdauer *f*; **~e** [pɜːsɪ'vɪə] beharren; aushalten.

per·sist [pə'sɪst] beharren, bestehen (*in* auf *dat.*); fortdauern, anhalten; **~sis·tence**, **~sis·ten·cy** [~əns, ~sɪ] Beharrlichkeit *f*; Hartnäckigkeit *f*; Ausdauer *f*; **~sis·tent** □ [~ənt] beharrlich, ausdauernd; anhaltend.

per·son ['pɜːsn] Person *f* (*a. gr.*, 🎭); **~age** [~ɪdʒ] (hohe *od.* bedeutende) Persönlichkeit *f*; **~al** □ [~l] persönlich (*a. gr.*); *attr.* Personal...; Privat...; **~ data** *pl.* Personalien *pl.*; **~al·i·ty** [pɜːsə'nælətɪ] Persönlichkeit *f*; **personalities** *pl.* anzügliche *od.* persönliche Bemerkungen *pl.*; **~i·fy** [pɜː'sɒnɪfaɪ] verkörpern; **~nel** [pɜːsə'nel] Personal *n*, Belegschaft *f*; ✗ Mannschaften *pl.*; ⚓, ✈ Besatzung *f*; **~ department** Personalabteilung *f*; **~ manager**, **~ officer** Personalchef *m*.

per·spec·tive [pə'spektɪv] Perspektive *f*; Ausblick *m*, Fernsicht *f*.

per·spic·u·ous □ [pə'spɪkjʊəs] klar.

per·spi·ra·tion [pɜːspə'reɪʃn] Schwitzen *n*; Schweiß *m*; **~spire** [pə'spaɪə] (aus)schwitzen.

per·suade [pə'sweɪd] überreden; überzeugen; **~sua·sion** [~ʒn] Überredung *f*; Überzeugung *f*, (*feste*) Meinung; Glaube *m*; **~sua·sive** □ [~sɪv] überredend; überzeugend.

pert □ [pɜːt] keck (*a. fig. Hut*), vorlaut, frech, naseweis.

per·tain [pɜː'teɪn] (*to*) gehören (*dat. od. zu*); betreffen (*acc.*).

per·ti·na·cious □ [pɜːtɪ'neɪʃəs] hartnäckig, zäh.

per·ti·nent □ ['pɜːtɪnənt] sachdienlich, relevant, zur Sache gehörig.

per·turb [pə'tɜːb] beunruhigen.

pe·rus·al [pə'ruːzl] sorgfältige Durchsicht; **~e** [~z] (sorgfältig) durchlesen; prüfen.

per·vade [pə'veɪd] durchdringen.

per·verse □ [pə'vɜːs] *psych.* pervers; eigensinnig, verstockt; vertrackt (*Sache*); **~ver·sion** [~ʃn] Verdrehung *f*; Abkehr *f*; *psych.* Perversion *f*; **~ver·si·ty** [~ɔtɪ] *psych.* Perversität *f*; Eigensinn *m*, Verstocktheit *f*.

per·vert 1. [pə'vɜːt] verdrehen; verführen; **2.** *psych.* ['pɜːvɜːt] perverser Mensch.

pes·si·mis·m ['pesɪmɪzəm] Pessimismus *m*.

pest [pest] lästiger Mensch, Nervensäge *f*; lästige Sache, Plage *f*; *zo.* Schädling *m*; △ *nicht* Pest (*Seuche*).

pes·ter ['pestə] belästigen.

pes·ti·lent □ ['pestɪlənt], **~len·tial** □ [pestɪ'lenʃl] *bsd. veraltet* schädlich; *mst co.* ekelhaft, abscheulich.

pet¹ [pet] **1.** (*zahmes*) (Haus)Tier; Liebling *m*; **2.** Lieblings...; Tier...; **~ dog** Schoßhund *m*; **~ name** Kosename *m*; **~ shop** Tierhandlung *f*, Zoogeschäft *n*; **3.** (*-tt-*) (ver)hätscheln; streicheln, liebkosen; F Petting machen.

pet² [~]: *in a* **~** verärgert.

pet·al ♥ ['petl] Blütenblatt *n*.

pe·ti·tion [pɪ'tɪʃn] **1.** Bittschrift *f*, Eingabe *f*; Gesuch *n*; **2.** bitten, ersuchen; ein Gesuch einreichen (*for* um), e-n Antrag stellen (*for* auf *acc.*).

pet·ri·fy ['petrɪfaɪ] versteinern.

pet·rol ['petrəl] Benzin *n*; △ *nicht* Petroleum; (~) **pump** Zapfsäule *f*; **~ station** Tankstelle *f*.

pe·tro·le·um 🜨 [pɪ'trəʊljəm] Petroleum *n*, Erd-, Mineralöl *n*; **~ refinery** Erdölraffinerie *f*.

pet·ti·coat ['petɪkəʊt] Unterrock *m*.

pet·ting F ['petɪŋ] Petting *n*.

pet·tish □ ['petɪʃ] launisch, reizbar.

pet·ty □ ['petɪ] (*-ier, -iest*) klein, geringfügig, Bagatell...; **~ cash** Portokasse *f*; **~ larceny** 🎭 einfacher Diebstahl.

pet·u·lant □ ['petjʊlənt] gereizt.

pew [pjuː] Kirchenbank *f*.

pew·ter ['pjuːtə] Zinn *n*; Zinngeschirr *n*; Zinnkrug *m*.

phan·tom ['fæntəm] Phantom *n*, Trugbild *n*; Gespenst *n*.

phar·ma·cy ['fɑːməsɪ] Pharmazie *f*; Apotheke *f*.

phase [feɪz] Phase *f*.

pheas·ant *zo.* ['feznt] Fasan *m*.

phe·nom·e·non [fɪ'nɒmɪnən] (*pl. -na* [-ə]) Phänomen *n*, Erscheinung *f*.

phi·al ['faɪəl] Phiole *f*, Fläschchen *n*.

phi·lan·thro·pist [fɪ'lænθrəpɪst] Philanthrop *m*, Menschenfreund *m*.

phi·lol·o·gist [fɪ'lɒlədʒɪst] Philolog|e *m*, -in *f*; **~·gy** [~ɪ] Philologie *f*.

phi·los·o·pher [fɪ'lɒsəfə] Philosoph *m*; **~·phize** [~aɪz] philosophieren; **~·phy** [~ɪ] Philosophie *f*.

phlegm [flem] Schleim *m*; Phlegma *n*.

phone F [fəʊn] = *telephone*.

pho·net·ics [fə'netɪks] *sg.* Phonetik *f*, Lautlehre *f*.

pho·n(e)y *sl.* ['fəʊnɪ] **1.** Fälschung *f*; Schwindler(in) *f*; **2.** (*-ier, -iest*) falsch, unecht.

phos·pho·rus 🜍 ['fɒsfərəs] Phosphor *m*.

pho·to F ['fəʊtəʊ] (*pl. -tos*) Foto *n*, Bild *n*.

pho·to- [~] Licht..., Photo..., Foto...; **~·cop·i·er** Fotokopiergerät *n*; **~·cop·y 1.** Fotokopie *f*; **2.** fotokopieren.

pho·to·graph ['fəʊtəgrɑːf] **1.** Fotografie *f* (*Bild*); △ *nicht Fotograf*; **2.** fotografieren; **~·tog·ra·pher** [fə'tɒgrəfə] Fotograf(in) *f*; **~·tog·ra·phy** [~ɪ] Fotografie *f*; △ *nicht Fotografie* (*Bild*).

phras·al ['freɪzl]: **~** *verb* Verb *n* mit Adverb (und Präposition); **phrase** [freɪz] **1.** (Rede)Wendung *f*, Redensart *f*, (idiomatischer) Ausdruck; △ *nicht Phrase (leere Redensart)*; **~·book** Sprachführer *m*; **2.** ausdrücken.

phys·i·cal □ ['fɪzɪkl] physisch; körperlich; physikalisch; **~** *education*, **~** *training* Leibeserziehung *f*; **~** *handicap* Körperbehinderung *f*; **~·ly** *handicapped* körperbehindert; **phy·si·cian** [fɪ'zɪʃn] Arzt *m*; △ *nicht Physiker*; **~·i·cist** ['fɪzɪsɪst] Physiker *m*; **~·ics** [~ɪks] *sg.* Physik *f*.

phy·sique [fɪ'ziːk] Körper(bau) *m*, Statur *f*; △ *nicht Physik*.

pi·an·o ['pjænəʊ] (*pl. -os*) Klavier *n*.

pi·az·za [pɪ'ætsə] Piazza *f*, (Markt-) Platz *m*; *Am.* (große) Veranda.

pick [pɪk] **1.** = *pickaxe*; (Aus)Wahl *f*; *take your* **~** suchen Sie sich etwas aus; **2.** (auf)hacken; (auf)picken (*Vogel*); entfernen; pflücken; *Knochen* abnagen; bohren *in* (*dat.*); *Schloß* mit e-m Dietrich öffnen, F knacken; *Streit* vom Zaun brechen; (sorgfältig) (aus)wählen; *Am.* ♪ *Saiten* zupfen, *Banjo* spielen; **~** *one's nose* in der Nase bohren; **~** *one's teeth* in den Zähnen (herum-) stochern; **~** *s.o.'s pocket* j-n bestehlen; *have a bone to* **~** *with s.o.* mit j-m ein Hühnchen zu rupfen haben; **~** *out et.* auswählen; heraussuchen; **~** *up* aufhacken; aufheben, -lesen, -nehmen; aufpicken (*Vogel*); *Spur* aufnehmen; *Täter* aufgreifen; F *et.* aufschnappen; sich *e-e Fremdsprache* aneignen; (*im Auto*) mitnehmen od. abholen; F *j-n* zufällig kennenlernen, auflesen; sich erholen; *a.* **~** *up speed mot.* schneller werden; **~·a·back** ['pɪkəbæk] huckepack; **~·axe**, *Am.* **~·ax** Spitzhacke *f*.

pick·et ['pɪkɪt] **1.** Pfahl *m*; ✕ Feldwache *f*; Steikposten *m*; **~** *line* Steikpostenkette *f*; **2.** mit Steikposten besetzen, Steikposten aufstellen vor (*dat.*); Steikposten stehen.

pick·ings ['pɪkɪŋz] *pl.* Überbleibsel *pl.*, Reste *pl.*; Ausbeute *f*; Profit *m*, (unehrlicher) Gewinn.

pick·le ['pɪkl] **1.** (Salz)Lake *f*; *mst* **~s** *pl.* Eingepökelte(s) *n*, Pickles *pl.*; F mißliche Lage; **2.** einlegen, (ein-)pökeln; **~d** *herring* Salzhering *m*.

pick·lock ['pɪklɒk] Einbrecher *m*; Dietrich *m*; **~·pock·et** Taschendieb *m*; **~·up** Anstiegen *n*; Tonabnehmer *m*; Kleinlieferwagen *m*; F Staßenbekanntschaft *f*.

pic·nic ['pɪknɪk] **1.** Picknick *n*; **2.** (*-ck-*) ein Picknick machen, picknicken.

pic·to·ri·al [pɪk'tɔːrɪəl] **1.** □ malerisch; illustriert; **2.** Illustrierte *f*.

pic·ture ['pɪktʃə] **1.** Bild *n*; Gemälde *n*; bildschöne Sache *od.* Person; Film *m*; *attr.* Bilder...; **~s** *pl. bsd.* *Brt.* Kino *n*; *put s.o. in the* **~** j-n ins Bild setzen, j-n informieren; **2.** abbilden; *fig.* schildern, beschreiben; *fig.* sich *et.* vorstellen; **~** *post·card* Ansichtskarte *f*; **pic·tur·esque** [pɪktʃə'resk] malerisch.

pie [paɪ] Pastete *f*; gedeckter Obstkuchen.

pie·bald ['paɪbɔːld] (bunt)scheckig.

piece [piːs] **1.** Stück *n*; Teil *m*, *n* (*e-r*

Maschine etc., ~-s Services); *Schach*: Figur f; *Brettspiel*: Stein m; *by the* ~ stückweise; im Akkord; a ~ *of advice* ein Rat; a ~ *of news* e-e Neuigkeit; *of* a ~ einheitlich; *give s.o.* a ~ *of one's mind* j-m gründlich die Meinung sagen; *take to* ~s zerlegen; 2. ~ *together* zusammensetzen, -stükkeln, -flicken; **~·meal** ['pi:smi:l] stückweise; **~·work** Akkordarbeit f; *do* ~ im Akkord arbeiten.

pier [pɪə] Pfeiler m; Pier m, Hafendamm m, Mole f; Landungsbrücke f.

pierce [pɪəs] durchbohren, -stechen, -stoßen; durchdringen; eindringen (in *acc.*).

pi·e·ty ['paɪətɪ] Frömmigkeit f; Pietät f.

pig [pɪg] *zo.* Schwein n (a. fig. F); *bsd. Am.* Ferkel n; *sl. contp.* Bulle m (*Polizist*).

pi·geon ['pɪdʒɪn] Taube f; **~·hole** 1. Fach n; 2. in Fächer einordnen.

pig·head·ed ['pɪg'hedɪd] dickköpfig; **~·i·ron** ['pɪgaɪən] Roheisen n; **~·skin** Schweinsleder n; **~·sty** Schweinestall m; **~·tail** (Haar)Zopf m.

pike [paɪk] ✕ *hist.* Pike f, Spieß m; *zo.* Hecht m; Schlagbaum m; Mautstraße f; Maut f.

pile [paɪl] 1. Haufen m; Stapel m, Stoß m; F Haufen m, Masse f; ⚡ Batterie f; Pfahl m; Flor m (*Stoff, Teppich*); ~s pl. ⚕ Hämorrhoiden pl.; (*atomic*) ~ Atommeiler m, (Kern)Reaktor m; 2. *oft* ~ *up*, ~ *on* (an-, auf)häufen, (auf)stapeln, aufschichten.

pil·fer ['pɪlfə] stehlen, F stibitzen.

pil·grim ['pɪlgrɪm] Pilger(in); **~·age** [~ɪdʒ] Pilger-, Wallfahrt f.

pill [pɪl] Pille f (a. fig.); *the* ~ die (Antibaby)Pille.

pil·lage ['pɪlɪdʒ] 1. Plünderung f; 2. plündern.

pil·lar ['pɪlə] Pfeiler m, Ständer m; Säule f; **~·box** *Brt.* Briefkasten m.

pil·li·on *mot.* ['pɪljən] Soziussitz m.

pil·lo·ry ['pɪlərɪ] 1. Pranger m; 2. an den Pranger stellen; *fig.* anprangern.

pil·low ['pɪləʊ] (Kopf)Kissen n; **~·case**, **~·slip** (Kopf)Kissenbezug m.

pi·lot ['paɪlət] 1. ✈ Pilot m; ♣ Lotse m; *fig.* Führer m; 2. Versuchs..., Probe..., Pilot...; **~ film** *TV* Pilotfilm m; **~ scheme** Versuchsprojekt n; 3. lotsen; steuern.

pimp [pɪmp] 1. Kuppler m; Zuhälter m; 2. sich als Kuppler betätigen; Zuhälter sein.

pim·ple ['pɪmpl] Pickel m, Pustel f.

pin [pɪn] 1. (Steck-, Krawatten-, Hut- *etc.*)Nadel f; ⊕ Pflock m, Bolzen m, Stift m, Dorn m; ♪ Wirbel m; *Kegeln*: Kegel m; *Bowling*: Pin m; (*clothes*) ~ *bsd. Am.* Wäscheklammer f; (*drawing-*) ~ *Brt.* Reißzwecke f; 2. (*-nn-*) (an)heften, anstecken (*to* an *acc.*), befestigen (*to* an *dat.*); pressen, drücken (*against*, *to* gegen, an *acc.*).

pin·a·fore ['pɪnəfɔː] Schürze f.

pin·cers ['pɪnsəz] *pl.* (a *pair of* ~ e-e) (Kneif)Zange.

pinch [pɪntʃ] 1. Kneifen n; Prise f (*Salz, Tabak etc.*); *fig.* Druck m, Not f; 2. *v/t.* kneifen, zwicken, (ein-) klemmen; drücken (*Schuh etc.*); F klauen; *v/i.* drücken (*Schuh, Not etc.*); *a.* ~ *and scrape* sich einschränken, knausern.

pin·cush·ion ['pɪnkuʃn] Nadelkissen n.

pine [paɪn] 1. ♀ Kiefer f, Föhre f; 2. sich abhärmen; sich sehnen (*for* nach); **~·ap·ple** ♀ ['paɪnæpl] Ananas f; **~·cone** ♀ Kiefernzapfen m.

pin·ion ['pɪnjən] 1. *zo.* Flügelspitze f; *zo.* Schwungfeder f; ⊕ Ritzel n (*Antriebsrad*); 2. die Flügel stutzen (*dat.*); fesseln (*to* an *acc.*).

pink [pɪŋk] 1. ♀ Nelke f; Rosa n; *be in the* ~ (*of condition od. health*) in Top- *od.* Hochform sein; 2. rosa(farben).

pin·mon·ey ['pɪnmʌnɪ] (selbstverdientes) Taschengeld (der Hausfrau).

pin·na·cle ['pɪnəkl] *arch.* Spitztürmchen n; (Berg)Spitze f; *fig.* Gipfel m, Höhepunkt m.

pint [paɪnt] Pint n (= 0,57 od. Am. 0,47 Liter); *Brt.* F Halbe f (*Bier*).

pi·o·neer [paɪə'nɪə] 1. Pionier m (a. ✕); 2. den Weg bahnen (für).

pi·ous □ ['paɪəs] fromm, religiös.

pip [pɪp] *vet.* Pips m; F miese Laune; (Obst)Kern m; Auge n (*auf Würfeln etc.*); ✕ *Brt.* F Stern m (*Rangabzeichen*); *kurzer, hoher Ton.*

pipe [paɪp] 1. Rohr n, Röhre f; Pfeife f (a. ♪); △ *nicht* (Triller)Pfeife; ♪ Flöte f; Pfeifen n, Lied n (*e-s Vogels*); Luftröhre f; Pipe f (*Weinfaß = 477, 3 Liter*); 2. (durch Rohre) leiten;

pfeifen; flöten; piep(s)en (*Vogel etc.*); **~·line** ['paɪplaɪn] Rohrleitung *f*; *Erdöl, Erdgas etc.*: Pipeline *f*; **~r** [~ə] Pfeifer *m*.

pip·ing ['paɪpɪŋ] **1.** pfeifend, schrill; **~** *hot* siedend heiß; **2.** Rohrleitung *f*, -netz *n*; *Schneiderei*: Paspel *f*, Biese *f*; Pfeifen *n*, Piep(s)en *n*.

pi·quant □ ['piːkənt] pikant.

pique [piːk] **1.** Groll *m*; **2.** kränken, reizen; **~** *o.s.* sich brüsten mit.

pi·ra·cy ['paɪərəsɪ] Piraterie *f*, Seeräuberei *f*; **pi·rate** [~ət] **1.** Pirat *m*, Seeräuber *m*; Piratenschiff *n*; **~** *radio station* Piratensender *m*.

piss ∨ [pɪs] pissen; **~** *off!* verpiß dich!, hau ab!

pis·tol ['pɪstl] Pistole *f*.

pis·ton ⊕ ['pɪstən] Kolben *m*; **~·rod** Kolben-, Pleuelstange *f*; **~·stroke** Kolbenhub *m*.

pit [pɪt] **1.** Grube *f* (*a.* 🅭, *anat.*); 🗡 Miete *f*; Fallgrube *f*, Falle *f*; *Motorsport*: Box *f*; *Sport*: Sprunggrube *f*; *thea. Brt.* Parterre *n*; *a. orchestra ~ thea.* Orchestergraben *m*; *Am.* (*Obst*)Stein *m*, Kern *m*; Pockennarbe *f*; **2.** (*-tt-*) 🗡 einmieten; mit Narben bedecken; *Am.* entsteinen, -kernen.

pitch [pɪtʃ] **1.** *min.* Pech *n*; *Brt.* Stand(platz) *m* (*Straßenhändler etc.*); ♪ Tonhöhe *f*; Grad *m*, Stufe *f*, Höhe *f*; Gefälle *n*, Neigung *f*; Wurf *m* (*a. Sport*); *bsd. Brt. Sport*: Spielfeld *n*, Platz *m*; ♴ Stampfen *n* (*Schiff*); **2.** *v/t.* werfen; schleudern; Zelt, Lager aufschlagen, -stellen; ♪ (an)stimmen; **~** *too high fig.* Erwartungen zu hoch stecken; *v/i.* 🗡 (sich) lagern; hinschlagen; ♴ stampfen (*Schiff*); **~** *into* F herfallen über (*acc.*); **~·black** ['pɪtʃ'blæk], **~·dark** pechschwarz; stockdunkel.

pitch·er ['pɪtʃə] Krug *m*; *Baseball*: Werfer *m*.

pitch·fork ['pɪtʃfɔːk] Heu-, Mistgabel *f*.

pit·e·ous □ ['pɪtɪəs] kläglich.

pit·fall ['pɪtfɔːl] Fallgrube *f*; *fig.* Falle *f*.

pith [pɪθ] Mark *n*; *fig.* Kern *m*; *fig.* Kraft *f*; **~·y** □ ['pɪθɪ] (*-ier, -iest*) markig, kernig.

pit·i·a·ble □ ['pɪtɪəbl] bemitleidenswert; erbärmlich; **~·ful** □ [~fl] bemitleidenswert; erbärmlich; jäm-

merlich (*a. contp.*); **~·less** □ [~lɪs] unbarmherzig.

pit·tance ['pɪtəns] Hungerlohn *m*.

pit·y ['pɪtɪ] **1.** Mitleid *n* (*on* mit); *it is a* ~ es ist schade; **2.** bemitleiden.

piv·ot ['pɪvət] **1.** ⊕ (Dreh)Zapfen *m*; *fig.* Dreh-, Angelpunkt *m*; **2.** sich drehen (*on, upon* um).

piz·za ['piːtsə] Pizza *f*.

pla·ca·ble □ ['plækəbl] versöhnlich.

plac·ard ['plækɑːd] **1.** Plakat *n*; Transparent *n*; **2.** anschlagen; mit e-m Plakat bekleben.

place [pleɪs] **1.** Platz *m*; Ort *m*; Stelle *f*; Stätte *f*; (*Arbeits*)Stelle *f*, (An-)Stellung *f*; Wohnsitz *m*, Haus *n*, Wohnung *f*; Wohnort *m*; *soziale* Stellung; **~** *of delivery econ.* Erfüllungsort *m*; *give* ~ *to* j-m Platz machen; *in* ~ *of* an Stelle (*gen.*); *out of* ~ fehl am Platz; **2.** stellen, legen, setzen; j-n ein-, anstellen; *Auftrag* erteilen (*with s.o.* j-m); *be* ~*d Sport*: sich placieren; *I can't* ~ *him fig.* ich weiß nicht, wo ich ihn hintun soll (*identifizieren*); **~·name** ['pleɪsneɪm] Ortsname *m*.

plac·id □ ['plæsɪd] sanft; ruhig.

pla·gia·rism ['pleɪdʒjərɪzəm] Plagiat *n*; **~·rize** [~raɪz] plagiieren.

plague [pleɪg] **1.** Seuche *f*; Pest *f*; Plage *f*; **2.** plagen, quälen.

plaice [pleɪs] *zo.* Scholle *f*.

plaid [plæd] Plaid *n*.

plain [pleɪn] **1.** □ klar; deutlich; einfach, schlicht; unscheinbar, wenig anziehend; häßlich (*Frau*); offen (u. ehrlich); einfarbig; rein (*Wahrheit, Unsinn etc.*); **2.** *adv.* klar, deutlich; **3.** Ebene *f*, Flachland *n*; *the Great* ~*s pl. Am.* die Prärien *pl.* (*im Westen der USA*); **~** *choc·olate* (zart)bittere Schokolade; **~·clothes man** ['pleɪn'kləʊðzmən] (*pl. -men*) Polizist *m* od. Kriminalbeamte(r) *m* in Zivil; **~** *deal·ing* Redlichkeit *f*; **~·s·man** (*pl. -men*) *Am.* Präriebewohner *m*.

plain·tiff 🕮 ['pleɪntɪf] Kläger(in). **~·tive** □ [~v] traurig, klagend.

plait [plæt, *Am.* pleɪt] **1.** (*Haaretc.*)Flechte *f*; Zopf *m*; **2.** flechten.

plan [plæn] **1.** Plan *m*; **2.** (*-nn-*) planen; entwerfen; ausarbeiten.

plane [pleɪn] **1.** flach, eben; **2.** Ebene *f*, (ebene) Fläche *f*; 🖳 Tragfläche *f*; Flugzeug *n*; ⊕ Hobel *m*; *fig.* Stufe *f*; Niveau *n*; *by* ~ mit dem Flugzeug, auf dem Luftweg; **3.** (ein)ebnen; ⊕ hobeln; ✈ fliegen.

plan·et *ast.* ['plænɪt] Planet *m*.

plank [plæŋk] **1.** Planke *f*, Bohle *f*, Diele *f*; *pol.* Programmpunkt *m*; **2.** dielen; verschalen; ∼ *down* F *et.* hinknallen; *Geld auf den Tisch* legen, blechen.

plant [plɑ:nt] **1.** ♀ Pflanze *f*; ⊕ Anlage *f*; Fabrik *m*; **2.** (an-, ein)pflanzen (*a. fig.*); bepflanzen; besiedeln; anlegen; (auf)stellen; *Schlag* verpassen; **plan·ta·tion** [plæn'teɪʃn] Pflanzung *f*, Plantage *f*; Besied(e)-lung *f*; ∼**er** ['plɑ:ntə] Pflanzer *m*; Plantagenbesitzer *m*; ⚓ Pflanzmaschine *f*; Übertopf *m*.

plaque [plɑ:k] (Schmuck)Platte *f*; Gedenktafel *f*; ⚕ Zahnbelag *m*.

plash [plæʃ] platschen.

plas·ter ['plɑ:stə] **1.** ⚕ Pflaster *n*; *arch.* (Ver)Putz *m*; *a.* ∼ *of Paris* Gips *m* (*a.* ⚕); Stuck *m*; **2.** verputzen; bekleben; ⚕ ein Pflaster legen auf (*acc.*); ∼ *cast* Gipsabdruck *m*, -abguß *m*; ⚕ Gipsverband *m*.

plas·tic ['plæstɪk] **1.** (∼*ally*) plastisch; Plastik...; **2.** *oft* ∼*s sg.* Plastik(material) *n*, Kunststoff *m*.

plate [pleɪt] **1.** Platte *f*; Teller *m*; (Bild)Tafel *f*; Schild *n*; (Kupfer-, Stahl)Stich *m*; (Tafel)Besteck *n*; *Baseball*: Heimbase *n*; ⊕ Grobblech *n*; **2.** plattieren; panzern.

plat·form ['plætfɔ:m] Plattform *f*; *geol.* Hochebene *f*; ⚑ Bahnsteig *m*; *Brt.* Plattform *f* (*bsd. am Busende, Am.* ⚑ *bsd. am Wagenende*); (Red-ner)Tribüne *f*, Podium *n*; ⊕ Rampe *f*, Bühne *f*; *pol.* Parteiprogramm *n*; *bsd. Am. pol.* Aktionsprogramm *n* (*im Wahlkampf*).

plat·i·num *min.* ['plætɪnəm] Platin *n*.

plat·i·tude *fig.* ['plætɪtju:d] Plattheit *f*.

pla·toon ✕ [plə'tu:n] Zug *m*.

plat·ter *Am. od. veraltet* ['plætə] (Servier)Platte *f*.

plau·dit ['plɔ:dɪt] Beifall *m*.

plau·si·ble □ ['plɔ:zəbl] glaubhaft.

play [pleɪ] **1.** Spiel *n*; Schauspiel *n*, (Theater)Stück *n*; ⊕ Spiel *n*; *fig.* Spielraum *m*; **2.** spielen; ⊕ Spiel (-raum) haben; ⊕ sich bewegen (*Kolben etc.*); ∼ *back* Ball zurück-spielen (*to zu*); *Tonband* abspielen; ∼ *off fig.* ausspielen (*against gegen*); ∼ *on*, ∼ *upon fig. j-s Schwächen* aus-

nutzen; ∼*ed out fig.* erledigt, erschöpft; ∼**-back** ['pleɪbæk] Playback *n*, Wiedergabe *f*, Abspielen *n*; ∼**bill** Theaterplakat *n*; *Am.* Programm (-heft) *n*; ∼**boy** Playboy *m*; ∼**er** [∼ə] (Schau)Spieler(in); Plattenspieler *m*; ∼**fel·low** Spielgefährt|e *m*, -in *f*; ∼**ful** □ [∼fl] verspielt; spielerisch, scherzhaft; ∼**girl** Playgirl *n*; ∼**go·er** [∼gəʊə] (*bsd.* häufige[r]) Theaterbe-sucher(in); ∼**ground** Spielplatz *m*; Schulhof *m*; ∼**house** *thea.* Schau-spielhaus *n*; Spielhaus *n* (*für Kin-der*); ∼**mate** = *playfellow*; Gespiel|e *m*, -in *f*; ∼**thing** Spielzeug *n*; ∼**wright** Dramatiker *m*.

plea [pli:] ⚖ Einspruch *m*; Ausrede *f*; Gesuch *n*; *on the* ∼ *of od. that* unter dem Vorwand (*gen.*) *od.* daß.

plead [pli:d] (∼*ed*, *bsd. schott., Am. pled*) *v/i.* ⚖ plädieren; ∼ *for* für *j-n* sprechen; sich einsetzen für; ∼ (*not*) *guilty* sich (nicht) schuldig bekennen; *v/t.* sich berufen auf (*acc.*), *et.* vorschützen; *Sache* vertreten; ⚖ (als Beweis) anführen; ∼**ing** ⚖ ['pli:dɪŋ] Plädoyer *n*.

pleas·ant □ ['plezənt] angenehm, erfreulich; freundlich; sympathisch; ∼**ry** [∼rɪ] Scherz *m*, Spaß *m*.

please [pli:z] *(j-m)* gefallen, angenehm sein; befriedigen; belieben; *bitte*; (*yes*) ∼ (ja,) bitte; (oh ja,) gerne; ∼ *come in!* bitte, treten Sie ein!; ∼ *yourself* (ganz) wie Sie wün-schen; ∼**d** erfreut, zufrieden; *be* ∼ *at* erfreut sein über (*acc.*); *be* ∼ *to do it.* gerne tun; ∼ *to meet you!* ange-nehm!; *be* ∼ *with* befriedigt sein von; Vergnügen haben an (*dat.*).

pleas·ing □ ['pli:zɪŋ] angenehm, ge-fällig.

plea·sure ['pleʒə] Vergnügen *n*, Freude *f*; Belieben *n*; *attr.* Vergnü-gungs...; *at* ∼ nach Belieben; ∼**boat** Vergnügungs-, Ausflugsdampfer *m*; ∼**ground** (Park)Anlage(n *pl.*) *f*; Vergnügungspark *m*.

pleat [pli:t] **1.** (Plissee)Falte *f*; **2.** fälteln, plissieren.

pled [pled] *pret. u. p.p. von plead.*

pledge [pledʒ] **1.** Pfand *n*; Zutrinken *n*, Toast *m*; Versprechen *n*, Gelöbnis *n*; **2.** verpfänden; *j-m* zutrinken; *he* ∼*d himself* er gelobte.

ple·na·ry ['pli:nərɪ] Voll..., Plenar...

plen·i·po·ten·tia·ry [plenɪpə'tenʃərɪ] (General)Bevollmächtigte(r *m*) *f*.

plen·ti·ful □ ['plentɪfl] reichlich.

plen·ty ['plentɪ] **1.** Fülle f, Überfluß m; ~ of reichlich; **2.** F reichlich.

pli·a·ble □ ['plaɪəbl] biegsam; fig. geschmeidig, nachgiebig.

pli·ers ['plaɪəz] pl. (a pair of ~ e-e) (Draht-, Kombi)Zange.

plight [plaɪt] (schlechter) Zustand, schwierige Lage, Notlage f.

plim·soll Brt. ['plɪmsəl] Turnschuh m.

plod [plɒd] (-dd-) a. ~ along, ~ on sich dahinschleppen; ~ away sich abplagen (at mit), schuften.

plop [plɒp] (-pp-) plumpsen od. (bsd. ins Wasser) platschen (lassen).

plot [plɒt] **1.** Stück n Land, Parzelle f, Grundstück n; (geheimer) Plan, Komplott n, Anschlag m, Intrige f; Handlung f (e-s Dramas etc.); **2.** (-tt-) v/t. auf-, einzeichnen; planen, anzetteln; v/i. sich verschwören (against gegen).

plough, Am. **plow** [plaʊ] **1.** Pflug m; **2.** (um)pflügen; **~share** ['plaʊʃeə] Pflugschar f.

pluck [plʌk] **1.** Rupfen n, Zupfen n, Zerren n, Reißen n; Zug m, Ruck m; Innereien pl.; fig. Mut m, Schneid m; **2.** pflücken; Vogel rupfen (a. fig.); zupfen, ziehen, zerren, reißen (at an dat.); ♪ Saiten zupfen; ~ up courage Mut fassen; **~·y** F □ ['plʌkɪ] (-ier, -iest) mutig.

plug [plʌg] **1.** Pflock m, Dübel m, Stöpsel m; ⚡ Stecker m; ⚡ F Steckdose f; Hydrant m; mot. (Zünd-) Kerze f; (Zahn)Plombe f; Priem m (Kautabak); Rundfunk, TV: F Empfehlung f, Tip m, Werbung f; **2.** v/t. (-gg-) Zahn plombieren; F im Rundfunk etc. (ständig) Reklame machen für; ~ away F arbeiten; ~ up zu-, verstopfen, zustöpseln; ~ in ⚡ Gerät einstecken.

plum [plʌm] ♀ Pflaume(nbaum m) f; Rosine f (a. fig.).

plum·age ['plu:mɪdʒ] Gefieder n.

plumb [plʌm] **1.** lot-, senkrecht; **2.** (Blei)Lot n; **3.** v/t. lotrecht machen; loten; sondieren (a. fig.); Wasser- od. Gasleitungen legen in; v/i. als Rohrleger arbeiten; **~·er** ['plʌmə] Klempner m, Installateur m; **~·ing** [~ɪŋ] Klempnerarbeit f; Rohrleitungen pl.; sanitäre Installation.

plume [plu:m] **1.** Feder f; Federbusch m; **2.** mit Federn schmücken;

das Gefieder putzen; ~ o.s. on sich brüsten mit.

plum·met ['plʌmɪt] Senkblei n.

plump [plʌmp] **1.** adj. drall, prall, mollig; F □ glatt (Absage etc.); △ nicht plump; **2.** a. ~ down (hin-) plumpsen (lassen); **3.** Plumps m; **4.** adv. F unverblümt, geradeheraus.

plum pud·ding ['plʌm'pʊdɪŋ] Plumpudding m.

plun·der ['plʌndə] **1.** Plünderung f; Raub m, Beute f; △ nicht Plunder; **2.** plündern.

plunge [plʌndʒ] **1.** (Ein-, Unter-) Tauchen n; (Kopf)Sprung m; Sturz m; take the ~ fig. den entscheidenden Schritt wagen; **2.** (ein-, unter-) tauchen; (sich) stürzen (into in acc.); e-e Waffe ins Herz etc. stoßen; ⚓ stampfen (Schiff).

plu·per·fect gr. ['plu:'pɜ:fɪkt] a. ~ tense Plusquamperfekt n, Vorvergangenheit f.

plu·ral gr. ['plʊərəl] Plural m, Mehrzahl f; **~·i·ty** [plʊə'rælətɪ] Mehrheit f, Mehrzahl f; Vielzahl f.

plus [plʌs] **1.** prp. plus; **2.** adj. positiv; Plus...; **3.** Plus n; Mehr n.

plush [plʌʃ] Plüsch m.

ply [plaɪ] **1.** Lage f, Schicht f (Stoff, Sperrholz etc.); Strähne f (Garn etc.); fig. Neigung f; three-~ dreifach (Garn etc.); dreifach gewebt (Teppich); **2.** v/t. handhaben, umgehen mit; fig. j-n zusetzen, j-n überhäufen (with mit); v/i. regelmäßig fahren (between zwischen); **~·wood** ['plaɪwʊd] Sperrholz n.

pneu·mat·ic [nju:'mætɪk] (~ally) Luft...; pneumatisch; ~ (tyre) ⊕ Luftreifen m.

pneu·mo·ni·a ⚕ [nju:'məʊnjə] Lungenentzündung f.

poach[1] [pəʊtʃ] wildern.

poach[2] [~] pochieren; ~ed eggs n. verlorene Eier pl.

poach·er ['pəʊtʃə] Wilddieb m, Wilderer m.

pock ⚕ [pɒk] Pocke f, Blatter f.

pock·et ['pɒkɪt] **1.** (Hosen- etc.)Tasche f; ⚓ = air pocket; **2.** einstecken (a. fig.); Am. pol. Gesetzesvorlage nicht unterschreiben; **3.** Taschen...; **~·book** Notizbuch n; Brieftasche f; Am. Geldbeutel m; Am. Handtasche f; Taschenbuch n; ~ **cal·cu·la·tor**

Taschenrechner *m*; **~-knife** (*pl. -knives*) Taschenmesser *n*.

pod ♀ [pɒd] Hülse *f*, Schale *f*, Schote *f*.

po·em ['pəʊɪm] Gedicht *n*.

po·et ['pəʊɪt] Dichter *m*; **~ess** [\~ɪs] Dichterin *f*; **~ic** [pəʊ'etɪk] (\~ally), **~i·cal** □ [\~kl] dichterisch; **~ics** [\~ks] *sg.* Poetik *f*; **~ry** ['pəʊɪtrɪ] Dichtkunst *f*; Dichtung *f*; *coll.* Dichtungen *pl.*, Gedichte *pl.*

poi·gnan·cy ['pɔɪnənsɪ] Schärfe *f*; **~t** [\~t] scharf; *fig.* bitter; *fig.* ergreifend.

point [pɔɪnt] 1. Spitze *f*; *geogr.* Landspitze *f*; *gr.*, Å, *phys. etc.* Punkt *m*; Å (Dezimal)Punkt *m*, Komma *n*; *phys.* Grad *m* (*e-r Skala*); ♫ Kompaßstrich *m*; Auge *n* (*auf Spielkarten etc.*); Punkt *m*, Stelle *f*, Ort *m*; springender Punkt; Zweck *m*, Ziel *n*; Pointe *f*; *fig.* hervorstechende Eigenschaft; **~s** *pl.* Brt. ✿ Weiche *f*; **~ of view** Stand-, Gesichtspunkt *m*; *the ~ is that ...* die Sache ist die, daß ...; *make a ~ of s.th.* auf e-r Sache bestehen; *there is no ~ in doing es* hat keinen Zweck, zu tun; *in ~ of* hinsichtlich (*gen.*); *to the ~* zur Sache (gehörig); *off* o*d. beside the ~* nicht zur Sache (gehörig); *on the ~ of ger.* im Begriff zu *inf.*; *beat s.o. on ~s* j-n nach Punkten schlagen; *win o*d. *lose on ~s* nach Punkten gewinnen *od.* verlieren; *winner on ~s* Punktsieger *m*; 2. *v/t.* (zu)spitzen; *~ at Waffe etc.* richten *auf* (*acc.*); (*mit dem Finger*) zeigen *auf* (*acc.*); **~ out** zeigen; *fig.* hinweisen auf (*acc.*); *v/i. ~ at* deuten, weisen auf (*acc.*); **~ to** nach *e-r Richtung* weisen; hinweisen auf (*acc.*); **~ed** □ ['pɔɪntɪd] spitz(ig); Spitz...; *fig.* scharf; **~er** [\~ə] Zeiger *m*; Zeigestock *m*; *zo.* Vorstehhund *m*; **~less** [\~lɪs] stumpf; witzlos; zwecklos.

poise [pɔɪz] 1. Gleichgewicht *n*; (Körper-, Kopf)Haltung *f*; 2. *v/t.* im Gleichgewicht halten; *Kopf etc.* tragen, halten; *v/i.* schweben.

poi·son ['pɔɪzn] 1. Gift *n*; 2. vergiften; **~ous** □ [\~əs] giftig (*a. fig.*).

poke [pəʊk] 1. Stoß *m*, Puff *m*; F Faustschlag *m*; 2. *v/t.* stoßen, puffen; *Feuer* schüren; *~ fun at* sich über *j-n* lustig machen; *~ one's nose into everything* F s-e Nase überall hineinstecken; *v/i.* stoßen, stochern.

pok·er ['pəʊkə] Feuerhaken *m*.

pok·y ['pəʊkɪ] (*-ier, -iest*) eng; schäbig.

po·lar ['pəʊlə] polar; **~ bear** *zo.* Eisbär *m*.

Pole¹ [pəʊl] Pole *m*, Polin *f*.

pole² [\~] Pol *m*; Stange *f*; Mast *m*; Deichsel *f*; *Sport:* (Sprung)Stab *m*.

pole·cat *zo.* ['pəʊlkæt] Iltis *m*; *Am* Skunk *m*, Stinktier *n*.

po·lem·ic [pə'lemɪk], *a.* **~i·cal** □ [\~kl] polemisch.

pole-star ['pəʊlstɑ:] *ast.* Polarstern *m*; *fig.* Leitstern *m*.

pole-vault ['pəʊlvɔ:lt] 1. Stabhochsprung *m*; 2. stabhochspringen; **~er** [\~ə] Stabhochspringer *m*; **~ing** [\~ɪŋ] Stabhochspringen *n*, -sprung *m*.

po·lice [pə'li:s] 1. Polizei *f*; △ *nicht Police*; 2. überwachen; **~man** (*pl. -men*) Polizist *m*; **~of·fi·cer** Polizeibeamte(r) *m*, Polizist *m*; **~ sta·tion** Polizeiwache *f*, -revier *n*; **~wom·an** (*pl. -women*) Polizistin *f*.

pol·i·cy ['pɒlɪsɪ] Politik *f*; Taktik *f*; Klugheit *f*; (Versicherungs)Police *f*; *Am.* Zahlenlotto *n*.

po·li·o ♀ ['pəʊlɪəʊ] Polio *f*, Kinderlähmung *f*.

Pol·ish¹ ['pəʊlɪʃ] 1. polnisch; 2. *ling.* Polnisch *n*.

pol·ish² ['pɒlɪʃ] 1. Politur *f*; Schuhcreme *f*; *fig.* Schliff *m*; 2. polieren; *Schuhe* putzen; *fig.* verfeinern.

po·lite □ [pə'laɪt] (*~r, ~st*) artig, höflich; **~ness** [\~nɪs] Höflichkeit *f*.

pol·i·tic □ ['pɒlɪtɪk] diplomatisch; klug; **po·lit·i·cal** □ [pə'lɪtɪkl] politisch; staatlich, Staats...; **~ti·cian** [pɒlɪ'tɪʃn] Politiker *m*; **~tics** ['pɒlɪtɪks] *oft sg.* Politik *f*.

pol·ka ['pɒlkə] Polka *f*; **~ dot** Punktmuster *n* (*auf Stoff*).

poll [pəʊl] 1. Wählerliste *f*; Stimmenzählung *f*; Wahl *f*; Stimmenzahl *f*; (Ergebnis *n* e-r) (Meinungs)Umfrage *f*; 2. *v/t.* Wahlstimmen erhalten; *v/i.* wählen.

pol·len ♀ ['pɒlən] Blütenstaub *m*.

poll·ing ['pəʊlɪŋ] Wählen *n*, Wahl *f*; **~booth** Wahlkabine *f*, -zelle *f*; **~ dis·trict** Wahlbezirk *m*; **~ place** *Am.*, **~ station** *bsd.* Brt. Wahllokal *n*.

poll-tax ['pəʊltæks] Kopfsteuer *f*.

pol·lut·ant [pə'lu:tənt] Schadstoff *m*; **~lute** [\~t] be-, verschmutzen; verunreinigen; *eccl.* entweihen; **~lu·tion** [\~ʃn] Verunreinigung *f* (der (Luft-, Wasser-, Umwelt)Verschmutzung *f*.

po·lo ['pəʊləʊ] *Sport:* Polo *n*; **~·neck** Rollkragen(pullover) *m*.

pol|yp *zo.*, **⚕** ['pɒlɪp], **~·y·pus ⚕** [~əs] (*pl. -pi* [-paɪ], *-puses*) Polyp *m*.

pom·mel ['pʌml] **1.** (Degen-, Sattel)Knopf *m*; **2.** (*bsd. Brt. -ll-, Am. -l-*) = *pummel*.

pomp [pɒmp] Pomp *m*, Prunk *m*.

pom·pous □ ['pɒmpəs] pompös, prunkvoll; aufgeblasen; schwülstig.

pond [pɒnd] Teich *m*, Weiher *m*.

pon·der ['pɒndə] *v/t.* erwägen; *v/i.* nachdenken; **~·a·ble** [~rəbl] wägbar; **~·ous** □ [~rəs] schwer(fällig).

pon·tiff ['pɒntɪf] Hohepriester *m*; Papst *m*.

pon·toon [pɒn'tuːn] Ponton *m*; **~ bridge** Pontonbrücke *f*.

po·ny *zo.* ['pəʊnɪ] Pony *n*, kleines Pferd; *Am.* Mustang *m*, (halb)wildes Pferd.

poo·dle *zo.* ['puːdl] Pudel *m*.

pool [puːl] **1.** Teich *m*; Pfütze *f*, Lache *f*; (Schwimm)Becken *n*; Pool *m*; *Karten:* Gesamteinsatz *m*; *econ.* Ring *m*, Kartell *n*; *mst* ~**s** *pl.* (Fußball- *etc.*)Toto *n*, *m*; **~·room** *Am.* Billardspielhalle *f*; Wettannahmestelle *f*; **2.** *econ.* ein Kartell bilden; *Geld, Unternehmen etc.* zusammenlegen.

poop ⚓ [puːp] Heck *n*; *a.* ~ **deck** (erhöhtes) Achterdeck.

poor □ [pʊə] arm(selig); dürftig; schlecht; **~·ly** [pʊəlɪ] **1.** *adj.* kränklich, unpäßlich; **2.** *adv.* arm(selig), dürftig; **~·ness** [~nɪs] Armut *f*.

pop¹ [pɒp] **1.** Knall *m*; F Limo *f* (*Limonade*); **2.** (*-pp-*) ~ *in:* knallen lassen; *Am.* Mais rösten; schnell *wohin* tun *od.* stecken; *v/i.* knallen; *mit adv.* huschen; ~ *in* hereinplatzen (*Besuch*).

pop² [~] **1.** *a.* ~ *music* Schlagermusik *f*; Pop(musik *f*) *m*; **2.** volkstümlich, beliebt; Schlager...; Pop...; ~ *concert* Popkonzert *n*; ~ *singer* Schlagersänger(in); ~ *song* Schlager *m*.

pop³ *Am.* F [~] Paps *m*, Papa *m*; Opa *m* (*alter Herr*).

pop·corn ['pɒpkɔːn] Popcorn *n*, Puffmais *m*.

pope [pəʊp] *mst* ♀ Papst *m*.

pop-eyed F [pɒp'aɪd] glotzäugig.

pop·lar ['pɒplə] Pappel *f*.

pop·py ♀ ['pɒpɪ] Mohn *m*; **~·cock** F Quatsch *m*, dummes Zeug.

pop·u|lace ['pɒpjʊləs] *die* breite Masse, *das* Volk; *contp.* Pöbel *m*; **~·lar** □ [~ə] Volks...; volkstümlich, populär, beliebt; **~·lar·i·ty** [pɒpjʊ'lærətɪ] Popularität *f*, Beliebtheit *f*.

pop·u|late ['pɒpjʊleɪt] bevölkern, besiedeln; *mst pass.* bewohnen; **~·la·tion** [pɒpjʊ'leɪʃn] Bevölkerung *f*; **~·lous** □ ['pɒpjʊləs] dichtbesiedelt, -bevölkert.

porce·lain ['pɔːslɪn] Porzellan *n*.

porch [pɔːtʃ] Vorhalle *f*, Portal *n*, Vorbau *m*; *Am.* Veranda *f*.

por·cu·pine *zo.* ['pɔːkjʊpaɪn] Stachelschwein *n*.

pore [pɔː] **1.** Pore *f*; **2.** ~ *over et.* eifrig studieren.

pork [pɔːk] Schweinefleisch *n*; **~·y** F ['pɔːkɪ] **1.** (*-ier, -iest*) fett; dick; **2.** *Am.* = *porcupine*.

porn F [pɔːn] = *porno*.

por|no F ['pɔːnəʊ] **1.** (*pl. -nos*) Porno (-film *m*) *m*; **2.** Porno...; **~·nog·ra·phy** [pɔː'nɒgrəfɪ] Pornographie *f*.

po·rous □ ['pɔːrəs] porös.

por·poise *zo.* ['pɔːpəs] Tümmler *m*.

por·ridge ['pɒrɪdʒ] Haferbrei *m*.

port¹ [pɔːt] Hafen(stadt *f*) *m*.

port² ⚓ ⚓ (Lade)Luke *f*; ⚓, ✈ Bullauge *n*.

port³ ⚓, ✈ [~] Backbord *n*.

port⁴ [~] Portwein *m*.

por·ta·ble ['pɔːtəbl] tragbar.

por·tal ['pɔːtl] Portal *n*, Tor *n*.

por·tent ['pɔːtent] (Vor)Zeichen *n*, Omen *n*; Wunder *n*; **~·ten·tous** □ [pɔː'tentəs] unheilvoll; wunderbar.

por·ter ['pɔːtə] (Gepäck)Träger *m*; *bsd. Brt.* Pförtner *m*, Portier *m*; *Am.* ⬜ Schlafwagenschaffner *m*; Porter (-bier *n*) *m*, *n*.

port·hole ⚓, ✈ ['pɔːthəʊl] Bullauge *n*.

por·tion ['pɔːʃn] **1.** (An)Teil *m*; Portion *f* (*Essen*); Erbteil *n*; Aussteuer *f*; *fig.* Los *n*; **2.** ~ *out* aus-, verteilen (*among* unter *acc.*).

port·ly ['pɔːtlɪ] (*-ier, -iest*) korpulent.

por·trait ['pɔːtrɪt] Porträt *n*, Bild *n*.

por·tray [pɔː'treɪ] (ab)malen, porträtieren; schildern; **~·al** [~əl] Porträtieren *n*; Schilderung *f*.

pose [pəʊz] **1.** Pose *f*; Haltung *f*; **2.** aufstellen; *Problem, Frage* stellen, aufwerfen; posieren; Modell sitzen *od.* stehen; ~ *as* sich ausgeben als *od.* für.

P

posh F [pɒʃ] schick, piekfein.
po·si·tion [pə'zɪʃn] Position *f*, Lage *f*,
Stellung *f* (*a. fig.*); Stand *m*; *fig.*
Standpunkt *m*.
pos·i·tive ['pɒzətɪv] **1.** □ bestimmt,
ausdrücklich; feststehend, sicher;
unbedingt; positiv; bejahend; überzeugt; rechthaberisch; **2.** *phot.* Positiv *n*.
pos|sess [pə'zes] besitzen, haben; be-
herrschen; *fig.* erfüllen; ~ *o.s. of et.*
in Besitz nehmen; **~sessed** besessen; **~ses·sion** [~ʃn] Besitz *m*; *fig.*
Besessenheit *f*; **~ses·sive** *gr.* [~sɪv]
1. □ possessiv, besitzanzeigend; ~
case Genitiv *m*; **2.** Possessivprono-
men *n*, besitzanzeigendes Fürwort;
Genitiv *m*; **~ses·sor** [~sə] Besit-
zer(in).
pos·si·bil·i·ty [pɒsə'bɪlətɪ] Möglichkeit *f*; **~ble** ['pɒsəbl] möglich; **~bly**
[~lɪ] möglicherweise, vielleicht; *if I ~
can* wenn ich irgend kann.
post [pəʊst] **1.** Pfosten *m*; Posten *m*;
Stelle *f*, Amt *n*; *bsd. Brt.* Post *f*; ~
exchange Am. Einkaufsstelle *f*; **2.**
Plakat etc. anschlagen; aufstellen,
postieren; eintragen; *bsd. Brt.* Brief
etc. einstecken, abschicken, aufgeben; ~ *up j-n* informieren.
post- [pəʊst] nach..., Nach...
post·age ['pəʊstɪdʒ] Porto *n*; ~
stamp Briefmarke *f*.
post·al □ ['pəʊstl] **1.** postalisch,
Post...; ~ *order Brt.* Postanweisung
f; **2.** *a.* ~ *card Am.* Postkarte *f*.
post|bag *bsd. Brt.* ['pəʊstbæg] Post-
sack *m*, -beutel *m*; **~box** *bsd. Brt.*
Briefkasten *m*; **~card** Postkarte *f*; *a.
picture* ~ Ansichtskarte *f*; **~code**
Brt. Postleitzahl *f*.
post·er ['pəʊstə] Plakat *n*; Poster *n*,
m.
pos·te·ri·or [pɒ'stɪərɪə] **1.** □ später
(*to* als); hinter; **2.** *oft* **~s** *pl.* Hinterteil *n*.
pos·ter·i·ty [pɒ'sterətɪ] Nachwelt *f*;
Nachkommen(schaft *f*) *pl.*
post-free *bsd. Brt.* ['pəʊst'friː] porto-
frei.
post-grad·u·ate ['pəʊst'grædjʊət] **1.**
nach dem ersten akademischen
Grad; **2.** *j.*, der nach dem ersten
akademischen Grad weiterstudiert.
post-haste ['pəʊst'heɪst] schnell-
stens.
post·hu·mous □ ['pɒstjʊməs] nach-
geboren; post(h)um.

post|man *bsd. Brt.* ['pəʊstmən] (*pl.
-men*) Briefträger *m*; **~mark 1.**
Poststempel *m*; **2.** (ab)stempeln;
~mas·ter Postamtsvorsteher *m*; ~
of·fice Post(amt *n*) *f*; **~of·fice box**
Post(schließ)fach *n*; **~paid** porto-
frei.
post·pone [pəʊst'pəʊn] ver-, aufschieben; **~ment** [~mənt] Verschiebung *f*, Aufschub *m*.
post·script ['pəʊsskrɪpt] Postskrip-
tum *n*.
pos·ture ['pɒstʃə] **1.** (Körper)Hal-
tung *f*, Stellung *f*; **2.** posieren, sich in
Positur werfen.
post-war ['pəʊst'wɔː] Nachkriegs...
po·sy ['pəʊzɪ] Sträußchen *n*.
pot [pɒt] **1.** Topf *m*; Kanne *f*; Tiegel
m; F *Sport:* Pokal *m*; *sl.* Hasch *n*
(*Haschisch*); *sl.* Grass *n* (*Marihuana*); **2.** (*-tt-*) in e-n Topf tun; einlegen.
po·ta·to [pə'teɪtəʊ] (*pl. -toes*) Kartoffel *f*; *s. chip 1, crisp 3.*
pot-bel·ly ['pɒtbelɪ] Schmerbauch *m.*
po·ten|cy ['pəʊtənsɪ] Macht *f*; Stärke
f; *physiol.* Potenz *f*; **~t** [~t] mächtig;
stark; *physiol.* potent; **~tial** [pə-
'tenʃl] **1.** potentiell; möglich; **2.** Potential *n*; Leistungsfähigkeit *f*.
poth·er ['pɒðə] Aufregung *f*.
pot-herb ['pɒthɜːb] Küchenkraut *n*.
po·tion ['pəʊʃn] (Arznei-, Gift-,
Zauber)Trank *m*.
pot·ter¹ ['pɒtə]: ~ *about* herumwer-
keln.
pot·ter² [~] Töpfer(in); **~y** [~rɪ] Töp-
ferei *f*; Töpferware(n *pl.*) *f*.
pouch [paʊtʃ] Tasche *f*; Beutel *m* (*a.
zo.*); *anat.* Tränensack *m.*
poul·ter·er ['pəʊltərə] Geflügel-
händler *m.*
poul·tice ✠ ['pəʊltɪs] Packung *f*.
poul·try ['pəʊltrɪ] Geflügel *n*.
pounce [paʊns] **1.** Satz *m*, Sprung *m*;
Herabstoßen *n* (*e-s Raubvogels*); **2.**
sich stürzen, *Raubvogel:* herabstoßen (*on, upon* auf *acc.*).
pound¹ [paʊnd] Pfund *n* (*Gewicht*);
~ (*sterling*) Pfund *n* (*Sterling*) (*abbr.
£ = 100 pence*).
pound² [~] Tierheim *n*; Abstellplatz
m (für polizeilich abgeschleppte
Fahrzeuge).
pound³ [~] (zer)stoßen, stampfen;
hämmern, trommeln, schlagen.
-pound·er ['paʊndə] ...pfünder *m*.
pour [pɔː] *v/t.* gießen, schütten; ~ *out*

Getränk eingießen; *v/i.* strömen, rinnen.

pout [paʊt] 1. Schmollen *n*; 2. *v/t.* *Lippen* aufwerfen; *v/i.* schmollen.

pov·er·ty [ˈpɒvətɪ] Armut *f*; Mangel *m*.

pow·der [ˈpaʊdə] 1. Pulver *n*; Puder *m*; 2. pulverisieren; (sich) pudern; bestreuen; ~**box** Puderdose *f*; ~**room** Damentoilette *f*.

pow·er [ˈpaʊə] 1. Kraft *f*; Macht *f*; Gewalt *f*; ⚖ Vollmacht *f*; ⚡ Potenz *f*; *in* ~ an der Macht, im Amt; 2. ⊕ antreiben; *rocket*-~ed raketengetrieben; ~**-cur·rent** ⚡ Starkstrom *m*; ~ **cut** ⚡ Stromsperre *f*; Strom-, Netzausfall *m*; ~**ful** □ [~fl] mächtig; kräftig; wirksam; ~**less** □ [~lɪs] macht-, kraftlos; ~**plant** = *power-station*; ~ **pol·i·tics** *oft sg.* Machtpolitik *f*; ~**-sta·tion** Elektrizitäts-, Kraftwerk *n*.

pow·wow *Am.* F [ˈpaʊwaʊ] Versammlung *f*.

prac·ti|ca·ble □ [ˈpræktɪkəbl] durchführbar; begeh-, befahrbar (*Weg*); brauchbar; ~**cal** □ [~l] praktisch; tatsächlich; sachlich; ~ *joke* Streich *m*; ~**cal·ly** [~lɪ] so gut wie.

prac·tice, *Am. a.* **-tise** [ˈpræktɪs] 1. Praxis *f*; Übung *f*; Gewohnheit *f*; Brauch *m*; Praktik *f*; *it is common* ~ es ist allgemein üblich; *put into* ~ in die Praxis umsetzen; 2. *Am.* = *practise*.

prac·tise, *Am. a.* **-tice** [~] *v/t.* in die Praxis umsetzen; ausüben; betreiben; üben; *v/i.* (sich) üben; praktizieren; ~ *on*, ~ *upon j-s Schwäche* ausnutzen; ~**d** geübt (*in* in *dat.*) (*Person*).

prac·ti·tion·er [præk'tɪʃnə]: *general* ~ praktischer Arzt; *legal* ~ Rechtsanwalt *m*.

prai·rie [ˈpreərɪ] Grasebene *f*; Prärie *f* (*in Nordamerika*); ~**-schoo·ner** *Am.* Planwagen *m*.

praise [preɪz] 1. Lob *n*; 2. loben, preisen; ~**wor·thy** [ˈpreɪzwɜːðɪ] lobenswert.

pram *bsd. Brt.* F [præm] Kinderwagen *m*.

prance [prɑːns] sich bäumen, steigen; tänzeln (*Pferd*); (einher)stolzieren.

prank [præŋk] Streich *m*.

prate [preɪt] 1. Gefasel *n*, Geschwafel *n*; 2. faseln, schwafeln.

prat·tle [ˈprætl] 1. Geplapper *n*; 2. (*et. daher*)plappern.

prawn *zo.* [prɔːn] Garnele *f*.

pray [preɪ] beten; inständig (er)bitten; bitte!

prayer [preə] Gebet *n*; inständige Bitte; *oft* ~*s pl.* Andacht *f; the Lord's* ♀ das Vaterunser; ~**book** [ˈpreəbʊk] Gebetbuch *n*.

pre- [priː; prɪ] *zeitlich:* vor, vorher, früher als; *räumlich:* vor, davor.

preach [priːtʃ] predigen; ~**er** [ˈpriːtʃə] Prediger(in).

pre·am·ble [priːˈæmbl] Einleitung *f*.

pre·car·i·ous □ [prɪˈkeərɪəs] unsicher, bedenklich; gefährlich.

pre·cau·tion [prɪˈkɔːʃn] Vorkehrung *f*, Vorsicht(smaßregel, -smaßnahme) *f*; ~**a·ry** [~ʃnərɪ] vorbeugend.

pre|cede [priːˈsiːd] voraus-, vorangehen (*dat.*); ~**ce·dence**, ~**ce·den·cy** [~əns, ~sɪ] Vorrang *m*; ~**ce·dent** [ˈpresɪdənt] Präzedenzfall *m*.

pre·cept [ˈpriːsept] Grundsatz *m*.

pre·cinct [ˈpriːsɪŋkt] Bezirk *m*; *Am.* Wahlbezirk *m*, -kreis *m*; *Am.* (Polizei)Revier *n*; ~*s pl.* Umgebung *f*; Bereich *m*; Grenzen *pl.*; *pedestrian* ~ Fußgängerzone *f*.

pre·cious [ˈpreʃəs] 1. □ kostbar; edel (*Steine etc.*); F schön, nett, fein; 2. *adv.* F reichlich, herzlich.

pre·ci·pice [ˈpresɪpɪs] Abgrund *m*.

pre·cip·i|tate 1. [prɪˈsɪpɪteɪt] *v/t.* (hinab)stürzen; 🜍 (aus)fällen; *fig.* beschleunigen; *v/i.* 🜍 *meteor.* sich niederschlagen; 2. □ [~tət] überstürzt, hastig; 3. 🜍 [~] Niederschlag *m*; ~**ta·tion** [prɪsɪpɪˈteɪʃn] Sturz *m*; 🜍 Niederschlagen *n*; *meteor.* Niederschlag *m*; *fig.* Überstürzung *f*, Hast *f*; ~**tous** □ [prɪˈsɪpɪtəs] steil (abfallend), jäh.

pré·cis [ˈpreɪsiː] (*pl.* -*cis* [-siːz]) (gedrängte) Übersicht, Zusammenfassung *f*.

pre|cise □ [prɪˈsaɪs] genau; ~**ci·sion** [~ˈsɪʒn] Genauigkeit *f*; Präzision *f*.

pre·clude [prɪˈkluːd] ausschließen; *e-r Sache* vorbeugen; *j-n* hindern.

pre·co·cious □ [prɪˈkəʊʃəs] frühreif; altklug.

pre·con|ceived [ˈpriːkənˈsiːvd] vorgefaßt (*Meinung*); ~**cep·tion** [~ˈsepʃn] vorgefaßte Meinung.

pre·cur·sor [priːˈkɜːsə] Vorläufer(in).

pred·a·to·ry [ˈpredətərɪ] Raub...

pre·de·ces·sor ['priːdɪsesə] Vorgänger(in).

pre·des·ti·nate [priː'destɪneɪt] vorherbestimmen; ~**tined** auserwählt, vorherbestimmt.

pre·de·ter·mine ['priːdɪ'tɜːmɪn] vorher festsetzen; vorherbestimmen.

pre·dic·a·ment [prɪ'dɪkəmənt] mißliche Lage, Zwangslage f.

pred·i·cate 1. ['predɪkeɪt] behaupten; gründen, basieren (*on* auf *dat.*); **2.** *gr.* [~kət] Prädikat n, Satzaussage f.

pre·dict [prɪ'dɪkt] vorhersagen; ~**dic·tion** [~kʃn] Prophezeiung f.

pre·di·lec·tion [priːdɪ'lekʃn] Vorliebe f.

pre·dis·pose ['priːdɪ'spəʊz] *j-n* (im voraus) geneigt *od.* empfänglich machen (*to* für); ~**po·si·tion** [~pə'zɪʃn]: ~ *to* Neigung f zu; *bsd.* 🐾 Anfälligkeit f für.

pre·dom·i·nance [prɪ'dɒmɪnəns] Vorherrschaft f; Vormacht(stellung) f; *fig.* Übergewicht n; ~**nant** □ [~t] vorherrschend; ~**nate** [~eɪt] die Oberhand haben; vorherrschen.

pre·em·i·nent □ [priː'emɪnənt] hervorragend.

pre·emp·tion [priː'empʃn] Vorkauf(srecht n) m; ~**tive** [~tɪv] Vorkaufs...; ⚔ Präventiv...

pre·ex·ist ['priːɪg'zɪst] vorher dasein.

pre·fab F ['priːfæb] Fertighaus n.

pre·fab·ri·cate ['priː'fæbrɪkeɪt] vorfabrizieren.

pref·ace ['prefɪs] **1.** Vorrede f, Vorwort n, Einleitung f; **2.** einleiten.

pre·fect ['priːfekt] Präfekt m; *Schule: Brt.* Aufsichts-, Vertrauensschüler(in).

pre·fer [prɪ'fɜː] (-*rr*-) vorziehen, bevorzugen, lieber haben *od.* mögen *od.* tun; ⚖ *Klage* einreichen; befördern.

pref·e|ra·ble □ ['prefərəbl] (*to*) vorzuziehen(d) (*dat.*), besser (als); ~**ra·bly** [~lɪ] vorzugsweise, besser; ~**rence** [~əns] Vorliebe f; Vorzug m; ~**ren·tial** □ [prefə'renʃl] bevorzugt; Vorzugs...

pre·fer·ment [prɪ'fɜːmənt] Beförderung f.

pre·fix ['priːfɪks] Präfix n, Vorsilbe f.

preg·nan|cy ['pregnənsɪ] Schwangerschaft f; Trächtigkeit f (*Tier*); *fig.* Bedeutung(sgehalt m) f, Tragweite

f; ~**t** □ [~t] schwanger; trächtig (*Tier*); *fig.* ideenreich; *fig.* bedeutungsvoll; △ *nicht* **prägnant**.

pre·judge ['priː'dʒʌdʒ] im voraus *od.* vorschnell be- *od.* verurteilen.

prej·u|dice ['predʒʊdɪs] **1.** Voreingenommenheit f, Vorurteil n; Nachteil m, Schaden m; **2.** *j-n* (günstig *od.* ungünstig) beeinflussen, einnehmen (*in favour of* für; *against* gegen); benachteiligen; *e-r Sache* Abbruch tun; ~**d** (vor)eingenommen; ~**di·cial** □ [predʒʊ'dɪʃl] nachteilig.

pre·lim·i·na·ry [prɪ'lɪmɪnərɪ] **1.** □ vorläufig; einleitend; Vor...; **2.** Einleitung f; Vorbereitung f.

prel·ude ['preljuːd] Vorspiel n.

pre·ma·ture [premə'tjʊə] vorzeitig, verfrüht; *fig.* vorschnell.

pre·med·i·tate [priː'medɪteɪt] vorher überlegen; ~**d** vorsätzlich; ~**ta·tion** [priːmedɪ'teɪʃn] Vorbedacht m.

prem·i·er ['premjə] **1.** erste(r, -s); **2.** Premierminister m.

prem·is·es ['premɪsɪz] *pl.* Grundstück n, Gebäude n *od. pl.*, Anwesen n; Lokal n.

pre·mi·um ['priːmjəm] Prämie f; *econ.* Agio n; Versicherungsprämie f; *at a* ~ über pari; *fig.* sehr gefragt.

pre·mo·ni·tion [priːmə'nɪʃn] (Vor-) Warnung f; (Vor)Ahnung f.

pre·oc·cu·pied [priː'ɒkjʊpaɪd] gedankenverloren; ~**py** [~aɪ] ausschließlich beschäftigen; *j-n* (völlig) in Anspruch nehmen.

prep F [prep] = *preparation, preparatory school.*

prep·a·ra·tion [prepə'reɪʃn] Vorbereitung f; Zubereitung f; **pre·par·a·to·ry** □ [prɪ'pærətərɪ] vorbereitend; ~ (*school*) Vor(bereitungs)schule f.

pre·pare [prɪ'peə] *v/t.* vorbereiten; zurechtmachen; (zu)bereiten; (aus-) rüsten; *v/i.* sich vorbereiten, sich anschicken; ~**d** □ bereit.

pre·pay ['priː'peɪ] (-*paid*) vorausbezahlen; frankieren.

pre·pon·de·rance [prɪ'pɒndərəns] Übergewicht n; ~**rant** [~t] überwiegend; ~**rate** [~reɪt] überwiegen.

prep·o·si·tion *gr.* [prepə'zɪʃn] Präposition f, Verhältniswort n.

pre·pos·sess [priːpə'zes] einnehmen; ~**ing** □ [~ɪŋ] einnehmend, anziehend.

pre·pos·ter·ous [prɪ'pɒstərəs] absurd; lächerlich, grotesk.

pre·req·ui·site ['priː'rekwɪzɪt] Vorbedingung f, (Grund)Voraussetzung f.

pre·rog·a·tive [prɪ'rɒɡətɪv] Vorrecht n.

pres·age ['presɪdʒ] **1.** (böses) Vorzeichen; (Vor)Ahnung f; **2.** (vorher) ankündigen; prophezeien.

pre·scribe [prɪ'skraɪb] vorschreiben; ♣ verschreiben.

pre·scrip·tion [prɪ'skrɪpʃn] Vorschrift f, Verordnung f; ♣ Rezept n.

pres·ence ['prezns] Gegenwart f, Anwesenheit f; ~ of mind Geistesgegenwart f.

pres·ent¹ ['preznt] **1.** □ gegenwärtig; anwesend; vorhanden; jetzig; laufend (Jahr etc.); vorliegend (Fall etc.); ~ tense gr. Präsens n, Gegenwart f; **2.** Gegenwart f, gr. a. Präsens n; Geschenk n; at ~ jetzt; for the ~ vorläufig.

pre·sent² [prɪ'zent] (dar)bieten; thea., Film: bringen, zeigen; Rundfunk, TV: bringen, moderieren; vorlegen, (-)zeigen; j-n vorstellen; (über)reichen; (be)schenken.

pre·sen·ta·tion [prezən'teɪʃn] Schenkung f; Überreichung f; Geschenk n; Vorstellung f (Person); Schilderung f; thea., Film: Darbietung f; Rundfunk, TV: Moderation f; Einreichung (Gesuch); Vorlage f.

pres·ent-day [preznt'deɪ] heutig, gegenwärtig, modern.

pre·sen·ti·ment [prɪ'zentɪmənt] Vorgefühl n, (mst böse Vor)Ahnung f.

pres·ent·ly ['prezntlɪ] bald (darauf); Am. zur Zeit, jetzt.

pres·er·va·tion [prezə'veɪʃn] Bewahrung f, Schutz m, Erhaltung f (a. fig.); Konservierung f; Einmachen n, -kochen n; **pre·ser·va·tive** [prɪ'zɜːvətɪv] **1.** bewahrend; konservierend; **2.** Konservierungsmittel n.

pre·serve [prɪ'zɜːv] **1.** bewahren, behüten; erhalten; einmachen; Wild hegen; a. hunt. (Jagd)Revier n, (Jagd-, Fisch)Gehege n; fig. Reich n; mst ~s pl. das Eingemachte.

pre·side [prɪ'zaɪd] den Vorsitz führen (at, over bei).

pres·i·den·cy ['prezɪdənsɪ] Vorsitz m; Präsidentschaft f; **~·dent** [~t] Präsident(in); Vorsitzende(r m f); Rektor m; Am. econ. Direktor m.

press [pres] **1.** Druck m (a. fig.); (Wein- etc.)Presse f; Verlag m; Druck(en n) m; a. printing-~ Druckerpresse f; die Presse (Zeitungswesen); bsd. (Wäsche-)Schrank m; Bügeln n; Andrang m, (Menschen)Menge f; **2.** v/t. (aus)pressen; (zusammen)drücken; drücken auf (acc.); Kleider plätten, bügeln; (be)drängen; bestehen auf (dat.); aufdrängen (on dat.); be ~ed for time es eilig haben; v/i. pressen, drücken, plätten, bügeln; (sich) drängen; ~ for dringen od. drängen auf (acc.), fordern; ~ on (zügig) weitermachen; **~ a·gen·cy** Nachrichtenbüro n, Presseagentur f; **~ a·gent** Presseagent m; **~·but·ton** ⚡ ['presbʌtn] Druckknopf m; **~·ing** □ [~ɪŋ] dringend; **~·stud** Brt. Druckknopf m; **pres·sure** [~ʃə] Druck m (a. fig.); Bedrängnis f, Belastung f.

pres·tige [pre'stiːʒ] Prestige n.

pre·su·ma·ble □ [prɪ'zjuːməbl] vermutlich; **~me** [~'zjuːm] v/t. annehmen, vermuten, voraussetzen; sich et. herausnehmen; v/i. sich erdreisten; anmaßend sein; ~ on, ~ upon ausnutzen od. mißbrauchen (acc.).

pre·sump·tion [prɪ'zʌmpʃn] Vermutung f; Wahrscheinlichkeit f; Anmaßung f; **~·tive** □ [~tɪv] mutmaßlich; **~·tu·ous** □ [~tjʊəs] überheblich; vermessen.

pre·sup·pose ['priːsə'pəʊz] voraussetzen; **~·po·si·tion** ['priːsʌpə'zɪʃn] Voraussetzung f.

pre·tence, Am. **-tense** [prɪ'tens] Vortäuschung f; Vorwand m; Schein m, Verstellung f.

pre·tend [prɪ'tend] vorgeben; vortäuschen; heucheln; Anspruch erheben (to auf acc.); **~·ed** □ angeblich.

pre·ten·sion [prɪ'tenʃn] Anspruch m (to auf acc.); Anmaßung f.

pre·ter·it(e) gr. ['pretərɪt] Präteritum n, erste Vergangenheit.

pre·text ['priːtekst] Vorwand m.

pret·ty ['prɪtɪ] **1.** □ (-ier, -iest) hübsch; niedlich; nett; **2.** adv. ziemlich.

pre·vail [prɪ'veɪl] die Oberhand haben od. gewinnen; (vor)herrschen; maßgebend od. ausschlaggebend sein; ~ on od. upon s.o. to do s.th. j-n dazu bewegen, et. zu tun; **~·ing** □ [~ɪŋ] (vor)herrschend.

prev·a·lent □ ['prevələnt] (vor)herr-schend, weitverbreitet.

pre·var·i·cate [prɪ'værɪkeɪt] Ausflüchte machen.

pre|vent [prɪ'vent] verhindern, -hüten, *e-r Sache* vorbeugen; *j-n* hindern; **~·ven·tion** [~ʃn] Verhinderung *f*, Verhütung *f*; **~·ven·tive** □ [~tɪv] *bsd.* ♪ vorbeugend.

pre·view ['priː·vjuː] Vorschau *f*; Vorbesichtigung *f*.

pre·vi·ous □ ['priːvjəs] vorher-, vorausgehend, Vor...; voreilig; ~ *to* bevor, vor (*dat.*); ~ *knowledge* Vorkenntnisse *pl.*; **~·ly** [~lɪ] vorher, früher.

pre·war ['priː'wɔː] Vorkriegs...

prey [preɪ] **1.** Raub *m*, Beute *f*; *beast of* ~ Raubtier *n*; *bird of* ~ Raubvogel *m*; *be od. fall a* ~ *to* die Beute (*gen.*) werden; *fig.* geplagt werden von; **2.** ~ *on, ~ upon zo.* Jagd machen auf (*acc.*), fressen (*acc.*); *fig.* berauben (*acc.*), ausplündern (*acc*); *fig.* nagen *od.* zehren an (*dat.*).

price [praɪs] **1.** Preis *m*; Lohn *m*; **2.** *Waren* auszeichnen; den Preis festsetzen für; *fig.* bewerten, schätzen; **~·less** ['praɪslɪs] von unschätzbarem Wert, unbezahlbar.

prick [prɪk] **1.** Stich *m*, ∨ Schwanz *m* (*Penis*); ~*s of conscience* Gewissensbisse *pl.*; **2.** *v/t.* (durch)stechen; *fig.* peinigen; *a.* ~ *out Muster* ausstechen; ~ *up one's ears* die Ohren spitzen; *v/i.* stechen; **~·le** ['prɪkl] Stachel *m*, Dorn *m*; **~·ly** [~lɪ] (*-ier*, *-iest*) stach(e)lig.

pride [praɪd] **1.** Stolz *m*; Hochmut *m*; *take (a)* ~ *in* stolz sein auf (*acc.*); **2.** ~ *o.s. on od. upon* stolz sein auf (*acc.*).

priest [priːst] Priester *m*.

prig [prɪg] Tugendbold *m*, selbstgefälliger Mensch; Pedant *m*.

prim □ [prɪm] (*-mm-*) steif; prüde.

pri·ma·cy ['praɪməsɪ] Vorrang *m*, **~·ri·ly** [~rəlɪ] in erster Linie; **~·ry** □ [~rɪ] **1.** ursprünglich; hauptsächlich; primär; elementar; höchst; Erst..., Ur..., Anfangs...; Haupt...; **2.** *a.* ~ *election Am. pol.* Vorwahl *f*; **~·ry school** *Brt.* Grundschule *f*.

prime [praɪm] **1.** □ erste(r, -s), wichtigste(r, -s), Haupt...; erstklassig, vorzüglich; ~ *cost econ.* Selbstkosten *pl.*; ~ *minister* Premierminister *m*, Ministerpräsident *m*; ~ *num-*

ber ♪ Primzahl *f*; ~ *time TV* Hauptsendezeit *f*, beste Sendezeit; **2.** *fig.* Blüte(zeit) *f*; *das Beste*, höchste Vollkommenheit; **3.** *v/t.* vorbereiten; *Pumpe* anlassen; instruieren; *paint.* grundieren.

prim·er ['praɪmə] Fibel *f*, Elementarbuch *n*.

pri·m(a)e·val [praɪ'miːvl] uranfänglich, Ur...

prim·i·tive □ ['prɪmɪtɪv] erste(r, -s), ursprünglich, Ur...; primitiv.

prim·rose ♀ ['prɪmrəʊz] Primel *f*.

prince [prɪns] Fürst *m*; Prinz *m*; **prin·cess** [prɪn'ses, *attr.* 'prɪnses] Fürstin *f*; Prinzessin *f*.

prin·ci·pal ['prɪnsəpl] **1.** □ erste(r, -s), hauptsächlich, Haupt...; △ *nicht prinzipiell*; **2.** Hauptperson *f*; Vorsteher *m*; (Schul)Direktor *m*, Rektor *m*; Chef(in); ⅗ Haupttäter(in); *econ.* (Grund)Kapital *n*; **~·i·ty** [prɪnsɪ'pælətɪ] Fürstentum *n*.

prin·ci·ple ['prɪnsəpl] Prinzip *n*, Grundsatz *m*; *on* ~ grundsätzlich, aus Prinzip.

print [prɪnt] **1.** *print.* Druck *m* (*a. Schriftart*); Druckbuchstaben *pl.*; (Finger- *etc.*)Abdruck *m*; bedruckter Kattun, Druckstoff *m*; (Stahl-, Kupfer)Stich *m*; *phot.* Abzug *m*; Drucksache *f*, *bsd. Am.* Zeitung *f*; *in* ~ gedruckt; *out of* ~ vergriffen; **2.** (ab-, be)drucken; in Druckbuchstaben schreiben; *fig.* einprägen (*on dat.*); ~ (*off od. out*) *phot.* abziehen; *Computer:* ~ *out Computer:* ausdrucken; **~·out** *Computer:* Ausdruck *m*; **~·ed matter** ♪ Drucksache *f*; **~·er** ['prɪntə] (Buch- *etc.*)Drucker *m*.

print·ing ['prɪntɪŋ] Druck *m*; Drucken *n*; *phot.* Abziehen *n*, Kopieren *n*; **~·ink** Druckerschwärze *f*; **~·of·fice** (Buch)Druckerei *f*; **~·press** Druckerpresse *f*.

pri·or ['praɪə] **1.** früher, älter (*to* als); **2.** *adv.* ~ *to* vor (*dat.*); **3.** *eccl.* Prior *m*; **~·i·ty** [praɪ'ɒrɪtɪ] Priorität *f*; Vorrang *m*; *mot.* Vorfahrt(srecht *n*) *f*.

prise *bsd. Brt.* [praɪz] = *prize²*.

pris·m ['prɪzəm] Prisma *n*.

pris·on ['prɪzn] Gefängnis *n*; **~·er** [~ə] Gefangene(r *m*) *f*, Häftling *m*; *take s.o.* ~ j-n gefangennehmen.

pri·va·cy ['prɪvəsɪ] Zurückgezogenheit *f*; Privatleben *n*; Intim-, Privatsphäre *f*; Geheimhaltung *f*.

pri·vate ['praɪvɪt] **1.** □ privat, Privat...; persönlich; vertraulich; geheim; ~ *parts pl.* Geschlechtsteile *pl.*; **2.** ✕ gemeiner Soldat; *in* ~ privat, im Privatleben; unter vier Augen.

pri·va·tion [praɪ'veɪʃn] Not *f*, Entbehrung *f.*

priv·i·lege ['prɪvɪlɪdʒ] Privileg *n*; Vorrecht *n*; **~d** privilegiert.

priv·y □ ['prɪvɪ] (*-ier, -iest*): ~ *to* eingeweiht in (*acc.*); ♀ *Council* Staatsrat *m*; ♀ *Councillor* Geheimer Rat (*Person*); ♀ *Seal* Geheimsiegel *n.*

prize¹ [praɪz] **1.** (Sieges)Preis *m*, Prämie *f*, Auszeichnung *f*; (Lotterie-) Gewinn *m*; **2.** preisgekrönt; Preis...; ~*winner* Preisträger(in); **3.** (hoch-) schätzen.

prize², *bsd. Brt.* **prise** [praɪz] (auf-) stemmen; ~ *open* aufbrechen.

pro¹ [prəʊ] für; △ *nicht pro = per.*

pro² □ [~] *Sport:* Profi *m.*

pro- [prəʊ] (eintretend) für, pro..., ...freundlich.

prob·a·bil·i·ty [prɒbə'bɪlətɪ] Wahrscheinlichkeit *f*; **~ble** □ ['prɒbəbl] wahrscheinlich.

pro·ba·tion [prə'beɪʃn] Probe *f*, Probezeit *f*; ⚖ Bewährung(sfrist) *f*; ~ *officer* Bewährungshelfer(in).

probe [prəʊb] **1.** ⚕, ⊕ Sonde *f*; *fig.* Sondierung *f*; △ *nicht Probe; lunar* ~ Mondsonde *f*; **2.** sondieren, untersuchen; △ *nicht proben, probieren.*

prob·lem ['prɒbləm] Problem *n*; ♣ Aufgabe *f*; **~at·ic** [~ə'mætɪk] (~*ally*), **~at·i·cal** □ [~kl] problematisch, zweifelhaft.

pro·ce·dure [prə'siːdʒə] Verfahren *n*; Handlungsweise *f.*

pro·ceed [prə'siːd] weitergehen (*a. fig.*); sich begeben (*to* nach); fortfahren; vor sich gehen; vorgehen; *Brt. univ.* promovieren; ~ *from* kommen *od.* ausgehen *od.* herrühren von; ~ *to* schreiten *od.* übergehen zu, sich machen an (*acc.*); **~ing** Vorgehen *n*; Handlung *f*; **~s** *pl.* ⚖ Verfahren *n*, (Gerichts)Verhandlung(en *pl.*) *f*; (Tätigkeits)Bericht *m*; **~s** ['prəʊsiːdz] *pl.* Erlös *m*, Ertrag *m*, Gewinn *m.*

pro|cess ['prəʊses] **1.** Fortschreiten *n*, Fortgang *m*; Vorgang *m*; Verlauf *m* (*der Zeit*); Prozeß *m*, Verfahren *n*; △ *nicht* ⚖ Prozeß; *in* ~ im Gange; *in* ~ *of construction* im Bau (befindlich); **2.** ⊕ bearbeiten; ⚖ gerichtlich belangen; △ *nicht prozessieren;* **~·ces·sion** [prə'seʃn] Prozession *f*; **~·ces·sor** ['prəʊsesə] Prozessor *m.*

pro·claim [prə'kleɪm] proklamieren, erklären, ausrufen.

proc·la·ma·tion [prɒklə'meɪʃn] Proklamation *f*, Bekanntmachung *f*; Erklärung *f.*

pro·cliv·i·ty *fig.* [prə'klɪvətɪ] Neigung *f.*

pro·cras·ti·nate [prəʊ'kræstɪneɪt] zaudern.

pro·cre·ate ['prəʊkrɪeɪt] (er)zeugen.

proc·u·ra·tor ⚖ ['prɒkjʊəreɪtə] Bevollmächtigte(r) *m.*

pro·cure [prə'kjʊə] *v/t.* be-, verschaffen; *v/i.* Kuppelei betreiben.

prod [prɒd] **1.** Stich *m*, Stoß *m*; *fig.* Ansporn *m*; **2.** (-*dd-*) stechen, stoßen; *fig.* anstacheln, anspornen.

prod·i·gal ['prɒdɪgl] **1.** □ verschwenderisch; *the* ~ *son* der verlorene Sohn; **2.** Verschwender(in).

pro·di·gious □ [prə'dɪdʒəs] erstaunlich, ungeheuer; **prod·i·gy** ['prɒdɪdʒɪ] Wunder *n* (*Sache od. Person*); *child od. infant* ~ Wunderkind *n.*

prod·uce¹ ['prɒdjuːs] (Natur)Erzeugnis(se *pl.*) *n*, (Landes)Produkte *pl.*; Ertrag *m*; ⊕ Leistung *f*, Ausstoß *m.*

pro|duce² [prə'djuːs] produzieren; erzeugen, herstellen; hervorbringen; *Zinsen etc.* (ein)bringen; heraus-, hervorziehen; (vor)zeigen; *Beweis etc.* beibringen; *Gründe* vorbringen; ♣ *Linie* ziehen; *Film* produzieren; *fig.* hervorrufen, erzielen; **~·duc·er** [~] Erzeuger(in), Hersteller(in); *Film, TV:* Produzent(in); *thea., Rundfunk: Brt.* Regisseur(in).

prod·uct ['prɒdʌkt] Produkt *n*, Erzeugnis *n.*

pro·duc|tion [prə'dʌkʃn] Produktion *f*; Erzeugung *f*, Herstellung *f*; Erzeugnis *n*; Hervorbringen *n*; Vorlegung *f*, Beibringung *f*; *thea. etc.* Inszenierung *f*; **~·tive** □ [~tɪv] produktiv; ertragreich, fruchtbar; schöpferisch; **~·tive·ness** [~nɪs], **~·tiv·i·ty** [prɒdʌk'tɪvətɪ] Produktivität *f.*

prof F [prɒf] Professor *m.*

pro|fa·na·tion [prɒfə'neɪʃn] Entweihung *f*; **~·fane** [prə'feɪn] **1.** □ profan, weltlich; gottlos, lästerlich; **2.** entweihen; **~·fan·i·ty** [~'fænətɪ] Gottlosigkeit *f*; Fluchen *n.*

P

pro·fess [prə'fes] (sich) bekennen (zu); erklären; beteuern; *Reue etc.* bekunden; *Beruf* ausüben; lehren; **~fessed** □ erklärt; angeblich; Berufs...; **~fes·sion** [~ʃn] Bekenntnis *n*; Erklärung *f*; Beruf *m*; **~fes·sion·al** [~nl] **1.** □ Berufs...; Amts...; professionell; beruflich; fachmännisch; freiberuflich; **~** *man* Akademiker *m*; **2.** Fachmann *m*; *Sport:* Berufsspieler(in), -sportler(in), Profi *m*; Berufskünstler(in); **~fes·sor** [~sə] Professor(in); *Am.* Dozent(in).

prof·fer ['prɒfə] **1.** anbieten; **2.** Anerbieten *n*.

pro·fi·cien·cy [prə'fɪʃənsɪ] Tüchtigkeit *f*; **~t** [~t] □ tüchtig; bewandert.

pro·file ['prəʊfaɪl] Profil *n*.

prof·it ['prɒfɪt] **1.** Gewinn *m*, Profit *m*; Vorteil *m*, Nutzen *m*; **2.** *v/t.* j-m nützen; *v/i.* **~** *from od. by* Nutzen ziehen aus; **~i·ta·ble** □ [~əbl] nützlich, vorteilhaft; gewinnbringend, einträglich; **~i·teer** [prɒfɪ'tɪə] **1.** Schiebergeschäfte machen; **2.** Profitmacher *m*, Schieber *m*; **~it·shar·ing** ['prɒfɪtʃeərɪŋ] Gewinnbeteiligung *f*.

prof·li·gate ['prɒflɪɡət] lasterhaft; verschwenderisch.

pro·found □ [prə'faʊnd] tief; tiefgründig, gründlich, profund.

pro·fuse □ [prə'fjuːs] verschwenderisch; (über)reich; **~fu·sion** *fig.* [~ʒn] Überfluß *m*, (Über)Fülle *f*.

pro·gen·i·tor [prəʊ'dʒenɪtə] Vorfahr *m*, Ahn *m*; **prog·e·ny** ['prɒdʒənɪ] Nachkommen(schaft *f*) *pl.*; *zo.* Brut *f*.

prog·no·sis ♂ [prɒg'nəʊsɪs] (*pl.* -*ses* [~siːz]) Prognose *f*.

prog·nos·ti·ca·tion [prəgnɒstɪ'keɪʃn] Vorhersage *f*.

pro·gram ['prəʊɡræm] **1.** *Computer:* Programm *n*; *Am.* = *Brt. programme* 1; **2.** (-*mm*-) *Computer:* programmieren; *Am.* = *Brt. programme* 2; **~er** [~ə] = programmer.

pro|gramme, *Am.* **-gram** ['prəʊɡræm] **1.** Programm *n*; *Rundfunk, TV: a.* Sendung *f*; **2.** (vor)programmieren; planen; **~gram·mer** [~ə] *Computer:* Programmierer(in).

pro|gress 1. ['prəʊgres] Fortschritt(e *pl.*) *m*; Vorrücken *n* (*a.* ✕); Fortgang *m*; *in* **~** im Gang; **2.** [prə'gres] fortschreiten; **~gres·sion** [~ʃn] Fort-

schreiten *n*; Weiterentwicklung *f*; ✕ Reihe *f*; **~gres·sive** [~sɪv] **1.** □ fortschreitend; fortschrittlich; **2.** *pol.* Progressive(r *m*) *f*.

pro·hib·it [prə'hɪbɪt] verbieten; verhindern; **~hi·bi·tion** [prəʊɪ'bɪʃn] Verbot *n*; Prohibition *f*; **~hi·bi·tion·ist** [~ʃənɪst] Prohibitionist *m*; **~hib·i·tive** □ [prə'hɪbɪtɪv] verbietend; Schutz...; unerschwinglich (*Preis*).

pro·ject¹ ['prɒdʒekt] Projekt *n*; Vorhaben *n*, Plan *m*.

pro·ject² [prə'dʒekt] *v/t.* planen, entwerfen; werfen, schleudern; projizieren; *v/i.* vorspringen, -ragen; **~jec·tile** [~aɪl] Projektil *n*, Geschoß *n*; **~jec·tion** [~kʃn] Werfen *n*; Entwurf *m*; Vorsprung *m*, vorspringender Teil *m*; ✕, *phot.* Projektion *f*; **~jec·tor** [~tə] Projektor *m*.

pro·le·tar·i·an [prəʊlɪ'teərɪən] **1.** proletarisch; **2.** Proletarier(in).

pro·lif·ic [prə'lɪfɪk] (*~ally*) fruchtbar.

pro·logue, *Am. a.* **-log** ['prəʊlɒg] Prolog *m*.

pro·long [prə'lɒŋ] verlängern.

prom·e·nade [prɒmə'nɑːd] **1.** (Strand)Promenade *f*; **2.** promenieren.

prom·i·nent □ ['prɒmɪnənt] vorstehend, hervorragend (*a. fig.*); *fig.* prominent.

pro·mis·cu·ous □ [prə'mɪskjʊəs] unordentlich; verworren; sexuell freizügig.

prom·ise ['prɒmɪs] **1.** Versprechen *n*; *fig.* Aussicht *f*; **2.** versprechen; **~is·ing** [~ɪŋ] vielversprechend; **~is·so·ry** [~ərɪ] versprechend; **~** *note econ.* Eigenwechsel *m*.

prom·on·to·ry ['prɒməntrɪ] Vorgebirge *n*.

pro|mote [prə'məʊt] *et.* fördern; *j-n* befördern; *Am. Schule:* versetzen; *parl.* unterstützen; *econ.* gründen; *Verkauf durch Werbung* steigern; *econ.* werben für; *Boxkampf etc.* veranstalten; **~mot·er** [~ə] Förderer *m*, Befürworter *m*; *Sport:* Veranstalter *m*; **~mo·tion** [~əʊʃn] Förderung *f*; Beförderung *f*; *econ.* Gründung *f*; *econ.* Verkaufsförderung *f*, Werbung *f*; △ *nicht* Promotion.

prompt [prɒmpt] **1.** □ umgehend, unverzüglich, sofort; bereit(willig); pünktlich; **2.** *j-n* veranlassen; *Gedanken* eingeben; *j-m* vorsagen, soufflieren; **~er** ['prɒmptə] Souffleu|r m, -se f; **~ness** [∧nɪs] Schnelligkeit f; Bereitschaft f.

prom·ul·gate ['prɒməlgeɪt] verkünden; verbreiten.

prone □ [prəʊn] (~r, ~st) mit dem Gesicht nach unten (liegend); hingestreckt; *be ~ to fig.* neigen zu.

prong [prɒŋ] Zinke f; Spitze f.

pro·noun *gr.* ['prəʊnaʊn] Pronomen n, Fürwort n.

pro·nounce [prə'naʊns] aussprechen; verkünden; erklären für.

pron·to F ['prɒntəʊ] fix, schnell.

pro·nun·ci·a·tion [prən∧nsɪ'eɪ∫n] Aussprache f.

proof [pru:f] **1.** Beweis m; Probe f; *print.* Korrekturfahne f, -bogen m; *print., phot.* Probeabzug m; **2.** fest; *in Zssgn:* ...fest, ...beständig, ...dicht, ...sicher; ~ **read** ['pru:fri:d] (*-read* [-red]) Korrektur lesen; **~read·er** Korrektor m.

prop [prɒp] **1.** Stütze f (a. *fig.*); **2.** (*-pp-*) a. **~ up** stützen; *sich, et.* lehnen (*against* gegen).

prop·a·gate ['prɒpəgeɪt] (sich) fortpflanzen; verbreiten; **~ga·tion** [prɒpə'geɪ∫n] Fortpflanzung f; Verbreitung f.

pro·pel [prə'pel] (*-ll-*) (vorwärts-, an)treiben; **~ler** [∧ə] Propeller m, (Schiffs-, Luft)Schraube f; **~ling pen·cil** [∧lɪ'pensl] Drehbleistift m.

pro·pen·si·ty *fig.* [prə'pensətɪ] Neigung f.

prop·er □ ['prɒpə] eigen(tümlich); passend; richtig; anständig, korrekt; zuständig; *bsd. Brt.* F ordentlich, tüchtig, gehörig; Eigen...; ~ *name* Eigenname m; **~ty** [∧tɪ] Eigentum n, Besitz m; Vermögen n; Eigenschaft f.

proph·e·cy ['prɒfɪsɪ] Prophezeiung f; **~sy** [∧aɪ] prophezeien, weissagen.

proph·et ['prɒfɪt] Prophet m.

pro·pi·ti·ate [prə'pɪ∫ɪeɪt] günstig stimmen, versöhnen; **~tious** □ [∧∫əs] gnädig; günstig.

pro·por·tion [prə'pɔ:∫n] **1.** Verhältnis n; Gleichmaß n; (An)Teil m; ~s pl. (Aus)Maße pl.; **2.** in das richtige Verhältnis bringen; **~al** □ [∧l] proportional; **~ate** □ [∧nət] im richtigen Verhältnis (*to* zu), angemessen.

pro·pos·al [prə'pəʊzl] Vorschlag m, (a. Heirats)Antrag m; Angebot n; **~e**

[∧z] *v/t.* vorschlagen; beabsichtigen, vorhaben; e-n Toast ausbringen auf (*acc.*); ~ *s.o.'s health* auf j-s Gesundheit trinken; *v/i.* e-n Heiratsantrag machen (*to dat*); **prop·o·si·tion** [prɒpə'zɪ∫n] Vorschlag m, Antrag m; *econ.* Angebot n; Behauptung f.

pro·pound [prə'paʊnd] *Frage etc.* vorlegen; vorschlagen.

pro·pri·e·ta·ry [prə'praɪətərɪ] Eigentümer..., Besitzer...; *econ.* gesetzlich geschützt (*Arznei, Ware*); **~tor** [∧ə] Eigentümer m, Geschäftsinhaber m; **~ty** [∧ɪ] Richtigkeit f; Schicklichkeit f, Anstand m; *the proprieties pl.* die Anstandsformen pl.

pro·pul·sion ⊕ [prə'p∧l∫n] Antrieb m.

pro·rate *Am.* [prəʊ'reɪt] anteilmäßig auf- od. verteilen.

pro·sa·ic *fig.* [prəʊ'zeɪɪk] (~ally) prosaisch, nüchtern, trocken.

prose [prəʊz] Prosa f.

pros·e·cute ['prɒsɪkju:t] (a. strafrechtlich) verfolgen; *Gewerbe etc.* betreiben; ʦ anklagen (*for* wegen); **~·cu·tion** [prɒsɪ'kju:∫n] Durchführung f (*e-s Plans etc.*); Betreiben n (*e-s Gewerbes etc.*); ʦ Strafverfolgung f, Anklage f; **~cu·tor** ʦ ['prɒsɪkju:tə] Ankläger m; *public* ~ Staatsanwalt m.

pros·pect 1. ['prɒspekt] Aussicht f (a. *fig.*); *econ.* Interessent m; △ *nicht* Prospekt; **2.** [prə'spekt]: ~ *for* ⚒ schürfen nach; bohren nach (*Öl*).

pro·spec·tive □ [prə'spektɪv] (zu-)künftig, voraussichtlich.

pro·spec·tus [prə'spektəs] (*pl. -tuses*) (Werbe)Prospekt m.

pros·per ['prɒspə] *v/i.* Erfolg haben; gedeihen, blühen; *v/t.* begünstigen; segnen; **~i·ty** [prɒ'sperətɪ] Gedeihen n, Wohlstand m, Glück n; *econ.* Wohlstand m, Konjunktur f, Blüte (-zeit) f; **~ous** □ ['prɒspərəs] erfolgreich, blühend; wohlhabend; günstig.

pros·ti·tute ['prɒstɪtju:t] Prostituierte f, Dirne f; *male* ~ Strichjunge m.

pros|trate 1. ['prɒstreɪt] hingestreckt; erschöpft; daniederliegend; demütig; gebrochen; **2.** [prɒ'streɪt] niederwerfen; erschöpfen; *fig.* niederschmettern; **~tra·tion** [∧∫n] Niederwerfen n, Fußfall m; Erschöpfung f.

P

pros·y *fig.* [ˈprəʊzɪ] (*-ier*, *-iest*) prosaisch; langweilig.
pro·tag·o·nist [prəʊˈtægənɪst] *thea.* Hauptfigur *f*; *fig.* Vorkämpfer(in).
pro|tect [prəˈtekt] (be)schützen; **~·tec·tion** [~kʃn] Schutz *m*; ⚖ (Rechts)Schutz *m*; *econ.* Schutzzoll *m*; ⚠ *nicht Protektion*; **~·tec·tive** [~tɪv] (be)schützend; Schutz...; *~ duty* Schutzzoll *m*; **~·tec·tor** [~ə] (Be)Schützer *m*; Schutz-, Schirmherr *m*; **~·tec·tor·ate** [~ərət] Protektorat *n*.
pro·test 1. [ˈprəʊtest] Protest *m*; Einspruch *m*; **2.** [prəˈtest] *v/i.* protestieren (*against* gegen); *v/t. Am.* protestieren gegen; beteuern.
Prot·es·tant [ˈprɒtɪstənt] **1.** protestantisch; **2.** Protestant(in).
prot·es·ta·tion [prɒteˈsteɪʃn] Beteuerung *f*; Protest *m* (*against* gegen).
pro·to·col [ˈprəʊtəkɒl] **1.** Protokoll *n*; **2.** (*-ll-*) protokollieren.
pro·to·type [ˈprəʊtətaɪp] Prototyp *m*, Urbild *n*.
pro·tract [prəˈtrækt] in die Länge ziehen, hinziehen.
pro|trude [prəˈtru:d] heraus-, (her-) vorstehen, -ragen, -treten; herausstrecken; **~·tru·sion** [~ʒn] Herausragen *n*, (Her)Vorstehen *n*, Hervortreten *n*.
pro·tu·ber·ance [prəˈtju:bərəns] Auswuchs *m*, Beule *f*.
proud □ [praʊd] stolz (*of* auf *acc.*).
prove [pru:v] (*proved*, *proved od. bsd. Am. proven*) *v/t.* be-, er-, nachweisen; prüfen; *v/i.* sich herausstellen *od.* erweisen (als); ausfallen; **prov·en** [ˈpru:vən] **1.** *Am. p.p. von prove*; **2.** be-, erwiesen; bewährt.
prov·e·nance [ˈprɒvənəns] Herkunft *f*.
prov·erb [ˈprɒvɜ:b] Sprichwort *n*.
pro·vide [prəˈvaɪd] *v/t.* besorgen, beschaffen, liefern; bereitstellen; versorgen, ausstatten; ⚖ vorsehen, festsetzen; *v/i.* (vor)sorgen; *~d (that)* vorausgesetzt, daß; sofern.
prov·i|dence [ˈprɒvɪdəns] Vorsehung *f*; Voraussicht *f*, Vorsorge *f*; **~·dent** □ [~t] vorausblickend, vorsorglich; haushälterisch; **~·den·tial** □ [prɒvɪˈdenʃl] durch die (göttliche) Vorsehung bewirkt; glücklich, günstig.
pro·vid·er [prəˈvaɪdə] Ernährer *m* (*der Familie*); *econ.* Lieferant *m*.
prov·ince [ˈprɒvɪns] Provinz *f*; *fig.* Gebiet *n*; *fig.* Fach *n*, Aufgabenbereich *m*; **pro·vin·cial** [prəˈvɪnʃl] **1.** □ Provinz..., provinziell; kleinstädtisch; **2.** Provinzbewohner(in).
pro·vi·sion [prəˈvɪʒn] Beschaffung *f*; Vorsorge *f*; ⚖ Bestimmung *f*; Vorkehrung *f*, Maßnahme *f*; **~s** *pl.* (Lebensmittel)Vorrat *m*, Proviant *m*, Lebensmittel *pl.*; ⚠ *nicht Provision*; **~·al** □ [~l] provisorisch.
pro·vi·so [prəˈvaɪzəʊ] (*pl. -sos, Am. a. -soes*) Bedingung *f*, Vorbehalt *m*.
prov·o·ca·tion [prɒvəˈkeɪʃn] Herausforderung *f*; **pro·voc·a·tive** [prəˈvɒkətɪv] herausfordernd; aufreizend.
pro·voke [prəˈvəʊk] reizen; herausfordern; provozieren.
prov·ost [ˈprɒvəst] Rektor *m* (*gewisser Colleges*); *schott.* Bürgermeister *m*; ⚔ [prəˈvəʊ]: *~ marshal* Kommandeur *m* der Militärpolizei.
prow ⚓ [praʊ] Bug *m*.
prow·ess [ˈpraʊɪs] Tapferkeit *f*.
prowl [praʊl] **1.** *v/i. a. ~ about*, *~ around* herumstreichen; *v/t.* durchstreifen; **2.** Herumstreifen *n*; **~ car** *Am.* [ˈpraʊlkɑ:] (Funk)Streifenwagen *m*.
prox·im·i·ty [prɒkˈsɪmətɪ] Nähe *f*.
prox·y [ˈprɒksɪ] (Stell)Vertreter(in); (Stell)Vertretung *f*, Vollmacht *f*; *by ~* in Vertretung.
prude [pru:d] prüder Mensch; *be a ~* prüde sein.
pru|dence [ˈpru:dns] Klugheit *f*, Vernunft *f*; Vorsicht *f*; **~·dent** □ [~t] klug, vernünftig; vorsichtig.
prud|er·y [ˈpru:dərɪ] Prüderie *f*; **~·ish** □ [~ɪʃ] prüde, spröde.
prune [pru:n] **1.** Backpflaume *f*; **2.** ✂ beschneiden (*a. fig.*); *a. ~ away*, *~ off* wegschneiden.
pru·ri·ent □ [ˈprʊərɪənt] geil, lüstern.
pry[1] [praɪ] neugierig gucken *od.* sein; *~ about* herumschnüffeln; *~ into* s-e Nase stecken in (*acc.*).
pry[2] [~] = *prize*[2].
psalm [sɑ:m] Psalm *m*.
pseu·do- [ˈpsju:dəʊ] Pseudo..., falsch.
pseu·do·nym [ˈpsju:dənɪm] Pseudonym *n*, Deckname *m*.
psy·chi·a|trist [saɪˈkaɪətrɪst] Psychiater *m*; **~·try** [~ɪ] Psychiatrie *f*.

psy|chic ['saɪkɪk] (~ally), ~**chi·cal** □ [~kl] psychisch, seelisch.

psy|cho·log·i·cal □ [saɪkə'lɒdʒɪkl] psychologisch; ~**chol·o·gist** [saɪ'kɒlədʒɪst] Psychologe m, -in f; ~**chol·o·gy** [~ɪ] Psychologie f.

pub Brt. F [pʌb] Pub n, Kneipe f.

pu·ber·ty ['pjuːbətɪ] Pubertät f.

pu·bic anat. ['pjuːbɪk] Scham...; ~ **bone** Schambein n; ~ **hair** Schamhaare pl.

pub·lic ['pʌblɪk] **1.** □ öffentlich; staatlich, Staats...; allgemein bekannt; ~ **spirit** Gemein-, Bürgersinn m; **2.** Öffentlichkeit f; die Öffentlichkeit, das Publikum, die Leute; △ nicht Publikum = audience.

pub·li·can bsd. Brt. ['pʌblɪkən] Gastwirt m.

pub·li·ca·tion [pʌblɪ'keɪʃn] f; Bekanntmachung f; Veröffentlichung f; Verlagswerk n; monthly ~ Monatsschrift f.

pub·lic| con·ve·ni·ence Brt. ['pʌblɪk kən'viːnjəns] öffentliche Bedürfnisanstalt; ~ **health** öffentliches Gesundheitswesen; ~ **hol·i·day** gesetzlicher Feiertag; ~ **house** Brt. s. pub.

pub·lic·i·ty [pʌb'lɪsətɪ] Öffentlichkeit f; Reklame f, Werbung f.

pub·lic| li·bra·ry ['pʌblɪk 'laɪbrərɪ] Leihbücherei f; ~ **re·la·tions** pl. Public Relations pl., Öffentlichkeitsarbeit f; ~ **school** Brt. Public School f (exklusives Internat); Am. staatliche Schule.

pub·lish ['pʌblɪʃ] bekanntmachen; veröffentlichen; Buch etc. herausgeben, verlegen; ~**ing house** Verlag m; ~**er** [~ə] Herausgeber m, Verleger m; ~**s** pl. Verlag(sanstalt f) m.

puck·er ['pʌkə] **1.** kleine Falte; **2.** a. ~ **up** Lippen, Mund: (sich) verziehen od. spitzen; Stirn: (sich) runzeln; Falten bilden in (dat.) od. werfen.

pud·ding ['pʊdɪŋ] Pudding m; (feste) Süßspeise, Nachspeise f, -tisch m; (Art) Fleischpastete f; black ~ Blutwurst f; white ~ Preßsack m.

pud·dle ['pʌdl] Pfütze f.

pu·er·ile ['pjʊəraɪl] kindisch.

puff [pʌf] **1.** kurzer Atemzug, Schnaufer m; leichter Windstoß, Hauch m; Zug m (beim Rauchen); (Dampf-, Rauch)Wölkchen n; (Puder)Quaste f; **2.** (auf)blasen; pusten; paffen; schnauben, schnaufen, keuchen; ~ **out**, ~ **up** sich (auf)blähen; ~ed **eyes** geschwollene Augen; ~ed **sleeve** Puffärmel m; ~ **pas·try** ['pʌf 'peɪstrɪ] Blätterteiggebäck n; ~**y** [~ɪ] (-ier, -iest) böig; kurzatmig; geschwollen; aufgedunsen; bauschig.

pug zo. [pʌg] a. ~**dog** Mops m.

pug·na·cious □ [pʌg'neɪʃəs] kampflustig; streitsüchtig.

pug-nose ['pʌgnəʊz] Stupsnase f.

puke sl. [pjuːk] (aus)kotzen.

pull [pʊl] **1.** Ziehen n, Zerren n; Zug m; Ruck m; print. Fahne f, (Probe-) Abzug m; Ruderpartie f; Griff m; Zug m (at an e-r Zigarette etc.); Schluck m (at aus e-r Flasche); fig. Einfluß m, Beziehungen pl., Vorteil m; **2.** ziehen; zerren; reißen; zupfen; pflücken; rudern; ~ **about** herumzerren; ~ **ahead of** vorbeiziehen an (dat.), überholen (acc.) (Auto etc.); ~ **away** anfahren (Bus etc.); sich losreißen (from von); ~ **down** niederreißen; ~ **in** einfahren (Zug); anhalten (Fahrzeug, Boot); ~ **off** F zustande bringen, schaffen; ~ **out** herausfahren (of aus), abfahren (Zug etc.); ausscheren (Fahrzeug); fig. sich zurückziehen, aussteigen; ~ **over** (s-n Wagen) an die od. zur Seite fahren; ~ **round** Kranken durchbringen; durchkommen (Kranker); ~ **through** j-n durchbringen; ~ o.s. **together** sich zusammennehmen, sich zusammenreißen; ~ **up** Fahrzeug, Pferd anhalten; (an)halten; ~ **up with**, ~ **up to** j-n einholen.

pul·ley ⊕ ['pʊlɪ] Rolle f; Flaschenzug m; Riemenscheibe f.

pull-in Brt. ['pʊlɪn] Raststätte (bsd. a. für Fernfahrer); ~**o·ver** Pullover m; ~**up** Brt. = pull-in.

pulp [pʌlp] Brei m; Fruchtfleisch n; ⊕ Papierbrei m; ~ **magazine** Schundblatt n.

pul·pit ['pʊlpɪt] Kanzel f.

pulp·y □ ['pʌlpɪ] (-ier, -iest) breiig; fleischig.

pul·sate [pʌl'seɪt] pulsieren, schlagen; **pulse** [pʌls] Puls(schlag) m.

pul·ver·ize ['pʌlvəraɪz] v/t. pulverisieren; v/i. zu Staub werden.

pum·mel ['pʌml] (bsd. Brt. -ll-, Am. -l-) mit den Fäusten bearbeiten, verprügeln.

pump [pʌmp] **1.** Pumpe f; Pumps m; **2.** F j-n aushorchen, -fragen; ~ **up** Reifen etc. aufpumpen; ~ **at·tend·ant** Tankwart m.

pump·kin ♀ ['pʌmpkɪn] Kürbis *m*.
pun [pʌn] 1. Wortspiel *n*; 2. (*-nn-*) ein Wortspiel machen.
Punch¹ [pʌntʃ] Kasperle *n*, *m*; ~-and-Judy show Kasperletheater *n*.
punch² [~] 1. Locheisen *n*; Locher *m*; Lochzange *f*; (Faust)Schlag *m*; Punsch *m*; 2. aus)stanzen; lochen; aufnehmen (*auf Lochkarten*); *bsd.* Am. Kontrolluhr stechen, Karte stempeln; schlagen (*mit der Faust*), boxen; (ein)hämmern auf (*acc.*); Am. Rinder treiben; ~(ed) card Lochkarte *f*; ~(ed) tape Lochstreifen *m*.
punc·til·i·ous □ [pʌŋk'tɪlɪəs] peinlich genau; (übertrieben) förmlich.
punc·tu·al □ ['pʌŋktjʊəl] pünktlich; ~·i·ty [pʌŋktjʊ'ælɪtɪ] Pünktlichkeit *f*.
punc·tu|ate *gr.* ['pʌŋktjʊeɪt] interpunktieren; ~·a·tion *gr.* [pʌŋktjʊ'eɪʃn] Interpunktion *f*, Zeichensetzung *f*; ~ mark Satzzeichen *n*.
punc·ture ['pʌŋktʃə] 1. (Ein)Stich *m*, Loch *n*; Reifenpanne *f*; 2. durchstechen; ein Loch machen in (*dat. od. acc.*); platzen (*Ballon*); *mot.* e-n Platten haben.
pun·gen|cy ['pʌndʒənsɪ] Schärfe *f*; ~t [~t] stechend, beißend, scharf.
pun·ish ['pʌnɪʃ] (be)strafen; ~·a·ble □ [~əbl] strafbar; ~·ment [~mənt] Strafe *f*; Bestrafung *f*.
punk [pʌŋk] *sl.* kleiner *od.* junger Ganove; Punk *m* (*a. ♪*), Punker *m*; ~ rock(er) ♪ Punkrock(er) *m*.
pu|ny □ ['pjuːnɪ] (-*ier*, -*iest*) winzig; schwächlich.
pup *zo.* [pʌp] Welpe *m*, junger Hund.
pu·pa *zo.* ['pjuːpə] (*pl.* -*pae* [-piː], -*pas*) Puppe *f*.
pu·pil ['pjuːpl] *anat.* Pupille *f*; Schüler(in); Mündel *m*, *n*.
pup·pet ['pʌpɪt] Marionette *f* (*a. fig.*); △ *nicht Puppe* = *doll*; ~·show Puppenspiel *n*.
pup·py ['pʌpɪ] *zo.* Welpe *m*, junger Hund; *fig.* Schnösel *m*.
pur|chase ['pɜːtʃəs] 1. (An-, Ein)Kauf *m*; ⚖ Erwerb(ung *f*) *m*; Anschaffung *f*; ⊕ Hebevorrichtung *f*; Halt *m*; make ~s Einkäufe machen; 2. (er)kaufen; ⚖ erwerben; ⊕ hochwinden; ~·chas·er [~ə] Käufer(in).
pure □ [pjʊə] (~*r*, ~*st*) rein; pur; ~bred ['pjʊəbred] reinrassig.
pur·ga|tive ♂ ['pɜːgətɪv] 1. abfüh-

rend; 2. Abführmittel *n*; ~·to·ry [~ərɪ] Fegefeuer *n*.
purge [pɜːdʒ] 1. ♂ Abführmittel *n*; *pol.* Säuberung *f*; 2. *mst fig.* reinigen; *pol.* säubern; ♂ abführen.
pu·ri·fy ['pjʊərɪfaɪ] reinigen; läutern.
pu·ri·tan ['pjʊərɪtən] (*hist.* ♀) 1. Puritaner(in); 2. puritanisch.
pu·ri·ty ['pjʊərətɪ] Reinheit *f* (*a. fig.*).
purl [pɜːl] murmeln (*Bach*).
pur·lieus ['pɜːljuːz] *pl.* Umgebung *f*.
pur·loin [pɜː'lɔɪn] entwenden.
pur·ple ['pɜːpl] 1. purpurn, purpurrot; 2. Purpur *m*; 3. (sich) purpurn färben.
pur·port ['pɜːpət] 1. Sinn *m*, Inhalt *m*; 2. behaupten, vorgeben.
pur·pose ['pɜːpəs] 1. Absicht *f*, Vorhaben *n*; Zweck *m*; Entschlußkraft *f*; for the ~ of *ger.* um zu *inf.*; on ~ absichtlich; to the ~ zweckdienlich; to no ~ vergebens; 2. beabsichtigen, vorhaben; ~·ful □ [~fl] zweckmäßig; absichtlich; zielbewußt; ~·less □ [~lɪs] zwecklos; ziellos; ~·ly [~lɪ] absichtlich.
purr [pɜː] schnurren (*Katze*); summen (*Motor*).
purse [pɜːs] 1. Geldbeutel *m*, -börse *f*; *Am.* (Damen)Handtasche *f*; Geldgeschenk *n*; Siegprämie *f*; *Boxen:* Börse *f*; 2. ~ (*up*) one's lips die Lippen schürzen.
pur·su|ance [pə'sjuːəns]: in (the) ~ of bei der Ausführung *od.* Ausübung (*gen.*); ~·ant □ [~t]: ~ to gemäß *od.* entsprechend (*dat.*).
pur|sue [pə'sjuː] verfolgen (*a. fig.*); streben nach; *Beruf* nachgehen; *Studium* betreiben; fortsetzen, -fahren in (*dat.*); ~·su·er [~ə] Verfolger (-in); ~·suit [~t] Verfolgung *f*; *mst* ~s *pl.* Beschäftigung *f*.
pur·vey [pə'veɪ] *Lebensmittel* liefern; ~·or [~ə] Lieferant *m*.
pus [pʌs] Eiter *m*.
push [pʊʃ] 1. (An-, Vor)Stoß *m*; Schub *m*; Druck *m*; Notfall *m*; Anstrengung *f*, Bemühung *f*; F Schwung *m*, Energie *f*, Tatkraft *f*; 2. stoßen; schieben; drängen; *Knopf* drücken; (an)treiben; *a.* ~ through durchführen; *Anspruch* etc. durchsetzen; F verkaufen, *Rauschgift* pushen; ~ s.th. on s.o. j-m et. aufdrängen; ~ one's way sich durch- *od.* vordrängen; ~ along, ~ on, ~ forward

weitermachen, -gehen, -fahren *etc.*; **~but·ton** ⊕ ['pʊʃbʌtn] Druckknopf *m*, -taste *f*; **~chair** *Brt.* (Falt)Sportwagen *m* (*für Kinder*); **~er** F [~ə] Pusher *m* (*Rauschgifthändler*); **~o·ver** Kinderspiel *n*, Kleinigkeit *f*; *be a ~ for* auf *j*-n *od. et.* hereinfallen.

pu·sil·lan·i·mous □ [pju:sɪˈlænɪməs] kleinmütig.

puss [pʊs] Mieze *f*, Kätzchen *n*, Katze *f* (*alle a. fig.* = *Mädchen*); **pus·sy** ['pʊsɪ], *a.* **~cat** Mieze *f*, Kätzchen *n*; **pus·sy·foot** F leisetreten, sich nicht festlegen.

put [pʊt] (*-tt-*; *put*) *v/t.* setzen, legen, stellen, stecken, tun; bringen (*ins Bett*); verwenden; *Frage* stellen, vorlegen; *Sport: Kugel* stoßen; werfen; ausdrücken, sagen; *~ to school* zur Schule schicken; *~ s.o. to work* *j*-n an die Arbeit setzen; *~ about* Gerüchte verbreiten; ⚓ den Kurs (*e-s Schiffes*) ändern; *~ across* Idee *etc.* an den Mann bringen, verkaufen; *~ back* zurückstellen (*a. Uhr*), -tun; *fig.* aufhalten; *~ by* Geld zurücklegen; *~ down v/t.* hin-, niederlegen, -setzen, -stellen; *j*-n absetzen, aussteigen lassen; (auf-, nieder-) schreiben; eintragen; eintragen (*to dat.*); *Aufstand* niederschlagen; *Mißstand* unterdrücken; (*a. v/i.*) ✈ landen, aufsetzen; *~ forth* Kräfte aufbieten; *Knospen etc.* treiben; *~ forward* Uhr vorstellen; *Meinung etc.* vorbringen; *~ o.s. forward* sich bemerkbar machen; *~ in v/t.* hereinhineinlegen, -setzen, -stellen, -stecken; hineintun; *Anspruch* erheben; *Gesuch* einreichen; *Urkunde* vorlegen; *Antrag* stellen; *j*-n einstellen; *Bemerkung* einwerfen; *v/i.* einkehren (*at* in *dat.*); ⚓ einlaufen (*at* in *dat.*); *~ off v/t. Kleider* ablegen (*a. fig.*); aufverschieben; vertrösten; *j*-n abbringen; hindern; *Passagiere* aussteigen lassen; *v/i.* ⚓ auslaufen; *~ on Kleider* anziehen, *Hut, Brille* aufsetzen; *Uhr* vorstellen; *Tempo* beschleunigen; an-, einschalten; vortäuschen, -spie-

len; *~ on airs* sich aufspielen; *~ on weight* zunehmen; *~ out v/t.* ausmachen, (-)löschen; verrenken; (her-) ausstrecken; verwirren; ärgern; *j*-m Ungelegenheiten bereiten; *Kraft* aufbieten; *Geld* ausleihen; *v/i.* ⚓ auslaufen; *~ right* in Ordnung bringen; *~ through teleph.* verbinden (*to* mit); *~ together* zusammensetzen; zusammenstellen; *~ up v/t.* hinauflegen, -stellen; hochheben, -schieben, -ziehen; *Bild etc.* aufhängen; *Haar* hochstecken; *Schirm* aufspannen; *Zelt etc.* aufstellen; errichten, bauen; *Ware* anbieten; *Preis* erhöhen; *Widerstand* leisten; *Kampf* liefern; *Gäste* unterbringen, (bei sich) aufnehmen; *Bekanntmachung* anschlagen; *v/i.* ~ *up at* einkehren *od.* absteigen in (*dat.*); *~ up for* kandidieren für, sich bewerben um; *~ up with* sich gefallen lassen, sich abfinden mit.

pu·tre·fy ['pju:trɪfaɪ] verwesen.

pu·trid □ ['pju:trɪd] faul, verfault, -west; *sl.* scheußlich, saumäßig; **~i·ty** [pju:ˈtrɪdətɪ] Fäulnis *f*.

put·ty ['pʌtɪ] **1.** Kitt *m*; **2.** kitten.

put-you-up *Brt.* F ['pʊtjuːʌp] Schlafcouch *f*, -sessel *m*.

puz·zle ['pʌzl] **1.** Rätsel *n*; schwierige Aufgabe; Verwirrung *f*; Geduld(s)-spiel *n*; **2.** *v/t.* verwirren; *j*-m Kopfzerbrechen machen; *~ out* austüfteln; *v/i.* verwirrt sein; sich den Kopf zerbrechen; **~head·ed** konfus.

pyg·my ['pɪɡmɪ] Pygmäe *m*; Zwerg *m*; *attr.* zwergenhaft.

py·ja·ma *Brt.* [pəˈdʒɑːmə] Schlafanzugs..., Pyjama...; **~s** *Brt.* [~əz] *pl.* Schlafanzug *m*, Pyjama *m*.

py·lon ['paɪlən] (Leitungs)Mast *m*.

pyr·a·mid ['pɪrəmɪd] Pyramide *f*.

pyre ['paɪə] Scheiterhaufen *m*.

Py·thag·o·re·an [paɪθæɡəˈrɪən] **1.** pythagoreisch; **2.** Pythagoreer *m*.

py·thon *zo.* ['paɪθn] Pythonschlange *f*.

pyx *eccl.* [pɪks] Hostienbehälter *m*.

Q

quack¹ [kwæk] **1.** Quaken n; **2.** quaken.

quack² [~] **1.** Scharlatan m; a. ~ doctor Quacksalber m, Kurpfuscher m; **2.** quacksalberisch; **3.** quacksalbern (an dat.); **~·er·y** ['kwækərɪ] Quacksalberei f.

quad·ran|gle ['kwɒdræŋgl] Viereck n; viereckiger Innenhof (e-s College); **~·gu·lar** □ [kwɒ'dræŋgjʊlə] viereckig.

quad·ren·ni·al □ [kwɒ'drenɪəl] vierjährig; vierjährlich (wiederkehrend).

quad·ru|ped ['kwɒdrʊped] Vierfüß(l)er m; **~·ple** [~pl] **1.** □ vierfach; Vierer...; **2.** (sich) vervierfachen; **~·plets** [~plɪts] pl. Vierlinge pl.

quag·mire ['kwægmaɪə] Sumpf(land n) m, Moor n; Morast m.

quail¹ zo. [kweɪl] Wachtel f.

quail² [~] verzagen; (vor Angst) zittern (before vor dat.; at bei).

quaint □ [kweɪnt] anheimelnd, malerisch; wunderlich, drollig.

quake [kweɪk] **1.** zittern, beben (with, for vor dat.); **2.** F Erdbeben n.

Quak·er ['kweɪkə] Quäker m.

qual·i|fi·ca·tion [kwɒlɪfɪ'keɪʃn] Qualifikation f, Eignung f, Befähigung f; Einschränkung f; gr. nähere Bestimmung; **~·fy** ['kwɒlɪfaɪ] (sich) qualifizieren; befähigen; bezeichnen; gr. näher bestimmen; einschränken; abschwächen, mildern; **~·ty** [~ɒtɪ] Eigenschaft f; Beschaffenheit f; econ. Qualität f.

qualm [kwɑːm] Übelkeit f; oft ~s pl. Skrupel m, Bedenken n; △ nicht Qualm.

quan·da·ry ['kwɒndərɪ] verzwickte Lage, Verlegenheit f.

quan·ti·ty ['kwɒntətɪ] Quantität f, Menge f; große Menge.

quan·tum ['kwɒntəm] (pl. -ta [-tə]) Quantum n, Menge f; phys. Quant n.

quar·an·tine ['kwɒrəntiːn] **1.** Quarantäne f; **2.** unter Quarantäne stellen.

quar|rel ['kwɒrəl] **1.** Streit m; **2.** (bsd. Brt. -ll-, Am. -l-) (sich) streiten; **~·some** □ [~səm] zänkisch, streitsüchtig.

quar·ry ['kwɒrɪ] **1.** Steinbruch m; hunt. (Jagd)Beute f; fig. Fundgrube f; **2.** Steine brechen.

quart [kwɔːt] Quart n (= 1,136 l).

quar·ter ['kwɔːtə] **1.** Viertel n, vierter Teil; Viertel(stunde f) n; Vierteljahr n, Quartal n; Viertelpfund n; Viertelzentner m; Am. Vierteldollar m (= 25 Cents); Sport: (Spiel)Viertel n; (bsd. Hinter)Viertel n (e-s Schlachttiers); (Stadt)Viertel n; (Himmels-, Wind)Richtung f; Gegend f, Richtung f; × Gnade f, Pardon m; ~s pl. Quartier n (a. ×); Unterkunft f; a ~ (of an hour) eine Viertelstunde; a ~ to (Am. of) od. a ~ past (Am. after) Uhrzeit: (ein) Viertel vor od. nach; at close ~s in od. aus nächster Nähe; from official ~s von amtlicher Seite; **2.** vierteln, in vier Teile teilen; beherbergen; × einquartieren; **~·back** American Football: wichtigster Spieler der Angriffsformation; **~·day** Quartalstag m; **~·deck** ⌖ Achterdeck n; **~·fi·nal** Sport: Viertelfinalspiel n; ~s pl. Viertelfinale n; **~·ly** [~lɪ] **1.** vierteljährlich; **2.** Vierteljahresschrift f; **~·mas·ter** × Quartiermeister m.

quar·tet(te) ♪ [kwɔː'tet] Quartett n.

quar·to ['kwɔːtəʊ] (pl. -tos) Quart (-format) n.

quartz min. [kwɔːts] Quarz m; ~ clock Quarzuhr f; ~ watch Quarzarmbanduhr f.

qua·si ['kweɪzaɪ] gleichsam, sozusagen; Quasi..., Schein...

qua·ver ['kweɪvə] **1.** Zittern n; ♪ Triller m; **2.** mit zitternder Stimme sprechen od. singen; ♪ trillern.

quay [kiː] Kai m.

quea·sy □ ['kwiːzɪ] (-ier, -iest) empfindlich (Magen, Gewissen); I feel ~ mir ist übel od. schlecht.

queen [kwiːn] Königin f (a. zo.); Karten, Schach: Dame f; sl. Schwule(r) m, Homo m; ~ bee Bienenkönigin f; **~·like** ['kwiːnlaɪk], **~·ly** [~lɪ] wie e-e Königin, königlich.

queer [kwɪə] sonderbar, seltsam; wunderlich; komisch; F schwul (homosexuell).

quench [kwentʃ] Flammen, Feuer (aus)löschen; Durst etc. löschen, stillen; Hoffnung zunichte machen.

quer·u·lous □ ['kwerʊləs] quengelig, mürrisch, verdrossen.

que·ry ['kwɪərɪ] **1.** Frage(zeichen n) f;

Zweifel *m*; **2.** (be)fragen; (be-, an-)zweifeln.

quest [kwest] **1.** Suche *f*; **2.** suchen (*for* nach).

ques·tion ['kwestʃən] **1.** Frage *f*; Problem *n*, (Streit)Frage *f*, (Streit-)Punkt *m*; Zweifel *m*; Sache *f*, Angelegenheit *f*; *beyond* (*all*) ~ ohne Frage; *in* ~ fraglich; *call in* ~ *et.* anbezweifeln; *that is out of the* ~ das kommt nicht in Frage; **2.** (be)fragen; ⚡ vernehmen, -hören; *et.* an-, bezweifeln; ~**·a·ble** □ [~əbl] fraglich; fragwürdig; ~**er** [~ə] Fragesteller (-in); ~ **mark** Fragezeichen *n*; ~**mas·ter** Brt. Quizmaster *m*; ~**naire** [kwestɪə'neə] Fragebogen *m*.

queue [kjuː] **1.** Reihe *f* (*von Personen etc.*), Schlange *f*; **2.** *mst* ~ *up* Schlange stehen; anstehen; sich anstellen.

quib·ble ['kwɪbl] **1.** Spitzfindigkeit *f*, Haarspalterei *f*; **2.** spitzfindig sein; ~ *with s.o. about od. over s.th.* sich mit j-m über et. herumstreiten.

quick [kwɪk] **1.** schnell, rasch; prompt; aufgeweckt, wach (*Verstand*); scharf (*Auge, Gehör*); lebhaft; hitzig, aufbrausend; *be* ~! mach schnell!; **2.** lebendes Fleisch; *cut* ~ *os. to the* ~ j-n tief verletzen; ~**·en** ['kwɪkən] anregen, beleben; (sich) beschleunigen; ~**freeze** (-*froze*, -*frozen*) einfrieren, tiefkühlen; ~**·ie** F [~ɪ] auf die schnelle gemachte Sache; kurze Sache; ~**·ly** [~lɪ] schnell, rasch; ~**·ness** [~nɪs] Schnelligkeit *f*; rasche Auffassungsgabe; Schärfe *f* (*des Auges etc.*); Lebhaftigkeit *f*; Hitzigkeit *f*; ~**·sand** Treibsand *m*; ~**·set hedge** *bsd. Brt.* lebende Hecke; Weißdornhecke *f*; ~**·sil·ver** Quecksilber *n*; ~**·wit·ted** geistesgegenwärtig; schlagfertig.

quid[1] [kwɪd] Priem *m* (*Kautabak*).

quid[2] *Brt. sl.* [~] (*pl.* ~) Pfund *n* (*Sterling*).

qui·es·cence [kwaɪ'esns] Ruhe *f*, Stille *f*; ~**·cent** □ [~t] ruhend; *fig.* ruhig, still.

qui·et ['kwaɪət] **1.** □ ruhig, still; *be* ~! sei still!; **2.** Ruhe *f*; *on the* ~ heimlich (, still u. leise); **3.** *bsd. Am.* = ~**·en** *bsd. Brt.* [~tn] *v/t.* beruhigen; *v/i. mst* ~ *down* sich beruhigen; ~**·ness** [~nɪs], **qui·e·tude** ['kwaɪɪtjuːd] Ruhe *f*, Stille *f*.

quill [kwɪl] *a.* ~**-feather** *zo.* (Schwung-, Schwanz)Feder *f*; *a.*

~**·pen** Federkiel *m*; *zo.* Stachel *m* (*des Stachelschweins*).

quilt [kwɪlt] **1.** Steppdecke *f*; **2.** steppen; wattieren.

quince ❧ [kwɪns] Quitte *f*.

quin·ine [kwɪ'niːn, *Am.* 'kwaɪnaɪn] Chinin *n*.

quin·quen·ni·al □ [[kwɪn'kwenɪəl] fünfjährig; fünfjährlich.

quin·sy ⚕ ['kwɪnzɪ] Mandelentzündung *f*.

quin·tal ['kwɪntl] Doppelzentner *m*.

quin·tes·sence [kwɪn'tesns] Quintessenz *f*; Inbegriff *m*.

quin·tu·ple ['kwɪntjʊpl] **1.** □ fünffach; **2.** (sich) verfünffachen; ~**·plets** [~lɪts] *pl.* Fünflinge *pl.*

quip [kwɪp] **1.** geistreiche Bemerkung; Stichelei *f*; **2.** (-*pp*-) witzeln, spötteln.

quirk [kwɜːk] Eigenart *f*, seltsame Angewohnheit; Laune *f* (*des Schicksals etc.*); *arch.* Hohlkehle *f*.

quit [kwɪt] **1.** (-*tt*-; *Brt.* ~*ted od.* ~, *Am. mst* ~) *v/t.* verlassen; *Stellung* aufgeben; aufhören mit; *v/i.* aufhören; weggehen; ausziehen (*Mieter*); *give notice to* ~ j-m kündigen; **2.** *pred. adj.* frei, los.

quite [kwaɪt] ganz, völlig, vollständig; ziemlich, recht; ganz, sehr, durchaus; ~ *nice* ganz *od.* recht nett; ~ (*so*!) ganz recht; ~ *the thing* F ganz große Mode; *she's a beauty* sie ist e-e wirkliche Schönheit.

quits *pred. adj.* [kwɪts]: *be* ~ *with s.o.* mit j-m quitt sein.

quit·ter F ['kwɪtə] Drückeberger *m*.

quiv·er[1] ['kwɪvə] zittern, beben.

quiv·er[2] [~] Köcher *m*.

quiz [kwɪz] **1.** (*pl. quizzes*) Prüfung *f*, Test *m*; Quiz *n*; **2.** (-*zz*-) ausfragen; j-n prüfen; ~**·mas·ter** *bsd. Am.* ['kwɪzmɑːstə] Quizmaster *m*; ~**·zi·cal** □ [~ɪkl] spöttisch; komisch.

quoit [kɔɪt] Wurfring *m*; ~*s sg.* Wurfringspiel *n.*

quo·rum ['kwɔːrəm] beschlußfähige Anzahl *od.* Mitgliederzahl.

quo·ta ['kwəʊtə] Quote *f*, Anteil *m*, Kontingent *n.*

quo·ta·tion [kwəʊ'teɪʃn] Anführung *f*, Zitat *n*; Beleg(stelle *f*) *m*; *econ.*: (Börsen-, Kurs)Notierung *f*; Preis (-angabe *f*) *m*; Kostenvoranschlag *m*; ~ **marks** *pl.* Anführungszeichen *pl.*

quote [kwəʊt] anführen, zitieren;

econ. Preis nennen, berechnen; *Börse:* notieren (*at* mit).

quoth *veraltet* [kwəʊθ]: ~ *I* sagte ich.

quo·tid·i·an [kwɒ'tɪdɪən] täglich.

quo·tient Ⱥ ['kwəʊʃnt] Quotient *m.*

R

rab·bi ['ræbaɪ] Rabbiner *m.*

rab·bit ['ræbɪt] Kaninchen *n.*

rab·ble ['ræbl] Pöbel *m,* Mob *m;* ~ **rous·er** [~ə] Aufrührer *m,* Demagoge *m;* ~**rous·ing** □ [~ɪŋ] aufwieglerisch, demagogisch.

rab·id □ ['ræbɪd] tollwütig (*Tier*); *fig.* wild, wütend.

ra·bies *vet.* ['reɪbiːz] Tollwut *f.*

rac·coon *zo.* [rə'kuːn] Waschbär *m.*

race¹ [reɪs] Rasse *f;* Geschlecht *n,* Stamm *m;* Volk *n,* Nation *f;* (Menschen)Schlag *m.*

race² [~] 1. Lauf *m* (*a. fig.*); (Wett-)Rennen *n;* Strömung *f;* ~s *pl.* Pferderennen *n;* 2. rennen; rasen; um die Wette laufen *od.* fahren (mit); ⊕ durchdrehen; ~**course** ['reɪskɔːs] Rennbahn *f,* -strecke *f;* ~**horse** Rennpferd *n;* **rac·er** ['reɪsə] Läufer (-in); Rennpferd *n;* Rennboot *n;* Rennwagen *m;* Rennrad *n.*

ra·cial □ ['reɪʃl] rassisch; Rassen...

rac·ing ['reɪsɪŋ] (Wett)Rennen *n;* (Pferde)Rennsport *m; attr.* Renn...

rack [ræk] 1. Gestell *n;* Kleiderständer *m;* Gepäcknetz *n;* Raufe *f,* Futtergestell *n;* Folter(bank) *f; go to* ~ *and ruin* verfallen (*Gebäude, Person*); dem Ruin entgegentreiben (*Land, Wirtschaft*); 2. strecken; foltern, quälen (*a. fig.*); ~ *one's brains* sich den Kopf zermartern.

rack·et ['rækɪt] 1. (*Tennis*)Schläger *m;* Lärm *m;* Trubel *m;* F Schwindel (-geschäft *n*) *m,* Gaunerei *f;* Strapaze *f;* 2. lärmen; sich amüsieren.

rack·e·teer [rækə'tɪə] Gauner *m,* Erpresser *m;* ~**ing** [~ərɪŋ] Gaunereien *pl,* Beutelschneiderei *f.*

ra·coon *Brt. zo.* [rə'kuːn] = *raccoon.*

rac·y [□ ['reɪsɪ] (-*ier, -iest*) kraftvoll, lebendig; stark; würzig; urwüchsig; gewagt.

ra·dar ['reɪdə] Radar(gerät) *n.*

ra·di·ance ['reɪdjəns] Strahlen *n,* strahlender Glanz (*a. fig.*); ~**ant** □ [~t] strahlend, leuchtend (*a. fig. with* vor *dat.*).

ra·di·ate ['reɪdɪeɪt] (aus)strahlen; strahlenförmig ausgehen; ~**a·tion** [reɪdɪ'eɪʃn] (Aus)Strahlung *f;* ~**a·tor** ['reɪdɪeɪtə] Heizkörper *m; mot.* Kühler *m.*

rad·i·cal ['rædɪkl] 1. □ ⚛, Ⱥ Wurzel...; Grund...; radikal, drastisch; eingewurzelt; *pol.* radikal; 2. *pol.* Radikale(r *m*) *f;* Ⱥ Wurzel *f;* ⚛ Radikal *n.*

ra·di·o ['reɪdɪəʊ] (*pl. -os*) 1. Radio (-apparat *m*) *n;* Funk(spruch) *m;* Funk...; ~ *play* Hörspiel *n;* ~ *set* Radiogerät *n; by* ~ über Funk; *on the* ~ im Radio; 2. funken; ~**ac·tive** radioaktiv; ~ *waste* Atommüll *m;* ~**ac·tiv·i·ty** Radioaktivität *f;* ~**ther·a·py** Strahlen-, Röntgentherapie *f.*

rad·ish ⚕ ['rædɪʃ] Rettich *m;* (*red*) ~ Radieschen *n.*

ra·di·us ['reɪdjəs] (*pl. -dii* [-dɪaɪ], *-uses*) Radius *m.*

raf·fle ['ræfl] 1. Tombola *f,* Verlosung *f;* 2. verlosen.

raft [rɑːft] 1. Floß *n;* 2. flößen; ~**er** ⊕ ['rɑːftə] (Dach)Sparren *m;* ~**s·man** (*pl. -men*) Flößer *m.*

rag¹ [ræg] Lumpen *m;* Fetzen *m;* Lappen *m; in* ~s zerlumpt; ~**and-bone man** *bsd. Brt.* Lumpensammler *m.*

rag² *sl.* [~] 1. Unfug *m;* Radau *m;* Schabernack *m;* 2. (*-gg-*) *j-n* aufziehen; *j-n* anschnauzen; *j-m* e-n Schabernack spielen; herumtollen; Radau machen.

rag·a·muf·fin ['rægəmʌfɪn] zerlumpter Kerl; Gassenjunge *m.*

rage [reɪdʒ] 1. Wut(anfall *m*) *f,* Zorn *m,* Raserei *f;* Wüten *n,* Toben *n* (*der Elemente etc.*); Sucht *f,* Gier *f* (*for* nach); Manie *f;* Ekstase *f; it is* (*all*)

the ~ es ist jetzt die große Mode; **2.**
wüten, rasen (*a. fig.*).

rag·ged □ ['rægɪd] rauh; zottig;
zackig; zerlumpt; ausgefranst.

raid [reɪd] **1.** (feindlicher) Überfall,
Streifzug *m*; (Luft)Angriff *m*; Razzia *f*; **2.** einbrechen in (*acc.*); überfallen; plündern.

rail¹ [reɪl] schimpfen.

rail² [~] **1.** Geländer *n*; Stange *f*; ⚓
Reling *f*; ⛟ Schiene *f*; (Eisen)Bahn
f; *by* ~ mit der Bahn; *off the* ~s *fig.*
aus dem Geleise, durcheinander;
verrückt; *run off (leave, jump) the* ~s
entgleisen; **2.** *a.* ~ *in* mit e-m Geländer umgeben; *a.* ~ *off* durch ein
Geländer (ab)trennen.

rail·ing ['reɪlɪŋ], *a.* ~*s pl.* Geländer *n.*

rail·ler·y ['reɪlərɪ] Neckerei *f*, Stichelei *f*.

rail·road *Am.* ['reɪlrəʊd] Eisenbahn
f.

rail·way *bsd. Brt.* ['reɪlweɪ] Eisenbahn *f*; ~·**man** (*pl.* -men) Eisen-
bahner *m*.

rain [reɪn] **1.** Regen *m*; ~s *pl.* Regenfälle *pl.*; *the* ~s *pl.* die Regenzeit (*in
den Tropen*); ~ *or shine* bei jedem
Wetter; **2.** regnen; *it never* ~s *but it
pours* es kommt immer gleich knüp-
peldick; ein Unglück kommt selten
allein; ~·**bow** ['reɪnbəʊ] Regenbo-
gen *m*; ~·**coat** Regenmantel *m*; ~·**fall**
Regenmenge *f*; ~·**proof 1.** regen-
wasserundurchlässig; imprägniert
(*Stoff*); **2.** Regenmantel *m*; ~·**y** □
['reɪnɪ] (-*ier*, -*iest*) regnerisch;
Regen...; *a* ~ *day fig.* Notzeiten *pl.*

raise [reɪz] *oft* ~ *up* (auf-, hoch-)
heben; (*oft fig.*) erheben; errichten;
erhöhen (*a. fig.*); *Geld etc.* aufbringen; *Anleihe* aufnehmen; *Familie*
gründen; *Kinder* aufziehen; (auf)er-
wecken; anstiften; züchten; ziehen;
Belagerung etc. aufheben.

rai·sin ['reɪzn] Rosine *f*.

rake [reɪk] **1.** Rechen *m*, Harke *f*;
Wüstling *m*; Lebemann *m*; **2.** *v/t.*
(glatt)harken, (-)rechen; *fig.* durch-
stöbern; *v/i.* ~ *about* (herum)stö-
bern; ~·**off** F ['reɪkɒf] (Gewinn)An-
teil *m*.

rak·ish □ ['reɪkɪʃ] schnittig; liederlich, ausschweifend; verwegen, keck.

ral·ly ['rælɪ] **1.** Sammeln *n*; Treffen *n*;
(Massen)Versammlung *f*; Kund-
gebung *f*; Erholung *f*; *mot.* Rallye *f*;
2. (sich ver)sammeln; sich erholen;

ram [ræm] **1.** *zo.* Widder *m*, Schaf-
bock *m*; ♈ *ast.* Widder *m*; ⊕, ⚓
Ramme *f*; **2.** (-*mm-*) (fest)rammen;
⚓ rammen; ~ *s.th. down s.o.'s
throat fig.* j-m et. eintrichtern.

ram|ble ['ræmbl] **1.** Streifzug *m*;
Wanderung *f*; **2.** umherstreifen; abschweifen; ~·**bler** [~ə] Wanderer *m*;
a. ~ *rose* ♣ Kletterrose *f*; ~·**bling**
[~ɪŋ] abschweifend; weitschwei-
fend; weitläufig.

ram·i·fy ['ræmɪfaɪ] (sich) verzweigen.

ramp [ræmp] Rampe *f*.

ram·pant □ ['ræmpənt] wuchernd;
fig. zügellos.

ram·part ['ræmpɑːt] Wall *m*.

ram·shack·le ['ræmʃækl] baufällig;
wack(e)lig; klapp(e)rig.

ran [ræn] *pret. von* run 1.

ranch [rɑːntʃ, *Am.* ræntʃ] Ranch *f*,
Viehfarm *f*; ~·**er** ['rɑːntʃə, *Am.*
'ræntʃə] Rancher *m*, Viehzüchter *m*;
Farmer *m*.

ran·cid □ ['rænsɪd] ranzig.

ran·co(u)r ['ræŋkə] Groll *m*, Haß *m*.

ran·dom ['rændəm] **1.** *at* ~ aufs Geratewohl, blindlings; **2.** ziel-, wahllos; zufällig; willkürlich.

rang [ræŋ] *pret. von* ring¹ 2.

range [reɪndʒ] **1.** Reihe *f*; (Berg-)
Kette *f*; *econ.* Kollektion *f*, Sortiment *n*; Herd *m*; Raum *m*; Umfang
m, Bereich *m*; Reichweite *f*; Schußweite *f*; Entfernung *f*; (ausgedehnte)
Fläche; Schießstand *m*; offenes
Weidegebiet; *at close* ~ aus nächster
Nähe; *within* ~ *of vision* in Sichtweite; *a wide* ~ *of* ... eine große
Auswahl an ...; **2.** *v/t.* (ein)reihen,
ordnen; *Gebiet etc.* durchstreifen;
v/i. in e-r Reihe *od.* Linie stehen;
(umher)streifen; sich erstrecken,
reichen; zählen, gehören (*among,
with* zu); ~ *from* ... *to* ..., ~ *between*
... *and* ... sich zwischen ... und ...
bewegen (*von Preisen etc*); **rang·er**
['reɪndʒə] Förster *m*; Aufseher *m* e-s
Forsts *od.* Parks; Angehörige(r) *m*
e-r berittenen Schutztruppe.

rank [ræŋk] **1.** Reihe *f*, Linie *f*; ✕
Glied *n*; Klasse *f*; Rang *m*, Stand *m*;
~*s pl.*, *the* ~ *and file* die Mannschaften *pl.*; *fig.* die gemeine Masse; **2.** *v/t.*
einreihen, (ein)ordnen; einstufen;
v/i. sich reihen, sich ordnen; gehören (*among, with* zu); e-n Rang *od.*
e-e Stelle einnehmen (*above* über

dat.); ~ *as* gelten als; **3.** üppig; ranzig; stinkend; scharf; kraß; △ *nicht rank* (= *slim, slender*).

ran·kle *fig.* ['ræŋkl] nagen, weh tun.

ran·sack ['rænsæk] durchwühlen, -stöbern, -suchen; ausrauben.

ran·som ['rænsəm] **1.** Lösegeld *n*; Auslösung *f*; **2.** loskaufen, auslösen.

rant [rænt] **1.** Schwulst *m*; **2.** Phrasen dreschen; mit Pathos vortragen.

rap¹ [ræp] **1.** Klaps *m*; Klopfen *n*; (**-pp-**) schlagen; pochen, klopfen.

rap² *fig.* [~] Heller *m*, Deut *m*.

ra·pa·cious □ [rə'peɪʃəs] habgierig; (raub)gierig; **~·ci·ty** [rə'pæsətɪ] Habgier *f*; (Raub)Gier *f*.

rape¹ [reɪp] **1.** Notzucht *f*, Vergewaltigung *f* (*a. fig.*); **2.** rauben; vergewaltigen.

rape² ♀ [~] Raps *m*.

rap·id ['ræpɪd] **1.** □ schnell, rasch, rapid(e); steil; **2.** ~*s pl.* Stromschnelle(n *pl.*) *f*; **ra·pid·i·ty** [rə'pɪdətɪ] Schnelligkeit *f*.

rap·proche·ment *pol.* ['ræ'prɒʃmɑ̃ː] Wiederannäherung *f*.

rapt □ [ræpt] entzückt; versunken; **rap·ture** ['ræptʃə] Entzücken *n*; *go into* ~ in Entzücken geraten.

rare □ [reə] (~*r*, ~*st*) selten; *phys.* dünn (*Luft*); halbgar, nicht durchgebraten (*Fleisch*); F ausgezeichnet, köstlich.

rare·bit ['reəbɪt]: *Welsh* ~ überbackener Käsetoast.

rar·e·fy ['reərɪfaɪ] (sich) verdünnen; **rar·i·ty** ['reərɪtɪ] Seltenheit *f*; Rarität *f*.

ras·cal ['rɑːskəl] Schuft *m*; *co.* Gauner *m*, Schlingel *m*; **~·ly** [~lɪ] schuftig; erbärmlich.

rash¹ □ [ræʃ] hastig, vorschnell; übereilt; unbesonnen; waghalsig; △ *nicht rash*.

rash² ♂ [~] (Haut)Ausschlag *m*.

rash·er ['ræʃə] Speckscheibe *f*.

rasp [rɑːsp] **1.** Raspel *f*; **2.** raspeln; kratzen; krächzen.

rasp·ber·ry ♀ ['rɑːzbərɪ] Himbeere *f*.

rat [ræt] *zo.* Ratte *f*; *pol.* Überläufer *m*; *smell a* ~ Lunte *od.* den Braten riechen; ~*s! sl.* Quatsch!

rate [reɪt] **1.** (Verhältnis)Ziffer *f*; Rate *f*; Verhältnis *n*; (Aus)Maß *n*; Satz *m*; Preis *m*, Gebühr *f*; Taxe *f*; (Gemeinde)Abgabe *f*, (Kommunal-)Steuer *f*; Grad *m*, Rang *m*, Klasse *f*; Geschwindigkeit *f*; *at any* ~ auf

jeden Fall; ~ *of exchange* (Umrechnungs-, Wechsel)Kurs *m*; ~ *of interest* Zinssatz *m*, -fuß *m*; **2.** (ein)schätzen; besteuern; △ *nicht raten*; ~ *among* rechnen, zählen zu (*dat.*).

ra·ther ['rɑːðə] eher, lieber; vielmehr; besser gesagt; ziemlich, fast; ~! F und ob!, allerdings!; *I had od. would* ~ (*not*) *go* ich möchte lieber (nicht) gehen.

rat·i·fy *pol.* ['rætɪfaɪ] ratifizieren.

rat·ing ['reɪtɪŋ] Schätzung *f*; Steuersatz *m*; ♣ Dienstgrad *m*; ♣ (Segel-)Klasse *f*; Matrose *m*; *TV* Einschaltquote *f*.

ra·ti·o ♣ ['reɪʃɪəʊ] (*pl.* **-os**) Verhältnis *n*.

ra·tion ['ræʃn] **1.** Ration *f*, Zuteilung *f*; **2.** rationieren.

ra·tion·al □ ['ræʃənl] vernunftgemäß; vernünftig; (*a.* ♣) rational; △ *nicht rationell*; **~·i·ty** [ræʃə'nælətɪ] Vernunft *f*; **~·ize** *econ.* ['ræʃnəlaɪz] rationalisieren.

rat race ['rætreɪs] harter (Konkurrenz)Kampf.

rat·tle ['rætl] **1.** Gerassel *n*; Geklapper *n*; Geplapper *n*; Klapper *f*; Röcheln *n*; **2.** rasseln (mit); klappern; rütteln; rattern; plappern; röcheln; ~ *off* herunterrasseln; **~·brain**, **~·pate** Hohl-, Wirrkopf *m*; Schwätzer(in); **~·snake** *zo.* Klapperschlange *f*; **~·trap** *fig.* Klapperkasten *m* (*Fahrzeug*).

rat·tling ['rætlɪŋ] **1.** *adj.* rasselnd; F schnell, flott; **2.** F *adv.* sehr, äußerst; ~ *good* prima.

rau·cous □ ['rɔːkəs] heiser, rauh.

rav·age ['rævɪdʒ] **1.** Verwüstung *f*; **2.** verwüsten; plündern.

rave [reɪv] rasen, toben; schwärmen (*about, of* von).

rav·el ['rævl] (*bsd. Brt.* **-ll-**, *Am.* **-l-**) *v/t.* verwickeln; ~ (*out*) auftrennen; *fig.* entwirren; *v/i. a.* ~ *out* ausfasern, aufgehen.

ra·ven *zo.* ['reɪvn] Rabe *m*.

rav·e·nous □ ['rævənəs] gefräßig; heißhungrig; gierig; raubgierig.

ra·vine [rə'viːn] Hohlweg *m*; Schlucht *f*; Klamm *f*.

rav·ings ['reɪvɪŋz] *pl.* irres Gerede; Delirien *pl.*

rav·ish ['rævɪʃ] entzücken; hinreißen; ~·ing □ [~ɪŋ] hinreißend, entzückend; ~·ment [~mənt] Entzükken *n*.

reason

raw □ [rɔː] roh; Roh...; wund; rauh (*Wetter*); ungefähr, unerfahren; **~boned** ['rɔːbəʊnd] knochig, hager; **hide** Rohleder *n*.

ray [reɪ] Strahl *m*; *fig.* Schimmer *m*.

ray·on ['reɪɒn] Kunstseide *f*.

raze [reɪz] *Haus etc.* abreißen; *Festung* schleifen; *fig.* ausmerzen, tilgen; **~** *s.th. to the ground* et. dem Erdboden gleichmachen.

ra·zor ['reɪzə] Rasiermesser *n*; Rasierapparat *m*; **~-blade** Rasierklinge *f*; **~-edge** *fig.* kritische Lage; *be on a* **~** auf des Messers Schneide stehen.

re- [riː] wieder, noch einmal, neu; zurück, wider.

reach [riːtʃ] **1.** Griff *m*; Reichweite *f*; Fassungskraft *f*; *beyond* **~**, *out of* **~** unerreichbar; *within easy* **~** leicht erreichbar; **2.** *v/i.* reichen; langen, greifen; sich erstrecken; △ *nicht* (*aus*)*reichen*; *v/t.* (hin-, her)reichen, (hin-, her)langen; erreichen, erzielen; *a.* **~** *out* ausstrecken.

re·act [rɪ'ækt] reagieren (*to auf acc.*); (ein)wirken (*on, upon auf acc.*).

re·ac·tion [rɪ'ækʃn] Reaktion *f* (*a.* ⚛ *pol.*); Rückwirkung *f*; **~·ar·y** [~nərɪ] **1.** reaktionär; **2.** Reaktionär(in).

re·ac·tor *phys.* [rɪ'æktə] (Kern-) Reaktor *m*.

read 1. [riːd] (*read* [red]) lesen; deuten; (an)zeigen (*Thermometer*); studieren; sich *gut etc.* lesen (lassen); lauten; **~** *to s.o.* j-m vorlesen; **~** *medicine* Medizin studieren; **2.** [red] *pret. u. p.p. von 1*; **~·a·ble** □ ['riːdəbl] lesbar; leserlich; lesenswert; **~·er** [~ə] (Vor)Leser(in); *typ.* Korrektor *m*; Lektor *m*; *univ.* Dozent *m*; Lesebuch *n*.

read·i·ly ['redɪlɪ] *adv.* gleich; leicht; bereitwillig, gern; **~·ness** [~nɪs] Bereitschaft *f*; Bereitwilligkeit *f*; Schnelligkeit *f*.

read·ing ['riːdɪŋ] Lesen *n*; Lesung *f* (*a. parl.*); Stand *m* (*des Thermometers*); Belesenheit *f*; Lektüre *f*; Lesart *f*; Auslegung *f*; Auffassung *f*; *attr.* Lese...

re·ad·just ['riːə'dʒʌst] wieder in Ordnung bringen; wieder anpassen; ⊕ nachstellen; **~·ment** [~mənt] Wiederanpassung *f*; Neuordnung *f*; ⊕ Korrektur.

read·y □ ['redɪ] (*-ier, -iest*) bereit, fertig; bereitwillig; im Begriff (*to do* zu tun); schnell; schlagfertig, gewandt; leicht; *econ.* bar; **~** *for use* gebrauchsfertig; *get* **~** (sich) fertig machen; **~** *cash*, **~** *money* Bargeld *n*; **~-made** fertig, Konfektions...

re·a·gent ⚗ [riː'eɪdʒənt] Reagens *n*.

real □ [rɪəl] wirklich, tatsächlich, real, wahr, eigentlich; echt; △ *nicht reell*; **~** *estate* Grundbesitz *m*, Immobilien *pl*.

re·al·is|m ['rɪəlɪzəm] Realismus *m*; **~t** [~ɪst] Realist *m*; **~·tic** [rɪə'lɪstɪk] (*~ally*) realistisch; sachlich; wirklichkeitsnah.

re·al·i·ty [rɪ'ælətɪ] Wirklichkeit *f*.

re·a·li·za·tion [rɪəlaɪ'zeɪʃn] Realisierung *f* (*a. econ.*); Verwirklichung *f*; Erkenntnis *f*; **~·ze** ['rɪəlaɪz] sich klarmachen; erkennen, begreifen, einsehen; verwirklichen; realisieren (*a. econ.*); zu Geld machen.

real·ly ['rɪəlɪ] wirklich, tatsächlich; **~!** ich muß schon sagen!

realm [relm] Königreich *n*; Reich *n*; Bereich *m*.

real·tor *Am.* ['rɪəltə] Grundstücksmakler *m*; **~·ty** ⚖ [~ɪ] Grundeigentum *n*, -besitz *m*.

reap [riːp] *Korn* schneiden; *Feld* mähen; *fig.* ernten; **~·er** ['riːpə] Schnitter(in); Mähmaschine *f*.

re·ap·pear ['riːə'pɪə] wieder erscheinen.

rear [rɪə] **1.** *v/t.* auf-, großziehen; züchten; (er)heben; *v/i. Pferd:* sich aufbäumen; **2.** Rück-, Hinterseite *f*; Hintergrund *m*; *mot.*, ⚓ Heck *n*; ✕ Nachhut *f*; *at* (*Am. in*) *the* **~** *of* hinter (*dat.*); **3.** Hinter..., Rück...; **~** *wheel drive* Hinterantrieb *m*; **~-ad·mi·ral** ⚓ ['rɪə'ædmərəl] Konteradmiral *m*; **~·guard** ✕ Nachhut *f*; **~-lamp**, **~-light** *mot.* Rücklicht *n*.

re·arm ✕ ['riː'ɑːm] (wieder)aufrüsten; **re·ar·ma·ment** ✕ [~'ɑːməmənt] (Wieder)Aufrüstung *f*.

rear|most ['rɪəməʊst] hinterste(r, -s); **~-view mir·ror** *mot.* Rückspiegel *m*; **~·ward** [~wəd] **1.** *adj.* rückwärtig; **2.** *adv. a.* **~s** rückwärts.

rea·son ['riːzn] **1.** Vernunft *f*; Verstand *m*; Recht *n*, Billigkeit *f*; Ursache *f*, Grund *m*; *by* **~** *of wegen*; *for this* **~** aus diesem Grund; *listen to* **~** Vernunft annehmen; *it stands to* **~** *that* es leuchtet ein, daß; **2.** *v/i.* vernünftig od. logisch denken; argumentieren; *v/t.* folgern, schließen (*from aus*); *a.* **~** *out* (logisch) durchdenken; ~ *away* wegdiskutieren; ~ *s.o. into (out of) s.th.* j-m et. ein(aus)reden; **rea·so·na·ble** □ [~əbl] vernünftig; angemessen; berechtigt.

re·as·sure ['ri:ə'ʃuə] (nochmals) versichern; beteuern; beruhigen.

re·bate ['ri:beit] *econ.* Rabatt *m*, Abzug *m*; Rückzahlung *f*.

reb·el¹ ['rebl] **1.** Rebell *m*; Aufrührer *m*; Aufständische(r) *m*; **2.** rebellisch, aufrührerisch.

re·bel² [ri'bel] rebellieren, sich auflehnen; **~·lion** [~ljən] Empörung *f*; **~·lious** [~ljəs] = *rebel*¹ **2.**

re·birth ['ri:'bɜ:θ] Wiedergeburt *f*.

re·bound [ri'baund] **1.** zurückprallen; **2.** [*mst* 'ri:baund] Rückprall *m*; *Sport:* Abpraller *m*.

re·buff [ri'bʌf] **1.** schroffe Abweisung, Abfuhr *f*; **2.** abblitzen lassen, abweisen.

re·build ['ri:'bild] (*-built*) wieder aufbauen.

re·buke [ri'bju:k] **1.** Tadel *m*; **2.** tadeln.

re·but [ri'bʌt] (*-tt-*) widerlegen, entkräften.

re·call [ri'kɔ:l] **1.** Zurückrufung *f*; Abberufung *f*; Widerruf *m*; *beyond ~, past ~* unwiderruflich; **2.** zurückrufen; ab(be)rufen; sich erinnern an (*acc.*); j-n erinnern (*to an acc.*); widerrufen; *econ. Kapital* kündigen.

re·ca·pit·u·late [ri:kə'pitjuleit] kurz wiederholen, zusammenfassen.

re·cap·ture ['ri:'kæptʃə] wieder ergreifen; ✕ zurückerobern; *fig.* wiedereinfangen.

re·cast ['ri:'kɑ:st] (*-cast*) ⊕ umgießen; umarbeiten, neu gestalten; *thea. Rolle* umbesetzen.

re·cede [ri'si:d] zurücktreten; receding fliehend (*Kinn, Stirn*).

re·ceipt [ri'si:t] **1.** Empfang *m*; Eingang *m* (*von Waren*); Quittung *f*; △ *nicht* 🍲, *Koch-Rezept*; **~s** *pl.* Einnahmen *pl.*; **2.** quittieren.

re·ceiv·a·ble [ri'si:vəbl] annehmbar; *econ.* ausstehend; **re·ceive** [~v] empfangen; erhalten, bekommen; aufnehmen; annehmen; anerkennen; **re·ceived** (allgemein) anerkannt; **re·ceiv·er** [~ə] Empfänger *m*; *teleph.* Hörer *m*; Hehler *m*; (*Steuer- etc.*) Einnehmer *m*; *official ~* ⚖️ Konkursverwalter *m*.

re·cent □ ['ri:snt] neu; frisch; modern; **~ events** *pl. die* jüngsten Ereignisse *pl.*; **~·ly** [~li] kürzlich, vor kurzem, neulich.

re·cep·ta·cle [ri'septəkl] Behälter *m*.

re·cep·tion [ri'sepʃn] Aufnahme *f* (*a. fig.*); Empfang *m* (*a. Rundfunk, TV*); Annahme *f*; **~ desk** Rezeption *f* (*im Hotel*); **~·ist** [~ist] Empfangsdame *f*, -chef *m*; Sprechstundenhilfe *f*; **~ room** Empfangszimmer *n*.

re·cep·tive □ [ri'septiv] empfänglich, aufnahmefähig (*of, to* für).

re·cess [ri'ses] Unterbrechung *f*, (*Am. a. Schul*)Pause *f*; *bsd. parl.* Ferien *pl.*; (entlegener) Winkel; Nische *f*; **~es** *pl. fig. das* Innere, Tiefe(n *pl.*) *f*; **re·ces·sion** [~ʃn] Zurücktreten *n*, Zurücktreten *n*; *econ.* Rezession *f*, Konjunkturrückgang *m*.

re·ci·pe ['resipi] (Koch)Rezept *n*.

re·cip·i·ent [ri'sipiənt] Empfänger *m*.

re·cip·ro·cal [ri'siprəkl] wechsel-, gegenseitig; **~·cate** [~eit] *v/i.* sich erkenntlich zeigen; ⊕ sich hin- und herbewegen; *v/t. Glückwünsche etc.* erwidern; **~·ci·ty** [resi'prosəti] Gegenseitigkeit *f*.

re·cit·al [ri'saitl] Bericht *m*; Erzählung *f*; ♪ (Solo)Vortrag *m*, Konzert *n*; **rec·i·ta·tion** [resi'teiʃn] Hersagen *n*; Vortrag *m*; **re·cite** [ri'sait] vortragen; aufsagen; berichten.

reck·less □ ['reklis] unbekümmert; rücksichtslos; leichtsinnig.

reck·on ['rekən] *v/t.* (er-, be)rechnen; *a. ~ for, ~ as* schätzen als, halten für; **~ up** zusammenzählen; *v/i.* rechnen; denken, vermuten; **~ on, ~ upon** sich verlassen auf (*acc.*); **~·ing** ['rekniŋ] Rechnen *n*; (Ab-, Be-) Rechnung *f*; *be out in one's ~* sich verrechnet haben.

re·claim [ri'kleim] zurückfordern; j-n bekehren, bessern; zivilisieren; urbar machen; ⊕ (zurück)gewinnen.

re·cline [ri'klain] (sich) (zurück)lehnen; liegen, ruhen; **~d** liegend.

re·cluse [ri'klu:s] Einsiedler(in) *m*.

rec·og·ni·tion [rekəg'niʃn] Anerkennung *f*; (Wieder)Erkennen *n*; **~ze** ['rekəgnaiz] anerkennen; (wieder-)erkennen; zugeben, einsehen.

re·coil 1. [ri'kɔil] zurückprallen; zurückschrecken; **2.** ['ri:kɔil] Rückstoß *m*, -lauf *m*.

rec·ol·lect¹ [rekə'lekt] sich erinnern an (*acc.*).

re·col·lect² ['ri:kə'lekt] wieder sammeln; ~ *o.s.* sich fassen.

rec·ol·lec·tion [rekə'lekʃn] Erinnerung *f* (*of an acc.*); Gedächtnis *n*.

rec·om·mend [rekə'mend] empfehlen; ~**men·da·tion** [rekəmen'deɪʃn] Empfehlung *f*; Vorschlag *m*.

rec·om·pense ['rekəmpens] **1.** Belohnung *f*, Vergeltung *f*; Entschädigung *f*; Ersatz *m*; **2.** belohnen, vergelten; entschädigen; ersetzen.

rec·on·cile ['rekənsaɪl] aus-, versöhnen; in Einklang bringen; schlichten; ~**cil·i·a·tion** [rekənsɪlɪ'eɪʃn] Ver-, Aussöhnung *f*.

re·con·di·tion ['ri:kən'dɪʃn] wieder herrichten; ⊕ überholen.

re·con·nais·sance [rɪ'kɒnɪsəns] ✗ Aufklärung *f*, Erkundung *f*; *fig.* Übersicht *f*; ~**noi·tre**, *Am.* ~**noi·ter** [rekə'nɔɪtə] erkunden, auskundschaften.

re·con·sid·er ['ri:kən'sɪdə] wieder erwägen; nochmals überlegen.

re·con·sti·tute ['ri:'kɒnstɪtju:t] wiederherstellen.

re·con·struct ['ri:kən'strʌkt] wiederaufbauen; ~**struc·tion** [~kʃn] Wiederaufbau *m*, Wiederherstellung *f*.

re·con·vert ['ri:kən'vɜ:t] umstellen.

rec·ord¹ ['rekɔ:d] Aufzeichnung *f*; Protokoll *n*; (*Gerichts*)Akte *f*; Urkunde *f*; Register *n*, Verzeichnis *n*; (schriftlicher) Bericht; Ruf *m*, Leumund *m*; Schallplatte *f*; *Sport*: Rekord *m*; *place on* ~ schriftlich niederlegen; ~ *office* Archiv *n*; *off the* ~ inoffiziell.

re·cord² [rɪ'kɔ:d] aufzeichnen, schriftlich niederlegen; *auf Schallplatte etc.* aufnehmen; ~**er** [~ə] Aufnahmegerät *n*, *bsd.* Tonband-Gerät *n*, *Kassetten*-Recorder *m*; ♪ Blockflöte *f*; ~**ing** [~ɪŋ] Rundfunk, *TV*: Aufzeichnung *f*, -nahme *f*; ~ **play·er** ['rekɔ:d-] Plattenspieler *m*.

re·count [rɪ'kaʊnt] erzählen.

re·coup [rɪ'ku:p] *j-n* entschädigen (*for für*); *et.* wiederbringen.

re·course [rɪ'kɔ:s] Zuflucht *f*; *have* ~ *to* (s-e) Zuflucht nehmen zu.

re·cov·er [rɪ'kʌvə] *v/t.* wiedererlangen, -bekommen, -finden; *Verluste* wiedereinbringen, wiedergutmachen; *Schulden etc.* eintreiben; *Fahrzeug, Schiff etc.* bergen; *be* ~*ed*

wiederhergestellt sein; *v/i.* sich erholen; genesen; ~**y** [~rɪ] Wiedererlangung *f*; Bergung *f*; Genesung *f*; Erholung *f*; *past* ~ unheilbar krank.

re·cre·ate ['rekrɪeɪt] *v/t.* erfrischen; *v/i. a.* ~ *o.s.* ausspannen, sich erholen; ~**a·tion** [rekrɪ'eɪʃn] Erholung *f*.

re·crim·i·na·tion [rɪkrɪmɪ'neɪʃn] Gegenbeschuldigung *f*.

re·cruit [rɪ'kru:t] **1.** Rekrut *m*; *fig.* Neuling *m*; **2.** ergänzen; *Truppe* rekrutieren; ✗ Rekruten ausheben.

rec·tan·gle ▲ ['rektæŋgl] Rechteck *n*.

rec·ti·fy ['rektɪfaɪ] berichtigen; verbessern; ∮ gleichrichten; ~**tude** [~tju:d] Geradheit *f*, Redlichkeit *f*.

rec·tor ['rektə] Pfarrer *m*; Rektor *m*; ~**to·ry** [~rɪ] Pfarre(i) *f*; Pfarrhaus *n*.

re·cum·bent □ [rɪ'kʌmbənt] liegend.

re·cu·per·ate [rɪ'kju:pəreɪt] sich erholen; *Gesundheit* wiedererlangen.

re·cur [rɪ'kɜ:] (*-rr-*) wiederkehren (*to* zu), sich wiederholen; zurückkommen (*to* auf *acc.*); ~**rence** [rɪ'kʌrəns] Rückkehr *f*, Wiederauftreten *n*; ~**rent** □ [~nt] wiederkehrend.

re·cy·cle ['ri:'saɪkl] *Abfälle* wiederverwerten; ~**cling** [~ɪŋ] Wiederverwertung *f*.

red [red] **1.** rot; ~ *heat* Rotglut *f*; ~ *tape* Bürokratismus *m*; **2.** Rot *n*; *bsd. pol.* Rote(r *m*) *f*; *be in the* ~ in den roten Zahlen sein.

red|·breast *zo.* ['redbrest] *a. robin* ~ Rotkehlchen *n*; ~**cap** Militärpolizist *m*; *Am.* Gepäckträger *m*; ~**den** ['redn] (sich) röten; erröten; ~**dish** [~ɪʃ] rötlich.

re·dec·o·rate ['ri:'dekəreɪt] *Zimmer* neu streichen *od.* tapezieren.

re·deem [rɪ'di:m] zurück-, loskaufen; ablösen; *Versprechen* einlösen; büßen; entschädigen für; erlösen; 2**er** *eccl.* [~ə] Erlöser *m*, Heiland *m*.

re·demp·tion [rɪ'dempʃn] Rückkauf *m*; Auslösung *f*; Erlösung *f*.

re·de·vel·op ['ri:dɪ'veləp] *Gebäude, Stadtteil* sanieren.

red|-hand·ed ['red'hændɪd]: *catch s.o.* ~ *j-n* auf frischer Tat ertappen; ~**head** Rotschopf *m*; ~**head·ed** rothaarig; ~**hot** rotglühend; *fig.* hitzig; 2 **In·di·an** Indianer(in); ~**let·ter day** Festtag *m*; *fig.* Freuden-, Glückstag *m*; denkwürdiger Tag; ~**ness** [~nɪs] Röte *f*; ~**nosed** rotnasig.

red·o·lent ['redələnt] duftend.

re·dou·ble [ˈriːˈdʌbl] (sich) verdoppeln.

re·dress [rɪˈdres] **1.** Abhilfe f; Wiedergutmachung f; ⚖ Entschädigung f; **2.** abhelfen (dat.); abschaffen, beseitigen; wiedergutmachen.

red-tap·ism [ˈredˈteɪpɪzəm] Bürokratismus m.

re·duce [rɪˈdjuːs] verringern, -mindern; einschränken; Preise herabsetzen; zurückführen, bringen (to auf, in acc., zu); verwandeln (to in acc.), machen zu; ♠, ♪ reduzieren; ✚ einrenken; ~ to writing schriftlich niederlegen; **re·duc·tion** [rɪˈdʌkʃn] Herabsetzung f, (Preis)Nachlaß m, Rabatt m; Verminderung f; Verkleinerung f; Reduktion f; Verwandlung f; ✚ Einrenkung f.

re·dun·dant □ [rɪˈdʌndənt] überflüssig; übermäßig; weitschweifig.

reed [riːd] ♣ Schilfrohr n; Rohrflöte f.

re·ed·u·ca·tion [ˈriːedjʊˈkeɪʃn] Umschulung f, Umerziehung f.

reef [riːf] (Felsen)Riff n; ⚓ Reff n.

ree·fer [ˈriːfə] Seemannsjacke f; sl. Marihuanazigarette f.

reek [riːk] **1.** Gestank m, unangenehmer Geruch; **2.** stinken, unangenehm riechen (of nach).

reel [riːl] **1.** Haspel f; (Garn-, Film-)Rolle f, Spule f; **2.** v/t. ~ (up) (auf-)wickeln, (-)spulen; v/i. wirbeln; schwanken; taumeln.

re·e·lect [ˈriːɪˈlekt] wiederwählen.

re·en·ter [ˈriːˈentə] wieder eintreten (in acc.).

re·es·tab·lish [ˈriːɪˈstæblɪʃ] wiederherstellen.

ref F [ref] = referee.

re·fer [rɪˈfɜː]: ~ to ver- od. überweisen an (acc.); sich beziehen auf (acc.); erwähnen (acc.); zuordnen (dat.); befragen (acc.), nachschlagen in (dat.); zurückführen auf (acc.), zuschreiben (dat.).

ref·er·ee [refəˈriː] Schiedsrichter m; Boxen: Ringrichter m.

ref·er·ence [ˈrefrəns] Referenz f, Empfehlung f, Zeugnis n; Verweis(ung f) m, Hinweis m; Erwähnung f, Anspielung f; Bezugnahme f; Beziehung f; Nachschlagen n, Befragen n; in od. with ~ to was ... betrifft, bezüglich (gen.); ~ book Nachschlagewerk n; ~ library Handbibliothek f; ~ number Aktenzei-

chen n; make ~ to et. erwähnen.

ref·er·en·dum [refəˈrendəm] Volksentscheid m.

re·fill 1. [ˈriːfɪl] Nachfüllung f; Ersatzpackung f; Ersatzmine f (Kugelschreiber etc.); **2.** [ˈriːˈfɪl] (sich) wieder füllen, auffüllen.

re·fine [rɪˈfaɪn] ⊕ raffinieren, veredeln; verfeinern, kultivieren; (sich) läutern; ~ on, ~ upon et. verfeinern, -bessern; **.~d** fein, vornehm; **~·ment** [~mənt] Vered(e)lung f; Verfeinerung f; Läuterung f; Feinheit f, Vornehmheit f; **re·fin·er·y** [~ərɪ] ⊕ Raffinerie f; metall. (Eisen)Hütte f.

re·fit ⚓ [ˈriːˈfɪt] (-tt-) v/t. ausbessern; neu ausrüsten; v/i. ausgebessert werden; neu ausgerüstet werden.

re·flect [rɪˈflekt] v/t. zurückwerfen, reflektieren; widerspiegeln (a. fig.); zum Ausdruck bringen; v/i. ~ on, ~ upon nachdenken über (acc.); sich abfällig äußern über (acc.); ein schlechtes Licht werfen auf (acc.); **re·flec·tion** [~kʃn] Reflexion f, Zurückstrahlung f; Widerspiegelung f (a. fig.); Reflex m; Spiegelbild n; Überlegung f; Gedanke m; abfällige Bemerkung; **re·flec·tive** □ [~tɪv] reflektierend, zurückstrahlend; nachdenklich.

re·flex [ˈriːfleks] **1.** Reflex...; **2.** Widerschein m, Reflex m (a. physiol.).

re·flex·ive □ gr. [rɪˈfleksɪv] reflexiv, rückbezüglich.

re·for·est [ˈriːˈfɒrɪst] aufforsten.

re·form¹ [rɪˈfɔːm] **1.** Verbesserung f, Reform f; **2.** verbessern, reformieren; (sich) bessern.

re·form² [ˈriːˈfɔːm] (sich) neu bilden; ✕ (sich) neu formieren.

ref·or·ma·tion [refəˈmeɪʃn] Reformierung f; Besserung f; eccl. ♀ Reformation f; **re·for·ma·to·ry** [rɪˈfɔːmətərɪ] **1.** Besserungs..., Reform...; **2.** Brt. veraltet, Am. Besserungsanstalt f; **re·form·er** [~ə] eccl. Reformator m; bsd. pol. Reformer m.

re·fract [rɪˈfrækt] Strahlen etc. brechen; **re·frac·tion** [~kʃn] (Strahlen-)Brechung f; **re·frac·to·ry** □ [~ktərɪ] widerspenstig; ♪ hartnäckig; ⊕ feuerfest.

re·frain [rɪˈfreɪn] **1.** sich enthalten (from gen.), unterlassen (from acc.); **2.** Kehrreim m, Refrain m.

re·fresh [rɪˈfreʃ] (o.s. sich) erfrischen, stärken; Gedächtnis etc. auffrischen; **~·ment** [~mənt] Erfrischung f (a. *Getränk etc.*).

re·fri·ge·rate [rɪˈfrɪdʒəreɪt] kühlen; **~·ra·tor** [~ə] Kühlschrank m, -raum m; ~ *van*, *Am.* ~ *car* ⊞ Kühlwagen m.

re·fu·el [ˈriːˈfjʊəl] (auf)tanken.

ref·uge [ˈrefjuːdʒ] Zuflucht(sstätte) f; Verkehrsinsel f; **~·u·gee** [refjʊˈdʒiː] Flüchtling m; ~ *camp* Flüchtlingslager n.

re·fund 1. [riːˈfʌnd] zurückzahlen; ersetzen; **2.** [ˈriːfʌnd] Rückzahlung f; Erstattung f.

re·fur·bish [ˈriːˈfɜːbɪʃ] aufpolieren (a. *fig.*).

re·fus·al [rɪˈfjuːzl] abschlägige Antwort; (Ver)Weigerung f; Vorkaufsrecht n (of auf *acc.*).

re·fuse[1] [rɪˈfjuːz] v/t. verweigern; abweisen, ablehnen; ~ *to do s.th.* sich weigern, etwas zu tun; v/i. sich weigern; verweigern (*Pferd*).

ref·use[2] [ˈrefjuːs] Ausschuß m; Abfall m, Müll m.

re·fute [rɪˈfjuːt] widerlegen.

re·gain [rɪˈɡeɪn] wiedergewinnen.

re·gal □ [ˈriːɡl] königlich, Königs...

re·gale [rɪˈɡeɪl] fürstlich bewirten; ~ *o.s. on* sich gütlich tun an (*dat.*), schwelgen in (*dat.*).

re·gard [rɪˈɡɑːd] **1.** (Hoch)Achtung f; Rücksicht f; Hinblick m, -sicht f; *with* ~ *to* hinsichtlich (*gen.*); ~s pl. Grüße pl. (*bsd. in Briefen*); *kind* ~s herzliche Grüße; **2.** ansehen; betrachten; (be)achten; betreffen; ~ *s.o. as* j-n halten für; *as* ~s *was* ... betrifft; **~·ing** □ [~ɪŋ] hinsichtlich (*gen.*); **~·less** □ [~lɪs]: ~ *of* ohne Rücksicht auf (*acc.*), ungeachtet (*gen.*).

re·gen·e·rate [rɪˈdʒenəreɪt] (sich) erneuern; (sich) regenerieren; (sich) neu bilden.

re·gent [ˈriːdʒənt] Regent(in); *Prince* ♀ Prinzregent.

reg·i·ment ✕ [ˈredʒɪmənt] **1.** Regiment n; **2.** [~ment] organisieren; reglementieren; **~·als** ✕ [redʒɪˈmentlz] pl. Uniform f.

re·gion [ˈriːdʒən] Gegend f, Gebiet n; fig. Bereich m; **~·al** □ [~l] regional; örtlich; *Regional*...., Orts...

re·gis·ter [ˈredʒɪstə] **1.** Register n, Verzeichnis n; ⊕ Schieber m, Ventil n; ♪ Register n; Zählwerk n; *cash* ~ Registrierkasse f; **2.** registrieren; (sich) eintragen od. -schreiben (las-

sen); (sich) anmelden; (an)zeigen, auf-, verzeichnen; einschreiben (lassen); *Postsache* einschreiben (lassen); *Brt. Gepäck* aufgeben; sich *polizeilich* melden; **~ed** *letter* Einschreibebrief m.

re·gis·trar [redʒɪˈstrɑː] Standesbeamte(r) m; **~·tra·tion** [~eɪʃn] Eintragung f; Anmeldung f; *mot.* Zulassung f; ~ *fee* Anmeldegebühr f; **~·try** [ˈredʒɪstrɪ] Eintragung f; Registratur f; Register n; ~ *office* Standesamt n.

re·gress [ˈriːɡres], **re·gres·sion** [rɪˈɡreʃn] Rückwärtsbewegung f; rückläufige Entwicklung.

re·gret [rɪˈɡret] **1.** Bedauern n; Schmerz m; **2.** (-tt-) bedauern; *Verlust* beklagen; **~·ful** □ [~fl] bedauernd; **~·ta·ble** □ [~əbl] bedauerlich.

reg·u·lar □ [ˈreɡjʊlə] regelmäßig; regulär, normal, gewohnt; geregelt; geordnet; genau, pünktlich; richtig, recht, ordentlich; F richtig(gehend); ✕ regulär; **~·i·ty** [reɡjʊˈlærətɪ] Regelmäßigkeit f; Richtigkeit f, Ordnung f.

reg·u·late [ˈreɡjʊleɪt] regeln, ordnen; regulieren; **~·la·tion** [reɡjʊˈleɪʃn] **1.** Regulierung f; ~s pl. Vorschrift f, Bestimmung f; **2.** herrschen, regieren.

re·hash fig. [ˈriːˈhæʃ] **1.** wiederaufwärmen; **2.** Aufguß m.

re·hears·al [rɪˈhɜːsl] thea., ♪ Probe f; Wiederholung f; **~·e** [rɪˈhɜːs] thea. proben; wiederholen; aufsagen.

reign [reɪn] **1.** Regierung f; a. fig. Herrschaft f; **2.** herrschen, regieren.

re·im·burse [ˈriːɪmˈbɜːs] j-n entschädigen; *Kosten* erstatten.

rein [reɪn] **1.** Zügel m; **2.** zügeln.

rein·deer zo. [ˈreɪndɪə] Ren(tier) n.

re·in·force [riːɪnˈfɔːs] verstärken; **~·ment** [~mənt] Verstärkung f.

re·in·state [ˈriːɪnˈsteɪt] wiedereinsetzen; wieder instand setzen.

re·in·sure [ˈriːɪnˈʃʊə] rückversichern.

re·it·e·rate [riːˈɪtəreɪt] (dauernd) wiederholen.

re·ject [rɪˈdʒekt] ab-, zurückweisen; abschlagen; verwerfen; ablehnen; **re·jec·tion** [~kʃn] Verwerfung f; Ablehnung f; Zurückweisung f.

re·joice [rɪˈdʒɔɪs] v/t. erfreuen; v/i. sich freuen (*at*, *over* über *acc.*); **re·joic·ing** [~ɪŋ] **1.** □ freudig; **2.** Freude f; ~s pl. Freudenfest n.

re·join [ˈriːˈdʒɔɪn] sich wieder ver-

Q R

einigen; wieder zurückkehren zu; [rɪˈdʒɔːn] erwidern.

re·ju·ve·nate [rɪˈdʒuːvɪneɪt] verjüngen.

re·kin·dle [ˈriːˈkɪndl] (sich) wieder entzünden.

re·lapse [rɪˈlæps] **1.** Rückfall *m*; **2.** zurückfallen, rückfällig werden; e-n Rückfall haben.

re·late [rɪˈleɪt] *v/t.* erzählen; in Beziehung bringen; *v/i.* sich beziehen (*to* auf *acc.*); **re·lat·ed** verwandt (*to* mit).

re·la·tion [rɪˈleɪʃn] Bericht *m*, Erzählung *f*; Verhältnis *n*; Verwandtschaft *f*; Verwandte(r *m*) *f*; ~*s pl.* Beziehungen *pl.*; *in* ~ *to* in bezug auf (*acc.*); ~**ship** [~ʃɪp] Verwandtschaft *f*; Beziehung *f*.

rel·a·tive [ˈrelətɪv] **1.** □ relativ, verhältnismäßig; bezüglich (*to gen.*); *gr.* Relativ…, bezüglich; entsprechend; **2.** *gr.* Relativpronomen *n*, bezügliches Fürwort; Verwandte(r *m*) *f*.

re·lax [rɪˈlæks] (sich) lockern; nachlassen (in *dat.*); (sich) entspannen, ausspannen; ~**a·tion** [riːlækˈseɪʃn] Lockerung *f*; Nachlassen *n*; Entspannung *f*, Erholung *f*.

re·lay[1] [ˈriːleɪ] Ablösung *f*; ⚡ Relais *n*; *Rundfunk*: Übertragung *f*; *Sport*: Staffel *f*; **2.** [riːˈleɪ] *Rundfunk*: übertragen.

re·lay[2] [ˈriːˈleɪ] *Kabel etc.* neu verlegen.

re·lay race [ˈriːleɪreɪs] *Sport*: Staffellauf *m*.

re·lease [rɪˈliːs] **1.** Freilassung *f*; Befreiung *f*; Freigabe *f*; *Film*: *oft first* ~ Uraufführung *f*; ⊕, *phot.* Auslöser *m*; **2.** freilassen; erlösen; freigeben; *Recht* aufgeben, übertragen; *Film* uraufführen; ⊕ auslösen.

rel·e·gate [ˈrelɪɡeɪt] verbannen; verweisen (*to an acc.*).

re·lent [rɪˈlent] sich erweichen lassen; ~**less** □ [~lɪs] unbarmherzig.

rel·e·vant □ [ˈreləvənt] sachdienlich; zutreffend; relevant, erheblich.

re·li·a|bil·i·ty [rɪlaɪəˈbɪlətɪ] Zuverlässigkeit *f*; ~**ble** □ [rɪˈlaɪəbl] zuverlässig.

re·li·ance [rɪˈlaɪəns] Vertrauen *n*; Zuversicht *f*.

rel·ic [ˈrelɪk] (Über)Rest *m*; Reliquie *f*.

re·lief [rɪˈliːf] Erleichterung *f*; (angenehme) Unterbrechung; Unter-

stützung *f*; ✕ Ablösung *f*; ✕ Entsatz *m*; Hilfe *f*; *arch. etc.* Relief *n*.

re·lieve [rɪˈliːv] erleichtern; mildern, lindern; *Arme etc.* unterstützen; ✕ ablösen; ✕ entsetzen; (ab)helfen (*dat.*); entlasten, befreien; (angenehm) unterbrechen, beleben; *to* ~ *o.s. od. nature* seine Notdurft verrichten.

re·li|gion [rɪˈlɪdʒən] Religion *f*; ~**gious** □ [~əs] Religions…; religiös, gewissenhaft.

re·lin·quish [rɪˈlɪŋkwɪʃ] aufgeben; verzichten auf (*acc.*); loslassen.

rel·ish [ˈrelɪʃ] **1.** (Wohl)Geschmack *m*; Würze *f*; Genuß *m*; *fig.* Reiz *m*; *with great* ~ mit großem Appetit; *fig.* mit großem Vergnügen, *bsd. iro.* mit Wonne; **2.** genießen; gern essen; Geschmack *od.* Gefallen finden an (*dat.*).

re·luc|tance [rɪˈlʌktəns] Widerstreben *n*; *bsd. phys.* Widerstand *m*; ~**tant** □ [~t] widerstrebend, widerwillig.

re·ly [rɪˈlaɪ]: ~ *on*, ~ *upon* sich verlassen auf (*acc.*), bauen auf (*acc.*).

re·main [rɪˈmeɪn] **1.** (ver)bleiben; übrigbleiben; **2.** ~*s pl.* Überbleibsel *pl.*, (Über)Reste *pl.*; *a. mortal* ~*s die* sterblichen Überreste *pl.*; ~**der** [~də] Rest *m*.

re·mand ⚖ [rɪˈmɑːnd] **1.** ~ *s.o.* (*in custody*) j-n in die Untersuchungshaft zurückschicken; **2.** *a.* ~ *in custody* Zurücksendung *f* in die Untersuchungshaft; *prisoner on* ~ Untersuchungsgefangene(r *m*) *f*; ~ *home centre Brt.* Untersuchungsgefängnis *n* für Jugendliche.

re·mark [rɪˈmɑːk] **1.** Bemerkung *f*; Äußerung *f*; **2.** *v/t.* bemerken; äußern; *v/i.* sich äußern (*on, upon über acc.*, *zu*); **re·mar·ka·ble** □ [~əbl] bemerkenswert; außergewöhnlich.

rem·e·dy [ˈremədɪ] **1.** (Heil-, Hilfs-, Gegen-, Rechts)Mittel *n*; (Ab)Hilfe *f*; **2.** heilen; abhelfen (*dat.*).

re·mem|ber [rɪˈmembə] sich erinnern an (*acc.*); denken an (*acc.*); beherzigen; ~ *me to her* grüße sie von mir; ~**brance** [~rəns] Erinnerung *f*; Gedächtnis *n*; Andenken *n*; ~*s pl.* Empfehlungen *pl.*, Grüße *pl.*

re·mind [rɪˈmaɪnd] erinnern (*of an acc.*); ~**er** [~ə] Mahnung *f*.

rem·i·nis|cence [remɪˈnɪsns] Erinnerung f; **~·cent** □ [~t] (sich) erinnernd.

re·miss [rɪ'mɪs] (nach)lässig; **re·mis·sion** [~ʃn] Vergebung f (der Sünden); Erlaß m (von Strafe etc.); Nachlassen n.

re·mit [rɪ'mɪt] (-tt-) Sünden vergeben; Schuld etc. erlassen; nachlassen in (dat.); überweisen; **~·tance** econ. [~əns] (Geld)Sendung f, Überweisung f, Rimesse f.

rem·nant ['remnənt] (Über)Rest m.

re·mod·el [ri:'mɒdl] umbilden.

re·mon·strance [rɪ'mɒnstrəns] Einspruch m; Protest m; **rem·on·strate** ['remənstreɪt] Vorhaltungen machen (about wegen; with s.o. j-m); protestieren.

re·morse [rɪ'mɔːs] Gewissensbisse pl.; Reue f; without ~ unbarmherzig; **~·less** □ [~lɪs] unbarmherzig.

re·mote □ [rɪ'məʊt] (~r, ~st) entfernt, entlegen; ~ control ⊕ Fernlenkung f, -steuerung f; Fernbedienung f; **~·ness** [~nɪs] Entfernung f.

re·mov·|al [rɪ'muːvl] Entfernen n; Beseitigung f; Umzug m; Entlassung f; ~ van Möbelwagen m; **~e** [~uːv] 1. v/t. entfernen; wegräumen, wegschaffen; beseitigen; entlassen; v/i. (aus-, um-, ver)ziehen; 2. Entfernung f; fig. Schritt m, Stufe f; (Verwandtschafts)Grad m; **~·er** [~ə] (Möbel)Spediteur m.

re·mu·ne·|rate [rɪ'mjuːnəreɪt] entlohnen; belohnen; entschädigen; vergüten; **~·ra·tive** □ [~rətɪv] lohnend.

Re·nais·sance [rə'neɪsəns] die Renaissance.

re·nas·|cence [rɪ'næsns] Wiedergeburt f; Erneuerung f; Renaissance f; **~·cent** [~nt] wiederauflebend, -erwachend.

ren·der ['rendə] berühmt, schwierig, möglich etc. machen; wiedergeben; Dienst etc. leisten; Ehre etc. erweisen; Dank abstatten; übersetzen; ♪ vortragen; thea. gestalten, interpretieren; Grund angeben; econ. Rechnung vorlegen; übergeben; machen zu; Fett auslassen; **~·ing** [~ərɪŋ] Wiedergabe f; Vortrag m; Interpretation f; Übersetzung f; Übertragung f; arch. Rohbewurf m.

ren·di·tion [ren'dɪʃn] Wiedergabe f; Interpretation f; Vortrag m.

ren·e·gade ['renɪgeɪd] Abtrünnige(r) m f.

re·new [rɪ'njuː] erneuern; Gespräch etc. wiederaufnehmen; Kraft etc. wiedererlangen; Vertrag, Paß verlängern; **~·al** [~əl] Erneuerung f; Verlängerung f.

re·nounce [rɪ'naʊns] entsagen (dat.); verzichten auf (acc.); verleugnen.

ren·o·vate ['renəʊveɪt] renovieren; erneuern.

re·nown [rɪ'naʊn] Ruhm m, Ansehen n; **re·nowned** berühmt, namhaft.

rent¹ [rent] Riß m; Spalte f.

rent² [~] 1. Miete f; Pacht f; △ nicht Rente; for ~ zu vermieten; 2. (ver-) mieten, (-)pachten; Auto etc. leihen; **~·al** [~rentl] Miete f; Pacht f; Leihgebühr f.

re·nun·ci·a·tion [rɪnʌnsɪ'eɪʃn] Entsagung f; Verzicht m (of auf acc.).

re·pair [rɪ'peə] 1. Ausbesserung f, Reparatur f; ~s pl. Reparaturarbeiten pl.; ~ shop Reparaturwerkstatt f; in good ~ in gutem Zustand, gut erhalten; out of ~ baufällig; 2. reparieren, ausbessern; wiedergutmachen.

rep·a·ra·tion [repə'reɪʃn] Wiedergutmachung f; Entschädigung f; ~s pl. pol. Reparationen pl.

rep·ar·tee [repɑː'tiː] schlagfertige Antwort; Schlagfertigkeit f.

re·past lit. [rɪ'pɑːst] Mahl(zeit f) n.

re·pay [riː'peɪ] (-paid) et. zurückzahlen; Besuch erwidern; et. vergelten; j-n entschädigen; **~·ment** [~mənt] Rückzahlung f.

re·peal [rɪ'piːl] 1. Aufhebung f (von Gesetzen); 2. aufheben; widerrufen.

re·peat [rɪ'piːt] 1. (sich) wiederholen; nachsprechen; aufsagen; nachliefern; aufstoßen (on dat.) (Essen); 2. Wiederholung f; ♪ Wiederholungszeichen n; oft ~ order econ. Nachbestellung f.

re·pel [rɪ'pel] (-ll-) Feind zurückschlagen; fig. zurückweisen; j-n abstoßen; **~·lent** [~ənt] abstoßend (a. fig.).

re·pent [rɪ'pent] bereuen; **re·pent·ance** [~əns] Reue f; **re·pen·tant** [~t] reuig, reumütig.

re·per·cus·sion [riːpə'kʌʃn] Rückprall m; mst pl ~s Auswirkungen pl.

rep·er·to·ry ['repətərɪ] thea. Repertoire n; fig. Fundgrube f.

rep·e·ti·tion [repɪ'tɪʃn] Wiederholung f; Aufsagen n; Nachbildung f.

re·place [rɪ'pleɪs] wieder hinstellen

od. -legen; ersetzen; an *j-s* Stelle
treten; ablösen; **~ment** [~mənt] Ersatz *m.*

re·plant ['ri:'plɑ:nt] umpflanzen.

re·plen·ish [rɪ'plenɪʃ] (wieder) auffüllen; ergänzen; **~ment** [~mənt] Auffüllung *f;* Ergänzung *f.*

re·plete [rɪ'pli:t] reich ausgestattet, voll(gepfropft) (*with* mit).

rep·li·ca ['replɪkə] *Kunst:* Originalkopie *f;* Nachbildung *f.*

re·ply [rɪ'plaɪ] **1.** antworten, erwidern (*to* auf *acc.*); **2.** Antwort *f,* Erwiderung *f; in ~ to* your letter in Beantwortung Ihres Schreibens; **~paid** envelope Freiumschlag *m.*

re·port [rɪ'pɔ:t] **1.** Bericht *m;* Meldung *f,* Nachricht *f;* Gerücht *n;* Ruf *m;* Knall *m;* (*school*) ~ (Schul)Zeugnis *n;* **2.** berichten (über *acc.*); (sich) melden; anzeigen; *it is ~ed that* es heißt (daß); *~ed speech gr.* indirekte Rede; **~er** [~ə] Reporter(in), Berichterstatter(in).

re·pose [rɪ'pəʊz] **1.** Ruhe *f;* **2.** *v/t.* (*o.s.* sich) ausruhen; (aus)ruhen lassen; ~ *trust, etc.* in Vertrauen *etc.* setzen auf *od.* in (*acc.*); *v/i.* (sich) ausruhen; ruhen; beruhen (*on* auf *dat.*).

re·pos·i·to·ry [rɪ'pɒzɪtərɪ] (Waren-)Lager *n; fig.* Fundgrube *f,* Quelle *f.*

rep·re·hend [reprɪ'hend] tadeln.

rep·re·sent [reprɪ'zent] darstellen; verkörpern; *thea.* Rolle darstellen, *Stück* aufführen; (fälschlich) hinstellen, darstellen (*as, to be* als); vertreten; **~·sen·ta·tion** [reprɪzen-'teɪʃn] Darstellung *f; thea.* Aufführung *f;* Vertretung *f;* **~·sen·ta·tive** □ [reprɪ'zentətɪv] **1.** darstellend (*of acc.*); (stell)vertretend; *a. parl.* präsentativ; typisch; **2.** Vertreter (-in); Bevollmächtigte(r *m) f;* Repräsentant(in); *parl.* Abgeordnete(r *m) f; House of ~s Am. parl.* Repräsentantenhaus *n.*

re·press [rɪ'pres] unterdrücken; *psych.* verdrängen; **re·pres·sion** [~ʃn] Unterdrückung *f; psych.* Verdrängung *f.*

re·prieve [rɪ'pri:v] **1.** Begnadigung *f;* (Straf)Aufschub *m; fig.* Gnadenfrist *f;* **2.** begnadigen; *j-m* Strafaufschub *od. fig.* e-e Gnadenfrist gewähren.

rep·ri·mand ['reprɪmɑ:nd] **1.** Verweis *m;* **2.** *j-m* e-n Verweis erteilen.

re·print [rɪ'prɪnt] neu auflegen *od.*

drucken, nachdrucken; **2.** ['ri:prɪnt] Neuauflage *f,* Nachdruck *m.*

re·pri·sal [rɪ'praɪzl] Repressalie *f,* Vergeltungsmaßnahme *f.*

re·proach [rɪ'prəʊtʃ] **1.** Vorwurf *m;* Schande *f;* **2.** vorwerfen (*s.o. with s.th.* j-m et.); Vorwürfe machen; **~ful** □ [~fl] vorwurfsvoll.

rep·ro·bate ['reprəbeɪt] **1.** verkommen, verderbt; **2.** verkommenes Subjekt; **3.** mißbilligen; verdammen.

re·pro·cess [rɪ'prəʊses] *Kernbrennstoffe* wiederaufbereiten; **~ing plant** Wiederaufbereitungsanlage *f.*

re·pro·duce [ri:prə'dju:s] (wieder-) erzeugen; (sich) fortpflanzen; wiedergeben, reproduzieren; **~·duc·tion** [~'dʌkʃn] Wiedererzeugung *f;* Fortpflanzung *f;* Reproduktion *f;* **~·duc·tive** [~ɪv] Fortpflanzungs...

re·proof [rɪ'pru:f] Tadel *m,* Rüge *f.*

re·prove [rɪ'pru:v] tadeln, rügen.

rep·tile *zo.* ['reptaɪl] Reptil *n.*

re·pub·lic [rɪ'pʌblɪk] Republik *f;* **~·li·can** [~ən] **1.** republikanisch; **2.** Republikaner(in).

re·pu·di·ate [rɪ'pju:dɪeɪt] nicht anerkennen; ab-, zurückweisen; *j-n* verstoßen.

re·pug·nance [rɪ'pʌgnəns] Abneigung *f,* Widerwille *m;* **~·nant** □ [~t] abstoßend; widerlich.

re·pulse [rɪ'pʌls] **1.** ✗ Abwehr *f;* Zurück-, Abweisung *f;* **2.** ✗ zurückschlagen, abwehren; zurück-, abweisen; **re·pul·sion** Abscheu *m,* Widerwille *m; phys.* Abstoßung *f;* **re·pul·sive** [~ɪv] abstoßend (*a. phys.*), widerwärtig.

rep·u·ta·ble □ ['repjʊtəbl] angesehen, achtbar; ehrbar, anständig; **~·tion** [repjʊ'teɪʃn] Ruf *m,* Ansehen *n;* **re·pute** [rɪ'pju:t] **1.** Ruf *m;* **2.** halten für; *be ~d* (*to be*) gelten als; **re·put·ed** vermeintlich; angeblich.

re·quest [rɪ'kwest] **1.** Bitte *f,* Gesuch *n;* Ersuchen *n; econ.* Nachfrage *f; by ~, on ~* auf Wunsch; *in* (*great*) ~ (sehr) gesucht *od.* begehrt; ~ *stop* Bedarfshaltestelle *f;* **2.** um *et.* bitten *od.* ersuchen; *j-n* (höflich) bitten um *od.* ersuchen.

re·quire [rɪ'kwaɪə] verlangen, fordern; brauchen, erfordern; *if ~d* falls notwendig; **~d** erforderlich; **~ment** [~mənt] (An)Forderung *f;* Erfordernis *n;* **~s** *pl.* Bedarf *m.*

req·ui·site [ˈrekwɪzɪt] **1.** erforderlich; **2.** Erfordernis *n*; (Bedarfs-, Gebrauchs)Artikel *m*; *toilet* ~*s pl.* Toilettenartikel *pl.*; △ *nicht (Bühnen-)Requisit*; ~·**si·tion** [rekwɪˈzɪʃn] **1.** Anforderung *f*; ✗ Requisition *f*; **2.** anfordern; ✗ requirieren.

re·quite [rɪˈkwaɪt] *j-m et.* vergelten.

re·sale [ˈriːseɪl] Wieder-, Weiterverkauf *m*; ~ *price* Wiederverkaufspreis *m*.

re·scind [rɪˈsɪnd] *Urteil* aufheben; *Vertrag* annullieren; **re·scis·sion** [rɪˈsɪʒn] Aufhebung *f*; Annullierung *f*.

res·cue [ˈreskjuː] **1.** Rettung *f*; Hilfe *f*; Befreiung *f*; **2.** retten; befreien.

re·search [rɪˈsɜːtʃ] **1.** Forschung *f*; Untersuchung *f*; Nachforschung *f*; **2.** forschen, Forschungen anstellen; *et.* untersuchen, erforschen; ~·**er** [~ə] Forscher(in).

re·sem|blance [rɪˈzembləns] Ähnlichkeit *f* (*to* mit); ~·**ble** [rɪˈzembl] gleichen, ähnlich sein (*dat.*).

re·sent [rɪˈzent] übelnehmen, sich ärgern über (*acc.*); ~·**ful** □ [~fl] übelnehmerisch; ärgerlich; ~·**ment** [~mənt] Ärger *m*; Groll *m*; △ *nicht Ressentiment.*

res·er·va·tion [rezəˈveɪʃn] Reservierung *f*, Vorbestellung *f* (*von Zimmern etc.*); Vorbehalt *m*; Reservat(ion *f*) *n*; *central* ~ *Brt.* Mittelstreifen *m* (*der Autobahn*).

re·serve [rɪˈzɜːv] **1.** Reserve *f* (*a.* ✗), Vorrat *m*; *econ.* Rücklage *f*; Zurückhaltung *f*; Vorbehalt *m*; *Sport:* Ersatzmann *m*; **2.** aufbewahren, aufsparen; (sich) vorbehalten; (sich) zurückhalten mit; *Platz etc.* reservieren (lassen), belegen, vorbestellen; ~**d** □ *fig.* zurückhaltend, reserviert.

res·er·voir [ˈrezəvwɑː] Behälter *m* (*für Wasser etc.*); Sammel-, Staubecken *n*; *fig.* Reservoir *n*.

re·side [rɪˈzaɪd] wohnen, ansässig sein, s-n Wohnsitz haben; ~ *in fig.* innewohnen (*dat.*).

res·i|dence [ˈrezɪdəns] Wohnsitz *m*, -ort *m*; Aufenthalt *m*; (Amts)Sitz *m*; (herrschaftliches) Wohnhaus; Residenz *f*; ~ *permit* Aufenthaltsgenehmigung *f*; ~·**dent** [~t] **1.** wohnhaft; ortsansässig; **2.** Ortsansässige(r *m*) *f*, Einwohner(in); Bewohner(in); Hotelgast *m*; *mot.* Anlieger *m*; ~·**den-**

tial [rezɪˈdenʃl] Wohn...; ~ *area* Wohngegend *f*.

re·sid·u·al [rɪˈzɪdjuəl] übrig(geblieben); zurückbleibend; restlich; **res·i·due** [ˈrezɪdjuː] Rest *m*; Rückstand *m*.

re·sign [rɪˈzaɪn] *v/t.* aufgeben; *Amt* niederlegen; überlassen; verzichten auf (*acc.*); ~ *o.s. to* sich ergeben in (*acc.*); sich abfinden mit; *v/i.* zurücktreten; **res·ig·na·tion** [rezɪɡˈneɪʃn] Rücktritt(sgesuch *n*) *m*; Resignation *f*; ~**ed** □ ergeben, resigniert.

re·sil·i|ence [rɪˈzɪlɪəns] Elastizität *f*; *fig.* Unverwüstlichkeit *f*; ~·**ent** [~t] elastisch; *fig.* unverwüstlich.

res·in [ˈrezɪn] **1.** Harz *n*; **2.** harzen.

re·sist [rɪˈzɪst] widerstehen (*dat.*); Widerstand leisten; sich widersetzen (*dat.*); ~·**ance** [~əns] Widerstand *m* (*a.* ⚡, *phys.*); *med.* Widerstandsfähigkeit *f*; *line of least* ~ Weg *m* des geringsten Widerstands; **re·sis·tant** [~nt] widerstandsfähig.

res·o|lute □ [ˈrezəluːt] entschlossen, energisch; ~·**lu·tion** [rezəˈluːʃn] Entschlossenheit *f*; Bestimmtheit *f*; Beschluß *m*; *pol.* Resolution *f*; Lösung *f*.

re·solve [rɪˈzɒlv] **1.** *v/t.* auflösen; *fig.* lösen; *Zweifel etc.* zerstreuen; beschließen, entscheiden; *v/i. a.* ~ *o.s.* sich auflösen; beschließen; ~ *on*, ~ *upon* sich entschließen zu; **2.** Entschluß *m*; Beschluß *m*; ~**d** □ entschlossen.

res·o|nance [ˈrezənəns] Resonanz *f*; ~·**nant** □ [~t] nach-, widerhallend.

re·sort [rɪˈzɔːt] **1.** Zuflucht *f*; Ausweg *m*; Aufenthalt(sort) *m*; Erholungsort *m*; *health* ~ Kurort *m*; *seaside* ~ Seebad *n*; *summer* ~ Sommerfrische *f*; **2.** ~ *to* oft besuchen; seine Zuflucht nehmen zu.

re·sound [rɪˈzaʊnd] widerhallen (lassen).

re·source [rɪˈsɔːs] Hilfsquelle *f*, -mittel *n*; Zuflucht *f*; Findigkeit *f*; ~*s pl.* (*natürliche*) Reichtümer *pl.*, Mittel *pl.*, Bodenschätze *pl.*; ~·**ful** □ [~fl] einfallsreich, findig.

re·spect [rɪˈspekt] **1.** Beziehung *f*, Hinsicht *f*; Achtung *f*, Respekt *m*; Rücksicht *f*; *with* ~ *to* ... was ... (an)betrifft; *in this* ~ in dieser Hinsicht; ~*s pl.* Empfehlungen *pl.*, Grüße *pl.*; *give my* ~*s to* ... grüßen Sie ...

von mir; **2.** *v/t.* achten, schätzen; respektieren; betreffen; *as ~s ... was ... (an)betrifft;* **re·spec·ta·ble** □ [~əbl] ehrbar; anständig; angesehen, geachtet (*Mensch*); ansehnlich, beachtlich (*Summe*); **~ful** □ [~fl] ehrerbietig; *yours ~ly* hochachtungsvoll; **~ing** [~ɪŋ] hinsichtlich (*gen.*).

re·spec·tive [rɪ'spektɪv] jeweilig; *we went to our ~ places* wir gingen jeder an seinen Platz; **~ly** [~lɪ] beziehungsweise.

res·pi·ra·tion [respə'reɪʃn] Atmung *f*; **~·tor** ⚕ [~] Atemgerät *n*.

re·spire [rɪ'spaɪə] atmen.

re·spite ['respaɪt] Frist *f*; Aufschub *m*; Stundung *f*; Ruhepause *f* (*from* von); *without (a) ~* ohne Unterbrechung.

re·splen·dent □ [rɪ'splendənt] glänzend, strahlend.

re·spond [rɪ'spɒnd] antworten, erwidern; *~ to* reagieren *od.* ansprechen auf (*acc.*).

re·sponse [rɪ'spɒns] Antwort *f*, Erwiderung *f*; *fig.* Reaktion *f*; *meet with little ~* wenig Anklang finden.

re·spon·si·bil·i·ty [rɪspɒnsə'bɪlətɪ] Verantwortung *f*; *on one's own ~* auf eigene Verantwortung; *sense of ~* Verantwortungsgefühl *n; take (accept, assume)* the *~* für die Verantwortung übernehmen für; **~ble** □ [rɪ'spɒnsəbl] verantwortlich; verantwortungsvoll.

rest¹ [rest] **1.** Ruhe *f*; Rast *f*; Pause *f*, Unterbrechung *f*; Erholung *f*; ⊕ Stütze *f*; (*Telefon*)Gabel *f*; *have od. take a ~* sich ausruhen; *be at ~* ruhig sein; **2.** *v/i.* ruhen; rasten; schlafen; (sich) lehnen, sich stützen (*on* auf *acc.*); *~ on, ~ upon* ruhen auf (*Blick, Last*); *fig.* beruhen auf (*dat.*); *~ with fig.* liegen bei (*Fehler, Verantwortung*); *v/t.* (aus)ruhen lassen; stützen (*on* auf); lehnen (*against* gegen).

rest² [~]: *the ~* der Rest; *and all the ~ of it* und so weiter und so fort; *for the ~* im übrigen.

res·tau·rant ['restərɔ̃:ŋ, ~rɒnt] Restaurant *n*, Gaststätte *f*.

rest·ful ['restfl] ruhig, erholsam.

rest·ing-place ['restɪŋpleɪs] Ruheplatz *m*; (letzte) Ruhestätte.

res·ti·tu·tion [restɪ'tjuːʃn] Wiederherstellung *f*; Rückerstattung *f*.

res·tive □ ['restɪv] widerspenstig.

rest·less □ ['restlɪs] ruhelos; rastlos; unruhig; **~ness** [~nɪs] Ruhelosigkeit *f*; Rastlosigkeit *f*; Unruhe *f*.

res·to·ra·tion [restə'reɪʃn] Wiederherstellung *f*; Wiedereinsetzung *f*; Restaurierung *f*; Rekonstruktion *f*; Nachbildung *f*; (Rück)Erstattung *f*; **~·tive** [rɪ'stɒrətɪv] **1.** stärkend; **2.** Stärkungsmittel *n*.

re·store [rɪ'stɔː] wiederherstellen; wiedereinsetzen (*to* in *acc.*); restaurieren; (rück)erstatten, zurückgeben; zurücklegen; *~ s.o. (to health)* j-n wiederherstellen.

re·strain [rɪ'streɪn] zurückhalten (*from* von); in Schranken halten; bändigen, zügeln; *Gefühle* unterdrücken; **~t** [~t] Zurückhaltung *f*; Beschränkung *f*, Zwang *m*.

re·strict [rɪ'strɪkt] be-, einschränken; **re·stric·tion** [~kʃn] Be-, Einschränkung *f*; *without ~s* uneingeschränkt.

re·sult [rɪ'zʌlt] **1.** Ergebnis *n*, Resultat *n*; Folge *f*; **2.** folgen, sich ergeben (*from* aus); *~ in* hinauslaufen auf (*acc.*), zur Folge haben.

re·sume [rɪ'zjuːm] wiederaufnehmen; fortsetzen; *Sitz* wieder einnehmen; **re·sump·tion** [rɪ'zʌmpʃn] Wiederaufnahme *f*; Fortsetzung *f*.

re·sur·rec·tion [rezə'rekʃn] Wiederaufleben *n*; ⌇ *eccl.* Auferstehung *f*.

re·sus·ci·tate [rɪ'sʌsɪteɪt] wiederbeleben; *fig.* wieder aufleben lassen.

re·tail 1. ['riːteɪl] Einzelhandel *m*; *by ~, adv. ~* im Einzelhandel; **2.** [~] Einzelhandels...; **3.** [riː'teɪl] im Einzelhandel verkaufen; **~er** [~ə] Einzelhändler(in).

re·tain [rɪ'teɪn] behalten; zurück(be)halten; beibehalten.

re·tal·i·ate [rɪ'tælɪeɪt] *v/t. Unrecht* vergelten; *v/i.* sich rächen; **~·a·tion** [rɪtælɪ'eɪʃn] Vergeltung *f*.

re·tard [rɪ'tɑːd] verzögern, aufhalten, hemmen; *(mentally) ~ed psych.* (geistig) zurückgeblieben.

retch [retʃ] würgen (*beim Erbrechen*).

re·tell [riː'tel] (*-told*) nacherzählen; wiederholen.

re·ten·tion [rɪ'tenʃn] Zurückhalten *n*; Beibehaltung *f*; Bewahrung *f*.

re·think [riː'θɪŋk] (*-thought*) *et.* nochmals überdenken.

ret·i·cent □ ['retɪsənt] verschwiegen; schweigsam; zurückhaltend.

ret·i·nue ['retɪnjuː] Gefolge *n*.

re·tire [rɪ'taɪə] v/t. zurückziehen; pensionieren; v/i. sich zurückziehen; zurück-, abtreten; sich zur Ruhe setzen; in Pension od. Rente gehen, sich pensionieren lassen; **~d** □ zurückgezogen; pensioniert, im Ruhestand (lebend); ~ **pay** Ruhegeld n; **~ment** [~mənt] Sichzurückziehen n; Ausscheiden n, Aus-, Rücktritt m; Ruhestand m; Zurückgezogenheit f; **re·tir·ing** [~rɪŋ] zurückhaltend; ~ **pension** Ruhegeld n.

re·tort [rɪ'tɔːt] **1.** (scharfe od. treffende) Erwiderung; **2.** (scharf od. treffend) erwidern.

re·touch ['riː'tʌtʃ] et. überarbeiten; phot. retuschieren.

re·trace [rɪ'treɪs] zurückverfolgen; ~ one's steps zurückgehen.

re·tract [rɪ'trækt] v/t. Angebot zurückziehen; Behauptung zurücknehmen; Krallen, ✈ Fahrgestell einziehen; v/i. eingezogen werden (Krallen, ✈ Fahrgestell).

re·train [riː'treɪn] umschulen.

re·tread 1. [riː'tred] Reifen runderneuern; **2.** ['riː'tred] runderneuerter Reifen.

re·treat [rɪ'triːt] **1.** Rückzug m; Zuflucht(sort m) f; Schlupfwinkel m; sound the ~ ✕ zum Rückzug blasen; **2.** sich zurückziehen.

ret·ri·bu·tion [retrɪ'bjuːʃn] Vergeltung f.

re·trieve [rɪ'triːv] wiederfinden, -bekommen; wiedergewinnen, -erlangen; wiedergutmachen; hunt. apportieren.

ret·ro· ['retrəʊ](zu)rück...; **~ac·tive** □ ✄ [retrəʊ'æktɪv] rückwirkend; **~grade** ['retrəʊɡreɪd] rückläufig; rückschrittlich; **~spect** [~spekt] Rückblick m; **~spec·tive** □ [retrəʊ'spektɪv] (zu)rückblickend; ✄ rückwirkend.

re·try ✄ ['riː'traɪ] wiederaufnehmen, neu verhandeln.

re·turn [rɪ'tɜːn] **1.** Rück-, Wiederkehr f; Wiederauftreten n; Brt. Rückfahrkarte f, ✈ Rückflugticket n; econ. Rückzahlung f; Rückgabe f; Entgelt n, Gegenleistung f; (amtlicher) Bericht; (Steuer)Erklärung f; parl. Wahl f (e-s Abgeordneten); Sport: Rückspiel n; Tennis etc. Rückschlag m, Return m; Erwiderung f; attr. Rück...; ~s pl. econ. Umsatz m; Ertrag m, Gewinn m;

many happy ~s of the day herzliche Glückwünsche zum Geburtstag; in ~ for (als Gegenleistung) für; by ~ (of post), by ~ mail Am. postwendend; ~ match Sport: Rückspiel n; ~ ticket Brt. Rückfahrkarte f, ✈ Rückflugticket n; **2.** v/i. zurückkehren, -kommen; wiederkommen; v/t. zurückgeben; Geld zurückzahlen; zurückschicken, -senden; zurückstellen, -bringen, -tun; Gewinn abwerfen; (zur Steuerveranlagung) angeben; parl. Abgeordneten wählen; Tennis etc.: Ball zurückschlagen, -geben; erwidern; vergelten; ~ a verdict of guilty ✄ j-n schuldig sprechen.

re·u·ni·fi·ca·tion pol. ['riːjuːnɪfɪ'keɪʃn] Wiedervereinigung f.

re·u·nion ['riː'juːnjən] Wiedervereinigung f; Treffen n, Zusammenkunft f.

re·val·ue econ. [riː'væljuː] Währung aufwerten.

re·veal [rɪ'viːl] enthüllen; offenbaren; **~ing** [~ɪŋ] aufschlußreich.

rev·el ['revl] (bsd. Brt. -ll-, Am. -l-) ausgelassen sein; ~ in schwelgen in (dat.); sich weiden an (dat.).

rev·e·la·tion [revə'leɪʃn] Enthüllung f; Offenbarung f.

rev·el·ry ['revlrɪ] lärmende Festlichkeit.

re·venge [rɪ'vendʒ] **1.** Rache f; bsd. Sport, Spiel: Revanche f; in ~ for als Rache für; **2.** rächen; **~ful** □ [~fl] rachsüchtig; **re·veng·er** [~ə] Rächer(in).

rev·e·nue econ. ['revənjuː] Staatseinkünfte pl., -einnahmen pl.

re·ver·be·rate phys. [rɪ'vɜːbəreɪt] zurückwerfen; zurückstrahlen; widerhallen.

re·vere [rɪ'vɪə] (ver)ehren.

rev·e·rence ['revərəns] **1.** Verehrung f; Ehrfurcht f; **2.** (ver)ehren; **~rend** [~d] **1.** ehrwürdig; **2.** Geistliche(r) m.

rev·e·rent □ ['revərənt], **~ren·tial** □ [revə'renʃl] ehrerbietig, ehrfurchtsvoll.

rev·er·ie ['revərɪ] (Tag)Träumerei f.

re·ver·sal [rɪ'vɜːsl] Umkehrung f, Umschwung m; **~e** [~ɜːs] **1.** Gegenteil n; Rück-, Kehrseite f; mot. Rückwärtsgang m; Rückschlag m; **2.** □ umgekehrt; Rück(wärts)...; in ~ order in umgekehrter Reihenfolge; ~ gear mot. Rückwärtsgang m; ~ side linke (Stoff)Seite f; **3.** umkehren; Ur-

teil umstoßen; **~·i·ble** □ [~əbl] doppelseitig (tragbar).

re·vert [rɪ'vɜːt] (*to*) zurückkehren (zu *dat.*); zurückkommen (auf *acc.*); wieder zurückfallen (in *acc.*); ⚖ zurückfallen (an *j-n*).

re·view [rɪ'vjuː] 1. Nachprüfung *f*, (Über)Prüfung *f*, Revision *f*; ✗ Parade *f*; Rückblick *m*; (Buch)Besprechung *f*, Kritik *f*, Rezension *f*; *pass s.th. in* ~ et. Revue passieren lassen; 2. (über-, nach)prüfen; ✗ besichtigen; *Buch etc.* besprechen, rezensieren; *fig.* überblicken, -schauen; **~·er** [~ə] Rezensent(in).

re·vise [rɪ'vaɪz] überarbeiten, durchsehen, revidieren; *Brt.* (den Stoff) wiederholen (*für e-e Prüfung*); **re·vi·sion** [rɪ'vɪʒn] Revision *f*; Überarbeitung *f*; *Brt.* Wiederholung *f* (des Stoffs) (*für e-e Prüfung*).

re·viv·al [rɪ'vaɪvl] Wiederbelebung *f*; Wiederaufleben *n*, -blühen *n*; Erneuerung *f*; *fig.* Erweckung *f*; **re·vive** [~aɪv] wiederbeleben; wiederaufleben (lassen); wiederherstellen; sich erholen.

re·voke [rɪ'vəʊk] widerrufen, zurücknehmen, rückgängig machen.

re·volt [rɪ'vəʊlt] 1. Revolte *f*, Aufstand *m*, -ruhr *m*; 2. *v/i.* sich auflehnen, revoltieren (*against* gegen); *v/t. fig.* abstoßen; **~·ing** □ [~ɪŋ] abstoßend; ekelhaft; scheußlich.

rev·o·lu·tion [revə'luːʃn] ⊕ Umdrehung *f*; *fig.* Revolution *f* (*a. pol.*), Umwälzung *f*, Umschwung *m*; **~·ar·y** [~ərɪ] 1. revolutionär; Revolutions...; 2. *pol. u. fig.* Revolutionär(in); **~·ize** *fig.* [~naɪz] revolutionieren.

re·volve [rɪ'vɒlv] *v/i.* sich drehen (*about, round* um); ~ *around fig.* sich um *j-n od. et.* drehen; *v/t.* drehen; **re·volv·ing** [~ɪŋ] sich drehend, Dreh...

re·vue *thea.* [rɪ'vjuː] Revue *f*; Kabarett *n*.

re·vul·sion *fig.* [rɪ'vʌlʃn] Abscheu *m*.

re·ward [rɪ'wɔːd] 1. Belohnung *f*; Entgelt *n*; 2. belohnen; **~·ing** □ [~ɪŋ] lohnend; dankbar (*Aufgabe*).

re·write ['riː'raɪt] (*-wrote, -written*) neu (*od.* um)schreiben. ♪

rhap·so·dy ['ræpsədɪ] ♪ Rhapsodie *f*; *fig.* Schwärmerei *f*, Wortschwall *m*.

rhe·to·ric ['retərɪk] Rhetorik *f*; *fig. contp.* leere Phrasen *pl.*

rheu·ma·tism ♂ ['ruːmətɪzəm] Rheumatismus *m*.

rhu·barb ♀ ['ruːbɑːb] Rhabarber *m*.

rhyme [raɪm] 1. Reim *m*; Vers *m*; *without* ~ *or reason* ohne Sinn u. Verstand; 2. (sich) reimen.

rhyth|m ['rɪðəm] Rhythmus *m*; **~·mic** [~mɪk] (*~ally*), **~·mi·cal** □ [~mɪkl] rhythmisch.

rib [rɪb] 1. *anat.* Rippe *f*; 2. (*-bb-*) F hänseln, aufziehen.

rib·ald ['rɪbəld] lästerlich, zotig.

rib·bon ['rɪbən] Band *n*; Ordensband *n*; Farbband *n*; Streifen *m*; ~*s pl.* Fetzen *pl.*

rib cage *anat.* ['rɪbkeɪdʒ] Brustkorb *m*.

rice ♀ [raɪs] Reis *m*.

rich [rɪtʃ] 1. □ reich (*in an dat.*); prächtig, kostbar; fruchtbar, fett (*Erde*); voll (*Ton*); schwer, nahrhaft (*Speise*); schwer (*Wein, Duft*); satt (*Farbe*); 2. *the* ~ *pl.* die Reichen *pl.*; **~·es** ['rɪtʃɪz] *pl.* Reichtum *m*, Reichtümer *pl.*

rick ⚘ [rɪk] (Stroh-, Heu)Schober *m*.

rick·ets ['rɪkɪts] *sg. od. pl.* Rachitis *f*; **rick·et·y** [~ɪ] ♂ rachitisch; wack(e)lig (*Möbel*).

rid [rɪd] (*-dd-*; *rid*) befreien, frei machen (*of von*); *get* ~ *of* loswerden.

rid·dance F ['rɪdəns]: *Good* ~ F! Den (die, das) wären wir (Gott sei Dank) los!

rid·den ['rɪdn] 1. *p.p. von ride 2*; 2. *in Zssgn:* geplagt von ...

rid·dle[1] ['rɪdl] Rätsel *n*.

rid·dle[2] [~] 1. grobes (Draht)Sieb; 2. durchsieben; durchlöchern.

ride [raɪd] 1. Ritt *m*; Fahrt *f*; Reitweg *m*; 2. (*rode, ridden*) *v/i.* reiten; fahren (*on a bicycle* auf e-m Fahrrad; *in, Am. on a bus* im Bus); *v/t. Pferd etc.* reiten; *Fahr-, Motorrad* fahren, fahren auf (*dat.*); **rid·er** ['raɪdə] Reiter(in).

ridge [rɪdʒ] 1. (Gebirgs)Kamm *m*, Grat *m*; *arch.* First *m*; ⚘ Rain *m*.

rid·i·cule ['rɪdɪkjuːl] 1. Spott *m*; 2. lächerlich machen, verspotten; **ri·dic·u·lous** □ [rɪ'dɪkjələs] lächerlich.

rid·ing ['raɪdɪŋ] Reiten *n*; *attr.* Reit...

riff-raff ['rɪfræf] Gesindel *n*.

ri·fle[1] ['raɪfl] Gewehr *n*; Büchse *f*.

ri·fle[2] [~] (aus)plündern, durchwühlen.

rift [rɪft] Riß *m*, Sprung *m*; Spalte *f*.

·ig¹ [rɪg] (*-gg-*) manipulieren.

·ig² [~] **1.** ♣ Takelage *f*; ⊕ Bohranlage *f*, -turm *m*; Förderturm *m*; F Aufmachung *f*; **2.** (*-gg-*) *Schiff* auftakeln; ~ **up** F (behelfsmäßig) herrichten, zusammenbauen; **~ging** ♣ ['rɪgɪŋ] Takelage *f*.

·ight [raɪt] **1.** □ recht; richtig; rechte(r, -s), Rechts...; *all* ~! in Ordnung!, gut!; *that's all* ~! das macht nichts!, schon gut!, bitte!; *I am perfectly all* ~ mir geht es ausgezeichnet; *that's* ~! richtig!, gut!, ganz recht!, stimmt!; *be* ~ recht haben; *put* ~, *set* ~ in Ordnung bringen; berichtigen, korrigieren; **2.** *adv.* rechts; recht; richtig; gerade(wegs), direkt; ganz (und gar); genau, gerade; ~ *away* sofort; ~ *on* geradeaus; *turn* ~ (sich) nach rechts wenden, rechts abbiegen; **3.** Recht *n*; Rechte *f* (*a. pol.*, *Boxen*), rechte Seite *od.* Hand; *by* ~ *of* auf Grund (*gen.*); *on od. to the* ~ rechts; **4.** aufrichten; *et.* wiedergutmachen; in Ordnung bringen; **~-down** ['raɪtdaʊn] regelrecht; **~eous** □ ['raɪtʃəs] rechtschaffen; selbstgerecht; gerecht(fertigt), berechtigt; **~ful** □ [~l] rechtmäßig; gerecht; **~hand** rechte(r, -s); ~ *drive* Rechtssteuerung *f*; **~hand·ed** rechtshändig; **~ly** [~lɪ] richtig; mit Recht; ~ **of way** Durchgangsrecht *n*; *mot.* Vorfahrt(srecht *n*) *f*; **~wing** *pol.* rechte(r, -s), rechtsgerichtet.

rig·id □ ['rɪdʒɪd] starr, steif; *fig.* streng, hart; **~i·ty** [rɪ'dʒɪdətɪ] Starrheit *f*; Strenge *f*, Härte *f*.

rig·ma·role ['rɪgmərəʊl] Geschwätz *n*.

rig·or·ous □ ['rɪgərəs] streng, rigoros; (peinlich) genau.

rig·o(u)r ['rɪgə] Strenge *f*, Härte *f*.

rile F [raɪl] ärgern, reizen.

rim [rɪm] Rand *m*; Krempe *f*; Felge *f*; Radkranz *m*; **~less** ['rɪmlɪs] randlos (*Brille*); **~med** mit (e-m) Rand.

rime *lit.* [raɪm] Rauhreif *m*.

rind [raɪnd] Rinde *f*, Schale *f*; (Speck)Schwarte *f*.

ring¹ [rɪŋ] **1.** Klang *m*; Geläut(e) *n*; Klingeln *n*, Läuten *n*; (Telefon)Anruf *m*; *give s.o. a* ~ j-n anrufen; **2.** (*rang*, *rung*) läuten; klingeln; klingen; erschallen; *bsd. Brt. teleph.* anrufen; ~ *the bell* läuten, klingeln; *bsd. Brt. teleph.*: ~ *back* zurückrufen;

~ *off* (den Hörer) auflegen, Schluß machen; ~ *s.o.* up j-n *od.* bei j-m anrufen.

ring² [~] **1.** Ring *m*; Kreis *m*; Manege *f*; (Box)Ring *m*; (Verbrecher-, Spionage- *etc.*)Ring *m*; **2.** umringen; beringen; **~bind·er** ['rɪŋbaɪndə] Ringbuch *n*; **~lead·er** Rädelsführer *m*; **~let** [~lɪt] (Ringel)Locke *f*; **~mas·ter** Zirkusdirektor *m*; ~ **road** *Brt.* Umgehungsstraße *f*; Ringstraße *f*; **~side:** *at the* ~ *Boxen*: am Ring; ~ *seat* Ringplatz *m*; Manegenplatz *m*.

rink [rɪŋk] (*bsd. Kunst*)Eisbahn *f*; Rollschuhbahn *f*.

rinse [rɪns] *oft* ~ *out* (ab-, aus)spülen.

ri·ot ['raɪət] **1.** Aufruhr *m*; Tumult *m*, Krawall *m*; *run* ~ randalieren; **2.** Krawall machen, randalieren; e-n Aufstand machen; **~er** [~ə] Aufrührer(in); Randalierer *m*; **~ous** □ [~əs] aufrührerisch; lärmend; ausgelassen, wild.

rip [rɪp] **1.** Riß *m*; **2.** (*-pp-*) (auf-, zer)reißen, (-)schlitzen; F sausen, rasen.

ripe □ [raɪp] reif; **rip·en** ['raɪpən] reifen (lassen), reif werden; **~ness** [~nɪs] Reife *f*.

rip·ple ['rɪpl] **1.** kleine Welle; Kräuselung *f*; Rieseln *n*; **2.** (sich) kräuseln; rieseln.

rise [raɪz] **1.** (An-, Auf)Steigen *n*; (Preis-, Gehalts-, Lohn)Erhöhung *f*; Steigung *f*; Anhöhe *f*; Ursprung *m*; *fig.* Aufstieg *m*; *give* ~ *to* verursachen, führen zu; **2.** (*rose*, *risen*) sich erheben, aufstehen; die Sitzung schließen; auf-, hoch-, emporsteigen; (an)steigen; sich erheben, emporragen; aufkommen (*Sturm etc.*); *eccl.* auferstehen; aufgehen (*Sonne, Samen*); entspringen (*Fluß*); (an-)wachsen; sich steigern; sich erheben, revoltieren; *beruflich etc.* aufsteigen; ~ *to the occasion* sich der Lage gewachsen zeigen; **~n** ['rɪzn] *p.p. von* rise 2; **ris·er** ['raɪzə]: *early* ~ Frühaufsteher(in).

ris·ing ['raɪzɪŋ] (An-, Auf)Steigen *n*; *ast.* Aufgehen *n*, -gang *m*; Aufstand *m*.

risk [rɪsk] **1.** Gefahr *f*, Wagnis *n*, Risiko *n* (*a. econ.*); *be at* ~ in Gefahr sein; *run the* ~ *of doing s.th.* Gefahr laufen, et. zu tun; *run od. take a* ~ ein Risiko eingehen; **2.** wagen, riskieren; **~y** □ ['rɪskɪ]

(-*ier*, -*iest*) riskant, gefährlich, gewagt.

rite [raɪt] Ritus *m*; Zeremonie *f*; **rit·u·al** ['rɪtʃʊəl] **1.** □ rituell; Ritual...; **2.** Ritual *n*.

ri·val ['raɪvl] **1.** Rival|e *m*, -in *f*, Konkurrent(in); **2.** rivalisierend, Konkurrenz...; **3.** (*bsd. Brt. -ll-, Am. -l-*) rivalisieren *od.* konkurrieren mit; ~**ry** [~rɪ] Rivalität *f*; Konkurrenz (-kampf *m*) *f*.

riv·er ['rɪvə] Fluß *m*, Strom *m* (*a. fig.*); ~**side 1.** Flußufer *n*; **2.** am Ufer (gelegen).

riv·et ['rɪvɪt] **1.** ⊕ Niet(e *f*) *m*, *n*; **2.** ⊕ (ver)nieten; *fig.* Blick *etc.* heften; *fig.* fesseln.

riv·u·let ['rɪvjʊlɪt] Flüßchen *n*.

road [rəʊd] (Auto-, Land)Straße *f*; *fig.* Weg *m*; on the ~ unterwegs; *thea.* auf Tournee; ~**ac·ci·dent** Straßenunfall *m*; ~**block** ['rəʊdblɒk] Straßensperre *f*; ~**map** Straßenkarte *f*; ~**safe·ty** Verkehrssicherheit *f*; ~**side 1.** Straßen-, Wegrand *m*; **2.** an der Landstraße (gelegen); ~**way** Fahrbahn *f*; ~**works** *pl.* Straßenbauarbeiten *pl.*; ~**wor·thy** *mot.* verkehrssicher.

roam [rəʊm] *v/i.* (umher)streifen, (-)wandern; *v/t.* durchstreifen.

roar [rɔː] **1.** brüllen; brausen, tosen, donnern; **2.** Brüllen *n*, Gebrüll *n*; Brausen *n*; Krachen *n*, Getöse *n*; schallendes Gelächter.

roast [rəʊst] **1.** Braten *m*; **2.** braten; rösten; **3.** gebraten; ~ beef Rost- *od.* Rinderbraten *m*.

rob [rɒb] (-*bb*-) (be)rauben; ~**ber** ['rɒbə] Räuber *m*; ~**ber·y** [~rɪ] Raub *m*; ~ with violence ᵗᵗᵗ schwerer Raub.

robe [rəʊb] (Amts)Robe *f*, Talar *m*; Bade-, Hausmantel *m*, Morgenrock *m*.

rob·in *zo.* ['rɒbɪn] Rotkehlchen *n*.

ro·bot ['rəʊbɒt] Roboter *m*.

ro·bust □ [rə'bʌst] robust, kräftig.

rock [rɒk] Fels(en) *m*; Klippe *f*; Gestein *n*; *Brt.* Zuckerstange *f*; △ *nicht* Rock; on the ~s mit Eiswürfeln (*Whisky etc.*); kaputt, in die Brüche gegangen (*Ehe*); ~ crystal Bergkristall *m*; **2.** schaukeln, wiegen; erschüttern (*a. fig.*).

rock·er ['rɒkə] Kufe *f*; *Am.* Schaukelstuhl *m*; *Brt.* Rocker *m*; off one's ~ *sl.* übergeschnappt.

rock·et ['rɒkɪt] Rakete *f*; *attr.* Rake ten...; ~**pro·pelled** mit Raketenar trieb; ~**ry** [~rɪ] Raketentechnik *f*.

rock·ing-**chair** ['rɒkɪntʃeə] Schau kelstuhl *m*; ~**horse** Schaukelpfer *n*.

rock·y ['rɒkɪ] (-*ier*, -*iest*) felsig, Fe sen...

rod [rɒd] Rute *f*; Stab *m*; ⊕ Stange

rode [rəʊd] *pret. von* ride 2.

ro·dent *zo.* ['rəʊdənt] Nagetier *n*.

ro·de·o [rəʊ'deɪəʊ] (*pl.* -os) Rodeo *n*

roe¹ *zo.* [rəʊ] Reh *n*.

roe² *zo.* [~] *a.* hard ~ Rogen *m*; *a.* so ~ Milch *f*.

rogue [rəʊg] Schurke *m*, Gauner *m* Schlingel *m*, Spitzbube *m*; **ro·guis** □ ['rəʊgɪʃ] spitzbübisch.

role, rôle *thea.* [rəʊl] Rolle *f* (*a. fig.*

roll [rəʊl] **1.** Rolle *f*; Brötchen *n* Semmel *f*; (*bsd.* Namens-, Anwesen heits)Liste *f*; Brausen *n*; (*Donner*-Rollen *n*; (*Trommel*)Wirbel *m*; ⊕ Schlingern *n*; **2.** *v/t.* rollen; wälzen walzen; *Zigarette* drehen; ~ u *Ärmel* hochkrempeln; *mot.* Fenste hochkurbeln; *v/i.* rollen; fahren sich wälzen; (g)rollen (*Donner* dröhnen; brausen; wirbeln (*Trom mel*); ⊕ schlingern; ~**call** ['rəʊlkɔ Namensaufruf *m*; ✕ Appell *m*.

roll·er ['rəʊlə] Rolle *f*, Walze *f* (Locken)Wickler *m*; ⊕ Sturzwelle *f* Brecher *m*; △ *nicht* Roller; ~**coast er** Achterbahn *f*; ~**skate** Rollschuh *m*; ~**skate** Rollschuh laufen; ~**skat·ing** Rollschuhlaufen *n*; ~**tow·el** Rollhandtuch *n*.

rol·lick·ing ['rɒlɪkɪŋ] übermütig.

roll·ing ['rəʊlɪŋ] rollend *etc.*; Roll... Walz...; ~**mill** ⊕ Walzwerk *n*; ~ *pir* Nudelholz *n*.

roll-neck ['rəʊlnek] **1.** Rollkragen (-pullover) *m*; **2.** Rollkragen...; ~**ed** [~t] Rollkragen...

Ro·man ['rəʊmən] **1.** römisch; **2.** Römer(in).

ro·mance¹ [rəʊ'mæns] **1.** (Ritter-Vers)Roman *m*; Abenteuer-, Liebesroman *m*; Romanze *f* (*a. fig.*); Romantik *f*, Zauber *m*.

Ro·mance² *ling.* [~] *a.* ~ languages die romanischen Sprachen *pl.*

Ro·ma·ni·an [ruː'meɪnjən] **1.** rumänisch; **2.** Rumän|e *m*, -in *f*; *ling.* Rumänisch *n*.

ro·man|tic [rə'mæntɪk] **1.** (~ally)

romantisch (veranlagt); 2. Romantiker(in); Schwärmer(in); **~·ti·cis·m** [~sɪzəm] Romantik f.

romp [rɒmp] 1. Tollen n, Toben n; Range f, Wildfang m; 2. a. ~ about, ~ around herumtollen, -toben; **~ers** ['rɒmpəz] pl. einteiliger Spielanzug.

roof [ruːf] 1. Dach n (a. fig.); ~ of the mouth anat. Gaumen m; 2. mit e-m Dach versehen; ~ in, ~ over überdachen; **~ing** ['ruːfɪŋ] 1. Material n zum Dachdecken; 2. Dach...; ~ felt Dachpappe f; ~ rack bsd. Brt. mot. Dachgepäckträger m.

rook [rʊk] 1. Schach: Turm m; zo. Saatkrähe f; 2. betrügen (of um).

room [ruːm] 1. Raum m; Platz m; Zimmer n; fig. Spielraum m; **~s** pl. (Miet)Wohnung f; 2. Am. wohnen; **~·er** ['ruːmə] bsd. Am. Untermieter(in); **~·ing-house** [~ɪŋhaʊs] Fremdenheim n, Pension f; **~·mate** Zimmergenosse m, -in f; **~·y** □ [~ɪ] (-ier, -iest) geräumig.

roost [ruːst] 1. Schlafplatz m (von Vögeln); Hühnerstange f; 2. sich zum Schlaf niederhocken (Vögel); **~·er** bsd. Am. zo. ['ruːstə] (Haus-) Hahn m.

root [ruːt] 1. Wurzel f; 2. v/i. Wurzeln schlagen; wühlen (for nach); ~ about, ~ around herumwühlen (among in dat.); v/t. tief einpflanzen; ~ out ausrotten; ~ up ausgraben; **~·ed** ['ruːtɪd] eingewurzelt; deeply ~ed tief verwurzelt; stand ~ to the spot wie angewurzelt stehen(bleiben).

rope [rəʊp] 1. Tau n; Seil n; Strick m; Schnur f (Perlen etc.); be at the end of one's ~ mit s-m Latein am Ende sein; know the ~s sich auskennen; 2. verschnüren; festbinden; ~ off (durch ein Seil) absperren od. abgrenzen; ~ **lad·der** Strickleiter f; **~·tow** Schlepplift m; **~·way** ['rəʊpweɪ] (Seil)Schwebebahn f.

ro·sa·ry eccl. ['rəʊzərɪ] Rosenkranz m.

rose[1] [rəʊz] 1. ⊕ Rose f; (Gießkannen-) Brause f; Rosa-, Rosenrot n.

rose[2] [~] pret. von rise 2.

ros·trum ['rɒstrəm] (pl. -tra [-trə], -trums) Rednertribüne f, -pult n.

ros·y □ ['rəʊzɪ] (-ier, -iest) rosig.

rot [rɒt] 1. Fäulnis f; Brt. F Quatsch m; 2. (-tt-) v/t. (ver)faulen lassen; v/i. (ver)faulen, (-)modern, verrotten.

ro·ta·ry ['rəʊtərɪ] rotierend, sich

drehend; Rotations...; **ro·tate** [rəʊˈteɪt] rotieren od. kreisen (lassen), (sich) drehen; ✶ die Frucht wechseln; **ro·ta·tion** [~ʃn] Rotation f, (Um)Drehung f, Umlauf m; Wechsel m, Abwechslung f.

ro·tor bsd. ✈ ['rəʊtə] Rotor m.

rot·ten □ ['rɒtn] verfault, faul(ig); morsch; mies; gemein; feel ~ sl. sich beschissen fühlen.

ro·tund □ [rəʊˈtʌnd] rundlich.

rough [rʌf] 1. adj. □ rauh; roh; grob; barsch; hart; holp(e)rig, uneben; grob, ungefähr (Schätzung); unfertig, Roh...; ~ copy erster Entwurf, Konzept n; ~ draft Rohfassung f; 2. adv. roh, rauh, hart; 3. Rauhe n, Grobe n; holp(e)riger Boden; Golf: Rough n; 4. a n.- aufrauhen; ~ it F primitiv od. anspruchslos leben; **~·age** ['rʌfɪdʒ] Ballaststoffe pl.; **~·cast** 1. ⊕ Rohputz m; 2. unfertig; 3. (-cast) ⊕ roh verputzen; roh entwerfen; **~·en** [~n] rauh werden; an-, aufrauhen; **~·neck** Am. F Grobian m; Ölbohrarbeiter m; **~·ness** [~nɪs] Rauheit f; rauhe Stelle; Roheit f; Grobheit f; **~·shod**: ride ~ over j-n rücksichtslos behandeln; rücksichtslos über et. hinweggehen.

round [raʊnd] 1. adj. □ rund; voll (Stimme etc.); abgerundet (Stil); unverblümt; a ~ dozen ein rundes Dutzend; in ~ figures auf- od. abgerundet (Zahlen); 2. adv. rund-, rings(her)um; überall, auf od. von od. nach allen Seiten; ask s.o. ~ j-n zu sich einladen; ~ about ungefähr; all the year ~ das ganze Jahr hindurch; the other way ~ umgekehrt; 3. prp. (rund)um; um (... herum) in od. auf (dat.) ... herum; 4. Rund n, Kreis m; Runde f; (Leiter)Sprosse f; Brt. Scheibe f (Brot etc.); (Dienst-) Runde f, Rundgang m; ✚ Visite f (in e-r Klinik); ♪ Kanon m; (Lachetc.)Salve f; 100 ~s × 100 Schuß (Munition); 5. rund machen od. werden; (herum)gehen od. (-)fahren um, biegen um; ~ off abrunden, fig. krönen, beschließen; ~ up Zahl etc. aufrunden (to auf acc.); Vieh zusammentreiben; Leute etc. zusammentrommeln, auftreiben; **~·a·bout** ['raʊndəbaʊt] 1. ~ way od. route Umweg m; in a ~ way fig. auf Umwegen; 2. Brt. Karussell n; Brt. Kreisverkehr m; **~·ish** [~ɪʃ] rundlich;

Q
R

~ trip Rundreise f; Am. Hin- u. Rückfahrt f, ✈ Hin- u. Rückflug m; **~trip:** ~ ticket Am. Rückfahrkarte, ✈ Rückflugticket n; **~-up** Zusammentreiben n (von Vieh).

rouse [raʊz] v/t. wecken; Wild aufjagen; j-n aufrütteln; j-n reizen, erzürnen; Zorn erregen; ~ o.s. sich aufraffen; v/i. aufwachen.

route [ru:t, ✕ a. raʊt] (Reise-, Fahrt)Route f, (-)Weg m; (Bahn-, Bus-, Flug)Strecke f; ✕ Marschroute f.

rou·tine [ru:'ti:n] 1. Routine f; 2. üblich, routinemäßig, Routine...

rove [rəʊv] umherstreifen, -wandern; durchstreifen, -wandern.

row¹ [rəʊ] Reihe f.

row² F [raʊ] 1. Krach m, Lärm m; (lauter) Streit, Krach m; 2. (sich) streiten.

row³ [rəʊ] 1. Rudern n; Ruderpartie f; 2. rudern; **~·boat** Am. ['rəʊbəʊt] Ruderboot n; **~·er** [~ə] Ruder|er m, -in f; **~·ing boat** Brt. [~ɪŋbəʊt] Ruderboot n.

roy·al □ ['rɔɪəl] königlich; **~·ty** [~tɪ] Königtum n; Königswürde f; coll. das Königshaus, die königliche Familie; Tantieme f.

rub [rʌb] 1. give s.th. a good ~ et. (ab)reiben; et. polieren; 2. (-bb-) v/t. reiben; polieren; (wund) scheuern; ~ down abschmirgeln, abschleifen; trockenreiben, (ab)frottieren; ~ in einreiben; ~ it in fig. F darauf herumreiten; ~ off ab-, wegreiben, ab-, wegwischen; ~ out Brt. ausradieren; ~ up aufpolieren; ~ s.o. up the wrong way j-n verstimmen; v/i. reiben (against, on an dat., gegen).

rub·ber ['rʌbə] 1. Gummi n, m; (Radier)Gummi m; Wischtuch n; **~s** pl. Am. (Gummi)Überschuhe pl.; Brt. Turnschuhe pl.; **~ band** Gummiband n; **~ cheque**, Am. **~ check** geplatzter Scheck; **~·neck** Am. F 1. Gaffer(in); 2. gaffen; **~·y** [~rɪ] gummiartig; zäh, wie Gummi (Fleisch).

rub·bish ['rʌbɪʃ] Schutt m; Abfall m, Müll m, Kehricht m; fig. Schund m; Quatsch m, Blödsinn m; **~ bin** Brt. Mülleimer m; **~ chute** Müllschlucker m.

rub·ble ['rʌbl] Schutt m.

ru·by ['ru:bɪ] Rubin(rot n) m.

ruck·sack ['rʌksæk] Rucksack m.

rud·der ['rʌdə] ⚓ (Steuer)Ruder n; ✈ Seitenruder n.

rud·dy □ ['rʌdɪ] (-ier, -iest) rot, rötlich; frisch, gesund.

rude □ [ru:d] (~r, ~st) unhöflich, grob; unanständig; heftig, wild; ungebildet; einfach, kunstlos.

ru·di|men·ta·ry [ru:dɪ'mentərɪ] elementar, Anfangs...; **~·ments** ['ru:dɪmənts] pl. Anfangsgründe pl.

rue·ful □ ['ru:fl] reuig.

ruff [rʌf] Halskrause f.

ruf·fi·an ['rʌfjən] Rüpel m, Grobian m; Raufbold m, Schläger m.

ruf·fle ['rʌfl] 1. Krause f, Rüsche f; Kräuseln n; 2. kräuseln; Haare, Federn sträuben; zerknüllen; fig. aus der Ruhe bringen; (ver)ärgern.

rug [rʌg] (Reise-, Woll)Decke f; Vorleger m, Brücke f, (kleiner) Teppich.

rug·ged □ ['rʌgɪd] rauh (a. fig.); wild, zerklüftet, schroff.

ru·in ['rʊɪn] 1. Ruin m, Verderben n, Untergang m; mst ~s pl. Ruine(n pl.) f, Trümmer pl.; 2. ruinieren, zugrunde richten, zerstören, zunichte machen, zerrütten; **~·ous** □ [~əs] verfallen; ruinös.

rule [ru:l] 1. Regel f; Spielregel f; Vorschrift f; Satzung f; Herrschaft f, Regierung f; Lineal n; as a ~ in der Regel; work to ~ Dienst nach Vorschrift tun; ~s pl. (Geschäfts-, Gerichts- etc.)Ordnung f; ~(s) of the road Straßenverkehrsordnung f; 2. v/t. beherrschen, herrschen über (acc.); lenken, leiten; anordnen, verfügen; liniieren; ~ out ausschließen; v/i. herrschen; **rul·er** ['ru:lə] Herrscher(in); Lineal n.

rum [rʌm] Rum m; Am. Alkohol m.

rum·ble ['rʌmbl] rumpeln, poltern, (g)rollen (Donner), knurren (Magen).

ru·mi|nant zo. ['ru:mɪnənt] 1. wiederkäuend; 2. Wiederkäuer m; **~·nate** [~eɪt] zo. wiederkäuen; fig. grübeln (about, over über acc.).

rum·mage ['rʌmɪdʒ] 1. gründliche Durchsuchung; Ramsch m; ~ sale Am. Ramschverkauf m; Wohltätigkeitsbasar m; 2. a. ~ about herumstöbern, -wühlen (among, in in dat.).

ru·mo(u)r ['ru:mə] 1. Gerücht n; 2. ⚠ nicht rumoren; it is ~ed man sagt od. munkelt, es geht das Gerücht.

rump [rʌmp] Steiß m, Hinterteil n, -keulen pl.

rum·ple [ˈrʌmpl] zerknittern, -knüllen, -wühlen; ⚠ *nicht rumpeln.*

run [rʌn] **1.** (*-nn-; ran, run*) *v/i.* laufen, rennen, eilen; fahren; verkehren, fahren, gehen (*Zug, Bus*); fließen, strömen; verlaufen (*Straße*), führen (*Weg*); ⊕ laufen; in Betrieb *od.* Gang sein; gehen (*Uhr etc.*); schmelzen (*Butter etc.*); zer-, auslaufen (*Farbe*); lauten (*Text*); gehen (*Melodie*); laufen (*Theaterstück, Film*), gegeben werden; ✍ gelten, laufen; *econ.* stehen auf (*dat.*) (*Preis etc.*); *bsd. Am. pol.* kandidieren (for für); ~ *across s.o.* j-n zufällig treffen, auf j-n stoßen; ~ *after* hinterher-, nachlaufen; ~ *along!* F ab mit dir!; ~ *away* davonlaufen; ~ *away with* durchbrennen mit; ~ *down* ablaufen (*Uhr etc.*); *fig.* herunterkommen; ~ *dry* austrocknen; ~ *into* (hinein)laufen *od.* (-)rennen in (*acc.*); fahren gegen; j-n zufällig treffen; geraten in (*Schulden etc.*); sich belaufen auf (*acc.*); ~ *low* knapp werden; ~ *off with* = ~ *away with*; ~ *out* ablaufen (*Zeit*); ausgehen, knapp werden; ~ *out of petrol* kein Benzin mehr haben; ~ *over* überlaufen, -fließen; überfliegen, durchgehen, -lesen; ~ *short* knapp werden; ~ *short of petrol* kein Benzin mehr haben; ~ *through* überfliegen durchgehen, -lesen; ~ *up to* sich belaufen auf (*acc.*); *v/t.* Strecke durchlaufen, *Weg* einschlagen; fahren; laufen lassen; *Zug, Bus* fahren *od.* verkehren lassen; *Hand etc.* gleiten lassen; *Geschäft* betreiben; *Betrieb* führen, leiten; fließen lassen; *Temperatur, Fieber* haben; ~ *down* an-, überfahren; *fig.* schlechtmachen; herunterwirtschaften; ~ *errands* Besorgungen *od.* Botengänge machen; ~ *s.o. home* F j-n nach Hause bringen *od.* fahren; ~ *in Auto* einfahren; F *Verbrecher* einbuchten; ~ *over* überfahren; ~ *s.o. through* j-n durchbohren; ~ *up Preis etc.* in die Höhe treiben; *Rechnung etc.* auflaufen lassen; **2.** Laufen *n*, Rennen *n*, Lauf *m*; Verlauf *m*; Fahrt *f*; Spazierfahrt *f*; Reihe *f*, Folge *f*, Serie *f*; *econ.* Ansturm *m*, Run *m*, stürmische Nachfrage; *Am.* Bach *m*; *Am.* Laufmasche *f*; Gehege *n*; Auslauf *m*, (Hühner)Hof *m*; *Sport:* Bob-, Rodelbahn *f*; (Ski)Abfahrt(sstrecke) *f*; freie Benutzung; *thea., Film:* Laufzeit *f*; *have a* ~ *of 20 nights thea.* 20mal nacheinander gegeben werden; *in the long* ~ auf die Dauer; *in the short* ~ fürs nächste; *on the* ~ auf der Flucht.

run|a·bout F *mot.* [ˈrʌnəbaʊt] kleiner leichter Wagen; **~·a·way** Ausreißer *m*.

rung¹ [rʌŋ] *p.p. von* **ring¹** 2.

rung² [~] (Leiter)Sprosse *f* (*a. fig.*).

run|let [ˈrʌnlɪt] Rinnsal *n*; **~·nel** [~l] Rinnsal *n*; Rinnstein *m*.

run·ner [ˈrʌnə] Läufer(in); Bote *m*; (Schlitten-, Schlittschuh)Kufe *f*; Schieber *m* (*am Schirm*); Läufer *m*; Tischläufer *m*; *Am.* Laufmasche *f*; ⚘ Ausläufer *m*; **~ bean** *Brt.* ⚘ Stangenbohne; **~·up** [ˈrʌnˈʌp] (*pl. runners-up*) *Sport:* Zweite(r *m*) *f*.

run·ning [ˈrʌnɪŋ] **1.** laufend; fließend; *two days* ~ zwei Tage hintereinander; **2.** Laufen *n*; Rennen *n*; **~·board** Trittbrett *n*.

run·way ≥ [ˈrʌnweɪ] Start-, Lande-, Rollbahn *f*.

rup·ture [ˈrʌptʃə] **1.** Bruch *m*; Riß *m*; (Zer)Platzen *n*; **2.** brechen; bersten, (zer)platzen.

ru·ral □ [ˈrʊərəl] ländlich, Land...

ruse [ruːz] List *f*, Kniff *m*, Trick *m*.

rush¹ [rʌʃ] Binse *f*.

rush² [~] **1.** Jagen *n*, Hetzen *n*, Stürmen *n*; Eile *f*; (An)Sturm *m*; Andrang *m*; *econ.* stürmische Nachfrage; Hetze *f*, Hochbetrieb *m*; **2.** *v/i.* stürzen, jagen, hetzen, stürmen; ~ *at* sich stürzen auf (*acc.*); ~ *in* hereinstürzen, -stürmen; *v/t.* jagen, hetzen, drängen, (an)treiben; losstürmen auf (*acc.*), angreifen; schnell (*wohin*) bringen; **~ hour** [ˈrʌʃaʊə] Hauptverkehrszeit *f*, Stoßzeit *f*; **~-hour traf·fic** Stoßverkehr *m*.

Rus·sian [ˈrʌʃn] **1.** russisch; **2.** Russe *m*, -in *f*; *ling.* Russisch *n*.

rust [rʌst] **1.** Rost *m*; Rostbraun *n*; **2.** (ver-, ein)rosten (lassen).

rus·tic [ˈrʌstɪk] **1.** (~*ally*) ländlich, rustikal; bäurisch; **2.** Bauer *m*.

rus·tle [ˈrʌsl] **1.** rascheln (mit *od.* in *dat.*); rauschen; *Am.* Vieh stehlen; **2.** Rascheln *n*.

rust|less [ˈrʌstlɪs] rostfrei; **~·y** □ [~I] (*-ier, -iest*) rostig; *fig.* eingerostet.

rut¹ [rʌt] Wagenspur *f*; *bsd. fig.* ausgefahrenes Geleise.

rut² *zo.* [~] Brunst *f*, Brunft *f*.
ruth·less □ ['ru:θlɪs] umbarmherzig; rücksichts-, skrupellos.

rut|ted ['rʌtɪd], **~ty** [~ɪ] (*-ier*, *-iest*) ausgefahren (*Weg*).
rye ♧ [raɪ] Roggen *m*.

S

sa·ble ['seɪbl] *zo.* Zobel *m*; Zobelpelz *m*; △ *nicht* Säbel.
sab·o·tage ['sæbətɑ:ʒ] 1. Sabotage *f*; 2. sabotieren.
sa·bre, *Am. mst* **-ber** ['seɪbə] Säbel *m*.
sack [sæk] 1. Plünderung *f*; Sack *m*; *Am.* (Einkaufs)Tüte *f*; Sackkleid *n*; *get the* ~ F entlassen werden; F den Laufpaß bekommen; *give s.o. the* ~ F j-n entlassen; F j-m den Laufpaß geben; 2. plündern; einsacken; F rausschmeißen, entlassen; F *j-m* den Laufpaß geben; **~cloth** ['sækklɒθ], **~ing** [~ɪŋ] Sackleinen *n*, -leinwand *f*.
sac·ra·ment *eccl.* ['sækrəmənt] Sakrament *n*.
sa·cred □ ['seɪkrɪd] heilig; geistlich.
sac·ri·fice ['sækrɪfaɪs] 1. Opfer *n*; *at a* ~ *econ.* mit Verlust; 2. opfern; *econ.* mit Verlust verkaufen.
sac·ri|lege ['sækrɪlɪdʒ] Sakrileg *n*; Entweihung *f*; Frevel *m*; **~·le·gious** □ [sækrɪ'lɪdʒəs] frevelhaft.
sad □ [sæd] traurig; jämmerlich, elend; schlimm; dunkel, matt.
sad·den ['sædn] traurig machen *od.* werden.
sad·dle ['sædl] 1. Sattel *m*; 2. satteln; *fig.* belasten; **~r** [~ə] Sattler *m*.
sa·dis·m ['seɪdɪzəm] Sadismus *m*.
sad·ness ['sædnɪs] Traurigkeit *f*.
safe [seɪf] 1. □ (~*r*, ~*st*) sicher; unversehrt; zuverlässig; 2. Safe *m*, *n*, Geldschrank *m*; Fliegenschrank *m*; **~ con·duct** freies Geleit; Geleitbrief *m*; **~guard** ['seɪfgɑ:d] 1. Schutz *m* (*against* gegen, vor *dat.*); 2. sichern, schützen (*against* gegen, vor *dat.*).
safe·ty ['seɪftɪ] Sicherheit *f*; Sicherheits...; **~belt** Sicherheitsgurt *m*; **~is·land** *Am.* Verkehrsinsel *f*; **~lock** Sicherheitsschloß *n*; **~pin** Sicherheitsnadel *f*; **~ra·zor** Rasierapparat *m*.
saf·fron ['sæfrən] Safran(gelb *n*) *m*.

sag [sæg] (*-gg-*) durchsacken; ⊕ durchhängen; abfallen, (herab)hängen; sinken, fallen, absacken.
sa·ga|cious □ [sə'geɪʃəs] scharfsinnig; **~·ci·ty** [sə'gæsətɪ] Scharfsinn *m*.
sage¹ [seɪdʒ] 1. □ (~*r*, ~*st*) klug, weise; 2. Weise(r) *m*.
sage² ♧ [~] Salbei *m*, *f*.
said [sed] *pret. u. p.p. von* say 1.
sail [seɪl] 1. Segel *n od. pl.*; (Segel-)Fahrt *f*; Windmühlenflügel *m*; (Segel)Schiff(e *pl.*) *n*; *set* ~ auslaufen (*for* nach); 2. *v/i.* segeln, fahren; auslaufen (*Schiff*); absegeln; *fig.* schweben; *v/t.* ♣ befahren; *Schiff* steuern; *Segelboot* segeln; **~boat** *Am.* ['seɪlbəʊt] Segelboot *n*; **~er** [~ə] Segler *m* (*Schiff*); **~ing-boat** *Brt.* [~ɪŋbəʊt] Segelboot *n*; **~ing-ship** [~ɪŋʃɪp], **~ing-ves·sel** [~ɪŋvesl] Segelschiff *n*; **~or** [~ə] Seemann *m*, Matrose *m*; *be a good* (*bad*) ~ (nicht) seefest sein; **~plane** Segelflugzeug *n*.
saint [seɪnt] 1. Heilige(r *m*) *f*; [*vor npr.* snt] Sankt ...; 2. heiligsprechen; **~ly** ['seɪntlɪ] heilig, fromm.
saith *veraltet od. poet.* [seθ] 3. *sg. pres. von* say 1.
sake [seɪk]: *for the* ~ *of* um ... (*gen.*) willen; *for my* ~ meinetwegen; *for God's* ~ um Gottes willen.
sa·la·ble ['seɪləbl] = saleable.
sal·ad ['sæləd] Salat *m*.
sal·a·ried ['sælərɪd] (fest)angestellt, (-)bezahlt; ~ *employee* Angestellte(r *m*) *f*, Gehaltsempfänger(in).
sal·a·ry ['sælərɪ] Gehalt *n*; **~ earn·er** [~ɜːnə] Angestellte(r *m*) *f*, Gehaltsempfänger(in).
sale [seɪl] Verkauf *m*; Ab-, Umsatz *m*; (Saison)Schlußverkauf *m*; Auktion *f*; *for* ~ zu verkaufen; *be on* ~ verkauft werden, erhältlich sein.
sale·a·ble *bsd. Brt.* ['seɪləbl] verkäuflich.

sales|clerk *Am.* ['seɪlzklɑːk] (Laden)Verkäufer(in); **~man** [~mən] (*pl. -men*) Verkäufer *m*; (Handels-)Vertreter *m*; **~wom·an** (*pl. -women*) Verkäuferin *f*; (Handels)Vertreterin *f*.

sa·li·ent □ ['seɪljənt] vorspringend; *fig.* ins Auge springend, hervorstechend.

sa·line ['seɪlaɪn] salzig, Salz...

sa·li·va [sə'laɪvə] Speichel *m*.

sal·low ['sæləʊ] blaß, gelblich, fahl.

sal·ly ['sælɪ]: ~ *forth*, ~ *out* sich aufmachen.

salm·on *zo.* ['sæmən] Lachs *m*, Salm *m*.

sa·loon [sə'luːn] Salon *m*; (Gesellschafts)Saal *m*; erste Klasse (*auf Schiffen*); *Am.* Kneipe *f*, Wirtschaft *f*, Saloon *m*; ~ (*car*) *Brt. mot.* Limousine.

salt [sɔːlt] **1.** Salz *n*; *fig.* Würze *f*; **2.** salzig; gesalzen, gepökelt; Salz...; Pökel...; **3.** (ein)salzen; pökeln; **~cel·lar** ['sɔːltselə] Salzfäßchen *n*, -streuer *m*; **~pe·tre**, *Am.* **~pe·ter** ↗ [~piːtə] Salpeter *m*; **~wa·ter** Salzwasser...; **~y** [~ɪ] (*-ier, -iest*) salzig.

sa·lu·bri·ous □ [sə'luːbrɪəs], **sal·u·ta·ry** □ ['sæljʊtərɪ] heilsam, gesund.

sal·u·ta·tion [sælju'teɪʃn] Gruß *m*, Begrüßung *f*; Anrede *f* (*im Brief*).

sa·lute [sə'luːt] **1.** Gruß *m*; ✕ Salut *m*; **2.** (be)grüßen; ✕ salutieren.

sal·vage ['sælvɪdʒ] **1.** Bergung(sgut *n*) *f*; Bergegeld *n*; **2.** bergen; retten.

sal·va·tion [sæl'veɪʃn] Erlösung *f*; (Seelen)Heil *n*; Rettung *f*; ♀ *Army* Heilsarmee *f*.

salve[1] [sælv] retten, bergen.

salve[2] [~] **1.** Salbe *f*; *fig.* Balsam *m*, Trost *m*; △ *nicht* Salve; **2.** *fig.* beschwichtigen, beruhigen.

same [seɪm]: *the* ~ der-, die-, dasselbe; *all the* ~ trotzdem; *it is all the* ~ *to me* es ist mir (ganz) gleich.

sam·ple ['sɑːmpl] **1.** Probe *f*, Muster *n*; **2.** probieren; kosten.

san·a·to·ri·um [sænə'tɔːrɪəm] (*pl. -ums, -a* [-ə]) Sanatorium *n*.

sanc·ti·fy ['sæŋktɪfaɪ] heiligen; weihen; **~ti·mo·ni·ous** □ [sæŋktɪ-'məʊnjəs] scheinheilig; **~tion** ['sæŋkʃn] **1.** Sanktion *f*; Billigung *f*, Zustimmung *f*; **2.** billigen; **~ti·ty** [~tətɪ] Heiligkeit *f*; **~tu·a·ry** [~jʊərɪ] Heiligtum *n*; *das* Allerheiligste; Asyl

n; Schutzgebiet *n* (*für Tiere*); *seek* ~ *with* Zuflucht suchen bei.

sand [sænd] **1.** Sand *m*; ~*s pl.* Sand (-fläche *f*) *m*; Sandbank *f*; **2.** mit Sand bestreuen; schmirgeln.

san·dal ['sændl] Sandale *f*.

sand|-glass ['sændglɑːs] Sanduhr *f*, Stundenglass *n*; **~hill** Sanddüne *f*; **~pip·er** *zo.* Strandläufer *m*; *common* ~ Flußuferläufer *m*.

sand·wich ['sænwɪdʒ] **1.** Sandwich *n*; **2.** einklemmen, -zwängen; *a.* ~ *in fig.* ein-, dazwischenschieben.

sand·y ['sændɪ] (*-ier, -iest*) sandig; rotblond.

sane [seɪn] (~*r*, ~*st*) geistig gesund; ⚖ zurechnungsfähig; vernünftig.

sang [sæŋ] *pret. von* sing.

san·gui·na·ry □ ['sæŋgwɪnərɪ] blutdürstig; blutig; **~guine** □ [~wɪn] leichtblütig; zuversichtlich; rot, frisch, blühend (*Gesichtsfarbe*).

san·i·tar·i·um *Am.* [sænɪ'teərɪəm] (*pl. -ums, -a* [-ə]) = *sanatorium*.

san·i·ta·ry □ ['sænɪtərɪ] Gesundheits..., gesundheitlich, sanitär... (*a.* ⊕); ~ *napkin Am.*, ~ *towel* Damenbinde *f*.

san·i·ta·tion [sænɪ'teɪʃn] Hygiene *f*; sanitäre Einrichtungen *pl.*

san·i·ty ['sænətɪ] geistige Gesundheit; ⚖ Zurechnungsfähigkeit *f*; gesunder Verstand.

sank [sæŋk] *pret. von* sink 1.

San·ta Claus ['sæntə'klɔːz] der Weihnachtsmann, der Nikolaus.

sap [sæp] **1.** Saft *m* (*in Pflanzen*); *fig.* Lebenskraft *f*; **2.** (*-pp-*) untergraben (*a. fig.*); **~less** ['sæplɪs] saft-, kraftlos; **~ling** [~lɪŋ] junger Baum.

sap·phire ['sæfaɪə] Saphir *m*.

sap·py ['sæpɪ] (*-ier, -iest*) saftig; *fig.* kraftvoll.

sar·cas·m ['sɑːkæzəm] Sarkasmus *m*.

sar·dine *zo.* [sɑː'diːn] Sardine *f*.

sash [sæʃ] Schärpe *f*; (schiebbarer) Fensterrahmen; **~win·dow** ['sæʃwɪndəʊ] Schiebefenster *n*.

sat [sæt] *pret. u. p.p. von* sit.

Sa·tan ['seɪtən] Satan *m*.

satch·el ['sætʃəl] Schulmappe *f*, -tasche *f*, -ranzen *m*.

sate [seɪt] übersättigen.

sa·teen [sæ'tiːn] (Baum)Wollsatin *m*.

sat·el·lite ['sætəlaɪt] Satellit *m*; *a.* ~ *state* Satellit(enstaat) *m*.

sa·ti·ate ['seɪʃɪeɪt] übersättigen.

sat·in ['sætɪn] (Seiden)Satin *m*.

satire 630

sat|ire ['sætaɪə] Satire f; ~ir·ist [~ərɪst] Satiriker(in); ~ir·ize [~raɪz] verspotten.

sat·is·fac|tion [sætɪs'fækʃn] Befriedigung f; Genugtuung f; Zufriedenheit f; eccl. Sühne f; Gewißheit f; ~·to·ry □ [~'fæktərɪ] befriedigend, zufriedenstellend.

sat·is·fy ['sætɪsfaɪ] befriedigen, zufriedenstellen; überzeugen; be satisfied with zufrieden sein mit.

sat·u·rate ⚗ u. fig. ['sætʃəreɪt] sättigen.

Sat·ur·day ['sætədɪ] Sonnabend m, Samstag m.

sat·ur·nine □ ['sætənaɪn] düster, finster.

sauce [sɔːs] 1. Soße f; △ nicht Bratensoße; Am. Kompott n; fig. Würze f, Reiz m; F Frechheit f; none of your ~! werd bloß nicht frech!; 2. F frech sein zu j-m; ~·boat ['sɔːsbəʊt] Soßenschüssel f; ~·pan Kochtopf m; Kasserolle f.

sau·cer ['sɔːsə] Untertasse f.

sauc·y □ ['sɔːsɪ] (-ier, -iest) frech; F flott, keß.

saun·ter ['sɔːntə] 1. Schlendern n, Bummel m; 2. schlendern, bummeln.

saus·age ['sɒsɪdʒ] Wurst f; a. small~ Würstchen n.

sav|age ['sævɪdʒ] 1. □ wild; roh, grausam; 2. Wilde(r m) f; Rohling m, Barbar(in); ~·age·ry [~rɪ] Wildheit f; Roheit f, Grausamkeit f.

sav·ant ['sævənt] Gelehrte(r) m.

save [seɪv] 1. retten; eccl. erlösen; bewahren; (auf-, er)sparen; schonen; 2. rhet. prp. u. cj. außer (dat.); ~ for bis auf (acc.); ~ that nur daß.

sav·er ['seɪvə] Retter(in); Sparer(in); it is a time~ es spart Zeit.

sav·ing ['seɪvɪŋ] 1. □ ...sparend; rettend, befreiend; 2. Rettung f; ~s pl. Ersparnisse pl.

sav·ings| ac·count ['seɪvɪŋzə'kaʊnt] Sparkonto n; ~ bank Sparkasse f; ~ de·pos·it Spareinlage f.

sa·vio(u)r ['seɪvjə] Retter m; the ⚬ eccl. der Erlöser, der Heiland.

sa·vo(u)r ['seɪvə] 1. (Wohl)Geschmack m; fig. Beigeschmack m; fig. Würze f, Reiz m; 2. fig. genießen; fig. schmecken, riechen (of nach); ~·y □ [~rɪ] schmackhaft; appetitlich, pikant.

saw¹ [sɔː] pret. von see¹.

saw² [~] Sprichwort n.

saw³ [~] 1. (~ed, ~n od. ~ed) sägen; 2. Säge f; ~·dust ['sɔːdʌst] Sägemehl n, -späne pl.; ~·mill Sägewerk n; ~n [sɔːn] p.p. von saw³ 1.

Sax·on ['sæksn] 1. sächsisch; ling. oft germanisch; 2. Sachse m, Sächsin f.

say [seɪ] 1. (said) sagen; auf-, hersagen; berichten; ~ grace das Tischgebet sprechen; what do you ~ to ...?, oft what ~ you to ...? was hältst du von ...?, wie wäre es mit ...?; it ~s lautet (Schreiben etc.); it ~s here hier heißt es; that is to ~ das heißt; (and) that's ~ing s.th. (und) das will was heißen; you don't ~ (so)! was Sie nicht sagen!; I ~ sag(en Sie) mal!; ich muß schon sagen!; he is said to be ... er soll ... sein; no sooner said than done gesagt, getan; 2. Rede f, Wort n; Mitspracherecht n; let him have his ~ laß(t) ihn (doch auch mal) reden od. s-e Meinung äußern; have a od. some (no) ~ in s.th. et. (nichts) zu sagen haben bei et.; ~·ing ['seɪɪŋ] Reden n; Sprichwort n, Redensart f; Ausspruch m; it goes without ~ es versteht sich von selbst; as the ~ goes wie es so schön heißt.

scab [skæb] ♂, ♀ Schorf m; vet. Räude f; sl. Streikbrecher m.

scab·bard ['skæbəd] (Schwert-) Scheide f.

scaf·fold ['skæfəld] (Bau)Gerüst n; Schafott n; ~·ing [~ɪŋ] (Bau)Gerüst n.

scald [skɔːld] 1. Verbrühung f; 2. verbrühen; Milch abkochen; ~ing hot kochendheiß; glühendheiß (Tag etc.).

scale¹ [skeɪl] 1. Schuppe f; Kesselstein m; ♂ Zahnstein m; 2. (sich) (ab)schuppen, ablösen; ⊕ Kesselstein abklopfen; ♂ Zähne vom Zahnstein reinigen.

scale² [~] 1. Waagschale f; (a pair of) ~s pl. (e-e) Waage; 2. wiegen.

scale³ [~] 1. Stufenleiter f; ♪ Tonleiter f; Skala f; Maßstab m; fig. Ausmaß n; 2. ersteigen; ~ up (down) maßstab(s)getreu vergrößern (verkleinern).

scal·lop ['skɒləp] 1. zo. Kammmuschel f; Näherei: Langette f; 2. ausbogen.

scalp [skælp] 1. Kopfhaut f; Skalp m; 2. skalpieren.

scal·y ['skeɪlɪ] (-ier, -iest) schuppig.

scamp [skæmp] **1.** Taugenichts *m*; **2.** pfuschen bei.

scam·per ['skæmpə] **1.** *a.* ~ *about*, ~ *around* (herum)tollen, herumhüpfen; hasten; **2.** (Herum)Tollen *n*, Herumhüpfen *n*.

scan [skæn] (*-nn-*) *Verse* skandieren; genau prüfen; forschend ansehen; *Horizont etc.* absuchen; *Computer, Radar, TV*: abtasten; *Überschriften etc.* überfliegen.

scan·dal ['skændl] Skandal *m*; Ärgernis *n*; Klatsch *m*; ~**ize** [~dəlaɪz]: *be* ~*d at s.th.* über et. empört sein. entrüstet sein; ~**ous** □ [~əs] skandalös, anstößig.

Scan·di·na·vi·an [skændɪ'neɪvjən] **1.** skandinavisch; **2.** Skandinavier(in); *ling.* Skandinavisch *n*.

scant □ [skænt] knapp, gering; ~**y** □ ['skæntɪ] (*-ier, -iest*) knapp, spärlich, kärglich, dürftig.

-scape [skeɪp] *in Zssgn*: ...landschaft, Bild.

scape·goat ['skeɪpɡəʊt] Sündenbock *m*; ~**grace** [~ɡreɪs] Taugenichts *m*.

scar [skɑː] **1.** Narbe *f*; *fig.* (Schand-) Fleck *m*, Makel *m*; Klippe *f*; **2.** (*-rr-*) e-e Narbe *od.* Narben hinterlassen (auf *dat.*); ~ *over* vernarben.

scarce [skeəs] (*~r, ~st*) knapp; rar, selten; ~**ly** [skeəslɪ] kaum; **scar·ci·ty** [~ətɪ] Mangel *m*, Knappheit *f* (*of* an *dat.*).

scare [skeə] **1.** erschrecken; ~ *away*, ~ *off* verscheuchen; *be* ~*d* (*of s.th.*) (vor et.) Angst haben; **2.** Schreck(en) *m*, Panik *f*; ~**crow** ['skeəkrəʊ] Vogelscheuche *f* (*a. fig.*).

scarf [skɑːf] (*pl.* **scarfs** [~fs], **scarves** [~vz]) Schal *m*, Hals-, Kopf-, Schultertuch *n*.

scar·let ['skɑːlət] **1.** Scharlach(rot *n*) *m*; **2.** scharlachrot; ~ *fever* ✿ Scharlach *m*; ~ *runner* ✿ Feuerbohne *f*.

scarred [skɑːd] narbig.

scarves [skɑːvz] *pl. von* scarf.

scath·ing *fig.* ['skeɪðɪŋ] vernichtend.

scat·ter ['skætə] (sich) zerstreuen; aus-, verstreuen; auseinanderstieben (*Vögel etc.*); ~**brain** F Schussel *m*; ~**ed** verstreut; vereinzelt.

sce·na·ri·o [sɪ'nɑːrɪəʊ] (*pl. -os*) Film: Drehbuch *n*.

scene [siːn] Szene *f*; Schauplatz *m*; ~**s** *pl.* Kulissen *pl.*; **sce·ne·ry** ['siːnərɪ] Szenerie *f*; Bühnenbild *n*, Kulissen *pl.*, Dekoration *f*; Landschaft *f*.

scent [sent] **1.** (*bsd.* Wohl)Geruch *m*, Duft *m*; *bsd.* Brt. Parfüm *n*; *hunt.* Witterung *f*; *gute etc.* Nase; Fährte *f* (*a. fig.*); **2.** wittern; *bsd.* Brt. parfümieren; ~**less** ['sentlɪs] geruchlos.

scep·tic, *Am.* **skep-** ['skeptɪk] Skeptiker(in); ~**ti·cal**, *Am.* **skep-** □ [~l] skeptisch.

scep·tre, *Am.* **-ter** ['septə] Zepter *n*.

sched·ule ['ʃedjuːl, *Am.* 'skedʒuːl] **1.** Verzeichnis *n*, Tabelle *f*; Plan *m*; *bsd. Am.* Fahr-, Flugplan *m*; *be ahead of* ~ dem Zeitplan voraus sein; *be behind* ~ Verspätung haben; im Rückstand sein; *be on* ~ (fahr)planmäßig *od.* pünktlich ankommen; **2.** (in e-e Liste *etc.*) eintragen; festlegen, -setzen, planen; ~**d** planmäßig (*Abfahrt etc.*); ~ *flight* ✈ Linienflug *m*.

scheme [skiːm] **1.** Schema *n*; Plan *m*, Projekt *n*, Programm *n*; Intrige *f*; **2.** *v/t.* planen; *v/i.* Pläne machen; intrigieren, Ränke schmieden.

schol·ar ['skɒlə] Gelehrte(r *m*) *f*; Gebildete(r *m*) *f*; *univ.* Stipendiat(in); *veraltet:* Schüler(in); ~**ly** *adj.* [~lɪ] gelehrt; ~**ship** [~ʃɪp] Gelehrsamkeit *f*; *univ.* Stipendium *n*.

school [skuːl] **1.** *zo.* Schwarm *m*; Schule *f* (*a. fig.*); *univ.* Fakultät *f*; *Am.* Hochschule *f*; *at* ~ auf *od.* in der Schule; **2.** schulen, ausbilden; *Tier* dressieren; ~**boy** [~lbɔɪ] Schüler *m*; ~**chil·dren** *pl.* Schulkinder *pl.*, Schüler *pl.*; ~**fel·low** Mitschüler(in); ~**girl** Schülerin *f*; ~**ing** [~lɪŋ] (Schul)Ausbildung *f*; ~**mas·ter** Lehrer *m*; ~**mate** Mitschüler(in); ~**mis·tress** Lehrerin *f*; ~**teach·er** Lehrer(in).

schoo·ner ['skuːnə] ⚓ Schoner *m*; *Am.* großes Bierglas; *Brt.* großes Sherryglas; *Am.* = *prairie schooner*.

sci·ence ['saɪəns] Wissenschaft *f*; *a. natural* ~ *die* Naturwissenschaft(en *pl.*); Kunst(fertigkeit) *f*, Technik *f*; ~ *fic·tion* Science-fiction *f*.

sci·en·tif·ic [saɪən'tɪfɪk] (~*ally*) (natur)wissenschaftlich; exakt, systematisch; kunstgerecht.

sci·en·tist ['saɪəntɪst] (Natur)Wissenschaftler(in).

scin·til·late ['sɪntɪleɪt] funkeln.

sci·on ['saɪən] Sproß *m*, Sprößling *m*.

scis·sors ['sɪzəz] *pl.* (*a pair of* ~ e-e) Schere.

scoff [skɒf] **1.** Spott *m*; **2.** spotten.

             S

scold [skəʊld] **1.** zänkisches Weib; **2.** (aus)schelten; schimpfen.

scol·lop [ˈskɒləp] = *scallop*.

scone [skɒn] weiches Teegebäck.

scoop [skuːp] **1.** Schaufel *f*, Schippe *f*; Schöpfkelle *f*; F Coup *m*, gutes Geschäft; *Zeitung*: F Exklusivmeldung *f*, Knüller *m*; **2.** schöpfen, schaufeln; ~ up (auf)schaufeln; hochheben, -nehmen; zusammenraffen.

scoot·er [ˈskuːtə] (Kinder)Roller *m*; (Motor)Roller *m*.

scope [skəʊp] Bereich *m*; Gesichtskreis *m*, (geistiger) Horizont; Spielraum *m*.

scorch [skɔːtʃ] *v/t.* versengen, -brennen; *v/i.* F (dahin)rasen.

score [skɔː] **1.** Kerbe *f*; Zeche *f*, Rechnung *f*; 20 Stück; *Sport*: (Spiel)Stand *m*, Punkt-, Trefferzahl *f*, (Spiel)Ergebnis *n*; große (An-)Zahl, Menge *f*; ♪ Partitur *f*; ~s of viele; *four* ~ achtzig; *run up a* ~ Schulden machen; *on the* ~ *of* wegen (*gen.*); **2.** einkerben; die Punkte anschreiben; *Sport*: *Punkte, Treffer* erzielen, *Tore* schießen; ♪ instrumentieren; *Am.* F scharf kritisieren.

scorn [skɔːn] **1.** Verachtung *f*; Spott *m*; **2.** verachten; verschmähen; ~ful □ [~nfl] verächtlich.

Scot [skɒt] Schotte *m*, -in *f*.

Scotch [skɒtʃ] **1.** schottisch; **2.** *ling.* Schottisch *n*; schottischer Whisky; *the* ~ die Schotten *pl.*; ~·man [ˈskɒtʃmən], ~·wom·an = *Scotsman, Scotswoman.*

scot-free [ˈskɒtˈfriː] ungestraft.

Scots [skɒts] = *Scotch*; *the* ~ *pl.* die Schotten *pl.*; ~·man [ˈskɒtsmən] (*pl. -men*) Schotte *m*; ~·wom·an (*pl. -women*) Schottin *f*.

Scot·tish [ˈskɒtɪʃ] schottisch.

scoun·drel [ˈskaʊndrəl] Schurke *m*.

scour[1] [ˈskaʊə] scheuern; reinigen.

scour[2] [~] durchsuchen, -stöbern.

scourge [skɜːdʒ] **1.** Geißel *f* (*a. fig.*); *fig.* Plage *f*; **2.** geißeln.

scout [skaʊt] **1.** *bsd.* ✗ Späher *m*, Kundschafter *m*; *Sport*: Spion *m*, Beobachter *m*; ⚓ Aufklärungskreuzer *m*; ✈ Aufklärer *m*; *Brt. mot.* motorisierter Pannenhelfer; (*boy*) ~ Pfadfinder *m*; (*girl*) ~ *Am.* Pfadfinderin *f*; *talent* ~ Talentsucher *m*; **2.** auskundschaften; *bsd.* ✗ auf Erkundung sein; ~ *about,*

~ *around* sich umsehen (*for* nach).

scowl [skaʊl] **1.** finsteres Gesicht; **2.** finster blicken.

scrab·ble [ˈskræbl] (be)kritzeln; scharren, krabbeln.

scrag *fig.* [skræg] Gerippe *n* (*dürrer Mensch etc.*).

scram·ble [ˈskræmbl] **1.** klettern; sich balgen (*for* um); ~*d eggs pl.* Rührei *n*; **2.** Kletterei *f*; Balgerei *f*; *fig.* Gerangel *n*.

scrap [skræp] **1.** Stückchen *n*, Fetzen *m*; (Zeitungs)Ausschnitt *m*, Bild *n* (*zum Einkleben*); Altmaterial *n*; Schrott *m*; ~s *pl.* Abfall *m* (*bsd. Speise*)Reste *pl.*; **2.** (-*pp-*) ausrangieren; verschrotten; ~·book [ˈskræpbʊk] Sammelalbum *n*.

scrape [skreɪp] **1.** Kratzen *n*, Scharren *n*; Kratzfuß *m*; Kratzer *m*, Schramme *f*; *fig.* Klemme *f*; **2.** schaben; kratzen; scharren; (*entlang-*) streifen.

scrap·heap [ˈskræphiːp] Abfall-, Schrotthaufen *m*; ~·i·ron, ~·met·al Alteisen *n*, Schrott *m*; ~·pa·per Schmierpapier *n*; Altpapier *n*.

scratch [skrætʃ] **1.** Kratzer *m*, Schramme *f*; Kratzen *n*; *Sport*: Startlinie *f*; **2.** zusammengewürfelt; improvisiert; *Sport*: ohne Vorgabe; **3.** (zer)kratzen; (zer)schrammen; (sich) kratzen, *Tier* krauen; ~ *out,* ~ *through,* ~ *off* aus-, durchstreichen; ~ **pad** *Am.* Notizblock *m*; ~ **pa·per** *Am.* Schmierpapier *n*.

scrawl [skrɔːl] **1.** kritzeln; **2.** Gekritzel *n*.

scraw·ny [ˈskrɔːnɪ] (*-ier, -iest*) dürr.

scream [skriːm] **1.** Schrei *m*; Gekreisch *n*; *he is a* ~ F er ist zum Schreien komisch; **2.** schreien, kreischen.

screech [skriːtʃ] = *scream*; ~·owl *zo.* [ˈskriːtʃaʊl] Schleiereule *f*.

screen [skriːn] **1.** Wand-, Ofen-, Schutzschirm *m*; (Film)Leinwand *f*; *der* Film, *das* Kino; *Radar, TV, Computer*: Bildschirm *m*; Sandsieb *n*; Fliegengitter *n*; *fig.* Schutz *m*, Tarnung *f*; **2.** abschirmen (*a.* ~ *off*) (*from gegen*); (be)schützen (*from vor dat.*); ✗ tarnen; *Sand etc.* (durch)sieben; *Bild* projizieren; *TV* senden; *Film* vorführen, zeigen; verfilmen; *fig. j-n* decken; *fig. Personen* überprüfen; ~·play [ˈskriːnpleɪ] Drehbuch *n*.

screw [skru:] **1.** Schraube *f*; (Flugzeug-, Schiffs-)Schraube *f*; Propeller *m*; **2.** schrauben; V bumsen, vögeln; ~ **up** zuschrauben; ~ **up** one's courage sich ein Herz fassen; ~**ball** *Am. sl.* ['skru:bɔ:l] komischer Kauz, Spinner *m*; ~**driv·er** Schraubenzieher *m*; ~**jack** Wagenheber *m*.

scrib·ble ['skrɪbl] **1.** Gekritzel *n*; **2.** kritzeln.

scrimp [skrɪmp], ~·**y** ['skrɪmpɪ] (-ier, -iest) = skimp(y).

script [skrɪpt] Schrift *f*; Handschrift *f*; *print.* Schreibschrift *f*; Manuskript *n*; *Film, TV:* Drehbuch *n*.

Scrip·ture ['skrɪptʃə]: (Holy) ~, The (Holy) ~s *pl.* die Heilige Schrift.

scroll [skrəʊl] Schriftrolle *f*; *arch.* Volute *f*; Schnecke *f* (am Geigenhals); Schnörkel *m*.

scro·tum *anat.* ['skrəʊtəm] (*pl.* -ta [-tə], -tums) Hodensack *m*.

scrub[1] [skrʌb] Gestrüpp *n*, Buschwerk *n*; Knirps *m*; *contp.* Null *f* (Person); *Am. Sport:* zweite (Spieler)Garnitur.

scrub[2] [~] **1.** Schrubben *n*, Scheuern *n*; **2.** (-bb-) schrubben, scheuern.

scru·ple ['skru:pl] **1.** Skrupel *m*, Zweifel *m*, Bedenken *n*; **2.** Bedenken haben; ~·**pu·lous** □ [~jʊləs] voller Skrupel; gewissenhaft; ängstlich.

scru·ti·nize ['skru:tɪnaɪz] (genau) prüfen; ~·**ny** [~ɪ] forschender Blick; genaue (*bsd.* Wahl)Prüfung.

scud [skʌd] **1.** (Dahin)Jagen *n*; (dahintreibende) Wolkenfetzen *pl.*; Bö *f*; **2.** (-dd-) eilen, jagen.

scuff [skʌf] schlurfen.

scuf·fle ['skʌfl] **1.** Balgerei *f*, Rauferei *f*; **2.** sich balgen, raufen.

scull [skʌl] **1.** Skull *n* (kurzes Ruder); Skullboot *n*; **2.** rudern, skullen.

scul·le·ry ['skʌlərɪ] Spülküche *f*.

sculp·tor ['skʌlptə] Bildhauer *m*; ~·**tress** [~trɪs] Bildhauerin *f*; ~·**ture** [~tʃə] **1.** Bildhauerei *f*, Skulptur *f*, Plastik *f*; **2.** (heraus)meißeln, formen.

scum [skʌm] (Ab)Schaum *m*; the ~ of the earth *fig.* der Abschaum der Menschheit.

scurf [skɜ:f] (Haut-, *bsd.* Kopf-) Schuppen *pl.*

scur·ri·lous □ ['skʌrɪləs] gemein, unflätig; △ *nicht* skurril.

scur·ry ['skʌrɪ] hasten, huschen.

scur·vy[1] ♣ ['skɜ:vɪ] Skorbut *m*.

scur·vy[2] □ [~] (-ier, -iest) (hunds-) gemein.

scut·tle ['skʌtl] **1.** Kohleneimer *m*; **2.** = scurry; sich hastig zurückziehen.

scythe ✔ [saɪð] Sense *f*.

sea [si:] See *f*, Meer *n* (*a. fig.*); hohe Welle; at ~ auf See; (all) at ~ *fig.* (völlig) ratlos; by ~ auf dem Seeweg, mit dem Schiff; ~**board** ['si:bɔ:d] Küste(ngebiet *n*) *f*; ~**coast** Meeresküste *f*; ~·**far·ing** ['si:feərɪŋ] seefahrend; ~·**food** Meeresfrüchte *pl.*; ~·**go·ing** ♦ (hoch)seetüchtig; (Hoch)See...; ~**gull** *zo.* (See)Möwe *f*.

seal[1] [si:l] **1.** Siegel *n*; Stempel *m*; ⊕ Dichtung *f*; *fig.* Bestätigung *f*; **2.** versiegeln; *fig.* besiegeln; ~ **off** *fig.* abriegeln; ~ **up** (fest) verschließen *od.* abdichten.

seal[2] *zo.* [~] **1.** Robbe *f*, Seehund *m*.

sea-lev·el ['si:levl] Meeresspiegel *m*, -höhe *f*.

seal·ing-wax ['si:lɪŋwæks] Siegellack *m*.

seam [si:m] **1.** Naht *f*, ♣ Fuge *f*; *geol.* Flöz *n*; Narbe *f*; △ *nicht* Saum; **2.** ~ together zusammennähen; ~ed with Gesicht: zerfurcht *vn.*

sea·man ['si:mən] (*pl.* -men) Seemann *m*, Matrose *m*.

seam·stress ['semstrɪs] Näherin *f*.

sea·plane ['si:pleɪn] Wasserflugzeug *n*; ~·**port** Seehafen *m*; Hafenstadt *f*; ~ **pow·er** Seemacht *f*.

sear [sɪə] versengen, -brennen; ✿ ausbrennen; verdorren (lassen) *fig.* verhärten.

search [sɜ:tʃ] **1.** Suche *f*, Suchen *n*, Forschen *n*; ⚖ Fahndung *f* (for nach); Unter-, Durchsuchung *f*; in ~ of auf der Suche nach; **2.** *v/t.* durch-, untersuchen; ✿ sondieren; *Gewissen* erforschen, prüfen; ~ me! F keine Ahnung!; *v/i.* suchen, forschen (for nach); ~ into untersuchen, ergründen; ~·**ing** □ ['sɜ:tʃɪŋ] forschend, prüfend; eingehend (*Prüfung etc.*); ~·**light** (Such)Scheinwerfer *m*; ~·**par·ty** Suchmannschaft *f*; ~·**war·rant** ⚖ Haussuchungs-, Durchsuchungsbefehl *m*.

sea|-shore ['si:ʃɔ:] See-, Meeresküste *f*; ~·**sick** seekrank; ~·**side**: at the ~ am Meer; go to the ~ ans Meer fahren; ~ place, ~ resort Seebad *n*.

sea·son ['si:zn] **1.** Jahreszeit *f*; (rechte) Zeit; Saison *f*; *Brt.* F = season-

ticket; *cherries are now in* ~ jetzt ist Kirschenzeit; *out of* ~ nicht (auf dem Markt) zu haben; *fig.* zur Unzeit; *with the compliments of the* ~ mit den besten Wünschen zum Fest; **2.** (aus)reifen (lassen); würzen; *Holz:* ablagern; abhärten (*to* gegen); **sea·so·na·ble** □ [~əbl] zeitgemäß; rechtzeitig; **~al** □ [~ənl] saisonbedingt, Saison...; **~ing** [~ŋ] Würze *f* (*a. fig.*); Gewürz *n*; **~tick·et** 🚂 Zeitkarte *f*; *thea.* Abonnement *n*.

seat [si:t] **1.** Sitz *m*; Sessel *m*, Stuhl *m*, Bank *f*; (Sitz)Platz *m*; Platz *m*, Sitz *m* (*im Theater etc.*); Landsitz *m*; Gesäß *n*; Hosenboden *m*; *fig.* Sitz *m* (*Mitgliedschaft*), *pol. a.* Mandat *m*; *fig.* Stätte *f*, Ort *m*, Schauplatz *m*; *s. take* 1; **2.** (hin)setzen; e-n (neuen) Hosenboden einsetzen in (*acc.*); fassen, Sitzplätze haben für; ~*ed* sitzend, ...sitzig; *be* ~*ed* sitzen; *be* ~*ed*! nehmen Sie Platz!; *remain* ~*ed* sitzen bleiben; **~belt** 🚗, *mot.* ['si:tbelt] Sicherheitsgurt *m*.

sea·ur·chin *zo.* ['si:3:tʃin] Seeigel *m*; **~ward** ['si:wəd] **1.** *adj.* seewärts gerichtet; **2.** *adv. a.* ~**s** seewärts; **~weed** ♀ (See)Tang *m*; **~wor·thy** seetüchtig.

se·cede [sɪ'si:d] sich trennen, abfallen (*from* von).

se·ces·sion [sɪ'seʃn] Abfall *m*, Abspaltung *f*, Sezession *f*; **~ist** [~ɪst] Abtrünnige(r *m*) *f*.

se·clude [sɪ'klu:d] abschließen, absondern; **se·clud·ed** einsam; zurückgezogen; abgelegen; **se·clu·sion** [~ʒn] Zurückgezogen-, Abgeschiedenheit *f*.

sec·ond ['sekənd] **1.** □ zweite(r, -s); ~ *to none* unübertroffen; *on* ~ *thought* nach reiflicher Überlegung; **2.** als zweite(r, -s), an zweiter Stelle; **3.** *der, die, das* Zweite; Sekundant *m*; Beistand *m*; Sekunde *f*; ~**s** *pl.* Ware(n *pl.*) *f* zweiter Wahl, zweite Wahl; **4.** sekundieren (*dat.*); unterstützen; **~a·ry** [~ərɪ] sekundär, untergeordnet; Neben...; Hilfs...; Sekundär..; ~ *education* höhere Schulbildung; ~ *modern (school) Brt.* (*etwa*) Kombination *f* aus Real- u. Hauptschule; ~ *school* höhere Schule; ~**hand** aus zweiter Hand; gebraucht; antiquarisch; **~ly** [~lɪ] zweitens; **~rate** zweitklassig.

se·cre|cy ['si:krɪsɪ] Heimlichkeit *f*;

Verschwiegenheit *f*; **~t** [~t] **1.** □ geheim; Geheim...; verschwiegen; verborgen; **2.** Geheimnis *n*; *in* ~ heimlich, insgeheim; *be in the* ~ eingeweiht sein; *keep s.th. a* ~ *from s.o.* j-m et. verheimlichen.

sec·re·ta·ry ['sekrətrɪ] Schriftführer *m*; Sekretär(in); ♀ *of State Brt.* Staatssekretär *m*; *Brt.* Minister *m*; *Am.* Außenminister *m*.

se·crete [sɪ'kri:t] verbergen; *biol.* absondern; **se·cre·tion** [~ʃn] Verbergen *n*; *biol.*, 🩺 Absonderung *f*; **se·cre·tive** [~tɪv] verschlossen, geheimnisturisch.

se·cret·ly ['si:krɪtlɪ] heimlich.

sec·tion ['sekʃn] 🩺 Sektion *f*; Schnitt *m*; Teil *m*; Abschnitt *m*; 🩺 Paragraph *m*; *print.* Absatz *m*; Abteilung *f*; Gruppe *f*.

sec·u·lar □ ['sekjʊlə] weltlich.

se·cure [sɪ'kjʊə] **1.** □ sicher; fest; gesichert; **2.** (sich *et.*) sichern; schützen; garantieren; befestigen; (fest) (ver)schließen; **se·cu·ri·ty** [~rətɪ] Sicherheit *f*; Sicherheitsmaßnahmen *pl.*; Sorglosigkeit *f*; Garantie *f*, Kaution *f*; Bürge *m*, Bürgin *f*; *securities pl.* Wertpapiere *pl.*; ~ *check* Sicherheitskontrolle *f*.

se·dan [sɪ'dæn] *Am. mot.* Limousine *f*; ~(-*chair*) Sänfte *f*.

se·date □ [sɪ'deɪt] gesetzt; ruhig.

sed·a·tive *mst* 🩺 ['sedətɪv] **1.** beruhigend; **2.** Beruhigungsmittel *n*.

sed·en·ta·ry □ ['sedntrɪ] sitzend; seßhaft.

sed·i·ment ['sedɪmənt] Sediment *n*; (Boden)Satz *m*; *geol.* Ablagerung *f*.

se·di·tion [sɪ'dɪʃn] Aufruhr *m*; **~tious** □ [~əs] aufrührerisch.

se·duce [sɪ'dju:s] verführen; **se·duc·er** [~ə] Verführer *m*; **se·duc·tion** [sɪ'dʌkʃn] Verführung *f*; **se·duc·tive** □ [~tɪv] verführerisch.

sed·u·lous □ ['sedjʊləs] emsig.

see¹ [si:] (*saw, seen*) *v/i.* sehen; nachsehen; (einsehen; sich überlegen; *I* ~*!* ich verstehe; ach so!; ~ *about so.* sich kümmern um; *I'll* ~ *about it* ich will es mir überlegen; ~ *into* untersuchen, nachgehen; ~ *through* j-n *od.* et. durchschauen; ~ *to* sich kümmern um; *v/t.* sehen; besuchen; dafür sorgen (, daß); j-n aufsuchen *od.* konsultieren; einsehen; ~ *s.o. home* j-n nach Hause bringen *od.* begleiten; ~ *you!* bis dann!, auf bald!; ~ *off* j-n verabschieden (*at* am *Bahnhof etc.*); ~ *out j-n* hinausbegleiten; *et.* zu Ende sehen *od.* erleben; ~ *through et.* durchhalten; *j-m* durchhelfen; *live to* ~ erleben.

see² [\~] (erz)bischöflicher Stuhl.

seed [si:d] **1.** Same(n) *m*, Saat(gut *n*) *f*; (Obst)Kern *m*; *coll.* Samen *pl.*; *mst* ~*s pl. fig.* Saat *f*, Keim *m*; *go od. run to* ~ schießen (*Salat etc.*); *fig.* herunterkommen; **2.** *v/t.* (be)säen; entkernen; *v/i.* in Samen schießen; ~**less** ['si:dlɪs] kernlos (*Obst*); ~**ling** [\~lɪŋ] Sämling *m*; ~**y** □ F [\~ɪ] (-*ier*, -*iest*) schäbig; elend.

seek [si:k] (*sought*) suchen; begehren; trachten nach.

seem [si:m] (er)scheinen; ~**ing** □ ['si:mɪŋ] scheinbar; ~**ly** [\~lɪ] (-*ier*, -*iest*) schicklich.

seen [si:n] *p.p. von* see¹.

seep [si:p] (durch)sickern.

seer [si:ə] Seher(in), Prophet(in).

see-saw ['si:sɔ:] **1.** Wippen *n*; Wippe *f*, Wippschaukel *f*; **2.** wippen; *fig.* schwanken.

seethe [si:ð] sieden; schäumen (*a. fig.*); *fig.* kochen.

seg·ment ['seɡmənt] Abschnitt *m*; Segment *n*.

seg·re·gate ['seɡrɪɡeɪt] absondern, (*a. nach Rassen, Geschlechtern etc.*); trennen; ~**ga·tion** [seɡrɪ'ɡeɪʃn] Absonderung *f*; Rassentrennung *f*.

seize [si:z] ergreifen, packen, fassen; an sich reißen; ✍ beschlagnahmen; *j-n* festnehmen, festhalten; (ein)nehmen, erobern; *fig.* erfassen.

sei·zure ['si:ʒə] Ergreifung *f*; ✍ Beschlagnahme *f*; 🖉 Anfall *m*.

sel·dom *adv.* ['seldəm] selten.

se·lect [sɪ'lekt] **1.** auswählen, -lesen, -suchen; **2.** ausgewählt; erlesen; exklusiv; **se·lec·tion** [\~kʃn] Auswahl *f*; Auslese *f*; ~**man** (*pl.* -*men*) Stadtrat *m* (*in den Neuenglandstaaten*).

self [self] **1.** (*pl.* selves [selvz]) Selbst *n*, Ich *n*; **2.** *pron.* selbst; *econ. od.* F = *myself, etc.*; ~**as·sured** ['selfə'ʃʊəd] selbstbewußt, -sicher; ~**cent(e)red** egozentrisch; ~**col·o(u)red** einheitlich in der Farbe; *bsd.* 🌿 einfarbig; ~**com·mand** Selbstbeherrschung *f*; ~**con·ceit** Eingenbildünkel *m*; ~**con·ceit·ed** eingebildet, überheblich; ~**con·fi·dence** Selbstvertrauen *n*, -bewußtsein *n*; ~**con·fi·dent** □ selbstsicher, -bewußt; ~

con·scious □ befangen, gehemmt, unsicher; ⚠ *nicht selbstbewußt*; ~**con·tained** (in sich) geschlossen, selbständig; *fig.* verschlossen; ~ *flat Brt.* abgeschlossene Wohnung; ~**con·trol** Selbstbeherrschung *f*; ~**de·fence**, *Am.* ~**de·fense** Selbstverteidigung *f*; in ~ in Notwehr; ~**de·ni·al** Selbstverleugnung *f*; ~**de·ter·mi·na·tion** *bsd. pol.* Selbstbestimmung *f*; ~**em·ployed** selbständig (*Handwerker etc.*); ~**ev·i·dent** selbstverständlich; ~**gov·ern·ment** *pol.* Selbstverwaltung *f*, Autonomie *f*; ~**help** Selbsthilfe *f*; ~**in·dul·gent** nachgiebig gegen sich selbst; zügellos; ~**in·struc·tion** Selbstunterricht *m*; ~**in·terest** Eigennutz *m*, eigenes Interesse; ~**ish** □ [\~ɪʃ] selbstsüchtig; ~**made** selbstgemacht; ~ *man* Selfmademan *m*; ~**pit·y** Selbstmitleid *n*; ~**pos·ses·sion** Selbstbeherrschung *f*; ~**re·li·ant** [\~rɪ'laɪənt] selbstsicher, -bewußt; ~**re·spect** Selbstachtung *f*; ~**right·eous** □ selbstgerecht; ~**serv·ice 1.** mit Selbstbedienung, Selbstbedienungs...; **2.** Selbstbedienung *f*; ~**willed** eigenwillig, -sinnig.

sell [sel] (*sold*) *v/t.* verkaufen (*a. fig.*); *j-m et.* aufschwatzen; *v/i.* sich verkaufen (lassen), gehen (*Ware*); verkauft werden (*at, for* für); ~ *off,* ~ *out econ.* ausverkaufen; ~**er** ['selə] Verkäufer(in); *good* ~ *econ.* gutgehender Artikel.

selves [selvz] *pl. von* self 1.

sem·blance ['sembləns] Anschein *m*; Gestalt *f*.

se·men *biol.* ['si:men] Samen *m*, Sperma *n*.

sem·i· ['semɪ] halb..., Halb...; ~**co·lon** Semikolon *n*, Strichpunkt *m*; ~**de·tached (house)** Doppelhaushälfte *f*; ~**fi·nal** *Sport:* Halb-, Semifinalspiel *n*; ~*s pl.* Halb-, Semifinale *n*, Vorschlußrunde *f*.

sem·i·nar·y ['semɪnərɪ] (Priester)Seminar *n*; *fig.* Schule *f*.

semp·stress ['sempstrɪs] Näherin *f*.

sen·ate ['senɪt] Senat *m*.

sen·a·tor ['senətə] Senator *m*.

send [send] (*sent*) senden, schicken, ✍ senden; (*mit adj. od. p.pr.*) machen; ~ *s.o. mad j-n* wahnsinnig machen; ~ *for* nach *j-m* schicken, *j-n* kommen lassen, *j-n* holen *od.* rufen (lassen); ~ **forth** aussenden, -strahlen; hervorbringen; veröffentlichen; ~ **in** einsenden, -schicken, -reichen; ~ **up** fig. Preise etc. steigen lassen, in die Höhe treiben; ~ **word to** s.o. j-m Nachricht geben; ~**er** ['sendə] Absender(in).

se·nile ['si:naɪl] greisenhaft, senil; **se·nil·i·ty** [sɪ'nɪlətɪ] Senilität f.

se·ni·or ['si:njə] **1.** nachgestellt: senior; älter; rang-, dienstälter; Ober...; ~ **citizens** pl. ältere Mitbürger pl., Senioren pl.; ~ **partner** econ. Seniorpartner m; **2.** Ältere(r m) f; Rang-, Dienstältere(r m) f; Senior(in); he is my ~ **by a year** er ist ein Jahr älter als ich; ~**i·ty** [si:nɪ'ɒrətɪ] höheres Alter od. Dienstalter.

sen·sa·tion [sen'seɪʃn] (Sinnes)Empfindung f; Gefühl n; Eindruck m; Sensation f; ~**al** □ [~l] sensationell; aufsehenerregend.

sense [sens] **1.** Sinn m (of für); Empfindung f, Gefühl n; Verstand m; Bedeutung f; Ansicht f; in (out of) one's ~s bei (von) Sinnen; bring s.o. to his od. her ~s j-n zur Vernunft bringen; make ~ Sinn haben; talk ~ vernünftig reden; **2.** spüren, fühlen.

sense·less □ ['senslɪs] bewußtlos; unvernünftig, dumm; sinnlos; ~**ness** [~nɪs] Bewußtlosigkeit f; Unvernunft f; Sinnlosigkeit f.

sen·si·bil·i·ty [sensɪ'bɪlətɪ] Sensibilität f, Empfindungsvermögen n; phys. etc. Empfindlichkeit f; sensibilities pl. Empfindsamkeit f, Zartgefühl n.

sen·si·ble □ ['sensəbl] vernünftig; spür-, fühlbar; △ nicht sensibel; be ~ **of** s.th. sich e-r Sache bewußt sein; et. empfinden.

sen·si·tive □ ['sensɪtɪv] empfindlich (to gegen); Empfindungs...; sensibel, empfindsam, feinfühlig; △ **tive·ness** [~nɪs], ~**tiv·i·ty** [sensɪ'tɪvətɪ] Sensibilität f; Empfindlichkeit f.

sen·sor ['sensə] Sensor m.

sen·su·al □ ['sensjʊəl] sinnlich.

sen·su·ous □ ['sensjʊəs] sinnlich; Sinnes...; sinnenfroh.

sent [sent] pret. u. p.p. von send.

sen·tence ['sentəns] **1.** ﷼ (Straf)Urteil n; gr. Satz m; serve one's ~ s-e Strafe absitzen; **2.** verurteilen.

sen·ten·tious □ [sen'tenʃəs] aufgeblasen, salbungsvoll.

sen·tient □ ['senʃnt] empfindungsfähig.

sen·ti·ment ['sentɪmənt] (seelische) Empfindung, Gefühl n; Meinung f; = sentimentality; ~**men·tal** □ [sentɪ'mentl] empfindsam; sentimental; ~**men·tal·i·ty** [sentɪmen'tælətɪ] Sentimentalität f.

sen·ti·nel ✕ ['sentɪnl], ~**try** ✕ [~rɪ] Wache f, (Wach[t])Posten m.

sep·a·ra·ble □ ['sepərəbl] trennbar; ~**rate 1.** □ ['seprət] (ab)getrennt, gesondert, separat; einzeln; **2.** ['sepəreɪt] (sich) trennen; (sich) absondern; (sich) scheiden; aufteilen (into in acc.); ~**ra·tion** [sepə'reɪʃn] Trennung f; Scheidung f.

sep·sis ✖ ['sepsɪs] (pl. -ses [-si:z]) Sepsis f (Blutvergiftung).

Sep·tem·ber [sep'tembə] September m.

sep·tic ✖ ['septɪk] (~ally) septisch.

se·pul·chral □ [sɪ'pʌlkrəl] Grab...; fig. düster, Grabes...

sep·ul·chre, Am. **-cher** ['sepəlkə] Grab(stätte f, -mal n) n.

se·quel ['si:kwəl] Folge f; Nachspiel n; (Roman- etc.)Fortsetzung f; a four-~ program(me) TV ein Vierteiler m, e-e vierteilige Serie.

se·quence ['si:kwəns] (Aufeinander-, Reihen)Folge f; Film: Szene f; ~ **of tenses** gr. Zeitenfolge f; **se·quent** [~t] (aufeinander)folgend.

se·ques·trate ﷼ [sɪ'kwestreɪt] Eigentum einziehen; beschlagnahmen.

ser·e·nade ♪ [serə'neɪd] **1.** Serenade f, Ständchen n; **2.** j-m ein Ständchen bringen.

se·rene □ [sɪ'ri:n] klar; heiter; ruhig; **se·ren·i·ty** [sɪ'renətɪ] Heiterkeit f; Ruhe f.

ser·geant ['sɑ:dʒənt] ✕ Feldwebel m; (Polizei)Wachtmeister m.

se·ri·al □ ['sɪərɪəl] **1.** serienmäßig, Reihen..., Serien..., Fortsetzungs...; **2.** Fortsetzungsroman m; (Hörspiel-, Fernseh)Folge f, Serie f.

se·ries ['sɪəri:z] (pl. -ries) Reihe f; Serie f; Folge f.

se·ri·ous □ ['sɪərɪəs] ernst; ernsthaft, ernstlich; △ nicht seriös; be ~ es ernst meinen (about mit); ~**ness** [~nɪs] Ernst(haftigkeit f) m.

ser·mon ['sɜ:mən] eccl. Predigt f; iro. (Moral-, Straf)Predigt f.

ser·pent zo. ['sɜ:pənt] Schlange f; ~**pen·tine** [~aɪn] schlangenförmig;

gewunden, kurvenreich, Serpentinen...

se·rum ['sɪərəm] *(pl. -rums, -ra [-rə])* Serum *n*.

ser·vant ['sɜːvənt] *a.* domestic ∼ Diener(in), Hausangestellte(r *m*) *f*, Dienstbote *m*, -mädchen *n*, Bedienstete(r *m*) *f*; *civil* ∼ *s.* civil; *public* ∼ Staatsbeamt|er, -in; Angestellte(r *m*) *f* im öffentlichen Dienst.

serve [sɜːv] **1.** *v/t.* dienen *(dat.)*; *Dienstzeit (a.* ✕*)* ableisten; *Lehre* machen; ⚖️ *Strafe* verbüßen; genügen *(dat.)*; *j-n, Kunden* bedienen; *Essen* servieren, auftragen, reichen; *Getränk* servieren, einschenken; versorgen (*with* mit) *j-n schändlich* behandeln; nützen, dienlich sein *(dat.)*; *Zweck* erfüllen; *Tennis etc.: Ball* aufschlagen; *Volleyball: Ball* aufgeben; *(it)* ∼*s him right* (das) geschieht ihm ganz recht; ∼ *out et.* aus-, verteilen; *v/i.* dienen *(a.* ✕*; as, for* als); *econ.* bedienen; nützen; genügen; *Tennis etc.:* aufschlagen; *Volleyball:* aufgeben; ∼ *at table* (bei Tisch) servieren, bedienen; **2.** *Tennis etc.:* Aufschlag *m*.

ser·vice ['sɜːvɪs] **1.** Dienst *m*; *econ. etc.* Bedienung *f*; Gefälligkeit *f*; Gottesdienst *m*; Versorgung(sdienst *m*, -sbetrieb *m*) *f*; ✕ (Wehr-, Militär-)Dienst *m*; ⊕ Wartung *f*, *mot. a.* Inspektion *f*; Service *m*, Kundendienst *m*; (Zug- etc.)Verkehr *m*; Service *n*; *Tennis etc.:* Aufschlag *m*; *Volleyball:* Aufgabe *f*; *be at s.o.'s* ∼ j-m zur Verfügung stehen; **2.** ⊕ warten, pflegen; ∼**vi·cea·ble** [∼əbl] brauchbar, nützlich, praktisch; strapazierfähig; ∼**ar·e·a** *Brt.* (Autobahn)Raststätte *f*; ∼ **charge** Bedienungsgeld *n*; Bearbeitungsgebühr *f*; ∼**sta·tion** Tankstelle *f*; (Reparatur)Werkstatt *f*.

ser·vile □ ['sɜːvaɪl] sklavisch *(a. fig.)*; unterwürfig, kriecherisch; ∼**vil·i·ty** [sɜːˈvɪlətɪ] Unterwürfigkeit *f*, Kriecherei *f*.

serv·ing ['sɜːvɪŋ] Portion *f*.

ser·vi·tude ['sɜːvɪtjuːd] Knechtschaft *f*; Sklaverei *f*.

ses·sion ['seʃn] Sitzung(speriode) *f*; *be in* ∼ ⚖️ *parl.* tagen.

set [set] **1.** *(-tt-; set)* *v/t.* setzen; stellen; legen; *in e-n Zustand* (ver-)setzen, bringen; veranlassen zu; ein-, herrichten, ordnen; ⊕ (ein-)

stellen; *Uhr, Wecker* stellen; *Edelstein* fassen; besetzen (*with* mit *Edelsteinen*); *Flüssigkeit* erstarren lassen; *Haar* legen; ✂️ *Bruch, Knochen* einrenken, -richten; ♪ *vertonen*; *print.* absetzen; *Aufgabe* stellen; *Zeitpunkt, Preis* festsetzen; *Rekord* aufstellen; ∼ *s.o. laughing* j-n zum Lachen bringen; ∼ *an example* ein Beispiel geben; ∼ *one's hopes on* s-e Hoffnung setzen auf *(acc.)*; ∼ *the table* den Tisch decken; ∼ *one's teeth* die Zähne zusammenbeißen; ∼ *at ease* beruhigen; ∼ *s.o.'s mind at rest* j-n beruhigen; ∼ *great (little) store by* großen (geringen) Wert legen auf *(acc.)*; ∼ *aside* beiseite legen, weglegen; ∼ *up* aufheben; *vorwerfen*; ∼ *forth* darlegen; ∼ *off* hervorheben; ∼ *up* errichten; aufstellen; einrichten, gründen; *Regierung* bilden; *j-n* etablieren; *v/i.* untergehen *(Sonne etc.)*; gerinnen, fest werden; erstarren *(a. Gesicht, Muskel)*; ✂️ sich einrenken; *hunt.* vorstehen *(Hund)*; ∼ *about doing s.th.* sich daranmachen, et. zu tun; ∼ *about s.o.* F über j-n herfallen; ∼ *forth* aufbrechen; ∼ *in* einsetzen (*beginnen*); ∼ *off* aufbrechen; ∼ *on* angreifen; ∼ *out* aufbrechen; ∼ *to* sich daran machen (*to do* zu tun); ∼ *up* sich niederlassen; ∼ *up as* sich ausgeben für; **2.** fest; starr; festgesetzt, bestimmt; bereit, entschlossen; vorgeschrieben; ∼ *fair Barometer:* beständig; ∼ *phrase* feststehender Ausdruck; ∼ *speech* wohlüberlegte Rede; **3.** Satz *m*, Garnitur *f*; Service *n*; Set *m*, Set *n* (*Platzdeckchen*); gesammelte Ausgabe (*e-s Autors*); (Schriften)Reihe *f*; (Artikel)Serie *f*; *Radio, TV:* Gerät *n*, Apparat *m*; *thea.* Bühnenausstattung *f*; *Film:* Szenenaufbau *m*; *Tennis:* Satz *m*; *hunt.* Vorstehen *n (Hund)*; ∼ (Personen-)Kreis *m*, *contp.* Clique *f*; Sitz *m*, Schnitt *m (Kleidung)*; *poet.* Untergang *m (Sonne)*; *fig.* Richtung *f*, Tendenz *f*; *have a shampoo and* ∼ sich die Haare waschen und legen lassen; ∼**back** *fig.* ['setbæk] Rückschlag *m*.

set·tee [seˈtiː] *kleines* Sofa.

set the·o·ry Ⓐ ['set ˈθɪərɪ] Mengenlehre *f*.

set·ting ['setɪŋ] Setzen *n*; Einrichten *n*; Fassung *f (Edelstein)*; Gedeck *n*; ⊕ Einstellung *f*; *thea.* Bühnenbild *n*;

Film: Ausstattung f; ♪ Vertonung f; (Sonnen- etc.)Untergang m; Umgebung f; Schauplatz m; fig. Rahmen m.

set·tle ['setl] **1.** Sitzbank f; **2.** v/t. vereinbaren, abmachen, festsetzen; erledigen, in Ordnung bringen, regeln; Frage etc. klären, entscheiden; Geschäft abschließen; Rechnung begleichen; econ. Konto ausgleichen; Streit beilegen; a. ~ down beruhigen; Kind versorgen; j-n beruflich, häuslich unterbringen; vermachen (on dat.); Rente aussetzen (on dat.); ansiedeln; Land besiedeln; ~ o.s. sich niederlassen; ~ one's affairs s-e Angelegenheiten (vor dem Tode) in Ordnung bringen; that ~s it F damit ist der Fall erledigt; that's ~d then das ist also klar; v/i. sich niederlassen od. setzen; a. ~ down sich ansiedeln od. niederlassen; sich (häuslich) niederlassen; sich senken (Grundmauern etc.); beständig werden (Wetter); a. ~ down fig. sich beruhigen, sich legen; sich setzen (Trübstoffe); sich klären (Flüssigkeit); sich legen (Staub); ~ back sich (gemütlich) zurücklehnen; ~ down to sich widmen (dat.); ~ in sich einrichten; sich einleben od. eingewöhnen; ~ on, ~ upon sich entschließen zu; ~d fest; geregelt (Leben); beständig (Wetter); **~·ment** [~mənt] (Be)Siedlung f; Klärung f, Erledigung f; Übereinkunft f, Abmachung f; Bezahlung f; Schlichtung f, Beilegung f; ᵗᵗᵗ (Eigentums)Übertragung f; **~r** [~ə] Siedler m.

sev·en ['sevn] **1.** sieben; **2.** Sieben f; **~·teen** [~'tiːn] **1.** siebzehn; **2.** Siebzehn f; **~·teenth** [~θ] siebzehnte(r, -s); **~th** ['sevnθ] **1.** □ sieb(en)te(r, -s); **2.** Sieb(en)tel n; **~th·ly** [~lı] sieb(en)tens; **~·ti·eth** [~tııθ] siebzigste(r, -s); **~·ty** [~tı] **1.** siebzig; **2.** Siebzig f.

sev·er ['sevə] (sich) trennen; zerreißen; fig. (auf)lösen.

sev·er·al □ ['sevrəl] mehrere, verschieden; einige; einzeln; eigen; getrennt; **~·ly** [~lı] einzeln, gesondert, getrennt.

sev·er·ance ['sevərəns] (Ab)Trennung f; fig. (Auf)Lösung f, Abbruch m.

se·vere □ [sı'vıə] (~r, ~st) streng; scharf; hart; rauh (Wetter); hart

(Winter); ernst, finster (Ausdruck etc.); heftig (Schmerz etc.); schlimm, schwer (Krankheit etc.); **se·ver·i·ty** [sı'verətı] Strenge f, Härte f; Heftigkeit f, Stärke f; Ernst m.

sew [səʊ] (sewed, sewn od. sewed) nähen; heften.

sew·age ['sjuːıdʒ] Abwasser n.

sew·er¹ ['səʊə] Näherin f.

sew·er² ['sjʊə] Abwasserkanal m; **~·age** ['sjʊərıdʒ] Kanalisation f.

sew·ing ['səʊıŋ] Nähen n; Näharbeit f; attr. Näh...; **~n** [səʊn] p.p. von sew.

sex [seks] Geschlecht n; Sexualität f; Sex m.

sex·ton ['sekstən] Küster m (u. Totengräber m).

sex·u·al □ ['seksjʊəl] geschlechtlich, Geschlechts..., sexuell, Sexual...; ~ intercourse Geschlechtsverkehr m; **~·y** [~ı] (-ier, -iest) sexy, aufreizend.

shab·by □ ['ʃæbı] (-ier, -iest) schäbig; gemein.

shack [ʃæk] Hütte f, Bude f.

shack·le ['ʃækl] **1.** Fessel f (fig. mst pl.); **2.** fesseln.

shade [ʃeıd] **1.** Schatten m (a. fig.); (Lampen- etc.)Schirm m; Schattierung f; Am. Rouleau n; Nuance f; fig. F Spur f; **2.** beschatten; verdunkeln (a. fig.); abschirmen; schützen; schattieren; ~ off allmählich übergehen (lassen) (into in acc.).

shad·ow ['ʃædəʊ] **1.** Schatten m (a. fig.); Phantom n; fig. Spur f; **2.** e-n Schatten werfen auf (acc.); fig. j-n beschatten, überwachen; **~·y** [~ı] (-ier, -iest) schattig, dunkel; unbestimmt, vage.

shad·y □ ['ʃeıdı] (-ier, -iest) schattenspendend; schattig, dunkel; fig. zweifelhaft.

shaft [ʃɑːft] Schaft m; Stiel m; poet. Pfeil m (a. fig.); poet. Strahl m; ⊕ Welle f; Deichsel f; ⚒ Schacht m.

shag·gy ['ʃægı] (-ier, -iest) zottig.

shake [ʃeık] **1.** (shook, shaken) v/t. schütteln; rütteln an (dat.); erschüttern; ~ down herunterschütteln; ~ hands sich die Hand geben od. schütteln; ~ off abschütteln (a. fig.); ~ up Bett aufschütteln; fig. aufrütteln; v/i. zittern, beben, wackeln, (sch)wanken (with vor dat.); ♪ trillern; ~ down kampieren; **2.** schütteln n; Erschütterung f; Beben n; ♪

Triller *m*; (*Milch- etc.*)Shake *m*;
~down ['ʃeɪkdaʊn] **1.** (Behelfs-)
Lager *n*; *Am.* F Erpressung *f*; *Am.* F
Durchsuchung *f*; **2.** *adj.*: ~ *flight* ✈
Testflug *m*; ~ *voyage* ⚓ Testfahrt *f*;
shak·en [~ən] **1.** *p.p. von* shake 1; **2.**
adj. erschüttert.

shak·y □ ['ʃeɪkɪ] (*-ier*, *-iest*)
wack(e)lig (*a. fig.*); (sch)wankend;
zitternd; zitt(e)rig.

shall *v/aux.* [ʃæl] (*pret.* should; *verneint:* ~ *not*, shan't) *ich, du etc.*
soll(st) *etc.*; *ich werde, wir* werden.

shal·low ['ʃæləʊ] **1.** □ seicht; flach;
fig. oberflächlich; **2.** seichte Stelle,
Untiefe *f*; **3.** (sich) verflachen.

sham [ʃæm] **1.** falsch; Schein...; **2.**
(Vor)Täuschung *f*, Heuchelei *f*; Fälschung *f*; Schwindler(in); △ *nicht*
Scham; **3.** (*-mm-*) *v/t.* vortäuschen;
v/i. sich verstellen; simulieren; ~
ill(ness) sich krank stellen.

sham·ble ['ʃæmbl] watscheln; **~s** *sg.*
Schlachtfeld *n*, wüstes Durcheinander, Chaos *n*.

shame [ʃeɪm] **1.** Scham *f*; Schande *f*;
for ~!, ~ *on you!* pfui!, schäm dich!;
put to ~ beschämen; **2.** beschämen;
j-m Schande machen; **~faced** □
['ʃeɪmfeɪst] schamhaft, schüchtern;
~ful □ [~fl] schändlich, beschä-
mend; **~less** □ [~lɪs] schamlos.

sham·poo [ʃæm'puː] **1.** Shampoo *n*,
Schampon *n*, Schampun *n*; Kopf-,
Haarwäsche *f*; *s. set* 3; **2.** *Kopf,
Haare* waschen; *j-m* den Kopf *od.*
die Haare waschen.

sham·rock ✤ ['ʃæmrɒk] Kleeblatt *n*.

shank [ʃæŋk] (Unter)Schenkel *m*,
Schienbein *n*; △ *nicht* (Ober)Schen-
kel; ✤ Stiel *m*; ⚓ Anker)Schaft *m*.

shan·ty ['ʃæntɪ] Hütte *f*, Bude *f*;
Seemannslied *n*.

shape [ʃeɪp] **1.** Gestalt *f*, Form *f* (*a.
fig.*); körperliche *od. geistige* Verfassung; **2.** *v/t.* gestalten, formen, bilden; anpassen (*to dat.*); *v/i. a.* ~ *up*
sich entwickeln; **~d** [~t] ...förmig;
~less □ ['ʃeɪplɪs] formlos; **~ly** [~lɪ]
(*-ier*, *-iest*) wohlgeformt.

share [ʃeə] **1.** (An)Teil *m*; Beitrag *m*;
econ. Aktie *f*; ✤ Kux *m*; ✎ Pflugschar *f*; *have a* ~ *in* Anteil haben an
(*dat.*); *go* ~s teilen; **2.** *v/t.* teilen; *v/i.*
teilhaben (*in an dat.*); **~crop·per**
['ʃeəkrɒpə] *kleiner* Farmpächter (*in
den USA*); **~hold·er** *econ.* Aktio-
när(in).

shark [ʃɑːk] *zo.* Hai(fisch) *m*; Gauner
m, Betrüger *m*; (*Kredit- etc.*)Hai *m*;
Am. sl. Kanone *f* (*Könner*).

sharp [ʃɑːp] **1.** □ scharf (*a. fig.*);
spitz; steil, jäh; schneidend, stechend; heftig; hitzig; beißend,
scharf; durchdringend, schrill;
schnell; pfiffig, schlau, gerissen; ♪
(*um e-n Halbton*) erhöht; *C* ~ ♪ *Cis n*;
2. *adv.* scharf; jäh, plötzlich; ♪ zu
hoch; pünktlich, genau; *at eight
o'clock* ~ Punkt 8 (Uhr); *look* ~! F
paß auf!, gib acht!; F *mach fix od.*
schnell!; **3.** ♪ Kreuz *n*; ♪ durch ein
Kreuz erhöhte Note; F Gauner *m*;
~en ['ʃɑːpən] (ver)schärfen; spitzen; verstärken; **~en·er** [~nə] (*Messer*)Schärfer *m*; (*Bleistift*)Spitzer *m*;
~er [~ə] Gauner *m*, Schwindler *m*;
Falschspieler *m*; **~eyed** [~'aɪd]
scharfsichtig; *fig. a.* scharfsinnig;
~ness [~nɪs] Schärfe *f* (*a. fig.*);
~shoot·er Scharfschütze *m*; **~-
sight·ed** [~'saɪtɪd] scharfsichtig; *fig.
a.* scharfsinnig; **~wit·ted** [~'wɪtɪd]
scharfsinnig.

shat·ter ['ʃætə] zerschmettern,
-schlagen; *Gesundheit, Nerven* zerstören, -rütten.

shave [ʃeɪv] **1.** (shaved, shaved *od.
als adj.* shaven) (sich) rasieren; (ab-)
schaben; (glatt)hobeln; streifen; *a.*
knapp vorbeikommen an (*dat.*); **2.**
Rasieren *n*, Rasur *f*; *have* (*od. get*) *a*
~ sich rasieren (lassen); *have a close
od. narrow* ~ mit knapper Not davonkommen *od.* entkommen; *that
was a close* ~ das ist gerade noch
einmal gutgegangen!; **shav·en**
['ʃeɪvn] *p.p. von* shave 1; **shav·ing**
[~ɪŋ] **1.** Rasieren *n*; **~s** *pl.* (*bsd.*
Hobel)Späne *pl.*; **2.** Rasier...

shawl [ʃɔːl] Umhängetuch *n*; Kopf-
tuch *n*.

she [ʃiː] **1.** sie; **2.** Sie *f*; *zo.* Weibchen
n; **3.** *adj. in Zssgn, bsd. zo.*: weiblich,
...weibchen *n*; **~dog** Hündin *f*; **~-
goat** Geiß *f*.

sheaf [ʃiːf] (*pl.* sheaves) ♪ Garbe *f*;
Bündel *n*.

shear [ʃɪə] **1.** (sheared, shorn *od.*
sheared) scheren; **2.** (*a pair of*) ~s *pl.*
(e-e) große Schere.

sheath [ʃiːθ] (*pl.* sheaths [~ðz])
Scheide *f*; Futteral *n*, Hülle *f*; **~e**
[ʃiːð] in die Scheide *od.* in ein Futteral stecken; *bsd.* ⊕ umhüllen.

sheaves [ʃiːvz] *pl. von* sheaf.

S

shebang

she·bang *bsd. Am. sl.* [ʃə'bæŋ]: *the whole* ~ der ganze Kram.

shed¹ [ʃed] (*-dd-*; *shed*) aus-, vergießen; verbreiten; *Blätter etc.* abwerfen.

shed² [~] Schuppen *m*; Stall *m*.

sheen [ʃiːn] Glanz *m* (*bsd. Stoff*).

sheep [ʃiːp] (*pl. sheep*) *zo.* Schaf *n*; Schafleder *n*; **~·dog** *zo.* ['ʃiːpdɔg] Schäferhund *m*; **~·fold** Schafhürde *f*; **~·ish** [~ɪʃ] einfältig; verlegen; **~·man** (*pl. -men*) *Am.*, **~·mas·ter** *Brt.* Schafzüchter *m*; **~·skin** Schaffell *n*; Schafleder *n*; *Am.* F Diplom *n*.

sheer [ʃɪə] rein; bloß; glatt; hauchdünn; steil; senkrecht; direkt.

sheet [ʃiːt] Bett-, Leintuch *n*, Laken *n*; (*Glas- etc.*)Platte *f*; ⊕ ...blech *n*; Blatt *n*, Bogen *m* (*Papier*); weite Fläche (*Wasser etc.*); ♣ Schot(e) *f*, Segelleine *f*; *the rain came down in* ~*s* es regnete in Strömen; ~ **i·ron** ⊕ Eisenblech *n*; ~ **light·ning** Wetterleuchten *n*.

shelf [ʃelf] (*pl. shelves*) (Bücher-, Wand- *etc.*)Brett *n*, Regal *n*, Fach *n*; Riff *n*; *on the* ~ *fig.* ausrangiert.

shell [ʃel] **1.** Schale *f*; ♀ Hülse *f*, Schote *f*; Muschel *f*; Schneckenhaus *n*; *zo.* Panzer *m*; Gerüst *n*, Gerippe *n*, *arch. a.* Rohbau *m*; ✕ Granate *f*; (Geschoß-, Patronen)Hülse *f*; *Am.* Patrone *f*; **2.** schälen; enthülsen; ✕ (mit Granaten) beschießen; **~·fire** ['ʃelfaɪə] Granatfeuer *n*; **~·fish** *zo.* Schal(en)tier *n*; ~ *pl.* Meeresfrüchte *pl.*; △ *nicht* Schellfisch; **~·proof** bombensicher.

shel·ter ['ʃeltə] **1.** Schutzhütte *f*, -raum *m*, -dach *n*; Zufluchtsort *m*; Obdach *n*; Schutz *m*, Zuflucht *f*; *take* ~ Schutz suchen; *bus* ~ Wartehäuschen *n*; **2.** *v/t.* (be)schützen; beschirmen; *j-m* Schutz *od.* Zuflucht gewähren; *v/i.* Schutz *od.* Zuflucht suchen.

shelve [ʃelv] *v/t.* in ein Regal stellen; *fig. et.* auf die lange Bank schieben; *fig. et.* zurückstellen; *v/i.* sanft abfallen (*Land*).

shelves [ʃelvz] *pl. von* shelf.

she·nan·i·gans F [ʃɪ'nænɪgəns] *pl.* Blödsinn *m*, Mumpitz *m*; übler Trick.

shep·herd ['ʃepəd] **1.** Schäfer *m*, Hirt *m*; **2.** hüten; führen, leiten.

sher·iff *Am.* ['ʃerɪf] Sheriff *m*.

shield [ʃiːld] **1.** (Schutz)Schild *m*;

Wappenschild *m*, *n*; *fig.* Schutz *m*; **2.** (be)schützen (*from vor dat.*); *j-n* decken.

shift [ʃɪft] **1.** Veränderung *f*, Verschiebung *f*, Wechsel *m*; Notbehelf *m*; List *f*, Kniff *m*, Ausflucht *f*; (Arbeits)Schicht *f*; *work in* ~*s* Schicht arbeiten; *make* ~ es fertigbringen (*to do* zu tun); sich behelfen; sich durchschlagen; **2.** *v/t.* (um-, aus)wechseln, verändern; *a. fig.* verlagern, -schieben, -legen; *Schuld etc.* (ab)schieben (*onto auf acc.*); ~ *gear(s) bsd. Am. mot.* schalten; *v/i.* wechseln; sich verlagern *od.* -schieben; *bsd. Am. mot.* schalten (*into, to* in *acc.*); ~ *from one foot to the other* von e-m Fuß auf den anderen treten; ~ *in one's chair* auf s-m Stuhl *ungeduldig etc.* hin u. her rutschen; ~ *for o.s.* sich selbst (weiter)helfen; **~·less** □ ['ʃɪftlɪs] hilflos; faul; **~·y** □ [~ɪ] (*-ier, -iest*) *fig.* gerissen; verschlagen; unzuverlässig.

shil·ling ['ʃɪlɪŋ] *altes englisches Währungssystem*: Schilling *m*.

shin [ʃɪn] **1.** *a.* **~-bone** Schienbein *n*; **2.** (*-nn-*) ~ *up* hinaufklettern.

shine [ʃaɪn] **1.** Schein *m*; Glanz *m*; **2.** *v/i.* (*shone*) scheinen; leuchten; *fig.* glänzen, strahlen; *v/t.* (*shined*) polieren, putzen.

shin·gle ['ʃɪŋgl] Schindel *f*; *Am.* F (Firmen)Schild *n*; grober Strandkies; ~*s sg.* ✿ Gürtelrose *f*.

shin·y ['ʃaɪnɪ] (*-ier, -iest*) blank, glänzend.

ship [ʃɪp] **1.** Schiff *n*; F Flugzeug *n*; F Raumschiff *n*; **2.** (*-pp-*) ♣ an Bord nehmen *od.* bringen; ♣ verschiffen; *econ.* transportieren, versenden; ♣ (an)heuern; ♣ sich anheuern lassen; **~·board** ♣ ['ʃɪpbɔːd]: *on* ~ an Bord; **~·ment** [~mənt] Verschiffung *f*; Versand *m*; Schiffsladung *f*; **~·own·er** Reeder *m*; **~·ping** [~ɪŋ] Verschiffung *f*; Versand *m*; *coll.* Schiffe *pl.*, Flotte *f*; *attr.* Schiffs...; Versand...; **~·wreck** Schiffbruch *m*; **~·wrecked 1.** *be* ~ schiffbrüchig werden *od.* sein; **2.** schiffbrüchig; *fig. a.* gescheitert; **~·yard** (Schiffs-)Werft *f*.

shire ['ʃaɪə, *in Zssgn*: ...ʃə] Grafschaft *f*.

shirk [ʃɜːk] sich drücken (*vor dat.*); **~·er** ['ʃɜːkə] Drückeberger(in).

shirt [ʃɜːt] **1.** (Herren-, Ober)Hemd *n*; *a.* ~ **blouse** Hemdbluse *f*; **~sleeve** ['ʃɜːtsliːv] **1.** Hemdsärmel *m*; **2.** hemdsärmelig; leger, ungezwungen; **~waist** *Am.* Hemdbluse *f*.

shit V [ʃɪt] **1.** Scheiße *f* (*a. fig.*); Scheißen *n*; **2.** (-*tt*-; *shit*) scheißen.

shiv·er ['ʃɪvə] **1.** Splitter *m*; Schauer *m*, Zittern *n*, Frösteln *n*; **2.** zersplittern; zittern, (er)schauern, frösteln; **~y** [~rɪ] fröstelnd.

shoal [ʃəʊl] **1.** Schwarm *m* (*bsd. von Fischen*); Masse *f*; Untiefe *f*, seichte Stelle; Sandbank *f*; **2.** flach(er) werden.

shock [ʃɒk] **1.** Garbenhaufen *m*; (Haar)Schopf *m*; (heftiger) Stoß; (*a. seelische*) Erschütterung; Schock *m*; Schreck *m*, (plötzlicher) Schlag (*to für*); *&* (Nerven)Schock *m*; **2.** erschüttern; *fig.* schockieren, empören; **~ab·sorb·er** ⊕ Stoßdämpfer *m*; **~ing** □ ['ʃɒkɪŋ] schockierend, empörend, anstößig; haarsträubend; F scheußlich.

shod [ʃɒd] *pret. u. p.p. von* shoe 2.

shod·dy ['ʃɒdɪ] **1.** Reißwolle *f*; *fig.* Schund *m*; **2.** (-*ier, -iest*) falsch; minderwertig, schäbig.

shoe [ʃuː] **1.** Schuh *m*; Hufeisen *n*; **2.** (*shod*) beschuhen; beschlagen; **~black** ['ʃuːblæk] Schuhputzer *m*; **~horn** Schuhanzieher *m*; **~mak·er** Schuhmacher *m*; **~shine** *bsd. Am.* Schuhputzen *n*; *boy Am.* Schuhputzer *m*; **~string** Schnürsenkel *m*.

shone [ʃɒn, *Am.* ʃəʊn] *pret. u. p.p. von* shine 2.

shook [ʃʊk] *pret. von* shake 1.

shoot [ʃuːt] **1.** Jagd *f*; Jagd(revier *n*) *f*; Jagdgesellschaft *f*; *&* Schößling *m*, (Seiten)Trieb *m*; **2.** (*shot*) *v/t.* (ab)schießen; erschießen; werfen, stoßen; fotografieren, aufnehmen, *Film* drehen; *unter e-r Brücke etc.* hindurchschießen, über *et.* hinwegschießen; *&* treiben; *&* (hinein)spritzen; ~ *up sl. Heroin etc.* drücken; *v/i.* schießen; jagen; stechen (*Schmerz*); (dahin-, vorbei- *etc.*)schießen, (-)jagen, (-)rasen; *&* sprießen, keimen; fotografieren; filmen; ~ *ahead of* überholen (*acc.*); **~er** ['ʃuːtə] Schütz|e, -in; F Schießeisen *n* (*Schußwaffe*).

shoot·ing ['ʃuːtɪŋ] **1.** Schießen *n*; Schießerei *f*; Erschießung *f*; Jagd *f*;

Film: Dreharbeiten *pl.*; **2.** stechend (*Schmerz*); **~gal·le·ry** Schießstand *m*, -bude *f*; **~range** Schießplatz *m*; **~ star** Sternschnuppe *f*.

shop [ʃɒp] **1.** Laden *m*, Geschäft *n*; Werkstatt *f*; Betrieb *m*; *talk* ~ fachsimpeln; **2.** (-*pp*-) *mst go* ~*ping* einkaufen gehen; *a.* ~ **as·sis·tant** *Brt.* ['ʃɒpəsɪstənt] Verkäufer(in); **~keep·er** Ladenbesitzer(in); **~lift·er** [~lɪftə] Ladendieb(in); **~lift·ing** [~lɪŋ] Ladendiebstahl *m*; **~per** [~ə] Käufer(in); **~ping** [~ɪŋ] **1.** Einkauf *m*, Einkaufen *n*; Einkäufe *pl.* (*Ware*); *do one's* ~ (s-e) Einkäufe machen; **2.** Laden..., Einkaufs...; **~ bag** *Am.* Trag(e)tasche *f*; **~ centre** (*Am. center*) Einkaufszentrum *n*; **~ street** Geschäfts-, Ladenstraße *f*; **~stew·ard** ['ʃtjʊəd] gewerkschaftlicher Vertrauensmann; **~walk·er** *Brt.* [~wɔːkə] Aufsicht(sperson) *f* (*im Kaufhaus*); **~win·dow** Schaufenster *n*.

shore [ʃɔː] **1.** Küste *f*, Ufer *n*, Strand *m*; Strebebalken *m*, Stütze *f*; *on* ~ an Land; **2.** ~ *up* abstützen.

shorn [ʃɔːn] *p.p. von* shear 1.

short □ [ʃɔːt] **1.** *adj.* kurz; klein; knapp; kurz angebunden, barsch (*with gegen*); mürbe (*Gebäck*); stark, unverdünnt (*alkoholisches Getränk*); *in* ~ kurz(um); ~ *of* knapp an (*dat.*); **2.** *adv.* plötzlich, jäh; abrupt; ~ *of* abgesehen von, außer (*dat.*); *come od. fall* ~ *of et.* nicht erreichen; *cut* ~ plötzlich unterbrechen; *stop* ~ plötzlich innehalten, stutzen; *stop* ~ *of* zurückschrecken vor (*dat.*); *s. run* 1; **~age** ['ʃɔːtɪdʒ] Fehlbetrag *m*; Knappheit *f*, Mangel *m* (*of an dat.*); **~com·ing** [~'kʌmɪŋ] Unzulänglichkeit *f*; Fehler *m*, Mangel *m*; **~ cut** Abkürzung(sweg *m*) *f*; *take a* ~ (*den Weg*) abkürzen; **~dat·ed** *econ.* kurzfristig; **~dis·tance** Nah...; **~en** ['ʃɔːtn] *v/t.* (ab-, ver)kürzen; *v/i.* kürzer werden; **~en·ing** [~ɪŋ] Backfett *n*; **~hand** ['ʃɔːthænd] Kurzschrift *f*; **~ typist** Stenotypistin *f*; **~ly** [~lɪ] *adv.* kurz; bald; **~ness** [~nɪs] Kürze *f*; Mangel *m*; Schroffheit *f*; **~s** *pl.* (*a pair of* ~*s*) Shorts *pl.*; *bsd. Am.* (e-e) (Herren)Unterhose; **~sight·ed** □ ['ʃɔːt'saɪtɪd] kurzsichtig (*a. fig.*); **~term** *econ.* ['ʃɔːtˈtɜːm] kurzfristig; **~ wave** *&* Kurzwelle *f*; **~ wind·ed** □ ['ʃɔːt'wɪndɪd] kurzatmig.

S

shot [ʃɒt] 1. *pret. u. p.p. von* shoot 2; 2. Schuß *m*; Abschuß *m*; Geschoß *n*, Kugel *f*; *a. small* ~ Schrot(kugeln *pl.*) *m*, *n*; Schußweite *f*; *guter etc.* Schütze; Fußball *etc.*: Schuß *m*, *Basketball etc.*: Wurf *m*, *Tennis*, *Golf*: Schlag *m*; *phot.*, *Film*: Aufnahme *f*; 💉 F Spritze *f*, Injektion *f*; Schuß *m* (*Drogeninjektion*); *fig.* Versuch *m*; *fig.* Vermutung *f*; *have a* ~ *at et.* versuchen; *not by a long* ~ F noch lange nicht; *big* ~ F großes Tier; ~**gun** [ˈʃɒtɡʌn] Schrotflinte *f*; ~ *marriage od. wedding* F Mußheirat *f*; ~**put** Sport: Kugelstoßen *n*; Stoß *m* (*mit der Kugel*); ~**put·ter** [~pʊtə] Sport: Kugelstoßer(in).

should [ʃʊd, ʃəd] *pret. von* shall.

shoul·der [ˈʃəʊldə] 1. Schulter *f* (*a. v. Tieren*; *fig. Vorsprung*); Achsel *f*; *Am.* Bankett *n* (*Straßenrand*); 2. auf die Schulter *od. fig.* auf sich nehmen; ✗ schultern; drängen; ~**blade** *anat.* Schulterblatt *n*; ~**strap** Träger *m* (*am Kleid etc.*); ✗ Schulter-, Achselstück *n*.

shout [ʃaʊt] 1. (*lauter*) Schrei *od.* Ruf; Geschrei *n*; 2. (*laut*) rufen; schreien.

shove [ʃʌv] 1. Schubs *m*, Stoß *m*; 2. schieben, stoßen.

shov·el [ˈʃʌvl] 1. Schaufel *f*; 2. (*bsd. Brt. -ll-, Am. -l-*) schaufeln.

show [ʃəʊ] 1. (*showed, shown od. showed*) *v/t.* zeigen; ausstellen; erweisen; beweisen; ~ *in* herein-, hineinführen; ~ *off* zur Geltung bringen; ~ *out* heraus-, hinausführen; ~ *round* herumführen; ~ *up* herauf-, hinaufführen; *j-n* bloßstellen; *et.* aufdecken; *v/i. a.* ~ *up* sichtbar werden *od.* sein; sich zeigen; zu sehen sein; ~ *off* angeben, prahlen; sich aufspielen; ~ *up* F auftauchen, sich blicken lassen; 2. (Her)Zeigen *n*; Zurschaustellung *f*; Ausstellung *f*; Vorführung *f*, -stellung *f*, Schau *f*; F (Theater-, Film-) Vorstellung *f*, (*Rundfunk-, Fernseh-*) Sendung *f*, Show *f*; *leerer Schein*; *on* ~ *zu besichtigen*; ~**biz** F [ˈʃəʊbɪz], ~ **busi·ness** Showbusineß *n*, Showgeschäft *n*, Vergnügungs-, Unterhaltungsbranche *f*; ~**case** Schaukasten *m*, Vitrine *f*; ~**down** Aufdecken *n* der Karten (*a. fig.*); *fig.* Kraftprobe *f*.

show·er [ˈʃaʊə] 1. (Regen- *etc.*) Schauer *m*; Dusche *f*; *fig.* Fülle *f*; 2. *v/t.* überschütten, -häufen; *v/i.* gießen; (sich) brausen *od.* duschen; ~ *down* niederprasseln; ~**y** [~rɪ] (*-ier, -iest*) regnerisch.

show|-jump·er [ˈʃəʊdʒʌmpə] Sport: Springreiter(in); ~**jump·ing** [~ɪŋ] Sport: Springreiten *n*; ~**n** [~n] *p.p. von* show 1; ~**room** Ausstellungsraum *m*; ~**win·dow** Schaufenster *n*; ~**y** □ [~ɪ] (*-ier, -iest*) prächtig; protzig.

shrank [ʃræŋk] *pret. von* shrink.

shred [ʃred] 1. Stückchen *n*; Fetzen *m* (*a. fig.*); *fig.* Spur *f*; 2. (*-dd-*) zerfetzen; in Streifen schneiden.

shrew [ʃruː] zänkisches Weib.

shrewd □ [ʃruːd] scharfsinnig; schlau.

shriek [ʃriːk] 1. schriller Schrei; Gekreisch *n*; 2. kreischen, schreien.

shrill [ʃrɪl] 1. □ schrill, gellend; 2. schrillen, gellen; *et.* kreischen.

shrimp [ʃrɪmp] zo. Garnele *f*, Krabbe *f*; *fig. contp.* Knirps *m*.

shrine [ʃraɪn] Schrein *m*.

shrink [ʃrɪŋk] (*shrank, shrunk*) (ein-, zusammen)schrumpfen (lassen); einlaufen; zurückweichen (*from* vor *dat.*); zurückschrecken (*from, at* vor *dat.*); ~**age** [ˈʃrɪŋkɪdʒ] Einlaufen *n*; (Ein-, Zusammen)Schrumpfen *n*; Schrumpfung *f*; *fig.* Verminderung *f*.

shriv·el [ˈʃrɪvl] (*bsd. Brt. -ll-, Am. -l-*) (ein-, zusammen)schrumpfen (lassen); (ver)welken (lassen).

shroud [ʃraʊd] 1. Leichentuch *n*; *fig.* Schleier *m*; 2. in ein Leichentuch (ein)hüllen; *fig.* hüllen.

Shrove|tide [ˈʃrəʊvtaɪd] Fastnachts-, Faschingszeit *f*; ~ **Tues·day** Fastnachts-, Faschingsdienstag *m*.

shrub [ʃrʌb] Strauch *m*; Busch *m*; ~**be·ry** [ˈʃrʌbərɪ] Gebüsch *n*.

shrug [ʃrʌg] 1. (*-gg-*) (die Achseln) zucken; 2. Achselzucken *n*.

shrunk [ʃrʌŋk] *p.p. von* shrink; ~**en** [ˈʃrʌŋkən] *adj.* (ein-, zusammen)geschrumpft.

shuck *bsd. Am.* [ʃʌk] 1. Hülse *f*, Schote *f*; ~*s!* F Quatsch!; 2. enthülsen.

shud·der [ˈʃʌdə] 1. schaudern; (er)zittern, (er)beben; 2. Schauder *m*.

shuf·fle [ˈʃʌfl] 1. *Karten*: mischen; schlurfen (mit); Ausflüchte machen; △ *nicht schaufeln*; ~ *off* Klei-

dung abstreifen; *fig. Verantwortung etc.* abwälzen (*on, upon auf acc.*); 2. (Karten)Mischen *n*; Schlurfen *n*; Umstellung *f*; (*Kabinetts*)Umbildung *f*; *fig.* Ausflucht *f*, Schwindel *m*.

shun [ʃʌn] (*-nn-*) (ver)meiden.

shunt [ʃʌnt] **1.** ⚙ Rangieren *n*; ⚙ Weiche *f*; ⚡ Nebenschluß *m*; 2. ⚙ rangieren; ⚡ nebenschließen; beiseite schieben; *fig. et.* aufschieben.

shut [ʃʌt] (*-tt-; shut*) (sich) schließen; zumachen; ~ *down Betrieb* schließen; ~ *off Wasser, Gas etc.* abstellen; ~ *up* einschließen; *Haus etc.* verschließen; einsperren; ~ *up!* F halt die Klappe!; ~**ter** [ˈʃʌtə] Fensterladen *m*; *phot.* Verschluß *m*; ~ *speed phot.* Belichtung(szeit) *f*.

shut-tle [ˈʃʌtl] **1.** ⊕ Schiffchen *n*; Pendelverkehr *m*; *s.* **space** ~; **2.** *etc.* pendeln; ~**cock** *Sport* Federball *m*; ~ **di·plo·ma·cy** *pol.* Pendeldiplomatie *f*; ~ **ser·vice** Pendelverkehr *m*.

shy [ʃaɪ] **1.** □ (~*er od.* **shier**, ~*est od.* **shiest**) scheu; schüchtern; **2.** scheuen (*at vor dat.*); ~ *away from fig.* zurückschrecken vor (*dat.*); ~**ness** [ˈʃaɪnɪs] Schüchternheit *f*; Scheu *f*.

Si·be·ri·an [saɪˈbɪərɪən] **1.** sibirisch; **2.** Sibirier(in).

sick [sɪk] krank (*of an dat.; with vor dat.*); überdrüssig (*of gen.*); *fig.* krank (*of von dat.; for nach*); *be* ~ sich übergeben (müssen); *be* ~ *of s.th.* et. satt haben; *fall* ~ krank werden; *I feel* ~ mir wird schlecht *od.* übel; *go* ~, *report* ~ sich krank melden; ~**ben·e·fit** *Brt.* [ˈsɪkbenɪfɪt] Krankengeld *n*; ~**en** [~ən] *v/i.* krank werden; kränkeln; ~ *at* sich ekeln vor (*dat.*); *v/t.* krank machen; anekeln.

sick·le [ˈsɪkl] Sichel *f*.

sick·leave [ˈsɪkliːv] Fehlen *n* wegen Krankheit; *be on* ~ wegen Krankheit fehlen; ~**ly** [~lɪ] (*-ier, -iest*) kränklich; schwächlich; bleich, blaß; ungesund (*Klima*); ekelhaft; matt (*Lächeln*); ~**ness** [~nɪs] Krankheit *f*; Übelkeit *f*.

side [saɪd] **1.** Seite *f*; ~ *by* ~ Seite an Seite; *take* ~*s with* Partei ergreifen für; **2.** Seiten...; Neben...; **3.** Partei ergreifen (*with für*); ~**board** [ˈsaɪdbɔːd] Anrichte *f*, Sideboard *n*; ~**car** *mot.* Beiwagen *m*; **sid·ed** ...seitig; ~-

dish Beilage *f* (*Essen*); ~**long 1.** *adv.* seitwärts; **2.** *adj.* seitlich; Seiten...; ~**road**, ~**street** Nebenstraße *f*; ~**stroke** *Sport*: Seitenschwimmen *n*; ~**track 1.** ⚙ Nebengleis *n*; **2.** ⚙ auf ein Nebengleis schieben; *fig.* ablenken; ~**walk** *Am.* Bürgersteig *m*; ~**ward(s)** [~wəd(z)], ~**ways** seitlich; seitwärts.

sid·ing [ˈsaɪdɪŋ] Nebengleis *n*.

si·dle [ˈsaɪdl]: ~ *up to s.o.* sich an j-n heranmachen.

siege [siːdʒ] Belagerung *f*; △ *nicht Sieg; lay* ~ *to* belagern; *fig.* j-n bestürmen.

sieve [sɪv] **1.** Sieb *n*; **2.** (durch)sieben.

sift [sɪft] sieben; *fig.* sichten, prüfen.

sigh [saɪ] **1.** Seufzer *m*; **2.** seufzen; sich sehnen (*for nach*).

sight [saɪt] **1.** Sehvermögen *n*, Sehkraft *f*; Auge(nlicht) *n*; Anblick *m*; Sicht *f* (*a. econ.*); Visier *n*; *fig.* Auge *n*; ~*s pl.* Sehenswürdigkeiten *pl.*; *at* ~, *on* ~ sofort; *at* ~ vom Blatt (*singen etc.*); *at the* ~ *of* beim Anblick (*gen.*); *at first* ~ auf den ersten Blick; *catch* ~ *of* erblicken; *know by* ~ vom Sehen kennen; *lose* ~ *of* aus den Augen verlieren; (*with*)*in* ~ in Sicht(weite); **2.** sichten, erblicken; (an)visieren; ~**ed** [ˈsaɪtɪd] ...sichtig; ~**ly** [~lɪ] (*-ier, -iest*) ansehnlich, stattlich; ~**see** (*-saw, -seen*): *go* ~*ing* eine Besichtigungstour machen; ~**see·ing** [~ɪŋ] Besichtigung *f* von Sehenswürdigkeiten; ~ *tour* Besichtigungstour *f*, (*Stadt*)Rundfahrt *f*; ~**se·er** [~ə] Tourist(in).

sign [saɪn] **1.** Zeichen *n*; Wink *m*; Schild *n*; *in* ~ *of* zum Zeichen (*gen.*); **2.** winken, Zeichen geben; (unter-)zeichnen, unterschreiben.

sig·nal [ˈsɪɡnl] **1.** Signal *n* (*a. fig.*); Zeichen *n*; **2.** bemerkenswert; außerordentlich; **3.** (*bsd. Brt.* -*ll*-, *Am.* -*l*-) (ein) Zeichen geben; signalisieren; ~**ize** [~nəlaɪz] auszeichnen; hervorheben.

sig·na|to·ry [ˈsɪɡnətərɪ] **1.** Unterzeichner(in); **2.** unterzeichnend; ~ *powers pl. pol.* Signatarmächte *pl.*; ~**ture** [~tʃə] Signatur *f*; Unterschrift *f*; ~ *tune Rundfunk, TV*: Kennmelodie *f*.

sign|board [ˈsaɪnbɔːd] (Aushänge-) Schild *n*; ~**er** [~ə] Unterzeichner(in).

sig·net [ˈsɪɡnɪt] Siegel *n*.

S

sig·nif·i·cance [sıg'nıfıkəns] Bedeutung *f*; **~·cant** □ [~t] bedeutsam; bezeichnend (*of* für); **~·ca·tion** [sıgnıfı'keıʃn] Bedeutung *f*, Sinn *m*.

sig·ni·fy ['sıgnıfaı] andeuten; zu verstehen geben; bedeuten.

sign·post ['saınpəʊst] Wegweiser *m*.

si·lence ['saıləns] **1.** (Still)Schweigen *n*; Stille *f*, Ruhe *f*; **~!** Ruhe!; *put od.* **reduce to ~ = 2.** zum Schweigen bringen; **si·lenc·er** [~ə] ⊕ Schalldämpfer *m*; *mot.* Auspufftopf *m*.

si·lent □ ['saılənt] still; schweigend; schweigsam; stumm; **~ partner** *Am. econ.* stiller Teilhaber.

silk [sılk] Seide *f*; *attr.* Seiden...; **~·en** ['sılkən] seiden, Seiden...; **~·stock·ing** *Am.* vornehm; **~·worm** *zo.* Seidenraupe *f*; **~·y** [~ı] (*-ier, -iest*) seidig, seidenartig.

sill [sıl] Schwelle *f*; Fensterbrett *n*.

sil·ly □ ['sılı] (*-ier, -iest*) albern, töricht, dumm, verrückt.

silt [sılt] **1.** Schlamm *m*; **2.** *mst ~ up* verschlammen.

sil·ver ['sılvə] **1.** Silber *n*; **2.** silbern, Silber...; **3.** versilbern; silb(e)rig *od.* silberweiß werden; **~ plate, ~ware** Tafelsilber *n*; **~·y** [~rı] silberglänzend; *fig.* silberhell.

sim·i·lar □ ['sımılə] ähnlich, gleich; **~·i·ty** [sımı'lærətı] Ähnlichkeit *f*.

sim·i·le ['sımılı] Gleichnis *n*.

si·mil·i·tude [sı'mılıtju:d] Gestalt *f*, Ebenbild *n*; Gleichnis *n*.

sim·mer ['sımə] leicht kochen, *od.* sieden (lassen); *fig.* kochen (*with* vor *dat.*), gären (*Gefühl, Aufstand*); **~ down** sich beruhigen *od.* abregen.

sim·per ['sımpə] **1.** einfältiges Lächeln; **2.** einfältig lächeln.

sim·ple □ ['sımpl] (*~r, ~st*) einfach; schlicht; einfältig; arglos, naiv; **~-heart·ed, ~-mind·ed** einfältig, arglos, naiv; **~·ton** [~tən] Einfaltspinsel *m*.

sim·plic·i·ty [sım'plısətı] Einfachheit *f*; Unkompliziertheit *f*; Schlichtheit *f*; Einfalt *f*; **~·fi·ca·tion** [sımplıfı'keıʃn] Vereinfachung *f*; **~·fy** ['sımplıfaı] vereinfachen.

sim·ply ['sımplı] einfach; bloß.

sim·u·late ['sımjʊleıt] vortäuschen; simulieren; ⚔, ⊕ *a.* Bedingungen, Vorgänge (wirklichkeitsgetreu) nachahmen.

sim·ul·ta·ne·ous □ [sıml'teınjəs] gleichzeitig, simultan.

sin [sın] **1.** Sünde *f*; **2.** (*-nn-*) sündigen.

since [sıns] **1.** *prp.* seit; **2.** *adv.* seitdem; **3.** *cj.* seit(dem); da (ja).

sin·cere □ [sın'sıə] aufrichtig, ehrlich, offen; *Yours* **~ly** *Briefschluß*: Mit freundlichen Grüßen; **sin·cer·i·ty** [~'serətı] Aufrichtigkeit *f*, Offenheit *f*.

sin·ew *anat.* ['sınju:] Sehne *f*; **~·y** [~ju:ı] sehnig; *fig.* kraftvoll.

sin·ful □ ['sınfl] sündig, sündhaft.

sing [sıŋ] (*sang, sung*) singen; **~ to** *s.o.* j-m vorsingen.

singe [sındʒ] (ver-, ab)sengen.

sing·er ['sıŋə] Sänger(in).

sing·ing ['sıŋıŋ] Gesang *m*, Singen *n*; **~ bird** Singvogel *m*.

sin·gle ['sıŋgl] **1.** □ einzig; einzeln; Einzel...; einzelne(r), unverheiratet; *bookkeeping by ~ entry* einfache Buchführung; *in ~ file* im Gänsemarsch; **2.** *Brt.* einfache Fahrkarte, ⚔ einfaches Ticket; Single *f* (*Schallplatte*); Single *m*, Unverheiratete(r *m*) *f*; *Brt.* Einpfund-; *Am.* Eindollarschein *m*; **~s** *sg.*, *pl. Tennis:* Einzel *n*; **3.** **~ out** auswählen, -suchen; **~-breast·ed** einreihig (*Jacke etc.*); **~-en·gined** ⚔ einmotorig; **~-hand·ed** eigenhändig, allein; **~-heart·ed** □, **~-mind·ed** □ aufrichtig; zielstrebig.

sin·glet *Brt.* ['sıŋglıt] ärmelloses Unterhemd *od.* Trikot.

sin·gle-track 🚆 ['sıŋgltræk] eingleisig; F *fig.* einseitig.

sin·gu·lar ['sıŋgjʊlə] **1.** □ einzigartig; eigenartig; sonderbar; **2.** *a. ~ number gr.* Singular *m*, Einzahl *f*; **~·i·ty** [sıŋgjʊ'lærətı] Einzigartigkeit *f*; Eigentümlich-, Seltsamkeit *f*.

sin·is·ter □ ['sınıstə] unheilvoll; böse.

sink [sıŋk] **1.** (*sank, sunk*) *v/i.* sinken; ein-, nieder-, unter-, versinken; sich senken; (ein)dringen, (-)sickern; *v/t.* (ver)senken; *Brunnen* bohren; *Geld* fest anlegen; **2.** Ausguß *m*, Spüle *f*; **~·ing** ['sıŋkıŋ] (Ein-, Ver)Sinken *n*; Versenken *n*; ⚕ Schwäche(gefühl *n*) *f*; *econ.* Tilgung *f*; **~-fund** (Schulden)Tilgungsfonds *m*.

sin·less □ ['sınlıs] sünd(en)los, sündenfrei.

sin·ner ['sınə] Sünder(in).

sin·u·ous □ ['sınjʊəs] gewunden.

sip [sıp] **1.** Schlückchen *n*; **2.** (*-pp-*)

v/t. nippen an (*dat.*) *od.* von; schlück-
chenweise trinken; *v/i.* nippen (*at* an
dat. od. von).

sir [sɜː] Herr *m* (*Anrede*); ♀ [sə] Sir *m*
(*Titel*).

sire ['saɪə] *mst poet.* Vater *m*; Vorfahr
m; *zo.* Vater(tier *n*) *m*.

si·ren ['saɪərən] Sirene *f*.

sir·loin ['sɜːlɔɪn] Lendenstück *n*.

sis·sy F ['sɪsɪ] Weichling *m*.

sis·ter ['sɪstə] (*a.* Ordens-, Ober-,
Kranken)Schwester *f*; **~hood**
[ˌhʊd] Schwesternschaft *f*; **~-in-
law** [ˌrɪnlɔ:] (*pl. sisters-in-law*)
Schwägerin *f*; **~·ly** [ˌlɪ] schwester-
lich.

sit [sɪt] (*-tt-*; *sat*) *v/i.* sitzen; e-e
Sitzung halten, tagen; *fig.* liegen,
stehen; *~ down* sich setzen; *~ in* ein
Sit-in veranstalten; *~ in for* für j-n
einspringen; *~ up* aufrecht sitzen;
aufbleiben; *v/t.* setzen; sitzen auf
(*dat.*).

site [saɪt] Lage *f*; Stelle *f*; Stätte *f*;
(Bau)Gelände *n*.

sit-in ['sɪtɪn] Sit-in *n*.

sit·ting ['sɪtɪŋ] Sitzung *f*; **~ room**
Wohnzimmer *n*.

sit·u·at·ed ['sɪtjʊeɪtɪd] gelegen; *be ~*
liegen, gelegen sein; **~·a·tion** [sɪt-
jʊ'eɪʃn] Lage *f*; Stellung *f*, Stelle *f*.

six [sɪks] 1. sechs; 2. Sechs *f*; **~teen**
['sɪks'ti:n] 1. sechzehn; 2. Sechzehn
f; **~·teenth** [ˌθ] sechzehnte(r, -s);
~th [sɪksθ] 1. sechste(r, -s); 2. Sech-
stel *n*; **~th·ly** ['sɪksθlɪ] sechstens;
~·ti·eth [ˌtɪθ] sechzigste(r, -s); **~·ty**
[ˌtɪ] 1. sechzig; 2. Sechzig *f*.

size [saɪz] 1. Größe *f*; Format *n*; 2.
nach Größe(n) ordnen; *~ up* F abschätzen; **~d** von *od.* in ... Größe.

siz(e)·a·ble □ ['saɪzəbl] (ziemlich)
groß.

siz·zle ['sɪzl] zischen; knistern; brutzeln; *sizzling (hot)* glühendheiß.

skate [skeɪt] 1. Schlittschuh *m*; Rollschuh *m*; 2. Schlittschuh laufen, eislaufen; Rollschuh laufen; **~·board**
['skeɪtbɔːd] 1. Skateboard *n*; 2.
Skateboard fahren; **skat·er** [ˌə]
Schlittschuhläufer(in); Rollschuh-
läufer(in); **skat·ing** [ˌɪŋ] Schlitt-
schuh-, Eislaufen *n*, Eislauf *m*; Roll-
schuhlauf(en *n*) *m*.

ske·dad·dle F [skɪ'dædl] abhauen.

skein [skeɪn] Strang *m*, Docke *f*.

skel·e·ton ['skelɪtn] Skelett *n*; Gerippe *n*; Gestell *n*; *attr.* Skelett...; ✕

Stamm...; *~ key* Nachschlüssel *m*.

skep|tic ['skeptɪk], **~·ti·cal** [ˌl] *Am.* =
sceptic(al).

sketch [sketʃ] 1. Skizze *f*; Entwurf *m*;
thea. Sketch *m*; 2. skizzieren; entwerfen.

ski [ski:] 1. (*pl. skis, ski*) Schi *m*, Ski
m; *attr.* Schi..., Ski...; 2. Schi *od.* Ski
laufen *od.* fahren.

skid [skɪd] 1. Bremsklotz *m*; ✕
(Gleit)Kufe *f*; *mot.* Rutschen *n*,
Schleudern *n*; *~ mark mot.* Brems-
spur *f*; 2. (*-dd-*) rutschen; schleudern.

skid-doo *Am. sl.* ['skɪ'du:] abhauen.

ski|er ['ski:ə] Schi-, Skiläufer(in); △
nicht Skier; **~·ing** [ˌɪŋ] Schi-, Ski-
lauf(en *n*) *m*, -fahren *n*, -sport *m*.

skil·ful □ ['skɪlfl] geschickt; geübt.

skill [skɪl] Geschicklichkeit *f*, Fertigkeit *f*; **~ed** geschickt; ausgebildet,
Fach...; *~ worker* Facharbeiter *m*.

skill·ful *Am.* □ ['skɪlfl] = *skilful*.

skim [skɪm] 1. (*-mm-*) abschöpfen;
Milch entrahmen; (hin)gleiten über
(*acc.*); *Buch* überfliegen; *~ through*
durchblättern; 2. *~ milk* Mager-
milch *f*.

skimp [skɪmp] *j-n* knapphalten; sparen an; knausern (*on* mit); **~·y** □
['skɪmpɪ] (*-ier, -iest*) knapp; dürftig.

skin [skɪn] 1. Haut *f*; Fell *n*; Schale *f*;
2. (*-nn-*) *v/t.* (*en*)häuten; abbalgen;
schälen; *v/i. a. ~ over* zuheilen; **~
deep** ['skɪn'di:p] (nur) oberflächlich; **~ div·ing** Sporttauchen *n*;
~·flint Knicker *m*; **~·ny** [ˌɪ] (*-ier,
-iest*) mager; **~·ny-dip** F nackt baden.

skip [skɪp] 1. Sprung *m*; 2. (*-pp-*) *v/i.*
hüpfen, springen; seilhüpfen; *v/t.*
überspringen.

skip·per ['skɪpə] ♣ Schiffer *m*; ♣,
✕, *Sport:* Kapitän *m*.

skir·mish ['skɜːmɪʃ] 1. ✕ *u. fig.* Ge-
plänkel *n*; 2. plänkeln.

skirt [skɜːt] 1. (Damen)Rock *m*;
(Rock)Schoß *m*; *oft ~s pl.* Rand *m*,
Saum *m*; 2. (um)säumen; (sich) ent-
langziehen an (*dat.*); **~·ing-board**
Brt. ['skɜːtɪŋbɔːd] Scheuerleiste *f*.

skit [skɪt] Stichelei *f*; Satire *f*; **~·tish**
□ ['skɪtɪʃ] ausgelassen; scheu
(*Pferd*).

skit·tle ['skɪtl] Kegel *m*; *play (at) ~s*
kegeln; **~·al·ley** Kegelbahn *f*.

skulk [skʌlk] (herum)schleichen;
lauern; sich drücken.

S

skull [skʌl] Schädel *m*.
skull(l)·dug·ge·ry F [skʌl'dʌgərɪ] Gaunerei *f*.
skunk *zo.* [skʌŋk] Skunk *m*, Stinktier *n*.
sky [skaɪ] *oft* **skies** *pl.* Himmel *m*; **~·jack** F ['skaɪdʒæk] *Flugzeug* entführen; **~·jack·er** F [~ə] Flugzeugentführer(in); **~·lab** *Am.* Raumlabor *n*; **~·lark** 1. *zo.* Feldlerche *f*; 2. F Blödsinn treiben; **~·light** Oberlicht *n*, Dachfenster *n*; **~·line** Horizont *m*, Silhouette *f*; **~·rock·et** F in die Höhe schießen (*Preise*), sprunghaft ansteigen; **~·scrap·er** Wolkenkratzer *m*; **~·ward(s)** [~wəd(z)] himmelwärts.
slab [slæb] Platte *f*, Fliese *f*; (dicke) Scheibe (*Käse etc.*).
slack [slæk] 1. □ schlaff; locker; (nach)lässig; flau (*a. econ.*); 2. ⚓ Lose *f* (*schlaffes Taustück*); Flaute *f* (*a. econ.*); Kohlengrus *m*; **~en** ['slækən] nachlassen; (sich) verringern; (sich) lockern; (sich) entspannen; (sich) verlangsamen; **~s** *pl.* Freizeithose *f*.
slag [slæg] Schlacke *f*.
slain [sleɪn] *p.p. von* **slay**.
slake [sleɪk] *Kalk* löschen; *Durst* löschen, stillen.
slam [slæm] 1. Zuschlagen *n*; Knall *m*; 2. (*-mm-*) *Tür etc.* zuschlagen, zuknallen; *et. auf den Tisch etc.* knallen.
slan·der ['slɑːndə] 1. Verleumdung *f*; 2. verleumden; **~ous** □ [~rəs] verleumderisch.
slang [slæŋ] 1. Slang *m*; Berufssprache *f*; lässige Umgangssprache; 2. *j-n* wüst beschimpfen.
slant [slɑːnt] 1. schräge Fläche; Abhang *m*; Neigung *f*; Standpunkt *m*, Einstellung *f*; Tendenz *f*; 2. schräg legen *od.* liegen; sich neigen; **~ing** *adj.* □ ['slɑːntɪŋ], **~wise** *adv.* [~waɪz] schief, schräg.
slap [slæp] 1. Klaps *m*, Schlag *m*; 2. (*-pp-*) *e-n* Klaps geben (*dat.*); schlagen; klatschen; **~·jack** *Am.* ['slæpdʒæk] *Art* Pfannkuchen *m*; **~·stick** (Narren)Pritsche *f*; **~ com·edy** *thea.* Slapstickkomödie *f*.
slash [slæʃ] 1. Hieb *m*; Schnitt(wunde *f*) *m*; Schlitz *m*; 2. (auf)schlitzen; schlagen, hauen; *fig.* scharf kritisieren.
slate [sleɪt] 1. Schiefer *m*; Schiefertafel *f*; *bsd. Am. pol.* Kandidatenliste *f*;

2. mit Schiefer decken; *Brt.* F heftig kritisieren; *Am.* F *Kandidaten* aufstellen; **~·pen·cil** ['sleɪt'pensl] Griffel *m*.
slat·tern ['slætən] Schlampe *f*.
slaugh·ter ['slɔːtə] 1. Schlachten *n*; *fig.* Blutbad *n*, Gemetzel *n*; 2. schlachten; *fig.* niedermetzeln; **~·house** Schlachthaus *n*, -hof *m*.
Slav [slɑːv] 1. Slaw|e *m*, -in *f*; 2. slawisch.
slave [sleɪv] 1. Sklav|e *m*, -in *f* (*a. fig.*); 2. sich (ab)placken, schuften.
slav·er ['slævə] 1. Geifer *m*, Sabber *m*; 2. geifern, sabbern.
sla·ve·ry ['sleɪvərɪ] Sklaverei *f*; Plackerei *f*; **slav·ish** □ [~ɪʃ] sklavisch.
slay *rhet.* [sleɪ] (**slew**, **slain**) erschlagen; töten; ⚠ *nicht* schlagen.
sled [sled] 1. = **sledge¹** 1; 2. (*-dd-*) = **sledge¹** 2.
sledge¹ [sledʒ] 1. Schlitten *m*; 2. Schlitten fahren, rodeln.
sledge² □ *a.* **~·hammer** Schmiedehammer *m*.
sleek [sliːk] 1. □ glatt, glänzend (*Haar, Fell*); geschmeidig; 2. glätten.
sleep [sliːp] 1. (**slept**) *v/i.* schlafen; **~** (up)on *od.* over *et.* überschlafen; **~** with *s.o.* mit j-m schlafen (*Geschlechtsverkehr haben*); *v/t.* schlafen; *j-n* für die Nacht unterbringen; **~** away *Zeit* verschlafen; 2. Schlaf *m*; get *od.* go to **~** einschlafen; put to **~** *Tier* einschläfern; **~·er** ['sliːpə] Schlafende(r *m*) *f*; ⚓ Schwelle *f*; ⚓ Schlafwagen *m*; **~·ing** [~ɪŋ] schlafend; Schlaf...; **♀·ing Beau·ty** Dornröschen *n*; **~·ing-car(·riage)** ⚓ Schlafwagen *m*; **~·ing part·ner** *Brt. econ.* stiller Teilhaber; **~·less** □ [~lɪs] schlaflos; **~·walk·er** Schlafwandler(in); **~·y** □ [~ɪ] (*-ier, -iest*) schläfrig; müde; verschlafen.
sleet [sliːt] 1. Schneeregen *m*; Graupelschauer *m*; 2. *it was* **~ing** es gab Schneeregen; es graupelte.
sleeve [sliːv] Ärmel *m*; ⊕ Muffe *f*; *Brt.* (Schall)Plattenhülle *f*; **~·link** ['sliːvlɪŋk] Manschettenknopf *m*.
sleigh [sleɪ] 1. (*bsd. Pferde*)Schlitten *m*; 2. (im) Schlitten fahren.
sleight [slaɪt]: **~** of hand (Taschenspieler)Trick *m*; Fingerfertigkeit *f*.
slen·der □ ['slendə] schlank; schmächtig; *fig.* schwach; dürftig.

slept [slept] *pret. u. p.p. von* sleep 1.

sleuth [slu:θ] *a.* ~**hound** Spürhund *m* (*a. fig. Detektiv*).

slew [slu:] *pret. von* slay.

slice [slaɪs] **1.** Schnitte *f*, Scheibe *f*, Stück *n*; (An)Teil *m*; **2.** (in) Scheiben schneiden; aufschneiden.

slick [slɪk] **1.** □ *adj.* glatt, glitschig; F geschickt, raffiniert; **2.** *adv.* direkt; **3.** Ölfleck *m*, -teppich *m*; ~**er** *Am.* F ['slɪkə] Regenmantel *m*; gerissener Kerl.

slid [slɪd] *pret. u. p.p. von* slide 1.

slide [slaɪd] **1.** (*slid*) gleiten (lassen); rutschen; schlittern; ausgleiten; ~ *into fig.* in *et.* hineinschlittern; *let things* ~ *fig.* die Dinge laufen lassen; **2.** Gleiten *n*, Rutschen *n*, Schlittern *n*; Rutschbahn *f*; Rutsche *f*; ⊕ Schieber *m*; *phot.* Dia(positiv) *n*; *Brt.* (Haar)Spange *f*; *a. land*~ Erdrutsch *m*; ~**rule** ['slaɪdru:l] Rechenschieber *m*.

slid·ing □ ['slaɪdɪŋ] gleitend, rutschend; Schiebe...; ~ *time Am. econ.* Gleitzeit *f*.

slight [slaɪt] **1.** □ leicht; schmächtig; schwach; gering, unbedeutend; **2.** Geringschätzung *f*; **3.** geringschätzig behandeln; beleidigen, kränken.

slim (*-mm-*) [slɪm] **1.** □ schlank, dünn; *fig.* gering, dürftig; **2.** e-e Schlankheitskur machen, abnehmen.

slime [slaɪm] Schlamm *m*; Schleim *m*; **slim·y** ['slaɪmɪ] (*-ier, -iest*) schlammig; schleimig; *fig.* schmierig; kriecherisch.

sling [slɪŋ] **1.** (Stein)Schleuder *f*; Schlinge *f* (*zum Tragen*); Tragriemen *m*; ✗ Schlinge *f*, Binde *f*; **2.** (*slung*) schleudern; auf-, umhängen; *a.* ~ *up* hochziehen; △ *nicht* schlingen.

slink [slɪŋk] (*slunk*) schleichen.

slip [slɪp] **1.** (*-pp-*) gleiten (lassen); rutschen; ausgleiten, -rutschen; (ver)rutschen; loslassen; ~ *away* wegschleichen, sich fortstehlen; ~ *in Bemerkung* dazwischenwerfen; ~ *into et.* hineinschlüpfen *od.* hineinschieben in (*acc.*); ~ *off* (*on*) *Ring, Kleid etc.* abstreifen (überstreifen); ~ *up* (e-n) Fehler machen; *have* ~**ped** *s.o.'s memory od. mind* j-m entfallen sein; **2.** (Aus)Gleiten *n*, (-)Rutschen *n*; Fehltritt *m* (*a. fig.*); (Flüchtigkeits-)Fehler *m*; Fehler *m*, Panne *f*; Strei-

fen *m*, Zettel *m*; *econ.* (Kontroll)Abschnitt *m*; (Kissen)Bezug *m*; Unterkleid *n*, -rock *m*; △ *nicht* Slip; *a* ~ *of a boy* (*girl*) ein schmächtiges Bürschchen (ein zartes Ding); ~ *of the tongue* Versprecher *m*; *give s.o. the* ~ j-m entwischen; ~**ped disc** ✗ [slɪpt 'dɪsk] Bandscheibenvorfall *m*; ~**per** ['slɪpə] Pantoffel *m*, Hausschuh *m*; ~**per·y** [~rɪ] (*-ier, -iest*) glatt, schlüpfrig; ~**road** *Brt.* Autobahnauffahrt *f*, -ausfahrt *f*; ~**shod** [~ʃɒd] schlampig, nachlässig.

slit [slɪt] **1.** Schlitz *m*, Spalt *m*; **2.** (*-tt-*; *slit*) (auf-, zer)schlitzen.

slith·er ['slɪðə] gleiten, rutschen.

sliv·er ['slɪvə] Splitter *m*.

slob·ber ['slɒbə] **1.** Sabber *m*, Geifer *m*; **2.** (be)geifern, (be)sabbern.

slo·gan ['sləʊgən] Slogan *m*; Schlagwort *n*; Werbespruch *m*.

sloop ✥ [slu:p] Schaluppe *f*.

slop [slɒp] **1.** Krankensüppchen *n*; ~*s pl.* Spül-, Schmutzwasser *n*; **2.** (*-pp-*) *v/t.* verschütten; *v/i.* ~ *over* überschwappen.

slope [sləʊp] **1.** (Ab)Hang *m*; Neigung *f*, Gefälle *n*; **2.** ⊕ abschrägen; abfallen; schräg halten *od.* stellen; (sich) neigen.

slop·py □ ['slɒpɪ] (*-ier, -iest*) naß, schmutzig; schlampig; labb(e)rig (*Essen*); *fig.* rührselig.

slot [slɒt] Schlitz *m*, (Münz)Einwurf *m*.

sloth [sləʊθ] Faulheit *f*; *zo.* Faultier *n*.

slot-ma·chine ['slɒtməʃi:n] (Waren-, Spiel)Automat *m*.

slouch [slaʊtʃ] **1.** krumm *od.* (nach-)lässig dastehen *od.* dasitzen; F (herum)latschen; **2.** schlaffe, schlechte Haltung; ~ *hat* Schlapphut *m*.

slough¹ [slaʊ] Sumpf(loch *n*) *m*.

slough² [slʌf] *Haut* abwerfen.

slov·en ['slʌvn] unordentlicher Mensch; Schlampe *f*; ~**ly** [~lɪ] schlampig.

slow [sləʊ] **1.** □ langsam; schwerfällig; träge; *be* ~ nachgehen (*Uhr*); **2.** *adv.* langsam; **3.** ~ *down*, ~ *up v/t.* *Geschwindigkeit* verlangsamen, -ringern; *v/i.* langsamer werden; ~**coach** ['sləʊkəʊtʃ] Langweiler *m*; ~**down (strike)** *Am. econ.* Bummelstreik *m*; ~ **mo·tion** *phot.* Zeitlupe *f*; ~**poke** *Am.* = slowcoach; ~**worm** *zo.* Blindschleiche *f*.

S

sludge [slʌdʒ] Schlamm *m*; Matsch *m*.

slug [slʌg] **1.** *zo.* Wegschnecke *f*; Stück *n* Rohmetall; *bsd. Am.* (Pistolen)Kugel *f*; *Am.* (Faust)Schlag *m*; **2.** (-gg-) *Am.* F *j-m* e-n harten Schlag versetzen.

slug|gard ['slʌgəd] Faulpelz *m*; ~**gish** □ [~ɪʃ] träge; *econ.* schleppend.

sluice ⊕ [sluːs] Schleuse *f*.

slum·ber ['slʌmbə] **1.** *mst* ~s *pl.* Schlummer *m*; **2.** schlummern.

slump [slʌmp] **1.** plumpsen; *econ.* fallen, stürzen (*Preise*); **2.** *econ.* (Kurs-, Preis)Sturz *m*; (starker) Konjunkturrückgang.

slums [slʌmz] *pl.* Slums *pl.*, Elendsviertel *n od. pl.*

slung [slʌŋ] *pret. u. p.p. von* sling 2.

slunk [slʌŋk] *pret. u. p.p. von* slink.

slur [sləː] **1.** (-rr-) verunglimpfen, verleumden; undeutlich (aus)sprechen; ♩ Töne binden; **2.** Verunglimpfung *f*, Verleumdung *f*; undeutliche Aussprache; ♩ Bindebogen *m*.

slush [slʌʃ] Schlamm *m*, Matsch *m*; Schneematsch *m*; Kitsch *m*.

slut [slʌt] Schlampe *f*; Nutte *f*.

sly □ [slaɪ] (~er, ~est) schlau, listig; hinterlistig; *on the* ~ heimlich.

smack [smæk] **1.** (Bei)Geschmack *m*; Schmatz *m* (*Kuß*); Schmatzen *n*; klatschender Schlag, Klatsch *m*, Klaps *m*; (Peitschen)Knall *m*; Spur *f*, Andeutung *f*; **2.** schmecken (*of* nach); klatschend schlagen; knallen (mit); *j-m* e-n Klaps geben; ~ *one's lips* schmatzen.

small [smɔːl] **1.** klein; gering; wenig; unbedeutend; bescheiden; (sozial) niedrig; kleinlich; △ *nicht schmal*; *feel* ~ sich schämen; sich ganz klein und häßlich vorkommen; *look* ~ beschämt *od.* schlecht dastehen; *the* ~ *hours* die frühen Morgenstunden *pl.*; *in a* ~ *way* bescheiden; **2.** ~ *of the back* anat. Kreuz *n*; ~*s pl. Brt.* F Unterwäsche *f*, Taschentücher *pl. etc.*; *wash one's* ~*s* kleine Wäsche waschen; ~ **arms** ['smɔː-laːmz] *pl.* Handfeuerwaffen *pl.*; ~ **change** Kleingeld *n*; ~**ish** [~ɪʃ] ziemlich klein; ~**pox** ✶ [~pɒks] Pocken *pl.*; ~ **talk** oberflächliche Konversation; ~**time** F unbedeutend.

smart [smaːt] **1.** □ klug; gewandt, geschickt; gerissen, raffiniert; elegant, schick, fesch; forsch; flink; hart, scharf; heftig; schlagfertig; ~ *aleck* F Klugscheißer *m*; **2.** stechender Schmerz; **3.** schmerzen; leiden; ~**ness** ['smaːtnɪs] Klugheit *f*; Gewandtheit *f*; Gerissenheit *f*; Eleganz *f*; Schärfe *f*.

smash [smæʃ] *v/t.* zerschlagen, -trümmern; (zer)schmettern; *fig.* vernichten; *v/i.* zersplittern; krachen; zusammenstoßen; *fig.* zusammenbrechen; **2.** heftiger Schlag; Zerschmettern *n*; Krach *m*; Zusammenbruch *m* (*a. econ.*); *Tennis etc.*: Schmetterball *m*; *a.* ~ *hit* F toller Erfolg; ~**ing** *bsd. Brt.* F [~ʃɪŋ] toll, sagenhaft; ~**up** Zusammenstoß *m*; Zusammenbruch *m*.

smat·ter·ing ['smætərɪŋ] oberflächliche Kenntnis.

smear [smɪə] **1.** (be-, ein-, ver-) schmieren; *fig.* verleumden; **2.** Schmiere *f*; Fleck *m*.

smell [smel] **1.** Geruch(ssinn) *m*; Duft *m*; Gestank *m*; **2.** (*smelt od. smelled*) *v/t.* riechen (*an dat.*); *v/i.* riechen (*at* an *dat.*); duften; stinken; ~**y** ['smelɪ] (-ier, -iest) übelriechend, stinkend.

smelt[1] [smelt] *pret. u. p.p. von* smell 2.

smelt[2] *metall.* [~] *Erz* (ein)schmelzen, verhütten.

smile [smaɪl] **1.** Lächeln *n*; **2.** lächeln; ~ *at j-n* anlächeln.

smirch [sməːtʃ] besudeln.

smirk [sməːk] grinsen.

smith [smɪθ] Schmied *m*.

smith·e·reens ['smɪðə'riːnz] *pl.* Stücke *pl.*, Splitter *pl*, Fetzen *pl.*

smith·y ['smɪðɪ] Schmiede *f*.

smit·ten ['smɪtn] betroffen, heimgesucht; *fig.* hingerissen (*with* von); *humor.* verliebt, -knallt (*with* in *acc.*).

smock [smɒk] Kittel *m*.

smog [smɒg] Smog *m*.

smoke [sməʊk] **1.** Rauch *m*; *have a* ~ (eine) rauchen; **2.** rauchen; qualmen; dampfen; räuchern; ~**dried** ['sməʊkdraɪd] geräuchert; **smok·er** [~ə] Raucher(in); ﷽ F Raucher(abteil *n*) *m*; ~**stack** ﷽, ♣ Schornstein *m*.

smok·ing ['sməʊkɪŋ] Rauchen *n*; *attr.* Rauch(er)...; ~**com·part·ment** ﷽ Raucherabteil *n*.

smok·y □ ['sməʊkɪ] (*-ier, -iest*) rauchig; verräuchert.

smooth [smu:ð] **1.** □ glatt; eben; ruhig (⊕, *Meer, Reise*); sanft (*Stimme*); flüssig (*Stil etc.*); mild (*Wein*); (aal)glatt, gewandt (*Benehmen*); **2.** glätten; *fig.* besänftigen; ~ *away fig.* wegräumen; ~ *down* sich glätten; glattstreichen; ~ *out Falte* glattstreichen; **~·ness** □ ['smu:ðnɪs] Glätte *f*.

smoth·er ['smʌðə] ersticken.

smo(u)l·der ['sməʊldə] schwelen.

smudge [smʌdʒ] **1.** (ver-, be)schmieren; schmutzig werden; **2.** Schmutzfleck *m*.

smug [smʌg] (*-gg-*) selbstgefällig.

smug·gle ['smʌgl] schmuggeln; **~r** [~ə] Schmuggler(in).

smut [smʌt] Ruß(fleck) *m*; Schmutzfleck *m*; *fig.* Zote(n *pl.*) *f*; △ *nicht* Schmutz; **2.** (*-tt-*) beschmutzen; **~·ty** □ ['smʌtɪ] (*-ier, -iest*) schmutzig.

snack [snæk] Imbiß *m*; *have a* ~ e-e Kleinigkeit essen; **~·bar** ['snækbɑ:] Snackbar *f*, Imbißstube *f*.

snaf·fle ['snæfl] *a.* ~ *bit* Trense *f*.

snag [snæg] (Ast-, Zahn)Stumpf *m*; *bsd. Am.* Baumstumpf *m* (*bsd. unter Wasser*); *fig.* Haken *m*.

snail *zo.* [sneɪl] Schnecke *f*.

snake *zo.* [sneɪk] Schlange *f*; △ *nicht* Schnecke.

snap [snæp] **1.** (Zu)Schnappen *n*, Biß *m*; Knacken *n*, Krachen *n*; Knacks *m*; Knall *m*; Schnappschloß *n*; F *phot.* Schnappschuß *m*; *fig.* F Schwung *m*, Schmiß *m*; *cold* ~ Kälteeinbruch *m*; **2.** (*-pp-*) *v/i.* schnappen (*at* nach); zuschnappen (*Schloß*); krachen; knacken; knallen; (zer)brechen; zerkrachen, -springen, -reißen; schnauzen; ~ *at s.o.* j-n anschnauzen; ~ *to it!, Am. a.* ~ *it up!* fix, mach schnell!, Tempo!; ~ *out of it!* hör auf (damit)!, komm, komm!; *v/t.* (er)schnappen, beißen; schnell greifen nach; knallen mit; (auf- *od.* zu)schnappen *od.* (-)knallen lassen; *phot.* knipsen; zerbrechen; j-n anschnauzen, anfahren; ~ *one's fingers* mit den Fingern schnalzen; ~ *one's fingers at fig.* j-n, *et.* nicht ernst nehmen; ~ *out Worte* hervorstoßen; ~ *up* wegschnappen; am sich reißen; **~·fas·ten·er** ['snæpfɑ:snə] Druckknopf *m*; **~·pish** □ [~ɪʃ] bissig; schnippisch; **~·py** [~ɪ] (*-ier, -iest*) bissig; F flott; F schnell; *make*

it ~!, *Brt. a. look* ~! F mach fix!; **~·shot** Schnappschuß *m*, Momentaufnahme *f*.

snare [sneə] **1.** Schlinge *f*, Falle *f* (*a. fig.*); **2.** fangen; *fig.* umgarnen.

snarl [snɑ:l] **1.** wütend knurren; **2.** Knurren *n*, Zähnefletschen *n*; Knoten *m*; *fig.* Gewirr *n*.

snatch [snætʃ] **1.** schneller Griff; Ruck *m*; Stückchen *n*; **2.** schnappen; ergreifen, *et.* an sich reißen; nehmen; ~ *at* greifen nach.

sneak [sni:k] **1.** *v/i.* schleichen; *Brt. sl.* petzen; *v/t. sl.* stibitzen; **2.** F Leisetreter *m*, Kriecher *m*; *Brt. sl.* Petze *f*; **~·ers** *bsd. Am.* ['sni:kəz] *pl.* Turnschuhe *pl.*

sneer [snɪə] **1.** höhnisches Grinsen; höhnische Bemerkung; **2.** höhnisch grinsen; spotten; *et.* höhnen.

sneeze [sni:z] **1.** niesen; **2.** Niesen *n*.

snick·er ['snɪkə] *bsd. Am.* kichern; *bsd. Brt.* wiehern.

sniff [snɪf] schnüffeln, schnuppern; *fig.* die Nase rümpfen.

snig·ger *bsd. Brt.* ['snɪgə] kichern.

snip [snɪp] **1.** Schnitt *m*; Schnipsel *m*, *n*; **2.** (*-pp-*) schnippeln, schnipseln.

snipe [snaɪp] **1.** *zo.* Schnepfe *f*; **2.** aus dem Hinterhalt schießen; **snip·er** ['snaɪpə] Heckenschütze *m*.

sniv·el ['snɪvl] (*bsd. Brt. -ll-, Am. -l-*) schniefen; schluchzen; plärren.

snob [snɒb] Snob *m*; **~·bish** □ ['snɒbɪʃ] versnobt.

snoop F [snu:p] **1.** ~ *about*, ~ *around* F *fig.* herumschnüffeln; **2.** Schnüffler(in).

snooze F [snu:z] **1.** Nickerchen *n*; *ein Nickerchen machen*; dösen.

snore [snɔ:] **1.** schnarchen; **2.** Schnarchen *n*.

snort [snɔ:t] schnauben; prusten.

snout [snaʊt] Schnauze *f*; Rüssel *m*.

snow [snəʊ] **1.** Schnee *m*; *sl.* Snow *m*, Schnee *m* (*Kokain, Heroin*); **2.** schneien; ~*ed in od.* up eingeschneit; *be* ~*ed under fig.* erdrückt werden; **~·bound** ['snəʊbaʊnd] eingeschneit; **~·capped**, **~·clad**, **~·cov·ered** schneebedeckt; **~·drift** Schneewehe *f*; **~·drop** ♀ Schneeglöckchen *n*; **~·white** schneeweiß; ♀ **White** Schneewittchen *n*; **~·y** □ [~ɪ] (*-ier, -iest*) schneeig; schneebedeckt, verschneit; schneeweiß.

snub [snʌb] **1.** (*-bb-*) j-n vor den Kopf stoßen, brüskieren; j-m über

S

den Mund fahren; *j-n* schneiden; **2.** Brüskierung *f*; **~-nosed** ['snʌb-nəʊzd] stupsnasig.

snuff [snʌf] **1.** Schnuppe *f* (*e-r Kerze*); Schnupftabak *m*; *take* ~ schnupfen; **2.** Kerze putzen; schnupfen.

snuf·fle ['snʌfl] schnüffeln; näseln.

snug □ [snʌg] (**-gg-**) geborgen; behaglich; enganliegend; **~·gle** ['snʌgl] sich anschmiegen *od.* kuscheln (*up to s.o.* an *j-n*).

so [səʊ] so; also; deshalb; *I hope* ~ ich hoffe es; *I think* ~ ich glaube *od.* denke schon; *are you tired?* – ~ *I am* bist du müde? Ja; *you are tired,* ~ *am I* du bist müde, ich auch; ~ *far* bisher.

soak [səʊk] *v/t.* einweichen; durchnässen; (durch)tränken; ~ *in* einsaugen; ~ *up* aufsaugen; *v/i.* sich vollsaugen; ein-, durchsickern.

soap [səʊp] **1.** Seife *f*; *soft* ~ Schmierseife *f*; *fig.* Schmeichelei *f*; **2.** ab-, einseifen; **~·box** ['səʊpbɒks] Seifenkiste *f*; improvisierte Rednerbühne; **~·y** □ [~ɪ] (**-ier, -iest**) seifig; *fig.* F schmeichlerisch.

soar [sɔː] (hoch) aufsteigen, sich erheben; in großer Höhe fliegen *od.* schweben; ≷ segeln, gleiten.

sob [sɒb] **1.** Schluchzen *n*; **2.** (**-bb-**) schluchzen.

so·ber ['səʊbə] **1.** □ nüchtern; **2.** ernüchtern; ~ *down,* ~ *up* nüchtern machen *od.* werden; **so·bri·e·ty** [səʊ'braɪətɪ] Nüchternheit *f*.

so-called ['səʊ'kɔːld] sogenannt.

soc·cer ['sɒkə] Fußball *m* (*Spiel*).

so·cia·ble ['səʊʃəbl] **1.** □ gesellig; gemütlich; **2.** geselliges Beisammensein.

so·cial ['səʊʃl] **1.** □ gesellig; gesellschaftlich; sozial; sozialistisch; Sozial...; **2.** geselliges Beisammensein; ~ *in·sur·ance* Sozialversicherung *f*.

so·cial·is·m ['səʊʃəlɪzəm] Sozialismus *m*; **~·ist** [~ɪst] **1.** Sozialist(in); **2.** = **~·is·tic** [səʊʃə'lɪstɪk] (**~ally**) sozialistisch; **~·ize** ['səʊʃəlaɪz] sozialisieren; verstaatlichen; gesellschaftlich verkehren (*with* mit).

so·cial | sci·ence ['səʊʃl'saɪəns] Sozialwissenschaft *f*; ~ **se·cu·ri·ty** Sozialhilfe *f*; *be on* ~ Sozialhilfe beziehen; ~ **serv·ic·es** *pl.* staatliche Sozialleistungen *pl.*; ~ **work** Sozialarbeit *f*; ~ **work·er** Sozialarbeiter(in).

so·ci·e·ty [sə'saɪətɪ] Gesellschaft *f*; Verein *m*, Vereinigung *f*.

so·ci·ol·o·gy [səʊsɪ'ɒlədʒɪ] Soziologie *f*.

sock [sɒk] Socke *f*; Einlegesohle *f*.

sock·et ['sɒkɪt] *anat.* (Augen-, Zahn-)Höhle *f*; *anat.* (Gelenk)Pfanne *f*; ⊕ Muffe *f*; ⨍ Fassung *f*; ⨍ Steckdose *f*; ⨍ (Anschluß)Buchse *f*.

sod [sɒd] Grasnarbe *f*; Rasenstück *n*.

so·da ['səʊdə] ⚗ Soda *f*, *n*; Soda (-wasser) *n*; **~-foun·tain** Siphon *m*; *Am.* Erfrischungshalle *f*, Eisbar *f*.

sod·den ['sɒdn] durchweicht; teigig.

soft [sɒft] **1.** □ weich; mild; sanft; sacht, leise; gedämpft (*Licht etc.*); leicht, angenehm (*Arbeit*); weichlich; *a.* ~ *in the head* F einfältig, doof; alkoholfrei (*Getränk*); weich (*Drogen*); **2.** *adv.* sanft, leise; **~·en** ['sɒfn] *v/t.* weich machen; *Farbe, Stimme etc.* dämpfen; *Wasser* enthärten; *j-n* erweichen; *fig.* mildern; *v/i.* weich(er) *od.* sanft(er) *od.* mild(er) werden; **~-head·ed** doof; **~-heart·ed** weichherzig; **~·land** *Raumfahrt:* weich landen; ~ **land·ing** *Raumfahrt:* weiche Landung; **~·ware** *Computer:* Software *f* (*Programme etc.*); *Sprachlabor:* Software *f*; Begleitmaterial *n*; **~·y** F [~ɪ] Trottel *m*; weichlicher Typ; Schwächling *m*.

sog·gy ['sɒgɪ] (**-ier, -iest**) durchnäßt, feucht.

soil [sɔɪl] **1.** Boden *m*, Erde *f*; Fleck *m*; Schmutz *m*; **2.** (be)schmutzen; schmutzig machen *od.* werden.

so·journ ['sɒdʒɜːn] **1.** Aufenthalt *m*; **2.** sich (vorübergehend) aufhalten.

sol·ace ['sɒləs] **1.** Trost *m*; **2.** trösten.

so·lar ['səʊlə] Sonnen...

sold [səʊld] *pret. u. p.p. von* sell.

sol·der ⊕ ['sɒldə] **1.** Lot *n*; **2.** löten.

sol·dier ['səʊldʒə] Soldat *m*; **~·like,** **~·ly** [~lɪ] soldatisch; **~·y** [~rɪ] Militär *n*, Soldaten *pl.*

sole¹ □ [səʊl] alleinig, einzig, Allein...; ~ *agent* Alleinvertreter *m*.

sole² [~] **1.** (Fuß-, Schuh)Sohle *f*; △ *nicht* Sole; **2.** besohlen.

sole³ *zo.* [~] Seezunge *f*.

sol·emn □ ['sɒləm] feierlich; ernst; **so·lem·ni·ty** [sə'lemnətɪ] Feierlichkeit *f*; **~·em·nize** ['sɒləmnaɪz] feiern; *Trauung* feierlich vollziehen.

so·lic·it [sə'lɪsɪt] (dringend) bitten (um); sich anbieten (*Prostituierte*).

so·lic·i·ta·tion [səlɪsɪ'teɪʃn] dringende Bitte; **~tor** [sə'lɪsɪtə] *Brt.* ⚖ *(nicht plädierender)* Anwalt; *Am.* Agent *m*, Werber *m*; **~tous** □ [~əs] besorgt *(about, for* um, wegen); **~ of** begierig nach; **~ to do** bestrebt zu tun; **~tude** [~ju:d] Sorge *f*, Besorgnis *f*.

sol·id ['sɒlɪd] **1.** □ fest; derb, kräftig; stabil; massiv; ⚖ körperlich, räumlich, Raum...; gewichtig, triftig; solid(e), gründlich; solid(e), zuverlässig *(Person)*; einmütig, solidarisch; **a ~ hour** e-e volle Stunde; **2.** fester Stoff; *geom.* Körper *m*; **~s** *pl.* feste Nahrung; **sol·i·dar·i·ty** [sɒlɪ'dærətɪ] Solidarität *f*.

so·lid·i·fy [sə'lɪdɪfaɪ] fest werden (lassen); verdichten; **~ty** [~tɪ] Solidität *f*.

so·lil·o·quy [sə'lɪləkwɪ] Selbstgespräch *n*; *bsd. thea.* Monolog *m*.

sol·i·taire [sɒlɪ'teə] Solitär *m*; *Am.* Karten: Patience *f*.

sol·i·ta·ry ['sɒlɪtərɪ] einsam; einzeln; einsiedlerisch; **~tude** [~ju:d] Einsamkeit *f*; Verlassenheit *f*; Öde *f*.

so·lo ['səʊləʊ] *(pl. -los)* Solo *n*; ✈ Alleinflug *m*; **~ist** ♪ [~ɪst] Solist(in).

sol·u·ble ['sɒljʊbl] löslich; *fig.* lösbar; **so·lu·tion** [sə'lu:ʃn] (Auf)Lösung *f*.

solve [sɒlv] lösen; **sol·vent** ['sɒlvənt] **1.** 🜊 (auf)lösend; *econ.* zahlungsfähig; **2.** 🜊 Lösungsmittel *n*.

som·bre, *Am.* **-ber** □ ['sɒmbə] düster, trüb(e); *fig.* trübsinnig.

some [sʌm, səm] (irgend)ein; *vor pl.*: einige, ein paar, manche; etwas; etwa; F beachtlich, vielleicht ein *(in Ausrufen)*; **~ 20 miles** etwa 20 Meilen; **to ~ extent** einigermaßen; **~·bod·y** ['sʌmbədɪ] (irgend) jemand, irgendeiner; **~·day** eines Tages; **~·how** irgendwie; **~ or other** irgendwie; **~·one** (irgend) jemand, irgendeiner; **~·place** *Am.* = **somewhere.**

som·er·sault ['sʌməsɔ:lt] **1.** Salto *m*; Purzelbaum *m*; **turn a ~ = 2.** e-n Salto machen; e-n Purzelbaum schlagen.

some·thing ['sʌmθɪŋ] (irgend) etwas; **~ like** so etwas wie, so ungefähr; **~·time 1.** irgendwann; **2.** ehemalige(r, -s); **~·times** manchmal; **~·what** etwas, ziemlich; **~·where** irgendwo(hin).

son [sʌn] Sohn *m*.

sonde [sɒnd] *Raumfahrt:* Sonde *f*.

song [sɒŋ] Lied *n*; Gesang *m*; Gedicht *n*; **for a ~** für ein Butterbrot; **~·bird** ['sɒŋbɜ:d] Singvogel *m*; **~·ster** [~stə] Singvogel *m*; Sänger *m*; **~·stress** [~strɪs] Sängerin *f*.

son·ic ['sɒnɪk] Schall...; **~ boom,** *Brt.* **a. ~ bang** Überschallknall *m*.

son-in-law ['sʌnɪnlɔ:] *(pl. sons-in-law)* Schwiegersohn *m*.

son·net ['sɒnɪt] Sonett *n*.

so·nor·ous □ [sə'nɔ:rəs] klangvoll.

soon [su:n] bald; früh; gern; *as od. so* **~ as** sobald als *od.* wie; **~·er** ['su:nə] eher; früher; lieber; **~ or later** früher oder später; *the ~ the better* je eher, desto besser; *no ~ ... than* kaum ... als; *no ~ said than done* gesagt, getan.

soot [sʊt] **1.** Ruß *m*; **2.** verrußen.

soothe [su:ð] beruhigen, besänftigen, beschwichtigen; lindern, mildern; **sooth·ing** □ ['su:ðɪŋ] besänftigend; lindernd; **sooth·say·er** ['su:θseɪə] Wahrsager(in).

soot·y □ ['sʊtɪ] *(-ier, -iest)* rußig.

sop [sɒp] **1.** eingetunkter *od.* -weicher Bissen; **2.** *(-pp-)* eintunken.

so·phis·ti·cat·ed [sə'fɪstɪkeɪtɪd] anspruchsvoll, kultiviert; intellektuell; blasiert; ⊕ hochentwickelt; ⊕ kompliziert; verfälscht; **soph·ist·ry** ['sɒfɪstrɪ] Spitzfindigkeit *f*.

soph·o·more *Am.* ['sɒfəmɔ:] College-Student(in) *od.* Schüler(in) e-r High-School vom zweiten Jahr.

sop·o·rif·ic [sɒpə'rɪfɪk] **1.** *(~ally)* einschläfernd; **2.** Schlafmittel *n*.

sor·cer|er ['sɔ:sərə] Zauberer *m*, Hexenmeister *m*; **~ess** [~ɪs] Zauberin *f*, Hexe *f*; **~·y** [~ɪ] Zauberei *f*, Hexerei *f*.

sor·did □ ['sɔ:dɪd] schmutzig; schäbig, elend, miserabel.

sore [sɔ:] **1.** □ *(~r, ~st)* schlimm, entzündet; wund, weh; gereizt; verärgert, böse; **a ~ throat** Halsschmerzen *pl.*; **2.** Wunde *f*, Entzündung *f*; **~·head** *Am.* F ['sɔ:hed] mürrischer Mensch.

sor·rel ['sɒrəl] **1.** rotbraun; **2.** *zo.* Fuchs *m (Pferd)*; ♣ Sauerampfer *m*.

sor·row ['sɒrəʊ] **1.** Kummer *m*, Leid *n*; Schmerz *m*, Jammer *m*; **2.** trauern; sich grämen; **~·ful** □ [~fl] traurig, betrübt.

sor·ry □ ['sɒrɪ] *(-ier, -iest)* betrübt, bekümmert; traurig, erbärmlich; *be ~ about s.th.* et. bereuen *od.* bedauern; *I am (so) ~!* es tut mir (sehr) leid, Verzeihung!; *~!* Verzeihung!,

Entschuldigung!; *I am ~ for him* er tut mir leid; *we are ~ to say* wir müssen leider sagen.

sort [sɔːt] **1.** Sorte *f*, Art *f*; *what ~ of* was für; *of a ~, of ~s* F so was wie; *~ of* F gewissermaßen; *out of ~s* F nicht auf der Höhe; **2.** sortieren; *~ out* (aus-)sortieren; *fig.* in Ordnung bringen.

sot [sɔt] Säufer *m*, Trunkenbold *m*.

sough [saʊ] **1.** Rauschen *n*; **2.** rauschen.

sought [sɔːt] *pret. u. p.p. von* **seek**.

soul [səʊl] Seele *f* (*a. fig.*); Inbegriff *m*; ♪ Soul *m*.

sound [saʊnd] **1.** □ gesund; intakt; *econ.* solid(e), stabil, sicher; vernünftig; (*t*) gültig; zuverlässig; kräftig, tüchtig; fest, tief (*Schlaf*); **2.** Ton *m*, Schall *m*, Laut *m*, Klang *m*; ♪ Sound *m*; ♂ Sonde *f*; Sund *m*, Meerenge *f*; Fischblase *f*; **3.** (er)tönen, (-)klingen; erschallen (lassen); *sich gut etc.* anhören; sondieren; ♨ (aus-)loten; ♂ abhorchen; **~ bar·ri·er** Schallgrenze *f*, -mauer *f*; **~film** ['saʊndfilm] Tonfilm *m*; **~ing** ♨ [ˌɪŋ] Lotung *f*; *~s pl.* lotbare Wassertiefe; **~·less** [ˌlɪs] lautlos; **~·ness** [ˌnɪs] Gesundheit *f* (*a. fig.*); **pol·lu·tion** Lärmbelästigung *f*; **~proof** schalldicht; **~·track** Film: Tonspur *f*; Filmmusik *f*; **~·wave** Schallwelle *f*.

soup [suːp] **1.** Suppe *f*; *(some) ~* e-e Suppe; **2.** *~ up* F *Motor* frisieren.

sour ['saʊə] **1.** □ sauer; *fig.* verbittert; **2.** *v/t.* säuern; *fig.* ver-, erbittern; *v/i.* sauer (*fig.* verbittert) werden.

source [sɔːs] Quelle *f*; Ursprung *m*.

sour·ish □ ['saʊərɪʃ] säuerlich; **~·ness** [ˌnɪs] Säure *f*; *fig.* Bitterkeit *f*.

souse [saʊs] eintauchen; (mit Wasser) begießen; *Fisch etc.* einlegen, -pökeln.

south [saʊθ] **1.** Süd(en *m*); **2.** südlich, Süd...; **~·east** ['saʊθ'iːst] **1.** Südosten *m*; **2.** südöstlich; **~·east·er** Südostwind *m*; **~·east·ern** südöstlich.

south·er·ly ['sʌðəlɪ], **~·n** [ˌn] südlich, Süd...; **~·n·most** südlichste(r, -s).

south·ward(s) *adv.* ['saʊθwəd(z)] südwärts, nach Süden.

south·west ['saʊθ'west] **1.** Südwesten *m*; **2.** südwestlich; **~·west·er** [ˌə] Südwestwind *m*; ♂ Südwester *m*; **~·west·er·ly**, **~·west·ern** südwestlich.

sou·ve·nir [suːvəˈnɪə] Souvenir *n*, Andenken *n*.

sove·reign ['sɒvrɪn] **1.** □ höchste(r, -s); unübertrefflich; unumschränkt, souverän; **2.** Herrscher(in); Monarch(in); Sovereign *m* (*alte brit. Goldmünze von 20 Shilling*); **~·ty** [ˌəntɪ] höchste (Staats)Gewalt; Souveränität *f*, Landeshoheit *f*.

So·vi·et ['səʊvɪət] Sowjet *m*; *attr.* sowjetisch, Sowjet...

sow[1] [saʊ] *zo.* Sau *f*, (Mutter-)Schwein *n*; ⊕ Sau *f*; ⊕ Massel *f*.

sow[2] [səʊ] (*sowed, sown od. sowed*) (aus)säen, ausstreuen; besäen; **~n** [ˌn] *p.p. von* **sow**[2].

spa [spɑː] Heilbad *n*; Kurort *m*.

space [speɪs] **1.** (Welt)Raum *m*; Raum *m*, Platz *m*; Abstand *m*, Zwischenraum *m*; Zeitraum *m*; **2.** *mst ~ out* *print.* sperren; **~·age** Weltraumzeitalter *m*; **~ cap·sule** ['speɪskæpsjuːl] Raumkapsel *f*; **~·craft** Raumfahrzeug *n*; **~ flight** (Welt)Raumflug *m*; **~·lab** Raumlabor *n*; **~·port** Raumfahrtzentrum *n*; **~ probe** (Welt)Raumsonde *f*; **~ re·search** (Welt)Raumforschung *f*; **~·ship** Raumschiff *n*; **~ shut·tle** Raumfähre *f*; **~ sta·tion** (Welt)Raumstation *f*; **~·suit** Raumanzug *m*; **~ walk** Weltraumspaziergang *m*; **~·wom·an** (*pl. -women*) (Welt)Raumfahrerin *f*.

spa·cious □ ['speɪʃəs] geräumig; weit; umfassend.

spade [speɪd] Spaten *m*; *Karten*: Pik *n*, Grün *n*; *king of ~s pl.* Pik-König *m*; *call a ~ a ~* das Kind beim (rechten) Namen nennen.

span [spæn] **1.** Spanne *f*; *arch.* Spannweite *f*; △ *nicht* Span; **2.** (*-nn-*) um-, überspannen; (aus)messen.

span·gle ['spæŋgl] **1.** Flitter *m*, Paillette *f*; **2.** mit Flitter *od.* Pailletten besetzen; *fig.* übersäen.

Span·iard ['spænjəd] Spanier(in).

Span·ish ['spænɪʃ] **1.** spanisch; **2.** *ling.* Spanisch *n*; *the ~ pl. coll.* die Spanier *pl.*

spank F [spæŋk] **1.** verhauen; **2.** Klaps *m*, Schlag *m*; **~·ing** ['spæŋkɪŋ] **1.** *adj.* □ schnell, flott; tüchtig, gehörig; **2.** *adv.:* *~ clean* blitzsauber; *~ new* funkelnagelneu; **3.** F Haue *f*, Tracht *f* Prügel.

span·ner ⊕ ['spænə] Schraubenschlüssel *m*.

spar [spɑː] **1.** ♂ Spiere *f*; ✕ Holm *m*; **2.** (*-rr-*) *Boxen*: sparren; *fig.* sich streiten.

speeding

spare [speə] **1.** ☐ sparsam; kärglich, mager; überzählig; überschüssig; Ersatz..., Reserve...; ~ *part* Ersatzteil *n*, *a*. *m*; ~ *room* Gästezimmer *n*; ~ *time od. hours* Freizeit *f*, Mußestunden *pl.*; ⊕ Ersatzteil *n*, *a*. *m*; **3.** (ver)schonen; erübrigen; entbehren; (übrig)haben (für); ersparen; sparen mit; scheuen; △ *nicht Geld etc. sparen.*

spar·ing ☐ ['speərɪŋ] sparsam.

spark [spɑːk] **1.** Funke(n) *m*; **2.** Funken sprühen; ~**ing-plug** *Brt. mot.* ['spɑːkɪŋplʌɡ] Zündkerze *f*.

spar·kle ['spɑːkl] **1.** Funke(n) *m*; Funkeln *n*; **2.** funkeln; blitzen; perlen (*Wein*); ~**kling** ☐ [~lɪŋ] funkelnd; sprühend; *fig.* geistsprühend, spritzig; ~ *wine* Schaumwein *m*.

spark-plug *Am. mot.* ['spɑːkplʌɡ] Zündkerze *f*.

spar·row *zo.* ['spærəʊ] Sperling *m*, Spatz *m*; ~**hawk** *zo.* Sperber *m*.

sparse ☐ [spɑːs] spärlich, dünn.

spas·m ['spæzəm] ⚕ Krampf *m*; Anfall *m*; **spas·mod·ic** [spæzˈmɒdɪk] (~*ally*) ⚕ krampfhaft, -artig; *fig.* sprunghaft.

spas·tic ⚕ ['spæstɪk] **1.** (~*ally*) spastisch; **2.** Spastiker(in).

spat [spæt] *pret. u. p.p. von* spit².

spa·tial ☐ ['speɪʃl] räumlich.

spat·ter ['spætə] (be)spritzen.

spawn [spɔːn] **1.** *zo.* Laich *m*; *fig. contp.* Brut *f*; **2.** *zo.* laichen; *fig.* hervorbringen.

speak [spiːk] (*spoke, spoken*) *v/i.* sprechen, reden (*to* mit; *about* über *acc.*); ~ *out*, ~ *up* laut u. deutlich sprechen; offen reden; ~ *to s.o.* j-n *od.* mit j-m sprechen; *v/t.* (aus)sprechen; sagen; äußern; *Sprache* sprechen (können); ~**er** ['spiːkə] Sprecher(in), Redner(in); ♀ *parl.* Sprecher *m*, Präsident *m*; *Mr* ♀! Herr Vorsitzender!

spear [spɪə] **1.** Speer *m*; Spieß *m*, Lanze *f*; **2.** durchbohren, aufspießen.

spe·cial ['speʃl] **1.** ☐ besondere(r, -s); speziell; Sonder...; Spezial...; ♂ Hilfspolizist *m*; Sonderausgabe *f*; Sonderzug *m*; *Rundfunk, TV:* Sondersendung *f*; *Am.* Tagesgericht *n* (*im Restaurant*); *Am. econ.* Sonderangebot *n*; *on* ~ *Am. econ.* im Angebot; ~**ist** [~lɪst] Spezialist(in), Fachmann *m*; ♂ Facharzt *m*, -ärztin

f; **spe·ci·al·i·ty** [speʃɪˈælətɪ] Besonderheit *f*; Spezialfach *n*; *econ.* Spezialität *f*; ~**ize** ['speʃəlaɪz] besonders anführen; (sich) spezialisieren; ~**ty** *bsd. Am.* [~tɪ] = speciality.

spe·cies ['spiːʃiːz] (*pl. -cies*) Art *f*, Spezies *f*.

spe·cif·ic [spɪˈsɪfɪk] (~*ally*) spezifisch; besondere(r, -s); bestimmt; ~**ci·fy** ['spesɪfaɪ] spezifizieren, einzeln angeben; ~**ci·men** [~mɪn] Probe *f*, Muster *n*; Exemplar *n*.

spe·cious ☐ ['spiːʃəs] blendend, bestechend; trügerisch; Schein...

speck [spek] Fleck(en) *m*; Stückchen *n*; △ *nicht Speck*; ~**le** ['spekl] Fleck(en) *m*, Sprenkel *m*, Tupfen *m*; ~**led** gefleckt, gesprenkelt, getüpfelt.

spec·ta·cle ['spektəkl] Schauspiel *n*; Anblick *m*; △ *nicht der Spektakel*; (*a pair of*) ~**s** *pl.* (e-e) Brille.

spec·tac·u·lar [spekˈtækjʊlə] **1.** ☐ spektakulär, sensationell, aufsehenerregend; **2.** große (Fernseh)Schau, Galavorstellung *f*.

spec·ta·tor [spekˈteɪtə] Zuschauer (-in).

spec·tral ☐ ['spektrəl] gespenstisch; ~**tre**, *Am.* ~**ter** [~ə] Gespenst *n*.

spec·u·late ['spekjʊleɪt] grübeln, nachsinnen; *econ.* spekulieren; ~**la·tion** [spekjʊˈleɪʃn] theoretische Betrachtung; Nachdenken *n*; Grübeln *n*; *econ.* Spekulation *f*; ~**la·tive** ☐ ['spekjʊlətɪv] grüblerisch; theoretisch; *econ.* spekulativ; ~**la·tor** [~eɪtə] *econ.* Spekulant *m*.

sped [sped] *pret. u. p.p. von* speed 2.

speech [spiːtʃ] Sprache *f*; Reden *n*, Sprechen *n*; Rede *f*, Ansprache *f*; *make a* ~ e-e Rede halten; ~**day** *Brt.* ['spiːtʃdeɪ] *Schule:* (Jahres-) Schlußfeier *f*; ~**less** ☐ [~lɪs] sprachlos.

speed [spiːd] **1.** Geschwindigkeit *f*, Tempo *n*, Schnelligkeit *f*, Eile *f*; ⊕ Drehzahl *f*; *mot.* Gang *m*; *phot.* Lichtempfindlichkeit *f*; *phot.* Belichtungszeit *f*; *sl.* Speed *n* (*Aufputschmittel*); **2.** (*sped*) *v/i.* (dahin)eilen, schnell fahren, rasen; ~ *up* (*pret. u. p.p. speeded*) die Geschwindigkeit erhöhen; *v/t.* rasch befördern; ~ *up* (*pret. u. p.p. speeded*) beschleunigen; ~**boat** ['spiːdbəʊt] Rennboot *n*; ~**ing** *mot.* [~ɪŋ] zu schnelles Fahren, Geschwindig-

S

keitsüberschreitung *f*; **~ lim·it** Geschwindigkeitsbegrenzung *f*, Tempolimit *n*; **~·o** F *mot.* [.ʒəʊ] (*pl. -os*) Tacho *m*; **~·om·e·ter** *mot.* [spɪ'dɒmɪtə] Tachometer *m, n*; **~·up** ['spi:dʌp] Beschleunigung *f*, Temposteigerung *f*; *econ.* Produktionserhöhung *f*; **~·way** *Sport:* Speedwayrennen *n*; Speedwaybahn *f*; *Am. mot.* Schnellstraße *f*; *Am. Sport: mot.* Rennstrecke *f*; **~·y** □ [.ɪ] (*-ier, -iest*) schnell, rasch.

spell [spel] **1.** Weile *f*, Weilchen *n*; Anfall *m*; Zauber(spruch) *m*; *fig.* Zauber *m*; **a ~ of** fine weather e-e Schönwetterperiode; **hot ~** Hitzewelle *f*; **2.** ~ s.o. at s.th. j-n bei et. ablösen; (*spelt od. Am. spelled*) buchstabieren; richtig schreiben; bedeuten; geschrieben werden, sich schreiben; **~·bound** ['spelbaʊnd] (wie) gebannt, fasziniert, gefesselt; **~·er** [.ə]: **be a good od. bad ~ in** Rechtschreibung gut od. schlecht sein; **~·ing** [.ɪŋ] Buchstabieren *n*; Rechtschreibung *f*; **~·ing-book** Fibel *f*.

spelt [spelt] *pret. u. p.p. von* spell 2.

spend [spend] (*spent*) verwenden; *Geld* ausgeben; verbrauchen; verschwenden; *Mühe* aufwenden; *Zeit* zu-, verbringen; **□ nicht spenden**; **~ o.s.** sich erschöpfen; **~·thrift** ['spendθrɪft] Verschwender(in).

spent [spent] **1.** *pret. u. p.p. von* spend; **2.** *adj.* erschöpft, matt.

sperm [spɜːm] Sperma *n*, Samen *m*.

sphere [sfɪə] Kugel *f*; Erd-, Himmelskugel *f*; *fig.* Sphäre *f*; (Wirkungs)Kreis *m*, Bereich *m*, Gebiet *n*; **spher·i·cal** □ ['sferɪkl] sphärisch; kugelförmig.

spice [spaɪs] **1.** Gewürz(e *pl.*) *n*; *fig.* Würze *f*; Anflug *m*; **2.** würzen.

spick and span ['spɪkən'spæn] blitzsauber; wie aus dem Ei gepellt; funkelnagelneu.

spic·y □ ['spaɪsɪ] (*-ier, -iest*) würzig; gewürzt; *fig.* pikant.

spi·der *zo.* ['spaɪdə] Spinne *f*.

spig·ot ['spɪgət] (Faß)Zapfen *m*; (Zapf-, *Am.* Leitungs)Hahn *m*.

spike [spaɪk] **1.** Stift *m*; Spitze *f*; Dorn *m*; Stachel *m*; ♀ Ähre *f*; *Sport:* Spike *m*; **~s** *pl.* Rennschuhe, *mot.*: Spikes *pl.*; **2.** festnageln; mit (Eisen-)Spitzen *etc.* versehen; **~ heel** Pfennigabsatz *m*.

spill [spɪl] **1.** (*spilt od. spilled*) *v/t.* ver-, ausschütten; *Blut* vergießen; verstreuen; *Reiter* abwerfen; *sl.* ausplaudern; *s. milk* 1; *v/i.* überlaufen; *sl.* auspacken, singen; **2.** Sturz *m* (*vom Pferd etc.*).

spilt [spɪlt] *pret. u. p.p. von* spill 1.

spin [spɪn] **1.** (*-nn-; spun*) *v/t.* spinnen; schnell drehen, (herum)wirbeln; *Wäsche* schleudern; *Münze* hochwerfen; *fig.* sich et. ausdenken, erzählen; **~ s.th. out** et. in die Länge ziehen, et. ausspinnen; *v/i.* spinnen; sich drehen; **✈** trudeln; *mot.* durchdrehen (*Räder*); **~ along** dahinrasen; **2.** schnelle Drehung; Schleudern *n* (*Wäsche*); **✈** Trudeln *n*; **go for a ~** e-e Spritztour machen.

spin·ach ♀ ['spɪnɪdʒ] Spinat *m*.

spin·al *anat.* ['spaɪnl] Rückgrat...; **~ column** Wirbelsäule *f*, Rückgrat *n*; **~ cord, ~ marrow** Rückenmark *n*.

spin·dle ['spɪndl] Spindel *f*.

spin|-dri·er ['spɪndraɪə] (Wäsche-) Schleuder *f*; **~-dry** *Wäsche* schleudern; **~-dry·er** = spin-drier.

spine [spaɪn] *anat.* Wirbelsäule *f*, Rückgrat *n*; *bot., zo.* Stachel *m*; (Gebirgs)Grat *m*; (Buch)Rücken *m*.

spin·ning-mill ['spɪnɪŋmɪl] Spinnerei *f*; **~-top** Kreisel *m*; **~-wheel** Spinnrad *n*.

spin·ster ['spɪnstə] ⚖ unverheiratete Frau; alte Jungfer.

spin·y ♀, *zo.* ['spaɪnɪ] (*-ier, -iest*) stach(e)lig.

spi·ral ['spaɪərəl] **1.** □ spiralig; Spiral...; gewunden; **~ staircase** Wendeltreppe *f*; **2.** Spirale *f*.

spire ['spaɪə] (Turm-, Berg- *etc.*)Spitze *f*; Kirchturm(spitze) *f* *m*.

spir·it ['spɪrɪt] **1.** Geist *m*; Schwung *m*; Elan *m*; Mut *m*; Gesinnung *f*; **🜊** Spiritus *m*; **~s** *pl.* alkoholische *od.* geistige Getränke *pl.*, Spirituosen *pl.*; **high** (**low**) **~s** *pl.* gehobene (gedrückte) Stimmung; **2.** **~ away** *od.* **off** wegschaffen, -zaubern; **~·ed** □ [.ɪd] lebhaft; energisch; feurig (*Pferd etc.*); geistvoll; **~·less** □ [.lɪs] geistlos; temperamentlos; mutlos.

spir·i·tu·al ['spɪrɪtjʊəl] **1.** □ geistig; geistlich; geistreich; **2.** ♪ (Neger-) Spiritual *n*; **~·is·m** [.ɪzəm] Spiritismus *m*.

spirt [spɜːt] = spurt².

spit¹ [spɪt] **1.** (Brat)Spieß *m*; *geogr.* Landzunge *f*; **2.** (*-tt-*) aufspießen.

spit² [~] **1.** Speichel *m*, Spucke *f*; Fauchen *n*; F Ebenbild *n*; **2.** (*-tt-*; *spat od.* spit) spucken; fauchen; sprühen (*fein regnen*); *a.* ~ *out* (aus)spucken.

spite [spaɪt] **1.** Bosheit *f*; Groll *m*; *in* ~ *of* trotz (*gen.*); **2.** *j-n* ärgern; ~**ful** □ [ˈspaɪtfl] boshaft, gehässig.

spit·fire [ˈspɪtfaɪə] Hitzkopf *m*.

spit·tle [ˈspɪtl] Speichel *m*, Spucke *f*.

spit·toon [spɪˈtuːn] Spucknapf *m*.

splash [splæʃ] **1.** Spritzer *m*, (Spritz-) Fleck *m*; Klatschen *n*, Platschen *n*; **2.** (be)spritzen; platschen; planschen; (hin)klecksen; ~ *down* wassern (*Raumkapsel*); ~**down** Wasserung *f*.

splay [spleɪ] **1.** Ausschrägung *f*; **2.** *v/t.* spreizen; ausschrägen; *v/i.* ausgeschrägt sein; ~**foot** [ˈspleɪfʊt] Spreizfuß *m*.

spleen [spliːn] *anat.* Milz *f*; schlechte Laune.

splen·did □ [ˈsplendɪd] glänzend, prächtig, herrlich; F großartig, hervorragend; ~**do(u)r** [~ə] Glanz *m*, Pracht *f*, Herrlichkeit *f*.

splice [splaɪs] spleißen; *Film* zusammenkleben.

splint [splɪnt] **1.** Schiene *f*; **2.** schienen.

splin·ter [ˈsplɪntə] **1.** Splitter *m*; **2.** (zer)splittern; ~ *off* (*fig.* sich) absplittern.

split [splɪt] **1.** Spalt *m*, Riß *m*, Sprung *m*; *fig.* Spaltung *f*; **2.** gespalten; **3.** (*-tt-*; *split*) *v/t.* (zer)spalten; zerreißen; sich *in et.* teilen; ~ *hairs* Haarspalterei treiben; ~ *one's sides laughing od.* with laughter sich totlachen; *v/i.* sich spalten; zerspringen, (-)platzen, (-)bersten; ~**ting** [ˈsplɪtɪŋ] heftig, rasend (*Kopfschmerz*).

splut·ter [ˈsplʌtə] (heraus)stottern; zischen; stottern (*Motor*).

spoil [spɔɪl] **1.** *mst* ~*s pl.* Beute *f*; *fig.* Ausbeute *f*, Gewinn *m*; **2.** (*spoilt od.* spoiled) verderben; ruinieren; *Kind* verwöhnen, -ziehen; ~**er** *mot.* [ˈspɔɪlə] Spoiler *m*; ~**sport** Spielverderber(in) *m*; ~**t** [~t] *pret. u. p.p. von* spoil **2**.

spoke¹ [spəʊk] Speiche *f*; (Leiter-) Sprosse *f*.

spoke² [~] *pret. von* speak; **spok·en** [ˈspəʊkən] **1.** *p.p. von* speak; **2.** gesprochen (*Sprache*); ~**s·man** [~smən] (*pl. -men*) Wortführer *m*,

Sprecher *m*; ~**s·wom·an** (*pl. -women*) Wortführerin *f*, Sprecherin *f*.

sponge [spʌndʒ] **1.** Schwamm *m*; F *fig.* Schmarotzer(in); Brt. = sponge-cake; **2.** *v/t.* mit e-m Schwamm (ab)waschen; ~ *off* weg-, abwischen; ~ *up* aufsaugen, -wischen; *v/i.* F *fig.* schmarotzen; ~**cake** [ˈspʌndʒkeɪk] Biskuitkuchen *m*; **spong·er** F *fig.* [~ə] Schmarotzer(in); **spong·y** [~ɪ] (*-ier*, *-iest*) schwammig.

spon·sor [ˈspɒnsə] **1.** Bürg|e *m*, -in *f*; (Tauf)Pat|e *m*, -in *f*; Förderer *m*, Gönner(in); Schirmherr(in); Geldgeber(in), Sponsor(in); **2.** bürgen für; fördern; die Schirmherrschaft (*gen.*) übernehmen; *Rundfunk-, TV-Sendung, Sportler* sponsern; ~**ship** [~ʃɪp] Bürgschaft *f*; Patenschaft *f*; Schirmherrschaft *f*; Unterstützung *f*, Förderung *f*.

spon·ta·ne|i·ty [spɒntəˈneɪətɪ] Spontaneität *f*, eigener Antrieb; Ungezwungenheit *f*; ~**ous** □ [spɒnˈteɪnjəs] spontan; unvermittelt; ungezwungen, natürlich; von selbst (entstanden); Selbst...

spook [spuːk] Spuk *m*; ~**y** [ˈspuːkɪ] (*-ier*, *-iest*) gespenstisch, Spuk...

spool [spuːl] Spule *f*; Rolle *f*; *a.* ~ *of thread Am.* Garnrolle *f*.

spoon [spuːn] **1.** Löffel *m*; **2.** löffeln; ~**ful** [ˈspuːnfʊl] (*ein*) Löffel(voll) *m*.

spo·rad·ic [spəˈrædɪk] (~*ally*) sporadisch, gelegentlich, vereinzelt.

spore ♧ [spɔː] Spore *f*, Keimkorn *n*.

sport [spɔːt] **1.** Sport(art *f*) *m*; Zeitvertreib *m*; Spaß *m*, Scherz *m*; F feiner Kerl; ~*s pl.* Sport *m*; Brt. *Schule:* Sportfest *n*; **2.** *v/i.* herumtollen; spielen; *v/t.* F stolz (zur Schau) tragen, protzen mit; **spor·tive** □ [ˈspɔːtɪv] verspielt; ~[~s] Sport...; ~**s·man** (*pl. -men*) Sportler *m*; ~**s·wom·an** (*pl. -women*) Sportlerin *f*.

spot [spɒt] **1.** Fleck *m*; Tupfen *m*; Makel *m*; Stelle *f*, Ort *m*; ♂ Leberfleck *m*; ♧ Pickel *m*; *Rundfunk, TV:* (Werbe)Spot *m*; Brt. F Tropfen *m*, Schluck *m*; *a.* ~ *of Brt.* F etwas; *on the* ~ auf der Stelle, sofort; **2.** *econ.* sofort liefer- *od.* zahlbar; **3.** (*-tt-*) beflecken; sprenkeln; entdecken, erspähen, erkennen; fleckig werden; ~**less** □ [ˈspɒtlɪs] fleckenlos; ~**light** *thea.*

S

Scheinwerfer(licht *n*) *m*; ~**ter** [~ə] Beobachter *m*; ⚔ Aufklärer *m*; ~**ty** [~ɪ] (*-ier*, *-iest*) fleckig; pickelig.

spouse [spaʊz] Gatt|e *m*, -in *f*.

spout [spaʊt] **1.** Tülle *f*, Schnabel *m*; Strahlrohr *n*; (Wasser)Strahl *m*; **2.** (heraus)spritzen; hervorsprudeln.

sprain ⚕ [spreɪn] **1.** Verstauchung *f*; **2.** sich *et.* verstauchen.

sprang [spræŋ] *pret. von* spring 2.

sprat *zo.* [spræt] Sprotte *f*.

sprawl [sprɔːl] sich rekeln; ausgestreckt daliegen; ♀ wuchern.

spray [spreɪ] **1.** Sprühregen *m*, Gischt *m*, Schaum *m*; Spray *m*, *n*; = *sprayer*; **2.** zerstäuben; (ver)sprühen; besprühen; *Haar* sprayen; ~**er** ['spreɪə] Zerstäuber *m*, Sprüh-, Spraydose *f*.

spread [spred] **1.** (*spread*) *v/t.* *a.* ~ *out* ausbreiten; ausstrecken; spreizen; ausdehnen; verbreiten; belegen; *Butter etc.* (auf)streichen; *Brot etc.* streichen; ~ *the table* den Tisch decken; *v/i.* sich aus- *od.* verbreiten; sich ausdehnen; **2.** Aus-, Verbreitung *f*; Ausdehnung *f*; Spannweite *f*; Fläche *f*; (*Bett*)Decke *f*; (*Brot*)Aufstrich *m*; ⅀ Festessen *n*.

spree F [spriː]: *go* (*out*) *on a* ~ e-e Sauftour machen; *go on a buying* (*shopping*, *spending*) ~ wie verrückt einkaufen.

sprig ♀ [sprɪg] kleiner Zweig.

spright·ly ['spraɪtlɪ] (*-ier*, *-iest*) lebhaft, munter.

spring [sprɪŋ] **1.** Sprung *m*, Satz *m*; ⊕ (Sprung)Feder *f*; Sprungkraft *f*, Elastizität *f*; Quelle *f*; *fig.* Triebfeder *f*; *fig.* Ursprung *m*; Frühling *m* (*a. fig.*), Frühjahr *n*; **2.** (*sprang od. Am. sprung*, *sprung*) *v/t.* springen lassen; (zer)sprengen; *Wild* aufjagen; ~ *a leak* ♨ leck werden; ~ *a surprise on s.o.* j-n überraschen; *v/i.* springen; entspringen (*from dat.*), *fig.* herkommen, stammen (*from* von); ♀ sprießen; ~ *up* aufkommen (*Ideen etc.*); ~**board** ['sprɪŋbɔːd] Sprungbrett *n*; ~**tide** Springflut *f*; *poet.*, ~**time** Frühling(szeit *f*) *m*, Frühjahr *n*; ~**y** [~ɪ] (*-ier*, *-iest*) federnd.

sprin|kle ['sprɪŋkl] (be)streuen; (be)sprengen; *impers.* sprühen (*fein regnen*); ~**kler** [~ə] Berieselungsanlage *f*; Sprinkler *m*; Rasensprenger *m*; ~**kling** [~ɪŋ] Sprühregen

m; *a* ~ *of fig.* ein wenig, ein paar.

sprint [sprɪnt] *Sport* **1.** sprinten; spurten; **2.** Sprint *m*; Spurt *m*; ~**er** ['sprɪntə] *Sport:* Sprinter(in), Kurzstreckenläufer(in).

sprite [spraɪt] Kobold *m*.

sprout [spraʊt] **1.** sprießen; wachsen (lassen); **2.** ♀ Sproß *m*; (*Brussels*) ~*s pl.* ♀ Rosenkohl *m*.

spruce[1] □ [spruːs] schmuck, adrett.

spruce[2] ♀ [~] *a.* ~ *fir* Fichte *f*, Rottanne *f*.

sprung [sprʌŋ] *pret. u. p.p. von* spring 2.

spry [spraɪ] munter, flink.

spun [spʌn] *pret. u. p.p. von* spin 1.

spur [spɜː] **1.** Sporn *m* (*a. zo.*, ♀); Vorsprung *m*, Ausläufer *m* (*e-s Berges*); *fig.* Ansporn *m*; △ *nicht Spur*; *on the* ~ *of the moment* der Eingebung des Augenblicks folgend, spontan; **2.** (*-rr-*) *e-m Pferd die Sporen geben*; *oft* ~ *on fig.* anspornen.

spu·ri·ous □ ['spjʊərɪəs] unecht, gefälscht.

spurn [spɜːn] verschmähen, verächtlich zurückweisen.

spurt[1] [spɜːt] **1.** plötzlich aktiv werden; *Sport:* spurten, sprinten; **2.** plötzliche Aktivität *od.* Anspannung; *Sport:* Spurt *m*, Sprint *m*.

spurt[2] [~] **1.** (heraus)spritzen; **2.** (*Wasser- etc.*)Strahl *m*.

sput·ter ['spʌtə] = splutter.

spy [spaɪ] **1.** Spion(in); Spitzel *m*; **2.** erspähen, entdecken; (aus)spionieren; ~ *on*, ~ *upon* j-m nachspionieren; j-n bespitzeln; *Gespräch etc.* abhören; ~**glass** ['spaɪglɑːs] Fernglas *n*; ~**hole** Guckloch *n*, Spion *m*.

squab·ble ['skwɒbl] **1.** Zank *m*, Kabelei *f*; **2.** sich zanken.

squad [skwɒd] Gruppe *f* (*a.* ⚔); *Polizei:* (*Überfall- etc.*)Kommando *n*; Dezernat *n*; ~ *car Am.* Streifenwagen *m*; ~**ron** ⚔ ['skwɒdrən] Schwadron *f*; (Panzer)Bataillon *n*; ⚓ Staffel *f*; ♨ Geschwader *n*.

squal·id □ ['skwɒlɪd] schmutzig, verwahrlost, -kommen, armselig.

squall [skwɔːl] **1.** *meteor.* Bö *f*; Schrei *m*; ~*s pl.* Geschrei *n*; **2.** schreien.

squal·or ['skwɒlə] Schmutz *m*.

squan·der ['skwɒndə] verschwenden, -geuden.

square [skweə] **1.** □ (vier)eckig; quadratisch, Quadrat...; ... im Quadrat; rechtwink(e)lig; vierschrötig (*Per-*

son); stimmend, in Ordnung; quitt, gleich; anständig, ehrlich, offen; F altmodisch, spießig; **2.** Quadrat *n*; Viereck *n*; Feld *n* (*-s* Brettspiels); *öffentlicher* Platz; Winkel(maß *n*) *m*; *sl.* altmodischer Spießer; **3.** quadratisch *od.* rechtwink(e)lig machen; *Zahl* ins Quadrat erheben; *Schultern* straffen; *Sport:* *Kampf* unentschieden beenden; *econ.* *Konten* ausgleichen; *econ.* *Schuld* begleichen; *fig.* in Einklang bringen *od.* stehen (*with* mit); anpassen (*to an acc.*); passen (*with* zu); **~built** ['skweə'bılt] vierschrötig; **~ dance** *bsd. Am.* Square dance *m*; **~ mile** Quadratmeile *f*; **~toed** *fig.* altmodisch, steif.

squash¹ [skwɒʃ] **1.** Gedränge *n*; Brei *m*, Matsch *m*; *Brt.* (*Orangen- etc.*) Saft *m*; *Sport:* Squash *n*; **2.** (*zer-, zusammen*)quetschen; zusammendrücken.

squash² 🌱 [~] Kürbis *m*.

squat [skwɒt] **1.** (*-tt-*) hocken, kauern; sich ohne Rechtstitel ansiedeln (*auf dat.*); *leerstehendes Haus* besetzen; **~ down** sich hinhocken; **2.** in der Hocke; untersetzt, vierschrötig; **~ter** ['skwɒtə] Squatter *m*, illegaler Siedler; Schafzüchter *m* (*in Australien*); Hausbesetzer(in) *f*; **~ movement** Hausbesetzerszene *f*.

squawk [skwɔːk] **1.** kreischen, schreien; **2.** Gekreisch *n*, Geschrei *n*.

squeak [skwiːk] quiek(s)en, piepen, piepsen; quietschen.

squeal [skwiːl] schreien, kreischen; quietschen, kreischen (*Bremsen etc.*); quiek(s)en, piep(s)en.

squeam·ish □ ['skwiːmɪʃ] empfindlich; mäkelig; heikel; penibel.

squeeze [skwiːz] **1.** (*aus-, zusammen*)drücken, (*-*)pressen, (*aus*)quetschen; sich zwängen *od.* quetschen; **2.** Druck *m*; Gedränge *n*; **squeez·er** ['skwiːzə] (*Frucht*)Presse *f*.

squelch *fig.* [skweltʃ] unterdrücken.

squid *zo.* [skwɪd] Tintenfisch *m*.

squint [skwɪnt] schielen; blinzeln.

squire ['skwaɪə] Großgrundbesitzer *m*, Gutsherr *m*.

squirm F [skwɜːm] sich winden.

squir·rel *zo.* F. ['skwɪrəl, *Am.* 'skwɜːrəl] Eichhörnchen *n*.

squirt [skwɜːt] **1.** Spritze *f*; Strahl *m*; F Wichtigtuer *m*; **2.** spritzen.

stab [stæb] **1.** Stich *m*, (*Dolch- etc.*)Stoß *m*; △ *nicht* Stab; **2.** (*-bb-*)

v/t. niederstechen; *et.* aufspießen; *v/i.* stechen (*at* nach).

sta·bil·i·ty [stə'bılətı] Stabilität *f*; Standfestig-, Beständigkeit *f*; **~ize** ['steɪbəlaɪz] stabilisieren.

sta·ble¹ □ ['steɪbl] stabil, fest.

sta·ble² [~] **1.** Stall *m*; **2.** in den Stall bringen; im Stall halten; im Stall stehen (*Pferd*).

stack [stæk] **1.** 🌾 (Heu-, Stroh-, Getreide)Schober *m*; Stapel *m*; F Haufen *m*; Schornstein(reihe *f*) *m*; **~s** *pl.* (Haupt)Magazin *n* (*e-r Bibliothek*); **2.** **~ up** (auf)stapeln.

sta·di·um ['steɪdjəm] (*pl. -diums, -dia* [-djə]) *Sport:* Stadion *n*.

staff [stɑːf] **1.** Stab *m* (*a.* ✗), Stock *m*; Stütze *f*; (*pl. staves* [steɪvz]) 🎵 Notensystem *n*; (Mitarbeiter)Stab *m*; Personal *n*, Belegschaft *f*; Beamtenstab *m*; Lehrkörper *m*; **2.** (*mit* Personal, Beamten *od.* Lehrern) besetzen; **~ mem·ber** Mitarbeiter(in) *f*; **~ room** Lehrerzimmer *n*.

stag *zo.* [stæg] Hirsch *m*.

stage [steɪdʒ] **1.** *thea.* Bühne *f*; *das* Theater; *fig.* Schauplatz *m*; Stufe *f*, Stadium *n*, Phase *f*; Teilstrecke *f*, Fahrzone *f* (*Bus etc.*); Etappe *f*; ⊕ Bühne *f*, Gerüst *n*; ⊕ Stufe *f* (*e-r Rakete*); **2.** inszenieren; veranstalten; **~coach** *hist.* ['steɪdʒkəutʃ] Postkutsche *f*; **~craft** dramaturgisches *od.* schauspielerisches Können; **~ de·sign** Bühnenbild *n*; **~ de·sign·er** Bühnenbildner(in) *f*; **~ di·rec·tion** Regieanweisung *f*; **~ fright** Lampenfieber *n*; **~ man·ag·er** Inspizient *m*; **~ prop·er·ties** *pl.* Requisiten *pl.*

stag·ger ['stægə] **1.** *v/i.* (sch)wanken, taumeln, torkeln; *fig.* (sch)wanken(d werden); *v/t.* ins Wanken bringen; *Arbeitszeit etc.* staffeln; *fig.* überwältigen, sprachlos machen; **2.** (Sch)Wanken *n*, Taumeln *n*; ✕ Staffelung *f*.

stag·nant □ ['stægnənt] stehend (*Gewässer*); stagnierend; stockend; *econ.* still, flau; *fig.* träge; **~nate** [stæg'neɪt] stagnieren, stillstehen, stocken.

staid □ [steɪd] gesetzt; ruhig.

stain [steɪn] **1.** Fleck *m*; Beize *f*; *fig.* Schandfleck *m*; **2.** *v/t.* beschmutzen, beflecken; färben; *Holz* beizen; *Glas* bemalen; *v/i.* Flecken verursachen; schmutzen; **~ed glass** Buntglas *n*;

S

~·less □ ['steɪnlɪs] rostfrei, nichtrostend; *bsd. fig.* fleckenlos.

stair [steə] Stufe *f*; ~s *pl.* Treppe *f*, Stiege *f*; **~·case** ['steəkeɪs], **~·way** Treppe(nhaus *n*) *f*.

stake [steɪk] **1.** Pfahl *m*, Pfosten *m*; Marterpfahl *m*; (Wett-, Spiel)Einsatz *m* (*a. fig.*); ~s *pl.* Pferderennen: Dotierung *f*; Rennen *n*; *pull up ~s bsd. Am. fig.* F s-e Zelte abbrechen; *be at* ~ *fig.* auf dem Spiel stehen; **2.** wagen, aufs Spiel setzen; ~ *off*, ~ *out* abstecken.

stale □ [steɪl] (~*r*, ~*st*) alt (*nicht frisch*); schal, abgestanden; verbraucht (*Luft*); *fig.* fad.

stalk[1] ♀ [stɔːk] Stengel *m*, Stiel *m*, Halm *m*.

stalk[2] [~] *v/i. hunt.* (sich an)pirschen; *oft* ~ *along* (einher)stolzieren; *v/t.* sich heranpirschen an (*acc.*); verfolgen, hinter *j-m* herschleichen.

stall[1] [stɔːl] **1.** Box *f* (*im Stall*); △ *nicht* Stall; (Verkaufs)Stand *m*, (Markt)Bude *f*; Chorstuhl *m*; ~s *pl. Brt. thea.* Parkett *n*; **2.** *v/t.* Tier in Boxen unterbringen; *Motor* abwürgen; *v/i.* absterben (*Motor*).

stall[2] [~] ausweichen; *a.* ~ *for time* Zeit schinden; *Sport:* auf Zeit spielen.

stal·li·on *zo.* ['stæljən] (Zucht-) Hengst *m*.

stal·wart □ ['stɔːlwət] stramm, kräftig; *bsd. pol.* treu.

stam·i·na ['stæmɪnə] Ausdauer *f*, Zähigkeit *f*; Durchhaltevermögen *n*, Kondition *f*.

stam·mer ['stæmə] **1.** stottern, stammeln; **2.** Stottern *n*.

stamp [stæmp] **1.** (Auf)Stampfen *n*; Stempel *m* (*a. fig.*); △ *nicht* Poststempel; (Brief)Marke *f*; *fig.* Gepräge *n*; *fig.* Art *f*; **2.** (auf)stampfen; aufstampfen mit; (ab)stempeln (*a. fig.*); frankieren; (auf)prägen; ~ *out* (aus)stanzen.

stam·pede [stæm'piːd] **1.** Panik *f*, wilde, panische Flucht; (Massen-) Ansturm *m*; **2.** *v/i.* durchgehen; *v/t.* in Panik versetzen.

stanch [stɑːntʃ] *s.* **staunch**[1,2].

stand [stænd] **1.** (*stood*) *v/i.* stehen; sich befinden; *fig.* festbleiben; *mst* ~ *still* stillstehen, stehenbleiben; *v/t.* stellen; aushalten; (v)ertragen; sich *et.* gefallen lassen; ertragen; sich *e-r Sache* unterziehen;

Probe bestehen; *e-e Chance* haben; F spendieren; ~ *a round* F e-e Runde schmeißen; ~ *about* herumstehen; ~ *aside* beiseite treten; ~ *back* zurücktreten; ~ *by* dabeistehen, -stehen; bereitstehen; *fig.* zu *j-m* halten *od.* stehen, helfen; ~ *for* kandidieren für; bedeuten; eintreten für; F sich *et.* gefallen lassen; ~ *in* einspringen (*for s.o.* für j-n); ~ *in for* Film: j-n doubeln; ~ *off* sich entfernt halten; *fig.* Abstand halten; ~ *on* (*fig.* be)stehen auf (*dat.*); ~ *out* hervorstehen, -treten; sich abheben (*against* gegen); aus-, durchhalten; *fig.* herausragen; standhalten (*dat.*); ~ *over* liegenbleiben; (sich) vertagen (*to auf acc.*); ~ *to* stehen zu, ⚔ in Bereitschaft stehen *od.* versetzen; ~ *up* aufstehen, sich erheben; sich aufrichten (*Stacheln etc.*); ~ *up for* eintreten für; ~ *up to* mutig gegenüberstehen (*dat.*); standhalten (*dat.*); ~ *upon* = ~ *on*; **2.** Stand *m*; Stillstand *m*; (Stand)Platz *m*, Standort *m*; Stand(platz) *m* (*für Taxis*); (Verkaufs-, Messe)Stand *m*; *fig.* Standpunkt *m*; Ständer *m*; Tribüne *f*; *bsd. Am.* Zeugenstand *m*; *make a* ~ *against* sich entgegenstellen (*dat.*).

stan·dard ['stændəd] **1.** Standarte *f*, Fahne *f*, Flagge *f*; Standard *m*, Norm *f*; Maßstab *m*; Niveau *n*, Stand *m*, Grad *m*; Münzfuß *m*; (*Gold- etc.*)Währung *f*; Ständer *m*; **2.** maßgebend; normal; Normal...; **~·ize** [~aɪz] norm(ier)en, standardisieren, vereinheitlichen.

stand·by ['stændbaɪ] **1.** (*pl. -bys*) Beistand *m*, Hilfe *f*; Bereitschaft *f*; Ersatz *m*; **2.** Not..., Ersatz..., Reserve...; Bereitschafts...; **~·in** Film: Double *n*; Ersatzmann *m*, Vertreter(in).

stand·ing ['stændɪŋ] **1.** stehend (*a. fig.*); (fest)stehend; *econ.* laufend; ständig; **2.** Stellung *f*, Rang *m*; Ruf *m*, Ansehen *n*; Dauer *f*; *of long* ~ alt; **~ or·der** *econ.* Dauerauftrag *m*; **~·room** Stehplatz *m*.

stand-off·ish ['stænd'ɒfɪʃ] reserviert, (sehr) ablehnend, zurückhaltend; **~·point** Standpunkt *m*; **~·still** Stillstand *m*; *be at a* ~ stocken, ruhen, an e-m toten Punkt angelangt sein; **~·up** stehend; im Stehen (eingenommen) (*Essen*); ~ *collar* Stehkragen *m*.

stay

stank [stæŋk] *pret. von* stink 2.

stan·za ['stænzə] Stanze *f*; Strophe *f*.

sta·ple[1] ['steipl] Haupterzeugnis *n*; Hauptgegenstand *m*; *attr.* Haupt...

sta·ple[2] [~] **1.** Krampe *f*; Heftklammer *f*; **2.** heften; △ *nicht* stapeln; **~r** [~ə] Heftmaschine *f*.

star [stɑː] **1.** Stern *m*; *thea.*, Film, Sport: Star *m*; △ *nicht zo.* Star; *The* ♀s *and Stripes pl.* das Sternenbanner (*der USA*); **2.** (-rr-) mit Sternen schmücken; die *od.* e-e Hauptrolle spielen; in *der od.* e-r Hauptrolle zeigen; *a film ~ring ...* ein Film mit ... in der Hauptrolle.

star·board ⚓ ['stɑːbəd] Steuerbord *n*.

starch [stɑːtʃ] **1.** (Wäsche)Stärke *f*; *fig.* Steifheit *f*; **2.** Wäsche stärken.

stare [steə] **1.** Starren *n*; starrer *od.* erstaunter Blick; **2.** (~ *at* an)starren; erstaunt blicken.

stark [stɑːk] **1.** *adj.* □ starr; rein, bar, völlig (*Unsinn*); △ *nicht* stark; **2.** *adv.* völlig.

star·light ['stɑːlait] Sternenlicht *n*.

star·ling *zo.* ['stɑːlɪŋ] Star *m*.

star·lit ['stɑːlɪt] stern(en)hell.

star|ry ['stɑːrɪ] (-ier, -iest) Stern(en)...; **~ry-eyed** F naiv; romantisch; **~span·gled** ['~spæŋgld] sternenbesät; *The* ♀ *Banner* das Sternenbanner (*Flagge u. Nationalhymne der USA*).

start [stɑːt] **1.** Auffahren *n*, -schrecken *n*; Schreck *m*; Start *m*; Aufbruch *m*, Abreise *f*, Abfahrt *f*, ✈ Abflug *m*, Start *m*; Beginn *m*, Anfang *m*; Sport: Vorgabe *f*; *fig.* Vorsprung *m*; *get the ~ of s.o.* j-m zuvorkommen; **2.** *v/i.* auffahren, hochschrecken; stutzen; sich auf den Weg machen, aufbrechen; abfahren (*Zug*), auslaufen (*Schiff*), ✈ abfliegen, starten; Sport: starten; ⊕ anspringen (*Motor*), anlaufen (*Maschine*); anfangen, beginnen; *~ from scratch* F ganz von vorne anfangen; *v/t.* in Gang setzen *od.* bringen, ⊕ *a.* anlassen; anfangen, beginnen; Sport: starten (lassen); **~er** ['stɑːtə] Sport: Starter *m*; *mot.* Anlasser *m*, Starter *m*; **~s** *pl.* F Vorspeise *f*.

start|le ['stɑːtl] erschrecken; aufschrecken; **~ling** [~lɪŋ] erschreckend; überraschend, aufsehenerregend.

starv|a·tion [stɑː'veiʃn] Hungern *n*;

Verhungern *n*, Hungertod *m*; *attr.* Hunger...; **~e** [stɑːv] verhungern (lassen); *fig.* verkümmern (lassen).

state [steit] **1.** Zustand *m*; Stand *m*; Staat *m*; *mst* ♀ *pol.* Staat *m*; *attr.* Staats...; *lie in ~* feierlich aufgebahrt liegen; **2.** angeben; erklären, darlegen; feststellen; festsetzen, -legen; ♀ **De·part·ment** *Am. pol.* Außenministerium *n*; **~ly** ['steitli] (-ier, -iest) stattlich; würdevoll; erhaben; **~ment** [~mənt] Angabe *f*; (Zeugen-*etc.*)Aussage *f*; Darstellung *f*; Erklärung *f*, Verlautbarung *f*, Statement *n*; Aufstellung *f*, *bsd. econ.* (Geschäfts-, Monats- *etc.*)Bericht *m*; ~ *of account* Kontoauszug *m*; **~room** Staatszimmer *n*; ⚓ (Einzel)Kabine *f*; **~side**, ♀**·side** *Am.* **1.** *adj.* USA-..., Heimat...; **2.** *adv.* in den Staaten; nach den *od.* in die Staaten (zurück); **~s·man** *pol.* [~smən] (*pl.* -men) Staatsmann *m*.

stat·ic ['stætɪk] (~ally) statisch.

sta·tion ['steiʃn] **1.** Platz *m*, Posten *m*; Station *f*; (Polizei- *etc.*)Wache *f*; (Tank- *etc.*)Stelle *f*; (Fernseh-, Rundfunk)Sender *m*; ✚ Bahnhof *m*; ⚓, ✗ Stützpunkt *m*; Stellung *f*, Rang *m*; **2.** aufstellen, postieren; ⚓, ✗ stationieren; **~·a·ry** □ [~əri] (still)stehend; fest(stehend); gleichbleibend; **~·er** [~ə] Schreibwarenhändler *m*; **~'s** (*shop*) Schreibwarenhandlung *f*; **~·er·y** [~rɪ] Schreibwaren *pl.*; Briefpapier *n*; **~·mas·ter** ✚ Stationsvorsteher *m*; **~ wag·on** *Am. mot.* Kombiwagen *m*.

sta·tis·tics [stə'tistiks] *pl. u. sg.* Statistik *f*.

stat|u·a·ry ['stætjʊəri] Bildhauer(-kunst *f*) *m*; **~·ue** [~uː] Standbild *n*, Plastik *f*, Statue *f*.

stat·ure ['stætʃə] Statur *f*, Wuchs *m*.

sta·tus ['steitəs] Zustand *m*; (Familien)Stand *m*; Stellung *f*, Rang *m*; Status *m*.

stat·ute ['stætjuːt] Statut *n*, Satzung *f*; Gesetz *n*.

staunch[1] [stɔːntʃ] Blut(ung) stillen.

staunch[2] □ [~] treu, zuverlässig.

stave [steiv] **1.** Faßdaube *f*; Strophe *f*; **2.** (staved *od.* stove) *mst* ~ *in* eindrücken; ein Loch schlagen in (*acc.*); ~ *off* abwehren.

stay [stei] **1.** ⊕ Strebe *f*, Stütze *f*; ⚓ Aufschub *m*; (vorübergehender) Aufenthalt; **~s** *pl.* Korsett *n*; **2.** blei-

S

ben (*with s.o.* bei j-m); sich (vorübergehend) aufhalten, wohnen (*at,
in* in *dat.*; *with s.o.* bei j-m); △ *nicht
stehen*; ~ *away* (*from*) fernbleiben
(*dat.*), wegbleiben (von); ~ *up* aufbleiben, wach bleiben.

stead [sted]: *in his* ~ an s-r Stelle;
~**fast** □ ['stedfəst] fest, unerschütterlich; standhaft; unverwandt
(*Blick*).

stead·y ['stedɪ] **1.** *adj.* □ (*-ier, -iest*)
fest; gleichmäßig, stetig, (be)stän-
dig; zuverlässig; ruhig, sicher; **2.**
adv.: *go* ~ *with s.o.* F (fest) mit j-m
gehen; **3.** festigen, fest *od.* sicher *od.*
ruhig machen *od.* werden; sich beruhigen; **4.** □ F feste Freundin, fester
Freund.

steak [steɪk] Steak *n.*

steal [stiːl] **1.** (*stole, stolen*) *v/t.* stehl-
len (*a. fig.*); *v/i.* stehlen; ~ *away* sich
davonstehlen.

stealth [stelθ]: *by* ~ heimlich, verstohlen; ~**y** □ ['stelθɪ] (*-ier, -iest*)
heimlich, verstohlen.

steam [stiːm] **1.** Dampf *m*; Dunst *m*;
attr. Dampf...; **2.** *v/i.* dampfen; ~ *up*
(sich) beschlagen (*Glas*); *v/t. Speisen*
dünsten, dämpfen; ~**er** ♣ ['stiːmə]
Dampfer *m*; ~**y** □ ['stiːmɪ] (*-ier, -iest*)
dampfig, dampfend; dunstig; beschlagen (*Glas*).

steel [stiːl] **1.** Stahl *m*; **2.** stählern;
Stahl...; **3.** *fig.* stählen, wappnen;
~**work·er** ['stiːlwɜːkə] Stahlarbeiter
m; ~**works** *sg.* Stahlwerk *n.*

steep [stiːp] **1.** □ steil, jäh; F toll; **2.**
einweichen; eintauchen; ziehen las-
sen; *be* ~*ed in s.th. fig.* von et.
durchdrungen sein.

stee·ple ['stiːpl] (spitzer) Kirchturm;
~**chase** *Pferdesport:* Hindernisren-
nen *n*; *Leichtathletik:* Hindernislauf
m.

steer¹ *zo.* [stɪə] junger Ochse; △ *nicht
Stier.*

steer² [~] steuern, lenken; ~**age** ♣
['stɪərɪdʒ] Steuerung *f*; Zwischen-
deck *n*; ~**ing col·umn** *mot.* [~ɪŋ-
kɒləm] Lenksäule *f*; ~**ing wheel** ♣
Steuerrad *n*; *mot. a.* Lenkrad *n.*

stem [stem] **1.** (Baum-, Wort)Stamm
m; Stiel *m*; Stengel *m*; **2.** (*-mm-*)
stammen (*from* von); eindämmen;
Blut(ung) stillen; ankämpfen gegen.

stench [stentʃ] Gestank *m.*

sten·cil ['stensl] Schablone *f*; *print.*
Matrize *f.*

ste·nog·ra·pher [ste'nɒgrəfə] Steno-
graph(in); ~**phy** [~ɪ] Stenographie *f.*

step [step] **1.** Schritt *m*; Tritt *m*; kurze
Strecke; (Treppen)Stufe *f*; Tritt-
brett *n*; *fig.* Fußstapfe *f*; (*a pair of*)
~*s pl.* (e-e) Trittleiter; *mind the* ~*!*
Vorsicht, Stufe!; *take* ~*s fig.* Schritte unternehmen; **2.** (*-pp-*) *v/i.* schreiten, treten; gehen; △ *nicht steppen*;
~ *out* forsch ausschreiten; *v/t.* ~ *off,* ~
out abschreiten; ~ *up* ankurbeln,
steigern.

step- [~] *in Zssgn:* Stief...; ~**fa·ther**
['stepfɑːðə] Stiefvater *m*; ~**moth·er**
Stiefmutter *f.*

steppe [step] Steppe *f.*

ster·e·o ['sterɪəʊ] (*pl. -os*) *Radio etc.:*
Stereo *n*; Stereogerät *n*; *attr.* Stereo...

ster·ile ['steraɪl] unfruchtbar; steril;
ste·ril·i·ty [ste'rɪlətɪ] Sterilität *f*; ~
il·ize ['sterəlaɪz] sterilisieren.

ster·ling ['stɜːlɪŋ] **1.** lauter, echt, gediegen; **2.** *econ.* Sterling *m* (*Währung*).

stern [stɜːn] **1.** □ ernst; finster,
streng, hart; **2.** ♣ *Naut.* Heck *n*; ~**ness**
['stɜːnnɪs] Ernst *m*; Strenge *f.*

stew [stjuː] **1.** schmoren, dämpfen; **2.**
Eintopf *m*, Schmorgericht *n*; *be in a*
~ in heller Aufregung sein.

stew·ard [stjʊəd] Verwalter *m*; ♣, ✈
Steward *m*; (Fest)Ordner *m*; ~**ess**
♣, ✈ ['stjʊədɪs] Stewardeß *f.*

stick [stɪk] **1.** Stock *m*; Stecken *m*;
trockener Zweig; Stengel *m*, Stiel *m*;
(*Lippen- etc.*)Stift *m*; Stab *m*; Stange
f; (*Besen- etc.*)Stiel *m*; ~*s pl.* Klein-
holz *n*; **2.** (*stuck*) *v/i.* stecken(bleib-
ben); (fest)kleben (*to an dat.*); sich
heften (*to an acc.*); ~ *at nothing* vor
nichts zurückschrecken; ~ *out* ab-,
hervor-, herausstehen; ~ *to* bleiben
bei; *v/t.* (ab)stechen; stecken, heften
(*to an acc.*); kleben; F Messer stoßen;
F *et., j-n* (v)ertragen, aussstehen; ~ *out*
herausst(r)ecken; ~ *it out* F durchhalten; ~**er** ['stɪkə] Aufkleber *m*;
antinuke ~ *sl.* Anti-Kernwaffen-
Aufkleber *m*; ~**ing plas·ter** [~ɪŋ-
plɑːstə] Heftpflaster *n.*

stick·y □ ['stɪkɪ] (*-ier, -iest*) klebrig;
schwierig, heikel.

stiff [stɪf] **1.** □ steif; starr; hart; fest;
mühsam; stark (*alkoholisches Ge-
tränk*); *be bored* ~ F zu Tode gelang-

weilt sein; *keep a ~ upper lip* Haltung bewahren; **2.** *sl.* Leiche *f;* **~en** ['stɪfn] (sich) versteifen; steif werden, erstarren; **~necked** [~'nekt] halsstarrig.

sti·fle ['staɪfl] ersticken; *fig.* unterdrücken.

stile [staɪl] Zauntritt *m.*

sti·let·to [stɪ'letəʊ] (*pl.* -tos, -toes) Stilett *n;* **~ heel** Pfennigabsatz *m.*

still [stɪl] **1.** *adj.* □ still; ruhig; unbeweglich; **2.** *adv.* noch (immer), (immer) noch; **3.** *cj.* und doch, dennoch; **4.** stillen; beruhigen; **5.** Destillierapparat *m;* **~born** ['stɪlbɔːn] totgeboren; **~ life** (*pl. still lifes od. lives*) *paint.* Stilleben *n;* **~ness** [~nɪs] Stille *f,* Ruhe *f.*

stilt [stɪlt] Stelze *f;* **~ed** □ ['stɪltɪd] gestelzt (*Stil*).

stim·u·lant ['stɪmjʊlənt] **1.** *✽* stimulierend; **2.** *✽* Reiz-, Aufputschmittel *n;* Genußmittel *n;* Anreiz *m;* **~late** [~eɪt] *✽* stimulieren (*a. fig.*), anregen, aufputschen; *fig. a.* anspornen; *j-n* knapphalten; **~la·tion** [stɪmjʊ'leɪʃn] Anreiz *m;* Reizung *f;* Anreiz *m,* Antrieb *m,* Anregung *f;* **~lus** ['stɪmjʊləs] (*pl. -li* [-liː]) *✽* Reiz *m;* (An)Reiz *m,* Antrieb *m.*

sting [stɪŋ] **1.** Stachel *m;* Stich *m,* Biß *m;* **2.** (*stung*) stechen; brennen; schmerzen; *fig.* anstacheln, reizen.

stin·gi·ness ['stɪndʒɪnɪs] Geiz *m;* **~gy** □ [~ɪ] (*-ier, -iest*) geizig, knaus(e)rig; dürftig.

stink [stɪŋk] **1.** Gestank *m;* **2.** (*stank od. stunk, stunk*) stinken.

stint [stɪnt] **1.** Einschränkung *f;* Arbeit *f;* **2.** knausern mit; einschränken; *j-n* knapphalten.

stip·u·late ['stɪpjʊleɪt] *a. ~ for* ausbedingen, ausmachen, vereinbaren; **~la·tion** [stɪpjʊ'leɪʃn] Abmachung *f;* Klausel *f,* Bedingung *f.*

stir [stɜː] **1.** Rühren *n;* Bewegung *f;* Aufregung *f,* Aufruhr *m;* Aufsehen *n;* **2.** (*-rr-*) (sich) rühren; (sich) bewegen; erwachen; (um)rühren; *fig.* erregen; *~ up* aufhetzen; *Streit etc.* entfachen.

stir·rup ['stɪrəp] Steigbügel *m.*

stitch [stɪtʃ] **1.** Stich *m;* Masche *f;* Seitenstechen *n;* **2.** nähen; heften.

stock [stɒk] **1.** (Baum)Strunk *m;* Pfropfunterlage *f;* Griff *m;* (Gewehr)Schaft *m;* △ *nicht* Stock; Stamm *m,* Familie *f,* Herkunft *f,*

Rohstoff *m;* (Fleisch-, Gemüse-) Brühe *f;* Vorrat *m;* *econ.* Waren(lager *n*) *pl.;* (Wissens)Schatz *m;* *a. live~* Vieh(bestand *m*) *n;* *econ.* Stammkapital *n;* *econ.* Anleihekapital *n;* *~s pl. econ.* Effekten *pl.;* Aktien *pl.;* Staatspapiere *pl.;* *in* (*out of*) *~ econ.* (nicht) vorrätig *od.* auf Lager; *take ~ econ.* Inventur machen; *take ~ of fig.* sich klarwerden über (*acc.*); **2.** vorrätig; Serien...; Standard...; *fig.* stehend, stereotyp; **3.** ausstatten, versorgen; *econ. Waren* führen, vorrätig haben.

stock·ade [stɒ'keɪd] Palisade(nzaun *m*) *f.*

stock|breed·er ['stɒkbriːdə] Viehzüchter *m;* **~brok·er** *econ.* Börsenmakler *m;* **~ex·change** *econ.* Börse *f;* **~farm·er** Viehzüchter *m;* **~hold·er** *bsd. Am. econ.* Aktionär(in).

stock·ing ['stɒkɪŋ] Strumpf *m.*

stock|job·ber *econ.* ['stɒkdʒɒbə] Börsenhändler *m;* *Am.* Börsenspekulant *m;* **~ mar·ket** *econ.* Börse *f;* **~still** stockstill, unbeweglich; **~tak·ing** *econ.* Bestandsaufnahme *f* (*a. fig.*), Inventur *f;* **~y** [~ɪ] (*-ier, -iest*) stämmig, untersetzt.

stok·er ['stəʊkə] Heizer *m.*

stole [stəʊl] *pret. von steal 1;* **sto·len** ['stəʊlən] *p.p. von steal 1.*

stol·id □ ['stɒlɪd] gleichmütig; stur.

stom·ach ['stʌmək] **1.** Magen *m;* Leib *m,* Bauch *m;* *fig.* Lust *f;* **2.** *fig.* (v)ertragen; **~ache** Magenschmerzen *pl.,* Bauchweh *n;* **~up·set** Magenverstimmung *f.*

stone [stəʊn] **1.** Stein *m;* (Obst)Stein *m,* (-)Kern *m;* (*pl. stone*) *Brt.* Gewichtseinheit (*= 14 lb. = 6,35 kg*); **2.** steinern; Stein...; **3.** steinigen; entsteinen, -kernen; **~blind** ['stəʊn'blaɪnd] stockblind; **~dead** mausetot; **~deaf** stocktaub; **~ma·son** Steinmetz *m;* **~ware** [~weə] Steinzeug *n.*

ston·y □ ['stəʊnɪ] (*-ier, -iest*) steinig; *fig.* steinern, kalt.

stood [stʊd] *pret. u. p.p. von stand 1.*

stool [stuːl] Hocker *m,* Schemel *m;* △ *nicht* Stuhl; *✽* Stuhl(gang) *m;* **~pigeon** ['stuːlpɪdʒɪn] Lockvogel *m;* Spitzel *m.*

stoop [stuːp] **1.** *v/i.* sich bücken; gebeugt gehen; *fig.* sich erniedrigen *od.* herablassen; *v/t.* neigen, beugen; **2.** gebeugte Haltung.

S

stop [stɒp] 1. (-pp-) v/t. aufhören (mit); stoppen; anhalten; aufhalten; hindern; *Zahlungen, Tätigkeit etc.* einstellen; *Zahn* plombieren; *Blut* stillen; *a.* ~ **up** ver-, zustopfen; v/i. (an)halten, stehenbleiben, stoppen; aufhören; bleiben; ~ *dead* plötzlich stehenbleiben *od.* aufhören; ~ **off** F kurz haltmachen; ~ **over** kurz haltmachen; Zwischenstation machen; ~ *short* plötzlich anhalten; 2. Halt *m*; Stillstand *m*; Ende *n*; Pause *f*; ✻ *etc.* Aufenthalt *m*; ~ Station *f*; (Bus-) Haltestelle *f*; ♣ Anlegestelle *f*; *phot.* Blende *f*; *mst full* ~ *gr.* Punkt *m*; **~gap** ['stɒpgæp] Notbehelf *m*; **~light** *mot.* Brems-, Stopplicht *n*; **~o·ver** *bsd. Am.* Zwischenstation *f*; ✈ Zwischenlandung *f*; **~page** [~ɪdʒ] Unterbrechung *f*; Stopp *m*; (Verkehrs)Stockung *f*, Stau *m*; Verstopfung *f* (Gehalts-, Lohn)Abzug *m*; Sperrung *f* (*e-s Schecks*); (Arbeits-, Zahlungs- *etc.*)Einstellung *f*; **~per** [~ə] Stöpsel *m*, Pfropfen *m*; **~ping** ✻ [~ɪŋ] Plombe *f*; **~sign** *mot.* Stoppschild *n*; **~watch** Stoppuhr *f*.

stor·age ['stɔːrɪdʒ] Lagerung *f*, Speicherung *f*; *Computer:* Speicher *m*; Lagergeld *n*; *attr.* Speicher... (*a. Computer*).

store [stɔː] 1. Vorrat *m*; Lagerhaus *n*; *Brt.* Kauf-, Warenhaus *n*; *bsd. Am.* Laden *m*, Geschäft *n*; *fig.* Fülle *f*, Reichtum *m*; △ *nicht* Store; in ~ vorrätig, auf Lager; 2. versorgen; *a.* ~ **up**, ~ **away** (auf)speichern, (ein)lagern; ✄, *Computer:* speichern; **~house** Lagerhaus *n*; *fig.* Fundgrube *f*; **~keep·er** Lagerverwalter *m*; *bsd. Am.* Ladenbesitzer (-in).

sto·rey, *bsd. Am.* **-ry** ['stɔːrɪ] Stock (-werk *n*) *m*.

-sto·reyed, *bsd. Am.* **-sto·ried** ['stɔːrɪd] mit ... Stockwerken, ...stöckig.

stork *zo.* [stɔːk] Storch *m*.

storm [stɔːm] 1. Sturm *m*; Unwetter *n*; Gewitter *n*; 2. stürmen; toben; **~y** □ ['stɔːmɪ] (-*ier*, -*iest*) stürmisch.

sto·ry[1] ['stɔːrɪ] Geschichte *f*; Erzählung *f*; *thea. etc.* Handlung *f*; F Lüge *f*, Märchen *n*; *short* ~ Kurzgeschichte *f*; Erzählung *f*.

sto·ry[2] *bsd. Am.* [~] = storey.

stout □ [staʊt] stark, kräftig; derb; dick; tapfer.

stove[1] [stəʊv] Ofen *m*, Herd *m*.

stove[2] [~] *pret. u. p.p. von* stave 2.

stow [stəʊ] (ver)stauen, packen; ~ **away** wegräumen; **~a·way** ♣, ✈ ['stəʊəweɪ] blinder Passagier.

strad·dle ['strædl] die Beine spreizen; rittlings sitzen auf (*dat.*).

strag·gle ['strægl] verstreut liegen *od.* stehen; herumstreifen; (hinterher-) bummeln; ✿ *etc.* wuchern; **~gly** [~ɪ] (-*ier*, -*iest*) verstreut (liegend); ✿ *etc.* wuchernd; unordentlich (*Haar*).

straight [streɪt] 1. *adj.* □ gerade; glatt (*Haar*); pur (*Whisky etc.*); aufrichtig, ehrlich, ehrlich; *put* ~ in Ordnung bringen; 2. *adv.* gerade(aus); gerade(wegs); direkt; klar (*denken*); ehrlich, anständig; *a.* ~ **out** offen, rundheraus; ~ **away** sofort; **~en** ['streɪtn] v/t. ge10cademachen, (gerade)richten; ~ **out** in Ordnung bringen; v/i. gerade werden; ~ **up** sich aufrichten; **~for·ward** □ [~'fɔː-wəd] ehrlich, redlich, offen; einfach.

strain [streɪn] 1. *biol.* Rasse *f*, Art *f*; (Erb)Anlage *f*, Hang *m*, Zug *m*; ⊕ Spannung *f*; (Über)Anstrengung *f*; Anspannung *f*; Belastung *f*; Druck *m*; ✻ Zerrung *f*; *fig.* Ton(art *f*) *m*; *mst* ~**s** *pl.* ♪ Weise *f*, Melodie *f*; 2. v/t. (an)spannen; (über)anstrengen; ✻ sich *et.* zerren *od.* verstauchen; *fig et.* strapazieren, überfordern; durchseihen, filtern; v/i. sich spannen; sich anstrengen (*after* um); zerren (*at an dat.*); **~ed** [~d] gezwungen, unnatürlich; **~er** ['streɪnə] Sieb *n*, Filter *m*.

strait [streɪt] (*in Eigennamen* 2*s pl.*) Meerenge *f*, Straße *f*; 2*s pl.* Not *f* (-lage) *f*; **~ened** ['streɪtnd]: *in* ~ *circumstances* in beschränkten Verhältnissen; **~jack·et** Zwangsjacke *f*.

strand [strænd] 1. Strang *m*; (Haar-) Strähne *f*; *poet.* Gestade *n*, Ufer *n*; △ *nicht* Strand; 2. auf den Strand setzen; *fig.* stranden (lassen).

strange □ [streɪndʒ] (~*r*, ~*st*) fremd; seltsam, sonderbar; **strang·er** ['streɪndʒə] Fremde(r *m*) *f*.

stran·gle ['stræŋgl] erwürgen.

strap [stræp] 1. Riemen *m*; Gurt *m*; Band *n*; Träger *m* (*Kleid*); 2. (-pp-) festschnallen; mit e-m Riemen schlagen.

strat·a·gem ['strætədʒəm] (Kriegs-) List *f*.

stra·te·gic [strə'tiːdʒɪk] (~*ally*) stra-

teg·isch; strat·e·gy ['strætɪdʒɪ] Strategie f.

stra·tum geol. ['strɑːtəm] (pl. -ta [-tə]) Schicht f (a. fig.), Lage f.

straw [strɔː] 1. Stroh(halm m) n; 2. Stroh...; ~**ber·ry** ♥ ['strɔːbərɪ] Erdbeere f.

stray [streɪ] 1. (herum)streunen; (herum)streifen; sich verirren; 2. verirrt, streunend; vereinzelt; 3. verirrtes od. streunendes Tier.

streak [striːk] 1. Strich m, Streifen m; fig. Spur f; fig. (Glücks- etc.)Strähne f; ~ of lightning Blitzstrahl m; 2. streifen; rasen, flitzen.

stream [striːm] 1. Bach m, Flüßchen n; Strom m, Strömung f; 2. strömen; tränen (Augen); triefen; flattern, wehen; ~**er** ['striːmə] Wimpel m; (flatterndes) Band.

street [striːt] Straße f; attr. Straßen...; in (Am. on) the ~ auf der Straße; ~**car** Am. ['striːtkɑː] Straßenbahn(wagen m) f.

strength [streŋθ] Stärke f, Kraft f; on the ~ of auf ... hin, auf Grund (gen.); ~**en** ['streŋθən] v/t. (ver)stärken; fig. bestärken; v/i. stark werden.

stren·u·ous □ ['strenjʊəs] rührig, emsig; eifrig; anstrengend.

stress [stres] 1. Ton m, Akzent m, Betonung f; fig. Nachdruck m; fig. Belastung f, Anspannung f, Druck m; Stress m; 2. betonen.

stretch [stretʃ] 1. v/t. strecken; (aus)dehnen; (an)spannen; recken; fig. übertreiben; fig. es nicht allzu genau nehmen mit; ~ out ausstrecken; v/i. sich erstrecken; sich dehnen (lassen); 2. Strecken n; Dehnen n; Anspannung f; Übertreibung f; Zeit (-raum m, -spanne) f; Strecke f, Fläche f; ~**er** ['stretʃə] (Kranken-) Trage f.

strew [struː] (strewed, strewn od. strewed) (be-, ver)streuen; ~**n** [~n] p.p. von strew.

strick·en adj. ['strɪkən] heimgesucht, schwer betroffen; ergriffen.

strict [strɪkt] streng; genau; ~**ly** speaking genaugenommen; ~**ness** ['strɪktnɪs] Genauigkeit f; Strenge f.

strid·den ['strɪdn] p.p. von stride 1.

stride [straɪd] 1. (strode, stridden) (a. ~ out a)schreiten; überschreiten; 2. großer Schritt.

strife [straɪf] Streit m, Hader m.

strike [straɪk] 1. econ. Streik m; (Öl-,

Erz)Fund m; ✕ (Luft)Angriff m; ✕ Atomschlag m; be on ~ streiken; go on ~ in (den) Streik treten; a lucky ~ ein Glückstreffer; 2. (struck) v/t. schlagen; treffen; stoßen; schlagen od. stoßen gegen od. auf (acc.); stoßen od. treffen auf (acc.); Flagge, Segel streichen; ♪ Ton anschlagen; Streichholz anzünden; ein Feuer machen; Zelt abbrechen; einschlagen in (acc.) (Blitz); Wurzel schlagen; j-n beeindrucken; j-m auf- od. einfallen; ~ off, ~ out (aus)streichen; ~ up ♪ anstimmen; Freundschaft schließen; v/i. schlagen; ✑ auflaufen (on auf acc.); econ. streiken; ~ home fig. ins Schwarze treffen; **strik·er** econ. ['straɪkə] Streikende(r m) f; **strik·ing** □ [~ɪŋ] Schlag...; auffallend; eindrucksvoll; treffend.

string [strɪŋ] 1. Schnur f; Bindfaden m; Band n; Faden m, Draht m; (Bogen)Sehne f; ♥ Faser f; Reihe f; Kette f; ♪ Saite f; ~s pl. ♪ Streichinstrumente pl., die Streicher pl.; pull the ~s fig. der Drahtzieher sein; no ~s attached ohne Bedingungen; 2. (strung) spannen; Perlen etc. aufreihen; ♪ besaiten, bespannen; (ver-, zu)schnüren; Bohnen abziehen; be strung up angespannt od. erregt sein; ~ **band** ♪ ['strɪŋbænd] Streichorchester n.

strin·gent □ ['strɪndʒənt] streng, scharf; zwingend; knapp.

string·y ['strɪŋɪ] (-ier, -iest) faserig; sehnig; zäh.

strip [strɪp] 1. (-pp-) entkleiden (a. fig.); a. ~ off abziehen, abstreifen, (ab)schälen; (sich) ausziehen; a. ~ down ⊕ zerlegen, auseinandernehmen; fig. entblößen, berauben; 2. Streifen m.

stripe [straɪp] Streifen m; ✕ Tresse f.

strip·ling ['strɪplɪŋ] Bürschchen n.

strive [straɪv] (strove, striven) streben; sich bemühen; ringen (for um).

striv·en ['strɪvn] p.p. von strive.

strode [strəʊd] pret. von stride 1.

stroke [strəʊk] 1. Schlag m; Streich m, Stoß m; Strich m; ✑ Schlag(anfall) m; ~ of (good) luck Glücksfall m; 2. streichen über; streicheln.

stroll [strəʊl] 1. schlendern, (herum)bummeln; herumziehen; 2. Bummel m, Spaziergang m; ~**er** ['strəʊlə] Bummler(in), Spaziergänger(in); Am. (Falt)Sportwagen m.

S

strong ☐ [strɒŋ] stark; kräftig; energisch; überzeugt; fest; stark, schwer (*Getränk etc.*); **~box** ['strɒŋbɒks] Geld-, Stahlkassette *f*; **~hold** Festung *f*; *fig.* Hochburg *f*; **~mind·ed** willensstark; **~room** Stahlkammer *f*, Tresor(raum) *m*.

strove [strəʊv] *pret. von* strive.

struck [strʌk] *pret. u. p.p. von* strike 2.

struc·ture ['strʌktʃə] Bau(werk *n*) *m*; Struktur *f*, Gefüge *n*; Gebilde *n*.

strug·gle ['strʌgl] **1.** sich (ab)mühen; kämpfen, ringen; sich winden, zappeln, sich sträuben; **2.** Kampf *m*, Ringen *n*; Anstrengung *f*.

strum [strʌm] (*-mm-*) klimpern (auf).

strung [strʌŋ] *pret. u. p.p. von* string 2.

strut [strʌt] **1.** (*-tt-*) *v/i.* stolzieren; *v/t.* ⊕ abstützen; **2.** Stolzieren *n*; ⊕ Strebe(balken *m*) *f*, Stütze *f*.

stub [stʌb] **1.** (Baum)Stumpf *m*; Stummel *m*; Kontrollabschnitt *m*; **2.** (*-bb-*) ~aus)roden; sich *die Zehe* anstoßen; ~ *out Zigarette etc.* ausdrücken.

stub·ble ['stʌbl] Stoppel(n *pl.*) *f*.

stub·born ☐ ['stʌbən] eigensinnig; widerspenstig; stur; hartnäckig.

stuck [stʌk] *pret. u. p.p. von* stick 2; **~up** F ['stʌk'ʌp] hochnäsig.

stud¹ [stʌd] **1.** Beschlagnagel *m*; Ziernagel *m*; Knauf *m*; Manschetten-, Kragenknopf *m*; **2.** (*-dd-*) mit Nägeln *etc.* beschlagen; übersäen.

stud² [~] Gestüt *n*; △ *nicht* Stute; *a.* **~horse** (Zucht)Hengst *m*; **~book** Gestütbuch *n*, **~farm** Gestüt *n*; **~mare** Zuchtstute *f*.

stu·dent ['stjuːdnt] Student(in); *Am.* Schüler(in).

stud·ied ☐ ['stʌdɪd] einstudiert; gesucht, gewollt; wohlüberlegt.

stu·di·o ['stjuːdɪəʊ] (*pl. -os*) Atelier *n*, Studio *n*; (Fernseh-, Rundfunk-) Studio *n*, Aufnahme-, Senderaum *m*.

stu·di·ous ☐ ['stjuːdjəs] fleißig; eifrig bemüht; sorgfältig, peinlich.

stud·y ['stʌdɪ] **1.** Studium *n*; Studier-, Arbeitszimmer *n*; *paint. etc.* Studie *f*; *studies pl.* Studium *n*, Studien *pl.*; *in a brown* ~ in Gedanken versunken, geistesabwesend; **2.** (ein)studieren; lernen; studieren, erforschen; sich bemühen um.

stuff [stʌf] **1.** Stoff *m*; Zeug *n*; **2.** *v/t.* (voll-, aus)stopfen; füllen; △ *nicht* stopfen (*ausbessern*); *v/i.* sich vollstopfen; **~ing** ['stʌfɪŋ] Füllung *f*; **~y** ☐ [~ɪ] (*-ier, -iest*) dumpf, muffig, stickig; langweilig, fad; F spießig; F prüde.

stum·ble ['stʌmbl] **1.** Stolpern *n*, Straucheln *n*; Fehltritt *m*; **2.** stolpern, straucheln; ~ *across*, ~ *on*, ~ *upon* zufällig stoßen auf (*acc.*).

stump [stʌmp] **1.** Stumpf *m*, Stummel *m*; **2.** *v/t.* F verblüffen; *v/i.* stampfen, stapfen; **~y** ☐ ['stʌmpɪ] (*-ier, -iest*) gedrungen; plump.

stun [stʌn] (*-nn-*) betäuben (*a. fig.*).

stung [stʌŋ] *pret. u. p.p. von* sting 2.

stunk [stʌŋk] *pret. u. p.p. von* stink 2.

stun·ning ☐ F ['stʌnɪŋ] toll, phantastisch.

stunt¹ [stʌnt] Kunststück *n*; (Reklame)Trick *m*; Sensation *f*; ~ *man* *Film:* Stuntman *m*, Double *m*.

stunt² [~] (im Wachstum *etc.*) hemmen; **~ed** ['stʌntɪd] verkümmert.

stu·pe·fy ['stjuːpɪfaɪ] betäuben; *fig.* verblüffen.

stu·pen·dous ☐ [stjuː'pendəs] verblüffend, erstaunlich.

stu·pid ☐ ['stjuːpɪd] dumm, einfältig; stumpfsinnig, blöd; **~i·ty** [stjuː'pɪdətɪ] Dummheit *f*; Stumpfsinn *m*.

stu·por ['stjuːpə] Erstarrung *f*, Betäubung *f*.

stur·dy ☐ ['stɜːdɪ] (*-ier, -iest*) robust, kräftig; *fig.* entschlossen.

stut·ter ['stʌtə] **1.** stottern; stammeln; **2.** Stottern *n*; Stammeln *n*.

sty¹ [staɪ] Schweinestall *m*.

sty², **stye** ✱ [~] Gerstenkorn *n*.

style [staɪl] **1.** Stil *m*; Mode *f*; (Mach)Art *f*; Titel *m*, Anrede *f*; **2.** nennen; entwerfen; gestalten.

styl·ish ☐ ['staɪlɪʃ] stilvoll; elegant; **~ish·ness** [~nɪs] Eleganz *f*; **~ist** [~st] Stilist(in).

suave ☐ [swɑːv] verbindlich; mild.

sub- [sʌb] Unter..., unter...; Neben..., untergeordnet; Hilfs...; fast ...

sub·di·vi·sion ['sʌbdɪvɪʒn] Unterteilung *f*; Unterabteilung *f*.

sub·due [səb'djuː] unterwerfen; bezwingen; bändigen; dämpfen.

sub·ject 1. ['sʌbdʒɪkt] unterworfen; untergeben; abhängig; untertan; ausgesetzt (*to dat.*); *be* ~ *to* neigen

successor

zu; ~ *to* vorbehaltlich (*gen.*); **2.** [~] Untertan(in); Staatsbürger(in), -angehörige(r *m*) *f*; *gr.* Subjekt *n*, Satzgegenstand *m*; Thema *n*, Gegenstand *m*; (Lehr-, Schul-, Studien-) Fach *n*; **3.** [səb'dʒekt] unterwerfen; *fig.* unterwerfen, -ziehen, aussetzen (*to dat.*); **~·jec·tion** [~kʃn] Unterwerfung *f*; Abhängigkeit *f*.

sub·ju·gate ['sʌbdʒʊgeɪt] unterjochen, -werfen.

sub·junc·tive *gr.* [səb'dʒʌŋktɪv] *a.* ~ *mood* Konjunktiv *m*.

sub|lease ['sʌb'li:s], **~let** (-*tt*-; -*let*) untervermieten.

sub·lime □ [sə'blaɪm] erhaben.

sub·ma·chine gun [sʌbmə'ʃi:n gʌn] Maschinenpistole *f*.

sub·ma·rine ['sʌbməri:n] **1.** unterseeisch, Untersee...; **2.** ♣, ⚔ Unterseeboot *n*.

sub·merge [səb'mɜ:dʒ] (unter)tauchen; überschwemmen.

sub·mis|sion [səb'mɪʃn] Unterwerfung *f*; Unterbreitung *f*; **~·sive** □ [~sɪv] unterwürfig; ergeben.

sub·mit [səb'mɪt] (-*tt*-) (sich) unterwerfen *od.* -ziehen; unterbreiten, vorlegen; sich fügen *od.* ergeben (*to dat. od.* in *acc.*).

sub·or·di·nate 1. □ [sə'bɔ:dɪnət] untergeordnet; nebensächlich; ~ *clause gr.* Nebensatz *m*; **2.** [~] Untergebene(r *m*) *f*; **3.** [~eɪt] unterordnen.

sub|scribe [səb'skraɪb] *v/t.* Geld stiften, spenden (*to* für); Summe zeichnen; mit *s-m* Namen unterzeichnen, unterschreiben mit; *v/i.* ~ *to Zeitung etc.* abonnieren; **~·scrib·er** [~ə] (Unter)Zeichner(in); Spender(in); Abonnent(in); *teleph.* Teilnehmer(in), Anschluß *m*.

sub·scrip·tion [səb'skrɪpʃn] Vorbestellung *f*, Subskription *f*; (Mitglieds)Beitrag *m*; Spende *f*.

sub·se·quent ['sʌbsɪkwənt] (nach-)folgend; später; **~·ly** nachher, später.

sub·ser·vi·ent □ [səb'sɜːvjənt] dienlich; unterwürfig.

sub|side [səb'saɪd] sinken; sich senken; sich setzen; sich legen (*Wind etc.*); ~ *into* verfallen in (*acc.*); **~·sid·i·a·ry** [~'sɪdjərɪ] **1.** □ Hilfs...; Neben...; untergeordnet; **2.** *econ.* Tochter(gesellschaft) *f*; **~·si·dize** ['sʌbsɪdaɪz] subventionieren; **~·si·dy** [~ɪ] Beihilfe *f*; Subvention *f*.

sub|sist [səb'sɪst] leben, sich ernähren (*on* von); **~·sis·tence** [~əns] Dasein *n*, Existenz *f*; (Lebens)Unterhalt *m*.

sub·stance ['sʌbstəns] Substanz *f*; das Wesentliche, Kern *m*, Gehalt *m*; Vermögen *n*.

sub·stan·dard ['sʌb'stændəd] unter der Norm; ~ *film* Schmalfilm *m*.

sub·stan·tial □ [səb'stænʃl] wesentlich; wirklich (vorhanden); beträchtlich; reichlich; kräftig; stark; solid; vermögend; namhaft (*Summe*).

sub·stan·ti·ate [səb'stænʃɪeɪt] beweisen, begründen.

sub·stan·tive *gr.* ['sʌbstəntɪv] Substantiv *n*, Hauptwort *n*.

sub·sti·tute ['sʌbstɪtjuːt] **1.** an die Stelle setzen *od.* treten (*for* von); ~ *s.th. for s.th.* et. durch et. ersetzen, et. gegen et. austauschen *od.* -wechseln; **2.** Stellvertreter(in), Vertretung *f*; Ersatz *m*; **~·tu·tion** [sʌbstɪ'tjuːʃn] Stellvertretung *f*; Ersatz *m*; *Sport:* Auswechslung *f*.

sub·ter·fuge ['sʌbtəfjuːdʒ] Vorwand *m*, Ausflucht *f*; List *f*.

sub·ter·ra·ne·an □ ['sʌbtə'reɪnjən] unterirdisch.

sub·ti·tle ['sʌbtaɪtl] Untertitel *m*.

sub·tle □ ['sʌtl] (~*r*, ~*st*) fein(sinnig); subtil; scharf(sinnig).

sub·tract ⚑ [səb'trækt] abziehen, subtrahieren.

sub·trop·i·cal ['sʌb'trɒpɪkl] subtropisch.

sub|urb ['sʌbɜːb] Vorstadt *f*, -ort *m*; **~·ur·ban** [sə'bɜːbən] vorstädtisch.

sub·ven·tion [səb'venʃn] Subvention *f*.

sub·ver|sion [səb'vɜːʃn] Umsturz *m*; **~·sive** □ [~sɪv] umstürzlerisch, subversiv; **~t** [~t] stürzen.

sub·way ['sʌbweɪ] (Straßen-, Fußgänger)Unterführung *f*; *Am.* Untergrundbahn *f*, U-Bahn *f*.

suc·ceed [sək'siːd] *v/i.* Erfolg haben; glücken, gelingen; ~ *to* folgen (*dat.*) *od.* auf (*acc.*), nachfolgen (*dat.*); *v/t.* (nach)folgen (*dat.*), *j-s* Nachfolger werden.

suc·cess [sək'ses] Erfolg *m*; **~·ful** □ [~fl] erfolgreich.

suc·ces|sion [sək'seʃn] (Nach-, Erb-, Reihen)Folge *f*; *in* ~ nacheinander; **~·sive** □ [~sɪv] aufeinanderfolgend; **~·sor** [~ə] Nachfolger(in).

suc·co(u)r ['sʌkə] 1. Hilfe f; 2. helfen.
suc·cu·lent □ ['sʌkjolənt] saftig.
suc·cumb [sə'kʌm] unter-, erliegen.
such [sʌtʃ] solche(r, -s); derartige(r, -s); so; ~ a man ein solcher Mann; ~ as diejenigen, welche; wie.
suck [sʌk] 1. saugen (an dat.); aussaugen; lutschen (an dat.); 2. Saugen n; ~**er** ['sʌkə] Saugorgan n; ♀ Wurzelschößling m; F Trottel m, Simpel m; ~**le** [~l] säugen, stillen; ~**ling** [~lɪŋ] Säugling m.
suc·tion ['sʌkʃn] (An)Saugen n; Sog m; attr. (An)Saug...
sud·den □ ['sʌdn] plötzlich; (all) of a ~ (ganz) plötzlich.
suds [sʌdz] pl. Seifenlauge f; Seifenschaum f; ~**y** ['sʌdzɪ] (-ier, -iest) schaumig.
sue [sjuː] v/t. verklagen (for auf acc., wegen); a. ~ out erwirken; v/i. nachsuchen (for um); klagen.
suede, suède [sweɪd] Wildleder n.
su·et ['sjoɪt] Nierenfett n, Talg m.
suf·fer ['sʌfə] v/i. leiden (from an, unter dat.); büßen; v/t. erleiden, erdulden; (zu)lassen; ~**ance** [~rəns] Duldung f; ~**er** [~ə] Leidende(r m) f; Dulder(in); ~**ing** [~ɪŋ] Leiden n.
suf·fice [sə'faɪs] genügen; ~ it to say es genügt wohl, wenn ich sage.
suf·fi·cien·cy [sə'fɪʃnsɪ] hinreichende Menge; Auskommen n; ~**t** [~t] genügend, genug, ausreichend; be ~ genügen, (aus)reichen.
suf·fix ['sʌfɪks] Suffix n, Nachsilbe f.
suf·fo·cate ['sʌfəkeɪt] ersticken.
suf·frage ['sʌfrɪdʒ] (Wahl)Stimme f; Wahl-, Stimmrecht n.
suf·fuse [sə'fjuːz] übergießen; überziehen.
sug·ar ['ʃogə] 1. Zucker m; 2. zuckern; ~**ba·sin**, bsd. Am. ~ **bowl** Zuckerdose f; ~**cane** ♀ Zuckerrohr n; ~**coat** überzuckern; fig. versüßen; ~**y** [~rɪ] zuckerig; fig. zuckersüß.
sug|gest [sə'dʒest, Am. a. səg'dʒest] vorschlagen, anregen; nahelegen; hinweisen auf (acc.); Gedanken eingeben; andeuten; denken lassen an (acc.); ~**ges·tion** [~tʃən] Anregung f, Vorschlag m; psych. Suggestion f; Eingebung f; Andeutung f; ~**ges·tive** □ [~tɪv] anregend; vielsagend; zweideutig; be ~ of s.th. auf et. hindeuten; an et. denken lassen; den Eindruck von et. erwecken.

su·i·cide ['sjoɪsaɪd] 1. Selbstmord m; Selbstmörder(in); commit ~ Selbstmord begehen; 2. Am. Selbstmord begehen.
suit [sjuːt] 1. (Herren)Anzug m; (Damen)Kostüm n; Anliegen n; Werben n (um e-e Frau); Karten: Farbe f; ⚖ Prozeß m; follow ~ fig. dem Beispiel folgen, dasselbe tun; 2. v/t. j-m passen, zusagen, bekommen; j-n kleiden, j-m stehen, passen zu; ~ oneself tun, was er-m beliebt; ~ yourself mach, was du willst; ~ s.th. to et. anpassen (dat.) od. an (acc.); be ~ed geeignet sein (for, to für, zu); v/i. passen; **sui·ta·ble** □ ['sjuːtəbl] passend, geeignet (for, to für, zu); ~**case** (Hand)Koffer m.
suite [swiːt] Gefolge n; ♪ Suite f; Zimmerflucht f, Suite f; (Möbel-, Sitz)Garnitur f, (Zimmer)Einrichtung f.
sui·tor ['sjuːtə] Freier m; ⚖ Kläger(in).
sul·fur ['sʌlfə] etc. Am. ['sʌlfə] s. sulphur, etc.
sulk [sʌlk] schmollen, eingeschnappt sein; ~**i·ness** ['sʌlkɪnɪs], ~**s** pl. Schmollen n; ~**y** [~ɪ] 1. □ (-ier, -iest) verdrießlich; schmollend; 2. Sport: Sulky m, Traberwagen m.
sul·len □ ['sʌlən] verdrossen, mürrisch; düster, trübe.
sul·ly mst fig. ['sʌlɪ] beflecken.
sul|phur ⚗ ['sʌlfə] Schwefel m; ~**phu·ric** ⚗ [sʌl'fjʊərɪk] Schwefel...
sul·tri·ness ['sʌltrɪnɪs] Schwüle f.
sul·try □ ['sʌltrɪ] (-ier, -iest) schwül; fig. heftig, hitzig.
sum [sʌm] 1. Summe f; Betrag m; Rechenaufgabe f; fig. Inbegriff m; do ~s rechnen; 2. (-mm-) ~ up zusammenzählen, addieren; j-n kurz einschätzen; Situation erfassen; zusammenfassen.
sum|ma·rize ['sʌməraɪz] zusammenfassen; ~**ma·ry** [~ɪ] 1. □ kurz (zusammengefaßt); ⚖ Schnell...; 2. (kurze) Inhaltsangabe, Zusammenfassung f.
sum·mer ['sʌmə] Sommer m; ~ school Ferienkurs m; ~**ly** [~lɪ], ~**y** [~rɪ] sommerlich.
sum·mit ['sʌmɪt] Gipfel m (a. fig.).
sum·mon ['sʌmən] auffordern; (einbe)rufen; ⚖ vorladen; ~ up Mut etc. zusammennehmen, auf-

supply

bieten; ~s Aufforderung f; ♙ Vorladung f.

sump·tu·ous □ ['sʌmptjʊəs] kostspielig; üppig, aufwendig.

sun [sʌn] **1.** Sonne f; *attr.* Sonnen...; **2.** (-nn-) der Sonne aussetzen; ~ (o.s.) sich sonnen; **~·bath** ['sʌnbɑ:θ] Sonnenbad n; **~·beam** Sonnenstrahl m; **~·burn** Sonnenbräune f; Sonnenbrand m.

sun·dae ['sʌndeɪ] Eisbecher m mit Früchten.

Sun·day ['sʌndɪ] Sonntag m; on ~ (am) Sonntag; on ~s sonntags.

sun·di·al ['sʌndaɪəl] Sonnenuhr f; **~·down** = sunset.

sun·dries ['sʌndrɪz] *pl.* Diverse(s) n, Verschiedene(s) n; **~·dry** [~ɪ] verschiedene.

sung [sʌŋ] *p.p. von* sing.

sun·glass·es ['sʌnglɑ:sɪz] *pl.* (a pair of ~ e-e) Sonnenbrille.

sunk [sʌŋk] *pret. u. p.p. von* sink 1.

sunk·en *adj.* ['sʌŋkən] versunken; tiefliegend; *fig.* eingefallen.

sun·ny □ ['sʌnɪ] (-ier, -iest) sonnig; **~·rise** Sonnenaufgang m; **~·set** Sonnenuntergang m; **~·shade** Sonnenschirm m; Markise f; **~·shine** Sonnenschein m; **~·stroke** ♨ Sonnenstich m; **~·tan** (Sonnen)Bräune f.

su·per F ['su:pə] super, toll, prima, Spitze, Klasse.

su·per- ['sju:pə] Über..., über...; Ober..., über...; Super..., Groß...; **~·a·bun·dant** □ [~rə'bʌndənt] überreichlich; überschwenglich; **~·an·nu·ate** [sju:pə'rænjʊeɪt] pensionieren; ~d pensioniert; veraltet.

su·perb □ [sju:'pɜ:b] prächtig, herrlich, großartig; ausgezeichnet.

su·per·charg·er *mot.* ['sju:pətʃɑ:dʒə] Kompressor m; **~·cil·i·ous** □ [~'sɪlɪəs] hochmütig; **~·fi·cial** □ [~'fɪʃl] oberflächlich; **~·fine** [~'faɪn] extrafein; **~·flu·i·ty** [~'flʊɪtɪ] Überfluß m; **~·flu·ous** [~'pɜ:flʊəs] überflüssig; überreichlich; **~·heat** ⊕ ['sju:pə'hi:t] überhitzen; **~·hu·man** □ [~'hju:mən] übermenschlich; **~·im·pose** [~rɪm'pəʊz] darauf-, darüberlegen; überlagern; **~·in·tend** [~rɪn'tend] die (Ober)Aufsicht haben über (*acc.*), überwachen; leiten; **~·in·tend·ent** [~ənt] **1.** Leiter m, Direktor m; (Ober)Aufseher m, Inspektor m; *Brt.* Kommissar (-in); *Am.* Polizeichef m; *Am.*

Hausverwalter m; **2.** aufsichtführend.

su·pe·ri·or [sju:'pɪərɪə] **1.** □ höhere(r, -s), höherstehend, vorgesetzt; besser, hochwertiger; überlegen (*to dat.*); hervorragend; **2.** Höherstehende(r m) f, bsd. Vorgesetzte(r m) f; *mst Father* ⚜ eccl. Superior m; *mst Lady* ⚜, *Mother* ⚜ eccl. Oberin f; **~·i·ty** [sju:pɪərɪ'ɒrətɪ] Überlegenheit f.

su·per·la·tive [sju:'pɜ:lətɪv] **1.** □ höchste(r, -s); überragend; **2.** a. ~ degree gr. Superlativ m.

su·per·mar·ket ['sju:pəmɑ:kɪt] Supermarkt m; **~·nat·u·ral** □ [~'nætʃrəl] übernatürlich; **~·nu·me·ra·ry** [~'nju:mərərɪ] **1.** überzählig; zusätzlich; **2.** Zusatzperson f, -sache f; *thea., Film:* Statist(in); **~·scrip·tion** [~'skrɪpʃn] Über-, Aufschrift f; **~·sede** [~'si:d] ersetzen; verdrängen; absetzen; ablösen; **~·son·ic** phys. [~'sɒnɪk] Überschall...; **~·sti·tion** [~'stɪʃn] Aberglaube m; **~·sti·tious** □ [~'stɪʃəs] abergläubisch; **~·vene** [~'vi:n] (noch) hinzukommen; dazwischenkommen; **~·vise** [~'vaɪz] beaufsichtigen, überwachen; **~·vi·sion** [~'vɪʒn] (Ober)Aufsicht f; Beaufsichtigung f, Überwachung f; **~·vi·sor** [~'vaɪzə] Aufseher(in); Leiter(in).

sup·per ['sʌpə] Abendessen n; *the (Lord's)* ⚜ *the* heilige Abendmahl.

sup·plant [sə'plɑ:nt] verdrängen.

sup·ple ['sʌpl] **1.** □ (~r, ~st) geschmeidig; **2.** geschmeidig machen.

sup·ple·ment 1. ['sʌplɪmənt] Ergänzung f; Nachtrag m; (Zeitungs- etc.)Beilage f; **2.** [~ment] ergänzen; **~·men·tal** □ [sʌplɪ'mentl], **~·men·ta·ry** [~ərɪ] ergänzend; nachträglich; Nachtrags...

sup·pli·ant ['sʌplɪənt] **1.** □ demütig bittend, flehend; **2.** Bittsteller(in).

sup·pli·cate ['sʌplɪkeɪt] demütig bitten; (an)flehen; **~·ca·tion** [sʌplɪ'keɪʃn] demütige Bitte.

sup·pli·er [sə'plaɪə] Lieferant(in); a. ~s pl. Lieferfirma f.

sup·ply [sə'plaɪ] **1.** liefern; *e-m Mangel* abhelfen; *e-e Stelle* ausfüllen; beliefern, ausstatten, versorgen; ergänzen; **2.** Lieferung f; Versorgung f; Zufuhr f; *econ.* Angebot n; (Stell)Vertretung f; *mst supplies pl.* Vorrat m; *econ.* Artikel m, Bedarf m;

parl. bewilligter Etat; ~ **and demand** *econ.* Angebot u. Nachfrage.

sup·port [sə'pɔːt] **1.** Stütze *f*; Hilfe *f*; ⊕ Träger *m*; Unterstützung *f*; (Lebens)Unterhalt *m*; **2.** tragen, (ab)stützen; unterstützen; unterhalten, sorgen für (*Familie etc.*); ertragen; ~**er** [~ə] Anhänger(in) (*a. Sport*), Befürworter(in).

sup·pose [sə'pəʊz] annehmen; voraussetzen; vermuten; *he is* ~*d to do* er soll tun; ~ *we go* gehen wir!; wie wär's, wenn wir gingen?; *what is that* ~ *to mean?* was soll denn das?; *I* ~ *so* ich nehme es an, vermutlich.

sup|**posed** □ [sə'pəʊzd] vermeintlich; ~**pos·ed·ly** [~ɪdlɪ] angeblich.

sup·po·si·tion [sʌpə'zɪʃn] Voraussetzung *f*; Annahme *f*, Vermutung *f*.

sup|**press** [sə'pres] unterdrücken; ~**pres·sion** [~ʃn] Unterdrückung *f*.

sup·pu·rate ⚕ ['sʌpjʊəreɪt] eitern.

su·prem|**a·cy** [sjʊ'preməsɪ] Oberhoheit *f*; Vorherrschaft *f*; Überlegenheit *f*; Vorrang *m*; ~**e** [~] [sjuː'priːm] höchste(r, -s); oberste(r, -s); Ober ...; ~ größte(r, -s).

sur·charge 1. [sɜː'tʃɑːdʒ] e-n Zuschlag *od.* ein Nachporto *etc.* erheben auf (*acc.*); **2.** ['sɜːtʃɑːdʒ] Zuschlag *m*; Nach-, Strafporto *n*; Über-, Aufdruck *m* (*auf Briefmarken*).

sure [ʃʊə] **1.** *adj.* □ (~, ~*st*): ~ (*of*) sicher, gewiß (*gen.*); überzeugt (von); *make* ~ *that* sich (davon) überzeugen, daß; **2.** *adv. Am.* F wirklich; *it* ~ *was cold Am.* F es war vielleicht kalt!; ~*!* klar!, aber sicher!; ~ *enough* ganz bestimmt; tatsächlich; ~**ly** ['ʃʊəlɪ] sicher(lich); **sure·ty** [~tɪ] Kaution *f*; Bürge *m*.

surf [sɜːf] **1.** Brandung *f*; **2.** *Sport:* surfen.

sur·face ['sɜːfɪs] *f*; (Ober)Fläche *f*; ✈ Tragfläche *f*; **2.** ♱ auftauchen (*U-Boot*).

surf|**board** ['sɜːfbɔːd] Surfbrett *n*; ~**boat** Brandungsboot *n*.

sur·feit ['sɜːfɪt] **1.** Übersättigung *f*; Überdruß *m*; **2.** (sich) übersättigen *od.* -füttern.

surf|**er** ['sɜːfə] *Sport:* Surfer(in), Wellenreiter(in); ~**ing** [~ɪŋ], ~**rid·ing** [~raɪdɪŋ] *Sport:* Surfen *n*, Wellenreiten *n*.

surge [sɜːdʒ] **1.** Woge *f*; **2.** wogen; (vorwärts)drängen; *a.* ~ *up* (auf)wallen (*Gefühle*).

sur|**geon** ['sɜːdʒən] Chirurg *m*; ~**ge·ry** [~rɪ] Chirurgie *f*; operativer Eingriff, Operation *f*; *Brt.* Sprechzimmer *n*; ~ *hours pl. Brt.* Sprechstunde(n *pl.*) *f*.

sur·gi·cal □ ['sɜːdʒɪkl] chirurgisch.

sur·ly □ ['sɜːlɪ] (*-ier, -iest*) mürrisch, grob.

sur·mise 1. ['sɜːmaɪz] Vermutung *f*; **2.** [sɜː'maɪz] vermuten.

sur·mount [sɜː'maʊnt] überwinden.

sur·name ['sɜːneɪm] Familien-, Nach-, Zuname *m*.

sur·pass *fig.* [sə'pɑːs] übersteigen, -treffen; ~**ing** [~ɪŋ] unvergleichlich.

sur·plus ['sɜːpləs] **1.** Überschuß *m*, Mehr *n*; **2.** überschüssig; Über(schuß) ...

sur·prise [sə'praɪz] **1.** Überraschung *f*; ✕ Überrump(e)lung *f*; **2.** überraschen; ✕ überrumpeln.

sur·ren·der [sə'rendə] **1.** Übergabe *f*; Kapitulation *f*; Aufgabe *f*, Verzicht *m*; Hingabe *f*; **2.** *v/t. et.* übergeben; aufgeben; *v/i.* sich ergeben (*to dat.*), kapitulieren; sich hingeben *od.* überlassen (*to dat.*).

sur·ro·gate ['sʌrəgɪt] Ersatz *m*; ~ *mother* Leihmutter *f*.

sur·round [sə'raʊnd] umgeben; ✕ umzingeln, -stellen; ~**ing** [~ɪŋ] umliegend; ~**ings** *pl.* Umgebung *f*.

sur·tax ['sɜːtæks] Steuerzuschlag *m*.

sur·vey 1. [sə'veɪ] überblicken; sorgfältig prüfen; begutachten; *Land* vermessen; **2.** ['sɜːveɪ] Überblick *m* (*a. fig.*); sorgfältige Prüfung; Inspektion *f*, Besichtigung *f*; Gutachten *n*; (Land)Vermessung *f*; (Lage-) Karte *f*, (-)Plan *m*; ~**or** [sə'veɪə] Landmesser *m*; (amtlicher) Inspektor.

sur|**viv·al** [sə'vaɪvl] Überleben *n*; Fortleben *n*; Überbleibsel *n*; ~ *kit* Überlebensausrüstung *f*; ~**vive** [~aɪv] überleben, am Leben bleiben; noch leben; fortleben; bestehen bleiben; ~**vi·vor** [~ə] Überlebende(r *m*) *f*.

sus·cep·ti·ble □ [sə'septəbl] empfänglich (*to* für); empfindlich (*to* gegen); *be* ~ *of et.* zulassen.

sus·pect 1. [sə'spekt] (be)argwöhnen; in Verdacht haben, verdächtigen; vermuten, befürchten; **2.** ['sʌspekt] Verdächtige(r *m*) *f*; **3.** [~] = ~**ed** [sə'spektɪd] verdächtig.

sus·pend [sə'spend] (auf)hängen;

aufschieben; in der Schwebe lassen; *Zahlung* einstellen; ⚖ *Verfahren etc.* aussetzen; suspendieren; *Sport: j-n* sperren; **~ed** [~ɪd] schwebend; hängend; ⚖ zur Bewährung ausgesetzt; suspendiert; **~er** [~ə] *Brt.* Strumpf-, Sockenhalter *m*; *(a. a pair of)* ~s *pl. Am.* Hosenträger *pl.*

sus|pense [sə'spens] *f.* Ungewißheit *f*; Unentschiedenheit *f*; Spannung *f*; **~pen·sion** [~ʃn] Aufhängung *f*; Aufschub *m*; (einstweilige) Einstellung; Suspendierung *f*, Amtsenthebung *f*; *Sport:* Sperre *f*; ~ **bridge** Hängebrücke *f*; ~ **railroad**, *bsd. Brt.* ~ **railway** Schwebebahn *f*.

sus·pi|cion [sə'spiʃn] Verdacht *m*; Mißtrauen *n*; *fig.* Spur *f*; **~cious** □ [~əs] verdächtig; mißtrauisch.

sus·tain [sə'steɪn] stützen, tragen; *et.* (aufrecht)erhalten; aushalten *(a. fig.)*; erleiden; *Familie* ernähren; *j-m* Kraft geben; ⚖ *e-m Einspruch* stattgeben.

sus·te·nance ['sʌstɪnəns] (Lebens-) Unterhalt *m*; Nahrung *f*.

swab [swɒb] **1.** Scheuerlappen *m*, Mop *m*; ✚ Tupfer *m*; ✚ Abstrich *m*; **2.** *(-bb-)* ~ *up* aufwischen.

swad·dle ['swɒdl] *Baby* wickeln; **~dling-clothes** [~ɪŋkləʊðz] *pl.* Windeln *pl.*

swag·ger ['swægə] stolzieren; prahlen, großtun.

swal·low¹ *zo.* ['swɒləʊ] Schwalbe *f*.

swal·low² [~] **1.** Schlund *m*; Schluck *m*; **2.** (hinunter-, ver)schlucken; *Beleidigung* einstecken, schlucken; F für bare Münze nehmen.

swam [swæm] *pret. von* swim 1.

swamp [swɒmp] **1.** Sumpf *m*; **2.** überschwemmen *(a. fig.)*; *Boot* vollaufen lassen; **~y** ['swɒmpɪ] *(-ier, -iest)* sumpfig.

swan *zo.* [swɒn] Schwan *m*.

swank F [swæŋk] **1.** Angabe *f*, Protzerei *f*; **2.** angeben, protzen; **~y** F ['swæŋkɪ] *(-ier, -iest)* protzig, angeberisch.

swap F [swɒp] **1.** Tausch *m*; **2.** *(-pp-)* (ein-, aus)tauschen.

swarm [swɔːm] **1.** (Bienen- *etc.*) Schwarm *m*; Haufen *m*, Schar *f*, Horde *f*; **2.** schwärmen *(Bienen)*; wimmeln *(with von)*.

swar·thy □ ['swɔːðɪ] *(-ier, -iest)* dunkel(häutig).

swash [swɒʃ] plan(t)schen.

swat [swɒt] *(-tt-)* *Fliege etc.* totschlagen.

sway [sweɪ] **1.** Schwanken *n*; Einfluß *m*; Herrschaft *f*; **2.** schwanken; (sich) wiegen; schwingen; beeinflussen; beherrschen.

swear [sweə] *(swore, sworn)* schwören; fluchen; ~ *s.o. in* j-n vereidigen.

sweat [swet] **1.** Schweiß *m*; Schwitzen *n*; *by the* ~ *of one's brow* im Schweiße seines Angesichts; *in a* ~, F *all of a* ~ in Schweiß gebadet *(a. fig.)*; **2.** *(sweated, Am. mst sweat)* *v/i.* schwitzen; *v/t.* (aus)schwitzen; in Schweiß bringen; *econ.* schuften lassen, ausbeuten; **~er** ['swetə] Sweater *m*, Pullover *m*; *econ.* Ausbeuter *m*; **~shirt** Sweatshirt *n*; ~ **suit** *Sport: bsd. Am.* Trainingsanzug *m*; **~y** □ [~ɪ] *(-ier, -iest)* verschwitzt.

Swede [swiːd] Schwed|e *m*, -in *f*.

Swed·ish ['swiːdɪʃ] **1.** schwedisch; **2.** *ling.* Schwedisch *n*.

sweep [swiːp] **1.** *(swept)* fegen *(a. fig.)*, kehren; gleiten *od.* schweifen über *(acc.)* *(Blick)*; (majestätisch) einherschreiten *od.* (dahin)rauschen; **2.** *(fig.* Dahin)Fegen *n*; Kehren *n*; schwungvolle Bewegung; Schwung *m*; Spielraum *m*, Bereich *m*; *bsd. Brt.* Schornsteinfeger *m*; *make a clean* ~ gründlich aufräumen *(of mit)*; *Sport:* überlegen siegen; **~er** ['swiːpə] (Straßen)Kehrer(in); Kehrmaschine *f*; **~ing** □ [~ɪŋ] schwungvoll; umfassend; **~ings** *pl.* Kehricht *m*, Müll *m*.

sweet [swiːt] **1.** □ süß; lieblich; freundlich; frisch; duftend; *have a* ~ *tooth* gern Süßes essen; **2.** *Brt.* Süßigkeit *f*, Bonbon *m*, *n*; *Brt.* Nachtisch *m*; Süße(r *m*) *f*, Schatz *m* *(als Anrede)*; **~en** ['swiːtn] (ver)süßen; **~heart** Schatz *m*, Liebste(r *m*) *f*; **~ish** [~ɪʃ] süßlich; **~meat** Bonbon *m*, *n*; kandierte Frucht; **~ness** [~nɪs] Süße *f*, Süßigkeit *f*; ~ **pea** ⚘ Gartenwicke *f*; **~shop** *Brt.* Süßwarenladen *m*.

swell [swel] **1.** *(swelled, swollen od. swelled)* *v/i.* (an)schwellen; sich (auf)blähen; sich bauschen; *v/t.* (an)schwellen lassen; aufblähen; **2.** *Am.* F prima; **3.** Anschwellen *n*; Schwellung *f*; ♩ Dünung *f*; **~ing** ['swelɪŋ] Schwellung *f*, Geschwulst *f*.

S

swel·ter ['sweltə] vor Hitze umkommen.

swept [swept] *pret. u. p.p. von* sweep 1.

swerve [swɜːv] 1. ausbrechen (*Auto, Pferd*); *mot.* das Steuer *od.* den Wagen herumreißen; schwenken (*Straße*); 2. *mot.* Schlenker *m*; Ausweichbewegung *f*; Schwenk *m* (*e-r Straße*).

swift □ [swift] schnell, eilig, flink; **~·ness** ['swiftnɪs] Schnelligkeit *f*.

swill [swil] 1. (Ab)Spülen *n*; Spülicht *n*; 2. (ab)spülen; F saufen.

swim [swim] 1. (-mm-; swam, swum) (durch)schwimmen; schweben; *my head ~s* mir ist schwind(e)lig; 2. Schwimmen *n*; *go for a ~* schwimmen gehen; *have od. take a ~* baden, schwimmen; *be in the ~* auf dem laufenden sein; **~·mer** ['swimə] Schwimmer(in); **~·ming** [~ɪŋ] 1. Schwimmen *n*; 2. Schwimm...; **~·bath(s** *pl.*) *Brt. bsd.* Hallenbad *n*; **~·pool** Schwimmbecken *n*, Swimmingpool *m*; Schwimmbad *n*; (*a pair of*) **~·trunks** *pl.* (e-e) Badehose; **~·suit** Badeanzug *m*.

swin·dle ['swindl] 1. beschwindeln; betrügen; △ *nicht* schwindeln; 2. Schwindel *m*, Betrug *m*.

swine [swain] Schwein *n*.

swing [swiŋ] 1. (swung) schwingen; schwenken; schlenkern; baumeln (lassen); (sich) schaukeln; sich (*in den Angeln*) drehen (*Tür*); F baumeln, hängen; 2. Schwingen *n*; Schwung *m*; Schaukel *f*; Spielraum *m*; *in full ~* in vollem Gange; **~·door** ['swiŋdɔː] Drehtür *f*.

swin·ish □ ['swainɪʃ] schweinisch.

swipe [swaip] 1. schlagen (*at* nach); F klauen; 2. harter Schlag.

swirl [swɜːl] 1. (herum)wirbeln, strudeln; 2. Wirbel *m*, Strudel *m*.

Swiss [swis] 1. schweizerisch, Schweizer...; 2. Schweizer(in); *the ~ pl.* die Schweizer *pl.*

switch [switʃ] 🚂 Gerte *f*; Am. 🚂 Weiche *f*; 🔌 Schalter *m*; falscher Zopf; 2. peitschen; *bsd. Am.* 🚂 rangieren; 🔌 (um)schalten; *fig.* wechseln, überleiten; **~ off** 🔌 ab-, ausschalten; **~ on** 🔌 an-, einschalten; **~·board** 🔌 ['switʃbɔːd] Schaltbrett *n*, -tafel *f*.

swiv·el ['swivl] 1. ⊕ Drehring *m*;

attr. Dreh...; 2. (*bsd. Brt.* -ll-, *Am.* -l-) (sich) drehen; schwenken.

swol·len ['swəʊlən] *p.p. von* swell 1.

swoon [swuːn] *veraltet* 1. Ohnmacht *f*; 2. in Ohnmacht fallen.

swoop [swuːp] 1. **~ down on** *od.* **upon** herabstoßen auf (*acc.*) (*Raubvogel*); *fig.* herfallen über (*acc.*); 2. Herabstoßen *n*; Razzia *f*.

swop F [swɒp] = swap.

sword [sɔːd] Schwert *n*; **~·man** ['sɔːdzmən] (*pl. -men*) Fechter *m*.

swore [swɔː] *pret. von* swear.

sworn [swɔːn] *p.p. von* swear.

swum [swʌm] *p.p. von* swim 1.

swung [swʌŋ] *pret. u. p.p. von* swing 1.

syc·a·more ♣ ['sikəmɔː] Bergahorn *m*; *Am.* Platane *f*.

syl·la·ble ['siləbl] Silbe *f*.

syl·la·bus ['siləbəs] (*pl. -buses, -bi* [-bai]) (*bsd.* Vorlesungs)Verzeichnis *n*; *bsd.* Lehrplan *m*.

sym·bol ['simbl] Symbol *n*, Sinnbild *n*; **~·ic** [sim'bɒlik], **~·i·cal** □ [~kl] sinnbildlich; **~·is·m** ['simbəlizəm] Symbolik *f*; **~·ize** [~aiz] symbolisieren.

sym·met·ric [si'metrik], **~·met·ri·cal** □ [~kl] symmetrisch, ebenmäßig; **~·me·try** ['simitri] Symmetrie *f*; Ebenmaß *n*.

sym·pa·thet·ic [simpə'θetik] (*~ally*) mitfühlend; △ *nicht* sympathisch; **~ strike** Sympathiestreik *m*; **~·thize** ['simpəθaiz] sympathisieren, mitfühlen; **~·thy** [~i] Anteilnahme *f*, Mitgefühl *n*; △ *nicht* Sympathie.

sym·pho·ny ♪ ['simfəni] Symphonie *f*.

symp·tom ['simptəm] Symptom *n*.

syn·chro·nize ['siŋkrənaiz] *v/i.* gleichzeitig sein; synchron gehen (*Uhr*) *od.* laufen (*Maschine*); *v/t.* Uhren, Maschinen, Film, TV synchronisieren; *Geschehen* aufeinander abstimmen; **~·nous** □ [~əs] gleichzeitig; synchron.

syn·di·cate ['sindikət] Syndikat *n*.

syn·o·nym ['sinənim] Synonym *n*; **sy·non·y·mous** □ [si'nɒniməs] synonym; gleichbedeutend.

sy·nop·sis [si'nɒpsis] (*pl. -ses* [-siːz]) Übersicht *f*, Zusammenfassung *f*.

syn·tax *gr.* ['sintæks] Syntax *f*.

syn·the·sis ['sinθəsis] (*pl. -ses* [-siːz]) Synthese *f*; **~·thet·ic** [sin'θetik], **~·thet·i·cal** □ [~kl] synthetisch.

take

sy·ringe ['sɪrɪndʒ] **1.** Spritze *f*; **2.** (be-, ein-, aus)spritzen.
syr·up ['sɪrəp] Sirup *m*.
sys|tem ['sɪstəm] System *n*;

physiol. Organismus *m*, Körper *m*; Plan *m*, Ordnung *f*; **~·te·mat·ic** [sɪstɪ'mætɪk] (~*ally*) systematisch.

T

ta *Brt. int.* F [tɑː] danke.
tab [tæb] Streifen *m*; Etikett *n*, Schildchen *n*, Anhänger *m*; Schlaufe *f*, (Mantel)Aufhänger *m*; F Rechnung *f*.
ta·ble ['teɪbl] **1.** Tisch *m*; Tafel *f*; Tisch-, Tafelrunde *f*; Tabelle *f*, Verzeichnis *n*; = *tableland*; *at ~* bei Tisch; *turn the ~s* den Spieß umdrehen (*on s.o.* j-m gegenüber); **2.** auf den Tisch legen; tabellarisch anordnen; **~·cloth** Tischtuch *n*, -decke *f*; **~·land** Tafelland *n*, Plateau *n*, Hochebene *f*; **~·lin·en** Tischwäsche *f*; **~·mat** Set *n*; *~ set* Rundfunk, *TV*: Tischgerät *n*; **~·spoon** Eßlöffel *m*.
tab·let ['tæblɪt] Tafelchen *n*; (Gedenk)Tafel *f*; (Schreib- *etc.*)Block *m*; Stück *n* (*Seife*); Tafel *f* (*Schokolade*); Tablette *f*; △ *nicht* Tablett.
table|top ['teɪbltɒp] Tischplatte *f*; **~·ware** Geschirr *n* u. Besteck *n*.
ta·boo [tə'buː] **1.** tabu, unantastbar; verboten; verpönt; **2.** Tabu *n*; **3.** *et.* für tabu erklären.
tab·u|lar □ ['tæbjʊlə] tabellarisch; **~·late** [~eɪt] tabellarisch (an)ordnen.
ta·cit □ ['tæsɪt] stillschweigend.
ta·ci·turn □ [~ɜːn] schweigsam.
tack [tæk] **1.** Stift *m*, Reißnagel *m*, Zwecke *f*; Heftstich *m*; ♣ Halse *f*; ♣ Gang *m* (*beim Lavieren*); *fig.* Weg *m*; **2.** *v/t.* heften (*to an acc.*); *v/i.* ♣ wenden; *fig.* lavieren.
tack·le ['tækl] **1.** Gerät *n*; ♣ Takel-, Tauwerk *n*; ⊕ Flaschenzug *m*; *Fußball*: Angreifen *n*; **2.** (an)packen; *Fußball*: angreifen; in Angriff nehmen; lösen, fertig werden mit.
tack·y ['tækɪ] (*-ier, -iest*) klebrig; *Am.* F schäbig.
tact [tækt] Takt *m*, Feingefühl *n*; **~·ful** □ ['tæktfl] taktvoll.
tac·tics ['tæktɪks] *pl. u. sg.* Taktik *f*.
tact·less □ ['tæktlɪs] taktlos.

tad·pole *zo.* ['tædpəʊl] Kaulquappe *f*.
taf·fe·ta ['tæfɪtə] Taft *m*.
taf·fy *Am.* ['tæfɪ] = *toffee*; F Schmus *m*, Schmeichelei *f*.
tag [tæg] **1.** (Schnürsenkel)Stift *m*; Schildchen *n*, Etikett *n*; loses Ende, Fetzen *m*, Lappen *m*; Redensart *f*, Zitat *n*; *a. question* ~ *gr.* Frageanhängsel *n*; Fangen *n* (*Kinderspiel*); **2.** (*-gg-*) etikettieren, auszeichnen; anhängen (*to, on to an acc.*); ~ *along* F mitkommen; ~ *along behind s.o.* hinter j-m hertrotten *od.* -zockeln.
tail [teɪl] **1.** Schwanz *m*; Schweif *m*; hinteres Ende, Schluß *m*; *~s pl.* Rückseite *f* (*e-r Münze*); *turn ~* davonlaufen; *~s up* in Hochstimmung, fidel; **2.** ~ *after s.o.* j-m hinterherlaufen; ~ *away, ~ off* abflauen, sich verlieren; nachlassen; **~·back** *mot.* ['teɪlbæk] Rückstau *m*; **~·coat** [~'kəʊt] Frack *m*; **~·light** *mot. etc.* [~laɪt] Rück-, Schlußlicht *n*.
tai·lor ['teɪlə] **1.** Schneider *m*; **2.** schneidern; *et.* gut *etc.* nach Maß...; **~·made** Schneider..., Maß...
taint [teɪnt] **1.** (Schand)Fleck *m*, Makel *m*; (verborgene) Anlage (*zu e-r Krankheit*); **2.** beflecken; verderben; ♠ anstecken; **3.** verderben, schlecht werden (*Fleisch etc.*).
take [teɪk] **1.** (*took, taken*) *v/t.* nehmen; (an-, ein-, entgegen-, heraus-, hin-, mit-, weg)nehmen; fassen; packen, ergreifen; fangen; ✕ gefangennehmen; sich aneignen, Besitz ergreifen von; (hin-, weg)bringen; △ *nicht herbringen*; *et. gut etc.* aufnehmen; *Beleidigung* hinnehmen; *et.* ertragen, aushalten; halten (*for* für); auffassen; *fig.* fesseln; *phot. et.* aufnehmen, *Aufnahme* machen; *Temperatur* messen; *Notiz* machen, nie-

derschreiben; *Prüfung* machen, ablegen; *Rast, Ferien etc.* machen; *Urlaub, ein Bad* nehmen; *Kleidergröße etc.* haben; sich *e-e Krankheit* holen; *Speisen* zu sich nehmen, *Mahlzeit* einnehmen; *Zeitung* beziehen; *Zug, Bus etc.* nehmen; *Weg* wählen; *j-n wohin* führen; *Preis* gewinnen; *Gelegenheit, Maßnahmen* ergreifen; *Vorsitz etc.* übernehmen; *Eid* ablegen; *Zeit, Geduld* erfordern, brauchen; *Zeit* dauern; *Mut* fassen; *Anstoß* nehmen; *I ~ it* that ich nehme an, daß; *~ it or leave it* F mach, was du willst; *~n all in all* im großen (u.) ganzen; *be ~n* besetzt sein; *be ~n ill od.* F *bad* krank werden; *be ~n with* begeistert *od.* entzückt sein von; *~ breath* verschnaufen; *~ comfort* sich trösten; *~ compassion on* Mitleid mit *j-m* haben; sich erbarmen (*gen.*); *~ counsel* beraten; *~ a drive* e-e Fahrt machen; *~ fire* Feuer fangen; *~ in hand* unternehmen; *~ hold of* ergreifen; *~ a look* e-n Blick tun *od.* werfen (*at* auf *acc.*); *Can I ~ a message?* Kann ich et. ausrichten?; *~ to pieces* auseinandernehmen, zerlegen; *~ pity on* Mitleid haben mit; *~ place* stattfinden; spielen (*Handlung*); △ *nicht* Platz nehmen; *~ a risk* ein Risiko eingehen *od.* auf sich nehmen; *~ a seat* Platz nehmen; *~ a walk* e-n Spaziergang machen; *~ my word for it* verlaß dich drauf; *~ along* mitnehmen; *~ apart* auseinandernehmen, zerlegen; *~ around j-n* herumführen; *~ away* wegnehmen; *... to ~ away* Brt. Schild: ... zum Mitnehmen; *~ down* herunternehmen; *Gebäude* abreißen; notieren; *~ from j-m* wegnehmen; *Å* abziehen von; *~ in* kürzer *od.* enger machen; *Zeitung* halten; aufnehmen (*als Gast etc.*); *Lage* überschauen; *fig.* einschließen; verstehen; erfassen; F *j-n* reinlegen; *be ~n in* reingefallen sein; *~ in lodgers* (Zimmer) vermieten; *~ off* ab-, wegnehmen; *Kleidungsstück* ablegen, ausziehen; *Hut etc.* abnehmen; *e-n Tag etc.* Urlaub machen; *~ on* an-, übernehmen; *Arbeiter etc.* einstellen; *Fahrgäste* zusteigen lassen; *~ out* heraus-, entnehmen; *Fleck* entfernen; *j-n* ausführen; *Versicherung* abschließen; *~ over Amt, Aufgabe, Idee etc.* übernehmen; *~ up* aufheben, -nehmen; sich befassen

mit; *Fall, Idee etc.* aufgreifen; *Raum, Zeit* in Anspruch nehmen; *v/i. ✈* wirken, anschlagen (*Medikament*) F gefallen, ankommen, ziehen; *~ after j-m* nachschlagen; *~ off* abspringen; *✈, Raumfahrt:* starten; *~ on* Anklang finden; *~ over* die Amtsgewalt *etc.* übernehmen; *~ to* sich hingezogen fühlen zu, Gefallen finden an; *~ to* allow *s.th.* anfangen et. zu tun; *~ up with* sich anfreunden mit; **2.** *Fischerei:* Fang *m*; (*Geld*)Einnahme(n *pl.*) *f*; *hunt.* Beute *f*; Anteil *m* (*of* an *dat.*); *Film:* Szene(naufnahme) *f*; **~away** ['teɪkəweɪ] **1.** zum Mitnehmen; **2.** Restaurant *n* mit Straßenverkauf; **~in** F [~ɪn] Schwindel *m*, Betrug *m*; **tak·en** [~ən] *p.p. von* take 1; **~off** [~ɒf] Absprung *m*; *✈, Raumfahrt:* Start *m*, Abflug *m*; Abheben *n*; F Nachahmung *f*.

tak·ing ['teɪkɪŋ] **1.** □ F anziehend, fesselnd, einnehmend; ansteckend; **2.** (An-, Ab-, Auf-, Ein-, Ent-, Hin-, Weg- *etc.*)Nehmen *n*; Inbesitznahme *f*; ✕ Einnahme *f*; F Aufregung *f*; **~s** *pl.* econ. Einnahme(n *pl.*) *f*.

tale [teɪl] Erzählung *f*; Geschichte *f*; Märchen *n*, Sage *f*; *tell* ~s klatschen; *it tells its own* ~ es spricht für sich selbst; **~bear·er** ['teɪlbeərə] Zuträger(in), Klatschmaul *n*.

tal·ent ['tælənt] Talent *n*, Begabung *f*, Anlage *f*; **~ed** talentiert, begabt.

talk [tɔːk] **1.** Gespräch *n*; Unterhaltung *f*; Unterredung *f*; Plauderei *f*; Vortrag *m*; Geschwätz *n*; Sprache *f*; Art *f* zu reden; **2.** sprechen; reden; plaudern; *~ to s.o.* mit j-m sprechen *od.* reden; **~a·tive** □ ['tɔːkətɪv] gesprächig, geschwätzig; **~er** [~ə] Schwätzer(in); Sprechende(r *m*) *f*; **~ show** *TV* Talk-Show *f*; **~show host** *TV* Talkmaster *m*.

tall [tɔːl] groß; lang; hoch; F übertrieben, unglaublich; *that's a ~ order* F das ist ein bißchen viel verlangt.

tal·low ['tæləʊ] Talg *m*.

tal·ly ['tælɪ] **1.** econ. (Ab-, Gegen-) Rechnung *f*; Kontogegenbuch *n*; Etikett *n*, Kennzeichen *n*; *Sport:* Punkt(zahl *f*) *m*; **2.** in Übereinstimmung bringen; übereinstimmen.

tal·on ['tælən] Kralle *f*, Klaue *f*.

tame [teɪm] **1.** □ (~*r*, ~*st*) zahm; folgsam; harmlos; lahm, fad(e); **2.** zähmen, bändigen.

tam·per ['tæmpə]: *~ with* sich (unbe-

fugt) zu schaffen machen an (dat.);
j-n zu bestechen suchen; *Urkunde*
fälschen.

tam·pon ⚓ ['tæmpən] Tampon m.

tan [tæn] **1.** Lohe f; Lohfarbe f;
(Sonnen)Bräune f; **2.** lohfarben; **3.**
(-nn-) gerben; bräunen; braun werden.

tang [tæŋ] scharfer Geruch od. Geschmack m; (scharfer) Klang; ⚓ See-
tang m.

tan·gent ['tændʒənt] ♣ Tangente f;
fly out go off at a ∼ plötzlich (vom
Thema) abschweifen.

tan·ge·rine ⚓ [tændʒə'ri:n] Mandarine f.

tan·gi·ble □ ['tændʒəbl] fühl-, greifbar; klar.

tan·gle ['tæŋgl] **1.** Gewirr n; fig. Verwirrung f, -wicklung f; **2.** (sich)
verwirren, -wickeln.

tank [tæŋk] **1.** mot., ✕ etc. Tank m;
(Wasser)Becken n, Zisterne f; **2.** ∼
(up) auf-, volltanken.

tank·ard ['tæŋkəd] Humpen m, bsd.
(Bier)Seidel n.

tank·er ['tæŋkə] ⚓ Tanker m; ✈
Tankflugzeug n; mot. Tankwagen m.

tan|ner ['tænə] Gerber m; ∼**ne·ry**
[∼rɪ] Gerberei f.

tan·ta·lize ['tæntəlaɪz] quälen.

tan·ta·mount ['tæntəmaʊnt] gleichbedeutend (to mit).

tan·trum ['tæntrəm] Wutanfall m.

tap [tæp] **1.** leichtes Klopfen; (Was-
ser-, Gas-, Zapf)Hahn m; Zapfen m;
Schankstube f; on ∼ vom Faß (Bier);
∼s pl. Am. ✕ Zapfenstreich m; **2.**
(-pp-) leicht pochen, klopfen, tippen
(on, at auf, an, gegen acc.); anzapfen
(a. Telefonleitung); abzapfen; ∼
dance ['tæpdɑ:ns] Steptanz m.

tape [teɪp] **1.** schmales Band, Streifen
m; Sport: Zielband n; tel. Papier-
streifen m; Computer, Fernschreiber:
Lochstreifen m; (Magnet-, Video-,
Ton)Band n; s. red tape; **2.** mit e-m
Band befestigen; mit Klebestreifen
verkleben; auf (Ton)Band aufnehmen; TV aufzeichnen; ∼ **cas·sette**
Tonbandkassette f; ∼ **deck** Tapedeck n; ∼ **li·bra·ry** Bandarchiv n; ∼
meas·ure Bandmaß n.

ta·per ['teɪpə] **1.** dünne Wachskerze;
2. adj. spitz (zulaufend); **3.** v/i. oft ∼
off spitz zulaufen; v/t. zuspitzen.

tape|-re·cord ['teɪprɪkɔ:d] auf (Ton-)
Band aufnehmen; ∼ **re·cord·er**

(Ton)Bandgerät n; ∼ **re·cord·ing**
(Ton)Bandaufnahme f; ∼ **speed**
Bandgeschwindigkeit f.

ta·pes·try ['tæpɪstrɪ] Gobelin m; △
nicht Tapete.

tape·worm zo. ['teɪpwɜ:m] Band-
wurm m.

tap·room ['tæprʊm] Schankstube f.

tar [tɑ:] **1.** Teer m; **2.** (-rr-) teeren.

tar·dy □ ['tɑ:dɪ] (-ier, -iest) langsam; Am. spät.

tare econ. [teə] Tara f.

tar·get ['tɑ:gɪt] (Schieß-, Ziel)Schei-
be f; ✕, Radar: Ziel n; fig. (Lei-
stungs- etc.)Ziel n, (-)Soll n; fig. Zielscheibe f (des Spottes etc.); ∼ **area** ✕
Zielbereich m; ∼ **group** econ. Werbung: Zielgruppe f; ∼ **language** ling.
Zielsprache f; ∼ **practice** Scheiben-,
Übungsschießen n.

tar·iff ['tærɪf] (bsd. Zoll)Tarif m.

tar·nish ['tɑ:nɪʃ] **1.** v/t. ⊕ matt od.
blind machen; fig. trüben; △ *nicht
tarnen*; v/i. matt od. trüb werden,
anlaufen; **2.** Trübung f; Belag m.

tar·ry ['tɑ:rɪ] (-ier, -iest) teerig.

tart [tɑ:t] **1.** □ sauer, herb; fig.
scharf, beißend; **2.** bsd. Brt. Obstkuchen m, (Obst)Torte f; sl. Flittchen n.

tar·tan ['tɑ:tn] Tartan m: Schotten-
tuch n; Schottenmuster n.

task [tɑ:sk] **1.** Aufgabe f; Arbeit f;
take to ∼ zur Rede stellen; **2.** beschäftigen; in Anspruch nehmen; ∼
force ⚓, ✕ Sonder-, Spezialeinheit
f; Sonderdezernat n (der Polizei).

tas·sel ['tæsl] Troddel f, Quaste f.

taste [teɪst] **1.** Geschmack m; (Kost-)
Probe f; Neigung f, Vorliebe f (for
für, zu); **2.** kosten; (ab)schmecken;
Essen anrühren; schmecken (of
nach); versuchen; ∼**ful** □ ['teɪstfl]
schmackhaft; fig. geschmackvoll;
∼**less** □ [∼lɪs] fad(e); fig. geschmacklos.

tast·y □ ['teɪstɪ] (-ier, -iest)
schmackhaft.

ta·ta int. F ['tæ'tɑ:] auf Wiedersehen!

tat·ter ['tætə] Fetzen m.

tat·tle ['tætl] **1.** klatschen, tratschen;
2. Klatsch m, Tratsch m.

tat·too [tə'tu:] **1.** (pl. -toos) ✕ Zapfenstreich m; Tätowierung f; **2.** fig.
trommeln; tätowieren.

taught [tɔ:t] pret. u. p.p. von teach.

taunt [tɔ:nt] **1.** Stichelei f, Spott m; **2.**
verhöhnen, -spotten.

T

taut □ [tɔːt] straff; angespannt.

tav·ern *veraltet* ['tævn] Wirtshaus *n*, Schenke *f*.

taw·dry □ ['tɔːdrɪ] (*-ier, -iest*) billig, geschmacklos; knallig.

taw·ny ['tɔːnɪ] (*-ier, -iest*) lohfarben.

tax [tæks] **1.** Steuer *f*, Abgabe *f*; *fig.* Inanspruchnahme *f* (*on, upon gen.*); **2.** besteuern; ⚖ *Kosten* schätzen; *fig.* stark in Anspruch nehmen; auf e-e harte Probe stellen; *j-n* zur Rede stellen; ~ *s.o. with s.th.* j-n e-r Sache beschuldigen; **~·a·tion** [tæk'seɪʃn] Besteuerung *f*; Steuer(n *pl.*) *f*; *bsd.* ⚖ Schätzung *f*.

tax·i F ['tæksɪ] **1.** *a.* ~*cab* Taxi *n*, Taxe *f*; **2.** (~*ing, taxying*) mit e-m Taxi fahren; ✈ rollen; ~ **driv·er** Taxifahrer(in); ~ **rank**, *bsd.* *Am.* ~ **stand** Taxistand *m*.

tax|pay·er ['tækspeɪə] Steuerzahler(in); ~ **re·turn** Steuererklärung *f*.

tea [tiː] Tee *m*; *s.* high tea; **~·bag** ['tiːbæg] Tee-, Aufgußbeutel *m*.

teach [tiːtʃ] (*taught*) lehren, unterrichten, *j-m et.* beibringen; **~·a·ble** ['tiːtʃəbl] gelehrig; lehrbar; **~·er** [~ə] Lehrer(in); **~·in** [~ɪn] Teach-in *n*.

tea|·co·sy ['tiːkəʊzɪ] Teewärmer *m*; **~·cup** Teetasse *f*; storm in a ~ *fig.* Sturm *m* im Wasserglas; **~·ket·tle** Tee-, Wasserkessel *m*.

team [tiːm] Team *n*, Arbeitsgruppe *f*; Gespann *n*; *Sport u. fig.*: Mannschaft *f*, Team *n*; **~·ster** *Am.* ['tiːmstə] LKW-Fahrer *m*; **~·work** Zusammenarbeit *f*, Teamwork *n*; Zusammenspiel *n*.

tea·pot ['tiːpɒt] Teekanne *f*.

tear[1] [teə] **1.** (*tore, torn*) zerren; (zer-) reißen; rasen, stürmen; **2.** Riß *m*.

tear[2] [tɪə] Träne *f*; *in* ~*s* weinend, in Tränen (aufgelöst); **~·ful** □ ['tɪəfl] tränenreich; weinend.

tea·room ['tiːrʊm] Teestube *f*.

tease [tiːz] necken, hänseln; ärgern.

teat [tiːt] *zo.* Zitze *f*; *anat.* Brustwarze *f* (*der Frau*); (Gummi)Sauger *m*.

tech·ni·cal □ ['teknɪkl] technisch; *fig.* rein formal; Fach...; **~·i·ty** [teknɪ'kælətɪ] technische Besonderheit *od.* Einzelheit; Fachausdruck *m*; reine Formsache.

tech·ni·cian [tek'nɪʃn] Techniker(in); Facharbeiter(in).

tech·nique [tek'niːk] Technik *f*, Verfahren *n*, Methode *f*; ⚠ *nicht Technik (Technologie)*.

tech·nol·o·gy [tek'nɒlədʒɪ] Technologie *f*.

ted·dy| bear ['tedɪbeə] Teddybär *m*; ₂ **boy** Halbstarke(r) *m*.

te·di·ous □ ['tiːdjəs] langweilig, ermüdend; weitschweifig.

teem [tiːm] wimmeln, strotzen (*with* von).

teen|-age(d) ['tiːneɪdʒ(d)] im Teenageralter; für Teenager; **~·ag·er** [~ə] Teenager *m*.

teens [tiːnz] *pl.* Teenageralter *n*; Teenager *pl.*; *be in one's* ~ ein Teenager sein.

tee·ny[1] F ['tiːnɪ] Teeny *m* (*Teenager*); **~·bopper** F junger Teenager (*bsd. Mädchen*), der alles mitmacht, was gerade `in' ist.

tee·ny[2] [~], *a.* **~·wee·ny** F [~'wiːnɪ] (*-ier, -iest*) klitzeklein, winzig.

tee shirt ['tiːʃɜːt] = T-shirt.

teeth [tiːθ] *pl. von* tooth; **~·e** [tiːð] zahnen, (die) Zähne bekommen.

tee·to·tal·(l)er [tiː'təʊtlə] Abstinenzler *m*.

tel·e·cast ['telɪkɑːst] **1.** Fernsehsendung *f*; **2.** (*-cast*) im Fernsehen übertragen *od.* bringen.

tel·e·course ['telɪkɔːs] Fernsehlehrgang *m*, -kurs *m*.

tel·e·gram ['telɪgræm] Telegramm *n*.

tel·e·graph ['telɪgrɑːf] **1.** Telegraf *m*; **2.** telegrafieren; **~·ic** [telɪ'græfɪk] (~*ally*) telegrafisch; im Telegrammstil.

te·leg·ra·phy [tɪ'legrəfɪ] Telegrafie *f*.

tel·e·phone ['telɪfəʊn] **1.** Telefon *n*, Fernsprecher *m*; **2.** telefonieren; anrufen; ~ **booth**, ~ **box** *Brt.* Telefon-, Fernsprechzelle *f*; **tel·e·phon·ic** [telɪ'fɒnɪk] (~*ally*) telefonisch; ~ **ki·osk** *Brt.* = telephone booth; **te·leph·o·ny** [tɪ'lefənɪ] Fernsprechwesen *n*.

tel·e·pho·to lens *phot.* ['telɪ'fəʊtəʊ 'lenz] Teleobjektiv *n*.

tel·e·print·er ['telɪprɪntə] Fernschreiber *m*.

tel·e·scope ['telɪskəʊp] **1.** Fernrohr *n*; **2.** (sich) ineinanderschieben.

tel·e·type·writ·er *Am.* [telɪ'taɪpraɪtə] Fernschreiber *m*.

tel·e·vise ['telɪvaɪz] im Fernsehen übertragen *od.* bringen.

tel·e·vi·sion ['telɪvɪʒn] Fernsehen *n*; *on* ~ im Fernsehen; *watch* ~ fernsehen; *a.* ~ set Fernsehapparat *m*, -gerät *n*.

tel·ex ['teleks] **1.** Telex n, Fernschreiben n; **2.** j-m et. telexen od. per Fernschreiben mitteilen.

tell [tel] (*told*) v/t. sagen, erzählen; erkennen; nennen; unterscheiden; zählen; ~ s.o. to do s.th. j-m sagen, er solle et. tun; ~ off abzählen; F abkanzeln; v/i. erzählen (of von; about über acc.); sich auswirken (on auf acc.); sitzen (*Hieb etc.*); ~ on s.o. j-n verpetzen; you never can ~ man kann nie wissen; ~**er** bsd. Am. (Bank)Kassierer m; ~**ing** □ [~ɪŋ] wirkungsvoll; aufschlußreich, vielsagend; ~**tale** ['telteɪl] **1.** Klatschbase f, Petze f; **2.** fig. verräterisch.

tel·ly Brt. F ['telɪ] Fernseher m.

te·mer·i·ty [tɪ'merətɪ] Verwegenheit f; Frechheit f.

tem·per ['tempə] **1.** mäßigen, mildern; ⊕ tempern; *Stahl* härten; **2.** ⊕ Härte(grad m) f; Temperament n, Charakter m, Laune f, Stimmung f; Wut f; keep one's ~ sich beherrschen; lose one's ~ in Wut geraten.

tem·pe·ra·ment ['tempərəmənt] Temperament n; ~**ra·men·tal** □ [tempərə'mentl] von Natur aus; launisch; ~**rance** ['tempərəns] Mäßigkeit f; Enthaltsamkeit f; ~**rate** □ [~rət] gemäßigt; zurückhaltend; maßvoll; mäßig; ~**ra·ture** [~prətʃə] Temperatur f.

tem|pest ['tempɪst] Sturm m; Gewitter n; ~**pes·tu·ous** □ [tem'pestjəs] stürmisch; ungestüm.

tem·ple ['templ] Tempel m; anat. Schläfe f.

tem·po|ral □ ['tempərəl] zeitlich; weltlich; ~**ra·ry** □ [~ərɪ] zeitweilig; vorläufig; vorübergehend; Not..., (Aus)Hilfs..., Behelfs...; ~**rize** [~raɪz] Zeit zu gewinnen suchen.

tempt [tempt] j-n versuchen; verleiten; (ver)locken; **temp·ta·tion** [temp'teɪʃn] Versuchung f; Reiz m; ~**ing** □ ['temptɪŋ] verführerisch.

ten [ten] zehn; **2.** Zehn f.

ten·a·ble ['tenəbl] haltbar (*Argument etc.*); verliehen (*Amt*).

te·na·cious □ [tɪ'neɪʃəs] zäh; gut (*Gedächtnis*); be ~ of s.th. zäh an et. festhalten; ~**ci·ty** [tɪ'næsətɪ] Zähigkeit f; Festhalten n; Verläßlichkeit f (*des Gedächtnisses*).

ten·ant ['tenənt] Pächter m; Mieter m.

tend [tend] v/i. sich bewegen, streben (to nach, auf ... zu); fig. tendieren, neigen (to zu); v/t. pflegen; hüten; ⊕ bedienen; **ten·den·cy** ['tendənsɪ] Tendenz f; Richtung f; Neigung f; Zweck m.

ten·der ['tendə] **1.** □ zart; weich; empfindlich; heikel (*Thema*); sanft, zart, zärtlich; **2.** Angebot n; econ. Kostenanschlag m; ⛴, ♣ Tender m; legal~ gesetzliches Zahlungsmittel; **3.** anbieten; *Entlassung* einreichen; ~**foot** (pl. -foots, -feet) Am. F Neuling m, Anfänger m, Greenhorn n; ~**loin** Filet n; ~**ness** [~nɪs] Zartheit f; Zärtlichkeit f.

ten·don anat. ['tendən] Sehne f.

ten·dril ♀ ['tendrɪl] Ranke f.

ten·e·ment ['tenɪmənt] Wohnhaus n; Mietwohnung f; a. ~ house Mietshaus n.

ten·nis ['tenɪs] Tennis n; ~ **court** Tennisplatz m.

ten·or ['tenə] Fortgang m, Verlauf m; Inhalt m; ♪ Tenor m.

tense [tens] **1.** gr. Zeit(form) f, Tempus n; **2.** □ (~r, ~st) gespannt (a. fig.); straff; (über)nervös, verkrampft; **ten·sion** ['tenʃn] Spannung f.

tent [tent] **1.** Zelt n; **2.** zelten.

ten·ta·cle zo. ['tentəkl] Fühler m; Fangarm m (e-s Polypen).

ten·ta·tive □ ['tentətɪv] versuchend; Versuchs...; vorsichtig, zögernd, zaghaft; ~**ly** versuchsweise.

ten·ter·hooks fig. ['tentəhʊks]: be on ~ wie auf (glühenden) Kohlen sitzen.

tenth [tenθ] **1.** zehnte(r, -s); **2.** Zehntel n; ~**ly** ['tenθlɪ] zehntens.

ten·u·ous □ ['tenjʊəs] dünn; zart, fein; fig. dürftig.

ten·ure ['tenjʊə] Besitz(art f, -dauer f) m; ~ of office Amtsdauer f.

tep·id □ ['tepɪd] lau(warm).

term [tɜːm] **1.** (bestimmte) Zeit, Dauer f; Frist f; Termin m; Zahltag m; Amtszeit f; ⚖ Sitzungsperiode f; Semester n, Quartal n, Trimester n; (Fach)Ausdruck m, Wort n, Bezeichnung f; Begriff m; ~s pl. (Vertrags)Bedingungen pl.; Beziehungen pl.; be on good (bad) ~s with gut (schlecht) stehen mit; they are not on speaking ~s sie sprechen nicht (mehr) miteinander; come to ~s sich einigen; **2.** (be)nennen; bezeichnen als.

ter·mi|nal ['tɜːmɪnl] **1.** □ End...;

letzte(r, -s); ✍ unheilbar; **~ly** zum
Schluß; **2.** Endstück n; ✍ Pol m; 🚇
etc. Endstation f; Terminal m, n:
Flughafenabfertigungsgebäude n;
Brt. Endstation der Zubringerlinie
zum u. vom Flughafen; Zielbahnhof
für Containerzüge; Computer: Terminal n, Datenendstation f, Abfra-
gestation f; **~nate** [~neɪt] begrenzen; beend(ig)en; Vertrag lösen,
kündigen; **~na·tion** [tɜːmɪˈneɪʃn]
Beendigung f; Ende n; gr. Endung f.

ter·mi·nus ['tɜːmɪnəs] (pl. -ni [-naɪ],
-nuses) Endstation f.

ter·race ['terəs] Terrasse f; Häuser-
reihe f (an erhöht gelegener Straße);
~d terrassenförmig (angelegt); **~d
house** Brt. = **~ house** Brt. Reihen-
haus n.

ter·res·tri·al [tɪˈrestrɪəl] irdisch;
Erd...; bsd. zo., ♣ Land...

ter·ri·ble □ ['terəbl] schrecklich.

ter·rif·ic F [təˈrɪfɪk] (~ally) toll, phantastisch; irre (Geschwindigkeit, Hitze
etc.).

ter·ri·fy ['terɪfaɪ] j-m Angst u.
Schrecken einjagen.

ter·ri·to·ri·al □ [terɪˈtɔːrɪəl] territorial, Land...; **~ry** ['terɪtərɪ] Territorium n, (Hoheits-/Staats)Gebiet n.

ter·ror ['terə] (tödlicher) Schrecken,
Entsetzen n; Terror m; **~is·m**
[~rɪzm] Terrorismus m; **~ist** [~rɪst]
Terrorist(in); **~ize** [~raɪz] terrorisie-
ren.

terse □ [tɜːs] (~r, ~st) knapp; kurz u.
bündig.

test [test] **1.** Probe f; Versuch m; Test
m; Untersuchung f; (Eignungs)Prü-
fung f; 🧪 Reagens n; **2.** probieren;
prüfen; testen; **3.** Probe..., Versuchs..., Test...

tes·ta·ment ['testəmənt] Testament
n; last will and **~** ⚖ Testament n.

tes·ti·cle anat. ['testɪkl] Hode(n m)
m, f.

tes·ti·fy ['testɪfaɪ] bezeugen; (als
Zeuge) aussagen.

tes·ti·mo·ni·al [testɪˈməʊnjəl] (Füh-
rungs)Zeugnis n; Zeichen n der Anerkennung; **~ny** ['testɪmənɪ] ⚖
Zeugenaussage f; Beweis m.

test tube ['testtjuːb] **1.** 🧪 Reagenz-
glas n; **2.** attr. Retorten...

tes·ty □ ['testɪ] (-ier, -iest) gereizt,
reizbar, kribbelig.

teth·er ['teðə] **1.** Haltestrick m; fig.
Spielraum m; at the end of one's **~**

fig. am Ende s-r Kräfte; **2.** anbinden.

text [tekst] Text m; Bibelstelle f;
~book ['tekstbʊk] Lehrbuch n.

tex·tile ['tekstaɪl] **1.** Textil..., Gewebe...; **2.** ~s pl. Webwaren pl., Textilien pl.

tex·ture ['tekstʃə] Gewebe n; Gefüge
n; Struktur f.

than [ðæn, ðən] als; △ nicht dann.

thank [θæŋk] **1.** danken (dat.); **~** you
danke; no, **~** you nein, danke; (yes,)
~ you ja, bitte; **2.** **~** s pl. Dank m; **~**s
danke (schön); no, ~s nein, danke;
~s to dank (dat. od. gen.); **~ful** □
['θæŋkfl] dankbar; **~less** □ [~lɪs]
undankbar; **~s·giv·ing** [~sgɪvɪŋ] bsd.
Dankgebet n; **2̲** (Day) Am. (Ernte-)
Dankfest n.

that [ðæt, ðət] **1.** pron. u. adj. (pl.
those [ðəʊz]) jene(r, -s), der, die,
das, der-, die-, dasjenige; solche(r,
-s); ohne n.: das; **2.** adv. F so, derma-
ßen; ~ much so viel; **3.** relative pron.
(pl. that) der, die, das, welche(r, -s);
4. cj. daß; damit; weil; da, als.

thatch [θætʃ] **1.** Dachstroh n; Stroh-
dach n; **2.** mit Stroh decken.

thaw [θɔː] **1.** Tauwetter n; (Auf-)
Tauen n; **2.** (auf)tauen.

the [ðiː; vor Vokalen: ðɪ; vor Konso-
nanten: ðə] **1.** bestimmter art. der, die,
das, pl. die; **2.** adv. desto, um so; ~ ...
~ ... je ... desto; s. sooner.

the·a·tre, Am. **-ter** ['θɪətə] Theater
n; fig. (Kriegs)Schauplatz m; **the·at-
ri·cal** □ [θɪˈætrɪkl] Theater...; fig.
theatralisch.

thee Bibel od. poet. [ðiː] dich; dir.

theft [θeft] Diebstahl m.

their [ðeə] pl. ihr(e); **~s** [~z] der (die,
das) ihrige od. ihre.

them [ðem, ðəm] sie (acc. pl.); ihnen.

theme [θiːm] Thema n.

them·selves [ðəmˈselvz] sie (acc. pl.)
selbst; sich (selbst).

then [ðen] **1.** adv. dann; damals; da;
denn; also, folglich; by ~ bis dahin;
inzwischen; every now and ~ ab u.
zu, gelegentlich; there and ~ sofort;
now ~ also (nun); **2.** attr. adj. dama-
lig.

thence lit. [ðens] daher; von da.

the·o·lo·gian [θɪəˈləʊdʒjən] Theolo-
ge m; **the·ol·o·gy** [θɪˈɒlədʒɪ] Theologie f.

the·o·ret·ic [θɪəˈretɪk] (~ally), **~ret·i-
cal** □ [~kl] theoretisch; **~ry** ['θɪərɪ]
Theorie f.

ther·a·peu·tic [θerə'pju:tɪk] **1.** (*~ally*) therapeutisch; **2.** *~s mst sg.* Therapeutik *f*; **~py** ['θerəpɪ] Therapie *f*.

there [ðeə] da, dort; darin; (da-, dort)hin; *int.* da!, na!; *~ is, pl. ~ are* es gibt, es ist, es sind; **~·a·bout(s)** ['ðeərəbaut(s)] da herum; so ungefähr; **~·aft·er** [ðeər'ɑ:ftə] danach; **~·by** ['ðeə'baɪ] dadurch; **~·fore** ['ðeəfɔ:] darum, deswegen, deshalb, daher; **~·up·on** [ðeərə'pɒn] darauf (-hin); **~·with** [ðeə'wɪð] damit.

ther·mal ['θɜ:ml] **1.** □ Thermal...; *phys.* thermisch, Wärme..., Hitze...; **2.** Thermik *f*.

ther·mom·e·ter [θə'mɒmɪtə] Thermometer *n*.

these [ði:z] *pl.* von this.

the·sis ['θi:sɪs] (*pl. -ses* [-si:z]) These *f*; Dissertation *f*.

they [ðeɪ] *pl.* sie; man.

thick [θɪk] **1.** □ dick; dicht; trüb; legiert (*Suppe*); heiser; dumm; F dick befreundet; *~ with* über u. über bedeckt von; voll von, voller; *that's a bit ~!* sl. das ist ein starkes Stück!; **2.** dickster Teil; *fig.* Brennpunkt *m*; *in the ~ of* mitten in (*dat.*); **~·en** ['θɪkən] (sich) verdicken (sich) verstärken; (sich) legieren; (sich) verdichten; dick(er) werden; **~·et** [~ɪt] Dickicht *n*; **~·head·ed** dumm; **~·ness** [~nɪs] Dicke *f*, Stärke *f*; Dichte *f*; **~·set** dicht(gepflanzt); untersetzt; **~·skinned** *fig.* dickfellig.

thief [θi:f] (*pl. thieves* [θi:vz]) Dieb(in *f*) *m*; **thieve** [θi:v] stehlen.

thigh *anat.* [θaɪ] (Ober)Schenkel *m*.

thim·ble ['θɪmbl] Fingerhut *m*.

thin [θɪn] **1.** □ (*-nn-*) dünn; licht; mager; spärlich; dürftig; schwach; fadenscheinig (*bsd. fig.*); **2.** (*-nn-*) verdünnen; (sich) lichten, abnehmen.

thine *Bibel od. poet.* [ðaɪn] dein(e); der (die, das) deinige *od.* deine.

thing [θɪŋ] Ding *n*; Sache *f*; Gegenstand *m*; Geschöpf *n*; *~s pl.* Sachen *pl.*; die Dinge *pl.* (*Umstände*); *the ~* das Richtige.

think [θɪŋk] (*thought*) *v/i.* denken (*of* an *acc.*); überlegen, nachdenken (*about* über *acc.*); meinen, glauben; *~ of* sich erinnern an (*acc.*); sich et. ausdenken; daran denken, beabsichtigen; *v/t. et.* denken; meinen, glauben; sich vorstellen; halten für; *et.* halten (*of* von); beabsichtigen, vor-

haben; *~ s.th. over* sich et. überlegen, über et. nachdenken.

third [θɜ:d] **1.** □ dritte(r, -s); **2.** Drittel *n*; **~·ly** ['θɜ:dlɪ] drittens; **~·rate** [~'reɪt] drittklassig.

thirst [θɜ:st] Durst *m*; **~·y** □ ['θɜ:stɪ] (*-ier, -iest*) durstig; dürr (*Boden*); *be ~* Durst haben, durstig sein.

thir·teen ['θɜ:'ti:n] **1.** dreizehn; **2.** Dreizehn *f*; **~·teenth** [~i:nθ] dreizehnte(r, -s); **~·ti·eth** ['θɜ:tɪɪθ] dreißigste(r, -s); **~·ty** ['θɜ:tɪ] **1.** dreißig; **2.** Dreißig *f*.

this [ðɪs] (*pl. these* [ði:z]) diese(r, -s); *~ morning* heute morgen; *~ is John speaking teleph.* hier (spricht) John.

this·tle ♀ ['θɪsl] Distel *f*.

thong [θɒŋ] (Leder)Riemen *m*.

thorn [θɔ:n] Dorn *m*; **~·y** ['θɔ:nɪ] (*-ier, -iest*) dornig; *fig.* schwierig; heikel.

thor·ough □ ['θʌrə] gründlich, genau; vollkommen; vollständig, völlig; vollendet; **~·bred** Vollblut (-pferd) *n*; *attr.* Vollblut...; **~·fare** Durchgangsstraße *f*, Hauptverkehrsstraße *f*; *no ~!* Durchfahrt verboten!; **~·go·ing** gründlich; kompromißlos; durch u. durch.

those [ðəuz] *pl.* von that 1.

thou *Bibel od. poet.* [ðau] du.

though [ðəu] obgleich, obwohl, wenn auch; zwar; jedoch, doch; *as ~* als ob.

thought [θɔ:t] **1.** *pret. u. p.p. von* think; **2.** Gedanke *m*, Einfall *m*; (Nach)Denken *n*; *on second ~s* nach reiflicher Überlegung; **~·ful** □ ['θɔ:tfl] gedankenvoll, nachdenklich; rücksichtsvoll (*of* gegen); **~·less** □ [~lɪs] gedankenlos, unbesonnen; rücksichtslos (*of* gegen).

thou·sand ['θauzənd] **1.** tausend; **2.** (*pl. ~, ~s*) Tausend *n*; **~·th** [~ntθ] **1.** tausendste(r, -s); **2.** Tausendstel *n*.

thrash [θræʃ] verdreschen, -prügeln; *Sport:* j-m e-e Abfuhr erteilen; *~ about, ~ around* sich *im Bett etc.* hin u. her werfen; um sich schlagen; zappeln (*Fisch*); *~ out fig.* gründlich erörtern; **~·ing** ['θræʃɪŋ] Dresche *f*, Tracht *f* Prügel.

thread [θred] **1.** Faden *m* (*a. fig.*); Zwirn *m*, Garn *n*; ⊕ (Schrauben-) Gewinde *n*; einfädeln; aufreihen; *fig.* sich durchwinden (durch); **~·bare** ['θredbeə] fadenscheinig (*a. fig.*); *fig.* abgedroschen.

threat [θret] (Be)Drohung f; **~en** ['θretn] (be-, an)drohen; **~en·ing** [~nɪŋ] drohend; bedrohlich.

three [θri:] **1.** drei; **2.** Drei f; **~fold** ['θri:fəʊld] dreifach; **~·pence** ['θrepəns] altes englisches Währungssystem: Dreipencestück n; **~·score** ['θri:'skɔ:] sechzig.

thresh ✧ [θreʃ] dreschen; **~er** ['θreʃə] Drescher m; Dreschmaschine f; **~ing** [~ɪŋ] Dreschen n; **~·ing-ma·chine** Dreschmaschine f.

thresh·old ['θreʃhəʊld] Schwelle f.

threw [θru:] pret. von throw 1.

thrice veraltet od. lit. [θraɪs] dreimal.

thrift [θrɪft] Sparsamkeit f; Wirtschaftlichkeit f; **~·less** □ ['θrɪftlɪs] verschwenderisch; **~·y** □ [~ɪ] (-ier, -iest) sparsam; poet. gedeihend.

thrill [θrɪl] **1.** v/t. erschauern lassen, erregen, packen; v/i. (er)beben, erschauern, zittern; **2.** Zittern n, Erregung f; (Nerven)Kitzel m, Sensation f; Beben n; **~er** ['θrɪlə] Reißer m, Thriller m (Kriminalfilm, -roman etc.); **~·ing** [~ɪŋ] spannend, aufregend.

thrive [θraɪv] (thrived od. throve, thrived od. thriven) gedeihen; fig. blühen; Erfolg haben; **~n** ['θrɪvn] p.p. von thrive.

throat [θrəʊt] Kehle f, Gurgel f, Schlund m; Hals m; clear one's ~ sich räuspern.

throb [θrɒb] **1.** (-bb-) (heftig) pochen, klopfen, schlagen; pulsieren; **2.** Pochen n; Schlagen n; Pulsschlag m.

throm·bo·sis ✧ [θrɒm'bəʊsɪs] (pl. -ses [-si:z]) Thrombose f.

throne [θrəʊn] Thron m.

throng [θrɒŋ] **1.** Gedränge n; (Menschen)Menge f; **2.** sich drängen (in dat.).

thros·tle zo. ['θrɒsl] Drossel f.

throt·tle ['θrɒtl] **1.** erdrosseln; ~ back, ~ down mot. ⊕ drosseln, Gas wegnehmen; **2.** a. ~·valve mot. ⊕ Drosselklappe f.

through [θru:] **1.** prp. durch; hindurch; Am. (von ...) bis; Monday ~ Friday Am. von Montag bis Freitag; **2.** adj. Durchgangs...; durchgehend; **2.** a. ~·train Am. von Montag bis Freitag;

durch und durch, ganz und gar, durchweg; **~·put** econ. Computer: Durchsatz m.

throve [θrəʊv] pret. von thrive.

throw [θrəʊ] **1.** (threw, thrown) (ab)werfen, schleudern; Am. Wettkampf etc. absichtlich verlieren; Würfel werfen; Zahl würfeln; ⊕ ein-, ausschalten; ~ over fig. aufgeben; ~ up hochwerfen; erbrechen, sich übergeben; fig. et. aufgeben, hinwerfen; **2.** Wurf m; **~·a·way** ['θrəʊəweɪ] **1.** et. zum Wegwerfen, z. B. Reklamezettel m; **2.** Wegwerf...; Einweg...; **~n** [θrəʊn] p.p. von throw 1.

thru Am. [θru:] = through.

thrum [θrʌm] (-mm-) klimpern auf (od. on auf) (dat.).

thrush zo. [θrʌʃ] Drossel f.

thrust [θrʌst] **1.** Stoß m; Vorstoß m; ⊕ Druck m, Schub m; **2.** (thrust) stoßen; stecken, schieben; ~ o.s. into sich drängen in (acc.); ~ upon s.o. j-m aufdrängen.

thud [θʌd] **1.** (-dd-) dumpf (auf-) schlagen, F bumsen; **2.** dumpfer (Auf)Schlag, F Bums m.

thug [θʌg] (Gewalt)Verbrecher m, Schläger m.

thumb [θʌm] **1.** Daumen m; **2.** ~ a lift od. ride per Anhalter fahren; ~ through a book ein Buch durchblättern; well-~ed Buch etc.: abgegriffen; **~·tack** Am. ['θʌmtæk] Reißzwecke f, -nagel m, Heftzwecke f.

thump [θʌmp] **1.** dumpfer Schlag; **2.** v/t. heftig schlagen od. hämmern od. pochen gegen od. auf (acc.); v/i. (auf)schlagen; (laut) pochen (Herz).

thun·der ['θʌndə] **1.** Donner m; **2.** donnern; **~·bolt** Blitz m (u. Donner m); **~·clap** Donnerschlag m; **~·ous** □ [~rəs] donnernd; **~·storm** Gewitter n; **~·struck** fig. wie vom Donner gerührt.

Thurs·day ['θɜ:zdɪ] Donnerstag m.

thus [ðʌs] so; also, somit.

thwart [θwɔ:t] **1.** durchkreuzen, vereiteln; **2.** Ruderbank f.

thy veraltet od. poet. [ðaɪ] dein(e).

tick¹ zo. [tɪk] Zecke f.

tick² [~] **1.** Ticken n; (Vermerk)Häkchen n, Haken m; **2.** v/i. ticken; v/t. anhaken; ~ off abhaken.

tick³ [~] Inlett n; Matratzenbezug m.

tick·er tape ['tɪkəteɪp] Lochstreifen

m; ~ *parade bsd. Am.* Konfettiparade *f*.

tick·et ['tɪkɪt] **1.** Fahrkarte *f*, -schein *m*; Flugkarte *f*, Ticket *n*; (Eintritts-, Theater- *etc.*)Karte *f*; *mot.* Strafzettel *m*, gebührenpflichtige Verwarnung; Etikett *n*, Schildchen *n*, (Preis- *etc.*)Zettel *m*; *bsd. Am. pol.* (Wahl-, Kandidaten)Liste *f*; **2.** etikettieren, *Ware* auszeichnen; ~ **can·cel·(l)ing ma·chine** (Fahrschein)Entwerter *m*; ~ **col·lec·tor** ⚓ (Bahnsteig)Schaffner *m*; (**au·to·mat·ic**) ~ **ma·chine** Fahrkartenautomat *m*; ~ **of·fice** ⚓ Fahrkartenschalter *m*; ~ *thea.* Kasse *f*.

tick·le ['tɪkl] kitzeln (*a. fig.*); ~**lish** □ [~lɪʃ] kitz(e)lig; *fig.* heikel.

tid·al ['taɪdl]: ~ **wave** Flutwelle *f*.

tid·bit *Am.* ['tɪdbɪt] = *titbit*.

tide [taɪd] **1.** Gezeiten *pl.*; Ebbe *f* u. Flut *f*; *fig.* Strom *m*, Strömung *f*; in *Zssgn*: Zeit *f*; **high** ~ Flut *f*; **low** ~ Ebbe *f*; **2.** ~ **over** *fig.* hinwegkommen *od. j-m* hinweghelfen über (*acc.*).

ti·dy ['taɪdɪ] **1.** □ (-*ier*, -*iest*) ordentlich, sauber, reinlich, aufgeräumt; F ganz schön, beträchtlich (*Summe*); **2.** Behälter *m*; Abfallkorb *m*; **3.** *a.* ~ **up** zurechtmachen; in Ordnung bringen; aufräumen.

tie [taɪ] **1.** (Schnür)Band *n*; Schleife *f*; Krawatte *f*, Schlips *m*; *fig.* Band *n*, Bindung *f*; *fig.* (lästige) Fessel, Last *f*; *Sport:* Punkt-, *parl.* Stimmengleichheit *f*; *Sport:* (Ausscheidungs)Spiel *n*; *Am.* ⚓ Schwelle *f*; **2.** *v/t.* (an-, fest-, *fig.* ver)binden; *v/i. Sport:* punktgleich sein; *mit Adverbien:* ~ **down** *fig.* binden (to an *acc.*); ~ **in with** passen zu; verbinden mit, koppeln mit; ~ **up** zu-, an-, ver-, zusammenbinden; ~**in** *econ.* ['taɪɪn] Kopplungsgeschäft *n*, -verkauf *m*; *a* **book movie** ~ *Am. etwa:* das Buch zum Film.

tier [tɪə] Reihe *f*; Rang *m*.

tie-up ['taɪʌp] (Ver)Bindung *f*; *econ.* Fusion *f*; Stockung *f*; *bsd. Am.* Streik *m*.

ti·ger *zo.* ['taɪgə] Tiger *m*.

tight [taɪt] **1.** □ dicht; fest; eng; knapp (sitzend); straff, (an)gespannt; *econ.* knapp; F blau, besoffen; F knick(e)rig, geizig; **be in a** ~ **corner** *od.* **place** *od.* F **spot** *fig.* in der Klemme sein; **2.** *adv.* fest; **hold** ~ festhalten; ~**en** ['taɪtn] fest-, anzie-

hen; *Gürtel* enger schnallen; *a.* ~ **up** (sich) zusammenziehen; ~**fist·ed** knick(e)rig, geizig; ~**ness** [~nɪs] Festigkeit *f*; Dichte *f*; Straffheit *f*; Knappheit *f*; Enge *f*; Geiz *m*; ~**s** [taɪts] *pl.* (Tänzer-, Artisten)Trikot *n*; *bsd. Brt.* Strumpfhose *f*.

ti·gress *zo.* ['taɪgrɪs] Tigerin *f*.

tile [taɪl] **1.** (Dach)Ziegel *m*; Kachel *f*; Platte *f*; Fliese *f*; **2.** mit Ziegeln *etc.* decken; kacheln; fliesen.

till[1] [tɪl] (Laden)Kasse *f*.

till[2] [~] **1.** *prp.* bis (zu); **2.** *cj.* bis.

till[3] [~] [~] bestellen, bebauen; ~**age** ['tɪldʒ] (Land)Bestellung *f*; Ackerbau *m*; Ackerland *n*.

tilt [tɪlt] **1.** (Wagen)Plane *f*; Kippen *n*; Neigung *f*; Stoß *m*; **2.** (um)kippen.

tim·ber ['tɪmbə] **1.** (Bau-, Nutz)Holz *n*; ⚓ Spant *m*; Baumbestand *m*, Bäume *pl.*; **2.** zimmern.

time [taɪm] **1.** Zeit *f*; Uhrzeit *f*; Frist *f*; Mal *n*; ♪ Takt *m*; Tempo *n*; ~**s** *pl.* mal, ...mal; ~ **is up** die Zeit ist um *od.* abgelaufen; **for the ~ being** vorläufig; **have a good** ~ sich gut unterhalten *od.* amüsieren; **what's the ~?**, **what ~ is it?** wieviel Uhr ist es?, wie spät ist es?; ~ **and again** immer wieder; **all the ~** ständig, immer; **at a** ~ auf einmal, zusammen; **at any** ~, **at all** ~**s** jederzeit; **at the same** ~ gleichzeitig, zur selben Zeit; **in** ~ rechtzeitig; **in no** ~ im Nu, im Handumdrehen; **on** ~ pünktlich; **2.** messen, (ab)stoppen; zeitlich abstimmen; timen (*a. Sport*), den richtigen Zeitpunkt wählen *od.* bestimmen für; ~ **card** Stechkarte *f*; ~ **clock** Stechuhr *f*; ~**hon·o(u)red** ['taɪmɒnəd] altehrwürdig; ~**ly** [~lɪ] (-*ier*, -*iest*) (recht)zeitig; ~**piece** Uhr *f*; ~ **sheet** Stechkarte *f*; ~ **sig·nal** Rundfunk, TV: Zeitzeichen *n*; ~**ta·ble** Terminkalender *m*; Fahr-, Flug-, Stundenplan *m*.

tim·id □ ['tɪmɪd], ~**or·ous** □ [~ərəs] ängstlich; schüchtern.

tin [tɪn] **1.** Zinn *n*; Weißblech *n*; *bsd. Brt.* (Konserven)Dose *f*, (-)Büchse *f*; **2.** (-*nn*-) verzinnen; *bsd. Brt.* (in Büchsen) einmachen, eindosen.

tinc·ture ['tɪŋktʃə] **1.** Farbe *f*; Tinktur *f*; *fig.* Anstrich *m*; **2.** färben.

tin·foil ['tɪn'fɔɪl] Stanniol(papier) *n*.

tinge [tɪndʒ] **1.** Tönung *f*; *fig.* Anflug m, Spur f; 2. tönen, färben; fig. e-n Anstrich geben (dat.).

tin·gle ['tɪŋgl] klingen; prickeln.

tink·er ['tɪŋkə] herumpfuschen, -basteln (at an dat.).

tin·kle ['tɪŋkl] klingeln (mit).

tin| **o·pen·er** bsd. Brt. ['tɪnˌəʊpnə] Dosenöffner m; ~ **plate** Weißblech n.

tin·sel ['tɪnsl] Flitter m; Lametta n.

tint [tɪnt] 1. (zarte) Farbe; (Farb)Ton m, Tönung f, Schattierung f; 2. (leicht) färben; tönen.

ti·ny □ ['taɪnɪ] (-ier, -iest) winzig, sehr klein.

tip [tɪp] 1. Spitze f; Filter m (e-r Zigarette); Trinkgeld n; Tip m, Wink m; leichter Stoß; Brt. Schuttabladeplatz m; 2. (-pp-) mit e-r Spitze versehen; (um)kippen; j-m ein Trinkgeld geben; a. ~ off j-m e-n Tip od. Wink geben.

tip·sy □ ['tɪpsɪ] (-ier, -iest) angeheitert.

tip·toe ['tɪptəʊ] 1. auf Zehenspitzen gehen; 2. on ~ auf Zehenspitzen.

tire¹ Am. ['taɪə] = tyre.

tire² [~] ermüden, müde machen od. werden; ~**d** □ müde; ~**less** □ ['taɪəlɪs] unermüdlich; ~**some** □ [~səm] ermüdend; lästig.

tis·sue ['tɪʃuː] Gewebe n; Papiertaschentuch n; = ~ **pa·per** Seidenpapier n.

tit¹ [tɪt] = teat.

tit² zo. [~] Meise f.

tit·bit bsd. Brt. ['tɪtbɪt] Leckerbissen m.

tit·il·late ['tɪtɪleɪt] kitzeln.

ti·tle ['taɪtl] (Buch-, Ehren- etc.)Titel m; Überschrift f; ⁿₜₛ Rechtsanspruch m; ~**d** ad(e)lig.

tit·mouse zo. ['tɪtmaʊs] (pl. -mice) Meise f.

tit·ter ['tɪtə] 1. kichern; 2. Kichern n.

tit·tle ['tɪtl]: not one od. a ~ of it kein od. nicht ein Jota (davon); ~**tat·tle** [~tætl] Schnickschnack m.

to [tuː, tʊ, tə] 1. prp. zu; gegen, nach; an, in, auf; bis zu, bis an (acc.); um zu; für; a quarter ~ one (ein) Viertel vor eins; from Monday ~ Friday Brt. von Montag bis Freitag; ~ me etc. mir etc.; I weep ~ think of it ich weine, wenn ich daran denke; here's ~ you! auf Ihr Wohl!, prosit!; 2. adv. zu, geschlossen; pull ~ Tür zuziehen; come ~ (wieder) zu

sich kommen; ~ and fro hin u. her, auf u. ab.

toad zo. [təʊd] Kröte f; ~**stool** ♀ ['təʊdstuːl] (größerer Blätter)Pilz; Giftpilz m; ~**y** [~ɪ] 1. Speichellecker(in); 2. fig. vor j-m kriechen.

toast [təʊst] 1. Toast m; Toast m, Trinkspruch m; 2. toasten; rösten; fig. wärmen; trinken auf (acc.).

to·bac·co [təˈbækəʊ] (pl. -cos) Tabak m; ~**nist** [~ənɪst] Tabakhändler m.

to·bog·gan [təˈbɒgən] 1. Rodelschlitten m; 2. rodeln.

to·day [təˈdeɪ] heute.

tod·dle ['tɒdl] auf wack(e)ligen Beinen gehen (bsd. Kleinkind); F (dahin)zotteln.

tod·dy ['tɒdɪ] Toddy m (Art Grog).

to-do F [təˈduː] Lärm m; Getue n, Aufheben n.

toe [təʊ] 1. anat. Zehe f; Spitze f (von Schuhen etc.); 2. mit den Zehen berühren.

tof·fee, a. ~**fy** ['tɒfɪ] Sahnebonbon m, n, Toffee n.

to·geth·er [təˈgeðə] zusammen; zugleich; Tage etc. nacheinander.

toil [tɔɪl] 1. mühselige Arbeit, Mühe f, Plackerei f; 2. sich plagen.

toi·let ['tɔɪlɪt] Toilette f; ~**pa·per** Toilettenpapier n.

toils fig. [tɔɪlz] pl. Schlingen pl., Netz n.

to·ken ['təʊkən] Zeichen n; Andenken n, Geschenk n; as a ~, in ~ of als od. zum Zeichen (gen.).

told [təʊld] pret. u. p.p. von tell.

tol·e·ra·ble □ ['tɒlərəbl] erträglich; ~**rance** [~ns] Toleranz f; Nachsicht f; ~**rant** □ [~t] tolerant (of gegen); ~**rate** [~eɪt] dulden; ertragen; ~**ra·tion** [tɒləˈreɪʃn] Duldung f.

toll [təʊl] 1. Straßenbenutzungsgebühr f, Maut f; Standgeld n (auf e-m Markt etc.); fig. Tribut m, (Zahl f der) Todesopfer pl.; the ~ of the road die Verkehrsopfer pl.; 2. läuten; ~**bar** ['təʊlbaː], ~**gate** Schlagbaum m.

to·ma·to ♀ [təˈmaːtəʊ, Am. təˈmeɪtəʊ] (pl. -toes) Tomate f.

tomb [tuːm] Grab(mal) n.

tom·boy ['tɒmbɔɪ] Wildfang m.

tomb·stone ['tuːmstəʊn] Grabstein m.

tom-cat zo. ['tɒmˈkæt] Kater m.

tom·fool·e·ry [tɒmˈfuːlərɪ] Unsinn m.

to·mor·row [tə'mɒrəʊ] morgen.

ton [tʌn] Tonne f (*Gewichtseinheit*); △ *nicht* Ton.

tone [təʊn] **1.** Ton m, Klang m, Laut m; (Farb)Ton m; **2.** (ab)tönen; ~ **down** (sich) abschwächen od. mildern.

tongs [tɒŋz] pl. (a pair of ~ e-e) Zange.

tongue [tʌŋ] anat. Zunge f; Sprache f; (Schuh)Lasche f; hold one's ~ den Mund halten; ~**tied** fig. ['tʌŋtaɪd] stumm, sprachlos.

ton·ic ['tɒnɪk] **1.** (~ally) tonisch; stärkend, belebend; **2.** ♪ Grundton m; Stärkungsmittel n, Tonikum n.

to·night [tə'naɪt] heute abend od. nacht.

ton·nage ♣ ['tʌnɪdʒ] Tonnage f.

ton·sil anat. ['tɒnsl] Mandel f; ~**li·tis** ⚕ [tɒnsl'laɪtɪs] Mandelentzündung f.

too [tuː] zu, allzu; auch, ebenfalls.

took [tʊk] pret. von take 1.

tool [tuːl] Werkzeug n, Gerät n; ~**bag** ['tuːlbæg] Werkzeugtasche f; ~**box** Werkzeugkasten m; ~**kit** Werkzeugtasche f.

toot [tuːt] **1.** blasen, tuten; hupen; **2.** Tuten n.

tooth [tuːθ] (pl. teeth [tiːθ]) Zahn m; ~**ache** ['tuːθeɪk] Zahnschmerzen pl.; ~**brush** Zahnbürste f; ~**less** □ [~lɪs] zahnlos; ~**paste** Zahnpasta f, -creme f; ~**pick** Zahnstocher m.

top¹ [tɒp] **1.** ober(st)es Ende; Oberteil n; Spitze f (a. fig.); Gipfel m (a. fig.); Wipfel m; Kopf(ende n) m; (Topf- etc.)Deckel m; mot. Verdeck n; Stulpe f (am Stiefel); at the ~ of one's voice aus vollem Halse; on ~ oben(auf); obendrein; on ~ of (oben) auf (dat.); **2.** oberste(r, -s), höchste(r, -s), Höchst..., Spitzen...; **3.** (-pp-) oben bedecken; überragen (a. fig.); an der Spitze e-r Liste etc. stehen; ~ up Tank etc. auf-, nachfüllen; ~ s.o. up j-m nachschenken.

top² [~] Kreisel m.

top| boots ['tɒp'buːts] pl. Stulpenstiefel pl.; ~ **hat** Zylinder(hut) m.

top·ic ['tɒpɪk] Gegenstand m, Thema n; ~**al** □ [~l] lokal; aktuell.

top|less ['tɒplɪs] oben ohne, Oben-ohne-...; ~**most** höchste(r, -s), oberste(r, -s).

top·ple ['tɒpl]: ~down, ~ over umkippen.

top·sy-tur·vy □ ['tɒpsɪ'tɜːvɪ] auf den Kopf (gestellt), das Oberste zuunterst; drunter u. drüber.

torch [tɔːtʃ] Fackel f; a. electric ~ bsd. Brt. Taschenlampe f; ~**light** ['tɔːtʃlaɪt] Fackelschein m; ~ **procession** Fackelzug m.

tore [tɔː] pret. von tear¹.

tor·ment 1. ['tɔːment] Qual f, Marter f; **2.** [tɔː'ment] quälen, peinigen, plagen.

torn [tɔːn] p.p. von tear¹.

tor·na·do [tɔː'neɪdəʊ] (pl. -does, -dos) Wirbelsturm m, Tornado m.

tor·pe·do [tɔː'piːdəʊ] (pl. -does) **1.** Torpedo m; **2.** ♣ torpedieren (a. fig.).

tor·pid □ ['tɔːpɪd] starr; gänzlich; träge; ~**i·ty** [tɔː'pɪdətɪ], ~**ness** [~nɪs], **tor·por** [~ə] Apathie f, Stumpfheit f; Erstarrung f, Betäubung f.

tor·rent ['tɒrənt] Sturz-, Wildbach m; reißender Strom; fig. Strom m, Schwall m; ~**ren·tial** [tə'renʃl]: ~ rain(s) sintflutartige Regenfälle.

tor·toise zo. ['tɔːtəs] Schildkröte f.

tor·tu·ous □ ['tɔːtjʊəs] gewunden.

tor·ture ['tɔːtʃə] **1.** Folter(ung) f; Tortur f; **2.** foltern.

toss [tɒs] **1.** Werfen n, Wurf m; Zurückwerfen n (Kopf); **2.** werfen, schleudern; a. ~ about (sich) hin- u. herwerfen; schütteln; ~ off Getränk hinunterstürzen; Arbeit hinhauen; a. ~ up hochwerfen; losen (for um) (durch Münzwurf).

tot F [tɒt] Knirps m (kleines Kind).

to·tal ['təʊtl] **1.** □ ganz, gänzlich; total; gesamt; **2.** Gesamtbetrag m, -menge f; **3.** (bsd. Brt. -ll-, Am. -l-) sich belaufen auf (acc.); ~**i·tar·i·an** [təʊtælɪ'teərɪən] totalitär; ~**i·ty** [təʊ'tælətɪ] Gesamtheit f.

tot·ter ['tɒtə] torkeln, (sch)wanken, wackeln.

touch [tʌtʃ] **1.** (sich) berühren; anrühren; anfassen; grenzen od. stoßen an (acc.); tip. rühren; erreichen; ♪ anschlagen; a bit ~ed fig. ein bißchen verrückt; ~ at ♣ anlegen in (dat.); ~ down ♣ aufsetzen; ~ up auffrischen; retuschieren; **2.** Berührung f; Tastsinn m, -gefühl n; Verbindung f, Kontakt m; leichter Anfall; Anflug m; besondere Note; ♪ Anschlag m; (Pinsel)Strich m; ~**and-go** ['tʌtʃən'gəʊ] gewagte Sache; *it is* ~ es steht auf des Messers Schneide; ~**ing** □ [~ɪŋ] rührend; ~**stone** Prüfstein *m*; ~**y** □ [~ɪ] (*-ier, -iest*) empfindlich; heikel.

tough □ [tʌf] zäh (*a. fig.*); robust, stark; hart, grob, brutal, übel; ~**en** ['tʌfn] zäh machen *od.* werden; ~**ness** [~nɪs] Zähigkeit *f*.

tour [tʊə] **1.** (Rund)Reise *f*, Tour *f*; Rundgang *m*, -fahrt *f*; *thea.* Tournee *f* (*a. Sport*); *s. conduct 2*; **2.** (be)reisen; ~**ist** ['tʊərɪst] Tourist(in); ~ *agency*, ~ *bureau*, ~ *office* Reisebüro *n*; Verkehrsverein *m*; ~ *season* Reisesaison *f*, -zeit *f*.

tour·na·ment ['tʊənəmənt] Turnier *n*.

tou·sle ['taʊzl] (zer)zausen.

tow [təʊ] **1.** Schleppen *n*; *take in* ~ ins Schlepptau nehmen; **2.** (ab)schleppen; treideln; ziehen.

to·ward(s) [təˈwɔːd(z)] gegen; nach ... zu, auf (*acc.*) ... zu; (*als Beitrag*) zu.

tow·el ['taʊəl] **1.** Handtuch *n*; **2.** (*bsd. Brt. -ll-, Am. -l-*) (ab)trocknen; (ab)reiben.

tow·er ['taʊə] **1.** Turm *m*; *fig.* Stütze *f*, Bollwerk *n*; *a.* ~ *block* (Büro-, Wohn)Hochhaus *n*; **2.** (hoch)ragen, sich erheben; ~**ing** □ ['taʊərɪŋ] (turm)hoch; rasend (*Wut*).

town [taʊn] **1.** Stadt *f*; **2.** Stadt...; städtisch; ~ **cen·tre**, *Am.* ~ **cen·ter** Innenstadt *f*, City *f*; ~ **clerk** *Brt.* städtischer Verwaltungsbeamter; ~ **coun·cil** *Brt.* Stadtrat *m* (*Versammlung*); ~ **coun·ci(l)·lor** *Brt.* Stadtrat *m*, -rätin *f*; ~ **hall** Rathaus *n*; ~**s·folk** ['taʊnzfəʊk] *pl.* Städter *pl.*; ~**ship** Stadtgemeinde *f*; Stadtgebiet *n*; ~**s·man** (*pl. -men*) Städter *m*; (Mit-) Bürger *m*; ~**s·peo·ple** *pl.* = *townsfolk*; ~**s·wom·an** *pl.* (*-women*) Städterin *f*; (Mit)Bürgerin *f*.

tox·ic ['tɒksɪk] (~*ally*) giftig; Gift...; ~**in** [~ɪn] Giftstoff *m*.

toy [tɔɪ] **1.** Spielzeug *n*; Tand *m*; ~*s pl.* Spielsachen *pl.*, -waren *pl.*; **2.** Spielzeug...; Miniatur...; Zwerg...; **3.** spielen.

trace [treɪs] **1.** Spur *f* (*a. fig.*); **2.** nachspüren (*dat.*), *j-s* Spur folgen; verfolgen; herausfinden; (auf)zeichnen; (durch)pausen.

trac·ing ['treɪsɪŋ] Pauszeichnung *f*.

track [træk] **1.** Spur *f*, Fährte *f*; 🚂 Gleis *n*, Geleise *n u. pl.*; Pfad *m*;

Computer, Tonband: Spur *f*; (Raupen)Kette *f*; *Sport*: (Renn-, Aschen-) Bahn *f*; ~-*and-field Sport*: Leichtathletik...; ~ *events pl. Sport*: Laufdisziplinen *pl.*; ~ *suit* Trainingsanzug *m*; **2.** nachgehen, -spüren (*dat.*); verfolgen; ~ *down*, ~ *out* aufspüren; ~*ing station Raumfahrt*: Bodenstation *f*.

tract [trækt] Fläche *f*, Strecke *f*, Gegend *f*; Traktat *n*, Abhandlung *f*.

trac·ta·ble □ ['træktəbl] lenk-, fügsam.

trac|tion ['trækʃn] Ziehen *n*, Zug *m*; ~ *engine* Zugmaschine *f*; ~**tor** ⊕ [~tə] Trecker *m*, Traktor *m*.

trade [treɪd] **1.** Handel *m*; Gewerbe *n*, Beruf *m*, Handwerk *n*; **2.** Handel treiben, handeln; ~ *on* ausnutzen; ~ **mark** Warenzeichen *n*; ~ **price** Großhandelspreis *m*; ~ **trad·er** ['treɪdə] Händler *m*; ~**s·man** [~zmən] (*pl. -men*) (Einzel)Händler *m*; ~**(s) un·i·on** Gewerkschaft *f*; ~**(s) un·i·on·ist** Gewerkschaftler(in); ~ *wind* Passat(wind) *m*.

tra·di·tion [trəˈdɪʃn] Tradition *f*; Überlieferung *f*; ~**al** □ [~l] traditionell.

traf·fic ['træfɪk] **1.** Verkehr *m*; Handel *m*; **2.** (*-ck-*) (*a. illegal*) handeln (*in* mit).

traf·fi·ca·tor *Brt. mot.* ['træfɪkeɪtə] (Fahrt)Richtungsanzeiger *m*, Blinker *m*.

traf·fic| cir·cle *Am.* ['træfɪkˈsɜːkl] Kreisverkehr *m*; ~ **jam** (Verkehrs-) Stau *m*, Verkehrsstockung *f*; ~ **light(s** *pl.*) Verkehrsampel *f*; ~ **sign** Verkehrszeichen *n*, -schild *n*; ~ **sig·nal** = *traffic light(s)*; ~ **war·den** *Brt.* Politesse *f*.

tra|ge·dy ['trædʒɪdɪ] Tragödie *f*; ~**gic** [~ɪk] (~*ally*), **trag·i·cal** □ [~kl] tragisch.

trail [treɪl] **1.** Schleppe *f*; Spur *f*; Pfad *m*, Weg *m*; *fig.* Schweif *m*; **2.** *v/t.* hinter sich herziehen; verfolgen; *j-n* beschatten; *v/i.* schleifen; sich schleppen; ~ *kriechen, sich ranken; ~**er** ['treɪlə] 💐 Kriechpflanze *f*; *mot.* Anhänger *m*; *Am. mot.* Wohnwagen *m*, Wohnanhänger *m*, Caravan *m*; *Film, TV*: (Programm)Vorschau *f*.

train [treɪn] **1.** (Eisenbahn)Zug *m*; *allg.* Zug *m*; Gefolge *n*; Reihe *f*, Folge *f*, Kette *f*; Schleppe *f* (*am Kleid*); **2.** erziehen; (sich) schulen;

abrichten; (sich) ausbilden; *Sport:*
trainieren; sich üben; **~·ee** [treɪˈniː]
in der Ausbildung Stehende(r *m*) *f;*
Auszubildende(r *m*) *f;* **~·er** [ˈtreɪnə]
Ausbilder *m; Sport:* Trainer *m;*
~·ing [-ɪŋ] Ausbildung *f;* Üben *n;*
bsd. Sport: Training *n.*

trait [treɪ] (Charakter)Zug *m.*

trai·tor [ˈtreɪtə] Verräter *m.*

tram(·car) *Brt.* [ˈtræm(kɑː)] Stra-
ßenbahn(wagen *m*) *f.*

tramp [træmp] **1.** Getrampel *n;*
Wanderung *f;* Tramp *m,* Landstreicher *m;* **2.** trampeln, treten; (durch-)
wandern; **tram·ple** [ˈtræmpl] (her-
um-, zer)trampeln.

trance [trɑːns] Trance *f.*

tran·quil □ [ˈtræŋkwɪl] ruhig; gelassen; **~·(l)i·ty** [træŋˈkwɪlɪti] Ruhe *f;*
Gelassenheit *f;* **~·(l)ize** [ˈtræŋ-
kwɪlaɪz] beruhigen; **~·(l)iz·er** [-aɪzə]
Beruhigungsmittel *n.*

trans- [trænz] jenseits; durch; über.

trans|act [trænˈzækt] abwickeln, ab-
machen; **~·ac·tion** [-kʃn] Erledigung *f;* Geschäft *n,* Transaktion *f.*

trans·al·pine [ˈtrænzˈælpaɪn] trans-
alpin(isch).

trans·at·lan·tic [ˈtrænzətˈlæntɪk]
transatlantisch, Übersee...

tran|scend [trænˈsend] überschrei-
ten, hinausgehen über (*acc.*); übertreffen; **~·scen·dence,** **~·scen·den·**
cy [-ɔns, -ɔsɪ] Überlegenheit *f; phls.*
Transzendenz *f.*

tran·scribe [trænˈskraɪb] abschreiben; *Kurzschrift* übertragen.

tran|script [ˈtrænskrɪpt], **~·scrip·**
tion [trænˈskrɪpʃn] Abschrift *f;* Umschrift *f.*

trans·fer 1. [trænsˈfɜː] (*-rr-*) *v/t.*
übertragen; versetzen; *Geld*
überweisen; *Sport: Spieler* transfe-
rieren (*to zu*), abgeben (*to an acc.*);
v/i. übertreten; *Sport:* wechseln
(*Spieler*); 🚗 *etc.* umsteigen; **2.**
[ˈtrænsfɜː] Übertragung *f;* Verset-
zung *f,* -legung *f; econ.* (Geld)Über-
weisung *f; Sport:* Transfer *m,* Wechsel *m; Am.* 🚗 *etc.* Umsteigefahr-
schein *m;* **~·a·ble** [trænsˈfɜːrəbl]
übertragbar.

trans·fig·ure [trænsˈfɪɡə] umgestalten; verklären.

trans|fix [trænsˈfɪks] durchstechen;
~ed *fig.* versteinert, starr (*with* vor
dat.)

trans|form [trænsˈfɔːm] umformen;

um-, verwandeln; **~·for·ma·tion**
[trænsfəˈmeɪʃn] Umformung *f;*
Um-, Verwandlung *f.*

trans|fuse [trænsˈfjuːz] *Blut* über-
tragen; **~·fu·sion** ♠ [-ʒn] (Blut-)
Übertragung *f,* (-)Transfusion *f.*

trans|gress [trænsˈɡres] *v/t.* über-
schreiten; *Gesetze etc.* übertreten,
verletzen; *v/i.* sich vergehen;
~·gres·sion [-ʃn] Überschreitung *f;*
Übertretung *f;* Vergehen *n;* **~·gres·**
sor [-sə] Übeltäter(in); Rechtsbre-
cher(in).

tran·sient [ˈtrænzɪənt] **1.** □ = *tran-*
sitory; **2.** *Am.* Durchreisende(r *m*) *f.*

tran·sis·tor [trænˈsɪstə] Transistor
m.

tran·sit [ˈtrænsɪt] Durchgang *m;*
Transit-, Durchgangsverkehr *m;*
econ. Transport *m (von Waren).*

tran·si·tion [trænˈsɪʒn] Übergang *m.*

tran·si·tive □ *gr.* [ˈtrænsɪtɪv] transitiv.

tran·si·to·ry □ [ˈtrænsɪtəri] vorübergehend; vergänglich, flüchtig.

trans|late [trænsˈleɪt] übersetzen;
fig. umsetzen; **~·la·tion**
[-ʃn] Übersetzung *f,* -tragung *f;*
~·la·tor [-ə] Übersetzer(in).

trans·lu·cent □ [trænzˈluːsnt] licht-
durchlässig.

trans·mi·gra·tion [ˈtrænzmaɪ-
ˈɡreɪʃn] Seelenwanderung *f.*

trans·mis·sion [trænzˈmɪʃn] Übermittlung *f;* Übertragung *f; biol.* Vererbung *f; phys.* Fortpflanzung *f;*
mot. Getriebe *n; Rundfunk, TV:*
Sendung *f.*

trans·mit [trænzˈmɪt] (*-tt-*) übermit-
teln, -senden; übertragen; *Rund-*
funk, TV: senden; *biol.* vererben;
phys. (weiter)leiten; **~·ter** [-ə] Über-
mittler(in); *tel. etc.* Sender *m.*

trans·mute [trænzˈmjuːt] um-, verwandeln.

trans·par·ent □ [trænsˈpærənt]
durchsichtig (*a. fig.*).

tran·spire [trænˈspaɪə] ausdünsten,
-schwitzen; *fig.* durchsickern.

trans|plant [trænsˈplɑːnt] umpflan-
zen; verpflanzen (*a.* ♠); **~·plan·ta·**
tion [ˈtrænsplɑːnˈteɪʃn] Verpflan-
zung *f (a.* ♠).

trans|port 1. [trænsˈpɔːt] transpor-
tieren, befördern, fortschaffen; *fig.*
j-n hinreißen; **2.** [ˈtrænspɔːt] Transport *m,* Beförderung *f;* Versand *m;*
Verkehr *m;* Beförderungsmittel *n;*

Transportschiff *n*, -flugzeug *n*; *in a ~ of rage* außer sich vor Wut; *be in ~s* of außer sich sein vor (*Freude etc.*); **~·por·ta·tion** ['trænspɔ'teɪʃn] Transport *m*, Beförderung *f*.

trans·pose [trænsˈpəʊz] versetzen, umstellen; ♪ transponieren.

trans·verse □ ['trænzvɜːs] querlaufend; Quer...

trap [træp] **1.** Falle *f* (*a. fig.*); ⊕ Klappe *f*; *sl.* Schnauze *f* (*Mund*); *keep one's ~ shut sl.* die Schnauze halten; *set a ~ for s.o.* j-m e-e Falle stellen; **2.** (*-pp-*) (in e-r Falle) fangen; *fig.* in e-e Falle locken; **~·door** ['træpdɔː] Falltür *f*; *thea.* Versenkung *f*.

tra·peze [trəˈpiːz] Trapez *n*.

trap·per ['træpə] Trapper *m*, Fallensteller *m*, Pelztierjäger *m*.

trap·pings *fig.* ['træpɪŋz] *pl.* Schmuck *m*, Putz *m*, Drum u. Dran *n*.

trash [træʃ] *bsd. Am.* Abfall *m*, Abfälle *pl.*, Müll *m*; Unsinn *m*, F Blech *n*; Gesindel *n*; Kitsch *m*; **~ can** *Am.* Abfall-, Mülleimer *m*; *Am.* Abfall-, Mülltonne *f*; **~·y** □ ['træʃɪ] (*-ier, -iest*) wertlos, kitschig.

trav·el ['trævl] **1.** (*bsd. Brt. -ll-, Am. -l-*) *v/i.* reisen; sich bewegen; *bsd. fig.* schweifen, wandern; *v/t.* bereisen; **2.** *das* Reisen; ⊕ (Kolben)Hub *m*; *~s pl.* Reisen *pl.*; **~ a·gen·cy, ~ bu·reau** Reisebüro *n*; **~·(l)er** [~ə] Reisende(r *m*) *f*; **~'s cheque** (*Am. check*) Reisescheck *m*.

tra·verse ['trævəs] durch-, überqueren; durchziehen; führen über (*acc.*).

trav·es·ty ['trævɪstɪ] **1.** Travestie *f*; Karikatur *f*, Zerrbild *n*; **2.** travestieren; ins Lächerliche ziehen.

trawl ♧ [trɔːl] **1.** (Grund)Schleppnetz *n*; **2.** mit dem Schleppnetz fischen; **~·er** ♧ ['trɔːlə] Trawler *m*.

tray [treɪ] (Servier)Brett *n*, Tablett *n*; Ablagekorb *m*.

treach·er·|ous □ ['tretʃərəs] verräterisch, treulos; (heim)tückisch; trügerisch; **~·y** [~ɪ] (*to*) Verrat *m* (an *dat.*), Treulosigkeit *f* (gegen).

trea·cle ['triːkl] Sirup *m*.

tread [tred] **1.** (*trod, trodden od. trod*) treten; (be)schreiten; trampeln; **2.** Tritt *m*, Schritt *m*; ⊕ Lauffläche *f*; *mot.* Profil *n*; **trea·dle** ['tredl] Pedal

n; Tritt *m*; **~·mill** Tretmühle *f* (*a. fig.*).

trea·|son ['triːzn] Verrat *m*; **~·so·na·ble** □ [~əbl] verräterisch.

treas·|ure ['treʒə] **1.** Schatz *m*, Reichtum *m*; **~ trove** Schatzfund *m*; **2.** sehr schätzen; **~ up** *Schätze* sammeln, anhäufen; **~·ur·er** [~rə] Schatzmeister *m*; Kassenwart *m*.

treas·ur·y ['treʒərɪ] Schatzkammer *f*; ⊕ Finanzministerium *n*; **⊕ Bench** *Brt. parl.* Regierungsbank *f*; **⊕ De·part·ment** *Am.* Finanzministerium *n*.

treat [triːt] **1.** *v/t.* behandeln, umgehen mit; betrachten; **~ *s.o. to s.th.*** j-m et. spendieren; *v/i.* ~ *of* handeln von; ~ *with* verhandeln mit; **2.** Vergnügen *n*; *school* ~ Schulausflug *m*, -fest *n*; *it is my* ~ es geht auf meine Rechnung.

trea·tise ['triːtɪz] Abhandlung *f*.

treat·ment ['triːtmənt] Behandlung *f*.

trea·ty ['triːtɪ] Vertrag *m*.

tre·ble ['trebl] **1.** □ dreifach; **2.** ♪ Diskant *m*, Sopran *m*; *Radio*: Höhen *pl.*; **3.** (sich) verdreifachen.

tree [triː] Baum *m*.

tre·foil ♧ ['trefɔɪl] Klee *m*.

trel·lis ['trelɪs] **1.** ✔ Spalier *n*; **2.** vergittern; ✔ am Spalier ziehen.

trem·ble ['trembl] zittern.

tre·men·dous □ [trɪˈmendəs] schrecklich, ungeheuer, gewaltig; F enorm.

trem·or ['tremə] Zittern *n*; Beben *n*.

trem·u·lous □ ['tremjʊləs] zitternd, bebend.

trench [trentʃ] **1.** ⚔ (Schützen)Graben *m*; Furche *f*; **2.** *v/t.* mit Gräben durchziehen; *v/i.* ⚔ (Schützen)Graben ausheben.

tren·chant □ ['trentʃənt] scharf.

trend [trend] **1.** Richtung *f*; *fig.* (Ver)Lauf *m*; *fig.* Trend *m*, Entwicklung *f*, Tendenz *f*; **2.** tendieren, neigen; **~·y** *bsd. Brt.* F ['trendɪ] (*-ier, -iest*) modern.

trep·i·da·tion [trepɪˈdeɪʃn] Zittern *n*; Angst *f*, Beklommenheit *f*.

tres·pass ['trespəs] **1.** ⚖ unbefugtes Betreten; Vergehen *n*; **2.** ~ (*up*)*on* ⚖ widerrechtlich betreten; über Gebühr in Anspruch nehmen; *no ~ing* Betreten verboten; **~·er** ⚖ [~ə] Rechtsverletzer *m*; Unbefugte(r *m*) *f*.

tres·tle ['tresl] Gestell n, Bock m.

tri·al ['traɪəl] 1. Versuch m; Probe f, Prüfung f (a. fig.); ⚖ Prozeß m, Verhandlung f; fig. Plage f; on ~ auf od. zur Probe; give s.th. od. s.o. a ~ e-n Versuch mit et. od. j-m machen; be on ~ ⚖ angeklagt sein; put s.o. on ~ ⚖ j-n vor Gericht bringen; 2. Versuchs..., Probe...

tri·an·gle ['traɪæŋgl] Dreieck n; **~gu·lar** □ [traɪ'æŋgjʊlə] dreieckig.

tribe [traɪb] (Volks)Stamm m; contp. Sippe f; ♀, zo. Klasse f.

tri·bu·nal ⚖ [traɪ'bjuːnl] Gericht(s-hof m) n; **trib·une** ['trɪbjuːn] Tribun m; Tribüne f.

trib·u·ta·ry ['trɪbjʊtərɪ] 1. □ zins-pflichtig; tributär; geogr. Neben...; 2. Nebenfluß m; **~ute** [~juːt] Tribut m (a. fig.), Zins m; Anerkennung f.

trice [traɪs]: in a ~ im Nu.

trick [trɪk] 1. Kniff m, List f, Trick m; Kunststück n; Streich m; (schlechte) Angewohnheit; play a ~ on s.o. j-m e-n Streich spielen; 2. überlisten, F hereinlegen; **~e·ry** ['trɪkərɪ] Betrügerei f.

trick·le ['trɪkl] tröpfeln, rieseln.

trick|ster ['trɪkstə] Gauner(in); **~y** □ [~ɪ] (-ier, -iest) verschlagen; F heikel; verzwickt, verwickelt, schwierig.

tri·cy·cle ['traɪsɪkl] Dreirad n.

tri·dent ['traɪdənt] Dreizack m.

tri|fle ['traɪfl] 1. Kleinigkeit f, Lappalie f; a ~ ein bißchen, ein wenig, etwas; 2. v/i. spielen; spaßen; v/t. ~ away verschwenden; **~fling** □ [~ɪŋ] geringfügig; unbedeutend.

trig·ger ['trɪgə] Abzug m (am Gewehr); phot. Auslöser m.

trill [trɪl] 1. Triller m; gerolltes r; 2. trillern; bsd. das r rollen.

tril·lion ['trɪljən] Brt. Trillion f; Am. Billion f.

trim [trɪm] 1. □ (-mm-) ordentlich; schmuck; gepflegt; 2. (guter) Zustand; Ordnung f; in good ~ in Form; 3. (-mm-) zurechtmachen, in Ordnung bringen; (a. ~ up heraus-)putzen, schmücken; Kleider etc. besetzen; stutzen, trimmen, (be-)schneiden; ⚓, ✈ trimmen; **~ming** ['trɪmɪŋ]: ~s pl. Besatz m; Zutaten pl., Beilagen pl. (e-r Speise).

Trin·i·ty eccl. ['trɪnɪtɪ] Dreieinigkeit f.

trin·ket ['trɪŋkɪt] wertloses Schmuckstück.

trip [trɪp] 1. (kurze) Reise, Fahrt f; Ausflug m, Spritztour f; Stolpern n, Fallen n; Fehltritt m (a. fig.); fig. Versehen n, Fehler m; F Trip m (Drogenrausch); 2. (-pp-) v/i. trippeln; stolpern; fig. (e-n) Fehler machen; v/t. a. ~ up j-m ein Bein stellen (a. fig.).

tri·par·tite [traɪ'pɑːtaɪt] dreiteilig.

tripe [traɪp] Kaldaunen pl., Kutteln pl.

trip|le □ ['trɪpl] dreifach; ~ jump Sport: Dreisprung m; **~lets** [~ɪts] pl. Drillinge pl.

trip·li·cate 1. ['trɪplɪkɪt] dreifach; 2. [~keɪt] verdreifachen.

tri·pod ['traɪpɒd] Dreifuß m; phot. Stativ n.

trip·per bsd. Brt. ['trɪpə] Ausflügler(in).

trite □ [traɪt] abgedroschen, banal.

tri|umph ['traɪəmf] 1. Triumph m, Sieg m; 2. triumphieren; **~um·phal** [traɪ'ʌmfl] Sieges..., Triumph...; **~um·phant** □ [~ənt] triumphierend.

triv·i·al □ ['trɪvɪəl] bedeutungslos; unbedeutend, trivial; alltäglich.

trod [trɒd] pret. u. p.p. von tread 1; **~den** ['trɒdn] p.p. von tread 1.

trol·l(e)y ['trɒlɪ] Brt. Handwagen m, Gepäckwagen m, Kofferkuli m, Einkaufswagen m, Sackkarre(n m) f; Golf: Caddie m; Brt. ⚙ Draisine f; Brt. Tee-, Servierwagen m; ✦ Kontaktrolle f (e-s Oberleitungsfahrzeugs); Am. Straßenbahn(wagen m) f; **~bus** O(berleitungs)bus m.

trol·lop ['trɒləp] F Schlampe f; leichtes Mädchen, Hure f.

trom·bone ♪ [trɒm'bəʊn] Posaune f.

troop [truːp] 1. Trupp m, Haufe(n) m; ~s pl. ⚔ Truppen pl.; 2. sich scharen; (herein- etc.)strömen, marschieren; ~ away, ~ off abziehen; ~ the colours Brt. ⚔ e-e Fahnenparade abhalten; **~er** ⚔ ['truːpə] Kavallerist m.

tro·phy ['trəʊfɪ] Trophäe f.

trop|ic ['trɒpɪk] 1. Wendekreis m; ~s pl. Tropen pl.; 2. (~ally), **~i·cal** □ [~kl] tropisch.

trot [trɒt] 1. Trott m, Trab m; 2. (-tt-) trotten; traben (lassen).

trou·ble ['trʌbl] 1. Mühe f, Plage f, Last f, Belästigung f, Störung f;

Unannehmlichkeiten *pl.*, Schwierigkeiten *pl.*, Scherereien *pl.*, Ärger *m*; *ask od.* **look for** ~ unbedingt Ärger haben wollen; *take (the)* ~ sich (die) Mühe machen; **2.** stören, beunruhigen, belästigen; quälen, plagen; *j-m* Mühe machen; (sich) bemühen; bitten (*for* um); *don't* ~ *yourself* bemühen Sie sich nicht; *what's the* ~? was ist los?; ~**mak·er** Unruhestifter(in); ~**some** □ [~səm] beschwerlich; lästig.

trough [trɒf] Trog *m*; Rinne *f*; Wellental *n*.

trounce [traʊns] verprügeln.

troupe *thea.* [tru:p] Truppe *f*.

trou·ser [ˈtraʊzə]: (*a pair of*) ~s *pl.* (e-e) (lange) Hose; Hosen *pl.*; *attr.* Hosen...; ~ **suit** Hosenanzug *m*.

trous·seau [ˈtru:səʊ] Aussteuer *f*.

trout *zo.* [traʊt] Forelle(n *pl.*) *f*.

trow·el [ˈtraʊəl] Maurerkelle *f*.

tru·ant [ˈtru:ənt] Schulschwänzer(in); *play* ~ (die Schule) schwänzen.

truce ✗ [tru:s] Waffenstillstand *m*.

truck [trʌk] **1.** 🚃 offener Güterwagen; *bsd. Am.* Last(kraft)wagen *m*, Lkw *m*; Transportkarren *m*; Tausch(handel) *m*; *Am.* Gemüse *n*; **2.** (ver)tauschen; ~**er** *Am.* [ˈtrʌkə] Lastwagen-, Fernfahrer *m*; ~ **farm** *Am.* Gemüsegärtnerei *f*.

truc·u·lent [ˈtrʌkjʊlənt] wild, roh, grausam; gehässig.

trudge [trʌdʒ] sich (mühsam dahin-) schleppen, (mühsam) stapfen.

trun·dle [ˈtrʌndl] rollen.

trunk [trʌŋk] (Baum)Stamm *m*; Rumpf *m*; Rüssel *m*; (Schrank)Koffer *m*, Truhe *f*; *Am. mot.* Kofferraum *m*; ~**call** *Brt. teleph.* [ˈtrʌŋkɔ:l] Ferngespräch *n*; ~**line** 🚃 Hauptlinie *f*; *teleph.* Fernleitung *f*; ~**s**

[trʌŋks] *pl.* Turnhose *f*; Badehose *f*; *Sport:* Shorts *pl.*; *bsd. Brt.* (Herren-) Unterhose *f*.

truss [trʌs] **1.** Bündel *n*, Bund *n*; 🏥 Bruchband *n*; *arch.* Träger *m*, Fachwerk *n*; **2.** (zs.-)binden; *arch.* stützen.

trust [trʌst] **1.** Vertrauen *n*; Glaube *m*; Kredit *m*; Pfand *n*; Verwahrung *f*; ⚖️ Treuhand *f*; ⚖️ Treuhandvermögen *n*; *econ.* Trust *m*; econ. Kartell *n*; ~ **company** 🏦 Treuhandgesellschaft *f*; *in* ~ zu treuen Händen; **2.** *v/t.* (ver)trauen (*dat.*); anvertrauen, übergeben (*s.o. with s.th., s.th. to s.o.* j-m et.); zuversichtlich hoffen; *v/i.* vertrauen (*in, to* auf *acc.*); ~**ee** ⚖️ [trʌsˈti:] Sach-, Verwalter *m*; Treuhänder *m*; ~**ful** □ [ˈtrʌstfl], ~**ing** □ [~ɪŋ] vertrauensvoll; ~**wor·thy** □ [~wɜ:ði] vertrauenswürdig, zuverlässig.

truth [tru:θ] (*pl.* ~s [tru:ðz, tru:θs]) Wahrheit *f*; Wirklichkeit *f*; Genauigkeit *f*; ~**ful** □ [ˈtru:θfl] wahr(-heitsliebend).

try [traɪ] **1.** versuchen; probieren; prüfen; ⚖️ verhandeln über et. *od.* gegen *j-n*; vor Gericht stellen; *die Augen etc.* angreifen; sich bemühen *od.* bewerben (*for* um); ~ *on Kleid* anprobieren; ~ *out* ausprobieren; **2.** Versuch *m*; ~**ing** □ [ˈtraɪɪŋ] anstrengend; kritisch.

tsar *hist.* [zɑ:] Zar *m*.

T-shirt [ˈti:ʃɜ:t] T-Shirt *n*.

tub [tʌb] **1.** Faß *n*; Zuber *m*, Kübel *m*; *Brt.* F (Bade)Wanne *f*; *Brt.* F (Wannen)Bad *n*.

tube [tju:b] Rohr *n*; ⚡ Röhre *f*; Tube *f*; (*inner* ~ Luft)Schlauch *m*; Tunnel *m*; *die* (Londoner) U-Bahn; *the* ~ *Am.* F die Röhre, die Glotze (*Fernseher*); ~**less** [ˈtju:blɪs] schlauchlos.

tu·ber 🌿 [ˈtju:bə] Knolle *f*.

tu·ber·cu·lo·sis 🏥 [tju:bɜ:kjʊˈləʊsɪs] Tuberkulose *f*.

tu·bu·lar □ [ˈtju:bjʊlə] röhrenförmig.

tuck [tʌk] **1.** Biese *f*; Abnäher *m*; **2.** stecken; ~ *away* weg-, verstecken; ~ *in,* ~ *up* (warm) zudecken; *s.o.* ~ *up in bed* j-n ins Bett packen; ~ *up Rock* schürzen; *Ärmel* hochkrempeln.

Tues·day [ˈtju:zdɪ] Dienstag *m*.

tuft [tʌft] Büschel *n*; (Haar)Schopf *m*.

tug [tʌg] **1.** Zerren, heftiger Ruck; *a.*

T

trump [trʌmp] **1.** Trumpf(karte *f*) *m*; **2.** übertrumpfen; ~ *up* erfinden.

trum·pet [ˈtrʌmpɪt] **1.** 🎵 Trompete *f*; **2.** trompeten; *fig.* ausposaunen.

trun·cheon [ˈtrʌntʃən] (Gummi-) Knüppel *m*, Schlagstock *m*.

tru·ly [ˈtru:lɪ] wirklich; wahrhaft; aufrichtig; genau; treu; *Yours* ~ *Briefschluß:* Hochachtungsvoll.

~**boat** ⚓ Schlepper *m*; *fig.* Anstrengung *f*; **2.** (*-gg-*) ziehen, zerren; ⚓ schleppen; sich mühen; ~ **of war** Tauziehen *n*.

tu·i·tion ['tjuːˈɪʃn] Unterricht *m*; Schulgeld *n*.

tu·lip ♀ ['tjuːlɪp] Tulpe *f*.

tum·ble ['tʌmbl] **1.** fallen; stürzen; purzeln; taumeln; sich wälzen; **2.** Sturz *m*; Wirrwarr *m*; ~**down** baufällig; ~**r** [~ə] Becher *m*; *zo.* Tümmler *m*.

tu·mid □ ['tjuːmɪd] geschwollen.

tum·my F ['tʌmɪ] Bäuchlein *n*.

tu·mo(u)r ♀ ['tjuːmə] Tumor *m*.

tu·mult ['tjuːmʌlt] Tumult *m*; **tu·mul·tu·ous** □ [tjuːˈmʌltjʊəs] lärmend; stürmisch.

tun [tʌn] Faß *n*.

tu·na *zo.* ['tuːnə] Thunfisch *m*.

tune [tjuːn] **1.** Melodie *f*; ♪ (Ein-)Stimmung *f*; *fig.* Harmonie *f*; *in* ~ (gut)gestimmt; *out of* ~ verstimmt; **2.** ♪ stimmen; ~ *in v/i.* (das Radio *etc.*) einschalten; *v/t.* das Radio *etc.* einstellen (*to* auf *acc.*); ~ *up* die Instrumente stimmen; *Motor* tunen; ~**ful** □ ['tjuːnfl] melodisch; ~**less** □ [~lɪs] unmelodisch.

tun·er ['tjuːnə] *Radio*, *TV*: Tuner *m*.

tun·nel ['tʌnl] **1.** Tunnel *m*; ⚒ Stollen *m*; **2.** (*bsd. Brt. -ll-*, *Am. -l-*) e-n Tunnel bohren (*durch*).

tun·ny *zo.* ['tʌnɪ] Thunfisch *m*.

tur·bid □ ['tɜːbɪd] trüb; dick(flüssig); *fig.* verworren, wirr.

tur·bine ⊕ ['tɜːbaɪn] Turbine *f*.

tur·bot *zo.* ['tɜːbət] Steinbutt *m*.

tur·bu·lent □ ['tɜːbjʊlənt] unruhig; ungestüm; stürmisch, turbulent.

tu·reen [təˈriːn] Terrine *f*.

turf [tɜːf] **1.** (*pl.* ~*s*, *turves*) Rasen *m*; Torf *m*; *the* ~ die (Pferde)Rennbahn; der Pferderennsport *m*; **2.** mit Rasen bedecken.

tur·gid □ ['tɜːdʒɪd] geschwollen.

Turk [tɜːk] Türk|e *m*, -in *f*.

tur·key ['tɜːkɪ] *zo.* Truthahn *m*, -henne *f*, Pute(*r m*) *f*; *talk* ~ *bsd. Am.* F offen *od.* sachlich reden.

Turk·ish ['tɜːkɪʃ] **1.** türkisch; **2.** *ling.* Türkisch *n*.

tur·moil ['tɜːmɔɪl] Aufruhr *m*, Unruhe *f*; Durcheinander *n*.

turn [tɜːn] **1.** *v/t.* (um-, herum)drehen; (um)wenden; *Seite* umdrehen, -blättern; lenken, richten; verwandeln; *j-n* abbringen (*from* von); ab-

wenden; *Text* übertragen, -setzen; bilden, formen; ⊕ drechseln; *Laub* verfärben; ~ *a corner* um eine Ecke biegen; ~ *loose* los-, freilassen; ~ *s.o. sick* j-n krank machen; ~ *sour Milch* sauer werden lassen; *s. somersault*; ~ *s.o. against* j-n aufhetzen gegen; ~ *aside* abwenden; ~ *away* abwenden; abweisen; ~ *down* umbiegen; *Kragen* umschlagen; *Bett* aufdecken; *Decke* zurückschlagen; *Gas etc.* klein(er) stellen; *Radio etc.* leiser stellen; *j-n, et.* ablehnen; ~ *in bsd. Am.* einreichen, -senden; ~ *off Gas*, *Wasser etc.* abdrehen; *Licht*, *Radio etc.* ausschalten, -machen; ~ *on Gas*, *Wasser etc.* aufdrehen; *Gerät* anstellen; *Licht*, *Radio etc.* anmachen, einschalten; F antörnen; F anmachen (*a. sexuell*); ~ *out econ.* Waren produzieren; hinausjagen; = *turn off*; ~ *over econ.* Waren umsetzen; umdrehen; *Seite* umblättern; umwerfen; übergeben (*to dat.*); überlegen; ~ *up* nach oben drehen *od.* biegen; *Kragen* hochschlagen; *Ärmel* hochkrempeln; *Hose etc.* auf-, umschlagen; *Gas etc.* aufdrehen; *Radio etc.* lauter stellen; *v/i.* sich drehen (lassen); sich (um-, herum)drehen; *mot.* wenden; sich (ab-, hin-, zu)wenden; (ab-, ein)biegen; e-e Biegung machen (*Straße etc.*); sich (ver)wandeln; umschlagen (*Wetter etc.*); *Christ*, *grau etc.* werden; ~ (*sour*) sauer werden (*Milch*); ~ *about* sich umdrehen; ⚔ kehrtmachen; ~ *aside*, ~ *away* sich abwenden; ~ *back* zurückkehren; ~ *in* F ins Bett gehen; ~ *off* abbiegen; ~ *out gut etc.* ausfallen, -gehen; sich herausstellen (*als*); ~ *over* sich umdrehen; ~ *to nach rechts etc.* abbiegen; sich zuwenden (*dat.*); sich an *j-n* wenden; *fig.* auftauchen; **2.** (Um)Drehung *f*; Biegung *f*, Kurve *f*, Kehre *f*; (einzelne) Windung (*e-s Kabels etc.*); *fig.* Wendung *f*; Wendepunkt *m* (*a. fig.*); Wende *f*; Wechsel *m*; Gestalt *f*, Form *f*; (kurzer) Spaziergang *m* (kurze) Fahrt; Reihe(nfolge) *f*; Dienst *m*, Gefallen *m*, Zweck *m*; Neigung *f*, Talent *n*; F Schrecken *m*; ~ (*of mind*) Denkart *f*, -weise *f*; *at every* ~ auf Schritt und Tritt; *by* ~*s* abwechselnd; *in* ~ der Reihe nach; *it is my* ~ ich bin an der Reihe; *take* ~*s* (mit-)einander *od.* sich (gegenseitig) abwechseln (*at* in *dat.*, bei); *does it serve your* ~? ist Ihnen damit gedient?; ~**coat** ['tɜːnkəʊt] Abtrünnige(r) *m*, Überläufer(in); ~**er** [~ə] Drechsler *m*; Dreher *m*.

turn·ing ['tɜːnɪŋ] ⊕ Drehen *n*, Drechseln *n*; Biegung *f*; Straßenecke *f*; (Weg)Abzweigung *f*; Querstraße *f*; ~**point** *fig.* Wendepunkt *m*.

tur·nip ♥ ['tɜːnɪp] (*bsd.* Weiße) Rübe.

turn·out ['tɜːnaʊt] Aufmachung *f*, *bsd.* Kleidung *f*; Teilnahme *f*, Besucher(zahl *f*) *pl.*, Beteiligung *f*, *econ.* Gesamtproduktion *f*; ~**o·ver** ['tɜːnəʊvə] *econ.* Umsatz *m*; Personalwechsel *m*, Fluktuation *f*; ~**pike** *a.* ~ *road Am.* gebührenpflichtige Schnellstraße; ~**stile** Drehkreuz *n*; ~**ta·ble** ⑯ Drehscheibe *f*; Plattenteller *m*; ~**up** *Brt.* Hosenaufschlag *m*.

tur·pen·tine ⚗ ['tɜːpəntaɪn] Terpentin *m*.

tur·pi·tude ['tɜːpɪtjuːd] Verworfenheit *f*.

tur·ret ['tʌrɪt] Türmchen *n*; ✕ ⚓ Geschützturm *m*.

tur·tle *zo.* ['tɜːtl] (See)Schildkröte *f*; ~**dove** *zo.* Turteltaube *f*; ~**neck** Rollkragen *m*; *a.* ~ *sweater* Rollkragenpullover *m*.

tusk [tʌsk] Fangzahn *m*; Stoßzahn *m*; Hauer *m*.

tus·sle ['tʌsl] **1.** Rauferei *f*, Balgerei *f*; **2.** raufen, sich balgen.

tus·sock ['tʌsək] (Gras)Büschel *n*.

tut *int.* [tʌt] ach was!; Unsinn!

tu·te·lage ['tjuːtɪlɪdʒ] ⚖ Vormundschaft *f*; (An)Leitung *f*.

tu·tor ['tjuːtə] **1.** Privat-, Hauslehrer *m*; *Brt. univ.* Tutor *m*; *Am. univ.* Assistent *m* (*mit Lehrauftrag*); **2.** unterrichten; schulen; erziehen; **tu·to·ri·al** [tjuːˈtɔːrɪəl] **1.** *Brt. univ.* Tutorenkurs *m*; **2.** Tutor(en)...

tux·e·do *Am.* [tʌkˈsiːdəʊ] (*pl.* -dos, -does) Smoking *m*.

TV F ['tiːˈviː] **1.** TV *n*, Fernsehen *n*; Fernseher *m*, Fernsehapparat *m*; *on* ~ im Fernsehen; **2.** Fernseh...

twang [twæŋ] **1.** Schwirren *n*; *mst nasal* ~ näselnde Aussprache; **2.** schwirren (lassen); näseln; klimpern *od.* kratzen auf (*dat.*), zupfen.

tweak [twiːk] zwicken, kneifen.

tweet [twiːt] zwitschern.

tweez·ers ['twiːzəz] *pl.* (*a pair of* ~ e-e) Pinzette *f*.

twelfth [twelfθ] **1.** zwölfte(r, -s); **2.** Zwölftel *n*; **2·night** ['twelfθnaɪt] Dreikönigsabend *m*.

twelve [twelv] **1.** zwölf; **2.** Zwölf *f*.

twen|ti·eth ['twentɪɪθ] zwanzigste(r, -s); ~**ty** [~ɪ] **1.** zwanzig; **2.** Zwanzig *f*.

twice [twaɪs] zweimal.

twid·dle ['twɪdl] herumdrehen (an *dat.*); (herum)spielen mit (*od. with* mit).

twig [twɪg] dünner Zweig, Ästchen *n*.

twi·light ['twaɪlaɪt] Zwielicht *n*; (*bsd.* Abend)Dämmerung *f*; *fig.* Verfall *m*.

twin [twɪn] **1.** Zwillings...; doppelt; **2.** Zwilling *m*; ~*s pl.* Zwillinge *pl.*; *attr.* Zwillings...; ~*s pl.* -**bedded room**, Zweibettzimmer *n*; ~ **brother** Zwillingsbruder *m*; ~**engined** ✈ zweimotorig; ~**jet** ✈ zwei-, doppelstrahlig; ~**lens reflex camera** *phot.* Spiegelreflexkamera *f*; ~ **sister** Zwillingsschwester *f*; ~ **town** Partnerstadt *f*; ~ **track** Doppelspur *f* (*e-s Tonbands*).

twine [twaɪn] **1.** Bindfaden *m*, Schnur *f*; Zwirn *m*; **2.** zs.-drehen; verflechten; (sich) schlingen *od.* winden; umschlingen, -ranken.

twinge [twɪndʒ] stechender Schmerz, Zwicken *n*, Stich *m*.

twin·kle ['twɪŋkl] **1.** funkeln, blitzen; huschen; zwinkern; **2.** Funkeln *n*, Blitzen *n*; (Augen)Zwinkern *n*, Blinzeln *n*.

twirl [twɜːl] **1.** Wirbel *m*; **2.** wirbeln.

twist [twɪst] **1.** Drehung *f*; Windung *f*; Biegung *f*; (Gesichts)Verzerrung *f*; Twist *m*, Garn *n*; Kringel *m*, Zopf *m* (*Backwaren*); ♪ Twist *m*; *fig.* Entstellung *f*; *fig.* (ausgeprägte) Neigung *od.* Veranlagung *f*; **2.** (sich) drehen *od.* winden; zs.-drehen; verdrehen; (sich) verziehen *od.* -zerren; ♪ twisten, Twist tanzen.

twit *fig.* [twɪt] *j-n* aufziehen.

twitch [twɪtʃ] **1.** zupfen (an *dat.*); zucken mit (*od. with* vor); **2.** Zuckung *f*.

twit·ter ['twɪtə] **1.** zwitschern; **2.** Gezwitscher *n*; *in a* ~, *all of a* ~ aufgeregt.

two [tuː] **1.** zwei; *in* ~*s* zu zweit, zu zweien; *in* ~ entzwei; *put* ~ *and* ~ *together* sich einen Vers darauf machen; **2.** Zwei *f*; ~**bit** *Am.* F ['tuːbɪt] 25-Cent-...; *fig.* unbedeutend, klein; ~**cy·cle** *Am.* ⊕ Zweitakt...; ~

edged ['tu:'edʒd] zweischneidig; **∼fold** ['tu:fəʊld] zweifach; **∼pence** Brt. ['tʌpəns] zwei Pence pl.; **∼pen·ny** Brt. ['tʌpnɪ] zwei Pence wert; **∼piece** ['tu:pi:s] **1.** zweiteilig; **2.** a. ∼ dress Jackenkleid; a. ∼ swimming-costume Zweiteiler m; **∼seat·er** mot., ✈ ['tu:'si:tə] Zweisitzer m; **∼stroke** bsd. Brt. ⊕ ['tu:strəʊk] Zweitakt...; **∼way** Doppel..., ∼ adapter ⚡ Doppelstecker m; ∼ traffic Gegenverkehr m.

ty·coon Am. F [taɪ'ku:n] Industriemagnat m; oil ∼ Ölmagnat m.

type [taɪp] **1.** Typ m; Urbild n; Vorbild n; Muster n; Art f, Sorte f; print. Type f, Buchstabe m; true to ∼ artgemäß, typisch; set in ∼ print. setzen; **2.** v/t. et. mit der Maschine (ab-)schreiben, (ab)tippen; v/i. maschineschreiben, tippen; **∼writ·er**

['taɪpraɪtə] Schreibmaschine f; ∼ ribbon Farbband n.

ty·phoid ✿ ['taɪfɔɪd] **1.** typhös; ∼ fever = **2.** (Unterleibs)Typhus m.

ty·phoon [taɪ'fu:n] Taifun m.

ty·phus ✿ ['taɪfəs] Flecktyphus m, -fieber n; △ nicht Typhus.

typ·i·cal □ ['tɪpɪkl] typisch; bezeichnend, kennzeichnend (of für); **∼fy** [∼faɪ] typisch sein für; versinnbildlichen.

typ·ist ['taɪpɪst] Maschinenschreiber(in); Schreibkraft f.

ty·ran·nic [tɪ'rænɪk] (∼ally), **∼ni·cal** □ [∼kl] tyrannisch.

tyr·an·nize ['tɪrənaɪz] tyrannisieren; **∼ny** [∼ɪ] Tyrannei f.

ty·rant ['taɪərənt] Tyrann(in).

tyre Brt. ['taɪə] (Rad-, Auto)Reifen m.

Ty·ro·lese [tɪrə'li:z] **1.** Tiroler(in); **2.** tirolisch, Tiroler...

tzar hist. [zɑ:] Zar m.

U

u·biq·ui·tous □ [ju:'bɪkwɪtəs] allgegenwärtig, überall zu finden(d).

ud·der ['ʌdə] Euter n.

ug·ly □ ['ʌglɪ] (-ier, -iest) häßlich; schlimm; gemein; widerwärtig, übel.

ul·cer ✿ ['ʌlsə] Geschwür n; **∼ate** ✿ [∼reɪt] eitern (lassen); **∼ous** ✿ [∼rəs] eiternd.

ul·te·ri·or □ [ʌl'tɪərɪə] jenseitig; weiter; tiefer(liegend), versteckt.

ul·ti·mate □ ['ʌltɪmət] äußerste(r, -s), letzte(r, -s); End...; **∼ly** [∼lɪ] letztlich; schließlich.

ul·ti·ma·tum [ʌltɪ'meɪtəm] (pl. -tums, -ta [-tə]) Ultimatum n.

ul·tra ['ʌltrə] übermäßig; extrem; super...; Ultra..., ultra...; **∼fashion·a·ble** [∼'fæʃənəbl] hypermodern; **∼mod·ern** hypermodern.

um·bil·i·cal cord anat. [ʌm'bɪlɪkl kɔ:d] Nabelschnur f.

um·brel·la [ʌm'brelə] Regenschirm m; ✕, ✈ Abschirmung f; fig. Schutz m.

um·pire ['ʌmpaɪə] **1.** Schiedsrichter m; **2.** als Schiedsrichter fungieren

(bei); schlichten; Sport: a. Spiel leiten.

un- [ʌn] un..., Un...; ent...; nicht...

un·a·bashed ['ʌnə'bæʃt] unverfroren; unerschrocken.

un·a·bat·ed ['ʌnə'beɪtɪd] unvermindert.

un·a·ble ['ʌn'eɪbl] unfähig, außerstande, nicht in der Lage.

un·ac·com·mo·dat·ing ['ʌnə'kɒmədeɪtɪŋ] unnachgiebig; ungefällig.

un·ac·coun·ta·ble □ ['ʌnə'kaʊntəbl] unerklärlich, seltsam.

un·ac·cus·tomed ['ʌnə'kʌstəmd] ungewohnt; ungewöhnlich.

un·ac·quaint·ed ['ʌnə'kweɪntɪd]: be ∼ with s.th. et. nicht kennen, mit e-r Sache nicht vertraut sein.

un·ad·vised □ ['ʌnəd'vaɪzd] unbesonnen, unüberlegt; unberaten.

un·af·fect·ed □ ['ʌnə'fektɪd] unberührt; ungerührt; ungekünstelt.

un·aid·ed ['ʌn'eɪdɪd] ohne Unterstützung, (ganz) allein; bloß (Auge).

un·al·ter·a·ble □ [ʌn'ɔ:ltərəbl] unveränderlich; **un·al·tered** ['ʌn'ɔ:ltəd] unverändert.

U
V

u·na·nim·i·ty [ju:nəˈnɪmətɪ] Einmütigkeit *f;* **u·nan·i·mous** □ [ju:ˈnænɪməs] einmütig, -stimmig.

un·an·swe·ra·ble □ [ʌnˈɑ:nsərəbl] unwiderleglich; **un·an·swered** [ʌnˈɑ:nsəd] unbeantwortet.

un·ap·proa·cha·ble □ [ˈʌnəˈprəʊtʃəbl] unzugänglich, unnahbar.

un·apt □ [ʌnˈæpt] ungeeignet.

un·a·shamed □ [ˈʌnəˈʃeɪmd] schamlos.

un·asked [ʌnˈɑ:skt] ungefragt; ungebeten; uneingeladen.

un·as·sist·ed [ˈʌnəˈsɪstɪd] ohne Hilfe *od.* Unterstützung.

un·as·sum·ing [ˈʌnəˈsju:mɪŋ] anspruchslos, bescheiden.

un·at·tached [ˈʌnəˈtætʃt] nicht gebunden; ungebunden, ledig, frei.

un·at·trac·tive □ [ˈʌnəˈtræktɪv] wenig anziehend, reizlos, unattraktiv.

un·au·thor·ized [ʌnˈɔ:θəraɪzd] unberechtigt; unbefugt.

un·a·vai·la·ble □ [ˈʌnəˈveɪləbl] nicht verfügbar; **un·a·vail·ing** [~ɪŋ] vergeblich.

un·a·void·a·ble □ [ʌnəˈvɔɪdəbl] unvermeidlich.

un·a·ware [ˈʌnəˈweə]: *be ~ of et.* nicht bemerken; **~s** [~z] unversehens, unvermutet; versehentlich.

un·backed [ʌnˈbækt] ohne Unterstützung; ungedeckt (*Scheck*).

un·bal·anced [ʌnˈbælənst] unausgeglichen; *of ~ mind* geistesgestört.

un·bear·a·ble □ [ʌnˈbeərəbl] unerträglich.

un·beat·en [ʌnˈbi:tn] ungeschlagen, unbesiegt; unübertroffen.

un·be·com·ing □ [ˈʌnbɪˈkʌmɪŋ] unkleidsam; unpassend, unschicklich.

un·be·known(st) [ˈʌnbɪˈnəʊn(st)] (*to*) ohne (*j-s*) Wissen; unbekannt (*to dat.*).

un·be·lief *eccl.* [ˈʌnbɪˈli:f] Unglaube *m.*

un·be·lie·va·ble □ [ˈʌnbɪˈli:vəbl] unglaublich; **un·be·liev·ing** □ [ˈʌnbɪˈli:vɪŋ] ungläubig.

un·bend [ʌnˈbend] (-*bent*) (sich) entspannen; aus sich herausgehen, auftauen; **~·ing** □ [~ɪŋ] unbiegsam; *fig.* unbeugsam.

un·bi·as(s)ed □ [ʌnˈbaɪəst] unvoreingenommen; ⚖ unbefangen.

un·bid·(·den) [ʌnˈbɪd(n)] unaufgefordert; ungebeten; ungeladen.

un·bind [ʌnˈbaɪnd] (-*bound*) losbinden, befreien; lösen; den Verband abnehmen von.

un·blush·ing □ [ʌnˈblʌʃɪŋ] schamlos.

un·born [ˈʌnˈbɔ:n] (noch) ungeboren; (zu)künftig, kommend.

un·bos·om [ʌnˈbuzəm] offenbaren.

un·bound·ed □ [ˈʌnˈbaʊndɪd] unbegrenzt; *fig.* grenzen-, schrankenlos.

un·bri·dled *fig.* [ʌnˈbraɪdld] ungezügelt; *~ tongue* lose Zunge.

un·bro·ken □ [ˈʌnˈbrəʊkən] ungebrochen; unversehrt; ununterbrochen; nicht zugeritten (*Pferd*).

un·bur·den [ʌnˈbɜ:dn]: *~ o.s.* (to *s.o.*) (j-m) sein Herz ausschütten.

un·but·ton [ʌnˈbʌtn] aufknöpfen.

un·called-for [ʌnˈkɔ:ldfɔ:] unerwünscht; unverlangt; unpassend.

un·can·ny □ [ʌnˈkænɪ] (-*ier*, -*iest*) unheimlich.

un·cared-for [ˈʌnˈkeədfɔ:] unbeachtet; vernachlässigt; ungepflegt.

un·ceas·ing □ [ʌnˈsi:sɪŋ] unaufhörlich.

un·ce·re·mo·ni·ous □ [ˈʌnserɪˈməʊnjəs] ungezwungen; grob; unhöflich.

un·cer·tain □ [ʌnˈsɜ:tn] unsicher; ungewiß; unbestimmt; unzuverlässig; **~·ty** [~tɪ] Unsicherheit *f.*

un·chal·lenged [ʌnˈtʃæləndʒd] unangefochten.

un·change·a·ble □ [ʌnˈtʃeɪndʒəbl] unveränderlich, unwandelbar; **un·changed** [ʌnˈtʃeɪndʒd] unverändert; **un·chang·ing** □ [ʌnˈtʃeɪndʒɪŋ] unveränderlich.

un·char·i·ta·ble □ [ʌnˈtʃærɪtəbl] lieblos; unbarmherzig; unfreundlich.

un·checked [ʌnˈtʃekt] ungehindert; unkontrolliert.

un·civ·il □ [ʌnˈsɪvl] unhöflich; **un·civ·i·lized** [~vəlaɪzd] unzivilisiert.

un·claimed [ʌnˈkleɪmd] nicht beansprucht; unzustellbar (*bsd. Brief*).

un·clasp [ʌnˈklɑ:sp] auf-, loshaken, auf-, losschnallen; aufmachen.

un·cle [ʌŋkl] Onkel *m.*

un·clean [ʌnˈkli:n] unrein.

un·close [ʌnˈkləʊz] (sich) öffnen.

un·come·ly [ʌnˈkʌmlɪ] (-*ier*, -*iest*) unattraktiv, unschön; reizlos; unpassend.

un·com·for·ta·ble □ [ʌnˈkʌmfətəbl]

unbehaglich, ungemütlich; unangenehm.

un·com·mon ☐ [ʌnˈkɒmən] ungewöhnlich.

un·com·mu·ni·ca·tive ☐ [ˈʌnkə-ˈmjuːnɪkətɪv] wortkarg, verschlossen.

un·com·plain·ing ☐ [ˈʌnkəmˈpleɪ-nɪŋ] klaglos, ohne Murren, geduldig.

un·com·pro·mis·ing ☐ [ʌnˈkɒm-prəmaɪzɪŋ] kompromißlos.

un·con·cern [ʌnkənˈsɜːn] Unbekümmertheit f; Gleichgültigkeit f; **~ed** ☐ unbekümmert; unbeteiligt; gleichgültig; uninteressiert (with an dat.).

un·con·di·tion·al ☐ [ˈʌnkənˈdɪʃənl] bedingungs-, vorbehaltlos.

un·con·firmed [ˈʌnkənˈfɜːmd] unbestätigt; eccl. nicht konfirmiert.

un·con·nect·ed ☐ [ˈʌnkəˈnektɪd] unverbunden; unzusammenhängend.

un·con·quer·a·ble ☐ [ʌnˈkɒŋkərəbl] unüberwindlich, unbesiegbar; **un·con·quered** [ʌnˈkɒŋkəd] unbesiegt.

un·con·scio·na·ble ☐ [ʌnˈkɒnʃnəbl] gewissen-, skrupellos; F unverschämt, unmäßig, übermäßig.

un·con·scious ☐ [ʌnˈkɒnʃəs] unbewußt; ǂ bewußtlos; **~·ness** ǂ [~nɪs] Bewußtlosigkeit f.

un·con·sti·tu·tion·al ☐ [ˈʌnkɒnstɪ-ˈtjuːʃənl] verfassungswidrig.

un·con·trol·la·ble ☐ [ˈʌnkənˈtrəʊ-ləbl] unkontrollierbar; unbeherrscht; **un·con·trolled** [ˈʌn-kənˈtrəʊld] unbeaufsichtigt; unbeherrscht.

un·con·ven·tion·al ☐ [ˈʌnkən-ˈvenʃənl] unkonventionell; unüblich; ungezwungen.

un·con·vinced [ˈʌnkənˈvɪnst] nicht überzeugt (of von); **un·con·vinc·ing** [~ɪŋ] nicht überzeugend.

un·cork [ʌnˈkɔːk] entkorken.

un·count|a·ble [ʌnˈkaʊntəbl] unzählbar; **~·ed** ungezählt.

un·cou·ple [ʌnˈkʌpl] ab-, aus-, loskoppeln.

un·couth ☐ [ʌnˈkuːθ] ungehobelt.

un·cov·er [ʌnˈkʌvə] aufdecken, freilegen; entblößen.

unc|tion [ˈʌŋkʃn] Salbung f (a. fig.); Salbe f; **~·tu·ous** ☐ [~tjʊəs] fettig, ölig; fig. salbungsvoll.

un·cul·ti·vat·ed [ʌnˈkʌltɪveɪtɪd], **un·cul·tured** [~tʃəd] unkultiviert.

un·dam·aged [ʌnˈdæmɪdʒd] unbeschädigt, unversehrt, heil.

un·daunt·ed ☐ [ʌnˈdɔːntɪd] unerschrocken, furchtlos.

un·de·ceive [ʌndɪˈsiːv] j-m die Augen öffnen; j-n aufklären.

un·de·cid·ed ☐ [ʌndɪˈsaɪdɪd] unentschieden, offen; unentschlossen.

un·de·fined [ʌndɪˈfaɪnd] unbestimmt; unbegrenzt.

un·de·mon·stra·tive ☐ [ʌndɪˈmɒn-strətɪv] zurückhaltend, reserviert.

un·de·ni·a·ble ☐ [ʌndɪˈnaɪəbl] unleugbar; unbestreitbar.

un·der [ˈʌndə] **1.** adv. unten; darunter; **2.** prp. unter; **3.** adj. untere(r, -s); in Zssgn: unter..., Unter...; ungenügend, zu gering; **~·bid** [ʌndəˈbɪd] (-dd-; -bid) unterbieten; **~·brush** [ˈʌndəbrʌʃ] Unterholz n; **~·car·riage** [ˈʌndəkærɪdʒ] ☒ Fahrwerk n, -gestell n; mot. Fahrgestell n; **~·clothes** [ˈʌndəkləʊðz] pl., **~·cloth·ing** [~ðɪŋ] Unterkleidung f, -wäsche f; **~·cut** [ʌndəˈkʌt] (-tt-; -cut) Preise unterbieten; **~·dog** [ˈʌndədɒg] Verlierer m, Unterlegene(r m) f; der sozial Schwächere od. Benachteiligte; **~·done** [ʌndəˈdʌn] nicht gar, nicht durchgebraten; **~·es·ti·mate** [ʌndəˈestɪmeɪt] unterschätzen; **~·fed** [ʌndəˈfed] unterernährt; **~·go** [ʌndəˈgəʊ] (-went, -gone) durchmachen; erdulden; sich unterziehen (dat.); **~·grad·u·ate** [ʌndəˈgræd-jʊət] Student(in); **~·ground 1.** unterirdisch; Untergrund...; **2.** bsd. Brt. Untergrundbahn f, U-Bahn f; **~·growth** [ˈʌndə-grəʊθ] Unterholz n; **~·hand** [ʌndə-ˈhænd] unter der Hand; heimlich; **~·lie** [ʌndəˈlaɪ] (-lay, -lain) zugrunde liegen (dat.); **~·line** [ʌndəˈlaɪn] unterstreichen; **~·ling** contp. [ˈʌn-dəlɪŋ] Untergebene(r m) f; **~·mine** [ˈʌndəˈmaɪn] unterminieren; fig. untergraben; schwächen; **~·most** [ˈʌn-dəməʊst] unterste(r, -s); **~·neath** [ʌndəˈniːθ] **1.** prp. unter(halb); **2.** adv. unten; darunter; **~·pass** [ˈʌn-dəpɑːs] Unterführung f; **~·pin** [ʌn-dəˈpɪn] (-nn-) untermauern (a. fig.); **~·plot** [ˈʌndəplɒt] Nebenhandlung f; **~·priv·i·leged** [ʌndəˈprɪvɪlɪdʒd] benachteiligt; **~·rate** [ʌndəˈreɪt] unterschätzen; **~·sec·re·ta·ry** [ˈʌndə-ˈsekrətərɪ] Staatssekretär m; **~·sell** econ. [ʌndəˈsel] (-sold) j-n unter-

U V

bieten; *Ware* verschleudern; **~shirt**
Am. ['ʌndəʃɜːt] Unterhemd *n*;
~signed ['ʌndəsaɪnd]: *the* ~ der, die
Unterzeichnete; **~size(d)** [ʌndə-
ˈsaɪz(d)] zu klein; **~skirt** ['ʌndə-
skɜːt] Unterrock *m*; **~staffed** ['ʌn-
dəˈstɑːft] Unterbesetzt; **~stand** [ʌndəˈstænd] (*-stood*) verstehen; sich verstehen auf (*acc.*); (als
sicher) annehmen; erfahren, hören;
(sinngemäß) ergänzen; *make o.s.*
understood sich verständlich machen; *an understood thing* e-e abge-
machte Sache; **~stand·a·ble** [~əbl]
verständlich; **~stand·ing** [~ɪŋ] Verstand *m*; Einvernehmen *n*; Verständigung *f*, Abmachung *f*, Einigung *f*;
Voraussetzung *f*; **~state** [ʌndəˈsteɪt]
zu gering angeben; abschwächen;
~state·ment [~mənt] Understate-
ment *n*, Untertreibung *f*; **~take**
[ʌndəˈteɪk] (*-took, -taken*) unternehmen; übernehmen; sich verpflichten; **~tak·er** ['ʌndəteɪkə] Leichenbestatter *m*; Beerdigungs-, Be-
stattungsinstitut *n*; △ *nicht Unter-
nehmer*; **~tak·ing** [ʌndəˈteɪkɪŋ]
Unternehmen *n*; Zusicherung *f*;
['ʌndəteɪkɪŋ] Leichenbestattung *f*;
~tone ['ʌndətəʊn] leiser Ton; *fig.*
Unterton *m*; **~val·ue** [ʌndəˈvæljuː]
unterschätzen; **~wear** ['ʌndəweə]
Unterkleidung *f*, -wäsche *f*; **~wood**
['ʌndəwʊd] Unterholz *n*.

un·de·served □ ['ʌndɪˈzɜːvd] unverdient; **un·de·serv·ing** □ [~ɪŋ] unwürdig.

un·de·signed □ ['ʌndɪˈzaɪnd] unbeabsichtigt, unabsichtlich.

un·de·sir·a·ble □ ['ʌndɪˈzaɪərəbl] **1.** □
unerwünscht; **2.** unerwünschte Person.

un·de·vel·oped ['ʌndɪˈveləpt] uner-
schlossen (*Gelände*); unentwickelt.

un·de·vi·at·ing □ ['ʌnˈdiːvɪeɪtɪŋ]
unentwegt.

un·dies F ['ʌndɪz] *pl.* (Damen)Unter-
wäsche *f*.

un·dig·ni·fied □ [ʌnˈdɪɡnɪfaɪd] unwürdig, würdelos.

un·dis·ci·plined [ʌnˈdɪsɪplɪnd] undiszipliniert; ungeschult.

un·dis·guised □ ['ʌndɪsˈɡaɪzd] nicht
verkleidet; *fig.* unverhohlen.

un·dis·put·ed □ ['ʌndɪsˈpjuːtɪd] un-
bestritten.

un·do ['ʌnˈduː] (*-did, -done*) aufmachen; (auf)lösen; ungeschehen ma-

chen, aufheben; vernichten; **~ing**
[~ɪŋ] Aufmachen *n*; Ungeschehen-
machen *n*; Vernichtung *f*; Verderben *n*; **un·done** ['ʌnˈdʌn] zugrunde
gerichtet, ruiniert, erledigt.

un·doubt·ed □ [ʌnˈdaʊtɪd] unzweifelhaft, zweifellos.

un·dreamed [ʌnˈdriːmd], **un-
dreamt** [ʌnˈdremt]: *~-of* ungeahnt.

un·dress ['ʌnˈdres] (sich) entkleiden
od. ausziehen; **~ed** unbekleidet.

un·due □ ['ʌnˈdjuː] unpassend;
übermäßig; *econ.* noch nicht fällig.

un·du·late ['ʌndjʊleɪt] wogen, wallen; wellenförmig verlaufen; **~la-
tion** [ʌndjʊˈleɪʃn] wellenförmige
Bewegung.

un·du·ti·ful □ ['ʌnˈdjuːtɪfl] ungehorsam; pflichtvergessen.

un·earth ['ʌnˈɜːθ] ausgraben; *fig.*
aufstöbern; **~ly** [ʌnˈɜːθlɪ] überirdisch; unheimlich; *at an ~ hour* F zu
e-r unchristlichen Zeit.

un·eas·i·ness [ʌnˈiːzɪnɪs] Unruhe *f*;
Unbehagen *n*; **~y** □ [ʌnˈiːzɪ] (*-ier,
-iest*) unbehaglich; unruhig; unsicher.

un·ed·u·cat·ed ['ʌnˈedjʊkeɪtɪd] ungebildet.

un·e·mo·tion·al □ ['ʌnɪˈməʊʃənl]
leidenschaftslos; passiv; nüchtern.

un·em·ployed ['ʌnɪmˈplɔɪd] **1.** arbeitslos; ungenützt; **2.** *the* ~ *pl.*
die Arbeitslosen *pl.*; **~ploy·ment**
[~mənt] Arbeitslosigkeit *f*.

un·end·ing □ [ʌnˈendɪŋ] endlos.

un·en·dur·a·ble □ ['ʌnɪnˈdjʊərəbl]
unerträglich.

un·en·gaged ['ʌnɪnˈɡeɪdʒd] frei.

un·e·qual □ ['ʌnˈiːkwəl] ungleich;
nicht gewachsen (*to dat.*); **~(l)ed**
unerreicht, unübertroffen.

un·er·ring □ ['ʌnˈɜːrɪŋ] unfehlbar.

un·es·sen·tial ['ʌnɪˈsenʃl] unwesentlich, unwichtig.

un·e·ven □ ['ʌnˈiːvn] uneben; un-
gleich(mäßig); ungerade (*Zahl*).

un·e·vent·ful □ ['ʌnɪˈventfl] ereig-
nislos; ohne Zwischenfälle.

un·ex·am·pled ['ʌnɪɡˈzɑːmpld] beispiellos.

un·ex·cep·tio·na·ble □ ['ʌnɪkˈsep-
ʃnəbl] untadelig; einwandfrei.

un·ex·pec·ted □ ['ʌnɪkˈspektɪd] unerwartet.

un·ex·plained ['ʌnɪkˈspleɪnd] uner-
klärt.

un·fad·ing [ʌnˈfeɪdɪŋ] nicht wel-

unimportant

kend; unvergänglich; echt (*Farbe*).

un·fail·ing ☐ [ʌnˈfeɪlɪŋ] unfehlbar, nie versagend; unerschöpflich; *fig.* treu.

un·fair ☐ [ʌnˈfeə] unfair; ungerecht; unehrlich.

un·faith·ful ☐ [ʌnˈfeɪθfl] un(ge)-treu, treulos; nicht wortgetreu.

un·fa·mil·i·ar [ʌnfəˈmɪljə] ungewohnt; unbekannt; nicht vertraut (*with* mit).

un·fas·ten [ʌnˈfɑːsn] aufmachen; lösen; ~ed unbefestigt, lose.

un·fath·o·ma·ble ☐ [ʌnˈfæðəməbl] unergründlich.

un·fa·vo(u)·ra·ble ☐ [ʌnˈfeɪvərəbl] ungünstig; unvorteilhaft.

un·feel·ing ☐ [ʌnˈfiːlɪŋ] gefühllos.

un·fil·i·al ☐ [ʌnˈfɪljəl] respektlos, pflichtvergessen (*Kind*).

un·fin·ished [ʌnˈfɪnɪʃt] unvollendet; unfertig; unerledigt.

un·fit [ʌnˈfɪt] **1.** ☐ ungeeignet, untauglich; *Sport:* nicht fit, nicht in (guter) Form; **2.** (*-tt-*) ungeeignet *od.* untauglich machen.

un·fix [ʌnˈfɪks] losmachen, lösen.

un·fledged [ʌnˈfledʒd] ungefiedert, (noch) nicht flügge; *fig.* unreif.

un·flinch·ing ☐ [ʌnˈflɪntʃɪŋ] entschlossen, unnachgiebig; unerschrocken.

un·fold [ʌnˈfəʊld] (sich) entfalten *od.* öffnen; [ʌnˈfəʊld] darlegen, enthüllen.

un·forced [ʌnˈfɔːst] ungezwungen.

un·fore·seen [ʌnfɔːˈsiːn] unvorhergesehen, unerwartet.

un·for·get·ta·ble ☐ [ʌnfəˈɡetəbl] unvergeßlich.

un·for·giv·ing [ʌnfəˈɡɪvɪŋ] unversöhnlich, nachtragend.

un·for·got·ten [ʌnfəˈɡɒtn] unvergessen.

un·for·tu·nate [ʌnˈfɔːtʃnət] **1.** ☐ unglücklich; **2.** Unglückliche(r *m*) *f*; ~**ly** [~lɪ] unglücklicherweise, leider.

un·found·ed ☐ [ʌnˈfaʊndɪd] unbegründet, grundlos.

un·friend·ly [ʌnˈfrendlɪ] (*-ier, -iest*) unfreundlich; ungünstig.

un·furl [ʌnˈfɜːl] entfalten, aufrollen.

un·fur·nished [ʌnˈfɜːnɪʃt] unmöbliert.

un·gain·ly [ʌnˈɡeɪnlɪ] unbeholfen, plump, linkisch.

un·gen·er·ous ☐ [ʌnˈdʒenərəs] nicht freigebig; kleinlich; unfair.

un·god·ly ☐ [ʌnˈɡɒdlɪ] gottlos; F scheußlich; *at an* ~ *hour* F zu e-r unchristlichen Zeit.

un·gov·er·na·ble ☐ [ʌnˈɡʌvənəbl] unlenksam; zügellos, wild.

un·grace·ful ☐ [ʌnˈɡreɪsfl] ungraziös, ohne Anmut; unbeholfen.

un·gra·cious ☐ [ʌnˈɡreɪʃəs] ungnädig; unfreundlich.

un·grate·ful ☐ [ʌnˈɡreɪtfl] undankbar.

un·guard·ed ☐ [ʌnˈɡɑːdɪd] unbewacht; ungeschützt; unvorsichtig.

un·guent *pharm.* [ˈʌŋɡwənt] Salbe *f*.

un·ham·pered [ʌnˈhæmpəd] ungehindert.

un·hand·some ☐ [ʌnˈhænsəm] unschön.

un·han·dy ☐ [ʌnˈhændɪ] (*-ier, -iest*) unhandlich; ungeschickt; unbeholfen.

un·hap·py ☐ [ʌnˈhæpɪ] (*-ier, -iest*) unglücklich.

un·harmed [ʌnˈhɑːmd] unversehrt.

un·health·y ☐ [ʌnˈhelθɪ] (*-ier, -iest*) ungesund.

un·heard-of [ʌnˈhɜːdɒv] unerhört; beispiellos.

un·heed·ed ☐ [ʌnˈhiːdɪd] unbeachtet; ~**ing** [~ɪŋ] sorglos.

un·hes·i·tat·ing ☐ [ʌnˈhezɪteɪtɪŋ] ohne Zögern; anstandslos.

un·ho·ly [ʌnˈhəʊlɪ] (*-ier, -iest*) unheilig; gottlos; F *s. ungodly*.

un·hook [ʌnˈhʊk] auf-, loshaken.

un·hoped-for [ʌnˈhəʊptfɔː] unverhofft, unerwartet.

un·hurt [ʌnˈhɜːt] unverletzt.

u·ni [ˈjuːnɪ] uni..., ein..., einzig.

u·ni·corn [ˈjuːnɪkɔːn] Einhorn *n*.

u·ni·fi·ca·tion [juːnɪfɪˈkeɪʃn] Vereinigung *f*; Vereinheitlichung *f*.

u·ni·form [ˈjuːnɪfɔːm] **1.** ☐ gleichförmig, -mäßig, gleich; einheitlich; **2.** Uniform *f*, Dienstkleidung *f*; **3.** uniformieren; ~**i·ty** [juːnɪˈfɔːmətɪ] Gleichförmigkeit *f*; Einheitlichkeit *f*, Übereinstimmung *f*.

u·ni·fy [ˈjuːnɪfaɪ] verein(ig)en; vereinheitlichen.

u·ni·lat·er·al ☐ [ˈjuːnɪˈlætərəl] einseitig.

un·i·mag·i·na|ble ☐ [ˈʌnɪˈmædʒɪnəbl] unvorstellbar; ~**tive** ☐ [ˈʌnɪˈmædʒɪnətɪv] phantasie-, einfallslos.

un·im·por·tant ☐ [ˈʌnɪmˈpɔːtənt] unwichtig, unbedeutend.

U
V

un·im·proved [ˈʌnɪmˈpruːvd] nicht kultiviert, unbebaut (*Land*); unverbessert.

un·in·formed [ˈʌnɪnˈfɔːmd] nicht unterrichtet *od.* eingeweiht.

un·in·hab·i·ta·ble [ˈʌnɪnˈhæbɪtəbl] unbewohnbar; **~·it·ed** [~tɪd] unbewohnt.

un·in·jured [ˈʌnˈɪndʒəd] unbeschädigt, unverletzt.

un·in·tel·li·gi·ble □ [ˈʌnɪnˈtelɪdʒəbl] unverständlich.

un·in·ten·tion·al □ [ˈʌnɪnˈtenʃənl] unabsichtlich, unbeabsichtigt.

un·in·te·rest·ing □ [ˈʌnˈɪntrɪstɪŋ] uninteressant.

un·in·ter·rupt·ed □ [ˈʌnɪntəˈrʌptɪd] ununterbrochen.

un·ion [ˈjuːnjən] Vereinigung *f*; Verbindung *f*; Union *f*; Verband *m*, Verein *m*, Bund *m*; *pol.* Vereinigung *f*, Zusammenschluß *m*; Gewerkschaft *f*; **~·ist** [~ɪst] Gewerkschaftler(in); ♀ **Jack** Union Jack *m* (*britische Nationalflagge*); **~ suit** *Am.* Hemdhose *f* (mit langem Bein).

u·nique □ [juːˈniːk] einzigartig, einmalig.

u·ni·son ♪ *u. fig.* [ˈjuːnɪzn] Einklang *m.*

u·nit [ˈjuːnɪt] Einheit *f*; ⊕ (Bau)Einheit *f*; ⚔ Einer *m.*

u·nite [juːˈnaɪt] (sich) vereinigen, (sich) verbinden; **u·nit·ed** vereinigt, vereint; **u·ni·ty** [ˈjuːnətɪ] Einheit *f*; Einigkeit *f*, Eintracht *f.*

u·ni·ver·sal □ [juːnɪˈvɜːsl] allgemein; allumfassend; Universal...; Welt...; **~·i·ty** [ˈjuːnɪvɜːˈsælətɪ] Allgemeinheit *f*; umfassende Bildung; Vielseitigkeit *f.*

u·ni·verse [ˈjuːnɪvɜːs] Weltall *n*, Universum *n.*

u·ni·ver·si·ty [juːnɪˈvɜːsətɪ] Universität *f*; **~ graduate** Akademiker *m.*

un·just □ [ˈʌnˈdʒʌst] ungerecht; **un·jus·ti·fi·a·ble** □ [ˈʌnˈdʒʌstɪfaɪəbl] nicht zu rechtfertigen(d), unentschuldbar.

un·kempt [ˈʌnˈkempt] ungekämmt, zerzaust; ungepflegt.

un·kind □ [ˈʌnˈkaɪnd] unfreundlich.

un·know·ing □ [ˈʌnˈnəʊɪŋ] unwissend; unbewußt; **un·known** [~n] **1.** unbekannt; **~ to me** ohne mein Wissen; **2.** der, die, das Unbekannte.

un·lace [ˈʌnˈleɪs] aufschnüren.

un·latch [ˈʌnˈlætʃ] *Tür* aufklinken.

un·law·ful □ [ˈʌnˈlɔːfl] ungesetzlich, widerrechtlich, illegal.

un·lead·ed [ˈʌnˈledɪd] bleifrei.

un·learn [ˈʌnˈlɜːn] (-ed *od.* -learnt) verlernen.

un·less [ənˈles] wenn ... nicht, außer wenn ..., es sei denn, daß ...

un·like [ˈʌnˈlaɪk] **1.** *adj.* □ ungleich; **2.** *prp.* unähnlich (*s.o.* j-m); anders als; im Gegensatz zu; **~·ly** [ˈʌnˈlaɪklɪ] unwahrscheinlich.

un·lim·it·ed [ˈʌnˈlɪmɪtɪd] unbegrenzt.

un·load [ˈʌnˈləʊd] ent-, ab-, ausladen; ♧ *Ladung* löschen.

un·lock [ˈʌnˈlɒk] aufschließen; **~ed** unverschlossen.

un·looked-for [ˈʌnˈlʊktfɔː] unerwartet, überraschend.

un·loose, un·loos·en [ˈʌnˈluːs, ʌnˈluːsn] lösen; lockern; losmachen.

un·love·ly [ˈʌnˈlʌvlɪ] reizlos, unschön; **un·lov·ing** □ [~ɪŋ] lieblos.

un·luck·y □ [ˈʌnˈlʌkɪ] (-ier, -iest) unglücklich; unheilvoll; **be ~** Pech haben.

un·make [ˈʌnˈmeɪk] (-made) aufheben, widerrufen, rückgängig machen; umbilden; j-n absetzen.

un·man [ˈʌnˈmæn] (-nn-) entmannen; entmutigen; **~ned** *Raumflug:* unbemannt.

un·man·age·a·ble □ [ˈʌnˈmænɪdʒəbl] unkontrollierbar.

un·mar·ried [ˈʌnˈmærɪd] unverheiratet, ledig.

un·mask [ˈʌnˈmɑːsk] (sich) demaskieren; *fig.* entlarven.

un·matched [ˈʌnˈmætʃt] unerreicht, unübertroffen, unvergleichlich.

un·mean·ing □ [ʌnˈmiːnɪŋ] nichtssagend.

un·mea·sured [ʌnˈmeʒəd] ungemessen; unermeßlich.

un·mer·it·ed [ʌnˈmerɪtɪd] unverdient.

un·mind·ful □ [ʌnˈmaɪndfl]: **be ~ of** nicht achten auf (*acc.*); nicht denken an (*acc.*).

un·mis·ta·ka·ble □ [ˈʌnmɪˈsteɪkəbl] unverkennbar; unmißverständlich.

un·mit·i·gat·ed [ʌnˈmɪtɪgeɪtɪd] ungemildert; **an ~ scoundrel** ein Erzhalunke.

un·mo·lest·ed [ˈʌnməˈlestɪd] unbelästigt.

un·mount·ed [ˈʌnˈmaʊntɪd] unberitten; ungefaßt (*Schmuckstein*); nicht aufgezogen (*Bild*).

un·moved ['ʌn'muːvd] unbewegt, ungerührt.

un·named ['ʌn'neɪmd] ungenannt.

un·nat·u·ral □ [ʌn'nætʃrəl] unnatürlich.

un·nec·es·sa·ry □ [ʌn'nesəsərɪ] unnötig; überflüssig.

un·neigh·bo(u)r·ly [ʌn'neɪbəlɪ] nicht gutnachbarlich; unfreundlich.

un·nerve [ʌn'nɜːv] entnerven.

un·no·ticed [ʌn'nəʊtɪst] unbemerkt.

un·ob·jec·tio·na·ble □ ['ʌnəb'dʒek-ʃnəbl] einwandfrei.

un·ob·serv·ant □ ['ʌnəb'zɜːvənt] unachtsam; **un·ob·served** □ [~d] unbemerkt.

un·ob·tai·na·ble ['ʌnəb'teɪnəbl] unerreichbar.

un·ob·tru·sive □ ['ʌnəb'truːsɪv] unaufdringlich, bescheiden.

un·oc·cu·pied ['ʌn'ɒkjʊpaɪd] unbesetzt; unbewohnt; unbeschäftigt.

un·of·fend·ing ['ʌnə'fendɪŋ] harmlos.

un·of·fi·cial □ ['ʌnə'fɪʃl] nichtamtlich, inoffiziell.

un·op·posed ['ʌnə'pəʊzd] ungehindert.

un·os·ten·ta·tious □ ['ʌnɒstən-'teɪʃəs] anspruchslos; unauffällig; schlicht.

un·owned ['ʌn'əʊnd] herrenlos.

un·pack ['ʌn'pæk] auspacken.

un·paid ['ʌn'peɪd] unbezahlt.

un·par·al·leled [ʌn'pærəleld] einmalig, beispiellos, ohnegleichen.

un·par·don·a·ble □ [ʌn'pɑːdnəbl] unverzeihlich.

un·per·ceived □ ['ʌnpə'siːvd] unbemerkt.

un·per·turbed ['ʌnpə'tɜːbd] ruhig, gelassen.

un·pick [ʌn'pɪk] *Naht etc.* auftrennen.

un·placed [ʌn'pleɪst]: *be* ~ *Sport:* sich nicht placieren können.

un·pleas·ant □ [ʌn'pleznt] unangenehm, unerfreulich; unfreundlich; **~·ness** [~nɪs] Unannehmlichkeit *f*; Unstimmigkeit *f*.

un·pol·ished [ʌn'pɒlɪʃt] unpoliert; *fig.* ungehobelt, ungebildet.

un·pol·lut·ed ['ʌnpə'luːtɪd] unverschmutzt, unverseucht, sauber (*Umwelt*).

un·pop·u·lar □ ['ʌn'pɒpjʊlə] unpopulär, unbeliebt; **~·i·ty** ['ʌn-pɒpjʊ'lærətɪ] Unbeliebtheit *f*.

un·prac·ti·cal □ [ʌn'præktɪkl] unpraktisch; **~·tised**, *Am.* **~·ticed** [ʌn-'præktɪst] ungeübt.

un·pre·ce·dent·ed □ [ʌn'presɪdən-tɪd] beispiellos; noch nie dagewesen.

un·prej·u·diced □ [ʌn'predʒʊdɪst] unbefangen, unvoreingenommen.

un·pre·med·i·tat·ed □ ['ʌnprɪ'me-dɪteɪtɪd] unüberlegt; nicht vorsätzlich.

un·pre·pared □ ['ʌnprɪ'peəd] unvorbereitet.

un·pre·ten·tious □ ['ʌnprɪ'tenʃəs] bescheiden, schlicht.

un·prin·ci·pled [ʌn'prɪnsəpld] ohne Grundsätze; gewissenlos.

un·prof·i·ta·ble □ [ʌn'prɒfɪtəbl] unrentabel.

un·proved, un·prov·en [ʌn'pruːvd, 'ʌn'pruːvn] unbewiesen.

un·pro·vid·ed ['ʌnprə'vaɪdɪd]: ~ *with* nicht versehen mit, ohne; ~ *for* unversorgt, mittellos.

un·pro·voked □ ['ʌnprə'vəʊkt] ohne Anlaß, grundlos.

un·qual·i·fied ['ʌn'kwɒlɪfaɪd] unqualifiziert, ungeeignet; uneingeschränkt.

un·ques·tio·na·ble □ [ʌn'kwestʃə-nəbl] unzweifelhaft, fraglos; **~·tion·ing** □ [~ɪŋ] bedingungslos, blind.

un·quote ['ʌn'kwəʊt]: ~! Ende des Zitats!

un·rav·el [ʌn'rævl] (*bsd. Brt. -ll-, Am. -l-*) auftrennen; (sich) entwirren.

un·re·al □ ['ʌn'rɪəl] unwirklich, irreal; **un·re·a·lis·tic** ['ʌnrɪə'lɪstɪk] (*~ally*) wirklichkeitsfremd, unrealistisch.

un·rea·so·na·ble □ [ʌn'riːznəbl] unvernünftig; unsinnig; unmäßig.

un·rec·og·niz·a·ble □ [ʌn'rekəg-naɪzəbl] nicht wiederzuerkennen(d).

un·re·deemed □ ['ʌnrɪ'diːmd] *eccl.* unerlöst; nicht eingelöst (*Rechnung, Pfand*); ungetilgt (*Schuld*).

un·re·fined ['ʌnrɪ'faɪnd] nicht raffiniert, roh, Roh...; *fig.* unkultiviert.

un·re·flect·ing □ ['ʌnrɪ'flektɪŋ] gedankenlos, unüberlegt.

un·re·gard·ed ['ʌnrɪ'gɑːdɪd] unbeachtet; unberücksichtigt.

un·re·lat·ed ['ʌnrɪ'leɪtɪd] ohne Beziehung (*to* zu).

U V

un·re·lent·ing □ [ˈʌnrɪˈlentɪŋ] erbarmungslos; unvermindert.

un·re·li·a·ble □ [ˈʌnrɪˈlaɪəbl] unzuverlässig.

un·re·lieved □ [ˈʌnrɪˈliːvd] ungemildert; ununterbrochen.

un·re·mit·ting □ [ʌnrɪˈmɪtɪŋ] unablässig, unaufhörlich; unermüdlich.

un·re·quit·ed □ [ˈʌnrɪˈkwaɪtɪd]: ~ love unerwiderte Liebe.

un·re·served □ [ˈʌnrɪˈzɜːvd] rückhaltlos; frei, offen; nicht reserviert.

un·re·sist·ing □ [ˈʌnrɪˈzɪstɪŋ] widerstandslos.

un·re·spon·sive □ [ˈʌnrɪˈspɒnsɪv] unempfänglich (to für); teilnahmslos.

un·rest [ˈʌnˈrest] Unruhe f, pol. a. Unruhen pl.

un·re·strained □ [ˈʌnrɪˈstreɪnd] ungehemmt; uneingeschränkt.

un·re·strict·ed □ [ˈʌnrɪˈstrɪktɪd] uneingeschränkt.

un·right·eous □ [ˈʌnˈraɪtʃəs] ungerecht; unredlich.

un·ripe [ˈʌnˈraɪp] unreif.

un·ri·val(l)ed [ʌnˈraɪvld] unvergleichlich, unerreicht, einzigartig.

un·roll [ˈʌnˈrəʊl] ent-, aufrollen; sich entfalten.

un·ruf·fled [ʌnˈrʌfld] glatt; fig. gelassen, ruhig.

un·ru·ly [ʌnˈruːlɪ] (-ier, -iest) ungebärdig, widerspenstig.

un·safe □ [ˈʌnˈseɪf] unsicher.

un·said [ʌnˈsed] unausgesprochen.

un·sal(e)·a·ble [ʌnˈseɪləbl] unverkäuflich.

un·san·i·tar·y [ʌnˈsænɪtərɪ] unhygienisch.

un·sat·is·fac·to·ry □ [ˈʌnsætɪsˈfæktərɪ] unbefriedigend, unzulänglich; **~fied** [ʌnˈsætɪsfaɪd] unbefriedigt; **~fy·ing** □ [~ɪŋ] = unsatisfactory.

un·sa·vo(u)r·y □ [ˈʌnˈseɪvərɪ] unappetitlich (a. fig.), widerwärtig.

un·say [ʌnˈseɪ] (-said) zurücknehmen, widerrufen.

un·scathed [ˈʌnˈskeɪðd] unversehrt, unverletzt.

un·schooled [ˈʌnˈskuːld] ungeschult, nicht ausgebildet; unverbildet.

un·screw [ˈʌnˈskruː] v/t. ab-, los-, aufschrauben; v/i. sich abschrauben lassen.

un·scru·pu·lous □ [ʌnˈskruːpjʊləs] bedenken-, gewissen-, skrupellos.

un·sea·soned [ʌnˈsiːznd] nicht abgelagert (Holz); ungewürzt; fig. nicht abgehärtet.

un·seat [ʌnˈsiːt] Reiter abwerfen; j-n s-s Postens entheben; j-m s-n Sitz (im Parlament) nehmen.

un·see·ing □ [ʌnˈsiːɪŋ] fig. blind; with ~ eyes mit leerem Blick.

un·seem·ly [ʌnˈsiːmlɪ] ungehörig.

un·self·ish □ [ʌnˈselfɪʃ] selbstlos, uneigennützig; **~ness** [~nɪs] Selbstlosigkeit f.

un·set·tle [ʌnˈsetl] durcheinanderbringen; beunruhigen; aufregen; erschüttern; **~d** unbeständig, veränderlich (Wetter).

un·shak·en [ʌnˈʃeɪkən] unerschüttert; unerschütterlich.

un·shaved, un·shav·en [ʌnˈʃeɪvd, ~n] unrasiert.

un·ship [ʌnˈʃɪp] ausschiffen.

un·shrink·a·ble [ʌnˈʃrɪŋkəbl] nicht einlaufend (Stoff); **~ing** □ [ʌnˈʃrɪŋkɪŋ] unverzagt, furchtlos.

un·sight·ly [ʌnˈsaɪtlɪ] häßlich.

un·skil(l)·ful □ [ˈʌnˈskɪlfl] ungeschickt; **un·skilled** ungelernt.

un·so·cia·ble □ [ʌnˈsəʊʃəbl] ungesellig; **un·so·cial** [~l] unsozial; asozial; work ~ hours Brt. außerhalb der normalen Arbeitszeit arbeiten.

un·sol·der [ʌnˈsɒldə] los-, ablöten.

un·so·lic·it·ed [ˈʌnsəˈlɪsɪtɪd] unaufgefordert; ~ goods econ. unbestellte Ware(n).

un·solv·a·ble [ʌnˈsɒlvəbl] ⚛ unlöslich; fig. unlösbar; **un·solved** [~d] ungelöst.

un·so·phis·ti·cat·ed [ˈʌnsəˈfɪstɪkeɪtɪd] ungekünstelt, natürlich, naiv.

un·sound □ [ˈʌnˈsaʊnd] ungesund; verdorben; wurmstichig, morsch; nicht stichhaltig (Beweis); verkehrt; of ~ mind ⚖ unzurechnungsfähig.

un·spar·ing □ [ʌnˈspeərɪŋ] freigebig; schonungslos, unbarmherzig.

un·spea·ka·ble □ [ʌnˈspiːkəbl] unsagbar, unbeschreiblich, entsetzlich.

un·spoiled, un·spoilt [ʌnˈspɔɪld, ~t] unverdorben; nicht verzogen (Kind).

un·spo·ken [ʌnˈspəʊkən] ungesagt; ~of unerwähnt.

un·stead·y □ [ʌnˈstedɪ] (-ier, -iest) unsicher; schwankend, unbeständig; unregelmäßig; fig. unsolide.

un·strained [ˈʌnˈstreɪnd] unfiltriert; fig. ungezwungen.

un·strap [ˈʌnˈstræp] (*-pp-*) ab-, auf-, losschnallen.

un·stressed *ling.* [ˈʌnˈstrest] unbetont.

un·strung [ˈʌnˈstrʌŋ] ♪ saitenlos; ♪ entspannt (*Saite*); *fig.* zerrüttet, entnervt (*Person*).

un·stuck [ˈʌnˈstʌk]: *come* ~ sich lösen, abgehen; *fig.* scheitern (*Person, Plan*).

un·stud·ied [ˈʌnˈstʌdɪd] ungekünstelt, natürlich.

un·suc·cess·ful □ [ˈʌnsəkˈsesfl] erfolglos, ohne Erfolg.

un·suit·a·ble □ [ˈʌnˈsjuːtəbl] unpassend; unangemessen.

un·sure [ˈʌnˈʃɔː] (*~r*, *~st*) unsicher.

un·sur·passed [ˈʌnsəˈpɑːst] unübertroffen.

un·sus·pect|ed □ [ˈʌnsəˈspektɪd] unverdächtig; unvermutet; **~ing** □ [~ɪŋ] nichts ahnend; arglos.

un·sus·pi·cious □ [ˈʌnsəˈspɪʃəs] nicht argwöhnisch, arglos; unverdächtig.

un·swerv·ing □ [ʌnˈswɜːvɪŋ] unbeirrbar.

un·tan·gle [ˈʌnˈtæŋgl] entwirren.

un·tapped [ˈʌnˈtæpt] ungenutzt (*Reserven, Energie*).

un·teach·a·ble [ˈʌnˈtiːtʃəbl] unbelehrbar (*Person*); nicht lehrbar (*Sache*).

un·ten·a·ble [ˈʌnˈtenəbl] unhaltbar (*Theorie etc.*).

un·ten·ant·ed [ˈʌnˈtenəntɪd] unbewohnt.

un·thank·ful □ [ˈʌnˈθæŋkfl] undankbar.

un·think|a·ble [ʌnˈθɪŋkəbl] undenkbar; **~ing** □ [ˈʌnˈθɪŋkɪŋ] gedankenlos.

un·thought [ˈʌnˈθɔːt] unüberlegt; **~of** unvorstellbar; unerwartet.

un·ti·dy □ [ʌnˈtaɪdɪ] (*-ier*, *-iest*) unordentlich.

un·tie [ˈʌnˈtaɪ] aufknoten, *Knoten etc.* lösen; losbinden.

un·til [ənˈtɪl] **1.** *prp.* bis; **2.** *cj.* bis (*daß*); *not* ~ erst als od. wenn.

un·time·ly [ʌnˈtaɪmlɪ] vorzeitig; ungelegen.

un·tir·ing □ [ʌnˈtaɪərɪŋ] unermüdlich.

un·to [ˈʌntʊ] = *to*.

un·told [ˈʌnˈtəʊld] unerzählt; ungesagt; unermeßlich; unsäglich.

un·touched [ˈʌnˈtʌtʃt] unberührt (*Essen etc.*); *fig.* ungerührt.

un·trou·bled [ˈʌnˈtrʌbld] ungestört; ruhig.

un·true □ [ˈʌnˈtruː] unwahr, falsch.

un·trust·wor·thy [ˈʌnˈtrʌstwɜːðɪ] unzuverlässig, nicht vertrauenswürdig.

un·truth·ful □ [ˈʌnˈtruːθfl] unwahr; unaufrichtig; falsch.

un·used[1] [ˈʌnˈjuːzd] unbenutzt, ungebraucht.

un·used[2] [ˈʌnˈjuːst] nicht gewöhnt (*to an acc.*); nicht gewohnt (*to doing* zu tun).

un·u·su·al □ [ʌnˈjuːʒʊəl] ungewöhnlich.

un·ut·ter·a·ble □ [ʌnˈʌtərəbl] unaussprechlich.

un·var·nished *fig.* [ʌnˈvɑːnɪʃt] ungeschminkt.

un·var·y·ing □ [ʌnˈveərɪɪŋ] unveränderlich.

un·veil [ʌnˈveɪl] entschleiern; *Denkmal etc.* enthüllen.

un·versed [ʌnˈvɜːst] unbewandert, unerfahren (*in* in *dat.*).

un·want·ed [ˈʌnˈwɒntɪd] unerwünscht.

un·war·rant·ed [ʌnˈwɒrəntɪd] ungerechtfertigt, unberechtigt.

un·wel·come [ʌnˈwelkəm] unwillkommen.

un·well [ʌnˈwel]: *she is od. feels* ~ sie fühlt sich unwohl od. unpäßlich, sie ist unpäßlich.

un·whole·some [ʌnˈhəʊlsəm] ungesund (*a. fig.*).

un·wield·y □ [ʌnˈwiːldɪ] unhandlich, sperrig; unbeholfen.

un·will·ing □ [ˈʌnˈwɪlɪŋ] widerwillig; ungern; *be* ~ *to do et.* nicht wollen.

un·wind [ˈʌnˈwaɪnd] (*-wound*) auf-, loswickeln; (sich) abwickeln; F sich entspannen, abschalten.

un·wise □ [ˈʌnˈwaɪz] unklug.

un·wit·ting □ [ʌnˈwɪtɪŋ] unwissentlich, unabsichtlich.

un·wor·thy □ [ʌnˈwɜːðɪ] unwürdig; *he is* ~ *of it* er verdient es nicht, er ist es nicht wert.

un·wrap [ˈʌnˈræp] auswickeln, auspacken, aufwickeln.

un·writ·ten [ˈʌnrɪtn]: ~ *law* ungeschriebenes Gesetz.

un·yield·ing □ [ʌnˈjiːldɪŋ] starr, fest; *fig.* unnachgiebig.

un·zip [ʌnˈzɪp] (*-pp-*) den Reißverschluß öffnen (*gen.*).

up [ʌp] **1.** *adv.* nach oben, hoch, (her-, hin)auf, in die Höhe, empor, aufwärts; von ... an; flußaufwärts; in der *od.* in die (*bsd.* Haupt-)Stadt; *Brt. bsd.* in *od.* nach London; in (*dat.*) (*up North*); aufrecht, gerade; *Baseball:* am Schlag; ~ *to* hinauf nach *od.* zu; bis (zu); **2.** *adj.* aufwärts..., nach oben; hoch; aufgegangen (*Sonne*); gestiegen (*Preise*); abgelaufen, um (*Zeit*); auf (-gestanden); ~ *and about* wieder auf den Beinen; *it is* ~ *to him* es liegt an ihm; es hängt von ihm ab; *what are you* ~ *to?* was machst du (*there* da)?; *what's* ~? was ist los?; ~ *train* Zug *m* nach der Stadt; **3.** *prp.* hinauf; ~ *(the) country* landeinwärts; **4.** *(-pp-)* *v/i.* aufstehen, sich erheben; *v/t.* *Preise etc.* erhöhen; **5.** *the* ~*s and downs* das Auf u. Ab, die Höhen u. Tiefen (*of life* des Lebens).

up-and-com·ing [ˈʌpənˈkʌmɪŋ] aufstrebend, vielversprechend.

up·bring·ing [ˈʌpbrɪŋɪŋ] Erziehung *f.*

up·com·ing *Am.* [ˈʌpkʌmɪŋ] bevorstehend.

up·coun·try [ˈʌpˈkʌntrɪ] landeinwärts; im Inneren des Landes (gelegen).

up·date [ʌpˈdeɪt] auf den neuesten Stand bringen.

up·end [ʌpˈend] hochkant stellen; *Gefäß* umstülpen.

up·grade [ʌpˈgreɪd] *j-n* (im Rang) befördern.

up·heav·al *fig.* [ʌpˈhiːvl] Umwälzung *f.*

up·hill [ˈʌpˈhɪl] bergauf; *fig.* mühsam.

up·hold [ʌpˈhəʊld] *(-held)* aufrechterhalten, unterstützen; ⚖ bestätigen.

up|hol·ster [ʌpˈhəʊlstə] *Möbel* polstern; ~·**hol·ster·er** [~rə] Polsterer *m*; ~·**hol·ster·y** [~rɪ] Polsterung *f*; (Möbel)Bezugsstoff *m*; Polstern *n*; Polsterei *f.*

up·keep [ˈʌpkiːp] Instandhaltung(s-kosten *pl.*) *f*; Unterhalt(ungskosten *pl.*) *m.*

up·land [ˈʌplənd] *mst* ~*s pl.* Hochland *n.*

up·lift *fig.* [ʌpˈlɪft] aufrichten, erbauen.

up·on [əˈpɒn] = *on; once* ~ *a time there was* es war einmal.

up·per [ˈʌpə] obere(r, -s), höhere(r, -s), Ober...; ~·**most 1.** *adj.* oberste(r, -s), höchste(r, -s); **2.** *adv.* obenan, ganz oben.

up·raise [ʌpˈreɪz] er-, hochheben.

up·right [ˈʌpraɪt] **1.** □ aufrecht; *fig.* rechtschaffen; **2.** (senkrechte) Stütze, Träger *m.*

up·ris·ing [ˈʌpraɪzɪŋ] Erhebung *f,* Aufstand *m.*

up·roar [ˈʌprɔː] Aufruhr *m*; ~·**i·ous** □ [ʌpˈrɔːrɪəs] lärmend, laut, tosend (*Beifall*), schallend (*Gelächter*).

up·root [ʌpˈruːt] entwurzeln; (her-) ausreißen.

up·set [ʌpˈset] *(-set)* umwerfen, (um)stürzen, umkippen, umstoßen; durcheinanderbringen (*a. fig.*); *Magen* verderben; *fig. j-n* aus der Fassung bringen; *be* ~ aufgeregt sein, aus der Fassung sein, durcheinander sein.

up·shot [ˈʌpʃɒt] Ergebnis *n.*

up·side down [ˈʌpsaɪdˈdaʊn] das Oberste zuunterst; verkehrt (herum).

up·stairs [ˈʌpˈsteəz] die Treppe hinauf, (nach) oben.

up·start [ˈʌpstɑːt] Emporkömmling *m.*

up·state *Am.* [ˈʌpsteɪt] im Norden (des Bundesstaates).

up·stream [ˈʌpˈstriːm] fluß-, stromaufwärts.

up·tight F [ˈʌptaɪt] nervös.

up-to-date [ˈʌptəˈdeɪt] modern; auf dem neuesten Stand.

up·town *Am.* [ˈʌpˈtaʊn] im *od.* in das Wohn- *od.* Villenviertel.

up·turn [ˈʌptɜːn] Aufschwung *m.*

up·ward(s) [ˈʌpwəd(z)] aufwärts (gerichtet).

u·ra·ni·um ⚛ [jʊəˈreɪnjəm] Uran *n.*

ur·ban [ˈɜːbən] städtisch, Stadt...; ~**e** □ [ɜːˈbeɪn] höflich; gebildet.

ur·chin [ˈɜːtʃɪn] Bengel *m.*

urge [ɜːdʒ] **1.** *j-n* (be)drängen (*to do* zu tun); dringen auf *et.*; *Recht* geltend machen; *oft* ~ *on* *j-n* drängen, (an)treiben; **2.** Drang *m*; **ur·gen·cy** [ˈɜːdʒənsɪ] Dringlichkeit *f*; Drängen *n*; **ur·gent** □ [~t] dringend; dringlich; eilig.

u·ri·nal [ˈjʊərɪnl] Harnglas *n*; (Männer)Toilette *f*, Pissoir *n*; ~·**nate** [~eɪt] urinieren; **u·rine** [~ɪn] Urin *m*, Harn *m.*

urn [ɜ:n] Urne *f*; Tee-, Kaffeemaschine *f*.

us [ʌs, əs] uns; *all of* ~ wir alle; *both of* ~ wir beide.

us·age ['ju:zɪdʒ] Brauch *m*, Gepflogenheit *f*; Sprachgebrauch *m*; Behandlung *f*; Verwendung *f*, Gebrauch *m*.

use 1. [ju:s] Gebrauch *m*, Benutzung *f*, Verwendung *f*; Gewohnheit *f*, Übung *f*, Brauch *m*; Nutzen *m*; (*of*) *no* ~ nutz-, zwecklos; *have no* ~ *for* keine Verwendung haben für; *Am.* F nicht mögen; **2.** [ju:z] gebrauchen, benutzen, ver-, anwenden; handhaben; ~ *up* ver-, aufbrauchen; *I* ~*d to do* ich pflegte zu tun, früher tat ich; ~**d** [ju:zd] ge-, verbraucht; [ju:st] gewöhnt (*to an acc.*), gewohnt (*to zu od. acc.*); ~**ful** □ ['ju:sfl] brauchbar, nützlich; Nutz...; ~**less** □ ['ju:slɪs] nutz-, zwecklos, unnütz.

ush·er ['ʌʃə] **1.** Türhüter *m*, Pförtner *m*; Gerichtsdiener *m*; Platzanweiser *m*; **2.** *mst.* ~ *in* herein-, hineinführen; ~**ette** ['ʌʃə'ret] Platzanweiserin *f*.

u·su·al □ ['ju:ʒʊəl] gewöhnlich, üblich, gebräuchlich.

u·sur·er ['ju:ʒərə] Wucherer *m*.

u·surp [ju:'zɜ:p] sich *et.* widerrechtlich aneignen, an sich reißen; ~**er** [~ə] Usurpator *m*.

u·su·ry ['ju:ʒʊrɪ] Wucher(zinsen *pl.*) *m*.

u·ten·sil [ju:'tensl] Gerät *n*.

u·te·rus *anat.* ['ju:tərəs] (*pl. -ri* [-raɪ]) Gebärmutter *f*.

u·til·i·ty [ju:'tɪlətɪ] **1.** Nützlichkeit *f*, Nutzen *m*; *utilities pl.* Leistungen *pl.* der öffentlichen Versorgungsbetriebe; **2.** Gebrauchs...

u·ti·li·za·tion [ju:tɪlaɪ'zeɪʃn] (Aus-) Nutzung *f*, Verwertung *f*, -wendung *f*; ~**lize** ['ju:tɪlaɪz] (aus)nutzen, verwerten, -wenden.

ut·most ['ʌtməʊst] äußerste(r, -s).

U·to·pi·an [ju:'təʊpjən] **1.** utopisch; **2.** Utopist *m*.

ut·ter ['ʌtə] **1.** □ *fig.* äußerste(r, -s), völlig; **2.** äußern; *Seufzer etc.* ausstoßen, von sich geben; *Falschgeld etc.* in Umlauf setzen; ~**ance** ['ʌtərəns] Äußerung *f*, Ausdruck *m*; Aussprache *f*; ~**most** ['ʌtəməʊst] äußerste(r, -s).

U-turn ['ju:tɜ:n] *mot.* Wende *f*; *fig.* Kehrtwendung *f*.

u·vu·la *anat.* ['ju:vjʊlə] (*pl. -lae* [-li:], *-las*) (Gaumen)Zäpfchen *n*.

V

va·can·cy ['veɪkənsɪ] Leere *f*; freies Zimmer (*Hotel*); offene *od.* freie Stelle; *fig.* geistige Leere; ~**cant** □ [~t] leer (*a. fig.*); frei (*Zimmer, Sitzplatz*); leer(stehend), unbewohnt (*Haus*); offen, frei (*Stelle*); unbesetzt, vakant (*Amt*); *fig.* geistesabwesend.

va·cate [və'keɪt, *Am.* 'veɪkeɪt] räumen, *Stelle* aufgeben, aus *e-m Amt* scheiden, *Amt* niederlegen; **va·ca·tion** [və'keɪʃn, *Am.* veɪ'keɪʃn] **1.** *bsd. Am.* Schulferien *pl.*; *univ.* Semesterferien *pl.*; ⅞ Gerichtsferien *pl.*; *Am.* Urlaub *m*, Ferien *pl.*; *be on* ~ *bsd. Am.* im Urlaub sein, Urlaub machen; *take a* ~ *bsd. Am.* sich Urlaub nehmen, Urlaub machen; **2.** *bsd. Am.* Urlaub machen;

va·ca·tion·ist *bsd. Am.* [~ʃənɪst] Urlauber(in).

vac·cin·ate ['væksɪneɪt] impfen; ~**cin·a·tion** [væksɪ'neɪʃn] (Schutz-) Impfung *f*; ~**cine** ≈ ['væksi:n] Impfstoff *m*.

vac·il·late *mst fig.* ['væsɪleɪt] schwanken.

vac·u·ous □ *fig.* ['vækjʊəs] leer, geistlos.

vac·u·um ['vækjʊəm] **1.** (*pl. -uums*, *-ua* [-jʊə]) *phys.* Vakuum *n*; ~ *bottle* Thermosflasche *f*; ~ *cleaner* Staubsauger *m*; ~ *flask* Thermosflasche *f*; ~*packed* vakuumverpackt; **2.** *v/t.* (*mit dem Staubsauger*) saugen; *v/i.* (staub)saugen.

vag·a·bond ['vægəbɒnd] Landstreicher(in).

U
V

va·ga·ry ['veɪgərɪ] wunderlicher Einfall; Laune *f*, Schrulle *f*.

va·gi|na *anat.* [vəˈdʒaɪnə] Vagina *f*, Scheide *f*; **~nal** *anat.* [~nl] vaginal, Vaginal..., Scheiden...

va|grant ['veɪgrənt] **1.** □ wandernd, vagabundierend; *fig.* unstet; **2.** Landstreicher(in).

vague □ [veɪg] (*~r*, *~st*) vage, verschwommen; unbestimmt; unklar.

vain □ [veɪn] eitel, eingebildet; nutzlos, vergeblich; *in ~* vergebens, vergeblich, umsonst.

vale [veɪl] *poet. od. in Namen:* Tal *n*.

val·e·dic·tion [vælɪˈdɪkʃn] Abschied(sworte *pl.*) *m*.

val·en·tine ['væləntaɪn] Valentinsgruß *m* (*am Valentinstag, 14. Februar, gesandt*); am Valentinstag erwählte(r) Liebste(r).

va·le·ri·an ♀ [vəˈlɪərɪən] Baldrian *m*.

val·et ['vælɪt] (Kammer)Diener *m*; Hoteldiener *m*.

val·e·tu·di·nar·i·an [vælɪtjuːdɪˈneərɪən] **1.** kränklich; hypochondrisch; **2.** kränklicher Mensch; Hypochonder *m*.

val·i·ant □ ['væljənt] tapfer, mutig.

val|id □ ['vælɪd] triftig, stichhaltig; berechtigt; gültig; *be ~* gelten; *become ~* Rechtskraft erlangen; **~·i·date** ⅓ [~eɪt] für gültig erklären, bestätigen; **~·id·i·ty** [vəˈlɪdətɪ] (⅓ Rechts)Gültigkeit *f*; Stichhaltigkeit *f*; Richtigkeit *f*.

va·lise [vəˈliːz] Reisetasche *f*.

val·ley ['vælɪ] Tal *n*.

val·o(u)r ['vælə] Mut *m*, Tapferkeit *f*.

val·u·a·ble ['væljʊəbl] **1.** □ wertvoll; **2.** ~*s pl.* Wertsachen *pl.*

val·u·a·tion [væljʊˈeɪʃn] Bewertung *f*, Schätzung *f*; Schätz-, Taxwert *m*.

val·ue ['væljuː] **1.** Wert *m*; *econ.* Währung *f*; *mst ~s pl. fig. (kulturelle od. sittliche)* Werte *pl.*; *at ~ econ.* zum Tageskurs; *give* (*get*) *good ~ for money econ.* reell bedienen (bedient werden); **2.** (ab)schätzen, veranschlagen; *fig.* schätzen, bewerten; **~·ad·ded tax** *econ.* (*abbr.* VAT) Mehrwertsteuer *f*; **~d** veranschlagt; geschätzt; **~·less** [~jʊlɪs] wertlos.

valve [vælv] ⊕ Ventil *n*; (*Herz- etc.*) Klappe *f*; *Brt.* ♫ (Radio-, Fernseh-) Röhre *f*.

vam·pire ['væmpaɪə] Vampir *m*.

van¹ [væn] Lieferwagen *m*; *bsd. Brt.*

⚙ Güter-, Gepäckwagen *m*; Wohnwagen *m*.

van² ✕ [~] = *vanguard*.

van·dal·ize ['vændəlaɪz] wie die Vandalen hausen in (*dat.*), mutwillig zerstören, verwüsten.

vane [veɪn] Wetterfahne *f*; (Propeller)Flügel *m*; ⊕ Schaufel *f*.

van·guard ✕ ['vænɡɑːd] Vorhut *f*.

va·nil·la [vəˈnɪlə] Vanille *f*.

van·ish ['vænɪʃ] verschwinden.

van·i·ty ['vænətɪ] Eitelkeit *f*; Nichtigkeit *f*; ~ *case* Kosmetiktäschchen *n*; ~ *case* Kosmetikkoffer *m*.

van·quish ['væŋkwɪʃ] besiegen.

van·tage [ˈvɑːntɪdʒ] *Tennis:* Vorteil *m*; **~·ground** günstige Stellung.

vap·id □ ['væpɪd] schal; fad(e).

va·por·ize ['veɪpəraɪz] verdampfen, verdunsten (lassen).

va·po(u)r ['veɪpə] Dampf *m*, Dunst *m*; ~ *trail* ✈ Kondensstreifen *m*.

var·i|a·ble ['veərɪəbl] **1.** □ veränderlich, wechselnd, unbeständig; ⊕ ver-, einstellbar; **2.** veränderliche Größe; **~·ance** [~ns]: *be at ~ with* uneinig sein (mit *j-m*), anderer Meinung sein (als *j-d*); im Widerspruch stehen (zu); **~·ant** [~nt] **1.** abweichend, verschieden; **2.** Variante *f*; **~·a·tion** [veərɪˈeɪʃn] Schwankung *f*, Abweichung *f*; Variation *f*.

var·i·cose veins ♣ ['værɪkəʊs veɪnz] *pl.* Krampfadern *pl.*

var·ied □ ['veərɪd] verschieden, mannigfaltig; verändert.

va·ri·e·ty [vəˈraɪətɪ] Mannigfaltigkeit *f*, Vielzahl *f*, Abwechslung *f*; *econ.* Auswahl *f*; Sorte *f*, Art *f*; Spielart *f*, Variante *f*; *for a ~ of reasons* aus den verschiedensten Gründen; ~ *show* Varietévorstellung *f*; ~ *theatre* Varieté(theater) *n*.

var·i·ous □ ['veərɪəs] verschiedene, mehrere; verschiedenartig.

var·mint F ['vɑːmɪnt] *zo.* Schädling *m*; Halunke *m*.

var·nish ['vɑːnɪʃ] **1.** Firnis *m*; Lack *m*; Politur *f*; *fig.* Tünche *f*; **2.** firnissen; lackieren; *Möbel* (auf)polieren; *fig.* beschönigen.

var·si·ty ['vɑːsətɪ] *Brt.* F Uni *f* (*Universität*); *a.* ~ *team Am.* Universitäts-, College-, Schulmannschaft *f*.

var·y ['veərɪ] (sich) (ver)ändern; variieren; wechseln (mit *et.*); abweichen *od.* verschieden sein (*from* von); **~·ing** □ [~ɪŋ] unterschiedlich.

verify

vase [vɑːz, *Am.* veɪs, veɪz] Vase *f*.

vast □ [vɑːst] ungeheuer, gewaltig, riesig, umfassend, weit.

vat [væt] Faß *n*, Bottich *m*.

vau·de·ville *Am.* ['vəʊdəvɪl] Varieté *n*.

vault[1] [vɔːlt] 1. (Keller)Gewölbe *n*; Wölbung *f*; Stahlkammer *f*, Tresorraum *m*; Gruft *f*; 2. (über)wölben.

vault[2] [~] 1. *bsd. Sport:* Sprung *m*; 2. *v/i.* springen (*over* über *acc.*); *v/t.* überspringen, springen über (*acc.*); **~ing-horse** ['vɔːltɪŋhɔːs] *Turnen:* Pferd *n*; **~ing-pole** *Stabhochsprung:* Sprungstab *m*.

've *abbr.* [v] = *have*.

veal [viːl] Kalbfleisch *n*; ~ **chop** Kalbskotelett *n*; ~ **cutlet** Kalbsschnitzel *n*; roast ~ Kalbsbraten *m*.

veer [vɪə] (sich) drehen; *Auto:* a. plötzlich die Richtung ändern, ausscheren.

vege·ta·ble ['vedʒtəbl] 1. Gemüse...; pflanzlich; 2. Pflanze *f*; *mst* ~s *pl.* Gemüse *n*.

veg·e|tar·i·an [vedʒɪˈteərɪən] 1. Vegetarier(in); 2. vegetarisch; **~tate** *fig.* ['vedʒɪteɪt] (dahin)vegetieren; **~ta·tive** □ [~tətɪv] vegetativ; wachstumsfördernd.

ve·he|mence ['viːɪməns] Heftigkeit *f*, Gewalt *f*; **~ment** □ [~t] heftig; ungestüm.

ve·hi·cle ['viːɪkl] Fahrzeug *n*, Beförderungsmittel *n*; *fig.* Vermittler *m*, Träger *m*; *fig.* Ausdrucksmittel *n*.

veil [veɪl] 1. Schleier *m*; 2. (sich) verschleiern; *fig.* verbergen.

vein [veɪn] *anat.* Vene *f*; Ader *f* (*a. fig.*); *fig.* Veranlagung *f*, Neigung *f*; *fig.* Stimmung *f*.

ve·loc·i·pede *Am.* [vɪˈlɒsɪpiːd] (Kinder)Dreirad *n*.

ve·loc·i·ty ⊕ [vɪˈlɒsətɪ] Geschwindigkeit *f*.

vel·vet ['velvɪt] 1. Samt *m*; 2. aus Samt, Samt...; **~y** [~ɪ] samtig.

ve·nal ['viːnl] käuflich; bestechlich; korrupt.

vend [vend] verkaufen; **~er** ['vendə] (Straßen)Händler *m*, (-)Verkäufer *m*; **~ing-ma·chine** ['vendɪŋməˈʃiːn] (Verkaufs)Automat *m*; **~or** [~ɔː] *bsd.* ⚖ Verkäufer(in); (Verkaufs)Automat *m*.

ve·neer [vəˈnɪə] 1. Furnier *n*; *fig.* äußerer Anstrich, Tünche *f*; 2. furnieren.

ven·e|ra·ble □ ['venərəbl] ehrwürdig; **~rate** [~eɪt] (ver)ehren; **~ra·tion** [venəˈreɪʃn] Verehrung *f*.

ve·ne·re·al [vɪˈnɪərɪəl] Geschlechts...; ~ **disease** ⚕ Geschlechtskrankheit *f*.

Ve·ne·tian [vɪˈniːʃn] 1. venezianisch; ♀ **blind** (Stab)Jalousie *f*; 2. Venezianer(in).

ven·geance ['vendʒəns] Rache *f*; with a ~ *F* wie verrückt, ganz gehörig.

ve·ni·al □ ['viːnjəl] verzeihlich; *eccl.* läßlich (Sünde).

ven·i·son ['venɪzn] Wildbret *n*.

ven·om ['venəm] (*bsd.* Schlangen-) Gift *n*; *fig.* Gift *n*, Gehässigkeit *f*; **~ous** □ [~əs] giftig (*a. fig.*).

ve·nous ['viːnəs] Venen...; venös.

vent [vent] 1. (Abzugs)Öffnung *f*; Luft-, Spundloch *n*; Schlitz *m*; give ~ to = 2. *v/t. fig.* s-m Zorn etc. Luft machen, s-e Wut etc. auslassen, abreagieren (on an *dat.*).

ven·ti|late ['ventɪleɪt] ventilieren, (be-, ent-, durch)lüften; *fig.* erörtern; **~la·tion** [ventɪˈleɪʃn] Ventilation *f*, Lüftung *f*; *fig.* Erörterung *f*; **~la·tor** ['ventɪleɪtə] Ventilator *m*.

ven·tril·o·quist [venˈtrɪləkwɪst] Bauchredner *m*.

ven·ture ['ventʃə] 1. Wagnis *n*, Risiko *n*; Abenteuer *n*; *econ.* Unternehmen *n*; *econ.* Spekulation *f*; at a ~ auf gut Glück; 2. (sich) wagen; riskieren.

ve·ra·cious □ [vəˈreɪʃəs] wahrhaftig; wahrheitsgemäß.

verb *gr.* [vɜːb] Verb *n*, Zeitwort *n*; **~al** □ ['vɜːbl] wörtlich; mündlich; **ver·bi·age** ['vɜːbɪɪdʒ] Wortschwall *m*; **ver·bose** □ [vɜːˈbəʊs] wortreich, langatmig.

ver·dant □ ['vɜːdənt] grün; *fig.* unreif.

ver·dict ['vɜːdɪkt] ⚖ (Urteils)Spruch *m* (der Geschworenen); *fig.* Urteil *n*; bring in od. return a ~ of guilty auf schuldig erkennen.

ver·di·gris ['vɜːdɪgrɪs] Grünspan *m*.

ver·dure ['vɜːdʒə] (frisches) Grün.

verge [vɜːdʒ] 1. Rand *m*, Grenze *f*; Bankett *n* (Straße); on the ~ of am Rande (*gen.*), dicht vor (*dat.*); on the ~ of despair (tears) der Verzweiflung (den Tränen) nahe; 2. ~ (up)on grenzen an (*acc.*) (*a. fig.*).

ver·i·fy ['verɪfaɪ] (nach)prüfen; beweisen; bestätigen.

U
V

ver·i·si·mil·i·tude [verısı'mılıtjuːd] Wahrscheinlichkeit f.

ver·i·ta·ble □ ['verıtəbl] wahr, wirklich.

ver·mi·cel·li [vɜːmı'selı] Fadennudeln pl.

ver·mic·u·lar [vɜː'mıkjʊlə] wurmartig.

ver·mi·form ap·pen·dix anat. ['vɜːmıfɔːm ə'pendıks] Wurmfortsatz m.

ver·mil·ion [və'mıljən] **1.** Zinnoberrot n; **2.** zinnoberrot.

ver·min ['vɜːmın] Ungeziefer n; Schädling(e pl.) m; fig. Gesindel n, Pack n; **~ous** [~əs] voller Ungeziefer.

ver·nac·u·lar [və'nækjʊlə] **1.** □ einheimisch; Volks...; **2.** Landes-, Volkssprache f; Jargon m.

ver·sa·tile □ ['vɜːsətaıl] vielseitig; flexibel.

verse [vɜːs] Vers(e pl.) m; Strophe f; Dichtung f; **~d** [~t] bewandert; be (well) ~ in sich (gut) auskennen in (dat.).

ver·si·fy ['vɜːsıfaı] v/t. in Verse bringen; v/i. Verse machen.

ver·sion ['vɜːʃn] Übersetzung f; Fassung f, Darstellung f; Lesart f; ⊕ Ausführung f, Modell n (Auto etc.).

ver·sus ['vɜːsəs] ⚖, Sport: gegen.

ver·te·bra anat. ['vɜːtıbrə] (pl. -brae [~riː]) Wirbel m; **~brate** zo. [~rət] Wirbeltier n.

ver·ti·cal □ ['vɜːtıkl] vertikal, senkrecht.

ver·tig·i·nous □ [vɜː'tıdʒınəs] schwindlig; schwindelnd (Höhe).

ver·ti·go ['vɜːtıgəʊ] (pl. -gos) Schwindel(anfall) m.

verve [vɜːv] Schwung m, Begeisterung f.

ver·y ['verı] **1.** adv. sehr; vor sup.: aller...; the ~ best die allerbeste; **2.** adj. gerade, genau; bloß; rein; die-, dasselbe; the ~ same ebenderselbe; in the ~ act auf frischer Tat; gerade dabei; the ~ thing genau das (richtige); the ~ thought der bloße Gedanke (of an acc.).

ves·i·cle ['vesıkl] Bläschen n.

ves·sel ['vesl] Gefäß n (a. anat., ⚕, fig.); ⚓ Fahrzeug n, Schiff n.

vest [vest] Brt. Unterhemd n; Am. Weste f.

ves·ti·bule ['vestıbjuːl] anat. Vorhof m; (Vor)Halle f; Am. 🚃 (Harmonika)Verbindungsgang m; ~ train Am.

🚃 Zug m mit (Harmonika)Verbindungsgängen.

ves·tige fig. ['vestıdʒ] Spur f.

vest·ment ['vestmənt] Amtstracht f, Robe f.

ves·try eccl. ['vestrı] Sakristei f; Gemeindesaal m.

vet F [vet] **1.** Tierarzt m; Am. ⚔ Veteran m; **2.** (-tt-) co. verarzten; gründlich prüfen.

vet·er·an ['vetərən] **1.** altgedient; erfahren; **2.** Veteran m.

vet·er·i·nar·i·an Am. [vetərı'neərıən] Tierarzt m.

vet·er·i·na·ry ['vetərınərı] **1.** tierärztlich; **2.** a. ~ surgeon Brt. Tierarzt m.

ve·to ['viːtəʊ] **1.** (pl. -toes) Veto n; **2.** sein Veto einlegen gegen.

vex [veks] ärgern; schikanieren; **~a·tion** [vek'seıʃn] Verdruß m; Ärger(nis) n; **~a·tious** [~ʃəs] ärgerlich.

vi·a ['vaıə] über, via.

vi·a·duct ['vaıədʌkt] Viadukt m, n.

vi·al ['vaıəl] Phiole f, Fläschchen n.

vi·brate [vaı'breıt] vibrieren; zittern; **vi·bra·tion** [~ʃn] Schwingung f; Zittern n, Vibrieren n.

vic·ar eccl. ['vıkə] Vikar m; **~age** [~rıdʒ] Pfarrhaus n.

vice¹ [vaıs] Laster n; Untugend f; Fehler m; ~ squad Sittenpolizei f, -dezernat n.

vice² Brt. ⊕ [~] Schraubstock m.

vice³ prp. ['vaısı] an Stelle von.

vice⁴ F [vaıs] Vize m; attr. stellvertretend, Vize...; **~roy** ['vaısrɔı] Vizekönig m.

vi·ce ver·sa ['vaısı'vɜːsə] umgekehrt.

vi·cin·i·ty [vı'sınətı] Nachbarschaft f; Nähe f.

vi·cious □ ['vıʃəs] lasterhaft; bösartig; boshaft; fehlerhaft.

vi·cis·si·tude [vı'sısıtjuːd] Wandel m, Wechsel m; **~s** pl. Wechselfälle pl., das Auf u. Ab.

vic·tim ['vıktım] Opfer n; **~ize** [~aız] (auf)opfern; schikanieren; (ungerechterweise) bestrafen.

vic|tor ['vıktə] Sieger(in); **2to·ri·an** hist. [vık'tɔːrıən] Viktorianisch; **~to·ri·ous** □ [~əs] siegreich; Sieges...; **~to·ry** ['vıktərı] Sieg m.

vict·ual ['vıtl] **1.** (bsd. Brt. -ll-, Am. -l-) (sich) verpflegen od. verproviantieren; **2.** mst **~s** pl. Lebensmittel pl.,

Proviant *m*; ~**(l)er** [~ə] Lebensmittellieferant *m*.

vid·e·o ['vɪdɪəʊ] **1.** (*pl.* -os) Video(gerät *n*, -recorder *m*) *n*; *Computer:* Bildschirm-, Bildsicht-, Datensichtgerät *n*; *Am.* Fernsehen *n*; **2.** Video...; *Am.* Fernseh...; ~ **cas·sette** Videokassette *f*; ~ **disc** Bildplatte *f*; ~ **game** Videospiel *n*; ~**phone** Bildtelefon *n*; ~**tape 1.** Videoband *n*; **2.** auf Videoband aufnehmen; ~**tape re·cord·er** Videorecorder *m*.

vie [vaɪ] wetteifern (*with* mit; *for* um).

Vi·en·nese [vɪə'niːz] **1.** Wiener(in); **2.** wienerisch, Wiener...

view [vjuː] **1.** Sicht *f*, Blick *m*; Besichtigung *f*; Aussicht *f* (*of* auf *acc.*); Anblick *m*; Ansicht *f* (*a. fig.*); Absicht *f*; *in* ~ sichtbar, zu sehen; *in* ~ *of* im Hinblick auf (*acc.*); angesichts (*gen.*); *on* ~ zu besichtigen; *with a* ~ *to inf. od. of ger.* in der Absicht zu *inf.*; *have* (*keep*) *in* ~ im Auge haben (behalten); **2.** *v/t.* ansehen, besichtigen; *fig.* betrachten; *v/i.* fernsehen; ~ **da·ta** *pl.* Bildschirmtext *m*; ~**er** ['vjuːə] Fernsehzuschauer(in), Fernseher(in); ⊕ Diabetrachter *m*; ~**find·er** *phot.* [,faɪndə] (Bild)Sucher *m*; ~**less** [~lɪs] ohne eigene Meinung; *poet.* unsichtbar; ~**point** Gesichts-, Standpunkt *m*.

vig·il ['vɪdʒɪl] Nachtwache *f*; ~**i·lance** [~əns] Wachsamkeit *f*; ~**i·lant** □ [~t] wachsam.

vig·or·ous □ ['vɪgərəs] kräftig; energisch; nachdrücklich; ~**o(u)r** ['vɪgə] Kraft *f*; Vitalität *f*; Energie *f*; Nachdruck *m*.

Vi·king ['vaɪkɪŋ] **1.** Wiking(er) *m*; **2.** wikingisch, Wikinger...

vile □ [vaɪl] gemein; abscheulich.

vil·lage ['vɪlɪdʒ] Dorf *n*; ~ **green** Dorfanger *m*, -wiese *f*; ~**lag·er** [~ə] Dorfbewohner(in).

vil·lain ['vɪlən] Schurke *m*, Schuft *m*, Bösewicht *m*; ~**ous** □ [~əs] schurkisch; F scheußlich; ~**y** [~ɪ] Schurkerei *f*.

vim F [vɪm] Schwung *m*, Schmiß *m*.

vin·di·cate ['vɪndɪkeɪt] rechtfertigen; rehabilitieren; ~**ca·tion** [vɪndɪ-'keɪʃn] Rechtfertigung *f*.

vin·dic·tive □ [vɪn'dɪktɪv] rachsüchtig, nachtragend.

vine [vaɪn] Wein(stock) *m*, (Wein-)Rebe *f*; △ *nicht* Wein (*Getränk*).

vin·e·gar ['vɪnɪgə] (Wein)Essig *m*.

vine|-grow·ing ['vaɪngrəʊɪŋ] Weinbau *m*; ~**yard** ['vɪnjəd] Weinberg *m*.

vin·tage ['vɪntɪdʒ] **1.** Weinlese *f*; (Wein)Jahrgang *m*; **2.** klassisch; erlesen; altmodisch; ~ *car mot.* Oldtimer *m*; ~**tag·er** [~ə] Weinleser(in).

vi·o·la ♪ [vɪ'əʊlə] Bratsche *f*.

vi·o·late ['vaɪəleɪt] verletzen; *Eid etc.* brechen; vergewaltigen; ~**la·tion** [vaɪə'leɪʃn] Verletzung *f*; (Eid- *etc.*-) Bruch *m*; Vergewaltigung *f*.

vi·o·lence ['vaɪələns] Gewalt(tätigkeit) *f*; Heftigkeit *f*; ~**lent** □ [~t] gewaltsam, -tätig; heftig.

vi·o·let ♀ ['vaɪələt] Veilchen *n*.

vi·o·lin ♪ [vaɪə'lɪn] Violine *f*, Geige *f*.

VIP F ['viː'aɪ'piː] prominente Persönlichkeit.

vi·per *zo.* ['vaɪpə] Viper *f*, Natter *f*.

vi·ra·go [vɪ'rɑːgəʊ] (*pl.* -gos, -goes) Zankteufel *m*, Drachen *m*.

vir·gin ['vɜːdʒɪn] **1.** Jungfrau *f*; **2.** *a.* ~**al** □ [~l] jungfräulich; Jungfern...; ~**i·ty** [və'dʒɪnətɪ] Jungfräulichkeit *f*.

vir·ile ['vɪraɪl] männlich; Mannes...; **vi·ril·i·ty** [vɪ'rɪlətɪ] Männlichkeit *f*; *physiol.* Mannes-, Zeugungskraft *f*.

vir·tu·al □ ['vɜːtjʊəl] eigentlich; ~**ly** [~l] praktisch.

vir·tue ['vɜːtjuː] Tugend *f*; Vorzug *m*; *in od. by* ~ *of* kraft, vermöge (*beide gen.*); *make a* ~ *of necessity* aus der Not e-e Tugend machen; ~**tu·os·i·ty** [vɜːtjʊ'ɒsətɪ] Virtuosität *f*; ~**tu·ous** □ ['vɜːtjʊəs] tugendhaft; rechtschaffen; △ *nicht* virtuos.

vir·u·lent □ ['vɪrʊlənt] ✿ (sehr) giftig, bösartig (*a. fig.*).

vi·rus ✿ ['vaɪərəs] Virus *n*, *m*; *fig.* Gift *n*.

vi·sa ['viːzə] Visum *n*, Sichtvermerk *m*; ~**ed**, ~**'d** [~d] mit e-m Sichtvermerk *od.* Visum (versehen).

vis·cose ['vɪskəʊs] Viskose *f*; ~ *silk* Zellstoffseide *f*.

vis·count ['vaɪkaʊnt] Vicomte *m*; ~**ess** [~ɪs] Vicomtesse *f*.

vis·cous □ ['vɪskəs] zähflüssig.

vise *Am.* ⊕ [vaɪs] Schraubstock *m*.

vis·i·bil·i·ty [vɪzɪ'bɪlətɪ] Sichtbarkeit *f*; Sichtweite *f*; ~**ble** □ ['vɪzəbl] sichtbar; *fig.* (er)sichtlich; *pred.* zu sehen (*Sache*); zu sprechen (*Person*).

vi·sion ['vɪʒn] Sehvermögen *n*, -kraft *f*; *fig.* Seherblick *m*; Vision *f*; ~**a·ry** [~ərɪ] **1.** phantastisch; **2.** Hellseher(in); Phantast(in).

vis·it ['vɪzɪt] **1.** *v/t.* besuchen; aufsuchen; besichtigen; *fig.* heimsuchen; ~ *s.th. on s.o. eccl.* j-n für et. (be)strafen; *v/i.* e-n Besuch *od.* Besuche machen; *Am.* plaudern (*with* mit); **2.** Besuch *m*; △ *nicht* ♮ Visite (*im Krankenhaus*); **~i·ta·tion** [vızı-'teɪ∫n] Besuch *m*; Besichtigung *f*; *fig.* Heimsuchung *f*; **~it·or** ['vɪzɪtə] Besucher(in), Gast *m*.

vi·sor ['vaɪzə] Visier *n*; (Mützen-) Schirm *m*; *mot.* Sonnenblende *f*.

vis·ta ['vɪstə] (Aus-, Durch)Blick *m*.

vis·u·al □ ['vɪzjʊəl] Seh..., Gesichts...; visuell; ~ *aids pl.* Schule: Anschauungsmaterial *n*; ~ *display unit Computer:* Bildschirm-, Bildsicht-, Datensichtgerät *n*; ~ *instruction Schule:* Anschauungsunterricht *m*; **~ize** [~aɪz] sich vorstellen, sich ein Bild machen von.

vi·tal □ ['vaɪtl] **1.** Lebens...; lebenswichtig; wesentlich; (hoch)wichtig; vital; ~ *parts pl.* = **2.** ~**s** *pl.* lebenswichtige Organe *pl.*, edle Teile *pl.*; **~i·ty** [vaɪ'tælətɪ] Lebenskraft *f*, Vitalität *f*; **~ize** ['vaɪtəlaɪz] beleben.

vit·a·min ['vɪtəmɪn] Vitamin *n*; ~ *deficiency* Vitaminmangel *m*.

vi·ti·ate ['vɪʃɪeɪt] verderben; beeinträchtigen.

vit·re·ous □ ['vɪtrɪəs] Glas..., gläsern.

vi·va·cious □ [vɪ'veɪ∫əs] lebhaft; **vi·vac·i·ty** [vɪ'væsətɪ] Lebhaftigkeit *f*.

viv·id □ ['vɪvɪd] lebhaft, lebendig.

vix·en ['vɪksn] Füchsin *f*; zänkisches Weib, Drachen *m*.

V-neck ['vi:nek] V-Ausschnitt *m*; **V-necked** [~t] mit V-Ausschnitt.

vo·cab·u·la·ry [və'kæbjʊlərɪ] Wörterverzeichnis *n*; Wortschatz *m*.

vo·cal □ ['vəʊkl] stimmlich, Stimm...; laut; ♪ Vokal..., Gesang...; klingend; *ling.* stimmhaft; **~ist** [~əlɪst] Sänger(in); **~ize** [~aɪz] (*ling.* stimmhaft) aussprechen.

vo·ca·tion [vəʊ'keɪ∫n] Berufung *f*; Beruf *m*; **~al** □ [~ənl] beruflich, Berufs...; ~ *adviser* Berufsberater *m*; ~ *education* Berufsausbildung *f*; ~ *guidance* Berufsberatung *f*; ~ *school Am.* (*etwa*) Berufsschule *f*; ~ *training* Berufsausbildung *f*.

vo·cif·er·ate [və'sɪfəreɪt] schreien; **~ous** □ [~əs] schreiend; lautstark.

vogue [vəʊg] Mode *f*; *be in* ~ (in) Mode sein.

voice [vɔɪs] **1.** Stimme *f*; *active* (*passive*) ~ *gr.* Aktiv *n* (Passiv *n*); *give* ~ *to* Ausdruck geben *od.* verleihen (*dat.*); **2.** äußern, ausdrücken; *ling.* (stimmhaft) (aus)sprechen.

void [vɔɪd] **1.** leer; ♯ (rechts)unwirksam, ungültig; ~ *of* frei von, arm an (*dat.*), ohne; **2.** Leere *f*; *fig.* Lücke *f*.

vol·a·tile ['vɒlətaɪl] ♠ flüchtig (*a. fig.*); flatterhaft.

vol·ca·no [vɒl'keɪnəʊ] (*pl.* -noes, -nos) Vulkan *m*.

vo·li·tion [və'lɪ∫n] Wollen *n*, Wille(nskraft *f*) *m*; *of one's own* ~ aus eigenem Entschluß.

vol·ley ['vɒlɪ] **1.** Salve *f*; (*Geschoß-etc.*)Hagel *m*; *fig.* Schwall *m*; *Tennis:* Flugball *m*; **2.** *mst* ~ *out* e-n Schwall von *Worten etc.* von sich geben; e-e Salve *od.* Salven abgeben; *fig.* hageln; dröhnen; **~ball** *Sport:* Volleyball(spiel *n*) *m*.

volt ♯ [vəʊlt] Volt *n*; **~age** ♯ ['vəʊltɪdʒ] Spannung *f*; **~me·ter** ♯ Volt-, Spannungsmesser *m*.

vol·u·bil·i·ty [vɒljʊ'bɪlətɪ] Redegewandtheit *f*; **~ble** □ ['vɒljʊbl] (rede)gewandt.

vol·ume ['vɒlju:m] Band *m* (*e-s Buches*); Volumen *n*; *fig.* Masse *f*, große Menge; (*bsd.* Stimm)Umfang *m*; ♯ Lautstärke *f*; **vo·lu·mi·nous** □ [və'lju:mɪnəs] vielbändig; umfangreich, voluminös.

vol·un·ta·ry □ ['vɒləntərɪ] freiwillig; **~teer** [vɒlən'tɪə] **1.** Freiwillige(r *m*) *f*; *v/i.* freiwillig dienen; sich freiwillig melden; sich erbieten; *v/t.* Dienste etc. freiwillig anbieten; sich *e-e Bemerkung* erlauben.

vo·lup·tu·a·ry [və'lʌptjʊərɪ] Lüstling *m*; **~ous** □ [~əs] wollüstig; üppig; sinnlich.

vom·it ['vɒmɪt] **1.** *v/t.* (er)brechen; *v/i.* (sich er)brechen; **2.** Erbrochene(s) *n*; Erbrechen *n*.

vo·ra·cious □ [və'reɪ∫əs] gefräßig, gierig, unersättlich; **vo·rac·i·ty** [vɒ'ræsətɪ] Gefräßigkeit *f*, Gier *f*.

vor·tex ['vɔ:teks] (*pl.* -texes, -tices [-tɪsi:z]) Wirbel *m*, Strudel *m* (*mst fig.*).

vote [vəʊt] **1.** (Wahl)Stimme *f*; Abstimmung *f*; Stimm-, Wahlrecht *n*; Beschluß *m*, Votum *n*; ~ *of no confidence* Mißtrauensvotum *n*; *take a* ~ *on s.th.* über et. abstimmen; **2.** *v/t.* wählen; bewilligen; *v/i.* abstimmen;

waken

wählen; ~ *for* stimmen für; F für *et.*
sein; **vot·er** ['vəʊtə] Wähler(in).

vot·ing ['vəʊtɪŋ] Abstimmung *f*,
Stimmabgabe *f*; *attr.* Wahl...; ~
pa·per Stimmzettel *m*.

vouch [vaʊtʃ]: ~ *for* (sich ver)bürgen
für; **~·er** ['vaʊtʃə] Beleg *m*, Unterlage *f*; Gutschein *m*; **~·safe** [vaʊtʃ'seɪf]
gewähren; geruhen (*to do* zu tun).

vow [vaʊ] **1.** Gelübde *n*; (Treu-)
Schwur *m*; *take a* ~, *make a* ~ ein
Gelübde ablegen; **2.** geloben.

vow·el *ling.* ['vaʊəl] Vokal *m*, Selbst-
laut *m*.

voy|age ['vɔɪdʒ] **1.** *längere* (See-,

Flug)Reise; **2.** *lit.* reisen; **~·ag·er**
['vɔɪədʒə] (See)Reisende(r *m*) *f*.

vul·gar □ ['vʌlgə] gewöhnlich, unfein, ordinär; vulgär; pöbelhaft; geschmacklos; ~ *tongue* Volkssprache
f; **~·i·ty** [vʌl'gærətɪ] ungehobeltes
Wesen; Ungezogenheit *f*; Ge-
schmacklosigkeit *f*.

vul·ne·ra·ble □ ['vʌlnərəbl] ver-
wundbar (*a. fig.*); ✕, *Sport*: ungeschützt, offen; *fig.* angreifbar.

vul·pine ['vʌlpaɪn] Fuchs..., fuchsartig; schlau, listig.

vul·ture *zo.* ['vʌltʃə] Geier *m*.

vy·ing ['vaɪɪŋ] wetteifernd.

W

wad [wɒd] **1.** (*Watte*)Bausch *m*;
Pfropf(en) *m*; Banknotenbündel *n*;
2. (*-dd-*) wattieren, auspolstern; zu
e-m Bausch zusammenpressen;
~·ding ['wɒdɪŋ] Einlage *f*, Füllmate-
rial (*zum Verpacken etc.*); Wattierung *f*; Watte *f*.

wad·dle ['wɒdl] **1.** watscheln; **2.** watsch-
elnder Gang, Watscheln *n*.

wade [weɪd] *v/i.* waten; ~ *through fig.*
F sich (hin)durcharbeiten; *v/t.*
durchwaten.

wa·fer ['weɪfə] Waffel *f*; Oblate *f*;
eccl. Hostie *f*.

waf·fle¹ ['wɒfl] Waffel *f*.

waf·fle² *Brt.* F [~] schwafeln.

waft [wɑːft] **1.** wehen; **2.** Hauch *m*.

wag [wæg] **1.** (*-gg-*) wackeln *od.* wedeln (mit); **2.** Schütteln *n*; Wedeln *n*;
Spaßvogel *m*.

wage¹ [weɪdʒ] *Krieg* führen, *Feldzug*
unternehmen (*on, against* gegen).

wage² [~] *mst* ~*s pl.* (Arbeits)Lohn *m*;
~·earn·er *econ.* ['weɪdʒɜːnə] Lohn-
empfänger(in) *f*; **~ freeze** *econ.* Lohnstopp *m*; **~ pack·et** *econ.* Lohntüte *f*.

wa·ger ['weɪdʒə] **1.** Wette *f*; **2.** wetten.

wag·gish □ ['wægɪʃ] schelmisch.

wag·gle ['wægl] wackeln (mit).

wag·(g)on ['wægən] (Last-, Roll-)
Wagen *m*; *Brt.* 🚆 (offener) Güterwagen; **~·er** [~ə] Fuhrmann *m*.

wag·tail *zo.* ['wægteɪl] Bachstelze *f*.

waif *lit.* [weɪf] verlassenes *od.* ver-
wahrlostes Kind.

wail [weɪl] **1.** (Weh)Klagen *n*; **2.**
(weh)klagen; schreien, wimmern,
heulen (*a. Wind*).

wain·scot ['weɪnskət] (Wand)Täfe-
lung *f*.

waist [weɪst] Taille *f*; schmalste
Stelle; ⚓ Mitteldeck *n*; **~·coat**
['weɪskəʊt] Weste *f*; **~·line** ['weɪst-
laɪn] *Schneiderei:* Taille *f*.

wait [weɪt] **1.** *v/i.* warten (*for* auf
acc.); *a.* ~ *at* (*Am.* on) *table* bedienen, servieren; ~ *on*, ~ *upon j-n*
bedienen; *fig.* ~*t.* abwarten; **2.** Warten
n; *lie in* ~ *for s.o.* j-m auflauern; **~·er**
['weɪtə] Kellner *m*; ~, *the bill* (*Am.*
check), *please!* (Herr) Ober, bitte
zahlen!

wait·ing ['weɪtɪŋ] Warten *n*; Dienst
m; *in* ~ diensttuend; **~·room** Wartezimmer *n*; 🚆 *etc.* Wartesaal *m*.

wait·ress ['weɪtrɪs] Kellnerin *f*, Bedienung *f*; ~, *the bill* (*Am.* check),
please! Fräulein, bitte zahlen!

waive [weɪv] verzichten auf (*acc.*).

wake [weɪk] **1.** ⚓ Kielwasser *n* (*a.*
fig.); *in the* ~ *of im* Kielwasser (*e-s*
Schiffes); *fig.* im Gefolge (*gen.*); **2.**
(*woke od. waked, woken od. waked*)
v/i. a. ~ *up* aufwachen; *v/t. a.* ~ *up*
(auf)wecken; *fig.* wachrufen; **~·ful**
□ ['weɪkfl] wachsam; schlaflos;
wak·en [~ən] = **wake** 2.

wale [weɪl] Strieme(n *m*) *f*.
walk [wɔːk] **1.** *v/i.* gehen (*a. Sport*), zu Fuß gehen, laufen, spazierengehen; wandern; im Schritt gehen; ~ **out** *econ.* streiken; ~ **out on** F im Stich lassen; *v/t.* (zu Fuß) gehen; führen; *Pferd* im Schritt gehen lassen; begleiten; durchwandern; auf u. ab gehen in *od.* auf (*dat.*); **2.** (Spazier-) Gang *m*; Spazierweg *m*; ~ **of life** (soziale) Schicht; Beruf *m*; **~er** ['wɔːkə] Spaziergänger(in); *Sport:* Geher *m*; *be a good* ~ gut zu Fuß sein.
walk·ie-talk·ie ['wɔːkɪ'tɔːkɪ] Walkie-talkie *n*, tragbares Funksprechgerät.
walk·ing ['wɔːkɪŋ] (Zufuß)Gehen *n*; Spazierengehen *n*, Wandern *n*; *attr.* Spazier...; Wander...; ~ **pa·pers** *pl.* *Am.* F Laufpaß *m* (*Entlassung*); **~stick** Spazierstock *m*; **~tour** Wanderung *f*.
walk|-out *econ.* ['wɔːkaʊt] Ausstand *m*, Streik *m*; **~over** Spaziergang *m*, leichter Sieg; **~up** *Am.* (Miets-) Haus *n* ohne Fahrstuhl; Wohnung *f* in e-m Haus ohne Fahrstuhl.
wall [wɔːl] **1.** Wand *f*; Mauer *f*; **2.** *a.* ~ **in** mit e-r Mauer umgeben; ~ **up** zumauern.
wal·let ['wɒlɪt] Brieftasche *f*.
wall·flow·er *fig.* ['wɔːlflaʊə] Mauerblümchen *n*.
wal·lop F ['wɒləp] *j-n* verdreschen.
wal·low ['wɒləʊ] sich wälzen.
wall|-pa·per ['wɔːlpeɪpə] **1.** Tapete *f*; **2.** tapezieren; **~sock·et** ⚡ (Wand-) Steckdose *f*; **~to-~:** ~ *carpet* Spannteppich *m*; ~ *carpeting* Teppichboden *m*.
wal·nut ♀ ['wɔːlnʌt] Walnuß(baum *m*) *f*.
wal·rus *zo.* ['wɔːlrəs] Walroß *n*.
waltz [wɔːls] **1.** Walzer *m*; **2.** Walzer tanzen.
wan □ [wɒn] (*-nn-*) blaß, bleich, fahl.
wand [wɒnd] Zauberstab *m*.
wan·der ['wɒndə] herumgehen, -laufen, umherstreifen; △ *nicht in e-m Gebiet wandern = hike*; *fig.* abschweifen; irregehen; phantasieren.
wane [weɪn] **1.** abnehmen (*Mond*); *fig.* schwinden; **2.** Abnehmen *n*.
wan·gle F ['wæŋgl] *v/t.* deichseln, hinkriegen; *v/i.* mogeln.
want [wɒnt] Mangel *m* (*of an dat.*);

Bedürfnis *n*; Not *f*; **2.** *v/i.* ermangeln (*for gen.*); *he* ~*s for nothing* es fehlt ihm an nichts; *v/t.* wünschen, (haben) wollen; bedürfen (*gen.*), brauchen; nicht (genug) haben; *it* ~*s s.th.* es fehlt an et. (*dat.*); *he* ~*s energy* es fehlt ihm an Energie; ~*ed* gesucht; **~-ad** F ['wɒntæd] Stellenangebot *n*, -gesuch *n*; **~ing** [~ɪŋ]: *be* ~ es fehlen lassen (*in an dat.*); unzulänglich sein.
wan·ton ['wɒntən] **1.** □ mutwillig; ausgelassen; **2.** herumtollen.
war [wɔː] **1.** Krieg *m*; *attr.* Kriegs...; *make od. wage* ~ Krieg führen (*on, against* gegen); **2.** (*-rr-*) streiten, kämpfen.
war·ble ['wɔːbl] trillern; trällern.
ward [wɔːd] **1.** (Krankenhaus)Station *f*, Abteilung *f*; Krankenzimmer *n*; (Gefängnis)Trakt *m*; Zelle *f*; (Stadt-, Wahl)Bezirk *m*; ⚖ Mündel *n*; *in* ~ ⚖ unter Vormundschaft (stehend); **2.** ~ **off** abwehren; **war·den** ['wɔːdn] Aufseher *m*; *univ.* Rektor *m*; *Am.* (Gefängnis)Direktor *m*; **~er** ['wɔːdə] *Brt.* Aufsichtsbeamte(r) *m* (*im Gefängnis*).
war·drobe ['wɔːdrəʊb] Garderobe *f*; Kleiderschrank *m*; ~ *trunk* Schrankkoffer *m*.
ware [weə] *in Zssgn:* Ware(n *pl.*) *f*, Artikel *m od. pl.*; △ *nicht* (*Einkaufs*-) *Ware*.
ware·house 1. ['weəhaʊs] (Waren-) Lager *n*; Lagerhaus *n*, Speicher *m*; △ *nicht Warenhaus*; **2.** [~z] auf Lager bringen, (ein)lagern.
war|fare ['wɔːfeə] Krieg(führung *f*) *m*; **~head** ✗ Spreng-, Gefechtskopf *m* (*e-r Rakete etc.*).
war·i·ness ['weərɪnɪs] Vorsicht *f*.
war·like ['wɔːlaɪk] kriegerisch.
warm [wɔːm] **1.** □ warm (*a. fig.*); heiß; *fig.* hitzig; **2.** *et.* Warmes; (Auf-, An)Wärmen *n*; **3.** *v/t. a.* ~ **up** (auf-, an-, er)wärmen; *v/i. a.* ~ **up** warm werden, sich erwärmen; warmlaufen (*Motor etc.*); **~th** [~θ] Wärme *f*.
warn [wɔːn] warnen (*of, against* vor *dat.*); verwarnen; ermahnen; verständigen; **~ing** ['wɔːnɪŋ] (Ver-) Warnung *f*; Mahnung *f*; Kündigung *f*; *attr.* warnend, Warn...
warp [wɔːp] *v/i.* sich verziehen (*Holz*); *v/t. fig.* verdrehen, -zerren; beeinflussen; *j-n* abbringen (*from* von).

war|rant ['wɒrənt] **1.** Vollmacht *f*; Rechtfertigung *f*; Berechtigung *f*; ⚡ (Vollziehungs-, Haft- *etc*.) Berechtigungsschein *m*; ~ *of arrest* ⚡ Haftbefehl *m*; **2.** bevollmächtigen; rechtfertigen; verbürgen, garantieren; ~**ran·ty** *econ*. [~tɪ]: *it's still under* ~ darauf ist noch Garantie.

war·ri·or ['wɒrɪə] Krieger *m*.

wart [wɔːt] Warze *f*; Auswuchs *m*.

war·y □ ['weərɪ] (*-ier, -iest*) wachsam, vorsichtig.

was [wɒz, wəs] *1. und 3. sg. pret. von* be: war; *pret. pass. von* be: wurde.

wash [wɒʃ] **1.** *v/t.* waschen; (ab)spülen; ~ *up* abwaschen, abspülen; *v/i.* sich waschen (lassen); *vom Wasser* gespült *od.* geschwemmt werden; ~ *up Brt.* Geschirr spülen; **2.** Waschen *n*; Wäsche *f*; Wellenschlag *m*; Spülwasser *n*; *mouth~* Mundwasser *n*; **3.** Wasch...; ~**a·ble** ['wɒʃəbl] waschbar; ~**and-wear** bügelfrei; pflegeleicht; ~**ba·sin** Waschbecken *n*; ~**cloth** *Am*. Waschlappen *m*; ~**er** ['wɒʃə] Wäscherin *f*; Waschmaschine *f*; = *dishwasher*; ⊕ Unterlegscheibe *f*; ~**er·wom·an** (*pl. -women*) Waschfrau *f*; ~**ing** ['wɒʃɪŋ] **1.** Waschen *n*; Wäsche *f*; ~*s pl.* Spülwasser *n*; **2.** Wasch...; ~**ing ma·chine** Waschmaschine *f*; ~**ing pow·der** Waschpulver *n*, -mittel *n*; ~**ing-up** *Brt.* Abwasch *m*; ~**rag** *Am*. Waschlappen *m*; ~**y** ['wɒʃɪ] (*-ier, -iest*) wässerig, wäßrig.

wasp *zo*. [wɒsp] Wespe *f*.

wast·age ['weɪstɪdʒ] Verlust *m*; Vergeudung *f*.

waste [weɪst] **1.** wüst, öde; unbebaut; überflüssig; Abfall...; *lay* ~ verwüsten; **2.** Verschwendung *f*, -geudung *f*; Abfall *m*; Ödland *n*, Wüste *f*; **3.** *v/t.* verwüsten; verschwenden; verzehren; *v/i.* verschwendet werden; ~**ful** □ ['weɪstfl] verschwenderisch; ~ **paper** Abfallpapier *n*; Altpapier *n*; ~**pa·per bas·ket** [weɪst'peɪpəbɑːs-kɪt] Papierkorb *m*; ~ **pipe** ['weɪst-paɪp] Abflußrohr *n*.

watch [wɒtʃ] **1.** Wache *f*; (Taschen-, Armband)Uhr *f*; **2.** *v/i.* zusehen, zuschauen; wachen; ~ *for* warten auf (*acc.*); ~ *out (for)* aufpassen, achtgeben (auf *acc.*); sich hüten (vor *dat.*); ~ *out!* Achtung!, Vorsicht!; *v/t.* bewachen; beobachten; achtgeben auf

(*acc.*); *Gelegenheit* abwarten; ~**dog** ['wɒtʃdɒg] Wachhund *m*; *fig.* Überwacher(in); ~**ful** □ [~fl] wachsam; ~**mak·er** Uhrmacher *m*; ~**man** [~mən] (*pl. -men*) (Nacht)Wächter *m*; ~**word** Kennwort *n*, Parole *f*.

wa·ter ['wɔːtə] **1.** Wasser *n*; Gewässer *n*; *drink the* ~*s* Brunnen trinken; **2.** *v/t.* bewässern; (be)sprengen; (be)gießen; mit Wasser versorgen; tränken; verwässern (*a. fig.*); *v/i.* wässern (*Mund*); tränen (*Augen*); ~**clos·et** (Wasser)Klosett *n*; ~**col·o(u)r** Wasser-, Aquarellfarbe *f*; Aquarell(malerei *f*) *n*; ~**course** Wasserlauf *m*; Fluß-, Strombett *n*; Kanal *m*; ~**cress** ♣ Brunnenkresse *f*; ~**fall** Wasserfall *m*; ~**front** an ein Gewässer grenzender Stadtbezirk, Hafengebiet *n*, -viertel *n*; ~ **ga(u)ge** ⊕ Wasserstand(san)zeiger *m*; Pegel *m*; ~**hole** Wasserloch *n*.

wa·ter·ing ['wɔːtərɪŋ] Bewässern *n*; (Be)Gießen *n*; Tränken (*von Vieh*); ~**can** Gießkanne *f*; ~**place** Wasserstelle *f*; Tränke *f*; Bad(eort *m*) *n*; Seebad *n*; ~**pot** Gießkanne *f*.

wa·ter| lev·el ['wɔːtəlevl] Wasserspiegel *m*; Wasserstand(slinie *f*) *m*; ⊕ Wasserwaage *f*; ~**logged** [~lɒgd] ♣ voll Wasser (*Boot*); vollgesogen (*Erdreich*); ~ **main** ⊕ Hauptwasserrohr *n*; ~**mark** Wasserzeichen *n* (*Papier*); ~**mel·on** ♣ Wassermelone *f*; ~ **pol·lu·tion** Wasserverschmutzung *f*; ~ **po·lo** *Sport*: Wasserball(spiel *n*) *m*; ~**proof 1.** wasserdicht; **2.** Regenmantel *m*; **3.** imprägnieren; ~**shed** *geogr.* Wasserscheide *f*; *fig.* Wendepunkt *m*; ~**side** Fluß-, Seeufer *n*; ~ **ski·ing** *Sport*: Wasserski(laufen) *n*; ~**tight** wasserdicht; *fig.* unanfechtbar; stichhaltig (*Argument*); ~**way** Wasserstraße *f*; ~**works** *oft sg.* Wasserwerk *n*; *turn on the* ~ *fig.* F losheulen; ~**y** [~rɪ] wässerig, wäßrig.

watt ⚡ [wɒt] Watt *n*.

wave [weɪv] **1.** Welle *f* (*a. phys.*); Woge *f*; Winken *n*; **2.** *v/t.* wellen; schwingen; schwenken; ~ *s.o. aside* j-n beiseite winken; *v/i.* wogen; wehen, flattern; ~ *at od. to s.o.* j-m (zu)winken, j-m ein Zeichen geben; ~**length** ['weɪvleŋθ] *phys.* Wellenlänge *f* (*a. fig.*).

wa·ver ['weɪvə] (sch)wanken; flakkern.

wav·y □ ['weɪvɪ] (-ier, -iest) wellig; wogend.

wax¹ [wæks] **1.** Wachs *n*; Siegellack *m*; Ohrenschmalz *n*; **2.** wachsen; bohnern.

wax² [~] zunehmen (*Mond*).

wax|en *fig.* ['wæksən] wächsern; **~works** Wachsfigurenkabinett *n*; **~y** [~ɪ] (-ier, -iest) wachsartig; weich.

way [weɪ] **1.** Weg *m*; Straße *f*; Art *f* u. Weise *f*; (Eigen)Art; Strecke *f*; Richtung *f*; *fig.* Hinsicht *f*; ~ **in** Eingang *m*; ~ **out** Ausgang *m*; *fig.* Ausweg *m*; *right of* ~ 🚊 Wegerecht *n*; *bsd. mot.* Vorfahrt(srecht *n*) *f*; *this* ~ hierher, hier entlang; *by the* ~ übrigens; *by* ~ *of* durch; *on the* ~, *on one's* ~ unterwegs; *out of the* ~ ungewöhnlich; *under* ~ in Fahrt; *give* ~ zurückweichen; *mot.* die Vorfahrt lassen (*to dat.*); nachgeben; abgelöst werden (*to von*); sich hingeben (*to dat.*); *have one's* ~ s-n Willen haben; *lead the* ~ vorangehen; **2.** *adv.* weit; **~·bill** ['weɪbɪl] Frachtbrief *m*; **~·far·er** *veraltet od. lit.* [~feərə] Wanderer *m*; **~·lay** [weɪ'leɪ] (-laid) *j-m* auflauern; *j-n* abfangen, abpassen; **~·out** F äußerst ungewöhnlich; toll, super; **~·side** ['weɪsaɪd] **1.** Wegrand *m*; **2.** am Wege; ~ **sta·tion** *Am.* Zwischenstation *f*; ~ **train** *Am.* Bummelzug *m*; **~·ward** [~wəd] launisch; eigensinnig.

we [wiː, wɪ] wir.

weak □ [wiːk] schwach; schwächlich; dünn (*Getränk*); **~·en** [wiːkən] *v/t.* schwächen; *v/i.* schwach werden; **~·ling** [~lɪŋ] Schwächling *m*; **~·ly** [~lɪ] (-ier, -iest) schwächlich; **~·mind·ed** [wiːk'maɪndɪd] schwachsinnig; **~·ness** ['wiːknɪs] Schwäche *f*.

weal [wiːl] Strieme(n *m*) *f*.

wealth [welθ] Reichtum *m*; *econ.* Besitz *m*, Vermögen *n*; *fig.* Fülle *f*; **~·y** □ ['welθɪ] (-ier, -iest) reich; wohlhabend.

wean [wiːn] entwöhnen; ~ *s.o. from s.th.* j-m et. abgewöhnen.

weap·on ['wepən] Waffe *f*.

wear [weə] **1.** (*wore, worn*) *v/t.* am Körper tragen; zur Schau tragen; *a.* ~ *away*, ~ *down*, ~ *off*, ~ *out* Kleidung *etc.* abnutzen, abtragen, verschleißen, *Reifen* abfahren; *a.* ~ *out* ermüden; *j-s* Geduld erschöpfen; *a.* ~ *away*, ~ *down* zermürben; entkräften; *v/i.* sich *gut etc.* tragen od. halten; *a.* ~ *away*, ~ *down*, ~ *off*, ~ *out* sich abnutzen *od.* abtragen, verschleißen; sich abfahren (*Reifen*); ~ *off fig.* sich verlieren; ~ *on* sich dahinschleppen (*Zeit etc.*); ~ *out fig.* sich erschöpfen; **2.** Tragen *n*; (Be-)Kleidung *f*; Abnutzung *f*; *for hard* ~ strapazierfähig; *the worse for* ~ abgetragen; **~ and tear** Verschleiß *m*; **~·er** ['weərə] Träger(in).

wear|i·ness ['wɪərɪnɪs] Müdigkeit *f*; Überdruß *m*; **~·i·some** □ [~səm] ermüdend; langweilig; **~·y** ['wɪərɪ] **1.** □ (-ier, -iest) müde; überdrüssig; ermüdend; anstrengend; **2.** ermüden; überdrüssig werden (*of gen.*).

wea·sel *zo.* ['wiːzl] Wiesel *n*.

weath·er ['weðə] **1.** Wetter *n*, Witterung *f*; **2.** *v/t.* dem Wetter aussetzen; ⚓ *Sturm* abwettern; *fig.* überstehen; *v/i.* verwittern; **~·beat·en** vom Wetter mitgenommen; **~ bu·reau** Wetteramt *n*; ~ **chart** Wetterkarte *f*; ~ **fore·cast** Wetterbericht *m*, -vorhersage *f*; **~·worn** verwittert.

weave [wiːv] (*wove, woven*) weben; flechten; *fig.* ersinnen, erfinden; **weav·er** ['wiːvə] Weber *m*.

web [web] Gewebe *n*, Netz *n*; *zo.* Schwimm-, Flughaut *f*; **~·bing** ['webɪŋ] Gurtband *n*.

wed [wed] (-dd-; *wedded od. selten: wed*) heiraten; *fig.* verbinden (*to* mit); **~·ding** ['wedɪŋ] **1.** Hochzeit *f*; **2.** Hochzeits..., Braut..., Trau...; ~ *ring* Ehe-, Trauring *m*.

wedge [wedʒ] **1.** Keil *m*; **2.** (ver)keilen; (ein)keilen, (-)zwängen (*in in acc.*).

wed·lock ['wedlɒk]: *born in (out of)* ~ ehelich (unehelich) geboren.

Wednes·day ['wenzdɪ] Mittwoch *m*.

wee [wiː] klein, winzig; *a* ~ *bit* ein klein wenig.

weed [wiːd] **1.** Unkraut *n*; **2.** jäten; säubern (*of von*); ~ *out fig.* aussondern, -sieben; **~·kill·er** ['wiːdkɪlə] Unkrautvertilgungsmittel *n*; **~s** [wiːdz] *pl. mst widow's* ~ Witwenkleidung *f*; **~·y** ['wiːdɪ] (-ier, -iest) voll Unkraut, verunkrautet; F schmächtig.

week [wiːk] Woche *f*; *this day* ~ heute in *od.* vor e-r Woche; **~·day** ['wiːkdeɪ] Wochentag *m*; **~·end** [wiːk'end] Wochenende *n*; **~·end·er** [~ə] Wo-

chenendausflügler(in); **~ly** ['wi:klɪ]
1. wöchentlich; Wochen...; **2.** a. ~
paper Wochenblatt n, Wochen-
(zeit)schrift f.

weep [wi:p] (wept) weinen; tropfen;
~ing ['wi:pɪŋ]: ~ willow ♥ Trauer-
weide f; **~y** F [~ɪ] (-ier, -iest) weiner-
lich; rührselig, sentimental.

weigh [weɪ] v/t. (ab)wiegen; fig. ab-
erwägen; ~ anchor ♣ den Anker
lichten; ~ed down niedergedrückt;
v/i. wiegen (a. fig.); ausschlaggebend sein; ~ on, ~ upon lasten auf
(dat.).

weight [weɪt] **1.** Gewicht n (a. fig.);
Last f; fig. Bedeutung f; put on ~,
gain ~ zunehmen; lose ~ abnehmen;
2. beschweren; belasten; **~·less** ['weɪtlɪs] schwere-
los; **~·less·ness** [~nɪs] Schwerelosig-
keit f (a. Raumfahrt); **~ lift·ing**
[~lɪftɪŋ] Sport: Gewichtheben n; **~·y**
□ [~ɪ] (-ier, -iest) (ge)wichtig;
wuchtig.

weir [wɪə] Wehr n; Fischreuse f.

weird □ [wɪəd] Schicksals...; unheimlich; F sonderbar, seltsam.

wel·come ['welkəm] **1.** willkommen;
you are ~ to inf. es steht Ihnen frei,
zu inf.; (you are) ~! nichts zu danken!, bitte sehr!; **2.** Willkomm(en n)
m; **3.** willkommen heißen; fig. begrüßen.

weld ⊕ [weld] (ver-, zusammen-)
schweißen.

wel·fare ['welfeə] Wohl(ergehen) n;
Sozialhilfe f; Wohlfahrt f; ~ state
pol. Wohlfahrtsstaat m; ~ work So-
zialarbeit f; ~ work·er Sozialarbei-
ter(in).

well[1] [wel] **1.** Brunnen f; Quelle f; ⊕
Bohrloch n; Fahrstuhl-, Licht-,
Luftschacht m; **2.** quellen.

well[2] [~] **1.** (better, best) wohl; gut;
ordentlich; gründlich; gesund; be ~,
feel ~ sich wohl fühlen; be ~ off in
guten Verhältnissen leben, wohlha-
bend sein; **2.** int. nun!, na!; **~·bal·anced** [wel'bælənst] ausgewo-
gen (Diät); (innerlich) ausgeglichen;
~·be·ing Wohl(befinden) n; **~·born**
aus guter Familie; **~·bred** wohlerzo-
gen; **~·de·fined** deutlich; klar um-
rissen; **~·done** gutgemacht; (gut)
durchgebraten (Fleisch); **~·in·ten·**
tioned [~ɪn'tenʃnd] wohlmeinend;
gutgemeint; **~·known** bekannt; **~·**
man·nered mit guten Manieren;

~·nigh ['welnaɪ] beinahe; **~·off**
[wel'ɒf] wohlhabend; **~·read** bele-
sen; **~·timed** (zeitlich) günstig, im
richtigen Augenblick; Sport: gutge-
timed (Paß etc.); **~·to-do** wohlhabend; **~·worn** abgetragen; fig. abgedroschen.

Welsh [welʃ] **1.** walisisch; **2.** ling.
Walisisch n; the ~ pl. die Waliser pl.;
~ **rab·bit**, ~ **rare·bit** überbackener
Käsetoast.

welt [welt] Strieme(n m) f.

wel·ter ['weltə] Wirrwarr m, Durcheinander n.

wench veraltet [wentʃ] (bsd. Bauern-)
Mädchen n.

went [went] pret. von go 1.

wept [wept] pret. u. p.p. von weep.

were [wɜ:, wə] **1.** pret. von be: du
warst, Sie waren, wir, sie waren, ihr
wart; **2.** pret. pass. von be: wurde(n);
3. subj. pret. von be: wäre(n).

west [west] **1.** West(en m); a. Westen
m, westlicher Landesteil; the ♀ der
Westen, die Weststaaten pl. (der
USA); pol. der Westen; **2.** West...,
westlich; **3.** westwärts, nach Westen; **~·er·ly** ['westəlɪ] westlich;
~·ern [~ən] **1.** westlich; **2.** Western
m, Wildwestfilm m; **~·ward(s)**
[~wəd(z)] westwärts.

wet [wet] **1.** naß, feucht; **2.** Nässe f,
Feuchtigkeit f; **3.** (-tt-; wet od wet-
ted) naß machen, anfeuchten.

weth·er zo. ['weðə] Hammel m.

wet-nurse ['wetnɜ:s] Amme f.

whack [wæk] (knallender) Schlag; F
(An)Teil m; **~ed** [~t] fertig, erledigt
(erschöpft); **~·ing** ['wækɪŋ] **1.** F
Mords...; **2.** (Tracht f) Prügel pl.

whale zo. [weɪl] Wal m; **~·bone**
['weɪlbəʊn] Fischbein n; **~ oil** Tran
m.

whal·er ['weɪlə] Walfänger m (a.
Schiff); **~·ing** [~ɪŋ] Walfang m.

wharf [wɔ:f] (pl. wharfs, wharves
[~vz]) Kai m.

what [wɒt] **1.** was; wie; was für ein(e),
welche(r, -s), vor pl.: was für; (das,)
was; know ~'s ~ Bescheid wissen; ~
about ...? wie steht's mit ...?; ~ for?
wozu?; ~ of it?, so ~? na und?; ~
next? was sonst noch?; iro. sonst
noch was?; ~ a blessing! was für ein Segen!; ~ with
..., ~ with ... teils durch ..., teils
durch ...; **2.** int. was!, wie!;
fragend: was?, wie?; **~·(so·)ev·er**

[wɒt(səʊ)'evə] was (auch immer); alles, was.

wheat [wi:t] Weizen m.

whee·dle ['wi:dl] beschwatzen; ~ s.th. out of s.o. j-m et. abschwatzen.

wheel [wi:l] **1.** Rad n; Steuer(rad) n; Lenkrad n; bsd. Am. F (Fahr)Rad n; Töpferscheibe f; Drehung f; ⚔ Schwenkung f; **2.** rollen, fahren, schieben; sich drehen; ⚔ schwenken; bsd. Am. F radeln; ~**bar·row** ['wi:lbærəʊ] Schubkarre(n m) f; ~**chair** Rollstuhl m; ~**ed** mit Rädern; fahrbar; in Zssgn: ...räd(e)rig. **-wheel·er** ['wi:lə] in Zssgn: Wagen od. Fahrzeug mit ... Rädern.

wheeze [wi:z] schnaufen, keuchen.

whelp [welp] **1.** zo. Welpe m; Junge(s) n; F Balg m, n (ungezogenes Kind); **2.** (Junge) werfen.

when [wen] **1.** wann; **2.** wenn; als; während, obwohl, wo ... (doch).

whence [wens] woher, von wo.

when·(so·)ev·er [wen(səʊ)'evə] (immer) wenn, sooft (als); fragend: wann denn.

where [weə] wo; wohin; ~ ... from? woher?; ~ ... to? wohin?; ~**a·bouts 1.** [weərə'baʊts] wo etwa; **2.** ['weərəbaʊts] Aufenthalt(sort) m, Verbleib m; ~**as** [weər'æz] wohingegen, während (doch); ~**at** [ˌr'æt] woran, wobei, worauf; ~**by** [weə'baɪ] wodurch; ~**fore** ['weəfɔ:] weshalb; ~**in** [weər'ɪn] worin; ~**of** [ˌr'ɒv] wovon; ~**·up·on** [ˌrə'pɒn] worauf(hin); **wher·ev·er** [ˌr'evə] wo(hin) (auch) immer; ~**with·al** ['weəwɪðɔ:l] die (nötigen) Mittel pl., das nötige (Klein)Geld.

whet [wet] (-tt-) wetzen, schärfen; fig. anstacheln.

wheth·er ['weðə] ob; ~ or no so oder so.

whet·stone ['wetstəʊn] Schleifstein m.

whey [weɪ] Molke f.

which [wɪtʃ] **1.** welche(r, -s); **2.** der, die, das; was; ~**·ev·er** [ˌ'evə] welche(r, -s) (auch) immer.

whiff [wɪf] **1.** Hauch m; Duftwolke f, Geruch m; F Zigarillo m, n; Zug m (beim Rauchen); have a few ~s ein paar Züge machen; **2.** paffen; F duften (unangenehm riechen).

while [waɪl] **1.** Weile f, Zeit f; for a ~ e-e Zeitlang; **2.** mst ~ away sich die Zeit vertreiben; verbrin-

gen; **3.** a. **whilst** [waɪlst] während.

whim [wɪm] Laune f, Grille f.

whim·per ['wɪmpə] **1.** wimmern, winseln; **2.** Wimmern n, Winseln; △ nicht Wimper.

whim·si·cal □ ['wɪmzɪkl] wunderlich; launisch (a. Wetter etc.); ~**sy** ['wɪmzɪ] Grille f, Laune f.

whine [waɪn] winseln; wimmern.

whin·ny ['wɪnɪ] wiehern.

whip [wɪp] **1.** (-pp-) v/t. peitschen; geißeln (a. fig.); j-n verprügeln; schlagen; a. Eier, Sahne schlagen; ~**ped cream** Schlagsahne f, -rahm m; ~**ped eggs** pl. Eischnee m; v/i. sausen, flitzen; **2.** Peitsche f; (Reit-) Gerte f.

whip·ping ['wɪpɪŋ] (Tracht f) Prügel pl.; ~**top** Kreisel m.

whip·poor·will zo. ['wɪppʊəwɪl] Ziegenmelker m.

whirl [wɜ:l] **1.** wirbeln; (sich) drehen; **2.** Wirbel m, Strudel m; ~**pool** ['wɜ:lpu:l] Strudel m; ~**wind** [ˌwɪnd] Wirbelwind m, -sturm m.

whir(r) [wɜ:] (-rr-) schwirren.

whisk [wɪsk] **1.** schnelle od. heftige Bewegung; Wisch m; Staubwedel m; Küche: Schneebesen m; **2.** v/t. (ab-, weg)wischen, (ab-, weg)fegen; mit dem Schwanz schlagen; Eier schlagen; ~ away schnell verschwinden lassen, wegnehmen; v/i. huschen, flitzen. **whis·ker** ['wɪskə] Barthaar n; ~**s** pl. Backenbart m.

whis·per ['wɪspə] **1.** flüstern; **2.** Flüstern n, Geflüster n; in a ~, in ~s flüsternd, im Flüsterton.

whis·tle ['wɪsl] **1.** pfeifen; **2.** Pfeife f; Pfiff m; F Kehle f; ~ **stop** Am. 🚃 Bedarfshaltestelle f; Kleinstadt f; pol. kurzes Auftreten (e-s Kandidaten im Wahlkampf).

Whit [wɪt] in Zssgn: Pfingst...

white [waɪt] **1.** (~r, ~st) weiß; rein; F anständig; Weiß...; **2.** Weiß(e) n; Weiße(r m) f (Rasse); ~**-col·lar** [waɪt'kɒlə] Büro...; ~ **worker** (Büro-) Angestellte(r m) f; ~ **heat** Weißglut f; ~ **lie** Notlüge f, fromme Lüge; **whit·en** ['waɪtn] weiß machen od. werden; weiß werden; ~**ness** [ˌnɪs] Weiße f; Blässe f; ~**wash 1.** Tünche f; **2.** weißen, tünchen; fig. reinwaschen.

whit·ish ['waɪtɪʃ] weißlich.

Whit·sun ['wɪtsn] Pfingst...; ~**tide** Pfingsten n od. pl.

wind

whit·tle ['wɪtl] schnitze(l)n; ~ away schwächen, beschneiden, herabsetzen, kürzen.

whiz(z) [wɪz] (-zz-) zischen, sausen.

who [huː, hʊ] wer; welche(r, -s), der, die, das.

who·dun(n)·it F [huː'dʌnɪt] Krimi m (*Kriminalroman, -stück, -film*).

who·ev·er [huː'evə] wer (auch) immer.

whole [həʊl] 1. □ ganz; voll(ständig); heil, unversehrt; 2. Ganze(s) n; *the* ~ *of London* ganz London; *on the* ~ im großen (u.) ganzen; im allgemeinen; **~·heart·ed** □ aufrichtig; **~ meal** ['həʊlmiːl] Vollkorn...; ~ *bread* Vollkornbrot n; **~·sale** 1. *econ.* Großhandel m; 2. *econ.* Großhandels...; *fig.* Massen...; ~ *dealer* = **~·sal·er** [~ə] *econ.* Großhändler m; **~·some** □ [~səm] gesund; ~ *wheat bsd. Am.* = wholemeal.

whol·ly *adv.* ['həʊlɪ] ganz, gänzlich.

whom [huːm, hʊm] *Objektkasus von* who.

whoop [huːp] 1. (*bsd.* Freuden)Schrei m; ✞ Keuchen n (*bei Keuchhusten*); 2. schreien, *a.* ~ *with joy* jauchzen; ~ *it up* F auf den Putz hauen (*ausgelassen feiern*); **~·ee** F ['wʊpiː]: *make* ~ auf den Putz hauen (*ausgelassen feiern*); **~·ing-cough** ✞ ['huːpɪŋkɒf] Keuchhusten m.

whore [hɔː] Hure f.

whose [huːz] *gen. sg. u. pl. von* who.

why [waɪ] 1. warum, weshalb; ~ *so?* wieso?; 2. *int.* nun (gut); ja doch.

wick [wɪk] Docht m.

wick·ed □ ['wɪkɪd] böse, schlecht, schlimm; **~·ness** [~nɪs] Bosheit f.

wick·er ['wɪkə] aus Weiden geflochten, Weiden..., Korb...; ~ *basket* Weidenkorb m; ~ *bottle* Korbflasche f; ~ *chair* Korbstuhl m; **~·work** Korbwaren pl.; Flechtwerk n.

wick·et ['wɪkɪt] Pförtchen n; *Kricket:* Dreistab m, Tor n.

wide [waɪd] *adj.* □ *u. adv.* weit; ausgedehnt; großzügig; breit; weitab; ~ *awake* völlig (*od.* hell)wach; aufgeweckt, wach; *3 feet* ~ 3 Fuß breit; **wid·en** ['waɪdn] (sich) verbreitern; (sich) erweitern (*Wissen etc.*); **~·o·pen** ['waɪd'əʊpən] weitgeöffnet; *Am.* äußerst großzügig (*in der Gesetzesdurchführung*); **~·spread** weitverbreitet; ausgedehnt.

wid·ow ['wɪdəʊ] Witwe f; *attr.* Witwen...; **~·ed** verwitwet; **~·er** [~ə] Witwer m.

width [wɪdθ] Breite f, Weite f.

wield [wiːld] *Einfluß etc.* ausüben.

wife [waɪf] (*pl.* wives [~vz]) (Ehe-) Frau f, Gattin f.

wig [wɪg] Perücke f.

wild [waɪld] 1. *adj.* □ wild; toll; rasend; wütend; ausgelassen; planlos; ~ *about* (ganz) verrückt nach; 2. *adv.:* *run* ~ verwildern (*Garten etc.*; *a. fig. Kinder etc.*); *talk* ~ (wild) drauflosreden; dummes Zeug reden; 3. *a.* ~**s** *pl.* Wildnis f; **~·cat** ['waɪldkæt] 1. *zo.* Wildkatze f; *econ. Am.* Schwindelunternehmen n; 2. wild (*Streik*); *econ. Am.* Schwindel...; **wil·der·ness** ['wɪldənɪs] Wildnis f, Wüste f; **~·fire** ['waɪldfaɪə]: *like* ~ wie ein Lauffeuer; **~·life** *coll.* wildlebende Tiere (u. wildwachsende Pflanzen).

wile [waɪl] List f; ~**s** *pl. a.* Schliche pl.

will [wɪl] 1. Wille m; Wunsch m; Testament n; *of one's own free* ~ aus freien Stücken; 2. *v/aux.* (*pret.* would; *verneint:* ~ *not, won't*) *ich, du etc.* will(st) *etc.*; *ich werde, wir werden; wollen; werden;* 3. wollen; durch Willenskraft zwingen; entscheiden; ⚖ʇʇ vermachen.

wil·l·ful □ ['wɪlfl] eigensinnig; absichtlich, *bsd.* ⚖ʇʇ vorsätzlich.

will·ing □ ['wɪlɪŋ] *pred.* gewillt, willens, bereit; (bereit)willig.

will-o'-the-wisp ['wɪləðə'wɪsp] Irrlicht n.

wil·low ♀ ['wɪləʊ] Weide f; **~·y** *fig.* [~ɪ] geschmeidig; gertenschlank.

will·pow·er ['wɪlpaʊə] Willenskraft f.

wil·ly-nil·ly ['wɪlɪ'nɪlɪ] wohl oder übel.

wilt [wɪlt] (ver)welken.

wi·ly □ ['waɪlɪ] (-ier, -iest) listig, gerissen.

win [wɪn] 1. (-nn-; won) *v/t.* gewinnen; erringen; erlangen; erreichen; *j-n* dazu bringen (*to do* zu tun); ~ *s.o. over* od. *round* j-n für sich gewinnen; *v/i.* gewinnen, siegen; 2. *Sport:* Sieg m.

wince [wɪns] (zusammen)zucken.

winch [wɪntʃ] Winde f; Kurbel f.

wind[1] [wɪnd] 1. Wind m; Atem m, Luft f; ✞ Blähung(en pl.) f; *the* ~ *sg. od. pl.* ♪ die Bläser; 2. *hunt.* wittern.

W

außer Atem bringen; verschnaufen lassen.

wind² [waɪnd] *(wound)* v/t. winden, wickeln, schlingen; kurbeln; *(winded od. wound)* Horn blasen; **~ up** Uhr aufziehen; *Rede etc.* beschließen; v/i. sich winden; sich schlängeln; **~ up** *(bsd. ~ Rede)* schließen *(by saying mit den Worten)*; F enden, landen.

wind|bag ['wɪndbæg] Schwätzer m; **~fall** Fallobst n; Glücksfall m.

wind·ing ['waɪndɪŋ] **1.** Windung f; **2.** sich windend; **~ stairs** pl. Wendeltreppe f; **~ sheet** Leichentuch n.

wind-in·stru·ment ♪ ['wɪndɪnstrʊmənt] Blasinstrument n.

wind·lass ⊕ ['wɪndləs] Winde f.

wind·mill ['wɪndmɪl] Windmühle f.

win·dow ['wɪndəʊ] Fenster n; Schaufenster n; Schalter m; **~ dress·ing** Schaufensterdekoration f; *fig.* Aufmachung f, Mache f; **~ shade** Am. Rouleau n; **~ shop·ping** Schaufensterbummel m; **go ~ing** e-n Schaufensterbummel machen.

wind|pipe anat. ['wɪndpaɪp] Luftröhre f; **~screen**, Am. **~shield** mot. Windschutzscheibe f; **~ wiper** Scheibenwischer m; **~surf·ing** Sport: Windsurfing n, -surfen n.

wind·y □ ['wɪndɪ] *(-ier, -iest)* windig *(a. fig. inhaltslos)*; geschwätzig.

wine [waɪn] Wein m; **~press** ['waɪnpres] (Wein)Kelter f.

wing [wɪŋ] **1.** Flügel m *(a. ⚔ u. arch., Sport, pol.)*; Schwinge f; Brt. mot. Kotflügel m; ✈ Tragfläche f; ✈, ⚔ Geschwader n; **~s** pl. thea. Seitenkulisse f; **take ~** weg-, auffliegen; **on the ~** im Flug; **2.** fliegen; *fig.* beflügeln.

wink [wɪŋk] **1.** Blinzeln n, Zwinkern n; **not get a ~ of sleep** kein Auge zutun; s. forty; **2.** blinzeln od. zwinkern (mit); blinken *(Licht)*; △ *nicht winken*; **~ at** j-m zublinzeln; *fig.* ein Auge zudrücken bei et.

win|ner ['wɪnə] Gewinner(in); Sieger(in); **~ning** ['wɪnɪŋ] **1.** □ einnehmend, gewinnend; **2.** **~s** pl. Gewinn m.

win|ter ['wɪntə] **1.** Winter m; **2.** überwintern; den Winter verbringen; **~ter sports** pl. Wintersport m; **~try** [~rɪ] winterlich; *fig.* frostig.

wipe [waɪp] (ab-, auf)wischen; reinigen; (ab)trocknen; **~ out** auswischen; wegwischen, (aus)löschen;

fig. vernichten; **~ up** aufwischen; *Geschirr* abtrocknen; **wip·er** mot. ['waɪpə] Scheibenwischer m.

wire ['waɪə] **1.** Draht m; ⚡ Leitung f; F Telegramm n; **pull the ~s** der Drahtzieher sein; s-e Beziehungen spielen lassen; **2.** (ver)drahten; telegrafieren; **~drawn** spitzfindig; **~less** [~lɪs] **1.** □ drahtlos, Funk...; **2.** Brt. Radio(apparat m) n; **on the ~** im Radio od. Rundfunk; **3.** funken; **~ net·ting** [waɪə'netɪŋ] Maschendraht m; **~tap** ['waɪətæp] *(-pp-)* Telefongespräche abhören, die Telefonleitung anzapfen.

wir·y □ ['waɪərɪ] *(-ier, -iest)* drahtig, sehnig.

wis·dom ['wɪzdəm] Weisheit f, Klugheit f; **~ tooth** Weisheitszahn m.

wise¹ □ [waɪz] *(~r, ~st)* weise, klug; verständig; erfahren; **~ guy** F Klugscheißer m.

wise² *veraltet* [~] Weise f, Art f.

wise·crack F ['waɪzkræk] **1.** witzige Bemerkung; **2.** witzeln.

wish [wɪʃ] **1.** wünschen; wollen; **~ for** (sich) et. wünschen; **~ s.o. well (ill)** j-m Gutes (Böses) wünschen; **2.** Wunsch m; **~ful** □ ['wɪʃfʊl] sehnsüchtig; **~ thinking** Wunschdenken n.

wish·y-wash·y ['wɪʃɪ'wɒʃɪ] wäßrig, dünn; *fig.* seicht, saft- u. kraftlos.

wisp [wɪsp] Bündel n; Strähne f.

wist·ful □ ['wɪstfʊl] sehnsüchtig.

wit¹ [wɪt] Geist m, Intelligenz f, Witz m; **a. ~s** pl. Verstand m; geistreicher Mensch; △ *nicht Witz = joke*; **be at one's ~s od. ~s' end** mit s-r Weisheit am Ende sein; **keep one's ~s about one** e-n klaren Kopf behalten.

wit² [~]: **to ~** bsd. ⚖ nämlich, das heißt.

witch [wɪtʃ] Hexe f, Zauberin f; **~craft** ['wɪtʃkrɑːft], **~e·ry** [~ərɪ] Hexerei f; **~hunt** pol. Hexenjagd f (for, against auf acc.).

with [wɪð] mit; nebst; bei; von; durch; vor *(dat.)*; **~ it** F up to date, modern.

with·draw [wɪð'drɔː] *(-drew, -drawn)* v/t. ab-, ent-, zurückziehen; zurücknehmen; *Geld* abheben; v/i. sich zurückziehen; zurücktreten; *Sport:* auf den Start verzichten; **~al** [~əl] Zurückziehung f, -nahme f; Rücktritt m; bsd. ⚔ Ab-, Rückzug m; econ. Abheben n *(von Geld)*; *Sport:*

Startverzicht *m*; ☞ Entziehung *f*; ~ *cure* ☞ Entziehungskur *f*; ~ *symptoms pl.* ☞ Entzugserscheinungen *pl.*

with·er ['wɪðə] *v/i.* (ver)welken, verdorren, austrocknen; *v/t.* welken lassen.

with·hold [wɪð'həʊld] (*-held*) zurückhalten; ~ *s.th. from s.o.* j-m et. vorenthalten.

with·in [wɪ'ðɪn] **1.** *adv.* im Innern, drin(nen); zu Hause; **2.** *prp.* in(nerhalb); ~ *doors* im Hause; ~ *call* in Rufweite; **~·out** [wɪ'ðaʊt] **1.** *adv.* (dr)außen; äußerlich; **2.** *prp.* ohne.

with·stand [wɪð'stænd] (*-stood*) widerstehen (*dat.*).

wit·ness ['wɪtnɪs] **1.** Zeuge *m*, -in *f*; *bear* ~ *to* Zeugnis ablegen von, et. bestätigen; **2.** bezeugen; Zeuge sein von et.; beglaubigen; ~ **box**, *Am.* ~ **stand** Zeugenstand *m*.

wit·ti·cis·m ['wɪtɪsɪzəm] witzige Bemerkung; **~·ty** □ [~ɪ] (*-ier, -iest*) witzig; geistreich.

wives [waɪvz] *pl. von* wife.

wiz·ard ['wɪzəd] Zauberer *m*; Genie *n*, Leuchte *f*.

wiz·en(ed) ['wɪzn(d)] schrump(e)lig.

wob·ble ['wɒbl] schwanken, wackeln.

woe [wəʊ] Weh *n*, Leid *n*; ~ *is me!* wehe mir!; **~·be·gone** ['wəʊbɪɡɒn] jammervoll; **~·ful** □ ['wəʊfl] jammervoll, traurig, elend.

woke [wəʊk] *pret. u. p.p. von* wake 2; **wok·en** ['wəʊkən] *p.p. von* wake 2.

wold [wəʊld] hügeliges Land.

wolf [wʊlf] **1.** (*pl.* wolves [~vz]) *zo.* Wolf *m*; **2.** *a.* ~ *down* (gierig) ver- *od.* hinunterschlingen; **~·ish** □ ['wʊlfɪʃ] wölfisch, Wolfs-.

wom·an ['wʊmən] **1.** (*pl.* women ['wɪmɪn]) Frau *f*; F (Ehe)Frau *f*; F Freundin *f*; F Geliebte *f*; **2.** weiblich; ~ *doctor* Ärztin *f*; ~ *student* Studentin *f*; **~·hood** [~hʊd] die Frauen *pl.*; Weiblichkeit *f*; **~·ish** □ [~ɪʃ] weibisch; **~·kind** [~'kaɪnd] die Frauen (-welt *f*) *pl.*; **~·like** [~laɪk] fraulich; **~·ly** [~lɪ] weiblich.

womb [wu:m] Gebärmutter *f*; Mutterleib *m*; *fig.* Schoß *m*.

wom·en ['wɪmɪn] *pl. von* woman; ♀'s *Liberation (Movement)*, a. F ♀'s *Lib* [lɪb] Frauenemanzipationsbewegung *f*; **~·folk**, **~·kind** die Frauen *pl.*; F Weibervolk *n*.

won [wʌn] *pret. u. p.p. von* win 1.

won·der ['wʌndə] **1.** Wunder *n*; Verwunderung *f*, Erstaunen *n*; *work* ~*s* Wunder wirken; **2.** sich wundern; gern wissen mögen, sich fragen; *I* ~ *if you could help me* vielleicht können Sie mir helfen; **~·ful** □ [~fl] wunderbar, -voll; **~·ing** □ [~rɪŋ] staunend, verwundert.

wont [wəʊnt] **1.** gewohnt; *be* ~ *to do* gewohnt sein zu tun, zu tun pflegen; **2.** Gewohnheit *f*; *as was his* ~ wie es s-e Gewohnheit war.

won't [~] = will not.

wont·ed ['wəʊntɪd] gewohnt.

woo [wu:] werben um; locken.

wood [wʊd] Holz *n*; *oft* ~*s pl.* Wald *m*, Gehölz *n*; Holzfaß *n*; = *woodwind*; *touch* ~*!* unberufen!, toi, toi, toi!; *he cannot see the* ~ *for the trees* er sieht den Wald vor lauter Bäumen nicht; **~·cut** ['wʊdkʌt] Holzschnitt *m*; **~·cut·ter** Holzfäller *m*; *Kunst:* Holzschnitzer *m*; **~·ed** [~ɪd] bewaldet; **~·en** □ [~n] hölzern, aus Holz, Holz...; *fig.* ausdruckslos; **~·man** [~mən] (*pl. -men*) Förster *m*; Holzfäller *m*; **~·peck·er** *zo.* [~pekə] Specht *m*; **~s·man** [~zmən] (*pl. -men*) Waldbewohner *m*; **~·wind** ♪ [~wɪnd] Holzblasinstrument *n*; *the* ~ *sg. od. pl.* die Holzbläser *pl.*; **~·work** Holzwerk *n*; **~·y** [~ɪ] (*-ier, -iest*) waldig; holzig.

wool [wʊl] Wolle *f*; **~·gath·er·ing** ['wʊlɡæðərɪŋ] Verträumtheit *f*; **~·(l)en** ['wʊlən] **1.** wollen, Woll...; **2.** ~*s pl.* Wollsachen *pl.*; **~·ly** ['wʊlɪ] **1.** (*-ier, -iest*) wollig; Woll...; verschwommen (*Ideen*); **2.** *woollies pl.* F Wollsachen *pl.*

word [wɜ:d] **1.** Wort *n*; Vokabel *f*; Nachricht *f*; ✗ Losung(swort *n*) *f*; Versprechen *n*; Befehl *m*; Spruch *m*; ~*s pl.* Wörter *pl.*; Worte *pl.*; *fig.* Wortwechsel *m*, Streit *m*; Text *m* (*e-s Liedes*); *have a* ~ *with* mit j-m sprechen; **2.** (in Worten) ausdrücken, (ab)fassen; **~·ing** ['wɜ:dɪŋ] Wortlaut *m*, Fassung *f*; **~ or·der** *gr.* Wortstellung *f* (*im Satz*); **~ pro·cess·ing** *Computer:* Textverarbeitung *f*; **~ pro·ces·sor** *Computer:* Textverarbeitungsanlage *f*, -system *n*; **~·split·ting** Wortklauberei *f*.

word·y □ ['wɜ:dɪ] (*-ier, -iest*) wortreich; Wort...

wore [wɔ:] *pret. von* wear 1.

work [wɜ:k] **1.** Arbeit *f*; Werk *n*; *attr.*

Arbeits...; ~s *pl.* ⊕ (Uhr-, Feder-) Werk *n*; ✗ Befestigungen *pl.*; ~s *sg.* Werk *n*, Fabrik *f*; ~ *of art* Kunstwerk *n*; *at* ~ bei der Arbeit; *be in* ~ Arbeit haben; *be out of* ~ arbeitslos sein; *set to* ~, *set od. go about one's* ~ an die Arbeit gehen; ~s *council* Betriebsrat *m*; **2.** *v/i.* arbeiten (*at*, *on an dat.*); ⊕ funktionieren, gehen; wirken; *fig.* gelingen, klappen; ~ *to rule econ.* Dienst nach Vorschrift tun; *v/t.* ver-, bearbeiten; *Maschine etc.* bedienen; betreiben; *fig.* bewirken; ~ *one's way* sich durcharbeiten; ~ *off* ab-, aufarbeiten; *Gefühl* abreagieren; *econ. Ware* abstoßen; ~ *out Plan* ausarbeiten; *Aufgabe* lösen; ausrechnen; ~ *up* verarbeiten (*into* zu); *Interesse* wecken; ~ *o.s. up* sich aufregen.

wor·ka·ble □ ['wɜːkəbl] bearbeitungs-, betriebsfähig; ausführbar.

work·a·day ['wɜːkədeɪ] Alltags...; ~**bench** ⊕ Werkbank *f*; ~**book** *Schule:* Arbeitsheft *n*; ~**day** Werktag *m*; *on* ~ *s* werktags; ~**er** [~ə] Arbeiter(in).

work·ing ['wɜːkɪŋ]**1.** ~s *pl.* Arbeitsweise *f*, Funktionieren *n*; **2.** arbeitend; Arbeits...; Betriebs...; ~**class** Arbeiter...; ~**day** Werk-, Arbeitstag *m*; ~ **hours** *pl.* Arbeitszeit *f*.

work·man ['wɜːkmən] (*pl.* *-men*) Arbeiter *m*; Handwerker *m*; ~**like** [~laɪk] kunstgerecht, fachmännisch; ~**ship** [~ʃɪp] Kunstfertigkeit *f*.

work·out ['wɜːkaʊt] F *Sport:* (Konditions)Training *n*; Erprobung *f*; ~**shop** Werkstatt *f*; Werkraum *m*; ~**shy** arbeitsscheu, faul; ~**to-rule** *econ.* Dienst *m* nach Vorschrift; ~**woman** (*pl.* *-women*) Arbeiterin *f*.

world [wɜːld] Welt *f*; *a* ~ *of e-e* Unmenge (*von*); *bring* (*come*) *into the* ~ zur Welt bringen (kommen); *think the* ~ *of* große Stücke halten auf (*acc.*); ~**class** (von) Weltklasse, von internationalem Format (*Sportler, etc.*); ♀ **Cup** Fußballweltmeisterschaft *f*; *Skisport:* Weltcup *m*.

world·ly ['wɜːldlɪ] (*-ier*, *-iest*) weltlich; Welt...; ~**wise** weltklug.

world pow·er *pol.* ['wɜːldpaʊə] Weltmacht *f*; ~**wide** weltweit, weltumspannend; Welt...

worm [wɜːm] **1.** *zo.* Wurm *m* (*a. fig.*); **2.** *ein Geheimnis* entlocken (*out of dat.*); ~ *o.s.* sich schlängeln; *fig.* sich

einschleichen (*into in acc.*); ~**eat·en** ['wɜːmiːtn] wurmstichig; *fig.* veraltet, altmodisch.

worn [wɔːn] *p.p. von wear 1*; ~**out** ['wɔːn'aʊt] abgenutzt; abgetragen; verbraucht (*a. fig.*); müde, erschöpft; abgezehrt; verhärmt.

wor·ried □ ['wʌrɪd] besorgt, beunruhigt.

wor·ry ['wʌrɪ] **1.** (sich) beunruhigen, (sich) ängstigen, sich sorgen, sich aufregen; ärgern; zerren an (*dat.*), (ab)würgen; plagen, quälen; *don't* ~! keine Angst od. Sorge!; **2.** Unruhe *f*; Sorge *f*; Ärger *m*.

worse [wɜːs] (*comp. von bad*) schlechter, schlimmer, ärger; ~ *luck!* leider!; *um so* schlimmer!; **wors·en** ['wɜːsn] (sich) verschlechtern.

wor·ship ['wɜːʃɪp] **1.** Verehrung *f*; Gottesdienst *m*; Kult *m*; **2.** (*bsd. Brt.* *-pp-*, *Am.* *-p-*) *v/t.* verehren; anbeten; *v/i.* den Gottesdienst besuchen; ~**(p)er** [~ə] Verehrer(in); Kirchgänger(in).

worst [wɜːst] **1.** *adj.* (*sup. von bad*) schlechteste(r, -s), schlimmste(r, -s), ärgste(r, -s); **2.** *adv.* (*sup. von badly*) am schlechtesten, am schlimmsten, am ärgsten; **3.** *der, die, das* Schlechteste *od.* Schlimmste *od.* Ärgste; *at* (*the*) ~ schlimmstenfalls.

wor·sted ['wʊstɪd] Kammgarn *n*.

worth [wɜːθ] **1.** wert; ~ *reading* lesenswert; **2.** Wert *m*; ~**less** □ ['wɜːθlɪs] wertlos; unwürdig; ~**while** [~'waɪl] der Mühe wert; ~**y** □ ['wɜːðɪ] (*-ier*, *-iest*) würdig; wert.

would [wʊd] *pret. von will 2*; *I* ~ *like* ich hätte gern; ~**be** ['wʊdbiː] Möchtegern...; angehend, zukünftig.

wound[1] [wuːnd] **1.** Wunde *f*, Verletzung *f* (*beide a. fig.*), Verwundung *f*; *fig.* Kränkung *f*; **2.** verwunden, verletzen (*beide a. fig.*).

wound[2] [waʊnd] *pret. u. p.p. von wind*[2].

wove [wəʊv] *pret. von weave*; **wov·en** ['wəʊvn] *p.p. von weave*.

wow *int.* F [waʊ] Mensch!, toll!

wran·gle ['ræŋgl] **1.** sich streiten *od.* zanken; **2.** Streit *m*, Zank *m*.

wrap [ræp] **1.** (*-pp-*) *v/t.* oft ~ *up* (ein)wickeln; *fig.* (ein)hüllen; *be* ~*ped up in* gehüllt sein in (*acc.*); ganz aufgehen in (*dat.*); *v/i.* ~ *up* sich einhüllen *od.* -packen; **2.** Hülle *f*;

Decke *f*; Schal *m*; Mantel *m*; **~per** ['ræpə] Hülle *f*, Umschlag *m*; *a.* postal ~ Streifband *m*; **~ping** [~ɪŋ] Verpackung *f*; **~paper** Einwickel-, Pack-, Geschenkpapier *n*.

wrath *lit.* [rɔːθ] Zorn *m*, Wut *f*.

wreak *lit.* [riːk] *Rache* üben, *Wut etc.* auslassen (*on*, *upon* an *j-m*).

wreath [riːθ] (*pl.* **wreaths** [~ðz]) (Blumen)Gewinde *n*, Kranz *m*, Girlande *f*; Ring *m*, Kreis *m*; **~e** [riːð] *v/t.* (um)winden; *v/i.* sich ringeln *od.* kräuseln.

wreck [rek] **1.** Wrack *n*; Trümmer *pl.*; Schiffbruch *m*; *fig.* Untergang *m*; **2.** zertrümmern, -stören; zugrunde richten, ruinieren; *be* ~ed ⚓ scheitern, Schiffbruch erleiden; *in* Trümmer gehen; ⚙ entgleisen; **~age** ['rekɪdʒ] Trümmer *pl.*; Wrackteile *pl.*; **~ed** [rekt] schiffbrüchig; ruiniert; **~er** ['rekə] ⚓ Bergungsschiff *n*, -arbeiter *m*; *bsd. hist.* Strandräuber *m*; Abbrucharbeiter *m*; *Am. mot.* Abschleppwagen *m*; **~ing** [~ɪŋ] *bsd. hist.* Strandraub *m*; ~ company *Am.* Abbruchfirma *f*; ~ service *Am. mot.* Abschleppdienst *m*.

wren *zo.* [ren] Zaunkönig *m*.

wrench [rentʃ] **1.** reißen, zerren, ziehen; entwinden (*from s.o.* j-m); ⚙ verrenken, -stauchen; ~ *open* aufreißen; **2.** Ruck *m*; ⚙ Verrenkung *f*, -stauchung *f*; *fig.* Schmerz *m*; ⊕ Schraubenschlüssel *m*.

wrest [rest] reißen; ~ *s.th. from s.o.* j-m et. entreißen.

wres|tle ['resl] ringen (mit); **~tler** [~ə] *bsd. Sport:* Ringer *m*; **~tling** [~ɪŋ] *bsd. Sport:* Ringen *n*.

wretch [retʃ] Elende(r *m*) *f*; Kerl *m*.

wretch·ed □ ['retʃɪd] elend.

wrig·gle ['rɪgl] sich winden *od.* schlängeln; ~ *out of s.th.* sich aus e-r Sache herauswinden.

-wright [raɪt] *in Zssgn:* ...macher *m*, ...bauer *m*.

wring [rɪŋ] (*wrung*) *Hände* ringen; (aus)wringen, pressen; *Hals* umdrehen; abringen (*from s.o.* j-m); ~ *s.o.'s heart* j-m zu Herzen gehen.

wrin·kle ['rɪŋkl] **1.** Runzel *f*, Falte *f*; **2.** (sich) runzeln.

wrist [rɪst] Handgelenk *n*; **~watch** Armbanduhr *f*; **~band** ['rɪstbænd] Bündchen *n*, (Hemd)Manschette *f*; Armband *n*.

writ [rɪt] Erlaß *m*; gerichtlicher Befehl; *Holy* ♀ die Heilige Schrift.

write [raɪt] (*wrote*, *written*) schreiben; **~ down** auf-, niederschreiben; **writ·er** ['raɪtə] Schreiber(in); Verfasser(in); Schriftsteller(in).

writhe [raɪð] sich krümmen.

writ·ing ['raɪtɪŋ] Schreiben *n* (*Tätigkeit*); Aufsatz *m*; Werk *n*; (Hand-)Schrift *f*; Schriftstück *n*; Urkunde *f*; Stil *m*; *attr.* Schreib...; *in* ~ schriftlich; **~case** Schreibmappe *f*; ~ **desk** Schreibtisch *m*; ~ **pad** Schreibblock *m*; ~ **pa·per** Schreibpapier *n*.

writ·ten ['rɪtn] **1.** *p.p. von* write; **2.** *adj.* schriftlich.

wrong [rɒŋ] **1.** □ unrecht; verkehrt, falsch; *be* ~ unrecht haben; nicht in Ordnung sein; falsch gehen (*Uhr*); *go* ~ schiefgehen; *be on the* ~ *side of sixty* über 60 (Jahre alt) sein; **2.** Unrecht *n*; Beleidigung *f*; Irrtum *m*, Unrecht *n*; *be in the* ~ unrecht haben; **3.** Unrecht tun (*dat.*); ungerecht behandeln; **~do·er** ['rɒŋduːə] Übeltäter(in); **~ful** □ [~fl] ungerecht; unrechtmäßig.

wrote [rəʊt] *pret. von* write.

wrought|i·ron [rɔːt'aɪən] Schmiedeeisen *n*; **~i·ron** ['rɔːt'aɪən] schmiedeeisern.

wrung [rʌn] *pret. u. p.p. von* wring.

wry □ [raɪ] (*-ier*, *-iest*) schief, krumm, verzerrt.

X

X·mas F ['krɪsməs] = *Christmas*.

X-ray ['eks'reɪ] **1.** ~*s pl.* Röntgenstrahlen *pl.*; **2.** Röntgen...; **3.** durch-leuchten, röntgen.

xy·lo·phone ♪ ['zaɪləfəʊn] Xylophon *n*.

Y

yacht ⚓ [jɒt] **1.** (Segel-, Motor)Jacht f; (Renn)Segler m; **2.** auf e-r Jacht fahren; segeln; **~club** [ˈjɒtklʌb] Segel-, Jachtklub m; **~ing** [ˌʌŋ] Segelsport m; attr. Segel...

Yan·kee F [ˈjæŋkɪ] Yankee m (Spitzname für Nordamerikaner).

yap [jæp] (-pp-) kläffen; F quasseln; F meckern.

yard [jɑːd] Yard n (= 0,914 m); ⚓ Rah(e) f; Hof m; (Bau-, Stapel)Platz m; Am. Garten m; **~ meas·ure** [ˈjɑːdmeʒə], **~stick** Yardstock m, -maß n.

yarn [jɑːn] Garn n; F Seemannsgarn n; abenteuerliche Geschichte.

yawl ⚓ [jɔːl] Jolle f.

yawn [jɔːn] **1.** gähnen; **2.** Gähnen n.

yea F [jeɪ] ja.

year [jɜː] Jahr n; **~ly** [ˈjɜːlɪ] jährlich.

yearn [jɜːn] sich sehnen (for nach); **~ing** [ˈjɜːnɪŋ] **1.** Sehnen n, Sehnsucht f; □ sehnsüchtig.

yeast [jiːst] Hefe f; Schaum m.

yell [jel] **1.** (gellend) schreien; aufschreien; **2.** (gellender) Schrei; Anfeuerungs-, Schlachtruf m.

yel·low [ˈjeləʊ] **1.** gelb; F hasenfüßig (feig); Sensations...; **2.** Gelb n; **3.** (sich) gelb färben; **~ed** vergilbt; **~ fe·ver** 🜬 Gelbfieber n; **~ish** [ˌʌɪʃ] gelblich; **~ pag·es** pl. teleph. die gelben Seiten, Branchenverzeichnis n.

yelp [jelp] **1.** (auf)jaulen (Hund etc.); aufschreien; **2.** (Auf)Jaulen n; Aufschrei m.

yeo·man [ˈjəʊmən] (pl. -men) freier Bauer.

yep F [jep] ja.

yes [jes] **1.** ja; doch; **2.** Ja n.

yes·ter·day [ˈjestədɪ] gestern.

yet [jet] **1.** adv. noch; schon (in Fragen); sogar; as ~ bis jetzt; not ~ noch nicht; **2.** cj. aber (dennoch), doch.

yew 🜬 [juː] Eibe f.

yield [jiːld] **1.** v/t. (ein-, hervor)bringen; Gewinn abwerfen; v/i. 🜬 tragen; sich fügen, nachgeben; **2.** Ertrag m; **~ing** □ [ˈjiːldɪŋ] nachgebend; fig. nachgiebig.

yip·pee int. F [jɪˈpiː] hurra!

yo·del [ˈjəʊdl] **1.** Jodler m; **2.** (bsd. Brt. -ll-, Am. -l-) jodeln.

yoke [jəʊk] **1.** Joch n (a. fig.); Paar n (Ochsen); Schulterträge f; **2.** an-, zusammenspannen; fig. paaren (to mit).

yolk [jəʊk] (Ei)Dotter m, n, Eigelb n.

yon [jɒn], **~·der** lit. [ˈjɒndə] da od. dort drüben.

yore [jɔː]: of ~ ehemals, ehedem.

you [juː; jʊ] du, ihr, Sie; man.

young [jʌŋ] **1.** □ jung; jung, klein; **2.** (Tier)Junge pl.; the ~ die Jungen, die Jugend; with ~ trächtig; **~·ster** [ˈjʌŋstə] Junge m.

your [jɔː] dein(e), euer(e), Ihr(e); **~s** [jɔːz] deine(r, -s), euer, euere(s), Ihre(r, -s); 🜬, Bill Briefschluß: Dein Bill; **~·self** [jɔːˈself] (pl. yourselves [ˌvz]) du, ihr, Sie selbst; dir, dich, euch, sich; by ~ allein.

youth [juːθ] (pl. ~s [ˌðz]) Jugend f; junger Mann, Jüngling m; **~ hostel** Jugendherberge f; **~·ful** □ [ˈjuːθfl] jugendlich.

Yu·go·slav [juːgəʊˈslɑːv] **1.** jugoslawisch; **2.** Jugoslaw|e m, -in f.

yule·tide bsd. poet. [ˈjuːltaɪd] Weihnachten, Weihnachtszeit f.

Z

zeal [ziːl] Eifer m; **~·ot** [ˈzelət] Eiferer m; **~·ous** □ [ˈzeləs] eifrig; eifrig bedacht (for auf acc.); innig, heiß.

ze·bra zo. [ˈziːbrə] Zebra n; **~ cross·ing** [ˈzebrə-] Zebrastreifen m (Fußgängerübergang).

ze·nith [ˈzenɪθ] Zenit m; fig. Höhepunkt m.

ze·ro [ˈzɪərəʊ] **1.** (pl. -ros, -roes) Null f; Nullpunkt m; **2.** Null...; ~ (economic) growth Nullwachstum n; ~ option pol. Nullösung f; have ~

interest in s.th. F null Bock auf et. haben.

zest [zest] **1.** Würze *f* (*a. fig.*); Lust *f*, Freude *f*; Genuß *m*; **2.** würzen.

zig·zag [ˈzɪgzæg] **1.** Zickzack *m*; Zickzacklinie *f*, -kurs *m*, -weg *m*; **2.** im Zickzack laufen *od.* fahren *etc.*

zinc [zɪŋk] **1.** *min.* Zink *n*; **2.** verzinken.

zip [zɪp] **1.** Schwirren *n*; F Schwung *m*; = *zip-fastener*; **2.** (*-pp-*): ~ *s.th. open* den Reißverschluß von et. öffnen; ~ *s.o. up* j-m den Reißverschluß zumachen; ~ **code** *Am.* Postleitzahl *f*; **~-fas·ten·er** *bsd.* Brt.

[ˈzɪpfɑːsnə], **~·per** *Am.* [~ə] Reißverschluß *m.*

zo·di·ac *ast.* [ˈzəʊdɪæk] Tierkreis *m.*

zone [zəʊn] Zone *f*; *fig.* Gebiet *n.*

zoo [zuː] (*pl.* ~s) Zoo *m.*

zo·o·log·i·cal □ [zəʊəˈlɒdʒɪkl] zoologisch; ~ *garden*(*s*) zoologischer Garten.

zo·ol·o·gy [zəʊˈɒlədʒɪ] Zoologie *f.*

zoom [zuːm] **1.** surren; ✈ steil hochziehen; F sausen; *phot. Film:* zoomen; ~ *in on s.th. phot. Film:* et. heranholen; ~ *past* F vorbeisausen; **2.** Surren *n*; ✈ Steilflug *m.*

APPENDIX

German Proper Names

Aachen ['ɑːxən] *n* Aachen, Aix-la-Chapelle.

Adenauer ['ɑːdənaʊər] *first chancellor of the German Federal Republic.*

Adler ['ɑːdlər] *Austrian psychologist.*

Adria ['ɑːdria] *f* Adriatic Sea.

Afrika ['ɑːfrika] *n* Africa.

Ägypten [ɛ'gʏptən] *n* Egypt.

Albanien [al'bɑːnjən] *n* Albania.

Algerien [al'geːrjən] *n* Algeria.

Algier ['alʒiːr] *n* Algiers.

Allgäu ['algɔʏ] *n* Al(l)gäu (*region of Bavaria*).

Alpen ['alpən] *pl.* Alps *pl.*

Amerika [a'meːrika] *n* America.

Anden ['andən] *pl. the* Andes *pl.*

Antillen [an'tilən] *f/pl.* Antilles *pl.*

Antwerpen [ant'vɛrpən] *n* Antwerp.

Apenninen [ape'niːnən] *m/pl. the* Apennines *pl.*

Argentinien [argɛn'tiːnjən] *n* Argentina, the Argentine.

Ärmelkanal ['ɛrmǝlkanɑːl] *m* English Channel.

Asien ['ɑːzjən] *n* Asia.

Athen [a'teːn] *n* Athens.

Äthiopien [ɛti'oːpjən] Ethiopia.

Atlantik [at'lantik] *m* Atlantic.

Australien [aʊ'strɑːljən] *n* Australia.

Bach [bax] *German composer.*

Baden-Württemberg ['bɑːdən-'vʏrtəmbɛrk] *n Land of the German Federal Republic.*

Barlach ['barlax] *German sculptor.*

Basel ['bɑːzəl] *n* Bâle, Basle.

Bayern ['baɪərn] *n* Bavaria (*Land of the German Federal Republic*).

Becher ['bɛçər] *German poet.*

Beckmann ['bɛkman] *German painter.*

Beethoven ['beːtoːfən] *German composer.*

Belgien ['bɛlgjən] *n* Belgium.

Belgrad ['bɛlgrɑːt] *n* Belgrade.

Berg [bɛrk] *Austrian composer.*

Berlin [bɛr'liːn] *n* Berlin.

Bermuda-Inseln [bɛr'muːdaˀinzəln] *f/pl.* Bermudas *pl.*

Bern [bɛrn] *n* Bern(e).

Bismarck ['bismark] *German statesman.*

Bloch [blɔx] *German philosopher.*

Böcklin ['bœkliːn] *German painter.*

Bodensee ['boːdənzeː] *m* Lake of Constance.

Böhm [bøːm] *Austrian conductor.*

Böhmen ['bøːmən] *n* Bohemia.

Böll [bœl] *German author.*

Bonn [bɔn] *n capital of the German Federal Republic.*

Brahms [brɑːms] *German composer.*

Brandt [brant] *German politician.*

Brasilien [bra'ziːljən] *n* Brazil.

Braunschweig ['braʊnʃvaɪk] *n* Brunswick.

Brecht [brɛçt] *German dramatist.*

Bremen ['breːmən] *n Land of the German Federal Republic.*

Bruckner ['bruknər] *Austrian composer.*

Brüssel ['brʏsəl] *n* Brussels.

Budapest ['buːdapɛst] *n* Budapest.

Bukarest ['buːkarɛst] *n* Bucharest.

Bulgarien [bul'gɑːrjən] *n* Bulgaria.

Calais [ka'lɛ] *n: Straße von ~* Straits of Dover.

Calvin [kal'viːn] *Swiss religious reformer.*

Chile ['tʃiːlə] *n* Chile.

China ['çiːna] *n* China.

Christus ['kristus] *m* Christ.

Daimler ['daɪmlər] *German inventor.*

Dänemark ['dɛːnəmark] *n* Denmark.

Deutschland ['dɔʏtʃlant] *n* Germany.

Diesel ['diːzəl] *German inventor.*

Döblin [dø'bliːn] *German author.*

Dolomiten [dolo'miːtən] *pl. the* Dolomites *pl.*

Donau ['doːnaʊ] *f* Danube.

Dortmund ['dɔrtmunt] *n industrial city in West Germany.*

Dresden ['dre:sdən] *n capital of Saxony.*

Dublin ['dʌblin] *n* Dublin.

Dünkirchen ['dy:nkirçən] *n* Dunkirk.

Dürer ['dy:rər] *German painter.*

Dürrenmatt ['dyrənmat] *Swiss dramatist.*

Düsseldorf ['dysəldɔrf] *n capital of North Rhine-Westphalia.*

Ebert ['e:bərt] *first president of the Weimar Republic.*

Egk [ek] *German composer.*

Eichendorff ['aiçəndɔrf] *German poet.*

Eiger ['aigər] *Swiss mountain.*

Einstein ['ainʃtain] *German physicist.*

Elbe ['ɛlbə] *f German river.*

Elsaß ['ɛlzas] *n* Alsace.

Engels ['ɛŋəls] *German philosopher.*

England ['ɛŋlant] *n* England.

Essen ['esən] *n industrial city in West Germany.*

Europa [ɔy'ro:pa] *n* Europe.

Feldberg ['fɛltbɛrk] *German mountain.*

Finnland ['finlant] *n* Finland.

Florenz [flo'rɛnts] *n* Florence.

Fontane [fɔn'ta:nə] *German author.*

Franken ['fraŋkən] *n* Franconia.

Frankfurt ['fraŋkfurt] *n* Frankfort.

Frankreich ['fraŋkraiç] *n* France.

Freud [frɔyt] *Austrian psychologist.*

Frisch [friʃ] *Swiss author.*

Garmisch ['garmiʃ] *n health resort in Bavaria.*

Genf [gɛnf] *n* Geneva; ~er See *m* Lake of Geneva.

Genua ['gɛ:nua] *n* Genoa.

Gibraltar [gi'braltar] *n* Gibraltar.

Goethe ['gø:tə] *German poet.*

Grass [gras] *German author.*

Graubünden [grau'byndən] *n* the Grisons.

Griechenland ['gri:çənlant] *n* Greece.

Grillparzer ['grilpartsər] *Austrian dramatist.*

Grönland ['grø:nlant] *n* Greenland.

Gropius ['gro:pjus] *German architect.* [Great Britain.\

Großbritannien [gro:sbri'tanjən] *n]*

Großglockner [gro:s'glɔknər] *Austrian mountain.*

Grünewald ['gry:nəvalt] *German painter.*

Haag [ha:k]: *Den* ~ The Hague.

Habsburg *hist.* ['ha:psburk] *n* Hapsburg *(German dynasty).*

Hahn [ha:n] *German chemist.*

Hamburg ['hamburk] *n Land of the German Federal Republic.*

Händel ['hɛndəl] Handel *(German composer).*

Hannover [ha'no:fər] *n* Hanover *(capital of Lower Saxony).*

Hartmann ['hartman] *German composer.*

Harz [ha:rts] *m* Harz Mountains *pl.*

Hauptmann ['hauptman] *German dramatist.*

Haydn ['haidən] *Austrian composer.*

Hegel ['he:gəl] *German philosopher.*

Heidegger ['haidegər] *German philosopher.*

Heidelberg ['haidəlbɛrk] *n university town in West Germany.*

Heine ['hainə] *German poet.*

Heinemann ['hainəman] *president of the German Federal Republic.*

Heisenberg ['haizənbɛrk] *German physicist.*

Heißenbüttel ['haisənbytəl] *German poet.*

Helgoland ['hɛlgolant] *n* Heligoland.

Helsinki ['hɛlziŋki] *n* Helsinki.

Henze ['hɛntsə] *German composer.*

Hesse ['hesə] *German poet.*

Hessen ['hesən] *n* Hesse *(Land of the German Federal Republic).*

Heuß [hɔys] *first president of the German Federal Republic.*

Hindemith ['hindəmit] *German composer.*

Hohenzollern *hist.* [ho:ən'tsɔlərn] *n German dynasty.*

Hölderlin ['hœldərli:n] *German poet.*

Holland ['hɔlant] *n* Holland.

Indien ['indjən] *n* India.

Inn [in] *m affluent of the Danube.*

Innsbruck ['insbruk] *n capital of the Tyrol.*

Irak [i'ra:k] *m* Iraq, *a.* Irak.

Irland ['irlant] *n* Ireland.

Island ['i:slant] *n* Iceland.

Israel ['israɛl] *n* Israel.

Italien [i'ta:ljən] *n* Italy.

Japan ['jɑːpan] *n* Japan.
Jaspers ['jaspərs] *German philosopher.*
Jesus ['jeːzus] *m* Jesus.
Jordanien [jɔr'dɑːnjən] *n* Jordan.
Jugoslawien [jugo'slɑːvjən] *n* Yugoslavia.
Jung [juŋ] *Swiss psychologist.*
Jungfrau ['juŋfrau] *f* Swiss mountain.

Kafka ['kafka] *Czech author.*
Kanada ['kanada] *n* Canada.
Kant [kant] *German philosopher.*
Karajan ['kɑːrajan] *Austrian conductor.*
Karlsruhe [karls'ruːə] *n city in South-Western Germany.*
Kärnten ['kɛrntən] *n* Carinthia.
Kassel ['kasəl] *n* Cassel.
Kästner ['kɛstnər] *German author.*
Kiel [kiːl] *n capital of Schleswig-Holstein.*
Kiesinger ['kiːziŋər] *German politician.*
Klee [kleː] *Swiss-born painter.*
Kleist [klaist] *German poet.*
Klemperer ['klempərər] *German conductor.*
Koblenz ['koːblɛnts] *n* Coblenz, Koblenz.
Kokoschka [ko'kɔʃka] *Austrian painter.*
Köln [kœln] *n* Cologne.
Kolumbien [ko'lumbjən] *n* Columbia.
Kolumbus [ko'lumbus] *m* Columbus.
Königsberg ['køːniçsbɛrk] *n capital of East Prussia.*
Konstanz ['kɔnstants] *n* Constance.
Kopenhagen [kopən'hɑːgən] *n* Copenhagen.
Kordilleren [kɔrdil'jeːrən] *f/pl. the* Cordilleras *pl.*
Kreml ['kreːməl] *m the* Kremlin.

Leibniz ['laibnits] *German philosopher.*
Leipzig ['laiptsiç] *n* Leipsic.
Lessing ['lɛsiŋ] *German poet.*
Libanon ['liːbanɔn] *m* Lebanon.
Liebig ['liːbiç] *German chemist.*
Lissabon ['lisabɔn] *n* Lisbon.
London ['lɔndɔn] *n* London.
Lothringen ['loːtriŋən] *n* Lorraine.
Lübeck ['lyːbɛk] *n city in West Germany.*

Luther ['lutər] *German religious reformer.*
Luxemburg ['luksəmburk] *n* Luxemb(o)urg.
Luzern [lu'tsɛrn] *n* Lucerne.

Maas [mɑːs] *f* Meuse.
Madrid [ma'drit] *n* Madrid.
Mahler ['mɑːlər] *Austrian composer.*
Mailand ['mailant] *n* Milan.
Main [main] *m German river.*
Mainz [maints] *n* Mayence (*capital of Rhineland-Palatinate*).
Mann [man] *name of three German authors.*
Marokko [ma'rɔko] *n* Morocco.
Marx [marks] *German philosopher.*
Matterhorn ['matərhɔrn] *Swiss mountain.*
Meißen ['maisən] *n* Meissen.
Meitner ['maitnər] *Austrian-born female physicist.*
Memel ['meːməl] *f frontier river in East Prussia.*
Menzel ['mɛntsəl] *German painter.*
Mexiko ['mɛksiko] *n* Mexico.
Mies van der Rohe ['miːsfandər-'roːə] *German architect.*
Mittelamerika ['mitəlʔa'meːrika] *n* Central America.
Mitteleuropa ['mitəlʔɔy'roːpa] *n* Central Europe.
Mittelmeer ['mitəlmeːr] *n* Mediterranean (Sea).
Moldau ['mɔldau] *f Bohemian river.*
Mörike ['møːrikə] *German poet.*
Mosel ['moːzəl] *f* Moselle.
Mössbauer ['mœsbauər] *German physicist.*
Moskau ['mɔskau] *n* Moscow.
Mozart ['moːtsart] *Austrian composer.*
München ['mynçən] *n* Munich (*capital of Bavaria*).

Neapel [ne'ɑːpəl] *n* Naples.
Neisse ['naisə] *f German river.*
Neufundland [nɔy'funtlant] *n* Newfoundland.
Neuseeland [nɔy'zeːlant] *n* New Zealand.
Niederlande ['niːdərlandə] *n/pl. the* Netherlands *pl.*
Niedersachsen ['niːdərzaksən] *n* Lower Saxony (*Land of the German Federal Republic*).
Nietzsche ['niːtʃə] *German philosopher.*

724

Nil [ni:l] *m* Nile.
Nordamerika ['nɔrtᵛa'me:rika] *n* North America.
Nordrhein-Westfalen ['nɔrtraɪn-vest'fa:lən] *n* North Rhine-Westphalia (*Land of the German Federal Republic*).
Nordsee ['nɔrtze:] *f* German Ocean, North Sea.
Norwegen ['nɔrve:gən] *n* Norway.
Nürnberg ['nyrnbɛrk] *n* Nuremberg.

Oder ['o:dər] *f* German river.
Orff [ɔrf] German composer.
Oslo ['ɔslo] *n* Oslo.
Ostasien ['ɔst'a:zjən] *n* Eastern Asia.
Ostende [ɔst'endə] *n* Ostend.
Österreich ['ø:stəraɪç] *n* Austria.
Ostsee ['ɔstze:] *f* Baltic.

Palästina [palɛ'sti:na] *n* Palestine.
Paris [pa'ri:s] *n* Paris.
Persien ['perzjən] *n* Persia.
Pfalz [pfalts] *f* Palatinate.
Philippinen [fili'pi:nən] *f/pl.* Philippines *pl.*, Philippine Islands *pl.*
Planck [plaŋk] German physicist.
Polen ['po:lən] *n* Poland.
Pommern ['pɔmərn] *n* Pomerania.
Porsche ['pɔrʃə] German inventor.
Portugal ['pɔrtugal] *n* Portugal.
Prag [pra:g] *n* Prague.
Preußen hist. ['prɔysən] *n* Prussia.
Pyrenäen [pyre'nɛ:ən] *pl.* Pyrenees *pl.*

Regensburg ['re:gənsburk] *n* Ratisbon.
Reykjavik ['raɪkjavi:k] *n* Reykjavik.
Rhein [raɪn] *m* Rhine.
Rheinland-Pfalz ['raɪnlant'pfalts] *n* Rhineland-Palatinate (*Land of the German Federal Republic*).
Rilke ['rilkə] Austrian poet.
Rom [ro:m] *n* Rome.
Röntgen ['rœntgən] German physicist.
Ruhr [ru:r] *f* German river; Ruhrgebiet ['ru:rgəbi:t] *n* industrial centre of West Germany.
Rumänien [ru'mɛ:njən] *n* Ro(u)mania.
Rußland ['ruslant] *n* Russia.

Saale ['za:lə] *f* German river.
Saar [za:r] *f* affluent of the Moselle; Saarbrücken [za:r'brykən] *n*

capital of the Saar; Saarland ['za:rlant] *n* Saar (*Land of the German Federal Republic*).
Sachsen ['zaksən] *n* Saxony.
Scherchen ['ʃɛrçən] German conductor.
Schiller ['ʃilər] German poet.
Schlesien ['ʃle:zjən] *n* Silesia.
Schleswig-Holstein ['ʃle:sviç'hɔl-ʃtaɪn] *n* Land of the German Federal Republic.
Schönberg ['ʃø:nbɛrk] Austrian composer.
Schottland ['ʃɔtlant] *n* Scotland.
Schubert ['ʃu:bərt] Austrian composer.   [poser.\
Schumann ['ʃu:man] German com-\
Schwaben ['ʃva:bən] *n* Swabia.
Schwarzwald ['ʃvartsvalt] *m* Black Forest.
Schweden ['ʃve:dən] *n* Sweden.
Schweiz [ʃvaɪts] *f*: die ~ Switzerland.
Sibirien [zi'bi:rjən] *n* Siberia.
Siemens ['zi:məns] German inventor.
Sizilien [zi'tsi:ljən] *n* Sicily.
Skandinavien [skandi'na:vjən] *n* Scandinavia.
Sofia ['zɔfja] *n* Sofia.
Sowjetunion [zɔ'vjetᵛunjo:n] *f* the Soviet Union.
Spanien ['ʃpa:njən] *n* Spain.
Spitzweg ['ʃpitsve:k] German painter.   [losopher.\
Spranger ['ʃpraŋər] German phi-\
Steiermark ['ʃtaɪərmark] *f* Styria.
Stifter ['ʃtiftər] Austrian author.
Stockholm ['ʃtɔkhɔlm] *n* Stockholm.
Storm [ʃtɔrm] German poet.
Strauß [ʃtraus] Austrian composer.
Strauss [ʃtraus] German composer.
Stresemann ['ʃtre:zəman] German statesman.
Stuttgart ['ʃtutgart] *n* capital of Baden-Württemberg.
Südamerika ['zy:tᵛa'me:rika] *n* South America.
Sudan [zu'da:n] *m* S(o)udan.
Syrien ['zy:rjən] *n* Syria.

Themse ['tɛmzə] *f* Thames.
Thoma ['to:ma] German author.
Thüringen ['ty:riŋən] *n* Thuringia.
Tirana [ti'ra:na] *n* Tirana.
Tirol [ti'ro:l] *n* the Tyrol.
Trakl ['tra:kəl] Austrian poet.

Tschechoslowakei [tʃɛçoslovaˈkaɪ] *f*: *die* ~ Czechoslovakia.
Türkei [tyrˈkaɪ] *f*: *die* ~ Turkey.

Ungarn [ˈuŋgarn] *n* Hungary.
Ural [uˈraːl] *m* Ural (Mountains *pl.*).

Vatikan [vatiˈkaːn] *m the* Vatican.
Venedig [veˈneːdiç] *n* Venice.
Vereinigte Staaten [vərˈaɪnɪçtə ˈʃtaːtən] *m/pl. the* United States *pl.*
Vierwaldstätter See [fiːrˈvaltʃtɛtər ˈzeː] *m* Lake of Lucerne.

Wagner [ˈvaːgnər] *German composer.*
Wankel [ˈvaŋkəl] *German inventor.*
Warschau [ˈvarʃau] *n* Warsaw.

Weichsel [ˈvaɪksəl] *f* Vistula.
Weiß [vaɪs] *German dramatist.*
Weizsäcker [ˈvaɪtszɛkər] *German physicist.*
Werfel [ˈvɛrfəl] *Austrian author.*
Weser [ˈveːzər] *f German river.*
Westdeutschland *pol.* [ˈvɛstdɔʏtʃlant] *n* West Germany.
Wien [viːn] *n* Vienna.
Wiesbaden [ˈviːsbaːdən] *n capital of Hesse.*

Zeppelin [ˈtsɛpəliːn] *German inventor.*
Zuckmayer [ˈtsukmaɪər] *German dramatist.*
Zweig [tsvaɪg] *Austrian author.*
Zürich [ˈtsyːrɪç] *n* Zurich.
Zypern [ˈtsyːpərn] *n* Cyprus.

German Abbreviations

a. a. O. *am angeführten Ort* in the place cited, *abbr.* loc. cit., l. c.

Abb. *Abbildung* illustration.

Abf. *Abfahrt* departure, *abbr.* dep.

Abg. *Abgeordnete* Member of Parliament, *etc.*

Abk. *Abkürzung* abbreviation.

Abs. *Absatz* paragraph; *Absender* sender.

Abschn. *Abschnitt* paragraph, chapter. [dept.]

Abt. *Abteilung* department, *abbr.*

a. D. *außer Dienst* retired.

Adr. *Adresse* address.

AG *Aktiengesellschaft* joint-stock company, *Am.* (stock) corporation.

allg. *allgemein* general.

a. M. *am Main* on the Main.

Ank. *Ankunft* arrival.

Anm. *Anmerkung* note.

a. O. *an der Oder* on the Oder.

a. Rh. *am Rhein* on the Rhine.

Art. *Artikel* article.

atü *Atmosphärenüberdruck* atmospheric excess pressure.

Aufl. *Auflage* edition.

b. *bei* at; with; *with place names:* near, *abbr.* nr; care of, *abbr.* c/o.

Bd. *Band* volume, *abbr.* vol.; **Bde.** *Bände* volumes, *abbr.* vols.

beil. *beiliegend* enclosed.

Bem. *Bemerkung* note, comment, observation.

bes. *besonders* especially.

betr. *betreffend, betrifft, betreffs* concerning, respecting, regarding.

Betr. *Betreff, betrifft letter:* subject, re. [reference to.]

bez. *bezahlt* paid; *bezüglich* with

Bez. *Bezirk* district.

Bhf. *Bahnhof* station. [sionally.]

bisw. *bisweilen* sometimes, occa-

BIZ *Bank für Internationalen Zahlungsausgleich* Bank for International Settlements.

Bln. *Berlin* Berlin.

BRD *Bundesrepublik Deutschland* Federal Republic of Germany.

BRT *Bruttoregistertonnen* gross register tons.

b. w. *bitte wenden* please turn over, *abbr.* P.T.O.

bzw. *beziehungsweise* respectively.

C *Celsius* Celsius, *abbr.* C.

ca. *circa, ungefähr, etwa* about, approximately, *abbr.* c.

cbm *Kubikmeter* cubic met|re, *Am.* -er.

ccm *Kubikzentimeter* cubic centimet|re, *Am.* -er, *abbr.* c.c.

CDU *Christlich-Demokratische Union* Christian Democratic Union.

cm *Zentimeter* centimet|re, *Am.* -er.

Co. *Kompagnon* partner; *Kompanie* Company.

CSU *Christlich-Soziale Union* Christian Social Union.

d. Ä. *der Ältere* senior, *abbr.* sen.

DB *Deutsche Bundesbahn* German Federal Railway.

DDR *Deutsche Demokratische Republik* German Democratic Republic.

DGB *Deutscher Gewerkschaftsbund* Federation of German Trade Unions.

dgl. *dergleichen, desgleichen* the like.

d. Gr. *der Große* the Great.

d. h. *das heißt* that is, *abbr.* i. e.

d. i. *das ist* that is, *abbr.* i. e.

DIN, Din *Deutsche Industrie-Norm* (-en) German Industrial Standards.

Dipl. *Diplom* diploma.

d. J. *dieses Jahres* of this year; *der Jüngere* junior, *abbr.* jr, jun.

DM *Deutsche Mark* German Mark.

d. M. *dieses Monats* instant, *abbr.* inst.

do. *dito* ditto, *abbr.* do.

d. O. *der (die, das) Obige* the abovementioned.

dpa, DPA *Deutsche Presse-Agentur* German Press Agency.

Dr. *Doktor* Doctor, *abbr.* Dr; **~ jur.** *Doktor der Rechte* Doctor of Laws (LL.D.); **~ med.** *Doktor der Me-*

dizin Doctor of Medicine (M.D.);
~ **phil.** *Doktor der Philosophie* Doctor of Philosophy (D. ph[il]., Ph. D.); ~ **theol.** *Doktor der Theologie* Doctor of Divinity (D. D.).
DRK *Deutsches Rotes Kreuz* German Red Cross.
dt(sch). *deutsch* German.
Dtz., Dtzd. *Dutzend* dozen.
d. Verf. *der Verfasser* the author.

ebd. *ebenda* in the same place.
ed. *edidit = hat* (es) *herausgegeben.*
eig., eigtl. *eigentlich* properly.
einschl. *einschließlich* including, inclusive, *abbr.* incl.
entspr. *entsprechend* corresponding.
Erl. *Erläuterung* explanation, (explanatory) note.
ev. *evangelisch* Protestant.
e. V. *eingetragener Verein* registered association, incorporated, *abbr.* inc.
evtl. *eventuell* perhaps, possibly.
EWG *Europäische Wirtschaftsgemeinschaft* European Economic Community, *abbr.* EEC.
exkl. *exklusive* except(ed), not included.
Expl. *Exemplar* copy.

Fa. *Firma* firm; *letter:* Messrs.
FDGB *Freier Deutscher Gewerkschaftsbund* Free Federation of German Trade Unions.
FDP *Freie Demokratische Partei* Liberal Democratic Party.
FD(-Zug) *Fernschnellzug* long-distance express.
ff. *sehr fein* extra fine; *folgende Seiten* following pages.
Forts. *Fortsetzung* continuation.
Fr. *Frau* Mrs.
frdl. *freundlich* kind.
Frl. *Fräulein* Miss.

g *Gramm* gram(me).
geb. *geboren* born; *geborene ...* née; *gebunden* bound.
Gebr. *Gebrüder* Brothers.
gef. *gefällig(st)* kind(ly).
gegr. *gegründet* founded.
geh. *geheftet* stitched.
gek. *gekürzt* abbreviated.
Ges. *Gesellschaft* association, company; society.   [registered.
ges. gesch. *gesetzlich geschützt*
gest. *gestorben* deceased.

gez. *gezeichnet* signed, *abbr.* sgd.
GmbH *Gesellschaft mit beschränkter Haftung* limited liability company, *abbr.* Ltd., *Am.* closed corporation under German law.

ha *Hektar* hectare.
Hbf. *Hauptbahnhof* central *or* main station.
Hbg. *Hamburg* Hamburg.
h. c. *honoris causa* = ehrenhalber *academic title:* honorary.
Hr., Hrn. *Herr(n)* Mr.
hrsg. *herausgegeben* edited, *abbr.* ed.
Hrsg. *Herausgeber* editor, *abbr.* ed.

i. *im, in* in.
i. A. *im Auftrage* for, by order, under instruction.
i. allg. *im allgemeinen* in general, generally speaking.
i. Durchschn. *im Durchschnitt* on an average.   [sive.
inkl. *inklusive, einschließlich* inclu-
i. J. *im Jahre* in the year.
Ing. *Ingenieur* engineer.
Inh. *Inhaber* proprietor.
'Interpol *Internationale Kriminalpolizei-Kommission* International Criminal Police Commission, *abbr.* ICPC.   [substitute.
i. V. *in Vertretung* by proxy, as a

Jb. *Jahrbuch* annual.
jr., jun. *junior, der Jüngere* junior *abbr.* jr, jun.

Kap. *Kapitel* chapter.
kath. *katholisch* Catholic.
Kfm. *Kaufmann* merchant.
kfm. *kaufmännisch* commercial.
Kfz. *Kraftfahrzeug* motor vehicle.
kg *Kilogramm* kilogram(me).
KG *Kommanditgesellschaft* limited partnership.
Kl. *Klasse* class; *school:* form.
km *Kilometer* kilomet|re, *Am.* -er.
'Kripo *Kriminalpolizei* Criminal Investigation Department, *abbr.* CID.
Kto. *Konto* account, *abbr.* a/c.
kW *Kilowatt* kilowatt, *abbr.* kw.
kWh *Kilowattstunde* kilowatt hour.

l *Liter* lit|re, *Am.* -er.
LDP *Liberal-Demokratische Partei* Liberal Democratic Party.

lfd. *laufend* current, running.

lfde. Nr. *laufende Nummer* consecutive number.

Lfg., Lfrg. *Lieferung* delivery; instalment, part.

Lit. *Literatur* literature.

Lkw. *Lastkraftwagen* lorry, truck.

lt. *laut* according to.

m *Meter* met|re, *Am,* -er.

m. A. n. *meiner Ansicht nach* in my opinion.

M. d. B. *Mitglied des Bundestages* Member of the Bundestag.

m. E. *meines Erachtens* in my opinion.

MEZ *mitteleuropäische Zeit* Central European Time.

mg *Milligramm* milligram(me[s]), *abbr.* mg.

Mill. *Million(en)* million(s).

mm *Millimeter* millimet|re, *Am,* -er.

möbl. *möbliert* furnished.

MP *Militärpolizei* Military Police.

mtl. *monatlich* monthly.

m. W. *meines Wissens* as far as I know.

N *Nord(en)* north.

nachm. *nachmittags* in the afternoon, *abbr.* p. m.

n. Chr. *nach Christus* after Christ, *abbr.* A. D.

n. J. *nächsten Jahres* of next year.

n. M. *nächsten Monats* of next month.

No., Nr. *Numero, Nummer* number, *abbr.* N°.

NS *Nachschrift* postscript, *abbr.* P. S.

O *Ost(en)* east.

o. B. *ohne Befund* 𝆕 without findings.

od. *oder* or.

OEZ *osteuropäische Zeit* time of the East European zone.

OHG *Offene Handelsgesellschaft* ordinary partnership.

o. J. *ohne Jahr* no date.

p. Adr. *per Adresse* care of, *abbr.* c/o.

Pf *Pfennig German coin:* pfennig.

Pfd. *Pfund German weight:* pound.

PKW, Pkw. *Personenkraftwagen* (motor) car.

P. P. *praemissis praemittendis* omitting titles, to whom it may concern.

p.p., p.pa., ppa. *per procura* by proxy, *abbr.* per pro.

Prof. *Professor* professor.

PS *Pferdestärke(n)* horse-power, *abbr.* H.P., h.p.; *postscriptum, Nachschrift* postscript, *abbr.* P. S.

qkm *Quadratkilometer* square kilomet|re, *Am,* -er.　　[*Am.* -er.]

qm *Quadratmeter* square met|re,

Reg. Bez. *Regierungsbezirk* administrative district.

Rel. *Religion* religion.

resp. *respektive* respectively.

S *Süd(en)* south.

S. *Seite* page.

s. *siehe* see, *abbr.* v., vid. (= *vide*).

s. a. *siehe auch* see also.

Sa. *Summa, Summe* sum, total.

s. d. *siehe dies* see this.

SED *Sozialistische Einheitspartei Deutschlands* United Socialist Party of Germany.

sen. *senior, der Ältere* senior.

sm *Seemeile* nautical mile.

s. o. *siehe oben* see above.

sog. *sogenannt* so-called.

SPD *Sozialdemokratische Partei Deutschlands* Social Democratic Party of Germany.

St. *Stück* piece; *Sankt* Saint.

St(d)., Stde. *Stunde* hour, *abbr.* h.

Str. *Straße* street, *abbr.* St.

s. u. *siehe unten* see below.

s. Z. *seinerzeit* at that time.

t *Tonne* ton.

tägl. *täglich* daily, per day.

Tel. *Telephon* telephone; *Telegramm* wire, cable.

TH *Technische Hochschule* technical university *or* college.

u. *und* and.

u. a. *und andere(s)* and others; *unter anderem or anderen* among other things, inter alia.

u. ä. *und ähnliche(s)* and the like.

U.A.w.g. *Um Antwort wird gebeten* an answer is requested, *répondez s'il vous plaît, abbr.* R.S.V.P.

u. dgl. (m.) *und dergleichen (mehr)* and the like.

u. d. M. *unter dem Meeresspiegel* below sea level; **ü. d. M.** *über dem Meeresspiegel* above sea level.

UdSSR *Union der Sozialistischen Sowjetrepubliken* Union of Soviet Socialist Republics.

u. E. *unseres Erachtens* in our opinion.   [following.)

u. f., u. ff. *und folgende* and the)

UKW *Ultrakurzwelle* ultra-short wave, very high frequency, *abbr.* VHF.

U/min. *Umdrehungen in der Minute* revolutions per minute, *abbr.* r.p.m.

urspr. *ursprünglich* original(ly).

US(A) *Vereinigte Staaten (von Amerika)* United States (of America).

usw. *und so weiter* and so on, *abbr.* etc.   [stances permitting.)

u. U. *unter Umständen* circum-)

v. *von, vom* of; from; by.

V *Volt* volt; *Volumen* volume.

V. *Vers* line, verse.

v. Chr. *vor Christus* before Christ, *abbr.* B. C.

VEB *Volkseigener Betrieb* People's Own Undertaking.

Verf., Vf. *Verfasser* author.

Verl. *Verlag* publishing firm; *Verleger* publisher.

vgl. *vergleiche* confer, *abbr.* cf.

v.g.u. *vorgelesen, genehmigt, unterschrieben* read, confirmed, signed.

v. H. *vom Hundert* per cent.

v. J. *vorigen Jahres* of last year.

v. M. *vorigen Monats* of last month.

vorm. *vormittags* in the morning, *abbr.* a. m.; *vormals* formerly.

Vors. *Vorsitzender* chairman.

v. T. *vom Tausend* per thousand.

VW *Volkswagen* Volkswagen, People's Car.

W *West(en)* west; *Watt* watt(s).

WE *Wärmeeinheit* thermal unit.

WEZ *westeuropäische Zeit* Western European time (Greenwich time).

WGB *Weltgewerkschaftsbund* World Federation of Trade Unions, *abbr.* WFTU.

Wwe. *Witwe* widow.

Z. *Zahl* number; *Zeile* line.

z. *zu, zum, zur* at; to.

z. B. *zum Beispiel* for instance, *abbr.* e. g.

z. H(d). *zu Händen* attention of, to be delivered to, care of, *abbr.* c/o.

z. S. *zur See* of the navy.

z. T. *zum Teil* partly.

Ztg. *Zeitung* newspaper.

Ztr. *Zentner* centner.

Ztschr. *Zeitschrift* periodical.

zus. *zusammen* together.

zw. *zwischen* between; among.

z. Z(t). *zur Zeit* at the time, at present, for the time being.

American and British Proper Names

Aberdeen [æbə'di:n] *Stadt in Schottland.*

Adam ['ædəm] Adam *m.*

Adelaide ['ædəleɪd] *Stadt in Australien.*

Aden ['eɪdn] *Hauptstadt des Südjemen.*

Africa ['æfrɪkə] Afrika *n.*

Aix-la-Chapelle [eɪksla:ʃæ'pel] Aachen *n.*

Alabama [ælə'bæmə] *Staat der USA.*

Alaska [ə'læskə] *Staat der USA.*

Alberta [æl'bɜ:tə] *Provinz in Kanada.*

Alderney ['ɔ:ldənɪ] *e-e der Kanalinseln.*

Alleghany ['ælɪgeɪnɪ] *Fluß u. Gebirge in USA.*

Alsace [æl'sæs] Elsaß *n.*

America [ə'merɪkə] Amerika *n.*

Andes ['ændi:z] *die Anden.*

Andrew ['ændru:] Andreas *m.*

Ann(e) [æn] Anna *f.*

Anthony ['æntənɪ, 'ænθənɪ] Anton *m.*

Antilles [æn'tɪli:z] *die Antillen.*

Appalachians [æpə'leɪtʃjənz] *die* Appalachen (*Gebirge in USA*).

Arizona [ærɪ'zəʊnə] *Staat der USA.*

Arkansas ['ɑ:kənsɔ:] *Fluß u. Staat der USA.*

Arlington ['ɑ:lɪŋtən] *Nationalfriedhof bei Washington.*

Ascot ['æskət] *Stadt in England mit berühmter Rennbahn.*

Asia ['eɪʃə] Asien *n.*

Athens ['æθɪnz] Athen *n.*

Atlantic [ət'læntɪk] *der* Atlantik.

Auckland ['ɔ:klənd] *Hafenstadt in Neuseeland.*

Austen ['ɒstɪn] *engl. Autorin.*

Australia [ɒ'streɪljə] Australien *n.*

Austria ['ɒstrɪə] Österreich *n.*

Avon ['eɪvən] *Fluß u. Grafschaft in England.*

Azores [ə'zɔ:z] *die* Azoren.

Bahamas [bə'hɑ:məz] *die* Bahamainseln.

Balkans ['bɔ:lkənz] *der* Balkan.

Balmoral [bæl'mɒrəl] *Königsschloß in Schottland.*

Basle [bɑ:l] Basel *n.*

Baltimore ['bɔ:ltɪmɔ:] *Hafenstadt in USA.*

Bath [bɑ:θ] *Badeort in England.*

Bavaria [bə'veərɪə] Bayern *n.*

Bedfordshire ['bedfədʃə] *Grafschaft in England.*

Belfast [bel'fɑ:st] *Hauptstadt von Nordirland.*

Belgium ['beldʒəm] Belgien *n.*

Ben Nevis [ben'nevɪs] *höchster Berg in Großbritannien.*

Berkshire ['bɑ:kʃə] *Grafschaft in England.*

Berlin [bɜ:'lɪn] Berlin *n.*

Bermudas [bə'mju:dəz] *die* Bermudainseln.

Bern(e) [bɜ:n] Bern *n.*

Bess(ie) ['bes(ɪ)] *Kurzform von Elizabeth.*

Bill(y) ['bɪl(ɪ)] *Kurzform von William.*

Birmingham ['bɜ:mɪŋəm] *Industriestadt in England.*

Bob [bɒb] *Kurzform von Robert.*

Boston ['bɒstən] *Stadt in USA.*

Bournemouth ['bɔ:nməθ] *Seebad in England.*

Bridget ['brɪdʒɪt] Brigitte *f.*

Brighton ['braɪtn] *Seebad in England.*

Bristol ['brɪstl] *Hafenstadt in England.*

British Columbia ['brɪtɪʃ kə'lʌmbɪə] *Provinz in Kanada.*

Britten ['brɪtn] *engl. Komponist.*

Brontë ['brɒntɪ] *Name dreier engl. Autorinnen.*

Brooklyn ['brʊklɪn] *Stadtteil von New York.*

Brussels ['brʌslz] Brüssel *n.*

Buckingham Palace ['bʌkɪŋəm 'pælɪs] *Königsschloß in London.*

Buckinghamshire ['bʌkɪŋəmʃə] *Grafschaft in England.*

Buddha ['bʊdə] Buddha *m.*

Burma ['bɜ:mə] Birma *n.*

Burns [bɜ:nz] *schott. Dichter.*

Byron ['baɪərən] *engl. Dichter.*

732

Calcutta [kæl'kʌtə] Kalkutta n.
California [kælɪ'fɔːnjə] Kalifornien n
(Staat der USA).
Cambridge ['keɪmbrɪdʒ] 1. engl.
Universitätsstadt; 2. Stadt in USA,
Sitz der Harvard-Universität; 3. a.
~shire [~ʃə] Grafschaft in England.
Canada ['kænədə] Kanada n.
Canary Islands [kə'neərɪ 'aɪləndz]
die Kanarischen Inseln.
Canberra ['kænbərə] Hauptstadt von
Australien.
Canterbury ['kæntəbərɪ] Stadt in
England, Erzbischofssitz.
Capetown ['keɪptaʊn] Kapstadt n.
Cardiff ['kɑːdɪf] Hauptstadt von
Wales.
Carinthia [kə'rɪnθɪə] Kärnten n.
Carlyle [kɑː'laɪl] schott. Autor.
Carnegie [kɑː'neɡɪ] amer. Industriel-
ler.
Caroline ['kærəlaɪn] Karoline f.
Carrie ['kærɪ] Kurzform von Caro-
line.
Carter ['kɑːtə] Präsident der USA.
Catherine ['kæθərɪn] Katharina f.
Cecil ['sesl, 'sɪsl] männlicher Vorna-
me.
Cecilia [sɪ'sɪljə], Cecily ['sɪsɪlɪ, 'sesɪlɪ]
Cäcilie f.
Ceylon [sɪ'lɒn] Ceylon n.
Chamberlain ['tʃeɪmbəlɪn] Name
mehrerer brit. Staatsmänner.
Charlemagne ['ʃɑːləmeɪn] Karl der
Große.
Charles [tʃɑːlz] Karl m.
Chaucer ['tʃɔːsə] engl. Dichter.
Cheshire ['tʃeʃə] Grafschaft in Eng-
land.
Chesterfield ['tʃestəfiːld] Industrie-
stadt in England.
Cheviot Hills ['tʃevɪət 'hɪlz] Grenz-
gebirge zwischen England u. Schott-
land.
Chicago [ʃɪ'kɑːɡəʊ] Industriestadt in
USA.
China ['tʃaɪnə] China n.
Churchill ['tʃɜːtʃɪl] brit. Staatsmann.
Cincinatti [sɪnsɪ'nætɪ] Stadt in USA.
Cissie ['sɪsɪ] Cilli f.
Cleveland ['kliːvlənd] 1. Grafschaft
in England; 2. Industrie- u. Hafen-
stadt in USA.
Clyde [klaɪd] Fluß in Schottland.
Coleridge ['kəʊlərɪdʒ] engl. Dichter.
Cologne [kə'ləʊn] Köln n.
Colorado [kɒlə'rɑːdəʊ] Name zweier
Flüsse u. Staat der USA.

Columbia [kə'lʌmbɪə] Fluß in USA.
Connecticut [kə'netɪkət] Fluß u.
Staat der USA.
Constance ['kɒnstəns] 1. Konstanze
f; 2. Konstanz n; Lake ~ Bodensee
m.
Cooper ['kuːpə] amer. Autor.
Copenhagen [kəʊpn'heɪɡən] Ko-
penhagen n.
Cordilleras [kɔː'dɪljeərəz] die Kor-
dilleren (amer. Gebirge).
Cornwall ['kɔːnwəl] Grafschaft in
England.
Coventry ['kɒvəntrɪ] Industriestadt
in England.
Cromwell ['krɒmwəl] engl. Staats-
mann.
Cumbria ['kʌmbrɪə] Grafschaft in
England.
Cyprus ['saɪprəs] Zypern n.
Czechoslovakia ['tʃekəʊsləʊ'vækɪə]
die Tschechoslowakei.

Dallas ['dæləs] Stadt in USA.
Daniel ['dænjəl] Daniel m.
Danube ['dænjuːb] Donau f.
Darwin ['dɑːwɪn] engl. Naturfor-
scher.
David ['deɪvɪd] David m.
Defoe [dɪ'fəʊ] engl. Autor.
Delaware ['deləweə] Fluß u. Staat
der USA.
Denmark ['denmɑːk] Dänemark n.
Denver ['denvə] Stadt in USA.
Derbyshire ['dɑːbɪʃə] Grafschaft in
England.
Detroit [də'trɔɪt] Industriestadt in
USA.
Devon(shire) ['devn(ʃə)] Grafschaft
in England.
Diana [daɪ'ænə] Diana f.
Dick [dɪk] Kurzform von Richard.
Dickens ['dɪkɪnz] engl. Autor.
Disraeli [dɪs'reɪlɪ] engl. Staatsmann.
District of Columbia ['dɪstrɪkt əv
kə'lʌmbɪə] Bezirk um Washington,
Bundesdistrikt der USA.
Dorset(shire) ['dɔːsɪt(ʃə)] Grafschaft
in England.
Dover ['dəʊvə] Hafenstadt in Eng-
land.
Downing Street ['daʊnɪŋ striːt]
Straße in London mit der Amtswoh-
nung des Prime Minister.
Doyle [dɔɪl] schott. Autor.
Dublin ['dʌblɪn] Hauptstadt der Re-
publik Irland.
Dunkirk [dʌn'kɜːk] Dünkirchen n.

Durham ['dʌrəm] *Grafschaft in England.*

East Sussex ['iːst 'sʌsɪks] *Grafschaft in England.*
Edinburgh ['edɪnbərə] Edinburg *n.*
Edison ['edɪsn] *amer. Erfinder.*
Egypt ['iːdʒɪpt] Ägypten *n.*
Eire ['eərə] *irischer Name der Republik Irland.*
Eisenhower ['aɪznhauə] *Präsident der U.S.A.*
Eliot ['eljət] **1.** *engl. Autorin;* **2.** *engl. Dichter, geboren in U.S.A.*
Elizabeth [ɪ'lɪzəbəθ] Elisabeth *f.*
Emerson ['eməsn] *amer. Philosoph.*
England ['ɪŋglənd] England *n.*
Epsom ['epsəm] *Stadt in England mit Pferderennplatz.*
Erie ['ɪərɪ]: *Lake* ~ Eriesee *m (e-r der fünf Großen Seen Nordamerikas).*
Essex ['esɪks] *Grafschaft in England.*
Ethel ['eθl] *weiblicher Vorname.*
Ethiopia [iːθɪ'əupjə] Äthiopien *n.*
Eton ['iːtn] *berühmte Public School.*
Europe ['juərəp] Europa *n.*
Eve [iːv] Eva *f.*

Falkland Islands ['fɔːlklənd 'aɪləndz] *die Falklandinseln.*
Faulkner ['fɔːknə] *amer. Autor.*
Fawkes [fɔːks] *Haupt der Pulververschwörung (1605).*
Finland ['fɪnlənd] Finnland *n.*
Florida ['flɒrɪdə] *Staat der U.S.A.*
Folkestone ['fəukstən] *Hafenstadt in England.*
Ford [fɔːd] **1.** *amer. Industrieller;* **2.** *Präsident der U.S.A.*
France [frɑːns] Frankreich *n.*
Frances ['frɑːnsɪs] Franziska *f.*
Francis ['frɑːnsɪs] Franz *m.*
Franklin ['fræŋklɪn] *amer. Staatsmann u. Physiker.*

Gainsborough ['geɪnzbərə] *engl. Maler.*
Galveston(e) ['gælvɪstən] *Hafenstadt in U.S.A.*
Geneva [dʒɪ'niːvə] Genf *n;* *Lake* ~ Genfer See *m.*
Geoffrey ['dʒefrɪ] Gottfried *m.*
George [dʒɔːdʒ] Georg *m.*
Georgia ['dʒɔːdʒjə] *Staat der U.S.A.*
Germany ['dʒɜːmənɪ] Deutschland *n.*
Gershwin ['gɜːʃwɪn] *amer. Komponist.*

Gettysburg ['getɪzbɜːg] *Stadt in U.S.A.*
Gibraltar [dʒɪ'brɔːltə] Gibraltar *n.*
Giles [dʒaɪlz] Julius *m.*
Gill [gɪl] *weiblicher Vorname.*
Gladstone ['glædstən] *brit. Staatsmann.*
Glasgow ['glɑːsgəu] *Hafenstadt in Schottland.*
Gloucester ['glɒstə] *Stadt in England;* *a.* ~shire [-ʃə] *Grafschaft in England.*
Great Britain ['greɪt 'brɪtn] Großbritannien *n.*
Greece [griːs] Griechenland *n.*
Greene [griːn] *engl. Autor.*
Greenland ['griːnlənd] Grönland *n.*
Greenwich ['grɪnɪdʒ] *Vorort von London.*
Guernsey ['gɜːnzɪ] *e-e der Kanalinseln.*
Guy [gaɪ] Guido *m,* Veit *m.*

Hague [heɪg]: *The* ~ Den Haag.
Halifax ['hælɪfæks] *Name zweier Städte in England u. Kanada.*
Hampshire ['hæmpʃə] *Grafschaft in England.*
Hanover ['hænəuvə] Hannover *n.*
Harlem ['hɑːləm] *Stadtteil von New York.*
Harrow ['hærəu] *berühmtl. Stadtbezirk Groß-Londons mit berühmter Public School.*
Harvard University ['hɑːvəd juːnɪ'vɜːsətɪ] *amer. Universität.*
Harwich ['hærɪdʒ] *Hafenstadt in England.*
Hawaii [hə'waɪiː] *Staat der U.S.A.*
Hebrides ['hebrɪdiːz] *die Hebriden.*
Heligoland [he'lɪgəulænd] Helgoland *n.*
Helsinki ['helsɪŋkɪ] Helsinki *n.*
Hemingway ['hemɪŋweɪ] *amer. Autor.*
Henry ['henrɪ] Heinrich *m.*
Hereford and Worcester ['herɪfədən'wustə] *Grafschaft in England.*
Hertfordshire ['hɑːfədʃə] *Grafschaft in England.*
Hogarth ['həugɑːθ] *engl. Maler.*
Hollywood ['hɒlɪwud] *Filmstadt in Kalifornien, U.S.A.*
Houston ['hjuːstən] *Stadt in U.S.A.*
Hudson ['hʌdsn] *Fluß in U.S.A.*
Hugh [hjuː] Hugo *m.*
Hull [hʌl] *Hafenstadt in England.*

Humberside ['hʌmbəsaɪd] *Grafschaft in England.*
Hungary ['hʌŋgərɪ] *Ungarn n.*
Huron ['hjuːərən]: *Lake ~ Huronsee m (e-r der fünf Großen Seen Nordamerikas).*
Huxley ['hʌkslɪ] *engl. Autor.*

Iceland ['aɪslənd] *Island n.*
Idaho ['aɪdəhəʊ] *Staat der USA.*
Illinois [ɪlɪ'nɔɪ] *Fluß u. Staat der USA.*
India ['ɪndjə] *Indien n.*
Indiana [ɪndɪ'ænə] *Staat der USA.*
Indies ['ɪndɪz]: *East ~ Ostindien n; West ~ Westindien n.*
Iowa ['aɪəʊə] *Staat der USA.*
Iran [ɪ'rɑːn] *Iran m.*
Iraq [ɪ'rɑːk] *Irak m.*
Ireland ['aɪələnd] *Irland n.*
Isle of Man ['aɪləv'mæn] *Insel in der Irischen See.*
Isle of Wight ['aɪləv'waɪt] *Insel u. Grafschaft vor der Südküste Englands.*
Israel ['ɪzreɪəl] *Israel n.*
Italy ['ɪtəlɪ] *Italien n.*

Jack [dʒæk] *Kurzform von James.*
James [dʒeɪmz] *Jakob m.*
Jane [dʒeɪn] *Johanna f.*
Japan [dʒə'pæn] *Japan n.*
Jefferson ['dʒefəsn] *Präsident der USA, Verfasser der Unabhängigkeitserklärung von 1776.*
Jeremy ['dʒerɪmɪ] *männlicher Vorname.*
Jersey ['dʒɜːzɪ] *e-e der Kanalinseln; ~ City Stadt in USA.*
Jesus (Christ) ['dʒiːzəs ('kraɪst)] *Jesus (Christus) m.*
Jim [dʒɪm] *Kurzform von James.*
Joan [dʒəʊn] *Johanna f.*
Job [dʒəʊb] *Hiob m.*
Joe [dʒəʊ] *Kurzform von Joseph.*
John [dʒɒn] *Johann(es) m, Hans m.*
Johnson ['dʒɒnsn] **1.** *engl. Autor;* **2.** *Präsident der USA.*
Joseph ['dʒəʊzɪf] *Joseph m.*
Joule [dʒuːl] *engl. Physiker.*
Joyce [dʒɔɪs] *irischer Autor.*

Kansas ['kænzəs] *Fluß u. Staat der USA.*
Karachi [kə'rɑːtʃɪ] *Hafenstadt in Pakistan.*
Kashmir [kæʃ'mɪə] *Kaschmir n.*
Kate [keɪt] *Käthe f.*

Keats [kiːts] *engl. Dichter.*
Kennedy ['kenɪdɪ] *Präsident der USA; ~ Airport Flughafen von New York.*
Kent [kent] *Grafschaft in England.*
Kentucky [ken'tʌkɪ] *Fluß u. Staat der USA.*
King [kɪŋ] *amer. Bürgerrechtskämpfer.*
Kipling ['kɪplɪŋ] *engl. Dichter.*
Klondike ['klɒndaɪk] *Fluß u. Landschaft in Kanada u. Alaska.*
Kremlin ['kremlɪn] *der Kreml.*

Labrador ['læbrədɔː] *Halbinsel Nordamerikas.*
Lancashire ['læŋkəʃə] *Grafschaft in England.*
Lancaster ['læŋkəstə] *Name zweier Städte in England u. USA; s. Lancashire.*
Lawrence ['lɒrəns] *engl. Autor.*
Lebanon ['lebənən] *der Libanon.*
Leeds [liːdz] *Industriestadt in England.*
Leicester ['lestə] *Stadt in England; a. ~shire [~ʃə] Grafschaft in England.*
Leslie ['lezlɪ] *männlicher u. weiblicher Vorname.*
Lewis ['luːɪs] *Ludwig m.*
Libya ['lɪbɪə] *Libyen n.*
Lincoln ['lɪŋkən] **1.** *Präsident der USA;* **2.** *Stadt in USA;* **3.** *Stadt in England;* **4.** *a. ~shire [~ʃə] Grafschaft in England.*
Lisbon ['lɪzbən] *Lissabon n.*
Liverpool ['lɪvəpuːl] *Hafen- u. Industriestadt in England.*
London ['lʌndən] **1.** *London n;* **2.** *amer. Autor.*
Los Angeles [lɒs'ændʒɪliːz] *Stadt in USA.*
Louisiana [luːiːzɪ'ænə] *Staat der USA.*
Lucerne [luː'sɜːn] *Luzern n; Lake of ~ Vierwaldstätter See m.*
Luxembourg ['lʌksəmbɜːg] *Luxemburg n.*

Mabel ['meɪbl] *weiblicher Vorname.*
Mackenzie [mə'kenzɪ] *Strom in Nordamerika.*
Madge [mædʒ] *weiblicher Vorname.*
Madrid [mə'drɪd] *Madrid n.*
Maine [meɪn] *Staat der USA.*
Malta ['mɔːltə] *Malta n.*
Manchester ['mæntʃɪstə] *Industriestadt u. Grafschaft in England.*

Manhattan [mænˈhætn] *Stadtteil von New York.*

Manitoba [mænɪˈtəubə] *Provinz in Kanada.*

Margaret [ˈmɑːgərɪt] Margarete *f.*

Mark [mɑːk] Markus *m.*

Mary [ˈmeərɪ] Maria *f.*

Maryland [ˈmeərɪlænd] *Staat der USA.*

Massachusetts [mæsəˈtʃuːsɪts] *Staat der USA.*

Mat(h)ilda [məˈtɪldə] Mathilde *f.*

Ma(t)thew [ˈmæθjuː] Matthäus *m.*

Maud [mɔːd] *Kurzform von Mat(h)ilda.*

Maugham [mɔːm] *engl. Autor.*

Maurice [ˈmɒrɪs] Moritz *m.*

May [meɪ] *Kurzform von Mary.*

Melbourne [ˈmelbən] *Stadt in Australien.*

Merseyside [ˈmɜːzɪsaɪd] *Grafschaft in England.*

Miami [maɪˈæmɪ] *Badeort in Florida, USA.*

Michigan [ˈmɪʃɪgən] *Staat der USA;* Lake ~ Michigansee *m (e-r der fünf Großen Seen Nordamerikas).*

Miller [ˈmɪlə] *amer. Dramatiker.*

Millicent [ˈmɪlɪsnt] *weiblicher Vorname.*

Milton [ˈmɪltən] *engl. Dichter.*

Milwaukee [mɪlˈwɔːkiː] *Stadt in USA.*

Minneapolis [mɪnɪˈæpəlɪs] *Stadt in USA.*

Minnesota [mɪnɪˈsəutə] *Staat der USA.*

Mississippi [mɪsɪˈsɪpɪ] *Strom u. Staat der USA.*

Missouri [mɪˈzuərɪ] *Fluß u. Staat der USA.*

Mohammed [məʊˈhæmed] Mohammed *m.*

Monroe [mənˈrəʊ] **1.** *Präsident der USA;* **2.** *amer. Filmschauspielerin.*

Montana [mɒnˈtænə] *Staat der USA.*

Montgomery [məntˈgʌmərɪ] *brit. Feldmarschall.*

Montreal [mɒntrɪˈɔːl] *Stadt in Kanada.*

Moore [mʊə] *engl. Bildhauer.*

Morocco [məˈrɒkəʊ] Marokko *n.*

Moscow [ˈmɒskəʊ] Moskau *n.*

Moselle [məʊˈzel] Mosel *f.*

Munich [ˈmjuːnɪk] München *n.*

Nancy [ˈnænsɪ] *weiblicher Vorname.*

Nebraska [nɪˈbræskə] *Staat der USA.*

Nelson [ˈnelsn] *engl. Admiral.*

Netherlands [ˈneðələndz] *die Niederlande.*

Nevada [neˈvɑːdə] *Staat der USA.*

New Brunswick [njuːˈbrʌnzwɪk] *Provinz in Kanada.*

Newcastle [ˈnjuːkɑːsl] *Hafenstadt in England.*

New Delhi [njuːˈdelɪ] *Hauptstadt von Indien.*

New England [njuːˈɪŋglənd] Neuengland *n.*

Newfoundland [ˈnjuːfəndlənd] Neufundland *n.*

New Hampshire [njuːˈhæmpʃə] *Staat der USA.*

New Jersey [njuːˈdʒɜːzɪ] *Staat der USA.*

New Mexico [njuːˈmeksɪkəʊ] Neumexiko *n (Staat der USA).*

New Orleans [njuːˈɔːlɪəns] *Hafenstadt in USA.*

Newton [ˈnjuːtn] *engl. Physiker.*

New York [njuːˈjɔːk] *Stadt u. Staat der USA.*

New Zealand [njuːˈziːlənd] Neuseeland *n.*

Niagara [naɪˈægərə] Niagara *m (Fluß zwischen Erie- u. Ontariosee).*

Nicholas [ˈnɪkələs] Nikolaus *m.*

Nixon [ˈnɪksən] *Präsident der USA.*

Norfolk [ˈnɔːfək] *Grafschaft in England.*

Northampton [nɔːˈθæmptən] *Stadt in England; a.* ~shire [~ʃə] *Grafschaft in England.*

North Carolina [ˈnɔːθ kærəˈlaɪnə] Nordkarolina *n (Staat der USA).*

North Dakota [ˈnɔːθ dəˈkəʊtə] Norddakota *n (Staat der USA).*

Northumberland [nɔːˈθʌmbələnd] *Grafschaft in England.*

Northwest Territories [nɔːθˈwest ˈterɪtərɪz] Nordwestterritorien *pl. (Kanada).*

North Yorkshire [ˈnɔːθ ˈjɔːkʃə] *Grafschaft in England.*

Norway [ˈnɔːweɪ] Norwegen *n.*

Norwich [ˈnɒrɪdʒ] *Stadt in England.*

Nottingham [ˈnɒtɪŋəm] *Stadt in England; a.* ~shire [~ʃə] *Grafschaft in England.*

Nova Scotia [ˈnəʊvəˈskəʊʃə] *Provinz in Kanada.*

Oceania [əʊʃɪˈeɪnɪə] Ozeanien *n.*

Ohio [əʊ'haɪəʊ] *Fluß u. Staat der USA.*

Oklahoma [əʊklə'həʊmə] *Staat der USA.*

Oliver ['ɒlɪvə] *männlicher Vorname.*

Omaha ['əʊməhɑː] *Stadt in USA.*

O'Neill [əʊ'niːl] *amer. Dramatiker.*

Ontario [ɒn'teərɪəʊ] *Provinz in Kanada;* Lake ∼ *Ontariosee m (e-r der fünf Großen Seen Nordamerikas).*

Oregon ['ɒrɪgən] *Staat der USA.*

Orkney Islands ['ɔːknɪ 'aɪləndz] *die Orkneyinseln.*

Orwell ['ɔːwəl] *engl. Autor.*

Osborne ['ɒzbən] *engl. Dramatiker.*

Ostend [ɒ'stend] *Ostende n.*

Ottawa ['ɒtəwə] *Hauptstadt von Kanada.*

Oxford ['ɒksfəd] *engl. Universitätsstadt; a.* ∼shire [∼ʃə] *Grafschaft in England.*

Pacific [pə'sɪfɪk] *der Pazifik.*

Pakistan [pɑːkɪ'stɑːn] *Pakistan n.*

Paris ['pærɪs] *Paris n.*

Patricia [pə'trɪʃə] *weiblicher Vorname.*

Patrick ['pætrɪk] *männlicher Vorname.*

Paul [pɔːl] *Paul m.*

Pearl Harbor ['pɜːl 'hɑːbə] *Hafenstadt auf Hawaii.*

Peg(gy) ['peg(ɪ)] *Kurzform von Margaret.*

Pennsylvania [pensɪl'veɪnjə] *Pennsylvanien n (Staat der USA).*

Peter ['piːtə] *Peter m.*

Philadelphia [fɪlə'delfjə] *Stadt in USA.*

Philippines ['fɪlɪpiːnz] *die Philippinen.*

Pittsburgh ['pɪtsbɜːg] *Stadt in USA.*

Plymouth ['plɪməθ] *Hafenstadt in England.*

Poe [pəʊ] *amer. Autor.*

Poland ['pəʊlənd] *Polen n.*

Portsmouth ['pɔːtsməθ] *Hafenstadt in England.*

Portugal ['pɔːtjʊgl] *Portugal n.*

Potomac [pə'təʊmək] *Fluß in USA.*

Prague [prɑːg] *Prag n.*

Prince Edward Island [prɪns'edwəd 'aɪlənd] *Provinz in Kanada.*

Pulitzer ['pʊlɪtsə] *amer. Journalist.*

Purcell ['pɜːsl] *engl. Komponist.*

Quebec [kwɪ'bek] *Provinz u. Stadt in Kanada.*

Reagan ['reɪgən] *Präsident der USA.*

Reynolds ['renldz] *engl. Maler.*

Rhine [raɪn] *Rhein m.*

Rhode Island [rəʊd'aɪlənd] *Staat der USA.*

Rhodesia [rəʊ'diːzjə] *Rhodesien n.*

Richard ['rɪtʃəd] *Richard m.*

Robert ['rɒbət] *Robert m.*

Rockefeller ['rɒkɪfelə] *amer. Industrieller.*

Rocky Mountains ['rɒkɪ'maʊntɪnz] *Gebirge in USA.*

Roger ['rɒdʒə] *männlicher Vorname.*

Romania [ruː'meɪnjə] *Rumänien n.*

Rome [rəʊm] *Rom n.*

Roosevelt ['rəʊzəvelt] *Name zweier Präsidenten der USA.*

Rugby ['rʌgbɪ] *berühmte Public School.*

Russell ['rʌsl] *engl. Philosoph.*

Russia ['rʌʃə] *Rußland n.*

Salinger ['sælɪndʒə] *amer. Autor.*

Salop ['sæləp] *Grafschaft in England.*

Sam [sæm] *Kurzform von Samuel.*

Samuel ['sæmjʊəl] *Samuel m.*

San Francisco [sænfrən'sɪskəʊ] *Hafenstadt in USA.*

Saskatchewan [səs'kætʃɪwən] *Provinz in Kanada.*

Scandinavia [skændɪ'neɪvjə] *Skandinavien n.*

Scotland ['skɒtlənd] *Schottland n;* ∼ *Yard Polizeipräsidium in London.*

Seattle [sɪ'ætl] *Hafenstadt in USA.*

Shakespeare ['ʃeɪkspɪə] *engl. Dichter.*

Shaw [ʃɔː] *engl. Dramatiker.*

Shelley ['ʃelɪ] *engl. Dichter.*

Shetland Islands ['ʃetlənd 'aɪləndz] *die Shetlandinseln.*

Sillitoe ['sɪlɪtəʊ] *engl. Autor.*

Singapore [sɪŋgə'pɔː] *Singapur n.*

Snowdon ['snəʊdn] *Berg in Wales.*

Somerset(shire) ['sʌməsɪt(ʃə)] *Grafschaft in England.*

South Carolina ['saʊθ kærə'laɪnə] *Südkarolina n (Staat der USA).*

South Dakota ['saʊθ də'kəʊtə] *Süddakota n (Staat der USA).*

South Yorkshire ['saʊθ 'jɔːkʃə] *Grafschaft in England.*

Spain [speɪn] *Spanien n.*

Staffordshire ['stæfədʃə] *Grafschaft in England.*

Stevenson ['stiːvnsn] *schott. Autor.*

St. Lawrence [snt'lɒrəns] *der St.-Lorenz-Strom.*

St. Louis [snt'luɪs] *Industriestadt in USA.*

Stratford ['strætfəd]: ~-on-Avon *Geburtsort Shakespeares.*

Styria ['stɪrɪə] *Steiermark f.*

Suffolk ['sʌfək] *Grafschaft in England.*

Superior [su:'pɪərɪə]: *Lake* ~ *Oberer See m (e-r der fünf Großen Seen Nordamerikas).*

Surrey ['sʌrɪ] *Grafschaft in England.*

Susan ['su:zn] *Susanne f.*

Sweden ['swi:dn] *Schweden n.*

Swift [swɪft] *engl. Autor.*

Switzerland ['swɪtsələnd] *die Schweiz.*

Sydney ['sɪdnɪ] *Hafen- u. Industriestadt in Australien.*

Tennessee [tenə'si:] *Fluß u. Staat der USA.*

Tennyson ['tenɪsn] *engl. Dichter.*

Texas ['teksəs] *Staat der USA.*

Thackeray ['θækərɪ] *engl. Autor.*

Thames [temz] *Themse f.*

Thatcher ['θætʃə] *engl. Politikerin.*

Thomas ['tɒməs] *Thomas m.*

Tokyo ['təʊkɪəʊ] *Tokio n.*

Tom(my) ['tɒm(ɪ)] *Kurzform von Thomas.*

Toronto [tə'rɒntəʊ] *Stadt in Kanada.*

Trafalgar [trə'fælgə] *Vorgebirge bei Gibraltar (Seesieg Nelsons 1805).*

Truman ['tru:mən] *Präsident der USA.*

Turkey ['tɜ:kɪ] *die Türkei.*

Turner ['tɜ:nə] *engl. Maler.*

Twain [tweɪn] *amer. Autor.*

Tyne and Wear ['taɪnən'wɪə] *Grafschaft in England.*

Tyrol ['tɪrəl] *Tirol n.*

Ulster ['ʌlstə] *Ulster n (Nordirland).*

United States of America [ju:'naɪtɪd 'steɪtsəvə'merɪkə] *die Vereinigten Staaten von Amerika.*

Utah ['ju:tɑ:] *Staat der USA.*

Vancouver [væn'ku:və] *Stadt in Kanada.*

Vatican ['vætɪkən] *Vatikan m.*

Venice ['venɪs] *Venedig n.*

Vermont [vɜ:'mɒnt] *Staat der USA.*

Vienna [vɪ'enə] *Wien n.*

Virginia [və'dʒɪnjə] *Staat der USA.*

Vivian ['vɪvɪən] *männlicher u. weiblicher Vorname.*

Wales [weɪlz] *Wales n.*

Wallace ['wɒlɪs] *engl. Autor.*

Wall Street ['wɔ:l stri:t] *Straße u. Finanzzentrum in New York.*

Warsaw ['wɔ:sɔ:] *Warschau n.*

Warwickshire ['wɒrɪkʃə] *Grafschaft in England.*

Washington ['wɒʃɪŋtən] **1.** *Präsident der USA;* **2.** *Staat der USA;* **3.** *Bundeshauptstadt der USA.*

Waterloo [wɔ:tə'lu:] *Dorf in Belgien (Niederlage Napoleons 1815).*

Watt [wɒt] *schott. Erfinder.*

Wellington ['welɪŋtən] **1.** *engl. Feldherr u. Staatsmann;* **2.** *Hauptstadt von Neuseeland.*

West Midlands ['west 'mɪdləndz] *Grafschaft in England.*

West Sussex ['west 'sʌsɪks] *Grafschaft in England.*

West Virginia ['west və'dʒɪnjə] *Staat der USA.*

West Yorkshire ['west 'jɔ:kʃə] *Grafschaft in England.*

White House ['waɪt haʊs] *das Weiße Haus (Amtssitz des Präsidenten der USA).*

Whitman ['wɪtmən] *amer. Dichter.*

Wilde [waɪld] *engl. Autor u. Dramatiker.*

Wilder ['waɪldə] *amer. Dramatiker.*

Will [wɪl] *Kurzform von William.*

William ['wɪljəm] *Wilhelm m.*

Wilson ['wɪlsn] **1.** *Präsident der USA;* **2.** *brit. Politiker.*

Wiltshire ['wɪltʃə] *Grafschaft in England.*

Wimbledon ['wɪmbldən] *Vorort von London (Tennisturniere).*

Winnipeg ['wɪnɪpeg] *See u. Stadt in Kanada.*

Wisconsin [wɪs'kɒnsɪn] *Fluß u. Staat der USA.*

Wolfe [wolf] *amer. Autor.*

Woolf [wolf] *engl. Autorin.*

Worcester ['wʊstə] *Industriestadt in England.*

Wordsworth ['wɜ:dzwəθ] *engl. Dichter.*

Wyoming [waɪ'əʊmɪŋ] *Staat der USA.*

Yale University ['jeɪl ju:nɪ'vɜ:sətɪ] *amer. Universität.*

Yellowstone ['jeləʊstəʊn] *Fluß u. Nationalpark der USA.*

York [jɔ:k] *Stadt in England;* ~shire [~ʃə] *Grafschaft in England.*

Yosemite [jəʊˈsemɪtɪ] *Nationalpark der USA.*

Yugoslavia [juːgəʊˈslɑːvjə] *Jugoslawien n.*

Yukon [ˈjuːkɒn] *Fluß und Territorium in Kanada.*

Zimbabwe [zɪmˈbɑːbwɪ] *Simbabwe n.*

American and British Abbreviations

abbr. *abbreviated* abgekürzt; *abbreviation* Abk., Abkürzung *f.*

ABC *American Broadcasting Company* (*amer. Rundfunkgesellschaft*).

AC *alternating current* Wechselstrom *m.*

A/C *account* (Bank)Konto *n.*

acc(t). *account* Konto *n,* Rechnung *f.*

AEC *Atomic Energy Commission* Atomenergie-Kommission *f.*

AFL-CIO *American Federation of Labor & Congress of Industrial Organizations* (größter *amer. Gewerkschaftsverband*).

AFN *American Forces Network* (*Rundfunkanstalt der amer. Streitkräfte*).

AI *Amnesty International.*

AL *Alabama.*

Alta *Alberta.*

AK *Alaska.*

AM *amplitude modulation* MW, Mittelwelle *f.*

a.m. *ante meridiem* (*lateinisch = before noon*) vormittags.

AP *Associated Press* (*amer. Nachrichtenbüro*).

AR *Arkansas.*

ARC *American Red Cross* Amer. Rotes Kreuz.

arr. *arrival* Ank., Ankunft *f.*

ASA *American Standards Association* Amer. Normungs-Organisation *f.*

AZ *Arizona.*

BA *Bachelor of Arts* Bakkalaureus *m* der Philosophie; *British Airways* (*brit. Fluggesellschaft*).

BBC *British Broadcasting Corporation* (*brit. Rundfunkgesellschaft*).

BC *British Columbia.*

B/E *bill of exchange* Wechsel *m.*

Beds. *Bedfordshire.*

Benelux *Belgium, Netherlands, Luxembourg* (*Zollunion*).

Berks. *Berkshire.*

BFN *British Forces Network* (*Sender der brit. Streitkräfte in Deutschland*).

BL *Bachelor of Law* Bakkalaureus *m* des Rechts.

bldg *building* Gebäude *n.*

BM *Bachelor of Medicine* Bakkalaureus *m* der Medizin.

BO *body odour* Körpergeruch *m.*

BOT *Board of Trade* Handelsministerium *n* (*in Großbritannien*).

BR *British Rail* (*Eisenbahn in Großbritannien*).

Brit. *Britain* Großbritannien *n*; *British* britisch.

Bros. *brothers* Gebrüder *pl.* (*in Firmenbezeichnungen*).

BS *Bachelor of Science* Bakkalaureus *m* der Naturwissenschaften; *British Standard* Brit. Norm *f.*

BSI *British Standards Institution* Brit. Normungs-Organisation *f.*

Bucks. *Buckinghamshire.*

C *Celsius, centigrade* (*Thermometereinteilung*).

c. *cent(s)* Cent *m od. pl.*; *circa* ca., ungefähr, zirka; *cubic* Kubik...

CA *California.*

C/A *current account* Girokonto *n.*

Cambs. *Cambridgeshire.*

Can. *Canada* Kanada *n*; *Canadian* kanadisch.

CBS *Columbia Broadcasting System* (*amer. Rundfunkgesellschaft*).

CD *compact disc* CD-Platte *f*, Kompaktschallplatte *f.*

cf. *confer* vgl., vergleiche.

Ches. *Cheshire.*

CIA *Central Intelligence Agency* (*amer. Geheimdienst*).

CID *Criminal Investigation Department* (*brit. Kriminalpolizei*).

c.i.f. *cost, insurance, freight* Kosten, Versicherung und Fracht einbegriffen.

CO *Colorado.*

Co. *Company* Gesellschaft *f*; *County* Grafschaft *f*, Kreis *m.*

c/o *care of* p.A., per Adresse, bei.

COD *cash* (*Am. collect*) *on delivery* Zahlung bei Empfang, gegen Nachnahme.

C of E *Church of England (englische Staatskirche).*
Corn. *Cornwall.*
cp. *compare* vgl., vergleiche.
CT *Connecticut.*
Cumb. *Cumberland.*
cwt. *hundredweight (etwa 1)* Zentner *m.*

DC *direct current* Gleichstrom *m.*
D.C. *District of Columbia (mit der amer. Hauptstadt Washington).*
DE *Delaware.*
dep. *departure* Abf., Abfahrt *f.*
Dept. *Department* Abt., Abteilung *f.*
Derby. *Derbyshire.*
Devon. *Devonshire.*
disc. *discount* Diskont *m,* Abzug *m.*
div. *dividend* Dividende *f.*
DJ *disc jockey* Diskjockey *m.*
Dors. *Dorsetshire.*
doz. *dozen* Dutzend *n od. pl.*
Dpt. *Department* Abt., Abteilung *f.*
Dur(h). *Durham.*
dz. *dozen* Dutzend *n od. pl.*

E *east* Ost(en *m*); *eastern* östlich; *English* englisch.
ea. *each* jeder.
ECU *European Currency Unit* europäische Währungseinheit.
Ed., ed. *edition* Auflage *f; edited* hrsg., herausgegeben; *editor* Hrsg., Herausgeber *m.*
EDP *electronic data processing* EDV, elektronische Datenverarbeitung.
EEC *European Economic Community* EWG, Europäische Wirtschaftsgemeinschaft.
EFTA *European Free Trade Association* EFTA, Europäische Freihandelsgemeinschaft *od.* -zone.
e.g. *exempli gratia (lateinisch = for instance)* z. B., zum Beispiel.
Enc. *enclosure(s)* Anlage(n *pl.*) *f.*
Ess. *Essex.*

F *Fahrenheit (Thermometereinteilung).*
f. *feminine* weiblich; *foot, pl. feet* Fuß *m od. pl.*; *following* folgend.
FAO *Food and Agricultural Organization* Organisation *f* für Ernährung und Landwirtschaft *(der UN).*
FBI *Federal Bureau of Investigation (Bundeskriminalamt der USA).*

fig. *figure(s)* Abb., Abbildung(en *pl.*) *f.*
FL *Florida.*
FM *frequency modulation* UKW, Ultrakurzwelle *f.*
FO *Foreign Office* Brt. Auswärtiges Amt.
f.o.b. *free on board* frei Schiff.
fol. *folio* Folio *n,* Seite *f.*
fr. *franc(s)* Franc(s *pl.*) *m.*
ft *foot, pl. feet* Fuß *m od. pl.*

g *gramme* g, Gramm *n.*
GA *Georgia.*
gal. *gallon* Gallone *f.*
GATT *General Agreement on Tariffs and Trade* Allgemeines Zoll- und Handelsabkommen.
GB *Great Britain* Großbritannien *n.*
GI *government issue* von der Regierung ausgegeben; Staatseigentum *n; fig.* amer. Soldat.
Glos. *Gloucestershire.*
GMT *Greenwich Mean Time* WEZ, Westeuropäische Zeit.
GP *general practitioner* Arzt *m* (Ärztin *f*) für Allgemeinmedizin.
GPO *General Post Office* Hauptpostamt *n.*
gr. *gross* brutto.

h. *hour(s)* Std., Stunde(n *pl.*) *f.*
Hants. *Hampshire.*
HBM *His (Her) Britannic Majesty* Seine (Ihre) britannische Majestät.
H.C. *House of Commons* Unterhaus *n.*
Herts. *Hertfordshire.*
hf. *half* halb.
HI *Hawaii.*
H.L. *House of Lords* Oberhaus *n.*
H.M. *His (Her) Majesty* Seine (Ihre) Majestät.
H.M.S. *His (Her) Majesty's Ship (Steamer)* Seiner (Ihrer) Majestät Schiff *n* (Dampfschiff *n*).
H.O. *Home Office* Brt. Innenministerium *n.*
H.P., hp *horsepower* PS, Pferdestärke *f.*
H.Q., Hq. *Headquarters* Stab(squartier *n*) *m,* Hauptquartier *n.*
H.R. *House of Representatives* Repräsentantenhaus *n (der USA).*
H.R.H. *His (Her) Royal Highness* Seine (Ihre) Königliche Hoheit.

IA *Iowa.*
ICBM *intercontinental ballistic missile* interkontinentaler ballistischer Flugkörper.
ID *Idaho.*
I.D. *Intelligence Department* Nachrichtenamt *n.*
i.e. *id est (lateinisch = that is to say)* d. h., das heißt.
IL *Illinois.*
IMF *International Monetary Fund* Internationaler Währungsfonds.
IN *Indiana.*
in. *inch(es)* Zoll *m od. pl.*
Inc. *Incorporated* (amtlich) eingetragen.
inst. *instant* d. M., dieses Monats.
IOC *International Olympic Committee* Internationales Olympisches Komitee.
I of W *Isle of Wight.*
IOU *I owe you* Schuldschein *m.*
Ir. *Ireland* Irland *n; Irish* irisch.
IRC *International Red Cross* Internationales Rotes Kreuz.

JP *Justice of the Peace* Friedensrichter *m.*
Jr *junior* jr., jun., der Jüngere.

k.o. *knock(ed) out* Boxen: k.o. (ge)schlagen; *fig.* erledigt.
KS *Kansas.*

l. *litre(s)* Liter *n, m od. pl.*
£ *pound sterling* Pfund *n* Sterling *(Währung).*
LA *Louisiana.*
Lab *Labrador.*
Lancs. *Lancashire.*
lb. *pound(s)* Pfund *n od. pl. (Gewicht).*
L/C *letter of credit* Kreditbrief *m.*
Leics. *Leicestershire.*
Lincs. *Lincolnshire.*
LP *long playing record* LP, Langspielplatte *f.*
Ltd. *limited* mit beschränkter Haftung.

m. *male* männlich; *metre* m, Meter *n, m; mile* Meile *f; minute* Min., Minute *f.*
MA *Massachusetts.*
M.A. *Master of Arts* Magister *m* der Philosophie.
Man *Manitoba.*
MD *Maryland.*
M.D. *Medicinae Doctor (lateinisch =*

Doctor of Medicine) Dr. med., Doktor *m* der Medizin.
ME *Maine.*
MI *Michigan.*
MN *Minnesota.*
MO *Missouri.*
M.O. *money order* Postanweisung *f.*
Mon. *Monmouthshire.*
MP, M.P. *Member of Parliament* Parlamentsabgeordnete(r *m) f; Military Police* Militärpolizei *f.*
m.p.h. *miles per hour* Stundenmeilen *pl.*
Mr *Mister* Herr *m.*
MRP *manufacturer's recommended price* unverbindliche Preisempfehlung.
Mrs *Mistress* Frau *f.*
MS *Mississippi; manuscript* Manuskript *n.*
Ms *Anrede für Frauen ohne Berücksichtigung des Familienstandes.*
Mt *Mount* Berg *m.*

N *north* Nord(en *m); northern* nördlich.
n. *noon* Mittag *m.*
NASA *National Aeronautics and Space Administration* NASA *f (amer. Luftfahrt- und Raumforschungsbehörde).*
NATO *North Atlantic Treaty Organization* NATO *f,* Nordatlantikpakt-Organisation *f.*
NB *New Brunswick.*
N.B. *nota bene (lateinisch = note well)* NB, notabene.
NBC *National Broadcasting Company (amer. Rundfunkgesellschaft).*
NC *North Carolina.*
ND *North Dakota; Newfoundland.*
NE *north-east* Nordost(en *m); north-eastern* nordöstlich; *Nebraska.*
NH *New Hampshire.*
N.H.S. *National Health Service* Nationaler Gesundheitsdienst *(in Großbritannien).*
NJ *New Jersey.*
NM *New Mexico.*
Norf. *Norfolk.*
Northants. *Northamptonshire.*
Northumb. *Northumberland.*
Notts. *Nottinghamshire.*
NS *Nova Scotia.*
NV *Nevada.*
NW *north-west* Nordwest(en *m); north-western* nordwestlich.

742

NY *New York.*
N.Y.C. *New York City* Stadt *f* New York.

o/a *on account of* für Rechnung von.
OAS *Organization of American States* Organisation *f* amerikanischer Staaten.
O.E.C.D. *Organization for Economic Cooperation and Development* Organisation *f* für wirtschaftliche Zusammenarbeit und Entwicklung.
OH *Ohio.*
O.H.M.S. *On His (Her) Majesty's Service* im Dienste Seiner (Ihrer) Majestät; Dienstsache *f*.
OK *Oklahoma.*
O.K. o.k., in Ordnung.
Ont *Ontario.*
OPEC *Organization of Petroleum-Exporting Countries* Organisation *f* erdölexportierender Staaten.
OR *Oregon.*
Oxon. *Oxfordshire.*
oz. *ounce* Unze.

p *(new) penny od. pence* Penny *m*.
PA *Pennsylvania.*
p.a. *per annum (lateinisch = yearly)* jährlich.
Pan Am *Pan American World Airways (amer. Fluggesellschaft).*
PC *Personal Computer* PC, Personalcomputer *m*.
P.C. *police constable* Schutzmann *m*.
p.c. *per cent* %, Prozent *n od. pl.*
pd. *paid* bezahlt.
P.E.N., *mst* **PEN Club** *Poets, Playwrights, Editors, Essayists, and Novelists* Pen-Club *m (Internationale Vereinigung von Dichtern, Dramatikern, Redakteuren, Essayisten und Romanschriftstellern).*
Ph.D. *Philosophiae Doctor (lateinisch = Doctor of Philosophy)* Dr. phil., Doktor *m* der Philosophie.
PM *Prime Minister* Premierminister(in).
p.m. *post meridiem (lateinisch = after noon)* nachmittags, abends.
P.O. *Post Office* Postamt *n*; *postal order* Postanweisung *f*.
POD *pay on delivery* Nachnahme *f*.
P.S. *postscript* PS, Nachschrift *f*.
pt *pint* Pinte *f (etwa ¹/₂ l).*

P.T.O., p.t.o. *please turn over* b.w., bitte wenden.
PX *Post Exchange* Verkaufsläden *pl (der amer. Streitkräfte).*

Que *Quebec.*
qt *quart* Quart *n (etwa 1 l).*

R.A.F. *Royal Air Force* Königlich-Brit. Luftwaffe *f*.
RAM *Computer: random access memory* Speicher *m* mit wahlfreiem Zugriff, Direktzugriffsspeicher *m*.
RC *Roman Catholic* rk, r.-k., römisch-katholisch.
Rd. *Road* Str., Straße *f*.
ref. *(in) reference (to)* (mit) Bezug *m* (auf); Empfehlung *f*.
regd. *registered* eingetragen; eingeschrieben.
reg.tn. *register ton* RT, Registertonne *f*.
resp. *respective(ly)* bzw., beziehungsweise.
ret. *retired* i.R., im Ruhestand.
Rev. *Reverend* Pfarrer *m*.
rev *revolution* Umdrehung *f*.
RI *Rhode Island.*
R.N. *Royal Navy* Königlich-Brit. Marine *f*.
ROM *Computer: read only memory* Nur-Lese-Speicher *m*, Fest(wert)-speicher *m*.
R.R. *Railroad Am.* Eisenbahn *f*.
RSVP *répondez s'il vous plaît (französisch = please reply)* u.A.w.g., um Antwort wird gebeten.

S *south* Süd(en *m*); *southern* südlich.
s. *second(s)* Sek., Sekunde(n *pl.*) *f*.
† *dollar* Dollar *m*.
S.A. *South Africa* Südafrika *n*; *South America* Südamerika *n*; *Salvation Army* Heilsarmee *f*.
Salop. *Shropshire.*
Sask *Saskatchewan.*
SC *South Carolina*; *Security Council* Sicherheitsrat *m (der UN).*
SD *South Dakota.*
SE *south-east* Südost(en *m*); *southeastern* südöstlich; *Stock Exchange* Börse *f*.
SEATO *South East Asia Treaty Organization* Südostasienpakt-Organisation *f*.
Soc. *society* Gesellschaft *f*; Verein *m*.
Som. *Somersetshire.*

Sq. *Square* Platz *m.*
sq. *square* ... Quadrat...
Sr *senior* sen., der Ältere.
S.S. *steamship* Dampfer *m.*
St(.) *Saint* ... Sankt ...; *Station* Bahnhof *m; Street* Straße *f.*
Staffs. *Staffordshire.*
St.Ex. *Stock Exchange* Börse *f.*
stg. *sterling* Sterling *m (brit. Währungseinheit).*
Suff. *Suffolk.*
SW *south-west* Südwest(en *m); south-western* südwestlich.
Sx *Sussex.*
Sy *Surrey.*

t *ton(s)* Tonne(n *pl.) f.*
TM *trademark* Warenzeichen *n.*
TMO *telegraph money order* telegraphische Geldanweisung.
TN *Tennessee.*
TO *Telegraph (Telephone) Office* Telegraphen-(Fernsprech)amt *n.*
TU *Trade(s) Union(s)* Gewerkschaft(en *pl.) f.*
TUC *Trade(s) Union Congress* brit. Gewerkschaftsverband *m.*
TV *television* Fernsehen *n.*
TWA *Trans World Airlines (amer. Fluggesellschaft).*
TX *Texas.*

UK *United Kingdom* Vereinigtes Königreich *(England, Schottland, Wales und Nordirland).*
UN(O) *United Nations (Organization)* UN(O) *f,* (Organisation *f* der) Vereinte(n) Nationen *pl.*
UNESCO *United Nations Educational, Scientific, and Cultural Organization* Organisation *f* der Vereinten Nationen für Erziehung, Wissenschaft und Kultur.
UNICEF *United Nations International Children's Emergency Fund* Weltkinderhilfswerk *n* der UNO.
UPI *United Press International (amer. Nachrichtenagentur).*

US(A) *United States (of America)* US(A) *pl.,* Vereinigte Staaten *pl.* (von Amerika).
UT *Utah.*

v. *verse* Vers *m; versus (lateinisch = against)* gegen; *vide (lateinisch = see)* s., siehe.
VA *Virginia.*
VAT *value-added tax* Mehrwertsteuer *f.*
VF *video frequency* Videofrequenz *f.*
viz. *videlicet (lateinisch = namely)* nämlich.
vol(s). *volume(s)* Band *m* (Bände *pl.).*
VT *Vermont.*

W *west* West(en *m); western* westlich.
WA *Washington.*
Warks. *Warwickshire.*
WC *water closet* WC *n,* Wasserklosett *n.*
W.F.T.U. *World Federation of Trade Unions* Weltgewerkschaftsbund *m.*
W.H.O. *World Health Organization* Weltgesundheitsorganisation *f (der UN).*
WI *Wisconsin.*
W.I. *West Indies* Westindien *n.*
Wilts. *Wiltshire.*
Worcs. *Worcestershire.*
wt. *weight* Gewicht *n.*
W.V. *West Virginia.*
WY *Wyoming.*

Xmas *Christmas* Weihnachten *n.*

yd(s). *yard(s)* Elle(n *pl.) f.*
Y.M.C.A. *Young Men's Christian Association* CVJM, Christlicher Verein Junger Männer.
Yorks. *Yorkshire.*
Y.W.C.A. *Young Women's Christian Association* Christlicher Verein Junger Mädchen.

Alphabetical List of the German Irregular Verbs

Infinitive – Preterite – Past Participle

backen - backte (buk) - gebacken
bedingen - bedang (bedingte) - bedungen (*conditional:* bedingt)
befehlen - befahl - befohlen
beginnen - begann - begonnen
beißen - biß - gebissen
bergen - barg - geborgen
bersten - barst - geborsten
bewegen - bewog - bewogen
biegen - bog - gebogen
bieten - bot - geboten
binden - band - gebunden
bitten - bat - gebeten
blasen - blies - geblasen
bleiben - blieb - geblieben
bleichen - blich - geblichen
braten - briet - gebraten
brauchen - brauchte - gebraucht (*v/aux.* brauchen)
brechen - brach - gebrochen
brennen - brannte - gebrannt
bringen - brachte - gebracht
denken - dachte - gedacht
dreschen - drosch - gedroschen
dringen - drang - gedrungen
dürfen - durfte - gedurft (*v/aux.* dürfen)
empfehlen - empfahl - empfohlen
erlöschen - erlosch - erloschen
erschrecken - erschrak - erschrocken
essen - aß - gegessen
fahren - fuhr - gefahren
fallen - fiel - gefallen
fangen - fing - gefangen
fechten - focht - gefochten
finden - fand - gefunden
flechten - flocht - geflochten
fliegen - flog - geflogen
fliehen - floh - geflohen
fließen - floß - geflossen
fressen - fraß - gefressen
frieren - fror - gefroren
gären - gor (*esp. fig.* gärte) - gegoren (*esp. fig.* gegärt)
gebären - gebar - geboren

geben - gab - gegeben
gedeihen - gedieh - gediehen
gehen - ging - gegangen
gelingen - gelang - gelungen
gelten - galt - gegolten
genesen - genas - genesen
genießen - genoß - genossen
geschehen - geschah - geschehen
gewinnen - gewann - gewonnen
gießen - goß - gegossen
gleichen - glich - geglichen
gleiten - glitt - geglitten
glimmen - glomm - geglommen
graben - grub - gegraben
greifen - griff - gegriffen
haben - hatte - gehabt
halten - hielt - gehalten
hängen - hing - gehangen
hauen - haute (hieb) - gehauen
heben - hob - gehoben
heißen - hieß - geheißen
helfen - half - geholfen
kennen - kannte - gekannt
klingen - klang - geklungen
kneifen - kniff - gekniffen
kommen - kam - gekommen
können - konnte - gekonnt (*v/aux.* können)
kriechen - kroch - gekrochen
laden - lud - geladen
lassen - ließ - gelassen (*v/aux.* lassen)
laufen - lief - gelaufen
leiden - litt - gelitten
leihen - lieh - geliehen
lesen - las - gelesen
liegen - lag - gelegen
lügen - log - gelogen
mahlen - mahlte - gemahlen
meiden - mied - gemieden
melken - melkte (molk) - gemolken (gemelkt)
messen - maß - gemessen
mißlingen - mißlang - mißlungen
mögen - mochte - gemocht (*v/aux.* mögen)

müssen - mußte - gemußt (*v/aux.* müssen)
nehmen - nahm - genommen
nennen - nannte - genannt
pfeifen - pfiff - gepfiffen
preisen - pries - gepriesen
quellen - quoll - gequollen
raten - riet - geraten
reiben - rieb - gerieben
reißen - riß - gerissen
reiten - ritt - geritten
rennen - rannte - gerannt
riechen - roch - gerochen
ringen - rang - gerungen
rinnen - rann - geronnen
rufen - rief - gerufen
salzen - salzte - gesalzen (gesalzt)
saufen - soff - gesoffen
saugen - sog - gesogen
schaffen - schuf - geschaffen
schallen - schallte (scholl) - geschallt (*for erschallen a.* erschollen)
scheiden - schied - geschieden
scheinen - schien - geschienen
schelten - schalt - gescholten
scheren - schor - geschoren
schieben - schob - geschoben
schießen - schoß - geschossen
schinden - schund - geschunden
schlafen - schlief - geschlafen
schlagen - schlug - geschlagen
schleichen - schlich - geschlichen
schleifen - schliff - geschliffen
schließen - schloß - geschlossen
schlingen - schlang - geschlungen
schmeißen - schmiß - geschmissen
schmelzen - schmolz - geschmolzen
schneiden - schnitt - geschnitten
schrecken - schrak - † geschrocken
schreiben - schrieb - geschrieben
schreien - schrie - geschrie(e)n
schreiten - schritt - geschritten
schweigen - schwieg - geschwiegen
schwellen - schwoll - geschwollen
schwimmen - schwamm - geschwommen
schwinden - schwand - geschwun-den [gen]
schwingen - schwang - geschwun-
schwören - schwor - geschworen
sehen - sah - gesehen
sein - war - gewesen
senden - sandte - gesandt
sieden - sott - gesotten
singen - sang - gesungen

sinken - sank - gesunken
sinnen - sann - gesonnen
sitzen - saß - gesessen
sollen - sollte - gesollt (*v/aux.* sollen)
spalten - spaltete - gespalten (gespaltet)
speien - spie - gespie(e)n
spinnen - spann - gesponnen
sprechen - sprach - gesprochen
sprießen - sproß - gesprossen
springen - sprang - gesprungen
stechen - stach - gestochen
stecken - steckte (stak) - gesteckt
stehen - stand - gestanden
stehlen - stahl - gestohlen
steigen - stieg - gestiegen
sterben - starb - gestorben
stieben - stob - gestoben
stinken - stank - gestunken
stoßen - stieß - gestoßen
streichen - strich - gestrichen
streiten - stritt - gestritten
tragen - trug - getragen
treffen - traf - getroffen
treiben - trieb - getrieben
treten - trat - getreten
triefen - triefte (troff) - getrieft
trinken - trank - getrunken
trügen - trog - getrogen
tun - tat - getan
verderben - verdarb - verdorben
verdrießen - verdroß - verdrossen
vergessen - vergaß - vergessen
verlieren - verlor - verloren
verschleißen - verschliß - verschlissen
verzeihen - verzieh - verziehen
wachsen - wuchs - gewachsen
wägen - wog (↖ wägte) - gewogen (↖ gewägt)
waschen - wusch - gewaschen
weben - wob - gewoben
weichen - wich - gewichen
weisen - wies - gewiesen
wenden - wandte - gewandt
werben - warb - geworben [den*)
werden - wurde - geworden (wor-
werfen - warf - geworfen
wiegen - wog - gewogen
winden - wand - gewunden
wissen - wußte - gewußt [wollen)
wollen - wollte - gewollt (*v/aux.*
wringen - wrang - gewrungen
ziehen - zog - gezogen
zwingen - zwang - gezwungen

* only in connexion with the past participles of other verbs, *e.g.* er ist gesehen worden he has been seen.

Alphabetical List of the English Irregular Verbs

Infinitive – Preterite – Past Participle

Irregular forms marked with asterisks (*)
can be exchanged for the regular forms.

arise (*sich erheben*) - arose - arisen
awake (*erwachen*) - awoke* - awoken*
be (*sein*) - was - been
bear (*tragen; gebären*) - bore - getragen: borne - *geboren*: born
beat (*schlagen*) - beat - beat(en)
become (*werden*) - became - become
beget (*zeugen*) - begot - begotten
begin (*anfangen*) - began - begun
bend (*beugen*) - bent - bent
bereave (*berauben*) - bereft* - bereft*
beseech (*dringend bitten*) - besought - besought
bet (*wetten*) - bet* - bet*
bid (*gebieten*) - bade, bid - bid(den)
bide (*abwarten*) - bode* - bided
bind (*binden*) - bound - bound
bite (*beißen*) - bit - bitten
bleed (*bluten*) - bled - bled
bless (*segnen; preisen*) - blest* - blest*
blow (*blasen*) - blew - blown
break (*brechen*) - broke - broken
breed (*aufziehen*) - bred - bred
bring (*bringen*) - brought - brought
build (*bauen*) - built - built
burn (*brennen*) - burnt* - burnt*
burst (*bersten*) - burst - burst
buy (*kaufen*) - bought - bought
cast (*werfen*) - cast - cast
catch (*fangen*) - caught - caught
choose (*wählen*) - chose - chosen
cleave (*[sich] spalten*) - cleft, clove* - cleft, cloven*
cling (*sich [an]klammern*) - clung - clung
clothe (*[an-, be]kleiden*) - clad* - clad*
come (*kommen*) - came - come
cost (*kosten*) - cost - cost
creep (*kriechen*) - crept - crept
crow (*krähen*) - crew* - crowed
cut (*schneiden*) - cut - cut
deal (*handeln*) - dealt - dealt
dig (*graben*) - dug - dug
dive (*[unter]tauchen*) - dived, *Am. a.* dove - dived
do (*tun*) - did - done
draw (*ziehen*) - drew - drawn
dream (*träumen*) - dreamt* - dreamt*
drink (*trinken*) - drank - drunk
drive (*treiben; fahren*) - drove - driven
dwell (*wohnen*) - dwelt* - dwelt*
eat (*essen*) -ate - eaten
fall (*fallen*) - fell - fallen
feed (*füttern*) - fed - fed
feel (*fühlen*) - felt - felt
fight (*kämpfen*) - fought - fought
find (*finden*) - found - found
fit (*[an]passen*) - fitted, *Am. a.* fit - fitted, *Am. a.* fit
flee (*fliehen*) - fled - fled
fling (*schleudern*) - flung - flung
fly (*fliegen*) - flew - flown
forbid (*verbieten*) - forbade - forbidden
forget (*vergessen*) - forgot - forgotten
forsake (*aufgeben; verlassen*) - forsook - forsaken
freeze (*[ge]frieren*) - froze - frozen
get (*bekommen*) - got - got, *Am.* gotten
gild (*vergolden*) - gilt* - gilt*
give (*geben*) - gave - given
go (*gehen*) - went - gone
grind (*mahlen*) - ground - ground
grow (*wachsen*) - grew - grown
hang (*hängen*) - hung - hung
have (*haben*) - had - had
hear (*hören*) - heard - heard
heave (*heben*) - hove* - hove*
hew (*hauen, hacken*) - hewed - hewn*
hide (*verbergen*) - hid - hidden
hit (*treffen*) - hit - hit
hold (*halten*) - held - held
hurt (*verletzen*) - hurt - hurt
keep (*halten*) - kept - kept
kneel (*knien*) - knelt* - knelt*
knit (*stricken*) - knit* - knit*

know (*wissen*) - knew - known
lay (*legen*) - laid - laid
lead (*führen*) - led - led
lean ([*sich*] [*an*]*lehnen*) - leant* - leant*
leap ([*über*]*springen*) - leapt* - leapt*
learn (*lernen*) - learnt* - learnt*
leave (*verlassen*) - left - left
lend (*leihen*) - lent -lent
let (*lassen*) - let - let
lie (*liegen*) - lay - lain
light (*anzünden*) - lit* - lit*
lose (*verlieren*) - lost - lost
make (*machen*) - made - made
mean (*meinen*) - meant - meant
meet (*begegnen*) - met - met
mow (*mähen*) - mowed - mown*
pay (*zahlen*) - paid - paid
plead (*plädieren*) - pleaded, *bsd. schott., Am.* pled - pleaded, *bsd. schott., Am.* pled
put (*setzen, stellen*) - put - put
read (*lesen*) - read - read
rid (*befreien*) - rid - rid
ride (*reiten*) - rode - ridden
ring (*läuten*) - rang - rung
rise (*aufstehen*) - rose - risen
run (*laufen*) - ran - run
saw (*sägen*) - sawed - sawn*
say (*sagen*) - said - said
see (*sehen*) - saw - seen
seek (*suchen*) - sought - sought
sell (*verkaufen*) - sold - sold
send (*senden*) - sent - sent
set (*setzen*) - set - set
sew (*nähen*) - sewed - sewn*
shake (*schütteln*) - shook - shaken
shave ([*sich*] *rasieren*) - shaved - shaven*
shear (*scheren*) - sheared - shorn
shed (*ausgießen*) - shed - shed
shine (*scheinen*) - shone - shone
shit (*scheißen*) - shit - shit
shoe (*beschuhen*) - shod - shod
shoot (*schießen*) - shot - shot
show (*zeigen*) - showed - shown*
shrink ([*ein*]*schrumpfen*) - shrank - shrunk
shut (*schließen*) - shut - shut
sing (*singen*) - sang - sung
sink (*sinken*) - sank - sunk
sit (*sitzen*) - sat - sat
slay (*erschlagen*) - slew - slain
sleep (*schlafen*) - slept - slept
slide (*gleiten*) - slid - slid
sling (*schleudern*) - slung - slung
slink (*schleichen*) - slunk - slunk

slit (*schlitzen*) - slit - slit
smell (*riechen*) - smelt* - smelt*
sow ([*aus*]*säen*) - sowed - sown*
speak (*sprechen*) - spoke - spoken
speed (*eilen*) - sped* - sped*
spell (*buchstabieren*) - spelt* - spelt*
spend (*ausgeben*) - spent - spent
spill (*verschütten*) - spilt* - spilt*
spin (*spinnen*) - spun - spun
spit ([*aus*]*spucken*) - spat - spat
split (*spalten*) - split - split
spoil (*verderben*) - spoilt* - spoilt*
spread (*verbreiten*) - spread - spread
spring (*springen*) - sprang, *Am.* sprung - sprung
stand (*stehen*) - stood - stood
stave (*den Boden einschlagen*) - stove* - stove*
steal (*stehlen*) - stole - stolen
stick (*stecken*) - stuck - stuck
sting (*stechen*) - stung - stung
stink (*stinken*) - stank, stunk - stunk
strew ([*be*]*streuen*) - strewed - strewn*
stride (*über-, durchschreiten*) - strode - stridden
strike (*schlagen*) - struck - struck
string (*spannen*) - strung - strung
strive (*streben*) - strove - striven
swear (*schwören*) - swore - sworn
sweat (*schwitzen*) - sweat* - sweat*
sweep (*fegen*) - swept - swept
swell ([*an*]*schwellen*) - swelled - swollen
swim (*schwimmen*) - swam - swum
swing (*schwingen*) - swung - swung
take (*nehmen*) - took - taken
teach (*lehren*) - taught - taught
tear (*ziehen*) - tore - torn
tell (*sagen*) - told - told
think (*denken*) - thought - thought
thrive (*gedeihen*) - throve* - thriven*
throw (*werfen*) - threw - thrown
thrust (*stoßen*) - thrust - thrust
tread (*treten*) - trod - trodden, trod
wake (*wachen*) - woke* - woke(n)*
wear ([*Kleider*] *tragen*) - wore - worn
weave (*weben*) - wove - woven
wed (*heiraten*) - wedded, *selten* wed - wedded, *selten* wed
weep (*weinen*) - wept - wept
wet (*nässen*) - wet* - wet*
win (*gewinnen*) - won - won
wind (*winden*) - wound - wound
wring ([*aus*]*wringen*) - wrung - wrung
write (*schreiben*) - wrote - written

Numerals

Cardinal Numbers

0 null *nought, zero, cipher*
1 eins *one*
2 zwei *two*
3 drei *three*
4 vier *four*
5 fünf *five*
6 sechs *six*
7 sieben *seven*
8 acht *eight*
9 neun *nine*
10 zehn *ten*
11 elf *eleven*
12 zwölf *twelve*
13 dreizehn *thirteen*
14 vierzehn *fourteen*
15 fünfzehn *fifteen*
16 sechzehn *sixteen*
17 siebzehn *seventeen*
18 achtzehn *eighteen*
19 neunzehn *nineteen*
20 zwanzig *twenty*
21 einundzwanzig *twenty-one*
22 zweiundzwanzig *twenty-two*
23 dreiundzwanzig *twenty-three*
30 dreißig *thirty*
31 einunddreißig *thirty-one*
40 vierzig *forty*
41 einundvierzig *forty-one*
50 fünfzig *fifty*

51 einundfünfzig *fifty-one*
60 sechzig *sixty*
61 einundsechzig *sixty-one*
70 siebzig *seventy*
71 einundsiebzig *seventy-one*
80 achtzig *eighty*
81 einundachtzig *eighty-one*
90 neunzig *ninety*
91 einundneunzig *ninety-one*
100 hundert *a or one hundred*
101 hundert(und)eins *a hundred and one*
200 zweihundert *two hundred*
300 dreihundert *three hundred*
572 fünfhundert(und)zweiundsiebzig *five hundred and seventy-two*
1000 tausend *a or one thousand*
1972 neunzehnhundertzweiundsiebzig *nineteen hundred and seventy-two*
500 000 fünfhunderttausend *five hundred thousand*
1 000 000 eine Million *a or one million*
2 000 000 zwei Millionen *two million*
1 000 000 000 eine Milliarde *a or one milliard (Am. billion)*

Ordinal Numbers

1. erste *first (1st)*
2. zweite *second (2nd)*
3. dritte *third (3rd)*
4. vierte *fourth (4th)*
5. fünfte *fifth (5th)*, etc.
6. sechste *sixth*
7. siebente *seventh*
8. achte *eighth*
9. neunte *ninth*
10. zehnte *tenth*

11. elfte *eleventh*
12. zwölfte *twelfth*
13. dreizehnte *thirteenth*
14. vierzehnte *fourteenth*
15. fünfzehnte *fifteenth*
16. sechzehnte *sixteenth*
17. siebzehnte *seventeenth*
18. achtzehnte *eighteenth*
19. neunzehnte *nineteenth*
20. zwanzigste *twentieth*

21. einundzwanzigste *twenty-first*
22. zweiundzwanzigste *twenty-second*
23. dreiundzwanzigste *twenty-third*
30. dreißigste *thirtieth*
31. einunddreißigste *thirty-first*
40. vierzigste *fortieth*
41. einundvierzigste *forty-first*
50. fünfzigste *fiftieth*
51. einundfünfzigste *fifty-first*
60. sechzigste *sixtieth*
61. einundsechzigste *sixty-first*
70. siebzigste *seventieth*
71. einundsiebzigste *seventy-first*
80. achtzigste *eightieth*
81. einundachtzigste *eighty-first*

90. neunzigste *ninetieth*
100. hundertste *(one) hundredth*
101. hundert(und)erste *(one) hundred and first*
200. zweihundertste *two hundredth*
300. dreihundertste *three hundredth*
572. fünfhundert(und)zweiundsiebzigste *five hundred and seventy-second*
1000. tausendste *(one) thousandth*
1970. neunzehnhundert(und)siebzigste *nineteen hundred and seventieth*
500000. fünfhunderttausendste *five hundred thousandth*
1000000. millionste *(one) millionth*
2000000. zweimillionste *two millionth*

Fractional Numbers and other Numerical Values

$1/2$ halb *one* or *a half*
$1/2$ eine halbe Meile *half a mile*
$1^1/2$ anderthalb *or* eineinhalb *one and a half*
$2^1/2$ zweieinhalb *two and a half*
$1/3$ ein Drittel *one* or *a third*
$2/3$ zwei Drittel *two thirds*
$1/4$ ein Viertel *one fourth, one* or *a quarter*
$3/4$ drei Viertel *three fourths, three quarters*
$1^1/4$ ein und eine viertel Stunde *one hour and a quarter*
$1/5$ ein Fünftel *one* or *a fifth*
$3^4/5$ drei vier Fünftel *three and four fifths*
0,4 null Komma vier *point four (.4)*
2,5 zwei Komma fünf *two point five (2.5)*

einfach *single*
  zweifach *double, twofold*
  dreifach *threefold, treble, triple*
  vierfach *fourfold, quadruple*
  fünffach *fivefold, quintuple*

einmal *once*
  zweimal *twice*
  drei-, vier-, fünfmal *three* or *four* or *five times*
  zweimal soviel(e) *twice as much* or *many*

erstens, zweitens, drittens *first(ly), secondly, thirdly; in the first* or *second* or *third place*

$2 \times 3 = 6$ zwei mal drei ist sechs, zwei multipliziert mit drei ist sechs *twice three are* or *make six, two multiplied by three are* or *make six*

$7 + 8 = 15$ sieben plus acht ist fünfzehn *seven plus eight are fifteen*

$10 - 3 = 7$ zehn minus drei ist sieben *ten minus three are seven*

$20 : 5 = 4$ zwanzig (dividiert) durch fünf ist vier *twenty divided by five make four*

German Weights and Measures

I. Linear Measure

1 mm Millimeter millimet|re, *Am.* -er = 0.039 inch

1 cm Zentimeter centimet|re, *Am.* -er = 10 mm = 0.394 inch

1 m Meter met|re, *Am.* -er = 100 cm = 1.094 yards = 3.281 feet

1 km Kilometer kilomet|re, *Am.* -er = 1000 m = 0.621 mile

1 sm Seemeile nautical mile = 1852 m

II. Square Measure

1 mm² Quadratmillimeter square millimet|re, *Am.* -er = 0.002 square inch

1 cm² Quadratzentimeter square centimet|re, *Am.* -er = 100 mm² = 0.155 square inch

1 m² Quadratmeter square met|re, *Am.* -er = 10 000 cm² = 1.196 square yards = 10.764 square feet

1 a Ar are = 100 m² = 119.599 square yards

1 ha Hektar hectare = 100 a = 2.471 acres

1 km² Quadratkilometer square kilomet|re, *Am.* -er = 100 ha = 247.11 acres = 0.386 square mile

III. Cubic Measure

1 cm³ Kubikzentimeter cubic centimet|re, *Am.* -er = 1000 mm³ = 0.061 cubic inch

1 m³ Kubikmeter cubic met|re, *Am.* -er = 1000 000 cm³ = 35.315 cubic feet = 1.308 cubic yards

1 RT Registertonne register ton = 2,832 m³ = 100 cubic feet

IV. Measure of Capacity

1 l Liter lit|re, *Am.* -er = 1.760 pints = *U.S.* 1.057 liquid quarts *or* 0.906 dry quart

1 hl Hektoliter hectolit|re, *Am.* -er = 100 l = 2.75 bushels = *U.S.* 26.418 gallons

V. Weight

1 g Gramm gram(me) = 15.432 grains

1 Pfd. Pfund pound (German) = 500 g = 1.102 pounds avdp.

1 kg Kilogramm kilogram(me) = 1000 g = 2.205 pounds avdp. = 2.679 pounds troy

1 Ztr. Zentner centner = 100 Pfd. = 0.984 hundredweight = 1.102 *U.S.* hundredweights

1 dz Doppelzentner = 100 kg = 1.968 hundredweights = 2.204 *U.S.* hundredweights

1 t Tonne ton = 1000 kg = 0.984 long ton = *U.S.* 1.102 short tons

American and British Weights and Measures

1. Linear Measure

1 inch (in.) = 2,54 cm
1 foot (ft)
   = 12 inches = 30,48 cm
1 yard (yd)
   = 3 feet = 91,439 cm
1 perch (p.)
   = $5^1/_2$ yards = 5,029 m
1 mile (m.)
   = 1,760 yards = 1,609 km

2. Nautical Measure

1 fathom (f., fm)
   = 6 feet = 1,829 m
1 nautical mile
   = 6,080 feet = 1853,18 m

3. Square Measure

1 square inch (sq. in.)
   = 6,452 cm²
1 square foot (sq. ft)
   = 144 square inches
   = 929,029 cm²
1 square yard (sq. yd)
   = 9 square feet = 8361,26 cm²
1 square perch (sq. p.)
   = $30^1/_4$ square yards = 25,293 m²
1 rood
   = 40 square perches = 10,117 a
1 acre (a.) = 4 roods = 40,47 a
1 square mile
   = 640 acres = 258,998 ha

4. Cubic Measure

1 cubic inch (cu. in.)
   = 16,387 cm³
1 cubic foot (cu. ft)
   = 1,728 cubic inches = 0,028 m³
1 cubic yard (cu. yd)
   = 27 cubic feet = 0,765 m³
1 register ton (reg. ton)
   = 100 cubic feet = 2,832 m³

5. Measure of Capacity
Dry and Liquid Measure

1 British or imperial gill (gl, gi.)
   = 0,142 l
1 British or imperial pint (pt)
   = 4 gills = 0,568 l
1 British or imperial quart (qt)
   = 2 pints = 1,136 l
1 British or imp. gallon (imp. gal.)
   = 4 imperial quarts = 4,546 l

Dry Measure

1 British or imperial peck (pk)
   = 2 imperial gallons = 9,092 l
1 Brit. or imp. bushel (bu., bus.)
   = 8 imperial gallons = 36,366 l
1 Brit. or imp. quarter (qr)
   = 8 imperial bushels = 290,935 l

Liquid Measure

1 Brit. or imp. barrel (bbl, bl)
   = 36 imperial gallons = 163,656 l

*

1 U.S. dry pint = 0,551 l
1 U.S. dry quart
   = 2 dry pints = 1,101 l
1 U.S. dry gallon
   = 4 dry quarts = 4,405 l
1 U.S. peck
   = 2 dry gallons = 8,809 l
1 U.S. bushel
   = 8 dry gallons = 35,238 l
1 U.S. gill = 0,118 l
1 U.S. liquid pint
   = 4 gills = 0,473 l
1 U.S. liquid quart
   = 2 liquid pints = 0,946 l
1 U.S. liquid gallon
   = 8 liquid pints = 3,785 l
1 U.S. barrel
   = 31½ liquid gallons = 119,228 l

1 U.S. barrel petroleum
= 42 liquid gallons = 158,97 l

= 50,802 kg (*U.S.A.* 100 pounds
= 45,359 kg)

6. Avoirdupois Weight

1 grain (gr.) = 0,065 g
1 dram (dr.)
= 27.344 grains = 1,772 g
1 ounce (oz.)
= 16 drams = 28,35 g
1 pound (lb.)
= 16 ounces = 453,592 g
1 quarter (qr)
= 28 pounds = 12,701 kg
(*U.S.A.* 25 pounds
= 11,339 kg)
1 hundredweight (cwt.)
= 112 pounds

1 ton (t.)
(*a.* long ton) = 20 hundredweights = 1016,05 kg (*U.S.A.*,
a. short ton, = 907,185 kg)
1 stone (st.) = 14 pounds = 6,35 kg

7. Troy Weight

1 grain = 0,065 g
1 pennyweight (dwt.)
= 24 grains = 1,555 g
1 ounce
= 20 pennyweights = 31,103 g
1 pound = 12 ounces = 373,242 g